D0271437

AN A TO Z

TO

almost
OF EVERYTHING

AUTHOR'S NOTE

This is the first A–Z of Everything. I hope you are entertained and edified by it. There are three points I ought to make about the book. First, there is often a time lag in the compilation of statistics – especially government figures – but those I have presented are the latest available to me. Second, since this is a British book, there may be a preponderance of British data, but I have attempted to give the book a global reach. Finally, and most important, although I have done my utmost to achieve one hundred per cent accuracy, with a project of this magnitude covering such a wide range of facts, it seems unavoidable that mistakes will be made, for which I apologize. I would be delighted to have these pointed out to ensure that future editions of An A–Z of almost Everything are as precise as can be. If you wish to do so or wish to suggest new ideas for the book, please write to Trevor Montague c/o Little, Brown and Company.

CONTENTS

ABOUT THE AUTHOR

Trevor Montague is perhaps one of the best known general knowledge buffs in the country. A veteran of numerous radio and television programmes, in 1997 alone he won a dozen shows, including the Grand Finals of both *15–to–1* (Channel 4) and *Today's the Day* (BBC). Trevor won a Gold Medal at the 1998 Mind Sports Olympiad and the following year founded the British Quiz Association which held its first ever championship in 1999 at Olympia in London. The second British Quiz Championships was held at Alexandra Palace in 2000 and Trevor has set the questions for both events as well as co-hosted them alongside Magnus Magnusson. He also sets questions for television quiz shows and compiles quizzes for Internet companies. Trevor had previously had a very successful sporting career but lists his proudest moments as his third place in the Peugeot Zest National Fitness Championship in 2000, from an entry of over 10,000 (at the age of forty-six!) and his tenth placing in his first ever open cycle race in March 2001 that made the pages of *Cycling Weekly* magazine – a desired prize for any budding cyclist.

Introduction by Magnus Magnusson kbe

Trevor Montague is a Masterminder. That is to say, in 1995 he became one of the 1,231 bravehearts who appeared on the television *Mastermind* during its twenty-five-year run. But Trevor Montague is much more than that: he is that not-quite-so-rare-now animal, a quiz addict.

Trevor is also a begetter of quiz-teams. There is an unofficial Mastermind Mafia which meets every month in the Grape Street wine bar in London, and from its regulars Trevor puts together formidable scratch teams of veteran Masterminders to take part in all and any quiz challenges. Trevor is also the question-setter of the fledgling British Quiz Championship which is a part of the annual Mind Sports Olympiad at London's Olympia.

That in itself is a sign of the immense and growing popularity of quizzes of all kinds on television, on radio, in pubs, in the Civil Service, and now even on the Internet. And it has given rise to Trevor's most ambitious project yet – *An A–Z of almost Everything*: a massive factfile of information calculated to be of value to anyone and everyone interested in quizzes.

But how does one define 'General Knowledge' as opposed to 'Specialised Knowledge'? Indeed, when does 'Specialised Knowledge' become 'General Knowledge'? With the staggering growth of pub quiz-teams and television game-shows over recent years, the reservoir of what used to be considered 'General Knowledge' has expanded out of all recognition. Over the twenty-five years of Mastermind, for instance, questions which would once have come into the specialised category became demoted to the General Knowledge sets. I tried to make that very point, as subtly as possible, in the last round of the last Final of the last *Mastermind* series (in Kirkwall Cathedral, Orkney, in 1997): the last question echoed the very first question I had asked, in the University of Liverpool back in 1972:

Q: During the Spanish Civil War, which town in the Basque country was destroyed by German bombers, an event which was commemorated in a painting by Picasso?

A: Guernica

When that question was first asked in 1972, it was in a set of specialised questions on 'The Visual Arts'; in 1997 it was in a General Knowledge set.

So, what exactly makes up an A–Z of Everything? For Trevor, everything is grist to his insatiable mill. He has produced a monster factfile on an astonishing array of subjects from abbreviations to zodiac, embracing Americanisms, animal adjectives, assassination attempts, *Carry On* films, dubbed singing voices, famous dogs, gestation periods, London postal areas, middle names, nursery rhymes, obituaries, pub names, quantum theory, Schrodinger's cat, sculptors, trains, Visigoth rulers and zip codes.

I can think of few subjects which has been omitted, except perhaps for some of the classic *Mastermind* offerings which never made it to the screen: 'orthopaedic bone cement in total hip-replacement'; 'self-service petrol stations from 1963–68'; 'perfect squares from 992–9801'; and 'motorway routes to anywhere in mainland Britain from Letchworth'.

To put together this weighty tome, Trevor called upon his network of friends and colleagues in the Mastermind Club – that remarkable association of survivors of the Black Chair. The Club membership represents an astonishing reservoir of knowledge which its owners are always ready to impart to others. Many is the time I found myself marooned in a hotel without reference books and phoned friends in the Club to check on some vital detail which I needed for an occasion in the next morning.

The quiz cognoscenti who will avidly devour this book may well start off feeling superior ('I know that, of course!'), but I am pretty sure that even they will find much to intrigue them in this shrine of serendipity.

ABBREVIATIONS

A & P   Advertising and Promotion
A & R   Artists and Repertoire / Recording
AA   Automobile Association; Alcoholics Anonymous
AAA   Amateur Athletic Association; Anti-Aircraft Artillery
AAM   Air-to-Air Missile
ABC   Atomic, Biological and Chemical; American Broadcasting Company; Australian Broadcasting Commission
ABM   Anti-Ballistic Missile
ABRACADABRA   ABbreviations and Related ACronyms Associated with Defense, Astronautics, Business and RAdio-electronics
ABS   Anti-lock Braking System
ABTA   Association of British Travel Agents
AC   Alternating Current
ACAS   Advisory Conciliation and Arbitration Service
ACCA   Association of Certified and Corporate Accountants
ACLU   American Civil Liberties Union
ACM   Air Chief Marshal
ACPO   Association of Chief Police Officers
ACT   Advance Corporation Tax
ACTT   Association of Cinematograph, Television and Allied Technicians
ACV   Air-Cushion Vehicle
AD   Anno Domini
ADC   Aide-De-Camp
ADCM   Archbishop of Canterbury's Diploma in Church Music
AEEU   Amalgamated Engineering and Electrical Union
AEGIS   Aid for the Elderly in Government InstitutionS
AEU   Amalgamated Engineering Union
AFP   Agence France Presse
AFV   Armoured Fighting Vehicle
AGM   Air-to-Ground Missile; Annual General Meeting
AGR   Advanced Gas-cooled Reactor
AH   Anno Hegirae (from 622 AD, the start of the Muslim calendar)
AI   Artificial Intelligence; Amnesty International
AID   Artificial Insemination by Donor
AIDS   Acquired Immune Deficiency Syndrome
AIM   Alternative Investment Market
AKA   Also Known As
ALGOL   ALGOrithmic Language
ALICE   Autistic and Language-Impaired Children's Education
ALWR   Advanced Light Water Reactor
AM   Ante Meridiem; Amplitude Modulation
AMCST   Associate, Manchester College of Science and Technology
AMICE   Associate Member of the Institute of Civil Engineers
ANC   African National Congress
ANZAC   Australian and New Zealand Army Corps
AP   Associated Press, Artist's Proof
APEX   Advance Purchase EXcursion; Association of Professional, EXecutive, Clerical and Computer Staff
APR   Annual / Annualised Percentage Rate

APT   Advanced Passenger Train
APWR   Advanced Pressurised Water Reactor
ARCO   Associate of the Royal College of Organists
ARCS   Associate of the Royal College of Science
ARP   Association of Retired Persons; Air-Raid Precautions
ASA   Advertising Standards Authority; Amateur Swimming Association
ASBM   Air-to-Surface Ballistic Missile
ASCII   American Standard Code for Information Interchange
ASDA   ASsociated DAiries
ASDE   Airport Surface Detection Equipment
ASDIC   Anti-Submarine Detection Investigation Committee
ASEAN   Association of South East Asian Nations
ASH   Action on Smoking and Health
ASLEF   Associated Society of Locomotive Engineers and Firemen
ASSC   Accounting Standards Steering Committee
ASSR   Autonomous Soviet Socialist Republic
ASTMS   Association of Scientific, Technical and Managerial Staff
AT & T   American Telephone and Telegraph Company
ATC   Air Traffic Control; Air Training Corps
ATOL   Air Travel Organisers Licence
ATS   Auxiliary Territorial Service
ATV   Associated TeleVision
AUEW   Amalgamated Union of Engineering Workers (now AEU)
AUT   Association of University Teachers
AVR   Army Volunteer Reserve
AWACS   Airborne Warning And Control System
AWOL   Absent WithOut Leave / Absent Without Official Leave
AWP   Amusement With Prizes
AWRE   Atomic Weapons Research Establishment

BA   Bachelor of Arts; British Airways
BAA   British Airports Authority
BAC   British Aircraft Corporation
BACS   Bankers' Automated Clearing Service
BACUP   British Association of Cancer-United Patients
BAFTA   British Academy of Film and Television Arts
BALPA   British AirLine Pilots' Association
BAOR   British Army Of the Rhine
BARB   British Audience Research Bureau; Broadcasters' Audience Research Board
BART   Baronet
BART   Bay Area Rapid Transit
BASIC   Beginners All-Purpose Symbolic Instruction Code
BAT   British American Tobacco Company
BBBC   British Boxing Board of Control
BBC   British Broadcasting Corporation
BBFC   British Board of Film Censors / Classification (new title)
BC   Before Christ
BCC   British Chamber of Commerce

BCE   Before Common / Christian Era
BCh(D) / BDS   Bachelor of Dental Surgery
BEC   Building Employers' Confederation
BECTU   Broadcasting, Entertainment and Cinematograph Technicians Union
BEF   British Expeditionary Force
BEM   British Empire Medal
BES   Business Expansion Scheme
BEST   British Expertise in Science and Technology
BFI   British Film Institute
BFPO   British Forces Post Office
BHF   British Heart Foundation
BHI   British Horological Institute
BIFU   Banking, Insurance and Finance Union
BIM   British Institute of Management
BLitt   Bachelor of Letters
BMA   British Medical Association
BMJ   British Medical Journal
BMR   Basal Metabolic Rate
BMX   Bicycle Motocross
BOAC   British Overseas Airways Corporation
BPD   Barrels Per Day
BRCS   British Red Cross Society
BSA   Birmingham Small Arms
BSAD   British Sports Association for the Disabled
BSB   British Satellite Broadcasting
BSc   Bachelor of Science
BSI   British Standards Institution
BSW   British Standard Whitworth
Bt   Baronet
BUNA   BUtadiene and NAtrium (synthetic rubber)
BUPA   British United Provident Association
BWIA   British West Indian Airways
BWR   Boiling Water Reactor
BYO   Bring Your Own

CAA   Civil Aviation Authority
CAFOD   CAtholic Fund for Overseas Development
CAMRA   CAMpaign for Real Ale
CAN   Christian Advertising Network
Cantab   Cantabrigiensis (of Cambridge)
CARE   Co-operative for American Relief Everywhere
CAT   Computerised Axial Tomography
CB   Companion of the order of the Bath
CBC   Canadian Broadcasting Corporation
CBE   Commander of the Order of the British Empire
CBI   Confederation of British Industry
CBS   Columbia Broadcasting System
CCTV   Closed Circuit TeleVision
CDI   Compact Disc Interactive
CERN   Conseil Européen pour la Recherche Nucléaire
CFC   ChloroFluoroCarbon
CFS   Chronic Fatigue Syndrome (see ME)
CGM   Conspicuous Gallantry Medal
CH   Companion of Honour
CHP   Combined Heat and Power
CIA   Central Intelligence Agency
CICB   Criminal Injuries Compensation Board
CID   Criminal Investigations Department
CIS   Commonwealth of Independent States (former Soviet republics)
CITES   Convention on International Trade in Endangered Species

CIWF   Compassion In World Farming
CLA   Country Landowners' Association
CM   Chirurgiae Magister (Master of Surgery)
CMEA   Council for Mutual Economic Assistance
CND   Campaign for Nuclear Disarmament
CNN   Cable News Network
COBOL   COmmon Business-Oriented Language
COD   Cash On Delivery
COI   Central Office of Information
COMECON   COuncil for Mutual ECONomic aid / assistance
COMINTERN   COMmunist INTERNational
CPRE   Council for the Protection of Rural England
CPS   Crown Prosecution Service
CPSA   Civil and Public Services Association
CRE   Commission for Racial Equality
CS (gas)   Carson and Staughton
CSA   Child Support Agency
CSO   Central Statistical Office
CTO   Cancelled To Order (Philately)
CTT   Capital Transfer Tax
CURE   Care, Understanding, REsearch
CVD   Compact Video Disc
CVO   Commander of the Royal Victorian Order
CVP   Climate, Vegetation and Productivity
CWU   Communication Workers' Union

DA   District Attorney
DAGMAR   Defining Advertising Goals for Measured Advertising Results
D & C   Dilatation and Curettage
DAR   Daughters of the American Revolution
DAT   Digital Audio Tape
DBE   Dame Commander of the Order of the British Empire
DBS   Direct Broadcasting by Satellite
DC   Direct Current; District of Columbia
DCL   Doctor of Civil Law
DCM   Distinguished Conduct Medal
DCMG   Dame Commander of the Order of St Michael and St George
DD   Doctor of Divinity
DDS   Doctor of Dental Surgery
DDT   DichloroDiphenylTrichloroethane
DERV   Diesel-Engined-Road Vehicle
DFC   Distinguished Flying Cross
DFM   Distinguished Flying Medal
DINKY   Double Income No Kids Yet
DipSW   Diploma in Social Work
DLitt   Doctor of Letters
DLR   Docklands Light Railway
DNA   DeoxyriboNucleic Acid
DORA   Defence Of the Realm Act (1914)
DOS   Disc Operating System
DSA   Driving Standards Agency
DSC   Distinguished Service Cross
DSM   Distinguished Service Medal
DSO   Distinguished Service Order
DSS   Department of Social Security
DTP   Desk-Top Publishing
DVM   Doctor of Veterinary Medicine
DWI   Drinking Water Inspectorate
DWT   Denarius WeighT (pennyweight); Dead Weight Tonnage

ECG   ElectroCardioGram / Graph
ECGD   Export Credit Guarantee Department
ECO   English Chamber Orchestra
ECSC   European Coal and Steel Community
ECT   Electro-Convulsive Therapy
ECU   European Currency Unit
EDM   Early Day Motion
EDP   Electronic Data Processing
EEC   European Economic Community
EEG   ElectroEncephaloGram / Graph
EFA   European Fighter Aircraft
EFTA   European Free Trade Association
e.g.   exempli gratia (for example)
EHF   Extremely High Frequency
EIB   European Investment Bank
EIS   Educational Institute of Scotland
EMF   Electro-Motive Force; European Monetary Fund
EMI   Electro-Magnetic Interference
EMS   European Monetary System
EMU   ElectroMagnetic Unit; European Monetary Union
ENEA   European Nuclear Energy Agency
ENG   Electronic News Gathering
ENO   English National Opera
ENSA   Entertainments National Service Association
ENT   Ear, Nose and Throat
EOC   Equal Opportunities Commission
EPCOT   Experimental Prototype Community Of Tomorrow
ER   Elizabeth Regina
ERA   Engine Room Artificer (navy)
ERM   Exchange Rate Mechanism
ERNIE   Electronic Random Number Indicator Equipment
ESA   European Space Agency
ESF   European Social Fund
ESP   ExtraSensory Perception
ESSO   Standard Oil
et seq.   et sequentia (and the following)
ETA   Estimated Time of Arrival; Euzkadi Ta Askatasuna (Basque separatist organisation)
ETD   Estimated Time of Departure
EU   European Union
EWCB   England and Wales Cricket Board

FANY   First Aid Nursing Yeomanry
FAO   Food and Agriculture Organisation
Fax   Facsimile transmission
FBI   Federal Bureau of Investigation
FBOU   Fellow of the British Ornithologists' Union
FGS   Fellow of the Geographical Society
FHS   Fellow of the Heraldry Society
FIA   Fellow of the Institute of Actuaries
FICE   Fellow of the Institution of Civil Engineers
FIFA   Fédération Internationale de Football Association
FIRST   Fixed Interest Rate Savings Tax free
FMCG   Fast Moving Consumer Goods
FOIA   Freedom Of Information Act
FOREST   Freedom Organisation for the Right to Enjoy Smoking Tobacco
FORTRAN   Formula Translation
FRAM   Fellow of the Royal Academy of Music
FRAS   Fellow of the Royal Astronomical Society
FRBS   Fellow of the Royal Botanical Society

FRCGP   Fellow of the Royal College of General Practitioners
FRCM   Fellow of the Royal College of Music
FRCOG   Fellow of the Royal College of Obstetricians and Gynaecologists
FRCP   Fellow of the Royal College of Physicians
FRHS   Fellow of the Royal Horticultural Society
FTSE   Financial Times Stock Exchange

GAA   Gaelic Athletic Association
GATT   General Agreement on Tariffs and Trade
GBE   Knight or Dame Grand Cross of the Order of the British Empire
GC   George Cross
GCB   Knight or Dame Grand Cross of the Order of the Bath
GCHQ   Government Communications Headquarters
GCSE   General Certificate of Secondary Education
GCVO   Knight or Dame Grand Cross of the Royal Victorian Order
GDBA   Guide Dogs for the Blind Association
GDP   Gross Domestic Product
Gestapo   GEheime STAatsPOlizei
GIFT   Gamete IntraFallopian Transfer
GMB   Grand Master Bowman
GNP   Gross National Product
GNVQ   General National Vocational Qualification
GPMU   Graphical, Paper and Media Union
GPS   Global Positioning System
GRAS   Generally Regarded As Safe
GRU   Glavnoye Razvedyvatelnoye Upravleniye (Military counterpart of KGB)

HB   Hard Black (pencil)
HBM   Her / His Britannic Majesty
HCF   Highest Common Factor
HDRA   Henry Doubleday Research Association (Gardening)
HDTV   High-Definition TeleVision
HGV   Heavy Goods Vehicle
HJ   Hic Jacet (here lies, seen on gravestones)
HOLMES   Home Office Large Major Enquiry System (police computer system)
HMSO   Her / His Majesty's Stationery Office
HRH   Her/His Royal Highness
HSH   Her / His Serene Highness
HSV   Herpes Simplex Virus
HWM   High Water Mark

IATA   International Air Transport Association
ib.   ibidem (in the same place)
IBA   International Broadcasting Authority
ibid.   Ibidem (in the same place)
ICAEW   Institute of Chartered Accountants of England and Wales
ICAO   International Civil Aviation Organisation
ICBM   InterContinental Balistic Missile
IDDS   Insulin Dependent Diabetic Syndrome
i.e.   id est (that is)
IFAW   International Fund for Animal Welfare
IFOR   Implementation FORce
IFS   Institute for Fiscal Studies
IGC   Inter-Governmental Conference
ILO   International Labour Organisation
IMO   International Maritime Organisation

INRI Iesus Nazarenus Rex Iudaeorum (Jesus of Nazareth King of the Jews)
INSET INSErvice Training
INTERPOL INTERnational Criminal POLice Organisation
IOM Isle Of Man
IOW Isle Of Wight
IPA International Phonetic Alphabet
IQ Intelligence Quotient
IRS Internal Revenue Service
IRSF Inland Revenue Staff Federation
ITA Initial Teaching Alphabet
ITC Independent Television Commission
ITU International Telecommunications Union
ITV Independent TeleVision
IVF In Vitro Fertilisation
IWC International Whaling Commission

J & B Justerni and Brooks
JCR Junior Common Room
JCS Joint Chiefs of Staff
JPL Jet Propulsion Laboratory
JRDF Joint Rapid Deployment Force

KBE Knight Commander of the Order of the British Empire
KCVO Knight Commander of the Royal Victorian Order
KG Knight of the Order of the Garter
KGB Komitet Gosudarstvennoi Bezopasnosti (State Security Committee)
KT Knight of the Order of the Thistle

LACS League Against Cruel Sports
LAN Local Area Net (computer Internet)
LASER Light Amplification by Stimulated Emission of Radiation
LAUTRO Life Assurance and Unit Trust Regulatory Organisation
LBO Leveraged BuyOut
LCE London Commodities Exchange
LCJ Lord Chief Justice
LCM Lowest Common Multiple
LDOS Lords Day Observance Society
LDV Local Defence Volunteers (Home Guard)
LIDAR Light Detection And Ranging
LIFFE London International Financial Futures and options Exchange
LIFT London International Festival Theatre
LLD Doctor of Laws
LMS / LMSR London, Midland and Scottish Railway
LNER London and North Eastern Railway
LORAN Long Range Navigation
LSD Librae Solidi Denarii; LySergic Acid Diethylamide
LSE London School of Economics
LSO London Symphony Orchestra
LWM Low Water Mark

M & B May and Baker (forerunner of antibiotics)
MADD Mothers Against Drunk Driving
MAFF Ministry of Agriculture Fisheries and Food
MANWEB Merseyside And North Wales Electricity Board
MASER Microwave Amplification by Stimulated Emission of Radiation

MBA Master of Business Administration
MBE Member of the Order of the British Empire
MBO Management BuyOut
MCC Marylebone Cricket Club
MCS Marine Conservation Society
ME Myalgic Encephalomyelitis (see CFS)
MEP Member of the European Parliament
MFH Master of Fox Hounds
MFN Most Favoured Nation
M. ft. mistura fiat (let a mixture be made)
MIDAS Missile Defence Alarm System
MIG Mortgage Indemnity Guarantee
MIPS Millions of Instructions Per Second
MIRAS Mortgage Income Relief At Source
MIRV Multiple Independently targeted Re-entry Vehicle
MIT Massachusetts Institute of Technology
MKS Metre Kilogram Second
MLR Minimum Lending Rate
MM Messieurs; Military Medal
MNR Marine Nature Reserve
MOMA Museum Of Modern Art
MOMI Museum Of Moving Image
MORI Market and Opinion Research Institute
MP Member of Parliament
MPLA Movimento Popular de Libertação de Angola (Popular Movement for the Liberation of Angola)
MPV Multi-Purpose Vehicle
MSF Manufacturing, Science and Finance (Union)
MSP Member of Scottish Parliament
MST Mountain Standard Time
MWGM Most Worthy Grand Master (Masons)

NAACP National Association for the Advancement of Colored People
NAAFI Navy, Army, and Air Force Institutes
NACODS National Association of Colliery Overmen, Deputies and Shotfirers
NACRO National Association for the Care and Resettlement of Offenders
NAO National Audit Office
NARAS National Academy of Recording Arts and Sciences
NASA National Aeronautics and Space Administration
NATO North Atlantic Treaty Organisation
NB Nota Bene (note well)
NBC National Broadcasting Company
NBL National Book League
NCCL National Council for Civil Liberties
NCDL National Canine Defence League
NCIS National Criminal Intelligence Service
NCVO National Council for Voluntary Organisations
NCVQ National Council for Vocational Qualifications
NEDC National Economic Development Council (Neddy)
NFT National Film Theatre
NFU National Farmers' Union
NGA National Graphical Association (now merged with SOGAT to form GPMU)
NHI National Health Insurance
NIDDS Non-Insulin-Dependent Diabetic Syndrome
NIMBY Not In My Back Yard
NIREX Nuclear Industry Radioactive waste EXecutive

NORWICH   (K)Nickers Off Ready When I Come Home
NP   Notary Public
NPT   Non-Proliferation Treaty
NRA   National Rifle Association; National Rivers Authority
NSPCC   National Society for the Prevention of Cruelty to Children
NUCPS   National Union of Civil and Public Servants
NUJ   National Union of Journalists
NUMAST   National Union of Marine, Aviation and Shipping Transport Officers
NUS   National Union of Students
NUT   National Union of Teachers
NYO   National Youth Orchestra
NYT   National Youth Theatre

O & M   Organisation and Method
OAPEC   Organisation of Arab Petroleum-Exporting Countries
OAS   Organisation of American States
OAU   Organisation of African Unity
OBE   Officer of the Order of the British Empire; Out-of-Body Experience
OBO   Ore Bulk Oil (carrier)
OECD   Organisation for Economic Co-operation and Development
OED   Oxford English Dictionary
OFFER   OFFice of Electricity Regulation
OFGAS   OFfice of GAS Supply
OFSTED   OFfice for STandards in EDucation
OFTEL   OFfice of TELecommunications
OFWAT   Office of Water Services
OHMS   On Her / His Majesty's Service
OM   Order of Merit
OMOV   One Member One Vote
OPCS   Office of Population Censuses and Surveys
OPEC   Organisation of Petroleum-Exporting Countries
OS   Old Style; Ordnance Survey
OST   Office of Science and Technology
OUDS   Oxford University Dramatic Society
OXFAM   OXford Committee for FAMine Relief
Oxon   Oxoniencis (of Oxford)

P & O   Peninsular and Oriental Steamship Company
PACE   Police And Criminal Evidence act
parSec   parallax second (3.26 light-years)
PAS   Power-Assisted Steering
PAYE   Pay As You Earn
PBX   Private Branch eXchange
PCA   Police Complaints Authority
PCB   Printed Circuit Board
PDSA   People's Dispensary for Sick Animals
PCP   Personal Equity Plan
pH   potential of Hydrogen ions
PIA   Personal Investment Authority (replaced LAUTRO)
PIN   Personal Identification Number
PLA   Port of London Authority
PLC   Public Limited Company
PLO   Palestine Liberation Organisation
PLR   Public Lending Rights
PMT   Pre-Menstrual Tension
PNMPB   Police National Missing Persons Bureau

POS   Point Of Sale
POW   Prisoner Of War
PP   Per Procurationem (by proxy)
PPS   Parliamentary Private Secretary
PPV   Pay Per View
pro tem.   pro tempore (for the time being)
PROM   Programmable Read Only Memory
PRP   Profit-Related Pay
PRS   Performing Rights Society
PS   Post Scriptum
PSBR   Public Sector Borrowing Requirement
PSDR   Public Sector Debt Repayment
PSV   Public Service Vehicle
PTI   Physical Training Instructor
PTSD   Post-Traumatic Stress Disorder
PVC   PolyVinylChloride

QANTAS   Queensland And Northern Territory Aerial Service
QARANC   Queen Alexandra's Royal Army Nursing Corps
QARNNS   Queen Alexandra's Royal Naval Nursing Service
QBD   Queen's Bench Division
QC   Queen's Counsel
QED   Quod Erat Demonstrandum (which was to be demonstrated)
QGM   Queen's Gallantry Medal
QMG   QuarterMaster General
QMV   Qualified Majority Voting
QPM   Queen's Police Medal
QSO   Quasi-Stellar Object (quaser)
QUANGO   QUasi-Autonomous Non-Governmental Organisation
qv   quod vide (which see)

RAC   Royal Automobile Club
RADA   Royal Academy of Dramatic Art
RAEC   Royal Army Educational Corps
RAFVR   Royal Air Force Voluntary Reserve
RAM   Random-Access Memory
RAMC   Royal Army Medical Corps
RAOC   Royal Army Ordnance Corps
RBA   Royal Society of British Artists
RCA   Radio Corporation of America
RCM   Royal College of Music
RCMP   Royal Canadian Mounted Police
RCN   Royal College of Nursing
REM   Rapid Eye Movement
REME   Royal Electrical and Mechanical Engineers
RFA   Royal Fleet Auxiliary
RFDS   Royal Flying Doctor Service
RH   Relative Humidity
RHA   Regional Health Authority
RHS   Royal Historical / Horticultural / Humane Society
RKO   Radio-Keith-Orpheum
RMT   (National Union of) Rail, Maritime and Transport Workers
RNA   RiboNucleic Acid
RNAS   Royal Naval Air Service
RNIB   Royal National Institute for the Blind
RNID   Royal National Institute for the Deaf
RNLI   Royal National Lifeboat Institution
RNR   Royal Naval Reserve

ROC Royal Observer Corps
ROI Return On Investment
ROM Read-Only Memory
ROSPA ROyal Society for the Prevention of Accidents
RP Received Pronunciation
RPI Retail Price Index
RSI Repetitive Stress Injury
RSPB Royal Society for the Protection of Birds
RSPCA Royal Society for the Prevention of Cruelty to Animals
RSV Revised Standard Version (Bible)
RSVP Répondez S'il Vous Plaît
RTE Radio Telefis Eireann
RTS Royal Television Society
RTZ Rio Tinto Zinc Corporation Ltd
RUC Royal Ulster Constabulary
RYS Royal Yacht Squadron

SA Sociedad Anónima (Spanish: limited company); Société Anonyme (French: limited company)
SAD Seasonal Affective Disorder
SAFE Saving Animals From Extinction
SALT Strategic Arms Limitation Talks
SANE Schizophrenia – A National Emergency
SAS Special Air Service
SATB Soprano, Alto, Tenor, Bass
SBS Special Boat Squadron; Sick Building Syndrome
SCM State Certified Midwife
SCO Scottish Chamber Orchestra
SCR Senior Common Room
SCREAM Society for the Control and Registration of Estate Agents and Mortgage brokers
SCUBA Self-Contained Underwater Breathing Apparatus
SDA Severe Disability Allowance
SDI Strategic Defence Initiative
SDLP Social Democratic and Labour Party
SDP Social Democratic Party
SEA Single European Act
SEC Securities Exchange Commission
SEN Special Educational Needs; State Enrolled Nurse
SERPS State Earnings-Related Pension Scheme
SETI Search for Extra-Terrestrial Intelligence
SFO Serious Fraud Office
SHAPE Supreme Headquarters Allied Powers in Europe
SHF Super High Frequency
SI Système International (of units)
SIB Securities and Investments Board
SIG Special Interest Group
SJ Society of Jesus (Jesuits)
SLBM Submarine-Launched Ballistic Missile
SLDP Social and Liberal Democratic Party
SMMT Society of Motor Manufacturers and Traders
SNAFU Situation Normal All Fouled / Fucked Up
SNCF Société Nationale des Chemins de Fer français
SOGAT Society Of Graphical and Allied Trades (now merged with NGA to form GPMU)
SONAR SOund Navigation And Ranging
SOWETO SOuth WEstern TOwnships (South Africa)
SP Sine Prole (without issue)

SPCK Society for Promoting Christian Knowledge
SPF Sun Protection Factor
SPG Special Patrol Group
SPQR Senatus PopulusQue Romanus (the Senate and People of Rome)
SRA Squash Rackets Association
SRN State Registered Nurse
SS SchutzStaffel
SSP Statutory Sick Pay
SST SuperSonic Travel
START STrategic Arms Reduction Talks
STD Subscriber Trunk Dialling; Sexually Transmitted Disease
STOL Short TakeOff and Landing
STRIVE Society for The Preservation of Rural Industrial and Village Enterprises
STROBE Satellite TRacking Of Balloons and Emergencies
STV Single Transferable Vote
SWALK Sealed With A Loving Kiss
SWAPO South West African People's Organisation
SWAT Special Weapons And Tactics

TAMBA Twins And Multiple Births Association
TASS Technical, Administrative and Supervisory Section (of AUEW); Telegrafnoye Agentsvo Sovetshkovo Soyuza (news agency)
TAURUS Transfer and AUtomated Registration of Uncertified Stock
TAVR Territorial and Army Volunteer Reserve
TAVRA Territorial Auxiliary and Volunteer Reserve Association
TBA To Be Advised / Agreed / Announced / Arranged
TCCB Test and County Cricket Board
TEC Training and Enterprise Corporation
TELEX TELeprinter EXchange
TES Times Educational Supplement
TGWU Transport and General Workers Union
TIFF Tag Image File Format (computing)
TIROS Television and InfraRed Observation Satellite
TLR Twin Lens Reflex
TLS Times Literary Supplement
TM Transcendental Meditation
TNT TriNitroToluene
Toc H Talbot House (Christian aid organisation)
TT Tuberculin Tested; Tourist Trophy
TUC Trades Union Congress
TVP Textured Vegetable Protein

UAE United Arab Emirates
UCATT Union of Construction, Allied Trades and Technicians
UCCA Universities Central Council on Admissions
UCLA University of California Los Angeles
UDC Urban Development Corporation (e.g. Docklands) Urban District Council
UDI Unilateral Declaration of Independence
UDM Union of Democratic Mineworkers
UDP United Democratic Party
UDR Ulster Defence Regiment
UEFA Union of European Football Associations
UFC Universities' Funding Council
UFO Unidentified Flying Object
UGC University Grants Committee
UHT Ultra High Temperature Ultra Heat Treatment

UKAEA   United Kingdom Atomic Energy Authority
ULCC   Ultra Large Crude Carrier
ULTRA   Unrelated Live Transplant Regulatory Authority
UMIST   University of Manchester Institute of Science and Technology
UNCTAD   United Nations Conference on Trade And Development
UNESCO   United Nations Educational, Scientific and Cultural Organisation
UNHCR   United Nations High Commission for Refugees
UNICEF   United Nations Children's Fund
UNITA   União Nacional para a Independencia Total de Angola (National Union for the Total Independence of Angola)
UNITAR   United Nations Institute for Training And Research
UNPROFOR   United Nations Protection Force
UNRRA   United Nations Relief and Rehabilitation Administration
UPC   Universal Product Code
UPU   Universal Postal Union
USDAW   Union of Shop, Distributive and Allied Workers
USSR   Union of Soviet Socialist Republics

VASCAR   Visual Average Speed Computer And Recorder
VC   Victoria Cross
VDU   Video Display Unit
VHF   Very High Frequency
VHS   Video Home System
vix.   vixit (she / he lived)
viz.   videlicet (namely)
VOD   Video On Demand
VR   Virtual Reality
VRY   ViceRoY
VSO   Voluntary Service Overseas
VSOP   Very Special Old Pale
VTOL   Vertical TakeOff and Landing

WAN   Wide Area Net (computer Internet)
WASP   White Anglo-Saxon Protestant
WCC   World Council of Churches
WDCS   Whales and Dolphins Conservation Society

WEA   Workers' Educational Association
WEU   Western European Union
WFP   World Food Programme
WFTU   World Federation of Trade Unions
WHAM   Winning Hearts And Minds (Vietnam propaganda slogan)
WHO   World Health Organisation
WIBF   Women's International Boxing Federation
WIMP   Windows Icons Menus Pointing (computing); Weakly Interacting Massive Particle
WMO   World Meteorological Organisation
WOMAN   World Organisation for Mothers of All Nations
WORM   Write Once Read Many (times)
WPBSA   World Professional Billiards and Snooker Association
WRAC   Women's Royal Army Corps
WRAF   Women's Royal Air Force
WRNS   Women's Royal Naval Service
WRP   Worker's Revolutionary Party
WRVS   Women's Royal Voluntary Service
WSPA   World Society for the Protection of Animals
WTO   World Trade Organisation
WVS   Women's Voluntary Service
WWF   World Wide Fund for Nature (formerly World Wildlife Fund)
WWW   World Weather Watch; World Wide Web
WYSIWYG   What You See Is What You Get

YCNAC   Young Conservative National Advisory Committee
YHA   Youth Hostels Association
YMCA   Young Men's Christian Association
YOC   Young Ornithologists' Club
YUPPIE   Young Upwardly mobile / Urban Professional
YWCA   Young Women's Christian Association

ZANU   Zimbabwe African National Union
ZAPU   Zimbabwe African People's Union
ZEBRA   Zero-Energy Breeder-Reactor Assembly
ZEG   Zero Economic Growth
ZENITH   Zero-Energy NITrogen-Heated thermal reactor
ZPG   Zero Population Growth

ABBREVIATIONS

ARCHITECTURE

Famous Architects

Aalto, Alvar (1898–1976) Finnish architect and designer whose work included the Hall of Residence, Massachusetts Institute of Technology, the Finlandia Concert Hall, Helsinki and Nordic Centre in Reykjavik. He also invented bent plywood furniture in 1932.

Abercrombie, (Sir) Patrick (1879–1957) English architect and pioneer of town planning in Britain, brother of the poet Lascelles Abercrombie. His major work was the replanning of London (County of London Plan, 1943, and Greater London Plan, 1944).

Adam, Robert (1728–92) Scottish architect and interior designer, leader of the British Neo-Classical revival. Famous works include the interiors of Harewood House, Luton Hoo, Syon House and Osterley Park. He worked with his brother James Adam, on the Adelphi near Charing Cross, largely rebuilt in 1936.

Barry, (Sir) Charles (1795–1860) British architect of the Neo-Gothic Houses of Parliament (1840–60) which was completed after his death by his son Edward Middleton Barry. Other works included the church of St Peter, Brighton; Travellers' Club, Pall Mall; the Reform Club, London; King Edward's School, Birmingham, and the Manchester Athenaeum. His fifth son Sir John Wolfe-Barry (1836–1918) was engineer of Tower Bridge and Barry Docks.

Bramante, Donato (1444–1514) Italian High Renaissance architect, born near Urbano. Designed the new Basilica of St Peter's as well as the Belvedere courtyard, the Tempietto di S Pietro in Montorio and the Palazzo Caprini.

Brown, Lancelot (1716–83) English landscape-gardener and architect, nicknamed 'Capability' due to his stock reply to clients that their gardens had 'excellent capabilities'. Works include the gardens at Blenheim, Kew, Stowe, and Warwick Castle.

Brunel, Isambard Kingdom (1806–59) English engineer and inventor, born in Portsmouth, son of Sir Marc Isambard Brunel. His numerous works include the original Thames Tunnel, Clifton and Hungerford Suspension Bridges, and the Saltash Bridge over the Tamar. His ship designs include the *Great Western* (1838), the *Great Britain* (1845) and the *Great Eastern*, in collaboration with John Scott Russell.

Chambers, (Sir) William (1723–96) Swedish-born, Scottish architect. He popularised Chinese influence (Kew Garden pagoda) and designed Somerset House, London (1776).

Cockerell, Charles Robert (1788–1863) English architect, son of Samuel Pepys Cockerell. He designed the Taylorian Institute at Oxford, Fitzwilliam Museum at Cambridge, and Ashmolean Museum, Oxford.

Foster, Norman (Lord Foster of Thames Bank) (1935–) British architect of the high-tech school. His best-known buildings include the Willis Faber office, Ipswich (1975), the Sainsbury Centre for the visual arts, Norwich (1978), and the Hong Kong and Shanghai Bank, Hong Kong (1986).

Fuller, Richard Buckminster (1895–1983) American architect who invented the Geodesic Dome. Examples of his works are at the Union Tank Car Repair Shop, Louisiana (1958), and the US Pavilion, Montreal Exhibition (1967).

Gaudí, Antonio (1852–1926) Spanish architect, noted for his flamboyant style. His work on the Church of the Holy Family in Barcelona begun in 1883 was unfinished at his death.

Gibbs, James (1682–1754) Scottish Neo-Classical architect whose works include St Martin-in-the-Fields, London (1722), and the Radcliffe Camera, Oxford (1737).

Hawksmoor, Nicholas (1661–1736) English architect born in Nottingham. He designed many London churches including St George's, Bloomsbury, and Christ Church, Spitalfields. Assisted Vanbrugh at Blenheim Palace and Castle Howard and was clerk to Wren.

Jones, Inigo (1573–1652) English architect, born in London. The founder of Classical English architecture whose innovations include the introduction of the proscenium arch and movable scenery to the English stage. In 1616 he designed the Queen's House at Greenwich. Other commissions included the rebuilding of the Banqueting Hall at Whitehall, the nave and transepts and a large Corinthian portico of old St Paul's, Marlborough Chapel, the Double-Cube room at Wilton, and possibly the York Water Gate. Jones also laid out Covent Garden and Lincoln's Inn Fields.

Lasdun, (Sir) Denys Louis (1914–) English architect whose works include the Royal College of Physicians, London; University of East Anglia, Norwich; National Theatre, London; and the European Investment Bank in Luxembourg.

Le Corbusier (1887–1965) Pseudonym of Charles Édouard Jeanneret, Swiss-born French architect, famous for his proclamation that the house is a habitable machine to be designed to functional criteria. His works include the Palace of the Nations, Geneva; and Cité Radieuse, Marseilles; as well as the town plan for Chandigarh, India.

Lutyens, (Sir) Edwin Landseer (1869–1944) English architect whose designs ranged from the picturesque of his early country houses, including Marsh Court, Stockbridge, and the restoration of Lindisfarne Castle, which owed much to the Arts and Crafts movement, to those in the Renaissance style such as Heathcote, Ilkley and Salutation, Sandwich. He finally evolved a classical style exhibited in the Cenotaph, Whitehall, which reached its height in his design – never built – for Liverpool Roman Catholic Cathedral. Other works include the Viceroy's House, New Delhi and the British Embassy in Washington.

Mackintosh, Charles Rennie (1868–1928) Scottish architect, designer, and water colourist. Outstanding exponent of the Art Nouveau style in Scotland. Born in Glasgow, the son of a police superintendent, he married Margaret Mackintosh in 1900. His output included the Glasgow School of Art, Cranston tearooms, and houses such as Hill House in Helensburgh. By the end of World War I he had given up architecture for a career in water colours, mainly in France.

Mies Van Der Rohe, Ludwig (1886–1969) German-born, American architect, born in Aachen. A pioneer of glass skyscrapers and high-rise flats, he also designed tubular-steel furniture, particularly the 'Barcelona Chair'. Became professor of architecture at the Illinois Institute of Technology in Chicago and designed two glass apartment towers on Lake Shore Drive, and the Seagram Building in New York. He also designed the Washington DC Public Library and two art galleries in Berlin.

Nash, John (1752–1835)　British architect who designed Regent's Park and its terraces, Regent Street and Marble Arch. He also recreated Buckingham Palace from old Buckingham House and rebuilt Brighton Pavilion in oriental style. Trafalgar Square and St James' Park were also laid out by Nash.

Paxton, (Sir) Joseph (1801–65)　British architect and garden superintendent to the Duke of Devonshire. By far his most famous work was the design of the Great Exhibition Building of 1851, the Crystal Palace, the first example of a prefabricated industrialised building on a large scale.

Pei, Ieoh Meng (1917–)　Chinese born, American architect whose works included the John Hancock Tower, Boston; the Mile High Center, Denver and the glass pyramid at the Louvre.

Rogers, Richard (Lord Rogers of Riverside) (1933–)　Florence-born, British architect whose works include the Pompidou Centre in Paris (1977) and the Lloyd's building, London (1986). Founder member with Norman Foster and their wives of 'Team 4'.

Saarinen, Eero (1910–61)　Finnish-born, American architect whose works include the American Embassy in London, and Dulles Airport near Wasington DC.

Scott, (Sir) George Gilbert (1811–78)　English architect, born in Gawcott, Bucks. His works include the Albert Memorial, St Pancras station, and the Episcopal Cathedral in Edinburgh.

Scott, (Sir) Giles Gilbert (1880–1960)　English architect, grandson of Sir George Gilbert Scott. Won a competition in 1903 for the design of the Anglican Cathedral in Liverpool (consecrated 1924). Other works include the new Bodleian Library at Oxford and the new Cambridge University Library. He also planned the new Waterloo Bridge and was responsible for the rebuilding of the House of Commons after World War II.

Shaw, Norman (1831–1912)　English architect born in Edinburgh. Worked with his partner William Eden Nesfield (1835–88) in many styles ranging from Gothic Revival to Neo-Baroque, but became an acknowledged leader in the trend away from the Victorian style back to traditional Georgian design, leading to the English Domestic Revival. His major

buildings include the Old Swan House, Chelsea (1876), New Scotland Yard (1888), the Gaiety Theatre, Aldwych (1902, now demolished), and Piccadilly Hotel (1905). He also designed the garden suburb at Bedford Park, London

Smirke, (Sir) Robert (1781–1867)　English architect, son of Robert Smirke (1752–1845) the painter and book illustrator. His works (destroyed) in London include Covent Garden Theatre, British Museum, King's College and the Royal College of Physicians.

Soane, (Sir) John (1753–1837)　English architect, born near Reading, the son of a mason. His works included the Bank of England, the Dulwich Picture Gallery and his own house in Lincoln's Inn Fields, London which he bequeathed to the nation.

Spence, (Sir) Basil Urwin (1907–76)　Scottish architect, born in India. His works include the conversions at Queen's College, Cambridge; the pavilions for the Festival of Britain and the British Embassy in Rome. His best-known work is his prize design for the new Coventry Cathedral (1951)

Tange, Kenzo (1913–)　Japanese architect who designed the National Gymnasium for the Tokyo Olympics and the city plan for the new Nigerian capital of Abuja (completed 1986).

Vanbrugh, (Sir) John (1664–1726)　English playwright and Baroque architect, born in London, the son of a tradesman. Educated in France and commissioned into Lord Huntingdon's regiment, he suffered imprisonment in the Bastille as a suspected spy. His major architectural work was Blenheim Palace at Woodstock, Oxfordshire, which was so disliked by the Duchess of Marlborough that she refused to pay him for some time.

Wren, Christopher (1632–1723)　Wren was educated at Westminster School and Wadham College, Oxford, and became a fellow of All Souls, Oxford. He became professor of astronomy at Gresham College, London, 1657, before returning to Oxford to take up a similar position. The chapel at Pembroke College, Cambridge, 1663, was the first design of Wren's to be built and later that year he began designs for Sheldonian Theatre at Oxford. Following the Great Fire he designed over 50 London churches including St Paul's (1675–1710). Other works included the Ashmolean Museum at Oxford, Chelsea Hospital, Greenwich Observatory, parts of Hampton Court Palace, Royal Exchange, and parts of the Royal Naval College, Greenwich. Wren was a founder of the Royal Society, was knighted in 1673, and became MP for Plympton in 1685, Windsor in 1689, and finally, Weymouth in 1701.

A
R
C
H
I
T
E
C
T
U
R
E

Architectural Terms

Acanthus　Conventionalised acanthus leaf used to decorate Corinthian and Composite capitals

Architrave　Lowest part of an entablature, resting immediately upon the abacus (flat slab) on the capital of a column. The term also describes the moulding around the exterior of an arch or the various parts surrounding a door or window

Bauhaus　German school of architecture and design founded by Walter Gropius in 1919 and closed in 1933

Brickwork: **Types**　English Bond: Bricklaying with

alternate courses of headers and stretchers. Flemish Bond: Bricklaying with courses of alternate headers and stretcher. Monk Bond: Bricklaying with courses alternating with pairs of stretchers

Buildings, New　Bridgewater Hall, Manchester: International concert hall opened in September 1996. Experimental Office Building for Building Research Establishment, Garston, near Watford, Herts: latest addition to the BRE site. River and Rowing Museum, Henley, Oxfordshire: opened in 1997. St Barnabas Church, Dulwich, London:

rebuilding of Victorian church destroyed by fire in 1992. Waterfront Hall, Lanyon Place, Laganside Belfast: conference centre opened Jan 17th 1997

Buttress   Structure of wood, stone or brick built against a wall to strengthen or support it

Campanile   A free-standing bell-tower

Capital   Head of a column, usually featuring mouldings or carvings

Cartouche   Scroll-shaped ornament or corbel. Term also describes a tablet representing a scroll with rolled-up ends or edges, with or without an inscription

Caryatid   Female figure used as a pillar to support an entablature

Column   Tall, often slightly tapering, cylinder usually surmounted by an entablature and forming part of an arcade or colonnade, or standing alone as a monument

Console   Ornamental flat-sided bracket or corbel, usually incorporating a volute at each end

Corbel   Projection of stone or timber jutting out from a wall to support weight

Cornice   Horizontal, usually moulded projection crowning the outside of a building or structure, especially the uppermost part of an entablature, above the frieze. Term also applies to an ornamental moulding running round the wall of a room near the ceiling

Cupola   Rounded vault or dome forming part of a roof of a building. Term also describes the ceiling of a dome

Dado   The plain portion of a pedestal between the base and the cornice. Term also describes the lower part of an interior wall when faced or coloured differently from the upper part

Dome: Geodesic   Invented by Richard Buckminster Fuller, the geodesic dome built with lightweight rods arranged as linked hexagons, is the only practical kind of building that has no limiting dimensions, i.e. beyond which the structural strength must be insufficient

Fanlight   Fan-shaped window over a door or other window

Flying Buttress   Buttress, usually on an arch, which slants upwards to a wall from a pier or other support

Gargoyle   Grotesque carving, usually in the form of a human or real or fantastic animal mouth, head, or body, projecting from the gutter of a building, especially in Gothic architecture, and used as a spout to drain off rainwater

Gazebo   Building or structure that commands a view, i.e. a summer-house or balcony

Gothic   Style of architecture prevalent in western Europe from the 12th to the 16th century, of which familiar features include the pointed arch and the flying buttress

Greek Orders   The three original classical orders of architecture, i.e. Doric, Ionic, and Corinthian

Groin   The edge formed by the intersection of two vaults. Term also describes an arch supporting a vault

Hypocaust   Hollow space under the floor where hot air was sent from a furnace to provide heating in Roman houses

Keystone   The wedge-shaped block or central voussoir at the summit of an arch built of stone

Kouros   Sculptured representation of a youth on Ionic architecture

Lancet   High, narrow window with a lancet arch

Lancet Arch   An arch with a head resembling the blade of a lancet (surgical knife)

Mansard   Roof in which each face has two slopes, the lower one steeper than the upper

Mezzanine   Low storey between two others in a building, usually between the ground floor and the floor above. Term also describes the floor beneath the stage in a theatre, from which the traps are worked

Mullion   Vertical bar dividing the lights in a window, especially in Gothic architecture

Niche   An artificially constructed wall recess often holding a statue or urn

Ogee   Moulding consisting of a continuous double curve, especially with the upper part concave and the lower part convex

Ogee Arch   An arch formed by two contrasted ogees which meet at its apex, often called a pointed or Gothic arch

Ogive   The diagonal groin or rib of a vault, two of which cross each other at the vault's centre; or any pointed arch

Oriel   Porch or balcony at the head of an outdoor staircase

Oriel Window   Large polygonal recess with a window, projecting from upper storey of a building, and supported from the ground or on corbels

Pediment   Triangular part crowning the front of a building in the classical style, usually situated over a portico and consisting of a flat recessed field, framed by a cornice and often ornamented with sculptures

Pier   Solid support designed to sustain vertical pressure, e.g. a doorpost or gatepost; also a massive supporting column, holding up a nave or a bridge

Portico   Formal entrance to a classical temple, church, or other building, consisting of columns at regular intervals supporting a roof often in the form of a pediment, a covered walkway

Porticus   Addition on north or south side of a church of the Anglo-Saxon period, resembling an aisle or transept and containing a chapel

Purlin   Horizontal beam along the length of a roof, resting on principals (pairs of angled supporting beams that meet at the top) and supporting the common rafters

Rib   A curved member supporting a vault or defining its form. The term also describes the curved pieces of stone, timber or metal strips forming the framework of a dome or the arched or flat beam or girder supporting a bridge

Roman Orders   The two classical orders of architecture, i.e. Tuscan and Composite, which were added to the earlier Greek orders

Rotunda   Building with a circular interior and plan, especially one with a dome, e.g. the Pantheon in Rome

Rustication   Style of masonry in which the surface of the blocks is roughened. Rustication also refers to masonry cut in massive blocks separated from each other by deep joints

Spandrel   Originally, a space between timbers supporting a building, but now refers to the almost triangular space between one side of the outer curve of an arch and the rectangle formed by the mouldings enclosing it. The term also applies to the area of support between a set of steps and the ground

Stucco   Fine plaster usually made from gypsum and pulverised marble, for covering walls and ceilings

Stupa   Domed structure erected as a Buddhist burial mound

Styles   Regency, Baroque, Palladian, Rococo, International

Telamon   Male figure used as a pillar to support an entablature or other structure

Tracery   Ornamentation in the upper part of a Gothic window, consisting of a perforated design or of an intersecting pattern, formed by the elaboration of the mullions. Tracery also refers to the interlaced work of a vault or panel

Transom   Horizontal supporting or strengthening crossbar in any structure but usually refers to a window frame

Tuscan Order   Simplest of the five classical orders of architecture, resembling the Doric, but devoid of all ornaments

Vault   Continuous arch, or a series of arches radiating from a central point or line, used to form a roof over a space inside a building

Venetian Window   Composite window with three separate openings, the central one being arched and taller than the others

Volute   Spiral scroll characteristic of Ionic capitals and also used in Corinthian and Composite capitals

Voussoir   Each of the wedge-shaped or tapered stones forming an arch or vaulting

Wonders of the World: Ancient   Colossus of Rhodes: bronze statue of Apollo erected c 280 BC; Hanging Gardens of Babylon: adjoining Nebuchadnezzar's palace 60 miles south of Baghdad; Pharos of Alexandria: lighthouse erected c 270 BC; Pyramids of Gizeh (Giza) near Cairo: Zoser, at Saqqara built c 2650 BC; Cheops built c 2580 BC (both still standing); Statue of Zeus: marble statue, built by Phidias c 430 BC, in the plains of Elis, Olympia; Temple of Artemis at Ephesus: Ionic temple built c 350 BC and burned by the Goths in AD 262; Tomb of Mausolus at Halicarnassus: built by the widowed Queen Artemisia c 350 BC

Wonders of the World: Modern   The seven modern wonders of the world are the Colosseum of Rome; Catacombs of Alexandria; Great Wall of China; Stonehenge; Leaning Tower of Pisa; Porcelain Tower of Nanking; Mosque of St Sophia at Constantinople

A
R
C
H
I
T
E
C
T
U
R
E

ART

Famous Artists

Abbate, Niccolo dell' (c1512–71)   Italian Mannerist landscapist.

Selected work: *Rape of Proserpine* (Louvre, Paris).

Albers, Josef (1888–1976)   German Bauhaus painter who founded the American Bauhaus in 1933 and took US citizenship in 1939.

Selected work: *Homage to the Square* series (Museum of Modern Art, New York).

Alma-Tadema, (Sir) Lawrence (1836–1912)   Dutch-born, British painter of Classical genre paintings.

Selected works: *The Visit* (Victoria and Albert Museum, London); *Pheidias and the Frieze of the Parthenon, Athens* (Birmingham City Gallery).

Altdorfer, Albrecht (c1480–1538)   German landscape painter and engraver, a pioneer of copperplate etching.

Selected works: *Landscape with a Bridge* (National Gallery, London); *St George* (Alte Pinakothek, Munich).

Andrea del Sarto (1486–1530)   Florentine High Renaissance painter. His original name was Andrea D'Agnolo, but his father's family (from Lanfranchi) were tailors, hence del Sarto.

Selected works: *Madonna of the Harpies* (Uffizi, Florence); *St John the Baptist* (Pitti Palace, Florence); *A Young Man* (National Gallery, London).

Angelico, Fra (c1387–1455)   Florentine religious painter and Dominican (monastic name Giovanni da Fiesole).

Selected works: *Annunciation* (Convent of San Marco, Florence); *St Lawrence Receiving the Treasure of the Church* (Vatican Museum, Rome).

Antonello da Messina (c1430–79)   Sicilian Renaissance landscapist and master of the oil-painting rather than tempora.

Selected works: *St Sebastian* (Gemäldegalerie, Dresden); *Salvator Mundi* his first dated work (1465); *A Man* (both National Gallery, London).

Appel, Karel (1921–)   Dutch Abstract Expressionist who founded the CoBrA group.

Selected work: *The Horseman* (Stedelijk Van Abbe-Museum, Eindhoven).

Avercamp, Hendrick (1585–1634)   Deaf and dumb Dutch landscapist who specialised in winter scenes.

Selected works: *Ice Skating in a Village* (Rijksmuseum Kröller-Müller, Otterlo); *Winter Landscape with Ice Skaters* (Rijksmuseum, Amsterdam); *Winter Scene* (National Gallery, London).

Bacon, Francis (1909–92)   Dublin-born figurative painter, influenced by Surrealism and violent imagery; studied under Graham Sutherland. A good collection of his work is in the Tate Gallery, London, including *Three Studies for a Crucifixion*.

Selected work: triptych inspired by the *Oresteia* trilogy of Aeschylus (Scottish National Gallery of Modern Art, Edinburgh).

Baldung (aka Grien), Hans (1484–1545)   German religious painter of the macabre.

Selected works: *A Man* (National Gallery, London); *Allegorical Figure* (Alte Pinakothek, Munich).

Balla, Giacomo (1871–1958)   Italian Futurist who

signed the Futurist Manifesto (1910) but by 1930 adopted a more conventional style of painting.

Selected work: *Dynamism of a Dog on a Leash* (Museum of Modern Art, New York).

Barocci, Federico (1530–1612)   Religious painter from Urbino who developed a very personal colour scheme of vivid reds and yellows.

Selected works: *The Circumcision* (Louvre, Paris); *Madonna of the Rosary* (Ashmolean Museum, Oxford); *Ecce Homo* (Pinacoteca di Brera, Milan).

Bassano, Jacopo (c1510/17–92)   Italian Mannerist and specialist in religious scenes. An important collection of his works and those of his followers is in the Museo Civico, Bassano del Grappa.

Selected works: *The Holy Family* (Castle Howard, North Yorkshire); *The Adoration of the Magi* (National Gallery of Scotland, Edinburgh); *The Good Samaritan* (National Gallery, London).

Beardsley, Aubrey Vincent (1872–98)   English illustrator, born in Brighton. Became famous for his fantastic posters and illustrations for *Morte d'Arthur*, Wilde's *Salome*, *Pope's Rape of the Lock*, as well as for the *Yellow Book* magazine (1894–6) and his own *Book of Fifty Drawings*. With Wilde he is regarded as leader of the 'Decadents' of the 1890s. Died of TB at Menton, France, having embraced Catholicism.

Beckmann, Max (1884–1950)   German Expressionist figurative painter and draughtsman who emigrated to the USA in 1947.

Selected work: *Night* (Kunstsammlung Nordrhein-Westfalen, Düsseldorf).

Bellini Family (fifteenth-century)   Jacopo (c1400–70) was founder of Venetian Renaissance art. His sons were Gentile (1429–1507), a portrait and panorama painter, and Giovanni (c1430–1516), the first Renaissance master of Venetian art, who taught both Giorgione and Titian.

Works (Giovanni):   *Descent into Limbo* (City of Bristol Art Gallery); *Doge Leonardo Loredan* (National Gallery, London); *Pietà* (Brera, Milan).

Bellotto, Bernardo (1720–80)   Venetian topographical artist, nephew of Canaletto. Painted a masterly interior of King's College Chapel, Cambridge.

Selected work: *View of Dresden* (Gemäldegalerie, Dresden).

Bernini, Gian Lorenzo (1598–1680)   Italian sculptor, architect and painter, born in Naples. Patronised by Cardinal Scipione Borghese. He designed the monumental baldacchino (choir canopy) for Saint Peter's in the Vatican. Although frequently used by Pope Urban VIII he was less popular with Innocent X, who preferred Alessandro Algardi. His most famous works include the Cornaro Chapel in the church of Santa Maria della Vittoria, the tomb of Alexander VII in Saint Peter's and the small Jesuit church of San Andrea al Quirinale, all in Rome. He was buried in Rome in the church of Santa Maria Maggiore.

Bewick, Thomas (1753–1828)   English wood engraver, born a farmer's son in Ovingham, Northumberland. His *History of British Birds* (1797–1804) was his masterpiece and the Bewick's Swan was named in his honour shortly after his death.

Blake, Peter (1932–)   British Pop artist during the 1960s and now more conventional.

Selected work: *Toy Shop* (Tate Gallery, London).

Blake, William (1757–1827)   English Romantic painter, poet and visionary.

Selected works: 20 illustrations to Dante's *Divine Comedy* (Tate Gallery, London); *Heads of the Poets* (18 pictures) (Manchester City Art Gallery); *The Circle of the Lustful* (Birmingham City Art Gallery).

Bonington, Richard Parkes (1802–28)   English topographical watercolourist.

Selected work: *View of Normandy* (Tate Gallery, London).

Bonnard, Pierre (1867–1947)   French landscape painter who also specialised in domestic scenes. Bonnard joined the Nabis, who included Denis and Vuillard, with whom he formed the Intimiste group.

Selected work: *Women with a Dog* (Phillips Collection, Washington DC).

Bosch, Hieronymus (c1450–1516)   Netherlands painter of the macabre and master of fantasy.

Selected works: *The Ship of Fools* (Louvre, Paris); *Christ Mocked* (National Gallery, London); altarpiece *The Garden of Earthly Delights* (Prado, Madrid).

Botticelli, Sandro (1445–1510)   Florentine Renaissance allegorical painter with distinctive linear style.

Selected works: *Mars and Venus* (National Gallery, London); *La Primavera*; *The Birth of Venus* (both Uffizi, Florence).

Boucher, François (1703–70)   French Rococo court painter and decorator to Louis XV; also director of the famous French tapestry workshop the Gobelins.

Selected works: *Diana after her Bath* (Louvre, Paris); *Reclining Girl* (Alte Pinakothek, Munich); *Madame de Pompadour* (Wallace Collection, London).

Boudin, Eugène Louis (1824–98)   French 'plein-airiste', painting in particular the fashionable French resorts of Trouville and Deauville in the 1860's. Collections of his work are in the Musée de Doctor Faure, Aix-les-Bains, and the Musée des Beaux-Arts Jules Chéret, Nice.

Selected works: *Deauville* (Tate Gallery, London); *Harbour of Trouville* (National Gallery, London); *Corvette Russe* (Luxembourg, Paris); *Beach Scene* (Leeds Castle, Kent).

Brancusi, Constantin (1876–1957)   Romanian sculptor, born in Pestisani, near Turgujiu. In his youth he was a shepherd boy in the Carpathians. Brancusi worked in Rodin's atelier and produced his *The Kiss* (1908) 22 years after Rodin's. His *Sleeping Muse* (1910) also shows Rodin's influence, but is the first of his characteristic highly polished egg-shaped carvings. The *Prodigal Son* (1925) shows the influence of African sculpture. Brancusi was a pioneer of modern abstract sculpture.

Selected works: *Adam and Eve*; *Flying Turtle* (both Guggenheim Museum, New York).

Brangwyn, Sir Frank (1867–1956)   Welsh painter, initially apprenticed to the Socialist designer William Morris. He presented à collection of his work to the city of Bruges in 1936 which is now housed in the Brangwyn Museum, and there is a substantial collection in the McManus Gallery, Dundee, and Brangwyn Hall, Swansea.

Selected work: *British Empire Panels* (Swansea Guildhall).

Braque, Georges (1882–1963)   French pioneer of Cubism, with Picasso, who designed scenes for two Diaghilev ballets, *Les Fâcheux* and *Zéphyr et Flore*. Braque was a Grand Officier of the Légion d'Honneur and was awarded an honorary doctorate by Oxford University in 1956. He was the first man to have his work exhibited in the Louvre during his lifetime.

Selected works: *Still Life* (Musée National d'Art Moderne, Paris); *Still Life with Playing Cards* (Rijksmuseum Kröller-Müller, Otterlo); *The Woman Musician* (Kunstmuseum, Basel); *The Candlestick* (Scottish National Gallery of Modern Art, Edinburgh).

Bronzino, Agnolo (1503–72)   Florentine Mannerist and portraitist.

Selected works: *Noli Me Tangere* (Louvre, Paris); *Venus, Cupid, Folly and Time* (National Gallery, London); *Portrait of Don Garzia de Medici* (Ashmolean Museum, Oxford); *Eleanora da Toledo with Her Son*; *Christ in Limbo* (both Uffizi, Florence).

Brouwer, Adriaen (c1605–38)   Flemish-born low-life painter who studied at Haarlem under Frans Hals and is regarded as 'culturally' Dutch, although eventually settling in Antwerp, where he died of the plague.

Selected works: *A Boor Asleep* (Wallace Collection, London); *Interior of an Alehouse* (Dulwich Picture Gallery, London); *Man with a Pointed Hat* (Museum Boymans-van Beuningen, Rotterdam).

Brown, Ford Madox (1821–93)   French-born British painter associated with Pre-Raphaelites and William Morris in particular. He completed twelve frescoes for Manchester Town Hall, just before his death. His most famous picture, *Work* was first exhibited at a retrospective exhibition held in London but is now hung in Manchester. Brown was the early tutor of Dante Gabriel Rossetti.

Selected work: *The Last of England* (Birmingham Museum & Art Gallery).

Brueghel, Jan (1568–1625)   Flemish landscape and flower painter; son of 'Peasant' Brueghel.

Selected works: *The Tower of Babel* (Koninklijk Museum voor Schone Kunsten, Antwerp); *Still Life with Garland of Flowers* (Musées Royaux des Beaux Arts, Brussels); *Vase of Flowers* (Ashmolean Museum, Oxford).

Brueghel the Elder, Pieter (c1520–69)   Flemish allegorical and religious painter, nicknamed 'Peasant' Brueghel.

Selected works: *Adoration of the Magi* (National Gallery, London); *Peasant Dance* (Kunsthistorisches Museum, Vienna).

Brueghel the Younger (c1564–1638)   Flemish painter nicknamed 'Hell' because he painted scenes of diablerie; son of Pieter 'Peasant' Brueghel.

Burne-Jones, Sir Edward Coley (1833–98)   British painter associated with Pre-Raphaelites and the Arts and Crafts Movement.

Selected works: *Perseus* series (Southampton Art Gallery); *The Legend of the Briar Rose* series (Buscot Park, Oxfordshire); *King Cophetua and the Beggar Maid* (Tate Gallery, London).

Canaletto, Antonio (1697–1768)   Venetian topographical artist who was the uncle of Bellotto. Canaletto was associated with his views of London and Venice, where the entrepreneur Joseph Smith was responsible for popularising his work.

Selected works: *View of the Grand Canal*, Venice (Uffizi, Florence); *View of the City of London from Richmond House* (Goodwood House, Sussex); *Stonemason's Yard* (National Gallery, London).

A
R
T

Caravaggio, Michelangelo Merisi da (c1573–1610) Italian Baroque painter who specialised in painting chiaroscuro. He fled Rome in 1606 after killing a man and spent the rest of his life as a refugee, moving between Naples, Sicily and Malta.

Selected works: *The Young Bacchus* (Uffizi, Florence); *Beheading of St John* (Cathedral of St John, Valletta, Malta); *Supper at Emmaus* (National Gallery, London).

(Sir) Anthony Caro (1924–   ) English sculptor. Assistant to Henry Moore between 1951 and 1953 and specialising in clay figures. From 1953 he was influenced by the American sculptor David Smith and began to use steel as his medium. He was knighted in 1987.

Selected works: *The Tower of Discovery* (Tate Gallery, London).

Carpaccio, Vittore (c1450–1525) Venetian early Renaissance religious painter. His most characteristic work is seen in the nine subjects from the life of St Ursula, and in his masterpiece, *the Presentation in the Temple*, both now in the Accademia, Venice.

Selected works: *The Preaching of St Stephen* (Louvre, Paris); *Courtesans* (Civico Museo Correr, Venice).

Carrà, Carlo (1881–1966) Italian Futurist who founded the Metaphysical School with de Chirico in 1917.

Carracci, Annibale (1560–1609) Most important of the family of Bolognese Mannerists.

Selected works: *The Butcher's Shop* (Christchurch Picture Gallery, Oxford); *Bacchus and Silenus* (National Gallery, London); *Coronation of the Virgin* (Staatliche Museen, Berlin).

Castagno, Andrea del (c1420–57) Florentine Early Renaissance fresco painter.

Selected works: *Dante* (Convent of S. Apollonia, Florence); *The Youthful David* (National Gallery of Art, Washington DC).

Cézanne, Paul (1839–1906) French Post-Impressionist who married Hortense Fiquet (subject of many of his paintings) in 1886, the year his friendship with Émile Zola ended, due to the publication of Zola's *L'Oeuvre*, in which the central figure is unflatteringly Cézanne.

Selected works: *Self portrait* (National Gallery, London); *The Lake at Annecy* (Courtauld Institute Galleries, London); *Card Players* (Metropolitan Museum of Art, New York).

Chagall, Marc (1887–1985) Russian-born figurative painter, active in France and the USA. The Musée Marc Chagall in Nice is entirely devoted to his work.

Selected works: *The Dead Man* (Marc Chagall Collection, Saint-Paul, France); *I and the Village* (Museum of Modern Art, New York); *Self Portrait with Seven Fingers* (Stedelijk Museum, Amsterdam).

Champaigne, Phillippe de (1602–74) Brussels-born, French Baroque court painter to Louis XIII who was patronised by Cardinal Richelieu. After 1647 he was associated with the Jansenists, a strict Roman Catholic sect.

Selected works: *Ex Voto of 1662*; *Cardinal Richelieu* (both Louvre, Paris).

Chardin, Jean-Baptiste Siméon (1699–1779) French still-life genre painter.

Selected works: *Grace before Meat*; *Housewife* (both Louvre, Paris); *The Young Schoolmistress* (National Gallery, London); *Still Life* (Badische Kunsthalle, Karlsruhe).

Chirico, Giorgio de (1888–1978) Italian Surrealist and co-founder of Metaphysical School with Carlo Carrà.

Selected work: *The Pink Tower* (Guggenheim Foundation, Venice).

Cimabue, Giovanni (c1240–1302) Florentine fresco painter who is accepted as the teacher of Giotto.

Selected work: *Madonna and Child* (Louvre, Paris).

Claude (le) Lorrain (1600–82) French Classical landscapist (born Claude Gellée).

Selected works: *Village Fête* (Louvre, Paris); *Aeneas at Delos* (National Gallery, London); *Ascanius Shooting the Stag of Sylvia* (Ashmolean Museum, Oxford).

Clouet the Younger, Jean (c1485–1541) French court painter to François I.

Selected work: *Guillaume Budé* (Metropolitan Museum of Art, New York).

Clouet, François (c1510–72) French court painter to Francis I, Henri II, Francis II, and Charles IX.

Selected works: *Elizabeth of Austria* (Louvre, Paris); *Mary Queen of Scots* (Scottish National Portrait Gallery, Edinburgh); *Portrait of Henri II* (Uffizi, Florence).

Constable, John (1776–1837) English landscapist, born in East Bergholt, Suffolk, the county where many of his most famous works are set.

Selected works: *Dedham Vale* (National Gallery of Scotland, Edinburgh); *The Haywain* (National Gallery, London); *Harnham Ridge from Archdeacon Fisher's House, Salisbury* (National Gallery of Ireland, Dublin).

Copley, John Singleton (1738–1815) American portraitist and history painter working in England from 1775.

Selected works: *Hugh Montgomery, 12th Earl of Eglinton* (Scottish National Portrait Gallery, Edinburgh); *The Siege of Gibraltar* (Guildhall Art Gallery, London); *The Copley Family* (National Gallery of Art, Washington DC); *Brook Watson and the Shark* (National Gallery of Art, Washington DC).

Corot, Jean-Baptiste Camille (1796–1875) French landscapist.

Selected works: *Louis Robert as a Child* (Louvre, Paris); *Avignon* (National Gallery, London).

Correggio, Antonio Allegri da (c1490–1534) Italian High Renaissance painter, active mainly in Parma.

Selected works: *Ecce Homo* (National Gallery, London); *The Agony in the Garden* (Wellington Museum, London); *St Mary Magdalen* (National Gallery, London); *Danae* (Borghese Gallery, Rome).

Cortona, Pietro Berrettini da (1596–1669) Italian painter and architect, creator of Roman High Baroque.

Selected works: *The Rape of the Sabines* (Capitoline Gallery, Rome); *Allegory of Divine Providence and Barbarian Power* (ceiling frescoe in the Galleria Nazionale, Rome).

Cotman, John Sell (1782–1842) English landscapist, co-founder of the Norwich School.

Selected works: *The Devil's Elbow* (Castle Museum, Norwich); *Greta Bridge* (British Museum, London); *Seashore with Boats* (Tate Gallery, London).

Courbet, Gustave (1819–77) French Realist who joined the Paris Commune, was imprisoned for his part in the destruction of the Vendôme Column and died in exile in Switzerland.

Selected works: *Studio of the Painter: an Allegory of Realism* (Louvre, Paris); *Les Demoiselles de Village* (Leeds City Art Gallery); *Bonjour, Monsieur Courbet* (Musée Fabre, Montpellier); *Stream in a Ravine* (Louvre, Paris); *Young Women on the Banks of the Seine* (Musée du Petit Palais, Paris).

Cranach the Elder, Lucas (1472–1553) German court painter to the Elector of Saxony. A number of his works are in the collection at Jagdschloss Grunewald, Berlin. He had three sons, one of them Lucas the Younger (1515–86), whose works are hard to distinguish from his father's.
Selected works: *A Young Girl* (Louvre, Paris); *Adam and Eve* (Courtauld Institute Galleries, London); *A Crucifixion* (Stadtkirche, Weimar); *Martin Luther* (Bristol City Art Gallery).

Crome, John (1768–1821) English topographical artist and founding member of the Norwich Society (1803), now known as the Norwich School.
Selected works: *Yarmouth Jetty* (Castle Museum, Norwich); *The Beaters* (National Gallery of Scotland, Edinburgh); *Marlingford Grove* (Lady Lever Art Gallery, Port Sunlight).

Cuyp, Aelbert (1620–91) Dutch landscapist who was greatly influenced by Jan van Goyen. He also painted animals, seascapes and still lifes.
Selected works: *River Scene with a View of Dordrecht* (Manchester City Art Gallery); *River Scene with a View of Dordrecht* (Wallace Collection, London); *Sunset after Rain* (Fitzwilliam Museum, Cambridge); *Resting Horsemen in a Landscape* (Dordrecht Museum).

Daddi, Bernardo (c1290–1348) Florentine Early Renaissance contemporary of Giotto.
Selected work: *Virgin and Child* (Museu de Arte de São Paolo 'Assis Chateaubriand', Brazil).

Dali, Salvador (1904–89) Spanish Surrealist. Born in Figueras but lived in Paris and, from 1940, in the USA. Dali collaborated with Luis Buñuel on such Surrealist films as *Le Chien Andalou* (1928) and *L'Age d'Or* (1930). His painting *The Persistence of Memory* in New York's Museum of Modern Art was known as 'The Limp Watches'.
Selected works: *Christ of St John of the Cross* (Glasgow Art Gallery & Museum); *Inventions of the Monsters* (Art Institute of Chicago); *Galacidalacideoxyribonucleicacid* (New England Merchant Bank, Boston, Mass.).

Daubigny, Charles-François (1817–78) French landscapist of the Barbizon School who was a pupil of Paul Delaroche.
Selected work: *Evening Landscape* (Metropolitan Museum of Art, New York).

David, Gerard (c1460–1523) Netherlandis painter who became dean of the Painters' Guild of Bruges in 1501.
Selected works: *The Transfiguration* (Lieve Vrouwkerk, Bruges); *The Marriage at Cana* (Louvre, Paris); *The Tree of Jesse* (Musée des Beaux-Arts, Lyons).

David, Jacques-Louis (1748–1825) French Neo-classicist who voted in the National Convention for the death of Louis XVI and after Robespierre's death was twice imprisoned. He produced his masterpiece *The Rape of the Sabines* in 1799 and in 1804 became court painter to Napoleon, but was eventually banished as a regicide after the Bourbon restoration.
Selected works: *The Death of Marat* (Musées Royaux des Beaux Arts, Brussels); *Death of

Socrates (Metropolitan Museum of Art, New York); *Madame Récamier* (Louvre, Paris); *Napoleon Crowning Josephine* (Musée de l'Histoire de la France, Versailles).

Degas, Edgar (1834–1917) French Impressionist painter and sculptor who specialised in dancers.
Selected works: *Miss La La at the Cirque Fernando* (National Gallery, London); *The Dancing Class* (Musée du Jeu de Paume, Paris); *L'Absinthe* (Louvre, Paris).

Delacroix, Eugène (1798–1863) French Romantic painter. Delacroix's Paris studio-apartment is now a museum for his work.
Selected works: *The Death of Sardanapalus* (Louvre, Paris); *Battle of Taillebourg* (Galerie des Batailles, Versailles); Baron Schwiter (National Gallery, London; *The Massacre at Chios* (Louvre, Paris); *The Execution of Faliero* (Wallace Collection, London); *Liberty Leading the People* (Louvre, Paris).

Delaunay, Robert (1885–1941) French Cubist and exponent of Orphism, husband of the pioneer abstract painter Sonia Delauney Terk (1885–1979).
Selected works: *La Tour Eiffel* (Kunstmuseum, Basel); *L'Equipe de Cardiff* (Scottish National Gallery of Modern Art, Edinburgh).

Delvaux, Paul (1897–1994) Belgian Neo-Impressionist, Expressionist and Surrealist.
Selected work: *Sleeping Venus* (Tate Gallery, London).

Denis, Maurice (1870–1943) French painter, founder of the 'Nabis'.
Selected work: *Hommage à Cézanne* (Musée d'Art Moderne, Paris).

Derain, André (1880–1954) French Fauvist painter and sculptor.
Selected works: *Mountains at Collioure* (Scottish National Gallery of Modern Art, Edinburgh); *Blackfriars* (Glasgow Art Gallery & Museum).

Dix, Otto (1891–1969) German Expressionist painter, a leader of theNeue Sachlichkeit group.
Selected works: *Sylvia von Harden* (Musée National d'Art Moderne, Paris); *Nude Girl in a Fur* (Scottish National Gallery of Modern Art, Edinburgh).

Dobson, William (c1610–46) English portrait painter who succeeded Van Dyck as painter to the exiled Charles I (1641).
Selected work: *Endymion Porter* (Tate Gallery, London).

Doesburg, Theo van (1883–1931) Dutch artist and architect. Leader of De Stijl movement with Mondrian and devotee of a severe form of geometrical abstraction known as Neo-Plasticism. He was originally called Christian Emil Marie Kupper.

Domenichino (1581–1641) Bolognese landscapist and portrait painter.
Selected works: *Portrait of Monsignor Agucchi* (York Art Gallery); *Sibyl* (Borghese Gallery, Rome); *Last Communion of St Jerome* (Vatican Palace, Rome); Tobias (National Gallery, London).

Domenico Veneziano (c1400–61) Florentine Early Renaissance painter.
Selected work: *St Lucy Altarpiece* (Uffizi, Florence).

Dongen, Kees van (1877–1968) Dutch painter active in Paris. Fauvist and member of Die Brücke (The Bridge).
Selected work: *Women on the Balcony* (Musée del'Annonciade, St Tropez).

A
R
T

Dossi, Dosso (c1479–1542)   Ferrarese fresco painter.

Selected works: *The Christ Child Learning to Walk* (Nottingham Castle); *The Sorceress Circe* (Borghese Gallery, Rome).

Dou, Gerrit (or Gerard) (1613–75)   Dutch painter and former collaborator with Rembrandt. Started the 'Fijnschilder' (fine painter) School in Laiden.

Selected works: *A Woman at a Window* (Fitzwilliam Museum, Cambridge); *Rembrandt's Mother*; *Self Portrait* (both Rijksmuseum, Amsterdam); *A Poulterer's Shop* (National Gallery, London); *The Astronomer* (Stedtlijk Museum 'De Lakenhal', Leiden).

Duccio di Buoninsegna   (c1260–c1318)   Sienese painter.

Selected works: *Maestà* (Cathedral Museum, Siena); *Rucellai Madonna* (Uffizi, Florence); *Christ Healing the Blind Man*; *The Annunciation* (both National Gallery, London).

Duchamp, Marcel (1887–1968)   French-born American painter and sculptor, brother of Jacques Villon. Inventor of the 'Ready-Made' and leader of the New York Dadaists.

Selected work: *The Bride Stripped Bare by her Bachelors, Even*, also known as *The Large Glass* (Philadelphia Museum of Art).

Dufy, Raoul (1877–1953)   French artist and designer, born in Le Havre. Dufy played a big part in popularising Fauvism. In 1911 he illustrated Guillaume Apollinaire's *Bestiary*.

Selected work: *Château and Horses* (Philips Collection, Washington DC).

Dürer, Albrecht (1471–1528)   German painter and graphic artist, born in Nuremberg, the son of a Hungarian goldsmith. Dürer is often considered the inventor of etching and was a supreme master of the woodcut.

Selected works: *Self Portrait in a Fur-collared Robe* (Alte Pinakothek, Munich); *A Young Man* (Hampton Court Palace, London); *Adoration of the Magi* (Uffizi, Florence).

Dyck, (Sir) Anthony van (1599–1641)   Anglo-Flemish court painter to Charles I of England and pupil of Rubens.

Selected works: *Triple Portrait of Charles I* (Windsor Castle); *Portrait of the Earl of Strafford* (Petworth House, Sussex); *The Lornellini Family* (National Gallery of Scotland, Edinburgh).

Eakins, Thomas (1844–1916)   American painter and photographer, born in Philadelphia. His composite plates inspired Duchamp's *Nude Descending a Staircase*.

Selected works: *Max Schmitt in a Single Scull*; *Chess Players* (both Metropolitan Museum of Art, New York).

Elsheimer, Adam (1578–1610)   German painte,r on copper, of night scenes and landscapes.

Selected works: *St Paul on Malta* (National Gallery, London); *Judith and Holofernes* (Wellington Museum, London); *Tobias and the Angel* (Historisches Museum, Frankfurt am Main).

Emin, Tracey (1963–)   British Modern Artist, who may be best described as Contraversalist. Typical work includes *The Hut* and *My Bed*. Her best-selling autobiography was entitled *Exploration of the Soul*.

Selected work: *Every Part of Me's Bleeding* (Lehman Maupin Gallery, New York).

Ensor, James (1860–1949)   Belgian painter of the macabre and precursor of Surrealism.

Selected work: *Entry of Christ into Brussels* (Casino Communal, Belgium).

Epstein, (Sir) Jacob (1880–1959)   American-born British sculptor, born a Russian-Polish Jew in New York. His early commissions included 18 nude figures for the façade of the British Medical Association building in the Strand (1907–8) and *Night and Day* (1929) for the London Transport Building in Westminster. These and later symbolic sculptures, such as the marble *Genesis* (1930) the *Ecce Homo* (1934) and the alabaster *Adam* (1939), resulted in accusations of indecency and blasphemy. His last two large commissioned works were *Christ in Majesty* (Llandaff Cathedral) and *St Michael and the Devil* (Coventry Cathedral).

Ernst, Max (1891–1976)   German painter and sculptor who was a founder of the Surrealist movement. He invented the technique of frottage (pencil rubbings on canvas).

Selected works: *The Elephant Celebes* (Tate Gallery, London); *Le Grand Amoureux* (Scottish National Gallery of Modern Art, Edinburgh).

Etty, William (1787–1849)   English portrait painter who specialised in nudes.

Selected works: *Monk Bar, York* (York City Art Gallery); *The Combat* (National Gallery of Scotland, Edinburgh); *Somnolency* (Aberdeen Art Gallery); *The Fairy of the Fountain* (Tate Gallery, London).

Eyck, Jan van (c1389–1441)   Netherlands painter, probably born near Maastricht; successively in the service of John of Bavaria, the Count of Holland and Philip the Good of Burgundy.

Selected works: *The Arnolfini Wedding* (National Gallery, London); *Adoration of the Lamb* (Church of St Bavo, Ghent); *The Madonna with Chancellor Rolin* (Louvre, Paris); *Man in a Red Turban* (National Gallery, London).

Fabritius, Carel (1622–54)   Dutch painter of still lifes and street-scenes. Worked under Rembrandt around 1641 and lived mainly at Delft, where he was killed in the explosion of the municipal ammunition depot.

Selected works: *View of Delft* (National Gallery, London); *An Old Man* (Walker Art Gallery, Liverpool); *The Goldfinch* (Mauritshuis, The Hague); *Self-portrait* (Museum Boymans-van Beuningen, Rotterdam).

Fantin-Latour, Henri (1836–1904)   French genre, still-life and Symbolist painter, born in Grenoble.

Selected works: *Flowers and Fruit* (Louvre, Paris); *Homage to Delacroix* (Musé du Jeu de Paume, Paris).

Feininger, Lyonel (1871–1956)   American artist and cartoonist, born in New York of German immigrant parents. Taught at the Bauhaus at Weimar and Dessau, but when the Nazis came to power he returned to the USA and, with Gropius and Mies van der Rohe, founded the Chicago Bauhaus.

Selected works: *Sailing Boats* (Collection Tannahill, Detroit); *Gelmeroda III* (Scottish National Gallery of Modern Art, Edinburgh).

Fouquet, Jean (c1420–81)   French court painter to Louis I. Pope Eugenius IV commissioned a portrait from him, now lost.

Selected works: *Etienne Chevalier with St Stephen* (Staatliche Museen, Berlin); *Madonna and Child* (Musée des Beaux Arts, Antwerp); *Charles VII* (Louvre, Paris).

Fragonard, Jean-Honoré (1732–1806)   French Rococo painter.

Selected works: *The Swing* (Wallace Collection, London); *Bathers* (Louvre, Paris).

Frankinthaler, Helen (1928–) American Abstract Expressionist painter, who devised a technique for straining unprimed canvases with washes of colour.
Selected work: *Blue Territory* (Whitney Museum, New York City).

Freud, Lucien (1922–) German-born, English figurative painter. In his early years he was one of the Neo-Romantic group along with Minton, Craxton, Sutherland and Piper; but from the 1950s he developed a realist style. One of the most respected artists since World War II. Freud's work does not lend itself to be pigeon-holed in any particular style and includes portraits ranging from *Francis Bacon* in the Tate (stolen in 1988 whilst on exhibition in Germany) to the painting of a man in a raincoat with a yucca – *Interior in Paddington* (Walker Art Gallery, Liverpool). Sigmund Freud was the artist's grandfather.

Friedrich, Caspar David (1774–1840) German Romantic painter of nature, and particularly forest scenes. His works are included in the German Romantic collection in the Schinkel Pavilion at Schloss Charlottenburg and in the Neue National Galerie, both in Berlin.
Selected works: *Man and Woman Gazing at the Moon* (Staatliche Museen, Berlin); *Wreck of the Hope* (Kunsthalle, Hamburg).

(Dame) Elizabeth Frink (1930–1993) English sculptress. The horror of war ran through her entire oeuvre and is best depicted in *Gogglehead*.
Selected works: *Arrival at Canterbury* (Royal Museum and Art Gallery, Canterbury).

Frith, William Powell (1819–1909) English genre painter who became the wealthiest painter of his time by selling both paintings and their copyright.
Selected works: *The Derby Day* (Tate Gallery, London); *The Railway Station* (Royal Holloway College, Egham, Surrey).

Fuseli, Henry (1741–1825) Swiss Romantic fantasy painter who took British citizenship and became professor of painting at the Royal Academy, and Keeper in 1804.
Selected works: *Lady Macbeth Sleepwalking* (Louvre, Paris); *Titania and Bottom* (Tate Gallery, London); *The Three Witches from Macbeth* (Kunsthaus, Zurich); *The Nightmare* (Detroit Institute of Art).

Gaddi, Taddeo (c1300–66) Florentine painter and mosaicist who was Giotto's best pupil and also his godson.
Selected work: *Life of the Virgin* (Baroncelli Chapel, Church of S. Croce, Florence).

Gainsborough, Thomas (1727–88) English portrait and landscape painter, born in Sudbury, Suffolk. Married Margaret Burr, the illegitimate daughter of the 4th Duke of Beaufort.
Selected works: *Harvest Wagon* (Barber Institute, University of Birmingham); *Self Portrait* (National Portrait Gallery, London); *Portrait of Mary, Countess Howe* (Iveagh Bequest, Kenwood House, London); *The Watering Place* (Tate Gallery, London); *Mrs Graham* (National Gallery of Scotland, Edinburgh); *George III and Queen Charlotte* (Windsor Castle).

Gaudier-Brzeska, Henri (1891–1915) French cubist sculptor born in St Jean de Braye. Henri Gaudier came to England in 1911 with his childhood sweetheart Sophie Brzeska and founded the London Group of Sculpture. In 1914 he signed the Vorticist

Manifesto. He joined the French army at the outbreak of WWI and was killed in action.
Selected work: *Armour* (Tate Gallery, London).

Gauguin, Paul (1848–1903) French Post-Impressionist who gave up a stockbroking career to devote himself to painting. He evolved a style known as 'Synthetism' in a reaction against Impressionism. Lived in Tahiti 1891–1901 and then the Marquesas Islands. Fell out with his friend Van Gogh at Arles in 1888.
Selected works: *The Vision after the Sermon* (National Gallery of Scotland, Edinburgh); *Tahitian Women* (Metropolitan Museum of Art, New York); *La Seine au Pont d'Iéna* (Louvre, Paris).

Gentile da Fabriano (c1370–1427) Italian International Gothic painter (properly, Niccolo di Giovanni di Massio).
Selected work: *Adoration of the Magi* (Uffizi, Florence).

Gentileschi, Artemisia (c1597–c1651) Italian painter, daughter of the Bolognese painter Orazio Gentileschi.
Selected works: *Self-portrait as Pittura* (Kensington Palace, London); *Susannah and the Elders* (Schloss Eissenstein, Pommersfelden).

Géricault, Théodore (1791–1824) French Romantic history painter. He died following a fall from his horse. His tomb in Père Lachaise cemetry, Paris, has a brass relief of *The Raft of the Medusa*.
Selected works: *The Raft of the Medusa*; *The Wounded Cuirassier* (both Louvre, Paris); *Mad Woman with a Mania of Envy* (Musée des Beaux Arts, Lyons).

Gheeraerts, Marcus, the Younger (c1561–1636) Flemish portraitist. Court painter to Elizabeth I and James I of England (VI of Scotland). Portrait of Arabella Stuart in the Scottish National Portrait Gallery is possibly by Gheeraerts.
Selected works: *The Ditchley Portrait of Elizabeth I* (National Portrait Gallery, London); *Sir Thomas Lee* (Tate Gallery, London); *William Camden* (Bodleian Library, Oxford).

Ghirlandaio, Domenico (1449–94) Florentine Renaissance fresco painter (properly, Domenico di Tommaso Bigordi).
Selected works: *Life of the Virgin* (Strozzi Chapel, S. Maria Novella, Florence); *Visitation of the Virgin* (Louvre, Paris); *Old Man and His Grandson* (Louvre, Paris).

Gilbert, (Sir) Alfred (1854–1934) English sculptor and goldsmith who was a leader of the New Sculpture movement. The Clarence Memorial in Windsor is considered the climax of his work. Other works include the Alexandra Memorial in Marlborough Road, London, and the *Queen Victoria* statue in Winchester.
Selected works: *Eros* (Piccadilly Circus, London); *Perseus Arming* (Victoria and Albert Museum, London); *Joule* (Manchester Town Hall).

Gill, Eric (1882–1940) English sculptor, engraver, writer and typographer, born in Brighton, the son of a clergyman. In 1909 he carved his first stone figure *The Madonna and Child*. Through the influence of Augustus John he exhibited at the Chenil Galleries, Chelsea (1911). He maintained a steady output for the rest of his life, during which he designed the classic typeface Gill. Joined the Fabian movement but eventually became Catholic.
Selected works: *Mankind* (Tate Gallery, London); *Stations of the Cross* (Westminster Cathedral,

London); *Prospero and Ariel* (BBC Broadcasting House, London).

Gillray, James (1756–1815)   English political and social caricaturist and printmaker, born in Chelsea, the son of a Lanark trooper. Gillray had a life-long partnership with the publisher Mrs Humphrey. From 1810 until his death he was hopelessly insane.

Giordano, Luca (1634–1705)   Neapolitan decorative painter, precursor of Rococo and court painter to Charles II of Spain. Renowned for his speed of working, hence his nickname 'Luca Fa Presto' (Luke Go Quickly).
   Selected work: *Apotheosis of the Medici* (ballroom ceiling, Palazzo Medici-Riccardi, Florence).

Giorgione (c1478–1510)   Venetian Renaissance painter (properly, Giorgio Barbarelli).
   Selected works: *The Adultress before Christ* (Glasgow Art Gallery & Museum); *The Adoration of the Magi* (National Gallery, London); *The Tempest* (Galleria dell'Accademia, Venice).

Giotto di Bondone (c1266–1337)   Florentine painter who introduced sculptural solidity into painting and heralded the Renaissance. He was a pupil of Cimabue, but because of confusion as to his early life it is not known for sure if the St Francis of Assisi frescoes were attributable to him. Often called the 'Father of Modern Painting'. Both he and Cimabue are mentioned by Dante. Legend says he drew a perfect circle freehand for the Pope.
   Selected works: the Arena Chapel murals (S. Maria Annunziata dell'Arena, Padua); *Ognissant Madonna* (Uffizi, Florence).

Giulio Romano (1492–1546)   Roman Mannerist painter and architect. an indication of his fame is a mention in Shakespeare's *Winter's Tale*.
   Selected works: *Isabella d'Este* (Hampton Court Palace, London); *Allegory of Immortality* (Alnwick Castle, Northumberland); fresco decorations at the Palazzo del Te, Mantua).

Goes, Hugo van der (c1440–82)   Flemish master painter, mostly of religious subjects.
   Selected works: *Adoration of the Shepherds* (Uffizi, Florence); *Death of the Virgin* (Musée Communal, Bruges); *Adoration of the Magi* (Museum Dahlem, Berlin).

Gogh, Vincent van (1853–90)   Dutch Post-Impressionist. The Rijksmuseum Vincent van Gogh in Amsterdam houses over 700 of his paintings and drawings.
   Selected works: *Cornfield and Cypress Trees* (National Gallery, London); *Self Portrait* (Saint-Rémy, 1889: Louvre, Paris); *The Potato Eaters* (Rijksmuseum Vincent van Gogh, Amsterdam); *Sunflowers* (Tate Gallery, London).

Gore, Spencer Frederick (1878–1914)   English painter, born in Epsom, Surrey. Gore was a founder member and first president of the Camden Town Group (1911).
   Selected work: *From a Window in Cambrian Road, Richmond* (Tate Gallery, London).

Gorky, Arshile (1904–48)   Armenian-born US painter influenced by Cubism, Surrealism and Abstract Expressionism. Original name: Vosdanig Manoog Adoian.
   Selected work: *The Liver Is the Cock's Comb* (Albright-Knox Art Gallery, Buffalo, NY State).

Goya y Lucientes, Francisco (1746–1828)   Spanish Romantic artist who was court painter to Charles IV of Spain. His series of etchings, *The Disasters of War*, describe the horrors of the Penninsular war in Spain.

Selected works: *Family of Charles IV*; *The Naked Maja* (both Prado, Madrid); *The Duke of Wellington* (National Gallery, London).

Goyen, Jan van (1596–1656)   Dutch realistic landscapist.
   Selected works: *Cottages and Fishermen by a River* (Glasgow City Art Gallery); *Leiden from the North-East* (Stedelijk Museum 'De Lakenhal', Leiden); *View of Dordrecht from Papendrecht* (Mauritshuis, The Hague).

Gozzoli, Benozzo (c1421–97)   Florentine fresco painter, a pupil of Fra Angelico.
   Selected works: frescoes (Medici Palace, Florence); *Journey of the Magi* (chapel of the Palazzo Medici-Riccardi, Florence).

Greco, El (1541–1614)   Cretan-born Spanish Mannerist (properly, Domenico Theotocopoulos).
   Selected works: *The Saviour* (National Gallery of Scotland, Edinburgh); *The Tears of St Peter* (Bowes Museum, Barnard Castle, Durham); The Disrobing of Christ (Toledo Cathedral).

Greuze, Jean-Baptiste (1725–1805)   French genre and portrait painter.
   Selected works: *The Broken Pitcher* (Louvre, Paris); *Girl with Doves* (Wallace Collection, London).

Gris, Juan (1887–1927)   Spanish Cubist (properly, José Victoriano González).
   Selected works: *Still Life with Dice* (Musée National d'Art Moderne, Paris); *The Glass* (Glasgow Art Gallery & Museum).

Grosz, George (1893–1959)   German-born American Expressionist and Dadaist whose depictions of the depravity of war were so graphic that the Nazis called him 'Cultural Bolshevist Number One'. Although starting as a Dadaist, he was a co-founder of the Neue Sachlichkeit movement.
   Selected works: *Kristallnacht* (Leicester Museum & Art Gallery, Leicester); *To Oskar Panizza* (Staatsgalerie, Stuttgart).

Grünewald, Matthias (c1470/80–1528)   German visionary artist (properly, Mathis Gothardt – although he occasionally added his wife's surname Neithardt to his own). Grünewald is the 'Mathis der Maler' of Hindemith's opera of that name.
   Selected works: *The Isenheim Altarpiece* (Musée d'Unterlinden, Colmar, France); *The Mocking of Christ* (Alte Pinakothek, Munich); *The Miracle of the Snow* (Aschaffenburg Altarpiece, Augustinermuseum, Freiburg-in-Breisgau).

Guardi, Francesco (1712–93)   Italian topographical artist, born in Pinzolo. Pupil of Canaletto, and like his master famous for his views of Venice.
   Selected works: *Ascent in a Balloon* (Staatliche Museen, Berlin); *The Doge Embarking on the Bucintoro* (Louvre, Paris); *The Doge's Palace* (National Gallery, London).

Guercino (1591–1666)   Bolognese early Baroque painter (properly, Gian-Francesco Barbieri).
   Selected works: *The Incredulity of St Thomas* (National Gallery, London); Susanna Bathing (Prado, Madrid).

Hals, Frans (c1580–1666)   Dutch genre and portrait painter, born in Antwerp.
   Selected works: *The Laughing Cavalier* (Wallace Collection, London); *Married Couple in a Garden* (Rijksmuseum, Amsterdam); *Aletta Hannemans* (Mauritshuis, The Hague); *The Merry Toper* (Rijksmuseum, Amsterdam).

Hamilton, Richard (1922–)   English artist who

became a pioneer of Pop Art after attending the *This is Tomorrow* exhibition in Whitechapel Art Gallery, London, in 1956. He reconstructed Duchamp's *Bride Stripped Bare by her Bachelors, Even*, by consulting the original notes and studies by the artist (Tate Gallery, London).

Selected work: *Just What Is It That Makes Today's Homes So Different, So Appealing* (Private Collection, California).

Hepworth, (Dame) Jocelyn Barbara (1903–75) English sculptor, born in Wakefield, West Yorkshire. Her first marriage was to fellow sculptor John Skeaping and her second to painter Ben Nicholson. Hepworth was noted for the strength and formal discipline of her carving, e.g. *Contrapuntal Forms*, exhibited at the Festival of Britain, 1951. Such pieces as *Wave* (1944) and *Mr & Mrs Ashley* (Havinden Collection, England) became increasingly open, hollowed out and variously perforated, so that the interior space became as important as the mass surrounding it.

Selected works: *Pelagos* (Tate Gallery); and *Pendour* (Hirshhorn Museum, Washington DC).

Hilliard, Nicholas (1537–1619) English miniature-painter at the courts of Elizabeth I and James I of England.

Selected works: *Young Man among Roses* (Vicoria and Albert Museum, London); *Elizabeth I Playing a Lute* (Berkeley Castle, Gloucester); *Self-portrait Aged 31* (Drumlanrig Castle, Dumfriesshire).

Hobbema, Meindert (1638–1709) Dutch landscapist and pupil of Jacob von Ruysdael.

Selected works: *The Avenue at Middleharnis* (National Gallery, London); *A Watermill* (Rijksmuseum, Amsterdam); *A Peasant Cottage on a Water* Course (Historisches Museum, Amsterdam).

Hockney, David (1937–) English Pop artist, born in Bradford.

Selected works: *My Parents and Myself* (Cartwright Hall Art Gallery, Bradford); *Rocky Mountains and Tired Indians* (Scottish National Gallery of Modern Art, Edinburgh).

Hogarth, William (1697–1764) English painter and satirist, born in Smithfield, the son of a teacher. Studied under Sir James Thornhill and married Thornhill's daughter in 1729.

Selected works: *Lord George Graham in His Cabin* (National Maritime Museum, London); *The Rake's Progress* series (Sir John Soane's Museum, London); *Self-portrait with His Pug* (Tate Gallery, London).

Hokusai, Katsushika (1760–1849) Japanese watercolourist whose work became extremely popular in England after the Anglo-Japanese trade agreements of the 1880s. His work influenced Whistler.

Selected work: *Thirty-six Views of Mount Fuji* series (Art Institute of Chicago).

Holbein the Younger, Hans (c1497–1543) German realist portraitist who was court painter to Henry VIII. His father, Hans Holbein the Elder (c1460–1524), was also a painter of note.

Selected works: *The Ambassadors* (National Gallery, London); *Sir Thomas Moore*; (Frick Collection, New York); *Jane Seymour* (Mauritshuis, The Hague).

Homer, Winslow (1836–1910) American painter, born in Boston. Began as an illustrator for magazines such as *Harper's Weekly* and *Ballou's Pictorial*. Worked for many years at his Prouts Neck

studio in Maine, where the local sea area became a favourite subject for depiction.

Selected works: *Fog Warning* (Museum of Fine Arts, Boston, Mass.); *Pitching Quoits* (Fogg Art Museum, Cambridge, Mass.).

Honthorst, Gerrit van (1590–1656) Dutch genre and night-scene painter who was the court painter to the Stadholder of Holland and Charles I of England.

Selected works: *Winter Queen* (Elizabeth of Bohemia) (National Portrait Gallery, London); *Willem II, Prince of Orange* (Mauritshuis, The Hague); *The Death of Seneca* (Centraal Museum, Utrecht).

Hooch (or Hoogh), Pieter de (1629–84) Dutch genre painter.

Selected works: *A Musical Party* (Wellington Museum, Apsley House, London); *Interior with a Woman Delousing a Child's Hair* (Rijksmuseum, Amsterdam); *A Courtyard in Delft* (Mauritshuis, The Hague).

Hopper, Edward (1882–1967) American realist painter, mostly of urban scenes, born in New York.

Selected works: *Early Sunday Morning* (Whitney Museum of American Art, New York); *Room in Brooklyn* (Museum of Fine Arts, Boston, Mass.).

Hunt, William Holman (1827–1910) English painter and founder member of the Pre-Raphaelite Brotherhood.

Selected works: *The Scapegoat* (Lady Lever Gallery, Port Sunlight); *Claudio and Isabella* (Tate Gallery, London); *The Light of the World* (Keble College, Oxford).

Hunt, William Morris (1824–79) American Romantic painter who created a fashion in the USA for the luminous, atmospheric painting of the Barbizon School.

Selected work: *Girl at a Fountain* (Metropolitan Museum of Art, New York).

Huysum, Jan van (1682–1749) Dutch still-life painter.

Selected work: *Fruit, Flowers and Insects* (Alte Pinakothek, Munich).

Ingres, Jean Auguste Dominique (1780–1867) French Classical painter of portraits and history pictures. Ingres bequeathed much of his work to his home town of Montauban, and the collection is now housed in the town's Musée Ingres. His motto was 'A thing well drawn is well enough painted'. Ingres was awarded the Légion d'Honneur and made a senator in 1862.

Selected works: *Madame Moitessier* (National Gallery, London); *The Turkish Bath* (Louvre, Paris).

Inness, George (1825–94) American landscapist, later influenced by the Barbizon School.

Selected works: *The Delaware Valley* (Metropolitan Museum of Art, New York); *Rainbow after a Storm* (Chicago Art Institute).

Jawlensky, Alexej von (1864–1941) Russian Expressionist working in Munich from 1896 and France from 1905. In 1924 he co-founded Der Blaue Vier (Blue Four group) with Kandinsky, Klee and Feininger.

Selected work: *Head of a Woman* (Scottish National Gallery of Modern Art, Edinburgh).

John, Augustus Edwin (1878–1961) Welsh painter, born in Tenby. Graduated from the Slade School of Art, London, with his elder sister, Gwen John. His favourite themes were gypsies, fishing folk and wild, lovely, yet regal women.

Selected works: *Smiling Woman* (Tate Gallery,

A
R
T

London); *Richard Hughes* (Tenby Museum & Picture Gallery).

John, Gwen (1876–1939)   Welsh painter and elder sister of Augustus John. Worked as an artist's model and became Rodin's mistress.
Selected works: *Self-portrait* (Tate Gallery, London); *A Corner of the Artist's Room* (Cannon Hall, Barnsley).

Johns, Jasper (1930–)   American Neo-Dadaist and strong influence on of Pop Art whose sculptures are of everyday items.
Selected work: *Zero Through Nine* (Tate Gallery, London).

Jordaens, Jacob (1593–1678)   Flemish low-life and religious painter. Pupil of Rubens.
Selected works: *Commerce and Industry Protecting the Fine Arts* (Koninklijk Museum voor Schone Kunsten, Antwerp); *Presentation in the Temple* (Rubenshuis, Antwerp); *The Fruit Seller* (Glasgow City Art Gallery).

Jorn, Asger Oluf (1914–73)   Danish Expressionist (properly, Asger Jorgensen). Founded the CoBrA group, which was named after COpenhagen, BRussels, Amsterdam.
Selected work: *The Lost World* (Stedelijk Van Abbe-Museum, Eindhoven).

Kandinsky, Wassily (1866–1944)   Russian pioneer of abstract art who was influenced by the Fauves, Bauhaus, and Surrealists. He founded Der Blaue Reiter group with Franz Marc.
Selected works: *First Abstract Watercolour* (Nina Kandinsky Collection, Neuilly-sur-Seine); *First Abstract Watercolour* (Musée National d'Art Moderne, Paris); *Blue Mountain* (Solomon R. Guggenheim Museum, New York).

Kauffmann, Angelica (1741–1807)   Swiss Neo-classical painter in England who co-founded the Royal Academy (1768). She married the Venetian painter Antonio Zucchi.
Selected works: *Self Portraits* (National Portrait Gallery & Tate Gallery, London); *Rinaldo and Armida* (Kenwood House, London); *Euphrosyne Complains to Venus of the Wounds of Cupid* (Attingham Park, Shropshire).

Kirchner, Ernst Ludwig (1880–1938)   German Expressionist, influenced by Neo-Impressionism, Fauvism and Primitive art.
Selected works: *Die Brücke painters – portraits of Otto Muller, Erich Heckel, Schmidt-Rotluff and Kirchner* (Wallraf-Richartz Museum / Museum Ludwig, Cologne); *Japanisches Theater* (Scottish National Gallery of Modern Art, Edinburgh).

Kitaj, Ron B. (1932–)   American Pop artist, introducing cultural and political elements. Active in the UK.
Selected work: *If Not . . . Not* (Scottish National Gallery of Modern Art, Edinburgh).

Klee, Paul (1879–1940)   Swiss painter and etcher. Blaue Reiter member and teacher at the Bauhaus. Described his work as 'taking a line for a walk'. A large collection of his work from 1906 to 1938 is housed in the Kunstsammlung Nordrhein-Westfalen at Düsseldorf.
Selected works: *Death and Fire* (Kunstmuseum, Berne); *Around the Fish* (Museum of Modern Art, New York); *Ad Marginem* (Kunstrunum, Basell).

Klein, Yves (1928–62)   French revolutionary Minimalist, painting only in blue. Klein was a celebrated exponent of judo and lived in Japan in 1952–3.

Selected work: *ANT 143 The Handsome Teuton* (London Arts Gallery).

Klimt, Gustav (1862–1918)   Austrian Art Nouveau painter, founder member of the Vienna Secession, 1898, artists who resigned as a group from conventional academic bodies.
Selected works: *Salome* (Galleria d'Arte Moderna, Ca' Pesaro, Venice); *The Kiss* (Österreichische Galerie, Vienna).

Kneller, (Sir) Godfrey (1646–1723)   German portrait painter in England, court painter to William III and George I. Famous for painting 42 portraits of the members of the literary association called the Kit-Kat Club, now in the National Portrait Gallery, London. These pictures were painted between 1700 and 1720 and are of a size (36" x 28") now known as 'Kit-Kat' size.
Selected works: *Isaac Newton* (National Gallery, London); *James, Duke of Monmouth* (Goodwood House, Sussex).

Kokoschka, Oskar (1886–1980)   Austrian Expressionist working in England and Switzerland.
Selected works: *Still Life with Tortoise and Hyacinth* (Österreichische Galerie, Vienna); *The Tempest* (Kunstmuseum, Basel).

Koninck, Philips de (1619–88)   Dutch panoramic landscapist.
Selected work: *Landscape* (Hunterian Art Gallery, Glasgow).

Kooning, Willem de (1904–97)   Dutch-born American Abstract Expressionist.
Selected work: *Woman I* (Museum of Modern Art, New York).

La Tour, Georges de (1593–1652)   French painter of candle-lit scenes, active entirely in Lorraine.
Selected works: *St Joseph the Carpenter* (Louvre, Paris); *The Dice Players* (Middlesbrough Art Gallery); *St Jerome* (Musée de Grenoble).

La Tour, Maurice Quentin de (1704–88)   French pastellist and portrait painter whose works are celebrated in the Musée Antoine Lecuyer in Saint-Quentin, France.
Selected works: *Mr and Mrs Angerstein*; *Madame de Pompadour* (both Louvre, Paris).

Lancret, Nicholas (1690–1743)   French Rococo genre and *fêtes galantes* painter in the style of Watteau.
Selected work: *Mademoiselle Camargo Dancing* (Wallace Collection, London).

Landseer, (Sir) Edwin Henry (1802–73)   English animal painter and engraver – a favourite of Queen Victoria. Landseer is famous for his *Monarch of the Glen* and for sculpting the lions at the foot of Nelson's Column. Buried in St Paul's Cathedral, London.
Selected works: *Dignity and Impudence*; *The Rout of Comus* (both Tate Gallery, London).

Lawrence, (Sir) Thomas (1769–1830) English painter, born in Bristol, the son of an innkeeper. In 1792 he became painter to George III.
Selected work: *Queen Charlotte* (National gallery, London).

Le Nain Brothers Antoine (c1588–1648), Louis (c1593–1648) and Mathieu (c1607–70). French painters, born in Laon. All painted scenes of peasant life but did not sign work with their initials, thus making attributions almost impossible.
Selected works: *Peasant Children* (Burrell Collection, Glasgow); *A Blacksmith in His Forge* (Louvre, Paris).

Léger, Fernand (1881–1955)   French Cubist who has a museum dedicated to him at Boit on the Côte d'Azur.

Selected works: *Homage to David* (Musée National d'Art Moderne, Paris); *Woman and Still Life* (Scottish National Gallery of Modern Art, Edinburgh).

Leighton, (Lord) Frederick (1830–96)   English painter of classical subjects, who became the 1st Baron Leighton of Stretton, the first British artist to be awarded a peerage; Leighton is buried in St Paul's Cathedral, London.

Selected work: *The Garden of the Hesperides* (Lady Lever Gallery, Port Sunlight).

Lely, (Sir) Peter (1618–80)   Dutch portrait painter working in England. Court painter to Charles II.

Selected works: *Ladies of the Lake Family* (Tate Gallery, London); *The Windsor Beauties* (Hampton Court Palace, London).

Leonardo da Vinci (1452–1519)   Italian painter, sculptor, scientist and creator of the High Renaissance style. Worked in the pay of Cesare Borgia, son of Pope Alexander VI, as senior military architect and general engineer, and then for François of France.

Selected works: *Mona Lisa* (aka La Gioconda) (Louvre, Paris); *The Virgin of the Rocks* (National Gallery, London); *The Last Supper* (Convent of S. Maria delle Grazie, Milan).

Leyster, Judith (1609–60)   Dutch genre and portrait painter, pupil of Hals. She married and worked with the painter Jan Molenaer (c1609–68).

Selected work: *The Lute-Playing Fool* (Rijksmuseum, Amsterdam).

Lichtenstein, Roy (1923–97)   American Pop artist, whose works were inspired by comic strips.

Selected works: *Whaam!* (Tate Gallery, London); *In the Car* (Scottish National Gallery of Modern Art, Edinburgh).

Limbourg Bothers (early 15th-century)   Flemish family of miniature painters in the International Gothic style. The three brothers were Pol, Jehanequin and Hermann de Limbourg.

Selected work: *Les Très Riches Heures* (Musée Condé, Chantilly).

Lippi, Filippino (c1457–1504)   Florentine painter of the transition from Early to High Renaissance. Son of Fra Filippo Lippi.

Selected work: *Vision of St Bernard* (Badia, Florence).

Lippi, Fra Filippo (c1406–69)   Florentine fresco painter, influenced by Masaccio and Gothic art. Aka 'Fra Lippo Lippi'.

Selected works: *Annunciation* (Church of S. Lorenzo, Florence); *The Adoration of the Magi* (National Gallery, Washington DC).

Lissitzky, Eleazar M. (1890–1941)   Russian Constructivist painter, influenced by Malevich.

Selected work: *Victory over the Sun* (Tatel Gallery, London).

Lorenzetti, Ambrogio (c1290/1300–c1348)   Sienese landscapist and realist.

Selected work: *frescoes in the Palazzo Pubblico*, Siena.

Lotto, Lorenzo (c1480–1556)   Italian Renaissance painter.

Selected works: *Portrait of Andreas Odoni* (Hampton Court Palace, London); *Madonna and Child with Saints* (National Gallery, Rome); *A*

Gentleman in His Study (Galleria dell'Accademia, Venice).

Louis, Morris (1912–62)   American Cubist until 1952 and then influenced by Jackson Pollock. He pioneered Colorfield painting, using bands of colour. Louis was further influenced by Helen Frankenthaler's *Mountains and Sea*, which prompted him to throw acrylic paint onto unprimed canvases to create brilliant patches of abstract colour.

Selected work: *Alpha-Phi* (Tate Gallery, London).

Low, (Sir) David (1891–1963)   New Zealand-born British political cartoonist. Joined the *Evening Standard* in 1927. His most famous creation was 'Colonel Blimp', an embodiment of the die-hard British bigot.

Lowry, Laurence Stephen (1887–1976)   Salford painter famous for his 'matchstick'-like men and women. Lowry was only ever a part-time painter and worked most of his life as a clerk.

Selected work: *The Pond* (Tate Gallery, London).

Mabuse, Jan (c1478–1532)   Flemish Mannerist allegorical painter (properly, Jan Gossaert).

Selected work: *The Adoration of the Kings*; *Little Girl* (both National Gallery, London).

Maes, Nicolaes (1634–93)   Dutch portrait and genre painter, pupil of Rembrandt.

Selected works: *The Idle Servant* (National Gallery, London).

Magritte, René (1898–1967)   Belgian Surrealist, influenced by de Chirico.

Selected work: *Black Flag* (Scottish National Gallery of Modern Art, Edinburgh).

Malevich, Kasimir (1878–1935)   Russian Suprematist, producing the first strictly geometrical art of the 20th century.

Selected work: *Woman with Water Pails* (Museum of Modern Art, New York).

Manet, Edouard (1832–83)   French precursor of Impressionism.

Selected works: *Music in the Tuileries Garden* (Hugh Lane Municipal Gallery, Dublin); *A Bar at the Folies Bergère* (Courtauld Institute Galleries, London); *Olympia* (Musée du Jeu de Paume, Paris); *Déjeuner sur l'herbe, Le* (Louvre, Paris).

Mantegna, Andrea (1431–1506)   Italian Renaissance painter working in Padua and Mantua. Mantegna married a daughter of Jacopo Bellini.

Selected works: *The Triumph of Caesar* (Hampton Court Palace, London); *Crucifixion* (Louvre, Paris); frescoes in the Camera degli Sposi, Palazzo Ducale, Mantua.

Marc, Franz (1880–1916)   German Expressionist and leading member of Der Blaue Reiter. Marc was killed at Verdun.

Selected works: *Large Blue Horses* (Walker Art Center, Minneapolis); *Red Woman* (Leicester Museum and Art Gallery).

Martini, Simone (c1280–1344)   Artist of the Sienese School.

Selected works: *Madonna with Angels and Saints, Maesta* (Palazzo Pubblico, Siena); *Christ Returns to his Parents* (Walker Art Gallery, Liverpool).

Masaccio (1401–28)   Florentine painter (properly Tommaso di Ser Giovanni di Simone dei Guidi), whose nickname literally means 'Hulking Tom'.

Selected works: frescoes in the Brancacci Chapel, S. Maria del Carmine, Florence; *Madonna and Child* (National Gallery, London); *Crucifixion* (Capodimonte, Naples).

A
R
T

Massys, Quentin (c1465–1530) Netherlandis portrait and religious-subject painter, influenced by Italian art.
Selected works: *Jesus and the Infant St John Embracing* (Chatsworth House, Derbyshire); *The Virgin and Child with Angels* (National Gallery, London); *Altarpiece of the Lamentation* (Koninklijk Museum voor Schone Kunsten, Antwerp).

Matisse, Henri (1869–1954) French painter who was leader of the Fauves, 1905–6, before changing his style. The Chapelle de Rosaire in Vence, France, was entirely designed and decorated by him. The Musée Matisse in Nice houses a collection donated by the artist's family.
Selected works: *The Painting Lesson* (Scottish National Gallery of Modern Art, Edinburgh); *Interior with Aubergines* (Musée de Peinture, Grenoble).

Memling, Hans (c1430–94) Flemish biblical and portrait painter. A good collection of his work is housed in the Memlingmuseum in Bruges.
Selected works: *Bathsheba* (Staatsgalerie, Stuttgart); *St John* (National Gallery, London); *The Adoration of the Magi* (Memlingmuseum, Bruges).

Mengs, Anton-Raphael (1728–79) German painter, born in Bohemia, the son of a Danish artist. Precursor of Neo-Classicism.
Selected works: *Maria Luisa of Parma* (Prado, Madrid); *Richard Wilson* (National Museum of Wales, Cardiff).

Metsu, Gabriel (1629–67) Dutch genre painter, particularly of domestic scenes, a pupil of Dou.
Selected works: *The Sick Child* (Rijksmuseum, Amsterdam); *The Music Lesson* (National Gallery, London); *Woman at the Spinet* (Museum Boymans-van Beuningen, Rotterdam).

Michelangelo Buonarotti (1475–1564) High Renaissance and later Mannerist painter, sculptor and architect, born near Florence, where he grew up. Patronised by Pope Julius II, for whom he decorated the ceiling of Sistine Chapel (1508–12).
Selected works: *The Last Judgement* (Sistine Chapel, Vatican Palace, Rome); *Holy Family* (Uffizi, Florence); *The Entombment* (National Gallery, London); *David* (Accademia, Florence).

Millais, (Sir) John Everett (1829–96) English co-founder of the Pre-Raphaelite Brotherhood. Born in Southampton. In 1840 he became the youngest ever student at the Royal Academy, and its President in 1896.
Selected works: *The Blind Girl* (Birmingham City Museum & Art Gallery); *Christ in the House of His Parents* (Tate Gallery, London); *The Return of the Dove to the Ark* (Ashmolean Museum, Oxford); *Ophelia* (Tate Gallery, London); *Autumn Leaves* (Manchester City Art Gallery).

Millet, Jean François (1814–75) French realist painter of peasant life. Worked at Barbizon from 1849.
Selected works: *The Gleaners* (Louvre, Paris); *La Famille du Paysan* (National Museum of Wales, Cardiff).

Miró, Joàn (1893–1983) Spanish Abstract painter,sculptor and ceramicist, influenced by Cubism and Surrealism.
Selected works: *Samurai* (Cannon Hall, Barnsley); *The Egg* (Foundation Macghet, Saint-Paul-de Venice).

Modigliani, Amadeo (1884–1920) Italian painter and sculptor, working in Paris from 1906.
Selected work: *Seated Nude* (Courtauld Institute, London).

Moholy-Nagy, László (1895–1946) Hungarian-born, American experimental artist and photographer, influenced by Lissitzky and Constructivism. He developed kinetic art and taught at the Bauhaus and in Chicago.
Selected work: *Z IV* (Marlborough Gallery, London).

Mondrian, Piet (1872–1944) Dutch member of De Stijl and developer of Neo-Plasticism, who influenced the Bauhaus School.
Selected works: *Broadway Boogie Woogie* (Museum of Modern Art, New York); *Composition in Black and White* (Rijksmuseum Kröller-Müller, Otterlo); *The Grey Tree* (Haags Gemeentemuseum, The Hague).

Monet, Claude (1840–1926) Father of Impressionism, whose *Impression: Sunrise* gave its name to the movement. Monet's *Déjeuner sur l'herbe* (Luncheon on the Grass) should not be confused with Manet's.
Selected works: *Field with Poppies* (Louvre, Paris); *The Beach at Trouville* (Tate Gallery, London); *Rouen Cathedral: Sunset* (Museum of Fine Arts, Boston, Mass.).

Moore, Henry Spencer (1898–1986) English sculptor, born in Castleford, Yorkshire, the son of a coal-miner. Moore is best known for his reclining female figures, carved in wood and stone or cast in bronze. He was an official war artist 1940–42, during which time he produced a famous series of drawings of air-raid shelter scenes. His principal commissions included the *Madonna and Child* in St Matthew's Church, Northampton; the decorative frieze on the Time-Life building, London; and the massive reclining figures for the UNESCO building in Paris and the Lincoln Center in New York. Moore was awarded the Order of Merit in 1963.

Moreau, Gustave (1826–98) French Symbolist painter whose Paris home and studio is now the Musée Gustave Moreau.
Selected work: *The Apparition* (Louvre, Paris).

Morisot, Berthe (1841–95) French Impressionist, granddaughter of Fragonard, who married Eugène, the brother of Manet.
Selected work: *Cradle* (Louvre, Paris).

Moro, Antonio (c1519–76) Dutch court painter to the Habsburgs and Mary I of England, who knighted him as Sir Anthony More.
Selected works: *Queen Anna of Spain* (Kunsthistorisches Museum, Vienna); *Sir Henry Lee* (National Portrait Gallery, London).

Morse, Samuel (1791–1872) American painter and first President of the National Academy (1826), but better known for his invention of the electric telegraph.
Selected works: *House of Representatives* (Corcoran, Washington DC); *Lafayette* (Brooklyn Museum, New York).

Motherwell, Robert Burns (1915–91) American Abstract Expressionist who married fellow Expressionist Helen Frankenthaler in 1955.
Selected works: *Elegy to the Spanish Republic XXXIV* (Albright-Knox Art Gallery, Buffalo, NY).

Mucha, Alphonse (1860–1939) Czech painter, graphic artist and designer, chiefly known for his Art Nouveau illustration style, especially the posters for the actress Sarah Bernhardt.
Selected work: *Job and Lorenzaccio* (Victoria and Albert Museum, London).

Munch, Edvard (1863–1944) Norwegian Expressionist. Important collections of his work are at the Rasmus Meyers Samlinger, Bergen, and the Munch Museum and the National Gallery, Oslo.

Selected works: *The Scream* (Nasjonalgalleriet, Oslo); *Vampire* (Munch-Museet, Oslo); *Ashes* (Nasjonalgalleriet, Oslo).

Murillo, Bartolomé Esteban (c1618–82)   Spanish Baroque painter of religious and genre subjects. Born in Seville, Murillo fell from a scaffold when painting an altarpiece at Cadiz, and died shortly afterwards in Seville.

Selected works: *Virgin of the Rosary* (Archbishop's Palace, Seville); *The Two Trinities*, aka *The Holy Family* (National Gallery, London); *Boys with Fruit* (Alte Pinakothek, Munich).

Nash, Paul (1889–1946)   English painter and co-founder of the Modern Movement. Nash was an official war artist in both world wars.

Selected works: *Landscape of the Vernal Equinox* (Scottish National Gallery of Modern Art, Edinburgh); *Pillar and Moon*; *Totes Meer* (Dead Sea) (both Tate Gallery, London).

Nicholson, Ben (1894–1982)   English Abstract painter who used a restricted palette of greys and muted tones. Married three times; his second wife was the sculptor Barbara Hepworth.

Selected works: *Still Life* (Glasgow Art Gallery & Museum); *White Relief* (Tate Gallery, London).

Nolde, Emil (1867–1956)   German Expressionist and printmaker (properly, Emil Hansen). His Art Nouveau house in Seebull, Germany, is now a museum.

Selected works: *Doubting Thomas* (Nolde-Museum, Seebull); *Death of Mary* (Museum Folkwang, Essen); *The Flower Garden* (Wallraf-Richartz Museum, Cologne).

O'Keeffe, Georgia (1887–1986)   American Surrealist and Abstract painter who married photographer Alfred Stieglitz.

Selected work: *Black Iris* (Metropolitan Museum of Art, New York).

Oliver, Isaac (c1560–1617)   French-born English miniaturist who married the half-sister of Marcus Gheeraerts the Younger. Oliver's work included a famous miniature of Elizabeth I of England that displeased her immensely.

Selected work: *Self Portrait* (National Portrait Gallery, London).

Opie, John (1761–1807)   Cornish portrait and history painter, son of a carpenter. Nicknamed the 'Cornish Wonder'.

Patronised by John Wolcot (the political satirist Peter Pindar). His first exhibited historical work was *The Assassination of James I of Scotland* (1786), followed by *The Murder of Rizzio* (1787), both destroyed by bombing in 1941.

Selected work: *Mary Wollstonecraft* (Tate Gallery, London).

Oudry, Jean-Baptist (1686–1755)   French still-life painter.

Selected works: *The Dog* (Burrell Collection, Glasgow); *The Calling of the Hounds* (tapestry) (Pitti Palace, Florence).

Palma Vecchio (c1480–1528)   Venetian painter of *sacra conversazione* altarpieces (properly, Jacopo Palma).

Selected works: *Venus and Cupid* (Fitzwilliam Museum, Cambridge); *Polyptych of St. Barbara* (S. Maria Formosa, Venice); *The Assumption* (Galleria dell'Accademia, Venice).

Palmer, Samuel (1805–81)   English landscapist and etcher, influenced by William Blake.

Selected work: *Coming from Evening Church* (Tate Gallery, London).

Parmigianino, Il (1503–40)   Italian early Mannerist (properly, Girolamo Francesco Maria Mazzola).

Selected works: *The Marriage of St Catherine* (National Gallery, London); *Madonna with the Long Neck* (Uffizi, Florence); frescoes in S. Maria della Steccata, Parma.

Pasmore, Victor (1908–98)   English portrait, still-life and landscape painter. Co-founder of the Euston Road School. In the late 1940s he turned towards abstract art.

Selected works: *Inland Sea* (Tate Gallery, London); *Wine Red* (Bristol City Art Gallery).

Pechstein, Max Hermann (1881–1955)   Co-founder of German Expressionism and member of Die Brücke from 1906 before helping to found the rival Neue Sezession (New Secession).

Selected work: *Indian and Woman* (Morton D. May Collection).

Perugino, Pietro (c1445–1523)   Umbrian Renaissance painter (properly, Pietro di Cristoforo Vannucci). Perugino was the master of Raphael).

Selected work: *Virgin and Child* (National Gallery, London).

Piazzetta, Giovanni Battista (1682–1754)   Venetian painter, illustrator and designer.

Selected works: *Fortune Teller* (Accademia, Venice); fresco *The Crucificxion* (Church of S. Maddalena de' Pazzi, Florence).

Picabia, Francis (1879–1953)   French Cubist, Dadaist and Surrealist who also dabbled in Futurism.

Selected work: *Udnie* (Musée d'art Moderne, Paris).

Picasso, Pablo (1881–1973)   Spanish painter and sculptor who embraced Cubism, Surrealism and Expressionism. Born in Malaga, Picasso, along with Braque, pioneered Cubism. Picasso's blue period was from 1902 to 1904, followed by his pink period (1904–6) and then a short brown period (1905–6). He was director of the Prado during the Spanish Civil War and joined the Communist Party in 1944. Picasso died in Mougins, France. The Musée Picasso in Antibes was decorated by him in 1946, and many works are in the Musée Picasso, Paris. His mural *War and Peace* is housed in the Musée National Picasso in Vallauris, and *Man with a Lamb* is in the public square. The Museo Pablo Picasso in Barcelona holds early works donated by the painter in 1970.

Selected works: *Three Dancers* (Tate Gallery, London); *Les Demoiselles d'Avignon* (Museum of Modern Art, New York); *Guernica* (Prado, Madrid).

Piero della Francesca (c1419–92)   Umbrian painter, scientist and mathematician.

Selected works: *The Nativity* (National Gallery, London); *Constantine's Dream* (Legend of the Holy Cross) (S. Francesco, Arezzo); *Federigo da Montrefeltro* (Uffizi, Florence).

Piper, John (1903–92)   English artist, born in Epsom, Surrey. Originally an abstract painter, he turned to Romantic realism under the influence of Palmer and the earlier English topographical painters. As an official war artist (1940–42), he painted many successful war pictures, but his design of the stained glass windows for Coventry Cathedral and Eton are his best-known works.

Pisanello, Antonio (c1390–1455)   Italian painter and follower of the International Gothic style of Gentile da Fabriano.
Selected works: *The Vision of St Eustace* (National Gallery, London); *Lionello d'Este* (Accademia Carrara, Bergamo); *St George and the Princess* (Church of S. Anastasia, Verona).

Pisano, Andrea (c1290–c1349)   Italian sculptor born in Pontadera and trained in Pisa. Considered the founder of the Florentine School of sculpture. Best known for his relief panels on the bronze south door of the Florence Baptistry.
Selected works: *Weaver* (Campanile, Florence cathedral); *Noah* (Museo dell'Opers del Duomo, Florence).

Pissarro, Camille (1830–1903)   French Impressionist and Pointillist, born in St Thomas, West Indies.
Selected works: *Boulevard Montmartre by Night*; *Lower Norwood, London, Snow* (both National Gallery, London).

Pollaiuolo, Antonio (c1431–c1498)   Florentine painter, sculptor, goldsmith and engraver, properly Antonio di Jacopo d'Antonio Benci, but took his name from his father's profession as a poulterer. Collaborated with his brother Piero (c1443–c1496) on the bronze tomb of Sixtus IV and the monument to Pope Innocent VIII, both in Saint Peter's, Rome. Other notable works include the bronze statuette *Hercules and Antaeus* in the Bargello, Florence, and the signed engraving *Battle of the Ten Nude Gods*. It is not always clear which brother should be credited with some of their oeuvre, but Piero, principally a painter, is thought to be responsible for at least three of the *Seven Virtues* in the Uffizi, Florence; three others were probably as collaborations with Antonio, and the seventh by Bottizelli.

Pollock, Jackson (1912–56)   American Abstract Expressionist and early exponent of tachisme (action painting). Full Fathom Five was probably the first work of this controversial 'poured painting' style. Alcoholism and his death in a car crash added to Pollock's notoriety.
Selected works: *Enchanted Wood* (Guggenheim Foundation, Venice); *Summertime: Number 9a* (Tate Gallery, London).

Pontormo, Jacopo Carrucci (1494–1557) Florentine early Mannerist.
Selected works: *Four Scenes from the Life of Joseph* (National Gallery, London); frescoes in S. Felicita, Florence; *Cosimo I de Medici* (Uffizi, Florence).

Poussin, Nicolas (1594–1665)   French Classical landscapist who was court painter to Louis XIII. His oeuvre included mythological works and biblical subjects; he was an early exponent of history painting.
Selected works: *The Nurture of Jupiter* (Dulwich Gallery, London); *Tancred and Erminia* (Barber Institute, University of Birmingham); *Inspiration of the Poet* (Louvre, Paris); *The Adoration of the Golden Calf* (National Gallery, London).

Primaticcio, Francesco (1504–70)   Italian Mannerist painter, sculptor and architect. A collection of his drawings is in the Louvre.
Selected works: *The Rape of Helen* (Bowes Museum, Barnard Castle); Fontainebleau Palace decorations, France.

Puvis de Chavannes, Pierre (1824–98)   French decorative, symbolic painter, noted for his murals. A number of huge canvases are set in to the walls of the grand staircase of the Musée de Picardie, Amiens.
Selected work: *Poor Fisherman* (Louvre, Paris).

Raeburn, (Sir) Henry (1756–1823)   Scottish portraitist, elected to the Royal Academy in 1815 and knighted by George IV in 1822.
Selected works: *Reverend Robert Walker Skating on Duddingston Loch* (National Gallery of Scotland, Edinburgh); *Self Portrait* (National Gallery of Scotland, Edinburgh); *Lady Dalrymple* (Tate Gallery, London).

Raphael (1483–1520)   Italian High Renaissance painter who worked on a number of Papal commissions. Raphael (properly, Raffaello Santi or Sanzio) was born in Urbino. Leo X selected him to succeed Donato Bramante (a relative) as architect of St Peter's in 1514. His last work, the *Transfiguration* was left unfinished when he died.
Selected works: *Pope Julius II* (National Gallery, London); *The Madonna of the Goldfinch* (Uffizi, Florence); frescoes in the Vatican Palace, Rome.

Redon, Odilon (1840–1916)   French Symbolist painter and graphic artist; a precursor of Surrealism.
Selected work: *Violette Heyman* (Cleveland Museum of Art, Ohio).

Rembrandt Harmenszoon van Rijn (1606–69) Dutch painter, etcher and graphic artist whose home is now a museum in Amsterdam. Born in Leiden, the son of a prosperous miller, his first wife was Saskia van Ulenburgh (d. 1642). He failed to achieve financial security and, despite being the most famous painter of his time, died a pauper.
Selected works: *Self Portrait* (Walker Art Gallery, Liverpool); *Portrait of Titus* (Wallace Collection, London); *The Night Watch – The Militia Company of Captain Frans Banning Cocq* (Rijksmuseum, Amsterdam).

Reni, Guido (1575–1642)   Bolognese Classical painter of Baroque religious works.
Selected work: *St John the Baptist* (Dulwich Gallery , London).

Renoir, Pierre Auguste (1841–1919)   French Impressionist, born in Limoges. He visited Italy in 1880 and during the next few years painted a series of *Bathers* in a colder, more classical style, influenced by Ingres and Raphael. He then returned to hot reds, orange and gold to portray nudes in sunlight. Renoir's hands were crippled by arthritis in later years. His son Jean (1894–1979) became a great film director.
Selected works: *Umbrellas* (Hugh Lane Municipal Gallery of Modern Art, Dublin); *Umbrellas* (National Gallery, London); *Moulin de la Galette* (Louvre, Paris); *Madame Charpentier and Her Children* (Metropolitan Museum of Art, New York).

Reynolds, (Sir) Joshua (1723–92)   English portraitist and art theorist. Co-founder and first President of the Royal Academy, 1768. Principal painter to George III of England, 1784.
Selected works: *Self-portrait,* c1753 (National Portrait Gallery, London); *Three Ladies Adorning a Term of Hymen: The Montgomerie Sisters* (Tate Gallery, London); *Admiral Lord Anson* (Shugborough, Staffordshire).

Ribera, Jusepe de (c1591–1652)   Spanish Baroque painter, known as Lo Spagnoletto (The Little Spaniard).
Selected work: *Martyrdom of St Bartholomew* (Prado, Madrid).

Richter, Hans (1888–1976)   American painter,

sculptor and film-maker, born in Berlin. Member of the Zurich Dadaists, 1917.

Rigaud, Hyacinthe (1659–1743)   French Rococo painter. Portraitist to Louis XIV and Louis XV of France. A small collection of his works is housed in the Musée Rigaud, Perpignan.

Selected works: *Cardinal de Bouillon* (Musée Rigaud, Perpignan); *Louis XIV; Louis XV* (both Musée de l'Histoire de la France, Versailles).

Riley, Bridget (1931–)   English Op artist since the early 1960s.

Selected work: *Crest* (Rowan Gallery, London).

Rodin, Auguste (1840–1917)   French sculptor, born in Paris, the son of a clerk. Produced his first great work in 1864, *L'Homme au nez cassé*. In 1877 he made a tour of the French cathedrals and published *Les Cathédrales de la France* in 1914. From 1886 to 1895 he worked on *Les Bourgeois de Calais*. His statues include a nude Victor Hugo and Balzac in a dressing gown. His works are represented in the Musée Rodin, Paris; the Rodin Museum, Philadelphia; and the Victoria and Albert Museum, London, where there is a collection of his bronzes that he presented to the British nation in 1914.

Selected works: *Le Penseur* (The Thinker) (Musée Rodin, Paris); *Le Baiser* (The Kiss) (Tate Gallery, London).

Romney, George (1734–1802)   English portraitist and history painter, born in Lancashire. At the height of his fame he rivalled both Reynolds and Gainsborough and his later history paintings and portraits of Emma Hart (later Lady Hamilton) enhanced his reputation, but he eventually died insane.

Selected work: *Self-portrait* (National Gallery, London).

Rosa, Salvator (1615–73)   Neapolitan Baroque and macabre painter.

Selected work: *Landscape* (National Gallery, London).

Rossetti, Dante Gabriel (1828–1882)   Anglo-Italian painter and poet, brother of the poet Christina Rossetti. DG Rossetti was born in London and his mother was Frances Mary Lavinia Polidori, daughter of Gaetano Polidori and sister of Lord Byron's physician, Dr John Polidori. Rossetti was fascinated by the Middle Ages and was a co-founder of the Pre-Raphaelite Brotherhood.

Selected works: *St George and the Princess Sabra; Ecce Ancilla Domini* (both Tate Gallery, London); *The Blessed Damozel* (Lady Lever Art Gallery, Port Sunlight).

Rothko, Mark (1903–70)   American Abstract Expressionist and co-founder of Colorfield painting. Latvian-born (properly, Marcus Rothkovitch).

Selected work: *Two Openings in Black over Wine* (Tate Gallery, London).

Rouault, Georges (1871–1958)   French Expressionist painter often on religious themes. Many of his works were acquired by the art dealer Ambroise Vollard.

Selected works: *Head of Christ* (Musée National d'Art Moderne, Paris); *Two Nudes* (Metropolitan Museum of Art, New York).

Rousseau, Henri (1844–1910)   French Primitive painter, known as 'Le Douanier' due to his early occupation as a tax collector in the Paris customs office.

Selected works: *The Child among Rocks* (Philadelphia Museum of Art); *The Sleeping Gypsy* (Museum of Modern Art, New York).

Rubens, (Sir) Peter Paul (1577–1640)   Enormously successful and productive Flemish Baroque painter and diplomat. Rubens's Antwerp home is now a museum. He married his first wife, Isabella Brandt, in 1609 (d. 1626) and his second, Hélèna Fourment, in 1630.

Selected works: *The Judgement of Paris* (National Gallery, London); *Descent from the Cross* (Antwerp Cathedral); *Peace and War* (National Gallery, London); *Portrait of Isabella Brandt* (Wallace Collection, London); *Apotheosis of James I* (Whitehall Banqueting House, London); *Hélèna Fourment with Two of Her Children* (Louvre, Paris).

Ruysdael, Jacob van (1628–82)   Dutch landscapist whose work was only appreciated after his death.

Selected works: *The Jewish Cemetery* (Gemäldegalerie, Dresden); *View on the Amstel Looking toward Amsterdam* (Fitzwilliam Museum, Cambs); *The Windmill at Wijk bij Duurstede* (Rijksmuseum, Amsterdam).

Ruysdael, Salomon van (c1600–70)   Dutch realist landscapist, properly, Salomon de Goyer. Uncle of Jacob van Ruysdael.

Selected works: *River Scene* (Leicester City Art Gallery); *River Scene near Utrecht* (Gemeentemuseum, Arnhem); *Landscape with a Carriage and Horsemen at a Pool. (National Gallery, London).*

Saenredam, Pieter Janszoon (1597–1665)   Dutch architectural painter.

Selected works: *Interior of the Grote Kerk at Haarlem* (National Gallery, London); *Interior of the Nieuwe Kerk* (Frans Hals Museum, Haarlem); *Interior of the Janskerk*, Utrecht (Centraal Museum, Utrecht).

Sargent, John Singer (1856–1925)   American portraitist of fashionable London society from 1884. Born in Florence, Sargent was an official war artist during World War I.

Selected works: *Carnation, Lily, Lily, Rose* (Tate Gallery, London); *Madame Gautreau* (Metropolitan Museum of Art, New York); *The Three Vickers Sisters* (Mappin Art Gallery, Sheffield); *Gassed* (Imperial War Museum, London)..

Sassetta, Stefano di Giovanni (c1392–1450)   Sienese painter.

Selected works: *St Francis Renounces His Earthly Father* (National Gallery, London); *Journey of the Magi* (Metropolitan Museum of Art, New York).

Sebastiano del Piombo (c1485–1547)   Venetian painter influenced by Giorgione and Michelangelo.

Selected works: *The Raising of Lazarus* (National Gallery, London); *The Madonna and Child with SS. Catherine and John the Baptist* (Galleria dell'Accademia, Venice).

Seurat, Georges Pierre (1859–91)   French Neo-Impressionist and developer of Pointillism.

Selected works: *Sunday Afternoon on the Island of the Grande Jatte* (Art Institute of Chicago); *Circus* (Louvre, Paris); *Bathers at Asnières* (National Gallery, London).

Sickert, Walter Richard (1860–1942)   German-born, English painter, influenced by Degas and Whistler. Co-founder of the Camden Town Group.

Selected works: *The Lion of St Mark* (Fitzwilliam Museum, Cambridge); *View at Ramsgate* (Huddersfield Art Gallery).

Sisley, Alfred (1839–99)   French landscape Impressionist of British parentage, noted for his subtle treatment of skies.

ART

Selected works: *Flood at Port Marly*; *The Boat during the Flood* (both Louvre, Paris).

Snyders, Frans (1579–1657)   Flemish painter, born in Antwerp. Pupil of Pieter Brueghel the Younger. He specialised in still life and animals, often assisting Rubens in hunting scenes. In 1611 he married Margaretha de Vos, the sister of the Flemish painters Cornelis and Paul de Vos.

Selected work: *Stag Hunt* (Prado, Madrid).

Soutine, Chaim (1893–1943)   Lithuanian painter, in Paris from 1913, influenced by Cézanne and Die Brücke group.

Selected work: *Les Gorges du Loup sur Vence* (Scottish National Gallery of Modern Art, Edinburgh).

Spencer, (Sir) Stanley (1891–1959)   English painter of portraits, landscapes and religious works. Born in Cookham, Berkshire. Spencer was an official war artist in World War II.

Selected works: Sandham Memorial Chapel murals, Burghclere; *The Garden at Cookham Rise* (Huddersfield Art Gallery).

Steen, Jan (c1626–79)   Dutch painter of low-life scenes and still-life subjects.

Selected works: *The Effects of Intemperence* (National Gallery, London); *Self-portrait* (Rijksmuseum, Amsterdam); *Romping Couple* (Stedelijk Museum 'De Lakenhal', Leiden).

Steer, Philip Wilson (1860–1942)   English landscapist. Member of the New English Art Club.

Selected works: *Mrs Cyprian Williams and Her Daughters* (Tate Gallery, London); *The Last Chapter* (Cartwright Hall, Bradford); *Self Portrait, The Music Room* (Tate Gallery, London).

Stella, Frank (1936–)   American Abstract Expressionist and Minimalist.

Selected work: *Hyena Stomp* (Tate Gallery, London).

Streeter, Robert (1624–79)   Pepys's famous history painter who became Charles II's serjeant-painter in 1660. The ceiling of Oxford's Sheldonian Theatre is one of his few remaining decorative works.

Stubbs, George (1724–1806)   English animal painter and engraver, born in Liverpool. Stubbs specialised in painting horses.

Selected works: *Mares and Foals in a River Landscape* (Tate Gallery, London); *Self-portrait* (National Portrait Gallery, London); *Molly Long Legs with a Jockey* (Walker Art Gallery, Liverpool).

Sutherland, Graham Vivian (1903–80)   English portraitist and official war artist, WW2. His official portrait of Sir Winston Churchill was destroyed by Lady Churchill, as she detested it. The Graham Sutherland Gallery in Haverfordwest is devoted almost entirely to his work.

Selected work: *Somerset Maugham* (Tate Gallery, London); *Christ in Majesty* (tapestry in Coventry Cathedral)..

Tanguy, Yves (1900–55)   French Surrealist in the USA from 1939, influenced by de Chirico.

Selected work: *The furniture of time* (Collection Soby, New Canaan, Connecticut).

Teniers the Younger, David (1610–90)   Flemish genre painter. Curator of Archduke Leopold Wilhelm's picture gallery in Brussels, and copyist of many of its masterpieces.

Selected works: *Archduke Leopold Wilhelm in His Gallery* (Musées Royaux des Beaux Arts, Brussels); *The Dentist* (Manchester City Art Gallery); *Interior with a Peasant* (Nottingham Castle Museum).

Terborch, Gerard (1617–81)   Dutch genre painter of domestic scenes.

Selected works: *A Man* (Museum de Waag, Deventer); *A Woman Playing a Theorbo to Two Men* (National Gallery, London); *Woman at a Mirror* (Rijksmuseum, Amsterdam).

Terbrugghen, Hendrick (c1588–1629)   Dutch religious and genre painter, influenced by Caravaggio.

Selected work: *Jacob, Laban and Leah* (National Gallery, London).

Thornhill, (Sir) James (1675–1734)   English Baroque painter, born in Melcombe Regis, Dorset. His paintings for the dome of St Paul's (1707), the hall at Blenheim Palace, Hampton Court and the Painted Hall at Greenwich Hospital – on a scale unrivalled in Britain in the 15th century – made his reputation. He was the father-in-law of William Hogarth. Knighted by George I (1720) and appointed serjeant-painter; from 1722 became MP for Melcombe Regis.

Thornycroft, (Sir) William Hamo (1850–1925)   English sculptor, born in London.

Selected works: public statues of General Gordon in Trafalgar Square; John Bright in Rochdale; and Cromwell outside the Houses of Parliament.

Tiepolo, Giambattista (1696–1770)   Venetian Rococo decorative painter. His work is prominent in palaces and churches throughout Europe.

Selected works: *Finding of Moses* (National Gallery of Scotland, Edinburgh); frescoes in the Residenz, Würzburg, and the Royal Palace, Madrid.

Tintoretto (1518–94)   Venetian Mannerist (properly, Jacopo Robusti). The son of a silk dyer (*tintore*), hence his nickname of Tintoretto (Little Dyer).

Selected works: *St George Killing the Dragon* (National Gallery, London); *Miracle of S. Marco* (Galleria dell'Accademia, Venice); *The Washing of the Feet* (Wilton House, Wiltshire).

Titian (c1487–1576)   Venetian painter (properly, Tiziano Vecellio); renowned for his use of colour. The Prado in Madrid has a superb collection of his work, particularly the paintings done under the patronage of the Holy Roman Emperor, Charles V. Titian was buried in the Church of S. Maria dei Frari, Venice.

Selected works: *The Three Ages of Man* (National Gallery of Scotland, Edinburgh); *Venus, Cupid and a Lute Player* (Fitzwilliam Museum, Cambridge); *Ecce Homo* (National Gallery of Ireland); *The Assumption* (S. Maria dei Frari, Venice).

Toulouse-Lautrec, Henri de (1864–1901)   French painter, graphic artist and lithographer who forsook his noble origins for the cafés of Montmartre. He was influenced by Degas and by Japanese prints. Much of his work is housed in the Musée Toulouse-Lautrec et Galerie d'Art Moderne, Albi, France.

Selected works: *Jane Avril at the Moulin Rouge* (Courtauld Institute, London); *La Toilette* (Louvre, Paris); *The Artist's Mother* (Musée Toulouse-Lautrec, Albi); *At the Moulin Rouge*; *In the Circus Fernando: The Ringmaster* (both Art Institute of Chicago); *At the Moulin de la Galette* (Stedelijk Museum, Amsterdam); *Jane Avril Dansant* (Louvre, Paris).

Turner, Joseph Mallord William (1775–1851)   English Romantic landscapist and precursor of Impressionism. A superb collection of Turner's work is in the Clore Gallery, attached to the Tate Gallery, London. Turner entered the Royal Academy at the age of 14 and was patronised by Lord Egremont of

Petworth. He died in temporary lodgings in Chelsea under the assumed name of Booth.

Selected works: *Battle of Trafalgar* (National Maritime Museum, London); *Norham Castle, Sunrise* (Tate Gallery, London); *The Fall of the Clyde* (Lady Lever Art Gallery, Port Sunlight).

Uccello, Paolo (1397–1475) Florentine painter noted for his sophisticated use of perspective.

Selected works: *The Hunt* (Ashmolean Museum, Oxford); *The Battle of San Romano* (National Gallery, London); *The Deluge* (Church of S. Maria Novella, Florence).

Utrillo, Maurice (1883–1955) French painter, born in Montmartre, Paris, the illegitimate son of painter Suzanne Valadon. Adopted by the Spanish writer Miguel Utrillo, he began to paint at Montmagny in 1902. Utrillo specialised in Paris street scenes. Despite acute alcoholism and drug addiction, his output was astonishing. His 'White Period' paintings of about 1908–14 are much sought after. He signed his works 'Maurice Utrillo V' incorporating the initial of his mother's family name.

Vasarely, Victor (1908–97) Hungarian-born, French precursor of Op art. The 16th century Château de Gordes in Vaucluse, France, is now the Musée Didactique Vasarely.

Selected works: *Sirius II* (Galerie Denise René, Paris); *Ondho* (Museum of Modern Art, New York); *Supernovae* (Tate Gallery, London).

Vasari, Giorgio (1511–74) Italian Mannerist fresco painter, architect and biographer. His *Lives of the Artists* was first published in Florence in 1550. The Casa Vasari in Arezzo was decorated by him.

Selected works: *Allegory of the Immaculate Conception* (Ashmolean Museum, Oxford); *Lorenzo the Magnificent* (Uffizi, Florence).

Velazquez, Diego Rodriguez de Silva y (1599–1660) Spanish Baroque genre and royal portrait painter to Philip IV of Spain. Born in Seville and pupil of Francisco Pacheco, whose daughter he married in 1618.

Selected works: *Las Meninas* (aka *Maids of Honour*) (Prado, Madrid); *An Old Woman Cooking Eggs* (National Gallery of Scotland, Edinburgh); *The Toilet of Venus*, known as *The Rokeby Venus* (National Gallery, London).

Velde, Esaias van de (c1591–1630) Dutch realistic landscapist who was the master of Jan van Goyen.

Selected work: *Ice Scene* (Alte Pinakothek, Munich).

Vermeer, Jan (1632–75) Dutch genre painter of domestic scenes. Born in Delft, the son of an art dealer, he married Caterina Bolnes, who was to bear him eleven children. Fewer than 40 of his paintings are known. During World War II, forged Vermeers were produced by Jan Van Meegeren, who for some time deceived the experts.

Selected works: *A Young Woman Standing at a Virginal* (National Gallery, London); *A Lady Reading a Letter* (Rijksmuseum, Amsterdam); *Head of Girl with a Pearl Earring* (Mauritshuis, The Hague).

Veronese (c1528–88) Venetian biblical and allegorical painter (properly, Paolo Caliari).

Selected works: *Hermes, Herse and Aglauros* (Fitzwilliam Museum, Cambridge); *Mars and Venus* (National Gallery of Scotland, Edinburgh); frescoes in the Palazzo Ducale, Venice.

Vigé-Lebrun, Elisabeth Louise (1755–1842) French painter famous for her female subjects such as Marie Antoinette. She did paint male subjects, notably the Prince of Wales and Lord Byron.

Villon, Jacques (1875–1963) French painter (real name Gaston Duchamp) who specialised in Cubist works.

Vlaminck, Maurice de (1876–1958) French Fauve who was also a noted violinist, author and racing cyclist.

Selected work: *Woody River Scene* (Glasgow Art Gallery and Museum).

Vouet, Simon (1590–1649) French Baroque history and portrait painter who was influenced by Caravaggio. Court painter to Louis XIII.

Selected work: *La Richesse* (Louvre, Paris).

Vuillard, Edouard (1868–1940) French portrait and domestic genre painter. Member of the Nabis in the 1890s.

Selected works: *The Mantelpiece* (National Gallery, London); *The Open Window* (Scottish National Gallery of Modern Art, Edinburgh).

Warhol, Andy (1928–87) American Pop Art painter, graphic artist and film-maker who was famous for the Campbell soup-can labels and magazine illustrations directly reproduced by silk-screen. His controversial films included *Sleep* (1963) and *Chelsea Girls* (1966). In 1968 he was shot and wounded by Valerie Solanis, an actress in one of his films.

Selected work: *Green Coca-Cola Bottles* (Whitney Museum of American Art, New York).

Watteau, Jean-Antoine (1684–1721) French Rococo painter of *fêtes galantes*.

Selected works: *The Music Party* (Wallace Collection, London); *Gilles* (Louvre, Paris); *Mezzetin* (Metropolitan Museum of Art, New York); *L'Enseigne de Gerseint* (Gerseint's Signboard) (Schloss Charlottenburg, Berlin).

Watts, George Frederick (1817–1904) English portrait and allegorical painter who first drew attention with his cartoon of Caractacus in the competition for murals for the new Houses of Parliament. In 1864 he married actress Ellen Terry but parted from her within a year.

Selected works: *Found Drowned* (Watts Gallery, Compton, Surrey); *Hope* (Tate Gallery, London).

West, Benjamin (1738–1820) American Neo-classical painter, in England from 1763. Founding member of the Royal Academy and its President in 1792. Court painter to George III of England, who patronised him for 40 years.

Selected works: *The Death of General Wolfe* (National Gallery of Canada, Ottawa); *The Apotheosis of Lord Nelson* (National Maritime Museum, London); *Mrs Worrall as Hebe* (Tate Gallery, London).

Westmacott, (Sir) Richard (1775–1856) A leading Neo-classical sculptor of public monuments and statues. After studying in Italy he returned to London and became a favourite sculptor of the Committee of Taste. His most accomplished monument was a public subscription commission commemorating Charles James Fox, in Westminster Abbey. His bronze public monuments include the *Achilles* at Hyde Park Corner, Park Lane.

Weyden, Rogier van der (c1399–1464) Netherlandis painter of portraits and altarpieces, noted for his technical brilliance and emotional intensity.

Selected works: *Lamentation* (*Pietà*) over the dead Christ (National Gallery, London); *Antoine de Bourgogne* (Musées Royaux des Beaux Arts, Brussels); *Deposition* (Prado, Madrid); *Bladelin Altarpiece* (Museum Dahlem, Berlin).

ART

Whistler, James Abbott McNeill (1834–1903)
American painter who lived in London and Paris. The
critic John Ruskin's vitriolic criticism of his
contributions to the Grosvenor Gallery exhibition of
1877, accusing him of 'flinging a pot of paint in the
public's face', provoked the famous lawsuit in which
Whistler was awarded a farthing's damages. Famous
for his evening scenes, called nocturnes, such as the
well-known impression of Battersea Bridge in the
Tate Gallery, London. Whistler often dressed as the
typical stereotype of an artist.

Selected works: *Thomas Carlyle* (Glasgow Art
Gallery); *Little White Girl: Symphony in White No. II*
(Tate Gallery, London); *Arrangement in Grey and
Black, No. I: The Artist's Mother* (Louvre, Paris).

Wilson, Richard (1714–82)   Welsh Classical
landscapist, influenced by Claude and Poussin. The
National Museum of Wales, Cardiff, holds an
important collection of his British and Italian
landscapes. In 1776 he became librarian to the
Royal Academy.

Selected works: *Caernarvon Castle* (National
Museum of Wales, Cardiff); *Flora Macdonald*
(Scottish National Portrait Gallery, Edinburgh);
Hadrian's Villa (Tate Gallery, London, and
Manchester City Art Gallery).

Wright, Joseph (1734–97)   English genre and
portrait painter who specialised in fireside portraits
and industrial scenes. A large number of his works
are in his home town at Derby Art Gallery; he is
known as Wright of Derby.

Selected works: *A Philosopher Giving a Lecture at
the Orrery* (Derby Museum & Art Gallery); *An
Experiment on a Bird in the Air Pump* (National

Gallery, London); *Sir Brooke Boothby* (Tate Gallery,
London).

Wyeth, Andrew Newell (1917–97)   American
figurative painter of scenes in Pennsylvania. His
Christina's World in the Museum of Modern Art, New
York, is probably the most famous American picture
of the 20th century.

Selected work: *Young America* (Pennsylvania
Academy of Fine Arts, Philadelphia).

Yeats, Jack Butler (1870–1957)   Irish painter, born in
London, brother of the poet William Butler Yeats.
Jack Yeats is considered as his country's greatest
modern artist.

Selected works: *Grief* (National Gallery of Ireland,
Dublin); *The Two Tavellers* (Tate Gallery, London)

Zoffany, Johann (1733–1810)   German portraitist
working in England from 1758, Italy from 1772 and
India from 1783. Patronised by George III of
England and a founder member of the Royal
Academy.

Selected works: *Garrick, Ackman and Bransby in
Lethe* (Birmingham City Art Gallery); *Self Portrait*
(National Portrait Gallery, London); *The Bradshaw
Family* (Tate Gallery, London); *Charles Towneley
among His Marbles* (Towneley Hall Art Gallery,
Burnley).

Zurbarán, Francisco de (1598–1664)   Spanish
Baroque religious painter whose earliest known
painting, *Immaculate Conception* dated 1616,
suggests he was schooled in the same naturalistic
style as his contemporary Velázquez.

Selected works: *The Vision of St Peter Nolasco*
(Prado, Madrid); *Death of St Bonaventure* (Louvre,
Paris).

Painting Movements and Terms

Abstract Art   Non-representational forms, relying on
line, form and colour, rather than realistic depiction.
Originally formulated by Kandinsky c1912, the art
form was embraced by all media, including
sculpture. The early years of English Abstract art are
represented in the Jim Ede collection at Kettle's
Yard, Cambridge, which includes a large collection
by Henri Gaudier-Brzeska and works by Nicholson
and Brancusi.

Abstract Expressionism   American painting
movement developed in the 1940s from Surrealism,
in which the idea is to make painting a spontaneous
act, devoid of premeditation. Jackson Pollock and
Willem de Kooning are the foremost exponents of
Action Painting (or Tachisme, as it is called in
France), using riotous swirls and splatters of colour.
Rothko, Motherwell and Gorky were also Abstract
Expressionists.

Academic Painting   Traditional and figurative
painting, often representing the work of a school or
academy.

Action Painting   see Abstract Expressionism.

Alla Prima   Describes the technique, general since
the 19th century but considered freakish and
slapdash before then, of completing the picture
surface in one session in full colour and with such
opacity that neither any previous drawing nor
underpainting (if in existence) modifies the final
effect. The French term is 'Au Premier Coup'.

Altarpiece   Decorated screen or panel placed behind
an altar. The number of panels is indicated by the

words diptych (2), triptych (3) or polyptych (many).

Armory Show, 1913   This exhibition introduced New
York to modern European painting and sculpture,
including the work of Marcel Duchamp.

Arts and Crafts   English aesthetic movement that
grew out of disenchantment at the mass-produced
and trite decorative arts that followed the Industrial
Revolution. By 1861, the social reformer, poet and
designer William Morris had co-founded a firm of
interior decorators dedicated to recapturing the
essence and quality of medieval craftmanship.
Together with artists Edward Burne-Jones and Ford
Madox Brown, and architect Philip Webb, Morris set
out to produce hand-crafted jewellery, wallpaper,
textiles, furniture and books. Many of Morris's
wallpaper and furniture designs continue to be
popular today.

Art Brut (Raw Art)   Term coined by Jean Dubuffet
'Raw Art' referring to spontaneous and untrained
artworks, often by criminals or the mentally ill.

Art Nouveau (New Art)   Art and design style
developed at the end of the 19th century,
incorporating angular or sinuous vegetable forms
into furniture and architecture. The style had its roots
in the Arts and Crafts Movement and was popular all
over Europe and North America. Samuel Bing
coined the term when he opened his Paris gallery
under the name L'Art Nouveau in 1895, although in
Germany it was known as 'Jugendstil', in Italy as
'Stile Floreale' or 'Stile Liberty', in Spain as
'Modernismo' and in Austria as 'Sezession'. Leading

exponents included René Lalique (glassware), Louis Comfort Tiffany (lamps and jewellery), Alphonse Mucha (graphic design), Alfred Gilbert (sculpture), Charles Rennie Mackintosh (interiors, buildings, furniture), Victor Horta and Hector Guimard (architecture), and Klimt, Beardsley, Jan Toorop and Ferdinand Hodler (art).

Ashcan School   Painting group preoccupied with depicting the low-life of New York in the early 20th century. George Wesley Bellows and his master, Robert Henri, were leading exponents.

Attribution   An artwork is 'attributed' to an artist when its provenance has not been proven.

Au Premier Coup   see Alla Prima.

Automatism   The method of producing a painting spontaneously and without conscious control. Used by the Surrealists such as Miró and Abstract Expressionists such as Pollock.

Avant-garde   Literally 'Vanguard'. In the forefront of artistic development, often with a conscious rejection of traditional methods or prior art forms.

Barbizon School   Mid-19th-century French school of landscape painting based in the village of Barbizon, near Fontainebleau. Members included Théodore Rousseau, Narcisse Diaz, Daubigny and Millet. As the precursors of Impressionism they painted *en plein air* observing light.

Baroque   European style of art and architecture following the High Renaissance and Mannerism, c1600–1740. It was a particularly Catholic style, popular in Italy, France and Spain in churches and public buildings, and encouraged as an integral part of the Counter-Reformation to appeal to the emotions and the senses of a still largely illiterate population. It was also eminently suitable for dramatising the idea of the divine right of kingship, and was adopted by many monarchs, such as Louis XIV of France. Exponents included the sculptor Bernini and the painters Rubens and da Cortona.

Bauhaus   School of modern art and design originally based in Weimar, founded and headed by the architect Walter Gropius in 1919. Its policy was to explore the avante-garde and to reforge the link between art and design and industry, which the Arts and Crafts Movement had largely surrendered. The Bauhaus moved to Dessau in 1925, and then to Berlin, where it was closed by the Nazis in 1933. The new Bauhaus was set up by László Moholy-Nagy in Chicago in 1937.

Blaue Reiter, Der (Blue Rider)   German Expressionist group that exhibited in Munich in 1911 and 1912. Among its members was the Russian émigré Kandinsky, who developed one of the earliest forms of abstract painting, and Franz Marc. It was an early titlework of Kandinsky's which provided the name. Other Key Members were Georges Braque, Robert Delaunay, André Derain, Paul Klee, August Macke, Henri Rousseau and Maurice de Vlaminck. Representative works are at the Kunsthalle, Bielefeld, Germany.

Bloomsbury Group   British group of the 1920s and 1930s, influenced by French Post-Impressionism and later developments. Members included Vanessa Bell, Roger Fry and Duncan Grant. Roger Fry staged the first Post-Impressionist exhibition in London in 1910.

Brücke, Die (The Bridge)   Among the earliest of the German Expressionist groups, Die Brücke was founded in Dresden in 1905, and included the artists van Dongen, Erich Heckel, Kirchner, Nolde and Karl Schmidt-Rottluff. The group disbanded in 1913. Two of the best collections of artworks by Die Brücke are housed in the Brücke-Museum, Berlin, and the Kunsthalle at Bielefeld. Kirchner's portrait series of the Die Brücke members is in the Wallraf-Richartz Museum / Ludwig Museum, Cologne.

Cabinet Picture   Small easel picture, usually not more than about 3 or 4 feet across, and often much less. The minor Dutch masters were the principal painters of this type of furniture picture at its best.

Camera Obscura   Mechanical means of securing accuracy in drawing, particularly of topographical detail. Invented in the 16th century and consisting of an arrangement of lenses and mirrors in a darkened tent or box. The view seen through the lens is reflected through the mirrors on to a sheet of paper, so that all the observer has to do is to trace round the edges. Canaletto is known to have used the device in making studies for his 'Vedute' (views). Camera Lucida is a more sophisticated optical instrument incorporating a prism.

Camden Town Group   British group formed in 1911 and influenced by the Post-Impressionists. Members included Sickert, Gore, Augustus John, Harold Gilman, Charles Ginner Lucien Pissaro and Robert Bevan.

Capriccio   A picture in which real scenes, forms and figures are rearranged to suit a particular composition.

Caravaggisti   Those artists heavily influenced by the style of Caravaggio, particularly in his use of chiaroscuro – contrasting light and dark. A strong Dutch Caravaggist school in the 17th century included van Honthorst, Terborch and Dirk van Baburen.

Cartoon   Originally a full-size preparatory drawing of an intended artwork (painting, fresco or tapestry).

Chiaroscuro (Italian, light and dark)   Defined contrast of light and dark most particularly in candle-lit scenes. Term used to describe works by Rembrandt and Caravaggio.

Classicism   The imitation of Classical art, i.e. the style of Ancient Greece or Rome. An ordered style based on the harmony of perspective and composition, devised in the early Renaissance period by Filippo Brunelleschi. Classicism influenced thinking in the Renaissance period, leading to the philosophies of Platonism and Humanism, and the stories of Homer and other ancients provided a host of popular subjects which were applied to portraits, history subjects (Titian, Jaques-Louis David) and landscape (Poussin, Claude) into the 18th century. The Stoicism of ancient Rome provided the inspiration for the Neo-classical reaction to the Rococo style in the 1780s. In the 19th century the more mundane details of life in ancient Greece or Rome became the vehicle for finely executed decorative works by Leighton, Alma-Tadema and Albert Moore.

CoBrA   Painting group that drew members from Copenhagen, Brussels and Amsterdam, including Appel and Jorn; founded in 1948. Their style incorporated violent figurative forms with Action Painting. Collections are in the Stedelijk Museum, Amsterdam. the Stedelijk Van Abbe-Museum, Eindhoven, and the Museum voor Schone Kunsten, Ghent.

Collage   Picture built up wholly or partly from pieces of paper, cloth or other material stuck on to the canvas or other ground. The word comes from the French *coller* (to stick). The device was much used by the early Cubists and by the Dadaists, such as

A
R
T

Kurt Schwitters. In his last years Matisse used pieces of coloured paper as a complete substitute for painting.

Colorfield Painting   American offshoot of Abstract Expressionism and Minimalism, exploring monochromes or restricted contrasts in paint. The original of this idea was Malevich's *Black Square* of 1913. Rothko and Klein were typical exponents.

Constructivism   Russian abstract sculptural and architectural movement from 1917 to 1921, founded by Vladimir Tatlin and developed by Naum Gabo and Antoine Pevsner, whose interest centred on movement in space and a reflection of the modern age.

Counterproof   Mirror-image reproduction made by damping an original drawing or engraving, laying a damp sheet of clean paper on it, and then running both through a press. It is sometimes done by an artist in order to bring a fresh eye to his/her work by seeing it in reverse, but it is also the commonest method of faking 'original' drawings. Such fakes are obviously easily detectable because of the reversal. An offset is the same as a counterproof but has a wider meaning, for example in printing.

Cubism   In 1907 Picasso and Braque began what was perhaps the first major development in painting away from figurative art. They were influenced by African tribal masks and by Cézanne, who looked at the world in terms of subtle coloured planes. This was the basis of Facet Cubism (1907–9). Analytical Cubism (1910–12) further fragmented basic shapes from all angles, and Synthetic Cubism (1913–14) totally recreated new objects. Delaunay (see Orphism), Léger and Gris were prominent Cubists. Although, as a particular style of art, Cubism developed into other things, it changed forever the way objects, and even the human form, were looked at.

Dada   Formulated as an anarchic form of Expressionism during World War I in Zurich, 1916, possibly by the poet Tristan Tzara. The main centres of Dada in Germany were in Berlin, Hanover and Cologne. Its purpose was to discomfit and enrage the viewer. One of its major exponents was Kurt Schwitters, whose *Elterwater Merz* is in the Hatton Gallery at the University of Newcastle upon Tyne. Other exponents included Man Ray, Jean Arp, Duchamp, Ernst, Hannah Hoch and Picabia. Dada eventually developed into Surrealism.

Euston Road School   Originally known as the Fitzroy Street School, this was a London-based school of painting and drawing, 1937–9, established by Pasmore, Claude Rogers and William Coldstream. It aimed to counteract the tendencies of Surrealism and abstract art by returning to more figurative and natural forms of expression. Exponents included Vanessa Bell, Eric Gill, Duncan Grant, Augustus John, Kenneth Martin, John Nash and Fred Uhlman.

Expressionism   Early 20th-century painting movement that expressed highly charged emotions and thoughts through colour, violence, distortion and exaggeration. The German Expressionist groups were among the first so to characterise their work, which itself developed further into Dada and Abstract Expressionism.

Fauves (Wild Beasts)   An initially derogatory label applied by the critics of artists such as Derain, Matisse, Rouault and Vlaminck when their work was exhibited in one room at the Paris Salon d'Automne of 1905. The distortion and flat patterns, along with the intensity of the colour, created a furore, and the Fauves were born. Matisse came to be regarded as their leader, although the movement itself had fallen apart by 1908 as a number of its members defected to Cubism.

Fête champêtre   Typical Rococo scene of lovers in an ideal setting, as epitomised by Lancret and Fragonard.

Fêtes galant   Pastoral masquerade in dreamlike settings, as painted by Lancret and Watteau.

Figurative Art   Artworks that contain recognisable objects.

Found Object (objet trouvé)   A Dadaist and Surrealist technique of taking any given object and displaying it as an art form, as in *Bicycle Wheel*.

Fresco   Wall-painting using water-based paints on damp plaster, particularly in European churches and ancient Greek and Egyptian temples. Giotto was one of the masters of fresco painting.

Futurism   Italian art movement developed in Venice c1909–15, embracing the machine and new technology. Balla, Carrà, Umberto Boccioni and Gino Severini were its leading exponents. The term was born in Paris, in an article in *Le Figaro* by the poet Filippo Marinetti (1876–1944). Although Futurism is sometimes used to mean any art more recent than 1900, as a discrete aesthetic movement it died early in World War I.

Genre   Type of subject painting or, more particularly, paintings of everyday life in a naturalistic style, reported without idealisation. Extremely popular in 17th-century Holland.

German Expressionism   Much of German Expressionism grew out of a painterly reaction to modernity, but most particularly to the horrors of World War I. Die Brücke was one of the first Expressionist groups, and the movement also embraced Der Blaue Reiter and Dada. Representative artists include Ernst Barlach, Beckmann, Grosz, Kirchner and Nolde.

German Romantic Painting   Early 19th -century forerunner of the English Pre-Raphaelite school. Artists were inspired by the collection of 14th and 15th century painting at the home of Bernhard August von Lindenau, now the Staatliches Lindenau-Museum, Altenburg. Friedrich, Philip Otto Runge and the Nazarenes are typical exponents.

Gothic   A generic term first used in the Renaissance period to describe the style of the 11th to 15th centuries. It was initially a critical term implying barbarism because the style made no reference to Classical precedents. In the 19th century medieval architecture and painting 'pre-Raphael' became the inspiration for a Victorian resurgence, led by the critic John Ruskin and the architect-designer A. W. Pugin, which produced 'Gothic' fantasies far removed from the original inspiration. William Morris, whilst also taking the medieval Gothic period for inspiration, went back to basics and developed the culture of craftsmanship and simple forms.

Grisaille   A painting done in tones of grey to define shadows or modelling. Often used in *trompe l'oeil*

Happening   An art form developed from the 1960s in which an artist participates in an action that encompasses the whole purpose of the piece, and once over is gone. Similar to Performance Art. Largely developed by Joseph Beuys.

High Victorian Art   The British art of the 1870s until the turn of the century, epitomised by the languid classical beauties of Albert Moore, Leighton and

Alma-Tadema – fabulously painted, very beautiful and often low on meaning. Fine collections are in the Lady Lever Art Gallery, Port Sunlight; Birmingham Museum and Art Gallery; and the Tate Gallery, London, as well as at Leighton's House in Holland Park Road, London.

History Painting After portraiture, the painting of uplifting scenes from history, the Bible or allegory was the highest form of art according to Reynolds. It was also used very effectively for propaganda purposes by the Neo-Classical painters such as Jacques-Louis David. (See his *Death of Marat*.)

Hudson River School 19th-century American landscape painting school, highly Romantic in feeling and glorifying the wonders of nature. The name is properly applied to the period after 1825 when leading exponent Thomas Cole, painter of *The Voyage of Life*, settled in New York. Other members include Albert Bierstadt, Asher B. Osmond and Frederick Church.

Impasto Word used to describe the thickness of the paint applied to a canvas or panel. When the paint is so heavily applied that it stands up in lumps, with the tracks of the brush clearly evident, it is said to be 'heavily' impasted.

Impressionism Essentially the painting of light and its effects on nature and objects. Developed in France in the late 19th century and influential all over Europe. Monet's *Impression: Sunrise* (Musée Marmottan, Paris) of 1872 was the work that suggested the name of the movement. Other leading protagonists included Cézanne, Degas, Morisot, Pissarro, Renoir and Sisley. The Impressionist exhibitions were held between 1874 and 1886. Seurat and Paul Signac took Impressionism a stage further with Pointillism.

International Gothic Late 14th-century form of Gothic which spread throughout Europe. Leading exponents were Gentile da Fabriano and Pisanello.

Kinetic Art Art that relies on real or apparent movement.

Land Art, Earth Art Arrangements of earth mounds or natural elements in situ, often in rural areas. Developed in the USA from the 1960s as a reaction to materialistic Pop Art. Richard Long is a leading exponent. Grizedale Forest in Cumbria is one of the foremost sculpture parks here, specialising in sculpture within natural settings.

Maestà (Majesty) A term used to describe a painting of the Virgin and Child enthroned, with saints or angels.

Mannerism The style that succeeded the High Renaissance, c1520–1600, exemplified by exaggerated figure drawing. Bronzino, El Greco, Michelangelo, Parmigianino and Pontormo were all Mannerists.

Metaphysical School Surrealist art group formed in Ferrara in 1917 by de Chirico and Carrà, which survived until 1920.

Minimalism American art movement in painting and sculpture, essentially paring ideas down to bare essentials. Exponents include Carl Andre and Richard Serra.

Mobile A form of sculpture invented in 1932 by Alexander Calder, and named by Marcel Duchamp. Essentially a mobile consists of a series of shapes cut from wood or sheet metal and connected by wires or rods of metal so that a gentle touch will cause the whole to revolve like a planetarium, giving an ever-changing sequence of planes, solids and colours, sometimes sounds, in three-dimensional movement.

Modern Art Accepted as the course of art in the 20th century from Impressionism up to the present day, embracing all major artistic developments including Cubism, Expressionism, Surrealism, Abstract Art, Pop Art, Minimalism and Performance Art. Excellent British public collections are in the Tate Galleries in London, Liverpool and St Ives; and the Scottish National Gallery of Modern Art in Edinburgh.

Nabis (Prophets) French anti-Impressionist art group inspired by Paul Gauguin's use of outline and flat colour which exhibited from 1892 to 1899. Members included Bonnard, Denis, Paul Sérusier and Vuillard.

Nazarenes Group of early 19th-century German and Austrian Romantic religious painters, founded by Friedrich Overbeck and Franz Pforr

Neo-classicism Often described as the art of the French Revolution, it was a late 18th-century reaction to the fussiness of the Rococo, embracing noble simplicity and stoic grandeur. Jacques-Louis David was its leading exponent in painting, and Antonio Canova in sculpture.

Neo-Impressionism A pre-Cubist movement which examined Impressionism from a scientific standpoint rather than an aesthetic one. An offshoot of Neo-Impressionism was Pointillism.

Neo-Plasticism Mondrian's term for his style of pure abstract art, first used in *De Stijl* magazine in 1917.

Neue Sachlichkeit An inter-war German brutal realism art style represented by Dix, Grosz and Christian Schad. The literal meaning is 'New Objectivity'.

New English Art Club British art group founded in 1886, which included George Clausen, Stanhope Forbes, Sargent, Steer and Edward Stott's work. The Club is well represented in the collection at Cartwright Hall, Bradford.

Norwich School A group of early 19th-century landscape painters led by Cotman and Crome.

Objet trouvé see Found Object.

Omega Workshops Co-operative workshop-cum-showroom at 33 Fitzroy Square, London, run by Roger Fry from 1913 to 1919, for the production of painted furniture, textiles, artefacts and decorative commissions.

Op Art (short for Optical Art) is a style of painting which manipulates overall patterns, using repeated shapes or undulating lines which give an optical illusion of movement and often dazzles the beholder. Victor Vasarély (1908–1997) is often considered a precursor of the op art movement with his black and white geometrical paintings but the movement became established in the early 1960s by Bridget Riley when she began to use colour in her optical paintings. The term became popularised following the 1965 New York City exhibition 'The Responsive Eye' at the Museum of Modern Art.

Perspective Quasi-mathematical system for the representation of three-dimensional objects in spatial recession on a two-dimensional surface, i.e. for the creation of an independent pictorial space as a microcosm of nature. The basic assumption of all perspective systems is that parallel lines never meet, but they appear to do so; and that, further, all parallel lines going in any one direction meet at a single point on the horizon, known as a vanishing point.

Pietà (Pity) Painting or sculpture showing the dead Christ cradled in the lap of the Virgin Mary.

A
R
T

Plein air 19th and 20th century landscape painting carried out in the open air, depicting nature and light as realistically as possible, as opposed to the deliberate Classicism of Old Masters such as Claude Lorrain and Poussin. Plein airists included the Barbizon School, the Impressionists, the Pre-Raphaelites, Millais, Ford Madox Brown and William Holman Hunt.

Pointillism Also known as 'Divisionism'. Seurat developed the Neo-Impressionist technique of using tiny dots of colour to build up form and subject; most notably used in his *Sunday Afternoon on the Island of the Grand Jatte*.

Pop Art American-formulated art form embracing painting, graphic design and sculpture, and preoccupied with modern technology, materialism and advertising. Exponents included Warhol, Blake, Johns, Robert Rauschenberg, Hamilton, Hockney, Lichtenstein and Claes Oldenburg.

Post-Impressionism Roger Fry of the Bloomsbury Group coined the term when he staged the 'Manet and the Post-Impressionists' Exhibition in London in 1910. They were artists whose chief feature in common was that they had rejected naturalism in various ways, through form, colour and subject, and included Cézanne, Denis, Gaughin, van Gogh, Picasso, Rouault, Seurat, Paul Sérusier, and Vlaminck.

Pre-Raphaelite Brotherhood The dream of a new generation to return art to its original purity of form and colour by preferring truth to nature to the stylised ideals of the Royal Academy and the ground rules laid down by its first president, Reynolds. The group was formed in London in 1848 by the painters Dante Gabriel Rossetti, William Holman Hunt, Millais and James Collinson, the art critics William Michael Rossetti and Frederick Stephens, and the sculptor Thomas Woolner. The group itself was shortlived, as its members were following separate artistic paths by 1853, but its impact on contemporary Victorian art was far more longlasting. Pre-Raphaelitism strongly influenced Ford Madox Brown, Burne-Jones, Augustus Egg, Frith, Hubert Herkomer, Watts, among others, and formed the basis of High Victorian Art. It was also a foundation stone of the Arts and Crafts Movement, led by William Morris, and the English Art Nouveau of Charles Rennie Mackintosh and the Glasgow School, Scottish painters of the late 19th century. The style also opened the way for a new class of art collectors in the form of major industrialists based in the north, important contemporary art galleries such as the Grosvenor Gallery, and satire in the form of Gilbert and Sullivan's *Patience* and the cartoons in *Punch*. Subject matter varies from the willowy and lush allegorical beauties of Rossetti and Burne-Jones to the real-life and religious ideals of Holman Hunt and Ford Madox Brown. Major collections of Pre-Raphaelite art are in the Tate Gallery, London; Walker Art Gallery, Liverpool; Lady Lever Art Gallery, Port Sunlight; Birmingham Museum and Art Gallery, and Manchester City Art Gallery.

Primitive Term applied to pre-Renaissance art and provincial or naive art by untrained artists.

Provenance The history – and hence authenticity of an artwork: who created it, who owned it, etc.

Ready-Made Term coined by Duchamp for his found objects, such as the urinal he exhibited at the 1913 Armory Show, signed 'R. Mutt'.

Realism Term applied to the realistic painting of artists such as Courbet, using a precision of detail and natural colour without idealisation.

Renaissance The 're-birth' of art and ideas in Italy after the Dark Ages and Gothic art, starting in the 14th century. It had repercussions around the known world on artistic expression, intellectual discussion, religious thought and scientific experiment. It was inspired by the rediscovery of the Classicism of the ancient civilisations of Rome and Greece in Italy and the rise of humanism. The Early Renaissance period, up to c1500, includes the artists Giotto, Duccio and Uccello, and the first experiments in art with perspective and painterly modelling. The High Renaissance saw the development of architecture, sculpture and painting by men such as Michelangelo, Leonardo, Raphael and Titian, leading to Mannerism and the late Renaissance of Correggio, Veronese and the sculptor Benvenuto Cellini. Dürer was responsible for introducing new ideas into Germany, and Holbein the Younger into England. France embraced Renaissance ideals following the rise of Italian influence after the marriage of Catherine de' Medici to the future Henri II in 1533.

Rococo 18th-century French decorative style, epitomised by the paintings of Rigaud, Boucher, Fragonard and Watteau. It illustrated the dream world in which the nobility wished to live, of sunlit *fêtes galantes*, garden swings, cherry-picking and whimsical shepherdesses. The French Revolution forced them to face an unpleasant reality. Rococo also influenced painters, architects and sculptors in Austria , Germany and Italy.

Romanticism The early 19th-century reaction to the cold formality of Neo-classicism, the style introduced a new depth of colour, expression and passion into painting not seen since Titian, particularly in the works of Delacroix and Géricault. Stylistically different Romanticists were William Blake, Constable, Friedrich, Fuseli, Turner, the Nazarenes and the Pre-Raphaelites.

Sacra conversazione A painting of the Virgin and Child, often with saints or family in an informal setting, first depicted by Fra Angelico in the 15th-century. The term literally means 'Holy Conversation'.

Slade School of Art London art school, founded 1871, that in the 1890s and under the professorship in 1918–30 of Henry Tonks produced some of the most important painters of British 20th-century art. Slade teachers and graduates included David Bomberg, Mark Gertler, Harold Gilman, Spencer Gore, Duncan Grant, Augustus John, Gwen John, Wyndham Lewis, Ambrose McEvoy, Paul Nash, C.R.W. Nevinson, Ben Nicholson, William Orpen, William Rothenstein, Matthew Smith, Stanley Spencer and Edward Wadsworth.

Socialist Realism A realistic if stylised art form officially sponsored and sanctioned for propaganda purposes in the Soviet Union of the 1930s and 40s, and later in China and Cuba.

Stijl, De ('The style') Dutch 20th-century art movement which embraced painting, sculpture, graphic design, interior design and architecture. Exponents include Mondrian, van Doesburg, Bart van der Leck and the architects Rietveld and Jacobus Oud. De Stijl architecture includes the Zonnestraal Sanatorium by Johannes Duiker, and Rietveld's Schröder house at Utrecht.

Suprematism Malevich produced his first non-representational Suprematist painting in 1913, *Black Square*, exploring elementary forms and restricted contrasts of colour which in turn influenced Expressionism, Abstract Art and Colorfield Painting.

Surrealism   Art of the inner reality, of objects out of context, and spontaneous writing, developed from Dada, founded in 1924 by the poet André Breton and influenced by Sigmund Freud's ideas. Exponents included de Chirico, Dali, Ernst, Klee, Magritte, Miró, Man Ray and Tanguy.

Symbolism   Late figurative style of painting, associated with the Art Nouveau period. Jan Toorop, Johan Thorn Prikker, Munch, Arnold Böcklin, Redon, Puvis de Chavannes, Rouault and Moreau were all exponents.

Tempera   Although this term actually means any kind of binder which will serve to 'temper' powder colour and make it workable, in practice it is confined to egg tempera (using the yolk of the egg), which was until the late 15th-century the commonest technique of painting easel pictures.

Tenebrism   Name given to painting in a very low key, particularly to the works of those early 17th-century painters, mostly Neapolitan and Spanish, who were much influenced by Caravaggio. The term literally means 'Dark colouring'.

Trompe l'oeil   Illusionistic painting effect, such as painting a ceiling to look as if it is open to the sky. The term literally means 'Deceive the eye'.

Veduta (View)   Detailed topographical painting of an existing place. Leading 'Vedutisti' were Guardi and Canaletto.

Vernissage   A custom, once widespread in academies, of allowing painters in to an exhibition after the pictures had been hung but before it was open to the public, so that they could nominally varnish (retouch) their pictures. Turner was notorious for submitting his pictures incomplete and taking advantage of Vernissage (Varnishing Day).

Nowadays the custom is merely to invite one's best patrons to see the pictures before the public are allowed in.

Vorticism   Brief English movement from 1914 with similar influences to Futurism, led by Percy Wyndham Lewis.

Watercolour   The English landscapists were particularly strong in their use of watercolour, especially the artists of the Norwich School, William Blake, Girtin, Bonington and Turner. Dante Gabriel. Rossetti brought a new jewel-like richness to watercolour painting in the 1850s, which raised the medium from insipidity.

Artists (not listed in main table)

Amigoni, Jacopo (c1682–1752)   Venetian history and portrait painter. The altarpiece of Emmanuel College, Cambridge, is his.

André, Carl (1935–)   American Minimalist sculptor famous for his 120 bricks (*Equivalent VIII*) in the Tate.

Arp, Jean (1887–1966)   French artist and co-founder of Dadaism.

Avercamp, Hendrick (1585–1634)   Dutch landscape painter who specialised in winter-scenes.

Baily, Edward Hodges (1788–1867)   English sculptor whose most famous work is his *Nelson* for the column in Trafalgar Square.

Beechey, Sir William (1753–1839)   English portraitist who was knighted for *George III and the Prince of Wales Reviewing Troops*.

Beerbohm, Max (1872–1956)   English writer and caricaturist famous for his watercolours of Oscar Wilde and Edward VII.

Bell, Vanessa (1879–1961)   English painter and decorative designer, sister of the writer Virginia Woolf.

Calder, Alexander (1898–1976)   American kinetic sculptor, abstract painter and illustrator of children's books. Calder invented the mobile.

Canova, Antonio (1757–1822)   Venetian Neoclassicist sculptor whose work includes *The Three Graces* and *Daedalus and Icarus*.

Christo (1935–)   Bulgarian-born, American sculptor famous for his 'wrappings', e.g. of the Reichstag building. His full name is Javacheff Christo.

Cooper, Samuel (c1608–72)   English miniaturist whose *Oliver Cromwell* (Buccleuch College) was his most famous work.

Cuyp, Jacob (1594–1651)   Dutch landscape and animal painter, many of whose works are housed in the Dulwich Gallery, London.

Dadd, Richard (1817–86)   English literary painter whose *Fairy Feller's Master-Stroke* is in the Tate. He murdered his father and was confined in an asylum.

Daumier, Honoré (1808–79)   French caricaturist and political satirist.

Delaroche, Paul (1797–1859)   French history painter whose *Children of King Edward* is housed in the Louvre.

Donatello (c1386–1466)   Florentine sculptor whose work included his *David* and *St George Killing the Dragon* (properly, Donato di Niccolò.)

Dyce, William (1806–64)   Scottish painter and pioneer of state art education in Great Britain.

Eyck, Hubert van (c1366–1426)   Flemish painter; the brother of Jan van Eyck.

Gabo, Naum (1890–1977)   Russian born, US artist; the brother of Antoine Pevsner, with whom he founded Constructivism.

Gérard, Baron François (1770–1837)   French artist, born in Rome; his *Cupid and Psyche* is housed in the Louvre.

Giacometti, Alberto (1901–66)   Swiss sculptor and painter best known for his attenuated sculptures of solitary figures.

Gibson, John (1790–1866)   Welsh Neo-classical sculptor whose *Tinted Venus* is in the Walker Art Gallery, Liverpool.

Gilbert & George (1943– / 1942–)   English avant-garde artists, noted for painting their faces gold and wearing identical outfits. Their full names are Gilbert Proesch and George Passmore.

Guardi, Giovanni (1699–1760)   Venetian painter, born in Vienna, brother of Francesco Guardi.

Hamilton, Gavin (1723–98)   Scottish painter in Rome, who pioneered the depiction of Homeric subjects in a severe manner.

Heartfield, John (1891–1968)   German painter, originally Helmut Herzfelde, a leading member of Berlin Dada and a lifelong pacifist.

Hirst, Damien (1965–)   English installation artist noted for his explorations of mortality, often via the use of dead animals.

Hoppner, John (1758–1810)   English portraitist whose masterpiece was *The Countess of Oxford*.

Hughes, Arthur (1830–1915)   English painter associated with the Pre-Raphaelite Brotherhood, although never formally.

ART

Ibbetson, Julius Caesar (1759–1817) English landscapist who specialised in the scenery of the Lakes and his native Yorkshire.

Judd, Donald (1928–1994) American Minimalist artist and sculptor who has geometric boxes built especially to use in his work.

Kiefer, Anselm (1945–) German avant-garde artist whose work tends to concentrate on German history.

Kline, Franz Joseph (1910–62) American artist who became an Abstract Expressionist around 1950, using black shapes on white canvas.

Le Brun, Charles (1619–90) French historical painter; the first director of the Gobelins tapestry works (1662).

Lear, Edward (1812–88) English landscape painter, youngest of 21 children, famous for his nonsense verse.

Liebermann, Max (1847–1935) German painter and etcher, leader of the German Impressionist school.

Lorenzo, Monaco (the Monk) (c1370–1425) Sienese painter in the International Gothic style who took holy orders in 1391.

Macke, August (1887–1914) German painter and leader of Der Blaue Reiter group killed in action in WWI.

Masson, André (1896–1987) French Surrealist painter and graphic artist who was famous for working whilst in a state of trance.

Moses, Anna Mary ('Grandma') (1860–1961) American Primitive artist who did not start to paint until she was 75 years old.

Newman, Barnett (1905–70) American painter who founded the 'subject of the Artist' school with William Baziotes, Rothko and Motherwell.

Nolan, (Sir) Sidney (1917–92) Australian artist noted for his series of Ned Kelly paintings, begun in 1946.

Oldenburg, Claes Thure (1929–) Swedish-born, US sculptor specialising in representing giant foodstuffs, such as hamburgers.

Pevsner, Antoine (1886–1962) Russian born, French Constructivist painter, brother of Naum Gabo.

Quelling, Arnold (1653–1686) English sculptor who collaborated with Grinling Gibbons on many works.

Rackham, Arthur (1867–1939) English artist best known for his illustrations of *Peter Pan* and of Hans Christian Andersen's fairy tales.

Ramsay, Allan (1713–84) Scottish portrait painter to George III of England.

Rauschenberg, Robert (1925–) American avant-garde artist specialising in works constructed from everyday rubbish. also a noted Pop silk-screenist.

Ray, Man (1890–1976) American painter, photographer and film-maker; he co-founded the New York Dadaist movement.

Rousseau, Théodore (1812–67) French landscape painter whose best known work was *The Forest of Compiègne*.

Schiele, Egon (1890–1918) Austrian Expressionist painter who died in the influenza epidemic of 1918.

Signac, Paul (1863–1935) French painter akin to Seurat, but using mosaic-like patches of colour as opposed to dots.

Smith, David Roland (1906–65) American sculptor who specialised in welded metal pieces.

Tàpies, Antoni (1923–) Spanish painter; a founder member of the Dau al Set (Die with the Seven) and El Paso groups.

Tatlin, Vladimir (1885–1953) Russian painter and designer, the founder of Constructivism, whose model *Monument to the Third International* was never built.

Teniers, the Elder, David (1582–1649) Flemish genre painter whose best known work is *Temptation of St Anthony*.

Tenniel, (Sir) John (1820–1914) English illustrator and political satirist (especially in *Punch*), best known for his illustrations of Lewis Caroll's *Alice in Wonderland* and *Through the Looking Glass*.

Tinguely, Jean (1925–91) Swiss sculptor who pioneered kinetic and auto-destructive art.

Twygge, Richard (1476–1510) English painter on glass whose work can be seen in many Malvern buildings.

Van Loo, Charles André (Carle) (1705–65) Prolific French artist and Rococo decorator; principle painter to Louis XV from 1762; the most talented of the artistic Van Loo family.

Van Loo, Jean-Baptiste (1684–1745) French portrait painter in England also notable for historical subjects. Brother of Charles André.

Wilkie, (Sir) David (1785–1841) Scottish painter famous for his genre pictures in the Dutch style eg, *Card Players*, and *Penny Wedding*.

Zincke, Christian Frederick (c1683–1767) German enamel portraitist in London from 1714.

Famous Works of Art

Paintings	Artist	Situation
Abduction of Rebecca, The	Delacroix	Louvre, Paris
Absinthe Drinker, The	Manet	Copenhagen
Accommodations of Desire	Dali	Mr & Mrs Julien Levy Collection, Bridgewater, Connecticut
Adam and Eve	Dürer	Prado, Madrid
Adam and Eve in Paradise	Brueghel	Mauritshuis, The Hague
Adoration of the Kings, The	Brueghel The Elder (Pieter)	Musées Royaux des Beaux-Arts, Brussels
Adoration of the Kings, The	Correggio	Brera, Milan
Adoration of the Kings, The	Veronese	National Gallery, London
Adoration of the Lamb, The	Jan van Eyck	Altarpiece of St Bavo Cathedral, Ghent
Adoration of the Magi, The	Bassano	Kunsthistorisches Museum, Vienna
Adoration of the Magi, The	Bosch	Johnson Collection, Philadelphia
Adoration of the Magi, The	Botticelli	Uffizi, Florence (1475) & Washington National Gallery, DC (1482)

Paintings	Artist	Situation
Adoration of the Magi, The (1500)	Dürer	Uffizi, Florence
Adoration of the Magi, The	Leonardo da Vinci	Uffizi, Florence
Adoration of the Magi, The (1446)	Lippi	National Gallery, Washington DC
Adoration of the Magi, The (1479)	Memling	Memling Museum, Bruges
Adoration of the Magi, The	Velásquez	Prado, Madrid
Adoration of the Magi, The (tapestry)	Burne-Jones	Exeter College, Oxford
Adoration of the Shepherds, The	Bassano	Hampton Court Palace, London
Adoration of the Shepherds, The	Caravaggio	Museo Nazionale, Messina
Allegory of Fortitude and Wisdom	Tiepolo	Ca' Rezzonico, Venice
Allegory of Spring (aka *La Prima vera*)	Botticelli	Uffizi, Florence
Ambassadors, The	Holbein the Younger	National Gallery, London
Anatomy Lesson of Dr Jan Deyman	Rembrandt	Rijksmuseum, Amsterdam
Anatomy Lesson of Dr Nicolaes Tulp	Rembrandt	Mauritshuis, The Hague
Andromeda	Rembrandt	Mauritshuis, The Hague
Angelus, The	Millet	Louvre, Paris
Anna Selbdritt	Dürer	Metropolitan Museum of Art, New York
Anne of Cleves	Holbein the Younger	Victoria and Albert Museum, London
Annunciation, The	Duccio di Buoninsegna	National Gallery, London
Annunciation, The	Jan van Eyck	National Gallery, Washington DC
Annunciation, The	Goya	Private Spanish Collection
Annunciation, The	Leonardo da Vinci	Versions in the Uffizi, Florence and Louvre, Paris
Anthony and Cleopatra	Steen	Kunstsammlung der Universität, Göttingen, Germany
Antibes	Monet	Toledo Museum of Art
Aristotle Contemplating the Bust of Homer	Rembrandt	Metropolitan Museum of Art, New York
Arnolfini Wedding, The	van Eyck, Jan	National Gallery, London
Around the Fish	Klee	Museum of Modern Art, New York
Arrangement in Grey and Black; No. 1: The Artist's Mother	Whistler	Louvre, Paris
Arrangement in Grey and Black; No. 2: Thomas Carlyle	Whistler	Glasgow Art Gallery
Artist and His Wife, The	Metsu	Metropolitan Museum of Art, New York
Ascension of Christ, The	Correggio	San Giovanni Church, Parma
Assumption	Titian	S. Maria dei Frara, Venice
Assumption of the Virgin	Correggio	Parma Cathedral
Assumption of the Virgin	El Greco	Church of Santo Domingo el Antiguo, Toledo, Spain
At the Bar	Toulouse-Lautrec	Kunsthaus, Zürich
At the Linen Closet	Hooch	Rijksmuseum, Amsterdam
At the Moulin Rouge	Toulouse-Lautrec	Art Institute of Chicago
At the Nouveau Cirque: Five Stuffed Shirts	Toulouse-Lautrec	Philadelphia Museum of Art
At the Races	Degas	Fogg Art Museum, Cambridge, Mass.
Avenue at Middelharnis, The	Hobbema	National Gallery, London
Backgammon Players	de Hooch	National Gallery of Ireland, Dublin
Balaam's Ass and the Angel	Rembrandt	Cognacq-Jay Museum, Paris
Ballet Scene, The	Degas	National Gallery, Washington DC
Banker Jabach and His Family, The	Le Brun	Staatliche Museen Preussischer Kulturbesitz, Berlin
Banks of the Seine, The	Henri Rousseau	Private Collection, Paris
Banquet of Anthony and Cleopatra	Tiepolo	Palazzo Labia, Venice
Baptism of Christ, The	Piero della Francesca	National Gallery, London
Bar at the Folies-Bergère, A	Manet	Courtauld Institute Galleries, London
Baron Schwiter	Delacroix	National Gallery, London
Bather	Renoir	Albright-Knox Art Gallery, Buffalo, NY (1879–90) and Sterling and Francine Clark Art Institute, Williamstown, Mass. (1881)
Bather, The	Cézanne	Museum of Modern Art, New York
Bathers	Renoir	Tyson Collection, Philadelphia
Bathsheba	Rembrandt	Louvre, Paris
Battle between Two Stags	Courbet	Louvre, Paris
Battle of Austerlitz	François Gérard	Versailles
Beach at Trouville, The	Monet	Tate Gallery, London
Beggar's Opera, The	Hogarth	Tate Gallery, London

Paintings	Artist	Situation
Belle Jardinière, La	Raphael	Louvre, Paris
Belshazzar's Feast	Rembrandt	National Gallery, London
Bentheim Castle	Jacob van Ruysdael	National Gallery of Ireland, Dublin
Bicycle Wheel	Duchamp	Museum of Modern Art
Birth of Venus, The	Botticelli	Uffizi, Florence
Blind Girl, The	Millais	Birmingham City Museum & Art Gallery
Blonde with Bare Breasts	Manet	Louvre, Paris
Blue Boy, The	Gainsborough	Huntington Library & Gallery, San Marino, California
Blue Mountain	Kandinsky	Guggenheim Museum, New York
Blue Rider, The	Kandinsky	Ernst Bührle Collection, Zürich
Blue Vase, The	Cézanne	Louvre, Paris
Boat during the Flood, The	Sisley	Louvre, Paris
Boatbuilding near Flatford Mill	Constable	Victoria and Albert Museum, London
Boy Bitten by a Lizard	Caravaggio	Louvre, Paris
Boy in a Red Waist-Coat	Cézanne	Mr & Mrs Paul Mellon Collection, Upperville, Vancouver
Boyhood of Raleigh, The	Millais	Tate Gallery, London
Breaking Wave of Kanagawa, The	Hokusai	One of 36 Views of Mt Fuji series, Art Institute of Chicago
Broadway Boogie Woogie	Mondrian	Museum of Modern Art, New York
Bubbles	Millais	Lever Foundation Collection
Burial of the Count de Orgaz	El Greco	Church of Santo Tomé, Toledo, Spain
Calling of St Matthew, The	Caravaggio	Contarelli Chapel, S. Luigi dei Francesci, Rome
Calvary	Bassano	Fitzwilliam Museum, Cambridge
Capt Woodes Rogers and Family	Hogarth	National Maritime Museum, Greenwich
Capture of Samson	Rembrandt	Dahlem Museums, Berlin
Card Players	Cézanne	Metropolitan Museum of Art, New York
Cardinal Richelieu	Champaigne	Louvre, Paris
Carrying of the Cross	Van Dyck	St Paul's, Antwerp
Cascade, The	Henri Rousseau	Art Institute of Chicago
Chair and the Pipe, The (aka Van Gogh's Chair)	Van Gogh	Tate Gallery, London
Chancellor Séguier, The	Le Brun	Louvre, Paris
Charge of the Mamelukes, The	Goya	Prado, Madrid
Charging Chasseur, The	Géricault	Louvre, Paris
Charles Brandon	Holbein the Younger	Windsor Castle
Charles I and Henrietta Maria with Their Children	Van Dyck	Windsor Castle
Charles I, King of England	Van Dyck	Louvre, Paris
Charles VII	Fouquet	Louvre, Paris
Chess Players, The	Duchamp	Philadelphia Museum of Art
Child among Rocks, The	Henri Rousseau	Philadelphia Museum of Art
Children of Edward	Delaroche	Louvre, Paris
Christ among the Doctors	Veronese	Prado, Madrid
Christ before Pilate	Rembrandt	National Gallery, London
Christ Crowned With Thorns	Titian	Louvre, Paris
Christ Healing the Blind Man	Duccio	National Gallery, London
Christ in the House of His Parents	Millais	Tate Gallery, London
Christ Nailed to the Cross	Gerard David	National Gallery, London
Christ on the Cross	Goya	Prado, Madrid
Christ on the Cross	Velásquez	Prado, Madrid
Christ Taking Leave of His Mother	Correggio	National Gallery, London
Christina of Denmark, Duchess of Milan	Holbein the Younger	National Gallery, London
Church at Auvers, The	Van Gogh	Louvre, Paris
Church at Blainville	Duchamp	Philadelphia Museum of Art
Clothed Maja, The	Goya	Prado, Madrid
Colossus, The	Goya	Prado, Madrid
Composition in Black and White	Mondrian	Rijksmuseum Kröller-Müller, Otterlo, Netherlands
Composition in Diamond Shape	Mondrian	Rijksmuseum Kröller-Müller, Otterlo, Netherlands
Composition II	Kandinsky	State Tretyakov Gallery, Moscow
Conversion of St Paul, The	Michelangelo	Pauline Chapel, Vatican
Conversion of St Paul, The	Caravaggio	Sta. Maria del Popolo, Rome

Paintings	Artist	Situation
Conversion of St Paul, The	Brueghel the Elder (Pieter)	Kunsthistorisches Museum, Vienna
Cornfield (etching)	Jacob van Ruysdael	Petit-Palais, Paris
Cornfield, The	Constable	National Gallery, London
Coronation of the Virgin, The	Fra Angelico	Uffizi, Florence
Coronation of the Virgin, The	Raphael	Vatican Museum, Rome
Country Festival near Antwerp	Teniers the Younger	National Gallery, London
Cripples, The	Brueghel the Elder,(Pieter)	Louvre, Paris
Crowning with Thorns, The	Bosch	Versions in the National Gallery, London & Escorial, Madrid
Crucifixion of St Peter	Caravaggio	Sta. Maria del Popolo, Rome
Crucifixion of St Peter	Michelangelo	Pauline Chapel, Vatican
Cupid and Psyche	Van Dyck	Buckingham Palace, London
Cupid and Psyche	François Gérard	Louvre, Paris
Cure of Folly, The	Bosch	Prado, Madrid
Danae	Correggio	Borghese Gallery, Rome
Danae	Rembrandt	Hermitage, St Petersburg
Dance of Four Breton Women	Gauguin	Neue Pinakothek, Munich
Dancer	Renoir	National Gallery of Art, Washington DC
Dancers, The	Degas	Toledo Museum of Art, Toledo, Ohio
Dead Man, The	Chagall	Marc Chagall Collection, Saint-Paul, France
Death and Fire	Klee	Kunstunseum, Berne
Dead Marat, The	Jaques-Louis David	Louvre, Paris
Death of the Virgin	Brueghel the Elder (Pieter)	National Gallery, London
Death of the Virgin	Caravaggio	Louvre, Paris
Dedham Lock and Mill	Constable	Victoria and Albert Museum, London
Déjeuner sur l'herbe, Le	Manet	Louvre, Paris
Demoiselles d'Avignon, Les	Picasso	Museum of Modern Art, New York
Deposition in the Tomb, The	Weyden	Uffizi, Florence
Descent from the Cross	Rembrandt	Alte Pinakothek, Munich
Descent from the Cross	Rubens	Antwerp Cathedral
Dignity and Impudence	Landseer	Tate Gallery, London
Dinner Table, The	Matisse	Stavros Niarchos Collection, London
Duchess of Cleveland	Lely	Courtauld Institute, London
Duet, The	Metsu	National Gallery, London
Duke of Wellington, The	Goya	National Gallery, London
Dunes	Jacob van Ruysdael	Louvre, Paris
Early Sunday Morning	Hopper	Whitney Museum of American Art, New York
Ecce Homo	Bosch	Stadelsches Kunstinstitut, Frankfurt-am-Main
Ecce Homo	Caravaggio	Galleria di Palazzo Rosso, Genoa
Ecce Homo	Correggio	National Gallery, London
Ecstasy of St Diego of Alcalá	Murillo	Louvre, Paris
Education of Cupid	Correggio	National Gallery, London
Emmanuel Philibert	Van Dyck	Dulwich Gallery, London
Entombment of the Lord, The	Massys	Musée Royal des Beaux-Arts, Antwerp
Entry into Jerusalem, The	Van Dyck	Herron Museum of Art, Indianapolis,
Erasmus	Holbein the Younger	Louvre, Paris
Erasmus in the Roundel	Holbein the Younger	Kunstmuseum, Basel,
(L') Estaque, l'embarcadère	Braque	Musée National d'Art Moderne, Paris
Evening Hour, The	Munch	Munch Museet, Oslo
Ex Voto of 1662	Champaigne	Louvre, Paris
Execution of Faliero	Delacroix	Wallace Collection, London
Fable of Arachne, The (aka The Spinners)	Velásquez	Prado, Madrid
Feast of the Rose Garlands, The	Dürer	St Bartholomew Church, Venice
Field of Waterloo, The	Turner	Tate Gallery, London
Fight between Carnival and Lent, The	Brueghel the Elder (Pieter)	Kunsthistorisches Museum, Vienna
Fighting Temeraire, The	Turner	National Gallery, London
First Abstract Watercolour	Kandinsky	Nina Kandinsky Collection, Neuilly-sur-Seine
Fishing Party, A	Hogarth	Dulwich Gallery, London
Flatford Mill on the River Stour	Constable	Tate Gallery, London
Flight into Egypt	Bassano	Bassano, Italy
Football Players	Henri Rousseau	Guggenheim Museum, New York

A
R
T

Paintings	Artist	Situation
Fortune-Teller (aka La Zingara)	Caravaggio	Louvre, Paris
Four Saints	Correggio	Metropolitan Museum of Art, NewYork
Frau Adele Bloch-Bauer	Klimt	Österreichische Galerie, Vienna
Frau Fritza Riedler	Klimt	Österreichische Galerie, Vienna
Fuji in Spring	Hokusai	Art Institute of Chicago
Galacidalacideoxyribonucleicacid	Dali	New England Merchant Bank, Boston, Mass.
Garden of Earthly Delights, The	Bosch	Prado, Madrid
Gardener, The	Cézanne	Tate Gallery, London
Garrick in the Character of Richard III	Hogarth	Earl of Feversham Collection
Gilles and His Family	Watteau	Wallace Collection, London
Gioconda, La (aka Mona Lisa)	Leonardo da Vinci	Louvre, Paris
Girl Asleep, A	Vermeer	Metropolitan Museum of Art, New York
Girl Balancing on a Ball	Picasso	Pushkin Museum, Moscow
Girl Drinking Wine with a Gentleman	Vermeer	Staatliche Museen Preussischer Kulturbesitz, Berlin
Girl in the Artist's Studio	Toulouse-Lautrec	Kunsthalle, Bremen
Girl with Bare Feet	Picasso	Picasso Museum, Paris
Gleaners, The	Millet	Louvre, Paris
Golconda	Magritte	D and J de Menil Collection, Houston, Texas
Goldfish and Sculpture	Matisse	Museum of Modern Art, New York
Good Samaritan, The	Hogarth	St Bartholomew's Hospital, London
Graham Children, The	Hogarth	National Gallery, London Hague
Greenwich Hospital from the North Bank of the Thames	Canaletto	National Maritime Museum, Greenwich
Grey Tree, The	Mondrian	Haags Gemeentemuseum, The Hague
Guernica	Picasso	Prado, Madrid
Guillaume Budé	Clouet the Younger	Metropolitan Museum of Art, New York
Gypsy Girl	Hals	Louvre, Paris
Half-Past Three	Chagall	Philadelphia Museum of Art
Hamlet (aka Young Man Holding a Skull)	Hals	Richard Proby Collection, Peterborough
Hay Wain, The	Bosch	Prado, Madrid
Haywain, The	Constable	National Gallery, London
Haystacks at Giverny	Monet	Josef Rosensaft Collection, New York
Henry VIII	Holbein the Younger	Thyssen-Bornemisza Collection, Castagnola, Switzerland
Hercules and Antaeus	Cranach the Elder	Private Collection, Garmisch-Partenkirchen, Germany
Hercules Killing the Stymphalis Birds	Dürer	Germanisches Nationalmuseum, Nürnberg
Holy Family	Michelangelo	Uffizi, Florence
Holy Family	Turner	Tate Gallery, London
Holy Family on the Steps	Poussin	National Gallery, Washington DC
Holy Family with St James	Correggio	Hampton Court Palace, London
Holy Family (aka The Two Trinities)	Murillo	National Gallery, London
Hope	Watts	Tate Gallery, London
Horatius Cocles Defending Rome	Le Brun	Dulwich Gallery, London
House by the Railroad	Hopper	Museum of Modern Art, New York
Hunters in the Snow	Brueghel the Elder (Pieter)	Kunsthistorisches Museum, Vienna
Hyde Park, London	Monet	Philadelphia Museum of Art
I and the Village	Chagall	Museum of Modern Art, New York
(L')île de Cythère	Watteau	J. Heugel Collection, Paris
Impression: Sunrise	Monet	Musée Marmottan, Paris
In the Circus Fernando: The Ringmaster	Toulouse-Lautrec	Art Institute of Chicago
In the Field	Van Gogh	Rijksmuseum, Vincent Van Gogh, Amsterdam
Inventions of the Monsters	Dali, Salvador	Art Institute of Chicago
Jane Seymour	Holbein the Younger	Kunsthistorisches Museum, Vienna
Jewish Bride, The	Rembrandt	Rijksmuseum, Amsterdam
Jewish Cemetery	Jacob van Ruysdael	Gemäldegalerie, Dresden

Paintings	Artist	Situation
Job and His Wife	Dürer	Wallraf-Richartz-Museum, Cologne
Josephine Bonaparte	François Gérard	Louvre, Paris
Judgement of Paris, The	Cranach the Elder	Kunsthalle, Karlsruhe,
Judgement of Paris, The	Rubens	National Gallery, London
Judgement of Solomon	Giorgione	Uffizi, Florence
Juggler, The	Chagall	Art Institute of Chicago
Jupiter and Io	Correggio	Kunsthistorisches Museum, Vienna
King Charles on Horseback	Van Dyck	National Gallery, London
King Cophetua and the Beggar Maid	Burne-Jones	Tate Gallery, London
King's Wife, The (aka Women with Mangoes)	Gauguin	Pushkin Museum, Moscow
Kiss, The	Klimt	Österreichische Galerie, Vienna
Kitchen-Maid, The (1658)	Vermeer	Rijksmuseum, Amsterdam
Liberty Leading the People	Delacroix	Louvre, Paris
Lady Reading a Letter at an Open Window, A	Vermeer	Gemäldegalerie, Dresden
Lamentation	Giotto	S. Maria Annunziata dell'Arena, Padua
Lamentation for Christ	Van Dyck	Alte Pinakothek, Munich
Lamentation over St Sebastian	La Tour	Staatliche Museen Preussischer Kulturbesitz, Berlin
Landscape with a Bridge	Altdorfer	National Gallery, London
Large Glass, The	Duchamp	Philadelphia Museum of Art; replica by Richard Hamilton in the Tate Gallery, London
Last Judgement, The	Michelangelo	Sistine Chapel, Vatican
Last Supper, The	Dali	National Gallery, Washington DC
Last Supper, The	Holbein the Younger	Kunstmuseum, Basel, Switzerland
Last Supper, The (mural)	Leonardo da Vinci	convent of S. Maria delle Grazie, Milan
Laughing Cavalier, The	Hals	Wallace Collection, London
Leaping Horse, The	Constable	Royal Academy of Arts, London
Leda	Correggio	Berlin Museum
Light of the World, The	Holman Hunt	Keble College, Oxford
Linlithgow Palace	Turner	Walker Gallery, Liverpool
Little Street, The	Vermeer	Rijksmuseum, Amsterdam
Loge, La (ak The Theatre Box)	Renoir	Courtauld Institute, London
Lucretia	Dürer	Alte Pinakothek, Munich
Luncheon, The	Manet	Neue Staatsgalerie, Munich
Luncheon of the Boating Party, The	Renoir	Phillips Collection, Washington DC
Lute Player, The	Caravaggio	Hermitage, St Petersburg
MacNab, The	Raeburn	John Dewar & Sons Collection
Mad Woman with a Mania of Envy	Géricault	Musée des Beaux-Arts, Lyons
Madame Charpentier and Her Children	Renoir	Metropolitan Museum of Art, New York
Mademoiselle Gachet at the Piano	Van Gogh	Kunstmuseum, Basel
Madhouse, The	Goya	Dallas, Texas
Madonna in Glory, The	Giotto	Uffizi, Florence
Madonna of St Jerome, The	Correggio	National Gallery, Parma
Madonna of the Basket, The	Correggio	National Gallery, London
Madonna of the Goldfinch, The	Raphael	Uffizi, Florence
Madonna of the Rosary	Van Dyck	Oratorio del Rosario, Palermo
Madonna of the Star	FraAngelico	Museo di San Marco, Florence
Madonna with Angels and Saints	Gerard David	Musée des Beaux-Arts, Rouen
Madonna with Chancellor Rolin, The	Janvan Eyck	Louvre, Paris
Madonna with Musical Angels	Dürer	Staatliche Museen Preussischer Kulturbesitz, Berlin
Madonna with the Carnation	Leonardo da Vinci	Alte Pinakothek, Munich
Maestà	Duccio di Buoninsegna	Cathedral Museum, Siena
Maids of Honour, The (aka Las Meninas)	Velázquez	Prado, Madrid
Man with a Straw Hat, The	Cézanne	Metropolitan Museum of Art, New York
Market Cart, The	Gainsborough	Tate Gallery, London
Marriage at Cana	Veronese	Louvre, Paris
Marriage of Isaac and Rebecca, The (aka The Mill)	Claude Lorrain	National Gallery, London
Mars and Venus	Botticelli	National Gallery, London
Marsh in the Woods	Jacob van Ruysdael	Hermitage, St Petersburg
Massacre at Chios, The	Delacroix	Louvre, Paris
Massacre of the Innocents, The	Brueghel the Elder (Pieter)	Hampton Court Palace, London
Meninas, Las (aka Maids of Honour)	Velázquez	Prado, Madrid
Merlin and Nimue	Burne-Jones	Victoria and Albert Museum, London

ART

Paintings	Artist	Situation
Merry Company, The	Hals	Metropolitan Museum of Art, New York
Merry Drinker, The	Hals	Rijksmuseum, Amsterdam
Militia Company of Captain Frans Banning Cocq, The (aka Night Watch)	Rembrandt	Rijksmuseum, Amsterdam
Milkmaid, The (1844)	Millet	Louvre, Paris
Milkmaid of Bordeaux, The	Goya	Prado, Madrid
Mill, The (aka The Marriage of Isaac and Rebecca)	Claude Lorrain	National Gallery, London
Miracle of St Bavo	Rubens	St Bavo Cathedral, Ghent
Miss Cicely Alexander: Harmony in Grey and Green	Whistler	Tate Gallery, London
Miss Harriet Cholmondeley	Hoppner	Tate Gallery, London New York
Mocker Mocked, The	Klee	Museum of Modern Art, New York
Model Reading	Hopper	Art Institute of Chicago
Mona Lisa (aka La Gioconda)	Leonardo da Vinci	Louvre, Paris
Mona Lisa with Moustache and Goatee	Duchamp	Ready Made (Photograph) – various venues
Money Changer and His Wife, The	Massys	Louvre, Paris
Morning Walk, The	Gainsborough	National Gallery, London
Mother beside a Cradle, A	Hooch	Staatliche Museen Preussischer Kulturbesitz, Berlin
Moulin Rouge, The	Toulouse-Lautrec	Národni Gallery, Prague
Mr and Mrs Andrews	Gainsborough	National Gallery, London
Mrs Robinson (aka Perdita)	Gainsborough	Wallace Collection, London
Mrs Siddons	Gainsborough	National Gallery, London
Mrs Siddons as the Tragic Muse	Reynolds	Henry E. Huntington Library, San Marino, California
Music Lesson, The	Metsu	Metropolitan Museum of Art, New York
Naked Maja, The	Goya	Prado, Madrid
Nativity	Correggio	Brera, Milan
Night-School	Gerrit Dou	Rijksmuseum, Amsterdam
Night Watch, The (aka The Militia)	Rembrandt	Rijksmuseum, Amsterdam
Nighthawks	Hopper	Art Institute of Chicago
Nocturne in Black and Gold: The Falling Rocket	Whistler	Detroit Institute of Arts
Nocturne in Blue and Gold: Old Battersea Bridge:	Whistler	Tate Gallery, London
Nude Descending a Staircase, Nos 1–4	Duchamp	Philadelphia Museum of Art (No. 2 is most famous)
Nurse and Child	Hals	Staatliche Museen Preussischer Kulturbesitz, Berlin
Oath of the Tennis Court	David	Louvre, Paris
Odalisque	Renoir	National Gallery of Art, Washington DC
Oedipus and the Sphinx	Ingres	Louvre, Paris
Officer and Laughing Girl	Vermeer	Frick Collection, New York
Old Man and the Courtesan, The	Massys	Pourtalès Collection, Paris
Old Walton Bridge	Canaletto	Dulwich Gallery, London
Old Woman Cooking Eggs, An	Velázquez	National Gallery of Scotland, Edinburgh
Old Woman Praying	Rembrandt	Residenz Gallery, Salzburg
Old Women of Arles	Gauguin	Art Institute of Chicago
Open Window	Matisse	John Hay Whitney Collection, New York
Order of Release, The	Millais	Tate Gallery, London
Oswolt Krel	Dürer	Alte Pinakothek, Munich
Painter's Daughters Chasing a Butterfly, The	Gainsborough	National Gallery, London
Pantry, The	Hooch	Rijksmuseum, Amsterdam
Paradise	Cranach the Elder	Kunsthistorisches Museum, Vienna
Parapluies, Les (aka Umbrellas)	Renoir	National Gallery, London
Paris through the Window	Chagall	Guggenheim Museum, New York
Parting of Hero and Leander, The	Turner	National Gallery, London
Pastoral	Bassano	Lugano, Switzerland
Payment, The	Cranach the Elder, Lucas	Nationalmuseum, Stockholm
Peasant Wedding	Brueghel the Elder (Pieter)	Kunsthistorisches Museum, Vienna
Peasant Woman in a Red Bonnet	Van Gogh, Vincent	Rijksmuseum Vincent Van Gogh,

Paintings	Artist	Situation
		Amsterdam
Peasants Playing Music	Teniers the Younger	Alte Pinakothek, Munich
Peasants Returning from Market	Gainsborough	Toledo Museum of Art, Ohio
Pembroke Family, The	Reynolds	Wilton House, Wiltshire
Perdita (aka Mrs Robinson)	Gainsborough	Wallace Collection, London
Peter Denying Christ	Rembrandt	Rijksmuseum, Amsterdam
Pheidias and the Frieze of the Parthenon, Athens	Alma-Tadema	Birmingham City Gallery
Piano and Lute	Braque	Guggenheim Museum, New York
Piazza San Marco and the Colonnade of the Procuratie Nuove	Canaletto	National Gallery, London
Piazza San Marco Looking East from South of the Central Line	Canaletto	Fogg Art Museum, Cambridge, Mass.
Pipe and Bandaged Ear (Self-portrait)	Van Gogh	Leigh B. Block Collection, Chicago
Pluto and Proserpina	Rembrandt	Dahlem Museums, Berlin
Portrait of a Young Man	Dürer	Alte Pinakothek, Munich
Potato Eaters, The	Van Gogh	Rijksmuseum Vincent Van Gogh, Amsterdam
Poulterer's Shop, A	Dou	National Gallery, London
Primavera, La (aka Allegory of Spring)	Botticelli	Uffizi, Florence
Princess Charlotte and her Two Sisters (aka Three Eldest Princesses)	Gainsborough	Buckingham Palace, London
Rabbi of Vitebsk (aka The Praying Jew)	Chagall	Art Institute of Chicago
Raft of the Medusa, The	Géricault	Louvre, Paris
Rain, Steam and Speed	Turner	National Gallery, London
Raising of Lazarus	Rembrandt	Los Angeles County Museum of Art
Raisng the Cross	Rubens	Antwerp Cathedral
Rake's Progress, The	Hogarth	Sir John Soane's Museum, London
Rape of Proserpine	dell Abbate	Louvre, Paris
Rape of the Sabine Women, The	Poussin	Louvre, Paris
Red Cloud, The	Mondrian	Haags Gemeentemuseum, The Hague
Red Tree, The	Mondrian	Haags Gemeentemuseum, The Hague
Rembrandt's Mother	Dou	Rijksmuseum, Amsterdam
Republic, The	Daumier	Louvre, Paris
Repudiation of Hagar	Tiepolo	Rasini Collection, Milan
Rest on the Flight into Egypt	Bassano	Milan
Return of the Dove to the Ark, The	Millais	Ashmolean Museum, Oxford
Return of the Prodigal Son	Rembrandt	Hermitage, St Petersburg
Rio dei Mendicanti	Guardi	Accademia Carrara, Bergamo
River, The	Monet	Art Institute of Chicago
Roffey Family	Reynolds	City of Birmingham Museum and Art Gallery
Rokeby Venus, The (aka The Toilet of Venus)	Velázquez	National Gallery, London
Room in Brooklyn	Hopper	Museum of Fine Arts, Boston, Mass.
Rouen Cathedral: Sunset	Monet	Museum of Fine Arts, Boston, Mass.
Rout of Comus, The	Landseer	Tate Gallery, London
Rout of San Romano, The	Uccello	National Gallery, London
Rucellai Madonna	Ducio	Uffizi, Florence
Ruins of Brederode Castle, The	Hobbema	National Gallery, London
Sabines, Les	Jacques-Louis David	Louvre, Paris
Sacrifice of Abraham (aka Sacrifice of Isaac)	Tiepolo	S. Maria dei Derelitti, Venice
Sacrifice of Isaac	Caravaggio	Uffizi, Florence
Sacrifice of Isaac	Rembrandt	Hermitage St Petersburg, and Alte Pinakothek, Munich
Sacrifice of Isaac (aka Sacrifice of Abraham)	Tiepolo	S. Maria dei Derelitti, Venice
Sad Young Man in a Train	Duchamp	Peggy Guggenheim Collection, Venice
St Ildefonso	El Greco	Hospital de la Caridad, Illescas, Spain
St Jerome Curing the Lion	Dürer	Kunstmuseum, Basel
St Joseph the Carpenter	La tour	Louvre, Paris
St Lawrence Receiving the Treasure of the Church	Fra Angelico	Vatican Museum, Rome
St Luke Painting the Virgin	Weyden	Museum of Fine Arts, Boston, Mass.
St Mawes at the Pilchard Season	Turner	Tate Gallery, London

ART

Paintings	Artist	Situation
St Michael Vanquishing Satan	Raphael	Louvre, Paris
Salisbury Cathedral from the Bishop's Grounds	Constable	Victoria and Albert Museum, London
Salisbury Cathedral from the Meadows	Constable	Lord Ashton of Hyde Collection, Moreton-in-Marsh
Salvator Mundi	Antonello da Messina	National Gallery, London
Samson and Delilah	Van Dyck	Kunsthistorisches Museum, Vienna
School of Athens	Raphael	Stanza della Segnatura, the Vatican, Rome
School of Love, The	Correggio	National Gallery, London
Scream, The	Munch	Nasjonalgalleriet, Oslo
Seine au Pont d'Iéna, La	Gauguin	Louvre, Paris
Self Portrait with Seven Fingers	Chagall	Stedelijk Museum, Amsterdam
Semiramis Founding Babylon	Degas	Louvre, Paris
Serenade	Steen	Národní Galerie, Prague
Seven Deadly Sins, The	Boschs	Prado, Madrid
Shoeing	Landseer	Tate Gallery, London
Shrimp Girl, The	Hogarth	National Gallery, London
Sick Child, The	Munch	Nasjonalgalleriet, Oslo
Sir Stanley Unwin	Kokoschka	Allen and Unwin Collection, London
Sir Thomas More	Holbein the Younger	Frick Collection, New York
Sistine Chapel ceiling	Michelangelo	Sistine Chapel, Vatican
Skating	Manet	Fogg Art Museum, Cambridge, Mass.
Skittle Players outside an Inn	Steen	National Gallery, London
Skull with a Cigarette	Van Gogh	Rijksmuseum Vincent Van Gogh, Amsterdam
Sleeping Gypsy, The	Henri Rousseau	Museum of Modern Art, New York
Smiling Woman	Augustus John	Tate Gallery, London
Snow, Moon and Flowers	Hokusai	Art Institute of Chicago
Soldier Drinks, The	Chagall	Guggenheim Museum, New York
Solitude	Chagall	Tel Aviv Museum
Sojourn in Egypt, The	Correggio	Uffizi, Florence
Soup, The	Picasso	Art Gallery of Ontario, Toronto
Sower, The	Millet	Various locations
Spanish Singer	Manet	Metropolitan Museum of Art, New York
Spinners, The (aka The Fable of Arachne)	Velázquez	Prado, Madrid
Stag Hunt of the Elector Frederick the Wise	Cranach the Elder	Kunsthistorisches Museum, Vienna
Starry Night, The	van Gogh	Museum of Modern Art, New York
Still Life with Gingerpot	Mondrian	Haags Gemeentemuseum, The Hague
Still Life with Playing Cards	Braque	Rijksmuseum Kröller-Müller, Otterlo
Still Life with Tortoise and Hyacinth	Kokoschka	Österreichische Galerie, Vienna
Stoning of St Stephen	Rembrandt	Museum of Fine Arts, Lyons
Storm at Sea, The	Bruege the Elder (Pieter)	Kunsthistorisches Museum, Vienna
Street in Tahiti	Gauguin	Toledo Museum of Art, Ohio
Street Singer, The	Manet	Museum of Fine Arts, Boston, Mass.
Suicide's House, The	Cézanne	Louvre, Paris
Sunday Afternoon on the Island of La Grande Jatte	Seurat	Art Institute of Chicago
Sunflowers and Pears	Gauguin	Private Collection, Paris
Susannah and the Elders	Bassano	Bassano, Italy
Swineherd, The	Gauguin	N. Simon Collection, Los Angeles
Symphony in Grey and Green: The Ocean	Whistler	Frick Collection, New York
Symphony in White No. 1: The White Girl	Whistler	National Gallery, Washington DC
Taking of Christ, The	Van Dyck	Prado, Madrid
Tempered Elan	Kandinsky	Nina Kandinsky Collection, Neuilly-sur-Seine
Tempest, The	Kokoschka	Kunstmuseum, Basel
Tête-à-Tête Supper, The	Toulouse-Lautrec	Courtauld Institute, London
Theatre Box, The (aka La Loge)	Renoir	Courtauld Institute, London
Thirty-Six Views of Mt Fuji (series)	Hokusai	Art Institute of Chicago
Threatening Weather	Magritte	Penrose Collection, London

Paintings	Artist	Situation
Three Dancers	Picasso	Tate Gallery, London
Three Eldest Princesses (aka Princess Charlotte and Her Two Sisters)	Gainsborough	Buckingham Palace, London
Three Graces	Raphael	Musée Condé, Chantilly
Three Lawyers in Conversation	Daumier	Phillips Collection, Washington DC
Three Women of Ghent	Jacques-Louis David	Louvre, Paris
Toilet of Venus, The (aka The Rokeby Venus)	Velázquez	National Gallery, London
Toilette, La	Toulouse-Lautrec	Louvre, Paris
Topers, The (aka Triumph of Bacchus)	Velázquez	Prado, Madrid
Tour Eiffel, La	Delaunay	Kunstmuseum, Basel
Tower of Babel	Brueghel the Elder (Pieter)	Kunsthistorisches Museum, Vienna
Transfiguration	Duccio	National Gallery, London
Trial of Moses	Giorgione	Uffizi, Florence
Trinity	El Greco	Prado, Madrid
Triumph of Bacchus (aka The Topers)	Velázquez	Prado, Madrid
Triumph of the Innocents, The	Holman Hunt	Tate Gallery, London
Tropical Forest with Monkeys	Rousseau, Henri	John Hay Whitney Collection, New York
Tuna Fishing	Dali	Paul Ricard Collection, Paris
Turkish Bath, The	Ingres	Louvre, Paris
Twittering Machine	Klee	Museum of Modern Art, New York
Two Haystacks	Monet	Art Institute of Chicago
Two Trinities, The (aka Holy Family)	Murillo	National Gallery, London
Ugolino	Reynolds	Knole House, Sevenoaks, Kent
Umbrellas (aka Les Parapluies)	Renoir	National Gallery, London
Uncle Dominic as a Monk	Cézanne	Private Collection, New York
Vampire	Munch	Munch-Museet, Oslo
Van Gogh's Chair	Van Gogh	National Gallery, London
Venus and Adonis	Titian	Prado, Madrid
Venus and Adonis	Turner	Tate Gallery, London
Venus and Cupid	Cranach the Elder	Staatliche Museen Preussischer Kulturbesitz, Berlin
Venus of Urbino	Titian	Uffizi, Florence
Victory Boogie Woogie	Mondrian	Burton Tremaine Collection, Meriden, Conn.
View of Delft	Vermeer	Mauritshuis, The Hague
View of Naples	Brueghel the Elder (Pieter)	Galleria Doria-Pamphili, Rome
Village Fête, The	Teniers the Younger, David	Hermitage, St Petersburg
Violin and Jug	Braque	Kunstmuseum, Basel
Virgin and Child with Saints	Duccio di Buoninsegna	National Gallery, London
Virgin and Child with Saints and Donor	Gerard David	National Gallery, London
Virgin in Prayer, The	Massys	Musée Royal des Beaux-Arts, Antwerp
Virgin of the Rocks	Leonardo da Vinci	Louvre, Paris and National Gallery, London
Virgin of the Rosary	Murillo	Archbishop's Palace, Seville
Vision of St Bernard	Lippi, Filippino	Badia, Florence
Visit, The	Alma-Tadema	Victoria and Albert Museum, London
Washerwoman, The	Daumier, Honoré	Louvre, Paris
Water-Lily Pool	Monet	Louvre, Paris
Water Mill, The	Hobbema	Wallace Collection, London
Way to Calvary, The	Brueghel the Elder, Pieter	Kunsthistorisches Museum, Vienna
Wedding Dance, The	Brueghel the Elder, Pieter	Detroit Institute of Arts
Wedding of Stephen Beckingham & Mary Cox	Hogarth	Metropolitan Museum of Art, New York
Whaam!	Lichtenstein	Tate Gallery, London
Wheatfields	van Ruysdael, Jacob	Metropolitan Museum of Art, New York
When Shall We Be Married	Gauguin	Kunstmuseum, Basel
Whistler's Mother (aka Arrangement in Grey and Black No. 1)	Whistler	Louvre, Paris
White Crucifixion	Chagall	Art Institute of Chicago
White Line	Kandinsky	Nina Kandinsky Collection, Neuilly-sur-Seine
Wild Poppies	Monet	Louvre, Paris
William Warham, Archbishop of Canterbury	Holbein the Younger	Louvre, Paris

A
R
T

Paintings	Artist	Situation
Windmill in Sunlight	Mondrian	Haags Gemeentemuseum, The Hague
Windsor Beauties, The	Lely	Hampton Court Palace, London
Woman and Her Maid in a Court	Hooch	National Gallery, London
Woman in an Armchair	Picasso	Picasso Museum, Paris
Woman Musician, The	Braque	Kunstmuseum, Basel
Woman Weighing Gold, A	Vermeer	National Gallery of Art, Washington DC
Woman with Pears	Picasso	Pushkin Museum, Moscow
Woman with the Hat	Matisse	Walter A. Haas Collection, San Francisco
Women in a Brothel	Toulouse-Lautrec	Szépmüvészeti Museum, Budapest
Women of Algiers in Their Apartment	Delacroix	Louvre, Paris
Women with Mangoes (aka The King's Wife)	Gauguin	Pushkin Museum, Moscow
Woodcutter Courting a Milkmaid, The	Gainsborough	Woburn Abbey, Bedfordshire
Woods near Oele	Mondrian	Haags Gemeentemuseum, The Hague
World Upside-down, The	Steen	Kunsthistorisches Museum, Vienna
Wounded Cuirassier, The	Géricault	Louvre, Paris
Wounded Heron, The	Watts	Watts Gallery, Compton, Surrey
Wreck of a Transport Ship	Turner	Gulbenkian Foundation, Lisbon
Young Bacchus, The	Caravaggio	Uffizi, Florence
Young Lady with a Pearl Necklace	Vermeer	Staatliche Museen Preussischer Kulturbesitz, Berlin
Young Man Holding a Skull (aka Hamlet)	Hals	Richard Proby Collection, Peterborough
Young Man in a Garden	Hilliard	Victoria and Albert Museum, London
Young Mother, The	Dou	Mauritshuis, The Hague
Young Virgin Auto-Sodomized by Her Own Chastity	Dali	Carlos B. Alemany Collection, New York
Young Woman Holding a Powder-Puff	Seurat	Courtauld Institute, London
Young Woman Standing at a Virginal, A	Vermeer	National Gallery, London
Yellow Christ, The	Gauguin	Albright-Knox Art Gallery, Buffalo, NY
Young Woman with a Water Jug, A	Vermeer	Metropolitan Museum of Art, New York
Young Women on the Banks of the Seine	Courbet	Musée du Petit Palais, Paris
Zingara, La (aka The Fortune-Teller)	Caravaggio	Louvre, Paris
Zoological Garden	Klee	Klee Foundation, Berne

NB: There are a number of points to be considered with reference to this section. The history of art is a complex subject and although it is traditional to fix a label on artists and their works, in fact not only is it often impossible to identify a painter with any one group, it is also just as precarious to attach one term to the whole oeuvre of an artist Even the historical styles overlap in many instances. The problem is that painters do not like to be pigeonholed, as styles and moods change and very often one style or school may become defunct or develop into something else. In researching this section I have also found that the nationalities of artists, especially those of the Low Countries, are open to interpretation, dependent not only on place of birth or naturalisation but also on style. I have endeavoured to qualify any contentious entries so as to give a more complete picture of the nature of the artist and his or her work

A problem when listing artworks is that not only are particular subjects covered as 'stock' pieces by numerous artists (such as The Adoration of the Magi) but also many individual artists often paint more than one version of a particular work – for example, Cézanne painted several versions of The Card Players and Millet painted several versions of The Sower. The final observation I have to offer in this web of intrigue is that when I came to list paintings in alphabetical order it occurred to me that many have alternative titles. For instance Vermeer's The Kitchen-Maid is listed in reputable sources with the alternative titles of The Milkmaid, The Maid with a Milk Jug, The Cook, The Maid-Servant Pouring Milk and The Servant Pouring Milk. I have listed only the most common variants in the table.

Art Movements and Schools: Some Members and Founders

Members / Founders (F)	Art Movements & Schools	Members / Founders (F)	Art Movements & Schools
Arp, Jean (F)	Dada	Klee, Paul	Blaue Reiter (Blue Rider)
Ball, Hugo	Dada	Knight, Laura	Newlyn School
Beardsley, Aubrey	Art Nouveau	'Grandma' Moses	Primitivism
Bell, Vanessa	Omega Workshops	Kokoschka, Oscar	Expressionism
Bellows, George	Ashcan School	Kooning, Willem de (F)	Aabstract Expressionism
Blake, Peter	Pop Art	Ladbrooke, Robert	Norwich School
Bleyl, Fritz (F)	Die Brücke (The Bridge)	Larionov, Mikhail (F)	Rayonnism
Bomberg, David	Kitchen Sink School	Léger, Fernand	Cubism
Bonnard, Pierre	Nabis	Lewis, Wyndham (F)	Vorticism
Braque, Georges (F)	Cubism	Lichtenstein, Roy (F)	Pop Art
Braque, Georges (F)	Fauvism	Mackintosh, Charles Rennie (F)	Glasgow School
Bratby, John	Kitchen Sink School		
Brown, Ford Madox	Pre-Raphaelite Brotherhood	Magritte, René	Surrealism
Brueghel the Elder, Pieter	Antwerp School	Malevich, Kasimir (F)	Suprematism
Burne-Jones, Edward	Arts and Crafts Movement	Manet, Edouard	Impressionism
Burne-Jones, Edward	Pre-Raphaelite Brotherhood	Marc, Franz (F)	Blaue Reiter (Blue Rider)
Carrà, Carlo (F)	Metaphysical school	Matisse, Henri (F)	Fauvism
Cézanne, Paul	Impressionism	Millais, John Everett (F)	Pre-Raphaelite Brotherhood
Cézanne, Paul	Post-Impressionism	Mondrian, Piet	Cubism
de Chirico, Giorgio	Metaphysical School	Mondrian, Piet (F)	De Stijl
Church, F. E.	Hudson River School	Mondrian, Piet (F)	Neo-Plasticism
Coldstream, William (F)	Euston Road School	Monet, Claude (F)	Impressionism
Cole, Thomas	Hudson River School	Moreau, Gustave	Symbolism
Cotman, John (F)	Norwich School	Morris, William	Arts and Crafts Movement
Crome, John (F)	Norwich School	Morris, William	Pre-Raphaelite Brotherhood
Dali, Salvador	Surrealism	Munch, Edvard	Expressionism
Degas, Edgar	Impressionism	Nicholson, Ben	St Ives Painters
Delaunay, Robert (F)	Orphism	Overbeck, Friedrich (F)	Nazarenes
Delaunay Terk, Sonia (F)	Orphism	Parmigianino, Francesco	Mannerism
Delaunay, Robert	Synchronism	Pasmore, Victor (F)	Euston Road School
Denis, Maurice (F)	Nabis	Pechstein, Max	Expressionism
Derain, André (F)	Fauvlsm	Pforr, Franz	Nazarenes
Dix, Otto	Neue Sachlichkeit	Picasso, Pablo (F)	Cubism
van Doesburg, Theo (F)	De Stijl	Piper, John	Neo-Romanticism
van Doesburg, Theo	Neo-Plasticism	Pissarro, Camille	Impressionism
van Dongen, Kees	Post-Impressionism	Pollock, Jackson (F)	Abstract Expressionism
Duccio di Buoninsegna (F)	Sienese School	Puvis de Chavannes,	Symbolism
Duchamp, Marcel	Dada	Redon, Odilon	Symbolism
van Dyck, Anthony	Antwerp School	Renoir, Pierre	Impressionism
Ernst, Max	Dada (1)	Riley, Bridget (F)	Op Art
Ernst, Max	Surrealism (2)	Rossetti, Dante Gabriel (F)	Pre-Raphaelite Brotherhood
Forbes, Stanhope	Newlyn School	Rothko, Mark	Abstract Expressionism
Fry, Roger (F)	Omega Workshops	Rouault, Georges	Expressionism
Funi, Achille	Novecento Italiano	Rouault, Georges (F)	Fauvism
Gauguin, Paul	Pont-Aven School	Rousseau, Henri	Primitivism
Gauguin, Paul	Post-Impressionism	Rousseau, Théodore	Barbizon School
Gilman, Harold (F)	Camden Town Group	Rubens, Peter Paul	Antwerp School
Ginner, Charles (F)	Camden Town Group	Schmidt-Rottluff, Karl (F)	Die Brücke (The Bridge)
Giulio Romano	Mannerism	Seurat, Georges (F)	Pointillism
van Gogh, Vincent	Post-Impressionism	Sickert, Walter (F)	Camden Town Group
Goncharova, Natalia	Rayonnism	Sisley, Alfred	Impressionism
Gore, Spencer (F)	Camden Town Group	Sluijters, Jan	Post-Impressionism
Gowing, Lawrence	Euston Road School	Stella, Frank	Post-Painterly Abstraction
Grant, Duncan	Omega Workshops	Stokes, Adrian	St Ives Painters
El Greco	Mannerism	Sutherland, Graham	Neo-Romanticism
Grosz, George	Neue Sachlichkeit	Tatlin, Vladimir (F)	Constructivism
Hamilton, Richard	Pop Art	Tintoretto	Mannerism
Heckel, Erich (F)	Die Brücke, The Bridge	de Vlaminck, Maurice (F)	Fauvism
Hepworth, Barbara	St Ives Painters	Vuillard, Edouard	Nabis
Hunt, William Holman (F)	Pre-Raphaelite Brotherhood	Warhol, Andy (F)	Pop Art
Kandinsky, Wassily (F)	Blaue Reiter (Blue Rider)	Watteau, Jean-Antoine	Rococo
Kirchner, Ernst Ludwig (F)	Die Brücke (The Bridge)		

A R T

NB: The table above should be taken as a quick reference for identifying artists and groups.
As has been stated previously, there is a distinct grey area in attempting to categorise painters – e.g. although Peter Blake was certainly identified with Pop Art in his early career, whether he would consider himself as such nowadays is debatable.

Art: General Information

Action Painting: aka	Abstract Expressionism
Adoration of the Magi (Botticelli)	The Medici family are depicted as the Magi
Arrangement in Grey and Black: Nickname	Whistler's Mother
Art Deco	Refers to a decorative style of the 1920s and 1930s
Art Gallery: Largest	The Hermitage in St Petersburg
Beggarstaff Brothers	Sir William Nicholson (1872–1949) and James Pryde (1866–1941) still-life and poster painters
Blue Boy: depiction of	Master Jonathan Buttall a friend of the artist Gainsborough
Blue Period: Picasso	Between 1901 and mid-1904
Brueg(h)el: Nicknames	Pieter (The Elder) – Peasant, Pieter (The Younger) – Hell, Jan - Velvet
Brueg(h)el: Spelling	Pieter the Elder spelt the name with an 'H' until 1559 and his children resorted back to original spelling
Bubbles: Subject	Millais' Grandson, the future Admiral William James
Churchill Portrait (Sutherland)	Destroyed by Churchill's wife
Cire Perdue	Modern bronzes are made either in sand moulds or by the 'cire perdue' (lost wax) method, it consists of a model which is smaller than the mould, the space between being filled with wax and vent pipes inserted, the molten bronze is poured in the top taking the place of the wax which has been melted out
Claude Lorrain Glass	Black convex glass used by artists to reflect the landscape in miniature and, in doing so, to merge details and reduce the strength of colour so that the artist is presented with a broad picture of the scene
Collage	Objects such as newspaper, string or cloth which are pasted onto paper or canvas. Picasso's 'Still Life with Chair Caning' may have been the first example of collage
Constructivism	Russian art movement initiated by Vladimir Tatlin in 1913 concerning the use of a 'Culture of Materials' which resulted in an art which had social purpose
Correggio	Named from the town in Modena where he was born
Cranach the Elder, Lucas: Epitaph	Pictor Celerrimus (swiftest of painters) is how Cranach is described on his tombstone
Cubism: First picture	Les Demoiselles d'Avignon by Picasso
Customs Officer: Former	Henri Rousseau (Hence his byname 'Le Douanier')
Dada: Formed Where	In a night club in Zurich (Cabaret Voltaire) 1916
Duke of Wellington (Goya)	Stolen in 1961 but later found
Fakers: Famous	Tom Keating faked the Samuel Palmer paintings and Hans van Meegeren the Vermeer
Frottage	Technique employed by Surrealists such as Max Ernst, which involves placing a piece of paper over an object and rubbing the paper with chalk or charcoal
Hay-Wain, The: Farm	Willy Lott's farm
I Want You: Recruiting Poster	James Montgomery Flagg
Intaglio	Term used to describe types of printing such as etching and engraving whereby the design is incised as opposed to relief printing, such as wood cutting, where the raised portion creates the design
Killed a man in argument	Caravaggio in 1606 forced to flee Rome after killing a man in fit of temper
Knighted by Britain & Spain	Sir Peter Paul Rubens
Libel Action Against John Ruskin	James Whistler, for Ruskin's attack on his 'Falling Rocket' (won the case but received only one farthing)
Madonna Rucellai	Now attributed to Duccio Di Buoninsegna: formerly thought to be a work of Cimabue (Vasari's attribution)
Magic Realism	Refers to a type of painting which combines a realistic technique with fanciful designs, as in the paintings of René Magritte and other surrealists. In its strict sense it refers to German realist art of the 1920s
Montage	Form of collage but refers specifically to the use of components which are complete in themselves
Murdered His Father	Richard Dadd
Myra (Hindley): painter	Marcus Harvey painted this controversial painting on display at the 'Sensations' exhibition of 1997
Neo-Expressionism	Refers to an International art movement of the late 1970s and 1980s involving revival of expressionist concerns
Neo-Plasticism	Name used by Mondrian & van Doesburg for a type of art which

	avoids representation in favour of abstraction
Neo-Romanticism	British art movement existing before the Second World War which revived the interest in the Romantic landscapes of William Blake and Samuel Palmer
New Objectivity	Name coined by G.F. Artlaub to describe a group of German artists who rejected abstract culture of the 1920s
Novecento Italiano	Italian art movement of the 1920s which encouraged a return to the renaissance art
Novembergruppe	Formed in Berlin 1918 and advocating art for the masses
Obscene: Exhibition closed as	Modigliani
Orphism	Term coined by poet, Apollinaire in 1912 to distinguish the fragmented use of colour from the Cubist approach
Painting: Highest price at auction	Van Gogh's 'Portrait of Dr Gachet' fetched £44,378,696 in May 1990
Patina	Term used to describe the beautiful greenish surface alteration on a bust or statue caused by age
Pears Soap Advertisement	Bubbles by Sir John Everett Millais
Pentimento	Phenomenon of earlier painting showing through a layer or layers of paint on a canvas
Pop Art: Term Coined by	The critic Lawrence Alloway
Post-Painterly Abstraction	Term coined by the critic Clement Greenberg in 1964 to refer to non-objective artists who were not members of the Abstract Expressionist movement
Primary Colours	The colours from which all other colours are made up i.e. Blue, Yellow and Red
Purism	Term coined in 1918 by Amédée Ozenfant in 'Après le Cubisme' which rejected decorative qualities of Cubism
Putto	A plump naked boy used as a decorative addition to painting and sculpture, especially in the Baroque
Quattrocento	The 15th Century, especially with reference to Renaissance Italian Art (Lit four hundred i.e. short for 14 hundred)
Rayonism	Russian art movement described as a combination of Cubism, Futurism and Orphism
Renoir's Nude Sitter	Renoir's maid, Gabrielle, would often sit as nude model for his paintings
Rheumatism Sufferer	In later life Renoir was forced to paint with the brush tied to his fingers
Rokeby Venus (Velasquez)	Slashed by suffragette in the National Gallery
Rose Period: Picasso	Late 1904 to 1906
Saturday Evening Post	Norman Rockwell was famous for the covers
Scumbling	Term used to describe the effect when an opaque colour is applied over another colour but allows the original colour to show through
Secondary Colours	Aka Complementary Colours; Produced when two Primary Colours are mixed together i.e. Green, Orange & Violet
Sensations	Charles Saatchi's controversial 1997 exhibition at the Royal Academy which includes such items as Damien Hirst's 'Tiger Shark', 'Bisected Pig' & 'Thousand Years'; Marcus Harvey's 'Myra', and Tracey Emin's 'Everyone I have ever slept with'
Signed Paintings 'OK'	Oscar Kokoschka signed many of his paintings 'OK' making them look like they had been vandalised
Stole Mona Lisa 1914	Vincenzo Perugia (Sentenced to one year, 15 days imprisonment)
Stolen from National Gallery	The Scream (Stolen in 1994 but returned 2 months later)
Surrealism	Term coined in 1922 by André Breton to describe the real and unreal world of waking and dreaming as depicted by the artist. Breton chose term from earlier description of a Chagall work by Guillaume Apollinaire
Tachisme	Term often used synonymously with Abstract Expressionism but it strictly refers to a French movement of the 1950s which consisted of paintings composed of large blobs of colour
Tempest, The (Kokoschka)	Depicts the artist and Alma Mahler resting in a huge cockleshell in the midst of a raging sea
Thousand Years	Damien Hirst's Rotting cow head in a smear of blood, beset by flies
Van Gogh: Only painting sold	Red Vineyard was the only painting he sold in his lifetime

ASTRONOMY

Constellations

Latin name	English name	Latin name	English name	Latin name	English name
Andromeda	Andromeda	Crux	Southern Cross	Orion	Orion
Antlia	Air Pump			Pavo	Peacock
Apus	Bird of Paradise	Cygnus	Swan	Pegasus	Winged Horse
		Delphinus	Dolphin	Perseus	Perseus
Aquarius	Water Bearer	Dorado	Swordfish or Goldfish	Phoenix	Phoenix
Aquila	Eagle			Pictor	Painter
Ara	Altar	Draco	Dragon	Pisces	Fishes
Aries	Ram	Equuleus	Foal	Piscis Austrinus	Southern Fish
Auriga	Charioteer	Eridanus	River Eridanus	Puppis	Poop or Stern
Boötes	Herdsman	Fornax	Furnace	Pyxis	Mariner's Compass
Caelum	Chisel	Gemini	Twins		
Camelopardalis	Giraffe	Grus	Crane	Reticulum	Net
Cancer	Crab	Hercules	Hercules	Sagitta	Arrow
Canes Venatici	Hunting Dogs	Horologium	Clock	Sagittarius	Archer
Canis Major	Great Dog	Hydra	Sea Serpent	Scorpius	Scorpion
Canis Minor	Little Dog	Hydrus	Water Snake	Sculptor	Sculptor
Capricornus	Sea Goat	Indus	Indian	Scutum	Shield
Carina	Keel	Lacerta	Lizard	Serpens	Serpent
Cassiopeia	Cassiopeia	Leo	Lion	Sextans	Sextant
Centaurus	Centaur	Leo Minor	Little Lion	Taurus	Bull
Cepheus	Cepheus	Lepus	Hare	Telescopium	Telescope
Cetus	Whale	Libra	Scales	Triangulum	Triangle
Chamaeleon	Chameleon	Lupus	Wolf	Triangulum Australe	Southern Triangle
Circinus	Compasses	Lynx	Lynx		
Columba	Dove	Lyra	Lyre	Tucana	Toucan
Coma Berenices	Berenice's Hair	Mensa	Table	Ursa Major	Great Bear
		Microscopium	Microscope	Ursa Minor	Little Bear
Corona Australis	Southern Crown	Monoceros	Unicorn	Vela	Sails
		Musca	Fly	Virgo	Virgin
Corona Borealis	Northern Crown	Norma	Level	Volans	Flying Fish
		Octans	Octant	Vulpecula	Fox
Corvus	Crow	Ophiuchus	Serpent Bearer		
Crater	Cup				

The Planets

Planetary data	Diameter km	miles	Maximum distance from Sun (millions) km	miles	Minimum distance from Sun (millions) km	miles	Sidereal period	Axial rotation period
Mercury	4878	3031	69.4	43	46.8	29	88 days	58d 16h
Venus	12104	7521	109	67.6	107.6	66.7	224.7 days	243 days
Earth	12756	7927	152.6	94.6	147.4	91.4	365.26 days	23h 56m
Mars	6794	4222	249.2	154.5	207.3	128.5	687 days	24h 37m 23s
Jupiter	142800	88700	817.4	506.8	741.6	459.8	11.86 years	9h 50m 30s
Saturn	120000	74600	1512	937.6	1346	834.6	29.46 years	10h 14m
Uranus	52000	32300	3011	1867	2740	1699.0	84.01 years	16-28 hours
Neptune	48400	30000	4543	2817	4466	2769.0	164.79 years	18-20 hours
Pluto	2300	1430	7364	4566	4461	2766.0	248.5 years	6d 9h

Astronomers Royal

John Flamsteed	1675–1719	Sir Frank Dyson	1910–1933	
Edmund Halley	1720–1742	Sir Harold Jones	1933–1955	
James Bradley	1742–1762	Sir Richard Woolley	1956–1971	
Nathaniel Bliss	1762–1764	Sir Martin Ryle	1972–1982	
Nevil Maskelyne	1765–1811	Sir Francis Graham–Smith	1982–1990	
John Pond	1811–1835	Sir Arnold Wolfendale	1991–1995	
Sir George Airy	1835–1881	Sir Martin Rees	1995–	
Sir William Christie	1881–1910			

Until 1972 the title of Astronomer Royal was given to the director of Greenwich Observatory. It is now an honorary title for an outstanding astronomer, who receives a stipend of approximately £100 per year

Planetary Satellites

		Discovered	Diameter km	miles			Discovered	Diameter km	miles
Earth	Moon		3476	2160		Pandora	1980	100	60
Mars	Phobos	1877	27	17		Atlas	1980	40	25
	Deimos	1877	15	9		Calypso	1980	30	19
Jupiter	Ganymede	1610	5260	3270		Telesto	1980	24	15
	Callisto	1610	4800	3000		Dione B	1982	15	9
	Io	1610	3650	2268		Prometheus	1980	10	6
	Europa	1610	3138	1950	**Uranus**	Oberon	1787	1600	1000
	Amalthea	1892	270	168		Titania	1787	1600	1000
	Himalia	1904	180	110		Ariel	1851	1300	800
	Elara	1905	80	50		Umbriel	1851	1100	700
	Pasiphae	1908	50	30		Miranda	1948	400	250
	Sinope	1914	40	25		Puck	1986	170	105
	Carme	1938	40	25		Portia	1986	90	55
	Lysithea	1938	40	25		Cressida	1986	70	40
	Metis	1979	40	25		Juliet	1986	70	40
	Ananke	1951	30	19		Belinda	1986	50	30
	Adrastea	1979	24	15		Bianca	1986	50	30
	Leda	1974	20	12		Desdemona	1986	50	30
	Thebe	1979	100	62		Rosalind	1986	50	30
Saturn	Titan	1655	5150	3200		Ophelia	1986	20	12
	Rhea	1672	1530	950		Cordelia	1986	15	9
	Iapetus	1671	1440	900	**Neptune**	Triton	1846	2700	1678
	Dione	1684	1120	700		Proteus	1989	415	260
	Tethys	1684	1050	650		Nereid	1949	300	190
	Enceladus	1789	500	310		Larissa	1989	190	118
	Hyperion	1848	400	250		Galatea	1989	160	100
	Mimas	1789	390	240		Despina	1989	150	95
	Phoebe	1898	220	135		Naiad	1989	50	30
	Janus	1966	200	120		Thalassa	1989	50	30
	Epimetheus	1980	140	90	**Pluto**	Charon	1978	1000	620
	Helene	1980	100	60					

Astronomy and Space: Selected Data

Albedo   Reflecting power of a planet or other non-luminous body

American in Space: 1st   Alan Shepard in Freedom 7 (May 5th 1961); duration of flight 15 minutes 28 seconds

American to Orbit the Earth: 1st   John Glenn in Friendship 7 (Feb 20th 1962); for 3 orbits, duration of flight 4 hrs 55 mins 23 secs

Aphelion   Furthest distance of a planet from the Sun

Apogee   Furthest point of the Moon from the Earth

Apollo 13: Crew   James Lovell, Jack Swigert and Fred Haise. The service module exploded 55 hrs into the mission to the Moon, but the lunar module was used to reach home safely on Apr 17th 1970)

Asteroid   Another name for a minor planet. Eros, discovered in 1898, comes closer to the Earth (every 37 years) than anything except the Moon

Asteroid: Brightest   Vesta

Asteroid: Largest   1. Ceres 2. Pallas 3. Vesta 4. Hygeia

Asteroid Belt   The 4,000-plus minor planets (asteroids) that orbit the Sun between Mars and Jupiter

Astrolabe   Ancient instrument used to measure altitudes of celestial bodies

Astronomical Unit   Mean distance between the Earth and the Sun: 149,598,500 km

Baikonur   Launch site for manned Soviet space flights in Kazakhstan

Baily's Beads   Brilliant points seen around the Moon just before and after a total solar eclipse

Big Bang Theory   First advanced by Georges Lemaitre: the idea that the universe began, around 15 to 17 billion years ago, as a point of superdense matter that exploded and has been expanding ever since

Black hole   Region of immense gravitational pull around a massive collapsed star from which not even light can escape

Bolide   A brilliant exploding meteor

Brightest Stars   1. Sirius 2. Canopus 3. Alpha Centauri 4. Arcturus 5. Vega

British National Space Centre   Head Office at 151 Buckingham Palace Road, London SWI 9SS

Cassini's Division   Dark gap between rings A and B of Saturn discovered by Gian Domenico Cassini, among others

Celestial Equator   Projection of the Earth's equator on to the celestial sphere

Celestial Sphere   Imaginary sphere surrounding the Earth on which all heavenly bodies appear to move, and whose centre is the same as that of the Earth's globe

Challenger   US space shuttle exploded 72 seconds after lift-off on Jan 28th 1986, killing all 7 crew members, including schoolteacher Christa McAuliffe

Chromosphere   Part of the Sun's atmosphere that lies above the photosphere

A
S
T
R
O
N
O
M
Y

Coldest Planet   Pluto

Comet: Shortest known orbital period Encke's Comet, 3.3 years

Comet: Meaning   From the Latin 'Coma' which means hair

Constellations   31 in Northern and 52 in Southern hemisphere, with 5 'floaters' overlapping. **Largest**: Hydra. **Smallest**: Crux Australis

Corona   Outermost part of the Sun's atmosphere visible with the naked eye only during a total solar eclipse

Cosmogony   Study of the origin and evolution of the universe

Cosmology   Study of the universe considered as a whole

Declination   Angular distance of celestial body north or south of celestial equator, corresponding to latitude on the Earth

Doppler Effect   Apparent change in wavelength of the light from a luminous body in motion relative to the observer

Earth: Mean distance from Sun: 150 million kms (93 million miles)

Ecliptic   Apparent yearly path of the Sun among the stars

Ephemeris   Table showing the predicted positions of a celestial body such as a planet, comet or asteroid

Equinox   Equinoxes are two points at which the ecliptic cuts the celestial equator; vernal equinox Mar 21st, autumnal Sep 22nd

European Space Agency   Created 1975 by merger of European Space Research Organisation and European Launcher Development Organisation. Members are Austria, Belgium, Denmark, Finland, France, Germany, Ireland, Italy, Netherlands, Norway, Spain, Sweden, Switzerland and the UK. Canada being non-European is deemed a co-operating state. Head Office is at 8–10 Rue Mario Nikis, 75738 Paris, France

Exosphere   Outermost part of a planet's atmosphere

Expanding Universe   Observation made by Edwin Hubble in 1929 that the universe appears to be expanding; this confirms the Big Bang Theory

Flocculi   Patches on the Sun's surface: bright (calcium) and dark (hydrogen)

Galaxies   Systems made up of stars, nebulae and interstellar matter, forming star families held together by their own gravitational pull and separate from other such galaxies

Gibbous Phase   Phase of the Moon or planet when between half and full

Great Red Spot   Enormous red feature in the atmosphere of Jupiter, visible since the 17th century

Hertzsprung-Russell Diagram   Diagram in which stars are plotted according to their spectral types and their absolute magnitudes

Hottest Planet   Venus

Hubble Space Telescope   Placed in the Earth's orbit by the space shuttle Discovery (April 24th 1990)

Inferior Planets   Mercury and Venus: closer to the Sun than the Earth is

Inner Planets   The 4 planets that orbit the Sun within the Asteroid Belt; i.e. Mercury, Venus, Earth, Mars

Ionosphere   Region of the Earth's atmosphere lying above the stratosphere

Jupiter   Mean distance from Sun: 778.34 million km (486 million miles). Galileo discovered satellites Callisto, Europa, Ganymede and Io. Atmosphere: hydrogen, ammonia and methane. Temperature can be as low as -200º C. Probes: Pioneer 10 and 11 (1973/4); Voyagers 1 and 2 (1979); Galileo (1995)

Largest Planet   Jupiter

Light year   Distance travelled by light in one year: 9.4607 million million km. Light travels at 186,000 miles per second (7 1/2 times round the Earth)

Local Group   Group of more than two dozen galaxies, including our own galaxy. Largest member is the Andromeda Galaxy, M.31

Lunar Eclipse   Passage of the Moon through the shadow cast by the Earth

Magnitude   Measurement unit for the brightness of a star or planet

Mars   Mean distance from the Sun: 227.94 million km (142 million miles). Atmosphere nearest to our own, but there is no water on Mars. Probes: Mariner 4, 6, 7, 8, 9, (1965–71); and 1 and 2 landed 1976; Pathfinder landed 1997

Mercury   Mean distance from the Sun: 57.9 million kms (36.2 million miles). Atmosphere: non-existent – burnt off by closeness to Sun. Probe: Mariner 10 (1974 & 1975)

Meteor   Particle or small rock moving around Sun and destroyed when entering atmosphere

Meteorite   Larger object that reaches the ground without being destroyed

Milky Way   The galaxy of which our Sun is a member. It contains approximately 100,000 million stars of which 5776 are visible to the naked eye

Mir   Advanced type of space station 1st launched by the Soviet Union in 1986

Moon   Mean distance from Earth: 384,000 km (239,900 miles). Diameter: 3,476 km (2,160 miles). Revolves around the Earth from west to east. First soft landing by Soviet Luna 9, launched on Jan 31st 1966, land Feb 3rd. First manned flight around the Moon: Apollo 8 in Dec 1968 First manned landing and walk: Apollo 11 on Jul 20th 1969 Last man on the Moon was Eugene Cernan in Apollo 17 on Dec 11th 1972

Moon's Rotation   Rotates about its own axis in 29 1/2 days, which is about the same time it takes to orbit the Earth. Hence the same face of the Moon is always presented to the Earth

Nadir   Point on the celestial sphere directly below the observer, diametrically opposite the zenith

Nearest Galaxy   Andromeda (2.3 million light years)

Nearest Planet to Earth   Venus

Nearest Star to Earth   Sun

Nearest Stars to Sun   1. Proxima Centauri (4.26 light years) 2. Alpha Centauri (4.34) 3. Barnard's Star (5.88)

Nebula   Cloud of gas and dust in space

Neptune   Mean distance from the Sun: 4496.7 million km (2810 million miles) Discovered by J. G. Galle in 1846. Atmosphere: hydrogen, helium, methane, ammonia. First suggested name was 'Janus'. Probe: Voyager 2 (1989)

Neutron Star   Remnant of a massive star that once exploded as a supernova

Nova   Star that suddenly flares up to many times its normal brilliancy and then fades back to obscurity

Occultation   The obscuring of one celestial body by another

Ophiuchus   Often called the 13th constellation of the Zodiac

Orrery   Model showing the Sun and the orbiting planets, capable of being moved mechanically to scale

Outer Planets   The 5 planets that orbit the Sun beyond the Asteroid belt; i.e. Jupiter, Saturn, Uranus, Neptune, Pluto

Parsec   Basic unit used to measure large astronomic distances: 3.26 light years

Perigee   Position of the Moon in its orbit when closest to the Earth

Perihelion   Position in orbit of a planet when closest to the Sun

Photosphere   The bright surface of the Sun

Planet   Large body orbiting a star; the name means 'Wanderer' in Greek

Pluto   Mean distance from the Sun: 5,900 million km (3687 million miles). Atmosphere: tenuous. Discovered by Clyde Tombaugh 1930; named by Venetia Burney

Polaris   Also called the Pole Star, it is 680 light years from the Earth

Quadrant   Ancient astronomical instrument used for measuring the apparent positions of celestial bodies

Reversing Layer   Gaseous layer above the Sun's photosphere

Rings of Saturn   Discs composed of ice and rock, in sizes ranging from tiny particles to massive boulders, orbiting Jupiter, Neptune and Uranus, and most spectaculary Saturn

Rotating Backwards   Venus (east to west)

Saturn   Mean distance from the Sun: 1427 million km (891 million miles). Atmosphere: mostly hydrogen and helium, some methane and ammonia. Christiaan Huygens discovered the rings in 1655. Cassini discovered 4 of the satellites. The satellite Phoebe revolves in the opposite direction to the others. Probes: Voyager 1 and 2, 1980–81

Sirius   Also called the 'Dog Star' it is 8.7 light years from the Earth

Solar Cycle   Discovered by H. Schwabe in 1826. He found that there is an 11-year solar cycle of sunspot activity

Solar Eclipse   Blotting out of the Sun by the Moon, so that the Moon is directly between the Earth and the Sun

Solar Flares   Brilliant eruptions of hydrogen in outer part of Sun's atmosphere

Solar Wind   Flow of ionised hydrogen and helium from the Sun

Solstices   Times when Sun is at its maximum declination of 23 1/2 degrees

Space Flight: 1st   Yuri Gagarin in Vostok 1 (Apr 12th 1961); duration of flight 1 hr 48 mins

Space Flight: 1st Briton   Helen Sharman (May 18th 1991)

Space Walk: 1st Briton   Michael Foale

Space Walk: 1st Untethered   Bruce McCandless of the USA (Feb 3rd 1984)

Space Walk: 1st Woman   Svetlana Savitskaya of the USSR (Jul 17th 1984)

Stratosphere   Region of the Earth's atmosphere lying above the troposphere and below the ionosphere

Sun   Distance from the Earth: 149,597,900 km on average. Diameter: 1,392,000 km. Light takes 8 minutes 14.2 seconds to reach the Earth

Sunspot   Region of lower temperature and therefore less brilliance, on the surface of the Sun

Superior Planets   Those whose orbits lie outside the Earth's: Mars, Jupiter, Saturn, Uranus,Neptune, Pluto.

Supernova   Cataclysmic explosion of a very massive star, which ends its career as a patch of expanding gas with a neutron star at its centre

Syzygy   Position of the Moon in its orbit when new or full

Telescope: Largest   Mount Semirodriki, Caucasus, with a 600 cm (236.2 in) reflector

Troposphere   Lowest part of the Earth's atmosphere, reaching to about 11km

Umbra   Main cone of shadow cast by Earth. Also darkest part of a sunspot

Uranus   Mean distance from Sun: 2869.6 million kms (1793 million miles). Atmosphere: hydrogen and helium. Discovered by William Herschel 1781. Probe: Voyager 2 (1986)

Van Allen Radiation Belts   Zones of charged particles around the Earth, held captive by the Earth's magnetic field

Venus   Mean distance from Sun: 108.2 million km (67.2 million miles). Atmosphere is largely carbon dioxide. Probes: Russian Venera series (1962–71); US Mariners 2, 5, and 10 ; Magallen (1990). Other names: Hesperus (evening star), Phosphorus (morning star)

Voyager   A pair of unmanned US interplanetary probes launched to observe and transmit to Earth data about the outer planetary system. Voyager runs out of power around 2020. Voyager 1 was Launched on Sep 5th 1977, flew by Jupiter in March 1979, reached Saturn in Nov 1980, then proceeded out of the solar system. Voyager 2 was launched on Aug 20th 1977. It flew by Jupiter (Jul 1979), Saturn (Aug 1981), Uranus (Jan 1986) and Neptune (Aug 1989), then on into interstellar space

Walk in Space: 1st   Alexei Leonov (Mar 18th 1965)

Woman in Space: 1st   Valentina Tereshkova (June 16th 1963)

Zenith   Point on the celestial sphere directly above the observer (altitude 90 degrees)

Zodiac   Belt stretching around the sky 8 degrees to either side of ecliptic. The constellations Aries, Taurus, Gemini, Cancer, Leo, Virgo, Libra, Scorpius, Sagittarius, Capricornus, Aquarius and Pisces lies within this belt, and so do the apparent paths of the Sun and all the planets except Pluto, which sometimes moves outside it

ASTRONOMY

BRITAIN

United Kingdom: Administration Centres

A restructure of the old County boundaries is ongoing throughout the UK and is unlikely to be finalised for at least another year or possibly two. Formerly there were 46 English County Councils, but this has been reduced to 35, all of which have the same Administrative Headquarters as before.

The other ten Counties, along with parts of still existing Counties, have been restructured and are now known officially as Unitary Authorities. There are 82 such authorities at present, plus the 32 London Boroughs and the City of London Corporation.

A similar position exists in Scotland, Wales and Northern Ireland, although it remains unclear if all the district councils are to become Counties.

Northern Ireland's six Counties have been rationalised across 26 districts (the same number as there are Counties of the Irish Republic), although at present only the traditional six Counties plus Belfast City and Londonderry City have Lord-Lieutenants.

As this is an area of uncertainty none of the District Councils and their respective Administration Headquarters have been entered in the very comprehensive list of 'Capitals', and only the long-established Counties have been listed.

English County Councils (as at July 31st 2001)

County	Admin Headquarters	County	Admin Headquarters
Bedfordshire	Bedford	Leicestershire	Leicester
Buckinghamshire	Aylesbury	Lincolnshire	Lincoln
Cambridgeshire	Cambridge	Norfolk	Norwich
Cheshire	Chester	Northamptonshire	Northampton
Cornwall	Truro	Northumberland	Morpeth
Cumbria	Carlisle	North Yorkshire	Northallerton
Derbyshire	Matlock	Nottinghamshire	Nottingham
Devon	Exeter	Oxfordshire	Oxford
Dorset	Dorchester	Shropshire	Shrewsbury
Durham	Durham	Somerset	Taunton
East Sussex	Lewes	Staffordshire	Stafford
Essex	Chelmsford	Suffolk	Ipswich
Gloucestershire	Gloucester	Surrey	Kingston-upon-Thames
Hampshire	Winchester		
Hertfordshire	Hertford	Warwickshire	Warwick
Isle of Wight	Newport	West Sussex	Chichester
Kent	Maidstone	Wiltshire	Trowbridge
Lancashire	Preston	Worcestershire	Worcester

NB: The five inhabited islands of the Scillies i.e. St Mary's (Admin HQ), Tresco, Bryher, St Agnes and St Martin's although not constituting a separate County, do however have their own Council

London Boroughs

(These are also Unitary Authorities)

Council	Admin Headquarters	Council	Admin Headquarters
Barking & Dagenham	Dagenham	Hounslow	Hounslow
Barnet	Hendon	* Islington	Islington
Bexley	Bexleyheath	* Kensington and Chelsea #	Kensington
Brent	Wembley	Kingston-upon-Thames #	Kingston-upon-Thames
Bromley	Bromley		
* Camden	Camden	* Lambeth	Lambeth
City of London	Guildhall, London	* Lewisham	Catford
Croydon	Croydon	Merton	Morden
Ealing	Ealing	Newham	East Ham
Enfield	Enfield	Redbridge	Ilford
* Greenwich	Woolwich	Richmond-upon-Thames	Twickenham
* Hackney	Hackney	* Southwark	Southwark
* Hammersmith & Fulham	Hammersmith	Sutton	Sutton
Haringey	Wood Green	* Tower Hamlets	Tower Hamlets
Harrow	Harrow	Waltham Forest	Walthamstow
Havering	Romford	* Wandsworth	Wandsworth
Hillingdon	Uxbridge	* Westminster City	Westminster

* denotes Inner London Borough   # denotes Royal Borough

Unitary Authorities (as at July 2001)

Authority	Headquarters	Authority	Headquarters
Barnsley*	Barnsley	Nottingham	Nottingham
Bath and North East Somerset	Bath	Oldham*	Oldham
Birmingham*	Birmingham	Peterborough	Peterborough
Blackburn with Darwen	Blackburn	Plymouth	Plymouth
Blackpool	Blackpool	Poole	Poole
Bolton*	Bolton	Portsmouth	Portsmouth
Bournemouth	Bournemouth	Reading	Reading
Bracknell Forest	Bracknell	Redcar and Cleveland	Redcar
Bradford	Bradford	Rochdale*	Rochdale
Brighton and Hove	Brighton	Rotherham*	Rotherham
Bristol	Bristol	Rutland*	Oakham
Bury*	Bury	St Helens*	St Helens
Calderdale*	Halifax	Salford*	Swinton
Coventry*	Coventry	Sandwell*	West Bromwich
Darlington	Darlington	Sefton*	Southport
Derby	Derby	Sheffield*	Sheffield
Doncaster*	Doncaster	Slough*	Slough
Dudley*	Dudley	Solihull*	Solihull
East Riding of Yorkshire	Beverley	Southampton	Southampton
Gateshead*	Gateshead	Southend	Southend
Halton	Widnes	South Gloucestershire	Thornbury
Hartlepool	Hartlepool	South Tyneside*	South Shields
Herefordshire	Hereford	Stockport*	Stockport
Isle of Wight	Newport	Stockton-on-Tees	Stockton-on-Tees
Kingston-upon-Hull	Kingston-upon-Hull		
Kirklees*	Huddersfield	Stoke-on-Trent	Stoke-on-Trent
Knowsley*	Huyton	Sunderland*	Sunderland
Leeds*	Leeds	Swindon	Swindon
Leicester	Leicester	Tameside*	Ashton-under-Lyme
Liverpool*	Liverpool		
Luton	Luton	Thurrock	Grays
Manchester*	Manchester	Torbay	Torquay
Medway Towns	Rochester	Trafford*	Stretford
Middlesbrough	Middlesbrough	Wakefield*	Wakefield
Milton Keynes	Milton Keynes	Walsall*	Walsall
Newbury	Newbury	Warrington	Warrington
Newcastle-upon-Tyne*	Newcastle-upon-Tyne	West Berkshire	Newbury
		Windsor and Maidenhead	Maidenhead
North East Lincolnshire	Grimsby	Wigan*	Wigan
North Lincolnshire	Brigg	Wirral*	Wallasey
North Somerset	Weston-Super-Mare	Wokingham	Wokingham
		Wolverhampton*	Wolverhampton
North Tyneside*	North Shields	Wrekin	Telford
		York	York

* denotes Metropolitan Authorities

Scottish Districts

Council	Admin Headquarters	Council	Admin Headquarters
Aberdeen	Aberdeen	Highland	Inverness
Aberdeenshire	Aberdeen	Inverclyde	Greenock
Angus	Forfar	Midlothian	Dalkeith
Argyll and Bute	Lochgilphead	Moray	Elgin
Clackmannanshire	Alloa	North Ayrshire	Irvine
Comhairlenan Eilean Siar	Stornoway	North Lanarkshire	Motherwell
Dumfries and Galloway	Dumfries	Orkney	Kirkwall
Dundee	Dundee	Perth and Kinrosshire	Perth
East Ayrshire	Kilmarnock	Renfrewshire	Paisley
East Dunbartonshire	Kirkintilloch	Scottish Borders	Melrose
East Lothian	Haddington	Shetland	Lerwick
East Renfrewshire	Glasgow	South Ayrshire	Ayr
Edinburgh	Edinburgh	South Lanarkshire	Hamilton
Falkirk	Falkirk	Stirling	Stirling
Fife	Glenrothes	West Dunbartonshire	Dunbarton
Glasgow City	Glasgow	West Lothian	Livingston

BRITAIN

Welsh Districts

District Council	Admin Headquarters	District Council	Admin Headquarters
Aberconway	Colwyn Bay	Merthyr Tydfil	Merthyr Tydfil
Anglesey	Llangefni	Monmouth	Cwmbran
Blaenau Gwent	Ebbw Vale	Neath Port Talbot	Port Talbot
Bridgend	Bridgend	Newport	Newport
Caerphilly	Hengoed	Pembrokeshire	Haverfordwest
Cardiff	Cardiff	Powys	Llandrindod Wells
Carmarthenshire	Carmarthen	Rhondda, Cynon, Taff	Cardiff
Ceredigion	Aberystwyth	Swansea	Swansea
Denbighshire	Ruthin	Torfaen	Pontypool
Flintshire	Mold	Vale of Glamorgan	Barry
Gwynedd	Caernarfon	Wrexham	Wrexham

Northern Ireland Districts

District Council	Admin Headquarters	District Council	Admin Headquarters
Antrim	Antrim	Down	Downpatrick
Ards	Newtownards	Dungannon	Dungannon
Armagh	Armagh	Fermanagh	Enniskillen
Ballymena	Ballymena	Larne	Larne
Ballymoney	Ballymoney	Limavady	Limavady
Banbridge	Banbridge	Lisburn	Hillsborough
Belfast	Belfast	Magherafelt	Magherafelt
Carrickfergus	Carrickfergus	Moyle	Ballycastle
Castlereagh	Cregagh	Newry and Mourne	Newry
Coleraine	Coleraine	Newtownabbey	Ballyclare
Cookstown	Cookstown	North Down	Bangor
Craigavon	Craigavon	Omagh	Omagh
Derry	Derry	Strabane	Strabane

Shopping Centres

by Towns and Cities

Aberdeen	Bredero	Horsham	Swan Walk
Bedford	Harpur	Hull	North Point
Belfast	Castle Court	Ilford	Exchange
Birmingham	Bull Ring	Lancaster	St Nicholas; Markgate
Bolton	Crompton Place	Leatherhead	Swan Centre
Bradford	Kirkgate	Leeds	Bramley Centre
Bristol	Galleries	Leicester	Shires
Bromley	Glades	Lincoln	Waterside
Cambridge	Grafton Centre	Manchester	Arndale
Cardiff	St Davids	Mansfield	Four Seasons
Cheltenham	Regent Arcade	Morecambe	Arndale
Chester	Grosvenor	Newcastle	Eldon Gardens
Colchester	Culver Square	Northampton	Grosvenor Centre
Coventry	Cannon Park	Norwich	Castle Mall
Crawley	County Mall	Nottingham	Broadmarsh; Victoria
Croydon	Whitgift	Oxford	Westgate
Dartford	Orchards	Peterborough	Queensgate
Derby	Eagle	Poole	Dolphin
Dorking	St Martin's Walk	Portsmouth	Bridge
Dundee	Wellgate	Preston	Fishergate
Durham	Milburngate	Sheffield	Meadowhall
Eastbourne	Arndale	Southend	Royals
Exeter	Guildhall	Stockton	Teeside Park
Gateshead	MetroCentre	Stoke-on-Trent	Potteries
Glasgow	St Enoch; Sauchiehall Centre	Sunderland	Bridges
Gloucester	Kings Square	Sutton (Surrey)	St Nicholas
Grimsby	Freshney Place	Swansea	St Davids
Guildford	Friary	Swindon	Brunel
Harlow	Harvey Centre	Thurrock	Lakeside

| Wandsworth | Arndale | Winchester | Brooks |
| Watford | Harlequin Centre | York | Coppergate |

by Shopping Centres

Arndale	Eastbourne; Manchester; Morecambe; Wandsworth	Harlequin Centre	Watford
		Harpur	Bedford
Bramley Centre	Leeds	Harvey Centre	Harlow
Bredero	Aberdeen	Kings Square	Gloucester
Bridge	Portsmouth	Kirkgate	Bradford
Bridges	Sunderland	Lakeside	Thurrock
Broadmarsh	Nottingham	Markgate	Lancaster
Brooks	Winchester	Meadowhall	Sheffield
Brunel	Swindon	MetroCentre	Gateshead
Bull Ring	Birmingham	Milburngate	Durham
Cannon Park	Coventry	North Point	Hull
Castle Court	Belfast	Orchards	Dartford
Castle Mall	Norwich	Potteries	Stoke-on-Trent
Coppergate	York	Queensgate	Peterborough
County Mall	Crawley	Regent Arcade	Cheltenham
Crompton Place	Bolton	Royals	Southend
Culver Square	Colchester	Sauchiehall Centre	Glasgow
Dolphin	Poole	Shires	Leicester
Eagle	Derby	St Davids	Cardiff; Swansea
Eldon Gardens	Newcastle	St Enoch	Glasgow
Exchange	Ilford	St Martin's Walk	Dorking
Fishergate	Preston	St Nicholas	Lancaster; Sutton
Four Seasons	Mansfield	Swan Centre	Leatherhead (Surrey)
Freshney Place	Grimsby	Swan Walk	Horsham (Sussex)
Friary	Guildford	Teeside Park	Stockton
Galleries	Bristol	Victoria	Nottingham
Glades	Bromley	Waterside	Lincoln
Grafton Centre	Cambridge	Wellgate	Dundee
Grosvenor	Chester	Westgate	Oxford
Grosvenor Centre	Northampton	Whitgift	Croydon
Guildhall	Exeter		

B
R
I
T
A
I
N

NB: Many cities have more than one shopping precinct e.g. Leeds. This is purely a list of some of the best-known.

Pub Names

Blind Beggar	Situated in Whitechapel Road, London and famous as the site of Ronald Kray's murder of George Cornell.
Crown	Second most popular pub name in Britain.
Five Alls	Sign depicts a king with the caption 'I rule for all', a parson with 'I pray for all', a lawyer with 'I plead for all' a soldier with 'I fight for all' and a labourer with 'I work for all'.
Greyhound	Situated in Tinsley Green, Crawley and famous for hosting the World Marbles Championships at Easter.
Marquis of Granby	Named after John Manners, Marquis of Granby (1721-70). C-in-C of the British army in 1766
Red Lion	Most popular pub name in Britain.
Royal Oak	Named after the oak tree that Charles II hid in after the battle of Worcester in 1651, the third most popular pub name in Britain.
Tan Hill Inn	Situated in Arkengarthdale, near Reeth, N. Yorks, the highest pub in Britain.
Trip to Jerusalem	Situated in the Brewhouse Yard, Nottingham, possibly the oldest pub in Britain.
White Hart	Named after Richard II's heraldic symbol.
White Lion	Named after Edward IV's heraldic symbol.

There are approximately 55,000 pubs in Britain and since 1988 they can remain open any time between 11am and 11pm.

Prisons

Name	Location	Name	Location
* Aberdeen	Aberdeen	Grendon	Aylesbury, Bucks
Acklington	Morpeth, Northumberland	Guys Marsh	Shaftesbury, Dorset
Albany	Newport, Isle of Wight	Haslar	Gosport, Hants
Aldington	Ashford, Kent	Hatfield	Hatfield, Doncaster
** Altcourse	Liverpool	Haverigg	Millom, Cumbria
Armley	Leeds	Hewell Grange	Redditch, Worcs
Ashfield	Bristol	High Down	Sutton, Surrey
Ashwell	Oakham, Leics	* Highpoint	Newmarket, Suffolk
* Askham Grange	Askham Richard, York	Hindley	Wigan, Lancs
Aylesbury	Aylesbury, Bucks	Hollesley Bay	Woodbridge, Suffolk
Barlinnie	Glasgow	* Holloway	Parkhurst Rd, London
	(holds the most prisoners	Holme House	Stockton-on-Tees
	in GB, approx 1150)	Hull	Hull, Yorks
Bedford	Bedford	Hydebank Wood	Belfast
Belmarsh	Thamesmead, London	Kilmarnock	Kilmarnock
** Blakenhurst	Redditch, Worcs	Kingston	Portsmouth
Blantyre House	Cranbrook, Kent	Kirkham	Preston, Lancs
Blundeston	Lowestoft, Suffolk	Kirklevington Grange	Yarm, Cleveland
Brinsford	Wolverhampton	Lancaster	Lancaster
Bristol	Bristol	Lancaster Farms	Lancaster
Brixton	Brixton, London	Latchmere House	Richmond, Surrey
* Brockhill	Redditch, Worcs	Leicester	Leicester
** Buckley Hall	Rochdale, Lancs	Lewes	Lewes, East Sussex
Bullingdon	Bicester, Oxon	Leyhill	Wotton-under-Edge, Glos
* Bullwood Hall	Hockley, Essex	Lincoln	Lincoln
Camp Hill	Newport, Isle of Wight	Lindholme	Doncaster
Cardiff	Cardiff, South Wales	Littlehey	Huntingdon
Castington	Morpeth	Liverpool	Liverpool
Castle Huntly	Longforgan, nr Dundee	Long Lartin	Evesham, Worcs
Channings Wood	Newton Abbott, Devon	Longport	Canterbury, Kent
* Chelmsford	Chelmsford, Essex	Longriggend	Airdrie
Coldingley	Woking, Surrey	** Lowdham Grange	Lowdham, Notts
* Cookham Wood	Rochester, Kent	Low Moss	Glasgow
* Cornton Vale	Stirling	* Low Newton	Brasside, Durham
Crumlin Road	Belfast	Maghaberry	Lisburn, Co Antrim
Dartmoor	Princetown, Yelverton,	Magilligan	Londonderry
	Devon	Maidstone	Maidstone
Deerbolt	Barnard Castle	Manchester	Manchester
** Doncaster	Marshgate, Doncaster	Maze (formerly	Lisburn, Co Antrim
Dorchester	North Square, Dorchester	'Long Kesh')	
Dover	Dover, Kent	Moorland	Doncaster
Downview	Sutton, Surrey	Morton Hall	Lincoln
* Drake Hall	Eccleshall, Staffs	Mount	Hemel Hempstead
* Dumfries	Dumfries	Mountjoy	Dublin
Dungavel	Strathaven, Lanark	Mousehold	Norwich
* Durham	Old Elvet, Durham	* New Hall	Wakefield, Yorks
* East Sutton Park	Maidstone, Kent	Noranside	Angus
* Eastwood Park	Falfield	Northallerton	Northallerton, N. Yorks
Edinburgh	Edinburgh	North Sea Camp	Boston, Lincs
Elmley	Sheerness, Kent	Norwich	Norwich
Erlestoke House	Devizes, Wilts	Nottingham	Nottingham
Everthorpe	Brough, Yorks	Onley	Rugby, Warks
Exeter	Exeter	** Parc	Bridgend, S. Wales
Featherstone	Featherstone,	Parkhurst	Newport, Isle of Wight
	Wolverhampton	Penninghame	Newton Stewart
Ford	Arundel, West Sussex	Pentonville	London
* Foston Hall	Ashbourne, Derby	Perth	Perth
Frankland	Brasside, Durham	Peterhead	Aberdeenshire
Friarton	Perth	Polmont	Falkirk
Full Sutton	Full Sutton, Yorks	Portland	Portland, Dorset
Garth	Preston, Lancs	* Porterfield	Inverness
Gartree	Market Harborough, Leics	Prescoed	Pontypool
Gateside	Greenock	Preston	Preston, Lancs
Glenochil	Clackmannanshire	Ranby	Retford, Notts
Glen Parva	Leicester	Reading	Reading
Gloucester	Barrack Square,	* Risley	Warrington
	Gloucester	Rochester	Rochester, Kent

Name	Location	Name	Location
Send	Woking, Surrey	Wandsworth	London
Shepton Mallet	Somerset		(holds the most prisoners
Shotts	Shotts		in England, approx 900)
Shrewsbury	The Dana, Shrewsbury	Wayland	Thetford, Norfolk
Stafford	Gaol Rd, Stafford	Wealston	Wetherby, W. Yorks
Standford Hill	Sheerness, Kent	Weare	Portland Harbour, Dorset
Stocken	Stretton, Leics	Wellingborough	Wellingborough, Northants
Stoke Heath	Market Drayton, Shrops	Werrington	Stoke-on-Trent
* Styal	Wilmslow, Cheshire	Wetherby	Wetherby, Yorks
Sudbury	Sudbury, Derbyshire	Whatton	Notts
Swaleside	Isle of Sheppey, Kent	Whitemoor	March, Cambs
Swansea	Swansea	* Winchester	Winchester, Hants
Swinfen Hall	Lichfield, Staffs	Winson Green	Birmingham
Thorn Cross	Warrington	** Wolds, The	Brough, Yorks
Usk	Usk, Gwent	Woodhill	Milton Keynes
Verne, The	Portland, Dorset	Wormwood Scrubs	DuCane Rd, London
Wakefield	Wakefield, Yorks		(built in 1874, the Scrubs is
			the largest prison in GB)
		Wymott	Preston, Lancs

* denotes women's prison (or women's wing attached)
** denotes private prison

British Castles

Name	Location	General Information
Abergavenny	Gwent	Norman Motte & Bailey castle founded by Hamelin of Ballon between 1087 & 1100, rebuilt in stone C12, captured by Welsh. c1172, recaptured by William de Braose c1175, ordered to be destroyed by Charles I in 1645.
Aberystwyth	Dyfed	Edwardian concentric castle erected 1277–90 under aegis of Edmund Crouchback and Master Giles of St George (after destruction in 1282 by Welsh). Held by Glyndwr 1404–9, slighted by Parliament in 1649.
Abinger	Surrey	Norman Motte & Bailey castle erected c1100. Wooden Donjon on stilts, excavated 1947–9.
Aboyne	Grampian	Motte castle erected C13, stone additions by 1300.
Acton Burnell	Shropshire	Fortified manor founded by Bishop Burnell c1284–90.
Airlie	Tayside	Enclosure castle founded by Ogilvy family c1432.
Allington	Kent	Founded by Stephen of Penchester 1281 beside site of Norman Motte & Bailey. Altered at end of C15 by Sir Henry Wyatt, restored by Lord Conway 1905–30. Now a Carmelite nunnery.
Alnwick	Northumberland	Norman Castle founded by Gilbert de Tesson, C12 shell keep, seat of Percy family since 1309, remodelled by Salvin C19.
Amberley	West Sussex	Built for the Bishops of Chichester, licence to crenellate 1377. Partially ruined, now a private residence.
Anstey	Herts	C12 Motte & Bailey, now lost.
Appleby	Cumbria	Norman castle erected C12 by Henry II, restored by Lady Anne Clifford 1651.
Ardrossan	Strathclyde	Courtyard castle founded late C13, gatehouse improved C15/16.
Arundel	West Sussex	Norman castle, founded 1069 by Roger of Montgomery, C12 shell keep, seat of Dukes of Norfolk.
Ashby de la Zouch	Leicestershire	Norman hall founded C12 by Zouch family. Converted into a castle 1474 by Lord Hastings, slighted by Parliament 1648. Now owned by English Heritage.
Auchen	Dumfries & Galloway	Castle founded C13, slighted by Bruce, rebuilt C14 as quadrangular castle.
Ayr	Strathclyde	Castle founded C12 by William the Lion, besieged by English 1298.
Balvenie	Grampian	Enclosure castle founded late C13 by Douglases, remodelled C16 by 4th Earl of Atholl.
Bamburgh	Northumberland	Norman castle with C12 tower keep erected by Henry II, besieged in 1095, 1462 and 1464, 'restored' by Lord Armstrong 1894–1905.
Bampton	Oxfordshire	Quadrangular castle founded 1315 by Aymer de Valence, now lost.
Banbury	Oxfordshire	Norman castle built early C12 by Bishops of Lincoln, extended 1400 into concentric plan, now lost.
Barnard Castle	Durham	Norman castle erected by Guy de Balliol c1100, C13 round keep,

B
R
I
T
A
I
N

Name	Location	General Information
		dismantled 1630 by Sir Henry Vane, now owned by English Heritage.
Barnstaple	Devon	Norman Motte & Bailey castle erected C11 by Judhael, C12 shell keep now lost.
Barnwell	Northants	Norman castle founded 1132 by Reginald de Moine. Rebuilt c1265, now ruined.
Bass of Inverurie	Grampian	Motte & Bailey castle founded c1180 by David, Earl of Huntingdon.
Beaumaris	Gwynedd	Concentric Edwardian castle erected by Master James of St George 1295–1330.
Bedford	Bedfordshire	Norman Motte & Bailey castle founded late C11, modified and enlarged C12, besieged by Henry III 1224 and destroyed shortly after.
Beeston	Cheshire	Built by Ranulf of Chester c1220, slighted in Civil War, owned by English Heritage.
Belvoir	Lincolnshire	Gothic style C19 castle, seat of Dukes of Rutland on site of Norman Motte & Bailey castle founded by Robert de Todeni C11, destroyed by King John.
Berkeley	Gloucestershire	Norman castle founded by William Fitz Osbern pre-1086, current building erected 1154 by Robert Fitzhardinge.
Berkhamsted	Hertfordshire	Norman Motte & Bailey castle founded by Robert of Mortain, rebuilt by Thomas Becket 1155–65 and King John, rare double moat, now owned by English Heritage.
Berry Pomeroy	Devon	Norman castle probably founded C12.
Bickleigh	Devon	Norman Motte & Bailey castle dismantled mid-C12; Courtenay family built fortified mansion on site C14.
Bishop's Stortford	Hertfordshire	Norman Motte & Bailey castle, now lost.
Blackness	Lothian	Tower castle founded C15, extended C16 with plan resembling that of a ship.
Blair	Tayside	Tower founded c1270, last castle to be besieged (1746), C18 mansion, seat of Dukes of Atholl.
Bodiam	East Sussex	Quadrangular moated castle built by Edward Dalyngrigge 1386, restored by Lord Curzon. National Trust property.
Bolingbroke	Lincolnshire	Built by Ranulf Earl of Chester c1220, now ruined.
Bolsover	Derbyshire	Norman castle founded by William Peverel, rebuilt by Smythson in Jacobean Romantic style, owned by English Heritage.
Bolton	North Yorkshire	Quadrangular castle built by Lord Scrope c1381–99, slighted during Civil War.
Bothwell	Strathclyde	Castle founded in 1270s by Moravia family, captured by Scots 1297, English 1301 & 1331, dismantled by Sir Andrew de Moravia 1337, rebuilt by Black Douglas in 1360s.
Bowes	County Durham	Tower castle built by the Earl of Richmond 1170–87, now owned by English Heritage.
Bramber	West Sussex	Norman castle founded by William de Braose c1070, slighted during Civil War, now owned by National Trust.
Brecon	Powys	Norman castle founded 1090 by Bernard de Neufmarche, extended and fortified in stone C12, unsuccessfully besieged by Welsh 1216, 1233 & 1404.
Bridgnorth	Shropshire	Norman castle founded by Robert de Belleme C11, C12 keep erected by Henry II, slighted during Civil War.
Bristol	Avon	Norman Motte & Bailey castle founded after Conquest; Tower Keep erected C12 by Stephen, destroyed in 1650s.
Bronllys	Powys	Norman Motte & Bailey castle founded C12, cylindrical tower added c1176 after a fire.
Brough	Cumbria	Norman castle founded by William Rufus c1095 in ruins of a Roman Fort, destroyed 1174 by William the Lion, rebuilt by Theobald de Valoires, restored C17 by Lady Anne Clifford. Now owned by English Heritage.
Brougham	Cumbria	Norman castle built C12 by Hugh d'Albini, pulled down c1700, now owned by English Heritage.
Buckingham	Buckinghamshire	Norman Motte & Bailey castle now covered by a church.
Builth	Powys	Norman Motte & Bailey castle founded by Philip de Braose c1100, destroyed by Llywelyn ap Gruffyd 1260, rebuilt 1277–82 by Edward I under direction of Master James of St. George, severely damaged by Glyndwr.
Bungay	Suffolk	Norman castle founded by Roger Bigod c1105, demolished 1176, shell keep & bailey erected c1295 by Roger Bigod.
Caerlaverock	Dumfries	Built c1280 to a triangular plan, captured by Edward I 1300, slighted by Bruce, rebuilt C15, now owned by Historic Scotland.
Caerleon	Gwent	Norman Motte & Bailey castle erected c1086, great tower added. 1158–73.

Name	Location	General Information
Caernarvon	Gwynedd	Norman Motte & Bailey castle erected 1093 by Earl Hugh of Chester, destroyed by Welsh 1115, Edwardian castle on site constructed by Master James of St George 1283–1330, designed to resemble walls of Constantinople.
Caerphilly	Mid Glamorgan	Built by Gilbert de Clare, Earl of Gloucester 1271–80 after original castle of 1267–70 destroyed by Llywelyn, now owned by Welsh Historic Mons.
Cainhoe	Bedfordshire	Norman castle founded by Nigel d'Albini, motte and 3 bailleys.
Caister	Norfolk	Built by Sir John Fastolf 1432–36, made of brick and surrounded by a moat.
Caldicot	Gwent	Norman Motte & Bailey castle founded by Walter Fitzroger early C12, developed by de Bohun Earls of Hereford late C12/early C13, gatehouse extended c1385, repaired late C19.
Cambridge	Cambs	Norman castle founded by William I 1068, rebuilt 1284–98, slighted in 1647.
Canterbury	Kent	Norman Motte & bailey castle founded by William I 1066, Keep erected early C12.
Cardiff	South Glamorgan	Norman Motte built C1080 by Robert Fitzhamon on site of Roman fort, shell keep erected C12, further additions by Gilbert de Clare C13, castle remodelled by William Burges for 3rd Marquess of Bute C19.
Cardigan	Dyfed	Norman Castle founded c1093, captured by Welsh c1170 and converted to stone, sold to John 1199, destroyed by Llywelyn the Great 1231, new castle built near original site by English in 1240s.
Carew	Dyfed	Norman Motte & Bailey castle founded by Gerald de Windsor 1105, extended by Nicholas de Carew in C13, damaged by Parliamentary forces in 1645.
Carisbrooke	Isle of Wight	Norman castle founded by William Fitz Osbern c1070, extended by Baldwin de Redvers in 1130s gatehouse erected c1335, now owned by English Heritage.
Carlisle	Cumbria	Norman castle built by William Rufus in 1192, improved by David I of Scotland, rebuilt 1541 for Henry VIII by Stefan von Hashenperg, now owned by English Heritage.
Carmarthen	Dyfed	Norman Motte & Bailey castle founded early C12, captured by Llywelyn the Great 1215, rebuilt and extended by English during C13, held by Glyndwr 1403–9.
Carreg Cennen	Dyfed	Courtyard castle built in C13 on site of Roman fort, demolished by Yorkists 1462.
Castell y Bere	Gwynedd	Enclosure castle founded c1221 by Llywelyn the Great, captured by Edward I 1283, restored 1286–90, adandoned by 1300.
Castle Acre, priory	Norfolk	Norman castle founded by William de Warenne C11, stone keep rebuilt C1140, now owned by English Heritage.
Castle Bytham	Lincolnshire	Norman castle founded c1169, besieged and demolished 1221, rebuilt by William de Colville 1220s.
Castle Drogo	Devon	Granite castle designed by Edwin Lutyens 1910–30.
Castle Hedingham	Essex	Tower keep built by Aubrey de Vere III 1141 on site of late C11 timber castle, now owned by English Heritage.
Castle Rising	Norfolk	Tower keep built by William II d'Albini c1140, now owned by English Heritage.
Cause	Shropshire	Norman Motte & Bailey castle founded by Roger Fitz Corbet, fortified in stone C12, demolished 1645.
Cawdor	Inverness	Built 1454, Seat of Earls of Cawdor.
Chepstow	Gwent	Norman castle with stone keep founded by William Fitz Osbern 1070, extended C13, disused from 1690, now owned by Welsh Historic Monuments.
Chester	Cheshire	Norman Motte & Bailey castle built on site of Roman fortress, improved C13, now lost.
Chilham	Kent	Norman castle founded by Fulbert of Dover, octagonal keep built for Henry II 1171–5.
Chirk	Clwyd	Motte & Bailey castle founded mid-C12, new castle founded nearby by Roger Mortimer 1274–1310.
Christchurch	Dorset	Norman Motte & Bailey castle founded by Richard de Redvers c1100, ruins now owned by English Heritage.
Cilgerran	Dyfed	Norman Enclosure castle founded by Gerald of Windsor c1110, rebuilt and extended c1233.
Clare	Suffolk	Norman Motte & Bailey castle founded by Richard Fitzgilbert, improved by Gilbert de Clare.
Clavering	Essex	Norman castle founded by Robert Fitz Wimarc c1050.
Claypotts	Tayside	Built C16.
Clifford's Tower	York	Quatrefoil keep on motte founded by Henry III 1245 on site of

Name	Location	General Information
		Norman castle of 1069, burnt down 1190 whilst housing Jewish refugees, rebuilt and blown down 1228, now owned by English Heritage.
Clitheroe	Lancashire	Norman castle founded by Roger de Poitou.
Clun	Shropshire	Norman castle founded by Roger de Say, tower keep built in motte C12 by William Fitz Alan.
Cockermouth	Cumbria	Built C13 by William de Fortibus, rebuilt by Anthony de Lucy in 1360, slighted in Civil War.
Coity	Mid Glamorgan	Norman castle founded by Payn de Turberville, extended late C12, altered C14.
Colchester	Essex	Norman castle founded by William the Conqueror 1076–80; largest Norman tower keep, partly demolished 1683.
Conisborough	Yorkshire	Norman castle founded by William de Warenne, rebuilt with cylindrical tower keep by Hamelin, Earl of Surrey c1180, now owned by English Heritage.
Conwy	Gwynedd	Edwardian castle erected by Master James of St George 1283–7.
Cooling	Kent	Double Quadrangular castle founded in 1380s, erected by Henry Yevele.
Corfe	Dorset	Norman castle founded by William I c1080, great tower erected by Henry I, gloriette erected by John, dismantled in Civil War (1646), now owned by National Trust.
Coulthalley	Strathclyde	Founded C12, rebuilt c1375, altered c1415 and c1520, rebuilt after siege 1557.
Craignethan	Strathclyde	Built in C16 by Sir James Hamilton, fortified courtyards with provision for artillery surrounding tower house, slighted 1579.
Criccieth	Gwynedd	Enclosure castle founded early C13, probably by Llywelyn the Great, Edwardian additions to site 1290, ruined by Glyndwr 1404.
Crichton	Lothian	Castle founded by John de Crichton late C14, extended C15.
Croft	Herefordshire	Medieval Quadrangular castle of C14, named after family who built it, now owned by National Trust.
Cruggleton	Dumfries & Galloway	Motte & Bailey castle founded C12, reinforced in stone C13.
Dartmouth	Devon	Artillery fort built 1481 by Dartmouth corporation to protect town now owned by English Heritage.
Deal	Kent	Henrician artillery fort built in 1539–40, besieged 1648, now owned by English Heritage.
Deganwy	Gwynedd	Double Motte & Bailey castle founded c1090, taken by Henry III 1241 and rebuilt/extended,destroyed by Llywelyn 1257.
Denbigh	Clywd	Edwardian castle built by Henry de Lacy, designed by Master James of St George, 1282–1311, destroyed in 1650s.
Devizes	Wiltshire	Norman castle founded late C11, used as prison by Henry II and Henry III, demolished in Civil War.
Dinefwr	Dyfed	Castle founded C12, rebuilt with cylindrical donjon C13, damaged by fire C18, modern castle constructed 1856.
Dirleton	Lothian	Founded by de Vaux family C12, stone buildings built C13, extended C14/C15.
Dolbadarn	Gwynedd	Castle with cylindrical donjon erected by Llywelyn the Great early C13, partially dismantled by Edward I in 1284.
Dolwyddelan	Gwynedd	Castle founded by Iorwerth Trwyndwn c1170, captured by English 1282 and repaired.
Donnington	Berkshire	Enclosure castle founded late C14 by Richard de Adderbury, destroyed in 1646, now owned by English Heritage.
Doune	Perth & Kinrosshire	Enclosure castle founded by Duke of Albany late 14th Century.
Dover	Kent	Norman castle founded 1066 by William I, rebuilt with tower keep designed by Maurice the Engineer for Henry II in 1180–9, concentric fortifications built at same time, besieged 1216, extra fortifications added C19.
Dudley	West Midlands	Norman Motte & Bailey castle founded by William Fitzansculf, destroyed by Henry II 1175, rebuilt c1270 by John de Somery, extended early C14 by John de Somery, slighted 1647.
Duffus	Grampian	Motte & Bailey castle founded by Freskin de Moravia C12, rebuilt c1300 in stone, north-west corner of Donjon slid down motte late C14.
Dumbarton	Strathclyde	Built upon Dumbarton Rock.
Dundonald	Strathclyde	Founded by Walter Stewart c1250, expanded by Robert II, 1371–90.
Dunstaffnage	Strathclyde	Enclosure castle built by MacDougall in the 13th Century.
Dunstanburgh	Northumberland	Enclosure castle founded by Thomas, 2nd Earl of Lancaster 1313–16, altered by John of Gaunt, now owned by English Heritage.
Dunster	Somerset	Norman castle founded by William de Mohun, fortified manor built on site C14, owned by Luttrells from 1376, remodelled by Salvin C19, now owned by National Trust.

Name	Location	General Information
Dunvegan	Skye	Home of the Chiefs of Clan Macleod since foundation in C13.
Durham	County Durham	Norman castle founded by William I c1072, rebuilt C12 in stone, keep C14, rebuilt 1840, now used by University of Durham.
Edinburgh	Lothian	Wooden fortress founded by Malcolm III C11, rebuilt C12/13, taken by Edward I 1296, taken by Earl of Moray and destroyed 1313, rebuilt C14.
Edlingham	Northumberland	Castle founded by Sir William Felton late C12, triangular enclosure with separate great tower.
Egremont	Cumbria	Norman castle built by William de Meschines in 1130.
Eilean Donan	Western Ross	Built in C13, probably by Alexander II, rebuilt in C20.
Etal	Northumberland	Castle with donjon and gatehouse tower at opposing corners, founded 1342 by Manners family, captured 1513 by James IV.
Ewloe	Clwyd	Castle founded 1146 by Owain Gwynedd, rebuilt in stone c1200 by Llywelyn the Great.
Ewyas Harold	Herefordshire	Norman castle built c1050, refortified by William FitzOsbern.
Exeter	Devon	Norman castle founded by William I in 1067 in corner of Roman walls, largely demolished in 1744, stone gatehouse c1068 still extant.
Eynsford	Kent	Norman Enclosure castle fortified in stone c1088, extended C12.
Farleigh Hungerford	Somerset	Castle erected c1370–83 by Sir Thomas Hungerford, enlarged C15 by Walter Hungerford, now owned by English Heritage.
Farnham	Surrey	Norman Motte & Bailey castle founded by Henry de Blois C12, slighted by Henry II 1155, rebuilt late C12 with stone encasing motte, slighted 1648, now owned by English Heritage.
Flint	Clwyd	Edwardian castle erected by Master James of St George 1277–80, donjon separate from rest of castle, slighted 1646.
Ford	Northumberland	Quadrangular castle founded 1338 by William Heron, attacked by Scots 1385, 1513, 1549, rebuilt 1861 by Marchioness of Waterford.
Fotheringhay	Northants	Norman Motte & Bailey castle, famous as the site of Mary Queen of Scots' beheading.
Framlingham	Suffolk	Norman castle founded c1100 by Roger Bigod, destroyed by Henry II 1175, rebuilt as enclosure castle by Roger II Bigod c1189–1200.
Gloucester	Gloucestershire	Norman Motte & Bailey castle founded by William I, Great Tower built by Henry I c1112.
Goodrich	Hereford and Worcester	Keep built mid-C12, converted into quadrangular castle by de Valence family late C13. Barbican erected C14, slighted 1646, now owned by English Heritage.
Grosmont	Gwent	Castle founded late C11, rebuilt in stone c1210, extended by Hubert de Burgh 1220–40.
Guildford	Surrey	Norman Motte & Bailey castle, keep erected on side of motte mid-C12.
Hadleigh	Essex	Enclosure castle founded by Hubert de Burgh C13, extended by Edward III 1361–70, now owned by English Heritage.
Hailes	Lothian	Founded C13, owned from C14 by Hepburns, who extended castle, besieged by Percies c1400.
Hallaton	Leicestershire	Norman Motte & Bailey castle, motte almost as large as bailey.
Harbottle	Northumberland	Motte & Bailey castle with shell keep erected 1159–60 by Robert d'Umfraville.
Harlech	Gwynedd	Edwardian concentric castle erected 1283–9 by Master James of St George, besieged 1294, 1401–5, 1408–9, 1468, 1647, now owned by Welsh Historic Monuments.
Hastings	East Sussex	Norman Motte & Bailey castle founded by William I 1066, appears in Bayeux Tapestry, later converted to stone, only C13 ruins extant.
Haughley	Suffolk	Norman Motte & Bailey castle, one of largest in Britain, dismantled by Henry II c1173.
Haverfordwest	Dyfed	Norman castle founded c1120 by Gilbert de Clare, strengthened by William de Valence C13, besieged by Glyndwr 1405.
Hawarden	Clwyd	Norman Motte & Bailey castle, fortified in stone early C13, destroyed by Llywelyn 1265, rebuilt 1277, slighted 1647/8.
Hay–on–Wye	Powys	Norman Motte & Bailey castle founded early C12 by William Revell, destroyed by King John, C13 replacement built on different site, destroyed by Glyndwr.
Helmsley	North Yorkshire	Norman castle founded by Robert de Mortain, held by Walter l'Espec and de Roos family, who constructed current structure 1186–1227. Enclosure castle with keep, keep heightened early C14, slighted 1644/5.
Hereford	Hereford and Worcester	Norman Motte & Bailey castle possibly founded c1050, held by William Fitz Osbern 1066–71, stoneworks C13 with tower on motte, now destroyed.

Name	Location	General Information
Hermitage	Borders	Founded early C14, captured by Scots 1338, owned by the Douglases, who extended it C14/15.
Herstmonceux	East Sussex	Brick quadrangular castle founded 1441 by Sir Roger Fiennes, restored C20.
Hertford	Herts	Norman Motte & Bailey castle founded c1067 by William I, major works on castle C15, demolished C17.
Hever	Kent	Manor house founded 1270s, fortified 1340 by William de Hever and in 1384 by Sir John Cobham, bought by Boleyn family 1462 and modified, restored by Viscount Astor 1903–7.
Holt	Clwyd	Edwardian enclosure castle founded by John de Warenne 1280s, demolished late C17.
Hopton	Shropshire	Norman Motte & Bailey castle founded C12, donjon built on motte by Walter de Hopton c1300.
Huntingdon	Cambridgeshire	Norman Motte & Bailey castle founded 1069 by William I, 2nd motte added C12, demolished 1174 by Henry II.
Huntly	Grampian	Motte & Bailey castle founded C12, rebuilt in stone and extended by 1st Earl of Huntly C15, blown up by James VI 1594, rebuilt by 1st Marquis of Huntly c1600–06.
Inverlochy	Highland	Enclosure castle founded c1270–80.
Inverness	Highland	Founded C12, later reclad in stone. Destroyed by Young Pretender 1746.
Jedburgh	Borders	Motte & Bailey castle founded C12 by David I, destroyed c1410 by Regent Albany.
Kenilworth	Warwickshire	Enclosure castle with motte & donjon founded c1120 by William de Clinton, donjon rebuilt later C12, water defences added C13, besieged for 6 months 1266, remodelled by John of Gaunt 1370s, slighted 1649, now owned by English Heritage.
Kidwelly	Dyfed	Norman castle founded by Roger, Bishop of Salisbury c1106, burnt by Welsh 1215, enclosure castle built 1270s, concentric curtain added C14.
Kiessimut	Barra, Western Isles	Enclosure castle of late C12/early C13, restored by MacNeils.
Kildrummy	Grampian	Enclosure castle of C13 on site of C12 Motte & Bailey castle.
Kirby Muxloe	Leicestershire	Unfinished quadrangular castle built by Lord Hastings c1480–3, now owned by English Heritage.
Knaresborough	North Yorkshire	Norman castle built C12 by Eustace Fitzjohn, improved by Edward II and III 1307–50, slighted 1648.
Lancaster	Lancashire	Norman castle built early C12 by Roger de Poitou, extended by King John, improved by Henry IV, partially demolished 1649.
Laugharne	Dyfed	Castle founded C12, rebuilt in C13 and 14 including cylindrical keep.
Launceston	Cornwall	Norman Motte & Bailey castle of Dunheved, built by Robert of Mortain, rebuilt with shell keep C13 by Richard of Cornwall. George Fox imprisoned in gatehouse 1656, owned by English Heritage.
Leeds	Kent	Norman castle founded by the de Crevecoeur family, rebuilt by Edward I after 1278, restored C19.
Leicester	Leicestershire	Norman Motte & Bailey castle founded c1068, fortified in stone by 2nd Earl of Leicester mid-C12, improved by Henry IV and V.
Lewes	East Sussex	Norman double Motte & Bailey castle built by William de Warenne c1069–70, shell keep added C13, barbican added C14.
Lincoln	Lincolnshire	Norman Double Motte & Bailey castle founded by William 1 1068, shell keep (Lucy Tower) added C12.
Llandovery	Dyfed	Norman Motte & Bailey castle founded early C12 by Robert Fitzpons, captured by Welsh 1116, recovered c1158, stonework added late C12, slighted by Cromwell.
Llanstephan	Dyfed	Enclosure castle founded C12, captured by Welsh 1146, retaken by Henry II, given to William de Camville, strengthened c1192, extended C13, captured by Glyndwr 1403.
Loch Doon	Strathclyde	Enclosure castle of late C13 erected on an island; moved to western shore of loch 1934–5.
Longtown	Hereford & Worcester	Norman Motte & Bailey castle founded late C11, cylindrical donjon added on motte early C14.
Ludgershall	Wiltshire	Norman Motte & Bailey castle founded late C11, unfinished donjon added mid-C12, replacement tower added c1200, now owned by English Heritage.
Ludlow	Shropshire	Norman Enclosure castle with flanking towers erected c1086 by Roger de Lacy.
Lydford	Devon	Norman castle founded C11, donjon added C12 and extended with motte built around base C13.
Lympne	Kent	Norman castle founded 1080s, reconstructed C14.

Name	Location	General Information
Manorbier	Dyfed	Norman Enclosure castle founded by Otto de Barri late C11, strengthened C12, birthplace of Giraldus Cambrensis 1146.
Marlborough	Wiltshire	Norman Motte & Bailey castle, extended by Henry II, shell keep added by King John and added to by Henry III.
Middleham	North Yorkshire	Norman Motte & Bailey castle founded c1086, tower keep built on nearby site by Robert Fitzranulph c1170, quadrangular curtain added C13, slighted in Civil War, now owned by English Heritage.
Monmouth	Gwent	Norman Motte & Bailey castle founded by William FitzOsbern c1070, keep added on motte c1120–30, birthplace of Henry V 1387, slighted during Civil War.
Montacute	Somerset	Norman Motte & Bailey castle founded by Robert of Mortain 1069/70, dismantled C12 by Cluniac monks of Montacute Priory.
Montfichet	London	Norman Motte & Bailey castle founded by William I 1066/7, dismantled C13.
Montgomery (I) (Hen Domen)	Powys	Norman Motte & Bailey castle built by Roger de Montgomery c1071, dismantled C12.
Montgomery (II)	Powys	Enclosure castle founded 1223 by Baldwin de Boller, slighted 1649.
Morpeth	Northumberland	Norman Motte & Bailey castle founded late C11, destroyed by King John 1215, castle rebuilt in bailey mid-C13.
Mountsorrell	Leicestershire	Norman Motte & Bailey castle, dismantled 1217.
Neroche	Somerset	Norman Enclosure castle founded C11 by Robert of Mortain, motte added early C12, shell keep added mid-C12.
Nether Stowey	Somerset	Norman Motte & 2 Bailey castle, tower keep added on motte mid-C12.
Newark	Nottinghamshire	Norman Enclosure castle built by Bishop of Lincoln 1130s, major reconstruction early C13, slighted 1646.
New Buckenham	Norfolk	Built by William II d'Albini c1140, cylindrical tower keep (first in Britain), demolished by Sir Philip Knyvey 1649.
Newcastle	Tyne & Wear	Norman Motte & Bailey castle founded c1080, rebuilt with keep designed by Maurice the Engineer 1068–77.
Newport	Gwent	Norman castle founded C12, rebuilt C13, sacked by Glyndwr and rebuilt C15.
Norham	Northumberland	Norman Motte & Bailey castle founded c1120 by Ranulf Flambard, destroyed by Scots 1140s, rebuilt by Bishop Hugh of Durham 1158–74, taken by Scots 1513, now owned by English Heritage.
Northampton	Northants	Norman Motte & Bailey castle founded c1080, enlarged by Henry I. tower keep added c1170.
Norwich	Norfolk	Norman Motte & Bailey castle founded by William FitzOsbern for William I 1067, tower keep added on motte 1125–35, stone curtain added 1268–70, keep restored by Salvin 1834–9, now serving as museum (since 1894).
Nottingham	Nottinghamshire	Norman Motte & Bailey castle founded 1068 by William I, modified by Henry II. Keep built 1213, demolished 1651 by Colonel Hutchinson, renovated 1878 by the Corporation and now a museum.
Nunney	Somerset	Rectangular moated Great Tower with cylindrical towers at corners built 1373 by Sir John de la Mare, slighted 1645, now owned by English Heritage.
Oakham	Rutland	Norman Motte & Bailey castle, stone added C12, Great Hall built by Wakelin de Ferrers c1180 still extant.
Odiham	Hampshire	Octagonal keep built by King John 1207–12.
Ogmore	Mid–Glamorgan	Norman castle founded c1110, stone donjon built late C12, fortified in stone C13.
Okehampton	Devon	Norman Motte & Bailey castle founded by Baldwin Fitzgilbert c1070, extended and tower built on motte early C14.
Ongar	Essex	Norman Motte & Bailey castle founded early C12 by de Lucy family, stone tower built on motte 1150s.
Orford	Suffolk	Castle with polygonal keep founded by Henry II 1165–72, now owned by English Heritage.
Oswestry	Shropshire	Norman Motte & Bailey castle founded late C11 by Rainald de Bailleul, shell keep built C12.
Oxford	Oxfordshire	Norman Motte & Bailey castle founded c1071 by Robert d'Oilly, St George's Tower built on motte late C11, shell keep built on motte C12.
Oystermouth	West Glamorgan	Norman castle built c1100, destroyed 1215, rebuilt C13 by William de Braose.
Peel of Lumphanan	Grampian	Motte & Bailey castle founded C12, shell keep erected early C13.
Pembridge	Hereford & Worcester	Castle founded C13 by Ralph de Pembridge, includes moat and cylindrical donjon, ruined in Civil War.

Name	Location	General Information
Pembroke	Dyfed	Norman Enclosure castle founded c1090 by Arnulf de Montgomery, extended and cylindrical donjon built by William Marshal early C13, slighted by Cromwell 1648/9.
Pendennis	Cornwall	Henrician artillery fort built to protect Falmouth, now owned by English Heritage.
Penhow	Gwent	Enclosure castle founded early C13 by Sir William St Maur.
Penrice	West Glamorgan	Norman Enclosure castle founded c1100, stone castle raised on nearby site mid-C13, cylindrical donjon.
Penrith	Cumbria	Tower built C14, quadrangular castle erected on site c1397–9 by William Strickland, Bishop of Carlisle.
Pevensey	East Sussex	Norman castle built within the site of old Roman fort, founded C11 by Robert of Mortain, donjon added c1100 by William of Mortain, strengthened early C13, now owned by English Heritage.
Peveril	Derbyshire	Norman castle founded by William Peverel, also known as Peak Castle, improved by Henry II, tower keep erected 1176, now owned by English Heritage.
Pickering	North Yorkshire	Norman Motte & Bailey castle founded c1100, shell keep built c1218–36, improved early C14.
Picton	Dyfed	Norman Motte & Bailey castle founded c1090 by William de Picton, enclosure castle built on nearby site mid-C13.
Pleshey	Essex	Norman Motte & Bailey castle founded early C12, destroyed 1157, refortified 1167–80, donjon on motte.
Pontefract	West Yorkshire	Norman Motte & Bailey castle founded 1069 by Ilbert de Lacy, improved by Thomas, Earl of Lancaster and John of Gaunt C14, destroyed 1649.
Portchester	Hampshire	Norman castle founded by Henry I c1120 in corner of old Roman fort, keep raised by Henry II, palace constructed for Richard II 1396–9, now owned by English Heritage.
Powis	Powys	Castle founded C13 by Gruffydd, Baron de la Pole, destroyed in 1270s by Llywelyn the Last and rebuilt, modified by the Herberts after purchase in 1587, now owned by the National Trust.
Raglan	Gwent	Norman Motte & Bailey castle founded c1070 by the Bloet family, major reconstruction C15, hexagonal Yellow Tower of Gwent constructed by Sir William ap Thomas, other works 1450–69 by Sir William Herbert, slighted 1646, now owned by Welsh Historic Monuments.
Ravenscraig	Fife	Coastal artillery fortress founded 1460 by James II, erected 1460–3.
Restormel	Cornwall	Norman castle founded C11 by Baldwin FitzUrstin, C12 shell keep built by Robert of Cardinham, now owned by English Heritage.
Rhuddlan	Clwyd	Norman Motte & Bailey castle founded c1070, Edwardian concentric castle erected nearby by Master James of St George 1282, slighted 1648.
Richards Castle	Hereford & Worcester	Norman Motte & Bailey castle founded by Richard Fitzscrub pre-Conquest, stone tower built on motte c1175.
Richmond	North Yorkshire	Norman Enclosure castle founded by Count of Penhievre 1071, late C11 stone hall (Scolland's Hall) built by Alan the Red, great tower added by Conan, Duke of Brittany c1150–70, now owned by English Heritage.
Ripley	Harrogate, North Yorks	C19 castle owned by Sir Thomas Ingilby, a baronet, who inherited the stately home on his 18th birthday.
Rochester	Kent	Norman Motte & Bailey castle founded c1080 and built by Bishop Gundulf, stone curtain added c1088, stone keep built c1126–40 by William de Corbeuil, besieged and taken by John 1215, recaptured by Louis of France 1216, keep repaired c1225 with cylindrical corner added, besieged by de Montfort 1264, captured by Wat Tyler 1381, now owned by English Heritage.
Rockingham	Northants	Norman Motte & Bailey castle founded by William I, improved by Henry II, gatehouse built by Edward I c1280, damaged in Civil War, alterations by Salvin C19.
Rothesay	Isle of Bute, Strathclyde	Motte & Bailey castle founded C12, shell keep erected C13.
Roxburgh	Borders	Motte & Bailey castle founded early C12, captured 1314 by Scots and demolished, rebuilt by Edward III 1335–7, extended by Richard II, taken by Scots 1460 with loss of James II and destroyed.
Ruthin	Clwyd	Edwardian castle founded 1277, held by Prince Dafydd to 1282 when taken by Reginald de Grey, slighted 1647, converted into a hotel C19.
Saffron Walden	Essex	Norman Motte & Bailey castle founded C11 by Geoffrey de Mandeville, flint tower added C12.
St Andrews	Fife	Castle founded late C12, slighted by Andrew Moray 1337, rebuilt

Name	Location	General Information
		late C14, extended early C16, besieged and damaged 1546–7, John Knox amongst besieged.
St Briavels	Gloucestershire	Norman Enclosure castle founded C12 by Milo Fitzwalter, tower added mid-C12, gatehouse built by Edward I c1292–3, keep collapsed 1752.
St Donats	South Glamorgan	Double enclosure castle founded by the Stradlings c1300.
St Mawes	Cornwall	Henrician artillery fort built 1540 to protect Falmouth, now owned by English Heritage.
Saltwood	Kent	Norman Enclosure castle founded by Henry of Essex c1150–60, improved by Archbishop Courtenay of Canterbury 1380s, designed by Henry Yevele, rendered uninhabitable by an earthquake 1580, formerly owned by Alan Clark MP.
Sandal	West Yorkshire	Norman Motte & Bailey castle founded c1157, converted to stone c1200–80, besieged 1645 and slighted 1646.
Sauvey	Leicestershire	Motte & Bailey castle founded by King John early C13, disused from 1260s.
Scarborough	North Yorkshire	Norman castle founded c1136 by William of Aumale, keep built by Henry II, barbican added c1240, Piers Gaveston besieged 1312, now owned by English Heritage.
Scotney	Kent	Moated castle founded late C14 by Roger Ashburnham, only cylindrical turret remaining, now owned by National Trust.
Sherborne	Dorset	Norman Enclosure castle founded by Roger, Bishop of Salisbury c1107–35, I-shaped donjon added mid-C12, besieged and ruined 1645, now owned by English Heritage.
Shrewsbury	Shropshire	Norman Motte & Bailey castle founded by Roger de Montgomery c1067–9, converted to stone by Henry II, tower on motte collapsed c1270, altered by Thomas Telford C18 for Sir William Pulteney.
Skenfrith	Gwent	Norman Motte & Bailey castle founded late C11, cylindrical donjon and stone curtain walls built c1220–40 by Hubert de Burgh.
Skipsea	East Yorkshire	Norman Motte & Bailey castle founded c1086, motte separated from bailey by a marsh, destroyed by Henry III.
Skipton	North Yorkshire	Norman D-shaped Enclosure castle founded c1080, extended with six round towers added by Robert Clifford c1310–14, besieged and severely damaged 1645, renovated by Lady Anne Clifford C17.
Southampton	Hampshire	Norman Motte & Bailey castle founded early C12, refortified C14 by Richard II with tower built by Henry Yevele.
South Mimms	Hertfordshire	Norman Motte & Bailey castle founded c1140–2 by Geoffrey de Mandeville, motte built around base of tower.
Stafford	Staffordshire	Norman Motte & Bailey castle founded c1070, destroyed by 1086, restored late C11, tower built on motte 1348 by Ralph, 1st Earl of Stafford, decayed C16.
Stamford	Lincolnshire	Norman Motte & Bailey castle founded late C11, shell enclosure built on motte C12, extended late C12.
Stirling	Stirling	Timber castle founded C12, taken 1296, 1297, 1298, 1299, 1304, 1314 (whence dismantled), rebuilt under the Stewarts C15.
Stogursey	Somerset	Norman Enclosure castle founded late C11, improved by de Courcys C12, demolished c1216.
Stokesay	Shropshire	Fortified manor house crenellated by Lawrence de Ludlow 1291.
Sulgrave	Northants	Norman triangular enclosure castle founded late C11, stone tower added early C12.
Sutton Valence	Kent	Castle founded mid-C12 with great tower, altered by William de Valence C13.
Swansea	West Glamorgan	Norman Motte & Bailey castle founded by Henry Beaumont, burned 1115/6, C12 Enclosure castle constructed nearby, rebuilt early C14, damaged by Glyndwr.
Sween	Strathclyde	Castle founded by McSwine family early C12, earliest stone castle in Scotland. Remodelled by Earls of Menteith C13 and extended by Lords of the Isles C14.
Tamworth	Staffordshire	Norman castle with shell enclosure founded early C12 by the Marmions.
Tantallon	Lothian	Founded by the 1st Earl of Douglas c1360, besieged by Stewarts 1492 and 1526, damaged by General Monck 1651.
Tattershall	Lincolnshire	Castle with Great Tower built in brick by Ralph, Lord Cromwell 1433–43, rescued by Lord Curzon 1911, now owned by National Trust.
Taunton	Somerset	Norman Enclosure castle founded c1110 by William Gifford, tower and other buildings raised by Henry de Blois mid-C12, improved 1207.
Tenby	Dyfed	Norman castle founded after 1153, sacked by Welsh 1187 and 1260.

BRITAIN

Name	Location	General Information
Thetford	Norfolk	Norman Motte & Bailey castle founded C11, destroyed by Henry II 1174.
Thornbury	Avon	Last military castle built in England c1511 by Edward Stafford, Duke of Buckingham, never completed.
Threave	Dumfries and Galloway	Founded by Archibald, 3rd Earl of Douglas c1370, extended c1454, taken by James II 1455.
Tickhill	South Yorkshire	Norman Motte & Bailey castle founded late C11 by Robert de Belleme, 11-sided tower built on motte c1178–80 by Henry II.
Tintagel	Cornwall	Norman castle built c1145 by Reginald, Earl of Cornwall, modified by Richard, Earl of Cornwall C13, now owned by English Heritage.
Tonbridge	Kent	Norman Motte & Bailey castle founded 1080s by Richard Fitzgilbert, shell enclosure added C12, gatehouse built by Gilbert de Clare C13.
Totnes	Devon	Norman Motte & Bailey castle founded C11 by the Nonants, shell keep added C13.
Tower of London	London	Norman Enclosure castle founded by William I 1067, White Tower built by Gundulf of Rochester 1078–c1100, concentric fortifications added C13 by Henry III & Edward I.
Trematon	Cornwall	Norman Motte & Bailey castle founded C11, Shell keep added C12.
Tretower	Powys	Norman Motte & Bailey castle founded by Sir Miles Picard c1100, shell keep added by Simon Picard mid-C12, cylindrical donjon added by Roger Picard c1220.
Turnberry	Strathclyde	Cylindrical Tower castle of C13, childhood home of Robert Bruce.
Tutbury	Staffordshire	Norman Motte & Bailey castle founded by Henry de Ferrers, improved by John of Gaunt from 1350, added to C15, slighted 1646.
Tynemouth	Tyne and Wear	Enclosure castle crenellated by Robert de Mowbray 1296, gatehouse added 1390s.
Urquhart	Highland	Motte & Bailey castle founded c1150, taken by Edward I, in 1313 passed to Randolph, Earl of Moray, extended C14.
Usk	Gwent	Norman Earthwork castle founded by de Clares c1138, rebuilt C14, slighted in Civil War.
Wakefield	West Yorkshire	Motte & 2 Bailey castle erected c1140–50, possibly by William de Warenne.
Wallingford	Oxfordshire	Norman Motte & Bailey castle erected c1071, stonework added C12, demolished 1652.
Wardour	Wiltshire	Old Wardour castle - Hexagonal construction founded by John, 5th Lord Lovell 1393, damaged after siege 1644 New Wardour 'Castle' built 1769–76.
Wareham	Dorset	Norman castle with keep founded by Henry I, destroyed in Civil War.
Wark	Northumberland	Norman Motte & Bailey castle dismantled by David I of Scotland 1138, rebuilt by Henry II 1158, decayed C14.
Warkworth	Northumberland	Norman Motte & Bailey castle founded by Henry, Earl of Northumberland c1140, taken by William the Lion 1173, rebuilt by Clavering family C13, multangular tower added by Henry Percy mid-C14, owned by Percys 1332–1922, now owned by English Heritage.
Warwick	Warwickshire	Norman Motte & Bailey castle founded by William I 1068, shell keep added C12, rebuilt C14 by Thomas Beauchamp, unfinished additions by Richard III C15, repaired by Fulke Greville C17.
West Malling	Kent	Stone Tower built c1100 by Bishop Gundulf of Rochester, now ruined.
White Castle	Gwent	Norman castle founded by Pain Fitzjohn, stone fortifications built c1184–6 by William de Braose, refortified by Edward I 1260s.
Whittington	Shropshire	Norman Motte & Bailey castle, improved by Fulke de Warenne from 1219 with tower built on motte.
Wigmore	Hereford & Worcester	Norman Motte & Bailey castle founded c1067 by William FitzOsbern, shell keep built C12, reconstructed C14.
Winchester	Hampshire	Norman Motte & Bailey castle founded 1067 by William I, Domesday Book originally housed in castle, site destroyed 1141, rebuilt shortly after, donjon added by Henry II, cylindrical tower on motte and Great Hall added by Henry III, only the Great Hall presently remains.
Windsor	Berkshire	Norman Motte & 2 Bailey castle founded 1067 by William I, shell keep added by Henry I, site rebuilt in stone and keep improved by Henry II, major rebuilding by Edward III c1350–77 with keep raised, alterations by Wyatville for George IV C19, damaged by fire 1992.
Wolvesey	Hampshire	Ecclesiastical castle-palace founded c1100, rebuilt in quadrangular form with great tower by Henry of Blois c1135–70.
Worcester	Hereford & Worcester	Norman Motte & Bailey castle founded c1069, burned down 1113,

Name	Location	General Information
		rebuilt C12, motte levelled 1830.
Wressle	East Yorkshire	Quadrangular enclosure castle founded c1380 by Sir Thomas Percy, damaged in Civil War.
Yester	Lothian	Motte & Bailey castle founded C12, C13 tower erected on motte, extended C15.
York	North Yorkshire	Norman Motte & Bailey castle on Baile Hill founded by William I 1068–9, destroyed 1069 and rebuilt, now lost.

Castles: General Information

Adulterine Castles	Unlicensed private castles built by barons primarily during the Anarchy (1135–54) of King Stephen's reign.
Berkeley Castle	Edward II murdered in south tower
Bolingbroke Castle	Henry IV born Apr 1366
Caernarfon Castle	Edward II born Apr 25th 1284
Cardiff Castle	Built on the site of a Roman fort. Robert Curthose imprisoned for 28 years
Carisbrooke Castle	Prison of Charles I 1647–8
Carlisle Castle	Prison of Mary Queen of Scots when she first entered England
Castle: Terms	
allure	Wall-walk along the top of the battlements: the basic fighting platform for archers and crossbowmen
bailey	A courtyard in a castle
barbican	An outer fortification in front of the gate of a castle
bartizan	Turret projecting from a tower or wall
bastion	Tower projecting from a wall length or junction of two walls, designed to cover dead ground
battlement	Parapet or wall with indentures or embrasures, originally for shooting through
berm	Space between curtain wall and moat
buttery	One of the 2 service rooms (the other is the kitchen), used for dispensing drinks
caponier	A covered gallery running across a ditch, housing guns to fire along the ditch
casemate	Armoured compartment in which guns are mounted
concentric	Possessing more than one curtain wall
counterscarp	Outer side of the moat
crenel	Openings formed in top of a wall or parapet between the merlons, having slanting sides as in a battlement
curtain wall	Wall around the perimeter of a castle or one of its courtyards
drawbridge	Bridge that may be raised to prevent access
embrasure	The opening in a wall behind a window or an arrow loop
forebuilding	Structure protecting the entrance to a tower
garderobe	Latrine
gatehouse	Guarded building above or beside an entrance gate
great tower	Most important tower also called the donjon and, since the 16th century, the keep
hourd	(also Hoarding) Timber gallery carried on beams outside the battlements. Stones could be dropped on attackers via holes in the floor
keep	see great tower
loop	Slit in wall for firing arrows
machicolation	Permanent stone version of a hourd
mangonel	Stone-throwing siege machine
merlon	Length of protective parapet between the openings of a battlement
mews	Building or yard where the hawks are kept
moat	Wide, often water-filled ditch surrounding a castle preventing land access
motte	Large, usually round flat-topped mound which supported a tower
murder hole	Opening over an entrance passage
oubliette	Dungeon or pit under the floor, usually below ground level, reached by a trap-door
palisade	Strong wooden fence
portcullis	Iron or wooden grating hanging vertically in gateway of castle, set in grooves and able to be raised and lowered
postern	Subsidiary gate in the outer wall
rampart	Surrounding embankment of a castle
revetment	Facing of stones or sandbags to protect a wall or embankment
scarp	Side of a moat surrounding a castle cut nearest to and immediately below a rampart
trebuchet	Stone-throwing siege engine powered by counterpoise weights; successor to the mangonel, and far more powerful
turret	Small tower that projects from the wall of a castle
ward	Courtyard in a castle
Dover Castle	Known as the 'Key of England'
First Castles	Imported by the Normans after 1066, although four possible sites c1050 built by Norman friends of Edward the Confessor
Flint Castle	Richard II formally surrendered his crown to Henry Bolingbroke

B
R
I
T
A
I
N

Fotheringhay Castle	Richard III born Oct 2nd 1452; Mary Queen of Scots executed Feb 8th 1587
Framlingham Castle	Mary Tudor proclaimed Queen while staying there
Henry VIII's reign: built	Calshot, Camber, Deal, Hurst, Pendennis, St Mawes, Sandgate, Southsea, Walmer
Keep: largest	Colchester castle
Largest Castle : England	Windsor
Scotland	Doune
Wales	Caerphilly
Leaning Keep	Bridgnorth, Shropshire
Lewes Castle	Two mottes
Ludlow Castle	King Edward IV made Royal property when he ascended the throne
Marlborough Castle	John Lackland was married in the castle chapel and Henry III was married in the chapel
Newark Castle	King John died of dysentery Oct 19th 1216
Oldest inhabited, UK	Berkeley, Gloucestershire
Pembroke Castle	Birthplace of Henry VII
Pontefract Castle	Richard II died cFeb 14th 1400
Powys Castle	Clive of India Museum
Roman forts: built in	Pevensey and Portchester Castles built within old Roman forts
Sherborne Castle	Once owned by Sir Walter Raleigh
Stone-built: first	Chepstow, Gwent
Stone keep: first	Tower of London (White Tower) 1078; Colchester built c1087
Thornbury Castle	Last built for military purposes
Tintagel Castle	Linked with Arthurian Legend
Towers of similar design :	Colchester and White Tower, London
	Castle Rising, Norwich and Falaise (Normandy)
	Castle Hedingham and Rochester
	Dover and Newcastle
Walmer Castle	Lord Warden of the Cinque Ports resides there; it houses a Madame Tussaud's Waxworks
Windsor Castle	Queen Mary's dolls' house, St George's Chapel, Royal Mausoleum Frogmore. Oldest royal residence still in regular use. Edward III born Nov 13th 1312. George III, George IV, William IV all died there

British Cathedrals

Name	Location	General Information
Aberdeen	Grampian	Dedicated to St Andrew. Seat of Episcopal diocese of Aberdeen and Orkney.
Aberdeen	Grampian	Dedicated to St Machar. RC cathedral founded 1424.
Arundel	West Sussex	Dedicated to Our Lady and St Philip Howard. RC since 1965 for see of Arundel and Brighton, designed by J.A. Hansom.
Ayr	Ayrshire	RC cathedral, seat of Bishop of Galloway.
Bangor	Gwynedd	Founded by and dedicated to St Deiniol and extensively restored in 1866.
Beverley Minster	Humberside	Destroyed by Danes, refounded by King Athelstan c935.
Birmingham	West Midlands	Dedicated to St Philip. Built by Thomas Archer 1715, became a cathedral 1905.
Birmingham	West Midlands	Dedicated to St Chad. RC cathedral from 1850, designed by Augustus Pugin 1841.
Blackburn	Lancashire	Dedicated to St Mary, became Anglican cathedral 1927.
Bradford	West Yorkshire	Dedicated to St Peter, designed by Sir Edward Maufe, became Anglican cathedral 1914.
Brecon	Powys	Benedictine priory of St John the Evangelist became cathedral 1923 for the see of Swansea and Brecon.
Brentwood	Essex	Dedicated to St Mary and St Helen, RC cathedral from 1917.
Bristol	Avon	Dedicated to the Holy Trinity, Anglican cathedral founded 1142 but rebuilt by G.E. Street.
Bristol	Avon	Dedicated to SS. Peter and Paul, RC cathedral, seat of Bishop of Clifton since 1850.
Bury St Edmunds	Suffolk	Dedicated to St James, Anglican cathedral designed by John Wastell / Gilbert Scott 1914, seat of Bishop of St Edmonsbury and Ipswich.
Canterbury	Kent	Dedicated to Christ, rebuilt 1174 by William of Sens.
C	Glamorgan	Dedicated to St David, RC cathedral from 1920, replacing Belmont, designed by Edward Pugin.
	Cumbria	Dedicated to the Holy Trinity, original site of Church of the Augustinian priory, founded 1093.
	Essex	Dedicated to SS. Mary, Peter and Cedd, refurbished by Charles Nicholson 1913, became cathedral 1951.
	Cheshire	Dedicated to Christ and Blessed Virgin Mary, Henry VIII gave Cathedral status in 1541.

Name	Location	General Information
Chichester	West Sussex	Dedicated to the Holy Trinity, founded by Bishop Ralph de Luffa 1108.
Coventry	West Midlands	Dedicated to St Michael, designed by Basil Spence, dedicated 1962.
Derby	Derbyshire	Dedicated to All Saints, became Anglican cathedral 1927, designed by James Gibbs.
Dundee	Central	Dedicated to St Paul. Seat of Episcopal Bishop of Brechin.
Dundee	Central	RC cathedral, seat of Bishop of Dunkeld.
Durham	Durham	Dedicated to Christ and Blessed Mary the Virgin c1093.
Edinburgh	Lothian	Dedicated to St Giles. High Kirk & National Church of Scotland.
Edinburgh	Lothian	Dedicated to St Mary. Episcopal Cathedral.
Edinburgh	Lothian	RC cathedral, seat of Bishop of St Andrews and Edinburgh.
Elgin	Moray	Founded in 1224, rebuilt in form of Jerusalem cross, now ruined.
Ely	Cambridgeshire	Dedicated to the Holy Trinity, founded by Simeon, Abbot of Ely, became cathedral 1109.
Exeter	Devon	Dedicated to St Peter, consecrated 1133 and rebuilt c1275.
Glasgow	Strathclyde	Dedicated to St Mary. Seat of Episcopal Bishop of Glasgow and Galloway.
Glasgow	Strathclyde	Dedicated to St Mungo (St Kentigern). Built in C12.
Gloucester	Gloucestershire	Dedicated to St Peter and Holy Trinity, founded 681 became cathedral 1541.
Guildford	Surrey	Dedicated to the Holy Spirit, Anglican cathedral designed by Sir Edward Maufe, completed 1968.
Hereford	Hereford and Worcester	Dedicated to the Blessed Virgin Mary and St Ethelbert, founded 676 by Bishop Putta, restored 1908.
Inverness	Moray	Dedicated to St Andrew. Seat of Episcopal Bishop of Moray, Ross and Caithness.
Kirkwall	Orkney	Dedicated to St Magnus. Founded in 1137 by St Rognvald, a Viking ruler, in honour of his martyred uncle.
Lancaster	Lancashire	Dedicated to St Peter, built 1859, became RC cathedral 1924.
Leeds	West Yorkshire	Dedicated to St Anne, RC cathedral from 1878.
Leicester	Leicestershire	Dedicated to St Martin, redesigned by Sir Charles Nicholson 1927.
Lichfield	Staffordshire	Dedicated to the Blessed Virgin Mary and St Chad. Built in C13/14.
Lincoln	Lincolnshire	Dedicated to the Blessed Virgin Mary. Norman cathedral built by Geoffrey de Noiers.
Liverpool	Merseyside	Dedicated to Christ Neo-Gothic Anglican cathedral founded 1904 but completed 1978.
Liverpool	Merseyside	Dedicated to Christ the King. Roman Catholic Metropolitan cathedral completed 1967. Nicknamed 'Paddy's Wigwam'. Original design by Lutyens rejected on grounds of cost.
Llandaff	Cardiff	Dedicated to St Peter and St Paul. Founded by St Teilo, rebuilt by Bishop Urban C12.
London	London	Dedicated to St Paul. Designed by Sir Christopher Wren, built 1675–1710.
Manchester	Greater Manchester	Dedicated to St Mary, St Denys and St George. Cathedral founded 1847.
Middlesbrough	Cleveland	Dedicated to St Mary. RC cathedral completed 1986.
Millport	Great Cumbrae Island, Ayrshire	Collegiate Church of the Holy Spirit. Anglican church known as the Cathedral of the Isles.
Motherwell	Strathclyde	Roman Catholic cathedral designed by Edward Pugin.
Newcastle	Tyne & Wear	Dedicated to St Nicholas. C14 cathedral rebuilt by R.J. Johnson.
Newcastle	Tyne & Wear	Dedicated to St Mary. RC cathedral from 1850, seat of Bishop of Hexham and Newcastle.
Newport	Newport	Dedicated to St Woolos. Seat of Bishop of Monmouth.
Northampton	Northamptonshire	Dedicated to Our Lady and St Thomas. RC cathedral completed in 1864.
Norwich	Norfolk	Dedicated to the Holy Trinity. Norman cathedral founded by William I in 1068.
Norwich	Norfolk	Dedicated to St John the Baptist. RC cathedral from 1976, seat of Bishop of East Anglia.
Nottingham	Nottinghamshire	Dedicated to St Barnabas. RC cathedral from 1850, designed by Augustus Pugin 1842.
Oban	Strathclyde	Dedicated to St John. Seat of Episcopal Bishop of Argyll and the Isles.
Oban	Strathclyde	Roman Catholic Cathedral, seat of Bishop of Argyll and the Isles
Oxford	Oxfordshire	Dedicated to St Frideswide. Smallest cathedral in England, also known as Christ Church.
Paisley	Glasgow	Roman Catholic cathedral built in the 1930s.
Perth	Perthshire	Dedicated to St Ninian. Seat of Episcopal Bishop of St Andrew Dunkeld & Dunblane. Built between 1850–1890.

Name	Location	General Information
Peterborough	Cambs	Dedicated to St Peter, St Paul and St Andrew. Consecrated 1238 and became cathedral 1541.
Plymouth	Devon	Dedicated to St Mary and St Boniface. RC cathedral completed 1858.
Portsmouth	Hampshire	Dedicated to St Thomas of Canterbury. Founded in C12, became a Cathedral in 1927.
Portsmouth	Hampshire	Dedicated to St John the Evangelist. RC Cathedral from 1882.
Ripon	North Yorkshire	Dedicated to St Peter and St Wilfred. Built in the C15.
Rochester	Kent	Dedicated to Christ and the Blessed Virgin Mary. Medieval church renovated by Bishop Gundulf 1125–30.
Salford	Greater Manchester	Dedicated to St John the Evangelist. RC cathedral from 1850, designed by Matthew Hadfield.
Salisbury	Wiltshire	Dedicated to the Blessed Virgin Mary. Founded 1220 by Richard Poore replacing prior foundation at Old Sarum.
Sheffield	South Yorkshire	Dedicated to St Peter and St Paul. Built by Charles Nicholson.
Sheffield	South Yorkshire	Dedicated to Saint Marie. RC Cathedral from 1980, designed by Matthew Hadfield. Seat of the Bishop of Hallam.
Shrewsbury	Shropshire	Dedicated to Our Lady Help of Christians and St Peter of Alcontara. RC cathedral built by Edward Pugin, completed 1856.
Southwark	London	Dedicated to St Saviour and St Mary Overie. Sir Arthur Blomfield rebuilt 1890s.
Southwark	London	Dedicated to St George. RC cathedral from 1850, rebuilt 1858.
Southwell	Nottinghamshire	Dedicated to the Blessed Virgin Mary.
St Albans	Hertfordshire	Dedicated to St Alban. Built in 1077 and designated a cathedral in 1877.
St Andrews	Fife	Medieval Cathedral completed in 1144, now ruined.
St Asaph	Clwyd	Dedicated to St Asaph. Restored C19 by Gilbert Scott.
St Davids	Dyfed	Dedicated to St David & St Andrew. Norman Cathedral restored in C19.
Swansea	Swansea	Dedicated to St Joseph. RC cathedral 1875, seat of Bishop of Menevia.
Truro	Cornwall	Dedicated to St Mary. Designed by J.L. Pearson 1879–1910.
Wakefield	West Yorkshire	Dedicated to All Saints. Designed by F.L. Pearson.
Wells	Somerset	Dedicated to St Andrew. Built C12 by Reginald de Bohun.
Westminster	London	Dedicated to the Most Precious Blood. RC cathedral designed by James Bentley 1895.
Winchester	Hampshire	Dedicated to Holy Trinity, St Peter, St Paul and St Swithin. Restored by Bishop Walkelin c1090.
Worcester	Hereford and Worcester	Dedicated to Christ and Blessed Virgin Mary. Wulfstan restored Worcester Cathedral 1084, improved C19.
Wrexham	Clwyd	Dedicated to Our Lady of Sorrows. RC cathedral built by Edward Pugin.
York Minster	North Yorkshire	Dedicated to St Peter. Thomas of Bayeux built St Peter's church c1070; restored C13.

NB: Although St Giles is known as Ediburgh Cathedral it does not have a cathedra so is technically a church. However, it is included in the listing because it has the same standing in Scotland as Westminster Abbey in England.

British Cathedrals: General Information

Arundel Screen   Part of Chichester Cathedral.
Bell Harry Tower   Tower of Canterbury Cathedral erected 1490.
Bell-tower: detached   Chichester.
Birmingham Cathedral   Edward Burne-Jones designed four windows in 1880 and William Morris made them.
~hop's eye window   Lincoln Cathedral.
ck stone fonts   Lincoln and Winchester both ‌ave black stone fonts from Belgium.
terbury Cathedral   Tombs for Henry IV and ‌|ward the Black Prince and Trinity Chapel Shrine ‌Thomas Becket. William of Sens fell from ‌|ffolding and work completed by William the ‌|lishman. T.S. Eliot's play *Murder in the Cathedral* performed in the Chapter House in 1935. ‌|royed by fire in 1174, rebuilt by William of Sens ‌Stone from Caen. Based on the Monastic

Church of St Etienne in Caen where Lanfranc had been Abbot.
Carlisle Cathedral   Sir Walter Scott was married there.
Cathedral: definition   Church that contains a cathedra, or throne of the bishop of the diocese.
Cathedral: longest   Winchester 556 ft.
Cathedral: widest in England   Manchester at 114 ft.
Cathedrals: shape   Cruciform, traditionally.
Chichester Cathedral   Houses tomb for Bishop Robert Sherburne, who died in 1536. Houses monument for Walter Huskisson, Chichester MP (dressed as Roman).
Chichester: windows   Designed by Marc Chagall.
Christ Church Gateway   Canterbury Cathedral.
Clock with no face   Salisbury Cathedral.
Coventry Cathedral   Tapestry of the Risen Christ by Graham Sutherland 1952. Statue of Christ being

doomed (behold the man) by Jacob Epstein. Windows by John Piper. Benjamin Britten's *War Requiem* first performed.

Coventry Cathedral: Old   Destroyed by bombing 1940.

Durham Cathedral   Completed by Ranulf Flambard and houses Tomb of St Cuthbert.

Gloucester Cathedral   Contains tomb of Edward II, murdered in Berkeley Castle; also tomb of Robert Curthose, Duke of Normandy.

Great Paul   17-ton bell in St Paul's.

Hedda Stone: Sculpture   Peterborough Cathedral.

Hereford Cathedral   Map of the World (Mappa Mundi) by Richard of Haldingham and Lafford C13, based on C5 work of Orosius. Africa is labelled as Europe, and vice versa. Jerusalem is centre of the world. Largest chained library (1450 books) includes *Anglo-Saxon Chronicle*. Restored by Lewis Cottingham and Sir George Gilbert Scott. Houses shrine of St Thomas Cantilupe. Highpoint of Hereford is a tower, not a spire.

Highest Spire   Salisbury Cathedral 404 ft; 2nd highest spire is Norwich at 315 ft.

Inverted Arches   Wells Cathedral.

Largest Gothic Church   York Minster, in England.

Lichfield Cathedral   Houses the Sleeping Children Statue. Three spires named The Ladies of the Vale. Name means Field of the Dead (Emperor Diocletian martyred 1000 Christians). Previous name – Bishopric called the diocese of 'Lichfield and Coventry' until 1836.

Lincoln   Highest spire 524 ft until it was blown down in 1584.

Liverpool Anglican   Designed by Sir Giles Gilbert Scott after winning competition.

Llandaff Cathedral   Houses *Christ in his Majesty* by Jacob Epstein.

Longest Nave   St Albans has England's longest nave at 275½ feet.

Magna Carta: copies   Lincoln and Salisbury cathedrals; the other two are in the British Library.

Mostyn Christ   Bangor Cathedral.

Nelson's Column   Hereford Cathedral had a Nelson's Column long before the London monument.

New Cathedrals of 1927   Isle of Wight and South Hampshire became Anglican Diocese, creating many new cathedrals.

Norwich Cathedral   Edith Cavell buried. It also has the largest cloisters in England.

Old St Paul's   The Norman cathedral was 600 ft long; its spire was 490 ft high.

Oldest clock (1380)   Salisbury Cathedral (no dial).

Peterborough Cathedral   Catherine of Aragon buried there 1536 and Mary Queen of Scots 1587 (moved to Westminster Abbey).

Priest and people: face   East, traditionally.

Ribbed Vault 1st   Durham Cathedral.

Ripon Cathedral   Crypt by St Wilfred and Reredos by Ninian Comper.

Scott, Sir George Gilbert   Restored Westminster Abbey, Ely, Lichfield and Salisbury cathedrals.

Smallest Cathedral   St Asaph's, Clwyd.

Southwark Cathedral   John Harvard, founder of Harvard University, baptised 1607. Bunyan and Chaucer windows.

St Albans: dedicatee   St Alban, Britain's first Christian Martyr (executed circa 209).

St Augustine's Chair   Canterbury Cathedral.

St David's Cathedral   Based on the Spanish Santiago de Compostela.

St Giles Cathedral   Jenny Geddes flung stool at preacher for reading an Anglican text. John Knox, the religious reformer, was buried there in 1572. White stork's nest was recorded on roof in 1416, the only British breeding occurrence.

St Lucy's Chapel   Oxford Cathedral.

St Paul's Cathedral   Henry Moore's statue *Mother and Child*. Bombed in December 1940. Statue of Queen Anne outside. St Paul's destroyed by fire in 1666. All Souls Chapel is memorial to Kitchener and other casualties of World War I. Whispering Gallery is famous for its acoustics. Frescoes on the inside of the dome by Sir James Thornhill. Houses Wellington's monument by Alfred Stevens and Nelson's statue by John Flaxman.

Three Spires   Lichfield, Truro and St Mary's Edinburgh.

Triforium 1st   Canterbury Cathedral.

Twenty-four-hour clock   Wells Cathedral.

Wastell's Tower   Canterbury Cathedral.

Westminster Abbey   Not a cathedral as such, as it lacks a Bishop's Throne. Official name is the Collegiate Church of St Peter. George II was last Sovereign to be buried in the Abbey, as Windsor Castle was subsequently used. Tombs include Henry III, Edward I, Edward III, Henry V, Elizabeth I, Mary Queen of Scots and the Unknown Warrior.

Westminster Cathedral   Houses Eric Gill's *14 Stations of the Cross*.

Whispering Gallery   St Paul's Cathedral.

Winchester Cathedral   Canute and other Danish kings are buried here. So are Jane Austen and Izaak Walton. When St Swithin's remains were transferred in 971 it rained for 40 days. Nave was built C14 by William of Wykeham and William of Edington.

Worcester Cathedral   Houses the tomb of King John.

Wren's tomb inscription   Lector, simonumentum requiris, circumspice – 'Reader, if you seek his monument, look around you.'

York Minster   Great East window by John Thornton 1405–8; St Cuthbert's (bishop in 685) window 1440.

B
R
I
T
A
I
N

CALENDAR

Wedding Anniversaries

1	Cotton / Paper	8	Bronze / Pottery	15	Crystal	50	Golden
2	Paper / Cotton	9	Pottery / Willow	20	China	55	Emerald
3	Leather	10	Tin	25	Silver	60	Diamond
4	Fruit / Flowers	11	Steel	30	Pearl	65	Blue Sapphire
5	Wood	12	Silk / Linen	35	Coral	70	Platinum
6	Sugar	13	Lace	40	Ruby	75	Gold or Diamond
7	Wool / Copper	14	Ivory	45	Sapphire		

NB: Wedding anniversaries are an area of frustration for quiz players because there are slight variations to many of the gifts that are traditionally given on wedding anniversaries, and to complicate matters even more, some of the gifts have changed over the years: e.g. diamonds were traditionally given on a 75th wedding anniversary but after Queen Victoria celebrated her 'Diamond' Jubilee in 1897, this became the established gift for a 60th anniversary, and the 75th which was previously Diamond then became Gold, as opposed to 'Golden' for a 50th. A more common cause of frustration is the gift for a first anniversary. Cotton was traditionally given, as the 'binding' of two people who have tied the knot, but as in the case of so many infrequently used customs it has become traditional to think of a first anniversary as a paper one, after the certificate of marriage. Neither is right or wrong, as they have never been observed for any reason other than a convenient question to ask in a quiz. In fairness, it would be better for quiz-setters to avoid the more controversial anniversaries – e.g. 1st, 2nd, 75th – or if insisting on using them, it would be advisable to phrase the question in the form 'If paper is a first anniversary, what is a second?'

Months of the French Revolutionary Calendar

Vendémiaire	(Grape harvest)	Sep 23rd–Oct 22nd	Germinal	(Buds)	Mar 22nd–Apr 20th	
Brumaire	(Mist)	Oct 23rd–Nov 21st	Floréal	(Flowers)	Apr 21st–May 20th	
Frimaire	(Frost)	Nov 22nd–Dec 21st	Prairial	(Meadows)	May 21st–Jun 19th	
Nivôse	(Snow)	Dec 22nd–Jan 20th	Messidor	(Harvest)	Jun 20th–Jul 19th	
Pluviôse	(Rain)	Jan 21st–Feb 19th	Thermidor	(Heat)	Jul 20th–Aug 18th	
Ventôse	(Wind)	Feb 20th–Mar 21st	Fructidor	(Fruit)	Aug 19th–Sep 22nd	

Months of the Jewish Calendar

Tishri	30 days	Adar*	29 days	Tammuz	29 days
Marheshvan	29 / 30 days	Ve-Adar†	30 days	Av	30 days
Kislev	29 / 30 days	Nisan	30 days	Elul	29 days
Tevet	29 / 30 days	Iyyar	29 days		
Shevat	30 days	Sivan	30 days		

*30 days in a leap year
†13th month every 3rd, 6th, 8th, 11th, 14th, 17th, & 19th year of a 19-year cycle
NB: The Jewish calendar places the creation at 3761 BCE

Months of the Muslim Calendar

1	Muharram	30 days	5	Jumâda I	30 days	9	Ramadan	30 days
2	Safar	29 days	6	Jumâda II	29 days	10	Shawwal	29 days
3	Rabia I	30 days	7	Rajab	30 days	11	Dhâl-Qa'da	30 days
4	Rabia II	29 days	8	Shaaban	29 days	12	Dhâl-Hijja	29 days*

*30 days in a leap year
NB: The Muslim calendar starts in 622 CE. 1 Muharram of the year I was 16 July 622; it marks the Prophet's move from Mecca to Medina

Other Calendars

Indian	Vikrama Era	Dates from Feb 23rd 57 BC
	Saka Era	Dates from Mar 3rd AD 78
	Buddhist Era	Dates from 543 BC
	Jain Era	Dates from 527 BC (Death of Vardhamana)
	Parsee Era	Dates from Jun 16th AD 632

Coptic   Egypt and Ethiopia; Dates from Aug 29th AD 284

Japanese Days (months are numbered)	Nichiyobi	Sun-day
	Getsuyobi	Moon-day
	Kayobi	Fire-day
	Suiyobi	Water-day
	Mokuyobi	Wood-day
	Kinyobi	Metal-day
	Doyobi	Earth-day

Commemorative Days

Advent Sunday	Sunday nearest to Nov 30th
All Saints' Day	Nov 1st
All Souls' Day	Nov 2nd
Andrew's Day, St	Nov 30th
Ascensiontide	Ascension day to Whitsun Eve (10 days)
Ash Wednesday	The 1st day of Lent
Assumption	Aug 15th
Australia Day	Jan 26th
Barnabas's Day, St	Jun 11th
Bartholomew's Day, St	Aug 24th
Bastille Day	Jul 14th
Burns Night	Jan 25th
Calends / Kalends	First day of each month in ancient Roman Calendar
Cecilia's Day, St	Nov 22nd
Commonwealth Day	2nd Monday in March
Corpus Christi	Thursday after Trinity Sunday
Crispin's Day, St	Oct 25th
David's Day, St	Mar 1st
Easter Sunday	The 1st Sunday after the full moon following the vernal equinox
Epiphany	Jan 6th
First day of year pre-1752	Mar 25th
Francis of Assisi's Day, St	Oct 4th
George Washington Day	Feb 17th (USA)
George's Day, St	Apr 23rd
Giles' Day, St	Sept 1st
Good Friday	Day before Easter Saturday
Holy Saturday	Last day of Lent
Immaculate Conception Day	Dec 8th
Independence Day (USA)	Jul 14th
John the Baptist's Day, St	Jun 24th
John the Evangelist's, St	Dec 27th
Labor Day (USA)	Equivalent to our May Day, First Monday of September
Lady Day	Mar 25th
Lent	The 40 days between Ash Wednesday and Easter Saturday

Low Sunday	The 1st after Easter
Luke's Day, St	Oct 18th
Maggie Thatcher Day	Jan 10th on Falkland Islands
Mark's Day, St	Apr 25th
Martin Luther King Day	Jan 15th (USA)
Martin's Day, St	Nov 11th
Matthew's Day, St	Sept 21st
Maundy Thursday	Day before Good Friday
May Day	Became public holiday in 1978
Michael's Day, St	Sept 29th
Mothering Sunday	4th in Lent and 3rd before Easter
New Year's Day	Became public holiday in 1974
Nicholas' Day, St	Dec 6th
Nones (Roman Calendar)	The 9th day before the ides of each month i.e. 7th of March, May, July and October and 5th of other months
Orangeman's Day	Celebrated by Irish protestants on July 12th
Palm Sunday	Sunday before Easter Sunday
Passion Sunday	Sunday before Palm Sunday
Patrick's Day, St	Mar 17th
Paul's Day, St	Jun 29th
Pentecost (Whit Sunday)	7th Sunday after Easter Sunday
Peter's Day, St	Jun 29th
Shrove Tuesday	Day before Ash Wednesday
Stephen's Day, St	Dec 26th
Swithin's Day, St	Jul 15th
Sylvester's Day, St	Dec 31st
Thomas' Day, St	Dec 21st
Trafalgar Day	Oct 21st
Trinity Sunday	1st Sunday after Whitsun
Twelfth Night	Jan 5th
United Nations Day	Oct 24th
Valentine's Day, St	Feb 14th

excluding Sundays

CALENDAR

English Quarter Days

Lady Day	March 25th
Midsummer Day	June 24th
Michaelmas	September 29th
Christmas Day	December 25th

NB: A useful mnemonic for remembering English Quarter Days is that three of the days end with the same number as letters in the month e.g. March has five letters so Lady Day is the 25th, June has four letters so Midsummer Day is 24th, September has nine letters so Michaelmas is 29th. Christmas Day should never be forgotten.

Scottish Quarter Days

Candlemas	February 28th
Whitsuntide	May 28th
Lammas	August 28th
Martinmas	November 28th

NB: Although the names of the four Scottish Quarter Days have remained the same, the dates changed in 1991. Candlemas used to be on Feb 2nd, Lammas was Aug 1st and Martinmas was on Nov 11th. The date of Whitsuntide varied.

Birthstones

January	Garnet
February	Amethyst
March	Bloodstone or Aquamarine
April	Diamond
May	Emerald
June	Pearl, Agate Moonstone, or Alexandrite
July	Ruby or Cornelian
August	Sardonyx or Peridot
September	Sapphire or Chrysolite
October	Opal or Tourmaline
November	Topaz
December	Turquoise or Zircon

NB: Birthstones are also controversial, as once again some months have more than one stone. Attempts to introduce birthstones for each sign of the Zodiac have fallen largely out of use.

Chinese Years

Snake	1989
Horse	1990
Sheep	1991
Monkey	1992
Chicken	1993
Dog	1994
Pig	1995
Rat	1996
Ox	1997
Tiger	1998
Rabbit	1999
Dragon	2000

NB: The calendar goes in 12-year cycles, so it continues Snake, 2001; Horse, 2002; and so on.

Watches at sea

First Watch	8pm–Midnight
Middle Watch	Midnight–4am
Morning Watch	4am–8am
Forenoon Watch	8am–Midday
Afternoon Watch	Midday–4pm
First Dog Watch	4pm–6pm
Last Dog Watch	6pm–8pm

NB: A bell is rung every half-hour during a watch, which therefore ends on eight bells or four for a dog watch. The New Year is brought in with 16 bells. Incidentally 'Dog' is thought to be a corruption of 'dodge', which was introduced to enable easier rostering.

Zodiac

Aries	Mar 21–Apr 19
Taurus	Apr 20–May 20
Gemini	May 21–Jun 21
Cancer	Jun 22–Jul 22
Leo	Jul 23–Aug 22
Virgo	Aug 23–Sep 22
Libra	Sep 23–Oct 23
Scorpio	Oct 24–Nov 21
Sagittarius	Nov 22–Dec 21
Capricorn	Dec 22–Jan 19
Aquarius	Jan 20–Feb 18
Pisces	Feb 19–Mar 20

CINEMA (A–Z OF OUTSTANDING FILMS)

À Nous la Liberté (1931) Raymond Cordy, Henri Marchand. Factory owner is blackmailed about his past and is helped by an old prison friend. US Title: *Freedom for Us*. *Dir*. René Clair.

Abbott & Costello Go to Mars (1953) Bud Abbott, Lou Costello, Mari Blanchard, Martha Hyer, Robert Paige. Despite the title, they land first in Louisiana and then on Venus! *Dir*. Charles Lamont.

Abbott & Costello Meet Captain Kidd (1952) Bud Abbott, Lou Costello, Charles Laughton, Leif Erickson. *Dir*. Charles Lamont.

Abbott & Costello Meet Dr Jekyll & Mr Hyde (1953) Bud Abbott, Lou Costello, Boris Karloff, Craig Stevens. This film starring Boris Karloff was given an 'X' certificate in its day. *Dir*. Charles Lamont.

Abbott & Costello Meet Frankenstein (1948) Bud Abbott, Lou Costello, Bela Lugosi, Lon Chaney Jnr. Dracula and the Wolf Man also feature. GB Title: *Abbott & Costello Meet the Ghosts*. *Dir*. Charles Barton.

Abbott & Costello Meet the Killer, Boris Karloff (1948) Bud Abbott, Lou Costello, Boris Karloff, Gary Moore. Boris Karloff is not the killer and appears very little. *Dir*. Charles Barton.

Abe Lincoln in Illinois (1940) Raymond Massey (Abraham Lincoln), Ruth Gordon. GB Title: *Spirit of the People*. *Dir*. John Cromwell.

Abominable Dr Phibes, The (1971) Vincent Price, Joseph Cotten, Terry-Thomas. Dr Phibes, a disfigured musical genius, avenges his wife's death at the hands of surgeons. Sequel: *Dr Phibes Rises Again* (1972), starred Price, Terry-Thomas, Beryl Reid, John Thaw. *Dir*. Robert Fuest.

Abominable Snowman, The (1957) Peter Cushing, Forrest Tucker, Richard Wattis. US Title: *The Abominable Snowman of the Himalayas*. *Dir*. Val Guest.

Above and Beyond (1952) Robert Taylor (Colonel Paul Tibbets, who dropped the first atomic bomb on Japan). *Dir*. Melvin Frank and Norman Panama.

Absence of Malice (1981) Paul Newman, Sally Field. *Dir*. Sydney Pollack.

Absent-Minded Professor, The (1961) Fred MacMurray, Tommy Kirk, Keenan Wynn, Ed Wynn. Lighter than air substance called 'Flubber' allows the Professor's Model-T Ford to fly. Sequel *Son of Flubber*. *Dir*. Robert Stevenson.

Absolute Beginners (1986) Eddie O'Connell, Patsy Kensit, David Bowie (Vendice Partners), Ray Davies, James Fox, Steven Berkoff, Mandy Rice Davies, Robbie Coltrane, Irene Handl, Eric Sykes, Lionel Blair. Teen life in 1958 London. *Dir*. Julien Temple.

Absolute Power (1997) Clint Eastwood, Gene Hackman (President Richmond), Ed Harris, EG Marshall, Laura Linney, Judy Davis. *Dir*. Clint Eastwood.

Accident (1967) Dirk Bogarde, Stanley Baker, Vivien Merchant, Michael York. Screenplay by Harold Pinter. *Dir*. Joseph Losey.

Accidental Hero (1992) Dustin Hoffman (Bernie Laplante), Geena Davis (Gale Gayley), Andy Garcia (John Bubber). Screenplay by David Webb Peoples, the writer of *Unforgiven* and *Blade Runner*. *Dir*. Stephen Frears.

Accidental Tourist, The (1988) William Hurt, Kathleen Turner, Geena Davis. Geena Davis won Academy Award for Best Supporting Actress. *Dir*. Lawrence Kasdan.

Accused, The (1988) Kelly McGillis (Kathryn Murphy), Jodie Foster (Sarah Tobias), Bernie Coulson. Jodie Foster won Academy Award for Best Actress. *Dir*. Jonathan Kaplan.

Ace in the Hole (1951) Kirk Douglas (Chuck Tatum), Jan Sterling (Lorraine), Porter Hall (Boot), Ray Teal (Sheriff). In order to boost newspaper sales a journalist delays the rescue of a man trapped in a cave. Aka: *The Big Carnival*. *Dir*. Billy Wilder.

Ace Ventura, Pet Detective (1994) Jim Carrey, Courteney Cox, Sean Young, Tone Loc. Ace is hired to recover the Miami Dolphins' dolphin mascot. *Dir*. Tom Shadyac.

Ace Ventura, When Nature Calls (1995) Jim Carrey, Ian McNeice, Simon Callow, Adewalé. Ace goes to Africa to find a sacred white bat. *Dir*. Steve Oedekerk.

Across the Pacific (1942) Humphrey Bogart (Rick Leland), Mary Astor (Alberta Marlow), Sydney Greenstreet (Dr Lorenz). Huston was called up mid-film and it was eventually completed by Vincent Sherman. *Dir*. John Huston.

Actress, The (1928) Norma Shearer, Ralph Forbes. This film was the opening attraction at London's Empire Theatre, Leicester Square. GB Title: *Trelawney of the Wells*. *Dir*. Sidney Franklin.

Adam's Rib (1949) Spencer Tracy, Katharine Hepburn, Judy Holliday. *Dir*. George Cukor.

Addams Family, The (1991) Anjelica Huston (Morticia), Raul Julia (Gomez), Christopher Lloyd (Uncle Fester). Impostor arrives at the Addams family home purporting to be a long-lost elder brother. *Dir*. Barry Sonnenfeld.

Addams Family Values (1993) Anjelica Huston (Morticia), Raul Julia (Gomez), Christopher Lloyd (Uncle Fester). Sequel in which the Addams children try, unsuccessfully, to kill the new baby. *Dir*. Barry Sonnenfeld.

Addicted To Love (1997) Meg Ryan (Maggie), Matthew Broderick (Sam), Kelly Preston (Linda), Tcheky Karyo (Anton) *Dir*. Griffin Dunne.

Addiction, The (1996) Christopher Walken, Lili Taylor. *Dir*. Abel Ferrara.

Admirable Crichton, The (1957) Kenneth More, Cecil Parker, Sally Ann Howes, Diane Cilento, Peter Graves, Gerald Harper. US Title: *Paradise Lagoon*. *Dir*. Lewis Gilbert.

Adolf Hitler – My Part In His Downfall (1972) Jim Dale (Spike Milligan), Spike Milligan (Milligan's father), Arthur Lowe, Bill Maynard. Notable for appearance of Spike Milligan playing the part of his father. *Dir*. Norman Cohen.

Adventure of Sherlock Holmes' Smarter Brother, The (1975) Gene Wilder, Marty Feldman, Madeline Kahn, Thorley Walters. *Dir*. Gene Wilder.

Adventures of Arsène Lupin, The (1956) Robert Lamoureux, Lisolotte Pulver, Otto Hasse. Based on the Jewel Thief character created by Maurice Leblanc. *Dir*. Jacques Becker.

Adventures of Baron Munchausen (1989) John Neville, Eric Idle, Sarah Polley, Oliver Reed, Uma Thurman. *Dir*. Terry Gilliam.

Adventures of Barry Mackenzie, The (1972) Barry Crocker, Barry Humphries (Edna Everage), Peter

Cook, Spike Milligan, Dennis Price. *Private Eye* comic strip fantasy. (The 1974 sequel was called *Barry Mackenzie Holds His Own*.) Bruce Beresford.

Adventures of Captain Marvel (1941) Tom Tyler (Billy Batson alias Captain Marvel). Assistant radio operator on scientific trip to Siam is endowed with superpowers by the mysterious 'Shazam' and battles against the evil 'Scorpion'. *Dir*. John English & William Witney.

Adventures of Mark Twain (1944) Fredric March (Twain), Alexis Smith, Alan Hale. *Dir*. Irving Rapper.

Adventures of Milo and Otis (1986) Narrated by Dudley Moore, the tale of a puppy in search of his friend, a kitten. This film was the second most popular film ever made in Japan. *Dir*. Masanori Hata.

Adventures of Pinocchio, The (1996) Martin Landau, Jonathan Taylor Thomas, Geneviève Bujold, Griff Rhys Jones, Dawn French. *Dir*. Steve Barron.

Adventures of Priscilla Queen of the Desert (1994) Terence Stamp, Hugo Weaving, Bill Hunter, Guy Pearce. Two transvestites and a transsexual drive a bus from Sydney to Alice Springs for a cabaret gig. *Dir*. Stephan Elliott.

Adventures of Robin Hood, The (1938) Errol Flynn (Robin), Basil Rathbone (Guy of Gisbourne), Claude Rains (Prince John), Olivia de Havilland (Marian), Alan Hale (Little John), Ian Hunter (King Richard), Melville Cooper (Sheriff of Nottingham). Won Academy Awards for Music and Editing. *Dir*. William Keighley and Michael Curtiz.

Adventures of Robinson Crusoe, The (1953) Dan O'Herlihy (Crusoe), Jaime Fernandez (Friday). *Dir*. Luis Buñuel.

Adventures of Sherlock Holmes, The (1939) Basil Rathbone, Nigel Bruce, George Zucco (Moriarty), Mary Gordon (Mrs Hudson). GB Title: *Sherlock Holmes*. *Dir*. Alfred Werker.

Adventures of Tom Sawyer, The (1938) Tommy Kelly (Tom), Jackie Moran (Huck), Ann Gillis (Becky Thatcher). *Dir*. Norman Taurog.

Advise and Consent (1962) Charles Laughton, Henry Fonda, Walter Pidgeon, Don Murray. *Dir*. Otto Preminger.

African Queen, The (1951) Humphrey Bogart (Charlie Allnutt), Katharine Hepburn (Rose Sayer), Robert Morley. Based on the CS Forester novel. Humphrey Bogart awarded the Best Actor Oscar. *Dir*. John Huston.

Agatha (1979) Vanessa Redgrave (Agatha Christie), Dustin Hoffman, Timothy Dalton. Tells the story of Agatha Christie's disappearance in 1926. *Dir*. Michael Apted.

Age of Innocence, The (1993) Daniel Day-Lewis, Michelle Pfeiffer, Winona Ryder, Richard E Grant. Wealthy lawyer falls in love with his wife's cousin. *Dir*. Martin Scorsese.

Agony and the Ecstasy, The (1965) Charlton Heston (Michelangelo), Rex Harrison (Pope Julius II). Based on the Irving Stone novel. *Dir*. Carol Reed.

Aida (1953) Sophia Loren, Lois Maxwell. Based on Verdi's opera. *Dir*. Clemente Fracassi.

Airborne (1993) Shane McDermott, Seth Green, Brittney Powell. Surfer moves to Cincinnati and becomes a rollerblade champion. *Dir*. Rob Bowman.

Airforce One (1997) Harrison Ford (President James Marshall), Jurgen Prochnow (General Radek), Gary Oldman (Korshunov) *Dir*. Wolfgang Petersen.

Airplane! (1980) Robert Stack, Lloyd Bridges, Leslie Nielsen, Peter Graves, Kareem Abdul-Jabbar, Julie Hagerty. (The 1982 sequel, '*Airplane II*, was directed by Ken Finkleman.) *Dir*. J. Abrahams, David and Jerry Zucker.

Airport (1970) Burt Lancaster, Dean Martin, Jean Seberg, Helen Hayes (Best Supporting Actress Oscar). Based on the Arthur Hailey novel. *Dir*. George Seaton.

Al Capone (1959) Rod Steiger (Capone), Fay Spain, Nehemiah Persoff, Martin Balsam. *Dir*. Richard Wilson.

Aladdin (1992) Voices of Robin Williams (Genie), Linda Larkin (Jasmine), Scott Weinger (Aladdin). 'Whole New World' won Best Song Oscar (music by Alan Menken, lyrics by Tim Rice) *Dir*. John Musker and Ron Clements.

Alamo, The (1960) John Wayne (Davy Crockett), Richard Widmark (Jim Bowie), Laurence Harvey (Travis), Frankie Avalon (Smitty), Richard Boone (Houston) *Dir*. John Wayne.

Albert RN (1953) Jack Warner, Anthony Steel, Robert Beatty, Anton Diffring. POWs build a life-like dummy to cover the absence of escapers. US Title: *Break to Freedom*. *Dir*. Lewis Gilbert.

Albino Alligator (1997) Faye Dunaway, Matt Dillon. Villains hold a group of New Yorkers hostage in a bar. *Dir*. Kevin Spacey.

Alexander the Great (1956) Richard Burton (Alexander), Fredric March, Claire Bloom. *Dir*. Robert Rossen.

Alexander's Ragtime Band (1938) Tyrone Power, Alice Faye, Don Ameche, Ethel Merman. *Dir*. Henry King.

Alf Garnett Saga, The (1972) Warren Mitchell, Dandy Nichols. The Una Stubbs and Tony Booth parts were played by Adrienne Posta and Mike Angelis. *Dir*. Bob Kellett.

Alfie (1966) Michael Caine (Alfie), Vivien Merchant, Shirley Anne Field, Jane Asher, Millicent Martin, Shelley Winters. Theme song sung by Cher. *Dir*. Lewis Gilbert.

Alfie Darling (1975) Alan Price, Jill Townsend, Joan Collins, Annie Ross, Hannah Gordon, Rula Lenska. Alan Price takes over the Michael Caine role as well as contributing the music. *Dir*. Ken Hughes.

Algiers (1938) Charles Boyer, Hedy Lamarr, Alan Hale. The famous line 'Come with me to the Casbah' was never actually said in this film. *Dir*. John Cromwell.

Alice (1990) Mia Farrow, Joe Mantegna, Alec Baldwin, William Hurt. *Dir*. Woody Allen.

Alice Doesn't Live Here Any More (1974) Ellen Burstyn, Kris Kristofferson, Jodie Foster, Diane Ladd, Alfred Lutter. Ellen Burstyn won Academy Award for Best Actress. *Dir*. Martin Scorsese.

Alice in Wonderland (1933) Charlotte Henry (Alice), WC Fields (Humpty Dumpty), Cary Grant (Mock Turtle), Gary Cooper (White Knight). Ida Lupino was brought from the UK for the title role but ultimately not used. *Dir*. Norman Z McLeod.

Alice's Adventures in Wonderland (1972) Fiona Fullerton (Alice), Michael Crawford (White Rabbit), Robert Helpmann (Mad Hatter), Dudley Moore (Dormouse), Spike Milligan (Gryphon), Peter Sellers (March Hare), Michael Hordern (Mock Turtle), Ralph Richardson (Caterpillar) *Dir*. William Sterling.

Alice's Restaurant (1969) Arlo Guthrie, Pat Quinn, James Broderick. *Dir*. Arthur Penn.

Alien (1979) Tom Skerritt, Sigourney Weaver, John Hurt, Ian Holm, Harry Dean Stanton. *Dir*. Ridley Scott.

Alien Resurrection (1997) Sigourney Weaver, Winona Ryder, Dominique Pinou, Ron Perlman. *Dir*. Jean-Pierre Jeunet.

Aliens (1986) Sigourney Weaver, Carrie Henn, Michael Biehn, Bill Paxton. Sequel to *Alien* which won Academy Award for Special Visual Effects. *Dir.* James Cameron.

Alien 3 (1992) Sigourney Weaver, Charles S. Dutton, Charles Dance, Paul McGann. *Dir.* David Fincher.

All about Eve (1950) Bette Davis (Margo Channing), George Sanders (Addison de Witt; Best Supporting Actor, Anne Baxter (Eve), Marilyn Monroe (Miss Caswell). Won Best Film Oscar. As well as Oscars above, Joseph L Mankiewicz won Academy Awards for Writing & Directing. *Dir.* Joseph L Mankiewicz.

All Creatures Great and Small (1974) Anthony Hopkins, Simon Ward, TP McKenna. Sponsored by *Reader's Digest*. *Dir.* Claude Whatham.

All of Me (1984) Steve Martin (Roger Cobb), Lily Tomlin (Edwina Cutwater), Victoria Tennant (Terry Hoskins) *Dir.* Carl Reiner.

All Quiet on the Western Front (1930) Lew Ayres (Paul Baumer), Louis Wolheim (Katczinsky). Based on novel by Erich Maria Remarque. *Dir.* Lewis Milestone.

All That Jazz (1979) Roy Scheider, Jessica Lange, Ann Reinking, Leland Palmer, Ben Vereen. Semi autobiographical musical which won Oscars for Editing, Art Direction, Musical Adaptation & Costume Design. *Dir.* Bob Fosse.

All That Money Can Buy (1941) Walter Huston (Mr Scratch), Edward Arnold (Daniel Webster). Bernard Herrmann won Oscar for his music for this Faustian version of Stephen Vincent Benet's *The Devil and Daniel Webster*. *Dir.* William Dieterle.

All the Fine Young Cannibals (1960) Robert Wagner, Natalie Wood, Pearl Bailey. A fine young pop group took their name from the title of this film. *Dir.* Michael Anderson.

All the King's Men (1949) Broderick Crawford, Joanne Dru John Ireland, Mercedes McCambridge. (Best Film Oscar). Academy Awards for Broderick Crawford (Best Actor) and Mercedes McCambridge (Best Supporting Actress). *Dir.* Robert Rossen.

All the President's Men (1976) Robert Redford, Dustin Hoffman, Jason Robards Jnr. Reconstruction of the White House link with the Watergate affair by the *Washington Post*. *Dir.* Alan J Pakula.

Almost an Angel (1990) Paul Hogan (Terry Dean), Elias Koteas (Steve), Linda Kozlowski (Rose Garner) *Dir.* John Cornell.

Alphabet Murders, The (1965) Tony Randall, Robert Morley, Anita Ekberg, Margaret Rutherford (cameo role as Miss Marple). Based on *The ABC Murders* by Agatha Christie. This film is notable for the fact that Tony Randall plays several characters as well as Poirot. *Dir.* Frank Tashlin.

Always (1989) Richard Dreyfuss, Holly Hunter, Audrey Hepburn. Remake of the 1944 film *A Guy Named Joe* about a dead pilot's ghostly return to matchmake his girlfriend. *Dir.* Steven Spielberg.

Amadeus (1984) F Murray Abraham (Salieri), Tom Hulce (Mozart), Elizabeth Berridge (Constance Mozart). Filmed mainly in Prague. The part of Constance was originally Meg Tilly's but she was injured in a soccer match the day before shooting began. *Dir.* Milos Forman.

American Beauty (1999) Kevin Spacey (Lester Burnham), Annette Bening, Thora Birch, Wes Bentley. *Dir.* Sam Mendes.

American Gigolo (1980) Richard Gere, Lauren Hutton. Music by Giorgio Moroder. Christopher Reeve allegedly refused $1 million to play the lead. *Dir.* Paul Schrader.

American Graffiti (1973) Richard Dreyfuss, Ron Howard, Candy Clark. Film was set in 1962 California. *Dir.* George Lucas.

American in Paris, An (1951) Gene Kelly, Oscar Levant, Leslie Caron. *Dir.* Vincente Minnelli.

Amityville Horror, The (1979) James Brolin, Margot Kidder, Rod Steiger, Don Stroud. (The 1982 film *Amityville II: The Possession* was in fact a prequel. *Dir.* Stuart Rosenberg.

Anaconda (1997) Jennifer Lopez, Ice Cube, Jon Voight, Eric Stoltz. *Dir.* Luis Llosa.

Anastasia (1956) Ingrid Bergman, Yul Brynner, Helen Hayes. Bergman's award winning performance was all the more noteworthy as this was her comeback after being ostracised for 'immoral behaviour'. *Dir.* Anatole Litvak.

Anchors Aweigh (1945) Frank Sinatra, Gene Kelly, Katherine Grayson. Notable for the homophonic spelling of the title and a memorable dance scene between Gene Kelly & Jerry Mouse. *Dir.* George Sidney.

And God Created Woman (1988) Rebecca DeMornay (Robin Shay), Frank Langella (Jim Tiernan), Donovan Leitch (Pete Moran). Remake of the 1957 classic starring Brigitte Bardot. *Dir.* Roger Vadim.

And Soon The Darkness (1970) Michele Dotrice, Pamela Franklin, Sandor Eles, John Nettleton. Cult film about 2 young nurses on a cycling holiday in France. *Dir.* Robert Fuest.

And Then There Were None (1945) Walter Huston, Barry Fitzgerald, Richard Haydn, Queenie Leonard. GB Title: *Ten Little Niggers* (after the novel it was based on by Agatha Christie) *Dir.* René Clair.

And Then There Were None (1974) Oliver Reed, Richard Attenborough, Elke Sommer, Charles Aznavour, Herbert Lom. US Title: *Ten Little Indians*. The writer Peter Welbeck is in fact Harry Alan Towers, a curious character who has made a living out of remaking this film. *Dir.* Peter Collinson.

Angels With Dirty Faces (1938) James Cagney, Pat O'Brien, Dead End Kids, Ann Sheridan, Humphrey Bogart. Memorable final scenes when the gangster goes to the electric chair. *Dir.* Michael Curtiz.

Animal Crackers (1930) Groucho Marx (Captain Spaulding), Chico, Harpo, Zeppo, and Margaret Dumont. Thieves covet a valuable oil painting unveiled at a swank party. *Dir.* Victor Heerman.

Anna and the King of Siam (1946) Irene Dunne, Rex Harrison, Linda Darnell. In 1862 an English governess arrives in Bangkok to teach the 67 children of the King. *Dir.* John Cromwell.

Anna Christie (1930) Greta Garbo, Charles Bickford, Marie Dressler. Prostitute falls in love with a seaman. This was the film in which Garbo first talked. *Dir.* Clarence Brown.

Anna Karenina (1935) Greta Garbo (Anna), Fredric March (Count Vronsky). Based on the Tolstoy novel. A 1948 British version starring Vivien Leigh was less successful. *Dir.* Clarence Brown.

Anne of Green Gables (1934) Anne Shirley (Anne), Tom Brown. Based on the LM Montgomery novel set on Prince Edward Island and notable for the fact that its star changed her name from Dawn O'Day to Anne Shirley to play the part. *Dir.* George Nicholls Jnr.

Anne of the Thousand Days (1969) Richard Burton (Henry VIII), Geneviève Bujold (Boleyn) John Colicos (Thomas Cromwell). Highly acclaimed film with many Oscar nominations but no awards. *Dir.* Charles Jarrott.

Annie Get Your Gun (1950) Betty Hutton (Annie Oakley), Howard Keel, Edward Arnold. Judy Garland was originally cast but was fired after her displays of temperament. *Dir.* George Sidney.

Annie Hall (1977)   Woody Allen, Diane Keaton, Paul Simon, Shelley Duvall. Oscars for Best Picture, Script, Direction Actress. Classic line by Woody Allen: 'Hey, don't knock masturbation. It's sex with someone I love'. *Dir.* Woody Allen.

Another Woman (1988)   Gena Rowlands, Mia Farrow, Ian Holm, Gene Hackman. *Dir.* Woody Allen.

Anthony Adverse (1936)   Fredric March, Olivia de Havilland, Claude Rains, Akim Tamiroff. Based on the novel by Hervey Allen, this film won minor Academy Awards. *Dir.* Mervyn Le Roy.

Antonia's Line (1995)   Willeke van Ammelrooy, Els Dottemans, Jan Decleir. *Dir.* Marleen Gorris.

Antony and Cleopatra (1972)   Charlton Heston, Hildegarde Neil, Fernando Rey, John Castle (Octavius). Based on Shakespeare's play. Both Olivier and Orson Welles were sought for the lead. *Dir.* Charlton Heston.

Antz (1998) Voices of Woody Allen, Dan Aykroyd, Anne Bancroft, Sharon Stone, Sylvester Stallone. *Dir.* Eric Darnell and Tim Johnson.

Anything Goes (1936)   Bing Crosby, Ethel Merman, Charles Ruggles, Ida Lupino. PG Wodehouse adapted much of the script from the successful Broadway show but only 3 of Cole Porter's songs were retained. *Dir.* Lewis Milestone.

Anything Goes (1956)   Bing Crosby, Donald O'Connor, Zizi Jeanmaire, Mitzi Gaynor. Same story of the stars of a musical comedy each signing a different female lead. *Dir.* Robert Lewis.

Apartment, The (1960)   Jack Lemmon (CC Baxter), Shirley Maclaine (Fran Kubelik), Fred MacMurray (Jeff D Sheldrake). Insurance co. name: Consolidated Life. Last line of film by Miss Kubelik: 'Shut up and deal'. *Dir.* Billy Wilder.

Apocalypse Now (1979)   Martin Sheen, Robert Duvall, Marlon Brando, Harrison Ford. Vittorio Storaro won Oscar for Photography. Harvey Keitel originally played Willard but was replaced by Martin Sheen. *Dir.* Francis Coppola.

Apollo 13 (1995)   Tom Hanks, Bill Paxton, Kevin Bacon, Ed Harris, Emile Ann Lloyd. Won Oscar for Sound Effects. *Dir.* Ron Howard.

Aria (1987)   Theresa Russell, Nicola Swain, Jack Kyle, Marion Peters, Beverley D'Angelo, Elizabeth Hurley, John Hurt, Bridget Fonda. Ten episodes each based on a different opera. Ten Directors: Nicolas Roeg, Jean-Luc Godard, Charles Sturridge, Julien Temple, Bruce Beresford, Robert Altman, Franc Roddam, Ken Russell, Derek Jarman, Bill Bryden.

Around the World in Eighty Days (1956)   David Niven, Cantinflas, Robert Newton, Shirley Maclaine. Although, winning a Best Film Oscar, this film is more notable for the galaxy of stars that had cameos., e.g. Sinatra, George Raft, John Mills, Noël Coward, Buster Keaton, Marlene Dietrich. *Dir.* Mike Anderson and Kevin McClory.

Arsenic and Old Lace (1942) released 1944. Cary Grant (Mortimer Brewster) Josephine Hull (Abby) Jean Adair (Martha), Raymond Massey (Jonathan), John Alexander (Teddy), Peter Lorre (Dr Einstein), Grant Mitchell (Rev Harper). Two old ladies poison unsuspecting visitors with elderberry wine and have their mad brother, who believes they are yellow fever victims, bury them in the cellar. Raymond Massey was imitating Boris Karloff. *Dir.* Frank Capra.

Arthur (1981)   Dudley Moore (Arthur Bach), John Gielgud (Hobson), Liza Minnelli (Linda Marolla). Gielgud won Oscar as Best Supporting Actor and 'Best That You Can Do' won Best Song Oscar. *Dir.* Steve Gordon.

Arthur 2: On the Rocks (1988)   Dudley Moore (Arthur Bach), John Gielgud (Hobson), Liza Minnelli (Linda Marolla Bach). Brogan Lane, the ex-Mrs Moore, appears briefly as 'Cindy'. *Dir.* Bud Yorkin.

As Good As it Gets (1997)   Jack Nicholson (Best Actor Oscar), Helen Hunt (Best Actor Oscar), Greg Kinnear. *Dir.* James L Brooks.

Ashanti (1979)   Michael Caine, Omar Sharif, Peter Ustinov, Rex Harrison, William Holden. Wife of a member of the World Health Organisation is seized by slave traders in West Africa. *Dir.* Richard Fleischer.

Ask a Policeman (1938)   Will Hay, Graham Moffatt, Moore Marriott. Classic written by Val Guest and remade by him in 1983 as the somewhat less popular The Boys in Blue starring Cannon and Ball. *Dir.* Marcel Varnel.

Asphalt Jungle, The (1950)   Sterling Hayden (Dix Handley), Louis Calhern (Alonzo D Emmerich), Marilyn Monroe (Angela Phinlay) *Dir.* John Huston.

Assassination Bureau, The (1968)   Oliver Reed, Diana Rigg, Telly Savalas, Curt Jurgens. In 1906, a woman journalist breaks up an international gang of professional killers by falling in love with their leader. *Dir.* Basil Dearden.

Assassins (1995)   Sylvester Stallone, Antonio Banderas, Julianne Moore. Hitman decides to quit but is menaced by a younger rival. *Dir.* Richard Donner.

Associate, The (1996)   Whoopi Goldberg (Laurel Ayres and 'male' alter ego Robert S. Cutty), Dianne Wiest (Sally), Tim Daly, Eli Wallach. *Dir.* Donald Petrie.

Asterix and the Big Fight (1989)   Voices of Bill Oddie, Bernard Bresslaw, Ron Moody, Sheila Hancock, Brian Blessed, Peter Hawkins. Asterix attempts to restore the village soothsayer's memory in order to make a potion to defeat the invading Romans. *Dir.* Philippe Grimond.

Attila the Hun (1954)   Anthony Quinn, Sophia Loren. *Dir.* Pietro Francisci.

August (1995)   Anthony Hopkins, Leslie Phillips, Kate Burton. *Dir.* Anthony Hopkins.

Austin Powers: International Man of Mystery (1997)   Mike Myers, Elizabeth Hurley, Michael York, Mimi Rogers, Robert Wagner, Seth Green. *Dir.* Jay Roach.

Austin Powers: The Spy Who Shagged Me (1999)   Mike Myers (Austin Danger Powers/Dr Evil/Fat Bastard), Robert Wagner (No 2), Elizabeth Hurley (Vanessa Kensington Powers), Heather Graham (Felicity Shagwell), Michael York (Basil Exposition), Rob Lowe (Young No. 2), Seth Green (Scott Evil). *Dir.* Jay Roach.

Autumn Leaves (1956)   Joan Crawford, Cliff Robertson, Lorne Greene, Vera Miles. Spinster marries a young man who turns out to be a pathological liar and tries to murder her. *Dir.* Robert Aldrich.

Awakening, The (1980)   Charlton Heston, Susannah York, Jill Townsend, Stephanie Zimbalist. Based on the Bram Stoker novel Jewel of the Seven Stars about an archaeologist who believes the spirit of an Egyptian queen has entered the soul of his daughter. *Dir.* Mike Newell.

Awakenings (1990)   Robert De Niro (Leonard Lowe) Robin Williams (Dr Sayer) Max Von Sydow (Dr Ingham). Based on factual development in treatment of mental illness. Robin Williams broke De Niro's nose accidentally. *Dir.* Penny Marshall.

Awfully Big Adventure, An (1994)   Georgina Cates, Hugh Grant, Alan Rickman, Peter Firth, Prunella Scales, Nicola Pagett. Romance in a Liverpool repertory theatre in 1947. *Dir.* Mike Newell.

Babe (1995) James Cromwell, Magda Szubanski, Roscoe Lee Browne (Narrator). Orphaned piglet is adopted by a sheepdog. Based on a book by Dick King-Smith. *Dir.* Chris Noonan.

Babe, The (1992) John Goodman, Kelly McGillis, Bruce Boxleitner. *Dir.* Arthur Hiller.

Babette's Feast (1987) Stéphane Audran, Jean-Philippe Lafont, Jarl Kulle Birgitte Federspiel. Best Foreign Language Oscar for this Danish film about a Lottery winner laying on an enormous banquet. The original story on which the film was based was written by Karen Blixen. *Dir.* Gabriel Axel.

Baby Doll (1956) Karl Malden, Eli Wallach, Carroll Baker. *Dir.* Elia Kazan.

Back to the Future (1985) Michael J Fox (Marty McFly), Christopher Lloyd (Dr Emmett Brown), Crispin Glover (George McFly). Notable for cameo roles by Billy Zane as Match, and Huey Lewis, who sings 'Power of Love'. *Dir.* Robert Zemeckis.

Back to the Future II (1989) Michael J Fox (Marty McFly), Christopher Lloyd (Dr Emmett Brown), Lea Thompson (Lorraine Baines). Crispin Glover refused to take part for less than $1 million so lookalikes were used. *Dir.* Robert Zemeckis.

Back to the Future III (1990) Michael J Fox (Marty / Seamus McFly), Christopher Lloyd (Dr Emmett Brown), Lea Thompson (Lorraine Baines / Maggie McFly). Set in the Wild West of the 1880s. *Dir.* Robert Zemeckis.

Backdraft (1991) Kurt Russell (Stephen McCaffrey), William Baldwin (Brian McCaffrey), Rebecca DeMornay (Helen McCaffrey) Robert De Niro (Donald Rimgale) Donald Sutherland (Ronald Bartel). Two brothers track down an arsonist and expose corruption in the fire department. *Dir.* Ron Howard.

Bad and the Beautiful, The (1952) Kirk Douglas (Jonathan Shields), Lana Turner (Georgia Lorrison), Walter Pidgeon (Harry Pebbel), Dick Powell (James Lee Bartlow). A director, a star, a screenwriter and an executive recall their experiences at the hands of a go-getting Hollywood producer. *Dir.* Vincente Minnelli.

Bad Day at Black Rock (1955) Spencer Tracy, Robert Ryan, Lee Marvin, Walter Brennan. Action takes place within 24 hours and concerns a one-armed stranger greeted with hostility by a town with something to hide. *Dir.* John Sturges.

Bad Influence (1990) Rob Lowe (Alex), James Spader (Michael Ball). Notable scene where Lowe tries to blow up a car by connecting a broken tail-light with a petrol tank is apparently a terrorist trick from which one important step was omitted. *Dir.* Curtis Hanson.

Badlands (1973) Martin Sheen, Sissy Spacek, Warren Oates. Teenage girl and garbage collector wander across America leaving a trail of murder. *Dir.* Terrence Malick.

Ballad of the Sad Café, The (1991) Vanessa Redgrave (Miss Amelia Evans), Keith Carradine (Marvin Macy), Rod Steiger (Reverend Willin). Tale of a Southern town run by the despotic Redgrave, based on the novella by Carson McCullers. The film was shot at Willie Nelson's farm. *Dir.* Simon Callow.

Bananas (1971) Woody Allen, Louise Lasser, Carlos Montalban, Sylvester Stallone (walk-on as mugger). When asked why he called the film *Bananas*, Allen replied, 'Because there are no bananas in it.' *Dir.* Woody Allen.

Bandit Queen (1994) Seema Biswas, Nirmal Pandey, Manjoj Baipal. Story of Phoolan Devi, a real-life Indian bandit and rape victim. *Dir.* Sheka Kapur.

Bank Dick, The (1940) WC Fields, Franklin Pangborn, Shemp Howard, Jack Norton. Fields wrote the script using his nom de plume of Mahatma Kane Jeeves, which derived from characters in old English plays. They would say 'M'Hat, M'cane, Jeeves'. GB Title: *The Bank Detective. Dir.* Eddie Cline.

Barabbas (1962) Anthony Quinn, Silvano Mangano, Ernest Borgnine, Jack Palance. The eclipse of the Sun at the beginning was a real one filmed in Nice. *Dir.* Richard Fleischer.

Barb Wire (1996) Pamela Anderson Lee, Temuera Morrison, Victoria Rowell. Set in civil-war-ravaged USA in the year 2017. *Dir.* David Hogan.

Barbarella (1967) Jane Fonda, John Phillip Law, Milo O'Shea, David Hemmings, Marcel Marceau. Beautiful 40th-century astronaut prevents positronic ray from getting into the wrong hands. *Dir.* Roger Vadim.

Barbarosa (1981) Willie Nelson (Barbarosa), Gary Busey (Karl), Isela Vega (Josephina). Old-style Western that was well received by critics. *Dir.* Fred Schepisi.

Barbary Coast (1935) Edward G Robinson, Miriam Hopkins, Joel McCrea, Walter Brennan. Set during the San Francisco gold rush. *Dir.* Howard Hawks.

Barefoot Contessa, The (1954) Humphrey Bogart (Harry Dawes), Ava Gardner (Maria Vargas), Edmond O'Brien (Muldoon). O'Brien won Best Supporting Actor Oscar. *Dir.* Joseph L Mankiewicz.

Barefoot in the Park (1967) Robert Redford (Paul Bratter), Jane Fonda (Corie Bratter), Charles Boyer (Victor Velasco), Mildred Natwick (Ethel Banks). Based on Neil Simon's play. *Dir.* Gene Saks.

Barkleys of Broadway, The (1949) Fred Astaire, Ginger Rogers, Oscar Levant. Judy Garland was originally cast but withdrew through illness. *Dir.* Charles Walters.

Barretts of Wimpole Street, The (1934) Norma Shearer (Elizabeth Barrett), Fredric March (Robert Browning), Charles Laughton (Edward Moulton-Barrett), Maureen O'Sullivan (Henrietta). The 1956 remake starred Jennifer Jones and Bill Travers. *Dir.* Sidney Franklin.

Basic Instinct (1992) Michael Douglas (Nick Curran), Sharon Stone (Catherine Tramell), George Dzundza (Gus), Jeanne Tripplehorn (Dr Beth Garner), Leilani Sarelle (Roxy). Famous for a scene where the knickerless Stone crosses her legs. *Dir.* Paul Verhoeven.

Basket Case (1982) Kevin Van Hentenryck, Terri Susan Smith, Beverly Bonner. First of 3 (to date) cult films – followed by *Basket Case II* (1990) and *Basket Case 3: The Progeny* (1992) – depicting Siamese twins with attitude. *Dir.* Frank Henenlotter.

Batman (1989) Michael Keaton (Batman), Jack Nicholson (Joker), Kim Basinger (Vicki, Vale), Jerry Hall (Alicia) Jack Palance (Grissom). *Batman Returns* (1992) starred Danny De Vito as Penguin (Oswald Cobblepot). *Dir.* Tim Burton.

Batman and Robin (1997) George Clooney (Batman), Chris O'Donnell (Robin), Alicia Silverstone (Batgirl), Arnold Schwarzenegger (Mr Freeze), Uma Thurman (Poison Ivy). Schwarzenegger line: 'Revenge is a dish best served cold' see *Star Trek: The Wrath of Khan. Dir.* Joel Schumacher.

Batman Forever (1995) Val Kilmer (Batman), Tommy Lee Jones (Harvey Two-Face), Jim Carrey (Riddler), Chris O'Donnell (Robin), Nicole Kidman, Drew Barrymore. *Dir.* Joel Schumacher.

Battle of Britain (1969) Laurence Olivier (Dowding), Robert Shaw, Michael Caine, Christopher Plummer,

Kenneth More, Susannah York, Trevor Howard, Ralph Richardson, Michael Redgrave, Edward Fox. *Dir.* Guy Hamilton.

Battle of the Bulge (1965)   Henry Fonda, Robert Shaw, Robert Ryan, Telly Savalas, Ty Hardin. Story of the German counter-attack in the Ardennes in December 1944. *Dir.* Ken Annakin.

Battle of the River Plate (1956)   John Gregson, Anthony Quayle, Peter Finch. US Title: *Pursuit of the Graf Spee. Dir.* Emeric Pressburger & Michael Powell.

Beaches (1988)   Bette Midler (CC Bloom), Barbara Hershey (Hillary Whitney Essex). Singer visits her dying friend, a lawyer, and recalls their long and volatile friendship. *Dir.* Garry Marshall.

Bean (1997)   Rowan Atkinson, Peter MacNicol, Pamela Reed, Burt Reynolds, John Mills, Peter Egan, Harris Yulin, Richard Gant, Tricia Vessey, Peter Capaldi, Andrew Lawrence. *Dir.* Mel Smith.

Beau Brummell (1954)   Stewart Granger, Elizabeth Taylor, Robert Morley (George III), Peter Ustinov (Prince of Wales). Remake of the 1924 film starring John Barrymore and Mary Astor. *Dir.* Curtis Bernhardt.

Beau Geste (1939)   Gary Cooper, Ray Milland, Brian Donlevy, Susan Hayward. Remake of the 1926 film starring Ronald Colman and based on PC Wren's novel. *Dir.* William Wellman.

Beauty and the Beast (1991)   Voices of Robby Benson (Beast), Paige O'Hara (Belle) Angela Lansbury (Mrs Potts). Disney classic which became the best-selling video of all time in the USA. *Dir.* Gary Trousdale & Kirk Wise.

Beavis and Butthead Do America (1996)   Created by animator Mike Judge. Voices include Robert Stack and Bruce Willis. *Dir.* Mike Judge.

Becket (1964)   Richard Burton (Becket), Peter O'Toole (Henry II), John Gielgud, Sian Phillips. Based on Jean Anouilh's bitter stage play. *Dir.* Peter Glenville.

Bed Sitting Room, The (1969)   Ralph Richardson, Rita Tushingham, Michael Hordern, Arthur Lowe, Spike Milligan, Harry Secombe, Peter Cook, Dudley Moore. After a nuclear war, motley survivors turn into bed sitting rooms, cupboards and parakeets. *Dir.* Richard Lester.

Bedazzled (1967)   Peter Cook, Dudley Moore, Michael Bates, Raquel Welch, Eleanor Bron. *Dir.* Stanley Donen. Short-order cook is saved from suicide by Mr Spiggott, who offers him seven wishes in exchange for his soul.

Bedknobs and Broomsticks (1971)   Angela Lansbury, David Tomlinson, Bruce Forsyth, Tessie O'Shea. *Dir.* Robert Stevenson.

Beetlejuice (1988)   Alec Baldwin (Adam), Geena Davis (Barbara), Michael Keaton (Betelgeuse), Winona Ryder (Lydia Deetz). *Dir.* Tim Burton.

Beguiled, The (1971)   Clint Eastwood, Geraldine Page, Elizabeth Hartman, Darleen Carr. Wounded Union soldier hides out in a Confederate girls' school. *Dir.* Don Siegel.

Beijing Bastards (1993)   Cui Jian, Li Wei, Wu Gang, Bian Tianshuo. Original title: *Beijing Zazhong.* Story of disillusionment by the young Chinese. *Dir.* Zhang Yuan.

Being Human (1994)   Robin Williams, John Turturro, Anna Galiena, Theresa Russell (as narrator). Box office flop about a father who fails to provide for his family in five historic eras. *Dir.* Bill Forsyth.

Being John Malkovich (1999)   John Cusack, Cameron Diaz, Catherine Keener, John Malkovich. *Dir.* Spike Jonze.

Being There (1979)   Peter Sellers, Shirley MacLaine, Melvyn Douglas. Melvyn Douglas won Best Supporting Actor Oscar for this film about a simple gardener who becomes philosopher and sage to the American people. *Dir.* Hal Ashby.

Bell, Book and Candle (1958)   James Stewart, Kim Novak, Jack Lemmon, Hermione Gingold. Publisher slowly realises that his girlfriend is a witch. *Dir.* Richard Quine.

Belles of St Trinian's, The (1954)   Alastair Sim, George Cole (Flash Harry), Joyce Grenfell, Beryl Reid, Irene Handl. Based on Ronald Searle's cartoons. *Dir.* Frank Launder.

Bells of St Mary's, The (1945)   Bing Crosby (Father O'Malley), Ingrid Bergman (Sister Benedict). Sequel to *Going My Way. Dir.* Leo McCarey.

Belstone Fox, The (1973)   Eric Porter, Rachel Roberts, Dennis Waterman, Jeremy Kemp, Bill Travers. Based on the novel *The Ballad of the Belstone Fox* by David Rook. *Dir.* James Hill.

Ben Hur (1925)   Ramon Novarro, Francis X Bushman, Carmel Myers. Based on the Lew Wallace novel. Originally, Charles Brabin was director and George Walsh the star; both were replaced when Louis Mayer saw the first rushes. *Dir.* Fred Niblo.

Ben Hur (1959)   Charlton Heston, Haya Harareet, Jack Hawkins, Stephen Boyd, Hugh Griffith. Multi-award-winning film but critics generally regard the 1925 silent epic as the definitive. *Dir.* William Wyler.

Beneath the Planet of the Apes (1970)   James Franciscus, Charlton Heston, Linda Harrison, Kim Hunter. Sequel to *Planet of the Apes. Dir.* Ted Post.

Benji (1974)   Peter Breck, Edgar Buchanan, Christopher Connelly. Popular film about a stray mongrel dog who saves two kidnapped children. *Dir.* Joe Camp.

Benny Goodman Story (1955)   Steve Allen (Goodman), Donna Reed, Berta Gersten, Harry James, Gene Krupa, Sammy Davis Snr. Steve Allen went on to host one of America's leading variety shows on television. *Dir.* Valentine Davies.

Bequest to the Nation (1973)   Peter Finch, Glenda Jackson, Michael Jayston, Margaret Leighton, Anthony Quayle. US Title: *The Nelson Affair.* Story of Nelson's long affair with the tempestuous Lady Hamilton. *Dir.* James Cellan Jones.

Bespoke Overcoat, The (1956)   Alfie Bass, David Kossoff. Won Academy Award for Best Short Film and launched its stars as successful TV actors. *Dir.* Jack Clayton.

Best Years of Our Lives, The (1946)   Fredric March, Myrna Loy, Teresa Wright, Dana Andrews, Virginia Mayo, Hoagy Carmichael. Multi-award-winning film notable for the performance of Harold Russell, a veteran who had lost his hands; he had no previous acting experience. *Dir.* William Wyler.

Beverly Hillbillies, The (1993)   Diedrich Bader, Dabney Coleman, Erika Elaniak, Cloris Leachman, Buddy Ebsen, Zsa Zsa Gabor, Dolly Parton. *Dir.* Penelope Spheeris.

Beverly Hills Cop (1984)   Eddie Murphy (Axel Foley), Judge Reinhold (Det Billy Rosewood), Steven Berkoff (Victor Maitland). Detroit cop races to Los Angeles to track down the killers of his best friend. *Dir.* Martin Brest.

Beverly Hills Cop 2 (1987)   Eddie Murphy (Axel Foley), Judge Reinhold (Det Billy Rosewood), Brigitte Nielsen (Karla Fry). Ironically Sylvester Stallone was to play Axel Foley in the original film and his ex Brigitte Nielsen appears in this sequel. *Dir.* Tony Scott.

Beverly Hills Cop 3 (1994)   Eddie Murphy (Axel

Foley), Judge Reinhold (Det Billy Rosewood), John Saxon. Cop discovers that the head of security at a Los Angeles theme park is a murderer. *Dir.* Tony Scott.

Beyond Bedlam (1994)   Craig Fairbrass, Elizabeth Hurley, Keith Allen, Anita Dobson, Georgina Hale. *Dir.* Vadim Jean.

Beyond the Poseidon Adventure (1979)   Michael Caine, Telly Savalas, Karl Malden, Sally Field. Not so much a sequel, more an alternative ending to the original. *Dir.* Irwin Allen.

Bible, The (1966)   Michael Parks (Adam), Ulla Bergryd (Eve), Richard Harris (Cain), John Huston (Noah), George C Scott (Abraham), Peter O'Toole (the 3 Angels). Remembered for Huston's whispered commentary and the eye-catching photography as well as Toshiro Mayuzumi's musical interpretation. *Dir.* John Huston.

Big (1988)   Tom Hanks (Josh Baskin), Elizabeth Perkins (Susan), Robert Loggia (MacMillan). Story of 12-yr-old who wishes he were 'Big' and wakes up 20 yrs older. Steven Spielberg was originally going to direct and Harrison Ford to star. *Dir.* Penny Marshall.

Big Business (1929)   Oliver Hardy, Stan Laurel, James Finlayson. Laurel & Hardy classic about their failure to sell a Christmas tree to a belligerent householder. Memorable for the scene of mutual destruction. *Dir.* James W Horne.

Big Business (1988)   Bette Midler (Sadie Shelton / Ratcliff), Lily Tomlin (Rose Shelton / Ratcliff). Story of twins mixed up at birth. *Dir.* Jim Abrahams.

Big Chill, The (1983)   Tom Berenger (Sam), Glenn Close (Sarah), William Hurt (Nick), Jeff Goldblum (Michael), Kevin Kline (Harold), Meg Tilly (Chloe). Story of a students' reunion after the suicide of one of them. Kevin Costner plays the corpse, Alex, although only his hands, torso and legs are seen in the final version. *Dir.* Lawrence Kasdan.

Big Country, The (1958)   Gregory Peck, Jean Simmons, Charlton Heston, Burl Ives, Carol Baker, Charles Bickford, Chuck Connors. Story of the Terills' and the Hannesseys' feud over water rights. Burl Ives won Best Supporting Actor Oscar. *Dir.* William Wyler.

Big Hand For the Little Lady, A (1966)   Henry Fonda, Joanne Woodward, Jason Robards, Kevin McCarthy, Charles Bickford, Burgess Meredith. GB Title: *Big Deal at Dodge City* (though the action, in fact, takes place in Laredo) *Dir.* Fielder Cook.

Big Man, The (1990)   Liam Neeson, Joanne Whalley-Kilmer, Billy Connolly, Ian Bannen. Unemployed miner becomes a bare-knuckle fighter. *Dir.* David Leland.

Big Sleep, The (1946)   Humphrey Bogart (Philip Marlowe), Lauren Bacall (Vivian Sherwood Rutledge). John Ridgely (Eddie Mars), Martha Vickers (Carmen Sternwood). Based on Raymond Chandler's Novel but adapted by William Faulkner, Leigh Brackett and Jules Furthman. (Alternative version with 18 minutes of different footage exists.) *Dir.* Howard Hawks.

Big Sleep, The (1978)   Robert Mitchum (Philip Marlowe), Sarah Miles, Richard Boone, Candy Clark, James Stewart, Edward Fox, Oliver Reed, Richard Todd. Remake of the 1946 film but set in London. *Dir.* Michael Winner.

Big Trouble in Little China (1986)   Kurt Russell (Jack Burton), Kim Cattrall (Gracie Law). *Dir.* John Carpenter.

Bill and Ted's Excellent Adventure (1989)   Keanu Reeves (Ted 'Theodore' Logan), Alex Winter (Bill S Preston). Napoleon, Billy the Kid, Socrates, Freud, Genghis Khan, Joan of Arc and Abe Lincoln are some of the famous people met on their journey. *Dir.* Stephen Herek.

Billy Bathgate (1991)   Dustin Hoffman, Nicole Kidman, Bruce Willis. Based on El Doctorow's novel. Teenager becomes an assistant to top gangster Dutch Schultz. *Dir.* Robert Benton.

Billy Budd (1962)   Peter Ustinov, Robert Ryan, Terence Stamp, Melvyn Douglas, David McCallum. Based on Herman Melville's novel about the young Billy Budd, who kills the sadistic master-at-arms of a British warship in 1797. *Dir.* Peter Ustinov.

Billy Liar (1963)   Tom Courtenay, Julie Christie, Wilfred Pickles, Leonard Rossiter. Written by Keith Waterhouse and inspired by *The Secret Life of Walter Mitty. Dir.* John Schlesinger.

Birdcage, The (1996)   Robin Williams, Nathan Lane, Gene Hackman, Dianne Wiest. Remake of French film, *La Cage aux Folles*. Son of a homosexual club-owner persuades his father to act the heterosexual with his future very conservative in-laws. *Dir.* Mike Nichols.

Birdman of Alcatraz (1962)   Burt Lancaster (Robert Stroud), Karl Malden, Thelma Ritter, Edmond O'Brien, Neville Brand, Telly Savalas. True story of Robert Stroud, who spent nearly 60 years in prison and made a name for himself as an ornithologist. *Dir.* John Frankenheimer.

Birds, The (1963)   Rod Taylor, Tippi Hedren, Jessica Tandy, Suzanne Pleshette. Birds turn against humans. Action takes place at Bodega Bay, California. *Dir.* Alfred Hitchcock.

Birdy (1984)   Matthew Modine (Birdy), Nicolas Cage (Al Columbato). *Dir.* Alan Parker.

Birth of a Nation (1915)   Lillian Gish, Henry B Walthall, Mae Marsh, Donald Crisp. Originally *The Clansman*, this story of US Civil War strife was the first big screen epic. *Dir.* DW Griffith.

Black Beauty (1994)   Alan Cummings (voice), Sean Bean, David Thewlis, Jim Carter, Peter Davison, Eleanor Bron, Peter Cook. Story is told by the horse itself. *Dir.* Caroline Thompson.

Black Narcissus (1946)   Deborah Kerr, Sabu, Jean Simmons, Flora Robson. Anglo-Catholic nuns in the Himalayas have trouble with climate and morale. *Dir.* Michael Powell & Emeric Pressburger.

Black Robe (1991)   Lothaire Bluteau, Aden Young, Sandrine Holt. Jesuit priest travels through Quebec to convert the Indians in the 17th century. *Dir.* Bruce Beresford.

Blackboard Jungle, The (1955)   Glenn Ford, Anne Francis, Louis Calhern, Sidney Poitier, Vic Morrow. Notable for the music of Bill Haley and the Comets. *Dir.* Richard Brooks.

Blackmail (1929)   Anny Ondra, Sara Allgood, Charles Paton. Hitchcock's first talkie involves a Scotland Yard inspector who finds his girl is involved in a murder but conceals the fact and is blackmailed. *Dir.* Alfred Hitchcock.

Blade Runner (1982)   Harrison Ford (Deckard), Rutger Hauer (Roy Batty), Sean Young (Rachel), Daryl Hannah (Pris). Set in LA in 2019. Ridley Scott released his 'Director's Cut' in 1992 which had a more satisfactory conclusion. Based on the novel *Do Androids Dream of Electric Sheep?* by Philip K Dick. *Dir.* Ridley Scott.

Blair Witch Project, The (1999)   Heather Donahue, Michael C. Williams, Joshua Leonard. *Dir.* Daniel Myrick and Eduardo Sanchez.

Blair Witch 2: Book of Shadows (2000)   Tristen Skyler, Stephen B. Turner, Jeffery Donovan.*Dir.* Joe Berlinger

Blazing Saddles (1974)   Cleavon Little, Gene Wilder,

Slim Pickens, Mel Brooks, Madeline Kahn. Black railroad worker and an alcoholic ex-gunfighter foil a crooked attorney. Famous for its beans scene. *Dir.* Mel Brooks.

Blob, The (1958)   Steve McQueen, Aneta Corseaut, Earl Rowe. GB Title: *Dir.* Irwin S Yeaworth.

Blockheads (1938)   Oliver Hardy, Stan Laurel, Billy Gilbert. Twenty years after WW1, Stan is still guarding a trench because nobody told him to stop. *Dir.* John G Blystone.

Blondie (1938)   Arthur Lake, Penny Singleton, Daisy the Dog, Jonathan Hale. Mr & Mrs Small Town America, Dagwood Bumstead and wife Blondie, spawned many sequels. *Dir.* Frank R Strayer.

Blow Up (1966)   David Hemmings, Sarah Miles, Vanessa Redgrave. London fashion photographer thinks he sees a murder, but the evidence disappears. *Dir.* Michelangelo Antonioni.

Blue Angel, The (1930)   Emil Jannings, Marlene Dietrich (Lola). Story of a professor's infatuation with a nightclub singer. *Dir.* Josef von Sternberg.

Blue Bird, The (1940)   Shirley Temple, Johnny Russell, Gale Sondergaard (the cat), Eddie Collins (the dog). Two children of a poor woodcutter seek the bluebird of happiness. *Dir.* Walter Lang.

Blue Bird, The (1976)   Elizabeth Taylor (Mother, Maternal Love, Light & The Witch), Ava Gardner, Jane Fonda, George Cole. Remake of the 1940 classic. *Dir.* George Cukor.

Blue Dahlia (1946)   Alan Ladd, Veronica Lake, William Bendix, Howard de Silva. Raymond Chandler story of a returning war veteran who finds his faithless wife murdered and himself suspected. *Dir.* George Marshall.

Blue Lagoon (1949)   Jean Simmons, Donald Houston, Cyril Cusack. Shipwrecked boy and girl grow up on a desert island. *Dir.* Frank Launder.

Blue Lagoon (1980)   Brooke Shields, Christopher Atkins, Leo McKern. Remake of the 1949 film. *Dir.* Randal Kleiser.

Blue Lamp, The (1949)   Jack Warner, Jimmy Hanley, Dirk Bogarde, Dora Bryan. Famous for its opening shooting scene and the subsequent reincarnation of George Dixon for *Dixon of Dock Green*, which ran for 20 years on Television. *Dir.* Basil Dearden.

Blue Max, The (1966)   George Peppard, James Mason, Ursula Andress, Jeremy Kemp. *Dir.* John Guillermin.

Blues Brothers, The (1980)   John Belushi (Jake), Dan Aykroyd (Elwood), Carrie Fisher, Cab Calloway. *Dir.* John Landis.

Bob and Carol and Ted and Alice (1969)   Robert Culp, Natalie Wood, Elliott Gould, Dyan Cannon. *Dir.* Paul Mazursky.

Body Heat (1981)   William Hurt, Kathleen Turner, Richard Crenna, Ted Danson. Florida lawyer becomes involved with a married woman and they plot to kill her husband. *Dir.* Lawrence Kasdan.

Bodyguard, The (1992)   Kevin Costner (Frank Farmer), Whitney Houston (Rachel Marron), Gary Kemp (Sy Spector). *Dir.* Mick Jackson.

Bonfire of the Vanities (1990)   Tom Hanks (Sherman McCoy), Bruce Willis (Peter Fallow), Melanie Griffith (Maria Ruskin). Based on Tom Wolfe's novel of the same name. *Dir.* Brian de Palma.

Bonnie and Clyde (1967)   Warren Beatty (Clyde Barrow), Faye Dunaway (Bonnie Parker), Gene Hackman (Buck), Estelle Parsons, Michael J Pollard, Gene Wilder. Estelle Parsons won Academy Award for Best Supporting Actress. *Dir.* Arthur Penn.

Boom! (1968)   Elizabeth Taylor, Richard Burton, Noël Coward. Based on Tennessee Williams's play *The*

Milk Train Doesn't Stop Here Anymore. Dir. Joseph Losey.

Born on the Fourth of July (1989)   Tom Cruise (Ron Kovic), Kyra Sedgwick (Donna), Willem Dafoe, Tom Berenger. *Dir.* Oliver Stone.

Box of Moonlight (1996)   John Turturro (Al Fountain), Sam Rockwell (The Kid). *Dir.* Tom DiCillo.

Boxing Helena (1993)   Julian Sands, Sherilyn Fenn, Bill Paxton, Art Garfunkel. Most memorable for Kim Basinger being sued for changing her mind over starring in it. Court ordered her to pay $8 million but studio settled for $3 million. *Dir.* Jennifer Chambers Lynch.

Boys Don't Cry (1999)   Peter Sarsgaard (John), Brendan Sexton III (Tom), Alison Folland (Kate). *Dir.* Kimberly Peirce

Boys from Brazil, The (1978)   Gregory Peck (Josef Mengele), Laurence Olivier, James Mason, Lilli Palmer. Based on the Ira Levin novel. *Dir.* Franklin Schaffner.

Brassed Off (1996)   Peter Postlethwaite (Danny), Tara Fitzgerald (Gloria), Ewan McGregor. *Dir.* Mark Herman.

Braveheart (1995)   Mel Gibson, Sophie Marceau, Patrick McGoohan, Ian Bannen. *Dir.* Mel Gibson.

Brazil (1985)   Jonathan Pryce, Robert De Niro, Michael Palin, Peter Vaughan, Bob Hoskins. *Dir.* Terry Gilliam.

Breaking the Waves (1996)   Emily Watson, Stellan Skarsgard, Katrin Cartlidge, Jean-Marc Barr. Award-winning film set in Scotland a concern a woman who humiliates herself in the hope of saving the life of her husband, paralysed in an oil rig accident. *Dir.* Lars von Trier.

Bridge on the River Kwai (1957)   Alec Guinness (Colonel Nicholson), Sessue Hayakawa (Colonel Saito), William Holden (Shears), Jack Hawkins (Major Warden). Based on the novel by Pierre Boulle. *Dir.* David Lean.

Bridges of Madison County (1995)   Clint Eastwood, Meryl Streep, Annie Corley. Written by Richard LaGravenese. *Dir.* Clint Eastwood.

Bridget Jones's Diary (2001)   Renée Zellweger, Hugh Grant, Colin Firth, Gemma Jones, Jim Broadbent. Cameo performances by Jeffrey Archer and Salman Rushdie. *Dir.* Sharon Maguire

Brief Encounter (1945)   Celia Johnson (Laura Jesson), Trevor Howard (Alec Harvey), Stanley Holloway, Joyce Carey. Based on a Noël Coward play, *Still Life*. The theme music was Rachmaninov's Piano Concerto No 2 and the railway station was Carnforth. *Dir.* David Lean.

Brigadoon (1954)   Gene Kelly, Cyd Charisse, Van Johnson. Scottish village awakens only once every hundred years. *Dir.* Vincente Minnelli.

Bringing Up Baby (1938)   Katharine Hepburn (Susan), Cary Grant (David Huxley), May Robson. The baby of the title was, in fact, a leopard. *Dir.* Howard Hawks.

Broken Arrow (1996)   John Travolta, Christian Slater, Samantha Mathis. *Dir.* John Woo.

Browning Version, The (1951)   Michael Redgrave, Jean Kent, Nigel Patrick, Wilfrid Hyde-White, Bill Travers. Based on Terence Rattigan's one-act play. *Dir.* Anthony Asquith.

Browning Version, The (1994)   Albert Finney, Greta Scacchi, Matthew Modine, Julian Sands, Michael Gambon. Ronald Howard's adaptation of Terence Rattigan play. *Dir.* Mike Figgis.

Brubaker (1980)   Robert Redford, Yaphet Kotto, Jane Alexander, Morgan Freeman, Murray Hamilton. Setting: Wakefield Prison Farm. *Dir.* Stuart Rosenberg.

Bugsy Malone (1976)   Scott Baio, Jodie Foster, Florrie Dugger. All the parts are played by children and the guns fire ice cream. *Dir.* Alan Parker.

Bullitt (1968)   Steve McQueen, Jacqueline Bisset, Robert Vaughan, Robert Duvall. Based on the novel *Mute Witness* by Robert L Pike. *Dir.* Peter Yates.

Burbs, The (1989)   Tom Hanks, Bruce Dern, Carrie Fisher, Corey Feldman. *Dir.* Joe Dante.

Buster (1988)   Phil Collins, Julie Walters (June Edwards), Larry Lamb, Stephanie Lawrence, Martin Jarvis. *Dir.* David Green.

Butch Cassidy and the Sundance Kid (1969)   Paul Newman, Robert Redford, Katharine Ross. 'Raindrops Keep Falling on My Head' won Oscar for Best Song. *Dir.* George Roy Hill.

Butterfield 8 (1960)   Elizabeth Taylor, Laurence Harvey, Eddie Fisher. Taylor won Best Actress Oscar for her role as a society call girl. The title *Butterfield 8* was her telephone number. *Dir.* Daniel Mann.

Cabaret (1972)   Liza Minnelli, Joel Grey, Michael York. Based on the novel *Goodbye to Berlin* by Christopher Isherwood and John Van Druten's play *I Am a Camera. Dir.* Bob Fosse.

Cabin in the Sky (1943)   Eddie 'Rochester' Anderson (Little Joe), Lena Horne (Georgia Brown), Ethel Waters (Petunia), Louis Armstrong. All black cast. *Dir.* Vincente Minnelli.

Cable Guy, The (1996)   Jim Carrey, Matthew Broderick, George Segal. *Dir.* Ben Stiller.

Cactus Jack (1979)   Kirk Douglas, Arnold Schwarzenegger, Ann-Margret. US Title: *The Villain. Dir.* Hal Needham.

Caesar and Cleopatra (1945)   Claude Rains, Vivien Leigh, Stewart Granger, Flora Robson. Britain's most expensive film to this date was based on George Bernard Shaw's comedy. *Dir.* Gabriel Pascal.

Caine Mutiny, The (1954)   Humphrey Bogart (Capt Queeg), José Ferrer (Lt Barney Greenwald), Van Johnson (Lt Steve Maryk), Fred MacMurray (Lt Tom Keefer), Lee Marvin (Meatball), Claude Akins (Horrible). Based on Herman Wouk's novel. *Dir.* Edward Dmytryk.

Calamity Jane (1953)   Doris Day, Howard Keel. Memorable for its opening rendition of 'The Deadwood Stage' and the Oscar-winning song 'Secret Love'. *Dir.* David Butler.

California Suite (1978)   Michael Caine, Maggie Smith, Walter Matthau, Alan Alda, Jane Fonda, Bill Cosby, Richard Pryor. Misadventures of 4 groups of guests at the Beverly Hills Hotel. *Dir.* Herbert Ross.

Caligula (1979)   Malcolm McDowell, John Gielgud, Peter O'Toole, Helen Mirren. *Dir.* Tinto Brass.

Callan (1974)   Edward Woodward, Eric Porter, Carl Mohner, Catherine Schell, Peter Egan, Russell Hunter. Aka: *The Neutralizer. Dir.* Don Sharp.

Camille (1936)   Greta Garbo (Marguerite Gautier), Robert Taylor (Armand Duval), Lionel Barrymore, Henry Daniell. Based on Alexandre Dumas' novel. *Dir.* George Cukor.

Candyman (1992)   Virginia Madsen, Tony Todd, Xander Berkeley, Vanessa Williams. Story of a mythical hook-handed serial killer which had an unsuccessful 1995 sequel *Candyman: Farewell to the Flesh. Dir.* Bernard Rose.

Cape Fear (1991)   Robert De Niro (Max Cady), Nick Nolte (Sam Bowden), Jessica Lange (Leigh Bowden), Robert Mitchum (Lt Elgart), Gregory Peck (Lee Heller). Notable for cameo roles of Mitchum, Peck and Martin Balsam, who were all in original 1962 film. *Dir.* Martin Scorsese.

Captain America (1944)   Dick Purcell, Lionel Atwill, Lorna Gray. District Attorney in guise of Capt America battles The Scarab (in guise of a museum curator). *Dir.* John English.

Captain America (1989)   Matt Salinger, Ronny Cox, Ned Beatty, Bill Mumy. Captain America is freed from his deep-ice captivity to battle arch-enemy The Red Skull. *Dir.* Albert Pyun.

Captain Corelli's Mandolin (2001)   Nicholas Cage (Corelli), Penelope Cruz, John Hurt, Christian Bale, David Morrissey. *Dir.* John Madden.

Captains Courageous (1937)   Spencer Tracy, Lionel Barrymore, Freddie Bartholomew, Mickey Rooney. Spoiled rich boy falls off a cruise liner and lives for a while among fisherfolk. *Dir.* Victor Fleming.

Caravaggio (1986)   Nigel Terry, Sean Bean, Tilda Swinton, Robbie Coltrane. *Dir.* Derek Jarman.

Caretaker, The (1964)   Alan Bates, Robert Shaw, Donald Pleasence. Based on Pinter's play about 2 men who invite a tramp to share their attic. US Title: *The Guest. Dir.* Clive Donner.

Carnal Knowledge (1971)   Jack Nicholson, Art Garfunkel, Candice Bergen, Ann-Margret, Rita Moreno. *Dir.* Mike Nichols.

Carousel (1956)   Gordon Macrae, Shirley Jones, Cameron Mitchell. *Dir.* Henry King.

Carpetbaggers, The (1964)   George Peppard, Alan Ladd, Carroll Baker, Martin Balsam, Elizabeth Ashley, Lew Ayres, Archie Moore, Leif Erickson. *Dir.* Edward Dmytryk.

Carrie (1952)   Laurence Olivier, Jennifer Jones, Eddie Albert. Based on Theodore Dreiser's novel *Sister Carrie. Dir.* William Wyler.

Carrie (1976)   Sissy Spacek, Piper Laurie, Amy Irving, John Travolta. Based on the Stephen King novel. *Dir.* Brian De Palma.

Carrington (1995)   Emma Thompson (Carrington), Jonathan Pryce (Strachey), Janet McTeer (Vanessa Bell). Based on Lytton Strachey's book. *Dir.* Christopher Hampton.

Carry On Columbus (1992)   Jim Dale (Chris Columbus), Bernard Cribbins (Mort), Maureen Lipman (Countess Esmerelda), Alexei Sayle, Julian Clary, Rik Mayall. Last of the series of Carry Ons. *Dir.* Gerald Thomas.

Carry On Sergeant (1958)   Bob Monkhouse, William Hartnell, Kenneth Williams, Charles Hawtrey, Shirley Eaton, Kenneth Connor. First of the series of 30 *Carry Ons. Dir.* Gerald Thomas.

Carve Her Name With Pride (1958)   Virginia McKenna (Violette Szabo), Paul Scofield, Jack Warner, Sydney Tafler. Based on RJ Minney's book about young British WW2 spy shot by a German firing squad. *Dir.* Lewis Gilbert.

Casablanca (1942)   Humphrey Bogart (Rick Blaine), Ingrid Bergman (Ilse Lund), Paul Henreid (Victor Laszlo), Claude Rains (Captain Louis Renault), Sydney Greenstreet (Ferrari), Peter Lorre (Ugarte), Conrad Veidt (Major Strasser), Dooley Wilson (Sam). Closing line, 'Louis, I think this is the beginning of a beautiful friendship.' Ronald Reagan and Ann Sheridan were originally cast as the leads. *Dir.* Michael Curtiz.

Casanova (1976)   Donald Sutherland, Tina Aumont, Cicely Browne. Aka Fellini's Casanova. *Dir.* Federico Fellini.

Casino (1995)   Sharon Stone, Robert De Niro, Joe Pesci, James Woods. *Dir.* Martin Scorsese.

Casino Royale (1967)   David Niven, Deborah Kerr, Orson Welles, Peter Sellers, Ursula Andress, Woody Allen, William Holden, Charles Boyer, Jean-Paul Belmondo, Peter O'Toole, John Huston, George Raft. Sir James Bond is called out of retirement to tackle the power of 'SMERSH'. Joe McGrath was

C
I
N
E
M
A

originally the sole director but was fired after Sellers walked out and Huston, Ken Hughes, Robert Parrish, Val Guest and Richard Talmadge finished the film. This was the first James Bond book but clearly not the first film. *Dir.* John Huston & others.

Cassandra Crossing, The (1976)   Sophia Loren, Richard Harris, Ava Gardner, Burt Lancaster, Martin Sheen, OJ Simpson. *Dir.* George Pan Cosmatos.

Cast a Dark Shadow (1955)   Dirk Bogarde, Margaret Lockwood. Wife-murderer marries an ex-barmaid and tries again. *Dir.* Lewis Gilbert.

Cast a Giant Shadow (1966)   Kirk Douglas, Angie Dickinson, Chaim Topol, John Wayne, Frank Sinatra, Yul Brynner, Gordon Jackson, Jeremy Kemp, Michael Hordern. Biopic of Colonel David Marcus's fight against the Arabs in the Israel of 1947. *Dir.* Melville Shavelson.

Castaway (1987)   Oliver Reed (Gerald Kingsland), Amanda Donohue, Georgina Hale, John Sessions. Based on Lucy Irvine's autobiographical book. *Dir.* Nicolas Roeg.

Casualties of War (1989)   Michael J Fox (Eriksson), Sean Penn (Sgt Meserve). Story of the gang rape of a Vietnamese girl. *Dir.* Brian De Palma.

Cat and the Canary, The (1939)   Bob Hope (Wally Campbell), Paulette Goddard (Joyce Norman), Gale Sondergaard (Miss Lu). *Dir.* Elliott Nugent.

Cat Ballou (1965)   Jane Fonda, Lee Marvin, Nat King Cole, Stubby Kaye. Oscar-winning performances by Lee Marvin as twin brothers. *Dir.* Elliot Silverstein.

Cat on a Hot Tin Roof (1958)   Paul Newman (Brick), Burl Ives (Big Daddy), Elizabeth Taylor (Maggie). Based on the play by Tennessee Williams. *Dir.* Richard Brooks.

Cat People (1942)   Simone Simon, Tom Conway, Kent Smith. Yugoslavian girl believes she can turn into a panther and deaths follow, although the monster is never seen. *Dir.* Jacques Tourneur.

Cat People (1982)   Nastassja Kinski, Malcolm McDowell. Kinky version of the 1942 classic. *Dir.* Paul Schrader.

Catch My Soul (1973)   Richie Havens, Lance LeGault, Season Hubley, Tony Joe White. Rock and country musical version of *Othello*. *Dir.* Patrick McGoohan.

Catch 22 (1970)   Alan Arkin (Yossarian), Martin Balsam, Richard Benjamin, Art Garfunkel, Bob Newhart, Orson Welles, Martin Sheen, Jon Voight, Anthony Perkins. Based on Joseph Heller's novel. *Dir.* Mike Nichols.

Catholic Boys (1985)   Donald Sutherland (Brother Thadeus), John Heard (Brother Timothy). Originally called: *Heaven Help Us*. *Dir.* Michael Dinner.

Celebrity (1998)   Kenneth Branagh, Hank Azaria, Judy Davis, Leonardo DiCaprio, Melanie Griffith, Winona Ryder. *Dir.* Woody Allen.

Celia (1989)   Rebecca Smart (Celia), Nicholas Eadie (Ray). *Dir.* Ann Turner.

Cemetery Man (1994)   Rupert Everett, Francois Hadji-Lazaro, Anna Falci. *Dir.* Michele Soavi.

Central Station (1998)   Fernanda Montenegro, Marilia Pera, Vinicius de Oliveira, Soia Lira, Othon Bastos. *Dir.* Walter Salles.

Chain Reaction (1996). Keanu Reeves, Morgan Freeman, Rachel Weisz. *Dir.* Andrew Davis.

Chamber, The (1996)   Gene Hackman (Sam Cayhall), Chris O'Donnell (Adam Hall), Faye Dunaway. *Dir.* James Foley.

Champ, The (1931)   Wallace Beery, Jackie Cooper. Frances Marion won Oscar for Best Original Story. *Dir.* King Vidor.

Champ, The (1979)   Jon Voight, Faye Dunaway, Ricky

Schroeder. Remake of the 1931 classic. *Dir.* Franco Zeffirelli.

Champions (1983)   John Hurt (Bob Champion), Edward Woodward (Josh Gifford). Story of a jockey's fight against cancer and his subsequent Grand National success in 1981. *Dir.* John Irvin.

Chance of a Lifetime (1950)   Bernard Miles, Kenneth More, Hattie Jacques. *Dir.* Bernard Miles.

Chaplin (1992)   Robert Downey Jnr, Dan Aykroyd (Mack Sennett), Geraldine Chaplin (Hannah Chaplin), Kevin Dunn (J Edgar Hoover), Kevin Kline (Douglas Fairbanks), John Thaw (Fred Karno), Marisa Tomei (Mabel Normand). *Dir.* Richard Attenborough.

Chariots of Fire (1981)   Ben Cross (Harold Abrahams), Ian Charleson (Eric Liddell), Nigel Havers. Oscars include: Best Film, Costume Design, Music and Script (Colin Welland). *Dir.* Hugh Hudson.

Charley Varrick (1973)   Walter Matthau, Joe Don Baker. Story of a bank robber who discovers he has stolen mafia money. *Dir.* Don Siegel.

Charley's Aunt (1941)   Jack Benny, Kay Francis, Anne Baxter, Laird Cregar. Based on play by Brandon Thomas. *Dir.* Archie Mayo.

Charlie Chan (Series)   Warner Oland (1931–37), Sidney Toler (1938–1947), Roland Winters (1947–49). Based on Earl Derr Biggers's character. *Dir.* Various.

Che! (1969)   Omar Sharif (Che Guevara), Jack Palance (Castro). *Dir.* Richard Fleischer.

Cheech and Chong's Next Movie (1980)   Cheech Marin, Thomas Chong, Evelyn Guerrero. GB Title: *High Encounters of the Ultimate Kind. Dir.* Thomas Chong.

Cheyenne Autumn (1964)   Richard Widmark, Carroll Baker, Karl Malden, Dolores del Rio, Sal Mineo, Edward G Robinson, James Stewart (Wyatt Earp). *Dir.* John Ford.

Chicago Joe and the Showgirl (1990)   Kiefer Sutherland (Ricky Allen), Emily Lloyd (Georgina Grayson), Patsy Kensit (Joyce Cook). *Dir.* Bernard Rose.

Children of a Lesser God (1986)   William Hurt (James), Marlee Matlin (Sarah), Piper Laurie (Mrs Norman). Deaf woman falls in love with her speech therapist. *Dir.* Randa Haines.

Child's Play (1988)   Catherine Hicks (Karen Barclay), Chris Sarandon (Mike Norris). Dying killer Brad Dourif's soul passes into a Chucky Doll. *Dir.* Tom Holland.

China Syndrome, The (1979)   Jane Fonda, Jack Lemmon, Michael Douglas. *Dir.* James Bridges.

Chinatown (1974)   Jack Nicholson, Faye Dunaway, John Huston, Roman Polanski, Diane Ladd. *Dir.* Roman Polanski.

Chitty Chitty Bang Bang (1968)   Dick Van Dyke, Sally Ann Howes (Truly Scrumptious), Lionel Jeffries, Benny Hill, Robert Helpmann, Gert Frobe, James Robertson Justice. Roald Dahl adapted the original Ian Fleming story. *Dir.* Ken Hughes.

Chorus Line, A (1985)   Michael Douglas (Zach), Alyson Reed (Cassie), Terrence Mann (Larry). *Dir.* Richard Attenborough.

Chorus of Disapproval (1989)   Anthony Hopkins (Dafydd Ap Llewellyn), Jeremy Irons (Guy Jones), Prunella Scales (Hannah), Jenny Seagrove (Fay Hubbard). *Dir.* Michael Winner.

Christopher Columbus: The Discovery (1992)   Marlon Brando (Torquemada), Tom Selleck (King Ferdinand), Georges Corraface (Columbus), Rachel Ward (Queen Isabella), Catherine Zeta Jones (Beatriz). *Dir.* John Glen.

Cincinnati Kid, The (1965)   Steve McQueen, Edward G Robinson, Karl Malden, Ann-Margret, Tuesday Weld. Based on Richard Jessup's novel concerning battle for supremacy among stud poker experts. *Dir.* Norman Jewison.

Citadel, The (1938)   Robert Donat, Rosalind Russell, Ralph Richardson, Rex Harrison. Based on AJ Cronin's novel, which also spawned the TV series *Dr Finlay's Casebook*. *Dir.* King Vidor.

Citizen Kane (1941)   Orson Welles (Kane), Joseph Cotten (Jedediah Leland), Agnes Moorehead (Kane's mother). Based loosely on the newspaper magnate William Randolph Hearst. Welles also co-wrote the script with Herman J Mankiewicz. *Dir.* Orson Welles.

City Hall (1996)   Al Pacino, John Cusack, Bridget Fonda, Danny Aiello. *Dir.* Harold Becker.

City Heat (1984)   Clint Eastwood (Lt Speer), Burt Reynolds (Mike Murphy), Madeline Kahn (Caroline Howley). Reynolds broke his jaw when a prop chair turned out to be a real one!. *Dir.* Richard Benjamin.

City of Industry (1997)   Harvey Keitel, Stephen Dorff, Timothy Hutton. *Dir.* John Irvin.

City Slickers (1991)   Billy Crystal (Mitch Robbins), Daniel Stern (Phil Berquist), Jack Palance (Curly). Oscar for Jack Palance as Best Supporting Actor. *Dir.* Ron Underwood.

Class Act (1992)   Christopher Reid, Christopher Martin, Karyn Parsons. Two students swop identities. *Dir.* Randall Miller.

Class Action (1991)   Gene Hackman, Mary Elizabeth Mastrantonio, Colin Friels. Father and daughter, both lawyers, find themselves on opposing sides in the courtroom. *Dir.* Michael Apted.

Cleopatra (1934)   Claudette Colbert, Henry Wilcoxon (Antony), Warren William (Caesar). *Dir.* Cecil B de Mille.

Cleopatra (1963)   Elizabeth Taylor, Richard Burton, Rex Harrison. *Dir.* Joseph L Mankiewicz.

Clockers (1995)   Harvey Keitel, John Turturro, Delroy Lindo, Mekhi Phifer, Pee Wee Love, Sticky Fingaz. A clocker is a small-time crack dealer working on the streets. *Dir.* Spike Lee.

Clockwise (1986)   John Cleese (Timpson), Alison Steadman (Gwenda), Penelope Wilton (Pat Garden). *Dir.* Christopher Morahan.

Clockwork Orange, A (1971)   Malcolm McDowell, Adrienne Corri, Patrick Magee, Michael Bates, Warren Clarke. Based on Anthony Burgess's novel. *Dir.* Stanley Kubrick.

Close Encounters of the Third Kind (1977)   Richard Dreyfuss, François Truffaut, Teri Garr. *Dir.* Steven Spielberg.

Coal Miner's Daughter (1980)   Sissy Spacek (Loretta Lynn), Tommy Lee Jones. *Dir.* Michael Apted.

Cocktail (1988)   Tom Cruise (Brian Flanagan), Bryan Brown (Doug Coughlin), Elizabeth Shue (Jordan Mooney). *Dir.* Roger Donaldson.

Cocoanuts, The (1929)   Four Marx Brothers, Margaret Dumont. First of the Marx Brothers films. *Dir.* Robert Florey and Joseph Santley.

Cocoon (1985)   Don Ameche (Art Selwyn), Steve Guttenberg (Jack Bonner), Jessica Tandy (Alma Finley), Tahnee Welch, (Kitty). There was a 1988 sequel *Cocoon: The Return*. *Dir.* Ron Howard.

Cold Comfort Farm (1995)   Kate Beckinsale (Flora Poste), Joanna Lumley, Stephen Fry, Eileen Atkins, Ian McKellen. *Dir.* John Schlesinger.

Color of Money, The (1986)   Paul Newman (Eddie Felson), Tom Cruise (Vincent), Mary Elizabeth Mastrantonio (Carmen).Sequel to *The Hustler*. *Dir.* Martin Scorsese.

Color of Night (1994)   Bruce Willis, Jane March, Ruben Blades, Lesley Ann Warren, Scott Bakula. Psychiatrist takes over a group that includes the person who murdered a colleague. *Dir.* Richard Rush.

Color Purple, The (1985)   Whoopi Goldberg (Celie), Danny Glover (Albert Johnson) Oprah Winfrey (Sofia), Willard Pugh (Harpo). Based on the novel by Alice Walker. *Dir.* Steven Spielberg.

Comfort and Joy (1984)   Bill Paterson (Alan), Eleanor David (Maddy), CP Grogan (Charlotte). Ice cream empires are called 'Mr McCool' and 'Mr Bunny' and the music is by Mark Knopfler. *Dir.* Bill Forsyth.

Coming Home (1978)   Jane Fonda, Jon Voight, Bruce Dern. *Dir.* Hal Ashby.

Commitments, The (1991)   Robert Arkins (Jimmy Rabbitte), Andrew Strong (Deco Cuffe), Michael Aherne (Steve Clifford). Story of a Dublin soul band. *Dir.* Alan Parker.

Con Air (1997)   Nicolas Cage, John Cusack, John Malkovich. *Dir.* Simon West.

Conspiracy Theory (1997)   Mel Gibson (Jerry Fletcher), Julia Roberts (Alice Sutton)

Contact (1997)   Jodie Foster (Ellie). Based on Carl Sagan's book. *Dir.* Robert Zemeckis.

Cook, the Thief, His Wife and Her Lover, The (1989)   Richard Bohringer (Richard the Cook), Michael Gambon (Albert the Thief), Helen Mirren (Georgina, His Wife), Alan Howard (Michael, Her Lover). *Dir.* Peter Greenaway.

Cool Hand Luke (1967)   Paul Newman (Lucas Jackson), George Kennedy, Jo Van Fleet. Luke was imprisoned for sawing off a parking meter. Famous scene where Luke swallows 50 eggs in an hour. *Dir.* Stuart Rosenberg.

Cotton Club, The (1984)   Richard Gere (Dixie Dwyer), Gregory Hines (Sandman Williams), Bob Hoskins (Owney Madden), Nicolas Cage (Vincent Dwyer). *Dir.* Francis Ford Coppola.

Courage under Fire (1996)   Denzel Washington (Colonel Serling), Meg Ryan (Captain Karen Walden). *Dir.* Edward Zwick.

Courtneys of Curzon Street, The (1947)   Anna Neagle, Michael Wilding, Michael Medwin. *Dir.* Herbert Wilcox.

Cousins (1989)   Ted Danson (Larry Kozinski), Isabella Rossellini (Maria Hardy), Sean Young (Tish Kozinski), Lloyd Bridges (Uncle Vince). *Dir.* Joel Schumacher.

Cowboy Way, The (1994)   Woody Harrelson, Kiefer Sutherland, Ernie Hudson. *Dir.* Gregg Champion.

Craft, The (1996)   Robin Tunney, Fairuza Balk. *Dir.* Andrew Fleming.

Crash (1996)   James Spader (James), Deborah Unger (Catherine), Holly Hunter (Helen). *Dir.* David Cronenberg.

Crimes and Misdemeanors (1989)   Caroline Aaron (Barbara), Alan Alda (Lester), Woody Allen (Cliff Stern), Claire Bloom (Miriam Rosenthal), Mia Farrow (Halley Reed), Anjelica Huston (Dolores Paley). *Dir.* Woody Allen.

Crimes of the Heart (1986)   Diane Keaton (Lenny Magrath), Jessica Lange (Meg), Sissy Spacek (Babe). Three kooky sisters argue about which one of them is going to go completely mad, first. *Dir.* Bruce Beresford.

Critters (1986)   Dee Wallace Stone, M Emmet Walsh, Billy Green Bush. Hair-ball creatures arrive from an asteroid and devastate Kansas. *Dir.* Stephen Herek.

Crocodile Dundee (1986)   Paul Hogan (Mick Dundee), Linda Kozlowski (Sue Charlton), John

Meillon (Wally Reilly). As so often the case with sequels, *Crocodile Dundee II* was not as big a hit. *Dir.* Peter Faiman.

Cromwell (1970)   Richard Harris, Alec Guinness, Frank Finlay, Robert Morley. *Dir.* Ken Hughes.

Crossing Guard, The (1995)   Jack Nicholson, David Morse, Anjelica Huston, Piper Laurie. Alcoholic jeweller plans to kill the man who killed his daughter in a drink driving incident. *Dir.* Sean Penn.

Crouching Tiger, Hidden Dragon (1999)   Nichelle Khan, Chang Chen, Zhang Ziyi, Chow Yun-Fat. *Dir.* Ang Lee

Crow, The (1994)   Brandon Lee, Ernie Hudson, Michael Wincott. Brandon Lee died in a shooting accident during filming. *Dir.* Alex Proyas.

Cruel Sea, The (1953)   Jack Hawkins, Donald Sinden, Stanley Baker. Eric Ambler adapted the novel of Nicholas Monsarrat. *Dir.* Charles Frend.

Crumb (1994)   Robert Crumb, Charles Crumb, Maxon Crumb, Dana Crumb, Beatrice Crumb, Aline Kominsky. Documentary about the creator of Fritz the Cat and Mr Natural. *Dir.* Terry Zwigoff.

Cry Freedom (1987)   Kevin Kline (Donald Woods), Denzel Washington (Steve Biko). *Dir.* Richard Attenborough.

Cry in the Dark, A (1988)   Meryl Streep (Lindy Chamberlain), Sam Neill (Michael). True story of a mother, convicted of killing her baby, who maintained a dingo had run off with it. *Dir.* Fred Schepisi.

Crying Freeman (1995)   Mark Dacascos, Julie Condra (Emu O'Hara). *Dir.* Christophe Gans.

Crying Game, The (1992)   Stephen Rea (Fergus), Miranda Richardson (Jude), Forest Whitaker (Jody). *Dir.* Neil Jordan.

Curse of the Pink Panther, The (1983)   David Niven (Sir Charles Litton), Robert Wagner (George Litton), Herbert Lom (Dreyfus), Joanna Lumley (Chandra), Capucine (Lady Litton). David Niven's voice was dubbed by Rich Little. *Dir.* Blake Edwards.

Cutthroat Island (1995)   Geena Davis (Morgan), Matthew Modine (William Shaw), Frank Langella. *Dir.* Renny Harlin.

Cyrano de Bergerac (1990)   Gérard Depardieu, Anne Brochet, Vincent Perez. *Dir.* Jean-Paul Rappeneau.

Daddy Longlegs (1931)   Janet Gaynor, Warner Baxter. Orphan girl grows up to fall in love with a mysterious benefactor. *Dir.* Alfred Santell.

Daddy Longlegs (1955)   Fred Astaire, Leslie Caron, Fred Clark. Musical remake of the 1931 film. *Dir.* Jean Negulesco.

Daleks: Invasion Earth 2150 AD (1966)   Peter Cushing, Bernard Cribbins. *Dir.* Gordon Flemyng.

Dam Busters, The (1954)   Michael Redgrave (Barnes Wallis), Richard Todd (Guy Gibson). *Dir.* Michael Anderson.

Damien: Omen Two (1978)   William Holden, Lee Grant, Jonathan Scott-Taylor, Sylvia Sidney. *Dir.* Don Taylor.

Dance with a Stranger (1985)   Miranda Richardson (Ruth Ellis), Rupert Everett (David Blakely), Ian Holm, Stratford Johns. *Dir.* Mike Newell.

Dances with Wolves (1990)   Kevin Costner (Lt John J Dunbar), Mary McDonnell (Stands With a Fist), Graham Greene (Kicking Bird). *Dir.* Kevin Costner.

Dangerous Ground (1997)   Elizabeth Hurley, Ice Cube. *Dir.* Darrell James Roodt.

Dangerous Liaisons (1988)   Glenn Close (Marquise de Merteuil), John Malkovich (Vicomte de Valmont), Michelle Pfeiffer (Madame de Tourvel), Keanu Reeves (Chevalier Danceny), Uma Thurman (Cecile de Volanges). *Dir.* Stephen Frears.

Danny the Champion of the World (1989)   Jeremy Irons (William Smith), Samuel Irons (Danny), Robbie Coltrane (Victor Hazell). Based on a Roald Dahl book. *Dir.* Gavin Millar.

Dante's Peak (1997)   Pierce Brosnan, Linda Hamilton. *Dir.* Roger Donaldson.

Darkman (1990)   Liam Neeson (Peyton Westlake / Darkman). Scientist left for dead by thugs re-emerges as Darkman. *Dir.* Sam Raimi.

Darling (1965)   Julie Christie, Dirk Bogarde, Laurence Harvey. *Dir.* John Schlesinger.

Dave (1993)   Kevin Kline, Sigourney Weaver, Frank Langella, Ben Kingsley. US President suffers a stroke and a Baltimore businessman is hired to impersonate him. *Dir.* Ivan Reitman.

David Copperfield (1934)   Freddie Bartholemew (young David), Frank Lawton (David as a man), WC Fields (Micawber). Charles Laughton was original choice for Micawber but resigned after 2 days. *Dir.* George Cukor.

Day at the Races, A (1937)   First of the high-budget Marx Brothers films. *Dir.* Sam Wood.

Day of the Beast (1995)   Alex Angulo, Armando de Razza, Santiago Segura. Priest attempts to track down the Anti-Christ who is to be born in Madrid. *Dir.* Alex de la Iglesia.

Day of the Jackal, The (1973)   Edward Fox, Michael Lonsdale, Alan Badel, Eric Porter. *Dir.* Fred Zinnemann.

Day of the Triffids, The (1962)   Howard Keel, Kieron Moore, Janette Scott, Nicole Maurey. *Dir.* Steve Sekely.

Daylight (1996)   Sylvester Stallone, Amy Brenneman, Viggo Mortensen, Karen Young, Claire Bloom. Diverse group of people are trapped in Manhattan's Holland Tunnel. *Dir.* Rob Cohen.

Days of Thunder (1990)   Tom Cruise (Cole Trickle), Robert Duvall (Harry Hogge), Nicole Kidman (Dr Claire Lewicki). *Dir.* Tony Scott.

Dead Again (1991)   Kenneth Branagh (Roman Strauss / Mike), Andy Garcia (Gray Baker), Derek Jacobi (Franklyn Madson), Emma Thompson (Margaret Strauss / Grace). *Dir.* Kenneth Branagh.

Dead Calm (1989)   Sam Neill (John Ingram), Nicole Kidman (Rae Ingram), Billy Zane (Hughie Warriner). *Dir.* Phillip Noyce.

Dead Man Walking (1995)   Susan Sarandon (Sister Helen Prejean), Sean Penn (Matthew Poncelet). *Dir.* Tim Robbins.

Dead Men Don't Wear Plaid (1982)   Steve Martin, Rachel Ward, Carl Reiner, Reni Santoni. Bogart, Ladd, Bacall, Stanwyck also appear in film-clip editing. *Dir.* Carl Reiner.

Dead Poets Society (1989)   Robin Williams (John Keating), Robert Sean Leonard, Ethan Hawke, Josh Charles. Keating's motto: 'Carpe Diem (Seize the Day)'. *Dir.* Peter Weir.

Dead Pool, The (1988)   Clint Eastwood (Harry Callahan), Patricia Clarkson, Liam Neeson, Evan C. Kim. Famous scene of a car chase involving a toy car. Jim Carrey has small part as a murder victim. *Dir.* Buddy van Horn.

Dead Ringers (1988)   Jeremy Irons (Beverly / Elliot Mantle), Geneviève Bujold (Claire Niveau). Concerns identical twins, gynaecologists. *Dir.* David Cronenberg.

Dealers (1989)   Paul McGann (Daniel Pasco), Rebecca DeMornay (Anna Schuman), Derrick O'Connor (Robby Barrell). TV series *Capital City* was a spin-off. *Dir.* Colin Bucksey.

Dear Diary (1994)   Jennifer Beals, Nanni Moretti, Alexandre Rockwell. *Dir.* Nanni Moretti.

Death in Venice (1971) Dirk Bogarde, Bjorn Andresen, Silvana Mangano Gustav Mahler's music is memorable. *Dir.* Luchino Visconti.

Death of a Salesman (1985) Dustin Hoffman (Willy Loman), Charles Durning (Charley), Kate Reid (Linda), Stephen Lang (Happy), John Malkovich. Screenplay: Arthur Miller. Film was made for cable TV. *Dir.* Volker Schlondorff.

Death on the Nile (1978) Peter Ustinov, Bette Davis, Mia Farrow, David Niven, Maggie Smith. Agatha Christie novel with Hercule Poirot. *Dir.* John Guillermin.

Death Race 2000 (1975) David Carradine, Simone Griffeth, Sylvester Stallone. *Dir.* Paul Bartel.

Death Wish (1974) Charles Bronson, Hope Lange, Vincent Gardenia. Four follow-on films – 1981, 1985, 1987 – similar plots. *Dir.* Michael Winner.

Deathtrap (1982) Michael Caine, Christopher Reeve, Dyan Cannon. From the play by Ira Levin. *Dir.* Sidney Lumet.

Deepstar Six (1989) Taurean Blacque, Nancy Everhard, Greg Evigan. Underwater thriller. *Dir.* Sean Cunningham.

Deer Hunter, The (1978) Robert De Niro, John Savage, Christopher Walken, Meryl Streep. Vietnam thriller that won 3 Oscars. *Dir.* Michael Cimino.

Defence of the Realm (1985) Gabriel Byrne (Nick Mullen), Greta Scacchi (Nina Beckman), Denholm Elliott (Vernon Bayliss), Robbie Coltrane (Leo McAskey). *Dir.* David Drury.

Defiant Ones, The (1958) Tony Curtis, Sidney Poitier, Theodore Bikel, Lon Chaney Jnr. Prison escape drama, with black and white prisoners chained together, that won 3 Oscars. *Dir.* Stanley Kramer.

Delinquents, The (1989) Notable only being Kylie Minogue's debut feature. *Dir.* Chris Thomson.

Deliverance (1972) Burt Reynolds, Jon Voight, Ned Beatty. From James Dickey's novel. *Dir.* John Boorman.

Demolition Man (1993) Sylvester Stallone (John Spartan), Wesley Snipes (Simon Phoenix), Lori Petty, Nigel Hawthorne, Melinda Dillon. Futuristic thriller with Stallone as former cop released from suspended animation. *Dir.* Marco Brambilla.

Dennis the Menace (1993) Walter Matthau, Mason Gamble, Joan Plowright, Christopher Lloyd, Lea Thompson. Story of the 6-yr-old menace. *Dir.* Nick Castle.

Desert Fox, The (1951) James Mason, Jessica Tandy, Cedric Hardwicke. Biography of Erwin Rommel. *Dir.* Henry Hathaway.

Desert Rats, The (1953) James Mason (Rommel), Richard Burton, Robert Newton. *Dir.* Robert Wise.

Desperado (1995) Antonio Banderas, Salma Hayek, Joaquin de Almeida, Cheech Marin, Quentin Tarantino. Man with guitar case full of weapons walks into a Mexican town and starts shooting. *Dir.* Robert Rodriguez.

Desperate Hours (1990) Mickey Rourke (Michael Bosworth), Anthony Hopkins (Tim Cornell), Mimi Rogers (Nora). *Dir.* Michael Cimino.

Desperate Measures (1998) Michael Keaton, Andy Garcia. Detective Frank Connor is forced to choose between his badge and his son. *Dir.* Barbet Schroeder.

Desperately Seeking Susan (1985) Madonna, Aidan Quinn, Rosanna Arquette. Madonna's first starring role. *Dir.* Susan Seidelman.

Destiny Turns on the Radio (1995) James LeGros, Dylan McDermott, Quentin Tarantino, James Belushi,

Nancy Travis. Bank robber gets out of jail and travels to Las Vegas to reclaim his loot. *Dir.* Jack Baran.

Devil Rides Out, The (1968) Christopher Lee, Charles Gray, Patrick Mower. From Dennis Wheatley's novel. *Dir.* Terence Fisher.

Devils, The (1970) Vanessa Redgrave, Oliver Reed, Dudley Sutton, Gemma Jones. *Dir.* Ken Russell.

Devil's Own, The (1997) Harrison Ford (Tom O'Meara), Brad Pitt (Frankie McGuire). *Dir.* Alan J Pakula.

Diabolique (1996) Sharon Stone, Isabelle Adjani, Kathy Bates. Wife and mistress of unpleasant schoolmaster conspire to murder him. *Dir.* Jeremiah Chechnik.

Dial M for Murder (1954) Ray Milland, Grace Kelly, Robert Cummings. Shot in 3D but never released in 3D form. *Dir.* Alfred Hitchcock.

Diamonds are Forever (1971) Sean Connery, Charles Gray (Blofeld), Jill St John (Tiffany Case), Lana Wood (Plenty O'Toole). Theme song sung by Shirley Bassey. *Dir.* Guy Hamilton.

Dick Tracy (1990) Warren Beatty, Madonna (Breathless Mahoney), Dick Van Dyke, Al Pacino (Big Boy Caprice), Dustin Hoffman (Mumbles), Charlie Korsmo (Kid), Kathy Bates (Mrs Green), James Caan (Spaldini). Won 3 Oscars. *Dir.* Warren Beatty.

Die Hard (1988) Bruce Willis (John McClane), Bonnie Bedelia (Holly Gennaro McClane), Alan Rickman (Hans Gruber). 3 sequels followed. *Dir.* John McTiernan.

Diner (1982) Steve Guttenberg (Eddie), Daniel Stern (Shrevie), Mickey Rourke (Boogie), Kevin Bacon (Fenwick), Ellen Barkin (Beth), Timothy Daly (Billy). Five men on verge of manhood hang out at Fells Point Diner. *Dir.* Barry Levinson.

Dirty Dancing (1987) Patrick Swayze (Johnny Castle), Jennifer Grey (Baby Houseman). Variant on *Saturday Night Fever. Dir.* Emile Ardolino.

Dirty Dingus Magee (1970) Frank Sinatra, George Kennedy. Western comedy. *Dir.* Burt Kennedy.

Dirty Dozen, The (1967) Lee Marvin, Robert Ryan, Charles Bronson, Telly Savalas, Ernest Borgnine, Jim Brown, John Cassavetes, George Kennedy, Richard Jaeckel, Trini Lopez, Ralph Meeker, Clint Walker, Donald Sutherland. *Dir.* Robert Aldrich.

Dirty Mary, Crazy Larry (1974) Peter Fonda, Susan George, Roddy McDowall (uncredited). *Dir.* John Hough.

Dirty Rotten Scoundrels (1988) Steve Martin (Freddie Benson), Michael Caine (Lawrence Jamieson). Remake of *Bedtime Story* (1964) *Dir.* Frank Oz.

Distinguished Gentleman, The (1992) Eddie Murphy (Thomas Jefferson Johnson), Lane Smith (Dick Dodge), James Garner. *Dir.* Jonathan Lynn.

DOA (1950) Edmond O'Brien, Pamela Britton, Neville Brand, Luther Adler. Title stands for 'Dead on Arrival' and concerns a professor, who has been poisoned by a slow-acting drug, in a race against time to track down his 'murderer'. *Dir.* Rudolph Maté.

DOA (1988) Dennis Quaid (Dexter Cornell), Meg Ryan (Sydney Fuller), Charlotte Rampling (Mrs Fitzwaring). Remake of the 1950 classic. *Dir.* Rocky Morton and Annabel Jankel.

Doc Hollywood (1991) Michael J Fox (Dr Benjamin Stone), Julie Warner (Lou), Bridget Fonda (Nancy Lee), George Hamilton (Dr Halberstrom). Famous scene of Warner urinating to throw hunters off their prey's scent. *Dir.* Michael Caton-Jones.

Doctor and the Devils (1986)   Timothy Dalton (Dr Thomas Rock), Jonathan Pryce (Robert Fallon), Twiggy (Jenny Bailey), Beryl Reid, TP McKenna, Patrick Stewart. Screenplay by Dylan Thomas. *Dir.* Freddie Francis.

Dr Doolittle (1967)   Rex Harrison, Anthony Newley, Samantha Eggar, Richard Attenborough. Oscars for Best Song ('Talk to the Animals') and Special Effects. LB Abbott. *Dir.* Richard Fleischer.

Doctor in the House (1954)   Dirk Bogarde, Kenneth More, Kay Kendall, Donald Sinden. First of many *Doctor* stories, followed by TV series. *Dir.* Ralph Thomas.

Doctor No (1962)   Sean Connery, Ursula Andress (Honeychile Rider), Joseph Wiseman (Dr No), Jack Lord. First of the James Bond stories to be filmed (James Bond theme by Monty Norman). *Dir.* Terence Young.

Dr Strangelove (1963)   Peter Sellers, George C Scott. Black comedy Peter Sellers plays 3 parts. *Dir.* Stanley Kubrick.

Dr Who and the Daleks (1965)   Peter Cushing, Roy Castle, Roberta Tovey, Jennie Linden. First Dr Who film; sequel in 1966. *Dir.* Gordon Flemyng.

Doctor Zhivago (1965)   Omar Sharif, Julie Christie, Rod Steiger, Alec Guinness, Rita Tushingham, Geraldine Chaplin, Tom Courtenay, Adrienne Corri. Oscars for Maurice Jarre (Music), Freddie Young (Photography), and Robert Bolt (Screenplay). *Dir.* David Lean.

Dog Day Afternoon (1975)   Al Pacino, John Cazale, Charles Durning, Chris Sarandon, Sully Boyar. *Dir.* Sidney Lumet.

Dolores Claiborne (1995)   Kathy Bates, Jennifer Jason Leigh, Judy Parfitt, Christopher Plummer. Housekeeper acquitted of murder is then arrested for killing her boss. *Dir.* Taylor Hackford.

Donnie Brasco (1997)   Al Pacino (Ben 'Lefty' Ruggiero), Johnny Depp (Donnie Brasco / Joe Pistone), Michael Madsen (Sonny). *Dir.* Mike Newell.

Don't Look Now (1973)   Donald Sutherland, Julie Christie. Daphne du Maurier story, set in Venice. *Dir.* Nicolas Roeg.

Doors, The (1991)   Val Kilmer (Jim Morrison), Meg Ryan (Pamela Courson), Billy Idol (Cat). *Dir.* Oliver Stone.

Down and Out in Beverly Hills (1986)   Nick Nolte (Jerry Baskin), Richard Dreyfuss (Davie Whiteman), Bette Midler (Barbara Whiteman), Little Richard (Orvis Goodnight). *Dir.* Paul Mazursky.

Downhill Racer (1969)   Robert Redford, Gene Hackman, Camilla Sparv. Plotless film about a skier. *Dir.* Michael Ritchie.

Dracula (1931)   Bela Lugosi, Helen Chandler, David Manners. Numerous follow-on films from this Bram Stoker novel. *Dir.* Tod Browning.

Dragnet (1987)   Dan Aykroyd (Joe Friday), Tom Hanks (Streebek), Christopher Plummer (Whirley), Harry Morgan (Bill Gannon). *Dir.* Tom Mankiewicz.

Dragon: The Bruce Lee Story (1993)   Jason Scott Lee, Robert Wagner, Michael Learned, Lauren Holly, Nancy Kwan. *Dir.* Rob Cohen.

Dragonheart (1996)   Dennis Quaid, David Thewlis, Pete Postlethwaite, voice of Sean Connery. *Dir.* Rob Cohen.

Dream Team, The (1989)   Michael Keaton (Billy Caulfield), Christopher Lloyd (Henry Sikorsky), Peter Boyle (Jack McDermott), Stephen Furst (Albert Ianuzzi). Four mental patients have to fend for themselves in Manhattan. *Dir.* Howard Zieff.

Dreamscape (1984)   Dennis Quaid (Alex), Max Von Sydow (Paul), Christopher Plummer (Bob), Kate Capshaw (Jane), George Wendt (Charlie). *Dir.* Joseph Ruben.

Dressed to Kill (1980)   Michael Caine, Angie Dickinson, Nancy Allen. Michael Caine plays a transvestite killer. *Dir.* Brian De Palma.

Dresser, The (1983)   Albert Finney (Sir), Tom Courtenay (Norman), Edward Fox (Oxenby). *Dir.* Peter Yates.

Driving Miss Daisy (1989)   Jessica Tandy (Daisy Werthan), Morgan Freeman (Hoke Colburn), Dan Akroyd (Boolie). Won 4 Oscars. *Dir.* Bruce Beresford.

Drugstore Cowboy (1989)   Matt Dillon (Bob Hughes), Kelly Lynch (Dianne Hughes), Heather Graham (Nadine), William S Burroughs (Tom the Priest). *Dir.* Gus Van Sant.

Dry White Season, A (1989)   Donald Sutherland (Ben Du Toit), Janet Suzman (Susan), Susan Sarandon (Melanie Bruwer), Marlon Brando (Ian McKenzie), Set in apartheid South Africa. *Dir.* Euzhan Palcy.

Duck Soup (1933)   The Marx Brothers, Margaret Dumont. According to *Time Out* the best Marx Bros film. *Dir.* Leo McCarey.

Duet for One (1986)   Julie Andrews (Stephanie Anderson), Alan Bates (David Cornwallis), Max Von Sydow (Dr Louis Feldman), Liam Neeson (Totter). Famous violinist develops multiple sclerosis. *Dir.* Andrei Konchalovsky.

Duke Wore Jeans, The (1958)   Tommy Steele, June Laverick, Michael Medwin. *Dir.* Gerald Thomas.

Dune (1984)   Kyle MacLachlan (Paul Atreides), Francesca Annis (Lady Jessica), Sting (Feyd Rautha), Kenneth McMillan (Baron Harkonnen). Based on Frank Herbert's epic SF novel. *Dir.* David Lynch.

Dunkirk (1958)   John Mills, Richard Attenborough, Bernard Lee. Directed by Barry Norman's father factual story. *Dir.* Leslie Norman.

Eagle Has Landed, The (1976)   Michael Caine, Donald Sutherland, Jenny Agutter, Robert Duvall, Donald Pleasence (Himmler). Involves a Nazi plot to kill Churchill. *Dir.* John Sturges.

Earth Girls Are Easy (1988)   Geena Davis (Valerie Dale), Jeff Goldblum (Mac), Jim Carrey (Wiploc), Julie Brown (Candy Pink). *Dir.* Julien Temple.

Earthquake (1974)   Charlton Heston, Ava Gardner, Lorne Greene, George Kennedy. First film to use 'Sensurround'. Big box-office hit. *Dir.* Mark Robson.

East of Sudan (1964)   Anthony Quayle, Sylvia Syms, Jenny Agutter. *Dir.* Nathan Juran.

Easter Parade (1948)   Fred Astaire, Judy Garland, Ann Miller. Music by Irving Berlin. *Dir.* Charles Walters.

Easy Street (1917)   Charles Chaplin, Edna Purviance, Albert Austin. Tramp is reformed by missionary and becomes a policeman. *Dir.* Charles Chaplin.

Eddie (1996)   Whoopi Goldberg (Eddie), Frank Langella (Wild Bill Burgess), Dennis Farina (John Bailey). *Dir.* Steve Rash.

Educating Rita (1983)   Michael Caine (Dr Frank Bryant), Julie Walters (Rita), Maureen Lipman (Trish), Michael Williams (Brian). From the play by Willie Russell; shot in Ireland for tax reasons. *Dir.* Lewis Gilbert.

Edward Scissorhands (1990)   Johnny Depp, Winona Ryder (Kim Boggs), Dianne Wiest (Peg), Alan Arkin (Bill), Vincent Price (Inventor). *Dir.* Tim Burton.

Eiger Sanction, The (1975)   Clint Eastwood, George Kennedy, Vonetta McGee. Art teacher returns to CIA post as an exterminator. *Dir.* Clint Eastwood.

Eight and a Half (1963)   Marcello Mastroianni, Claudia Cardinale, Anouk Aimée. Fellini self portrait. Best Foreign Film Oscar. (The 8 1/2 refers to the number of films Fellini had then made). *Dir.* Federico Fellini.

18 Again! (1988)   George Burns (Jack Watson), Charlie Schlatter (David Watson), Tony Roberts (Arnold). *Dir.* Paul Flaherty.

84 Charing Cross Road (1987)   Anne Bancroft (Helene), Anthony Hopkins (Frank Doel), Judi Dench (Nora Doel). Based on a true story of the late Helene Hanff. *Dir.* David Jones.

Elephant Boy (1937)   Sabu, Wilfrid Hyde-White. Based on a Kipling novel, made a star of Sabu. *Dir.* Robert Flaherty.

Elephant Man, The (1980)   Anthony Hopkins, John Hurt (John Merrick), Anne Bancroft, John Gielgud. *Dir.* David Lynch.

Elmer Gantry (1960)   Burt Lancaster, Jean Simmons, Arthur Kennedy, Shirley Jones. Oscars for Lancaster, Jones and Brooks (writer). *Dir.* Richard Brooks.

Emma (1996)   Gwyneth Paltrow, Toni Collette, Ewan McGregor, Greta Scacchi, Sophie Thompson, Phyllida Law. Rachel Portman won Oscar for Music. *Dir.* Douglas McGrath.

Emmanuelle (1974)   Sylvia Kristel, Marika Green, Daniel Sarky. Big soft-porn cinema hit, spawned 6 sequels. *Dir.* Just Jaeckin.

Empire of the Sun (1987)   Christian Bale (Jim), John Malkovich (Basie), Miranda Richardson (Mrs Victor), Screenplay by Tom Stoppard, from JG Ballard's autobiographical novel. *Dir.* Steven Spielberg.

Empire Strikes Back, The (1980)   Mark Hamill, Harrison Ford, Carrie Fisher. Second of the *Star Wars* films. *Dir.* Irvin Kershner.

Enchanted April (1991)   Miranda Richardson (Rose Arbuthnot), Joan Plowright (Mrs Fisher), Alfred Molina (Mellersh Wilkins), Josie Lawrence (Lottie Wilkins). A quartet of Edwardian ladies go on holiday in an Italian villa. *Dir.* Mike Newell.

Endless Summer, The (1966)   Study of surfing round the world. Documentary which has become a cult among surfers. *Dir.* Bruce Brown.

Enforcer, The (1976)   Clint Eastwood, Tyne Daly, Bradford Dillman. Third of the *Dirty Harry* films. *Dir.* James Fargo.

English Patient (1996)   Ralph Fiennes (Count Almasy), Kristin Scott-Thomas, Juliette Binoche, Willem Dafoe, Colin Firth. Dying Hungarian count recalls his doomed affair with the English wife of a colleague. Based on Michael Ondaatje's book. Won 9 Academy Awards. *Dir.* Anthony Minghella.

Entertainer, The (1960)   Laurence Olivier, Joan Plowright, Alan Bates, Albert Finney. *Dir.* Tony Richardson.

Equinox (1992)   Matthew Modine, Lara Flynn Boyle, Marisa Tomei, Fred Ward, Lori Singer. Timid garage mechanic discovers he has a killer brother. *Dir.* Alan Rudolph.

Eraser (1996)   Arnold Schwarzenegger, James Caan, James Coburn, Vanessa Williams. Agent for the Federal Witness Protection Program discovers he can trust no one. *Dir.* Charles Russell.

Erik the Viking (1989)   Tim Robbins (Erik), Mickey Rooney (Erik's grandfather), Eartha Kitt (Freya), Terry Jones (King Arnulf), John Cleese. *Dir.* Terry Jones.

Erin Brockovich (1999)   Julia Roberts, Aaron Eckhart, Albert Finney, Marg Helgenberger, Cherry Jones, Peter Coyote, Veanne Cox. *Dir.* Steven Soderbergh. (The film was made in late 1999, too late for the 2000 Oscars) True story of a twice-divorced single parent lawyer who took on the might of the Pacific Gas and Electric, accusing them of contaminating a town's water supply.

Escape from Alcatraz (1979)   Clint Eastwood, Patrick McGoohan, Jack Thibeau. *Dir.* Don Siegel.

Escape from LA (1996)   Kurt Russell (Snake Plissken), Steve Buscemi. Set in year 2013. *Dir.* John Carpenter.

ET – The Extra Terrestrial (1982)   Dee Wallace (Mary), Henry Thomas (Elliott), Drew Barrymore (Gertie). ET was 3 million light years from home. *Dir.* Steven Spielberg.

Ethan Frome (1993)   Liam Neeson, Patricia Arquette, Joan Allen. Massachusetts community is setting for story of minister and his crippled driver. *Dir.* John Madden.

Eureka (1983)   Gene Hackman, Theresa Russell, Rutger Hauer, Jane Lapotaire, Mickey Rourke, Joe Pesci. Gold prospector strikes it rich, but at a price. *Dir.* Nicolas Roeg.

Every Which Way but Loose (1978)   Clint Eastwood, Sondra Locke, Ruth Gordon. The 1980 sequel *Any Which Way you Can* is the same story. *Dir.* James Fargo.

Everyone Says I Love You (1996)   Woody Allen, Julia Roberts, Drew Barrymore, Alan Alda, Goldie Hawn. *Dir.* Woody Allen.

Evil That Men Do, The (1984)   Charles Bronson (Holland), Theresa Saldana, José Ferrer. *Dir.* J. Lee Thompson.

Evil under the Sun (1982)   Peter Ustinov, James Mason, Diana Rigg, Maggie Smith, Roddy McDowall. Agatha Christie novel starring Hercule Poirot. *Dir.* Guy Hamilton.

Evita (1996)   Madonna, Antonio Banderas, Jonathan Pryce, Jimmy Nail. Best Song Oscar: 'You Must Love Me' (Andrew Lloyd-Webber & Tim Rice). *Dir.* Alan Parker.

Executive Suite (1954)   Fredric March, William Holden, June Allyson, Barbara Stanwyck, Walter Pidgeon, Shelley Winters. Boardroom battle. *Dir.* Robert Wise.

Exorcist, The (1973)   Ellen Burstyn, Max Von Sydow, Linda Blair, Lee J Cobb. *Dir.* William Friedkin.

Expresso Bongo (1959)   Cliff Richard, Laurence Harvey, Sylvia Sums, Gilbert Harding. *Dir.* Val Guest.

Eyes Wide Shut (1999)   Tom Cruise (Dr Bill Hayard), Nicole Kidman, Madison Eginton, Marie Richardson. *Dir.* Stanley Kubrick.

Fabulous Baker Boys, The (1989)   Jeff Bridges (Jack Baker), Beau Bridges (Frank), Michelle Pfeiffer (Susie Diamond). Pianist brothers ginger up their act by taking on a singer. *Dir.* Steve Kloves.

Face (1997)   Robert Carlyle, Ray Winstone, Damon Albarn. Five criminals undertake a robbery, one of them is a traitor. *Dir.* Antonia Bird.

Face Off (1997)   John Travolta, Nicolas Cage. *Dir.* John Woo.

Faithful (1996)   Cher, Chazz Palminteri, Ryan O'Neal, Paul Mazursky, Amber Smith. Hitman chats to his victim whilst waiting for the signal to kill. *Dir.* Paul Mazursky.

Falling Down (1993)   Michael Douglas (D-Fens), Robert Duvall (Prendergast), Barbara Hershey (Beth), Tuesday Weld (Mrs Prendergast). *Dir.* Joel Schumacher.

Fan, The (1996)   Robert De Niro (Gil Renard), Wesley Snipes (Bobby Rayburn), Ellen Barkin. Baseball fan kidnaps the son of a star player. *Dir.* Tony Scott.

Fantasia (1940)   Cartoon characters to music of Bach, Tchaikovsky, Dukas, Stravinsky, Beethoven, Ponchielli, Schubert and Mussorgsky. *Dir.* Ben Sharpsteen.

Fantastic Voyage (1966)   Stephen Boyd, Raquel Welch, Edmond O'Brien, Donald Pleasence, Arthur O'Connell, Arthur Kennedy. *Dir.* Richard Fleizcher.

Far from the Madding Crowd (1967)   Julie Christie, Peter Finch, Alan Bates, Terence Stamp (Sgt Troy). Set in Victorian Wessex. *Dir.* John Schlesinger.

Farewell My Lovely (1944)   Dick Powell, Claire Trevor, Anne Shirley, Mike Mazurki, Otto Kruger. Aka: *Murder My Sweet. Dir.* Edward Dmytryk.

Farewell My Lovely (1975)   Robert Mitchum, Charlotte Rampling, John Ireland, Sylvia Miles. Remake of the Raymond Chandler classic. *Dir.* Dick Richards.

Fargo (1996)   Frances McDormand, William H Macy, Steve Buscemi, Harve Presnell, Peter Stormare. Car salesman with money troubles hires criminals to kidnap his wife for ransom. Nothing goes to plan. *Dir.* Joel Coen.

Fatal Attraction (1987)   Michael Douglas (Dan Gallagher), Glenn Close (Alex Forrest), Anne Archer (Beth Gallagher), Fred Gwynne (Arthur). *Dir.* Adrian Lyne.

Father of the Bride (1950)   Spencer Tracy, Elizabeth Taylor, Leo G Carroll. *Dir.* Vincente Minnelli.

Father of the Bride (1991)   Steve Martin (George Banks), Diane Keaton (Nina Banks), Kimberly Williams (Annie Banks). Remake of the Spencer Tracy classic. *Dir.* Charles Shyer.

Father's Day (1997)   Robin Williams (Dale), Billy Crystal (Jack), Nastassja Kinski (Colette), Charlie Hofheimer (Scott), Mel Gibson. *Dir.* Ivan Reitman.

Fear (1996)   Reese Witherspoon, Mark Wahlberg. *Dir.* James Foley.

Ferris Bueller's Day Off (1986)   Matthew Broderick (Ferris Bueller), Alan Ruck (Cameron Frye), Mia Sara (Sloane Peterson). *Dir.* John Hughes.

Fever Pitch (1996)   Colin Firth, Ruth Gemmell, Neil Pearson. Obsession with Arsenal FC creates romantic problems for teacher. *Dir.* David Evans.

Few Good Men, A (1992)   Tom Cruise (Lt JG Kaffee), Jack Nicholson (Colonel Jessep), Demi Moore (Lt Cdr Galloway), Kevin Bacon (Capt Ross), Kiefer Sutherland (Lt Kendrick). *Dir.* Rob Reiner.

Fiddler on the Roof (1971)   Topol, Norma Crane, Molly Picon. Topol recreates his classic stage role. *Dir.* Norman Jewison.

Field, The (1990)   Richard Harris (Bull McCabe), Sean Bean (Tadgh McCabe), Frances Tomelty (Widow), Brenda Fricker (Maggie McCabe), John Hurt (Bird O'Donnell), Tom Berenger (The American). *Dir.* Jim Sheridan.

Field of Dreams (1989)   Kevin Costner (Ray Kinsella), Amy Madigan (Annie), James Earl Jones (Terence Mann), Burt Lancaster (Dr Moonlight Graham), Ray Liotta (Shoeless Joe Jackson). Famous line: 'If you build it, he will come'. *Dir.* Phil Alden Robinson.

Fierce Creatures (1997)   John Cleese, Jamie Lee Curtis, Kevin Kline, Michael Palin, Ronnie Corbett,

Robert Lindsay. Fred Schepisi replaced Young as director for three weeks whilst refilming the final scenes. *Dir.* Robert Young.

Fifth Element, The (1997)   Gary Oldman (Zorg), Bruce Willis (Will Dallas), Milla Jovovich (Leeloo), Ian Holm (Cornelius). Costumes by Jean-Paul Gaultier. *Dir.* Luc Besson.

Fight Club (1999) Brad Pitt, Edward Norton, Helena Bonham Carter, Meatloaf. *Dir.* David Fincher.

Finian's Rainbow (1968)   Fred Astaire, Petula Clark, Tommy Steele. Tommy Steele plays a leprechaun. *Dir.* Francis Ford Coppola.

Firm, The (1993)   Tom Cruise (Mitch Deere), Gene Hackman, Jeanne Tripplehorn. Cruise is the new boy at a Memphis law firm run, unknown to him, by the Mafia. Based on bestseller by John Grisham. *Dir.* Sydney Pollack.

First Blood (1982)   Sylvester Stallone (John Rambo), Richard Crenna (Trautman), Brian Dennehy (Teasle). Q Moonblood on the writing credits is Stallone. *Dir.* Ted Kotcheff.

First Great Train Robbery, The (1978)   Sean Connery, Donald Sutherland, Lesley-Anne Down. Wayne Sleep makes his first movie appearance. *Dir.* Michael Crichton.

First Knight (1995)   Sean Connery, Richard Gere, Julia Ormond, Ben Cross, John Gielgud. King Arthur story that lost money at the box office. *Dir.* Jerry Zucker.

Fish Called Wanda, A (1988)   John Cleese (Archie Leach), Jamie Lee Curtis (Wanda), Kevin Kline (Otto), Michael Palin (Ken). Big box office hit, Oscar for Kevin Kline. *Dir.* Charles Crichton.

Fisher King, The (1991)   Robin Williams (Parry), Jeff Bridges (Jack Lucas), Amanda Plummer (Lydia), Ted Ross (Limo Bum), Tom Waits. *Dir.* Terry Gilliam.

Five Easy Pieces (1970)   Jack Nicholson, Karen Black, Fannie Flagg. Jack Nicholson plays a pianist. *Dir.* Bob Rafelson.

Flash Gordon (1980)   Topol, Max Von Sydow, Brian Blessed, Timothy Dalton. Music by Queen. *Dir.* Michael Hodges.

Flashdance (1983)   Jennifer Beals (Alex Owens), Michael Nouri (Nick Hurley), Lilia Skala (Hanna Long). *Dir.* Adrian Lyne.

Flatliners (1990)   Kiefer Sutherland (Nelson Wright), Julia Roberts (Rachel Mannus), Kevin Bacon (David Labraccio), William Baldwin (Joe Hurley). *Dir.* Joel Schumacher.

Fletch (1985)   Chevy Chase (Fletch), Joe Don Baker (Chief Karlin). Sequel: *Fletch Lives* (1989). *Dir.* Michael Ritchie.

Flintstones, The (1994)   John Goodman, Elisabeth Perkins, Rick Moranis, Rosie O'Donnell, Elizabeth Taylor. *Dir.* Brian Levant.

Fly, The (1958)   David Hedison, Patricia Owens, Vincent Price, Herbert Marshall. Classic horror film. *Dir.* Kurt Neumann.

Fly, The (1986)   Jeff Goldblum (Seth Brundle), Geena Davis (Veronica Quaife). David Cronenberg makes a cameo performance as the gynaecologist. *Dir.* David Cronenberg.

Fools Rush In (1997)   Matthew Perry, Salma Hayek, Jon Tenney, Jill Clayburgh. *Dir.* Andy Tennant.

Footloose (1984)   Kevin Bacon (Ren), Lori Singer (Ariel), John Lithgow (Reverend Shaw Moore). *Dir.* Herbert Ross.

For Me and My Gal (1942)   Judy Garland, Gene Kelly, George Murphy. *Dir.* Busby Berkeley.

For the Boys (1991)   Bette Midler (Dixie Leonard), James Caan (Eddie Sparks), George Segal (Art Silver). *Dir*. Mark Rydell.

For Your Eyes Only (1981)   Roger Moore, Topol, Carole Bouquet (Melina), Julian Glover (Kristatos). Ian Fleming does not get credit of any kind for this film. (Theme song: Sheena Easton.) *Dir*. John Glen.

Forbidden Planet (1956)   Walter Pidgeon, Anne Francis, Leslie Nielsen, Warren Stevens, Jack Kelly. Set in AD 2200 and follows the plot of Shakespeare's *The Tempest. Dir*. Fred M Wilcox.

Forever Amber (1947)   Linda Darnell, Cornel Wilde, George Sanders (Charles II), Richard Greene, Jessica Tandy. Costume drama set in the reign of Charles II. *Dir*. Otto Preminger.

Forever Young (1992)   Mel Gibson (Daniel), Jamie Lee Curtis (Claire), Elijah Wood (Nat), George Wendt (Harry). *Dir*. Steve Miner.

Forrest Gump (1994)   Tom Hanks, Robin Wright, Gary Sinise, Sally Field, Hanna R Hall. Won 6 Oscars. *Dir*. Robert Zemeckis.

Fort Apache (1948)   Henry Fonda, John Wayne, Shirley Temple, Victor McLaglen, Ward Bond. *Dir*. John Ford.

Fort Apache, the Bronx (1980)   Paul Newman, Ed Asner, Ken Wahl, Danny Aiello. *Dir*. Daniel Petrie.

Fortune Cookie, The (1966)   Walter Matthau, Jack Lemmon. GB Title: *Meet Whiplash Willie. Dir*. Billy Wilder.

48 Hrs (1982)   Nick Nolte (Jack Cates), Eddie Murphy (Reggie Hammond), Annette O'Toole (Elaine). Sequel: *Another 48 Hrs* (1990). *Dir*. Walter Hill.

49th Parallel (1941)   Eric Portman, Laurence Olivier, Leslie Howard, Raymond Massey, Glynis Johns. US Title: *The Invaders. Dir*. Michael Powell.

Foul Play (1978)   Goldie Hawn, Chevy Chase, Burgess Meredith, Rachel Roberts, Dudley Moore. Two innocents in San Francisco get involved in plot to assassinate the Pope. *Dir*. Colin Higgins.

Four for Texas (1963)   Dean Martin, Frank Sinatra, Anita Ekberg, Ursula Andress, Charles Bronson, Victor Buono, 3 Stooges. *Dir*. Robert Aldrich.

Four Horsemen of the Apocalypse, The (1921)   Rudolph Valentino, Alice Terry, Alan Hale, Wallace Beery. Young Argentinian fights for his father's country, France, in WWI. 1961 remake starred Glenn Ford. *Dir*. Rex Ingram.

Four Musketeers, The (Revenge of Milady), (1974)   Michael York, Oliver Reed, Frank Finlay, Richard Chamberlain, Raquel Welch, Faye Dunaway, Charlton Heston. *Dir*. Richard Lester.

Four Weddings and a Funeral (1994)   Hugh Grant, Andie MacDowell, Kristin Scott Thomas, Simon Callow. *Dir*. Mike Newell.

1492: Conquest of Paradise (1992)   Gérard Depardieu (Columbus), Armand Assante (Sanchez), Sigourney Weaver (Queen Isabel). *Dir*. Ridley Scott.

Fourth Protocol, The (1987)   Michael Caine (John Preston), Pierce Brosnan (Petrofsky), Joanna Cassidy (Vassileva). Thriller by Frederick Forsyth. *Dir*. John Mackenzie.

Fox, The (1968)   Anne Heywood, Sandy Dennis, Keir Dullea. Based on DH Lawrence's novella. *Dir*. Mark Rydell.

Francis (1949)   Donald O'Connor, Patricia Medina, Chill Wills (as voice of Francis the Mule). Series of sequels followed. *Dir*. Arthur Lubin.

Frankenstein (1931)   Boris Karloff, Colin Clive, Mae Clarke, Edward Van Sloan. Series of sequels followed. *Dir*. James Whale.

Frankie and Johnny (1966)   Elvis Presley, Donna Douglas, Nancy Kovack. *Dir*. Frederick De Cordova.

Frankie and Johnny (1991)   Al Pacino (Johnny), Michelle Pfeiffer (Frankie). *Dir*. Garry Marshall.

Frantic (1988)   Harrison Ford (Richard Walker), Betty Buckley (Sondra Walker), Emmanuelle Seigner. American cardiologist searching for his kidnapped wife in Paris becomes embroiled with Arabs. *Dir*. Roman Polanski.

Freebie and the Bean (1974)   Alan Arkin, James Caan, Loretta Swit. *Dir*. Richard Rush.

French Connection, The (1971)   Gene Hackman (Popeye Doyle), Roy Scheider, Fernando Rey. As well as Friedkin and Hackman, Ernest Tidyman was awarded Oscar for Screenplay. *Dir*. William Friedkin.

French Lieutenant's Woman (1981)   Meryl Streep, Jeremy Irons, Leo McKern, Peter Vaughan. Harold Pinter adaption of John Fowles's novel. *Dir*. Karel Reisz.

Frenzy (1972)   Barry Foster, Jon Finch, Alec McCowen, Vivien Merchant, Anna Massey, Billie Whitelaw. Anthony Shaffer adapted *Goodbye Piccadilly, Farewell Leicester Square* by Arthur La Bern. *Dir*. Alfred Hitchcock.

Freshman, The (1990)   Marlon Brando (Carmine Sabatini), Matthew Broderick (Clark Kellogg), Maximilian Schell (Larry London). *Dir*. Andrew Bergman.

Freud (1962)   Montgomery Clift, Larry Parks, Susannah York, David McCallum. *Dir*. John Huston.

Friday the 13th (1980)   Betsy Palmer, Adrienne King, Jeannine Taylor, Robbi Morgan. Others in series include part 4 *The Final Chapter* and the last (part 8), *Jason Takes Manhattan. Dir*. Sean S. Cunningham.

Fried Green Tomatoes at the Whistle Stop Cafe (1992)   Kathy Bates (Evelyn Couch), Jessica Tandy (Ninny Threadgoode). *Dir*. Jon Avnet.

Friendly Persuasion (1956)   Gary Cooper, Dorothy McGuire, Anthony Perkins. No script credit (the writer, Michael Wilson, was blacklisted). *Dir*. William Wyler.

Fright Night (1985)   Chris Sarandon (Jerry Dandridge), Roddy McDowall (Peter Vincent). William Ragsdale (Charley Brewster). Present-day vampires. McDowall's character named as tribute to Peter Cushing and Vincent Price. *Dir*. Tom Holland.

Fright Night Part 2 (1988)   Roddy McDowall, William Ragsdale. *Dir*. Tommy Lee Wallace.

Frisco Kid, The (1979)   Gene Wilder, Harrison Ford, Leo Fuchs. *Dir*. Robert Aldrich.

Fritz the Cat (1971)   First 'X'-rated cartoon, about the adventures of an alleycat in New York. *Dir*. Ralph Bakshi.

From Here to Eternity (1953)   Burt Lancaster, Deborah Kerr, Frank Sinatra, Montgomery Clift. *Dir*. Fred Zinnemann.

From Russia with Love (1963)   Sean Connery, Robert Shaw (Red Grant), Daniela Bianchi (Tatiana Romanova), Lotte Lenya (Rosa Kleb), Bernard Lee, Lois Maxwell, Pedro Armendariz.Theme song sung by Matt Monro. *Dir*. Terence Young.

Front Page, The (1931) Adolph Merjon, Pat O'Brien, Mary Brian, Walter Catlett, Edward Everett Horton. *Dir*. Lewis Milestone.

Front Page, The (1974)   Walter Matthau, Jack Lemmon, Susan Sarandon, David Wayne, Vincent Gardenia. *Dir*. Billy Wilder.

Fugitive, The (1993) Harrison Ford (Dr Richard Kimble), Tommy Lee Jones (Lt Gerard). *Dir.* Andrew Davis.

Full Metal Jacket (1987) Matthew Modine (Private Joker), Adam Baldwin (Animal Mother), Dorian Harewood (Eightball), Vincent D'Onofrio (Private Pyle). *Dir.* Stanley Kubrick.

Full Monty, The (1997) Robert Carlyle (Gaz), Mark Addy (Dave), Tom Wilkinson (Gerald), Hugo Speer (Guy), Paul Barber (Horse), Steve Huison (Lomper). Unemployed Sheffield welders decide to become male strippers. *Dir.* Peter Cattaneo.

Funeral, The (1996) Christopher Walken, Isabelle Adjani, Chris Penn, Annabella Sciorra. *Dir.* Abel Ferrara.

Funeral in Berlin (1967) Michael Caine (Harry Palmer), Oscar Homolka, Eva Renzi, Hugh Burden. *Dir.* Guy Hamilton.

Funny Girl (1968) Barbra Streisand (Fanny Brice), Omar Sharif, Walter Pidgeon, Kay Medford. *Dir.* William Wyler.

Funny Lady (1975) Barbra Streisand, James Caan, Ben Vereen, Omar Sharif, Roddy McDowall. *Dir.* Herbert Ross.

Funny Thing Happened on the Way to the Forum, A (1966) Zero Mostel, Phil Silvers, Michael Crawford, Michael Hordern, Buster Keaton. *Dir.* Richard Lester.

Futureworld (1976) Peter Fonda, Blythe Danner, Yul Brynner, Arthur Hill, Stuart Margolin. *Dir.* Richard T Heffron.

Game, The (1997) Michael Douglas (Nicholas Van Orton), Sean Penn (Conrad Van Orton). *Dir.* David Fincher.

Games, The (1970) Stanley Baker, Michael Crawford, Ryan O'Neal, Charles Aznavour. Four men take part in the Rome Olympics marathon. *Dir.* Michael Winner.

Gandhi (1982) Ben Kingsley (Gandhi), Candice Bergen (Margaret Bourke-White), Edward Fox (General Dyer), Daniel Day Lewis (Colin). *Dir.* Richard Attenborough.

Gardens of Stone (1987) James Caan (Clell Hazard), Anjelica Huston (Samantha Davis), James Earl Jones (Goody Nelson). Vietnam War from the perspective of soldiers guarding Arlington National Cemetery. *Dir.* Francis Ford Coppola.

Gaslight (1940) Anton Walbrook, Diana Wynyard, Frank Pettingell, Robert Newton, Jimmy Hanley. Victorian schizophrenic tries to drive his wife insane because of his guilty past. *Dir.* Thorold Dickinson.

Gaslight (1944) Charles Boyer, Ingrid Bergman, Joseph Cotten, Angela Lansbury. Remake of the 1940 film. *Dir.* George Cukor.

Genevieve (1953) Dinah Sheridan, John Gregson, Kay Kendall, Kenneth More, Joyce Grenfell. Genevieve was a classic car (Darracq). *Dir.* Henry Cornelius.

Genghis Khan (1964) Omar Sharif, Stephen Boyd, James Mason, Telly Savalas, Françoise Dorléac. *Dir.* Henry Levin.

Gentleman Jim (1942) Errol Flynn, Alan Hale, Ward Bond. Based on the life of world heavyweight boxing champion Jim Corbett. *Dir.* Raoul Walsh.

Gentlemen Marry Brunettes (1955) Jane Russell, Jeanne Crain, Alan Young, Rudy Vallee. Sequel to *Gentlemen Prefer Blondes*. *Dir.* Richard Sale.

Gentlemen Prefer Blondes (1953) Jane Russell, Marilyn Monroe, Charles Coburn. Based on Anita Loos's novel. *Dir.* Howard Hawks.

Geordie (1955) Bill Travers, Alastair Sim, Norah Gorsen, Stanley Baxter. Sickly Scottish boy becomes Olympic hammer thrower. *Dir.* Frank Launder.

George Raft Story, The (1961) Ray Danton, Julie London, Jayne Mansfield, Frank Gorshin, Neville Brand (Al Capone). GB Title: *Spin of a Coin*. *Dir.* Joseph M Newman.

Georgy Girl (1966) James Mason, Lynn Redgrave, Charlotte Rampling, Alan Bates, Rachel Kempson. *Dir.* Silvio Narizzano.

Gerald McBoing Boing (1951) Cartoon written by Dr Seuss (Theodore Geisel), which won an Oscar. *Dir.* Robert Cannon.

Get Carter (1971) Michael Caine, John Osborne, Ian Hendry, Britt Ekland. Based on Ted Lewis's novel *Jack's Return Home*. *Dir.* Mike Hodges.

Get Shorty (1995) John Travolta, Gene Hackman, Rene Russo, Danny De Vito. Miami debt collector for the mob goes to Las Vegas and discovers a talent for film production. *Dir.* Barry Sonnenfeld.

Getaway, The (1972) Steve McQueen, Ali MacGraw, Ben Johnson, Sally Struthers, Slim Pickens. *Dir.* Sam Peckinpah.

Getaway, The (1994) Alec Baldwin, Kim Basinger, Michael Madsen, James Woods. *Dir.* Roger Donaldson.

Ghost (1990) Patrick Swayze (Sam Wheat), Demi Moore (Molly Jensen), Whoopi Goldberg (Oda Mae Brown). *Dir.* Jerry Zucker.

Ghost in the Machine (1993) Karen Allen, Chris Mulkey, Ted Marcoux, Nancy Fish. *Dir.* Rachel Talalay.

Ghostbusters (1984) Bill Murray (Dr Peter Venkman), Dan Aykroyd (Dr Raymond Stantz), Harold Ramis (Dr Egon Spengler), Sigourney Weaver (Dana Barrett), Rick Moranis (Louis Tully). *Ghostbusters II* (1989), was sequel. Ramis and Aykroyd also wrote the screenplay. *Dir.* Ivan Reitman.

Ghosts from the Past (1997) Alec Baldwin (DeLaughter), Whoopi Goldberg (Myrlie), James Woods (Byron De La Beckwith). Original Title: *Ghosts of Mississippi*. *Dir.* Rob Reiner.

GI Jane (1997) Demi Moore (Lt Jordan O'Neill), Anne Bancroft (Senator Lillian DeHaven). *Dir.* Ridley Scott.

Giant (1956) Rock Hudson, Elizabeth Taylor, James Dean, Mercedes McCambridge, Carroll Baker, Chill Wills, Rod Taylor, Earl Holliman. *Dir.* George Stevens.

Gigi (1958) Leslie Caron, Louis Jourdan, Maurice Chevalier, Hermione Gingold, Eva Gabor. *Dir.* Vincente Minnelli.

Gilda (1946) Rita Hayworth, Glenn Ford, George Macready. *Dir.* Charles Vidor.

Girl 6 (1996) Theresa Randle, Isaiah Washington, Spike Lee. Unsuccessful actress is employed as a sex chat operator. *Dir.* Spike Lee.

Girls Girls Girls (1962) Elvis Presley, Stella Stevens, Laurel Goodwin. *Dir.* Norman Taurog.

Give My Regards to Broad Street (1984) Paul McCartney, Bryan Brown, Ringo Starr, Barbara Bach, Tracey Ullman, Ralph Richardson. *Dir.* Peter Webb.

Gladiator (2000) Russel Crowe (Maximus), Joaquin Phoenix (Commodus), Connie Nielson, Derek Jacobi, Richard Harris (Emperor Marcus Aurelius), Oliver Reed (Proximo). *Dir.* Ridley Scott.

Glass Menagerie, The (1950) Gertrude Lawrence,

Jane Wyman, Kirk Douglas, Arthur Kennedy. Shy, crippled girl seeks escape from her shabby life in St Louis. *Dir.* Irving Rapper.

Glass Menagerie, The (1987)　Joanne Woodward, John Malkovich, Karen Allen. Remake of earlier version of Tennessee Williams' play. *Dir.* Paul Newman.

Glass Mountain, The (1949)　Michael Denison, Dulcie Gray, Tito Gobbi. Nino Rota's music score is memorable and haunting. *Dir.* Henry Cass.

Gleaming the Cube (1988)　Christian Slater, Steven Bauer, Richard Herd. Skateboarding film. *Dir.* Graeme Clifford.

Glenn Miller Story, The (1954)　James Stewart, June Allyson, Harry Morgan, Charles Drake, Louis Armstrong, Gene Krupa. *Dir.* Anthony Mann.

Gloria (1980)　Gena Rowlands, John Adames, Buck Henry. *Dir.* John Cassavetes.

Glory (1989)　Matthew Broderick (Col Robert G Shaw), Denzel Washington (Private Trip), Cary Elwes (Maj Cabot Forbes), Morgan Freeman (Sgt Maj John Rawlins). *Dir.* Edward Zwick.

Go-Between, The (1970)　Alan Bates, Julie Christie, Michael Redgrave, Dominic Guard, Michael Gough, Margaret Leighton, Edward Fox. Harold Pinter adaptation of LP Hartley's novel. *Dir.* Joseph Losey.

Godfather, The (1972).　Marlon Brando, Al Pacino, James Caan, Robert Duvall, Diane Keaton, Richard Conte. *Dir.* Francis Ford Coppola.

Godfather Part II, The (1974)　Al Pacino, Robert De Niro, Diane Keaton, Robert Duvall, Lee Strasberg, Troy Donahue. The first sequel to win a Best Picture Oscar (and 5 others). *Dir.* Francis Ford Coppola.

Godfather Part III, The (1990)　Al Pacino, Diane Keaton, Talia Shire, Andy Garcia, Eli Wallach, Sofia Coppola. *Dir.* Francis Ford Coppola.

Godzilla (1955)　Raymond Burr, Takashi Shimura, Momoko Kochi. *Dir.* Inoshiro Honda.

Goin' South (1978)　Jack Nicholson, Mary Steenburgen, Christopher Lloyd, John Belushi. *Dir.* Jack Nicholson.

Going My Way (1944)　Bing Crosby (Father O'Malley), Barry Fitzgerald, Rise Stevens, Gene Lockhart. *Dir.* Leo McCarey.

Goldfinger (1964)　Sean Connery, Honor Blackman, Gert Fröbe (Auric Goldfinger), Harold Sakata (Oddjob), Bernard Lee, Lois Maxwell, Desmond Llewellyn, Shirley Eaton. Theme song sung by Shirley Bassey. *Dir.* Guy Hamilton.

Gone with the Wind (1939)　Clark Gable, Vivien Leigh, Olivia de Havilland, Leslie Howard, Thomas Mitchell, Hattie McDaniel, Butterfly McQueen. *Dir.* Victor Fleming (with George Cukor, Sam Wood, B Reeves Eason).

Good Earth, The (1937)　Paul Muni, Luise Rainer, Keye Luke. Chinese peasant grows rich but loses his wife. *Dir.* Sidney Franklin.

Good Morning, Vietnam (1987)　Robin Williams (Adrian Cronauer), Forest Whitaker (Edward Garlick). *Dir.* Barry Levinson.

Good Mother, The (1988)　Diane Keaton (Anna), Liam Neeson (Leo). *Dir.* Leonard Nimoy.

Good Son, The (1993)　Macaulay Culkin, Elijah Wood, Wendy Crewson, Quinn Culkin. Ten-year-old boy is a sadistic killer. *Dir.* Joseph Ruben.

Good, the Bad and the Ugly, The (1966)　Clint Eastwood, Eli Wallach, Lee Van Cleef. *Dir.* Sergio Leone.

Good Will Hunting (1997)　Robin Williams, Matt Damon (Will Hunting), Ben Affleck, Minnie Driver, Stellan Skarsgard. Janitor is spotted as a mathematical genius. *Dir.* Gus Van Sant.

Goodbye, Columbus (1969)　Richard Benjamin, Ali MacGraw, Jack Klugman. Jewish librarian has an affair with daughter of a nouveau riche family. *Dir.* Larry Peerce.

Goodbye Girl, The (1977)　Richard Dreyfuss, Marsha Mason, Quinn Cummings. Neil Simon story. *Dir.* Herbert Ross.

Goodbye, Mr Chips (1939)　Robert Donat, Greer Garson, Paul Henreid, John Mills. James Hilton's novel adapted by RC Sherriff, Claudine West & Eric Maschwitz. *Dir.* Sam Wood.

Goodbye, Mr Chips (1969)　Peter O'Toole, Petula Clark, Michael Redgrave, Sian Phillips. Musical remake of the 1939 classic. *Dir.* Herbert Ross.

Goodfellas (1990)　Robert De Niro (James Conway), Ray Liotta (Henry Hill), Joe Pesci (Tommy De Vito), Lorraine Bracco (Karen Hill), Catherine Scorsese (Tommy's mother). *Dir.* Martin Scorsese.

Goonies, The (1985)　Sean Astin (Mickey), Josh Brolin (Brand), Jeff Cohen (Chunk), Corey Feldman (Mouth). Screenplay by Chris Columbus, based on a Steven Spielberg story. *Dir.* Richard Donner.

Gorillas in the Mist (1988)　Sigourney Weaver (Diane Fossey), Bryan Brown (Bob Campbell). *Dir.* Michael Apted.

Gorky Park (1983)　William Hurt (Arkady Renko), Lee Marvin (Jack Osborne). Filmed mainly in Helsinki. *Dir.* Michael Apted.

Grace of My Heart (1996)　Illeana Douglas, John Turturro, Eric Stoltz, Patsy Kensit, Bridget Fonda, Matt Dillon. Based loosely on Carole King, with Illeana Douglas's voice dubbed by Kristen Vigard. *Dir.* Allison Anders.

Graduate, The (1967)　Dustin Hoffman (Benjamin Braddock), Anne Bancroft (Mrs Robinson), Katharine Ross, William Daniels. *Dir.* Mike Nichols.

Grand Canyon (1991)　Danny Glover, Kevin Kline, Steve Martin. Black truck driver and white lawyer form an unlikely friendship. *Dir.* Lawrence Kasdan.

Grand Hotel (1932)　Greta Garbo (Grusinskaya), John Barrymore, Lionel Barrymore, Joan Crawford. Famous Garbo line: 'I want to be alone'. *Dir.* Edmund Goulding.

Grand Prix (1966)　James Garner, Eva Marie Saint, Yves Montand. *Dir.* John Frankenheimer.

Grande Illusion, La (1937)　Pierre Fresnay, Erich Von Stroheim, Jean Gabin. Three captured French WWI pilots have uneasy relationship with their German commandant. *Dir.* Jean Renoir.

Grapes of Wrath, The (1940)　Henry Fonda, Jane Darwell, John Carradine, Grant Mitchell. From the John Steinbeck novel. Oklahoma farmers trek to California after dust bowl disaster of the Thirties. *Dir.* John Ford.

Grease (1978)　John Travolta, Olivia Newton-John, Stockard Channing, Frankie Avalon, Jeff Conaway, Sha Na Na, Eve Arden, Sid Caesar. School: Rydell High. *Dir.* Randal Kleiser.

Grease 2 (1982)　Maxwell Caulfield, Michelle Pfeiffer, Lorna Luft, Eve Arden, Sid Caesar. *Dir.* Patricia Birch.

Great Balls of Fire (1989)　Dennis Quaid (Jerry Lee Lewis), Winona Ryder (Myra Gale Lewis), John Doe (JW Brown). Peter Cook is 'First English Reporter'. *Dir.* Jim McBride.

Great Caruso, The (1951)　Mario Lanza, Ann Blyth, Jarmila Novotna, Alan Napier. *Dir.* Richard Thorpe.

Great Escape, The (1963)   James Garner, Steve McQueen, Richard Attenborough, Charles Bronson, Donald Pleasence, James Coburn, David McCallum, Gordon Jackson, John Leyton. *Dir.* John Sturges.

Great Expectations (1934)   Phillip Holmes (Pip), Jane Wyatt (Estella), Henry Hull (Magwitch), Alan Hale (Joe Gargery), Francis L Sullivan (Jaggers), Florence Reed (Miss Havisham). *Dir.* Stuart Walker.

Great Expectations (1946)   John Mills, Bernard Miles, Finlay Currie, Martita Hunt, Valerie Hobson, Jean Simmons, Alec Guinness, Francis L Sullivan. *Dir.* David Lean.

Great Gatsby, The (1949)   Alan Ladd, Macdonald Carey, Barry Sullivan. Based on novel by F. Scott Fitzgerald. *Dir.* Elliott Nugent.

Great Gatsby, The (1974)   Robert Redford, Mia Farrow, Karen Black, Sam Waterston, Lois Chiles. Screenplay by Francis Ford Coppola. Nelson Riddle gained Oscar for music. *Dir.* Jack Clayton.

Great Muppet Caper, The (1981)   Diana Rigg, Charles Grodin, John Cleese, Peter Ustinov, Robert Morley, Trevor Howard. Peter Falk has cameo as a tramp. *Dir.* Jim Henson.

Great St Trinian's Train Robbery, The (1966) Frankie Howerd, Dora Bryan, Reg Varney, George Cole. *Dir.* Frank Launder.

Great Santini, The (1979)   Robert Duvall, Michael O'Keefe, Blythe Danner, Julie Anne Haddock. *Dir.* Lewis John Carlino.

Great Scout and Cathouse Thursday, The (1976) Lee Marvin, Oliver Reed, Kay Lenz, Robert Culp, Elizabeth Ashley, Sylvia Miles, Strother Martin. *Dir.* Don Taylor.

Great Waldo Pepper, The (1975)   Robert Redford, Bo Svenson, Bo Brundin, Susan Sarandon. *Dir.* George Roy Hill.

Great Waltz, The (1938)   Fernand Gravet, Luise Rainer, Miliza Korjus. Biopic of Johann Strauss the Younger. *Dir.* Julien Duvivier.

Great White Hope, The (1970)   James Earl Jones, Jane Alexander, Lou Gilbert, Hal Holbrook. Jack Johnson story (he's called Jefferson in the film). *Dir.* Martin Ritt.

Great White Hype, The (1996)   Samuel L Jackson, Jeff Goldblum, John Rhys-Davies. *Dir.* Reginald Hudlin.

Great Ziegfeld, The (1936)   William Powell, Luise Rainer (Anna Held), Myrna Loy (Billie Burke), Frank Morgan, Ray Bolger, Fanny Brice. Biopic of impresario Florenz Ziegfeld. *Dir.* Robert Z Leonard.

Greatest, The (1977)   Muhammad Ali, Ernest Borgnine, Robert Duvall, Ben Johnson, James Earl Jones. *Dir.* Tom Gries.

Greatest Show on Earth, The (1952)   Betty Hutton, Cornel Wilde, Charlton Heston, James Stewart, Dorothy Lamour, John Ringling North. *Dir.* Cecil B de Mille.

Greatest Story Ever Told, The (1965)   Max Von Sydow, Dorothy McGuire, Claude Rains, José Ferrer, David McCallum, Charlton Heston, Sidney Poitier, John Wayne, Pat Boone, Telly Savalas, Angela Lansbury. Famous John Wayne line: 'Truly this man was the Son of God'. *Dir.* George Stevens.

Greed (1925)   Gibson Gowland, Zasu Pitts, Jean Hersholt. Ex-miner dentist kills his wife and later in Death Valley kills her lover but is bound to him by handcuffs. Re-edited by June Mathis, this film is memorable for its original length of nearly 9 hours. *Dir.* Erich Von Stroheim.

Green Berets, The (1968)   John Wayne, David Janssen, Jim Hutton, Aldo Ray, Patrick Wayne. Vietnam War film. *Dir.* John Wayne.

Gremlins (1984)   Zach Galligan (Billy), Hoyt Axton (Rand Peltzer), Phoebe Cates (Kate), Keye Luke (Grandfather), Judge Reinhold (Gerald). Don't get them wet and never feed them after midnight. Sequel: *Gremlins II (The New Batch)*. *Dir.* Joe Dante.

Greystoke: The Legend of Tarzan, Lord of the Apes (1984)   Christopher Lambert (John Clayton / Tarzan), Ralph Richardson (Lord Greystoke), Andie MacDowell (Jane Porter). *Dir.* Hugh Hudson.

Gridlock'd (1997)   Tim Roth (Stretch), Tupac Shakur (Spoon), Thandie Newton (Cookie). *Dir.* Vondie Curtis-Hall.

Grifters, The (1990)   Anjelica Huston (Lily Dillon), John Cusack (Roy Dillon), Annette Bening (Myra Langtry). *Dir.* Stephen Frears.

Groundhog Day (1993)   Bill Murray (Phil), Andie MacDowell (Rita). Weatherman Murray is cursed to live the same day over and over. *Dir.* Harold Ramis.

Groundstar Conspiracy, The (1972)   George Peppard, Michael Sarrazin, James Olson. *Dir.* Lamont Johnson.

Group, The (1966)   Joanna Pettet, Candice Bergen, Jessica Walter, Joan Hackett, Elizabeth Hartman, Kathleen Widdoes, Larry Hagman, Hal Holbrook, Robert Emhardt. *Dir.* Sidney Lumet.

Guarding Tess (1994)   Shirley MacLaine, Nicolas Cage, Austin Pendleton, Richard Griffiths. Secret Service agent engages in battle of wills with a former First Lady. *Dir.* Hugh Wilson.

Guess Who's Coming to Dinner (1967)   Spencer Tracy, Katherine Hepburn, Sidney Poitier, Katharine Houghton. Katherine Houghton is the niece of Katharine Hepburn. *Dir.* Stanley Kramer.

Gunfight at the OK Corral (1957)   Burt Lancaster, Kirk Douglas, Jo Van Fleet, Rhonda Fleming, John Ireland. *Dir.* John Sturges.

Gunfighter, The (1950)   Gregory Peck, Helen Westcott, Karl Malden. *Dir.* Henry King.

Guns of Navarone (1961)   Gregory Peck, David Niven, Stanley Baker, Anthony Quinn, Anthony Quayle, James Darren, James Robertson Justice, Richard Harris. *Dir.* J Lee Thompson.

Guys and Dolls (1955)   Frank Sinatra, Marlon Brando, Jean Simmons, Vivian Blaine, Stubby Kaye. *Dir.* Joseph L Mankiewicz.

Gypsy (1962)   Rosalind Russell, Natalie Wood, Karl Malden. *Dir.* Mervyn Le Roy.

Hairspray (1988)   Sonny Bono (Franklin Von Tussle), Ruth Brown (Motormouth Maybell), Divine (Edna Turnblad / Arvin Hodgepile), Deborah Harry (Velma Von Tussle), Ricki Lake (Tracy Turnblad), Pia Zadora (Beatnik chick). *Dir.* John Waters.

Half Moon Street (1986)   Sigourney Weaver (Lauren Slaughter), Michael Caine (Lord Bullbeck). *Dir.* Bob Swaim.

Halloween (1978)   Jamie Lee Curtis, Donald Pleasence (Dr Loomis). *Dir.* John Carpenter.

Halloween 2 (1981)   Jamie Lee Curtis, Donald Pleasence (Dr Loomis). *Dir.* Rick Rosenthal.

Halloween 3: Season of the Witch (1983)   Tom Atkins, Stacey Nelkin, Dan O'Herlihy. *Dir.* Tommy Lee Wallace.

Halloween 4: The Return of Michael Myers (1988) Donald Pleasence, Ellie Cornell, Danielle Harris. *Dir.* Dwight H Little.

Hamlet (1948)   Laurence Olivier, Eileen Herlie, Jean

Simmons, Peter Cushing, Patrick Troughton. *Dir.* Laurence Olivier.

Hamlet (1990)   Mel Gibson, Glenn Close, Alan Bates, Paul Scofield, Helen Bonham Carter, Ian Holm. *Dir.* Franco Zeffirelli.

Hand that Rocks the Cradle, The (1992)   Rebecca DeMornay (Peyton Flanders), Annabella Sciorra (Claire Bartel), Matt McCoy (Michael Bartel). *Dir.* Curtis Hanson.

Handful of Dust (1988)   James Wilby (Tony Last), Kristin Scott Thomas (Brenda Last), Anjelica Huston (Mrs Rattery), Stephen Fry (Reggie), Alec Guinness (Mr Todd), Judi Dench (Mrs Beaver). *Dir.* Charles Sturridge.

Hang 'em High (1967)   Clint Eastwood, Inger Stevens, Pat Hingle. *Dir.* Ted Post.

Hannah and Her Sisters (1986)   Woody Allen (Micky), Michael Caine (Elliot), Mia Farrow (Hannah), Carrie Fisher (April), Barbara Hershey (Lee), Maureen O'Sullivan (Hannah's mother). *Dir.* Woody Allen.

Hannibal Brooks (1968)   Oliver Reed, Michael J Pollard. *Dir.* Michael Winner.

Hanover Street (1979)   Harrison Ford, Lesley-Anne Down, Christopher Plummer, Alec McCowen, Max Wall. *Dir.* Peter Hyams.

Hans Christian Andersen (1952)   Danny Kaye, Zizi Jeanmaire, Farley Granger. *Dir.* Charles Vidor.

Happiest Days of Your Life, The (1950)   Alastair Sim, Margaret Rutherford, Joyce Grenfell, Richard Wattis. *Dir.* Frank Launder.

Happy Hooker, The (1975)   Lynn Redgrave (Xaviera Hollander). *Dir.* Nicholas Sgarro.

Hard Day's Night, A (1964)   Beatles, Wilfrid Brambell, John Junkin, Norman Rossington, Victor Spinetti, Brian Epstein. *Dir.* Richard Lester.

Hard Way, The (1991)   Michael J Fox (Nick Lang), James Woods (John Moss), Annabella Sciorra (Susan). *Dir.* John Badham.

Harder They Fall, The (1956)   Humphrey Bogart, Rod Steiger, Max Baer, Jan Sterling. Bogart's last film. *Dir.* Mark Robson.

Hardy Family (1936–58)   Mickey Rooney, Lewis Stone, Fay Holden, Cecilia Parker, Sara Haden, Spring Byington, Lionel Barrymore. Howard Koch directed the last of the series: *Andy Hardy Comes Home. Dir.* George B Seitz.

Harry and Tonto (1974)   Art Carney, Ellen Burstyn, Chief Dan George, Larry Hagman. Tonto was a cat. *Dir.* Paul Mazursky.

Harvey (1950)   James Stewart (Elwood P Dowd), Josephine Hull (Veta Louise), Victoria Horne. *Dir.* Henry Koster.

Hawk the Slayer (1980)   Jack Palance, John Terry, Bernard Bresslaw. *Dir.* Terry Marcel.

Head (1968)   Monkees, Victor Mature. Written by Jack Nicholson & Bob Rafelson. *Dir.* Bob Rafelson.

Hear My Song (1992)   Ned Beatty (Josef Locke: voice of Vernon Midgley), Adrian Dunbar (Mickey O'Neill), Shirley Anne Field (Cathleen Doyle), David McCallum (Jim Abbott). *Dir.* Peter Chelsom.

Heart is a Lonely Hunter, The (1968)   Alan Arkin, Sondra Locke, Stacy Keach. Based on Carson McCullers's story of a deaf mute. *Dir.* Robert Ellis Miller.

Heartbreak Ridge (1986)   Clint Eastwood (Highway), Marsha Mason (Aggie). *Dir.* Clint Eastwood.

Heartburn (1986)   Meryl Streep (Rachel), Jack Nicholson (Mark), Jeff Daniels (Richard), Stockard Channing (Julie). *Dir.* Mike Nichols.

Heat (1995)   Al Pacino, Robert De Niro, Val Kilmer, Jon Voight. Based on TV movie: *L.A. Takedown.* First film in which the 2 stars actually filmed scenes together. *Dir.* Michael Mann.

Heathers (1989)   Winona Ryder (Veronica Sawyer), Christian Slater (JD), Shannen Doherty (Heather Duke), Lisanne Falk (Heather McNamara), Kim Walker (Heather Chandler). *Dir.* Michael Lehmann.

Heaven and Earth (1993)   Tommy Lee Jones, Joan Chen, Haing S Ngor, Debbie Reynolds. Vietnamese woman endures hardships and torments from both sides during the war. *Dir.* Oliver Stone.

Heaven Can Wait (1943)   Don Ameche, Gene Tierney, Laird Cregar, Charles Coburn. *Dir.* Ernst Lubitsch.

Heaven Can Wait (1978)   Warren Beatty, Julie Christie, James Mason (Mr Jordan), Dyan Cannon, Vincent Gardenia. Remake of *Here Comes Mr Jordan* (1941). *Dir.* Warren Beatty.

Heaven Knows, Mr Allison (1957)   Robert Mitchum, Deborah Kerr. Marine and nun marooned on Pacific island during WW2. *Dir.* John Huston.

Heavenly Creatures (1994)   Melanie Lynskey, Kate Winslet, Diane Kent. *Dir.* Peter Jackson.

Heavens Above (1963)   Peter Sellers, Isabel Jeans, Ian Carmichael, Irene Handl, Eric Sykes, Bernard Miles. *Dir.* John Boulting.

Heaven's Gate (1980)   Kris Kristofferson, Christopher Walken, John Hurt, Jeff Bridges. Famous Western, remembered as a box office disaster. *Dir.* Michael Cimino.

Hedda (1975)   Glenda Jackson, Peter Eyre, Jennie Linden, Patrick Stewart, Timothy West. *Dir.* Trevor Nunn.

Heidi (1937)   Shirley Temple, Jean Hersholt, Arthur Treacher. Based on Johanna Spyri's novel. *Dir.* Allan Dwan.

Heiress, The (1949)   Olivia de Havilland, Ralph Richardson, Montgomery Clift, Miriam Hopkins, Ray Collins. Based on Henry James's novel *Washington Square* and the play of the same name by Ruth and Augustus Goetz. *Dir.* William Wyler.

Helen Morgan Story, The (1957)   Ann Blyth, Paul Newman, Walter Woolf King (Ziegfeld). GB Title: *Both Ends of the Candle. Dir.* Michael Curtiz.

Hellfire Club, The (1960)   Keith Michell, Peter Arne, Adrienne Corri, Peter Cushing, David Lodge. *Dir.* Robert S Baker and Monty Berman.

Hello Dolly (1969)   Barbra Streisand, Walter Matthau, Michael Crawford, Marianne McAndrew, Tommy Tune. Based on Thornton Wilder's play *The Matchmaker. Dir.* Gene Kelly.

Hell's Angels (1930)   Ben Lyon, James Hall, Jean Harlow. *Dir.* Howard Hughes.

Hellzapoppin (1942)   Ole Olsen, Chic Johnson, Hugh Herbert, Martha Raye, Mischa Auer. Montage of Mirth and Madness. *Dir.* HC Potter.

Help! (1965)   Beatles, Leo McKern, Eleanor Bron, Victor Spinetti. *Dir.* Dick Lester.

Henry and June (1990)   Fred Ward (Henry Miller), Uma Thurman (June Miller), Maria De Medeiros (Anaïs Nin). Censors created a new 'NC-17' rating to cover rude but artistically worthwhile films. *Dir.* Philip Kaufman.

Henry V (1944)   Laurence Olivier, Robert Newton, Leslie Banks, Esmond Knight, Renée Asherson. *Dir.* Laurence Olivier.

Henry V (1989)   Kenneth Branagh, Derek Jacobi, Brian Blessed, Ian Holm, Alec McCowen, Robbie

Coltrane (Falstaff), Emma Thompson (Katherine). *Dir.* Kenneth Branagh.

Henry VIII and His Six Wives (1972) Keith Michell, Frances Cuka (Aragon), Charlotte Rampling (Boleyn), Jane Asher (Seymour), Jenny Bos (Cleves), Lynne Frederick (Howard), Barbara Leigh-Hunt (Parr). *Dir.* Waris Hussein.

Hercules (1997) Voices of: Tate Donovan (Hercules), Rip Torn (Zeus), James Woods (Hades), Danny De Vito (Philoctetes), Susan Egan (Meg). Cartoons by Gerald Scarfe. *Dir.* John Musker & Ron Clements.

Here Come the Huggetts (1948) Jack Warner, Kathleen Harrison, Susan Shaw, Petula Clark, Jimmy Hanley, Diana Dors. Britain's answer to the Hardys. *Dir.* Ken Annakin.

Here Comes Mr Jordan (1941) Robert Montgomery, Evelyn Keyes, Claude Rains. Much copied plot about a prizefighter cum saxophonist arriving in heaven too early. *Dir.* Alexander Hall.

Heroes of Telemark, The (1965) Kirk Douglas, Richard Harris, Ulla Jacobsson, Roy Dotrice, Michael Redgrave. *Dir.* Anthony Mann.

High Anxiety (1977) Mel Brooks, Madeline Kahn, Cloris Leachman. Psychologist suspects his predecessor was murdered. *Dir.* Mel Brooks.

High Noon (1952) Gary Cooper (Will Kane), Grace Kelly, Thomas Mitchell, Lloyd Bridges, Lon Chaney. Tex Ritter sang Dimitri Tiomkin's theme tune. Action takes place during the 85 minutes of running time. *Dir.* Fred Zinnemann.

High School High (1996) Jon Lovitz (Mr Clark), Tia Carrere (Victoria). School is Marion Berry High. *Dir.* Hart Bochner.

Highlander (1986) Christopher Lambert (Connor MacLeod), Roxanne Hart (Brenda Wyatt), Sean Connery (Ramirez). *Highlander II: The Quickening* was the 1990 sequel. *Dir.* Russell Mulcahy.

His Girl Friday (1940) Cary Grant, Rosalind Russell, Ralph Bellamy, Gene Lockhart. Remake of *The Front Page* (1931). *Dir.* Howard Hawks.

History of Mr Polly, The (1949) John Mills, Sally Ann Howes, Megs Jenkins, Finlay Currie. Based on HG Wells's novel. *Dir.* Anthony Pelissier.

Hit, The (1984) John Hurt, Terence Stamp, Tim Roth, Laura Del Sol, Fernando Rey. *Dir.* Stephen Frears.

Hitler – The Last Ten Days (1973) Alec Guinness, Simon Ward, Doris Kunstmann, Diane Cilento, Eric Porter, Joss Ackland. *Dir.* Ennio de Concini.

Hobson's Choice (1953) Charles Laughton, Brenda de Banzie, John Mills, Helen Haye, Prunella Scales. Based on Harold Brighouse's play. *Dir.* David Lean.

Hoffa (1992) Jack Nicholson, Danny De Vito, Armand Assante. *Dir.* Danny De Vito.

Holiday Inn (1942) Bing Crosby, Fred Astaire, Walter Abel, Marjorie Reynolds. Won Oscar for the song 'White Christmas'. *Dir.* Mark Sandrich.

Hollywood or Bust (1956) Dean Martin, Jerry Lewis, Pat Crowley, Anita Ekberg. Last of the Martin & Lewis films. *Dir.* Frank Tashlin.

Home Alone (1990) Macaulay Culkin (Kevin McCallister), Joe Pesci (Harry), Daniel Stern (Marv), John Candy (Gus). *Dir.* Chris Columbus.

Home Alone 2: Lost in New York (1992) Macaulay Culkin (Kevin McCallister), Joe Pesci (Harry), Daniel Stern (Marv), Brenda Fricker (Pigeon Lady). *Dir.* Chris Columbus.

Homeboy (1988) Mickey Rourke (Johnny Walker), Christopher Walken (Wesley), Kevin Conway (Grazziano). *Dir.* Michael Seresin.

Honey, I Blew up the Kid (1992) Rick Moranis (Wayne Szalinski), Lloyd Bridges (Clifford Sterling), Marcia Strassman (Diane). 'Blew up' in as much as the baby grows to 100 feet tall. *Dir.* Randal Kleiser.

Honey, I Shrunk the Kids (1989) Rick Moranis (Wayne Szalinski), Matt Frewer (Big Russ Thompson), Marcia Strassman (Diane), Kristine Sutherland (Mae Thompson). *Dir.* Joe Johnston.

Honkytonk Man (1982) Clint Eastwood (Red Stovall), Kyle Eastwood (Whit), John McIntire (Grandpa). *Dir.* Clint Eastwood.

Honorary Consul, The (1983) Michael Caine (Charley Fortnum), Richard Gere (Dr Plarr), Bob Hoskins (Col Perez). US Title: *Beyond the Limit*. *Dir.* John MacKenzie.

Hook (1991) Dustin Hoffman (Capt Hook), Robin Williams (Peter Banning / Pan), Julia Roberts (Tinkerbell), Bob Hoskins (Smee). *Dir.* Steven Spielberg.

Hoop Dreams (1994) William Gates, Arthur Agee, Emma Gates. *Dir.* Steve James.

Hooper (1978) Burt Reynolds, Sally Field, Brian Keith, Jan Michael Vincent, Adam West. Ageing stuntman decides on one last sensational stunt. *Dir.* Hal Needham.

Hoosiers (1986) Gene Hackman, Barbara Hershey, Dennis Hopper, Sheb Wooley. Triumphs of an Indiana high school basketball team. *Dir.* David Anspaugh.

Horse Feathers (1932) Groucho (Wagstaff), Chico, Zeppo, Harpo Marx, Thelma Todd. College football team needs to win. *Dir.* Norman Z. McLeod.

Hound of the Baskervilles (1939) Basil Rathbone, Nigel Bruce, Richard Greene, John Carradine. *Dir.* Sidney Lanfield.

Hound of the Baskervilles (1959) Peter Cushing, André Morell, Christopher Lee, John Le Mesurier. *Dir.* Terence Fisher.

Hound of the Baskervilles (1977) Peter Cook (Sherlock Holmes), Dudley Moore (Watson), Denholm Elliott (Stapleton), Terry-Thomas (Mortimer), Max Wall, Spike Milligan, Penelope Keith. *Dir.* Paul Morrissey.

Houseboat (1958) Cary Grant, Sophia Loren, Martha Hyer, Harry Guardino. *Dir.* Melville Shavelson.

Housesitter (1992) Steve Martin (Davis), Goldie Hawn (Gwen). One-night stand turns into a comic fatal attraction. *Dir.* Frank Oz.

How Green Was My Valley (1941) Walter Pidgeon, Maureen O'Hara, Roddy McDowall. Based on Richard Llewellyn's novel. *Dir.* John Ford.

How I Won the War (1967) Michael Crawford, John Lennon, Roy Kinnear, Lee Montague, Michael Hordern. *Dir.* Richard Lester.

How the West Was Won (1962) Debbie Reynolds, Carroll Baker, Lee J Cobb, Henry Fonda, James Stewart, Gregory Peck. Spencer Tracy was the narrator. *Dir.* Henry Hathaway, John Ford, George Marshall.

How to Marry a Millionaire (1953) Lauren Bacall, Marilyn Monroe, Betty Grable, William Powell, Cameron Mitchell. *Dir.* Jean Negulesco.

Howard's End (1992) Anthony Hopkins (Henry Wilcox), Vanessa Redgrave (Ruth), Helen Bonham Carter (Helen), Emma Thompson (Margaret Schlegel). The Howard's End of the title is a house. *Dir.* James Ivory.

Howling, The (1980) Dee Wallace, Patrick Macnee, Kevin McCarthy. *Dir.* Joe Dante.

Howling II: Your Sister is a Werewolf (1985) Christopher Lee, Annie McEnroe, Reb Brown. Filmed in Czechoslavakia and not a sequel to *The Howling*. *Dir*. Philippe Mora.

Hud (1963) Paul Newman, Patricia Neal, Melvyn Douglas, Brandon De Wilde. *Dir*. Martin Ritt.

Hue and Cry (1946) Alastair Sim, Jack Warner, Harry Fowler. First of the 'Ealing comedies concerns crooks passing information in a boys' paper. *Dir*. Charles Crichton.

Hunchback of Notre Dame, The (1939) Charles Laughton, Cedric Hardwicke, Maureen O'Hara, Edmond O'Brien, Thomas Mitchell. Remake of the Lon Chaney 1923 film. *Dir*. William Dieterle.

Hunchback of Notre Dame, The (1956) Anthony Quinn, Gina Lollobrigida. French / Italian production of the classic story. *Dir*. Jean Delannoy.

Hunger, The (1983) Catherine Deneuve (Miriam), David Bowie (John), Susan Sarandon (Sarah Roberts). *Dir*. Tony Scott.

Hunt for Red October, The (1990) Sean Connery (Capt Marko Ramius), Alec Baldwin (Jack Ryan), Sam Neill (Capt Borodin). *Dir*. John McTiernan.

Hunter, The (1980) Steve McQueen, Eli Wallach, Ben Johnson. McQueen's last film. *Dir*. Buzz Kulik.

Hurlyburly (1998) Sean Penn (Eddie), Kevin Spacey (Mickey), Robin Wright Penn, Garry Shandling, Meg Ryan, Chazz Pálminteri, Anna Paquin. *Dir*. Anthony Drazan.

Husbands and Wives (1992) Woody Allen (Gabe Roth), Judith Lewis (Rain), Blythe Danner (Rain's mother), Mia Farrow (Judy Roth), Judy Davis (Sally). *Dir*. Woody Allen.

Hustler, The (1961) Paul Newman, Jackie Gleason, George C Scott, Piper Laurie. *Dir*. Robert Rossen.

Hustler White (1996) Tony Ward, Bruce LaBruce, Kevin Kramer. *Dir*. Bruce LaBruce.

I Accuse (1958) José Ferrer (Dreyfus), Anton Walbrook (Esterhazy), Emlyn Williams (Zola). Written by Gore Vidal. *Dir*. José Ferrer.

I Am a Camera (1955) Julie Harris, Laurence Harvey, Shelley Winters, Anton Diffring. John Collier adaptation of Isherwood stories and the stage play by John Van Druten. *Dir*. Henry Cornelius.

I Am a Fugitive from a Chain Gang (1932) Paul Muni, Glenda Farrell, Helen Vinson, Preston Foster. *Dir*. Mervyn Le Roy.

I Confess (1953) Montgomery Clift, Anne Baxter, Brian Aherne, Karl Malden. Priest hears confession of a murderer and has a dilemma. *Dir*. Alfred Hitchcock.

I Married a Witch (1942) Fredric March, Veronica Lake, Cecil Kellaway, Susan Hayward, Elizabeth Patterson. *Dir*. René Clair.

I Wanna Hold Your Hand (1978) Nancy Allen, Bobby diCicco, Marc McClure. *Dir*. Robert Zemeckis.

I Want to Live (1958) Susan Hayward, Simon Oakland, Virginia Vincent, Theodore Bikel. Based on the Barbara Graham story of a prostitute executed despite doubts as to her guilt. *Dir*. Robert Wise.

I Was a Male War Bride (1949) Cary Grant, Ann Sheridan, Marion Marshall. *Dir*. Howard Hawks.

I Was Monty's Double (1958) John Mills, Cecil Parker, ME Clifton-James. US Title: *Hell, Heaven and Hoboken*. *Dir*. John Guillermin.

Ice Cold in Alex (1958) John Mills, Sylvia Syms, Anthony Quayle, Harry Andrews. *Dir*. J Lee Thompson.

Ice Station Zebra (1968) Rock Hudson, Patrick McGoohan, Ernest Borgnine, Jim Brown. Based on the Alistair MacLean story. *Dir*. John Sturges.

Ideal Husband, An (1999) Cate Blanchett, Minnie Driver, Rupert Everett, Peter Vaughan, Julianne Moore. *Dir*. Oliver Parker.

If (1968) Malcolm McDowell, David Wood, Richard Warwick, Arthur Lowe. *Dir*. Lindsay Anderson.

If These Walls Could Talk (1996) Demi Moore, Cher. TV movie. *Dir*. Nancy Savoka and Cher.

I'm All Right Jack (1959) Ian Carmichael, Peter Sellers, Irene Handl, Richard Attenborough, Terry-Thomas, Dennis Price, Margaret Rutherford. *Dir*. John Boulting.

Importance of Being Earnest, The (1952) Michael Redgrave, Michael Denison, Edith Evans, Margaret Rutherford, Dorothy Tutin. *Dir*. Anthony Asquith.

In Search of the Castaways (1961) Maurice Chevalier, Hayley Mills, George Sanders, Wilfrid Hyde-White, Wilfrid Brambell. *Dir*. Robert Stevenson.

In the Bleak Midwinter (1995) Michael Maloney, Richard Briers, Julia Sawalha, Joan Collins, Jennifer Saunders. Story of a production of *Hamlet* in a village church. *Dir*. Kenneth Branagh.

In the Heat of the Night (1967) Sidney Poitier, Rod Steiger, Warren Oates. *Dir*. Norman Jewison.

In Which We Serve (1942) Noël Coward, Bernard Miles, John Mills, Richard Attenborough, Celia Johnson, Michael Wilding. Viewed as one of the best propaganda wartime films. *Dir*. Noël Coward and David Lean.

Inchon (1981) Laurence Olivier (General MacArthur), Jacqueline Bisset, David Janssen, Ben Gazzara, Richard Roundtree. *Dir*. Terence Young.

Incredible Journey, The (1963) Disney cartoon about 2 dogs and a cat and their 250-mile journey home after being separated from their owners. *Dir*. Fletcher Markle.

Incredible Shrinking Man, The (1957) Grant Williams, Randy Stuart, April Kent. Radioactive mist is the cause of the shrinking. *Dir*. Jack Arnold.

Incredible Shrinking Woman, The (1981) Lily Tomlin, Charles Grodin, Ned Beatty, Henry Gibson. A new perfume causes the diminution in this case. *Dir*. Joel Schumacher.

Indecent Proposal (1993) Robert Redford (John Gage), Demi Moore (Diana Murphy), Woody Harrelson (David Murphy), Billy Connolly (Auction MC). *Dir*. Adrian Lyne.

Independence Day (1996) Will Smith (Capt Steve Hiller), Bill Pullman (President Whitmore), Jeff Goldblum, Judd Hirsch, Harry Connick Jnr, Brent Spiner. Pilot and computer expert battle an alien force. *Dir*. Roland Emmerich.

Indiana Jones and the Last Crusade (1989) Harrison Ford, Sean Connery (Professor Henry Jones), Denholm Elliott (Marcus Brody), John Rhys-Davies (Sallah), Julian Glover (Walter Donovan). *Dir*. Steven Spielberg.

Indiana Jones and the Temple of Doom (1984) Harrison Ford, Kate Capshaw (Willie Scott), Ke Huy Quan (Short Round). Prequel to *Raiders of the Lost Ark* (action takes place in 1935). *Dir*. Steven Spielberg.

Indiscreet (1958) Cary Grant, Ingrid Bergman, Phyllis Calvert, Cecil Parker, David Kossoff, Megs Jenkins. Not very indiscreet as it happens as the loving couple are both single. *Dir*. Stanley Donen.

Informer, The (1935) Victor McLaglen, Heather Angel, Margot Grahame, Una O'Connor. Story of IRA allegiances. *Dir*. John Ford.

Inherit the Wind (1960)   Spencer Tracy, Fredric March, Dick York, Florence Eldridge, Gene Kelly. Fictionalised account of the Scopes Monkey Trial of 1925 when a teacher was accused of teaching Darwin's Theory of Evolution and, consequently, blasphemy. *Dir.* Stanley Kramer.

Inn of the Sixth Happiness, The (1958)   Ingrid Bergman, Curt Jurgens, Robert Donat. Biopic of the missionary Gladys Aylward and her work in China. *Dir.* Mark Robson.

Inner Circle, The (1991)   Tom Hulce (Ivan Sanshin), Lolita Davidovich (Anastasia), Bob Hoskins (Beria), Alexandre Zbruev (Stalin). Cinema projectionist goes to work for Stalin. *Dir.* Andrei Konchalovsky.

Innerspace (1987)   Dennis Quaid (Lt Tuck Pendleton), Martin Short (Jack Putter), Meg Ryan (Lydia Maxwell), Kevin McCarthy (Victor Scrimshaw). Version of *The Fantastic Voyage*. *Dir.* Joe Dante.

Insider, The (1999)   Al Pacino (Lowell Bergman), Russell Crowe (Jeffrey Wigand), Rip Torn (John Scanlon), Christopher Plummer (Mike Wallace), Diane Venora (Liare Wigand) Michael Gambon (Thomas Sandefor).   *Dir.* Michael Mann.

Insignificance (1985)   Gary Busey (The Ballplayer), Tony Curtis (The Senator), Michael Emil (The Professor), Theresa Russell (The Actress), Will Sampson (The Elevator Attendant). Four people resembling Monroe, Einstein, McCarthy & Di Maggio meet in New York hotel. *Dir.* Nicolas Roeg.

Inspector Calls, An (1954)   Alastair Sim, Jane Wenham, Bryan Forbes, Arthur Young. *Dir.* Guy Hamilton.

International Velvet (1978)   Nanette Newman, Tatum O'Neal, Anthony Hopkins, Christopher Plummer. *Dir.* Bryan Forbes.

Intersection (1994)   Sharon Stone, Richard Gere, Martin Landau. *Dir.* Mark Rydell.

Intolerance (1916)   Mae Marsh, Lillian Gish, Constance Talmadge. Four stories depicting intolerance and persecution through the ages. *Dir.* DW Griffith.

Invasion of the Body Snatchers (1956)   Kevin McCarthy, Dana Wynter, Larry Gates, King Donovan, Carolyn Jones, Sam Peckinpah. Small American town is taken over by aliens. *Dir.* Don Siegel.

Invasion of the Body Snatchers (1978)   Donald Sutherland, Brooke Adams, Leonard Nimoy, Jeff Goldblum, Kevin McCarthy, Don Siegel. San Francisco becomes the venue for the remake of the 1956 classic. *Dir.* Philip Kaufman.

Invisible Man, The (1933)   Claude Rains (Dr Griffin), Gloria Stuart, Una O'Connor. *Dir.* James Whale.

Ipcress File, The (1965)   Michael Caine (Harry Palmer), Nigel Green, Sue Lloyd, Gordon Jackson. The Michael Caine character was never named in the novel by Len Deighton. *Dir.* Sidney J Furie.

IQ (1994)   Tim Robbins, Meg Ryan, Walter Matthau (Einstein), Stephen Fry, Keene Curtis (Eisenhower). *Dir.* Fred Schepisi.

Irma La Douce (1963)   Shirley MacLaine, Jack Lemmon, Lou Jacobi. Paris policeman falls for a prostitute and becomes her pimp. *Dir.* Billy Wilder.

Ishtar (1987)   Warren Beatty (Lyle Rogers), Dustin Hoffman (Chuck Clarke), Isabelle Adjani (Shirra Assel). Second biggest flop of all time. *Dir.* Elaine May.

Island of Dr Moreau (1977)   Burt Lancaster, Michael York, Nigel Davenport, Barbara Carrera. Story of shipwrecked sailors on a Pacific Island in 1911. *Dir.* Don Taylor.

It Happened One Night (1934)   Clark Gable, Claudette Colbert, Walter Connolly, Alan Hale, Ward Bond. Earned Oscars for both its stars. *Dir.* Frank Capra.

It Takes Two (1995)   Kirstie Alley, Steve Guttenberg, Mary-Kate and Ashley Olsen. *Dir.* Andy Tennant.

Italian Job, The (1969)   Michael Caine, Noël Coward, Benny Hill, Rossano Brazzi, Irene Handl, Fred Emney, John Le Mesurier, Simon Dee, Robert Powell. Crooks stage a traffic jam in Turin to pull off a robbery. *Dir.* Peter Collinson.

It's a Mad Mad Mad Mad World (1963)   Spencer Tracy, Jimmy Durante, Mickey Rooney, Phil Silvers, Terry-Thomas, Peter Falk, Buster Keaton, The 3 Stooges. Buried loot is the instigator of mayhem. *Dir.* Stanley Kramer.

It's a Wonderful Life (1946)   James Stewart, Henry Travers (Clarence), Donna Reed, Lionel Barrymore, Thomas Mitchell. James Stewart's favourite film and many believe Frank Capra's finest. *Dir.* Frank Capra.

It's a Wonderful World (1939)   James Stewart, Claudette Colbert, Frances Drake, Guy Kibbee. *Dir.* WS Van Dyke II.

Jack (1996)   Robin Williams, Diane Lane, Jennifer Lopez, Bill Cosby. *Dir.* Francis Ford Coppola.

Jack the Bear (1993)   Danny De Vito, Robert J Steinmiller Jnr, Miko Hughes. *Dir.* Marshall Herskovitz.

Jackal, The (1997)   Bruce Willis (The Jackal), Richard Gere (Declan Mulqueen), Sidney Poitier (Preston), Diane Venora (Valentina Koslova), Mathilda May (Isabella). *Dir.* Michael Caton-Jones.

Jackie Brown (1998)   Pam Grier (Jackie Brown), Samuel L Jackson (Ordell Robbie), Robert Forster (Max Cherry), Michael Keaton, Michael Bowen, Robert De Niro (Louis Gara). Air stewardess smuggles cash into America for a gun-runner. *Dir.* Quentin Tarantino.

Jagged Edge (1985)   Jeff Bridges (Jack Forrester), Glenn Close (Teddy Barnes), Robert Loggia (Sam Ransom). *Dir.* Richard Marquand.

James and the Giant Peach (1996)   Paul Terry, Joanna Lumley, Pete Postlethwaite. *Dir.* Henry Selick.

Jaws (1975)   Robert Shaw, Roy Scheider, Richard Dreyfuss, Lorraine Gary. Long Island resort: Amity. *Dir.* Steven Spielberg.

Jaws 2 (1978)   Roy Scheider, Lorraine Gary. *Dir.* Jeannot Szwarc.

Jaws 3-D (1983)   Dennis Quaid (Mike), Bess Armstrong (Kathryn), Simon MacCorkindale (Philip), Louis Gossett Jr (Calvin). *Dir.* Joe Alves.

Jaws: the Revenge (1987)   Lorraine Gary (Ellen Brody), Lance Guest (Michael), Mario Van Peebles (Jake), Karen Young (Carla), Michael Caine (Hoagie). *Dir.* Joseph Sargent.

Jazz Singer, The (1927)   Al Jolson, May McAvoy, Warner Oland. Notable for being the first talkie. *Dir.* Alan Crosland.

Jean de Florette (1987)   Yves Montand (Cesar Soubeyran), Gérard Depardieu (Jean de Florette), Daniel Auteuil (Ugolin), Elisabeth Depardieu (Aimée), Ernestine Mazurowna (Manon). Sequel: *Manon des Sources*. *Dir.* Claude Berri.

Jennifer 8 (1992)   Andy Garcia (John Berlin), Uma Thurman (Helena Robertson). Serial killer preys on blind women. *Dir.* Bruce Robinson.

Jerry Maguire (1996)   Tom Cruise, Cuba Gooding Jnr. *Dir.* Phillip Noyce.

Jesus Christ Superstar (1973)   Ted Neeley, Carl

Anderson, Yvonne Elliman. Melvyn Bragg wrote the screenplay with Jewison. *Dir.* Norman Jewison.

Jewel of the Nile (1985)   Michael Douglas (Jack), Kathleen Turner (Joan), Danny De Vito (Ralph). Film is dedicated to Diane Thomas, the writer of *Romancing the Stone. Dir.* Lewis Teague.

Jezebel (1938)   Bette Davis, Henry Fonda. US Civil War epic. *Dir.* William Wyler.

JFK (1991)   Kevin Costner (Jim Garrison), Sissy Spacek (Liz Garrison), Tommy Lee Jones (Clay Shaw), Joe Pesci (David Ferrie), Gary Oldman (Lee Harvey Oswald), Brian Doyle-Murray (Jack Ruby). *Dir.* Oliver Stone.

Jim Thorpe, All-American (1951)   Burt Lancaster (Thorpe), Charles Bickford, Phyllis Thaxter. Truish story of the Native American who became a star footballer. *Dir.* Michael Curtiz.

Jingle All the Way (1996)   Arnold Schwarzenegger (Howard Langston), Rita Wilson (Liz Langston), Jake Lloyd (Jamie Langston), Sinbad, James Belushi. *Dir.* Brian Levant.

Joan of Arc (1948)   Ingrid Bergman, José Ferrer, Francis L Sullivan. *Dir.* Victor Fleming.

John Paul Jones (1959)   Robert Stack, Charles Coburn (Benjamin Franklin), Bette Davis (Catherine the Great). Notable for its unending list of star cameos. *Dir.* John Farrow.

Johnny Belinda (1948)   Jane Wyman, Lew Ayres, Charles Bickford, Agnes Moorehead. Deaf mute is raped and the local doctor is suspected of being the father of the baby. *Dir.* Jean Negulesco.

Joker is Wild, The (1957)   Frank Sinatra, Mitzi Gaynor, Eddie Albert, Jeanne Crain. The song 'All the Way' won an Academy Award. *Dir.* Charles Vidor.

Jokers, The (1967)   Michael Crawford, Oliver Reed, Harry Andrews, James Donald, Daniel Massey, Michael Hordern, Frank Finlay, Rachel Kempson. Two brothers decide to 'borrow' and replace the crown jewels. *Dir.* Michael Winner.

Jolson Story, The (1946)   Larry Parks (voice of Jolson), Evelyn Keyes. *Dir.* Alfred E Green.

Journey into Fear (1942)   Joseph Cotten, Dolores del Rio, Orson Welles. Munitions expert finds himself in danger from assassins in Istanbul. *Dir.* Norman Foster.

Journey to Shiloh (1967)   James Caan, Michael Sarrazin, Brenda Scott, Paul Petersen, Don Stroud, Harrison Ford. Seven young Texans leave home to fight in the Civil War. *Dir.* William Hale.

Journey to the Center of the Earth (1959)   James Mason, Arlene Dahl, Pat Boone, Diane Baker. Film ends with the team being catapulted out of Stromboli. *Dir.* Henry Levin.

Judge Dredd (1995)   Sylvester Stallone, Armand Assante, Diane Lane, Ian Dury, Max Von Sydow. Set in Mega City One in AD 2139. *Dir.* Danny Cannon.

Judgment at Nuremberg (1961)   Spencer Tracy, Marlene Dietrich, Burt Lancaster, Richard Widmark, Maximilian Schell, Judy Garland, Montgomery Clift, William Shatner. *Dir.* Stanley Kramer.

Judgment in Berlin (1988)   Martin Sheen (Herbert J Stern), Sam Wanamaker (Bernard Hellring). Director is Sean Penn's father. *Dir.* Leo Penn.

Juggernaut (1974)   Richard Harris, David Hemmings, Omar Sharif, Anthony Hopkins. Transatlantic liner is threatened by a mad bomber. *Dir.* Richard Lester.

Julia (1977)   Jane Fonda, Vanessa Redgrave, Jason Robards Jnr, Maximilian Schell, Hal Holbrook. Based on Lillian Hellman's book *Pentimento. Dir.* Fred Zinnemann.

Julius Caesar (1953)   John Gielgud, Marlon Brando, James Mason, Greer Garson, Deborah Kerr. *Dir.* Joseph L Mankiewicz.

Jumanji (1995)   Robin Williams, Bonnie Hunt, Kirsten Dunst. Two children play a mysterious board game that releases, after 25 years, a child and some ferocious animals. *Dir.* Joe Johnston.

Jumpin' Jack Flash (1986)   Whoopi Goldberg (Terry Doolittle), Tracey Ullman, James Belushi, Jonathan Pryce. *Dir.* Penny Marshall.

Jungle Fever (1991)   Wesley Snipes (Flipper Purify), Annabella Sciorra (Angela Tucci), Spike Lee (Cyrus), Anthony Quinn (Lou Carbone), Samuel L Jackson (Gator Purify). *Dir.* Spike Lee.

Jurassic Park (1993)   Richard Attenborough, Jeff Goldblum, Sam Neill, Laura Dern, Samuel L. Jackson, Bob Peck. *Dir.* Steven Spielberg.

Just a Gigolo (1978)   David Bowie, Sydne Rome, Kim Novak, Marlene Dietrich, David Hemmings, Curt Jurgens. *Dir.* David Hemmings.

K-9 (1989)   James Belushi (Thomas Dooley), Mel Harris (Tracy), Kevin Tighe (Lyman). Not the same K-9 as in Dr Who. *Dir.* Rod Daniel.

Kaleidoscope (1966)   Warren Beatty, Susannah York, Clive Revill, Eric Porter. Playboy breaks into card factory to mark the cards and so enable him to clean up. *Dir.* Jack Smight.

Kansas City (1996)   Jennifer Jason Leigh, Miranda Richardson, Harry Belafonte. Woman kidnaps a politician's drug addicted wife in a bid to get her husband released by the gangsters holding him. *Dir.* Robert Altman.

Karate Kid, The (1984)   Ralph Macchio (Daniel), Pat Morita (Miyagi), Elisabeth Shue (Ali), Martin Kove (Kreese), William Zabka (Johnny). *Dir.* John G Avildsen.

Karate Kid Part II, The (1986)   Ralph Macchio, Pat Morita, Nobu McCarthy (Yukie), Danny Kamekona (Sato). *Dir.* John G. Avildsen.

Karate Kid III, The (1989)   Ralph Macchio, Pat Morita (Miyagi), Robyn Lively (Jessica Andrews). *Dir.* John G Avildsen.

Kelly's Heroes (1970)   Clint Eastwood, Telly Savalas, Don Rickles, Donald Sutherland. *Dir.* Brian G Hutton.

Kentuckian, The (1955)   Burt Lancaster, Dianne Foster, Walter Matthau, John McIntire. *Dir.* Burt Lancaster.

Kes (1969)   David Bradley, Lynne Perrie, Colin Welland, Brian Glover. *Dir.* Ken Loach.

Key Largo (1948)   Humphrey Bogart, Lauren Bacall, Claire Trevor, Edward G. Robinson, Lionel Barrymore. *Dir.* John Huston.

Kickboxer (1989)   Jean Claude Van Damme, Dennis Alexio, Tong Po (Michel Qissi). *Dir.* Mark DiSalle and David Worth.

Kid, The (1921)   Charles Chaplin, Jackie Coogan, Edna Purviance. *Dir.* Charles Chaplin.

Kid for Two Farthings, A (1955)   Celia Johnson, Diana Dors, David Kossoff, Primo Carnera, Sydney Tafler. *Dir.* Carol Reed.

Kid from Brooklyn, The (1946)   Danny Kaye, Virginia Mayo, Eve Arden, Walter Abel. Timid milkman becomes a prizefighter. *Dir.* Norman Z McLeod.

Kid Galahad (1937)   Edward G Robinson, Bette Davis, Humphrey Bogart, Harry Carey. *Dir.* Michael Curtiz.

Kid Galahad (1962)   Elvis Presley, Lola Albright, Gig Young, Charles Bronson. *Dir.* Phil Karlson.

Kidnapped (1971)   Michael Caine, Lawrence Douglas, Trevor Howard, Jack Hawkins, Donald Pleasence, Gordon Jackson. Other versions starred Warner Baxter and Freddie Bartholomew (1938), and Peter Finch and James MacArthur (1959). *Dir.* Delbert Mann.

Kids (1995)   Lee Fitzpatrick, Sarah Henderson, Justin Pearce. Day in the life of teenagers includes sex and skateboarding. *Dir*. Larry Clark.

Killers, The (1946)   Burt Lancaster, Edmond O'Brien, Ava Gardner. *Dir*. Robert Siodmak.

Killers, The (1964)   John Cassavetes, Lee Marvin, Clu Gulager, Angie Dickinson, Ronald Reagan. Ronald Reagan's last film and the first in which he played a bad guy. *Dir*. Don Siegel.

Killer: A Journal of Murder (1996)   James Woods (Carl Panzram), Robert Sean Leonard (Henry Lesser). True story set in Leavenworth Prison, Kansas. *Dir*. Tim Metcalfe.

Killing Fields, The (1984)   Sam Waterston (Sydney Schanberg), Haing S Ngor (Dith Pran), John Malkovich (Al Rockoff). *Dir*. Roland Joffé.

Killing of Sister George, The (1969)   Beryl Reid, Susannah York, Coral Browne, Patricia Medina, Roland Fraser. *Dir*. Robert Aldrich.

Kind Hearts and Coronets (1949)   Dennis Price, Alec Guinness, Valerie Hobson, Joan Greenwood, Arthur Lowe. Alec Guinness plays the 8 members of the D'Ascoyne family. *Dir*. Robert Hamer.

Kind of Loving, A (1962)   Alan Bates, June Ritchie, Thora Hird, Bert Palmer. Keith Waterhouse & Willis Hall adapted Stan Barstow's story. *Dir*. John Schlesinger.

Kindergarten Cop (1990)   Arnold Schwarzenegger (John Kimble), Penelope Ann Miller (Joyce Paulmarie), Pamela Reed (Phoebe O'Hara), Linda Hunt (Miss Schlowski). *Dir*. Ivan Reitman.

King and I, The (1956)   Yul Brynner, Deborah Kerr, Rita Moreno. *Dir*. Walter Lang.

King and I, The (1999)   Voices of Miranda Richardson, Ian Richardson, Martin Vidnovic, Darrell Hammond. *Dir*. Richard Rich.

King David (1985)   Richard Gere (David), Edward Woodward (Saul), Alice Krige (Bathsheba), Dennis Quilley (Samuel). *Dir*. Bruce Beresford.

King Kong (1933)   Fay Wray, Robert Armstrong (Carl Denham), Bruce Cabot. *Dir*. Merian C Cooper & Ernest B Schoedsnack.

King Kong (1976)   Jeff Bridges, Charles Grodin, Jessica Lange. This Dino de Laurentiis production was something of a spoof. *Dir*. John Guillermin.

King of Comedy, The (1983)   Robert De Niro (Rupert Pupkin), Jerry Lewis (Jerry Langford), Diahnne Abbott (Rita). *Dir*. Martin Scorsese.

King of Kings (1961)   Jeffrey Hunter, Robert Ryan, Siobhan McKenna. *Dir*. Nicholas Ray.

King Ralph (1991)   John Goodman (Ralph Jones), Peter O'Toole (Sir Cedric Willingham), John Hurt (Lord Graves), Joely Richardson (Princess Anna), Leslie Phillips (Gordon), Julian Glover (King Gustav), Judy Parfitt (Queen Katherine). The whole of the Royal Family are wiped out, leaving a lounge pianist as King. *Dir*. David S Ward.

King Rat (1965)   George Segal, Tom Courtenay, John Mills, James Fox, Leonard Rossiter. Based on James Clavell novel about collaboration in Changi POW camp during WW2. *Dir*. Bryan Forbes.

King Solomon's Mines (1950)   Stewart Granger, Deborah Kerr, Richard Carlson. *Dir*. Compton Bennett.

King Solomon's Mines (1985)   Richard Chamberlain, Sharon Stone, Herbert Lom, John Rhys-Davies. *Dir*. J Lee Thompson.

King's Row (1941)   Ann Sheridan, Robert Cummings, Ronald Reagan (Drake), Claude Rains. Reagan took the name of his autobiography from a line in this film. *Dir*. Sam Wood.

Kipps (1941)   Michael Redgrave, Phyllis Calvert, Diana Wynyard, Michael Wilding. Later turned into a musical as *Half a Sixpence*. *Dir*. Carol Reed.

Kismet (1955)   Howard Keel, Ann Blyth, Vic Damone, Sebastian Cabot. Musical based on Borodin. *Dir*. Vincente Minnelli.

Kiss Me Kate (1953)   Howard Keel, Kathryn Grayson, Ann Miller, Keenan Wynn. Musical version of *The Taming of the Shrew*. *Dir*. George Sidney.

Kiss of the Spider Woman (1985)   William Hurt (Molina), Raul Julia (Valentin), Sonia Braga (Leni Lamaison / Marta). Flamboyant gay shares South American prison cell with a radical activist. *Dir*. Hector Babenco.

Kissin' Cousins (1963)   Elvis Presley, Arthur O'Connell, Glenda Farrell, Jack Albertson. Presley plays 2 parts. *Dir*. Gene Nelson.

Kitty Foyle (1940)   Ginger Rogers, Dennis Morgan, James Craig, Eduardo Ciannelli. *Dir*. Sam Wood.

Klansman, The (1974)   Lee Marvin, Richard Burton, Cameron Mitchell, OJ Simpson, Linda Evans. *Dir*. Terence Young.

Klute (1971)   Jane Fonda, Donald Sutherland, Roy Scheider. *Dir*. Alan J Pakula.

Knack, The (1965)   Michael Crawford, Ray Brooks, Rita Tushingham. *Dir*. Richard Lester.

Kotch (1971)   Walter Matthau, Deborah Winter. *Dir*. Jack Lemmon.

Krakatoa, East of Java (1968)   Maximilian Schell, Diane Baker, Brian Keith, Rossano Brazzi, Sal Mineo. Krakatoa is actually west of Java. *Dir*. Bernard Kowalski.

Kramer versus Kramer (1979)   Dustin Hoffman, Justin Henry, Meryl Streep, Jane Alexander, Howard Duff. Based on an Avery Corman novel. *Dir*. Robert Benton.

Krays, The (1990)   Gary Kemp (Ronnie), Martin Kemp (Reggie), Billie Whitelaw (Violet), Susan Fleetwood (Rose), Jimmy Jewell (Cannonball Lee), Tom Bell (Jack 'The Hat' McVitie). *Dir*. Peter Medak.

L-Shaped Room, The (1962)   Leslie Caron, Tom Bell, Brock Peters, Cicely Courtneidge, Bernard Lee, Avis Bunnage, Pat Phoenix, Emlyn Williams. *Dir*. Bryan Forbes.

La Bamba (1987)   Lou Diamond Phillips (Ritchie Valens), Esai Morales (Bob Morales), Rosana De Soto (Connie Valenzuela). *Dir*. Luis Valdez.

LA Confidential (1997)   Danny De Vito (Sid Hudgens), Kim Basinger (Lynn Bracken), Kevin Spacey (Jack Vincennes), Russell Crowe (Bud White), Guy Pearce (Ed Exley). Hooker with a facial similarity to Veronica Lake gets mixed up in murder investigation. *Dir*. Curtis Hanson.

LA Story (1991)   Steve Martin (Harris K Telemacher), Victoria Tennant (Sara McDowel), Iman (Cynthia), Richard E Grant (Roland), Marilu Henner (Trudi), Patrick Stewart (Maître d' at L'Idiot). *Dir*. Mick Jackson.

Labyrinth (1986)   David Bowie (Jareth), Jennifer Connelly (Sarah), Toby Froud (Toby), Shelley Thompson (Stepmother). *Dir*. Jim Henson.

Lady Caroline Lamb (1972)   Sarah Miles, Jon Finch, Richard Chamberlain (Byron), Margaret Leighton, John Mills (Canning), Ralph Richardson (George III), Laurence Olivier (Wellington). *Dir*. Robert Bolt.

Lady Sings the Blues (1972)   Diana Ross (Billie Holliday), Billy Dee Williams, Richard Pryor. *Dir*. Sidney J Furie.

Lady Vanishes, The (1938)   Margaret Lockwood, Michael Redgrave, Dame May Whitty, Googie Withers. A 1979 remake starring Cybill Shepherd and Elliott Gould flopped. *Dir*. Alfred Hitchcock.

Lady with the Lamp, The (1951)   Anna Neagle, Michael Wilding. *Dir.* Herbert Wilcox.

Ladykillers, The (1955)   Alec Guinness, Katie Johnson, Peter Sellers, Herbert Lom, Frankie Howerd. *Dir.* Alexander Mackendrick.

Lamerica (1994)   Enrico Lo Verso, Michele Placido. *Dir.* Gianni Amelio.

Land and Freedom (1995)   Ian Hart, Rosana Pastor, Iciar Bollain. *Dir.* Ken Loach.

Lara Croft: Tomb Raider (2001)   Angelina Jolie (Lara), Iain Glen, Noah Taylor, Leslie Philips, Chris Barrie, Daniel Craig. *Dir.* Simon West. Angelina Jolie's father Jon Voight is cast as her on screen father in this film.

Lassie Come Home (1943)   Roddy McDowall, Elizabeth Taylor, Donald Crisp. Based on an Eric Knight story. *Dir.* Fred M Wilcox.

Last Action Hero, The (1993)   Arnold Schwarzenegger, Mercedes Ruehl, F Murray Abraham, Art Carney, Anthony Quinn. *Dir.* John McTiernan.

Last Boy Scout, The (1992)   Bruce Willis (Joe Hallenbeck), Damon Wayans (Jimmy Dix), Chelsea Field (Sarah Hallenbeck). *Dir.* Tony Scott.

Last Dance (1996)   Sharon Stone (Cindy Liggett), Rob Morrow (Rick Hayes). *Dir.* Bruce Beresford.

Last Detail, The (1973)   Jack Nicholson, Otis Young, Randy Quaid, Clifton James. *Dir.* Hal Ashby.

Last Emperor, The (1987)   John Lone (Pu Yi), Peter O'Toole (RJ), Joan Chen (Wan Jung). *Dir.* Bernardo Bertolucci.

Last Exit to Brooklyn (1990)   Stephen Lang (Harry Black), Jennifer Jason Leigh (Tralala), Burt Young (Big Joe), Peter Dobson (Vinnie). *Dir.* Uli Edel.

Last Hard Men, The (1976)   Charlton Heston, James Coburn, Barbara Hershey, Christopher Mitchum. *Dir.* Andrew V McLaglen.

Last Man Standing (1996)   Bruce Willis, Christopher Walken, Bruce Dern, Alexandra Powers. Set in Texas during the Depression of the 1930s, it concerns a gunman on the run and rival bootleggers. *Dir.* Walter Hill.

Last of the Dogmen (1995)   Tom Berenger, Barbara Hershey, Kuttwood Smith, Steve Reevis. Bounty hunter discovers a group of Cheyenne in Montana. *Dir.* Tab Murphy.

Last of the Mohicans, The (1992)   Daniel Day-Lewis (Hawkeye), Madeleine Stowe (Cora), Russell Means (Chingachgook), Eric Schweig (Uncas). *Dir.* Michael Mann.

Last Picture Show, The (1971)   Timothy Bottoms, Jeff Bridges, Cybill Shepherd, Ben Johnson, Cloris Leachman, Ellen Burstyn. *Dir.* Peter Bogdanovich.

Last Seduction, The (1994)   Linda Fiorentino, Peter Berg, Bill Nunn, Bill Pullman. Woman leaves her husband taking with her a million dollars he made from a drug deal. *Dir.* John Dahl.

Last Summer (1969)   Barbara Hershey, Richard Thomas, Bruce Davison, Cathy Burns, Ralph Waite. *Dir.* Frank Perry.

Last Tango in Paris (1972)   Marlon Brando, Maria Schneider. *Dir.* Bernardo Bertolucci.

Last Temptation of Christ, The (1988)   Willem Dafoe (Jesus), Harvey Keitel (Judas), Barbara Hershey (Mary Magdalene), David Bowie (Pontius Pilate). *Dir.* Martin Scorsese.

Last Tycoon, The (1976)   Robert De Niro, Robert Mitchum, Tony Curtis, Jeanne Moreau, Jack Nicholson, Donald Pleasence. *Dir.* Elia Kazan.

Lavender Hill Mob, The (1951)   Alec Guinness, Stanley Holloway, Sid James, Alfie Bass, Audrey Hepburn. Bank clerk masterminds bullion robbery by moulding Eiffel Towers in gold to be smuggled to France. *Dir.* Charles Crichton.

Lawrence of Arabia (1962)   Peter O'Toole, Omar Sharif, Arthur Kennedy, Jack Hawkins, Alec Guinness. Screenplay by Robert Bolt. *Dir.* David Lean.

League of Gentlemen, The (1960)   Jack Hawkins, Richard Attenborough, Roger Livesey, Bryan Forbes, Nigel Patrick, Nanette Newman. *Dir.* Basil Dearden.

Leaving Las Vegas (1995)   Nicolas Cage, Elisabeth Shue, Julian Sands, Richard Lewis. Alcoholic writer goes to Las Vegas to drink himself to death. *Dir.* Mike Figgis.

Left-Handed Gun, The (1958)   Paul Newman (Billy the Kid), John Dehner (Pat Garrett). *Dir.* Arthur Penn.

Legend of the Lone Ranger, The (1981)   Klinton Spilsbury, Michael Horse, Christopher Lloyd, Matt Clark. *Dir.* William A Fraker.

Lemon Drop Kid, The (1951)   Bob Hope, Marilyn Maxwell, Lloyd Nolan. Based on a Damon Runyon story. *Dir.* Sidney Lanfield.

Lenny (1974)   Dustin Hoffman (Lennie Bruce), Valerie Perrine. *Dir.* Bob Fosse.

Les Misérables (1995)   Jean-Paul Belmondo, Michel Boujenah, Rufus. *Dir.* Claude Lelouch.

Lethal Weapon (1987)   Mel Gibson (Martin Riggs), Danny Glover (Roger Murtaugh), Gary Busey (Joshua). Vietnam veteran turned cop is unhinged by his wife's death and has a death wish. *Dir.* Richard Donner.

Lethal Weapon 2 (1989)   Mel Gibson, Danny Glover, Joe Pesci (Leo Getz), Patsy Kensit (Rika Van Den Haas), Joss Ackland. South African drug runners unfortunately meet Martin Riggs. *Dir.* Richard Donner.

Lethal Weapon 3 (1992)   Mel Gibson, Danny Glover, Joe Pesci, Rene Russo (Lorna Cole). *Dir.* Richard Donner.

Let's Make Love (1960)   Yves Montand, Marilyn Monroe, Tony Randall, Wilfrid Hyde-White, Frankie Vaughan, Bing Crosby, Gene Kelly. Multi-millionaire learns he is to be burlesqued, so joins the cast. *Dir.* George Cukor.

Letter to Brezhnev (1985)   Alfred Molina (Sergei), Peter Firth (Peter), Margi Clarke (Teresa), Tracy Lea (Tracy). Liverpool lass falls in love with a Russian sailor. *Dir.* Chris Bernard.

Liar Liar (1997)   Jim Carrey (Fletcher Reede), Amanda Donohoe, Justin Cooper, Jennifer Tilly. (Out-takes shown as end credits roll.) *Dir.* Tom Shadyac.

Licence to Kill (1989)   Timothy Dalton, Carey Lowell (Pam Bouvier), Anthony Zerbe (Milton Krest), Robert Davi (Frank Sanchez), Caroline Bliss (Moneypenny), Robert Brown (M), Talisa Soto (Lupe Lamora). Book title: *Licence Revoked*. Title song by Gladys Knight. *Dir.* John Glen.

Licensed to Kill (1965)   Tom Adams, Veronica Hurst, Karel Stepanek. US Title: *The Second Best Secret Agent in the Whole Wide World*. *Dir.* Lindsay Shonteff.

Life at the Top (1965)   Laurence Harvey (Joe Lampton), Jean Simmons, Honor Blackman, Michael Craig, Margaret Johnston. *Dir.* Ted Kotcheff.

Life is Beautiful (1997)   Roberto Benigni, Nicoletta Braschi, Giustino Durano, Horst Buchholz. *Dir.* Roberto Benigni

Limelight (1952)   Charlie Chaplin, Claire Bloom, Buster Keaton, Sydney Chaplin. *Dir.* Charlie Chaplin.

Lion in Winter, The (1968)   Katharine Hepburn (Eleanor of Aquitaine), Peter O'Toole (Henry II), Anthony Hopkins. *Dir.* Anthony Harvey.

Lion King, The (1994)   Voices of Matthew Broderick, Rowan Atkinson, Whoopi Goldberg, Jeremy Irons, Robert Guillaume, James Earl Jones. Songs include: 'Can You Feel the Love Tonight', 'Circle of Life' & 'Hakuna Matata'. (Music by Elton John, lyrics by Tim Rice.) *Dir.* Roger Allers.

Liquidator, The (1965)   Rod Taylor, Trevor Howard, David Tomlinson, Wilfrid Hyde-White, Derek Nimmo. *Dir.* Jack Cardiff.

List of Adrian Messenger, The (1963)   George C Scott, Kirk Douglas, Clive Brook, Dana Wynter, Robert Mitchum, Frank Sinatra, Tony Curtis, Burt Lancaster. The cameos by the last 4 listed stars are debatable as they are unrecognisable. *Dir.* John Huston.

Lisztomania (1975)   Roger Daltrey, Sara Kestelman, Paul Nicholas, Fiona Lewis, Ringo Starr. *Dir.* Ken Russell.

Little Big Man (1970)   Dustin Hoffman, Martin Balsam, Faye Dunaway, Chief Dan George. *Dir.* Arthur Penn.

Little Caesar (1931)   Edward G Robinson, Douglas Fairbanks Jnr, Glenda Farrell. *Dir.* Mervyn Le Roy.

Little Dorrit (1987)   Derek Jacobi (Arthur Clennam), Alec Guinness (William Dorrit), Max Wall (Flintwinch). There are 211 people named on the cast list, which is a record for a British film. *Dir.* Christine Edzard.

Little Foxes, The (1941)   Bette Davis, Herbert Marshall, Teresa Wright, Dan Duryea. Based on a Lillian Hellman story. *Dir.* William Wyler.

Little Giants (1994)   Rick Moranis, Ed O'Neil, John Madden. Wimp decides to create a young football team full of misfits. *Dir.* Duwayne Dunham.

Little Shop of Horrors (1986)   Rick Moranis (Seymour Krelborn), Ellen Greene (Audrey), Vincent Gardenia (Mushnik), Steve Martin (Orin Scrivello, DDS). Voice of the plant (Audrey II): Levi Stubbs of the Four Tops. *Dir.* Frank Oz.

Little Women (1933)   Katharine Hepburn, Paul Lukas, Joan Bennett, Frances Dee, Spring Byington. *Dir.* George Cukor.

Little Women (1949)   June Allyson, Elizabeth Taylor, Peter Lawford, Margaret O'Brien, Janet Leigh, Mary Astor. *Dir.* Mervyn Le Roy.

Little Women (1994)   Winona Ryder, Gabriel Byrne, Trini Alvarado, Samantha Mathis, Susan Sarandon. *Dir.* Gillian Armstrong.

Live and Let Die (1973)   Roger Moore, Yaphet Kotto (Dr Kananga), Jane Seymour (Solitaire). Paul McCartney wrote and performed theme song. *Dir.* Guy Hamilton.

Living Daylights (1987)   Timothy Dalton, Maryam d'Abo (Kara Milovy), Jeroen Krabbe (Gen Georgi Koskov), Joe Don Baker (Brad Whitaker), John Rhys-Davies (Gen Leonid Pushkin), Robert Brown (M), Desmond Llewellyn (Q), Caroline Bliss (Moneypenny), John Terry (Felix Leiter). Theme Song by A-Ha. *Dir.* John Glen.

Local Hero (1983)   Burt Lancaster (Happer), Peter Riegert (Mac), John Gordon Sinclair (Ricky). TV series *Northern Exposure* was strongly influenced by this film. *Dir.* Bill Forsyth.

Loch Ness (1995)   Ted Danson, Joely Richardson, Ian Holm, John Savident. US scientist tries to debunk the monster myth. *Dir.* John Henderson.

Lock Up (1989)   Sylvester Stallone (Frank Leone), Donald Sutherland (Warden Drumgoole). *Dir.* John Flynn.

Logan's Run (1976)   Michael York, Richard Jordan, Jenny Agutter, Farrah Fawcett-Majors, Peter Ustinov. Based on SF novel by William F Nolan. *Dir.* Michael Anderson.

Lolita (1962)   James Mason, Shelley Winters, Sue Lyon, Peter Sellers. Lolita is 14 years old. *Dir.* Stanley Kubrick.

London Kills Me (1991)   Justin Chadwick, Steven Mackintosh, Emer McCourt, Roshan Seth, Fiona Shaw. Down on his luck drug pusher is told he can have a job as a waiter if he can acquire a decent pair of shoes. *Dir.* Hanif Kureishi.

Loneliness of the Long Distance Runner, The (1962)   Tom Courtenay, Michael Redgrave, James Bolam, Avis Bunnage. *Dir.* Tony Richardson.

Lonely are the Brave (1962)   Kirk Douglas, Walter Matthau, Gena Rowlands, Carroll O'Connor. Modern technology is pitted against a last rebel cowboy. *Dir.* David Miller.

Long and the Short and the Tall, The (1960)   Laurence Harvey, Richard Todd, David McCallum, Richard Harris. US Title: *Jungle Fighters.* *Dir.* Leslie Norman.

Long Good Friday, The (1980)   Bob Hoskins, Helen Mirren, Dave King, Bryan Marshall, Eddie Constantine, Stephen Davis. *Dir.* John Mackenzie.

Long Goodbye, The (1973)   Elliott Gould, Nina Van Pallandt, Sterling Hayden, Mark Rydell, Henry Gibson. *Dir.* Robert Altman.

Long Kiss Goodnight, The (1996)   Geena Davis, Samuel L Jackson, Patrick Malahide. *Dir.* Renny Harlin.

Long Riders, The (1980)   Stacy Keach, James Keach, David Carradine, Keith Carradine, Robert Carradine, Dennis Quaid, Randy Quaid. Story of the Younger, Miller and James boys. *Dir.* Walter Hill.

Longest Day, The (1962)   John Wayne, Robert Mitchum, Henry Fonda, Robert Ryan, Roddy McDowall, Robert Wagner, Paul Anka, Fabian, Jeffrey Hunter, Rod Steiger, Red Buttons, Richard Burton, Sean Connery. *Dir.* Andrew Marton.

Look Back in Anger (1959)   Richard Burton, Mary Ure, Claire Bloom, Edith Evans, Donald Pleasence. *Dir.* Tony Richardson.

Look Who's Talking (1989)   John Travolta (James), Kirstie Alley (Mollie), Olympia Dukakis (Rosie), George Segal (Albert). Bruce Willis was the voice of Mikey. *Dir.* Amy Heckerling.

Look Who's Talking Too (1990)   John Travolta, Kirstie Alley, Olympia Dukakis, Roseanne Arnold (voice of Julie), Mel Brooks (voice of Mr Toilet Man), Bruce Willis (voice of Mikey). *Dir.* Amy Heckerling.

Loot (1970)   Richard Attenborough, Lee Remick, Hywel Bennett, Milo O'Shea, Dick Emery. *Dir.* Silvio Narizzano.

Lord of the Flies (1963)   James Aubrey, Tom Chapin, Hugh Edwards. Remake in 1990 was directed by Harry Hook. *Dir.* Peter Brook.

Lost Highway (1997)   Bill Pullman, Patricia Arquette, Balthazar Getty. *Dir.* David Lynch.

Lost Horizon (1937)   Ronald Colman, HB Warner, Thomas Mitchell, Sam Jaffe. Remade in 1972 with Peter Finch in Colman role. *Dir.* Frank Capra.

Lost Weekend, The (1945)   Ray Milland (Don Birnam), Jane Wyman, Howard da Silva. *Dir.* Billy Wilder.

Lost World, The: Jurassic Park (1997)   Jeff Goldblum (Dr Ian Malcolm), Julianne Moore, Pete Postlethwaite, Richard Attenborough (John Hammond). *Dir.* Steven Spielberg.

Love is a Many-Splendored Thing (1955)   Jennifer Jones, William Holden, Torin Thatcher. Sammy Fain & Paul Francis Webster won an Academy Award for the title song. *Dir.* Henry King.

Love Me Tender (1956)   Richard Egan, Debra Paget,

Elvis Presley, Neville Brand, James Drury. *Dir.* Robert D Webb.

Love Me Tonight (1932)   Maurice Chevalier, Jeanette MacDonald, Charles Butterworth, Myrna Loy. *Dir.* Rouben Mamoulian.

Love on the Dole (1941)   Deborah Kerr, Clifford Evans, George Carney. Based on Walter Greenwood's novel. *Dir.* John Baxter.

Love Story (1970)   Ali MacGraw, Ryan O'Neal (Oliver Barrett IV), Ray Milland. 1978 sequel: *Oliver's Story*. *Dir.* Arthur Hiller.

Lust for Life (1956)   Kirk Douglas (Vincent Van Gogh), Anthony Quinn (Paul Gauguin). *Dir.* Vincente Minnelli.

Mad Dog and Glory (1992)   Robert De Niro, Uma Thurman, Bill Murray. Timid cop is given a present of a beautiful girl for a week by a gangster. *Dir.* John McNaughton.

Mad Max (1979)   Mel Gibson, Joanne Samuel. *Dir.* George Miller.

Mad Max 2 (1981)   Mel Gibson, Bruce Spence, Vernon Wells. *Dir.* George Miller.

Mad Max beyond Thunderdome (1985)   Mel Gibson, Tina Turner, Angelo Rossitto, Helen Buday. *Dir.* George Miller.

Madame Bovary (1949)   Jennifer Jones, Van Heflin, James Mason, Louis Jourdan. A 1991 remake starring Isabelle Huppert kept to the original plot a little better. *Dir.* Vincente Minnelli.

Made in America (1993)   Whoopi Goldberg, Ted Danson, Will Smith. Black teenager, born by artificial insemination, discovers her father is a white car salesman. *Dir.* Richard Benjamin.

Madness of King George, The (1994)   Nigel Hawthorne, Helen Mirren, Ian Holm, Amanda Donohoe, Rupert Everett, Rupert Graves. *Dir.* Nicholas Hytner.

Magic Christian (1969)   Peter Sellers, Ringo Starr, Richard Attenborough, Laurence Harvey, Spike Milligan, Raquel Welch, John Cleese. Yul Brynner cameo as a transvestite nightclub singer. *Dir.* Joseph McGrath.

Magnificent Seven, The (1960)   Yul Brynner, Steve McQueen, Robert Vaughan, James Coburn, Charles Bronson, Brad Dexter, Horst Buchholz. *Dir.* John Sturges.

Malcolm X (1992)   Denzil Washington, Angela Bassett, Albert Hall, Al Freeman Jnr, Spike Lee. Based on the book *Autobiography of Malcolm X as told to Alex Haley*. *Dir.* Spike Lee.

Mame (1974)   Lucille Ball, Beatrice Arthur, Robert Preston, Bruce Davison. *Dir.* Gene Saks.

Man and a Woman, A (1966)   Anouk Aimée, Jean-Louis Trintignant. Best Foreign Film Oscar Concerns a racing driver and a script girl who fall in love. *Dir.* Claude Lelouch.

Man Called Horse, A (1970)   Richard Harris, Judith Anderson, Jean Gascon, Manu Tupou. Sequels: *Return of a Man Called Horse* (1976), & *Triumphs of a Man Called Horse* (1984). *Dir.* Elliot Silverstein.

Man for All Seasons, A (1966)   Paul Scofield, Wendy Hiller, Susannah York, Robert Shaw, Orson Welles, John Hurt, Corin Redgrave. Events leading to the execution of Sir Thomas More. *Dir.* Fred Zinnemann.

Man in the Iron Mask, The (1939)   Louis Hayward, Warren William (D'Artagnan), Alan Hale, Bert Roach, Joseph Schildkraut. King Louis XIV keeps his twin brother prisoner. *Dir.* James Whale.

Man of the Year (1995)   Dirk Shafer, Vivian Paxton, Deidra Shafer. Documentary about events surrounding the homosexual Dirk Shafer's awarding of the 1992 *Playgirl* magazine's Man of the Year. *Dir.* Dirk Shafer.

Man Who Came to Dinner, The (1941)   Bette Davis, Monty Woolley, Ann Sheridan, Jimmy Durante (spoofing Harpo Marx). *Dir.* William Keighley.

Man Who Could Work Miracles, The (1936)   Roland Young, Ralph Richardson, Ernest Thesiger, George Sanders. Based on the HG Wells story. *Dir.* Lothar Mendes.

Man Who Fell to Earth, The (1976)   David Bowie, Rip Torn, Candy Clark. *Dir.* Nicolas Roeg.

Man Who Knew too Much, The (1934)   Leslie Banks, Edna Best, Peter Lorre. *Dir.* Alfred Hitchcock.

Man Who Knew too Much, The (1956)   James Stewart, Doris Day, Bernard Miles. Remake of the 1934 film. *Dir.* Alfred Hitchcock.

Man Who Shot Liberty Valance, The (1962)   John Wayne, James Stewart, Lee Marvin, Vera Miles. John Wayne shot Liberty Valance. *Dir.* John Ford.

Man Who Would Be King, The (1975)   Sean Connery, Michael Caine, Christopher Plummer (Kipling), Shakira Caine, Saeed Jaffrey. Based on a Rudyard Kipling story. *Dir.* John Huston.

Man with the Golden Arm (1956)   Frank Sinatra, Kim Novak, Eleanor Parker, Arnold Stang. Golden Arm refers to the card-dealing expertise of the lead character. *Dir.* Otto Preminger.

Man with the Golden Gun (1974)   Roger Moore, Christopher Lee (Scaramanga), Britt Ekland (Mary Goodnight), Maud Adams (Andrea Anders), Hervé Villechaize, Clifton James, Richard Loo. Title song performed by Lulu. *Dir.* Guy Hamilton.

Man without a Face, The (1993)   Mel Gibson, Margaret Whitton, Fay Masterson, Viva. Boy remembers how he was helped to enter a military academy by a disfigured former teacher. *Dir.* Mel Gibson.

Mandy (1952)   Jack Hawkins, Terence Morgan, Phyllis Calvert, Mandy Miller. Little deaf girl is sent to a special school. *Dir.* Alexander Mackendrick.

Manhattan (1979)   Woody Allen, Diane Keaton, Meryl Streep, Mariel Hemingway. *Dir.* Woody Allen.

Manhattan Murder Mystery (1993)   Woody Allen, Alan Alda, Anjelica Huston, Diane Keaton. *Dir.* Woody Allen.

Marathon Man (1976)   Dustin Hoffman, Laurence Olivier, Roy Scheider, William Devane. *Dir.* John Schlesinger.

Marnie (1964)   Tippi Hedren, Sean Connery, Martin Gabel, Diane Baker. Rich man marries a kleptomaniac who sees red when she sees red! *Dir.* Alfred Hitchcock.

Mars Attacks! (1996)   Jack Nicholson, Glenn Close, Annette Bening, Michael J Fox, Pierce Brosnan, Rod Steiger, Danny De Vito, Tom Jones. *Dir.* Tim Burton.

Marty (1955)   Ernest Borgnine, Betsy Blair, Jerry Paris. *Dir.* Delbert Mann.

Mary of Scotland (1936)   Katharine Hepburn, Fredric March, Donald Crisp. *Dir.* John Ford.

Mary Poppins (1964)   Julie Andrews, Dick Van Dyke, Glynis Johns, David Tomlinson, Elsa Lanchester, Arthur Treacher. Among many other awards, the song 'Chim Chim Cheree' won the Oscar for Best Song. *Dir.* Robert Stevenson.

Mary Queen of Scots (1971)   Vanessa Redgrave, Glenda Jackson, Trevor Howard, Patrick McGoohan, Nigel Davenport. *Dir.* Charles Jarrott.

M*A*S*H (1970)   Donald Sutherland, Elliott Gould, Sally Kellerman, Robert Duvall, Gary Burghoff. *Dir.* Robert Altman.

Mask, The (1994)   Jim Carrey, Amy Yasbeck, Peter Riegert. *Dir.* Charles Russell.

Matilda (1997) Danny De Vito, Mara Wilson (Matilda), Rhea Perlman, Pam Ferris. Based on Roald Dahl's bestseller. *Dir.* Danny De Vito.

Matter of Life and Death, A (1946) David Niven, Roger Livesey, Kim Hunter, Marius Goring, Raymond Massey, Abraham Sofaer. US Title: *Stairway to Heaven*. *Dir.* Michael Powell.

Maverick (1994) Mel Gibson, Jodie Foster, James Garner, Graham Greene, James Coburn, Alfred Molina. *Dir.* Richard Donner.

Mean Streets (1973) Robert De Niro, Harvey Keitel, Amy Robinson. *Dir.* Martin Scorsese.

Meet Me in St Louis (1944) Judy Garland, Margaret O'Brien, Tom Drake, Mary Astor. *Dir.* Vincente Minnelli.

Men, The (1950) Marlon Brando, Teresa Wright, Everett Sloane, Jack Webb. Reissue Title: *Battle Stripe*. *Dir.* Fred Zinnemann.

Men of Respect (1990) John Turturro, Katherine Borowitz, Dennis Farina, Peter Boyle, Rod Steiger. Gangster setting for Shakespeare's *Macbeth*. *Dir.* William Reilly.

Mercury Rising (1998) Bruce Willis, Alec Baldwin, Miko Hughes, Chi McBride, Kim Dickens, Robert Stanton, Carrie Preston, Bodhi Pine Elfman, LL Ginter, John Carroll Lynch, Peter Stormare. *Dir.* Harold Becker.

Mermaids (1990) Cher, Bob Hoskins, Winona Ryder. Daughter, torn between becoming a nun and her feelings for a handsome boy, resolves her difficulties with her flirtatious mother. *Dir.* Richard Benjamin.

Merry Christmas, Mr Lawrence (1982) David Bowie, Tom Conti, Ryuichi Sakamoto, Takeshi. *Dir.* Nagisa Oshima.

Metro (1997) Eddie Murphy (Scott Roper), Michael Rapaport, Kim Miyori. *Dir.* Thomas Carter.

Miami Rhapsody (1995) Sarah Jessica Parker, Gil Bellows, Antonio Banderas, Mia Farrow, Paul Mazursky, Naomi Campbell. Woman contemplating marriage observes the marital errors being committed by her siblings and friends. *Dir.* David Frankel.

MIB (Men in Black), (1997) Tommy Lee Jones (K), Will Smith (J), Linda Fiorentino (Dr Weaver), Rip Torn (Zed). SF film in which Will Smith performs title track & Snoop Doggy Dogg the soundtrack album. *Dir.* Barry Sonnenfeld.

Michael Collins (1996) Liam Neeson (Michael Collins), Aidan Quinn (Harry Boland), Julia Roberts (Kitty Kiernan). *Dir.* Neil Jordan.

Microcosmos (1996) French documentary film revolving around stag beetles' attempts to gain control of a twig. *Dir.* Marie Perennau & Claude Nuridsany.

Midnight Cowboy (1969) Dustin Hoffman, Jon Voight, Brenda Vaccaro, Sylvia Miles. *Dir.* John Schlesinger.

Midnight Express (1978) John Hurt, Brad Davis, Randy Quaid, Bo Hopkins. *Dir.* Alan Parker.

Midsummer Night's Dream, A (1935) James Cagney, Dick Powell, Jean Muir, Mickey Rooney, Olivia de Havilland. *Dir.* Max Reinhardt.

Midsummer Night's Dream, A (1996) Lindsay Duncan, Alex Jennings, Alfred Burke. *Dir.* Adrian Noble.

Mighty, The (1998) Sharon Stone, Gena Rowlands Harry Dean Stanton, Gillian Anderson, Meatloaf. *Dir.* Peter Chelsom.

Mighty Aphrodite (1995) Woody Allen, Helena Bonham Carter, Mira Sorvino, F Murray Abraham, Olympia Dukakis, Peter Weller, Claire Bloom, Michael Rapaport. Sportswriter's attempt to rescue the mother of his adopted son from life as a prostitute. *Dir.* Woody Allen.

Mighty Ducks, The (1992) Emilio Estevez, Joss Ackland, Lane Smith, Heidi King. Lawyer on community service for drink-driving adopts a hockey team. (GB Title: *Champions*). *Dir.* Stephen Herek.

Mighty Quinn, The (1989) Denzel Washington, James Fox, Mimi Rogers, M Emmet Walsh, Norman Beaton. Caribbean police investigate the murder of an American. *Dir.* Carl Shenkel.

Million Pound Note, The (1953) Gregory Peck, Jane Griffiths, Ronald Squire, Joyce Grenfell, Wilfrid Hyde-White. Based on a Mark Twain story. *Dir.* Ronald Neame.

Miracle on 34th Street (1994) Richard Attenborough, Elizabeth Perkins, Robert Prosky. Remake of the 1947 film starring Edmund Gwenn & Maureen O'Hara. *Dir.* Les Mayfield.

Miracle Worker, The (1962) Anne Bancroft, Patty Duke, Victor Jory. *Dir.* Arthur Penn.

Miranda (1947) Glynis Johns, Griffith Jones, Googie Withers, Margaret Rutherford, David Tomlinson. Sequel to this mermaid movie was *Mad About Men*, starring Johns and Donald Sinden. *Dir.* Ken Annakin.

Misery (1990) James Caan, Kathy Bates, Richard Farnsworth, Lauren Bacall. Disturbed fan kidnaps an injured novelist and forces him to write a novel. *Dir.* Rob Reiner.

Misfits, The (1961) Clark Gable, Marilyn Monroe, Montgomery Clift, Eli Wallach, Kevin McCarthy. Film about cowboys in the Nevada desert roping mustangs but more famous for its co-stars' imminent deaths. *Dir.* John Huston.

Mission, The (1986) Robert De Niro, Jeremy Irons, Ray McAnally, Liam Neeson, Cherie Lunghi. Music by Ennio Morricone. *Dir.* Roland Joffe.

Mission Impossible (1996) Tom Cruise, Jon Voight, Kristin Scott-Thomas, Vanessa Redgrave. *Dir.* Brian De Palma.

Missionary, The (1983) Michael Palin, Maggie Smith, Trevor Howard, Michael Hordern, Denholm Elliott. *Dir.* Richard Loncraine.

Mississippi Burning (1988) Gene Hackman, Willem Dafoe, Frances McDormand. *Dir.* Alan Parker.

Missouri Breaks (1976) Marlon Brando, Jack Nicholson, Randy Quaid, Kathleen Lloyd. *Dir.* Arthur Penn.

Moby Dick (1956) Gregory Peck, Richard Basehart, Orson Welles, James Robertson Justice. Based on Herman Melville's novel. *Dir.* John Huston.

Mommie Dearest (1981) Faye Dunaway, Diana Scarwid, Steve Forrest, Howard da Silva (Louis B Mayer). Joan Crawford life story. *Dir.* Frank Perry.

Mona Lisa (1986) Bob Hoskins, Cathy Tyson, Michael Caine, Robbie Coltrane. *Dir.* Neil Jordan.

Money Train (1995) Wesley Snipes, Woody Harrelson, Jennifer Lopez. *Dir.* Joseph Ruben.

Monty Python and the Holy Grail (1975) John Cleese, Graham Chapman, Terry Gilliam, Eric Idle, Michael Palin, Terry Jones. *Dir.* Terry Gilliam and Terry Jones.

Monty Python's Life of Brian (1979) John Cleese, Graham Chapman, Terry Gilliam, Eric Idle, Michael Palin, Terry Jones. *Dir.* Terry Jones.

Monty Python's The Meaning of Life (1983) John Cleese, Graham Chapman, Terry Gilliam, Eric Idle, Michael Palin, Terry Jones. *Dir.* Terry Jones.

Moon is Blue, The (1953) Maggie McNamara, David Niven, William Holden, Tom Tully, Dawn Addams. *Dir.* Otto Preminger.

Moonlighting (1982) Jeremy Irons, Eugene Lipinski, Jiri Stanislaw. Four Polish building workers arrive in

London to renovate a house and hear of social unrest at home. *Dir.* Jerzy Skolimowski.

Moonraker (1979) Roger Moore, Lois Chiles (Holly Goodhead), Michael Lonsdale (Hugo Drax). Title song performed by Shirley Bassey. *Dir.* Lewis Gilbert.

Moonstruck (1987) Cher, Nicolas Cage, Vincent Gardenia, Olympia Dukakis, Danny Aiello. Young widow falls for the estranged brother of her husband-to-be. *Dir.* Norman Jewison.

Moonwalker (1988) Michael Jackson, Joe Pesci, Sean Lennon. *Dir.* Colin Chilvers.

Mouse on the Moon, The (1963) Margaret Rutherford, Ron Moody, Bernard Cribbins, David Kossoff, Terry-Thomas, Michael Crawford. Sequel to *The Mouse that Roared;* concerning home-made wine making excellent rocket-fuel. *Dir.* Richard Lester.

Mouse that Roared, The (1959) Peter Sellers (three roles), Jean Seberg, David Kossoff, William Hartnell, Leo McKern. Tiny Duchy of Grand Fenwick is bankrupt, so decides to declare war on USA, be defeated, and then accept aid. *Dir.* Jack Arnold.

Move over Darling (1963) Doris Day, James Garner, Polly Bergen, Chuck Connors. Wife returns home after shipwreck to find her husband remarried. *Dir.* Michael Gordon.

Mr and Mrs Bridge (1990) Paul Newman, Joanne Woodward, Robert Sean Leonard, Blythe Danner, Simon Callow. Inhibited lawyer gradually erodes his wife's personality. *Dir.* James Ivory.

Mr Deeds Goes to Town (1936) Gary Cooper, Jean Arthur, Raymond Walburn, Margaret Seddon. Small-town poet inherits fortune and sets New York on its heels with his honesty. *Dir.* Frank Capra.

Mr Jones (1993) Richard Gere, Lena Olin, Anne Bancroft. Manic depressive begins an affair with his psychiatrist. *Dir.* Mike Figgis.

Mr Smith Goes to Washington (1939) James Stewart, Claude Rains, Jean Arthur, Thomas Mitchell, Edward Arnold. Senator exposes corruption in high places. *Dir.* Frank Capra.

Mrs Brown (1997) Billy Connolly (John Brown), Dame Judi Dench (Queen Victoria). *Dir.* John Madden.

Mrs Dalloway (1998) Vanessa Redgrave, Rupert Graves, Natascha McElhone, Michael Kitchen. *Dir.* Marleen Gorris.

Mrs Doubtfire (1993) Robin Williams, Sally Field, Pierce Brosnan, Robert Prosky. *Dir.* Chris Columbus.

Mrs Miniver (1942) Greer Garson, Walter Pidgeon, Teresa Wright. Multi-award winning film. *Dir.* William Wyler.

Mrs Pollifax – Spy (1970) Rosalind Russell, Darren McGavin. Written by CA McKnight who was, in fact, Rosalind Russell. *Dir.* Leslie Martinson.

Much Ado about Nothing (1993) Kenneth Branagh, Emma Thompson, Richard Briers, Michael Keaton, Denzel Washington. *Dir.* Kenneth Branagh.

Mudlark, The (1950) Alec Guinness, Irene Dunne, Andrew Ray, Anthony Steel, Finlay Currie. Scruffy boy from the docks breaks into Windsor Castle to visit Queen Victoria. *Dir.* Jean Negulesco.

Mulholland Falls (1996) Nick Nolte, Melanie Griffith, Treat Williams, John Malkovich, Bruce Dern. *Dir.* Lee Tamahori.

Multiplicity (1996) Michael Keaton, Andie MacDowell, Ann Cusack. *Dir.* Harold Ramis.

Mummy, The (1932) Boris Karloff, Zita Johann, David Manners, Arthur Byron, Edward Van Sloan. Boris Karloff was billed as 'Karloff the Uncanny'. *Dir.* Karl Freund.

Mummy Returns, The (2001) Brendan Fraser, Rachel Weisz, John Hannah, Arnold Vosloo (The Mummy), Kevin O'Conner. *Dir.* Stephen Sommers. Acting debut of wrestling superstar 'The Rock' as The Scorpian King.

Mummy, The (1959) Peter Cushing, Christopher Lee, Yvonne Furneaux, Eddie Byrne, Felix Aylmer, Raymond Huntley, John Stuart. *Dir.* Terence Fisher.

Mummy, The (1999) Brendan Fraser, Rachel Weisz, John Hannah, Arnold Vosloo, Kevin O'Connor. *Dir.* Stephen Sommers.

Muppet Movie, The (1979) Charles Durning, Edgar Bergen, Bob Hope, Milton Berle, Mel Brooks, James Coburn, Dom DeLuise, Elliott Gould, Cloris Leachman, Telly Savalas, Orson Welles. *Dir.* James Frawley.

Muppets Take Manhattan, The (1984) Dabney Coleman, Art Carney, James Coco, Joan Rivers, Gregory Hines, Linda Lavin. *Dir.* Frank Oz.

Murder by Decree (1978) Christopher Plummer, James Mason, Anthony Quayle, David Hemmings, Susan Clark, John Gielgud, Donald Sutherland, Frank Finlay, Geneviève Bujold. Sherlock Holmes investigates the murders of 'Jack the Ripper'. *Dir.* Bob Clark.

Murder Most Foul (1964) Margaret Rutherford, Ron Moody, Charles Tingwell, Andrew Cruickshank, Megs Jenkins, Ralph Michael, James Bolam, Stringer Davis, Francesca Annis, Dennis Price, Terry Scott. Based on the Agatha Christie novel *Mrs McGinty's Dead*. *Dir.* George Pollock.

Murder on the Orient Express (1974) Albert Finney, Ingrid Bergman, Lauren Bacall, Wendy Hiller, Sean Connery, Vanessa Redgrave, Michael York, Martin Balsam, Richard Widmark, Jacqueline Bisset, Jean-Pierre Cassel, Rachel Roberts, George Coulouris, John Gielgud, Anthony Perkins, Colin Blakely, Jeremy Lloyd, Denis Quilley. Hercule Poirot solves this Agatha Christie story. *Dir.* Sidney Lumet.

Murders in the Rue Morgue (1932) Bela Lugosi, Sidney Fox, Leon Ames, Bert Roach, Brandon Hurst. *Dir.* Robert Florey.

Murders in the Rue Morgue (1971) Jason Robards Jnr, Herbert Lom, Lilli Palmer, Adolfo Celi, Michael Dunn, Christine Kaufmann. *Dir.* Gordon Hessler.

Muriel's Wedding (1994) Toni Collette, Bill Hunter, Rachel Griffiths, Jeanie Drynan. *Dir.* PJ Hogan.

Murphy's Law (1986) Charles Bronson, Carrie Snodgress, Kathleen Wilhoite, Robert F Lyons, Richard Romanus. *Dir.* J Lee Thompson.

Murphy's War (1971) Peter O'Toole, Sian Phillips, Philippe Noiret, Horst Janson. *Dir.* Peter Yates.

Music Lovers, The (1970) Richard Chamberlain, Glenda Jackson, Christopher Gable, Max Adrian, Isabelle Telezynska, Maureen Pryor, Andrew Faulds. Screenplay written by Melvyn Bragg. *Dir.* Ken Russell.

Music Man, The (1962) Robert Preston, Shirley Jones, Buddy Hackett, Hermione Gingold, Pert Kelton, Paul Ford. *Dir.* Morton da Costa.

Mutiny on the Bounty (1935) Charles Laughton, Clark Gable, Franchot Tone, Movita, Dudley Digges. *Dir.* Frank Lloyd.

Mutiny on the Bounty (1962) Trevor Howard, Marlon Brando, Richard Harris, Hugh Griffith, Tarita, Richard Haydn, Gordon Jackson. *Dir.* Lewis Milestone.

My Beautiful Laundrette (1985) Saeed Jaffrey, Roshan Seth, Daniel Day-Lewis, Shirley Anne Field. Based on the Hanif Kureishi work. *Dir.* Stephen Frears.

My Favourite Martian (1999) Christopher Lloyd, Jeff Daniels, Elizabeth Hurley, Daryl Hannah, Ray

Walston. *Dir.* Donald Petrie. Based on the TV series starring Ray Walston and Bill Bixby.

Mysterious Dr Fu Manchu, The (1929)   Warner Oland played the Sax Rohmer character in early films in the series. *Dir.* Various.

Naked (1993)   David Thewlis, Lesley Sharp, Katrin Cartlidge, Greg Cruttwell. *Dir.* Mike Leigh.

Naked Edge, The (1961)   Gary Cooper, Deborah Kerr, Peter Cushing, Michael Wilding, Diane Cilento. *Dir.* Michael Anderson.

Naked Gun, The: From the Files of Police Squad (1988)   Leslie Nielsen, Priscilla Presley, Ricardo Montalban, OJ Simpson, George Kennedy. *Dir.* David Zucker.

Naked Gun 2 1/2, The: The Smell of Fear (1991)   Leslie Nielsen, Priscilla Presley, Robert Goulet, OJ Simpson, George Kennedy. *Dir.* David Zucker.

Naked Gun 33 1/3, The: The Final Insult (1994)   Leslie Nielsen, Priscilla Presley, Fred Ward, OJ Simpson, George Kennedy, Anna Nicole Smith. *Dir.* Peter Segal.

Naked in New York (1993)   Eric Stoltz, Mary-Louise Parker, Ralph Macchio, Jill Clayburgh, Tony Curtis, Kathleen Turner, Timothy Dalton, Whoopi Goldberg, Quentin Crisp. *Dir.* Dan Algrant.

Naked Lunch (1991)   Peter Weller, Judy Davis, Ian Holm, Roy Scheider, Julian Sands. Drug-addicted writer emulates William Tell with fatal results. *Dir.* David Cronenberg.

Name of the Rose, The (1986)   Sean Connery (William of Baskerville), F Murray Abraham (Bernardo Gui), Christian Slater (Adso of Melk), Feodor Chaliapin (Jorge de Burgos), William Hickey (Ubertino de Casale). Based on Umberto Eco novel. *Dir.* Jean-Jacques Annaud.

Narrow Margin (1952)   Charles McGraw, Marie Windsor, Jacqueline White, Queenie Leonard. Police try to guard a witness on a train from Chicago to LA. The 1990 remake starred Gene Hackman and Anne Archer. *Dir.* Richard Fleischer.

National Lampoon's Animal House (1978)   John Belushi, Tim Matheson, Donald Sutherland, John Vernon. First of the series which continued with *Movie Madness* (1981), *Class Reunion* (1982), *Vacation* (1983), *European Vacation* (1985), *Christmas Vacation* (1989), *Loaded Weapon* (1993), and *Senior Trip* (1995). The Chevy Chase character in 3 of the films was Clark Griswold. *Dir.* John Landis.

National Velvet (1945)   Mickey Rooney, Elizabeth Taylor, Anne Revere, Donald Crisp, Angela Lansbury. *Dir.* Clarence Brown.

Natural, The (1984)   Robert Redford (Roy Hobbs), Robert Duvall (Max Mercy), Glenn Close (Iris), Kim Basinger (Memo Paris), Barbara Hershey (Harriet Bird), Robert Prosky (Judge), Joe Don Baker (The Whammer). Ups and downs of a baseball star. *Dir.* Barry Levinson.

Natural Born Killers (1994)   Woody Harrelson, Juliette Lewis, Robert Downey Jnr, Tommy Lee Jones. Young couple become mass murderers while winning the affection of the media. *Dir.* Oliver Stone.

Ned Kelly (1970)   Mick Jagger, Allen Bickford, Geoff Gilmour, Mark McManus. Story of the 19th-century Australian outlaw. *Dir.* Tony Richardson.

Nell (1994)   Jodie Foster, Liam Neeson, Natasha Richardson. Two doctors endeavour to talk to a young woman who speaks a solitary language. *Dir.* Michael Apted.

Net, The (1995)   Sandra Bullock, Jeremy Northam, Dennis Miller, Diane Baker. *Dir.* Irwin Winkler.

Network (1976)   Peter Finch (Howard Beale), William Holden (Max Schumacher), Faye Dunaway, Robert Duvall, Ned Beatty. Peter Finch was awarded a posthumous Academy Award. *Dir.* Sidney Lumet.

Nevada Smith (1966)   Steve McQueen, Karl Malden, Brian Keith, Suzanne Pleshette. Scenes from the early life of the *Carpetbaggers* character. *Dir.* Henry Hathaway.

Never Been Kissed (1998)   Drew Barrymore, David Arquette, Michael Vartan, Leelee Sobieski, Jeremy Jordan. *Dir.* Raja Gosnell.

Never on Sunday (1959)   Melina Mercouri, Jules Dassin. Original title: *Pote tin Kyriaki*. *Dir.* Jules Dassin.

Never Say Never Again (1983)   Sean Connery, Klaus Maria Brandauer (Largo), Max Von Sydow (Blofeld), Alec McCowen (Q), Kim Basinger (Domino), Edward Fox, Rowan Atkinson, Barbara Carrera (Fatima). Remake of *Thunderball*, so titled because Connery vowed he would never make another Bond movie after *Diamonds are Forever*. *Dir.* Irvin Kershner.

New York, New York (1977)   Liza Minnelli, Robert De Niro, Lionel Stander, Barry Primus. *Dir.* Martin Scorsese.

New York Stories (1989)   *Life Lessons*: Nick Nolte, Patrick O'Neal, Rosanna Arquette, Steve Buscemi, Debbie Harry, Peter Gabriel. *Dir.* Martin Scorsese. *Life without Zoe*: Talia Shire, Giancarlo Giannini, Heather McComb, Carmine Coppola. *Dir.* Francis Ford Coppola. *Oedipus Wrecks*: Woody Allen, Mia Farrow, Julie Kavner, Mae Questel, Mayor Ed Koch. *Dir.* Woody Allen.   Teacher sets the 3 top boys an essay – topic: 'My Story about New York' and the 3 separately directed stories follow.

Next of Kin (1989)   Patrick Swayze (Truman Gates), Liam Neeson (Briar Gates), Adam Baldwin (Joey Rosselini). *Dir.* John Irvin.

Niagara (1952)   Joseph Cotten, Jean Peters, Marilyn Monroe. *Dir.* Henry Hathaway.

Nicholas and Alexandra (1971)   Michael Jayston, Janet Suzman, Laurence Olivier, Jack Hawkins, Tom Baker, Michael Redgrave. Life of Tsar Nicholas II from 1904 until the execution of his family in 1918. *Dir.* Franklin Schaffner.

Nickelodeon (1976)   Ryan O'Neal, Burt Reynolds, Tatum O'Neal, Brian Keith, Stella Stevens. Events leading up to the premiere of *The Birth of a Nation*. *Dir.* Peter Bogdanovich.

Night and Day (1946)   Cary Grant (Cole Porter), Alexis Smith, Monty Woolley, Mary Martin, Jane Wyman, Eve Arden. *Dir.* Michael Curtiz.

Night and the City (1992)   Robert De Niro (Harry Fabian), Jessica Lange (Helen Nasseros), Alan King (Boom Boom Grossman). Remake of the 1950 classic starring Richard Widmark and Gene Tierney. *Dir.* Irwin Winkler.

Night at the Opera, A (1935)   Groucho Marx, Chico Marx, Harpo Marx, Margaret Dumont. *Dir.* Sam Wood.

Night Crossing (1982)   John Hurt, Jane Alexander, Beau Bridges, Ian Bannen. East Germans escape to the West via air balloon. *Dir.* Delbert Mann.

Night Falls on Manhattan (1997)   Andy Garcia (Sean Casey), Ian Holm. *Dir.* Sidney Lumet.

Night in Casablanca, A (1946)   Groucho Marx (Kornblow), Chico Marx, Harpo Marx, Lisette Verea (Beatrice). *Dir.* Archie Mayo.

Night of the Hunter (1955)   Robert Mitchum, Shelley Winters, Lillian Gish, Peter Graves. Psychopathic preacher on the trail of hidden loot. *Dir.* Charles Laughton.

Night of the Iguana (1964)   Richard Burton, Deborah

Kerr, Ava Gardner, Sue Lyon. Disbarred clergyman becomes a courier in Mexico and is chased by teenage nymphomaniac. *Dir.* John Huston.

Night on Earth (1992)   Winona Ryder (Corky), Gena Rowlands (Victoria Snelling), Giancarlo Esposito (Yo Yo). Five people take simultaneous taxi rides in 5 cities, i.e. LA, New York, Paris, Rome & Helsinki. *Dir.* Jim Jarmusch.

Night Porter, The (1973)   Dirk Bogarde, Charlotte Rampling. Wife of opera conductor recognises porter as a former SS officer. *Dir.* Liliana Cavani.

Night Shift (1982)   Henry Winkler, Michael Keaton, Shelley Long, Gina Hecht, Kevin Costner (Frat Boy). *Dir.* Ron Howard.

Night They Raided Minsky's, The (1968)   Jason Robards, Britt Ekland, Norman Wisdom, Bert Lahr. *Dir.* William Friedkin.

Night to Remember, A (1958)   Kenneth More, Honor Blackman, David McCallum. *Dir.* Roy Baker.

Nightmare Before Christmas, The (1993)   Voices of Danny Elfman, Chris Sarandon, William Hickey, Catherine O'Hara. Based on a Tim Burton story. *Dir.* Henry Selick.

Nightmare on Elm Street, A (1984)   John Saxon, Ronee Blakley, Robert Englund (Freddie). *Dir.* Wes Craven.

Nightmare on Elm Street, A, 2: Freddy's Revenge (1985)   Mark Patton, Clu Gulager, Hope Lange, Kim Myers, Robert Englund (Freddie). *Dir.* Jack Sholder.

Nightmare on Elm Street, A, 3: Dream Warriors (1987)   Heather Langenkamp, Patricia Arquette, Robert Englund (Freddie). *Dir.* Chuck Russell.

Nightmare on Elm Street, A, 4: The Dream Master (1988)   Rodney Eastman, Danny Hassel, Robert Englund (Freddie). *Dir.* Renny Harlin.

Nightmare on Elm Street, A: The Dream Child (1989)   Lisa Wilcox, Kelly Jo Minter, Danny Hassel, Robert Englund (Freddie). Last of the series called *Freddy's Dead: The Final Nightmare* (1991). *Dir.* Stephen Hopkins.

Nil by Mouth (1997)   Ray Winstone (Ray), Kathy Burke (Valerie). *Dir.* Gary Oldman.

Nine and a Half Weeks (1986)   Mickey Rourke, Kim Basinger. *Dir.* Adrian Lyne.

976–EVIL (1988)   Stephen Geoffreys (Hoax), Sandy Dennis (Aunt Lucy). The title refers to the Devil's freephone number. *Dir.* Robert Englund.

9/30/55 (1977)   Richard Thomas, Susan Tyrrell, Dennis Quaid. Title refers to the death of James Dean and the effect on an Arkansas student. *Dir.* James Bridges.

Nine to Five (1980)   Jane Fonda, Dolly Parton, Lily Tomlin, Dabney Coleman, Sterling Hayden. Three office women plot to get rid of their boss. *Dir.* Colin Higgins.

1984 (1984)   John Hurt (Winston Smith), Richard Burton (O'Brien), Suzanna Hamilton (Julia), Cyril Cusack (Carrington). A 1955 version starred Michael Redgrave and Edmond O'Brien. *Dir.* Michael Radford.

1941 (1979)   Dan Aykroyd, Ned Beatty, John Belushi, Christopher Lee, Robert Stack, Lorraine Gary. Farce concerning a stray Japanese submarine terrorising Hollywood after Pearl Harbor. *Dir.* Steven Spielberg.

Ninotchka (1939)   Greta Garbo, Melvyn Douglas, Bela Lugosi. *Dir.* Ernst Lubitsch.

Nixon (1995)   Anthony Hopkins (Nixon), Joan Allen (Pat Nixon), Powers Boothe (Alexander Haig), Ed Harris (E. Howard Hunt), Paul Sorvino (Henry Kissinger). *Dir.* Oliver Stone.

Nobody's Fool (1994)   Paul Newman, Jessica Tandy,

Bruce Willis, Melanie Griffith. A 60-yr-old handyman has a chance to make up for a disappointing life. *Dir.* Robert Benton.

Noises Off (1992)   Carol Burnett (Dotty Otley / Mrs Clackett), Michael Caine (Lloyd Fellowes), Denholm Elliott, Julie Hagerty, Marilu Henner, Christopher Reeve. Adaptation of Michael Frayn's farce about a second-rate touring company. *Dir.* Peter Bogdanovich.

No Place To Go (Die Unberüehrbare) (2001)   Hannelore Elsner (Hanna), Vadim Glowna, Tonio Arango, Michael Gwisdek, Bernd Stempel. *Dir.* Oskar Röhler.

North by Northwest (1959)   Cary Grant, Eva Marie Saint, James Mason. *Dir.* Alfred Hitchcock.

North Dallas Forty (1979)   Nick Nolte, Mac Davis, Charles Durning, Bo Svenson. Gruelling life of an American football player. *Dir.* Ted Kotcheff.

Notorious (1946)   Cary Grant, Ingrid Bergman, Claude Rains, Louis Calhern. Lady marries a Nazi in Rio to help the American government. *Dir.* Alfred Hitchcock.

Notting Hill (1999)   Julia Roberts, Hugh Grant, Hugh Bonneville, Emma Chambers, Alec Baldwin. *Dir.* Roger Michell.

Nuns on the Run (1990)   Eric Idle, Robbie Coltrane, Janet Suzman, Doris Hare. *Dir.* Jonathan Lynn.

Nun's Story, The (1959)   Audrey Hepburn, Peter Finch, Edith Evans, Peggy Ashcroft. Belgian girl joins a strict order of nuns. *Dir.* Fred Zinnemann.

Nurse Edith Cavell (1939)   Anna Neagle, George Sanders. Based on Reginald Berkeley's novel *Dawn*. *Dir.* Herbert Wilcox.

Nutty Professor, The (1996)   Eddie Murphy (plays 7 roles), James Coburn, Jada Pinkett. *Dir.* Tom Shadyac.

Object of Beauty, The (1991)   John Malkovich, Andie MacDowell, Joss Ackland, Bill Paterson, Jack Shepherd. *Dir.* Michael Lindsay-Hogg.

Objective Burma! (1945)   Errol Flynn, James Brown, William Prince. Exploits of a US platoon during the Burma campaign. The film caused a furore among the Burma Star Organisation and nearly created a diplomatic fallout by failing to mention the British contribution. *Dir.* Raoul Walsh.

Obsession (1976)   Cliff Robertson, Geneviève Bujold, John Lithgow. Widower meets the double of his dead wife. *Dir.* Brian De Palma.

Ocean's Eleven (1960)   Frank Sinatra, Peter Lawford, Sammy Davis Jnr, Dean Martin, Richard Conte, Ilka Chase, Cesar Romero, Joey Bishop, Patrick Wymore, Akim Tamiroff, Henry Silva, Angie Dickenson. *Dir.* Lewis Milestone.

Octopussy (1983)   Roger Moore, Maud Adams (Octopussy), Louis Jourdan (Prince Kamel Khan), Steven Berkoff (Orlov), Robert Brown (M), Desmond Llewelyn (Q). Tennis player Vijay Amritraj appeared in a cameo role. Title song performed by Rita Coolidge. *Dir.* John Glen.

Odd Couple, The (1968)   Jack Lemmon (Felix Unger), Walter Matthau (Oscar Goldman). Written by Neil Simon. *Dir.* Gene Saks.

Odessa File, The (1974)   Jon Voigt, Maria Schell, Maximilian Schell, Derek Jacobi. *Dir.* Ronald Neame.

Of Mice and Men (1939)   Burgess Meredith, Lon Chaney Jnr, Betty Field, Charles Bickford. Itinerant worker looks after his immensely strong but mentally retarded cousin. The 1992 remake starred John Malkovich and Gary Sinise. *Dir.* Lewis Milestone.

Officer and a Gentleman, An (1982)   Richard Gere (Zack Mayo), Debra Winger, Lou Gossett Jnr, David Keith, Lisa Blount. Oscars for Lou Gossett Jnr (Best

Supporting), and song ('Up Where We Belong').
Dir. Taylor Hackford.

Oh What a Lovely War (1969)   Ralph Richardson, Meriel Forbes, John Gielgud, Kenneth More, John Clements, Joe Melia, Paul Daneman, Jack Hawkins, Maggie Smith, John Mills, Michael Redgrave, Laurence Olivier, Susannah York, Dirk Bogarde, Phyllis Calvert, Vanessa Redgrave. Musical fantasia of World War I. *Dir.* Richard Attenborough.

O.H.M.S. (1936)   John Mills, Wallace Ford, Anna Lee. British forces in China are joined by an American gangster on the run, who dies a hero. US Title: *You're in the Army Now. Dir.* Raoul Walsh.

Oklahoma (1955)   Gordon Macrae, Shirley Jones, Rod Steiger, Eddie Albert. *Dir.* Fred Zinnemann.

Oklahoma Kid, The (1939)   James Cagney, Humphrey Bogart, Rosemary Lane, Donald Crisp, Ward Bond. *Dir.* Lloyd Bacon.

Old Gringo (1989)   Jane Fonda (Harriet Winslow), Gregory Peck (Ambrose Bierce), Jimmy Smits (Tomas Arroyo). *Dir.* Luis Puenzo.

Old Man and the Sea, The (1958)   Spencer Tracy, Felipe Pazos, Harry Bellaver. *Dir.* John Sturges.

Old Mother Riley (1935–52)   Arthur Lucan (Old Mother Riley), Kitty McShane (his daughter). Series of films with Lucan and his real-life wife playing mother and daughter. *Stars on Parade* was the first of the series and *Mother Riley Meets the Vampire* the last. *Dir.* Maclean Rogers.

Oliver! (1968)   Ron Moody, Oliver Reed, Harry Secombe, Mark Lester, Shani Wallis, Jack Wild. *Dir.* Carol Reed.

Oliver Twist (1948)   Alec Guinness, Robert Newton, Francis L Sullivan, John Howard Davies, Anthony Newley, Diana Dors, Mary Clare, Kay Walsh. *Dir.* David Lean.

Oliver's Story (1978)   Ryan O'Neal, Candice Bergen, Nicola Pagett, Ray Milland. *Dir.* John Korty.

Omega Man, The (1971)   Charlton Heston, Rosalind Cash, Anthony Zerbe. Based on the novel *I am Legend* by Richard Matheson. Set in 1977 Los Angeles after a germ warfare plague has decimated the world's population. *Dir.* Boris Sagal.

Omen, The (1976)   Gregory Peck, Lee Remick, David Warner, Billie Whitelaw, Leo McKern, Patrick Troughton. Three inferior sequels were made. *Dir.* Richard Donner.

On Deadly Ground (1994)   Steven Seagal, Michael Caine, Joan Chen, Chief Irvin Brink. *Dir.* Steven Seagal.

On Golden Pond (1981)   Henry Fonda, Katharine Hepburn, Jane Fonda, Dabney Coleman, Doug McKeon. *Dir.* Mark Rydell.

On Her Majesty's Secret Service (1969)   George Lazenby, Diana Rigg (Tracy Vicenzo née Draco), Telly Savalas (Blofeld). *Avengers* fans note: not only does Diana Rigg become Mrs Bond but Joanna Lumley is one of the lovelies in the Swiss Alps and Honor Blackman is visible in a clip from *Goldfinger* in the opening titles. *Dir.* Peter Hunt. Theme song: 'We have all the time in the World' performed by Louis Armstrong.

On the Beach (1959)   Gregory Peck, Ava Gardner, Fred Astaire, Anthony Perkins, Donna Anderson. Crew of serving American submarine wait for the devastation of atomic war to catch up with them in Australia. *Dir.* Stanley Kramer.

On the Buses (1971)   Reg Varney, Doris Hare, Anna Karen, Michael Robbins, Stephen Lewis. Sequels: *Mutiny on the Buses* (1972), and *Holiday on the Buses* (1973). *Dir.* Harry Booth.

On the Double (1961)   Danny Kaye, Dana Wynter,

Wilfrid Hyde-White, Diana Dors, Margaret Rutherford, Allan Cuthbertson, Jesse White. American private is asked to impersonate a British Intelligence officer. *Dir.* Melville Shavelson.

On the Fiddle (1961)   Alfred Lynch, Sean Connery, Wilfrid Hyde-White, Kathleen Harrison, Cecil Parker, Alan King, Eleanor Summerfield, Eric Barker, John Le Mesurier, Terence Longdon. US Title: *Operation Snafu.* Wide boy and slow-witted gypsy's adventures in the RAF. *Dir.* Cyril Frankel.

On the Town (1949)   Frank Sinatra, Gene Kelly, Jules Munshin, Ann Miller, Vera-Ellen, Betty Garrett. Gene Kelly directed the dance scenes. *Dir.* Stanley Donen.

On the Waterfront (1954)   Marlon Brando, Eva Marie Saint, Rod Steiger, Lee J Cobb, Karl Malden. *Dir.* Elia Kazan.

Once a Jolly Swagman (1948)   Dirk Bogarde, Renée Asherson, Bonar Colleano, Bill Owen. US Title: *Maniacs on Wheels.* Factory worker becomes a speedway rider. *Dir.* Jack Lee.

Once Around (1991)   Richard Dreyfuss, Holly Hunter, Danny Aiello, Gena Rowlands, Laura San Giacomo. *Dir.* Lasse Hallstrom.

Once Bitten (1985)   Lauren Hutton, Jim Carrey, Karen Kopins, Cleavon Little. Teenage sex problems are complicated by a visiting vampiress. *Dir.* Howard Storm.

Once More with Feeling (1960)   Yul Brynner, Kay Kendall, Geoffrey Toone, Maxwell Shaw, Mervyn Johns. Volatile private life of an orchestral conductor. *Dir.* Stanley Donen.

Once Upon a Crime (1992)   John Candy, James Belushi, Cybill Shepherd, Sean Young, Joss Ackland. *Dir.* Eugene Levy.

Once Upon a Horse (1958)   Dan Rowan, Dick Martin, Martha Hyer, Leif Erickson, Nita Talbot, James Gleason. Two cowboys steal a herd of cattle but can't afford to feed them. The two stars later went on to revolutionise TV comedy with their *Laugh-in* shows. *Dir.* Hal Kanter.

Once Upon a Time in America (1984)   Robert De Niro (Noodles), James Woods (Max), Elizabeth McGovern (Deborah), Treat Williams (Jimmy O'Donnell), Tuesday Weld (Carol), Joe Pesci (Frankie), Danny Aiello (Police Chief Aiello), William Forsythe (Cockeye). Story of four Jewish gangsters known as the 'Kosher Nostra', from 1922 to 1968. It is a 228-minute film which has a 147-minute version. *Dir.* Sergio Leone.

Once Upon a Time in the West (1969)   Henry Fonda, Claudia Cardinale, Jason Robards, Charles Bronson. Notable for its opening credits which last for the first 12 minutes of film time. *Dir.* Sergio Leone.

Once Were Warriors (1994)   Rena Owen, Temuera Morrison. This film is the top NZ film as regards box office takings. *Dir.* Lee Tamahori.

One-Eyed Jacks (1961)   Marlon Brando, Karl Malden, Pina Pellicer, Katy Jurado, Slim Pickens, Ben Johnson. Based on the novel *The Authentic Death of Hendry Jones* by Charles Neider. *Dir.* Marlon Brando.

One False Move (1992)   Bill Paxton (Dale 'Hurricane' Dixon), Cynda Williams (Fantasia / Lila), Michael Beach (Pluto), Billy Bob Thornton (Ray Malcolm), Jim Metzler (Dud Cole). Two killers on the run with their black girlfriend go to Alabama where the sheriff is waiting. Cynda Williams and Billy Bob Thornton fell in love on set and married soon after. *Dir.* Carl Franklin.

One Fine Day (1996)   Michelle Pfeiffer, George Clooney, Charles Durning, Mae Whitman. Two busy single parents fall in love with each other. *Dir.* Michael Hoffman.

One from the Heart (1982)   Frederic Forrest (Hank), Teri Garr (Frannie), Raul Julia (Ray), Nastassja Kinski (Leila). Rebecca DeMornay's screen debut in the restaurant scene with the line: 'Excuse me, I think those are my waffles'. First film for Coppola's Zoetrope studios. *Dir.* Francis Ford Coppola.

187 (1997)   Samuel L Jackson (Trevor Garfield), Tony Plana. Title refers to the Californian penal code for murder. School: John Quincy Adams High. *Dir.* Kevin Reynolds.

101 Dalmatians (1996)   Glenn Close, Jeff Daniels, Joan Plowright, Joely Richardson, Hugh Laurie. Live-action remake of the 1961 animated film. *Dir.* Stephen Herek. The sequel *102 Dalmations* was released in 2000.

One Hundred Men and a Girl (1937)   Deanna Durbin was the girl and the men were an orchestra. *Dir.* Henry Koster.

One Million Years BC (1966)   John Richardson, Raquel Welch, Robert Brown. *Dir.* Don Chaffey.

One Woman or Two (1985)   Gérard Depardieu (Julien Chayssac), Sigourney Weaver (Jessica Fitzgerald), Dr Ruth Westheimer (Mrs Heffner). Advertising woman uses an archaeologist as basis for a new campaign and falls in love. *Dir.* Daniel Vigne.

Onibaba (1964)   Nobuko Otowa, Jitsuko Yoshimura, Kei Sato. Mother and daughter live by preying on stray soldiers. Aka: *The Hole*. *Dir.* Kaneto Shindo.

Operation Crossbow (1965)   George Peppard, Tom Courtenay, John Mills, Sophia Loren, Lilli Palmer, Trevor Howard. *Dir.* Michael Anderson.

Ordinary People (1980)   Donald Sutherland, Mary Tyler Moore, Timothy Hutton, Judd Hirsch. Oscars for Hutton, Redford and Alvin Sargent (screenplay). *Dir.* Robert Redford.

Othello (1965)   Laurence Olivier, Frank Finlay, Maggie Smith, Derek Jacobi. The 1995 Oliver Parker film starred Laurence Fishburne and Ken Branagh (Iago). *Dir.* Stuart Burge.

Our Man Flint (1965)   James Coburn, Lee J Cobb. *Dir.* Daniel Mann.

Our Man in Havana (1965)   Alec Guinness, Noël Coward, Burl Ives, Maureen O'Hara, Ralph Richardson. *Dir.* Carol Reed.

Out of Africa (1985)   Robert Redford (Denys), Meryl Streep (Karen Blixen), Klaus Maria Brandauer, Michael Gough. *Dir.* Sydney Pollack.

Outbreak (1995)   Dustin Hoffman, Rene Russo, Morgan Freeman, Donald Sutherland, Kevin Spacey. *Dir.* Wolfgang Petersen.

Outland (1981)   Sean Connery, Peter Boyle, Kika Markham. *Dir.* Peter Hyams.

Outlaw Josey Wales, The (1976)   Clint Eastwood, Chief Dan George, Sondra Locke. *Dir.* Clint Eastwood.

Outrageous Fortune (1987)   Bette Midler (Sandy), Shelley Long (Lauren), Robert Prosky, Peter Coyote. *Dir.* Arthur Hiller.

Outsiders, The (1983)   Matt Dillon (Dallas Winston), Ralph Macchio (Johnny Cade), Patrick Swayze (Darrel Curtis), Robb Lowe (Sodapop Curtis), Emilio Estevez (Two-Bit Matthews), Tom Cruise (Steve Randle). *Dir.* Francis Ford Coppola.

Over the Top (1987)   Sylvester Stallone (Lincoln Hawk), Robert Loggia (Jason Cutler), Susan Blakely (Chris Hawk). *Dir.* Menahem Golan.

Overboard (1987)   Goldie Hawn (Joanna / Annie), Kurt Russell (Dean Proffitt), Roddy McDowall (Andrew). *Dir.* Garry Marshall.

Owl and the Pussycat, The (1970)   Barbra Streisand, George Segal, Robert Klein, Allen Garfield. *Dir.* Herbert Ross.

Paint Your Wagon (1969)   Lee Marvin, Clint Eastwood (Pardner), Jean Seberg, Harve Presnell, Ray Walston. *Dir.* Joshua Logan.

Pal Joey (1957)   Frank Sinatra, Rita Hayworth, Kim Novak. *Dir.* George Sidney.

Pale Rider (1985)   Clint Eastwood (Preacher), Michael Moriarty, Carrie Snodgrass, Chris Penn, Richard Kiel. *Dir.* Clint Eastwood.

Paleface, The (1948)   Bob Hope, Jane Russell, Robert Armstrong. Song 'Buttons and Bows' (music by J Livingston, lyrics by Ray Evans) won Oscar. Sequel was *Son of Paleface* and 1968 remake was *The Shakiest Gun in the West*. *Dir.* Norman Z. Mcleod.

Pallbearer (1996)   David Schwimmer, Gwyneth Paltrow, Michael Rapaport, Barbara Hershey. *Dir.* Matt Reeves.

Palm Beach Story, The (1942)   Claudette Colbert, Joel McCrea, Rudy Vallee (Hackensacker), Robert Dudley (Weenie King). Engineer's wife travels to Florida with her sights set on a millionaire. *Dir.* Preston Sturges.

Palookaville (1996)   Adam Trese (Jerry), William Forsythe (Sid), Vincent Gallo (Russ), Frances McDormand. Story of 3 bungling would-be criminals. *Dir.* Alan Taylor.

Panther (1995)   Kadeem Hardison, Bokeem Woodbine, Joe Don Baker, Nefertiti. Black Vietnam vet recalls his role in the Black Panther movement. *Dir.* Mario Van Peebles.

Paper, The (1994)   Michael Keaton, Glenn Close, Marisa Tomei, Robert Duvall, Randy Quaid. *Dir.* Ron Howard.

Paper Chase, The (1973)   Timothy Bottoms, Lindsay Wagner, John Houseman, Graham Bickel. Based on John Jay Osborn Jnr novel. Houseman won Oscar and film spawned a successful TV series of the same name. *Dir.* James Bridges.

Paper Moon (1973)   Ryan O'Neal, Tatum O'Neal, Madeline Kahn, John Hillerman. Tatum O'Neal won an Oscar. *Dir.* Peter Bogdanovich.

Paper Tiger (1975)   David Niven, Toshiro Mifune, Hardy Kruger, Ando, Ronald Fraser, Ivan Desny. Englishman becomes tutor to the son of a Japanese ambassador. *Dir.* Ken Annakin.

Papillon (1973)   Dustin Hoffman, Steve McQueen. *Dir.* Franklin Schaffner.

Paradise (1991)   Melanie Griffith (Lily Reed), Don Johnson (Ben Reed), Elijah Wood, Louise Latham. The first film that Griffith and Johnson starred in together. Remake of *Le Grand Chemin* directed in 1987 by Jean-Loup Hubert. *Dir.* Mary Agnes Donoghue.

Parallax View, The (1974)   Warren Beatty, Paula Prentiss, William Daniels. Witnesses to political assassination are systematically killed. *Dir.* Alan J. Pakula.

Parenthood (1989)   Steve Martin (Gil), Mary Steenburgen (Karen), Dianne Wiest (Helen), Jason Robards (Frank), Rick Moranis (Nathan), Tom Hulce (Larry), Keanu Reeves (Tod), Leaf Phoenix (Gary). Four generations of a large family have different approaches to parenthood. *Dir.* Ron Howard.

Passage to India, A (1984)   Judy Davis (Adela Quested), Victor Banerjee (Dr Aziz), Peggy Ashcroft (Mrs Moore), James Fox (Richard Fielding), Alec Guinness (Godbole), Nigel Havers, Art Malik Richard Wilson (Turton), Saeed Jaffrey, Clive Swift, Roshan Seth. David Lean's first film for 14 years. It was also his last. *Dir.* David Lean.

Pat and Mike (1952) Spencer Tracy, Katharine Hepburn, Aldo Ray. Small-time sports promoter takes on a female intellectual multi-champion. *Dir*. George Cukor.

Patriot Games (1992) Harrison Ford (Jack Ryan), Anne Archer, Patrick Bergin, Sean Bean, Samuel L Jackson James Fox, Richard Harris, James Earl Jones, Thora Birch. *Dir*. Philip Noyce.

Patton (1969) George C Scott, Karl Malden, Michael Bates. Famous for Scott's refusal to collect his Oscar. *Dir*. Franklin Schaffner.

Patty Hearst (1988) Natasha Richardson, William Forsythe, Ving Rhames, Frances Fisher. *Dir*. Paul Schrader.

Peacemaker, The (1997) Nicole Kidman (Dr Julia Kelly), George Clooney (Lt Col Thomas Devoe). First film from Steven Spielberg's Dreamworks Studio. *Dir*. Mimi Leder.

Pearl Harbor (2001) Ben Affleck, Josh Hartnett, Kate Beckinsale, Cuba Gooding, Jon Voight, Dan Aykroyd, Alec Baldwin, James King, Tom Sizemore, *Dir*. Michael Bay.

Pearl of Death, The (1944) Basil Rathbone (Holmes), Nigel Bruce (Watson), Dennis Hoey, Miles Mander, Rondo Hatton. Based on Conan Doyle's *The Six Napoleons*. *Dir*. Roy William Neill.

Peggy Sue Got Married (1986) Kathleen Turner (Peggy Sue), Nicolas Cage (Charlie Bodell), Jim Carrey (Walter Getz), Barry Miller, Catherine Hicks, Joan Allen, Helen Hunt (Beth Bodell). *Dir*. Francis Ford Coppola.

Pelican Brief, The (1993) Julia Roberts, Denzel Washington, Sam Shepard, John Heard, Robert Culp. Law student is stalked by hitmen after she suspects their involvement in murder of 2 judges. *Dir*. Alan J Pakula.

People vs Larry Flint, The (1996) Woody Harrelson (Larry Flynt, the self styled King of Sleaze), Courteney Love, Edward Norton. Biopic of the publisher of soft porn mag, *Hustler*. *Dir*. Milos Forman.

Perez Family, The (1995) Marisa Tomei, Alfred Molina, Anjelica Huston. *Dir*. Mira Nair.

Perfect (1985) John Travolta (Adam), Jamie Lee Curtis (Jessie), Anne De Salvo (Frankie). Journalist falls in love with aerobics teacher he is investigating. *Dir*. James Bridges.

Perfect Storm, The (1999) George Clooney, Mark Wahlberg, Diane Lane, Mary Elizabeth Mastrantonio, Michael Ironside, *Dir*. Wolfgang Peterson. Six Massachusetts fishermen encounter a raging storm in their boat 'Andrea Gail'.

Perfect World, A (1993) Clint Eastwood, Kevin Costner, Laura Dern. *Dir*. Clint Eastwood.

Performance (1970) James Fox, Mick Jagger, Anita Pallenberg, Allan Cuthbertson. *Dir*. Nicolas Roeg & Donald Cammell.

Perils of Pauline, The (1934) Betty Hutton, John Lund, Billy de Wolfe. The career of silent serial queen Pearl White. *Dir*. George Marshall.

Personal Services (1987) Julie Walters (Christine Painter), Alec McCowen (Wing Commander Morton), Shirley Stellfox. Read 'Cynthia Payne' for Christine Painter. *Dir*. Terry Jones.

Peter's Friends (1992) Kenneth Branagh (Andrew), Alphonsia Emmanuel (Sarah), Stephen Fry (Peter), Hugh Laurie (Roger), Phyllida Law (Vera), Rita Rudner (Carol), Emma Thompson (Maggie). *Dir*. Kenneth Branagh.

Phantom of the Opera (1925) Lon Chaney, Mary Philbin, Norman Kerry. Remakes include 1943 version with Claude Rains, 1962 film with Herbert Lom and 1989 version with Robert Englund. *Dir*. Rupert Julian.

Phenomenon (1996) John Travolta, Kyra Sedgwick, Robert Duvall, Forest Whitaker, Brent Spiner. Simpleton is struck by a strange light which raises his IQ and his sensitivity. *Dir*. James Cameron.

Philadelphia (1993) Tom Hanks, Denzel Washington, Jason Robards, Mary Steenburgen, Antonio Banderas, Joanne Woodward, Robert Ridgely. Homosexual lawyer with AIDS sues his firm for unfair dismissal. *Dir*. Jonathan Demme.

Philadelphia Story, The (1940) Katharine Hepburn, Cary Grant, James Stewart, Ruth Hussey. *Dir*. George Cukor.

Piano, The (1993) Holly Hunter, Harvey Keitel, Sam Neill, Genevieve Lemon. *Dir*. Jane Campion.

Picnic (1955) William Holden, Kim Novak, Rosalind Russell, Susan Strasberg. *Dir*. Joshua Logan.

Picnic at Hanging Rock (1975) Rachel Roberts, Dominic Guard, Helen Morse, Vivian Gray. *Dir*. Peter Weir.

Picture of Dorian Gray, The (1945) Hurd Hatfield (Gray), George Sanders (Sir Henry), Donna Reed, Angela Lansbury. *Dir*. Albert Lewin.

Pillow Talk (1959) Doris Day, Rock Hudson, Tony Randall, Thelma Ritter. First of the partnership films of Day and Hudson, this one concerning a party line love affair. *Dir*. Michael Gordon.

Pink Panther, The (1963) David Niven, Peter Sellers, Capucine, Claudia Cardinale, Robert Wagner. The seven sequels were *A Shot in the Dark*, *Inspector Clouseau*, *Return of the Pink Panther*, *The Pink Panther Strikes Again*, *The Revenge of the Pink Panther*. *Trail of the Pink Panther* and *Son of the Pink Panther*. *Dir*. Blake Edwards.

Pit and the Pendulum, The (1961) Vincent Price, Barbara Steele, John Kerr. *Dir*. Roger Corman.

Place in the Sun, A (1951) Montgomery Clift, Elizabeth Taylor, Shelley Winters, Raymond Burr. Man is offered the chance of a rich wife, but allows himself to be convicted and executed for the accidental death of his former fiancée. *Dir*. George Stevens.

Planes, Trains and Automobiles (1987) Steve Martin (Neal Page), John Candy (Del Griffith), Laila Robbins, Kevin Bacon. Yuppie attempts to get home to his family for a snowy Thanksgiving. *Dir*. John Hughes.

Planet of the Apes (1968) Charlton Heston, Roddy McDowall, Kim Hunter, James Whitmore. John Chambers won Oscar for Make-up. Sequels included *Beneath the Planet of the Apes* (1969), *Escape from the Planet of the Apes* (1970), *Conquest of the Planet of the Apes* (1972), and *Battle for the Planet of the Apes* (1973). *Dir*. Franklin Schaffner.

Platoon (1986) Tom Berenger (Sgt Barnes), Willem Dafoe (Sgt Elias), Charlie Sheen (Chris), Johnny Depp (Lerner), Forest Whitaker (Big Harold). *Dir*. Oliver Stone.

Play Misty for Me (1971) Clint Eastwood, Jessica Walter, Donna Mills, John Larch. *Dir*. Clint Eastwood.

Player, The (1992) Tim Robbins (Griffin Mill), Greta Scacchi (June Gudmundsdottir), Fred Ward (Walter Stuckel), Whoopi Goldberg (Det. Avery), Richard E Grant (Tom Oakley), Sydney Pollack (Dick Mellen). This satire on Hollywood also starred 65 other stars who accepted nominal fees, including, Steve Allen, Cher, James Coburn, Peter Falk, Teri Garr, Jeff Goldblum, Elliott Gould, Joel Grey, Anjelica Huston, Sally Kellerman, Jack Lemmon, Marlee Matlin, Nick Nolte, Malcolm McDowell, Burt Reynolds, Julia Roberts, Mimi Rogers, Annie Ross, Jill St John,

Susan Sarandon, Rod Steiger, Lily Tomlin, Robert Wagner, Bruce Willis. *Dir.* Robert Altman.

Ploughman's Lunch, The (1983) Jonathan Pryce (James Penfield), Tim Curry (Jeremy Hancock), Charlie Dore (Sue Barrington). British journalist furthers his career by rewriting history. *Dir.* Richard Eyre.

Pocahontas (1995) Voices of Mel Gibson, Irene Bedard, David Ogden Stiers, Judy Kuhn, Billy Connolly. *Dir.* Mike Gabriel and Eric Goldberg.

Point Blank (1967) Lee Marvin, Angie Dickinson, Keenan Wynn, Carroll O'Connor. Based on the novel *The Hunter* by Richard Stark. *Dir.* John Boorman.

Point Break (1991) Patrick Swayze (Bodhi), Keanu Reeves (Johnny Utah), Gary Busey, Lori Petty. FBI man Reeves infiltrates a gang of surfers to investigate bank robberies. *Dir.* Kathryn Bigelow.

Police Academy (1984) Steve Guttenberg (Carey), Kim Cattrall (Karen), Bubba Smith (Moses), GW Bailey (Lt. Harris), David Graf (Tackleberry), Donovan Scott (Leslie). Sequels include *2: Their First Assignment*; *3: Back in Training*; *4: Citizens on Patrol*; *5: Assignment Miami Beach*; *6: City under Siege*. *Dir.* Hugh Wilson.

Poltergeist (1982) JoBeth Williams, Craig T Nelson, Beatrice Straight, Oliver Robbins, Dominique Dunne. Two inferior sequels were made. *Dir.* Tobe Hooper.

Pope Joan (1972) Liv Ullmann, Trevor Howard, Olivia de Havilland, Franco Nero, Maximilian Schell. *Dir.* Michael Anderson.

Pope Must Die, The (1991) Robbie Coltrane, Beverly D'Angelo, Herbert Lom, Alex Rocco, Annette Crosbie. *Dir.* Peter Richardson.

Popeye (1980) Robin Williams, Shelley Duvall, Ray Walston. *Dir.* Robert Altman.

Postcards From the Edge (1990) Meryl Streep, Shirley MacLaine, Dennis Quaid, Gene Hackman, Richard Dreyfuss, Annette Bening. *Dir.* Mike Nichols.

Postman Always Rings Twice, The (1981) Jack Nicholson, Jessica Lange, Anjelica Huston. Remake of the 1946 film starring Lana Turner & John Garfield. *Dir.* Bob Rafelson.

Predator (1987) Arnold Schwarzenegger (Dutch), Carl Weathers (Dillon), Kevin Peter Hall (The Predator). *Predator 2* starred Danny Glover and Gary Busey. *Dir.* John McTiernan.

Prêt-à-Porter (1994) Anouk Aimée, Lauren Bacall, Kim Basinger, Sophia Loren, Marcello Mastroianni, Julia Roberts, Teri Garr, Tracey Ullman, Richard E Grant. Aka: *Ready to Wear*. *Dir.* Robert Altman.

Pretty Woman (1990) Richard Gere (Edward Lewis), Julia Roberts (Vivian Ward), Ralph Bellamy (James Morse). *Dir.* Garry Marshall.

Prick up Your Ears (1987) Gary Oldman (Joe Orton), Alfred Molina (Kenneth Halliwell), Vanessa Redgrave (Peggy), Julie Walters (Elsie Orton), Lindsay Duncan (Anthea Lahr). *Dir.* Stephen Frears.

Prime of Miss Jean Brodie, The (1969) Maggie Smith, Robert Stephens, Pamela Franklin, Celia Johnson, Gordon Jackson. *Dir.* Ronald Neame.

Prince and the Pauper (1937) Errol Flynn, Claude Rains, Billy and Bobby Mauch, Montagu Love (Henry VIII). Edward VI changes place with a street urchin. The 1977 remake starred Mark Lester, Oliver Reed and Raquel Welch (dir. Richard Fleischer). *Dir.* William Keighley.

Prince and the Showgirl (1957) Laurence Olivier, Marilyn Monroe, Sybil Thorndike. *Dir.* Laurence Olivier.

Prince of Tides, The (1991) Nick Nolte (Tom Wingo), Barbra Streisand (Susan Lowenstein), Blythe Danner, Kate Nelligan. *Dir.* Barbra Streisand.

Prisoner of Zenda (1952) Stewart Granger, James Mason, Deborah Kerr, Louis Calhern. Remake of the 1937 classic starring Ronald Colman and Douglas Fairbanks Jnr. A further remake of 1979 starred Peter Sellers and Lynne Frederick. *Dir.* Richard Thorpe.

Private Function, A (1984) Michael Palin, Maggie Smith, Denholm Elliott, Richard Griffiths, Betty the Pig. *Dir.* Malcolm Mowbray.

Private Life of Henry VIII, The (1933) Charles Laughton, Elsa Lanchester, Robert Donat, Merle Oberon. *Dir.* Alexander Korda.

Private Parts (1996) Howard Stern (as himself), Mary McCormack (Alison). Screen biography of top US disc jockey. *Dir.* Betty Thomas.

Prizzi's Honor (1985) Jack Nicholson, Kathleen Turner, Robert Loggia, Anjelica Huston. *Dir.* John Huston.

Producers, The (1968) Zero Mostel, Gene Wilder, Kenneth Mars. The play within the film *Springtime for Hitler*. *Dir.* Mel Brooks.

Prospero's Books (1991) John Gielgud, Michael Clark, Tom Bell, Mark Rylance. *Dir.* Peter Greenaway.

Psycho (1960) Anthony Perkins, Vera Miles, Janet Leigh, John Gavin, Martin Balsam. Shower stabbing scene was directed by Saul Bass. Two sequels also starring Perkins in 1983 and 1986. *Dir.* Alfred Hitchcock.

Pulp Fiction (1994) John Travolta, Samuel L Jackson, Uma Thurman, Harvey Keitel, Tim Roth, Bruce Willis, Rosanna Arquette. *Dir.* Quentin Tarantino.

Punchline (1988) Sally Field (Lilah Krytsick), Tom Hanks (Steven Gold), John Goodman (John Krytsick), Mark Rydell (Romeo), Kim Greist (Madeline Urie). As the title suggests the film examines the world of a stand-up comedian. *Dir.* David Seltzer.

Quadrophenia (1979) Phil Daniels, Mark Wingett, Philip Davis, Sting, Leslie Ash, Toyah Wilcox. *Dir.* Frank Roddam.

Queen Christina (1933) Greta Garbo, John Gilbert, Ian Keith, Lewis Stone, Reginald Owen. Queen of Sweden roams the country to escape a political marriage. *Dir.* Rouben Mamoulian.

Quick and the Dead, The (1995) Sharon Stone, Gene Hackman, Leonard DiCaprio. *Dir.* Sam Raimi.

Quiet Man, The (1952) John Wayne, Maureen O'Hara, Barry Fitzgerald, Victor McLaglen, Ward Bond. *Dir.* John Ford.

Quigley Down Under (1990) Tom Selleck, Laura San Giacomo, Alan Rickman, Chris Haywood. In 1860s Australia, an American hired gun is outlawed. *Dir.* Simon Wincer.

Quiller Memorandum, The (1966) George Segal, Max Von Sydow, Alec Guinness, Senta Berger, George Sanders. *Dir.* Michael Anderson.

Quiz Show (1994) John Turturro, Ralph Fiennes, Rob Morrow, Paul Scofield, Martin Scorsese. *Dir.* Robert Redford.

Quo Vadis (1951) Robert Taylor, Deborah Kerr, Peter Ustinov, Leo Genn. *Dir.* Mervyn Le Roy.

Radio Days (1987) Woody Allen (Narrator), Mia Farrow (Sally White), Seth Green (Little Joe), Julie Kavner (Mother), Michael Tucker (Father), Diane Keaton (New Year's singer). *Dir.* Woody Allen.

Rage, The: Carrie 2 (1999) Emily Bergl, Jason London, Dylan Bruno, Amy Irving, John Doe, Zachery Ty Bryan. *Dir.* Katt Shea.

Rage in Harlem, A (1991) Forest Whitaker, Gregory Hines, Robin Givens, Danny Glover. *Dir.* Bill Duke.

Raging Bull (1980)   Robert De Niro, Cathy Moriarty, Joe Pesci. *Dir.* Martin Scorsese.

Raiders of the Lost Ark (1981)   Harrison Ford, Karen Allen, John Rhys-Davies, Denholm Elliott. *Dir.* Steven Spielberg.

Railway Children, The (1970)   Dinah Sheridan, William Mervyn, Jenny Agutter, Sally Thomsett, Bernard Cribbins. *Dir.* Lionel Jeffries.

Rain Man (1988)   Dustin Hoffman (Raymond Babbitt), Tom Cruise (Charles Babbitt), Valerie Golino (Susanna). *Dir.* Barry Levinson.

Raising Arizona (1987)   Nicolas Cage (HI), Holly Hunter (Ed), Trey Wilson (Nathan Arizona Sr), John Goodman (Gale). *Dir.* Joel Coen.

Rambo: First Blood Part II (1985)   Sylvester Stallone, Richard Crenna, Steven Berkoff. Written by Sylvester Stallone & James Cameron. *Dir.* George Pan Cosmatos.

Rambo III (1988)   Sylvester Stallone, Richard Crenna, Marc de Jonge. Written by Sylvester Stallone and Sheldon Lettich. *Dir.* Peter MacDonald.

Ran (1985)   Tatsuya Nakadai, Satoshi Terao. Japanese version of *King Lear*. *Dir.* Akiro Kurosawa.

Reach for the Sky (1956)   Kenneth More (Douglas Bader), Muriel Pavlow. *Dir.* Lewis Gilbert.

Rear Window (1954)   James Stewart, Grace Kelly, Raymond Burr. *Dir.* Alfred Hitchcock.

Rebecca (1940)   Laurence Olivier, Joan Fontaine, George Sanders. *Dir.* Alfred Hitchcock.

Rebel without a Cause (1955)   James Dean, Natalie Wood, Jim Backus, Sal Mineo, Dennis Hopper. *Dir.* Nicholas Ray.

Red Heat (1988)   Arnold Schwarzenegger (Ivan Danko), James Belushi (Art Ridzik), Peter Boyle (Lou Donnelly). *Dir.* Walter Hill.

Red Sonja (1985)   Arnold Schwarzenegger (Kalifor), Brigitte Nielsen (Red Sonja). *Dir.* Richard Fleischer.

Reds (1981)   Warren Beatty (John Reed), Diane Keaton, Edward Herrmann, Jerzy Kosinski, Jack Nicholson. *Dir.* Warren Beatty.

Relic, The (1997)   Tom Sizemore (D'Agosta), Penelope Ann Miller (Dr Margo Green)

Remains of the Day, The (1993)   Anthony Hopkins, Emma Thompson, James Fox, Christopher Reeve, Peter Vaughan, Hugh Grant. *Dir.* James Ivory.

Repulsion (1965)   Catherine Deneuve, Ian Hendry, John Fraser, Patrick Wymark. *Dir.* Roman Polanski.

Reservoir Dogs (1991)   Lawrence Tierney, Harvey Keitel (Mr White), Tim Roth (Mr Orange), Eddie Bunker (Mr Blue), Michael Madsen (Mr Blonde), Steve Buscemi (Mr Pink), Quentin Tarantino (Mr Brown). *Dir.* Quentin Tarantino.

Return of Swamp Thing, The (1989)   Louis Jourdan (Dr Anton Arcane), Heather Locklear (Abby Arcane), Dick Durock (Swamp Thing). *Dir.* Jim Wynorski.

Return of the Jedi (1983)   Mark Hamill, Harrison Ford, Carrie Fisher, Billy Dee Williams. *Dir.* Richard Marquand.

Revenge (1990)   Kevin Costner (Jay Cochran), Anthony Quinn (Tiburon), Madeleine Stowe (Miryea). *Dir.* Tony Scott.

Revenge of the Pink Panther (1978)   Peter Sellers, Herbert Lom, Dyan Cannon. *Dir.* Blake Edwards.

Reversal of Fortune (1990)   Jeremy Irons (Claus Von Bulow), Glenn Close (Sunny Von Bulow), Julie Hagerty (Alexandra). *Dir.* Barbet Schroeder.

Revolution (1985)   Al Pacino (Tom Dobb), Donald Sutherland (Sgt Major Peasy), Nastassja Kinski (Daisy). Notable for being the biggest flop of all time. *Dir.* Hugh Hudson.

Rhapsody in Blue (1945)   Robert Alda (George Gershwin), Joan Leslie, Alexis Smith. *Dir.* Irving Rapper.

Richard III (1995)   Ian McKellen, Annette Bening, Jim Broadbent, Robert Downey Jnr, Kristin Scott-Thomas, Maggie Smith, Nigel Hawthorne. Ian McKellen wrote the screenplay. *Dir.* Richard Loncraine.

Rififi (1955)   Jean Servais, Carl Mohner, Jules Dassin. Famous for its 25 minutes of silence whilst robbery is taking place. *Dir.* Jules Dassin.

Right Stuff, The (1983)   Sam Shepard (Chuck Yeager), Barbara Hershey (Glennis), Scott Glenn (Alan Shepard), Ed Harris (John Glenn), Fred Ward (Gus Grissom), Dennis Quaid (Gordon Cooper). *Dir.* Philip Kaufman.

Rising Sun (1993)   Sean Connery, Harvey Keitel, Wesley Snipes, Mako. *Dir.* Philip Kaufman.

Road House (1989)   Patrick Swayze, Kelly Lynch, Sam Elliott, Ben Gazzara, Marshall Teague. *Dir.* Rowdy Herrington.

Road to Hong Kong (1962)   Bob Hope, Bing Crosby, Dorothy Lamour, Joan Collins, Peter Sellers, Frank Sinatra, Dean Martin, David Niven. Last of the seven *Road* films. *Dir.* Norman Panama.

Road to Singapore (1940)   Bob Hope, Bing Crosby, Dorothy Lamour, Anthony Quinn. First of the seven *Road* films, destination followed by Zanzibar, Moscow, Utopia, Rio, Bali and Hong Kong. *Dir.* Victor Schertzinger.

Rob Roy (1995)   Liam Neeson, Jessica Lange, John Hurt, Tim Roth. *Dir.* Michael Caton-Jones.

Robe, The (1953)   Richard Burton, Jean Simmons, Michael Rennie, Victor Mature, Richard Boone. *Dir.* Henry Koster.

Robin Hood (1991)   Patrick Bergin, Uma Thurman, Edward Fox. *Dir.* John Irvin.

Robin Hood: Men in Tights (1993)   Cary Elwes, Richard Lewis, Roger Rees, Tracey Ullman, Mel Brooks, Isaac Hayes, Patrick Stewart. *Dir.* Mel Brooks.

Robin Hood: Prince of Thieves (1991)   Kevin Costner, Morgan Freeman, Christian Slater, Alan Rickman, Sean Connery (uncredited). Title song: 'Everything I Do I Do for You' by Bryan Adams. *Dir.* Kevin Reynolds.

Robocop (1987)   Peter Weller, Nancy Allen, Ronny Cox. *Dir.* Paul Verhoeven.

Rock, The (1996)   Sean Connery, Nicolas Cage, Ed Harris. *Dir.* Michael Bay.

Rocking Horse Winner, The (1949)   John Mills, Valerie Hobson, John Howard Davies, Cyril Smith. Based on a DH Lawrence short story. *Dir.* Anthony Pelissier.

Rocky (1976)   Sylvester Stallone, Burgess Meredith, Talia Shire, Carl Weathers,. Written by Sylvester Stallone. *Dir.* John G Avildsen.

Rocky II (1979)   Stallone, Meredith, Shire, Weathers. Written and directed by Stallone.

Rocky III (1982)   Stallone, Meredith, Shire, Weathers, Mr T, Hulk Hogan. Written and directed by Stallone.

Rocky IV (1985)   Stallone, Dolph Lundgren, T Shire, Weathers, Brigitte Nielsen. Written and directed by Stallone.

Rocky V (1990)   Stallone, Meredith, Shire, Burt Young, Sage Stallone. Written by Stallone. *Dir.* John G Avildsen.

Rocky Horror Picture Show, The (1975)   Tim Curry, Susan Sarandon, Meat Loaf, Little Nell. *Dir.* Jim Sharman.

Roman Holiday (1953)   Gregory Peck, Audrey Hepburn, Eddie Albert, Hartley Power. *Dir.* William Wyler.

Roman Scandals (1933)   Eddie Cantor, Gloria Stuart, Ruth Etting, Edward Arnold. *Dir.* Frank Tuttle.

Romancing the Stone (1984)   Michael Douglas, Kathleen Turner, Danny De Vito, Zack Norman. *Dir.* Robert Zemeckis.

Rookie, The (1990)   Clint Eastwood (Nick Pulovski), Charlie Sheen (David Ackerman), Raul Julia (Strom). *Dir.* Clint Eastwood.

Rookie of the Year (1993)   Gary Busey, Thomas Ian Nicholas, Albert Hall, John Candy (uncredited). Young boy becomes pitcher for the Chicago Cubs after his arm is injured in an accident. *Dir.* Daniel Stern.

Room at the Top (1959)   Laurence Harvey, Simone Signoret, Heather Sears, Donald Wolfit. Based on John Braine's novel. *Dir.* Jack Clayton.

Room with a View, A (1986)   Maggie Smith (Charlotte Bartlett), Helena Bonham Carter (Lucy Honeychurch). Opens in Italy in 1907. *Dir.* James Ivory.

Rope (1948)   James Stewart, John Dall, Farley Granger, Joan Chandler. Two homosexuals murder a friend for the thrill of it and hide his body in a trunk from which they serve cocktails to a party. *Dir.* Alfred Hitchcock.

Rose, The (1979)   Bette Midler, Alan Bates, Frederic Forrest, Harry Dean Stanton. *Dir.* Mark Rydell.

Rosencrantz and Guildenstern are Dead (1990)   Gary Oldman (Rosencrantz), Tim Roth (Guildenstern), Iain Glen (Prince Hamlet). *Dir.* Tom Stoppard.

Running Man, The (1987)   Arnold Schwarzenegger (Ben Richards), Maria Conchita Alonso (Amber Mendez), Yaphet Kotto (Laughlin), Jim Brown (Fireball). *Dir.* Paul Michael Glaser.

Russia House, The (1990)   Sean Connery, Michelle Pfeiffer, Roy Scheider, James Fox. *Dir.* Fred Schepisi.

Ruthless People (1986)   Bette Midler, Danny De Vito, Judge Reinhold, Helen Slater. *Dir.* Jim Abrahams.

Ryan's Daughter (1970)   Robert Mitchum, Sarah Miles, John Mills, Trevor Howard. *Dir.* David Lean.

Saint, The (1997)   Val Kilmer (Simon Templar), Elisabeth Shue (Emma Russell). Roger Moore's voice heard on car radio. *Dir.* Phillip Noyce.

Santa Claus: The Movie (1985)   Dudley Moore (Patch), John Lithgow (BZ), David Huddleston (Claus), Burgess Meredith (Elf). *Dir.* Jeannot Szwarc.

Saturday Night and Sunday Morning (1960)   Albert Finney, Shirley Anne Field, Rachel Roberts. Nottingham factory worker is dissatisfied with his lot. *Dir.* Karel Reisz.

Saturday Night Fever (1977)   John Travolta, Karen Lynn Gorney, Barry Miller. *Dir.* John Badham.

Saving Private Ryan (1998)   Tom Hanks, Edward Burns, Tom Sizemore, Matt Damon, Ted Danson, Harve Presnell. *Dir.* Steven Spielberg. Author's Note: I believe this is the first work to be published which highlights a subtle continuity error. After losing one of the eight original platoon members all eight can be seen marching across a field, but fortunately become seven again on arrival at a radar station!

Scandal (1989)   John Hurt (Stephen Ward), Joanne Whalley-Kilmer (Christine Keeler), Bridget Fonda (Mandy Rice-Davies), Ian McKellen (John Profumo), Leslie Phillips, Britt Ekland, Jean Alexander, Jeroen Krabb, Michael Ironside. *Dir.* Michael Caton-Jones.

Scanners (1981)   Stephen Lock, Jennifer O'Neill, Patrick McGoohan, Michael Ironside. *Dir.* David Cronenberg.

Scanners II: The New Order (1991)   David Hewlett, Yvan Ponton, Raoul Trujillo. *Dir.* Christian Duguay.

Scanners III: The Takeover (1992)   Liliana Komorowska, Valerie Valcis, Steve Parrish, Harry Hill. *Dir.* Christian Duguay.

Scarface (1983)   Al Pacino (Tony Montana), Steven Bauer (Manny Ray), Michelle Pfeiffer (Elvira), Mary Elizabeth Mastrantonio (Gina), Robert Loggia (Frank Lopez), F Murray Abraham (Omar). *Dir.* Brian De Palma.

Scarlet Letter, The (1995)   Demi Moore, Gary Oldman, Robert Duvall, Robert Prosky, Joan Plowright. Set in C17 Massachusetts; a settler's wife gives birth to an illegitimate daughter. Based on the Nathaniel Hawthorne novel, the scarlet letter is 'A' for adultery. *Dir.* Roland Joffé.

Scenes from a Mall (1991)   Bette Midler, Woody Allen, Paul Mazursky. *Dir.* Paul Mazursky.

Scent of a Woman (1992)   Al Pacino, Chris O'Donnell, Gabrielle Anwar. Blind ex-officer takes young man under his wing. *Dir.* Martin Brest.

Schindler's List (1993)   Liam Neeson, Ben Kingsley, Ralph Fiennes. *Dir.* Steven Spielberg.

Scream (1996)   David Arquette, Neve Campbell (Sidney), Courteney Cox (Gale Weathers), Drew Barrymore. *Dir.* Wes Craven.

Screamers (1996)   Peter Weller, Roy Dupuis, Jennifer Rubin, Ron White. Set in 2078 on the planet Sirius 6B where killer robots run amok. *Dir.* Christian Duguay.

Sea of Love (1989)   Al Pacino (Frank Keller), Ellen Barkin (Helen Cruger), John Goodman (Sherman Touhy). Cop investigating murders of lonely hearts advertisers places an ad himself. *Dir.* Harold Becker.

Sebastiane (1976)   Leonardo Treviglio, Barney James, Neil Kennedy, Ken Hicks. Title character is banished by Emperor Diocletian and suffers further tragedy. Dialogue is in Latin with English subtitles. *Dir.* Derek Jarman and Paul Humfress.

Secrets and Lies (1995)   Timothy Spall, Phyllis Logan, Brenda Blethyn, Claire Rushbrook, Marianne Jean-Baptiste. *Dir.* Mike Leigh.

See No Evil, Hear No Evil (1989)   Gene Wilder (Dave Lyons), Richard Pryor (Wally Karew). Pryor is blind and Wilder is deaf. *Dir.* Arthur Hiller.

Seize the Day (1986)   Robin Williams, Joseph Wiseman. Based on a Saul Bellow novel. *Dir.* Fielder Cook.

Sense and Sensibility (1995)   Emma Thompson, Alan Rickman, Kate Winslet, Hugh Grant, Hugh Laurie, Gemma Jones. Emma Thompson wrote the screenplay. *Dir.* Ang Lee.

September (1987)   Denholm Elliott (Howard), Dianne Wiest (Stephanie), Mia Farrow (Lane), Elaine Stritch. *Dir.* Woody Allen.

Sgt Bilko (1996)   Steve Martin, Dan Aykroyd. *Dir.* Jonathan Lynn.

Sgt Pepper's Lonely Hearts Club Band (1978)   Peter Frampton, Bee Gees, George Burns, Frankie Howerd, Donald Pleasence, Paul Nicholas, Alice Cooper, Steve Martin, Earth Wind & Fire, Sandy Farina. *Dir.* Michael Schultz.

Seven (1995)   Brad Pitt, Morgan Freeman, Richard Roundtree, Kevin Spacey. *Dir.* David Fincher.

Seven Brides for Seven Brothers (1954)   Howard Keel, Jane Powell, Jeff Richards, Russ Tamblyn. *Dir.* Stanley Donen.

Seven Year Itch, The (1955)   Tom Ewell, Marilyn Monroe, Sonny Tufts, Evelyn Keyes. *Dir.* Billy Wilder.

Seven Years in Tibet (1997)   Brad Pitt, David Thewlis, BD Wong. *Dir.* Jean-Jacques Annaud.

Shadow, The (1994)   Alec Baldwin, Penelope Ann Miller, Tim Curry. In the 1930s a former criminal battles against a descendant of Genghis Khan. *Dir.* Russell Mulcahy.

Shakespeare in Love (1998)   Gwyneth Paltrow, Joseph Fiennes, Geoffrey Rush, Colin Firth, Ben Affleck, Judi Dench, Rupert Everett, Simon Callow, Martin Clunes, Antony Sher, Imelda Staunton. *Dir.* John Madden, Judi Dench won Best Supporting Actor Oscar although only on screen for eight minutes. Daniel Day-Lewis and Julia Roberts turned down the lead roles.

Shadowlands (1993)   Anthony Hopkins, Debra Winger, John Wood. Biopic of CS Lewis and his love for an American woman. *Dir.* Richard Attenborough.

Shawshank Redemption, The (1994)   Tim Robbins, Morgan Freeman, Bob Gunton, James Whitmore. *Dir.* Frank Darabont.

Sheena, Queen of the Jungle (1984)   Tanya Roberts, Ted Wass, Donovan Scott. *Dir.* John Guillermin.

Shine (1996)   Armin Mueller-Stahl, Geoffrey Rush, Noah Taylor, Lynn Redgrave, Googie Withers, John Gielgud. Based on the life of pianist David Helfgott. *Dir.* Scott Hicks.

Ship of Fools (1965)   Vivien Leigh, Simone Signoret, Oskar Werner, Lee Marvin. German line *Vera Cruz* leaves for Bremerhaven with a mixed bag of passengers. *Dir.* Stanley Kramer.

Shirley Valentine (1989)   Pauline Collins, Tom Conti, Julia McKenzie, Alison Steadman, Joanna Lumley, Bernard Hill. *Dir.* Lewis Gilbert.

Shooting Fish (1997)   Dan Futterman, Stuart Townsend, Kate Beckinsale, Annette Crosbie, Jane Lapotaire, Phyllis Logan. *Dir.* Stefan Schwartz.

Shooting Party, The (1984)   James Mason (Ralph Nettleby), Dorothy Tutin, Edward Fox, Cheryl Campbell, John Gielgud. *Dir.* Alan Bridges.

Shootist, The (1976)   John Wayne, Lauren Bacall, James Stewart, Ron Howard, Hugh O'Brian. *Dir.* Don Siegel.

Short Cuts (1993)   Andie MacDowell, Bruce Davison, Jack Lemmon, Robert Downey Jnr. Lives of 9 dysfunctional suburban couples intertwine. *Dir.* Robert Altman.

Silence of the Lambs (1991)   Jodie Foster (Clarice Starling), Anthony Hopkins (Dr Hannibal Lecter), Scott Glen. *Dir.* Jonathan Demme.

Silkwood (1983)   Meryl Streep, Cher, Kurt Russell. Female worker in nuclear processing plant mysteriously dies before she denounces safety aspects of the plant. *Dir.* Mike Nichols.

Silverado (1985)   Scott Glen, Kevin Costner, John Cleese, Kevin Kline, Rosanna Arquette, Danny Glover. *Dir.* Lawrence Kasdan.

Single White Female (1992)   Bridget Fonda (Allison Jones), Jennifer Jason Leigh (Hedra Carlson), Steven Weber. *Dir.* Barbet Schroeder.

Sirens (1994)   Hugh Grant, Tara FitzGerald, Sam Neill, Elle MacPherson. *Dir.* John Duigen.

Sister Act (1992)   Whoopi Goldberg, Maggie Smith, Harvey Keitel. *Dir.* Emile Ardolino.

Sister Act 2: Back in the Habit (1993)   Whoopi Goldberg, Maggie Smith, James Coburn. *Dir.* Bill Duke.

Sixth Sense, The (1999)   Bruce Willis (Malcolm Crowe), Toni Collette, Haley Joel Osment (Cole). *Dir.* M. Night Shyamalan.

Sleeper (1973)   Woody Allen, Diane Keaton, John Beck. *Dir.* Woody Allen.

Sleeping with the Enemy (1990)   Julia Roberts, Patrick Bergin. *Dir.* Joseph Ruben.

Sleepless in Seattle (1993)   Tom Hanks, Meg Ryan, Ross Malinger. *Dir.* Nora Ephron.

Sleepy Hollow (1999)   Johny Depp (Ichabod Crane), Christina Ricci (Katrina Van Tassel), Michael Gambon (Bactus Van Tassel), Christopher Lee (Burgomaster), Christopher Walken (Hessian Horseman). *Dir.* Tim Burton.

Sliding Doors (1998)   Gwyneth Paltrow, John Hannah, John Lynch, Jeanne Tripplehorn, Virginia McKenna. *Dir.* Peter Howitt.

Sliver (1993)   Sharon Stone, William Baldwin, Tom Berenger, Martin Landau. Based on an Ira Levin novel. *Dir.* Philip Noyce.

Smilla's Feeling for Snow (1997)   Julia Ormond (Smilla), Gabriel Byrne, Richard Harris (Tork), Vanessa Redgrave, Bob Peck, Jim Broadbent, Robert Loggia. *Dir.* Bille August.

Sneakers (1992)   Robert Redford, Dan Aykroyd, Ben Kingsley, River Phoenix, Sidney Poitier. Experts hired to recover electronic device that can penetrate the government's most secure computer systems. *Dir.* Phil Alden Robinson.

Snow White: A Tale of Terror (1997)   Monica Keena (Lilli), Sam Neill (Baron Hoffman), Sigourney Weaver (Claudia).

Somebody up There Likes Me (1956)   Paul Newman (Rocky Graziano), Pier Angeli, Sal Mineo, Steve McQueen. *Dir.* Robert Wise.

Some Like it Hot (1939)   Bob Hope, Shirley Ross, Una Merkel, Gene Krupa. Sideshow owner runs out of money. *Dir.* George Archainbaud.

Some Like it Hot (1959)   Tony Curtis, Jack Lemmon, Marilyn Monroe, Joe E Brown, George Raft. *Dir.* Billy Wilder.

Sommersby (1993)   Richard Gere, Jodie Foster. Remake of *The Return of Martin Guerre*. *Dir.* Jon Amiel.

Son of Lassie (1945)   Peter Lawford, Donald Crisp, Nigel Bruce. The first sequel to *Lassie Come Home*; many more followed. *Dir.* S Sylvan Simon.

Son of the Pink Panther (1993)   Robert Benigni, Herbert Lom, Claudia Cardinale, Burt Kwouk. *Dir.* Blake Edwards.

Song of Bernadette, The (1943)   Jennifer Jones, Charles Bickford, William Eythe. *Dir.* Henry King.

Song to Remember, A (1944)   Cornel Wilde, Merle Oberon, Paul Muni. Life and death of Chopin. *Dir.* Charles Vidor.

Sophie's Choice (1982)   Meryl Streep, Kevin Kline, Josh Mostel. *Dir.* Alan J Pakula.

Sound of Music, The (1965)   Julie Andrews, Christopher Plummer, Richard Haydn, Marni Nixon. *Dir.* Robert Wise.

Soylent Green (1973)   Charlton Heston, Edward G Robinson, Leigh Taylor-Young. Set in 2022, the Soylent Green of the title is synthetic food. *Dir.* Richard Fleischer.

Space Jam (1996)   Michael Jordan, Bugs Bunny, voice of Danny De Vito. *Dir.* Joe Pytka.

Space Truckers (1997)   Dennis Hopper, Stephen Dorff, Debi Mazar, Charles Dance. Set in 2196; BMW's Bio-Mechanical Warriors. *Dir.* Stuart Gordon.

Specialist, The (1994)   Sharon Stone, Sylvester Stallone, Rod Steiger, James Woods. *Dir.* Luis Llosa.

Speed (1994)   Sandra Bullock, Keanu Reeves, Dennis Hopper, Jeff Daniels. *Dir.* Jan de Bont.

Spiceworld (1997)   Spice Girls, Richard E Grant. Originally called: *Five*. *Dir.* Bob Spiers.

Spitfire Grill, The (1996)   Ellen Burstyn, Marcia Gay Harden, Alison Elliott. *Dir.* Lee David Zlotoff.

Splash! (1984)   Tom Hanks (Allen Bauer), Daryl Hannah (Madison), John Candy, Eugene Levy. *Dir.* Ron Howard.

Splitting Heirs (1993)   Rick Moranis (Henry), Eric

Idle (Tommy Patel), Barbara Hershey, Catherine Zeta Jones, John Cleese (Raoul P Shadgrind), Stratford Johns, Eric Sykes. *Dir*. Robert Young.

Spy Hard (1996)   Leslie Nielsen (Agent WD-40), Andy Griffith, Nicollette Sheridan. *Dir*. Rick Friedberg.

Spy Who Loved Me, The (1977)   Roger Moore, Barbara Bach (Major Anya Amasova), Curt Jurgens (Stromberg). Theme song 'Nobody Does it Better' performed by Carly Simon. *Dir*. Lewis Gilbert.

Stagecoach (1939)   John Wayne, Claire Trevor, Thomas Mitchell, Andy Devine. The 1966 remake starred Ann-Margret & Bing Crosby. *Dir*. John Ford.

Stalag 17 (1953)   William Holden, Don Taylor, Otto Preminger, Peter Graves, Neville Brand. *Dir*. Billy Wilder.

Stanley and Iris (1990)   Jane Fonda, Robert De Niro. *Dir*. Martin Ritt.

Star! (1968)   Julie Andrews, Richard Crenna, Daniel Massey (Noël Coward), Bruce Forsyth, Beryl Reid. Biopic of Gertrude Lawrence. *Dir*. Robert Wise.

Star is Born, A (1937)   Janet Gaynor, Fredric March, Adolphe Menjou, Andy Devine. *Dir*. William A Wellman.

Star is Born, A (1954)   Judy Garland, James Mason, Charles Bickford. *Dir*. George Cukor.

Star is Born, A (1976)   Barbra Streisand, Kris Kristofferson, Gary Busey, Paul Mazursky. *Dir*. Frank Pierson.

Star Trek: First Contact (1996)   Patrick Stewart, Jonathan Frakes, Brent Spiner, Michael Dorn, LeVar Burton. *Dir*. Jonathan Frakes.

Star Trek: Generations (1994)   Patrick Stewart, William Shatner, Malcolm McDowell, Jonathan Frakes, Brent Spiner, Whoopi Goldberg. *Dir*. David Carson.

Star Trek: The Motion Picture (1979)   William Shatner, Leonard Nimoy, DeForest Kelley, Persis Khambatta. *Dir*. Robert Wise.

Star Trek II: The Wrath of Khan (1982)   William Shatner, Leonard Nimoy, DeForest Kelley, Ricardo Montalban. Sequel to TV episode 'Space Seed'. *Dir*. Nicholas Meyer.

Star Trek III: The Search for Spock (1984)   William Shatner, Leonard Nimoy, DeForest Kelley, Robert Hooks. *Dir*. Leonard Nimoy.

Star Trek IV: The Voyage Home (1986)   William Shatner, Leonard Nimoy, DeForest Kelley, Catherine Hicks, Jane Wyatt. *Dir*. Leonard Nimoy.

Star Trek V: The Final Frontier (1989)   William Shatner, Leonard Nimoy, DeForest Kelley, David Warner. *Dir*. William Shatner.

Star Trek VI: The Undiscovered Country (1991) William Shatner, Leonard Nimoy, DeForest Kelley, David Warner, Christian Slater, Christopher Plummer. *Dir*. Nicholas Meyer.

Star Wars (1977)   Mark Hamill, Harrison Ford, Alec Guinness, Carrie Fisher, Anthony Daniels (C3PO), Kenny Baker (R2D2), Dave Prowse. *Dir*. George Lucas.

Star Wars Episode 1: The Phantom Menace (1999) Liam Neeson, Ewan McGregor, Natalie Portman, Jake Lloyd, Frank Oz, Ray Park, Ian McDiarmid, Samuel L Jackson, Brian Blessed, Sofia Coppola, Pernilla August. *Dir*. George Lucas.

Starman (1984)   Jeff Bridges, Karen Allen. Alien arrives in Wisconsin. *Dir*. John Carpenter.

Starship Troopers (1997)   Casper van Dien, Dina Meyer, Denise Richards, Jake Busey, Michael Ironside. *Dir*. Paul Verhoeven.

Stay Hungry (1976)   Jeff Bridges, Sally Field, Arnold Schwarzenegger, Robert Englund. *Dir*. Bob Rafelson.

Staying Alive (1983)   John Travolta, Cynthia Rhodes, Finola Hughes, Steve Inwood. Sequel to *Saturday Night Fever*, Tony Manero becomes a Broadway dancer. *Dir*. Sylvester Stallone.

Steaming (1985)   Vanessa Redgrave (Nancy), Sarah Miles (Sarah), Diana Dors (Violet), Patti Love, Brenda Bruce. *Dir*. Joseph Losey.

Steel Magnolias (1989)   Sally Field, Dolly Parton, Shirley MacLaine, Daryl Hannah, Olympia Dukakis, Julia Roberts, Tom Skerritt. *Dir*. Herbert Ross.

Stepford Wives, The (1974)   Katharine Ross, Paula Prentiss, Nanette Newman, Patrick O'Neal. *Dir*. Bryan Forbes.

Sting, The (1973)   Paul Newman, Robert Redford, Robert Shaw. *Dir*. George Roy Hill.

Stormy Monday (1988)   Melanie Griffith (Kate), Tommy Lee Jones (Cosmo), Sting (Finney), Sean Bean (Brendan). *Dir*. Mike Figgis.

Strange Days (1995)   Ralph Fiennes (Lenny Nero). *Dir*. Mike Newell.

Strangers on a Train (1951)   Farley Granger, Robert Walker, Ruth Roman, Patricia Hitchcock. *Dir*. Alfred Hitchcock.

Straw Dogs (1971)   Dustin Hoffman, Susan George, Peter Vaughan, David Warner, TP McKenna. Based on Gordon M Williams novel *The Siege of Trencher's Farm*. *Dir*. Sam Peckinpah.

Striptease (1996)   Demi Moore (Erin Grant), Burt Reynolds (David Dilbeck). Strip club name: The Eager Beaver. *Dir*. Andrew Bergman.

Substitute, The (1996)   Tom Berenger, Ernie Hudson, Diane Venora. Commando-trained man takes over teaching position when his girlfriend is beaten up. *Dir*. Robert Mandel.

Sudden Impact (1983)   Clint Eastwood (Callahan), Sondra Locke (Jennifer Spencer), Pat Hingle. *Dir*. Clint Eastwood.

Suddenly Last Summer (1959)   Katharine Hepburn, Elizabeth Taylor, Mongomery Clift. *Dir*. Joseph L Mankiewicz.

Summer Holiday (1962)   Cliff Richard, Lauri Peters, Melvyn Hayes, Una Stubbs. *Dir*. Peter Yates.

Summer of '42 (1971)   Jennifer O'Neill, Gary Grimes, Jerry Houser. *Dir*. Robert Mulligan.

Sunday, Bloody Sunday (1971)   Glenda Jackson, Peter Finch, Murray Head. *Dir*. John Schlesinger.

Sundowners, The (1960)   Robert Mitchum, Deborah Kerr, Glynis Johns, Peter Ustinov. *Dir*. Fred Zinnemann.

Sunset (1988)   Bruce Willis (Tom Mix), James Garner (Wyatt Earp), Malcolm McDowell. *Dir*. Blake Edwards.

Sunset Boulevard (1950)   William Holden, Gloria Swanson, Erich Von Stroheim, Cecil B de Mille, Buster Keaton, Hedda Hopper. *Dir*. Billy Wilder.

Super Mario Brothers (1993)   Bob Hoskins, Dennis Hopper, John Leguizamo. *Dir*. Rocky Morton and Annabel Jankel.

Supergirl (1984)   Faye Dunaway (Selena), Helen Slater (Supergirl / Linda Lee), Peter O'Toole (Zeitar), Peter Cook, Simon Ward, Brenda Vaccaro, Mia Farrow. *Dir*. Jeannot Szwarc.

Superman (1978)   Christopher Reeve, Marlon Brando, Susannah York, Margot Kidder, Glenn Ford, Gene Hackman, Trevor Howard. *Dir*. Richard Donner.

Superman 2 (1980)   Christopher Reeve, Susannah York, Margot Kidder, Gene Hackman, Ned Beatty, Terence Stamp. *Dir*. Richard Lester.

Superman 3 (1983)   Christopher Reeve, Richard Pryor, Jackie Cooper, Margot Kidder, Pamela Stephenson, Robert Vaughn. *Dir*. Richard Lester.

Superman 4: The Quest for Peace (1987)

Christopher Reeve, Gene Hackman, Jackie Cooper, Margot Kidder. *Dir.* Sidney J Furie.

Surviving Picasso (1996)   Anthony Hopkins (Picasso), Natascha McElhone (Françoise). *Dir.* James Ivory.

Swallows and Amazons (1974)   Virginia McKenna, Ronald Fraser, Simon West, Sophie Neville. *Dir.* Claude Whatham.

Sweet Charity (1969)   Shirley MacLaine, Ricardo Montalban, Chita Rivera, Stubby Kaye, Sammy Davis Jnr. *Dir.* Bob Fosse.

Sweet Liberty (1986)   Alan Alda, Michael Caine, Michelle Pfeiffer, Lilian Gish, Bob Hoskins. College professor is alarmed as he watches the Hollywood filming of his historical novel. *Dir.* Alan Alda.

Swing Shift (1984)   Goldie Hawn, Kurt Russell, Fred Ward, Christine Lahti. *Dir.* Jonathan Demme.

Swiss Family Robinson, The (1960)   John Mills, Dorothy McGuire, James MacArthur, Janet Munro. *Dir.* Ken Annakin.

Sword of Sherwood Forest (1960)   Richard Greene, Peter Cushing, Richard Pasco, Niall MacGinnis, Oliver Reed. *Dir.* Terence Fisher.

Taking of Pelham 123, The (1974)   Walter Matthau, Robert Shaw, Martin Balsam, Hector Elizondo. Four gunmen hold a New York subway train to ransom. *Dir.* Joseph Sargent.

Tale of Two Cities, A (1958)   Dirk Bogarde, Dorothy Tutin, Christopher Lee, Donald Pleasence, Alfie Bass. Remake of 1935 classic. *Dir.* Ralph Thomas.

Talented Mr Ripley, The (1999)   Matt Damon (Tom Ripley), Jude Law (Dickie Greenleaf), Gwyneth Paltrow (Marge Sherwood), Cate Blanchett (Meredith Logue), Philip Seymour Hoffman (Freddie Miles). *Dir.* Anthony Minghella. Anthony Minghella wrote the screen play based on Patricia Highsmith's novel.

Tales from the Darkside: The Movie (1991)   Debbie Harry is a cannibal waiting to eat a young boy once he has told her 3 stories. *The Wraparound Story*: Deborah Harry (Betty), Matthew Lawrence (Timmy). *Lot 249*: Christian Slater, Steve Buscemi, Robert Sedgwick, Julianne Moore. *Cat from Hell*: David Johansen, William Hickey. *Lover's Vow*: James Remar, Rae Dawn Chong, Robert Klein. *Dir.* John Harrison.

Talk Radio (1988)   Eric Bogosian (Barry Champlain), Ellen Greene, Leslie Hope, Alec Baldwin. *Dir.* Oliver Stone.

Tall Guy, The (1989)   Jeff Goldblum (Dexter King), Emma Thompson (Kate Lemon), Rowan Atkinson (Ron Anderson). *Dir.* Mel Smith.

Tango and Cash (1989)   Kurt Russell, Sylvester Stallone, Jack Palance, Teri Hatcher, Michael J Pollard. *Dir.* Andrei Konchalovsky.

Tank Girl (1994)   Lon Petty, Ice T, Naomi Watts, Malcolm McDowell. *Dir.* Rachel Talalay.

Tank Malling (1988)   Ray Winstone, Jason Connery, Amanda Donohoe, John Conteh, Terry Marsh, Nick Berry. *Dir.* James Marcus.

Tap (1989)   Gregory Hines, Suzanne Douglas, Sammy Davis Jnr (Little Mo). *Dir.* Nick Castle.

Taps (1981)   Timothy Hutton, George C Scott, Sean Penn, Tom Cruise. *Dir.* Harold Becker.

Taras Bulba (1962)   Yul Brynner, Tony Curtis, Christine Kaufmann, Sam Wanamaker. *Dir.* J Lee Thompson.

Tarzan the Apeman (1981)   Bo Derek, Miles O'Keeffe (Tarzan), Richard Harris, John Phillip Law, Wilfrid Hyde-White. *Dir.* John Derek.

Taste of Honey, A (1961)   Rita Tushingham, Dora Bryan, Murray Melvin. Based on Shelagh Delaney play. *Dir.* Tony Richardson.

Taxi Driver (1976)   Robert De Niro (Travis Bickle), Jodie Foster, Cybill Shepherd, Harvey Keitel. *Dir.* Martin Scorsese.

Teenage Mutant Ninja Turtles (1990)   Judith Hoag (April O'Neil), Elias Koteas (Casey Jones), Josh Pais (Raphael), Michelan Sisti (Michelangelo), Leif Tilden (Donatello), David Forman (Leonardo). Michael Pressman's 1991 sequel: *Teenage Mutant Ninja Turtles II: The Secret of the Ooze*. *Dir.* Steve Barron.

Ten Commandments, The (1956)   Charlton Heston (Moses), Yul Brynner, Edward G Robinson, Anne Baxter, Yvonne De Carlo. *Dir.* Cecil B de Mille.

Ten Little Indians (1965)   Wilfrid Hyde-White, Dennis Price, Stanley Holloway, Shirley Eaton, Hugh O'Brian, Daliah Lavi, Fabian, Mario Adorf. Based on Agatha Christie's novel. *Dir.* George Pollock.

Ten Rillington Place (1971)   Richard Attenborough, John Hurt, Judy Geeson. Account of the Christie murders of the 1940's. *Dir.* Richard Fleischer.

10 Things I Hate About You (1999)   Heath Ledger, Julia Stiles, Joseph-Gordon Levitt, Andrew Keegan, Susan May Pratt. *Dir.* Gil Junger. Teenage comedy loosely based on Shakespeare's *The Taming of the Shrew*.

10 to Midnight (1983)   Charles Bronson (Leo Kessler), Lisa Eilbacher (Laurie), Andrew Stevens, Gene Davis. *Dir.* J Lee Thompson.

Tender Mercies (1982)   Robert Duvall, Tess Harper, Betty Buckley. Robert Duvall sang the songs himself. *Dir.* Bruce Beresford.

Tequila Sunrise (1988)   Mel Gibson (McKussic), Michele Pfeiffer, Kurt Russell, Raul Julia. *Dir.* Robert Towne.

Terminator, The (1984)   Arnold Schwarzenegger, Linda Hamilton, Michael Biehn. *Dir.* James Cameron.

Terminator 2: Judgment Day (1991)   Arnold Schwarzenegger, Linda Hamilton, Edward Furlong. *Dir.* James Cameron.

Terms of Endearment (1983)   Shirley MacLaine, Jack Nicholson, Debra Winger, Danny De Vito. *Dir.* James L Brooks.

Texas Chainsaw Massacre, The (1974)   Marilyn Burns, Allen Danziger, Paul A Partain. *Dir.* Tobe Hooper.

Thelma and Louise (1991)   Susan Sarandon (Louise Sawyer), Geena Davis (Thelma Dickinson), Harvey Keitel, Brad Pitt. *Dir.* Ridley Scott.

There's No Business Like Show Business (1954)   Ethel Merman, Dan Dailey, Marilyn Monroe, Donald O'Connor, Johnny Ray, Mitzi Gaynor, Hugh O'Brian. *Dir.* Walter Lang.

They Died with Their Boots On (1941)   Errol Flynn, Olivia de Havilland, Arthur Kennedy, Anthony Quinn, Sidney Greenstreet. Biopic of General Custer. *Dir.* Raoul Walsh.

They Shoot Horses, Don't They? (1969)   Gig Young, Jane Fonda, Susannah York, Red Buttons. Tragedy during a six-day marathon dance contest in the 1930s. *Dir.* Sydney Pollack.

Thin Man, The (1934)   William Powell, Myrna Loy, Maureen O'Sullivan. *Dir.* WS Van Dyke.

Thing, The (1951)   Robert Cornthwaite, Kenneth Tobey, James Arness (the Thing). GB Title: *The Thing from Another World*. *Dir.* Christian Nyby.

Thing, The (1982)   Kurt Russell, A Wilford Brimley, TK Carter. Remake of the 1951 film, although this 'Thing' is a metamorphic creature that can now enter and take over the protagonists. *Dir.* John Carpenter.

Things To Do in Denver When You're Dead (1995)   Andy Garcia (Jimmy the Saint), Christopher Walken, Christopher Lloyd. *Dir.* Gary Fleder.

Thinner (1987)   Robert John Burke (William Halleck). Stephen King wrote the novel under the pseudonym Richard Bachman. *Dir.* Tom Holland.

Third Man, The (1949)   Orson Welles (Harry Lime), Joseph Cotten, Trevor Howard, Alida Valli, Bernard Lee, Wilfrid Hyde-White. *Dir.* Carol Reed.

Thirty-Nine Steps, The (1935)   Robert Donat, Madeleine Carroll, Peggy Ashcroft. *Dir.* Alfred Hitchcock.

Thirty-Nine Steps, The (1959)   Kenneth More, Taina Elg, Barry Jones. *Dir.* Ralph Thomas.

Thirty-Nine Steps, The (1978)   Robert Powell, Karen Dotrice, John Mills. *Dir.* Don Sharp.

This is Spinal Tap (1984)   Michael McKean (David St Hubbins), Christopher Guest (Nigel Tufnel), Harry Shearer (Derek Smalls), RJ Parnell (Mick Shrimpton), Rob Reiner (Marti DiBerti). Cameos by Anjelica Huston, Patrick Macnee and Billy Crystal. *Dir.* Rob Reiner.

This Sporting Life (1963)   Richard Harris, Rachel Roberts, Alan Badel, William Hartnell, Arthur Lowe, Colin Blakely. *Dir.* Lindsay Anderson.

Thomas Crown Affair, The (1968)   Steve McQueen, Faye Dunaway, Yaphet Kotto. *Dir.* Norman Jewison.

Thoroughly Modern Millie (1967)   Julie Andrews, Mary Tyler Moore, James Fox. *Dir.* George Roy Hill.

Three Amigos! (1986)   Chevy Chase (Dusty Bottoms), Steve Martin (Lucky Day), Martin Short (Ned Nederlander). *Dir.* John Landis.

Three Colours: Blue (1993)   Juliette Binoche, Benoît Régent, Florence Pernel. First part of trilogy based on the colours of the French tricolour. *Dir.* Krzysztof Kieslowski.

Three Colours: Red (1994)   Juliette Binoche, Irene Jacob, Jean-Louis Trintignant, Julie Delpy. Third part of trilogy based on the colours of the French tricolour. *Dir.* Krzysztof Kieslowski.

Three Colours: White (1993)   Zbigniew Zamachowski, Julie Delpy, Juliette Binoche, Florence Pernel. Second part of trilogy based on the colours of the French tricolour. *Dir.* Krzysztof Kieslowski.

Three Days of the Condor (1975)   Robert Redford, Faye Dunaway, Cliff Robertson, Max Von Sydow. *Dir.* Sydney Pollack.

Three Faces of Eve, The (1957)   Joanne Woodward, Lee J Cobb. Introduced by Alistair Cooke. *Dir.* Nunnally Johnson.

Three Fugitives (1989)   Nick Nolte (Dan Lucas), Martin Short (Ned Perry), Sarah Rowland Doroff, James Earl Jones. *Dir.* Francis Veber.

Three Kings (1999)   George Clooney (Major Archie Gates), Ice Cube (Chief Elgin), Mark Wahlberg (Sgt Barlow). *Dir.* David O. Russell.

Three Men and a Baby (1987)   Tom Selleck (Peter), Steve Guttenberg (Michael), Ted Danson (Jack), Nancy Travis. *Dir.* Leonard Nimoy.

Three Men and a Little Lady (1990)   Tom Selleck, Steve Guttenberg, Ted Danson, Nancy Travis, Sheila Hancock. *Dir.* Emilio Ardelino.

Three Men in a Boat (1956)   David Tomlinson, Jimmy Edwards, Laurence Harvey, Shirley Eaton, Jill Ireland. *Dir.* Ken Annakin.

Three Musketeers, The (1993)   Charlie Sheen, Kiefer Sutherland, Chris O'Donnell, Rebecca DeMornay. *Dir.* Stephen Herek.

Three Musketeers, The (The Queen's Diamonds), (1973)   Michael York, Oliver Reed, Richard Chamberlain, Frank Finlay, Raquel Welch, Geraldine Chaplin, Spike Milligan, Faye Dunaway, Charlton Heston, Christopher Lee. *Dir.* Richard Lester.

Throw Momma from the Train (1987)   Danny De Vito (Owen), Billy Crystal (Larry), Kim Greist (Beth),

Anne Ramsey (Momma), Kate Mulgrew, Rob Reiner, Annie Ross, Oprah Winfrey (as herself). *Dir.* Danny De Vito.

Thunderball (1965)   Sean Connery, Adolfo Celi (Emilio Largo), Claudine Auger (Domino). Title song performed by Tom Jones. *Dir.* Terence Young.

Thunderbolt and Lightfoot (1974)   Clint Eastwood, Jeff Bridges, George Kennedy, Catherine Bach. *Dir.* Michael Cimino.

THX 1138 (1970)   Robert Duvall, Donald Pleasence. *Dir.* George Lucas.

Tiger Bay (1959)   Hayley Mills, John Mills, Horst Buchholz, Megs Jenkins. *Dir.* J Lee Thompson.

Tightrope (1984)   Clint Eastwood (Wes Block), Geneviève Bujold (Beryl Thibodeax), Alison Eastwood (Amanda). *Dir.* Richard Tuggle.

Time after Time (1980)   Malcolm McDowell, David Warner, Mary Steenburgen. Jack the Ripper in modern San Francisco via HG Wells's time machine. *Dir.* Nicholas Meyer.

Time Bandits (1981)   John Cleese (Robin Hood), Sean Connery (Agamemnon), Ian Holm (Napoleon), Ralph Richardson (God), David Warner (Satan). *Dir.* Terry Gilliam.

Time Machine, The (1960)   Rod Taylor, Yvette Mimieux, Alan Young, Sebastian Cabot. Victorian scientist builds a machine which transports him to the year 802701. *Dir.* George Pal.

Time of Your Life (1948)   James Cagney, William Bendix, Jeanne Cagney, Wayne Morris, Broderick Crawford, Ward Bond. Group of eccentrics meet in a San Francisco bar. *Dir.* HC Potter.

Time to Kill, A (1996)   Sandra Bullock, Matthew McConaughey, Samuel L Jackson, Donald & Kiefer Sutherland. Ku Klux Klan still has power in small Mississippi town. *Dir.* Joel Schumacher.

Tin Cup (1996)   Kevin Costner, Rene Russo, Don Johnson. *Dir.* Ron Shelton.

Tin Men (1987)   Richard Dreyfuss (Bill 'BB' Babowsky), Danny De Vito (Ernie Tilley), Barbara Hershey (Nora). *Dir.* Barry Levinson.

Titanic (1997)   Kate Winslet, Leonardo DiCaprio. Equalled the record of Ben Hur by gaining 11 Oscars (14 nominations). *Dir.* James Cameron.

To Be or Not to Be (1983)   Mel Brooks (Frederick Bronski), Anne Bancroft (Anna), Tim Matheson (Lt Andre Sobinski), Charles Durning (Col Erhardt), José Ferrer (Prof Siletski), Christopher Lloyd (Capt Schultz). *Dir.* Alan Johnson.

To Catch a Thief (1955)   Cary Grant, Grace Kelly. *Dir.* Alfred Hitchcock.

To Die For (1995)   Nicole Kidman, Matt Dillon, Joaquin Phoenix, David Cronenberg, George Segal (uncredited). Fame-obsessed weather woman on local TV station describes how she murdered her husband. *Dir.* Gus Van Sant.

To Have and Have Not (1945)   Humphrey Bogart, Lauren Bacall, Walter Brennan, Hoagy Carmichael. US charter boat captain in Martinique gets involved with Nazis. *Dir.* Howard Hawks.

To Sir with Love (1967)   Sidney Poitier, Judy Geeson, Suzy Kendall, Lulu. *Dir.* James Clavell.

Tom Brown's Schooldays (1940)   Freddie Bartholomew, Jimmy Lydon, Cedric Hardwicke, Billy Halop, Gale Storm. The 1951 remake starred Robert Newton and John Howard Davies (Tom). *Dir.* Robert Stevenson.

Tom Horn (1979)   Steve McQueen, Linda Evans, Slim Pickens. *Dir.* William Wiard.

Tombstone (1993)   Kurt Russell, Val Kilmer, Sam Elliott, Charlton Heston. Narrated by Robert Mitchum. *Dir.* George P Cosmatos.

Tomorrow Never Dies (1997)   Pierce Brosnan (James Bond), Teri Hatcher (Paris Carver), Jonathan Pryce. Theme song sung by Sheryl Crow. *Dir.* Roger Spottiswoode.

Too Hot to Handle (1991)   Kim Basinger (Vicki Rosemary Anderson), Alec Baldwin (Charley Raymond Pearl), Robert Loggia, Elisabeth Shue, Armand Assante. *Dir.* Jerry Rees.

Tootsie (1982)   Dustin Hoffman (Michael Dorsey / Dorothy), Teri Garr, Dabney Coleman, Jessica Lange, Charles Durning, Bill Murray, Sydney Pollack, Geena Davis. *Dir.* Sydney Pollack.

Top Gun (1986)   Tom Cruise (Maverick), Kelly McGillis (Charlie), Val Kilmer (Ice), Tom Skerritt (Viper), Anthony Edwards (Goose), Michael Ironside (Jester), John Stockwell (Cougar), Meg Ryan (Carole), Tim Robbins (Merlin), Barry Tubb (Wolfman), Clarence Gilyard (Sundown). *Dir.* Tony Scott.

Top Hat (1935)   Fred Astaire, Ginger Rogers. *Dir.* Mark Sandrich.

Tora! Tora! Tora! (1970)   Martin Balsam, Joseph Cotten, Jason Robards. Events leading up to Pearl Harbor. *Dir.* Richard Fleischer.

Torn Curtain (1966)   Paul Newman, Julie Andrews. *Dir.* Alfred Hitchcock.

Total Eclipse (1995)   Leonardo DiCaprio (Arthur Rimbaud the 18th century poet), David Thewlis (Verlaine). *Dir.* Agnieszka Holand.

Total Recall (1990)   Sharon Stone, Arnold Schwarzenegger (Doug Quaid), Rachel Ticotin, Michael Ironside. *Dir.* Paul Verhoeven.

Tough Guys (1986)   Burt Lancaster (Harry Doyle), Kirk Douglas (Archie Long), Charles Durning, Eli Wallach. *Dir.* Jeff Kanew.

Towering Inferno, The (1974)   Paul Newman, Steve McQueen, William Holden, Faye Dunaway, Fred Astaire, OJ Simpson, Robert Wagner, Jennifer Jones, Robert Vaughn, Richard Chamberlain. *Dir.* John Guillermin.

Toxic Avenger, The (1985)   Andree Maranda, Mitchell Cohen, Pat Ryan Jnr. Archetypal Troma trash-fest. Ron Fazio took over the role of the supercharged weakling in the sequels. *Dir.* Michael Herz.

Toy Story (1995)   Voices of Tom Hanks, Don Rickles, Jim Varney, Tim Allen. First full length computer-animated feature film. Song: 'You've Got a Friend in Me' (music and lyrics by Randy Newman). *Dir.* John Lasseter.

Toy Story 2 (1999)   Voice of Woody (Tom Hanks), Tim Allen, Joan Cusack. *Dir.* Ash Brannan and John Lasseter.

Toys (1992)   Robin Williams, Michael Gambon, LL Cool J, Joan Cusack, Donald O'Connor. *Dir.* Barry Levinson.

Trading Places (1983)   Dan Aykroyd, Eddie Murphy, Ralph Bellamy, Don Ameche, Jamie Lee Curtis, Denholm Elliott. *Dir.* John Landis.

Trail of the Pink Panther (1982)   Peter Sellers, Joanna Lumley, Herbert Lom, David Niven. *Dir.* Blake Edwards.

Trainspotting (1996)   Ewan McGregor, Ewen Bremner, Jonny Lee Miller, Robert Carlyle, Kelly MacDonald. *Dir.* Danny Boyle.

Trapeze (1956)   Burt Lancaster, Tony Curtis, Gina Lollobrigida, Sid James. *Dir.* Carol Reed.

Treasure Island (1990)   Charlton Heston, Oliver Reed, Christian Bale, Christopher Lee, Richard Johnson. *Dir.* Raúl Ruiz. Earlier versions 1934 (*Dir.* Victor Fleming); 1950 (*Dir.* Byron Haskin).

Treasure of the Sierra Madre, The (1948)   Humphrey Bogart, Walter Huston, Tim Holt, John Huston. *Dir.* John Huston.

Trial, The (1962)   Orson Welles, Jeanne Moreau, Anthony Perkins. Joseph K is tried and condemned for an unspecified crime. 1992 remake starred Anthony Hopkins & Kyle MacLachlan. *Dir.* Orson Welles.

Trials of Oscar Wilde, The (1960)   Peter Finch, Yvonne Mitchell, John Fraser, James Mason. US title: *The Man with the Green Carnation. Dir.* Ken Hughes.

Trouble with Girls, The (1969)   Elvis Presley, Marlyn Mason, Vincent Price. Manager of an educational medicine show (a chautauqua) gets involved in a murder. *Dir.* Peter Tewksbury.

True Grit (1969)   John Wayne, Kim Darby, Glen Campbell, Robery Duvall, Dennis Hopper. *Dir.* Henry Hathaway.

True Lies (1994)   Arnold Schwarzenegger, Jamie Lee Curtis, Tom Arnold, Charlton Heston. US secret agent pretends to be a computer salesman to his wife. *Dir.* James Cameron.

True Romance (1993)   Christian Slater, Patricia Arquette, Dennis Hopper, Val Kilmer, Brad Pitt, Gary Oldman, Christopher Walken. Quentin Tarantino story about a shop assistant and a callgirl who go on the run with a case full of cocaine. *Dir.* Tony Scott.

True Stories (1986)   David Byrne (Narrator), John Goodman (Louis Fyne), Annie McEnroe (Kay Culver). Famous for the club scene where a multitude of characters mime to Byrne's voice. *Dir.* David Byrne.

Truly, Madly, Deeply (1990)   Juliet Stevenson (Nina), Alan Rickman (Jamie), Bill Paterson, Michael Maloney. *Dir.* Anthony Minghella.

Truman Show, The (1998)   Jim Carrey, Laura Linney, Noah Emmerich, Ed Harris, Natascha McElhone. *Dir.* Peter Weir.

Tunes of Glory (1960)   Alec Guinness, John Mills, Susannah York, Dennis Price, Kay Walsh, Duncan Macrae. *Dir.* Ronald Neame.

Turbulence (1997)   Lauren Holly (Teri Halloran), Ray Liotta (Ryan Weaver), Brenda Gleeson (Stubbs). *Dir.* Robert Butler.

Turner & Hooch (1989)   Tom Hanks, Mare Winningham, John McIntire. Cop teams up with a dog to solve a murder. *Dir.* Roger Spottiswoode.

Turning Point, The (1977)   Anne Bancroft, Shirley MacLaine, Mikhail Baryshnikov, Tom Skerritt. *Dir.* Herbert Ross.

Twelfth Night (1996)   Helena Bonham Carter, Richard E. Grant, Nigel Hawthorne, Mel Smith, Imogen Stubbs. *Dir.* Trevor Nunn.

Twelve Angry Men (1957)   Henry Fonda, Lee J Cobb, EG Marshall, Jack Warden, Ed Begley, George Voskovec, Jack Klugman, John Fiedler, Martin Balsam, Robert Webber, Edward Binns, Joseph Sweeney. *Dir.* Sidney Lumet.

Twelve Monkeys (1995)   Bruce Willis, Brad Pitt, Madeleine Stowe, Christopher Plummer. Set in 2035; a convict is sent back to 1996 to discover cause of pandemic disease. *Dir.* Terry Gilliam.

Twelve O'Clock High (1949)   Gregory Peck, Hugh Marlowe, Gary Merrill, Dean Jagger. *Dir.* Henry King.

Twenty Thousand Leagues under the Sea (1954)   Kirk Douglas, James Mason, Paul Lukas, Peter Lorre. *Dir.* Richard Fleischer.

Twilight Zone: The Movie (1983)   Dan Aykroyd, Vic Morrow, Scatman Crothers, Kevin McCarthy. Four supernatural stories. *Dir.* John Landis, Steven Spielberg, Joe Dante, George Miller.

Twin Town (1997)   Rhys Ifans, Llyr Evans, Keith Allen. *Dir.* Kevin Allen.

Twinky (1969)   Charles Bronson, Susan George, Trevor Howard. 16-yr-old schoolgirl marries a dissolute 40-yr-old American author. *Dir.* Richard Donner.

Twins (1988)   Arnold Schwarzenegger (Julius Benedict), Danny De Vito (Vincent Benedict). *Dir.* Ivan Reitman.

Twister (1996)   Helen Hunt, Bill Paxton, Lois Smith. *Dir.* Jan de Bont.

Two Days in the Valley (1996)   Danny Aiello, James Spader, Jeff Daniels, Teri Hatcher, Louise Fletcher, Keith Carradine. *Dir.* John Herzfeld.

Two Much (1996)   Antonio Banderas, Melanie Griffith, Danny Aiello, Daryl Hannah. Art dealer, engaged to wealthy woman, invents a twin brother so that he can marry her sister. *Dir.* Fernando Trueba.

Two Mules for Sister Sara (1969)   Clint Eastwood, Shirley MacLaine. *Dir.* Don Siegel.

2001: A Space Odyssey (1968)   Keir Dullea, Gary Lockwood, Leonard Rossiter, Robert Beatty, Douglas Rain (voice of Hal). Film based on Arthur C Clarke story 'The Sentinel'. Computer: Hal 9000 stands for Holistic Algorithmic. Journeyed to moon of Jupiter, although it was to the rings of Saturn in the book. *Dir.* Stanley Kubrick.

2010 (1984)   Roy Scheider, Helen Mirren, John Lithgow, Keir Dullea. *Dir.* Peter Hyams.

Two-Way Stretch (1960)   Peter Sellers, Wilfrid Hyde-White, Lionel Jeffries, Bernard Cribbins, David Lodge, Beryl Reid, Irene Handl. Three convicts break out of jail to do a robbery. *Dir.* Robert Day.

Ultimate Warrior, The (1975)   Yul Brynner, Max Von Sydow, Joanna Miles. Set in New York AD 2012. *Dir.* Robert Clouse.

Unforgiven (1992)   Clint Eastwood, Gene Hackman, Morgan Freeman, Richard Harris. *Dir.* Clint Eastwood.

Unforgiven, The (1960)   Burt Lancaster, Audrey Hepburn, Audie Murphy. *Dir.* John Huston.

Universal Soldier (1992)   Jean-Claude Van Damme, Dolph Lundgren. *Dir.* Roland Emmerich.

Unsinkable Molly Brown, The (1964)   Debbie Reynolds, Harve Presnell, Ed Begley. *Dir.* Charles Walters.

Untouchables, The (1987)   Kevin Costner, Sean Connery (Jim Malone), Robert De Niro (Al Capone), Andy Garcia. *Dir.* Brian De Palma.

Uptown Saturday Night (1974)   Sidney Poitier, Bill Cosby, Harry Belafonte, Flip Wilson, Richard Pryor. Friends pursue crooks who have stolen a winning lottery ticket. *Dir.* Sidney Poitier.

Urban Cowboy (1980)   John Travolta, Debra Winger. *Dir.* James Bridges.

Used Cars (1980)   Kurt Russell, Gerrit Graham, Jack Russell. *Dir.* Robert Zemeckis.

Usual Suspects, The (1995)   Gabriel Byrne, Stephen Baldwin, Kevin Spacey, Pete Postlethwaite. *Dir.* Bryan Singer.

Valentino (1977)   Rudolf Nureyev, Leslie Caron, Michelle Phillips. *Dir.* Ken Russell.

Valley of the Dolls (1967)   Barbara Parkins, Patty Duke, Susan Hayward, Sharon Tate, Martin Milner. *Dir.* Mark Robson.

Verdict, The (1982)   Paul Newman, James Mason, Charlotte Rampling. *Dir.* Sidney Lumet.

Very Important Person (1961)   James Robertson Justice, Stanley Baxter, Leslie Phillips. *Dir.* Ken Annakin.

Vice Versa (1988)   Judge Reinhold, Fred Savage, Corinne Bohrer. *Dir.* Brian Gilbert.

Victor / Victoria (1982)   James Garner, Julie Andrews, Robert Preston, John Rhys-Davies. *Dir.* Blake Edwards.

View to a Kill, A (1985)   Roger Moore, Christopher Walken (Max Zorin), Grace Jones (May Day), Tanya Roberts (Stacey Sutton), Patrick MacNee, Fiona Fullerton, David Yip. Title song performed by Duran Duran. *Dir.* John Glen.

Vikings, The (1958)   Kirk Douglas, Tony Curtis, Janet Leigh, Ernest Borgnine. Orson Welles was the narrator. *Dir.* Richard Fleischer.

Village of the Damned (1960)   George Sanders, Barbara Shelley, Laurence Naismith. Village women simultaneously give birth to fair-haired, genius level, telepathic children with eerie results. *Dir.* Wolf Rilla.

Village of the Damned (1995)   Christopher Reeve, Kirstie Alley, Linda Kozlowski, Mark Hamill. *Dir.* John Carpenter.

Villain (1971)   Richard Burton, Ian McShane, Nigel Davenport, TP McKenna. *Dir.* Michael Tuchner.

VIPs, The (1963)   Richard Burton, Elizabeth Taylor, Rod Taylor, Maggie Smith, Orson Welles, Louis Jourdan, Lance Percival. *Dir.* Anthony Asquith.

Virginian, The (1929)   Gary Cooper, Walter Huston. 1946 remake starred Joel McCrea & Brian Donlevy. *Dir.* Victor Fleming.

Viva Las Vegas (1964)   Elvis Presley, Ann-Margret. Presley plays the part of a sports car racer. *Dir.* George Sidney.

Viva Zapata (1952)   Marlon Brando, Anthony Quinn, Jean Peters, Joseph Wiseman. *Dir.* Elia Kazan.

Volcano (1997)   Tommy Lee Jones (Mike Roark), Gaby Hoffmann, Don Cheadle, Anne Heche (Dr Amy Barnes)

Von Ryan's Express (1965)   Frank Sinatra, Trevor Howard, Sergio Fantoni. *Dir.* Mark Robson.

Voyage to the Bottom of the Sea (1961)   Walter Pidgeon, Robert Sterling, Joan Fontaine, Peter Lorre, Barbara Eden. Spawned a long-running TV series. *Dir.* Irwin Allen.

Wag the Dog (1998)   Dustin Hoffman, Robert De Niro. *Dir.* Barry Levinson.

Wages of Fear, The (1953)   Yves Montand, Folco Lulli, Peter Van Eyck, Charles Vanel. Nitro-glycerine is the substance transported over dangerous roads to put out oil well fire. *Dir.* Henri-Georges Clouzot.

Wait until Dark (1967)   Audrey Hepburn, Alan Arkin, Richard Crenna, Efrem Zimbalist Jnr. *Dir.* Terence Young.

Walkabout (1970)   Jenny Agutter, Lucien John, David Gulpilil. *Dir.* Nicolas Roeg.

War, The (1994)   Kevin Costner, Elijah Wood, LaToya Chisholm. *Dir.* Jon Avnet.

War Games (1983)   Matthew Broderick, Dabney Coleman, John Wood. *Dir.* John Badham.

War of the Roses, The (1989)   Michael Douglas, Kathleen Turner, Danny De Vito. *Dir.* Danny De Vito.

Waterworld (1995)   Kevin Costner, Dennis Hopper, Jeanne Tripplehorn. *Dir.* Kevin Reynolds.

Way We Were, The (1973)   Robert Redford, Barbra Streisand, Patrick O'Neal. *Dir.* Sydney Pollack.

Wedding Banquet, The (1993)   Mitchell Lichtenstein, Winston Chao, May Chin. *Dir.* Ang Lee.

Welcome II The Terrordome (1994)   Suzette Llewellyn, Saffron Burrows. *Dir.* Ngozi Onwurah.

Welcome to the Dollhouse (1995)   Heather Matarazzo, Victoria Davis. *Dir.* Todd Solondz.

We're No Angels (1954)   Humphrey Bogart, Peter Ustinov, Aldo Ray, Basil Rathbone. *Dir.* Michael Curtiz.

We're No Angels (1989)   Robert De Niro, Sean Penn, Demi Moore. Remake of the 1954 film. *Dir.* Neil Jordan.

West Side Story (1961)   Natalie Wood, Richard Beymer, Russ Tamblyn, George Chakiris, Rita Moreno. *Dir*. Robert Wise.

Westerner, The (1940)   Gary Cooper, Walter Brennan, Charlton Heston. *Dir*. William Wyler.

Westworld (1973)   Yul Brynner, Richard Benjamin, James Brolin. *Dir*. Michael Crichton.

Whatever Happened to Baby Jane? (1962)   Bette Davis, Joan Crawford, Victor Buono. *Dir*. Robert Aldrich.

What's New Pussycat? (1965)   Peter O'Toole, Peter Sellers, Woody Allen, Ursula Andress, Capucine. *Dir*. Woody Allen.

What's Up Doc? (1972)   Barbra Streisand, Ryan O'Neal. *Dir*. Peter Bogdanovich.

When Saturday Comes (1996)   Sean Bean (Jimmy Muir), Emile Lloyd (Annie Doherty), Pete Postlethwaite. *Dir*. Maria Giese.

When We Were Kings (1996)   Documentary of Muhammad Ali's defeat of George Foreman in Zaïre. *Dir*. Leon Gast.

Where Eagles Dare (1969)   Richard Burton, Clint Eastwood, Mary Ure. Seven Allied agents land in Bavarian Alps to rescue officer from impregnable castle during World War II. *Dir*. Brian G. Hutton.

Whistle down the Wind (1961)   Hayley Mills, Bernard Lee, Alan Bates, Norman Bird. Three children think a murderer on the run is Jesus. *Dir*. Bryan Forbes.

White Christmas (1954)   Bing Crosby, Danny Kaye, Rosemary Clooney, Dean Jagger. *Dir*. Michael Curtiz.

White Heat (1949)   James Cagney, Edmond O'Brien, Margaret Wycherly, Virginia Mayo. *Dir*. Raoul Walsh.

White Hunter, Black Heart (1990)   Clint Eastwood (John Wilson), Jeff Fahey (Pete Verrill), Marisa Berenson (Kay Gibson), Timothy Spall (Hodkins). Fictionalised account of John Huston during the shooting of *The African Queen*. *Dir*. Clint Eastwood.

White Men Can't Jump (1992)   Wesley Snipes, Woody Harrelson, Rosie Perez. *Dir*. Ron Shelton.

White Mischief (1987)   Charles Dance, Greta Scacchi, John Hurt, Sarah Miles, Trevor Howard. *Dir*. Michael Radford.

White Nights (1985)   Mikhail Baryshnikov, Gregory Hines, Helen Mirren, Isabella Rossellini. Best Song Oscar for 'Say You, Say Me' by Lionel Richie. *Dir*. Taylor Hackford.

White Squall (1996)   Jeff Bridges (Christopher 'Skipper' Sheldon). Boat: *The Albatross*. *Dir*. Ridley Scott.

Who Framed Roger Rabbit? (1988)   Bob Hoskins (Eddie Valiant) Animation synchronised with live action. Christopher Lloyd (Judge Doom). Jessica Rabbit's speaking voice was Kathleen Turner and singing voice was Amy Irving. *Dir*. Robert Zemeckis.

Whoops Apocalypse (1986)   Loretta Swit (President Adams), Peter Cook (Sir Mortimer Chris). *Dir*. Tom Bussmann.

Who's Afraid of Virginia Woolf? (1966)   Richard Burton, Elizabeth Taylor, George Segal, Sandy Dennis. Based on Edward Albee's play. *Dir*. Mike Nichols.

Wicked Lady, The (1945)   Margaret Lockwood, James Mason, Michael Rennie. The 1983 remake starred Faye Dunaway in the Lockwood role. *Dir*. Leslie Arliss.

Wild Bunch, The (1969)   William Holden, Ernest Borgnine, Robert Ryan, Warren Oates, Edmond O'Brien. *Dir*. Sam Peckinpah.

Wild One, The (1954)   Marlon Brando, Lee Marvin, Mary Murphy. The Garutso lens created the sharpness of photography. *Dir*. Laslo Benedek.

Willard (1971)   Bruce Davison, Elsa Lanchester, Ernest Borgnine, Sondra Locke. Shy, introverted man breeds and trains rats to kill his enemies. *Dir*. Daniel Mann.

William Shakespeare's Romeo and Juliet (1996)   Leonardo DiCaprio, Claire Danes, Brian Dennehy, Pete Postlethwaite. *Dir*. Baz Luhrmann.

Wind in the Willows, The (1996)   Steve Coogan (Mole), Eric Idle (Rat), Terry Jones (Toad), Stephen Fry, Julia Sawalha. *Dir*. Terry Jones.

Winslow Boy, The (1948)   Robert Donat, Cedric Hardwicke, Margaret Leighton, Wilfrid Hyde-White, Kathleen Harrison. Father endeavours to prove the innocence of naval cadet son, expelled for stealing postal order. *Dir*. Anthony Asquith.

Wish You Were Here (1987)   Emily Lloyd, Tom Bell, Clare Clifford. *Dir*. David Leland.

Witches of Eastwick, The (1987)   Jack Nicholson, Cher, Susan Sarandon, Michelle Pfeiffer. *Dir*. George Miller.

Witness (1985)   Harrison Ford, Kelly McGillis, Lukas Haas, Alexander Godunov. *Dir*. Peter Weir.

Witness for the Prosecution (1957)   Charles Laughton, Tyrone Power, Marlene Dietrich, Elsa Lanchester. *Dir*. Billy Wilder.

Wiz, The (1978)   Diana Ross, Michael Jackson, Lena Horne, Richard Pryor. *Dir*. Sidney Lumet.

Wizard of Oz, The (1939)   Judy Garland, Frank Morgan, Bert Lahr (Lion), Jack Haley (Tin Man), Ray Bolger (Scarecrow). *Dir*. Victor Fleming.

Wolf (1994)   Jack Nicholson, Michelle Pfeiffer, James Spader, Kate Nelligan, Christopher Plummer. *Dir*. Mike Nichols.

Woman in a Dressing Gown (1957)   Yvonne Mitchell, Anthony Quayle, Sylvia Syms, Andrew Ray. *Dir*. J Lee Thompson.

Women in love (1969)   Glenda Jackson, Jennie Linden, Alan Bates, Oliver Reed. Famous for its nude wrestling scene between Bates and Reed. *Dir*. Ken Russell.

Working Girl (1988)   Harrison Ford, Sigourney Weaver, Melanie Griffith, Alec Baldwin, Olympia Dukakis. *Dir*. Mike Nichols.

Working Girls (1986)   Louise Smith, Ellen McElduff, Amanda Goodwin. *Dir*. Lizzie Borden.

World is Not Enough, The (1999)   Pierce Brosnan, Robert Carlyle, Sophie Marceau, Denise Richards, Judi Dench (M) Robbie Coltrane, John Cleese (R). Theme song performed by Shirley Manson of Garbage. *Dir*. Michael Apted.

World of Suzie Wong, The (1960)   William Holden, Nancy Kwan, Sylvia Syms, Michael Wilding, Jackie Chan. *Dir*. Richard Quine.

Wrong Box, The (1966)   Ralph Richardson, John Mills, Michael Caine, Peter Cook, Dudley Moore, Peter Sellers, Tony Hancock, Nanette Newman. Two Victorian brothers are last survivors of a tontine agreement and try to kill each other. *Dir*. Bryan Forbes.

Wrong Man, The (1957)   Henry Fonda, Vera Miles, Anthony Quayle. *Dir*. Alfred Hitchcock.

Wuthering Heights (1939)   Laurence Olivier, Merle Oberon, David Niven, Flora Robson. *Dir*. William Wyler.

Wuthering Heights (1970)   Timothy Dalton, Anna Calder-Marshall, Ian Ogilvy. *Dir*. Robert Fuest.

Wyatt Earp (1994)   Kevin Costner, Dennis Quaid, Gene Hackman, Mark Harmon, Isabella Rossellini. *Dir*. Lawrence Kasdan.

Xanadu (1980)   Olivia Newton-John, Gene Kelly, Michael Beck. *Dir*. Robert Greenwald.

Yankee Doodle Dandy (1942)   James Cagney,

Walter Huston, Eddie Foy Jnr. Life story of dancer George M Cohan. *Dir.* Michael Curtiz.

Yanks (1979)   Vanessa Redgrave, Richard Gere, Rachel Roberts. *Dir.* John Schlesinger.

Year of the Dragon, The (1985)   Mickey Rourke, John Lone, Ariane. *Dir.* Michael Cimino.

Yearling, The (1946)   Gregory Peck, Jane Wyman. *Dir.* Clarence Brown.

Yellow Rolls Royce, The (1964)   Rex Harrison, Jeanne Moreau, Omar Sharif, Ingrid Bergman, Shirley MacLaine. Aristocrat, gangster and millionairess in turn own an expensive car. *Dir.* Anthony Asquith.

Yellowbeard (1983)   Graham Chapman, Peter Cook, Marty Feldman, Eric Idle, John Cleese, Spike Milligan, Beryl Reid, Susannah York. *Dir.* Mel Damski.

Yentl (1983)   Barbra Streisand, Mandy Patinkin, Amy Irving, Nehemiah Persoff. Barbra Streisand also co-wrote with Jack Rosenthal. *Dir.* Barbra Streisand.

You Only Live Twice (1967)   Sean Connery, Tetsuro Tamba, Charles Gray, Donald Pleasence (Blofeld), Bernard Lee, Mie Hama (Kissy Suzuki). Theme song sung by Nancy Sinatra. *Dir.* Lewis Gilbert.

Young Bess (1953)   Jean Simmons, Stewart Granger, Charles Laughton (Henry VIII), Kay Walsh, Deborah Kerr. *Dir.* George Sidney.

Young Frankenstein (1974)   Gene Wilder, Marty Feldman, Madeline Kahn, Gene Hackman. *Dir.* Mel Brooks.

Young Guns (1988)   Emilio Estevez, Kiefer Sutherland, Charlie Sheen, Terence Stamp, Jack Palance, Patrick Wayne. *Dir.* Christopher Cain.

Young Guns II (1990)   Emilio Estevez, Kiefer Sutherland, Lou Diamond Phillips, Christian Slater, James Coburn. *Dir.* Geoff Murphy.

Zardoz (1974)   Sean Connery, Charlotte Rampling, John Alderton. Set in the year 2293. *Dir.* John Boorman.

Ziegfeld Follies (1946)   Fred Astaire, Lucille Ball, Jimmy Durante, Fanny Brice, Lena Horne, Esther Williams, Judy Garland, Red Skelton, Gene Kelly. *Dir.* Vincente Minnelli.

Zorba the Greek (1964)   Anthony Quinn, Alan Bates, Lila Kedrova. *Dir.* Michael Cacoyannis.

Zorro the Gay Blade (1981)   George Hamilton, Lauren Hutton, Brenda Vaccaro, Ron Leibman, James Booth. *Dir.* Peter Medak.

Zulu (1964)   Stanley Baker, Jack Hawkins, Michael Caine, James Booth, Ivor Emmanuel. *Dir.* Cy Endfield.

Zulu Dawn (1979)   Burt Lancaster, Denholm Elliott, Peter O'Toole, John Mills. *Dir.* Douglas Hickox. Famous for being the last listed film in 'Halliwell's' Film Guide'.

NB: It is hoped that this is a fairly representative catalogue of cinematic history but it is inevitable that some films of quality will not be listed.

Films: General Information

Abba hits featured   *Muriel's Wedding.*

Acromegaly: sufferer   Rondo Hatton (d.1946), often billed as 'The Brute Man' or 'The Creeper', suffered from this enlargement of the bones.

Archers: nickname   Film makers Michael Powell and Emeric Pressburger (and name of their film company).

Bafta President   Princess Anne, The Princess Royal.

Barons   Richard Attenborough (Richmond on Thames), Laurence Olivier (Brighton).

Benchley shorts   Popular one-reel shorts delivered by Robert Benchley, sitting behind a desk, pontificating on aspects of modern living.

Bowery Boys   Leo Gorcey, Huntz Hall, Bob Jordan, Gabriel Dell, Bernard Gorcey, David Gorcey, Billy Benedict, Bennie Bartlett.

Carry On Cleo: US video title   Caligula's Funniest Home Videos.

Carry On films   *Carry On Sergeant* (1958), *Carry On Nurse* (1959), *Carry On Teacher,* (1959), *Carry On Constable* (1960), *Carry On Regardless* (1961), *Carry On Cruising* (1962), *Carry On Cabby* (1963), *Carry On Cleo* (1964), *Carry On Spying* (1964), *Carry On Jack* (US Title: Carry On Venus), (1964), *Carry On Cowboy* (1965), *Carry On – Don't Lose Your Head* (1966), *Carry On – Follow that Camel* (1966), *Carry On Screaming* (1966), *Carry On Doctor* (1968), *Carry On Up the Khyber* (1968), *Carry On Again Doctor* (1969), *Carry On Camping* (1969), *Carry On Up the Jungle* (1970), *Carry On Loving* (1970), *Carry On Henry* (1971), *Carry On at Your Convenience* (1971), *Carry On Abroad* (1972), *Carry On Matron* (1972), *Carry On Girls* (1973), *Carry On Dick* (1974), *Carry On Behind* (1975), *Carry On England* (1976), *Carry On Emmanuelle* (1978), *Carry On Columbus* (1992).

Celluloid film: innovator   William Friese-Greene (1888).

Cinéma verité   Film technique that utilises raw, natural sound, hand-held cameras and little rehearsal.

Cinemascope: first film   *The Robe* (1953).

Cinematic projections: early examples   Stroboscope, zoetrope, thaumatrope and praxinoscope.

Cinerama: invented   New York 1952.

Directors: film with 10   *Aria* (1988).

Documentary film: pioneer   John Grierson.

Dolby Stereo: invented   1980.

Film à clef   Film that appears to be a fictional work, but is in fact based on a true story.

Film festival: first   Venice, 1932.

Film: first British feature   *Oliver Twist* (Aug 1912).

Film: first before paying audience   *Young Griffo v Battling Charles Barnett* (New York, May 20th 1895).

Film: first over one hour long   *The Story of the Kelly Gang* (Melbourne, Dec 24th 1906).

Film: most expensive shot in Britain   *The Fifth Element* (1997).

Gulf War story   *Courage under Fire.*

Hitchcock cameos   *The Lodger* (1926) Seen seated at desk in a newsroom, and later he's one of the onlookers watching arrest of Ivor Novello. *Blackmail* (1929) Bothered by a young boy on the Underground as he is trying to read a book. *Murder!* (1930), He is a passer-by on the street. *The Thirty-Nine Steps* (1935) Again, he is a passer-by on the street. *Young and Innocent* (1937) Appears as a clumsy press photographer. *The Lady Vanishes* (1938) Appears in a London railway station. *Rebecca* (1940) Appears standing outside a telephone booth while George Sanders is making a call. *Foreign Correspondent* (1940) Reading newspaper on the street, before Joel

McCrea meets Van Meer (Albert Basserman). *Mr & Mrs Smith* (1941) On the street, unaware of Robert Montgomery. *Saboteur* (1942) At the news-stand. *Shadow of a Doubt* (1943) Holding a full house whilst playing poker on a train. *Lifeboat* (1944) Pictured in a before-and-after weight reduction advertisement in paper read by William Bendix. *Spellbound* (1945) Getting out of a crowded hotel lift. *Notorious* (1946) Drinking champagne at a party. *The Paradine Case* (1948) Carrying a cello case. *Rope* (1948) Crossing the street during the opening credits. *Under Capricorn* (1949) Seen first at Governor's house and then on steps of Government House. *Stage Fright* (1950) Turning round in the street to look at Jane Wyman, who's talking to herself. *Strangers on a Train* (1951) Boarding a train carrying a bass violin. *I Confess* (1953) Crossing the screen at the top of a long staircase. *Dial M for Murder* (1954) In a class reunion photo. *Rear Window* (1954) Winding a clock in the musician's apartment. *To Catch a Thief* (1955) On a bus, next to Cary Grant. *The Trouble with Harry* (1955) At an outdoor exhibition. *The Man who Knew too Much* (1956) Watching Arab acrobats in Marrakesh marketplace. *Vertigo* (1958) Crossing the street. *North by Northwest* (1959) Running to catch a bus, with the door slamming in his face. *Psycho* (1960), Standing outside the real-estate office, wearing a ten gallon hat. *The Birds* (1963) Exiting a pet shop, with 2 Scottie dogs. *Marnie* (1964) Coming out of a hotel room. *Torn Curtain* (1966) In hotel lobby with baby on his lap (his theme tune playing softly). *Topaz* (1969) Wheelchair-bound being attended by a nurse (in an airport). *Frenzy* (1972) Spectator in a crowd scene. *Family Plot* (1976) In silhouette behind the door of the Office of Vital Statistics.

Hollywood studio: first Centaur Film Company (Horsley).

Latin dialogue *Sebastiane* (directed by Derek Jarman).

Marilyn Monroe: film shooting when died *Something's Gotta Give.*

Monarch acted in film Edward VIII (whilst Prince of Wales), *The Power of Right* & *The Warrior Strain* (1919). Prince Charles was the first member of the Royal Family to speak in a fiction film: *Grime Goes Green* (1990).

Movie camera: first patent William Friese-Greene (1888).

Nicolas Cage: famous relation Nephew of Francis Ford Coppola.

Oscar: first British Charles Laughton for *Private Life of Henry VIII* in 1934.

Oscar nominations: most without winning *The Color Purple* and *The Turning Point* each had 11 Oscar nominations but failed to win a single award.

Oscar statuettes Designed by Cedric Gibbons and sculpted by George Stanley.

Oscars: film with most awards *Ben Hur* (1959), and *Titanic* (1997): 11.

Oscars: films with most nominations *All About Eve* (1950), and *Titanic* (1998), each nominated in 14 categories.

Pamela Stephenson: film sued for £3.5m *Hello, She Lied* (renamed *Miami Hustle*); replaced by Kathy Ireland.

Pearl and Dean: music called Asteroid.

Picasso painting in lieu of cash Robin Williams received a $7 million Picasso in lieu of earnings for Aladdin.

Road films: first in colour *Road to Bali* (1952).

Road films: order Singapore, Zanzibar, Morocco, Utopia, Rio, Bali, Hong Kong.

Ronald Reagan films: include *Accidents Will Happen* (1938), *Angels Wash their Faces* (1939), *Bedtime for Bonzo* (1951), *Hellcats of the Navy* (1957), *Cattle Queen of Montana* (1954), *The Killers* (1964).

Smell-O-Vision: first film *The Scent of Mystery* (1959).

Sound film: first *Jazz Singer* (1927).

Tarzan: actors played Johnny Weismuller 1932–48, Lex Barker 1949-1953, Gordon Scott 1955–1960, Jock Mahoney 1962–3, Mike Henry 1966–8. Also Miles O'Keeffe, Buster Crabbe, Frank Merrill, Christopher Lambert.

Third Man: famous quote 'In Italy for 30 years under the Borgias they had warfare, terror, murder and bloodshed, but they produced Michelangelo, Leonardo da Vinci and the Renaissance. In Switzerland, they had brotherly love, they had 500 years of democracy and peace – and what did they produce? The cuckoo clock.'

Triangle Film Corporation Formed in 1915 by DW Griffiths, Thomas Ince and Mack Sennett.

United Artists Formed in 1919 by Mary Pickford, Douglas Fairbanks, Charlie Chaplin and DW Griffiths.

Videodrome: presenters Alex Cox, Mark Cousins.

Western film: first in USA *The Great Train Robbery* (directed by Edwin Porter, 1903).

First Films

Actor	Film
Danny Aiello	*Bang the Drum Slowly* (1973)
Claude Akins	*A Place in the Sun* (1951)
Alan Alda	*Gone Are the Days* (1963)
Woody Allen	*What's New Pussycat* (1965)
Kirstie Alley	*One More Chance* (1981)
June Allyson	*All Girl Revue* (1937)
Mädchen Amick	*The Borrower* (1989)
Dana Andrews	*Lucky Cisco Kid* (1938)
Harry Andrews	*Red Beret, The* (1952)
Julie Andrews	*Mary Poppins* (1964) As extra: *The Reluctant Debutante* (1958) Voice only: *Rose of Baghdad* (1952)
Gabrielle Anwar	*Manifesto* (1988)
Anne Archer	*The All-American Boy* (1970; released 1973)
Eve Arden	*Song of Love* (1929)
Alan Arkin	*Calypso Heat Wave* (1957)
George Arliss	*Devil, The* (1921)
Edward Arnold	*The Heart of Virginia Keep* (1916) Short: *When the Man Speaks* (1916)
Rosanna Arquette	*More American Graffiti* (1979) TV film: *Having Babies II* (1977)
Jean Arthur	*Cameo Kirby* (1923) Short: *Somebody Lied* (1923)

Actor	Film
Armand Assante	*The Lords of Flatbush* (1974)
Fred Astaire	*Dancing Lady* (1933)
	Short: *Municipal Bandwagon* (1932)
Mary Astor	*Hope* (1922)
	Short: *The Beggar Maid* (1921)
Rowan Atkinson	*The Secret Policeman's Ball* (1979)
Richard Attenborough	*In Which We Serve* (1942)
Gene Autry	*In Old Santa Fe* (1934)
Dan Aykroyd	*Love at First Sight* (1976)
	Short and voice only: *The Gift of Winter* (1974)
Lew Ayres	*The Sophomore* (1929)
Charles Aznavour	*Les Disparus de Saint-Agil* (1938) US title: *Boys' School*
Lauren Bacall	*To Have and Have Not* (1944)
Kevin Bacon	*National Lampoon's Animal House* (1978)
Carroll Baker	*Easy to Love* (1953)
Joe Don Baker	*Cool Hand Luke* (1967)
Stanley Baker	*Undercover* (1943)
Alec Baldwin	*Forever Lulu* (1987)
	TV film: *Sweet Revenge* (1984)
William Baldwin	*Born on the Fourth of July* (1989)
Martin Balsam	*On the Waterfront* (1954)
Anne Bancroft	*Don't Bother to Knock* (1952)
Theda Bara	*A Fool There Was* (1914)
Brigitte Bardot	*Le Trou Normand* (1952)
Ellen Barkin	*The Diner* (1982)
Drew Barrymore	*Altered States* (1980)
Ethel Barrymore	*The Nightingale* (1914)
John Barrymore	*An American Citizen* (1913)
Lionel Barrymore	*Men and Women* (1914)
	Short: *Friends* (1969)
Kim Basinger	*Hard Country* (1981)
Alan Bates	*It's Never Too Late* (1956)
Kathy Bates	*Taking Off* (1971)
Anne Baxter	*Twenty Mule Team* (1940)
Warren Beatty	*Splendor in the Grass* (1961)
Bonny Bedelia	*The Gypsy Moths* (1969)
Harry Belafonte	*Bright Road* (1953)
Ralph Bellamy	*The Secret Six* (1931)
William Bendix	*Woman of the Year* (1942)
Tom Berenger	*The Sentinel* (1976)
Candice Bergen	*The Group* (1966)
Ingrid Bergman	*Munkbrogreven* (1934)
Juliette Binoche	*Liberty Belle* (1981)
Jacqueline Bisset	*The Knack* (1964)
Honor Blackman	*Daughter of Darkness* (1947)
Claire Bloom	*The Blind Goddess* (1948)
Dirk Bogarde	*Dancing With Crime* (1947)
	As extra: *Come on George* (1939)
Humphrey Bogart	*A Devil with Women* (1930).
	As extra: *The Dancing Team* (1928)
Ernest Borgnine	*China Corsair* (1951)
Clara Bow	*Beyond the Rainbow* (1921)
Stephen Boyd	*Lilacs in the Spring* (1954) US title: *Let's Make Up*
Charles Boyer	*L'Homme du Large* (1920)
Kenneth Branagh	*High Season* (1986)
Marlon Brando	*The Men* (1950)
Walter Brennan	*Watch Your Wife* (1926)
Beau Bridges	*No Minor Vices* (1948)

Actor	Film
Jeff Bridges	*The Company She Keeps* (1950) (as baby)
Lloyd Bridges	*They Dare Not Love* (1941)
Charles Bronson	*You're in the Navy Now* (1951) Aka: *USS Teakettle* (as Charles Buchinski)
Mel Brooks	*Putney Swope* (1969)
	As narrator: *The Critic* (1963)
Pierce Brosnan	*The Long Good Friday* (1980)
	Short: *Resting Rough* (1979)
Yul Brynner	*Port of New York* (1949)
Sandra Bullock	*A Fool and His Money* (1988)
George Burns	*Lamb Chops* (1929)
Raymond Burr	*San Quentin* (1946)
Richard Burton	*The Last Days of Dolwyn* (1948)
Max Bygraves	*Bless 'em All* (1949)
Gabriel Byrne	*The Outsider* (1979)
	BFI 'Art' film: *On a Paving Stone Mounted* (1978)
James Caan	*Irma La Douce* (1963)
Nicolas Cage	*Fast Times at Ridgemont High* (1982).
	TV film: *The Best of Times* (1981) as Nicolas Coppola (both)
James Cagney	*Sinner's Holiday* (1930)
Michael Caine	*A Hill in Korea* (1956)
Simon Callow	*Amadeus* (1984)
John Candy	*Class of '44* (1973)
Claudia Cardinale	*Goha* (1957)
	Short: *Chaines d'Or* (1956)
Ian Carmichael	*Bond Street* (1948)
Leslie Caron	*An American in Paris* (1951)
David Carradine	*Taggart* (1965)
Keith Carradine	*A Gunfight* (1970)
Jim Carrey	*Introducing Janet* (1982)
	TV film: *Rubberface* (1981)
Richard Chamberlain	*The Secret of the Purple Reef* (1960)
Lon Chaney	*Storm and Sunshine* (1910)
Charlie Chaplin	*Charlie as a Piano Mover* (1910)
Cyd Charisse	*Something to Shout About* (1942).
	Short: *Rhumba Serenade* (1941)
Cher	*Wild on the Beach* (1965)
Maurice Chevalier	*Le Mauvais Garçon* (1921)
	Short: *Trop Crédule* (1908)
Julie Christie	*Crooks Anonymous* (1962)
John Cleese	*Interlude* (1968)
Montgomery Clift	*The Search* (1948)
George Clooney	*Grizzly II – The Predator* (1982)
Glenn Close	*The World According to Garp* (1982)
	TV film: *Orphan Train* (1979)
James Coburn	*Ride Lonesome* (1959)
Claudette Colbert	*For the Love of Mike* (1927)
George Cole	*Cottage to Let* (1941)
Joan Collins	*Lady Godiva Rides Again* (1951)
Ronald Colman	*The Toilers* (1919)
	Short: *The Live Wire* (1917)
Sean Connery	*Lilacs in the Spring* (1954)
Tom Conti	*Flame* (1974)
Jackie Coogan	*Skinner's Baby* (1916)
Gary Cooper	*Blind Justice* (1923)
Harry H Corbett	*Never Look Back* (1952)

CINEMA

Actor	Film	Actor	Film
Kevin Costner	Night Shift (1982) (Sizzle Beach, USA made in late 70s but not shown till 1986)	Kirk Douglas	The Strange Love of Martha Ivers (1946)
Joseph Cotten	Citizen Kane (1941)	Michael Douglas	Hail, Hero (1969)
	Unreleased: Too Much Johnson (1938)		TV film: The Experiment (1968)
Tom Courtenay	Loneliness of the Long Distance Runner (1962)	Richard Dreyfuss	The Graduate (1967)
		Faye Dunaway	The Happening (1967)
Noël Coward	Hearts of the World (1918)	Deanna Durbin	Three Smart Girls (1936)
Broderick Crawford	Woman Chases Man (1937)		Short: Every Sunday (1936)
Joan Crawford	Lady of the Night (1925)	Robert Duvall	To Kill a Mockingbird (1962)
	Short: Miss MGM (1925)		TV film: John Brown's Raid (1960)
Michael Crawford	Soap Box Derby (1957)	Clint Eastwood	Revenge of the Creature (1955).
Bing Crosby	King of Jazz (1930)		Short: A Day in a Hollywood Star Factory (1955)
	Short: Ripstitch the Tailor (1930)		
Tom Cruise	My Bodyguard (1980)	Edith Evans	A Honeymoon for Three (1915)
Billy Crystal	Rabbit Test (1978)	Douglas Fairbanks	The Lamb (1915)
	TV film: Death Flight (1977)	Douglas Fairbanks Jr	Stephen Steps Out (1923)
Macaulay Culkin	Rocket Gibraltar (1988)	Peter Falk	Wind across the Everglades (1958)
Jamie Lee Curtis	Halloween (1978)		
	TV film: Operation Petticoat (1977)	Mia Farrow	John Paul Jones (1959)
Tony Curtis	Criss Cross (1948)	Marty Feldman	The Bed Sitting Room (1969)
John Curtis	Class (1983)	Sally Field	Moon Pilot (1962)
Peter Cushing	The Man in the Iron Mask (1939)	Gracie Fields	Sally in Our Alley (1931)
		WC Fields	Janice Meredith (1924)
Willem Dafoe	Heaven's Gate (1980)		GB title: The Beautiful Rebel (1915)
Jim Dale	6.5 Special (1958)		Short: Pool Sharks (1915)
Timothy Dalton	The Lion in Winter (1968)	Ralph Fiennes	Emily Bronte's Wuthering Heights (1992)
Charles Dance	The Spy Who Loved Me (1977)		A Dangerous Man – Lawrence after Arabia (1991) was a TV film never released in cinemas
Jeff Daniels	Ragtime (1981)		
Ted Danson	The Onion Field (1979)		
Kim Darby	The Restless Ones (1965)	Peter Finch	Dad and Dave Come to Town (1938).
	As extra: Bye Bye Birdie (1963)		Unreleased: Magic Shoes (1935)
Sammy Davis Jnr	The Benny Goodman Story (1956)		
	Short: Rufus Jones for President (1933)	Albert Finney	The Entertainer (1960)
		Errol Flynn	Dr H. Erben's New Guinea Expedition (1932)
Bette Davis	Bad Sister (1931)	Henry Fonda	The Farmer Takes a Wife (1935)
Geena Davis	Tootsie (1982)	Jane Fonda	Tall Story (1960)
Nancy Davis	Shadow on the Wall (1950)	Joan Fontaine	No More Ladies (1935) (as Joan Burfield)
Daniel Day-Lewis	Sunday, Bloody Sunday (1971)		
Doris Day	Romance on the High Seas (1948) GB title: It's Magic	Glenn Ford	Heaven With a Barbed Wire Fence (1939).
	Short: My Lost Horizon (1941)		Short: Night in Manhattan
Yvonne De Carlo	Harvard Here I Come (1941) GB title: Here I Come		(1937)
	Short: I Look at You (1941)	Harrison Ford	Dead Heat on a Merry-Go-Round (1966)
Olivia De Havilland	A Midsummer Night's Dream (1935)	George Formby	By the Shortest of Heads (1915)
		Jodie Foster	Napoleon and Samantha (1972)
Rebecca DeMornay	One From the Heart (1982)	Edward Fox	The Mind Benders (1962)
Robert De Niro	Trois Chambres à Manhattan (1966)	James Fox	The Miniver Story (1950) (as William Fox)
Danny De Vito	Dreams of Glass (1969)	Michael J Fox	Letters From Frank (1979)
James Dean	Sailor Beware (1951)	Tony Franciosa	A Face in the Crowd (1957)
Judi Dench	The Third Secret (1964)	Clark Gable	Forbidden Paradise (1924)
Catherine Deneuve	Les Collégiennes (1956)	Greta Garbo	Fortune Hunter (1921)
Gérard Depardieu	Le Beatnik et le Minet (1965)		Short: How Not to Dress (1921)
Johnny Depp	A Nightmare on Elm Street (1984)	Andy Garcia	Blue Skies Again (1983)
Leonardo DiCaprio	Critters 3 (1991)		TV film: Hill Street Blues (1980) Pilot for series
Marlene Dietrich	So Sind die Männer (1922) Aka: Der Kleine Napoleon	Ava Gardner	HM Pulham Esq (1941)
Matt Dillon	Over the Edge (1979)		Short: Fancy Answers (1941)
Robert Donat	Men of Tomorrow (1932)	Judy Garland	Pigskin Parade (1936)
Amanda Donohoe	Foreign Body (1986)		GB title: Harmony Parade.
	Castaway (1986) released at the same time		Short: The Meglin Kiddie Revue (1929) (billed as a Gumm sister)
Diana Dors	The Shop at Sly Corner (1946)		

Actor	Film	Actor	Film
James Garner	*Toward the Unknown* (1956) GB title: *Brink of Hell*	Wendy Hiller	*Lancashire Luck* (1937)
Greer Garson	*Goodbye Mr Chips* (1939) As extra: *21 Days* (1937) US title: *21 Days Together*	Dustin Hoffman	*The Tiger Makes Out* (1967)
		Paul Hogan	*Fatty Finn* (1980)
		William Holden	*Prison Farm* (1938)
Richard Gere	*Report to the Commissioner* (1974). GB title: *Operation Undercover*	Judy Holliday	*Greenwich Village* (1944) Unreleased: *Too Much Johnson* (1938)
Mel Gibson	*Summer City* (1977)	Stanley Holloway	*The Rotters* (1921)
John Gielgud	*Who is the Man?* (1924)	Ian Holm	*Girls at Sea* (1958)
Lillian Gish	*Judith of Bethulia* (1914) Short: *Oil and Water* (1912)	Bob Hope	*The Big Broadcast of 1938* (1938) Short: *Paree, Paree* (1934)
Whoopi Goldberg	*Citizen (1982)* (released 1983)	Anthony Hopkins	*The Lion in Winter* (1968) Short: *Changes* (1963)
Jeff Goldblum	*Death Wish (1974)*	Dennis Hopper	*Johnny Guitar* (1954)
Elliott Gould	*The Confession (1964)* GB title: *Quick, Let's Get Married!*	Bob Hoskins	*Up the Front* (1972)
		Leslie Howard	*The Happy Warrior* (1917) Short: *The Heroine of Mons* (1914)
Betty Grable	*Happy Days* (1929)		
Stewart Granger	*A Southern Maid* (1933) As stand-in: *I Spy* (1933)	Trevor Howard	*Volga-Volga* (1944) (dubbed voice)
Cary Grant	*This is the Night* (1932)	Frankie Howerd	*The Runaway Bus* (1954)
Hugh Grant	*Privileged* (1982)	Rock Hudson	*Fighter Squadron* (1948)
Richard E Grant	*Withnail and I* (1986) TV film: *Honest, Decent and True* (1985)	Holly Hunter	*The Burning* (1981)
		Jeffrey Hunter	*A Date with Judy* (1948)
		Isabelle Huppert	*Faustine et le Bel Été* (1971) GB title: *Faustine*
Richard Greene	*Four Men and a Prayer* (1938)	John Hurt	*The Wild and the Willing* (1962)
Sydney Greenstreet	*The Maltese Falcon* (1941)	William Hurt	*Altered States* (1980) TV film: *Verna the USO Girl* (1978)
John Gregson	*Saraband for Dead Lovers* (1948)		
Melanie Griffith	*Smith!* (1969)	Anjelica Huston	*Sinful Davey* (1969)
Charles Grodin	*Rosemary's Baby* (1968) TV film: *The Meanest Men in the West* (1962)	John Huston	*The Shakedown* (1928)
		Jeremy Irons	*Nijinsky* (1980)
		Burl Ives	*Smoky* (1946)
Alec Guinness	*Great Expectations* (1946) As extra: *Evensong* (1934)	Glenda Jackson	*The Extra Day* (1956)
Gene Hackman	*Mad Dog Coll* (1961)	Gordon Jackson	*The Foreman Went to France* (1942)
Larry Hagman	*Ensign Pulver* (1964) TV film: *The Member of the Wedding* (1958)	Derek Jacobi	*Othello* (1965)
		Sid James	*Black Memory* (1947)
Susan Hampshire	*The Woman in the Hall* (1947)	Martin Jarvis	*Secrets of a Windmill Girl* (1965)
Tony Hancock	*Orders Are Orders* (1954)	Lionel Jeffries	*Stage Fright* (1950)
Tom Hanks	*He Knows You're Alone* (1980)	Celia Johnson	*Dirty Work* (1934)
Daryl Hannah	*The Fury* (1978)	Don Johnson	*Good Morning ... and Goodbye!* (1967) GB title: *The Lust Seekers* (Russ Meyer epic!)
Oliver Hardy	*Outwitting Dad* (1913)		
Jean Harlow	*Moran of the Marines* (1928)		
Woody Harrelson	*Harper Valley PTA* (1978)		
Ed Harris	*Coma* (1977) TV film: *The Amazing Howard Hughes* (1977)	Al Jolson	*The Jazz Singer* (1927) Short: *April Showers* (1926)
		Tommy Lee Jones	*Love Story* (1970)
Richard Harris	*Alive and Kicking* (1958)	Louis Jourdan	*Le Corsaire* (1939)
Rex Harrison	*The Great Game* (1930)	Boris Karloff	*The Dumb Girl of Portici* (1916)
Laurence Harvey	*House of Darkness* (1948)	Danny Kaye	*Up in Arms* (1944) Short: *Dime a Dance* (1937)
Rutger Hauer	*Repelstweltje* (1973)		
Jack Hawkins	*Birds of Prey* (1930)	Stacy Keach	*The Heart is a Lonely Hunter* (1968)
Goldie Hawn	*The One and Only Genuine Original Family Band* (1968)	Buster Keaton	*The Saphead* (1920) Short: *A Reckless Romeo* (1917)
Will Hay	*Those Were the Days* (1934) Short: *Know Your Apples* (1933)		
		Diane Keaton	*Lovers and Other Strangers* (1970)
Susan Hayward	*Hollywood Hotel* (1937)	Michael Keaton	*Night Shift* (1982)
Rita Hayworth	*Cruz Diablo* (1934) Short: *La Fiesta* (1926) (as Rita Cansino)	Howard Keel	*The Small Voice* (1948) (as Harold Keel)
Van Heflin	*A Woman Rebels* (1936)	Harvey Keitel	*Who's That Knocking at My Door* (1968) Unreleased: *Bring on the Dancing Girls* (1965)
David Hemmings	*Night and the City* (1950)		
Ian Hendry	*Simon and Laura* (1955)		
Audrey Hepburn	*Nederlan in 7 Lessen* (1948)		
Katharine Hepburn	*A Bill of Divorcement* (1932)	Gene Kelly	*For Me and My Gal* (1942) GB title: *For Me and My Girl*
Barbara Hershey	*With Six You Get Egg Roll* (1968)		
Charlton Heston	*Peer Gynt* (1941)		

C
I
N
E
M
A

Actor	Film
Grace Kelly	*Fourteen Hours* (1951)
George Kennedy	*The Little Shepherd of Kingdom Come* (1961)
Patsy Kensit	*For the Love of Ada* (1972)
Deborah Kerr	*Major Barbara* (1941) *Contraband* (1940) first film but scene was cut
Nicole Kidman	*Bush Christmas* (1982)
Val Kilmer	*Top Secret!* (1984)
Ben Kingsley	*Fear is the Key* (1972)
Nastassja Kinski	*Falsche Bewegung* (1975) GB title: *Wrong Movement*
Eartha Kitt	*Casbah* (1948)
Kevin Kline	*Sophie's Choice* (1982)
Kris Kristofferson	*The Last Movie* (1971)
Alan Ladd	*Once in a Lifetime* (1932)
Veronica Lake	*All Women Have Secrets* (1939) (as Constance Keane)
Hedy Lamarr	*Geld auf der Strasse* (1930) (as Hedy Kiesler)
Christopher Lambert	*Le Bar du Téléphone* (1981)
Dorothy Lamour	*The Jungle Princess* (1936) Short: *The Stars Can't Be Wrong* (1936)
Burt Lancaster	*The Killers* (1946)
Michael Landon	*I Was A Teenage Werewolf* (1957)
Jessica Lange	*King Kong* (1976) Short: *Home is Where the Heart Is* (1970)
Angela Lansbury	*Gaslight* (1944). GB title: *The Murder in Thornton Square*
Mario Lanza	*Winged Victory* (1944)
Charles Laughton	*Piccadilly* (1929) Short: *Bluebottles* (1928)
Stan Laurel	*Lucky Dog* (1917)
Peter Lawford	*Poor Old Bill* (1930)
Bruce Lee	*Golden Gate Girl / Tears of S. Francisco* (1941, aged 3 months) *The Birth of Mankind* (1946, first professional role)
Christopher Lee	*Corridor of Mirrors* (1948)
Gypsy Rose Lee	*You Can't Have Everything* (1937) (as Louise Hovick)
Janet Leigh	*The Romance of Rosy Ridge* (1947)
Jennifer Jason Leigh	*Eyes of a Stranger* (1981)
Vivien Leigh	*Things are Looking Up* (1934)
Jack Lemmon	*It Should Happen to You* (1953)
Jerry Lewis	*My Friend Irma* (1949)
Juliette Lewis	*Any Which Way You Can* (1980)
Emily Lloyd	*Wish You Were Here* (1987)
Harold Lloyd	*Samson and Delilah* (1913)
Margaret Lockwood	*Lorna Doone* (1934)
Gina Lollobrigida	*L'Aguila Nera* (1946)
Herbert Lom	*Zena Pod Krizem* (1937)
Carole Lombard	*A Perfect Crime* (1921) (as Jane Peters)
Sophia Loren	*Cuori Sul Mare* (1950) (as Sofia Scicolone)
Peter Lorre	*Bomben auf Monte Carlo* (1931)
Rob Lowe	*The Outsiders* (1983) TV film: *Thursday's Child* (1982)
Myrna Loy	*Pretty Ladies* (1925)
Bela Lugosi	*Alarscobal* (1917)
Dolph Lundgren	*For Your Eyes Only* (1981)
Ida Lupino	*The Love Race* (1932)
David McCallum	*Ill Met By Moonlight* (1956)
Jeanette MacDonald	*The Love Parade* (1929)

Actor	Film
Roddy McDowall	*Grime Doesn't Pay* (1935)
Andie MacDowell	*Greystoke: The Legend of Tarzan Lord of Apes* ('84)
Malcolm McDowell	*If* (1968). *Poor Cow* (1967) first film but scene was cut
Kelly McGillis	*Reuben, Reuben* (1983)
Patrick McGoohan	*The Dam Busters* (1954)
Ali MacGraw	*A Lovely Way to Die* (1968) GB title: *A Lovely Way to Go*
Virginia McKenna	*Father's Doing Fine* (1952)
Kyle MacLachlan	*Dune* (1984)
Victor McLaglen	*The Call of the Road* (1920)
Shirley MacLaine	*The Trouble with Harry* (1955)
Fred MacMurray	*Girls Gone Wild* (1929)
Patrick MacNee	*Sailors Three* (1940)
Steve McQueen	*Somebody up There Likes Me* (1956)
Ian McShane	*The Wild and the Willing* (1962)
Madonna	*A Certain Sacrifice* (1978)
Anna Magnani	*Scampolo* (1927)
Lee Majors	*Strait-Jacket* (1964) (as Lee Yeary)
Karl Malden	*They Knew What They Wanted* (1940)
John Malkovich	*Places in the Heat* (1984) TV film: *Word of Honor* (1981)
Jayne Mansfield	*Prehistoric Women* (1950)
Fredric March	*The Devil* (1920)
Dean Martin	*My Friend Irma* (1949)
Steve Martin	*Sgt Pepper's Lonely Heart's Club Band* (1978) Short: *The Absent-Minded Waiter* (1977)
Lee Marvin	*Teresa* (1950)
Marx Brothers	*The Cocoanuts* (1929) Limited release: *Humorist* (1926)
Harpo Marx	*Too Many Kisses* (1925)
James Mason	*Late Extra* (1935) (The name of his fan club's news letter)
Raymond Massey	*The Crooked Billet* (1929) Aka: *International Spy*
Marcello Mastroianni	*I Miserabili* (1947) As extra: *Marionette* (1938)
Walter Matthau	*The Kentuckian* (1955)
Jessie Matthews	*The Beloved Vagabond* (1923)
Victor Mature	*The Housekeeper's Daughter* (1939)
Virginia Mayo	*Stand by for Action* (1942) GB title: *Cargo of Innocents*
Melina Mercouri	*Stella* (1954)
Ethel Merman	*Follow the Leader* (1930)
Bette Midler	*Hawaii* (1966)
Toshiro Mifune	*Shin Baka Jidai* (1946)
Sarah Miles	*Term of Trial* (1962)
Ray Milland	*The Plaything* (1929) (as Spike Milland)
Max Miller	*The Good Companions* (1933)
Spike Milligan	*Penny Points to Paradise* (1951)
Hayley Mills	*Tiger Bay* (1959)
John Mills	*The Midshipmaid* (1932) Limited release: *Words and Music* (1932)
Juliet Mills	*In Which We Serve* (1942) (as baby)
Liza Minnelli	*Easter Parade* (1948) (as baby)
Carmen Miranda	*A Voz do Carnaval* (1933)
Helen Mirren	*Herostratus* (1967)
Robert Mitchum	*Hoppy Serves a Writ* (1943)

Actor	Film	Actor	Film
Tom Mix	The Heart of Texas Ryan (1917). Short: On the Little Big Horn (1909)	Leslie Phillips	A Lassie from Lancashire (1935)
		River Phoenix	Explorers (1985) TV film: Surviving (1985)
Marilyn Monroe	The Shocking Miss Pilgrim (1946)	Mary Pickford	Through the Breakers (1909)
Yves Montand	Etoile sans Lumière (1945)	Walter Pidgeon	Mannequin (1925)
Demi Moore	Choices (1981)	Brad Pitt	Cutting Class (1989) TV film: A Stoning in Fulham County (1988)
Dudley Moore	The Wrong Box (1966) As narrator: The Hat (1964)	Donald Pleasence	The Beachcomber (1954)
Roger Moore	Caesar and Cleopatra (1945)	Christopher Plummer	Wind Across the Everglades (1958)
Jeanne Moreau	Dernier Amour (1948)	Sidney Poitier	From Whence Cometh My Help (1949)
Kenneth More	Look up and Laugh (1935)		
Robert Morley	Marie Antoinette (1938)	Eric Portman	The Girl from Maxim's (1933)
Zero Mostel	DuBarry Was a Lady (1943)	Dick Powell	Street Scene (1931)
Paul Muni	The Valiant (1929)	Robert Powell	Robbery (1967)
Eddie Murphy	48 Hrs (1982)	William Powell	When Knighthood Was In Flower (1922)
Audie Murphy	Beyond Glory (1948)		
Bill Murray	Meatballs (1979) Short: The Hat Act (1976) Voice only: Jungle Burger (1975)	Tyrone Power	Tom Brown of Culver (1932)
		Stefanie Powers	Tammy Tell Me True (1961)
		Elvis Presley	Love Me Tender (1956)
Anna Neagle	Those Who Love (1929) (as Marjorie Robertson)	Robert Preston	King of Alcatraz (1938)
		Dennis Price	A Canterbury Tale (1944) As extra: No Parking (1938)
Liam Neeson	Excalibur (1981)		
Sam Neill	Ashes (1975)	Vincent Price	Service de Luxe (1938)
Anthony Newley	The Little Ballerina (1947) Short: Dusty Bates (1947)	Richard Pryor	The Busy Body (1966)
		Bill Pullman	Ruthless People (1986)
Paul Newman	The Silver Chalice (1954)	Dennis Quaid	Crazy Mama (1975)
Jack Nicholson	The Cry Baby Killer (1958)	Anthony Quayle	Moscow Nights (1935)
Leslie Nielsen	The Vagabond King (1956)	Aidan Quinn	Reckless (1984)
David Niven	There Goes the Bride (1932)	Anthony Quinn	The Milky Way (1936)
Nick Nolte	The Feather Farm (1965)	George Raft	Queen of the Night Clubs (1929)
Chuck Norris	The Wrecking Crew (1968)		
Kim Novak	The Veils of Baghdad (1953)	Luise Rainer	Ja, der Himmel über Wien (1930)
Ivor Novello	Call of the Blood (1919)		
Warren Oates	Up Periscope! (1958)	Claude Rains	Build Thy House (1920)
Merle Oberon	The Three Passions (1929)	Charlotte Rampling	The Knack and How to Get it (1965)
Edmond O'Brien	Prison Break (1938)		
Pat O'Brien	Compliments of the Season (1930)	Basil Rathbone	Innocent (1921)
		Ronald Reagan	Love is on the Air (1937) GB title: The Radio Murder Mystery
Donald O'Connor	Melody for Two (1937)		
Maureen O'Hara	Kicking the Moon Around (1938) as Maureen Fitzsimmons	Robert Redford	War Hunt (1962). TV film: In the Presence of Mine Enemies (1960). (Charles Laughton played a rabbi in this film!)
Gary Oldman	Remembrance (1982)		
Laurence Olivier	Too Many Crooks (1930)		
Ryan O'Neal	The Big Bounce (1969) TV film: This Rugged Land (1962)		
		Lynn Redgrave	Tom Jones (1963)
		Michael Redgrave	Secret Agent (1936)
Tatum O'Neal	Paper Moon (1973)	Vanessa Redgrave	Behind the Mask (1958)
Maureen O'Sullivan	Song o' My Heart (1930)	Oliver Reed	Value for Money (1955)
Richard O'Sullivan	Dance Little Lady (1954)	Christopher Reeve	Gray Lady Down (1977)
Peter O'Toole	The Savage Innocents (1959)	Keanu Reeves	The Prodigal (1984). Video only: Act of Vengeance (1984)
Al Pacino	Me Natalie (1969)		
Jack Palance	Panic in the Streets (1950) (as Walter Palance)	Lee Remick	A Face in the Crowd (1957)
		Burt Reynolds	Angel Baby (1961)
Lilli Palmer	Crime Unlimited (1935)	Debbie Reynolds	June Bride (1948)
Dolly Parton	The Nashville Sound (1970)	Cliff Richard	Serious Charge (1959)
Gregory Peck,	Days of Glory (1944)	Joely Richardson	The Charge of the Light Brigade (1968)
Sean Penn	Taps (1981) TV film: The Killing of Randy Webster (1980)		
		Miranda Richardson	Dance with a Stranger (1984)
George Peppard	The Strange One (1957) GB title: End as a Man	Natasha Richardson	The Charge of the Light Brigade (1968)
Anthony Perkins	The Actress (1953)	Ralph Richardson	The Ghoul (1933)
Joe Pesci	Hey, Let's Twist (1961) (as Joe Ritchie)	Brian Rix	Reluctant Heroes (1951)
		Jason Robards Jnr	The Journey (1958)
Michelle Pfeiffer	Falling in Love Again (1979)	Tim Robbins	No Small Affair (1984)

C
I
N
E
M
A

Actor	Film	Actor	Film
Julia Roberts	Blood Red (1988 but released 1990).		Judd for the Defense: The Holy Ground (1969) was a made-for-TV film series
	Baja Oklahoma (shown in selected cinemas) 1988	Peter Sellers	Penny Points to Paradise (1951)
Rachel Roberts	Valley of Song (1953)		As extra: Oliver Twist (1948)
Cliff Robertson	Corvette K-225 (1943)		Voice only: The Black Rose
	GB title: The Nelson Touch		(1950)
Dale Robertson	The Boy with Green Hair (1948)	Jane Seymour	Oh What a Lovely War (1969)
Paul Robeson	Body and Soul (1924)	Omar Sharif	The Blazing Sun (1954) (as Omar el Cherif)
Edward G Robinson	Arms and the Woman (1916)		
Flora Robson	Gentleman of Paris (1931)	William Shatner	The Brothers Karamazov (1958)
Ginger Rogers	Queen High (1930)		
	Short: Campus Sweethearts (1929)		TV film: The Defenders (1957)
Roy Rogers	Way Up Thar (1935) (as Dick Weston)	Robert Shaw	The Lavender Hill Mob (1951)
		Norma Shearer	Way Down East (1920)
	Short: Slightly Static (1935) (as Leonard Slye)	Charlie Sheen	Grizzly II: The Predator (1982)
Will Rogers	Laughing Bill Hyde (1918)		TV film: The Execution of Private Slovik (1974)
Gilbert Roland	The Lady Who Lied (1925)	Martin Sheen	The Incident (1967)
Cesar Romero	The Shadow Laughs (1933)	Sam Shepard	Renaldo and Clara (1977)
Mickey Rooney	Orchids and Ermine (1927)		Voice only: Easy Rider (1969)
	Short: Not to Be Trusted (1926)	Cybill Shepherd	The Last Picture Show (1971)
Katharine Ross	Shenandoah (1965)	Ann Sheridan	Search for Beauty (1934) (as Clara Lou Sheridan)
Isabella Rossellini	A Matter of Time (1976)		
Leonard Rossiter	The Two-Headed Spy (1958)	Dinah Sheridan	I Give My Heart (1934)
Tim Roth	Meantime (1983)	Brooke Shields	Communion / Alice Sweet Alice (1977)
	TV film: Made in Britain (1983)		
Richard Roundtree	What Do You Say to a Naked Lady (1969)	Dinah Shore	Thank Your Lucky Stars (1943)
		Simone Signoret	Le Prince Charmant (1942)
Mickey Rourke	1941 (1979).	Phil Silvers	Hit Parade of 1941 (1940)
	TV film: Panic on Page One (1979)		Short: Here's Your Hat (1937)
		Alicia Silverstone	The Crush (1993)
	Aka City in Fear		TV film: Scattered Dreams (1992)
Gena Rowlands	The High Cost of Loving (1958)		
Jane Russell	The Outlaw (1943)	Alastair Sim	Riverside Murder (1935)
Kurt Russell	The Absent-Minded Professor (1961)	Jean Simmons	Give Us the Moon (1944)
		Frank Sinatra	Las Vegas Nights (1941) GB title: The Gray City
Rosalind Russell	Forsaking All Others (1934)		
Theresa Russell	The Last Tycoon (1976)		Short: Major Bowes' Amateur Theatre of the Air (1935)
Rene Russo	Major League (1989)		
Margaret Rutherford	Talk of the Devil (1936)		
Meg Ryan	Rich and Famous (1981)	Donald Sinden	Portrait from Life (1948)
Robert Ryan	The Ghost Breakers (1940)	Christian Slater	The Legend of Billie Jean (1985).
Winona Ryder	Lucas (1986)		
George Sanders	Love, Life and Laughter (1934)		TV film. Living Proof: The Hank Williams Jr Story (1983)
Susan Sarandon	Joe (1970)		
Telly Savalas	The Young Savages (1961)	Maggie Smith	Child in the House (1956)
John Saxon	It Should Happen to You (1953)	Jimmy Smits	Running Scared (1986)
Greta Scacchi	Das Zweite Gesicht (1982)		TV film: Rockabye (1986)
	Short: Dead on Time (1981)	Wesley Snipes	Wildcats (1986)
Roy Scheider	The Curse of the Living Corpse (1963) as Roy R Scheider	Elke Sommer	Das Totenschiff (1958)
		Ann Sothern	Broadway Nights (1927)
		Sissy Spacek	Prime Cut (1972)
			As extra: Trash (1970)
Maximilian Schell	Die Letzte Brucke (1954)	James Spader	Team-Mates (1978)
Romy Schneider	Wenn der Weisse Flieder Wieder Blüht (1953)	Robert Stack	First Love (1939)
		Sylvester Stallone	Party at Kitty and Studs (1970)
Arnie Schwarzenegger	Hercules Goes Bananas (1969) (as Arnold Strong)		Re-released as: The Italian Stallion
Paul Scofield	That Lady (1955)	Terence Stamp	Billy Budd (1962)
Kristin Scott-Thomas	Under the Cherry Moon (1986)	Barbara Stanwyck	Broadway Nights (1927)
Randolph Scott	Sharp Shooters (1928)	Anthony Steel	Quartet (1948)
George C Scott	The Hanging Tree (1959)	Tommy Steele	Kill Me Tomorrow (1957)
Steven Seagal	Above the Law (1988) GB title: Nico	Mary Steenburgen	Goin' South (1978)
		Rod Steiger	Teresa (1951)
Jean Seberg	Saint Joan (1957)	Inger Stevens	Man on Fire (1957)
Harry Secombe	Hocus Pocus (1948)	Stella Stevens	Say One for Me (1959)
George Segal	The Young Doctors (1961)	James Stewart	The Murder Man (1935)
Tom Selleck	Myra Breckinridge (1970)		Short: Important News (1935)

Actor	Film
Sting	*Quadrophenia* (1979)
Eric Stoltz	*Fast Times at Ridgemont High* (1982). TV film: *The Grass is Always Greener over the Septic Tank* (1978)
Sharon Stone	*Stardust Memories* (1980)
The 3 Stooges	*Hollywood on Parade* (1930)
Meryl Streep	*Julia* (1977) Voice only: *Everybody Rides a Carousel* (1976)
Barbra Streisand	*Funny Girl* (1968)
Donald Sutherland	*The World Ten Times Over* (1963)
Kiefer Sutherland	*Max Dugan Returns* (1983)
Gloria Swanson	*Her Decision* (1918) Short: *The Romance of an American Duchess* (1915)
Patrick Swayze	*Skatetown USA* (1979)
Eric Sykes	*Orders Are Orders* (1954)
Sylvia Syms	*My Teenage Daughter* (1955)
Russ Tamblyn	*Boy with Green Hair* (1948) (as Rusty Tamblyn)
Jacques Tati	*Retour à la Terre* (1938) Short: *Oscar, Champion de Tennis* (1932)
Elizabeth Taylor	*One Born Every Minute* (1942) Short: *Man or Mouse* (1942)
Robert Taylor	*Handy Andy* (1934)
Rod Taylor	*The Sturt Expedition* (1951) (as Rodney Taylor)
Shirley Temple	*The Red-Haired Alibi* (1932) Short: *War Babies* (1932)
Terry Thomas	*It's Love Again* (1936)
Emma Thompson	*The Tall Guy* (1989)
Sybil Thorndike	*Moth and Rust* (1921)
Uma Thurman	*Kiss Daddy Good Night* (1987)
Gene Tierney	*The Return of Frank James* (1940)
Richard Todd	*For Them That Trespass* (1948)
Lily Tomlin	*Nashville* (1975)
David Tomlinson	*Garrison Follies* (1940) Short: *Name, Rank and Number* (1940)
Spencer Tracy	*Up the River* (1930) Short: *Taxi Talks* (1930)
Bill Travers	*Conspirator* (1950)
John Travolta	*The Devil's Rain* (1975)
Claire Trevor	*Life in the Raw* (1933)
Tommy Trinder	*Almost a Honeymoon* (1938)
Jean-Louis Trintignant	*Si Tous les Gars du Monde* (1955) GB title: *Race for Life* Short: *Pechinef* (1955)
Forrest Tucker	*The Westerner* (1940)
Kathleen Turner	*Body Heat* (1981)
Lana Turner	*A Star is Born* (1937)
Rita Tushingham	*A Taste of Honey* (1961)
Twiggy	*The Boy Friend* (1971)
Liv Ullman	*Fjol til Fjells* (1957)
Peter Ustinov	*Hullo Fame!* (1940)
Rudolph Valentino	*My Official Wife* (1914)
Rudy Vallee	*Vagabond Lover* (1929) Short: *Radio Rhythm* (1929)
Lee Van Cleef	*The Showdown* (1950)
Jean-Claude Van Damme	*Rue Barbar* (1983) US Title: *Street of the Damned*
Dick Van Dyke	*Bye Bye Birdie* (1963)
Frankie Vaughan	*Ramsbottom Rides Again* (1957)

Actor	Film
	Singing commentary: *Escape in the Sun* (1956)
Robert Vaughn	*The Ten Commandments* (1956)
Conrad Veidt	*Der Spion* (1916)
Monica Vitti	*Ridere, Ridere, Ridere* (1955)
Jon Voight	*The Hour of the Gun* (1967)
Erich Von Stroheim	*Captain McLean* (1914)
Max Von Sydow	*Bara en Mor* (1949)
Robert Wagner	*The Happy Years* (1950)
Christopher Walken	*Me and My Brother* (1968)
Clint Walker	*Mighty Joe Young* (1949) (as Norman Walker)
Eli Wallach	*Baby Doll* (1956) TV film: *Danger* (1952)
Julie Walters	*Educating Rita* (1983) Short: *Occupy!* (1976)
Rachel Ward	*Night School* (1980) GB Title: *Terror Eyes*
Simon Ward	*If* (1968)
David Warner	*Loneliness of the Long Distance Runner* (1962)
Jack Warner	*The Dummy Talks* (1943)
Denzel Washington	*Carbon Copy* (1981) TV film: *Wilma* (1977)
Dennis Waterman	*Night Train for Inverness* (1959)
John Wayne	*Brown of Harvard* (1926)
Dennis Weaver	*Riders of Vengeance* (1952)
Sigourney Weaver	*Annie Hall* (1977)
Clifton Webb	*Polly with a Past* (1920)
Johnny Weissmuller	*Glorifying the American Girl* (1929)
Raquel Welch	*Roustabout* (1964)
Tuesday Weld	*The Wrong Man* (1956)
Orson Welles	*Citizen Kane* (1941) Short: *The Hearts of Age* (1934) (Home-made) Unreleased: *Too Much Johnson* (1938). As narrator: *Swiss Family Robinson* (1940)
Mae West	*Night after Night* (1932) Short: *unidentified 'Screen Snapshot'* (1930)
Joanne Whalley-Kilmer	*The Wall* (1982)
Billie Whitelaw	*The Fake* (1953)
Pearl White	*The Life of Buffalo Bill* (1910)
Richard Widmark	*Kiss of Death* (1947)
Gene Wilder	*Bonnie and Clyde* (1967)
Cornel Wilde	*The Lady With Red Hair* (1940)
Michael Wilding	*Heads We Go* (1933) As extra: *Bitter Sweet* (1933)
Nicol Williamson	*Inadmissible Evidence* (1968) Short: *The Six-Sided Triangle* (1963)
Emlyn Williams	*The Frightened Lady* (1932)
Esther Williams	*Andy Hardy's Double Life* (1942)
Kenneth Williams	*Trent's Last Case* (1952)
Robin Williams	*Can I Do it 'til I Need Glasses* (1977)
Bruce Willis	*The First Deadly Sin* (1980) TV film: *Ziegfeld – The Man & His Women* (1978)
Barbara Windsor	*Belles of St Trinian's* (1954)
Oprah Winfrey	*The Color Purple* (1985)
Debra Winger	*Slumber Party '57* (1976)
Kate Winslet	*Heavenly Creatures* (1994)

CINEMA

Actor	Film	Actor	Film
Shelley Winters	*What a Woman!* (1943) GB Title: The Beautiful Title		Sarah Jane Fulks)
		Michael York	*The Mind Benders* (1962)
Norman Wisdom	*A Date with a Dream* (1948)	Susannah York	*Tunes of Glory* (1960)
Googie Withers	*The Girl in the Crowd* (1934)	Gig Young	*Misbehaving Husbands* (1940)
Sir Donald Wolfit	*Down River* (1931)		(as Byron Barr)
Natalie Wood	*Happy Land* (1943) (as Natasha Gurdin)	Loretta Young	*The Only Way* (1917) (as Gretchen Young)
James Woods	*The Visitors* (1971)	Robert Young	*The Black Camel* (1931)
Edward Woodward	*Where There's a Will* (1955)	Sean Young	*Stripes* (1981).
Joanne Woodward	*Count Three and Pray* (1955)		TV film: *Jane Austen in*
Fay Wray	*What Price Goofy* (1925)		*Manhattan* (1980)
	Short: *Gasoline Love* (1923)	Pia Zadora	*Santa Claus Conquers the*
Teresa Wright	*The Little Foxes* (1941)		*Martians* (1964)
Jane Wyman	*The Kid from Spain* (1932) (as	Mai Zetterling	*Lasse-Maja* (1941)

NB: This is an area where many fine sources of information will inevitably differ, depending on the definition given of 'first film'. To give an example of the inherent dangers in answering questions on screen debuts, we can look at the early career of Orson Welles.

The 1941 classic, *Citizen Kane*, is often considered to be Welles's first film performance; but whilst it was certainly his first feature film, he did in fact do various film work before this. His potential was first spotted in his home-made film of 1934, *The Hearts of Age*, a film short that never went on general release. The unreleased film *Too Much Johnson* (1938) was shown to private audiences, although it was eventually lost to the world in a fire at Welles's Spanish home.

If narration is considered a film role, then the 1940 film *Swiss Family Robinson*, starring Thomas Mitchell and Freddie Bartholomew, could also be regarded as his big screen debut.

The approach taken in listing these is to cite an actor's debut in a film on general release and to mention prior work underneath. Many jobbing screen actors start their careers making 'film shorts', often shown before a main feature, but these films are rarely listed in cinema catalogues and are only included here if they predate a debut in a full-length feature. 'Made for television' films are treated in a similar vein.

Last Films

Actor	Film	Actor	Film
Fred Astaire	*Ghost Story* (1981)	Jackie Coogan	*The Prey* (1983)
Mary Astor	*Hush, Hush, Sweet Charlotte* (1964)	Gary Cooper	*The Naked Edge* (1961)
		Harry H Corbett	*Silver Dream Racer* (1980)
Gene Autry	*It's Showtime* (1976)	Joseph Cotten	*Rambo Sfida la Citta* (1982)
Lew Ayres	*Letters from Frank* (1979)	Noël Coward	*The Italian Job* (1969)
	TV film: *Cast the First Stone* (1989)	Broderick Crawford	*Liar's Moon* (1981)
		Joan Crawford	*Trog* (1970)
Ingrid Bergman	*Autumn Sonata* (1978)		TV film: *We're Going to Scare You to Death* (1975)
	TV film: *A Woman Called Golda* (1982)	Bing Crosby	*That's Entertainment* (1974)
Humphrey Bogart	*The Harder They Fall* (1956)	Peter Cushing	*Biggles* (1986)
Stephen Boyd	*The Squeeze* (1977)	Bette Davis	*Wicked Stepmother* (1989)
Charles Boyer	*A Matter of Time* (1976)		Short: *Hairway to the Stars* (1989)
Yul Brynner	*Futureworld* (1976)		
George Burns	*Radioland Murders* (1994)	Sammy Davis Jnr	*Tap* (1988)
Raymond Burr	*Delirious* (1991)		TV film: *The Kid Who Loved Christmas* (1990)
	TV film: *Perry Mason: The Case of the Killer Kiss* (1993)	James Dean	*Giant* (1956)
Richard Burton	*1984* (1984)	Marlene Dietrich	*Marlene* (1984)
	TV film: *Ellis Island* (1984)	Robert Donat	*The Inn of the Sixth Happiness* (1958)
James Cagney	*Ragtime* (1981)	Diana Dors	*Steaming* (1985)
	TV film: *Terrible Joe Moran* (1984)	Edith Evans	*Nasty Habits* (1976)
John Candy	*Canadian Bacon* (1995)	Douglas Fairbanks	*The Private Life of Don Juan* (1934)
Lon Chaney	*The Unholy Three* (1930)		
Charlie Chaplin	*A Countess from Hong Kong* (1966)	Marty Feldman	*Yellowbeard* (1983)
		Gracie Fields	*Madame Pimpernel* (1945)
Maurice Chevalier	*Monkeys Go Home* (1967)	WC Fields	*Sensations of 1945* (1944)
	Voice only: *The Aristocats* (1970)	Peter Finch	*Network* (1976)
			TV film: *Raid on Entebbe* (1977)
Montgomery Clift	*The Defector* (1966)		
Claudette Colbert	*Parrish* (1961)	Errol Flynn	*Cuban Rebel Girls* (1959)
	TV film: *The Two Mrs Grenvilles* (1987)	Henry Fonda	*On Golden Pond* (1981)
			TV film: *Summer Solstice* (1981)
Ronald Colman	*The Story of Mankind* (1957)		

Actor	Film
George Formby	*George in Civvy Street* (1946)
Clark Gable	*The Misfits* (1961)
Greta Garbo	*Two-Faced Woman* (1941)
Ava Gardner	*Roma Regina* (1982)
Judy Garland	*I Could Go on Singing* (1963)
Greer Garson	*Directed by William Wyler* (1986)
Lillian Gish	*The Whales of August* (1987)
Betty Grable	*How to Be Very Very Popular* (1955)
Stewart Granger	*Oro Fina (Fine Gold)* (1988)
	TV film: *Chameleons* (1989)
Cary Grant	*Elvis – That's the Way It Is* (1970)
Sydney Greenstreet	*Malaya* (1949).
	GB title: *East of the Rising Sun*
John Gregson	*The Tiger Lily* (1975)
Tony Hancock	*The Wrong Box* (1966)
Oliver Hardy	*Meet Bela Lugosi and Oliver Hardy* (1952)
Jean Harlow	*Saratoga* (1937)
Rex Harrison	*A Time to Die* (1983). Aka *Seven Graves for Rogan*
Jack Hawkins	*The Last Lion* (1973)
	TV film: *QB VII* (1974)
Susan Hayward	*The Revengers* (1972)
	TV film: *Say Goodbye, Maggie Cole* (1972)
Rita Hayworth	*Circle* (1976)
Will Hay	*My Learned Friend* (1943)
Van Heflin	*The Big Bounce* (1969)
	TV film: *The Last Child* (1971)
Audrey Hepburn	*Always* (1989)
William Holden	*S.O.B.* (1981)
	TV film: *Mysteries of the Sea* (1981) (as narrator)
Judy Holliday	*Bells Are Ringing* (1960)
Stanley Holloway	*Journey into Fear* (1976)
Leslie Howard	*The First of the Few* (1942)
Trevor Howard	*The Dawning* (1988) Died whilst filming *Stille Nacht*, about the author of the carol 'Silent Night'
Frankie Howerd	*Sgt Pepper's Lonely Heart's Club Band* (1978)
Rock Hudson	*The Ambassador* (1984)
	TV film: *The Vegas Strip Wars* (1985)
Jeffrey Hunter	*Mafia Mob* (1969)
John Huston	*John Huston and the Dubliners* (1987)
Burl Ives	*Two Moon Junction* (1988)
Gordon Jackson	*The Whistle Blower* (1986)
	TV film: *The Lady and the Highwayman* (1989)
Sid James	*Carry On Dick* (1974)
Celia Johnson	*The Prime of Miss Jean Brodie* (1968)
	TV film: *The Hostage Tower* (1980)
Al Jolson	*Rhapsody in Blue* (1945) Voice only: *Jolson Sings Again* (1949)
Boris Karloff	*The Incredible Invasion* (1969). Limited release: *House of Evil* (1972) Unseen footage: *Transylvania Twist* (1989)
Danny Kaye	*The Madwoman of Chaillot*

Actor	Film
	(1969)
	Short: *Pied Piper* (1972)
	TV film: *Once They Marched through a Thousand Towns* (1981) US title: *Skokie*
Buster Keaton	*A Funny Thing Happened on the Way to Forum* (1966)
	Short: *The Scribe* (1966)
Gene Kelly	*That's Entertainment III* (1994)
Grace Kelly	*Invitation to Monte Carlo* (1959) As narrator: *The Children of Theatre Street* (1978)
Alan Ladd	*The Carpetbaggers* (1964)
Veronica Lake	*Flesh Feast* (1970)
Dorothy Lamour	*Creepshow 2* (1987)
Burt Lancaster	*Field of Dreams* (1989) TV film: *Separate but Equal* (1991)
Mario Lanza	*For the First Time* (1959)
Charles Laughton	*Advise and Consent* (1962)
Stan Laurel	*Atoll K* (1951). GB title: *Robinson Crusoeland*
Peter Lawford	*Where is Parsifal?* (1984)
Bruce Lee	*Game of Death* (1978; posthumously)
Gypsy Rose Lee	*The Trouble with Angels* (1966). TV film: *The Over the Hill Gang* (1969)
Vivien Leigh	*Ship of Fools* (1965)
Harold Lloyd	*The Sins of Harold Diddlebock* (1947) GB Title: *Mad Wednesday*
Margaret Lockwood	*The Slipper and the Rose* (1976)
Carole Lombard	*To Be or Not to Be* (1942)
Peter Lorre	*Muscle Beach Party* (1964)
Myrna Loy	*Just Tell Me What You Want* (1980). TV film: *Summer Solstice* (1981)
Bela Lugosi	*Plan 9 from Outer Space* (1957)
Ida Lupino,	*Deadhead Miles* (1982)
Jeanette MacDonald	*The Sun Comes Up* (1948) TV film: *Charley's Aunt* (1957)
Victor McLaglen	*The Italians Are Crazy* (1958)
Fred MacMurray	*The Swarm* (1978)
Anna Magnani	*Fellini's Roma* (1972)
Jayne Mansfield	*Mondo Hollywood* (1967)
Fredric March	*The Iceman Cometh* (1973)
Dean Martin	*Cannonball Run II* (1983) TV film: *Half Nelson* (1985)
Lee Marvin	*The Delta Force* (1986)
Marx Brothers	*Love Happy* (1950) Guest appearances in separate episodes of *The Story of Mankind* (1957) TV film: *The Incredible Jewel Robbery* (1960) Later films did not include all 3 main brothers
James Mason	*The Assisi Underground* (1984)
Raymond Massey	*MacKenna's Gold* (1969) TV film: *The President's Plane is Missing* (1973)
Marcello Mastroianni	*Journey to the Beginning of the World* (1996)
Jessie Matthews	*Never Never Land* (1980)
Victor Mature	*Firepower* (1979) TV film: *Samson and Delilah* (1984)

C
I
N
E
M
A

Actor	Film
Steve McQueen	*The Hunter* (1980)
Melina Mercouri	*Keine Zufallige Geschichte* (1983) US Title: *Not by Coincidence*
Ethel Merman	*Airplane!* (1980)
Ray Milland	*The Sea Serpent* (1985)
Max Miller	*Asking for Trouble* (1943)
Carmen Miranda	*Scared Stiff* (1953)
Robert Mitchum	*Waiting for Sunset* (1997)
Tom Mix	*Rustlers' Roundup* (1933) Short film Series: *The Miracle Rider* (1935)
Marilyn Monroe	*The Misfits* (1961) (Uncompleted) *Something's Got to Give*
Yves Montand	*IP5: L'Ile aux Pachydermes* (1992)
Kenneth More	*The Spaceman and King Arthur* (1979). TV film: *A Tale of Two Cities* (1981)
Robert Morley	*Istanbul* (1989). TV film: *The Lady and the Highwayman* (1989)
Zero Mostel	*Best Boy* (1979)
Paul Muni	*The Last Angry Man* (1959)
Audie Murphy	*A Time for Dying* (1969)
Anna Neagle	*The Lady is a Square* (1959)
David Niven	*Curse of the Pink Panther* (1983)
Ivor Novello	*Autumn Crocus* (1934)
Warren Oates	*Blue Thunder* (1983)
Merle Oberon	*Interval* (1973)
Edmond O'Brien	*Dream No Evil* (1976)
Pat O'Brien	*Ragtime* (1981)
Laurence Olivier	*War Requiem* (1988)
Lili Palmer	*The Holcroft Covenant* (1985) TV film: *Peter the Great* (1986)
George Peppard	*The Tigress* (1992)
Anthony Perkins	*The Mummy Lives* (1992) TV film: *In the Deep Woods* (1992)
River Phoenix	*The Thing Called Love* (1993) Uncompleted: *Dark Blood* (1994)
Mary Pickford	*Star Night at the Cocoanut Grove* (1935)
Walter Pidgeon	*Sextette* (1977)
Donald Pleasence	*Halloween 6: The Curse of Michael Myers* (1995) Uncompleted: *Fotogrammi Mortal* (1996) (aka *Fatal Frames*). After he died his role was played by an actor in his face mask (as was Rossano Brazzi's, who also died). David Warbeck (the 'Milk Tray' man) died soon after the release of the film
Eric Portman	*Deadfall* (1968)
Dick Powell	*Susan Slept Here* (1954)
William Powell	*Mister Roberts* (1955)
Tyrone Power	*Witness for the Prosecution* (1957)
Elvis Presley	*That's the Way it is* (1970) TV film: *Elvis on Tour* (1972).
Robert Preston	*The Last Starfighter* (1984) TV film: *Outrage* (1986)
Dennis Price	*Theatre of Blood* (1973) Unreleased: *Son of Dracula*

Actor	Film
	(1974) Aka *Count Downe* (also starred Ringo Starr)
Vincent Price	*Edward Scissorhands* (1990). TV film: *The Heart of Justice* (1992) Voice only: *The Thief and the Cobbler* (1995) Aka *Arabian Knight*
Anthony Quayle	*King of the Wind* (1989)
George Raft	*The Man with Bogart's Face* (1979)
Claude Rains	*The Greatest Story Ever Told* (1965)
Basil Rathbone	*Hillbillies in a Haunted House* (1968)
Ronald Reagan	*The Killers* (1964)
Michael Redgrave	*Nicholas and Alexandra* (1971). As narrator: Roosevelt: *The Power behind the Smile* (1975)
Lee Remick	*The Vision* (1987)
Ralph Richardson	*Directed by William Wyler* (1986) (posthumously)
Rachel Roberts	*Charlie Chan and the Curse of the Dragon Queen* (1980) TV film: *The Hostage Tower* (1980)
Paul Robeson	*Paul Robeson: Tales of Manhattan* (1979)
Edward G Robinson	*Soylent Green* (1973)
Flora Robson	*Clash of the Titans* (1981)
Ginger Rogers	*The Confession* (1964) GB title: *Let's Get Married* TV film: *Harlow* (1964)
Will Rogers	*In Old Kentucky* (1935)
Gilbert Roland	*Barbarosa* (1982)
Cesar Romero	*The Player* (1992)
Rosalind Russell	*Mrs Pollifax – Spy* (1970) TV film: *The Crooked Hearts* (1972)
Margaret Rutherford	*Arabella* (1969)
Robert Ryan	*The Outfit* (1973)
George Sanders	*Psychomania* (1972)
Telly Savalas	*Backfire* (1994)
Romy Schneider	*La Passante du Sans-Souci* (1981)
Randolph Scott	*Ride the High Country* (1962). GB title: *Guns in the Afternoon*
Jean Seberg	*The Wild Duck* (1976)
Peter Sellers	*Trail of the Pink Panther* (1982) (posthumous)
Robert Shaw	*Avalanche Express* (1979) (posthumous)
Norma Shearer	*Her Cardboard Lover* (1942)
Ann Sheridan	*Triangle on Safari* (1957) TV film: *Without Incident* (1957)
Dinah Shore	*Health* (1979) TV film: *Death Car on the Freeway* (1979)
Simone Signoret	*L'Etoile du Nord* (1982): As narrator: *Des 'Terroristes' à la Retraite* (1983)
Phil Silvers	*Hollywood Blue* (1980) Aka *The Happy Hooker Goes to Hollywood*
Alastair Sim	*Escape from the Dark* (1976)
Barbara Stanwyck	*The Night Walker* (1965) TV film: *The Thorn Birds* (1983)
James Stewart	*A Tale of Africa* (1981)

Actor	Film
	TV film: *North and South II* (1986)
	Voice only: *An American Tail 2: Fievel Goes West* (1991)
The 3 Stooges	*Dr Death – Seeker of Souls* (1973)
Gloria Swanson	*Airport 1975* (1974)
Jacques Tati	*Traffic* (1971)
	Limited release: *Parade* (1974)
Robert Taylor	*The Glass Sphinx* (1968)
Shirley Temple	*A Kiss for Corliss* (1949)
Terry Thomas	*Happy Birthday Harry!* (1981)
Sybil Thorndike	*Uncle Vanya* (1963)
Gene Tierney	*The Pleasure Seekers* (1964). TV film: *Daughter of the Mind* (1969)
Spencer Tracy	*Guess Who's Coming to Dinner* (1967)
Bill Travers	*Christian the Lion* (1973)
	TV film: *Bloody Ivory* (1979)
Tommy Trinder	*Barry McKenzie Holds His Own* (1974)
Lana Turner	*Witches' Brew* (1978; released 1985)
Rudolph Valentino	*Son of the Sheik* (1926)
Rudy Vallee	*The Perfect Woman* (1978)
Lee Van Cleef	*Speed Zone* (1989)
Conrad Veidt	*Above Suspicion* (1943)
Erich Von Stroheim	*L'Homme Aux Cent Visages* (1956).

Actor	Film
	GB title: *Man of a Thousand Faces*
Jack Warner	*Dominique* (1978)
John Wayne	*The Shootist* (1976)
Clifton Webb	*Satan Never Sleeps* (1962)
Johnny Weissmuller	*Devil Goddess* (1955)
	Guest appearance: *That's Entertainment II* (1976)
Orson Welles	*Someone to Love* (1987) (posthumous)
Mae West	*Sextette* (1977)
Pearl White	*Perils of Paris* (1925)
Cornel Wilde	*Vultures in Paradise / Flesh and Bullets* (1983)
Michael Wilding	*Lady Caroline Lamb* (1972)
	TV film: *Frankenstein: The True Story* (1973)
Emlyn Williams	*The Walking Stick* (1970)
	TV film: *Past caring* (1985)
Kenneth Williams	*Carry On Emmanuelle* (1978)
Sir Donald Wolfit	*The Charge of the Light Brigade* (1968)
Natalie Wood	*Brainstorm* (1981; released posthumously, 1983)
Fay Wray	*Summer Love* (1957). TV film: *Gideon's Trumpet* (1980)
Gig Young	*Game of Death* (1978)

C
I
N
E
M
A

Oscars (Academy Awards)

*Year	Best Film	Best Actor	Best Actress	Best Director
1929	Wings (1927)	Emil Jannings (The Way of All Flesh)	Janet Gaynor (Seventh Heaven)	Frank Borzage (Seventh Heaven) / Lewis Milestone (Two Arabian Knights)†
1930	The Broadway Melody	Warner Baxter (In Old Arizona)	Mary Pickford (Coquette)	Frank Lloyd (The Divine Lady)
1931	All Quiet on the Western Front	George Arliss (Disraeli)	Norma Shearer (The Divorcee)	Lewis Milestone (All Quiet on the Western Front)
1932	Cimarron (1930)	Lionel Barrymore (A Free Soul)	Marie Dressler (Min and Bill)	Norman Taurog (Skippy)
1933	Grand Hotel	Fredric March (Dr Jekyll and Mr Hyde) / Wallace Beery (The Champ)	Helen Hayes (The Sin of Madelon Claudet)	Frank Borzage (Bad Girl)
1934	Cavalcade (1932)	Charles Laughton (Private Life of Henry VIII)	Katharine Hepburn (Morning Glory)	Frank Lloyd (Cavalcade)
1935	It Happened One Night	Clark Gable (It Happened One Night)	Claudette Colbert (It Happened One Night)	Frank Capra (It Happened One Night)
1936	Mutiny on the Bounty	Victor McLaglen (The Informer)	Bette Davis (Dangerous)	John Ford (The Informer)
1937	The Great Ziegfeld	Paul Muni (The Story of Louis Pasteur)	Luise Rainer (The Great Ziegfeld)	Frank Capra (Mr Deeds Goes to Town)
1938	The Life of Emile Zola	Spencer Tracy (Captains Courageous)	Luise Rainer (The Good Earth)	Leo McCarey (The Awful Truth)
1939	You Can't Take It with You	Spencer Tracy (Boys Town)	Bette Davis (Jezebel)	Frank Capra (You Can't Take It With You)
1940	Gone with the Wind	Robert Donat (Goodbye Mr Chips)	Vivien Leigh (Gone with the Wind)	Victor Fleming (Gone with the Wind)
1941	Rebecca	James Stewart (The Philadelphia Story)	Ginger Rogers (Kitty Foyle)	John Ford (The Grapes of Wrath)
1942	How Green Was My Valley	Gary Cooper (Sergeant York)	Joan Fontaine (Suspicion)	John Ford (How Green Was My Valley)
1943	Mrs Miniver	James Cagney (Yankee Doodle Dandy)	Greer Garson (Mrs Miniver)	William Wyler (Mrs Miniver)
1944	Casablanca (1942)	Paul Lukas (Watch on the Rhine)	Jennifer Jones (The Song of Bernadette)	Michael Curtiz (Casablanca)
1945	Going My Way	Bing Crosby (Going My Way)	Ingrid Bergman (Gaslight)	Leo McCarey (Going My Way)
1946	The Lost Weekend	Ray Milland (The Lost Weekend)	Joan Crawford (Mildred Pearce)	Billy Wilder (The Lost Weekend)
1947	The Best Years of Our Lives	Fredric March (The Best Years of Our Lives)	Olivia de Haviland (To Each His Own)	William Wyler (The Best Years of Our Lives)
1948	Gentleman's Agreement	Ronald Colman (A Double Life)	Loretta Young (The Farmer's Daughter)	Elia Kazan (Gentleman's Agreement)
1949	Hamlet	Laurence Olivier (Hamlet)	Jane Wyman (Johnny Belinda)	John Huston (The Treasure of the Sierra Madre)
1950	All the King's Men	Broderick Crawford (All the King's Men)	Olivia De Havilland (The Heiress)	Joseph L Mankiewicz (A Letter To Three Wives)
1951	All about Eve	José Ferrer (Cyrano de Bergerac)	Judy Holliday (Born Yesterday)	Joseph L Mankiewicz (All about Eve)
1952	An American In Paris	Humphrey Bogart (The African Queen)	Vivian Leigh (A Streetcar Named Desire)	George Stevens (A Place in the Sun)
1953	The Greatest Show on Earth	Gary Cooper (High Noon)	Shirley Booth (Come Back Little Sheba)	John Ford (The Quiet Man)
1954	From Here to Eternity	William Holden (Stalag 17)	Audrey Hepburn (Roman Holiday)	Fred Zinnemann (From Here to Eternity)
1955	On the Waterfront	Marlon Brando (On the Waterfront)	Grace Kelly (The Country Girl)	Elia Kazan (On the Waterfront)
1956	Marty	Ernest Borgnine (Marty)	Anna Magnani (The Rose Tattoo)	Delbert Mann (Marty)
1957	Around the World in Eighty Days	Yul Brynner (The King and I)	Ingrid Bergman (Anastasia)	George Stevens (Giant)
1958	The Bridge on the River Kwai	Alec Guinness (The Bridge on The River Kwai)	Joanne Woodward (The Three Faces of Eve)	David Lean (The Bridge on the River Kwai)
1959	Gigi	David Niven (Separate Tables)	Susan Hayward (I Want To Live)	Vincente Minnelli (Gigi)
1960	Ben Hur	Charlton Heston (Ben Hur)	Simone Signoret (Room at the Top)	William Wyler (Ben Hur)
1961	The Apartment	Burt Lancaster (Elmer Gantry)	Elizabeth Taylor (Butterfield 8)	Billy Wilder (The Apartment)
1962	West Side Story	Maximilian Schell (Judgment at Nuremberg)	Sophia Loren (Two Women)	Jerome Robbins & Robert Wise (West Side Story)

*Year	Best Film	Best Actor	Best Actress	Director
1963	Lawrence of Arabia	Gregory Peck (To Kill a Mockingbird)	Anne Bancroft (The Miracle Worker)	David Lean (Lawrence of Arabia)
1964	Tom Jones	Sidney Poitier (Lilies of the Field)	Patricia Neal (Hud)	Tony Richardson (Tom Jones)
1965	My Fair Lady	Rex Harrison (My Fair Lady)	Julie Andrews (Mary Poppins)	George Cukor (My Fair Lady)
1966	The Sound of Music	Lee Marvin (Cat Ballou)	Julie Christie (Darling)	Robert Wise (The Sound of Music)
1967	A Man for All Seasons	Paul Scofield (A Man for All Seasons)	Elizabeth Taylor (Who's Afraid of Virginia Woolf)	Fred Zinnemann (A Man for All Seasons)
1968	In the Heat of the Night	Rod Steiger (In the Heat of the Night)	Katharine Hepburn (Guess Who's Coming To Dinner)	Mike Nichols (The Graduate)
1969	Oliver!	Cliff Robertson (Charly)	Katherine Hepburn (The Lion in Winter)† Barbra Streisand (Funny Girl)†	Carol Reed (Oliver!)
1970	Midnight Cowboy	John Wayne (True Grit)	Maggie Smith (The Prime of Miss Jean Brodie)	John Schlesinger (Midnight Cowboy)
1971	Patton	George C Scott (Patton) refused Oscar	Glenda Jackson (Women in Love)	Franklin Schaffner (Patton)
1972	The French Connection	Gene Hackman (The French Connection)	Jane Fonda (Klute)	William Friedkin (The French Connection)
1973	The Godfather	Marlon Brando (The Godfather, refused Oscar)	Liza Minnelli (Cabaret)	Bob Fosse (Cabaret)
1974	The Sting	Jack Lemmon (Save the Tiger)	Glenda Jackson (A Touch of Class)	George Roy Hill (The Sting)
1975	The Godfather Part II	Art Carney (Harry and Tonto)	Ellen Burstyn (Alice Doesn't Live Here Any More)	Francis Ford Coppola (The Godfather Part II)
1976	One Flew over the Cuckoo's Nest	Jack Nicholson (One Flew over the Cuckoo's Nest)	Louise Fletcher (One Flew Over the Cuckoo's Nest)	Milos Forman (One Flew over the Cuckoo's Nest)
1977	Rocky	Peter Finch (Network: posthumously awarded)	Faye Dunaway (Network)	John G. Avildsen (Rocky)
1978	Annie Hall	Richard Dreyfuss (The Goodbye Girl)	Diane Keaton (Annie Hall)	Woody Allen (Annie Hall)
1979	The Deer Hunter	Jon Voight (Coming Home)	Jane Fonda (Coming Home)	Michael Cimino (The Deer Hunter)
1980	Kramer versus Kramer	Dustin Hoffman (Kramer versus Kramer)	Sally Field (Norma Rae)	Robert Benton (Kramer versus Kramer)
1981	Ordinary People	Robert De Niro (Raging Bull)	Sissy Spacek (Coal Miner's Daughter)	Robert Redford (Ordinary People)
1982	Chariots of Fire	Henry Fonda (On Golden Pond)	Katharine Hepburn (On Golden Pond)	Warren Beatty (Reds)
1983	Gandhi	Ben Kingsley (Gandhi)	Meryl Streep (Sophie's Choice)	Richard Attenborough (Gandhi)
1984	Terms of Endearment	Robert Duvall (Tender Mercies)	Shirley MacLaine (Terms of Endearment)	James L Brooks (Terms of Endearment)
1985	Amadeus	F Murray Abraham (Amadeus)	Sally Field (Places in the Heart)	Milos Forman (Amadeus)
1986	Out of Africa	William Hurt (Kiss of the Spider Woman)	Geraldine Page (The Trip to Bountiful)	Sydney Pollack (Out of Africa)
1987	Platoon	Paul Newman (The Color of Money)	Marlee Matlin (Children of a Lesser God)	Oliver Stone (Platoon)
1988	The Last Emperor	Michael Douglas (Wall Street)	Cher (Moonstruck)	Bernardo Bertolucci (The Last Emperor)
1989	Rain Man	Dustin Hoffman (Rain Man)	Jodie Foster (The Accused)	Barry Levinson (Rain Man)
1990	Driving Miss Daisy	Daniel Day Lewis (My Left Foot)	Jessica Tandy (Driving Miss Daisy)	Oliver Stone (Born on the Fourth of July)
1991	Dances with Wolves	Jeremy Irons (Reversal of Fortune)	Kathy Bates (Misery)	Kevin Costner (Dances with Wolves)
1992	Silence of the Lambs	Anthony Hopkins (Silence of the Lambs)	Jodie Foster (Silence of the Lambs)	Jonathan Demme (Silence of the Lambs)
1993	Unforgiven	Al Pacino (Scent of a Woman)	Emma Thompson (Howard's End)	Clint Eastwood (Unforgiven)
1994	Schindler's List	Tom Hanks (Philadelphia)	Holly Hunter (The Piano)	Steven Spielberg (Schindler's List)
1995	Forrest Gump	Tom Hanks (Forrest Gump)	Jessica Lange (Blue Sky)	Robert Zemeckis (Forrest Gump)
1996	Braveheart	Nicolas Cage (Leaving Las Vegas)	Susan Sarandon (Dead Man Walking)	Mel Gibson (Braveheart)
1997	The English Patient	Geoffrey Rush (Shine)	Frances McDormand (Fargo)	Anthony Minghella (The English Patient)
1998	Titanic	Jack Nicholson (As Good As it Gets)	Helen Hunt (As Good As it Gets)	James Cameron (Titanic)
1999	Shakespeare in Love	Roberto Benigni (Life is Beautiful)	Gwyneth Paltrow (Shakespeare in Love)	Steven Spielberg (Saving Private Ryan)

CINEMA

*Year	Best Film	Best Actor	Best Actress	Director
2000	American Beauty	Kevin Spacey (American Beauty)	Hilary Swank (Boy's Don't Cry)	Sam Mendes (American Beauty)
2001	Gladiator	Russell Crowe (Gladiator)	Julia Roberts (Erin Brockovich)	Steven Soderbergh (Traffic)

* Probably the most frustrating question for any quiz player is in determining what a question setter means when asking a question about the Oscars. The confusion arises because the Oscars are awarded for films made the previous year, which means the question must be qualified – e.g. the 1997 Best Film Oscar was awarded to The English Patient, which was a 1996 film release. It must be said that the real confusion lies in the fact that after, even when the question is qualified, bad research will cause a wrongly given answer by an unaware question setter.

The suggested phraseology to use in such a question would be: 'At the 1996 Oscar ceremony, which film was awarded the Best Film Oscar?'. The answer is Braveheart. However, if the question was: 'Which 1996 film won the Oscar for Best Film' then the answer would clearly be The English Patient. The problem with the question 'Which film won the Best Film Oscar in 1996?' is that although seemingly unambiguous, as clearly only one Oscar ceremony took place in 1996, many sources refer to the film release date, quite wrongly. I can only suggest that question setters take more care with such questions or that an appropriately qualified answer must be accepted. All of the above films were premiered in the year prior to the award unless the date is specifically given – as on rare occasions a film has been released too late for consideration for a nomination, as in the case of Casablanca.

† Separate award for Comedy Director.

COMPUTERS

Common Terms

Artificial Intelligence A word coined in the USA in 1956 as the ultimate aim for electronic processing ability. Although great strides have been made towards a device that would stimulate human thought processes, as yet, no such device exists and the term is used to describe advanced programs such as PROLOG which allows empirical evidence to guide future decisions.

ASCII American Standard Code for Information Interchange (computer code for representing alphanumeric characters.

bit (binary digit) Smallest unit of data manageable by a computer.

bootstrap Technique for loading the first few program instructions into a computer main store to enable the rest of the program to be introduced from an input device.

busbar Group of electrical conductors maintained at low voltage, used for carrying data in binary form between the various parts of a computer or it's peripherals.

byte Equivalent of eight bits (generally makes up a character of information). It is possible to have a six-bit byte.

computer: definition A machine that carries out a programmed sequence of instructions by translation of coded data. Digital computers use binary code which is represented by eletrical current being turned off and on. Analogue computers use continuous variables as opposed to the discreet data of digital machines. A simple example of an analogue computer would be a set of scales.

computer generations The developement of computers is sometimes viewed as falling into several phases or generations. First generation began with the ENIAC (electronic numerical integrator and calculator) modern computers designed by J. Presper Eckert and John W Mauchly, both of the University of Pennsylvania. Completed in 1946, this was first all-purpose, all-electronic digital computer. A special-purpose, all-electronic computing machine called Colossus had earlier been developed at Bletchley Park, in England, and was in operation by December 1943. The Colossus was designed (by the computer genius Alan Turing) to decipher codes generated by the German electromechanical enciphering devices known as Enigma machines. The successor to ENIAC was EDVAC (Electronic Discrete Variable Automatic Computer).

The 'second generation' of modern computers began in 1959, when machines employing semiconductor devices known as transistors became commercially available.

The 'third generation' of modern computers began in the late 1960s, when integrated circuits were imprinted on silicon chips. This permitted the construction of large 'mainframe' computers with much higher operating speeds.

The 'fourth generation' of modern computers began in the 1980s. This and subsequent generations have continued to develop very large-scale integration (VLSI) and have promoted the advancement of virtual reality (VR) and computer aided design (CAD).

Computer Programming languages (high-level)

ADA Designed for dealing with real-time processing problems and used for military and other systems. It was named after Augusta Ada Byron, Lady Lovelace (assistant to Charles Babbage), and developed in the late 1970s by the US Defense Department.

AED Algol Extended for Design.

ALGOL ALGorithmic Orientated Language, principally used for scientific and mathematical problems (types: ALGOL 60 and ALGOL 68).

APL A Programming Language.

APT Automatically Programmed Tools.

BASIC Beginners All-purpose Symbolic Instruction Code.

BCPL Basic Computer Programming Language.

C Introduced at Bell Laboratories in 1974 and originally developed for use in the UNIX operating system.

COBOL COmmon Business-Oriented Language (developed in 1959).

COGO CO-ordinate GeOmetry.

COMAL COMmon Algorithmic Language.

CORAL Computer On-line ReAL time.

FORTH Name derives from an intention to provide a language for fourth-generation computers. It uses a notation called reverse polish, in which an operator is always preceded by its arguments. FORTH is popularly used for writing video game programs.

FORTRAN FORmula TRANslation (Invented in 1956).

GPSS General Purpose Systems Simulation.

LISP LISt Processor (introduced in 1960). Its basic entity is an s-expression (symbolic expression) which is either an atomic symbol or a list structure.

LOGO A simple, interactive language which is compact enough to run on most microcomputers but also embodies powerful programming facilities. It is used extensively for teaching programming to children.

ML Meta Language.

PASCAL ALGOL-related language named after the scientist-philosopher Blaise Pascal (1623–62). Pascal is a teaching language developed in the late 1960s.

PL/1 Programming Language 1, a multipurpose programming language designed for solving both business and scientific problems.

PL/M Programming Language for Micro Computers.

PROLOG PROgramming in LOGic. There the emphasis is on description rather than on action, eg to find the greater of two input numbers, one would describe what 'greater of' meant and then query it with the given numbers as data.

SIMULA SIMUlation LAnguage.

SNOBOL StriNg-Oriented symBOlic Languagem, provides facilities for the manipulation of strings of characters by pattern-matching expressions. SNOBOL is particularly applicable for text editing, linguistics and the compiling and symbolic manipulation of algebraic expressions.

SQL Structured Query Language.

computer: makes and models: Commodore: Amiga and Pe; Apple: Macintosh; Sinclair: Spectrum and ZX80 / 1; Packard Bell:Legend; DEC:Vax; IBM:PS/2; Acorn:BBC Micro; Digital:Equipment Corporation-PDP Series.

computer: mechanical pioneers Charles Babbage (1791–1871) who designed computing machines that he called the 'Difference Engine' and 'Analytical Engine' in the 1820s and 30s. They were never built but the first practical programmed computer built by Georg Scheutz of Stockholm and exhibited at the Paris Exposition of 1855 was based on Babbage's Difference Engine. The mechanical adding machine developed by Blaise Pascal in 1642 which used a 10:1 gearing ratio to represent decimal columns, can be regarded as the ancestor of the computer.

computer programmer: first Ada Byron, Countess Lovelace, assistant to Charles Babbage (see computer mechanical pioneers) is generally recognised as the first 'computer programmer'.The first proposal for a computer language, however, was by German philosopher Gottfried Leibniz (1646–1716), who devised a system allowing logic statements to be dealt with mathematically, using the digit 0 for false and 1 for true.)

computer: types Micro, mini, mainframe (computers can also be categorised as digital and analog).

CPU Central Processing Unit; the electronic decision making device within a computer.

DTP Desktop Publishing; the production of high-quality printed matter using a desktop computer and a laser printer. Some examples of packages are Pagemaker and QuarkXpress, Adobe Illustrator, Microsoft Publisher, Corel Draw, GST and Serif.

gigabyte one billion characters of information.

GIGO Garbage In, Garbage Out. Computer user's proverb meaning if you use unreliable data you will get unreliable results.

Hardware The electronic and mechanical components of a computer are called the hardware; this includes the processing unit.

high-level language Computer programming language that is closer to human language or mathematical notation than to machine language.

home computer: first Apple-1; created by Steve Wozniak and Steve Jobs in 1977.

k Kilobyte (1,024 bytes).

Internet An international computer network linking computers from educational institutions, government agencies, and industry.

Lara Croft Heroine of the video game 'Tomb Raider'.

Laptops: first Became prevalent in 1987, although the first laptop machine with a full colour screen was developed in 1990.

Laser printer developed in 1987 using the principle of the Xerox copier.

LCD Liquid Crystal Display

low-level language Computer-programming language that is closer to machine language than to human language.

m Megabyte (1,024 kilobytes).

microprocessor: first Intel 4004.

modem Acronym for MOdulator DEModulator, a device used to enable computers to communicate with one another via telephone lines.

motherboard Printed circuit board through which all hardware and software devise send electronic to talk to each other.

MS-DOS MicroSoft Disc Operating System.

network Group of computers connected in order to share and exchange information.

nibble Equivalent of four bits.

OS Operating System: a program that controls the overall operation of a computer system, typically by performing such tasks as memory allocation, job scheduling and input/output control.

pixel Picture element: one of the number of very small dots that make up the picture on a visual display unit.

port Socket used to connect a computer to other devices.

punched card: inventor The American Dr Herman Hollerith (1860–1929) invented the punched-card system in 1890; his company, the Tabulating Machine Co. became IBM in 1924. Hollerith's device enabled a census to be taken in six weeks rather than the six years required by manual analysis. Mechanical punched cards had been suggested earlier by Charles Babbage; and the 'Jacquard Loom' of 1801 is an even earlier example of punched card principles but Hollerith patented the system and was the first to use electrical contacts.

RAM Random Access Memory; temporary storage space that is lost when the computer is switched off.

ROM Read-Only Memory; permanent storage device that holds data that cannot be altered by the user.

software the programs and operating information used by a computer.

spreadsheets: first The first spreadsheet program Visicalc was developed on the Apple-2 in 1979.

terabyte Approxiamately a thousand billion characters of information.

Turing Test Test for successful artificial intelligence that depends on a human not knowing that he or she is communicating with a computer. No computer has ever passed the Turing Test.

VGA Video Graphics Array (Super VGA is the advanced array).

video games: 1st Pong (established in Italy in the early 1970's).

Video games: famous Super Mario Brothers by Nintendo, Sonic the Hedgehog by Sega, Donkey Kong by Atari, Tomb Raider by Eios, Duke Nukem by 3D Realms, and Doom by Idoh.

Windows User-friendly operating system created by Microsoft.

NB: Many computer acronyms (eg AI, DOS, WYSIWYG, VDU, and MIPS) can be found listed in the Abbreviations section.

CURRENT AFFAIRS

Daily Record 1999

January 1999

1   Radio 4's *Today* listeners voted William Shakespeare as 'Personality of the Millenium'.
4   Charlie Whelan, the Chancellor of the Exchequer's press secretary, was forced to resign after allegations that he leaked details of Peter Mandelson's controversial loan.
5   Lord Falconer of Thoroton began his first day as the new Dome Minister.
8   Trade Secretary, Stephen Byers, admitted he had a son when he was 17-years-old.
10   Tintin, the Belgian cartoon character, celebrated his 70th birthday.
11   A large section of Beachy Head crumbled into the sea causing a lighthouse to be joined to the cliffs.
12   President Clinton sent a cheque for $850,000 to Paula Jones to settle her claims of sexual harassment.
13   A 1965 episode of *Dr Who*, 'The Lion', thought to be wiped by the BBC, materialised in New Zealand.
14   President Clinton's impeachment hearing began, the first such hearing for 131 years.
15   Jeff and Jennifer Bramley who ran away with their foster children, made contact with PR man, Max Clifford, to discuss the possibility of selling their story.
17   HMS *Norfolk*, the British warship dispatched to support West African troops in Sierra Leone, arrived off the coast of Freetown.
19   Jonathan Aitken admitted perjury and perverting the course of justice and faced a lengthy prison sentence.
20   Paddy Ashdown announced that he would stand down as Liberal Democrat leader in the summer.
25   Greg Cordell and Carla Germaine, the couple who won a Birmingham radio blind date competition, were married after meeting for the first time at the altar.
27   Chris Brocklesby, 17, won the world line-dancing championship in Texas.
28   The Prince of Wales and Camilla Parker Bowles left the Ritz together after a 50th birthday party for Mrs Parker Bowles's sister, Annabel Elliott.
29   In a new set of legal rules published today, and in operation from April 26th, old terms such as writ and plaintiff will be replaced by 'claim forms' and 'claimant'.
31   Chimpanzees slaughtered for food in west Central Africa were the source of Aids, according to a team of scientists who traced the initial outbreak to the sub-species 'Pan troglodytes troglodytes'.

February 1999

1   Monica Lewinsky spent the day giving a deposition in the impeachment trial of President Clinton.
2   Louise Sullivan, an Australian nanny, was sentenced at the Old Bailey to fifteen months' imprisonment, suspended for two years, for the manslaughter of a six-month-old baby, Caroline Jongen, in her care in April 1997.
3   The Zinoviev Letter, which helped to bring down Ramsay MacDonald's government in the 1920s, was explained by Gill Bennett, the chief historian at the Foreign Office. The conclusion was that the letter was written by White Russians living in Latvia.
4   An attempt by the family and memorial fund of Diana, Princess of Wales, to turn her face into a trademark was turned down by the Patent Office.
7   King Abdullah I I succeeded his father, King Hussein, as the King of Jordan.
8   Laurent Fabius, the former French Prime Minister, began a manslaughter trial for his role in the blood scandal that spread Aids to more than 4,000 people.
9   The British film *Shakespeare in Love* was nominated for 13 Oscars.
10   Only 'Island Line' of the 25 train companies, qualified for top marks under a new grading system that measures punctuality and performance.
11   The BBC suspended three programme makers amid the controversy surrounding the Vanessa Feltz daytime chat show fakes.
12   President Clinton was cleared of high crimes and misdemeanours by the Senate.
14   Eve Enster's controversial play *Vagina Monologues* opened at the Old Vic, London.
16   Negla Kanteper, the 15-year-old daughter of a Kurdish refugee, set herself alight outside the Greek embassy in London.
     Robbie Williams won three Brit awards i.e. best male singer, best single and best video.
     Chinese people celebrated the lunar festival ushering in the year of the rabbit.
17   Israeli security guards shot dead three Kurdish protesters and injured 16 people after an attempt to storm Israel's consulate in Berlin.
18   The occupation of the Greek embassy in London ended peacefully, after 60 hours, when 77 Kurdish demonstrators gave themselves up to police.
19   Spice Girl Melanie Brown gave birth to a daughter, Phoenix Chi.
21   Mike Tyson, serving a year for assault, was put in isolation after throwing a television set against cell bars.
22   Doctor Harold Shipman, 53, was charged with the murder of another seven women patients bringing the tally to fifteen.
23   It was announced that the RAF and Royal Navy squadrons of Harrier fighters and bombers are to be combined in a plan to place them under a single command known as Joint Force 2000.
24   *The Man from Beyond*, a feature film made by Harry Houdini in 1922, was found and will be restored and shown at the Bradford film festival.
25   It was announced that Richard Dearlove, the director of operations and assistant chief of MI6, is to succeed David Spedding as the chief of the intelligence service, codenamed 'C'.
26   It was announced that *Kavanagh QC* would be the first programme to replace *News at Ten* on Monday, March 8th.
28   The first edition of *The Beano* was sold for £6,200, the largest amount ever paid for a comic in Britain.

March 1999
1   Peter Clowes, the disgraced financier, was jailed for four months for making false benefit claims.
2   Tony McCarroll, ex Oasis drummer, was awarded £600,000 compensation by the courts for his dismissal.
4   Spice Girl Victoria Adams and footballer David Beckham became the parents of a son, Brooklyn Joseph.
5   Sir Elton John won a landmark ruling that his privacy was invaded when newspapers published long-lens photographs of David Beckham and Victoria Adams at his house. The Press Complaints Commission upheld his complaint although he was not himself in the published photographs.
9   It was announced that Mortgage Interest Relief At Source (Miras) will be scrapped from April 6th 2000.
11   Paratrooper, Lee Clegg, was cleared of the 1990 murder of a Belfast joyrider.
        Oskar Lafontaine, the German Finance Minister, resigned.
14   Caspians Intrepid, an Irish setter, was crowned Best in Show at Crufts.
15   Bertie Ahern, the Irish Prime Minister, gained critical praise for his published poem 'Whoseday is it Today ?'
16   Tony Blair introduced a teaching strategy 'Maths Year 2000' in an attempt to raise the standard in schools.
17   Fabian Alarcon, former president of Ecuador, was arrested on charges of creating a payroll of 1,000 fictional employees.
19   Brian Jones, 51, pilot of Breitling Orbiter 3, and his co-pilot Bertrand Piccard became the first people to complete a circumnavigation by balloon.
23   Pauline Lyon, 56, gave birth to her second test-tube baby; she was the oldest British test-tube mother four years ago.
24   Gaby Vernoff gave birth to a girl in a Los Angeles hospital after being impregnated by sperm from her dead husband.
25   Charlotte Church, 13, became the youngest solo artist to enter the American top 30 album chart.
26   America's stealth bomber, the bat-wing B2, capable of dropping sixteen 2,000lb bombs to near perfect accuracy was introduced for the Kosovo military operation.
29   Benecol became the first food to go on sale in Britain with a claim it can cut cholesterol by up to 10 %
30   The peace mission to Belgrade by Yevgeny Primakov, the Russian Prime Minister, failed to produce an end to the Serb aggression in Kosovo.
31   The future of Britain's biggest car plant at Longbridge, Birmingham, was safeguarded when a deal between the British government and Germany's BMW saved the Rover plant.

April 1999
2   David Smith, 30, was arrested and charged with inventing 'Melissa' the computer virus that had been infecting e-mail systems for the past week.
6   The two Libyans suspected of blowing up Pan Am Flight 103 sat in the dock whilst all 270 names of the Lockerbie victims were read out.
7   Edgar Pearce admitted he was the Mardi Gra bomber who extorted money from Barclays bank and Sainsbury's.
9   Viviana Durante, the prima ballerina with the Royal Ballet, was dropped from the company's Japanese tour following differences with Bruce Sansom.
10   Linda McCartney was honoured at the Royal Albert Hall by a concert in aid of the Animaline charity.
11   Bafta winners: Best film: Shakespeare in Love, Best Actress: Cate Blanchett (*Elizabeth*), Best Actor: Roberto Benigni (*La Vita e Bella*), Best Supporting Actress: Dame Judi Dench (*Shakespeare in Love*) Best Supporting Actor: Geoffrey Rush (*Shakespeare in Love*), Academy Fellowship: Liz Taylor. Best film not in English: *Central Do Brasil*, Best Short Animated Film: *The Canterbury Tales*. Best Sound: *Saving Private Ryan*, David Lean Award for Direction: Peter Weir (*The Truman Show*). Best Short Film: *Home*.
12   Women's Institute members in Rylstone, near Skipton, raised their profile by posing for a nude calendar.
13   Jack Kevorkian, alias Dr Death, was sentenced to between 10 and 25 years imprisonment for murdering a terminally ill man by lethal injection.
14   A Japanese Maglev train, with 17 engineers on board, broke the world speed record when it recorded a top speed of 343 mph near Tokyo.
15   Benazir Bhutto and her husband Asif Ali Zardari were both sentenced to five years in jail and fined £5 million on corruption charges.
16   Abdelaziz Bouteflika became president of Algeria after the other six candidates withdrew following rigging allegations.
18   The Queen and Prince Philip began their fourth consecutive Asian tour with a visit to Seoul, South Korea.
19   The German parliament met for the first time in the new glass domed Reichstag, designed by Lord Norman Foster.
20   Two men in black trench-coats walked into a Denver High School and shot students indiscriminately. The death toll was believed to be 25. The men later turned their guns on themselves.
21   Andy Stevens, alias Kooky the Clown, was declared international clown of the year.
22   Ex pop singer, Sinead O'Connor, was ordained a priest in a secret ceremony near the Holy Shrine at Lourdes and will be known as Mother Bernadette.
23   Five passers-by were shot by gunmen trying to escape police in a chase across the M6 and into Rochdale.
24   Veteran Radio 2 disc jockey Johnnie Walker was suspended after drug taking allegations.
25   Alben Maksuti, aged four, became the first Kosovan from the Balkan refugee camps to set foot on British soil when he landed at Leeds-Bradford Airport. Woody Allen and his wife Soon-Yi Previn paraded their new-born baby, Bechet Dumaine Allen, up Madison Avenue, NY
26   Jill Dando, the presenter of Crimewatch UK, was shot and killed in broad daylight outside her home in Fulham.
27   Unilever, which owns Bird's Eye and Wall's, announced plans to remove genetically modified (GM) ingredients from their foodstuffs.

28	Simon Armitage was appointed poet-in-residence of the Millenium Dome.
29	The High Court re-instated Fiona Jones as Labour MP for Newark after her suspension over election rigging allegations.
30	Dame Shirley Porter, the former leader of Westminster city council, was successful in the Appeal Court over the alleged 'homes for votes' scandal.

May 1999

2	David Copeland was charged with the three recent nail bomb attacks in London.
3	The body of George Mallory, who disappeared with Andrew Irvine in 1924 whilst climbing Everest, was found 2000 feet from the summit.
5	Air Stewardess, Andrea O'Neill, stripped on a British Airways flight to Genoa as a result of a bet.
6	Mohamed Al Fayed, the owner of Harrods, was refused British citizenship by Home Secretary, Jack Straw.
7	The Labour party gained victory in the Scottish, and Welsh devolution votes although the proportional representation system meant there was no overall majority. Donald Dewar became first Minister for Scotland and Alun Michael is to become his Welsh equivalent.
9	Prince Rainier of Monaco celebrated 50 years of rule; he is second only to King Bhumibol of Thailand as the longest reigning monarch.
10	Jonathan Aitken, the former Tory cabinet minister who faces a jail sentence for perjury, declared himself bankrupt.
12	It was announced that Chris Patten would replace Sir Leon Brittan as a European Commissioner in September.
15	Binyamin Netenyahu resigned as Israeli Prime Minister to leave the way clear for Ehud Barak.
16	Terry Keane, a former gossip columnist with the *Sunday Independent*, announced she had a 27-year affair with Charles Haughey, the former Irish Prime Minister.
17	In the latest Cabinet reshuffle John Reid became Scottish Secretary and Helen Liddell became Transport Minister. Donald Dewar's first Cabinet included Jim Wallace (Minister for Justice), Henry McLeish (Minister for Enterprise and Lifelong Learning), Wendy Alexander (Minister for Social Inclusion, Local Government and Housing), Sam Galbraith (Minister for Children, Education, Culture, Arts and Sport), Sarah Boyack (Minister for Transport and the Environment), Ross Finnie (Minister for Rural Affairs), Jack McConnell (Minister for Finance), Susan Deacon (Minister for Health and Community Care), Tom McCabe (Business Manager), Lord Hardie (Lord Advocate).
18	Andrew Motion succeeded Ted Hughes as Poet Laureate.
19	Martin Flynn, a teacher who spanked his daughter for refusing to have a tooth extracted at the dentist, was found guilty of using unreasonable force.
21	Insurance Company, Sun Life of Canada, offered all its employees, aged 50 or over, early retirement. The *Star Wars* prequel, *Episode One: The Phantom Menace*, earned more than $1 million on its opening day.
24	The first Burke's Peerage for 30 years went on sale with illegitimate members of the aristocracy included.
25	Tony Blair announced that Alastair Goodlad was to become the next High Commissioner to Australia.
26	Kara Noble, an employee of Heart FM, was dismissed from her job for allowing the *Sun* newspaper to publish a topless photograph of Sophie Rhys-Jones with Chris Tarrant.
	The Queen opened the National Assembly for Wales.
27	After the shooting down of two Indian MiG aircraft over Pakistani-controlled Kashmir, the Indian Prime Minister, Atal Bihari Vajpayee, called for a state of emergency.
28	The Victoria and Albert Museum agreed to give the Tate Gallery up to 20 paintings by John Constable as part of a scheme to share the nation's art treasures.
29	James Major, son of former Prime Minister John Major, married TV presenter Emma Noble.
30	The mystery surrounding the disappearance of President John F Kennedy's coffin which carried his body from Dallas to Washington was apparently solved when US officials announced it was dropped into the Atlantic.

June 1999

1	Sir Anthony Dowell announced his retirement as director of the Royal Ballet from August 2001.
2	Colin Follows drove his jet-propelled car 'Vampire' to a new British land speed record of 269.09 mph in New York.
3	Slobodan Milosevic declared his intention to end the war in Kosovo, however, the bombing will continue until there are clear signs of a Serb withdrawal.
4	It was announced that the Tory party treasurer, Michael Ashcroft, was funding the party at a rate of £360,000 per month.
7	Mark Elder was appointed music director of the Hallé Orchestra.
8	Jonathan Aitken was sentenced to 18 months imprisonment for perjury, his sentence to begin at Belmarsh prison, London.
9	Serb generals signed a military pact setting out terms for their forces' withdrawal from Kosovo and an end to Nato strikes.
11	It was announced that Her Majesty, The Queen, will be sending greeting cards in the post for centenarians, instead of the telemessage, which replaced the telegram in 1982.
13	The Kosovan capital of Pristina was liberated on its east and west sides by British troops.
15	William Hague announced his new shadow cabinet as follows: Francis Maude (Chancellor), Michael Ancram (Chairman), Ann Widdecombe (Home Affairs), John Maples (Foreign Affairs), Sir George Young (Leader of the Commons and Constitutional Affairs), John Redwood (Environment, Transport and the Regions), David Heathcoat-Amory (Chief Secretary to the Treasury), Iain Duncan Smith (Defence), Lord Strathclyde (Leader of the House of Lords) Andrew MacKay (Northern Ireland), David Willetts (Social Security), Dr Liam Fox (Health), Peter Ainsworth (Culture, Media and Sport), Gary Streeter (International Development), Tim Yeo (Agriculture, Fisheries & Food), Angela Browning (Trade and Industry), Theresa May (Education and

CURRENT AFFAIRS

Employment), Andrew Lansley (Cabinet Office and Policy Renewal), Bernard Jenkin (Transport), James Arbuthnot (Chief Whip in Commons), Lord Henley (Chief Whip in Lords), not a member of cabinet but attends meetings Edward Garnier (Attorney General)

18   Andrew Motion published his first poem as Laureate 'Epithalamium' for the Royal wedding. The first line is 'One day, the tissue-light through stained glass falls'.

19   Prince Edward married Sophie Rhys-Jones at St George's Chapel, Windsor.

20   The Earl and Countess of Wessex flew to Balmoral to begin their honeymoon.

22   The new £20 note went on the market with Edward Elgar's depiction replacing Michael Faradays.

23   It was announced that Jeffrey and Jennifer Bramley, the foster parents that absconded with their wards, Hannah and Jade Bennett are to be allowed to keep their charges for at least two years.

       Sir Simon Rattle became the first British conductor of the Berlin Philharmonic Orchestra and will replace Claudio Abbado as its chief conductor in 2002.

25   The funeral of Cardinal Basil Hume at Westminster Cathedral was attended by prominent Catholics including recent converts the Duchess of Kent, Ann Widdecombe, and John Gummer, as well as the most eminent Catholic family in England, the Fitzalan-Howards, the family name of the Dukes of Norfolk.

27   Tony Benn announced he would stand down from his Chesterfield constituency at the next election.

30   Duty-free shopping within the European Union ended.

July 1999

1   The Good Friday peace accord passed its ratification dead-line as both Gerry Adams and Tony Blair had sticking points.

3   Nick Leeson, the man who broke Barings Bank, was released from prison in Singapore and was immediately involved in controversy over his deal with the *Daily Mail* for his story.

4   David Beckham and Victoria Adams were married in Luttrellstown Castle, near Dublin

5   The Automobile Association announced its intention to pay £240 to each of its members after being taken over by Centrica.

8   It was announced that the Post Office is to become a plc although its shares will be wholly owned by the Government.

9   Sir Elton John had a pacemaker fitted at the Wellington hospital in London.

11   The first-ever televised Teacher Awards took place in London and were the brainchild of Lord Puttnam.

12   Ernie Ross, a senior Labour MP, was suspended from the House of Commons for ten days for breaking parliamentary rules by leaking a select committee report to the Government.

13   Ilona Staller, the porn star and former Italian MP known as La Cicciolina, claimed that she acted as a secret agent in her native Hungary during the Cold War.

14   Jacques Santer, president of the European Commission, took his seat in the European Parliament as a Luxembourg Christian Democrat. Vice-president Manuel Martin took the chair until Romano Prodi is confirmed in office in September.

15   Sir Andrew Davis, chief conductor of the BBC Symphony Orchestra, opened the 105th season of the BBC Proms.

17   John F. Kennedy Jr was missing presumed dead when the aircraft carrying Mr Kennedy, his wife and sister-in-law, was seen descending towards the sea off Martha's Vineyard.

18   The Ministry of Defence announced that this year's Field Gun Competition at the annual Royal Tournament will be the last.

19   Tim Westwood, a Radio One disc jockey, was shot by a hitman as he sat in his car at traffic lights. Police suspect he was hit by a jealous faction in the world of rap.

20   James Major, 24, the son of the former Prime Minister, was reported to have been fitted with a heart pacemaker.

21   The West Bengal Assembly announced it is to change the name of Calcutta to Kolkata from August 24th.

22   The Mothers' Union announced the appointment of Reg Bailey, 49, as its chief executive, the first man to hold the post in the 120-year history of the union.

23   Pop star Phil Collins married his 27-year-old girlfriend Orianne Cevey in a secret ceremony in Lausanne, Switzerland.

25   Nick Brown, the Agriculture Minister, announced the delay of the pilot scheme for pet passports to replace Britain's quarantine controls, until next April.

28   Bruce Grobbelaar, the former Liverpool goalkeeper, was awarded £85,000 damages by a libel jury over allegations in the *Sun* newspaper, that he took bribes. (This decision was overturned on January 18th 2001.)

30   *The Big Breakfast* presenter Kelly Brook resigned amid reports that she was about to be sacked from the programme.

August 1999

1   General Wesley Clark, Nato supreme commander, and Lieutenant-General Sir Michael Jackson, commander on the ground in Kosovo, were reported to have had heated differences on the approach to the Kosovo crisis. The British general was reported to have said 'I'm not going to start the Third World War for you'.

2   Des Lynam, who was under contract to the BBC until next year, defected to ITV under a £5 million four-year deal.

3   The US Government paid $16 million to the heirs of Abraham Zapruder for the 26-second home movie footage of the assassination of President Kennedy.

4   George Robertson was formally approved by nineteen alliance governments as the next Secretary-General of Nato.

5   Rod Richards stood down as Conservative leader in the Welsh Assembly after he was charged with assaulting a woman.

8   Judge Anthony Leonard, QC, made a ground-breaking ruling that lip-reading evidence, crucial in analysing closed circuit television, was admissible.

9   Paul Arthurs, guitarist with pop group Oasis, announced he was quitting the band.

10   India's armed forces were put on high alert after two of their combat planes shot down a Pakistani Navy aircraft, killing all 16 people on board.

11   A total eclipse of the Sun was seen all over Great Britain at approximately 11.11am

13   The 21-year relationship of the model Jerry Hall and Mick Jagger came to an official end when their Hindu wedding in Bali was declared null and void.

16   Tony Blair attended the Palio of Siena bareback horse race which has seen the deaths of 43 horses since 1970.

17   An earthquake measuring 7.5 on the Richter scale devastated western areas of Turkey; the death toll was over 2000.

18   The Home Secretary Jack Straw was reported to the Commission for Racial Equality after describing 'travellers' as 'crooks who thought they had a licence to commit crime'.

19   The Rail Regulator announced that Railtrack will be hit with fines of up to £42 million if it fails to vastly improve its performance in cutting train delays.

20   Fausta Mareno, a 41-year-old mexican woman, died while trying to swim the English Channel, becoming the fourth person killed in an attempt since 1875.

21   BBC Radio Breakfast Show host Zoe Ball married Norman Cook (aka Fatboy Slim) at Babington House in Somerset.

22   Hurricane Bret, the biggest storm to hit Texas in nearly 20 years, caused devastation and flooding to property.

23   A National Canine Defence League commissioned MORI survey showed that 22,000 dogs were destroyed in the past year because owners could not be found.

24   A Taiwanese container ship Ever Decent collided with a cruise ship Norwegian Dream in the English Channel, 15 miles off the Kent coast.

25   John Stevens was named as successor to Sir Paul Condon as Metropolitan Police Commissioner from next January.

26   Nirav Gathaniwas, 7, became the youngest pupil to pass a full GCSE by gaining a B grade in computing.

27   The King of Buganda, Ronald Mutebi, married British-born Sylvia Nagginda Luswata. Buganda is a 600-year-old kingdom of Uganda which has recently been restored.

29   Eight-year-old David Howell became the youngest person to beat a chess grandmaster when he defeated Dr John Nunn at the Mind Sports Olympiad at Olympia, London.

30   Microsoft was forced to shut down 'Hotmail', the free e-mail service, when a webpage allowed users to access messages of any of the 40 million users worldwide. Hackers Unite, a group of seven programmers based in Sweden, admitted they were responsible for the breach of Microsoft's Hotmail security system.

September 1999

3   Two French judges ruled that the car crash that killed Diana, Princess of Wales was caused solely by her drunken driver and not the photographers that pursued her.

5   Anti-independence militiamen rampaged through Dili, the capital of East Timor, killing 20 and forcing thousands to become refugees.

7   Joe Smith, 65, a former lifeguard, became the oldest Briton to swim the English Channel.

8   The Archbishop of Canterbury, Dr George Carey, endorsed the use of the morning-after pill as part of the way to deal with the rise in teenage pregnancies.

10   Melita Norwood, 87, was unmasked by Christopher Andrew, a Cambridge professor, as a KGB spy for over 40 years.

12   The Home Office announced that no charges would be brought against Melita Norwood as no useful purpose would be served by prosecuting her.

15   Veterans of the Battle of Britain gathered at the RAF Museum in Hendon, North London, to celebrate the launch of a book by Kenneth Flynn detailing the lives of The Few.

17   Robin Pearson, a University of Hull lecturer, was named by the BBC as a former agent for the East German Stasi security police.

19   A Tesco store in Kensington, London, opened the first 'cyberzone' site whereby goods not available in the shop can be ordered via the Internet.

20   The Home Secretary Jack Straw announced that mental patients will be able to vote in future general elections.

22   Singer, Diana Ross was arrested at Heathrow Airport for allegedly assaulting a female security guard. She was later released after being cautioned.

23   Marco Pierre White, the youngest recipient of three Michelin stars, retired from cooking at 37 to expand his restaurant empire, which includes Mirabelle and Quo Vadis in London.

24   Rebecca Edmonds, a trainee barrister, won a High Court ruling that pupils over the age of 26 are 'workers' and are entitled to a minimum wage of up to £8,000 per annum.

26   Morecambe and Wise were named as the finest double act of the century at a British Comedy Society tribute and had a blue plaque unveiled in the Hall of Fame at Pinewood studios.

27   Mark Dixon, 39, Chief Executive of Regus Business Centres, was named Entrepreneur of the Year.

28   Larry Harrison apologised to the bereaved families and the 147 injured in the Southall rail crash; the train driver admitted he was packing a bag moments before the crash.

October 1999

1   Manjit Basuta, a British childminder, was sentenced to 25 years in jail in Los Angeles for causing the death of a 13-month old boy by shaking him vigorously.

CURRENT AFFAIRS

Jeffrey Archer became the Tory candidate for London mayor after beating his rival Steven Norris by a clear majority.

3   It was announced that Liz Varlow, a viola player with the London Symphony Orchestra, who has been profoundly deaf since she was 16, will receive the Frink Award for overcoming her disability.

4   Scottish Nationalists and historians accused the Royal Mail of snubbing the Scottish hero Robert the Bruce by featuring him on second-class stamps; Oliver Cromwell being preferred on first-class.

5   A train crash near Paddington between a Great Western express and a commuter train to Great Bedwyn was thought to have been caused by a missed red signal at Ladbroke Grove.

6   On the eve of National Poetry Day, Jo Shapcott won Britain's biggest poetry award, the £10,000 Forward Prize, for her third collection, *My Life Asleep.*

7   A previously unknown manuscript by Beethoven, lasting 52 seconds and containing 23 bars, was discovered in the collection of the Molesworth St Aubyn family at Pencarrow in Cornwall.

8   Rail safety inspectors ordered Railtrack to make immediate improvements to 22 signals around the country which train drivers have repeatedly passed at red.

10   The Millennium Wheel, known as the London Eye, was raised to the near vertical of its 450 feet full height.

11   Tony Blair's Cabinet reshuffle included the return of Peter Mandelson into the Government as replacement for Mo Mowlam who became Minister to the Cabinet Office replacing Dr Jack Cunningham. Lord Robertson, who leaves the Cabinet to become Nato secretary-general, was replaced as Defence Secretary by Geoffrey Hoon. Frank Dobson joined the race to become London's mayor and was replaced as Health Secretary by Alan Milburn who in turn was replaced as Chief Secretary to the Treasury by Employment minister Andrew Smith. Non-Cabinet appointments were Tessa Jowell as New Deal Minister, Yvette Cooper as Public Health Minister, Keith Vaz as Minister for Europe and Jane Kennedy as Parliamentary Under Secretary in the Lord Chancellor's Department.

12   The Government of Nawaz Sharif of Pakistan was overthrown in a military coup following the dismissal of his Army Chief of Staff, General Pervaiz Musharraf.

15   Winston Silcott, who was convicted but later cleared of the murder of PC Blakelock during the Broadwater Farm riot, in Tottenham, northeast London, 14 years ago, accepted a £50,000 out-of-court settlement from Scotland Yard after he sued for false imprisonment and malicious prosecution.

17   The entire body of a woolly mammoth was exhumed from the ice of Siberia, 20,000 years after it perished.

18   President Jiang Zemin arrived in Britain; the first visit by a Chinese head of state.

19   Lord's cricket ground was named as building of the year by the Royal Institute of British Architects.

20   Elizabeth Dole dropped out of the race to be American President because of lack of funds.

21   The Rear of the Year, a 23-year-old award, was won jointly by Denise van Outen and Robbie Williams.

22   Gordon Brown was accused of undermining the impartiality of the Civil Service after he promoted his closest political aide, Ed Balls, to the post of chief economic adviser to the Treasury.

24   Tracey Emin's Turner Prize final entry 'My Bed', consisting of an unmade bed strewn with debris, was jumped on by two Chinese performance artists who proceeded to have a pillow fight until security guards at the Tate apprehended them.

26   The House of Lords voted 221 to 81 to back the Government's plans to expel hereditary peers from Parliament. Richard Bingham, 7th Earl of Lucan, missing since the murder of his family's nanny in 1974, was officially declared dead.

27   Vazgen Sarkisyan, the Armenian Prime Minister, was assassinated in the Armenian parliament building.

28   The flesh-coloured evening dress worn by Marilyn Monroe when she sang 'Happy Birthday' to John F Kennedy was sold at auction for $1.5 million.

31   All 217 passengers and crew of an Egypt Air Boeing 767 were killed when the plane crashed into the sea 60 miles off the coast of Massachusetts, USA.

November 1999

1   Tim Gilbert and Martin Rutty flew into the record books with a 39-day helicopter trip from England to Australia.

4   The Queen presented the first of a newly created medal for members of the reserves; the Queen's Volunteer Reserves Medal will be awarded for 'exemplary meritorious service'.

5   Lord Montague of Oxford, 67, collapsed and died in the House of Lords as the names of the 75 surviving life peers were read out.
     The film *Notting Hill* became the highest grossing British film of all time beating the previous record of *The Full Monty.*

7   The Australian people voted to 're-elect' the Queen as their Head of State.

8   The Queen started a two-day state visit to Ghana before departing for South Africa to open a Commonwealth summit.

9   Chancellor Gordon Brown's mini-budget included free television licences for the over 75s and an annual £100 winter fuel payment for all pensioners.

10   Drama teacher Renate Williams, 32, was cleared of seducing a 15-year-old pupil on a school trip to Wales.

11   The 17-year-old American pop sensation, Britney Spears, won four awards at the MTV Europe Music Awards.

12   The pop star Gary Glitter was jailed for four months after admitting amassing a 'library' of child pornography downloaded on to his computer from the Internet.

14   Astronomers in America announced the sighting of a new planet outside our solar system in the constellation Pegasus.

15   President Kuchma of the Ukraine was elected for a second five-year term of office.

16   Johnny Morris, the popular host of BBC's Animal Magic, cut his family and animal charities out of his will; he left his house to close friend and fellow presenter Terry Nutkins.

17   A statue of Sir Winston Churchill, who is regarded by many Czechs as a symbol of freedom, was unveiled in Prague by Baroness Thatcher.

20   Jeffrey Archer resigned as the Tory candidate to be Mayor of London amid allegations that he asked his friend, Ted Francis, to lie for him in a legal matter.
21   The World Health Organisation announced the influx of fruit-flavoured cigarettes into the UK; 'Bidies' are made in India and are aimed at the teenage market.
22   William Hague withdrew the Conservative whip in the House of Lords from Jeffrey Archer, to effectively end his political career.
23   The Queen awarded the George Cross to the Royal Ulster Constabulary for 30 years of fighting terrorism.
24   The advance of DNA techniques led to the conviction of John Taft, who was found guilty and jailed for life for the 'Beauty in the Bath' murder of Cynthia Bolshaw in 1983.
28   James Sutton, 13, became the youngest father of twins in Britain when his girlfriend Sarah Drinkwater gave birth to two girls, Leah and Louise.
29   Martin McGuinness, a former IRA commander, was appointed Minister for Education in the Northern Ireland government.
30   The 7th Earl of Clanwilliam, expelled from the House of Lords under the hereditary peer reform vote, still attended debates because of the little-known right of Irish peers to sit on the steps of the throne and follow proceedings in the chamber.

December 1999
1   The Queen attended the opening ceremony of the refurbished Royal Opera House, Covent Garden; the £214 million renovation has taken three years to complete.
2   The Eire government dropped its territorial claim to Northern Ireland in a move that British prime minister Tony Blair called 'the hand of history'.
3   A High Court judge refused an injunction brought by fashion chain 'French Connection' for copyright infringement against a website calling itself 'fcuk'.
5   Yukta Mookhey, 20, a zoology graduate from Bombay, beat 93 rivals to become Miss World at Olympia, London.
6   A teacher, Michael Turnbull, was cleared of assaulting a pupil by clipping her around the head with a schoolbook.
8   France refused to lift a ban on British beef despite a directive from the European Commission to ease the 1996 embargo.
9   The Church of Scientology was barred from charitable status after the Charity Commission ruled that it failed to promote the 'moral and spiritual welfare' of the community.
10   President Fernando de la Rua of Argentina was sworn into office.
12   It was announced that the ban on homosexuals serving in the armed forces will be lifted next month.
13   Modern Croatia's founding President, Franjo Tudjman, was laid to rest in Zagreb although Suleyman Demirel, the Turkish President, was the only world statesman present.
14   Paul McCartney returned to the Cavern Club in Liverpool where he performed for the first time in 36 years.
15   Charles Schulz announced his retirement from drawing his 'Peanuts' comic strip; the final strip will run on January 4th 2000.
16   The European Court of Justice ruled that men as well as women would receive the £100 winter fuel payment, at aged 60.
17   Clare Barwick, 35, became Britain's first-ever quiz show millionaire, on the Virgin Radio Breakfast Show.
19   The former Portuguese enclave of Macau was officially handed over to China after 442 years of colonial rule.
20   The Solicitor-General reiterated that Melita Norwood, code-named 'Hola', would not be prosecuted although the self-styled 'Bolshevik of Bexleyheath' admitted she had no regrets about betraying the nation's nuclear secrets as a Soviet spy.
      Rabbi Shmuley Boteach won the Preacher of the Year award.
21   Former Tory minister, Neil Hamilton, lost his five-year crusade to clear his name of the 'cash for questions' allegations.
      The most popular names in Britain for 1999 were Jack and Chloe according to the Office for National Statistics.
22   President Bandaranaike Kumaratunga of Sri Lanka was re-elected after being injured in a recent suicide bomber attack.
23   President Bouteflika of Algeria, named Senator Ahmed Benbitour as his new Prime Minister.
24   Ian Woodley became Britain's first-ever television quiz millionaire on *TFI Friday*.
26   Despite torrential rain the meteorological office declared it a white Christmas and bookies will pay out at odds of 50–1.
27   The last No 1 hit of the millennium in Britain was 'I have a dream' by Westlife.
29   Scientific researchers claimed that smoking a cigarette will take 11 minutes off a person's life expectancy.
30   Former Beatle George Harrison was stabbed in the chest by an intruder, Michael Abram, at his Henley-on-Thames home.
31   The last New Year's Honours List of the millennium included knighthoods for Henry Cooper, Stirling Moss, Sean Connery, Richard Branson and Norman Wisdom. Elizabeth Taylor, Shirley Bassey and Julie Andrews became Dames.
      Boris Yeltsin resigned as Russian President and was replaced by Vladimir Putin, 47.

CURRENT AFFAIRS

Daily Record 2000

January 2000
3   Opera singer Luciano Pavarotti agreed to pay the Italian authorities £1.6 million after losing his appeal against tax evasion.
4   Pop group Oasis announced the setting up of their own record company, Big Brother, following their split with Alan McGee, the founder of Creation records.
5   The bestselling British book of 1999 by volume sold was *Harry Potter and the Philosopher's Stone* and by value was *The Guinness World Records 2000*.
6   The longest place name in Britain was given a special allowance to exceed the maximum 26 letters to become the longest Internet site address. The full address is
     www.llanfairpwllgwyngyllgogerychwyrndrobwilliantysiliogogogoch.wales.com
7   John Lennon's childhood home in Mendip Avenue, Liverpool, was honoured with an English Heritage blue plaque.
9   Lord Lloyd-Webber bought the Stoll Moss theatre company in an £87.5 million deal to increase the theatres owned by the Really Useful Group from three to thirteen.
10   America Online, one of the world's largest Internet companies, merged with the media group Time Warner.
11   Comic character Ali G, aka Sacha Baron Cohen, was criticised by black comics Curtis Walker and Felix Dexter for racism.
12   Teenage diva Charlotte Church controversially ended her association with her manager Jonathan Shalit.
13   Presenter and disc jockey Chris Evans sold his 51 per cent share of the Ginger Media Group to the Scottish Media Group.
16   James Boyle, the Controller of Radio 4, announced his retirement from the BBC.
17   Hugo Williams won the TS Eliot Prize for Poetry for his autobiographical collection of poems *Billy's Rain*.
19   Bones found in southern Patagonia were thought to be from the largest dinosaur ever recorded. The herbivore, which lived during the Cretaceous period 105 million years ago, appeared to have been between 157ft and 167ft long.
21   Hasbro, the makers of the table top football game Subbuteo, announced that it could no longer compete with computer games and will not be made in the future.
23   Al Gore, the US Vice-President, and George W Bush, his Republican presidential rival, spent the day campaigning in Iowa before the first important vote of the 2000 election. Mr Gore has a 37-point lead over fellow Democrat Bill Bradley and Mr Bush leads his Republican challenger Steve Forbes by 20 points.
27   Meg Matthews, the wife of pop star Noel Gallagher, gave birth to a 7lb 2oz baby-girl, Anais, named after Ms Matthew's favourite author Anais Nin.
28   A man wielding a samurai sword killed an MP's assistant who was trying to defend Nigel Jones, the Liberal Democrat Member for Cheltenham, during a surgery. The man was named as Robert Ashman.
30   Peter Kilfoyle resigned his position as Defence Minister.
31   The Greater Manchester GP Harold Shipman was convicted of murdering 15 elderly woman patients although police believe the final tally may be considerably more.

February 2000
1   In a Shadow Cabinet reshuffle Michael Portillo replaced Francis Maude as Shadow Chancellor. Maude replaced John Maples as Shadow Foreign Secretary and former Asda chief Archie Norman replaced John Redwood in the Environment.
     The London Eye carried its first fare-paying passengers although only 10 of its 32 capsules were operational.
4   Within hours of the formation of the new Austrian Government, Jörg Haider threatened to bring the European Union to a standstill by wielding the country's veto at every chance.
8   The Prince of Wales cancelled a trip to open a trade show in Austria on advice from the Foreign Office in protest against the new coalition government which includes Jörg Haider's ultra-right Freedom Party.
     Lynne Brindley was named as the replacement for Brian Lang as chief executive of the British Library from July 1st.
9   Alun Michael, the First Secretary of Wales, resigned shortly before being defeated in a vote of no confidence. Natwest, once Britain's biggest bank, was taken over by the Royal Bank of Scotland.
10   Cyclist Bruce Bursford, who set a world record of 207.9mph on a rolling treadmill in 1995, was killed in a cycling accident near his home town of Dereham, Norfolk.
11   Rhodri Morgan was confirmed as the Labour party's choice as First Secretary of Wales.
12   Episodes of *The Cook Report* were exposed by *News of the World* reporters.
13   The Chechen capital of Grozny lay in ruins as the constant Russian bombing made the city uninhabitable.
16   Queen Margrethe of Denmark met her British counterpart at Windsor at the beginning of her three-day state visit to Britain.
17   Charles Bronson, the category A prisoner who has spent most of the last 25 years in solitary confinement, was given a further life sentence for taking a teacher hostage during a siege.
18   At the Laurence Olivier Awards Janie Dee was named best actress for her role as a sexy robot in Alan Ayckbourn's *Comic Potential*. Henry Goodman won best actor and Peter OToole a special award for oustanding achievements.
20   Ken Livingstone (46.0%) was defeated by Frank Dobson (49.6%) in the race to become the official Labour

candidate for the position of London Mayor. Glenda Jackson's votes (4.4%) were redistributed to give Dobson (51.53%) a 3 per cent victory.

24   Conservative MP Michael Colvin and his wife Nichola were killed during a blaze at their country home of Tangley House, near Andover, Hampshire.

25   It was announced that all 300,000 British Armed Forces SA80 standard rifle issues are to be recalled for modifications.

26   It was reported that the Queen has cut off Prince Edward's £141,000-a-year allowance because he does so little royal work.

March 2000

1   Helen Boaden, a former Woman's Hour presenter, was appointed Controller of Radio 4 as replacement for James Boyle.

2   General Augusto Pinochet left Britain bound for Santiago following medical opinion that he was not fit to stand trial.

3   Jimmy Wray, the MP for Glasgow Bailieston, was awarded £60,000 in damages against Associated Newspapers for an article in *The Mail on Sunday* suggesting he was a wife-beater and loud-mouthed control freak.

4   Andrew Motion, the Poet Laureate, published a poem on bullying. 'The Game' was commissioned by the children's charity Child Line.

5   Tony Blair and his wife Cherie sought an injunction against their former nanny Rosalind Mark for breach of a confidentiality agreement following her revelations in *The Mail on Sunday*.
The world's first cloned pigs were produced by PPL Therapeutics, the Edinburgh company responsible for Dolly the sheep. The five female piglets were named Alexis, Carrel, Christa, Dotcom and Millie.

6   Ken Livingstone was suspended from the Labour Party and announced his intention of running for London Mayor as an independent candidate.

8   Stephen King announced he would be releasing his latest book *Riding the Bullet* over the Internet.

9   Former Conservative politician Edwina Currie was awarded £30,000 damages plus costs from *The Express* for an article branding her 'the vilest lady in Britain'.

10   World Book Day was celebrated with a national poll to find Britain's favourite author. Roald Dahl came out top closely followed by JK Rowling.

15   Sir Paul McCartney confirmed that he and former model Heather Mills were an 'item'.

20   The Pope began his historic visit to the Holy Land by standing on Mount Nebo in Jordan, the peak from where Moses is said to have seen the Promised Land.

21   Gordon Brown's Budget speech included marginal income tax benefits and increased Winter Fuel Payments for the elderly. The three tax bands for year ending April 2001 are: Taxable Income £0–£1,520 @ 10%, £1,521–£28,400 @ 22%, over £28,400 @ 40%. A single person's tax allowance up to the age of 65 will rise to £4,385, and the married couple's allowance is abolished for the year ending April 2001.

23   The Tate Gallery in Millbank, Central London, was officially renamed Tate Britain and will specialise in British art of the past five centuries.

26   The pre-Oscars Golden Raspberry Foundation Awards (Razzies), which recognise the worst achievements in film, were held in Hollywood.

27   Actress Kathleen Turner received a standing ovation for her portrayal of Mrs Robinson at the Gielgud Theatre when she appeared nude in the bathroom scene.

29   Pete Goss and his six-man crew were forced to abort their round-the-world record attempt for the Jules Verne Trophy when their catamaran, officially named *Team Philips* by the Queen, foundered 27 miles off the Isles of Scilly.

31   Television presenter Sara Cox launched her Radio 1 Breakfast Show, as replacement for Zoe Ball.

April 2000

2   One of Germany's original Enigma coding machines was stolen from the Bletchley Park Museum.

3   Microsoft, the software company whose Windows programs run 95% of the world's personal computers, was found to have abused its monopoly to stifle competition. The US Federal Court verdict caused a $12 billion loss of Microsoft's stock value.

5   Marco Pierre White, chef and proprietor of the Mirabelle restaurant in Mayfair, was awarded £75,000 in a libel action against *The New York Times* and *International Herald Tribune*, that claimed he had a 'well-publicised bout with drugs and alcohol'.

6   Senior Church of England bishops at the House of Lords unveiled the Church's new prayer book, Common Worship, dubbed the 'little black book' by the Church Times.

7   Lord Archer of Weston-super-Mare was arrested in a South London police station for attempting to pervert the course of justice by asking a friend, Ted Francis, to lie for him before his 1987 libel trial.

9   British Academy of Film and Television Arts winners included Annette Bening and Kevin Spacey as Best Actress and Actor for *American Beauty*.

12   The first British police officers to go on duty wearing roller skates patrolled London's Hyde Park and Kensington Gardens.

14   Kenneth Noye, once dubbed Public Enemy Number One, was sentenced to life imprisonment for the murder of Stephen Cameron, 21, in a so-called road-rage attack.

16   Zimbabwe was on the brink of civil war after an entire white farming community of 50 families was driven from its land.

19   Tony Martin, a farmer who shot dead a teenage burglar, was sentenced to life imprisonment at Norwich Crown Court.

21   Fords announced that their Dagenham plant was to cease production from next year.

27   Michael Heseltine, the former Deputy Prime Minister, announced he would retire as an MP at the next election.

May 2000

2   Formula One racing driver David Coulthard survived the crash of a privately-owned Learjet, which killed the two pilots, at Lyons-Satolas airport in France.

4   A computer virus sent by e-mail created havoc throughout the world. The 'I Love You' bug appeared to come from a friend but if accessed wiped out important files.

5   Ahmet Necdet Sezer, the candidate of Bulent Ecevit, the Prime Minister, was elected as Turkish President.

8   Al Gore defeated Bill Bradley in the race for the American Democratic presidential nomination.

9   The Queen inaugurated London's newest bridge over the Thames. The 370 metres long Millennium Bridge, linking St Paul's Cathedral to the Tate Modern art gallery, was designed by Foster & Partners, Ove Arup & Partners and sculptor Sir Anthony Caro. It is the first new crossing in Central London since Tower Bridge was opened in 1894.
         British author Nicola Barker won the world's richest literary prize, the £75,000 International IMPAC Dublin Literary award, for her novel *Wide Open*.

11   The Queen opened the new Tate Modern art gallery on the site of the former Bankside power station.

16   Actresses Julie Andrews and Elizabeth Taylor were invested as Dame Commanders of the Most Excellent Order of the British Empire.

17   French actress Laetitia Casta was chosen to represent Marianne, the bare-breasted symbol of the French Republic, on their latest stamp issue.

19   Rudolph Giuliani, the Mayor of New York, bowed to health and personal problems and withdrew from the race for the US Senate, leaving Hillary Clinton as favourite to win the seat.

20   Prime Minister's wife Cherie Blair gave birth to a 6lb 12oz baby boy, Leo.

21   Icelandic pop singer Björk was voted best actress at the Cannes film festival for her performance in *Dancer in the Dark*.

22   The British Library launched its 'adopt a book' scheme whereby a donation of £15 upwards ensures the donor's name or message is recorded on a permanent bookplate.

23   Bob Ayling resigned as chairman of the New Millennium Experience Company.

25   Iceland, the food retailer, announced a near £1 billion merger with Booker, the cash-and-carry firm that sponsors the Booker literary prize.

26   Following Fiona Shaw's portrayal of Richard III and Mark Rylance's Cleopatra, Vanessa Redgrave made her debut as Prospero at Shakespeare's Globe.

27   Cellist Guy Johnston, 18, became the BBC Young Musician of the Year 2000 despite snapping the A string of his cello during his performance of Shostakovich's Cello Concerto No 1 at the Bridgewater Hall, Manchester.

28   Ezer Weizman announced he would be standing down as President of Israel on July 10th.

June 2000

1   Millionaire businessman Malcolm Horsman, 66, was jailed for life for suffocating his wife after she had accused him of being mean.

5   British actress Jennifer Ehle won the Tony Award for Best Actress defeating her mother Rosemary Harris who was nominated for the ninth time.

6   Commonwealth foreign ministers partially suspended Fiji's membership and warned the Solomon Islands that it faces similar action unless democracy is restored.

7   British Prime Minister Tony Blair was heckled, jeered and slow-handclapped during a speech to the Women's Institute.

11   Tens of thousands of thrill-seekers queued to walk across the new Millennium Bridge over the Thames amid reports of a swaying effect.

12   The Millennium Bridge was shut at 10pm due to the uncomfortable swaying effect experienced by pedestrians.

14   Conservative MP Julie Kirkbride, wife of Shadow Northern Ireland Secretary Andrew MacKay, awoke to find a knife-wielding burglar in her bedroom. The burglar fled when the pregnant MP let out some 'blood-curdling screams'.

15   A two-mile cortège of 800 motorcycles brought traffic on the A2 to a standstill behind the hearse of Ian 'Maz' Harris, a founding father of the British Hell's Angels.

16   Actor Michael Caine was awarded a knighthood in the Queen's Birthday Honours List.

19   58 illegal Chinese immigrants were found dead from suffocation in an articulated lorry container, by custom officials at Dover.

20   The Prince of Wales and Camilla Parker Bowles attended their first official function together when they opened the headquarters of the Prince's Foundation in Shoreditch.

22   A fire in the Palace Backpackers Hostel in Childers, Queensland, Australia, claimed the lives of six young British men and women.

23   The death toll in the Queensland hostel fire climbed to 15 as police began the hunt for a suspected arsonist.

26   Gerard Hemsworth won the Charles Wollaston Award for the most distinguished work in the Royal Academy's Summer Exhibition with his *Between Heaven and Hell* a simplistic painting of a rabbit.

28   Elian Gonzales, the Cuban shipwreck survivor who became the centre of an international custody tug-of-war, finally left his Washington refuge and flew home to Havana.
         Robert Long, 37, the prime suspect in the Australian hostel blaze, was shot in the arm and arrested after a five-day manhunt.

29   Theatre director Barrie Rutter won the richest arts prize in Britain, the £100,000 Creative Britons, for his adaptation of Shakespeare's plays for northern audiences.

30   David Copeland, the neo-nazi who planted devastating bombs in Soho, Brixton and Brick Lane in London, was given six life sentences at the Old Bailey.

July 2000

4   Tony Blair announced details of the Civil List which was set at £7.9 million in 1990 and will remain as such until 2010.

5   Actor Sean Connery received a knighthood at an investiture at the Palace of Holyrood in Edinburgh.

7   Actress Patsy Kensit announced she had separated from pop musician Liam Gallagher.

9   The annual Drumcree parade by Portadown Orangemen was blocked by protesters at Garvaghy Road. The route has been followed since 1807, until it was banned in 1998.

10   Israeli prime minister Ehud Barak narrowly retained power after scraping through a vote of no-confidence in the Knesset.

11   JK Rowling's fourth book about the trainee magician, *Harry Potter and the Goblet of Fire*, set a sales record of 372,775 on its first day of publication.

13   Boris Johnson, editor of *The Spectator*, was chosen to succeed Michael Heseltine as the parliamentary candidate for Henley-on-Thames when the MP stands down at the next election.

14   The First Night of the Proms included works by Aaron Copland to celebrate the centenary of his birth and JS Bach on the 250th anniversary of his death.

15   The British Apache, the army's new attack helicopters, were grounded from public demonstration flights due to technical problems.

17   The body of the missing eight-year-old Sarah Payne was found dumped in a field by the A29 at Pulborough, West Sussex.
      Alex Salmond announced he will stand down as leader of the Scottish National Party in September.

18   Poet Laureate Andrew Motion published a poem 'Picture This' for the 100th birthday of Queen Elizabeth the Queen Mother.

20   The world's largest maze was opened at Tulley's Farm, near Crawley, West Sussex. The castle-shaped maize maze has three miles of passage-ways.

21   A major fire broke out on a theme park ride and led to the evacuation of Thorpe Park in Surrey.
      The last Ford Escort rolled off the production line at Ford's Halewood plant thus ending its 32-year history.

25   At least 113 people were killed when an Air France Concorde crashed into a hotel two minutes after taking off from Charles de Gaulle Airport, Paris.

27   Sagle Bernstein who died aged 82 bequeathed £11 million to her local NHS hospital in Cromer, Norfolk.

28   Eighty-six convicted terrorists were released from the Maze prison in Northern Ireland under the provisions of the Good Friday agreement.
      Channel 4's *Big Brother* became the hit television show of the summer with an ever-increasing audience. Sada Walkington became the first inmate to be voted out of the house.
      Emma Noble, daughter-in-law of former prime minister John Major, gave birth to an 8lb 13oz baby boy, Harrison Major.

29   Actor Brad Pitt married *Friends* star Jennifer Aniston in a private ceremony in Los Angeles.

31   Jerry Hall, former wife of pop star Mick Jagger, made her debut as Mrs Robinson in *The Graduate* at the Gielgud Theatre.

August 2000

4   Queen Elizabeth the Queen Mother received a congratulatory message from her daughter at Clarence House before celebrating her 100th birthday at Buckingham Palace.
      Andrew Davidson became the second person to be voted out of the Channel 4 *Big Brother* house.

7   King Mswati III of Swaziland married his seventh wife,18-year-old Liphovela Senteni Masango.

8   Actress Catherine Zeta-Jones gave birth to a 7lb 7oz baby, Dylan. Actor Michael Douglas is the father.

9   A team of six British rowers set a world record for crossing the English Channel from Greve de Lecq, Jersey, to Poole, Dorset. The 91.5 mile journey was completed in under 15 hours.

10   British back-packer Kirsty Sara Jones was murdered in the northern Thai capital of Chiang Mai.

11   Pop star Madonna gave birth to a boy, Rocco, providing a brother for her daughter, Lourdes. British film director Guy Ritchie is the father.
      Caroline became the third person to be voted out of the Channel 4 *Big Brother* house.

13   Ten-year-old Tyla Green became the first child in Britain to contract tetanus for more than a decade.

15   The entire British Airways Concorde fleet was grounded following an investigation by the Civil Aviation Authority into their airworthiness.
      Iman, the 45-year-old Somalian supermodel, gave birth to a baby daughter, Alexandria Zahra Jones. David Bowie her rock star husband cut the umbilical cord.
      The Queen appointed Sir Richard Luce as Lord Chamberlain, the effective head of the royal household.

16   Official statistics indicated unemployment figures totalled 1.07 million, the lowest level since early 1980.

17   Producers of the Channel 4 programme *Big Brother* ejected Nick Bateman from the house for cheating. Claire Strutton, 25, was announced as his replacement.

18   Nichola, the Bolton textile artist, became the latest evacuee of the *Big Brother* house.

20   President Putin announced on state television the loss of the crew of the Russian nuclear submarine 'Kursk' after they had been entombed for eight days at the bottom of the Barents Sea, victims of a faulty hatch.

21   Warner Bros announced that Daniel Radcliffe, 11, would play the title role in the Chris Columbus film *Harry Potter and the Sorcerer's Stone*.

22   Oftel, the television watchdog, criticised America's Alta Vista for announcing a free Internet access service in the UK but not being able to fund the launch.

23   Chinese officials drowned a healthy baby in the village of Caidian, Hubei province, to uphold its one-child policy.

24   An estimated 51 million Americans watched Richard Hatch become the $1 million winner of their top-rated show *Survivor*

25   Thomas became the fifth evacuee of the *Big Brother* house.

27   Home Secretary Jack Straw announced that gangster Reggie Kray would be granted compassionate parole to end his days as a free man.
      Moscow's Ostankino Tower, at 1,780 feet, the tallest structure in Europe, was badly damaged by fire.
28   American stock markets began quoting prices in decimals rather than the long established fraction method.
30   French fishermen blockaded Mediterranean and Atlantic ports in a marine fuel price protest.
31   Two carriages collided on the world's tallest rollercoaster, the Pepsi Max Big One, injuring over 20 people at the Blackpool Pleasure Beach.

September 2000
1   Marjorie Evans, headmistress of a South Wales primary school, won her appeal against the suspended sentence she received for allegedly slapping an unruly pupil.
      Claire Strutton became the sixth person voted out of the *Big Brother* house.
3   The Metropolitan Police failed to prevent an illegal rave by more than 2,000 New Age travellers in Tolworth, Surrey.
4   Rafik Hariri, a billionaire building tycoon, was voted in as the new Lebanese Prime Minister.
5   Tony Blair flew out to New York to join more than 150 world leaders for the United Nations Millennium Summit.
6   Princess Beatrice, 12, began the first day at her new school, St George's, Ascot, Berkshire.
      Peter Houghton, 64, became the first person in Britain to have an artificial heart implanted permanently.
7   Nancy Reagan published a collection of love letters from her husband that revealed he referred to her as 'Mommie Poo Pants'.
      Protesters against the heavy government taxation on fuel, picketed oil depots causing many petrol stations to run dry.
8   Melanie Hill became the final evacuee from the Channel 4 *Big Brother* house when 3.3 million people voted her out.
10   Six British soldiers held hostage in the Sierra Leone jungle for 16 days were recovered unharmed.
11   British comedian Eddie Izzard won two Emmy variety awards in Los Angeles for writing and performing his one-man show Eddie Izzard: Dress to Kill
14   The week-long siege of the country's oil depots and refineries ended peacefully.
15   Craig Phillips won Channel 4's *Big Brother* programme when he pipped Anna Nolan to the £70,000 first prize
16   Actress Angelina Jolie began work as Lara Croft on the new *Tomb Raider* movie at Pinewood Studios.
18   The Liberal Democrats voted overwhelmingly to legalise 'gay marriages' at their annual conference in Bournemouth.
19   Former *Coronation Street* actress Jane Danson (Leanne Battersby) and television presenter Graham Norton were declared to have the rears of the year in a London awards ceremony.
20   Lord Melchett and 27 Greenpeace protesters who destroyed genetically modified maize crops in Norfolk were cleared of criminal charges at Norwich Crown Court.
      Two explosions rocked the MI6 headquarters in central London but no casualties were reported.
22   The Court of Appeal ruled that the operation to separate the Siamese twins known as Mary and Jodie should go ahead despite the inevitable death of Mary.
      Former gangland leader Reginald Kray, was discharged from a secure hospital and transported to a riverside hotel in Norwich.
23   The funeral of Paula Yates ended with her rendition of 'These Boots Are Made for Walking' as she was laid to rest in her favourite white mink bikini.
24   Pop star Liam Gallagher and actress Patsy Kensit were granted a divorce in the High Court in London.
26   A Greek ferry, the *Express Samina*, sank off the island of Paros killing at least 72 people. Reports confirm that staff were watching a Panathinaikos football match against SV Hamburg during the crisis.
      The premiere of Andrew Lloyd Webbers and Ben Elton's new musical *The Beautiful Game* at the Cambridge Theatre was attended by John Major and Albert Reynolds.
28   Denmark voted 53 per cent to 47 per cent against the introduction of the euro.
29   Prince William gave a press conference at Highgrove in which he criticised author Patrick Jephson for remarks made about his mother in a recent biography.

October 2000
1   Former gangland boss Reginald Kray, died of bladder cancer in the Beefeater Town House Hotel, Thorpe St Andrew, Norwich.
2   A British team of aviation enthusiasts broke the world altitude record for an amateur rocket flight in the Nevada desert. The Phoebos Exo-Atmospheric Vehicle flew to a height of almost seven miles.
4   Dame Helena Shovelton, the chairman of the Lottery Commission, resigned following the controversy over the initial exclusion of Camelot from negotiations from the next seven-year licence. She was replaced by Ms Harriet Spicer.
      Ann Widdecombe's plan to impose £100 fixed penalty fines on soft drug users was criticised by party leader William Hague.
5   The Yugoslav presidential election result was annulled by the country's supreme court and tens of thousands of protesters demonstrated in Belgrade. Slobodan Milosevic was eventually forced to hand over power to Vojislav Kostunica who polled 52 per cent of the vote in last month's elections.
      On National Poetry Day, the same poem, *Word*, by Patience Agbabi, was read out at many school assemblies at 9.10am.
      The world's largest liner, the 142,000-tonne *Explorer of the Seas*, sailed into Southampton to prepare for her maiden cruise.

7   Seven members of the shadow Cabinet admitted they had taken narcotics. Francis Maude, Archie Norman, Bernard Jenkin, Lord Strathclyde, Peter Ainsworth, Oliver Letwin and David Willetts all smoked cannabis as students and Peter Ainsworth admitted to trying harder drugs.

9   Tim Yeo, the Shadow Agriculture Minister, became the eighth member of the shadow Cabinet to admit he once smoked pot.

11   The First Minister of Scotland, Donald Dewar, died of a brain haemorrhage following a fall on the pavement outside his official residence, Bute House in Edinburgh.

13   It was reported that the parents of Stephen Lawrence settled for a £320,000 out-of-court settlement in compensation for the bungled police inquiry into their son's murder seven years ago.

15   Carl Gill, 27, became the first person in Great Britain to be cautioned for being drunk in charge of a fold-up micro-scooter.

17   A broken rail caused a train crash in Hatfield in which four died and 35 were injured.
        Broadcaster Jeremy Paxman received a parcel from a 'P Smith', the contents being the stolen Enigma coding machine.

18   Pop star George Michael was announced as the person who paid £1.45 million for John Lennon's piano, on which he composed the pop-classic *Imagine*.

19   London Mayor Ken Livingstone told the Greater London Authority that statues of Sir Henry Havelock and Sir Charles Napier should be removed from Trafalgar Square and replaced by contemporary heroes.

22   Lorde Holme of Cheltenham, the Liberal Democrat peer, resigned as chairman of the Broadcasting Standards Commission following the disclosure of an affair with a woman 36 years his junior.

23   Michael Martin, MP for Glasgow Springburn, was elected as the new Speaker of the House of Commons.

24   Sir Edward Heath, the former Conservative Prime Minister, announced his retirement from the Commons at the next election. Billionaire Tory party treasurer Michael Ashcroft took his seat in the House of Lords as Lord Ashcroft of Chichester.

25   American businessman Gary Tanaka donated £27 million to Imperial College, London. The donation was the second highest to a British educational institution behind Bill Gates's donation of £150 million to Cambridge University.

26   Following the Hatfield crash, almost 2000 cracked rails were exposed and speed restrictions were implemented indefinetely.

27   The Most Reverend John Ward, Roman Catholic Archbishop of Wales, was under pressure to resign following the second priest in his diocese to be convicted of paedophilia.

31   A Singapore Airlines 747 jumbo jet crashed on take-off from Chiang Kai Shek Airport, Taipei, killing up to 95 people on board.

November 2000

1   Michael Portillo and Francis Maude resigned from the Thatcherite No Turning Back group in protest over leaks which they regard as 'a fundamental breach of trust'.

2   Vladimir Kramnik became the fourteenth world chess champion when he drew the penultimate game with Garry Kasparov.
        Chris Woodhead, the Chief Inspector of Schools, resigned his position to become a columnist with the *Daily Telegraph*.

3   The fear of further action by fuel protesters caused panic buying throughout Britain and forced many filling stations to close.

6   The Siamese twins known as Jodie and Mary were separated at St Mary's hospital in Manchester. As expected Mary died during the operation.

7   The world's biggest armed robbery was foiled by police when a gang smashed their way into the Millennium Dome aboard a JCB bulldozer. The police had known of the robbery for months and Operation Magician was instigated to prevent the theft of 12 diamonds worth £350 million.
        Hillary Clinton defeated the Republican candidate Rick Lazio to gain her seat in the United States Senate.

8   Gordon Brown, the Chancellor of the Exchequer, announced in his mini-budget that state pensions would rise by £5 for a single person and £8 for a married couple.

9   The American Presidential Election was plunged into uncertainty following the Democratic candidate Al Gore calling for a second recount in Florida.

11   A fire which swept through a ski-train in a tunnel in the Austrian Alps claimed the lives of at least 155 people including the world freestyle skiing champion Sandra Schmitt of Germany.

14   The Church of England's new service book, Common Worship, received the royal seal of approval when the Queen opened the first session of the newly elected General Synod in Westminster.

15   Michael Abram, 34, who repeatedly stabbed former Beatle George Harrison at his mansion last December, was ordered to be held indefinitely in a secure psychiatric hospital.

16   A report in the New Scientist disclosed that the bowhead whale can live to an age in excess of 200-years-old, making it by far the oldest mammal and possibly the longest-lived creature in the world.

17   Gerald Corbett, the chief executive of Railtrack, resigned with an estimated £1 million payoff.

18   Actor Michael Douglas married actress Catherine Zeta-Jones at the New York Plaza Hotel. The couple signed a £1 million picture deal with *OK!* magazine.

19   The Press Complaints Commission ruled that *OK!* magazine was guilty of harassing Prince William by photographing him during his visit to Chile.

20   Judith Keppel, a distant cousin of Camilla Parker Bowles, became the first contestant to win £1 million on the 122nd episode of *Who Wants To Be A Millionaire*.
        Tyneside's Millennium footbridge was successfully installed by the Asian Hercules II, one of the world's

CURRENT AFFAIRS

largest floating cranes. The design of the £22 million structure allows it to pivot along its axis to enable large vessels to reach the upper river. The bridge is nicknamed 'The Blinking Eye'.

21   The Oxford Street Christmas lights were officially switched on by singer Charlotte Church.

27   The Netherlands became the first country to legalise euthanasia when its parliament voted 104–40 in favour of doctors immunity from prosecution for mercy killings.

28   German-born art photographer Wolfgang Tillmans won the Turner Prize for a set of 57 photo images ranging from flowers in a jam jar to naked body parts.

30   At the Unesco meeting in Cairns, Australia, the World Heritage Committee added the Blaenavon Industrial Centre to its list of 691 World Heritage sites.

December 2000

3   A science conference in Argentina announced that the hole in the ozone layer which is currently 11 million square miles, will close almost completely within 50 years.

6   Colonel Margaret Hay won the Preacher of the Year award at Walsall Central Hall Methodist Church.

8   Television soap opera *Coronation Street* celebrated its 40th anniversary with a live episode with cameo performances from Prince Charles and rock singer Noddy Holder.

9   Claire Swire, the author of a salacious e-mail sent to her boyfriend Bradley Chait, became hot property when Mr Chait forwarded the mail to several friends who did likewise, and the sexually explicit love letter was ultimately read globally.

12   Vauxhall announced the end of car production at its Luton plant with the possible loss of 6,000 jobs.

13   Al Gore finally conceded defeat to George W Bush in the US Presidential Election race.

14   The 73-year-old popular music magazine *Melody Maker* was merged into its 48-year-old rival *New Musical Express*.

15   Television presenter Zoe Ball gave birth to a baby boy at the Portland Hospital. Ms Ball and husband Norman Cook, alias Fat Boy Slim, named the baby, Woody.

18   It was announced that Wolverhampton, Brighton and Hove, and Inverness would be the three new Millennium Cities.

19   Camelot held on to their franchise to run the National Lottery for the next seven years despite the strong challenge of Sir Richard Branson's People's Lottery.

22   Pop singer and actress Madonna married film director Guy Ritchie at Skibo Castle, near Dornoch in Sutherland. Their son Rocco was baptised there yesterday.

25   The coveted Christmas No 1 chart-topper was 'Can we fix it' by Bob the Builder, the children's television character voiced by Neil Morrissey. In the video that accompanies the song the 'can we fix it' refrain is answered by a resounding 'Yes we can' as Bob beavers away accompanied by his friends Lofty the Crane, Scoop the Digger, Muck the Bulldozer and Pilchard the Cat.

27   Michael McDermott, 42, appeared in court in Wakefield, a suburb of Boston, Massachusetts, accused of killing seven co-workers at Edgewater Technology, an Internet consulting firm.

28   A 36-year-old Australian, Brett De La Mare, was arrested for landing a motor-assisted paraglider at Buckingham Palace.
    John Kufuor won the presidential election in Ghana.

29   A deranged passenger aboard British Airways 747–400 flight 2069 from Gatwick to Nairobi caused the plane to drop 10,000 feet during a struggle with the pilot,Captain William Hagan. All 379 passengers, which included pop star Bryan Ferry and Jemima Khan, escaped shaken but otherwise uninjured.
    In the New Year's Honours List there were knighthoods for actor Tom Courtenay, astronomer Patrick Moore and an honorary knighthood for comedian and writer Spike Milligan.

Obituaries 1999

January 1999

2   Sebastian Haffner, German author, born Dec 27th 1907

3   Duke of Rutland, Charles John Robert Manners, born May 28th 1919
    Jerry Quarry, heavyweight boxer, born May 15th 1945

4   Iron Eyes Cody, native American actor, born 1904

6   Michel Petrucciani, jazz pianist, born Dec 28th 1962

7   Prince Rostislav Romanov I I I, born Dec 3rd 1938

9   Jim Peters, marathon runner, born Oct 24th 1918

10   Sheila Hawkins, painter and illustrator, born Aug 20th 1905
    Marquess of Bristol, born Sept 15th 1954

11   Naomi Mitchison, author, born Nov 1st 1897
    Brian Moore, novelist, born Aug 25th 1921

14   Robin Bailey, actor, born Oct 5th 1919

15   Marion Ryan, singer, born in Leeds 1931
    Betty Box, film producer, born Sept 25th 1915

19   Jacques Lecoq, mime artist and theatre director, born Dec 15th 1921

20   John Golding, politician, born Mar 9th 1931

21   Charles Brown, rhythm and blues vocalist, born Sept 13th 1922
    Leslie French, actor (inspiration for Eric Gill's *Prospero and Ariel*), born Apr 23rd 1904
    Susan Strasberg, actress, born May 22nd 1938

23   Admiral of the Fleet, Lord Lewin, Chief of Defence Staff 1979–82, born Nov 19th 1920

25   Robert Shaw, conductor, born Apr 30th 1916

| 26 | Rt Revd Patrick Casey, Roman Catholic Bishop of Brentwood, born Nov 20th 1913 |
| 30 | Michael McGahey, former vice-president of the NUM, born May 29th 1925 |

February 1999
2	Paul Mellon, philanthropist and owner of Derby-winning racehorse 'Mill Reef', born June 11th 1907
	Robin Nedwell, actor, born Sept 27th 1946
3	Alfred Janes, artist, born June 30th 1911
5	Colin Purbrook, jazz pianist and double bass player, born Feb 26th 1936
	Herbert Kline, documentary film pioneer, born Mar 13th 1909
6	Lt-Col Randal Plunkett, 19th Lord Dunsany, born Aug 25th 1906
7	King Hussein of Jordan, born Nov 14th 1935
	Al Phillips, Former European and British Empire featherweight boxing champion, born Jan 25th 1920
8	Dame Iris Murdoch, novelist and philosopher, born July 15th 1919
9	Bryan Mosley, actor, born Aug 25th 1931
10	Joseph Rank, businessman, born Apr 24th 1918
11	Xiao Qian, writer, born Jan 27th 1910
15	John Ehrlichman, aide to President Nixon, born Mar 20th 1925
16	Petre Crowder, QC, politician, born July 18th 1919
17	Tom Carr, artist, born Sept 21st 1909
19	Lady Pansy Lamb, writer, born May 18th 1904
20	Sarah Kane, playwright, born in 1971
21	Father Walter Lini, prime minister of Vanuatu, born in 1942
23	Ruth Gipps, composer and conductor, born Feb 20th 1921
24	Derek Nimmo, actor, born Sept 19th 1932
25	King Opoku Ware I I of Ashanti, born Nov 30th 1919
26	Lord Dean of Beswick, politician, born in 1922
28	Christine Glanville (Nancy Fletcher), puppeteer, born Oct 24th 1924

March 1999
2	Dusty Springfield, pop singer, born Apr 16th 1939
5	Lord Denning, former Master of the Rolls, born Jan 23rd 1899
6	Dennis Viollet, Manchester United footballer, born Sept 20th 1933
	Sheikh Isa bin Sulman al-Khalifa, Emir of Bahrain, born June 3rd 1933
7	Stanley Kubrick, film-maker, born July 26th 1928
8	Joe DiMaggio, baseball player, born Nov 25th 1914
	Lowell Fulson, blues singer and guitarist, born Mar 31st 1921
9	Arnold Machin, sculptor and designer of the portrait of The Queen on postage stamps since 1967, born in 1911
10	Adrian Love, radio disc jockey, born Aug 3rd 1944
12	Yehudi Menuhin, violinist and conductor, born Apr 22nd 1916
	Bidu Sayao, Brazilian soprano, born May 11th 1902
13	Garson Kanin, film director and playwright, born Nov 24th 1912
14	Kirk Alyn, actor (first cinema 'Superman'), born Oct 8th 1910
15	Harry Callahan, photographer, born Oct 22nd 1912
17	Rod Hull, entertainer, born Aug 13th 1935
18	Sid Green, comedy scriptwriter, born Jan 24th 1928
20	Norman McCann, musician, impresario and collector, born Apr 24th 1920
21	Ernie Wise, comedian, born Nov 27th 1925
22	Lord Max Beloff, historian, born July 2nd 1913
23	Dorothy Brooking, children's-television producer, born Dec 7th 1916
24	Lord Henry Brandon of Oakbrook, Law Lord, born June 3rd 1920
25	Ryszard Bakst, pianist, born Apr 6th 1926
26	Edward North, 9th Earl of Guildford, born Sept 22nd 1933
29	Joe Williams, jazz singer, born Dec 12th 1918

April 1999
2	Andrew Gardner, newscaster, born Sept 25th 1932
3	Lionel Bart, composer, born Aug 1st 1930
4	Bob Peck, actor, born Aug 23rd 1945
6	Red Norvo, jazz musician, born Mar 31st 1908
8	Dickie Ritchie, tennis player, born Apr 22nd 1910
9	Mary Lutyens, writer, born July 31st 1908
	Bert Firman, dance-band leader, born Feb 3rd 1906
11	Frank Tuohy, writer, born May 2nd 1925
12	Lecil Travis Martin (Boxcar Willie), born Sept 1st 1931
13	Harvey Postlethwaite, grand prix car designer, born Mar 4th 1944
14	Anthony Newley, entertainer, born Sept 24th 1931
16	Skip Spence, singer and guitarist, born Apr 18th 1946
18	Michael Melford, sports journalist, born Nov 19th 1916
19	Dame Kathlen Raven, former Chief Nursing Officer of the United Kingdom, born Nov 9th 1910
20	Señor Wences, ventriloquist, born Apr 20th 1896
21	Buddy Rogers, film actor and bandleader, born Aug 13th 1904
	Tim Forster, racehorse trainer, born Feb 27th 1934

23	Henrietta Branford, children's author, born Jan 12th 1946
24	Arthur Boyd, artist, born July 24th 1920
25	Lord Killanin, former President of the International Olympic Committee, born July 30th 1914
26	Jill Dando, television presenter, born Nov 9th 1961
27	Al Hirt, trumpeter, born Nov 7th 1922
	Cyril Washbrook, Lancashire and England cricketer, born Dec 6th 1914
28	Sir Alf Ramsey, manager of the England football team 1963–74, born Jan 22nd 1920
	Rory Calhoun, actor, born Aug 8th 1922
	Arthur Schawlow, co-inventor of the laser (with Charles Townes), born May 5th 1921
29	Elspeth March, actress, born Mar 5th 1911

May 1999

2	Oliver Reed, actor, born Feb 13th 1938
3	Godfrey Evans, cricketer, born Aug 18th 1920
6	Ernest John (Johnny) Morris, broadcaster, born June 20th 1916
7	Rt Revd Joseph Gray, Roman Catholic Bishop of Shrewsbury, born Oct 20th 1919
8	Dirk Bogarde, actor, born Mar 28th 1921
9	Derek Fatchett, MP for Leeds Central, born Aug 22nd 1945
11	Birdy Sweeney, actor, born June 14th 1931
12	Saul Steinberg, artist, born June 15th 1914
13	Gene Sarazen, golfer, born Feb 27th 1902
15	Rt Revd Kenneth Riches, Bishop of Lincoln, born Sept 20th 1908
17	James Broughton, film-maker, born Nov 10th 1913
18	Elizabeth Robinson, athlete (first woman Olympic gold medallist in 1928), born Aug 23rd 1911
19	James Blades, percussionist, born Sept 9th 1901
21	Norman Rossington, actor, born Dec 24th 1928
23	Arthur Ellis, football referee, born July 8th 1914
	Gerald Palmer, car designer, born Jan 30th 1911
25	Freda Brilliant, sculptress, born Apr 7th 1904
27	Violet Webb, athlete, born Feb 3rd 1915
28	Joao Carlos De Oliveira, Brazilian athlete, born May 28th 1954
30	Terri Rogers, ventriloquist, born May 4th 1937

June 1999

1	Christopher Cockerell, inventor of the hovercraft, born June 4th 1910
3	Peter Brough, ventriloquist, born Feb 26th 1916
5	Mel Tormé, singer, born Sept 13th 1925
6	Anne Haddy, actress (Helen Daniels in *Neighbours*), born Oct 5th 1927
7	Hugh Astor, deputy chairman of *The Times* 1959–67, born Nov 20th 1920
8	Christina Foyle, bookseller, born Jan 30th 1911
11	DeForest Kelley, actor, born Jan 20th 1920
12	Professor Sydney Urry, engineer, born Jan 23rd 1925
14	Sir George Labouchere, former British Ambassador to Belgium and Spain, born Dec 2nd 1905
15	John Glashan, cartoonist and painter, born Dec 24th 1927
16	David (Screaming Lord) Sutch, founder of the Monster Raving Loony Party, born Nov 12th 1940
17	Cardinal Basil Hume, Archbishop of Westminster 1976–99, born Mar 2nd 1923
19	Henri d'Orleans, Comte de Paris, born July 5th 1908
23	Buster Merryfield, actor, born Nov 27th 1920
	Yvonne Kapp, author, born Apr 17th 1903
24	Jim Allen, playwright and scriptwriter, born Oct 7th 1926
25	Fred Feast, actor, born Oct 5th 1929
	Frank Tarloff, film director, born Feb 4th 1916
26	Harry Blacker, cartoonist and commercial artist, born May 1st 1910
27	George Papadopoulos, former dictator of Greece, born May 15th 1919
28	Sir John Woolf, film and television producer, born Mar 15th 1913

July 1999

1	Viscount Whitelaw, politician, born June 28th 1918
	Joshua Nkomo, Zimbabwean Politician, born June 7th 1917
	Sylvia Sidney (Sophia Kosow), actress, born Aug 8th 1910
	Guy Mitchell, singer, born Feb 22nd 1927
2	Mario Puzo, novelist, born Oct 15th 1920
3	Igor Belsky, dancer and choreographer, born Mar 28th 1925
4	Jack Watson, actor, born May 15th 1915
6	Joaquin Rodrigo, Spanish composer of Concierto de Aranjuez, born Nov 22nd 1901
7	ML Jaisimha, Indian Test cricketer, born Mar 3rd 1939
8	Pete Conrad, astronaut, born June 2nd 1930
9	Lord Howard de Walden and Seaford, racehorse owner and breeder, born Nov 27th 1912
11	Helen Forrest, jazz singer, born Apr 12th 1918
12	Bill Owen, actor, born Mar 14th 1914
14	Dick Richardson, former European heavyweight boxing champion, born June 1st 1934
	Gordon Fowler, former Chief Inspector of Prisons, born June 10th 1923

16	John F Kennedy Jr, lawyer and magazine proprietor, born Nov 25th 1960
17	Donal McCann, actor, born May 7th 1943
18	Reg Tweedie, National Hunt trainer, born July 6th 1911
19	A Stanley Tretick, photographer, born July 21st 1921
20	Katharine Church, artist, born July 4th 1910
22	Mary Kerridge, actress, born Apr 3rd 1914
23	King Hassan II of Morocco, born July 9th 1929
25	Philipa Gail, actress, born Aug 16th 1942
26	John Watkins, philosopher, born July 31st 1924
27	Harry 'Sweets' Edison, jazz trumpeter, born Oct 10th 1915
29	Werner Haftmann, art historian, born Apr 28th 1912
30	Olive Dodds, casting director, born Feb 1st 1912

August 1999

1	Nirad C Chaudhuri, author, born Nov 23rd 1897
2	Naomi Sim, actress and writer, born Nov 30th 1913
3	Richard Olney, writer on food and wine, born Apr 12th 1927
4	Victor Mature, actor, born Jan 29th 1913
	Carl Toms, theatrical designer, born May 29th 1927
5	Sir Leonard Crossland, Chairman of Ford 1968–72, born Mar 2nd 1914
7	Brian Connell, journalist, newscaster and author, born Apr 12th 1916
8	Clifford Hanley, writer, born Oct 28th 1922
9	Helen Rollason, television sports presenter, born Mar 11th 1956
10	Jennifer Paterson, broadcaster and cook, born Apr 3rd 1928
11	Don Mosey, cricket journalist and broadcaster, born Oct 4th 1924
12	David Graham, broadcaster, born Aug 16th 1911
	Joe Black, comedian, born May 6th 1918
13	Nathaniel Kleitman, sleep scientist, born Apr 26th 1895
14	Paddy Devlin, Northern Ireland politician, born Mar 8th 1925
15	Sir Hugh Casson, architect, born May 23rd 1910
16	Carlos Moreira de Castro, King of Samba, born Aug 2nd 1902
19	Lord Orr-Ewing, former MP and businessman, born Feb 10th 1912
21	Len Lowe, actor and comedian, born Dec 17th 1915
23	Norman Wexler, screenwriter, born Aug 6th 1926
26	Group Captain Bill Dixon, wartime bomber pilot, born July 29th 1920
27	Hellmut Feisenberger, bookseller, born Mar 14th 1909
28	Edie Atkins, cyclist, born Feb 2nd 1920
31	Marguerite Chapman, actress, born Mar 1st 1918

September 1999

1	Doreen Valiente, author and witch, born Jan 4th 1922
3	Paul Dessau, artist, born Feb 15th 1909
4	Lord Oram, Labour and Co-Operative MP for East Ham 1955–74, born Aug 13th 1913
5	Alan Clark, politician, born Apr 13th 1928
6	Ilse Wolf, singer and teacher, born June 7th 1921
8	Birgit Cullberg, choreographer, born Aug 3rd 1908
9	Chili Bouchier, actress (Britain's 'It' girl), born Sept 12th 1909
10	Alfredo Kraus, Spanish tenor, born Nov 24th 1927
11	Janet Adam Smith, literary editor, author and mountaineer, born Dec 9th 1905
13	Victoria Sladen, soprano, born May 24th 1910
14	Charles Crichton, film director, born Aug 6th 1910
15	The Right Rev William Westwood, Bishop of Peterborough 1984–95, born Dec 28th 1925
16	John Hadjipateras, shipowner, born Sept 11th 1926
17	Frankie Vaughan, singer, born Feb 3rd 1928
18	Leo Valiani, senator and founding father of the Italian Republic, born Feb 9th 1909
20	Raisa Gorbachev, wife of the former Soviet President, born Jan 5th 1932
21	Frank Gollins, architect, born May 14th 1910
22	Clive Jenkins, former gen sec of the Association of Scientific, Technical and Managerial Staffs, born May 2nd 1926
	George C Scott, actor, born Oct 18th 1927
28	Sir Nigel Broackes, chairman of Trafalgar House, 1969–92, born July 21st 1934
30	The Right Rev Thomas Holland, Roman Catholic Bishop of Salford, born June 11th 1908

October 1999

1	Lena Zavaroni, singer, born Nov 4th 1964
	Noël Johnson, actor and the first radio Dick Barton, born Dec 28th 1916
2	Georg Tintner, conductor, born May 22nd 1917
4	Emil Schumacher, artist, born Aug 29th 1912
	Bernard Buffet, artist, born July 10th 1928
7	Derek Guyler, actor, born Apr 29th 1914
	Richard Hough, author, born May 15th 1922
9	Milt Jackson, jazz musician, born Jan 1st 1923
10	John Hadfield, author and publisher, born June 16th 1907

13   Gertrude Shilling, famous for her hats at Royal Ascot, born Mar 3rd 1910
14   Julius Nyerere, President of Tanzania 1964–85, born Apr 13th 1922
      Josef Locke, singer and entertainer, born Mar 23rd 1912
17   Lord Grey of Naunton, former Governor of Northern Ireland, born Apr 15th 1910
19   Nathalie Sarraute, French author, born July 18th 1900
      Penelope Mortimer, novelist and biographer, born Sept 19th 1918
20   Jack Lynch, former Taoiseach of the Republic of Ireland, born Aug 15th 1917
21   John Bromwich, Australian tennis player, born Nov 14th 1918
22   Martin Donnelly, former New Zealand cricketer and England rugby player, born Oct 17th 1917
23   Bobby Willis, showbusiness manager and husband of Cilla Black, born Jan 25th 1942
      Andras Hegedus, former Prime Minister of Hungary, born Oct 31st 1922
24   Philip Sansom, artist and anarchist, born Sept 19th 1916
25   Payne Stewart, golfer, born Jan 30th 1957
27   John 'Budgie' Byrne, footballer, born May 13th 1939
29   Sir Robin Black, former Governor of Hong Kong and Singapore, born June 3rd 1906
31   Lord Jakobovits, Chief Rabbi of the United Hebrew Congregations of the British Commonwealth, born Feb 8th 1921

November 1999
2   Clifford Harker, organist, conductor and composer, born Feb 5th 1912
3   Ian Bannen, actor, born June 29th 1928
4   Malcolm Marshall, cricketer, born Apr 18th 1958
5   Lord Montague of Oxford, businessman, born Mar 10th 1932
6   George V Higgins, novelist, born Nov 13th 1939
7   Primo Nebiolo, President of the International Athletic Federation, born July 14th 1923
8   Lester Bowie, jazz trumpeter, born Oct 11th 1941
9   Sir Murray Fox, former Lord Mayor of London, born June 7th 1912
11   Sir Vivian Fuchs, polar explorer, born Feb 11th 1908
13   Donald Mills, singer, born Apr 29th 1915
      Lady Margaret Casson, architect, born Sept 26th 1913
14   Minna Keal, composer, born Mar 22nd 1909
15   Sir Harry Llewellyn, showjumper, born July 18th 1911
18   Horst P Horst, photographer, born Aug 14th 1906
20   Amintore Fanfani, six-times Prime Minister of Italy, born Feb 6th 1908
21   Quentin Crisp, author, born Dec 25th 1908
22   Ian Messiter, inventor of the radio panel game 'Just a Minute', born Apr 2nd 1920
25   Kathleen Farrell, novelist, born Aug 4th 1912
26   John Skelton, sculptor, born July 8th 1923
27   I-Roy, reggae singer and disc jockey, born in 1944
29   Sidney Patterson, cyclist, born Aug 14th 1927

December 1999
1   Angela Fox, author and mother of a theatrical dynasty, born June 17th 1912
3   Madeline Kahn, actress, born Sept 29th 1942
4   Sylvester Clarke, cricketer, born Dec 11th 1954
5   Alexander Baron, novelist and television writer, born Dec 4th 1917
7   Kenny Baker, jazz musician, born Mar 1st 1921
8   Sir Rupert Hart-Davis, publisher, born Aug 28th 1907
10   Franjo Tudjman, President of Croatia, born May 14th 1922
11   Christopher Wren, actor and choreographer, born July 3rd 1947
12   Joseph Heller, author, born May 1st 1923
13   Jill Craigie, documentary film director and wife of Michael Foot, born Mar 7th 1914
14   Gré Brouwenstijn, soprano, born Aug 26th 1915
16   George Elrick, musician and disc jockey, born Dec 29th 1903
17   Grover Washington Jr, jazz saxophonist and bandleader, born Dec 12th 1943
18   Robert Dougall, newsreader, born Nov 27th 1913
19   Desmond Llewelyn, actor (Q in the James Bond films), born Sept 12th 1914
20   Hank Snow, country singer, born May 9th 1914
23   Baroness White, former Labour government minister, born Nov 7th 1909
24   Maurice Couve de Murville, French prime minister 1968–9, born Jan 24th 1907
25   Peter Jeffrey, actor, born Apr 18th 1929
26   Prunella Clough, painter, born Nov 14th 1919
      Curtis Mayfield, singer and songwriter, born 1942
27   Eva Neurath, publisher, born Aug 22nd 1908
28   Clayton Moore, actor (famous for playing the Lone Ranger), born Sept 14th 1914
      Dame Josephine Barnes, first woman president of the BMA, born Aug 18th 1912
30   Sir John Lawrence, author, born May 27th 1907
      Eli Goren, violinist and founder of the Allegri String Quartet, born Jan 23rd 1923

Obituaries 2000

January 2000
1	Victor Serebriakoff, International President of Mensa, born Oct 17th 1912
2	Patrick O'Brian, novelist, born Richard Russ, Dec 12th 1914
3	June Brae, ballerina, born May 18th 1917
5	Holcombe Douglas 'Hopper' Read, cricketer, born Jan 28th 1910
9	Leonard Marchant, artist, born Oct 23rd 1929
10	Stephen Mitchell, theatre impresario, born Aug 31st 1907
11	Professor Hilde Behrend, economic psychologist, born Aug 13th 1917
16	Irving Rapper, film director, born Jan 16th 1904
17	Elisabeth Collins, artist, born Oct 31st 1904
18	Rex Willis, rugby player, born Oct 25th 1924
	Frankie Durr, jockey and trainer, born Nov 10th 1925
19	Hedy Lamarr, actress, born Nov 9th 1914
	Bettino Craxi, Italian Prime Minister, 1983–87, born Feb 24th 1934
22	EW Swanton, cricket writer and broadcaster, born Feb 11th 1907
23	Willie Hamilton, anti-royalist Labour politician, born June 26th 1917
	Kay Cavendish, entertainer, born Oct 1st 1908
26	Kathleen Hale, writer and illustrator of *Orlando the Marmalade Cat*, born May 24th 1898
	Donald Budge, tennis player, born June 13th 1915
27	Friedrich Gulda, pianist and composer, born May 16th 1930
28	Jean Metcalfe, broadcaster, born in 1923
	Lauris Edmond, poet, born Apr 2nd 1924
	Kenneth Waller, actor, born Nov 5th 1927
31	Gil Kane, comic book artist, born Apr 26th 1926

February 2000
1	Bill Holroyd, cartoonist, born Mar 21st 1919
2	Francis Stuart, novelist, poet and playwright, born Apr 29th 1902
4	Edgar Bowers, poet, born Mar 2nd 1924
5	Claude Autant-Lara, film-maker and politician, born Aug 5th 1901
6	Derroll Adams, folk singer, born Nov 27th 1925
7	VH Drummond, author, illustrator and artist, born July 30th 1911
	Doug Henning, illusionist, born in 1947
9	Bruce Bursford, cyclist and cycling designer, born Apr 29th 1958
	Beau Jack, world lightweight boxing champion, 1943 and 1944, born Apr 21st 1921
11	Roger Vadim, film director, born Jan 26th 1928
	Aldwyn Roberts, calypso singer as Lord Kitchener, born Apr 18th 1922
12	Charles Schulz, cartoonist, born Nov 26th 1922
16	Lila Kedrova, actress, born Oct 9th 1919
	Karsten Solheim, inventor of the Ping putter, born Sept 15th 1911
19	Josef Herman, artist, born Jan 3rd 1911
21	Lord Annan, writer and administrator, born Dec 25th 1916
	Constance Cummings-John, campaigner for African women's rights, born Jan 7th 1918
23	Sir Stanley Matthews, footballer, born Feb 1st 1915
	Ofra Haza, singer, born Nov 19th 1957
24	Michael Colvin, MP, born Sept 27th 1932
25	Michael Houseman, ballroom dancer, born Apr 9th 1930
26	Queen Giovanna of the Bulgarians, widow of King Boris, born Nov 13th 1907
	Roger Longrigg, author, born May 1st 1929
28	Kariel Gardosh, cartoonist, born Apr 15th 1921
29	James Bailey, proprietor of Drum magazine, born Oct 23rd 1919

March 2000
1	Betsie Verwoerd, widow of Hendrik Verwoerd, born May 17th 1901
5	Abe Yanofsky, the Commonwealth's first chess grandmaster, born Mar 26th 1925
6	Chris Balderstone, cricketer, footballer and umpire, born Nov 16th 1940
7	Charles Gray, actor, born Aug 29th 1928
9	Sir Francis Dashwood, premier Baronet of Great Britain, born Aug 7th 1925
10	Barbara Cooney, author and illustrator, born Aug 6th 1917
11	Will Roberts, painter, born Dec 21st 1907
12	Cardinal Ignatius Kung, Roman Catholic Bishop of Shanghai, born Aug 2nd 1901
13	Cab Kaye, jazz singer and pianist, born Sept 3rd 1921
15	Robert Welch, designer, born May 21st 1929
	Frederic Kelly, dancer and choreographer, brother of Gene Kelly, born June 29th 1916
16	Thomas Ferebee, American bombadier who dropped the atomic bomb on Hiroshima, born Nov 9th 1918
19	Fraser Kerr, actor, born Feb 25th 1931
20	Gerald Kingsland, journalist and castaway, born Mar 8th 1930
21	Rex Reid, dancer and choreographer, born Jan 14th 1921

22	Carlo Parola, footballer who invented the 'bicycle kick', born Sept 20th 1921
26	Dr Alex Comfort, physician, poet and novelist, born Feb 10th 1920
27	Ian Dury, singer, songwriter and actor, born May 12th 1942
28	Anthony Powell, novelist, born Dec 28th 1905
29	Anna Sokolow, dancer and choreographer, born Feb 9th 1910
30	Rudolf Kirchschlager, President of Austria, 1974–86, born Mar 20th 1915
31	Gisèle Freund, photographer, born Nov 19th 1908

April 2000

2	Margrethe Woxholt, actress as Greta Gynt, born Nov 15th 1916
	Leslie Bear, Editor of *Hansard*, 1954–72, born June 16th 1911
4	Marian Nowakowski, opera singer, born Aug 3rd 1912
5	Jeremy James, dancer and choreographer, born Aug 4th 1961
6	William Stobbs, illustrator, born June 27th 1914
	Habib Bourguiba, President of Tunisia, 1957–87, born Aug 3rd 1903
7	Meriel Forbes, actress, born Sept 13th 1913
	Heinz G Burt, singer and actor, born July 24th 1942
8	Bernie Grant, Labour MP for Tottenham since 1987, born Feb 17th 1944
	Claire Trevor, actress, born Mar 8th 1909
10	Peter Jones, actor and writer, born June 12th 1920
	Larry Linville, actor, born Sept 29th 1939
11	Andre Deutsch, publisher, born Nov 15th 1917
12	Ronald Lockley, writer and naturalist, born Nov 8th 1903
13	Inglis Gundry, composer, born May 8th 1905
14	Wilf Mannion, footballer, born May 16th 1918
	Phillip Katz, computer software pioneer (creator of the compression program PKZIP), born Nov 3rd 1962
15	Edward Gorey, writer, illustrator and theatrical designer, born Feb 22nd 1925
16	Henry Bird, artist, born July 15th 1909
19	Louis Applebaum, composer, born Apr 3rd 1918
24	Major Derek Allhusen, equestrian Olympic gold medallist, born Jan 9th 1914
25	Niels Bentzon, composer, born Aug 24th 1919
27	Clifford Forsythe, MP for Antrim South since 1983, born Aug 24th 1929
28	Penelope Fitzgerald, novelist, born Dec 17th 1916
29	Pham Van Dong, Prime Minister of North Vietnam, 1955–76 and Vietnamese Socialist Republic, 1976–86, born Mar 1st 1906
30	Poul Hartling, Prime Minister of Denmark, 1973–75, born Aug 14th 1914

May 2000

1	Steve Reeves, actor and bodybuilder, born Jan 21st 1926
4	Diana Ross, artist and storyteller, born July 8th 1910
5	Gino Bartali, cyclist who won the Tour de France on two occasions, born July 18th 1914
7	Douglas Fairbanks Jr, actor, born Dec 9th 1909
9	Barry MacSweeney, poet, born July 17th 1948
11	Mervyn Mills, author, born Feb 23rd 1906
14	Karl Shapiro, poet, born Nov 10th 1913
15	Geoff Goddard, songwriter ('Johnny Remember Me' and 'Just Like Eddie'), born Nov 17th 1937
16	Richard Dormer, fashion photographer, born Feb 12th 1913
17	The Right Rev Lord Coggan, Archishop of Canterbury, 1974–80, born Oct 9th 1909
18	Denis Gifford, artist and author, born Dec 26th 1927
	Sir Larry Lamb, former editor of the *Sun* newspaper, born July 15th 1929
20	Jean-Pierre Rampal, flautist, born Jan 7th 1922
21	Sir John Gielgud, actor, born Apr 14th 1904
	Dame Barbara Cartland, novelist, born July 9th 1901
	Mahmoud al-Zoubi, former Prime Minister of Syria, born in 1938
23	Sally Harrison, choreographer, born Sept 17th 1938
25	Elizabeth Durack, painter, born July 6th 1915
	Nicholas Clay, actor, born Sept 18th 1946
	Francis Lederer, actor, born Nov 1899
27	Maurice 'Rocket' Richard, ice-hockey player, born Aug 4th 1921
29	Doris Hare, actress, born Mar 1st 1905
30	Gordon 'Tex' Beneke, saxophonist who led the Glenn Miller Band after the founder's death, born Feb 12th 1914
31	Joe Puma, jazz guitarist, born Aug 13th 1927
	Andrew Faulds, actor and politician, born Mar 1st 1923

June 2000

1	Oskar Czerwenka, opera singer, born July 5th 1924
3	William Simon, banker (inventor of leveraged buyouts), born Nov 27th 1927
	Peter Myers, co-founder of Abbey Records, born Dec 2nd 1928
4	General Sir James Glover, Commander-in-Chief UK Land Forces 1985–7, born Mar 25th 1929
5	Lord Mostyn, landowner, born Apr 17th 1920
7	Eric Doitch, artist and teacher, born May 17th 1923

9	Abe Lincoln, jazz trombonist, born Mar 29th 1907
	Shay Brennan, footballer, born May 6th 1937
10	Hafez al-Assad, President of Syria, born Oct 6th 1930
11	Brian Statham, cricketer, born June 17th 1930
	George Segal, sculptor, born Nov 26th 1924
14	Attilio Bertolucci, poet, born Nov 18th 1911
15	Jules Roy, writer, born Oct 22nd 1907
16	Nagako, The Dowager Empress of Japan (wife of Hirohito), born Mar 6th 1903
19	Noboru Takeshita, Prime Minister of Japan, 1987–89, born Feb 26th 1924
20	Mary Benson, anti-apartheid campaigner, born Dec 8th 1919
22	Veronica Bamfield, writer and broadcaster, born Nov 22nd 1908
23	Jerome Richardson, jazz saxophonist and flautist, born Nov 15th 1920
25	Judith Wright, poet, born May 31st 1915
29	John Aspinall, zoo owner and casino proprietor, born June 11th 1926
	Vittorio Gassman, actor, born Sept 1st 1922
30	Lt-Commander Peter Lamb, naval aviator and test pilot, born May 7th 1923

July 2000

1	Walter Matthau, actor, born Oct 1st 1920
2	Joey Dunlop, motorcyclist, born Feb 25th 1952
5	Franta Belsky, sculptor, born Apr 6th 1921
7	Ruth Werner, spy, born May 15th 1907
9	Henri Gault, restaurant critic who coined the phrase 'nouvelle cuisine', born Nov 4th 1929
10	John Morgan, author, born May 28th 1959
	Frank Berni, restaurateur, born Oct 30th 1903
11	The Right Reverend Lord Runcie, Archbishop of Canterbury, 1980–91, born Oct 2nd 1921
12	Ras Shorty (Garfield Blackman), calypso and soca singer, born Oct 6th 1941
14	Sir Mark Oliphant, physicist, born Oct 8th 1901
15	Paul Young, singer with Sad Cafe and Mike and the Mechanics, born June 17th 1947
16	Gyorgy Petri, poet, born Dec 22nd 1943
17	Aligi Sassu, painter and sculptor, born July 17th 1912
	Edna Ginesi, artist, born Feb 15th 1902
18	Paul Coverdell, US Senator, born Jan 20th 1939
19	Harry Legge, conductor, born Apr 24th 1914
21	Iain Hamilton, composer, born June 6th 1922
22	Claude Sautet, film director, born Feb 23rd 1924
23	Jock Cameron, helicopter pioneer, born Oct 14th 1916
24	Oscar Shumsky, violinist, born Mar 23rd 1917
	Thea Porter, fashion designer, born Dec 24th 1927
27	Lorely Dyer, soprano, born Dec 15th 1907
28	Professor Sir Leslie Martin, architect, born Aug 17th 1908
	John Wells, artist, born July 27th 1907
29	Alan Boon, publisher, born Sept 28th 1913
30	Derek Hill, painter, born Dec 6th 1916

August 2000

4	Bill Ward, artist, born Nov 8th 1918
5	Sir Alec Guinness, actor, born Apr 2nd 1914
	Nanik (Lala) Amarnath, first Indian cricketer to score a Test century, born Sept 11th 1911
6	Sir Robin Day, television presenter, born Oct 24th 1923
7	Otto Wiener, opera singer, born Feb 13th 1911
8	Lt-General Sir Peter Hudson, Deputy Commander-in-Chief UK Land Forces 1977–80, born Sept 14th 1923
9	Professor John Harsanyi, economist, philosopher and Nobel Laureate, born May 29th 1920
10	Joan Marsh (real name Nancy Ann Rosher), actress, born July 10th 1913
11	Loretta Young, actress, born Jan 6th 1913
15	Edward Craven Walker, inventor of the lava lamp, born July 4th 1918
	Lancelot Ware, founder of Mensa, born June 5th 1915
16	Alan Caddy, guitarist with the 60s group The Tornados, born Feb 2nd 1940
17	Franco Donatoni, composer, born June 9th 1927
18	Michael Copus, muralist, born Oct 7th 1936
	Jack Walker, owner of Blackburn Rovers FC, born May 19th 1929
20	Vice-Admiral Sir Peter Compston, Deputy Supreme Allied Commander Atlantic 1968–79, born Sept 12th 1915
21	Rod Griffith, television presenter (inspiration for Viz magazine Roger Mellie), born Apr 21st 1926
22	Rina Gigli, soprano, born Jan 30th 1916
25	Carl Barks, cartoonist (Donald Duck), born Mar 27th 1901
26	Bunny Austin, tennis player, born Aug 26th 1906
31	Euan Uglow, painter, born Mar 10th 1932

September 2000

| 2 | Audrey Wise, Labour MP for Coventry South West 1974–79 and Preston since 1987, born Jan 4th 1935 |
| 3 | Godfrey Talbot, broadcaster, born Oct 8th 1908 |

CURRENT AFFAIRS

4 Mary Shepard, artist and illustrator, born Dec 25th 1909
5 Roy Fredericks, cricketer, born Nov 11th 1942
   Julian Baring, investment fund manager, born Dec 9th 1935
6 Donald Gallup, bibliographer of TS Eliot, born May 12th 1913
   Desmond Wilcox, broadcaster, born May 21st 1931
7 Bruce Gyngell, television executive, born July 8th 1929
9 Sir Julian Critchley, author and Conservative MP, born Dec 8th 1930
   Bill Waddington, actor, born June 10th 1916
11 Phillip Glasier, founder of the National Birds of Prey Centre, born Dec 22nd 1915
12 Stanley Turrentine, jazz saxophonist and bandleader, born Apr 5th 1934
   Konrad Kujau, forger of the so-called Hitler Diaries, born June 27th 1938
17 Paula Yates, television presenter, born Apr 24th 1960
20 Gherman Titov, cosmonaut, born Sept 11th 1935
   Jeanloup Sieff, photographer, born Nov 30th 1933
22 Sir Anthony Pilkington, businessman, born June 20th 1935
24 Antony Darnborough, film producer, born Oct 6th 1913
25 RS Thomas, poet, born Mar 29th 1913
26 Carl Sigman, composer of 'Pennsylvania 6–5000' and 'Robin Hood, Robin Hood, Riding through the Glen', born Sept 24th 1909
   Tommy Reilly, harmonica player, born Aug 21st 1919
   Baden Powell, Brazilian guitarist, born Aug 6th 1937
27 Keith Roberts, science fiction writer, born Sept 20th 1935
28 Pierre Trudeau, prime minister of Canada 1968–79, 1980–87, born Oct 18th 1919
30 Sir Fred Pontin, founder of Pontin's holiday camps, born Oct 24th 1906
   Howard Winstone, boxer, born April 15th 1939

October 2000
1 Pat Pottle, anti-war campaigner, born Aug 8th 1938
3 Benjamin Orr, rock musician, born Aug 9th 1947
5 Mireille Johnston, author and television cook, born Oct 4th 1935
6 Richard Farnsworth, actor and stuntman, born Sept 1st 1920
8 Sheila Holland, author known as Charlotte Lamb, born Dec 22nd 1937
10 Sirimavo Bandaranaike, former Prime Minister of Sri Lanka, born Apr 17th 1916
11 Donald Dewar, PC, First Minister of the Scottish Executive, born Aug 21st 1937
13 Brit Woodman, jazz trombonist, born June 4th 1920
   Lady Sarah Spencer-Churchill, socialite, born Dec 17th 1921
   Jean Peters, film actress, born Oct 15th 1926
14 Jennifer Dawson, novelist, born Jan 21st 1928
15 Brian Kay, founder of the *Eikoka News Digest*, born Aug 2nd 1946
16 David Golub, pianist and conductor, born Mar 22nd 1950
17 Walter Shenson, film producer, born June 22nd 1919
   Ivan Owen, creator of Basil Brush, born Aug 19th 1927
18 Julie London, singer and actress, born Sept 26th 1926
19 Katherine Faning, editor of *The Christian Science Monitor*, 1983–88, born Oct 18th 1927
20 Judy Fryd, founder of Mencap, born Oct 31st 1909
21 Barbara Tribe, sculptor, born June 20th 1913
22 The Reverend Fred Pratt Green, hymn writer and poet, born Sept 2nd 1903
25 Mike Rawson, athlete, born May 26th 1934
26 Walter Berry, bass-baritone, born Apr 8th 1929
27 Air Commodore Bob Weighill, rugby union administrator, born Sept 9th 1920
28 Josef Felder, German politician, born Aug 24th 1900
30 Steve Allen, original presenter of America's 'Tonight' show, born Dec 26th 1921
31 George Armstrong, footballer, born Aug 9th 1944

November 2000
1 Sir Steven Runciman, historian, born July 7th 1903
2 Baroness Ryder of Warsaw, social worker, born July 3rd 1923
4 Stephanie Lawrence, actress and singer, born Dec 16th 1949
5 Jimmie Davis, songwriter and former Governor of Louisiana, born Sept 10th 1899
6 Roger Peyrefitte, author, born Aug 17th 1907
7 Queen Ingrid of Denmark, the Danish Queen Mother, born Mar 28th 1910
8 Dick Morrissey, jazz tenor-saxophonist, born May 9th 1940
9 Eric Morley, impresario, born Sept 26th 1918
   Hugh Paddick, actor, born Aug 1915
10 Jacques Chaban-Delmas, Prime Minister of France, 1969–72, born Mar 7th 1915
13 Llewelyn Thomas, advertising copywriter and son of Dylan Thomas, born Jan 30th 1939
14 Bernard Gadney, rugby player, born July 16th 1909
15 Alexander Schindler, leader of America's Jewish Reform Movement, born Oct 4th 1925
16 Russ Conway, pianist, born Sept 2nd 1925
17 Bim Sherman, reggae singer, born Feb 2nd 1950
22 Emil Zatopek, athlete, born Sept 19th 1922
   Caroline Benn, author and educationalist, born Oct 13th 1926

23   Rayner Unwin, publisher, born Dec 23rd 1925
        Bernard Vorhaus, film director, born Dec 25th 1904
26   Ralph Bates, author, born Nov 3rd 1899
27   Sir Malcolm Bradbury, novelist and Professor of American Studies at the University of East Anglia 1970–94,
        born Sept 7th 1932
28   Len Shackleton, footballer, born May 22nd 1922
29   Liam Hamilton, Chief Justice of Ireland, 1994–2000, born Dec 30th 1928

December 2000
 2   Jack Hemingway, fisherman, writer and conservationist, born Oct 10th 1923
        Arthur Oglesby, angler, born Dec 23rd 1923
 3   Eli Frankham, Romany leader, born Nov 26th 1928
 4   Lord Cowdrey of Tonbridge, born Dec 24th 1932
 5   Norman Swallow, pioneer of television documentaries, born Feb 17th 1921
 7   Lord Aldington, soldier and politician, born May 25th 1914
 8   Rosemarie Frankland, Britain's first Miss World (1961), born in 1943
 9   ER Thompson, journalist and broadcaster, born Aug 19th 1907
11   Henry Clother, journalist, born Jan 9th 1931
12   Goetz Friedrich, opera producer, born Aug 4th 1930
        George Montgomery, actor, born Aug 29th 1916
13   Sir Hubert Bennett, architect to the GLC, 1956–71, born Sept 4th 1909
15   George Alcock, astronomer, born Aug 28th 1912
16   Pauline Curley, actress, born Dec 10th 1903
18   Kirsty MacColl, singer and songwriter, born Oct 10th 1959
19   Sir Laurence Whistler, artist and poet, born Jan 21st 1912
20   Adrian Henri, poet and painter, born Apr 10th 1932
21   Al Gross, inventor of the walkie-talkie, born Feb 22nd 1918
23   Victor Borge, entertainer, born Jan 3rd 1909
        Sir Jimmy Shand, accordionist and band leader, born Jan 28th 1908
        Allan Smethurst, the singing postman, born Nov 19th 1927
24   John Cooper, automobile engineer, born July 17th 1923
26   Jason Robards, actor, born July 26th 1922
30   Julius Epstein, screenwriter, born Aug 22nd 1909

Sporting Record 1999

January 1999
 1   Czech tennis player Petr Korda announced he would not retire following his nandrolone conviction and
        subsequent ban.
 2   Darren Gough took a hat trick as Australia were bowled out for 322 on the first day of the final Test in
        Sydney.
 3   Phil Taylor won his seventh darts world championship by beating Peter Manley 6–2 in the final at Purfleet.
 4   Keith Wiseman resigned as chairman of the Football Association. Vice-chairman Geoff Thompson took over
        temporarily.
 5   Australia defeated England by 98 runs in the final test match in Sydney to win the series 3–1 and retain the
        Ashes.
 6   The National Basketball Association ended its 191 day dispute, which began on July 1st 1998, when owners
        locked out players in protest at their huge salary demands.
 7   The mayor of Marbella and owner of Atlético Madrid, Jésus Gil y Gil, was jailed for funnelling town hall
        money to the club.
 8   Ron Atkinson became the new manager of Nottingham Forest FC.
 9   Tim Henman was beaten in the final of the Qatar Open by Rainer Schuttler.
10   Raymond Barneveld of Holland retained his Embassy World Dart's Championship by beating Ronnie Baxter
        6–5.
11   David Duval won the PGA Mercedes Golf Championship in Hawaii by a record nine strokes from Mark
        O'Meara.
12   The Chicago Bulls basketball star, Michael Jordan, announced his retirement.
13   Ben Ainslie won the Laser class at the World Sailing Championships in Melbourne. Jason Prince made a
        maximum 147 break against Ian Brumby in the British Snooker Open but lost the match 5–4.
14   Jack Nicklaus announced he is to have a hip replacement which will mean missing the Masters for the first
        time in 40 years.
15   Arsenal FC signed the Nigerian striker Nwanko Kanu.
16   Graham Thorner retired as a racehorse trainer.
17   Mike Tyson knocked out Francois Botha in his comeback fight but was far from impressive.
18   England were expelled from the Five Nations Rugby Championship after a dispute over television rights.
        South Africa defeated the West Indies by 351 runs to inflict a 5–0 series whitewash.
19   England were re-instated to the Five Nations Rugby Championship.
20   The N. Ireland FA were jointly awarded FIFA's Fair Play Award for 1998 for their contribution to community
        relations. The other joint winners were Iran and the USA.
21   Nationwide announced plans to sponsor the England team in a four-year deal with the Football Association.

24   Six members of the International Olympic Committee were expelled over the 'votes for favours' scandal which surrounded the controversial allocation of the 2002 Winter Olympics to Salt Lake City. Alex Marshall won the world indoor bowls championship.

25   David Duval scored a 59 during the final round of the Bob Hope Classic to win by one stroke.

26   The European 200 metres champion Doug Walker, was found to have nandrolone in his urine sample.

27   West Ham signed Paolo Di Canio from Sheffield Wednesday and Marc-Vivien Foe from Lens.

28   The Sri Lankan cricket captain Arjuna Ranatunga, received a six-match suspended ban after his unsporting behaviour in the international against England.

29   Aberdeen Asset Management announced its plans to sponsor the University Boat Race for the next three years.

31   Pakistan defeated India by 12 runs in an enthralling Test match in Madras to take a 1–0 series lead.

February 1999

1   John Hartson, the Wimbledon and Wales forward, was fined £20,000 by the FA and suspended for three matches for his attack on Eyal Berkovic, his former West Ham team-mate.

2   Glenn Hoddle was sacked as England football coach after his alleged comments about disabled people paying for the sins of a previous life.

3   Mark Taylor, the Australian cricket captain, announced his retirement from international cricket.

5   Mike Tyson was sentenced to a year in jail for attacking two men after a traffic incident.

7   Anil Kumble became the second man in 122 years of Test cricket to take all ten wickets in an innings when he bowled out Pakistan single-handedly in Delhi to square the series 1–1.

8   Tony Drago defeated Stephen Hendry in the Benson and Hedges Snooker Masters.

9   Teeton Mill, the favourite for the Cheltenham Gold Cup, was allotted top weight of 12 stone for the Grand National.

10   England lost 2–0 to world champions France in Howard Wilkinson's first match as caretaker England football coach.

11   Andre Agassi was disqualified from the Sybase Open in California for repeatedly using obscenities.

12   The latest edition of the regulations of the MCC stated that women's shoulders should be covered in the Lord's pavilion.

13   Arsenal were ordered to replay their FA Cup 5th round victory over Sheffield Utd after Arsene Wenger, the winning manager, appealed for fair-play. Joe Calzaghe defeated Robin Reid by the narrowest of margins to retain his WBO super-middleweight boxing title.

14   Leeds Rhinos defeated Wigan Warriors in the Silk Cup Challenge Cup despite having a man sent off.

15   Nick Faldo made the field of 64 for the Andersen Consulting Match Play Championship although he is presently ranked 65 in the world; Jumbo Ozaki pulled out at the last minute.

16   Three racehorses were killed in a freak accident at Sedgefield when they careered into first fence fallers.

17   Kevin Keegan was named as England's football team coach, but only for the next four internationals. Muhammad Ali was given a hero's welcome in Brixton, as he campaigned for the Jubilee 2000 movement.

19   Graham Rix, the Chelsea FC assistant manager, faced jail after admitting unlawful sex with a 15-year-old girl.

20   England defeated Scotland 24–21 in the Five Nations Rugby Championship and Ireland defeated Wales 29–23.

21   Stephen Hendry beat Graeme Dott 9–1 in the final of the Scottish Snooker Open.

23   Bint Allayl, the favourite for the 1,000 Guineas, was put down after suffering a leg fracture on the gallops. Arsenal defeated Sheffield Utd 2–1 in their replayed FA Cup tie.

24   Nick Faldo was beaten by Tiger Woods in the first round of the Arthur Andersen Match Play Championship.

25   The South African cricket board announced its decision to take action against racial terms in cricket such as 'coolie creeper' for a ball that bounces twice.

26   Amelie Mauresmo gained revenge for her defeat in the Australian Open when she beat Martina Hingis in the quarter-finals of the Paris Open.

27   Former world champion Colin McRae won the Safari Rally. Richard Krajicek defeated Greg Rusedski in the final of the Guardian Direct tennis tournament.

28   The first lifestyle magazine, *The Players' Journal* was delivered free to an elite of 1,000 football league players.

March 1999

1   It was announced that the Cambridge University boat crew will be the tallest in the history of the race, with Josh West, at six feet nine inches, the tallest rower ever to take part.

2   Geoff Allott, the New Zealand No 11, scored the longest duck in history, it lasted 101 minutes.

6   The English lacrosse selectors gave James Perrin, David Middleton-Egan and Mark Reynolds one month to prove their fitness for the under-19 world championships.

7   Jamie Baulch and Ashia Hansen won gold medals at the seventh World Indoor Athletics Championships. Eddie Irvine won the Australian Formula One Grand Prix in Melbourne.

8   Jim Farry, chief executive of the Scottish Football Association, was dismissed over the delay of Jorge Cadete to Celtic.

9   Paul Foster, last years world indoor bowls champion, won the British Championship beating Jamie Mills in the final.

11   Wembley Stadium was sold for £103 million to a consortium headed by the Football Association.

12   Hampton won the 54th Head of the River race on the Thames in London.

13   Lennox Lewis drew with Evander Holyfield in their heavyweight unification title bout in a fight that most impartial observers thought Lewis had clearly won.

14   Serena Williams defeated Steffi Graf in the final of the Evert Cup.

15	Carlos Moya officially became the number one mens tennis player according to the latest computer rankings.
16	Former England cricket captains Rachael Heyhoe-Flint and Carole Cornthwaite were among the first women members of the MCC to enter the Long Room at Lords. Istabraq won his second Champion Hurdle title at Cheltenham as Jenny Pitman announced her retirement.
17	Call Equiname won the two-mile Champion Chase at Cheltenham.
18	See More Business won the Cheltenham Gold Cup.
21	Tottenham Hotspur won the Worthington Cup beating Leicester City 1–0. Sheffield Steelers beat Nottingham Panthers in the final of the Superleague Ice Hockey Challenge Cup.
22	Darren Gough was named Cornhill English Cricketer of the Year.
23	David Lloyd announced he will stand down as England cricket coach after the World Cup.
24	Aston Villa announced that Stan Collymore, who is suffering from depression, would be out for the rest of the season.
27	England beat Poland 3–1 in the European Championship qualifiers thanks to a hat trick by Paul Scholes.
28	Venus Williams defeated her sister, Serena, in the final of the Lipton Championship in Key Biscayne, Florida. Paul Tergat won his fifth consecutive World Cross Country Championship in Belfast.
29	Jamie Osborne announced his retirement as a National Hunt jockey.
30	Snooker player, Dean Reynolds, was electronically tagged whilst playing his opponent in the seventh round of the world championship, due to a motoring conviction. Brian Lara scored 153 to lead the West Indies to a one-wicket victory against Australia to take a 2–1 series lead.
31	Doug Walker, the European 200 metres champion, was suspended after drug allegations.

April 1999

4	The USA defeated Great Britain in a Davis Cup tennis tie.
5	Richard Dunwoody became the leading NH jockey of all time when he broke Peter Scudamore's record of 1,678 victories.
6	Parma won the first leg of their Uefa Cup semi-final against Atletico Madrid but Marseilles only drew with Bologna.
9	Robbie Fowler was banned for six games and fined £32,000 for taunting Graeme Le Saux and pretending to snort cocaine after scoring a goal. The Government blocked BSkyB's proposed £623 million takeover of Manchester Utd.
10	Bobbyjo, ridden by Paul Carberry, won the Grand National at 10–1. Prince Naseem Hamed retained his WBO featherweight title with an 11th round stoppage of Paul Ingle.
11	José Maria Olazabal won the US Masters by two strokes from Davis Love III. Feargal O'Brien defeated Anthony Hamilton in the British Snooker Open to win his first major tournament. Scotland won the last Five Nations Rugby Championship after Wales defeated England 32–31 in a dramatic finale. Mika Hakkinen won the Brazilian Formula One Grand Prix. Newcastle Utd defeated Spurs 2–0 in the semi-final of the FA Cup.
12	Britain were drawn at home in the Davis Cup relegation play-off against South Africa. Trevor Brooking was named as the new chairman of Sport England, previously called the English Sports Council.
13	Sunderland returned to the FA Carling Premiership after beating Bury 5–2. Michael Owen, the Liverpool striker, signed a million pound deal with HarperCollins for a three-book deal.
14	Manchester Utd defeated Arsenal in the FA Cup semi-final to keep their treble hopes alive.
16	Sergio Garcia, who was the top amateur at last weeks US Masters, turned professional.
17	Young Kenny, ridden by Brendan Powell and trained by Philip Beaumont, won the Scottish Grand National at Ayr.
18	The mens London Marathon winner was Moroccan Abdelkader El Mouaziz, whilst Joyce Chepchumba of Kenya won the women's race. Chepchumba earnt £210,000 for breaking the London Marathon 'world record' although Tegla Loroupe posted a faster time in the Rotterdam (mixed) Marathon on the same day.
19	Ethiopian Fatuma Roba won the women's Boston Marathon for the third successive year.
20	Michelle Martin of Australia, the world number one, won her 50th championship squash title.
21	Manchester Utd beat Juventus to reach the final of the European Cup. Bayern Munich defeated Dynamo Kiev to earn the right to face Manchester Utd in the European Cup final.
22	Real Mallorca beat Chelsea 1–0 and 2–1 on aggregate to reach the Cup Winners' Cup final.
23	Katja Seizinger, three time Olympic gold medal-winner, retired from skiing due to injury.
24	Paula Radcliffe broke her own world best time for 5 miles at Balmoral when she ran 24min 47secs. Ron Atkinson announced he is to quit Nottingham Forest at the end of the season and retire from football.
25	Tim Henman and Olivier Delaitre won the Monte Carlo Open doubles title.
27	David Ginola of Spurs was voted the English football's Players' Player of the Year.
28	England drew 1–1 in the friendly with Hungary and Kevin Keegan announced he would like to stay on as coach.
30	Dundee FC announced they would not be selling the club to Giovanni di Stefano and that they were on schedule to complete the ground improvements necessary by the July 31st deadline.

May 1999

1	Island Sands, trained by Saeed Bin Suroor and ridden by Frankie Dettori, won the 2000 Guineas.
2	Wince, trained by Henry Cecil and ridden by Keiren Fallon, won the 1000 Guineas. Michael Schumacher won the San Marino Formula One Grand Prix.
3	Stephen Hendry won his seventh Snooker World Championship by defeating Mark Williams in the final 18–11.
6	David Ginola became the Football Writers' Footballer of the Year to go with his recent Players' award.
9	Ian Stark riding Jaybee won the 50th Badminton Horse Trials title. Sunderland won the Nationwide First Division title with a record points tally of 105. Marcelo Rios defeated Mariano Zabaleta of Argentina to win the German Tennis Open.

13   Bernie Ecclestone's bid to have the British Formula 1 Grand Prix returned to Brands Hatch was successful; the Kent circuit will hold the race from 2002.

15   Peta Beckett, a member of last years World Championship equestrian team, died after a fall during a competition on Lord Cardigan's estate in Wiltshire.

16   Manchester Utd won their fifth FA Carling Premiership title in seven years after coming from behind to beat Spurs 2–1. Michael Schumacher won the Monaco Grand Prix after overtaking Mika Hakkinen in the run up to the first corner. Colin Montgomerie won the Benson and Hedges Golf International.

17   Wales lock Craig Quinnell joined Cardiff from Richmond in a four-year deal worth £400,000.

18   Roy Keane, the Manchester Utd captain, was arrested and detained for allegedly attacking two women.

21   Steve Collins, former WBO super-middleweight champion, was forced to abandon his comeback after suffering a blackout.

22   Manchester Utd defeated Newcastle 2–0 in the FA Cup final to remain on course for the treble. Saffron Waldon, ridden by Olivier Peslier and trained by AP O'Brien, won the Irish 2000 Guineas.

23   Hula Angel, ridden by Michael Hills and trained by his father Barry, won the Irish 1000 Guineas. Wrestler Owen Hart whose latest nickname was 'Blue Blazer' was killed in a stunt whilst entering the ring.

25   Polly Phillips's horse Coral Cove tested positive for too-high a level of salicylic acid resulting in the Great Britain equestrian team losing last year's World Cup bronze medal.

26   Manchester Utd completed the treble by defeating Bayern Munich 2–1 in the European Cup final in Barcelona. Sourav Ganguly and Rahul Dravid of India achieved a world record international one-day partnership of 318 against Sri Lanka.

27   Ian Wright was fined £17,500 and suspended for West Ham's first three matches of next season after trashing the referee's dressing room after a recent football match against Leeds.

30   England failed to make the Super Six stage of the cricket World Cup after losing to India, and Zimbabwe beating South Africa. Mika Hakkinen led all the way to win the Spanish Formula One Grand Prix. Manchester City beat Gillingham 3–1 on penalties to gain promotion to next seasons Division.

31   Watford won their first division play-off against Bolton 2–0 and will take their place in next season's Premiership. Scottish golfer Colin Montgomerie won the Volvo PGA Championship. Dean Macey scored 8,347 points to become the second highest-ever scoring decathlete in Britain.

June 1999

1   It was announced that Egil Olsen, the former coach of the Norwegian national team, would replace Joe Kinnear as manager of Wimbledon Football Club.

2   Ireland refused the Yugoslav football team entry visas into the country to play their European Championship qualifying match.

4   Ramruna, ridden by Kieren Fallon and trained by Henry Cecil, won the Vodaphone Oaks.

5   Kieren Fallon and Henry Cecil landed an Oaks / Derby double when Oath landed the Epsom Classic. Steffi Graf defeated Martina Hingis in the final of the French Open. England drew 0–0 with Sweden and Paul Scholes became the first Englishman to be sent off at Wembley in an Internatonal. The Scotland football team could only manage a 1–1 draw against the Faeroe Islands.

6   Andre Agassi beat Andrei Medvedev in five sets to win the French Open and become the fifth man to win all four grand-slams. Darren Clarke won the Compass English Open by two shots from John Bickerton.

7   Michelle de Bruin (née Smith) lost her appeal against a four-year ban for urine tampering.

9   Alan Shearer recaptured his scoring touch with a 15th minute goal against Bulgaria but the game ended in a 1–1 draw.

10   Golfer Justin Rose opened his season on the Challenger Tour with a six-under par 64 to take the lead in the Diners' Club Austrian Open. Rose failed to make the cut in 20 consecutive tournaments since the British Open.

11   Alex Ferguson, the Manchester Utd manager, was awarded a knighthood.

13   Mika Hakkinen won the Canadian Grand Prix where for the first time the race ended behind the safety car. Dwain Chambers became the second Englishman to break ten seconds for 100 metres when he ran 9.99sec in Nuremberg.

14   Tim Henman was seeded six, and Greg Rusedski nine, for the Wimbledon Championships.

16   Pakistan defeated New Zealand by nine wickets to reach Sunday's World Cup final. Maurice Greene of the USA broke the world record for the 100 metres dash when he recorded 9.79 in Athens.

17   Australia went through to face Pakistan in the World Cup final after a tie with South Africa, both teams scoring 213. Enzeli, ridden by J Murtagh and trained in Ireland by John Oxx, won the Ascot Gold Cup.

18   Ross Baillie, a young International hurdler, died after suffering an allergic reaction to peanuts in a chicken sandwich.

20   Australia defeated Pakistan by eight wickets to win the cricket World Cup; Shane Warne was Man of the Match and Lance Klusener was Man of the Series.

22   Martina Hingis of Switzerland was beaten 6–2, 6–0 by Jelena Dokic, a Belgrade-born Australian 16-year-old, in the first round at Wimbledon.

23   Holland defeated Durham in the third round of the NatWest Trophy in Amsterdam.

24   Nasser Hussain was appointed as the new England cricket captain.

26   Herbie Hide was stopped in the second round by Vitali Klitschko of the Ukraine in defence of his WBO heavyweight title.

27   Heinz-Harald Frentzen, in a Jordan, won the French Formula One Grand Prix at Magny Cours, despite a broken leg.

28   Damon Hill announced he will retire after the British Grand Prix at Silverstone.

29   Tim Henman's victory over Jim Courier at Wimbledon was finally completed after the third day of play.

30   Manchester Utd announced they would not defend the FA Cup next season as they would contest the inaugural World Club Championships in Brazil to boost England's chances of hosting the World Cup Finals in 2006. Greg Rusedski was beaten in the quarter-finals at Wimbledon by Mark Philippoussis.

July 1999
1   David Platt took over as player-manager of Nottingham Forest.
2   Jason Gardner recorded 9.98 seconds in Lausanne to become the third sub ten-second British 100 metre runner.
3   Tim Henman was defeated by Pete Sampras in four sets in the Wimbledon semi-finals.
4   Pete Sampras defeated Andre Agassi 6–3, 6–4, 7–5 to claim his sixth Wimbledon singles title. Steffi Graf was beaten 6–4, 7–5, in her last Wimbledon visit, by Lindsay Davenport, who won her first Grand Slam title.
5   Chelsea signed Chris Sutton from Blackburn for £10 million.
6   Milton, the greatest showjumper that Great Britain has produced, died at the age of 22.
7   Hicham El Guerrouj of Morocco broke the world mile record in Rome with a time of 3min 43.13sec.
10   Mario Cipollini won his fourth consecutive stage win of the Tour de France.
11   The British Grand Prix was won by David Coulthard, as Michael Schumacher broke his right leg in a high-speed crash. The Traxdata King George V Cup was won by Nick Skelton on Hopes Are High. Ramruma won the Irish Oaks to complete the English / Irish Oaks double.
12   Iwan Thomas, the European 400 metres champion, underwent surgery on his injured left ankle.
13   The Champagne Mumm Admiral's Cup, the unofficial world championship of offshore yacht racing, was in chaos as the French team withdrew in protest at the handicapping.
14   David Graveney was confirmed as chairman of the England cricket selectors for a further two years.
15   It was announced that Phil Neale will manage the England cricket team on their tour of South Africa as administrative assistant to Duncan Fletcher, the new coach.
16   The Pakistan Cricket Board was suspended by the Government and replaced by a two-man committee amid allegations of deliberately losing the World Cup final.
18   Paul Lawrie of Scotland won the British Open Golf Championship at Carnoustie, in a play-off with Justin Leonard and Jean Van de Velde. The Frenchman began the final round ten strokes ahead of Lawrie but squandered a three stroke cushion on the final hole.
24   Jason Gardener ran the fastest 100 metres ever seen on British soil when he won the AAA Championship in a wind-assisted time of 10.02sec
25   Lance Armstrong, who was suffering from cancer three years ago, won the Tour de France cycle race. Eddie Irvine won the Austrian Formula One Grand Prix.
26   Paul Palmer of Great Britain won the 400 metres freestyle at the European swimming championships in Istanbul. Patrick Rafter became the first Australian to top the world tennis rankings.
28   Susan Rolph became the first British woman since 1962 to win a European swimming title when she won the 100 metres freestyle in Istanbul.
29   Kate Hoey, an Arsenal supporter, replaced Tony Banks as Sports Minister.
30   Chief shareholder of the Hull Sharks rugby league team, David Lloyd, the British Davis Cup captain, cut the players' wages following poor results.

August 1999
1   Eddie Irvine captured the lead in the world drivers' championship by winning the German Formula One Grand Prix.
2   Lee Westwood won the Smurfit European Open Golf Championship at The K Club, Co. Kildare.
4   Linford Christie faced allegations that he took a banned drug before an indoor athletic meeting in Dortmund on February 13.
5   Matthew Syed was beaten in the third round of the World Table Tennis Championships, in Eindhoven, by Liu Guoliang, of China, the Olympic champion.
6   Essex batsman Ronnie Irani, who was stumped by Steve Marsh of Kent, was controversially given not out as the batsman was not informed that Marsh was standing up to the stumps.
10   Graham Gooch and Mike Gatting were removed from the England cricket team selection panel.
12   Henry Cecil announced that Richard Quinn would replace Keiren Fallon as stable jockey for the next flat-race season.
15   Sherri Steinhauer of the USA retained the Weetabix Women's British Open Golf Championship at Woburn. Tiger Woods won the US PGA Championship by a stroke from Sergio Garcia of Spain, at Medinah Country Club, Chicago. Mika Hakkinen won the Hungarian Grand Prix to come within two points of Eddie Irvine at the top of the drivers' table.
16   The United States Ryder Cup captain Ben Crenshaw chose Tom Lehman and Steve Pate as his wild card entries.
17   Adrian Morley, the Leeds Rhinos and Great Britain rugby league forward, was suspended for three matches for butting Paul Rowley of Halifax Blue Sox.
18   British cycling suffered a setback when Prudential announced it was to withdraw its sponsorship for the 2000 Tour of Britain.
19   Robbie Keane became Britain's most expensive teenage player when he joined Coventry City from Wolverhampton Wanderers for nearly £6 million.
20   Pete Sampras's 24-match winning streak ended when he was forced to retire from the RCA championship in Indianapolis with a hip injury.
21   Graham Thorpe, the Surrey batsman, announced he would not be available to tour South Africa this winter. Nick Faldo was informed by Ryder Cup captain Mark James that he would not be in his team.
22   Maurice Greene and Marion Jones of the USA duly won the men's and women's 100 metres titles in Seville but Dwain Chambers gained a surprise bronze for Britain. Andrew Coltart was a surprise inclusion in the European Ryder Cup team. Equestrian star Polly Phillips was killed when her horse fell on top of her.
23   Marion Jones of the USA, winner of the 100 metres world title, could only manage a bronze medal in the long jump.
24   Hicham El Guerrouj of Morocco won the 1,500 metres at the World Athletics Championships in Seville,

Spain. Haile Gebrselassie of Ethiopia won the 10,000 metres at the World Athletics Championships in Seville, Spain.

25   Colin Jackson won Britain's first gold medal at the World Athletics Championships when he won the 110 metres hurdles. Dean Macey from Canvey Island, Essex, won a silver medal in the decathlon at the World Athletics Championships.

26   Michael Johnson broke the 400 metres world record when he ran 43.18secs to win the world title in Seville, Spain.

27   Maurice Greene and Inger Miller of the USA won the mens and women's 200 metres world titles in Seville, Spain.

28   Great Britain won the coxless fours world championship title in Canada; Steve Redgrave, Matthew Pinsent, Jamie Cracknell and Ed Goode beat an Australia four.

29   Gloucester beat Somerset by 50 runs to win the Natwest Trophy final at Lord's. David Coulthard won the Belgian Grand Prix at Spa-Francorchamps.

30   Bernard Barmasai, the world record holder for the 3,000 metres steeplechase was stripped of his chance to share in the $1 million Golden League bonanza after he admitted he had asked his friend Christopher Koskei to let him win an earlier race in the series.

September 1999
2   Surrey won the cricket county championship for the first time since 1971. Bobby Robson became the manager of Newcastle Utd. At 66-years-old, he is the oldest manager in the football league, and the oldest Premiership manager ever.

4   Alan Shearer scored a hat-trick in England's 6–0 win over Luxembourg in a Euro 2000 qualifying match.

6   Linford Christie was cleared by UK Athletics of drug allegations although the International Amateur Athletic Federation remain firm that there is a case to answer.

7   Athletes Gabriela Szabo and Wilson Kipketer shared the $ million bonus for winning all seven races in the Golden League.

8   England drew 0–0 with Poland in a Euro 2000 qualifying game and must now rely on Sweden beating Poland in the final group five match next month.

12   Serena Williams defeated Martina Hingis to win the US Open Tennis Championship. Lancashire won the CGU National League first division cricket championship. Carl Fogarty won his fourth World Superbike Championship. Heinz-Harald Frentzen won the Italian Formula One Grand Prix. Annaliese Heard of Cardiff won the junior women's world triathlon title.

13   Andre Agassi defeated Todd Martin 6–4, 6–7, 6–7, 6–3, 6–2, to win the US Open Tennis Championship.

18   Australian cricket star Shane Warne signed a one-year contract to play for Hampshire.

19   Golfer Pierre Fulke of Sweden won the Lancome Trophy. Newcastle United striker Alan Shearer scored five goals in an 8–0 demolition of Sheffield Wednesday.

21   Rob Andrews retired from rugby union following a recurrence of a shoulder injury. Barry Pinches had a maximum 147 break during the Regal Welsh Open but lost his match 5–4 to Joe Johnson.

22   Manchester Utd beat Sturm Graz 3–0 and Arsenal beat AIK of Stockholm 3–1 in European Championship League matches.

23   Tony Pigott resigned as chief executive of Sussex cricket club.

24   British boxer Michael Watson, who suffered brain damage during a world title fight eight years ago, won his compensation claim against the BBBC.

25   Manchester Utd striker Andy Cole was dropped by record company Warner following his debut rap song 'Unbelievable' only reaching No 59 in the charts.

26   The United States won the Ryder Cup from Europe 14.5 to 13.5 after winning the final single matches 8 1/2 to 3 1/2 Johnny Herbert won the Formula One Grand Prix of Europe; a maiden victory for Jackie Stewart's Stewart-Ford team. Great Britain defeated South Africa 4–1 in the Davis Cup to retain their place in the world group. Tegla Loroupe, of Kenya, clipped four seconds off her own world marathon best in Berlin but her 2hr 20min 43secs was in a mixed race and so will not be ratified.

30   It was announced that the New Zealand rugby union hooker, Anton Oliver, failed a drugs test.

October 1999
2   The Tote Cambridgeshire was run over the July course of 1 mile 2 furlongs and was won by Irish trained She's Our Mare.

3   Montjeu, ridden by Mick Kinane, won the Prix de L'Arc de Triomphe at Longchamps. British tennis player Greg Rusedski earned £800,000 when he won the Grand Slam Cup final in Munich. Chelsea thrashed Manchester Utd 5–0, the European champions' first league defeat since December 1998.

4   Peter Nicol of Scotland became the world number one squash player on the latest ranking list.

5   Scotland qualified for the Euro 2000 football play-offs; a John Collins penalty gave them a 1–0 victory over Bosnia.

6   Jan Ullrich, of Germany, won the world cycling time-trial championship in Treviso, Italy; Chris Boardman, of Great Britain gained a bronze medal.

8   Graeme Randall of Great Britain won the light-middleweight gold medal in the world judo championships in Birmingham.

9   Sweden beat Poland 2–0 in group five of Euro 2000; a result which meant England gain entry into the European championship play-offs.

10   Spanish golfers won the Alfred Dunhill Cup with a 2–1 victory over Australia.

11   Billy Schwer was named as domestic boxer of the year at the British Boxing Awards in London.

12   Wilt Chamberlain, who once scored 100 points in a basketball game for Philadelphia Warriors, died aged 63.

15   England had a record 101–10 victory over Tonga in the Rugby Union World Cup at Twickenham.

16   Top Cees, ridden by Keiren Fallon, won the Tote Cesarewitch at Newmarket.

17   Eddie Irvine won the Malaysian Formula 1 Grand Prix but was disqualified for a rule infringement in the
          design of his Ferrari. Venus Williams beat Martina Hingis 6–3, 6–4 in the final of the European indoor tennis
          championship in Zurich.
18   Adrian Dodson was banned for 18 months and fined £1,000 for biting his opponent during a Commonwealth
          middleweight boxing title fight.
20   England and Scotland reached the quarter-finals of the Rugby Union World Cup by beating Fiji and Samoa
          respectively.
21   The British cycling trio of Chris Hoy, Craig MacLean and Jason Queally won silver medals in the final of the
          world championship Olympic sprint, in Berlin.
23   Eddie Irvine was re-instated as winner of the Malaysian Grand Prix and takes a four point lead into the final
          Formula One Grand Prix at Suzuka, Japan. Australia defeated Wales 24–9 in the quarter-finals of the Rugby
          Union World Cup. Mike Tyson's latest comeback fight was declared a no-contest after he punched his
          opponent, Orlin Norris, after the bell.
24   South Africa beat England 44–21 to reach the Rugby Union World Cup semi-final. In other quarter-finals
          New Zealand beat Scotland 30–18 and France beat Argentina 47–26. Khalid Khannouchi of Morocco set a
          world best of 2hr 5min 42secs to win the Chicago Marathon.
25   A Learjet with five people on board including the US Open golf champion Payne Stewart, crashed in South
          Dakota; there were no survivors. Cassie Campion of Great Britain won the women's World Squash Open.
26   The FIA, announced that the Formula One British Grand Prix at Silverstone will be held in April next year
          instead of July.
27   Arsenal were defeated 1–0 by Fiorentina in group B of the European Cup Champions' League and exit the
          tournament but Manchester Utd qualified in group D.
28   Arsenal footballer Patrick Vieira was suspended for six games and fined £45,000 for spitting at West Ham's
          Neil Ruddock and swearing at a policeman.
30   Australia defeated South Africa 27–21 in extra time, after the match finished 18–18 in normal time, to reach
          the final of the Rugby Union World Cup.
31   France defeated New Zealand 43–31 to reach the final of the Rugby Union World Cup. Mika Hakkinen
          retained his Formula One world driver's championship by winning the Japanese Grand Prix at Suzuka.

November 1999
1   Cassie Campion, of England, the new world squash champion, defeated Michelle Martin of Australia 9–4,
          9–4, 4–9, 9–3 to win the Women's US Open.
2   Rogan Josh, trained by Bart Cummings, won the Foster's Melbourne Cup from Frankie Dettori's mount
          Central Park.
3   Brian Kidd was dismissed by Blackburn Rovers FC after less than a year as their manager.
4   Karl Burrows made the ninth break of 147 in professional competition this year but was defeated 5–3 by
          Adrian Rosa in the Benson and Hedges snooker championship.
5   French Holly, a leading fancy for the Cheltenham Gold Cup, was killed in a schooling accident at Middleham
          stables.
6   Australia defeated France 35–12 in the final of the Rugby Union World Cup at the Millennium Stadium,
          Cardiff.
7   Daylami, ridden by Frankie Dettori, won the Breeders Cup turf race at Gulfstream Park, Florida. Phil Taylor,
          the Professional Darts Council world champion defeated Raymond Barneveld, the British Darts
          Organisation world champion, in a special match sponsored by Skol. Tommy Makinen won his fourth world
          rally championship in succession by finishing third in Rally Australia.
8   The Football Association announced that because of Manchester United's withdrawal from the FA Cup, a
          second-round loser would receive a wild card entry into the third round.
9   Project Oarsome was launched at the London Regatta Centre; its aim is to bring rowing into 100 non-rowing
          schools to enhance Britain's success in the sport.
11   The Newcastle and England rugby union wing Tony Underwood announced his retirement due to persistent
          knee injuries.
12   Race-horse trainer David Nicholson announced his retirement; his assistant Alan King will take over his
          stables.
13   England defeated Scotland 2–0 in the first leg of the Euro 2000 play-offs at Hampden Park; Paul Scholes
          scored both goals. National hunt jockey Graham Bradley announced his retirement after winning the 2.00 at
          Haydock aboard Ontheboil.
14   Lennox Lewis beat Evander Holyfield on points to become the first British heavyweight boxer this century to
          win the undisputed world title.
16   Race-horse trainer Philip Mitchell was involved in controversy when his Running Stag was beaten in a lowly
          all-weather race at Lingfield after winning grade two events in the USA.
17   England qualified for the Euro 2000 finals, losing 1–0 to Scotland at Wembley but winning 2–1 on
          aggregate.
21   The International Amateur Athletic Federation (IAAF) named Carl Lewis and Fanny Blankers-Koen as the
          male and female athletes of the century.
22   Justin Rose, who came fourth in the British Open as a 17-year-old amateur golfer, won his European Tour
          card in southern Spain, but Philip Walton failed to qualify.
23   Richard Burns, in a Subaru, won the Network Q Rally for the second year in a row, beating Juha
          Kankkunen.
26   Peter Marshall, the Nottingham-based squash player who has been suffering from chronic fatigue
          syndrome, won the Pakistan Open title in Karachi.
27   Ever Blessed, ridden by Tommy Murphy and trained by Mark Pitman, won the Hennessy Cognac Gold Cup
          at Newbury.

28   Australian Aaron Baddeley, 18, became the first amateur to win the Australian Open golf championship since Bruce Devlin in 1960. Pete Sampras beat Andre Agassi 6–1, 7–5, 6–4 in the final of the ATP Tour world tennis championship.

29   Billy Schwer, the Luton-based boxer, was beaten by Stevie Johnston on points for the World Boxing Council lightweight championship at Wembley.

30   Manchester Utd won the Intercontinental Cup by beating Palmeiras 1–0 in Tokyo.

December 1999

1   Darlington FC received the wildcard entry into the FA Cup and despite losing to Gillingham, in the second round, will play Aston Villa in the third round. Sam Torrance, an assistant at the 1999 match, was named as the captain of the European Ryder Cup team in 2001.

2   Frank Endacott, the New Zealand rugby league coach, joined Wigan Warriors as replacement for Andy Goodway.

3   Darren Burnett beat Mark McMahon 7–0, 3–7, 7–1, 7–2 in the final of the Glasgow Bowls Classic at the Kelvin Hall.

4   Ernie Els won the Sun City Million Dollar golf challenge.

5   The Australian men's tennis team defeated France 3–2 to win the Davis Cup.

6   Roy Keane became the highest-paid footballer in Britain when he signed a new contract with Manchester United.

7   England were drawn in the same group as Germany for World Cup 2002; Albania, Finland and Greece complete group nine.

10   Australian Steve Waugh became the first cricketer to score centuries against all eight other Test-playing nations when he scored 117 not out against India.

12   England were drawn in the same group as Germany in the European football championship finals; Romania and Portugal are the other teams in the group.

13   England and South Africa cricket teams drew the second Test match at Port Elizabeth.

14   Richard Dunwoody, who rode a record 1,699 National Hunt winners, retired from racing because of a chronic arm injury.

18   The Football League ordered West Ham to replay their Worthington Cup quarter-final match against Aston Villa after fielding an ineligible player, striker Manny Omoyimni. West Ham won the original match.

19   Ronnie O'Sullivan won the China Open snooker title beating Stephen Lee 9–2 in the final.

20   Barcelona footballer Rivaldo was named as European Footballer of the Year.

21   The British Boxing Board of Control was put into administration after the successful compensation claim by Michael Watson.

22   Cornhill Insurance announced they are to stop sponsoring cricket Test matches.

23   A professional lap dancer, Yvonne Robb, 21, was fined a total of £600 on four charges, including streaking on the final day of the British Open golf championship and kissing Tiger Woods on the 18th green.

25   Greg Rusedski announced he would not play in the Australian Open tennis championship following surgery on his right foot.

27   England cricket captain Nasser Hussain scored an unbeaten 146 on the second day of the third Test against South Africa. See More Business, won the Pertemps King George VI Chase at Kempton but a bomb scare meant the abandonment of the rest of the card.

28   South Africa were forced to follow on as Andy Caddick took seven wickets on the third day of the third Test match. The Coral Welsh Grand National was won by Edmond.

30   Gary Kirsten of South Africa scored 275 runs to earn his team a draw against England in the third Test match.

Sporting Record 2000

January 2000

5   South Africa beat England by an innings and 37 runs in the fourth Test at Newlands, to take a 2–0 lead in the series.

6   Emma Carrick-Anderson of Great Britain scored World Cup slalom-skiing points when she came 28th in Maribor, Slovenia.

8   Graeme Hick was announced as the England cricket captain for the next tour match against a South African Invitation XI.

9   Sheffield Sharks defeated Manchester Giants 89–80 in the final of the Sainsbury's Classic Cola national basketball cup.

10   British tennis-player Jamie Delgado was ranked 17th in the new ATP Champion's race, one place ahead of Tim Henman.

12   Gary Croft, 25, the Ipswich Town defender, became the first professional footballer to play a match while wearing an electronic tag.

15   Andy Goodway resigned as Great Britain rugby league coach.

16   Ted 'The Count' Hankey defeated Ronnie Baxter to become the Embassy World Darts Champion at Frimley Green's Lakeside Country Club, Surrey.

18   England beat South Africa by two wickets in the final Test at Centurion Park, South Africa.

21   John Higgins scored the first maximum 147 break recorded in a professional team competition during the Nations' Cup at the Hexagon Theatre in Reading. Hermann Maier of Austria won his third successive super giant slalom race at Kitzbühl.

23   Tim Henman was beaten in the fourth round of the Australian Open tennis championships in Melbourne by Chris Woodruff of the USA.

24   Jenson Button, 20, replaced Stirling Moss as the youngest-ever British Formula One racing-driver after
        signing a five-year contract with BMW-Williams.
28   Glenn Hoddle became the new manager of Southampton FC.
29   Boxer Mike Tyson knocked out British heavyweight Julius Francis in the second round in Manchester.
30   John Higgins defeated Stephen Lee 9–8 in the final of the Regal Welsh Open snooker championship.
31   John Leslie became the new captain of the Scottish rugby union team.

February 2000
2   The IOC announced the ten cities that submitted formal applications to host the 2008 Summer Olympics. In
        alphabetical order they were Bangkok, Beijing, Cairo, Havana, Istanbul, Kuala Lumpur, Osaka, Paris, Seville
        and Toronto.
5   In the Six-Nations Rugby Union Championship, England defeated Ireland 50–18, France beat Wales 36–3
        and Italy beat Scotland 34–20.
6   Jacqui Frazier-Lyde, daughter of the former heavyweight boxing champion Joe Frazier, made a successful
        professional boxing debut at the age of 38.
10   John Barnes was sacked as Celtic manager and replaced temporarily by Kenny Dalglish. Stan Collymore
        was transferred from Aston Villa to Leicester City FC.
13   South Africa defeated England by 38 runs in the final of a triangular one-day cricket series in Johannesburg.
14   Paul Gascoigne broke his left arm whilst playing for Middlesbrough against Aston Villa.
16   The Leicester City football team were thrown out of their training camp at La Manga in Spain after team
        members let off a fire extinguisher in a busy bar. Controversial new signing Stan Collymore was at the
        centre of the fracas and was warned by manager Martin O'Neill as to his future conduct.
17   Matthew Syed of England retained his Commonwealth table tennis title in Singapore.
18   Tony McCoy beat his own record for the fastest 200 winners in a season when Mr Cool won the first race at
        Sandown Park.
19   In the Six-Nations Rugby Union Championship, England defeated France 15–9, Wales beat Italy 47–16 and
        Ireland beat Scotland 44–22.
20   Hailu Mekkonen of Ethiopia broke the world indoor two mile record with a time of 8min 09.66secs at the
        CGU Grand Prix in Birmingham. Wilson Kipketer the Kenyan-born Dane also broke a world record at the
        National Indoor Arena with a time of 2min 14.96secs for 1,000 metres.
23   In international football friendlies England drew 0–0 with Argentina, Wales beat Qatar 1–0, Ireland beat
        Czech Republic 3–2 and N. Ireland beat Luxembourg 3–1.
26   Christian Malcolm of Great Britain won the European indoor 200 metres title in Ghent, Belgium.
27   Leicester City beat Tranmere Rovers 2–1 in the Worthington Cup final at Wembley. Darren Clarke defeated
        Tiger Woods 4 and 3 in the final of the Andersen Consulting World Match Play championship at La Costa,
        California.
29   Roger Taylor began his tenure as the British Davis Cup captain.

March 2000
1   Twelve cricketers were given six-month contracts with the England cricket team in a deal that means the
        players will only be released to play for their counties at the discretion of Duncan Fletcher, the coach. The
        twelve players are Nasser Hussain, Mike Atherton, Andrew Caddick, Darren Gough, Alec Stewart, Graeme
        Hick, Mark Ramprakash, Andrew Flintoff, Craig White, Dean Headley, Michael Vaughan and Chris Schofield.
3   Greyhound El Tenor won a record 100th open race when he won the 10.18 at Romford Stadium.
4   In the Six-Nations Rugby Union Championship, England defeated Wales 46–12, France beat Scotland
        28–16 and Ireland beat Italy 60–13.
7   400 metre runner Mark Richardson was suspended by UK Athletics over an adverse finding in a routine drugs
        test.
10   Striker Emile Heskey was transferred from Leicester City to Liverpool Football Club for a club record £11 million.
11   Ellery Hanley was sacked as coach to St Helens rugby league club.
12   Michael Schumacher won the Australian Formula One Grand Prix in Melbourne.
14   Istabraq, ridden by Charlie Swan and trained by A. P. O'Brien, won the Smurfit Champion Hurdle at
        Cheltenham for the third successive year.
16   Looks Like Trouble, ridden by Richard Johnson and trained by Noel Chance, won the Cheltenham Gold Cup.
17   Swimmer Mark Foster of Britain won his fourth world short-course title over 50 metres freestyle in Athens.
18   Derartu Tulu of Ethiopia won the women's world cross-country championship in Vilamoura, Portugal.
        Britain's Paula Radcliffe could only finish fifth.
19   In the Six-Nations Rugby Union Championship, England defeated Italy 59–12, Wales beat Scotland 26–18
        and Ireland beat France 27–25 Mohammed Mourhit of Belgium won the men's world cross-country
        championship in Vilamoura, Portugal.
20   Ahmed Barada, the world No 3 squash player, was stabbed twice in the back by an unidentified assailant
        and is in intensive care in a Cairo hospital.
24   Michael Johnson set a world record of 30.85 seconds for the 300 metres at the Engen athletics Grand Prix
        in Pretoria.
25   John Ferneley, ridden by Jimmy Fortune and trained by Paul Cole, won the Worthington Lincoln Handicap at
        Doncaster. Oxford won the University Boat Race for the first time since 1992.
26   Michael Schumacher won the Brazilian Formula One Grand Prix at Interlagos, São Paulo.
27   West Indian pace bowler Courtney Walsh became the world's leading Test match wicket-taker when Henry
        Olonga of Zimbabwe was caught by Wavell Hinds to become his 435th victim.
28   Stephen Maguire, 19, became the youngest snooker player to compile a 147 break in a professional
        tournament.
30   France defeated Scotland 2–0 and Finland beat Wales 2–1 in friendly football internationals.

CURRENT AFFAIRS

April 2000

1   In the Six-Nations Rugby Union Championship, Wales defeated Ireland 23–19 and France beat Italy 42–31 to ensure that England win the championship. Michelle Kwan of the USA regained her world figure skating title in Nice.

2   Scotland defeated England 19–13 in the final match of the Six-Nations Rugby Union Championship.

3   The International Amateur Athletic Association chose Birmingham as hosts of the 2003 world indoor championships and London as the venue for the 2005 world championships.

4   David Coulthard's appeal against his disqualification from second place in the Brazilian Grand Prix was thrown out.

8   Papillon, ridden by Ruby Walsh and trained by his father Ted Walsh, won the Grand National at Aintree.

9   Golfer Vijay Singh of Fiji won the US Masters at Augusta. Michael Schumacher won the San Marino Formula One Grand Prix at Imola. Ronnie O'Sullivan defeated Mark Williams 9–1 in the final of the Regal Scottish Open snooker championship at the Aberdeen Exhibition and Conference Centre.

11   Hansie Cronje was sacked as the South African cricket captain after allegedly admitting receiving money from an illegal Indian bookmaker to 'fix' a match.

15   Bowler Jeremy Henry, 26, of Ireland became the youngest world outdoor singles champion when he beat Steve Glasson of Australia 21–14 in Johannesburg.

16   Portugal's Antonio Pinto won his third London Marathon with a European record of 2 hrs 6 mins and 37 secs. Tegla Loroupe of Kenya won the women's race. Stuart Bingham defeated Stephen Hendry 10–7 in the first round of the Embassy World Snooker Championship.

17   David Gray defeated Ronnie O'Sullivan in the first round of the Embassy World Snooker Championship in Sheffield.

18   Chelsea were beaten 6–4 on aggregate in the European Cup quarter-finals after losing the second-leg 5–1 against Barcelona.

19   Manchester United lost 3–2 to Real Madrid in the European Cup quarter-final second leg and 3–2 on aggregate.

20   Leeds drew 2–2 with Galatasaray in the Uefa Cup semi-final second leg but lost 4–2 on aggregate.

22   Boxer Laila Ali, daughter of Muhammad Ali, stopped Kristia King in the fourth round in Guangzhou, China.

23   David Coulthard won the British Formula One Grand Prix at Silverstone.

26   Jimmy White was beaten 13–7 by Matthew Stevens in the quarter-finals of the World Professional Snooker Championship.

28   PSV Eindhoven forward Ruud van Nistelrooy ruptured the cruciate ligament of his right knee in a training accident which prevented his transfer to Manchester Utd for a record £18.25 million.

29   Lennox Lewis knocked out Michael Grant in the second round to retain his WBC and IBF heavyweight boxing titles.

30   Marat Safin of Russia defeated Juan Carlos Ferrero of Spain 6–3, 6–3, 6–4, to win the Barcelona Open tennis championship.

May 2000

1   Mark Williams beat Matthew Stevens 18–16 to win the World Professional Snooker Championship at the Crucible Theatre.

5   It was announced that British Superleague ice hockey matches will ensure clear winners next season by introducing a penalty shoot-out in drawn matches.

6   King's Best, trained by Michael Stoute and ridden by Kieren Fallon, won the Sagitta 2000 Guineas and it was announced that the horse will be known as Kings Best in future (i.e. no apostrophe)

7   Lahan, trained by John Gosden and ridden by Richard Hills, won the Sagitta 1000 Guineas Stakes at Newmarket. Stephen Hendry beat Mark Williams 9–5 to win the Alto Digital Premier Snooker League title. Mika Hakkinen won the Spanish Formula One Grand Prix in Barcelona.

13   Wasps defeated Northampton 31–23 to win the Tetley's Bitter Rugby Union Cup at Twickenham.

14   Golfer Padraig Harrington was disqualified in the Benson and Hedges International Open for failing to sign his card after the first round. Harrington was five strokes clear after the third round when the mistake came to light.

17   Galatasaray defeated Arsenal 4–1 on penalties in the UEFA Cup final in Copenhagen after drawing 0–0 at 90 minutes.

20   Chelsea defeated Aston Villa 1–0 in the FA Cup Final at Wembley; the winning goal was scored by Roberto Di Matteo.

21   Michael Schumacher won the European Formula One Grand Prix at the Nürburgring in Germany. England cricketers beat Zimbabwe by an innings and 209 runs in the first Test match at Lord's.

24   Real Madrid beat Valencia 3–0 in the European Cup final at the Stade de France.

27   Rangers beat Aberdeen 4–0 to add the Scottish Cup to their league title triumph. Northampton beat Munster 9–8 in the Heineken Cup rugby union final at Twickenham. Bachir, ridden by Frankie Dettori and trained by Saeed bin Suroor, won the Entenmann's Irish 2,000 Guineas at the Curragh.

28   Crimplene, ridden by Philip Robinson and trained by Clive Brittain, won the Entenmann's Irish 1,000 Guineas at the Curragh.

30   Scotland defeated Ireland 2–1 in a friendly international football match.

31   England defeated Ukraine 2–0 in a friendly international football match with goals from Robbie Fowler and Tony Adams.

June 2000

1   Jockeys Frankie Dettori and Ray Cochrane were injured in a plane crash at Newmarket racecourse which killed the pilot, Patrick Mackey.

4   David Coulthard won the Monaco Formula One Grand Prix at Monte Carlo. Stefano Garzelli of Italy won the Giro d'Italia (Tour of Italy) cycle race from his countryman Francesco Casagrande. Neil Coles became the first golfer to win a professional tournament in six different decades when he won the Jersey Seniors Open at La Moye.

5   England drew the second Test match against Zimbabwe at Trent Bridge.

6   Golfer Shigeki Maruyama of Japan shot a tour record 13-under par 58 at Woodmont Country Club, Rockville, Maryland. The record will not be ratified as it was in a qualifying round for a US PGA event.

9   Love Divine ridden by Richard Quinn and trained by Henry Cecil won the Vodaphone Oaks at Epsom.

10 Sinndar ridden by Johnny Murtagh and trained by John Oxx, won the Vodaphone Derby.

11 The New Jersey Devils won ice hockey's Stanley Cup after a 2–1 overtime victory against the Dallas Stars in Texas.

12 England were defeated 3–2 by Portugal in their opening game in the European Football Championship in Eindhoven.

14 Phil Tufnell joined Allan Donald, Phil DeFreitas and Devon Malcolm as the only cricketers to have taken 900 county championship wickets.

15 Former South African cricket captain Hans Cronje admitted that he had accepted bribes to throw a Test match.

17 The England football team gained their first competitive victory over Germany since the 1966 World Cup Final with a 1–0 win in Charleroi.

18 Michael Schumacher won the Canadian Formula One Grand Prix in Montreal The Le Mans 24-hour race was won by the Audi team led by Frank Biela. His co-drivers were Tom Kristensen and Emmanuele Pirro.

20 England were beaten 3–2 by Romania to end their involvement in Euro 2000 at the group stage.

22 Kayf Tara, ridden by Michael Kinane and trained by Saeed Bin Suroor, won the Ascot Gold Cup

23 New Zealander Graham Henry was named as the coach for the forthcoming British Lions tour of Australia.

26 Greg Rusedski was beaten in the first round at Wimbledon by American Vince Spadea who had lost his last 22 matches.

28 France defeated Portugal 2–1 on the golden goal rule to reach the final of the European football championship.

July 2000

1   England defeated the West Indies by two wickets in the second Test match at Lord's. Scotland's David Millar won the first stage of the Tour De France, a 16.5 kilometre time trial.

2   France defeated Italy 2–1 on the golden goal rule to win the European football championship. David Coulthard won the French Formula One Grand Prix at Magny-Cours. Sinndar, ridden by Johnny Murtagh and trained by John Oxx, won the Budweiser Irish Derby. John McEnroe defeated Bjorn Borg in a special challenge match held at Buckingham Palace.

3   Mark Phillipoussis beat Tim Henman 6–1, 5–7, 6–7, 6–3, 6–4 in the fourth round at Wimbledon.

5   Snooker player Steve Davis created the greatest upset in the history of nine-ball pool when he recovered from 8–2 down to beat world champion Efran Reyes 9–8.

6   FIFA announced that Germany would host the 2006 World Cup after a 12–11 victory vote over South Africa.

7   Pat Rafter beat Andre Agassi 7–5, 4–6, 7–5, 4–6, 6–3 to reach the Wimbledon singles final. Pete Sampras beat Vladimir Voltchkov 7–6, 6–2, 6–4 in the other semi-final.

8   Venus Williams defeated Lindsay Davenport 6–3, 7–6 to win the Wimbledon ladies singles crown. Mark Woodforde and Todd Woodbridge, affectionately known as 'The Woodies', won their sixth Wimbledon doubles title.

9   Pete Sampras defeated Pat Rafter 6–7, 7–6, 6–4, 6–2 to win the Wimbledon singles crown for the seventh time.

10 Venus and Serena Williams defeated Julie Halard-Decugis and Ai Sugiyama 6–3, 6–2 to win the Wimbledon doubles title.

13 Oxford University won the second annual cross-Channel relay swim against Cambridge in 8 hours 18 minutes.

14 Tim Henman defeated Luis Morejon to draw level with Ecuador in the Davis Cup tie after Greg Rusedski had earlier lost to Nicolas Lapenti. Rusedski subsequently withdrew from the tie with an injury.

15 Tim Henman and Arvind Parmar lost the Davis Cup doubles rubber against Nicolas and Giovanni Lapenti to trail 2–1. Lennox Lewis stopped Francois Botha of South Africa in the second round at the London Arena to retain his undisputed Heavyweight Boxing Crown. Mika Hakkinen won the Austrian Formula One Grand Prix at the A-1 Ring circuit in Spielberg.
    The Great Britain men's athletic team won the European Cup by half a point from Germany.

16 Great Britain were relegated from the Davis Cup elite nations following Arvind Parmar's defeat by Giovanni Lapenti of Ecuador. Tim Henman had earlier levelled the tie when he beat Nicolas Lapenti in straight sets.

17 Alex Corretja of Spain defeated Mariano Puerta of Argentina 6–1, 6–3 to win the Swiss Open tennis championship in Gstaad.

18 In the wake of Great Britain's Davis Cup defeat, Richard Lewis departed as director of tennis at the LTA.

19 Middlesex won their appeal against the eight-point penalty imposed for a poor pitch during their championship match against Glamorgan at Southgate last week.

20 The West Indies defeated England by three runs in the final qualifying match of the triangular NatWest cricket tournament despite a century from Alec Stewart.

21 Jack Nicklaus held a final photo shoot on the Swilcan Bridge on the 18th hole at St Andrews as he failed to make the cut in the Open golf championship.

22 England cricketers defeated Zimbabwe by six wickets to win the first triangular NatWest series.

23 Tiger Woods won the British Open golf championship by eight strokes from Ernie Els and Thomas Bjorn. Lance Armstrong won his second consecutive Tour de France. Both Michael Johnson and Maurice Greene pulled up injured during the 200 metres at the US Olympic athletics trials.

24 The world record football transfer fee was broken when the Portuguese midfield player Luis Figo was transferred from Barcelona to Real Madrid for £41 million.

27   Craig MacLean won his fourth consecutive British sprint title at the National cycling championships in Manchester.

29   Phil Taylor defeated Alan Warriner 18–12 to win the Stan James World Matchplay Darts Championship in Blackpool. Martin Dugard of Eastbourne, a wild card entry, created an upset by winning the British Speedway Grand Prix at Coventry.

30   Rubens Barrichello of Brazil won the German Formula One Grand Prix at Hockenheim, his first victory in his 123rd race.

31   Sussex cricketer Michael Bevan became the first batsman to score 1000 first-class runs for the season.

August 2000

4   Alec Stewart, who along with Mike Atherton was playing in his 100th Test match, scored a century on the second day of the third Test against the West Indies at Old Trafford.

5   Tayseer, ridden by Richard Hughes and trained by David Nicholls, won the Vodafone Steward's Cup at Goodwood.

6   Golfer Lee Westwood won the Volvo Scandanavian Masters.

7   The third Test between England and the West Indies at Old Trafford ended in a draw.

8   Golfer Mark James resigned as one of Sam Torrance's vice-captains for the Ryder Cup match at the Belfry next year following the controversy over remarks made about Nick Faldo in his recent book 'Into The Bear Pit'.

11   Tim Henman defeated Pete Sampras for the first time to reach the final of the Masters Series tennis tournament in Cincinnati.

12   Evander Holyfield became the first heavyweight boxer to win the world title for a fourth time when he outpointed John Ruiz for the vacant WBA crown. Joe Calzaghe retained his WBO super-middleweight title when he stopped Omar Sheika in the fifth round.

13   Thomas Enqvist defeated Tim Henman 7–6, 7–4 to win the Masters Series tennis tournament in Cincinnati.

17   The West Indian fast bowler Curtley Ambrose took his 400th Test match wicket.

18   England beat the West Indies in two days at Headingley to lead the current cricket Test series 2–1.

19   Boxer Naseem Hamed won his 35th professional fight when he knocked out Augie Sanchez in the fourth round.

21   Athletes Linford Christie, Dougie Walker and Gary Cadogan were banned for two years by the IAAF arbitration panel for alleged drug offences.

22   Giant's Causeway, ridden by Mick Kinane and trained by Aiden O'Brien, won his fourth group one horse race in nine weeks when he won the Juddmonte Stakes at York.

23   Petrushka, ridden by Johnny Murtagh and trained by Michael Stoute, won the Yorkshire Oaks at York.

27   Mika Hakkinen won the Belgian Formula One Grand Prix to extend his lead in the driver's championship to six points. John Whitaker riding Virtual Village Welham won the Peugeot Showjumping Derby at Hickstead. Tiger Woods won the NEC Invitational golf championship by 11 shots.

28   Dwaine Chambers defeated world record holder Maurice Greene over 100 metres in the Norwich Union Classic at Gateshead.

29   Beijing, Paris, Toronto, Istanbul and Osaka were named as the shortlisted cities for the 2008 Summer Olympic Games.

31   Mike Atherton and Marcus Trescothick shared a record first wicket partnership of 159 against the West Indies at the Oval.

September 2000

3   Andrew Nicholson of New Zealand riding Mr Smiffy won the Burghley Horse Trial.

4   England cricketers were victorious in the final Test match at the Oval to gain a 3–1 series win, the first over the West Indies since 1969. Curtley Ambrose subsequently announced his retirement from Test match cricket.

6   It was announced that a design fault meant that the gold, silver and bronze medals to be awarded at the Sydney Olympics depict the Colosseum in Rome rather than the Parthenon in Athens.

9   Venus Williams defeated Lindsay Davenport 6–4, 7–5 to win the US Open ladies singles title at Flushing Meadows. Millenary, ridden by Richard Quinn and trained at Arundel by John Dunlop, won the Rothmans Royals St Leger at Doncaster.

10   Marat Safin of Russia defeated Pete Sampras 6–4, 6–3, 6–3 to win the US Open mens singles title at Flushing Meadows. Michael Schumacher won the Italian Formula One Grand Prix at Monza but the race was marred by the death of a marshal, Paolo Ghislimberti, after a first-lap crash

12   Chelsea FC manager Gianluca Vialli was sacked by chairman Ken Bates.

13   Surrey won the county cricket championship for the second successive year.

15   The Sydney Olympic Games opened in colourful fashion with 400 metre runner Cathy Freeman igniting the Olympic flame.

16   Britain won Olympic gold on the first day of the games when cyclist Jason Queally won the kilometre race in 61.609 secs.

17   Ian Peel won Britain's second medal in Sydney when he took silver in the men's Olympic trap shooting competition. Britain's Olympic sprint team of Jason Queally, Chris Hoy and Craig Maclean won a silver medal in Sydney.

18   Yvonne McGregor, 39, won a bronze medal for Britain in the 3,000 metres cycling pursuit in Sydney. Eric Moussambani of Equatorial Guinea, nicknamed Eric the eel, won a standing ovation following his solo 100 metres freestyle swim at the Sydney Olympics, the first time he had completed the distance!

19   Richard Faulds won Great Britain's second gold medal of the Sydney Olympics in the men's double trap shooting. The British 4,000 metres cycling pursuit team won a bronze medal in the Sydney velodrome.

20   Four-time World Superbike Champion Carl Fogarty announced his retirement from the sport. Britain's equestrian team won silver in the Sydney three-day event. Simon Archer and Joanne Goode won a bronze medal in the badminton mixed doubles in Sydney.

21   Kate Howey won the only British judo medal when she gained a silver in the women's judo 70 kg class. Paul Ratcliffe won a silver medal for Britain in the men's K1 canoe slalom.

22   Steven Redgrave won his fifth consecutive Olympic rowing gold medal and Matthew Pinsent his third when the coxless fours narrowly defeated the Italians. Tim Foster and James Cracknell completed the four.

23   Steve Backley broke the Olympic javelin record but only gained the silver medal behind Jan Zelezny of the Czech Republic.

24   Great Britain won its second rowing gold medal of the Sydney Games when the men's coxed eight succeeded despite having to row in the repechage. Denise Lewis also won a gold medal for Great Britain, in the heptathlon. The women's quadruple sculling team won a silver medal but had to wait ten minutes for confirmation. Michael Schumacher won the US Grand Prix at Indianapolis to extend his lead in the Formula One Drivers' Championship.

25   Jonathan Edwards won gold in the men's triple jump. Katharine Merry (400 mts) and Kelly Holmes (800 mts) won bronzes. Andreea Raducan of Romania, the 16-year-old gold medal winning gymnast, tested positive for pseudoephedrine, a prohibited drug, and her medal was withdrawn.

27   Martin Johnson, the Leicester lock, was confirmed as England's rugby union captain for the coming season.

28   Darren Campbell earnt a surprise silver medal for Great Britain in the men's 200 metres sprint at the Sydney Olympics.

29   Shirley Robertson in the Europe dinghy class and Ben Ainslie in the laser class won two more sailing golds for Britain.

30   Iain Percy won gold in the men's Finn class to ensure Great Britain topped the table in the sailing medals. Katy Nowaitee, ridden by John Reid and trained by Peter Harris, won the Tote Cambridgeshire at Newmarket.

October 2000

1   Great Britain won two gold medals on the final day of the Sydney Olympics. Audley Harrison won the super heavyweight boxing title and Stephanie Cook the modern pentathlon. Sinndar, ridden by Johnny Murtagh and trained by John Oxx, won the Prix de L'arc de Triomphe at Longchamps.

7   England were defeated 1–0 by Germany in a football World Cup qualifier at Wembley. Kevin Keegan immediately resigned as coach and was replaced temporarily by Howard Wilkinson. In other World Cup group matches Scotland beat San Marino 2–0, Northern Ireland drew with Denmark 1–1, and Wales drew with Norway 1–1.

8   Michael Schumacher won the Japanese Grand Prix to win the Formula One world championship for the third time. European Lady golfers defeated the United States 14 1/2 points to 11 1/2 points to regain the Solheim Cup at Loch Lomond. Peter Ebdon defeated Jimmy White 9–6 to win the British Open snooker championship.

9   Golfer Lee Westwood defeated Colin Montgomerie at the 38th hole to win the Cisco World Matchplay Championship.

10   The FA banned Arsenal manager Arsène Wenger from the touchline for 12 matches following an alleged confrontation with an official in the tunnel after his teams 1–0 defeat by Sunderland at the Stadium of Light on the opening day of the season. Naseem Hamed relinquished his WBO featherweight boxing title but will still be rated the world number one.

11   England footballers drew with Finland 0–0 in Helsinki which left them bottom of World Cup qualifying group nine. In other group matches Scotland drew 1–1 with Croatia, Iceland beat Northern Ireland 1–0, and Wales drew with Poland 0–0.

12   *The Guinness Book of Records'* latest entry involves footballer Lee Todd, who was sent off after two seconds for swearing when he heard the whistle for the start of the match. Colin Edwards of the USA won the World Superbike Championship.

13   Nicole Cooke, a 17-year-old cyclist from Glamorgan, became the first Briton to win the junior women's title at the World Road Race Championships held in Plouay, France.

14   Heros Fatal, ridden by Gary Carter and trained by Martin Pipe, won the Tote Cesarewitch at Newmarket.

15   Tim Henman defeated Tommy Haas of Germany 6–4, 6–4, 6–4 to win the CA Trophy in Vienna. Spanish golfers retained the Alfred Dunhill Cup at St Andrews by defeating South Africa in the final. David Evans defeated Paul Price 15–11, 15–6, 15–10 to win the British Open Squash Championship.

17   The New York Mets defeated the St Louis Cardinals 4–1 in the best of seven National League baseball championship series.

18   Mark Lewis-Francis of Great Britain won the 100 metres in the world junior athletic championships in a time of 10.12 seconds. The New York Yankees baseball team defeated the Seattle Mariners 4–2 in the best of seven American League series.

19   John Higgins beat Terry Murphy in the Telford snooker Grand Prix but then scratched in order to attend his brother's wedding.

20   Boxer Mike Tyson beat Andrew Golota in Detroit after the Pole controversially refused to come out for the third round.

21   Great Britain swimmers Giles Long, Jody Cundy and Emily Jennings won gold medals at the Sydney Paralympic Games.

26   The Great Britain cycling pursuit team won a silver medal at the World Track Championships at the Manchester velodrome.

27   Tanni Grey-Thompson claimed her fourth gold medal at the Paralympics in the T53 400 metres to add to her victories in the 100, 200 and 800 metres. The New York Yankees beat the New York Mets 4–1 to win the baseball World Series. Chris Boardman cycled 49.441 kilometres to beat Eddy Merckx's one-hour record on a standard bike.

28   Yvonne McGregor won the women's 3000 metres cycling pursuit world championship in Manchester.

29   Rob Hayles won the bronze medal in the 4000 metres pursuit at the world cycling championships in Manchester.

31   Britain's top Olympian Steve Redgrave announced that he was retiring from international rowing. The
        Football Association announced that Sven-Goran Eriksson would be the next England football team coach.

November 2000
2   The wet weather caused the first-ever cancellation of the 47th Fours Head of the River rowing event from
        Mortlake to Putney.
3   Boxer Steve Robinson was beaten by Cassius Baloyi of South Africa for the WBU featherweight
        championship in Ebbw Vale.
4   Kalanisi, ridden by Johnny Murtagh and trained by Sir Michael Stoute, won the Breeders Cup Turf Race in
        Kentucky. Kevin Darley won the flat-race jockeys' riding championship.
5   Pierre Fulke of Sweden won the Volvo Masters Golf Championship from Darren Clarke of Northern Ireland.
6   Rodney Eyles, president of the Professional Squash Association and a former world champion, announced
        his retirement.
7   Brew, ridden by Kerrin McEvoy, won the Melbourne Cup, Australia's richest horse-race.
8   Jamie Delgado, the national tennis champion, was beaten in the second round of this year's competition by
        Luke Milligan.
9   Caretaker England football manager Peter Taylor announced his decision to cap the age of squad members
        at 30 for the forthcoming match against Italy.
11   Lennox Lewis defeated David Tua of Samoa to retain his WBC and IBF World Heavyweight Boxing titles, in
        Las Vegas. Lady Cricket, ridden by Tony McCoy and trained by Martin Pipe, won the Thomas Pink Gold Cup
        at Cheltenham, the race formerly known as the Murphy's Gold Cup and originally the Mackeson Gold Cup.
12   English golfer Lee Westwood won the European Order of Merit following his second place to Canadian Mike
        Weir in the American Express Championship.
15   Italy defeated England 1–0 in a football friendly under new temporary coach Peter Taylor, the Leicester City
        manager.
16   Surrey batsman Graham Thorpe scored his maiden Test century for England on the second day of the first
        Test against Pakistan in Lahore.
18   Skier Heinz Schilchegger of Austria won his first-ever world cup slalom victory at Park City Mountain Resort,
        Utah.
19   Allan Donald became the first South African bowler to take 300 Test wickets when he had Shayne O'Connor
        of New Zealand leg before wicket.
20   John McEnroe resigned as captain of the United States Davis Cup team citing frustration with the failure of
        top players to make themselves available. McEnroe's brother, Patrick, was named as his replacement.
22   England's rugby union players ended a 24-hour strike over pay following an ultimatum from team manager
        Clive Woodward.
23   Goran Ivanisevic was forced to retire from the Samsung International Tennis Tournament after breaking all
        three of his rackets during a match.
25   Australia defeated New Zealand 40–12 to win the Rugby League World Cup Final. King's Road, ridden by
        Jamie Goldstein and trained by Nigel Twiston-Davies, won the Hennessy Gold Cup at Newbury.
26   Tim Henman defeated Dominik Hrbaty of Slovakia 6–2, 6–2 to win the Samsung International Tennis
        Tournament in Brighton. Richard Burns of Great Britain won the Network Q RAC Rally but runner-up Marcus
        Grönholm of Finland won the rally driver's world championship
30   Petra Haltmayer of Germany won the opening downhill event of the season and captured the first World Cup
        Skiing victory of her career.

December 2000
1   Top British Showjumper John Whitaker underwent surgery for a cerebral haemorrhage after collapsing in a
        Stockholm hotel.
3   England and Pakistan drew the second Test match in Faisalabad. John Higgins beat Mark Williams 10–4 to
        win the Liverpool Victoria UK snooker championship at Bournemouth. Gustavo Kuerten ensured ending the
        year as world number one tennis player following his win in the Master's Cup in Lisbon.
4   Former England football coachTerry Venables was appointed as temporary first-team coach at
        Middlesbrough FC although Bryan Robson retains the position of manager.
5   Mohammad Azharuddin, the former Indian cricket captain, and batsman Ajay Sharma, were banned for life
        for match-fixing.
6   Regine Cavagnoud of France won her first World Cup super giant slalom of the season in Val d'Isère.
10   Five-time Olympic gold medal-winning rower Steve Redgrave became BBC Sports Personality of the Year.
        Spain defeated Australia 3–1 in Barcelona to win the Davis Cup final.
11   England cricketers beat Pakistan by six wickets in Karachi to win the series 1–0.
14   Spain's Paralympic basketball team were asked to hand back their gold medals after ten squad members
        were found to have no disability.
16   Boxer Paul Ingle was rushed to hospital for a life-saving brain operation after being knocked out in the last
        round of his IBF featherweight title defence.
17   The American pool players defeated Europe for the fifth year running in the Mosconi Cup in Bethnal Green,
        London.
19   Alain Baxter of Scotland took a career-best eighth place in the World Cup slalom in Madonna di Campiglio, Italy.
21   British tennis players Lee Childs and James Nelson became the world's number one ranked junior doubles
        pair in the world.
26   First Gold, ridden by Thierry Doumen and trained by Francois Doumen, won the King George VI Chase at
        Kempton.
27   Jocks Cross, ridden by Brian Crowley and trained by Venetia Williams, won the Coral Eurobet Welsh
        National at Chepstow.

28   Martin Johnson, captain of the England rugby union team, was suspended for five weeks for foul play during the Tetley's Bitter Cup quarter-final on December 9th.

29   Five-time Olympic gold-medal-winning rower Steve Redgrave was knighted in the New Year's Honours List. Martin Schmitt of Germany won the first event of the Four Hills tournament in Oberstdorf with a ski jump record of 133 metres.

30   Richard Virenque, a five-time Tour de France King of the Mountains, was suspended by the Swiss Cycling Federation for nine months after admitting taking performance-enhancing drugs. Muttiah Muralitharan of Sri Lanka became the seventeenth bowler to take 300 Test wickets when he had Shaun Pollock caught at silly point.

Birthdays 2000

Every effort has been made in verifying every entry below, but in the course of my research I soon realised what a veritable minefield of misinformation was apparent in any list of people's birthdays. The problem is that, even when the source is the person themself, it cannot infallibly be relied upon. To give an example of the intrinsic difficulties of drafting such a list I cite Ms Katharine Hepburn as having the most interesting and oft-most mistaken birth date. The multiple Oscar-winning actress is documented as being born on 9th November 1909 in many reputable sources, including those that bothered to contact Ms Hepburn directly. However, in her autobiography she gives her date of birth as 12th May 1907. Further research shows that Ms Hepburn had a devoted brother, Tom, who died tragically aged 14, and out of respect for him she usurped his birth date as her own. Not to add further to the confusion, this entry, and all other controversial entries, have been omitted from my list. I apologise in advance for any persons listed that are no longer living, it is inevitable that with the passing of time from the start of the year until the publication date, a sad few will have passed away. I hope living relatives will not be offended by their inclusion in these circumstances.

January 2000

1   JD Salinger, author, 81; Lawrence Rowe, West Indian cricketer, 51; Zena Marshall, actress, 73

2   David Bailey, photographer, 62; Roger Miller, singer and composer, 64

3   Sir George Martin, composer and record producer, 74; Michael Schumacher, racing driver, 31; John Thaw, actor, 58; Mel Gibson, actor and director, 44

4   Floyd Patterson, boxer, 65; Iain Cuthbertson, actor, 70; Margaret Marshall, singer, 51; Dyan Cannon, actress, 61; Rick Stein, chef and broadcaster, 53

5   Diane Keaton, actress, 54; General Sir Michael Rose, soldier, 60; Robert Duvall, actor, 69; King Juan Carlos of Spain, 62; Eusebio, footballer, 57

6   Rowan Atkinson, comedian, 45; Kapil Dev, cricketer, 41; Nancy Lopez-Melton, golfer, 43; Barry John, rugby union player, 55; Angus Deayton, broadcaster, 45; Terry Venables, footballer, 57; Sacha Distel, singer, 68; Sylvia Sims, actress, 66; Michael Foale, British-born astronaut, 43

7   Ian Le Frenais, screenwriter, 63; Ross Norman, squash player, 41; Helen Worth, actress, 49; Nicolas Cage, actor, 36

8   David Bowie, singer and songwriter, 53; Shirley Bassey, singer, 63; Stephen Hawking, physicist, 58; Ron Moody, actor, 76

9   Joan Baez, singer, 59; Joely Richardson, actress, 35; Susannah York, actress, 58; Clive Dunn, actor, 78

10   Rod Stewart, singer, 55; Derek Hammond-Stroud, operatic baritone, 74; Freddie Starr, comedian, 56; Anton Rodgers, actor, 67

11   Bryan Robson, footballer, 43; John Sessions, actor and comedian, 47; Arthur Scargill, trade unionist, 62

12   Kirstie Alley, actress, 45; Anthony Andrews, actor, 52; Michael Aspel, broadcaster, 67; Pieter Willem Botha, South African politician, 84; Joe Frazier, boxer, 56; Des O'Connor, entertainer, 68; Brendan Foster, athlete, 52; Anne Howells, opera singer, 59

13   Michael Bond, author, 74; Stephen Hendry, snooker player, 31; Ronan Rafferty, golfer, 36; Tim Flavin, entertainer, 41

14   Faye Dunaway, actress, 59; Trevor Nunn, theatre director, 60; Warren Mitchell, actor, 74; Maina Gielgud, ballerina, 55; Richard Briers, actor, 66

15   Margaret Beckett, politician, 57; Chuck Berry, singer, 74; Frank Bough, broadcaster, 67; Princess Michael of Kent, 55; Gareth Hale, comedian, 47

16   Christine Truman, tennis player, 59; Cliff Thorburn, snooker player, 52; Keith Shackleton, artist and naturalist, 77

17   Muhammad Ali, boxer, 58; Vidal Sassoon, hair stylist, 72; Paul Young, singer, 44; Gillian Weir, concert organist, 59; Moira Shearer, ballerina, 74

18   Kevin Costner, actor and director, 45; John Boorman, film director, 67; Dr David Bellamy, botanist, 67; Raymond Briggs, illustrator, 66; Jane Horrocks, actress, 36; Mark Rylance, artistic director of the Globe Theatre, 40

19   Stefan Edberg, tennis player, 34; Dolly Parton, singer, 54; Simon Rattle, conductor, 45; Michael Crawford, actor and singer, 58; Phil Everly, singer, 61; Richard Lester, film director, 68; Julian Barnes, novelist, 54; Robert Palmer, singer, 51; Javier Pérez de Cuéllar, Secretary-General of the United Nations, 1982–91, 80

20   Liza Goddard, actress, 50; Edwin 'Buzz' Aldrin, astronaut, 70; Tom Baker, actor, 64; Malcolm McLaren, impressario, 53; The Countess of Wessex, 35

21   Placido Domingo, operatic tenor, 59; Jack Nicklaus, golfer, 60; Paul Scofield, actor, 78; Martin Shaw, actor, 55; Emma Lee Bunton, singer, 24

22   Nigel Benn, boxer, 36; George Foreman, boxer, 52; Linda Blair, actress, 41; John Hurt, actor, 60; Nyree Dawn Porter, actress, 64; Claire Rayner, writer, 69; Mary Hayley Bell, playwright, 89; Gillian Shepherd, politician, 60; Piper Laurie, actress, 68

CURRENT AFFAIRS

23   Princess Caroline of Monaco, 43; Jeanne Moreau, actress, 72; Rutger Hauer, actor, 56
24   Neil Diamond, singer, 59; Bamber Gascoigne, author and broadcaster, 65; Desmond Morris, zoologist, 72;
      Nastassya Kinski, actress, 39
25   Corazon Aquino, former President of the Phillipines, 67; Angela Thorne, actress, 61; Emma Freud,
      broadcaster, 38; Raymond Baxter, broadcaster, 78; David Ginola, footballer, 33
26   Paul Newman, actor, 75; Eartha Kitt, singer, 72; Ronald Allison, author and broadcaster, 68; Christopher
      Hampton, playwright, 54
27   Right Reverend HD Halsey, former Bishop of Carlisle, 81; Lord Rix of Whitehall, actor, 76; Michael Craig,
      actor and playwright, 71
28   Mikhail Baryshnikov, ballet dancer, 52; Robert Wyatt, rock musician, 55; Professor John Tavener, composer,
      56; Alan Alda, actor, 64
29   Germaine Greer, author, 61; Tom Selleck, actor, 55; John Junkin, actor, 70; Raymond Keene, chess player,
      51; Oprah Winfrey, television presenter, 46
30   Phil Collins, rock singer, 49; Vanessa Redgrave, actress, 63; Victoria Principal, actress and writer, 50; Gene
      Hackman, actor, 68
31   Queen Beatrix of the Netherlands, 62; Jean Simmons, actress, 71; Christopher Chataway, athlete and
      politician, 69

February 2000
1   Boris Yeltsin, former Russian President, 69; Don Everly, singer, 63; Princess Stephanie of Monaco, 34;
      Renata Tebaldi, soprano, 78
2   Andrew Davis, conductor, 56; Valéry Gisgard d'Estaing, former French President, 74; David Jason, actor, 60;
      Norman Fowler, politician, 62
3   Val Doonican, singer, 71; Jeremy Kemp, actor, 65; Gillian Ayres, painter, 70; Bobby Simpson, Australian
      cricketer, 64
4   Richard Ryder, politician, 51; Norman Wisdom, actor and comedian, 83; Russell Hoban, author, 75
5   Charlotte Rampling, actress, 54; Susan Hill, novelist and playwright, 58; John Nettleton, actor, 71; Barbara
      Hershey, actress, 52
6   Patrick MacNee, actor, 78; Ronald Reagan, US President, 89; Denis Norden, writer and broadcaster, 78;
      Jimmy Tarbuck, comedian, 60; Fred Trueman, cricketer, 69; Francois Truffaut, film director, 68; Keith
      Waterhouse, writer, 71; Gayle Hunnicutt, actress, 57
7   Peter Jay, broadcaster, 63; Dora Bryan, actress, 76; Gareth Hunt, actor, 57; Sammy Lee, footballer, 41;
      Gerald Davies, rugby player, 55
8   Jack Lemmon, actor, 75; John Williams, composer and conductor, 68; Osian Ellis, harpist, 72
9   Mia Farrow, actress, 55; Sandy Lyle, golfer, 42; Ben E King, singer, 58; Janet Suzman, actress, 61; Clive
      Swift, actor, 64
10   Larry Adler, musician, 86; Greg Norman, golfer, 45; Mark Spitz, swimmer, 50; Roberta Flack, singer, 62;
      Robert Wagner, actor, 70
11   Jennifer Aniston, actress, 31; Dennis Skinner, politician, 68; Mary Quant, fashion designer, 66; Leslie
      Nielsen, actor, 74; Burt Reynolds, actor, 64
12   Fergus Slattery, rugby player, 49; Steve Backley, javelin thrower, 31; Annette Crosbie, actress, 66; Simon
      MacCorkindale, actor, 48
13   Liam Brady, footballer, 44; Kim Novak, actress, 67; George Segal, actor, 66; Robbie Williams, singer, 26;
      Jerry Springer, talk-show host, 56
14   Prince Hans Adam II of Liechtenstein, 55; Kevin Keegan, footballer, 49; Alan Parker, film director, 56;
      Manuela Maleeva, tennis player, 33
15   Claire Bloom, actress, 69; Jane Seymour, actress, 49; Clare Short, politician, 54; Gerald Harper, actor, 71
16   Anthony Dowell, ballet dancer, 57; John McEnroe, tennis player, 41; John Schlesinger, film director, 74; Ian
      Lavender, actor, 54
17   Ruth Rendell, author, 70; Patricia Routledge, actress, 71; Prunella Gee, actress, 50; Gene Pitney, singer, 59;
      Julia McKenzie, actress and singer, 59; Barry Humphries, actor and comedian, 66; Yasser Arafat, Arab
      leader, 71
18   Bobby Robson, football manager, 67; Cybil Shepherd, actress, 50; Greta Scacchi, actress, 40; John
      Travolta, actor, 46; Yoko Ono Lennon, 66
19   Hana Mandlikova, tennis player, 38; Smokey Robinson, singer, 60; HRH The Duke of York, 40; Gwen Taylor,
      actress, 61
20   Robert Altman, film director, 73; Jimmy Greaves, footballer, 60; Mike Leigh, dramatist, 57; Sidney Poitier,
      actor, 73
21   Harald V, King of Norway, 63; Robert Mugabe, Zimbabwe politician, 76; Alan Rickman, actor, 54; Nina
      Simone, singer, 66
22   Bruce Forsyth, entertainer, 72; Sir John Mills, actor, 92; The Duchess of Kent, 67; Julie Walters, actress, 50;
      Niki Lauda, racing driver, 51
23   Helena Sukova, tennis player, 35; Pam Blundell, fashion designer, 33; Sylvie Guillem, ballerina, 35; Peter
      Fonda, actor, 60
24   Brian Close, cricketer, 69; Denis Law, footballer, 60; Alain Prost, racing driver, 45; Michel Legrand, composer
      and conductor, 68
25   Elkie Brooks, singer, 55; George Harrison, musician, 57; David Puttnam, film producer, 59; Tom Courtenay,
      actor, 63
26   Johnny Cash, singer, 68; Everton Weekes, cricketer, 75; Sandie Shaw, singer, 53
27   Paddy Ashdown, politician, 59; Ralph Nader, consumer protection pioneer, 66; Elizabeth Taylor, actress, 68;
      Antoinette Sibley, ballerina, 61; Kenzo Takada, fashion designer, 61; Joanne Woodward, actress, 70
28   Peter Alliss, golfer and broadcaster, 69; Stephanie Beacham, actress, 51; Robin Cook, politician, 54; Barry

McGuigan, boxer, 39; Brian Moore, football commentator, 68; Barry Fantoni, novelist, cartoonist and jazz musician, 60

29   Joss Ackland, actor, 72, and Mario Andretti, racing driver, 60

March 2000
1   Harry Belafonte, singer, 73; David Broome, showjumper, 60; Roger Daltrey, actor and singer, 56; Mike Read, radio and television presenter, 49
2   Margaret Barbieri, ballerina, 53; Mikhael Gorbachev, Russian statesman, 69; Ian Woosnam, golfer, 42; John Peter Rhys Williams, rugby player, 51; Dame Naomi James, yachtswoman, 52; Lou Reed, rock singer, 56; Jon Bon Jovi, rock singer, 38
3   Miranda Richardson, actress, 42; Fatima Whitbread, athlete, 39; Peter O'Sullevan, racing commentator, 82
4   Kenny Dalglish, footballer, 49; Patrick Moore, astronomer, 77; Bernard Haitink, violinist and conductor, 71; Shakin' Stevens, pop singer, 52
5   Elaine Page, singer, 48; Sir Anthony Hedges, composer, 69; Samantha Eggar, actress, 61; Dean Stockwell, actor, 64; Richard Hickox, conductor, 52
6   Valentina Tereshkova, first woman in space, 63; Dame Kiri Te Kanawa, operatic soprano, 56; Jean Boht, actress, 64
7   Viv Richards, cricketer, 48; Sir Ranulph Fiennes, explorer, 56; Ivan Lendl, tennis player, 40; The Earl of Snowdon, photographer, 70; Mickey Dolenz, actor, 55
8   Lynn Redgrave, actress, 57; Douglas Hurd, politician, 70; Gyles Brandreth, politician, 52; Gary Numan, musician, 42; Lynn Seymour, ballerina, 61
9   Bill Beaumont, rugby player and sports commentator, 48; Bobby Fischer, chess player, 57
10   Prince Edward of Wessex, 36; Fou Ts'ong, concert pianist, 66; Hugh Johnson, wine connoisseur, 61; Terry Holmes, rugby player, 43
11   Lord Lawson of Blaby, 68; Rupert Murdoch, chairman of the News Corporation, 69; David Gentleman, designer and painter, 70
12   Liza Minnelli, actress and singer, 54; David Mellor, politician and broadcaster, 51; Willie Duggan, rugby player, 50
13   Neil Sedaka, singer and composer, 61; Sir Robert Mark, former Police Commisioner, 83; Joe Bugner, boxer, 50
14   Pam Ayres, poet, 53; Michael Caine, actor, 67; Rita Tushingham, actress, 58; Quincy Jones, bandleader and impressario, 67; Tessa Sanderson, 44, athlete; Jasper Carrott, comedian and actor, 55
15   Ben Okri, author, 41; Sunetra Gupta, authoress, 35; John Duttine, actor, 51; Ry Cooder, guitarist, 53
16   Bernardo Bertolucci, film director, 59; Leo McKern, actor, 80; Kate Nelligan, actress, 49; Matthew Bannister, BBC executive, 43
17   Sir Robin Knox-Johnston, yachtsman, 61; Kurt Russell, actor, 49; Penelope Lively, writer, 67; Alexander McQueen, fashion designer, 31; Lesley-Anne Down, actress, 46; Patrick Duffy, actor, 51; Professor John Lill, concert pianist, 56
18   Ron Atkinson, football manager, 61; Alex Higgins, snooker player, 51; Pat Eddery, jockey, 48; Ingemar Stenmark, slalom skier, 44; Kenny Lynch, entertainer, 61; John Hoyer Updike, novelist, 68
19   Glenn Close, actress, 53; Patrick McGoohan, actor, 72; Bruce Willis, actor, 45; Ursula Andress, actress, 64; Philip Roth, novelist, 67
20   William Hurt, actor, 50; Dame Vera Lynn, singer, 83; Brian Mulroney, Canadian politician, 61; Madan Lal, Indian cricketer, 49
21   Brian Clough, football manager, 65; Timothy Dalton, actor, 54; Alvin Kallicharran, cricketer, 51; Michael Heseltine, politician, 67; Lord Oaksey, jockey, 71
22   George Benson, guitarist and singer, 57; Sir Andrew Lloyd Webber, composer, 52; Marcel Marceau, mime artist, 77; Mary Tamm, actress, 50; Stephen Sondheim, composer and lyricist, 70; William Shatner, actor, 69; Leslie Thomas, author, 69
23   Princess Eugenie of York, 10; Mike Atherton, cricketer, 32; Barry Cryer, writer and comedian, 65; Roger Bannister, athlete and neurologist, 71
24   Barbara Daly, make-up artist, 55; Benjamin Luxon, baritone, 63; Alan Sugar, businessman, 53; Patrick Malahide, actor, 55; Peter Powell, disc jockey, 49
25   Aretha Franklin, singer, 58; Elton John, musician, 53; Nick Lowe, musician, 51; Penelope Gilliatt, author, 68
26   Pierre Boulez, composer and conductor, 75; Leonard Nimoy, actor, 69; Diana Ross, singer, 56; Kyung-wha Chung, violinist, 52; James Caan, actor, 61
27   Lord Callaghan of Cardiff, politician, 88; Maria Ewing, opera singer, 50; Michael York, actor, 58; Mariah Carey, singer, 30; Quentin Tarantino, film director, 37
28   Neil Kinnock, politician, 58; Richard Stilgoe, musician, 57; Michael Parkinson, journalist and chat-show host, 65
29   Richard Rodney Bennett, composer, 64; Jennifer Capriati, tennis player, 24; Eric Idle, actor, 57; John Major, politician, 57; Lord Tebbit, politician, 69; Lucy Lawless, actress, 32; Elle Macpherson, model and actress, 36
30   Warren Beatty, actor, 63; Eric Clapton, guitarist, 55; Tom Sharpe, novelist, 72; Lord MacLaurin of Knebworth, 63; Rolf Harris, entertainer, 70; Celine Dion, singer, 32
31   Richard Chamberlain, actor, 64; John Fowles, writer, 73; Lord Steel of Aikwood, politician, 61; Herb Alpert, musician, 64 Shirley Jones, actress, 65

April 2000
1   David Gower, cricketer, 43; George Baker, actor, 69; Steve Race, musician and broadcaster, 79; Ali MacGraw, actress, 62; Debbie Reynolds, actress, 68
2   Linford Christie, athlete, 40; Penelope Keith, actress, 61; Sue Townsend, writer, 54
3   Alec Baldwin, actor, 42; Anthony Wedgwood Benn, politician, 75; John Virgo, snooker player and television

presenter, 54; Marlon Brando, actor, 76; Eddie Murphy, actor, 39; Doris Day, actress, 76; Jonathan Lynn, director, author and actor, 57

4   Paul Parker, footballer, 36; Dave Sexton, football manager, 70; Margaret Dupont, tennis player, 82; Anthony Perkins, actor, 68; Robert Downey Jr, actor, 35

5   Jane Asher, actress and author, 54; Tom Finney, footballer, 78; Gregory Peck, actor, 84; Agnetha Faltskog, singer, 50; Nigel Hawthorne, actor, 71

6   Andre Previn, conductor, 71; Rory Bremner, impressionist, 39; Paul Daniels, magician, 62; Roger Cook, broadcaster, 57

7   Francis Ford Coppola, film director, 61; David Frost, television presenter, 61; James Garner, actor, 72; Pandit Ravi Shankar, sitar player, 80; Jackie Chan, actor, 46; Gerry Cottle, circus proprietor, 55; Martyn Lewis, newsreader and presenter, 55; Gordon Kaye, actor, 59; Ian Richardson, actor, 66; Russell Crowe, actor, 36

8   Kofi Annan, Secretary General of the UN, 62; Tony Banks, politician, 57; Ian Smith, Rhodesian politician, 81; Vivian Westwood, fashion designer, 59; Julian Lennon, musician, 37; Hywel Bennett, actor, 56; Dorothy Tutin, actress, 69; Eric Porter, actor, 72; Patricia Arquette, actress, 32

9   Severiano Ballesteros, golfer, 43; Alan Knott, cricketer, 54; Dennis Quaid, actor, 46; Hannah Gordon, actress, 59; Jean-Paul Belmondo, actor, 67

10   Gloria Hunniford, radio and television presenter, 60; Omar Sharif, actor, 68; Paul Theroux, writer, 59; David Moorcroft, athlete, 47

11   Gervase de Peyer, clarinettist, 73; James Alan Ferman, former Director of British Board of Film Classification, 70; Jill Gascoigne, actress, 62

12   Sir Alan Ayckbourn, playwright, 61; Montserrat Caballé, opera singer, 67; George Robertson, politician, 54; David Cassidy, singer and actor, 51

13   Seamus Heaney, Poet, 61; Garry Kasparov, Chess Player, 37; Edward Fox, actor, 63; Peter Davison, actor, 49

14   Julie Christie, actress, 60; David Hope, Archbishop of York, 60; Rod Steiger, actor, 75; Julian Lloyd Webber, cellist, 49; Robert Carlyle, actor, 39

15   Lord Archer of Weston-super-Mare, 60; Claudia Cardinale, Actress, 62; Neville Marriner, Conductor, 76; Emma Thompson, Actress, 41; Marty Wilde, pop singer, 61; Samantha Fox, singer and model, 34

16   Queen Margrethe II of Denmark, 60; Spike Milligan, comedian, writer and actor, 82; Peter Ustinov, actor, writer and wit, 79; Ruth Madoc, actress, 57; Joan Bakewell, television presenter, 67; Vince Hill, singer, 68

17   Victoria Addams, singer, 26; Clare Francis, novelist and yachtswoman, 54; James Last, bandleader, 71; Olivia Hussey, actress, 49

18   Hayley Mills, actress, 54; Teddy Taylor, politician, 63; Nick Farr-Jones, rugby player, 38

19   Sue Barker, tennis player and broadcaster, 44; Dickie Bird, cricket umpire, 67; Dudley Moore, musician and comic actor, 65; Alan Price, musician, 58; Ruby Wax, comedienne, 47

20   Nicholas Lyndhurst, actor, 39; Alan Beith, politician, 57; Ray Brooks, actor, 61; Ryan O'Neal, actor, 59; Peter Snow, broadcaster, 62

21   HM the Queen, 74; Anthony Quinn, actor, 85; John Mortimer, QC, author and playwright, 75; Srinivas Venkataraghavan, Indian cricketer, 54

22   George Cole, actor, 75; Jack Nicholson, actor, 63; Lloyd Honeyghan, boxer, 40; Peter Frampton, rock musician, 50; Glen Campbell, singer, 62

23   Lady Gabriella Windsor, 19; Shirley Temple Black, actress and diplomat, 72; Bill Cotton, television executive, 72; Lee Majors, actor, 60; The Hon. Victoria Glendinning, author, 63; Tessa Wyatt, actress, 52

24   Jean Paul Gaultier, fashion designer, 46; Barbra Streisand, actress and singer, 58; Bridget Riley, artist, 69; John Williams, guitarist, 59; Richard Jarman, opera-house director, 51; Shirley Maclaine, actress, 66; Sir Clement Freud, politician and writer, 76; Ralph Brown, sculptor, 72

25   The Earl of Lichfield, photographer, 61; Eric Bristow, darts player, 43; Al Pacino, actor, 60; Dr John Nunn, chess player, 45; William Roache, actor, 68

26   Peter Schaufuss, ballet dancer, 50; Derek Waring, actor, 70; David Coleman, sports commentator, 74

27   Darcey Bussell, ballerina, 31; Igor Oistrakh, violinist, 69; Michael Fish, meteorologist, 56; Sheena Easton, singer, 41; Anouk Aimée, actress, 68

28   Lady Helen Taylor, 36; Duane Eddy, guitarist, 62; Ann-Margret, actress, 59; Nicola Le Fanu, composer, 53

29   Andre Agassi, tennis player, 30; Daniel Day-Lewis, actor, 43; Lonnie Donegan, musician, 69; Zizi Jeanmaire, dancer, 76; Zubin Mehta, conductor, 64; Saddam Hussein, tyrannical president of Iraq, 63; Lt General Sir Peter de la Billière, 66; Cheryl Kennedy, actress, 53; Ann Bell, actress, 60; Michelle Pfeiffer, actress, 43; Uma Thurman, actress, 30; Jerry Seinfeld, comedy actor, 46

30   King Carl XVI of Sweden, 54; Leslie Grantham, actor, 54; Dickie Davies, sports commentator, 67; Jill Clayburgh, actress, 56

May 2000

1   Joanna Lumley, actress, 54; Una Stubbs, actress, 63; Steve Cauthen, jockey,40; Lady Sarah Chatto, 36; Rita Coolidge, actress, 55

2   David Beckham, footballer, 24; Jimmy White, snooker player, 38; Brian Lara, cricketer, 31; Engelbert Humperdinck, singer, 64

3   James Brown, soul singer, 67; Henry Cooper, boxer, 66; Ben Elton, author, 41; Allan Wells, athlete, 48; Kathy Cook, athlete, 40

4   Michael Barrymore, entertainer, 48; Eric Sykes, comedian and writer, 77; John Watson, racing driver, 54; Professor Marisa Robles, harpist, 63

5   Michael Palin, broadcaster, comedian and author, 57; Roger Rees, actor, 56; Dilys Watling, actress, 54

6   Anna Walker, Deputy Director General Oftel, 47; Alessandra Ferri, ballerina, 37; Susan Brown, actress, 54; Joanna Dunham, actress, 64; Alexander Thynn, 7th Marquess of Bath, 68; Tony Blair, politician 47; Graham Souness, football manager, 47; George Clooney, actor, 39

7   Scobie Breasley, jockey, 85; Peter Carey, writer, 57; Elisabeth Soderstrom, soprano, 73; Mary Spillane, founder of 'Colour Me Beautiful', 50

8   Sir David Attenborough, naturalist and broadcaster, 74; Norman Lamont, politician, 58; Dr John Reid, politician, 53; Gary Wilmot, entertainer, 44; Jack Charlton, footballer, 65; Felicity Lott, soprano, 53; Heather Harper, soprano, 70

9   Alan Bennett, playwright, 66; Albert Finney, actor, 64; Glenda Jackson, actress and politician, 64; Billy Joel, singer, 51; Matthew Kelly, actor and presenter, 50; Patrick Ryecart, actor, 48; Terry Downes, boxer, 64; James L Brookes, film producer, 60

10   Jonathan Edwards, athlete, 34; Maureen Lipman, actress, 54; Barbara Taylor Bradford, author, 67; Sir Denis Thatcher, businessman, 85; Bono, singer, 40

11   John Parrott, snooker player, 36; Jeremy Paxman, broadcaster, 50; Judith Weir, composer, 46; Natasha Richardson, actress, 37; Eric Burdon, singer, 59

12   Burt Bacharach, composer, 71; Chris Patten, politician, 56; Miriam Stoppard, broadcaster, 63; Susan Hampshire, actress, 58; Alan Ball, footballer, 55

13   Bea Arthur, actress, 74; Trevor Baylis, inventor, 63; Harvey Keitel, actor, 61; Stevie Wonder, singer, 50; Joe Brown, singer, 59; Selina Scott, broadcastter, 49; Dr Jane Glover, conductor, 51; Zoë Wanamaker, actress, 51; Tim Pigott-Smith, actor, 54; Richard Madeley, broadcaster, 44

14   Francesca Annis, actress, 55; George Lucas, film director, 56; Sian Phillips, actress, 66; Chay Blyth, yachtsman, 60; Cate Blanchett, actress, 31; Tim Roth, actor, 39

15   Zara Phillips, 19; Ted Dexter, cricketer, 65; Anthony and Peter Shaffer, playwrights, 74; Mike Oldfield, musician, 47; Brian Eno, musician, 52

16   Judy Finnegan, broadcaster, 52; Roy Hudd, comedian and actor, 64; Pierce Brosnan, actor, 49; Janet Jackson, singer, 34

17   Simon Hughes, politician, 49; Sugar Ray Leonard, boxer, 44; Birgit Nilsson, soprano, 82; Sue Carpenter, television presenter and journalist, 44; Andrea Corr, singer, 26

18   Pope John Paul II, 80; John Bruton, Irish politician, 53; Perry Como, singer, 88; Jacques Santer, former European Commisson President, 63; Nobby Stiles, footballer, 58; Toyah Willcox, singer and actor, 42; Rick Wakeman, musician and raconteur, 51

19   Victoria Wood, comedienne and writer, 47; Edward De Bono, lateral thinker, 67; David Jacobs, broadcaster, 74; Pete Townshend, musician, 55; Robert Kilroy-Silk, television presenter and politician, 58; James Fox, actor, 61; Mel Calman, cartoonist, 69

20   Lynn Davies, long jumper, 60; Charles, Earl Spencer, 38; Cher, singer and actress, 54

21   Malcolm Fraser, Australian politician, 70; Rosalind Plowright, soprano, 51; Mary Robinson, Irish politician, 56

22   Cheryl Campbell, actress, 51; Menzies Campbell, politician and athlete, 59; George Best, footballer, 54; Richard Benjamin, actor, 62; Naomi Campbell, model, 30

23   Anatoly Karpov, chess player, 49; Nigel Davenport, actor, 72; Joan Collins, actress, 67

24   Stanley Baxter, comedian, 74; Eric Cantona, footballer, 34; Bob Dylan, musician, 59; Arnold Wesker, playwright, 68

25   Alastair Campbell, political press secretary, 43; Sir Ian McKellen, actor, 61; Beverly Sills, soprano, 71; David Jenkins, athlete, 48

26   Helena Bonham-Carter, actress, 34; Zola Budd, athlete, 34; Roy Dotrice, actor, 75; Peggy Lee, singer, 80; Michael Portillo, politician, 47

27   Cilla Black, entertainer, 57; Paul Gascoigne, footballer, 33; Thea Musgrave, composer, 72; Sam Snead, golfer, 88; Christopher Lee, actor, 78; Pat Cash, tennis player, 35; Henry Kissinger, US statesman, 77; Duncan Goodhew, swimmer, 43; John Conteh, boxer, 49; Joseph Fiennes, actor, 30

28   Thora Hird, actress, 84; Rachel Kempson, actress, 90; Richard Van Allan, opera singer, 65; Faith Brown, impressionist, 53; Sue Holderness, actress, 51

29   Bob Hope, comedian, 97; Francis Rossi, musician, 51; Noel Gallagher, singer, 33; Linda Esther Gray, opera singer, 52; Michael Berkeley, composer, 52

30   Harry Enfield, comedian, 39; Tim Waterstone, bookseller, 61; Bob Willis, cricketer, 51; Ray Cooney, theatrical producer, 68; Clint Walker, actor, 73

31   Prince Rainier III of Monaco, 77; Clint Eastwood, actor and director, 70; John Prescott, politician, 62; Debbi Moore, chairman of Pineapple Dance Studio, 54; Terry Waite, Anglican emissary, 61; Lynda Bellingham, actress, 52

June 2000

1   Lord Foster of Thames Bank, architect, 65; Bob Monkhouse, comedian, 72; Paco Peña, flamenco guitarist, 58; Jonathan Pryce, actor, 58; Robert Powell, actor, 56; Gerald Scarfe, artist, 64; Gemma Craven, actress, 50; Edward Woodward, actor, 70; Pat Boone, actor and singer, 66; Morgan Freeman, actor, 63; Alanis Morissette, singer, 26

2   King Constantine of the Hellenics, 60; Marvin Hamlisch, composer, 56; Charlie Watts, drummer with the Rolling Stones, 59; Stacy Keach, actor, 59

3   Tony Curtis, actor, 75; Alain Resnais, film director, 78; Penelope Wilton, actress, 53; Suzi Quattro, singer and actress, 50; Anita Harris, singer, 58

4   Bob Champion, jockey and racehorse trainer, 52; Andrea Jaeger, tennis player, 35; Dennis Weaver, actor, 76; Geoffrey Palmer, actor, 73

5   Nigel Rees, author, 56; Moira Anderson, singer, 60; David Hare, playwright, 53; Chris Finnegan, boxer, 56; Margaret Drabble, novelist, 61

6   David Blunkett, politician, 53; Bjorn Borg, tennis player, 44; Ninette de Valois, ballerina, 102; Frank Tyson, cricketer, 70; Billie Whitelaw, actress, 68

7   James Ivory, film director, 72; Tom Jones, singer, 60; Liam Neeson, actor, 48; Curtis Robb, Athlete, 28;

Virginia McKenna, actress, 69; Anna Kournikova, tennis player, 19; Artist formerly known as Prince, song writer and performer, 42

8 Francis Crick, biologist, 84; Derek Underwood, cricketer, 55; Norma Shaw, bowler, 63; Colin Baker, actor, 57; Doug Mountjoy, snooker player, 58; Nancy Sinatra, actress and singer, 60; Millicent Martin, actress and singer, 66; Ray Illingworth, cricketer, 68; Joan Rivers, comedienne, 67

9 Michael J Fox, actor, 39; Johnny Depp, actor, 37; Edgar Evans, tenor, 88; David Troughton, actor, 50; Charles Saatchi, advertising executive, 57

10 HRH Prince Philip, Duke of Edinburgh, 79; Saul Bellow, author, 85; Lionel Jeffries, actor and director, 74

11 Jackie Stewart, racing driver, 61; Gene Wilder, actor, 65; Lindsey de Paul, singer, 50; Jenny Pitman, racehorse trainer, 54; Elizabeth Hurley, actress, 34

12 George Bush, US President, 76; Vic Damone, singer, 72; Oliver Knussen, composer, 48; Pat Jennings, footballer, 55; Brigid Brophy, novelist, 71

13 Malcolm McDowell, actor, 57; Tom King, politician, 67; Peter Scudamore, jockey, 42; Mary Whitehouse, campaigner against pornography, 90

14 Steffi Graf, tennis player, 31; Sir James Black, pharmacologist, 76; Paul Boateng, politician, 49; Nigel Short, chess player, 35; Boy George, singer, 39

15 Simon Callow, actor, 51; John Redwood, politician, 50; Richard Baker, broadcaster, 75; Courtney Cox Arquette, actress, 36; Nicola Pagett, actress, 55

16 James Bolam, actor, 62; Professor Erich Segal, classicist and writer, 63; Simon Williams, actor, 54; Eileen Atkins, actress, 66

17 Ken Livingstone, politician, 55; Kenneth Loach, film director, 64; Barry Manilow, musician, 54; Venus Williams, tennis player, 20

18 Ian Carmichael, actor, 80; Paul McCartney, musician, 58; Delia Smith, cookery expert, 60; Alison Moyet, singer, 39; Linda Thorsen, actress, 53; Isabella Rossellini, actress, 48; Michael Blakemore, film and theatre director, 72

19 Aung San Suu Kyi, Nobel Peace Laureate, 55; Salman Rushdie, writer, 53; Kathleen Turner, actress, 46; Paula Abdul singer, 38

20 Wendy Craig, actress, 66; Stephen Frears, film director, 59; John Goodman, actor, 48; Lionel Richie, singer, 51; Alan Lamb, cricketer, 46; Nicole Kidman, actress, 33

21 Prince William of Wales, 18; Benazir Bhutto, politician, 47; Ian McEwan, author, 52; Jane Russell, actress, 80; Maurice Saatchi, advertising executive, 54

22 Bruce Kent, CND campaigner, 71; Esther Rantzen, broadcaster, 60; Dame Cicely Saunders, founder of St Christopher's Hospice, Sydenham, 82; Billy Wilder, film director, 94; Meryl Streep, actress, 51; Prunella Scales, actress, 68; Kris Kristofferson, singer and actor, 64; Cyndi Lauper, singer, 47

23 Mr Kim Begley, tenor, 48; Lord Irvine of Lairg, 60; Martin Rees, astronomer, 58; John Prebble, writer, 85; Adam Faith, singer and actor, 60

24 Anita Desai, novelist, 61; Betty Jackson, fashion designer, 51; Jeff Beck, musician, 56; Mick Fleetwood, musician, 58

25 Eddie Large, comedian, 58; George Michael, Singer, 37; Roy Marsden, actor, 59; Carly Simon, singer and songwriter, 55

26 Willie Hamilton, politician, 83; Robert McLennan, politician, 64; Georgie Fame, musician, 57; Claudio Abbado, conductor, 67; Greg Lemond, cyclist, 39

27 Shirley Ann Field, actress, 62; Tommy Cannon, comedian, 62; Alan Coren, journalist and broadcaster, 62

28 Kathy Bates, actress, 52; Harold Evans, former editor of *Times* and *Sunday Times*, 71; Mel Brooks, actor and director, 74

29 The Hon. Charlotte Bingham, playwright and novelist, 58; Sir Rex Hunt, Diplomat, 74; Michael McIntyre, yachtsman, 44

30 Lena Horne, singer, 83; CH Lloyd, Surveyor of the Queen's Pictures, 53; Mike Tyson, boxer, 34; Tony Hatch, songwriter and lyricist, 61

July 2000

1 Dan Aykroyd, actor, 48; Leslie Caron, actress, 69; Debbie Harry, singer, 55; Carl Lewis, athlete, 39; Genevieve Bujold, actress, 58; Pamela Anderson, actress, 33

2 Ann Taylor, politician, 53; Lord David Owen, politician, 62; John Timpson, broadcaster, 72; Lord Mackay of Clashfern, former Lord Chancellor, 73

3 Tom Cruise, actor, 38; Sir Richard Hadlee, cricketer, 49; Ken Russell, film director, 73; Tom Stoppard, playwright, 63; Susan Penhaligon, actress, 50

4 Gina Lollobrigida, actress, 73; Neil Simon, playwright, 73; Alec and Eric Bedser, cricketers, 82; Colin Welland, playwright, 66; Prince Michael of Kent, 58

5 Elizabeth Emanuel, fashion designer, 47; Philip Madoc, actor, 66; Mark Cox, tennis player, 57; Warren Oates, actor, 72

6 Dave Allen, comedian, 64; Vladimir Ashkenazy, pianist, 63; Sylvester Stallone, actor, 54; Geraldine James, actress, 50

7 Pierre Cardin, fashion designer, 78; Jeremy Guscott, rugby player, 35; Michael Howard, QC, politician, 59; Tony Jacklin, golfer, 56; Gianluca Vialli, footballer, 36; Ringo Starr, musician, 60; Gian Carlo Menotti, composer, 89; Charles Dyer, playwright and actor, 72

8 Mal Meninga, rugby league player, 40; Pauline Quirke, actress, 41; Brian Walden, politician and broadcaster, 68; Neil Jennings, rugby union player, 29; Keith Fielding, rugby league player, 51; Bruce Gyngell, former managing director, TV-am, 71; Anjelica Huston, actress, 49

9 John Ainsley, tenor, 37; Tom Hanks, actor, 44; Michael Williams, actor, 65; Richard Wilson, actor, 64; Kelly McGillis, actress, 43

10 Virginia Wade, tennis player, 55; James Aldridge, author, 82; Sunil Gavaskar, cricketer, 51; Ian Wallace, actor, broadcaster and singer, 81

11   Giorgio Armani, fashion designer, 66; Richard Chartres, Bishop of London, 53; Gough Whitlam, politician, 84
12   Sir Alastair Burnet, broadcaster, 72; Gareth Edwards, rugby player, 53; Baroness Ramsay of Cartvale, 64; Bill Cosby, actor and comedian, 63; Frank Windsor, actor, 73
13   Moss Evans, trade unionist, 75; Patrick Stewart, actor, 60; Ian Hislop, editor, *Private Eye*, 40; Bryan Murray, actor, 51; Harrison Ford, actor, 58; Sir Garfield Todd, former Prime Minister of Southern Rhodesia, 92; Larry Gomes, cricketer, 47
14   Bruce Oldfield, designer, 50; Betty Kenward, 'Jennifer' of *Tatler*, 94; Sue Lawley, television presenter, 54
15   The Sultan of Brunei, 54; Sir Harrison Birtwistle, composer, 66; Julian Bream, guitarist and lutenist, 67; Linda Ronstadt, singer, 54; Trevor Horn, songwriter, 51
16   Dr Anita Brookner, author and art historian, 72; Margaret Court, tennis player, 58; Pinchas Zukerman, violinist and conductor, 52
17   Hardy Amies, designer, 91; Marques de Samaranch, President of the Olympic Committee, 80; Wayne Sleep, dancer, 52; Donald Sutherland, actor, 66
18   Richard Branson, entrepreneur, 50; Nick Faldo, golfer, 43; Senator John Glenn, astronaut, 79; Denis Lillee, cricketer, 51; Jim Watt, boxer, 52; Nelson Mandela, South African politician, 82; Yevgeny Yevtushenko, poet, 67
19   Evelyn Glennie, percussionist, 35; Brian May, guitarist, 53; Ilie Nastase, tennis player, 54; Adrian Noble, artistic director, Royal Shakespeare Company, 50
20   Jacques Delors, former President, Commission of the European Community, 75; Sir Edmund Hillary, first man to climb Mt Everest, 81; Dame Diana Rigg, actress, 62; Desmond Douglas, table tennis player, 45
21   Norman Jewison, film director, 74; Dr. Jonathan Miller, film theatre and opera director, 66; Karel Reisz, film director, 74; Bill Pertwee, actor, 74; Robin Williams, actor and comedian, 48; Cat Stevens, singer, 52; Barry Richards, cricketer, 55; Julian Pettifer, broadcaster, 65
22   Willem Dafoe, actor, 45; Bryan Forbes, film director and author, 74; Bonnie Langford, actress, 36; Terence Stamp, actor and director, 62; Jimmy Hill, broadcaster, 72; Danny Glover, actor, 53
23   David Essex, singer, 53; Michael Foot, politician, 87; Clive Rice, cricketer, 51; Graham Gooch, cricketer, 47
24   Chris Smith, politician, 49; Quinlan Terry, architect, 63; Peter Yates, film director and producer, 71; Jennifer Lopez, actress and singer, 30
25   James Butler, sculptor, 69; Right Rev Barry Rogerson, Bishop of Bristol, 64; Dallas Bower, television producer and director, 93; Lynne Frederick, actress, 46
26   Blake Edwards, film producer, 78; John Howard, Australian politician, 61; Mick Jagger, rock singer, 57; Helen Mirren, actress, 55; Susan George, actress, 50; Lance Percival, entertainer, 67; Kevin Spacey, actor, 41; Sandra Bullock, actress, 36
27   Michael Ball, singer, 38; Allan Border, cricketer, 45; Christopher Dean, ice skater, 42; Jack Higgins, novelist, 71; Baroness Williams of Crosby, 70
28   Phil Walker, editor of the *Daily Star*, 56; Ian McCaskill, meteorologist, 62; Sir Garfield Sobers, cricketer, 64
29   Kay Dick, writer, 85; Max Faulkner, golfer, 84; Sally Gunnell, athlete, 34; Joe Johnson, snooker player, 48; Mikis Theodorakis, composer, 75
30   Kate Bush, singer, 42; Peter Bogdanovich, film director, 61; Arnold Schwarzenegger, actor, 53; Teresa Cahill, opera singer, 56; Lisa Kudrow, actress, 37; Daley Thompson, actor, 42; Richard Johnson, actor, 73; Harriet Harman, politician, 50; Paul Anka, singer and songwriter, 59
31   Yvonne Cawley, tennis player, 49; Jonathan Dimbleby, broadcaster, 56; Milton Friedman, economist, 88; Peter Nichols, playwright, 73; JK Rowling, children's writer, 35; Dean Cain, actor, 34; Wesley Snipes, actor, 38; Geraldine Chaplin, actress, 56

August 2000
1   Yves Saint Laurent, fashion designer, 64; Right Rev Professor Stephen Sykes, Bishop of Ely, 61; Professor Laurie Taylor, sociologist, 64
2   Peter O'Toole, actor, 68; Rose Tremain, novelist and playwright, 57; Alan Whicker, broadcaster, 75; Lord Waddington, QC, politician, 71
3   Tony Bennett, singer, 74; Steven Berkoff, actor and director, 63; Martin Sheen, actor, 60; Jack Straw, politician, 54; Terry Wogan, broadcaster, 62
4   Queen Elizabeth the Queen Mother, 100; Georgina Hale, actress, 57; Martin Jarvis, actor, 59; David Lange, NZ politician, 58; David Bedford, composer, 63
5   Professor Neil Armstrong, first man on the moon, 70; John Saxon, actor, 65; Barbara Flynn, actress, 52; Rodney Pattisson, yachtsman, 57
6   Sir Chris Bonington, mountaineer, 66; Ron Davies, politician, 54; Frank Finlay, actor, 74; Sir Freddie Laker, businessman, 78; Geri Estelle Halliwell, singer, 28; Barbara Windsor, actress, 63; Dom Mintoff, former Prime Minister of Malta, 84; Jack Parnell, drummer, 77; Charles Wood, writer, 68
7   Kenneth Kendall, broadcaster, 76; Sue Lloyd, actress, 61; Alexei Sayle, comedian, 48; Walter Swinburn, jockey, 39; Greg Chappell, cricketer, 52
8   Princess Beatrice of York, 12; Nigel Mansell, racing driver, 47; Dustin Hoffman, actor, 63; Connie Stevens, singer and actress, 62
9   Melanie Griffith, actress, 43; Whitney Houston, singer, 37; Rod Laver, tennis player, 62; Gillian Anderson, actress, 32; Posy Simmonds, cartoonist, 55
10   Roy Keane, footballer, 29; Kate O'Mara, actress, 61; Rosanna Arquette, actress, 41; Anita Lonsborough, swimmer, 59; Antonio Banderas, actor, 40
11   Anna Massey, actress, 63; Tamas Vasary, pianist and conductor, 67; Don Boyd, film director, 52; Professor Alun Hoddinott, composer, 71
12   Mark Knopfler, singer, songriter and guitarist, 51; Norris McWhirter, founder editor, *Guinness Book of Records*, 75; Pete Sampras, tennis player, 29

CURRENT AFFAIRS

13   Marie Helvin, model, 49; Tony Jarrett, athlete, 33; Dr Frederick Sanger, biochemist, 83; Alan Shearer, footballer, 31; George Shearing, pianist, 82; Dr Fidel Castro, president of Cuba, 75; Sheila Armstrong, soprano, 60; Susan Jameson, actress, 59

14   Sarah Brightman, singer, 40; Buddy Greco, singer, 75; Steve Martin, actor and comedian, 56; Frederic Raphael, author, 70

15   Dame Wendy Hiller, actress, 88; Oscar Peterson, jazz pianist, 75; Anne, the Princess Royal, 50; Rita Hunter, soprano, 67

16   Bruce Beresford, film director, 60; Most Rev Sean Brady, Archbishop of Armagh and Primate of All Ireland, 61; Sir Trevor McDonald, broadcaster, 61; John Standing, actor, 66; Madonna, singer, 42; Katharine Hamnett, fashion designer, 53; Jeff Thomson, cricketer, 50

17   Robin Cousins, ice-skater, 43; Robert De Niro, actor, 57; George Melly, jazz singer, 74; Alan Minter, boxer, 49; Nelson Piquet, racing driver, 48

18   Brian Aldiss, science fiction writer, 75; Roman Polanski, film director, 67; Robert Redford, actor and director, 63; Patrick Swayze, actor, 46; Caspar Weinberger, former American Secretary of Defence, 83; Shelley Winters, actress, 78

19   Bill Clinton, US President, 54; Richard Ingrams, editor, *The Oldie*, 63; David Lodge, actor, 79; Willie Shoemaker, jockey, 69; Matthew Perry, actor, 31

20   Robert Plant, singer with Led Zeppelin, 52; William Woollard, television presenter, 61; Finlay Calder, rugby player, 43; John Emburey, cricketer, 48

21   Dame Janet Baker, opera singer, 67; Chris Brasher, athlete, 72; Barry Norman, broadcaster, 67; Princess Margaret, 70

22   Ray Bradbury, author, 80; Steve Davis, snooker player, 43; Donald MacLeary, ballet dancer, 63; General Norman Schwarzkopf, 66; Karlheinz Stockhausen, composer and conductor, 72; Boris Schapiro, former world bridge champion, 91; Mats Wilander, tennis player, 36

23   Geoff Capes, shot putter and former strongman, 51; Peter Lilley, politician, 57; John Rocha, fashion designer, 46; Willy Russell, author, 53

24   Dame Antonia Byatt, writer, 64; Stephen Fry, actor, writer and comedian, 43; Jean-Michel Jarre, musician, 52; Yasser Arafat, PLO leader, 71

25   Anne Archer, actress, 53; Sean Connery, actor, 70; Frederick Forsyth, writer, 62; Nell Moody, soprano, teacher and librettist, 91

26   Alison Steadman, actress, 54; Chris Boardman, cyclist, 32; The Duke of Gloucester, 56; Macaulay Culkin, actor, 20

27   Gerhard Berger, racing driver, 41; Sir Donald Bradman, cricketer, 92; Lady Antonia Fraser, writer, 68; Michael Holroyd, writer, 65; Denise Lewis, heptathlete, 28; John Lloyd, tennis player, 46; Jeanette Winterson, writer, 41; Bernhard Langer, golfer, 43

28   Emlyn Hughes, footballer, 53; The Duke of Argyll, 63; Imogen Cooper, concert pianist, 51; Sir Godfrey Hounsfield, inventor of the EMI-scanner, 81

29   Lennie Henry, comedian, 42; Lord Attenborough, actor and director, 77; Dame Mary Donaldson, former Lord Mayor of London, 79; Michael Jackson, entertainer, 42; Elliott Gould, actor, 62; William Friedkin, film director, 61

30   Lord Healey, Chancellor of the Exchequer 1974–79, 83; Countess of Longford, author, 94; Sydney Wooderson, athlete, 85; John Peel, broadcaster, 61; Cameron Diaz, actress, 28; Jean-Claude Killy, skier, 57

31   Liz Forgan, writer and broadcaster, 56; Serge Blanco, rugby player, 42; Van Morrison, singer and songwriter, 55; Bryan Organ, painter, 65; Clive Lloyd, cricketer, 56; Richard Gere, actor, 51; Ed Moses, athlete, 45

September 2000

1   Gloria Estefan, singer, 43; Margaret Ewing, politician, 55; Barry Gibb, pop singer and writer, 54; Lord Parkinson, politician, 69; Ruud Gullit, footballer, 38

2   Jimmy Connors, tennis player, 48; Lennox Lewis, boxer, 35; Keanu Reeves, actor, 36; Victor Spinetti, actor, 67

3   Pauline Collins, actress, 60; Charlie Sheen, actor, 35; Susan Milan, flautist, 53; Al Jardine, singer, 58

4   Tom Watson, golfer, 51; Joan Aitken, novelist, 76; Bill Kenwright, theatrical impresario, 55; Dinsdale Landen, actor, 68

5   Johnny Briggs, actor, 65; George Tremlett, author, 61; Tracy Edwards, yachtswoman, 38; Dick Clement, scriptwriter, 63; Raquel Welch, actress, 60

6   Greg Rusedski, tennis player, 27; Tim Henman, tennis player, 26; Monica Mason, ballerina, 59; Roger Knight, secretary, MCC, 54; Britt Ekland, actress, 57

7   Sir Paul Getty, philanthropist, 68; Elia Kazan, director and author, 91

8   Jack Rosenthal, playwright, 69; Sir Peter Maxwell Davies, composer, 66; Michael Frayn, playwright and novelist, 67; Sir Harry Secombe, comedian, 79; Sir Denys Lasdun, CH, architect of the National Theatre, 86; Anne Diamond, broadcaster, 46; Geoff Miller, cricketer, 48

9   Edward Upward, writer, 97; Hugh Grant, actor, 40; Michael Keaton, actor, 49; Raine Countess Spencer, 71; Chaim Topol, actor and singer, 65

10   John Entwistle, rock musician, 56; Beryl Cook, painter, 74; Amy Irving, actress, 47; Arnold Palmer, golfer, 71; José Feliciano, guitarist, 55

11   Franz Beckenbauer, footballer, 55; Brian De Palma, film director, 56; Barry Sheene, motorcycle racer, 50; Roger Uttley, rugby player, 51

12   Bertie Ahern, Eire politician, 46; Maria Aitken, actress, 55; Ian Holm, actor, 69; Barry White, singer, 56; Rachel Ward, actress, 43

13   Jacqueline Bisset, actress, 56; Goran Ivanisevic, tennis player, 29; Shane Warne, cricketer, 31; Carol Barnes, broadcaster, 56

14   Amanda Barrie, actress, 61; Ray Wilkins, footballer, 44; Martyn Hill, tenor, 56; Sandra Blow, painter, 75; Michael Howard, composer, 78; Sam Neill, actor, 53

15   Tommy Lee Jones, actor, 54; Prince Henry of Wales, 16; Jessye Norman, soprano, 55; Oliver Stone, film director, 54; Graham Taylor, football manager, 56

16   Lauren Bacall, actress, 76; Charles Haughey, Eire politician, 75; Lee Kuan Yew, Singapore politician, 77; Mickey Rourke, actor, 44; BB King, guitarist, 75

17   Anne Bancroft, actress, 69; Damon Hill, motor racing driver, 40; Des Lynam, broadcaster, 58; Stirling Moss, motor racing driver, 71

18   John Fashanu, footballer, 38; Darren Gough, cricketer, 30; Peter Shilton, footballer, 51; Marjorie (Mo) Mowlam, politician, 51; Lance Armstrong, cyclist, 29

19   Jarvis Cocker, pop singer, 37; Kate Adie, broadcaster, 55; Jeremy Irons, actor, 52; Twiggy, actress, 51; David McCallum, actor, 67; Michael Elphick, actor, 54; Captain Jim Fox, modern pentathlete, 59; Austin Mitchell, politician and broadcaster, 66; Zandra Rhodes, fashion designer, 60

20   Johnny Dankworth, jazz musician, 73; Sophia Loren, actress, 66; Jane Manning, soprano, 62; Jose Rivero, golfer, 45

21   Leonard Cohen, singer, poet and composer, 66; Shirley Conran, writer, 68; Liam Gallagher, pop singer, 28; Stephen King, novelist, 53; Simon Mayo, broadcaster, 42; Sir Bernard Williams, philosopher, 71; Jimmy Young, broadcaster, 77; Bill Murray, actor, 50; Larry Hagman, actor, 69

22   Fay Weldon, writer, 69; Andrea Bocelli, opera singer,42; Captain Mark Phillips, equestrian trainer, 52; Gina Fratini, fashion designer, 69; Joan Jett, singer, 40

23   Ray Charles, singer, 70; Julio Iglesias, singer, 57; Mickey Rooney, actor, 80; Bruce Springsteen, singer, 51

24   Brian Glanville, author and journalist, 69; John Rutter, composer and conductor, 55; Jack Dee, comedian, 39

25   Felicity Kendall, actress, 54; Ronnie Barker, comedy actor, 71; Michael Douglas, actor, 56; Leon Brittan, politician, 61; Colin Davis, conductor, 73; Catherine Zeta-Jones, actress, 31; Will Smith, actor and singer, 32; Heather Locklear, actress, 39; Mark Hamill, actor, 49

26   Ian Chappell, cricketer, 57; Bryan Ferry, singer and musician, 55; Lucette Aldous, ballerina, 62; Olivia Newton-John, singer and actress, 52

27   Josephine Barstow, opera singer, 60; Barbara Dickson, singer and actress, 52; Gwyneth Paltrow, actress, 28; Diane Abbott, politician, 47

28   Brigitte Bardot, actress and animal rights campaigner, 66; Mika Hakkinen, racing driver, 32; Gwyneth Paltrow, actress, 28; Helen Shapiro, singer, 54

29   Patricia Hodge, actress, 54; Richard Bonynge, opera conductor, 70; Sebastian Coe, athlete and politician, 44; Colin Dexter, author, 70; Lech Walesa, former President of Poland, 57; Michelangelo Antonioni, film director, 88; Jerry Lee Lewis, musician, 65

30   Martina Hingis, tennis player, 20; Deborah Kerr, actress, 79; Angie Dickinson, actress, 69; Teresa Gorman, politician, 69; Ian Ogilvy, actor, 57

October 2000

1   Jimmy Carter, American President, 1977–81, 76; Julie Andrews, singer and actress, 65; Philip de Glanville, rugby player, 32

2   Trevor Brooking, footballer and commentator, 52; Sting (Gordon Sumner), musician, 49; Donna Karan, fashion designer, 52

3   Shridath (Sonny) Ramphal, secretary-general of the Commonwealth 1975–90, 72; Gore Vidal, author, 75

4   Jackie Collins, novelist, 63; Alicia Silverstone, actress, 24; Charlton Heston, actor, 76; Susan Sarandon, actress, 54; Anneka Rice, broadcaster, 42

5   Bob Geldof, rock singer, 46; The Right Rev Robert Hardy, Bishop of Lincoln, 64; Vaclav Havel, Czech politician, 64; Kate Winslet, actress, 25

6   Richie Benaud, cricket commentator, 70; Lord Bragg, arts commentator and novelist, 61; Thor Heyerdahl, explorer, 86; Britt Ekland, actress, 58

7   Clive James, broadcaster, 61; Thomas Keneally, writer, 65; Jayne Torvill, ice dancer, 43; The Right Rev Desmond Tutu, 69; Vladimir Putin, Russian politician, 48; Yo-Yo Ma, French cellist, 45

8   Betty Boothroyd, politician, 71; Sigourney Weaver, actress, 51; Alasdair Milne, Director-General, BBC, 1982–87, 70; Bel Mooney, writer, 54; Bill Maynard, actor, 72; Ray Reardon, snooker player, 68; David Carradine, actor, 64; Chevy Chase, actor, 57; Paul Hogan, actor, 61

9   Brian Blessed, actor, 63; Steve Ovett, athlete, 45; John Pilger, journalist and author, 61; Sir Donald Sinden, actor, 77; Sally Burgess, classical singer, 47

10   Tony Adams, footballer, 34; Charles Dance, actor, 54; Harold Pinter, playwright, 70; Chris Tarrant, broadcaster, 54; Ben Vereen, actor, 54; Nicholas Parsons, television personality, 72; Midge Ure, singer, 47

11   Maria Bueno, tennis player, 61; Sir Bobby Charlton, footballer, 63; Dawn French, comedienne, 43; David Rendall, tenor, 52

12   Angela Rippon, broadcaster, 56; Magnus Magnusson, broadcaster and presenter of *Mastermind* 1972–97, 71; Luciano Pavarotti, tenor, 65; Rick Parfitt, rock musician, 52; Jaroslav Drobny, tennis player, 79; Marion Jones, athlete, 25

13   Lord Bingham of Cornhill, Lord Chief Justice, 67; Edwina Currie, politician, 54; Paul Simon, singer and songwriter, 59; Baroness Thatcher, politician, 75; John Snow, cricketer, 59; John Regis, athlete, 34; Marie Osmond, singer, 41

14   Ralph Lauren, fashion designer, 61; Steve Cram, athlete, 40; Roger Moore, actor, 73; Sir Cliff Richard, singer, 60

15   Sarah Ferguson, the Duchess of York, 41; Craig Chalmers, rugby player, 32 David Trimble, politician, 56

16   Peter Bowles, actor, 64; Max Bygraves, entertainer, 78; Gunter Grass, writer, 73; Angela Lansbury, actress, 75; William Webb, conductor, 53

17   Margot Kidder, actress, 52; Sir Cameron Mackintosh, musical producer, 54; Arthur Miller, playwright, 85; Harry Carpenter, broadcaster, 75; Eminem, rap artist, 26

18   Michael Stich, tennis player, 32; Jean-Claude Van Damme, actor, 40; Martina Navratilova, tennis player, 44;
      Melina Mercouri, actress and political activist, 75
19   Michael Gambon, actor, 60; Bernard Hepton, actor, 75; Mavis Nicholson, broadcaster, 70; Evander
      Holyfield, boxer, 38
20   The Hon Chris Cowdrey, cricketer, 43; Lord Montagu of Beaulieu, 74; Allan Donald, cricketer, 34; Ian Rush,
      footballer, 39; Emma Tennant, writer, 63
21   Geoffrey Boycott, cricketer, 60; Sir Malcolm Arnold, composer, 79; David Campese, rugby player, 38; Peter
      Mandelson, politician, 47
22   Derek Jacobi, actor, 62; Catherine Deneuve, actress, 57; Joan Fontaine, actress, 83; Jeff Goldblum, actor,
      48; Doris Lessing, author, 81
23   Johnny Carson, broadcaster, 75; Pele, footballer, 60; Anita Roddick, founder of the Body Shop, 58
24   Luciano Berio, composer, 75; Sena Jurinac, opera singer, 79; Bill Wyman, Rolling Stones' guitarist, 64; Kevin
      Kline, actor, 53; Jonathan Davies, rugby player, 38
25   Joe Mercer, jockey, 66; Michael Lawrence, chief executive, the London Stock Exchange 1994–96, 57; Glynis
      Barber, actress, 45; Helen Reddy, singer, 58
26   Bob Hoskins, actor, 58; Hillary Clinton, United States senator, 53; Shaw Taylor, broadcaster, 76; Gyorgy
      Pauk, violinist, 64
27   John Cleese, comedy actor, 61; David Bryant, flat-green bowler, 69; Glenn Hoddle, footballer, 43;
      AN Wilson, author, 50; Simon le Bon, singer, 42
28   Julia Roberts, actress, 33; Carl Davis, conductor, 64; David Dimbleby, broadcaster, 62; Bill Gates, chairman
      of Microsoft, 45; Hank Marvin, guitarist with the Shadows, 59; Joan Plowright (Lady Olivier), actress, 71;
      Cleo Laine, singer, 73
29   Richard Dreyfuss, actor, 53; Winona Ryder, actress, 29; Robert Hardy, actor, 75; Jon Vickers, opera singer,
      74; Jack Shepherd, actor, 60
30   Michael Winner, film producer and director, 65; Juliet Stevenson, actress, 44; Richard Alston,
      choreographer, 52; Henry Winkler, actor, 55
31   Michael Collins, astronaut, 70; Dick Francis, jockey and author, 80; Charles Moore, editor of the *Daily
      Telegraph*, 44; Jimmy Savile, broadcaster, 74

November 2000
 1   Gary Player, golfer, 65; Sharron Davies, swimmer, 38; Nigel Dempster, journalist, 59; Lyle Lovett, musician,
      43
 2   KD Lang, singer, 39; Bruce Welch, guitarist with the Shadows, 59; Stefanie Powers, actress, 58; Ken
      Rosewall, tennis player, 66; Alan Jones, racing driver, 54
 3   Viscount Linley, 39; Lord Baker of Dorking, Home Secretary 1990–92, 66; Charles Bronson, actor, 78; Ian
      Wright, footballer, 37; Lulu, singer, 52; Albert Reynolds, former Prime Minister of Eire, 68; Roseanne Arnold,
      actress, 48; Adam Ant, singer, 46
 4   Walter Cronkite, broadcaster, 84; Michael Meacher, politician, 61; Sean 'Puff Daddy' Combs, record producer,
      30
 5   Bryan Adams, singer, 41; Art Garfunkel, singer and songwriter, 59; Lester Piggott, jockey, 65; Tatum O'Neal,
      actress, 37
 6   Sally Field, actress, 54; Frank Carson, comedian, 74; Mike Nichols, film director, 69; PJ Proby, singer, 62;
      Bernat Klein, designer, 78
 7   John Barnes, footballer, 37; Dame Gwyneth Jones, soprano, 64; Billy Graham, evangelist, 82; Rio
      Ferdinand, footballer, 22; Dame Joan Sutherland, soprano, 74; Helen Suzman, South African politician, 83;
      Su Pollard, actress, 51
 8   Professor Christiaan Barnard, heart surgeon, 78; Ken Dodd, entertainer, 69; Tamàs Vasary, pianist and
      conductor, 67; Martin Peters, footballer, 57; Rupert Allason, author and politician, 49; Alain Delon, actor, 65;
      Rifat Ozbek, fashion designer, 47; Iain Sproat, politician, 62; Kazuo Ishiguro, author, 46
 9   Hedy Lamarr, actress, 87; Tom Weiskopf, golfer, 58; Tony Slattery, writer and actor, 41; Lord Brabourne, film
      and television producer, 76
10   Sir Tim Rice, lyricist, 56; Robert Carrier, cookery writer and broadcaster, 77; Eddie Irvine, racing driver, 35;
      Roy Scheider, actor, 65
11   June Whitfield, actress, 75; Ron Greenwood, England football manager 1977–82, 79; Lord Jenkins of
      Hillhead, Chancellor of the Exchequer 1967–70, 80; Daniel Ortega, President of Nicaragua 1984–90, 55;
      Demi Moore, actress, 38; Kurt Vonnegut, author, 78; Leonardo DiCaprio, actor, 26
12   Nadia Comaneci, gymnast and first to be awarded a perfect 10, at the 1976 Olympics, 39; David
      Schwimmer, actor, 34; Neil Young, musician, 55
13   The Most Rev George Carey, Archbishop of Canterbury, 65; Whoopi Goldberg, actress, 46; Sir Ewart Bell,
      head of the N. Ireland Civil Service 1979–84, 76
14   Dr Boutros Boutros Ghali, Secretary-General of the United Nations 1992–6, 78; Michael Dobbs, novelist, 52;
      Stefano Gabbana, fashion designer, 38; HRH the Prince of Wales, 52; Bernard Hinault, cyclist, 46
15   Daniel Barenboim, pianist and conductor, 58; Peter Phillips, 23; J. G. Ballard, novelist, 70; Petula Clark,
      singer and actress, 66; Ed Asner, actor, 71; Aleksander Kwasniewski, President of Poland, 46; Tim Pears,
      writer, 44; Tibor Fischer, author, 41
16   Frank Bruno, boxer, 39; Willie Carson, jockey, 58; Griff Rhys Jones, actor and writer, 47; Professor Sir Magdi
      Yacoub, cardiothoracic surgeon, 65
17   Martin Scorsese, film director, 58; Danny DeVito, actor, 56; Jonathan Ross, television personality, 40;
      Fenella Fielding, actress, 66
18   David Hemmings, actor and director, 59; Admiral of the Fleet, Sir Henry Leach, 77; Brian Quinn, executive
      director of the Bank of England 1988–96, 64
19   Jodie Foster, actress, 38; Lady Davina Windsor, 23; Calvin Klein, fashion designer, 58; Meg Ryan, actress, 39

20   Alistair Cooke, journalist and broadcaster, 92; Nadine Gordimer, author, 77; Dulcie Gray, actress, 80; Bo Derek, actress, 44

21   Beryl Bainbridge, author, 66; Goldie Hawn, actress, 55; Natalia Markova, ballerina, 60; Roy Boulting, film producer, 87; Malcolm Williamson, Master of the Queen's Music, 69

22   Boris Becker, tennis player, 33; Jamie Lee Curtis (Lady Haden-Guest), actress, 42; Billie Jean King, tennis player, 57; Tom Conti, actor, 58; Terry Gilliam, film animator, 60; Sir Peter Hall, drama director, 70; John Bird, actor and writer, 64; Robert Vaughan, actor, 68

23   Most Reverend Patrick Kelly, Archbishop of Liverpool, 62; Alan Mullery, footballer, 59; Michael Gough, actor, 83; Diana Quick, actress, 54

24   Ian Botham, cricketer, 45; Billy Connolly, comedian, 58; Marquess of Blandford, 45; David Kossoff, actor, 81; Vivien Saunders, golfer, 54

25   Lord Weatherill, Speaker of the House of Commons 1979–83, 80; Charles Kennedy, politician, 41; Richard Seifert, architect, 90

26   John Gummer, politician, 61; Tina Turner, singer, 61; General Pinochet, President of Chile 1973–90, 85; Earl of Gowrie, former chairman of the Arts Council, 61

27   John Alderton, actor, 60; Rodney Bewes, actor, 63; Verity Lambert, film and television producer, 65

28   Kriss Akabusi, athlete, 42; Keith Miller, Australian cricketer, 81; Alistair Darling, politician, 47; Fiona Armstrong, broadcaster, 44; Stephen Roche, cyclist, 41

29   Jacques Chirac, President of France, 68; Ryan Giggs, footballer, 27; John Mayall, singer, 67; Dame Shirley Porter, Lord Mayor of Westminster 1991–2, 70

30   Gary Lineker, footballer, 40; Marguerite Porter, ballerina, 52; Max Reinhardt, publisher, 85; Radu Lupu, pianist, 55; David Mamet, writer, 53

December 2000
1   Woody Allen, actor and director, 65; Dame Alicia Markova, ballerina, 90; Bette Midler, entertainer, 55; Lee Trevino, golfer, 61; Richard Pryor, actor, 60; Andy Ripley, rugby player and rower, 53; Stephen Poliakoff, playwright, 48; Eva Evdokimova, ballerina, 52; Harry Fowler, actor, 74

2   General Alexander Haig, American Secretary of State 1981–2, 78; Monica Seles, tennis player, 27; Peter Harding, Marshal of the RAF, 67; David Batty, footballer, 32; Alex Smith, politician, 57; Nigel Calder, science writer, 69; Britney Spears, pop star, 19

3   Darryl Hannah, actress, 40; Jean-Luc Godard, film director, 70; Andy Williams, singer, 70; Craig Raine, poet, 56; Franz Klammer, skier, 47; Mel Smith, comedian, actor and director, 48; Trevor Bailey, cricketer, 77; Paul Nicholas, actor and singer, 50; Ozzy Osbourne, rock star, 52

4   Jeff Bridges, actor, 51; Ronnie Corbett, comedian, 70; Deanna Durbin, actress, 79; Pamela Stephenson, comedienne and actress, 50

5   Jose Carreras, tenor, 54; Hanif Kureishi, writer, 46; Little Richard, singer and pianist, 65; Sheridan Morley, author and broadcaster, 59

6   Gerry Francis, footballer, 49; Nicholas Lyell, QC, 62; Dave Brubeck, jazz musician, 80; Jonathan King, impressario, 56

7   Ellen Burstyn, actress, 68; Eli Wallach, actor, 85; Helen Watts, opera singer, 73; Sir Sydney Samuelson, British Film Commissioner 1991–7, 75

8   Kim Basinger, actress, 47; Les Ferdinand, footballer, 34; Lucien Freud, painter, 78; James Galway, flautist, 61; Sir Geoff Hurst, footballer, 59

9   Dame Elizabeth Schwarzkopf, soprano, 85; Dame Judi Dench, actress, 66; Kirk Douglas, actor, 84; Joanna Trollope, writer, 57; John Malkovich, actor, 47; Susan Bullock, soprano, 42; Bob Hawke, Austrlian politician, 71; Donny Osmond, singer, 43

10   Sir John Birt, former Director-General of the BBC, 56; Jahangir Khan, squash player, 37; Kenneth Branagh, actor and director, 40

11   Carlo Ponti, film producer, 87; Alexander Solzhenitsyn, author, 82; Sir Edward Ashmore, Admiral of the Fleet, 81

12   Tracy Austin, tennis player, 40; Lionel Blair, dancer, 69; Will Carling, rugby player, 35; Jasper Conran, fashion designer, 41; Dionne Warwick, singer, 59

13   Prince Karim, the Aga Khan, 64; John Francome, jockey, 48; Anouska Hempel (Lady Weinberg), actress and hotelier, 59; Dick Van Dyke, actor, 75

14   Stan Smith, tennis player, 54; Barbara Leigh-Hunt, actress, 65; Rosalyn Tureck, conductor, 86; Michael Owen, footballer, 21; Patty Duke, actress, 54

15   Frankie Dettori, jockey, 30; Carl Hooper, cricketer, 34; Don Johnson, actor, 51; Edna O' Brien, author, 64

16   Sir Arthur C Clarke, science-fiction writer, 83; Trevor Pinnock, harpsichordist and conductor, 54; Joel Garner, cricketer, 48; Liv Ullmann, actress, 62

17   Tommy Steele, entertainer, 64; Christopher Cazenove, actor, 55; Bernard Hill, actor, 56; Kerry Packer, businessman, 63; Robert Robinson, broadcaster, 73

18   Annette Page, ballerina, 68; Keith Richard, Rolling Stones' guitarist, 57; Steven Spielberg, film-maker, 53; Christina Aguilera, singer, 20; Brad Pitt, actor, 37

19   Upamanyu Chatterje, novelist, 41; Steven Isserlis, cellist, 42; Syd Little, comedian, 58; Tim Parks, novelist, 46; Jennifer Beals, actress, 37

20   Lord Howe of Aberavon, Deputy Prime Minister 198–0, 74; Michael Beaumont, Seigneur of Sark, 73; Jenny Agutter, actress, 48; Billy Bragg, singer, 42

21   Jane Fonda, actress, 63; Michael Tilson Thomas, conductor, 56; Dr Kurt Waldheim, President of Austria, 1986–92, 82; Chris Evert, tennis player, 46; Kiefer Sutherland, actor, 34; Samuel L Jackson, actor, 52

22   Duke of Westminster, 49; Maurice and Robin Gibb, singers, 51; James Burke, broadcaster, 64; Chris Old, cricketer, 52; Noel Edmonds, broadcaster, 52

23   Helmut Schmidt, former German Chancellor, 82; Graham Kelly, chief executive of the FA 1989–99, 55; Belinda Lang, actress, 47; Emperor Akihito of Japan, 67

C
U
R
R
E
N
T

A
F
F
A
I
R
S

24   Professor Anthony Clare, psychiatrist, 58; Carol Vorderman, television presenter, 40; Thea Porter, designer, 73; Ricky Martin, pop singer, 29
25   Princess Alexandra, 64; Annie Lennox, singer, 46; Ismael Merchant, film producer, 64; Sissy Spacek, actress, 51
26   Jane Lapotaire, actress, 56; Professor Thea King, clarinettist, 75; Harry Christophers, conductor, 47; Denis Quilley, actor, 73
27   Polly Toynbee, journalist, 54; Right Rev AMA Turnbull, Bishop of Durham, 65; Janet Street-Porter, broadcaster, 54; Gérard Depardieu, actor, 52
28   Dame Maggie Smith, actress, 66; Nigel Kennedy, violinist, 44; Denzel Washington, actor, 46; Noel Johnson, radio's Dick Barton, 84
29   Harvey Smith, showjumper, 62; Ted Danson, actor, 53; Martin Offiah, rugby player, 34; Jon Voight, actor, 62; Marianne Faithfull, actress, 54; Jude Law, actor, 28
30   Tiger Woods, golfer, 25; Tracey Ullman, actress, 41; Davey Jones, former 'Monkee', 55; Mike Nesmith, musician and former 'Monkee', 58
31   Sir Alex Ferguson, manager of Manchester United FC, 59; Sir Anthony Hopkins, actor, 63; Ben Kingsley, actor, 57; Alex Salmond, politician, 46; Val Kilmer, actor, 41; Donna Summer, singer dubbed the 'Disco Queen', 52; Sarah Miles, actress, 59

EDUCATION

Public Schools	Founded
King's School, Canterbury, Kent	600
King's School, Rochester, Kent	604
St Alban's	948
King's School, Ely	973
Winchester	1382
Eton	1440
City of London	1442
Loughborough	1495
St Paul's	1509
Manchester Grammar	1515
Bristol Grammar	1532
Berkhamstead, Herts	1541
Christ College, Brecon	1541
King's Worcester	1541
Bristol Cathedral	1542
Bedford	1552
Christ's Hospital, Horsham	1553
Tonbridge	1553
Shrewsbury	1552
Gresham's School, Holt, Norfolk	1555
Oundle, Northants	1556
Repton, Derby	1557
Merchant Taylors', Northwood	1560
Westminster	1560
Kingston	1561
Felsted, Dunmow, Essex	1564
Rugby	1567
Harrow	1571
Uppingham, Oakham	1584
Stonyhurst, RC, Clitheroe	1593
Wellingborough, Northants	1595
Trinity School, Croydon	1596
Whitgift School, Croydon	1596
Blundell's, Tiverton	1604
Downside, RC, Somerset	1607
Charterhouse, Godalming	1611
Douai, RC	1615
Dulwich College	1619
Merchant Taylors', Liverpool	1620
Haberdashers' Aske's, Herts	1690
Dame Allan's Boys', Newcastle upon Tyne	1705
Churcher's College, Petersfield	1722
Robert Gordon, Aberdeen	1729
James Allen's Girls' School	1741
Ampleforth, RC, North Yorkshire	1802
Wellington School, Somerset	1837
Cheltenham	1841
Marlborough College, Wiltshire	1843

Public Schools	Founded
Radley College, Abingdon	1847
Brighton	1847
Lancing	1848
Hurstpierpoint, West Sussex	1849
Bradfield, Reading	1850
City of London Freemen's, Ashtead	1854
Cheadle Hulme, Cheshire	1855
Ardingly, West Sussex	1858
Oratory School, RC, Woodcote, Berks	1859
Wellington College, Crowthorne, Berks	1856
King's, Tynemouth	1860
Clifton, Bristol	1862
Haileybury, Hertford	1862
Cranleigh	1863
Fettes, Edinburgh	1870
Leys, Cambridge	1875
John Lyon, Harrow, Middlesex	1876
Alleyn's School	1882
Roedean	1885
Merchant Taylors' Girls, Liverpool	1888
Bedales, Petersfield	1893
Benenden, Cranbrook, Kent	1923
Cranford, Wimbourne	1923
Stowe, Buckinghamshire	1923
Gordonstoun, Elgin	1934
Millfield, Street, Somerset	1935

British Universities Founded

	Founded
Oxford	1249
Cambridge	1284
St Andrew's	1411
Glasgow	1451
Aberdeen	1495
Edinburgh	1583
UMIST	1824
Durham	1832
London	1836
Manchester	1851
Newcastle Upon Tyne	1852
Wales, Cardiff	1893
Birmingham	1900
Liverpool	1903
Leeds	1904
Sheffield	1905
Queen's, Belfast	1908
Bristol	1909
Reading	1926
Nottingham	1948
Southampton	1952
Hull	1954
Exeter	1955
Leicester	1957

British Universities	Founded
Sussex	1961
Keele	1962
East Anglia	1963
York	1963
Lancaster	1964
Essex	1964
Strathclyde, Glasgow	1964
Warwick, Coventry	1965
Kent	1965
Ulster	1965
Loughborough	1966
Heriot-Watt, Edinburgh	1966
Surrey, Guildford	1966
Bradford	1966
Bath	1966
Brunel, Uxbridge	1966
City	1966
Aston, Birmingham	1966
Stirling	1967
Dundee	1967
Salford	1967
Open	1969
Cranfield	1969
Buckingham	1976

British Universities: Former Polytechnics

	Founded
Leeds Metropolitan	1992
Kingston	1992
Huddersfield	1992
Hertfordshire	1992
Greenwich	1992
North London	1992
Wolverhampton	1992
Glamorgan	1992
Westminster	1992
West of England (Bristol)	1992
Paisley	1992
Plymouth	1992
Portsmouth	1992
Robert Gordon (Aberdeen)	1992
Sheffield Hallam	1992
South Bank	1992
Staffordshire	1992
Sunderland	1992
Teesside	1992
Thames Valley	1992
Northumbria at Newcastle	1992
Nottingham Trent	1992
Liverpool John Moores	1992
Manchester Metropolitan	1992
Middlesex	1992
Napier (Edinburgh)	1992
De Montfort (Leicester)	1992
Anglia Polytechnic (Chelmsford)	1992
Bournemouth	1992

British Universities: Former Polytechnics	Founded
Brighton	1992
Coventry	1992
Central England (Perry Barr)	1992
Central Lancashire (Preston)	1992
London Guildhall	1993
Luton	1993
Oxford Brookes	1993
Derby	1993
Glasgow Caledonian	1993
East London	1993
Abertay Dundee	1994
Lincoln and Humberside	1996

University of Cambridge

College	Founded
Peterhouse	1284
Clare	1326
Pembroke	1347
Gonville and Caius	1348
Trinity Hall	1350
Corpus Christi	1352
King's	1441
Queen's	1448
St Catherine's	1473
Jesus	1496
Christ's	1505
St John's	1511
Magdalene	1542
Trinity	1546
Emmanuel	1584
Sidney Sussex	1596
Downing	1800

University of Cambridge College	Founded
Homerton	1824
Girton	1869
Newnham	1871
Selwyn	1882
Hughe's Hall	1885
St Edmund's	1896
New Hall	1954
Churchill	1960
Darwin	1964
Lucy Cavendish	1965
Wolfson	1965
Clare Hall	1966
Fitzwilliam	1966
Robinson	1977

University of Oxford

College	Founded
University	1249
Balliol	1263
Merton	1264
St Edmund Hall	1278
Exeter	1314
Oriel	1326
Queens	1340
New College	1379
Lincoln	1427
All Souls	1438
Magdalen	1458
Brasenose	1509
Corpus Christi	1517
Christ Church	1546
Trinity	1554
St John's	1555
Jesus	1571

University of Oxford College	Founded
Wadham	1612
Pembroke	1624
Worcester	1714
Harris Manchester	1786
*Regents Park	1810
Keble	1868
Hertford	1874
*Wycliffe Hall	1877
Lady Margaret Hall	1878
Somerville	1879
St Hugh's	1886
Mansfield	1886
*Champion Hall	1896
*St. Benet's Hall	1897
*Greyfriars	1910
*Blackfriars's	1921
St Peter's	1929
Nuffield	1937
St Hilda's	1938
St Antony's	1950
St Anne's	1952
Linacre	1962
St Catherine's	1962
St Cross	1965
Templeton	1965
Wolfson	1966
Green	1979
**Kellogg	1990

*classified as Permanent Private Halls
**from 1990–94 called Rewley House

University of London
College
Birkbeck College
Charing Cross and Westminster Medical
Goldsmith's College
Heythrop College
Imperial College of Science
King's College London
London Business School
London Hospital Medical College
London School of Economics and Political Science
London School of Hygiene and Tropical Medicine
London School of Jewish Studies
Queen Mary and Westfeld College
Royal Free Hospital School of Medicine
Royal Holloway
Royal Postgraduate Medical School
Royal Veterinary College
School of Oriental and African Studies
School of Pharmacy
St Bartholomew's and the Royal London School
    of Medicine and Dentistry
St George's Hospital Medical School
United Medical and Dental Schools of Guy's and
    St Thomas' Hospitals
University College London
Wye College

University of Durham
College
Collingwood
Graduate Society
Grey
Hatfield
Neville's Cross
St Aidan's
St Chad's
St Cuthbert's
St Hild & St Bede
St John's
St Mary's
Trevelyan
University (Durham)
University (Stockton)
Ushaw
Van Mildert

Miscellaneous Information

Baker Days	Part of the controversial education reform bill, during Kenneth Baker's tenancy as Education Minister 1986–89. His legislation on the in-service training days for teachers came to be known as Baker Days.
City Technology Colleges	Set up in the 1980s in an attempt to widen the choices of secondary education in disadvantaged urban areas. There are seven CTCs at present and they are state-aided.
Dulwich College	Founded by the English actor Edward Alleyn in 1619 but a distinct school from Alleyn's School, founded in 1882. Old Boys of Dulwich College are however known as Old Alleynians.
GCSE	General Certificate of Secondary Education.
GNVQ	General National Vocation Qualification (Further Education).
Gordonstoun	Founded by Kurt Hahn in 1934.
Grant-Maintained Schools	Came into being as a result of the 1988 Education Act which permits schools with more than 300 pupils to opt out of local authority control if the majority of parents wish to do so. These schools are funded by central government.
Independent Schools	Receive no grants from Public Funds and are funded by fees and contributions, and run by trusts.
Lyceum school	Founded by Aristotle.
Mottoes	Eton – Floreat Etona (May Eton Flourish), Rugby – Orando Laborando (By Praying and by Working), Winchester – Manners Makyth Man, Ampleforth College – Dieu le Ward (God Protect Him), The Ridings, Calderdale – Together We Make the Difference.
National Curriculum	Under the 1988 Education Act the National Curriculum was set out in four Key Stages of a child's development. Key Stage 1 and 2 concerned 5–11-year-olds and stated that Core Subjects would include English, (Welsh in Welsh-speaking schools) Maths and Science; and the Foundation Subjects would be Design & Technology, Information Technology, History, Geography, Art, Music and PE. Key Stage 3 caters for 11–14-year-olds and states that a Modern Foreign Language must be included. Key Stage 4 concerns 14–16-year olds. The Act states that the child must be tested at the end of each Key Stage i.e. 7, 11, and 14-years-old. 16-year-olds only require testing if staying in education.
Newnham College: 1st Male Fellow	Dr Rachel Padman (who had a sex change operation in 1982).
Parents Charter	Booklet informing parents about the education system.
Public Schools: Famous Founders	John Lyon (Harrow) Elizabeth I (Westminster) William of Wykeham (Winchester) Henry VI (Eton) Thomas Sutton (Charterhouse) Edward Alleyne (Dulwich College) Lawrence Sheriff (Rugby) John Colet (St Paul's) Edward VI (Shrewsbury).
Public Schools: Meaning	In recent years the term 'Pubic School' applies to those Independent Schools in membership of the Headmasters' and Headmistresses' Conference, the Governing Bodies Association or the Governing Bodies of Girl's Schools Association. Historically Public Schools were fee-paying private boarding schools, for pupils aged 13 years and above, which gained sufficient reputation to attract pupils from backgrounds of social worthiness. Public schools were contrasted with 'Private Schools' which were run for the profit of their proprietors. In Scotland, the term Public School refers to a free state school, open to all.
School Age Limits	In Great Britain schooling is compulsory between the ages of 5 and 16 (4 and 16 in Northern Ireland).
Scotvec	Scottish Vocational Education Council (Further Education).
St Andrews: Colleges	United College of St Salvator & St Leonard, College of St Mary.
Subfusc	Formal academic dress, especially at Oxford University.
University: Most Students	Open University has the most registered students although London University has most on campus.

NB: There are currently over 1,000 Independent Schools (Public Schools).
The list here is not a comprehensive list of all of them, rather more a cross-section of the better known ones.

EDUCATION

FAMOUS PEOPLE

Alternative Occupations

Aesop Slave
Prince Albert Musician
Woody Allen Jazz Clarinettist
Idi Amin British Army Sergeant
Kingsley Amis University Lecturer
Clive Anderson Barrister
John Arlott Policeman
Paddy Ashdown Commando
Isaac Asimov Biochemist
Clement Attlee Lawyer and Social Worker
Alfred Austin Lawyer
Mily Balakirev Railway Official
Hastings Banda Physician
Roger Bannister, Roger Doctor
Brendan Behan Painter and Decorator
Aphra Behn Secret agent
Hilaire Belloc MP
Alexander Graham Bell Speech Therapist to the Deaf
Arnold Bennett Solicitor's Clerk
Jorge Luis Borges Librarian
Alexander Borodin Chemist
Jim Bowen Teacher
John Buchan Lawyer, Publisher and Statesman
Robert Burns Excise Officer and Farmer
Michael Caine Billingsgate Fish Porter
James Callaghan Tax Official
Geoff Capes Policeman
LewisCarroll Mathematics Lecturer
Jimmy Carter Peanut Farmer
Casanova Librarian, Spy and Lottery Director
Miguel de Cervantes Professional Soldier
Geoffrey Chaucer Customs Officer and MP
Perry Como Barber
Sean Connery Coffin Polisher and RN Sailor
Billy Connolly Docker
Tommy Cooper Guardsman
André Courréges Civil Engineer
AJ Cronin Inspector of Mines
CésarCui Military Engineer
Alighieri Dante Embassy Official
Walter De La Mare Oil Company Worker
Christopher Dean Policeman
Dave Dee Policeman
Daniel Defoe Brickmaker and Shopkeeper
Charles Dickens Court Stenographer and Shoe Black Factory Worker
Benjamin Disraeli Novelist
John Boyd Dunlop Vet
Albrecht Dürer Draughtsman
Clint Eastwood Swimming Instructor
Thomas Alva Edison Telegraph Operator and Newsboy
Albert Einstein Patent Office Clerk
TS Eliot Clerk with Lloyds Bank
Juan Fangio Bus Driver
Michael Faraday Bookseller and Lab Technician
William Faulkner Postmaster
Kathleen Ferrier Telephone Operator

Frank Finlay Butcher
Scott Fitzgerald Hollywood Scriptwriter
Ian Fleming Intelligence Officer and Journalist
Gerald Ford Male Model
George Foreman Minister of Religion
George Formby Jockey
Benjamin Franklin Printer
Frederick II, the Great Musician
Billy Fury Tugboat Worker
Clark Gable Lumberjack
Greta Garbo Milliner's Model
Graeme Garden Doctor
Giuseppe Garibaldi Candlemaker and Privateer
James Garner Swimsuit Model
David Garrick Wine Merchant
Paul Gauguin Stockbroker and Labourer on Panama Canal
Jean Genet Professional Criminal and Male Prostitute
William S Gilbert Barrister and Cartoonist
Joseph Goebbels Newspaper Editor
Johann von Goethe Fire Chief, Newspaper Critic and Court Official
WG Grace Doctor
Kenneth Grahame Secretary to Bank of England
Cary Grant, Acrobat
Zane Grey Dentist
Terry Griffiths Postman
Ernesto 'Che' Guevara Doctor
Gareth Hale PE Teacher
Thomas Hardy, Architect
Bob Harris, Policeman
Russell Harty Teacher
Alex Harvey Lion Tamer
AP Herbert, Oxford University MP
William Herschel, Music Teacher
Benny Hill Milkman
Adolf Hitler Painter of Postcards
Ho Chi Minh Hotel Worker and Pastry Cook
Bob Hoskins Market Porter, Fire-Eater, Steeplejack and Seaman
AE Housman Classics Teacher
Rod Hull Electrician
Gareth Hunt Merchant Seaman
Henrik Ibsen Pharmacist
Julio Iglesias Goalkeeper
Charles Ives Insurance Executive
David Jason Electrician
Andrew Johnson Tailor
Wassily Kandinsky Lawyer
Harvey Keitel US Marine
Charles Kingsley Cambridge History Professor
Burt Lancaster Circus Acrobat
Eddie Large Electrician
Philip Larkin Librarian
Antoine Laurent Lavoisier Tax Collector
Kuan Yew Lee Barrister
Vladimir Ilich Lenin Lawyer
Leopold I of Habsburg Musician

Franz Liszt Priest
Little Richard Minister of Religion
Syd Little Decorator
Luke, St Painter and Physician
Harold MacMillan Publisher
André Malraux Archaeologist and Pilot
Thomas Malthus Clergyman
Christopher Marlowe Secret agent
Nelson Mandela Lawyer
Karl Marx Newspaper Correspondent
Marcello Mastroianni Draughtsman
St Matthew Tax Collector
William Somerset Maugham Surgeon and Spy
Herman Melville Customs Officer
Gregor Mendel Monk
Jonathan Miller Doctor
John Mills Toilet Paper Salesman
Robert Mitchum Miner
Matt Monroe Bus Driver
Samuel Morse Artist
Modest Musorgsky Civil Servant
Arthur Mullard Professional Boxer
Dame Anna Neagle Dance Instructor
Jawaharlal Nehru Lawyer
Thomas Newcomen Blacksmith
Bob Newhart Accountant
Isaac Newton Warden of the Mint and MP
Julius Nyerere Teacher
Milton Obote Labourer, Clerk and Salesman
Sean O'Casey Building Labourer
Tom O'Connor Teacher
Bruce Oldfield Art Teacher
George Orwell Policeman
David Owen Doctor
Norman Pace PE Teacher
Peter the Great Shipwright
François André Philidor Chess Master and Composer
Enoch Powell Greek Professor
Magnus Pyke Nutritionist
Sir Walter Raleigh Poet and Explorer
Charles Reade Lawyer
Reagan Ronald Actor
Ray Reardon Policeman and Miner
Paul Revere Silversmith
Arthur Rimbaud Gun Runner and Merchant
Joan Rivers Fashion Co-ordinator for Bond Stores
Peter Roget Doctor
Leonard Rossiter Insurance Agent
Henri Rousseau Customs Officer
Salman Rushdie Actor and Advertising Copywriter
Willie Rushton Cartoonist and Playwright
Sir Walter Scott Lawyer
WilliamShakespeare Actor

Richard Sheridan MP
Nevil Shute Engineer (worked on R100)
Sir Philip Sidney Professional Soldier
Norodom Sihanouk Musician
Delia Smith Hairdresser and Norwich City FC Director
Benjamin Spock Naval Officer and Rower
Jerry Springer Lawyer
Stalin Trainee Monk
Freddie Starr Bricklayer
Tommy Steele Merchant Seaman
Laurence Sterne Clergyman
Rod Stewart Gravedigger
David Storey Rugby League Professional
Jonathan Swift Clergyman
Charles Talleyrand-Périgord Abbot
Jimmy Tarbuck Milkman
Shirley Temple US Ambassador to Ghana
Valentina Tereshkova Cotton Mill worker
Margaret Thatcher Research Chemist and Barrister
John Thaw Market Porter
JRR Tolkien Oxford English Professor
Anthony Trollope Post Office Worker
Harry S Truman Haberdasher
Desmond Tutu Schoolteacher
Liv Ullmann UNICEF Ambassador
John Vanbrugh Playwright and Architect
Vincent Van Gogh Evangelist
Jules Verne Librettist
King Vidor Cinema Projectionist and Cameraman
Kurt Vonnegut Soldier
Lech Walesa Electrician
Lew Wallace Soldier
Noah Webster Lawyer
Orson Welles Picador
HG Wells Draper's Assistant and Teacher
Walt Whitman Teacher and Printer
Billy Wilder Journalist and Crime Reporter
Tennessee Williams Waiter and Cinema Usher
Ludwig Wittgenstein Hospital Porter and Gardener
Terry Wogan Bank Clerk
Ermanno Wolf-Ferrari Artist
William Wordsworth Stamp Distributor
Harry Worth Miner
Sir Christopher Wren Astronomy Professor
Tammy Wynette Beautician
JR Wyss Swiss National Anthem Writer
Yohji Yamamoto Lawyer
Andrew John Young Poet and Clergyman
Lazarus Zamenhof Oculist
Franco Zeffirelli Actor and Costume Designer
Count Ferdinand von Zeppelin US Civil War Soldier
Émile Zola Journalist

F
A
M
O
U
S

P
E
O
P
L
E

NB: The list gives only the 'lesser known' professions. In cases where the person is equally well known in two different professions, however, both professions are given (e.g. Vanbrugh). Most of the alternative professions were fee-earning, but some are listed primarily as items of curiosity rather than serious professions.

Assassinations

681BC   *Sennacherib of Assyria*   Murdered by his two sons.

514BC   *Hipparchus of Athens*   Killed by Harmodius and Aristogeiton, two Athenians.

465BC   *Xerxes I of Persia*   Killed by members of his court, led by Artabanus.

336BC   *Philip II of Macedon*   Killed by Pausanias, a Spartan regent and general.

330BC   *Darius III (Codomannus) of Persia*   Slain by a satrap, Arterxes (Ardashir), whilst fleeing Alexander the Great.

44BC   *Julius Caesar*   (*Roman dictator*)   Stabbed by Brutus, Cassius and others in the Senate.

41   *Caligula*   (*Roman emperor*)   Murdered by Cassius Chaerea, an officer of his guard.

54   *Claudius I*   (*Roman Emperor*)   Ate poisoned mushrooms served by his wife, Agrippina the Younger.

96   *Domitian*   (*Roman dictator*)   Stabbed in his bedroom by Stephanus, a freed slave.

192   *Commodus*   (*Roman Emperor*)   Strangled by wrestler Narcissus, at the behest of his mistress, Marcia.

978   *Edward the Martyr (King of England)*   Murdered at Corfe Castle by his younger half-brother Ethelred's household, led by Elfthryth.

1057   *Macbeth*   (*King of Scotland*)   Killed by Malcolm III, Canmore, at Lumphanan (15 August).

1170   *Thomas à Becket*   Killed by four knights, Fitzurse, Tracy, De Merville and Le Breton in Canterbury Cathedral.

1192   *Conrad, King of Jerusalem*   Killed by members of the militant Islamic sect, the Assassins, who gave assassination their name.

1327   *Edward II, of England*   Murdered in Berkeley Castle possibly with a red hot poker at the instigation of his wife, Isabella, and her lover Roger de Mortimer; possible perpetrators were De Gournay and Maltravers.

1437   *James I, of Scotland*   Murdered in court residence, a Dominican monastery, by assassins led by Sir Robert Graham.

1471   *Henry VI, of England*   Murdered in the Tower of London, possibly by Richard of Gloucester the future Richard III.

1488   *James III of Scotland*   Murdered following defeat of royal army at Sauchieburn by unknown.

1533   *Atahualpa*   (*Last Inca ruler*)   Strangled by Spanish forces under Francisco Pizarro.

1541   *Francisco Pizarro*   Murdered at his home in Lima, possibly by Juan de Rada at the instigation of Diego de Almagro.

1567   *Henry, Lord Darnley*   (*husband of Mary, Queen of Scots*)   Strangled by Scottish nobles after explosion at Kirk O' Field.

1584   *William the Silent*   (*aka William of Orange*)   Shot at Delft by Balthasar Gerard.

1589   *Henry III, of France*   Stabbed by Jacques Clément, a fanatical Dominican.

1610   *Henry IV, of France*   Murdered by François Ravaillac, a Catholic fanatic.

1628   *Duke of Buckingham*   Stabbed at Portsmouth en route for La Rochelle by John Felton, a discontented subaltern.

1634   *Prince Wallenstein*   (*German general*)   Killed by Devereux.

1762   *Peter III, Tsar of Russia*   Strangled in captivity by Count Aleksei Orlov, the lover of his wife and future empress, Catherine.

1793   *Jean Paul Marat*   (*French Revolutionary*)   stabbed in his bath by Charlotte Corday.

1801   *Paul I, of Russia*   Strangled by army officers who had conspired to force his abdication.

1812   *Spencer Perceval (PM)*   Shot while entering lobby of the House of Commons by John Bellingham, a bankrupt Liverpool broker.

1865   *Abraham Lincoln*   Shot by actor John Wilkes Booth in Ford's Theater, Washington, while watching *Our American Cousin.*

1872   *Richard Burke, Earl of Mayo*   Stabbed to death by Shere Ali, a convict, while inspecting the settlement at Port Blair on the Andaman Islands.

1881   *James A Garfield*   (*US President*)   Shot in a station by Charles Guiteau, a disappointed office-seeker.

1881   *Alexander II, of Russia*   Died from injuries after a bomb was thrown near his palace by Nihilists, led by Sophia Perovskaya.

1882   *Lord Frederick Cavendish*   (*Chief Secretary for Ireland*)   Murdered by 'Irish invincibles' in Phoenix Park, Dublin.

1894   *Marie François Carnot*   (*French President*)   Stabbed by anarchist, Cesare Giovanni Santo Caserio.

1897   *Antonio Cánovas del Castillo*   (*Spanish Premiere*)   Shot by Italian anarchist Angiolillo at the bath of Santa Agueda, Vitoria.

1900   *Umberto I, of Italy*   Murdered by anarchist G. Bresci in Monza.

1901   *William McKinley*   (*US President*)   Shot by anarchist Leon Czolgosz in Buffalo, NY.

1903   *Alexander Obrenovich*   (*King of Serbia*)   Murdered by military conspirators, along with his wife, Draga.

1913   *George I, of Greece*   Murdered by a Greek, Schinas, in Salonika.

1914   *Archduke Franz Ferdinand*   Shot in a car by Gavrilo Princip in Sarajevo (28 June); the assassination helped to precipitate World War I.

1914   *Jean Jaurès*   (*French Socialist*)   Shot by nationalist, Raoul Villain, in café.

1916   *Rasputin, (Russian monk)*   Killed and dumped in River Neva by group of nobles led by Prince Feliks Yusupov and Grand Duke Dimitry Pavlovich, revenging his influence over Tsarina Alexandra.

1922   *Michael Collins*   (*Sinn Fein leader*)   Killed in an ambush between Bandon and Macroom in the Irish Republic.

1923   *Pancho Villa*   (*Mexican Revolutionary*)   Assassinated on his ranch at Parral, Mexico (20 June).

1934   *Dr Englebert Dollfuss   (Austrian Chancellor)*   Shot by Nazis in the Chancellery.

1934   *Sergey Mironovich Kirov   (Russian Communist)*   Shot by Leonid Nikolayev at the Communist Party HQ (1 December); Stalin subsequently purged Leningrad of all suspected anti-Stalinists.

1934   *Alexander I, of Yugoslavia   (King of the Serbs, Croats and Slovenes)*   Murdered in Marseilles by a Macedonian terrorist.

1935   *Huey Long   (US politician)*   Murdered by Dr Carl Austin Weiss.

1940   *Leon Trotsky   (Exiled Russian leader)*   Killed with an ice pick in Mexico by Ramón Mercader.

1942   *Reinhard Heydrich   (second-in-command in the Nazi Secret Police)*   Murdered by Czech resistance fighters.

1943   *Isoruku Yamamoto (Japanese Admiral)*   Plane intercepted and shot down by US P-38 fighter squad after Japanese naval code was broken.

1948   *Mohandas Gandhi   (Indian leader)*   Shot by Hindu fanatic, Nathuran Godse at Birla House, New Delhi.

1948   *Count Folke Bernadotte   (Swedish diplomat)*   Murdered by Jewish extremists in ambush in Jerusalem.

1951   *Abdullah 1 of Jordan*   Murdered by member of Jihad faction.

1951   *Liaquat Ali Khan   (Pakistani PM)*   Murdered in Rawalpindi by fanatics advocating war with India.

1958   *Faisal II, of Iraq*   Murdered with his entire household during a military coup.

1959   *Solomon Bandaranaike   (Sri Lankan statesman)*   Murdered by Buddhist monk, Talduwe Somarama.

1959   *Rafael Trujillo Molina   (Dominican Republic dictator)*   Machine-gunned in car by assassins including General JT Diaz.

1963   *John F Kennedy   (US President)*   Shot while riding in open Lincoln Continental in Dallas, Texas, by rifleman Lee Harvey Oswald (22 Nov).

1963   *Malcolm X   (Black Muslim leader)*   Shot at political rally.

1966   *Hendrik Verwoerd   (South African Premier)*   Stabbed by parliamentary messenger, Dimitri Tsafendas.

1968   *Martin Luther King   (civil rights leader)*   Shot on hotel balcony by James Earl Ray in Memphis, Tennessee.

1968   *Robert F Kennedy   (US Senator)*   Shot by Jordanian Arab immigrant Sirhan Bishara Sirhan in the Hotel Ambassador, Los Angeles.

1975   *King Faisal of Saudi Arabia*   Murdered by his nephew, Prince Faisal.

1976   *Christopher Ewart-Biggs   (British Ambassador to Eire)*   Car blown up by IRA landmine.

Georgi Markov (Bulgarian dissident)   Infected with poisoned pellet on Westminster Bridge by Bulgarian agent.

1978   *Aldo Moro, former Italian PM*   Kidnapped by Red Brigade and later found dead.

Wafizulah Amin (President of Afghanistan)   Killed with his mistress in the presidential palace, Kabul, by KGB commandos.

1979   *Airey Neave, MP*   Killed by IRA bomb in House of Commons car park.

1979   *Lord Mountbatten*   Killed by IRA bomb in sailing boat while fishing off County Sligo, Ireland.

1979   *Park Chung Hee   (South Korean President)*   Shot in restaurant by chief of Korean Central Intelligence Agency.

1980   *John Lennon   (former Beatle)*   Shot by Mark Chapman outside his apartment in New York.

1980   *Oscar Romero   (Salvadorean RC Prelate)*   Murdered by government troops.

1981   *Anwar Sadat   (Egyptian President)*   Shot by rebel soldier Khalid Ahmed Shawki and others while reviewing military parade.

1981   *Zia ur-Rahman   (Bangladeshi President)*   Shot by military and replaced as President by Abdus Sattar.

1983   *Benigno Aquino   (Filipino politician)*   Shot in the head at Manila airport by a government-backed assassin.

1984   *Indira Gandhi   (Indian PM)*   Murdered by members of her Sikh bodyguard (Satwant and Beant Singh).

1986   *Olaf Palme   (Swedish PM)*   Shot in Stockholm as he walked home from cinema by unknown hand.

1988   *General Zia ul-Haq   (Pakistani leader)*   Killed in air crash owing to sabotage.

1991   *Rajiv Gandhi   (Former Indian PM)*   Blown up during an election campaign by Thanu.

1992   *Muhammad Boudiaf   (President of Algeria's High State Council)*   Murdered during a speech.

1995   *Yitzhak Rabin   (Israeli PM)*   Murdered by Yigal Amir.

F
A
M
O
U
S

P
E
O
P
L
E

Attempted Assinations

Count Otto von Bismarck   Attempts by Kulimann (1874) and Blind (1866).

Queen Elizabeth I   Numerous plots to replace Elizabeth on the her throne by Mary Queen of Scots, notably the Ridolfi and Babington plots, but the only person to be put to death for an alleged direct attempt was Dr Lopez, her physician, in 1594.

Gerald Ford   Assassination attempt by Lynette 'Squeaky' Fromme, member of Charles Manson's 'family' (1975).

Henry Frick   Steel magnate who was shot and stabbed by anarchist Alexander Berkman (1892).

George III   James Hadfield attempted assassination in 1800 but was acquitted due to insanity.

Hitler   Bomb planted by Colonel Von Stauffenberg at his Wolf's Lair HQ in E Prussia in 1944 exploded but failed to kill him.

John Paul II   Shot by Mehmet Ali Agca in 1981.

Lenin   Assassination attempt by Fanny Kaplan in 1918 caused his health to go into steady decline.

Leopold II   Gennaro Rubino made an attempt on the life of the Belgian king in 1902.

Napoleon III   Felice Orsini made an attempted assassination, but Napoleon eventually died of a gall bladder infection.

Prince of Wales   Jean Baptiste Sipido made an

attempt on the life of the future King Edward VII (1900).

Ronald Reagan Shot by John Hinckley in 1981.

Theodore Roosevelt Attempt on life by Weilbrenner in 1903.

Shah of Persia Francois Salsou made an attempt on the life of the Shah in 1900.

Margaret Thatcher The IRA Grand Hotel bombing in

Brighton (Oct 1984) was an attempt on her life.

Queen Victoria Attempts by Edward Oxford (1840), Bean (1840), John Francis (1842), William Hamilton (1849) and R. Maclean (1882).

George Wallace Left paralysed after being shot by Arthur Bremer in 1972.

Andy Warhol Shot by Valerie Solaris, one of his starlets, in 1968.

Catchphrases and Slogans

NB: The list below shows a phrase and the most identifiable body to that phrase. In most cases the details are self-explanatory and where the phrase has actually been coined by a person then his information is given. Many phrases will be of doubtful origin and no attempt has been made to authenticate entries as original spoutings. To give Robert Walpole as an example from my list; the phrase 'every man has his price' is identified with the prime minister but the phrase was almost certainly used as a maxim centuries earlier although impossible to research. Many more catchphrases associated with household products will be found in the TV Advert section.

a good idea . . . son Max Bygraves (as Archie Andrew's tutor in *Educating Archie*)

all human life is there News of the World (advertising slogan from a Henry James novel)

all done in the best possible taste Kenny Everett (in the guise of the leggy Miss Cupid Stunt)

a man of my cal-aye-ber Tony Hancock (originally coined in *Hancock's Half-Hour*)

and now for something completely different John Cleese (in *Monty Python*)

and that's the way it is Walter Cronkite (in concluding his CBS TV *Evening News* programme)

and the next Tonight will be tomorrow night Cliff Michelmore (at the end of the nightly BBC magazine programme)

are you looking for a punch up the bracket Tony Hancock (originally coined in *Hancock's Half-Hour*)

are you sitting comfortably ? Julia Lang (on BBC radio's *Listen with Mother*)

as it happens Jimmy Savile

ask the audience Chris Tarrant (in *Who Wants to be a Millionaire*)

as the art mistress said to the gardener Monica (Beryl Reid) as Archie Andrew's posh friend in *Educating Archie*

aw don't embarrass me Lenny the Lion (ventriloquist Terry Hall's creation)

awight at the back (sic) Michael Barrymore (at the start of many of his shows)

beam me up, Scotty Attributed to Captain Kirk (William Shatner) in *Star Trek*

because it is there George Leigh Mallory (on being asked why he wanted to climb Mt Everest)

before you can say Jack Robinson Richard Brinsley Sheridan (in the Commons to avoid using a fellow MP's name)

before your very eyes Arthur Askey (from the name of his first television series as a proof of live TV)

be like dad, keep mum 1941 propaganda slogan advising civilians to not talk about war-related issues)

be prepared Pears' Soap usurped the slogan from the motto of the Boy Scout movement

Bernie, the bolt Bob Monkhouse (in the *Golden Shot*) Bernie's real name was Derek Young

better red than dead Bertrand Russell (in a 1958 article stating Communism was preferable over death)

bet you can't eat three Ian Botham (used in an advertising campaign for Shredded Wheat)

Beulah, peel me a grape Mae West (first said by the actress to a black maid in the film *I'm No Angel*)

Big Bang, the Nickname for the London Stock Exchange deregulation of 27 October 1986

Big Brother is watching you George Orwell in his novel *Nineteen Eighty-Four* first coined this cry for democracy

big-hearted Arthur, that's me Arthur Askey (introducing himself on radio's *Band Waggon*)

black is beautiful Stokely Carmichael (at a civil rights rally in Memphis in 1966)

black power Usually attributed to Stokely Carmichael after shooting of James Meredith in 1966

blonde bombshell Jean Harlow (not so much a catchphrase more a description and nickname)

book 'em Danno Steve McGarrett (Jack Lord) to Detective 'Danno' Williams in *Hawaii Five O*

boom, boom Billy Bennett (the comedian coined the phrase to underline the punchline of a gag) Basil Brush and Eric Morecambe usurped Billy Bennett's catchphrase in their acts

born 1820, still going strong Johnnie Walker whisky slogan first used in 1908

British are coming, the Colin Welland (after collecting an Oscar for the film *Chariots of Fire*)

buck stops here, the Harry S. Truman (from a sign on his desk in the Oval Office)

bumper bundle Coined by Jean Metcalfe whilst introducing *Two-Way Family Favourites* The phrase denotes a large number of requests for the same record

can I do you now sir Mrs Mopp (Dorothy Summers) in *ITMA* i.e. *It's That Man Again*

can we talk ? Joan Rivers (interjection used by the comedienne to link her jokes)

can you hear me, mother ? Sandy Powell (coined in 1932, probably the first radio catchphrase that caught on)

carry on London Freddie Grisewood (at the end of BBC radio's *In Town Tonight*)

clap hands, here comes Charley Charlie Kunz (became the signature tune of the *American pianist*)

clunk, click, every trip Jimmy Savile (from a seat-belt campaign launched in 1971)

come on down The Price is Right (originated in America when the popular show began in 1957)

come up and see me sometime   Mae West (originally said as 'Why don't you come up sometime and see me)

come with me to the Casbah   Charles Boyer (attributed to the 1938 film *Algiers* although not in the final cut)

customer is always right, the   H. Gordon Selfridge (the American pioneer of the large department store)

daft as a brush   Ken Platt (comedian who corrupted the northern phrase 'soft as a brush')

day war broke out, the   Robb Wilton (after WWII the comedian substituted 'peace' for 'war')

dead as a door-nail   From Langland's *Piers Plowman* (door-nail was a knob on which a knocker struck)

did you spot this week's deliberate mistake   Lionel Gamlin (from his BBC radio series *Monday Night at Seven*)

didn't he do well   Bruce Forsyth (at the end of the conveyor belt finale of the *Generation Game*)

dig for victory   Sir Reginald Dorman Smith (slogan asking people to grow food during WWII)

disgusted . . . Tunbridge Wells   Stock phrase used when the writer does not want to give their name

dodgy   Norman Vaughan (the phrase was accompanied by a thumbs-down gesture)

doesn't it make you want to spit   Arthur Askey (from the radio show *Band Waggon*)

don't forget the fruit gums mum   Roger Musgrave (the copywriter coined the phrase for Rowntree's Fruit Gums)

don't spit, remember the Johnstown flood   US admonition against spitting (citing the 1889 flood caused by a dam bursting)

don't touch me   Julian Clary (said by the comedian when any contact is made on his person)

don't worry, be happy   George Bush (unofficial campaign slogan used in the 1988 presidential election)

do you know the Bishop of Norwich ?   An allusion to a port drinker who is holding on to the bottle and not passing it round

Drinka Pinta Milka Day   Bertrand Whitehead (the Executive Officer of the National Milk Publicity Council)

economical with the truth   Sir Robert Armstrong (whilst being cross-examined in 1986 regarding MI5 secrets)

elementary, my dear Watson   Sherlock Holmes (attributed to him but not to be seen in Conan Doyle's writings)

eleventh commandment, the   George Whyte-Melville (cites 'thou shalt not be found out' in his book *Holmby House*)

'er indoors   Arthur Daley (George Cole) in the ITV series *Minder*

evening all   George Dixon (Jack Warner) in *Dixon of Dock Green*

ever-open door, the   Dr Barnardo's Homes (slogan used to describe the homes in the 1950s)

everybody out   Paddy (Miriam Karlin) as the shop steward in the BBC's *The Rag Trade*

everybody wants to get into the act   Jimmy Durante (subsequently changed to everybody wants to get in on the act)

every man has his price   Often attributed to Robert Walpole

every picture tells a story   Appears to originate in

1904 as a slogan for Doan's Bachache and Kidney Pills
The slogan was accompanied by a picture of a person bent over with back pain

everything in the garden's lovely   Marie Lloyd (from the title of one of her popular songs)

expletive deleted   Made famous by the Watergate transcripts but a general US term in documents

exterminate . . . exterminate   Daleks (in the BBC television series *Dr Who*)

eyes and ears of the world, the   Slogan promoting the cinema newsreel, *Paramount News* from 1927–57

fifty fifty   Chris Tarrant (in *Who Wants to be a Millionaire*)

fleet's lit up, the   Cdr Tommy Woodrooffe (the BBC radio commentator coined the phrase in 1937)

flippin' kids   Tony Hancock (as Archie Andrew's tutor in *Educating Archie*)

Flying Fickle Finger of Fate Award, the   Prize in a mock talent contest in Rowan and Martin's *Laugh In*

F. T. A. (Fuck The Army)   Popular American graffiti used since 1960 among US Army recruits to express a dislike for orders especially in the Vietnam conflict. Protestants use F. T. P. to express their dislike for the Pope and N. Irish patriots use F. T. Q. for the Queen

fully paid-up member of the human race   Kenneth Clarke (described as such by the Observer on 31 July 1988)

get out of that   Eric Morecambe (whilst pressing his down-turned palm under Ernie Wise's chin)

gis a job   Yosser Hughes (Bernard Hill) in *Boys from the Blackstuff*

give 'em the money Barney   Wilfred Pickles (*Have a Go*) to Barney Colehan

give 'em the money Mabel   Wilfred Pickles (to his wife Mabel in radio's *Have a Go*)

go ahead, make my day   Harry Callahan (Clint Eastwood) originally in the 1983 film *Sudden Impact* Ronald Reagan (in an address to the 1985 American Business Conference)

Godfrey Daniel   W. C. Fields (used in place of 'God, damn you' to comply with the strict Hay's Code)

gone for a Burton   RAF expression of WWII denoting a presumed dead person had gone for a drink

good game, good game   Bruce Forsyth (at the end of each round of the *Generation Game*)

good morning sir; was there something   Sam Costa (in the radio programme *Much Binding in the Marsh*)

goodnight children everywhere   Uncle Mac (Derek McCulloch) in BBC radio's *Children's Hour*

goodnight, Mrs Calabash . . . wherever you are   Jimmy Durante (when ending his radio and television appearances)

goody, goody gumdrops   Humphrey Lestocq (presenter of BBC television's *Whirligig* in the 1950s)

greatest show on earth, the   P. T. Barnum (describing the merger of his circus with Bailey's in 1881)

happy as a sandboy   The phrase alludes to the happiness of the door-to-door sellers of sand during the nineteenth century. Sand was bought as an absorber of liquids and scourer

happy as Larry   An Australian expression of delight referring to the boxer Larry Foley 1847–1917

hat-trick   Originating in cricket parlance whereby the perpetrator would be awarded a new hat for his feat. The term is now used for any triple successes

have a gorilla   Neddie Seagoon (Harry Secombe)

offering a cigarette in the *Goon Show*

haves and the have-nots   Sancho Panza (in Miguel Cervantes' *Don Quixote*)

he can't fart and chew gum at the same time   President Lyndon Johnson's insulting description of President Gerald Ford

he can't walk and chew gum at the same time   Revision of Lyndon Johnson's words when Ford became President in 1974

Heinz the Bolt   Jackie Rae (in television's the *Golden Shot*) Heinz later became Bernie the Bolt

hello folks   Tommy Handley (eponymous hero of *It's That Man Again*)

hello folks and world   Neddie Seagoon (Harry Secombe) in the *Goon Show*

hello, good evening, and welcome   David Frost (coined in the *Frost Programme* but has become his stock greeting)

hello, it's me, Twinkletoes   Bernard Bresslaw (as Archie Andrew's tutor in *Educating Archie*)

hello my darlings   Charlie Drake (usual opening greeting of the diminutive funny man)

hello peeps   Stavros (Harry Enfield)

hello playmates   Arthur Askey (introducing himself on radio's *Band Waggon*)

hello possums   Dame Edna Everage (Barry Humphries)

hello sailor   Minnie Bannister (Spike Milligan) in the classic Goon's script *Tales of Men's Shirts*
The phrase has entered the language as a camp double-entendre

here and now, before your very eyes   Arthur Askey (original catchphrase from the series *Before Your Very Eyes*)

here's another fine mess you've gotten me into   Oliver Hardy (invariably to his long-suffering partner Stan Laurel)

here's a pretty kettle of fish   Queen Mary (to Stanley Baldwin referring to the abdication crisis of 1936)

here's Johnny   Ed McMahon (introduction to Johnny Carson on NBC's *Tonight show*)

here's looking at you kid   Rick Blaine (Humphrey Bogart) in *Casablanca*. The phrase is used four times

here we are again   Joey the Clown (Joseph Grimaldi) one of the oldest attributable catchphrases

he's fallen in the water   Little Jim (Spike Milligan) in the *Goon Show*

he's loo-vely, Mrs Hoskins . . . .he's loo-oo-vely   Ivy (Ted Ray) in the comedian's hit radio programme Ray's a Laugh

hi there pop pickers   Alan Freeman (Australian disc-jockey) whilst presenting *Pick of the Pops*

how's about that then, guys and gals   Jimmy Savile (phrase used by the disc-jockey after a particularly good record)

how tickled I am   Ken Dodd (whilst usually shoving a tickling stick between his legs from behind)

I am the greatest   Muhammad Ali (Cassius Clay) usurped the phrase from wrestler Gorgeous George

I could do that   Yosser Hughes (Bernard Hill) in *Boys from the Blackstuff*

I didn't get where I am today . . .   CJ (John Barron) in *The Fall and Rise of Reginald Perrin*

I do not like this game   Bluebottle (Peter Sellers) in the *Goon Show*

I don't mind if I do   Colonel Chinstrap (Jack Train) in *ITMA* whenever a drink was offered him

if it ain't broke, why fix it   Bert Lance (President Carter's Director of the Office of Management and Budget) speaking on the subject of governmental reorganization

If it's up there I'll give you the money myself   Les Dennis (in *Family Fortunes*)

If you can't stand the heat, get out of the kitchen   Harry S.Truman (when he gave his reason for not standing in the 1952 elections)
Truman himself was quoting Major-General Harry Vaughan

I got a horse   Ras Prince Monlulu (Peter Carl McKay) racing pundit of the 1930s to the 1950s

I'll be leaving you now, sir   Claud Snudge (Bill Fraser) in Granada Television's *Bootsie and Snudge*

illegitimi non carborundum   General 'Vinegar Joe' Stilwell used this motto during WWII under the false assumption that it meant 'don't let the bastards grind you down'

I'll give it foive   Janice Nicholls; a member of the public who took part in *Thank Your Lucky Stars* Spin-a-Disc panel and became famous when she gave a maximum five

I'll give you the results in reverse order   Eric Morley (giving *Miss World* results)

I'm a little worried about Jim   Mrs Dale (in *Mrs Dale's Diary*)

I mean that most sincerely, friends   Hughie Green (phrase usually accompanied by a clenched fist gesture)

I'm in charge   Bruce Forsyth (whilst introducing the Beat the Clock section at the Palladium)

I'm not a number, I'm a free man   The Prisoner (Patrick McGoohan) spoken in defiance of his number 6 nomenclature

I'm smarter than the average bear   Yogi Bear (whilst constantly out-witting ranger John Smith in Jellystone Park)

in like Flynn   Errol Flynn (alluding to his legendary bedroom prowess)

I only arsked (sic)   Popeye Popplewell (Bernard Bresslaw) in *The Army Game*

I say, I say, I say   Murray and Mooney; a famous double act of the 1930s in which Harry Mooney would utter the immortal words and Harry Murray would invariably reply with 'I don't wish to know that, kindly leave the stage'

I say, what a smasher   Charlie Chester (from the BBC radio programme *Stand Easy*)

is she a friend of Dorothy ?   An allusion to a homosexual (from Judy Garland's character in *The Wizard of Oz*)
The phrase arose from Judy Garland's friendships within male homosexual circles

I thang you (sic)   Arthur Askey (from the radio show *Band Waggon*)

I think the answer lies in the soil   Arthur Fallowfield (Kenneth Williams) in *Beyond Our Ken*

I think we should be told   Attributed to John Junor by *Private Eye* in a parody of his opinion column in the *Sunday Express*. Although the column invariably used the phrase it is doubtful whether Junor ever actually used the phrase himself

it'll play in Peoria   Coined by John Ehrlichman during the Nixon election campaign of 1969
The phrase was an allusion to whether policies would appeal to 'Middle America'
Peoria is in Illinois and was chosen as it had four syllables and scanned well

it never rains, but it pours John Arbuthnot (the inventor of 'John Bull' coined this phrase in 1726)

it's goodnight from me . . . and it's goodnight from him Ronnie Barker and Ronnie Corbett (*The Two Ronnies*)

it's only a bloody game Magnus Magnusson would invariably say this to settle the nerves of contenders of *Mastermind*; of course, this ice-breaker was only for the ears of the audience and participants

it's the way I tell 'em Frank Carson (full phrase is 'you've heard them all before but it's the way I tell 'em')

it's turned out nice again George Formby (invariably opened his act with this phrase)

I've arrived, and to prove it, I'm here Max Bygraves (as Archie Andrews tutor in *Educating Archie*)

I've found it, I've found the lost chord Jimmy Durante (whilst playing the piano he would feign this new discovery)

I've got a million of 'em Jimmy Durante (after telling a joke) Max Miller later used this phrase

I've got his pecker in my pocket Lyndon B. Johnson (dates from his time as Senate Majority leader in Washington)

I've started so I'll finish Magnus Magnusson would say this if he had started asking a question on the BBC's *Mastermind* programme but the time had elapsed and the hooter sounded

I wanna tell you a story Max Bygraves (as Archie Andrew's tutor in *Educating Archie*)

I want me tea Grandma Grove (Nancy Roberts) who often made this demand in the *Grove Family*

I want to be alone Greta Garbo never actually spoke these words off-set although she was very reclusive. The most often quoted origin of these words on screen is in the 1932 film *Grand Hotel*, however she utters the immortal words in the earlier 1929 film *The Single Standard* but as it was a silent film it was subtitled

I won't take me coat off; I'm not stopping Ken Platt, the northern comedians catchphrase was coined by Ronnie Taylor producer of radio's *Variety Fanfare* in 1951

jolly hockey sticks Monica (Beryl Reid) as Archie Andrew's posh friend in *Educating Archie*

just give me the facts, ma'am Joe Friday (Jack Webb) in *Dragnet*

just like that Tommy Cooper (sometimes the master comedian would say 'not like that, like that')

K-E-Y-N-S-H-A-M Horace Batchelor, the football pools export on Radio Luxembourg would always end his advert by spelling out his address in Bristol

Kilroy was here Phrase used in WWII to allude to the US Air Transport Command

The phrase is of doubtful origin but it is beloved of graffiti writers

kiss of death, the Stock phrase deriving from the kiss of betrayal given by Judas to Christ

lady bountiful George Farquhar coined the phrase from the name of a character in his 1707 work *The Beaux Stratagem* but phrase is now applied to a woman who is conspicuously generous to others less fortunate than herself

laugh and the world laughs with you From Ella Wheeler Wilcox poem 'Solitude' it continues 'weep and you weep alone'

left hand down a bit Leslie Phillips (in *The Navy*

Lark) Jon Pertwee would reply 'left hand down it is, sir'

let's get outta here In a survey of stock film phrases this is the most often said in film history

life begins at forty William B. Pitkin (Professor of Journalism at Columbia University in a 1932 book)

listening bank, the Midland Bank (advertising slogan used from 1980 onwards)

little of what you fancy does you good, a Marie Lloyd popularised the phrase in a song written by Fred W. Leigh and George Arthurs. The phrase was invariably accompanied by a suggestive wink

Lloyd George knew my father Tommy Rhys Roberts, whose father did indeed know Lloyd George, popularised the phrase which became a Welsh standard song which was sung to the tune of Onward Christian Soldier

loadsamoney Harry Enfield character (first seen in *Friday Night Live*) who was a plasterer by trade

loook Alf Garnett (Warren Mitchell) in *Till Death Us Do Part*

love me, love my dog St Bernard of Clairvaux first espoused this philosophical metaphor which meant in effect, you must love me warts and all. Incidentally St Bernard of Clairvaux is not the St Bernard (of Menthon) that the breed of Alpine dog is named

love you madly Duke Ellington often said 'We'd like you to know that the boys in the band all . . .

man for all season, a Robert Bolt's title for his 1960 play about Sir Thomas More has entered the language to describe an adaptable, all round accomplished person

man on the Clapham omnibus, the Lord Bowen first coined this phrase in 1903 when summing up a case. The phrase has entered the modern idiom to represent the ordinary man in the street

man they couldn't gag, the Peter Wilson (nickname of the *Daily Mirror* sports columnist)

man you love to hate, the Erich von Stroheim (epithet rather than catchphrase)

Martini . . . shaken not stirred James Bond (The line is first spoken in *Goldfinger* but does not appear in the books)

mean! moody! magnificent Jane Russell (epithet rather than catchphrase) first used as slogan for *The Outlaw*

mind how you go George Dixon (Jack Warner) in *Dixon of Dock Green*

mind my bike Jack Warner popularised this unlikely hit phrase on radio

moment of truth, the The phrase derives from a Spanish bullfighting term 'El momento de la verdad' in in which the final sword thrust kills the animal

Mounties always get their man, the Unofficial motto of the Royal Canadian Mounted Police first coined by John J. Healy although the official motto since 1873 is 'Maintain the Right'

Mr Big Ian Fleming coined the phrase in his second novel *Live and Let Die* (1954)

The characters name was Buonaparte Ignace Gallia, hence Mr Big

The phrase has come to mean any top man in an organization

Mr Clean James Baker the American Secretary of State was given this epithet

Much Binding in the Marsh Not so much a catchphrase but this popular radio programme, that grew out of an edition of *Merry-Go-Round* and starring Kenneth Horne and Richard Murdoch, became the instigator of many catchphrases and a song of the same title

mum, mum, they are laughing at me Arthur English (whilst playing his cockney spiv character and unfurling his kipper tie)

my flabber has never been so gasted Frankie Howard coined this ridiculous phrase that became an essential part of his act. He would say 'I'm flabbergasted, in fact my flabber has never been so gasted'

my name's Monica Beryl Reid (as Archie Andrew's posh friend in *Educating Archie*)

nah . . . Luton airport Lorraine Chase (in a famous advert for Campari)

never change / swap horses in midstream Abraham Lincoln is identified with the phrase in a citation of 1864

never knowingly undersold John Lewis Partnership (slogan) devised by John Spedan Lewis in 1920

nice 'ere innit Lorraine Chase (in a famous advert for Campari)

nice to see you, to see you nice Bruce Forsyth (originally from the *Generation Game* but often used in other shows)

night of the long knives, the Originally referred to the night of 2 July 1934 when Hitler, aided by Himmler's black-shirted SS, liquidated the leadership of the brown-shirted SA

The phrase has entered modern vernacular to mean a surprise bloodless purge for example Harold Macmillan's wholesale reorganization of his cabinet in 1962

nine days' wonder Possibly traced back to Geoffrey Chaucer and more recently alluding to the fact that a puppy is blind for the first nine days of its life.
The phrase has come to mean anything of short-lived appeal

no such thing as a free lunch The Nobel Prize-Winning Economist Milton Friedman is identified with the saying and he wrote a book of this name, but the phrase dates back to the 19th century

not a lot Paul Daniels (usually before doing a trick he would say 'you're going to like this . . .')

not 'arf Alan Freeman would say this phrase out of context which perhaps gave it appeal

not tonight, Josephine Napoleon I (attributed but never actually said)

now that's magic Paul Daniels (after successfully performing a slick trick)

nudge nudge, wink wink, say no more squire Eric Idle (in *Monty Python*) showing suspect pictures to Terry Jones

often a bridesmaid, but never a bride Milton Feasley wrote this slogan for Listerine mouthwash in 1923

oh hello, I'm Julian, and this is my friend Sandy Hugh Paddick (referring to Kenneth Williams in *Round the Horne*)

old soldiers never die, they simply fade away General Douglas MacArthur whilst addressing congress on 19 April 1951 after being dismissed by President Truman. The phrase originated much earlier

one foot in the grave Jonathan Swift in *Gulliver's Travels* (1726) made the phrase popular in connection with the Struldbruggs of Laputa

one small step for man Neil Armstrong's exact words when walking on the moon were 'That's one small step for a man, one giant leap for mankind'

only the names have been changed Narrator of the detective series *Dragnet* would continue . . . .to

protect the innocent

on with the motley (vesti la giubba) From Leoncavallo's opera *I Pagliacci* relating to the fact that the clown must carry on despite a broken heart

on your bike Norman Tebbit, addressing the Conservative Party conference on 15 Oct 1981
He related how his father was brought up with unemployment but instead of rioting got on his bike and looked for work

ooh Betty Frank Spencer (Michael Crawford) in *Some Mothers do 'ave 'em*

ooh you are awful, but I like you Mandy (Dick Emery) accompanied by a slap on the interviewer's shoulder

oooo arr, me ol' pal, me ol' beauty Walter Gabriel (Chris Gittins) in the *Archers*

orft we jolly well go Jimmy Young (after finishing the link with Terry Wogan would utter these words)

pass The stock reply of contenders on the BBC's *Mastermind* programme to save time if the answer did not immediately spring to mind

pass the sick-bag, Alice John Junor (used in his Sunday Express column and parodied by *Private Eye*)

phone a friend Chris Tarrant (in *Who Wants to be a Millionaire*)

pile it high, sell it cheap Sir John Cohen, founder of Tesco supermarkets, coined this phrase

play it again Sam attributed to Humphrey Bogart as Rick Blaine in *Casablanca* although he never actually said these words

pop goes the weasel W. R. Mandale wrote the rhyme 'Up and down the City Road, In and out the Eagle, That's the way the money goes, Pop goes the weasel
The meaning of the rhyme is uncertain but 'Pop' means to pawn

probably the best lager in the world Carlsberg (1973 advertising slogan voiced by Orson Welles)

public enemy No. 1 John Dillinger (Attorney General Homer Cummings gave this name to the murderer)

Queen Anne's dead Phrase of uncertain origin but used to put down someone who delights in telling you some very old news or what you knew already

quick and the dead, the Phrase of uncertain origin but likely to be from the gunslinging days of the wild west
The quick in this context meant the living

read my lips George Bush popularised this phrase in his acceptance speech for the Republican nomination on 19 August 1988. The rest of the line was 'no new taxes'

real thing, it's the Coca-Cola (advertising slogan dating from 1942)

refreshes the parts other beers cannot reach Heineken (advertising slogan for the lager)

right monkey Al Read (the popular northern comedian also used 'cheeky monkey' in his act)

rock on, Tommy Bobby Ball (the comedian would often tug his braces at the same time)

Rodney, you plonker Del Boy (David Jason) to his younger brother in *Only Fools and Horses*

roses grow on you Norman Vaughan (advertising campaign for Roses Chocolates)

say goodnight Dick Dan Rowan (in *Rowan and Martin's Laugh In*) to his co-star Dick Martin

say goodnight Gracie George Burns (to his wife and co-star Gracie Allen)

say it with flowers   Patrick O' Keefe an advertising agent coined the phrase in 1917

shame, shame   Bruce Forsyth (usually accompanied by a cuddle from him)

she who must be obeyed   Horace Rumpole (Leo McKern) referring to his wife in John Mortimer's *Rumpole of the Bailey*. The original expression came from Henry Rider Haggard's novel 'She' and referred to the all-powerful Ayesha

short, fat, hairy legs   Eric Morecambe (referring to Ernie Wise)

shut that door   Larry Grayson (turning towards the wings and intimating a draught)

silly old moo   Alf Garnett (Warren Mitchell) referring to Elsie, his wife, in *Till Death Us Do Part*

sit (sssit)   Barbara Woodhouse (whilst demonstrating her methods of training dogs)

slow, slow, quick, quick, slow   Victor Sylvester popularised this quickstep tempo in his radio and television series

smile, you're on . . .   Candid Camera (first coined by Allen Funt in the original American version)

sock it to me   Judy Carne (in *Rowan and Martin's Laugh In*)

somebody up there likes me   Rocky Graziano (world champion boxer had a film and book about him with this title)

some mothers do 'ave 'em   Jimmy Clitheroe (corruption of the phrase 'don't some mothers have 'em')

somewhere to the right of Genghis Khan   Arthur Scargill relating a political standpoint to John Mortimer

speak as you find, that's my motto   Nola Purvis (Pat Coombs) in the radio series *Hello Playmates*

spend, spend, spend, I'm going to   Viv Nicholson (after winning £152,000 on Littlewoods football pools in 1961)

stone me   Tony Hancock (originally coined in *Hancock's Half-Hour*)

stop me and buy one   Lionel and Charles Rodd came up with this slogan for Wall's ice-cream in 1923 although in those days it was for ice-cream tricycles rather than vans

stop messin' abaht (sic)   Kenneth Williams (originally coined by Williams in *Hancock's Half-Hour*)

suck it and see   Charlie Naughton of the Crazy Gang coined this phrase which meant 'try it'

sweet Fanny Adams   The phrase originates from the murder of an eight-year-old child in 1867. Fanny Adams was the victim of Frederick Booth, a solicitor's clerk, who grotesquely mutilated her body. As these things tend to go, at around the same time, the Royal Navy issued tinned meat which sailors flippantly said probably contained the remains of the little girl. Fanny Adams became slang for mutton or stew and later any worthless item

In modern day vernacular 'Sweet F. A.' can also mean sweet fuck-all

swinging   Norman Vaughan (the phrase was accompanied by a thumbs-up gesture)

ten, four   Dan Matthews (Broderick Crawford) in the American detective series Highway Patrol

The phrase signified agreement and was always being bellowed into the radio

thank you music lovers   Spike Jones, the American musician would murder a classic piece of music along the same lines as Les Dawson or Eric Morecambe and then proceed to say . . .

that'll do nicely, sir   American Express (advertising slogan originating in the late 1970s)

that's all folks   Merry Melodies (Warner Brothers cartoons) written at the end of their cartoons

that's magic   Paul Daniels (after completion of a successful trick or illusion)

the ranger ain't gonna like it Yogi   Booboo bear (when Yogi bear had inventive ideas for stealing picker-nick baskets)

there's more   Jimmy Cricket (whilst telling a joke in his act)

there's no answer to that   Eric Morecambe (cleverly used if the quick-witted comedian was stuck for words)

thinking man's crumpet, the   Frank Muir coined this phrase about television presenter Joan Bakewell

this is Funf speaking   Funf the spy (in *ITMA* i.e. *Its That Man Again*)

today is the first day of the rest of your life   Charles Dederich (founder of anti-heroin centres in the USA)

too little, too late   Professor Allan Nevins wrote this in an article in Current History (1935) referring to the Nazi menace in Germany and the lack of remedial action

T. T. F. N. (ta-ta for now)   Mrs Mopp (Dorothy Summers) in *ITMA*

Jimmy Young adopted this phrase in his popular Radio Two morning show

turn on, tune in, drop out   Dr Timothy Leary coined this pro drug phrase in 1967 although he himself suggests that he stole the phrase from Marshall McLuhan

unacceptable face of capitalism   Edward Heath coined this phrase in 1973 when replying to a question from Jo Grimond in the House of Commons

up and under   Eddie Waring (the much imitated rugby commentator was synonymous with the phrase)

very interesting, but stupid   Arte Johnson (in *Rowan and Martin's Laugh In*) dressed as a German soldier and smoking a cigarette in a holder

wakey, wakey   Billy Cotton (a fanfare of *Somebody Stole My Gal* would precede this cry)

walkies   Barbara Woodhouse (whilst demonstrating her methods of training dogs)

weekend starts here, the   Ready Steady Go (the Friday night pop show was always preceded by these words)

week is a long time in politics, a   Harold Wilson (also deliberated that 48 hours was a long time in politics)

well, he would, wouldn't he   Mandy Rice-Davies (referring to Lord Astor's denial of involvement with her)

were you truly wafted here from paradise?   Terry Howard wrote this Campari advert which made Lorraine Chase a star

what do you think of it so far   Eric Morecambe would rhetorically ask this question whilst either performing one of Ernie's plays or during a lull between sketches. The stock reply by Eric himself was 'rubbish', which was often said through an inanimate object by way of him throwing his voice or saying it between clenched teeth

what's new pussycat ?   Warren Beatty (coined the phrase and had the film originally written for him)

what's on the table Mabel ?   Wilfred Pickles (to his wife Mabel in radio's *Have a Go*)

what's up, doc ?   Bugs Bunny originally said these

words to his adversary Elmer J. Fudd, a doctor, but eventually would say this as a form of greeting to almost everyone

The full phrase was 'er, what's up doc' followed by a crunch on a carrot

when the going gets tough, the tough get going Joseph P. Kennedy, the father of John F. Kennedy, used this phrase in the bringing up of his sons, in an effort to help them through adversity

who dares wins, Rodney Del Boy (David Jason) in *Only Fools and Horses*

who loves ya, baby Theo Kojak (Telly Savalas) in the popular American detective series, *Kojak*

wind of change, the Harold Macmillan used this phrase, written by Sir David Hunt, in describing the change of political standing in Africa in 1960

winter of discontent, the The phrase originates as the opening words of the eponymous Richard of Gloucester in Shakespeare's Richard III, however the term is now used as a description of the winter of 1978/79 when industrial action became rife due to the Labour Government's endeavours to curb pay rises

without hesitation, deviation or repetition Just a Minute (the popular radio panel game meant guests had to speak for a minute)

world's favourite airline, the British Airways slogan

wot, no Chad The phrase was very common in Britain during WWII and was accompanied by a depiction of a bald-headed man appearing over a wall and inquiring 'wot, no . . . .' the blank being filled in by any commodity in short supply. Its origin is uncertain

yaroooo Billy Bunter (created by Frank Richards)

you ain't heard nothin' yet Al Jolson (the most often mis-quoted catchphrase of all. The line is from the *Jazz Singer*)

you ain't seen nothin' yet President Ronald Reagan used this phrase as a slogan during his 1984 re-election bid

you bet your sweet bippy Dick Martin (in *Rowan and Martin's Laugh In*) popular 1960s US comedy show

you cannot be serious John McEnroe (much caricatured phrase that the tennis player often said on court)

you can run but you can't hide Joe Louis (said of Billy Conn, a nifty heavyweight of the day who Louis knocked out)

you can't see the join Eric Morecambe (talking about Ernie Wise's fictitious wig)

you dirty old man Harold Steptoe (Harry H Corbett) addressing his father in *Steptoe and Son*

you dirty rat Cagney, James (dirty, double crossing rat were actual words in *Blonde Crazy* 1931)

you dirty rotten swine, you Bluebottle (Peter Sellers) in the *Goon Show*

you lucky people Tommy Trinder used this phrase whilst compering the *Sunday Night at the London Palladium* shows and it became his stock phrase identified with him

your starter for ten Bamber Gascoigne (an on the buzzer question to teams in *University Challenge*)

you too can have a body like mine Charles Atlas (slogan used for his mail-order body-building lessons)

you've never had it so good Harold MacMillan (actually said 'most of our people have never had it so good')

Causes of Death

Ace, Johnny Rhythm and blues act, died playing Russian roulette (1954).

Alexander the Great Died aged 32 after a prolonged banquet and drinking bout (323 BC).

Alkan, Charles-Henri Valentin French pianist and composer who died when bookshelf collapsed on him whilst reaching for the Talmud (1888).

Antony, Mark Roman triumvir, committed suicide by running onto his sword in 31 BC (misled by a false report of Cleopatra's death).

Archer, Fred English champion jockey, shot himself during an attack of typhoid (1886).

Astor, John Jacob American financier, went down in the *Titanic* in 1912.

Bach, Johann Sebastian German composer, suffered stroke following unsuccessful eye operation (1750).

Ballard, Florence Supremes vocalist, died of a heart attack aged 32 yrs 7 mths.

Barnett, Lady Isobel Committed suicide in her bathroom on 20, October, 1980. One week after being found guilty of shoplifting.

Bartók, Bela Hungarian composer, died of leukaemia (1945).

Beethoven, Ludwig van German compuser, died of cirrhosis of the liver (lupus erythematosus is sometimes considered an alternative cause) (1827).

Belushi, John American actor, died of drug-related illness, aged 33 yrs 1 mth (1982).

Berg, Alban Austrian composer, died from infection from a septic insect bite (1935).

Berlioz, Hector French composer, died following brain haemorrhage (1869).

Billy the Kid Pseudonym of Henry McCarty, aka William H Bonney, American bandit, shot by sheriff Pat Garrett in 1881.

Bizet, Georges French composer, died of angina pectoris complicated by rheumatoid arthritis (1875).

Bolan, Marc T Rex singer, died in car crash aged 30 yrs 2 mths (1977).

Bonham, John Led Zeppelin member, died of alcohol poisoning, aged 32 yrs 3 mths (1980).

Brahms, Johannes German composer, died of liver cancer (1897).

Brooke, Rupert English poet, died of septicaemia, aged 27 yrs (1915).

Brown, Grace Murdered by Chester Gillett in 1906; formed basis for Theodore Dreiser's book *An American Tragedy*.

Calmette, Gaston Editor of *Le Figaro*, shot by Madame Caillaux, wife of the French Finance Minister, accusing her husband of fraud; she was later acquitted (1914).

Calvi, Robert Italian banker, found hanging from scaffolding under Blackfriars Bridge (18 June 1982).

Carpenter, Karen American vocalist and drummer, died aged 32 yrs 11 mths from heart attack caused by anorexia nervosa (1983).

Castlereagh, Viscount British statesman, stabbed himself with a penknife (1822).

Chausson, Ernest   French composer, died in a bicycle accident (1899).

Childers, Erskine   Irish nationalist, was executed in 1922 by the Irish Free State authorities.

Chopin, Fryderyk   Polish composer, died of pulmonary tuberculosis (1849).

Clarke, Ossie   Fashion designer, murdered by his flatmate Diego Cogolato (7 August 1996).

Cleopatra   Queen of Egypt, allegedly committed suicide by allowing an asp to bite her breast (30 BC).

Cline, Patsy   Top American country singer, died in a plane crash aged 30 yrs 5 mths (1963).

Clive, Robert (of Plassey)   English soldier, committed suicide (after several attempts) by shooting himself (1774).

Kurt Cobain   Lead singer of Nirvana, shot himself dead aged 27 yrs 1 mth (1994).

Cogan, Alma   English singer, died of cancer aged 34 yrs 5 mths (1966).

Cooke, Sam   American soul singer, shot dead aged 33 yrs 9 mths (1964).

Crane, Harold Hart   American poet, committed suicide by leaping from a steamboat into the Caribbean (1932).

Davison, Emily   Suffragette, threw herself under the King's horse in the 1913 Epsom Derby.

Dean, James   American actor, died in a car crash in 1955, aged 24.

Debussy, Claude   French composer, died of cancer of the rectum (1918).

Delius, Frederick   English composer, died of syphilis in 1934.

Diana, Princess of Wales   Died in Paris car crash (31st Aug 1997).

Dvořák, Antonín   Czech composer, died of a brain haemorrhage (1904).

Eastman, George   American inventor of the Kodak camera, shot himself in 1932.

Elgar, Edward   English composer, died of a brain tumour in 1934.

Elliot, 'Mama' Cass   American singer, died of a heart attack, aged 32 yrs 10 mths (1974).

Epstein, Brian   Manager of the Beatles, died of a drugs overdose in 1967.

Fayed, Dodi   Son of Harrods director, died in Paris car crash (31st Aug 1997).

Freud, Sigmund   Austrian neurologist and founder of psychoanalysis, died of cancer in 1939.

Garland, Judy   American entertainer, died of a drugs overdose in 1969.

Genovese, Kitty   Famous New York murder whereby nobody answered her calls for help.

Gershwin, George   American composer, died of a brain tumour (1937).

Gibb, Andy   Brother of the Bee Gees, died aged 30 of drug-related illness (1988).

Granados, Enrique   Spanish composer, died when his ship SS *Sussex* was torpedoed by a German sub in the English Channel (1916).

Grieg, Edvard   Norwegian composer, died from coronary artery disease with angina pectoris (1907).

Hamm, Pete   Badfinger member and co-writer of 'Without You', committed suicide after depression brought on possibly by royalty problems (1975).

Hancock, Tony   Birmingham-born comedian, took a drug overdose in a Sydney hotel room in 1968.

Hannibal   Carthaginian soldier, committed suicide by poison when the Romans demanded his surrender (182bc).

Haydn, Franz Joseph   Austrian composer, died of arteriosclerosis (1809).

Hemingway, Ernest   American novelist, shot himself in the mouth in Ketchum, Idaho (1961).

Hendrix, Jimi   American guitarist, suffocated in his own vomit after mixing drugs and alcohol aged 27 yrs 9 mths (1970).

Hickok, Wild Bill   American gunfighter, shot from behind by Jack McCall whilst playing poker in 1876. Hickok's hand was a queen and 2 pair aces over eights (Deadman's hand).

Himmler, Heinrich   German Nazi leader, committed suicide with a cyanide phial concealed in his mouth (1945).

Holly, Buddy   Rock and roll pioneer, died aged 22 yrs 5 months in a plane crash (with Ritchie Valens, 17 yrs 9 mths, and Big Bopper, 29 yrs 4 mths) in 1959.

Hutchence, Michael   Lead singer with INXS, found hanging in a Sydney hotel room (21st Nov 1997).

Ingram, Herbert   English journalist, founder of the *Illustrated London News* and MP for Boston from 1856, drowned in a boat collision on Lake Michigan in 1860.

Ireton, Henry   English Parliamentarian soldier, died of the plague in 1651.

Irving, Laurence   Novelist son of actor Sir Henry Irving, drowned in the *Empress of Ireland* disaster in 1914.

James, Jesse   Wild West robber, shot in the back of the head by Bob Ford (1882).

Jones, Brian   Member of the Rolling Stones, drowned in a swimming pool (aged 27 yrs 4 mths) soon after leaving the group in 1969.

Joplin, Janis   American folk singer, died aged 27 yrs 8 mths of heroin overdose (1970).

Klee, Paul   Swiss artist, died of a heart attack (1940).

Koestler, Arthur and Cynthia   Hungarian-born British author and his wife, committed suicide together in 1983 when he became terminally ill.

Leclair, Jean Marie   French composer, stabbed in his own home, possibly by his wife (1764).

Liszt, Franz   Hungarian composer, died of pneumonia (1886).

London, Jack   American novelist, committed suicide by taking poison in 1916.

Lully, Jean-Baptiste   French composer, died of gangrene and blood poisoning after he struck himself in the foot whilst conducting with a pointed cane (1687).

Lynott, Phil   Thin Lizzy vocalist and guitarist, died of drug-related illness aged 34 yrs 4 mths (1986).

Markov, Georgi   Bulgarian defector, famously murdered by the poison 'ricin' dispensed from the tip of an umbrella (1978).

Marten, Maria   Mole-catcher's daughter, murdered by William Corder in May 1827 at the Red Barn at Polstead nr Ipswich.

Mendelssohn, Felix   German composer, died of brain haemorrage (1847).

Milk, Harvey   US gay rights activist and politician, killed alongside San Francisco Mayor, George Moscone, by ex-city employee Dan White (1978).

Mishima, Yukio   Japanese writer, born Hiraoka Kimitake, committed Seppuku in 1970.

Monroe, Marilyn   American model and actress, died from an overdose of sleeping pills in 1962.

Moon, Keith Who drummer, died of alcoholic poisoning aged 32 (in the same flat that Mama Cass died, owned by Harry Nilsson) in 1978.

Morrison, Jim Doors vocalist, died of drug related illness in 1971 (aged 27 yrs 6 mths); buried in Paris.

Mozart, Wolfgang Austrian composer died of heated military fever (nowadays usually considered to be Bright's Disease) (1791).

Murrell, Hilda Famous botanist (rose grower) and peace campaigner, found stabbed in a wood (1984) in suspicious circumstances as she was linked with documents about the sinking of the *General Belgrano*.

Niven, David English actor, died of motor neurone disease (1983).

Orton, Joe English dramatist, struck by hammer wielded by lover Kenneth Halliwell (1967), who subsequently committed suicide.

Owen, Wilfred English poet, killed on the bank of the Oise-Sambre Canal, nr Ors, one week before the armistice was signed in 1918.

Palach Jan Czech philosophy student, set fire to himself in Jan 1969 in protest at the Russian invasion of Czechoslovakia the previous year.

Pasolini, Pier Paolo Italian writer and director, murdered, possibly as a result of a homosexual encounter, by Giuseppe Pelosi (1975).

Plath, Sylvia Poet wife of Ted Hughes, committed suicide by gassing herself (1963).

Pliny the Elder Roman writer, died in Stabiae (Castellamare) in 79 AD overcome by fumes from Vesuvius.

Presley, Elvis American singer, died of drug-related illnesses in 1977.

Prokofiev, Sergei Russian composer, died of brain haemorrage (1953).

Puccini, Giacomo Italian composer, died of throat cancer (1924).

Quisling, Vidkun Norwegian Fascist leader and puppet PM in occupied Norway, executed in May 1945.

Rachmaninov, Sergei Russian composer and pianist, died of malignant melanoma (1943).

Ravel, Maurice French composer, died of brain tumour (1937).

Redding, Otis Soul singer, died aged 26 yrs 3 mths in a plane crash (1967).

Relf, Keith Yardbirds musician, electrocuted himself, aged 33 yrs 1 mth (1976).

Rimsky-Korsakov, Nikolai Russian composer, died of coronary artery disease with angina pectoris (1908).

Riperton, Minnie American singer, died of cancer aged 31 yrs 8 mths (1979).

Rivett, Sandra Children's nanny, probably murdered by Lord Lucan in 1974 (convicted in absentia 19th June 1975).

Rizzio, David Italian courtier to Mary Queen of Scots, murdered by Scottish noblemen including the Earls of Morton and Lindsay, at the instigation of Lord Darnley (1566).

Robsart, Amy Wife of the Earl of Leicester (favourite of Elizabeth I), found dead at the bottom of a flight of stairs at Cumnor Place, Berkshire (1560).

Rossini, Gioacchino Italian composer, died of cancer of the rectum (1868).

Rothko, Mark Latvian-born American painter, committed suicide by slashing his wrists (1970).

Schubert, Franz Austrian composer, died of typhoid fever (1828).

Scriabin, Alexander Russian composer, died of an infection of a facial carbuncle (1915).

Shannon, Del American pop singer, shot himself whilst depressed (1990).

Siddall, Elizabeth Wife of Dante Gabriel Rossetti, took overdose of laudanum (1862).

Silkwood, Karen US nuclear activist, died in a car crash; her car was suspected to have been forced off the road (1973).

Stradella, Alessandro Italian composer, murdered by persons unknown (1682).

Tchaikovsky, Piotr Russian composer, died of cholera in 1893.

Tone, Wolfe Irish nationalist, cut his throat with a penknife whilst awaiting hanging in Dublin (1798).

Tyler, Wat Leader of the Peasants' Revolt of 1381, wounded by William Walworth, Mayor of London and subsequently dragged from his hospital bed (St Bartholomew's) and beheaded.

Van Gogh, Vincent Dutch painter, shot himself whilst depressed (1890).

Versace, Gianni Murdered outside his Miami home (15th July 1997) by serial killer Andrew Cunanan, committed suicide shortly afterwards.

Wagner, Richard German composer, died of coronary artery disease with angina pectoris (1883).

Wallace, William Scottish patriot, famously depicted in the film *Braveheart*. After being hanged, drawn and quartered by the British, his quarters were sent to Newcastle, Berwick, Stirling and Perth, as a reminder of his insurrection (1305).

Webern, Anton von Austrian composer, shot and killed by an American military policeman whilst out after curfew (1945).

Weber, Carl German composer, died of pulmonary tuberculosis and ulcerated larynx (1826).

Westbrook, Harriet First wife of the poet PB Shelley, committed suicide by drowning herself in the Serpentine, Hyde Park (1816).

Woolf, Virginia English novelist, drowned herself in the River Ouse, near her home at Rodmell in Sussex (1941).

Yamamoto, Isoruku Japanese naval officer who directed the attack on Pearl Harbor; his plane was shot down over the Soloman Islands in 1943.

Zweig, Stefan Austrian-born British writer, committed suicide with his second wife in 1942.

NB: This section gives only a selective list; further death details may be found in other sections, eg Assassinations and Monarchs.

Countries of Birth

John Dalberg, 1st Baron Acton (Italy) English Historian

Joy Adamson (Austria) British Naturalist

Shmuel Yosef Agnon (Poland) Israeli Writer

Viscount Alanbrooke (France) British Soldier

Josef Albers (Germany) American Painter

Alexander Alekhine (Russia) French Chess master

Gubby Allen (Australia) English Cricketer

Peter Alliss (Germany) British Golfer

Jeanette Altwegg (India) British Skating Gold Medallist

Lawrence Alma-Tadema (Holland) British Painter

Leopold Amery (India) English Tory Politician

Lindsay Anderson (India) British Film Director

Mario Andretti (Italy) US Racing Driver

Edward Ardizzone (Vietnam) British Illustrator

Michael Arlen (Bulgaria) British Novelist

Pamela Armstrong (Borneo) British Newscaster

Paddy Ashdown (India) English Politician

Vladimir Ashkenazy (Russia) Icelandic Pianist

Frederick Ashton (Ecuador) English Choreographer

John Jacob Astor (Germany) American Financier

Nancy Astor (USA) British Politician

WH Auden (England) American Writer

John Audubon (Haiti) American Ornithologist

Frank Auerbach (Germany) British Artist

Charles Aznavour (Armenia) French Singer

Leo Baekland (Belgium) American Chemist

Bruce Bairnsfather (India) British Cartoonist

George Baker (Bulgaria) British Actor

JG Ballard (China) British Writer

Daniel Barenboim (Argentina) Israeli Pianist

Victor Barna (Hungary) British Table-Tennis Champion

John Barnes (Jamaica) English Footballer

Raymond Barre (Réunion) French Politician

Lord Beaverbrook (Canada) British Newspaper Magnate

Bee Gees (Isle of Man) Australian Pop Group

Menachem Begin (Poland [now Russia]) Israeli Statesman

Georg von Bekesy (Hungary) US Physiologist

Hilaire Belloc (France) British Writer

Saul Bellow (Canada) US Writer

Baruj Benacerraf (Venezuela) US Immunologist

Floella Benjamin (Trinidad) British TV Presenter

Jill Bennett (Straits Settlement, now Malaysia) British Actress

Irving Berlin (Russia) US Composer

Isaiah Berlin (Latvia) British Philosopher

Pete Best (India) British Musician

Hans A Bethe (Germany [Strasbourg, now France]) US Physicist

Lord Beveridge (India) British Economist

Zulfikar Ali Bhutto (India) Pakistani Statesman

Isla Blair (India) British Actress

George Blake (Netherlands) British Spy (for Soviet Union)

Nicolas Bloembergen (Netherlands) US Physicist

Paul Boateng (Ghana) British Politician

Andrew Bonar Law (Canada) English Prime Minister

Alan Bond (England) Australian Businessman

Daniel Bovet (Switzerland) Italian Pharmacologist

Anne Bradstreet (England) US Poet

Gyles Brandreth (West Germany) British Author and Politician

Frank Brangwyn (Belgium) Welsh Painter

Chris Brasher (British Guiana) British Athlete

Walter Houser Brattain (China) US Physicist

Fenner Brockway (India) English Politician

Joseph Brodsky (Russia) US Poet

Ford Madox Brown (France) English Painter

Herbert C Brown (England) US Chemist

Yul Brynner (Russia) US Actor

Frances Hodgson Burnett (England) US Novelist

Terry Butcher (Singapore) English Footballer

Andrew Caddick (New Zealand) English Cricketer

Maria Callas (United States) Greek Soprano

Albert Camus (Algeria) French Writer

Jacques Canetti (Bulgaria) French Record Producer

Frank Capra (Sicily) US Film Director

Claudia Cardinale (Tunisia) Italian Actress

Barbara Carrera (Nicaragua) US Actress

Anna Carteret (India) British Actress

Gian Domenico Cassini (Genoa) French Astronomer

Marc Chagall (Russia) French Artist

Ernst Boris Chain (Germany) British Biochemist

William Chambers (Sweden) Scottish Architect

Phillipe de Champaigne (Belgium) French Painter

Subrahmanyan Chandrasekhar (India [Lahore, now Pakistan]) US Astrophysicist

Louis Chevrolet (Switzerland) US Automobile Engineer

Erskine Childers (England) Irish Writer and Nationalist

Glynn Christian (New Zealand) British TV Broadcaster

Julie Christie (India) English Actress

Linford Christie (Jamaica) British Olympic Gold Medallist

Christo (Bulgaria) American Artist

Elizabeth Connell (South Africa) Irish Soprano

Joseph Conrad (Poland) English Novelist

Alistair Cooke (UK) American Journalist and Broadcaster

Harry H Corbett (Burma) English Actor

Carl Ferdinand Cori (Czechoslovakia) US Biochemist

Allan Cormack (South Africa) US Physicist

John Cornforth (Australia) British Chemist

Sir Michael Costa (Italy) British Conductor

André Frédéric Cournand (France) US Physicist

Cicely Courtneidge (Australia) English Actress

Colin Cowdrey (India) English Cricketer

Frederic Cowen (Jamaica) English Composer

Kid Creole (Canada) US Singer

Cyril Cusack (South Africa) Irish Actor

György Cziffra (Hungary) French Pianist

Frank Damrosch (Germany) US Conductor

Walter Damrosch (Germany) US Conductor
Dana (Rosemary Scallon) (England) Irish Singer
Edward Dannreuther (Alsace) English Pianist
Nyree Dawn Porter (New Zealand) British Actress
Edward De Bono (Malta) British Psychologist
Chris De Burgh (Argentina) British Singer
Christian R De Duve (England) Belgian
  Biochemist
Hans Dehmelt (Germany) US Physicist
Max Delbruck (Germany) US Biophysicist
Eamon De Valera (USA) Irish Politician
Ted Dexter (Italy) English Cricketer
Thomas Dolby (Egypt) British Musician
Gabrielle Drake (Pakistan) British Actress
Marcel Duchamp (France) American artist
Renato Dulbecco (Italy) American Biologist
George Du Maurier (France) English Writer
Lawrence and Gerald Durrell (India) English
  Writers
Sophie-Carmen Eckhardt-Gramatté (Russia)
  Canadian Composer
Glynn Edwards (Malaya) British Actor
Albert Einstein (Germany) Swiss physicist
Brian Elias (India) English Composer
Iso Elinson (Russia) British Pianist
TS Eliot (USA) British Poet
Mary Ellis (USA) English Soprano
Gloria Estefan (Cuba) American Singer
Eusebio (Mozambique) Portuguese Footballer
Enrico Fermi (Italy) US Nuclear Physicist
Edmond H Fischer (China) US Chemist
Bob Fitzsimmons (England) American Boxer
Errol Flynn (Tasmania) American Actor
CS Forester (Egypt) British Writer
Malcolm Forsyth (South Africa)
  Canadian Composer
Harry Freedman (Poland) Canadian Composer
Lucien Freud (Germany) British Artist
Marya Freund (Poland) French Soprano
Géza Frid (Hungary) Dutch Composer
Oskar Fried (Germany) Russian Conductor
Fiona Fullerton (Nigeria) British Actress
Henry Fuseli (Switzerland) British Painter
Dennis Gabor (Hungary) British Physicist
Ivan Galamian (Iran) US Violinist
Sandy Gall (Malaya) British Newsreader
Lamberto Gardelli (Italy) Swedish Conductor
Baron Francois Gérard (Italy) French Painter
Ivar Giaever (Norway) US Physicist
Mel Gibson (USA) Australian Actor
Werner Wolf Glaser (Germany) Swedish
  Composer
Vinko Globokar (France) Yugoslav Trombonist
Alma Gluck (Romania) American Soprano
Maria Goeppert-Mayer (Germany [Katowice, now
  Poland]) US Physicist
James Goldsmith (France) British Tycoon
Adam Lindsay Gordon (Azores) Australian Poet
Arshile Gorky (Armenia) US Painter
Bryan Gould (New Zealand) British Politician
Ragnar Granit (Finland) Swedish Physiologist
Bernie Grant (British Guiana) English Politician
Cary Grant (England) US Actor
El Greco (Crete (Candia)) Spanish Painter
Silvia Greenberg (Romania) Israeli Soprano

Tony Greig (South Africa) English Cricketer
André Grétry (Belgium) French Composer
Dulcie Grey (Malaya) British Actress
Frederick Grinke (Canada) British Violinist
Walter Gropius (Germany) US Architect
Georg Grosz (Germany) US Painter
Giovanni Guardi (Austria) Venetian Painter
Roger Guillemin (France) US Physiologist
Richard Hageman (Holland) US Composer
Thomas Duffus Hardy (Jamaica) English Archivist
Friedrich von Hayek (Austria) British Economist
Jascha Heifetz (Lithuania) US Violinist
László Heltay (Hungary) British Conductor
Victor Hely-Hutchinson (South Africa) English
  Composer
Audrey Hepburn (Belgium) American Actress
William Herschel (Germany) British Astronomer
Gerhard Herzberg (Germany) Canadian Physical
  Chemist
Rudolf Hess (Egypt) German Politician
Victor Hess (Austria) US Physicist
Hermann Hesse (Germany) Swiss Novelist
Dorothy Hodgkin (Egypt) English Chemist
Roald Hoffmann (Poland) US Chemist
Adam Hollioake (Australia) English Cricketer
Ben Hollioake (Australia) England Cricketer
Bob Holness (South Africa) British Presenter
Gordon Honeycombe (India [now Pakistan])
  British TV Presenter
Bob Hope (England) US Comedian
Harry Houdini (Hungary) US Escapologist
John Houseman (Hungary) US Actor / Director
Charles B Huggins (Canada) American Surgeon
William Morris Hughes (Wales) Australian
  Statesman
Olivia Hussey (Argentina) British Actress
Anjelica Huston (Ireland) American Actress
Alec Issigonis (Turkey) British Automobile
  Designer
Eddie Izzard (Yemen) English Comedian
Sid James (South Africa) British Actor
Karl Jaspers (Germany) Swiss Philosopher
Niels K Jerne (England) Danish Immunologist
Ruth Prawer Jhabvala (Germany) British Novelist
Alexander Johnson (England) American
  Philosopher
Vasily Kandinsky (Russia) French Painter
Anna Karen (South Africa) British Actress
Boris Karloff (England) US Actor
Yousef Karsh (Turkey) Canadian Photographer
Kenneth Kendall (India) British TV Presenter
Har Gobind Khorana (India [Raipur, now Pakistan])
  US Molecular Chemist
Wilson Kipketer (Kenya) Danish Athlete
Rudyard Kipling (India) English Writer
Henry Kissinger (Germany) US Politician
Aaron Klug (Lithuania) British Biophysicist
Godfrey Kneller (Germany) British Artist
Arthur Koestler (Hungary) British Author
Oskar Kokoschka (Austria) British Artist
Tjalling Koopmans (Netherlands) US Economist
Alexander Korda (Hungary) British Film Producer
Alexis Korner (France) British Musician
Hans Adolf Krebs (Germany) British Biochemist
Polykarp Kusch (Germany) US Physicist

Simon Kuznets (Russia) US Economist
John Lang (Scotland) Australian Clergyman
Angela Lansbury (England) US Actress
Danny La Rue (Ireland) British Entertainer
Charles Laughton (England) US Actor
Stan Laurel (England) US Actor / Comedian
Sir Austen Layard (France) English Archaeologist
Bernard Leach (Hong Kong) English Potter
Vivien Leigh (India) British Actress
Peter Lely (Netherlands) British Painter
Philipp EA Lenard (Hungary) German Physicist
Wassily Leontief (Russia) US Economist
Doris Lessing (Persia [now Iran]) British Writer
W Arthur Lewis (St Lucia) British Economist
Wyndham Lewis (Canada) English Novelist / Painter
Eric Liddell (China) Scottish Athlete
Basil Liddell Hart (France) English Historian
Fritz A Lipmann (Germany) US Biochemist
David Lloyd George (England) Welsh Politician
Margaret Lockwood (India) British Actress
Frederick Loewe (Austria) US Composer
Peter Lorre (Hungary) US Actor
David Low (New Zealand) British Political Cartoonist
Henry Luce (China) US Magazine Publisher
Bela Lugosi (Lugos Hungary [Lugos, now Romania]) US Actor
Jean-Baptiste Lully (Italy) French Composer
Joanna Lumley (Kashmir) British Actress
Salvador Luria (Italy) US Biologist
Rosa Luxemburg (Poland) German Revolutionary
Roddy McDowall (England) US Actor
John McEnroe (West Germany) US Tennis Player
Thomas McGee (Ireland) Canadian Writer
Patrick McGoohan (USA) British Actor
Shane MacGowan (England) Irish Musician
Donald McIntyre (New Zealand) English Bass-Baritone
Leo McKern (Australia) British Actor
Jean-Paul Marat (Switzerland) French Revolutionary
Ann- Margret (Sweden) US Actress
Raymond Massey (Canada) US Actor
William Somerset Maugham (France) British Writer
Robert Maxwell (Czechoslovakia) British Businesman
Jules Mazarin (Italy) French Prelate
Peter B Medawar (Brazil) British Zoologist
Golda Meir (Ukraine) Israeli Politician
Gian-Carlo Menotti (Italy) US Composer
Freddie Mercury (Zanzibar) British Singer
William Mervyn (Kenya) British Actor
Albert Michelson (Germany) US Physicist
Bette Midler (Hawaii [now US State]) US Singer
Ludwig Mies Van Der Rohe (Germany) USA Architect
Spike Milligan (India) British Comedian
Guy Mitchell (Yugoslavia) US Singer
Franco Modigliani (Italy) US Economist
Yves Montand (Italy) French Actor and Singer
Lola Montez (Eire) US Dancer
Benjamin Mottelson (USA) Danish Physicist
Vladimir Nabokov (Russia) US Novelist

Sam Neill (New Zealand) Australian Actor
Olivia Newton-John (UK) Australian Actress
Mike Nichols (Germany) US Film Director
Harold Nicolson (Persia [now Iran]) British Diplomat
Merle Oberon (India) British Actress
Severo Ochoa (Spain) US Biochemist
Jacques Offenbach (Germany) French Composer
Claes Oldenburg (Sweden) US Sculptor
Isaac Oliver (France) English Painter
Charles Chadwick Oman (India) English Historian
Lars Onsager (Norway) US Physical Chemist
Eugene Ormandy (Hungary) US Conductor
George Orwell (India) British Novelist
Thomas Paine (England) US Writer and Revolutionary
George Palade (Romania) US Biologist
Lili Palmer (Austria) French Actress
Adelina Patti (Spain) Italian Soprano
IM Pei (China) US Architect
Susan Penhaligon (Philippines) British Actress
Arno Penzias (Germany) US Astrophysicist
Max F Perutz (Austria) British Biochemist
Antoine Pevsner (Russia) French Painter
Harry Philby (Ceylon [Sri Lanka]) English Arabist and Explorer
Kim Philby (India) British Spy (for Soviet Union)
HRH Prince Philip (Greece) British Duke and Consort to the Queen
Camille Pissarro (West Indies [St Thomas]) French Painter
Sidney Poitier (Bahamas) US Actor
Roman Polanski (France) Polish Film Maker
Vladimir Prelog (Bosnia) Swiss Chemist
Emeric Pressburger (Hungary) British Film Writer
Ilya Prigogine (Russia) Belgian Chemist
Victoria Principal (Japan) US Actress
Juliet Prowse (South Africa) US Dancer
Anthony Quinn (Mexico) US Actor
Peter Rachman (Poland) British Property Developer
Stamford Raffles (Jamaica [at sea]) English Colonial Administrator
Basil Rathbone (South Africa) British Actor
Cyril Regis (French Guiana) English Footballer
Elisabeth Rethberg (Germany) US Soprano
Cliff Richard (India) British Vocalist
Frederick Sleigh Roberts (India) English Soldier
Edward G Robinson (Romania) US Actor
Richard Rogers (Italy) English Architect
Ronald Ross (India) British Physician
Mark Rothko (Latvia) US Painter
Eero Saarinen (Finland) US Architect
Albert Sabin (Poland) American Physician
Andrew Sachs (Germany) British Actor
Nelly Leonie Sachs (Germany) Swedish Poet and Playwright
Yves Saint Laurent (Algeria) French Fashion Designer
Pamela Salem (India) British Actress
George Sanders (Russia) British Actor
Tessa Sanderson (Jamaica) British Olympic Gold Medallist
John Singer Sargent (Italy) US Painter
Andrew Schally (Poland) US Biochemist

Elsa Schiaparelli   (Italy)   French Fashion Designer
Shaun Scott   (Canada)   British Actor
Emilio Segre   (Italy)   US Physicist
Harry Selfridge   (USA)   British Merchant
Aloys Senefelder   (Czechoslovakia)   German Printer and Inventor
Robert Service   (England)   Canadian Poet
Yitzhak Shamir   (Poland)   Israeli Politician
William Bradford Shockley   (England)   US Physicist
Walter Sickert   (Germany)   English Artist
Claude Simon   (Madagascar)   French Novelist
Isaac Bashevis Singer   (Poland)   US Writer
Israel Singer   (Poland)   US Writer
Elaine Smith   (Scotland)   Australian Actress
Sydney Smith   (New Zealand)   British Poet
George Solti   (Hungary)   British Conductor
Basil Spence   (India)   Scottish Architect
Sheila Steafel   (South Africa)   British Actress
Brian Stein   (South Africa)   English Footballer
Max Steiner   (Austria)   US Composer
Edward Stourton   (Nigeria)   UK TV Presenter
Robert Swinhoe   (India)   English Naturalist
Yves Tanguy   (France)   US Painter
WM Thackeray   (India)   British Author
Mother Teresa   (Yugoslavia)   Indian Roman Catholic Nun
Roy Thomson   (Canada)   British Newspaper Magnate
Angela Thorne   (India [now Pakistan])   British Actress

Debbie Thrower   (Kenya)   British TV Presenter
Dmitri Tiomkin   (Russia)   US Composer
Richard Todd   (Ireland)   English Actor
JRR Tolkien   (South Africa)   English Novelist
Walter Trog   (Canada)   British Cartoonist
Liv Ullmann   (Japan)   Norwegian Actress
Rudolph Valentino   (Italy)   American Actor
Victor Vasarely   (Hungary)   French Painter
Hendrik Verwoerd   (Holland)   South African Politician
Colin Viljoen   (South Africa)   English Footballer
Selman A Waksman   (Russia)   US Biochemist
Hugh Walpole   (New Zealand)   British Novelist
Max Weber   (Russia)   US Painter
Vanessa-Mae   (Singapore)   British Violinist
Victor Weisz   (Germany)   British Political Cartoonist
Benjamin West   (USA)   English Painter
Alan Whicker   (Egypt)   British Broadcaster
Joseph Blanco White   (Spain)   English Poet
Patrick White   (England)   Australian Author
Terence Hanbury White   (India)   British Novelist
Roger Whitaker   (Kenya)   South African Singer
Eugene Paul Wigner   (Hungary)   US Physicist
Billy Wilder   (Austria)   US Film Maker
David Wilkie   (Sri Lanka)   Scottish Swimmer
John Williams   (Australia)   British Guitarist
Malcolm Williamson   (Australia)   British Composer
Bruce Willis   (Germany)   US Actor
Orde Wingate   (India)   British Soldier
William Wyler   (Germany [Mulhausen now France])   US Film Maker

Dying Words

Independence for ever   **John Adams**   *US President*

It is the last of Earth, I am content   **John Quincy Adams**   *US President*

See in what peace a christian can die   **Joseph Addison**   *Essayist*

Kurt   **Alfred Adler**   *Psychologist*

If I feel in good form I shall take the difficult way up. If I do not, I shall take the easy one. I shall join you in an hour   **Albert I**   *King of Belgium*

I have had wealth, rank and power, but if these were all I had, how wretched I would be   **Prince Albert**   *Queen Victoria's Consort*

I have such sweet thoughts   **Prince Albert**   *Queen Victoria's Consort*

Is it not meningitis ?   **Louisa M Alcott**   *American writer*

I am sweeping through the gates, washed in the blood of the lamb   **Alexander II**   *Russian Tsar*

Clasp my hand dear friend, I am dying   **Vittorio Alfieri**   *Italian Poet*

Haircut!   **Albert Anastasia**   *US gangster*

Give the boys a holiday   **Anaxagoras**   *Philosopher*

Monsieur, I beg your pardon. I did not do it on purpose   **Marie Antoinette**   *French Queen*

I see my God He calls me to Him   **Antony of Padua**   *Monk*

Wait till I have finished my problem   **Archimedes**   *Greek Mathematician*

May God forgive me for putting on any other   **Benedict Arnold**   *American Traitor*

I desire to die and be with Christ   **Roger Ascham**   *Elizabeth I's tutor*

Am I dying, or is this my birthday?   **Nancy Astor**   *British Politician*

Do you think I have played my part pretty well through the farce of life?   **Augustus**   *Roman Emperor*

The murder of the Queen has been represented to me as a deed; lawful and meritorious, I die a firm Catholic   **Anthony Babington**   *Plotter against Elizabeth I*

My name and memory I leave to men's charitable speeches, to foreign nations and to the next age   **Francis Bacon**   *Statesman and philosopher*

Oh God, here I go ...   **Max Baer**   *Heavyweight Boxer*

Let me have my own fidgets   **Walter Bagehot**   *Economist*

I can't sleep   **JM Barrie**   *Scottish Author*

I am a priest, fie, fie! All is gone   **Cardinal Beaton**   *Scottish prelate*

I am prepared to die for Christ and his Church   **Thomas à Becket**   *Archbishop of Canterbury*

Gloria Patri et Filio et Spiritu Sancto   **Venerable St Bede**   *Theologian and historian*

It is well, you have said the truth, it is indeed   **Venerable St Bede**   *Theologian and historian*

Now comes the mystery   **Henry Ward Beecher**   *US Clergyman*

Too bad, too bad! It's too late   **Ludwig Van Beethoven**   *Composer*

I shall hear in heaven   **Ludwig van Beethoven**   *Composer*

I thank God for having enabled me to meet my fate with so much fortitude and resignation **John Bellingham** *Assassin of Spencer Perceval*

One thousand greetings to Balakirev **Hector Berlioz** *Composer*

I want to live because there are a few things I want to do **Aneurin Bevan** *British Politician*

Who's there? **Billy the Kid** *American Outlaw*

I do not fear death **Thomas Blood** *Irish Adventurer*

My belief is rooted in hope **Léon Blum** *French Prime Minister*

I should never have switched from scotch to Martinis **Humphrey Bogart** *Film Actor*

It is a great consolation to a poet on the point of death that he has never written a line injurious to good morals **Nicolas Boileau** *French Poet*

The executioner is, I believe, very expert; and my neck is very slender **Anne Boleyn** *Queen Consort*

Take my baggage on board the frigate **Simon Bolivar** *Venezuelan Revolutionary*

Goodbye and God bless you, I'll see you again, tomorrow **Horatio Bottomley** *British Politician*

At least one knows that death will be easy **Bertold Brecht** *German Playwright*

A slight knock at the window pane, then ... then puddle it, puddle it and puddle it again **James Brindley** *Engineer*

Take courage Charlotte, take courage **Anne Brontë** *Author*

If you will send for the doctor I will see him now **Emily Brontë** *English Writer*

Decay is inherent in all component things **Buddha (Prince Gautama Siddhartha)** *Founder of Buddhism*

I wish Johnny would come **Buffalo Bill** *American Frontiersman*

Well I think it is about time to go to bed now **Sir Redvers Buller** *Colonial Administrator*

World without end **John Bunyan** *Religious Writer*

With the best that was in me I have tried to write more happiness into the world **Frances Hodgson Burnett** *American Novelist*

Don't let the awkward squad fire over my grave **Robert Burns** *Scottish Poet*

I must sleep now **Lord George Byron** *English Poet*

Now I shall go to sleep **Lord George Byron** *English Poet*

Et tu, Brute **Julius Caesar** *Roman Statesman*

I am still alive! **Caligula** *Roman Emperor*

Spain and Portugal **George Canning** *British Prime Minister*

So this is death, well ... **Thomas Carlyle** *Historian and essayist*

Take away those pillows, I shall need them no more **Lewis Carroll** *Author*

Bankhead, let me fall into your arms. It is all over **Viscount Robert Castlereagh** *British statesman*

Stand by me, Tom, and we will die together **Robert Catesby** *Gunpowder Plotter*

Lord, into thy hands I commend my spirit **Catherine of Aragon** *Henry VIII's first wife*

Now I am master of myself **Marcus Porcius Cato (The Younger)** *Roman statesman*

Patriotism is not enough. I must have no hatred or bitterness towards anyone **Edith Cavell** *Nurse*

Italy is made – all is safe **Camillo Cavour** *Italian Patriot*

Pontier! Pontier! **Paul Cezanne** *French artist*

Approaching dissolution brings relief **Neville Chamberlain** *British Prime Minister*

Lord, into thy hands I commend my spirit **Charlemagne** *King of the Franks*

Remember **Charles I** *British King*

I have been a most unconscionable time a-dying, but I hope you will excuse it **Charles II** *English King*

Do not, do not let poor Nelly starve **Charles II** *English King*

Nurse, Nurse, what murder, what blood! Oh! I have done wrong, God pardon me **Charles IX** *French King*

I hope never again to commit a mortal sin, nor even a venial one, if I can help it **Charles VIII** *French King*

Give Dayrolles a chair **Philip Dormer Chesterfield** *English Statesman*

The issue now is clear, it is between light and darkness and everyone must choose his side **GK Chesterton** *British Essayist*

Glory to God for all things **St John Chrysostom** *Syrian Churchman*

Oh I'm so bored with it all **Winston Churchill** *British Prime Minister*

Strike **Marcus Tullius Cicero** *Roman Statesman*

Doctor, do you think it could have been the sausage? **Paul Claudel** *French writer*

I Wish to be buried standing – facing Germany **Georges Clemenceau** *French Premier*

Thy kingdom come, thy will be done **Edward Coke** *English Jurist*

Honour these grey hairs young man **Admiral Gaspard Coligny** *French Huguenot Leader*

I am signing my death warrant **Michael Collins** *Irish Patriot*

Lord, into thy hands I commend my spirit **Christopher Columbus** *Italian Explorer*

What an irreparable loss **Auguste Comte** *French Philosopher*

My time has come to die **Confucius** *Chinese Philosopher*

You, Jess, I am better this morning. I can always get a rise out of you **Joseph Conrad** *British Author*

Now, O Lord, set thy servant free **Nicolas Copernicus** *Polish Astronomer*

That was the best ice-cream soda I ever tasted **Lou Costello** *American Comedian*

Goodnight my darlings, I'll see you tomorrow **Noël Coward** *British Playwright*

That unworthy hand! **Thomas Cranmer** *Archbishop of Canterbury*

My design is to make what haste I can to be gone **Oliver Cromwell** *Lord Protector of England*

That was a great game of golf, fellers **Bing Crosby** *American Singer*

Benteen - come on - big village - be quick - bring packs **George Custer** *US soldier*

Nurse, it was I that discovered that leeches had red blood **Georges Cuvier** *French naturalist*

Be sure you show the mob my head, it will be a long time before they see it's like **Georges Danton** *French Revolutionary Leader*

I am not in the least afraid to die **Charles Darwin** *English Naturalist*

My fun days are over **James Dean** *American Film Star*

Lord, into thy hands I commend my spirit **Robert Devereaux** *Earl of Essex*

The bullet hasn't been made that can kill me **Legs Diamond** *Gangster*

On the ground! **Charles Dickens** *Author*

The first step towards philosophy is incredulity **Denis Diderot** *French man of letters*

Dammit! put them back on. This is funny **Doc Holliday** *Gambler and gunfighter*

I have deserved a thousand deaths **John Dudley** *Duke of Northumberland*

Adieu my friends, I go on to glory **Isadora Duncan** *Dancer*

It is very beautiful over there **Thomas Alva Edison** *American Inventor*

Carry my bones before you on your march, for the rebels will not be able to endure the sight of me; **Edward I** *King of England*

Trust in god and you need not fear **Jonathan Edwards** *American Philosopher*

All my possessions for a moment of time **Elizabeth I** *Queen of England*

I die for my king and for France **Louis Duke of Enghien** *French soldier*

Dear God! **Desiderius Erasmus** *Dutch Humanist*

Now I'll have eine kleine pause **Kathleen Ferrier** *Opera Singer*

On the whole, I'd rather be in Philadelphia **WC Fields** *American Comedian*

The nourishment is palatable **Millard Fillmore** *US President*

I've had a hell of a lot of fun and I've enjoyed every minute of it **Errol Flynn** *Actor*

I am a dead man, Lord have mercy upon me **Gaston de Foix** *French Soldier*

I suffer nothing, but I feel a sort of difficulty in living longer **Bernard Fontenelle** *French Author*

It don't signify, my dearest, dearest Liz **Charles James Fox** *English Statesman*

Never heed! The Lord's power is over all weakness and death **George Fox** *English Religious Leader*

We are all going to Heaven and Van Dyke is of the company **Thomas Gainsborough** *English landscape painter*

Yet it still moves **Galileo Galilei** *Astronomer*

Feed them when I am gone **Giuseppe Garibaldi** *Italian Patriot*

Wally, what is this? It is death, my boy. They have deceived me **George IV** *British King*

Bugger Bognor **George V** *British King*

How is the Empire? **George V** *British King*

Put your hands on my shoulders and don't struggle **WS Gilbert** *Librettist*

Let's do it **Gary Gilmore** *American Murderer*

Light, more light **Johann Wolfgang Goethe** *German poet and dramatist*

Where is the Mahdi ? **Charles Gordon** *British general*

I want nobody distressed on my account **Ulysses S Grant** *American Soldier and Statesman*

It is done **Horace Greeley** *American Politician*

Lord, into thy hands I commend my spirit **Lady Jane Grey** *English Queen*

Well if it must be so **Edvard Grieg** *Composer*

I hope to see you on Tuesday at 10.30 am **Earl Douglas Haig** *British General*

I regret that I have but one life to give for my country **Nathan Hale** *American Soldier*

Remember, my Eliza, you are a Christian **Alexander Hamilton** *American Politician*

The rest is silence **Hamlet** *Shakespearean Character*

Let us now relieve the Romans of their fears by the death of a feeble old man **Hannibal** *Carthaginian Soldier*

That's good. Go on, read some more **Warren Harding** *US President*

Four sixes to beat **John Wesley Hardin** *American Outlaw*

I am about the extent of a tenth of a gnat's eyebrow better **Joel Chandler Harris** *American Author*

Cheer up, children, I'm all right **Franz Joseph Haydn** *Composer*

I know I'm going where Lucy is **Rutherford B Hayes** *US President*

Monks! Monks! Monks! **Henry VIII** *King of England*

One more summer and another winter **Hermann Hesse** *German Novelist*

Moderately, I am continuing to orbit **Richard Hillary** *English fighter pilot and writer*

And I wish myself the joy of your fellowship at Whitsuntide **Gustav Holst** *Composer*

I am tired of fighting. I guess this thing is going to get me **Harry Houdini** *Escapologist*

I'll tell that story on the golden floor **AE Housman** *Poet*

Texas, Texas, Margaret **Sam Houston** *Texan patriot*

I die a Queen, but I would rather die the wife of Culpepper. **Catherine Howard** *Henry VIII's Fifth Wife*

God have mercy on my soul. good people, I beg you pray for me. I see the black light **Victor Hugo** *French Poet*

Truth, truth **Anne Hyde** *Duchess of York*

Let us cross over the river and sit in the shade of the trees **Thomas Jackson** *US Civil War General*

It came with a lass and it will go with a lass **James V** *King of Scotland*

Do not hack me as you did my Lord Russell **James, Duke of Monmouth** *James II's Son*

That picture is crooked **Jesse James** *Train Robber*

Jesus Jesus Jesus, blessed be God **Joan of Arc** *French Patriot*

I commit my soul to god and my body to Saint Alstane **John** *King of England*

This is it, I'm going, I'm going **Al Jolson** *Singer*

Napoleon! Elba! Marie Louise! **Josephine** *French Empress*

Give me another horse, Howard! **Edmund Kean** *British Actor*

Such is life **Ned Kelly** *Australian Outlaw*

I wish to god you had heard them as I have heard them, and I praise God of that heavenly sound **John Knox** *Scottish Church Reformer*

Ah well, it is not the first time an innocent man has been condemned **Henri Landru** *French Murderer*

We shall this day light such a candle, by God's grace, in England, as I trust shall never be put out **Hugh Latimer** *Protestant Martyr*

I think it is time for morphine **DH Lawrence** *British Author*

Strike the tent **Robert E Lee** *Confederate General*

Now I have finished with all earthly business, and high time too. **Franz Lehar** *Hungarian Composer*

Yes, yes, my dear child, now comes death. They won't think anything about it **Abraham Lincoln** *US President*

Tristan! **Franz Liszt** *Composer*

Jerusalem, Jerusalem **Louis IX** *French King*

Why weep you? Did you think I would live for ever? I thought dying was harder **Louis XIV** *French King*

Repeat those words, Monsieur Almoner, repeat them **Louis XV** *French King*

Frenchmen I Die guiltless of the crimes imputed to me. Pray God my blood falls not on France **Louis XVI** *French King*

I shall drink the cup to the last dregs **Louis XVI** *French King*

A king should die standing up **Louis XVIII** *French King*

Marty **Lucky Luciano** *US gangster*

Keep Paddy behind the big mixer **Alfred MacAlpine** *British building tycoon*

Lay on Macduff, and damned be him that first cries 'hold enough' **Macbeth** *Shakespearean Character*

Now all is over, let the piper play 'Return no More' **Rob Roy MacGregor** *Scottish Outlaw*

I love my country more than my soul **Niccolo Machiavelli** *Italian Statesman*

We are all going, we are all going ... oh dear! **William McKinley** *US President*

Mozart! **Gustav Mahler** *Composer*

Let's cool it, brothers **Malcolm X** *Black Muslim Leader*

I love the rain, I want the feeling of it on my face **Katherine Mansfield** *Writer*

Act in accordance with past principles **Mao Tse Zedong** *Chinese Ruler*

Last words are for fools who haven't said enough **Karl Marx** *Philosopher*

My Lord, why do you not go on? I am not afraid to die **Mary II** *English Queen*

When I am dead and opened, you shall find Calais lying in my heart **Mary Tudor** *English Queen*

Thank you, Monsieur **Mata Hari** *Dutch Spy*

Dying is a very dull, dreary affair. My advice to you is to have nothing whatever to do with it. **William Somerset Maugham** *British Writer*

Lotte! **Ferdinand-Joseph Maximilian** *Mexican Emperor*

I am crossing a beautiful wide river and the opposite shore is coming nearer and nearer **George Meade** *US Civil War General*

Ah, my God, I am dead **Catherine de Medici** *Florentine Ruler*

God bless Captain Vere **Herman Melville** *US Author*

Forgive some sinner and wink your eye at some homely girl **HL Mencken** *American Essayist*

Weary, very weary **Felix Mendelssohn** *Composer*

My soul I resign to God, my body to the Earth, My worldly goods to my next of kin **Michelangelo** *Italian sculptor and painter*

O Allah! Pardon my sins. Yes I come **Muhammad** *Founder of Islam*

For all my misfortunes, Malinche, I bear you no ill will **Montezuma II** *Aztec Emperor*

Commend your souls to God, for our bodies are the foe's **Simon de Montfort** *British Aristocrat*

See me safe up; for my coming down let me shift for myself **Thomas More** *English Statesman*

Did I not tell you I was writing this for myself **Wolfgang Amadeus Mozart** *Composer*

Put that bloody cigarette out **HH Munro** *British Author*

But, but, Mr Colonel .... **Benito Mussolini** *Italian Dictator*

France! Army! Head of the army! Josephine! **Napoleon 1** *French Emperor*

I don't need anything more ... Poultices **Napoleon II** *Duke of Reichstadt*

Were you at Sedan? **Napoleon III** *French Emperor*

Thank God I have done my duty, kiss me, Hardy **Horatio Nelson** *British Naval commander*

What an artist the world is losing in me **Nero** *Roman Emperor*

I seem to have been only a boy playing on the seashore and diverting myself in now and then finding a smoother pebble or prettier shell than the ordinary whilst the great ocean of truth lay all undiscovered before me **Isaac Newton** *Scientist*

I am just going outside and I may be some time **Captain Lawrence Oates** *Explorer*

Die, my dear doctor, that's the last thing I shall do **Viscount Palmerston** *British Prime Minister*

Get my swan costume ready **Anna Pavlova** *Ballerina*

What is the scaffold? A short cut to Heaven **Charles Peace** *Murderer*

To be like Christ is to be a Christian **William Penn** *English Quaker*

Murder! **Spencer Perceval** *British Prime Minister*

Do not weep, do not grieve **Henri Pétain** *French Soldier*

Drink to me **Pablo Picasso** *Spanish Artist*

The hearse, the horse, the driver and – enough **Luigi Pirandello** *Italian Dramatist*

I think I could eat one of Bellamy's veal pies **William Pitt (the younger)** *British Prime Minister*

Oh my country, how I leave thee **William Pitt (the younger)** *British Prime Minister*

Lord help my soul **Edgar Allan Poe** *Writer*

I am dying, sir, of a hundred good symptoms **Alexander Pope** *Poet*

Turn up the lights, I don't want to go home in the dark **William Porter (O'Henry)** *US Short Story Writer*

I am going to sleep like you, but we shall all awake together and, I trust to everlasting happiness **Joseph Priestley** *Chemist*

I have such sweet thoughts **Prince Albert** *Prince Consort*

My poor Elvira, my poor wife **Giacomo Puccini** *Composer*

Sister, sister, sister **Thomas de Quincey** *British Writer*

I could wish this tragic scene were over, but I hope to go through it with becoming dignity **James Quin** *Irish Actor*

Let down the curtain, the farce is over **François Rabelais** *French writer*

I am going to seek the great, perhaps **François Rabelais** *French writer*

It matters little how the head lies, so the heart be right

Walter Raleigh   *English Explorer and Statesman*

I look like a moor   **Maurice Ravel**   *French Composer*

I know that all things on earth must have an end, and now I am come to mine   **Joshua Reynolds**   *English Artist*

Turn me over, Jack   **Cecil Rhodes**   *South African Statesman*

So little done, so much to do   **Cecil Rhodes**   *South African Statesman*

Take off his chains, give him a hundred shillings, and let him go   **Richard I**   *King of England*

Treason, treason!   **Richard III**   *King of England*

I have no enemies save those of the state   **Cardinal Richelieu**   *French Statesman*

Don't you think I'll be back?   **Manfred von Richthofen**   *German Air Ace*

O Liberty! What crimes are committed in thy name   **Madame Marie Roland**   *French Revolutionary*

I have a terrific headache   **FDR Roosevelt**   *US President*

We are the first victims of American fascism   **Ethel Rosenberg**   *Alleged Atom Spy*

There is God! Yes, God Himself, who is opening his arms and inviting me to taste at last that eternal and unchanging joy that I had so long desired   **Jean-Jacques Rousseau**   *French Political Theorist*

You can keep the things of bronze and stone and give me one man to remember me just once a year   **Damon Runyon**   *American Writer*

The bitterness of death is now past   **Lord William Russell**   *English Whig Statesman*

Of all his victories, realms and riches, nothing remains to him but this   **Saladin**   *Sultan of Egypt and Syria*

I am leaving you with your worries, good luck   **George Sanders**   *British Film Star*

Ah, my children, you cannot cry for me so much as I have made you laugh   **Paul Scarron**   *French Writer*

Many things are growing plain and clear to my understanding. One look at the sun   **Johann Von Schiller**   *German Dramatist*

Here, here is my end   **Franz Schubert**   *Composer*

French Canadian bean soup. I want to pay. Let them leave me alone   **Dutch Schultz**   *New York Gangster*

God bless you all, I feel myself again   **Sir Walter Scott**   *British Novelist*

I can't live any longer with my nerves   **Jean Seberg**   *US Film Star*

They couldn't hit an elephant at this dist ...   **John Sedgwick**   *US General*

I am absolutely undone   **Richard Brinsley Sheridan**   *Irish Writer and Statesman*

I believe we must adjourn the meeting to some other place   **Adam Smith**   *Economist*

Let me go   **Capt EJ Smith**   *Captain of SS Titanic*

That's right Brother Taylor, parry them off as well as you can   **Joseph Smith**   *Mormon Martyr*

Beautifully done   **(Sir) Stanley Spencer**   *British Artist*

Four o'clock. How strange, so that is time. Strange, enough!   **Sir Henry Stanley**   *Explorer*

I feel faint   **Adlai Stevenson**   *American Politician*

If this is dying, I don't think much of it   **Lytton Strachey**   *Biographer*

Put not your trust in princes   **Thomas Strafford**   *English Statesman*

Thy necessity is yet greater than mine   **Philip Sydney**   *British Soldier and Poet*

Lord, into thy hands I commend my spirit   **Torquato Tasso**   *Italian Poet*

How sweet it is to rest   **John Taylor**   *English Poet*

I have tried to do my duty, and am not afraid to die. I am ready   **Zachary Taylor**   *US President*

Brother warriors, we are about to enter an engagement from which I will not return. My body will remain on the field of battle   **Tecumseh**   *Indian Chief*

I have opened it   **Lord Alfred Tennyson**   *Poet*

Gentlemen of the jury, you may retire   **Charles Tenterden**   *Lord Chief Justice*

And my heart throbbed with an exquisite bliss   **William Thackeray**   *British Novelist*

To the health of the fair critias   **Theramenes**   *Athenian Statesman*

I shall soon know the grand secret   **Arthur Thistlewood**   *English Conspirator*

I've had 18 straight whiskies, I think that's a record ... after 39 yrs this is all I've done   **Dylan Thomas**   *Poet*

I leave this world without a regret   **Henry Thoreau**   *American Essayist*

God bless ... god damn   **James Thurber**   *American humorist*

I'll be shot if I don't believe I'm dying   **Edward Thurlow**   *English Politician*

Oh look, see how the cherry blossoms fall mutely   **Hidekio Tojo**   *Japanese Politician and Soldier*

The enemy have demanded a surrender and I have answered the summons with a cannon shot and our flag still waves proudly from the walls   **W Barrett Travis**   *Commander of the Alamo*

Now I stretch out my hand, and from the further shore I bid adieu to all who have cared to read any among the many words I have written   **Anthony Trollope**   *British Novelist*

I feel here that this time they have succeeded   **Leon Trotsky**   *Russian Leader*

The sun is God   **JMW Turner**   *British Artist*

Death, the only immortal, who treats us all alike, whose peace and whose refuge are for all, the soiled and the pure, the rich and the poor, the loved and unloved   **Mark Twain**   *American Novelist*

Lord forgive my sins. Especially my sins of omission   **James Ussher**   *Archbishop of Armagh*

I want the sunlight to greet me   **Rudolph Valentino**   *Film star*

I shall never get rid of this depression   **Vincent Van Gogh**   *Artist*

I suppose I am now becoming a God   **Vespasian**   *Roman Emperor*

Oh that peace may come   **Victoria**   *British Queen*

Do let me die in peace   **Voltaire**   *French Author and Philosopher*

I am fond of them, of the inferior beings of the abyss, of those who are full of longing   **Richard Wagner,**   *Composer*

It is well, I die hard, but am not afraid to go   **George Washington**   *US President*

A last interview ...   **Ethel Waters**   *US Blues Singer*

Life, life, death, death, how curious it is   **Daniel Webster**   *American Statesman*

Go away, I'm all right   **HG Wells**   *Author*

I shall be satisfied with thy likeness – satisfied   **Charles Wesley**   *English Hymn Writer*

I am dying as I have lived: beyond my means   **Oscar Wilde**   *Dramatist*

Either this wallpaper goes or I do   **Oscar Wilde** *Dramatist*

O my God, have mercy upon this poor people   **William the Silent**   *Stadholder of the Netherlands*

Edith   **Woodrow Wilson**   *US President*

I fear not this fire   **George Wishart**   *Scottish Reformer*

Give me back my youth   **John Wolcot**   *English Satirist*

What! do they run already? Then I die happy   **James**

Wolfe   *English General*

Had I but served god as diligently as I have served the King, He would not have given me over in my grey hairs   **Thomas Wolsey**   *English Prelate*

Is that you Dora?   **William Wordsworth**   *Poet*

Mind your own business   **Percy Wyndham-Lewis**   *British artist*

Better fighting death than a slave's life   **Emiliano Zapata**   *Mexican Revolutionary*

Make my skin into drumheads for the Bohemian cause   **John Ziska**   *Bohemian Hussite Leader*

NB: This is an area of uncertainty and vagueness and cannot be said to be true and exact glossary of last words. The reason for this is because quite often there would be some contoversy over the reported words uttered before death by a solitary witness, and even when witnessed by many people there would often be a conflict of opinion, hence the need for double entries for various persons. It is thought, perhaps, that some of the more witty sayings were possibly the sort of thing that a particular person would have said and it is in the way of a tribute to a person that not too many questions would be asked. The point to remember about these last utterances is not so much the truth of the speech *per se*, but rather the fact that the words are universally identifiable with these people. Several persons have more than one entry for the reasons stated above.

First names
(of people better known by other names)

Alvar Aalto – Hugo   *Finnish Architect*

Patrick Abercrombie – Leslie   *English Architect*

Pepper Anderson – Suzanne   *TV character (Police Woman)*

Antonioni – Michelangelo   *Film Director*

Corazon Aquino – Maria   *Filipino President*

Yasser Arafat – Mohammed   *Palestinian Resistance Leader*

Louis Armstrong – Daniel   *Jazz Musician*

Cash Asmussen – Brian Keith   *US Jockey*

Avon – Kerr   *Blake 7 character*

Balakirev – Mily   *Russian Composer*

Balzac – Honoré de   *French Writer*

Banacek – Thomas   *TV Character*

Batista – Fulgencio   *Cuban President*

Max Beerbohm – Henry   *English Writer and Caricaturist*

Bix Beidebecke – Leon   *Jazz Cornet Player*

Hilaire Belloc – Joseph   *French-born Writer*

Arnold Bennett – Enoch   *English Novelist*

Ingmar Bergman – Ernst   *Film Director*

Busby Berkeley – William   *Choreographer and Director*

Hector Berlioz – Louis   *French Composer*

Ali Bhutto – Zulfikar   *Pakistani Statesman*

John Biffen – William   *English Politician*

Laurence Binyon – Robert   *Poet*

Bizet – Georges Alexandre Césare Léopold   *French Composer*

Blake – Roj   *'Blake's 7' Character*

Boccaccio – Giovanni   *Italian Writer*

Bodie and Doyle – William and Ray   *TV Characters ('The Professionals')*

Bootsie (Pte 'excused boots' Bisley) – Montague   *TV Character ('The Army Game')*

Lord Byron – George   *English Poet*

Calamity Jane – Martha   *Wild West Heroine*

James Callaghan – Leonard   *British Politician*

Callan – David   *TV Character*

Hoss Cartwright – Eric   *TV Western Hero*

('Bonanza')

Casanova – Giovanni Jacopo   *Poet and Libertine*

Casey Jones – John Luther   *TV Character based on Ballad*

Emmanuel Chabrier – Alexis   *French Composer*

Paddy Chayevsky – Sidney   *Playwright*

Chekov – Pavel   *Star Trek Character*

Erskine Childers – Robert   *Anglo-Irish Writer*

Colette – Sidonie   *French Novelist*

Colin Cowdrey – Michael   *English Cricketer*

Crane – Richard   *TV Character*

Sonny Crockett – James   *Miami Vice Character*

Cui – César   *Russian Composer*

Robert Cummings – Charles   *US Actor*

Bette Davis – Ruth   *US Actress*

Debussy – Achille-Claude   *French Composer*

Edgar Degas – Hilaire-Germain   *French Artist*

Paul Delaroche – Hippolyte   *French Painter*

Delibes – Léo   *French Composer*

Delius – Frederick   *English Composer*

Legs Diamond – Jack   *Gangster*

Fats Domino – Antoine   *US Vocalist*

Lonnie Donegan – Anthony   *Skiffle Musician*

Donizetti – Gaetano   *Italian Composer*

Faye Dunaway – Dorothy   *US Actress*

Dvorak – Antonin   *Czech Composer*

Samantha Eggar – Victoria   *US Actress*

Erasmus – Desiderius   *Dutch Humanist*

Escoffier – Auguste   *French Chef*

Private Fender – Sam   *TV Character ('Bilko')*

Figgis – Roy   *TV Character ('Only When I Laugh')*

Finlay, Dr – Alan (Bill Simpson)   *TV Character*

Finlay, Dr – John (David Rintoul)   *TV Character*

Private Fraser – James   *'Dad's Army' Character*

Paul Gaughin – Eugène   *French Post-Impressionist*

Gigli – Beniamino   *Italian Tenor*

Gill, Eric – Arthur   *English Sculptor*

Glinka – Mikhail   *Russian Composer*

Glover – Archie   *TV Character ('Only When I Laugh')*

Gluck – Christoph   *German Composer*
Private Godfrey – Charles   *'Dad's Army' Character*
Joseph Goebbels – Paul   *Nazi Leader*
Pancho Gonzales – Richard   *US Tennis Player*
Gounod – Charles   *French Composer*
Goya – Francisco   *Spanish Painter*
Ulysses S Grant – Hiram   *US President*
Florence Griffith-Joyner – Delorez   *US Athlete*
Brothers Grimm – Jacob and Wilhelm   *Folktale collectors*
Che Guevara – Ernesto   *Argentinian Revolutionary Leader*
Colonel Hall – John   *TV Character ('Bilko')*
Mrs Hall – Nell   *TV Character ('Bilko')*
Dashiell Hammett – Samuel   *US Novelist*
Learned Hand – Billings   *American Jurist*
Patsy Hendren – Elias   *England Cricketer*
Barbara Hepworth – Jocelyn   *English Sculptor*
William Herschel – Frederick   *British Astronomer*
Rudolf Hess – Richard   *Nazi Leader*
Patricia Highsmith – Mary   *US Novelist*
Hinge and Bracket – Dr Evadne and Dame Hilda   *comic duo*
Doc Holliday – John   *Western gunfighter*
Holman Hunt – William   *English Painter*
Honegger – Arthur   *Swiss Composer*
Ron L Hubbard – Lafayette   *SF Writer and Scientology Founder*
John Humphreys – Desmond   *TV and Radio Presenter*
Lauren Hutton – Mary   *US Actress*
Ivanhoe – Wilfred   *Literary Character*
Jacuzzi – Candido   *Inventor of luxury bath*
Janáček – Leoš   *Czech Composer*
Jeeves – Reginald   *PG Wodehouse character (named after Warwickshire Cricketer)*
Corporal Jones – Jack   *'Dad's Army' Character*
Miss Jones – Ruth   *TV Character ('Rising Damp')*
Khachaturian – Aram   *Armenian Composer*
Kookie – Gerald (Lloyd Kookson III)   *TV Character ('77 Sunset Strip')*
Lucky Luciano – Charles   *Gangster*
Lugg – Magersfontein   *Literary Character: Campion's Manservant*
Lytton Strachey – Giles   *Biographer*
Harold Macmillan – Maurice   *British Prime Minister*
Magnificent Evans – Plantagenet   *TV Character*
Mr Magoo – Quincy   *Cartoon Character*
Captain Mainwaring – George   *Dad's Army Character*
Paul McCartney – James   *Beatle*
Campbell Menzies – Walter   *MP and Former Athlete*
Mrs Merton – Dorothy   *TV Character*
Miles Van Der Rohe – Ludwig   *Architect*
Milhaud – Darius   *French Composer*
Monteverdi – Claudio   *Italian Composer*
Morse – Endeavour   *Fictional detective*
Angela Mortimer – Florence   *British Wimbledon Champion*
Mulder and Scully – Fox and Dana   *TV Characters ('X Files')*
Brian Mulroney – Martin   *Canadian Politician*
Murillo – Bartolomé   *Spanish Painter*
Mussorgsky – Modest   *Russian Composer*
Ogden Nash – Frederic   *American Poet*
Birgit Nilsson – Märta   *Swedish Soprano*

Captain Oates – Lawrence   *Explorer*
Milton Obote – Apollo   *Ugandan Politician*
Offenbach – Jacques   *French Composer*
King Oliver – Joseph   *American Cornet-player*
Palestrina – Giovanni   *Italian Composer*
Captain Peacock – Stephen   *TV Character*
Petrocelli – Tony   *TV Character*
Graeme Pollock – Robert   *South African Cricketer*
Jackson Pollock – Paul   *American Action Painter*
Ponchielli – Amilcare   *Italian Composer*
Potsie Weber – Warren   *TV Character (Happy Days)*
Beatrix Potter – Helen   *English Children's Writer*
Enoch Powell – John   *British Politician*
Pressburger and Powell – Emeric and Michael   *Film Makers*
Princip – Gavrilo   *Assassin*
Prokofiev – Sergey   *Russian Composer*
Puccini – Giacomo   *Italian Composer*
Captain Pugwash – Horatio   *TV Character*
Professor Quatermass – Bernard   *TV Character*
Dan Quayle – James   *US Vice-President*
Rachmaninoff – Sergey   *Russian Composer*
Sonny Ramphal – Shridath   *Secretary-General of the Commonwealth*
Ravel – Maurice   *French Composer*
Django Reinhardt – Jean Baptiste   *Belgian Guitarist*
Viv Richards – Isaac   *West Indian Cricketer*
Cardinal Richelieu – Armand   *French politician-prelate*
Rigsby – Rupert   *TV Character ('Rising Damp')*
Rimsky-Korsakov – Nikolay   *Russian Composer*
Sergeant Ritzik – Rupert   *TV Character ('Bilko')*
Auguste Rodin – René-François   *French Sculptor*
Rossini – Gioachino   *Italian Composer*
Rostropovich – Mstislav   *Russian Musician*
Mr Rumbold – Cuthbert   *TV Character*
Salman Rushdie – Ahmed   *British Novelist*
Anwar Sadat – Mohamed   *Egyptian President*
Saint-Saens – Charles Camille   *French Composer*
Vicario Sanchez – Arantxa   *Tennis Player*
Savonarola – Girolamo   *Italian Religious Reformer*
Schubert – Franz Peter   *Austrian Composer*
Schumann – Robert   *German Composer*
Paul Scofield – David   *English Actor*
Scottie – Montgomery   *'Star Trek' Character*
Norman Shaw – Richard   *English Architect*
Shelley – James   *TV Character*
Phones (Sheridan) – George   *TV Character ('Stingray')*
Shostakovich – Dmitry   *Russian Composer*
Sibelius – Jean   *Finnish Composer*
Mrs Slocombe – Betty   *TV Character*
Smetana – Bedrich   *Czech Composer*
Colonel Hannibal Smith – John   *TV Character*
Snudge – Claude   *TV Character ('Army Game')*
Leland Stanford – Amasa   *US Railway Magnate*
Starsky and Hutch – David and Ken   *TV policemen*
Nobbie Stiles – Norbert   *Footballer*
Stockhausen – Karlheinz   *German Composer*
August Strindberg – Johann   *Swedish Playwright*
Sulu – Hikaru   *'Star Trek' character*
Booth Tarkington – Newton   *US Author*
Tchaikovsky – Pyotr   *Russian Composer*
Tinker – Edward Sexton   *Blake's Assistant*

Daley Thompson – Francis   *Athlete*
Wolfe Tone – Theobald   *Irish Nationalist*
Topol – Chaim   *Israeli Actor*
Uccello – Paolo   *Florentine Painter*
Verdi – Giuseppe   *Italian Composer*
Vivaldi – Antonio   *Italian Composer*
Richard Wagner – Wilhelm   *German Composer*
Private Walker – James   *'Dad's Army' Character*
Dionne Warwick – Marie   *US Singer*
Dr Watson – John   *Literary Character*

Weber – Carl   *German Composer*
Webern – Anton   *Austrian Composer*
Orson Welles – George   *Film Maker and Actor*
Andy Williams – Howard   *US Singer*
Harold Wilson – James   *British Prime Minister*
Debra Winger – Marie   *US Actress*
Terry Wogan – Michael   *Broadcaster*
Wolf-Ferrari – Ermanno   *Italian Composer*
Roy Wood – Ulysses   *Pop Musician*
Virginia Woolf – Adeline   *English Novelist*

Firsts

Air Hostess Ellen Church		1930
Airmail (GB) Sept 9th		1911
Airmail Stickers Aug 17th		1918
Appendix Operation		
George Thomas Morton		1887
Athlete to use Crouch Start		
Charles Sherrill		1888
Atom Bomb		
Alamogordo Air Base, New Mexico (July 16th)		1945
Atom Bomb (UK)		
Monte Bello Islands off West Australia		1952
Atomic Power Station (large-scale)		
Calder Hall, Cumbria		1956
Atomic Research Centre (UK)		
Harwell in Berkshire		1946
Baronet Nicholas Bacon of Redgrove		1611
Bikini June 24th		1950
Blood transfusion		
Montpelier University, France		1667
Boy Scout Movement		
Brownsea Island, Poole, Dorset		1907
Breakfast Cereal (ready to eat)		
Shredded Wheat		1893
Bus Conductress Kate Barton		1909
Bus Service (scheduled) Shillibeer's		
Marylebone to Euston Rd Service		1829
Capital Gains Tax April 6th		1965
Car Tax Discs		
On windowscreen from Jan 1st		1921
Casino (UK) Metropole in Brighton		1962
Catamaran		
Experiment, built for Sir William Petty: adaptation from traditional Polynesian design		1662
Channel Swim: both ways (UK)		
Kevin Murphy (non-stop) in 35 hrs 10 mins		1970
Chelsea Flower Show		
May 20th-22nd by Royal Horticultural Society		1913
Christmas Card John Calcott Horsley		
designed for Henry Cole		1843
Christmas Speech of Sovereign		
Elizabeth II		1957
Christmas Tree From German idea		1605
Circumnavigation of Earth		
Juan de Elcano in *Vittoria* (Magellan killed en route)		1522
Circumnavigation of Earth: Non-stop Solo		
Robin Knox-Johnston in *Suhaili*		1969
Club Colours		
Black, Red, Gold of I Zingari Cricket Club		1845

Coeducational School		
Henry Morley opened Marine Terrace, Cheshire		1849
Comic *Comic Cuts* an 8-page weekly		1890
Comic Strip in Newspaper		
Richard Outcault's 'Yellow Kid'		1897
Credit Card Diners Club, New York		1950
Cremation (UK)		
Honoretta Pratt		1769
Cub Scouts		
Robertsbridge, Sussex (Feb 2nd)		1914
Daylight Saving (UK) Clocks put forward I hour		1916
Detective Story Edgar Allan Poe's *Murder in the Rue Morgue*		1841
Diet (scientifically planned)		
Dr Harvey for undertaker William Banting		1862
Dinner Jacket		
Worn by G Lorillard, Tuxedo Park Country Club, NY		1886
Dresswear hire firm (UK)		
Moss Bros of Covent Garden		1860
Driving tests (UK) Leslie Hore-Belisha instigated voluntary tests		1935
Duke (UK)		
Edward, Duke of Cornwall		1337
Electric lamp J Lindsay developed but did not patent lamp		1835
Electric oven Installed Hotel Bernina, Samaden, Switzerland		1889
Electric power station		
Central Power Station, Godalming, Surrey		1881
Escalator (UK)		
Harrods Department Store		1898
Family allowance June 15th (5s per child)		1945
Film festival Hotel Excelsior Venice, Italy		1932
Fire brigade (UK)		
Nicholas Barbon established in London		1684
Fixed penalty parking ticket (UK)		
Sept 19th		1961
Football: televised live (UK)		
Wembley Cup Final		1938
Four-minute mile		
Roger Bannister in 3: 59.4 (Oxford)		1954
Fruit machine		
Liberty Bell designed by Charles Frey		1889
GCE 'O' and 'A' Levels		
Introduced to replace School Certificate		1950
GCSE Introduced to replace CGE 'O' Level		1988
Girl Guide Allison Cargill		1908
Gold disc		
Glen Miller's 'Chattanooga Choo Choo'		1941

Greetings card   Designer W Harvey
engraved by J Thompson   1829
Heart Transplant
Christiaan Barnard, Groote Schuur Hospital   1967
Helicopter (free flight)   Twin-rotor machine
designed by Paul Cornu   1907
Hydrofoil (UK)
'Miranda III' by John Thornycroft   1909
Hydrogen bomb   Detonated by USA
at Eniwetok, Marshall Isles   1952
Indianapolis 500   Won by Ray Harroun
(May 30th)   1911
In-flight movie   Conan Doyle's *The Lost World*   1925
Isle of Man TT Races
Won by Charles Collier on a Matchless   1907
Jazz band   Led by Buddy Bolden,
New Orleans   1900
Jukebox   Installed at Palais Royal Saloon,
San Francisco   1889
Life insurance policy   Taken out by London
Alderman Richard Martin   1583
Lighthouse (UK)   Spurn Point, Yorkshire   1427
Lord Mayor's Show   Instigated by
Sir John Norman   1453
Loudspeaker
Auxetophone by Horace Short   1900
Luncheon Vouchers (UK)   January 1st   1955
Meteorological satellite   Tiros I   1960
Miss World Contest   April 19th   1951
Monarch to Abdicate: English   Richard II   1399
MOT test   September 12th   1960
Motorway   Avus Autobahn, Germany   1921
Moving staircase (UK)   Earls Court Station   1911
National park   Yellowstone, Wyoming   1872
National park: GB   Peak District   1950
National Savings stamps
On sale from July 8th   1918
Newspaper colour supplement (UK)
Sunday Times   1962
North Sea gas   Piped ashore by BP   1967
Nuclear merchant vessel
Savannah (launched in New Jersey)   1962
Old age pensions
Bismarck introduced in Germany   1889
Old age pensions (UK)
Introduced on January 1st   1909
Old school tie   Old Etonian, of narrow
blue and broad black stripes   1900
Opera
Jacopo Peri's *Dafne*, libretto by Rinuccini   1597
Oral contraceptive (UK)
Marketed on Aug 18th (invented 1954)   1960
Parachute jump (aeroplane)
Albert Berry from a height of 1,500 feet   1912
Parachute jump (balloon)   Andre-Jacques
Garnerin from a height of 2,230 feet   1797
Parcel post   Introduced on Aug 1st   1883
Parking meter (UK)
(America had them from 1935)   1958
Parking ticket (UK)
Dr Thomas Creighton was first victim   1960
Pedestrian crossing (UK)
Parliament Square, London   1926
Photo finish: horse race
Introduced by Ernest Marks, New Jersey   1888
Photographic process
Louis Daguerre first commercial success   1839

Pneumatic motor car tyres
Michelin fitted first tyre to a 4hp Daimler   1895
Policewoman
Mrs Alice Stebbins Wells of the LAPD   1910
Policewoman (UK)   Nov 27th   1914
Postage stamp (adhesive)
James Chalmers of Dundee printed first   1834
Postage stamp (perforations)
Penny Red, issued in February   1854
Postal orders (UK)
Introduced on 1 January   1881
Postcard (UK)   Introduced on 1 October   1870
Premium Bonds
On sale from 1 November   1956
Prince of Wales: English
Edward of Caernarvon, later Edward 11   1301
Prisoner of War camp
Norman X Depot, Stilton, for French PoWs   1797
Public library (UK)
Jerrom Goodwyn Library, Norwich   1608
Recorded delivery   Feb 1st   1961
Registered letters
Introduced by GPO on Jan 1st   1878
Row across the Atlantic
Capt John Ridgway and Sgt Chay Blyth   1966
Row across the Atlantic (solo)
Tom McLean in 20 ft dory *Super Silver*   1969
Sex Change Operation   George/Christine
Jorgensen by Dr K Hamburger   1952
Space Flight (manned)
Vostok I, piloted by Yuri Gagarin   1961
Space flight (by woman)
Vostok VI, piloted by Valentina Tereshkova   1963
Space walk
Aleksey Leonov, from Voshkod II   1965
Spacecraft on the Moon   Luna II   1959
Spiritualist mediums
Margaretta and Kate Fox from New York   1848
Starting stalls: horse race (UK)
Newmarket on 8th July   1965
Tape recorder
Telagraphone by Valdemar Poulsen   1898
Telegrams
I shilling for 20 words (1st worldwide in 1843) 1870
Telephone directory (UK)
Published by London Telephone Co   1880
Telephone speaking clock (UK)
Aka TIM was voice of Ethel Cain for 20 yrs   1936
Television announcer (UK)   Leslie Mitchell 1936
Television commercial, black and white (UK)
Gibbs SR Toothpaste   1955
Television commercial, colour (UK)
Birds Eye Peas   1969
Television licence (UK)   Cost of £2   1946
Television communications satellite
Bell Telephone 'Telstar'   1962
Traffic lights   Parliament Square, London   1868
Traffic lights: electric (UK)   July   1926
Traffic lights: automatic (UK)   Nov 5th   1927
Traffic wardens (UK)
Sept 15th in London   1960
Train accident fatality
William Huskisson MP, run down by *Rocket*   1830
Traveller's cheques
Introduced on Jan 1st   1772
Underground railway (UK)
Metropolitan Line Paddington to Farringdon   1863

Underground railway (electric)	
City branch of the Northern line	1890
Undergound map	
Albert Stanley, Lord Ashfield instigated	1908
Underground (Tube) train (automatic)	
Central Line Woodford to Hainault	1964
Vending machine	
So-called 'Honesty' tobacco boxes, 1d a go	1615
Vending machine (automatic)	
Patented by Carl Ade in Germany	1867
Victoria Cross Mate Charles Lucas, for action aboard HMS *Hecla*	1854
Voting rights for women	
New Zealand was 1st country to allow Finland 1st in Europe 1906	1893
Windscreen wipers (mechanical)	
Introduced in the USA	1916
Windscreen wipers (electrical)	
The 'Berkshire', produced in the USA	1923

Woman cabinet minister (UK)	
Margaret Bondfield, Minister of Labour	1929
Woman doctor (US) Elizabeth Blackwell	1849
Woman doctor (UK)	
Elizabeth Garrett Anderson	1859
Woman MP (UK) Constance, Countess Markievicz, Sinn Fein MP	1918
Woman MP (to take seat)	
Nancy Astor for Plymouth Sutton	1919
Woman novelist	
Lady Murasaki, Japan	c1004
Woman novelist (UK) Aphra Ben	1687
Woman pilot Baronne Elise de la Roche	1909
Woman prime minister	
Mrs Sirimavo Bandaranaike of Ceylon	1960
Women's Institute	
Stoneycreek, Ontario, Canada	1897
Yellow lines restricting parking Laid in Slough	1956
Zebra crossing Oct 31st	1951

NB: Although this topic of 'firsts' has been listed in the Famous People section, many of the entries relate to inanimate objects. This is purely a matter of expediency and is not an oversight on the part of the author.

Initials: Known by

WH Auden Wystan Hugh
British Poet

AJ Ayer Alfred Jules
English Philosopher

CPE Bach Carl Philipp Emanuel
German composer

JC Bach Johann Christian
German composer

JS Bach Johann Sebastian
German composer

RM Ballantyne, Robert Michael
Scottish author

JG Ballard James Graham
British writer

JC Bamford Joseph Cyril
Founder of JCB Company

BA Baracus Bad Attitude
Fictional TV character ('A Team')

PT Barnum Phineas Taylor
US showman

JM Barrie James Matthew
Scottish novelist

HE Bates Herbert Ernest
English novelist

CC Beck Clarence
US Graphic Artist

AC Benson Arthur Christopher
English author and poet

EF Benson Edward Frederic
English author

EC Bentley Edmund Clerihew
English journalist and novelist

RD Blackmore Richard
Doddridge *English novelist*

PW Botha Pieter Willem
South African Politician

RA Butler Richard Austen
British Politician

AS Byatt Antonia Susan
English novelist and critic

GK Chesterton Gilbert Keith
English novelist

JM Coetzee John Michael
South African novelist

AE Coppard Alfred Edgar
English poet and writer

AJ Cronin Archibald Joseph
Scottish novelist

ee cummings Edward Estlin
American writer and painter

WH Davies William Henry
British Poet

JW De Forest John William *US novelist and Historian*

FW De Klerk, Frederik Willem
South African Politician

RF Delderfield Ronald Frederick
English Playwright

EL Doctorow Edgar Lawrence
US novelist

JP Donleavy James Patrick
Irish novelist

TS Eliot Thomas Stearns
poet and Dramatist

JK Ewers John Keith *Australian writer*

JR Ewing John Ross
Fictional TV character ('Dallas')

JG Farrell James Gordon
English novelist

EH Fellowes Edmund Horace
English musicologist

WC Fields William Claude
American comedy actor

CS Forester Cecil Scott
British writer

EM Forster Edward Morgan
English novelist

AJ Foyt Anthony Joseph
US Racing Driver

CB Fry Charles Burgess
English sportsman

JK Galbraith John Kenneth
Economist

TS Garp Technical Sergeant
John Irving character

WS Gilbert William Schwenck
English operetta librettist

KC Gillette King Camp
American inventor

WE Gladstone William Ewart
British politician

EW Godwin Edward William
English architect and designer

HL Gold Horace Leonard
Science fiction writer

WG Grace William Gilbert
English cricketer

DW Griffith David Wark
American film director

AB Guthrie Alfred Bertram
US writer

MC Hammer Master of
Ceremonies *US rap artist*

WC Handy William Christopher
US Blues composer

LP Hartley Leslie Poles
English author

HJ Heinz Henry John
US food manufacturer

WE Henley William Ernest
English poet and Critic

GA Henty George Alfred
English novelist

AP Herbert Alan Patrick
English writer

AD Hope Alec Derwent
Australian poet

EW Hornung Ernest William
English writer

AE Housman Alfred Edward
 English poet
CLR James Cyril Lionel Robert
 Trinidadian writer
MR James Montague Rhodes
 Ghost story writer
PD James Phyllis Dorothy
 English writer
WE Johns William Earl
 English writer and aviator
MM Kaye Mary Margaret
 British writer
HRF Keating Henry Raymond
 Fitzwalter *UK detective
 story writer*
BB King Blues Boy
 Singer/guitarist
WP Kinsella William Patrick
 Canadian writer
RB Kitaj Ronald Brooks
 American painter
RD Laing Ronald David
 Scottish psychiatrist
CJ Lamb Cara Jean
 *Fictional TV character
 (LA Law)*
kd lang Kathryn Dawn
 Canadian singer
DH Lawrence David Herbert
 English novelist
TE Lawrence Thomas Edward
 British soldier and writer
FR Leavis Frank Raymond
 English literary critic
CS Lewis Clive Staples
 Irish writer
HP Lovecraft Howard Phillips
 US Science fiction writer
LS Lowry Laurence Stephen
 English artist
HL Mencken Henry Louis
 US journalist
AA Michelson Albert Abraham
 US physicist
AA Milne Alan Alexander
 Children's writer

LM Montgomery Lucy Maud
 Canadian novelist
CL Moore Catherine Lucille *US
 science fiction writer*
JP Morgan John Pierpoint
 US financier
JB Morton John Bingham
 British journalist (Beachcomber)
HH Munro Hector Hugh
 English writer (Saki)
VS Naipaul Vidiadhar
 Surajprasad *Trinidadian
 novelist*
RK Narayan Rasipuram
 Kirshnaswamy *Indian novelist*
PH Newby Percy Howard
 British novelist
TV Olsen Theodore Victor
 US Westerns writer
PJ O'Rourke Patrick John
 US journalist
CJ Parker Casey Jean
 *Fictional TV character
 ('Baywatch')*
SJ Perelman Sydney Joseph
 US writer
JB Priestley John Boynton
 English novelist
VS Pritchett Victor Sawdon
 English writer
JD Rockefeller John Davison
 US businessman
AV Roe Alliot Verdon
 English aviation pioneer
JK Rowling Joanne Kathleen
 English children's writer
JD Salinger Jerome David
 US novelist
EH Shepard Ernest Howard
 English illustrator
RC Sherriff Robert Cedric
 English novelist
OJ Simpson Orenthal James
 US sportsman
VP Singh Vishwanath Pratap
 Indian politician

BF Skinner Burrhus Fredric
 US psychologist
EE 'Doc' Smith Edward Elmer
 US science fiction writer
WH Smith William Henry
 English Newsagent
CP Snow Charles Percy
 English novelist
HM Stanley Henry Morton
 Journalist and explorer
JIM Stewart John Innes
 Mackintosh *English writer*
JEB Stuart James Ewell Brown
 Confederate general
JM Synge John Millington *Irish
 Dramatist*
AJP Taylor Alan John Percivale
 English historian
DM Thomas Donald Michael
 English writer
JRR Tolkien John Ronald Reuel
 Philologist and author
PL Travers Pamela Lyndon
 Author of Mary Poppins
AE Van Vogt Alfred Elton
 Science fiction writer
HG Wells Herbert George
 English novelist
EB White Elwyn Brooks
 US essayist and novelist
TH White Terence Hanbury
 English novelist
JPR Williams John Peter Rhys
 Welsh rugby player
WD and HO Wills William Day
 and Henry Overton
 Tobacco manufacturers
PG Wodehouse Pelham Grenville
 English novelist
FW Woolworth Frank Winfield
 US businessman
PC Wren Percy Christopher
 English novelist
WB Yeats William Butler
 Irish poet

Inventions and Discoveries

Adding machine *Blaise Pascal*	1642	
Aeroplane (steam powered) *Clement Ader*	1886	
Aeroplane *Wright Brothers*	1903	
Aerosol *Erik Rotheim*	1926	
Air Pump *Otto Von Guericke*	1654	
Airship (non-rigid) *Henri Giffard*	1852	
Airship (rigid) *Ferdinand Von Zeppelin*	1900	
Ambulance *Baron Dominique Jean Larrey*	1792	
Anaesthesia *William Morton*	1846	
Antiseptic surgery *Joseph Lister*	1867	
Aqualung *Cousteau and Gagnan*	1943	
Aspirin (synthesization) *Kolbe, Heinrich*	1859	
Aspirin (intro into medicine) *H Dresser of Bayer AG*	1899	
Assembly line *Samuel Colt*	1855	
Atom bomb *Frisch, Bohr, Peierls*	1939	
Baby incubator *Dr Alexandre Lion*	1891	
Bakelite *Leo H Baekeland*	1907	
Balloon *Montgolfier Brothers*	1783	
Balloons: rubber *Michael Faraday*	1824	
Balloons: toy *JG Ingram*	1847	
Ball-point pen *John T Loud*	1888	
Ball-point pen (mass-produced) *László Biro*	1938	
Barbed wire (manufacture) *Joseph Glidden*	1874	
Barbed wire (patent) *Lucien B Smith*	1867	
Barometer *Evangelista Torricelli*	1643	
Battery (electric) *Alessandro Volta*	1800	
Bell (electric) *Joseph Henry*	1831	
Betatron *Donald Kerst*	1940	
Bicycle *Kirkpatrick MacMillan*	1839	
Bicycle (spoked wheels) *James Starley*	1870	
Bifocal Lens *Benjamin Franklin*	1780	

Bikini *Louis Reard*	1946	
Boy Scout movement Sir Robert		
Baden-Powell	1907	
Bra (cantilevered) *Robard Howard Hughes*	1943	
Breakfast cereal (ready to eat) *Henry D*		
Perky	1893	
Bunsen burner *Robert Wilhelm Bunsen*	1855	
Burglar alarm *Edwin T Holmes*	1858	
Cable-car *W Ritter*	1866	
Calculating clock *Wilhelm Schickard*	1623	
Calculus *Leibniz and Newton*	1684	
Canning *Nicholas Appert*	1795	
Car (3 process wheel steam tractor)		
Nicolas Cugnot	1769	
Car (petrol) *Karl Benz*	1888	
Car speedometer *Thorpe and Salter*	1902	
Carbon fibres *Courtaulds*	1964	
Carbon paper *Ralph Wedgewood*	1806	
Carburettor *Gottlieb Daimler*	1876	
Carpet sweeper *Melville R Bissell*	1876	
Cash register *James Ritty*	1879	
Cats' eyes *Percy Shaw*	1933	
Cellophane *Dr Jacques Brandenberger*	1908	
Celluloid *Alexander Parkes*	1861	
Cement (Portland) *Joseph Aspdin*	1824	
Centigrade thermometer *Anders Celsius*	1742	
Chewing gum (commercial) *John Curtis*	1848	
Chocolate (solid) *Francois-Louis Cailler*	1819	
Christmas card *Sir Henry Cole*	1843	
Chronometer *John Harrison*	1735	
Cinematography *Lumière brothers*	1895	
Circulation of the blood *William Harvey*	1628	
Clock (mechanical) *I-Hsing and Liang-Tsan*	725	
Clock (quartz) *Warren Alvin Marrison*	1929	
Cloud chamber *Charles Thomson*		
Rees Wilson	1927	
Cluedo *Anthony Pratt*	1948	
Coca-Cola *Dr John Pemberton*	1886	
Coffee (instant) *Nestles*	1937	
Compact disc *Philips and Sony*	1979	
Computer *Charles Babbage*	1835	
Computer (electronic) *Eckert and*		
Mauchly	1946	
Concrete (reinforced) *François*		
Hennebique	1892	
Condensed milk *Gail Borden*	1858	
Condom *Gabriel Fallopius*	1560	
Contact lens *Adolph E Fick*	1887	
Contraceptive pill *Dr Gregory Pincus*	1950	
Cordite *Dewar and Abel*	1905	
Corrugated iron *Pierre Carpentier*	1853	
Credit card *Ralph Scheider*	1950	
Crossword puzzle *Arthur Wynne*	1913	
Cyclotron *James Chadwick*	1935	
DDT *Paul Muller*	1939	
Decompression chamber *Robert H*		
Davis	1929	
Disc brake *Dr F Lanchester*	1902	
Diving suit *Andrew Becker*	1715	
DNA structure *Francis Crick and James*		
Watson	1953	
Dome (geodesic) *Richard Buckminster*		
Fuller	1945	
Double-entry bookkeeping *Lucas Paciolus*	1495	
Doughnut (with hole) *Hanson Gregory*	1847	
Drill (electric) *Wilhelm Fein*	1895	
Drill (pneumatic) *Germain Sommelier*	1861	
Dry-cleaning *M Jolly-Bellin*	1849	
Dynamite *Alfred Nobel*	1863	
Dynamo *Hippolyte Pixii*	1832	
Elastic bands *Stephen Perry*	1845	
Electric chair *Harold Brown and*		
EA Kenneally	1890	
Electric fan *Dr Schuyler Skaats*	1882	
Electric flat iron *HW Seeley*	1882	
Electric generator *Michael Faraday*	1831	
Electric guitar *Rickenbacker, Barth and*		
Beauchamp	1931	
Electric heating system *Dr W Leigh*		
Burton	1887	
Electric lamp *Independently invented*		
by Joseph, Swan and Thomas Alva Edison	1879	
Electric motor (AC) *Nikola Tesla*	1888	
Electric motor (DC) *Zenobe Gramme*	1873	
Electrocardiography *Willem Einthoven*	1903	
Electromagnet *William Sturgeon*	1824	
Electron *JJ Thomas*	1897	
Electronic computer (dedicated) *Alan*		
Turing	1943	
Electronic computer (general purpose)		
Eckert and John Mauchly	1946	
Electronic computer (commercially		
available) *Eckert and Mauchly*	1951	
Endoscope *Pierre Segalas*	1827	
Equals sign (mathematics) *Robert*		
Record	1557	
Escalator *Jesse W Reno*	1892	
Esperanto *Dr Ludovic Zamenhof*	1887	
Exclamation mark *J Day*	1553	
Facsimile machine (Fax) *Arthur Korn*	1907	
Ferrofluids *Ronald Rosensweig*	1968	
Film (Moving outlines) *Louis Le Prince*	1885	
Film (Talking) *Engl, Mussolle and Vogt*	1922	
Film (Musical sound) *Lee De Forest*	1923	
Fingerprint classification *Francis Galton*	1891	
Fire extinguisher *M Fuches*	1734	
Flying doctor service *KH Vincent Welsh*	1928	
Foam rubber *John Boyd Dunlop*	1929	
Food processor *Kenneth Wood*	1947	
Fountain pen *Lewis Edson Waterman*	1884	
Frozen food *Clarence Birdseye*	1930	
Galvanometer *Andre-Marie Ampere*	1834	
Gas fire *Philippe Lebon*	1799	
Gas lighting *William Murdock*	1792	
Gas meter *William Clegg*	1815	
Gearbox (automatic) *Hermann Fottinger*	1910	
Genetics *Gregor Mendel*	1865	
Geodesic dome *Richard Buckminster*		
Fuller	1945	
Gift coupons *Benjamin Talbert Babbit*	1865	
Girl Guides *Robert and Agnes*		
Baden-Powell	1910	
Glider *Sir George Cayley*	1853	
Golliwog *Florence K Upton*	1895	
Gramophone *Thomas Alva Edison*	1878	
Gravitation, laws of *Isaac Newton*	1684	
Gun cotton *Christian Friedrich Schönbein*	1845	
Gyro-compass *Elmer Sperry*	1911	
Gyroscope *Leon Foucault*	1852	
Half-tone process *Carl Gustaf Wilhelm*		
Carleman	1871	
Hearing aid (electric) *Miller Reese*		
Hutchinson	1901	
Heart (artificial) *Vladimir Demikhov*	1937	
Helicopter *Louis and Jacques Breguet*	1907	
Holography *Dennis Gabor*	1947	
Hovercraft *Christopher Cockerell*	1955	
Hydrofoil *Comte de Lambert*	1897	

Ice-cream cones *Italo Marcioni*	1896
Identikit *Hugh McDonald*	1959
Insulin *Frederick Grant Banting and Charles Herbert Best*	1921
Intelligence test (IQ) *Alfred Binet*	1896
Iron Lung *Philip Drinker*	1927
Jeans *Levi Strauss*	1850
Jet engine *Sir Frank Whittle*	1937
Jigsaw puzzle *George Spilsbury*	1767
Jukebox (pre-selective) *John C Dunton*	1905
Kaleidoscope *Sir David Brewster*	1816
Knitting machine *William Lee*	1589
Laser *Theodore Maiman*	1960
Lathe, screw-cutting *Henry Maudslay*	1800
Launderette *JF Cantrell*	1934
Lawn mower *Edwin Budding and John Ferrabee*	1830
Lie detector *John Larson*	1928
Lift (mechanical) *Elisha G Otis*	1852
Lightning conductor *Benjamin Franklin*	1752
Linoleum *Frederick Walton*	1860
Lithography *Aloys Senefelder*	1796
Locomotive *Richard Trevithick*	1804
Logarithms *John Napier*	1614
Loom, power *Edmund Cartwright*	1785
Loudspeaker *Horace Short*	1898
Loudspeaker (electric) *Miller Reece Hutchinson*	1906
Machine gun *James Puckle*	1718
Margarine *Hippolyte Mège-Mouriés*	1869
Maser *Charles H Townes*	1953
Match *Robert Boyle*	1680
Match (friction) *John Walker*	1826
Match (safety) *JE Lundstrom*	1855
Metronome *Dietrich Nikolaus Winkel*	c1800
Microchip *Jack Saint Clair Kilby*	1958
Microphone *Alexander Graham Bell*	1876
Micro-processor *Moore and Hoff Noyce*	1971
Microscope *Zacharias Janssen*	1590
Microscope (electron) *EAF Ruska*	1933
Microwave oven *Percy Spencer*	1945
Miner's safety lamp *Sir Humphry Davy*	1816
Missile (air-to-air) *Herbert Wagner*	1943
Monopoly *Charles Darrow*	1931
Motor cycle *Gottlieb Daimler*	1885
Neon lamp *Georges Claude*	1910
Neptune (planet) *Johann Gottfried Galle*	1846
Neutron *James Chadwick*	1935
Non-stick pan *Marc Gregoir*	1954
Nylon *Wallace Carothers*	1937
Optical fibres *Navinder Kapany*	1955
Oven (electric) *Bernina Hotel, Switzerland*	1889
Ozone *Christian Friedrich Schönbein*	1840
Pacemaker (implantable) *Wilson Greatbach*	1956
Paint (acrylic) *Reeves Ltd*	1964
Paint (fluorescent) *Joe and Bob Switzer*	1933
Paper *Tsai Lun*	105
Paper (from wood pulp) *Gottlab Keller*	1844
Paper clip *Johann Vaaler*	1900
Parachute *Jean-Pierre Blanchard*	1785
Parachute (patent) *André-Jacques Garnerin*	1802
Parking meter *Carlton Magee*	1935
Pasteurisation *Louis Pasteur*	1863
Pen (ball-point) *Laszlo Biro*	1938
Pen (fountain) *Lewis Waterman*	1884
Pencil (using pulverised graphite lead)	

Nicolas Jacques Conté	1795
Pendulum clock *Christiaan Huygens*	1656
Penicillin *Sir Alexander Fleming*	1928
Periodic table *Dmitri Mendelev*	1866
Photoelectric cell *Johann Phillip Elster and Hans F Geitel*	1896
Photographic lens *William H Wollaston*	1812
Photography (on pewter plate) *Joseph Nicephore Niepce*	1826
Photography (on paper) *William Henry Fox Talbot*	1835
Photography (colour) *James Clerk Maxwell*	1861
Photography (on film) *John Carbutt*	1888
Pianoforte *Bartolomeo Cristofori*	1709
Pillar box (UK) *Anthony Trollope*	1851
Plastics *Alexander Parkes*	1852
Pluto (planet) *Clyde Tombaugh*	1930
Plutonium *GT Seaborg, JW Kennedy and AC Wahl*	1940
Pneumatic bicycle tyres *John Boyd Dunlop*	1887
Pneumatic tyres *RW Thompson.*	1845
Pocket calculator *Kilby, Tassell and Merryman*	1972
Polio vaccine (injection) *Jonas Salk*	1952
Polio vaccine (oral) *Albert Sabin*	1957
Polythene *RO Gibson*	1933
Potato crisps *George Crum*	1853
Pressure cooker *Denis Papin*	1679
Printing press (wooden) *Johann Gutenberg*	1455
Printing (rotary) *Richard Hoe*	1846
Propeller (boat, hand-operated) *David Bushnell*	1775
Propeller (ship) *Francis Smith*	1837
Propeller (ship), patent *Isambard Kingdom Brunel*	1844
Proton *Ernest Rutherford*	1920
Pyramid *Imhotop*	2650BC
Radar (application) *Taylor and Young*	1930
Radar (theory) *Nikola Tesla*	1900
Radar (UK) *Robert Watson-Watt*	1935
Radio telegraphy *Mahlon Loomis*	1864
Radio telegraphy (transatlantic) *Guglielmo Marconi*	1901
Radioactivity *Henri Becquerel*	1896
Rails (iron) *Abraham Darby*	1738
Railway airbrake *George Westinghouse*	1863
Railway (electric) *Ernst Siemens*	1878
Railway (underground) *Charles Pearson*	1843
Rayon *Joseph Swan*	1883
Razor (safety) *King Camp Gillette*	1895
Razor (electric) *Jacob Schick*	1931
Record (flat disc) *Emil Berliner*	1888
Record (LP) *Peter Goldmark*	1948
Refrigerator *James Harrison and Alexander Catlin Twinning*	1850
Revolver *Samuel Colt*	1835
Rickshaw *Jonathan Scobie*	1869
Roller Skates *Joseph Merlin*	1760
Roulette Wheel *Blaise Pascal*	1647
Rubber (latex foam) *Dunlop Rubber Co*	1928
Rubber (tyres) *Thomas Hancock*	1846
Rubber (vulcanised) *Charles Goodyear*	1841
Rubber (waterproof) *Charles Macintosh*	1823
Rubik cube *Erno Rubik*	1975
Safety pin *Walter Hunt*	1849
Scooter *Walter Lines*	1897
Scotch tape *Richard Drew*	1930

Scrabble *James Brunot*	1950
Sealing wax *Gerard Hermann*	1554
Seismographic scale *Charles Francis Richter*	1935
Self-starter motor (UK) *Charles F Kettering*	1911
Sewing machine *Thomas Saint*	1790
Shorthand *Marcus Tullius Tiro*	63BC
Shorthand (modern world) *Timothy Bright*	1588
Skyscraper *William Le Baron Jenny*	1882
Slide rule *William Oughtred*	1621
Snooker *Sir Neville Chamberlain*	1875
Spectacles *Salvino degli Armati and Alessandro delle Spina*	c1280
Spinning frame *Richard Arkwright*	1769
Spinning jenny *James Hargreaves*	1764
Spinning mule *Samuel Crompton*	1779
Spirit level *JM Thevenot*	1666
Stamp (perforations) *Henry Archer*	1854
Stapler *Charles Henry Gould*	1868
Steam engine *Thomas Savery*	1698
Steam engine (condenser) *James Watt*	1765
Steam engine (piston) *Thomas Newcomen*	1712
Steamship *JC Perier*	1775
Steamturbine (ship's) *Charles Parsons*	1894
Steel production *Henry Bessemer*	1855
Steel (stainless) *Harry Brearley*	1913
Stereotype *William Ged*	1725
Stethoscope *Rene Laennec*	1816
Stopwatch *Jean Moyse*	1776
Submarine *Cornelius Jacobszoon Drebbel*	1624
Sun-tan cream *Eugene Schueller*	1936
Syringe (hypodermic) *Charles Gabriel Pravaz*	1835
Table tennis *James Gibb*	1890
Tampon *Earl Hass*	1830
Tank *Ernest Swinton*	1914
Tape Recorder *Louis Blattner*	1929
Telegraph (electric) *George Louis Lesage*	1774
Telegraph *M Lammond*	1787
Telegraph code *Samuel Morse*	1837
Telephone *Antonio Meucci*	1849
Telephone (patent) *Alexander Graham Bell*	1876
Telephone switchboard *Almon B Strowger*	1889
Telescope (refractor) *Hans Lippershey*	1608
Television (mechanical) *John Logie Baird*	1926
Tennis *Walter G Wingfield*	1873
Terylene *JR Whinfield and JT Dickson*	1941

Thermometer *Galileo Galilei*	1593
Thermometer (mercury) *Gabriel Fahrenheit*	1714
Thimble *Nicolas Van Benschoten*	1684
Toothbrush *William Addis*	1649
Top hat *John Hetherington*	1797
Torpedo (UK) *Robert Whitehead*	1866
Traffic lights *JP Knight*	1868
Traffic lights (automatic) *Alfred Benesch*	1914
Transformer *Michael Faraday*	1831
Transistor *John Bardeen, William Bradley Shockley and Walter Brattain*	1948
Travel agency *Thomas Cook*	1841
Travellers cheques *Robert Herries*	1772
Travellers cheques (commercial) *American Express*	1891
Tubercle bacillus *Robert Koch*	1882
Tuning fork *John Shore*	1711
Turbojet *Frank Whittle*	1928
Typewriter *Pellegrine Tarri*	1808
Typewriter (patent) *William Burt*	1829
Typewriter (mass production) *Christopher Sholes*	1874
Ultrasonography (obstetric) *Ian Donald*	1979
Uranus *William Herschel*	1781
Vaccination *Edward Jenner*	1770
Vacuum cleaner (electric) *Hubert Cecil Booth*	1901
Vacuum cleaner (steam) *Ives McGaffrey*	1871
Vacuum flask *James Dewar*	1892
Vending machine *Percival Everitt*	1883
Ventilator *Théophile Guibal*	1858
Video recorder *Ampex Co*	1956
Videophone *American Telegraph and Telephone Co*	1927
Vulcanised rubber *Charles Goodyear*	1839
Washing machine (electric) *Hurley Machine Co*	1907
Watch *Bartholomew Manfredi*	1462
Watch (waterproof) *Rolex*	1927
Water closet *Sir John Harrington*	1589
Welder (electric) *Elisha Thomson*	1877
Wheel *Mesopotamians*	c3500BC
White road markings *Edward Norris Hines*	1911
Wire recorder (mechanical) *Valdemar Poulsen*	1898
Xerox copier *Chester Carlson*	1938
X-ray *Wilhelm Konrad Röntgen*	1895
Zip fastener *Whitcomb L Judson*	1891

FAMOUS PEOPLE

Marriages: By Female Spouse

Diahnne Abbott	Actress	**Robert De Niro**	Actor
Paula Abdul (2)	Singer	**Emilio Estevez**	Actor
Victoria Adams	Spice girl	**David Beckham**	Footballer
Princess Adelaide of Saxe-Coburg Meiningen	German noblewoman	**William IV**	British king
Agrippina	Roman noblewomen	**Claudius**	Roman emperor
Pauline de Ahna	Soprano	**Richard Strauss**	Composer
Anouk Aimée (2)	Actress	**Albert Finney (5)**	Actor
Aisha	Muhammad's favourite wife	**Muhammad**	Founder of Islam
Maria Aitken	Actress	**Nigel Davenport**	Actor
Nadiya Aja (2)	Saudi tycoon's daughter	**Omar Sharif**	Actor and bridge player
Kitty Aldridge	Actress	**Mark Knopfler**	Musician
Princess Alexandra of Schlesung-Holstein-Sorderburg	Danish princess	**Edward VII**	British king

Princess Alexandra	British princess	Angus Ogilvy	Businessman
Alison Allen	TV producer	Keith Allen	Actor
Catherine Allen	Secretary	Frankie Dettori	Jockey
Gracie Allen	Comedienne	George Burns	Comedian and actor
Lorraine Allen (2)	Singer	Xavier Cugat	Band leader
June Allyson (2)	Actress	Dick Powell	Actor
Amphitrite	Greek mythical sea nymph	Poseidon	Greek God of the Sea
Debra Anderson (1)	Childhood sweetheart	Sean Bean	Actor
Loni Anderson (2)	Actress	Burt Reynolds (3)	Actor
Pamela Anderson (3)	Actress	Tommy Lee	Singer
Nina Andreevskaya	Moscow socialite	Wassily Kandinsky	Russian artist
Ursula Andress (1)	Actress	John Derek	Actor and director
Julie Andrews	Actress/singer	Blake Edwards (2)	Film director
Marie Angel	Australian soprano	David Freeman	Opera director
Princess Anne	British princess	Mark Phillips (1)	Equestrian rider
		Tim Laurence (2)	Naval Officer
Princess Anne	Danish princess	James I	British king
Anne of Bohemia (1)	Emperor Charles IV's daughter	Richard II	English king
Queen Anne	British queen	George of Denmark	Danish Prince
Marie Antoinette	French princess	Louis XVI	King of France
Aphrodite	Greek goddess of Love	Hephaestus	Greek god of fire
Frances Appleton	Socialite	Henry W Longfellow	US poet
Ariadne	Mythical daughter of King Minos of Crete	Dionysus	Greek god of wine
Jean Armour	Socialite	Robert Burns	Poet
Patricia Arquette	Actress	Nicholas Cage	Actor
Debbie Ash (1)	Actress	Eddie Kidd	Stunt motorcyclist
Leslie Ash	Actress	Lee Chapman	Footballer
Jane Asher	Cook	Gerald Scarfe	Cartoonist
Edwina Ashley	Heiress and charity worker	Louis Mountbatten	Naval commander
Elizabeth Ashley	Actress	James Farentino (1)	Actor
		George Peppard (2)	Actor
Atalanta	Mythical Greek huntress	Milanion	Mythical Greek athlete
Rosalind Ayres	Actress	Martin Jarvis	Actor
Lauren Bacall	Actress	Humphrey Bogart (1)	Actor
		Jason Robards (2)	Actor
Barbara Bach (2)	Actress	Ringo Starr	Musician
Maria Barbara Bach (1)	Cousin of JS Bach	JS Bach	Composer
Enid Bagnold	Author	Sir G Roderick Jones	MD of Reuters
Lilian Bailey	American soprano	George Henschel	Baritone
Barbara Bain	Actress	Martin Landau	Actor
Shakira Baksh (2)	Actress and model	Sir Michael Caine	Actor
Jill Balchin	Actress	Cecil Day-Lewis	Poet
Caroline Balestier	Publishing heiress	Rudyard Kipling	Novelist and poet
Lucille Ball	Comedienne and actress	Desi Arnaz	Musician and actor
Zoe Ball	TV presenter	Norman Cook	Musician
Rose Bampton	Soprano	Wilfred Pelletier	Conductor
Anne Bancroft	Actress	Mel Brooks	Actor/producer
Glynis Barber	Actress	Michael Brandon (2)	Actor
Emma Bardac (2)	Socialite	Claude Debussy	Composer
Brigitte Bardot (1)	Actress	Roger Vadim	Film director
Margherita Barezzi (1)	Daughter of Verdi's sponsor	Giuseppe Verdi	Composer
Ellen Barkin	Actress	Gabriel Byrne	Actor
Nora Barnacle	Socialite	James Joyce	Irish writer
Pinkie Barnes	Table tennis international	Sam Kydd	Actor
Roseanne Barr	Actress	Tom Arnold (2)	Actor
	Actress	Ben Thomas (3)	Actor
Elizabeth Barrett	Poet	Robert Browning	Poet
Kim Basinger	Actress	Alec Baldwin (2)	Actor
Elizabeth Batts	Captain's wife	James Cook	Seaman and explorer
Stephanie Beacham	Actress	John McEnery	Actor
Priscilla Beaulieu	Actress	Elvis Presley	Singer
Mary Hayley Bell	Playwright	John Mills	Actor
Annette Bening	Actress	Warren Beatty	Actor
Jill Bennett	Actress	John Osborne (1)	Playwright
		Willis Hall (2)	
Veronica Bennett	Singer	Phil Spector	Record producer
Berengaria	Princess of Navarre	Richard 1	English king
Candice Bergen (3)	Actress	Louis Malle	Director
Ingrid Bergman (2)	Actress	Roberto Rossellini (2)	Director
Joy Beverley	Singer	Billy Wright	Footballer

Female spouse		Male spouse	
Anne Birley (3)	Lady Annabel Vane-Tempest Stewart	*James Goldsmith*	Tycoon
Blanche of Lancaster (1)	English noblewoman	*John of Gaunt*	English prince
Renate Blauel	Actress	*Elton John*	Vocalist and composer
Joan Blondell	Actress	*Dick Powell (1)*	Actor
		Mike Todd (2)	Showman and film producer
Claire Bloom	Actress	*Rod Steiger (1)*	Actor
		Philip Roth (3)	Novelist
Maureen Blott (2)	Actress	*Harry H. Corbett*	Actor
Jean Boht	Actress	*Carl Davis*	Composer
Cherie Booth	Barrister	*Tony Blair*	Politician
Connie Booth	Actress	*John Cleese*	Actor
Catherine Boucher	Illiterate pauper	*William Blake*	Poet and painter
Boudicca	Queen of Iceni	*Prasutagus*	King of Iceni
Margaret Bourke-White	Photo-journalist	*Erskine Caldwell*	US author
Jacqueline Bouvier	Socialite	*John F Kennedy (1)*	US president
Elizabeth Bowen	Irish novelist	*Alan Charles Cameron*	Businessman
Marjory Bowes (1)	John Knox's 1st wife	*John Knox*	Religious reformer
Patti Boyd	Model	*George Harrison (1)*	Musician
		Eric Clapton (2)	Musician
Elizabeth Boyle	Socialite	*Edmund Spenser*	English poet
Philippa Braithewaite (2)	TV Producer	*Martin Clunes*	Actor
Sarah Brightman (2)	Singer	*Andrew Lloyd Webber (2)*	Composer
Cosima Von Bülow	Franz Liszt's daughter	*Hans von Bülow (1)*	Conductor
Christie Brinkley (2)	Model	*Billy Joel (2)*	Singer
May Britt	Actress	*Sammy Davis Jnr*	Entertainer
Vera May Brittain	Writer	*George Catlin*	Professor of politics
Charlotte Brontë	Writer	*Arthur Bell Nicholls*	Curate
Janet Brown	Impressionist	*Peter Butterworth*	Actor
Melanie Brown	Spice girl	*Jimmy Gulzar*	Musician
Coral Browne	Actress	*Vincent Price*	Actor
Jill Browne	Actress	*John Alderton (1)*	Actor
		Brian Wolfe (2)	Theatre producer
Anna Brueghel	Daughter of Jan Brueghel	*David Teniers the Younger*	Flemish painter
Sheila Buckley	Secretary	*John Stonehouse*	Politician
Cosima von Bülow (2)	Franz Liszt's daughter	*Richard Wagner*	Composer
Fanny Burney	English novelist	*General D'Arblay*	French émigré
Margaret Burr	Daughter of 4th Duke of Beaufort	*Thomas Gainsborough*	English painter
Irene Busch	Musician	*Rudolf Serkin*	Pianist
Penny Calvert	Dancer	*Bruce Forsyth (1)*	Entertainer
		Peter Murray Hill (2)	Actor and bookseller
Dyan Cannon (4)	Actress	*Cary Grant*	Actor
Sarah Caplin	TV executive	*Nick Ross*	Broadcaster
Kate Capshaw (2)	Actress	*Steven Spielberg (2)*	Director
Mariah Carey	Singer	*Tommy Mottola*	President of Sony Music
Judy Carne	Actress	*Burt Reynolds*	Actor
Caroline of Ansbach	German noblewoman	*George II*	British king
Caroline of Brunswick	German noblewoman	*George IV*	British king
Caroline of Monaco	Princess	*Pierre Junot (1)*	Businessman
		Stefano Casiraghi (2)	Businessman
		Prince Ernst August (3)	Hanoverian Prince
Leslie Caron	Actress	*Peter Hall*	Theatre director
Theresa Carreño (1)	Pianist	*Eugène D'Albert*	Composer and pianist
June Carter	Singer	*Johnny Cash*	Singer
Martita Casals	Pablo Casals' widow	*Eugene Istomin*	Pianist
Carmen Castillo (1)	Singer	*Xavier Cugat*	Bandleader
Phoebe Cates	Actress	*Kevin Kline*	Actor
Princess Catherine	Valois princess	*Owen Tudor (1)*	Grandfather of Henry V11
Catherine I	Russian empress	*Peter the Great (2)*	Russian Tsar
Catherine II (the Great)	Russian empress	*Peter III*	Russian Tsar
Catherine de-Medici	Queen of France	*Henry II*	French king
Catherine of Braganza	Portuguese princess	*Charles II*	English king
Catherine of Valois	French princess	*Henry V (2)*	English king
Anna Cermakova	Socialite	*Antonin Dvorák*	Composer
Alice Charigot	Socialite	*Pierre-Auguste Renoir*	French painter
Charlotte Sophia	German noblewoman	*George III*	British king
Charlotte Charpentier	Daughter of French émigré	*Walter Scott*	Scottish novelist
Cher	Actress/Singer	*Sonny Bono (1)*	Actor and politician
		Greg Allmann (2)	Musician
Helen Cherry	Actress	*Trevor Howard*	Actor

Name	Role	Partner	Partner's Role
Chiang Ching (3)	Actress	*Mao Zedong Tse Tsung*	*Chinese leader*
Agatha Christie	Writer	*Max Mallowan*	*Archaeologist*
Diane Cilento (1)	Actress	*Sean Connery*	*Actor*
Cleopatra VII	Queen of Egypt	*Ptolemy XIII (1)*	*Egyptian Ruler*
		Mark Antony (2) ?	*Roman General*
Rosemary Clooney	Singer	*José Ferrer*	*Actor*
Clotilda	Queen of the Franks	*Clovis I*	*King of the Franks*
Clytemnestra	Mythical Queen of Mycenae	*Agamemnon*	*Mythical King of Mycenae*
Isabella Colbran (1)	Spanish soprano	*Gioacchino Rossini*	*Composer*
Venetia Collett-Barrett (1)	Actress	*Edward Woodward*	*Actor*
Joan Collins (1)	Actress	*Anthony Newley (1)*	*Actor and singer*
Pauline Collins (2)	Actress	*John Alderton*	*Actor*
Jane Colt (1)	Farmer's daughter	*Thomas More*	*Chancellor of England*
Shirley Conran	Authoress	*Terence Conran*	*Businessman*
Constance of Castile (2)	Castilian princess	*John of Gaunt*	*English prince*
Sarah Cook	Schoolgirl (13 when married)	*Musa Komeagac*	*Turkish waiter*
Rita Coolidge (2)	Singer	*Kris Kristofferson*	*Actor*
Dolores Costello	Actress	*John Barrymore*	*Actor*
Cicely Courtneidge	Actress	*Jack Hulbert*	*Actor*
Maureen Cox (1)	Childhood sweetheart	*Ringo Starr*	*Musician*
Charlotte Mary Craddock (1)	Socialite	*Henry Fielding*	*English novelist*
Jill Craigie	TV scriptwriter and author	*Michael Foot*	*Politician*
Gemma Craven (1)	Actress	*Frazer Hines*	*Actor*
Cindy Crawford	Supermodel	*Richard Gere*	*Actor*
Joan Crawford	Actress	*Douglas Fairbanks Jnr (2)*	*Actor*
Creusa	Mythical Roman character	*Aeneas*	*Mythical Trojan prince*
Christina	Spanish Infanta	*Inaki Vrdangarin*	*Handball player*
Abigail Cruttenden (3)	Actress	*Sean Bean*	*Actor*
Cynthia Curzon (1)	English noblewoman	*Oswald Mosley*	*Politician*
Sinead Cusack	Actress	*Jeremy Irons*	*Actor*
Martha Custis	Socialite	*George Washington*	*President of USA*
Sasha Czack (1)	Theatre usher	*Sylvester Stallone*	*Actor*
Bebe Daniels	Radio comedienne	*Ben Lyon*	*Radio comedian*
Mary Daniel (2)	Maid	*Henry Fielding*	*English novelist*
Lili Damita (1)	Socialite	*Errol Flynn*	*Actor*
Joy Davidman	Poet	*CS Lewis*	*Author*
Geena Davis	Actress	*Renny Harlin (1)*	*Film director*
		Jeff Goldblum (2)	*Actor*
Nancy Davis (2)	Actress	*Ronald Reagan*	*US president*
Sharron Davis	Swimmer	*Derek Redmond*	*Athlete*
Isabel Dean	Actress	*William Fairchild*	*Playwright*
Sandra Dee	Actress	*Bobby Darin*	*Singer*
Judi Dench	Actress	*Michael Williams*	*Actor*
Catherine Deneuve (2)	Actress	*David Bailey*	*Photographer*
Bo Derek (3)	Actress	*John Derek*	*Actor and director*
Donna D'Errico	'Baywatch' actress	*Nikki Sixx*	*Motley Crue guitarist*
Félicité Desmousseaux	Actress	*César Franck*	*Composer*
Colleen Dewhurst	Socialite	*George C Scott*	*Actor*
Angie Dickinson (2)	Actress	*Burt Bacharach (2)*	*Composer*
Sandra Dickinson	Actress	*Peter Davidson*	*Actor*
Marlene Dietrich	Actress	*Rudolf Seiber (1)*	*Production assistant*
Kitty Dobbs	Niece of Beatrice Webb	*Malcolm Muggeridge*	*Journalist*
Hilda Doolittle	US Poet	*Richard Aldington*	*Poet and novelist*
Diana Dors	Actress	*Alan Lake (3)*	*Actor*
		Dickie Dawson (2)	*US comedian*
Michele Dotrice (2)	Actress	*Edward Woodward*	*Actor*
Angela Douglas	Irish actress	*Kenneth More*	*Actor*
Lesley-Anne Down (2)	Actress	*William Friedkin (1)*	*Film director*
Margaret Drabble	Novelist	*Clive Swift (1)*	*Author*
		Michael Holroyd (2)	*Biographer*
Isadora Duncan (1)	Dancer	*Sergei Yessenin*	*Poet*
Jacqueline Du Pré	Cellist	*Daniel Barenboim*	*Pianist*
Otilie Dvorák	Daughter of Antonin Dvorák	*Josef Suk*	*Violinist*
Linda Eastman	Photographer	*Paul McCartney (2)*	*Musician*
Nora Eddington (3)	Actress	*Errol Flynn*	*Actor*
Martha Eggerth	Soprano	*Jan Kiepura*	*Tenor*
Britt Ekland	Actress	*Peter Sellers (1)*	*Actor*
		Slim Jim Phantom McDonnell (2)	*Musician*

Anita Ekberg	Actress	*Anthony Steele*	*Actor*
		Peter Sellers	*Actor*
Eleanor of Aquitaine	French noblewoman	*Louis VII (1)*	*French king*
		Henry II	*English king*
Eleanor of Castile	Castilian princess	*Edward I*	*English king*
Eleanor of Provence	French noblewoman	*Henry III*	*English king*
George Eliot	Authoress	*John Walter Cross*	*Banker*
Elizabeth Bowes-Lyon	Earl of Strathmore's daughter	*George VI*	*British king*
Elizabeth of York	English princess	*Henry VII*	*English King*
Elizabeth Woodville	English noblewoman	*Edward IV*	*English King*
Jill Esmond (1)	Actress	*Laurence Olivier*	*Actor*
Eudoxia	Russian noblewoman	*Peter the Great (1)*	*Russian Tsar*
Dale Evans	Actress and singer	*Roy Rogers*	*Actor and singer*
Linda Evans (2)	Actress	*John Derek*	*Actor and director*
Chris Evert	Tennis player	*John Lloyd (1)*	*Tennis player*
Siobhan Fahey	Singer	*Dave Stewart*	*Musician*
Mia Farrow	Actress	*Frank Sinatra (1)*	*Singer*
		André Previn (2)	*Conductor*
Farrah Fawcett (2)	Actress	*Lee Majors (1)*	*Actor*
		Ryan O'Neal (2)	*Actor*
Gracie Fields	Singer	*Monty Banks*	*Film director*
Judy Finnegan	TV Presenter	*Richard Madeley*	*TV presenter*
Carina Fitzalan-Howard (2)	Noble woman	*David Frost*	*Broadcaster*
Carrie Fisher (2)	Actress	*Paul Simon*	*Singer and composer*
Jennifer Flavin (3)	Model	*Sylvester Stallone*	*Actor*
Jane Fonda (2)	Actress	*Roger Vadim*	*Film Director*
Anna Ford	Broadcaster	*Mark Boxer*	*Cartoonist and journalist*
Margaret Forster	Author	*Hunter Davies*	*Author*
Helen Frankenthaler	US artist	*Robert Motherwell*	*US Artist*
Lady Antonia Fraser (2)	Authoress	*Harold Pinter*	*Playwright*
Lynne Frederick	Actress	*Peter Sellers (1)*	*Actor*
		David Frost (2)	*Broadcaster*
Dido Freire (2)	Brazilian film-maker's daughter	*Jean Renoir*	*Film director*
Dawn French	Comedienne	*Lenny Henry*	*Comedian*
Agnes Frey	Merchant's daughter	*Albrecht Dürer*	*German painter*
Edith Fricker	Socialite	*Robert Southey*	*Poet*
Sarah Fricker	Socialite	*Samuel Taylor Coleridge*	*Poet*
Fiona Fullerton (1)	Actress	*Simon MacCorkindale*	*Actor*
Zsa Zsa Gabor	Actress	*Conrad Hilton (2)*	*Businessman*
Magda Gabor (4)	Actress	*George Sanders*	*Actor*
Myte Garcia	Belly dancer	*Prince (Symbol)*	*Singer*
Ava Gardner (2)	Actress	*Mickey Rooney (1)*	*Actor*
		Artie Shaw (2)	*Bandleader*
		Frank Sinatra (3)	*Singer*
Judy Garland	Actress	*Vincente Minnelli (2)*	*Film director*
		Sid Luft (3)	*Entertainer*
Jill Gascoigne (1)	Actress	*Alfred Molina (2)*	*Actor*
Elvira Gemignani	Socialite	*Giacomo Puccini*	*Composer*
Susan George (2)	Actress	*Simon MacCorkindale*	*Actor*
Robin Givens (1)	Actress	*Mike Tyson (2)*	*Boxer*
Alma Gluck	Soprano	*Efrem Zimbalist*	*Violinist*
Liza Goddard	Actress	*Colin Baker (1)*	*Actor*
		Alvin Stardust (3)	*Pop singer*
Paulette Goddard (3)	Actress	*Charlie Chaplin (2)*	*Actor*
		Burgess Meredith (3)	*Actor*
		Erich Maria Remarque (4)	*Author*
Lady Godiva	Countess of Mercia	*Leofric*	*Earl of Mercia*
Beatrix Godwin	Widow of EW Godwin (architect)	*James McNeill Whistler*	*Artist*
Mary Godwin	Writer	*Percy Bysshe Shelley*	*Poet*
Jane Goldman	Writer	*Jonathan Ross*	*TV presenter*
Stephanie Goldner	Harpist	*Eugene Ormandy*	*Conductor*
Jemima Goldsmith	Heiress	*Imran Khan*	*Cricketer*
Betty Grable	Actress	*Jackie Coogan (1)*	*Actor*
		Harry James (2)	*Musician*
Dulcie Gray	Actress	*Michael Denison*	*Actor*
Effie Gray	Artist	*John Ruskin (1)*	*Art Critic*
		John Everett Millais (2)	*Artist*
Elspet Gray	Actress	*Brian Rix*	*Actor*
Alex Greaves	Jockey	*David Nicholls*	*Horseracing trainer*

Sarah Greene	TV presenter	Mike Smith	TV presenter
Debbie Greenwood	TV presenter (former Miss UK)	Paul Coia	TV presenter
Lady Jane Grey	English noblewoman	Lord Guildford Dudley	English nobleman
Lita Grey (2)	Actress	Charlie Chaplin	Actor
Melanie Griffith	Actress	Don Johnson (1) + (3)	Actor
		Antonio Banderas (4)	Actor
Tammie Grimes	Actress	Christopher Plummer	Actor
Diana Guinness (2)	Nancy Mitford's sister	Oswald Mosley	Politician
Nina Hagerup	Singer (Grieg's Cousin)	Edvard Grieg	Composer
Geneviève Halévy	Composer's daughter	Georges Bizet	Composer
Faten Hamama (1)	Actress	Omar Sharif	Actor and bridge player
Alana Hamilton (1)	Model	Rod Stewart (2)	Singer
Sheila Hancock	Actress	John Thaw (2)	Actor
Sue Hanson	Actress	Carl Wayne	Actor and Singer
Harriet Harman	British politician	Jack Dromey	Trade unionist
Harmonia	Mythical daughter of Ares and Aphrodite	Cadmus	Mythical founder of Thebes
Mildred Harris (1)	Actress	Charlie Chaplin	Actor
Deborah Harry	Singer	Chris Stein	Guitarist
Teri Hatcher	Actress	Jon Tenney	Actor
Ann Hathaway	Farmer's daughter	William Shakespeare	Playwright
June Haver	Actress	Fred MacMurray	Actor
Jacquetta Hawkes	Archaeologist	JB Priestley	Author
Goldie Hawn	Actress	Kurt Russell	Actor
Anne Hayes (1)	Housewife	Peter Sellers	Actor
Rita Hayworth	Actress	Orson Welles (2)	Actor and director
		Aly Khan (3)	Middle Eastern prince
Patty Hearst	Heiress	Bernard Shaw	Bodyguard
Lillian Hellman	Playwright	Dashiell Hammett	Author
Heloise	Abelard's wife	Peter Abelard	French philosopher
Marie Helvin (3)	Model	David Bailey	Photographer
Anouska Hempel	Actress	Mark Weinberg	Businessman
Henrietta Maria	French princess	Charles I	British king
Audrey Hepburn	Actress	Mel Ferrer	Actor
Barbara Hepworth	Sculptor	John Skeaping (1)	Sculptor
		Ben Nicholson (2)	Artist
Hera (3)	Sister of Zeus	Zeus	Greek supreme god
Lady Herries	Racehorse trainer	Colin Cowdrey	Cricketer
Irene Hervey	Actress	Allan Jones	Singer and actor
Eva Herzigova	Model	Tico Torres	Pop musician (Bon Jovi)
Andrée Heurschling (1)	Artist's model	Jean Renoir	Film director
Hildegarde	Queen of the Franks	Charlemagne	King of the Franks
Melanie Hill (2)	Actress ('Bread')	Sean Bean	Actor
Tracy Hilton	Housewife	Jim Davidson	Comedian
Gill Hinchcliffe	TV Production assistant	David Jason	Actor
Liz Hobbs (2)	Waterskier	Frazer Hines	Actor
Valerie Hobson	Actress and dancer	John Profumo (2)	Politician
Chaatal Hochuli (1)	Swiss Heiress	Ernst August	Prince of Hanover
Catherine Hogarth	Newspaper magnate's daughter	Charles Dickens	Author
Alison Holloway	Presenter	Jim Davidson	Comedian
Lauren Holly	Actress	Jim Carrey	Actor
Marilyn Horne	Mezzo-soprano	Henry Lewis	Conductor
Whitney Houston	Singer	Bobby Brown	Singer
Elizabeth Jane Howard	Novelist	Kingsley Amis	Novelist and poet
Clementine Hozier	Charity worker	Winston Churchill	Politician
Mabel Hubbard	Deaf student	Alexander Graham Bell	Inventor
Benita Hume	Actress	Ronald Culman (1)	Actor
		George Sanders (2)	Actor
Kirsty Hume	Model	Donovan Leitch	Actor
Gayle Hunnicut	Actress	David Hemmings	Actor
Rachel Hunter (2)	Model	Rod Stewart	Singer
Anjelica Huston	Actress and director	Robert Graham	Sculptor
Mary Hutchinson	Socialite	William Wordsworth	Poet
Barbara Hutton (2)	Actress	Cary Grant	Actor
Judy Huxtable (2)	Actress	Peter Cook	Comedian and writer
Anne Hyde (1)	Daughter of Earl of Clarendon	James II	English King
Georgie Hyde-Lees	Socialite	WB Yeats	Poet
Ildico	Consort of Attila	Attila the Hun	Hunnish ruler
Iman	Model	David Bowie (2)	Singer/composer

Jill Ireland	Actress	*David McCallum (1)*	*Actor*
		Charles Bronson (2)	*Actor*
Isabella	Daughter of Philip IV of France		
		Edward II	*English king*
Isabella of Angoulême (2)	French noblewoman	*John*	*King of England*
Isabelle (2)	Daughter of Charles VI of France		
		Richard II	*English king*
Hattie Jacques	Actress	*John Le Mesurier*	*Actor*
Susan Jameson	Actress	*James Bolam*	*Actor*
Samantha Janus	Actress	*Mauro Mantovani*	*Actor*
Aino Järnefelt	General's daughter	*Jean Sibelius*	*Composer*
Cécile Jeanrenaud	Clergyman's daughter	*Felix Mendelssohn*	*Composer*
Ffion Jenkins	Ex-civil servant	*William Hague*	*Politician*
Jenny Jerome	Daughter of NY businessman	*Lord Randolph Churchill*	*Politician*
Jezebel	Queen of Israel	*Ahab*	*King of Israel*
Amy Johnson	Aviator	*Jim Mollison*	*Aviator*
Jennifer Jones	Actress	*Robert Walker (1)*	*Actor*
		David O'Selznick (2)	*Director*
Joséphine de Beauharnais	French noblewoman	*Napoleon I*	*French emperor*
Yootha Joyce	Actress	*Glyn Edwards*	*Actor*
Angelica Kauffmann	Swiss painter	*Antonio Zucchi*	*Venetian painter*
Ruby Keeler	Actress	*Al Jolson*	*Entertainer*
Maria Anna Keller	Hairdresser's daughter	*Franz Joseph Haydn*	*Composer*
Barbara Kelly	Actress and presenter	*Bernard Braden*	*Actor and presenter*
Margaret Kempson (1)	Housewife	*Denis Thatcher*	*Businessman*
Rachel Kempson	Actress	*Michael Redgrave*	*Actor*
Kay Kendall (3)	Actress	*Rex Harrison*	*Actor*
Suzy Kendall (1)	Actress	*Dudley Moore*	*Entertainer*
Cherly Kennedy	Actress	*Tom Courtenay*	*Actor*
Jacqueline Kennedy	Socialite	*Aristotle Onassis (2)*	*Businessman*
Patsy Kensit	Actress	*Jim Kerr (2)*	*Musician*
		Liam Gallagher (3)	*Pop musician*
Nicole Kidman (2)	Actress	*Tom Cruise*	*Actor*
Carole King	Singer/composer	*Gerry Goffin*	*Composer*
Henrietta Knight	Racehorse trainer	*Terry Biddlecombe*	*Jockey*
Vivienne Knight (3)	Scriptwriter	*Patrick Campbell*	*Irish writer and wit*
Gertrud Kolisch (2)	Musician	*Arnold Schoenberg*	*Composer*
Cleo Laine	Jazz singer	*John Dankworth (2)*	*Jazz musician*
Elsa Lanchester	Actress	*Charles Laughton*	*Actor*
Abbe Lane (3)	Singer	*Xavier Cugat*	*Bandleader*
Brogan Lane (3)	Actress	*Dudley Moore*	*Entertainer*
Horg Lanse	Actress	*Alan J Pakula (2)*	*Director*
Louise Lasser (2)	Actress	*Woody Allen*	*Actor/director*
Sue Lawley	Broadcaster	*Hugh Williams*	*TV magnate*
Evelyn Lear	Soprano	*Thomas Stewart*	*Baritone*
Kelly Le Brock	Actress	*Steven Seagal (2)*	*Actor*
Michelle Lee (2)	Actress and singer	*James Farentino*	*Actor*
Jane Leeves	Actress	*Marshall Coben*	*US television executive*
Margaret Leighton	Actress	*Laurence Harvey (2)*	*Actor*
		Michael Wilding (3)	*Actor*
Janet Leigh	Actress	*Tony Curtis (3)*	*Actor*
Vivien Leigh (2)	Actress	*Laurence Olivier (2)*	*Actor*
Rula Lenska (3)	Actress	*Dennis Waterman (2)*	*Actor*
Lotte Lenya	Actress/singer	*Kurt Weill (1)*	*Composer*
Kay Lenz	Actress	*David Cassidy*	*singer*
Tea Leoni	Actress	*David Duchovny (2)*	*Actor*
Lyubov Leonidovna (2)	Russian ballerina	*Marius Petipa*	*French choreographer*
Ginette Lery (2)	Secretary	*JamesGoldsmith*	*Tycoon*
Astriel Lindstrom (2)	Model	*Bill Wyman*	*Musician*
Muriel Ling (1)	Model	*Harold Robbins*	*Writer*
Elizabeth Linley	Composer's daughter	*Richard Brinsley Sheridan*	*Irish dramatist*
Maureen Lipman	Actress	*Jack Rosenthal*	*Playwright*
Constance Lloyd	Socialite	*Oscar Wilde*	*Playwright/novelist*
Sue Lloyd	Actress	*Ronald Allen*	*Actor*
Lina Llubera	Spanish singer	*Sergei Prokofiev*	*Composer*
Heather Locklear (2)	Actress	*Tommy Lee*	*Singer*
Victoria Lockwood	Model	*Earl Charles Spencer*	*English nobleman*
Carole Lombard (1)	Actress	*William Powell (1)*	*Actor*
		Clark Gable (2)	*Actor*

FAMOUS PEOPLE

Name	Role	Name	Role
Claudine Longet	Actress	*Andy Williams*	*Singer*
Anita Lonsborough	Swimmer	*Hugh Porter*	*Cyclist*
Lydia Lopokova	Ballerina	*John Maynard Keynes*	*Economist*
Sophia Loren	Actress	*Carlo Ponti*	*Film producer*
Courtney Love	Actress/singer	*Kurt Cobain (2)*	*Musician (Nirvana)*
Sarah Lowndes	Poet	*Bob Dylan*	*Musician*
Lorna Luft	Singer	*Colin Freeman*	*Musical director*
Linda Lusardi	Actress and model	*Sam Kane*	*Actor*
Emma Lyon	Blacksmith's daughter	*William Hamilton*	*Scottish diplomat*
Lulu	Singer	*Maurice Gibb*	*Singer*
Carol McGiffin	Radio DJ	*Chris Evans*	*Television presenter*
Cathy McGowan	Broadcaster	*Hywel Bennett*	*Actor*
Ali McGraw	Actress	*Steve McQueen (2)*	*Actor*
Heather McIntyre	Actress and playwright	*William Hartnell*	*Actor*
Virginia McKenna	Actress	*Denholm Elliott (1)*	*Actor*
		Bill Travers (2)	*Actor*
Alison McNair	Doctor's daughter	*Donald Dewar (1)*	*British politician*
		Alexander AM Irvine (2)	*Lord Chancellor*
Kitty McShane	Music-hall artist	*Arthur Lucan*	*Music-hall artist*
Madonna	Singer and actress	*Sean Penn (1)*	*Actor*
		Guy Ritchie (2)	*Film director*
Justine Mahler	Sister of Gustav Mahler	*Arnold Rosé*	*Austrian violinist*
Madame de Maintenon	Louis X1V's 2nd wife	*Louis XIV*	*King of France*
Maria Malibran	Contralto	*Charles de Bériot*	*Violinist and composer*
Erika Mann	Writer	*WH Auden*	*Poet and essayist*
Jayne Mansfield	Actress	*Mickey Hargitay*	*Body-builder*
Katherine Mansfield	NZ writer	*George Bowden (1)*	*Businessman*
		John Middleton Murry	*Writer and critic*
Leslie Manville (1)	Actress	*Gary Oldman*	*Actor*
Margaret of Anjou	French noblewoman	*Henry VI*	*English king*
Princess Margaret	Elizabeth II's sister	*Anthony Armstrong Jones*	*Photographer*
Maria Theresa	Spanish princess	*Louis XIV*	*King of France*
Marie Louise	Austrian archduchess	*Napoleon I*	*French emperor*
Marsh Jean (1)	Actress	*Jon Pertwee*	*Actor*
Marion Marshall (2)	Actress	*Robert Wagner*	*Actor*
Barbara Marx (4)	Actress	*Frank Sinatra*	*Singer*
Mary II	British queen	*William III*	*British king*
Mary of Guise	French noblewoman	*James V*	*King of Scotland*
Mary of Modena (2)	Italian noblewoman	*James II*	*British king*
Mary of Teck	German noblewoman	*George V*	*British king*
Mary Stewart	Queen of Scots	*Francis II (1)*	*French Dauphin then king*
		Henry Darnley (2)	*English nobleman*
		Earl of Bothwell (3)	*Scottish nobleman*
Anna Massey	Actress	*Jeremy Brett*	*Actor*
Meg Matthews	Record company secretary	*Noel Gallagher*	*Pop musician*
Luisa Mattioli (2)	Housewife	*Roger Moore*	*Actor*
Sharon Maughan	Actress	*Trevor Eve*	*Actor*
Patricia Maynard (2)	Actress	*Dennis Waterman*	*Actor*
Patricia Medina	Actress	*Richard Greene*	*Actor*
Wilnelia Merced (3)	Beauty queen	*Bruce Forsyth*	*Entertainer*
Vivien Merchant (1)	Actress	*Harold Pinter*	*Playwright*
Melina Mercouri	Actress	*Jules Dassin*	*Film director*
Ethel Merman	Singer	*Ernest Borgnine (3)*	*Actor*
Messallina (3)	Roman noblewoman	*Nero*	*Roman emperor*
Jean Metcalfe	Broadcaster	*Cliff Michelmore*	*Broadcaster*
Metis (1)	Greek sea nymph	*Zeus*	*Greek supreme god*
Alice Middleton (2)	Widow of London mercer	*Thomas More*	*Chancellor of England*
Annabella Milbanke	Heiress	*Lord Byron*	*Poet*
Sarah Miles	Actress	*Robert Bolt*	*Playwright*
Antonina Miliukova	Pupil of Tchaikovsky	*Pyotr Tchaikovsky*	*Composer*
Rebecca Miller	Actress (Arthur Miller's daughter)	*Daniel Day-Lewis*	*Actor*
Elizabeth Minshull (3)	Milton's 3rd wife	*John Milton*	*Poet*
Marilyn Monroe	Actress	*Jim Dougherty (1)*	*Policeman*
		Joe Di Maggio (2)	*Baseball player*
		Arthur Miller (3)	*Playwright*
Margaret Montgomerie	Socialite	*James Boswell*	*Biographer*
Elizabeth Montgomery (3)	Actress	*Gig Young*	*Actor*
LM Montgomery	Canadian novelist	*Ewan Macdonald*	*Presbyterian minister*
Fanny Moody	English soprano	*Charles Manners*	*Irish bass and impresario*
Bel Mooney	Writer and broadcaster	*Jonathan Dimbleby*	*Broadcaster*

Female	Description	Male	Description
Demi Moore	Actress	*Bruce Willis*	*Actor*
Jeanne Moreau (1)	Actress	*William Friedkin (3)*	*Film director*
Anne Morrow	Writer	*Charles Lindbergh*	*Aviator*
Angela Mortimer	British Wimbledon champion	*John Barrett*	*Tennis commentator*
Iris Murdoch	Writer	*John Bayley*	*Professor of literature*
Patricia Neal	Actress	*Roald Dahl*	*Writer*
Nefertiti	Egyptian queen	*Akhenaton*	*Egyptian king*
Hildegarde Neil (2)	Actress	*Brian Blessed*	*Actor*
Wendy Neuss	Producer ('Star Trek')	*Patrick Stewart*	*Actor (StarTrek)*
Anne Nevill	English Noblewoman	*Richard III*	*English king*
Nanette Newman	Actress	*Bryan Forbes*	*Actor and director*
Mary Ellen Nicolls (1)	Daughter of Thomas Love Peacock	*George Meredith*	*English novelist*
Sue Nichols	Actress	*Mark Eden*	*Actor*
Brigitte Nielsen (2)	Actress	*Sylvester Stallone*	*Actor*
Frances Nisbet	Doctor's widow	*Horatio Nelson*	*English naval hero*
Catherine Nossenko (1)	Stravinsky's cousin	*Igor Stravinsky*	*Composer*
Kim Novak	Actress	*Richard Johnson (1)*	*Actor*
Jane Nugent	Secretary	*Edmund Burke*	*British statesman*
Merle Oberon (2)	Actress	*Alexander Korda*	*Film director*
Octavia (1)	Roman noblewoman	*Nero*	*Roman emperor*
Octavia (1)	Emperor Augustus' sister	*Marc Antony*	*Roman General*
Georgia O'Keefe	US painter	*Alfred Stieglitz*	*US photographer*
Tamsin Olivier	Pub owner	*Simon Dutton*	*Actor*
Julia Trevelyan Oman	Designer	*Roy Strong*	*Writer and historian*
Tatum O'Neal	Actress	*John McEnroe*	*Tennis player*
Oona O'Neill (4)	Playwright's daughter	*Charlie Chaplin*	*Actor*
Yoko Ono (2)	Artist	*John Lennon (2)*	*Musician*
Dorothy Osborne	Daughter of governor of Guernsey	*William Temple*	*Diplomat and essayist*
Fanny Osbourne	Actress	*Robert Louis Stevenson*	*Author*
Ann Packer	Athlete	*Robbie Brightwell*	*Athlete*
Grace Palermo (5)	Socialite	*Harold Robbins*	*Writer*
Lilli Palmer (2)	Actress	*Rex Harrison (1)*	*Actor*
Pandora	First woman of Greek myth	*Epimetheus*	*Titan*
Euphrosyne Parepa	Soprano	*Karl Rosa*	*German conductor*
Mary Parker	Actress	*Harold French*	*Actor and theatre director*
Isabel Patiño (1)	Bolivian tin magnate's daughter	*James Goldsmith*	*Tycoon*
Charlotte Payne-Townshend	Heiress	*George Bernard Shaw*	*Dramatist*
Rhea Pearlman	Actress	*Danny De Vito*	*Actor*
Olympie Pélissier (2)	Parisian hostess	*Gioacchino Rossini*	*Composer*
Penelope	Daughter of King Icarius of Sparta	*Odysseus*	*Mythical king of Ithaca*
Christine Perfect	Singer	*John McVie*	*Musician*
Jean Peters	Actress	*Howard Hughes*	*Businessman*
Sandy Pflueger (2)	Equestrian rider	*Mark Phillips*	*Equestrian rider*
Maggie Philbin	TV presenter	*Keith Chegwin*	*TV presenter*
Philippa Hainault	Dutch noblewoman	*Edward III*	*English king*
Fiona Phillips	GMTV presenter	*Martin Frizell*	*GMTV presenter*
Siân Phillips	Actress	*Peter O'Toole (2)*	*Actor*
Pat Phoenix (2)	Actress	*Anthony Booth (3)*	*Actor*
Paloma Picasso	Beautician and businesswoman	*Rafael Lopez-Cambil*	*Argentinian playwright*
Evelyn Pickering	Pre-Raphaelite artist	*William Frend De Morgan*	*Pre-Raphaelite artist*
Mary Pickford (2)	Actress	*Douglas Fairbanks Snr*	*Actor*
Billie Piper	Pop singer	*Chris Evans*	*Disc Jockey*
Valerie Pitts	TV presenter	*Georg Solti*	*Conductor*
Minna Planer (1)	Opera singer and actress	*Richard Wagner (1)*	*Composer*
Sylvia Plath	Poet	*Ted Hughes*	*Poet*
Joan Plowright (3)	Actress	*Laurence Olivier*	*Actor*
Pocahontas	Princess	*John Rolfe*	*English colonist*
Lily Pons	Soprano	*André Kostelanetz*	*Conductor*
Poppaea (2)	Roman noblewoman	*Nero*	*Roman emperor*
Elizabeth Porter	Schoolteacher	*Samuel Johnson*	*Writer and lexicographer*
Beatrix Potter	Author and illustrator	*William Heelis*	*Solicitor*
Eleanor Powell (3)	Actress	*Glenn Ford*	*Actor*
Mary Powell (1)	Royalist sympathiser	*John Milton*	*Poet*
Stefanie Powers	Actress	*Gary Lockwood*	*Actor*

FAMOUS PEOPLE

Lisa Presley (1)	Actress	*Michael Jackson*	*Entertainer*
Kelly Preston	Actress	*John Travolta*	*Actor*
Soon-Yi Previn (3)	Personal assistant	*Woody Allen*	*Actor/director*
Libby Purves	Broadcaster	*Paul Heiney*	*Broadcaster*
Pyrrha	Daughter of Epimetheus and Pandora	*Deucalion*	*Son of Prometheus*
Miranda Quarry (3)	Actress	*Peter Sellers*	*Actor*
Gilda Radner	Psychotherapist	*Gene Wilder*	*Actor*
Anna Raeburn	Agony Aunt	*Nick Lilley*	*Businessman*
Charlotte Rampling	Actress	*Jean-Michel Jarre*	*Musician*
Esther Rantzen	Broadcaster	*Desmond Wilcox*	*Producer*
Anthea Redfern (2)	Presenter	*Bruce Forsyth*	*Entertainer*
Vanessa Redgrave	Actress	*Franco Nero (1)*	*Actor*
		Tony Richardson (2)	*Film producer*
Alma Reville	Actress	*Alfred Hitchcock*	*Film director*
Debbie Reynolds (2)	Actress	*Eddie Fisher*	*Singer*
Ingeborg Rhosea (2)	Novelist	*Jon Pertwee*	*Actor*
Anneka Rice	TV Presenter	*Nick Allott*	*Theatre producer*
Frieda von Richthofen	Socialite	*DH Lawrence*	*Writer*
Rachel Robards	Colonel's daughter	*Andrew Jackson*	*US president*
Amy Robbins	Student	*HG Wells*	*Author*
Margaret Roberts (2)	Politician	*Dennis Thatcher*	*Businessman*
Rachel Roberts (4)	Actress	*Rex Harrison*	*Actor*
Amy Robsart	Socialite	*Robert Dudley*	*Earl of Leicester*
Julie Rogers	Singer	*Michael Black*	*Theatrical agent*
Mimi Rogers (1)	Actress	*Tom Cruise*	*Actor*
Wenda Rogerson	Fashion model	*Norman Parkinson*	*Photographer*
Primula Rollo	Cipher clerk	*David Niven*	*Actor*
Micheline Roquebrune (2)	Artist	*Sean Connery*	*Actor*
Isabella Rosellini (4)	Actress	*David Lynch (1)*	*Actor*
		Martin Scorsese (2)	*Director*
Jelka Rosen	Singer	*Frederick Delius*	*Composer*
Hannah Rothschild	Heiress	*Lord Rosebery*	*Scottish statesman*
Nicole Rothschild (4th)	Actress	*Dudley Moore*	*Entertainer*
Debbie Rowe (2)	Nurse	*Michael Jackson*	*Entertainer*
Geena Rowlands	Actress	*John Cassavettes*	*Actor*
Roxana	Queen of Macedon	*Alexander the Great*	*King of Macedon*
Sue Ryder	Philanthropist	*Leonard Cheshire*	*Philanthropist*
Vita Sackville-West	Poet and novelist	*Harold Nicolson*	*Diplomat*
Carol Bayer Sager (3)	Singer	*Burt Bacharach*	*Composer*
Beatrice Salkeld	Illustrator	*Brendan Behan*	*Irish writer*
Jill St John	Actress	*Jack Jones (1)*	*Singer*
		Robert Wagner (2)	*Actor*
Olga Samaroff (1)	Pianist	*Leopold Stokowski*	*Conductor*
Susan Sarandon	Actress	*Tim Robbins (2)*	*Actor*
Meg Ryan (2)	Actress	*Dennis Quaid*	*Actor*
Maria Elena Santiago	Secretary	*Buddy Holly*	*Musician*
Susan Sarandon	Actress	*Tim Robbins (2)*	*Actor*
Jennifer Saunders	Comedienne	*Ade Edmondson*	*Comedian*
Zelda Sayre	Socialite	*Francis Scott Fitzgerald*	*Novelist*
Prunella Scales	Actress	*Timothy West*	*Actor*
Alma Maria Schindler	Artist and musician	*Gustav Mahler (1)*	*Composer*
		Walter Gropius (2)	*Architect*
		Franz Werfel (3)	*Writer*
Elizabeth Schumann	German soprano	*Carl Alwin*	*German pianist/conductor*
Coretta Scott	Music graduate	*Martin Luther King*	*Civil rights leader*
Janette Scott (3)	Actress	*Mel Torme (1)*	*Singer*
		Jackie Rae (3)	*TV presenter*
Kyra Sedgwick	Actress	*Kevin Bacon*	*Actor*
Phyllis Sellick	Pianist	*Cyril Smith*	*Pianist*
Sandie Shaw	Singer	*Jeff Banks*	*Fashion designer*
Moira Shearer	Ballet dancer	*Ludovic Kennedy*	*Broadcaster*
Evgenia Shelepin (2)	Trotsky's secretary	*Arthur Ransome*	*Writer*
Dinah Sheridan	Actress	*Jimmy Hanley (2)*	*Entertainer*
		Sir John Davis (2)	*Rank chairman*
Brooke Shields	Actress	*Andre Agassi*	*Tennis player*
Elizabeth Siddal	Model	*Dante Gabriel Rossetti*	*Poet and painter*
Simone Signoret	Actress	*Yves Montand (2)*	*Actor*
Sheila Sim	Actress	*Richard Attenborough*	*Actor*
Jean Simmons	Actress	*Stewart Granger*	*Actor*
Carly Simon	Singer	*James Taylor*	*Composer*
Carole Smillie	TV presenter	*Alex Knight*	*Restaurateur*

Anna Nicole Smith	Actress	*J Howard Marshall II*	Oil Tycoon
Delia Smith	Cookery writer	*Michael Wynn Jones*	Publisher
Maggie Smith	Actress	*Robert Stephens*	Actor
Mandy Smith (3)	Model	*Bill Wyman*	Rolling Stone
Michelle Smith	Irish swimmer	*Erik De Bruin*	Dutch discus thrower
Harriet Smithson	Irish actress	*Hector Berlioz*	Composer
Wendy Snowden	Actress	*Peter Cook*	Comedian and writer
Sophia Dorothea	German noblewoman	*George I*	British king
Dorothy Squires (1)	Singer	*Roger Moore (2)*	Actor
Barbara Stanwick	Actress	*Robert Taylor*	Actor
Jann Stapp (6)	Businesswoman	*Harold Robbins*	Writer
Alison Steadman	Actress	*Mike Leigh*	Dramatist
Sheila Steafel (1)	Actress	*Harry H Corbett*	Actor
Marion Stein	Musician	*7th Earl of Harewood (1)*	English nobleman
		Jeremy Thorpe (2)	Politician
Pamela Stephenson	Actress and comedienne	*Nicholas Ball (1)*	Actor
		Billy Connolly (2)	Scottish comedian
Virginia Stephen	Novelist	*Leonard Woolf*	Publisher and writer
Margaret Stewart (2)	Lord Ochiltree's daughter	*John Knox*	Religious reformer
Miriam Stoppard	TV presenter and journalist	*Christopher Hogg (2)*	Industrialist
Susan Stranks	Presenter	*Robin Ray*	Broadcaster
Barbra Streisand	Singer and actress	*Elliot Gould (1)*	Actor
		James Brolin (2)	Actor
Giuseppina Strepponi (2)	Soprano	*Giuseppe Verdi*	Composer
Imogen Stubbs (3)	Actress	*Trevor Nunn*	Artistic director
Una Stubbs	Actress	*Peter Gilmore (1)*	Actor
		Nicky Henson (2)	Entertainer
Trudie Styler (2)	Actress	*Sting*	Singer
Vera de Bosset Sudekeine (2)	Ballet dancer	*Igor Stravinsky*	Composer
Margaret Sullavan	Actress	*William Wyler*	Film director
Anna Beth Sully (1)	Actress	*Douglas Fairbanks Snr*	Actor
Mariya Surovshchikova (1)	Russian ballerina	*Marius Petipa*	French choreographer
Joan Sutherland	Soprano	*Richard Bonynge*	Conductor
Janet Suzman (1)	Actress	*Trevor Nunn*	Artistic director
Gloria Swanson	Actress	*Wallace Beery*	Actor
Catherine Swynford (3)	Former mistress	*John of Gaunt*	English Prince
Jessica Tandy	Actress	*Jack Hawkins (1)*	Actor
		Hume Cronyn (2)	Actor
Sharon Tate (2)	Actress	*Roman Polanski*	Director
Elizabeth Taylor	Actress	*Nicky Hilton (1)*	Hotelier
		Michael Wilding (2)	Actor
		Mike Todd (3)	Film producer
		Eddie Fisher (4)	Singer
		Richard Burton(5 and 6)	Actor
		John Warner (7)	Senator
		Larry Fortensky (8)	Builder
Kiri Te Kanawa	Opera singer	*Desmond Park*	Mining engineer
Victoria Tennant	English actress	*Steve Martin*	US actor
Ellen Terry	English actress	*George Frederick Watts (1)*	English painter
		James Carew (2)	US actor
		Charlie Kelly (3)	Actor
Josephine Tewson	Actress	*Leonard Rossiter*	Actor
Rosalie Texier (1)	Dressmaker	*Claude Debussy*	Composer
Themis (2)	Daughter of Gaia and Uranus	*Zeus*	Greek supreme god
Theodora	Actress	*Justinian*	East Roman emperor
Thetis	Mythical sea nymph (Nereid)	*Peleus*	Mythical King of Phthia
Emma Thompson	Actress	*Kenneth Branagh*	Actor
Elspeth Thomson	Socialite	*Kenneth Grahame*	Children's writer
Sybil Thorndike	Actress	*Lewis Casson*	Actor and manager
Hester Thrale	Writer	*Gabriel Piozzi*	Musician
Julia Thuillier	Socialite	*Walter Savage Landor*	Writer
Uma Thurman	Actress	*Gary Oldman (1)*	Actor
		Ethan Hawke (2)	Actor
Pauline Tiltson	Businesswoman	*John Prescott*	British politician
Ann Todd	Actress	*David Lean*	Film director
Mary Todd	Socialite	*Abraham Lincoln*	US president
Frances Tomelty (1)	Actress	*Sting*	Singer
Wanda Toscanini	Musician	*Vladimir Horowitz*	Pianist

Ludmilla Touréscheva	Gymnast	*Valeri Borzov*	*Athlete*
Marie Truffot	Socialite	*Camille Saint-Saëns*	*Composer*
Ivana Trump	Former wife of Donald Trump	*Ricardo Mazzucchelli (2)*	*Italian businessman*
Anthea Turner	TV presenter	*Peter Powell (1)*	*Disc jockey and producer*
		Grant Bovey (2)	*Businessman*
Cora Turner	Opera singer	*Hawley Crippen*	*Murderer*
Lana Turner	Actress	*Lex Barker (5)*	*Actor*
		Artie Shaw (1)	*Bandleader*
Martha Turner	Farmer's daughter	*John Clare*	*Poet*
Monica Turner (2)	Actress	*Mike Tyson (1)*	*Boxer*
Twiggy	Model and actress	*Leigh Lawson (2)*	*Actor*
Cathy Tyson	Actress	*Craig Charles*	*Actor*
Mary Ure	Actress	*John Osborne (1)*	*Playwright*
		Robert Shaw (2)	*Actor*
Saskia Uylenburgh	Burgomaster's daughter	*Rembrandt Van Rijn*	*Dutch painter*
Joanna Van Gyseghem (1)	Actress	*Ralph Bates*	*Actor*
Eva Marie Violetti	Viennese dancer	*David Garrick*	*Actor*
Galina Vishnevskaya	Soprano	*Mstislav Rostropovich*	*Cellist and conductor*
Carol Vorderman	TV presenter	*Paddy King*	*Businessman*
Marie Vulliamy (2)	Socialite	*George Meredith*	*English novelist*
Lindsay Wagner	Actress	*Alan Rider (1)*	*Music publisher*
		Michael Brandon (2)	*Actor*
		Henry Kingi (3)	*Stuntman*
		Lawrence Mortoff (4)	*Producer*
Lillias Walker (2)	Actress	*Peter Vaughan*	*Actor*
Lalla Ward (2)	Actress	*Tom Baker*	*Actor*
Rachel Ward	Actress	*Bryan Brown*	*Australian actor*
Sophie Ward	Actress	*Paul Hobson*	*Vet*
Sandra Warfield	Soprano	*James McCracken*	*Tenor*
Wallis Simpson	American socialite	*Edward VIII*	*British king*
Lavinia Warren	Circus performer	*Tom Thumb*	*Circus performer*
Jan Waters (2)	Actress	*Peter Gilmore (1)*	*Actor*
Ruby Wax	Comedienne	*Edward Bye*	*Producer*
Constance Weber	Singer	*Wolfgang Amadeus Mozart*	*Composer*
Denise Welch	Actress	*Tim Healy*	*Actor*
Tuesday Weld (2)	Actress	*Dudley Moore (2)*	*Entertainer*
Jane Baillie Welsh	Doctor's daughter	*Thomas Carlyle*	*Essayist*
Joanne Whalley	Actress	*Val Kilmer*	*Actor*
Billie Whitelaw (1)	Actress	*Peter Vaughan*	*Actor*
Clara Wieck	Pianist	*Robert Schumann*	*Composer*
Cynda Williams	Actress	*Billy Bob Thornton*	*Actor*
Esther Williams (4)	Actress	*Tony Franciso (2)*	*Actor*
Shelley Winters	Actress	*Fernando Lamas (4)*	*Actor*
Penelope Wilton (4)	Actress	*Ian Holm*	*Actor*
Catherine Woodcock (2)	Commoner	*John Milton*	*Poet*
Catherine Woodville	Sister-in-law of Edward IV	*Henry Stafford*	*2nd Duke of Buckingham*
Joanne Woodward	Actress	*Paul Newman*	*Actor*
Natalie Wood	Actress	*Robert Wagner*	*Actor*
Victoria Wood	Comedienne	*Geoffrey Durham*	*Comedian*
Helen Worth	Actress	*Michael Angelis*	*Actor*
Syreeta Wright	Singer	*Stevie Wonder*	*Musician*
Anna Magdalena Wülken (2)	Soprano	*JS Bach*	*Composer*
Tessa Wyatt	Actress	*Tony Blackburn*	*Disc jockey*
Jane Wyman (1)	Actress	*Ronald Reagan (3)*	*US president*
Patrice Wymore (2)	Actress	*Errol Flynn*	*Actor*
Xanthippe	Athenian	*Socrates*	*Philosopher*
Paula Yates	Broadcaster	*Bob Geldof*	*Singer*
Cecilia Young	Singer	*Thomas Arne*	*Composer*
Mathilde von Zemlinsky (1)	Musician	*Arnold Schoenberg*	*Composer*
Marta Ziegler	Socialite	*Béla Bartók*	*Composer*
Anna Zimmerman	Housewife	*Charles Gounod*	*Composer*

Marriages: By Male Spouse

Male spouse		Female spouse	
Peter Abelard	French philosopher	Heloise	Abelard's Roman wife
Aeneas	Mythical Trojan prince	Creusa	Mythical character
Agamemnon	Mythical king of Mycenae	Clytemnestra	Mythical queen of Mycenae
André Agassi	Tennis player	Brooke Shields	Actress
Ahab	King of Israel	Jezebel	Queen of Israel
Akhenaton	Egyptian king	Nefertiti	Egyptian queen
John Alderton	Actor	Jill Browne (1)	Actress
		Pauline Collins (2)	Actress
Richard Aldington	Poet/novelist	Hilda Doolittle	US poet
Alexander the Great	King of Macedon	Roxana	Queen of Macedon
Keith Allen	Actor	Alison Allen	Television producer
Ronald Allen	Actor	Sue Lloyd	Actress
Woody Allen	Actor and director	Louise Lasser (2)	Actress
		Soon-Yi Previn (3)	Personal assistant
Greg Allmann (2)	Musician	Cher	Actress and singer
Nick Allott	Theatre producer	Anneka Rice	TV presenter
Carl Alwin	German pianist and conductor	Elizabeth Schumann	German soprano
Kingsley Amis	Novelist and poet	Elizabeth Jane Howard	Novelist
Michael Angelis	Actor	Helen Worth	Actress
Marc Antony	Roman general	Octavia (1)	Emperor Augustus' sister
		Cleopatra VII	Queen of Egypt
Thomas Arne	Composer	Cecilia Young	Singer
Desi Arnez	Musician and actor	Lucille Ball	Comedienne and actress
Tom Arnold (2)	Actor	Roseanne Barr	Actress
Richard Attenborough	Actor	Sheila Sim	Actress
Attila the Hun	Hunnish ruler	Ildico	Consort of Attila
WH Auden	Poet and essayist	Erika Mann	Writer
Burt Bacharach	Composer	Angie Dickinson	Actress
		Carol Bayer Sager (3)	Singer
JS Bach	Composer	Maria Barbara Bach (1)	Cousin of JS Bach
		Anna Magdalena Wülken (2)	Soprano
Kevin Bacon	Actor	Kyra Sedgwick	Actress
David Bailey	Photographer	Marie Helvin (3)	Model
		Catherine Deneuve (2)	Actress
Colin Baker (1)	Actor	Liza Goddard (1)	Actress
Tom Baker	Actor	Lalla Ward (2)	Actress
Alec Baldwin (2)	Actor	Kim Basinger	Actress
Nicholas Ball (1)	Actor	Pamela Stephenson	Actress and comedienne
Antonio Banderas (4)	Actor	Melanie Griffith (2)	Actress
Jeff Banks	Fashion designer	Sandie Shaw	Singer
Monty Banks	Film director	Gracie Fields	Singer
Daniel Barenboim	Pianist	Jacqueline Du Pré	Cellist
Lex Barker (5)	Actor	Lana Turner (3)	Actress
John Barrett	Tennis commentator	Angela Mortimer	British Wimbledon champion
John Barrymore	Actor	Dolores Costello	Actress
Béla Bartók	Composer	Marta Ziegler	Socialite
Ralph Bates	Actor	Joanna Van Gyseghem (1)	Actress
John Bayley	Professor of literature	Iris Murdoch	Writer
Sean Bean	Actor	Debra Anderson (1)	Childhood sweetheart
		Melanie Hill (2)	Actress ('Bread')
		Abigail Cruttenden (3)	Actress ('Sharpe')
Warren Beatty	Actor	Annette Bening	Actress
David Beckham	Footballer	Victoria Adams	Spice Girl
Wallace Beery	Actor	Gloria Swanson	Actress
Brendan Behan	Irish writer	Beatrice Salkeld	Illustrator
Alexander Graham Bell	Inventor	Mabel Hubbard	Deaf student
Hywel Bennett	Actor	Cathy McGowan	Broadcaster
Charles de Beriot	Violinist	Maria Malibran	Contralto
Hector Bérlioz	Composer	Harriet Smithson	Irish actress
Terry Biddlecombe	Jockey	Henrietta Knight	Racehorse trainer
Georges Bizet	Composer	Geneviève Halévy	Composer's daughter
Tony Blackburn	Disc jockey	Tessa Wyatt	Actress
Michael Black	Theatrical agent	Julie Rogers	Singer

FAMOUS PEOPLE

Tony Blair	Politician
William Blake	English poet and painter
Brian Blessed	Actor
Humphrey Bogart (1)	Actor
James Bolam	Actor
Robert Bolt	Playwright
Sonny Bono (1)	Actor and politician
Richard Bonynge	Conductor
Anthony Booth (3)	Actor
Ernst Borgnine (3)	Actor
Valeri Borzov	Athlete
James Boswell	Biographer
Earl of Bothwell (3)	Scottish nobleman
Grant Bovey (2)	Businessman
George Bowden (1)	Businessman
David Bowie (2)	Singer and composer
Mark Boxer	Cartoonist
Bernard Braden	Actor and presenter
Kenneth Branagh	Actor
Michael Brandon (2)	Actor
Jeremy Brett	Actor
Robbie Brightwell	Athlete
Charles Bronson (2)	Actor
James Brolin (2)	Actor
Mel Brooks	Actor and producer
Robert Browning	Poet
Bobby Brown	Singer
Bryan Brown	Australian actor
Hans von Bülow (1)	Conductor
Edmund Burke	British statesman
George Burns	Comedian and actor
Robert Burns	Poet
Richard Burton (5 and 6)	Actor
Peter Butterworth	Actor
Edward Bye	Producer
Gabriel Byrne	Actor
Lord Byron	Poet
Cadmus	Mythical founder of Thebes
Nicholas Cage	Actor
David Cassidy	singer
Michael Caine	Actor
Erskine Caldwell	American author
Alan Charles Cameron	Businessman
Patrick Campbell	Irish writer and wit
James Carew (2)	US Actor
Thomas Carlyle	Essayist
Jim Carrey	Actor
Johnny Cash	Singer
Stefano Casiraghi (2)	Businessman
John Cassavettes	Actor
Lewis Casson	Actor and manager
George Catlin	Professor of politics
Charlie Chaplin	Actor
Lee Chapman	Footballer
Charlemagne	King of the Franks
Charles I	British king
Charles II	British king
Craig Charles	Actor
Keith Chegwin	TV presenter
Leonard Cheshire	Philanthropist
Lord Randolph Churchill	Politician
Winston Churchill	Politician
Eric Clapton (2)	Musician
John Clare	Poet
Claudius	Roman emperor
John Cleese	Actor

Cherie Booth	*Barrister*
Catherine Boucher	*Illiterate pauper*
Hildegarde Neil (2)	*Actress*
Lauren Bacall (4)	*Actress*
Susan Jameson	*Actress*
Sarah Miles	*Actress*
Cher (2)	*Actress and singer*
Joan Sutherland	*Soprano*
Pat Phoenix (2)	*Actress*
Ethel Merman (3)	*Singer*
Ludmilla Tourischeva	*Gymnast*
Margaret Montgomerie	*Socialite*
Mary Stewart	*Queen of Scots*
Anthea Turner	*TV presenter*
Katherine Mansfield	*NZ writer*
Iman	*Model*
Anna Ford	*Broadcaster*
Barbara Kelly	*Actress and presenter*
Emma Thompson	*Actress*
Glynis Barber	*Actress*
Lindsay Wagner	*Actress*
Anna Massey	*Actress*
Ann Packer	*Athlete*
Jill Ireland (2)	*Actress*
Barbara Streisand (3)	*Singer and actress*
Anne Bancroft	*Actress*
Elizabeth Barrett	*Poet*
Whitney Houston	*Singer*
Rachel Ward	*Actress*
Cosima von Bülow	*Franz Liszt's daughter*
Jane Nugent	*Secretary*
Gracie Allen	*Comedienne*
Jean Armour	*Socialite*
Elizabeth Taylor	*Actress*
Janet Brown	*Impressionist*
Ruby Wax	*Comedienne*
Ellen Barkin	*Actress*
Annabella Milbanke	*Heiress*
Harmonia	*Daughter of Ares and Aphrodite*
Patricia Arquette	*Actress*
Kay Lenz	*Actress*
Shakira Baksh (2)	*Actress and model*
Margaret Bourke-White	*Photo-journalist*
Elizabeth Bowen	*Irish novelist*
Vivienne Knight (3)	*Scriptwriter*
Ellen Terry	*English actress*
Jane Baillie Welsh	*Doctor's daughter*
Lauren Holly	*Actress*
June Carter	*Singer*
Caroline of Monaco	*Princess*
Geena Rowlands	*Actress*
Sybil Thorndike	*Actress*
Vera May Brittain	*Writer*
Mildred Harris (1)	*Actress*
Lita Grey (2)	*Actress*
Paulette Goddard (3)	*Actress*
Oona O'Neil (4)	*Playwright's daughter*
Leslie Ash	*Actress*
Hildegarde	*Queen of the Franks*
Henrietta Maria	*French princess*
Catherine of Braganza	*Portuguese princess*
Cathy Tyson	*Actress*
Maggie Philbin	*TV presenter*
Baroness Sue Ryder	*Philanthropist*
Jenny Jerome	*Daughter of NY businessman*
Clementine Hozier	*Charity worker*
Patti Boyd (1)	*Model*
Martha Turner	*Farmer's daughter*
Agrippina	*Roman noblewomen*
Connie Booth	*Actress*

Clovis 1	King of the Franks	*Clotilda*	Queen of the Franks
Martin Clunes	Actor	*Philippa Braithewaite (2)*	TV producer
Kurt Cobain (2)	Musician (Nirvana)	*Courtney Love*	Actress and singer
Marshall Coben	US television executive	*Jane Leeves*	Actress
Jackie Codgan	Actor	*Betty Gradle*	Actress
Paul Coia	TV presenter	*Debbie Greenwood*	TV presenter (former Miss UK)
Samuel Taylor Coleridge	Poet	*Sarah Fricker*	Socialite
Ronald Colman	Actor	*Benita Hume (2)*	Actress
Sean Connery	Actor	*Diane Cilento (1)*	Actress
		Micheline Roquebrune (2)	Artist
Billy Connolly (2)	Scottish comedian	*Pamela Stephenson*	Actress and comedienne
Terence Conran	Businessman	*Shirley Conran*	Authoress
Jackie Coogan (1)	Actor	*Betty Grable*	Actress
James Cook	British seaman and explorer	*Elizabeth Batts*	Captain's wife
Norman Cook	Musician	*Zoe Ball*	TV presenter
Peter Cook	Comedian and writer	*Wendy Snowden (1)*	Actress
		Judy Huxtable (2)	Actress
Harry H Corbett	Actor	*Sheila Steafel (1)*	Actress
		Maureen Blott (2)	Actress
Tom Courtenay	Actor	*Cheryl Kennedy*	Actress
Colin Cowdrey	Cricketer	*Lady Herries*	Racehorse trainer
Hawley Crippen	Murderer	*Cora Turner*	Opera singer
Hume Cronyn (2)	Actor	*Jessica Tandy*	Actress
John Walter Cross	Banker	*George Eliot*	Authoress
Tom Cruise	Actor	*Mimi Rogers (1)*	Actress
		Nicole Kidman (2)	Actress
Xavier Cugat	Bandleader	*Carmen Castillo (1)*	Singer
		Lorraine Allen (2)	Singer
		Abbe Lane (3)	Singer
Tony Curtis (3)	Actor	*Janet Leigh*	Actress
Roald Dahl	Writer	*Patricia Neal*	Actress
Eugène D'Albert	Composer and pianist	*Theresa Carreño (1)*	Pianist
John Dankworth (2)	Jazz musician	*Cleo Laine*	Jazz singer
General D'Arblay	French émigré	*Fanny Burney*	English novelist
Bobby Darin	Singer	*Sandra Dee*	Actress
Henry Darnley (2)	English nobleman	*Mary Stewart*	Queen of Scots
Jules Dassin	Film director	*Melina Mercouri*	Actress
Nigel Davenport	Actor	*Maria Aitken*	Actress
Jim Davidson	Comedian	*Tracy Hilton*	Housewife
		Alison Holloway	TV presenter
Peter Davidson	Actor	*Sandra Dickinson*	Actress
Hunter Davies	Author	*Margaret Forster*	Author
Carl Davis	Composer	*Jean Boht*	Actress
Sir John Davis (2)	Rank chairman	*Dinah Sheridan*	Actress
Sammy Davis Jnr	Entertainer	*May Britt*	Actress
Dickie Dawson (2)	US Comedian	*Diana Dors*	Actress
Cecil Day-Lewis	Poet	*Jill Balchin*	Actress
Daniel Day-Lewis	Actor	*Rebecca Miller*	Actress (Arthur Miller's daughter)
Erik De Bruin	Dutch discus thrower	*Michelle Smith*	Irish swimmer
William Frend De Morgan	Pre-Raphaelite artist	*Evelyn Pickering*	Pre-Raphaelite artist
Robert De Niro	Actor	*Diahnne Abbott*	Actress
Danny De Vito	Actor	*Rhea Pearlman*	Actress
Claude Debussy	Composer	*Rosalie Texier (1)*	Dressmaker
		Emma Bardac (2)	Socialite
Frederick Delius	Composer	*Jelka Rosen*	Singer
Michael Denison	Actor	*Dulcie Gray*	Actress
John Derek	Actor and director	*Ursula Andress (1)*	Actress
		Linda Evans (2)	Actress
		Bo Derek (3)	Actress
Frankie Dettori	Jockey	*Catherine Allen*	Secretary
Deucalion	Son of Prometheus	*Pyrrha*	Daughter of Epimetheus and Pandora
Donald Dewar (1)	British politician	*Alison McNair*	Doctor's daughter
Joe Di Maggio (2)	Baseball player	*Marilyn Monroe (2)*	Actress
Charles Dickens	Author	*Catherine Hogarth*	Newspaper magnate's daughter
Jonathan Dimbleby	Broadcaster	*Bel Mooney*	Writer and broadcaster
Dionysus	Greek god of wine	*Ariadne*	Mythical daughter of King Minos of Crete
Jim Dougherty (1)	Polieman	*Marilyn Monroe*	Actress

Jack Dromey	Trade unionist	*Harriet Harman*	*British politician*
David Duchovny (2)	Actor	*Tea Leoni*	*Actress*
Lord Guilford Dudley	English nobleman	*Lady Jane Grey*	*English noblewoman*
Robert Dudley	Earl of Leicester	*Amy Robsart*	*Socialite*
Albrecht Dürer	German painter	*Agnes Frey*	*Merchant's daughter*
Geoffrey Durham	Comedian	*Victoria Wood*	*Comedienne*
Simon Dutton	Actor	*Tamsin Olivier*	*Pub owner*
Antonín Dvořák	Composer	*Anna Cermakova*	*Socialite*
Bob Dylan	Musician	*Sarah Lowndes*	*Poet*
Mark Eden	Actor	*Sue Nicholls*	*Actress*
Ade Edmondson	Comedian	*Jennifer Saunders*	*Comedienne*
Edward I	English king	*Eleanor*	*Castilian princess*
Edward II	English king	*Isabella*	*Daughter of Philip IV of France*
Edward III	English king	*Philippa Hainault*	*Dutch noblewoman*
Edward IV	English king	*Elizabeth Woodville*	*English noblewoman*
Edward VII	British king	*Alexandra*	*Danish princess*
Edward VIII	British king	*Wallis Simpson*	*American socialite*
Blake Edwards (2)	Film director	*Julie Andrews*	*Actress and singer*
Glyn Edwards	Actor	*Yootha Joyce*	*Actress*
Denholm Elliott (1)	Actor	*Virginia McKenna*	*Actress*
Epimetheus	Greek Titan	*Pandora*	*First woman of Greek myth*
Ernst August of Hanover (3)	Hanoverian prince	*Chantal Hochuli (1)*	*Swiss Heiress*
		Caroline of Monaco (2)	*Princess*
Emilio Estevez	Actor	*Paula Abdul (2)*	*Singer*
Chris Evans	Disc jockey	*Carol McGiffin (1)*	*Radio DJ*
		Billie Piper (2)	*Pop singer*
Trevor Eve	Actor	*Sharon Maughan*	*Actress*
Douglas Fairbanks Jnr (2)	Actor	*Joan Crawford*	*Actress*
Douglas Fairbanks Snr	Actor	*Anna Beth Sully (1)*	*Actress*
Douglas Fairbanks Snr (2)	Actor	*Mary Pickford (2)*	*Actress*
William Fairchild	Playwright	*Isabel Dean*	*Actress*
James Farentino	Actor	*Elizabeth Ashley (1)*	*Actress*
		Michele Lee (2)	*Actress and singer*
José Ferrer	Actor	*Rosemary Clooney*	*Singer*
Mel Ferrer	Actor	*Audrey Hepburn*	*Actress*
Henry Fielding	English novelist	*Charlotte Mary Craddock (1)*	*Socialite*
Henry Fielding	English novelist	*Mary Daniel (2)*	*Maid*
Albert Finney (5)	Actor	*Anouk Aimée (2)*	*Actress*
Eddie Fisher (1)	Singer	*Debbie Reynolds (2)*	*Actress*
		Elizabeth Taylor (3)	*Actress*
		Connie Stevens (4)	*Actress*
Francis Scott Fitzgerald	Novelist	*Zelda Sayre*	*Socialite*
Errol Flynn	Actor	*Patrice Wymore*	*Actress*
		Lili Damita	*Socialite*
Michael Foot	Politician	*Jill Craigie*	*TV scriptwriter and author*
Glenn Ford	Actor	*Eleanor Powell (3)*	*Actress*
Bryan Forbes	Actor and director	*Nanette Newman*	*Actress*
Bruce Forsyth	Entertainer	*Wilnelia Merced (3)*	*Beauty queen*
		Penny Calvert (1)	*Dancer*
		Anthea Redfern (2)	*presenter*
Larry Fortensky (8)	Builder	*Elizabeth Taylor*	*Actress*
Francis II (1)	French Dauphin then king	*Mary Stewart*	*Queen of Scots*
Tony Francioso (2)	Actor	*Shelley Winters*	*Actress*
César Franck	Composer	*Félicité Desmousseaux*	*Actress*
Colin Freeman	Musical director	*Lorna Luft*	*Singer*
David Freeman	Operatic director	*Marie Angel*	*Australian soprano*
French Harold	Actor and theatre director	*Mary Parker*	*Actress*
William Friedkin	Film director	*Lesley-Anne Down (2)*	*Actress*
		Jeanne Moreau (1)	*Actress*
Martin Frizell	GMTV presenter	*Fiona Phillips*	*GMTV presenter*
David Frost	Broadcaster	*Lynne Frederick (1)*	*Actress*
		Carina Fitzalan Howard (2)	*Noblewoman*
Clark Gable (2)	Actor	*Carole Lombard (3)*	*Actress*
Thomas Gainsborough	English painter	*Margaret Burr*	*Daughter of 4th Duke of Beaufort*
Liam Gallagher (3)	Pop musician	*Patsy Kensit*	*Actress and singer*
Noel Gallagher	Pop artist	*Meg Matthews*	*Record company secretary (Creation)*
David Garrick	Actor	*Eva Marie Violetti*	*Viennese dancer*
Bob Geldof	Singer	*Paula Yates*	*Broadcaster*

George I	British king	Dorothea Sophia	German noblewoman
George II	British king	Caroline of Ansbach	German noblewoman
George III	British king	Charlotte Sophia	German noblewoman
George IV	British king	Caroline of Brunswick	German noblewoman
George of Denmark	Danish Prince	Queen Anne	British queen
George V	British king	Mary of Teck	German noblewoman
George VI	British king	Elizabeth Bowes-Lyon	Earl of Strathmore's daughter
Maurice Gibb	Musician	Lulu	Singer
Richard Gere	Actor	Cindy Crawford	Supermodel
Peter Gilmore (1)	Actor	Jan Waters (2)	Actress
		Una Stubbs (1)	Actress
Gerry Goffin	Composer	Carole King	Singer and composer
Jeff Goldblum (2)	Actor	Geena Davis	Actress
James Goldsmith	Tycoon	Ginette Lery (2)	Secretary
		Isabel Patiño (1)	Bolivian tin magnate's daughter
		Anne Birley (3)	Lady Annabel Vane-Tempest Stewart
Elliot Gould (1)	Actor	Barbra Streisand	Singer and actress
Charles Gounod	Composer	Anna Zimmerman	Housewife
Kenneth Grahame	Children's writer	Elspeth Thomson	Socialite
Robert Graham	Sculptor	Anjelica Huston	Actress and director
Stewart Grainger	Actor	Jean Simmons	Actress
Cary Grant	Actor	Barbara Hutton (2)	Actress
		Dyan Cannon (4)	Actress
Richard Greene	Actor	Patricia Medina	Actress
Edvard Grieg	Composer	Nina Hagerup	Singer (Grieg's cousin)
Walter Gropius (2)	Architect	Alma Maria Schindler (1)	Musician
Jimmy Gulzar	Musician	Melanie Brown	Spice Girl
William Hague	Politician	Ffion Jenkins	Ex Civil Servant
Peter Hall	Theatre director	Leslie Caron	Actress
Willis Hall	Writer	Jill Bennett (2)	Actress
William Hamilton	Scottish diplomat	Emma Lyon	Blacksmith's daughter
Dashiell Hammett	Author	Lillian Hellman	Playwright
Jimmy Hanley	Entertainer	Dinah Sheridan (1)	Actress
7th Earl of Harewood (1)	English nobleman	Marion Stein	Musician
Hargitay (2)	Body-builder	Jayne Mansfield	Actress
Renny Harlin (1)	Film director	Geena Davis	Actress
George Harrison (1)	Musician	Patti Boyd (1)	Model
Rex Harrison	Actor	Lilli Palmer (2)	Actress
		Kay Kendall (3)	Actress
		Rachel Roberts (4)	Actress
William Hartnell	Actor	Heather McIntyre	Actress and playwright
Laurence Harvey (2)	Actor	Margaret Leighton	Actress
Ethan Hawke (2)	Actor	Uma Thurman	Actress
Jack Hawkins (1)	Actor	Jessica Tandy	Actress
Franz Joseph Haydn	Composer	Maria Anna Keller	Hairdresser's daughter
Tim Healy	Actor	Denise Welch	Actress
William Heelis	Solicitor	Beatrix Potter	Author and illustrator
Paul Heiney	Broadcaster	Libby Purves	Broadcaster
David Hemmings	Actor	Gayle Hunnicutt	Actress
Henry II	French king	Catherine de Medici	Queen of France
Henry II (2)	English king	Eleanor of Aquitaine	French noblewoman
Henry III	English king	Eleanor of Provence	French noblewoman
Henry V (2)	English king	Catherine of Valois	French princess
Henry VI	English king	Margaret of Anjou	French noblewoman
Henry VII	English king	Elizabeth of York	English princess
Lenny Henry	Comedian	Dawn French	Comedienne
George Henschel	Baritone	Lilian Bailey	American soprano
Nicky Henson (2)	Entertainer	Una Stubbs	Actress
Hephaestus	Greek god of fire	Aphrodite	Greek Goddess of Love
Peter Murray Hill	Actor and bookseller	Phyllis Calvert	Actress
Conrad Hilton (2)	Hotelier	Zsa Zsa Gabor	Actress
Nicky Hilton Jnr	Hotelier	Elizabeth Taylor	Actress
Frazer Hines	Actor	Gemma Craven (1)	Actress
		Liz Hobbs (2)	Waterskier
Alfred Hitchcock	Film director	Alma Reville	Actress
Paul Hobson	Vet	Sophie Ward	Actress
Christopher Hogg (2)	Industrialist	Miriam Stoppard	TV presenter and journalist
Buddy Holly	Musician	Maria Elena Santiago	Secretary
Ian Holm	Actor	Penelope Wilton (4)	Actress

F
A
M
O
U
S

P
E
O
P
L
E

Michael Holroyd (2)	Biographer	*Margaret Drabble*	*Novelist*
Vladimir Horowitz	Pianist	*Wanda Toscanini*	*Musician*
Trevor Howard	Actor	*Helen Cherry*	*Actress*
Howard Hughes	Businessman	*Jean Peters*	*Actress*
Ted Hughes	Poet	*Sylvia Plath*	*Poet*
Jack Hulbert	Actor	*Cicely Courtneidge*	*Actress*
Timothy Hutton	Actor	*Debra Winger*	*Actress*
Jeremy Irons	Actor	*Sinead Cusack*	*Actress*
Alexander Irvine (2)	Irvine of Lairg	*Alison McNair*	*Doctor's daughter*
Eugene Istomin	Pianist	*Martita Casals*	*Pablo Casals' widow*
Andrew Jackson	US president	*Rachel Robards*	*Colonel's daughter*
Michael Jackson	Entertainer	*Lisa-Marie Presley (1)*	*Nurse*
		Debbie Rowe (2)	*Actress*
James I	English king	*Anne*	*Danish princess*
James II	English king	*Anne Hyde (1)*	*Daughter of the Earl of Clarendon*
		Mary of Modena (2)	*Italian noblewoman*
James V	King of Scotland	*Mary of Guise*	*French noblewoman*
Harry James	Musician	*Betty Grable*	*Actress*
Jean-Michel Jarre	Musician	*Charlotte Rampling*	*Actress*
Martin Jarvis	Actor	*Rosalind Ayres*	*Actress*
David Jason	Actor	*Gill Hinchcliffe*	*TV production assistant*
Billy Joel (2)	Singer	*Christie Brinkley (2)*	*Model*
John	King of England	*Isabella of Angoulême (2)*	*French noblewoman*
John of Gaunt	English prince	*Blanche of Lancaster (1)*	*English noblewoman*
		Constance of Castile (2)	*Castilian princess*
		Catherine Swynford (3)	*Former mistress*
Don Johnson (1) & (3)	Actor	*Melanie Griffith*	*Actress*
Richard Johnson (1)	Actor	*Kim Novak*	*Actress*
Samuel Johnson	Writer and lexicographer	*Elizabeth Porter*	*Schoolteacher*
Elton John	Vocalist and composer	*Renate Blauel*	*Actress*
Al Jolson	Entertainer	*Ruby Keeler*	*Actress*
Allan Jones	Singer and actor	*Irene Hervey*	*Actress*
Anthony Armstrong Jones	Photographer	*Princess Margaret*	*Elizabeth II's sister*
Sir G Roderick Jones	MD of Reuters	*Enid Bagnold*	*Authoress*
Jack Jones (2)	Singer	*Jill St John (2)*	*Actress*
James Joyce	Irish writer	*Nora Barnacle*	*Socialite*
Pierre Junot	Businessman	*Caroline of Monaco*	*Princess*
Justinian	East Roman emperor	*Theodora*	*Actress*
Wassily Kandinsky	Russian artist	*Nina Andreevskaya*	*Moscow socialite*
Sam Kane	Actor	*Linda Lusardi*	*Actress and model*
Charles Kelly (2)	Actor	*Ellen Terry*	*Actress*
John F Kennedy (1)	US president	*Jacqueline Bouvier*	*Socialite*
Ludovic Kennedy	Broadcaster	*Moira Shearer*	*Ballet dancer*
Jim Kerr (2)	Musician	*Patsy Kensit*	*Actress*
John Maynard Keynes	Economist	*Lydia Lopokova*	*Ballerina*
Aly Khan (3)	Middle Eastern prince	*Rita Hayworth (1)*	*Actress*
Imran Khan	Cricketer	*Jemima Goldsmith*	*Heiress*
Eddie Kidd	Stunt motorcyclist	*Debbie Ash (1)*	*Actress*
Jan Kiepura	Tenor	*Martha Eggerth*	*Soprano*
Val Kilmer	Actor	*Joanne Whalley*	*Actress*
Martin Luther King	Civil rights leader	*Coretta Scott*	*Music graduate*
Paddy King	Businessman	*Carol Vorderman*	*TV presenter*
Henry Kingi (3)	Stuntman	*Lindsay Wagner*	*Actress*
Rudyard Kipling	Novelist and poet	*Caroline Balestier*	*Publishing heiress*
Kevin Kline	Actor	*Phoebe Cates*	*Actress*
Alex Knight	Restaurateur	*Carole Smillie*	*TV presenter*
Mark Knopfler	Musician	*Kitty Aldridge*	*Actress*
John Knox	Religious reformer	*Marjory Bowes (1)*	*John Knox's 1st wife*
		Margaret Stewart (2)	*Lord Ochiltree's daughter*
Musa Komeagac	Turkish waiter	*Sarah Cook*	*Schoolgirl (13 when married)*
Alexander Korda	Film director	*Merle Oberon (2)*	*Actress*
André Kostelanetz	Conductor	*Lily Pons*	*Soprano*
Kris Kristofferson	Actor	*Rita Coolidge (2)*	*Singer*
Sam Kydd	Actor	*Pinkie Barnes*	*Table tennis international*
Alan Lake (3)	Actor	*Diana Dors*	*Actress*
Fernando Lamas (4)	Actor	*Esther Williams (4)*	*Actress*
Martin Landau	Actor	*Barbara Bain*	*Actress*
Walter Savage Landor	Writer	*Julia Thuillier*	*Socialite*
Charles Laughton	Actor	*Elsa Lanchester*	*Actress*

Tim Laurence (2)	Naval officer	Princess Anne	British Princess
DH Lawrence	Writer	Frieda von Richthofen	Socialite
Leigh Lawson (2)	Actor	Twiggy	Model and actress
David Lean	Film director	Ann Todd	Actress
John Le Mesurier	Actor	Hattie Jacques	Actress
Tommy Lee	Singer	Heather Locklear (2)	Actress
		Pamela Anderson (3)	Actress
Mike Leigh	Dramatist	Alison Steadman	Actress
Donovan Leitch	Actor	Kirsty Hume	Model
John Lennon (2)	Musician	Yoko Ono (2)	Artist
Leofric	Earl of Mercia	Lady Godiva	Countess of Mercia
CS Lewis	Author	Joy Davidman	Poet
Henry Lewis	Conductor	Marilyn Horne	Mezzo-soprano
Nick Lilley	Businessman	Anna Raeburn	Agony aunt
Abraham Lincoln	US president	Mary Todd	Socialite
Charles Lindbergh	Aviator	Anne Morrow	Writer
Andrew Lloyd Webber (2)	Composer	Sarah Brightman (2)	Singer
John Lloyd (1)	Tennis player	Chris Evert	Tennis player
Gary Lockwood	Actor	Stefanie Powers	Actress
Henry W Longfellow	US poet	Frances Appleton	Socialite
Rafael Lopez-Cambil	Argentinian playwright	Paloma Picasso	Beautician and businesswoman
Louis VII (1)	King of France	Eleanor of Aquitaine	French noblewoman
Louis XIV	King of France	Maria Theresa (1)	Spanish princess
		Madame de Maintenon (2)	Louis X1V's 2nd wife
Louis XVI	King of France	Marie Antoinette	French princess
Lucan Arthur	Music-hall artist	Kitty McShane	Music-hall artist
Sid Luft (3)	Entertainer	Judy Garland	Actress
Ben Lyon	Radio comedian	Bebe Daniels	Radio comedienne
David Lynch	Director	Isabella Rosellini (3)	Actress
Simon MacCorkindale	Actor	Fiona Fullerton (1)	Actress
		Susan George (2)	Actress
Ewan Macdonald	Presbyterian minister	LM Montgomery	Canadian novelist
Fred MacMurray	Actor	June Haver	Actress
Richard Madeley	TV presenter	Judy Finnegan	TV presenter
Gustav Mahler	Composer	Alma Maria Schindler (1)	Musician
Lee Majors	Actor	Farrah Fawcett (2)	Actress
Max Mallowan	Archaeologist	Agatha Christie	Writer
Louis Malle	Director	Candice Bergen (3)	Actress
Charles Manners	Irish bass and impresario	Fanny Moody	English soprano
Mauro Mantovani	Actor	Samantha Janus	Actress
Mao Zedong	Chinese leader	Chiang Ching	Actress
J Howard Marshall II	Oil tycoon	Anna Nicole Smith	Actress
Steve Martin	Actor	Victoria Tennant	Actress
Slim Jim Phantom McDonnell	Musician	Britt Ekland (1)	Actress
Ricardo Mazzucchelli (2)	Italian businessman	Ivana Trump	Former wife of Donald Trump
David McCallum (1)	Actor	Jill Ireland	Actress
Paul McCartney (2)	Musician	Linda Eastman	Photographer
James McCracken	Tenor	Sandra Warfield	Soprano
John McEnery	Actor	Stephanie Beacham	Actress
John McEnroe	Tennis player	Tatum O'Neal	Actress
Steve McQueen (2)	Actor	Ali McGraw	Actress
John McVie	Musician	Christine Perfect	Singer
Felix Mendelssohn	Composer	Cécile Jeanrenaud	Clergyman's daughter
Burgess Meredith (3)	Actor	Paulette Goddard	Actress
George Meredith	English novelist	Mary Ellen Nicolls (1)	Daughter of Thomas Love Peacock
		Marie Vulliamy (2)	Socialite
Cliff Michelmore	Broadcaster	Jean Metcalfe	Broadcaster
Milanion	Mythical Greek athlete	Atalanta	Mythical Greek huntress
John Everett Millais (2)	Artist	Effie Gray	Artist
Arthur Miller (3)	Playwright	Marilyn Monroe	Actress
John Mills	Actor	Mary Hayley Bell	Playwright
John Milton	Poet	Mary Powell (1)	Royalist sympathiser
		Catherine Woodcock (2)	Second wife
		Elizabeth Minshull (3)	Third wife
Vincente Minnelli (2)	Film director	Judy Garland	Actress
Alfred Molina (2)	Actor	Jill Gascoigne (1)	Actress
Jim Mollison	Aviator	Amy Johnson	Aviator

FAMOUS PEOPLE

Yves Montand (2)	Actor	*Simone Signoret*	*Actress*
Dudley Moore	Entertainer	*Suzy Kendall (1)*	*Actress*
		Tuesday Weld (2)	*Actress*
		Brogan Lane (3)	*Actress*
		Nicole Rothschild (4th)	*Actress*
Roger Moore	Actor	*Dorothy Squires (1)*	*Singer*
		Luisa Mattioli (2)	*Housewife*
Kenneth More	Actor	*Angela Douglas*	*Irish actress*
Thomas More	Chancellor of England	*Jane Colt (1)*	*Farmer's daughter*
		Alice Middleton (2)	*Widow of London mercer*
Lawrence Mortoff (4)	Producer	*Lindsay Wagner*	*Actress*
Oswald Mosley	Politician	*Cynthia Curzon (1)*	*English noblewoman*
		Diana Guinness (2)	*(Nancy Mitford's sister)*
Robert Motherwell	US artist	*Helen Frankenthaler*	*US artist*
Tommy Mottola	President of Sony Music	*Mariah Carey*	*Singer*
Louis Mountbatten	Naval commander	*Edwina Ashley*	*Heiress and charity worker*
Wolfgang Amadeus Mozart	Composer	*Constance Weber*	*Singer*
Malcolm Muggeridge	Journalist	*Kitty Dobbs*	*Niece of Beatrice Webb*
Muhammad	Founder of Islam	*Aisha*	*Muhammad's favourite wife*
John Middleton Murry (2)	Writer and critic	*Katherine Mansfield*	*NZ short story writer*
Napoleon I	French emperor	*Josephine de Beauharnais (1)*	*French empress*
		Marie Louise (2)	*Austrian archduchess*
Liam Neeson (2)	Actor	*Natasha Richardson*	
Horatio Nelson	English naval hero	*Frances Nisbet*	*Doctor's widow*
Nero	Roman emperor	*Octavia (1)*	*Roman noblewoman*
		Poppaea (2)	*Roman noblewoman*
		Messalina (3)	*Roman noblewoman*
Franco Nero (1)	Actor	*Vanessa Redgrave*	*Actress*
Anthony Newley (1)	Actor and singer	*Joan Collins (1)*	*Actress*
Paul Newman	Actor	*Joanne Woodward*	*Actress*
Arthur Bell Nicholls	Curate	*Charlotte Brontë*	*Writer*
David Nicholls	Horseracing trainer	*Alex Greaves*	*Jockey*
Ben Nicholson (2)	Artist	*Barbara Hepworth*	*Sculptor*
Harold Nicolson	Diplomat	*Vita Sackville-West*	*Poet and novelist*
David Niven	Actor	*Primula Rollo*	*Cipher Clerk*
Trevor Nunn	Artistic director	*Janet Suzman (1)*	*Actress*
		Imogen Stubbs (3)	*Actress*
Odysseus	Mythical king of Ithaca	*Penelope*	*Daughter of King Icarius of Sparta*
Angus Ogilvy	Businessman	*Princess Alexandra*	*British princess*
Gary Oldman	Actor	*Leslie Manville (1)*	*Actress*
		Uma Thurman (2)	*Actress*
Laurence Olivier	Actor	*Jill Esmond (1)*	*Actress*
		Vivien Leigh (2)	*Actress*
		Joan Plowright (3)	*Actress*
Aristotle Onassis (2)	Businessman	*Jacqueline Kennedy*	*Socialite*
Ryan O'Neal (2)	Actor	*Farrah Fawcett*	*Actress*
Eugene Ormandy	Conductor	*Stephanie Goldner*	*Harpist*
David O'Selznick (2)	Director	*Jennifer Jones (2)*	*Actress*
Peter O'Toole (2)	Actor	*Sian Phillips*	*Actress*
John Osborne	Playwright	*Mary Ure (2)*	*Actress*
		Jill Bennett (4)	*Actress*
Owen Tudor (1)	Grandfather of Henry V11	*Catherine*	*Valois princess*
Alan J Pakula (2)	Director	*Hope Lange*	*Actress*
Desmond Park	Mining engineer	*Kiri Te Kanawa*	*Opera singer*
Norman Parkinson	Photographer	*Wenda Rogerson*	*Model*
Peleus	Mythical king of Phthia	*Thetis*	*Mythical sea nymph (Nereid)*
Wilfred Pelletier	Conductor	*Rose Bampton*	*Soprano*
Sean Penn (1)	Actor	*Madonna*	*Singer and actress*
George Peppard (2)	Actor	*Elizabeth Ashley*	*Actress*
Jon Pertwee	Actor	*Jean Marsh (1)*	*Actress*
	Actor	*Ingeborg Rhosea (2)*	*Novelist*
Peter the Great (1)	Russian tsar	*Catherine I*	*Russian empress*
		Eudoxia	*Russian noblewoman*
Peter III	Russian tsar	*Catherine II (the Great)*	*Russian empress*
Marius Petipa	French choreographer	*Mariya Surovshchikova (1)*	*Russian ballerina*
		Lyubov Leonidovna (2)	*Russian ballerina*
Mark Phillips	Equestrian rider	*Sandy Pflueger (2)*	*Equestrian rider*
		Princess Anne (1)	*British princess*

Harold Pinter	Playwright	*Vivien Merchant (1)*	*Actress*
		Lady Antonia Fraser (2)	*Authoress*
Gabriel Piozzi	Musician	*Hester Thrale*	*Writer*
Christopher Plummer	Actor	*Tammie Grimes*	*Actress*
Roman Polanski	Director	*Sharon Tate (2)*	*Actress*
Carlo Ponti	Film producer	*Sophia Loren*	*Actress*
Hugh Porter	Cyclist	*Anita Lonsborough*	*Swimmer*
Poseidon	Greek god of the sea	*Amphitrite*	*Mythical Greek sea nymph*
Dick Powell	Actor	*Joan Blondell (1)*	*Actress*
		June Allyson (2)	*Actress*
Peter Powell (1)	Disc jockey and producer	*Anthea Turner*	*TV presenter*
William Powell	Actor	*Carole Lombard*	*Actress*
Prasutagus	King of Iceni	*Boudicca*	*Queen of Iceni*
John Prescott	British politician	*Pauline Tiltson*	*Businesswoman*
Elvis Presley	Singer	*Priscilla Beaulieu*	*Actress*
Andre Previn (2)	Conductor	*Mia Farrow (3)*	*Actress*
Vincent Price	Actor	*Coral Browne*	*Actress*
JB Priestley	Author	*Jacquetta Hawkes*	*Archaeologist*
Prince (Symbol)	Singer	*Myte Garcia*	*Belly dancer*
John Profumo	Politician	*Valerie Hobson*	*Actress and dancer*
Sergei Prokofiev	Composer	*Lina Llubera*	*Spanish singer*
Ptolemy XII	Egyptian ruler	*Cleopatra III*	*Queen of Egypt*
Ptolemy XIII (1)	Egyptian Ruler	*Cleopatra VII*	*Queen of Egypt*
Giacomo Puccini	Composer	*Elvira Gemignani*	*Socialite*
Dennis Quaid	Actor	*Meg Ryan (2)*	*Actress*
Jackie Rae (3)	TV presenter	*Janette Scott*	*Actress*
Arthur Ransome	Writer	*Evgenia Shelepin (2)*	*Trotsky's secretary*
Robin Ray	Broadcaster	*Susan Stranks*	*TV presenter*
Ronald Reagan	US president	*Jane Wyman (1)*	*Actress*
		Nancy Davis (2)	*Actress*
Michael Redgrave	Actor	*Rachel Kempson*	*Actress*
Derek Redmond	Athlete	*Sharron Davis*	*Swimmer*
Erich Maria Remarque (4)	Author	*Paulette Goddard*	*Actress*
Rembrandt Van Rijn	Dutch painter	*Saskia Uylenburgh*	*Burgomaster's daughter*
Jean Renoir	Film director	*Andrée Heurschling (1)*	*Artist's model*
		Dido Freire (2)	*Brazilian film-maker's daughter*
Pierre-Auguste Renoir	French painter	*Alice Charigot*	*Socialite*
Burt Reynolds	Actor	*Judy Carne (1)*	*Actress*
		Loni Anderson (2)	*Actress*
Richard I	English king	*Berengaria*	*Princess of Navarre*
Richard II	English king	*Anne of Bohemia (1)*	*Emperor Charles 1V's daughter*
		Isabelle (2)	*Daughter of Charles VI of France*
Richard III	English king	*Anne Nevill*	*English noblewoman*
Tony Richardson (2)	Film producer	*Vanessa Redgrave*	*Actress*
Shane Richie	Comedian	*Coleen Nulan*	*Singer*
Guy Ritchie (2)	Film director	*Madonna*	*Singer and Actress*
Allan Rider (1)	Music publisher	*Lindsay Wagner*	*Actress*
Brian Rix	Actor	*Elspet Gray*	*Actress*
Jason Robards (2)	Actor	*Lauren Bacall (3)*	*Actress*
Harold Robbins	Writer	*Muriel Ling (1)*	*Model*
		Grace Palermo (5)	*Socialite*
		Jann Stapp (6)	*Businesswoman*
Tim Robbins (2)	Actor	*Susan Sarandon*	*Actress*
Roy Rogers	Actor and singer	*Dale Evans*	*Actressand singer*
John Rolfe	English Colonist	*Pocahontas*	*Indian princess*
Mickey Rooney	Actor	*Ava Gardner*	*Actress*
Karl Rosa	German conductor	*Euphrosyne Parepa*	*Soprano*
Arnold Rosé	Violinist	*Justine Mahler*	*Sister of Gustav Mahler*
Lord (Primrose) Rosebery	Scottish statesman	*Hannah Rothschild*	*Heiress*
Jack Rosenthal	Playwright	*Maureen Lipman*	*Actress*
Jonathan Ross	TV presenter	*Jane Goldman*	*Writer*
Nick Ross	Presenter	*Sarah Caplin*	*TV executive*
Roberto Rossellini (2)	Director	*Ingrid Bergman (2)*	*Actress*
Dante Gabriel Rossetti	Poet and painter	*Elizabeth Siddal*	*Model*
Gioacchino Rossini	Composer	*Isabella Colbran (1)*	*Spanish soprano*
		Olympie Pélissier (2)	*Parisian hostess*
Leonard Rossiter	Actor	*Josephine Tewson*	*Actress*

Mstislav Rostropovich	Cellist and conductor	
Philip Roth	Novelist	
John Ruskin (1)	Art Critic	
Kurt Russell	Actor	
Camille Saint-Saëns	Composer	
George Sanders	Actor	
Gerald Scarfe	Cartoonist	
Arnold Schoenberg	Composer	
Robert Schumann	Composer	
Martin Scorsese	Director	
George C Scott	Actor	
Walter Scott	Scottish novelist	
Steven Seagal (2)	Actor	
Rudolf Seiber (1)	Production assistant	
Peter Sellers	Actor	
Rudolf Serkin	Pianist	
William Shakespeare	Playwright	
Omar Sharif	Actor and bridge player	
Artie Shaw	Bandleader	
Bernard Shaw	Bodyguard	
George Bernard Shaw	Dramatist	
Robert Shaw (2)	Actor	
Percy Bysse Shelley	Poet	
Richard Brinsley Sheridan	Irish dramatist	
Jean Sibelius	Composer	
Paul Simon	Singer and composer	
Frank Sinatra	Singer	
Nikki Sixx	Motley Crue guitarist	
John Skeaping (1)	Sculptor	
Cyril Smith	Pianist	
Mike Smith	TV presenter	
Socrates	Philosopher	
David Solkin	Businessman	
Georg Solti	Conductor	
Robert Southey	Poet	
Phil Spector	Record producer	
Earl Charles Spencer	English nobleman	
Edmund Spenser	English poet	
Steven Spielberg (2)	Director	
Henry Stafford	2nd Duke of Buckingham	
Sylvester Stallone	Actor	
Alvin Stardust (3)	Pop singer	
Ringo Starr	Musician	
Rod Steiger (1)	Actor	
Anthony Steele	Actor	
Chris Stein	Guitarist	
Robert Stephens	Actor	
Robert Louis Stevenson	Author	
Dave Stewart	Musician	
Patrick Stewart	Actor ('Startrek')	
Rod Stewart	Singer	
Thomas Stewart	Baritone	
Alfred Stieglitz	US photographer	
Sting	Singer	

Galina Vishnevskaya	*Soprano*
Claire Bloom	*Actress*
Effie Gray	*Artist*
Goldie Hawn	*Actress*
Marie Truffot	*Socialite*
Zsa Zsa Gabor (2)	*Actress*
Benita Hume (3)	*Actress*
Magda Gabor (4)	*Actress*
Jane Asher	*Actress and cook*
Mathilde von Zemlinsky (1)	*Musician*
Gertrud Kolisch (2)	*Musician*
Clara Wieck	*Pianist*
Isabella Rossellini (4)	*Actress*
Colleen Dewhurst	*Socialite*
Charlotte Charpentier	*Daughter of French émigré*
Kelly Le Brock	*Actress*
Marlene Dietrich	*Actress*
Anne Hayes (1)	*Housewife*
Britt Ekland (2)	*Actress*
Miranda Quarry (3)	*Actress*
Lynne Frederick (4)	*Actress*
Irene Busch	*Musician*
Ann Hathaway	*Farmer's daughter*
Faten Hamama (1)	*Actress*
Nadiya Aja (2)	*Saudi tycoon's daughter*
Lana Turner (1)	*Actress*
Ava Gardner (2)	*Actress*
Patty Hearst	*Heiress*
Charlotte Payne-Townshend	*Heiress*
Mary Ure	*Actress*
Mary Godwin	*Writer*
Elizabeth Linley	*Composer's daughter*
Aino Järnefelt	*General's daughter*
Carrie Fisher (2)	*Actress*
Ava Gardner (2)	*Actress*
Mia Farrow (3)	*Actress*
Barbara Marx (4)	*Actress*
Donna D'Errico	*'Baywatch' actress*
Barbara Hepworth	*Sculptor*
Phyllis Sellick	*Pianist*
Sarah Greene	*TV presenter*
Xanthippe	*Athenian*
Janet Street-Porter	*TV presenter*
Valerie Pitts	*TV presenter*
Edith Fricker	*Socialite*
Veronica Bennett	*Singer*
Victoria Lockwood	*Model*
Elizabeth Boyle	*Socialite*
Kate Capshaw (2)	*Actress*
Amy Irving (1)	*Actress*
Catherine Woodville	*Sister-In-law of Edward 1V*
Sasha Czatv (1)	*Theatre usher*
Brigitte Nielsen (2)	*Actress*
Jennifer Flavin (3)	*Model*
Liza Goddard	*Actress*
Maureen Cox (1)	*Childhood sweetheart*
Barbara Bach (2)	*Actress*
Claire Bloom	*Actress*
Anita Ekber	*Actress*
Deborah Harry	*Singer*
Maggie Smith	*Actress*
Fanny Osbourne	*Actress*
Siobhan Fahey	*Singer*
Wendy Neuss	*Producer ('Startrek')*
Alana Hamilton (1)	*Model*
Rachel Hunter (2)	*Model*
Evelyn Lear	*Soprano*
Georgia O' Keeffe	*US Painter*
Frances Tomelty (1)	*Actress*
Trudie Styler (2)	*Actress*

Leopold Stokowski	Conductor	Olga Samaroff (1)	Pianist
John Stonehouse	Politician	Sheila Buckley	Secretary
Richard Strauss	Composer	Pauline de Ahna	Soprano
Igor Stravinsky	Composer	Catherine Nossenko (1)	Stravinsky's cousin
		Vera de Bosset Sudekeine (2)	Ballet dancer
Roy Strong	Writer and historian	Julia Trevelyan Oman	Designer
Josef Suk	Violinist	Otilie Dvorák	Daughter of Antonin Dvorák
Clive Swift (1)	Author	Margaret Drabble	Novelist
James Taylor	Composer	Carly Simon	Singer
Robert Taylor	Actor	Barbara Stanwyck	Actress
Pyotr Tchaikovsky	Composer	Antonina Miliukova	Pupil of Tchaikovsky
William Temple	Diplomat and essayist	Dorothy Osborne	Daughter of governor of Guernsey
David Teniers the Younger	Flemish painter	Anna Brueghel	Daughter of Jan Brueghel
Jon Tenney	Actor	Teri Hatcher	Actress
Denis Thatcher	Businessman	Margaret Kempson (1)	Housewife
John Thaw (2)	Actor	Margaret Roberts (2)	Politician
		Sheila Hancock	Actress
Ben Thomas (2)	Actor	Roseanne Barr	Actress
Billy Bob Thornton	Actor	Cynda Williams	Actress
Jeremy Thorpe (2)	Politician	Marion Stein	Musician
Tom Thumb	Circus performer	Lavinia Warren	Circus performer
Mike Todd	Showman	Elizabeth Taylor (3)	Actress
		Joan Blondell (2)	Actress
Mel Torme (1)	Singer	Janette Scott (3)	
Tico Torres	Pop musician (Bon Jovi)	Eva Herzigova	Model
Bill Travers	Actor	Virginia McKenna (2)	Actress
John Travolta	Actor	Kelly Preston	Actress
Mike Tyson	Boxer	Robin Givens (1)	Actress
		Monica Turner (2)	Actress
Inaki Urdangarin	Handball player	Christina	Spanish Infanta
Roger Vadim	Film director	Brigitte Bardot (1)	Actress
		Jane Fonda (2)	Actress
Peter Vaughan	Actor	Billie Whitelaw (1)	Actress
		Lillias Walker (2)	Actress
Giuseppe Verdi	Composer	Margherita Barezzi (1)	Daughter of Verdi's sponsor
		Giuseppina Strepponi (2)	Soprano
Richard Wagner	Composer	Minna Planer (1)	Opera singer and actress
		Cosima Von Bülow (2)	Franz Liszt's daughter
Robert Wagner	Actor	Natalie Wood (1) and (3)	Actress
		Marion Marshall (2)	Actress
		Jill St John (4)	Actress
John Warner (7)	Senator	Elizabeth Taylor	Actress
Robert Walker (1)	Actor	Jennifer Jones	Actress
George Washington	US president	Martha Custis	Socialite
Dennis Waterman	Actor	Patricia Maynard (2)	Actress
		Rula Lenska (3)	Actress
George Frederick Watts (1)	English painter	Ellen Terry	English actress
Carl Wayne	Actor and singer	Sue Hanson	Actress
Kurt Weill	Composer	Lotte Lenya	Actress and singer
Mark Weinberg	Businessman	Anouska Hempel	Actress
Orson Welles (2)	Actor and director	Rita Hayworth (2)	Actress
HG Wells	Author	Amy Robbins	Student
Franz Werfel (3)	Writer	Alma Maria Schindler	Musician
Timothy West	Actor	Prunella Scales	Actress
James McNeill Whistler	Artist	Beatrix Godwin	Widow of EW Godwin (architect)
Desmond Wilcox	Producer	Esther Rantzen	Broadcaster
Herbert Wilcox	Film director	Anna Neagle	Actress
Gene Wilder	Actor	Gilda Radner	Psychotherapist
Oscar Wilde	Playwright and novelist	Constance Lloyd	Socialite
Michael Wilding	Actor	Elizabeth Taylor (2)	Actress
		Margaret Leighton (4)	Actress
William III	British king	Mary II	British queen
William IV	British king	Adelaide	German noblewoman
Andy Williams	Singer	Claudine Longet	Actress
Hugh Williams	TV magnate	Sue Lawley	Broadcaster
Michael Williams	Actor	Judi Dench	Actress
Bruce Willis	Actor	Demi Moore	Actress

Brian Wolfe (2)	Theatre producer	*Jill Browne*	*Actress*
Stevie Wonder	Musician	*Syreeta Wright*	*Singer*
Edward Woodward	Actor	*Venetia Barrett (1)*	*Actress*
		Michelle Dotrice (2)	*Actress*
Leonard Woolf	Publisher and writer	*Virginia Stephen*	*Novelist*
William Wordsworth	Poet	*Mary Hutchinson*	*Socialite*
Billy Wright	Footballer	*Joy Beverley*	*Singer*
William Wyler	Film director	*Margaret Sullavan*	*Actress*
Bill Wyman	Rolling Stone	*Astrid Lundstrom (2)*	*Model*
		Mandy Smith (3)	*Model*
Michael Wynn Jones	Publisher	*Delia Smith*	*Cookery writer*
WB Yeats	Poet	*Georgie Hyde-Lees*	*Socialite*
Sergei Yessenin	Poet	*Isadora Duncan (1)*	*Dancer*
Gig Young	Actor	*Elizabeth Montgomery (3)*	*Actress*
Zeus	Greek supreme god	*Metis (1)*	*Greek sea nymph*
		Themis (2)	*Daughter of Gaia and Uranus*
		Hera (3)	*Sister of Zeus*
Efrem Zimbalist	Violinist	*Alma Gluck*	*Soprano*
Antonio Zucchi	Venetian painter	*Angelica Kaufmann*	*Swiss painter*

Middle Names: Ordered by Middle Name

First Name	*Middle Name(s)*	*Surname*	
Søren	**Aabye**	KIERKEGAARD	Danish philosopher
Herbert	**Aaron**	HAUPTMAN	US physicist
Elvis	**Aaron**	PRESLEY	US singer
Selman	**Abraham**	WAKSMAN	US biochemist
James	**Abram**	GARFIELD	US president
Claude	**Achille**	DEBUSSY	Composer
John	**Addington**	SYMONDS	Author
Hans	**Adolph**	KREBS	British biochemist
Walter	**Adolf**	GROPIUS	Architect
Henry	**Agard**	WALLACE	US vice-president
Robin	**Airling**	HANBURY-TENISON	Explorer
Chester	**Alan**	ARTHUR	US president
Bob	**Alan**	DYLAN	Singer and composer
Graham	**Alan**	GOOCH	Cricketer
James	**Albert**	MICHENER	Author
Francis (Frank)	**Albert**	SINATRA	Singer
Hans	**Albrecht**	BETHE	US physicist
John	**Alden**	CARPENTER	Musician and businessman
Gene	**Alden**	HACKMAN	Actor
Nelson	**Aldrich**	ROCKEFELLER	US vice-president
Nicholas	**Alexander**	FALDO	Golfer
Alan	**Alexander**	MILNE	Author
Robert	**Alexander**	RUNCIE	Archbishop of Canterbury
Peter	**Alexander**	USTINOV	Actor and writer
Henry	**Alfred**	KISSINGER	US statesman
Marcus	**Algernon**	ADAMS	Photographer
Enid	**Algerine**	BAGNOLD	Author
Ellen	**Alice**	TERRY	Actress
Charles	**Allston**	COLLINS	Artist
Tony	**Aloysius**	HANCOCK	TV character
James	**Aloysius**	HANSOM	Designer
Glenn	**Alton**	MILLER	Musician
Thomas	**Alva**	EDISON	Inventor
Pedro	**Alvarez**	CABRAL	Navigator
Elmer	**Ambrose**	SPERRY	US inventor
Billy	**Ambrose**	WRIGHT	Footballer
Meyer	**Amschel**	ROTHSCHILD	German financier
Nikolai	**Andreievich**	RIMSKY-KORSAKOV	Composer
Michael J	**Andrew**	FOX	Actor
Miguel	**Angel**	ASTURIAS	Guatemalan poet
George	**Anthony**	NEWLEY	Actor and singer
Giacomo	**Antonio**	PUCCINI	Composer
Hendrik	**Antoon**	LORENTZ	Dutch physicist
Benjamin	**Apthorp**	GOULD	US astronomer
Spangler	**Arlington**	BROUGH	Actor

First Name	Middle Name(s)	Surname	
Enoch	**Arnold**	BENNETT	Author
Philip	**Arnold**	HESELTINE	Composer
Eric	**Arthur**	BLAIR	Author
Kenneth	**Arthur**	DODD	Comedian
Cliff	**Arthur**	MICHELMORE	Broadcaster
Robert	**Arthur Talbot**	CECIL	British prime minister
Pierre	**Athanase**	LAROUSSE	French publisher
George	**Augustus**	ARLISS	Actor
Charles	**Augustus**	LINDBERGH	US aviator
Francis	**Aungier**	LONGFORD	Prison reformer
Richard	**Austen**	BUTLER	Politician
Henry	**Austin**	DOBSON	Poet
Erik	**Axel**	KARLFELDT	Swedish poet
Julia	**Babette Sarah**	NEUBERGER	Rabbi
Thomas	**Babington**	MACAULAY	Author
Brian	**Baden**	MOORE	Football commentator
Thomas	**Bailey**	ALDRICH	Author
Jane	**Baillie**	CARLYLE	Wife of Thomas Carlyle
Lyndon	**Baines**	JOHNSON	US president
Ronnie	**Balfour**	CORBETT	Comedian
Robert	**Banks**	JENKINSON	British prime minister
Robert	**Bannatyne**	FINLAY	Politician
Jocelyn	**Barbara**	HEPWORTH	Sculptor
Ruth	**Barbara**	RENDELL	Crime novellist
Peter	**Barker Howard**	MAY	Cricketer
John	**Barry**	HUMPHRIES	Comedian and writer
Isaac	**Bashevis**	SINGER	Writer
George	**Basil**	HUME	Cardinal
Upton	**Beall**	SINCLAIR	US novelist
Claire	**Berenice**	RAYNER	Broadcaster
Alan	**Beresford**	B' STARD	TV character ('New Statesman')
Norman	**Beresford**	TEBBIT	Politician
Colin	**Berkeley**	MOYNIHAN	Politician
Henry	**Bernard**	LEVIN	Journalist and author
George	**Bernard**	SHAW	Author
John (Jack)	**Berry**	HOBBS	English cricketer
George	**Biddell**	AIRY	Astronomer
Rutherford	**Birchard**	HAYES	US president
John	**Bird**	SUMNER	Archbishop of Canterbury
John ('Dizzy')	**Birks**	GILLESPIE	Jazz trumpeter
Bill	**Blackledge**	BEAUMONT	Rugby union player
Joseph	**Blanco**	WHITE	English poet
Cecil	**Blount**	DE MILLE	Film director
John	**Bodkin**	ADAMS	Doctor and murder suspect
Christian	**Boehmer**	ANFINSEN	US biochemist
Wilson	**Boit**	KIPKETER	Kenyan s/chase WR 13/8/97
Ulrich	**Bonnell**	PHILLIPS	US historian
Ernst	**Boris**	CHAIN	German biochemist
Arthur	**Bowden**	ASKEY	Comedian
Richard	**Bowdler**	SHARPE	Ornithologist
Lester	**Bowles**	PEARSON	Canadian politician
Leslie	**Bowyer**	CHARTERIS	Author
John	**Boyd**	DUNLOP	Inventor
John	**Boynton**	PRIESTLEY	Author
William	**Bradford**	SHOCKLEY	American physicist
James	**Branch**	CABELL	Novelist
Charles	**Brenton**	HUGGINS	American surgeon
William	**Bridges**	ADAMS	Engineer
George	**Brinton**	McCLELLAN	US soldier
Roy	**Broadbent**	FULLER	Poet
Amos	**Bronson**	ALCOTT	Transcendentalist
Susan	**Brownell**	ANTHONY	Suffragette
Lawrence	**Bruno Nero**	DALLAGLIO	Rugby player
Lee	**Buck**	TREVINO	American golfer
Matthew	**Bunker**	RIDGWAY	US soldier
Charles	**Burgess**	FRY	Sportsman
Walter	**Burley**	GRIFFIN	US architect
Lawrence	**Burnett**	GOWING	Painter
Robert	**Burns**	WOODWARD	American chemist
Stephen	**Burton**	LANCASTER	Actor

First Name	Middle Name(s)	Surname	
Paul	**Bustill Le Roy**	ROBESON	Actor
William	**Butler**	YEATS	Author
James	**Byron**	DEAN	Actor
Percy	**Bysshe**	SHELLEY	Poet
John	**Cabell**	BRECKINRIDGE	US vice-president
Henry	**Cabot**	LODGE	US senator
Ben	**Caine**	HOLLIOAKE	English cricketer
John	**Caldwell**	CALHOUN	US vice-president
Hugh	**Callum**	LAURIE	Actor and comedian
John	**Calvin**	COOLIDGE	US president
Edward	**Calvin**	KENDALL	American chemist
John	**Cameron**	MORTON	Journalist
King	**Camp**	GILLETTE	Inventor
Donald	**Campbell**	DEWAR	British politician
Patricia	**Campbell**	HEARST	Heiress
Archibald	**Campbell**	TAIT	Archbishop of Canterbury
Christopher	**Carandini**	LEE	Actor
John	**Carew**	ECCLES	Australian neurophysiologist
Peter	**Carl**	FABERGÉ	Russian goldsmith
Peter	**Carl**	GOLDMARK	Inventor
Wilhelm	**Carl**	GRIMM	Folklorist
Linus	**Carl**	PAULING	Scientist
Daniel	**Carleton**	GAJDUSEK	US virologist
Hugh	**Carleton**	GREENE	Journalist and broadcaster
Percy	**Carlyle**	GILCHRIST	Metallurgist
Gertrude	**Caroline**	EDERLE	US swimmer
Hugh	**Caswell Tremenheere**	DOWDING	RAF chief
Maureen	**Catherine**	CONNOLLY	Tennis Pro
George	**Catlett**	MARSHALL	US soldier and statesman
Lawrence (Larry)	**Cecil**	ADLER	Musician
James	**Cellan**	JONES	Film director
Thomas	**Chandler**	HALIBURTON	Canadian writer
Joel	**Chandler**	HARRIS	Author
Samuel	**Chao Chung**	TING	US physicist
Frederick	**Chapman**	ROBBINS	US physiologist
Kenneth	**Charles**	BRANAGH	Actor
Tjalling	**Charles**	KOOPMANS	US economist
Anthony	**Charles Lynton**	BLAIR	Politician
Richard	**Charles Nicholas**	BRANSON	Entrepreneur
Denis	**Charles Scott**	COMPTON	Cricketer
Rodney	**Charlton**	TROTTER	'Fools and Horses' character
Walter	**Chauncy**	CAMP	American footballer
Rupert	**Chawner**	BROOKE	Poet
Johann	**Christian**	BACH	Composer
Patrick	**Christopher**	STEPTOE	Gynaecologist
Dennis	**Christopher George**	POTTER	Playwright
Chris	**Clairmonte**	LEWIS	Cricketer
Herbert	**Clark**	HOOVER	US president
William	**Claude**	FIELDS	Comedian and actor
Roy	**Claxton**	ACUFF	Country musician
Harold	**Clayton**	LLOYD	US film comedian
Thomas	**Clayton**	WOLFE	Novelist
Elizabeth	**Cleghorn**	GASKELL	Writer
Edmund	**Clerihew**	BENTLEY	Writer
Marcus	**Cocceius**	NERVA	Roman emperor
John	**Cody Fiddler**	SIMPSON	News reporter
Michael	**Colin**	COWDREY	Cricketer
Norman	**Colin**	DEXTER	Author
Stephen	**Collins**	FOSTER	US songwriter
Mel	**Columcille**	GIBSON	Actor
Louis	**Comfort**	TIFFANY	Glassmaker
Milner	**Connorton**	GRAY	Graphic designer
Gianfranco	**Corsi**	ZEFFIRELLI	Film director
Alfred	**Cort**	HADDON	Anthropologist
Ingvar	**Costa**	CARLSSON	Swedish politician
Reginald	**Cotterell**	BUTLER	Sculptor
John	**Couch**	ADAMS	Astronomer
Ludovic	**Coverley**	KENNEDY	Broadcaster
John	**Cowdery**	KENDREW	English biochemist
Cornelius	**Crane**	CHASE	Actor

First Name	Middle Name(s)	Surname	
Elzie	**Crisler**	SEGAR	US strip cartoonist
Betsy	**Cromer**	BYARS	Novelist
John	**Crowe**	RANSOM	US poet and critic
Dorothy	**Crowfoot**	HODGKIN	Scientist
William	**Cullen**	BRYANT	Poet
Gene	**Curran**	KELLY	Dancer
Gordon	**Cuthbert**	GREENIDGE	Cricketer
Len	**Cyril**	DEIGHTON	Novelist
Herman	**Cyril**	McNEILE	Author
Gabriel	**Daniel**	FAHRENHEIT	Physicist
Arnold	**Daniel**	PALMER	Golfer
Dwight	**David**	EISENHOWER	US president
Benny	**David**	GOODMAN	US Jazz clarinetist
Jerome	**David**	SALINGER	Author
Joan	**Dawson**	BAKEWELL	Broadcaster
Alfred	**Day**	HERSHEY	US biologist
Humphrey	**De Forest**	BOGART	Actor
Everton	**Decourcey**	WEEKES	West Indian cricketer
Franklin	**Delano**	ROOSEVELT	US president
William	**Denby**	HANNA	US animated cartoonist
Danny	**Dennio**	BLANCHFLOWER	Footballer
Michael	**Denzil Xavier**	PORTILLO	Politician
Earl	**Derr**	BIGGERS	US novelist
Henri	**Desire**	LANDRU	French murderer
Andrew	**Dewar**	GIBB	Scottish jurist
Miles	**Dewey**	DAVIS	Jazz musician
James	**Dewey**	WATSON	US biologist
Maureen	**Diane**	LIPMAN	Actress
Michael	**Dibdin**	HESELTINE	Politician
John	**Dickson**	CARR	US detective writer
Richard	**Doddridge**	BLACKMORE	Author
Juan	**Domingo**	PERÓN	Argentinian president
Frederick	**Donald**	COGGAN	Archbishop of Canterbury
Harry	**Donald**	SECOMBE	Comedian and singer
Alan	**Donald**	WHICKER	Broadcaster
Stella	**Dorothea**	GIBBONS	Writer
Phyllis	**Dorothy**	JAMES	Authoress
Heber	**Doust**	CURTIS	US astronomer
Henry	**Drysdale**	DAKIN	Chemist
Donald	**Duart**	MACLEAN	English traitor
Thomas	**Duffus**	HARDY	Archivist
Charlie	**Dunbar**	BROAD	Philosopher
John	**Dunmore**	LANG	Clergyman
Bob	**Dylan**	WILLIS	Cricketer
Anthony	**Dymoke**	POWELL	English novelist
James	**Earl**	CARTER	US president
Alfred	**Edgar**	COPPARD	Writer
John	**Edgar**	HOOVER	FBI director
Billy	**Edmund**	BUTLIN	Businessman
Ferdinand	**Edralin**	MARCOS	Filipino president
Lewis	**Edson**	WATERMAN	Inventor
Alfred	**Edward**	HOUSMAN	Author
Thomas	**Edward**	LAWRENCE	Author and soldier
Jonas	**Edward**	SALK	Biologist
Joseph	**Eggleston**	JOHNSTON	US soldier
Michael	**Elias**	BALCON	Film producer
Walt	**Elias**	DISNEY	Film producer
Gottlieb	**Eliel**	SAARINEN	Finnish/US architect
Mary	**Elizabeth**	PETERS	Pentathlete
Mai	**Elizabeth**	ZETTERLING	Actress and director
James	**Elroy**	FLECKER	Poet
Douglas	**Elton**	FAIRBANKS (Snr)	Actor
Charles	**Elwood**	YEAGER	US test pilot
George	**Emil**	PALADE	US biologist
Angelina	**Emily**	GRIMKE	US feminist
Barry	**Emmanuel**	TUCKWELL	Australian musician
John	**Enoch**	POWELL	British politician
George	**Eric**	NEWBY	Author
Oswald	**Ernald**	MOSLEY	British politician
Herbert	**Ernest**	BATES	Author

First Name	Middle Name(s)	Surname	
John	**Ernest**	STEINBECK	US novelist
Nigel	**Ernest James**	MANSELL	Racing driver
Robert	**Erskine**	CHILDERS	Writer
Richard	**Erskine Frere**	LEAKEY	Palaeontologist and naturalist
Bartolomé	**Estebàn**	MURILLO	Spanish painter
Maria	**Esther**	BUENO	Tennis player
Linda	**Esther**	GRAY	Scottish soprano
Willis	**Eugene**	LAMB	American physicist
Richard	**Evelyn**	BYRD	Explorer
Norman	**Everard**	BROOKES	Tennis player
William	**Ewart**	GLADSTONE	British prime minister
Adlai	**Ewing**	STEVENSON	US politician
Charles	**Farrar**	BROWNE	Humorist and writer
Pearl	**Fay**	WHITE	US actress
Igor	**Fedorovich**	STRAVINSKY	Composer
Isidor	**Feinstein**	STONE	US journalist
David	**Feodorovich**	OISTRAKH	Violinist
Carl	**Ferdinand**	CORI	American biochemist
Max	**Ferdinand**	PERUTZ	British biochemist
Ana	**Fidelia**	QUIROT	Cuban athlete
Dwight	**Filley**	DAVIS	Founder of Davis Cup
Oscar	**Fingal O'Flahertie Wills**	WILDE	Writer
Robin	**Finlayson**	COOK	Politician
Samuel	**Finley Breese**	MORSE	US inventor
Harlan	**Fiske**	STONE	US judge
John	**Fitzgerald**	KENNEDY	US president
Harry	**Flood**	BYRD	Politician
Lillian	**Florence**	HELLMAN	US playwright
Sarah	**Flower**	ADAMS	English poet
Chester	**Floyd**	CARLSON	US inventor
Sade	**Folasade**	ADU	Singer
Leopoldo	**Fortunato**	GALTIERI	Argentinian politician
Norman	**Foster**	RAMSEY	US physicist
Geoffrey	**Francis**	FISHER	Archbishop of Canterbury
Robert	**Francis**	KENNEDY	US politician
Donald	**Francis**	TOVEY	Pianist and composer
Daley	**Francis Morgan**	THOMPSON	Athlete
James	**Franciscus**	DURANTE	Entertainer
Charles	**François**	GOUNOD	Composer
Anatole	**François**	THIBAULT	Author
John	**Franklin**	CANDY	Actor
Samuel	**Franklin**	CODY	Aviator
John	**Franklin**	ENDERS	US bacteriologist
Billy	**Franklin**	GRAHAM	US evangelist
Robert	**Franklin**	STROUD	Birdman of Alcatraz
William	**Frederick**	CODY	Showman
Ronald	**Frederick**	DELDERFIELD	Author
Alexander	**Frederick**	DOUGLAS-HOME	British prime minister
Spencer	**Frederick**	GORE	Painter
George	**Frederick**	HANDEL	Composer
Walter	**Frederick (Fritz)**	MONDALE	US vice-president
Thomas	**Frognall**	DIBDIN	Librarian
Robert	**Gabriel**	MUGABE	Zimbabwean president
Mario	**Gabriele**	ANDRETTI	Racing driver
Sidonie	**Gabrielle**	COLETTE	Authoress
Matthew	**Galbraith**	PERRY	US naval officer
Warren	**Gamaliel**	HARDING	US president
Gabriel	**Garcia**	MARQUEZ	Columbian author
Jan	**Garrigue**	MASARYK	Czech statesman
Charles	**Gates**	DAWES	US vice-president
Johannes	**Gensfleisch**	GUTENBERG	German Printer
Billy	**George**	BUNTER	Fictional character
Lawrence	**George**	DURRELL	Novelist
Rodney	**George**	LAVER	Tennis player
Roger	**George**	MOORE	Actor
Andre	**George**	PREVIN	Conductor
William	**Gerald**	GOLDING	Novelist
John	**Gerard**	BRAINE	Novelist
William	**Gershom**	COLLINGWOOD	Artist
Roger	**Gilbert**	BANNISTER	Athlete

First Name	Middle Name(s)	Surname	
William	**Gilbert**	GRACE	Cricketer
Ian	**Gillett**	CARMICHAEL	Actor
Eugene	**Gladstone**	O'NEILL	US playwright
William	**Gladstone**	STEWART	TV broadcaster/producer
Charles	**Glover**	BARKLA	English physicist
Robson	**Golightly**	GREEN	Actor
Dean	**Gooderham**	ACHESON	US statesman
Sydney	**Goodsir**	SMITH	Poet
James	**Gordon**	BROWN	Politician
George	**Gordon**	BYRON	Poet
Neil	**Gordon**	KINNOCK	Politician
Harry	**Gordon**	SELFRIDGE	British merchant
Norman	**Graham**	HILL	Racing driver
Robert	**Graeme**	POLLOCK	Cricketer
James	**Graham**	BALLARD	Author
Frederick	**Grant**	BANTING	Physiologist
Lewis	**Grassic**	GIBBON	Novelist
Elisha	**Graves**	OTIS	Inventor
Charles	**Greely**	ABBOT	Astrophysicist
Emily	**Greene**	BALCH	US social reformer
Eldred	**Gregory**	PECK	Actor
Pelham	**Grenville**	WODEHOUSE	Author
Jack	**Griffith**	LONDON	US novelist
Thomas	**Griffiths**	WAINEWRIGHT	Art critic and murderer
Samuel	**Griswold**	GOODRICH	US publisher
Stephen	**Grover**	CLEVELAND	US president
James	**Grover**	THURBER	Humorist
Carl	**Gustav**	JUNG	Swiss psychiatrist
Magdi	**Habib**	YACOUB	Surgeon
Edvard	**Hagerup**	GRIEG	Norwegian composer
William	**Hale**	WHITE	Writer
Barbara	**Hamilton**	CARTLAND	Writer
George	**Hamilton**	GORDON	British prime minister
Charles	**Hamilton**	SORLEY	Poet
Glen	**Hammond**	CURTISS	US air pioneer
Terence	**Hanbury**	WHITE	Novelist
Fred	**Handel**	ELLIOTT	'Coronation Street' character
John	**Hanning**	SPEKE	Explorer
Martin	**Harcourt**	CHIVERS	Footballer
Charles	**Hard**	TOWNES	American physicist
Terence (Terry)	**Hardy**	WAITE	Religious adviser
Maurice	**Harold**	MACMILLAN	British prime minister
James	**Harold**	WILSON	British prime minister
Emma	**Harriet**	NICHOLSON	Politician
Roy	**Harris**	JENKINS	Politician
Kenneth	**Harry**	CLARKE	Politician
Francis	**Harry Compton**	CRICK	Biologist
Hawley	**Harvey**	CRIPPEN	Murderer
John	**Harvey**	KELLOGG	Inventor
Willis	**Haviland**	CARRIER	US inventor
Alfred	**Hawthorne**	HILL	Comedian
Mary	**Hayley**	BELL	Playwright
David	**Hayward**	BOWIE	Musician
Oliver	**Hazard**	PERRY	US naval officer
Publius	**Helvius**	PERTINAX	Roman emperor
Joan	**Henrietta**	COLLINS	Actress
Herbert	**Henry**	ASQUITH	British prime minister
William	**Henry**	CAVENDISH-BENTINCK	British prime minister
Augustus	**Henry**	FITZROY	British prime minister
William	**Henry**	HARRISON	US president
Fiorello	**Henry**	LA GUARDIA	US politician
Richard	**Henry Simpson**	STILGOE	Songwriter and broadcaster
Robert	**Hepler**	LOWE	Actor
Horatio	**Herbert**	KITCHENER	Irish soldier and statesman
David	**Herbert**	LAWRENCE	Author
George	**Herbert Walker**	BUSH	US president
Elton	**Hercules**	JOHN	Singer and composer
John	**Herschel**	GLENN	US astronaut and politician
Cyrus	**Herzl**	GORDON	US Hebrew scholar
Margaret	**Hilda**	THATCHER	British prime minister

First Name	Middle Name(s)	Surname	
Virginia	**Hilda Brunette Maxwell**	BOTTOMLEY	Politician
Henry	**Hinchcliffe**	AINLEY	Actor
Dag	**Hjalmar Agne Carl**	HAMMARSKJÖLD	Swedish statesman
Arthur	**Holly**	COMPTON	Physicist
Eric	**Honeywood**	PARTRIDGE	Lexicographer
James	**Hopwood**	JEANS	Physicist and astronomer
Hubert	**Horatio**	HUMPHREY	US vice-president
Walter	**Houser**	BRATTAIN	American physicist
Jeffrey	**Howard**	ARCHER	Author
Tasker	**Howard**	BLISS	Soldier and statesman
William	**Howard**	STEIN	US biochemist
William	**Howard**	TAFT	US president
Bernard	**Howell**	LEACH	English potter
William	**Howson**	TAYLOR	Potter
George	**Hoy**	FORMBY	Singer and musician
John	**Hoyer**	UPDIKE	Author
Elinor	**Hoyt**	WYLIE	US author
Thomas	**Huckle**	WELLER	US physiologist
Wystan	**Hugh**	AUDEN	Poet
Michael	**Hugh**	MEACHER	Politician
Hector	**Hugh**	MUNRO	Author
Mark	**Hume**	McCORMACK	Promoter
David	**Hunter**	HUBEL	US neurophysiologist
William	**Hunter Fisher**	CARSON	Jockey
Robert	**Hutchings**	GODDARD	US rocket pioneer
Leonid	**Ilich**	BREZHNEV	USSR president
Vladimir	**Ilyich**	LENIN	Russian revolutionary
Pyotr	**Ilyich**	TCHAIKOVSKY	Composer
Rupert	**Iolanthe**	RIGSBY	TV character ('Rising Damp')
Alexander	**Isaevich**	SOLZHENITSYN	Author
Jeremy	**Israel**	ISAACS	Arts mogul
George	**Ivan**	MORRISON	Singer and composer
James	**Jackson**	JEFFRIES	Boxing champion
Paul	**Jackson**	POLLOCK	US artist
Samuel	**Jackson**	SNEAD	Golfer
Lucinda	**Jane**	GREEN	Three-day eventer
Kiri	**Janette**	TE KANAWA	Opera singer
Abel	**Janszoon**	TASMAN	Navigator
Stanley	**Jasspon**	KUNITZ	US poet
William	**Jefferson**	HAGUE	Politician
William	**Jefferson Blyth**	CLINTON	US president
Michael	**Jeffrey**	JORDAN	US basketball player
Ada	**Jemima**	CROSSLEY	Australian contralto
John	**Jeremy**	THORPE	Politician
Gary	**Jim**	PLAYER	Golfer
Barbra	**Joan**	STREISAND	Singer
Liv	**Johanne**	ULLMANN	Norwegian actress
Stephen	**John**	FRY	Actor and author
Tony	**John**	HANCOCK	Comedy Actor
Arthur	**John**	GIELGUD	Actor
Frederick	**John**	ROBINSON	British prime minister
Henry	**John**	TEMPLE	British prime minister
Jeremy	**John Durham**	ASHDOWN	Politician
Charles	**John Huffam**	DICKENS	Author
Ralph	**Johnson**	BUNCHE	American economist
Angelina	**Jolie**	VOIGHT	Actress
Irene	**Joliot**	CURIE	Nuclear Physicist
Anders	**Jonas**	ANGSTROM	Physicist
Samuel	**Jones**	TILDEN	US politician
Richard	**Jordan**	GATLING	Inventor
Michael	**Joseph**	CAINE	Actor
Archibald	**Joseph**	CRONIN	Author
Bruce	**Joseph**	FORSYTH	Entertainer
Israel	**Joshua**	SINGER	Writer
Stephen	**Joshua**	SONDHEIM	Composer and lyricist
River	**Jude**	PHOENIX	Actor
Diane	**Julie**	ABBOT	Politician
Ferdinand	**Julius**	COHN	Botanist
Annie	**Jump**	CANNON	US astronomer
Seamus	**Justin**	HEANEY	Poet

First Name	Middle Name(s)	Surname	
Aimo	Kaarlo	CAJANDER	Finnish politician
Niels	Kai	JERNE	Danish immunologist
Julius	Kambarage	NYERERE	Tanzanian president
Hastings	Kamuzu	BANDA	Malawi politician
Mohandas	Karamchand	GANDHI	Indian leader
Uma	Karuna	THURMAN	Actress
Haldan	Keffer	HARTLINE	US physiologist
Gilbert	Keith	CHESTERTON	Author
Will	Keith	KELLOGG	Inventor
Dennis	Keith	LILLEE	Australian cricketer
Lester	Keith	PIGGOTT	Jockey
Michael	Kemp	TIPPETT	Composer
Edward ('Duke')	Kennedy	ELLINGTON	Composer and pianist
Tom	Kennerley	WOLFE	Novelist
Laurence	Kerr	OLIVIER	Actor
Philip	Kindred	DICK	US writer
Henry	Kirke	BROWN	Sculptor
Ragnar	Kittil	FRISCH	Norwegian economist
Jerome	Klapka	JEROME	Author
Hablot	Knight	BROWNE	Illustrator
James	Knox	POLK	US president
Sally	Kristen	RIDE	US astronaut
Ian	Lancaster	FLEMING	English novelist
Raymond	Landry	POINCARÉ	French statesman
Edwin	Landseer	LUTYENS	English architect
Samuel	Langhorne	CLEMENS	Author
Mervyn	Laurence	PEAKE	Author and artist
Bernard	Law	MONTGOMERY	Field Marshall
Edward	Lawrie	TATUM	US biochemist
James	Leathes	PRIOR	Politician
George	Ledyard	STEBBINS	US botanist
Sheldon	Lee	GLASHOW	US physicist
Dustin	Lee	HOFFMAN	Actor
Arthur	Lehman	GOODHART	US jurist
Walter	Leland	CRONKITE	US broadcaster
James	Leonard	CALLAGHAN	British prime minister
George	Leonard	CAREY	Archbishop
Geoffrey	Leonard	CHESHIRE	Philanthropist
Aldous	Leonard	HUXLEY	Novelist
Winston	Leonard Spencer	CHURCHILL	British prime minister
Nelly	Leonie	SACHS	Swedish poet and playwright
Mstislav	Leopoldovich	ROSTROPOVICH	Cellist
John	Leslie	PRESCOTT	Politician
Bob	Leslie Townes	HOPE	Comedian
Basil	Lewis	D'OLIVEIRA	Cricketer
David	Lewis	JACOBS	Broadcaster
Harry (Bing)	Lillis	CROSBY	Vocalist and actor
Adam	Lindsay	GORDON	Australian poet
John	Liptrot	HATTON	Composer
Chris	Livingstone	EUBANK	Boxer
Adam	Llewellyn De Vere	ADAMANT	Fictional TV character
James	Logie	ROBERTSON	Poet
Val	Logsdon	FITCH	US physicist
Hugh	Longbourne	CALLENDAR	Physicist
Ezra	Loomis	POUND	Poet
Carl	Lotus	BECKER	US historian
John	Loughborough	PEARSON	Architect
Esther	Louise	RANTZEN	TV presenter
Thomas	Love	PEACOCK	Novelist and poet
Thomas	Lovell	BEDDOES	Poet and physiologist
Verney	Lovett	CAMERON	Explorer
Anita	Lucia	RODDICK	Businesswoman
Jacques	Lucien Jean	DELORS	European politician
Caroline	Lucretia	HERSCHEL	Astronomer
Lazarus	Ludwig	ZAMENHOF	Inventor of Esperanto
Jacob	Ludwig Carl	GRIMM	Folklorist
Maria	Lurdes	MUTOLA	Mozambique athlete
Jean	Lyndsey Torren	MARSH	Actress
Kenneth	Mackenzie	CLARK	Art historian
Michael	Mackintosh	FOOT	Politician

First Name	Middle Name(s)	Surname	
William	Maddock	BAYLISS	Physiologist
Eartha	Mae	KITT	Singer
William	Makepeace	THACKERAY	Author
onald	Malcolm	CAMPBELL	Car and boat racer
Gerald	Malcolm	DURRELL	Writer and naturalist
James	Mallahan	CAIN	Writer
Alice	Malsenior	WALKER	US novelist
Gerard	Manley	HOPKINS	Poet
Vosdanig	Manoog	ADOIAN	Painter
Cassius	Marcellus	CLAY	Boxer
Leon	Marcus	URIS	US author
William	Marcy	TWEED	US politician and criminal
Penelope	Margaret	LIVELY	Writer
Erich	Maria	REMARQUE	Author
Victor	Marie	HUGO	French writer
Dylan	Marlais	THOMAS	Poet
John	Marlan	POINDEXTER	US naval officer
David	Martin Scott	STEEL	Politician
John	Marwood	CLEESE	Actor
Meryl	Mary Louise	STREEP	Actress
Thomas	Massa	ALSAGER	Newspaper manager
Thomas	Masterman	HARDY	Naval officer
Kenneth	Mathieson	DALGLISH	Footballer
Alan	Mathison	TURING	Mathematician
James	Matthew	BARRIE	Author
Gerald	Maurice	EDELMAN	US biochemist
Hugh	Maxwell	CASSON	Architect
Liza	May	MINNELLI	Singer
Quintin	McGarel	HOGG	Politician
James	McGill	BUCHANAN	American economist
Edwin	McMasters	STANTON	US statesman
Frank	Meadow	SUTCLIFFE	Photographer
Alexander	Meigs	HAIG	US soldier
Friedrich	Melchior	GRIMM	Journalist
Maria	Meneghini	CALLAS	Operatic soprano
Richard	Mentor	JOHNSON	US vice-president
Isaac	Merritt	SINGER	US inventor
Robert	Merton	SOLOW	American economist
William	Mervyn	PICKWOAD	Actor
Ian	Michael	CHAPPELL	Cricketer
Arthur	Michael	RAMSEY	Archbishop of Canterbury
Arthur	Michell	RANSOME	Author
Frank	Michler	CHAPMAN	Ornithologist
John	Middleton	MURRY	Writer and critic
George	Mifflin	DALLAS	US vice-president
Richard	Milhous	NIXON	US president
Ernest	Millar	HEMINGWAY	American novelist
Dorothy	Miller	RICHARDSON	English novelist
John	Millington	SYNGE	Author
Thomas	Milner	GIBSON	Politician
Philip	Milton	ROTH	Novelist
Samora	Moises	MACHEL	Mozambique president
Charles	Monroe	SCHULZ	US cartoonist
Augustus	Montague	TOPLADY	Clergyman and hymnist
Edward	Montgomery	CLIFF	Actor
Sarah	Moore	GRIMKE	US feminist
Edward	Moore	KENNEDY	US politician
Edward	Morgan	FORSTER	Author
Barry	Morris	GOLDWATER	US politician
Bill	Morris	LAWRY	Australian cricketer
Jack	Morris	ROSENTHAL	Playwright
Frank	Mortimer Magilinne	WORRELL	Cricketer
Henry	Morton	STANLEY	Explorer and journalist
John	Moses	BROWNING	Gunsmith and inventor
Stephen	Moulton	BABCOCK	US agricultural chemist
Kenesaw	Mountain	LANDIS	Baseball commissioner
Desmond	Mpilo	TUTU	South African prelate
Joshua	Mqabuko Nyongolo	NKOMO	Zimbabwean politician
Nicholas	Murray	BUTLER	US educationist
Christopher	Murray	GRIEVE	Poet

First Name	Middle Name(s)	Surname	
Michael	**Murray**	HORDERN	Actor
John	**Nance**	GARNER	US vice-president
Maggie	**Natalie**	SMITH	Actress
Christian	**Neethling**	BARNARD	Surgeon
Pablo	**Neftali Reyes**	NERUDA	Poet
Leon	**Neil**	COOPER	US physicist
Omar	**Nelson**	BRADLEY	US soldier
Johann	**Nepomuk**	HUMMEL	Austrian pianist
Johann	**Nepomuk**	MAELZEL	German inventor
Bob	**Nesta**	MARLEY	Musician
Arthur	**Neville**	CHAMBERLAIN	Politician
Sebastian	**Newbold**	COE	Athlete and politician
Godfrey	**Newbold**	HOUNSFIELD	English electrical engineer
Edith	**Newbold**	WHARTON	Author
Joseph	**Nicéphore**	NIEPCE	Inventor
Conrad	**Nicholson**	HILTON	Businessman
Louis	**Nicolas**	VAUQUELIN	Chemist
Herbert	**Nigel**	GRESLEY	Locomotive engineer
Florence	**Nightingale**	GRAHAM	Beautician
Boris	**Nikolayevich**	YELTSIN	Russian president
Dirk	**Niven**	BOGARDE	Actor
Alfred	**North**	WHITEHEAD	Philosopher and mathematician
Cyril	**Northcote**	PARKINSON	Political scientist
Oliver	**Norville**	HARDY	Actor
William	**Nunn**	LIPSCOMB	US chemist
Thomas	**Octave Murdoch**	SOPWITH	Aircraft designer
Frederick	**Ogden**	NASH	Poet
Donald	**Olding**	HEBB	Canadian Psychologist
Robert	**Oliver**	REED	British Actor
David	**Oliver**	SELZNICK	US cinema mogul
Donald	**Oliver**	SOPER	Methodist minister
Judi	**Olivia**	DENCH	Actress
Henri	**Omer**	PÉTAIN	French statesman
James	**Orchard**	HALLIWELL-PHILLIPPS	Shakespearean scholar
Ronald	**Ossary**	DUNLOP	Irish painter
Hamilton	**Othanel**	SMITH	US molecular biologist
Selma	**Ottiliana Lovisa**	LAGERLOF	Swedish novelist
George	**Paget**	THOMSON	English physicist
Richard	**Palethorpe**	TODD	Actor
Publius	**Papinius**	STATIUS	Roman poet
David	**Paradine**	FROST	Interviewer and presenter
Clifton	**Parmelee**	WEBB	Actor
Levi	**Parsons**	MORTON	US vice-president
James	**Patrick**	DONLEAVY	Author
Nigel	**Paul**	KENNEDY	Violinist
James	**Paul**	MCCARTNEY	Musician and composer
Anton	**Pavlovich**	CHEKHOV	Russian author
George	**Peabody**	GOOCH	Politician
Walter	**Percy**	CHRYSLER	Automobile manufacturer
Charles	**Percy**	SNOW	Author
Vladimir	**Petrovich**	KUTS	Russian athlete
Francis	**Peyton**	ROUS	American pathologist
Anthony	**Philip**	HOPKINS	Actor
Archibald	**Philip**	PRIMROSE	British prime minister
Georg	**Philipp**	TELEMANN	Composer
Harry	**Philmore**	LANGDON	US comedian
Noël	**Pierce**	COWARD	Actor and dramatist
Samuel	**Pierpont**	LANGLEY	US aeronautic pioneer
Hilaire	**Pierre**	BELLOC	Writer
Lionel	**Pigot**	JOHNSON	Poet
Leslie	**Poles**	HARTLEY	Author
Klas	**Pontus**	ARNOLDSON	Swedish politician
James	**Prescott**	JOULE	Physicist
John	**Presper**	ECKERT	American inventor
Bob	**Primrose**	WILSON	Goalkeeper and broadcaster
Bob	**Prometheus**	FITZSIMMONS	Boxer
Arthur	**Quiller**	COUCH	Man of letters
John	**Quincy**	ADAMS	US president
Edward (Ted)	**Ralph**	DEXTER	Cricketer
James	**Ramsay**	MACDONALD	British prime minister

F
A
M
O
U
S

P
E
O
P
L
E

First Name	Middle Name(s)	Surname	
William	**Randal**	CREMER	Nobel laureate
Leroy	**Randle**	GRUMMAN	US aircraft pioneer
Joseph	**Randolf**	ACKERLEY	Author
Philip	**Ranulph**	DE GLANVILLE	Rugby Union player
Clement	**Raphael**	FREUD	Liberal politician
Michael	**Ray Dibdin**	HESELTINE	Politician
Tyrus	**Raymond**	COBB	Baseball player
Anna	**Raymond**	MASSEY	Actress
Daniel	**Raymond**	MASSEY	Actor
Brian	**Rayner**	COOK	English baritone
Miller	**Reece**	HUTCHINSON	Inventor
Edward	**Regan**	MURPHY	US Comedian
Georges	**Remi**	HERGÉ	Belgian cartoonist
Jaques	**René**	CHIRAC	Prime minister
Christian	**René**	DE DUVE	Belgian biochemist
John	**Richard**	SCHLESINGER	Film director
Humphrey	**Richard Adeane**	LYTTELTON	Musician
Nigel	**Richard Patton**	DEMPSTER	Gossip columnist
Henry	**Rider**	HAGGARD	Novelist
Howard	**Robard**	HUGHES	Businessman
Ian	**Robert**	MAXWELL	Businessman
Sheridan	**Robert**	MORLEY	Author and broadcaster
Trevor	**Robert**	NUNN	Theatre director
Christopher	**Robert**	SMITH	British politician
Henry	**Robinson**	LUCE	US magazine publisher
Joseph	**Roland**	BARBERA	US animated cartoonist
Nelson	**Rolihlahla**	MANDELA	South African president
Kenneth	**Ronald**	ROSEWALL	Tennis player
John	**Ronald Revel**	TOLKIEN	Author
Elizabeth	**Rosemond**	TAYLOR	Actress
Henry	**Rowley**	BISHOP	Composer
John	**Roy**	MAJOR	British prime minister
Benjamin	**Roy**	MOTTELSON	Danish physicist
Johann	**Rudolf**	WYSS	Swiss writer
Gerald	**Rudolph**	FORD	US president
William	**Rufus de Vane**	KING	US vice-president
Keith	**Rupert**	MURDOCH	Businessman
John	**Rushworth**	JELLICOE	Naval commander
David	**Russell**	LANGE	New Zealand politician
Steve	**Russell**	RACE	Broadcaster
Carlos	**Saavedra**	LAMAS	Argentinian jurist
Garfield	**St Auburn**	SOBERS	Cricketer
Ahmed	**Salman**	RUSHDIE	Author
Richard	**Samuel**	ATTENBOROUGH	Actor
Baruch	**Samuel**	BLUMBERG	US biochemist
Robert	**Sanderson**	MULLIKEN	American chemist
Cherilyn (Cher)	**Sarkisian**	LAPIERRE	Singer
Arthur	**Sarsfield**	WARD	Author
Carlos	**Saul**	MENEM	Argentinian politician
Walter	**Savage**	LANDOR	Writer
Victor	**Sawdon**	PRITCHETT	Writer and critic
Wilfrid	**Scawen**	BLUNT	Poet
James	**Schoolcraft**	SHERMAN	US vice-president
William	**Schwenck**	GILBERT	Librettist
Jimmy	**Scott**	CONNORS	Tennis player
Cecil	**Scott**	FORESTER	Author
Michael	**Scudamore**	REDGRAVE	Actor
Peter	**Seamus**	O'TOOLE	Irish actor
Johann	**Sebastian**	BACH	Composer
John	**Selwyn**	GUMMER	Politician
Tiberius	**Sempronius**	GRACCHUS	Roman statesman
Sergei	**Sergeyevich**	PROKOFIEV	Composer
William	**Seward**	BURROUGHS	Author
Clarence	**Seward**	DARROW	US lawyer
Frederick (Freddy)	**Sewards**	TRUEMAN	Cricketer
Robert	**Seymour**	BRIDGES	Poet
Jane	**Seymour**	FONDA	Actress
Arthur	**Seymour**	SULLIVAN	Composer
Hugh	**Seymour**	WALPOLE	Novelist
Edward	**Sheriff**	CURTIS	US photographer

First Name	Middle Name(s)	Surname	
Charles	**Sherwood**	STRATTON	Circus performer
Philip	**Showalter**	HENCH	American physician
Ulysses	**Simpson**	GRANT	US president
Harry	**Sinclair**	LEWIS	US Novelist
Frederick	**Sleigh**	ROBERTS	British soldier
Simon	**Smith**	KUZNETS	US economist
Aristotle	**Socrates**	ONASSIS	Shipping magnate
Canaan	**Sodindo**	BANANA	Zimbabwe president
William	**Somerset**	MAUGHAM	Author
Richard	**Southwell**	BOURKE	Earl of Mayo
John	**Spedan**	LEWIS	Businessman
Charlie	**Spencer**	CHAPLIN	Comedy actor
Herbert	**Spencer**	GASSER	US physiologist
Henry	**Spencer**	MOORE	Sculptor
Elizabeth	**Sprague**	COOLIDGE	American pianist
Stavros	**Spyros**	NIARCHOS	Greek ship owner
Richard	**Stafford**	CRIPPS	Politician
Thomas	**Stamford**	RAFFLES	Colonial Administrator
Clive	**Staples**	LEWIS	Author
Thomas	**Stearns**	ELIOT	Poet
Gavin	**Steel**	STRANG	Politician
Greg	**Stephen**	CHAPPELL	Cricketer
Laurence	**Stephen**	LOWRY	Artist
Robert	**Strange**	McNAMARA	Businessman
John	**Stuart**	BLACKIE	Scholar
Jenny	**Susan**	PITMAN	Racehorse trainer
Henrietta	**Swan**	LEAVITT	US astronomer
Pearl	**Sydenstricker**	BUCK	Author
William	**Sydney**	PORTER	Author
John	**Taliaferro**	THOMPSON	US soldier and inventor
Booker	**Taliaferro**	WASHINGTON	US educationalist
William	**Tatem**	TILDEN	US tennis player
Phineas	**Taylor**	BARNUM	Showman
Barbara	**Taylor**	BRADFORD	Novelist
Samuel	**Taylor**	COLERIDGE	Poet
Charles	**Taze**	RUSSELL	Religious leader
William	**Tecumseh**	SHERMAN	General
Joseph	**Teodor**	CONRAD	Author
Ernesto	**Teodoro**	MONETA	Italian journalist
Michael	**Terence**	ASPEL	Broadcaster
Ian	**Terence**	BOTHAM	Cricketer
Michael	**Terence**	WOGAN	Broadcaster
Spiro	**Theodore**	AGNEW	US vice-president
René	**Théophile Hyacinthe**	LAENNEC	French physician
Randall	**Thomas**	DAVIDSON	Archbishop of Canterbury
Alfred	**Thompson**	DENNING	Law lord
Wednesday	**Thursday**	ADDAMS	'Addams Family' character
James	**Tiberius**	KIRK	Starship captain ('Star Trek')
Hugh	**Todd Naylor**	GAITSKELL	Politician
Rex	**Todhunter**	STOUT	US detective writer
Roger	**Tory**	PETERSON	US ornithologist
Marcus	**Tullius**	TIRO	Inventor
William	**Turner**	WALTON	Composer
Ranulph	**Twistleton-Wykeham**	FIENNES	Explorer
Bobby	**Tyre**	JONES	US golfer
Gabriel	**Urbain**	FAURE	Composer
Basil	**Urwin**	SPENCE	Architect
Comer	**Vann**	WOODWARD	US historian
Sergey	**Vasilyevich**	RACHMANINOV	Composer
Ralph	**Vaughan**	WILLIAMS	Composer
Nicholas	**Verity**	KNIGHT	Cricketer
Eddie	**Vernon**	RICKENBACKER	Fighter pilot
Eugene	**Victor**	DEBS	US politician
Mia	**Villiers**	FARROW	Actress
Michael	**Vincent**	O'BRIEN	Racehorse trainer
Sarah	**Virginia**	WADE	Tennis player
Adeline	**Virginia**	WOOLF	Novelist
Henry	**Wager**	HALLECK	US soldier
Ralph	**Waldo**	EMERSON	US poet
King	**Wallis**	VIDOR	Film director

First Name	Middle Name(s)	Surname	
Luis	**Walter**	ALVAREZ	US physicist
John	**Warcup**	CORNFORTH	British chemist
David	**Wark**	GRIFFITH	Film director
Henry	**Warren**	BEATY	Actor
Dave	**Warren**	BRUBECK	Jazz musician
Charles	**Warren**	FAIRBANKS	US vice-president
Marshall	**Warren**	NIRENBERG	US biochemist
Jimmy	**Warren**	WHITE	Snooker player
George	**Washington**	CABLE	Novelist
Norman	**Washington**	MANLEY	Jamaican politician
James	**Watson**	CRONIN	US physicist
Charles	**Watson**	WENTWORTH	British prime minister
Richard	**Wayne**	PENNIMAN	Musician
George	**Wells**	BEADLE	US biochemical geneticist
Rainer	**Werner**	FASSBINDER	Film director
Marthinus	**Wessels**	PRETORIUS	South African general
William	**Wetmore**	STORY	Poet and sculptor
Edward	**Wheewall**	HOLDEN	Motor pioneer
Alan	**Whipper**	WELLS	Athlete
Jack	**Whitaker**	STRAW	Politician
Edward	**White**	BENSON	Archbishop of Canterbury
Arnold	**Whittaker**	WOLFENDALE	Astronomer
Caryl	**Whittier**	CHESSMAN	Convict and author
Bertie	**Wilberforce**	WOOSTER	Fictional character
Robert	**Wilhelm**	BUNSEN	Physicist
William	**Wilkie**	COLLINS	Novelist
Caspar	**Willard**	WEINBERGER	US politician
Johnnie	**William**	CARSON	US TV personality
Jack	**William**	NICKLAUS	Golfer
Brian	**Wilson**	ALDISS	Science fiction writer
Woodrow (Woodie)	**Wilson**	GUTHRIE	US folk singer
Ronald	**Wilson**	REAGAN	US president
Joseph	**Wilson**	SWAN	Physicist
James (Jimmy)	**Wilson Vincent**	SAVILE	Broadcaster
Frank	**Winfield**	WOOLWORTH	US businessman
Arthur	**Wing**	PINERO	Playwright
Gary	**Winston**	LINEKER	Footballer
John	**Winston (then Ono)**	LENNON	Musician and composer
Wells	**Wintemute**	COATES	Architect
John	**Winthrop**	HACKETT	Soldier and academic
Victor	**Witter**	TURNER	Anthropologist
Roger	**Wolcott**	SPERRY	US neuroscientist
Jonathan	**Wolfe**	MILLER	Broadcaster
Theobald	**Wolfe**	TONE	Irish nationalist
Robert	**Woodrow**	WILSON	US physicist
Thomas	**Woodrow**	WILSON	US president
Dickinson	**Woodruff**	RICHARDS	American physician
Ronald	**Wreyford**	NORRISH	English chemist
William	**Wymark**	JACOBS	Short story writer
William	**Wyndham**	GRENVILLE	British prime minister
Franz	**Xaver**	HABERL	German musicologist
Denis	**Yates**	WHEATLEY	Novelist
Paul	**Yaw**	BOATENG	Politician
Susannah	**Yolande**	YORK	Actress
Shmuel	**Yosef**	AGNON	Israeli novelist
Konrad	**Zacharias**	LORENZ	Austrian zoologist

Middle Names: Ordered by Surname

First Name	Middle Name(s)	Surname	
Charles	**Greely**	ABBOT	Astrophysicist
Diane	**Julie**	ABBOT	Politician
Dean	**Gooderham**	ACHESON	American statesman
Joseph	**Randolf**	ACKERLEY	Author
Roy	**Claxton**	ACUFF	Country musician
Adam	**Llewellyn De Vere**	ADAMANT	Fictional TV character
John	**Bodkin**	ADAMS	Doctor and murder suspect

First Name	Middle Name(s)	Surname	
John	**Couch**	ADAMS	Astronomer
John	**Quincy**	ADAMS	US president
Marcus	**Algernon**	ADAMS	Photographer
Sarah	**Flower**	ADAMS	English poet
William	**Bridges**	ADAMS	Engineer
Wednesday	**Thursday**	ADDAMS	'Addams Family' character
Lawrence (Larry)	**Cecil**	ADLER	Musician
Vosdanig	**Manoog**	ADOIAN	Painter
Sade	**Folasade**	ADU	Singer
Spiro	**Theodore**	AGNEW	US vice-president
Shmuel	**Yosef**	AGNON	Israeli novelist
Henry	**Hinchcliffe**	AINLEY	Actor
George	**Biddell**	AIRY	Astronomer
Amos	**Bronson**	ALCOTT	Transcendentalist
Brian	**Wilson**	ALDISS	Science fiction writer
Thomas	**Bailey**	ALDRICH	Author
Thomas	**Massa**	ALSAGER	Newspaper manager
Luis	**Walter**	ALVAREZ	US physicist
Mario	**Gabriele**	ANDRETTI	Racing driver
Christian	**Boehmer**	ANFINSEN	US biochemist
Anders	**Jonas**	ANGSTROM	Physicist
Susan	**Brownell**	ANTHONY	Suffragette
Jeffrey	**Howard**	ARCHER	Author
George	**Augustus**	ARLISS	Actor
Klas	**Pontus**	ARNOLDSON	Swedish politician
Chester	**Alan**	ARTHUR	US president
Jeremy	**John Durham**	ASHDOWN	Politician
Arthur	**Bowden**	ASKEY	Comedian
Michael	**Terence**	ASPEL	Broadcaster
Herbert	**Henry**	ASQUITH	British prime minister
Miguel	**Angel**	ASTURIAS	Guatemalan poet
Richard	**Samuel**	ATTENBOROUGH	Actor
Wystan	**Hugh**	AUDEN	Poet
Alan	**Beresford**	B'STARD	TV character ('New Statesman')
Stephen	**Moulton**	BABCOCK	US agricultural chemist
Johann	**Christian**	BACH	Composer
Johann	**Sebastian**	BACH	Composer
Enid	**Algerine**	BAGNOLD	Author
Joan	**Dawson**	BAKEWELL	Broadcaster
Emily	**Greene**	BALCH	US social reformer
Michael	**Elias**	BALCON	Film producer
James	**Graham**	BALLARD	Author
Canaan	**Sodindo**	BANANA	Zimbabwean president
Hastings	**Kamuzu**	BANDA	Malawi politician
Roger	**Gilbert**	BANNISTER	Athlete
Frederick	**Grant**	BANTING	Physiologist
Joseph	**Roland**	BARBERA	US animated cartoonist
Charles	**Glover**	BARKLA	English physicist
Christian	**Neethling**	BARNARD	Surgeon
Phineas	**Taylor**	BARNUM	Showman
James	**Matthew**	BARRIE	Author
Herbert	**Ernest**	BATES	Author
William	**Maddock**	BAYLISS	Physiologist
George	**Wells**	BEADLE	US biochemical geneticist
Henry	**Warren**	BEATY	Actor
Bill	**Blackledge**	BEAUMONT	Rugby Union player
Carl	**Lotus**	BECKER	US historian
Thomas	**Lovell**	BEDDOES	Poet and physiologist
Mary	**Hayley**	BELL	Playwright
Hilaire	**Pierre**	BELLOC	Writer
Enoch	**Arnold**	BENNETT	Author
Edward	**White**	BENSON	Archbishop of Canterbury
Edmund	**Clerihew**	BENTLEY	Writer
Ernst	**Ingmar**	BERGMAN	Film producer
Hans	**Albrecht**	BETHE	US physicist
Earl	**Derr**	BIGGERS	US novelist
Henry	**Rowley**	BISHOP	Composer
John	**Stuart**	BLACKIE	Scholar
Richard	**Doddridge**	BLACKMORE	Author
Anthony	**Charles Lynton**	BLAIR	Politician

First Name	Middle Name(s)	Surname	
Eric	Arthur	BLAIR	Author
Danny	Dennio	BLANCHFLOWER	Footballer
Tasker	Howard	BLISS	Soldier and statesman
Baruch	Samuel	BLUMBERG	US biochemist
Wilfrid	Scawen	BLUNT	Poet
Paul	Yaw	BOATENG	Politician
Dirk	Niven	BOGARDE	Actor
Humphrey	De Forest	BOGART	Actor
Ian	Terence	BOTHAM	Cricketer
Virginia	Hilda Brunette Maxwell	BOTTOMLEY	Politician
Richard	Southwell	BOURKE	Earl of Mayo
David	Hayward	BOWIE	Musician and singer
Barbara	Taylor	BRADFORD	Novelist
Omar	Nelson	BRADLEY	US soldier
John	Gerard	BRAINE	Novelist
Kenneth	Charles	BRANAGH	Actor
Richard	Charles Nicholas	BRANSON	Entrepreneur
Walter	Houser	BRATTAIN	US physicist
John	Cabell	BRECKINRIDGE	US vice-president
Leonid	Ilich	BREZHNEV	USSR president
Robert	Seymour	BRIDGES	Poet
Charlie	Dunbar	BROAD	Philosopher
Rupert	Chawner	BROOKE	Poet
Norman	Everard	BROOKES	Tennis player
Spangler	Arlington	BROUGH	Actor
Henry	Kirke	BROWN	Sculptor
James	Gordon	BROWN	Politician
Charles	Farrar	BROWNE	Humorist and writer
Hablot	Knight	BROWNE	Illustrator
John	Moses	BROWNING	Gunsmith and inventor
Dave	Warren	BRUBECK	Jazz musician
William	Cullen	BRYANT	Poet
James	McGill	BUCHANAN	American economist
Pearl	Sydenstricker	BUCK	Author
Maria	Esther	BUENO	Tennis player
Ralph	Johnson	BUNCHE	American economist
Robert	Wilhelm	BUNSEN	Physicist
Billy	George	BUNTER	Fictional character
William	Seward	BURROUGHS	Author
George	Herbert Walker	BUSH	US president
Nicholas	Murray	BUTLER	US educationist
Reginald	Cotterell	BUTLER	Sculptor
Richard	Austen	BUTLER	Politician
Billy	Edmund	BUTLIN	Businessman
Betsy	Cromer	BYARS	Novelist
Richard	Evelyn	BYRD	Explorer
Harry	Flood	BYRD	Politician
George	Gordon	BYRON	Poet
James	Branch	CABELL	Novelist
George	Washington	CABLE	Novelist
Pedro	Alvarez	CABRAL	Navigator
James	Mallahan	CAIN	Writer
Michael	Joseph	CAINE	Actor
Aimo	Kaarlo	CAJANDER	Finnish politician
John	Caldwell	CALHOUN	US vice-president
James	Leonard	CALLAGHAN	British prime minister
Maria	Meneghini	CALLAS	Operatic soprano
Hugh	Longbourne	CALLENDAR	Physicist
Verney	Lovett	CAMERON	Explorer
Walter	Chauncy	CAMP	American footballer
Donald	Malcolm	CAMPBELL	Car and boat racer
John	Franklin	CANDY	Actor
Annie	Jump	CANNON	US astronomer
George	Leonard	CAREY	Archbishop
Chester	Floyd	CARLSON	US inventor
Ingvar	Costa	CARLSSON	Swedish politician
Jane	Baillie	CARLYLE	Wife of Thomas Carlyle
Ian	Gillett	CARMICHAEL	Actor
John	Alden	CARPENTER	Musician and businessman
John	Dickson	CARR	US Detective writer

First Name	Middle Name(s)	Surname	
Willis	Haviland	CARRIER	US inventor
Johnnie	William	CARSON	US TV personality
William	Hunter Fisher	CARSON	Jockey
James	Earl	CARTER	US president
Barbara	Hamilton	CARTLAND	Writer
Hugh	Maxwell	CASSON	Architect
William	Henry	CAVENDISH-BENTINCK	British prime minister
Robert	Arthur Talbot	CECIL	British prime minister
Ernst	Boris	CHAIN	German biochemist
Arthur	Neville	CHAMBERLAIN	Politician
Charlie	Spencer	CHAPLIN	Comedy actor
Frank	Michler	CHAPMAN	Ornithologist
Greg	Stephen	CHAPPELL	Cricketer
Ian	Michael	CHAPPELL	Cricketer
Leslie	Bowyer	CHARTERIS	Author
Cornelius	Crane	CHASE	Actor
Anton	Pavlovich	CHEKHOV	Russian author
Geoffrey	Leonard	CHESHIRE	Philanthropist
Caryl	Whittier	CHESSMAN	Convict and author
Gilbert	Keith	CHESTERTON	Author
Robert	Erskine	CHILDERS	Writer
Jaques	René	CHIRAC	French prime minister
Martin	Harcourt	CHIVERS	Footballer
Walter	Percy	CHRYSLER	Automobile manufacturer
Winston	Leonard Spencer	CHURCHILL	British prime minister
Kenneth	Mackenzie	CLARK	Art historian
Kenneth	Harry	CLARKE	Politician
Cassius	Marcellus	CLAY	Boxer
John	Marwood	CLEESE	Actor
Samuel	Langhorne	CLEMENS	Author
Stephen	Grover	CLEVELAND	US president
Edward	Montgomery	CLIFT	Actor
William	Jefferson Blyth	CLINTON	US president
Wells	Wintemute	COATES	Architect
Tyrus	Raymond	COBB	Baseball player
Samuel	Franklin	CODY	Aviator
William	Frederick	CODY	Showman
Sebastian	Newbold	COE	Athlete and politician
Frederick	Donald	COGGAN	Archbishop of Canterbury
Ferdinand	Julius	COHN	Botanist
Samuel	Taylor	COLERIDGE	Poet
Sidonie	Gabrielle	COLETTE	Authoress
William	Gershom	COLLINGWOOD	Artist
Charles	Allston	COLLINS	Artist
Joan	Henrietta	COLLINS	Actress
William	Wilkie	COLLINS	Novelist
Arthur	Holly	COMPTON	Physicist
Denis	Charles Scott	COMPTON	Cricketer
Maureen	Catherine	CONNOLLY	Tennis player
Jimmy	Scott	CONNORS	Tennis player
Joseph	Teodor	CONRAD	Author
Brian	Rayner	COOK	English baritone
Robin	Finlayson	COOK	Politician
Elizabeth	Sprague	COOLIDGE	American pianist
John	Calvin	COOLIDGE	US president
Leon	Neil	COOPER	US physicist
Alfred	Edgar	COPPARD	Writer
Ronnie	Balfour	CORBETT	Comedian
Carl	Ferdinand	CORI	American biochemist
John	Warcup	CORNFORTH	British chemist
Arthur	Quiller	COUCH	Man of letters
Noel	Pierce	COWARD	Actor and dramatist
Michael	Colin	COWDREY	Cricketer
William	Randal	CREMER	Nobel Laureate
Francis	Harry Compton	CRICK	Biologist
.Hawley	Harvey	CRIPPEN	Murderer
Richard	Stafford	CRIPPS	Politician
Archibald	Joseph	CRONIN	Author
James	Watson	CRONIN	US physicist
Walter	Leland	CRONKITE	US broadcaster

First Name	Middle Name(s)	Surname	
Harry (Bing)	Lillis	CROSBY	Singer and actor
Ada	Jemima	CROSSLEY	Australian contralto
Irene	Joliot	CURIE	Nuclear physicist
Heber	Doust	CURTIS	US astronomer
Edward	Sheriff	CURTIS	US photographer
Glen	Hammond	CURTISS	US air pioneer
Henry	Drysdale	DAKIN	Chemist
Kenneth	Mathieson	DALGLISH	Footballer
Lawrence	Bruno Nero	DALLAGLIO	Rugby player
George	Mifflin	DALLAS	US vice-president
Clarence	Seward	DARROW	US Lawyer
Randall	Thomas	DAVIDSON	Archbishop of Canterbury
Dwight	Filley	DAVIS	Founder of Davis Cup
Miles	Dewey	DAVIS	Jazz musician
Charles	Gates	DAWES	US vice-president
Christian	René	DE DUVE	Belgian biochemist
Philip	Ranulph	DE GLANVILLE	Rugby Union player
Cecil	Blount	DE MILLE	Film director
James	Byron	DEAN	Actor
Eugene	Victor	DEBS	US politician
Claude	Achille	DEBUSSY	Composer
Len	Cyril	DEIGHTON	Novelist
Ronald	Frederick	DELDERFIELD	Author
Jacques	Lucien Jean	DELORS	European politician
Nigel	Richard Patton	DEMPSTER	Gossip columnist
Judi	Olivia	DENCH	Actress
Alfred	Thompson	DENNING	Law lord
Donald	Campbell	DEWAR	British politician
Norman	Colin	DEXTER	Author
Edward (Ted)	Ralph	DEXTER	Cricketer
Thomas	Frognall	DIBDIN	Librarian
Philip	Kindred	DICK	US writer
Philip	Kindred	DICK	US science fiction writer
Charles	John Huffam	DICKENS	Author
Walt	Elias	DISNEY	Film producer
Henry	Austin	DOBSON	Poet
Kenneth	Arthur	DODD	Comedian
Basil	Lewis	D'OLIVEIRA	Cricketer
James	Patrick	DONLEAVY	Author
Alexander	Frederick	DOUGLAS-HOME	British prime minister
Hugh	Caswell Tremenheere	DOWDING	RAF chief
John	Boyd	DUNLOP	Inventor
Ronald	Ossary	DUNLOP	Irish painter
James	Franciscus	DURANTE	Entertainer
Gerald	Malcolm	DURRELL	Writer and naturalist
Lawrence	George	DURRELL	Novelist
Bob	Alan	DYLAN	Singer and composer
John	Carew	ECCLES	Australian neurophysiologist
John	Presper	ECKERT	American inventor
Gerald	Maurice	EDELMAN	US biochemist
Gertrude	Caroline	EDERLE	US swimmer
Thomas	Alva	EDISON	Inventor
Dwight	David	EISENHOWER	US president
Thomas	Stearns	ELIOT	Author
Edward ('Duke')	Kennedy	ELLINGTON	Pianist
Fred	Handel	ELLIOTT	'Coronation Street' character
Ralph	Waldo	EMERSON	US poet
John	Franklin	ENDERS	US bacteriologist
Chris	Livingstone	EUBANK	Boxer
Peter	Carl	FABERGÉ	Russian goldsmith
Gabriel	Daniel	FAHRENHEIT	Physicist
Charles	Warren	FAIRBANKS	US vice-president
Douglas	Elton	FAIRBANKS (Snr)	Actor
Nicholas	Alexander	FALDO	Golfer
Mia	Villiers	FARROW	Actress
Rainer	Werner	FASSBINDER	Film director
Gabriel	Urbain	FAURÉ	Composer
William	Claude	FIELDS	Comedian and actor
Ranulph	Twistleton-Wykeham	FIENNES	Explorer
Robert	Bannatyne	FINLAY	Politician

First Name	Middle Name(s)	Surname	
Geoffrey	Francis	FISHER	Archbishop of Canterbury
Val	Logsdon	FITCH	US physicist
Augustus	Henry	FITZROY	British prime minister
Bob	Prometheus	FITZSIMMONS	Boxer
James	Elroy	FLECKER	Poet
Ian	Lancaster	FLEMING	English novelist
Jane	Seymour	FONDA	Actress
Michael	Mackintosh	FOOT	Politician
Gerald	Rudolph	FORD	US president
Cecil	Scott	FORESTER	Author
George	Hoy	FORMBY	Vocalist and musician
Edward	Morgan	FORSTER	Author
Bruce	Joseph	FORSYTH	Entertainer
Stephen	Collins	FOSTER	US songwriter
Michael J	Andrew	FOX	Actor
Clement	Raphael	FREUD	Liberal politician
Ragnar	Kittil	FRISCH	Norwegian economist
Kermit	The	FROG	Muppet
David	Paradine	FROST	Interviewer and presenter
Charles	Burgess	FRY	Sportsman
Stephen	John	FRY	Actor and author
Roy	Broadbent	FULLER	Poet
Hugh	Todd Naylor	GAITSKELL	Politician
Daniel	Carleton	GAJDUSEK	US virologist
Leopoldo	Fortunato	GALTIERI	Argentinian politician
Mohandas	Karamchand	GANDHI	Indian leader
James	Abram	GARFIELD	US president
John	Nance	GARNER	US vice-president
Elizabeth	Cleghorn	GASKELL	Writer
Herbert	Spencer	GASSER	US physiologist
Richard	Jordan	GATLING	Inventor
Andrew	Dewar	GIBB	Scottish jurist
Lewis	Grassic	GIBBON	Novelist
Stella	Dorothea	GIBBONS	Writer
Mel	Columcille	GIBSON	Actor
Thomas	Milner	GIBSON	Politician
Arthur	John	GIELGUD	Actor
William	Schwenck	GILBERT	Librettist
Percy	Carlyle	GILCHRIST	Metallurgist
John	Birks	GILLESPIE	Jazz trumpeter
King	Camp	GILLETTE	Inventor
William	Ewart	GLADSTONE	British prime minister
Sheldon	Lee	GLASHOW	US physicist
John	Herschel	GLENN	US astronaut and politician
Robert	Hutchings	GODDARD	US rocket pioneer
William	Gerald	GOLDING	Novelist
Peter	Carl	GOLDMARK	Inventor
Barry	Morris	GOLDWATER	US politician
George	Peabody	GOOCH	Politician
Graham	Alan	GOOCH	Cricketer
Arthur	Lehman	GOODHART	US jurist
Benny	David	GOODMAN	US jazz clarinetist
Samuel	Griswold	GOODRICH	US publisher
Adam	Lindsay	GORDON	Australian poet
Cyrus	Herzl	GORDON	US Hebrew scholar
George	Hamilton	GORDON	British prime minister
Spencer	Frederick	GORE	Painter
Benjamin	Apthorp	GOULD	US astronomer
Charles	François	GOUNOD	Composer
Lawrence	Burnett	GOWING	Painter
Tiberius	Sempronius	GRACCHUS	Roman statesman
William	Gilbert	GRACE	Cricketer
Billy	Franklin	GRAHAM	US evangelist
Florence	Nightingale	GRAHAM	Beautician
Ulysses	Simpson	GRANT	US president
Milner	Connorton	GRAY	Graphic designer
Linda	Esther	GRAY	Scottish soprano
Lucinda	Jane	GREEN	Three-day eventer
Robson	Golightly	GREEN	Actor
Hugh	Carleton	GREENE	Journalist and broadcaster

F
A
M
O
U
S

P
E
O
P
L
E

First Name	Middle Name(s)	Surname	
Gordon	**Cuthbert**	GREENIDGE	Cricketer
William	**Wyndham**	GRENVILLE	British prime minister
Herbert	**Nigel**	GRESLEY	Locomotive engineer
Edvard	**Hagerup**	GRIEG	Norwegian composer
Christopher	**Murray**	GRIEVE	Poet
Walter	**Burley**	GRIFFIN	US architect
David	**Wark**	GRIFFITH	Film director
Angelina	**Emily**	GRIMKE	US feminist
Sarah	**Moore**	GRIMKE	US feminist
Friedrich	**Melchior**	GRIMM	Journalist
Jacob	**Ludwig Carl**	GRIMM	Folklorist
Wilhelm	**Carl**	GRIMM	Folklorist
Walter	**Adolph**	GROPIUS	Architect
Leroy	**Randle**	GRUMMAN	US aircraft pioneer
John	**Selwyn**	GUMMER	Politician
Johannes	**Gensfleisch**	GUTENBERG	German printer
Woodrow	**Wilson**	GUTHRIE	US folk singer
Franz	**Xaver**	HABERL	German musicologist
John	**Winthrop**	HACKETT	Soldier and academic
Gene	**Alden**	HACKMAN	Actor
Alfred	**Cort**	HADDON	Anthropologist
Henry	**Rider**	HAGGARD	Novelist
William	**Jefferson**	HAGUE	Politician
Alexander	**Meigs**	HAIG	US soldier
Thomas	**Chandler**	HALIBURTON	Canadian writer
Henry	**Wager**	HALLECK	US soldier
James	**Orchard**	HALLIWELL-PHILLIPPS	Shakespearean scholar
Dag	**Hjalmar Agne Carl**	HAMMARSKJÖLD	Swedish statesman
Robin	**Airling**	HANBURY-TENISON	Explorer
Tony	**Aloysius**	HANCOCK	TV character
Tony	**John**	HANCOCK	Comedy actor
George	**Frederick**	HANDEL	Composer
William	**Denby**	HANNA	US animated cartoonist
James	**Aloysius**	HANSOM	Designer
Warren	**Gamaliel**	HARDING	US president
Oliver	**Norville**	HARDY	Comedy actor
Thomas	**Duffus**	HARDY	Archivist
Thomas	**Masterman**	HARDY	Naval officer
Joel	**Chandler**	HARRIS	Author
William	**Henry**	HARRISON	US president
Leslie	**Poles**	HARTLEY	Author
Haldan	**Keffer**	HARTLINE	US physiologist
John	**Liptrot**	HATTON	Composer
Herbert	**Aaron**	HAUPTMAN	US physicist
Rutherford	**Birchard**	HAYES	US president
Seamus	**Justin**	HEANEY	Poet
Patricia	**Campbell**	HEARST	Heiress
Donald	**Olding**	HEBB	Canadian psychologist
Lillian	**Florence**	HELLMAN	US playwright
Ernest	**Millar**	HEMINGWAY	US novelist
Philip	**Showalter**	HENCH	US physician
Jocelyn	**Barbara**	HEPWORTH	Sculptor
Georges	**Remi**	HERGÉS	Belgian cartoonist
Caroline	**Lucretia**	HERSCHEL	Astronomer
Alfred	**Day**	HERSHEY	US biologist
Michael	**Ray Dibdin**	HESELTINE	Politician
Philip	**Arnold**	HESELTINE	Composer
Alfred	**Hawthorne**	HILL	Comedian
Norman	**Graham**	HILL	Racing driver
Conrad	**Nicholson**	HILTON	Businessman
John (Jack)	**Berry**	HOBBS	English cricketer
Dorothy	**Crowfoot**	HODGKIN	Scientist
Dustin	**Lee**	HOFFMAN	Actor
Quintin	**McGarel**	HOGG	Politician
Edward	**Wheewall**	HOLDEN	Motor pioneer
Ben	**Caine**	HOLLIOAKE	English cricketer
Herbert	**Clark**	HOOVER	US president
John	**Edgar**	HOOVER	FBI director
Bob	**Leslie Townes**	HOPE	Comedian
Gerard	**Manley**	HOPKINS	Poet

First Name	Middle Name(s)	Surname	
Anthony	Philip	HOPKINS	Actor
Michael	Murray	HORDERN	Actor
Godfrey	Newbold	HOUNSFIELD	English electrical engineer
Alfred	Edward	HOUSMAN	Author
David	Hunter	HUBEL	US neurophysiologist
Charles	Brenton	HUGGINS	US surgeon
Howard	Robard	HUGHES	Businessman
Victor	Marie	HUGO	French writer
George	Basil	HUME	Cardinal
Johann	Nepomuk	HUMMEL	Austrian pianist
Hubert	Horatio	HUMPHREY	US vice-president
John	Barry	HUMPHRIES	Comedian and writer
Miller	Reece	HUTCHINSON	Inventor
Aldous	Leonard	HUXLEY	Novelist
Jeremy	Israel	ISAACS	Arts mogul
David	Lewis	JACOBS	Broadcaster
William	Wymark	JACOBS	Short story writer
Phyllis	Dorothy	JAMES	Authoress
James	Hopwood	JEANS	Physicist and astronomer
James	Jackson	JEFFRIES	Boxing champion
John	Rushworth	JELLICOE	Naval commander
Roy	Harris	JENKINS	Politician
Robert	Banks	JENKINSON	British prime minister
Niels	Kai	JERNE	Danish immunologist
Jerome	Klapka	JEROME	Author
Elton	Hercules	JOHN	Vocalist and composer
Lyndon	Baines	JOHNSON	US president
Lionel	Pigot	JOHNSON	Poet
Richard	Mentor	JOHNSON	US vice-president
Joseph	Eggleston	JOHNSTON	US soldier
James	Cellan	JONES	Film director
Bobby	Tyre	JONES	US golfer
Michael	Jeffrey	JORDAN	US basketball player
James	Prescott	JOULE	Physicist
Carl	Gustav	JUNG	Swiss psychiatrist
Erik	Axel	KARLFELDT	Swedish poet
John	Harvey	KELLOGG	Inventor
Will	Keith	KELLOGG	Inventor
Gene	Curran	KELLY	Dancer
Edward	Calvin	KENDALL	US chemist
John	Cowdery	KENDREW	English biochemist
Edward	Moore	KENNEDY	US politician
John	Fitzgerald	KENNEDY	US president
Ludovic	Coverley	KENNEDY	Broadcaster
Nigel	Paul	KENNEDY	Violinist
Robert	Francis	KENNEDY	US politician
Søren	Aabye	KIERKEGAARD	Danish philosopher
William	Rufus de Vane	KING	US vice-president
Neil	Gordon	KINNOCK	Politician
Wilson	Boit	KIPKETER	Athlete
James	Tiberius	KIRK	Starship captain ('Star Trek')
Henry	Alfred	KISSINGER	USA statesman
Horatio	Herbert	KITCHENER	Irish soldier and statesman
Eartha	Mae	KITT	Singer
Nicholas	Verity	KNIGHT	Cricketer
Tjalling	Charles	KOOPMANS	US economist
Hans	Adolf	KREBS	British biochemist
Stanley	Jasspon	KUNITZ	US poet
Vladimir	Petrovich	KUTS	Russian athlete
Simon	Smith	KUZNETS	US economist
Fiorello	Henry	LA GUARDIA	US politician
René	Théophile Hyacinthe	LAENNEC	French physician
Selma	Ottiliana Lovisa	LAGERLOF	Swedish novelist
Carlos	Saavedra	LAMAS	Argentinian jurist
Willis	Eugene	LAMB	US physicist
Stephen	Burton	LANCASTER	Actor
Kenesaw	Mountain	LANDIS	Baseball commissioner
Walter	Savage	LANDOR	Writer
Henri	Désiré	LANDRU	French murderer
John	Dunmore	LANG	Clergyman

First Name	Middle Name(s)	Surname	
Harry	Philmore	LANGDON	US Comedian
David	Russell	LANGE	New Zealand politician
Samuel	Pierpont	LANGLEY	US aeronautic pioneer
Cherilyn (Cher)	Sarkisian	LAPIERRE	Singer
Pierre	Athanase	LAROUSSE	French publisher
Hugh	Callum	LAURIE	Actor and comedian
Rodney	George	LAVER	Tennis player
Thomas	Edward	LAWRENCE	Author and soldier
David	Herbert	LAWRENCE	Author
Bill	Morris	LAWRY	Australian cricketer
Bernard	Howell	LEACH	English potter
Richard	Erskine Frere	LEAKEY	Palaeontologist and naturalist
Henrietta	Swan	LEAVITT	US astronomer
Christopher	Carandini	LEE	Actor
Vladimir	Ilyich	LENIN	Russian revolutionary
John	Winston (then Ono)	LENNON	Musician and composer
Henry	Bernard	LEVIN	Journalist and author
Harry	Sinclair	LEWIS	US novelist
Chris	Clairmonte	LEWIS	Cricketer
Clive	Staples	LEWIS	Author
John	Spedan	LEWIS	Businessman
Dennis	Keith	LILLEE	Australian cricketer
Charles	Augustus	LINDBERGH	US aviator
Gary	Winston	LINEKER	Footballer
Maureen	Diane	LIPMAN	Actress
William	Nunn	LIPSCOMB	US chemist
Penelope	Margaret	LIVELY	Writer
Harold	Clayton	LLOYD	US film comedian
Henry	Cabot	LODGE	US senator
Jack	Griffith	LONDON	US novelist
Francis	Aungier	LONGFORD	Prison reformer
Hendrik	Antoon	LORENTZ	Dutch physicist
Konrad	Zacharias	LORENZ	Austrian zoologist
Robert	Hepler	LOWE	Actor
Laurence	Stephen	LOWRY	Artist
Henry	Robinson	LUCE	US magazine publisher
Edwin	Landseer	LUTYENS	English architect
Humphrey	Richard Adeane	LYTTELTON	Musician
Thomas	Babington	MACAULAY	Author
George	Brinton	McCLELLAN	US soldier
Mark	Hume	McCORMACK	Promoter
James	Ramsay	MACDONALD	British prime minister
Samora	Moises	MACHEL	Mozambique president
Donald	Duart	MACLEAN	English traitor
James	Paul	McCARTNEY	Musician and composer
Maurice	Harold	MACMILLAN	British prime minister
Robert	Strange	McNAMARA	Businessman and politician
Herman	Cyril	McNEILE	Author
Johann	Nepomuk	MAELZEL	German inventor
John	Roy	MAJOR	British prime minister
Nelson	Rolihlahla	MANDELA	South African president
Norman	Washington	MANLEY	Jamaican prime minister
Nigel	Ernest James	MANSELL	Racing driver
Ferdinand	Edralin	MARCOS	Filipino president
Bob	Nesta	MARLEY	Musician
Gabriel	Garcia	MARQUEZ	Columbian author
Jean	Lyndsey Torren	MARSH	Actress
George	Catlett	MARSHALL	American soldier and statesman
Jan	Garrigue	MASARYK	Czech statesman
Anna	Raymond	MASSEY	Actress
Daniel	Raymond	MASSEY	Actor
William	Somerset	MAUGHAM	Author
Ian	Robert	MAXWELL	Businessman
Peter	Barker Howard	MAY	Cricketer
Michael	Hugh	MEACHER	Politician
Carlos	Saul	MENEM	Argentinian politician
Cliff	Arthur	MICHELMORE	Broadcaster
James	Albert	MICHENER	Author
Glenn	Alton	MILLER	Musician
Jonathan	Wolfe	MILLER	Broadcaster

First Name	Middle Name(s)	Surname	
Alan	**Alexander**	MILNE	Author
Liza	**May**	MINNELLI	Singer
Walter	**Frederick (Fritz)**	MONDALE	US vice-president
Ernesto	**Teodoro**	MONETA	Italian journalist
Bernard	**Law**	MONTGOMERY	Field Marshal
Brian	**Baden**	MOORE	Football commentator
Henry	**Spencer**	MOORE	Sculptor
Roger	**George**	MOORE	Actor
Sheridan	**Robert**	MORLEY	Author and broadcaster
George	**Ivan (Van)**	MORRISON	Singer and composer
Samuel	**Finley Breese**	MORSE	US inventor
John	**Cameron**	MORTON	Journalist
Levi	**Parsons**	MORTON	US vice-president
Oswald	**Ernald**	MOSLEY	British politician
Benjamin	**Roy**	MOTTELSON	Danish physicist
Colin	**Berkeley**	MOYNIHAN	Politician
Robert	**Gabriel**	MUGABE	Zimbabwean president
Robert	**Sanderson**	MULLIKEN	American chemist
Hector	**Hugh**	MUNRO	Author
Keith	**Rupert**	MURDOCH	Businessman
Bartolomé	**Esteban**	MURILLO	Spanish painter
Edward	**Regan**	MURPHY	US comedian
John	**Middleton**	MURRY	Writer and critic
Maria	**Lurdes**	MUTOLA	Mozambique athlete
Frederic	**Ogden**	NASH	Poet
Pablo	**Neftali Reyes**	NERUDA	Poet
Marcus	**Cocceius**	NERVA	Roman emperor
Julia	**Babette Sarah**	NEUBERGER	Rabbi
George	**Eric**	NEWBY	Author
George	**Anthony**	NEWLEY	Actor and singer
Stavros	**Spyros**	NIARCHOS	Greek shipowner
Emma	**Harriet**	NICHOLSON	Politician
Jack	**William**	NICKLAUS	Golfer
Joseph	**Nicéphore**	NIEPCE	Inventor
Marshall	**Warren**	NIRENBERG	US biochemist
Richard	**Milhous**	NIXON	US president
Joshua	**Mqabuko Nyongolo**	NKOMO	Zimbabwean politician
Ronald	**Wreyford**	NORRISH	English chemist
Trevor	**Robert**	NUNN	Theatre director
Julius	**Kambarage**	NYERERE	Tanzanian president
Michael	**Vincent**	O'BRIEN	Racehorse trainer
David	**Feodorovich**	OISTRAKH	Violinist
Laurence	**Kerr**	OLIVIER	Actor
Aristotle	**Socrates**	ONASSIS	Shipping magnate
Eugene	**Gladstone**	O'NEILL	US playwright
Elisha	**Graves**	OTIS	Inventor
Peter	**Seamus**	O'TOOLE	Irish actor
George	**Emil**	PALADE	US biologist
Arnold	**Daniel**	PALMER	Golfer
Cyril	**Northcote**	PARKINSON	Political scientist
Eric	**Honeywood**	PARTRIDGE	Lexicographer
Linus	**Carl**	PAULING	Scientist
Thomas	**Love**	PEACOCK	Novelist and poet
Mervyn	**Laurence**	PEAKE	Author and artist
John	**Loughborough**	PEARSON	Architect
Lester	**Bowles**	PEARSON	Canadian politician
Eldred	**Gregory**	PECK	Actor
Richard	**Wayne**	PENNIMAN	Musician
Juan	**Domingo**	PERÓN	Argentinian president
Matthew	**Galbraith**	PERRY	US naval officer
Oliver	**Hazard**	PERRY	US naval officer
Publius	**Helvius**	PERTINAX	Roman emperor
Max	**Ferdinand**	PERUTZ	British biochemist
Henri	**Omer**	PÉTAIN	French statesman
Mary	**Elizabeth**	PETERS	Pentathlete
Roger	**Tory**	PETERSON	US ornithologist
Ulrich	**Bonnell**	PHILLIPS	US historian
River	**Jude**	PHOENIX	Actor
William	**Mervyn**	PICKWOAD	Actor
Lester	**Keith**	PIGGOTT	Jockey

First Name	Middle Name(s)	Surname	
Arthur	Wing	PINERO	Playwright
Jenny	Susan	PITMAN	Racehorse trainer
Gary	Jim	PLAYER	Golfer
Raymond	Landry	POINCARÉ	French statesman
John	Marlan	POINDEXTER	US naval officer
James	Knox	POLK	US president
Robert	Graeme	POLLOCK	Cricketer
Paul	Jackson	POLLOCK	US artist
William	Sydney	PORTER	Author
Michael	Denzil Xavier	PORTILLO	Politician
Dennis	Christopher George	POTTER	Playwright
Ezra	Loomis	POUND	Poet
Anthony	Dymoke	POWELL	English novelist
John	Enoch	POWELL	British politician
John	Leslie	PRESCOTT	Politician
Elvis	Aaron	PRESLEY	American singer
Marthinus	Wessels	PRETORIUS	South African general
André	George	PREVIN	Conductor
John	Boynton	PRIESTLEY	Author
Archibald	Philip	PRIMROSE	British prime minister
James	Leathes	PRIOR	Politician
Victor	Sawdon	PRITCHETT	Writer and critic
Sergei	Sergeyevich	PROKOFIEV	Composer
Giacomo	Antonio	PUCCINI	Composer
Ana	Fidelia	QUIROT	Cuban athlete
Steve	Russell	RACE	Broadcaster
Sergey	Vasilyevich	RACHMANINOV	Composer
Thomas	Stamford	RAFFLES	Colonial administrator
Arthur	Michael	RAMSEY	Archbishop of Canterbury
Norman	Foster	RAMSEY	US physicist
John	Crowe	RANSOM	US poet and critic
Arthur	Michell	RANSOME	Author
Esther	Louise	RANTZEN	TV presenter
Claire	Berenice	RAYNER	Broadcaster
Ronald	Wilson	REAGAN	US president
Michael	Scudamore	REDGRAVE	Actor
Robert	Oliver	REED	British actor
Erich	Maria	REMARQUE	Author
Ruth	Barbara	RENDELL	Crime novellist
Dickinson	Woodruff	RICHARDS	US physician
Dorothy	Miller	RICHARDSON	English novelist
Eddie	Vernon	RICKENBACKER	Fighter pilot
Sally	Kristen	RIDE	US astronaut
Matthew	Bunker	RIDGWAY	US soldier
Rupert	Iolanthe	RIGSBY	TV character
Nikolai	Andreievich	RIMSKY-KORSAKOV	Composer
Frederick	Chapman	ROBBINS	US physiologist
Frederick	Sleigh	ROBERTS	British soldier
James	Logie	ROBERTSON	Poet
Paul	Bustill Le Roy	ROBESON	Actor
Frederick	John	ROBINSON	British prime minister
Nelson	Aldrich	ROCKEFELLER	US vice-president
Anita	Lucia	RODDICK	Businesswoman
Franklin	Delano	ROOSEVELT	US president
Jack	Morris	ROSENTHAL	Playwright
Kenneth	Ronald	ROSEWALL	Tennis player
Mstislav	Leopoldovich	ROSTROPOVICH	Cellist
Philip	Milton	ROTH	Novelist
Meyer	Amschel	ROTHSCHILD	German financier
Francis	Peyton	ROUS	American pathologist
Robert	Alexander	RUNCIE	Archbishop of Canterbury
Ahmed	Salman	RUSHDIE	Author
Charles	Taze	RUSSELL	Religious leader
Gottlieb	Eliel	SAARINEN	Finnish–US architect
Nelly	Leonie	SACHS	Swedish poet and playwright
Jerome	David	SALINGER	Author
Jonas	Edward	SALK	Biologist
James	Wilson Vincent	SAVILE	Broadcaster
John	Richard	SCHLESINGER	Film director
Charles	Monroe	SCHULZ	US strip cartoonist

First Name	Middle Name(s)	Surname	
Harry	Donald	SECOMBE	Comedian and singer
Elzie	Crisler	SEGAR	US strip cartoonist
Harry	Gordon	SELFRIDGE	British merchant
David	Oliver	SELZNICK	US cinema mogul
Richard	Bowdler	SHARPE	Ornithologist
George	Bernard	SHAW	Author
Percy	Bysshe	SHELLEY	Poet
James	Schoolcraft	SHERMAN	US vice-president
William	Tecumseh	SHERMAN	General
William	Bradford	SHOCKLEY	US physicist
John	Cody Fiddler	SIMPSON	News reporter
Francis (Frank)	Albert	SINATRA	Singer
Upton	Beall	SINCLAIR	US novelist
Isaac	Bashevis	SINGER	Writer
Israel	Joshua	SINGER	Writer
Isaac	Merritt	SINGER	US inventor
Christopher	Robert	SMITH	British politician
Hamilton	Othanel	SMITH	US molecular biologist
Maggie	Natalie	SMITH	Actress
Sydney	Goodsir	SMITH	Poet
Samuel	Jackson	SNEAD	Golfer
Charles	Percy	SNOW	Author
Garfield	St Auburn	SOBERS	Cricketer
Robert	Merton	SOLOW	American economist
Aleksandr	Isaevich	SOLZHENITSYN	Author
Stephen	Joshua	SONDHEIM	Composer and lyricist
Donald	Oliver	SOPER	Methodist minister
Thomas	Octave Murdoch	SOPWITH	Aircraft designer
Charles	Hamilton	SORLEY	Poet
John	Hanning	SPEKE	Explorer
Basil	Urwin	SPENCE	Architect
Elmer	Ambrose	SPERRY	US inventor
Roger	Wolcott	SPERRY	US neuroscientist
Henry	Morton	STANLEY	Explorer and journalist
Edwin	McMasters	STANTON	US statesman
Publius	Papinius	STATIUS	Roman poet
George	Ledyard	STEBBINS	US botanist
David	Martin Scott	STEEL	Politician
William	Howard	STEIN	US biochemist
John	Ernest	STEINBECK	US novelist
Patrick	Christopher	STEPTOE	Gynaecologist
Adlai	Ewing	STEVENSON	US politician
William	Gladstone	STEWART	TV broadcaster and producer
Richard	Henry Simpson	STILGOE	Songwriter and broadcaster
Isidor	Feinstein	STONE	US journalist
Harlan	Fiske	STONE	US judge
William	Wetmore	STORY	Poet and sculptor
Rex	Todhunter	STOUT	US detective writer
Gavin	Steel	STRANG	Politician
Charles	Sherwood	STRATTON	Circus performer
Igor	Fedorovich	STRAVINSKY	Composer
Jack	Whitaker	STRAW	Politician
Meryl	Mary Louise	STREEP	Actress
Barbra	Joan	STREISAND	Singer
Arthur	Seymour	SULLIVAN	Composer
John	Bird	SUMNER	Archbishop of Canterbury
Frank	Meadow	SUTCLIFFE	Photographer
Joseph	Wilson	SWAN	Physicist
John	Addington	SYMONDS	Author
John	Millington	SYNGE	Author
William	Howard	TAFT	US president
Archibald	Campbell	TAIT	Archbishop of Canterbury
Abel	Janszoon	TASMAN	Navigator
Elizabeth	Rosemond	TAYLOR	Actress
Edward	Lawrie	TATUM	US biochemist
William	Howson	TAYLOR	Potter
Pyotr	Ilyich	TCHAIKOVSKY	Composer
Kiri	Janette	TE KANAWA	Opera Singer
Norman	Beresford	TEBBIT	Politician
George	Philipp	TELEMANN	Composer

First Name	Middle Name(s)	Surname	
Henry	John	TEMPLE	British prime minister
Ellen	Alice	TERRY	Actress
William	Makepeace	THACKERAY	Author
Margaret	Hilda	THATCHER	British prime minister
Anatole	François	THIBAULT	Author
Dylan	Marlais	THOMAS	Poet
Daley	Francis Morgan	THOMPSON	Athlete
John	Taliaferro	THOMPSON	US soldier and inventor
George	Paget	THOMSON	English physicist
John	Jeremy	THORPE	Politician
James	Grover	THURBER	Humorist
Uma	Karuna	THURMAN	Actress
Louis	Comfort	TIFFANY	Glassmaker
Samuel	Jones	TILDEN	US politician
William	Tatem	TILDEN	US tennis player
Samuel	Chao Chung	TING	US physicist
Michael	Kemp	TIPPETT	Composer
Marcus	Tullius	TIRO	Inventor
Richard	Palethorpe	TODD	Actor
John	Ronald Reuel	TOLKIEN	Author
Theobald	Wolfe	TONE	Irish nationalist
Augustus	Montague	TOPLADY	Clergyman and hymnist
Donald	Francis	TOVEY	Pianist and composer
Charles	Hard	TOWNES	American physicist
Lee	Buck	TREVINO	American golfer
Rodney	Charlton	TROTTER	'Fools and Horses' character
Frederick (Freddy)	Sewards	TRUEMAN	Cricketer
Barry	Emmanuel	TUCKWELL	Australian musician
Alan	Mathison	TURING	Mathematician
Victor	Witter	TURNER	Anthropologist
Desmond	Mpilo	TUTU	South African prelate
William	Marcy	TWEED	US politician and criminal
Liv	Johanne	ULLMANN	Norwegian actress
John	Hoyer	UPDIKE	Author
Leon	Marcus	URIS	US author
Peter	Alexander	USTINOV	Actor and writer
Louis	Nicolas	VAUQUELIN	Chemist
King	Wallis	VIDOR	Film director
Angelina	Jolie	VOIGHT	Actress
Sarah	Virginia	WADE	Tennis player
Thomas	Griffiths	WAINEWRIGHT	Art critic and murderer
Terence (Terry)	Hardy	WAITE	Religious adviser
Selman	Abraham	WAKSMAN	US biochemist
Alice	Malsenior	WALKER	US novelist
Henry	Agard	WALLACE	US vice-president
Hugh	Seymour	WALPOLE	Novelist
William	Turner	WALTON	Composer
Arthur	Sarsfield	WARD	Author
Booker	Taliaferro	WASHINGTON	US educationist
Lewis	Edson	WATERMAN	Inventor
James	Dewey	WATSON	US biologist
Clifton	Parmelee	WEBB	Actor
Everton	Decourcey	WEEKES	West Indian cricketer
Caspar	Willard	WEINBERGER	US politician
Thomas	Huckle	WELLER	US physiologist
Alan	Whipper	WELLS	Athlete
Charles	Watson	WENTWORTH	British prime minister
Edith	Newbold	WHARTON	Author
Denis	Yates	WHEATLEY	Novelist
Alan	Donald	WHICKER	Broadcaster
Jimmy	Warren	WHITE	Snooker player
Joseph	Blanco	WHITE	English poet
Pearl	Fay	WHITE	US actress
Terence	Hanbury	WHITE	Novelist
William	Hale	WHITE	Writer
Alfred	North	WHITEHEAD	Philosopher and mathematician
Oscar	Fingal O'Flahertie Wills	WILDE	Playwright and novelist
Ralph	Vaughan	WILLIAMS	Composer
Bob	Dylan	WILLIS	Cricketer
Bob	Primrose	WILSON	Goalkeeper and broadcaster

First Name	Middle Name(s)	Surname	
James	**Harold**	WILSON	British prime minister
Robert	**Woodrow**	WILSON	US physicist
Thomas	**Woodrow**	WILSON	US president
Pelham	**Grenville**	WODEHOUSE	Author
Michael	**Terence**	WOGAN	Broadcaster
Thomas	**Clayton**	WOLFE	Novelist
Tom	**Kennerley**	WOLFE	Novelist
Arnold	**Whittaker**	WOLFENDALE	Astronomer
Comer	**Vann**	WOODWARD	US historian
Robert	**Burns**	WOODWARD	American chemist
Adeline	**Virginia**	WOOLF	Novelist
Frank	**Winfield**	WOOLWORTH	US businessman
Bertie	**Wilberforce**	WOOSTER	Fictional character
Frank	**Mortimer Magilinne**	WORRELL	Cricketer
Billy	**Ambrose**	WRIGHT	Footballer
Elinor	**Hoyt**	WYLIE	US author
Johann	**Rudolf**	WYSS	Swiss writer
Magdi	**Habib**	YACOUB	Surgeon
Charles	**Elwood**	YEAGER	US test pilot
William	**Butler**	YEATS	Author
Boris	**Nikolayevich**	YELTSIN	Russian president
Susannah	**Yolande**	YORK	Actress
Lazarus	**Ludwig**	ZAMENHOF	Inventor of Esperanto
Gianfranco	**Corsi**	ZEFFIRELLI	Film director
Mai	**Elizabeth**	ZETTERLING	Actress and director

Nicknames

Joseph Addison   **Atticus**
Aeschylus   **Father of Greek Tragedy**
Mike Aherne ('Gladiator')   **Warrior**
Muhammed Ali   **Louisville Lip**
Queen Anne   **Brandy Nan**
Anne of Cleves   **Flanders Mare**
Lord George Anson   **Father of the Royal Navy**
Thomas Aquinas   **Angelic Doctor**
Aristophanes   **Father of Comedy**
Richard Arkwright   **Father of the Factory System**
Henry Armstrong   **Homicide Hank**
Louis Armstrong   **Satchmo (Satchel Mouth)**
Charles Atlas   **World's Most Perfectly Developed Man**
Attila the Hun   **Scourge of God**
Aurelian (Roman Emperor)   **Restorer of the World**
Stephen Babcock   **Father of Scientific Dairying**
Francis Bacon   **Father of Inductive Philosophy**
Roger Bacon   **Father of Philosophy, Admirable Doctor (Doctor Miralilis)**
John Logie Baird   **Father of Television**
Joan Bakewell   **Thinking Man's Crumpet** (by Frank Muir)
Theda Bara   **Vamp**
John Barbour   **Father of Scottish Poetry**
Sir John Barnard   **Father of London**
John Barrymore   **Great Profile**
Sir Edmund Barton   **Father of Australia**
Elyesa Bazna (Spy)   **Cicero**
Bill Beaumont   **Amiable Geronimo**
Alexander Graham Bell   **Father of the Telephone**
John Bell   **Father of Sunday Newspapers**
Aphra Ben   **Divine Astraea**
Jeremy Bentham   **Father of Utilitarianism**
Lavrenti Beria   **Himmler of Russia**
David Berkowitz   **Son of Sam**

Irving Berlin   **Father of Published Ragtime**
Sarah Bernhard   **Divine Sarah**
John Biddle   **Father of English Unitarianism**
Clarence Birdseye   **Father of Frozen Food**
Bismarck   **Iron Chancellor**
Dr Greene Valadiman Black   **Father of Modern Dentistry**
Simon Bolivar   **Liberator**
Peter Bonetti   **Cat**
Bononcini and Handel   **Tweedle Dee and Tweedle Dum**
Jean Borotra   **Bounding Basque**
James Boswell   **Will O' the Wisp**
Clara Bow   **It Girl**
Robert Boyle   **Father of Chemistry**
Bessie Braddock   **Workers' Champion**
William Bradford   **Father of American History**
James Brindley   **Father of Britain's Canals**
William Hill Brown   **Father of the American Novel**
William Cullen Bryant   **Father of American Poetry**
Martha Jane Burke   **Calamity Jane**
Robert Burns   **Bard of Ayrshire**
Richard Burton   **The Voice**
Francis X Bushman   **Handsomest Man in the World**
David Bushnell   **Father of the Submarine**
George Bush   **Wimp**
Caedmon   **Father of English Song**
Cab Calloway   **King of Hi de Ho**
Walter Chauncey Camp   **Father of American Football**
Martha Jane Canary (Burke)   **Calamity Jane**
Thomas Carlyle   **Sage of Chelsea**
Primo Carnera   **Ambling Alp**
Judy Carne   **Sock-it-to-me-girl**
Georges Carpentier   **Orchid Kid**
Jacques Cartier   **Father of Canada**
John Cartwright   **Father of Reform**

Johnny Cash   **Man in Black**
Nicholas Catinat   **Father Thoughtful**
William Caxton   **Father of English Printing**
Sir George Cayley   **Father of Aviation**
Craig Chalmers   **Sponge**
Wilton Chamberlain   **Wilt the Stilt**
Lon Chaney Snr   **Man of a thousand Faces**
Charles I   **Martyr King, Ahab of the Nation, Britain's Josiah, White King**
Charles II   **Blackbird, Old Rowley, Merry Monarch**
Eddie Charlton   **Steady Eddie**
Henri Charrière   **Papillon**
Chris Chataway   **Red Fox**
Geoffrey Chaucer   **Father of English Poetry**
Cicero   **Father of his Country**
Cassius Clay   **Louisville Lip**
Georges Clemenceau   **Tiger**
Daniel Cohn-Bendit   **Danny the Red**
Peter Cook   **Cambridge Rapist**
John Calvin Coolidge   **Silent Cal**
Jim Corbett   **Gentleman Jim**
Paul Cotton   **Poco**
Noël Coward   **The Master**
Colin Cowdrey   **Kipper**
Alexander Cozens   **Father of English Watercolour**
Brigadier-General Alfred Critchley   **Father of Greyhound Racing**
Oliver Cromwell   **Old Noll, Nose Almighty, Old Ironsides**
Richard Cromwell   **Tumbledown Dick**
James Crossley ('Gladiator')   **Hunter**
Alister Crowley   **Wickedest Man in the World**
Duke of Cumberland   **Butcher**
Laurie Cunningham   **Black Pearl**
Edwina Currie   **Vindaloo**
Clarence Darrow   **Attorney for the Damned**
Freddie Davies (Comedian)   **Parrot Face**
Sharon Davies ('Gladiator')   **Amazon**
William Henry Davies   **Supertramp**
Steve Davis   **Interesting**
William Morris Davis   **Father of Geomorphology**
Eamon De Valera   **Father of the Irish Republic**
Daniel Defoe   **Father of Modern Prose Fiction**
Jack Dempsey   **(heavyweight) Manassa Mauler**
Jack Dempsey   **(middleweight) Nonpareil**
Joe Di Maggio   **Yankee Clipper**
Nikki Diamond, ('Gladiator')   **Scorpio**
Mildred Didrikson   **Babe**
Graham Dilley (Cricketer)   **Picca**
Tommy Docherty   **Doc**
Antoine Domino   **Fats**
Rodrigo de Vivar   **El Cid**
General Abner Doubleday   **Father of Baseball**
Antony Dowell and Antoinette Sibley   **Golden Pair**
Jimmy Durante   **Schnozzle**
Valentine Dyall   **Man in Black**
Nelson Eddy and Jeanette MacDonald   **America's Sweethearts**
Thomas Alva Edison   **Wizard of Menlo Park**
Edward I   **Longshanks**
Edward II   **Ironside**
Edward III   **Father of English Commerce**
Edward V and brother Richard   **Princes in the Tower**
Edward (Son of Edward III)   **Black Prince**
Eddie Edwards   **Eagle**

George Edwards   **Father of Ornithologists**
Elizabeth I   **Virgin Queen**
Elizabeth II   **Brenda** (by *Private Eye*)
Elizabeth Stuart (of Bohemia)   **Winter Queen**
Empress Tzu Hsi   **Old Buddha**
Arthur English   **Prince of the Wide Boys**
Ethelred II   **Unready**
Eusebio   **Black Panther**
Eusebius of Caesarea   **Father of Ecclesiastical History**
Derrick Evans   **Mr Motivator**
Henry Fielding   **Father of the English Novel**
Tom Finney   **White Ghost**
Bob Fitzsimmons   **Cornishman, Antipodean**
George Formby Snr   **Wigan Nightingale**
Tregonwell Frampton   **Father of the English Turf**
Francis I of France   **Father of Letters**
John Francome   **Greatest Jockey (by John MaCririck)**
Frederick I   **Barbarossa**
Frederick II   **Wonder of the World**
William Frederick   **Great Elector (of Brandenburg)**
Alan Freeman   **Fluff**
Tony Galento   **Two Ton**
Gandhi   **Mahatma (Great Soul)**
Joel Garner   **Big Bird**
George III   **Farmer George**
George IV   **Adonis of Fifty**
Cass Gilbert   **Father of the Skyscraper**
Ian Gillis   **Mycroft**
Bernard Gilpin   **Father of the Poor**
Giotto Di Bondone   **Father of Modern Art**
Thomas Girtin   **Father of Modern Watercolour**
William Gladstone   **Grand Old Man (GOM)**
Captain Sir John Hawley Glover   **Father of the Hausas**
Major General Sir John Bagot Glubb   **Father of the Chin, Glubb Pasha**
Sir James Goldsmith   **Goldenballs** (*Private Eye*)
Barry Goldwater   **AuH2O**
Graham Gooch   **Zap**
Benny Goodman   **King of Swing**
Charles Goodnight   **Father of the Cowboys**
Betty Grable   **Million Dollar Legs**
Ulysses Simpson Grant   **Uncle Sam**
Zachary Grey   **Father of Modern Commentators**
Florence Griffith-Joyner   **Flo Jo**
Grock   **King of Clowns**
Marvin Hagler   **Marvellous (later became first name)**
Archie Hahn   **Milwaukee Meteor**
John George Haigh   **Acid Bath Murderer, Vampire Killer**
Handel and Bononcini   **Tweedle Dum and Tweedle Dee**
WC Handy   **Father of the Blues**
Harold I   **Harefoot**
Russell Harty   **Sooty**
Mark Hateley (footballer)   **Attila**
Sir Christopher Hatton   **Mutton, the Dancing Chancellor**
Franz Josef Haydn   **Father of the Symphony**
Edward Heath   **Grocer**
Henry I of England   **Beauclerc**
Henry IV of France   **Father of the People**

Henry V   **Bluff Prince Hal**
Herodotus   **Father of History**
Michael Heseltine   **Tarzan, Veronica Lake**, **Action Man, Goldilocks**
Alex Higgins   **Hurricane**
Jimmy Hill   **Rabbi**
Bernard Hinault (cyclist)   **Badger**
Hippocrates   **Father of Medicine**
Bob Hite (Canned Heat)   **Bear**
James Hogg   **Ettrick Shepherd**
Billie Holliday   **Lady Day**
John Philip Holland   **Father of the Military Submarine**
Homer   **Father of Epic Poetry**
Thomas Hooker   **Father of American Democracy**
Matthew Hopkins   **Witchfinder General**
Lesley Hornby   **Twiggy**
Geoffrey Howe   **Mogadon Man**
Edmond Hoyle   **Father of the Game of Whist**
George Hudson   **Railway King**
Cordell Hull   **Father of the United Nations**
Barbara Hutton   **Poor Little Rich Girl**
Hypatia   **Divine Pagan**
Thomas Ince   **Father of Westerns**
Andrew Jackson   **Old Hickory**
General Thomas Jackson   **Stonewall (Battle of Bull Run)**
Joseph Holson Jagger   **Man Who Broke the Bank at Monte Carlo**
James I   **Wisest Fool in Christendom (by Henry IV of France)**
James II   **King over the Water**
Thomas Jefferson   **Moonshine Philosopher**
James J Jeffries   **Boilermaker**
Edward Jenner   **Father of Immunology**
William Le Baron Jenney   **Father of the Skyscraper**
Gilbert Jessop (cricketer)   **The Croucher**
Joan of Arc   **Maid of Orleans**
Samuel Johnson   **Great Cham**
Sir John Harvey Jones   **Admiral**
Ben Jonson   **Father of Poets**
Janis Joplin   **Pearl**
Scott Joplin   **Father of Ragtime**
William Joyce   **Lord Haw Haw**
Alberto Juantorena   **White Lightning**
Helen Kane   **Boop a Doop Girl**
Nora Kaye   **Duse of the Dance**
Buster Keaton   **The Great Stone Face**
Joseph Keaton   **Buster** (*coined by Houdini*)
Fanny Kemble   **Anne of Swansea**
Rev Geoffrey Kennedy   **Woodbine Willie**
Ludovic Kennedy   **Uckers**
Admiral Sir Henry Keppel   **Father of the Fleet**
Graham Kerr   **Galloping Gourmet**
King John   **Lackland**
Peter Kurten   **Monster of Düsseldorf**
Henri Landru   **Bluebeard**
Allen Lane   **Father of Penguin Paperbacks**
Niki Lauda   **Clockwork Mouse**
Rod Laver   **Rockhampton Rocket**
Antoine Lavoisier   **Father of Modern Chemistry**
Florence Lawrence   **Biograph Girl**
Frances Lawrence (Novelist)   **Gidget**
John Lawrence   **Noble Lord** (*by John McCririck*)
Major General Stringer Lawrence   **Father of the Indian Army**
TE Lawrence   **Lawrence of Arabia**

Jean-Baptiste Le Moyne   **Father of Louisiana**
Jerry Lee Lewis   **Killer**
Mike Lewis ('Gladiators')   **Saracen**
Eric Liddell   **Flying Scotsman**
Fred Lillywhite   **Nonpareil Bowler** (*overarm pioneer*)
Jenny Lind   **Swedish Nightingale**
Charles Lindbergh   **Lone Eagle**
David Lloyd George   **Welsh Wizard**
Harry Longbaugh   **Sundance Kid**
Lord Longford   **Lord Porn**
Lorenzo de' Medici   **Father of Letters, The Magnificent**
Konrad Lorenz   **Father of Ethology**
Louis XII   **Father of the People**
Louis XIV   **Sun King**
Joe Louis   **Brown Bomber**
Lord Lucan   **Lucky**
Vera Lynn   **Forces Sweetheart**
Ma Rainey   **Mother of the Blues**
Mary McCauley   **Molly Pitcher**
Derek McCulloch   **Uncle Mac**
John McEnroe   **Superbrat**
Barry McGuigan   **Clones Cyclone**
Harold Macmillan   **Supermac**
McPartlin and Donnelly   **Ant and Dec**
Helen Madderson ('Gladiator')   **Panther**
James Madison   **Father of the Constitution**
Mary Mallon   **Typhoid Mary**
Rocky Marciano   **Brockton Blockbuster**
Frances Marion   **Swamp Fox**
Duchess of Marlborough   **Mrs Freeman**
Duke of Marlborough (1st)   **Anne's Great Captain**
Major William Martin   (WW2 decoy) **Man Who Never Was**
Mary I   **Bloody Mary**
Matilda   **Empress Maud**
Stanley Matthews   **Wizard of Dribble**
Colin Meads   **Pine Tree**
Bette Midler   **Divine Miss M**
Henry Miller   **Father of the Four Letter Word**
Joseph Miller   **Father of Jests**
Max Miller   **Cheekie Chappie**
Carmen Miranda   **Brazilian Bombshell**
Thelonius Monk   **High Priest of Bop**
Duke of Monmouth (James Scott)   **Absalom**
Jean Monnet   **Father of the Common Market**
Lady Mary Wortley Montague   **Sappho**
Helen Wills Moody   **Little Miss Poker Face**
Lewis Henry Morgan   **Father of American Anthropology**
Jedediah Morse   **Father of American Geography**
Charles Morton   **Father of Variety, Champagne, Father of the Halls**
Lord Louis Mountbatten   **Dickie**
Richard Murdoch   **Stinker**
Lindley Murray   **Father of English Grammar**
James Naismith   **Father of Basketball**
Renaldo Nehemiah (athlete)   **Skeets**
Jarwaharlal Nehru   **Pandit (Wise Man)**
Donald Neilson (Nappey)   **Black Panther**
Marshal Ney   **Bravest of the Brave**
Jack Nicklaus   **Golden Bear**
Florence Nightingale   **Lady with the Lamp**
Richard Nixon   **Tricky Dicky**
Kwame Nkrumah   **Showboy**

Greg Norman   **Great White Shark**
Senator George Norris   **Father of the 20th Amendment**
Paavo Nurmi   **Flying Finn**
Lord John Oaksey   **Noble Lord** (by John McCririck)
Ronald O'Bryan   **Candy Man Killer**
Chris Old (Cricketer)   **Chilly**
Sir Henry Oliver   **Father of Modern Navigation**
Christina Onassis   **Thunderthighs**
Dr Robert Oppenheimer   **Father of the Atom Bomb**
Count D'Orsay   **Last of the Dandies**
Countess Spencer   **Acid Raine**
Tessie O'Shea   **Two-Ton Tessie**
Richard Fellow Outcault   **Father of the Comic Strip**
Robert Owen   **Father of British Socialism**
Jesse Owens   **Ebony Antelope**
Palmerston, Lord Henry   **Pam**
Bonnie Parker   **Suicide Sal**
Charlie Parker   **Bird**
Archbishop Matthew Parker   **Nosey Parker**
General George Patton   **Old Blood and Guts**
Cynthia Payne   **Madame Sin**
Pele   **Black Pearl**
Vladimir Peniakoff (Belgian soldier)   **Popski**
Sir Henry Percy   **Hotspur**
Joseph Père   **Grey Eminence**
William Perry   **Refrigerator**
John Joseph Pershing   **Black Jack**
Marius Petipa   **Father of Classical Ballet**
Louis Philippe   **Citizen King**
Edith Piaf   **Little Sparrow**
Mary Pickford   **America's Sweetheart**
William Pitt   **Aeolus**
William Pitt the Elder   **Great Commoner**
Gary Player   **Man in Black**
John Playford   **Father of British Music Publishing**
Edgar Allen Poe   **Father of the Detective Story**
Alexander Pope   **Wasp of Twickenham**
Elvis Presley   **The Pelvis, The King**
Princess Michael of Kent   **Princess Pushy**
Ferenc Puskas   **Galloping Major**
Rufus Putnam   **Father of Ohio**
Max Quartermann   **Superhod**
Fabius Quintus   **Cunctator (Delayer)**
Rabelais   **Father of Ridicule**
Luise Rainer   **Viennese Teardrop**
Sonny Ramadhin   **Spin King**
Derek Randall (Cricketer)   **Arkle**
Maharajah Ranjit Singh   **Lion of the Punjab**
Ranulf de Glanvill   **Father of Jurisprudence**
John Ray   **Father of English Natural History**
Johnny Ray   **Prince of Wails**
Nancy Reagan   **Smiling Mamba**
Ronald Reagan   **Teflon President**
Ray Reardon   **Dracula**
John Redmond   **Vulcan**
John Reid   **Father of American Golf**
Richard I   **Lionheart, Yea and Nay**
Richard de Beauchamp   **Father of Courtesy**
Richard de Clare   **(2nd Earl of Pembroke) Strongbow**
Richard Neville   **(Earl of Warwick) Kingmaker**
Richard Duke of York and Edward V   **Princes in the Tower**
Samuel Richardson   **Father of the English Novel**

Cardinal Richelieu   **Red Eminence**
Manfred von Richthofen   **Red Baron**
John Rich   **Father of Harlequins, Father of English Pantomime**
Eddie Rickenbacker   **Ace of Aces**
Helen Riley ('Gladiator')   **Panther**
Robespierre   **Sea-Green Incorruptible**
George Robey   **Prime Minister of Mirth**
Derek Robinson   **Red Robbo**
Jimmie Charles Rodgers   **Father of Country Music**
Steve Rogers   **Captain America**
Erwin Rommel   **Desert Fox**
Ken Rosewall   **Muscles**
Stanley Rous   **Father of English Football**
William Hepburn Russell   **Father of the Pony Express**
Ernest Rutherford   **Father of Nuclear Physics**
Babe Ruth   **Sultan of Swat**
William Sacheverell   **First Whig**
St Anthony   **Father of Christian Monasticism**
St Ethelwold   **Father of Monks**
St Thomas Aquinas   **Father of Moral Philosophy**
Albert de Salvo   **Boston Strangler**
Sir Malcolm Sargent   **Flash Harry**
Sir Walter Scott   **Wizard of the North, Great Unknown, Ariosto of the North, Old Peveril**
William Shakespeare   **Swan of Avon, Bard of Avon**
Percy Bysshe Shelley   **Ariel**
Ann Sheridan   **Oomph Girl**
Manny Shinwell   **Sinbad the Tailor**
Willie Shoemaker (jockey)   **Shoe**
Antoinette Sibley and Anthony Dowell   **Golden Pair**
Igor Sikorsky   **Father of the Helicopter**
OJ Simpson   **The Juice**
Frank Sinatra   **The Voice**
Dennis Skinner   **Beast of Bolsover**
Adam Smith   **Father of Economics**
Bob Smith   **Wolfman Jack**
William Smith   **Father of English Geology**
Soeur Sourire   **Singing Nun**
John Philip Sousa   **March King**
Ursula Southiel   **Old Mother Shipton**
John Spencer   **Sniffer**
Bruce Springsteen   **The Boss**
Craig Stadler, (golfer)   **Walrus**
Sylvester Stallone   **Italian Stallion**
George Stephenson   **Father of Railways**
Sir Rowland Stephenson   **Father of Indian Railways**
Jenny Stoute ('Gladiators')   **Rebel**
Robert Franklin Stroud   **Birdman of Alcatraz**
Charles Edward Stuart   **Bonnie Prince Charlie, Young Pretender, Young Chevalier**
James Edward Stuart   **Old Pretender, Old Chevalier**
Peter Sutcliffe   **Yorkshire Ripper**
Thomas Tallis   **Father of English Church Music**
James T Tanner   **Father of Musical Comedy**
David Taylor (Snooker player)   **Silver Fox**
John Taylor   **Water Poet**
Edward Teach   **Blackbeard**
Norman Tebbit   **Chingford Skinhead**
Temujin   **Genghis Khan**
Alfred Lord Tennyson   **Merlin**
Margaret Thatcher   **Iron Lady, The Milk Snatcher, Attila the Hen**
Cliff Thorburn (Snooker player)   **Grinder**

William Tilden **Big Bill**
Timon (Athenian nobleman) **Misanthrope of Athens**
Thomas Tompion **Father of English Clockmaking**
Mel Torme **Velvet Fog**
Charles Townshend **Turnip**
Hugh Montague Trenchard **Father of the RAF**
Richard Trevethick **Father of the Locomotive**
Lee Trevino **Super-Mex**
Freddie Trueman **Fiery Fred**
Lyman Trumbell **Father of the 13th Amendment**
Sophie Tucker **Last of the Red Hot Mamas**
JMW Turner **Admiral Pugsy Booth, Blackbirdy**
Lana Turner **Sweater Girl**
William Turner, (Dean of Wells) **Father of English Botany**
Christopher Tye **Father of the Anthem**
Frank Tyson (cricketer) **Typhoon**
Mike Tyson **Catskill Thunder**
Uganda **Pearl of Africa**
US Defence Dept **Foggy Bottom**
Rudolph Valentino **Pink Powder Puff**
Rudy Vallee **Vagabond Lover**
Michael Van Wijk ('Gladiators') **Wolf**
Venerable Bede **Father of English History**
Queen Victoria **Widow of Windsor**
Horace Walpole **Autocrat of Strawberry Hill**
Rosalind P Walter **Rosie the Riveter**

Izaak Walton **Father of Angling**
George Washington **Father of his Country**
Isaac Watts **Father of English Hymnody**
James Watt **Father of Steam**
John Wayne **Duke**
Josiah Wedgwood **Father of English Pottery**
Duke of Wellington **Iron Duke, Old Nosey, Achilles of England**
Jimmy White **Whirlwind**
William White (US writer) **Sage of Emporia**
Ann Widdecombe **Doris Karloff**
Bishop Samuel Wilberforce **Soapy Sam**
William Willett **Father of Daylight Saving**
William I **Conqueror**
William I of Orange **Silent**
William II **Rufus**
William IV **Silly Billy**
Esther Williams **Hollywood's Mermaid**
Kim Williams ('Gladiators') **Lightning**
Walter Winchell **Father of the Gossip Column**
Orde Wingate **Robin Hood**
Sir Henry Wood **Old Timber**
Harry Wragg (Jockey) **The Head Waiter**
Philemon Wright **Father of Ottawa**
Francis Xavier **Apostle of the Indies**
Diane Youdale, ('Gladiators') **Jet**
Sandy Young ('Gladiators') **Phoenix**

Traditional Occupations and Hobbies

This list of definitions includes some now-defunct traditional occupations alongside hobbies, pastimes, and colloquial names for certain types of worker. It also lists some lesser-known meanings for familiar professions.

Actuary Person employed to assess risks for insurance companies, a statistician
Alderman Senior member of a local council (until 1974)
Ale conner Inspector of beer and bread
Almoner Hospital social worker
Amanuensis Secretary employed to take dictation or copy manuscripts
Artificer Serviceman trained in mechanics
Bhishti (bheesty) Formerly a water carrier, in India
Bibliophile Collector of books
Bibliopole Dealer in rare books
Boatswain/bosun Petty officer on a merchant ship or warrant officer on a warship, responsible for maintenance
Bowyer Person who makes or sells archery bows
Broderer Person who embroiders
Bumbailiff Formerly, an officer employed to collect debts and arrest non-payers
Bursar Official in charge of finance in educational institutions
Campanologist Bell ringer
Cartographer Person who draws maps
Cartomancer Person who tells fortunes by use of playing cards
Cartophilist Collector of cigarette cards
Cartwright Maker of carts
Chandler Maker or seller of candles; grocer
Charcutier Pork butcher
Cobbler Shoemaker
Colporteur Hawker of books, especially bibles

Conchologist Collector of shells
Cooper Maker of barrels
Cordwainer Shoemaker, leather worker
Costermonger Fruit and vegetable salesman (formerly an apple vendor)
Coxswain Helmsman of a boat
Curator Person in charge of a collection, e.g. in a museum or library
Currier Person who grooms horses or curries leather
Deltiologist Picture-postcard collector
Didactics The art or science of teaching
Draper Person who sells cloth and cloth goods
Ecdysiast Striptease artist
Equerry Formerly, an officer in the royal household responsible for the horses
Farrier Person who shoes horses
Fletcher Maker of arrows
Founder Maker of bells and castings
Franklin Substantial landowner of free but not noble birth (Middle Ages)
Fromologist Person who collects cheese labels
Funambulist Tightrope walker
Gatherer Glass blower, and formerly a bookbinder
Glaziers Person who fits windows, doors etc, with glass
Goliard Wandering scholar of 12th and 13th centuries, famed for riotous behaviour
Gombeen man An Irish moneylender
Gricer Person who seeks out and photographs unusual trains

Groom   Person employed to clean and generally look after horses

Haberdasher   Seller of sewing articles, e.g. buttons, needles, zips and ribbons

Haberdasher (USA)   Men's clothes outfitter

Hack   Run of the mill journalist

Hard hat   Construction worker

Horner   Person who made objects such as spoons and combs out of horn

Hosier   Person who sells stockings

Houseman   Junior doctor who is a member of the medical staff attached to a hospital

Ikebanist   Practitioner of the Japanese decorative art of flower arranging

Intern   North American equivalent to a houseman; it is also a US term for a student teacher

Ironmonger   Dealer in hardware Dealer, eg nuts, bolts and locks, etc

Jobber   Dealer in stocks and shares

Joiner   Person skilled in making finished woodwork, eg windows, doors and stairs

Kamikaze   Japanese pilot who performed suicide missions in World War II

Lepidopterist   Butterfly and moth collector

Locum tenens   Person who deputises for another in the same profession

Longshoreman   American equivalent of a docker or stevedore

Lorimer/loriner   Person who makes bits, spurs and other small metal objects

Matador   Principal bullfighter

Mercer   Textile dealer

Milliner   Person who makes or sells women's hats

Millwright   Engineer who designs, builds or repairs grain mills or mill machinery

Modiste   Fashionable dressmaker or milliner

Navvy   Labourer on a building site

Notary public   Solicitor licensed to prepare legal documents

Numismatist   Collector of coins and medals

Obstetrician   Physician who specialises in childbirth

Ocularist   Person who makes artificial eyes

Optometrist   Person qualified to examine the eyes and prescribe lenses; also called optician or ophthalmologist

Origamist   Person who folds paper into ornate figures and decorations

Paediatrician   Physician who specialises in children and their diseases

Paramedic   Person such as a laboratory technician who supplements the work of the medical profession

Pedagogue   A teacher or educator

Pedant   Archaic term for a teacher

Philatelist   Stamp collector

Phillumenist   Person who collects matchbox labels

Picador   In bullfighting or horseman who lances the bull in early stages in order to weaken it

Pilot   Person qualified to steer or guide a ship into or out of port

Potholer   Cave and underground passage explorer

Prestidigitator   Magician, especially one skilled in close sleight of hand

Publican   In Roman times, a tax collector

Purser   On a ship or plane, officer who keeps the accounts and attends to passenger welfare

Quantity surveyor   Person who estimates the cost of the materials and labour necessary for a construction job

Radiographer/radiologist   Person who takes X-rays

Recorder   Barrister or solicitor of at least ten years, standing appointed to sit as a judge in the Crown Court

Registrar   Hospital doctor, senior to a houseman but junior to a consultant

Roughneck   Worker in an oil-drilling operation

Saddler   Person who makes saddles, harnesses and other leather equipment for horses

Sandhog   North American term for person who works in underground or underwater construction projects

Scrivener   Formerly, a person who wrote out legal documents, a notary

Sempstress/seamstress   Woman who sews and makes clothes

Sensei   Japanese teacher of martial and other arts

Sexton   Church helper responsible for church upkeep

Shaman   Medicine man or witch doctor

Shipwright   Artisan skilled in shipbuilding

Spelunker   Cave explorer

Spodomancer   Person who makes prophecies by divination of ashes

Stationer   Person who sells stationery; formerly a publisher or bookseller

Steeplejack   Person skilled in construction and felling of steeples, spires, chimneys and towers

Stenographer   North American name for a shorthand typist

Stevedore   Person employed to load or unload a ship

Stoker   Person employed to tend a furnace, as on a steamship

Subaltern   Army officer below the rank of captain, usually a second lieutenant

Tanner   Person who tans skins and hides into leather

Topiarist   Person who shapes hedges into ornate shapes

Toreador   Rank-and-file bullfighter

Turner   Lathe operator

Upholsterer   Person who upholsters furniture

Vexillologist   Person who studies and collects information about flags

Vintner   Wine merchant

Vulcanologist   Person who studies volcanoes

Wainwright   Maker of wagons, wains and carts

Wheelwright/wheeler   Maker of wheels

Philosophers and Political Thinkers

Thales (c624–c545 BC)   Greek natural philosopher and astronomer, born in Miletus, traditionally seen as the founder of European philosophy. Thales identified water as the basis of the universe and also predicted the solar eclipse that took place in 585 BC. He was included in the traditional canon of 'Seven Wise Men' and was the original 'absent-minded professor', having allegedly fallen into a well whilst looking at the stars.

Anaximander (c611–546 BC)   Greek natural philosopher and astronomer, born in Miletus, and possibly a pupil of Thales. Anaximander is credited with producing the first maps. He was the second of the three great Milesian thinkers (the third was Anaximenes).

Pythagoras (c580– c500 BC)   Greek philosopher and mathematician, born in Samos, Ionia. He established his ethico-political academy at Croton (now Crotona) in southern Italy. Famous for his theorem concerning properties of right-angled triangles.

Heraclitus (554–483 BC)   Greek philosopher, born in Ephesus and nicknamed at various times 'the obscure' and 'the riddler'. Most famous doctrine is that everything is in a state of flux and that fire is the ultimate constituent of the world.

Confucius (551–479 BC)   Chinese philosopher, born in what is now Shantung province.His birthday is celebrated on 28 Sepember and is an official holiday in Taiwan ('Teacher's Day'). Although Confucius was not greatly revered in his lifetime, Confucianism, as expressed in his *Analects*, subsequently dominated Chinese life as both a religious and philosophical way of life.

Parmenides of Elea (510–483 BC)   Greek philosopher from southern Italy and founder of the Eleatic school, which included his pupils Zeno and Melissus. His great work *On Nature* was written in hexameter verse.

Empedocles (c490–c430 BC)   Greek philosopher, poet, statesman, religious teacher and physiologist, born in Acragas in Sicily. Empedocles held that the world is composed of four elements – air, fire, earth and water – which are governed by the opposing forces of love and discord. Heralded by his followers as a god, he allegedly died by leaping into the volcanic crater of Mount Etna whilst attempting to prove his divinity.

Socrates (469–399 BC)   Athenian philosopher, held in such esteem that all earlier Greek philosophy is known as pre Socratic. Little is known about him other than that he had an apparently shrewish wife, Xanthippe, and took part in military campaigns at Potidaea, Delium and Amphipolis. Socrates wrote nothing but was eulogised in the 'Dialogues' of his pupil, Plato. Socrates' approach was to question everything. He chose to pick holes in the deliberations of others and asked people to think for themselves. He was eventually charged with 'Impiety' and 'Corrupting the youth of Athens' and forced to die by drinking hemlock.

Democritus (c460–c370 BC)   Greek philosopher, born in Abdera in Thrace and known as the 'laughing philosopher' because of his wry amusement at human foibles. A prolific writer, he is best known for the atomistic theory he developed from Leucippus.

Plato (c428–348 BC)   Athenian philosopher who related the story of Socrates' trial in three of his *Dialogues*: the *Apology*, the *Crito* and the *Phaedo*. In c387 BC he founded the Academy, which became a famous establishment for philosophical, mathematical and scientific research. His writings comprise around 30 dialogues and a series of letters (only the seventh and eighth are likely to be genuine). The dialogue *Symposium* is an allegory of the search for love, and the *Republic* is an allegory of the search for justice. Plato was the teacher of Aristotle.

Aristotle (384–322 BC)   Greek philosopher and scientist, born in Stagira, son of the court physician to the King of Macedon. Aristotle is one of the two most important philosophers of the ancient world, and one of the four or five most important of any time or place. For twenty years he was a member of Plato's Academy. When Plato died, Speusippus became head of the academy and Aristotle left Athens and became tutor to Alexander the Great (then aged 13). He returned to Athens in 335 BC and founded his 'Lyceum', so called from its proximity to the temple of Apollo Lyceius. The 'Aristotelian corpus' (1462 pages of Greek text, including some spurious works) is probably derived from the lectures he gave in the Lyceum. Aristotle's followers became known as peripatetics (from his habit of walking around whilst lecturing). There is no doubt that many of the sub-categories of modern philosophy were formulated by Aristotle. He argued that although philosophy encompassed all areas of intellectual enquiry, there were distinct disciplines within this structure. Some areas in which Aristotle made a fundamental contribution in the expansion of philosophy as a science include logic, the study of nature, metaphysics, philosophy of mind,ethics and politics, and literary criticism and rhetorical theory. His works include the *Nicomachean Ethics, De Anima Politics, Poetics, Metaphysics*, and the *Organon* (treatises on logic).

Epicurus (341–270 BC)   Greek philosopher, born in Samos. His ethical philosophy was based on simple pleasures, friendship, and reflection. When Epicurus came to Athens in 306 BC he bought a house and established a school in the garden which became known as Ho Kepos (The Garden), where men and women of any background could attend. Like many of his predecessors he wrote treatises 'On Nature' but his best works were his ethical and theological dialogues which made him a revered figure long after his death.

Lucretius (c99–55 BC)   Roman philosopher and poet whose great works are his hexameter poem *Dererum natura* and his treatises attempting to separate philosophy from religion, which he denounced as the one great source of man's wickedness and misery. He was said to have died mad from the effects of a love potion administered by his wife, Lucilia.

Plotinus (c205–70)   Born in Egypt of Roman parentage. His prolific writings were posthumously edited and arranged by his pupil, Porphyry, into six 'groups of nine books' or *Enneads*. These established the foundations of Neoplatonism, which combined Platonic with Pythagorean, Aristotelian and Stoic doctrines.

St Augustine of Hippo (354–430)   Born in Tagaste

in Numidia (modern Tunisia) of Roman descent, he was converted to Christianity in 386 and described his conversion in his most famous work *Confessions*. His other masterpiece was *The City of God*.

Roger Bacon (c1214–92)   English philosopher and scientist, probably born near Ilchester, Somerset. His soubriquet 'Doctor Mirabilis' was gained because of his learning in magic and alchemy and he was the first European to describe the process for making gunpowder. Bacon held radical philosophical views and was imprisoned by the Franciscans for some time because of his suspected heretical teachings.

St Thomas Aquinas (c1225–74)   Italian Dominican philosopher and theologian, born in the castle of Roccasecca, near Aquino, Sicily. His early education was at the monastery of Monte Cassino and then the University of Naples. He was a pupil of the Dominican scholar, Albertus Magnus, at the University of Paris and from 1256 began teaching there himself. In 1259 he was appointed theological adviser to the papal Curia. His two major works are *Summa theologica* and *Summa contra gentiles*. Thomas was known as 'Doctor Angelicus' and canonized a saint in 1323 by Pope John XXII. Thomism was the standard teaching of the Dominican order and has recently had a revival.

John Duns Scotus (c1265–1308)   Scottish scholastic philiiosopher who became a Franciscan and was ordained a priest in St Andrew's Church, Northampton in 1291. He taught at Cologne, where he died and was buried. Duns Scotus was known by contemporaries as 'Doctor Subtilis' because of his extremely nuanced and technical resoning, but in the Renaissance the Scotists were dubbed 'Dunses' (hence the word 'dunce'). His important works include the *Opus Pariense* (Parisian Lectures), *Opus Oxiense* (Oxford Lectures, also known as the Ordinatio), *Tractatus de Primo Principio* and *Quaestiones Quodlibetales*.

William of Ockham (c1285–c1349)   English philosopher, theologian and political writer, born in Ockham, Surrey. William entered the Franciscan order after studying theology at Oxford, although he failed to graduate hence his nickname, 'the Venerable Inceptor'. He was excommunicated by John XXII and fled to Bavaria where he died of the Black Death. His works greatly upset the papacy and included *Summa Logicae, Quodlibeta Septem* and commentaries on the sentences of Peter Lombard and Aristotle His greatest philosophical contribution is 'Ockham's razor' or the 'Law of Parsimony', which states that entities are not to be multiplied beyond necessity. The principle was invoked previously by Durand de Saint-Pourcain but Ockhams freuent and sharp employment of the doctrine ensured that his name would be identified with the principle.

Nicholas of Cusa (1401–64)   German philosopher, scientist and churchman, born in Cues, Trier. He studied at Heidelberg and Padua, was ordained in 1430 and subsequently became a papal diplomat and Cardinal. Nicholas stressed the incomplete nature of man's knowledge of God and the universe. His main philosophical work is *De Docta Ignorantia* (1440) but he was the precursor of Copernicus as regards his non-geocentric theories.

Niccolò Machiavelli (1469–1527)   Italian political philosopher, statesman and writer, born in Florence. He rose to prominence after the demise of Savonarola's regime in 1498. He had a controversial career and was in and out of favour dependent on the political climate. His masterpiece, *The Prince*, was dedicated to Lorenzo de Medici and published 1532. This work epitomised his ethic of evil sometimes being necessary in order for good to prevail. Other works include *The Art of War*, and *Mandragola*, a comic play about seduction, as well as a discourse on Livy. He is buried in Santa Croce, Florence.

Giordano Bruno (1548–1600)   Italian philosopher, born in Nola, near Naples. He became a Dominican but came into conflict with the Inquisition due to his championing of Copernicus' heliocentricity theory, and his pantheistic views. He was eventually burned at the stake in Rome.

Sir Francis Bacon (1561–1626)   English philosopher and statesman who became Viscount St Albans. He was a leading proponent of Empiricism and rejected Aristotelian deductive logic. His works include *The Advancement of Learning, Novum Organum* and *The New Atlantis*. Bacon was also a leading parliamentarian and his methodical and logical approach was not trusted by his uncle, Lord Burghley. An example of his political expediency was to try to convict his former friend, the Earl of Essex. He apparently died from hypothermia caused while carrying out food preservation experiments on chickens.

Thomas Hobbes (1588–1679)   English political philosopher, born in Malmesbury (apparently prematurely, after his mother heard news of the approaching Spanish Armada). His first published work was a translation of Thucydides' *History* (1629); other works include *Elements of Law Natural and Politic* and his masterpiece '*Leviathan*' (1651), in which he argues that absolutist government is needed to ensure law and order. His later works were published in Holland, the most famous being 'Behemoth: a History of the causes of the Civil Wars of England'.

René Descartes (1596–1650)   French philosopher and mathematician, born near Tours in a town now called La-Haye, later renamed Descartes in his honour. He is often called the father of modern philosophy. Descartes was in Germany with the army of the Duke of Bavaria in 1619 when, on November 10th, he had a visionary dream in a stove-heated room, which revealed a scientific postulate that would link all possible human knowledge together into an all-embracing wisdom. Most of his major works were published shortly after the death of his illegitimate daughter, Francine, in 1640, the most famous being the *Discourse on Method* which framed the basis for Cartesian philosophy, the phrase '*Cogito ergo sum*' (I think therefore I am) encapsulating his rational methodology. He died of pneumonia and his last words were supposedly 'So my soul a time for parting'. He was buried in Stockholm but was later moved to Saint-Germain-des-Prés, Paris.

Baruch Spinoza (1632–77)   Dutch philosopher, born in Amsterdam. He was expelled from his Jewish community for heresy in 1656 and made a living grinding and polishing lenses (the glass dust was to cause his untimely death from consumption). His *Principia Philosophiae* was the only book published in his lifetime with his name on it. His main work, *Ethics*, was published posthumously. Spinoza is also known for his contributions to the development of an historical approach to the Bible.

John Locke (1632–74)   English empiricist

philosopher, born in Wrington, Somerset. Locke's *Essay Concerning Human Understanding* was the basis for the resurgence of Empiricism as an alternative to Cartesianism. He believed the mind at birth was a *tabula rasa*, as opposed to the Cartesian view that knowledge is derived from first principles.

Gottfried Wilhelm von Leibniz (1646–1716)
German philosopher and mathematician, born in Leipzig. His optimism and faith in enlightenment and reason was satirised by Voltaire in *Candide* ('all is for the best in the best of all possible worlds'). His most famous work is the *Monadology*, in which he argues that the world is made up of an infinite number of units (monads), the highest of which is God. Apart from his philosophical essays, Leibniz also invented differential calculus, although the Royal Society formally declared Newton as its inventor in 1711 (nowadays both are credited).

Giovanni Vico (1668–1744) Italian philosopher, born in Naples. His major work, *Scienza Nuova* (The New Science), is concerned with the differences between scientific and historical explanation.

George Berkeley (1685–1753) Irish Anglican bishop and philosopher, born at Dysert Castle, Kilkenny. Bishop Berkeley was Dean of Derry and then Bishop of Cloyne; in between he tried to establish a college in the Bermudas but only got as far as Rhode Island. His celebrated claim that 'to be is to be perceived', whereby the contents of the material world are 'ideas' that only exist when they are perceived by a mind, is set out in his *Essay Towards a New Theory of Vision* and *A Treatise Concerning the Principles of Human Knowledge*. His other major work is *Three Dialogues Between Hylas and Philanous*.

David Hume (1711–76) Scottish philosopher and historian, born in Edinburgh. Hume's life was dogged in its early stages with fits of depression which he came to terms with whilst tutoring the insane nobleman, the Marquis of Annandale. His major works, *A Treatise of Human Nature* and *Dialogues Concerning Natural Religion* had a profound effect on Immanuel Kant and provoked the Idealists to counter Hume's scepticism. Hume was a friend of Rousseau but became embroiled in a famously bitter quarrel with him.

Jean-Jacques Rousseau (1712–78) French political philosopher, born in Geneva (his mother died in childbirth). He worked as a secretary and music copier in his early life. After a brief affair with Mme Louise de Warens he formed a lifelong liaison with Thérèse le Vasseur, with whom he had five children and eventually married in 1768. In 1762 he published his masterpiece *The Social Contract* which begins, 'Man is born free; and everywhere he is in chains.' His text, with its slogan 'Liberty, Equality, Fraternity', became the Bible of the French Revolution. At the invitation of David Hume, he lived at Wootton Hall near Ashbourne in Derbyshire. Here he began his *Confessions* but became increasingly paranoiac and returned to Paris where he completed the work. He became seriously insane and died in Ermenonville. His remains were placed alongside Voltaire's in the Panthéon in Paris.

Denis Diderot (1713–84) French philosopher and man of letters, born in Langres in Champagne, the son of a master cutler. He was a precursor of the Romanticists and was patronised by Catherine II, (the Great) of Russia. In 1743 he married Antoinette Champion, daughter of a linendraper, although his father disapproved. Diderot set out a philosophy of the arts and sciences which took the progress of

civilisation to be a measure of mankind's moral improvement and perceived the Christian religion as morally harmful. From 1745 to 1772 Diderot served as chief editor of the *Encyclopédie*, one of the principal works of the Age of Enlightenment.

Immanuel Kant (1724–1804) German philosopher, born in Könisberg in Prussia (now Kaliningrad), the son of a saddler. He taught at the university and was known for his ordered way of life (locals allegedly set their watches by the time of his daily walks). Kant was a keen astronomer who predicted the existence of the planet Uranus before Herschel's discovery in 1781. Kant's most famous works, such as *Critique of Pure Reason* (1781), *Critique of Practical Reason* (1788) and *Critique of Judgement* (1790) were all pubished late in his life. Kant described his philosophy as 'transcendental' or 'critical' idealism.

Edmund Burke (1729–97) Irish philosopher and statesman, born in Dublin, and educated at a Quaker school and Trinity College. Burke's *Thoughts on the Present Discontents* and *Reflections on the French Revolution* were his masterpieces. Although a Whig all his life, Burke's political thought became, with Disraeli's, the philosophy of modern Conservatism.

Thomas Paine (1737–1809) English-born, American revolutionary philosopher and writer, born in Thetford, Norfolk, the son of a Quaker. He followed his father's trade as a corset maker before becoming, firstly a sailor, then a schoolmaster and ultimately an exciseman. It was during this period that he first showed his tendency to speak out against what he felt were injustices and was dismissed for disturbing the status quo by deriding the lack of pay increases. Benjamin Franklin helped him emigrate to America, where he settled in Philadelphia and became a radical journalist. He published a pamphlet *Common Sense* following the outbreak of the American Revolutionary War urging an immediate declaration of independence. He returned to England, after visiting France, and published *The Rights of Man* (1792) a reply to Burke's *Reflections on the French Revolution*. He was indicted for treason but fled to France whereupon he fell foul of Robespierre and was imprisoned but later freed on the grounds of his American citizenship (1795). His book *The Age of Reason* (1796) mostly written in prison, upset many of his American friends, including George Washington. He died alone and in poverty on his farm in New Rochelle, New York.

Jeremy Bentham (1748–1832) English philosopher, jurist and social reformer, born in London. Bentham is best known as a proponent of Utilitarianism, as seen in his pioneering works *A Fragment on Government* (1776) and *Introduction to the Principles of Morals and Legislation* (1789), in which he argued that the proper objective of all conduct and legislation is 'the greatest happiness of the greatest number'. He developed 'hedonic calculus' to estimate the effects of different actions. Bentham became an honorary French citizen in 1792 and published treatises on social and penal reform. He also planned a special prison (Panopticon) and school (Chrestomathia), helped start the *Westminster Review* (1823) and founded University College, where his clothed skeleton is preserved.

Johann Fichte (1762–1814) German philosopher, born in Rammenau, Saxony, the son of a ribbon weaver. In 1793 Fichte married Johanna Maria Rahn and in the same year published two anonymous works, the most important being *Contribution to the*

Correction of the Public's Judgments Regarding the French Revolution. He developed Kants' Critical philosophy into a system of his own, which he named 'Theory of Science' (Wissenschaftslehre).

Georg Hegel (1770–1831)   German Idealist philosopher, born in Stuttgart. After studying theology he became a lecturer at Jena but Napoleon's victory there in 1806 interrupted his career. Hegel worked temporarily as a newspaper editor at Bamberg and then headmaster of the gymnasium at Nuremberg. Hegel's first great work was *The Phenomenology of Mind* (1807), which describes the human mind's progression from mere consciousness through self-consciousness, reason, spirit and religion, to absolute knowledge. His second great work was *The Science of Logic* which gained him the chair at Heidelberg in 1816. Hegel's dialectic method of reasoning involved a sequence of thesis, antithesis and synthesis, and his doctrines influenced Karl Marx and contributed to the development of 'Modern Totalitarianism'. In 1818 he succeeded Fichte as professor in Berlin and remained there until his death from cholera.

Charles Fourier (1772–1837)   French philosopher and social theorist, born in Besançon. He published a number of utopian socialist works including *The Social Destiny of Man; or, Theory of the Four Movements* (1857). Fourier argued for the existence of a natural social order corresponding to Newton's ordering of the physical universe, claiming that both evolved in eight ascending periods. In Harmony, the highest stage, human emotions would be freely expressed. Fournier declared that this stage could be attained by dividing society into phalanges, each comprising a commune approximately 1,800 people within which all property would be collectively owned. His other works include *Treatise on Domestic Agricultural Association* and *The New Industrial World*.

Friedrich Schelling (1775–1854)   German idealist philosopher, born in Leonberg in Württemberg. His early work was influenced by Kant and Fichte, and included *On the Possibility and Form of Philosophy in General* and *Of the Ego as Principle of Philosophy* in which he discusses the theological concept of the 'Absolute'. Schelling's major work *System of Transcendental Idealism* was an attempt to unite his concept of nature having a spiritual separateness from man, with Fichte's philosophy that nature is merely a tool of man. Schelling spent time in Jena, where he replaced Fichte in his teaching post, and in 1803, married Caroline Schlegel, a leading German Romanticist. A disagreement with Hegel concerning the dispute with Fichte caused him to retreat to Munich. After the death of Caroline, he married her friend, Pauline Gotter.

Arthur Schopenhauer (1788–1860)   German philosopher, born in Danzig, and whose metaphysical doctrines of the will were in contrast to Hegelian idealism. He was strongly influenced firstly by Plato, and then by Immanuel Kant, and also became friendly with the playwright and poet Goethe, who invited his assistance with some problems concerning his 'Farbenlehre' (theory of colours). After finishing *On Vision and Colours*, Schopenhauer began his masterpiece *The World as Will and Idea*, which expounds his pessimismistic and atheistic views. The premise being that man's nature as willing beings inevitably leads to suffering and such a life is worse than non-existence.

Auguste Comte (1798–1857)   French philosopher and social theorist, born in Montpellier, and usually considered the founder of modern sociology and Positivism. Comte was nicknamed the 'Thinker' and was rebellious by nature. He was the first thinker to advocate the use of scientific procedures in the study of economics and politics. In a typical non conformist act he married a prostitute, Caroline Massin, in 1821. He then became increasingly depressed and mentally disturbed culminating in a suicide attempt in the Seine which seemed to bring him to his senses. His wife, however, resorted to her previous occupation and Comte formed an alliance with Clotilde de Vaux which lasted for two years until her death in 1846. Comte's major work was *The Positive Philosophy of Auguste Comte*, which became the bible for students of Positivism.

John Stuart Mill (1806–73)   English philosopher and social reformer, born in London, the son of Scottish philosopher, James Mill. He began publishing in *The Traveller* in 1822 and helped form the Utilitarian Society, which met in Jeremy Bentham's house, and he ultimately modified some of Bentham's doctrines. As with many philosophers, both before and after, Mill endured a phase of severe depression but in 1830 met and eventually married the bluestocking, Harriet Taylor, who influenced his future works. Mill's works include *System of Logic, On Liberty, Principles of Political Economy, Utilitarianism*, as well as a celebrated autobiography.

Søren Kierkegaard (1813–55)   Danish philosopher, born in Copenhagen, the son of a Jewish merchant. Kierkegaard is considered the founder of Existentialism. His most famous work is probably *Either-Or*, in which he opposes Hegel by arguing the importance of individual choice. He was a convert to Christianity, although he fought against the formal structure of religion and believed that God and some special disciples were above moral laws as we know them. His other works include *The Concept of Irony, Christian Discourses, Fear of Trembling*, and *The Sickness Unto Death*.

Karl Marx (1818–1883)   German social, political and economic theorist, born in Trier. His Jewish parents converted to Protestantism out of political expediency. Marx became the inspiration for international Communism. He studied at Bonn and then Berlin University, where he met the 'young Hegelians' who were chiefly concerned with the critique of religion. His doctoral dissertation was on 'The Difference between the Philosophies of Nature in Democritus and Epicurus'. Marx worked firstly as a journalist and then editor of the liberal Cologne paper *Rheinische Zeitung* but after the paper was suppressed by the government, Marx emigrated to Paris and became a communist. It was here that he first stated his belief that the proletariat must itself be the agent of revolutionary change in society, and wrote his first critique of capitalism, 'Economic and Philosophical Manuscripts of 1844 (not published until 1932). Marx had by now become friendly with Friedrich Engels and under political pressure they moved to Brussels where they wrote *German Ideology* and the famous *Communist Manifesto* (1848) which ends with the Communist rallying cry: 'The workers have nothing to lose but their chains. They have a world to win. Workers of all lands, unite!' Marx moved to London in 1849 and wrote the first volume of his most famous work *Das Kapital*, in 1867 (future volumes followed in 1884 and 1894) where he forecast the classless society. Marx is buried in Highgate cemetery, London.

Wilhelm Dilthey (1833–1911)   German philosopher, born in Biebrich, Hesse. His central theme was the radical distinction between the natural sciences (*Naturwissenshaften*) and human sciences (*Geisteswissenschaften*). He also developed a theory of hermeneutics for the interpretation of historical texts and wrote biographies of Hegel, Lessing, Schleiermacher, and Goethe.

Friedrich Wilhelm Nietzsche (1844–1900)   German philosopher, scholar and writer, born in Röcken, Saxony, son of a Lutheran pastor. He was seen by Nazi ideologists as a precursor of Nazism due to his doctrine of the superman (*Übermensch*) expounded in *Thus Spake Zarathustra* and *Beyond Good and Evil*. Nietzsche rejected Christianity by arguing that 'God is Dead'. His first work was *The Birth of Tragedy* which compared Dionysian and Apollonian values, and was dedicated to Richard Wagner, whose operas he regarded as the true successors to Greek tragedy. Other works include *On the Genealogy of Morals*, *Beyond Good and Evil*, *Untimely Meditations* and his autobiography *Ecce Homo* (published posthumously in 1908).

Henri Bergson (1859–1941)   French philosopher, born in Paris, son of a Polish Jewish musician and an English mother. Bergson claimed that time (which he calls duration), cannot be analysed as a set of moments, but is unitary. He claimed the same distribution between movement and the trajectory it covers. This became known as 'process philosophy'. He won the Nobel Prize for Literature in 1927. His major works include *Time and Freewill, Matter and Memory* and *Creative Evolution*.

Edmund Husserl (1859–1938)   German philosopher, born in Prossnitz in the Austrian empire, of Jewish parentage. He studied mathematics at Berlin and psychology at Vienna, under Franz Brentano a leading Aristotelian scholar. Husserl taught at Halle, Gottingen and Freiburg. He was the founder of the philosophical school of phenomenology which gave rise to Gestalt psychology. Works include *On the Goals and Problems of Metaphysics, Logical Investigations* (in which Husserl employed his Phenomenological methods) and *Ideas: General Introduction to Pure Phenomenology*.

Nishida Kitarō (1870–1945)   Japanese philosopher, born near Kanazawa, Ishikawa, son of a school teacher. Nishida is considered Japan's first original modern philosopher and his work typifies Japanese attempts to absorb Western philosophy into the oriental spiritual tradition. His memoirs, entitled *A Certain Professor's Statement upon Retirement from Kyoto Imperial University, December 1928* became a Japanese best-seller.

Bertrand Russell (1872–1970)   Welsh philosopher, mathematician and author, born in Trelleck, Gwent, and brought up by his grandmother (the widow of the Liberal PM) following the death of both his parents in his youth. Russell was educated at Trinity College, Cambridge and became British Embassy attaché in Paris. He married Alys Pearsall Smith in 1895 and wrote his first book, *German Social Democracy*, soon after. Russell's first major philosophical work was *The Problems of Philosophy* (1912), which is often heralded as the perfect introduction for students of the subject. His pacifism caused the loss of his Trinity fellowship in 1916 and his imprisonment in 1918, after which he visited the Soviet Union and met Lenin, Trotsky and Gorky. He subsequently wrote *Theory and Practice of Bolshevism*. Russell's philosophy was now based on the premise that scientific knowledge was the only factual knowledge. His other major philosophical work was *A History of Western Philosophy*. Russell was also the co-author (with AN Whitehead) of *Principia Mathematica*.

Otto Neurath (1882–1945)   Austrian socialist philosopher, economist and historian. Neurath was famous for creating the Isotype language for visual education. He was a founder member of the Vienna Circle.

György Lukács (1885–1971)   Hungarian Marxist philosopher and critic, born in Budapest, of a wealthy Jewish family. Early works include *Soul and Form*, and *Theory of the Novel*. He joined the Hungarian Communist Party in 1918 but after the defeat of the uprising in 1919 travelled to Vienna and then Moscow. His major work on Marxism, *History and Class Consciousness* (1923), was condemned by the Russian Communist party as heretical.

Ludwig Wittgenstein (1889–1951)   Austrian-born British philosopher, born in Vienna, son of an industrialist. Wittgenstein studied mechanical engineering at Berlin but became increasingly interested in mathematics and went to Cambridge to study under Bertrand Russell. He served in the Austrian army in WWI and was captured and held as a POW near Monte Cassino. Here he wrote *Tractatus Logico Philosophicus*, which expounded his 'picture theory' and the nature and limits of language whereby the deep truths of the nature of reality and representation cannot properly be said but can only be shown. Wittgenstein became a naturalised British citizen in 1938 and spent much of his time in Cambridge, although he worked as a porter in Guy's Hospital during World War II. Wittgenstein is undoubtedly one of the pre-eminent philosophers of the twentieth century.

Martin Heidegger (1889–1976)   German philosopher, born in Messkirch in Baden, son of a Catholic sexton. Heidegger was appointed rector at Freiburg in 1933 and pledged support for Hitler in his inaugural address. His writings concern the nature and predicament of human existence, the search for 'authenticity' and the distractions of Angst (anxiety). His major work, *Being and Time* (1927), although considered a masterpiece, is often misunderstood in philosophical circles due to its complexity. The essence of the work as a description of a fundamental ontology where he names the human entity 'Dasein' (the being) and argues that Dasein's own being is intrinsically temporal in as existential sense.

Rudolf Carnap (1891–1970)   German-born American philosopher of Logical Positivism. He was a prominent member of the Vienna Circle and made significant contributions to logic, the philosophy of science, model theory and probability. He was viewed as an 'enfant terrible' in his early career but became one of the most respected philosophers of the twentieth century. Carnap was a great advocate of international languages (e.g. Esperanto).

Hans-Georg Gadamer (1900–)   German philosopher, born in Marburg, Hesse. A pupil of Heidegger, his major work, *Truth and Method*, expounds his hermeneutic beliefs.

Karl Raimund Popper (1902–1994)   Austrian-born British philosopher. Popper's greatest contributions are in philosophy of sciences and in political and social philosophy. His 'falsificationism' reverses the

F
A
M
O
U
S

P
E
O
P
L
E

usual view that accumulated experience leads to scientific hypotheses. He was a member of the Vienna Circle.

Jean-Paul Sartre (1905–80)   French philosopher, dramatist and novelist, born in Paris. He studied at the Sorbonne with Simone de Beauvoir, with whom he had a lifelong relationship. He taught philosophy at Le Havre, Paris and Berlin but joined the French army in 1939 and became a POW in 1941. On his release he became a key member of the French Resistance. In 1946, Sartre and De Beauvoir founded the avant-garde monthly *Les Temps Modernes* and Sartre began to develop his Existentialist doctrines. He declined the 1964 Nobel Prize for Literature and campaigned against American involvement in Vietnam. Sartre's major works were *Being and Nothingness* and his semi-autobiographical work *Nausea*, and a later more detailed autobiography, *Words* (*Les Mots*).

Maurice Merleau-Ponty (1908–61)   French philosopher, born in Rochefort-sur-Mer, Charente-Maritime. Although, he was closely associated with Sartre and helped him and De Beauvoir found *Les Temps Modernes* in 1945 his philosophy was more akin to that of the German phenomenonologists Husserl and Heidegger. His major work was *The Phenomenology of Perception*.

Willard Quine (1908–   )   American philosopher, born in Akron, Ohio. He was professor of philosophy at Harvard from 1948 to 1978 and was much influenced by Carnap, the Vienna Circle and Empiricism. His major works include *Two Dogmas of Empiricism*, *Word and Object* and *The Roots of Reference*.

Sir Alfred Jules Ayer (1910–89)   English philosopher, born in London. Ayer was educated at Eton and Oxford and served in the Welsh Guards in World War II before becoming a professor at University College London in 1947 and professor at Oxford in 1947. His major work, which was also his first, was *Language, Truth & Logic* (1936) which reflected the views of the Vienna Circle and established him a the leading English representative of logical positivism. It was dubbed 'The Young Man's book'. Ayer was knighted in 1970. His other major work was *The Problem of Knowledge*.

Albert Camus (1913–60)   French writer, born in Mondovi, Algeria, son of a farm labourer. After studying philosophy at Algiers, Camus became an actor, schoolmaster, playwright and journalist before World War II, and subsequently became a French Resistance activist. He then became co-editor of the left-wing newspaper *Combat* and wrote his Existentialist novel *The Stranger*, after which he became identified with 'the absurd'. His other great work was *The Plague* in which a plague-stricken city, Oran, symbolises man's isolation. He was awarded the 1957 Nobel Prize for Literature for having 'illuminated the problems of the human conscience in our times.' He died in a car accident.

Michel Foucault (1926–84)   French philosopher, born in Poitiers. Foucault argued that social attitudes are manipulated by those in power, so that areas such as criminality, illness, sexuality and insanity have changing levels of acceptability dependent on the aims of government and others in positions of influence. His major works are *Madness and Civilization*, *The Order of Things*, and *The History of Sexuality*.

NB: The list above does not contain religious reformers such as John Calvin, or writers such as Voltaire. The people cited above have all made some contribution to the furtherance of philosophical theory. Although some writers are known for their philosophical utterances e.g. Proudhon's 'property is theft' or Voltaire's 'if God did not exist it would be necessary to invent him', this alone is not enough to warrant inclusion in this section. Karl Marx is a notable exception to this rule of thumb, it is true that he was not a philosopher by design but his words and deeds enhanced and expanded political and philosophical thought to such an extent that it would be crass to omit him. It should also be noted that many of the works listed above are English translations of foreign titles and as such are open to slight variations in interpretations.

An explanation of some philosophical terms

Dialectics   The philosophy of metaphysical contradictions and their solutions.

Empiricism   The belief that all knowledge derives from experience and that the mind cannot postulate in advance.

Existentialism   Modern philosophical movement that stresses the importance of personal experience and responsibility and the demands that they make on the individual, who is seen as a free agent in a derterministic and seemingly meaningless universe. Although Jean-Paul Sartre is often accredited as being the first person to name himself an existentialist, the works of Søren Kiekegaard have retrospectively been attributed as existential.

Hermeneutics   The art of interpretation of human behaviour and social institutions. Hermeneutics was originally the theory and method of interpreting the Bible and other theological texts but Wilhelm Dilthey extended it to the interpretation of all human acts and products.

Marxism   Marxism is a broad term that covers many different philosophical doctrines but ultimately relate to the various schools of thought that have flourished since the death of Karl Marx in 1883. Western Marxism usually includes those thinkers that were influenced by the Hegelian idea of dialectics and who focused their attention on the cultural as opposed to the economic aspects of capitalism.

Metaphysics   The branch of philosophy concerning first principles, especially of being and knowing. It is the study of the nature of reality and deals with such questions as the existence of God and the external world.

Nihilism   Philosophy of negation, rejection, or denial of some or all aspects of thought or life. An example would be moral nihilism whereby any possibility of justifying or criticising moral judgements is rejected because morality is a cloak for egoistic self-seeking and therefore a sham. Nihilism is an extreme form of scepticism.

Ontology   The branch of metaphysics that deals with the nature of being.

Pascal's Wager   The postulate that it is better to wager that God does exist rather than on his non-existence.

Phenomenology   Movement founded by Husserl that concentrates on the detailed description of conscious experience without recourse to explanation, metaphysical assumptions or traditional philosophical questions.

Positivism   Extreme form of empericism that rejects metaphysics and theology as seeking knowledge beyond the scope of experience and holds that experimental investigation and observation are the only sources of knowledge.

Sceptisim   The view that we fail to know anything and the rejection of the postulate that some term of positive epistemic appraisal applies to our beliefs.

Solopsism   The exreme form of scepticism which denies the possibility of any knowledge other than of one's own existence.

Sophist   Pre-Socratic itinerant teacher of oratory and argument who was prepared to debate any matter however specious.

Stoicism   Greek philosophical system founded by Zeno of Citium (334–262 BC) in Athens c3000 BC. It views the world as permeated by rationality and divinely planned as the best possible organisation of matter. Moral goodness and happiness are achieved by replicating a perfect rationality in oneself, and by enacting one's own assigned role in the cosmic scheme of things.

Thomism   The name derives from Thomas Aquinas and relates to a body of philosophical and theological ideas that seek to articulate the intellectual content of Catholic Christianity.

Totalitarianism   Term adopted in the 1920s by the Italian Giovanni Gentile to describe the ideal fascist state. Totalitarianism has attracted the attention of philosophers because a number of classical philosophical systems have been suspected of harbouring totalitarian aspirations.

Vienna Circle   Group of about thirty to forty thinkers drawn from the social and natural sciences, logic and mathematics who met regularly in Vienna between the two world wars to discuss philosophy. Its manifesto was published in 1929 *The Scientific Conception of the World: The Vienna Circle by Carnap, Hahn and Neurath*. The inner sanctum of the group were called the 'Schlick Circle', organised by the physics professor Moritz Schlick in 1924. Its members included Carnap, Neurath, Philipp Frank, Kurt Gödel, and Edgar Zilsel. Other eminent philosophers such as Ludwig Wittgenstein and Karl Popper often joined discussion groups. The public profile of the circle was provided by the Ernst Mach Society but in 1934 the society was suspended for political reasons and in 1936 Morlitz Schlick was murdered and the circle gradually disintegrated when many of its members were forced to leave Austria for racial and political reasons.

Real Names: By Original Name

NB: This is not intended to be a comprehensive listing of pseudonyms but a selection of some of the best-known and most intriguing examples. It is an area that is surrounded with much uncertainty and potential for error. Generally the 'Assumed Name' is the more familiar, but not always (for instance when authors adopt a pen-name for a particular kind of writing). For people who have acquired titles, the title is given as the 'Assumed Name', although in such cases the 'Original Name' is of course equally valid. There is necessarily some overlap between this section and that on Nicknames.

Original Name		Assumed Name		
Abbott	Janet	**Baker**	Janet	*Mezzo-Soprano*
Abelsohn	Frank	**Vaughan**	Frankie	*Vocalist*
Abruza	Sophie	**Tucker**	Sophie	*Music Hall Singer*
Adair	William Penn	**Rogers**	Will	*US Actor*
Adams	Nathaniel	**Cole**	Nat King	*Vocalist*
Aday	Marvin Lee	**Meatloaf**		*Vocalist*
Addington	Henry	**Sidmouth**	Viscount	*Prime Minister of Great Britain*
Addison	Joseph	**Atticus**	(Satirised by Pope)	*Essayist/Politician*
Adoian	Vosdanig Manoog	**Gorky**	Arshile	*US Painter*
Adu	Helen Folasade	**Sade**		*Vocalist*
Ahenobarbus	Lucius Domitius	**Nero**		*Roman Emperor*
Aherne	Michael	**Warrior**		*Gladiator*
Aken	Jerome van	**Bosch**	Hiëronymus	*Dutch Painter*
Albert	Harold	**Cathcart**	Helen	*Royal Biographer*
Alepoudelis	Odysseus	**Elytis**	Odysseus	*Greek Poet*
Alexeyev	Konstantin Sergeivitch	**Stanislavsky**		*Actor*
Allason	Rupert	**West**	Nigel	*MP and Author*
Allegri	Antonio	**Correggio**		*Artist*
Amis	Kingsley	**Markham**	Robert	*Novelist*
Anderson	Roberta Joan	**Mitchell**	Joni	*Vocalist/Composer*
Andrews	Augustus George	**Arliss**	George	*Actor*
Andrews	William Forrest	**Forrest**	Steve	*US Actor*
Anson	Thomas Patrick John	**Lichfield**	Lord	*Photographer*
Arango	Dovoteo	**Villa**	Pancho	*Mexican Patriot*
Arbuckle	Penelope	**Dripping**	Lizzie	*Literary Character*
Arbuckle	Roscoe (Fatty)	**Goodrich**	William B.	*Actor*
Arcelos	Raul Rafael Y	**Julia**	Raul	*Actor*
Arenson	Max	**Anderson**	Bronco Billy	*Entertainer*
Armstrong nee Mitchell	Helen Porter	**Melba**	Dame Nellie	*Opera Singer*
Armstrong-Jones	David Albert Charles	**Linley**	Viscount	*Furniture Maker*
Arouet	Francois Marie	**Voltaire**		*Philosopher*
Ashdown	Jeremy	**Ashdown**	Paddy	*Politician*
Ashton	Winifred	**Dane**	Clemence	*English Dramatist*
Ashurst	Anne	**Craven**	Sara	*Novelist and Mastermind Winner*
Asquith	Herbert	**Oxford**	Earl of	*Prime Minister of Great Britain*
Aurness	James	**Arness**	James	*US Actor*
Austerlitz	Frederick	**Astaire**	Fred	*Dancer/Actor*
Aznavurjal	Shahnovr	**Aznavour**	Charles	*Singer & Actor*
Bailey	William	**Rose**	Axl	*Pop Singer*
Baker	George	**Divine**	Father	*Religious Leader*
Baker	Tammy Marie	**Fox**		*TV Gladiator*
Baker	Norma Jean	**Monroe**	Marilyn	*Actress*
Balanchivadze	Georgi Melitonivich	**Balanchine**	George	*Choreographer*
Baldwin	Stanley	**Bewdley**	Earl of	*Prime Minister of Great Britain*
Baline	Israel	**Berlin**	Irving	*Composer*
Balsame	Guiseppe	**Cagliostro**	'Count'	*Italian Adventurer*
Barbarelli	Giorgio	**Giorgione**		*Artist*
Barbella	Rocco	**Graziano**	Rocky	*Boxer*
Barbieri	Gian-Francesco	**Guercino**		*Italian Painter*
Barker	Ronnie	**Wylie**	Gerald	*Writer*
Barr	Byron	**Young**	Gig	*Actor*
Barratt	Michael	**Stevens**	Shaking	*Vocalist*
Barrow	Joseph	**Louis**	Joe	*Boxer*
Bartholomew	John Eric	**Morecambe**	Eric	*Comedian*

Original Name		Assumed Name		
Basie	William	Basie	Count	Musician
Bates	Ellas	Diddley	Bo	Vocalist
Batson	Billy	Marvel	Captain	Comic Book Hero
Baumgartner	James	Garner	James	Actor
Beauchamp	Katherine	Mansfield	Katherine	NZ Writer
Bean	Frederick	Avery	Tex	Cartoonist
Beaty	Warren	Beatty	Warren	Actor
Beaty	Shirley	Maclaine	Shirley	Actress
Beedle	William	Holden	William	Actor
Begleiter	Lionel	Bart	Lionel	Composer
Benevetto	Anthony Dominic	Bennett	Tony	Vocalist
Bernard	Rosine	Bernhardt	Sarah	Actress
Bernardone	Giovanni de	Francis of Assisi	Saint	Religious Leader
Bernhard	Rosine	Bernhardt	Sarah	Actress
Bernstein	Morris	Louis	Morris	US Painter
Berra	Lawrence Peter	Berra	Yogi	Baseball Player
Berry	Mike	Bennett	Lennie	Comedian
Beyle	Marie-Henri	Stendhal		Author
Bickel	Frederick	March	Fredric	Actor
Biden	Edmund	Sturges	Preston	Writer/Director
Bingham	Richard John	Lucan	Lord	Suspected Murderer
Bingzhi	Jiang	Ding Ling		Chinese Novelist
Birnbaum	Nathan	Burns	George	Comedian
Blair	Eric Arthur	Orwell	George	Author
Blamauer	Karoline Wilhelmine	Lenya	Lotte	Austrian Actress
Blau	Jenö	Ormandy	Eugene	Musician
Blixen	Karen	Dinesen	Isak	Authoress
Blythe	Lionel	Barrymore	Lionel	Actor
Blythe	Ethel	Barrymore	Ethel	Actress
Blythe	John	Barrymore	John	Actor
Bogaerde	Derek van den	Bogarde	Dirk	Actor
Bojaxhiu	Agnes Gonxha	Theresa	Mother	Roman Catholic Nun
Bookbinder	Elaine	Brooks	Elkie	Vocalist
Booth	George Hoy	Formby Jnr	George	Music Hall Entertainer
Booth	James	Formby Snr	George	Music Hall Entertainer
Bottom	Charles	Bart	Black	Outlaw
Bourgeois	Jeanne Marie	Mistinguett		French Dancer
Breitenberger	Edward	Byrnes	Edd	Actor
Bright	Gerald	Geraldo		Musician
Broadbent	Shirley Ann	Barrie	Amanda	Actress
Broadbent	Dora	Bryan	Dora	Actress/Comedienne
Brodribb	John Henry	Irving	Henry	Actor
Bronstein	Lev Davidovitch	Trotsky	Leon	Russian Revolutionary
Bronte	Anne	Bell	Acton	Authoress
Bronte	Emily	Bell	Ellis	Authoress
Bronte	Charlotte	Bell	Currer	Authoress
Brophy	Brigid Antonia	Levey	Lady	Author/Playwright
Brough	Spangler	Taylor	Robert	Actor
Brown	Rosemary	Dana		Singer and Politician
Brown	Angeline	Dickinson	Angie	Actress
Browne	Hablot Knight	Phiz		Illustrator
Browne	Charles Farrar	Ward	Artemus	Humorist/writer
Broz	Josip	Tito	Marshal	Yugoslav Leader
Buchinski	Charles	Bronson	Charles	Actor
Bukht	Michael	Barry	Michael	Food Journalist
Bullock	Annie Mae	Turner	Tina	Vocalist
Bulsara	Frederick	Mercury	Freddie	Vocalist
Burgess	George	Meredith	Burgess	Actor
Burke	Martha Jane	Jane	Calamity	Frontierswoman
Burnett	Chester Arthur	Wolf	Howling	Vocalist/Composer
Burns	Ray	Sensible	Captain	Vocalist
Butterfield	Sylvia	Dawn	Elizabeth	Actress
Bygraves	Walter	Bygraves	Max	Entertainer
Byron	James	Dean	James	Actor
Caliari	Paolo	Veronese	Paolo	Venetian Painter
Calvin	George	Leno	Dan	English Comedian
Campbell	Patrick	Glenavy	Baron	Irish Writer & Wit
Canale	Giovanni Antonio	Canaletto		Artist
Cansino	Marguerita	Hayworth	Rita	Actress
Caplin	Alfred Gerald	Capp	Al	Cartoonist

FAMOUS PEOPLE

Original Name		Assumed Name		
Carpentier	Harlean	*Harlow*	Jean	*Actress*
Carr	John Dickson	*Dickson*	Carter	*US Detective Writer*
Carroll	Daniel	*La Rue*	Danny	*Female Impersonator*
Carter	Charlton	*Heston*	Charlton	*Actor*
Cassotto	Robert Walden	*Darin*	Bobby	*Vocalist*
Castellucio	Frank	*Valli*	Frankie	*Vocalist*
Cavendish	William	*Devonshire*	Duke of	*Prime Minister of Great Britain*
Cavendish-Bentinck	William Henry	*Portland*	Duke of	*Prime Minister of Great Britain*
Cecil	Robert Arthur Talbot	*Salisbury*	Marquis of	*Prime Minister of Great Britain*
Cernick	Al	*Mitchell*	Guy	*Vocalist*
Chalupek	Appolonia	*Negri*	Pola	*Actress*
Chambers	James	*Cliff*	Jimmy	*Vocalist*
Chapman	John	*Appleseed*	Johnny	*Missionary/Nurseryman*
Chauchoin	Lily	*Colbert*	Claudette	*Actress*
Chauvin/Cauvin	Jean	*Calvin*	Jean	*French Theologian*
Chavarri	Emperatriz	*Sumac*	Yma	*Musician*
Cheeseman	Patrick	*Wymark*	Patrick	*Actor*
Chomette	Rene Lucien	*Clair*	Rene	*Film Director*
Christie	Agatha	*Westmacott*	Mary	*Authoress*
Ciccone	Madonna Louise	*Madonna*		*Vocalist/Actress*
Clapp	Eric	*Clapton*	Eric	*Guitarist/Singer*
Clary	Julian	*Joan Collins' Fan Club*		*Entertainer*
Clay	Cassius Marcellus	*Ali*	Muhammed	*Boxer*
Clemens	Samuel Langhorne	*Twain*	Mark	*Author*
Cobbett	William	*Porcupine*	Peter	*Writer*
Cobblepot	Oswald	*Penguin*		*Batman Character*
Cochrane	Elizabeth	*Bly*	Nellie	*Aviatrix*
Cocozza	Alfredo	*Lanza*	Mario	*Opera Singer*
Cody	William	*Bill*	Buffalo	*Showman*
Cole	Maurice	*Everett*	Kenny	*Disc Jockey/Comedian*
Coles	Elizabeth	*Taylor*	Elizabeth	*Novelist*
Collins	Cathleen	*Derek*	Bo	*Actress*
Colon	Cristobel	*Columbus*	Christopher	*Explorer*
Compton	Spencer	*Wilmington*	Earl of	*Prime Minister of Great Britain*
Connery	Thomas	*Connery*	Sean	*Actor*
Connor	William	*Cassandra*	(Daily Mirror column)	*Journalist*
Cook	David	*Essex*	David	*Vocalist/Actor*
Cooper	Francis	*Cooper*	Gary	*Actor*
Coppola	Nicholas	*Cage*	Nicolas	*US Actor*
Cornwell	David	*Le Carré*	John	*Author*
Crabtree	Shirley	*Daddy*	Big	*Wrestler*
Craddock	Eugene Vincent	*Vincent*	Gene	*Vocalist*
Crane	Randolph	*Scott*	Randolph	*Actor*
Cripps	Bruce	*Welch*	Bruce	*Guitarist*
Cristillo	Louis	*Costello*	Lou	*Comedian*
Crocetti	Dino	*Martin*	Dean	*Actor*
Cromwell	Richard	*Clark*	John	*Lord Protector of England*
Crosby	Harry Lillis	*Crosby*	Bing	*Vocalist/Actor*
Crossley	James	*Hunter*		*Gladiator*
Culkin	Bonnie	*Bedelia*	Bonnie	*TV Actress*
Czaczkes	Shmuel Josef	*Agnon*	Shmuel Yosef	*Israeli Novelist*
Da Ponte	Giacomo	*Bassano*	Jacopo	*Italian Painter*
D'Abruzzo	Alfonso	*Alda*	Alan	*Actor*
Dallion	Susan	*Sioux*	Siouxsie	*Vocalist*
Daly	Sandra	*Khashoggi*	Soraya	*Millionairess*
Dannay	Frederick	*Queen*	Ellery	*Author*
		Ross	Barnaby	*Author*
D'Antonguolla	Rudolpho	*Valentino*	Rudolph	*Actor*
Darnell Browder	Thomas August	*Creole*	Kid	*Vocalist*
Davies	Sharron	*Amazon*		*TV Gladiator/Swimmer*
Davies	Robert	*Carrott*	Jasper	*Comedian*
Davies	David Ivor	*Novello*	Ivor	*Composer*
Davies	Nigel	*Villeneuve*	Justin de	*Hair Stylist*
De Havilland	Joan	*Fontaine*	Joan	*Actress*
Deeks	Barbara	*Windsor*	Barbara	*Actress*

Original Name		Assumed Name		
Demsky	Issar Danielovitch	*Douglas*	Kirk	*Actor*
Dénes	Gábor	*Gabor*	Dennis	*Physicist*
Denning	Alfred Thompson	*Whitchurch*	Baron of	*Law Lord*
Derbyshire	Tommy	*Cannon*	Tommy	*Comedy Straight Man*
Deutschendorf Jnr	Henry John	*Denver*	John	*Vocalist/Composer*
Dibley	Dwayne	*Cat*		*TV Character (Red Dwarf)*
Dickens	Charles	*Boz*	(Monthly Magazine)	*Author*
Dinh Khai	Phan	*Le Duc Tho*		*Vietnamese Politician*
Disraeli	Benjamin	*Beaconsfield*	Earl of	*Prime Minister of Great Britain*
Dodgson	Charles Lutwidge	*Carroll*	Lewis	*Author*
Donaghue	Patrick	*Magenta*	Captain	*TV Fictional Character*
Doolittle	Hilda	*HD*		*Authoress*
Dorleac	Catherine	*Deneuve*	Catherine	*Actress*
Dorsey	Arnold	*Dorsey*	Gerry	*Vocalist*
		Humperdinck	Englebert	*Vocalist*
Douglas	Michael	*Keaton*	Michael	*Actor*
Douglas-Home	Alec	*Hirsel*	Lord	*Prime Minister of Great Britain*
Dudevant	Amandine Lucie Dupin	*Sand*	George	*Authoress*
Dukenfield	William Claude	*Fields*	W.C.	*Comedian/Actor*
Dumble-Smith	Michael	*Crawford*	Michael	*Actor/Singer*
Dutt	Narendranath	*Vivekananda*	Swami	*Hindu Missionary*
Dwight	Reginald Kenneth	*John*	Elton Hercules	*Vocalist/Composer*
Dzhugashvili	Iosif Vissarionovich	*Stalin*	Joseph	*Russian Leader*
Eberst	Jakob	*Offenbach*	Jacques	*Composer*
Eden	Anthony	*Avon*	Earl of	*Prime Minister of Great Britain*
Egstrom	Norma	*Lee*	Peggy	*Vocalist*
Eichelbaum	Jack Leonard	*Warner*	Jack Leonard	*Film Mogul*
Einstein	Albert	*Brooks*	Albert	*Actor*
Elizabeth	of Romania	*Sylva*	Carmen	*Queen of Romania*
Enos	William	*Berkeley*	Busby	*Choreographer*
Ercolani	James	*Darren*	James	*US Actor*
Estevez	Ramon	*Sheen*	Martin	*Actor*
Evans	Ernest	*Checker*	Chubby	*Vocalist*
Evans	Dave	*Edge*	The	*Musician*
Evans	Mary Ann	*Eliot*	George	*Authoress*
Fagan	Eleanora	*Holiday*	Billie	*Vocalist*
Fairfield	Cicely Isabel	*West*	Rebecca	*Author*
Fawkes	Ernest	*Trog*	Walter	*Cartoonist*
Federkiewicz	Stefania	*Powers*	Stefanie	*Actress*
Feld	Marc	*Bolan*	Marc	*Vocalist/Musician*
Fellows	Graham	*John Shuttleworth*	Jilted John	*Pop Singer Creation*
Fields	W.C.	*Kane Jeeves*	Mahatma	*Comedian/Actor*
Fiersohn	Reba	*Gluck*	Alma	*American Soprano*
Filipepi	Alessandro	*Botticelli*	Sandro	*Artist*
Finklea	Tula Ellice	*Charisse*	Cyd	*Dancer*
Firbank	Louis	*Reed*	Lou	*Vocalist/Composer*
Fischman	Harve	*Bennett*	Harve	*US TV Producer*
Fitzroy	Augustus Henry	*Grafton*	Duke of	*Prime Minister of Great Britain*
Fitzsimmons	Maureen	*O'Hara*	Maureen	*Actress*
Flaccus	Quintus Horatius	*Horace*		*Poet*
Flegenheimer	Arthur	*Schultz*	Dutch	*Gangster*
Fletcher	Susannah	*York*	Susannah	*Actress*
Foe	Daniel	*Defoe*	Daniel	*Author*
Forte	Fabiano	*Fabian*		*Vocalist*
Fowles	Gloria	*Gaynor*	Gloria	*Vocalist*
Frahm	Karl Herbert	*Brandt*	Willy	*German Chancellor*
Francabilla	Marchesa Caterina de	*Boyle*	Katie	*TV Presenter*
Franconers	Concetta	*Francis*	Connie	*Vocalist*
Frankel	Bernice	*Arthur*	Beatrice	*US Actress*
Frankenberg	Joyce	*Seymour*	Jane	*Actress*
Frazier	Richard	*Ochre*	Captain	*TV Fictional Character*
Frece	Lady De	*Tilley*	Vesta	*Comedian*
Frewer	Matt	*Headroom*	Max	*TV Fictional Character*

FAMOUS PEOPLE

Original Name		Assumed Name		
Fries	Victor	Freeze	Mr	Fictional Super-Villain
Frith	Mary	Cutpurse	Moll	Pick Pocket/Robber
Fucini	Renato	Tanfucio	Neri	Italian Writer
Fuertes	Dolores Adios	Menken	Adah Isaacs	US Actress & Poet
Fuhrhop	Roland	Rowland	Tiny	Businessman
Fulks	Sarah Jane	Wyman	Jane	Actress
Furnier	Vincent	Cooper	Alice	Vocalist
Fyffe	Patrick	Bracket	Hilda	TV Transvestite
Gadd	Paul	Glitter	Gary	Vocalist
Gaines	Donna Andrea	Summers	Donna	Vocalist
Garfunkel	Art	Graph	Tom	Half of 'Tom & Jerry' Duo
Gassion	Edith	Piaf	Edith	Vocalist
Gazzimos	Brenda Gail	Gayle	Crystal	Vocalist
Geisel	Theodore Seuss	Seuss	Dr	Author
Gelee	Claude	Lorrain	Claude	Landscape Painter
Gellen	Arthur	Hunter	Tab	Singer/Actor
Gendre	Louis	Jordan	Louis	Actor
George III	(in Gardening Periodicals)	Robinson	Ralph	British King
Georgiou	Stephen	Stevens	Cat	Vocalist
Gettman	Leslie	Brooks	Louise	US Actress
Gheraerd	Gheraerd	Erasmus	Desiderius	Scholar
Gilbert	Maria Eliza (Délores)	Montez	Lola	American Dancer
Gilhooly	Brenda	Tuesday	Gayle	Comedienne
Gillis	Ian	Mycroft		Brain of Britain
Gillis	Lester	Nelson	Baby Face	Gangster
Gillorly	Edna	Burstyn	Ellen	Actress
Glitter	Gary	Raven	Paul	Vocalist
Glover	Brian	Arras	Leon	Professional Wrestler
Goddard	Stuart	Ant	Adam	Vocalist
Godfree	Edward	Aldington	Richard	English Poet
Goffage	John	Rafferty	Chips	Entertainer
Gold	Jacqueline	Summers	Ann	Businesswoman
Goldbert	Cyril Louis	Wyngarde	Peter	Actor
Goldenberg	Emmanuel	Robinson	Edward G	Actor
Goldenburger	Avron	Todd	Mike	Producer
Goldfish	Sam	Goldwyn	Sam	Film Producer
Goldstein	Elliott	Gould	Elliot	Actor
Gonne	Maud	MacBride	Maud	Irish Nationalist
Gonzalez	José Victoriano	Gris	Juan	Spanish Cubist Painter
Goodman	Theodosia	Bara	Theda	Vamp Actress
Goodrich	Samuel	Parley	Peter	US Publisher
Goodrich	Sandra	Shaw	Sandie	Vocalist
Gordon	George Hamilton	Aberdeen	Earl of	Prime Minister of Great Britain
Gorowicz	Vladimir	Horowitz	Vladimir	Russian Pianist
Gossart	Jan	Mabuse	Jan	Flemish Painter
Gothardt	Mathis	Grünewald	Mathias	German Painter
Goyathlay		Geronimo		Apache Indian Chief
Graham	Florence Nightingale	Arden	Elizabeth	Beautician
Grasemann	Ruth	Rendell	Ruth	Crime Novellist
Gravelet	Jean Francois	Blondin	Charles	French Acrobat
Gray	Charles	White	Colonel	TV Fictional Character
Grayson	Larry	Breen	Billy	Comedian
Grayson	Dick	Robin		Fictional Super Hero
Green	David	Ben-Gurion	David	Israeli Statesman
Greenbaum	Peter	Green	Peter	Musician
Greene	Gladys	Arthur	Jean	Actress
Gregson	Michael	Craig	Michael	Actor
Gretzky	Wayne	Great One	The	Ice Hockey Player
Grieve	Christopher Murray	MacDiarmid	Hugh	Poet
Griffith	John	London	Jack	Author
Griffiths	Seymour	Green	LT	TV Fictional Character
Grossell	Ira	Chandler	Jeff	Actor
Guiche	Lilian	Gish	Lilian	Actress
Guidi, Di Simone	Tommaso Di Giovanni	Masaccio		Florentine Painter
Guillerm	Nelly	Verdy	Violette	French Dancer
Gumm	Frances	Garland	Judy	Actress/Singer

Original Name		Assumed Name		
Guojonsson	Halldor	*Laxness*	Halldor	*Icelandic Novelist*
Gurdin	Natasha	*Wood*	Natalie	*Actress*
Gustaffson	Greta	*Garbo*	Greta	*Actress*
Gutteridge	John	*Pallo*	Jackie	*Wrestler*
Guttoveggio	Joseph	*Creston*	Paul	*Musician*
Guynes	Demi	*Moore*	Demi	*Actress*
Hackenbacker	Hiram J	*Brains*	(Thunderbirds)	*Scientist*
Hall	Diane	*Keaton*	Diane	*Actress*
Halliley	John Elton	*Le Mesurier*	John	*Actor*
Hamill	Christopher	*Limahl*	(Kajagoogoo)	*Vocalist*
Hamilton	Charles	*Conquest*	Owen	*Author*
		Richards	Frank	*Author*
Hansen	Emil	*Nolde*	Emil	*German Painter*
Hardin	Charles	*Holly*	Buddy	*Vocalist*
Haris	Derek	*Derek*	John	*Actor*
Harmsworth	Harold Sydney	*Rothermere*	Viscount	*Newspaper Magnate*
Harper	Robert	*Ball*	Bobby	*Comedian*
Harris	Joel Chandler	*Remus*	Uncle	*Author*
Harrison	Gerald	*Gee*	Dustin	*Impressionist*
Hartley	Vivien	*Leigh*	Vivien	*Actress*
Hartree	George	*Hawtrey*	Charles	*Actor*
Hatcher	Charles	*Starr*	Edwin	*Vocalist*
Haussman	Jacques	*Houseman*	John	*Actor*
Hawkins	Jack	*Hedley*	Jack	*Actor*
Hawkins	Anthony	*Hope*	Anthony	*Author*
Hawkins	Christian	*Slater*	Christian	*Actor*
Haynes	Brian	*Laine*	Denny	*Guitarist*
Healey-Kay	Patrick	*Dolin*	Anton	*Choreographer*
Hearne	Richard	*Pastry*	Mr	*Actor*
Heemstra	Edda Hepburn Van	*Hepburn*	Audrey	*Actress*
Heimberger	Eddie	*Albert*	Eddie	*US Actor*
Hensley	Virginia	*Kline*	Patsy	*Vocalist*
Herzstine	Barbara	*Hershey*	Barbara	*Actress*
Heseltine	Les	*Dennis*	Les	*Comedian*
Heseltine	Philip Arnold	*Warlock*	Peter	*Composer*
Hesketh-Harvey	Kit	*Kit*		*Musical act 'Kit and the Widow'*
Heurschling	Andrée	*Hessling*	Catherine	*Jean Renoir's Wife (actress)*
Hewson	Paul	*Bono*		*Vocalist*
Hickenlooper	Lucie	*Samaroff*	Olga	*Musician*
Hicks	Thomas	*Steele*	Tommy	*Entertainer*
Hieronymus	Eusebius Sophronius	*Jerome*	St	*Italian Scholar*
Higginbottom	Minnie	*Staff*	Kathy	*Actress*
Hill	Alfred Hawthorne	*Hill*	Benny	*Comedian*
Hinault	Bernard	*Badger (Le Blaireau)*		*Cyclist*
Hoch	Jan Ludvik	*Maxwell*	Robert	*Businessman*
Hogg	James	*Ettrick Shepherd*		*Poet*
Hogg	Quintin	*Hailsham of Marylebone*	Baron	*Politician*
Holden	Bradley	*Grey*	Captain	*TV Fictional Character*
Hollea	Terry	*Hogan*	Hulk	*Professional Wrestler and Actor*
Hollenbeck	Webb Parmelee	*Webb*	Clifton	*Actor*
Hook/Aherne	Caroline	*Merton*	Mrs	*Comedian*
Hookham	Margaret	*Fonteyn*	Margot	*Ballerina*
Hornby	Leslie	*Twiggy*		*Actress*
Horowitz	Winona	*Ryder*	Winona	*Actress*
Hovick	Rose Louise	*Rose Lee*	Gypsy	*Entertainer*
Howell	Vernon	*Koresh*	David	*Branch Davidian cult Leader*
Huffman	Barbara	*Eden*	Barbara	*US Actress*
Huggins	Peter Jeremy	*Brett*	Jeremy	*Actor*
Humphries	Barry	*Everage*	Dame Edna	*Comedian*
Humphries	Barry	*Patterson*	Sir Les	*Comedian*
Hunter	Evan	*McBain*	Ed	*Writer*
Hyde	Edward	*Clarendon*	Earl of	*Statesman*
Illingworth	Harry	*Worth*	Harry	*Comedian*
Ingolia	Concetta	*Stevens*	Connie	*Actress*

FAMOUS PEOPLE

Original Name		Assumed Name		
Irving	Washington	*Knickerbocker*	Diedrich	*Author*
Iskowitz	Edward	*Cantor*	Eddie	*Comedian*
Isley	Pamela	*Ivy*	Poison	*Fictional Super-Villainess*
Italiano	Anna Maria	*Bancroft*	Anne	*Actress*
Ivanhoe	Burl	*Ives*	Burl	*Actor/Singer*
Iyotake	Tatanka	*Sitting Bull*		*Sioux Indian Chief*
Jacob	Lee	*Cobb*	Lee J.	*Actor*
Jacobs	Rosetta	*Laurie*	Piper	*US Actress*
James	Michael	*Jayston*	Michael	*Actor*
Javal	Camille	*Bardot*	Brigitte	*Actress*
Jeanneret	Charles Edouard	*Corbusier*	Le	*Architect*
Jefferson	Arthur Stanley	*Laurel*	Stan	*Comedy Actor*
Jeffries	James Jackson	*Boilermaker*		*Boxing Champion*
Jenkins	Richard	*Burton*	Richard	*Actor*
Jenkins	Harold Lloyd	*Twitty*	Conway	*Vocalist*
Jenkinson	Robert Banks	*Liverpool*	Earl of	*Prime Minister of Great Britain*
Jensen	Anita	*Genée*	Adeline	*Ballerina*
Jewry	Bernard	*Fenton*	Shane	*Vocalist*
		Stardust	Alvin	*Vocalist*
Johnson	Carol Diahann	*Carroll*	Diahann	*Actress*
Johnson	Bruce	*Forsyth*	Bruce	*Entertainer*
Johnson	Caryn	*Goldberg*	Whoopi	*US Actress*
Johnson	Lawrence	*Naismith*	Laurence	*Actor*
Johnson	William Eugene	*Pussyfoot*		*US Reformer*
Johnson	Hewlett	*Red Dean*		*English Prelate*
Johnson	Mike	*York*	Michael	*Actor*
Jones	Magnolia	*Angel*	Melody	*Captain Scarlet Character*
Jones	David	*Bowie*	David	*Vocalist/Composer*
Jones	Edward	*German*	Edward	*English Composer*
Jones	Edith	*Wharton*	Edith	*Authoress*
Judkins	Steveland	*Wonder*	Stevie	*Vocalist/Composer*
Judson	Edward Zane	*Buntline*	Ned	*Inventor*
Kalageropoulos	Cecilia	*Callas*	Maria	*Operatic Soprano*
Kam	Lee Yuen	*Lee*	Bruce	*Actor/Martial Artist*
Kaminker	Henriette Charlotte	*Signoret*	Simone	*Actress*
Kaminsky	Melvin	*Brooks*	Mel	*Actor*
Kaminsky	Noah	*Diamond*	Neil	*Vocalist/Composer*
Kaminsky	David Daniel	*Kaye*	Danny	*Entertainer*
Kappelhoff	Doris Von	*Day*	Doris	*Actress/Singer*
Katz	Phoebe	*Cates*	Phoebe	*Actress*
Kaumeyer	Dorothy Mary	*Lamour*	Dorothy	*Actress*
Kaye	Paul	*Pennis*	Dennis	*Actor and Comedian*
Kazanjoglou	Elia	*Kazan*	Elia	*Film Director*
Keane	Molly	*Farrell*	MJ	*Irish Novelist*
Kemal	Mustafa	*Ataturk*	Kemal	*Turkish Statesman*
Khan Jnr	Taidje	*Brynner*	Yul	*Actor*
Khaury	Herbert	*Tim*	Tiny	*Vocalist*
Kiesler	Hedwig	*Lamarr*	Hedy	*Actress*
Kilminster	Ian	*Lemmy*	(Motorhead)	*Vocalist*
King	Leslie	*Ford*	Gerald	*President USA*
King	Jefferson	*Shadow*		*TV Gladiator*
Kingsley	Charles	*Lot*	Parson	*Author*
Klass	Eugene	*Barry*	Gene	*US Actor*
Klein	Carole	*King*	Carol	*Vocalist*
Konigsberg	Allen	*Allen*	Woody	*Actor*
Koreff	Nora	*Kaye*	Nora	*American Ballerina*
Korzeniowski	Jozef Teodor Konrad	*Conrad*	Joseph	*Author*
Kostrowitzky	Apollinaris	*Apollinaire*	Guillaume	*French Poet*
Kouyoumdjian	Dikran	*Arlen*	Michael	*British Novelist*
Kramer	Erich Maria	*Remarque*	Erich Maria	*Author*
Krampke	Hugh	*O'Brien*	Hugh	*Actor*
Kubelsky	Benjamin	*Benny*	Jack	*Comedian*
Kwan	Chan	*Angel*	Harmony	*Captain Scarlet Character*
Lake	Margaret	*Meg*	Mystic	*TV Personality*
Lamb	Charles	*Elia*		*Essayist*
Lamb	William	*Melbourne*	Viscount	*Prime Minister of Great Britain*
Lamburn	Richmal	*Crompton*	Richmal	*Authoress*
Landru	Henri	*Bluebeard*		*French Murderer*

Original Name		Assumed Name		
Lange	Cedric	Hawk	Jeremy	Actor and TV Presenter
Langemanke	Lucille	Astor	Mary	Actress
Lawrence	Thomas Edward	Ross	Aircraftsman John Hume	Soldier/Author
		Shaw	T. E. (Royal Tank Corps)	Soldier/Author
Lawrie	Marie McLaughlin	Lulu		Vocalist
Lawson	Nigel	Blaby	Lord	Politician
Leach	Archibald	Grant	Cary	Actor
Lee	Manfred B	Queen	Ellery	Author
		Ross	Barnaby	Author
Leger	Marie Rene	Saint-John Perse		French Poet
Leitch	Donovan	Donovan		Vocalist
Letz	George	Montgomery	George	Actor
Levitch	Joseph	Lewis	Jerry	Actor/Comedian
Levy	Marion	Goddard	Paulette	Actress
Levy	Ivo	Montand	Yves	Actor
Lewis	Cecil Day	Blake	Nicholas	Detective Writer
Lewis	CS	Hamilton	Clive	Irish Writer
Lewis	Mike	Saracen		TV Gladiator
Liddell	Eric	Flying Scotsman		Athlete
Little	Malcolm	X	Malcolm	Civil Rights Leader
Lloyd George	David	Gwynedd of Dwyfor	Viscount	Prime Minister of Great Britain
Loewenstein	Laszlo	Lorre	Peter	Actor
Logan	George	Hinge	Dr Evadne	TV Transvestite
Longbaugh	Henry	Sundance Kid		Outlaw
Lorimer	Maxwell George	Wall	Max	Actor and Comedian
Loughran	Angus	Statto		TV Soccer Pundit
Louis	Joe	Brown Bomber		Boxer
Louis	Marilyn	Fleming	Rhonda	Actress
Lubbertszoon	Meyndert	Hobbema	Meindert	Dutch Painter
Lubowitz	Michael	Mann	Manfred	Musician
Lucas	Matt	Dawes (He's a baby)	George	Comedian
Luta	Mahpiua	Red Cloud	Oglala Teton Dakota	(Sioux) Chief
Lydon	John	Rotten	Johnny	Vocalist
Lyon	Emma (Amy)	Hamilton	Emma	Lady
		Hart	Emma	Blacksmith's Daughter
Mabovitch	Golda	Meir	Golda	Israeli PM
McDaniel	Ellas	Diddley	Bo	Vocalist
McCarthy	Henry	Bonney	William	Billy the Kid
McGillicuddy	Cornelius	Mack	Connie	Baseball Player
McGregor	Robert	Roy	Rob	Scottish freebooter
McGuinness	Eddie	Large	Eddie	Comedian
McGurran	Aidan	Lottery	Lenny	National Lottery Expert
Mackay	Mary	Corelli	Marie	English Novelist
McLoughlin	Mark	Pellow	Marti	Vocalist
McManus	Declan	Costello	Elvis	Vocalist/Composer
McMasters	Luke	Haystacks	Giant	Wrestler
McMath	Virginia	Rogers	Ginger	Actress/Dancer
MacMillan	Harold	Stockton	Earl of	Prime Minister of Great Britain
McMurray	Barbara	Flynn	Barbara	Actress
McNeile	H.C.	Sapper		Author
McPherson	Graham	Suggs		Vocalist
Maddox	No-Name	Manson	Charles	Cult Leader
Mainwaring	Edward Stewart	Stewart	Ed	Disc Jockey
Makonnen	Ras Tafari	Selassie	Hailie	Ethiopian Emperor
Mapother	Tom Cruise	Cruise	Tom	Actor
Mariano	Agnolo di Cosimo	Bronzino	IL	Painter
Marks	Lilian Alice	Markova	Alicia	Ballerina
Maro	Publius Vergilius	Virgil		Poet
Martin	Paul	Merton	Paul	Comedian
Marx	Julius	Marx	Groucho	Actor
Marx	Herbert	Marx	Zeppo	Actor
Marx	Adolph	Marx	Harpo	Actor
Marx	Milton	Marx	Gummo	Actor
Marx	Leonard	Marx	Chico	Actor
Massaccesi	Aristide	D'Amato	Joe	Film Director

F
A
M
O
U
S

P
E
O
P
L
E

Original Name		Assumed Name		
Mathieu	Henri Donat	Saint-Laurent	Yves	French Designer
Matthews	Pauline	Dee	Kiki	Vocalist
Matuschanskavasky	Walter	Matthau	Walter	Actor
Mavor	Osborne Henry	Bridie	James	Dramatist
		Henderson	Mary	Dramatist
Mayer	David	Janssen	David	Actor
Mayson	Isabella	Beeton	Mrs Isabella	Cookery Writer
Mazzola	Girolamo Francesco M.	Parmigiano		Italian Painter
Mead	Cyril	Little	Syd	Comedian
Mellencamp	John	Cougar	John	Vocalist
Mendelssohn-Bartholdy	Felix	Mendelssohn	Felix	Composer
Menendez	Andres Arturo Garcia	Garcia	Andy	Actor
Mennini	Peter	Mennin	Peter	Musician
Mercer	Cecil William	Yates	Dornford	Novelist
Merisi	Michelangelo	Caravaggio		Artist
Meservey	Robert	Preston	Robert	Actor
Metcalfe	Paul	Scarlet	Captain	TV Animation Character
Micklewhite	Maurice	Caine	Michael	Actor
Middleton	Roger	Colbourne	Maurice	Actor
Middleton	Peggy	De Carlo	Yvonne	Actress
Mikhailovich	Sergius	Stepnyak		Russian Revolutionary
Millar	William	Boyd	Stephen	Actor
Miller	James	MacColl	Ewan	Folk Singer
Millet	Jean-Francois	Francisque		Belgian Painter
Milligan	Terence Alan	Milligan	Spike	Comedian/Writer
Mitchell	Ian	Finch	Peter	Actor
Mitchell	James Leslie	Gibbon	Lewis	Novelist
Mizell	George	Mitchell	Cameron	Actor
Modini	Robert	Stack	Robert	Actor
Moir	Jim	Reeves	Vic	Comedian
Molinsky	Joan	Rivers	Joan	Comedienne
Monro	Hector Hugh	Saki		Author
Montagu	John	Sandwich	Earl of	Inventor of Sandwich
Montgomery	Edward	Clift	Montgomery	Actor
Moodnick	Ronald	Moody	Ron	Actor
Morganfield	McKinley	Waters	Muddy	Vocalist
Morhange	Charles-Valentin	Alkan	Charles-Valentin	French Musician
Morrison	Jeanette	Leigh	Janet	Actress
Morrison	George Ivan	Morrison	Van	Vocalist/Composer
Morrison	Marion	Wayne	John	Actor
Morrow	Jennifer Lee	Leigh	Jennifer Jason	Actress
Morton	John Cameron	Beachcomber	(Daily Express column)	Journalist
Mostel	Samuel Joel	Mostel	Zero	Actor
Mozee	Phoebe	Oakley	Annie	Frontierswoman
Mulgrew	Jimmy	Cricket	Jimmy	Comedian
Müller	Lucas	Cranach	Lucas	German Painter
Müller	Johannes	Regiomontanus		German Mathematician
Munker	Ariane	Foster	Jodie	US Actress
Nakszynski	Natassja	Kinski	Natassia	Actress
Nankeville	Robert	Davro	Bobby	Comic Impressionist
Nascimento	Edson Arantes Do	Pele		Footballer
Needham	Yootha	Joyce	Yootha	Actress
Nelhams	Terry	Faith	Adam	Vocalist
Nelson	Benjamin	King	Ben E.	Vocalist
Nelson	Prince Rogers	Prince (formerly)		Vocalist/Composer
Nice	Stephen	Harley	Steve	Pop Singer
Niewoehner	Dirk	Benedict	Dirk	US Actor
Norway	Neville	Shute	Neville	Author
Oaxaca	Rudolph	Quinn	Anthony	US Actor
O'Brien	Mary	Springfield	Dusty	Vocalist
O'Day	Dawn	Shirley	Anne	Actress
O'Donovan	Michael	O'Connor	Frank	Irish Writer
O'Dowd	George	George	Boy	Vocalist
O'Fearna	Sean	Ford	John	Film Director
O'Flaherty	Katherine	Chopin	Kate	Author/Feminist
O'Grady	Paul	Savage	Lily	Female Impersonator
Ohm	Peter	Vaughan	Peter	Actor

Original Name		Assumed Name		
Original Name		*Assumed Name*		
Olden	Charles	*Ray*	Ted	Comedian
Olsson	Ann-Margret	*Margret*	Ann	Actress
O'Mahoney	Tynian	*Allen*	Dave	Comedian
O'Nolan	Brian	*O'Brien*	Flann	Irish Writer
Ord	Irene	*Larrigan*	Tex	Author of Westerns
Orowitz	Eugene Maurice	*Landon*	Michael	US Actor
Orrico	Carmen	*Saxon*	John	Actor
Orton	Joe	*Wellthorpe*	Edna	Fictional Letter Writer
Osterberg	James Jewel	*Pop*	Iggy	Vocalist
Ostlere	Gordon	*Gordon*	Richard	Doctor/Author
O'Sullivan	Raymond	*O'Sullivan*	Gilbert	Vocalist
Pakenham	Francis Aungier	*Longford*	Lord	Prison Reformer
Pal (Female)		*Lassie (Male)*		Dog
Palaniuk	Walter	*Palance*	Jack	Actor
Palmer	Vera Jane	*Mansfield*	Jayne	Actress
Panayiotou	Georgios	*Michael*	George	Vocalist/Composer
Papaceo	Anthony	*Franciosa*	Tony	Actor
Parker	Robert LeRoy	*Cassidy*	Butch	Outlaw Leader
Paton	Alison	*Siren*		TV Gladiator
Patterson	Henry	*Higgins*	Jack	Author
Paul	Maury	*Knickerbocker*	Cholly	NY Gossip Columnist
Paup	Theresa	*Russell*	Theresa	Actress
Peiser	Lili	*Palmer*	Lili	Actress
Pelham-Holles	Thomas	*Newcastle*	Duke of	Prime Minister of Great Britain
Penniman	Richard Wayne	*Richard*	Little	Vocalist/Musician
Penrose	Elizabeth	*Markham*	Elizabeth	Writer for Children
Perelmuth	Jacob Pincus	*Peerce*	Jan	Musician
Perez	Manuel Benitez	*Cordobes*	El	Matador
Perido	Nick	*Como*	Perry	Vocalist
Perks	William	*Wyman*	Bill	Musician
Perry	William	*Refrigerator*		American Footballer
Perske	Betty Joan	*Bacall*	Lauren	Actress
Peschkowsky	Michael	*Nichols*	Mike	US Film Director
Peshkov	Max	*Gorky*	Maxim	Author
Peters	Jane	*Lombard*	Carole	Actress
Petty-Fitzmaurice	William	*Shelburne*	Earl of	Prime Minister of Great Britain
Pickwoad	William	*Mervyn*	William	Actor
Pierre	Cherilyn Sarkisian La	*Cher*		Vocalist/Actress
Pietro/Fiesoli	Guido di	*Angelico*	Fra	Artist
Pisperikos	Elizabeth	*Perkins*	Elizabeth	Actress
Plemiannkov	Roger	*Vadim*	Roger	Film Director
Pointon	Juliette	*Angel*	Destiny	Captain Scarlet Character
Poire	Emmanuel	*D'Ache*	Caran	French Illustrator
Poliakov	Nikolai	*Coco*		Clown
Popley	Bernard	*Youens*	Bernard	Actor
Poquelin	Jean-Baptiste	*Moliere*		Playwright
Porter	William Sydney	*O'Henry*		Author
Pound	Ezra Loomis	*Atheling*	William	Poet
Powell	Clive	*Fame*	Georgie	Vocalist/Musician
Powles	Matilda Alice	*Tilley*	Vesta	Comedian
Pratt	Denis	*Crisp*	Quentin	Writer
Pratt	William Henry	*Karloff*	Boris	Actor
Prendergast	John Barry	*Barry*	John	Musician
Price	Ellen	*Wood*	Mrs Henry	English Novelist
Priestley	John Boynton	*Goldsmith*	Peter	Author
Primrose-Pechey	Phyllis	*Craddock*	Fanny	Television Cook
Prior-Palmer	Lucinda	*Green*	Lucinda	Three-Day Eventer
Pugh	Wynette	*Wynette*	Tammy	Vocalist
Quedens	Eunice	*Arden*	Eve	Actress
Quiller-Couch	Arthur	*Q*		Author
Quincey	Thomas	*De Quincey*	Thomas	Essayist
Quoirez	Francoise	*Sagan*	Francoise	Authoress
Rajan	John	*Lord*	Jack	Actor
Ramée, de la	Marie Louise	*Ouida*		English Novelist
Ranft	George	*Raft*	George	Actor
Rankin	Brian	*Marvin*	Hank	Guitarist
Ravenscroft	John	*Peel*	John	Disc jockey

F
A
M
O
U
S

P
E
O
P
L
E

Original Name		Assumed Name		
Reibnitz	Marie von	**Michael of Kent**	Princess	*Austrian Princess*
Relph	Harry	**Tich**	Little	*Comedian*
Relyea	Walter	**Hayden**	Sterling	*Actor*
Rendell	Ruth	**Vine**	Barbara	*Crime Novellist*
Richards	Pauline	**Rocket**		*TV Gladiator*
Richardson	Jiles Perry (JP)	**Bopper**	The Big	*Vocalist*
Riddle	James	**Hoffa**	Jimmy	*US Union Leader*
Riley	Helena	**Panther**		*TV Gladiator*
Ritchie	John	**Vicious**	Sid	*Vocalist*
Robbins	Anne Frances	**Davis**	Nancy	*Actress*
Roberts	Russ	**Abbot**	Russ	*Comedian*
Robertson	James Logie	**Haliburton**	Hugh	*Poet*
Robertson	Anna Mary	**Moses**	Grandma	*Artist*
Robertson	Marjorie	**Neagle**	Anna	*Actress*
Robinson	Ray Charles	**Charles**	Ray	*Vocalist*
Robinson	Frederick John	**Goderich**	Viscount	*Prime Minister of Great Britain*
Robusti	Jacopo	**Tintoretto**		*Artist*
Rolfe	Frederick William	**Corvo**	Baron	*Novelist*
Rosenbaum	Borge	**Borge**	Victor	*Comic Musician*
Rosenberg	Leonard	**Randall**	Tony	*Actor*
Rose-Price	Dennistoun Franklyn	**Price**	Dennis	*Actor*
Rothschild	Dorothy	**Parker**	Dorothy	*Authoress*
Rowlands	John	**Stanley**	Henry Morton	*Explorer*
Rubin	Lynsey	**De Paul**	Lynsey	*Vocalist*
Rubin	Harold	**Robbins**	Harold	*Author*
Ruiz	Pablo	**Picasso**	Pablo	*Artist*
Russell	George William	**AE**		*Irish Poet*
Ruston	Audrey	**Hepburn**	Audrey	*Actress*
Saillot	Félicité	**Desmousseaux**	Félicité	*Actress*
Samaniegos	Ramon	**Novarre**	Ramon	*Actor*
Samuel	Henry	**Seal**		*Vocalist*
Samuels	Miriam	**Karlin**	Miriam	*Actress*
Sánchez	Illich Ramirez	**Carlos the Jackal**		*Guerrilla*
Sandeman	Mary	**Aneka**		*Pop Singer*
Santi/Sanzio	Raffaello	**Raphael**		*Artist*
Sarstedt	Richard	**Kane**	Eden	*Vocalist*
Sättler	Elisabeth	**Rethberg**	Elisabeth	*Musician*
Scallon (nee Brown)	Rosemary	**Dana**		*Singer & Politician*
Scherer Jnr	Roy	**Hudson**	Rock	*Actor*
Schicklgruber	Adolf	**Hitler**	Adolf	*Dictator*
Schipani	Pia	**Zadora**	Pia	*Actress*
Schneider	Guenther	**Arnold**	Edward	*Actor*
Schrift	Shirley	**Winters**	Shelley	*Actress*
Schwabe	Cecil	**Parker**	Cecil	*Actor*
Schwartz	Bernard	**Curtis**	Tony	*Actor*
Schwatt	Aaron	**Buttons**	Red	*Actor*
Schweider	Alfred	**Bruce**	Lenny	*Comedian*
Scicolini	Sophia	**Loren**	Sophia	*Actress*
Scudery	Madeleine de	**Sappho**		*French Novelist*
Seagull	Barbara	**Hershey**	Barbara	*US Actress*
Sekolovich	Mladen	**Malden**	Karl	*Actor*
Shalhoub	Michael	**Sharif**	Omar	*Actor*
Sharpe	Alexander John	**Ellis**	Alexander John	*English Philologist*
Shaw	George Bernard	**Corno Di Bassetto**	(Music critic for 'Star')	*Author*
Siciliano	Angelo	**Atlas**	Charles	*Athlete*
Siddhartha	Gautama	**Buddha**		*Buddhism Founder*
Sieffert	Ernst	**Tauber**	Richard	*Austrian Tenor*
Sigursteinnson	Magnus	**Magnusson**	Magnus	*Broadcaster*
Silberman	Jerome	**Wilder**	Gene	*Actor*
Silverman	Belle	**Sills**	Beverly	*Musician*
Simon	Paul	**Landis**	Jerry	*Half of 'Tom & Jerry' Duo*
Sims	Diane	**Angel**	Rhapsody	*Captain Scarlet Character*
Sinnott	Michael	**Sennett**	Mack	*Film Producer*
Sisson	Richard	**Widow**		*Musical act 'Kit and the Widow'*
Skikne	Larushka Mischa	**Harvey**	Laurence	*Actor*
Sklodowska	Manya	**Curie**	Marie	*Physicist*
Skryabin	Vyacheslav	**Molotov**	Vyacheslav	*Russian Statesman*

Original Name		Assumed Name		
	Mikhaylovich		Mikhaylovich	
Skurnick	Estelle	Nicole		Renault Clio Advert
Slye	Leonard	Rogers	Roy	Actor
Smith	Robert	Jack	Wolfman	Disc Jockey
Smith	Gladys Mary	Pickford	Mary	Actress
Smith	James Marcus	Proby	PJ	Vocalist
Smith	Walker	Robinson	Sugar Ray	Boxer
Smith	Harold J	Silverheels	Jay	Actor
Smith	Reginald	Wilde	Marty	Vocalist
Smith	Kim	Wilde	Kim	Vocalist
Solberg	David	Soul	David	Actor
Sorya	Francoise	Aimee	Anouk	Actress
Southill	Ursula	Mother Shipton		Witch and Prophetess
Spartanero	Franco	Nero	Franco	Actor
Springall	Charles	Drake	Charlie	Comedian
Stainer	Leslie	Howard	Leslie	Actor
Stanley	Edward	Derby	Earl of	Prime Minister of Great Britain
Stanley	Henry Morton	Rowlands	John	Explorer/Journalist
Stansfield	Grace	Fields	Gracie	Actress/Singer
Starkey	Richard	Starr	Ringo	Drummer/Composer
Steele	Richard	Bickerstaffe	Isaac	Author
Stengland	Inger	Stevens	Inger	Actress
Stephens	Yvette Marie	Khan	Chaka	Vocalist
Stern	Miriam	Stoppard	Miriam	Broadcaster
Stevens	Cat	Islam	Yusuf	Vocalist/Composer
Stevens	Shaking	Kent	Clark	Vocalist
Stevens	Ruby	Stanwyck	Barbara	Actress
Stevens	Terry	Thomas	Terry	Comedy Actor
Stevenson	Elizabeth	Gaskell	Elizabeth	Writer
Stewart	Charles Edward	Burke	Betty	Scottish Pretender
Stewart	James	Granger	Stewart	Actor
Stewart	John	Innes	Michael	Author
Stoppelmoor	Cheryl	Ladd	Cheryl	Actress
Stoute	Jenny	Rebel		TV Gladiator
Stovenour	June	Haver	June	Actress
Strataki	Anastasia	Stratas	Teresa	Soprano
Stratemeyer	Edward	Dixon	Franklin W.	Author
Stratemeyer	Edward	Hope	Laura Lee	Author
Stratemeyer	Edward	Keene	Carolyn	Author
Stratton	Charles	Thumb	Tom	Circus Performer
Straussler	Thomas	Stoppard	Tom	Dramatist
Stringer	Lynne	Caine	Marti	Comedienne/Singer
Stuart	Charles Edward	Burke	Betty	Bonnie Prince Charlie
Stuart	John	Bute	Earl of	Prime Minister of Great Britain
Sueur	Lucille le	Crawford	Joan	Actress
Sullivan	Gaynor	Tyler	Bonnie	Vocalist
Sumner	Gordon	Sting		Vocalist/Musician
Svenson	Adam	Blue	Captain	TV Fictional Character
Svenson	Beryl	Grey	Beryl	Ballerina
Svensson	Gloria	Swanson	Gloria	Actress
Swift	Jonathan	Bickerstaffe	Isaac	Author
Sykes	Norma	Sabrina		Model
Tarpley	Brenda	Lee	Brenda	Vocalist
Tatischeff	Jacques	Tati	Jacques	Actor
Teach	Edward	Blackbeard		Pirate
Tejada	Raquel	Welch	Raquel	Actress
Temple	Henry John	Palmerston	Viscount	Prime Minister of Great Britain
Tennenbaum	Irving	Stone	Irving	US Novelist
Tennyson	Alfred Lord	Merlin		Poet
Terzi	Orhan	DJ Quicksilver		Turkish Pop Star
Thackeray	William Makepeace	Titmarsh	Michael Angelo	Author
Thann	Nguyen Van	Chi-Minh	Ho	Vietnamese Politician
Thatcher	Margaret	Kesteven	Lady	Prime Minister of Great Britain
Theotocopoulos	Domenico	Greco	El	Artist
Thibault	Anatole Francois	France	Anatole	Author
Thomas	George	Tonypandy	Viscount	Speaker of Commons

FAMOUS PEOPLE

Original Name		Assumed Name		
Thompson	Estelle	Oberon	Merle	Actress
Thornburg	Betty June	Hutton	Betty	US Comedy Actress
Thornley	Peter	Nagasaki	Kendo	Professional Wrestler
Ticker	Reuben	Tucker	Richard	Singer
Tidbury	Eldred	Gray	Donald	South African Actor
Titta	Ruffo	Ruffo	Titta	Baritone
Tomaling	Susan	Sarandon	Susan	Actress
Touchinsky	Alfred	Marks	Alfred	Actor/Comedian
Trendle	Doug	Bloodvessel	Buster	Vocalist
Trevorrow	Mark	Downe	Bob	Australian Comedian
Trimmler	Deborah	Kerr	Deborah	Actress
Truscott-Jones	Reginald	Milland	Ray	Actor
Tsering	Lhamo Thondup	Tenzin Gyatso		14th Dalai Lama
Tullius	Marcus	Cicero (from wart on nose)		Roman Statesman
Tureaud	Lawrence	T	Mr	Actor
Turner	Conrad	Black	Captain	Captain Scarlet Character
Ullman	Douglas	Fairbanks	Douglas	Actor
Ulyanov	Vladimir Ilyich	Lenin	Vladimir Ilyich	Russian revolutionary
Uttini	Guiseppe	Verdi		Vocalist
Valentino	Wladziu	Liberace		Pianist
Valenzuela	Ritchie	Valens	Ritchie	Vocalist
Van Aken	Jerome	Bosch	Hiëronymus	Dutch Painter
Van Den Bogaerde	Derek Niven	Bogarde	Dirk	Actor
Van der Faes	Pieter	Lely	Peter	British Painter
Van Varenberg	Jean-Claude	Van Damme	Jean-Claude	Actor
Vander Walt	Lize	Gold		TV Gladiator
Vecchio	Frank Lo	Laine	Frankie	Vocalist
Vecellio	Tiziano	Titian		Artist
Velline	Robert Thomas	Vee	Bobby	Vocalist
Vivar	Rodrigo diaz de	Cid	El	Spanish Warrior
Vliet	Don Van	Beefheart	Captain	Vocalist
Wainewright	Thomas Griffiths	Weathercock	Janus	Art Critic/Murderer
Wainwright	Karen	Angel	Symphony	Captain Scarlet Character
Walker	Edmund	Kemp	Jeremy	Actor
Waller	Thomas Wright	Waller	Fats	Jazz Pianist
Walpole	Robert	Orford	Earl of	Prime Minister of Great Britain
Walters	Mrs Daryl	Blyton	Enid	Author
Ward	Arthur Sarsfield	Rohmer	Sax	Author
Waters	Jack	Warner	Jack	Actor
Wayman	Eunice	Simone	Nina	Vocalist
Wayne	Bruce	Batman		Fictional Super Hero
Webb	Gary	Numan	Gary	Vocalist/Composer
Webb	Harold	Richard	Cliff	Singer
Weinstein	Bernie	Winters	Bernie	Comedian
Weiss	Ehrich	Houdini	Harry	Illusionist
Welch	Vera	Lynn	Vera	Singer
Wellesley	Arthur	Wellington	Duke of	Prime Minister of Great Britain
Wells	Julia	Andrews	Julie	Actress/Singer
Wentworth	Charles Watson	Rockingham	Marquis of	Prime Minister of Great Britain
Wesley	Arthur	Wellesley	Arthur	Prime Minister of Great Britain
Westcott	Fred	Karno	Fred	Impresario
Westover	Charles	Shannon	Del	Singer
Wettach	Adrien	Grock		Clown
White	Priscilla	Black	Cilla	Vocalist/Presenter
White	William	Grayson	Larry	Comedian
White	P.D.	James	P.D.	Authoress
White	David	Jason	David	Actor
White	William Hale	Rutherford	Mark	Writer
Whittaker	James	Bowen	Jim	Comedian
Wight	James	Herriot	James	Vet/Author
Wilde	Oscar	Melmoth	Sebastian	Author
Wilfred	Sir	Ivanhoe		Literary Character
Wilkens	Maybritt	Britt	May	Actress
Wilkie	Edward	Fawn	Doctor	Captain Scarlet Character
William	Walter	Maynard	Bill	Actor

Original Name		Assumed Name		
Williams	Kim	Lightning		Gladiator
Wilson	Barbara	Batgirl		Fictional Film Hero
Wilson	Anthony	Burgess	Anthony	Writer
Wilson	Harold	Rievaulx	Lord	Prime Minister of Great Britain
Windsor	Albert	George V1	King	Sovereign
Winogradsky	Boris	Delfont	Bernard	Impresario
Winogradsky	Louis	Grade	Lew	Impresario
Winter	Richard	Warwick	Richard	Actor
Wiseman	Ernest	Wise	Ernie	Comedian
Witko	Tasunko	Crazy Horse		Sioux Indian Chief
Wojtyla	Karol	John Paul 11	Pope	Bishop of Rome
Wolcot	John	Pindar	Peter	Satirist
Wood	Henry	Klenovsky	Paul	English Conductor
Wood	Mathilda	LLoyd	Marie	Actress
Woodward	Thomas	Jones	Tom	Vocalist
Worrell	Charles	I Spy	Big Chief	Author
Wright	Archibald	Moore	Archibald	Boxer
Wunderman	Leslie	Carlisle	Belinda	Vocalist
Wupperman	Frank	Morgan	Frank	Actor
Wycherly	Ronald	Fury	Billy	Vocalist
Yanks	Byron	Janis	Byron	Musician
Yeary	Harvey Lee	Majors	Lee	Actor
Yin	Leslie Charles Bowyer	Charteris	Leslie	Author
Youdale	Diane	Jet		TV Gladiator
Young	Sandy	Phoenix		Gladiator
Young	Leslie Ronald	Young	Jimmy	Broadcaster
Yule Jnr	Joseph	Rooney	Mickey	Actor
Ze Schluderpacheru	Herbert	Lom	Herbert	Actor
Zerby	Deborah	Darby	Kim	Actress
Zimmerman	Robert Alan	Dylan	Bob	Vocalist/Composer
Zogu	Ahmed Bey	Zog	King	Albanian King
Zoine	Vincento	Edwards	Vince	US Actor
Zwinge	James Randall	Randi	Amazing	Magician

Real Names: By Assumed Name

Assumed Name		Original Name		
Abbot	Russ	Roberts	Russ	Comedian
Aberdeen	Earl of	Gordon	George Hamilton	British Prime Minister
Sade		Adu	Helen Folasade	Singer
AE		Russell	George William	Irish poet
Agnon	Shmuel Yosef	Czaczkes	Shmuel Josef	Israeli novelist
Aimée	Anouk	Sorya	Françoise	Actress
Albert	Eddie	Heimberger	Eddie	US actor
Alda	Alan	D'Abruzzo	Alfonso	Actor
Aldington	Richard	Godfree	Edward	English poet
Ali	Muhammad	Clay	Cassius Marcellus	Boxer
Alkan	Charles-Valentin	Morhange	Charles-Valentin	French musician
Allen	Dave	O'Mahoney	Tynian	Comedian
Allen	Woody	Konigsberg	Allen	Actor/director
Amazon		Davies	Sharron	Swimmer and TV Gladiator
Anderson	Bronco Billy	Arenson	Max	Entertainer
Andrews	Julie	Wells	Julia	Actress/Singer
Aneka		Sandeman	Mary	Pop singer
Angel	Destiny	Pointon	Juliette	'Captain Scarlet' character
Angel	Harmony	Kwan	Chan	'Captain Scarlet' character
Angel	Melody	Jones	Magnolia	Captain Scarlet Character
Angel	Rhapsody	Sims	Diane	'Captain Scarlet' character
Angel	Symphony	Wainwright	Karen	'Captain Scarlet' character

FAMOUS PEOPLE

Assumed Name		Original Name		
Angelico	Fra	di Pietro	Guido di	Artist
Ant	Adam	Goddard	Stuart	Singer
Apollinaire	Guillaume	de Kostrowitzky	Wilhelm Apollinaris	French poet
Appleseed	Johnny	Chapman	John	Missionary nurseryman
Arden	Elizabeth	Graham	Florence Nightingale	Beautician
Arden	Eve	Quedens	Eunice	Actress
Arlen	Michael	Kouyoumdjian	Dikran	British novelist
Arliss	George	Andrews	Augustus George	Actor
Arness	James	Aurness	James	US actor
Arnold	Edward	Schneider	Guenther	Actor
Arras	Leon	Glover	Brian	Professional wrestler
Arthur	Beatrice	Frankel	Bernice	US actress
Arthur	Jean	Greene	Gladys	Actress
Astaire	Fred	Austerlitz	Frederick	Dancer and actor
Astor	Mary	Langemanke	Lucille	Actress
Ataturk	Kemal	Kemal	Mustafa	Turkish statesman
Atheling	William	Pound	Ezra Loomis	Poet
Atlas	Charles	Siciliano	Angelo	Athlete
Atticus		Addison	Joseph	Essayist and politician
Avery	Tex	Bean	Frederick	Cartoonist
Aznavour	Charles	Aznavurjal	Shahnovr	Singer and actor
Bacall	Lauren	Perske	Betty Joan	Actress
Badger (Le Blaireau)		Hinault	Bernard	Cyclist
Baker	Janet	Abbott	Janet	Mezzo-soprano
Balanchine	George	Balanchivadze	Georgi Melitonivich	Choreographer
Bancroft	Anne	Italiano	Anna Maria	Actress
Bara	Theda	Goodman	Theodosia	Actress
Bardot	Brigitte	Javal	Camille	Actress
Barrie	Amanda	Broadbent	Shirley Ann	Actress
Barry	Gene	Klass	Eugene	US actor
Barry	John	Prendergast	John Barry	Musician
Barry	Michael	Bukht	Michael	Food journalist
Barrymore	Ethel	Blythe	Ethel	Actress
Barrymore	John	Blythe	John	Actor
Barrymore	Lionel	Blythe	Lionel	Actor
Bart	Lionel	Begleiter	Lionel	Composer
Bart	Black	Bottom	Charles	Outlaw
Basie	Count	Basie	William	Musician
Bassano	Jacopo	Da Ponte	Giacomo	Italian painter
Batgirl		Wilson	Barbara	Comic and film heroine
Batman		Wayne	Bruce	Comic and film hero
Beachcomber	John	Morton	Cameron	Newspaper columnist
Beatty	Warren	Beaty	Warren	Actor
Bedelia	Bonnie	Culkin	Bonnie	Actress
Beefheart	Captain	Van Vliet	Don	Musician
Beeton	Mrs	Mayson	Isabella	Cookery writer
Bell	Acton	Brontë	Anne	Novelist
Bell	Currer	Brontë	Charlotte	Novelist
Bell	Ellis	Brontë	Emily	Novelist
Benedict	Dirk	Niewoehner	Dirk	US actor
Ben-Gurion	David	Green	David	Israeli statesman
Bennett	Harve	Fischman	Harve	US TV producer
Bennett	Lennie	Berry	Mike	Comedian
Bennett	Tony	Benevetto	Anthony Dominic	Vocalist
Benny	Jack	Kubelsky	Benjamin	Comedian
Berkeley	Busby	Enos	William	Choreographer
Berlin	Irving	Baline	Israel	Composer
Bernhardt	Sarah	Bernard	Rosine	Actress
Berra	Yogi	Berra	Lawrence Peter	Baseball player
Bickerstaffe (shared pen-name)	Isaac	Steele	Richard	Author (shared pen-name)
Bickerstaffe (shared pen-name)	Isaac	Swift	Jonathan	Author (shared pen-name)
Bill	Buffalo	Cody	William	Showman
Billy the kid		McCarty	Henry	Oulaw
Captain Black		Turner	Conrad	'Captain Scarlet' character

Assumed Name		Original Name		
Black	Cilla	White	Priscilla	Singer and TV presenter
Blackbeard		Teach	Edward	Pirate
Blake	Nicholas	Day-Lewis	Cecil	Detective writer
Blondin	Charles	Gravelet	Jean François	French acrobat
Bloodvessel	Buster	Trendle	Doug	Singer
Blue	Captain	Svenson	Adam	TV fictional character
Bluebeard		Landru	Henri	French murderer
Bly	Nellie	Cochrane	Elizabeth	Aviator
Blyton	Enid	Walters	Mrs Daryl	Author
Bogarde	Dirk	Van Den Bogaerde	Derek	Actor
Boilermaker		Jeffries	James Jackson	Boxing champion
Bolan	Marc	Feld	Marc	Musician
Bono		Hewson	Paul	Musician
Big Bopper		Richardson	Jiles Perry (JP)	Musician
Bonney	William	McCarthy	Henry	Outlaw Billy the Kid
Borge	Victor	Rosenbaum	Borge	Comic and musician
Bosch	Hieronymus	Van Aken	Jerome	Dutch painter
Botticelli	Sandro	Filipepi	Alessandro	Artist
Bowen	Jim	Whittaker	James	Comedian
Bowie	David	Jones	David	Musician
Boyd	Stephen	Millar	William	Actor
Boyle	Katie	Francabilla	Marchesa Caterina de	TV presenter
Boz		Dickens	Charles	Author (occasional pen-name)
Bracket	Hilda	Fyffe	Patrick	Entertainer
Brains		Hackenbacker	Hiram J	'Thunderbirds' character
Brandt	Willy	Frahm	Karl Herbert	German chancellor
Breen	Billy	Grayson	Larry	Comedian
Brett	Jeremy	Huggins	Peter Jeremy	Actor
Bridie	James	Mavor	Osborne Henry	Dramatist
Britt	May	Wilkens	Maybritt	Actress
Bronson	Charles	Buchinski	Charles	Actor
Bronzino	il	Mariano	Agnolo di Cosimo	Painter
Brooks	Albert	Einstein	Albert	Actor
Brooks	Elkie	Bookbinder	Elaine	Singer
Brooks	Louise	Gettman	Leslie	US actress
Brooks	Mel	Kaminsky	Melvin	Actor and director
Brown Bomber		Louis	Joe	Boxer
Bruce	Lenny	Schweider	Alfred	Comedian
Bryan	Dora	Broadbent	Dora	Actress and comedienne
Brynner	Yul	Khan Jnr	Taidje	Actor
Buddha		Siddhartha	Gautama	Founder of buddhism
Buntline	Ned	Judson	Edward Zane	Inventor
Burgess	Anthony	Wilson	Anthony	Writer
Burke	Betty	Stuart	Charles Edward	Bonnie Prince Charlie
Burns	George	Birnbaum	Nathan	Comedian
Burstyn	Ellen	Gillorly	Edna	Actress
Burton	Richard	Jenkins	Richard	Actor
Buttons	Red	Schwatt	Aaron	Actor
Bygraves	Max	Bygraves	Walter	Entertainer
Byrnes	Edd	Breitenberger	Edward	Actor
Cage	Nicolas	Coppola	Nicholas	US actor
Cagliostro	Count	Balsame	Giuseppe	Italian adventurer
Caine	Michael	Micklewhite	Maurice	Actor
Caine	Marti	Stringer	Lynne	Comedienne/ and singer
Callas	Maria	Kalageropoulos	Cecilia	Operatic soprano
Calvin	Jean	Chauvin/Cauvin	Jean	French theologian
Canaletto		Canale	Giovanni Antonio	Artist
Cannon	Tommy	Derbyshire	Tommy	Comedy straight man
Cantor	Eddie	Iskowitz	Edward	Comedian
Capp	Al	Caplin	Alfred Gerald	Cartoonist
Caravaggio		Merisi	Michelangelo	Artist
Carlisle	Belinda	Wunderman	Leslie	Vocalist
Carlos 'the Jackal'		Sánchez	Illich Ramirez	Revolutionary and assisin
Carroll	Diahann	Johnson	Carol Diahann	Actress
Carroll	Lewis	Dodgson	Charles Lutwidge	Author
Carrott	Jasper	Davies	Robert	Comedian
Cassandra		Connor	William	Journalist

FAMOUS PEOPLE

Assumed Name		Original Name		
Cassidy	Butch	Parker	Robert LeRoy	Outlaw leader
Cat		Dibley	Dwayne	TV character ('Red Dwarf')
Cates	Phoebe	Katz	Phoebe	Actress
Cathcart	Helen	Albert	Harold	Royal biographer
Chandler	Jeff	Grossell	Ira	Actor
Charisse	Cyd	Finklea	Tula Ellice	Dancer
Charles	Ray	Robinson	Ray Charles	Singer
Charteris	Leslie	Yin	Leslie Charles Bowyer	Author
Checker	Chubby	Evans	Ernest	Singer
Cher		La Pierre	Cherilyn Sarkisian	Singer and actress
Chi-Minh	Ho	Thann	Nguyen Van	Vietnamese politician
Chopin	Kate	O'Flaherty	Katherine	Author
Cicero		Tullius	Marcus	Roman statesman
Cid	El	Vivár	Rodrigo Díaz de	Spanish warrior
Clair	René	Chomette	René Lucien	Film director
Clapton	Eric	Clapp	Eric	Guitarist and singer
Clarke	John	Cromwell	Richard	Son of Oliver Cromwell
Cliff	Jimmy	Chambers	James	Singer
Clift	Montgomery	Montgomery	Edward	Actor
Cobb	Lee J	Jacob	Lee	Actor
Coco		Poliakov	Nikolai	Clown
Colbert	Claudette	Chauchoin	Lily	Actress
Colbourne	Maurice	Middleton	Roger	Actor
Cole	Nat King	Adams	Nathaniel	Singer
Como	Perry	Perido	Nick	Singer
Connery	Sean	Connery	Thomas	Actor
Conquest	Owen	Hamilton	Charles	Author
Conrad	Joseph	Korzeniowski	Jozef Teodor Konrad	Author
Cooper	Alice	Furnier	Vincent	Singer
Cooper	Gary	Cooper	Francis	Actor
Le Corbusier		Jeanneret	Charles Edouard	Architect
El Cordobes		Perez	Manuel Benitez	Matador
Corelli	Marie	Mackay	Mary	English novelist
Corno di Bassetto		Shaw	George Bernard	Author (as music critic)
Correggio		Allegri	Antonio	Artist
Corvo	Baron	Rolfe	Frederick William	Novelist
Costello	Elvis	McManus	Declan	Singer and composer
Costello	Lou	Cristillo	Louis	Comedian
Cougar	John	Mellencamp	John	Vocalist
Craddock	Fanny	Primrose-Pechey	Phyllis	Television cook
Craig	Michael	Gregson	Michael	Actor
Cranach	Lucas	Müller	Lucas	German painter
Craven	Sara	Ashurst	Anne	Novelist
Crawford	Joan	Le Sueur	Lucille	Actress
Crawford	Michael	Dumble-Smith	Michael	Actor and singer
Crazy Horse		Witko	Tasunko	Sioux Indian chief
Creole	Kid	Darnell Browder	Thomas August	singer
Creston	Paul	Guttoveggio	Joseph	Musician
Cricket	Jimmy	Mulgrew	James	Comedian
Crisp	Quentin	Pratt	Denis	Writer
Crompton	Richmal	Lamburn	Richmal	Author
Crosby	Bing	Crosby	Harry Lillis	Singer and actor
Cruise	Tom	Mapother	Tom Cruise	Actor
Curie	Marie	Sklodowska	Manya	Physicist
Curtis	Tony	Schwartz	Bernard	Actor
Cutpurse	Moll	Frith	Mary	Pickpocket and Robber
D'Ache	Caran	Poire	Emmanuel	French illustrator
Daddy	Big	Crabtree	Shirley	Wrestler
D'Amato	Joe	Massaccesi	Aristide	Film director
Dana		Scallon (nee Brown)	Rosemary	Singer and politician
Dane	Clemence	Ashton	Winifred	English dramatist
Darby	Kim	Zerby	Deborah	Actress
Darin	Bobby	Cassotto	Robert Walden	Singer
Darren	James	Ercolani	James	US actor
Davis	Nancy	Robbins	Anne Frances	Actress
Davro	Bobby	Nankeville	Robert	Comic impressionist

Assumed Name		Original Name		
Dawes (He's a baby)	George	**Lucas**	Matt	*Comedian*
Dawn	Elizabeth	**Butterfield**	Sylvia	*Actress*
Day	Doris	**Kappelhoff**	Doris Von	*Actressand singer*
De Carlo	Yvonne	**Middleton**	Peggy	*Actress*
De Paul	Lynsey	**Rubin**	Lynsey	*Singer*
De Quincey	Thomas	**Quincey**	Thomas	*Essayist*
Dean	James	**Byron**	James	*Actor*
Dee	Kiki	**Matthews**	Pauline	*Singer*
Defoe	Daniel	**Foe**	Daniel	*Author*
Delfont	Bernard	**Winogradsky**	Boris	*Impresario*
Deneuve	Catherine	**Dorléac**	Catherine	*Actress*
Dennis	Les	**Heseltine**	Les	*Comedian*
Denver	John	**Deutschendorf Jnr**	Henry John	*Singer and composer*
Derek	Bo	**Collins**	Cathleen	*Actress*
Derek	John	**Harris**	Derek	*Actor*
Desmousseaux	Félicité	**Saillot**	Félicité	*Actress*
Diamond	Neil	**Kaminsky**	Noah	*Singer and composer*
Dickinson	Angie	**Brown**	Angeline	*Actress*
Dickson	Carter	**Carr**	John Dickson	*US detective writer*
Diddley	Bo	**Bates**	Otha Ellas	*Singer*
Dinesen	Isak	**Blixen**	Karen	*Writer*
Ding Ling		**Bingzhi**	Jiang	*Chinese novelist*
Divine	Father	**Baker**	George	*Religious leader*
Dixon	Franklin W	**Stratemeyer**	Edward	*Author*
DJ Quicksilver		**Terzi**	Orhan	*Turkish pop star*
Dolin	Anton	**Healey-Kay**	Patrick	*Choreographer*
Donovan		**Leitch**	Donovan	*Singer*
Dorsey	Gerry	**Dorsey**	Arnold	*Singer*
Douglas	Kirk	**Demsky**	Issur Danielovitch	*Actor*
Downe	Bob	**Trevorrow**	Mark	*Australian comedian*
Drake	Charlie	**Springall**	Charles	*Comedian*
Dylan	Bob	**Zimmerman**	Robert Alan	*Singer and composer*
Eden	Barbara	**Huffman**	Barbara	*US actress*
Edge	The	**Evans**	Dave	*Musician*
Edwards	Vince	**Zoine**	Vincento	*US actor*
Elia		**Lamb**	Charles	*Essayist*
Eliot	George	**Evans**	Mary Ann	*Novelist*
Ellis	Alexander John	**Sharpe**	Alexander John	*English philologist*
Elytis	Odysseus	**Alepoudelis**	Odysseus	*Greek poet*
Erasmus	Desiderius	**Gheraerd**	Gheraerd	*Scholar*
Essex	David	**Cook**	David	*Singer and actor*
Everage	Dame Edna	**Humphries**	Barry	*Comedian*
Everett	Kenny	**Cole**	Maurice	*Disc jockey and comedian*
Fabian		**Forte**	Fabiano	*Singer*
Fairbanks	Douglas	**Ullman**	Douglas	*Actor*
Faith	Adam	**Nelhams**	Terry	*Singer*
Fame	Georgie	**Powell**	Clive	*Musician*
Farrell	MJ	**Keane**	Molly	*Irish novelist*
Fawn	Doctor	**Wilkie**	Edward	*'Captain Scarlet' character*
Fenton	Shane	**Jewry**	Bernard	*Singer*
Fields	WC	**Dukenfield**	William Claude	*Comedian/and actor*
Fields	Gracie	**Stansfield**	Grace	*Actress and singer*
Finch	Peter	**Mitchell**	Ian	*Actor*
Fleming	Rhonda	**Louis**	Marilyn	*Actress*
Flying Scotsman		**Liddell**	Eric	*Athlete*
Flynn	Barbara	**McMurray**	Barbara	*Actress*
Fontaine	Joan	**De Havilland**	Joan	*Actress*
Fonteyn	Margot	**Hookham**	Margaret	*Ballerina*
Ford	Gerald	**King**	Leslie	*US president*
Ford	John	**O'Fearna**	Sean	*Film director*
Formby Jnr	George	**Booth**	George Hoy	*Music hall entertainer*
Formby Snr	George	**Booth**	James	*Music hall entertainer*
Forrest	Steve	**Andrews**	William Forrest	*US actor*
Forsyth	Bruce	**Johnson**	Bruce	*Entertainer*
Foster	Jodie	**Munker**	Ariane	*US actress*
Fox		**Baker**	Tammy Marie	*TV Gladiator*
France	Anatole	**Thibault**	Anatole François	*Author*
Franciosa	Tony	**Papaceo**	Anthony	*Actor*
Francis	Connie	**Franconers**	Concetta	*Singer*

FAMOUS PEOPLE

Assumed Name		Original Name		
Francis of Assisi	Saint	de Bernardone	Giovanni	Religious leader
Francisque		Millet	Jean-François	Belgian painter
Freeze	Mr	Fries	Victor	Fictional super-villain
Fury	Billy	Wycherly	Ronald	Vocalist
Gabor	Dennis	Dénes	Gábor	Physicist
Garbo	Greta	Gustaffson	Greta Louisa	Actress
Garcia	Andy	Menendez	Andres Arturo Garcia	Actor
Garfunkel	Art	Graph	Tom	Half of 50s singing duo Tom & Jerry
Garland	Judy	Gumm	Frances	Actress and singer
Garner	James	Baumgartner	James	Actor
Gaskell	Elizabeth	Stevenson	Elizabeth	Writer
Gayle	Crystal	Gazzimos	Brenda Gail	Singer
Gaynor	Gloria	Fowles	Gloria	Singer
Gee	Dustin	Harrison	Gerald	Impressionist
Genée	Adeline	Jensen	Anita	Ballerina
George	Boy	O'Dowd	George	Singer
Geraldo		Bright	Gerald	Musician
German	Edward	Jones	Edward	English composer
Geronimo		Goyathlay		Apache Indian chief
Giant Haystacks		McMasters	Luke	Wrestler
Gibbon	Lewis	Mitchell	James Leslie	Novelist
Giorgione		Barbarelli	Giorgio	Artist
Gish	Lillian	Guiche	Lilian	Actress
Glitter	Gary	Gadd	Paul	Singer
Gluck	Alma	Fiersohn	Reba	American soprano
Goddard	Paulette	Levy	Marion	Actress
Gold		Vander Walt	Lize	TV Gladiator
Goldberg	Whoopi	Johnson	Caryn	US actress
Goldsmith	Peter	Priestley	John Boynton	Author
Goldwyn	Sam	Gelbfisz	Samuel	Film producer
Goodrich	William B	Arbuckle	Roscoe Conkling (Fatty)	Actor
Gordon	Richard	Ostlere	Gordon	Doctor and author
Gorky	Arshile	Adoian	Vosdanig Manoog	US painter
Gorky	Maxim	Peshkov	Max	Author
Gould	Elliott	Goldstein	Elliott	Actor
Grade	Lew	Winogradsky	Louis	Impresario
Granger	Stewart	Stewart	James	Actor
Grant	Cary	Leach	Archibald	Actor
Gray	Donald	Tidbury	Eldred	South African actor
Grayson	Larry	White	William	Comedian
Graziano	Rocky	Barbella	Rocco	Boxer
El Greco		Theotocopoulos	Domenico	Artist
L.T. Green		Griffiths	Seymour	TV Fictional character
Green	Lucinda	Prior-Palmer	Lucinda	Three-day eventer
Green	Peter	Greenbaum	Peter	Musician
Grey	Captain	Holden	Bradley	TV Fictional character
Grey	Beryl	Svenson	Beryl	Ballerina
Gris	Juan	González	Juan Victoriano	Cubist painter
Grock		Wettach	Adrien	Clown
Grünewald	Matthias	Gothardt	Mathis	German painter
Guercino		Barbieri	Gian-Francesco	Italian Painter
Haliburton	Hugh	Robertson	James Logie	Poet
Hamilton	Clive	Lewis	CS	British writer
Hamilton	Emma	Lyon	Emma	Lord Nelson's mistress
Harley	Steve	Nice	Stephen	Pop singer
Harlow	Jean	Carpentier	Harlean	Actress
Hart	Emma	Lyon	Emma (Amy)	Blacksmith's daughter
Harvey	Laurence	Skikne	Larushka Mischa	Actor
Haver	June	Stovenour	June	Actress
Hawk	Jeremy	Lange	Cedric	Actor and TV presenter
Hawtrey	Charles	Hartree	George	Actor
Hayden	Sterling	Relyea	Walter	Actor
Hayworth	Rita	Cansino	Marguerita	Actress
HD		Doolittle	Hilda	Writer
Headroom	Max	Frewer	Matt	Fictional TV character
Hedley	Jack	Hawkins	Jack	Actor
Henderson	Mary	Mavor	Osborne Henry	Dramatist

Assumed Name		Original Name		
Hepburn	Audrey	Van Heemstra	Edda Hepburn	Actress
Hepburn	Audrey	Ruston	Audrey	Actress
Herriot	James	Wight	James	Vet and author
Hershey	Barbara	Herzstein	Barbara	Actress
Hershey	Barbara	Seagull	Barbara	US actress
Hessling	Catherine	Heurschling	Andrée	Jean Renoir's wife (actress)
Heston	Charlton	Carter	Charlton	Actor
Higgins	Jack	Patterson	Henry	Author
Hill	Benny	Hill	Alfred Hawthorne	Comedian
Hinge	Evadne	Logan	George	Entertainer
Hitler	Adolf	Schicklgrüber	Adolf	Dictator
Hobbema	Meindert	Lubbertszoon	Meyndert	Dutch painter
Hoffa	Jimmy	Riddle	James	US union leader
Hogan	Hulk	Hollea	Terry	Professional wrestler and actor
Holden	William	Beedle	William	Actor
Holiday	Billie	Fagan	Eleanora	Singer
Holly	Buddy	Hardin	Charles	Singer
Hope	Anthony	Hawkins	Anthony	Author
Hope	Laura Lee	Stratemeyer	Edward	Author
Horowitz	Vladimir	Gorowicz	Vladimir	Russian pianist
Houdini	Harry	Weiss	Ehrich	Illusionist
Houseman	John	Haussman	Jacques	Actor
Howard	Leslie	Stainer	Leslie	Actor
Hudson	Rock	Scherer Jnr	Roy	Actor
Humperdinck	Engelbert	Dorsey	Arnold	Singer
Hunter		Crossley	James	Gladiator
Hunter	Tab	Gellen	Arthur	Singer and actor
Hutton	Betty	Thornburg	Betty June	US comedy actress
I Spy	Big Chief	Worrell	Charles	Author
Innes	Michael	Stewart	John	Author
Irving	Henry	Brodribb	John Henry	Actor
Islam	Yusuf	Stevens	Cat	Singer and composer
Ives	Burl	Ivanhoe	Burl	Actor and singer
Ivy	Poison	Isley	Pamela	Fictional super-villainess
Jack	Wolfman	Smith	Robert	Disc jockey
James	PD	White	PD	writer
Jane	Calamity	Canary	Martha Jane	Frontierswoman
Janis	Byron	Yanks	Byron	Musician
Janssen	David	Mayer	David	Actor
Jason	David	White	David	Actor
Jayston	Michael	James	Michael	Actor
Jet		Youdale	Diane	TV Gladiator
Joan Collins' Fan Club		Clary	Julian	Entertainer
John	Elton Hercules	Dwight	Reginald Kenneth	Singer and composer
John	Jilted	Fellows	Graham	Pop singer
John Paul II	Pope	Wojtyla	Karol	Pope
Jolie	Angelina	Voight	Angelina	Actress
Jones	Tom	Woodward	Thomas	Singer
Jordan	Louis	Gendre	Louis	Actor
Joyce	Yootha	Needham	Yootha	Actress
Julia	Raul	Rafael Y Arcelos	Raul	Actor
Kane	Eden	Sarstedt	Richard	Singer
Kane Jeeves	Mahatma	Fields	WC	Comedian and Actor
Karlin	Miriam	Samuels	Miriam	Actress
Karloff	Boris	Pratt	William Henry	Actor
Karno	Fred	Westcott	Fred	Impresario
Kaye	Danny	Kaminsky	David Daniel	Entertainer
Kaye	Nora	Koreff	Nora	Ballerina
Kazan	Elia	Kazanjoglou	Elia	Film director
Keaton	Diane	Hall	Diane	Actress
Keaton	Michael	Douglas	Michael	Actor (Batman actor)
Keene	Carolyn	Stratemeyer	Edward	Author
Kemp	Jeremy	Walker	Edmund	Actor
Kerr	Deborah	Trimmler	Deborah	Actress
Khan	Chaka	Stephens	Yvette Marie	Singer
Khashoggi	Soraya	Daly	Sandra	Millionairess
King	Ben E.	Nelson	Benjamin	Singer

Assumed Name		Original Name		
King	Carol	Klein	Carole	Singer
Kinski	Nastassia	Nakszynski	Nastassja	Actress
Kit		Hesketh-Harvey	Kit	Musical act 'Kit and the Widow'
Klenovsky	Paul	Wood	Henry	English conductor
Kline	Patsy	Hensley	Virginia	Singer
Knickerbocker	Cholly	Paul	Maury	NY gossip columnist
Knickerbocker	Diedrich	Irving	Washington	Author
Koresh	David	Howell	Vernon	Branch Davidian cult leader
La Rue	Danny	Carroll	Daniel	Female impersonator
Ladd	Cheryl	Stoppelmoor	Cheryl	Actress
Laine	Denny	Haynes	Brian	Guitarist
Laine	Frankie	Vecchio	Frank Lo	Vocalist
Lamarr	Hedy	Kiesler	Hedwig	Actress
Lamour	Dorothy	Kaumeyer	Dorothy Mary	Actress
Landis	Jerry	Simon	Paul	Half of 50s singing duo 'Tom & Jerry' duo
Landon	Michael	Orowitz	Eugene Maurice	US actor
Lanza	Mario	Cocozza	Alfredo	Opera singer
Large	Eddie	McGuinness	Eddie	Comedian
Larrigan	Tex	Ord	Irene	Author of westerns
Lassie (male)		Pal (female)		Film dog
Laurel	Stan	Jefferson	Arthur Stanley	Comedy actor
Laurie	Piper	Jacobs	Rosetta	US actress
Laxness	Halldor	Guojonsson	Halldor	Icelandic novelist
Le Carre	John	Cornwell	David	Author
Le Duc Tho		Dinh Khai	Phan	Vietnamese politician
Le Mesurier	John	Halliley	John Elton	Actor
Lee	Brenda	Tarpley	Brenda	Vocalist
Lee	Bruce	Kam	Lee Yuen	Actor and martial artist
Lee	Peggy	Egstrom	Norma	Vocalist
Leigh	Janet	Morrison	Jeanette	Actress
Leigh	Jennifer Jason	Morrow	Jennifer Lee	Actress
Leigh	Vivien	Hartley	Vivien	Actress
Lely	Peter	Van der Faes	Pieter	Artist
Lemmy		Kilminster	Ian	Singer (Motorhead)
Lenin	Vladimir Ilich	Ulyanov	Vladimir Ilich	Russian revolutionary
Leno	Dan	Calvin	George	English comedian
Lenya	Lotte	Blamauer	Karoline Wilhelmine	Austrian actress
Lewis	Jerry	Levitch	Joseph	Actor and comedian
Liberace		Valentino	Wladziu	Pianist and entertainer
Lightning		Williams	Kim	TV Gladiator
Limahl		Hamill	Christopher	Singer (Kajagoogoo)
Little	Syd	Mead	Cyril	Comedian
Lloyd	Marie	Wood	Mathilda	Actress
Lom	Herbert	Ze Schluderpacheru	Herbert	Actor
Lombard	Carole	Peters	Jane	Actress
London	Jack	Griffith	John	Author
Lord	Jack	Ryan	John Joseph	Actor
Loren	Sofia	Scicolone	Sofia	Actress
Lorraine	Claude	Gelée	Claude	Landscape painter
Lorre	Peter	Loewenstein	Laszlo	Actor
Lot	Parson	Kingsley	Charles	Author
Lottery	Lenny	McGurran	Aidan	National Lottery expert
Louis	Joe	Barrow	Joseph	Boxer
Louis	Morris	Bernstein	Morris	US painter
Lulu		Lawrie	Marie McLaughlin	Singer
Lynn	Vera	Welch	Vera	Singer
Mabuse	Jan	Gossart	Jan	Flemish painter
MacBride	Maud	Gonne	Maud	Irish nationalist
MacColl	Ewan	Miller	James	Folk singer
MacDiarmid	Hugh	Grieve	Christopher Murray	Poet
Mack	Connie	McGillicuddy	Cornelius	Baseball player
Maclaine	Shirley	Beaty	Shirley	Actress
Madonna		Ciccone	Madonna Louise	Singer
Magenta	Captain	Donaghue	Patrick	Fictional TV character
Magnusson	Magnus	Sigursteinnson	Magnus	Broadcaster
Majors	Lee	Yeary	Harvey Lee	Actor

Assumed Name		Original Name		
Malden	Karl	Sekolovich	Mladen	Actor
Mann	Manfred	Lubowitz	Michael	Musician
Mansfield	Jayne	Palmer	Vera Jane	Actress
Mansfield	Katherine	Beauchamp	Kathleen	NZ Writer
Manson	Charles	Maddox	No-Name	Cult Leader
March	Fredric	Bickel	Frederick	Actor
Margret	Ann	Olsson	Ann-Margret	Actress
Markham	Elizabeth	Penrose	Elizabeth	Writer for children
Markham	Robert	Amis	Kingsley	Novelist
Markova	Alicia	Marks	Lilian Alice	Ballerina
Marks	Alfred	Touchinsky	Alfred	Actor and comedian
Martin	Dean	Crocetti	Dino	Actor
Marvel	Captain	Batson	Billy	Comics hero
Marvin	Hank	Rankin	Brian	Guitarist
Marx	Chico	Marx	Leonard	Actor
Marx	Groucho	Marx	Julius	Actor
Marx	Gummo	Marx	Milton	Actor
Marx	Harpo	Marx	Adolph	Actor
Marx	Zeppo	Marx	Herbert	Actor
Masaccio	di Simone Guidi	de Giovanni	Tommaso	Florentine painter
Matthau	Walter	Matuschanskavasky	Walter	Actor
Maxwell	Robert	Hoch	Jan Ludvik	Businessman
Maynard	Bill	William	Walter	Actor
McBain	Ed	Hunter	Evan	Writer
Meatloaf		Aday	Marvin Lee	Singer
Meg	Mystic	Lake	Margaret	TV personality
Meir	Golda	Mabovitch	Golda	Israeli PM
Melba	Dame Nellie	Armstrong, née Mitchell	Helen Porter	Opera singer
Melbourne	Viscount	Lamb	William	British prime minister
Melmoth	Sebastian	Wilde	Oscar	Author
Mendelssohn	Felix	Mendelssohn -Bartholdy	Felix	Composer
Menken	Adah Isaacs	Fuertes	Dolores Adios	American actress/poet
Mennin	Peter	Mennini	Peter	Musician
Mercury	Freddie	Bulsara	Frederick	Singer
Meredith	Burgess	Burgess	George	Actor
Merlin		Tennyson	Alfred Lord	Poet
Merton	Mrs	Hook/Aherne	Caroline	Comedienne
Merton	Paul	Martin	Paul	Comedian
Mervyn	William	Pickwoad	William	Actor
Michael	George	Panayiotou	Georgios	Vocalist/composer
Michael of Kent	Princess	von Reibnitz	Marie	Princess
Milland	Ray	Truscott-Jones	Reginald	Actor
Milligan	Spike	Milligan	Terence Alan	Comedian/writer
Mistinguett		Bourgeois	Jeanne Marie	French dancer
Mitchell	Cameron	Mizell	George	Actor
Mitchell	Guy	Cernick	Al	Singer
Mitchell	Joni	Anderson	Roberta Joan	Singer/composer
Moliére		Poquelin	Jean-Baptiste	Playwright
Molotov	Vyacheslav Mikhaylovich	Skryabin	Vyacheslav Mikhaylovich	Russian statesman
Monroe	Marilyn	Baker	Norma Jean	Actress
Montand	Yves	Levy	Ivo	Actor
Montez	Lola	Gilbert	Maria Eliza (Délores)	American dancer
Montgomery	George	Letz	George	Actor
Moody	Ron	Moodnick	Ronald	Actor
Moore	Archibald	Wright	Archibald	Boxer
Moore	Demi	Guynes	Demi	Actress
Morecambe	Eric	Bartholomew	John Eric	Comedian
Morgan	Frank	Wupperman	Frank	Actor
Morrison	Van	Morrison	George Ivan	Singer/composer
Moses	Grandma	Robertson	Anna Mary	Artist
Mostel	Zero	Mostel	Samuel Joel	Actor
Mycroft		Gillis	Ian	'Brain of Britain'
Nagasaki	Kendo	Thornley	Peter	Professional wrestler
Naismith	Laurence	Johnson	Lawrence	Actor
Neagle	Anna	Robertson	Marjorie	Actress
Negri	Pola	Chalupek	Appolonia	Actress

FAMOUS PEOPLE

Assumed Name		Original Name		
Nelson	Baby Face	Gillis	Lester	*Gangster*
Nero		Ahenobarbus	Lucius Domitius	*Roman emperor*
Nero	Franco	Spartanero	Franco	*Actor*
Newcastle	Duke of	Pelham-Holles	Thomas	*British Prime Minister*
Nichols	Mike	Peschkowsky	Michael	*American film director*
Nicole		Skurnick	Estelle	*'Renault Clio' star of advert*
Nolde	Emil	Hansen	Emil	*German painter*
Novarre	Ramon	Samaniegos	Ramon	*Actor*
Novello	Ivor	Davies	David Ivor	*Composer*
Numan	Gary	Webb	Gary	*Vocalist/composer*
Oakley	Annie	Mozee	Phoebe	*Frontierswoman*
Oberon	Merle	Thompson	Estelle	*Actress*
O'Brien	Flann	O'Nolan	Brian	*Irish writer*
O'Brien	Hugh	Krampke	Hugh	*Actor*
Ochre	Captain	Frazier	Richard	*Fictional TV character*
O'Connor	Frank	O'Donovan	Michael	*Irish writer*
Offenbach	Jacques	Eberst	Jakob	*Composer*
O'Hara	Maureen	Fitzsimmons	Maureen	*Actress*
O'Henry		Porter	William Sydney	*Author*
Ormandy	Eugene	Blau	Jenö	*Musician*
Orwell	George	Blair	Eric Arthur	*Author*
O'Sullivan	Gilbert	O'Sullivan	Raymond	*Singer*
Ouida		Ramée, de la	Marie Louise	*English singer*
Palance	Jack	Palaniuk	Walter	*Actor*
Pallo	Jackie	Gutteridge	John	*Wrestler*
Palmer	Lilli	Peiser	Lilli	*Actress*
Panther		Riley	Helena	*TV Gladiator*
Parker	Dorothy	Rothschild	Dorothy	*Author*
Parker	Cecil	Schwabe	Cecil	*Actor*
Parley	Peter	Goodrich	Samuel	*US publisher*
Parmigianino	Il	Mazzola	Girolamo Francesco Maria	*Italian painter*
Pastry	Mr	Hearne	Richard	*Actor*
Patterson	Sir Les	Humphries	Barry	*Comedian*
Peel	John	Ravenscroft	John	*Disc jockey*
Peerce	Jan	Perelmuth	Jacob Pincus	*Musician*
Pele		do Nascimento	Edson Arantes Do	*Footballer*
Pellow	Marti	McLoughlin	Mark	*Singer*
Penguin		Cobblepot	Oswald	*Batman character*
Pennis	Dennis	Kaye	Paul	*Actor and comedian*
Perkins	Elizabeth	Pisperikos	Elizabeth	*Actress*
Phiz		Browne	Hablot Knight	*Illustrator*
Phoenix		Young	Sandy	*Gladiator*
Piaf	Edith	Gassion	Edith	*Singer*
Pickford	Mary	Smith	Gladys Mary	*Actress*
Pindar	Peter	Wolcot	John	*Satirist*
Pop	Iggy	Osterberg	James Jewel	*Singer*
Porcupine	Peter	Cobbett	William	*Writer*
Powers	Stefanie	Federkiewicz	Stefania	*Actress*
Preston	Robert	Meservey	Robert	*Actor*
Price	Dennis	Rose-Price	Dennistoun Franklyn	*Actor*
Prince		Nelson	Prince Rogers	*Singer and composer*
Proby	PJ	Smith	James Marcus	*Singer*
Pussyfoot		Johnson	William Eugene	*US reformer*
Q		Quiller-Couch	Arthur	*Author and onthologist*
Queen	Ellery	Dannay	Frederick	*Joint authors*
		Lee	Manfred B	
Quinn	Anthony	Oaxaca	Rudolph	*US Actor*
Rafferty	Chips	Goffage	John	*Entertainer*
Raft	George	Ranft	George	*Actor*
Randall	Tony	Rosenberg	Leonard	*Actor*
Randi	Amazing	Zwinge	James Randall	*Magician*
Ray	Ted	Olden	Charles	*Comedian*
Rebel		Stoute	Jenny	*TV Gladiator*
Red Cloud		Iuta	Mahpiua	*(Sioux) chief*
Reed	Lou	Firbank	Louis	*Singer and composer*
Reeves	Vic	Moir	Jim	*Comedian*
Regiomontanus		Müller	Johannes	*German mathematician*

Assumed Name		Original Name		
Remarque	Erich Maria	Kramer	Erich Maria	Author
Rendell	Ruth	Grasemann	Ruth	Crime novellist
Rethberg	Elisabeth	Sättler	Elisabeth	Musician
Richard	Cliff	Webb	Harold	Singer
Richard	Little	Penniman	Richard Wayne	Singer
Richards	Frank	Hamilton	Charles	Author
Rivers	Joan	Molinsky	Joan	Comedienne
Robbins	Harold	Rubin	Harold	Author
Robin		Grayson	Dick	Comics character
Robinson	Edward G	Goldenberg	Emmanuel	Actor
Robinson	Ralph	George III		British king (in Garden Periodicals)
Robinson	Sugar Ray	Smith	Walker	Boxer
Rocket		Richards	Pauline	TV Gladiator
Rogers	Ginger	McMath	Virginia	Actress and dancer
Rogers	Roy	Slye	Leonard	Actor
Rogers	Will	Adair	William Penn	US actor
Rohmer	Sax	Ward	Arthur Sarsfield	Author
Rooney	Mickey	Yule Jnr	Joseph	Actor
Rose	Axl	Bailey	William	Singer
Rose Lee	Gypsy	Hovick	Rose Louise	Entertainer
Ross	Aircraftsman John Hume	Lawrence	Thomas Edward	Soldier and author
Ross	Barnaby	Dannay	Frederick	Joint authors
		Lee	Manfred B	
Rotten	Johnny	Lydon	John	Singer
Rowland	Tiny	Fuhrhop	Roland	Businessman
Rowlands	John	Stanley	Henry Morton	Explorer/journalist
Roy	Rob	McGregor	Robert	Scottish outlaw
Ruffo	Titta	Titta	Ruffo	Baritone
Russell	Theresa	Paup	Theresa	Actress
Rutherford	Mark	White	William Hale	Writer
Ryder	Winona	Horowitz	Winona	Actress
Sabrina		Sykes	Norma	Model
Sade		Adu	Helen Folasade	Singer
Sagan	Françoise	Quoirez	Françoise	Novelist
Saint-John Perse	Léger	Marle René	Alexis Saint-Léger	French poet
Saint-Laurent	Yves	Mathieu	Henri Donat	French designer
Saki		Monro	Hector Hugh	Writer
Samaroff	Olga	Hickenlooper	Lucie	Musician
Sand	George	Dudevant	Amondine Lucie Dupin	Writer
Sapper		McNeile	Herman Cyril	Author
Sappho		de Scudéry	Madeleine	French novelist
Saracen		Lewis	Mike	TV Gladiator
Sarandon	Susan	Tomaling	Susan	Actress
Savage	Lily	O'Grady	Paul	Entertainer
Saxon	John	Orrico	Carmen	Actor
Scarlet	Captain	Metcalfe	Paul	Animated TV character
Schultz	Dutch	Flegenheimer	Arthur	Gangster
Scott	Randolph	Crane	Randolph	Actor
Seal		Samuel	Henry	Singer
Selassie	Hailie	Makonnen	Ras Tafari	Ethiopian emperor
Sennett	Mack	Sinnott	Michael	Film producer
Sensible	Captain	Burns	Ray	Singer
Dr Seuss		Geisel	Theodore Seuss	Author
Seymour	Jane	Frankenberg	Joyce	Actress
Shadow		King	Jefferson	TV Gladiator
Shannon	Del	Westover	Charles	Singer
Sharif	Omar	Shalhoub	Michael	Actor
Shaw	Sandie	Goodrich	Sandra	Singer
Shaw	TE	Lawrence	Thomas Edward	Soldier and author (in Royal Tank Corps)
Sheen	Martin	Estevez	Ramon	Actor
Shipton	Mother	Southill/Southiel	Ursula	Prophetess
Shirley	Anne	O'Day	Dawn	Actress
Shute	Neville	Norway	Neville	Author
Shuttleworth	John	Fellows	Graham	Singer and songwriter
Signoret	Simone	Kaminker	Henriette Charlotte	Actress
Sills	Beverly	Silverman	Belle	Musician

Assumed Name		Original Name		
Silverheels	Jay	Smith	Harold J	Actor
Simone	Nina	Wayman	Eunice	Singer
Sioux	Siouxsie	Dallion	Susan	Singer
Siren		Paton	Alison	TV Gladiator
Sitting Bull		Iyotanka	Tatanka	Sioux Hunkpapa chief
Slater	Christian	Hawkins	Christian	Actor
Soul	David	Solberg	David	Actor
Springfield	Dusty	O'Brien	Mary	Singer
Stack	Robert	Modini	Robert	Actor
Staff	Kathy	Higginbottom	Minnie	Actress
Stalin	Joseph	Dzhugashvili	Iosif Vissarionovich	Russian leader
Stanislavsky		Alexeyev Sergeivitch	Konstantin	Actor
Stanley	Henry Morton	Rowlands	John	Explorer
Stanwyck	Barbara	Stevens	Ruby	Actress
Stardust	Alvin	Jewry	Bernard	Singer
Starr	Edwin	Hatcher	Charles	Singer
Starr	Ringo	Starkey	Richard	Drummer and composer
Statto		Loughran	Angus	TV soccer pundit
Steele	Tommy	Hicks	Thomas	Entertainer
Stendhal		Beyle	Marie-Henri	Author
Stepniak		Kravchinski	Sergei Mikhailovich	Russian revolutionary
Stevens	Cat	Georgiou	Stephen	Singer
Stevens	Connie	Ingolia	Concetta	Actress
Stewart	Ed	Mainwaring	Edward Stewart	Disc jockey
Stevens	Inger	Stengland	Inger	Actress
Stevens	Shakin'	Barrett	Michael	Singer
Sting		Sumner	Gordon	Vocalist/and musician
Stone	Irving	Tennenbaum	Irving	US novelist
Stoppard	Miriam	Stern	Miriam	Broadcaster
Stoppard	Tom	Straussler	Thomas	Dramatist
Stratas	Teresa	Strataki	Anastasia	Soprano
Sturges	Preston	Biden	Edmund Preston	Writer and director
Suggs		McPherson	Graham	Singer (Madness)
Sumac	Yma	Chavarri	Emperatriz	Musician
Summer	Donna	Gaines	Donna Andrea	Singer
Summers	Ann	Gold	Jacqueline	Businesswoman
Sundance Kid		Longabaugh	Henry	Outlaw
Swanson	Gloria	Svensson	Gloria	Actress
Sylva	Carmen	Elizabeth	of Romania	Queen of Romania
T	T	Tureaud	Lawrence	Actor
Tanfucio	Neri	Fucini	Renato	Italian writer
Tati	Jacques	Tatischeff	Jacques	Actor
Tauber	Richard	Seiffert	Ernst	Austrian tenor
Taylor	Elizabeth	Coles	Elizabeth	Novelist
Taylor	Robert	Brough	Spangler	Actor
Tenzin Gyatso		Tsering	Lhamo Thondup	14th Dalai Lama
Theresa	Mother	Bojaxhiu	Agnes Gonxha	Roman Catholic nun
Thomas	Terry	Stevens	Terry	Comedy actor
Thumb	Tom	Stratton	Charles	Circus performer
Tich	Little	Relph	Harry	Comedian
Tilley	Vesta	Powles	Matilda Alice	Male impersonator
Tim	Tiny	Khaury	Herbert	Singer
Tintoretto		Robusti	Jacopo	Artist
Titmarsh	Michael Angelo	Thackeray	William Makepeace	Author
Tito		Broz	Josip	Yugoslav leader
Todd	Mike	Goldenburger	Avron	Producer
Trog		Fawkes	Walter Ernest	Cartoonist and clarinetist
Trotsky	Leon	Bronstein	Lev Davidovitch	Russian revolutionary
Tucker	Richard	Ticker	Reuben	Singer
Tucker	Sophie	Abruza	Sophie	Music hall singer
Tuesday	Gayle	Gilhooly	Brenda	Comedienne
Turner	Tina	Bullock	Annie Mae	Singer
Twain	Mark	Clemens	Samuel Langhorne	Author
Twiggy		Hornby	Leslie	Model/actress
Twitty	Conway	Jenkins	Harold Lloyd	Singer
Tyler	Bonnie	Sullivan	Gaynor	Singer

Assumed Name		Original Name		
Uncle Remus		Harris	Joel Chandler	Author
Vadim	Roger	Plemiannikov	Roger Vadim	Film director
Valens	Ritchie	Valenzuela	Ritchie	Singer
Valentino	Rudolph	D'Antonguolla	Rudolpho	Actor
Valli	Frankie	Castellucio	Frank	Singer
Van Damme	Jean-Claude	Van Varenberg	Jean-Claude	Actor
Vaughan	Frankie	Abelsohn	Frank	Singer
Vaughan	Peter	Ohm	Peter	Actor
Vee	Bobby	Velline	Robert Thomas	Singer
Verdy	Violette	Guillerm	Nelly	French dancer
Veronese	Paolo	Caliari	Paolo	Venetian painter
Vicious	Sid	Ritchie	John	Singer
Villa	Pancho	Arango	Doroteo	Mexican patriot
Villeneuve	Justin	Davies	Nigel	Hair stylist
Vincent	Gene	Craddock	Eugene Vincent	Singer
Vine	Barbara	Rendell	Ruth	novelist
Vivekananda	Swami	Dutt	Narendranath	Hindu missionary
Voltaire		Arouet	François-Marie	Philosopher
Wall	Max	Lorimer	Maxwell George	Actor and comedian
Ward	Artemus	Browne	Charles Farrar	Writer and humorist
Warlock	Peter	Heseltine	Philip Arnold	Composer
Warner	Jack	Waters	Jack	Actor
Warner	Jack Leonard	Eichelbaum	Jack Leonard	Film mogul
Warrior		Aherne	Michael	TV Gladiator
Warwick	Richard	Winter	Richard	Actor
Waters	Muddy	Morganfield	McKinley	Singer
Wayne	John	Morrison	Marion	Actor
Weathercock	Janus	Wainewright	Thomas Griffiths	Art critic and murderer
Webb	Clifton	Hollenbeck	Webb Parmalee	Actor
Welch	Bruce	Cripps	Bruce	Guitarist
Welch	Raquel	Tejada	Raquel	Actress
Wellthorpe	Edna	Orton	Joe	Dramatist (as fictional letter writer)
West	Nigel	Allason	Rupert	MP and author
West	Rebecca	Fairfield	Cicely Isabel	Author
Westmacott	Mary	Christie	Agatha	Author (as romantic novelist)
Wharton	Edith	Jones	Edith	Author
White	Colonel	Gray	Charles	fictional TV character
Widow		Sisson	Richard	Musical act 'Kit and the Widow'
Wilde	Kim	Smith	Kim	Singer
Wilde	Marty	Smith	Reginald	Singer
Wilder	Gene	Silberman	Jerome	Actor
Windsor	Barbara	Deeks	Barbara	Actress
Winters	Bernie	Weinstein	Bernie	Comedian
Winters	Shelley	Schrift	Shirley	Actress
Wise	Ernie	Wiseman	Ernest	Comedian
Wolf	Howling	Burnett	Chester Arthur	Singer and composer
Wonder	Stevie	Judkins	Steveland	Singer and composer
Wood	Mrs Henry	Price	Ellen	English novelist
Wood	Natalie	Gurdin	Natasha	Actress
Worth	Harry	Illingworth	Harry	Comedian
Wylie	Gerald	Barker	Ronnie	Writer
Wyman	Bill	Perks	William	Musician
Wyman	Jane	Faulks	Sarah Jane	Actress
Wymark	Patrick	Cheeseman	Patrick	Actor
Wynette	Tammy	Pugh	Wynette	Singer
Wyngarde	Peter	Goldbert	Cyril Louis	Actor
X	Malcolm	Little	Malcolm	Civil rights leader
Yates	Dornford	Mercer	Cecil William	Novelist
York	Michael	Johnson	Mike	Actor
York	Susannah	Fletcher	Susannah	Actress
Youens	Bernard	Popley	Bernard	Actor
Young	Gig	Barr	Byron	Actor
Young	Jimmy	Young	Leslie Ronald	Broadcaster
Zadora	Pia	Schipani	Pia	Actress

FAMOUS PEOPLE

NB: The area of pseudonyms is a veritable minefield for misinformation and errors and although an attempt has been made to verify as many entries as possible it is inevitable that there will be doubt relating to some entries. To give an example of the intricacies that make an infallible list almost impossible to compile, many sources refer to

Marlene Dietrich's original name as Von Losch, this is only partly true, as in fact her original name was Dietrich and only changed to von Losch when her mother remarried after the death of her father.

The format of the tables are basically Surnames followed by Christian names but where the person is titled or is known by just a single name, then the familiar name is in the left hand box. This is not meant to be a fully comprehensive listing as it would be possible to fill this whole book with pseudonyms and pen-names, but it is hoped that all the more common ones and a few less known but interesting ones are present. There is a small overlap between this section and the nicknames section as some of the entries warrant inclusion in both, as a nickname is sometimes adopted as the most famous title of a person.

Relationships

NB: Relations appear in alphabetical order within each category.
The relationship given is that of the second column to the first.

Arthur Conan Doyle	EW Hornung	*Brother-in-law*
Stanley Baldwin	Rudyard Kipling	*Cousin*
Richard Briers	Terry-Thomas	*Cousin*
Elizabeth I	Mary Queen of Scots	*Cousin*
King George V	Kaiser Wilhelm II	*Cousin*
Christopher Lee	Ian Fleming	*Cousin*
Patrick McNee	David Niven	*Cousin*
Ginger Rogers	Rita Hayworth	*Cousin*
Franklin D Roosevelt	Theodore Roosevelt	*5th cousin*
Herbert H Asquith	Violet Bonham-Carter	*Daughter*
Ingrid Bergman	Isabella Rossellini	*Daughter*
Vera Brittain	Shirley Williams	*Daughter*
William Jennings Bryan	Ruth Rohde	*Daughter*
Debbie Reynolds and Eddie Fisher	Carrie Fisher	*Daughter*
Judy Garland	Lorna Luft	*Daughter*
	Liza Minnelli	*Daughter*
Jeremy Hawk	Belinda Lang	*Daughter*
Tippi Hedren	Melanie Griffith	*Daughter*
Helios & Perse	Circe	*Daughter*
Roger Kemble	Sarah Siddons	*Daughter*
King Agenor and Queen Telephassa	Europa	*Daughter*
King Cepheus and Queen Cassiopeia	Andromeda	*Daughter*
King Priam and Queen Hecuba	Cassandra	*Daughter*
Phillida Law	Sophie Thompson	*Daughter*
	Emma Thompson	*Daughter*
Lord Longford	Lady Antonia Fraser	*Daughter*
Mary of Guise and James V	Mary Queen of Scots	*Daughter*
Arthur Miller	Rebecca Miller	*Daughter*
Muhammad	Fatima	*Daughter*
Thomas More	Margaret Roper	*Daughter*
Jawaharlal Nehru	Indira Gandhi	*Daughter*
Nanette Newman	Emma Forbes	*Daughter*
Tsar Nicholas II	Anastasia	*Daughter*
Oedipus and Jocasta	Antigone	*Daughter*
Maureen O'Sullivan	Mia Farrow	*Daughter*
Jon Voight	Angelina Jolie	*Daughter*
Zeus and Leda	Helen and Clytemnestra	*Daughters*
Zeus and Metis	Athene	*Daughter*
Zeus and Themis	Clotho (one of the 3 Fates)	*Daughter*
Emmeline Pankhurst	Christabel and Sylvia	*Daughters*
Sigmund Freud	Clement and Lucian	*Grandsons*
Genghis Khan	Kublai Khan	*Grandson*
Herbert Beerbohm Tree	Oliver Reed	*Grandson*
Queen Victoria	Queen Elizabeth II	*Great-great-granddaughter*
Queen Victoria	Duke of Edinburgh	*Great-great-grandson*
Bonnie Bedelia	Macaulay Culkin	*Nephew*
Francis Ford Coppola	Nicolas Cage	*Nephew*
Lord Salisbury	Arthur Balfour	*Nephew*
Carol Reed	Oliver Reed	*Nephew*
Ellen Terry	John Gielgud	*Nephew*
Circe	Medea	*Niece*
Echidne and Typhon	Cerberus, Chimaera, Hydra	*Offspring*

Poseidon and Medusa	Pegasus	*Offspring*
Dana Andrews	Steve Forrest	*Sibling*
Thomas Arne	Susanna Cibber	*Sibling*
Balarama	Krishna	*Sibling*
Warren Beatty	Shirley Maclaine	*Sibling*
David Broome	Liz Edgar	*Sibling*
Duggie Brown	Lynn Perrie	*Sibling*
Keith Chegwin	Janice Long	*Sibling*
Catherine Deneuve	Françoise Dorléac	*Sibling*
Adila Fachiri (violinist)	Jelly Arányi (violinist)	*Sibling*
Marty Feldman	Fenella Fielding	*Sibling*
Joan Fontaine	Olivia de Havilland	*Sibling*
Lady Antonia Fraser	Rachel Billington	*Sibling*
Crystal Gayle	Loretta Lynn	*Sibling*
Graham Greene	Hugh Carleton Greene	*Sibling*
Hannibal	Hasdrubal	*Sibling*
Eden Kane	Peter and Robin Sarstedt	*Siblings*
John Kemble	Sarah Siddons	*Sibling*
Jimmy Logan	Annie Ross	*Sibling*
Lord Rothermere	Lord Northcliffe	*Sibling*
Paul McCartney	Mike McGear	*Sibling*
John Mills	Annette Mills	*Sibling*
Liza Minnelli	Lorna Luft	*Sibling*
River Phoenix	Leaf, Rainbow, Summer, Liberty	*Siblings*
Brian Rix	Sheila Mercier	*Sibling*
Kate Robbins	Ted Robbins	*Sibling*
Eric Roberts	Julia Roberts	*Sibling*
Georhe Sanders	Tom Conway	*Sibling*
Julia Sawalha	Nadia Sawalha	*Sibling*
Talia Shire	Francis Ford Coppola	*Sibling*
Tanita Tikaram	Ramon Tikaram	*Sibling*
Jack Warner	Ethel and Doris Waters	*Siblings*
Virginia Woolf	Vanessa Bell	*Sibling*
Aeacus and Endeis	Peleus	*Son*
Anu and Ki	Enki and Enlil	*Sons*
Ares and Aphrodite	Eros	*Son*
Atreus and Aerope	Agamemnon	*Son*
David Carradine and Barbara Hershey	Frêe (changed to Tom)	*Son*
Charles Martel	Pepin the Short	*Son*
Cleopatra and Julius Caesar	Caesarion (Ptolemy XV)	*Son*
Cecil Day-Lewis	Daniel Day-Lewis	*Son*
Elizabeth and Zacharias	John the Baptist	*Son*
Erebos and Nyx	Charon	*Son*
Eric the Red	Leif Eriksson	*Son*
Indira Gandhi	Rajiv Gandhi	*Son*
Hamilcar	Hannibal	*Son*
Helios and Clymene	Phaethon	*Son*
Iapetus and Clymene	Prometheus, Atlas, Epimetheus, Menoetius	*Sons*
Jenny Jerome	Winston Churchill	*Son*
Jupiter and Latona	Apollo	*Son*
Rosa Kaufman (Pianist)	Boris Pasternak	*Son*
King Agenor and Queen Telephassa	Cadmus	*Son*
King Glaucus and Queen Eurynome	Bellerophon	*Son*
King Laius and Queen Jocasta	Oedipus	*Son*
Mary Martin	Larry Hagman	*Son*
Mary Queen of Scots	James VI (Scotland) I (England)	*Son*
Osiris and Nephthys	Anubis	*Son*
Norrie Paramour	John Paramour (golf director)	*Son*
Peleus and Thetis	Achilles	*Son*
Pepin the Short	Charlemagne	*Son*
Priam and Hecuba of Troy	Paris	*Son*
Martin Sheen	Emilio Estevez and Charlie Sheen	*Sons*
Ellen Terry and EW Godwin	Edward Gordon Craig	*Son*
Suzanne Valadon	Maurice Utrillo	*Son*
Zebedee	St John	*Son*
Zeus and Danaë	Perseus	*Son*
Zeus and Leda	Castor, Polydeuces	*Sons*
Zeus and Leto	Apollo	*Son*
De Mille, Cecil B	Anthony Quinn	*Son-in-law*

FAMOUS PEOPLE

Franz Liszt	Richard Wagner	*Son-in-law*
Thomas Mann	WH Auden	*Son-in-law*
Arthur Miller	Daniel Day Lewis	*Son-in-law*
Eugene O'Neill	Charlie Chaplin	*Son-in-law*
Peter Vaughan	Gregor Fisher	*Son-in-law*

aba   Loose gown worn in the Muslim world.

agal   fillet of twp or three cords used to fasten a keffiyeh on the head.

Agnès B   Born Agnès Troublé in Versailles, France, 1941, she worked as a junior editor on *Elle* magazine before opening her first boutique. Her style is characterised by precise tailoring, simple subdued colours, usually black, natural materials and casual looks. In 1987 she launched her 'Le B' perfume range and a maternity collection.

aigrette   Spray of gems worn on the head.

Alaia, Azzedine   Tunisian designer who was a leading light throughout the 1980s but is experiencing a revival with his merger with Prada.

alb   Long, white linen vestment with sleeves, usually worn by priests.

alpargata   Light canvas shoe with a plaited fibre sole; an espadrille.

amice   Rectangular piece of white linen worn by priests around the neck and shoulders under the alb, or formerly, on the head. Also a furred hood with long ends hanging down in front.

Armani, Giorgio   Italian fashion designer based in Milan and New York. Armani opened his first fashion house in 1974 and, although well respected within his industry, rose to fame after dressing Richard Gere in the 1980 film *American Gigolo*.

Ashley, Laura   Born in Merthyr Tydfil, South Wales (1925–85) as Laura Mountney. Married Bernard Ashley in 1949 and started a business manufacturing furnishing materials and wallpaper with patterns based upon document sources mainly from the 19th century. After giving up work to start a family she experimented with designing and making clothes, and this transformed the business into an international chain of boutiques, selling clothes, furnishing fabrics and wallpapers.

astrakhan wool   Obtained from the Karakul breed of sheep.

babouche   Turkish or oriental heelless slipper.

babushka   Headscarf tied under the chin and worn by Russian peasant women.

Badgley Mischka   American designers Mark Badgley and James Mischka. The duo are best known for their stellar beaded creations and 'aged look'. Their material is made in Italy and embroidered in Bombay, India.

balbriggan   Knitted, unbleached cotton fabric, from which underwear is often made.

baldric   Wide silk sash or leather belt worn over the opposite shoulder to the hip, for carrying a sword.

Balenciaga, Cristobal   Spanish fashion designer (1895–1972) opened the House of Balenciaga in Paris, 1937, and retired in 1968.

Balmain, Pierre   French fashion designer (1914–82) famous for his elegant simplicity. Immortalised by Peter Sarstedt in 'Where do you go to my lovely'.

Balmoral   Can be a laced walking shoe, a woollen petticoat, a Scottish brimless hat, traditionally made of dark blue wool with a cockade and plume, a cloak, a jacket or mantle – all these styles set by Queen Victoria and Prince Albert in the 1850s and 60s.

bandanna   Square of silk or cotton with spotted pattern, tied round the head or neck.

Banks, Jeff   Born in Wales, 1943, became widely known in the mid 70s when he launched the 'Warehouse' chain. Presenter of the first dedicated television fashion programme, *The Clothes Show*.

banyan   Loose-fitting shirt or jacket originally worn in India.

batiste   Fine plain-weave cotton or linen fabric, used for shirts and dresses.

batwing sleeve   Sleeve of a garment with a deep armhole and tight wrist.

bauchle   General term for an old, worn shoe.

Bebe   Top international brand name for designer shoes as in the name of their stores.

Benetton   Fashion empire based in Treviso, Italy and identified with its sponsorship of rugby, basketball and volleyball but especially Formula One racing team.

Biba founder   Barbara Hulanicki.

biggin   Plain, close-fitting cap, often tied under the chin, popular in 16th and 17th centuries based on coif-like caps worn by the Béguires lay sisters.

bijouterie   Costume jewellery or trinkets, particularly finger-rings, from which the name derives.

bikini designer   Louis Réard.

Bikkembergs, Dirk   Born in Cologne, Germany, 1959, of Belgian extraction, first came to prominence as a shoe designer before establishing himself as a top ready-to-wear designer. Along with Ann Demeulemeester, Dirk Van Saene, Walter Van Beirendonck, Dries Van Noten, and Martin Margiela, one of the so-called Anvers 'Group of Six'.

billycock   Any of several round-crowned brimmed hats of felt, named after William Coke, for whom it was first made in the 19th century.

biretta   Stiff clerical cap with either three or four upright pieces projecting outwards from the centre to the edge, coloured black for priests, purple for bishops, red for cardinals and white for certain members of religious orders.

Blahnik, Manolo   Born in the Canary Islands of a Spanish mother and Czech father, Blahnik is a British-based designer of fashion shoes.

Bloomers   Named after, and designed by Amelia Jenks Bloomer (1818–94), a New York campaigner for temperance and women's rights. Bloomers were originally the full-length Turkish trousers worn under a skirt in the 1850s, but evolved firstly into a knickerbock style, and made popular by lady cyclists in the 1890s, and subsequently into any loose-fitting ladies baggy undergarments.

boa   Woman's long round scarf, usually of feathers or fur.

bodkin   Blunt, large-eyed needle used for drawing tape through openwork, also a pin used in ancient times to fasten women's hair.

Body Shop founder   Anita Roddick.

bolero   Short jacket, just reaching the waist, as worn by men in Spain; also a woman's short, open jacket, with or without sleeves.

bonnet rouge   Red cap worn by ardent supporters of the French Revolution.

bowler   Hard felt hat with a rounded crown and a narrow curled brim, named after William Bowler in the US who designed it in 1850; in the US, a derby.

breeks   Scottish name for breeches.

British warm   Army officer's short, thick overcoat.

Brogue (1)   Rough shoe of untanned hide, formerly worn in Ireland but now having ornamental perforated bands and worn throughout the world.

brogue (2)   Waterproof leggings with feet, used by anglers.

buckram   Originally a fine cotton or linen fabric stiffened with size, later used in lining or stiffening clothes as well as bookbinding.

Bui, Barbara   French fashion designer best known for her clean lines and offbeat femininity that combines various cultural and ethnic influences.Daughter of a French mother and Vietnamese father, Bui first came to prominence when opening her 'Kabuki' boutique in the 1980s with her actor husband William Halimi. In 1998 she started her 'BB Initials' line and more recently has started a line in designer shoes.

buibui   Piece of black cloth worn as a shawl by Muslim women, especially on the North African coast.

bumfreezer   Short jacket ; also a slang name for an Eton jacket.

burberry   Drapery business opened in Basingstoke, Hampshire, England, in 1865 by 21-year old Thomas Burberry, producing waterproof garbardine raincoats. Since 1988 has enjoyed success with its youthful collections.

burlap   Coarse fabric woven from jute or hemp.

burnous   Arab or Moorish hooded cloak, now worn as a fashion accessory in the Western world.

busby   Tall, fur helmet with a bag hanging from the top to the right side as worn by certain soldiers, usually hussars; it is also another name for a bearskin.

buskin   Originally, a thick-soled boot worn by tragic actors in ancient Athenian theatre; now a half-boot.

bustle   Pad or frame worn to puff out the top of a woman's skirt at the back.

Busuuti   Long garment with short sleeves and square neckline, as worn by Ugandan women.

cagoule   Thin-hooded outer jacket, especially one that is windproof and waterproof, and worn by mountaineers and others following outdoor pursuits.

calash (also caléche)   Woman's folding, hooped hood, worn in 18th century.

calico   White or unbleached cotton fabric with no printed design (originally from 'Calicut, on the Malabar coast,' a town in India).

calotte   Skullcap worn by Roman Catholic clergy.

cambric   Originally a fine white linen fabric of the late Tudor and early Stuart period and imported from the French town of Cambrai. The lightness of the material made it popular as a decorative accompaniment to dress as ruffs, cuffs, bands and handkerchiefs. Modern cambric is made from high-quality American or Egyptian cotton and is identified with good-quality underwear.

camisole   Woman's under-bodice with shoulder straps, originally designed as a cover for a corset.

capote   Long cloak or soldier's coat, usually with a hood; also a kind of 19th-century bonnet.

capuchin   Woman's cloak and hood resembling the dress of a Capuchin friar.

casque   Piece of armour to cover the head; a helmet.

castor   Hat made of beaver fur.

Cerruti   Founded in 1881 in Biella, Milan, by Antonio Cerruti as a fabric mill company, Cerruti became fashionable when Nino Cerruti, grandson of the founder developed the business into a ready-to-wear fashion house in 1957 when he opened 'Hitman' in Milan. In 1967 Nino opened 'Cerruti 1881', a men's couture house in the centre of Paris and soon established an international reputation. In 1976 Cerruti developed a women's ready-to-wear market and is now established in all aspects of haute couture.

cestus (1)   Pugilist's gauntlet of bull's hide loaded or studded with metal.

cestus (2)   Girdle, named after the girdle of Aphrodite.

chador/chuddar   Large shawl or veil worn by Muslim or Hindu women that covers them from head to foot.

Chanel, Coco   French fashion designer (1883–1971), worked as a milliner until 1912 and following service as a nurse during World War I, opened a couture house in Paris. She revolutionised women's fashions during the 1920s, her designs including the 'chemise' dress, the collarless cardigan jacket, and the 'little black dress'. Her designer perfume Chanel No. 5 became the ultimate status symbol. Chanel retired in 1938 but made a successful comeback in 1954 and her innovations such as the vogue for costume jewellery and the evening scarf have maintained their popularity.

Ch'ao-fu   Pre-modern chinese man's robe with kimono-style upper body with long, close-fitting sleeves that terminated in the horse-hoof cuff introduced by the Manchus, and a closely-fitted neckband over which was worn a detached collar with wing-like tips that extended over the shoulders. The lower body consisted of a full, pleated skirt with a banded waist. Colours were dependent on rank.

chaplet   Ornamental wreath of flowers or beads worn on the head. Also a precious metal circlet, possibly set with gems.

chaps   protective leather trousers worn by American cowboys. The name comes from the Mexican 'chaparajos'.

chasuble   Long, sleeveless outer vestment worn by a priest when celebrating Mass.

chemise   Woman's loose-fitting undergarment or dress hanging straight from the shoulders.

cheongsam   Woman's garment with high neck and slit skirt, worn in China.

chiffon (1)   Light, diaphanous, plain-woven fabric of silk or nylon.

chiffon (2)   Trimmings or other adornments on a woman's dress.

chi-fu   Straight, kimono-sleeved robe, alternatively called lung-p'ao 'dragon robes', worn formally by both sexes in China under the Manchu empire.

chignon   Arrangement of long hair in a roll or knot at the back of the head.

ch'ima   Korean pleated skirt, as worn by women from the 15th century onward.

chintz   Brightly patterned cotton fabric with glazed finish (from a Hindi word that indicates a spatter or stain).

chiton   Long tunic worn in ancient Greece made of wool, linen or cotton.

chlamys   Short woollen cloak worn mostly by men in Ancient Greece.

choga   Loose Afghan garment with long sleeves.

chōgori   Traditional Korean jacket.

choli   Short-sleeved blouse worn under a sari.

clinquant   Imitation gold leaf worn as a fashion accessory.

cloche   Woman's close-fitting bell-shaped hat.

Clothes Show   BBC television programme that ran from 1985–8. Its presenters included Jeff Banks, Brenda Emmanus, Caryn Franklin, Tim Vincent and Margherita Taylor.

Coach   Leading brand name in the field of luxury customised handbags for all occasions.

codpiece   Bagged appendage to the fork of a man's breeches or close-fitting hose.

coif   Close-fitting cap, worn under a veil in the Middle Ages or under a chainmail hood and tied under the chin with strings, now worn only by nuns.

coiffeur   Professional hair-stylist.

coli   Short-sleeved breast-length jacket, usually worn by Muslim women over a ghaghra.

Cook, Emma   British designer who graduated in St Martins and like her classmates Stella McCartney and Alexander McQueen has become a leading light of the fashion industry. Formerly a consultant with Ghost, she is now freelance.

combinations   One-piece woollen undergarment with long sleeves and legs; known in the USA as a union suit.

cote hardie   Medieval close-fitting sleeved tunic, when worn by men long enough to cover the buttocks and belted around the hips; when worn by women, full-length and often unbelted..

cowl   A cap or hood especially on a monk's habit.

Cox, Patrick   Born in Canada, 1963, as a student he designed shoes for Vivian Westwood, Body Map and later for John Galliano. Cox introduced his own label 1987 and his fleurs-de-lis-logo is a sign of elegant fashion and quirky design.

cracowe   Long pointed shoe named after the Polish city of Cracow (Kraków). It is thought that the in 1382 was responsible for the fashion in England.

cravat   A scarf of silk or fine wool, worn round the neck, especially by men. Cravats were popularised by Croats in the French army during the Thirty Years' War and the name is a corruption of Croat.

crinoline   In the 1830s a stiff fabric made of horsehair and cotton or linen thread, used for linings, hats and skirts. Later a petticoat with steel hoops worn under a skirt to make it stand out from the body in a bell-shape.

cuisse   Piece of armour for the front of the thigh.

culottes   Woman's breeches that hang like a skirt but have separate legs.

cymar (also simar, cimarra)   Woman's loose gown, popular in the 17th and 18th centuries.

dalmatica   Wide-sleeved, tunic-like vestment, open at the sides, worn by deacons and bishops. Originally worn by Roman noblemen from the 2nd century on and made of white Dalmatian wool.

damask   Richly figured woven material, originally of silk, with a pattern visible on either side. It originated in Damascus in Syria.

dashiki   Loose brightly coloured shirt worn in West Africa and also in the USA.

décolleté   Low-cut neckline.

deerstalker   Cloth cap, peaked in front and behind, with earflaps that are usually tied up on the top.

De La Renta, Oscar   Born in the Dominican Republic, 1932, but became a naturalised American in the 1960s. He started his own company in 1965 with a reputation for opulent, ornately trimmed clothes, particularly evening dresses. In 1993 he became the first American to design for a French couture house, Pierre Balmain.

denim   Originally serge de nîmes, (named from Nîmes, in France), now a twilled, hard-wearing, cotton fabric used for jeans.

dernier cri   Latest fashion ('last cry').

dhoti   Loincloth worn by male Hindus. The ends are passed between the legs and tucked in at the waist.

Dinnigan, Collette   Born in South Africa to an Irish father and South African mother, she was brought up in New Zealand and after completing her education, emigrated to Australia. She started her own label in 1990 and in 1995 became the first Australian to have a full-scale ready-to-wear parade in Paris.

Dior, Christian   French fashion designer (1905–57). Founded his fashion house in 1945 and achieved worldwide fame with his long-skirted 'New Look' of 1947. His later designs included the 'H' line and the 'A' line.

dirndl   Dress in the style of an Alpine female peasant costume, with close-fitting bodice and full skirt.

Dolce & Gabbana   Founded in Milan in 1982 by Domenico Dolce, a shy bearded Sicilian, and the Venetian Stefano Gabbana. Throughout the 1990s they have expanded their operations into menswear and a popular youth line. A further division of their operations has created a White Line for day-to-day basics, and a Black Line for fantasy goods.

Dolly Varden   Woman's large hat, named after a Dickens' character in Barnaby Rudge; also a flowered dress.

dolman (1)   Long Turkish robe, open in the front and with narrow sleeves.

dolman (2)   Hussar's jacket worn with the sleeves hanging loose.

dolman (3)   Woman's mantle with dolman sleeves.

dolman sleeve   Loose sleeve made in one piece with the body of a coat; it has a wide armhole but a tight wrist.

domino (1)   Large, hooded cloak, worn with an eye mask at a masquerade.

domino (2)   The eye mask worn at masquerades.

Donna Karan   Born in New York as Donna Faske in 1948, she began her career as a designer for Anne Klein and subsequently took control on her death in 1974. Karan eventually began her own company with second husband Stephen Weis.

doublet   Close-fitting body garment with or without sleeves and a short skir, worn by men from the medieval times to the 17th century

duchesse   Soft, heavy kind of satin; also a type of chaise longue.

dundreary   Long sidewhiskers worn without a beard, named after Lord Dundreary, a character in Tom Taylor's comedy (1858).

dungaree   Coarse cotton fabric used chiefly for work clothes from a Hindi word.

durzi   An Indian tailor.

Emanuels   David, born 1952, and Elizabeth, born 1953, launched their label in 1975 but split up in the 1990s. Their most famous creation was the wedding dress of Diana, Princess of Wales. Co-author of Style for all Seasons.

Erotokritos   Cyprus-born, Paris-based fashion designer who launched his own label in 1994 and since his first Paris show in 1996 has built a reputation for chic yet casual clothing.

eton jacket   Waist-length jacket with a V-shaped back, open in the front, formerly worn by pupils of Eton College.

Etro   Italian company that specialises in selling extraordinary crafted, brightly coloured paisley (Etro's hallmark), foulard and brocade ties and vests, as well as finely tailored suits. Gimno Etro is the head of the empire and his three sons, Ippolito, Jacopo and Kean, are directors.

Farhi, Nicole   French-born Algerian designer known for her luxurious and sensual woman's collections. She opened her first store in 1983 as part of a Harvey Nichols and in 1984 opened a boutique in New York. Farhi's home shop is in Clifford Street London.

farjï   Long, gown-like coat with short sleeves, made of wool or cotton (silk is forbidden to men by the Koran), as worn by Muslim priests or high officials.

farthingale   Framework of hoops, or a hooped petticoat, used the 15th to 17th century to extend the skirts of a woman's dress.

Fendi   Established in Rome, 1918, as a leather and fur workshop by Adele Casagrande (d. 1978). The named changed in 1925 when Adele married Edoardo Fendi. Since the death of Edoardo in 1954 the company is being run by his five daughters, Alda, Anna, Carla, Franca and Paola, although a controlling interest is now shared by Prada and Louis Vuitton. Karl Lagerfeld has designed the Fendi fur collection since 1962.

Ferre, Gianfranco   Born in Legnano, Italy, 1944, he formed the Gianfranco Ferre company in 1978 with business partner Franco Mattioli. Unusually, Ferre has maintained a popularity in all aspects of the fashion industry having had successful women's, men's and children's clothing lines and fragrances.

fez   rimless felt or woollen cap, cylindrical in shape, usually red and with a tassel, usually worn by men in Muslim coutries and formerly the national head-dress of Turkey.

fichu   Woman's small triangular shawl of lace for the shoulders and neck. Late 18th to late 19th century.

filibeg / philibeg   Kilt worn by Scottish Highlanders.

finnesko   Boot of reindeer skin with the hair on the outside.

forage cap   Soldier's undress cap.

Ford Tom   Born in Texas 1962, he rose to prominence when taken on as Creative Director of Gucci and immmediately made an impact. Ford is sometimes know as the'It' Boy of the fashion world, or more recently the 'King of Cool'. He has often been targeted by animal rights activists for his refusal to stop using fur in his designs.

Franz Josef   Long sidewhiskers, merging into a moustache, named in honour of the emperor of Austria.

frippery   Originally old or second-hand clothes or tawdry adornment in dress; now means showy.

frog   Decorative braided coat-fastening, originally forming part of military dress, consisting of a spindle-shaped button and a loop and a braided loop that retains it.

furisode   Long-sleeved outer kimono traditionally worn by young, unmarried Japanese girls (married women wearing the short-sleeved kimono known as a kosode).

gabardine   Raincoat made from a smooth, durable, twill-woven cloth of worsted or cotton; also a long loose cloak.

gaberdine   Twill-weave worsted, cotton, or spun-rayon fabric.

Galliano, John   British fashion designer currently head of the Dior fashion empire.

galligaskins   Loose, wide breeches or hose, especially as worn by men in the 16th and 17th centuries; also the leather leggings worn in the 19th century.

gallus   Trouser braces of a type worn in the USA, where braces are called suspenders.

galosh   Originally a clog, or wooden sole attached to a shoe, but now an overshoe, usually made of rubber or plastic.

Garroudi, Pierre   Born in Tehran, Iran, 1959, and educated in Paris. He moved to New York in 1986 and opened his own fashion house in 1993. His designs are daring and innovative and his shows are erotic, witty and provocative.

georgette   Thin silk or crêpe dress material, named after Georgette de la Plante, a French dressmaker.

gewgaw   Worthless piece of frippery worn to be showy.

ghāghrā   Open-fronted pleated skirt, as worn by Muslim women.

Ghost   Tanya Sarne's 'Ghost' is well know for its trademark garment-dyed vintage-look viscose and ultra feminine garments. Its clothes are created by women for women.

Gibbs, Bill   Scottish fashion designer 1943–88, launched his own label in 1971 in partnership with Kate Franklin. Inspired by the vast diversity and volume of ethnic costume as well as Scottish Highland dress. His signature motif was the bee (B for Bill).

Gibson girl   Young woman typifying the fashionable ideal of around 1900, as represented in the work of Charles Dana Gibson (1867–1944) US artist.

gilet   Waist-length, sleeveless garment, usually quilted and fastened up the front, designed to be worn over a blouse and often worn as part of a ballet dancer's costume. Gilet literally means waistcoat in French.

gingham   Plain-woven cotton cloth, especially striped or checked (literally means 'striped' in Malay).

gipon   Close-fitting padded tunic, buttoned down the front, the sleeves long enough to cover the knuckles, the neck round and low. Originally worn under medieval body armour.

Givenchy, Hubert   Born in Beauvais, France, 1927, Hubert Givenchy opened his own house in 1952, producing ready-to-wear clothes under his Nouvelle Boutique label.

Gladstone bag   A light portmanteau opening into two equal compartments and named afer the British Prime Minister who carried such a bag.

Glengarry   Brimless Scottish hat with a cleft down the centre and two ribbons hanging down the back, chiefly worn as part of Highland dress.

gorget (1)   Collar-like piece of armour worn to protect the throat.

gorget (2)   Part of a wimple worn by women to cover the neck and shoulders, especially in the late Middle Ages.

greave   Piece of armour protecting the leg below the knee.

Gucci, Guccio   Italian fashion designer (1881–1953) born in Florence. He opened his first shop in Florence, 1920, and became known for his leather craftsmanship and accessories. His four sons joined the firm and in 1953 the first overseas shop opened in New York. The empire has had several corporate identities and after Gucci's grandson Maurizio's (1949–95) presidency from 1989 to 1993, the company was sold to the multinational Investcorp.

habergeon   Sleeveless coat of mail.

haik   Large cloak, usually white, worn by both sexes in North Africa.

hakama   Very full men's trousers, as worn in Japan from the 7th century onwards.

hauberk   Piece of defensive armour, for neck and shoulders at first, but soon developed into a long mail shirt or military tunic.

haute couture   High fashion, literally 'high dressmaking'; collectively the leading dressmakers and fashion houses or their products.

Hermès   Founded in 1837 by Thierry Hermès, the world famous fashion house began life as a manufacturer of equestrian accessories such as saddles, riding boots and bridles. The present regime is headed by Jean-Louis Dumas, the fifth family successor to the Hermès empire. The current head designer is Martin Margiela, who has expanded the repertoire into his trademark camel coats and grunge apparel but the reputation of Hermès is built upon the success of their silk scarf and handbag market. The 'Kelly' bag, as popularised by Grace Kelly, is still a best seller.

himation   Outer garment worn over the left shoulder, and under the right, in ancient Greece.

hitatare   The formal court dress of a Samurai.

hobble skirt   Skirt so narrow at the hem as to impede walking; introduced before World War I

Holland   Smooth hard-wearing linen fabric.

Homburg   Man's felt hat with a narrow curled brim and a lengthwise dent in the crown.

houppelande   Medieval tunic or gown worn by both sexes, with full sleeves and long train, belted at the waist. The collar was high, often with a dagged edge.

imperial   Pointed tuft of whiskers on the chin, named in honour of Napoleon III (Emperor of France 1852–70).

isar   Wide trousers, usually worn by Muslim men under the jāmah.

Jacquard   Method of weaving a design directly into the fabric instead of being printed or dyed on. The piece of apparatus used for this type of weave is called a Jacquard loom, after its French inventor Joseph M Jacquard (1752–1834).

Jāmah   Long-sleeved coat that reaches to, or below, the knees and has a belted waist; as worn by Muslim men.

jeans inventor   Levi Strauss.

Jimmy Choo   Born in 1961, his label was founded in 1996 in partnership with Tamara Yeardye and Sandra Choi, who is the Creative Director and designer of their popular fashion shoes which are affectionately known as 'Jimmys'.

Joseph   Founded by Joseph Ettedgui, born 1935, a highly influential retailer who provides a showcase for top designers

Jon, Anand   Indian fashion designer whose 'functional luxury' style is currently en vogue.

Juliet cap   Small net ornamental cap worn by brides etc.

Jungle Jap shops   Opened by Kenzo Takada in 1970.

juni hitoe   Japanese noblewoman's full court costume meaning 'twelve layer' but possibly with more.

karaginu   Outermost garment of the juni hitoe, consisting of a wide-sleeved jacket reaching only to the waist.

keffiyeh   Bedouin Arab's kerchief or larger square of wool cotton or linen worn as a headdress and held in place by an agal.

kebaya (1)   Light loose tunic of a type worn in SE Asia by both sexes.

kebaya (2)   Short tight-fitting long-sleeved jacket, together with a sarong the traditional dress of Malay and Indonesian women.

Kenzo   Popular name of Kenzo Takada, Japanese fashion designer, born in Kyoto. He had small success in his home country before moving to Paris and producing freelance collections in 1964. His Jungle Jap shop built his reputation as an innovator and his creations blend Oriental and Western influences with traditional designs. Kenzo is also a trendsetter in the field of knitwear.

képi   French military cap with a circular top and a horizontal peak.

kimono   A Japanese loose sashed ankle-length garment with wide sleeves. Literally means wear thing.

kirtle   Old English name for a woman's skirt or dress; also the name of a man's tunic or coat, usually reaching to the knees.

Klein Anne   Native New Yorker Anne Klein made her name when setting up her company in 1968 and introducing a sporty element into US fashion. Following her death in 1974, Donna Karen and Louis Dell'Olio continued as co-designers and Dell'Olio remains the head designer and the overseer of the company's latest manifestation, Anne Klein II.

Klein, Calvin   Born in New York, USA, in 1942. Opened his first store in 1968 in partnership with long-time friend and businessman Barry Schwartz. The simple but sophisticated style of his clothes soon gained him recognition and this became universal when actress Brooke Shields modelled his designer jeans in the late 1970s. Klein popularised designer mens underwear in 1982 and following the success of his fragrances, Obsession, Eternity and Escape, his CK One became the first of the unisex fragrances.

knickerbockers   Short, loose-fitting trousers gathered in at the knee or calf. Named after Diedrich Knickerbocker, fictitious author of a *History of New York* actually written by Washington Irving (1783–1859).

Lacroix, Christian   Born in 1951, the French fashion designer opened the House of Lacroix in Paris, 1987, and specialises in ornate and frivolous designs.

Lagerfeld, Karl   Born in 1939, Lagerfeld has been head of Chanel since 1983 and was previously chief designer of Chloe from 1963–84.

Lang, Helmut   Born in Vienna, Austria, 1956, Lang has become a pioneer in many areas of the fashion industry. He is known for his use of techno fabrics, minimalism and deconstructionism.

La Perla   Founded by Ada Masotti in Italy, 1954, and known for high-quality and luxurious, intimate apparel. Pioneered the wearing of bodysuits as outerwear, and sleepwear as casual clothes.

Laroche, Guy   French fashion designer (1923–89),

born in La Rochelle. He worked in millinery, first in Paris, then New York, before returning to Paris to start his own company. By 1961 he was producing both couture and ready-to-wear clothes. From 1966 his designs included menswear.

leghorn Hat made of fine plaited straw.

leg-of-mutton sleeve Sleeve which is full and loose on the upper arm but close-fitting on the forearm.

lei Polynesian garland made of flowers, feathers or shells; often given as a symbol of affection.

leotard Close-fitting one-piece garment named after Jules Léotard, a French trapeze artist (1830–70).

Levi's Proprietary name for a type of blue denim jeans, produced by Levi Strauss as working clothes in the 1860s.

Liripipe / Liripoop In medieval times, the extended tail of a hood which could be as much as five or six feet long; also a medieval slang name for a shoelace.

Louis Vuitton Founded in 1854 by luggage manufacturer Louis Vuitton Malletier, the label has become the most imitated of all top fashion houses. The reputation was founded on their luxurious leather bags, often using exotic leathers such as alligator, ostrich and lizard. In March 1987 Marc Jacobs became the artistic director.

mantelet / mantlet Women's short, loose, sleeveless cloak.

mantilla Light scarf, often made from black lace, worn over the head and shoulders, especially by Spanish women.

mantua Woman's loose gown of the 17th and 18th centuries. So spelled after an Italian city but originally from French manteau.

Marocain Dress fabric of ribbed crêpe.

McCartney, Stella Born in 1971, the daughter of Sir Paul McCartney, currently chief designer of the Chloe fashion house.

McQueen, Alexander Chief designer of the Gívenchy fashion house and a contemporary of Emma Cook and Stella McCartney

mignonette Light, fine, narrow lace used for trimming.

Missoni Founded in Gallarate, Varese, Italy, 1953, by Ottavio Missoni and his wife Rosita (née Jelmeni). The Missoni label, created in 1958, is known for its fluidity and colour of its creations, which have an affinity to art.

mitra / mitre (1) Headband worn by women in ancient Greece.

mitra / mitre (2) Tall Asian head-dress, regarded by the Romans as effeminate when worn by men; the ceremonial turban of a high priest. Also the deeply-cleft head-dress worn in the Christian Church by a bishop or abbot, especially as a symbol of episcopal office, forming in outline the shape of a pointed arch, and often made of embroidered white linen or satin.

Miyake, Issey Japanese fashion designer born in Hiroshima in 1938. His distinctive style combines Eastern and Western influences in his loose-fitting garments which have a theatrical quality to them by the use of dramatic assymetric outline and varied textures.

mo Women's pleated train, part of the formal court costume established in Japan by the time of the 8th century.

mob cap Large indoor cap covering all the hair, worn by women in 18th and 19th centuries.

moccasin Soft leather shoe, originally worn by Native Americans.

Monmouth Flat, round cap formerly worn by soldiers and sailors.

Montana, Claude Began his career in London with the Carnaby Street movement, where he designed jewellery made from large coloured stones embedded in papier mâché. On his return to Paris he became popular for his designer leather outfits and his 1976 show at the Angelina tea rooms in Paris caught the imagination of the fashion industry.

Montera / montero Spanish peaked travelling cap with a spherical crown and flaps for lowering over the ears;also the black hat worn by bullfighters.

muff Soft insulated covering, cylindrical, into which both hands may be thrusted at opposite ends to keep warm.

mutch Woman's or child's linen cap.

mutton chops Sidewhiskers narrow at the top and broad and rounded at the bottom.

muu-muu Woman's loose, brightly coloured dress from Hawaii.

Naga-Bakama Japanese formal undergarment made of a stiff red cloth and fastened high up under the breast and covering the feet at the front but extending out to a train at the back.

Napery Household linen, especially table linen.

New Look Christian Dior's 1947 creation of women's dress with narrow shoulders and long, full skirts.

Norfolk jacket Man's loose belted sporting jacket with box pleats.

Nutter, Tommy Welsh fashion designer 1943–92, revolutionised menswear by introducing high fashion to Savile Row in 1969, funded by pop singer Cilla Black.

nylons Stockings or tights made from a synthetic polymeric amid. The process was invented by Wallace Carothers in the 1930s and named after New York and London.

Oldfield, Bruce Born in 1950, launched his own label in 1975. Famous for his pretty and glamorous eveningwear.

Oxfords Can be a type of shoe, shirt, or trousers (Oxford bags).

Ozbek, Rifat Turkish-born, 1953, British fashion designer who bizarrely first came to prominence for his extraordinary resemblance to Diana Vreeland. His transposing of ethnically inspired clothes into a modern context such as Indonesian Ikat patterns printed on slinky lycra tube skirts, and his opulent Oriental brocades woven into the English gentleman's tailcoats are trademark Ozbek creations.

paji Traditional Korean trousers.

palisado During the reign of Elizabeth, women wore their hair turned back from the forehead over a pad or a wire known as a palisado.

palla Loose outer garment or outdoor wrap, usually worn by women in ancient Rome and Byzentium.

pallium (1) Man's large rectangular outdoor cloak worn in ancient Rome.

pallium (2) Woollen vestment conferred by the Pope on an archbishop Roman, consisting of a narrow circular band worn round the shoulders with a short flap hanging from front and back.

Panama Hat made originally from the plaited leaves of the jipijapa plant of Ecuador.

pannier Framework, used to extend and support the skirt of a woman's dress in the late 17th and 18th centuries, and usually made from osier reeds or whalebone.

parure   Matching set of jewels designed to be worn together.

pashmina   A cashmere shawl made from pashm, the underfur of various Tibetan animals but especially the goat.

patten   Shoe or clog with a raised sole, or set on an iron ring, for walking over mud or on uneven ground.

pauldron   Piece of shoulder armour.

pea-jacket   Sailor's short, double-breasted overcoat of coarse dark blue cloth, also pilot or reefer jacket.

pelerine   Woman's narrow cape with long, pointed ends in front (literally means 'pilgrim'); 18th and 19th century.

peplos   Half or full length loose outer robe often two lengths of fabric pinned at the shoulders worn by women in ancient Greece.

perizoma   Short pants worn by athletes in ancient Greece.

Perrin, Christina   New york-based designer of Swedish extraction. Popular in the late 1990s for her silhouettes in distinctive fabrications, avant-garde use of leather and fur, and her unusual tailoring and richness of colour.

Persian lamb   Silky, tightly curled fur of a breed of lamb called a Karakul, used in clothing.

peruke   Kind of wig worn in Europe from 1660 -1800. A skullcap covered with hair at first imitating the natural hair of the head, later often much more elaborate and imposing (also periwig, perruque).

petasos   Low-crowned, wide brimmed hat of ancient Greece, often with a cord which allowed it to be slung ove the wearer's back when the weather permitted.

Petersham (1)   Thick, corded, silk ribbon used for stiffening in dressmaking.

Petersham (2)   A heavy overcoat or the rough cloth (usually dark blue) from which it was made.

petticoat   Woman's undergarment, but also, in Elizabethan times, a small coat worn by men under the doublet.

Piccadilly Weepers   Long sidewhiskers, worn without a beard.

pickelhaube   German soldier's spiked helmet.

pileus   Brimless, close-fitting felt cap, worn in ancient Greece; a similar cap was called a pilos.

Pillbox   A small cylindrical hat worn at the back of the head and popularised by Jacqueline Kennedy in the 1960s.

pinking shears   Dressmaker's serrated shears in ancient Rome and Etruria for cutting a zigzag edge.

pith helmet   Light sun-helmet made of the dried pith of the sola plant.

plus-fours   Men's baggy knickerbockers reaching below the knee, now only worn for hunting or golf.

Poiret, Paul   French couturier (1879–1944), the most fashionable dress designer of pre-war Paris, and designer of the hobble skirt.

poleyn   Piece of armour for the knee.

poor boy   Type of pullover.

Prada   Since the mid 1990s there have been few status symbols as potent as the Prada-embossed silver triangle. Prada began life as a family-run leather goods business in Milan but enjoyed the patronage of a growing number of celebrities. The Prada empire has been run since 1978 by Patrizio Bertelli and his wife Miuccia Prada, the grand-daughter of the founder. In 1992 a youth-targeted 'Miu Miu' line was introduced as well as a 'Granello' and 'Prada Sport' range. Miuccia Prada has won

critical praise for her innovative experiments in both fabric design and use of colour and her businessman husband equal praise for his shrewd purchasing of large share-holdings of rival operations such as Gucci, Lang, Alaia and Sander.

praetexta   Toga with purple edge, worn by some Roman magistrates and pre-adult boys.

p'u-fu   Three-quarter-length coat worn by men and women in China over their ch'ao-fu or chi-fu.

puggaree (also pagari)   Indian word for a full turban; also a pleated scarf around the crown of some hats, especially sun hats.

puttee (1)   A strip of cloth wound round the leg from ankle to knee as a legging.

puttee (2)   Leather-legging.

Quant, Mary   Born in London, 1934, opened her first boutique in Chelsea in 1955, and married one of her partners, Alexander Plunket Greene. She was the inventor of the mini skirt in the 1960s and hot pants in the early 1970s.

Rabanne, Paco   Born in the Basque area of Spain in 1934, Rabanne's first collection in 1966 entitled 'Twelve Unwearable Dresses' set the scene for his unconventional career. He has designed in plastic, chain metal, fluorescent leather, ostrich feathers, aluminium, paper, laser discs, fibre optic wire, socks and doorknobs.

Ralph Lauren   Born in the Bronx, NY in 1939 as Ralph Lifshitz, Lauren introduced the Polo label in 1967 and became popular following the 1974 film *The Great Gatsby* after many of his designs were worn

reefer   An overcoat, as worn in North America, often called a gaitor or reefer jacket.

rerebrace   Piece of armour developed to cover the upper arm but later protecting to the shoulder and elbow.

Rhinegraves   Late 17th-century breeches, loose at the knee and wide like shorts, often with frilly embellishments.

Rhodes, Zandra   Born in 1940, first came to prominence when she opened the Fulham Road Clothes Shop in 1967. She is noted for her distinctive exotic designs in floating chiffons and silks.

roquelaure   Man's knee-length cloak with a cape collar, fashionable in the 18th century.

ruff   Decorative frill encircling the neck developed in mid-16th-century Spain and fashionable in Europe, in Jacobean and Elizabethan times. Also a frill around the sleave of a garment.

sabaton   Piece of armour for the foot.

sabot   Shoe made from a single block of wood; a clog or, in Holland, a klomp.

Saint-Laurent, Yves   Born in Oran, Algeria, 1936, he studied in Paris and joined the House of Dior in 1955 after winning a Wool Secretariat design competition. On Dior's death in 1957 he took over the house. In 1962 he opened his own house and launched the first of his 160 Rive Gauche boutiques in 1966, selling ready-to-wear clothes, a trend that was soon copied by other fashion houses. Saint-Laurent also creates costumes for theatre, ballet, and films, and in 1985 was awarded a Best Fashion Design Oscar.

Sander, Jill   Born in Wesselburen, Germany, 1943, Sander is best known for her long, lean silhouettes. She has brought minimalism in fashion to an art form and superfluous buttons and zips have been banished. The Prada corporation presently own a large shareholding in the Sander fashion empire.

sand-shoe   Light canvas shoe with a rubber sole; a plimsoll.

sari   Traditional garment of Indian women, worn over a choli and an underskirt, consisting of a length of cotton, silk, or other cloth wrapped around the waist and draped over one shoulder.

sarong   Traditional skirtlike garment of the Malay archipelago, Java, and some Pacific islands, consisting of a long strip of cloth worn tucked round the waist or under the armpits by both sexes. Popularised by actress Dorothy Lamour in the 'Road' series of films.

Sarong Kebaya   Traditional dress of Malay and Indonesian women, consisting of a sarong and a kebaya.

Schiaparelli, Elsa   Italian fashion designer (1896–1973) born in Rome. After studying philosophy she worked as a film scriptwriter in America before venturing to Paris in 1920 and receiving her first order for a black sweater knitted with a white bow, ironically from an American store. Her following designs were innovative and sensational, and she was noted for her use of colour, including 'shocking pink', and also for her outrageous hats and use of zippers and buttons.

seersucker   Material of linen or cotton with a puckered surface.

semmit   An undervest, as worn in Scotland.

serge   Durable woollen or worsted fabric.

shako   Tall, cylindrical, military peaked cap worn with a plume or pompom.

Shilling, David   Born in 1953, from the age of 12 he designed the extravagant headwear made famous by his mother Gertrude at Royal Ascot. Launched his own label in 1975. Author of *Thinking Rich – A Personal Guide to Luxury Living*.

Shitagasane   Kimono of white damask, worn under the ho, with an elongated train of up to 12 feet long.

sideburns   Short sidewhiskers, originally called Burnsides, after US Union General Ambrose Everett Burnside (1824–81) who wore them.

Siemens, Crystal   Canadian fashion designer who uses combinations of materials and colour to give an effect of light playing off the fabric.

Simons, Raf   Born in Belgium, 1968, his first show was in Milan in 1995. Subsequent shows in Paris and New York have highlighted his influence by pop culture, particularly David Bowie, and are described by himself as fashion, youth culture, music and performance parades.

skinny rib   Type of pullover.

smock-frock   Loose protective garment of coarse homepin linen or cotton reaching below the knees, traditionally worn by farm labourers before the machine age.

snood (1)   Pouchlike hat, often of net, loosely holding a woman's hair at the back.

snood (2)   Headband, formerly worn by young unmarried women in Scotland.

sokutai   Japanese court costume, exclusively worn by the emperor, with a yellow outer robe (ho) patterned with hō-ō birds and kilin, and baggy white damask trousers (ue-no-hakama).

soup and fish   Men's evening dress.

sou'wester   Waterproof hat with a very broad rim behind, worn especially by seamen.

spat   A short gaiter worn over the instep and reaching a little way above the ankle, worn to keep trousers or stockings clean, especially when riding.

Spat is an abbreviation for Spatterdash although nowadays a distinction is drawn between the fashion accessories.

spatterdash   Long gaiter or legging of leather or cloth, worn to keep trousers or stockings clean.

Stetson   Man's felt slouch hat with a broad brim and high crown, named after John Stetson (1830–1906), the hatter who designed it.

stock   Long white scarf worn with formal riding dress.

stomacher   Originally an ornamental 'V' or 'U' shaped piece of stiff material worn under a man's doublet to cover the chest and stomach. Later, an ornamental triangular panel filling the open front of a woman's dress, covering the breast and stomach, and often jewelled or embroidered.

suberakashi   The elaborate coiffure worn as part of the juni-hitoe, consisting of a lacquered, gold-sprinkled comb surmounted by a gold-lacquered chrysanthemum crest.

Sui, Anna   Born in Detroit, Michigan, USA, 1955, of Chinese extraction. Her baby-doll dresses of the early 1990s became in vogue with the inception of the grunge movement. Her designs are popular with pop musicians and models.

surplice   Loose, white linen vestment with wide sleeves, reaching to the knees or feet and worn over a cassock by clergy and choristers at church services.

surtout   Can be either a man's overcoat or a woman's hooded mantle.

tabard (1)   Coarse outer garment formerly worn by the peasantry or by monks and foot-soldiers.

tabard (2)   Short, open surcoat worn by a knight over his armour and emblazoned with armorial bearings.

taffeta   Fine, lustrous silk with a crisp texture, used for making formal dresses.

tallith   A shawl with fringed corners, traditionally worn by male jews whilst at prayer.

tam-o'-Shanter   Scottish, brimless woollen cap, with a bobble in the centre, usually worn pulled down at one side.

tammy   Glazed woollen or mixed fabric, used for linings or undergarments.

tarboosh   Cap, similar to a fez, usually of red felt with a tassel at the top, worn by Muslim men either alone or as part of a turban.

tasset   Piece of armour for the upper thigh.

tebenna   Forerunner of the Roman toga, as worn in ancient Greece.

tika dot   Mark on the forehead of Hindu women, indicating caste, or worn by both sexes as an ornament.

tiki   An amulet or figurine in the form of a carved representation of an ancestor, worn in some Polynesian cultures.

tippet (1)   In Elizabethan times, a long streamer-like part to a sleeve or hood. Also a woman's fur cape for the shoulders, often consisting of the whole fur of a fox or marten.

tippet (2)   The long stole worn by Anglican clergy during a service.

toga   Loose, flowing outer garment worn by Roman citizens and made of a single piece of cloth covering the whole body except the right arm.

toga virilis   White toga donned as a sign of manhood at the age of 14.

topi   Hat, originally Indian but now a type of pith helmet.

toque (1)   Woman's small, round, brimless hat, popular in Edwardian times.

toque (2)   Hat with a small brim and pouched crown, popular in the 16th century.

toque (3)   Canadian, close-fitting knitted hat, often with a tassel or pompom.

torchon   Coarse bobbin lace with geometrical designs.

toreador pants   Women's close-fitting, calf-length trousers.

trabea   Roman toga ornamented with horizontal purple stripes, worn as a state robe by kings, consuls and other men of rank in ancient Rome.

tricorn   Hat with the brim turned up on three sides.

trilby   Soft felt hat with a narrow brim and indented crown, resembling that worn in the stage version of Trilby by the eponymous heroine of George Du Maurier's novel of 1894.

trousseau   Clothes collected by a bride in preparation for her marriage.

turumagi   Traditional Korean overcoat.

Tuscan Straw   Fine yellow wheat straw used for hats.

tutu   Ballet dancer's skirt made up of layers of stiffened frills, very short and standing out from the legs.

tutulus   Head-dress formed by plaiting the hair in a cone above the forehead, worn especially by a flamen and his wife.

tuxedo   Dinner jacket, named after Tuxedo Park in New York, site of a country club where the garment was first worn.

tweed   Rough-surfaced woollen cloth of varying texture, usually of mixed flecked colours, originally made in Scotland.

uchikake   Outer kimono, fashionable in the Muromachi period (14th–16th centuries), sometimes with a short-sleeved kimono (kosode), but later (18th century) with a coloured sash (obi) around the waist and bunched at the back.

uwagi   Outer kimono, of rich brocade, under which it is usual to wear a plain purple kimono and generally a third kimono-type robe known as itsutsu-ginu (usually having five bands of coloured silks attached at the sleeves, neckline and hem).

Valentino   Popular name of Valentino Garavani, Italian fashion designer, born in Rome, 1933. He opened his first house in 1959 and achieved universal recognition following his Florence show in 1962.

vambrace   Piece of armour for the arm, especially the forearm.

Van Dyke   Broad, lace or linen collar or neckerchief, with an edge deeply cut into large points, and fashionable after the life of the painter (d. 1641) until the mid 18th century.

veldskoen   Strong suede or leather shoe or boot of South African origin.

vent   Opening or slit in a garment, especially in the lower edge of the back of a coat or skirt.

Versace, Donatella   Took over as head of the Versace empire following the murder of her brother in 1997. Under the terms of Gianni Versace's will Donatella was left a 20% shareholding, her brother Santo having a 35% shareholding and her daughter Allegra a 45% holding.

Versace, Gianni   Designer shot dead outside his Miami mansion by Andrew Cunanan (July 15th, 1997).

viyella   Fabric made from a twilled mixture of cotton and wool, named from Via Gellia, a valley in Derbyshire where it was first made.

Vreeland, Diana   Legendary fashion editor (1903–1989) of Harper's Bazaar and editor-in-chief of Vogue. Much parodied as the epitome of a fashion icon.

watteau gown   Loose gown, worn over a tight bodice, with long, vertical pleats falling from the shoulders to the ground, popular in the early 18th century and named after costumes depicted by the French artist.

Westwood, Vivienne   Born in 1941, and first came to prominence in 1971 when she began a 13-year collaboration with Malcolm McLaren. She became the first British designer to show in Paris since Mary Quant when her 'Bufalo Collection', based on Peruvian women's fashion, caught the imagination in 1982. She was active in the punk rock fashion of the 1970s and the pioneer of the 'New Romantic' style of the early 1980s. Her designs have included leather bondage gear, latex lounge dresses, flesh-coloured body suits, slashed t-shirts and mink g-strings

wide-awake   Soft felt hat with a low crown and wide brim.

Williamson, Matthew   Born and educated in London and known for his unique colour sense and exquisite embroidery and beading. His debut collection was in 1997 and his name is synonymous with 'The Karma Kit', a white leather clutch bag complete with leather flower, jasmine flower mist, a peppermint pulse-point balm, incense perfume and a pink travel candle

wimple   Piece of cloth draped around the head to frame the face, worn by women in the Middle Ages and still a part of the habit of some nuns.

winceyette   Lightweight napped flannelette used for nightclothes.

windcheater   Warm jacket, usually with a close-fitting knitted neck, cuffs and waistband.

Wong, Farida   Dress designer who has carved a niche as a high-quality designer of ballroom gowns for both amateurs and professionals.

Xuly Bët   Popular name of Kouyaté Lamine Badian, born in Bamako, Mali, 1962. His Xuly Bët (name means voyeur in his native wolof dialect) label is identified with cheap and cheerful but quality goods, often recycled but always with an aesthetic quality. Very popular with the French youth culture.

Yamamoto, Yohji   Born in Tokyo, 1943, he is the only Japanese fashion designer to be awarded the French Chevalier de l'Ordre des Arts et Lettres. Apart from his very successful clothing creations he also designs opera costumes and ballet sets.

yarmulka   Skullcap worn by Jewish men.

yashmak   Veil concealing the face, except the eyes, worn by some Muslim women when in public.

yukata   Cotton kimono, worn by both men and women, formerly after bathing but now as outdoor wear on hot summer evenings.

Zoller, Amy   Chicago-based fashion designer originally known for her minimalist silhouettes. Her reputation increased throughout the 1990s and she now has two shows a year in Chicago, Houston, New York and Los Angeles.

zucchetto   Skullcap worn by Roman Catholic ecclesiastics: black for priests, purple for bishops, red for cardinals, and white for the Pope.

NB: This section is simply an A–Z of historical costume and dress, plus a few interesting snippets of additional information relating to designers and materials.

FOOD AND DRINK

Dishes, Ingredients and Terms

Aemono   Japanes term for a salad; 'dressed things'. A dress aemono may include fish, shellfish and seaweeds, poultry and cooked vegetables or may be made of only one ingredient

Agemono   Japanese culinary term for something deep-fried

Aïoli   Provençal sauce, mayonnaise, seasoned with garlic

Alboni sauce   brown sauce with pine kernels and redcurrants, served with venison

Allumettes   French, vegetables cut into matchstick-sized strips

Armoricaine   in the Breton fashion, with wine, brandy and tomato sauce

Angels on horseback   oysters wrapped in bacon

Antipasto   Italian term meaning 'before the meal', comparable to the French hors d'oeuvres

Artsoppa   Swedish, dried pea soup with ham

Avgolemono   Greek, sauce made with egg and lemon

Babka   Polish bread similar to a fruit cake

Bagna cauda   Italian sauce of garlic, anchovy and olive oil

Baklava   Turkish/Greek filo (Phyllo) pastry filled with nuts (usually walnuts and almonds), honey flavoured

Bannock   Scottish dish of oatmeal, soda and salt usually served with butter, honey or jam

Barquettes   boat-shaped pastry moulds served with assorted fillings (lit. little boats)

Béarnaise   French, egg yolk and butter sauce

Béchamel   French, white sauce flavoured with onion

Beurre, au   French, cooked in butter

Bigarade   French, orange-flavoured sauce served with duck

Biltong   South African, dried meat

Bird's nest soup   Chinese soup, contains saliva of swiftlet

Biryani   Indian dish of pilau rice and meat or fish in spiced gravy

Bisque   creamy soup usually made with sea food and enriched with cream or egg yolks

Black pudding   sausage made of pig's blood and fat with oatmeal and seasoning

Blanquette   French, meat stew made with white sauce

Blini   Russian, stuffed pancake made with buckwheat flour and classically topped with sour cream and caviar

Blintz   Jewish, pancakes stuffed with various sweet or savoury fillings, then fried

Bloater   herring or sometimes a mackerel, that has been lightly smoked and cured (kipper is slit open, a bloater is not)

Blutwurst   German, blood sausage

Boeuf bourguignon   French beef dish in red wine sauce

Bombe   spherical dessert dish consisting of an outer layer of ice cream or sherbet and a softer, inner layer of custard or mousse

Bonne femme   French, in country style, or housewife style, homely, also sole poached in fish stock

Bordelaise   Sauce of red wine, artichokes or shallots and marrow fat

Börek   Turkish savoury pastry filled with spinach, eggs, pumpkin, cheese, meat or fruit

Borsch (1) borsht   Russian, beetroot soup served with a sour cream garnish

Bouillabaisse   French fish stew cooked in a highly flavoured stock with oil, spices and herbs

Bouillon   French broth made by simmering meat, chicken, fish or vegetables in water (derives from 'to boil')

Bourride   Provençal fish stew with aïoli sauce

Bratwurst   German, fried sausage, usually pork

Bretonne, à la   French, garnished with beans

Brochette, en   French, on a skewer

Brouillé   French, scrambled

Bruxelloise   garnish for meat, composed of Brussel sprouts and pommes château, i.e. barrel-shaped potatoes, cooked in butter to a golden brown colour

Bubble and squeak   Originally meat, cabbage and potatoes fried up as leftovers

Calamares   Spanish fried squid or cuttlefish

Cannelloni   Italian pasta stuffed with meat or cheese in cheese sauce

Carpetbag steak   Australian, thick cut of steak stuffed with oysters

Cassata   Italian, ice cream dish of two types, cassata gelata and cassata siciliana. The siciliana is filled with ricotta cheese, the gelate with chopped nuts or candied fruit

Cassoulet   French casserole with haricot beans, meat and vegetables

Ceviche   South American dish of marinated raw fish

Chapatti   Indian, bread pancake

Charlotte russe   cold dessert made in a mould with sponge fingers enclosing a mash of whipped cream, lemon jelly and glacé cherries (literal meaning 'Russian Charlotte)

Charlotte: apple   hot dessert of bread pudding with an apple filling

Charlotte: strawberry   cold dessert similar to a Charlotte Russe but with a strawberry base

Chasseur   French sauce of white wine, mushrooms and onions

Châteaubriand   thick fillet steak

Chawan-mushi   the most popular example of mushimono. Small pieces of poultry, fish or vegetables mixed with beaten eggs and dashi are steamed in a cup. Chawan-mushi literally means 'teacup steamed' and is the only Japanese dish to be eaten with a spoon

Chicken Kiev   boned and flattened chicken breast wrapped around chilled butter lightly flavoured with chives , dipped in egg and breadcrumbs and fried

Chicken Marengo   Italian fried chicken in a sauce of garlic, tomatoes and white wine supposedly named after Napoleonic battle when the owner of an inn was forced to use any food available to make a dish

Chicken Maryland   Fried chicken served cold, iced or chilled

Chilli con carne   Mexican minced beef with chilli and beans

Chop suey   Originally a Cantonese dish that literally means 'bits and pieces' a way of dealing with leftovers by stir-frying; widely adopted in the USA under this Americanised name

Chorizo   Spanish, spiced pork sausage

Chow mein   Chinese-American fried noodles served with diced chicken, pork or seafood

Chowder   fish or seafood thick soup or stew

Churro   Spanish choux pastry fritter usually, served with a mug of chocolate

Ciabatta   moist aerated Italian bread made from olive oil. Ciabatta literally means slipper (from the shape of the loaf)

Cocido   Spanish, meat and vegetable stew

Cock-a-leekie   Scottish, leek served onions and sometimes with prunes and chicken stew

Colbert   French with lemon sauce , parsley and madeira

Colcannon   Irish, potato and cabbage dish

Coleslaw   Dutch and then American, shredded cabbage salad

Compôte   dish of fruit cooked in a light sugar syrup and served hot or cold

Consommé   French, clear soup

Coquilles Saint-Jacques   French scallops

Coulibiac   Russian, fish pie with buckwheat and chopped up hard-boiled eggs

Coulis   French term meaning 'to strain' and often referring to a thin vegetable or fuit pureé

Couscous   North African, steamed wheat mixed with semolina to form pasta-like pellets

Crécy, a la   French, garnished with carrots

Crêpe suzette   French, pancake with orange syrup and liqueur (Curacao)

Croque-monsieur   French, toasted cheese sandwich with ham

Croûte, en   French, in pastry

Cumberland sauce   redcurrant-based sauce

Dashi   the basic Japanese soup stock consisting of dried bonito (Katsuobushi) and giant kelp (Kombu)

Daube, en   French, braised with vegetables in red wine and stock

Déglacer   French, deglaze, to add wine, cream or stock to juices in a pan, thereby making a gravy

Dente al   Italian, firm to the teeth

Devils on horseback   stuffed prunes wrapped in bacon

Dhall   general name for a variety of beans, peas and lentils used a staple in Indian cookery

Diablé   French, devilled

Dolmades   Greek/Turkish, vine leaves stuffed with meat and rice

Doner kebab   Middle Eastern, a block of seasoned, sliced lamb roasted on a spit

Doré   French, brushed with egg yolk

Duchesse   potatoes mashed in butter and egg shaped and then baked

Enchiladas   Mexican, fried, stuffed pancakes cooked with chilli-flavoured sauce

Entrecôte   steak cut from between two ribs

Espagnole   French, brown sauce (fat and flour cooked in oven to light brown colour with stock added)

Falafel   Middle Eastern, chickpea patties

Farci   French, stuffed

Fettucine   Italian, ribbon-shaped pasta

Filet mignons Henri IV   French, steak dish served

with potatoes, artichoke hearts and Béarnaise sauce

Financière   French sauce made with Madeira and truffles

Florentine   French, with spinach

Focaccia   a flat savoury Italian bread made with and usually seasoned with herbs

Fondue   Swiss, melted cheese in white wine eaten with bread dips

Forestière   French, with bacon, mushrooms and potatoes

Forno, à la   from the oven

Fricassée   French meat stew in white sauce

Frikadelle   Swedish boiled meat ball

Fritto misto   Italian, seafood fried in batter

Gado gado   Indonesian, dish of vegetables in white sauce

Galantine   chopped meat in calves-head jelly

Garni   French, garnished

Gaspacho   Spanish, cold vegetable soup

Glaze   French, glossy finish produced by brushing food with beaten egg, milk, jelly or sugar syrup

Gnocchi   Italian, savoury dumplings.

Goulash   Hungarian, paprika-flavoured meat stew

Granita   Italian, water ice

Gratin, au   French, browned with cheese and breadcrumbs

Gravlax   Scandinavian, raw pickled salmon with mustard and dill sauce

Grecque, à la   French, means ('Greek style'), cooked in oil and lemon juice (also an hors d'oeuvre with rice)

Guacamole   Mexican, avocado dip

Gumbo   stew with okra and rice

Haggis   Scottish, sheep's stomach filled with offal, oatmeal, suet and seasoning

Halva   Middle Eastern sesame seed, honey and almond sweet

Hoisin sauce   sauce made from soya beans

Hollandaise   French, sauce with egg yolk, vinegar, lemon juice

Hot dog   Frankfurter in bun

Hummus   chickpea, garlic and sesame purée

Indienne à la   French, curried

Jardinière   French, with garnish of fresh vegetables cut in julienne method

Julienne   French, vegetables cut in fine strips

Kebab   Turkish, lamb or mutton cooked on skewers (lit. on skewers)

Kedgeree   Originally Indian, rice and bean dish adapted as breakfast dish by the British with flaked fish and hard-boiled eggs

Korma   An Indian cooking instruction meaning 'to braise'

Kulfi   Indian ice cream made with reduced milk and nuts

Larding   threading strips of lard through lean meat to prevent dryness during roasting

Lasagne   flat pasta dish with minced meat, tomatoes and white cheese sauce

Laulau   Hawaiian, steamed pork and fish cooked in leaves

Lobscouse   fisherman's stew associated with Liverpool but similar dishes with similar names come from Denmark, Germany and Norway

Liaison   French, binding agent such as egg yolk or cream

F
O
O
D

A
N
D

D
R
I
N
K

Lyonnaise sauce with white wine and onions fried in butter

Macédoine French, mixture of fruit or vegetabeles cut into small pieces

Madeleine small sponge cake

Maître d'hotel French, sauce with butter, parsley, lemon and cayenne pepper (lit. headwaiter)

Marrons glacés French candied chestnuts

Melba sauce sauce made with fresh raspberries and served with peach melba

Melba toast thin toast named after opera singer Dame Nellie Melba by French chef Auguste Escoffier

Meringue baked pudding made with egg white and sugar

Meunière French, floured and cooked in butter with salt, pepper and lemon juice and garnished with parsley

Mez(z)e Selection of hot and cold dishes served as an hors d' oeuvres in Eastern Mediterranean regions

Miso a paste made from fermented soya beans and barley or rice malt, used in Japanese cookery

Mocha Arabian, a kind of coffee flavouring often with chocolate

Mornay French, béchamel sauce with grated Parmesan Cheese

Mortadella Italian, sausage from Bologna

Moussaka Greek, minced lamb, aubergine and tomato dish topped with cheese

Mulligatawny Indian, curried soup (means 'pepper water')

Mushimono Japanese culinary term for steamed dishes such as chicken, fish or vegetables, often treated with saké

Nabemono Japanese culinary term for one-pot dishes usually cooked at the table by the diners. Sukiyaki is a typical example of nabemono

Nan Wheatflour leavened bread cooked in a clay tandoor

Nasi goreng Indonesian, meat and fried rice dish

Neige, à la French, white of egg beaten stiffly (literally means 'snow')

Nimono Japanese culinary term meaning 'to simmer'

Nougat French, sweet made from almonds and honey

Okashi Japanese culinary term for accompaniments to tea. Okashi can be made from various ingredients but usually based on sweet bean paste made with azuki bean

Osso buco Italian, braised knuckle of veal dish cooked with wine and tomatoes

Paella Spanish, baked saffron rice with chicken, seafood and vegetables

Pancetta Italian cured belly of pork often used in pasta dressings. The name pancetta derives from the Italian for 'belly'

Papillote, en French, cooked in a greased paper bag

Parata Indian flaky unleavened bread smeared with ghee and rolled and stuffed before frying

Parisienne French, with round, ball artichoke hearts or other vegetables, shaped potatoes and leeks

Parmentier potato, diced and fried in butter (named from Baron Parmentier, who first introduced potatoes into France)

Pâté de foie gras French goose liver pâté

Paupiette French, thin slice of meat, or fillet of fish, rolled around a savoury filling

Pavlova fruit, cream and meringue dessert (named after ballerina Anna Pavlova)

Paysanne à la French, in peasant style

Peach melba dessert made of halved peaches and vanilla ice cream and topped with raspberry purée – named after opera singer Dame Nellie Melba by French chef Auguste Escoffier

Perigueux sauce made with Madeira and truffles

Pesto Italian, sauce of basil, garlic, pine nuts and cheese.

Petit four French small cakes or crystallised fruit or sweets (literally means 'little oven').

Pilau/pilaf The cleaning of surface starch by means of simmering and steaming of rice to ensure separate grains

Piperade Basque tomatoes and peppers with egg beaten to a fluffy consistency

Pirozhki Russian, small pies with filling

Pissaladière French, pastry flan with onion, anchovy and black olives

Pizza Italian, flat-baked dough with various coverings (lit. pie)

Plat du jour French, dish of the day

Polenta Italian dish of maize, flour and water

Poivre, au French, with pepper

Profiteroles choux pastry puffs, covered with chocolate, usually with cream filling

Prosciuto Italian, smoked ham

Provençale French, prepared with garlic, oil and often, tomatoes

Pumpernickel German, malted rye bread

Quiche lorraine French, savoury flan with egg, bacon and cheese filling

Ragoût meat and vegetable stew

Raita Indian yoghurt-based cucumber salad

Ratatouille French, dish of aubergine, courgette, onions, peppers and tomatoes stewed in oil

Ravioli Italian, small pasta casings with stuffing

Red cooked braised in soy sauce and wine

Rijsttafel Indonesian, a selection of dishes served with rice

Risotto Italian, rice dish cooked with stock

Rissole fried minced meat ball

Rogan josh Kashmiri, lamb curry with yoghurt

Rollmop German, raw herring with onion or gherkin pickled

Roux butter and flour cooked and constantly stirred until blended

Rum baba small sponge cake soaked in rum and syrup (invented by a Polish king: Stanislaus)

Sachertorte Austrian, chocolate sponge cake named after Sacher Hotel in Vienna

Salade niçoise tuna and anchovies

Saignant French, rare or underdone

Salmagundi English dish popular in 18th century and consisting of mixed salad items possibly with meat, eggs anchovies and onions

Salsa A spicy sauce especially served with Mexican food

Saltimbocca Italian, veal and ham dish

Sambal Indonesian spiced pickle

Samosa In Indian cuisine, small, crisp, flaky pastries, usually fried but may be baked. Samosas are stuffed with a variety of fillings such as cheese, egg, spiced minced meat, vegetables or sweets

Sashimi Japanese, raw fish

Satay Malaysian, grilled skewers of meat

Sauerkraut   German, pickled cabbage

Scotch broth: cereal used   barley.

Scotch woodcock   anchovies and eggs on toast

Searing   browning meat rapidly with fierce heat to seal in the juices

Shiromono   Generic Japanese culinary term describing all soups but thick soups in particular

Shish kebab   Turkish, skewered meat pieces

Smörgasbord   Swedish buffet including herring, seafood, cheese and crispbread

Smørrebrød   Danish, open sandwich

Solyanka   Russian, cucumber soup

Sorbet   water ice, used to cleanse palate between courses

Soubise   white sauce with onion or purée of onions and rice to accompany some cuts of meat

Soufflé   French, dish of eggs whisked and baked

Soufflé cheese   Parmesan and Gruyère are the two cheeses used traditionally

Steak à la tartare   raw minced beef bound with egg into rissoles

Stollen   German, fruit loaf

Stroganoff   Russian, dish of thin strips of fillet of beef cooked in butter with sour cream and shallots

Strudel   German, thin sheet of filled dough rolled up and baked (literally meaning 'eddy' or 'whirlpool')

Suimono   Generic Japanese culinary term describing all clear soups

Sukiyaki   Japanese dish of beef and vegetables in soy sauce

Sunomono   Japanese culinary term meaning 'vinegared things' and referring to salad items given a vinegar dressing

Sushi   Japanese, vinegared rice with fresh fish or other seafood

Syllabub   dish dates from Elizabethan times. One definition claims that a favourite white wine in those days came from 'Sillery' in the Champagne region of France; the slang term for a bubbly drink was 'bub'; therefore the mixture of still wine and frothy cream became known as a 'syllabub'

Tabouli   cracked wheat with lemon, parsley, tomato and mint

Taco   Mexican, stuffed fried pancake

Tagliatelle   Italian, ribbon-shaped pasta

Tandoori   dish in a clay oven

Tapas   Spanish small appetizers served in bars and varied according to season and locality

Taramasalata   Greek, grey mullet smoked cod roe dip.

Tartare   mayonnaise sauce mixed with hard-boiled egg yolks, onions or chives or herbs, capers and gherkins

Tempura   Japanese, fish or vegetables deep-fried in butter

Teriyaki   Japanese culinary term referring to a special glaze of soy sauce, saké, and mirin, applied to fish, meat or poultry when partly grilled

Terrine, en   French, potted

Tikka   Indian term referring to meat or poultry cooked on skewers

Tiramisu   Italian dessert consisting of layers of sponge cake soaked in coffee and brandy or liqueur with powdered chocolate and mascarpone cheese. Tiramisu literally means 'pick-me-up'

Toad in the hole   English sausage in batter

Tortillas   Mexican, pancakes cooked on a griddle

Tournedos Rossini   named after the composer by French chef Auguste Escoffier; thick round slices of fillet steak garnished with sliced sautéd truffles and foie gras

Tourtière   Pie dish, for small pies

Tsukemono   Japanese culinary term referring to various pickled vegetables and also for pickled umeboshi, a plum-like fruit

Tzatziki   Greek, cucumber in yoghurt

Veal escalope   veal fried in breadcrumbs

Velouté   French, smooth white sauce with added white meat or fish stock

Vichyssoise   potato and leek soup, usually cold

Vindaloo   Indian, hot vinegary pork curry

Vol au vent   puff pastry shell with a variety of filling

Waffle   crisp golden brown pancake with deep indentations caused by the waffle-iron it is cooked in, often served with maple syrup

Waldorf salad   American, celery, apples, mayonnaise and walnuts named after the Waldorf Astoria Hotel in New York City

Wellington   English or Irish beef (or often any meat or fish) cooked in pastry

Welsh rarebit   cheese on toast sometimes melted with mustard and with beer added

White sauce   a roux with added milk used as a base for numerous sauces

Wiener schnitzel   Austrian, breaded veal cutlet

Wonton   chinese, meat-filled dumplings

Yakimono   Japanese culinary term for something grilled

Zensai   Japanese culinary term for appetizers comparable to the French hors d'oeuvres

Zabaglione   Italian dessert made from egg yolks with marsala and sugar

FOOD AND DRINK

Fruit and Vegetable Varieties

Apple   Allington pippin, Api, Blenheim, Bramley, Braeburn Calville, blanche d'hiver, Cortland, Costard, Cox's Orange Pippin, Discovery, Ellison's Orange, Faro, Flower of Kent, Gillyflower, Gladstone, Golden Delicious, Granny Smith, Gravenstein, Idared, James Grieve, Jonathans, Laxton's Superb, McIntosh, Macoun, Mutsu, Newtown Pippin, Northern Spy, Pearmain Pippin, Reinette, Ribston Pippin, Rome Beauty ,Russet, Star Kings, Wealthy, White Joaneting, White Transparent, Winesnap, Worcester, York Imperial.

Beetroot   Cheltenham Green Top, Crimson Globe, Nutting's Red Globe.

Broad bean   Bonny Lad, Bunyard's Exhibition, Express, Green Windsor, Red Epicure, Sutton, White Windsor.

Brussel sprouts   Bedford-Fillbasket, Bedford Winter Harvest, Cambridge No 5, Early Half Tall, Fortress, Huizer's Late, Peer Gynt, Predora, Welland, Wellington, Widgen.

Cabbage   April, Christmas Drumhead, Derby Day, Durham Early, Golden Acre, Greyhound, Hargenger, Hispy, January King, June Star, Ormskirk, Quickstep, Rear Guard, Spivoy, Spring Hero,

Velocity, Winnigstadt, Wivoy.

Carrot Autumn King, Early Giant, Favourite, Figaro, Regulus Imperial, St Valery.

Cauliflower Alpha, Canberra, Dominant, Nevada, Snow Cap, Snow Crown.

Cherry Amarelle, Bigarreau, Bing, Black Tartarian, Bradbourne Black, Coe's Transparent, Early Rivers, Griotte, Guigne, May Duke, Montemorency, Morello, Napoleon, Rainier, Van.

Cucumber Bushcrop, Conqueror, King of the Ridge, Pacer, Pepita, Stockwood Ridge, Telegraph, Tokyo Slicer.

Dates Asharasi, Barhi, Deglet Noor, Fardh, Gundila, Halawi, Hilali, Khadrawi, Khalas, Khustawi, Khidri, Medjool, Mactoum, Naghal, Yatimeh, Zahidi.

French bean Cordon, Loch Ness, Long Bow, Masterpiece, Remus, Sprite, Tendergreen.

Grape Alicante, Almeria, Barbera, Baresana, Barlinka, Cabernet Franc, Cabernet Sauvignon, Cardinal, Cassidy, Catawba, Chasselas, Cinsaut, Chardonnay, Concord, Delaware, Emporer, Gamay, Hermitage, Gewürztraminer, Grenache, Hanepoot, Irikara, Italia, Kishmishi, Madeleine Royale, Malaga, Malvasia, Merlot, Montefiascone, Muscat, Nebbiolo, Niagara, Palamino,Perlette, Pinot Blanc, Pinot Gris, Pinot Noir, Portugieser, Red Emporer, Regina, Ribier, Riesling, Sangiovese, Sémillon, Shiraz, Simone, Sultanina, Syrah, Thompson's Seedless, Tokay, Ugni Blanc, Viognier, Waltham Cross, Zinfandel.

Grapefruit Duncan, Marsh.

Leek Catalina, Early Market, Giant Winter-Wila, Lyon Prizetaker, Musselburgh, Royal Favourite, Walton Mammoth.

Lettuce Arctic King, Density, Fortune, Lakeland, Little Gem, Lobjoit's Green, Sabin, Saladin, Sigmaball, Stanstead Park, Paris White, Tom Thumb, Unrivalled, Webb's Wonder White.

Nut Acorn, Almond, Beech, Brazil, Breadnut, Calumpang, Candlenut, Chestnut, Coco de Mer, Coconut, Dika, Gabon, Gingko, Gnetum, Groundnut, Hazelnut, Hickory, Illipe, Java Olive, Jojoba, Karaka, Kedrouvie, Kepayang, Kubuli, Macadamia, Madia, Manketti, Naras, Ngapi, Niger Seed, Okari, Olive, Oyster, Palm, Pecan, Pignut, Pili, Pine, Pistachio, Safflower, Sandalwood, Sapucaya, Sesame, Shea Butter, Souari, Sunflower, Walnut, Yeheb.

Onion Ailsa Craig, Autumn Queen, Bedfordshire Champion, Blood Red, Brunswick, Dobies Allrounder, Lancastrian, Marshall's Giant Fenglobe, North Holland Blood Red, Pearl Pickler, Ricardo, Southport Red Globe, Stuttgarter Giant, Sturon, Turbo.

Parsnip Improved Hollow Crown, The Student, Tender and True, White Gem.

Pea Feltham First, Histon Mini, Hurst Beagle, Hurst Green, Kelvedon Wonder, Little Marvel, Meteor, Onward, Semitar, Shaft.

Pear Abbé, Anjou, Bartlett, Beurré, Clapp Favourite, Comice Conference, Glou Morceau, Jargonelle, Josephine de Malines, Kaiser, Loiuse Bonne der Jersey, Olivier de Serres, Passe Crasanne, Seckel, Wardens, Williams, Winter Nelis.

Plum Ambarella, Bokhara, Brazil, Burbank, Chickasaw, Czar, Davidson's, Denniston's Superb, Early Rivers, El Dorado, Greengage, Hog, Imperial Gage, Jew, Laxton's Cropper, Pershore, President, Prince's Gage, Red Gage, Santa Rosa, Victoria, Warwickshire Drooper, Washington.

Potato Blue, Catriona, Craig's Royal, Desiree, Edgecote Purple, Esteema, Majestic, May Queen, Romano, Vanessa, Wilja, Arran Victory.

Raspberry Lloyd George, Newburgh, Norfolk Giant.

Runner bean Butler, Kelvedon Marvel, Mergoles.

Strawberry Baron Solemacher, Cambridge Vigour, Grandee.

Tomato Alfresco, Alicante, Big Boy, Dombito, Early Girl, Eurocross, Golden Boy, Herald, Marmande, Minibel, Piranto, Red Alert, Shirley, Tiny Tim, Supersonic.

Turnip Golden Ball, Green Globe, Model White, Veitch's Red Globe.

Fruit: Latin Names and Origin

English Name	Species	Origin
Apple	*Malus Sylvestris*	Temperate regions
Apricot	*Prunus armeniaca*	Asia
Avocado	*Persea americana*	Central America
Banana	*Musa various species*	India/Asia
Bilberry	*Vaccinium myrtillus*	Europe/Asia
Blackberry	*Rubus fruticosis and other species*	Europe/Asia
Blackcurrant	*Ribes nigrum*	Europe/Asia/Africa
Blueberry	*Vaccinium various species*	Europe/USA
Breadfruit	*Artocarpus atilis*	Malaysia
Carambola	*Averrhoa carambola*	Asia
Cherry (sour)	*Prunus cerasus*	Temperate regions
Cherry (sweet)	*Prunus avium*	Temperate regions
Clementine	*Citrus reticulata*	Mediterranean
Coconut	*Cocos nucifera*	Pacific
Cranberry	*Oxycoccus macrocarpus*	North America
Damson	*Prunus instititia*	Temperate regions
Date	*Phoenix dactylifera*	Persian Gulf
Fig	*Ficus carica*	Asia
Gooseberry	*Ribes grossularia*	Europe
Grape	*Vitis vinifera*	Asia
Grapefruit	*Citrus paradisi*	West Indies
Greengage	*Prunus domestica*	Temperate regions
Kiwi fruit	*Actinidia deliciosa*	China

English Name	Species	Origin
Kumquat	Fortunella margarita	China
Lemon	Citrus limon	Asia
Lime	Citrus aurantifolia	Asia
Loganberry	Rubus loganobaccus	America
Loquat	Eriobotrya japorica	China/Japan
Mandarin	Citrus reticulata	China
Mango	Mangifera indica	Asia
Medlar	mespilus Germanica	Europe/Asia
Mulberry	Morus nigra	Asia
Nectarine	Prunus persica	China
Olive	Olea europaea	East Mediterranean
Orange	Citrus sinensis	China
Passion fruit	Passiflora edulis	South America
Peach	Prunus persica	China
Pear	Pyrus cummunis	Middle East/Europe
Persimmon	Diospyros kaki	Far East
Pineapple	Ananas comosus	South America
Plum	Prunus domestica	Temperate regions
Pomegranate	Punica granatum	Persia
Pomelo	Citrus grandis	Asia
Quince	Cydonia oblonga	Persia
Raspberry	Rubus idaeus	Northern hemisphere
Redcurrant	Ribes rubrum	Worldwide
Rhubarb	Rheum rharbararum	Asia
Satsuma	Citrus nobilis	Japan
Strawberry	Fragaria x ananassa	Europe/Asia
Ugli fruit	Citrus reticulata	Jamaica
Watermelon	Citrullus lanatus	Africa
Whitecurrant	Ribes rubrum	Europe

Vegetables: Latin Names and Origin

English Name	Species	Origin
Artichoke, Chinese	Stachys affinis	China
Artichoke, globe	Cynara scolymus	Meditarranean
Artichoke, Jerusalem	Helianthus tuberosus	North America
Aubergine	Solanum melongena	Asia/Africa
Avocado	Persea americana	Central America
Bean sprout	Vigna radiata Glycirve maximus	China
Broad bean	Vicia faba	Africa/Europe
Kidney bean	Phaseolus vulgaris	America
Runner bean	Phaseolus coccineus	America
Soya bean	Glycine soja	East Asia
Beetroot	Beta vulgaris	Meditarranean
Broccoli	Brassica oleracea	Europe
Brussel sprout	Brassica oleracea	North Europe
Cabbage	Brassica oleracea	Europe/Asia
Celery	Apium graveolens	Europe/Africa/USA
Chick-pea	Cicer arietinum	West Asia
Chives	Allium schoenoprasum	Europe/USA
Courgette	Cucurbita pepo	Africa/S. America
Cucumber	Cucumis sativus	Uncertain
Fennel	Foeniculum vulgare	Italy
Garlic	Allium sativum	Uncertain
Gherkin	Cucumis anguria	Northern India
Kale	Brassica oleracea acephala	East Mediterranean
Kohlrabi	Brassica oleracea caulorapa	Asia
Leek	Allium porrum	Africa/Europe
Lettuce	Lactuca sativa	Middle East
Lettuce: lamb's tongue	Valerianella locusta	Europe
Mange-tout	Pisum sativum saccharatum	Near East
Mushroom	Agaricus campestris	Worldwide
Okra	Hibiscus esculentus	Africa
Onion	Allium cepa	Central Asia
Parsley	Petroselinum crispum	East Mediterranean
Parsnip	Pastinaca sativa	Europe
Pea	Pisum sativum	Asia/Europe

FOOD AND DRINK

English Name	Species	Origin
Pepper	*Capsicum annuum*	South America
Potato	*Solanum tuberosum*	South America
Pumpkin	*Cucurbita pepo*	South America
Radish	*Raphanus sativus*	China/Japan
Salsify	*Tragopogon porrifolius*	Europe
Sorrel	*Rumex acetosa*	Europe
Spinach	*Spinacia oleracea*	Persia
Squash, summer	*Cucurbita pepo*	America
Squash, winter	*Cucurbita maxima*	America
Swede	*Brassica napus*	Europe
Sweetcorn	*Zea mays*	Central & South America
Sweet potato	*Ipomaea batatas*	Central America
Tomato	*Lycopersicon esculentum*	South America
Turnip	*Brassica rapa*	Middle East
Water chestnut Chinese	*Eleocharis dulcis*	China
Watercress	*Nasturtium officinale*	Europe/Asia
White cabbage	*Brassica oleracea capitata*	East Mediterranean
Yam	*Dioscorea various species*	Tropics

Spices: Latin names and Origin

English Name	Species	Origin
Acitrón	*Echinocactus grandis*	Mexico
Agar wood	*Aquillaria agallocha*	Asia
Ajmud	*Trachyspermum roxburghianum*	Asia
Ajowan	*Trachyspermum ammi*	Asia
Alexanders	*Smyrnium olusatrum*	Meditarranean
Allspice	*Pimenta dioica*	West Indies
Angelica	*Angelica archangelica*	Europe
Anise	*Pimpinella anisum*	Meditarranean
Annatto	*Bixa orellana*	West Indies
Asafoetida	*Ferula assafoetida*	Asia
Ashanti pepper	*Piper guineense*	West Africa
Balm	*Melissa officinalis*	Meditarranean
Balsam	*Myroxylon balsamum*	Asia
Basil	*Ocimum basilicum*	Asia
Bay	*Laurus nobilis*	Mediterranean
Bergamot	*Monarda fistulosa*	Mexico
Bistort	*Polygonum bistorta*	Europe
Bitter berries	*Solanum aethiopicum*	North Africa
Black cumin	*Nigella sativa*	Asia
Borage	*Borago officinals*	Meditarranean
Burnet	*Sanguisorba officinals*	Europe
Calamint	*Calamintha sylvatica*	Europe
Caper	*Capparis spinosa*	Meditarranean
Caraway	*Carum carvi*	Europe/Asia
Cardamom	*Ellataria cardamomum*	Asia
Cassia	*Cinnamonum cassia*	Asia
Cayenne	*Capsicum frutescens*	America/Africa
Cherry laurel	*Laurocerasus officinalis*	Meditarranean
Chervil	*Anthriscus cerefolium*	Asia
Chinese keys	*Boesenbergia pandurata*	Asia
Cinnamon	*Cinnamomum zeylanicum*	Asia
Clary	*Salvia sclarea*	Europe
Cleavers	*Galium aparine*	Europe
Chilli pepper	*Capsicum annuum*	America
Cloves	*Syzygium aromaticum*	Moluccas
Coltsfoot (common)	*Tussilago farfara*	Europe
Coltsfoot (sweet)	*Petasites japonicus*	Japan
Comfrey	*Symphytum officinalis*	Europe
Coriander	*Coriandrum sativum*	Meditarranean
Corkwing	*Glehnia littoralis*	Asia
Costmary	*Tanacetum balsamita*	Asia
Costus	*Saussurea lappa*	Asia
Cowslip	*Primula veris*	Eurasia
Cubeb	*Piper cubeba*	Indonesia
Cumin seed	*Cuminum cyminum*	Meditarranean

English Name	Species	Origin
Curry leaf	*Murraya koenigii*	India
Daun salam	*Syzygium polyanthum*	Indonesia
Dill	*Anethum graveolens*	Asia
Elecampane	*Inula helenium*	Europe
Epazote	*Chenopodium ambrosioides*	Mexico
Fennel	*Foeniculum vulgare*	Europe
Fenugreek	*Trigonella foenum-graecum*	India/Europe
Galinggale/Galangal	*Alpinia galanga*	Asia
Garden mace	*Archillea decolorans*	Europe
Ginger	*Zingiber officinale*	Asia
Golden needles	*Hemerocallis fulva*	Asia
Grains of selim	*Xylopia aethiopica*	Africa
Ground Elder	*Aegopodium podagraria*	Europe
Guascas/huascas	*Galinsoga parviflora*	South America
Hedge garlic	*Alliaria petiolata*	Europe
Hogweed	*Heracleum sphondylium*	Eurasia
Horehound	*Marrubium vulgare*	Eurasia
Horseradish	*Armoracia rusticana*	Europe
Khus khus	*Vetiveria zizaniodes*	Asia
Lemon grass	*Cymbopogon citratus*	Asia
Lemon verbena	*Lippia triphyllos*	Europe
Lime flowers	*Tilia platyphyllos*	Europe
Lovage	*Levisticum officinalis*	Europe
Mace	*Myristica fragrans*	Moluccas
Marjoram (sweet)	*Origanum majorana*	Meditarranean
Marjoram (wild)	*Origanum vulgare*	Europe
Mastic	*Pistacia lentiscus*	Meditarranean
Meadowsweet	*Filipendula ulmaria*	Northern Hemisphere
Melegueta pepper	*Aframomum melegueta*	Africa
Mint (water)	*Mentha aquatica*	Worldwide
Mint (wild)	*Mentha arvensis*	Asia
Mitsuba	*Cryptotaenia japonica*	Japan
Mugwort	*Artemisa vulgaris*	Northern Hemisphere
Mustard, black	*Brassica nigrar*	Worldwide
Mustard, white	*Sinapis aba*	Europe/Asia
Nasturtium	*Tropaeolum majus*	South America
Nutmeg	*Myristica fragrans*	Moluccas
Palilo	*Escobedia scabrifolio*	Peru
Paprika	*Capsicum annuum*	South America
Parsley	*Petroselenum crispum*	Meditarranean
Pennyroyal	*Mentha pulegium*	Asia
Pepper	*Piper nigrum*	India
Rau ram	*Polygonum odoratum*	Brazil
Rosemary	*Rosmarinus officinalis*	Meditarranean
Rue	*Ruta graveolens*	Meditarranean
Saffron	*Crocus sativus*	Eurasia
Sage	*Salvia officinalis*	Eurasia
Samphire (marsh)	*Salicornia europaea*	Europe
Samphire (rock)	*Crithmum maritmum*	Meditarranean
Sandalwood	*Santalum album*	India/Australia
Sansho	*Zanthoxylum piperitum*	Asia
Sarsaparilla	*Smilax officinalis*	America
Savory (summer)	*Satureja hortensis*	Meditarranean
Savory (winter)	*Satureja montana*	Meditarranean
Shado béni	*Eryngium foetidum*	Carribean
Shiso	*Perilla frutescens*	Japan
Sichuan pepper	*Zanthoxylum silulans*	China
Smartweed	*Persicaria hydropiper*	Eurasia
Southernwood	*Artemisia abrotanum*	Europe
Spanish needles	*Bidens pilosa*	Worldwide
Spanish thyme	*Plectranthus amboinicus*	Uncertain
Spearmint	*Mentha spicata*	Meditarranean
Star anise	*Illicium verum*	China
Sweet cicely	*Myrrhis odorata*	Europe
Tansy	*Tanacetum vulgare*	Northern Hemisphere
Tarragon	*Artemisia dracunculus*	Eurasia
Thyme	*Thymus vulgaris*	Meditarranean
Turmeric	*Curcuma longa*	Asia
Vanilla	*Vanilla planifolia*	Central America
Vervain	*Verbena officinalis*	Europe

FOOD AND DRINK

English Name	Species	Origin
Wasabi	*Eutrema wasabi*	Japan
Water dropwort	*Oenanthe javanica*	Asia
Wintergreen	*Gaultheria procumbens*	North America
Woodruff	*Galium odoratum*	Eurasia
Wormwood (common)	*Artemisia absinthium*	Eurasia
Wormwood (Roman)	*Artemisia pontica*	Eurasia
Ylang-ylang	*Cananga odorata*	Asia
Zedoary	*Curcuma zedoaria*	Asia

Miscellaneous information

Abalone	shellfish
Aga: stoves from	Sweden (full name: Aktienbolagetgasackumalator)
Agurketid (Danish silly season)	literally means 'cucumber time': the season when they are served
Allspice: other name	pimento, Jamaican pepper
Associated with a place:	
Aberdeen	rowies (rolls) sausage
Arbroath	smokies
Bakewell	tart
Banbury	cake
Bath	bun, Oliver (biscuits)
Battenberg	cake
Berwick	cockles
Black Forest	gateau
Bologna	Bolognese sauce
Boston	baked beans, brown bread
Brussels	sprouts
Cayenne	pepper
Chelsea	bun
Cornish	pasty
Coventry	Godcakes
Cumberland	sausage, sauce
Denmark	pastries
Dublin	prawn
Dundee	cake
Eccles	cake
Frankfurt	sausage
Geneva	pudding
Genoa	fruit cake
Hamburg	hamburger
Hungary	goulash
Ireland	stew
Kendal	mint cake
Kiev	chicken
Lancashire	hot-pot
Lima	bean
Lorraine	quiche
Madeira	cake
Manchester	pudding
Maryland	chicken
Melton Mowbray	pork pie
Norway	lobster
Pontfract	liquorice cake
Seville	orange
Siena	cake
Switzerland (Swiss)	roll
Tabasco	sauce
Vichy	Vichyssoise soup
Vienna	loaf
Wales (Welsh)	(rabbit) rarebit
Whitestable	oysters
Windsor	bean
Worcester	sauce
Yorkshire	pudding
Bagel	doughnut-shaped roll cooked in water, then baked
Baine-Marie	large pan of boiling water in which a smaller pan is placed to help the

	cooking process
Baking powder	bicarbonate of soda, cream of tartar and starch
Banana: cooking variety	plantain
Bombay duck	fish
Bouquet garni	parsley, thyme, bay leaf, used as flavouring in stews etc.
Brawn	pig's head (occasionally sheep or cow's head)
Brisling	small herring-like fish
Caboc cheese	soft, Scottish cheese rolled in toasted oatmeal
Caviar	roe of sturgeon
Cendrés cheeses	coated with ashes originally from vine roots, later from industrial charcoal
Champignon	French name for mushrooms, but usually refers to button mushrooms
Charcuterie	French name for pork products (and for a shop that sells these)
Chayote	Mexican vegetable related to the gourd family also called choko, christifine, custard marrow, militon
Cheeses: blue veined	Gorgonzola, bleu d' Auvergnes, bleu de Bresse, Roquefort, Stilton
Cheese: holes formed by	carbon dioxide gas produced by bacteria in the milk sugar
Cheese: agent used to curdle milk for	rennet (from calf's stomach)
Cheese: largest producer	USA
Cheese: unusual types	
Feta	Greek, salted, based on sheep or goat's milk.
Emmental	Swiss, cheese with bigger holes than Gruyère
Gorgonzola	made from ewe's milk with blue veins (named after village near Milan)
Mozzarella	originally made from buffalo milk
Parmesan	made from skimmed milk
Ricotta	sweet cottage cheese
Roquefort	made from ewe's milk
Stilton	adds cream of one day to milk of next
Chef: 'Architect of French Cuisine'	Antonin Carême
Chewing gum: original base	chicle, the latex of the sapodilla tree
Cinnamon: from	bark of tree
Clementine: cross between	orange and tangerine
Coffee: source	pips of fruit (not beans)
Condensed milk: inventor	Gail Borden, US patent granted in 1856
Consumption: beer, most	Germany
Consumption: tea, most	Ireland
Consumption: wine, most	France consumes most wine overall but Portugal most per capita
Crab: how to tell if fresh	it should feel heavy but have no sound of water in it
Croissant	French, crescent-shaped roll
Croutons	toast pieces, fried in butter
Cuts of meat: beef neck	aka clod or sticking, it is usually used for stewing
beef sirloin	behind the neck (best beef for roasting)
beef topside	top of hind quarters of steer
Dariole (mould)	small and narrow with sloping sides used for setting creams and jellies or for steaming puddings
Denby Dale pie: created for	George III's recovery from an illness in 1788
Devon Garland cheese	layer of herbs pressed into the middle
Dredging	sprinkling with flour or icing sugar
E (European) numbers	code numbers used on food packaging which represent substances deemed safe by the EU
Edible grain crops: 9	wheat, barley, maize, oats, buckwheat, millet, rye, sorghum and rice
Eggs: brown or white more nutritious	no difference
Endive: English word for	chicory
Escargots	French, snails
Filbert: fruit of	hazel tree
Fines herbes	French, fresh chopped chives, chervil, parsley and tarragon but other fresh herbs may be added
Five-spice powder	Chinese, anise, pepper, cinnamon, cloves, fennel
Flageolet	a kind of haricot bean
Foodstuff: most extensively grown and eaten most generally by people	wheat (also used as animal fodder) rice
Fruit: nutrition	avocado is the most nutritious and cucumber the least
Gammon: part of pig from	thigh of legs (when salted and cured, this is ham)
Garam masala	mixed spices used in curry
Gas marks	Mark 1 – 250°F, Mark 2 – 275°F, Mark 3 – 300°F, Mark 4 – 325°F, Mark 5 – 350°F
Ghee	Indian clarified butter

F
O
O
D

A
N
D

D
R
I
N
K

Gohan	steamed rice
Grenadilla: aka	passion fruit
Grilling: Americans call	Broiling
Guinea pig: where eaten	Peru
Honey: nectar for 1 lb	from 2 million flowers
Indian bread	poori, chapati, naan
Indian cinnamon tea	masala chai
Indian prawn dish	jhinga
Indian rice: most often used	Basmati (grown in the Himalayan foothills)
Indian-style chicken	murghi
Insect: most eaten	grasshopper
Instant potato: invented	Edward Asselberg (1941)
Kipper	split smoked herring
Langouste	crayfish
Larousse Gastronomique: original author	Prosper Montagné
Licence: chefs require to prepare	fugu (puffer fish) in Japan, lethal if toxic parts are not completely removed
Loganberry	cross between a raspberry and a blackberry
Loquat: aka	Japanese medlar
Margarine: 1st ingredients	chopped sheep intestine, cow's udder, beef suet
Meat: cholesterol-free	kangaroo, possum
Milk: most protein	reindeer's milk contains three times as much protein as cow's milk
Milk: UHT; stands for	Ultra High Temperature
Miso	Japanese fermented soya bean paste
Mooli	long, parsnip-shaped vegetable, which tastes like radish
MSG	monosodium glutamate (used to intensify flavour)
Naan	Indian flat bread
Noisette	hazelnut (French)
Okra: called in Indian supermarkets	bhindi (aka ladies' fingers)
Omelette and a glass of wine, An	Elizabeth David book of the 1960s which challenged British eating habits
Onion family: smallest plant in	chive
Oranges: best for marmalade	Seville
Oysters: when to eat; saying	When there is an 'r' in the month
Palm trees: two fruits that grow on	coconuts and dates
Parboil	derived from old French for 'boiling thoroughly'; now means 'boiling preliminary to further cooking'
Pasteurisation: temperature	approx 63° C
Petits pois	small French green peas
Pitta	Middle Eastern flat bread
Potato: poisonous parts	leaves and fruit (tubers eaten)
Prosciutto	Italian smoked ham
Prunes: made from	dried plums
Quargel cheese: from	Austria (sharp cheese, caraway-flavoured)
Quotations:	
Clement Attlee	The House of Lords is like a glass of champagne that has stood for 5 days
James Beard	A gourmet who thinks of calories is like a tart who looks at her watch.
Paul Bocuse	Cuisine is like fireworks display, nothing remains. It is une fête, rapid, ephemeral.
Michel Bourdin	Cooking is a way of giving and making yourself desirable.
Mel Brooks	Where you eat is sacred.
George Burns	Actually, it only takes one drink to get me loaded. Trouble is, I can't remember if it's the thirteenth or the fourteenth
Robert Byrne	Anybody who believes that the way to man's heart is through his stomach flunked geography.
Lord Byron	Let us have wine and women, mirth and laughter, Sermons and soda water the day after
Titus Lucretius Carus	What is food to one man is bitter poison to others.
Malcolm de Chazal	Women eat when they talk, men talk when they eat.
Winston Churchill	(of champagne) In victory you deserve it, in defeat you need it
Shirley Conran	Life is too short to stuff a mushroom.
Alexandre Dumas (Père)	Le Montrachet [a top Burgundy] should be drunk on the knees with head bared
Edward VII	One not only drinks wine, one smells it, observes it, tastes it, sips it and – one talks about it
William M Evarts	It was a brilliant affair – water flowed like champagne (Description of a

	dinner given by teetotal President Rutherford B Hayes)
Clifton Fadiman	Cheese - milk's leap towards immortality.
Sir Alexander Fleming	If penicillin can cure those who are ill, Spanish sherry can bring the dead back to life
Clement Freud	If a bird says, "Cluk bik bik bik bik" and "Caw" you may kill it, eat it or ask Fortnums to pickle it in Napoleon brandy with wild strawberries. If it says, "tweet" it is a dear and precious friend and you'd better lay off it if you want to remain a member of the Boodles.
Gail Greene	Great food is like great sex, the more you have the more you want.
Galileo	Wine is sunlight, held together by water
Nubar Gulbenkian	The best number for a dinner party is two – myself and a damn good head waiter.
Philip W Haberman Jr	A gourmet is just a glutton with brains.
Ernest Hemingway	Wine is the most civilised thing in the world
Horace	Wine is Life
Jerome K Jerome	We drink one another's health and spoil our own
Dr Johnson	Claret is the liquor for boys; port for men; but he who aspires to be a hero must drink brandy
John Keats	Wine is only sweet to happy men
Prue Leith	When you get to fifty-two food becomes more important than sex.
Joe E Lewis	A man is never drunk if he can lie on the floor without holding on
Arnold Lobel	All's well that end with a good meal.
Martin Luther	Who loves not women, wine and song, remains a fool his whole life long
W Somerset Maugham	At a dinner party one should eat wisely but not too well, and talk well, butnot too wisely.
George Mikes	On the Continent people have good food, in England people have good table manners.
Robert Morley	No man is lonely while eating spaghetti.
Napoleon	Champagne banishes etiquette
Ogden Nash	Celery raw, develops the jaw; But celery stewed, Is more easily chewed
Louis Pasteur	Wine is the most healthful and most hygienic of beverages A meal without wine is like a day without sunshine
St Paul	Use a little wine for thy stomach's sake
Madame de Pompadour	Champagne is the only wine that leaves a woman beautiful after drinking it
Anthony Powell	Dinner at Huntercombes' possessed only two dramatic features - the wine was a farce and the food a tragedy.
William Shakespeare	The food that to him now is as luscious as locusts, shall be to him shortly as bitter as coloquintida.
Robert Louis Stevenson	Wine is bottled poetry
Jonathan Swift	I have been assured by a very knowing American of my acquaintance in London, that a young healthy child well nursed is at a year old a most delicious, nourishing and wholesome food, whether stewed, roasted, baked or boiled and I make no doubt that it will equally serve in a fricassee, or a ragout.
Raclette	Swiss mild cheese; also a dish made from it with potatoes, pickled onions and gherkins
Raisins: made from	dried grapes
Rambutan: aka	hairy lychee
Ramekin	small casserole dish
Ratafia	1. type of macaroon, small biscuit, 2. liqueur made from fruit juice and brandy, or essence of bitter almond
Restaurant guide: first European	Michelin 1900
Restaurant: first	Boulanger's, Paris (1765)
Sago	starch from the pith of a palm
Salami	Italian sausage flavoured with garlic (Latin for salted)
Sally Lunn: cake named after	legendary lady from Bath
Singin' hinny	Northumberland fruit loaf; it gets its name from the sound it makes as it cooks
Spam: name from	spiced ham
Spice: from same plant	nutmeg, mace
Spice: most expensive by weight	saffron
Stilton cheese	made in Leicester but became famous in the early 18th century, when it was sold in the Bell Inn, a coaching house on the Great North Road, at Stilton, Cambridgeshire
Sweetbread from	pancreas
Tabasco: name from	Mexican state
Tapioca: source	root of cassava (manioc)
Tartrazine	azo dye that produces a yellow colour (E102)

FOOD AND DRINK

Tava	concave cast-iron plate used for cooking bread
Tea: the Champagne of Tea	Darjeeling
Tea: country that produces most	India produces 30% of the world's tea crop annually
Tea: originally dried over burning ropes	lapsang souchong
Tea: spoon used for extracting floating tea leaves	mote spoon
Tea: weekly ration during WW2	2 oz per week
Terrine	pot used for pâté or savoury mixtures
Tofu	Japanese soya bean curd
Tripe	cow's, sheep's or other animal's stomach lining
Truffles: how found	detected by trained pigs in France; by dogs in N/W Italy
Turmeric: obtained from	rhizomes of curcuma plant
Ugli: fruit cross between	grapefruit, tangerine and orange
Vegetable: oldest known	broad bean (also called fava)
Wok	hemispherical pan used in Chinese stir-fry cookery
Worcester Sauce: origin	India
Yarg	Cornish cheese that is wrapped in nettles

Cocktails

Adonis dry sherry (2 parts), red vermouth (1 part), dash of orange bitters, twist of orange peel

Affinity scotch whisky (2 parts), dry vermouth (1 part), 2 dashes Angostura bitters

Afrodizzy white rum, banana liqueur, passion fruit juice, lemonade

Alaska gin (3 parts), yellow Chartreuse (1 part)

Alexander cognac (3 parts), crème de caçao (1 part) & cream (1 part)

Angel Face dry gin (1/3), apricot brandy (1/3), calvados (1/3)

Angel's Kiss sloe gin, dark crème de caçao, prunelle liqueur, whipping cream

Atta Boy gin, dry vermouth, grenadine

Bacardi white rum (2 parts), lemon juice (1 part), a dash of grenadine

Bamboo dry sherry (1/2), dry vermouth (1/2), a dash of orange bitters

Bellini champagne, peach juice

Bentley calvados (1/2), Dubonnet (1/2)

Between the Sheets Cointreau, brandy, rum, lemon juice

Black Russian vodka, Kahlúa, cola

Black Velvet champagne, stout (equal measures)

Black Widow white rum, Kahlúa

Block and Fall cognac (2 parts), Cointreau (2 parts), calvados (1 part), anisette (1 part)

Bloody Mary vodka, tomato juice, lemon juice, Worcester sauce, salt and pepper

Blue Star gin, dry vermouth, blue curaçao, orange juice

Bobby Burns whisky, sweet vermouth, Benedictine

Bombay brandy (2 parts), dry vermouth (1 part), red vermouth (1 part), dash of pastis, 2 dashes curaçao

Boomerang Canadian Club whiskey, Swedish punch, dry vermouth, lemon, Angostura

Bosom Caresser brandy, orange curaçao, grenadine, egg yolk

Bronx gin, sweet vermouth, dry vermouth, orange juice

Brooklyn rye whiskey (2 parts), red vermouth (1 part), 1 dash of maraschino, 1 dash of Amer Picon

Bucks Fizz champagne, orange juice, grenadine (optional)

Butt Wobbler gin, calvados, dry vermouth, Pernod, lemonade

Buttock Clencher tequila, gin, melon liqueur, pineapple juice, lemonade

Caruso gin, dry vermouth, green crème de menthe

Casino dry gin (9 parts), maraschino (1 part), lemon juice (1 part), orange bitters (1)

Champagne Cocktail champagne, brandy

Champs-Elysées brandy, Chartreuse, lemon juice, Angostura

Cinderella pineapple juice, orange juice, lemon juice, soda water, sugar

Claridge dry gin (2 parts), dry vermouth (2 parts), apricot brandy (1 part), Cointreau (1)

Clover Club gin, grenadine, lime juice, egg white

Corcovado tequila, Drambuie, blue curaçao, Lemonade

Corpse Reviver brandy, sweet vermouth, calvados

Crème Puff crème de menthe, milk, soda water

Cuba Libre rum, lime juice, cola.

Czarina vodka (2 parts), dry vermouth (1 part), apricot brandy (1 part), dash of Angostura bitters

Daiquiri rum (4 parts), lemon juice (1 part), or lime juice, sugar

Dempsey calvados, gin, Pernod, grenadine

Depth Charge brandy, calvados, grenadine, lemon juice

Derby dry gin (55ml, 2oz), 2 dashes of peach bitters, 2 sprigs of fresh mint

Diki-Diki calvados (4 parts), Swedish punch (1 part), grapefruit juice (1 part)

Double or Drop tequila, brandy, lime juice, honey

Dry Martini gin (4 parts), vermouth (1 part)

Duchess red vermouth (1 part), dry vermouth (1 part), pastis (1 part)

Earthquake whisky, gin, and Pernod

East-India brandy (6 parts), curaçao (1 part), orange juice (1 part)

Eclipse sloe gin, grenadine, gin, a cherry

Fair and Warmer white rum, sweet vermouth, orange curaçao

Fallen Angel   gin, lime juice, white crème de menthe, Angostura, lemonade

Floppy Dick   brandy, dry vermouth, sweet vermouth, triple sec, vermouth

Flu   Canadian Club whiskey, lemon juice, rock candy syrup, ginger brandy, Jamaican ginger

Fluffy Navel   brandy, dry vermouth, sweet vermouth, triple sec, Pernod

Fourth Degree   gin, sweet vermouth, dry vermouth, Pernod

Gibson   gin (4 parts), vermouth (1 part), served with a cocktail onion

Gimlet   gin, lime juice

Gin Fizz   gin (4parts), lemon juice (2parts), sugar, soda water

Gin Sling   gin, lemon juice, sugar (aka Pimm's No 1)

Gin Swizzle   gin, soda water, lime juice, sugar syrup, Angostura

Glad Eye   Pernod, crème de menthe

Grand Slam   Swedish punch, sweet vermouth, dry vermouth

Grasshopper   green crème de menthe, white crème de caçao, whipping cream

Green Dragon   champagne, Midori

Harvey Wallbanger   vodka (1 part), orange juice (2 parts), 2 teaspoons of Galliano (named after surfer, Tom Harvey)

Highball   whisky, Angostura bitters, ginger ale

Hoopla   brandy, Cointreau, dry vermouth, lemon juice

Hoots Mon   whisky, sweet vermouth, dry vermouth

Horse's Neck   brandy, Angostura, dry ginger ale

Hula Hula   gin, orange juice, Cointreau

Hurricane   rum, lime juice, passion fruit juice, orange juice, pineapple juice

John Collins   gin, lemon juice, spoonful of sugar, soda water

Jungle Juice   Pisang Ambon, Mandarine Napoléon, gin, orange juice, sugar

Kicker   Bacardi rum, calvados, sweet vermouth

Kir   glass of white wine with a teaspoon of crème de cassis stirred in

Kir Royale   glass of champagne with a teaspoon of crème de cassis stirred in

Knickerbocker   gin, dry vermouth, sweet vermouth

Knock Out Punch   gin, cider, Bénédictine, brandy, peach brandy, lemonade

Leap Year   gin, Grand Marnier, sweet vermouth, lemon juice

Macaroni   Pernod, sweet vermouth

Manhattan   rye whiskey (2 parts), sweet vermouth (1 part), bitters, maraschino cherry
    Named after a NY club and invented by Jenny Jerome (Winston Churchill's mother)

Margarita   tequila (2 parts), lemon juice (1 part), curaçao (1 part), glass is salted

Mary Pickford   white rum (1/2), natural pineapple juice (1/2), teaspoon grenadine, 6 dashes maraschino

Merry Widow   gin, dry vermouth, Bénédictine, Pernod, Angostura

Mikado   brandy (40 ml, 1 1/2oz), 2 drops curaçao, 2 drops crème de noyaux, 2 drops orange curaçao, 2 drops Orgeat, 2 drops Angostura bitters

Mint Julep   bourbon, sugar syrup, sprigs of mint

Monkey Gland   gin, orange juice, grenadine, 2 dashes of pastis

Monkey Wrench   white rum, grapefruit juice, lemon juice

Morning Glory   whisky, lemon juice, soda water, Angostura, sugar, egg white

Moscow Mule   Smirnoff vodka, lime juice, dry ginger ale

Negroni   red vermouth (1/3), Campari (1/3), dry gin (1/3)

Oh! Henry!   whisky, Bénédictine, ginger ale

Old Fashioned   bourbon, sugar cube, Angostura, 1/2 slice lemon, 1/2 slice orange, dash of soda water

Old Pal   rye whiskey (1/3), dry vermouth (1/3), Campari (1/3)

Orange Blossom   gin, orange juice, grenadine, orange bitters

Oriental   rye whiskey (1/2), red vermouth (1/4), white curaçao (1/4), 2 teaspoons fresh lemon juice

Paradise   gin, apricot brandy, orange juice

Parisian   dry gin (2 parts), dry vermouth (2 parts), créme de cassis (1 part)

Parisian Blonde   dark rum, triple sec, double cream, sugar syrup

Pimms 1–6   long drink with spirit base and fruit flavouring, bases as follows:
    (1) gin (2) whisky (3) brandy (4) rum (5) rye whisky (6) vodka

Pina Colada   rum, pineapple juice, coconut milk, whipping cream, sugar

Pink Elephant   bourbon, lemon juice, grenadine, egg white

Pink Lady   gin, grenadine, egg white

Planter's Punch   lime juice (1 part), sugar syrup (2 parts), rum (3 parts), Ice (4 parts), 2 dashes Angostura

Planter's Punch Rhyme   one of sour, two of sweet, three of strong, four of weak

Presto   brandy, sweet vermouth, orange juice, Pernod

Princeton   dry gin (2 parts), port (1 part), dash orange bitters, twist lemon peel

Prohibition   dry vermouth, gin, apricot brandy, orange juice

Purple Cactus   tequila, passion fruit juice, sweet sherry, grenadine

Rob Roy   Scotch whisky, vermouth, Angostura bitters

Rolls Royce   brandy, Cointreau, orange juice, egg white

Rose   dry vermouth (2 parts), Kirsch (1 part), dash strawberry syrup

Rusty Nail   whisky, Drambuie

Screwdriver   vodka orange juice

Sensation   gin, lemon juice, Maraschino, sprigs of mint

Sidecar   brandy, Cointreau, lemon juice

Singapore Sling   gin, Angostura bitters, lemon juice

Slow Comfortable Screw   vodka, Southern Comfort, sloe gin, orange juice

Snowball   Advocaat, lime juice, lemonade

Sporran Free   Drambuie, whisky, lemon juice, Angostura, soda water

Starboard Light   crème de menthe (9 parts), brandy (1 part)

Stinger   brandy, white crème de menthe

Tackety Boot   whisky, Drambuie, sweet vermouth, dry vermouth, lemonade

Tequila Sunrise   tequila, orange juice, grenadine

Third Degree   gin, dry vermouth, Pernod

Third Rail   white rum, brandy, calvados, Pernod

FOOD AND DRINK

TNT   tequila, Tia Maria, Mandarine Napoléon

Tom and Jerry   rum, eggs, cinammon, sugar, cloves, allspice, soda, brandy, milk, nutmeg

Tom Collins   gin (1 part), lemon juice (1 part), sugar syrup (1 teaspoon), soda water

Tonsil Teaser   Grand Marnier, crème de banane, coffee liqueur, cream

Torpedo   brandy, coffee liqueur, egg white

Triple Testosterone   dark rum, white rum, triple sec, lime juice, Grenadine

Trouser Rouser   whisky, mango juice, pineapple, lime juice, crème de banane, egg white

Wembley   whiskey, dry vermouth, pineapple juice

Whisky Mac   whisky, green ginger wine

White Lady   gin, Cointreau, lemon juice

Whizz Bang   whisky, dry vermouth, orange bitters, Absinthe, Grenadine

Za-Za   Dubonnet (1/2), dry gin (1/2), dash Angostura bitters

Zombie   white rum, dark rum, pineapple juice, sugar

Flavouring

Absinthe   green alcoholic drink, technically a gin, originally having high wormwood content

Aki   plum-flavoured alcoholic drink

Akvavit   Scandinavian spirit made from potatoes and flavoured with caraway

Amaretto   almond-flavoured alcoholic drink

Angostura bitters   bitter aromatic tonic made from gentian and various spices, the true angostura bitters being obtained from the angostura bark

Arrack   rice-based spirit with a coconut flavour from Eastern countries

Aurum   orange-flavoured alcoholic drink (literal meaning 'gold'), based on Italian brandy

Ava   Polynesian drink made from peppers

B & B   Brandy and Bénédictine based liqueur

Beer   barley, flavoured with hops and fermented with yeast

Brandy   spirit distilled from the grape (literal meaning 'burnt wine'), Dutch 'brandewijn'

Calvados   spirit distilled from apples grown in the Basse-Normandie region

Cassis   blackcurrant-flavoured spirit

Chartreuse   either of two liqueurs, green or yellow, with an orange flavour

Cider   alcoholic drink made from the fermented juice of apples

Cointreau   colourless liqueur with orange flavouring

Curaçao   orange-flavoured liqueur originally made on the Caribbean island of that name

Drambuie   Scottish liqueur made from whisky and heather honey (secret recipe given by Bonnie Prince Charlie to MacKinnon family in 1746)

Gin   distilled grain flavoured with juniper berries

Grand Marnier   French cognac-based liqueur with an orange flavour

Izarra   Basque herb liqueur on an armagnac base that may be green or yellow (basque word for 'star')

Kahlúa   Mexican coffee-flavoured liqueur

Kirsch   brandy distilled from cherries, made principally in the Black Forest

Kriek-Lambic   cherry-flavoured Belgian beer

Kumiss/Koumiss   fermented mare's milk

Kümmel   Dutch grain liqueur flavoured with cumin and aniseed

Kvass   barley-flavoured East European drink distilled from stale bread

Lassi   yoghurt-based drink served with either salt or sugar

Maraschino   liqueur-flavoured with kernels of the marasca cherry and tasting of bitter almonds

Mastic   aniseed-flavoured liquor which has additional flavour from mastic gum resin

Mead   wine made by fermenting a solution of honey

Mirabelle   plum-flavoured alcoholic drink

Ouzo   Greek spirit with a strong aniseed flavour

Pastis   aniseed-flavoured apéritif from France

Pernod   aniseed-flavoured apéritif from France

Perry   alcoholic drink made from the fermented juice of pears

Port   sweet fortified dessert wine distilled from grapes

Pulque   Mexican drink made from the juice of the maguey, a kind of agave plant, literal meaning 'decomposed', since it will only keep for a day

Raki/Rakee   strong spirit distilled in Turkey and Yugoslavia and flavoured with aniseed

Retsina   Greek wine flavoured with pine wood resin

Ricard   aniseed-flavoured alcoholic drink

Rum   spirit made from sugar cane and flavoured with molasses

Sake/Saki   Japanese alcoholic drink made from fermented rice

Samshu   Chinese alcoholic drink made from fermented rice

Sangria   orange-flavoured Spanish red wine with cinnamon and cloves (literal meaning 'a bleeding')

Sherry   fortified wine made from grapes, originally only made in Jerez and San Lucar, Spain

Shochu   alcoholic drink flavoured by sweet potatoes

Slivovitz   plum brandy from Eastern Europe, particularly Southern Slav regions

Southern Comfort   peach and orange-flavoured liqueur with Bourbon base

Tequila   Mexican drink made from the juice of the agave plant

Tia Maria   coffee-flavoured liqueur from the West Indies

Tisane   herbal infusion commonly with mint vervair or camomile. Literal meaning 'barley water'

Van der Hum   South African Cape brandy liqueur with tangerine and a touch of rum. Literal meaning 'What's his name' or 'So and So'

Vodka   alcoholic drink originating in Russia and distilled from either potato or grain

Whisky (grain)   spirit made by distilling various kinds of grain. Literal meaning 'water of life'

Whisky (malt)   spirit made by distilling barley. Literal meaning 'water of life'

Whiskey   Irish whiskey (spelt with an 'e' in Ireland); the same spelling is always used in the USA

Wine   alcoholic drink produced by fermenting grapes

General Information

Alcohol: coffee effect on	Makes worse
Alcohol content of beers and wines	on average, beers contain between 3 and 7% alcohol, whilst wines contain between 8 and 15%
Anjou rosé wine: from	Loire Valley
Asti Spumante: grape used	Muscat
Barbed wire	Australian term for lager, especially Castlemaine XXXX
Beer: highest alcohol content	barley wine
Bénédictine liqueur: distilled	Fécamp in Normandy (it is also distilled in the UK, where the most popular distillery is in Blackburn because a Lancashire regiment was stationed at Fécamp during the First World War)
Bottle sizes: Bordeaux	Magnum (2 bottles) Marie-Jeanne (3) Double Magnum (4) Jéroboam (6) Impériale (8)
Bottle sizes:other wines	Magnum (2) Jeroboam (4) Rehoboam (6) Methuselah (8) Salmanazar (12) Balthazar (16) Nebuchadnezzar (20)
Breweries, British: headquarters	Adnams – Suffolk; Badger – Dorset; Belhaven – Dunbar; Burtonwood – Warrington; Felinfoel – Llanelli; Greene King – Bury St Edmunds; Jennings – Cockermouth; King & Barnes – Horsham in Sussex; Marston's – Burton on Trent; Moorhouse's – Burnley; Morland – Abingdon; Rectory – Sussex; Wyre Piddle – Evesham, Worcs
Brewery: oldest in the world	Weihenstephan Brewery in Freising near Munich (founded 1040)
Cap Bon wine: from	Tunisia
Champagne: designations	brut (very dry), demi-sec (sweet), extra-sec (medium dry), Sec (medium sweet)
Champagne making: remuage	Process of tilting the bottle and tapping it to help the sediment fall to the cork for subsequent removal, previously a manual process but now mechanical
Coca-Cola: original constituent	cocaine (until 1903)
Coffee: types	Blue Mountain, Bourbon, Caturra, Maragogype, Mocha, Mysore and Teaberry
Cru :French wine term	refers to the product of a growth from a single vineyard
Drink: drinking once could cause excommunication	chocolate (Central America in the 18th century)
Firkin of beer	9 gallons
French wine: only region to name its wines after the grape used	Alsace, eg. Riesling, Gewürztraminer and Muscat
Gin: former names	geneva (From French for juniper); Hollands (because the Dutch were the first to distil it)
Halbtrocken	any medium-dry German wine
Huckle-my-buff	Sussex drink of beer, eggs and brandy
Iced tea: inventor	Richard Blechynden (St Louis World Fair, 1904)
Iskra sparkling wine: from	Bulgaria (Iskra, meaning 'spark', is also from Russia)
Johnnie Walker Red Label: malt whisky used in blending of	Talisker, a single malt whisky from the Isle of Skye
Kvass	traditional Russian drink similar to beer made from rye flour mixed with a little sprouted barley
Monbazillac wine: from	Bergerac region of France
Port: aka	'the Englishman's Wine', because it was originally produced by British traders settled there
Port: maturity	it can take 40 years for a vintage port to reach maturity
Port: name from	Oporto, Portugal
Prohibition in USA	Between 1920 and 1933
Pub name: most popular in England	King's Head
Pub name: most popular in UK	Red Lion
Real ales: names (examples)	Brewer's Droop, Double Dragon, How's Your Father, Nessie's Monster

FOOD AND DRINK

	Mash, Old Horny, Old Speckled Hen, Piddle in the Snow, Rector's Revenge, St Andrew's Witches' Brew, Snecklifter, Spingo, Workie Ticket
Red Stripe lager: from	Jamaica
Rioja	Northern Spanish wine-producing region divided into Alta, Alavesa and Baja
Scotch whisky: matured in	oak casks (formerly in sherry butts, now in casks sprayed with sherry concentrate)
Sheeps dip: aka	single malt Scotch whisky
Sherry: name from	Jerez, Spain
Sherry: standard cask	butt (contains 108 gallons)
Sherry: standard glass	copita (Tulip shaped)
Sherry: types	fino (dry, pale, young wine); oloroso (darker, heavier and fuller); amontillado (fuller both in colour and body and made by ageing finos); Manzanilla (palest and driest of finos)
Solera system	tiered system of blending wines in the making of sherry
Sparkling wine: invented by	Dom Pérignon (1639-1715), a Benedictine monk from Hautvillers Abbey
Spätlese	German term for 'late picked' wine; the riper grapes make the wine sweeter
Spingo beer: from	Helston in Cornwall
Spirit: best selling in the world	Bacardi
Stirrup cup	sloe gin is the traditional drink to take before hunting
Strega: liqueur from	Italy (literal meaning 'witch')
Table wine: Americans call	jug wine
Tea: bergamot-flavoured	Earl Grey
categories	black (fermented); green (unfermented); oolong (semi-fermented)
Chinese word for	cha
grades	orange pekoe (highest), pekoe, pekoe souchong, congou, pekoe dust, dust
Japanese ceremony	chanoyu
Original use	medicine
Used as currency	Siberia
Tiger beer: from	Singapore and Malaysia
Trocken	drier style of German wine
Tulip : glasses	best glass for serving cognac as balloon glass loses bouquet
Ullage	air gap between the cork and the wine, often found in very old wine; also refers to the space created in a wine barrel by evaporation
Vermouth: types	French has come to mean 'dry white', whilst Italian is 'sweet red'
VSOP	Very Special/Superior Old Pale: not more than 5 years old
Whisky: bourbon and rye contrast	bourbon comes from Kentucky, whilst rye comes from the USA and Canada; bourbon is aged in cold warehouses whilst rye is aged in heated rooms
Whisky: Johnnie Walker Black Label matured for	twelve years
Whisky: largest malt whisky distillery in the world	Suntory distillery at Hakushu, Japan
Whisky: meaning	water of life
Whisky: world's best-selling single-malt Scottish whisky	Glenfiddich
White Horse whisky: malt whisky used in blending of	Lagavulin
Wine: some famous Bordeaux districts	Entre-Deux-Mers, Graves, Margaux, Sauternes, St Emilion, Médoc, Pomerol
Wine: difference between English and British	English wine is made from grapes grown in England, British wine is made in Britain from concentrated grape juice imported from abroad and reconstituted with British water
Wine: difference between sweet & dry	sweet wine is taken from the vat before all the sugar is converted to alcohol by fermentation
Wine: grape colours	red and rosé wines are made with red grapes, but white wine may be made with red or white grapes
Wine labels: AC, control designation	Appellation Contrôlée (French quality-control designation)
Wine labels: Cava	found on best sparkling wines from Spain (not quite as good as champagne), mostly from Catalonia
Wine labels: DOC, control designation	Denominazione di Origine Controllata (Italian quality-control designation)
Wine: Lacrima Christi	made on the south slopes of Mt Vesuvius, near Naples

Wine: length of cork denotes	the longer the cork, the longer period of time the wine is intended to be laid down for
Wine: louse that attacks vine roots of vitis vinifera	Phylloxera vastatrix accidentally imported into Europe from the USA in the 1860s
Wine making: chapeau (hat)	term that refers to the layer of grape skins which rise to the surface during red wine fermentation
Wine making terms: must	unfermented grape juice seeds and skins; first stage in wine-making process or crushed grapes
Wine making: difference between red and white	skins of red grapes must be left in contact with the crushed grapes during fermentation, whilst the skins are removed before fermentation in production of white wine
Wine: marc	spirit distilled from grape skins and stalks
Wine: minimum alcohol content under EC laws	7%
Wine: off licence scale of sweetness	from 1 to 9: sweetest is 9 and driest is 1
Wine: origins	somewhere between the Black and Caspian seas, around 4000 BC
Wine producer: world's largest	Italy, in 8 years out of every 10, on average; otherwise France
Wine: rosé	basically white wine made from red grapes that causes it to be given a little colour and flavour by being left a short time with the skins
Wine: Sauternes, most expensive	Château Yquem
Wine: sparkling	sparkling wine is a wine which undergoes a second fermentation effervesces when poured
Wine: sparkling: production methods	méthode champenoise (bottle fermentation – method for best wines); cuve close; transfer system; transversage
Wine stored horizontally: reason	to keep cork in contact with the wine so that it does not shrink and admit air to the bottle
Wine: study of	oenology
Wine: some tasting terms:	
beefy	red wines high in alcohol, big, solid and chunky
buttery	refers to the soft, rich vanilla flavour imparted by new oak barrels
chewy	plenty of of tannin and a strong flavour
clean	no chemical or bacterial faults, and a straightforward, simple flavour
fat	heavy, perhaps clumsy
grapy	most common with Muscat, Gewürztraminer, and Müller-Thurgau, it denotes the flavour of the grape itself
green	unripe or tart
hard	red wines that have too much tannin
length	length of time and the way the flavour of wine continues to develop in the mouth after swallowing
prickly	refers to a wine with some residual gas left in it
stony	rather dull, empty dryness in either a red or white
tough	too much tannin
Wines: types:	
Amontillado	sherry
Amoroso	sherry
Asti Spumante	sparkling Italian wine from Muscat grape
Bull's Blood	Hungarian wine from Eger region
Chianti	Italian red wine from Tuscany
Claret	red Bordeaux wine (traditional English name for)
Fino	dry, light sherry
Hock	German Rhine wine (from the village called Hochheim)
Liebfraumilch	type of hock (blended wine from Rhine area)
Manzanilla	sherry (dry)
Marsala	Sicilian fortified wine
Moselle	German white wine
Oloroso	dark sherry
Retsina	Greek wine
Soave	white Italian wine
Tokay	Hungarian wine
Vinho Verde	white wine from the north of Portugal
Wine: vintage & non-vintage	vintage wine comes from a single harvest, whilst non-vintage is a blend of wines of more than one year
Wine: what it is	fermented juice of the grape; fermentation being a bio-chemical reaction in which sugar in grape juice is converted into ethyl alcohol and carbon dioxide gas
Wine: world's best-seller	Lambrusco (especially popular in USA)

FOOD AND DRINK

Geography

British Dependent Territories

Anguilla
Bermuda (Somers Islands)
British Antarctic Territory
British Indian Ocean Territory
British Virgin Islands
Cayman Islands
Falkland Islands

Gibraltar
Montserrat
Pitcairn Islands
St Helena and Dependencies
   (Ascension and Tristan Da Cunha)
South Georgia and South Sandwich Islands
Turks and Caicos Islands

Capitals

Country, State, County or Area	Capital or Admin Centre	Country, State, County or Area	Capital or Admin Centre
A'āli an-Nil (Upper Nile) (Sudan)	Malakāi	Amambay (Paraguay)	Pedro Juan Caballero
Aargau (Swiss canton)	Aarau		
Abaco and Mores Island (Bahamas)	Marsh Harbour	Amapá (Brazil)	Macapá
Abalang (Kiribati)	Tuarabu	Amazonas (Brazil)	Manaus
Abemama (Kiribati)	Kariatebike	Amazonas (Colombia)	Leticia
Abkhaziya (CIS)	Sukhumi	Amazonas (Peru)	Chachapoyas
Abruzzi (Italy)	L'Aquila	Ambae/Maéwo (Vanuatu)	Longana
Abyān (Yemen)	Zinjibār	Ambrym (Vanuatu)	Eas
Acklins Island (Bahamas)	Pompey Bay	**American Samoa**	Pago Pago
Acre (Brazil)	Rio Branco	Amou (Togo)	Amiamé
Adamous (Cameroon)	Ngaoundéré	An Giang (Vietnam)	Long Xuyen
Ad-Dagahliyah (Egypt)	Al-Mansurah	Anambra (Nigeria)	Enugu
Adrar (Mauritania)	Atar	Ancash (Peru)	Huaraz
Adygeya (Russia)	Maikop	Andalucia (Spain)	Seville
Afghanistan	Kabul	Andaman and Nicobar Islands	Port Blair
Agin-Buryat (Russia)	Aginskoe	Andhra Pradesh (India)	Hyderabad
Aichi (Japan)	Nagoya	**Andorra**	Andorra La Vella
Ain (France)	Bourg-en-Bresse	Andros Island (Bahamas)	Kemps Bay
Aisén del Gen Carlos Ibáñez del Campo (Chile)	Coihaique	**Angola**	Luanda
		Anhui (aka Anhwei) (China)	Hefei (aka Ho-fei)
Aisne (France)	Laon	An-Nil al-Azraq (Blue Nile) (Sudan)	Ad-Damazin
Akwa Ibom (Nigeria)	Uyo	**Antigua and Barbuda**	St John's
Alabama (USA)	Montgomery	Antioquia (Colombia)	Medellín
Alagoas (Brazil)	Maceió	Antofagasta (Chile)	Antofagasta
Al-Anbār (Iraq)	Ar-Ramādi	Antrim (NI)	Belfast
Alania (Russia)	Vladikavkaz	Anzoátegui (Venezuela)	Barcelona
Alaska (USA)	Juneau	Aorangi (NZ)	Timaru
Al-Bahr al-Ahmar (Egypt)	Al-Ghurdaqah	Appenzell Ausser-Rhoden (Swiss canton)	Herisau
Albania	Tirana		
Alberta (Canada)	Edmonton	Appenzell Inner-Rhoden (Swiss canton)	Appenzell
Al-Biqa (Lebanon)	Zahlah		
Al-Buhayrah (Egypt)	Damanhur	Apulia (Italy)	Bari
Alderney	St Annes	Apure (Venezuela)	San Fernando de Apure
Algeria	Algiers		
Al-Gharbiyah (Egypt)	Tanjā	Apurimac (Peru)	Abancay
Alifu (Maldives)	Mahibadhoo	Aqua Grande (São Tomé and Principe)	São Tomé
Al-Janub (Lebanon)	Sidon/Saydā		
Al-Lādhiqiyah (Syria)	Latakia	Aquitaine (France)	Bordeaux
Allier (France)	Moulins	Aragón (Spain)	Zaragoza
Al-Mahrah (Yemen)	Al-Ghaydah	Aragua (Venezuela)	Maracay
Al-Minufiyah (Egypt)	Shibin al-Kawm	Arakan/Rakhine (Burma)	Sittwe (aka Akyab)
Alpes-de-Haute-Provence (France)	Digne	Aranuka (Kiribati)	Takaeang
Alpes-Maritimes (France)	Nice	Araucanía (Chile)	Temuco
Al-Qalyubiyah (Egypt)	Banhā	Ardèche (France)	Privas
Alsace (France)	Strasbourg	Ardennes (France)	Charleville-Mézières
Attaisk Altai (Russia)	Gorno		
Alta Verapaz (Guatemala)	Cobán	**Argentina**	Buenos Aires
Alto Paraguay (Paraguay)	Fuerte Olimpio	Arges (Romania)	Pitesti
Alto Paraná (Paraguay)	Ciudad del Este	Arhangay (Mongolia)	Tsetserieg
Älvsborg (Sweden)	Vänersborg	Ariège (France)	Foix
Al-Wādi al-Jadid (Egypt)	Al-Kharijah	Arizona (USA)	Phoenix

Country, State, County or Area	Capital or Admin Centre	Country, State, County or Area	Capital or Admin Centre
Arkansas (USA)	Little Rock	Bas-Rhin (France)	Strasbourg
Armagh (NI)	Armagh	Basse-Kotto (Cape Verde)	Mobaye
Armenia	Yerevan	Basse-Normandie (France)	Caen
Arorae (Kiribati)	Roreti	Bas-Zaïre (Dem Rep of Congo)	Matadi
Arsi (Ethiopia)	Asela	Batha (Chad)	Ati
Artibonite (Haiti)	Gonaives	Bavaria (Germany)	Munich
Arua (Uganda)	Olaki	Bay (Somalia)	Baidoa
Aruba	Oranjestad		(Baydhabo)
Arunãchal Pradesh (India)	Itãnagar	Bay of Plenty (NZ)	Tauranga
Ascension	Georgetown	Bazéga (Burkina Faso)	Kombissiri
Ashanti (Ghana)	Kumasi	Bedfordshire (Eng)	Bedford
Ash-Shamãl (Lebanon)	Tripoli/Tarãbulus	Belait (Brunei)	Kuala Belait
Ash-Sharqiyah (Egypt)	Az-Zaqãziq	**Belgium**	Brussels
Assam (India)	Dispur	**Belize**	Belmopan
Assoli (Togo)	Bafilo	**Belorussia**	Minsk
Asturias (Spain)	Oviedo	Bendel (Nigeria)	Benin City
Atacama (Chile)	Copiapó	Bengo (Angola)	Caxito
Atacora (Benin)	Natitingou	Beni (Bolivia)	Trinidad
Atlántico (Colombia)	Barranquilla	**Benin**	Porto Novo (de
Atlántida (Honduras)	La Ceiba		facto Cotonou)
Atlantique (Benin)	Cotonou	Benue (Nigeria)	Makurdi
Aube (France)	Troyes	Berea (Lesotho)	Teyateyaneng
Aude (France)	Carcassonne	Berkshire (Eng)	Reading
Aust-Agder (Norway)	Arendal	**Bermuda**	Hamilton
Australia	Canberra	Berry Island (Bahamas)	Nicolls Town
Australian Capital Territory	Canberra	Beru (Kiribati)	Taubukinberu
Austria	Vienna	**Bhutan (aka Druk-Yul)**	Thimphu
Austurland (Iceland)	Egilsstadhir	Bié (Angola)	Kuito
Auvergne (France)	Clermont-Ferrand	Bihar (India)	Patna
Aveyron (France)	Rodez	Bihor (Romania)	Oradea
Avon (Eng)	Bristol	Bimini Islands (Bahamas)	Alice Town
Azerbaijan	Baku	Binah (Togo)	Pagouda
Azores (Portugal)	Ponta Delgada	Binh Dinh (Vietnam)	Quy Nhon
Azuay (Ecuador)	Cuenca	Binh Duong (Vietnam)	Thu Dau Mot
Ba Ria (Vietnam)	Vung Tau	Binh Phuoc (Vietnam)	Dung Xoai
Baa (Maldives)	Eydhafushi	Binh Thuan (Vietnam)	Phan Thiet
Bãbil (Iraq)	Al-Hillah	Bíobío (Chile)	Concepción
Bács-Kiskun (Hungary)	Kecskemét	Bioko (Equatorial Guinea)	Malabo
Baden-Württemberg (Germany)	Stuttgart	Biombo (Guinea-Bissau)	Bissau
Bahamas	Nassau	Blekinge (Sweden)	Karlskrona
Bahia (Brazil)	Salvador	Boavista (Cape Verde)	Sal Rei
Bahoruco (Dominican Republic)	Neiba	Bokeo (Laos)	Houayxay
Bahr al-Ghazãl (Sudan)	Wãu	Bolikhamxay (Laos)	Pakxan
Bahrain	Manama	Bolivar (Colombia)	Cartagena
Baja California Norte (Mexico)	Mexicali	Bolivar (Ecuador)	Guaranda
Baja California Sur (Mexico)	La Paz	Bolivar (Venezuela)	Ciudad Bolivar
Baja Verapaz (Guatemala)	Salamá	**Bolivia**	Sucre–judicial
Bakool (Somalia)	Oddur (Xuddur)		La Paz–
Bale (Ethiopia)	Goba		administrative
Balearic Islands (Spain)	Palma de	Bombali (Sierra Leone)	Makeni
	Mallorca	Bomi (Liberia)	Tubmanburg
Bali (Indonesia)	Denpassar	Bonaire (Netherland Antilles)	Kralendijk
Baluchistãn (Pakistan)	Quetta	Bong (Liberia)	Gbarnga
Bam (Burkina Faso)	Kongoussi	Bophuthatswana (South Africa)	Mmabatho
Bamingui-Bangoran (Cape Verde)	Ndélé	Boquerón (Paraguay)	Dr Pedro P. Peña
Banaadir (Somalia)	Mogadishu	Bora-Bora (French Polynesia)	Vaitape
	(Muqdisho)	Borders (Scotland)	Newtown St
Banaba (Kiribati)	Anteeren		Boswells
Bangladesh	Dhaka	Borgou (Benin)	Parakou
Banks/Torres (Vanuatu)	Sola	Borkou-Ennedi-Tibesti (Chad)	Faya
Baranya (Hungary)	Pécs	Bornholm (Denmark)	Renne
Barbados	Bridgetown	Borno (Nigeria)	Malduguri
Bari (Somalia)	Bender Cassim	Borsod-Abaúj-Zemplén (Hungary)	Miskolc
	(Boosaaso)	**Bosnia and Hercegovina**	Sarajevo
Barima/Waini (Guyana)	Mabaruma	**Botswana**	Gaborone
Basel-Landschaft (Swiss canton)	Liestal	Botswana (Central)	Serowe
Basel-Stadt (Swiss canton)	Basel	Botswana (North East)	Masunga
Bashkir (Russia)	Ufa	Botswana (South East)	Ramotswa
Basilicata (Italy)	Potenza	Bouches-du-Rhône (France)	Marseille
Basque Country (Spain)	Vitoria	Bouenza (Congo)	Madingou

Country, State, County or Area	Capital or Admin Centre
Bougouriba (Burkina Faso)	Diébougou
Boulgou (Burkina Faso)	Tenkodogo
Boulkiemde (Burkina Faso)	Koudougou
Bourgogne/Burgundy (France)	Dijon
Boyacá (Colombia)	Tunja
Brabant (Flemish)	Louvain (Leuven)
Brabant (Walloon)	Wavre
Brakna (Mauritania)	Aleg
Brandenburg (Germany)	Potsdam
Brava (Cape Verde)	Nova Sintra
Brazil	Brasilia
Bretagne/Brittany (France)	Rennes
British Columbia (Canada)	Victoria
Brong-Ahafo (Ghana)	Sunyani
Brunei	Bandar Seri Begawan
Buckinghamshire (Eng)	Aylesbury
Buenos Aires (Argentina)	La Plata
Bulgaria (aka Narodna Republic)	Sofia
Bumthang (Bhutan)	Jakar
Bundibugyo (Uganda)	Busaru
Burgenland (Austria)	Eisenstadt
Burkina Faso	Ouagadougou
Burundi	Bujumbura
Buryat (Russia)	Ulan-Ude
Bushenyi (Uganda)	Bumbaire
Buskerud (Norway)	Drammen
Caaguazú (Paraguay)	Coronel Oviedo
Cabañas (El Salvador)	Sensuntepeque
Cabo Delgado (Mozambique)	Pemba
Calabria (Italy)	Catanzaro
Caldas (Colombia)	Manizales
California (USA)	Sacramento
Calvados (France)	Caen
Cambodia	Phnom Penh
Cambridgeshire (Eng)	Cambridge
Cameroon	Yaoundé
Campania (Italy)	Naples
Canada	Ottawa
Cañar (Ecuador)	Azoques
Canary Islands (Spain)	Santa Cruz de Tenerife
Canendiyú (Paraguay)	Salto del Guairá
Cantabria (Spain)	Santander
Cantagaio (São Tomé and Principe)	Santana
Cantal (France)	Aurillac
Canterbury (NZ)	Christchurch
Cape Verde	Praia
Caprivi (Namibia)	Katima Mulilo
Caquetá (Colombia)	Florencia
Carabobo (Venezuela)	Valencia
Caras-Severin (Romania)	Resita
Carchi (Ecuador)	Tulcan
Carlow (Rep of Ireland)	Carlow
Caroni (Trinidad and Tobago)	Chaguanas
Casanare (Colombia)	Yopal
Castilla-La Mancha (Spain)	Toledo
Castilla-León (Spain)	Valladolid
Cat Island (Bahamas)	Arthur's Town
Catalonia (Spain)	Barcelona
Catamarca (Argentina)	San Fernando
Cauca (Colombia)	Popoyán
Caué (São Tomé and Principe)	São João Angolares
Cavan (Rep of Ireland)	Cavan
Cayman Islands	George Town
Cayo (Belize)	San Ignacio
Ceará (Brazil)	Fortaleza
Central (Scotland)	Stirling

Country, State, County or Area	Capital or Admin Centre
Central African Republic	Bangui
Central District (Israel)	Ramla
Central Islands (Solomon Isles)	Tulagi
Central Nepal	Kāthmāndu
Central Province (Fiji)	Suva
Central Province (Kenya)	Nyeri
Central Province (Zambia)	Kabwe
Central Region (Ghana)	Cape Coast
Central Region (Paraguay)	Asunción
Centrale Region (Togo)	Sokodé
Centre Département (Haiti)	Hinche
Centre Province (Cameroon)	Yaoundé
Cerro Largo (Uruguay)	Melo
Cesar (Colombia)	Valledupar
Chaco (Argentina)	Resistencia
Chaco (Paraguay)	Mayor Pablo Lagerenza
Chad	N'Djamena
Chagang-do (North Korea)	Kanggye
Champagne-Ardenne (France)	Châlons-sur-Marne
Champasak (Laos)	Pakxé
Charente (France)	Angoulême
Charente-Maritime (France)	La Rochelle
Chari-Baguirmi (Chad)	N'Djaména
Chechnya	Dzhohar
Cher (France)	Bourges
Cheshire (Eng)	Chester
Chiapas (Mexico)	Tuxtla Gutiérrez
Chile	Santiago
Chimborazo (Ecuador)	Riobamba
Chimbu (Papua New Guinea)	Kundiawa
Chin (Myanmar)	Hakha
China	Beijing (aka Peking)
Chirang (Bhutan)	Damphu
Chiriqui (Panama)	David
Chobe (Botswana)	Kasane
Chocó (Colombia)	Quibdó
Chõlla-namdo (South Korea)	Kwangju
Chõlla-pukto (South Korea)	Ch'õnju
Christmas Island (Aus)	Flying Fish Cove
Christmas Island/Kiritimati Atoll (Kiribati)	London
Chubut (Argentina)	Rawson
Chukut (Russia)	Anadyr
Chuquisaca (Bolivia)	Sucre
Chuvashia (Russia)	Cheboksary
Ciskei (South Africa)	Bisho
Citta (San Marino)	San Marino
Clare (Rep of Ireland)	Ennis
Clarendon (Jamaica)	May Pen
Cleveland (Eng)	Middlesbrough
Clwyd (Wales)	Mold
Coahuila (Mexico)	Saltillo
Coast Province (Kenya)	Mombasa
Coclé (Panama)	Penonomé
Cocos (aka Keeling Islands) (Aus)	West Island
Cojedes (Venezuela)	San Carlos
Colombia	Bogotá
Colón (Honduras)	Trujillo
Colorado (USA)	Denver
Commewijne (Suriname)	Nieuw Amsterdam
Comoé (Burkina Faso)	Banfora
Comoros Islands	Moroni
Congo: Democratic Republic	Kinshasa
Congo: People's Republic	Brazzaville
Connecticut (USA)	Hartford
Cook Islands (New Zealand)	Ararua

Country, State, County or Area	Capital or Admin Centre	Country, State, County or Area	Capital or Admin Centre
Copperbelt (Zambia)	Ndola	Dumfries and Galloway (Scotland)	Dumfries
Coquimbo (Chile)	La Serena	Dundgovi (Mongolia)	Mandalgov
Cordillera (Paraguay)	Caacupé	Durham (Eng)	Durham
Córdoba (Colombia)	Montería	Dyfed (Wales)	Carmarthen
Corfu	Kerkira	Dzavhan (Mongolia)	Uliastay
Cork (Rep of Ireland)	Cork	East Berbice/Corentyne (Guyana)	New Amsterdam
Cornwall (Eng)	Truro	East Cape (NZ)	Gisborne
Coronie (Suriname)	Totness	East Flanders (Belgium)	Ghent
Corrèze (France)	Tulle	East New Britain (Papua	
Corse-du-Sud (France)	Ajaccio	New Guinea)	Rabaul
Corsica (France)	Ajaccio	East Sepik (Papua New Guinea)	Wewak
Cortés (Honduras)	San Pedro Sula	East Sussex (Eng)	Lewes
Costa Rica	San José	Easter Island	Hanga Roa
Côte-d'Or (France)	Dijon	Eastern Equatoria (Sudan)	Jubā
Côtes-du-Nord (France)	Saint-Brieuc	Eastern Highlands (Papua	
Cotopaxi (Ecuador)	Latacunga	New Guinea)	Goroka
Covasna (Romania)	Sfintu Gheorghe	Eastern Nepal	Dhankutā
Crete	Khania	Eastern Province (Fiji)	Levuka
Creuse (France)	Guéret	Eastern Province (Kenya)	Embu
Croatia	Zagreb	Eastern Province (Sierra Leone)	Kenema
Crooked Island (Bahamas)	Colonel Hill	Eastern Province (Zambia)	Chipata
Cross River (Nigeria)	Calabar	Eastern Region (Ghana)	Koforidua
Csongrád (Hungary)	Szeged	Eastern Timor (Pacific)	Dili
Cuba	Havana	**Ecuador**	Quito
Cumbria (Eng)	Carlisle	Efaté (Vanuatu)	Vila
Cundinamarca (Colombia)	Bogotá	**Egypt**	Cairo
Cunene (Angola)	N'Giva	Ehime (Japan)	Matsuyama
Curaçao (Netherland Antilles)	Willemstad	El Oro (Ecuador)	Machala
Cuscatlán (El Salvador)	Cojutepeque	El Paraiso (Honduras)	Yuscarán
Cuvette (Congo)	Owando	**El Salvador**	San Salvador
Cuzco (Peru)	Cuzco	El-Acâba (Mauritania)	Kiffa
Cyprus	Nicosia	Emilia-Romagna (Italy)	Bologna
Czech Republic	Prague	Enga (Papua New Guinea)	Wabag
Dac Lac (Vietnam)	Buon Ma Thuot	**England**	London
Dadra and Nagar Haveli (India)	Silvassa	Entre Rios (Argentina)	Paraná
Dagestan (Russia)	Makhachkala	Epi (Vanuatu)	Ringdove
Dārfur (Sudan)	Al-Fāshir	Equateur (Dem Rep of Congo)	Mbandaka
Darién (Panama)	La Palma	**Equatorial Guinea**	Malabo
Delaware (USA)	Dover	**Eritrea**	Asmara
Demerara/Mahaica (Guyana)	Paradise	Erongo (Namibia)	Swakopmund
Denmark	Copenhagen	Espaillat (Dom Republic)	Moca
Derbyshire (Eng)	Matlock	Espirito Santo (Brazil)	Vitória
Des Plateaux (Togo)	Atakpamé	Essequibo Islands (Guyana)	Vreed-en-Hoop
Des Savanes (Togo)	Dapaong	Essex (Eng)	Chelmsford
Deux-Sèvres (France)	Niort	Essonne (France)	Évry
Devon (Eng)	Exeter	Est (Cameroon)	Bertoua
Dhaalu (Maldives)	Kudahuvadhoo	**Estonia**	Tallinn
Dhi Qār (Iraq)	An-Nāsiriyah	Estuaire (Gabon)	Libreville
Dibēr (Albania)	Peshkopi	**Ethiopia**	Addis Ababa
Dimashq (Syria)	Damascus	Eua (Tonga)	Ohonua
Dimbovita (Romania)	Tirgoviste	Eure (France)	Évreux
Djibouti	Djibouti	Eure-et-Loire (France)	Chartres
Dolj (Romania)	Craiova	Evenki (Russia)	Tura
Dominica	Roseau	Extremadura (Spain)	Mérida
Dominican Republic	Santo Domingo	Extrême-Nord (Cameroon)	Maroua
Donegal (Rep of Ireland)	Lifford	Faafu (Maldives)	Magoodhoo
Dong Nai (Vietnam)	Bien Hoa	**Faeroe Islands**	Thorshavn
Dong Thap (Vietnam)	Sa Dec	Falcón (Venezuela)	Coro
Dordogne (France)	Périgueux	**Falkland Islands**	Stanley
Dornod (Mongolia)	Choybaisan	Fanning/Tabuaeran (Kiribati)	Paelau
Dornogovi (Mongolia)	Saynshand	Fārs (Iran)	Shirāz
Dorset (Eng)	Dorchester	Far-Western Nepal	Dipāyal
Doubs (France)	Besançon	Fejér (Hungary)	Székesfehérvár
Doufelgou (Togo)	Niamtougou	Fermanagh (NI)	Enniskillen
Down (NI)	Downpatrick	Fife (Scotland)	Glenrothes
Drenthe (Netherlands)	Assen	**Fiji**	Suva
Drôme (France)	Valence	Finistère (France)	Quimper
Duarte (Dominican Republic)	San Francisco de Macoris	**Finland**	Helsinki
		Finnmark (Norway)	Vardø
Dublin (Rep of Ireland)	Dublin	Flevoland (Netherlands)	Lelystad

Country, State, County or Area	Capital or Admin Centre
Flores (Uruguay)	Trinidad
Florida (USA)	Tallahassee
Fogo (Cape Verde)	São Filipe
France	Paris
Francisco Morazán (Honduras)	Tegucigalpa
Frederiksborg (Denmark)	Hillerod
French Guiana	Cayenne
French Polynesia	Papeete
Friesland (Netherlands)	Leeuwarden
Friuli-Venezia Giulia (Italy)	Trieste
Fujian (aka Fukien) (China)	Fuzhou (aka Foochow)
Fyn (Denmark)	Odense
Gaafu-Alifu (Maldives)	Vilgili
Gaafu-Dhaalu (Maldives)	Thinadhoo
Gabon	Libreville
Galguduud (Somalia)	Dusa Marreb
(Dhuusamarreeb)	
Galicia (Spain)	Santiago de Compostela
Galway (Rep of Ireland)	Galway
Gambia	Banjul
Gambier Islands (French Polynesia)	Rikitea
Gansu (aka Kansu) (China)	Lanzhou (aka Lan-chou)
Ganzourgou (Burkina Faso)	Zorgho
Gard (France)	Nîmes
Gaza (Mozambique)	Xai-Xai
Gazankulu (South Africa)	Giyani
Gedo (Somalia)	Garbahaarrey
Gelderland (Netherlands)	Arnhem
Gemu Gofa (Ethiopia)	Arba Minch
Georgia	Tbilisi
Georgia (USA)	Atlanta
Germany	Berlin
Gers (France)	Auch
Ghana	Accra
Gia Lai (Vietnam)	Plei Ku
Gilān (Iran)	Rasht
Gilbert Isles (Kiribati)	Bairiki
Gironde (Aquitaine, France)	Bordeaux
Gloucestershire (Eng)	Gloucester
Gnagna (Burkina Faso)	Bogandé
Gnyaviyani (Maldives)	Foah Mulah
Goa (India)	Panaji
Goiás (Brazil)	Goiânia
Gojam (Ethiopia)	Debre Markos
Golfe (Togo)	Lomé
Gongola (Nigeria)	Yola
Gorgol (Mauritania)	Kaédi
Gorj (Romania)	Tirgu Jiu
Gotland (Sweden)	Visby
Gourma (Burkina Faso)	Fada N'Gourma
Gozo (Malta)	Victoria
Gracias a Dios (Honduras)	Puerto Lempira
Grampian (Scotland)	Aberdeen
Gran Canaria	Las Palmas
Grand Bahama	Freeport
Grand Bassa (Liberia)	Buchanan
Grand Cape Mount (Liberia)	Robertsport
Grand Gedeh (Liberia)	Zwedru
Grand Kru (Liberia)	Barclayville
Grande Anse (Haiti)	Jérémie
Granma (Cuba)	Bayamo
Graubunden (Swiss canton)	Chur
Greater Accra (Ghana)	Accra
Greater London (Eng)	London
Greater Manchester (Eng)	Manchester

Country, State, County or Area	Capital or Admin Centre
Greece	Athens
Greenland (aka Kalaallit Nunaat)	Godthaab (aka Nuuk)
Grenada	St George's
Gribingui-Economique (CA Rep)	Kaga-Bandoro
Guadalcanal (Solomon Isles)	Honiara
Guadeloupe	Basse-Terre
Guainia (Colombia)	Puerto Inirida
Guairá (Paraguay)	Villarica
Guam	Agana
Guanacaste (Costa Rica)	Liberia
Guangdong (aka Kwangtung) (China)	Guangzhou (aka Canton)
Guangxi Zhuang (aka Kwangsi Chuang) (China)	Nanning
Guárico (Venezuela)	San Juan de Los Morros
Guatemala	Guatemala City
Guayas (Ecuador)	Guayaquil
Guéra (Chad)	Mongo
Guernsey	St Peter Port
Guerrero (Mexico)	Chilpancingo
Guidimaka (Mauritania)	Sélibaby
Guinea	Conakry
Guinea-Bissau	Bissau
Guizhou (aka Kweichow) (China)	Guiyang (aka Kuei-yang)
Gujarāt (India)	Gāndhinagar
Gulf (Papua New Guinea)	Kerema
Gulu (Uganda)	Bungatira
Gumma (Japan)	Maebashi
Guyana	Georgetown
Gwent (Wales)	Cwmbran
Gwynedd (Wales)	Caernarfon
Ha Nan (Vietnam)	Phu Ly
Ha Tay (Vietnam)	Ha Dong
Haa-Alifu (Maldives)	Dhidhdhoo
Haa-Dhaalu (Maldives)	Nolhivaranfaru
Ha'apai (Tonga)	Pangai
Hadramawt (Yemen)	Al-Mukallā
Haho (Togo)	Notsé
Hainan (China)	Haikou
Hainaut (Belgium)	Mons
Haiti	Port-au-Prince
Hajdú-Bihar (Hungary)	Debrecen
Halab (Syria)	Aleppo
Halland (Sweden)	Halmstad
Häme (Finland)	Hämeenlinna
Hamgyong-namdo (North Korea)	Hamhung
Hamgyong-pukto (North Korea)	Ch'ŏngjin
Hampshire (Eng)	Winchester
Hanover (Jamaica)	Lucea
Hararge (Ethiopia)	Harer
Hardap (Namibia)	Mariental
Harghita (Romania)	Miercurea-Ciuc
Haryana (India)	Chandigarh
Hau Giang (Vietnam)	Can Tho
Haute-Corse (France)	Bastia
Haute-Garonne (France)	Toulouse
Haute-Kotto (CA Rep)	Bria
Haute-Loire (France)	Le Puy
Haute-Marne (France)	Chaumont
Haute-Normandie (France)	Rouen
Hautes-Alpes (France)	Gap
Haute-Sangha (CA Rep)	Berbérati
Haute-Saône (France)	Vesoul
Haute-Savoie (France)	Annecy
Hautes-Pyrénées (France)	Tarbes
Haute-Vienne (France)	Limoges
Haute-Zaïre (Dem Rep of Congo)	Kisangani

Country, State, County or Area	Capital or Admin Centre	Country, State, County or Area	Capital or Admin Centre
Haut-Mbomou (CA Rep)	Obo	Indre-et-Loire (France)	Tours
Haut-Ogooué (Gabon)	Masuku	Ingushetia (Russia)	Nazran
Haut-Rhin (France)	Colmar	Inner Mongolia (aka Nei Monggol)	Hu-ho-hao-t'e
Hauts-de-Seine (France)	Nanterre		(aka Hohhot)
Hawaii (USA)	Honolulu	Intibucá (Honduras)	La Esperanza
Hawke's Bay (NZ)	Napier	Iowa (USA)	Des Moines
Hebei (China)	Shijazhuang	**Iran**	Tehran
Hedmark (Norway)	Hamar	**Iraq**	Baghdad
Heilongjiang (China)	Harbin	**Ireland, Republic of**	Dublin
Henan (China)	Zhengzhou	Irian Jaya (Indonesia)	Jayapura
Hentiy (Mongolia)	Öndörhaan	Isabel (Solomon Isles)	Buala
Hérault (France)	Montpellier	Isère (France)	Grenoble
Hercegovina	Mostar	Ishikawa (Japan)	Kanazawa
Hereford and Worcester (Eng)	Worcester	Islas de la Bahia (Honduras)	Roatán
Herrera (Panama)	Chitré	Isle of Man	Douglas
Hertfordshire (Eng)	Hertford	Isle of Wight	Newport
Hessen (Germany)	Wiesbaden	**Israel**	Jerusalem
Heves (Hungary)	Eger	**Italy**	Rome
Hhohho (Swaziland)	Mbabane	Itapúa (Paraguay)	Encarnación
Hidalgo (Mexico)	Pachuca	**Ivory Coast**	Yamoussoukro–
Highland (Scotland)	Inverness		admin
Hiiraan (Somalia)	Beledweyne		Abidjan–
Himãchal Pradesh (India)	Shimla		legislative
Hims (Syria)	Homs	Iwate (Japan)	Morioka
Hodh-ech-Chargui (Mauritania)	Néma	Izabal (Guatemala)	Puerto Barrios
Hodh-el-Gharbi (Mauritania)	Ayoûn el-Atroûs	Jakarta Raya (Indonesia)	Jakarta
Höfudhborgarsvaedhi (Iceland)	Reykjavik	Jalisco (Mexico)	Guadalajara
Hokkaidõ (Japan)	Sapporo	**Jamaica**	Kingston
Honduras	Tegucigalpa	Jammu and Kashmir (India)	Srinagar (in
Hong Kong (aka Hsiang Kang)	Victoria (on Hong		summer)
	Kong Isle)		Jammu
Hordaland (Norway)	Bergen		(in winter)
Horowhenua (NZ)	Levin	Jämtland (Sweden)	Östersund
Houaphan (Laos)	Xam Nua	**Japan**	Tokyo
Houet (Burkina Faso)	Bobo-Dioulasso	Jawar Barat (Indonesia)	Bandung
Hövsgöl (Mongolia)	Mörön	Jawar Tengah (Indonesia)	Semarang
Hubei (China)	Wuhan	Jawar Timur (Indonesia)	Surabaya
Huila (Colombia)	Neiva	Jersey	St Helier
Huita (Angola)	Lubango	Jiangsu (aka Kiangsu) (China)	Nanjing (aka
Humberside (Eng)	Beverley		Nanking)
Hunan (China)	Changsha	Jiangxi (aka Kiangsi) (China)	Nanchang
Hunedoara (Romania)	Deva	Jilin (aka Kirin) (China)	Changchun
Hungary	Budapest	Johor (Malaysia)	Johor Baharu
Hwanghae-namdo (North Korea)	Haeju	**Jordan**	Amman
Hwanghae-pukto (North Korea)	Sariwõn	Jubbada Dhexe (Somalia)	Bu'aale
Hyõgo (Japan)	Kõbe	Jubbada Hoose (Somalia)	Chisimayu
Ialomita (Romania)	Siobozia		(Kismaayo)
Ibaraki (Japan)	Mito	Jujuy (Argentina)	San Salvador
Iceland	Reykjavik	Junin (Peru)	Huancayo
Idaho (USA)	Boise	Junquli (Jongley) (Sudan)	Bor
Iganga (Uganda)	Bulamogi	Jura (France)	Lons-le-Saunier
Île-de-France (France)	Paris	Jura (Swiss canton)	Delémont
Îles Australes (French Polynesia)	Mataura	Kaafu (Maldives)	Male
Îles du Vent (French Polynesia)	Papeete	Kabale (Uganda)	Rubale
Îles Marquises (French Polynesia)	Taiohae	Kabardino-Balkaria (Russia)	Nalchik
Îles sous le Vent (French Polynesia)	Uturoa	Kabarole (Uganda)	Karambe
Îles Tuamotu et Gambier		Kachin (Myanmar)	Myitkyinä
(French Polynesia)	Papeete	Kadiogo (Burkina Faso)	Ouagadougou
Ille-et-Vilaine (France)	Rennes	Kagawa (Japan)	Takamatsu
Illinois (USA)	Springfield	Kalimantan Barat (Indonesia)	Pontianak
Ilubabor (Ethiopia)	Metu	Kalimantan Selatan (Indonesia)	Banjarmasin
Imbabura (Ecuador)	Ibarra	Kalimantan Tengah (Indonesia)	Palangkaraya
Imo (Nigeria)	Owerri	Kalmuck (Russia)	Elista
Inagua, Great and Little	Matthew Town	Kamuli (Uganda)	Namendwa
Inchiri (Mauritania)	Akjoujt	Kanagawa (Japan)	Yokohama
Independencia (Dominican		Kanem (Chad)	Mao
Republic)	Jimani	KaNgwane (South Africa)	Louieville
India (aka Bharat)	New Delhi	Kangwõn-do (North Korea)	Wõnson
Indonesia	Jakarta	Kangwõn-do (South Korea)	Ch'unch'õn
Indre (France)	Châteauroux	Kansas (USA)	Topeka

GEOGRAPHY

Country, State, County or Area	Capital or Admin Centre	Country, State, County or Area	Capital or Admin Centre
Kao-hsiung (Taiwan)	Feng-shan	Kyŏngsang-pukto (South Korea)	Taegu
Kapchorwa (Uganda)	Rukoki	**Kyrgyzstan**	Bishkek
Karachai-Cherkessia (Russia)	Cherkesst	La Altagracia (Dominican Republic)	Higüey
Kara-Kalpak (Russia)	Nukus	La Estrelleta (Dominican Republic)	Elias Piña
Karas (Namibia)	Keetmanshoop	La Guajira (Colombia)	Riohacha
Karelian (Russia)	Petrozavodsk	La Habana (Cuba)	Havana
Karen (Myanmar)	Pa-an	La Libertad (El Salvador)	Nueva San
Karnataka (India)	Bangalore		Salvador
Kärnten (Austria)	Klagenfurt		
Kasai-Occidental (Dem		La Libertad (Peru)	Trujillo
Rep of Congo)	Kananga	La Pampa (Argentina)	Santa Rosa
Kasai-Oriental (Dem		La Paz (El Salvador)	Zacatecoluca
Rep of Congo)	Mbuji-Mayi	La Rioja (Spain)	Logrono
Kayah (Myanmar)	Loi-kaw	Laamu (Maldives)	Hithadhoo
Kazakhstan	Astana	Lac (Chad)	Bol
Kedah (Malaysia)	Alor Setar	Lacs (Togo)	Aného
Kefa (Ethiopia)	Jima	Lagos (Nigeria)	Lkeja
Kelantan (Malaysia)	Kota Bharu	Lai Chau (Vietnam)	Dien Bien
Kemo-Gribingui (CA Rep)	Sibut	Lakshadweep Islands (India)	Kavaratti Island
Kénédougou (Burkina Faso)	Orodara	Lam Dong (Vietnam)	Da Lat
Kent (Eng)	Maidstone	Lambayeque (Peru)	Chiclayo
Kentucky (USA)	Frankfort	Lampung (Indonesia)	Tanjung Karang
Kenya	Nairobi	Lancashire (Eng)	Preston
Kerala (India)	Trivandrum	Landes (France)	Mont-de-Marsan
Kéran (Togo)	Kandé	Languedoc-Roussillon (France)	Montpellier
Kerry (Rep of Ireland)	Tralee	Laois/Leix (Rep of Ireland)	Portlaoise
Keski-Suomi (Finland)	Jyväskylä	**Laos**	Vientiane
Kgalagadi (Botswana)	Tsabong	Lappi (Finland)	Rovaniemi
Kgatleng (Botswana)	Mochudi	Lara (Venezuela)	Barquisimeto
Khakassia (Russia)	Abakan	**Latvia**	Riga
Khammouan (Laos)	Thakhek	Lavalleja (Uruguay)	Minas
Khanh Hoa (Vietnam)	Nha Trang	Lazio (Italy)	Rome
Khanty-Mansi (Russia)	Khanty-Mansüsk	**Lebanon**	Beirut
Khomas (Namibia)	Windhoek	Lebowa (South Africa)	Lebowakgomo
Kien Giang (Vietnam)	Rach Gia	Leicestershire (Eng)	Leicester
Kildare (Rep of Ireland)	Naas	Leitrim (Rep of Ireland)	Carrick-on-
Kilimanjaro (Tanzania)	Moshi		Shannon
Kilkenny (Rep of Ireland)	Kilkenny	Lékoumou (Congo)	Sibiti
Kiribati	Bairiki on Tarawa	Lemba (São Tomé and Principe)	Neves
	Island	Lempira (Honduras)	Gracias
Kitgum (Uganda)	Labongo	Leribe (Lesotho)	Hiotse
Kloto (Togo)	Kpalimé	**Lesotho**	Maseru
Koinaduga (Sierra Leone)	Kabala	Lhaviyani (Maldives)	Naifaru
Kolonjë (Albania)	Ersekë	Liaoning (China)	Shenyang
Komárom (Hungary)	Tatabánya	**Liberia**	Monrovia
Kombo St Mary (Gambia)	Kanifing	Libertador Gen Bernardo	
Komi (Russia)	Syktyv-Kar	O'Higgins (Chile)	Rancagua
Komy Permyak (Russia)	Kudymkar	**Libya**	Tripoli
Kono (Sierra Leone)	Sefadu	**Liechtenstein**	Vaduz
Kopparberg (Sweden)	Falun	Liguria (Italy)	Genoa
Koryak (Russia)	Palana	Likouala (Congo)	Impfondo
Kosovo (Yugoslavia)	Pristina	Limburg (Belgium)	Hasselt
Kossi (Burkina Fasso)	Nouna	Limburg (Netherlands)	Maastricht
Kouilou (Congo)	Pointe-Noire	Limerick (Rep of Ireland)	Limerick
Kouritenga (Burkina Faso)	Koupéla	Limousin (France)	Limoges
Kozah (Togo)	Kara	Lincolnshire (Eng)	Lincoln
Kronoberg (Sweden)	Växjö	Line Isles (Kiribati)	Kiritimati
Kuando Kubango (Angola)	Menongue	**Lithuania**	Vilnius
Kuanza Norte (Angola)	N'Dalatando	Littoral (Cameroon)	Douala
Kuanza Sul (Angola)	Sumbe	Lobata (São Tomé and Principe)	Guadalupe
Kunene (Namibia)	Opuwo	Lobaye (CA Rep)	Mbaiki
Kuria (Kiribati)	Tabontebike	Lofa (Liberia)	Voinjama
Kuwait	Kuwait	Logone Occidental (Chad)	Moundou
KwaNdebele (South Africa)	Siyabuswa	Logone Oriental (Chad)	Doba
Kwara (Nigeria)	Llorin	Loire (France)	Saint-Etienne
KwaZulu (South Africa)	Ulundi	Loire-Atlantique (France)	Nantes
Kweneng (Botswana)	Molepolole	Loiret (France)	Orléans
Kymi (Finland)	Kouvola	Loir-et-Cher (France)	Blois
Kyŏnggi-do (South Korea)	Suwŏn	Lombardy (Italy)	Milan
Kyŏngsang-namdo (South Korea)	Masan	Londonderry (NI)	Londonderry
		Long An (Vietnam)	Tan An

Country, State, County or Area	Capital or Admin Centre	Country, State, County or Area	Capital or Admin Centre
Long Island (Bahamas)	Clarence Town	Markazi (Iran)	Arāk
Longford (Rep of Ireland)	Longford	Marlborough (NZ)	Blenheim
Loreto (Peru)	Iquitos	Marne (France)	Châlons-sur-Marne
Lorraine (France)	Metz		
Los Lagos (Chile)	Puerto Montt	Marowijne (Suriname)	Albina
Los Rios (Ecuador)	Babahoyo	**Marshall Islands**	Dalap-Uliga-Darrit
Los Santos (Panama)	Las Tablas	Martinique (France)	Fort-de-France
Lot (France)	Cahors	Maryland (Liberia)	Harper
Lot-et-Garonne (France)	Agen	Maryland (USA)	Annapolis
Lothian (Scotland)	Edinburgh	Masaka (Uganda)	Kaswa Bukoto
Louisiana (USA)	Baton Rouge	Mashonaland Central (Zimbabwe)	Bindura
Louth (Rep of Ireland)	Dundalk	Mashonaland East (Zimbabwe)	Marondera
Lower River (Gambia)	Mansakonko	Mashonaland West (Zimbabwe)	Chinhoyi
Lower Saxony (Germany)	Hanover	Masindi (Uganda)	Nyangeya
Lozère (France)	Mende	Massachusetts (USA)	Boston
Luapula (Zambia)	Mansa	Mat (Albania)	Burrel
Lubombo (Swaziland)	Siteki	Matabeleland North (Zimbabwe)	Bulawayo
Lunda Norte (Angola)	Lucapa	Matabeleland South (Zimbabwe)	Gwanda
Lunda Sol (Angola)	Saurimo	Mato Grosso (Brazil)	Cuiabá
Luxembourg	Luxembourg	Mato Grosso do Sul (Brazil)	Campo Grande
Luxembourg (Belgium)	Arlon	Matruh (Egypt)	Marsā Matruh
Macao (Portugal)	Macao	Maule (Chile)	Talca
MacCarthy Island (Gambia)	Kuntaur/ Georgetown	**Mauritania**	Nouakchott
		Mauritius	Port Louis
Macedonia	Skopje	Mayaguana (Bahamas)	Abraham's Bay
Macedonia (Greece)	Thessaloniki	Mayenne (France)	Laval
Madagascar	Antananarivo	Mayo (Rep of Ireland)	Castlebar
Madeira (Portugal)	Funchal	Mayo-Kebbi (Chad)	Bongor
Madhya Pradesh (India)	Bhopal	Mayotte (France)	Mamoudzou
Madre de Dios (Peru)	Puerto Maldonado	Maysān (Iraq)	Al-Amārah
		Māzandarān (Iran)	Sari
Magallanes y de la Antártica Chilena (Chile)	Punta Arenas	Mbale (Uganda)	Bunkoko
		Mbarara (Uganda)	Kakika
Magdalena (Colombia)	Santander	Mbomou (CA Rep)	Bangassou
Mahaica/Berbice (Guyana)	Fort Wellington	Meath (Rep of Ireland)	Trim
Maharashtra (India)	Bombay	Mecklenburg-West Pomerania (Germany)	Schwerin
Mahé (Seychelles)	Victoria		
Maiana (Kiribati)	Tebangetua	Meemu (Maldives)	Muli
Maine (USA)	Augusta	Meghālaya (India)	Shillong
Maine-et Loire (France)	Angers	Mehedinti (Romania)	Drobeta-Turnu-Severin
Maio (Cape Verde)	Porto Inglês		
Makira (Solomon Isles)	Kira Kira	Melaka (Malaysia)	Melaka
Malaita (Solomon Isles)	Auki	Merseyside (Eng)	Liverpool
Malawi	Lilongwe	Meta (Colombia)	Villavicencio
Malaysia	Kuala Lumpur	Metropolitan (Chile)	Santiago
Maldives	Malé	Meurthe-et-Moselle (France)	Nancy
Malekula (Vanuatu)	Lakatoro	Meuse (France)	Bar-le-Duc
Mali	Bamako	**Mexico**	Mexico City
Malta	Valletta	México (Mexican state)	Toluca
Maluku (Indonesia)	Ambon	Mé-zóchi (São Tomé and Principe)	Trinidade
Manabi (Ecuador)	Portoviejo		
Manawatu (NZ)	Palmerston North	Michigan (USA)	Lansing
Manche (France)	Saint-Lô	Michoacán (Mexico)	Morelia
Manchester (Jamaica)	Mandeville	**Micronesia**	Kolonia/Palikir
Manica (Mozambique)	Chimolo	Mid-Glamorgan (Wales)	Cardiff
Manicaland (Zimbabwe)	Mutare	Midi-Pyrénées (France)	Toulouse
Maniema (Dem Rep of Congo)	Kindu	Midland Province (Zimbabwe)	Gweru
Manipur (India)	Imphāl	Mid-Western Nepal	Surkhet
Manitoba (Canada)	Winnipeg	Mie (Japan)	Tsu
Manus (Papua New Guinea)	Lorengau	Milne Bay (Papua New Guinea)	Samarai
Mara (Tanzania)	Musoma	Minas Gerais (Brazil)	Belo Horizonte
Marakei (Kiribati)	Rawannawi	Minnesota (USA)	St Paul
Maramures (Romania)	Baia Mare	Minorca (Spain)	Mahon
Maranhão (Brazil)	São Luis	Miranda (Venezuela)	Los Teques
Marche (Italy)	Ancona	Mirditë (Albania)	Rrëshen
Margibi (Liberia)	Kakata	Misiones (Argentina)	Posadas
Maria Trinidad Sánchez (Dominican Republic)	Nagua	Misiones (Paraguay)	San Juan Bautista
Mari-El (Russia)	Yoshkar-Ola	Mississippi (USA)	Jackson
Maritime Region (Togo)	Lomé	Missouri (USA)	Jefferson City

GEOGRAPHY

Country, State, County or Area	Capital or Admin Centre	Country, State, County or Area	Capital or Admin Centre
Miyagi (Japan)	Sendai	New Ireland (Papua New Guinea)	Kavieng
Mizorām (India)	Āīzawi	New Jersey (USA)	Trenton
Moili (Comoros)	Fomboni	New Mexico (USA)	Santa Fe
Moldavia	Kishinev	New Providence (Bahamas)	Nassau
Moluccas (Indonesia)	Amboina	New South Wales	Sydney
Mon (Myanmar)	Moulmein	New York (USA)	Albany
Monaco	Monaco-Ville	**New Zealand**	Wellington
Monagas (Venezuela)	Maturin	Newfoundland (Canada)	St Johns
Monaghan (Rep of Ireland)	Monaghan	Ngamiland (Botswana)	Maun
Mongolia	Ulan Bator	Ngazidja (Comoros)	Moroni
Mono (Benin)	Lokossa	Nghe Tinh (Vietnam)	Vinh
Monseñor Nouel (Dominican Republic)	Bonao	Ngounié (Gabon)	Mouila
		Ngwaketse (Botswana)	Kanye
Montana (USA)	Helena	Niari (Congo)	Loubomo
Montenegro	Podgorica	Niassa (Mozambique)	Lichinga
Montserrado (Liberia)	Bensonville	**Nicaragua**	Managua
Montserrat	Plymouth	Nickerie (Suriname)	Nieuw Nickerie
Morazán (El Salvador)	San Francisco (Gotera)	Nicobar Islands (India)	Car Nicobar
		Nidwalden (Swiss canton)	Stans
Morbihan (France)	Vannes	Niederösterreich (Austria)	Sankt Pölten
Mordovia (Russia)	Saransk	Nièvre (France)	Nevers
Møre og Romsdal (Norway)	Molde	**Niger**	Niamey
Morelos (Mexico)	Cuernavaca	Niger (Nigeria)	Minna
Morobe (Papua New Guinea)	Lae	**Nigeria**	Abuja
Morocco	Rabat	Nikunau (Kiribati)	Rungata
Morona-Santiago (Ecuador)	Macas	Nimba (Liberia)	Sanniquellie
Moroto (Uganda)	Katikekile	Ninawā (Iraq)	Mosul
Moselle (France)	Metz	Ningxia Hui (China)	Yinchuan
Mouhoun (Burkina Faso)	Dédougou	Ninh Thuan (Vietnam)	Phan Rang
Moxico (Angola)	Lwena	Niuas (Tonga)	Hihifo
Moyen-Chari (Chad)	Sarh	Niue (New Zealand)	Alofi
Moyen-Ogooué (Gabon)	Lambaréné	Nógrád (Hungary)	Salgótarján
Mozambique	Maputo	Nonouti (Kiribati)	Teuabu
Mubende (Uganda)	Bageza	Noonu (Maldives)	Manadhoo
Mudug (Somalia)	Galcaio (Gaalkacyo)	Noord-Brabant (Netherlands)	s-Hertogenbosch
		Noord-Holland (Netherlands)	Haarlem
Mures (Romania)	Tirgu Mures	Nord (Cameroon)	Garoua
Musandam (Oman)	Khasab	Nord (France)	Lille
Myanmar (formerly Burma)	Yangon (Rangoon)	Nord (Haiti)	Cap-Haitien
		Nord-Est (Haiti)	Fort-Liberté
Nāgāland (India)	Kohima	Nordhurland eystra (Iceland)	Akureyri
Nahouri (Burkina Faso)	Pô	Nordhurland vestra (Iceland)	Saudhárkrókur
Namentenga (Burkina Faso)	Boulsa	Nordjylland (Denmark)	Alborg
Namibia	Windhoek	Nord-Kivu (Dem Rep of Congo)	Goma
Nana-Mambere (CA Rep)	Bouar	Nordland (Norway)	Bode
Napo (Ecuador)	Tena	Nord-Ouest (Cameroon)	Bamenda
Nariño (Colombia)	Pasto	Nord-Ouest (Haiti)	Port-de-Paix
Nariva/Mayaro (Trinidad and Tobago)	Rio Claro	Nord-Pas-de-Calais (France)	Lille
		Nord-Trønelag (Norway)	Steinkjer
Natal (South Africa)	Pietermaritsburg	Norfolk (Eng)	Norwich
National Capital District (Papua New Guinea)	Port Moresby	Norfolk Island (Aus)	Kingston
		Norrbotten (Sweden)	Luleå
Nauru	Yaren	Norte de Santander (Colombia)	Cúcuta
Navarre (Spain)	Pamplona	North Bank (Gambia)	Kerewan
Nayarit (Mexico)	Tepic	North Carolina (USA)	Raleigh
Ndzouani (Comoros)	Mutsamudu	North Dakota (USA)	Bismarck
Neamt (Romania)	Piatra Neamt	North Eastern Province (Kenya)	Garissa
Nebraska (USA)	Lincoln	**North Korea (aka Choson)**	Pyongyang
Ñeembucu (Paraguay)	Pilar	North Otago (NZ)	Dunedin
Negeri Sembilan (Malaysia)	Seremban	North Rhine–Westphalia (Germany)	Dusseldorf
Nelson Bays (NZ)	Nelson		
Nenets (Russia)	Naryan-Mar	North Solomons (Papua New Guinea)	Buka
Nepal	Kāthmāndu		
Netherlands Antilles	Willemstad	North West Frontier (Pakistan)	Peshāwar
Netherlands	Amsterdam	North Yorkshire (Eng)	Northallerton
Nevada (USA)	Carson City	Northamptonshire (Eng)	Northampton
Nevis (St Kitts and Nevis)	Charlestown	Northern District (Israel)	Tiberias
New Brunswick (Canada)	Fredericton	**Northern Ireland**	Belfast
New Caledonia (France)	Nouméa	Northern Mariana Islands (USA)	Chalan Kanoa
New Hampshire (USA)	Concorde	Northern Province (Fiji)	Labasa

Country, State, County or Area	Capital or Admin Centre	Country, State, County or Area	Capital or Admin Centre
Northern Province (Papua New Guinea)	Popondetta	Overijssel (Netherlands)	Zwolle
Northern Province (Sierra Leone)	Makeni	Övörhangay (Mongolia)	Arvayheer
Northern Province (Zambia)	Kasama	Oxfordshire (Eng)	Oxford
Northern Region (Ghana)	Tamale	Oyo (Nigeria)	Ibadan
Northern Territory (Aus)	Darwin	Paama (Vanuatu)	Liro
Northland (NZ)	Whangarei	Paguê (São Tomé and Principe)	Principe
Northumberland (Eng)	Morpeth	**Pakistan**	Islamabad
Northwest Territories (Canada)	Yellowknife	**Palau**	Koror Island
North-Western Province (Zambia)	Solwezi	**Panama**	Panama City
Norway	Oslo	Panama Canal Zone	Balboa Heights
Nottinghamshire (Eng)	Nottingham	Pando (Bolivia)	Cobija
Nova Scotia (Canada)	Halifax	**Papua New Guinea**	Port Moresby
Nueva Asunción (Paraguay)	General Eugenio A. Garay	Pará (Brazil)	Belém
		Para (Suriname)	Onverwacht
Nueva Esparta (Venezuela)	La Asunción	**Paraguay**	Asunción
Nuevo León (Mexico)	Monterrey	Paraíba (Brazil)	João Pessoa
Nugaal (Somalia)	Garoowe	Paraná (Brazil)	Curitiba
Nunavut (Canada)	Iqaluit	Pas-de-Calais (France)	Arras
Nusa Tenggara Barat (Indonesia)	Mataram	Passoré (Burkina Faso)	Yako
Nusa Tenggara Timur (Indonesia)	Kupang	Pastaza (Ecuador)	Puyo
Nyanga (Gabon)	Tchibanga	Paúl (Cape Verde)	Pombas
Nyanza (Kenya)	Kisumu	Pays de la Loire (France)	Nantes
Oberösterreich (Austria)	Linz	Pemba North (Tanzania)	Wete
Obwalden (Swiss canton)	Sarnen	Pemba South (Tanzania)	Chake Chake
Offaly (Rep of Ireland)	Tullamore	Penang/Pinang (Malaysia)	George Town
Ogooué-Ivindo (Gabon)	Makokou	P'eng-hu (Taiwan)	Ma-kung
Ogooué-Lolo (Gabon)	Koulamoutou	Pennsylvania (USA)	Harrisburg
Ogooué-Maritime (Gabon)	Port-Gentil	Pentecost (Vanuatu)	Loltong
Ogou (Togo)	Atakpamé	Peravia (Dominican Republic)	Bani
Ogun (Nigeria)	Abeokuta	Pernambuco (Brazil)	Recife
Ohangwena (Namibia)	Oshikango	**Peru**	Lima
Ohio (USA)	Columbus	Pest (Hungary)	Budapest
Oio (Guinea-Bissau)	Farim	Petén (Guatemala)	Ciudad Flores
Oise (France)	Beauvais	**Philippines**	Manila
Okavango (Namibia)	Rundu	Phoenix Isles (Kiribati)	Kanton
Okinawa (Japan)	Naha City	Phu Khanh (Vietnam)	Nha Trang
Oklahoma (USA)	Oklahoma City	Phu Tho (Vietnam)	Viet Tri
Olancho (Honduras)	Juticalpa	Phu Yen (Vietnam)	Tuy Hoa
Olt (Romania)	Slatina	Piauí (Brazil)	Teresina
Omaheke (Namibia)	Gobabis	Picardie (France)	Amiens
Oman	Muscat	Pichincha (Ecuador)	Quito
Ombella-Mpoko (CA Rep)	Bimbo	Piedmont (Italy)	Turin
Ömnögovi (Mongolia)	Dalandzadgad	Pitcairn Islands	Adamstown
Omusati (Namibia)	Outapi	Plateau (Nigeria)	Jos
Ondo (Nigeria)	Akure	Plateaux (Congo)	Djambala
Onotoa (Kiribati)	Buariki	Pohjois-Karjala (Finland)	Joensuu
Ontario (Canada)	Toronto	Poitou-Charentes (France)	Poitiers
Oppland (Norway)	Lillehammer	**Poland**	Warsaw
Orange Free State (South Africa)	Bloemfontein	Pomeroon/Supenaam (Guyana)	Anna Regina
Oregon (USA)	Salem	Poni (Burkina Faso)	Gaoua
Orissa (India)	Bhubaneswar	Pool (Congo)	Kinkala
Orkney Islands	Kirkwall	Portland (Jamaica)	Port Antonio
Orne (France)	Alen	**Portugal**	Lisbon
Oshana (Namibia)	Oshakati	Portuguesa (Venezuela)	Guanare
Oshikoto (Namibia)	Tsumeb	Powys (Wales)	Llandrindod Wells
Östergötland (Sweden)	Linköping	Prahova (Romania)	Ploiesti
Østfold (Norway)	Moss	President Hayes (Paraguay)	Pozo Colorado
Oti (Togo)	Sansanné-Mango	Prince Edward Island (Canada)	Charlottetown
Otjozondjupa (Namibia)	Grootfontein	Principe (São Tomé and Principe)	São António
Ouaddai (Chad)	Abéché	Provence-Alpes-Côte D'Azur	Marseille
Ouaka (CA Rep)	Bambari	**Puerto Rico (USA)**	San Juan
Oubritenga (Burkina Faso)	Ziniaré	Puglia (Italy)	Bari
Oudalan (Burkina Faso)	Gorom Gorom	Punjab (India)	Chandigarh
Oudomxay (Laos)	Xay	Punjab (Pakistan)	Lahore
Ouémé (Benin)	Porto-Novo	Putumayo (Colombia)	Mocoa
Ouest (Cameroon)	Bafoussam	Puy-de-Dôme (France)	Clermont-Ferrand
Ouest (Haiti)	Port-au-Prince	Pwani (Tanzania)	Dar es Salaam
Ouham (CA Rep)	Bossangoa	P'yongan-namdo (North Korea)	P'yŏngsan
Ouham-Pendé (CA Rep)	Bozoum	P'yongan-pukto (North Korea)	Sinujiu
		Pyrénées-Atlantiques (France)	Pau

GEOGRAPHY

Country, State, County or Area	Capital or Admin Centre	Country, State, County or Area	Capital or Admin Centre
Pyrénées-Orientales (France)	Perpignan	St Eustatius (Netherland Antilles)	Oranjestad
Qatar	Doha	St Helena	Jamestown
Qinghai (aka Tsinghai) (China)	Xining (aka Hsi-ning)	St James (Jamaica)	Montego Bay
		St Kitts (St Kitts and Nevis)	Basseterre
Quang Binh (Vietnam)	Dong Hoi	**St Kitts and Nevis**	Basseterre
Quang Nam (Vietnam)	Hoi An	**St Lucia**	Castries
Quang Nam-Hoi An (Vietnam)	Ha Long City	St Maarten (Netherland Antilles)	Philipsburg
Quang Ninh (Vietnam)	Ha Long City	St Martin and St Barthélemy	
Quang Tri (Vietnam)	Dong Ha	(Guadeloupe)	Marigot
Quebec (Canada)	Quebec	St Mary (Jamaica)	Port Maria
Queensland (Aus)	Brisbane	St Patrick (Trinidad and Tobago)	Siparia
Quiché (Guatemala)	Santa Cruz	St Thomas (Jamaica)	Morant Bay
Quinara (Guinea-Bissau)	Fulacunda	St Thomas and St John (US Virgins)	Charlotte Amalie
Quindio (Colombia)	Armenia	**St Vincent and Grenadines**	Kingstown
Quintana Roo (Mexico)	Chetumal	St-Pierre and Miquelon (France)	St-Pierre
Qwaqwa (South Africa)	Phuthaditjhaba	Saipan	Chalan Kanoa
Raa (Maldives)	Ugoofaaru	Saitama (Japan)	Urawa
Ragged Island (Bahamas)	Duncan Town	Sakha (Russia)	Yakutsk
Raiatea (French Polynesia)	Uturoa	Sakhalin Island	Yuzhno-Sakhalinsk
Rajasthan (India)	Jaipur		
Rakai (Uganda)	Byakabanda	Sal (Cape Verde)	Santa Maria
Región Autónoma del Atlántico		Salaj (Romania)	Zalău
Norte (Nicaragua)	Rosita	Salamat (Chad)	Am Timan
Región Autónoma del Atlántico		San Andrés y Providencia	San Andrés
Sur (Nicaragua)	Bluefields	**San Marino (Most Serene**	
Región 1 (Nicaragua)	Esteli	**Republic)**	San Marino
Región II (Nicaragua)	León	San Martín (Peru)	Moyobamba
Región III (Nicaragua)	Managua	San Salvador and Rum Cay	Cockburn Town
Región IV (Nicaragua)	Jinotepe	(Bahamas)	
Región V (Nicaragua)	Juigalpa	Sanaag (Somalia)	Erigavo (Ceerigaabo)
Región VI (Nicaragua)	Matagalpa		
Réunion (France)	Saint-Denis	Sánchez Ramirez (Dominican	Cotui
Rhineland Palatinate (Germany)	Mainz	Republic)	
Rhode Island (USA)	Providence	Sangha (Congo)	Ouesso
Rhodes (Greece)	Rhodes	Sangha-Économique (CA Rep)	Nola
Rhône (France)	Lyon	Sanguie (Burkina Faso)	Réo
Rhône-Alpes (France)	Lyon	Sanmatenga (Burkina Faso)	Kaya
Riau (Indonesia)	Pakanbaru	Santa Catarina (Brazil)	Florianópolis
Ribeira Grande (Cape Verde)	Ponta do Sol	Santa Catarina (Cape Verde)	Assomada
Rift Valley (Kenya)	Nakuru	Santa Cruz (Argentina)	Rio Gallegos
Rio Grande do Norte (Brazil)	Natal	Santa Cruz (Cape Verde)	Pedra Badejo
Rio Grande do Sul (Brazil)	Pôrto Alegre	Santa Rosa (Guatemala)	Cuilapa
Rio Muni (Equatorial Guinea)	Bata	Santander (Colombia)	Bucaramanga
Rio Negro (Argentina)	Viedma	Santiago (Dominican Republic)	Santiago de los Caballeros
Rio Negro (Uruguay)	Fray Bentos		
Risaraldo (Colombia)	Pereira	Santo/Maio (Vanuatu)	Luganville
Rivercess (Liberia)	Rivercess City	São Nicolau (Cape Verde)	Ribeira Brava
Rivers (Nigeria)	Port-Harcourt	**São Tomé and Príncipe**	São Tomé
Rogaland (Norway)	Stavanger	São Vicente (Cape Verde)	Mindelo
Romania	Bucharest	Saône-et-Loire (France)	Mâcon
Rondônia (Brazil)	Pôrto Velho	Saramacca (Suriname)	Groningen
Roraima (Brazil)	Boa Vista	Sarawak (Malaysia)	Kuching
Roscommon (Rep of Ireland)	Roscommon	**Sardinia (Italy)**	Cagliari
Rukungiri (Uganda)	Kagunga	Sarthe (France)	Le Mans
Rukwa (Tanzania)	Sumbawanga	Saskatchewan (Canada)	Regina
Russia	Moscow	**Saudi Arabia**	Riyadh
Ruvuma (Tanzania)	Songea	Savoie (France)	Chambéry
Rwanda	Kigali	Saxony (Germany)	Dresden
Ryukyu Islands (Japan)	Naha City (on Okinawa)	Saxony-Anhalt (Germany)	Magdeburg
		Schleswig-Holstein (Germany)	Kiel
Saarland (Germany)	Saarbrücken	Scilly Isles	Hugh Town
Saba (Netherland Antilles)	The Bottom	**Scotland**	Edinburgh
Sabah (Malaysia)	Kota Kinabalu	Seenu (Maldives)	Hithadoo
Sacatepéquez (Guatemala)	Antigua Guatemala	Seine-et-Marne (France)	Melun
		Seine-Maritime (France)	Rouen
St Andrew and St David (Trinidad and Tobago)	Sangre Grande	Seine-Saint-Denis (France)	Bobigny
St Catherine (Jamaica)	Spanish Town	Selenge (Mongolia)	Sühbaatar
St Croix (US Virgins)	Christiansted	**Senegal**	Dakar
St Elizabeth (Jamaica)	Black River	Sèno (Burkina Faso)	Dori
		Serbia	Belgrade

Country, State, County or Area	Capital or Admin Centre
Sergipe (Brazil)	Aracaju
Seychelles	Victoria
Shaanxi (aka Shensi)	Xi'an (aka Sian)
Shaba (Dem Rep of Congo)	Lubumbashi
Shabeellaha Dhexe (Somalia)	Giohar (Jawhar)
Shabeellaha Hoose (Somalia)	Merca (Marka)
Shabwah (Yemen)	Atãq
Shan (Myanmar)	Taunggyi
Shandong (aka Shantung) (China)	Jinan (aka Tsinan)
Shanxi (China)	Taiyuan
Shaviyani (Maldives)	Farukolhu Funadhoo
Shepherd (Vanuatu)	Morua
Shetland Islands	Lerwick
Shewa (Ethiopia)	Addis Ababa
Shiga (Japan)	Ōtsu
Shimane (Japan)	Matsue
Shiselweni (Swaziland)	Nhlangano
Shropshire (Eng)	Shrewsbury
Sichuan (China)	Chengdu
Sicily (Italy)	Palermo
Sidamo (Ethiopia)	Awasa
Sierra Leone	Freetown
Sikkim (India)	Gangtok
Sinã' al-Janubiyah (Egypt)	At-Tur
Sinã' ash-Shamãliyah (Egypt)	Al-'Arish
Sinaloa (Mexico)	Culiacán
Sind (Pakistan)	Karãchi
Singapore	Singapore
Sinoe (Liberia)	Greenville
Sissilli (Burkina Faso)	Léo
Sistãn va Baluchestãn (Iran)	Zãhedãn
Skaraborg (Sweden)	Mariestad
Skrapar (Albania)	Corovoda
Sligo (Rep of Ireland)	Sligo
Slovakia	Bratislava
Slovenia	Lubijana
Society Islands	Papeete
Socotra (Yemen)	Tamrida
Södermanland (Sweden)	Nyköping
Sofala (Mozambique)	Beira
Sogn og Fjordane (Norway)	Leikanger
Solomon Islands	Honiara
Somalia	Mogadishu
Somaliland	Berbera
Somerset (Eng)	Taunton
Somme (France)	Amiens
Somogy (Hungary)	Kaposvár
Sonderjylland (Denmark)	Abenra
Sonora (Mexico)	Hermosillo
Soriano (Uruguay)	Mercedes
Sor-Trøndelag (Norway)	Trondheim
Soum (Burkina Faso)	Djibo
Sourou (Burkina Faso)	Tougan
South Africa	Pretoria–admin Capetown–legislative Bloemfontein–judicial
South Australia	Adelaide
South Carolina (USA)	Columbia
South Dakota (USA)	Pierre
South Glamorgan (Wales)	Cardiff
South Korea	Seoul
South Yorkshire (Eng)	Barnsley
Southern District (Israel)	Beersheba
Southern Highlands (Papua New Guinea)	Mende
Southern Province (Sierra Leone)	Bo

Country, State, County or Area	Capital or Admin Centre
Southern Province (Zambia)	Livingstone
Southland (NZ)	Invercargill
Spain	Madrid
Sri Lanka	Colombo
Staffordshire (Eng)	Stafford
Stann Creek (Belize)	Dangriga
Steiermark (Austria)	Graz
Storstrom (Denmark)	Nykebing
Strathclyde (Scotland)	Glasgow
Suchitepéquez (Guatemala)	Mazatenango
Sucre (Colombia)	Sincelejo
Sucre (Venezuela)	Cumaná
Sud (Cameroon)	Ebolowa
Sud (Haiti)	Les Cayes
Sudan	Khartoum
Sud-Est (Haiti)	Jacmel
Sudhurland (Iceland)	Selfoss
Sudhurnes (Iceland)	Keflavik
Sud-Kivu (Dem Rep of Congo)	Bukavu
Sud-Ouest (Cameroon)	Buea
Suffolk (Eng)	Ipswich
Sühbaatar (Mongolia)	Baruun-urt
Sulawesi Selatan (Indonesia)	Ujung Pandang
Sulawesi Tengah (Indonesia)	Palu
Sulawesi Tenggara (Indonesia)	Kendari
Sulawesi Utara (Indonesia)	Menado
Sumatera Barat (Indonesia)	Padang
Sumatera Utara (Indonesia)	Medan
Suriname	Paramaribo
Surrey (Eng)	Kingston-upon-Thames
Swaziland	Mbabane
Sweden	Stockholm
Switzerland	Berne
Syria	Damascus
Szabics-Szatmár (Hungary)	Nyiregyháza
Tabasco (Mexico)	Villahermosa
Tabiteuea North (Kiribati)	Utiroa
Tabiteuea South (Kiribati)	Buariki
Táchira (Venezuela)	San Cristóbal
Taféa (Vanuatu)	Isangei
Tagant (Mauritania)	Tidjikdja
Tahiti (France)	Papeete
T'ai-chung (Taiwan)	Feng-yuan
Taimyr (Russia)	Dudinka
Tai-nan (Taiwan)	Hsin-ying
Tai-pei (Taiwan)	Pan-ch'iao
Taiwan	Taipei
Tajikistan	Dushanbe
Tamana (Kiribati)	Bakaka
Tamaulipas (Mexico)	Ciudad Victoria
Tamil Nadu (India)	Madras
Tandjilé (Chad)	Lai
Tanzania	Dodoma
Tapoa (Burkina Faso)	Diapaga
Taranaki (NZ)	New Plymouth
Tarapacá (Chile)	Iquique
Tarawa North (Kiribati)	Abaokoro
Tarawa South (Kiribati)	Bairiki
Tarn (France)	Albi
Tarn-et-Garonne (France)	Montauban
Tasmania (Aus)	Hobart
Tatarstan (Russia)	Kazan
Tayside (Scotland)	Dundee
Tchaoudjo (Togo)	Sokodé
Telemark (Norway)	Skien
Teleorman (Romania)	Alexandria
Temburong (Brunei)	Bangar
Temotu (Solomon Isles)	Santa Cruz
Tennessee (USA)	Nashville

GEOGRAPHY

Country, State, County or Area	Capital or Admin Centre	Country, State, County or Area	Capital or Admin Centre
Territoire de Belfort (France)	Belfort	Upper West (Ghana)	Wa
Texas (USA)	Austin	Uri (Swiss canton)	Altdorf
Thaa (Maldives)	Veymandhoo	**Uruguay**	Montevideo
Thailand	Bangkok	Ust-Ordyn-Buryat (Russia)	Ust-Ordynsk
Thames Valley (NZ)	Thames-Coromandel	Utah (USA)	Salt Lake City
		Uttar Pradesh (India)	Lucknow
Thua Thien (Vietnam)	Hue	Uusimaa (Finland)	Helsinki
Thurgau (Swiss canton)	Frauenfeld	Uvs (Mongolia)	Ulaangom
Thuringia (Germany)	Erfurt	**Uzbekistan**	Tashkent
Tibet (aka Xizang) (China)	Lhasa	Vaavu (Maldives)	Felidhoo
Ticino (Swiss canton)	Bellinzona	Vakaga (CA Rep)	Birao
Tien Giang (Vietnam)	My Tho	Valais (Swiss canton)	Sion
Tierra Del Fuego (Argentina)	Ushuaia	Val-de-Marne (France)	Créteil
Tigray (Ethiopia)	Mekele	Val-d'Oise (France)	Pontoise
Timis (Romania)	Timisoara	Valle (Honduras)	Nacaome
Timor Timur (Indonesia)	Dili	Valparaíso (Chile)	Valparaiso
Tipperary (Rep of Ireland)	Clonmel	Valverde (Dominican Republic)	Mao
Tiris Zemmour (Mauritania)	Fdérik	**Vanuatu**	Vila
Tirol (Austria)	Innsbruck	Var (France)	Toulon
Tobago (Trinidad and Tobago)	Scarborough	Värmland (Sweden)	Karlstad
Tocantins (Brazil)	Miracema do Tocantins	Vas (Hungary)	Szombathely
		Västerbotten (Sweden)	Umea
Tochigi (Japan)	Utsunomiya	Västernorrland (Sweden)	Härnösand
Togdheer (Somalia)	Burao (Burco)	Västmanland (Sweden)	Västerås
Togo	Lome	Vaucluse (France)	Avignon
Toledo (Belize)	Punta Gorda	Vaud (Swiss canton)	Lausanne
Tolima (Colombia)	Cali	Vaupés (Colombia)	Mitú
Tolna (Hungary)	Szekszárd	Vava'u (Tonga)	Neiafu
Tombali (Guinea-Bissau)	Catió	Venda (South Africa)	Thohoyandou
Tône (Togo)	Dapaong	Vendée (France)	La Roche-sur-Yon
Tonga	Nuku'alofa	**Venezuela**	Caracas
Tongariro (NZ)	Taupo	Veracruz (Mexico)	Jalapa
Tongatapu (Tonga)	Nuku'alofa	Veraguas (Panama)	Santiago
Tonkolili (Sierra Leone)	Magburaka	Vermont (USA)	Montpelier
Tororo (Uganda)	Sukulu	Vest-Agder (Norway)	Kristiansand
Töv (Mongolia)	Dzuunmod	Vestfirdhir (Iceland)	Isafjördhur
Transkei (South Africa)	Umtata	Vestfold (Norway)	Tønsberg
Transvaal (South Africa)	Pretoria	Vestjaelland (Denmark)	Sore
Trarza (Mauritania)	Rosso	Vesturland (Iceland)	Borgarnes
Trelawny (Jamaica)	Falmouth	Vichada (Colombia)	Puerto Carreño
Trinidad and Tobago	Port of Spain	Victoria (Aus)	Melbourne
Tripura (India)	Agartala	Victoria (Trinidad and Tobago)	Princes Town
Tristan da Cunha	Edinburgh	Vienne (France)	Poitiers
Tropojë (Albania)	Bajram	**Vietnam**	Hanoi
Trujillo (Venezuela)	Trujillo	Villa Clara (Cuba)	Santa Clara
Tucumán (Argentina)	San Miguel	Vinh Phuc (Vietnam)	Vinh Yen
Tungurahua (Ecuador)	Ambato	**Virgin Islands (British)**	Road Town
Tunisia	Tunis	**Virgin Islands (USA)**	Charlotte Amalie
Turkey	Ankara	Virginia (USA)	Richmond
Turkmenistan	Ashkhabad	Vo (Togo)	Vogan
Turks and Caicos Islands	Grand Turk	Vojvodina (Yugoslavia)	Novi Sad
Turku ja Pori (Finland)	Turku	Volta (Ghana)	Ho
Tuscany (Italy)	Florence	Vorarlberg (Austria)	Bregenz
Tuva (Russia)	Kyzyl	Vosges (France)	Épinal
Tuvalu	Fongafale (on Funafuti Isle)	Vrancea (Romania)	Focsani
		Waikato (NZ)	Hamilton
Tyne and Wear (Eng)	Newcastle-upon-Tyne	Wairarapa (NZ)	Masterton
		Wales	Cardiff
Tyrone (NI)	Omagh	Wallis and Futuna Islands (France)	Mata-Utu
Ucayali (Peru)	Pucallpa	Warwickshire (Eng)	Warwick
Udmurtia (Russia)	Izhevsk	Washington (USA)	Olympia
Uganda	Kampala	Wasit (Iraq)	Al-Kut
Ukraine	Kiev	Waterford (Rep of Ireland)	Waterford
Umbria (Italy)	Perugia	Wawa (Togo)	Badou
United Arab Emirates	Abu Dhabi	Welega (Ethiopia)	Nekemte
United Kingdom	London	Welo (Ethiopia)	Dese
United States of America	Washington DC	West Bengal (India)	Calcutta
Upper Demerara/Berbice (Guyana)	Linden	West Coast (NZ)	Greymouth
Upper East (Ghana)	Bolgatanga	West Flanders (Belgium)	Bruges
Upper River (Gambia)	Basse	West Glamorgan (Wales)	Swansea

Country, State, County or Area	Capital or Admin Centre	Country, State, County or Area	Capital or Admin Centre
West Midlands (Eng)	Birmingham	Xianghoang (Laos)	Phônsavan
West New Britain (Papua New Guinea)	Kimbe	Xinjiang Uighur (China)	Urumqi
West Sepik (Papua New Guinea)	Vanimo	Yamalo-Nenets (Russia)	Salekhard
West Sussex (Eng)	Chichester	Yamanashi (Japan)	Kōfu
West Virginia (USA)	Charleston	Yanggang-do (North Korea)	Hyesan
West Yorkshire (Eng)	Wakefield	Yaracuy (Venezuela)	San Felipe
Western Area (Sierra Leone)	Freetown	Yatenga (Burkina Faso)	Ouahigouya
Western Australia	Perth	**Yemen**	Sana'a
Western Division (Gambia)	Brikama	Yogyakarta (Indonesia)	Yogyakarta
Western Equatoria (Sudan)	Yambio	Yonne (France)	Auxerre
Western Highlands (Papua New Guinea)	Mount Hagen	Yoto (Togo)	Tabligbo
		Yucatán (Mexico)	Mérida
Western Isles (Scotland)	Stornaway (Lewis)	**Yugoslavia**	Belgrade
		Yukon Territory (Canada)	Whitehorse
Western Nepal	Pokharā	Yün-lin (Taiwan)	Tou-liu
Western Province (Fiji)	Lautoka	Yunnan (China)	Kunming
Western Province (Kenya)	Kakamega	Yvelines (France)	Versailles
Western Province (Papua New Guinea)	Daru	Zaïre (Angola)	M'Banza Kongo
		Zambézia (Mozambique)	Quelimane
Western Province (Solomon Isles)	Gizo	**Zambia**	Lusaka
Western Province (Zambia)	Mongu	Zamora-Chinchipe (Ecuador)	Zamora
Western Region (Ghana)	Sekondi-Takoradi	Zanzibar North (Tanzania)	Mkokotoni
Western Sahara	Laâyoune (El Aaiún)	Zanzibar South and Central (Tanzania)	Koani
		Zanzibar West (Tanzania)	Zanzibar
Western Samoa	Apia	Zeeland (Netherlands)	Middleburg
Westmeath (Rep of Ireland)	Mullingar	Zhejiang (aka Chekiang) (China)	Hangzhou (aka Hangchow)
Westmoreland (Jamaica)	Savanna-la-Mar		
Wexford (Rep of Ireland)	Wexford	**Zimbabwe**	Harare
Wicklow (Rep of Ireland)	Wicklow	Zio (Togo)	Tsévié
Wiltshire (Eng)	Trowbridge	Zona Especial III (Nicaragua)	San Carlos
Wisconsin (USA)	Madison	Zou (Benin)	Abomey
Woleu-Ntem (Gabon)	Oyem	Zoundwéogo (Burkina Faso)	Manga
Woqooyi Galbeed (Somalia)	Hargeysa	Zuid-Holland (Netherlands)	Hague
Wyoming (USA)	Cheyenne	Zulia (Venezuela)	Maracaibo
Xékong (Laos)	Thong		

Capitals

Capital or Admin Centre	Country, State, County or Area	Capital or Admin Centre	Country, State, County or Area
Aarau	Aargau (Swiss Canton)	Akjoujt	Inchiri (Mauritania)
Abancay	Apurimac (Peru)	**Akmola**	**Kazakhstan**
Abaokoro	Tarawa North (Kiribati)	Akure	Ondo (Nigeria)
Abéché	Ouaddai (Chad)	Akureyri	Nordhurland eystra (Iceland)
Abenra	Sonderjylland (Denmark)		
Abeokuta	Ogun (Nigeria)	Al-Amārah	Maysān (Iraq)
Aberdeen	Grampian (Scotland)	Al-'Arish	Sinā' ash-Shamāliyah (Egypt)
Abidjan-legislative	**Ivory Coast**		
Abomey	Zou (Benin)	Albany	New York (USA)
Abraham's Bay	Mayaguana (Bahamas)	Albi	Tarn (France)
Abu Dhabi	United Arab Emirates	Albina	Marowijne (Suriname)
Abuja	**Nigeria**	Alborg	Nordjylland (Denmark)
Accra	**Ghana**	Aleg	Brakna (Mauritania)
	Greater Accra (Ghana)	Alen	Orne (France)
Adamstown	Pitcairn Islands	Aleppo	Halab (Syria)
Ad-Damazin	An-Nil al-Azraq (Blue Nile) (Sudan)	Alexandria	Teleorman (Romania)
		Al-Fāshir	Dārfur (Sudan)
Addis Ababa	**Ethiopia**	Al-Ghaydah	Al-Mahrah (Yemen)
	Shewa (Ethiopia)	Al-Ghurdaqah	Al-Bahr al-Ahmar (Egypt)
Adelaide	South Australia	**Algiers**	**Algeria**
Agana	**Guam**	Al-Hillah	Bābil (Iraq)
Agartala	Tripura (India)	Alice Town	Bimini Islands (Bahamas)
Agen	Lot-et-Garonne (France)	Al-Kharijah	Al-Wādi al-Jadid (Egypt)
Aginskoe	Agin-Buryat (Russia)	Al-Kut	Wasit (Iraq)
Ajaccio	**Corsica (France)**	Al-Mansurah	Ad-Dagahliyah (Egypt)
	Corse-du-Sud (France)	Al-Mukallā	Hadramawt (Yemen)

GEOGRAPHY

Capital or Admin Centre	Country, State, County or Area	Capital or Admin Centre	Country, State, County or Area
Alofi	Niue (Pacific)	Avignon	Vaucluse (France)
Alor Setar	Kedah (Malaysia)	Awasa	Sidamo (Ethiopia)
Altdorf	Uri (Swiss Canton)	Aylesbury	Buckinghamshire (Eng)
Ālzawi	Mizorām (India)	Ayoûn el-Atroûs	Hodh-el-Gharbi
Am Timan	Salamat (Chad)		(Mauritania)
Ambato	Tungurahua (Ecuador)	Azoques	Cañar (Ecuador)
Amboina	Moluccas (Indonesia)	Az-Zaqāziq	Ash-Sharqiyah (Egypt)
Ambon	Maluku (Indonesia)	Babahoyo	Los Rios (Ecuador)
Amiamé	Amou (Togo)	Bac Giang	Ha Bac (Vietnam)
Amiens	Picardie (French Region)	Bac Lieu	Minh Hai (Vietnam)
	Somme (French	Badou	Wawa (Togo)
	Department)	Bafilo	Assoli (Togo)
Amman	**Jordan**	Bafoussam	Ouest (Cameroon)
Amsterdam	**Netherlands**	Bageza	Mubende (Uganda)
Anadyr	Chukut (Russia)	**Baghdad**	**Iraq**
Ancona	Marche (Italy)	Baia Mare	Maramures (Romania)
Andalucia	Seville (Spain)	Baidoa (Baydhabo)	Bay (Somalia)
Andorra La Vella	Andorra	**Bairiki on Tarawa Island**	**Kiribati**
Aného	Lacs (Togo)		Tarawa South (Kiribati)
Angers	Maine-et Loire (France)	Bairiki Islet	Gilbert Isles (Kiribati)
Angoulême	Charente (France)	Bajram	Tropojë (Albania)
Ankara	**Turkey**	Bakaka	Tamana (Kiribati)
Anna Regina	Pomeroon/Supenaam	**Baku**	**Azerbaijan**
	(Guyana)	Balboa Heights	Panama Canal Zone
Annapolis	Maryland (USA)	**Bamako**	**Mali**
An-Nāsiriyah	Dhi Qār (Iraq)	Bambari	Ouaka (C. A. Rep)
Annecy	Haute-Savoie (France)	Bamenda	Nord-Ouest (Cameroon)
Antananarivo	**Madagascar**	**Bandar Seri Begawan**	**Brunei**
Anteeren	Banaba (Kiribati)	Bandung	Jawar Barat (Indonesia)
Antigua Guatemala	Sacatepéquez (Guatemala)	Banfora	Comoé (Burkina Faso)
Apia	**Samoa**	Bangalore	Karnataka (India)
Appenzell	Appenzell Inner-Rhoden	Bangar	Temburong (Brunei)
	(Swiss Canton)	Bangassou	Mbomou (C. A. Rep)
Aracaju	Sergipe (Brazil)	**Bangkok**	**Thailand**
Arāk	Markazi (Iran)	**Bangui**	**Central African Republic**
Ararua	Cook Islands	Banhã	Al-Qalyubiyah (Egypt)
	(New Zealand)	Bani	Peravia (Dom Republic)
Arba Minch	Gemu Gofa (Ethiopia)	Banjarmasin	Kalimantan Selatan
Arendal	Aust-Agder (Norway)		(Indonesia)
Arlon	Luxembourg (Belgium)	**Banjul**	**Gambia**
Armagh	Armagh (N.I.)	Barcelona	Anzoátegui (Venezuela)
Armenia	Quindio (Colombia)	Barcelona	Catalonia (Spain)
Arnhem	Gelderland (Netherlands)	Barclayville	Grand Kru (Liberia)
Ar-Ramādi	Al-Anbār (Iraq)	Bari	Apulia a.k.a. Puglia (Italy)
Arras	Pas-de-Calais (France)	Bar-le-Duc	Meuse (France)
Arthur's Town	Cat Island (Bahamas)	Barnsley	South Yorkshire (Eng)
Arvayheer	Övörhangay (Mongolia)	Barquisimeto	Lara (Venezuela)
Asela	Arsi (Ethiopia)	Barranquilla	Atlántico (Colombia)
Ashkhabad	Turkmenistan	Baruun-urt	Sühbaatar (Mongolia)
Asmara	Eritrea	Basel	Basel-Stadt (Swiss Canton)
Assen	Drenthe (Netherlands)	Basse	Upper River (Gambia)
Assomada	Santa Catarina	**Basse-Terre**	**Guadeloupe**
	(Cape Verde)	Basseterre	St Kitts and Nevis
Asunción	**Paraguay**		St Kitts (St Kitts and
	Central Region (Paraguay)		Nevis)
Atakpamé	Des Plateaux (Togolese	Bastia	Haute-Corse (France)
	Region)	Bata	Rio Muni (Equatorial
	Ogou (Togolese Prefecture)		Guinea)
Atāq	Shabwah (Yemen)	Baton Rouge	Louisiana (USA)
Atar	Adrar (Mauritania)	Bayamo	Granma (Cuba)
Athens	**Greece**	Beauvais	Oise (France)
Ati	Batha (Chad)	Bedford	Bedfordshire (Eng)
Atlanta	Georgia (USA)	Beersheba	Southern District (Israel)
At-Tur	Sinā' al-Janubiyah (Egypt)	**Beijing (a.k.a. Peking)**	**China**
Auch	Gers (France)	Beira	Sofala (Mozambique)
Augusta	Maine (USA)	**Beirut**	**Lebanon**
Auki	Malaita (Solomon Isles)	Beledweyne	Hiiraan (Somalia)
Aurillac	Cantal (France)	Belém	Pará (Brazil)
Austin	Texas (USA)	**Belfast**	**Northern Ireland**
Auxerre	Yonne (France)		Antrim (N.I.)

Capital or Admin Centre	Country, State, County or Area
Belfort	Territoire de Belfort (France)
Belgrade	**Yugoslavia**
	Serbia
Bellinzona	Ticino (Swiss Canton)
Belmopan	**Belize**
Belo Horizonte	Minas Gerais (Brazil)
Bender Cassim (Boosaaso)	Bari (Somalia)
Benin City	Bendel (Nigeria)
Bensonville	Montserrado (Liberia)
Berbera	Somaliland
Berbérati	Haute-Sangha (C. A. Rep)
Bergen	Hordaland (Norway)
Berlin	**Germany**
Berne	**Switzerland**
Bertoua	Est (Cameroon)
Besancon	Doubs (France)
Beverley	Humberside (Eng)
Bhopal	Madhya Pradesh (India)
Bhubaneswar	Orissa (India)
Bien Hoa	Dong Nai (Vietnam)
Bimbo	Ombella-Mpoko (C. A. Rep)
Bindura	Mashonaland Central (Zimbabwe)
Birao	Vakaga (C. A. Rep)
Birmingham	West Midlands (Eng)
Bishkek	**Kyrgyzstan**
Bisho	Ciskei (South Africa)
Bismarck	North Dakota (USA)
Bissau	**Guinea-Bissau**
	Biombo (Guinea-Bissau)
Black River	St Elizabeth (Jamaica)
Blenheim	Marlborough (NZ)
Bloemfontein-judicial	**South Africa**
	Orange Free State (South Africa)
Blois	Loir-et-Cher (France)
Bluefields	Región Autónoma del Atlántico Sur (Nic)
Bo	Southern Province (Sierra Leone)
Boa Vista	Roraima (Brazil)
Bobigny	Seine-Saint-Denis (France)
Bobo-Dioulasso	Houet (Burkina Faso)
Bode	Nordland (Norway)
Bogandé	Gnagna (Burkina Faso)
Bogotá	**Colombia**
	Cundinamarca (Colombia)
Boise	Idaho (USA)
Bol	Lac (Chad)
Bolgatanga	Upper East (Ghana)
Bologna	Emilia-Romagna (Italy)
Bombay	Maharashtra (India)
Bonao	Monseñor Nouel (Dom Republic)
Bongor	Mayo-Kebbi (Chad)
Bor	Junquli (Jongley) (Sudan)
Bordeaux	Aquitaine (French Region) Gironde (French Department)
Borgarnes	Vesturland (Iceland)
Bossangoa	Ouham (C. A. Rep)
Boston	Massachusetts (USA)
Bouar	Nana-Mambere (C. A. Rep)
Boulsa	Namentenga (Burkina Faso)
Bourg-en-Bresse	Ain (France)
Bourges	Cher (France)

Capital or Admin Centre	Country, State, County or Area
Bozoum	Ouham-Pendé (CA Rep)
Brasilia	**Brazil**
Bratislava	**Slovakia**
Brazzaville	**Congo: People's Republic**
Bregenz	Vorarlberg (Austria)
Bria	Haute-Kotto (CA Rep)
Bridgetown	**Barbados**
Brikama	Western Division (Gambia)
Brisbane	Queensland (Aus)
Bristol	Avon (Eng)
Bruge	West Flanders (Belgium)
Brussels	**Belgium**
	Brabant (Belgium)
Bu'aale	Jubbada Dhexe (Somalia)
Buala	Isabel (Solomon Isles)
Buariki	Onotoa (Kiribati) Tabiteuea South (Kiribati)
Bucaramanga	Santander (Colombia)
Buchanan	Grand Bassa (Liberia)
Bucharest	**Romania**
Budapest	**Hungary**
	Pest (Hungary)
Buea	Sud-Ouest (Cameroon)
Buenos Aires	**Argentina**
Bujumbura	**Burundi**
Buka	North Solomons (Papua New Guinea)
Bukavu	Sud-Kivu (Dem Rep of Congo)
Bulamogi	Iganga (Uganda)
Bulawayo	Matabeleland North (Zimbabwe)
Bumbaire	Bushenyi (Uganda)
Bungatira	Gulu (Uganda)
Bunkoko	Mbale (Uganda)
Buon Me Thoat	Dac Lac (Vietnam)
Burao (Burco)	Togdheer (Somalia)
Burrel	Mat (Albania)
Busaru	Bundibugyo (Uganda)
Byakabanda	Rakai (Uganda)
Caacupé	Cordillera (Paraguay)
Caen	Basse Normandie (French Region) Calvados (French Department)
Caernarfon	Gwynedd (Wales)
Cagliari	**Sardinia (Italy)**
Cahors	Lot (France)
Cairo	**Egypt**
Calabar	Cross River (Nigeria)
Calcutta	West Bengal (India)
Cali	Tolima (Colombia)
Cambridge	Cambridgeshire (Eng)
Campo Grande	Mato Grosso do Sul (Brazil)
Can Tho	Hau Giang (Vietnam)
Canberra	**Australia**
	Australian Capital Territory
Cape Coast	Central Region (Ghana)
Capetown-legislative	**South Africa**
Cap-Haitien	Nord (Haiti)
Car Nicobar	Nicobar Islands
Caracas	**Venezuela**
Carcassonne	Aude (France)
Cardiff	**Wales**
	Mid-Glamorgan (Wales) South Glamorgan (Wales)
Carlisle	Cumbria (Eng)
Carlow	Carlow (Eire)

GEOGRAPHY

Capital or Admin Centre	Country, State, County or Area	Capital or Admin Centre	Country, State, County or Area
Carmarthen	Dyfed (Wales)	Clonmel	Tipperary (Eire)
Carrick-on-Shannon	Leitrim (Eire)	Cobán	Alta Verapaz (Guatemala)
Carson City	Nevada (USA)	Cobija	Pando (Bolivia)
Cartagena	Bolivar (Colombia)	Cockburn Town	San Salvador & Rum Cay
Castlebar	Mayo (Eire)	Cojutepeque	Cuscatián (El Salvador)
Castries	**Saint Lucia**	Colhaique (Chile)	Aisén del Gen Carlos
Catanzaro	Calabria (Italy)		Ibáñez del Campo
Catió	Tombali (Guinea-Bissau)	Colmar	Haut-Rhin (France)
Cavan	Cavan (Eire)	**Colombo**	**Sri Lanka**
Caxito	Bengo (Angola)	Colonel Hill	Crooked Island
Cayenne	**French Guiana**		(Bahamas)
Chachapoyas	Amazonas (Peru)	Columbia	South Carolina (USA)
Chaguanas	Caroni (Trinidad & Tobago)	Columbus	Ohio (USA)
Chake Chake	Pemba South (Tanzania)	**Conakry**	**Guinea**
Chalan Kanoa	Northern Mariana Islands	Conceptión	Bio-Bio (Chile)
	(Pacific)	Concorde	New Hampshire (USA)
Chalan Kanoa	Saipan	**Copenhagen**	**Denmark**
Châlons-sur-Marne	Champagne-Ardenne	Copiapó	Atacama (Chile)
	(French Region)	Cork	Cork (Eire)
	Marne (French	Coro	Falcón (Venezuela)
	Department)	Coronel Oviedo	Caaguazú (Paraguay)
Chambéry	Savoie (France)	Corovoda	Skrapar (Albania)
Chandigar	Haryana (India)	Cotonou	Atlantique (Benin)
Chandigar	Punjab (India)	Cotui	Sánchez Ramirez
Changchun	Jilin (aka Kirin)		(Dom Republic)
Changsha	Hunan (China)	Craiova	Dolj (Romania)
Charleston	West Virginia (USA)	Créteil	Val-de-Marne (France)
Charlestown	Nevis (St Kitts and Nevis)	Cúcuta	Norte de Santander
Charleville-Mézières	Ardennes (France)		(Colombia)
Charlotte Amalie	**Virgin Islands (U.S.A.)**	Cuenca	Azuay (Ecuador)
	St Thomas & St John	Cuernavaca	Morelos (Mexico)
	(US Virgins)	Cuiabá	Mato Grosso (Brazil)
Charlottetown	Prince Edward Island	Cuilapa	Santa Rosa (Guatemala)
	(Canada)	Culiacán	Sinaloa (Mexico)
Chartres	Eure-et-Loire (France)	Cumaná	Sucre (Venezuela)
Châteauroux	Indre (France)	Curitiba	Paraná (Brazil)
Chaumont	Haute-Marne (France)	Cuzco	Cuzco (Peru)
Cheboksary	Chuvasia (Russia)	Cwmbran	Gwent (Wales)
Chelmsford	Essex (Eng)	Da Lat	Lam Dong (Vietnam)
Chengdu	Sichuan (China)	**Dakar**	**Senegal**
Cherkesst	Karachai-Cherkessia	Dalandzadgad	Ömnögovi (Mongolia)
	(Russia)	Damanhur	Al-Buhayrah (Egypt)
Chester	Cheshire (Eng)	**Damascus**	**Syria**
Chetumal	Quintana Roo (Mexico)		Dimashq (Syria)
Cheyenne	Wyoming (USA)	Damphu (Bhutan)	Chirang
Chichester	West Sussex (Eng)	Dangriga	Stann Creek (Belize)
Chiclayo	Lambayeque (Peru)	Dapaong	Des Savanes (Togolese
Chilpancingo	Guerrero (Mexico)		Region)
Chimolo	Manica (Mozambique)		Tône (Togolese
Chinhoyi	Mashonaland West		Prefecture)
	(Zimbabwe)	Dar es Salaam	Pwani (Tanzania)
Chipata	Eastern Province (Zambia)	Darrit-Uliga-Dalap	
Chisimayu (Kismaayo)	Jubbada Hoose (Somalia)	(on Majuro isle)	Marshall Islands
Chitré	Herrera (Panama)	Daru	Western Province
Ch'öngjin	Hamgyong-pukto (North		(Papua New Guinea)
	Korea)	Darwin	Northern Territory (Aus)
Ch'önju	Chõlla-pukto (South Korea)	David	Chiriqui (Panama)
Choybaisan	Dornod (Mongolia)	Debre Markos	Gojam (Ethiopia)
Christchurch	Canterbury (NZ)	Debrecen	Hajdú-Bihar (Hungary)
Christiansted	St Croix (US Virgins)	Dédougou	Mouhoun (Burkina Faso)
Ch'unch'ön	Kangwõn-do (South Korea)	Delémont	Jura (Swiss Canton)
Chur	Graubunden (Swiss	**Denpassar**	**Bali (Indonesia)**
	Canton)	Denver	Colorado (USA)
Ciudad Bolivar	Bolivar (Venezuela)	Des Moines	Iowa (USA)
Ciudad del Este	Alto Paraná (Paraguay)	Dese	Welo (Ethiopia)
Ciudad Flores	Petén (Guatemala)	Deva	Hunedoara (Romania)
Ciudad Victoria	Tamaulipas (Mexico)	**Dhaka**	**Bangladesh**
Clarence Town	Long Island (Bahamas)	Dhankutä	Eastern Nepal
Clermont-Ferrand	Auvergne (Frech Region)	Dhidhdhoo	Haa-Alifu (Maldives)
Puy-de-Dôme	(French Department)	Diapaga	Tapoa (Burkina Faso)

Capital or Admin Centre	Country, State, County or Area
Diébougou	Bougouriba (Burkina Faso)
Dien Bien	Lai Chau (Vietnam)
Digne	Alpes-de-Haute-Provence (France)
Dijon	Bourgogne/Burgundy (French Region) Cote-d'Or (French Department)
Dili	Eastern Timor (Pacific)
Dili	Timor Timur (Indonesia)
Dipāyal	Far-Western Nepal
Dispur	Assam (India)
Djambala	Plateaux (Congo)
Djibo	Soum (Burkina Faso)
Djibouti	**Djibouti**
Doba	Logone Oriental (Chad)
Dodoma	**Tanzania**
Doha	**Qatar**
Dong Ha	Quang Tri (Vietnam)
Dong Hoi	Quang Binh (Vietnam)
Dorchester	Dorset (Eng)
Dori	Sèno (Burkina Faso)
Douala	Littoral (Cameroon)
Douglas	Isle of Man
Dover	Delaware (USA)
Downpatrick	Down (N.I.)
Dr Pedro P. Peña	Boquerón (Paraguay)
Drammen	Buskerud (Norway)
Dresden	Saxony (Germany)
Drobeta-Turnu-Severin	Mehedinti (Romania)
Dublin	**Republic of Ireland** Dublin (rep of Ireland)
Dudinka	Taimyr (Russia)
Dumfries	Dumfries and Galloway (Scotland)
Duncan Town	Ragged Island (Bahamas)
Dundalk	Louth (Eire)
Dundee	Tayside (Scotland)
Dunedin	North Otago (NZ)
Dungxoai	Binh Phuoc (Vietnam)
Durham	Durham (Eng)
Dusa Marreb (Dhuusamarreeb)	Galguduud (Somalia)
Dushanbe	**Tadzhikstan**
Düsseldorf	Nordrhein-Westfalen (Germany)
Dzhohar	Chechnya
Dzuunmod	Töv (Mongolia)
Eas	Ambrym (Vanuatu)
Ebolowa	Sud (Cameroon)
Edinburgh	**Scotland** Lothian (Scotland)
Edinburgh	Tristan da Cunha
Edmonton	Alberta (Canada)
Eger	Heves (Hungary)
Egilsstadhir	Austurland (Iceland)
Eisenstadt	Burgenland (Austria)
Elias Piña	La Estrelleta (Dom Republic)
Elista	Kalmuck (CIS)
Embu	Eastern Province (Kenya)
Encarnación	Itapúa (Paraguay)
Ennis	Clare (Eire)
Enniskillen	Fermanagh (N.I.)
Enugu	Anambra (Nigeria)
Épinal	Vosges (France)
Erfurt	Thuringia (Germany)
Erigavo (Ceerigaabo)	Sanaag (Somalia)
Ersekë	Kolonjë (Albania)
Esteli	Región 1 (Nicaragua)

Capital or Admin Centre	Country, State, County or Area
Évreux	Eure (France)
Évry	Essonne (France)
Exeter	Devon (Eng)
Eydhafushi	Baa (Maldives)
Fada N'Gourma	Gourma (Burkina Faso)
Falmouth	Trelawny (Jamaica)
Falun	Kopparberg (Sweden)
Farim	Oio (Guinea-Bissau)
Farukolhu Funadhoo	Shaviyani (Maldives)
Faya	Borkou-Ennedi-Tibesti (Chad)
Fdérik	Tiris Zemmour (Mauritania)
Felidhoo	Vaavu (Maldives)
Feng-shan	Kao-hsiung (Taiwan)
Feng-yuan	T'ai-chung (Taiwan)
Florence	Tuscany (Italy)
Florencia	Caquetá (Colombia)
Florianópolis	Santa Catarina (Brazil)
Flying Fish Cove	Christmas Island (Aus)
Foah Mulah	Gnyaviyani (Maldives)
Focsani	Vrancea (Romania)
Foix	Ariège (France)
Fomboni	Moili (Comoros)
Fongafale (on Funafuti atoll)	**Tuvalu**
Fort Wellington	Mahaica/Berbice (Guyana)
Fortaleza	Ceará (Brazil)
Fort-de-France	**Martinique (France)**
Fort-Liberté	Nord-Est (Haiti)
Franceville	Haut-Ogooué (Gabon)
Frankfort	Kentucky (USA)
Frauenfeld	Thurgau (Swiss Canton)
Fray Bentos	Rio Negro (Uruguay)
Fredericton	New Brunswick (Canada)
Freeport	Grand Bahama
Freetown	**Sierra Leone** Western Area (Sierra Leone)
Fuerte Olimpio	Alto Paraguay (Paraguay)
Fulacunda	Quinara (Guinea-Bissau)
Funchal	**Madeira**
Fuzhou (aka Foochow)	Fujian (aka Fukien)
Gabarone	**Botswana**
Galcaio (Gaalkacyo)	Mudug (Somalia)
Galway	Galway (Eire)
Gāndhinagar	Gujarāt (India)
Gangtok	**Sikkim (India)**
Gaoua	Poni (Burkina Faso)
Gap	Haute-Alpes (France)
Garbahaarrey	Gedo (Somalia)
Garissa	North Eastern Province (Kenya)
Garoowe	Nugaal (Somalia)
Garoua	Nord (Cameroon)
Gbarnga	Bong (Liberia)
General Eugenio A. Garay	Nueva Asunción (Paraguay)
Genoa	Liguria (Italy)
George Town	Penang/Pinang (Malaysia)
Georgetown	Ascension
Georgetown	**Cayman Islands**
Georgetown	**Guyana**
Ghent	East Flanders (Belgium)
Gibeon	Namaland (Namibia)
Giohar Jawhar	Shabeellaha Dhexe (Somalia)
Gibeon	Namaland (Namibia)
Giohar (Jawhar)	Shabeellaha Dhexe (Somalia)
Gisborne	East Cape (NZ)
Giyani	Gazankulu (South Africa)

GEOGRAPHY

Capital or Admin Centre	Country, State, County or Area	Capital or Admin Centre	Country, State, County or Area
Gizo	Western Province (Solomon Isles)	Harper	Maryland (Liberia)
		Harrisburg	Pennsylvania (USA)
Glasgow	Strathclyde (Scotland)	Hartford	Connecticut (USA)
Glenrothes	Fife (Scotland)	Hasselt	Limburg (Belgium)
Gloucester	Gloucestershire (Eng)	**Havana**	**Cuba**
Goba	Bale (Ethiopia)		La Habana (Cuba)
Gobabis	Omaheke (Namibia)	Hefei (aka Ho-fei)	Anhui (aka Anhwei)
Godthaab (a.k.a.Nuuk)	**Greenland (a.k.a. Kalaallit Nunaat)**	Helena	Montana (USA)
		Helsinki	**Finland**
Goiânia	Goiás (Brazil)		Uusimaa (Finland)
Goma	Nord-Kivu (Dem Rep of Congo)	Herisau	Appenzell Ausser-Rhoden (Swiss Canton)
Gonaives	Artibonite (Haiti)	Hermosillo	Sonora (Mexico)
Goroka	Eastern Highlands (Papua New Guinea)	Hertford	Hertfordshire (Eng)
		Higüey	La Altagracia (Dom Republic)
Gorom Gorom	Oudalan (Burkina Faso)		
Gracias	Lempira (Honduras)	Hihifo	Niuas (Tonga)
Grand Turk	**Turks and Caicos Islands**	Hillerod	Frederiksborg (Denmark)
Graz	Steiermark (Austria)	Hinche	Centre Departement (Haiti)
Greenville	Sinoe (Liberia)	Hiotse	Leribe (Lesotho)
Grenoble	Isère (France)	Hithadhoo	Laamu (Maldives)
Greymouth	West Coast (NZ)	Hithadoo	Seenu (Maldives)
Groningen	Saramacca (Suriname)	Ho	Volta (Ghana)
Grootfontein	Otjozondjupa (Nambia)	Hobart	Tasmania
Guadalajara	Jalisco (Mexico)	Hoi An	Quang Nam (Vietnam)
Guadalupe	Lobata (São Tomé & Principe)	Homs	Hims (Syria)
		Honiara	**Solomon Islands**
Guanare	Portuguesa (Venezuela)		Guadalcanal (Solomon Isles)
Guangzhou (aka Canton)	Guangdong (aka Kwangtung)	Honolulu	Hawaii (USA)
Guaranda	Bolivar (Ecuador)	Houayxay	Bokeo (Laos)
Guatemala City	**Guatemala**	Hsin-ying	Tai-nan (Taiwan)
Guayaquil	Guayas (Ecuador)	Huancayo	Junin (Peru)
Guéret	Creuse (France)	Huaraz	Ancash (Peru)
Guiyang (aka Kuei-yang)	Guizhou (aka Kweichow)	Hue	Bin Tri Thien (Vietnam)
Gwanda	Matabeleland South (Zimbabwe)	Hugh Town	Scilly Isles
		Hu-ho-hao-t'e (aka Hohhot)	Inner Mongolia (aka Nei Monggol)
Gweru	Midland Province (Zimbabwe)	Hyderabad	Andhra Pradesh (India)
Ha Dong	Ha Tay (Vietnam)	Hyesan	Yanggang-do (North Korea)
Ha Giang	Ha Tuyen (Vietnam)	Ibadan	Oyo (Nigeria)
Ha Long City	Quang Nam-Hoi An (Vietman)	Ibarra	Imbabura (Ecuador)
		Impfondo	Likouala (Congo)
Ha Long City	Quang Ninh (Vietman)	Imphāl	Manipur (India)
Haarlem	Noord-Holland (Netherlands)	Innsbruck	Tirol (Austria)
		Invercargill	Southland (NZ)
Haeju	Hwanghae-namdo (North Korea)	Inverness	Highland (Scotland)
		Ipswich	Suffolk (Eng)
Hague	Zuid-Holland (Netherlands)	Iqaluit	Nunavut (Canada)
Haikou	Hainan (China)	Iquique	Tarapacá (Chile)
Hakha	Chin (Myanmar)	Iquitos	Loreto (Peru)
Halifax	Nova Scotia (Canada)	Isafjördhur	Vestfirdhir (Iceland)
Halmstad	Halland (Sweden)	Isangei	Taféa (Vanuatu)
Hamar	Hedmark (Norway)	**Islamabad**	**Pakistan**
Hämeenlinna	Häme (Finland)	Itānagar	Arunāchal Pradesh (India)
Hamhung	Hamgyong-namdo (North Korea)	Izhevsk	Udmurtia (Russia)
		Jackson	Mississippi (USA)
Hamilton	**Bermuda**	Jacmel	Sud-Est (Haiti)
Hamilton	Waikato (NZ)	Jaipur	Rajasthan (India)
Hanga Roa	Easter Island	Jakar	Bumthang (Bhutan)
Hangzhou (aka Hangchow)	Zhejiang (aka Chekiang)	**Jakarta**	**Indonesia**
			Jakarta Raya (Indonesia)
Hanoi	**Vietnam**	Jalapa	Veracruz (Mexico)
Hanover	Niedersachsen (Germany)	Jamestown	St Helena
Harare	**Zimbabwe**	**Jayapura**	**Irian Jaya (Indonesia)**
Harbin	Heilongjiang (China)	Jefferson City	Missouri (USA)
Harer	Hararge (Ethiopia)	Jérémie	Grande Anse (Haiti)
Hargeysa	Woqooyi Galbeed (Somalia)	**Jerusalem**	**Israel**
		Jima	Kefa (Ethiopia)
Härnösand	Västernorrland (Sweden)	Jimani	Independencia (Dom

Capital or Admin Centre	Country, State, County or Area
	Republic)
Jinan (aka Tsinan)	Shandong (aka Shantung)
Jinotepe	Región IV (Nicaragua)
João Pessoa	Paraíba (Brazil)
Joensuu	Pohjois-Karjala (Finland)
Johor Baharu	Johor (Malaysia)
Jos	Plateau (Nigeria)
Jubã	Eastern Equatoria (Sudan)
Juigalpa	Región V (Nicaragua)
Juneau	Alaska (USA)
Juticalpa	Olancho (Honduras)
Jyväskylä	Keski-Suomi (Finland)
Kabala	Koinaduga (Sierra Leone)
Kabul	**Afghanistan**
Kabwe	Central Province (Zambia)
Kaédi	Gorgol (Mauritania)
Kaga-Bandoro	Gribingui-Economique (CA Rep)
Kagunga	Rukungiri (Uganda)
Kakamega	Western Province (Kenya)
Kakata	Margibi (Liberia)
Kakika	Mbarara (Uganda)
Kampala	**Uganda**
Kananga	Kasai-Occidental (Dem Rep of Congo)
Kanazawa	Ishikawa (Japan)
Kandé	Kéran (Togo)
Kanggye	Chagang-do (North Korea)
Kanifing	Kombo St. Mary (Gambia)
Kanton	Phoenix Isles (Kiribati)
Kanye	Ngwaketse (Botswana)
Kaposvár	Somogy (Hungary)
Kara	Kozah (Togo)
Karãchi	Sind (Pakistan)
Karambe	Kabarole (Uganda)
Kariatebike	Abemama (Kiribati)
Karlskrona	Blekinge (Sweden)
Karlstad	Värmland (Sweden)
Kasama	Northern Province (Zambia)
Kasane	Chobe (Botswana
Kaswa Bukoto	Masaka (Uganda)
Kãthmãndu	**Nepal** Central Nepal
Katikekile	Moroto (Uganda)
Katima Mulilo	Caprivi Oos (Namibia)
Kavaratti Island	Lakshadweep Islands (India)
Kavieng	New Ireland (Papua New Guinea)
Kaya	Sanmatenga (Burkina Faso)
Kazan	Tatarstan
Kecskemét	Bács-Kiskun (Hungary)
Keetmanshoop	Karas (Namibia)
Keflavik	Sudhurnes (Iceland)
Kemps Bay	Andros Island (Bahamas)
Kendari	Sulawesi Tenggara (Indonesia)
Kenema	Eastern Province (Sierra Leone)
Kerema	Gulf (Papua New Guinea)
Kerewan	North Bank (Gambia)
Kerkira	**Corfu**
Khania	**Crete**
Khartoum	**Sudan**
Khanty-Mansüsk	Kharty-Mansi (Russia)
Khasab	Musandam (Oman)
Khorixas	Damaraland (Namibia)
Kiel	Schleswig-Holstein (Germany)

Capital or Admin Centre	Country, State, County or Area
Kiev	**Ukraine**
Kiffa	El-Acâba (Mauritania)
Kigali	**Rwanda**
Kilkenny	Kilkenny (Eire)
Kimbe	West New Britain (Papua New Guinea)
Kindu	Maniema (Dem Rep of Congo)
Kingston	**Jamaica**
Kingston	Norfolk Island
Kingston-upon-Thames	Surrey (Eng)
Kingstown	St Vincent and Grenadines
Kinkala	Pool (Congo)
Kinsasha	**Congo: Democratic Republic**
Kira Kira	Makira (Solomon Isles)
Kiritimati	Line Isles (Kiribati)
Kirkwall	Orkney Islands
Kisangani	Haute-Zaire (Dem Rep of Congo)
Kishinev	**Moldavia**
Kisumu	Nyanza (Kenya)
Kizyl	Tuva (CIS)
Klagenfurt	Karnten (Austria)
Koani	Zanzibar South & Central (Tanzania)
Kõbe	Hyõgo (Japan)
Koforidua	Eastern Region (Ghana)
Kõfu	Yamanashi (Japan)
Kohima	Nãgãlaland (India)
Kolonia/Palikir	Micronesia (Pacific)
Kombissiri	Bazéga (Burkina Faso)
Kongoussi	Bam (Burkina Faso)
Koror Island	Palau (Pacific)
Kota Bharu	Kelantan (Malaysia)
Kota Kinabalu	Sabah (Malaysia)
Koudougou	Boulkiemde (Burkina Faso)
Koulamoutou	Ogooué-Lolo (Gabon)
Koupéla	Kouritenga (Burkina Faso)
Kouvola	Kymi (Finland)
Kpalimé	Kloto (Togo)
Kralendijk	Bonaire (Netherland Antilles)
Kristiansand	Vest-Agder (Norway)
Kuala Belait	Belait (Brunei)
Kuala Lumpur	**Malaysia**
Kuching	**Sarawak (Malaysia)**
Kudahuvadhoo	Dhaalu (Maldives)
Kudymkar	Komy Permyak (Russia)
Kuito	Bié (Angola)
Kumasi	Ashanti (Ghana)
Kundiawa	Chimbu (Papua New Guinea)
Kunming	Yunnan (China)
Kuntaur/Georgetown	MacCarthy Island (Gambia)
Kupang	Nusa Tenggara Timur (Indonesia)
Kuwait	**Kuwait**
Kwangju	Chõlla-namdo (South Korea)
La Asunción	Nueva Esparta (Venezuela)
La Ceiba	Atlántida (Honduras)
La Esperanza	Intibucá (Honduras)
La Palma	Darién (Panama)
La Paz	Baja California Sur (Mexico)
La Paz-admin	**Bolivia**
La Plata	Buenos Aires
La Rochelle	Charente-Maritime (France)
La Roche-sur-Yon	Vendée (France)
La Serena	Coquimbo (Chile)

GEOGRAPHY

Capital or Admin Centre	Country, State, County or Area	Capital or Admin Centre	Country, State, County or Area
Laâyone (El Aaiún)	Western Sahara	Loltong	Pentecost (Vanuatu)
Labasa	Northern Province (Fiji)	**Lomé**	**Togo**
Labongo	Kitgum (Uganda)		Golfe (Togolese
Lae	Morobe (Papua New		Prefecture)
	Guinea)		Maritime Region (Togo)
Lahore	Punjab (Pakistan)	London	Christmas Island/Kiritimati
Lai	Tandjilé (Chad)		Atoll (Kiribati)
Lakatoro	Malekula (Vanuatu)	**London**	**England**
Lambaréné	Moyen-Ogooué (Gabon)		Greater London (Eng)
Lansing	Michigan (USA)		United Kingdom
Lanzhou (aka Lan-chou)	Gansui (aka Kansu)	Londonderry	Londonderry (N.I.)
Laon	Aisne (France)	Long Xuyen	An Giang (Vietnam)
L'Aquila	Abruzzi (Italy)	Longana	Ambae/Maéwo (Vanuatu)
Las Palmas	Gran Canaria	Longford	Longford (Eire)
Las Tablas	Los Santos (Panama)	Lons-le-Saunier	Jura (France)
Latacunga	Cotopaxi (Ecuador)	Lorengau	Manus (Papua New
Latakia	Al-Lādhiqiyah (Syria)		Guinea)
Lausanne	Vaud (Swiss Canton)	Los Teques	Miranda (Venezuela)
Lautoka	Western Province (Fiji)	Loubomo	Niari (Congo)
Laval	Mayenne (France)	Louieville	KaNgwane (South Africa)
Le Mans	Sarthe (France)	Louvain (Leuven)	Brabant (Flemish)
Le Puy	Haute-Loire (France)	**Luanda**	**Angola**
Lebowakgomo	Lebowa (South Africa)	Lubango	Huita (Angola)
Leeuwarden	Friesland (Netherlands)	**Lubijana**	**Slovenia**
Leicester	Leicestershire (Eng)	Lubumbashi	Shaba (Dem Rep of Congo)
Leikanger	Sogn og Fjordane (Norway)	Lucapa	Lunda Norte (Angola)
Lelystad	Flevoland (Netherlands)	Lucea	Hanover (Jamaica)
Léo	Sissilli (Burkina Faso)	Lucknow	Uttar Pradesh (India)
León	Región II (Nicaragua)	Luganville	Santo/Maio (Vanuatu)
Lerwick	Shetland Islands	Luleá	Norrbotten (Sweden)
Les Cayes	Sud (Haiti)	**Lusaka**	**Zambia**
Leticia	Amazonas (Colombia)	**Luxembourg**	**Luxembourg**
Levin	Horowhenua (NZ)	Lwena	Moxico (Angola)
Levuka	Eastern Province (Fiji)	Lyon	Rhône (France)
Lewes	East Sussex (Eng)	Lyon	Rhône-Alpes (France)
Lhasa (China)	**Tibet (aka Xizang)**	Maastricht	Limburg (Netherlands)
Liberia	Guanacaste (Costa Rica)	Mabaruma	Barima/Waini (Guyana)
Libreville	**Gabon**	Macao	Macao (Portugal)
	Estuaire (Gabon)	Macapá	Amapá (Brazil)
Lichinga	Niassa (Mozambique)	Macas	Morona-Santiago (Ecuador)
Liestal	Basel-Landschaft (Swiss	Maceió	Alagoas (Brazil)
	Canton)	Machala	El Oro (Ecuador)
Lifford	Donegal (Eire)	Mâcon	Saône-et-Loire (France)
Lille	Nord (France)	Madingou	Bouenza (Congo)
Lille	Nord-Pas-de-Calais (France)	Madison	Wisconsin (USA)
Lillehammer	Oppland (Norway)	Madras	Tamil Nadu (India)
Lilongwe	**Malawi**	**Madrid**	**Spain**
Lima	**Peru**	Maebashi	Gumma (Japan)
Limerick	Limerick (Eire)	Magburaka	Tonkolili (Sierra Leone)
Limoges	Haute-Vienne (French	Magdeburg	Saxony-Anhalt (Germany)
	Department)	Magoodhoo	Faafu (Maldives)
	Limousin (French Region)	Mahibadhoo	Alifu (Maldives)
Lincoln	Lincolnshire (Eng)	Mahon	Minorca
Lincoln	Nebraska (USA)	Maidstone	Kent (Eng)
Linden	Upper Demerara/Berbice	Mainz	Rheinland-Pfalz (Germany)
	(Guyana)	Makeni	Bombali (Sierra Leone)
Linköping	Östergötland (Sweden)		Northern Province
Linz	Oberosterreich (Austria)		(Sierra Leone)
Liro	Paama (Vanuatu)	Makhachkala	Dagestan (CIS)
Lisbon	**Portugal**	Makokou	Ogooué-Ivindo (Gabon)
Little Rock	Arkansas (USA)	Ma-kung	P'eng-hu (Taiwan)
Liverpool	Merseyside (Eng)	Makurdi	Benue (Nigeria)
Livingstone	Southern Province	**Malabo**	**Equatorial Guinea**
	(Zambia)		Bioko (Equatorial
Lkeja	Lagos (Nigeria)		Guinea)
Llandrindod Wells	Powys (Wales)	Malakāi	A'āli an-Nil (Upper Nile)
Llorin	Kwara (Nigeria)		(Sudan)
Logrono	La Rioja (Spain)	Malduguri	Borno (Nigeria)
Loi-kaw	Kayah (Myanmar)	**Male**	**Maldives**
Lokossa	Mono (Benin)		Kaafu (Maldives)

Capital or Admin Centre	Country, State, County or Area	Capital or Admin Centre	Country, State, County or Area
Mamoudzou	**Mayotte**	Menado	Sulawesi Utara (Indonesia)
Manadhoo	Noonu (Maldives)	Mende	Lozère (France)
Managua	**Nicaragua**	Mende	Southern Highlands (Papua New Guinea)
Managua	Región III (Nicaragua)		
Manama	**Bahrain**	Menongue	Kuando Kubango (Angola)
Manaus	Amazonas (Brazil)	Merca (Marka)	Shabeellaha Hoose (Somalia)
Manchester	Greater Manchester (Eng)		
Mandalgov	Dundgovi (Mongolia)	Mercedes	Soriano (Uruguay)
Mandeville	Manchester (Jamaica)	Merida	Extremadura (Spain)
Manga	Zoundwéogo (Burkina Faso)	Mérida	Yucatán (Mexico)
		Metu	Ilubabor (Ethiopia)
Manila	**Philippines**	Metz	Lorraine (French Region)
Manizales	Caldas (Colombia)	Metz	Moselle (French Department)
Mansa	Luapula (Zambia)		
Mansakonko	Lower River (Gambia)	Mexicali	Baja California Norte (Mexico)
Mao	Kanem (Chad)		
Mao	Valverde (Dom Republic)	**Mexico City**	**Mexico**
Maputo	**Mozambique**	Middleburg	Zeeland (Netherlands)
Maracaibo	Zulia (Venezuela)	Middlesbrough	Cleveland (Eng)
Maracay	Aragua (Venezuela)	Miercurea-Ciuc	Harghita (Romania)
Mariestad	Skaraborg (Sweden)	Milan	Lombardy (Italy)
Marigot	St-Martin & St Barthelemy (Guadeloupe)	Minas	Lavalleja (Uruguay)
		Mindelo	São Vicente (Cape Verde)
Marondera	Mashonaland East (Zimbabwe)	Minna	Niger (Nigeria)
		Minsk	**Bellorussia**
Maroua	Extrême-Nord (Cameroon)	Miracema do Tocantins	Tocantins (Brazil)
Marsã Matruh	Matruh (Egypt)	Miskolc	Borsod-Abaúj-Zemplén (Hungary)
Marseille	Bouches-de-Rhône (French Department) Provence-Alpes-Côte D'Azur (Region)	Mito	Ibaraki (Japan)
		Mitú	Vaupés (Colombia)
		Mkokotoni	Zanzibar North (Tanzania)
Marsh Harbour	Abaco & Mores Island	Mmabatho	Bophuthatswana (South Africa)
Masan	Kyŏngsang-namdo (South Korea)		
		Mobaye	Basse-Kotto (Cape Verde)
Maseru	**Lesotho**	Moca	Espaillat (Dom Republic)
Masterton	Wairarapa (NZ)	Mochudi	Kgatleng (Botswana)
Masunga	Botswana (North East)	Mocoa	Putumayo (Colombia)
Matadi	Bas-Zaire (Dem Rep of Congo)	**Mogadishu (Muqdisho)**	**Somalia** Banaadir (Somalia)
Matagalpa	Región VI (Nicaragua)	Mold	Clwyd (Wales)
Mataram	Nusa Tenggara Barat (Indonesia)	Molde	Møre og Romsdal (Norway)
		Molepolole	Kweneng (Botswana)
Mataura	Îles Australes (French Polynesia)	Mombasa	Coast Province (Kenya)
		Monaco-Ville	**Monaco**
Mata-Utu	Wallis and Futuna Islands	**(aka Monaco)**	
Matlock	Derbyshire (Eng)	Monaghan	Monaghan (Eire)
Matsue	Shimane (Japan)	Mongo	Guéra (Chad)
Matsuyama	Ehime (Japan)	Mongu	Western Province (Zambia)
Matthew Town	Inagua, Great & Little		
Maturin	Monagas (Venezuela)	**Monrovia**	**Liberia**
Maun	Ngamiland (Botswana)	Mons	Hainaut (Belgium)
May Pen	Clarendon (Jamaica)	Montauban	Tarn-et-Garonne (France)
Mayor Pablo Lagerenza	Chaco (Paraguay)	Mont-de-Marsan	Landes (France)
Mazatenango	Suchitepéquez (Guatemala)	Montego Bay	St James (Jamaica)
		Montería	Córdoba (Colombia)
Mbabane	**Swaziland** Hhohho (Swaziland)	Monterrey	Nuevo León (Mexico)
		Montevideo	**Uruguay**
Mbaiki	Lobaye (CA Rep)	Montgomery	Alabama (USA)
Mbandaka	Equateur (Dem Rep of Congo)	Montpelier	Vermont (USA)
		Montpellier	Hérault (French Department) Languedoc-Roussillon (French Region)
M'Banza Kongo	Zaire (Angola)		
Mbuji-Mayi	Kasai-Oriental (Dem Rep of Congo)		
Medan	Sumatera Utara (Indonesia)	Morant Bay	St Thomas (Jamaica)
Medelin	Antioquia (Colombia)	Morelia	Michoacán (Mexico)
Mekele	Tigray (Ethiopia)	Morioka	Iwate (Japan)
Melaka	Melaka (Malaysia)	Mörön	Hövsgöl (Mongolia)
Melbourne	Victoria (Aus)	**Moroni**	**Comoros Island** Ngazidja (Comoros)
Melo	Cerro Largo (Uruguay)		
Melun	Seine-et-Marne (France)	Morpeth	Northumberland (Eng)

GEOGRAPHY

Capital or Admin Centre	Country, State, County or Area	Capital or Admin Centre	Country, State, County or Area
Morua	Shepherd (Vanuatu)	Neves	Lemba (São Tomé & Principe)
Moscow	**Russia**	New Amsterdam	East Berbice/Corentyne (Guyana)
Moshi	Kilimanjaro (Tanzania)	**New Delhi**	**India (a.k.a. Bharat)**
Moss	Østfold (Norway)	New Plymouth	Taranaki (NZ)
Mostar	**Hercegovina**	Newcastle-upon-Tyne	Tyne and Wear (Eng)
Mosul	Ninawā (Iraq)	Newport	Isle of Wight
Mouila	Ngounié (Gabon)	Newtown St Boswells	Borders (Scotland)
Moulins	Allier (France)	Ngaoundéré	Adamous (Cameroon)
Moulmein	Mon (Myanmar)	N'Giva	Cunene (Angola)
Moundou	Logone Occidental (Chad)	Nha Trang	Khanh Hoa (Vietnam)
Mount Hagen	Western Highlands (Papua New Guinea)	Nha Trang	Phu Khanh (Vietnam)
Moyobamba	San Martin (Peru)	Nhlangano	Shiselweni (Swaziland)
Muli	Meemu (Maldives)	**Niamey**	**Niger**
Mullingar	Westmeath (Eire)	Niamtougou	Doufelgou (Togo)
Munich	Bavaria (Germany)	Nice	Alpes-Maritimes (France)
Muscat	**Oman**	Nicolls Town	Berry Island (Bahamas)
Musoma	Mara (Tanzania)	**Nicosia**	**Cyprus**
Mutare	Manicaland (Zimbabwe)	Nieuw Amsterdam	Commewijne (Suriname)
Mutsamudu	Ndzouani (Comoros)	Nieuw Nickerie	Nickerie (Suriname)
My Tho	Tien Giang (Vietnam)	Nimes	Gard (France)
Myitkyinā	Kachin (Myanmar)	Niort	Deux-Sévres (France)
Naas	Kildare (Eire)	Nola	Sangha-Économique (CA Rep)
Nacaome	Valle (Honduras)	Nolhivaranfaru	Haa-Dhaalu (Maldives)
Nagoya	Aichi (Japan)	Northallerton	North Yorkshire (Eng)
Nagua	Maria Trinidad Sánchez (Dom Republic)	Northampton	Northamptonshire (Eng)
Naha City	Okinawa (Japan)	Norwich	Norfolk (Eng)
	Ryukyu Islands (Japan)	Notsé	Haho (Togo)
Naifaru	Lhaviyani (Maldives)	Nottingham	Nottinghamshire (Eng)
Nairobi	**Kenya**	**Nouakchott**	**Mauritania**
Nakuru	Rift Valley (Kenya)	Nouméa	New Caledonia (France)
Nalchik	Kabardino-Balkar (CIS)	Nouna	Kossi (Burkina Fasso)
Namendwa	Kamuli (Uganda)	Nova Sintra	Brava (Cape Verde)
Nanchang	Jiangxi (aka Kiangsi)	Novi Sad	Vojvodina (Yugoslavia)
Nancy	Meurthe-et-Moselle (France)	Nueva San Salvador	La Libertad (El Salvador)
Nanjing (aka Nanking)	Jiangsu (aka Kiangsu)	**Nuku'alofa**	**Tonga**
Nanning (China)	Kwangsi Chuang (aka Guangxi Zhuang)		Tongatapu (Tonga)
Nanterre	Hauts-de-Seine (France)	Nukus	Kara-Kalpak (CIS)
Nantes	Loire-Atlantique (French Department)	Nyangeya	Masindi (Uganda)
	Pays de la Loire (French Region)	Nyeri	Central Province (Kenya)
Napier	Hawke's Bay (NZ)	Nyiregyháza	Szabics-Szatmár (Hungary)
Naples	Campania (Italy)	Nykebing	Storstrom (Denmark)
Naryan-Mar	Nennets (Russia)	Nyköping	Södermanland (Sweden)
Nashville	Tennessee (USA)	Obo	Haut-Mbomou (CA Rep)
Nassau	**Bahamas**	Oddur (Xuddur)	Bakool (Somalia)
	New Providence (Bahamas)	Odense	Fyn (Denmark)
Natal	Rio Grande do Norte (Brazil)	Ohonua	Eua (Tonga)
Natitingou	Atacora (Benin)	Okakarara	Hereroland-Wes (Namibia)
N'Dalatando	Kuanza Norte (Angola)	Oklahoma City	Oklahoma (USA)
Ndélé	Bamingui-Bangoran (Cape Verde)	Olaki	Arua (Uganda)
		Olympia	Washington (USA)
N'Djamena	**Chad**	Omagh	Tyrone (N.I.)
	Chari-Baguirmi (Chad Prefecture)	Öndörhaan	Hentiy (Mongolia)
Ndola	Copperbelt (Zambia)	Onverwacht	Para (Suriname)
Neiafu	Vava'u (Tonga)	Opuwo	Kaokoland (Namibia)
Neiba	Bahoruco (Dom Republic)	Oradea	Bihor (Romania)
Neiva	Huila (Colombia)	**Oranjestad**	**Aruba**
Nekemte	Welega (Ethiopia)	Oranjestad	St Eustatius (Netherland Antilles)
Nelson	Nelson Bays (NZ)	Orléans	Loiret (France)
Néma	Hodh-ech-Chargui (Mauritania)	Orodara	Kénédougou (Burkina Faso)
		Oshakati	Oshana (Namibia)
Nevers	Nièvre (France)	Oshikango	Ohangwena (Namibia)
		Oslo	**Norway**
		Östersund	Jämtland (Sweden)
		Ōtsu	Shiga (Japan)
		Ottawa	**Canada**
		Ouagadougou	**Burkina Faso**

Capital or Admin Centre	Country, State, County or Area	Capital or Admin Centre	Country, State, County or Area
Ouagadougou	Kadiogo (Burkina Faso)	**Phnom Penh**	**Cambodia**
Ouahigouya	Yatenga (Burkina Faso)	Phoenix	Arizona (USA)
Ouesso	Sangha (Congo)	Phônsavan	Xianghoang (Laos)
Outapi	Omusati (Namibia)	Phu Ly	Ha Nan (Vietnam)
Oviedo	Asturias (Spain)	Phuthaditjhaba	Qwaqwa (South Africa)
Owando	Cuvette (Congo)	Piatra Neamt	Neamt (Romania)
Owerri	Imo (Nigeria)	Pierre	South Dakota (USA)
Oxford	Oxfordshire (Eng)	Pietermaritsburg	Natal (South Africa)
Oyem	Woleu-Ntem (Gabon)	Pilar	Ñeembucu (Paraguay)
Pa-an	Karen (Myanmar)	Pitesti	Arges (Romania)
Pachuca	Hidalgo (Mexico)	Plei Ku	Gia Lai (Vietnam)
Padang	Sumatera Barat (Indonesia)	Ploiesti	Prahova (Romania)
Paelau	Fanning/Tabuaeran (Kiribati)	**Plymouth**	**Montserrat**
		Pô	Nahouri (Burkina Faso)
Pago Pago	American Samoa	Pointe-Noire	Kouilou (Congo)
Pagouda	Binah (Togo)	Poitiers	Poitou-Charentes
Pakanbaru	Riau (Indonesia)	Poitiers	Vienne (France)
Pakxan	Bolikhamxay (Laos)	Pokharã	Western Nepal
Pakxé	Champasak (Laos)	Pombas	Paúl (Cape Verde)
Palana	Koryak (Russia)	Pompey Bay	Acklins Island (Bahamas)
Palangkaraya	Kalimantan Tengah (Indonesia)	Ponta Delgada	Azores
		Ponta do Sol	Ribeira Grande (Cape Verde)
Palermo	**Sicily (Italy)**		
Palma de Mallorca	Balearic Islands (Spain)	Pontianak	Kalimantan Barat (Indonesia)
Palmerston North	Manawatu (NZ)		
Palu	Sulawesi Tengah (Indonesia)	Pontoise	Val-d'Oise (France)
		Popondetta	Northern Province (Papua New Guinea)
Pamplona	Navarre (Spain)		
Panaji	Goa (India)	Popoyán	Cauca (Colombia)
Panama City	**Panama**	Port Antonio	Portland (Jamaica)
Pan-ch'iao	Tai-pei (Taiwan)	Port Blair	Andaman and Nicobar Islands
Pangai	Ha'apai (Tonga)		
Papeete	**French Polynesia**		
	Society Islands	**Port Louis**	**Mauritius**
	Tahiti	Port Maria	St Mary (Jamaica)
	Îles Tuamotu et Gambier (French Polynesia)	**Port Moresby**	**Papua New Guinea**
	Îles du Vent (French Polynesia)		National Capital District (PNG)
		Port of Spain	**Trinidad and Tobago**
Paradise	Demerara/Mahaica (Guyana)	**Port-au-Prince**	**Haiti**
			Ouest (Haiti)
Parakou	Borgou (Benin)	Port-de-Paix	Nord-Ouest (Haiti)
Paramaribo	**Suriname**	Port-Genttil	Ogooué-Maritime (Gabon)
Paraná	Entre Rios (Argentina)	Port-Harcourt	Rivers (Nigeria)
Paris	**France**	Portlaoise	Laois/Leix (Eire)
	Île-de-France (France)	Pôrto Alegre	Rio Grande do Sul (Brazil)
Pasto	Nariño (Colombia)	Porto Inglês	Maio (Cape Verde)
Patna	Bihar (India)	**Porto Novo**	
Pau	Pyrénées-Atlantiques (France)	**(de facto Cotonou)**	**Benin**
		Pôrto Velho	Rondônia (Brazil)
Pécs	Baranya (Hungary)	Porto-Novo	Ouémé (Benin)
Pedra Badejo	Santa Cruz (Cape Verde)	Portoviejo	Manabi (Ecuador)
Pedro Juan Caballero	Amambay (Paraguay)	Posadas	Misiones (Argentina)
Pemba	Cabo Delgado (Mozambique)	Potenza	Basilicata (Italy)
		Potsdam	Brandenburg (Germany)
Penonomé	Coclé (Panama)	Pozo Colorado	President Hayes (Paraguay)
Pereira	Risaralda (Colombia)		
Périgueux	Dordogne (France)	**Prague**	**Czech Republic**
Perpignan	Pyrénées-Orientales (France)	**Praia**	**Cape Verde**
		Preston	Lancashire (Eng)
Perth	Western Australia	Pretoria	Transvaal (South Africa)
Perugia	Umbria (Italy)	**Pretoria-admin**	**South Africa**
Peshãwar	North West Frontier (Pakistan)	Princes Town	Victoria (Trinidad & Tobago)
		Principe	Paguê (São Tomé & Principe)
Peshkopi	Dibër (Albania)		
Petrozavodsk	Karelian (CIS)	Pristina	Kosovo (Yugoslavia)
Phan Rang	Ninh Thuan (Vietnam)	Privas	Ardèche (France)
Phan Thiet	Thuan Hai (Vietnam)	Providence	Rhode Island (USA)
Philipsburg	St Maarten (Netherland Antilles)	Pucallpa	Ucayali (Peru)
		Puerto Barrios	Izabal (Guatemala)
		Puerto Carreño	Vichada (Colombia)

GEOGRAPHY

Capital or Admin Centre	Country, State, County or Area	Capital or Admin Centre	Country, State, County or Area
Puerto Inirida	Guainia (Colombia)	Roreti	Arorae (Kiribati)
Puerto Lempira	Gracias a Dios (Honduras)	Roscommon	Roscommon (Eire)
Puerto Maldonado	Madre de Dios (Peru)	**Roseau**	**Dominica**
Puerto Montt	Los Lagos (Chile)	Rosita	Región Autónoma del
Punta Arenas (Chile)	Magallanes y de la		Atlántico Norte (Nic)
	Antártica Chilena	Rosso	Trarza (Mauritania)
Punta Gorda	Toledo (Belize)	Rouen	Haute-Normandie (French
Puyo	Pastaza (Ecuador)		Region)
P'yŏngsan	P'yongan-namdo (North		Seine-Maritime (French
	Korea)		Department)
Pyongyang	**North Korea (a.k.a.**	Rovaniemi	Lappi (Finland)
	Choson)	Rrëshen	Mirditë (Albania)
Quebec	Quebec (Canada)	Rubale	Kabale (Uganda)
Quelimane	Zambézia (Mozambique)	Rukoki	Kapchorwa (Uganda)
Quetta	Baluchistān (Pakistan)	Rundu	Kavango (Namibia)
Qui Nhon	Nghia Binh (Vietnam)	Rungata	Nikunau (Kiribati)
Quibdó	Chocó ((Colombia)	Saarbrücken	Saarland (Germany)
Quimper	Finistère (France)	Sacramento	California (USA)
Quito	**Ecuador**	Sa Dec	Dong Thap (Vietnam)
	Pichincha (Ecuador)	St Annes	Alderney
Quy Nhon	Binh Dinh (Vietnam)	Saint-Brieuc	Côtes-du-Nord (France)
Rabat	**Morocco**	**Saint-Denis**	**Réunion**
Rabaul	East New Britain (Papua	Saint-Etienne	Loire (France)
	New Guinea)	**St George's**	**Grenada**
Rach Gia	Kien Giang (Vietnam)	St Helier	Jersey
Raleigh	North Carolina (USA)	**St Johns**	**Antigua and Barbuda**
Ramla	Central District (Israel)	Saint-Lô	Manche (France)
Ramotswa	Botswana (South East)	St Paul	Minnesota (USA)
Rancagua (Chile)	Libertador Gen Bernardo	St Peter Port	Guernsey
	O'Higgins	Sal Rei	Boavista (Cape Verde)
Rangoon (Yangon)	**Burma (now Myanmar)**	Salamá	Baja Verapaz (Guatemala)
Rasht	Gilān (Iran)	Salem	Oregon (USA)
Rawannawi	Marakei (Kiribati)	Salgótarján	Nógrád (Hungary)
Rawson	Chubut (Argentina)	Salt Lake City	Utah (USA)
Reading	Berkshire (Eng)	Saltillo	Coahuila (Mexico)
Recife	Pernambuco (Brazil)	Salto del Guairá	Canendiyú (Paraguay)
Regina	Saskatchewan (Canada)	Salvador	Bahia (Brazil)
Renne	Bornholm (Denmark)	Samarai	Milne Bay (Papua New
Rennes	Bretagne/Brittany (French		Guinea)
	Region)	San Andrés	San Andrés y Providencia
	Ille-et-Vilaine (French	San Carlos	Cojedes (Venezuela)
	Department)	San Carlos	Zona Especial III
Réo	Sanguie (Burkina Faso)		(Nicaragua)
Resistencia	Chaco (Argentina)	San Cristóbal	Táchira (Venezuela)
Resita	Caras-Severin (Romania)	San Felipe	Yaracuy (Venezuela)
Reykavik	**Iceland**	San Fernando	Catamarca (Argentina)
	Höfudhborgarsvaedhi	San Fernando de Apure	Apure (Venezuela)
	(Iceland)	San Francisco de Macoris	Duarte (Dom Republic)
		San Francisco (Gotera)	Morazán (El Salvador)
Rhodes	**Rhodes**	San Ignacio	Cayo (Belize)
Ribeira Brava	São Nicolau (Cape Verde)	**San José**	**Costa Rica**
Richmond	Virginia (USA)	**San Juan**	**Puerto Rico**
Riga	**Latvia**	San Juan Bautista	Misiones (Paraguay)
Rikitea	Gambier Islands	San Juan de Los Morros	Guárico (Venezuela)
Ringdove	Epi (Vanuatu)	**San Marino**	**San Marino (Most Serene**
Rio Branco	Acre (Brazil)		**Republic)**
Rio Claro	Nariva/Mayaro (Trinidad &		Citta (San Marino)
	Tobago)	San Miguel	Tucumán (Argentina)
Rio Gallegos	Santa Cruz (Argentina)	San Pedro Sula	Cortés (Honduras)
Riobamba	Chimborazo (Ecuador)	**San Salvador**	**El Salvador**
Riohacha	La Guajira (Colombia)	San Salvador	Jujuy (Argentina)
Rivercess City	Rivercess (Liberia)	**Sana**	**Yemen Republic**
Riyadh	**Saudi Arabia**	Sangre Grande	St Andrew & St David
Road Town	**Virgin Islands (British)**		(Trinidad & Tobago)
Roatán	Islas de la Bahia	Sankt Pölten	Niederösterreich (Austria)
	(Honduras)	Sanniquellie	Nimba (Liberia)
Robertsport	Grand Cape Mount	Sansanné-Mango	Oti (Togo)
	(Liberia)	Santa Clara	Villa Clara (Cuba)
Rodez	Aveyron (France)	Santa Cruz	Quiché (Guatemala)
Rome	**Italy**	Santa Cruz	Temotu (Solomon Isles)
	Lazio (Italy)		

Capital or Admin Centre	Country, State, County or Area	Capital or Admin Centre	Country, State, County or Area
Santa Cruz de Tenerife	Canary Islands (Spain)	Siparia	St Patrick (Trinidad & Tobago)
Santa Fe	New Mexico (USA)		
Santa Maria	Sal (Cape Verde)	Siteki	Lubombo (Swaziland)
Santa Rosa	La Pampa (Argentina)	Sittwe (a.k.a. Akyab)	Arakan/Rakhine (Burma)
Santana	Cantagaio (São Tomé & Principe)	Siyabuswa	KwaNdebele (South Africa)
		Skien	Telemark (Norway)
Santander	Cantabria (Spain)	**Skopje**	**Macedonia (Yugoslavia)**
Santander	Magdalena (Colombia)	Slatina	Olt (Romania)
Santiago	**Chile**	Sligo	Sligo (Eire)
Santiago	Metropolitan (Chile)	**Sofia**	**Bulgaria (a.k.a. Narodna Republic)**
Santiago	Veraguas (Panama)		
Santiago de Compostela	Galicia (Spain)	Sokodé	Centrale Region (Togo)
Santiago de los Caballeros	Santiago (Dom Republic)		Tchaoudjo (Togolese Prefecture)
Santo Domingo	**Dominican Republic**	Sola	Banks/Torres (Vanuatu)
São António	Principe (São Tomé & Principe)	Solwezi	North-Western Province (Zambia)
São Filipe	Fogo (Cape Verde)	Songea	Ruvuma (Tanzania)
São João Angolares	Caué (São Tomé & Principe)	Sore	Vestjaelland (Denmark)
		Spanish Town	St Catherine (Jamaica)
São Luis	Maranhão (Brazil)	Springfield	Illinois (USA)
São Tomé	**São Tomé and Príncipe**	Srinigar	Jammu and Kashmir (India)
	Aqua Grande (São Tomé & Principe)	Stafford	Staffordshire (Eng)
		Stanley	**Falkland Islands**
Sapporo	Hokkaidō (Japan)	Stans	Nidwalden (Swiss Canton)
Saransk	Mordovia (Russia)	Stavanger	Rogaland (Norway)
Sarayevo	**Bosnia and Hercegovina**	Steinkjer	Nord-Trønelag (Norway)
Sarh	Moyen-Chari (Chad)	Stirling	Central (Scotland)
Sari	Māzandarān (Iran)	**Stockholm**	**Sweden**
Sariwŏn	Hwanghae-pukto (North Korea)	Stornaway (Lewis)	Western Isles (Scotland)
		St-Pierre	St-Pierre and Miquelon
Sarnen	Obwalden (Swiss Canton)	Strasbourg	Alsace (French Region)
Saudhárkrókur	Nordhurland vestra (Iceland)		Bas-Rhin (French Department)
Saurimo	Lunda Sol (Angola)	Stuttgart	Baden-Württemberg (Germany)
Savanna-la-Mar	Westmoreland (Jamaica)		
Saynshand	Dornogovi (Mongolia)	St. Johns	Newfoundland (Canada)
Scarborough	Tobago	**Sucre-judicial**	**Bolivia**
Sefadu	Kono (Sierra Leone)		Chuquisaca (Bolivia)
Sekondi-Takoradi	Western Region (Ghana)	Sühbaatar	Selenge (Mongolia)
Selfoss	Sudhurland (Iceland)	Sukhumi	Abkhaziya (CIS)
Sélibaby	Guidimaka (Mauritania)	Sukulu	Tororo (Uganda)
Semarang	Jawar Tengah (Indonesia)	Sumbawanga	Rukwa (Tanzania)
Sendai	Miyagi (Japan)	Sumbe	Kuanza Sul (Angola)
Sensuntepeque	Cabañas (El Salvador)	Sunyani	Brong-Ahafo (Ghana)
Seoul	**South Korea**	Surabaya	Jawar Timur (Indonesia)
Seremban	Negeri Sembilan (Malaysia)	Surkhet	Mid-Western Nepal
Serowe	Botswana (Central)	Suva	Central Province (Fiji)
Seville	Andalucia (Spain)	**Suva**	**Fiji**
Sfintu Gheorghe	Covasna (Romania)	Suwŏn	Kyŏnggi-do (South Korea)
Shenyang	Liaoning (China)	Swakopmund	Erongo (Namibia)
s-Hertogenbosch	Noord-Brabant (Netherlands)	Swansea	West Glamorgan (Wales)
		Sydney	New South Wales
Shibin al-Kawm	Al-Minufiyah (Egypt)	Syktyv-Kar	Komi (CIS)
Shijazhuang	Hebei (China)	Szeged	Csongrád (Hungary)
Shillong	Meghālaya (India)	Székesfehérvár	Fejér (Hungary)
Shimla	Himāchal Pradesh (India)	Szekszárd	Tolna (Hungary)
Shirāz	Fārs (Iran)	Szombathely	Vas (Hungary)
Shrewsbury	Shropshire (Eng)	Tabligbo	Yoto (Togo)
Sibiti	Lékoumou (Congo)	Tabontebike	Kuria (Kiribati)
Sibut	Kemo-Gribingui (CA Rep)	Taegu	Kyŏngsang-pukto (South Korea)
Sidon/Saydā	Al-Janub (Lebanon)		
Silvassa	Dadra and Nagar Haveli (India)	Taiohae	Îles Marquises (French Polynesia)
Sincelejo	Sucre (Colombia)	**Taipei**	**Taiwan**
Singapore	**Singapore**	Taiyuan	Shanxi (China)
Sinujiu	P'yongan-pukto (North Korea)	Takaeang	Aranuka (Kiribati)
		Takamatsu	Kagawa (Japan)
Siobozia	Ialomita (Romania)	Talca	Maule (Chile)
Sion	Valais (Swiss Canton)	Tallahassee	Florida (USA)

Capital or Admin Centre	Country, State, County or Area	Capital or Admin Centre	Country, State, County or Area
Tallinn	**Estonia**	**Tripoli**	**Libya**
Tamale	Northern Region (Ghana)	Tripoli/Tarābulus	Ash-Shamāl (Lebanon)
Tamrida	Socotra (Yemen)	Trivandrum	Kerala (India)
Tan An	Long An (Vietnam)	Trondheim	Sor-Trøndelag (Norway)
Tanjã	Al-Gharbiyah (Egypt)	Trowbridge	Wiltshire (Eng)
Tanjung Karang	Lampung (Indonesia)	Troyes	Aube (France)
Tarbes	Haute-Pyrénées (France)	Trujillo	Colón (Honduras)
Tashkent	**Uzbekistan**	Trujillo	La Libertad (Peru)
Tatabánya	Komárom (Hungary)	Trujillo	Trujillo (Venezuela)
Taubukinberu	Beru (Kiribati)	Truro	Cornwall (Eng)
Taunggyi	Shan (Myanmar)	Tsabong	Kgalagadi (Botswana)
Taunton	Somerset (Eng)	Tsetserieg	Arhangay (Mongolia)
Taupo	Tongariro (NZ)	Tsévié	Zio (Togo)
Tauranga	Bay of Plenty (NZ)	Tsu	Mie (Japan)
Tbilisi	**Georgia (CIS)**	Tsumeb	Oshikoto (Namibia)
Tchibanga	Nyanga (Gabon)	Tsumkwe	Boesmanland (Namibia)
Tebangetua	Maiana (Kiribati)	Tuarabu	Abalang (Kiribati)
Tegucigalpa	**Honduras**	Tubmanburg	Bomi (Liberia)
	Francisco Morazán (Honduras)	Tulagi	Central Islands (Solomon Isles)
Tehran	**Iran**	Tulcan	Carchi (Ecuador)
Temuco	Araucania (Chile)	Tullamore	Offaly (Eire)
Tena	Napo (Ecuador)	Tulle	Corrèze (France)
Tenkodogo	Boulgou (Burkina Faso)	**Tunis**	**Tunisia**
Tepic	Nayarit (Mexico)	Tunja	Boyacá (Colombia)
Teresina	Piauí (Brazil)	Tura	Evenki (Russia)
Teuabu	Nonouti (Kiribati)	Turin	Piedmont (Italy)
Teyateyaneng	Berea (Lesotho)	Turku	Turku ja Pori (Finland)
Thakhek	Khammouan (Laos)	Tuxtla Gutiérrez	Chiapas (Mexico)
Thames-Coromandel	Thames Valley (NZ)	Tuy Hoa	Phu Yen (Vietnam)
The Bottom	Saba (Netherland Antilles)	Ufa	Bashkir (CIS)
Thessalonika	**Macedonia (Greece)**	Ugoofaaru	Raa (Maldives)
Thimphu	**Bhutan (a.k.a Druk-Yul)**	Ujung Pandang	Sulawesi Selatan (Indonesia)
Thinadhoo	Gaafu-Dhaalu (Maldives)		
Thohoyandou	Venda (South Africa)	Ulaangom	Uvs (Mongolia)
Thong	Xékong (Laos)	**Ulan Bator**	**Mongolia**
Thorshavn	**Faeroe Islands**	Ulan-Ude	Buryat (CIS)
Thu Dau Mot	Binh Duong (Vietnam)	Uliastay	Dzavhan (Mongolia)
Tiberias	Northern District (Israel)	Ulundi	KwaZulu (South Africa)
Tidjikdja	Tagant (Mauritania)	Umea	Västerbotten (Sweden)
Timaru	Aorangi (NZ)	Umtata	Transkei (South Africa)
Timisoara	Timis (Romania)	Urawa	Saitama (Japan)
Tirana	**Albania**	Urumchi (aka Urumqi)	Sinkiang Uighur (aka Xinjiang Uygur)
Tirgoviste	Dimbovita (Romania)	Ushuaia	Tierra Del Fuego (Argentina)
Tirgu Jiu	Gorj (Romania)		
Tirgu Mures	Mures (Romania)	Ust-Ordynsk	Ust-Ordyn-Buryat (Russia)
Titograd	**Montenegro**	Utiroa	Tabiteuea North (Kiribati)
Tokyo	**Japan**	Utsunomiya	Tochigi (Japan)
Toledo	Castilla-La-Mancha (Spain)	Uturoa	Îles sous le Vent (French Polynesia)
Toluca	México (Mexican State)		Raiatea (French Polynesia)
Tønsberg	Vestfold (Norway)		
Topeka	Kansas (USA)		
Toronto	Ontario (Canada)	Uyo	Akwa Ibom (Nigeria)
Totness	Coronie (Suriname)	**Vaduz**	**Liechenstein**
Tougan	Sourou (Burkina Faso)	Vaitape	Bora-Bora
Tou-liu	Yün-lin (Taiwan)	Valence	Drôme (France)
Toulon	Var (France)	Valencia	Carabobo (Venezuela)
Toulouse	Haute-Garonne (French Department)	Valladolid	Castilla-Leon (Spain)
	Midi-Pyrénées (French Region)	Valledupar	Cesar (Colombia)
		Valletta	**Malta**
Tours	Indre-et-Loire (France)	Valparaiso	Valparaiso (Chile)
Tralee	Kerry (Eire)	Vänersborg	Älvsborg (Sweden)
Trenton	New Jersey (USA)	Vanimo	West Sepik (Papua New Guinea)
Trieste	Friuli-Venezia Giulia (Italy)		
Trim	Meath (Eire)	Vannes	Morbihan (France)
Trinidad	Flores (Uruguay)	Vardø	Finnmark (Norway)
Trinidad	Beni (Bolivia)	Västerås	Västmanland (Sweden)
Trinidade	Mé-zóchi (São Tomé & Principe)	Växjö	Kronoberg (Sweden)
		Versailles	Yvelines (France)

Capital or Admin Centre	Country, State, County or Area	Capital or Admin Centre	Country, State, County or Area
Vesoul	Haute-Saône (France)		Curacao (Netherland Antilles)
Veymandhoo	Thaa (Maldives)		
Victoria	British Columbia (Canada)	Winchester	Hampshire (Eng)
Victoria	**Seychelles**	**Windhoek**	**Namibia**
	Mahé (Seychelles)	Windhoek	Khomas (Namibia)
Victoria (Guzo)	Malta	Winnipeg	Manitoba (Canada)
Victoria (on Hong Kong Island)	**Hong Kong (a.k.a. Hsiang Kang)**	Wŏnson	Kangwŏn-do (North Korea)
Viedma	Rio Negro (Argentina)	Worcester	Hereford and Worcester (Eng)
Vienna	**Austria**	Wuhan	Hubei (China)
Vientiane	**Laos**	Xai-Xai	Gaza (Mozambique)
Viet Tri	Phu Tho (Vietnam)	Xam Nua	Houaphan (Laos)
Vila	**Vanuatu**	Xay	Oudomxay (Laos)
	Efaté (Vanuatu)	Xi'an (aka Sian)	Shaanxi (aka Shensi)
Vilgili	Gaafu-Alifu (Maldives)	Xining (aka Hsi-ning)	Qinghai (aka Tsinghai)
Villahermosa	Tabasco (Mexico)	Yako	Passoré (Burkina Faso)
Villarica	Guairá (Paraguay)	Yakutsk	Yakut (CIS)
Villavicencio	Meta (Colombia)	Yambio	Western Equatoria (Sudan)
Vilnius	**Lithuania**	**Yamoussoukro-admin**	**Ivory Coast**
Vinh	Nghe Tinh (Vietnam)	**Yangon**	**Myanmar**
Vinh Yen	Vinh Phuc (Vietnam)	**Yaoundé**	**Cameroon**
Visby	Gotland (Sweden)		Centre Province (Cameroon)
Vitoria	Basque Country (Spain)		
Vitória	Espirito Santo (Brazil)	**Yaren**	**Nauru**
Vladikavkaz	Alania (Russia)	Yellowknife	Northwest Territories (Canada)
Vogan	Vo (Togo)		
Voinjama	Lofa (Liberia)	**Yerevan**	**Armenia**
Vreed-en-Hoop	Essequibo Islands (Guyana)	Yinchuan	Ningxia Hui (China)
Wa	Upper West (Ghana)	Yogyakarta	Yogyakarta (Indonesia)
Wabag	Enga (Papua New Guinea)	Yokohama	Kanagawa (Japan)
Wakefield	West Yorkshire (Eng)	Yola	Gongola (Nigeria)
Warsaw	**Poland**	Yopal	Casanare (Colombia)
Warwick	Warwickshire (Eng)	Yushkar-Ola	Mari-El (Russia)
Washington D.C.	**United States of America**	Yuscarán	El Paraiso (Honduras)
Waterford	Waterford (Eire)	Yuzhno-Sakhalinsk	Sakhalin Island
Wāu	Bahr al-Ghazal (Sudan)	Zacatecoluca	La Paz (El Salvador)
Wavre	Brabant (Walloon)	**Zagreb**	**Croatia**
Wellington	**New Zealand**	Zāhedān	Sistān va Baluchestān (Iran)
West Island	Cocos (a.k.a.Keeling Islands) (Aus)	Zahlah	Al-Biqa (Lebanon)
		Zalāu	Salaj (Romania)
Wete	Pemba North (Tanzania)	Zamora	Zamora-Chinchipe (Ecuador)
Wewak	East Sepik (Papua New Guinea)		
		Zanzibar	Zanzibar West (Tanzania)
Wexford	Wexford (Eire)	Zaragosa	Aragón (Spain)
Whangarei	Northland (NZ)	Zhengzhou	Henan (China)
Whitehorse	Yukon Territory (Canada)	Ziniaré	Oubritenga (Burkina Faso)
Wicklow	Wicklow (Eire)	Zinjibār	Abyăn (Yemen)
Wiesbaden	Hessen (Germany)	Zorgho	Ganzourgou (Burkina Faso)
Willemstad	**Netherland Antilles**	Zwedru	Grand Gedeh (Liberia)
		Zwolle	Overijssel (Netherlands)

GEOGRAPHY

NB: This section is a fully comprehensive listing of all the world's capital cities, chief towns, and administrative centres. It can be assumed that where a capital is not included in this section it is because the State, County or Area has a capital with the same name. To simplify the process of researching the more obscure capitals, when the continent or country is perhaps unknown, all areas, be it Country, State, Island or City, which have a capital, admin centre or chief town, have been sorted alphabetically. Similarly, any area which is the capital, chief town, or administrative centre, of a larger area, has also been sorted alphabetically. This methodology ensures that, as long as you know one half of the equation, the other half can be found very quickly. All countries, and some of the more significant islands and states, have been printed in bold type.

Capitals: former

Aachen Holy Roman Empire
Aarau (Switzerland) Helvetic Republic
Abeokuta (Nigeria) Egba State
Aden South Yemen
Agra India

Akmola Kazakhstan
Alexandria Egypt
Amarapura Burma
Angkor Thom Cambodia
Antigua Guatemala Guatemala

Antioch Ancient Syria		**Maribo** Lolland (Denmark)	
Anuradhapura Ceylon		**Marrakesh** Morocco	
Arras Artois Province		**Melbourne** Australia	
Ashur (Assur) Assyria		**Memphis** Ancient Egypt	
Auch Gascony		**Mocha** Yemen	
Auckland New Zealand		**M(o)ukden** Manchuria	
Augusta Georgia, USA		**Nanking** China	
Ava Burma		**Nara (Heijo-Kyo)** Japan	
Ayutthaya (Ayuthia) Thailand		**New Orleans** Louisiana (USA)	
Babylon Babylonia		**Nineveh** Assyria	
Baeza (Spain) Moorish Kingdom		**Olomouc** Moravia	
Bakhchisarai Crimean Khans		**Persepolis** Persia	
Bamburgh Northumbria		**Perth** Scotland	
Bastia Corsica		**Philadelphia** USA	
Belize Belize		**Quezon City** Philippines	
Bingerville Ivory Coast		**Rawalpindi** Pakistan	
Bucharest Walachia		**Rio de Janeiro** Brazil	
Calcutta India		**Rovigno** Istria	
Chan Chan Chimú Empire		**Saigon** South Vietnam	
Ctesiphon Parthia		**St George** Bermuda	
Cuzco Inca Empire		**St Mary's City** Maryland (USA)	
Danzig West Prussia		**St Petersburg** Russia	
Dar Es Salaam Tanzania		**Sardis** Lydia	
Dawson Yukon		**Scodra** Illyra	
Entebbe Uganda		**Sitka** Alaska	
Gondar Ethiopia		**Stettin** Pomerania	
Gordium Phrygia		**Susa** Elam (Persian Empire)	
Grozny Chechnya		**Sydney** Australia	
Guthrie Oklahoma (USA)		**Tenochtitlán** Aztec Empire	
Hague, The Netherlands		**Thebes** Ancient Egypt	
Hattusa Hittite Empire		**Toledo** Spain	
Hué Annam		**Toulouse** Languedoc	
Jerusalem Palestine		**Trondheim** Norway	
Karachi Pakistan		**Trujillo** Honduras	
Kaunas Lithuania		**Turku** Finland	
Kracow Poland		**Tyre** Phoenicia	
Kyoto Japan		**Vathy** Ithaca	
Kzyl-Orda Kazakhstan		**Winchester** England	
Lagos Nigeria		**Yasodharapura** Cambodia	
Levuka Fiji		**Zanzibar** Oman	
Livingstone Northern Rhodesia		**Zomba** Malawi	
Mandalay Burma			

Continents

Continents	Area (Sq Miles)	% of Earth's Land	Lowest Point	Estimated population mid-1990
Asia	16,988,000	29.9	Dead Sea (-400 m)	3,317,800,000
Africa	11,506,000	20.3	Lake Assal (-156 m)	654,600,000
North America	9,365,000	16.5	Death Valley (-86 m)	435,800,000
South America	6,820,000	12.0	Valdés Peninsula (-40 m)	299,900,000
Antarctica	5,400,000	9.5	ice-covered (-2538 m)	No indigenous population
Europe	3,745,000	6.6	Caspian Sea (-28 m)	684,400,000
Australia	2,941,526	5.2	Lake Eyre (-16 m)	17,800,000

Deserts: World's Largest

		Area (Sq Miles)				Area (Sq Miles)
1	Sahara	3,500,000	4	Arabian		470,000
2	Australian	600,000	5	Kalahari		225,000
3	Gobi	500,000	6	Sonoran		120,000

7	Kara Kum	120,000
8	Namib	110,000
9	Thar	100,000
10	Somali	100,000
11	Kyzyl Kum	100,000

12	Atacama	70,000
13	Dasht-e Lut	20,000
14	Mojave	13,500
15	Desierto de Sechura	10,000

NB: The Gobi Desert includes the Takla Makan area, comprising 125,000 sq miles. The Kara Kum and the Kyzyl Kum are often considered as one large desert, the Turkestan.

Earth's Extremes

coldest place	Plateau Station, Antarctica: annual average temperature -56.7 deg C
deepest canyon	Colca River Canyon, Peru: 3,625 m
driest place	Atacama Desert, Chile: rainfall negligible
greatest tides	Bay of Fundy, Nova Scotia: 16 m
highest waterfall	Angel, Venezuela: 3,212′ (979 m)
hottest place	Dalol, Danakil Depression, Ethiopia: annual average temperature 35 deg C
largest canyon	Grand Canyon, Colorado River, Arizona: 466 km long and 183 m to 29 km wide, about 1.6 km deep
longest reef	Great Barrier Reef, Australia: 2,012 km
most predictable geyser	Old Faithful, Wyoming: annual average interval 69 to 78 minutes
wettest place	Mount Waialeale, Hawaii: annual average rainfall 16,800 mm

Major Earthquakes

	Richter scale	Estimated deaths	Year
Antioch, Turkey		250,000	526
Corinth, Greece		45,000	856
Shensi Province, China		830,000	1556
Catania, Italy		60,000	1693
Calcutta, India		300,000	1737
Lisbon, Portugal		60,000	1755
Calabria, Italy		50,000	1783
San Francisco	8.3	452	1906
Messina	7.5	83,000	1908
Avezzano, Italy	7.5	29,980	1915
Gansu, China	8.6	100,000	1920
Tokyo	8.3	140,000	1923
Nan-Shan, China	8.3	200,000	1927
Gansu, China	7.6	70,000	1932
Quetta, India	7.5	30,000	1935
Erzincan, Turkey	7.9	30,000	1939
Chillán, Chile	8.3	28,000	1939
Assam, India	8.7	1,526	1950
USSR	7.3	110,000	1948
Agadir, Morocco	5.8	12,000	1960
Anchorage, Alaska	9.2	131	1964
Northern Peru	7.7	66,794	1970
Managua, Nicaragua	6.5	7,000	1971
Guatemala City	7.5	23,000	1976
Tangshan, China	8.2	242,000	1976
NE Iran	7.7	25,000	1978
El Asnam, Algeria	7.3	20,000	1980
Mexico	8.1	25,000	1985
Armenia, USSR	6.9	25,000	1988
San Francisco	7.1	300	1989
Roudhon, NW Iran	7.7	50,000	1990
Latur, India	6.5	9,748	1993
Kobe, Japan	7.2	5,500	1995
Neftegursk, Russia	7.5	1,989	1995
Qayen, NE Iran	7.1	4,000	1997
Ismit, Turkey	7.8	2,000+	1999

GEOGRAPHY

NB: The estimated deaths caused by these earthquakes are purely to indicate the devastation. It is very hard to draw accurate conclusions as government statistics are in some instances based on bodies actually recovered. To give Tokyo 1923 as an example, the official death toll was 99,330, but that figure does not take into account the deaths caused by fire, famine, pestilence, and shock in the aftermath or the persons missing presumed dead.

European Cities of Culture

1985	Athens
1986	Florence
1987	Amsterdam
1988	Berlin
1989	Paris
1990	Glasgow
1991	Dublin
1992	Madrid
1993	Antwerp
1994	Lisbon
1995	Luxemburg
1996	Copenhagen
1997	Thessaloniki
1998	Stockholm
1999	Weimar
2000	Avignon, Bergen, Bologna, Brussels, Helsinki, Krakow, Prague, Reykjavik, Santiago de Compostela (Spain)
2001	Rotterdam and Porto

NB: In 1999 the European Cities of Culture were renamed Cultural Capitals of Europe.

General Information

anabranch   Stream that leaves a river and re-enters it lower down, especially in Australia.

Appalachian trail   Public footpath that runs for over 2,000 miles between Mount Springer in Georgia and Mount Katahdin in Maine.

arroyo   Dry channel in a semi-arid area that may be subject to flash flooding during seasonal downpours.

atmospheric layers   Troposphere is the lowest layer, 11 miles thick at the equator. Stratosphere lies above the troposphere, contains most of the ozone layer. Mesosphere lies above the stratosphere and is often considered part of it. Thermosphere lies between the mesosphere and the exosphere reaching altitudes of 250 miles. Ionosphere is the area charged by the Sun's radiation, between 40 and 600 miles, and has 4 main layers: the D-layer (40–60 miles), E-layer (60–95 miles), F1 and F2-layers (95–250 miles). Exosphere is the outermost layer of the Earth's atmosphere.

berg   Hot, dry north wind of Cape Province and Natal.

bise   Cold, dry north wind prevalent in Switzerland and southern France.

bora   Strong northerly wind that blows in the northern Adriatic.

brickfielder   Hot, dry north wind of Australia.

bridge: longest by span   Akashi-Kaikyo, Shikoku, Japan (6,528′).

building: tallest inhabited   Chongqing Tower, China (1,499′). The 2nd tallest is the Petronas Towers, Kuala Lumpur (1,482′). One World Trade Center Tower is 1,368′ but with the television antennae is actually 1,710′ tall. Similarly, the Sears Tower, Chicago, is the 3rd tallest (1,454′) but with the television mast is 1,707′. Canary Wharf Tower, designed by Cesar Pelli, is currently the tallest British building (800′).

building: tallest uninhabited   Warszawa Radio Mast, Konstantynow, Poland (2,120′) although under repair after collapsing in 1991. 2nd tallest structure is KTHI-TV Mast, N. Dakota (2,063′). 3rd is the CN Tower, Toronto (1,822′).

buran   Snowstorm accompanied by high winds, chiefly prevalent in the Russian Steppes.

cataract   A large, rushing waterfall, usually over a precipice.

chinook   Warm dry wind that blows in the Rocky Mountain region of North America.

clouds: classification   *High cloud:* Cirrus – detached clouds resembling feathers, named from the Latin for 'lock of hair'. Cirrocumulus – rounded small clouds appearing in the form of grains or ripples. Cirrostratus – white veil of smooth fibrous ice crystals, often forming a halo of light. *Middle cloud:* Altocumulus – grey or white clouds having rounded shapes, sometimes touching. Altostratus – flat, grey sheet cloud, often obscuring the Sun and often bringing drizzle. Nimbostratus – flat, shapeless clouds which are the main source of rain and snow. *Low Cloud:* Cumulus – detached clouds that vary from small fleeces to large cauliflower shapes. Cumulonimbus – often anvil-shaped and noted for its accompaniment of thunder. Stratus – shapeless thin, grey cloud, often starting as fog. Stratocumulus – round-shaped patchy cloud often formed as Cumulus but thinning out.

coastline: longest   Canada (152,100 miles).

coastline: shortest   Monaco (3.5 miles).

continental extremities   west–east–north–south
Africa – Cape Vert, Senegal; Ras Hafun, Somalia; Cape Blanc, Tunisia; Cape Agulhas, South Africa. *Asia* – Cape Baba, Turkey; Cape Dezneva, Russia; Cape Celjuskin, Russia; Cape Piai, Malaysia. *Australia* – Steep Point; Cape Byron; Cape York; South East Point, Tasmania. *Europe* – Cape Roca, Portugal; Kara River; North Cape, Norway; Point Tarifa, Spain. *North America* – Cape Prince of Wales, Alaska; Cape Charles, Newfd; Boothia peninsula, NWT; SW Panama. *South America* – Punta Pariña, Peru; Cape Branco, Brazil; Punta Gallinas, Colombia; Cape Horn.

It should be noted that some countries are included in different continents from the country that administers them, e.g. Greenland is administered by Denmark, although part of North America.

cordillera System or group of parallel mountain ranges together with intervening plateaux, especially of the Andes and in Central America and Mexico.

Dams: Tallest Rogun Dam in Tajikistan (1,098′) is the tallest, followed by Nurek Dam in Tajikistan (984′). The 3rd tallest dam is the Grande Dixence in Switzerland (935′).

depression: deepest Dead Sea (1,296′ below sea level), Turfan Depression, China (505′), Qattara Depression, Egypt (436′).

desert: meaning From the Latin word *desertus* meaning 'abandoned'.

dictionary of places Gazetteer.

driest place on Earth Calama in the Atacama Desert, Chile, has no recorded rainfall.

Earth: composition The most abundant elements of the Earth's composition are iron (35.9%), oxygen (28.5%), magnesium and silicon (each about 15%). The most abundant elements of the Earth's crust are oxygen, silicon, and aluminium.

Earth: dimensions
Mass 5,974,000,000,000,000,000,000 metric tons.
Area 510,066,000 square Kilometres.
Land 148,429,000 square Kilometres (29.1%).
Water 361,637,000 square Kilometres (70.9%).
Population 5,420, 391,000 approximately.

Earth's layers crust, mantle, core.

El Niño Destructive climatic phenomenon involving a periodic change of direction in the prevailing trade winds and ocean currents flowing from the Americas to Asia across the southern Pacific.

Etesian Dry north wind blowing over the Aegean and eastern Mediterranean during the summer months (aka Meltemi).

Fö(e)hn Hot southerly wind on the northern slopes of the Alps.

footpaths Dales Way – runs for 81 miles from Ilkley in West Yorkshire to Bowness-on-Windermere. Icknield Way – most ancient road in Britain, 105 miles from Ridgeway to Peddars Way. Mid Shires Way – opened in 1994 covering 225 miles from Buckinghamshire to Greater Manchester. North Downs Way – stretches 141 miles from south-west of London (Farnham) to the Dover coast. Offa's Dyke – follows the English/Welsh border for 168 miles via the Wye Valley. Peddars Way – 94-mile stretch from Thetford to Cromer. Pembrokeshire Coastal Path – 186-mile stretch from Amroth on Carmarten Bay to west of Cardigan. Pennine Way – follows course of the Pennines from Edale in Derbyshire to Kirk Yetholm in the Borders. Ridgeway – runs 85 miles from Avebury to Ivinghoe Beacon. South Downs Way – 106-mile walk from Beachy Head to Winchester. South-west Coastal Path – runs 600 miles from Minehead in Somerset to Poole Harbour. West Highland Way – 95-mile route from Milngavie, near Glasgow to north of Fort William.

fumarole Opening in or near a volcano through which hot vapours emerge.

ghibli Hot, dry southerly wind of Libya.

glacier types continental, mountain, piedmont.

grasslands Africa – savannah; Argentina/Paraguay – pampas; North America – prairies; Russia – Steppes. In other South American countries the general term for a grassland is llanos. The Sahel of West Africa is a semi-arid transitional area between grassland and desert.

Green Line Boundary dividing Cyprus between Greek south and Turkish north since the 1974 Turkish invasion.

gregale Strong north-east wind blowing in the Mediterranean.

Gutenberg discontinuity The core–mantle boundary of the Earth.

haboob Violent and oppressive seasonal wind blowing in Sudan and causing fierce sand storms.

harmattan Parching dusty land-wind of the W African coast, blowing from the Sahara Desert.

helm Violent wind of the Lake District of England which often culminates in the formation of a cloud hanging over the mountain tops.

hypsography Description or mapping of the contours of the earth's surface.

isocheim Line on a map connecting places having the same average temperature in winter.

isohyet Line on a map connecting places having the same amount of rainfall in a given period.

Itaipu dam Joint project by Brazil and Paraguay on the River Parana. Largest hydro-electric dam in the world.

jungle: meaning From the Hindi *Jangal* meaning 'wilderness'.

Kanaks Native Melanesian population of the French overseas territory of New Caledonia.

Kashmir Territory in the north-west of the Indian subcontinent which has been the subject of rival claims by India and Pakistan and the cause of 2 wars between them in 1948 and 1965.

Kentish man West of the Medway.

khamsin Hot south or south-easterly wind occurring in Egypt for about 50 days in March, April and May.

Levant Area of the Mediterranean bordering Syria and the Lebanon.

lithosphere Rigid outer part of the earth consisting of the crust and upper mantle.

Maghreb Region of North Africa bordering the Mediterranean and comprising Morocco, Algeria, Tunisia and Libya.

man of Kent East of the Medway.

Mashriq Geographical region including Egypt, Sudan, Saudi Arabia, Yemen, Oman, Kuwait, UAE, Jordan, Lebanon, Syria and Iraq.

Medway towns Chatham, Gillingham, Rochester, Strood.

mistral Cold northerly wind that blows down the Rhone valley and southern France into the Mediterranean.

mofette Exhalation of vapour from a volcano. Sometimes used as an alternative name for the fumarole itself.

Moho Abbreviation for the Mohorovicic discontinuity, the boundary separating the earth's crust and mantle.

monsoon Seasonal wind of SW Asia and the Indian Ocean which brings heavy summer rain.

pampero Strong cold SW wind in S. America blowing from the Andes towards the Atlantic.

peninsulas Arabian is the largest (1,250,000 sq miles); second largest is the Southern Indian (800,000 sq miles).

permafrost General term for ground that is permanently frozen (see tundra).

Pig Island Australian and NZ slang word for New Zealand.

puna Cold, dry wind of the Andes in Peru.

rock: types Igneous, sedimentary, metamorphic.

Sargasso Sea Area of the North Atlantic, named after the 'Sargassum' seaweed that floats on the surface. The Sargasso lies south of Bermuda and is noted for having no land borders.

simoom Hot, suffocating wind of North Africa.

sirocco Hot, dusty wind blowing from North Africa across southern Europe via the Mediterranean.

solano Hot, dusty south-easterly wind of mainland Spain.

Sumatra Violent wind in the Straits of Malacca and the Malay peninsula blowing from the direction of Sumatra.

taiga (cold forest) Coniferous forests of sub-Arctic North America and Eurasia bordered by tundra and steppes.

tectonic plates Regions of the Earth's crust that may be oceanic or continental, and relate to the activity within the Earth, creating new surface material, moving the plates against or underneath each other, forming mountain ranges and causing earthquakes and volcanic activity.

temperature: highest recorded Al' Aziziyah, Libya, at 136 degrees Fahrenheit (58°C).

temperature: lowest recorded Vostock Station, Antarctica, at -129 degrees Fahrenheit (-89°C).

tombolo Narrow sand or shingle bar linking a small island with mainland.

tramontana Cold north wind in the Adriatic.

tundra Area south of the North Pole where the layers of soil are permanently frozen.

tunnels: longest vehicular Seikan Rail Tunnel, Japan (33.49 miles); Channel Tunnel, Cheriton,

Kent – Sangatte, Calais (31.03 miles).

tunnels: longest non-vehicular Delaware Aqueduct, NY State (105 miles).

twilight: types Civil, nautical, astronomical (6, 12 and 18 degrees angle of the sun below the horizon).

typhoon Tropical storm in the western Pacific.

volcanic eruptions: famous Krakatoa (1883); Mont Pelée, Martinique (1902); Mount St Helens, Washington State (1980).

volcano: classifications active, dormant, extinct.

volcano: highest Cotopaxi in Ecuador is the highest continuously active volcano (19,347'), although Guallatiri in Chile at 19,882' is the highest dormant and Aconcagua at 22,834', and also in the Andes, is the highest extinct volcano (excluding underwater volcanoes).

Volcano Islands Three small volcanic islands, San Alexander (Kita-Iō) Iwo Jima (Iō) San Augustino (Minami-Iō), of the West Pacific between the Bonin Islands and the Mariana Islands. Japan has claimed the islands since 1891, apart from a brief USA administration from 1951 to 1968.

volcano: types Fissure and central.

williwaw Sudden, strong cold wind originally describing the squall through the Straits of Magellan but now describing any sudden strong wind of Alaska and Canada.

Zanzibar Principal islands are Zanzibar and Pemba islands. Joined with Tanganyika in 1964 to become Tanzania. Zanzibar's African population call themselves 'Shirazi' after the ancient Persian principality of Shîrãz, as traders from the Persian Gulf began to settle there after the 7th century.

zonda Hot dusty north wind of Argentina.

Geological Ages

Era	Period	Epoch	Years ago (m)	Life forms
Cenozoic		Holocene	0.01	
	Quaternary	Pleistocene	1.64	humans appeared
		Pliocene	5.2	
		Miocene	23.5	
	Tertiary	Oligocene	35.5	
		Eocene	56.5	
		Palaeocene	65	mammals flourished
Mesozoic	Cretaceous		146	heyday of dinosaurs
	Jurassic		208	first birds
	Triassic		245	first mammals and dinosaurs
Palaeozoic	Permian		290	reptiles expanded
	Carboniferous		363	first reptiles
	Devonian		409	first amphibians
	Silurian		439	first land plants
	Ordovician		510	first fish
	Cambrian		570	first fossils
Precambrian	Proterozoic		3500	earliest living things
	Archaean		4600	

Ice Ages: years before present

Pleistocene	1.64m–10,000
Permo-Carboniferous	330–250m
Ordovician	440–430m
Varangian	615–570m
Sturtian	820–770m
Gnejsö	940–880m
Huronian	2700–1800m

Island Groups

Group	Administered by	Sea Area	Main Islands
Admiralty	Papua New Guinea	Pacific Ocean	Manus, Los Reyes, Rambutyo, Tong, Pak, Baluan. Lou Purdy Islands are a sub division of the Admiralty Islands.
Aeolian (aka Eolie)	Italy	Tyrrhenian Sea	Stromboli, Lipari, Vulcano, Salina, Filicudi, Panarea.
Åland	Finland	Gulf of Bothnia	Åland, Ahvenanmaa, Eckero, Lemland, Lumparland, Vardo.
Aleutian	Alaska, USA	Pacific Ocean	Andreanof, Adak, Amchitka, Atka, Attu, Fox, Kiska, Near, Rat, Seguam, Umnak, Unalaska, Unimak, Yunaska.
Alexander Archipelago	Alaska, USA	Gulf of Alaska	Baranof (chief city Sitka), Prince of Wales, Chichagof, Admiralty, Mitkof, Wrangell, Revillagigedo (chief city Ketchikan), Kupreanof, Zaremba, Kuiu, Kosciusko, Yakobi, Heceta.
Andaman (204)	India	Bay of Bengal	North, Middle and South Andaman Islands (collectively known as Great Andaman).
Andreanof	Alaska, USA	Pacific Ocean	Kanaga, Great Sitkin, Amlia, Atka, Adak, Tanaga, Delarof. Andreanof Islands are a sub-division of the Aleutians.
Antilles, Greater	Various	Caribbean Sea	Cuba, Jamaica, Hispaniola, Puerto Rico.
Antilles, Lesser	Various	Caribbean Sea	Windward, Leeward, Netherlands Antilles.
Azores	Portugal	Atlantic Ocean	Flores, Corvo, Terceira, Graciosa, São Jorge, Faial, Pico, Santa Maria, Formigar, São Miguel.
Bahamas (700)	UK	Atlantic Ocean	Great Abaco, Acklins, Andros, Berry, Cay, New Providence, Grand Bahama, Inagua, Long, Mayaguana, Bimini, Cat, Exuma, Ragged, Crooked, Eleuthera. Nassau, the capital, is on New Providence and it was here that Columbus made his first landfall in the New World, 12 Oct 1492. Highest point: Mt Alvernia (formerly Como Hill), 206', on Cat Island.
Balearic	Spain	Mediterranean	Ibiza, Majorca, Minorca, Formentera, Cabrera.
Banks	Vanuatu	Pacific Ocean	Vanua Lava, Santa Maria (Gaua), Mota, Mota Lava (Saddle).
Bay Islands	Honduras	Caribbean Sea	Utila, Roatan, Guanja.
Bismarck Archipelago	Papua New Guinea	Pacific Ocean	New Britain, New Ireland, Admiralty, Lavonga, New Hanover.
Bissagos	Guinea-Bissau	Atlantic Ocean	Orango, Formosa, Caravela, Roxa.
Canadian Arctic	Canada	Arctic Ocean	Baffin, Victoria, Queen Elizabeth, Banks.
Canaries	Spain	Atlantic Ocean	Tenerife, Gomera, Las Palmas, Lanzarote, Hierro, Fuerteventura, Gran Canaria.
Cape Verde Islands (10)	Cape Verde	Atlantic Ocean	Windward Islands: Barlavento, Santo Antão, São Vicente, São Nicolau, Boa Vista, Sal Sotavento, Santa Luzia. Leeward Islands: São Tiago, Maio Fogo, Brava.
Caroline (680)	USA	Pacific Ocean	Yap, Ponape (Ascension or Pohnpei), Truk, Kusac, Belau.
Chagos	UK	Indian Ocean	Diego Garcia, Peros, Banhos, Salomon.
Channel	UK	English Channel	Jersey, Guernsey, Alderney, Sark, Herm.
Channel (Santa Barbara)	USA	Pacific Ocean	San Miguel, Santa Rosa, Santa Cruz, Anacapa, Santa Barbara, San Nicolas, Santa Catalina, San Clemente.
Chonos Archipelago	Chile	Pacific Ocean	Chaffers, Benjamin, James, Melchior, Victoria, Luz.
Commander	Russia	Bering Sea	Bering, Medny.
Comoros	Comoros	Mozambique Channel	Grande Comore, Anjouan, Mohéli, Mayotte.
Cook	New Zealand	Pacific Ocean	Rarotonga, Palmerston, Mangaia, Aitutaki.
Crozet	France	Indian Ocean	Île de la Possession, Îles des Pingouins, Îles des Apôtres.
Cyclades (220)	Greece	Aegean Sea	Andros, Mikonos, Milos, Naxos, Paros, Kithnos, Serifos, Siros, Tinos.
Denmark	Denmark	Baltic Sea	Zealand, Fyn, Lolland, Falster, Sjael/Langeland, Bornholm.
Desolation	France	Indian Ocean	Kerguelen, Grande Terre.
Dodecanese	Greece	Aegean Sea	Kasos, Karpathos, Rhodes, Samos, Khalki, Tilos, Simi, Astipalaia, Kalimnos, Leros, Patmos, Kos.

GEOGRAPHY

Group	Administered by	Sea Area	Main Islands
Egadi (Aegadi)	Italy	Mediterranean	Favignana, Levanzo, Marettimo.
Ellice	Tuvalu	Pacific Ocean	Funafuti, Nukefetau, Nukulailai, Nanumea.
Falkland (200)	UK	Atlantic Ocean	West Falkland, East Falkland, South Georgia, South Sandwich.
Farne (Staple)	UK	North Sea	House, Long Stone (lighthouse was the home of Grace Darling). St Cuthbert died on House (Inner Farne) in 687. Nowadays the group is a bird sanctuary and home for grey seals.
Faroe (17 inhabited)	Denmark	Atlantic Ocean	Stromo (Streymoy), Ostero (Eysturoy), Vågø (Vágar), Sando (Sandoy), Bordo (Bordhoy), Sudero (Sudhuroy).
Fiji	Fiji	Pacific Ocean	Viti Levu, Vanua Levu.
Frisian, East	Germany and Denmark	North Sea	Borkum, Juist, Norderney, Langeoog, Spiekeroog, Wangerooge.
Frisian, North	Germany and Denmark	North Sea	Sylt, Fohr, Nordstrand, Pellworm, Amrum (German); Romo, Fano, Mando (Danish).
Frisian, West	Germany and Denmark	North Sea	Texel, Vlieland, Terschelling, Ameland, Schiermonnikoog.
Galapagos (19)	Ecuador	Pacific Ocean	San Cristobal, Santa Cruz, Isabela, Floreana, Santiago, San Salvador, Rabida, Darwin, Wolf, Pinta, Marchena, Genovesa, Española, Santa Maria, Santa Fe, Pinzon, Fernandina, Baltra. Isabela (Albemarle) is largest, Santa Cruz (Indefatigable) is 2nd. Highest point is Mt Azul.
Gilbert	Kiribati	Pacific Ocean	Tarawa, Makin, Abaiang, Abemama, Tabiteuea, Nonouti, Beru.
Gotland	Sweden	Baltic Sea	Gotland, Faro, Karlso.
Great Britain	United Kingdom	Atlantic Ocean	Isle of Wight, Orkneys, Shetlands, Hebrides, Scillies, Skomer, Ramsey, Skokholm, Caldey, Holy, Lundy, Brownsea, Rat, Sully, Flat Holm, Horsey, Osea, Skerries, Bardsey, Hilbre, Little Eye, Read's, Calf of Man, Ailsa Crag, Craigleith, Fidra, Bass Rock, May, St Serfs (in Loch Leven).
Greater Sunda	Indonesia	South China Sea	Sumatra, Java, Borneo, Celebes (Sulawesi), Belitung. North-west Borneo is not under Indonesian administration.
Greenland	Denmark	Atlantic/Arctic	Greenland, Disko.
Hawaiian	USA	Pacific Ocean	Hawaii, Oahu, Maui, Lanai, Kauai, Molokai, Kahoolawe, Niihau.
Heard and McDonald	Australia	Indian Ocean	Heard, McDonald, Shag.
Hebrides, Inner	UK	Atlantic Ocean	Skye (chief town is Portree; home of the Cuillin Hills; also famous as the refuge of the Young Pretender in 1746), Raasay, Mull (chief town is Tobermory; contains Ben More at 3,171'); Eigg, Coll, Tiree, Iona, Staffa, Jura, Islay, Rum, Muck, Arran (containing Goat Fell at 2,868'), Colonsay and Oronsay.
Hebrides, Outer	UK	Atlantic Ocean	Lewis with Harris, North and South Uist, Benbecula, Baleshare, Barra, Bernera, Berneray, Eriskay, Grimsay, Scalpay, Vatersay.
Indonesia (13,677)	Indonesia	Pacific Ocean	Java, Sumatra, Kalimantan, Celebes, Lesser Sundas, Moluccas, Rian-Lingga Archipelago, Irian Jaya.
Ionian	Greece	Aegean Sea	Kerkira, Kefallinia, Zakinthos, Levkas.
Japan	Japan	Pacific Ocean	Hokkaido, Honshu, Shikoku, Kyushu, Ryuku.
Juan Fernandez	Chile	Pacific Ocean	Mas a Tierra (Nearer Land Island, aka Robinson Crusoe Island), Mas Afuera (Farther Out Island, aka Alexander Selkirk Island).
Kermadec	New Zealand	South Pacific	Raoul (Sunday), Macauley, Curtis. Highest point is Mt Mumukai at 1723' on Raoul Island.
Kuril (56)	Russia	Pacific Ocean	Shumsu, Iturup, Urup, Paramushir, Onekotan, Shiaskhotan, Kunashir, Shimushir, Shikotanto.
Lakshadweep	India	Arabian Sea	Amindivi, Laccadive, Minikoy (Maliku), Androth, Kavaratti.
Leeward Islands	Lesser Antilles	Caribbean Sea	Virgin Islands, Anguilla, Saint-Martin, St Christopher and Nevis, Antigua and Barbuda, Montserrat, Guadeloupe. Highest point is Mt Soufrière (on Guadeloupe) at 4813'.

Group	Administered by	Sea Area	Main Islands
Lesser Sunda	Indonesia/Timor	Indian Ocean	Bali, Lombok, Sumbawa, Sumba, Flores, Timor, Alor.
Line	Kiribati	Pacific Ocean	Christmas, Fanning, Washington.
Lipari	Italy	Tyrrhenian Sea	see Aeolian Islands.
Lofoten	Norway	Norwegian Sea	Hinney, Austvagey, Vestvagey, Moskenes.
Madeira	Portugal	Atlantic Ocean	Madeira, Ilha do Porto Santo, Ilhas Desertas, Ilhas Selvagens.
Malay Archipelago	Malaysia	Pacific/Indian	Borneo, Celebes, Java, Luzon, Mindanao, New Guinea, Sumatra.
Maldives (200 inhabited)	Maldives	Indian Ocean	The atolls of the Maldives are listed in the 'capitals'. The word 'atoll' is, in fact, a Maldive word.
Malta	Malta	Mediterranean	Malta, Gozo, Comino.
Mariana (14)	USA	Pacific Ocean	Saipan, Tinian, Rota, Pagan, Guguan.
Marquesas	France	Pacific Ocean	Nuku Hiva, Ua Pu, Ua Huka, Hiva Oa, Tahuata, Fatu Hiva, Eiao Hatutu.
Marshall	Marshall	Pacific Ocean	Bikini, Wotha, Kwajalein, Eniwetok, Maiura, Jalut, Rogelap.
Mascarenes	France/Mauritius	Indian Ocean	Réunion, Mauritius, Rodrigues.
Melanesia	Various	Pacific Ocean	Solomon Islands, Bismarck Archipelago, New Caledonia, Papua New Guinea, Fiji, Vanuatu.
Mentawai	Indonesia	Indian Ocean	Siberut, Sipura, Pagai, Utara (North Pagai), Pagai Selatan Utara and Pagai Selatan (South Pagai), aka Nassau Islands.
Micronesia	Various	Pacific Ocean	Caroline, Gilberts, Marianas, Marshalls, Guam, Kiribati, Nauru.
Moluccas (Maluku)	Indonesia	Pacific Ocean	Halmahera, Bacan, Sula, Obi, Moratai, Ternate.
Mussau	Papua New Guinea	Pacific Ocean	Mussau, Emira, Tench, Emira, Emananus, Tabalo.
Near	Alaska, USA	Pacific Ocean	Agattu, Semichi, Attu, Alaid, Nizki, Shemya. Near Islands are a sub division of the Aleutians.
New Hebrides	Vanuatu	Pacific Ocean	Espiritu Santo, Malekula, Efate, Ambrim, Eromanga, Tanna, Epi, Pentecost, Aurora.
New Siberian	Russia	Arctic Ocean	Kotelny, Faddeyevski.
Newfoundland	Canada	Atlantic Ocean	Prince Edward, Anticosti.
Nicobar (12)	India	Bay of Bengal	Great Nicobar, Camorta with Nancowry, Car Nicobar, Teressa, Little Nicobar. Usually considered with the Andamans as a joint group.
Ninigo Islands	Papua New Guinea	Pacific Ocean	Manu, Aua, Wuvulu, Heina, Kaniet Islands, Hermit Islands.
Northern Land	Russia	Arctic Ocean	Komsomolets, Bolshevik, October Revolution.
Norway	Vietnam	Gulf of Tonkin	aka Xuy Nong Chao.
Novaya Zemlya	Russia	Arctic Ocean	North and South Novaya Zemlya.
Orkney	UK	North Sea	Mainland, North and South Ronaldsay, Stronsay, Papa Westray, Hoy, Shapinsay, Rousay, Sanday, Burray, Eday, Flotta and Fara, Westray.
Parry	NWT Canada	Arctic Ocean	Bathurst, Melville, Cornwallis, Devon.
Pelagian	Italy	Mediterranean	Lampedusa, Linosa, Lampione.
Philippines (7100)	Philippines	Pacific Ocean	Luzon, Mindanao, Samar, Palawan, Mindoro, Panay, Negros, Leyte, Masbate, Bohol, Cebu.
Polynesia	Various	Pacific Ocean	New Zealand, French Polynesia, Phoenix Islands, Hawaii, Line, Pitcairn, Tokelau, Tonga, Society, Easter, Samoa, Kiribati, Ellice, Cook.
Pribilof (Fur Seal)	Alaska, USA	Bering Sea	St Paul, St George, Walrus, Otter.
Prince Edward	South Africa	Indian Ocean	Prince Edward, Marion.
Queen Charlotte (150)	Canada	Pacific Ocean	Prince Rupert, Graham, Moresby, Louise, Lyell, Kunghit.
Queen Elizabeth	NWT Canada	Arctic Ocean	Ellesmere, Mackenzie King, Parry Islands, Zverdrup Islands.
Rat	Alaska, USA	Pacific Ocean	Kiska, Amchitka, Semisopochnoi, Little Sitkin, Little Kiska. Rat Islands are a subdivision of the Aleutians.
Santa Barbara	USA	Pacific Ocean	see Channel Islands.
São Tomé and Principe	São Tomé	Atlantic Ocean	São Tomé, Principe.
Scilly (150)	UK	English Channel	St Mary's, St Martin's, Tresco, St Agnes, Bryher.
Seychelles (115)	Seychelles	Indian Ocean	Praslin, La Digue, Silhouette, Mahé, Bird.
Shetland (100)	UK	North Sea	Mainland, Unst, Yell, Fetlar, Whalsay, Bressay,

GEOGRAPHY

Group	Administered by	Sea Area	Main Islands
			Muckle Roe, Trondra, West Burra, Housay, Fair Isle, East Burra.
Society	France	Pacific Ocean	Windward and Leeward, Tahiti.
Solomon	Solomon	Pacific Ocean	Choiseul, Guadalcanal, Malaita, New Georgia, San Cristobal, Santa Isabel, Vella Lavella, Kolombangara. Highest point is Mt Makarakomburu.
South Orkney	UK	Atlantic Ocean	Coronation, Signy, Laurie, Inaccessible.
South Shetland	UK	Atlantic Ocean	King George, Elephant, Clarence, Gibbs, Nelson, Livingstone, Greenwich, Snow.
Sri Lanka	Sri Lanka	Indian Ocean	Mannar, Sri Lanka.
Taiwan	China	China Sea/Pacific	Taiwan, Lan Hsu, Lu Tao, Quemoy, Pescadores.
Tasmania	Australia	Tasman Sea	Tasmania, King, Flinders, Bruny.
Tierra Del Fuego	Arg/Chile	Pacific Ocean	Tierra Del Fuego, Isla de los Estados, Hoste, Navarino, Wollaston, Desolación, Santa Ines, Clarence, Dawson, Diego Ramirez.
Tres Marias	Mexico	Pacific Ocean	Maria Madre, Maria Magdalena, Maria Cleofas, San Juanito.
Tristan da Cunha	UK	Atlantic Ocean	Tristan da Cunha, Gough, Inaccessible, Nightingale.
Tuamotu Archipelago	France	Pacific Ocean	Makatea, Fakarava, Rangiroa, Anaa, Hao, Reao, Gambier, Duke of Gloucester.
Vesterålen	Norway	Norwegian Sea	Hinnoy, Langoya, Andoya, Hadseloy.
Virgin	USA	Caribbean Sea	St Croix, St Thomas, St John.
Virgin	UK	Caribbean Sea	Tortola, Virgin Gorda, Anegada, Jost Van Dyke.
Visayas (Bisayas)	Philippines	Philippine/ Sulu Sea	Bohol, Cebu, Leyte, Masbate, Negros, Panay, Samar.
Windward Islands	Lesser Antilles	Caribbean Sea	Dominica, Martinique, St Lucia, St Vincent, Grenada, Grenadines.
Zanzibar	Tanzania	Indian Ocean	Zanzibar, Tumbatu, Kwale.
Zemlya Frantsa-Iosifa	Russia	Arctic Ocean	Graham Bell, Wilczekland, Georgeland, Hooker, Zemlya Alexsandry, Ostrov Rudol'fa.

Islands

Island	Area	Administered by	Sq Miles
Adelaide	British Antarctic Territory	Great Britain	1,400
Admiralty	Alexander Archipelago	Alaska, USA	1,709
Alderney	English Channel Nearest of the Channel Islands to France	Great Britain	3
Alexander I	British Antarctic Territory Largest island in Antarctica	Great Britain	16,700
Andros	Atlantic Ocean	Bahamas	2,300
Andros	Aegean Sea The 2nd largest island of the Cyclades	Greece	145
Anticosti	Gulf of St Lawrence	Quebec, Canada	3,066
Ascension (Pohnpei)	Pacific Ocean Highest peak is Mt Totolom at 2,595'	Micronesia	129
Ascension	Atlantic Ocean	Great Britain	34
Bali	Indian Ocean	Indonesia	2,147
Bananal	Goiás State World's largest inland island	Brazil	7,720
Banks	Beaufort Sea	NWT, Canada	27,038
Bathurst	Timor Sea	NT Australia	1,000
Bathurst	Arctic Ocean	NWT Canada	6,194
Bioko	Gulf of Guinea	Equatorial Guinea	779
Bolshevik	Arctic Ocean	Russia	4,368
Bougainville	Solomon Sea Highest peaks Mt Balbi 9,000', Mt Bagana 6,560', Mt Takuan 7,358'	Papua New Guinea	3,880
Bouvet	South Atlantic	France	23
Cape Breton	Nova Scotia	Canada	3,981
Cebu	Bohol Sea	Philippines	1,703
Chatham Island	South Pacific Chief town is Waitangi	New Zealand	348

Island	Area	Administered by	Sq Miles
Chiloé	Pacific Ocean	Chile	3,241
	Chief town is Castro		
Christmas	Indian Ocean	Australia	52
	Highest point is Murry Hill at 1,184′		
Christmas (Kiritimati)	Pacific Ocean	Kiribati	150
	Largest island of purely coral formation in the world		
Clipperton	Pacific Ocean	France	2
Coats	Northwest Territories	Canada	2,123
Cocos	Pacific Ocean	Costa Rica	9
Cornwallis	Northwest Territories	Canada	2,701
Corsica	Mediterranean	France	3,352
	Highest peak is Mont Cinto 8,890′		
Crete	Mediterranean	Greece	3,190
	Highest peak is Mt Idhi 8,058′		
Desolation Island	Indian Ocean	French Antarctica	2,239
	aka Kerguélen Island		
Devon	Northwest Territories	Canada	21,331
Disko	Davis Strait	Greenland	3,312
East Falkland	South Atlantic	Great Britain	2,550
	Highest peak is Mt Usborne, 2,312′		
Easter (Rapa Nui)	Pacific Ocean	Chile	63
	Famous for rongorongo hieroglyphs and stone statues in human form		
Éfaté	Pacific Ocean	Vanuatu	353
	aka Vaté or Sandwich, highest peak is Mt Macdonald, 2,123′		
Ellesmere	Northwest Territories	Canada	75,767
Euboea	Aegean Sea	Greece	1,412
	The 2nd largest island in Greece after Crete		
Flores	Indian Ocean	Indonesia	5,500
Flores	Azores	Portugal	55
	Highest peak is Morro Grande, 3,087′		
Fyn	Baltic Sea	Denmark	1,152
Gotland	Baltic	Sweden	1,212
Graham	British Columbia	Canada	2,456
Guernsey	English Channel	Great Britain	24
	The 2nd largest of the Channel Islands		
Hai-nan	Kwangtung	China	12,962
Halmahera	Moluccas	Indonesia	6,865
Heard	Indian Ocean	Australia	351
	Highest peak is Mt Mawson on Big Ben Mountain at 9,005′		
Hispaniola	Caribbean	Haiti/Dominican Republic	29,418
	Offshore islands include Gonâve and Tortuga Island		
Holy Island (Lindisfarne)	North Sea	Great Britain	2
	St Aidan established church and monastery in 635 and the 7th-century Lindisfarne Gospels are now housed in the British Museum. Of the other Holy Islands, the most notable is the one off the coast of Anglesey		
Hoste	Pacific Ocean	Chile	1,590
Ibiza	Mediterranean	Spain	221
	Highest point is La Atalaya at 1,558′		
Iturup	Sea of Okhotsk	Russia	2,596
Iwo Jima	West Pacific	Japan	8
	Famous photo of marines raising the US flag over Mt Suribachi in Feb 1945		
Jan Mayen	Greenland Sea	Norway	144
	Home of the Beerenberg volcano, 7,470′		
Jersey	English Channel	Great Britain	44
	Largest and southernmost of the Channel Islands		
Kangaroo	South Australia	Australia	1,680
Kerguélen	Indian Ocean	French Antarctica	2,239
	aka Desolation Island		
Kiritimati	Pacific Ocean	Kiribati	see Christmas Islands
Kodiak	Gulf of Alaska	Alaska, USA	3,588
Kyushu	Pacific	Japan	16,274
	Kyushu means 'the nine provinces'		

GEOGRAPHY

Island	Area	Administered by	Sq Miles
Lanzarote	Atlantic Ocean	Spain	307
	Easternmost of the Canary Islands		
Leyte	Philippine Sea	Philippines	2,785
Lindisfarne	North Sea	Great Britain	see Holy Island
Long Island	New York	USA	1,723
Lundy	Bristol Channel	Great Britain	1
Mackenzie King	Northwest Territories	Canada	1,949
Mactan	Bohol Strait	Philippines	24
	Ferdinand Magellan was killed here by Chief Lapulapu on 27 Apr 1521		
Majorca	Mediterranean	Spain	1,405
Mansel	Northwest Territories	Canada	1,228
Marajó	Atlantic Ocean	Brazil	15,500
Martinique	Caribbean	France	417
	Site of the Carbet Mountains: highest peaks Lacroix, 3,924′, Piquet, 3,806′; Dumauzé, 3,638′; Alma, 3,625′; Boucher, 3,510′		
Melville	Timor Sea	NT Australia	2,240
Milne Land	Arctic Ocean	Greenland	1,400
Minorca	Mediterranean	Spain	258
	The 2nd largest of the Balearics		
Náxos	Aegean Sea	Greece	165
	Largest island of the Cyclades, highest peak Mt Zeus at 3,377′		
Negros	Philippine Sea	Philippines	4,905
New Britain	Bismarck Archipelago	Papua New Guinea	14,100
New Caledonia	Coral Sea	Papua New Guinea	6,467
New Ireland	Bismarck Archipelago	Papua New Guinea	3,340
Norway	Beaufort Sea	NWT, Canada	13
Palawan	South China Sea	Philippines	4,550
Panay	Sulu Sea	Philippines	4,446
Pitcairn	Pacific Ocean	Great Britain	2
Pohnpei	Pacific Ocean	Micronesia	see Ascension
Prince Charles	Foxe Basin	NWT, Canada	3,676
Prince Edward	Gulf of St Lawrence	Canada	2,184
Prince of Wales	Alexander Archipelago	Alaska, USA	2,731
	Islands of the same name in Canada and Australia		
Puerto Rico	Caribbean	USA	3,435
Réunion	Indian Ocean	France	970
Riesco	Pacific Ocean	Chile	1,973
Roosevelt	East River	NY City, USA	1
Roosevelt	Ross Sea	NZ Antarctica	2,900
St Helena	South Atlantic	Great Britain	47
	Peaks include Mt Actaeon at 2,685′ and Diana Peak at 2,700′		
St Lawrence	Bering Sea	Alaska, USA	1,780
Samar	Philippine Sea	Philippines	5,050
Santa Catalina	Pacific Ocean	USA	74
	One of the Channel Islands, highest peak Mt Orizaba at 2,130′		
Sardinia	Mediterranean	Italy	9,194
Sark	English Channel	Great Britain	2
	Sark's area includes Brechou		
Seram (Ceram)	West Pacific	Indonesia	6,621
	Highest point is Mt Binaiyi 9,905′		
Shikoku	Pacific Ocean	Japan	7,261
Sicily	Mediterranean	Italy	9,830
Socotra	Indian Ocean	Yemen	1,400
Somerset	Northwest Territories	Canada	9,570
South Georgia	Falklands Islands	Great Britain	1,450
Southampton	Hudson Bay	NWT, Canada	15,913
Spitsbergen	Barents Sea	Norway	15,075
Stewart Island	Pacific Ocean	New Zealand	674
	Third largest NZ island after North and South		
Sumbawa	Indian Ocean	Indonesia	5,965
Taiwan (Formosa)	Pacific Ocean	Taiwan (Formosa)	13,851
Tasmania	Indian Ocean	Australia	24,868
	Other islands in the Tasmanian state include Bruny, King, Flinders and Macquarie		

Island	Area	Administered by	Sq Miles
Tenerife	Atlantic Ocean	Spain	795
	Largest of the Canary Islands		
Timor	Indian Ocean	Indonesia/Timor	11,883
Traill	Greenland Sea	Greenland	1,300
Vancouver	Pacific Ocean	BC, Canada	12,079
Vanua Levu	Pacific Ocean	Fiji	2,137
Viti Levu	Pacific Ocean	Fiji	4,011
Wellington	Pacific Ocean	Chile	2,549
West Falkland	South Atlantic	Great Britain	1,750
Wight	English Channel	Great Britain	147
	Largest British island outside the mainland		
Wrangel	Chukchi Sea	Russia	2,800
Yap	Pacific Ocean	USA Micronesia	21
	Highest peak is Mt Tabiwol at 568'		
Zealand (Sjaelland)	Baltic Sea	Denmark	2,713
Zemlya Aleksandry	Franz Josef Land	Russia	1,080
Zemlya Georga	Franz Josef Land	Russia	1,120

Islands: world's largest

		Area (Sq Miles)	Location
1	Greenland	840,000	Arctic Ocean
2	New Guinea	306,000	Western Pacific
3	Borneo	280,100	Western Pacific
4	Madagascar	226,658	Indian Ocean
5	Baffin Island	195,928	Arctic Ocean
6	Sumatra	165,000	Indian Ocean
7	Honshu	87,805	North Pacific
8	Great Britain	84,186	North Atlantic
9	Victoria Island	83,897	Arctic Ocean
10	Ellesmere Island	75,767	Arctic Ocean
11	Celebes (Sulawesi)	69,000	Indian Ocean
12	South Island (NZ)	58,305	South Pacific
13	Java	48,900	Indian Ocean
14	Cuba	44,218	North Atlantic
15	North Island (NZ)	44,035	South Pacific
16	Newfoundland	42,030	North Atlantic
17	Luzon	40,880	West Pacific
18	Iceland	39,770	North Atlantic
19	Mindanao	36,775	West Pacific
20	Ireland	31,839	North Atlantic
21	Hokkaido	30,077	North Pacific
22	Hispaniola	29,418	North Atlantic
23	Sakhalin	28,597	North Pacific
24	Tasmania	24,868	South Pacific
25	Sri Lanka	25,332	Indian Ocean

GEOGRAPHY

NB: What is the largest island in the world? This is the subject of constant frustration to the more enlightened quiz player. In fact, the answer is very simple when one understands that the dictionary defines an island as a body of land, smaller than a continent, that is wholly surrounded by water. The dictionary defines Australia as the smallest continent and consequently, although it is surrounded by water, it clearly should not be included in geographical listings of islands. If an island was to be considered any area of land wholly surrounded by water then the whole of mainland Eurasia would in fact be far larger than Australia!

Lakes: world's largest

		Location	Area Sq Miles	Details
1	Caspian Sea	Russia, Kazakhstan, Turkmenistan, Azerbaijan, Iran	143,552	classed as a brackish lake; although salinity rises to 32% in the Kara-Bogaz-Gol Gulf, it is negligible around the Volga area
2	Superior	Canada, USA	31,795	often considered the largest freshwater lake in the world, although the Caspian Sea is freshwater in parts; the largest of the Great Lakes of North America

			Location	Area Sq Miles	Details
3	Victoria		Uganda, Tanzania, Kenya	26,834	aka Victoria Nyanza, the chief reservoir of the Nile
4	Huron		Canada, USA	23,011	one of the Great Lakes, often considered as a single entity with Lake Michigan
5	Michigan		USA	22,394	one of the Great Lakes, often considered as a single entity with Lake Huron
6	Aral Sea		Uzbekistan, Kazakhstan	15,444	the largest true salt lake in the world, although its area has been severely diminished
7	Tanganyika		Dem Rep of Congo, Tanzania, Zambia, Burundi	12,703	at 410 miles it is the longest true freshwater lake in the world, and at 4,710' the second deepest in the world
8	Great Bear		Northwest Territories (Canada)	12,279	lying astride the Arctic Circle, it is the largest lake wholly in Canada
9	Baikal		Russia	11,776	world's deepest lake at 5,314'
10	Malawi (Nyasa)		Malawi, Tanzania, Mozambique	11,429	aka Lake Nyasa (which means 'lake')
11	Great Slave		Northwest Territories (Canada)	11,031	links the Mackenzie River to the Slave River
12	Erie		Canada, USA	9,910	one of the 5 Great Lakes of North America
13	Winnipeg		Manitoba (Canada)	9,417	named from the Cree Indian words for 'muddy water'
14	Ontario		Canada, USA	7,550	smallest of the Great Lakes of North America
15	Balkhash		Kazakhstan	7,115	shallow salt lake whose area has varied considerably over the years
16	Chad		Cameroon, Chad, Niger, Nigeria	6,875	freshwater lake whose area varies from about 4,000 to 10,000 sq miles
17	Ladoga (Ladozhskoye)		Russia	6,835	largest lake in Europe, situated near the Gulf of Finland; there is also a small lake in Indiana, USA, of the same name
18	Maracaibo		Venezuela	5,150	large brackish inlet of the Caribbean Sea, lying in the Maracaibo Basin
19	Bangweulu		Zambia	3,800	Bangweulu is Bantu for 'large water'
20	Onega		Russia	3,753	second-largest lake in Europe, situated between Lake Ladoga and the White Sea
21	Eyre		South Australia	3,600	dry for most of the year
22	Volta		Ghana	3,283	artificial lake
23	Titicaca		Peru, Bolivia	3,200	highest navigable lake in the world at 12,500' above sea level
24	Nicaragua		Nicaragua	3,190	freshwater lake, the largest lake of Central America
25	Athabasca		Saskatchewan, Alberta (Canada)	3,064	explored by Samuel Hearne in 1771, who named it 'Lake of the Hills'
26	Reindeer		Saskatchewan, Manitoba (Canada)	2,568	the Reindeer River links the lake to the Churchill River
27	Tonle Sap		Cambodia	2,525	linked to the Mekong by the Tonle Sap River
28	Rudolf		Ethiopia, Kenya	2,473	known as Lake Turkana in Kenya
29	Issyk Kul		Kyrgyzstan	2,408	salt lake
30	Torrens		South Australia	2,230	dry for most of the year
31	Albert		Uganda, Dem Rep of Congo	2,160	aka Albert Nyanza and since 1973 Lake Mobuto Sese Seko
32	Vänern		Sweden	2,156	largest lake in Sweden and a major source of hydroelectric power
33	Urmia		Iran	2,150	salt lake
34	Netilling		Northwest Territories (Canada)	2,140	situated in Baffin Island
35	Winnipegosis		Manitoba (Canada)	2,075	situated north of Lake Manitoba and west of Lake Winnipeg
36	Kariba		Zambia, Zimbabwe	2,000	artificial lake formed by the damming of the Zambesi River
37	Mweru		Zambia, Dem Rep of Congo	1,900	Mweru is the Bantu word for 'lake'
38	Nipigon		Ontario (Canada)	1,872	Nipigon is the Indian word for 'deep, clear water'
39	Gairdner		South Australia	1,845	dry for most of the year
40	Manitoba		Manitoba (Canada)	1,799	lies south of lakes Winnipeg and Winnipegosis
41	Koko Nor		Tsinghai (China)	1,770	salt lake, aka Ch'ing Hai or Tsing Hai
42	Taymyr		Russia	1,760	freshwater lake
43	Kyoga		Uganda	1,710	freshwater lake
44	Great Salt		Utah (USA)	1,700	salt lake that has varied from about 2,400 sq miles in 1873 to 950 sq miles in 1963 depending on the level of evaporation and the flow of the surrounding rivers; largest salt lake in the Western Hemisphere
	Iso Saimaa		Finland	1,700	Largest lake in Finland
46	Khana (Hsing-K'ai)		Russia, China	1,690	Freshwater lake

		Location	Area Sq Miles	Details
47	Lake of the Woods	Canada, USA	1,679	Situated where the provinces of Ontario and Manitoba and the US State of Minnesota meet
48	Dubawnt	Northwest Territories (Canada)	1,480	freshwater lake
49	Van	Turkey	1,434	salt lake
50	Tana	Ethiopia	1,418	freshwater lake
51	Peipus	Estonia, Russia	1,400	freshwater lake
52	P'o-yang	Kiangsi (China)	1,383	freshwater lake
53	Uvs	Mongolia	1,300	salt lake
54	Amadjuak	Northwest Territories (Canada)	1,203	freshwater lake
55	Tung-t-'ing	Hunan (China)	1,089	freshwater lake
56	Kivu	Rwanda, Dem Rep of Congo	1,040	freshwater lake
57	Wollaston	Saskatchewan (Canada)	1,035	freshwater lake
58	Alakol	Kazakhstan	1,025	salt lake
59	Hövsgöl	Mongolia	1,012	freshwater lake
60	Illamna	Alaska (USA)	1,000	freshwater lake
	Poopó	Bolivia	1,000	salt lake
	Rukwa	Tanzania	1,000	salt lake
	Chilwa	Malawi, Mozambique	1,000	salt lake
64	Edward (Idi Amin Dada)	Uganda, Dem Rep of Congo	970	freshwater lake
65	Chany	Russia	960	salt lake
66	Tangra (T'ang-ku-la-yu-mu)	Tibet, China	950	salt lake
67	T'ai	Chekiang, Kiangsu (China)	936	freshwater lake
68	Mistassini	Quebec (Canada)	902	freshwater lake
69	Frome	South Australia	900	dry for most of the year
70	Hu-lun	Inner Mongolia	894	freshwater lake
71	Leopold II (Mai-Ndombe)	Dem Rep of Congo	890	freshwater lake
72	Nueltin	Northwest Territories, Manitoba (Canada)	880	freshwater lake
73	Southern Indian	Manitoba (Canada)	868	freshwater lake
74	Buenos Aires	Chile, Argentina	865	freshwater lake
75	Michikamau	Newfoundland (Canada)	784	freshwater lake
76	Lama	Russia	772	freshwater lake
77	Lop Nor (Lo-pu)	Sinkiang (China)	770	dry for most of the year
78	Hung-tse	Anhwei, Kiangsu (China)	757	freshwater lake
79	Hamar	Iraq	750	freshwater lake
80	Na-mu (Nam)	Tibet, China	741	salt lake
81	Vättern	Finland	738	freshwater lake
82	Baker	Northwest Territories (Canada)	729	freshwater lake
83	Ch'i-lin (Zilling)	Tibet, China	720	salt lake
84	Chiquita	Argentina	714	salt lake
85	Okeechobee	Florida (USA)	700	freshwater lake
86	Martre	Northwest Territories (Canada)	686	freshwater lake
87	Har Us	Mongolia	680	freshwater lake
88	Williston	British Columbia (Canada)	641	freshwater lake
89	Seul	Ontario (Canada)	640	freshwater lake
90	Pontchartrain	Louisiana (USA)	625	usually considered a tidal lagoon, as it is connected to the Gulf of Mexico by the Rigolets
91	Tengiz	Kazakhstan	614	salt lake
92	Tuz	Turkey	580	salt lake
	Po-ssu-t'eng (Baghrash)	Sinkiang (China)	580	freshwater lake
94	Yathkyed	Northwest Territories (Canada)	559	freshwater lake
95	Claire	Alberta (Canada)	555	freshwater lake
96	Cree	Saskatchewan (Canada)	554	freshwater lake
97	Argentino	Argentina	546	freshwater lake
	Ronge	Saskatchewan (Canada)	546	freshwater lake
99	Hyargas	Mongolia	543	salt lake
100	Eau Claire	Quebec (Canada)	534	freshwater lake
101	Moose	Manitoba (Canada)	528	freshwater lake
102	Sevan	Armenia	525	freshwater lake
103	Cedar	Manitoba (Canada)	522	freshwater lake
104	Kasba	Northwest Territories (Canada)	518	freshwater lake
105	Bienville	Quebec (Canada)	482	freshwater lake
106	Island	Manitoba (Canada)	472	freshwater lake

G
E
O
G
R
A
P
H
Y

		Location	Area Sq Miles	Details
107	St Clair	Canada, USA	460	freshwater lake
108	Becharof	Alaska (USA)	458	freshwater lake
109	Lesser Slave	Alberta (Canada)	451	freshwater lake
	Red	Minnesota (USA)	451	freshwater lake
111	Abaya	Ethiopia	448	freshwater lake
112	Gods	Manitoba (Canada)	444	freshwater lake
113	Toba	Sumatra (Indonesia)	440	freshwater lake
	Mälaren	Sweden	440	freshwater lake
115	Champlain	Canada, USA	435	freshwater lake
116	Aberdeen	Northwest Territories (Canada)	425	freshwater lake
	Stefanie	Ethiopia	425	salt lake
118	Päyänne	Finland	421	freshwater lake
119	Viedma	Argentina	420	freshwater lake
120	Chapala	Mexico	417	freshwater lake
	Napaktulik	Northwest Territories (Canada)	417	freshwater lake
122	Mackay	Northwest Territories (Canada)	410	freshwater lake
123	Managua	Nicaragua	402	freshwater lake
124	Eyasi	Tanzania	400	salt lake
125	Dead Sea	Israel, Jordan	394	salt lake; the lowest body of water on Earth at 1,312' below sea level
126	San Martin (O'Higgins)	Argentina, Chile	391	freshwater lake
127	Saint-Jean	Quebec (Canada)	387	freshwater lake
128	Wei-shan	Kiangsu, Shantung (China)	386	freshwater lake
	Ebi	Sinkiang (China)	386	salt lake
	Inari	Finland	386	freshwater lake
131	Limen	Russia	379	freshwater lake
132	Pipmuacan	Quebec (Canada)	378	freshwater lake
133	Garry	Northwest Territories (Canada)	377	freshwater lake
134	Contwoyto	Northwest Territories (Canada)	370	freshwater lake
135	Abitibi	Ontario (Canada)	360	freshwater lake
	Rainy	Canada, USA	360	freshwater lake
137	Bay	Luzon (Philippines)	356	salt lake
138	Hottah	Northwest Territories (Canada)	354	freshwater lake
139	Natron	Tanzania	350	salt lake
140	Oulu	Finland	348	freshwater lake
141	Salton Sea	California (USA)	340	salt lake
	P'u-mo (Pomo)	Tibet, China	340	freshwater lake
	Amadeus	Northern Territories (Australia)	340	dry for most of the year
144	Llanquihue	Chile	330	freshwater lake
145	Pielinen	Finland	328	freshwater lake
146	Aylmer	Northwest Territories (Canada)	327	freshwater lake
147	Eskimo North	Northwest Territories (Canada)	324	freshwater lake
148	Nipissing	Ontario (Canada)	321	freshwater lake
149	Teshekpuk	Alaska (USA)	315	freshwater lake
150	Imandra	Russia	314	freshwater lake
151	Terinam (Cha-jih-nan-mu)	Tibet, China	313	freshwater lake
152	Colhué Huapi	Argentina	310	freshwater lake
153	Yamdrok (Yang-cho-yung)	Tibet, China	309	freshwater lake
	Ch'ao	Anhwei (China)	309	freshwater lake
155	Nonacho	Northwest Territories (Canada)	303	freshwater lake
156	Abe	Djibouti, Ethiopia	300	salt lake
	Peter Pond	Saskatchewan (Canada)	300	freshwater lake
	Seletyteniz	Kazakhstan	300	freshwater lake
159	Atlin	British Columbia, Yukon (Canada)	299	freshwater lake
160	Minto	Quebec (Canada)	294	freshwater lake
161	Cross	Manitoba (Canada)	292	freshwater lake

Other Notable Lakes	Location	Area Sq Miles	Details
Bala (Llyn Tegid)	Gwynedd, Wales	1.69	deepest lake in Wales (125')
Balaton	Hungary	230.96	largest lake of central Europe
Bassenthwaite Water	Cumbria, England	2.06	Lake District lake
Bitter Lakes	Suez Canal	219.86	named for its high concentrations of sodium sulphate, as opposed to alkali lakes which contain sodium carbonate

	Location	Area Sq Miles	Details
Coniston	Cumbria, England	1.89	famous for the water speed exploits of both Malcolm and his son Donald Campbell
Constance (Bodensee)	Switzerland, Germany, Austria	209.69	forms part of the River Rhine; first flight of the Zeppelin (2 July 1900) was from a floating hangar on Lake Constance
Crater	Oregon (USA)	28.14	deepest lake in USA (1,932')
Derwent Water	Cumbria, England	2.06	Lake District lake
Ellesmere	South Island (New Zealand)	69.76	brackish lake
Geneva (Lac Léman)	Switzerland, France	225.19	lake is formed by the Rhône River
Lomond	Strathclyde Region, Scotland	27.46	largest lake of mainland Britain
Mead	Arizona, Nevada	229.84	reservoir of Hoover Dam formed by the damming of the Colorado River, it forms, with Lake Powell, the extremities of the Grand Canyon National Park
Menteith	Central Region, Scotland	1.48	the only true Scottish lake, as all the others are lochs. The lake contains 3 islands including Inchmahome, the temporary hideaway of the young Mary, Queen of Scots after the Battle of Pinkie in 1547
Mono	California	87.62	devoid of any life due to its high alkalinity
Morar	Highlands, Scotland	10.33	deepest lake in Great Britain (1,017')
Neagh	Northern Ireland	147.39	largest lake in the British Isles; it borders all the 6 counties bar Co Fermanagh
Ness	Highlands, Scotland	21.87	famous for its monster legend
Ohrid	Albania, Former Yugoslav Rep of Macedonia	134.49	deepest lake in the Balkans (938')
Seneca	New York (USA)	67.44	largest and deepest (618') of the Finger Lakes
Tahoe	California, Nevada (USA)	193.79	freshwater lake
Tiberias (Sea of Galilee)	Israel	64.34	Old Testament name 'Kinneret', later 'Gennesaret'
Ullswater	Cumbria, England	3.44	the 2nd largest lake in England
Vyrnwy	Powys, Wales	1.75	largest lake in Wales
Wastwater	Cumbria, England	1.12	deepest lake in England (260')
Windermere	Cumbria, England	5.69	largest lake in England. Henry Segrave died on this lake in 1930 while attempting a water speed record
Zurich	Zurich (Switzerland)	34.11	freshwater lake

Mountains

10 Highest	Height (ft)	Height (m)	Range	First Climbed	By	Country
Everest	29,035	8,850	Himalaya	29 May 1953	Hillary (NZ) and Tenzing Norgay	Nepal/Tibet
K2 (Chogori)	28,250	8,610	Karakorum	31 July 1954	Compagnoni and Lacedelli (Italian)	Pakistan
Kanchenjunga	28,208	8,597	Himalaya	25 May 1955	Charles Evans (British)	Nepal/Sikkim
Lhotse	27,923	8,511	Himalaya	18 May 1956	Luchsinger and Reiss (Swiss)	Nepal/Tibet
Makalu 1	27,824	8,481	Himalaya	15 May 1955	Couzy and Terray (French)	Nepal/Tibet
Dhaulagiri 1	26,795	8,167	Himalaya	13 May 1960	Max Eiselin (Swiss)	Nepal
Manaslu 1 (Kutang)	26,760	8,156	Himalaya	9 May 1956	Japanese expeditions	Nepal
Cho Oyu	26,750	8,153	Himalaya	19 Oct 1954	Tichy and Jochler (Austrian)	Nepal/Tibet
Nanga Parbat (Diamir)	26,660	8,124	Himalaya	3 Jul 1953	Hermann Buhl (Austrian)	Pakistan
Annapurna 1	26,546	8,091	Himalaya	3 Jun 1950	Herzog and Lachenal (French)	Nepal

Highest subsidiary peaks	Height (ft)	Height (m)	Range	First Climbed
Everest South Summit	28,707	8,750	Himalaya	26 May 1953
Lhotse (Zemu gap peak)	27,591	8,410	Himalaya	Unclimbed
Kanchenjunga West	27,894	8,502	Himalaya	14 May 1973
Kanchenjunga South Peak	27,848	8,488	Himalaya	19 May 1978
Kanchenjunga Middle Peak	27,806	8,475	Himalaya	22 May 1978

Lhotse Shar	27,504	8,383	Himalaya	12 May 1970
Highest Continental Peaks	Height (ft)	Height (m)	Range	General Info
Africa – Kilimanjaro (Kibo peak)	19,340	5,895	Monarch	dormant Tanzanian volcano 1st climbed by Meyer and Purtscheller 1889.
Antarctica – Vinson Massif	16,864	5,140	Ellsworth	first climbed in 1966.
Asia – Everest	29,035	8,856	Himalaya	29 May 1953 Hillary (NZ) and Tenzing Norgay.
Europe, East – Elbrus	18,510	5,642	Caucasus	extinct volcano, first climbed in 1874.
Europe, West – Mt Blanc	15,771	4,807	Alps	first climbed by Jacques Balmat in 1786
North America – Mt McKinley	20,320	6,194	Alaska Range	known to local Indians as Denali and 1st climbed on 7 June 1913 by Stuck and Karstens, although smaller North Peak was climbed by Taylor and Anderson in 1910
Mainland North America – Whitney	14,494	4,418	Sierra Nevada	first climbed by AH Johnson, CD Begole, J Lucas in 1873
South America – Aconcagua	22,834	6,960	Andes	first climbed by Matthias Zurbriggen in 1897
Australia – Kosciusko	7,316	2,228	Great Dividing Range	named by Paul Strzelecki in 1840 in honour of Polish patriot

Mountain Ranges: longest

	Miles	Kilometres	High Point	Height (ft)
Andes	4,500	7,240	Aconcagua (Arg)	22,834
Rockies (Western America)	3,000	4,827	Mt Elbert (US)	14,433
Himalaya–Karakorum–Hindu Kush	2,400	3,861	Everest (China/Nepal)	29,035
Great Dividing Range (Aus)	2,250	3,620	Kosciusko	7,316
Trans-Antarctic Mts	2,200	3,540	Vinson	16,863
Brazilian Atlantic Coast Range	1,900	3,057	Bandeira	9,482
West Sumatran–Javan Range	1,800	2,896	Kerintji	12,484
Aleutian Range (Alaska)	1,600	2,574	Shishaldin	9,387
Tien Shan (Kyrgyzstan/China)	1,400	2,252	Pik Pobeda	24,406
Central New Guinea Range	1,250	2,011	Jayakusumu (Ngga Pulu)	16,503
Altai Mountains (Russia/Mongolia)	1,250	2,011	Gora Belukha	14,783
Urals (Russia)	1,250	2,011	Gora Narodnaya	6,214
Kamchatka (Russia)	1,200	1,930	Klyuchevskaya Sopka	15,910
Atlas (North Africa)	1,200	1,930	Jebel Toubkal (Morocco)	13,665
Verkhoyansk (Russia)	1,000	1,609	Gora Mas Khaya	9,708
Western Ghats (India)	1,000	1,609	Anai Madi	8,841
Sierra Madre Oriental (Mexico)	950	1,528	Orizaba (Citlaltépetl)	18,406
Zagros (Iran)	950	1,528	Zard Kuh	14,921
Scandinavian Range (Nor/Swed)	950	1,528	Galdhopiggen (Nor)	8,098
Semien Mountains (Ethiopia)	900	1,448	Ras Dashen	15,158
Sierra Madre Occidental (Mexico)	900	1,448	Nevado de Colima	13,993
Malagasy Range (Madagascar)	850	1,367	Tsaratanana	9,465
Drakensberg (S Africa)	800	1,287	Thabana Ntlenyana	11,425
Chersky Range (Russia)	800	1,287	Gora Pobeda (Mt Victory)	10,325
Caucasus (Geor/Rus/Azer)	750	1,206	Elbrus, West Peak	18,510
Alaska Range	700	1,126	McKinley, South Peak	20,320
Assam–Burma Range	700	1,126	Hkakabo Razi	19,296
Cascades (USA/Canada)	700	1,126	Rainier (US)	14,410
Crocker Range (Borneo)	700	1,126	Kinabalu (Mal)	13,455
Apennines (Italy)	700	1,126	Corno Grande	9,617
Appalachians (Eastern USA)	700	1,126	Mt Mitchell	6,684
Alps	650	1,045	Mt Blanc (Fr)	15,771
Elburz Mountains (Iran)	560	900	Mt Damavand	18,386
Allegheny Mountains (USA)	500	800	Spruce Knob	4,862
Pyrenees (France/Spain)	270	434	Mt Aneto (Spa)	11,178
Jura	225	360	Crêt de la Neige (Fr)	5,636

NB: A definition of a mountain is an upward projection of the Earth's surface with an altitude of at least 600 m (about 1,968'), often having a rocky surface.

Mountains that are not part of a designated range, e.g. Kilimanjaro, are known as monarchs.

The list of mountains and ranges that follow is a fair representation of the major peaks and systems in the world, but more information can be found in the World Geographical Gazetteer (see below).

The list also contains details of the major volcanic mountains. A few general terms are listed below.

Mountain Ranges: general

Name	Area	Details
Absaroka Range	USA	Situated in north-western Wyoming and southern Montana, highest point is Francs Peak
Adirondacks	USA	Situated in north-eastern New York state, highest peak being Mt Marcy
Aleutian Range	USA	Stretching across southern Alaska and north Pacific islands, highest peak being Shishaldin
Allegheny Mountains	USA	Part of the Appalachians extending south-southwestward for more than 500 miles from north-central Pennsylvania to south-western Virginia
Alps	Central Europe	Extending about 650 miles from the Gulf of Genoa in the south-west to Vienna in the north-east. Highest peak is Mont Blanc
Altai Mountains	Central Asia	Running in a southeast-northwest direction from the Gobi desert to the West Siberian Plain, through Chinese, Mongolian and Soviet territory. Highest peak is Belukha
Amambai Mountains	Brazil–Paraguay	Situated in western Mato Grosso do Sul state of Brazil, and eastern Paraguay
Andes	South America	Stretching the length of the South American continent from Lake Maracaibo in the north to the Tierra del Fuego archipelago in the south
Apennine Range	Italy	The backbone of peninsular Italy extending from the Colle di Cadibona, close to the maritime Alps in the north-west, as far as the Egadi Islands to the west of Sicily
Appalachians	USA	Extending from the Gaspé Peninsula in Quebec through eastern United States southward to central Alabama
Apuseni Range	Romania	Subgroup of the Western Carpathians, lying north of the Mures River in north-western Romania
Arāvalli Range	India	Situated in northern India and running north-easterly for 350 miles through Rājasthān state. Highest point is Guru Sikhar on Mount Abu
Armorican Massif	France	Flattened erosional upland encompassing the western French départements of Finistère, Côtes-du-Nord, Morbihan, and Ille-et-Vilaine and parts of Manche, Orne, Mayenne, Maine-et-Loire, Loire-Atlantique, and Vendée. Highest mountain in the Massif is Avaloirs, in Orne at 1,368′
Atherton Tableland	Australia	Also called the Atherton Plateau, part of the Great Dividing Range
Athos Range	Antarctica	Located in West Antarctica, joining the Lambert Glacier
Atlas	North Africa	Running north-east to south-west through the three countries of the Maghrib i.e. Morocco, Algeria, and Tunisia, the highest point Jebel Toubkal being in Morocco
Australian Alps	Australia	Part of the Great Dividing Range, occupying the south-easternmost corner of Australia, in eastern Victoria and south-eastern New South Wales
Balkan Mountains	Bulgaria	Extending from the Timok Valley near the Yugoslav border and stretching eastward towards the Black Sea, highest point is Botev Peak
Baranya Mountains	Hungary	See Mecsek Mountains
Beartooth Range	USA	North-eastern spur of the Absarokas, highest point is Granite Peak
Berkshire Hills	USA	Segment of the Appalachians in western Massachusetts, Mt Greylock being the highest point in the state
Black Mountain Range	Bhutan	Southern spur of the Assam Himalayas
Black Mountains	Wales	Situated in east Dyfed and west Powys, highest peak being Carmarthen Van
Black Mountains	Wales	Situated in east Gwent, highest peak being Waun Fach
Black Mountains	USA	Situated in Yancey County in western North Carolina, extending from the Blue Ridge Mountains
Blue Ridge Mountains	USA	Part of the Appalachians extending south-west from Carlisle, Pennsylvania, through Maryland, Virginia, N. Carolina, South Carolina, to Mt Oglethorpe in Georgia
Brecon Beacons	Wales	Red sandstone mountains
Cader Idris	Wales	Situated in Gwynedd, highest point is Pen-y-Gader (Cader Idris means 'chair of Idris')
Cariboo Mountains	Canada	Major subdivision of the Columbia Mountains in British Columbia, highest peak is Mt Sir Wilfrid Laurier
Carpathians	East Europe	Crescent-shaped continuation of the Alps running through parts of The Czech Republic, Poland, Hungary, Romania, and the Ukraine, highest peak being Mt Gerlach (Gerlachovsky Stit)
Cascades	USA - Canada	Extending 700 miles from Lassen Peak in northern California, through Oregon and Washington to the Fraser River in southern British Columbia

GEOGRAPHY

Name	Area	Details
Catskills	USA	Dissected segment of the Allegheny Plateau, and part of the Appalachians, lying mainly in Greene and Ulster counties of south-eastern New York. Highest point is Slide Mountain
Caucasus	East Europe	Situated between the Black Sea and the Caspian Sea on the border of russia, Georgia and Azerbaijan, highest point being Mt Elbrus
Cheviots	England	Range of rounded hills, mainly in Northumberland, forming the border between England and Scotland, highest point is Cheviot Peak
Chilterns	England	Range of chalk hills stretching 40 miles north-east from the Thames near Reading, highest point is Coombe Hill
Columbia Mountains	Canada – USA	Major mountain group of British Columbia that includes the Selkirk, Monashee, Cariboo, and Purcell ranges.
Dângrêk Mountains	Asia	Situated between Thailand and Cambodia
Darling Range	Australia	Situated on the south-west coast of Western Australia, highest peaks are Mt Cooke, Mt Solus and Mt Dale
Dartmoor	England	Area of high moorland in Devon, highest peak being High Willhays
Dauphiné Alps	France	Western spur of the Cottian Alps in south-eastern France
Dolomites	Italy	Eastern section of the northern Italian Alps, named after the 18th century French geologist, Dieudonné Dolomieu, highest peak being Marmolada
Dome Rock Mountains	USA	Situated in western Arizona in the Sonoran Desert region near the California border
Drakensberg	South Africa	Extends from north-eastern Transvaal, through Lesotho, to south-eastern Cape Province, highest peak being Mt Thabana Ntlenyana
Durack Range	Australia	Situated in northern Western Australia, forming the eastern edge of the Kimberley Plateau
Elburz Mountains	Iran	Situated in northern Iran, highest point Mt Damāvand
Exmoor	England	Area of high moorland on the border of Somerset and Devon, highest point being Dunkery Beacon
Fan Si Pan Mountains	Vietnam	Situated in northern Vietnam, the highest peak is Mt Fan Si Pan
Flinders Range	Australia	Situated in eastern South Australia between Lake Torrens and Lake Frome, highest peak is St Mary
Gawler Ranges	Australia	Situated in South Australia, the eastern sector is known as the Middleback Ranges; the highest peak is Mount Bluff
Ghāts	India	Two ranges, East and West, forming the eastern and western edges of the Deccan Plateau of peninsular India. Ghāts means 'river landing stairs'
Golan Heights	Middle East	Situated in south-western Syria, overlooking the upper Jordan Valley, occupied by Israel since 1967 and unilaterally annexed in 1981
Grampians	Scotland	Dividing the Highlands and Lowlands, and including Ben Nevis, highest peak in the UK, the Cairngorms & Schiehallion
Great Dividing Range	Australia	Parallels the coasts of Queensland, New South Wales, and Victoria
Great Smoky Mountains	USA	Western segment of the Appalachian Mountains between Asheville, North Carolina and Knoxville, Tennessee; they are sometimes considered part of the Unaka Mountains
Great Western Mountains	Australia	Situated in central Tasmania, highest peak is Ironstone Mountain
Hamersley Range	Australia	Situated in the Pilbara region, north-western Western Australia, highest peak Mt Bruce
Himalayas	Central Asia	Extends in a south-easterly arc from Nanga Parbat peak in Jammu and Kashmir, to Namcha Barwa peak in Tibet, it contains 9 of the 14 highest peaks in the world and touches India, China, Nepal, Sikkim, and Bhutan
Hindu Kush	Central Asia	Stretches 1000 miles from the Pakistan/Chinese border in the east to a south-westerly point in Afghanistan; highest point is Tirich Mir
Jura Mountains	Central Europe	Situated on the Franco-Swiss border from the Rhône River to the Rhine
Karakoram Range	Central Asia	Northern extension of the Himalayas stretching from easternmost Afghanistan south-eastward into Jammu and Kashmir, highest peak being K2
Kibara Mountains	Zaire	Reaching heights of 6,070' and situated in the Upemba National Park
King Leopold Ranges	Australia	Situated in northern Western Australia, forming the south-western edge of the Kimberley Plateau, highest peak is Mt Ord at just over 3,000'
Kipengere Range	Tanzania	Situated north of Lake Malawi
Kunlun Mountains	China	Extends from the Pamirs due east along the coast of Sinkiang to the Sino-Tibetan range of Tsinghai
Kwanto Range	Japan	Aka Kantō-sammyaku, situated on Honshu, the northern range is known as the Chichibu Mts
Kyrenia Mountains	Cyprus	Extending 100 miles east to west from Cape St Andreas to Cape Kormakiti, highest point being Mt Kyparissovouno

Name	Area	Details
Lofty Range	Australia	Situated on the Tropic of Capricorn in Western Australia
MacDonnell Ranges	Australia	Situated in south central Northern Territory, west of Alice Springs; Mt Ziel being the highest peak
Malverns	England	Granite ridge of Hereford and Worcester, high point being Worcester Beacon
Mealy Mountains	Canada	Situated south of Lake Melville in the Labrador peninsula of Newfoundland
Mecsek Mountains	Hungary	Aka Baranya Mts, situated in Baranya (Megye) county, southern Hungary. Highest peak is at Zengö
Monashee	Canada	Major subdivision of the Columbia Mountains in British Columbia
Mount Lofty Ranges	Australia	Situated in South Australia as a continuation of the Flinders range, highest point is Mt Byron
North Yolla Bolly Mountains	USA	California mountain range
Ore Mountains	East Europe	Situated on the border of Czech Republic and Eastern Germany highest peak is Klinovec at 4080′
Ozark Mountains	USA	Extends south-westward from St Louis, Missouri to the Arkansas River, highest point being Taum Sauk Mountain
Pamirs	Tajikistan	Often called 'The Roof of the World', highest point Communism Peak
Pare Range	Tanzania	Situated near the border with Kenya
Parecis Range	Brazil	Situated near the border with Bolivia
Peak District	England	Hill area in Derbyshire, forming the southern end of the Pennines, highest peak being Kinder Scout
Pennines	England	Range of limestone hills with a footpath stretching from Edale in Derbyshire to Kirk Yetholm in the Borders, highest point is Cross Fell
Pisgah Range	Jordan	Situated north-east of the Dead Sea, the ridge includes Mt Nebo
Przhevalsky Range (Arkatag)	Central Asia	Extension of the Kunlun Mountains, highest peak being Wu-Lu-k'o-mu-shih Ling
Purcell Range	Canada – USA	Major subdivision of the Columbia Mountains extending from British Columbia into northern Idaho
Queen Alexandra Range	Antarctica	Situated in the Ross Dependency (NZ admin), highest point Mt Kirkpatrick
Queen Elizabeth Range	Antarctica	Situated in the Ross Dependency (NZ admin), highest point Mt Miller
Queen Maud Range	Antarctica	Situated in the Ross Dependency (NZ admin), the range is a subdivision of the Transarctic Mountains
Rhodope Mountains	Balkan Peninsula	Situated mainly in Bulgaria, but extends into Macedonia, Greece, and Turkey, highest point being Golyam Perelik
Ring of Fire	Pacific	Not a mountain range but a colloquial name for the band of volcanoes that circle the Pacific and erupt frequently
Rockies	USA – Canada	Extending from British Columbia to New Mexico, highest peak is Mt Elbert
Ruwenzori Range	Zaire – Uganda	Highest mountain in the range is Mt Stanley, the highest peak being Margherita
Salt Range	Pakistan	Situated between the valleys of the Indus and Jhelum rivers of the northern Punjab, highest point being Mt Sakesar
San Bernardino Mountains	USA	Segment of the Pacific coast Ranges of southern California extending from Cajon Pass to Gorgonio Pass, highest point being San Gorgonio
San Francisco Peaks	USA	Three summits, Humphreys, Agassiz, and Fremont, on the ridge of an eroded volcano, 10 miles north of Flagstaff in north central Arizona
San Gabriel Mountains	USA	Segment of the Pacific coast Ranges of southern California extending from Newhall Pass to Cajon Pass, highest point being Mt San Antonio
San Jacinto Mountains	USA	Segment of the Pacific Coast Ranges of southern California extending from Gorgonio Pass to Santa Rosa Mountains
Sangro de Cristo Mountains	USA	Segment of the southern Rockies, extending south-eastward for about 250 miles, from Poncha Pass in south Colorado to north central New Mexico, highest point being Blanca Peak
Santa Marta Mountains	Colombia	Part of the Andes of northern Colombia, highest point Pico Cristóbal Colón is also the highest peak in Colombia
Sarykol Range	Central Asia	Borders Tajikistan and China, highest point being Mt Lyavirdyr
Sawatch Range	USA	Segment of the southern Rocky Mountains in central Colorado stretching from the Eagle River to Saguache, highest point being Mt Elbert
Selkirk Mountains	Canada – USA	Major subdivision of the Columbia Mountains extending for 200 miles from British Columbia into northern Idaho and Montana, highest peak is Mt Sir Stanford

GEOGRAPHY

Name	Area	Details
Sentinel Range	Antarctica	Located in West Antarctica, joining the Heritage Range, making up the Ellsworth Mountain Range, contains the Continent's highest peak, Vinson Massif
Sierra Madre	Mexico	Includes the 3 ranges, Sierra Madre Occidental, Sierra Madre Oriental, and Sierra Madre del Sur (to the south)
Sierra Madre de Chiapas	Mexico	Aka Sierra de Soconusco, and extending to the south-east along the Pacific Coast from the Isthmus of Tehuantepec to the Guatemalan border
Sierra Nevada	Spain	Highest division of the Penibético Mountain System of south-eastern Spain, highest point being Cerro de Mulhacén
Sierra Nevada Range	USA	Extending for more than 250 miles along the eastern edge of California, from the Mojave Desert in the south to the Cascades in the north, highest peak is Mt Whitney
Southern Alps	New Zealand	Situated on South Island and extending from Haast Pass, north-eastwards to Arthur's Pass, highest point being Mt Cook
Sperrin Mountains	N. Ireland	Situated 20 miles south-east of Londonderry, major peaks include, Mullaclogher, Sawel, and Mullaghaneany
St Elias Range	Canada	Situated in south-western Yukon Territory near the Pacific coast, highest peak is Mt Logan
Tatras	East Europe	Situated along the Slovak – Polish border, it is the highest range of the Central Carpathians, high point being Mt Gerlach
Transylvanian Alps	Romania	Aka Southern Carpathians, the section of the Carpathians between the Prahova River Valley and the gap between the Timis and Cerna rivers, highest point Mt Moldoveanu
Uinta Mountains	USA	Mountain range in N.E. Utah, part of the Rocky Mountains, the highest point being Kings Peak
Unaka Mountains	USA	Extending from south-west Virginia, along the Tennessee-North Carolina border, into northern Georgia. Unaka means 'white' in Cherokee
Urals	Russia	Extending from the Arctic Ocean to northern Kazakhstan, forming part of the boundary between Europe and Asia, highest peak Mt Narodnaya
Velikonda Range	India	Situated in Andhra Pradesh state of southern India
Virunga Range	Central Africa	Also spelled Birunga, and also called M'Fumbiro Mountains. The range straddles Zaire, Rwanda and Uganda, although, the highest peak, Karisimbi, borders Zaire & Rwanda
Vosges Mountains	France	Extending west of the Rhine River Valley in the Haut-Rhin, Bas-Rhin, and Vosges départements of eastern France; highest point Ballon de Guebwiller
White Mountains	USA	Segment of the Appalachians extending across New Hampshire and into western Maine, highest point is Mt Washington
Wilhelmina Gebergte	Suriname	Forming part of South America's granitic Precambrian Guiana Shield, highest point being Juliana Top
Wilson's Promontory	Australia	Not a range of mountains as such but the southernmost point of the Australian mainland, in Victoria; it is a mountainous area, highest point being Mt Latrobe
Wind River Range	USA	Situated in the central Rocky Mountains, west central Wyoming, the highest peak being Gannett Peak
Wrangell Mountains	USA	Segment of the Pacific Coast Range, extending southward in south-eastern Alaska for about 100 miles from the Copper River to the St Elias Mountains near the Yukon border; the highest point is Mt Blackburn
Yablonovy Range	Russia	Situated in the Transbaikalia region of Chita and Buryat, highest point being Mt Kusotuy
Zagros Mountains	Iran	Situated in south-west Iran, extending north-west to south-east from the Sirvān (Diyala) river to Shirāz, the highest peak being Zard Kuh
Zambales Mountains	Philippines	Situated in the south-western part of northern Luzon, from Lingayen Gulf in the north to the entrance to Manila Bay in the south, highest point being High Peak
Zeravshan Range	Tadzhik – Uzbek	Extends 230 miles as an east-west parallel to the Turkistan Range, highest point being Chimtorga

Mountain Passes, Valleys and Gorges

Arthur's   the lowest pass (3,038′) of the Southern Alps, west-central South Island, New Zealand, the Otira Tunnel crosses the Alps at this point

Berthoud   situated in the Front Range of the central Rocky Mountains at an altitude of 11,315′

Bran   situated to the west of Predeal Pass and linking Brasov to Cimpulung between the Bucegi Massif and the Fagaras Mountains, Romania

Brenner	lying on the Italian–Austrian border and at 4,498′ one of the lowest Alpine passes
Cameron	situated in the extreme southerly end of the Medicine Bow Mountains in Colorado at an altitude of 10,285′
Great Saint Bernard	lying on the Italian–Swiss border and at 8,100′ one of the highest Alpine passes
Gumal	situated between the Khyber pass and Bolān pass and connects Ghazni in eastern Afghanistan with Tānk and Dera Ismāil Khān in Pakistan
Iron Gate	last gorge of the Djerdap gorge system on the Danube River, dividing the Carpathian and Balkan mountains and forming part of the boundary between Yugoslavia and Romania. The gorge is two miles long and 530′ wide
Katára (Métsovo in Albania)	situated in the Pindus Mountains of northern Greece and southern Albania at an altitude of 5,593′
Khyber	Connecting Kābul, Afghanistan, with Peshāwar, Pakistan. The pass is extremely undulating and reaches 3,518′ at its highest point
Kicking Horse	situated on the Alberta–British Columbia border, the highest point on the Canadian Pacific Railway at 5,338′
Little Saint Bernard	at 7,178′ one of the highest passes of the French Alps. The road across the pass links France and Italy
Lolo	situated in the Bitteroot Range along the Idaho–Montana border at an altitude of 5,236′
Loveland	situated in the Front Range of the central Rocky Mountains at an altitude of 11,990 feet.
Marias	situated in the Lewis Range of the northern Rockies at an elevation of 5,216′
Métsovo (Katára in Greece)	situated in the Pindus Mountains of northern Greece and southern Albania at an altitude of 5,593′
Pajares	railway pass through the Cantabrian Mountains of northern Spain linking Oviedo and León at an altitude of 4,524′
Pele	cuts through the Black Mountain Range of the Assam Himalayas at an altitude of 11,055′
Plöcken (Passo di Monte Croce)	situated at an elevation of 4,462′ in the Carnic Alps on the Austrian–Italian border
Predeal	links the city of Brasov and the Birsei Depression to the north with the city of Ploiesti and the Danube Plain to the south, across the Transylvanian Alps (Southern Carpathians)
Predel	separates the Julian Alps at the Italian–Slovenian border at an altitude of 3,793′
Radstädter Tauern	situated in the Niedere Tauern Range at an elevation of 5,705′
Saint Gothard	a 16-mile-long pass situated in the Lepontine Alps of southern Switzerland. The pass has an altitude of 6,916′; the nine-mile-long St Gothard railway tunnel underneath the pass links Italy and Switzerland via Milan and Luzern; the ten-mile long St Gothard road tunnel links Göschenen and Airolo
Simplon	situated in the southern Swiss Alps at an altitude of 6,581′; the Simplon railway tunnel cuts through beneath the pass and connects Brig, Switzerland and Iselle, Italy
Uspallata	situated in the Andes, at 12,500′, connecting Mendoza, Argentina and Santiago, Chile

G
E
O
G
R
A
P
H
Y

Mountains (General)

Name	Area	Height (ft)	Details
Abu (Guru Sikhar)	India	5,650	highest mountain in the Arāvalli range of northern India
Aconcagua	Argentina	22,834	highest peak in the Andes and in the Western Hemisphere, first climbed in 1897
Adam's Peak	Sri Lanka	7,360	situated in south-western Sri Lanka, 11 miles north-east of Ratnapura; famous for its footprint (5′4″ x 2′6″) revered as the Buddha's, Adam's or Siva's, dependent on faith
Alverstone	North America	14,565	situated in the St Elias Mountains, on the Yukon/Alaska border, and first climbed in 1951
Ampato	Peru	20,702	situated in the Andes, first climbed in 1972
Anai Mudi	India	8,842	situated in Kottayam district, eastern Kerala state, SW India, in the Western Ghāts, highest point of peninsular India
Annapurna	Nepal	26,546	first peak above 26,000′ to be climbed to the summit, on 3 June 1950, by Maurice Herzog and Louis Lachenal
Apo	Philippines	9,690	volcanic mountain, the highest point of the Philippines, part of the Cordillera Central
Aragats	Armenia	13,418	highest point in both Armenia, and the Little Caucasus range
Ararat (Agri Dagi)	Turkey	17,011	extinct volcano, highest peak in Turkey. Little Ararat (Kucuk Agri Dagi) rises to 12,782′
Aspiring	New Zealand	9,932	situated in the Southern Alps of west central South Island, first climbed in 1909 by Major Bernard Head
Athos	Greece	6,670	situated in northern Greece, it is also the site of a semi-autonomous republic of Greek Orthodox monks
Backbone	USA	3,360	highest point in Maryland
Baden-Powell	USA	9,389	twin peak, with North Baldy, and situated in the San Gabriel Mountains
Baker	USA	10,778	volcano situated in the Cascade range in Washington

Name	Area	Height (ft)	Details
Ballon de Guebwiller	France	4,672	highest peak of the Vosges Mountains
Bandeira	Brazil	9,482	situated on the border of Espirito Santo and Minas Gerais states, eastern Brazil; until Neblina peak was discovered in 1962 Bandeira was the highest known peak in Brazil
Batu	Ethiopia	14,130	situated in the Eastern Highlands between the Genale and Shebele rivers
Bear	USA	14,831	situated in the Wrangell Mountains, first climbed in 1951
Belukha	Russia	14,783	highest peak in the Altai Mountain range
Ben Macdui	Scotland	4,296	highest peak of the Cairngorm Mountains and the second highest mountain in the British Isles
Ben Nevis	Scotland	4,406	highest mountain of the British Isles
Betling Sib	India	3,280	highest peak of the Tripura Hills of north-eastern India
Big Black Mountain	USA	4,150	highest peak of Kentucky
Blackburn	USA	16,523	highest point in Alaska's Wrangell Mountains, first climbed in 1912
Blanc	France/Italy	15,771	highest peak in the Alps
Blanca Peak	USA	14,345	highest peak in the Sangre de Cristo Mountains of Colorado/New Mexico
Blue Mountain Peak	Jamaica	7,402	highest peak of the Blue Mountains in eastern Jamaica
Bluff	Australia	1,550	highest peak of the Gawler ranges of South Australia
Bolivar	Venezuela	16,427	situated in the Sierra Nevada National Park of Mérida and Barinas states, north-western Venezuela; Pico Bolivar (Columna) is marginally higher than Humboldt and Bonpland and is the highest peak in Venezuela: the cable-car running from Mérida to nearby Pico Espejo (Mirror Peak), 15,600', is thought to be the highest in the world
Bona	USA	16,421	situated in the Wrangell Mountains, first climbed in 1930
Botev Peak	Bulgaria	7,795	highest point in the Balkan Mountain range
Boundary Peak	USA	13,140	highest point in Nevada
Brasstown Bald	USA	4,784	highest point in Georgia, part of the Unaka range of the Blue Ridge
Brown	USA	14,530	situated in the Alaska range
Bruce	Australia	4,056	highest peak in the Hamersley range, and the highest in Western Australia
Bukit Maxwell	Malaysia	3,399	situated in Taiping, West Malaysia, and formerly called Mazwells Hill
Byron	Australia	3,058	highest point of the Mount Lofty ranges of South Australia
Carrantuohill	Ireland	3,414	highest point of Macgillicuddy's Reeks in County Kerry and highest mountain in Ireland
Carmarthen Van	Wales	2,632	highest peak of the Black Mountains of east Dyfed
Carn Mairg	Scotland	3,087	highest peak of the Monadhliath Mountains in the Highlands between Loch Ness and the River Spey; aka Grey Hills
Chances Peak	Montserrat	3,002	situated east of the capital Plymouth in the Soufrière Hills
Cheaha	USA	2,407	highest point in Alabama
Cheviot Peak	England	2,676	highest point of the Cheviots of northern England
Chimborazo	Ecuador	20,561	extinct volcano in the Andes of central Ecuador
Chimtorga	Tajik/Uzbek	18,009	highest point of the Zeravshan range
Churchill	USA	15,638	situated in the Wrangell Mountains
Cleveland	USA–Canada	10,479	highest peak of the Lewis range in the northern Rockies
Clingman's Dome	USA	6,643	highest point in Tennessee, situated in the Great Smoky Mountains National Park
Cloud Peak	USA	13,165	highest peak of the Bighorn Mountains in the northern Rocky Mountains, southern Montana
Communism Peak	Tajikistan	24,590	highest point of the Pamirs, and highest point of Tajikistan
Cook	New Zealand	12,349	situated in the Southern Alps, the highest peak of New Zealand
Cooke	Australia	1,910	highest peak in the Darling range of Western Australia
Coombe Hill	England	825	highest peak of the Chilterns
Corn Ddu	Wales	2,863	twin peak, with Pen-y-Fan, of the Brecon Beacons
Cotopaxi	Ecuador	19,347	active volcano situated in the Andes, last eruption in 1975
Crêt de la Neige	France	5,636	situated in the French segment of the Jura Mountains
Cristóbal Colón	Colombia	18,947	situated in the Santa Marta Mountains and is the highest peak in Colombia
Cross Fell	England	2,930	highest peak in the Pennines
Curcubăta Marc	Romania	6,063	highest peak of the Bihor Massif in the Apuneni Mountains
Dandenong	Australia	2,077	highest peak in the Dandenong range of southern Victoria
Davis	USA	3,213	highest point in Pennsylvania, part of the Allegheny Mountains
Dhaulagiri	Nepal	26,795	Himalayan mountain; name means 'White Mountain' in Sanskrit
Djebel Chélia	Algeria	7,638	situated in the Aurès range of Northern Algeria
Doda Betta	India	8,652	highest peak in Tamil Nādu state, south-eastern India, and 2nd highest peak in the Western Ghāts

Name	Area	Height (ft)	Details
Dom Mountain	Indonesia	4,396	situated on the island of New Guinea, there is also a Dom Peak in the Apennines
Dome Fuji Peak	Antarctica	12,487	situated on Queen Maud Land
Dome Mountain	Canada	896	situated south of Lake Melville in Newfoundland
Dufourspitze	Switzerland	15,203	highest peak in Switzerland, in the Monte Rosa Massif
Dunkery Beacon	England	1,750	highest peak of Exmoor, on the border of Somerset and Devon
Eagle	USA	2,300	highest peak in Minnesota
Ebal	Palestine	3,084	situated in the West Bank just north of Mt Gerizim
Edith	USA	9,504	highest peak of the Big Belt Mountains, a segment of the northern Rocky Mountains
Egmont	New Zealand	8,260	extinct volcano on the Taranaki peninsula of North Island
Eiger	Switzerland	13,026	first climbed in 1858 by Charles Barrington and Christian Almer. The 6,000′ North Face was first climbed in July 1938 by Heinrich Harrer, Fritz Kasparek, Anderl Heckmair and Ludwig Vorg; the difficulty of this climb earned the Eiger Nordwand many nicknames, including 'The White Spider', 'The White Cobra' and 'Murder Wall'
El Capitan	USA	3,604	highest peak in Yosemite National Park, central California. El Capitan is a granite buttress, part of Sierra Nevada range
El Misti	Ecuador	19,233	volcano situated in the Ecuadorean Andes; last eruption in 1878
Elbert	USA	14,433	situated in the Sawatch range of the Rockies in central Colorado, the highest point in Colorado and the Rockies
Elbright Road	USA	442	situated in New Castle County, the highest point in Delaware
Elbrus	Russia	18,510	highest peak in the Caucasus and highest in Russia, just north of the Georgia border
Elgon	Kenya/Uganda	14,140	extinct volcano on the Kenya/Uganda border, first climbed by Sir Frederick Jackson and Ernest Gedge in 1890, highest peak is Wagagai
Encuolo	Ethiopia	14,144	situated in the Eastern Highlands north of the Shebele river
Erebus	Antarctica	12,448	volcano situated on Ross Island, discovered by Sir James Ross in 1841 and named after his ship
Etna	Italy	10,855	situated on the island of Sicily, this volcano, the highest in Europe, had a major eruption in 1669 when 20,000 people were killed and the city of Catania was devastated
Evans	USA	14,264	highest peak of the Front range in the central Rocky Mountains
Everest	Nepal/Tibet	29,035	highest point on Earth, named after George Everest, Surveyor General of India (1830–43), and called Peak XV until 1865; Dalai Lama 1st gave permission to climb in 1920 and Sir John Hunt led the 1953 successful expedition; Dougal Haston and Doug Scott in 1976 became the first British climbers; Reinhold Messner was the first to make a successful climb without oxygen; Junko Tabei of Japan became the first woman to climb Everest on 16 May 1975; Alison Hargreaves became first woman to climb Everest without oxygen but died soon after on K2; Everest is also called Goddess Mother of the World (Chomolungma in the Tibetan language); previously believed to be 29,028′; remeasured on 5 May 1999 with GPS equipment
Fairweather	North America	15,299	situated in the St. Elias Mountains, on the British Columbia/Alaska border, and first climbed in 1931
Fan Si Pan	Vietnam	10,308	highest peak in Vietnam
Fanthams Peak	New Zealand	6,438	extinct volcano on the Taranaki peninsula of North Island
Fichtelberg	Germany	3,983	highest peak on the German side of the Ore Mountains
Finsteraarhorn	Switzerland	14,022	highest peak of the Bernese Alps
Foraker	USA	17,400	situated in the Alaska range, and first climbed in 1934
Francs Peak	USA	13,140	highest peak of the Absaroka range of the northern Rocky Mountains in northwestern Wyoming and southern Montana
Fremont Peak	USA	13,730	situated in the Wind River range of Wyoming
Galtymore	Ireland	3,018	highest peak of the Galty Mountains of Western Ireland
Gannett Peak	USA	13,763	highest peak in the Wind River range and also the highest peak in Wyoming
Gerizim (Jabal At-Tur)	Palestine	2,890	Since 1967 has been part of the West Bank of Judaea and Samaria, under Israeli administration, it is twinned with Mt Ebal, which is just north of Gerizim
Gerlach	Slovakia	8,711	situated in the Tatra segment of the Carpathian Mountains and is the highest peak of the Carpathians
Glittertinden	Norway	8,110	situated in the Jotunheimen (Giant's Home) Mountain and although twelve feet higher than Galdhopiggen the peak is a 65 ft thick permanent, glacial ice cap
Golyam (Great) Perelik	Balkans	7,188	highest peak in the Rhodope Mountains

GEOGRAPHY

Name	Area	Height (ft)	Details
Goodsir	Canada	11,683	situated in the Yoho National Park of eastern British Columbia
Grandfather	USA	5,964	situated in North Carolina, part of the Blue Ridge Mountains
Granite Peak	USA	12,799	highest peak in Montana, part of the Beartooth range
Greylock	USA	3,491	situated in the Berkshire Hills, the highest point in Massachusetts
Guadalupe Peak	USA	8,749	highest point in Texas
Guge	Ethiopia	13,790	situated west of Lake Abaya
Guru Sikhar	India	5,650	See Mt Abu
Hagen	New Guinea	12,392	situated in the Central Highlands of New Guinea Island, Papua New Guinea
Harney Peak	USA	7,242	highest peak in South Dakota situated in the Black Hills
Hartz Mountain	Australia	4,111	highest peak of the Hartz Mountain range in Southern Tasmania
Harvard	USA	14,420	situated in the Sawatch Mountains, a segment of the Rockies running through Colorado
Hermon	Syria/Lebanon	9,232	aka Jabal ash-Shaikh, and situated west of Damascus, Hermon means 'Forbidden Place'
High Peak	Philippines	6,683	highest peak of the Zambales Mountains
High Point	USA	1,803	highest peak in New Jersey
High Willhays	England	2,039	highest peak in the Dartmoor National Park of Devon
Hochgolling	Austria	9,393	highest peak of the Niedere Tauern range of the Eastern Alps
Hood	USA	11,235	situated in the Cascade range, highest peak in Oregon
Huascarán	Peru	22,205	extinct volcano in west Peru, in the Peruvian Andes, highest peak in Peru
Hubbard	North America	15,015	situated in the St. Elias Mountains, on the Yukon/Alaska border, and first climbed in 1951
Humphrey's Peak	USA	12,633	one of the three San Francisco Peaks, the highest peak in Arizona
Hunter	USA	14,573	situated in the Alaska range
Ingleborough	England	2,376	one of the so called Three Peaks of the Yorkshire Dales National Park
Ironstone	Australia	4,736	highest peak of the Great Western Mountains in Tasmania
Isto	USA	9,058	highest peak of the Brooks range in the northern Rocky Mountains near the Canadian border
Iztaccíhuatl	Mexico	17,159	dormant volcano which last erupted in 1868, situated on the México-Puebla state line in central Mexico, 10 miles north of its twin, Popocatépetl
Jerimoth Hill	USA	812	highest peak in Rhode Island, less than a mile from the Connecticut border
Juliana Top	Suriname	4,199	highest peak of the Wilhelmina Gebergte range of central Suriname
Jungfrau	Switzerland	13,642	situated in the Bernese Alps 11 miles south-east of Interlaken; first climbed by two Swiss brothers, Rudolf and Hieronymus Meyer, in 1811
K2	Pakistan	28,250	situated in the Karakorum range in the Himalayas, on the western side of the Indian/Pakistani line of control in Jammu and Kashmir, first climbed by Compagnoni and Lacedelli in 1954 K2 is also known as Mt Godwin Austen, Dapsang, and Chogori
Kanchenjunga	Nepal/India	28,208	on the border of Nepal and Sikkim, the 3rd highest mountain in the world was first climbed in 1955, although Charles Evans stopped short of the summit in deference to Sikkimese religious beliefs; Kanchenjunga means 'Five Treasuries of the Great Snow' (Sikkim)
Karisimbi	Dem Rep Congo/ Rwanda	14,787	highest peak of the Virunga range
Katahdin	USA	5,268	highest peak in Maine
Kellerwand	Austria	9,121	highest peak of the Carnic Alps
Kennedy Peak	Myanmar	2,704	situated on the Tropic of Cancer near the Indian border
Kennesaw	USA	551	situated in Atlanta, Georgia
Kenya (Batian Peak)	Kenya	17,057	extinct volcano, first climbed in 1899 by Halford and Mackinder of Great Britain
Kerintji	Indonesia	12,484	highest peak in the West Sumatran/Java range
Kilimanjaro	Tanzania	19,340	Volcanic mountain near the Kenyan border, the Kibo peak being the highest point in Tanzania and probably the only snow-covered point on the equator; the other main peak is Mawenzi
Kimpō	Japan	8,514	situated in the Chichibu Mountains, the northern extension of the Kwanto range
Kinabalu	Malaysia	13,455	highest peak in the Malay Archipelago, situated on the island of Borneo, it was formerly known as St Peter's Mount
Kinder Scout	England	2,088	highest point in the Peak District
King	Canada	16,972	situated in the St Elias Mountains, Yukon Territory, and first climbed in 1952

Name	Area	Height (ft)	Details
Kings Peak	USA	13,528	highest point in Utah, situated in the Uintas range
Kirkpatrick	Antarctica	14,856	highest point of the Queen Alexandra range
Klinovec	Czech Republic	4,080	highest peak in the Ore Mountains
Klyuchevskaya Sopka Peninsula	Russia	15,584	highest active volcano in Asia, situated in Kamchatka
Kompasberg	South Africa	8,215	highest peak of the Sneeuberg (Snow Mountain) range in central Cape Province
Kosciusko	Australia	7,316	situated in the Snowy Mountains of New South Wales, the highest peak in Australia
Krakatoa	Indonesia	2,667	famous for the eruption of 1883 when 163 villages were destroyed and 36,417 people were killed. Despite the title of the 1968 film, Krakatoa is actually west of Java
Kriván	East Europe	8,182	one of the highest peaks of the High Tatras on the Poland/Slovakia border
Kusotuy	Russia	5,512	highest point of the Yablonovy range
Kyparissovouno	Cyprus	3,360	highest point of the Kyrenia Mountains
La Dôle	Switzerland	5,545	situated in the Swiss segment of the Jura Mountains
Lascar	Chile	18,508	Volcano situated in the Chilean Andes, last eruption in 1969
Lassen	USA	10,457	Volcano situated in the Cascade range in Washington
Latrobe	Australia	2,475	highest point of Wilson's Promontory in southern Victoria
Le Reculet	France	5,633	situated in the French segment of the Jura Mountains
Les Écrins	France	13,461	highest peak of the Dauphiné Alps
Lhotse (E)	Nepal/Tibet	27,923	situated just south of Everest, to which it is joined by a 25,000′ ridge; The 'E' of its original name stands for Everest
Llullaillaco	S America	22,058	Dormant volcano situated in the Andes on the Argentina/Chile border, last eruption in 1877
Logan	Yukon	19,550	2nd highest peak in North America, first climbed in 1925 by MacCarthy and Lambert; mountains with the same name in Quebec, Arizona and Washington
Lomnicky	East Europe	8,635	one of the highest peaks of the High Tatras on the Poland/Slovakia border
Lozère	France	5,584	highest peak of the Cévennes range of southern France
Lucania	Canada	17,146	situated in the St Elias Mountains, Yukon Territory, and first climbed in 1937
Lugnaquilla	Ireland	3,039	highest peak of the Wicklow Mountains
Lyavirdyr	Tajikistan	20,837	highest point of the Sarykol range
Magazine	USA	2,753	highest peak in Arkansas
Mansfield	USA	4,393	highest point in Vermont
Marcy	USA	5,344	highest peak of the Adirondacks, and the highest Peak of New York state
Mariveles	Philippines	4,659	Most southerly peak of the Zambales Mountains, lying opposite Manila Bay
Markham	Antarctica	14,272	highest point of the Queen Elizabeth range
Marmolada	Italy	10,964	highest peak in the Dolomites
Mary's Peak	USA	4,097	South-west of Corvallis, the highest point of the Oregon Coastal range
Massive	USA	14,421	situated in the Sawatch Mountains, a segment of the Rockies running through Colorado
Matterhorn	Switzerland/Italy	14,691	First climbed 14 Jul 1865 by British explorer Edward Whymper, although the Italian ridge was scaled 3 days later by Giovanni Carrel; Matterhorn was named after the Swiss city of Zermatt; Italian name is Monte Cervino
Mauna Kea	USA	13,796	Dormant volcano situated on Hawaii Island, the highest point in Hawaii state, in fact, its 32,000′ height from the seafloor makes it the world's highest peak from base to tip
Mauna Loa	USA	13,678	situated on Hawaii Island, the actual height of the volcano from its base on the seafloor is second only to Mauna Kea; last erupted in 1988
McIntyre	USA	5,114	situated in the Adirondack range of New York state; highest peak is Algonquin
McKinley	USA	20,320	situated in the Alaska range, and first climbed in 1913, the highest peak of North America
Mercedario	Argentina	22,211	situated in the Andes, first climbed in 1934
Meru	Tanzania	14,980	located near the Kenyan border, south-west of Kilimanjaro
Mikeno	Dem Rep Congo/ Rwanda	14,557	situated in the Virunga Mountains
Miller	Antarctica	13,646	situated in the Queen Elizabeth range
Mitchell	USA	6,684	highest point in North Carolina, situated in the Black Mountains, part of the Blue Ridge Mountains; highest peak east of the Mississippi

GEOGRAPHY

Name	Area	Height (ft)	Details
Moldoveanu	Romania	8,346	situated in the Transylvanian Alps, the highest peak in Romania
Mönch	Switzerland	13,448	flanked by the Eiger and Jungfrau in the Bernese Alps
Mount Darwin	Zimbabwe	4,951	situated in northern Zimbabwe, locals call it Pfura, meaning 'rhinoceros'
Mulhacén	Spain	11,421	situated in the Sierra Nevadas of southern Spain, the highest mountain of the Iberian Peninsula
Nanda Devi	India	25,643	situated in the Uttar Pradesh segment of the Himalayas
Nanga (Naked) Parbat	Kashmir	26,660	often regarded as the first major peak of the western Himalayas; the local name is Diamir (King of the Mountains)
Neblina	Brazil	9,889	situated in the Serra Tapirapeó, Amazonas state, highest peak in Brazil
Nebo	Jordan	2,631	highest point of the Pisgah Ridge, from which Moses viewed the Promised Land
North Baldy	USA	9,131	Twin peak, with Mt Baden-Powell, and situated in the San Gabriel Mountains of southern California
Ojos del Salado	S America	22,588	Although the mountain straddles the Chile/Argentina border, the highest peak is totally in Chile and is the highest point, first climbed in 1937. Ojos del Salado is also the highest active volcano in the world. It was previously designated as dormant but it started to 'steam' in 1981 and has recently produced vents
Olga	Australia	3,507	situated in Uluru National Park, Mt Olga is the most westerly of Australia's 3 giant tors, the others being Ayers Rock at 2,845' and Mt Conner
Orizaba (Citlaltépetl)	Mexico	18,406	dormant volcano situated in Altiplano de Mexico, last erupted in 1687, the highest point in Mexico
Pelée	Martinique	4,582	In 1902 the town of St Pierre was destroyed by this volcano's eruption, which killed all 26,000 inhabitants, except for a prisoner who survived in the thick-walled prison
Pen-y-Fan	Wales	2,906	highest point of the Brecon Beacons
Pen-y-Gader	Wales	2,927	highest point of the Cader Idris range
Pen-y-Ghent	England	2,278	one of the so called Three Peaks of the Yorkshire Dales National Park
Pinátubo	Philippines	5,723	situated in Luzon, this volcano last erupted in 1991, when 847 people were killed – the most lethal eruption of the 20th century
Pissis	Argentina	22,241	situated in the Andes, first climbed in 1937
Popocatépetl	Mexico	17,930	volcano which last erupted in 1997, the first eruption since 1802, although it does emit large clouds of smoke periodically; known locally as Nahuatl (smoking mountain)
Poroshiri	Japan	6,732	highest peak of the Hidaka–Sammyaku range on Hokkaido
Profitis	Greece	1,857	volcanic mountain on the island of Thera in the Cyclades, the highest point on the island
Punta Pora	Paraguay	2,296	second-highest peak in Paraguay
Puy de Sancy	France	6,184	highest peak of the Massif Central
Rainier	USA	14,410	dormant volcano, highest peak of the Cascade range and also the highest peak in Washington state, first climbed in 1870
Ramlo	Ethiopia	6,988	situated inland of the Red Sea coast, north of Djibouti
Revelstoke	Canada	6,375	situated in the Selkirk Mountains of south-eastern British Columbia
Rock Creek Butte	USA	9,105	highest peak of the Blue Mountains, situated on the Elkhorn Ridge on the Oregon/Washington border
Rogers	USA	5,729	highest point in Virginia, part of the Blue Ridge Mountains
Rosa	Switzerland/Italy	15,203	situated SE of Zermatt, often identified with Dufourspitze, although Monte Rosa has many other named peaks
Round	Australia	5,300	highest peak of the New England range, NSW
Ruapehu	New Zealand	9,177	active volcano and highest point on North Island
Rushmore	South Dakota	6,040	situated in the Black Hills, and famous for its carved faces (60' high) of Washington, Lincoln, Jefferson and Roosevelt, executed by Gutzon Borglum between 1927 and 1941
St Helens	USA	8,360	volcano situated in Washington state (Cascades); it erupted in 1980 after lying dormant from 1857
St Mary	Australia	3,825	highest peak in the Flinders ranges
Sajama	Bolivia	21,391	situated in the Andes, first climbed in 1939, the highest peak of Bolivia
Sakesar	Pakistan	4,992	highest peak of the Salt range in the northern Punjab
San Antonio	USA	10,080	Nicknamed 'Old Baldy' and the highest peak of the San Gabriel Mountains of southern California
San Bernardino	USA	10,630	situated in the San Bernardino Mountains of southern California
San Gorgonio	USA	11,502	situated in the San Bernardino Mountains, highest point in southern California

Name	Area	Height (ft)	Details
San Jacinto Peak	USA	10,804	highest point of the San Jacinto Mountains of southern California
San Pedro	Chile	20,339	volcano situated in the Chilean Andes, last eruption in 1960
Sanford	USA	16,237	situated in the Wrangell Mountains of south-eastern Alaska, first climbed in 1938
Santorini	Greece	1,960	See Thera
Sassafras	USA	3,560	highest point in South Carolina, part of the Blue Ridge Mountains
Scafell	England	3,162	South-west of Scafell Pike, the 2nd-highest peak in England
Scafell Pike	England	3,210	situated in the Lake District of Cumbria, highest point in England
Scott Peak	USA	11,394	highest peak of the Bitterroot range in the northern Rocky Mountains, Idaho
Shasta	USA	14,162	extinct volcano situated in the Cascade range of northern California
Shirane	Japan	10,472	highest mountain of the Japanese Alps, on Honshu island; the peak of the mountain is named Ontake
Shishaldin	USA	9,387	volcanic mountain in the Unimak Islands, the highest point in the Aleutian range of Alaska
Sierra Blanca	USA	12,003	highest peak of the Sacramento Mountains in the southern Rockies
Sinai	Egypt	7,497	situated on the Sinai Peninsula, under Israeli administration from the Six-Day War of 1967 until 1979, when it was returned to Egypt; God is purported to have given Moses the Ten Commandments here
Sir James McBrien	Canada	9,061	highest peak of the Mackenzie Mountains in the Yukon Territory
Sir Sanford	Canada	11,590	highest peak of the Selkirk Mountains
Sir Wilfrid Laurier	Canada	11,299	highest peak of the Cariboo range of British Columbia
Slide	USA	4,204	highest point of the Catskill Mountains
Slieve Donard	N Ireland	2,796	highest peak of the Mourne Mountains
Snaefell	Isle of Man	2,034	highest peak of the Isle of Man
Snowdon	Wales	3,560	situated in Snowdonia National Park, Clwyd and Gwynedd, highest peak in Wales
Solomon's Throne	Pakistan	18,481	situated in the Sulaimân range of central Pakistan
Spruce Knob	USA	4,862	highest point in West Virginia, part of the Allegheny Mountains
Stanley	Dern Rep Congo/ Uganda	16,795	highest mountain in the Ruwenzori range (highest peak named after Queen Margherita of Italy), first climbed in 1906 by Luigi Abruzzi
Steele	Canada	16,644	situated in the St Elias Mountains, Yukon Territory, and first climbed in 1935
Sugar Loaf	Brazil	1,325	overlooking the entrance of Guanabara Bay, south-eastern Brazil
Sunflower	USA	4,039	highest point in Kansas, situated south-east near the Colorado border
Table (Tafelberg)	South Africa	3,563	Flat-topped mountain overlooking Cape Town and Table Bay; the highest peak is Maclear's Beacon, subsidiary peaks include Lion's Head (2,195′) and Devil's Peak (3,281′)
Tahan	Malaysia	7,175	situated in Taman Negara National Park, West Malaysia
Tahat	Algeria	9,852	situated in the Hoggar Massif of the southern Saharan Atlas mountains
Talo	Ethiopia	14,478	situated in central Ethiopia in the Gojam Massif
Tambora	Indonesia	9,350	situated on Sumbawa and famous for its eruption of 1815 when over 90,000 people perished
Tapuaenuku	New Zealand	9,465	highest peak of the Kaikoura range on South Island
Taum Sauk	USA	1,772	highest peak of the Ozark Mountains, and highest point in Missouri
Teide	Spain	12,190	volcanic mountain situated on the island of Tenerife in the Canaries, last erupted in 1909
Tendre	Switzerland	5,550	situated in the Swiss segment of the Jura Mountains
Thabana Ntlenyana	Lesotho	11,425	highest peak in the Drakensberg Mountains
Thera	Greece	1,960	southernmost island of the Cyclades group, aka Santorini, and famous for its volcanic eruption c1550 BC which possibly gave rise to the legend of the lost city of Atlantis
Timpanogos	USA	12,008	highest peak of the Wasatch range in the south central Rocky Mountains
Tirich Mir	Pakistan	25,230	highest peak in the Hindu Kush range, lying 155 miles north of Peshawar
Titano	San Marino	2,424	highest peak and dominant feature of San Marino
Toluca	Mexico	4,577	volcano situated in Mexico state, central Mexico near Toluca, the crater partly filled by a lake

GEOGRAPHY

Name	Area	Height (ft)	Details
Triglav	Slovenia	9,396	highest peak of the Julian Alps of Slovenia, first climbed in 1778
Tsiafajavona	Madagascar	8,671	situated in the Ankaratra Mountain region, 2nd-highest peak of Madagascar
Tupungato	S. America	22,310	situated in the Andes, on the Argentina/Chile border, first climbed in 1897
Tyree	Antarctica	16,289	situated in the Sentinel range of the Ellsworth Mountains, first climbed in 1967
Vancouver	North America	15,700	situated in the St Elias Mountains, on the Yukon/Alaska border, and first climbed in 1949
Veleta	Spain	11,128	situated in the Sierra Nevadas of southern Spain, the 2nd highest mountain of mainland Spain
Vesuvius	Italy	4,198	volcano situated in the Bay of Naples, first major eruption in AD 79 and the last in 1944
Victoria	Myanmar	10,150	highest peak of the Arakan Yoma range separating Myanmar from the Indian subcontinent
Vikhren	Bulgaria	9,564	situated in the Rhodope Mountains; second-highest peak in Bulgaria
Vinson Massif	Antarctica	16,864	situated in the Sentinel range of the Ellsworth Mountains, first climbed in 1966
Waddington	Canada	13,104	highest peak of the Coast Mountains of British Columbia
Walsh	Canada	14,780	situated in the St Elias Mountains, Yukon Territory, and first climbed in 1941
Warren	USA	13,720	situated in the Wind River range of Wyoming
Washington	USA	6,288	highest peak in the Presidential range of the White Mountains, and the highest peak in New Hampshire
Waun Fach	Wales	2,660	highest peak of the Black Mountains of east Gwent
Wheeler Peak	USA	13,161	situated in the Sangre de Cristo Mountains, the highest point in New Mexico
Whernside	England	2,416	one of the so-called Three Peaks of the Yorkshire Dales National Park
White Butte	USA	3,506	highest peak in North Dakota
Whiteface	USA	4,865	situated in the Adirondacks of New York
Whitney	USA	14,494	highest peak of Sierra Nevada range in California and the highest peak of the 48 coterminous United States of America
Wilson	USA	5,710	situated in the San Gabriel Mountains of southern California
Wood	Canada	15,886	situated in the St Elias Mountains, Yukon Territory, and first climbed in 1941
Woodroffe	Australia	4,724	highest peak of South Australia situated in the Musgrave ranges
Worcester Beacon	England	1,395	highest peak of the Malverns
Wrangell	USA	14,163	situated in the Wrangell Mountains of south-eastern Alaska
Wu-t'ai	China	10,033	situated in north-east Shansi Province, the name meaning 'five terraces'
Yes Tor	England	2,028	situated in the Dartmoor National Park of Devon, and twinned with High Willhays
Zengö	Hungary	2,237	highest peak of the Mecsek Mountains of southern Hungary
Ziel	Australia	4,954	highest peak of the MacDonnell ranges of Australia
Zomba	Malawi	6,846	highest point of the Zomba Massif in southern Malawi
Zugspitze	Germany	9,721	part of the Wettersteingebirge in the Bavarian Alps, lying on the Austrian border, the highest point in Germany

Oceans

	Area (Sq Miles)	% of Earth's Water	Deepest Point
Pacific	64,186,300	46.0	Challenger Deep
Atlantic	33,420,000	23.9	Milwaukee Deep
Indian	28,350,500	20.3	Planet Deep
Arctic	5,105,700	3.6	Eurasia Basin

British Place Names:
meanings of suffixes and prefixes

Name	Meaning	Name	Meaning	Name	Meaning
aber	river mouth	dal	field	kyle	strait
ac	oak or acorn	dar	water	lade	river mouth
agh	field	dean	wooded vale	law	rising ground
aig	nook or creek	dearg	red	lea	meadow
aird	height	del	dale	leck	field of corpses
ald	old	den	wooded vale	lee	meadow
alt	brook	dene	wooded vale	leigh	woodland glade or meadow
alt	steep place	der	water		
an	terminal diminutive	dhu	black	ley	woodland glade or meadow
ard	height	don	hill or water		
ath	ford	dor	water	linn	waterfall
auch	field	dour	water	lis	enclosure
auchter	summit	drom	ridge	litch	field of corpses
avon	river	drum	ridge	llan	church
ax	water	dum	fortress	llech	smooth cliff
ay	island	dun	hill (england)	llwyd	grey or hoary
bal	village or town	dun	fortress (Scotland + Ireland)	llwyn	wood
balloch	pass			llyn	lake
bally	village or town	dur	water	loch	lake
ban	white or fair	dwfr	water	lough	lake
bar	point or projecting height	dyke	ditch	low	rising ground or mound
		ea	island	lynn	waterfall
beath	birch tree	eccles	church	madah	wolf
beck	brook	egles	church	madan	fair
bedd	grave	ennis	island	maen	stone
beg	little	esk	water	magh	plain
ben	mountain	ex	water	mawr	great
bere	barley	ey	island	mere	lake or marsh
blair	plain	fell	mountain	mickle	great or much
borough	fortified place	field	clearing	minster	monastic establishment
bourne	stream	fin	white or fair		
brae	promontory	fleet	river	moor	lake or marsh
bre	promontory	force	waterfall	mor	great
brogh	fortified place	gord	shallow river crossing	moss	bog
bruach	slope or brae	gair	short	mull	headland
bryn	ridge	garth	enclosure	nant	brook or valley
burg	fortified place	gate	passage	ness	promontory
burn	brook	ghyll	ravine	ock	water
bury	fortified place	gill	ravine	oke	water
by	village	glen	narrow valley	or	river or sea shore
caer	camp or fortified place	ham	home or enclosure	pen	hill or headland
cairn	pile of stones	hampton	home farm or village	pike	mountain summit
cambus	crooked	hanger	wood on hillside	pont	bridge
carn	pile of stones	haugh	meadow between hills	port	harbour
carrick	cliff	hause	pass or col	pwil	pool
caster	walled camp	hay	hedge	rath	round earthwork
cefn	ridge	head	headland or hill	rhos	moor
cester	walled camp	hithe	haven	rhyd	ford
cheap	market	holme	river island	rigg	ridge
chester	walled camp	holt	small wood	ross	promontory
chipping	market place	hoo	heel of land	royd	ridded of trees
clach	stone	hurst	thick wood on a hill	scar	cliff
clere	hill	inch	island	seat	cultivated place or dwelling
clon	meadow	ing	meadow		
coe	narrow	ing	son of	set	settlement
coln	colony	ing	people of	sex	saxon
combe	grassy hollow	innis	island	shan	mountain
cote	mud cottage	inver	river mouth	shaw	shady place
craig	rock or cliff	keld	spring	shot	protruding land
crick	cliff	ken	head	shott	protruding land
croe	sheepfold	kil	church	slievh	mountain
croft	enclosure	kirk	church	staple	store or market
cwm	grassy valley	knock	knoll	stead	place or holding
dal	dale	knoll	hill top	stock	palisaded place

Name	Meaning	Name	Meaning	Name	Meaning
stoke	palisaded place	ton	farm or town	walt	wood
stow	holy place or enclosure	tor	rocky hill	weald	wood
strat	roman road	tre	dwelling or small town	wich	marshy meadow
strath	broad valley	tree	post, cross or crucifix	wick	village or farm
tam	wide	try	dwelling	win	plain
thorpe	farm or village	twistle	boundary	wold	wood
thwaite	clearing	ty	house	worth	protected enclosure
tober	well	ux	water	ystrad	vale
toft	enclosure	wald	wood		

British Place Names: meanings

Name	Meaning	Name	Meaning
Accrington	Acorn Farm	Oundle	Non-sharing Ones
Crawley	Crows Wood	Pontypridd	Bridge by the Earthen House
Croydon	Saffron Valley	Powys	Provincial
Cumbernauld	Meeting of the Streams	Prestatyn	Priest's Village
Cumbria	Fellow Countrymen	Preston	Priest's Village
Derby	Deer Village	Prestwick	Priest's Outlying Farm
Derwent	Oak River	Purbeck	Bittern's Beak
Devizes	Boundaries	Purley	Pear-Tree Wood
Diss	Ditch	Ramsey	Land of Wild Garlic
Ely	Eel	Ramsgate	Raven's Gap
Epping	Look out Place	Redhill	Red Slope
Falkirk	Speckled Church	Reigate	Doe Gate
Gateshead	Goats Head	Renfrew	Current Point
Gatwick	Goat Farm	Rhondda	Noisy One
Harlow	Army Mound	Ribble	Tearing One
Harrogate	Heap of Stones Road	Rievaulx	Rye Valley
Harwich	Military Settlement	Salford	Willow-Tree Ford
Hendon	High Hill	Selby	Village by the Willows
Hythe	Landing Place	Sherborne	Bright Stream
Kesteven	Wood Meeting Place	Skye	Wing
Lampeter	St Peter's Church	Snaefell	Snow Mountains
Leatherhead	Grey Ford	Soho	Hunting Cry (named after)
Lerwick	Mud Bay	Solihull	Muddy Hill
Lichfield	Open Land by the Grey Forest	Staines	Stone
Llanfair-Pwllgwyngyllgogerychwyrndrobwillantysiliogogogoch	St Mary's Church in the hollow of the White Hazel	Stevenage	Place at the firm Oak
		Stranraer	Fat Peninsula
		Streatham	Home by a Roman Road
		Surrey	Southern District
Lundy	Puffin (Norse meaning)	Sussex	South Saxons
Malpas	Bad Step	Sutton	Southern Farm
March	Boundary	Swindon	Pig Hill
Margate	Sea Gate	Tay	Silent One
Matlock	Assembly Oak	Tees	Seething One
Melrose	Bare Moor	Tenby	Little Fort
Menai	Carrying	Tintagel	Throat Fort
Merton	Farm by a Pool	Tobermory	St Mary's Well
Morecambe	Curved Sea	Tranmere	Cranes
Morpeth	Murder Path	Tresco	Elder-Tree Farm
Moulton	Mule's Settlement	Tring	Tree-covered Hillside
Neasden	Nose-shaped Hill	Trossachs	Transverse Hills
Neath	Shining One	Unst	Abode of Eagles
Nottingham	Home of Snot's People		

World Place Names: meanings

Name	Meaning
Aachen	Water Springs
Acapulco	Conquered City
Accra	Ant
Aceldama	Field of Blood
Acropolis	Citadel
Addis Ababa	New Flower
Africa	People of the Dusty Land
Agadir	Wall
Agulhas, Cape	Needle
Ajaccio	Resting Place
Alamo	Cottonwood
Alaska	Great Land
Amritsar	Immortal Lake
Anatolia	Sunrise East
Angostura	Strait Narrows
Anguilla	Eel
Annapurna	Abundant Food
Antananarivo	City of a Thousand
Antofagasta	Hidden Copper
Antrim	One House
Antwerp	Wharfside
Appenzell	Abbot's Cell
Aquitaine	Water Land
Arabia	Tent Dweller
Aral Sea	Island Sea
Aran Islands	Kidney Islands
Ararat	Mountain of Sorrow
Ardennes	Land of Forests
Argentina	Land of Silver
Arizona	Dry Region
Arnhem	Sand Homestead
Asturias	Rock Water
Atacama	Black Duck
Australia	Southern Land
Austria	Eastern Borderland
Azores	Goshawks
Babylon	Gate of the Gods
Baden	Baths
Baghdad	Gift of God
Bahrain	Two Seas
Baku	Windward
Bangkok (see Krung Thep)	Region of Olive Trees
Bangui	Rapids
Banjui	Rope Matting
Barbados	Bearded
Basse-Terre	Low Land
Baton Rouge	Red Stick
Beijing	Northern Capital
Beirut	The Wells
Belfast	Mouth of the Sandbank
Belgrade	White City
Belorussia	White Russia
Bern	Bear
Bethany	House of Poverty
Bethlehem	House of Bread
Bethphage	House of Figs
Betws-y-Coed	Chapel in the Woods
Bhutan (see Druk Yul)	End of Tibet
Bihar	Monastery
Bikini	Surface Coconut
Bizerta	Stable Flowing Through
Bloemfontein	Fountain of Flowers
Boise	Wooded
Bosporus	Oxford
Brindisi	Deer
Brno	Clay

Name	Meaning
Bruges	Bridge
Brussels	Marsh Room
Bulawayo	Place of the Massacre
Bulgaria	Mixed Race
Burkina Faso	Land of the Worthy Men
Cairo	The Fort
Calvary	Skull
Cambrai	Crayfish
Canada	Camp
Canberra	Meeting Place
Carlow	Four Lakes
Carmel	Garden
Carthage	New Town
Casablanca	White House
Cayman Islands	Alligator
Ceylon	Lion
Chattanooga	Rock Rising to a Point
Chicago	Garlic Place
Chittagong	White Village
Clonmel	Meadow of Honey
Comoros	Moon
Conakry	Over the Water
Coney Island	Rabbit Island
Copenhagen	Merchant's Port
Cork	Marsh
Costa Dorada	Gold Coast
Costa Rica	Rich Coast
Cotonou	Dead Person Lagoon
Cotopaxi	Shining Mountain
Cyprus	Copper
Dahomey	On the Stomach of Dan
Dalmatia	Young Animal
Danube	River of Sheep
Dar es Salaam	House of Peace
Darjeeling	Diamond Island (literal) aka Place of the Thunderbolt
Davos	Behind
Deauville	Damp Plain
Dijon	Divine
Djibouti	Plate
Dnieper	Far River
Dodecanese	Twelve Islands
Dominica	Lord's Day
Donegal	Fort of Foreigners
Drakensberg	Dragon Mountain
Druk Yul (see Bhutan)	Land of the Dragon
Dublin	Black Pool
Dubrovnik	Oak Forest
Dumbarton	Fort of the Britons
Dunkirk	Dune Church
Dunsinane	Hill of the Teat
Dushanbe	Monday
Egypt	Temple of Soul Ptah
Eindhoven	End Property
Ephesus	Overseer
Eritrea	Red
Ethiopia	Burnt Appearance
Faeroes	Islands of Sheep
Fair Isle	Islands of Sheep
Formosa	Beautiful
Franche-Comté	Free County
Fray Bentos	Brother Benedict
Galapagos	Giant Tortoise
Gallipoli	Beautiful Town
Galway	Stony
Gangtok	Hill Summit

Name	Meaning	Name	Meaning
Geelong	Marshy Place	Lesbos	Wooded
Gelderland	Yellow Mountain	Levant	Rising
Georgia	Fertile Earth/Tilled Land	Lhasa	City of the Gods
Ghent	Confluence	Liepaja	Lime Tree
Gibraltar	Mountain of Tariq	Limburg	Lime-Tree Fortress
Grasse	Fat	Limerick	Bare Area of Ground
Graubunden	Grey League	Limoges	Elm-Tree Village
Graz	Small Fort	Limpopo	Crocodile River
Greece	Venerable	Linkoping	Flax Market
Gretna	Gravel Hill	Linz	Lime Tree
Groningen	Green	Lisburn	Fort of the Gamblers
Grozny	Awesome	Lodz	Boat
Guadalajara	River of Stones	Lofoten	Fox Foot
Guadalupe	River Wolf	Lombardy	Long Beards/Axes
Guatemala	Land of the Eagle	Longjumeau	New Market
Haarlem	Height Silt	Los Angeles	City of Angels
Haiphong	Sea Room	Luanda	Tax
Haiti	Mountain Land/Nest	Luxembourg	Little Fort
Hanoi	Inside the River	Machu Picchu	Old Man Peak
Hanover	High Bank	Malaga	Queen
Harbin	Place Where Fish is Dried	Malmo	Mineral Island
Harfleur	High Estuary	Managua	Rain Spirit
Harlech	Beautiful Rock	Manama	Place of Rest/Dreams
Harz	Forest	Mandalay	Circle
Hawaii	Place of the Gods	Marathan	Fennel
Hebron	To Unite	Marianske Lazne	Mary's Springs
Hekla	Cloak	Marmara	Marble
Hokkaido	North Sea Province	Marrakesh	Fortified
Holm	Island	Massachusetts	People of the Big Hill
Honshu	Main District	Mato Grosso	Dense Forest
Huang Hai	Yellow Sea	Matsuyama	Pine Mountain
Huang Ho	Yellow River	Mayo	Plain of the Yew Tree
Hunan	South of the Lake	Meath	Middle
Hyderabad	Lion Town	Mecca	Ruined/Sanctuary
Ibadan	Worship	Mechelen	Meeting Place
Ibiza	Island of Perfumes	Medina	The City
Inchon	Virtue River	Melanesia	Black Islands
Iona	Yew Tree	Memphis	His Beauty
Irian Jaya	Cloud-Covered Victory	Mesopotamia	Between the Rivers
Jaffa	Beautiful	Monaghan	Little Thickets
Japan	Sun Origin	Monte Carlo	Charles's Mountain
Jericho	Moon Month	Montenegro	Black Mountain
Johore	To Tie	Montreal	Royal Mountain
Kanchenjunga	Five Treasures of the Snow	Morocco	Far West
Kara Kum	Black Sands	Munich	Monk
Katmandu	Wooden Temples	Munster	Monastery
Kattegat	Boat Way	Muscat	Hidden
Kawasaki	River Cape	Myanmar	The Strong
Kazan	Cauldron	Nairobi	Marsh
Khartoum	End of Elephant's Trunk	Nanking	Southern Capital
Kildare	Church of the Oak	Narvik	Narrow Bay
Kilimanjaro	Mountain of the God of Cold	Natal	Christmas
		N'Djamena	Resting Place
Killarney	Church of the Sloes	Negev	South
Kobe	House of God	Nepal	Fly Down
Koblenz	Confluence	Netherlands	Lower Land
Kosovo	Blackbird	Neuchâtel	New Castle
Kronstadt	Crown City	Neustria	New Western Kingdom
Krung Thep (see Bangkok)	City of Angels	Nevada	Snowy
		New York (named after)	Future James II
Kuala Lumpur	Mouth of the Muddy River	Newry	Yew Tree
Kyushu	Nine Provinces	Nicosia	Victory
Kyzyl Kum	Red Sand	Nijmegen	New Market
Labrador	Labourer	Nîmes	Sanctuary
Lagos	Lakes	Norrkoping	Northern Trading Place
Las Vegas	Meadows	Nova Scotia	New Scotland
Latakia	People Ruler	Nullarbor	No Trees
Lebanon	White	Oahu	Place of Assembly
Leipzig	Lime Tree	Omaha	Those Who Live Upstream on the River
Leitrim	Grey Ridge		

Name	Meaning	Name	Meaning
Omsk	Calm	Saskatoon	Fruit of Tree of Many Branches
Orinoco	Place of Paddling	Schaffhausen	Sheep House
Oruro	Black and White	Shaba	Copper
Osnabrück	Current Bridge	Shikoku	Four Provinces
Pacific	Calm	Shiraz	Good Grape
Padua	Pine	Sichuan	Four Rivers
Pagalu	Father Cockerel	Sierra Leone	Lion Mountains
Pakistan	Land of the Pure	Sierra Madre	Mother Range
Palermo	Safe Anchorage	Sierra Nevada	Snowy Mountains
Palestine	Land of the Philistines	Sikkim	Summit
Pamplona	Pompey's City	Singapore	Lion House
Panmunjom	Floor Gate Shop	Smolensk	Tar
Papeete	Water Basket	Society Islands (after)	Royal Society
Pemba	Green Island	Solferino	Sulphur
Peshawar	Frontier Town	Soweto (acronym)	South Western Townships
Petra	Rock	Sporades	Disseminated
Philadelphia	Brotherly Love	Sri Lanka	Island of the Blessed
Philippines (named after)	Philip II of Spain	Srinagar	City of Happiness
Phnom Penh	Mountain of Plenty	Stromboli	Round
Picardy	Pike	Stuttgart	Mares Garden
Piedmont	Foot of the Mountain	Sudan	Land of the Blacks
Plovdiv	Philip's Town	Sulawesi	Spear Iron
Po	Pines	Surabaya	Hero Danger
Pomerania	By the Sea	Tabor	Navel
Pompeii	Five	Taipei	Northern Taiwan
Pont-L'Évêque	Bishop's Bridge	Taiwan	Terrace Bay
Popocatepetl	Smoking Mountain	Tegucigalpa	Silver Mountain
Port Louis (named after)	Louis XV of France	Tehran	Level
Portugal	Warm Harbour	Tel Aviv	Hill Spring
Potomac	Where Goods are Brought in	Temirtau	Mountain of Iron
Potsdam (Germany)	Under the Oaks	Teplice	Warm
Prague	Threshold	Texas	Friends
Praia	Beach	Thailand	Free People
Prince Edward Isle (named after)	Father of Queen Victoria	Tigris	Arrow
		Timor	East
Puerto Rico	Rich Harbour	Tiruchchirappalli	Town of the Sacred Rock
Punta Arenas	Sandy Point	Tokyo	Eastern Capital
Pusan	Pot Mountain	Topeka	A Good Place to Dig Potatoes
Pyongyang	Flat Land		
Quebec	Place Where Waters Narrow	Transylvania	Beyond the Forest
		Trieste	Trade Market
Quemoy	Golden Gate	Trinidad	Trinity
Rajasthan	Land of Kings	Tripoli	Three Towns
Reykjavik	Bay of Smoke	Tsushima	Pair of Horses
Rio de Janeiro	River of January	Turku	Market Place
Rio Muni	Silent River	Tuscany (named after)	Etruscans
Riyadh	Gardens	Tuvalu	Eight Standing Together
Robben Island	Seal Island	Tyre	Stone
Roncesvalles	Bramble Valley	Ukraine	Border Country
Roquefort	Strong Rock	Ulan Bator	Town of the Red Hero
Roscoff	Hill of the Blacksmith	Ulm	Marsh
Roubaix	Horse Stream	Utah	Mountain Men
Rub-al-Khali	Empty Quarter	Uttar Pradesh	North State
Ryukyu	Ball of Precious Stones	Xinjiang	New Frontier
'sHertogenbosch	Duke's Wood	Yucatan	Massacre
Sahara	Desert	Zagreb	Beyond the Bank
Sakhalin	Black River	Zamora	Emerald
Samos	Dune	Zanzibar	Black Coast
Santo Domingo	Holy Sunday	Zermatt	At the Pasture
Sapporo	Pavillion of Banknotes	Zhengzhou	Solemn Region
Saratov	Yellow Mountain	Zimbabwe	House of Stones
Sarayevo	Palace		
Saskatchewan	Rapid Flowing River		

GEOGRAPHY

Places: alternative names

Aachen	Aix-La-Chapelle
Almaty	Alma-Ata
Banaba	Ocean Island
Bangkok	Krung Thep
Bavaria	Bayern
Belarus	Belorussia
Belfast	Athens of Ireland
Bermuda	Somers Islands
Bhutan	Druk Yul
Bioko	Fernando Po
Bogotá	Santa Fé de Bogotá
Boston	Athens of the New World
Bulgaria	Narodna Republic
Burma	Myanmar
Cairo	Al-Qāhirah
China	Cathay
Christiansted	Bassin
Cordoba	Athens of the West
Croagh Patrick, Mt	Reek
Edinburgh	Athens of the North
Egypt	Misr
Florence	Firenze
Gambier Islands	Mangareva Islands
Godthaab	Nuuk
Golgotha	Calvary
Gravelly Hill Interchange	Spaghetti Junction
Grenada	Isle of Spice
Istanbul	Stamboul
Japan	Nihon – Nippon
K2	Godwin Austen
Korea	Choson
Lake Constance	Bodensee
Lake Geneva	Lac Léman
Lake Gennesaret	Sea of Galilee
Lake Tiberias	Sea of Galilee
Le Havre	Newhaven
Lhasa	Forbidden City
Liberec	Reichenburg
Lindisfarne	Holy Island
Livorno	Leghorn
London	The Smoke
Lushun	Port Arthur
Macao	Aomin
Munich	München
New Orleans	The Big Easy
New York	The Big Apple
New Zealand	Pig Island
Niue	Savage Island
Osaka	Venice of Japan
Peking	Beijing – Celestial City
Persian Gulf	Arabian Gulf
Regensburg	Ratisbon
Rio Grande	Rio Bravo
Rome	Eternal City
Sousse	Susa
Sweden	Sverige
Switzerland	Confederation of Helvetia
Sydney	The Big Smoke
Thessaloníki	Salonika
Turin	Torino
Victoria (Mt)	Tomaniivi (Fiji)

Places: former names

Albany (NY)	Fort Orange
Almaty	Zailiyskoye (1854–55), Verny (1855–1921)
Alvernia (Mt)	Como Hill (Bahamas)
Annapolis	Providence, Town of Proctor's, Town at the Severn, Anne Arundel Town
Astana	Akmola
Bangladesh	East Bengal (until 1947), East Pakistan (1947–70)
Belize	British Honduras (until 1973)
Benin	Dahomey (until 1975)
Bermuda	Somers Islands
Bioko	Macias Nguema Biyogo (1973–79)
Black Sea	The Euxine
Bodrum	Halicarnassus
Bolivia	Upper Peru
Botswana	Bechuanaland (until 1966)
Bujumbura	Usumbura
Burkina Faso	Upper Volta (until 1984)
Burundi	Urundi
Cambodia	Kampuchea, Khmer Empire
Canada	New France
Cape Horn	Elizabetha
Central African Republic	Ubanghi Shari
Congo, Dem Republic of	Zaïre, Belgian Congo, Congo Free State
Dardanelles	Hellespont
Djakarta	Sunda Kelapa
Djibouti	French Somaliland
Donetsk	Stalino
Duarte (Mt)	Trujillo (Dominican Republic)
Dunaujváros	Sztalinvaros (Hungary)
Dushanbe	Stalinabad
East Timor	Portuguese Timor
Edirne	Adrianople
Equatorial Guinea	Spanish Guinea
Ethiopia	Abyssinia
Frunze	Pishpek
Ghana	Gold Coast
Grenada	Conception
Guinea	French Guinea
Guinea-Bissau	Portuguese Guinea
Guyana	British Guiana
Harare	Salisbury
Hawaii	Sandwich Islands
Ho Chi Minh City	Saigon
Indonesia	Dutch East Indies
Iran	Persia
Iraq	Mesopotamia
Istanbul	Constantinople, Byzantium
Izmir	Smyrna
Iznik	Niacaea
Jordan	Transjordan
Kathmandu	Manju-Patan
Katowice	Stalinogrod
Kinshasa	Léopoldville (until 1966)
Kiribati	Gilbert Islands
Klagenfurt	Chlagenvurt
Klondyke	River of Fish
Kota Kinabalu	Jesselton

Kyrgyzstan	Khirgizia
Ladoga	Neva
Ladysmith	Windsor
Lahore	Lava
Lahti	Bay (Finland)
Le Mans	Cenomannis
Le Puy	Podium
Leningrad	St Petersburg (1703–1914 and 1991 to present), Petrograd (1914–24)
Lesotho	Basutoland
Malawi	Nyasaland
Mali	French Sudan
Maputo	Lourenço Marques
Marianske Lazne	Marienbad
Mariupol	Zhdanov
Marseille	Ville-sans-Nom
Mauritius	Île de France
Micronesia	Caroline Islands
Moldova	Moldavia, Bessarabia
Mongolian People's Republic	Outer Mongolia
Montreal	Ville Marie
Myanmar	Burma
Namibia	South West Africa
N'Djamena	Fort-Lamy
New Britain	Neu-Pommern
New York	New Amsterdam (1625–64)
Novokuznetsk	Stalinsk
Novomoskovsk	Stalinogorsk
Nuuk	Godthaab
Olympia	Smithfield
Oman	Muscat and Oman
Oslo	Kristiania
Ottawa	Bytown
Palm Beach	Palm City
Palm Springs	Agua Caliente
Palmyra	Tadmor
Pittsburgh	Fort Duquesne
Prince Edward Island	Île Saint-Jean
Princeton	Stony Brook
Puerto Rico	San Juan (Puerto Rico was then capital)
Réunion	Île Bonaparte Île Bourbon Île Mascareigne
Richmond (Eng)	Sheen
Seychelles	Seven Sisters
Shaba	Katanga
Shenyang	Mukden
Sofia	Serdica
Sousse	Hadrumetum
Sparta	Lacedaemonia
Sri Lanka	Ceylon
Stepanakert	Khankendy
Suriname	Dutch Guiana
Tahiti	King George III Island, Nouvelle-Cythère
Taiwan	Formosa
Tanzania	Tanganyika
Tasmania	Van Diemen's Land
Thailand	Siam
Tiruchchirappalli	Trichinopoly
Toronto	York
Troy	Ilium
Tuvalu	Ellice Islands
Ubangi-Shari	French Equatorial Africa
Ulyanovsk	Simbirsk
Uskudar	Scutari
United Arab Emirates	Trucial States
Vanuatu	New Hebrides
Volgograd	Tsaritsyn (1589–1925) Stalingrad (1925–61)
Western Sahara	Spanish Sahara
Yangon	Rangoon
Yemen	Aden
Zambia	Northern Rhodesia
Zanzibar	Shirazi
Zimbabwe	Southern Rhodesia (1911–64) Rhodesia (1964–79) Zimbabwe Rhodesia (1979–80)

G
E
O
G
R
A
P
H
Y

World's Longest Rivers

		Source	Length (miles)	Course and Outflow
1	Nile	Kagera River, Burundi	4,145	Tanzania/Uganda/Sudan/Egypt to eastern Mediterranean.
2	Amazon	Apurimac River, Peru	4,007	Colombia to Brazil to South Atlantic (Canal do Sul).
3	Mississippi-Missouri	Jefferson (Red Rock) River, Montana	3,710	N and S Dakota/Nebraska/Iowa/Missouri/Kansas/Illinois/Kentucky/Tennessee/Arkansas/Mississippi/Louisiana to Gulf of Mexico. Although the Missouri is a tributary of the Mississippi, it is also an extension via Lake Itasca (see individual entries), so the system is made up of the total length of the Missouri and 1,395 miles of the Mississippi.
4	Yenisey	Selenga River, Mongolia	3,442	Flows due north through central Russia to the Kara Sea.
5	Yangtze (Chang-Jiang)	Kunlun Mts, China	3,436	Flows in an easterly course across China to the East China Sea near Shanghai.
6	Yellow River (Huang Ho)	Qinghai, China	3,395	Flows north of the Yangtze in an easterly course to the Yellow Sea.
7	Ob'-Irtysh	Altai Mts, Russia	3,361	Northern course touching Kazakhstan and through Russia to Kara Sea.
8	Paraná	Paranáiba and Grande confluence, Brazil	3,032	Flows south via Paraguay border and Argentina into confluence with River Uruguay to the Rio de la Plata (River Plate) estuary in the South

	Source	Length (miles)	Course and Outflow
			Atlantic near Buenos Aires. The system is aka Rio de la Plata-Paraná.
9 Zaïre (Congo)	Chambeshi River, Zambia	2,920	Called Lualaba in Dem Rep of Congo. Runs along Congo border into Atlantic at Angola.
10 Amur-Argun	China	2,782	See individual entries of the 2 rivers.
11 Lena	Kirenga River, Siberia	2,734	Russia and northward to Laptev Sea in the Arctic Ocean.
12 Mackenzie-Peace	Finlay/Parsnip confluence, BC	2,635	Flows eastwards to Alberta and then north via NWT to Beaufort Sea. The system is linked by the Slave River between Lake Athabasca and the Great Slave Lake.
13 Mekong	Lants'ang, Tibet	2,600	China/Burma/Laos/Thailand/Cambodia/Vietnam to South China Sea.
14 Niger	Loma Mts, Guinea	2,590	Flows through Mali, Niger and along Benin border into Nigeria before discharging into the Gulf of Guinea in the Atlantic.
15 Murray-Darling	Cape Byron, NSW	2,330	See individual entries of the 2 rivers.
16 Zambesi	Kalene Hill, Zambia	2,200	Flows south across Angola and western Zambia, then north-eastward forming the border between Zambia and Zimbabwe, and finally south-eastward across Mozambique to its delta on the Indian Ocean.
17 Volga	Valdai Hills, nr Moscow	2,193	Flows generally south-eastward to discharge into the Caspian Sea in Russia. The Volga is considered the longest river in Europe as the longer Russian rivers flow east of the Urals which are considered the boundary into Asia.
18 Madeira	Mamoré and Beni Rivers, Bolivia	2,082	Joins the Amazon 90 miles east of Manaus, it is the 2nd longest tributary in the world.
19 Jurua	Puerto Portillo, Peru	2,040	Flows east and north into Brazil before joining the Amazon south of Fonte Boa.
20 Purus	Loreto Department, Peru	1,995	Flows north and east into Brazil to join the Amazon upstream from Manaus (Solimões River).

NB: A usual definition of a river might be 'a freshwater channelled body of water that flows from its source into another river, a lake, the sea, or an inland desert' in which case the Missouri and Mississippi Rivers would make the above listing as separate entries. However, the table above includes the system as a whole and both the rivers are dealt with individually below. The alphabetic listing is for ease of reference, as in many of the sections, but is in no way an attempt to be fully comprehensive; it is merely a useful gazetteer of some interesting rivers.

Other Notable Rivers

	Source	Length (miles)	Course and Outflow
Achelous (Akhelóös)	Pindus Mountains	140	Divides Aetolia from Acarnania and discharges into the Ionian Sea.
Amu Darya (Oxus)	Eastern Pamirs	1,578	Follows the Afghanistan/Tajikistan border and then the Turkmenistan/Uzbekistan border before discharging into the Aral Sea. The source of the Amu Darya is often thought to be the confluence of the Vakhsh and Pyandzh rivers but in fact its longest headstream is the Daryã-ye Vãkhjir in the Eastern Pamirs.
Amur	Russia/China	1,755	Tatar Strait of the Pacific Ocean.
Argun	Khingan range, China	1,007	Joins Amur at the confluence of the Shilka.
Arkansas	Sawatch range of Rocky Mountains	1,459	Flows east-southeastward to the Mississippi at Arkansas City via Kansas and Oklahoma.
Arno	Monte Falterona, Tuscan Apennines	150	Flows westwards via Florence and Pisa to the Ligurian Sea area of the Mediterranean.
Athabasca	Columbia Icefield, Canadian Rockies	765	Forms the southernmost part of the Mackenzie River system in northern Alberta and discharges into Lake Athabasca.
Avon	Devizes, Wiltshire	48	Aka Hampshire Avon or East Avon, flows generally south via Salisbury to the English Channel at Christchurch Harbour.
Avon (Lower)	Cotswolds	75	Aka Bristol Avon, flows through Gloucester,

	Source	Length (miles)	Course and Outflow
			Wiltshire, and Avon before entering the Bristol Channel via the Severn estuary, at Avonmouth, the ocean port of Bristol.
Avon (Upper)	Naseby, Leicester/Northants border	96	Aka Warwickshire Avon, flows generally south-westward through Northants, Leicestershire, Warwickshire, and Hereford and Worcester before joining the Severn at Tewkesbury, Gloucs.
Axe	Beaminster, Dorset	24	Flows westward to form the boundary between Dorset and Somerset before reaching Axminster in Devon and entering the English Channel south of Axmouth.
Bann	Co Down, NI	76	Longest river of Northern Ireland; flows into the Atlantic Ocean.
Black	Yunnan Province, China	498	Flows south-east into northern Vietnam parallel to the Red River, which it joins near Hanoi.
Black	Ozark Mountains, Missouri	280	Flows south-eastward to Poplar Bluff, Missouri, and then flows south-west before entering the White River near Newport, Arkansas.
Black Volta (Mouhoun)	Bobo Dioulasso, Burkina Faso	720	Flows along the border of Burkina Faso and Côte D'Ivoire with Ghana before discharging into Lake Volta in northern Ghana.
Boyne	Bog of Allen, Co Kildare	70	Flows north-east to enter the Irish Sea just south of Drogheda.
Brahmaputra	Tibetan Himalayas	1,800	Confluence with the Ganges as the Jamuna and into the Bay of Bengal in Bangladesh.
Bug	Western Ukraine	516	Flows into Poland via Brest in Belarus and discharges into the Vistula just south of Warsaw.
Camel	Davidstow, Cornwall	30	Generally flows northward into the Celtic Sea at Padstow.
Cher	North-west Massif Central, France	217	Flows north across the Combrailles Plateau, eventually reaching the Loire at Cinq-Mars-la-Pile.
Cimarron	Capulin Mt Monument, New Mexico	698	Flows eastwards past the Black Mesa peak in Oklahoma and into Kansas via Colorado before re-entering Oklahoma and discharging into the Arkansas River near Tulsa.
Clyde	Lowther Hills, Strathclyde	98	Flows north-westerly into the Firth of Clyde.
Colorado	Rockies, Colorado	1,450	Flows south-west to the Gulf of California.
Colorado	Grande and Barrancas confluence	530	Flows south-eastward across Patagonia and into the Atlantic Ocean south of Bahia Blanca.
Columbia	Rockies, British Columbia	1,243	Flows south through central Washington to the Oregon border and then due west before discharging into the Pacific Ocean.
Danube	Black Forest, Germany	1,775	Flows through Germany, Austria, Czech Republic, Hungary, Croatia, Yugoslavia, Bulgaria, Romania, Moldova, and into the Black Sea in the Ukraine.
Darling	Cape Byron, NSW	1,702	Follows the NSW/Queensland border into NSW to join the Murray at Wentworth, on the Victoria border. Longest river of Australia.
Dee	Cairngorms	87	Famous for its salmon, the Dee flows easterly to the North Sea at Aberdeen. The 17-mile stretch of the Dee between Braemar and Ballater has become known as 'Royal Deeside' because Balmoral Castle is a popular holiday retreat of the Royal Family.
Dee	Snowdonia National Park	70	Flows via Lake Bala and then north-east to Corwen and eastward past Llangollen before travelling northward to Chester and out to the Irish Sea at Flint.
Dee	Dumfries and Galloway	50	Flows south and enters the Solway Firth at Kircudbright.
Delaware	Schoharie County, New York	405	Flows along the border between New York and Pennsylvania, New Jersey and Pennsylvania, and Delaware and New Jersey before discharging into the Atlantic Ocean at Delaware Bay.
Demerara	Central Guyana	215	Flows northward to the Atlantic Ocean at Georgetown.
Derwent	Tasmania	107	Flows south-east to the Tasman Sea.
Derwent	Peak District	60	Flows south-east through Derby to the River Trent.
Derwent	Fylingdales Moor	57	Flows south joining the Ouse just west of the Humber estuary.

GEOGRAPHY

	Source	Length (miles)	Course and Outflow
Derwent	Borrowdale Fells, Cumbria	34	Flows north and west to the Irish Sea.
Dnestr	Carpathian Mountains	877	Flows south from Ukraine into Moldova before emptying into the Black Sea
Dnieper (Dnepr)	Valdai Hills, Smolensk	1,367	Flows through Russia, Belarus and the Ukraine into the Black Sea.
Don	Novomoskovsk, Russia	1,224	Flows south and discharges into the Gulf of Taganrog in the Sea of Azov.
Don	Grampians	78	Flows south-eastward into the North Sea at the Bridge of Don.
Douro	Sierra de Urbión, Spain	556	Flows across Spain and northern Portugal to the Atlantic Ocean at Foz do Douro.
Dunajec	Tatra Mountains, Czech/Polish border	156	Flows north-east across Poland into the Vistula.
Ebro	Fontibre, Cantabrian Mts	565	Longest river in Spain. Flows in a south-easterly direction via Zaragosa and into the Balearic Sea area of the Mediterranean.
Eden	Lake District Fells	90	Flows north-westward to the Irish Sea at the Solway Firth inlet.
Elbe	Czech/Polish border	724	Flows westward through Czech Republic (where it is known as the Labe) until it starts a north-westerly run east of Prague through Germany to discharge into the North Sea.
Euphrates	South-west Turkey	1,700	Flows in south-easterly direction through northern Syria and Iraq to the Persian Gulf.
Exe	The Chains, Somerset	60	Flows south across Devon and into the English Channel at Exmouth.
Forth	Ben Lomond	65	Flows eastward into the Firth of Forth, near Kincardine.
Frome	Evershot, Dorset	40	Flows eastward into Poole Harbour at Wareham.
Gambia	Guinea Republic	700	Flows westwards via the Gambia into the Atlantic Ocean.
Ganges	Indian Himalayas	1,553	Confluence with the Brahmaputra as the Jamuna and into the Bay of Bengal in Bangladesh.
Garonne	Spanish Pyrenees	357	Flows north-east to Toulouse then north-west to the Bay of Biscay via the Gironde estuary.
Great Ouse	Brackley, Northants	150	Flows through Buckinghamshire, Bedfordshire and Cambridgeshire before discharging into the North Sea at the Wash.
Hudson	Lake Tear of Clouds, New York State	315	Flows south-eastward to Corinth in Saratoga County and then north-eastwards to Hudson Falls before travelling south to New York Bay.
Hunter	Mt Royal Range, New South Wales	287	Flows south-west through Glenbawn Reservoir before entering the Tasman Sea at Newcastle.
Iguaçu	Serra do Mar, Brazil	808	Flows westward before joining the Paraná at border of Argentina, Brazil and Paraguay.
Indus	Tibet	1,790	Runs through Pakistan from north to south and discharges into the Arabian Sea.
Irrawaddy	Northern Myanmar	1,337	Flows south through Mandalay and eventually west of Yangon into the Andaman Sea.
Isar	Karwendelgebirge, Innsbruck, Austria	183	Flows into Germany at Scharnitz Pass then after travelling through Munich enters the Danube.
James	Jackson and Cowpasture confluence, Virginia	340	Flows in an easterly direction, crossing the Blue Ridge Mountains near Lynchburg and continuing past Richmond into the southern end of Chesapeake Bay at the Hampton Roads.
Jordan	Mount Hermon, Syria	223	Lowest river in the world, flows south across Israel and into Jordan before draining into the Dead Sea. The distance between the Sea of Galilee and the Dead Sea is approximately 100 miles and yet the Jordan's length is double that distance due to its meandering course. The Jordan became the cease-fire line during the Israeli-Jordanian hostilities.
Jumna (Yamuna)	Jamnotri, Himalayas	855	Flows from Uttar Pradesh along the border with Haryāna and then via Delhi to the Agra Canal before joining the Ganges at its most sacred point.
Liffey	Wicklow Mountains	50	Flows through Co Wicklow, Kildare and Dublin before entering the Irish Sea at Dublin Bay.
Limpopo	Witwatersrand, South Africa	1,100	Rises as the Crocodile River and flows in an arc first north-east and then east forming the border

Source	Length (miles)	Course and Outflow
		between Transvaal and Botswana and then Transvaal and Zimbabwe before veering south-east into Mozambique and into the Indian Ocean north of Maputo. It becomes the Limpopo at the Crocodile's confluence with the Marico on the Transvaal/Botswana border.
Loire	Southern Massif Central	634	Longest river in France. Flows north and west towards the Brittany peninsula, where it discharges into the Bay of Biscay in the Atlantic Ocean.
Mackenzie	Great Slave Lake, NWT, Canada	1,060	Beaufort Sea in Arctic Ocean.
Magdalena	Colombian Andes	930	Flows northward to the Caribbean Sea.
Manzanares	El Pardo Reservoir, Madrid	42	Minor river that discharges into a canal system south of Madrid, it is notable only for being the river on which Madrid stands (at over 2,100' the highest capital of Europe).
Marañón	Peruvian Andes	879	Flows northwest from northeast Peru before receiving the Huallaga River and combining with the Ucayali River, to form the Amazon.
Marne	Langres, Plateau de Langres, France	326	Flows north-northwest past Chaumont and Saint-Dizier, then turns west-northwest to Epernay before veering south of Paris and discharging into the Seine at Charenton.
Medina	St Catherine's Downs	13	Flows from the south of the Isle of Wight to its northern outflow into the Solent.
Medway	East Grinstead, West Sussex	70	Follows the Sussex/Kent boundary to Ashurst before turning north-east to the Thames at the Sheerness delta. Traditionally those born in Kent west of the Medway are called Kentish Men, and those born east of the Medway, Men of Kent.
Merrimack	White Mts, New Hampshire	110	Flows southward into Massachusetts before veering north-east to empty into the Atlantic.
Mersey	Confluence of Goyt, Etherow, Tame	70	Flows eastward to the Irwell and the Manchester Ship Canal.
Meuse	Pouilly, Plateau de Langres, France	590	Flowing north through Belgium and the Netherlands to the North Sea.
Mississippi	Lake Itasca, Minnesota	2,348	Gulf of Mexico.
Missouri (Big Muddy)	Beaverhead Co, Montana	2,315	Joins Mississippi 10 miles north of St Louis; it is the longest tributary in the world.
Motagua	Chichicastenango	250	Longest river in Guatemala, flowing east-north-east into the Gulf of Honduras.
Murray	Snowy Mts, NSW	1,609	Flows along the boundary of NSW and Victoria, bends south at Morgan, South Australia, and discharges into the Indian Ocean at Encounter Bay in the Great Australian Bight.
Negro	Eastern Colombia	1,400	Major tributary of the Amazon that follows the Colombian/Venezuelan border and into Brazil to join the Amazon at the Solimões confluence.
Negro	Bagé, Brazil	500	Flows south-westward into Uruguay before joining the Uruguay River at Soriano.
Negro	Chilean Andes	400	Flows south-eastward across northern Patagonia and discharges into the Atlantic Ocean south-east of Viedma and Carmen de Patagones.
Neisse (Nysa)	Sudeten Mountains	157	Forms part of the German/Polish frontier before joining the Oder River. There is another Neisse which also rises in the Sudeten Mountains but lies totally in Poland.
Nene	Northants/Leics	102	Flows north-easterly via Peterborough to the North Sea in the Wash.
Oder	Oder Mountains, Czechoslovakia	531	Flows north-east then north when it picks up the Neisse and flows into the Baltic Sea.
Ohio	Allegheny and Monongahela, Pittsburgh	981	Flows north-west out of Pennsylvania then south-westward, forming boundaries between Ohio/Kentucky, Indiana/Kentucky, and Illinois/Kentucky before joining the Mississippi at Cairo, Illinois.
Omo	Ethiopian Highlands	290	Flows south across Ethiopia before emptying into Lake Rudolf on the Ethiopia/Sudan border.
Orange	Sinqu River, Lesotho	1,300	Flows west along the Orange Free State/Cape

GEOGRAPHY

	Source	Length (miles)	Course and Outflow
			Province border through Upington and along the southern border of Namibia before discharging into the Atlantic Ocean at Alexander Bay.
Orinoco	Venezuela–Brazil border	1,700	Flows in a northern arc forming the boundary between Venezuela and Colombia before veering north-eastward across Venezuela and into the Atlantic Ocean near Trinidad.
Ouse	Swale and Ure Confluence	57	Flows south-east to the Humber estuary.
Parramatta	Sydney	15	Meaning 'plenty of eels', flows through Sydney and into Port Jackson on the Tasman Sea.
Patuca	Guayape and Guayambre confluence	200	Flows from north-eastern Honduras and crosses the Mosquito Coast before discharging into the Caribbean at Patuca Point.
Peace	Finlay River, BC, Canada	1,195	Slave River in Wood Buffalo National Park.
Pechora	Northern Urals	1,124	Flows south and then west and north across Russia before emptying into the Barents Sea.
Pecos	Mora County, New Mexico	735	Flows into Texas and empties into the Rio Grande at the Amistad National Recreation Area.
Piddle	Alton Pancras, Dorset	21	Aka the Trent, and flowing south-eastward to Poole Harbour.
Po	Monte Viso Mts, Cottian Alps	405	Longest river in Italy. Flows eastwards in its upper course then northward through Turin and finally eastward to its delta on the Gulf of Venice in the Adriatic area of the Mediterranean.
Potomac	Appalachian Mts, West Virginia	383	Forms boundary between Maryland and Virginia via Washington DC and into Chesapeake Bay.
Red River	New Mexican Plains	1,270	Flows south-eastward through Texas, Oklahoma and Louisiana and into the Gulf of Mexico via the Mississippi River near Baton Rouge.
Red River (Hong)	Yunnan Province, SW China	750	Principal river of northern Vietnam, flowing south-east across the Tonkin region through Hanoi before discharging into the Gulf of Tonkin.
Red Volta	NW of Ouagadougou, Burkina Faso	200	Flows south-south-east to join the White Volta near the Gambaga scarp, northern Ghana.
Rhine	Swiss Alps	865	Forms the boundary between Switzerland, Liechtenstein and Germany and then runs north, bordering France and Germany and finally north-westward towards the North Sea via the Netherlands.
Rhône	Swiss Alps	505	Flows into Lake Geneva and then through France, merging with the Saône at Lyons, before entering the Mediterranean west of Marseille in the Golfe du Lion.
Ribble	Gayle and Cam confluence, Yorkshire	75	Flows south into Lancashire after rounding Whernside, at 2,419′ the highest peak in the Yorkshire Dales National Park; on entering Preston it flows due west towards the Irish Sea near Lytham St Annes.
Rio Grande	Rockies, Colorado	1,885	Forms the boundary between Texas and Mexico before discharging into the Gulf of Mexico. The Rio Grande is known in Mexico as the Rio Bravo.
Salween	Eastern Tibet	1,500	Flows east and south through China and forms the border between Myanmar and Thailand before emptying into the Gulf of Martaban
São Francisco	Serra da Canastra, Minais Gerais, Brazil	1,811	The longest river totally in Brazil flows in a north easterly direction to the Atlantic.
Sava	Triglav Mts, Slovenia	584	Flows south-east through Slovenia and Croatia and follows border of Bosnia and Herzegovina into northern Yugoslavia to discharge into the Danube at Belgrade.
Scheldt	Northern France	270	Flows north and north-east through western Belgium to Antwerp, then north-west to the North Sea in the Netherlands.
Seine	Langres Plateau, nr Dijon	485	Flows north-westerly through Paris before emptying into the English Channel near Le Havre.
Severn	Finger Lakes, Ontario	610	Flows north-east through Severn Lake to Hudson Bay.

	Source	Length (miles)	Course and Outflow
Severn (Hafren)	Plynlimon, Northern Powys	220	Flows south via Shropshire, Worcestershire, Gloucestershire, and into Bristol Channel in the Atlantic Ocean. It is the longest river in Britain.
Shannon	Tiltinbane Mts, Co Cavan	240	Flows through Leitrim and boundaries of Roscommon, Longford, Westmeath, Offaly, Galway, Tipperary, Clare, Limerick, and discharges into the Atlantic Ocean at Loop Head, Co Clare.
Shenandoah	Virginia	370	Flows north to meet the Potomac at Harper's Ferry.
Spey	Corrieyairack Forest	107	Flows north-east across the Highlands into the North Sea, east of the Moray Firth.
Spree	Lusatian Mts, Germany	250	Rising near the Czech/Polish border, the Spree flows north through Berlin and into the Havel River, a tributary of the Elbe, at Spandau.
St Lawrence	St Louis River, Minnesota	1,945	Gulf of St Lawrence in Quebec. (The St Lawrence proper is 760 miles in length, as the remainder runs from its source via the Great Lakes, except Lake Michigan.)
Stour	East Cambridgeshire	47	Flows eastward through East Anglia, forming most of the Suffolk/Essex boundary, and discharges into the North Sea at Harwich.
Stour (Dorset)	Stourhead, Wiltshire	51	Flows south-eastward through Blandford Forum and into the English Channel at Christchurch Harbour.
Stour (Great)	South of Ashford	40	Aka Kentish Stour, flows through the Weald, past Ashford to Canterbury and Sandwich and into the English Channel.
Suir	Devil's Bit Mountains	114	Flows south across Co Tipperary through Thurles before discharging into Waterford Harbour.
Susquehanna	Otsego Lake, New York State	444	Flows south through western Pennsylvania and into Chesapeake Bay in Maryland.
Sutlej (Zaradros)	Lan-ka Ts'o, SW Tibet	900	Longest of the Punjab's 'Five Rivers', flowing into India and Pakistan, where it joins the Chenāb River, west of Bahāwalpur.
Swan	Corrigin, Western Australia	224	Rises as the Avon and flows through Perth to the Indian Ocean at Fremantle.
Syr Darya	Naryn and Karadarya confluence	1,374	The Syr Darya River is 1,876 miles long including the 500 miles of the Naryn. On leaving the Fergana Valley the river flows north-west via Kyrgyzstan and into the Aral Sea at Kazakhstan.
Taff	Brecon Beacons	38	Flows southwards through Merthyr Tydfil, Pontypridd and finally Cardiff.
Tagus	Sierra de Albarracin, Spain	626	Flows westward into Portugal before discharging into the Atlantic Ocean near Lisbon.
Tamar	Woolley, Morwenstow	61	Flows south along the border between Devon and Cornwall and into the English Channel at Plymouth Sound.
Tay	Ben Lui, southern Grampians	117	Longest river in Scotland flows out to the Firth of Tay in the North Sea.
Tees	Cross Fell, Pennines	70	Flows eastwards defining the boundary of Cumbria and Durham then into Cleveland, passing through Stockton and Middlesbrough and into the North Sea.
Teifi	Strata Florida, Cambrian Mts	56	Famous for the many castle ruins along its banks, the Teifi flows generally south-westward through Lampeter and Cenarth Falls, where salmon can be seen climbing the artificial ladder up the falls, before discharging into the bay at Cardigan.
Test	Overton, nr Basingstoke, Hants	45	Famous trout river that flows southward via Winchester into Southampton Water, the last 16 miles between Romsey and Southampton Water are famous for their salmon.
Thames	Cotswolds, Gloucs	215	Flows easterly into the North Sea at Tilbury. Tributaries include the Churn, Coln, Windrush, Evenlode, Cherwell, Ock, Thame, Kennett, Loddon, Colne, Wey and Mole.
Tiber (Tevere)	Monte Fumaiolo, Apennines	252	Flows in a southerly direction through the city of Rome and into the Tyrrhenian Sea area of the Mediterranean near Ostia Antica.

GEOGRAPHY

	Source	Length (miles)	Course and Outflow
Tigris	South-west Turkey	1,180	Flows south into Iraq, through Baghdad and joins Euphrates before discharging into the Persian Gulf between Iraq and Iran.
Towy (Tywi)	Rhandirmwyn, Cambrian Mts	65	The longest river wholly in Wales, although since the damming of its main headwater in 1972 to form Llyn Brianne Reservoir it is slightly shorter than before.
Trent	Pennines, Staffordshire	170	Historically the boundary between north and south England, running south-east through the Potteries and Stoke-on-Trent, then north-east via Burton-on-Trent and Nottingham before entering the North Sea by the Humber estuary.
Tweed	Peebles	96	Flows easterly into the North Sea.
Tyne	River Rede, nr Hexham	62	Flows eastward along the Northumberland/Co Durham border before discharging into the North Sea at the Tyne estuary in Newcastle.
Urubamba	Peruvian Andes	450	Flows northward to meet the Apurimac to become the Ucayali.
Uruguay	Southern Brazil	990	Flows west through Brazil and then south-westward forming the Argentina/Brazil border before veering southward to form the Argentina/Uruguay border and discharging into the Rio de la Plate estuary at its confluence with the Paraná.
Usk	Black Mountain, Brecon Beacons	57	Flows generally south via Abergavenny and into the Bristol Channel at Newport.
Vistula (Wisla)	Beskidy Mts, Poland	664	Longest river of Poland, flows northwards via Kracow and Warsaw before entering the Baltic Sea on the Gulf of Gdansk; it is the longest river that empties into the Baltic Sea.
Vltava (Moldau)	South-west Bohemia	270	Longest river of the Czech Republic, flows north through Prague before discharging into the Elbe (Labe) at Melnik, just north of Prague.
Volta	Black and White Voltas	1,000	The extension of the Black and White Voltas through Lake Volta, discharging into the Gulf of Guinea in Ghana, near the Togo border.
Wear	Waskerley Beck, Co Durham	65	Flows south-east towards Bishop Auckland then north-east to Durham before discharging into the North Sea at Sunderland.
White Volta (Nakambe)	Ouagadougou, Burkina Faso	400	Flows generally southward into Lake Volta in northern Ghana.
Witham	Leicestershire	80	Flows through Lincoln and then south-east into the North Sea at the Wash.
Wye	Plynlimon, Northern Powys	130	Rises within 2 miles of the Severn and flows south-west into England at Hay before travelling through Hereford and back into Wales just south of Monmouth and finally through Tintern and Chepstow to discharge into the Bristol Channel at the Severn estuary.
Yare	Norfolk Broads	55	Flows through the middle of Broadland into Yarmouth and the North Sea; its tributary the Wensum flows through Norwich City.
Yarqon	Rosh ha-'Ayin	16	Flows westward north of Tel Aviv via the Plain of Sharon to the Mediterranean.
Yarra	Mt Matlock, Victoria	153	Flows west to Melbourne and discharges into Hobson's Bay, at the head of Port Phillip Bay.
Yellowstone	Yount Peak, Wyoming	671	Flows northeasterly via the Yellowstone National Park into Montana before joining the Missouri River on the border of Montana and North Dakota.
Yukon	Tagish Lake, Yukon-BC	1,875	Flows north-west into Alaska and discharges into the Bering Sea at Norton Sound.
Zaradros (Sutlej)	Lan-ka Ts'o, SW Tibet	900	Longest of the Punjab's 'Five Rivers', flowing into India and Pakistan where it joins the Chenāb River, west of Bahāwalpur.
Zeravshan	Eastern Turkistan Range	545	Flows west through Tajikistan and south-eastern Uzbekistan to Chardzhou.

Seas of the World

	Details	Sq Miles	Ocean
Adriatic	arm of the Mediterranean between Italy, Slovenia, Croatia and Yugoslavia	50,590	inland
Aegean	arm of the Mediterranean between Greece and Turkey; Crete is its southern boundary	83,000	inland
Andaman	bounded by Myanmar, Thailand, Malay Peninsula, Sumatra and the Andaman and Nicobar Islands	218,100	Indian
Arabian	bounded to the east by India, to the north by Pakistan and Iran and to the west by the Arabian Peninsula and the Horn of Africa	1,490,000	Indian
Arafura	situated between the north coast of Australia, the Gulf of Carpentaria and the south coast of New Guinea, it lies east of the Timor Sea, from which it is separated by the Torres Strait	250,000	Pacific
Azov	inland sea north of the Black Sea between Ukraine and Russia	15,000	inland
Baltic	bordered by Norway, Sweden, Denmark, Germany, Poland, Lithuania, Latvia, Estonia, Russia and Finland	147,500	Atlantic
Banda	bounded by the Moluccas and Lesser Sunda Islands	180,000	Pacific
Barents	formerly known as the Murmean Sea, bounded by the Russian and Norwegian mainlands to the south, Franz Josef Land to the north, the Norwegian and Greenland seas to the west, Spitsbergen to the north-west and the Novaya Zemlya archipelago to the east	542,000	Arctic
Beaufort	situated north of Alaska and Canada	184,000	Arctic
Bering	separates the Asian and North American continents and contains St Lawrence Island, St Matthew Island, Nunivak Island and the Pribilof Islands and the northern border of the Aleutians	875,750	Pacific
Bismarck	lies north of the Solomon Sea off the north-east coast of Papua New Guinea	15,000	Pacific
Black	inland sea lying between Turkey, Bulgaria, Romania, Moldova, Ukraine, Russia and Georgia	196,100	inland
Caribbean	deepest sea in the world, average depth about 8,000' and maximum depth 30,249'	971,400	Atlantic
Celebes (Sulawesi)	bounded to the north by the Sulu Sea, to the east by the Sangi Islands, to the south by Celebes and to the west by Borneo	110,000	Pacific
Chukchi	situated north of the Bering Sea separating Alaska and Russia	225,000	Arctic
Coral	lies off the east coast of Australia north of the Tasman Sea	1,886,000	Pacific
East China	bounded by South Korea, Japan, Taiwan and China	256,600	Pacific
East Siberian	lying between the Laptev Sea and the Chukchi Sea	361,000	Arctic
English Channel	separates the southern coast of England from the northern coast of France; the French call the Channel 'La Manche' (the sleeve) and its minimum width of 21 miles lies between Dover and Calais	34,700	Atlantic
Flores	situated between the Lesser Sunda Islands to the south and Sulawesi (Celebes) Island to the north	93,000	Pacific
Greenland	borders Greenland to the west, Iceland and the Norwegian Sea to the south and the Arctic Ocean to the north	465,000	Arctic
Ionian	arm of the Mediterranean between Greece to the east, Sicily to the south-west and the Italian mainland to the west	49,500	inland
Irish	bounded by Scotland on the north, England on the east, Wales on the south and Ireland on the west	34,200	Atlantic
Japan	northern extension of the East China Sea, bounded by Japan and Sakhalin Island to the east and by Korea and Russia to the west	391,100	Pacific
Java	bounded by Borneo to the north and Java to the south	167,000	Pacific
Kara	situated off the northern coast of Russia between the Barents Sea and the Laptev Sea	340,000	Arctic
Laccadive	bordering the south-west coast of mainland India, Lakshadweep Islands and the Maldives	209,000	Indian
Laptev	until 1935 known as the Siberian Sea, lying between the Kara Sea and East Siberian Sea	276,000	Arctic
Ligurian	arm of the Mediterranean between the north-west coast of Italy and Corsica to the south	9,800	inland
Mediterranean	largest inland sea in the world, linked to the Atlantic in the west by the Strait of Gibraltar; it encompasses many named sea areas	966,500	inland
Molucca	merges with the Ceram Sea to the south-east and the Banda Sea to the south	77,000	Pacific
North	extends southward from the Norwegian Sea between Norway and the UK, connecting the Skagerrak with the English Channel	164,900	Atlantic
Norwegian	bordered by the Greenland and Barents seas, Norwegian mainland, Shetland and Faeroe islands, Icelandic mainland, Jan Mayen Island, North Sea and Atlantic Ocean	712,000	Atlantic
Okhotsk	bounded by the east Russian mainland, Japan and the Kuril Islands	537,500	Pacific

GEOGRAPHY

	Details	Sq Miles	Ocean
Philippine	lying east of the Philippines and Japan, its southern boundary includes the Caroline Islands, its western boundary includes Guam, and the northern boundary by the Volcano Islands to the north-east and Honshu to the north-west	400,000	Pacific
Red	inland sea extending from Suez in Egypt to the Straits of Bāb el-Mandeb in the south, it washes the shores of Egypt, Sudan, Eritrea, Ethiopia, Djibouti, Saudi Arabia and Yemen	174,900	inland
Savu	situated in the Lesser Sunda Islands between Timor and Sumba Islands	41,000	Pacific
Sea of Marmara (Propontis)	inland sea separating parts of Asian Turkey from European Turkey	4,429	inland
Solomon	lies north of the Coral Sea off the east coast of New Guinea	280,000	Pacific
South China	bounded by the Malay Peninsula, Taiwan, Philippines, Borneo, China and Vietnam	1,148,500	Pacific
Sulu	situated in the Philippine Islands north of the Celebes Sea	100,000	Pacific
Tasman	situated between the south-east coast of Australia and New Zealand	900,000	Pacific
Timor	lies south-west of the Arafura Sea off the north-west coast of Australia	235,000	Indian
Tyrrhenian	bounded by Sicily and the Italian mainland to the east and Corsica and Sardinia to the west	51,000	inland
White	lying south of the Barents Sea off the north-west coast of Russia	35,000	Arctic
Yellow	lying between the People's Republic of China to the north and west, and Korea to the east	113,500	Pacific
Zuiderzee (Southern Sea)	inlet of the North Sea washing the shores of the Netherlands	2,000	Atlantic

NB: The areas given for the above seas, as well as the following gulfs, straits and bays, are as produced by the latest world statistics, which are open to interpretation because it is not always clear at what point the waters merge. Most lists of seas only include those recognized by the International Hydrographic Bureau, and this is a controversial area as, although the reasoning is that seas not recognized are either parts of larger seas or oceans, in fact many of the seas that are recognized – e.g. the Caribbean – are also part of larger sea areas. Surely the Panama Canal links the Atlantic to the Pacific and not merely the Caribbean to the Pacific! The criterion used by the Bureau appears to be that a sea must be surrounded by large areas of land to enable it to be separately identifiable from the oceans but, apart from the inland seas noted above, all other seas are purely geographical markings. In order not to be too controversial I have given the best judgements possible of the areas usually considered as seas by cartographers in the list above, but have remained true to tradition when listing the seas by size elsewhere in this section. This will mean that although the South China Sea will be listed as the world's largest sea in the relevant section, this is inconsistent with the above table which shows the Coral Sea as the largest. If the question is asked, "What is the largest sea in the world?" then the safe answer would be the South China Sea, which is part of the much larger Malay Sea, no longer recognized by the Bureau, but one has to be aware that large sea areas such as the Coral Sea and Arafura Sea are, rather ambiguously, classed as parts of oceans.

Seas: world's largest

		Area (Sq Miles)
1	South China	1,148,500
2	Caribbean	971,400
3	Mediterranean	966,500
4	Bering	875,750
5	Gulf of Mexico	582,100
6	Okhotsk	537,500
7	Sea of Japan	391,100
8	Hudson Bay	281,900
9	East China	256,600
10	Andaman	218,100
11	Black	196,100
12	Red	174,900

NB: The Malay Sea, which embraced the South China Sea and the Straits of Malacca, is no longer recognized by the International Hydrographic Bureau. Similarly, many other large seas (e.g. the Coral and the Arafura) would normally be included in the list but are also not recognized by the Bureau.

Straits of the World

Bass — Named by English navigator Matthew Flinders after the surgeon-explorer George Bass, the strait is 180 miles in length with an area of 28,950 sq mi; it separates the Tasman Sea area of the Pacific from the Indian Ocean. Technically it is the Tasman Sea that separates Victoria from Tasmania, but the whole of the northern coast of Tasmania borders the waters of the Bass Strait.

Belle Isle Strait — Links the Atlantic to the Gulf of St Lawrence between Newfoundland and Labrador; it is 90 miles long.

Bosporus (Bosphorus) — Links the Black Sea and the Sea of Marmara, and separates part of Asian Turkey from European Turkey. The strait is 19 miles in length.

Cabot — A 60-mile-long channel linking the Gulf of St Lawrence to the Atlantic between Newfoundland and Nova Scotia.

Cook — Links the Tasman Sea to the South Pacific between North Island and South Island, New Zealand. The Cook Strait is 14 miles wide at its narrowest point.

Dardanelles (Hellespont) — Formerly called the Hellespont, they are 38 miles long and link the Aegean Sea with the Sea of Marmara.

Davis — Links Baffin Bay and the Labrador Sea between Greenland and Baffin Island, part of the Northwest Passage linking the Atlantic to the Pacific, it is approximately 400 miles long and wide.

Denmark — Links the Greenland Sea to the North Atlantic between Greenland and Iceland. The British battleship *Hood* was sunk by the German battleship *Bismarck* in the strait on 24 May 1941.

Florida — Links the Gulf of Mexico and the Atlantic between Florida and Cuba; it is 110 miles in length. The Spanish explorer Ponce de León was the first European to navigate the strait, in 1513.

Foveaux — Links the Tasman Sea to the South Pacific between South Island and Stewart Island, New Zealand.

Gibraltar — Links the Mediterranean Sea to the Atlantic Ocean. The western extreme is 27 miles wide between the capes of Trafalgar and Spartel and the eastern extreme is 14 miles wide between the Rock of Gibraltar (Pillars of Hercules) and Mount Hacho. The length of the strait is 36 miles and it is also known as Fretum Herculeum.

Hormuz — Links the Persian Gulf to the Gulf of Oman between Iran and the Arabian Peninsula.

Hudson — Links Hudson Bay and the Labrador Sea between Baffin Island and Quebec and is approximately 500 miles in length.

Johore — The northern arm of the Singapore Strait between Singapore Island and Johor State, Malaysia, it is 30 miles in length.

Kattegat — Links the Baltic to the North Sea (Skagerrak inlet) and separates Denmark and Sweden; it is 137 miles in length.

Magellan — Links the Atlantic and Pacific Oceans, between the mainland southern tip of South America and Tierra del Fuego. It is 350 miles in length.

Makassar — Links the Celebes Sea to the Java Sea between Borneo and Celebes; it stretches for approximately 500 miles.

Malacca — Links the Andaman Sea to the South China Sea between Sumatra and the Malay Peninsula; it is 500 miles in length and has an area of 25,000 sq miles.

Messina — Links the Tyrrhenian Sea and the Ionian Sea between Sicily and mainland Italy; it is 20 miles in length and ranges from 2 to 10 miles in width.

North Channel — Links the Irish Sea and the North Atlantic Ocean and washes the shores of Northern Ireland and Scotland. The minimum width of 13 miles lies between the Mull of Kintyre and Torr Head; it is 52 miles long.

Otranto — Links the Adriatic Sea and the Ionian Sea between Albania and Italy. Capo d'Otranto is the most easterly point in Italy and from that point the width of the strait is 40 miles.

St George's Channel — Links the Irish Sea to the Celtic Sea in the North Atlantic, its minimum width of 47 miles lies between Carnsore Point, near Rosslare, Ireland and St David's Head in Dyfed, Wales. It is 100 miles in length.

Singapore — Links the Strait of Malacca and the South China Sea between Singapore Island and the Riau Islands of Indonesia; it is 65 miles in length and 10 miles in width.

Taiwan (Formosa) — Links the South China Sea and the East China Sea between Fukien Province of China and Taiwan; its former name of Formosa means 'beautiful' in Portuguese.

Yucatán Channel — Although not actually called a strait, it links the Gulf of Mexico and the Caribbean Sea between Cuba and Mexico, and is 135 miles in length.

GEOGRAPHY

Towns and Cities on Rivers

Abbotsford	Tweed	Colchester	Colne	Jarrow	Tyne
Aberdeen	Dee and Don	Coldstream	Tweed	Kathmandu	Vishnumati
Adelaide	Torrens	Coleraine	Bann	Kelso	Tweed and
Albuquerque	Rio Grande	Cologne	Rhine		Teviot
Alexandria	Nile	Concord, NH	Merrimack	Khartoum	White Nile and
Alloa	Forth	Cork	Lee		Blue Nile
Amsterdam	Amstel	Cowes	Medina	Kidderminster	Stour
Anstruther	Forth	Delft	Schie	Kiev	Dnieper
Antwerp	Scheldt	Derby	Derwent	Kilkenny	Nore
Astrakhan	Caspian Sea	Derry	Foyle	Kilmarnock	Irvine
Augusta	Savannah	Detroit	Lake St Clair	King's Lynn	Great Ouse
Aviemore	Spey	Dewsbury	Calder	Lahore	Ravi
Avignon	Rhône	Doncaster	Don	Lancaster	Lune
Babylon	Euphrates	Dorchester	Frome	Langholm	Esk
Baghdad	Tigris	Dorking	Mole	Le Havre	Seine
Baku	Caspian Sea	Dresden	Elbe	Leamington Spa	Warwickshire
Balmoral	Dee	Dublin	Liffey		Avon
Bamako, Mali	Niger	Dumbarton	Clyde	Leeds	Aire
Bangkok	Chao Phraya	Dumfries	Nith	Leicester	Soar
Bangui	Ubangi	Dundee	Tay	Leipzig	Pleisse, Parthe,
Basel	Rhine	Dunoon	Clyde		Elster
Basra	Shatt al Arab	Durham	Wear	Lima	Rimac
Bath	Bristol Avon	Düsseldorf	Rhine	Limerick	Shannon
Baton Rouge	Mississippi	Edinburgh	Forth, Firth of	Limoges	Vienne
Bedford	Great Ouse	Ennis	Fergus	Lincoln	Witham
Belfast	Lagan	Enniskillen	Erne	Linz	Danube
Belgrade	Danube, Sava	Evesham	Warwickshire	Lisbon	Tagus
Benares	Ganges		Avon	Lisburn	Lagan
Berlin	Spree	Exeter	Exe	Littlehampton	Arun
Berne	Aare	Falmouth	Fa	Liverpool	Mersey
Berwick	Tweed	Florence	Arno	London	Thames
Birkenhead	Mersey	Frankfurt	Main	Loughborough	Soar
Blandford Forum	Dorset Stour	am Main		Louisville	Ohio
Bonn	Rhine and Seig	Frankfurt	Oder	Luton	Lea
Bootle	Mersey	an der Oder		Lyons	Rhône and
Bordeaux	Garonne	Fremantle	Swan		Saône
Bowness	Forth	Geneva	Rhône	Madrid	Manzanares
Bratislava	Danube	Geneva	Lake Geneva	Maidstone	Medway
Brecon	Usk	Gillingham	Medway	Maldon	Blackwater
Bremen	Weser	Glasgow	Clyde	Mallow	Blackwater
Brest, Belarus	Bug	Gloucester	Severn	Manchester	Irwell
Brighouse	Calder	Godalming	Wey	Manchester, NH	Merrimack
Bristol	Bristol Avon	Grantchester	Granta	Mandalay	Irrawaddy
Brussels	Senne	Grantham	Witham	Maputo	Delagoa Bay
Bucharest	Danube	Gravesend	Thames	Marlow	Thames
	tributary:	Greenock	Clyde	Melbourne	Yarra
	Dimbovita	Grenoble	Isère	Middlesbrough	Tees
Buckhaven	Forth	Grimsby	Humber	Midhurst	Rother
Buckingham	Ouse	Guangzhou	Zhujiang	Milan	Olono
Budapest	Danube	Guildford	Wey	Mold	Alyn
Buenos Aires	Rio de la Plata	Hamburg	Elbe	Montreal	St Lawrence
Buffalo	Lake Erie	Hanoi	Song-Koi (Red)		and Ottawa
Cairo	Nile (Rosetta	Harrogate	Nidd	Morpeth	Wansbeck
	and Damietta)	Harwich	Stour	Moscow	Moskva
Calcutta	Hoogly	Haverfordwest	Cleddau	Munich	Isar
Cambridge	Cam (aka	Hawick	Teviot and Slitrig	Nantes	Loire
	Granta)	Heidelberg	Neckar	Nantwich	Weaver
Canterbury	Stour	Helensburgh	Clyde	Nashville	Cumberland
Cardiff	Taff	Hereford	Wye	New Delhi	Jumna
Carlisle	Eden	Hertford	Lea	New Orleans	Mississippi
Carmarthen	Towy	Ho Chi-Minh City	Saigon		Gulf of Mexico
Chester	Dee	Hull	Humber	New York	Hudson
Chicago	Lake Michigan	Huntingdon	Ouse	Newbury	Kennet
Chichester	Lavant	Hyderabad	Indus	Newcastle	Tyne
Chongqing	Yangzi	Ilkley	Wharfe	Newport (Gwent)	Usk
Cincinnati	Ohio	Indianapolis	White	Newport (I of W)	Medina
Cockermouth	Derwent and	Inverness	Moray	Niamey, Niger	Niger
	Cocker	Ipswich	Orwell	Northampton	Nene

Norwich	Wensum	Rome	Tiber	Swansea	Tawe
Nottingham	Trent	Rotterdam	Rhine, Maas, Scheldt	Taunton	Tone
Nuneaton	Anker			Tewkesbury	Severn, Warwickshire Avon
Omdurman	Nile	Rugby	Warwickshire Avon		
Oporto	Douro			Thebes (Egypt)	Nile
Orléans	Loire	Rye	Rother	Tidmarsh	Pang
Oxford	Thames (Isis and Cherwell)	Salisbury	Hampshire Avon and Wily	Tintern Abbey	Wye
				Tipperary	Ara
		São Paulo	Tiete	Tiverton	Exe
Pangbourne	Thames	Seoul	Han	Tonbridge	Medway
Paris	Seine	Shanghai	Hwangpu	Totnes	Dart
Patna	Ganges	Sheffield	Don, and Sheaf	Turin	Po
Peebles	Tweed	Shoreham-by-Sea	Adur	Vienna	Danube
Perth, Australia	Swan			Wakefield	Calder
Perth, Scotland	Tay	Shrewsbury	Severn	Wareham	Frome
Peterborough	Nene	Sligo	Garavogue	Warsaw	Vistula
Philadelphia	Delaware	Southampton	Test, and Itchen	Warwick	Warwickshire Avon
Phnom Penh	Mekong	Southend-on-Sea	Thames		
Pisa	Arno	Spalding	Welland	Washington DC	Potomac
Pittsburgh	Ohio	St Albans	Ver	Waterford	Suir
Plock	Vistula	St Ives (Cambs)	Ouse	Whalley	Calder
Prague	Vltava	St Louis	Mississippi	Whitby	Esk
Preston	Ribble	St Petersburg	Neva	Wimborne	Stour and Allen
Quebec	St Lawrence, St Charles	Stafford	Sow	Winchester	Itchen
Reading	Thames and Kennet	Stoke	Trent	Windsor	Thames
		Strabane	Mourne	Worcester	Severn
Richmond (Yorks)	Swale	Strasbourg	Ill	Wuhan	Han and Yangzi
Richmond (Va)	James	Stratford	Warwickshire Avon	Yonkers	Hudson
Ripon	Ure			York	Ouse
Rochester	Medway	Stuttgart	Neckar	Zagreb	Sava
		Sunderland	Wear	Zurich	Limmat

GEOGRAPHY

Trenches: deepest

Trench	Deepest Point
Marianas Trench (Pacific)	Challenger Deep 35,840′
Puerto Rico Trench (Atlantic)	Milwaukee Deep 28,232′
Java Trench (Indian)	Planet Deep 23,376′
Eurasia Basin (Arctic)	Eurasia Basin 17,880′

Waterways

Aden Links the Red Sea to the Arabian Sea and borders Yemen to the north and Somalia to the south. The gulf is 920 miles in length and has an area of 205,000 sq miles.

Alaska Inlet of the North Pacific on the south coast of Alaska, and bordered by Kodiak Island to the west and Cape Spencer to the east, it has an area of 592,000 sq miles.

Aqaba North-eastern arm of the Red Sea between Saudi Arabia and the Sinai Peninsula. The gulf is 100 miles in length.

Alphonse XIII Canal Opened in 1926 and runs for 53 miles, linking Seville to the Atlantic via the Gulf of Cadiz.

Angel Falls Situated in the Guiana Highlands in Bolivar state, south-eastern Venezuela, on the Rio Churún, a tributary of the Caroni. At 3,212′ the falls are the highest in the world.

Baffin Bay Inlet of the North Atlantic with an area of 266,000 sq miles, situated between Greenland and Baffin Island.

Bengal, Bay of Inlet of the Indian Ocean bordering India, Myanmar, Sri Lanka, and the Andaman and Nicobar Islands; it occupies an area of 839,000 sq miles.

Biscay, Bay of Inlet of the North Atlantic bordering northern Spain and south-west France; it has an area of 86,000 sq miles.

Biscayne Bay Inlet of the Atlantic in south-eastern Florida; it is 40 miles in length and between 2 and 10 miles in width.

Bothnia Northern arm of the Baltic between Sweden on the west and Finland on the east.

Boyoma Falls Formerly called the Stanley Falls; situated on the Lualaba River in the Democratic Republic of Congo, it has a drop of 200′ and is the world's greatest waterfall by volume of water.

Bridgewater Canal Opened in 1761 and named after Francis Egerton, 3rd Duke of Bridgewater. The canal was built by James Brindley and originally ran for 10 miles, carrying barges over the Irwell at Barton; it was extended to Liverpool in 1776, joining the Mersey at Runcorn.

Bristol Channel Inlet of the Atlantic between South Wales and the English counties of Somerset, Devon and Cornwall.

Caledonian Canal Built by Thomas Telford in 1803–21 and opened in 1822, it has 29 locks and links the east and west coasts of Scotland via the lakes of the Great Glen.

California Aka Sea of Cortés and situated in northwestern Mexico, it is 750 miles in length and has an area of 62,000 sq miles.

Carpentaria Inlet of the Arafura Sea indenting the north-eastern coast of Australia. The gulf has an area of 120,000 sq miles.

Cauldron Snout Situated on the River Tees, Cumbria/Durham border, the highest waterfall in England (200′).

Churchill Falls Discovered in 1839 by John McLean and known as the Grand Falls until 1965, when they were renamed in honour of Winston Churchill. Situated on the Churchill River, in west Labrador, Newfoundland, the falls have a drop of 245′.

Corinth Inlet of the Ionian Sea separating the Peloponnese from mainland Greece.

Delagoa Bay Situated on the south-east coast of Mozambique, it is 19 miles in length and 16 miles wide.

Eas a' Chuàl Aluinn Situated in Sutherland in the Scottish Highlands in Glas Bheinn, the highest waterfall in the British Isles (658′).

False Bay Inlet of the Atlantic, south of Cape Town, South Africa.

Finland Eastern arm of the Baltic between Finland to the north, Estonia to the south, and Russia to the east.

Florida Bay Triangular-shaped body of water at the southern tip of mainland Florida stretching from Cape Sable in the west, Key Largo in the east and Long Key in the south.

Fundy, Bay of Inlet of the Atlantic between New Brunswick and Nova Scotia; it stretches for 94 miles.

Genoa Inlet of the Ligurian Sea stretching eastwards for 90 miles around the north-west coast of Italy from Imperia to La Spezia.

Grand Canal Waterway that splits the city of Venice from St Mark's Cathedral to Sta Chiara church; it is 2.1 miles in length.

Grand Canal (China) Often considered a river system rather than a canal system, but much of its 1,107 miles is artificial waterway made by damming rivers and lakes. Nowadays it is treated in the same fashion as the St Lawrence Seaway and not included in lists of canals. It runs from Beijing to Hangzhou, was opened in AD 610 and has been regularly reconstructed ever since.

Grand Union Canal Before 1929 was known as the Grand Junction Canal but was enlarged by amalgamating several canals and is now a main line between London and Birmingham and has several forks, the largest connecting to Leicester. The main sideshoots of the system are the Regent's Canal (Little Venice), the Paddington Arm to Brentford, the Aylesbury Arm, the Northampton Arm, and the Erewash Canal, which extends to the Leicester branch.

Great Australian Bight Inlet of the Indian Ocean extending eastwards from West Cape, Western Australia, to South-West Cape, Tasmania.

Guinea Inlet of the Atlantic washing the coasts of Liberia (Grain Coast), Cote D'Ivoire (Ivory), Ghana (Gold), Togo (Slave), Benin (Slave), Nigeria (Slave), Equatorial Guinea, Gabon, and Cameroon (Bight of Bonny).

Hauraki (North Wind) Inlet of the South Pacific indenting eastern North Island, New Zealand, covering an area of 884 sq miles.

Houston Canal Shipping channel running through Houston, Texas, into Galveston Bay and ultimately the Gulf of Mexico after a journey of 56.7 miles. The Houston Canal has no locks.

Hudson Bay Inland sea bordering Manitoba, Ontario, Quebec, and Northwest Territories; it has an area of 281,900 sq miles and contains Belcher Islands, Mansel Island, Coats Island and Southampton Island. The southern section has an inlet between Ontario and Quebec (James Bay).

Islands, Bay of Situated in the north of North Island, New Zealand, it has a shoreline of 500 miles.

James Bay Southern extension of the larger Hudson Bay; it is 275 miles in length and 135 miles in width and contains many islands the largest being, Akimiski.

Khone Falls Situated on the Mekong River, Laos, on the border with Cambodia, it has a drop of 45′ and is the world's second greatest waterfall by volume.

Kiel Canal (North Sea) Stretches for 60.9 miles and links the North Sea (at the mouth of the Elbe) to Kiel Harbour on the Baltic.

Love Canal Not a canal at all nowadays but an area of Niagara Falls, New York, which, in 1978, was the scene of the worst environmental disaster involving chemical wastes in US history. The area, which had become a dumping ground for nuclear waste, has become a byword for similar areas.

Manchester Ship Canal Opened in 1894 and runs for 39.7 miles linking Manchester to the Irish Sea.

Mexico, Gulf of Large body of water occupying an area of 582,000 square miles situated on the southeast coast of North America and connected to the Atlantic Ocean by the Straits of Florida and to the Caribbean Sea by the Yucatan Channel.

Mozambique Channel Channel of the Indian Ocean between Madagascar and Mozambique which stretches for about 1,000 miles.

Niagara Falls Situated on the Niagara River, the falls are divided into two cataracts divided by Goat Island. The larger cataract is called the Horseshoe Falls with its drop of 162′ and crest line of 2,600′; the smaller is called the American Falls with its drop of 167′ but much smaller crest line of 1,000′ across. Niagara Falls is the world's third greatest waterfall by volume of water.

Oman Northwestern arm of the Arabian Sea between Oman and Iran, it is 350 miles in length and is linked to the Persian Gulf via the Strait of Hormuz.

Panama Canal Connecting the Atlantic and Pacific oceans and stretching for 50.71 miles, the canal was begun by Ferdinand de Lesseps in 1879, but numerous difficulties caused its cancellation until the Hay-Bunau-Varilla Treaty of 1903 between Panama and the USA granted the United States the building rights. The engineer, John F. Stevens, drafted the final plan in 1906 but was succeeded as chief engineer by George Washington Goethals in 1907. The canal opened on 15 August 1914, and under the Carter-Torrijos Treaty of 1977 was officially handed back to Panama on 31 December 1999 by US President Bill Clinton. The 6 locks are the Gatún Locks (a set of three), Pedro Miguel Lock and Miraflores Locks (a set of two) . The Caribbean entrance is at Limón Bay and its southern entrance is in the Bay of Panama. Vessels cannot navigate the waters under their own power.

Persian Gulf Shallow body of water between the Arabian Peninsula and Iran. The surface area of this inlet of the Indian Ocean is approximately 88,800 square miles.

Pistyll-y-Llyn   Situated on the Powys/Dyfed border, at 240′ the highest waterfall in Wales.

Port Phillip Bay   Inlet of Bass Strait on the south central coast of Victoria, Australia. Its entrance is known as 'the Rip'.

Powerscourt Falls   Situated in the River Dargle, Co Wicklow, the highest waterfall in Ireland (350′).

Prince William Sound   Inlet of the Gulf of Alaska with Hinchinbrook and Montague islands at its entrance.

Princess Charlotte Bay   Inlet of the Coral Sea off the coast of Queensland; named after the daughter of George IV, it is bounded by Cape Melville to the east and Claremont Point to the west.

Ribbon Falls   Situated in the Yosemite National Park, California.

Riga   Inlet of the Baltic bounded by the northern coast of Latvia and the western coast of Estonia, it has an area of 7,000 sq miles.

Saint Lawrence   Truly, a sea area of 91,800 sq miles with borders on Quebec, Newfoundland, Nova Scotia and New Brunswick; and containing Prince Edward Island.

Saint Lawrence Seaway   Stretching from the Atlantic Ocean to the western end of the Great Lakes, the seaway was begun in August 1954, completed in April 1959 and measures 2,342 miles in length. It is a series of nearly 60 canals, of which the Welland is the longest.

Saint Vincent   Inlet of the Indian Ocean on the south-east coast of South Australia, it is 90 miles in length.

Saronic (Aegina)   Inlet of the Aegean Sea lying east of the Gulf of Corinth from which it is separated by the Corinth Canal.

Skagerrak   Arm of the North Sea between Norway and the Jutland peninsula of Denmark on the south.

Spencer   Inlet of the Great Australian Bight between the Eyre and Yorke peninsulas of South Australia, it contains many small islands including Gambier, Thistle, Sir Joseph Banks, and Neptune.

Suez   North-western arm of the Red Sea between Africa and the Sinai Peninsula, it is 195 miles in length and its most northerly point at Suez marks the beginning of the Suez Canal.

Suez Canal   The first fact to determine about the Suez Canal is its length, a subject that is one of the most frequently asked quiz questions. It is officially 100.6 miles long, but many reputable sources will have it listed anywhere between 100 and 105 miles; this difference is mainly due to alterations to accommodate larger vessels. The canal was built by Ferdinand de Lesseps (1805–94) and opened in 1869; its extremities are Port Said at the northern end and Suez to the south; it links two broad areas of sea, the Mediterranean and the Red Sea (via the Gulf of Suez), and is therefore technically, like many canals, a strait. It has no locks.

Sutherland Falls   Situated in the Arthur River near Milford Sound, Otago, South Island, New Zealand; at 1,904′ the fifth-highest waterfall in the world.

Tadjoura   Situated at the western end of the Gulf of Aden around the port of Djibouti. The gulf is 50 miles in length.

Taranto   Arm of the Ionian Sea in southern Italy between Cape Santa Maria di Leuca and Cape Colonne, forming the hollow in front of the 'boot' of Italy.

Thailand (Siam)   Bordering Thailand, Cambodia, and South Vietnam, the gulf is 350 miles wide and 450 miles in length.

Thérmai   Inlet of the Aegean Sea in north eastern Greece between Macedonia, Thessaly, and the Chalcidice Peninsula.

Tonkin   Inlet of the South China Sea bounded by China, Hainan Island, and North Vietnam. The gulf is 300 miles in length and 150 miles in width.

Tugela Falls   Situated in the Tugela River, Natal, South Africa; at 3,110′ the second highest cataract in the world.

Utigård Falls   Situated in the Jostedal Glacier, Nesdale, Norway, the highest of the many great waterfalls of Norway and with a total drop of 2,625′ the third highest in the world.

Victoria Falls   Truly breathtaking waterfall on the Zambesi River on the border between Zambia and Zimbabwe, its drop is 355′ and it is known locally as 'The Smoke That Thunders'.

Volga–Don Shipping Canal   Runs from Kalach on the Tsimlyansk Reservoir on the Don 62.2 miles to Krasnoarmeysk on the Volga; it was completed in 1952 and joins the Black Sea to the Caspian Sea.

Welland Canal   Completed in 1932 and now part of the St Lawrence Seaway, it is 27.6 miles in length and is situated in southern Ontario between Lake Erie to the south and Lake Ontario to the north; it was built as an alternative route through the River Niagara because of the impassable falls.

White Sea–Baltic Canal   Longest ship canal in the world (141 miles), between Povenets and Belomorsk in Russia; it has 19 locks and was opened in 1933 as the Stalin Canal.

Yosemite Falls   Situated in Yosemite National Park, central California, USA. The Upper Yosemite Fall drops 1,430′ and the Lower Falls 320′ with the cascades between making a total drop of 2,425′

G
E
O
G
R
A
P
H
Y

Definitions of Waterways

bay   a wide semicircular indentation of a shoreline, especially between two headlands or peninsulas.

canal   an artificial waterway constructed for navigational aid, irrigation, or hydro-electric power.

lake   a body of water, either freshwater or salt, completely surrounded by land.

ocean   very large stretch of sea, especially one of the 4 main oceans of the world, i.e. Pacific, Atlantic, Indian, Arctic. The Antarctic Ocean is made up of the southern extremities of the Atlantic, Pacific and Indian Oceans.

river   see definition in relevant section.

sea   a mass of salt water that may be part of one of the Earth's oceans or part of a larger sea area.

strait   a narrow channel of the sea, bordered by land and linking two larger sea areas. It is often confusing to think of a strait as connecting waters, as opposed to land, because it is usually the land boundaries of the strait that are better known. To give a typical example, most people realise that the Bass Strait lies between mainland Australia and Tasmania, but few will know that the strait links the Tasman Sea area of the Pacific and the Indian Ocean.

Sea Areas

Weather forecasts are broadcast on a regular basis for the Shipping Forecast Areas around the British coast and neighbouring countries. It should be noted that the areas listed below are the boundaries set by Britain and are not universally accepted by other countries who have their own boundary limits and names.

The areas will be described firstly by clockwise coastal areas around Great Britain, starting with the northernmost point of Scotland, and then the coastal regions of Ireland, starting with the northernmost point, before describing other areas and their locations relative to one another.

Around Great Britain

Fair Isle: southeast of Faroes, west of Viking, northeast of Hebrides, northwest of Forties
Cromarty: west of Forties
Forth: west of Forties
Tyne: west of Dogger
Humber: west of German Bight and touching the coast of the Netherlands
Thames: bordering the Netherlands and touching the coast of Belgium
Dover: bordering France and Belgium
Wight: bordering France
Portland: bordering France
Plymouth: east of Sole and bordering France
Lundy: east of Fastnet and touching the coast of Ireland
Irish Sea: surround Anglesey and the Isle of Man
Hebrides: east of Bailey, northeast of Rockall and containing the Outer Hebrides
Malin: east of Rockall and containing the Inner Hebrides

Around Ireland

Malin: east of Rockall and containing the Inner Hebrides
Irish Sea: surround Angelsey and the Isle of Man
Lundy: east of Fastnet and touching the coast of Ireland
Fastnet: north of Sole and bordering the southern coast of Ireland
Shannon: north of Sole
Rockall: south of Bailey and touching the western coast of Ireland

South-East Iceland: most northerly sea area; north of Bailey and northwest of Faeroes and bordering Iceland
Faeroes: southeast of S.E. Iceland, northwest of Fair Isle, northeast of Bailey, north of Hebrides
Viking: east of Fair Isle, west of North Utsire, north of Forties, northwest of South Utsire
North Utsire: east of Viking, north of South Utsire, and bordering the coast of Norway
South Utsire: southeast of Viking, south of North Utsire, north of Fisher and bordering the coast of Norway
Fisher: south of South Utsire, north of German Bight, east of Forties, and bordering the Skaggerak
Forties: bordered by Fair Isle, Viking, South Utsire, Fisher, Dogger, Forth, and Cromarty
German Bight: south of Fisher, east of Dogger, east of Humber, and bordering Denmark and Germany
Dogger: south of Forties, west of German Bight, north of Humber, east of Tyne
Biscay: south of Plymouth, east of Finisterre, and bordering France and Spain
Finisterre: west of Biscay, south of Sole, north of Trafalgar and bordering Spain
Trafalgar: south of Finisterre and bordering Spain and Portugal
Sole: west of Plymouth and south of Shannon and Fastnet
Bailey: south of S.E. Iceland, southwest of Faeroes, west of Hebrides, north of Rockall

Beaufort Scale

0	Calm
1	Light air
2	Light breeze
3	Gentle breeze
4	Moderate breeze
5	Fresh breeze
6	Strong breeze
7	Moderate gale
8	Fresh gale
9	Strong gale
10	Whole gale
11	Storm
12	Hurricane

(Devised in 1805 by Francis Beaufort. Force 13 to 17 were added in 1955 by the US Weather Bureau but are seldom used.)

Flags of the World

Afghanistan	horizontal bands of green, white and black, with the national arms in the centre in gold.
Albania	black double-headed eagle on a red background.
Algeria	red star and crescent on a green and white background split vertically.
Andorra	vertical stripes of blue, yellow (gold) and red, with the national arms in the central yellow band.
Angola	yellow (gold) star, machete and half cog wheel on a red and black background split horizontally.
Antigua & Barbuda	red with an inverted triangle divided horizontally black over blue over white, with a rising yellow (gold) sun on the black band.
Argentina	horizontal bands of blue, white and blue, with a yellow (gold) sun on white band.
Armenia	horizontal tricolour of red, blue and orange.
Aruba	blue with two narrow yellow (gold) horizontal bands near the bottom and a red four-pointed star, bordered white, in the top left hoist.
Australia	Union Flag in the canton, with five white stars of the Southern Cross in the fly, and the white Commonwealth star of seven points beneath the Union Flag.
Austria	horizontal bands of red, white and red, sometimes depicting the National emblem in the centre.
Azerbaijan	horizontal bands of blue, red and green, with a white crescent and eight-pointed star on the red band.
Bahamas	horizontal bands of blue, yellow (gold) and blue, with a black equilateral triangle on the hoist.
Bahrain	red, with vertical serrated white bar on the hoist.
Bangladesh	red circle on a green background.
Barbados	vertical stripes of blue, yellow (gold) and blue, with a trident head on central gold stripe.
Belarus	red, with a green horizontal band in the lower third, and a red and white ornamental vertical stripe on the hoist.
Belgium	vertical tricolour of black, yellow (gold) and red.
Belize	white disc containing the coat of arms surrounded by a green garland, the disc being on a blue background with a red edge top and bottom.
Benin	two horizontal bands of yellow (gold) over red with a larger vertical green stripe on the hoist.
Bermuda	red with a British Blue Ensign in the canton and shield of arms in the fly.
Bhutan	silver-grey dragon on a background of yellow (gold) over orange triangles split from top right to bottom left.
Bolivia	horizontal tricolour of red, yellow (gold) and green, occasionally showing the National emblem in centre.
Bosnia-Hercegovina	blue with a yellow (gold) triangle in the fly with a series of white stars running diagonally across the hypotenuse top left to bottom right. Prior to 1998 the flag was white with a blue shield in the centre with white diagonal and six yellow (gold) fleurs-de-lys.
Botswana	blue, with a horizontal black stripe in centre with a white edge top and bottom.
Brazil	green with yellow (gold) lozenge containing a blue sphere with a white girdle often displaying the motto Ordem e Progresso.
Brunei	yellow (gold), with two diagonal stripes white over black running from just below top left corner to just above bottom right hand corner, with the coat of arms in the centre.
Bulgaria	horizontal tricolour of white, green and red.
Burkina Faso	two horizontal bands of red over green with yellow (gold) star in the centre.
Burma/Myanmar	red with a dark blue canton containing a cogwheel and two rice ears surrounded by 14 white stars.
Burundi	white saltire with red background top and bottom and green background on fly and hoist, a central white disc containing a triangle of three red six-pointed stars edged in green.
Cambodia	horizontal bands of blue, red and blue, with the red of double width and containing a depiction of the temple of Angkor in white.
Cameroon	vertical tricolour of green, red and yellow (gold), with a five-pointed yellow (gold) star on the central red band.
Canada	red maple leaf in a white square, with vertical red stripes on fly and hoist.
Cape Verde	blue, with three horizontal narrow bands of white, red and white in the third quarter, and a circle of ten yellow (gold) stars running through the bands near the hoist.
Central African Republic	four horizontal bands of blue, white, green and yellow (gold), with a vertical red stripe in centre and a five-pointed yellow (gold) star in top left of blue band.
Chad	vertical tricolour of blue, yellow (gold) and red.
Chile	two horizontal bands of white over red, with a five-pointed white star in a blue square covering the first third of the white band.
China	red with large five-pointed yellow (gold) star in the upper left quarter, four smaller stars of the same colour forming an arc around the larger one.
Colombia	horizontal tricolour of yellow (gold), blue and red, the yellow (gold) band being twice the width of the other two.
Comoros	central vertical white crescent with four white stars between its horns and facing the fly, on a green background, the name of Allah in the upper fly and Muhammad in the lower hoist both in Arabic script.

Congo, Dem Rep of	blue, with a large yellow (gold) five-pointed star in the centre, with six smaller stars of the same colour running vertically down the hoist.
Congo, Republic of	green equilateral triangle over red equilateral triangle with a yellow (gold) diagonal stripe separating them running from the top right fly to the bottom left hoist.
Costa Rica	five horizontal bands of blue, white, red, white and blue, the red central band being twice the width of the others and containing the national emblem in the centre.
Croatia	horizontal bands of red, white and blue, with the national emblem in the centre.
Cuba	five horizontal bands of blue, white, blue, white and blue, with red equilateral triangle on hoist with white five-pointed star in centre.
Cyprus	white, with a yellow (gold) outline of Cyprus in the centre above a wreath of olive.
Czech Republic	two horizontal bands of white over red, with a blue equilateral triangle on the hoist.
Denmark	white cross on a red background, the vertical stripe being slightly nearer the hoist than the fly.
Djibouti	two horizontal bands of blue over green, with a white equilateral triangle on the hoist with a red five-pointed star in the centre.
Dominica	cross of yellow (gold), black and white stripes on a green background, and in the centre a red disc charged with a Sisserou parrot encircled by ten green stars.
Dominican Republic	blue and red quarters, with a white cross overlapping and the national emblem in the centre.
Ecuador	horizontal bands of yellow (gold), blue and red, the yellow (gold) band being twice the width of the other two and the national emblem in the centre.
Egypt	horizontal bands of red, white and black, with an eagle in the centre.
El Salvador	horizontal bands of blue, white and blue, with coat of arms on white band.
England	red cross of St George on a white background.
Equatorial Guinea	horizontal bands of green, white and red, with a blue equilateral triangle on the hoist and coat of arms in the centre.
Eritrea	red triangle with a yellow (gold) olive wreath on the hoist, green triangle over blue triangle on the fly.
Estonia	horizontal tricolour of blue, black and white.
Ethiopia	horizontal bands of green, yellow (gold), and red, with blue disc in the centre containing a yellow (gold) pentagram.
Faroe Islands	red cross, bordered blue on a white background the vertical stripe being nearer the hoist than the fly.
Fiji	Union flag in top left quarter on a blue background and the shield of Fiji in the fly.
Finland	blue cross on a white background, the vertical stripe being slightly nearer the hoist than the fly.
France	vertical tricolour of blue, white and red.
Gabon	horizontal tricolour of green, yellow (gold), and blue.
Gambia	five horizontal bands of red, white, blue, white and green, the white bands being much narrower than the others.
Georgia	cherry red, with a black over white rectangle in the upper hoist.
Germany	horizontal tricolour of black, red and yellow (gold).
Ghana	horizontal bands of red, yellow (gold) and green, with black five-pointed star in the centre.
Greece	nine blue and white horizontal stripes with a white cross on a blue background in the canton.
Greenland	two horizontal bands of white over red, with a large circle near the hoist and the colours reversed within, being red over white.
Grenada	two green equilateral triangles with apex towards the centre and separated by a yellow (gold) five-pointed star in a red disc, the area between the triangles is yellow (gold), the flag has a red border with three yellow (gold) stars on the top and three yellow (gold) stars on the bottom, the green triangle in the hoist has a nutmeg in its centre.
Guatemala	vertical stripes of blue, white and blue, with a coat of arms in the central white band.
Guinea	horizontal tricolour of red, yellow (gold) and green.
Guinea-Bissau	horizontal bands of yellow (gold) over green, with vertical red band in the hoist, charged with a black star.
Guyana	green with a yellow, white-bordered triangle from the hoist to the fly, with an equilateral red triangle on the hoist with a black border.
Haiti	two horizontal bands of blue over red, with the national emblem in the centre.
Honduras	horizontal bands of blue, white and blue, with five blue five-pointed stars arranged as a saltire in the white band.
Hong Kong	red ground with a white bauhinia flower of five petals in the centre, each petal containing a red star.
Hungary	horizontal tricolour of red, white and green.
Iceland	blue with a white-bordered red cross, the vertical stripe being nearer the hoist than the fly.
India	horizontal bands of saffron (orange-yellow), white and green, with a blue Asoka wheel in the central white band.
Indonesia	two horizontal bands of red over white.
Iran	horizontal tricolour of green, white and red, with the words Allahu Akbar repeated 22 times in white on the lower green and upper red bands, and the national emblem in red in the central white band.
Iraq	horizontal bands of red, white and black, with three green five-pointed stars in the central white band and the words Allahu Akbar written between the stars.
Ireland	vertical tricolour of green, white and orange.

Israel	two horizontal blue bands near the top and bottom with a blue shield of David in the centre, all on a white background.
Italy	vertical tricolour of green, white and red.
Ivory Coast	vertical tricolour of orange, white and green.
Jamaica	yellow (gold) diagonal cross forming background triangles of green top and bottom and black on the hoist and fly.
Japan	white with a large red disc representing the sun in the centre.
Jordan	horizontal bands of black, white and green, with a red equilateral triangle on the hoist containing a seven-pointed white star.
Kazakhstan	blue with a yellow (gold) sun in the centre and a soaring eagle wrapped around the lower hemisphere, a gold (yellow) stripe adorns the hoist.
Kenya	five horizontal bands of black, white, red, white and green, the white bands being much narrower than the others, a red and black oval shield adorns the centre with two white crossed spears behind the shield.
Kiribati	red representing the sky and six white and blue wavy lines representing the sea, a yellow (gold) rising sun in the centre with a flying frigate bird above in the same colour.
Korea, North (Chosun)	five horizontal bands of blue, white, red, white and blue, the white bands being much narrower than the others and the central red band being twice the width of the blue bands, a large red five-pointed star within a white circle adorns the central band on the hoist.
Korea, South	white with a red over blue yin-yang symbol in the centre, and four black trigrams emanating from the symbol diagonally.
Kuwait	horizontal bands of green, white and red, with a black trapezoid in the hoist.
Kyrgyzstan	red with a yellow (gold) sun in the centre containing a representation of a yurt.
Laos	horizontal bands of red, blue and red, the central blue band being twice the width of the other two and containing a white circle.
Latvia	horizontal bands of red, white and red, the central white band being half the width of the other two.
Lebanon	horizontal bands of red, white and red, the central white band being twice the width of the other two and containing a green and brown cedar tree.
Lesotho	split diagonally from bottom to top, the top half being white and the bottom half mainly green with a blue band at the top, the upper white triangle contains an assegai and knobkerrie behind a Basotho shield in brown, in the hoist.
Liberia	eleven alternate red and white horizontal bands (six red and five white), with a blue canton containing a white five-pointed star.
Libya	emerald green.
Liechtenstein	two horizontal bands of blue over red with a yellow (gold) crown in the blue band near the hoist.
Lithuania	horizontal tricolour of yellow (gold), green and red.
Luxembourg	horizontal tricolour of red, white and blue.
Macedonia	red with a yellow (gold) disc in the centre representing the sun and eight yellow (gold) flares emanating from the sun in the shape of a cross and saltire.
Madagascar	two horizontal bands of red over green with a broad white stripe in the hoist.
Malawi	horizontal tricolour of black, red and green with a red rising sun on the black band.
Malaysia	fourteen alternating horizontal bands of red and white with a yellow (gold) fourteen-pointed star inside a crescent of the same colour in a large blue canton.
Maldives	green with a large red border and a white crescent in the centre with horns facing the fly.
Mali	vertical tricolour of green, yellow (gold) and red.
Malta	two vertical stripes of white and red with a representation of the George Cross in the canton of the white stripe.
Marshall Islands	blue with a diagonal ray divided orange over white running from the lower hoist to the upper fly, a white sun in the canton.
Mauritania	green with a yellow (gold) crescent in the centre with horns facing the top, a five-pointed yellow (gold) star situated within the horns of the crescent.
Mauritius	four horizontal bands of red, blue, yellow (gold), and green.
Mexico	vertical stripes of green, white and red with the Mexican emblem of an eagle on a cactus devouring a snake in the centre.
Moldova	vertical stripes of blue, yellow (gold) and red with the national arms in the centre.
Monaco	horizontal bands or red over white.
Mongolia	vertical stripes of red, blue and red with the Soyombo symbol in yellow (gold) on the red band in the hoist.
Morocco	red with a green pentagram, representing the Seal of Solomon, in the centre.
Mozambique	horizontal bands of green, black and yellow (gold) with the central black band having a white border, a red equilateral triangle in the hoist charged with the national emblem.
Namibia	split diagonally from bottom to top by a red stripe with a white border, the upper blue triangle containing a yellow (gold) 12-pointed sun in the canton, and the lower triangle being plain green.
Nauru	blue ground with a yellow (gold) horizontal narrow band in the centre representing the equator, and a white 12-pointed star representing the 12 original Nauruan tribes in the lower hoist.
Nepal	double pennant of red with a blue border, the lower pennant containing a white rayed sun and the upper pennant containing a white recumbent crescent and quarter moon.
Netherlands	horizontal tricolour of red, white and blue.

New Zealand	blue ground with Union Flag in canton and four five-pointed red stars with white borders on the fly.
Nicaragua	horizontal bands of blue, white and blue, with the national coat of arms in the centre.
Niger	horizontal bands of orange, white and green, with an orange disc in the central white band.
Nigeria	vertical stripes of green, white and green.
Norway	blue cross bordered with white on a red background, the vertical stripe being slightly nearer the hoist than the fly.
Oman	red with a white panel in the upper fly and a green one in the lower fly, the national emblem in white in the upper hoist.
Pakistan	Green with a large white crescent with horns facing the upper fly in the centre and a small five-pointed white star in between the horns, a large white vertical stripe running along the hoist.
Palau	light blue with a large yellow (gold) disc just off centre near the hoist.
Panama	quartered, the white canton containing a five-pointed blue star, a red upper fly, blue lower staff and a white lower fly containing a five-pointed red star.
Papua New Guinea	diagonally split from upper hoist to lower fly red over black, a soaring Bird of Paradise in yellow (gold) in the red fly and five white stars of the Southern Cross on the black hoist.
Paraguay	horizontal bands of red, white and blue with the National seal in the central white band, and the Treasury seal on the reverse central white band. The Paraguayan flag is the only National flag to have different obverse and reverse designs.
Peru	vertical stripes of red, white and red with the national emblem in the central white stripe.
Philippines	two horizontal bands of blue over red, with a white equilateral triangle running the length of the hoist; the triangle containing a yellow (gold) sun in the centre and three small five-pointed stars of the same colour, one in each angle.
Poland	equal horizontal bands of white over red.
Portugal	vertical stripes of green and red, the green stripe being a little smaller than the red fly; the National emblem just off centre overlapping the two colours.
Qatar	maroon, with vertical serrated white bar on the hoist.
Romania	vertical tricolour of blue, yellow (gold) and red.
Russia	horizontal tricolour of white, blue and red.
Rwanda	vertical stripes of red, yellow (gold) and green with bold letter R in the yellow (gold) stripe.
St Christopher & Nevis (aka St Kitts)	green over red triangles divided by a diagonal black bar running from the staff to the upper fly, the black bar is bordered yellow (gold) and contains two white stars, one in the staff and one in the upper fly.
St Lucia	blue with three triangles in the centre, yellow (gold) over black over white, all with a common base, the white appearing to border the black but the yellow (gold) being right-angled at its apex.
St Vincent & Grenadines	vertical stripes of blue, yellow (gold) and green with the central yellow (gold) band being twice the width of the other two, and three green diamonds in the shape of a V in the centre.
Samoa	red with a blue canton of five white stars of the Southern Cross.
San Marino	equal horizontal bands of white over blue.
São Tomé & Principe	horizontal bands of green, yellow (gold) and green, with the yellow (gold) band wider than the other two and containing two large black five-pointed stars nearer the fly than the hoist; a red equilateral triangle runs along the hoist.
Saudi Arabia	green with a white scimitar in the centre with the Arabic writing 'There is no God but God and Muhammad is the Prophet of God' also in white, above the scimitar.
Scotland	white diagonal cross of St Andrew on a blue background.
Senegal	vertical tricolour of green, yellow (gold) and red with green five-pointed star in central yellow (gold) band.
Seychelles	five rays extending from the lower hoist, from left to right, blue, yellow (gold), red, white, and green.
Sierra Leone	horizontal tricolour of green, white and blue.
Singapore	equal horizontal bands of red over white with white crescent in the canton with horns facing the fly and five small white five-pointed stars in a pentagon shape between the horns.
Slovakia	horizontal tricolour of white, blue and red with the National coat of arms off centre near the hoist.
Slovenia	horizontal tricolour of white, blue and red with the National coat of arms over the white and blue bands in the upper hoist.
Solomon Islands	split diagonally from bottom to top by a yellow stripe, the upper blue triangle containing five white stars and the lower triangle being plain green.
Somalia	blue with a white five-pointed star in the centre.
South Africa	divided red over blue by a horizontal green Y bordered white, inside the V of the Y a black triangle bordered yellow (gold).
Spain	horizontal bands of red, yellow (gold) and red with the National emblem being optionally depicted on the yellow (gold) band near the hoist.
Sri Lanka	on a dark red field with yellow (gold) border a yellow (gold) lion passant holding a sword in its right paw, and a representation of a bo leaf in each corner; to its left two vertical stripes of green and saffron also with a yellow (gold) border.
Sudan	horizontal bands of red, white and black, with a green equilateral triangle on the hoist.
Suriname	five horizontal bands of green, white, red, white and green, the red band being twice the width of the green bands and the white bands being a mere border to the red; a yellow (gold) five-pointed star in the centre.

Swaziland	five horizontal bands of blue, yellow (gold), crimson, yellow (gold) and blue, the crimson band being twice the width of the blue bands and the yellow (gold) bands being a mere border to the crimson; an emblem of a shield and two spears is depicted all over the central band.
Sweden	yellow (gold) cross on a blue background, the vertical stripe being slightly nearer the hoist than the fly.
Switzerland	red square flag with a large central white cross.
Syria	horizontal bands of red, white and black, with two green five-pointed stars either side of the centre of the white band running horizontally.
Taiwan	red with a blue canton containing a 12-rayed white sun.
Tajikistan	horizontal bands of red, white and green, the white band being twice the width of the other two; a crown adorned with a crescent of seven yellow (gold) stars is depicted in the centre.
Tanzania	green over blue triangles divided by a diagonal black bar running from the staff to the upper fly, the bar having a yellow (gold) border.
Thailand	five horizontal bands of red, white, blue, white and red, the blue band being twice the width of the others.
Togo	five horizontal bands of green, yellow (gold), green, yellow (gold) and green, a large white five-pointed star within a red canton in the upper hoist.
Tonga	red with a white canton containing a red cross.
Trinidad & Tobago	red with a black diagonal bar, bordered white, running from right of the upper hoist to left of the bottom fly.
Tunisia	red with a central white disc containing a red five-pointed star within a red crescent, horns facing the fly.
Turkey	red with a central white skewed five-pointed star within a white crescent, horns facing the fly.
Turkmenistan	green with an ornamental carpet pattern running vertically near the hoist; a crescent and five stars in white are depicted to the right of the upper hoist, the horns facing the hoist and stars forming a diagonal cross within the horns.
Tuvalu	light blue with Union Flag in canton and nine yellow (gold) five-pointed stars in the fly.
Uganda	six horizontal bands of black, yellow (gold), red, black, yellow (gold), red; with a white disc in central two bands containing a depiction of a crested crane.
Ukraine	equal horizontal bands of blue over yellow (gold).
United Arab Emirates	horizontal bands of green, white and black, with a wide red stripe running down the hoist.
United Kingdom	Union Flag consisting of the English and Scottish flags and the red saltire of St Patrick on a white ground representing Northern Ireland.
USA	thirteen alternating horizontal bands of red and white with a blue canton containing fifty white stars in a six, five, six, five, six, five, six, five, six pattern, each star representing one of the fifty constituent states.
Uruguay	nine alternating horizontal bands of white and blue with a 16-rayed yellow (gold) sun in a white canton, the sun often depicted with eyes and full mouth.
Uzbekistan	horizontal bands of blue, white and green, the central white band being fimbriated with red, and the blue band containing a white crescent in the hoist, facing the fly and three rows of white stars, three, four, five, making 12 in all.
Vanuatu	divided red over green by a horizontal yellow (gold) Y bordered black, inside the V of the Y a black triangle containing a boar's tusk overlaid by two crossed fern leaves.
Vatican City	square flag divided vertically, yellow (gold) in the hoist and white in the fly; crossed keys and triple crown device in the centre of the white stripe.
Venezuela	vertical stripes of yellow (gold), blue and red, with an arc of seven white stars in the central blue band and the National emblem in the canton.
Vietnam	red with a large yellow (gold) five-pointed star in the centre.
Wales	equal horizontal bands of white over green with large red dragon all over the field.
Yemen	horizontal tricolour of red, white and black.
Yugoslavia	horizontal tricolour of blue, white and red.
Zambia	green with three vertical stripes of red, black and orange in the fly topped by a depiction of an eagle.
Zimbabwe	seven horizontal bands of green, yellow (gold), red, black, red, yellow (gold) and green; a white equilateral triangle running down the hoist, bordered black, and containing the National emblem.
Definition of terms	Canton: small rectangular charge in the top left hand corner.
	Charge: a shield or emblem within a field or canton.
	Field: the whole of the ground of a flag
	Fly: the outer edge of a flag away from the hoist.
	Hoist: the inner edge of a flag next to the staff.
	Staff: the flagpole.

G
E
O
G
R
A
P
H
Y

Roman Place Names

British Names	Roman Names	British Names	Roman Names
Alderney	*Riduna*	London	*Londinium*
Anglesey	*Mona*	Longjumeau	*Noviomagus*
Appenzell	*Abbatis Cella (Abbot's Cell)*	Lyon	*Lugdunum*
Arabia	*Arabia Felix*	Macon	*Matisco*
Arnhem	*Arenacum*	Man, Isle of	*Manavia*
Bath	*Aquae sulis*	Manchester	*Mancunium:Mamucium*
Budapest	*Aquincum*	Marseilles	*Massilia*
Cadiz	*Gades*	Milan	*Mediolanum*
Cambridge	*Granta*	Morocco	*Mauretania*
Canterbury	*Durovernum*	Newcastle	*Pons Aelius*
Carlisle	*Luguvalium*	Nijmegen	*Noviomagus*
Chelmsford	*Caesaromagus*	Oporto	*Portus Cale*
Chester	*Deva*	Orleans	*Aurelianum*
Chichester	*Noviomagus*	Padua	*Patavium*
Cirencester	*Corinium Dobunnorum*	Palestrina	*Praenestum*
Colchester	*Camulodonum*	Paris	*Lutetia*
Crete	*Candia*	Pevensey	*Anderetium*
Doncaster	*Danum*	Poissy	*Pinciacum*
Dorchester	*Durnovaria*	Poitiers	*Limonum*
Dover	*Dubris*	Portugal	*Lusitania*
Egypt	*Aegyptus*	Port-Vendres	*Portus Veneris*
England	*Albion*	Pozzuoli	*Puteoli*
Epernay	*Sparnacum*	Rimini	*Ariminum*
Exeter	*Isca Dumnoniorum*	Rochester	*Durobrivae*
Fecamp	*Fiscamnum*	Romania	*Dacia*
France	*Gallia*	Ruse	*Sexantaprista*
Gap	*Vapincum*	St Albans	*Verulamium*
Gascony	*Vasconia*	Salisbury	*Sorviodunum*
Germany	*Germania*	Sark	*Caesarea*
Gibraltar (Straits of)	*Freightum Herculaneum*	Scotland	*Caledonia*
Gloucester	*Glevum*	Sibiu	*Cibinium*
Grasse	*Crassus*	Silchester	*Calleva Atrebatum*
Great Yarmouth	*Gernemuta Magna*	Southampton	*Clausentum*
Greece	*Graecia*	Spain	*Hispania*
Guernsey	*Sarnia*	Switzerland	*Helvetia*
Gyor	*Arabona*	Thanet	*Ranatis/Tanatus*
Ireland	*Hibernia*	Turin	*Augusta Taurinorum*
Italy	*Italia*	Utrecht	*Trajectum Castrum*
Jersey	*Caesaria*	Vienna	*Vindobona*
Krk	*Curicum*	Wales	*Cambria*
Lancaster	*Lunecastrum*	Wight, Isle of	*Vectis*
Lausanne	*Lausodunum*	Winchester	*Venta Belgarum*
Leicester	*Ratae*	Worcester	*Vigornia*
Libya:Tunisia	*Africa*	Wroxeter	*Viroconium Cornoviorum*
Lincoln	*Lindum*	York	*Eboracum*
Lisbon	*Olisipo*	Zaragoza	*Caesarea Augusta*
Liverpool	*Esmeduna*	Zurich	*Turicum*
Lombardy	*Langobardus*		

World Table: Geographical Gazetteer

Country	GMT	Currency	Split into 100	UN Member	Common-wealth	Europe	Official Languages	Highest Point	Area Sq Km	Area Sq Miles	Population
Afghanistan	+4	afghani	puls	1946			Pashto, Dari Persian	Noshaq (24,581')	647,497	249,999	19,062,000
Albania	+1	Lek	qindarka	1955			Albanian	Korabi (9,028')	28,748	11,100	3,363,000
Algeria	+1	dinar	centimes	1962			Arabic, Berber, French	Tahat (9,852')	2,381,741	919,591	26,346,000
Andorra	+1	franc + peseta	centimos	1993			Catalan, French, Spanish	Pla del'Estany (9,678')	468	181	64,311
Angola	+1	kwanza	lweis	1976			Portuguese	Serra Moco (8,563')	1,246,700	481,351	10,609,000
Antigua and Barbuda	-4	East Caribbean dollar	cents	1981	1981		English	Boggy Peak (1,319')	440	170	65,962
Argentina	-3	peso	cents	1945			Spanish	Aconcagua (22,834')	2,766,889	1,068,297	32,370,298
Armenia	+4	dram	louma	1992			Armenian	Aragats (13,418')	29271	11,302	3,645,000
Australia	+8–11	dollar	cents	1945	1931		English	Kosciusko (7,316')	7,686,848	2,967,895	17,938,500
Austria	+1	schilling	groschen	1955		1995	German	Grossglockner (12,462')	83,849	32,374	8,015,000
Azerbaijan	+4	manat	gopik	1992			Azeri	Bazar-dyuzi (15,156')	86,600	33,436	7,400,900
Bahamas	-5	dollar	cents	1973	1973		English	Alvernia (on Cat Island) (206')	13,935	5,380	262,000
Bahrain	+3	dinar	fils (1,000)	1971			Arabic	Jabal ad-Dukhan (440')	622	240	533,000
Bangladesh	+6	taka	paisa	1974	1972		Bengali	Keokradong (4,034')	143,998	55,598	108,000,000
Barbados	-4	dollar	cents	1966	1966		English	Hillaby (1,115')	430	166	259,000
Belarus	+2	rouble	kopecks	1945			Belarussian	Dzerzhinsky (1,135')	207,600	80,154	10,280,000
Belgium	+1	franc	centimes	1945		1958	Dutch, French, German	Botrange (2,277')	30,513	11,781	10,068,319
Belize	-6	dollar	cents	1981	1981		English	Victoria Peak (3,681')	22,965	8,867	205,000
Benin	+1	franc	centimes	1960			French, Fon, Adja, Yoruba	Atacora Massif (2,103')	122,622	47,344	5,047,000
Bermuda	-4	dollar	cents				English	Gibb's Hill (245')	53	20	58,400
Bhutan	+6	ngultrum	chetrum	1971			Dzongkha, Bumthangka	Khula Kangri (24,784')	47,000	18,147	650,000
Bolivia	-4	boliviano	centavos	1945			Spanish, Quechua, Amyara	Nevado Sajama (21,391')	1,098,581	424,163	6,440,000
Bosnia-Hercegovina	+1	dinar	paras	1992			Bosnian	Bobotov Kuk (8,274')	51,129	19,741	2,900,000
Botswana	+2	pula	thebes	1966	1966		Setswana, English	Otse (4,886')	581,730	224,606	1326,796
Brazil	-2–5	real	centavos	1945			Portuguese	Pico da Bandeira (9,482')	8,511,965	3,286,473	156,275,000
Brunei	+8	dollar	sen	1984	1984		Malay, English	Bukit Belalong (3,098')	5,765	2,226	260,863
Bulgaria	+2	lev	stotinki	1955			Bulgarian	Musala (9,596')	110,912	42,823	8,963,000
Burkina Faso	0	franc	centimes	1960			French, Mossi	Tema (2,457')	274,200	105,869	9,490,000
Burundi	+2	franc	centimes	1962			Rundi, French, Swahili	Muramvya (8,809')	27,834	10,747	5,786,000
Cambodia	+7	riel	sen	1955			Khmer, French	Ka-Kup (5,722')	181,035	69,898	9,054,000
Cameroon	+1	franc	centimes	1960	1995		French, English	Cameroon (13,350')	475,442	183,568	12,198,000
Canada	-4–8	dollar	cents	1945	1931		English, French	Logan (19,550')	9,976,185	3,851,809	29,248,100
Cape Verde	-1	escudo	centavos	1975			Portuguese, Crioulo	Pico do Cano (9,285')	4,033	1,557	384,000
Central African Rep	+1	franc	centimes	1960			French, Sangho	Gaou (4,659')	622,984	240,534	3,173,000

GEOGRAPHY

Country	GMT	Currency	Split into 100	UN Member	Common-wealth	Europe	Official Languages	Highest Point	Area Sq Km	Area Sq Miles	Population
Chad	+1	franc	centimes	1960			French, Arabic	Emi Koussi (11,204')	1,284,000	495,753	5,961,000
Chile	-3--5	peso	centavos	1945			Spanish	Ojos del Salado (22,588')	756,945	292,257	13,599,000
China	+8	yuan	fen	1945			Mandarin Chinese	Everest (29,035')	9,596,961	3,705,390	1130,000,000
Colombia	-5	peso	centavos	1945			Spanish	Pico Cristobal Colon (18,947')	1,141,748	440,829	33,392,000
Comoros	+3	franc	centimes	1975			French, Arabic, Comoran	Kartala (7,746')	2,171	838	585,000
Congo, Dem Rep of	+1--2	zaire	makuta	1960			French, Lingala, Kiswahili	Stanley (Ngaliema) (16,795')	2,345,409	905,563	39,882,000
Congo, Rep of	+1	franc	centimes	1960			French	Foungouti (3,412')	342,000	132,046	2,368,000
Costa Rica	-6	colon	centimos	1945			Spanish	Chirripo (12,533')	50,700	19,575	3,194,000
Croatia	+1	kuna	lipas	1993			Croatian	Velika Peak (7,200')	56,538	21,829	4,760,344
Cuba	-5	peso	centavos	1945			Spanish	Pico Turquino (6,467')	110,861	42,803	10,811,000
Cyprus	+2	pound	cents	1960	1961		Greek, Turkish	Olympus (6,401')	9,251	3,572	725,000
Czech Republic	+1	koruna	haléru	1993		1973	Czech, Slovak	Snezka (5,256')	78,644	30,364	10,302,000
Denmark	+1	krone	ore	1945			Danish	Yding Skovhoj (568')	43,069	16,629	5,180,614
Djibouti	+3	franc	centimes	1977			French, Arabic, Afar, Somali	Mousa (6,769')	22,000	8,494	520,000
Dominica	-4	East Caribbean $	cents	1978	1978		English	Imray's View (4,747')	748	289	72,000
Dominican Republic	-4	peso	centavos	1945			Spanish	Pico Duarte (10,417')	48,734	18,816	7,459,000
Ecuador	-5	sucre	centavos	1945			Spanish	Chimborazo (20,561')	283,561	109,483	10,741,000
Egypt	+2	pound	piastres	1945			Arabic	Jebel Katherina (8,651')	1,001,449	386,660	57,850,000
El Salvador	-6	colon	centavos	1945			Spanish	Santa Ana (7,812')	21,041	8,124	5,376,000
Equatorial Guinea	+1	franc (was epkwele)	centimos	1968			Spanish	Moka (9,350')	28,051	10,831	369,000
Eritrea	+3	birr	cents	1993			English, Arabic	Ramlo (7,235')	93,679	36,169	3,500,000
Estonia	+2	kroon	sent	1991			Estonian	Munamagi (1,042')	45,125	17,423	1,526,177
Ethiopia	+3	birr (was dollar)	cents	1945			Amharic, Galla, Somali	Ras Dashen (15,158')	1,128,221	435,607	51,617,000
Fiji	+13	dollar	cents	1970 left 1987	1970		English, Fijian	Victoria (Tomanivi) 4,341'	18,274	7,056	715,373
Finland	+2	markka	penni	1955		1995	Finnish, Swedish	Haltiatunturi (4,344')	338,000	130,502	5,078,000
France	+1	franc	centimes	1945		1958	French	Blanc (15,771')	547,026	211,207	57,218,000
Gabon	+1	franc	centimes	1960			French, Fang, Eshira, Mbete	Iboundji (5,185')	267,667	103,346	1,237,000
Gambia	0	dalasi	butut	1965	1965		English	No land above 66'	11,295	4,361	909,000
Georgia	+4	lari	tetri	1992			Georgian, Russian, Armenian	Shkhara (16,627')	69,700	26,911	5,401,000
Germany	+1	deutschmark	pfennig	1973		1958	German	Zugspitze (9,721')	357,050	137,857	81,075,000
Ghana	0	cedi	pesewas	1957	1957		English, Asante, Ewe, Fante	Afadjato (2,860')	238,537	92,099	15,959,000
Greece	+2	drachma	leptae	1945		1981	Greek	Olympus (9,550')	131,944	50,944	10,256,464
Greenland	-3	krone	ore				Greenlandic, Danish	Gunnbjorns Field (12,139)	2,175,600	840,000	54,000
Grenada	-4	East Caribbean $	cents	1974	1974		English	St Catherine (2,756')	344	133	95,000

Country	GMT	Currency	Split into 100	UN Member	Commonwealth	Europe	Official Languages	Highest Point	Area Sq Km	Area Sq Miles	Population
Guatemala	-6	quetzal	centavos	1945			Spanish	Tajumulco (13,881')	108,889	42,042	9,745,000
Guinea	0	franc (was syli)	centimes	1958			French	Nimba (5,748')	245,857	94,925	6,116,000
Guinea-Bissau	0	peso	centavos	1974			Portuguese, Creole, Fulani	Fouta Djallon (600')	36,125	13,948	1,006,000
Guyana	-4	dollar	cents	1966	1966		English, Hindu, Urdu	Roraima (9,094')	214,969	83,000	808,000
Haiti	-5	gourde	centimes	1945			French, Creole	Pic La Selle (8,793')	27,750	10,714	6,764,000
Honduras	-6	lempira	centavos	1945			Spanish	Cerro Las Minas (9,400')	112,088	43,277	4,915,900
Hong Kong	+8	dollar	cents				Chinese, English	no named mountains	1,071	414	5,700,000
Hungary	+1	forint	filler	1955			Magyar	Kekes (3,330')	93,030	35,919	10,278,000
Iceland	+1	krona	aurar	1946			Icelandic	Hvannadalshnukur (6,952')	103,000	39,768	266,786
India	+5.5	rupee	paisa	1945	1947		Hindi, English	Nanda Devi (25,645')	3,287,590	1,269,340	846,302,688
Indonesia	+7–+9	rupiah	sen	1950			Bahasa Indonesia	Puncak Jaya (16,020')	1,904,569	735,355	191,170,000
Iran	+3.5	rial	dinars	1945			Farsi	Qolleh-ye Damavand (18,386')	1,648,000	636,293	66,000,000
Iraq	+3	dinar (= 5 riyals)	dirhams	1945			Arabic	Kurdistan Range (12,000')	434,924	167,924	19,290,000
Ireland	0	punt	pighne (pence)	1955	left 1949	1973	Irish, English	Carrantuohill (3,414')	70,283	27,136	3,525,719
Israel	+2	Shekel	Agorot	1949			Hebrew, Arabic	Atzmon (Har Meron) 3,963'	20,770	8,019	5,090,000
Italy	+1	lira	centesimi	1955		1958	Italian	Blanc (15,616')	301,225	116,303	56,777,000
Ivory Coast	0	franc	centimes	1960			French	Toukui (6,900')	322,463	124,503	12,190,000
Jamaica	-5	dollar	cents	1962	1962		English	Blue Mountain Peak (7,402')	10,991	4,244	2,460,700
Japan	+9	yen	sen	1956			Japanese	Fuji (12,388')	369,792	142,777	124,764,215
Jordan	+2	dinar	fils—1,000	1955			Arabic	Jabal Ramm (5755')	97,740	37,737	4,095,579
Kazakhstan	+4–+6	tenge	cents	1992			Kazakh, Russian	Khan-Tengri Peak (5,000')	2,717,300	1,049,151	16,963,600
Kenya	+3	shilling	cents	1963	1963		Swahili, English, Kikuyu	Kenya (17,057')	582,646	224,960	25,700,000
Kiribati	+12–+13	Australian $	cents	1979	1979		English, Kiribati (Gilbertese)	Banaba Peak (265')	728	281	74,000
Korea, North (Chosun)	+9	won	chon	1991			Korean	Pektu San (9,003')	120,538	46,540	22,618,000
Korea, South	+9	won	jeon	1991			Korean	Halla-san (6,398')	98,477	38,022	43,663,000
Kuwait	+3	dinar	fils—1000	1963			Arabic	Ash-Shaqaya (951')	17,818	6,880	1,695,128
Kyrgyzstan	+5	som		1992			Kirghiz, Russian	Victory Peak (24,406') (Pik Pobedy)	198,500	76,641	4,500,000
Laos	+7	kip	at	1955			Lao, French	Phou Bia (9252')	231,800	89,498	4,469,000
Latvia	+2	lat	santimes	1991			Latvian	Vidzeme (Livonia) 1020'	63,935	24,685	2,529,600
Lebanon	+2	pound (was livre)	piastres	1945			Arabic	Qurnat as-Sawda (10131')	10,400	4,015	2,838,000
Lesotho	+2	loti	lisente	1966	1966		Sesotho, English	Thabana Ntlenyana (11425')	30,355	11,720	1,836,000
Liberia	0	dollar	cents	1945			English	Peak of Mt Nimba (4500')	111,369	43,000	2,580,000
Libya	+1	dinar	dirhams-1000	1955			Arabic	Pico Bette (7500')	1,759,540	679,359	4,875,000
Liechtenstein	+1	Swiss franc	rappen/centimes	1993			German	Grauspitze (8526')	158	61	30,310
Lithuania	+2	litas		1991			Lithuanian	Juozapine (964')	65,200	25,174	3,724,000

GEOGRAPHY

Country	GMT	Currency	Split into 100	UN Member	Common-wealth	Europe	Official Languages	Highest Point	Area Sq Km	Area Sq Miles	Population
Luxembourg	+1	franc	centimes	1945		1958	French, German, Letzeburgesch	Bourgplatz (1833')	2,586	998	395,200
Macedonia	+1	macedonian denar	paras	1993			Macedonian, Albanian	Kajmakcalan (8271')	25,713	9,928	1,936,877
Madagascar	+3	franc	centimes	1960			Malagasy, French	Maromokotro (9436')	587,041	226,657	12,827,000
Malawi	+2	kwacha	tambala	1964	1964		English, Chichewa	Mlanje Sapitwa (9843')	118,484	45,747	8,823,000
Malaysia	+8	Malaysian $/ ringgit	sen/cents	1957	1957		Malay, Chinese, English	Kinabalu (13455')	329,749	127,316	19,959,000
Maldives	+5	rufiyaa	laaris	1965	1982		Divehi	no land above 8'	298	115	246,000
Mali	0	franc	centimes	1960			French, Bambara, Fulani	Hombori Tondo (3789')	1,240,000	478,764	9,818,000
Malta	+1	lira	cents	1964	1964		Maltese, English, Italian	Sceberras (816')	246	95	369,845
Marshall Islands	+12	US dollar	cents	1991			Marshallese, English	no land above 20'	181	70	50,000
Mauritania	0	ouguiya	khoums–5	1961			Arabic, French, Hassaniya	Kediet Ijill (3,002')	1,030,700	397,954	2,143,000
Mauritius	+4	rupee	cents	1968	1968		English	Black River Mountain (2,711')	2,045	790	1,082,998
Mexico	-6/-8	peso	centavos	1945			Spanish	Orizaba (18,406')	1,972,547	761,601	89,538,000
Moldova	+2	leu	bani	1992			Moldovan, Russian	Balaneshty (1,409')	33,700	13,012	4,359,000
Monaco	+1	franc	centimes	1992			French	On Chemin de Revoires (533')	1.9	0.73	29,972
Mongolia	+8	tugrik	möngö	1961			Khalkha Mongolian	Monh Hayrhan Uul (14,311')	1,565,000	604,247	2,156,000
Morocco	0	dirham	centimes	1956			Arabic, French, Berber	Jebel Toubkal (13,655')	446,550	172,413	27,575,000
Mozambique	+2	metical	centavos	1975	1995		Portuguese	Monte Binga (7,992')	801,590	309,494	14,872,000
Myanmar (Burma)	+6	kyat	pyas	1948			Burmese, English	Hkakado Razi (19,296')	676,552	261,217	43,668,000
Namibia	+2	namibian $	cents	1990	1990		Afrikaans, English	Brandberg (8,461')	824,292	318,259	1,534,000
Nauru	+12	Australian $	cents	1968	1968		English	Nauru Peak (225')	21	8	8,042
Nepal	+5.75	rupee	paisa	1955			Nepali	Everest (29,035')	140,747	54,342	20,577,000
Netherlands	+1	guilder/florin	cents	1945		1958	Dutch	Vaalserberg (1,053')	40,844	15,770	15,240,000
New Zealand	+13	dollar	cents	1945	1931		English, Maori	Cook (12,349)	268,867	103,810	3,516,539
Nicaragua	-6	cordoba	centavos	1945			Spanish	Pico Mogoton (6,913')	130,000	50,193	4,131,000
Niger	+1	franc	centimes	1960			French, Hausa, Tuareg	Greboun (6,562')	1,267,000	489,189	8,252,000
Nigeria	+1	naira	kobo	1960	1960		English, Hausa, Ibo, Yoruba	Dimlang (6,700')	923,768	356,667	115,664,000
Norway	+1	kroner	ore	1945			Norwegian	Galdhopiggen (8,098')	386,958	149,405	4,324,815
Oman	+4	rial omani	baizas–1000	1971			Arabic	Jabal ash Sham (10,400')	212,457	82,030	2,000,000
Pakistan	+5	rupee	paisa	1947	1947		Urdu	K2 (Godwin Austen) 28,250'	883,254	341,025	119,107,000
Panama	-5	balboa	centesimos	1945			Spanish	Chiriqui (11,467')	77,082	29,761	2,631,013
Papua New Guinea	+10	kina	toea	1975	1975		English, Pidgin, Moru	Wilhelm (15,400')	461,691	178,259	3,847,000
Paraguay	-3	guarani	céntimos	1945			Spanish, Guarani	Cerro Tatug (2,297')	406,752	157,047	4,519,000
Peru	-5	new sol	cents	1945			Spanish, Quechua	Huascaran (22,205')	1,285,216	496,222	22,465,000
Philippines	+8	peso	centavos	1945			Pilipino, English	Apo (9,690')	3000,00	115,830	64,259,000
Poland	+1	zloty	groszy	1945			Polish	Rysy (8,199')	312,677	120,725	38,300,000

Country	GMT	Currency	Split into 100	UN Member	Common-wealth	Europe	Official Languages	Highest Point	Area Sq Km's	Area Sq Miles	Population
Portugal	0	escudo	centavos	1955		1986	Portuguese	Estrela (6,539')	88,880	34,317	9,862,700
Qatar	+3	riyal	dirhams	1971			Arabic	no named mountains	11,000	4,247	453,000
Romania	+2	leu	bani	1955			Romanian	Moldoveanu (8,346')	237,500	91,699	22,760,449
Russia	+2–+12	rouble	kopeks	1991			Russian	Elbrus (18,510')	17,075,400	6,592,819	148,300,000
Rwanda	+2	franc	centimes	1962			French, Kinyarwanda	Karisimbi (14,787')	26,338	10,169	7,526,000
St Kitts and Nevis	-4	East Caribbean $	cents	1983	1983		English	Liamuiga Nevis (3,792')	269	104	42,000
St Lucia	-4	East Caribbean $	cents	1979	1979		English	Gimie (3,145')	616	238	137,000
St Vincent	-4	East Caribbean $	cents	1980	1979		English	Soufrière (4,048')	388	150	109,000
Samoa	-11	tala	sene	1976	1970		Samoan, English	Mauga Silisili (6,094')	1,714	662	162,000
San Marino	+1	lira	centesimi	1992			Italian	Titano (2,424')	61	24	24,801
São Tomé	0	dobra	centavos	1975			Portuguese	Pico Gago Coutinho (6,640')	964	372	124,000
Saudi Arabia	+3	riyal	halalah	1945			Arabic	Jebel Razikh (12,002')	2,149,640	829,977	16,929,294
Senegal	0	franc	centimes	1960			French, Wolof, Fulani	Gounou (4,970')	196,192	75,750	7,736,000
Seychelles	+4	rupee	cents	1976	1976		Creole, English, French	Seychellois (2,992')	456	176	72,000
Sierra Leone	0	leone	cents	1961	1961		English, Krio, Mende	Bintimani (6,390')	71,740	27,699	4,376,000
Singapore	+8	dollar	cents	1965	1965		Malay, Chinese, Tamil, English	Bukit Timah (581')	639	247	2,873,800
Slovak Republic	+1	koruna	haléru	1993			Slovak, Hungarian, Czech	Gerlachovsky (8,711')	49,035	18,932	5,336,455
Slovenia	+1	tolar	stotin	1993			Slovene, Hungarian	Triglav (9,396')	20,251	7,819	1,989,477
Solomon Islands	+11	dollar	cents	1978	1978		English, Pidgin	Makarakombou (8,028')	28,446	10,983	328,723
Somalia	+3	shilling	cents	1960			Somali, Arabic, English	Surud Ad (7,894')	637,657	246,200	9,204,000
South Africa	+2	rand	cents	1945	1931		Afrikaans, English, Xhosa, Zulu	Injasuti (11,182')	1,221,031	471,441	40,049,000
Spain	+1	peseta	centimos	1955		1986	Spanish	Teide (12,190') Canaries	504,782	194,897	38,872,268
Sri Lanka	+6	rupee	cents	1955	1948		Sinhalese, Tamil	Pidurutalagala (8,292')	65,610	25,332	17,619,000
Sudan	+3	dinar	pounds–10	1956			Arabic	Kinyeti (10,456')	2,505,813	967,495	26,656,000
Suriname	-3	guilder/florin	cents	1975			Dutch, Hindustani, Sranang Tongo	Julianatop (4,218')	163265	63,037	438,000
Swaziland	+2	lilangeni	cents	1968	1968		English, Swazi	Emlembe (6,113')	17,363	6,704	792,000
Sweden	+1	krona	ore	1946		1995	Swedish, Finnish	Kebnekaise (6,965')	449,964	173,731	8,745,109
Switzerland	+1	Swiss francs	centimes/rappen				German, French, Italian, Romansch	Dufourspitze (15,203')	41,293	15,943	6,907,959
Syria	+2	pound	piastres	1945			Arabic, Kurdish, Armenian	Jabal ash–Shaikh (Hermon) 13,113' (9,232')	185,180	71,498	12,958,000
Taiwan	+8	dollar	cents				Mandarin Chinese	Yu Shan (Morrison) 13,113'	35,742	13,800	20,894,522
Tajikistan	+5	rouble	tanga	1992			Tajik, Uzbek, Russian	Communism Peak (24,590)	143,100	55,251	5,513,400
Tanzania	+3	shilling	cents	1964	1961		English, Kiswahili	Kilimanjaro (19,340')	945,087	364,898	28,359,000
Thailand	+7	baht	satang	1946			Thai	Doi Inthanon (8,452')	514,000	198,456	58,336,072

GEOGRAPHY

Country	GMT	Currency	Split into 100	UN Member	Common-wealth	Europe	Official Languages	Highest Point	Area Sq Km's	Area Sq Miles	Population
Togo	0	franc	centimes	1960			French, Ewe, Kabiye	Baumann (3,235') aka Agou	56,785	21,925	3,763,000
Tonga	+14	pa'anga/dollar	seniti	1970	1970		Tongan, English	Kao (3,380')	699	270	97,000
Trinidad and Tobago	-4	dollar	cents	1962	1962		English, Hindi, French, Spanish	Cerro Aripo (3,085')	4,828	1864	1239,908
Tunisia	+1	dinar	millemes–1,000	1956			Arabic, French	Djebel Chambi (5,066')	164,150	63,378	8,401,000
Turkey	+2	lira	kurus	1945			Turkish	Buyuk Agridagi (Ararat) (17,011')	814,578	314,509	58,775,000
Turkmenistan	+5	manat		1992			Turkmenian, Russian, Uzbek	Koitendag Peak (11,293)	488,100	188,456	3,808,900
Tuvalu	+12	dollar	cents	1978	1978		Tuvaluan, English	no land above 15'	16	6	8,229
Uganda	+3	shilling	cents	1962	1962		English, Swahili, Luganda	Stanley (16,795')	236,036	91,134	18,674,000
Ukraine	+2	hryvna	kopiykas	1945			Ukrainian, Russian	Kamul (1,549')	603,700	233,089	52,100,000
United Arab Emirates	+4	dirham	fils	1971			Arabic	Western Al-Hajar (3,900')	83,600	32,278	2,310,000
United Kingdom	0	pound	pence	1945	1931		English	Ben Nevis (4,406')	240,883	93,005	58,191,000
USA	-5/–10	dollar	cents	1945			English	McKinley (20,320')	9,158,960	3,536,278	259,681,000
Uruguay	-3	peso	centesimos	1945			Spanish	Cerro de Las Animas (1,643')	176,215	68,037	3,116,802
Uzbekistan	+5	sum	tiyin	1992			Uzbek, Russian, Tajik	Beshtor (14,104')	447,400	172,741	21,206,800
Vanuatu	11	vatu	centimes	1981	1980		Bislama, French, English	Tabwebesana (6,195')	12,190	4,707	159,800
Vatican City	+1	lira	centesimi				Italian, Latin, Polish	none	0.44	0.17	1,000
Venezuela	-4	bolivar	centimos	1945			Spanish	La Pico Columna (Bolivar) (16,427')	912,050	352,143	20,249,000
Vietnam	+7	dong (=10 Hao)	xu	1977			Vietnamese	Fan si Pan (10,308')	329,556	127,242	71,267,000
Yemen	+3	riyal	fils	1947			Arabic	Jabalan Nabi Shu'ayb (12,336')	527,969	203,849	15,800,000
Yugoslavia	+1	dinar	paras	1945			Serbo Croat, Macedonian, Slovenic	Daravica (8,714')	102,350	39,517	10,410,000
Zambia	+2	kwacha	ngwee	1964	1964		English, Bemba, Nyanja	Muchinga (7,350')	752,614	290,585	8,638,000
Zimbabwe	+2	dollar	cents	1980	1980		English, Sindebele, Chishona	Inyangani (8,503')	390,580	150,803	10,583,000

NB: Of the 54 Commonwealth members, 16 have Queen Elizabeth II as head of state, 33 are republics and five have their own monarchies. Pakistan left the Commonwealth in 1972 but rejoined in 1989, however they were suspended on 18 October 1999. Tuvalu is a special member, with rights to attend commonwealth meetings but not to attend meetings of commonwealth heads of government.

Country	International Car Registration	Drives	International Civil Aircraft Markings	Type of Government	Religion	National Day	IDD Codes from UK	IDD Codes to UK
Afghanistan	AFG	right	YA	democratic republic	Islam	19 Aug	0093	operator
Albania	AL	right	ZA	socialist republic	Islam	11 Jan	00355	0044
Algeria	DZ	right	7T	democratic republic	Islam	1 Nov	00213	0044
Andorra	AND	right	C3	unicameral co-principality	RC	8 Sept	00376	0044
Angola		right	D2	people's republic	none	11 Nov	00244	0044
Antigua and Barbuda		left	V2	constitutional monarchy	none	1 Nov	001268	01144
Argentina	RA	right	LQ, and LV	federal republic	RC	25 May	0054	0044
Armenia		right		federal state	none	21 Sept	00374	81044
Australia	AUS	left	V8	federal parliamentary state	none	26 Jan	0061	001144
Austria	A	right	OE	federal republic	none	26 Oct	0043	0044
Azerbaijan		right		federal republic	Shia Muslim	28 May	00994	81044
Bahamas	BS	left	C6	constitutional monarchy	none	10 July	001242	01144
Bahrain	BRN	right	A9	monarchy	Islam	16 Dec	00973	044
Bangladesh	BD	left	S2	people's republic	Islam	26 Mar	00880	0044
Barbados	BDS	left	8P	constitutional monarchy	none	30 Nov	001246	01144
Belarus	BER	right		federal republic	RC	27 July	00375	81044
Belgium	B	right	OO	constitutional monarchy	RC	21 July	0032	0044
Belize	BH	right	V3	constitutional monarchy	none	21 Sept	00501	01144
Benin	DY	right	TY	people's republic	none	30 Nov	00229	0044
Bermuda			VR-B	British colony	none	17 Dec	001441	01144
Bhutan		right	A5	constitutional monarchy	Buddhism	6 Aug	00975	0044
Bolivia		right	CP	republic	RC	1 Mar	00591	9944
Bosnia-Hercegovina		right		federal republic	Islam	30 Sept	00396	0044
Botswana	RB	left	A2	republic	none	7 Sept	00267	0044
Brazil	BR	right	PP, and PT	federal republic	RC	23 Feb	0055	0144
Brunei	BRU	left	V8	monarchy (sultanate)	Islam	3 Mar	00673	0044
Bulgaria	BG	right	LZ	socialist republic	none	11 Dec	00359	0044
Burkina Faso	XT	right		military regime	none	1 July	00226	9044
Burundi	RU	right	9U	military regime	none	9 Nov	00257	0044
Cambodia	K	right	XU	people's republic	Buddhism	20 May	00855	0044
Cameroon	TJ	right		republic	none	1 July	00237	0044
Canada	CDN	right	CF, and CG	federal parliamentary state	none	1 July	001	01144
Cape Verde	D4	right		republic	RC	5 July	00238	044
Central African Rep	RCA	right	TL	republic	none	1 Dec	00236	0044
Chad	TT	right		military regime	none	13 Apr	00235	0044
Chile	RCH	right	CC	republic	RC	18 Sept	0056	0044
China	B	right		people's republic	none	1 Oct	0086	0044
Colombia	CO	right	HK	republic	RC	20 July	0057	0044
Comoros	D6	right		federal republic	Islam	6 July	00269	9044
Congo, Dem Rep of	ZRE	right	9Q	federal republic	RC	24 Nov	00243	1044
Congo, Rep of	RCB	right	TN	people's republic	RC	15 Aug	00242	0044

Country	International Car Registrations	Drives	International Civil A/C Markings	Type of government	Religion	National Day	IDD Codes from UK	IDD Codes to UK
Costa Rica	CR	right	TI	republic	RC	15 Sept	00506	0044
Croatia	HR	right		republic	RC	30 May	00385	9944
Cuba	C	right	CU	socialist republic	none	1 Jan	0053	11944
Cyprus	CY	left	5B	republic (unicameral parliament)	Greek Orthodox	1 Oct	00357	0044
Czech republic	CS	right	OK	federal republic	RC	28 Oct	00420	0044
Denmark	DK	right	OY	constitutional monarchy	Evangelical Lutheran	5 June	0045	0044
Djibouti			J2	republic	none	27 June	00253	0044
Dominica	WD	left	J7	republic	none	3 Nov	001809	01144
Dominican republic	DOM	right	HI	republic	none	27 Feb	001809	01144
Ecuador	EC	right	HC	republic	none	10 Aug	00593	0144
Egypt	ET	right	SU	republic	Islam	23 July	0020	0044
El Salvador	ES	right	YS	republic	none	15 Sept	00503	0044
Equatorial Guinea			3C	republic	none	12 Oct	00240	1944
Eritrea		right		republic	none	24 May	00291	operator
Estonia	EW	right	CCCP	unicameral republic	Lutheran	24 Feb	00372	80044
Ethiopia	E	right	ET	people's republic	none	28 May	00251	0044
Falkland Islands			VP-F		none		00500	0144
Fiji	FJI	left	DQ	republic	none	10 Oct	00679	0544
Finland	SF	right	OH	republic	none	6 Dec	00358	99044
France	F	right	F	republic	none	14 July	0033	0044
Gabon		right	TR	republic	none	17 Aug	00241	0044
Gambia	WAG	right	C5	republic	none	18 Feb	00220	0044
Georgia			GRU	republic	none	26 May	00995	81O44
Germany	D	right	D	republic	none	3 Oct	0049	0044
Ghana	GH	right	9G	republic	none	6 Mar	00233	0044
Gibraltar	GBZ	right	VR-G		none		00350	0044
Greece	GR	right	SX	republic	Eastern Orthodox	25 Mar	0030	0044
Greenland				constitutional monarchy (Denmark)	Evangelical Lutheran		00299	00944
Grenada	WG	left	J3	constitutional monarchy	none	7 Feb	001809	01144
Guatemala	GCA	right	TG	republic	none	15 Sept	00502	0044
Guinea			3X	republic	none	2 Oct	00224	0044
Guinea-Bissau			J5	republic	none	24 Sept	00245	operator
Guyana	GUY	left	8R	republic	none	26 May	00592	00144
Haiti	RH	right	HH	republic	none	1 Jan	00509	operator
Honduras			HR	republic	none	15 Sept	00504	0044
Hong Kong	HK	left	VR-H	territory of China	none	15 Mar, 20 Aug	00852	00144
Hungary	H	right	HA	people's republic	none	23 Oct	0036	0044
Iceland	IS	right	TF	republic	Evangelical Lutheran	17 June	00354	0044
India	IND	left	VT	republic	none	26 Jan	0091	0044
Indonesia	RI	left	PK	republic	Monotheism	17 Aug	0062	00144
Iran	IR	right	EP	republic	Islam	11 Feb	0098	0044

Country	International Car Registrations	Drives	International Civil A/C Markings	Type of government	Religion	National Day	IDD Codes from UK	IDD Codes to UK
Iraq	IRQ	right	YI	republic	Islam	17 July	00964	0044
Ireland	IRL	left	EI, and EJ	republic	none	17 Mar	00353	0044
Israel	IL	right	4X	republic	none		00972	0044
Italy	I	right	I	republic	none	2 June	0039	0044
Ivory Coast	CI	right	TU	republic	none	7 Dec	00225	0044
Jamaica	JA	left	6Y	constitutional monarchy	none	Aug 1st Mon	001879	01144
Japan	J	left	JA	constitutional monarchy	none	23 Dec	0081	00144
Jordan	HKJ	right	JY	hashemite kingdom	Islam	25 May	00962	0044
Kazakhstan			CCCP	republic	Islam	16 Dec	007	81044
Kenya	EAK	left	5Y	republic	none	12 Dec	00254	00044
Kiribati			T3	republic	none	12 July	00686	0044
Korea, North	P	right	P	democratic people's republic	none	8 Sept	00850	01044
Korea, South	ROK	right	HL	republic	none	15 Aug	0082	00144
Kuwait	KWT	right	9K	constitutional monarchy	Islam	25 Feb	00965	0044
Kyrgyzstan			CCCP	republic	Islam	31 Aug	00996	81044
Laos	LAO	right	RDPL	democratic people's republic	none	2 Dec	00856	operator
Latvia			CCCP	republic	Lutheran	18 Nov	00371	81044
Lebanon	RL	right	OD	republic	none	22 Nov	00961	0044
Lesotho	LS	right	7P	constitutional monarchy	none	4 Oct	00266	0044
Liberia	LB	right	EL	republic	none	26 July	00231	0044
Libya	LAR	right	5A	socialist republic	Islam	1 Sept	00218	0044
Liechtenstein	FL	right	HB	principality	RC	15 Aug	0041	0044
Lithuania			CCCP	republic	RC	16 Feb	00370	81044
Luxembourg	L	right	LX	grand duchy	none	23 June	00352	0044
Macedonia				republic	none	18 Sept	00389	9944
Madagascar	RM	right	5R	democratic republic	none	26 June	00261	0044
Malawi	MW	left	7Q	republic	none	6 July	00265	10144
Malaysia	MAL	left	9M	constitutional monarchy	Islam	31 Aug	0060	0044
Maldives			8Q	republic	Islam	26 July	00960	0044
Mali	RMM	right	TZ	republic	RC	22 Sept	00223	0044
Malta	M	left	9H	republic	none	31 Mar	00356	0044
Marshall Islands			MI	republic	none	21 Oct	00692	01244
Mauritania	RIM	right	5T	Islamic republic	Islam	28 Nov	00222	0044
Mauritius	MS	left	3B	constitutional monarchy	none	12 Mar	00230	0044
Mexico	MEX	right	XA, XB, XC	federal republic	none	16 Sept	0052	9844
Micronesia				federal states	none		00691	01144
Moldova			MOL	republic	none	27 Aug	00373	81044
Monaco	MC	right	3A	principality	none	19 Nov	0037793	0044
Mongolia				people's republic	none	11 July	00976	operator
Morocco	MA	right	CN	kingdom	Islam	3 Mar	00212	0044
Mozambique			C9	people's republic	none	25 June	00258	0044

Country	International Car Registrations	Drives	International Civil A/C Markings	Type of government	Religion	National Day	IDD Codes from UK	IDD Codes to UK
Myanmar (Burma)	BUR	right	XY, XZ	military regime	none	4 Jan	0095	044
Namibia	SWA	left		federal state	none	21 Mar	00264	0944
Nauru			C2	republic	none	31 Jan	00674	0044
Nepal			9N	kingdom	Hinduism	18 Feb	00977	0044
Netherlands	NL	right	PH	kingdom	none	30 April	0031	0044
New Zealand	NZ	left	ZK	constitutional monarchy	none	6 Feb	0064	0044
Nicaragua	NIC	right	YN	republic	none	15 Sept	00505	0044
Niger	RN	right	5U	republic	none	18 Dec	00227	0044
Nigeria	WAN	right	5N	federal republic	none	1 Oct	00234	00944
Norway	N	right	LN	constitutional monarchy	Evangelical Lutheran	17 May	0047	09544
Oman			A40	Sultanate	Islam	18 Nov	00968	0044
Pakistan	PAK	left	AP	republic	Islam	23 Mar & 14 Aug	0092	0044
Panama	PA	right	HP	republic	none	3 Nov	00507	0044
Papua New Guinea	PNG	left	P2	constitutional monarchy	none	16 Sept	00675	0544
Paraguay	PY	right	ZP	republic	RC	15 May	00595	00244
Peru	PE	right	OB	republic	RC	28 July	0051	0044
Philippines	RP	right	RP	republic	RC	12 June	0063	0044
Poland	PL	right	SP	republic	none	3 May	0048	0044
Portugal	P	right	CS	republic	RC	10 June	00351	0044
Qatar			A7	constitutional monarchy	Islam	3 Sept	00974	O44
Romania	RO	right	YR	republic	none	1 Dec	0040	0044
Russia	RUS		CCCP	federal republic	none	12 June	007	81044
Rwanda	RWA	right	9XR	republic	none	1 July	00250	0044
Samoa	WS	right	5W	constitutional monarchy	none	1 June	00685	144
San Marino	RSM	right	T7	serene republic	RC	3 Sept	00378	0044
São Tomé			S9	republic	RC	12 July	00239	0044
Saudi Arabia			HZ	kingdom	Islam	23 Sept	00966	0044
Senegal	SN	right	6V	republic	none	4 Apr	00221	0044
Seychelles	SY	left	S7	republic	RC	5 June	00248	044
Sierra Leone	WAL	right	9L	republic	none	27 Apr	00232	044
Singapore	SGP	left	9V	republic	none	9 Aug	0065	00544
Slovak republic			SQ	republic	RC	1 Jan	0042	0044
Slovenia			SLO	republic	RC	25 June	00386	0044
Solomon Islands			H4	constitutional monarchy	none	7 July	00677	0044
Somalia			6O	democratic republic	Islam	tba	00252	operator
South Africa	ZA	left	ZS	republic	none	27 April	0027	0944
Spain	E	right	EC	kingdom	none	12 Oct	0034	0744
Sri Lanka	CL	left	4R	democratic socialist republic	none	4 Feb	0094	0044
St Kitts and Nevis			VP-LKA/ LLZ	constitutional monarchy	none	19 Sept	001869	operator

Country	International Car Registrations	Drives	International Civil A/C Markings	Type of government	Religion	National Day	IDD Codes from UK	IDD Codes to UK
St Lucia	WL	left	J6	constitutional monarchy	none	22 Feb	001758	044
St Vincent	WV	left	J8	constitutional monarchy	none	27 Oct	001809	0044
Sudan			ST	republic	none	1 Jan	00249	0044
Surinam	SME	left	PZ	republic	none	25 Nov	00597	00144
Swaziland	SD	left	3D	kingdom	none	6 Sept	00268	0044
Sweden	S	right	SE	constitutional monarchy	Lutheran	6 June	0046	00744
Switzerland	CH	right	HB	federal republic	none	1 Aug	0041	0044
Syria	SYR	right	YK	republic	none	17 Apr	00963	0044
Taiwan	RC	right	B	republic	none	10 Oct	00886	00244
Tajikistan			CCCP	republic	Islam	9 Sept	007	81044
Tanzania	EAT/EAZ	left	5H	republic	none	26 Apr	00255	0044
Thailand	T	left	HS	constitutional monarchy	Buddhism	5 Dec	0066	00144
Togo	TG	right	5V	republic	none	13 Jan	00228	0044
Tonga			A3	constitutional monarchy	none	4 June	00676	0044
Trinidad and Tobago	TT	left	9Y	republic	none	31 Aug	001868	01144
Tunisia	TN	right	TS	republic	Islam	20 Mar	00216	0044
Turkey	TR	right	TC	republic	none	29 Oct	0090	0044
Turkmenistan			CCCP	republic	Islam	27 Oct	00993	81044
Tuvalu			T2	constitutional monarchy	Protestant	1 Oct	00688	0044
Uganda	EAU	left	5X	republic	None	9 Oct	00256	0044
UK	GB	left	G	constitutional monarchy				
Ukraine	UKR		CCCP	republic	RC	24 Aug	00380	81044
UAE			A6	federal monarchy	Islam	2 Dec	00971	0044
Uruguay	ROU	right	CX	republic	RC	25 Aug	00598	0044
USA	USA	right	N	federal republic	none	4 July	001	01144
Uzbekistan			CCCP	republic	Islam	1 Sept	007	81044
Vanuatu			YJ	republic	none	30 July	00678	0044
Vatican City				state	RC	22 Oct	003966982	0044
Venezuela	YV	right	YV	republic	none	5 July	0058	0044
Vietnam	VN	right	VN	socialist republic	none	2 Sept	0084	0044
Yemen	ADN	right	4W	people's democratic republic	Islam	22 May	00967	0044
Yugoslavia	YU	right	YU	socialist federal republic	none	29 Nov	00381	9944
Zambia	Z	left	9J	republic	none	24 Oct	00260	0044
Zimbabwe	ZW	left	Z	republic	none	18 Apr	00263	11044

NB: Any gaps in the World Geographical Gazetteer or table above indicate information that has not been verifiable.

GEOGRAPHY

National Anthems

Country	National Anthem
Afghanistan	Soroud-e-Melli First line: As long as the earth and heavens exist
Albania	The Flag that in Battle United Us
Algeria	Qassaman First line: We swear by the lightning that destroys
Andorra	Great Charlemagne, My Father
Angola	Angola Avante
Antigua and Barbuda	Fair Antigua and Barbuda
Argentina	Hear, Oh Mortals, the Sacred Cry of Liberty
Australia	Advance Australia Fair
Austria	Land of Mountains, Land on the River (from Mozart's 'Little Masonic Cantata')
Bahamas	March on, Bahamaland
Bangladesh	Amar Sonar Bangla First line: My golden Bengal, I love you
Barbados	In Plenty and in Time of Need
Belarus	Soviet anthem with words omitted
Belgium	La Brabançonne
Belize	O Land of the Free
Benin	The New Dawn
Bolivia	Oh Bolivia, Our Long-Felt Desires First line: Bolivians, propitious fate has crowned our hopes
Botswana	Fatshe Leno La Rona First line: Blessed be this noble land
Brazil	From Peaceful Ypiranga's Banks
Brunei	O God, Long Live Our Majesty the Sultan
Bulgaria	Stara Planina's Peaks Proudly Rise
Burkina Faso	Against the Humiliating Bars, a Thousand Years Ago
Burundi	Dear Burundi, O Pleasant Land
Cambodia	Nokoreach
Cameroon	O Cameroon Thou Cradle of Our Forefathers
Canada	O Canada, Our Home and Native Land
Chile	Dulce Patria, Recibe Los Votos
China	March of the Volunteers
Colombia	Oh Gloria Inmarcesible
Croatia	Our Beautiful Homeland
Cuba	To Battle, Men of Bayamo
Cyprus	Ode to Freedom
Czech Republic	Where is my Motherland
Denmark	King Christian Stood by the Lofty Mast
Dominica	Isle of Beauty
Dominican Rep	Brave men of Quisqueya, Let Us Raise Our Song
Egypt	Biladi
El Salvador	Let Us Proudly Hail the Fatherland
Estonia	My Fatherland
Ethiopia	Ityopya, Ityopya Kidemi
Fiji	God bless Fiji
Finland	Oi aamme Suomi (Our Land, Finland)
France	La Marseillaise
Gabon	Uni dans la Concorde
Gambia, The	For The Gambia, Our Homeland
Germany	Unity and Right and Freedom

Country	National Anthem
Ghana	God bless our Homeland, Ghana
Greece	Hymn to Freedom
Guatemala	Happy Guatemala
Guinea	People of Africa
Guyana	Dear land of Guyana
Haiti	La Dessalinienne
Honduras	Your Flag is a Heavenly Light
Hungary	God Bless the Hungarians
Iceland	O God of Our Country
India	Jana-gana-mana
Indonesia	Indonesia, Our Native Land
Iran	Sorood-e Jomhoori-e Eslami
Iraq	Salute of the Republic
Ireland	The Soldier's Song
Israel	The Hope (Hatikvah)
Italy	Inno di Mameli
Ivory Coast	L'Abidjanaise
Jamaica	First line: Jamaica, Land We Love
Japan	Kimi ga yo Wa (May Your Peaceful Reign Last Long) First line: The reign of our emperor
Jordan	Long Live the King
Kenya	Ee Mungu nguvu yetu (Oh God of all creation)
Kiribati	Stand up, Kiribati
Korea, North	Shine Bright O Dawn on This Land So Fair
Korea, South	Aegukka
Laos	Xatlao tangtae dayma Lao First line: thook thuana nentxoo soo tehay (for the whole of time the Lao people glorified their Fatherland)
Latvia	God Bless Latvia
Lebanon	We All Belong to the Homeland
Lesotho	Lesotho fatsela bontat'a rona (Lesotho, land of our fathers)
Liberia	All Hail, Liberia, Hail
Liechtenstein	High on the Rhine
Lithuania	Lietuva tevyne musu (Lithuania, Our land)
Luxembourg	Our Homeland
Macedonia	Today over Macedonia
Madagascar	Ry tanindrazanay Malala o (O beloved Fatherland)
Malawi	O God Bless our Land of Malawi
Malaysia	Negara-Ku (My Country)
Maldives	Qawmee Salaam
Mali	A ton appel, Mali (at your call Mali)
Malta	L-Innu Malti
Mauritius	Glory to Thee, Motherland
Mexico	Mexicans, the War Cry
Monaco	Hymne Monégasque
Morocco	Hymn of the Sharif
Mozambique	Long Live Frelimo
Myanmar (Burma)	We Shall Love Burma Evermore
Nepal	May Glory Crown Our Illustrious Sovereign
Netherlands	Wilhelmus van Nassaue
New Zealand	God Defend New Zealand/God Save the Queen
Nicaragua	Hail, Nicaragua
Nigeria	Arise, O Compatriots
Norway	Yes, We Love This Country
Oman	God Save Our Sultan Said
Pakistan	Quami Tarana
Panama	Victory Is Ours at Last

Country	National Anthem
Papua New Guinea	Arise, All You Sons of This Land
Paraguay	Paraguayans, Republic or Death
Peru	We Are Free, Let Us Remain So Forever
Philippines	Bayang Magiliw First line: Beloved land, pearl of the Orient
Poland	Poland Has Not Yet Been Destroyed
Portugal	A Portuguesa
Romania	Desteaptate, Romane, din somnul cel de moarte (wake up Romanians, from your deadly slumber)
Russia	Slavsya (Be Great)
Samoa	The Banner of Freedom
Saudi Arabia	Long Live Our Beloved King
Seychelles	Koste Seselwa (Seychelles Unite)
Sierra Leone	High We Exalt Thee, Realm of the Free
Singapore	Majulah Singapura
Slovak Republic	Storm over the Tatras
Slovenia	A Toast
Solomon Islands	God Bless our Solomon Islands
South Africa	The Call of South Africa, and God Bless South Africa
Spain	Marcha Real Española
Sri Lanka	Sri Lanka Matha, Apa Sri Lanka (Mother Sri Lanka, thy Sri Lanka)
St Kitts and Nevis	O Land of Beauty
St Lucia	Sons and Daughters of Saint Lucia
St Vincent	St Vincent, Land So Beautiful
Sudan	We Are the Army of God
Swaziland	Ingoma Yesive

Country	National Anthem
Sweden	Thou Ancient, Thou Freeborn
Switzerland	Step into the Rosy Dawn
Syria	Defenders of the Homeland, Greetings
Tanzania	God Bless Africa
Thailand	Pleng Chart
Togo	Terre de nos aieux (Land of our forefathers)
Tonga	Oh Almighty God Above
Trinidad and Tobago	Forged from the Love of Liberty
Tunisia	Humata Al Hima First line: Immortal and precious the blood we have shed
Turkey	The Independence March First line: Korkma Sünmez bu safaklarda yüzen al sancak (Be not afraid! Our flag will never fade)
Tuvalu	Tuvalu for the Almighty
Uganda	Oh, Uganda First line: Pearl of Africa
UK	God Save the Queen
Uruguay	Easterners, the Fatherland or Death
USA	The Star-Spangled Banner
Vanuatu	First line: Yumi, yumi, yumi i glat blong tale se, yumi, yumi, yumi i man blong Vanuatu (We, we, we are glad to tell, we, we we are the people of Vanuatu)
Venezuela	Glory to the Brave People
Vietnam	Soldiers of Vietnam, We Are Advancing
Yugoslavia	Oh Slavs, Our Ancestors' Words Still Live
Zambia	Stand and Sing of Zambia, Proud and Free
Zimbabwe	Blessed be the Country of Zimbabwe

GEOGRAPHY

HISTORY

Chronicles of World History

AD 1   The accepted year of Jesus' birth as calculated by Dionysius Exiguus in AD 525. (The more probable date is now considered to be 4 or possibly 6 BC.)
The King of the Trinovantes tribe, in Southern England, Addedomarus, dies and is succeeded by Dubnovellaunus.

2   Lucius Caesar (the 1st grandson of Augustus) dies.

3   The future Roman Emperor Galba is born.

4   Gaius Caesar (2nd grandson of Augustus) dies leaving Tiberius, the Emperor's newly adopted grandson, as heir.

5   Romans defeat the Lombard tribes on the lower Elbe.

6   Chinese initiate 'Civil Service' examinations for prospective politicians.

7   Ovid works on his masterpiece, *Metamorphoses*.

8   Ovid is exiled to Tomis (now Constanta, in present-day Romania) by the Emperor Augustus for reasons unknown.

9   Titus Livius (Livy), from Padua, completes his 142-volume *History of Rome*.

10   Cunobelinus (Cymbeline) rules over most of southern England from his HQ at Camulodunum (Colchester).

12   Gaius Caesar (later nicknamed Caligula, meaning 'little boots') is born.

13   Tiberius is appointed his successor by Augustus.

14   Death of Augustus. His adopted son Agrippa Postumus is immediately executed, and Tiberius becomes emperor.

15   The law of 'Maiestas', making it a crime to harm the interests of Rome, and therefore of the Emperor, is brought back by Tiberius to ensure that his sovereign power is not undermined.

16   An attempt to overthrow Tiberius is thwarted when a slave of Agrippa Postumus, named Clemens, is killed.

17   The poet Ovid dies in exile. Livy dies in Patavium (Padua).

18   In China, the usurper Emperor Wang Mang's forces fail to subdue the rebel band known as the Red Eyebrows At Shandong.

19   Tiberius' nephew Germanicus is poisoned in Syria, possibly by Gnaeus Calpurnius Piso, the governor of Syria.

20   Piso commits suicide during his trial.

21   A revolt by the Gallic tribes, the Treveri and the Aedui, is put down by Gaius Silius.

22   Wang Mang is defeated and killed, during a revolt by followers of the Han regime.

23   Drusus, the son of Tiberius, is poisoned by Lucius Aelius Sejanus, commander of the Praetorian Guard.

24   Tacfarinas, king of the Numidians, is killed by the Romans after a 7-year revolt.

25   Tiberius retires to Capri on the advice of the increasingly dominating Sejanus. Buddha is represented in human form for the first time at Gandhara.

26   Pontius Pilate becomes the 5th Roman procurator of Judaea and Samaria.

27   Tiberius leaves Rome and settles on Capri.

29   Agrippina, widow of Germanicus, is arrested on the orders of Tiberius.

30   Jesus of Nazareth is crucified at Golgotha. Dionysius Exiguus, the inventor of the Christian calendar, wrongly dated the birth of Jesus according to the Roman System, i.e. 754 years after the founding of Rome.

31   Sejanus is executed by Tiberius when the extent of his plotting emerges.

32   In Rome, interest rates rocket as a result of a currency shortage. The Emperor Otho is born.

35   Tiberius makes Caligula and Tiberius Gemellus heirs to his private estate.

36   The future Emperor Nerva is born.

37   Tiberius dies at Misenum and is succeeded by Gaius Caesar (Caligula). The Emperor Nero is born.

38   Drusilla, beloved sister and consort of Caligula, dies, and is deified.

39   Caligula puts down a conspiracy by the governor of higher Germany, Gaetulicus.

40   King Ptolemy of Mauretania is assassinated by order of Caligula.

41   Caligula declares himself a god and is assassinated shortly afterwards. Claudius succeeds him.

42   Cunobelinus, ruler of most of Southern England, dies.

43   The Romans, on the orders of Claudius, invade Britain.

44   James becomes the first Christian apostle to be martyred.

45   The philosopher Philo dies.

46   The kingdom of Thrace becomes a province of Rome.

47   Messalina, wife of the Emperor Claudius, is acquiring a reputation as a sexual profligate.

48   Emperor Guang Wudi re-establishes Chinese domination of the people of inner Mongolia. Claudius has Messalina executed for infidelity.

49   Claudius expels Jewish Christians from Rome.

50   Claudius adopts his stepson Nero.

51   Caractacus, son of Cunobelinus, is captured by the Romans at Ludlow.

52   The future Emperor Domitian is born.

53   Nero marries his stepsister Octavia.

54   Claudius dies after eating poisoned mushrooms administered by the Empress Agrippina. Nero succeeds him.

55   Britannicus, son of Claudius, dies, possibly poisoned by Nero.

57   Paul is arrested at Caesarea and held for trial.

58	Paul writes an epistle to the Romans.
59	Nero has his mother, Agrippina, killed.
60	Mark, a disciple of Jesus, chronicles the life of his master, from baptism by his cousin, John, to his eventual death.
61	During a rebellion led by Queen Boudicca of the Iceni, the Trinovantes and Iceni tribes sack Roman Colchester, St Albans and London. Boudicca commits suicide after defeat by Suetonius Paulinus.
62	Paul is put under 'house arrest' in Rome.
63	The Armenian throne is returned to Tiridates after the peace of Rhandeia.
64	Paul of Tarsus is executed, as is Peter the apostle. Fire destroys over half of the city of Rome.
65	Nero's pregnant wife dies after being kicked by him.
66	The courtier Gaius Petronius is accused of treason and has to commit suicide.
67	The Jews rise up against the Romans.
68	Nero commits suicide to end the Julio-Claudian line of Roman Emperors. He is succeeded by Servius Sulpicius Galba.
69	The year of 4 Roman emperors, Galba, Vitellius, Otho and Vespasian.
70	Vespasian's son, Titus, sacks Jerusalem, destroying most of the 3rd Temple; only the 'Wailing Wall' is left standing.
71	The 'Arch of Titus', in celebration of the sacking of Jerusalem, is erected in Rome.
73	Chinese forces under General Ban Chao gain control over the 'Oasis' states. After a two-year siege, the fortress of Masada in Judea falls to the Romans.
74	Vespasian institutes 'Latin Rights' which give inhabitants of towns identical civil rights to 'Citizens' except for holding public office.
75	Vespasian completes his Temple of Peace in Rome.
76	Johanan Ben Zakkai re-establishes the Sanhedrin, the Jewish religious court.
77	Gnaeus Julius Agricola arrives in Britain to complete the conquest.
78	Vima Kadphises, the Kushan king, who rules India from Benares, sends a delegation to Rome to arrange a surprise attack on the Parthians.
79	Vesuvius erupts, destroying Pompeii and the neighbouring towns of Herculaneum and Stabiae. Pliny the Elder is one of the victims. Vespasian dies, and his son Titus succeeds him.
80	The apostle Luke begins to write his gospel. The Colosseum is opened in Rome.
81	Titus dies of the plague and is succeeded by his brother, Titus Flavius Domitianus (Domitian). Domitian consecrates the triumphal arch to celebrate Titus's victory over the Jews.
82	Spanish poet Marcus Valerius Martialis (Martial) begins his *Epigrams*.
83	Agricola defeats the Caledonians at Mount Graupius.
84	Agricola is called back to Rome.
85	Domitian appoints himself censor for life, thereby giving himself complete control of the composition of the Senate.
86	The future Emperor Antoninus is born.
87	The Romans suffer a serious setback in the Dacian War.
88	The revolt of Saturninus, governor of Upper Germany, leads to Domitian declaring that only one legion is to be quartered in each Roman camp, to prevent any local commander from gaining excessive influence over troops.
89	Domitian is forced to sign a peace treaty with the Dacian king, Decebalus.
90	Domitian begins the persecution and execution of opponents.
91	Chinese general Ban Chao defeats the Indian Kushans.
92	The Iazyges, a nomadic tribe, invade Dacia. Domitian leads his soldiers in person and succeeds in repelling them.
94	General Ban Chao completes his conquest of the Tarim basin.
95	Malaria appears in rural areas around Rome.
96	Emperor Domitian is stabbed to death by plotters led by his wife, Domitia. Senator Marcus Cocceius Nerva succeeds him.
97	Emperor Nerva recalls General Marcus Ulpius Trajanus (Trajan) from Upper Germany and adopts him.
98	Emperor Nerva dies, and is succeeded by Trajan.
99	Julius Frontinus, a former governor of Britain, surveys and describes the aqueducts of Rome in his capacity as superintendent of Rome's water supply.
100	The Sun and Moon pyramids are begun at Teotihuacán in Mexico.
101	Trajan invades Dacia (in present-day Romania), fearing the increasing dominance of Decebalus.
102	Sarmizegethusa, capital of Dacia, is taken by Trajan; Decebalus agrees to become a Roman ally.
104	Martial dies at Bibilis, in Spain.
105	Tsai Lun, a Chinese eunuch, invents a kind of paper made from tree bark, hemp and rags.
106	Dacia becomes a Roman province after King Decebalus and his chiefs commit suicide.
110	Pliny the Younger is appointed governor of Bithynia. Juvenal publishes his first book of *Satires* in Rome, highlighting corruption, vice and the unjust treatment of the poor.
114	Trajan's Column and Basilica are built. Armenia is annexed to the Roman Empire.
115	Mesopotamia is occupied by the Romans.
116	Assyria is annexed to the Roman Empire.
117	Trajan dies and is succeeded by Publius Aelius Hadrianus (Hadrian). Cornelius Tacitus, the celebrated historian, dies.
120	Construction of the Pantheon in Rome is begun.
122	Construction of Hadrian's Wall is begun.
123	Emperor Hadrian meets the king of Parthia, thus averting war.
125	Plague and famine in North Africa.

128	The Greek physician Galen is born.
132	The Jewish population of Jerusalem revolts over the construction of a shrine to Jupiter on the site of the Temple.
135	The Romans retake and demolish Jerusalem; Jewish leader Simon Bar-Kokhba killed near Caesarea; diaspora begins.
138	Hadrian dies and is succeeded by his recently adopted son Antonius Pius.
139	The Romans advance northwards under governor Quintus Lollius Urbicus from Hadrian's Wall to the Clyde–Forth line.
142	Construction of the Antonine Wall is begun.
154	Brigantian revolt in Pennines put down by governor Julius Verus, but troops withdrawn from Caledonia as a result.
155	Partial destruction by indigenous Picts of the Antonine Wall.
161	Antonius dies and is succeeded by his adopted son Marcus Annius Verus (Marcus Aurelius).
163	Antonine Wall abandoned.
167	Barbarians attack Rome, but are repelled by Marcus Aurelius. The Marcomanni and Quadicross the Danube into Roman territory.
168	The Marcomanni, who have occupied North-western Italy, are conquered by Marcus Aurelius.
169	The Marcomanni revolt, but the revolt is crushed.
174	The Germanic Quadi tribe defeated by Marcus Aurelius.
175	Avidius Cassius encourages the legions in Asia to revolt, but is assassinated and his head sent to Marcus Aurelius.
177	Persecution of Christians recommences in Rome; they adopt the fish symbol as an emblem of their faith.
180	Marcus Aurelius dies and is succeeded by his son Commodus.
185	Mass mutiny of the Roman army in Britain eventually quelled by newly appointed governor Publius Helvius Pertinax.
192	Commodus murdered by his mistress and chamberlain, who found their names on an execution list.
193	Pertinax is chosen as emperor by the senate, but his strict rule leads to his assassination. Didius Julianus becomes emperor after an auction but has already been deposed and killed by the time that Septimius Severus, the Pannonian legate, invades Rome and is declared emperor.
197	Clodius Albinus, the British legate, revolts, but is defeated and killed by Severus at Lyons.
200	Japanese empress, Jingu, sends a fleet to invade Korea, which surrenders on sight of it.
205	Plotinus, founder of Neoplatonism, is born.
209	Roman legions under Severus and Caracalla march against the Caledonii, advancing as far as Aberdeen; forts built on Firths of Forth and Tay.
211	Septimus Severus dies at York; he is succeeded by his sons Caracalla and Geta.
212	Caracalla murders Geta and slaughters thousands of his brother's supporters. He extends Roman citizenship to all free inhabitants of the Empire by the Edict of Caracalla.
215	Manes, who develops the dualist philosophy known as Manichaeism, is born in southern Mesopotamia.
216	Britannia is divided into two provinces – Upper Britain (south and west) and Lower Britain (north).
217	Caracalla is murdered by his officers, and is succeeded by Macrinus.
218	Macrinus is defeated in battle near Antioch and executed. He is succeeded by Varius Avitus Bassianus, who takes the name Heliogabalus.
220	Fall of the Han Dynasty in China, which splits into a number of smaller states.
222	Heliogabalus is murdered by the Praetorian Guard. His cousin and adopted son Bassianus succeeds him, taking the name Severus Alexander.
225	Southern India breaks up into several kingdoms with the end of the Andgra dynasty.
226	The rebel prince Ardashir takes control of Persia, founding the Sassanid dynasty.
234	Severus Alexander decrees that bread, rather than grain, be given to Rome's poor.
235	The Alemanni invade Gaul, but are bought off by Severus Alexander. As a result, he is murdered by his army, who proclaim Maximinus as Emperor.
238	The African provinces set up Gordianus I, a descendant of Trajan, as Emperor. Gordianus commits suicide when his son is killed by supporters of Maximinus, but when Maximinus is assassinated by the Praetorian Guard, Gordianus' grandson, Gordianus III, becomes emperor.
244	Gordianus III defeats the Persians at Resaena, but soon after is murdered during a mutiny by Marcus Philippus, who replaces him and makes peace with the Persians.
248	Games are held to celebrate Rome's millennium.
249	Decius usurps the throne from Philippus, who is killed. The Goths cross the River Danube and lay waste several Roman provinces.
250	Decius initiates further persecution of Christians.
251	Decius dies in battle against the Goths; his successor Gallus bribes the Goths to return from whence they came.
253	Aemilian revolts against Gallus, who dies by the hand of his own troops. Aemilian dies and Valerianus becomes Emperor.
254	Origen, one of the leading Christian scholars, dies.
255	Plague sweeps across Europe.
257	The Goths move into the Black Sea area.
258	The Alemanni and Suevi invade Northern Italy, but are repulsed at Milan.
260	Valerianus seized by the Persians and dies in captivity; his son Gallienus succeeds him.
267	Prince Odenathus of Palmyra assassinated with Gallienus' complicity.
268	Gallienus murdered by his own troops at Milan. Claudius II becomes emperor.
269	The Goths invade the Balkans, sacking Athens, Sparta and Corinth, but are defeated in battle by Claudius II.

270	Claudius II dies. His brother Quintillus succeeds him, but commits suicide when his troops desert him. Aurelian becomes emperor.
271	Aurelian ejects the Alemanni from Italy, and rebuilds the walls of Rome.
272	Aurelian conquers the kingdom of Palmyra.
274	A rebellion at Châlons is put down by Aurelian, who returns to Rome in triumph.
275	The Romans pull back to the Danube and Rhine, which are established as the Empire's frontier. Aurelian is assassinated by his officers, and Tacitus succeeds him as emperor.
276	Tacitus killed by his own troops after defeating the Goths in Asia Minor. His brother Florianus succeeds, only to be killed also. Marcus Aurelius Probus becomes Emperor. Mani is crucified on the grounds of heresy.
282	The Franks and Alemanni invade Gaul, but are repulsed by Probus, who is killed by his troops in Egypt. Marcus Aurelius Carus replaces him.
283	Marcus Aurelius Carus dies, to be succeeded by his son Numerianus.
284	Numerianus is assassinated, to be replaced by Diocletian.
285	Diocletian partitions the Empire – he rules in the East, to counter the barbarian threat there, while Maximian is appointed to run the Western portion.
286	Carausius, commander of the Channel fleet, revolts and seizes Britain, where construction begins on a series of forts to guard the south-eastern coast (the Saxon Shore forts).
290	Construction begins on the amphitheatre in Verona.
291	Persian King Vahram II kills the manichaean sisih.
293	Carausius murdered by Allectus, his finance minister, who seizes power in Britain.
296	Allectus defeated and killed by Constantius Chlorus in battle near Silchester.
300	Diocletian builds a palace at Ragusa (later Dubrovnik).
301	Christianity proclaimed the state religion in Armenia.
303	The notary Genesius is martyred. Diocletian begins a general persecution of Christians.
304	The Kingdom of Cheng Han is founded in Sichuan.
305	Diocletian and his co-ruler Maximian abdicate and are succeeded by Galerius and Constantius Chlorus respectively.
306	Constantius Chlorus dies near York. His son Constantine is proclaimed Emperor, but Galerius raises Severus instead.
307	Severus dies; Galerius raises Licinius to co-Emperor.
308	Maxentius, son of Maximian, becomes despot in Rome.
311	Galerius attempts to expel Maxentius, but is defeated and dies soon after.
312	Constantine defeats Maxentius, his rival Western emperor, at the Milvian Bridge.
313	Christianity tolerated in the Roman Empire by the Edict of Milan.
316	The Xiongnu, later identified with the Huns, invade China.
323	Constantine and Licinius at war; Constantine victorious.
324	Licinius executed; Constantine becomes sole ruler. Christianity declared the official religion of the Roman Empire.
325	Council of Nicaea declares Christ and God are of the same substance – 'consubstantial'.
330	Constantinople (formerly Byzantine; known today as Istanbul) is dedicated as the new capital of the Roman Empire.
335	Church of the Holy Sepulchre consecrated in Jerusalem.
337	Constantine I dies, not long after taking Christian baptism; he is succeeded by his three sons, Constantine II, Constantius II and Constans.
338	Jewish calendar reformed by establishing variable year lengths.
340	Constantine II killed at Aquileia fighting Constans; Empire splits into East under Constantius II and West under Constans.
350	Constans murdered by General Magnentius in a coup.
352	Magnentius is defeated by Constantius II at Mursa in Mesopotamia.
353	Magnentius commits suicide. Constantius II reunites Empire.
356	All pagan temples in the Roman Empire ordered closed by Constantius II.
360	Lo-tsun founds the Caves of the Thousand Buddhas in Gansu, China. The Huns invade Europe for the first time.
361	Constantius II dies, and is succeeded by his pagan cousin Julian.
363	Julian dies in battle against the Persians; Jovian, captain of the Imperial Bodyguard, succeeds to the throne.
364	Jovian cedes Armenia to Shah Shapur II of Persia, and dies on his return. Valentinian I becomes emperor, and appoints his brother Valens to rule in the Eastern half.
367	Picts, Scots, Angles and Saxons invade Britain in a joint attack.
369	Theodosius, a Roman general, re-establishes order in Britain.
372	Buddhism reaches Korea from China.
375	Valentinian I dies. His 4-year-old son Valentinian II nominally succeeds him in the West but his older half-brother Gratian has effective control.
376	The Huns invade Russia and defeat the Visigoths. From now on, tribes pushed westward by the Huns press harder into the Roman Empire.
378	Visigoths defeat and kill the Emperor Valens at the battle of Adrianople.
379	Gratian's general, Theodosius becomes Emperor in the East.
382	Visigoths settled as Foederati (military allies) in the Balkans by Theodosius.
383	Magnus Maximus mutinies against Gratian, who is assassinated. Magnus rules in Britain, Gaul and Spain.
386	Hymn singing introduced by St Ambrose, Bishop of Milan.
388	Magnus Maximus invades Italy, to be defeated by Theodosius and murdered. Valentinian II established in power in the West.

391	The library at Alexandria is destroyed in a fire started by a Christian mob seeking to eradicate non-Christian works.
392	The Frankish general Arbogast organises the assassination of Valentinian II and replaces him with a puppet emperor, Eugenius.
394	Eugenius defeated and killed by Theodosius, who reunites the Empire. Arbogast commits suicide.
395	Theodosius dies, and the Roman Empire splits in two for good. His son Arcadius rules in the East, Honorius in the West.
396	Alaric the Visigoth invades Greece.
397	Stilicho, regent to Honorius, ejects the Visigoths from Greece and crushes a rebellion in North Africa.
401	The Visigoths invade Northern Italy.
402	Visigoths halted by Stilicho at the battle of Pollentia.
405	The Colosseum closed by Honorius.
406	Stilicho halts barbarian invasion of Italy. Vandals under Gunderic invade Gaul.
407	Roman troops depart Britain under the pretender Constantine III; Britain left to fend for itself.
408	Stilicho is murdered on Honorius' orders. Arcadius dies. His son Theodosius II becomes emperor in Constantinople.
409	The Vandals cross the Pyrenees and enter Spain.
410	Visigoths under Alaric sack Rome. Alaric dies shortly afterwards; his brother Ataulf takes command.
411	Constantine III defeated and executed by troops loyal to Honorius. Pelagius calls on St Augustine at Hippo but Augustine refuses to see him.
412	The Visigoths enter Gaul from Italy and establish a kingdom there.
415	Neoplatonist philosopher Hypatia is killed in Alexandria by a Christian mob who scraped her to death with oyster shells.
416	Vandal kingdom of Spain falls to the Visigoths.
418	Franks enter Gaul and settle.
420	Nanjing becomes the capital of northern China once more. Eastern Qin state in China is overthrown by its general Liu Yu, who founds the Liu Song state. St Jerome dies.
422	Theodosius II makes peace with Shah Varahran of Persia, and agrees an annual tribute with the Huns.
423	Death of Honorius, emperor of the West.
425	Constantinople University founded.
426	Yash Kukhmol arrives from Teotihuacán in Copán, founding a Mayan dynasty.
427	Korean capital moved to Pyongyang by King Changsu.
429	Vandals invade Africa, led by King Gaiseric. The British, led by Bishop Germanus, defeat barbarian invaders (the 'Alleluia Victory').
430	Cunedda, chief of the Gododdin, moves at the Welsh King Vortigern's behest from Scotland to Gwynedd, whose royal house he thereby founds.
431	Council of Ephesus deposes Patriarch Nestorius of Constantinople for his belief that Jesus had two natures, one human and one divine.
432	Saint Patrick sent as a missionary to Ireland.
433	Attila becomes co-ruler of the Huns.
439	Carthage taken by Gaiseric's Vandals, who make it their capital.
440	The town of Ys in Armorica (later Brittany) is submerged in a great flood. The Vandals invade Sicily.
441	Britain invaded by Angles, Saxons and Jutes.
443	The Alemanni settle in Alsace.
444	The wheelbarrow developed in China.
446	Britain told to fend for itself when it appeals to Rome for help against barbarian invaders.
450	Theodosius II dies, to be succeeded by Marcian, who refuses to continue paying tribute to the Huns to prevent them from attacking.
451	Huns defeated at battle of Châlons by Romans and Visigoths under Flavius Aetius.
452	Venice founded by refugees from the Huns.
453	Death of Attila on his wedding night.
455	The Vandals sack Rome.
457	Marcian dies, to be succeeded by Leo I.
460	Roman fleet destroyed by the Vandals off Cartagena.
461	Severus III becomes Western emperor.
466	Theodoric II of the Visigoths killed by his brother Euric, who succeeds him.
467	Anthemius elected Western emperor at Leo I's behest; they mount a joint expedition against the Vandals in North Africa.
468	The Vandals successfully repulse the Roman invasion.
471	Goths and Eastern Romans clash due to a feud caused by the failure of the expedition against the Vandals.
472	Ricimer the Visigoth captures Anthemius, and appoints Olybrius in his stead. Both Ricimer and Olybrius subsequently die; Gundobad the Burgundian takes control.
473	Gundobad names Glycerinus Western emperor, but he is deposed by Julius Nepos, a protégé of Leo I.
474	Leo I dies, to be succeeded by his son-in-law Zeno.
475	Orestes deposes Julius Nepos and makes his son Romulus Augustulus Western emperor.
476	Romulus Augustulus deposed by Odoacer at Ravenna; Western Roman Empire ends.
477	Sussex founded by Aelle, who lands with his sons at Selsey.
478	Shinto shrines appear in Japan.
481	At the age of 15, Clovis I succeeds his father Childeric I as king of the Franks.
484	Armenia revolts successfully against the Persians led by Vahan Mamikonian. Freedom of religious worship was restored to them by the Treaty of Nvarsag.

486	Clovis defeats governor Syragius at Soissons and takes control of Northern Gaul.
488	The Ostrogoths, led by Theodoric and prompted by Zeno, invade Italy, now ruled by Odoacer.
491	Zeno dies, to be succeeded by Anastasius, who marries his widow. The South Saxons under Aelle capture Pevensey Castle.
493	Odoacer surrenders to Theodoric at Ravenna after a siege, and is murdered by him. Theodoric founds the Ostrogoth kingdom of Italy.
495	Cerdic, founder of Wessex, lands near Southampton.
496	Clovis defeats the Alemanni near Strasbourg, and converts to Christianity, being baptised by Bishop Remigius of Rheims.
500	The Marcomanni invade Bavaria from Bohemia, which is settled by the Czechs. Incense is added to Christian services to cover the smell of unwashed worshippers.
502	King Gundobad of Burgundy issues a legal code that establishes equality before the law for Burgundians and Romans.
507	Clovis defeats the Visigoths, killing King Alaric II at Vouillé, near Poitiers, and goes on to conquer Southern Gaul.
508	The Ostrogoths under Theodoric conquer Provence and Septimania.
511	Death of Clovis.His kingdom of Francia is divided into four to provide kingdoms for his four sons.
516	The British comprehensively defeat the Saxons at Mons Badonicus.
517	Emperor Wudi introduces Buddhism to central China.
518	Emperor Anastasius I dies, to be succeeded by Justin I, chief of the imperial guard, who entrusts much imperial policy to his nephew Justinian.
519	Eastern and Western Churches reconciled.
520	Priscian codifies Latin grammar with his long treatise, the *Institutiones Grammaticae*.
522	The philosopher and statesman Boethius arrested on a charge of conspiring against Theodoric.
523	King Thrasamund of the Vandals dies and is succeeded by Hilderic.
524	Boethius writes *The Consolation of Philosophy* and is executed shortly after.
525	Yemen invaded by Abyssinians under Caleb. Dionysius Exiguus wrongly sets the date of Christ's birth as 25 December in the 753rd year of Rome.
526	Theodoric the Ostrogoth dies, and is succeeded by his 10-year-old grandson Athalaric.
527	Death of Justin I; his nephew Justinian succeeds him.
528	Hun King Grod converted to Christianity and was killed. The Korean state of Silla officially recognized Buddhism.
529	Benedict of Nursia founds the monastery of Monte Cassino. Justinian closes the non-Christian Academy at Athens.
530	The great Byzantine general Belisarius defeats the Persians at Dara. King Hilderic of the Vandals dies, to be succeded by Gelimer.
531	Chosroes I becomes Shah of Persia. The Franks conquer Thuringia.
532	Burgundy invaded by the Franks.
533	Belisarius conquers the Vandal kingdom of North Africa, reclaiming it for Byzantium.
534	Toledo made capital of the Visigoth kingdom of Spain. Malta captured by the Byzantine army.
535	Belisarius invades and captures Sicily, and moves into Southern Italy.
536	Belisarius takes Rome from the Ostrogoths.
537	Arthur and Medrault fall at the battle of Camlann.
539	Witigis, leader of the Ostrogoths, is captured by Belisarius at Ravenna. Belisarius recalled to Constantinople.
540	Totila, an Ostrogoth leader, expels the Byzantines from Italy. The Roman statesman and author Cassiodorus founds the monastery at Vivarium in Calabria and retires there.
541	Totila succeeds to the Ostrogothic throne on the death of his uncle Hildebad. The bubonic 'Plague of Justinian' pandemic starts in Constantinople.
542	The Welsh monk Gildas writes *De Excidio et Conquestu Britanniae*, a history of the Roman conquest and Anglo-Saxon invasion of Britain.
543	Justinian condemns the writings of Origen.
546	Totila captures Rome. Audoin establishes a new Lombard kingdom in Austria.
547	The Plague of Justinian reaches Britain. The Angle king Ida accedes to the throne of Bernicia, in north-east England.
549	The last games are held in Rome.
550	The Toltecs overrun Teotihuacán. St David converts the Welsh.
551	The Byzantines defeat an Ostrogothic fleet in a naval battle.
552	Totila killed at Taginae fighting the Byzantines under Narses. Justinian sends missionaries to China to smuggle silkworms out. Buddhism arrives in Japan from Korea.
553	Rome and Naples annexed by Narses for Byzantium.
554	Narses appointed Exarch of Italy.
558	Reunification of Francia by Chlothar I after the death of his brother Childebert I.
559	The Bulgars attack Constantinople, but are repelled by Belisarius.
560	Aethelbert I becomes king of Kent. Ceawlin becomes king of Wessex.
561	Death of Chlothar I – Francia again split in four by his sons.
563	Foundation of monastery on Iona by Columcille (Saint Columba).
565	St Columba subdues a monster on Loch Ness. Belisarius dies. Justinian I dies, and is succeeded by his nephew Justin II.
567	With the death of Charibert, Francia reorganised into Austrasia in the east, Neustria in the west and Burgundy in the south.
568	Alboin founds a Lombard kingdom in Northern and Central Italy.

570	Muhammad born in Mecca. The Persians take the Yemen from the Abyssinians.
571	Foundation of the kingdom of East Anglia.
572	War breaks out between Persia and Byzantium.
573	Sigebert of Austrasia attacks Chilperic of Neustria over the murder of Galswintha, sister of Sigebert's wife Brunhilda.
574	Aidan ordained king of the Argyll Scots by St Columba.
575	King Sigebert assassinated on the orders of Chilperic's wife and former mistress Fredegunde; Brunhilda seeks revenge.
577	Celtic kings Coinmail, Condidan and Farinmail killed at the battle of Dyrham by West Saxons under Cuthwine and Ceawlin.
578	Death of Justin II, to be succeeded by Tiberius II.
579	Death of Shah Chosroes of Persia.
581	China's Sui dynasty founded by Emperor Wendi (Yang Jian).
582	Death of Tiberius II, to be succeeded by his son-in-law Maurice.
583	Wendi moves into the new city of Chang'an, soon to become the world's largest city.
584	Death of Chilperic of Neustria, who is succeeded by his son Chlothar II.
585	King Leovigild of the Visigoths puts down a revolt by his son Hermenegild, whom he kills, and proceeds to conquer the rest of the Iberian peninsula.
586	King Leovigild dies, leaving the Visigothic throne to his son Recared. Disputes in Japan between Shinto and Buddhist adherents.
587	The Visigoths convert from Arianism to Catholicism. The first Buddhist monastery is built in Japan.
588	Shah Hormizd of Persia deposed and murdered after defeats by Byzantines; replaced by his son Chosroes II.
589	Wendi defeats the Chen at Jian-Kang and reunites China. Chosroes II deposed in Persia, fleeing to Constantinople.
590	Gregory I the Great becomes Pope and undertakes reforms in Rome, as well as helping to expel the plague from the city.
591	Maurice helps restore Chosroes II to the Persian throne in return for territorial concessions.
592	Ceawlin of Wessex deposed by Ceol. The Bretwaldaship (overlordship) of the English peoples south of the Humber passes to Aethelbert of Kent.
593	The newly crowned Aethelfrith unites Bernicia and Deira to create the kingdom of Northumbria.
594	The 'Plague of Justinian' pandemic comes to an end. Gregory of Tours dies.
596	St Augustine dispatched by Pope Gregory to convert Britain.
597	Saint Augustine arrives in Kent, converts King Aethelbert and founds the archdiocese of Canterbury.
600	Tibet begins to develop into a unitary state.
602	Emperor Maurice killed and replaced by Phocas.
603	Battle of Catraeth (Catterick): Aethelfrith of Northumbria defeats a coalition of British from Lothian, North Wales and North West England.
604	The Japanese code of Prince Shotoku Taishi demands the veneration of Buddha, his priests and his laws.
606	Harsha of Thanesar founds an empire in Northern India, the last indigenous ruler to do so for several centuries.
607	Horyuji temple and hospital, the oldest surviving wooden building in the world, constructed in Japan.
609	Consecration of the Pantheon in Rome.
610	Emperor Phocas deposed and killed by Heraclius. Muhammad has a vision of the angel Gabriel on Mount Hira.
611	Death of Ceolwulf of Wessex, succeeded by Cynegils.
612	Harsha of Thanesar takes the title of Emperor of the Five Indies. St Gall founds the hermitage, later a monastery of St Gallen in Switzerland.
613	Francia reunited under Chlothar II after his conquest of Austrasia.
614	Chlothar II issues the *Edictum Chlotacharii*, which defines the rights of kings, nobles and Church within Francia.
615	Jerusalem sacked by the Persians, who take the 'True Cross' as booty.
616	Aethelbert of Kent dies; Raedwald of East Anglia becomes Bretwalda; he kills Aethelfrith of Northumbria at the River Idle, replacing him by the exiled Edwin.
618	Sui dynasty replaced by the Tang.
619	Publication of the *Suan-Ching*, textbooks for use in public examinations in China.
620	Chosroes II takes Rhodes, thus restoring the Persian Empire to the extent it reached under Darius I.
622	In July Muhammad flees from Mecca to Medina (the hegira, from which the Islamic calendar year 1 is dated).
623	Samo, a Frankish merchant, frees Slav tribes in Carinthia from Avar overlordship and becomes their ruler.
625	Death of Raedwald; Edwin of Northumbria becomes Bretwalda.
626	Chinese Emperor Gaozu abdicates in favour of his son Taizong.
627	The Byzantines decisively defeat the Persians at Nineveh.
628	Chosroes II murdered by his son Kavadh II, who succeeds him.
629	Chlothar II dies, to be succeeded by his son Dagobert I. Emperor Heraclius recovers Jerusalem from the Persians.
630	Mecca falls to Muhammad who writes letters on the principles of Islam to various rulers.
632	Death of Muhammad; Abu Bakr chosen as Caliph.
633	Edwin of Northumbria killed by Mercian/Welsh forces at Hatfield. They proceed to ravage the kingdom, which splits back in two.
634	Abu Bakr dies; Umar becomes Caliph. Oswald re-establishes the kingdom of Northumbria and becomes Bretwalda.

635	Islamic forces take Damascus, which becomes the capital of the Caliphate. Harsha invades the land of the Chalukyas, but is repulsed.
638	Jerusalem falls to Islamic forces under Umar.
639	Dagobert I of Francia dies; the kingdom is split again.
641	Great Library at Alexandria destroyed in a fire.
642	Oswald of Northumbria dies in battle at Maserfelth (near Oswestry) fighting King Penda of Mercia; he is succeeded in Bernicia by Oswy. Persia is conquered and made subject to the Caliphate.
644	Byzantine forces capture Alexandria, which revolted against Islamic rule, but the Arabs retake it. Caliph Umar dies, to be succeeded by Uthman.
646	The Taikwa reform in Japan establishes centralised government under Imperial control.
647	Harsha of Thanesar dies, and his Northern Indian empire fragments as a result.
649	Cyprus falls to Islamic forces.
650	The Bulgarian Empire, then in Southern Russia, conquered by the Khazars.
652	Arabs come to an agreement with the Nubians, establishing Aswan as the southern limit of the Caliphate in Egypt.
653	The Visigothic king Recesswinth of Spain draws up a legal code for his domains, the *Liber Iudicorium*.
654	Penda of Mercia, Aethelhere of East Anglia and various other royals are killed in the battle of the River Winwaed by Oswy of Bernicia, who re-establishes Northumbria.
655	A Byzantine fleet led by Constans II defeated at Lycia by an Arab fleet.
656	Caliph Uthman is murdered in Medina. Muhammad's son-in-law Ali replaces him. Grimoald attempts to usurp the throne of Austrasia after the death of Clovis II.
657	Mercia released from Northumbrian rulership; Wulfhere son of Penda becomes king.
661	Ali deposed and murdered; the Umayyad dynasty, founded by Muawiya, assumes the Caliphate at Damascus.
664	The English Church adopts the Roman liturgy in preference to the Irish at the Synod of Whitby.
668	Emperor Constans II dies mysteriously in his bath at Syracuse.
669	Theodore of Tarsus ordained Archbishop of Canterbury, and proceeds to reform the English Church.
670	Death of Oswy of Northumbria, the last Bretwalda; his son Ecgfrith succeeds him.
671	The weapon Greek fire – an inflammable liquid that could be propelled through bronze tubes – invented by Kallinikos of Byzantium.
672	The see of Canterbury given authority over the church in England by the Synod of Hertford.
674	The Arabs penetrate as far as the Indus.
678	After several years' siege, the Arabs fail to take Constantinople and establish a 30-year peace with the Byzantine Empire.
680	Caliph Yaezid puts down a revolt by Hussain, son of Ali, who is killed.
682	Islamic forces overrun Tripoli, Carthage and Tangiers, expelling the Byzantines from North Africa.
685	Ecgfrith of Northumbria falls in battle against the Picts at Nechtanesmere; he is succeeded by Aldfrith.
687	Pepin II of Hérstal defeats his foes at Tertry and gains effective control of all of Francia. He and his successors rule as 'mayors of the palace', holding real power under figurehead Merovingian kings.
688	Caedwalla of Wessex resigns the kingship and goes on pilgrimage to Rome, succeeded by Ine.
689	Justinian II defeats Slavic forces in Thrace, and deports many of them to Anatolia.
690	Wihtred becomes King of Kent.
692	Brihtwold becomes the first native Archbishop of Canterbury; the Irish church accepts the authority of Rome at the Synod of Tara.
694	King Ine codifies the laws of Wessex.
695	Emperor Justinian II deposed by his officers, who cut off his nose and exile him; he is replaced by Leontius.
696	Paoluccio Anafesto is appointed the first doge of Venice.
697	Carthage destroyed by the Arabs.
698	Emperor Leontius deposed and replaced by Tiberius III.
700	The Agilofings, dukes of Bavaria, make Ratisbon their capital.
701	The Japanese emperor passes a law making him the sole proprietor of land in the country.
705	Justinian II restored as emperor.
709	Deaths of bishops Aldhelm of Sherborne, who converted Wessex, and St Wilfrid of Hexham.
710	Nara established as the capital of Japan.
711	Fall of the Visigothic kingdom in Spain to the invading Arab and Moorish forces after the defeat and death of King Roderick; only Asturias remains a Christian kingdom. Justinian II murdered by Philip Bardanes, who takes the throne as Philippicus.
712	The Arabs take Samarkand, where they discover the art of making paper, and Sind.
713	Emperor Philippicus deposed and replaced by Anastasius II.
714	Death of Pepin II in Francia. His son, Charles Martel, begins to unify the Frankish kingdom.
715	Winfrith, the future St Boniface, begins his missionary work among the Germans.
716	Emperor Anastasius II deposed; he is replaced by Theodosius III. Aethelbald becomes king of Mercia, succeeding Ceolred.
717	Theodosius III deposed by Leo III. The Arabs besiege Constantinople. Omar II becomes caliph and grants a tax exemption to true believers.
718	Constantinople fights off the Arab siege; Greek fire is spectacularly used to decimate the Arab fleet.
720	The Arabs conquer Sardinia and cross the Pyrenees, taking Narbonne.
722	St Boniface made the first bishop among the Germans.
725	The heathen Oak of Thor felled by St Boniface.
726	Ine of Wessex dies on pilgrimage in Rome; succeeded by Aethelheard.
730	Emperor Leo III excommunicated by Pope Gregory II over his iconoclastic policies, which forbid making images of Christ, the Virgin Mary or the saints.
731	Bede completes his *Ecclesiastical History of the English People*.

732	Charles Martel defeats the Arabs at the battle of Tours (or Poitiers), their furthest incursion into Europe.
735	Burgundy conquered by Charles Martel. The Venerable Bede dies.
737	Death of King Theuderic IV of Francia.
739	Bishoprics at Passau, Ratisbon and Salzburg founded by St Boniface. Charles Martel and his Lombard allies expel the Moors and Arabs from Provence.
741	Death of Charles Martel, who divides his mayoralty between his sons Carloman in Neustria and Pepin in Austrasia.
743	Childeric III becomes king of Francia after a six-year interregnum.
744	Swabia added to territory of Francia.
746	Constantine V retakes Cyprus from the Arabs. Carloman retires to a monastery, leaving Pepin as mayor of all of Francia.
748	The first printed newspaper published in what is now Beijing.
749	The Neighing Stallion sculpted out of fire-clay in China. As-saffah establishes Abbasid rule in Baghdad.
750	Umayyad Caliph Marwan II deposed and killed by the Abbasids, descended from the Prophet's uncle.
751	Childeric III, last Merovingian monarch, replaced as king by Pepin III the Short, who founds the Carolingian dynasty.
754	Pepin III assists Pope Stephen III against the Lombards.
756	Abd-al-Rahman establishes the Umayyad Emirate of Cordoba.
757	Offa succeeds Aethelbald as king of Mercia after the latter's murder.
758	King Edbriht of Northumbria abdicates to become a monk, succeeded by his son Osulf.
759	Narbonne retaken from the Moors by Frankish troops.
760	Turkish empire founded by a Tartar tribe in Armenia.
762	Caliph Mansur founds Baghdad as capital of the Abbasid Caliphate.
765	China invaded by a Tibetan army.
768	Pepin III dies; Francia is split between his sons Charles (later Charlemagne) and Carloman.
770	Death of the poet Tu Fu.
771	Carloman dies; kingdom reunited under Charlemagne.
772	Charlemagne invades and subdues Saxony.
773	Charlemagne invades and subdues Lombardy.
774	Charlemagne confirms the Donation of Pepin, a grant of lands made by his father to Pope Stephen II in 757, which creates the Papal States.
775	Tibet and China confirm a boundary agreement.
776	Kent gains temporary independence from Mercia as a result of winning the battle of Otford.
778	Roland, Lord of the Breton Marches, killed by Basques at Roncesvalles as Charlemagne's army withdraws from a venture in Spain.
779	Offa defeats Cynewulf of Wessex near Benson and becomes de facto ruler of England.
780	On the death of her husband, Leo IV, the Empress Irene becomes Regent of the Byzantine Empire and restores Image Worship.
781	Nestorian Christians in China develop monasteries.
782	Charlemagne executes 4,500 Saxon hostages at Verdun and annexes Saxony.
783	Widukind leads a Saxon revolt against Frankish rule.
784	Work commences on Offa's Dyke.
785	Widukind submits to Charlemagne and is baptised.
786	Harun al-Rashid becomes Caliph, succeeding his brother al-Hadi.
787	First Viking raid on England, near Wareham.
788	Charlemagne annexes Bavaria, deposing Duke Tassilo.
789	Frankish ports closed to English merchants due to a dispute between Charlemagne and Offa.
790	Irish monks sail to Iceland in skin-frame vessels.
792	Offa has King Aethelbert of East Anglia beheaded, and annexes his kingdom.
793	Lindisfarne and Jarrow sacked by the Vikings.
794	The Japanese capital moves from Nara to Heian (later known as Kyoto).
795	First Viking attacks on Ireland.
796	Death of Offa brings his son Ecgfrith to the throne. He dies soon after, and Cenwulf succeeds him.
797	Empress Irene of Byzantium deposes and blinds her son Constantine VI.
798	Revolt in Kent against Mercian rule subdued by King Cenwulf, who blinds the Kentish royal leader Eadbert and cuts off his hands.
799	Charlemagne captures and destroys Fiume.
800	Charlemagne crowned Holy Roman Emperor on Christmas Day.
802	Empress Irene deposed by her finance minister Nicephorus; Egbert succeds Brihtric as king of Wessex.
803	The Bulgarians free themselves from Tartar overlordship.
804	Charlemagne finally defeats the Saxons.
805	The Japanese Buddhist priest Saicho brings tea to Japan.
807	Monastery founded by Cellach of Iona at Kells.
808	Foundation of Fez, in Morocco, as a tent colony.
809	Death of Harun al-Rashid, succeeded by his son al-Amin.
810	Musa al-Khwarazmi writes a book on equations, introducing the Hindu numerals now known as Arabic.
812	Byzantine Empire recognizes Charlemagne as emperor in the West.
813	Al-Mamun murders and succeeds his brother Caliph al-Amin.
814	Death of Charlemagne. His son Louis the Pious succeeds him.
815	Cornwall conquered by Egbert of Wessex.
817	Louis the Pious partitions the Holy Roman Empire amongst his sons and makes Lothair, his eldest son, co-emperor.

821	Tibetan independence from China ratified by treaty at Chang'an.
825	Egbert of Wessex defeats Beornred of Mercia at Ellandun, near Swindon, and briefly controls all England.
826	Islamic pirates capture Crete and use it as a base for raids in the Aegean. Nominoë becomes Count of Brittany.
827	Sicily invaded by Arab forces.
829	Louis the Pious invests his son Charles the Bald with the dukedom of Swabia, upsetting the status quo.
830	The Great Moravian Empire founded by Prince Moimir.
831	Anskar is created bishop of Hamburg, with responsibility for converting Scandinavia.
832	Emperor Theophilus issues an edict banning the worship of images.
833	Louis the Pious defeated by his elder sons at Colmar and imprisoned.
834	Louis the Pious restored to his throne by loyalists; his eldest son Lothair retires to his Italian sub-kingdom.
838	The Arabs sack Marseilles and also cross to Southern Italy.
839	Egbert of Wessex dies, and is succeeded by his son Aethelwulf.
840	Death of Louis the Pious. The Holy Roman Empire splits into three, but the new emperor, Lothair, seeks to conquer his brothers' portions.
841	Lothair defeated by his brothers Louis the German and Charles the Bald at Fontenoy, thus frustrating his imperial plans. The Vikings found the city of Dublin in Ireland.
842	Emperor Theophilus dies, and is succeeded by his son Michael III. Under the regency of his mother, Theodora, image worship is restored.
843	Treaty of Verdun establishes the territories of the three remaining sons of Louis the Pious, thus dividing for good the lands of the Holy Roman Empire. Kenneth MacAlpin, king of Dalriada since 840, unites the Picts and Scots into a single kingdom (Alba), the forerunner of Scotland.
845	Buddhism suppressed in China by Emperor Wu Tsung.
846	Rome is attacked and badly damaged by Arab forces.
847	Al-Mutawakkil succeeds his brother al-Wathiq as caliph.
849	Birth of Alfred the Great of Wessex, at Wantage.
850	Rurik the Norseman becomes the ruler of Kiev.
851	The Vikings sack London and Canterbury, but are halted in their depredations by Aethelwulf of Wessex and his son Aethelbald at Aclea.
852	Muhammad I succeeds to the Emirate of Cordoba on the death of his father Abdul-Rahman II.
853	Kudawara Kudanari, the first major Japanese painter, dies.
855	Holy Roman Emperor Lothair I dies; his portion of the empire is divided amongst his three sons; Louis II succeeds his father as Emperor.
856	Aethelbald replaces Aethelwulf as king in Wessex, Kent, Surrey and Sussex. Vikings burn Paris.
857	Ergotism epidemics, caused by poisoned grain, begin to appear in Europe.
858	Death of Aethelwulf of Wessex. Aethelbald becomes sole king of Wessex but grants his brother Aethelbert an under-kingship.
859	Norse marauders enter the Mediterranean and cause havoc.
860	Aethelbald of Wessex dies, to be succeeded by his brother Aethelbert.
861	Cologne, Paris, Aix-la-Chapelle, Toulouse and Worms sacked by Viking raiders.
862	Novgorod, capital of Kiev Rus, founded by Rurik.
863	The Cyrillic alphabet is developed by Cyril and his brother Methodius in Moravia.
864	King Boris I of Bulgaria converts to Christianity.
865	Ivar the Boneless and his brother Halfdan arrive in England in an attempt to conquer the country. Aethelbert of Wessex dies; his brother Aethelred I succeeds him.
867	Basil I, the Macedonian, murders Michael III and becomes Byzantine emperor.
868	Ahmad ibn Tulun establishes the Tulunid dynasty in Egypt.
869	Malta captured by Islamic forces.
870	Martyrdom of King (later St) Edmund of East Anglia at the hands of the Vikings.
871	Vikings defeated by Wessex at Ashdown but victorious at Reading, Basing, Merton and Wilton. Alfred succeeds Aethelred I as king of Wessex.
874	The Vikings begin to colonise Iceland. Burgred, last independent English king of Mercia, forced to abdicate by the Vikings, who replace him with their puppet Ceolwulf II.
875	Holy Roman Emperor Louis II dies; his uncle Charles the Bald establishes himself as his successor.
876	Louis the German dies; his portion of the Holy Roman Empire is divided amongst his three sons.
877	Charles the Bald dies; he is succeeded as French king by his son Louis II the Stammerer. The imperial throne is left unfilled.
878	Alfred, after a period in hiding at Athelney, decisively defeats the Vikings at Edington, Wiltshire, and preserves Wessex as an English kingdom.
879	The treaty of Wedmore establishes the Danelaw in parts of England: Danish laws and customs will prevail there. Louis II dies; his sons Louis III and Carloman jointly succeed him.
880	Southern Italy reconquered from the Arabs by the Byzantine Emperor Basil.
881	Charles III, king of Swabia, crowned Holy Roman Emperor.
882	Louis III of France dies; his brother Carloman reigns alone. Kiev replaces Novgorod as capital of Kiev Rus under Oleg.
883	The Zenj rebellion of African slaves in Chaldea, which has lasted fourteen years, finally suppressed by al-Muwaffiq, brother of Caliph al-Mu'tamid.
884	Carloman of France dies while hunting. Emperor Charles III the Fat takes control, temporarily reuniting most of the Holy Roman Empire.
885	Ashot IV, Prince of Armenia, assumes the title King Ashot I.
886	Paris besieged by Vikings, who are paid off by Charles the Fat. London retaken by Alfred, who gives it and English Mercia to his son-in-law Aethelred.

887 Charles III deposed as emperor at Tribur; the Carolingian Empire falls apart.

888 Odo Count of Paris elected king of France; Berengar I of Friuli, grandson of Louis the Pious, becomes king of Italy. Rudolf I becomes king of a reformed Burgundy.

889 Donald II succeeds his cousin Eochaid as king of Scotland. Guido of Spoleto replaces Berengar I as king of Italy.

890 Alfred the Great establishes an English navy and militia. Harald I Finehair defeats his opponents at Hafursfjord and claims the sovereignty of Norway.

891 Guido of Spoleto crowned first non-Carolingian Holy Roman Emperor. Arnulf of Germany drives the Vikings from his country.

892 Caliph al-Mu'tamid dies; he is succeeded by his nephew al-Mu'tadid. The Vikings launch another invasion attempt on England.

893 The Vikings are decisively defeated by Alfred's son, Edward the Elder, at Farnham. Asser writes his life of Alfred.

894 Guido of Spoleto dies; his son Lambert succeeds him in Italy and as Emperor. Svatopluk I of Moravia, who has created the greater Moravian kingdom dies; his sons Moimir I and Svatopluk II jointly succeed him.

895 The Magyars, expelled from southern Russia, move under Arpad into Hungary.

896 By request of Pope Formosus, Arnulf of Germany replaces Lambert of Spoleto as Holy Roman Emperor, re-establishing Carolingian rule. Alfred defeats the Vikings at sea and ends their threat.

897 Pope Formosus' body is exhumed, dressed in papal vestments and tried for perjury; found guilty, it has three fingers cut off and is thrown into the Tiber.

898 Odo of France dies. The Carolingian pretender Charles III the Simple replaces him. Lambert of Spoleto dies and Berengar I reclaims the Italian crown.

899 Alfred the Great dies, and his son Edward succeeds him. Emperor Arnulf dies, and is succeeded in Germany by his son Louis III the Child.

900 Gunbjorn discovers Greenland. The Arab physician al-Razi identifies measles, smallpox, plague, consumption and rabies.

901 Louis III of Provence, grandson of Emperor Louis II, crowned Holy Roman Emperor. Edward the Elder takes the title 'King of the Angles and Saxons'.

902 With the fall of Taormina to the Arabs, Sicily is lost to Byzantium.

903 Pope Leo V is deposed after one month as Pontiff by Christopher, who lasts a year.

904 Leo of Tripoli commands an Arab fleet that sacks Thessalonica. The election of Pope Sergius III leads to a period of pornocracy in the Vatican.

905 Emperor Louis III surprised and blinded by insurgents, leading to his deposition from the imperial throne. Sancho I of Navarre succeeds his brother Fortun Garces and makes the county a kingdom. Shaiban succeeds his nephew Harun as king of Egypt, but is deposed shortly after; the Tulunid dynasty falls as a result.

906 Annam gains independence from China.

907 Fall of the Tang dynasty following conquest by Khitan Mongols. The Later Liang Dynasty under Taizu replaces it. The Magyars invade and destroy the Moravian empire of Moimir I, who perishes in the invasion.

909 The Fatimid dynasty is founded in Tunisia when al-Mahdi claims the caliphate.

910 The Byzantine Emperor Leo VI is forced to pay tribute to the Magyars. The kingdom of Asturias is renamed the kingdom of León its new capital. The Abbey of Cluny is founded.

911 Normandy established as a Norse province by the treaty of Saint-Clair-sur-Epte; Hrolf (Rollo) becomes duke. Louis III of Germany dies, the Carolingians die out and Conrad I of Franconia is elected king in his place.

912 Abdul-Rahman III succeeds his grandfather Abdullah as emir of Cordoba. The Byzantine Emperor Leo VI dies; his brother Alexander II succeeds him.

913 Emperor Alexander II dies; his nephew Constantine VII, still a child, succeeds him. Byzantium refuses to pay its tribute to Symeon of Bulgaria, who calls himself Emperor of the Romans but fails to take Constantinople.

914 With the death of Pope Lando, no Pope until John Paul I in 1978 will take a name that has not been used by a Pope before, starting with Lando's successor, John X.

915 Berengar I of Italy is crowned Holy Roman Emperor, the last Carolingian to hold the title.

916 Essex taken from the Vikings by king Edward the Elder.

917 Symeon of Bulgaria overruns Thrace and now controls the Balkans.

918 Deaths of Conrad I of Germany and Lady Aethelflaed of the Mercians. The latter acknowledge Edward the Elder as their king; he now controls all England south of the Humber.

919 Henry the Fowler, duke of Saxony, elected king of Germany. Ragnald the Viking seizes York, and makes himself king.

920 Edward the Elder acknowledged as overlord by the kings of Scotland, York and Strathclyde.

921 Sitric Caoch of Dublin succeeds Ragnald as king of York.

922 Charles III of France deposed by his barons, who elect Robert Capet, duke of Francia, king in his place; Charles raises an army to contest this.

923 Robert of France killed at the battle of Soissons, but Charles III is defeated and imprisoned; Duke Rudolf of Burgundy, Robert's son-in-law, is elected by the barons as king. Fall of the Later Liang dynasty in China, Li Cunxu of the Later Tang replacing Modi as emperor, taking the name Zhuengzong.

924 Edward the Elder of Wessex and England dies; his son Athelstan is hailed king in Mercia but Wessex disputes the succession. Symeon of Bulgaria unsuccessfully attacks Constantinople. Emperor Berengar, king of Italy, dies; the Imperial crown falls into abeyance.

925 Athelstan crowned king of England, having finally been accepted by Wessex. Henry the Fowler conquers Lorraine.

926 Symeon of Bulgaria defeated by Croat allies of the Byzantine Empire. Hugh of Arles becomes king of Italy after Rudolf II of Burgundy resigns the throne.

927	Symeon of Bulgaria dies. His son Peter succeeds him and signs a peace treaty with the Byzantines. Sitric of York dies. He is succeeded by his brother Guthfrith who is forced to flee when Athelstan conquers York and Southern Northumbria. The kings of Scotland and Strathclyde acknowledge Athelstan as their overlord.
928	Cornwall subdued by Athelstan, who sets the River Tamar as its boundary.
929	Duke Wenceslas of Bohemia murdered by non-Christians led by his brother Boleslav I, who succeeds him. Charles III of France dies, leaving Rudolf II as sole king. Emir Abdul-Rahman III of Corboba proclaims himself caliph.
930	The Black Stone stolen from the Kaaba in Mecca by the Carmathians, a Muslim sect.
931	Rameiro II succeeds his brother Alfonso IV as king of León.
932	William Longsword succeeds his father Rollo as duke of Normandy.
933	Henry the Fowler defeats Magyar raiders at the battle of Merseburg.
934	Scotland invaded by Athelstan, whose fleet ravages the coast as far as Caithness.
936	Louis IV (d'Outremer) returns from exile in England to be king of France after the death of Duke Rudolf of Burgundy. Henry the Fowler dies, and is succeeded by his son Otto I. The Tang dynasty falls in China; Shi Jing-tang of the Later Jin replaces Feidi as emperor, taking the name Gaozu.
937	Athelstan defeats a coalition of his foes at Brunanburh (whereabouts unknown), cementing his power in Britain. King Rudolf of Burgundy dies, his son Conrad succeeding him.
938	Yenching (later Peking and Beijing) founded as a Khitan capital.
939	Athelstan dies, and is succeeded by his half-brother Edmund (the Elder). Olaf Guthricson retakes York for the Vikings. Otto I defeats Eberhard of Franconia and his ducal allies at Andernach, confirming his monarchical authority in Germany.
940	Olaf of York invades the Midlands. By the treaty of Leicester much of the old Danelaw is ceded to him.
941	Igor of Kiev attacks Constantinople by way of the River Dnieper and the Black Sea, but his fleet is destroyed by Greek fire. Olaf of York dies; his cousin Olaf Sitricsson succeeds him.
942	Richard the Old succeeds his father William Longsword as duke of Normandy after the latter's murder by Arnold I of Flanders. The Five Boroughs of Derby, Leicester, Lincoln, Nottingham and Stamford are recovered by Edmund the Elder. Erik Bloodaxe succeeds his father Harald I Finehair as king of Norway on the latter's abdication at the age of 80.
943	Constantine I of Scotland abdicates and retires to a monastery, his son Malcolm I succeeds him. Byzantine troops recover the Mandylion.
944	Edmund the Elder recovers York, expelling Ragnald Guthricson, who had usurped the throne from his cousin Olaf the previous year.
945	Igor of Kiev dies; he is succeeded by his wife Olga. Mozambique attacked by Indonesians. Imad ibn-Buwayhid conquers Baghdad, keeping Caliph al-Mustaqfi as a figurehead. Louis IV taken prisoner by Hugh the Great, duke of France.
946	Caliph al-Mustaqfi deposed and blinded by the Buwayhids; his cousin al-Muti replaces him. Edmund the Elder and Otto I act in support of Louis IV, who is freed. Edmund the Elder assassinated at Pucklechurch; his brother Eadred succeeds him.
947	Eric Bloodaxe deposed as king of Norway by his brother Haakon I due to his violence. He flees to England where Wulfstan of York makes him king of that city. Hugh of Arles dies; his son Lothair of Arles succeeds him as king of Italy. The Later Jin dynasty falls in China, Emperor Chudi being replaced by Gaozu of the Later Han.
948	Eadred ravages Northumbria in response to their crowning of Eric Bloodaxe, who is forced to flee.
949	Olaf Sitricsson is invited to return as king of York.
950	Hywel Dda, prince of Deheubarth and Gwynedd and creator of a Welsh law code, dies; Gwynedd and Deheubarth separate. Mixcoatl, Toltec emperor, is assassinated and deified as a result; Lothair of Arles dies; Italy ruled jointly by Berengar II of Ivrea and his son Adalbert.
951	The Later Han dynasty falls in China; Emperor Yindi is replaced by Guo Wei of the Later Zhou, who takes the name Taizu.
952	Eric Bloodaxe returns to York and resumes the kingship.
954	Louis IV of France dies; his son Lothair succeeds him. Eric Bloodaxe forced to flee from York and is killed soon after; Eadred now rules all England.
955	Otto I decisively defeats the Magyars at the battle of Lechfeld. Eadred of England dies; his nephew Eadwig succeeds him.
956	St Dunstan, abbot of Glastonbury, exiled from England after a quarrel with King Eadwig.
957	Mercia and Northumbria rebel against Eadwig and choose his younger brother Edgar as their king.
959	Eadwig of Wessex dies; his brother Edgar the Peaceable succeeds him and reunites the kingdom of England. Emperor Constantine VII dies, his son Romanus II succeeds him.
960	Northern Song dynasty established by Zhao Kuangyin, who takes the name Taizu, replacing Gongdi of the Later Zhou. The kingdom of Poland created by King Mieszko I, who founds the Piast dynasty.
961	A Byzantine fleet commanded by Nicephorus Phocas recaptures Crete from the Arabs. Caliph Abdul-Rahman III of Cordoba dies; his son al-Hakam II succeeds him.
962	Otto I of Germany is crowned Holy Roman Emperor, re-establishing that title.
963	The Byzantine Emperor Romanus II is poisoned by his wife Theophano, who marries Nicephorus Phocas, elevating him to the imperial crown.
965	Cyprus recaptured from the Arabs by Byzantine forces. Al-Mutannabi, the Arab poet, is murdered by bandits.
966	Sancho I of León dies; he is succeeded by his son Ramiro III. King Dub of Scotland dies; he is succeeded by his third cousin Culen.
967	Duke Boleslav I of Bohemia dies; he is succeeded by his son Boleslav II.
968	Dinh Tien-Hoang De becomes king of North Vietnam, founding the Dinh dynasty.

969	Byzantine Emperor Nicephorus II Phocas murdered by his wife's lover, John Tzimisces, who rules in his stead. Cairo founded by the Fatimids, who have conquered Egypt.
970	Garcia II of Navarre dies, and is succeeded by his son Sancho II.
971	Culen of Scotland dies; he is succeeded by his third cousin Kenneth II. St Swithin reinterred inside Winchester Cathedral; 40 days of rain follow.
972	Boris II of Bulgaria forced to abdicate by the invading Byzantines, ending the Krum dynasty's reign in that country.
973	Holy Roman Emperor Otto I dies; he is succeeded by his son Otto II. Edgar of England crowned king at Bath.
975	Edgar dies, and is succeeded by his son Edward. Modern arithmetical notation introduced into Europe by the Arabs.
976	Byzantine Emperor John I Tzimisces dies; succeeded by Basil II, son of Romanus II. Leopold I of the house of Babenberg made Margrave of Austria. Caliph al-Hakam II of Cordoba dies; his son Hisham II succeeds him. Samuel makes himself Tsar of Bulgaria. Duke Henry the Quarrelsome of Bavaria deposed by Otto II.
978	Edward (the Martyr) assassinated at Corfe and succeeded by his half-brother Aethelred II (Unraed). Mohammad ibn abi-Amir al-Mansur, regent of Cordoba, takes effective control of the Caliphate there.
979	Dinh Tien-Hoang De of Dai Vet (Vietnam) dies; succeeded by his son Dinh De-Toan.
980	Le Dai-Hanh Hoang-De usurps the Dai Vet throne from Dinh De-Toan, establishing the Earlier Le Dynasty. Vladimir of Novgorod seizes Kiev from his brother Yaropolk I.
981	León made tributary to the Caliphate of Cordoba. Italy invaded by Arabs; Otto II marches against them but the Byzantines offer them support.
982	Otto II defeated by a combination of Byzantine and Arab forces at Basientello. Eric the Red settles in Greenland.
983	Emperor Otto II dies, his three-year-old son Otto III succeeds him.
984	Henry the Quarrelsome seizes Otto III in an attempt to make himself regent, but is thwarted by Otto II's widow Theophano of Byzantium.
985	Henry the Quarrelsome returned to the dukedom of Bavaria. Harald I Bluetooth of Denmark dies, and is succeeded by his son Sweyn I Forkbeard. Otto-William, a Carolingian prince, establishes the county of Burgundy.
986	Lothair of France dies, he is succeeded by his son Louis V. Sultan Sabuk-Tigan of Ghazni invades India. Bjarni Herjolfsson sights the coast of Labrador.
987	Louis V dies; the Carolingians are replaced as kings of France by the Capetians, when Hugh I is crowned King.
988	Vladimir of Kiev converts to Christianity, marries Anne, sister of Emperor Basil II, and sets about converting his subjects.
989	Emperor Basil II, with the aid of Russian troops, defeats Anatolian insurgents led by Bardas Phocas.
990	William IV of Aquitaine dies; succeeded by his son William V. Ghanaian forces take Awdaghost and establish the king of Ghana as the most powerful ruler in non-Islamic Africa.
991	Norsemen raid England led by Olaf Tryggvesson, defeating English forces under Ealdorman Byrhtnoth at Maldon; they are paid to leave by Danegeld.
992	Mieszko I of Poland dies, and is succeeded by his son Boleslav I the Brave, who invades Pomerania to gain access to the Baltic.
993	Khitan Mongols annex Korea .
994	Sweyn of Denmark, assisted by Olaf Tryggvesson, raids England, unsuccessfully besieges London and is paid off by Aethelred II. Olaf Tryggvesson converts to Christianity.
995	Syria retaken by the Byzantine Empire. Olaf Tryggvesson succeeds to the throne of Norway, and forcibly attempts to convert his subjects to Christianity.
996	Otto III crowned Holy Roman Emperor by his cousin Pope Gregory V. Hugh I of France dies, and is succeeded by his son Robert II. Richard I the Old, Duke of Normandy dies; succeeded by his son Richard II the Good. Emperor Basil II defeats the Bulgarians and recovers Greece.
997	Duke Geza of Hungary dies; succeeded by his son Stephen I. Sultan Sabuk-Tagin of Ghazni, in modern Afghanistan, dies; succeeded by his son Ismail.
998	Sultan Ismail of Ghazni dies; succeeded by his brother Mahmud.
999	Boleslav I of Poland conquers Silesia. Gerbert of Aurillac becomes Pope, taking the name Sylvester II; he is the first French Pope. Brian Boru conquers Dublin from the Norse settlers.
1000	Ceylon conquered by King Rajaraja of the Cholas. Stephen I of Hungary becomes king with Papal approval. Olaf Tryggvesson commits suicide after his defeat by the kings of Denmark and Sweden at the naval battle of Svolder; Erik Jarl of Lade replaces him as king of Norway.
1002	Emperor Otto III dies of malaria; succeeded by his cousin Henry II. Al-Mansur, chief minister of Cordoba dies, the Caliphate begins to decline. Aethelred II marries Emma, sister of Richard II of Normandy, and orders the massacre of Danish settlers in southern England.
1003	King Sweyn of Denmark raids England in revenge for the massacre of his countrymen, exacting tribute from Aethelred.
1004	China pays tribute to the Khitan Mongols as the result of a peace treaty. Emperor Henry II defeats Ardoin of Lombardy and is crowned king of that country.
1005	Kenneth III of Scotland is killed in battle against his cousin Malcolm II, who succeeds him.
1006	Islamic settlers arrive in north-western India. Mount Metrop erupts in Java, killing King Dharmawangs.
1007	Danegeld of £36,000 paid by Aethelred II to protect England from raids for two years.
1008	Sultan Mahmud of Ghazni defeats Hindu forces at Peshawar and expands his realms.
1009	Caliph al-Hakim of Egypt sacks the Church of the Holy Sepulchre in Jerusalem. Caliph Hisham II of Cordoba deposed by his cousin Muhammad II, who is deposed in his turn by his cousin Suleiman.
1010	The 'Peace of God' established in France by Robert II. Danish forces under Thorkell the Tall defeat the East

Anglians at Ringmere. Muhammad II regains the caliphate of Cordoba from Suleiman, but is ousted again, this time by a returning Hisham II.

1011	Canterbury taken by the Danes, who capture Archbishop Alphege.
1012	Danegeld of £48,000 paid to the Danes, who nevertheless kill Alphege before they leave. Thorkell the Tall defects to the English. Persecution of heretics in Germany commences.
1013	Sweyn Forkbeard conquers England, helped by Thorkell, who redefects. Aethelred II flees to Normandy. Hisham II of Cordoba dies, and is succeeded by Suleiman.
1014	Sweyn dies, and Aethelred returns from exile. Brian Boru wins the battle of Clontarf but is killed. Emperor Basil II seizes Western Bulgaria and blinds the resisting native army.
1015	Olaf II succeeds Eric as king of Norway and establishes its independence from Denmark. Cnut invades England and Wessex submits to him.
1016	Aethelred II dies, succession disputed between his son Edmund Ironside and Cnut. Cnut wins the battle of Ashingdon; Edmund allowed to reign in Wessex but dies shortly afterwards.
1017	Cnut divides England into four earldoms, Wessex, East Anglia, Mercia and Northumbria, for administrative purposes.
1018	The treaty of Bautzen ends the war between Germany and Poland. Macedonia regained by the Byzantines after the submission of the Bulgarians.
1019	Yaroslav I the Wise succeeds his brother Sviatopolk I as prince of Kiev. Cnut becomes king of Denmark on the death of his brother Harald II.
1020	Corsica annexed by Pisa. Faroes, Shetlands and Orkneys recognize Olaf II of Norway as king. Godwin becomes earl of Wessex.
1021	Emperor Basil II invades Armenia. An epidemic of St Vitus' Dance sweeps Europe.
1022	Emperor Henry II defeats a Byzantine army in Southern Italy. The Synod of Pavia decrees celibacy for higher clergy.
1023	Abdul-Rahman V becomes caliph of Cordoba, replacing the Hammudid al-Qasim of Malaga.
1024	Emperor Henry II dies. He is succeeded by his second cousin twice removed, Conrad II of Franconia. Boleslav I of Poland is crowned king of that country.
1025	Emperor Basil II dies, and is succeeded by his brother Constantine VIII. Boleslav I of Poland dies and is succeeded by his son Mieszko II and reverts to the title of prince.
1026	Cnut thwarts a combined Norwegian and Swedish attack at the sea battle of the Holy River. Guido d'Arezzo introduces solmization in music.
1027	Robert I the Devil becomes duke of Normandy on the death of his brother Richard III.
1028	Cnut conquers Norway and sends his son Sweyn to rule it. Emperor Constantine VIII dies, succeeded by his daughter Zoë. Romanus III becomes co-emperor upon marrying her. Sancho III of Navarre conquers Castile.
1030	Olaf II of Norway attempts to win back his throne, but is defeated and killed by Cnut's forces at Stiklestad. Sultan Mahmud of Ghazni dies, and is succeeded by his son Muhammad.
1031	Muhammad of Ghazni deposed and blinded by his brother Masud I. Caliph Hisham III deposed, ending the Umayyad Caliphate of Cordoba, which fragments. Robert II the Pious of France dies; succeeded by his son Henry I.
1032	Rudolf III of Burgundy dies without an heir, and Conrad II unites the kingdom with the Empire.
1033	Mieszko II of Poland defeated by combined German and Russian forces and his realm forced to become a fief of the Empire. Castile granted independence from Navarre.
1034	Empress Zoe murders Romanus III and marries Michael IV, who becomes co-Emperor. Mieszko of Poland dies; his son Kasimir I succeeds him but the country plunges into civil war. Malcolm II of Scotland dies, and is succeeded by his grandson Duncan I.
1035	Duke Robert the Magnificent of Normandy dies on pilgrimage to Jerusalem. His illegitimate son William (the future 'Conqueror') succeeds, sparking a succession dispute. Sancho III of Navarre dies, and is succeeded in Navarre by his son Garcia IV and in Castile by his son Ferdinand I. Cnut dies. Harthacnut succeeds him in Denmark and England, but his brother Harold seizes England for himself. Magnus I the Good, son of Olaf II, regains Norwegian independence, defeating Sweyn.
1036	Alfred, son of Aethelred II, returns to England but is murdered by Godwin of Wessex. Harold I (Harefoot) proclaimed Regent of England.
1037	Harold I proclaimed king of England. Ferdinand I of Castile conquers León, deposing Vermudo III. The Islamic philosopher and physician Avicenna dies.
1038	King Stephen of Hungary dies, and is succeeded by his nephew by marriage Peter Orseolo.
1039	Emperor Conrad II dies, succeeded by his son Henry III. Gruffydd ap Llywelyn, prince of Gwynedd, defeats an English invading force on the River Severn.
1040	Macbeth defeats and kills King Duncan of Scotland and assumes the crown. Harold I dies; Harthacnut successfully claims the English crown by right of succession.
1041	Samuel Aba usurps the Hungarian throne from Peter Orseolo. Co-Emperor Michael IV dies; his nephew Michael V fills the breach.
1042	Harthacnut dies; his half-brother Edward the Confessor is elected king whilst Magnus of Norway takes Denmark. Michael V imprisons the Empress Zoë, but a rebellion blinds him, locks him in a monastery and frees Zoë, who marries Constantine IX and makes him co-Emperor.
1043	Samuel Aba of Hungary invades Bavaria, where he is countered by Emperor Henry III. Coventry Abbey founded by Leofric of Mercia.
1044	Emperor Henry III defeats Samuel Aba's Hungarians and restores Peter Orseolo to his throne. Anawrata founds the Pagan dynasty in Burma.
1045	The deposed Pope Benedict IX retakes the throne from Sylvester III by force, and then sells it to Gregory VI.
1046	Peter Orseolo of Hungary deposed by his second cousin Andras I. Emperor Henry III forces Gregory VI to

abdicate on grounds of simony, ratifies the depositions of his two predecessors and installs Clement II at the Synod of Rome.

1047 Norman rebels defeated at Val-ès-Dunes by Duke William, who thus lies secure in his rule. King Magnus dies. Sweyn II, a nephew of Cnut, succeeds him in Denmark, whilst Harald III Hardrada, Magnus' uncle, succeeds him in Norway.

1048 Last Viking raid on south-east England, the raiders flee to Flanders, which is attacked by Edward the Confessor and Emperor Henry III.

1049 Leo IX elected Pope after the death of Damasus II.

1050 Empress Zoë dies, her older sister Theodora succeeding her. Robert of Jumièges becomes Archbishop of Canterbury.

1051 Earl Godwin of Wessex rebels unsuccessfully against Edward the Confessor, he and his family flee to Flanders.

1052 Earl Godwin and his family return to power in England. Stigand uncanonically becomes Archbishop of Canterbury as Archbishop Robert is forced to flee. Pisa takes Sardinia from the Arabs.

1053 Robert Guiscard defeats Papal forces at Civitate, capturing Leo IX, before taking Benevento from the Byzantines and founding a Norman state in Southern Italy. Godwin of Wessex dies, his son Harold succeeding him as earl.

1054 Final schism between Roman Catholic and Orthodox churches. Henry I of France invades Normandy and is defeated at Mortemer. Macbeth defeated by Malcolm Canmore and Earl Siward of Northumbria at Dunsinane.

1055 Seljuk Turks led by Togril-Beg enter Baghdad to liberate the Abbasid Caliphate from Shiite control; Togril-Beg makes himself the Caliph's temporal master. Co-Emperor Constantine IX dies, Theodora reigns alone. Earl Siward of Northumbria dies, and is succeeded six-year-old by Tostig Godwinson.

1056 Emperor Henry III dies, succeeded by his son Henry IV. Empress Theodora dies, ending the reign of the Macedonian dynasty in Byzantium. Michael VI succeeds her.

1057 Macbeth killed by Malcolm III Canmore at Lumphanan, but is succeeded by his stepson Lulach. Isaac Comnenus overthrows Emperor Michael VI.

1058 Lulach killed by Malcolm III Canmore, who becomes king of Scotland. Prince Kasimir I of Poland dies; succeeded by his son Boleslav II.

1059 By the treaty of Melfi Robert Guiscard becomes Duke of Apulia and Sicily and swears fealty to the Papacy. Emperor Isaac Comnenus abdicates in favour of Constantine X.

1060 Andras I of Hungary deposed by his brother Bela I. Henry I of France dies; succeeded by his son Philip I.

1061 Northumbria raided by Malcolm III of Scotland. Duke Spitihnev II of Bohemia dies, succeeded by his brother Vratislav II.

1062 By the Coup d'Etat of Kaiserswerth, Emperor Henry IV seized by Archbishop Anno of Cologne, who takes power in Germany alongside Archbishop Adalbert of Bremen.

1063 Gwynedd conquered by Earls Harold and Tostig; Prince Gruffydd killed by his own men. Bela I of Hungary dies, succeeded by his nephew Salomon, son of deposed king Andras. Alp Arslan succeeds his uncle Togril-Beg as sultan of the Seljuk Turks.

1064 Belgrade seized by the Hungarians from Byzantium. Armenia conquered by Alp Arslan.

1065 Ferdinand I of Castile and León dies; succeeded by his sons Sancho II in Castile and Alfonso VI in León. Westminster Abbey is consecrated.

1066 Death of Edward the Confessor causes succession dispute in England. Harold II Godwinson chosen king, defeats and kills Harald Hardrada at Stamford Bridge but is defeated and killed at Hastings by William of Normandy, who becomes king.

1067 Emperor Constantine X dies; his widow marries Romanus IV Diogenes, who becomes Emperor. Boleslav II of Poland captures Kiev. El Cid founds the world's first leper hospital in Castile.

1068 Earls Edwin and Morcar rebel against William I, but are defeated in York.

1069 Northumbrians and Mercians rebel, with Danish help, against William I, but the risings are put down and William devastates Northumbria ('the harrying of the North').

1070 The Order of the Knights of St John founded in Jerusalem by Amalfian merchants. Sweyn II of Denmark attacks England, but is bought off by William I, who puts down the revolt of Hereward the Wake.

1071 Robert Guiscard captures Bari, thus expelling the Byzantines from Italy. Byzantine forces heavily defeated at Manzikert under Alp Arslan, by Seljuk Turks who capture Emperor Romanus. When released he is blinded by the Byzantines, who select Michael VII as Emperor, and dies soon after. The Seljuqs now control Asia Minor.

1072 Sancho II of Castile murdered at the siege of Zamora whilst fighting Navarrese forces. He is succeeded by his brother Alfonso VI of León. Palermo taken by Robert and Roger Guiscard. Alp Arslan murdered by a captive while campaigning in Transoxiana; his son Malik Shah becomes sultan.

1073 Hildebrand of Soana elected Pope, taking the title Gregory VII.

1074 Salomon of Hungary deposed by his cousin Geza I. Robert Guiscard excommunicated by Gregory VII, who also excommunicates all married priests.

1075 Malik Shah subdues Syria and Palestine. Gregory VII bans simony and declares the Pope to be absolute sovereign of the Church.

1076 German bishops at the Synod of Worms declare Gregory VII deposed and Henry IV demands Gregory's abdication. Gregory excommunicates the bishops and Henry, whom he declares deposed. Thus the 'Investiture Contest' begins between Emperor and Pope, over the right of the Emperor to appoint bishops, who hold secular as well as spiritual power.

1077 When Henry IV does penance at Canossa to Gregory VII, the Germans declare him deposed and elect Rudolf of Swabia as anti-king. Geza I of Hungary dies, and is succeeded by his brother Ladislas I.

1078 Emperor Michael VII abdicates; Nicephorus III elected in his place.

1079 King Boleslav II of Poland excommunicated by Bishop (later Saint) Stanislas of Cracow, who is assassinated on Boleslav's orders. Gregory VII excommunicates Boleslav, who is deposed by a revolt by his nobles and succeeded by his brother Vladislav I Herman, who reverts to the title Prince.

1080 Anti-king Rudolf of Swabia defeated and killed by Henry IV's forces. Gregory VII again excommunicates and deposes Henry IV, who then seeks to depose Gregory, replacing him with the Archbishop of Ravenna as Clement III.

1081 Emperor Nicephorus III abdicates in favour of Alexius I Comnenus. Emperor Henry IV invades Italy seeking to establish Clement III as Pope.

1082 Bishop Odo, Earl of Kent, revolts against his half-brother William I, but is stripped of his earldom and imprisoned.

1083 The Kiyowara family revolt in northern Japan; Yoshiiye Minamoto sent to quell the rebellion.

1084 The Synod of Rome deposes Gregory VII and recognizes Clement III, but Henry IV and Clement III are forced to withdraw when Robert Guiscard advances in support of Gregory from Southern Italy.

1085 Toledo taken from the Arabs by Alfonso VI of Castile. Pope Gregory VII dies at Salerno. Robert Guiscard dies, and is succeeded as duke of Apulia by his son Roger Borsa. William I commissions the Domesday Book.

1086 Islamic rule in Southern Spain rejuvenated by the Almoravids of Morocco, who defeat Alfonso VI of Castile at Zallaka. The Domesday Book is compiled. Cnut IV of Denmark dies, ending an invasion threat to England. His brother Olaf IV succeeds him.

1087 William I dies of an injury sustained at the siege of Mantes, and is succeeded by his sons Robert in Normandy and William II Rufus in England.

1088 Urban II elected Pope, but only partially recognized. Bishop Odo and various Norman barons in England rebel against William II, but the revolt is crushed.

1089 Archbishop Lanfranc of Canterbury dies, but no successor is chosen, so William II can enjoy the revenues of the see.

1090 Count Roger Guiscard of Sicily captures Malta from the Arabs.

1091 William II of England and Robert of Normandy make their peace by the treaty of Caen. Malcolm III of Scotland invades Northumbria, but is repulsed by William and Robert and acknowledges William as his overlord.

1092 The Seljuk vizier Nizam al-Malik assassinated by the Ismailite sect, the Hashashin (Assassins). King Vratislav of Bohemia dies. He is succeeded for a short while by his brother Conrad and then his son Bretislav II, who reverts to the title Duke. William II takes Cumberland from the Scots and refounds Carlisle as his north-western outpost.

1093 William II falls gravely ill and appoints St Anselm to the see of Canterbury, recovering soon after. Malcolm III invades Northumbria again but is killed near Alnwick; his wife Margaret dies 4 days later. He is succeeded by his brother Donald III Bane.

1094 Rodrigo Diaz de Vivar, El Cid, takes Valencia from the Moors. Donald Bane is deposed from the Scottish throne by his nephew Duncan II, who dies after six months. Donald Bane returns to the throne.

1095 Ladislas I of Hungary conquers Croatia and Dalmatia but dies soon after, and is succeeded by his nephew Koloman. Olaf IV of Denmark dies, and is succeeded by his brother Erik I. First Crusade launched by Pope Urban II at the council of Clermont, aiming to take Jerusalem and the Holy Land from the Seljuk Turks.

1096 Peter the Hermit preaches the crusade in France and Germany, assembling a rag-tag force which goes East. Germans such as Ermich of Leiningen take advantage of crusade hysteria to persecute Jews in the Holy Roman Empire. Robert of Normandy leases his duchy to William II in order to go on crusade.

1097 Peter the Hermit's crusaders massacred near Nicaea in Asia Minor by Seljuk Turks, but the main crusading force wins major victories both there and at Dorylaeum. Donald Bane of Scotland deposed with William II's help, and replaced by his nephew Edgar.

1098 Robert de Molesme founds the monastery of Cîteaux, and thereby the Cistercian order. Magnus III of Norway seizes the Orkneys, Hebrides and Isle of Man. Crusaders take Antioch after a lengthy siege.

1099 Jerusalem captured by the crusaders; Godfrey of Bouillon becomes Advocate of the Holy Sepulchre. El Cid dies at Cuenca after defeat by the Almoravids.

1100 Godfrey of Bouillon dies, and his brother Baldwin succeeds him and founds the Kingdom of Jerusalem. William II of England dies whilst hunting, and is succeeded by his brother Henry I.

1101 Robert of Normandy invades England to take the throne from brother Henry, but is bought off by the treaty of Alton. Roger d'Hauteville, count of Sicily, dies; succeeded by his son Simon.

1102 Vladislav I of Poland abdicates, and is succeeded after a power struggle by his son Boleslav III. Alfonso VI of Castile raises the year-long siege of Valencia.

1103 Magnus III of Norway invades Ireland, but is killed in battle; his son Eysten I succeeds him. Bohemund of Otranto ransomed from captivity by the Danishmend Emir.

1104 Acre taken by crusaders under Baldwin I of Jerusalem. Mount Hekla in Iceland erupts violently.

1105 Emperor Henry IV is captured by his son Henry and is forced to abdicate in favour of him; when he breaks the terms of his abdication he is imprisoned.

1106 Henry IV escapes from prison but dies whilst raising an army against his son, who succeeds him. Henry of England defeats Robert of Normandy at Tinchebrai, dispossessing Robert of his duchy and imprisoning him.

1107 King Edgar of Scotland dies, and his succeeded by his brother Alexander I.

1108 Philip I of France dies, and is succeeded by his son Louis VI. Bohemund of Otranto defeated by the Emperor Alexius at Durazzo.

1109 Boleslav III of Poland defeats Emperor Henry V at Hundsfeld. Crusaders led by Raymond of St Gilles take Tripoli and Beirut; Raymond founds the County of Tripoli.

1110 The earliest known miracle play performed at Dunstable.

1111 Henry V crowned emperor under duress by Pope Paschal II. Bohemund of Otranto dies, and is succeeded as prince of Antioch by his nephew Tancred. Count Roger of Apulia dies; his son William II succeeds him.

1112 Emperor Henry V excommunicated. Tancred of Antioch dies, and is succeeded by his nephew Roger of Salerno. Henry of Burgundy, count of Portugal, dies, and is succeeded by his son Alfonso I.

1113 Pisa conquers the Balearic Islands. Sviatopolk of Kiev dies, and is succeeded by his cousin Vladimir II Monomach. The Knights Hospitaller resolve to defend the Holy Land.

1114 Pipe rolls introduced by Bishop Roger of Salisbury as a means of recording Exchequer accounts.

1115 St Bernard founds a monastery at Clairvaux and becomes its first abbot. The Juchens create the Chinese state of Jin under their chieftain Aguda.

1116 Coloman of Hungary dies; succeeded by his son Stephen II.

1117 St Magnus, earl of Orkney, murdered on the island of Egilsay on the orders of his cousin Earl Haakon.

1118 The Knights Templar founded in Jerusalem by Hugh de Payens. Emperor Alexius I dies, and is succeeded by his son John II. Baldwin I of Jerusalem dies, and is succeeded by his great-nephew Baldwin II. Alfonso I of Aragon takes Zaragoza from the Almoravids and makes it his capital.

1119 Count Baldwin VII of Flanders dies; succeeded by his cousin Charles the Good. Crusading armies are heavily defeated at the Field of Blood in Syria. Roger of Antioch is killed.

1120 Prince William, heir and only legitimate son of Henry I, drowns in the wreck of the *White Ship*.

1121 Peter Abelard's teachings on the Trinity condemned at the Synod of Soissons.

1122 Emperor John II wipes out the Pecheneg Turks in the Balkans. The Investiture Question is finally settled with the Concordat of Worms; Emperor Henry V renounces the right of investiture.

1123 Emperor John II defeats the Serbs in the Balkans. Marriage of priests banned by the First Lateran Council. The Augustinian canon Rahere founds St Bartholomew's Hospital in London.

1124 Emperor John II defeats the Hungarians. Alexander I of Scotland dies; succeeded by his brother David I.

1125 Emperor Henry V dies, leaving no successor; Lothair of Saxony is elected to succeed him. Morocco conquered by the Almohads.

1126 Emperor Lothair III makes his son-in-law, Henry X the Proud, duke of Bavaria, succeeding Henry's father, Henry IX. Chinese Emperor Huizong dies after being captured by the Jin; his son Qinzong succeeds him.

1127 The Jin overrun Northern China and Emperor Qinzong perishes; his brother Gaozong flees south and establishes the Southern Song dynasty. Count William III of Apulia dies, Roger of Sicily claims overlordship, but the inhabitants appeal to the Pope for protection. Roger is excommunicated.

1128 Count Charles the Good of Flanders is murdered; Louis VI attempts to impose Robert of Normandy on the county but the inhabitants install Thierry of Alsace, a cousin of Charles. The Templars gain papal recognition; St Bernard draws up their rule. Alfonso I of Portugal defeats Alfonso VII of Castile at São Mamede and shakes off Castilian overlordship. Pope Honorius accepts Roger of Sicily's claim to Apulia and invests him as count.

1129 First Cistercian abbey founded in England, at Waverley. Henry of Blois becomes Bishop of Winchester. Count Fulk V of Anjou resigns the county to his son Geoffrey and goes to Jerusalem to marry Melisande, heiress to King Baldwin II.

1130 Pope Honorius II dies. Innocent II is elected to succeed him but the election is disputed and an antipope, Anacletus II, is also elected. Innocent II flees to France, where he is championed by St Bernard, while Anacletus is backed by Roger II of Sicily, whom he crowns king of that country.

1131 Baldwin II of Jerusalem dies, and is succeeded by his son-in-law Fulk V. Rievaulx Abbey founded.

1132 Fountains Abbey founded.

1133 Lothair III crowned Emperor by Innocent II in the Lateran while the antipope Anacletus II is established in St Peter's. St Bartholomew's Fair founded in London.

1134 Emperor Lothair makes Albert the Bear margrave of Brandenburg and head of the North March.

1135 Henry I of England dies of a surfeit of lampreys; although he made his barons swear that his daughter Matilda would succeed him, his nephew Stephen of Blois engineers his own coronation as king.

1136 Emperor Lothair takes Apulia from Roger II of Sicily. Peter Abelard writes his *Historia calamitatum mearum*.

1137 Louis VI of France dies, and is succeeded by his son Louis VII. Gruffydd ap Cynan, prince of Gwynedd, dies, and is succeeded by his son Owain Gwynedd. Emperor Lothair III dies.

1138 Conrad III of Hohenstaufen elected emperor to succeed Lothair III. When Boleslav III of Poland dies, his country is divided amongst his four sons. David I of Scotland invades England in support of Matilda but is defeated at the battle of the Standard.

1139 The Second Lateran Council ends the schism in the Church. Innocent II is now universally recognized as Pope. Alfonso I crowned king of Portugal. Matilda lands at Arundel, staking her claim to the English throne; anarchy breaks out in the country.

1140 Prince Sobeslav I of Bohemia dies, and is succeeded by his son Vladislav II. Peter Abelard is condemned for heresy at the council of Sens, on a motion railroaded through by St Bernard.

1141 Stephen of England taken prisoner after defeat at Lincoln. Matilda proclaimed queen, but her high-handed behaviour alienates many, in particular London. Stephen is released in exchange for Robert, earl of Gloucester, and Matilda is forced back on the defensive.

1142 The duchy of Bavaria is conferred by Conrad III on Margrave Henry II of Austria. Peter Abelard dies, worn out by the Church's ill-treatment.

1143 Emperor John II of Byzantium dies, and is succeeded by his son Manuel I. Fulk V of Jerusalem dies; his son Baldwin III succeeds him.

1144 Geoffrey of Anjou subdues Normandy and is proclaimed duke. Imad-ud-Din Zangi, sultan of Mosul, captures Edessa, in eastern Turkey, causing alarm in Outremer and in Western Europe.

1145 Arnold of Brescia establishes a republic in Rome; the newly-crowned Pope Eugenius III is forced to flee. St Bernard takes the lead in proclaiming the Second Crusade, to avenge the fall of Edessa.

1146 Zangi of Mosul is murdered, and succeeded by his formidable son Nur-ud-Din, who consolidates the conquest of Edessa.

1147	The Second Crusade collapses in chaos as the crusaders attack Damascus, an ally of Jerusalem, thus alienating it. Lisbon however is taken from the Moors by King Alfonso of Portugal. Matilda leaves England; her son Henry is left to carry on the fight, though only fourteen.
1148	Sugar brought back from the Middle East by returning crusaders.
1149	Raymond of Poitiers, prince of Antioch, killed by Nur-ud-Din.
1150	The University of Paris is founded. *The Black Book of Carmarthen*, an anthology of ancient Welsh poetry, is compiled.
1151	Geoffrey of Anjou dies, and is succeeded in Anjou, Normandy and associated domains by his son Henry. Fire and plague insurance policies are developed in Iceland.
1152	Emperor Conrad III dies and is succeeded by his nephew Frederick I Barbarossa. Louis VII divorces Eleanor of Aquitaine, who promptly marries Henry of Anjou.
1153	David I of Scotland dies; succeeded by his grandson Malcolm IV. Ascalon falls to Baldwin III of Jerusalem. St Bernard of Clairvaux dies. The Treaty of Wallingford brings the English anarchy to an end by recognizing Henry of Anjou as Stephen's heir.
1154	Roger II of Sicily dies; succeeded by his son William I. Damascus surrenders to Nur-ud-Din, who now controls most of Syria. Stephen of England dies and is succeeded by Henry, who now rules half of France as well as England. On the death of Anastasius IV, Nicholas Breakspear is elected Pope, taking the name Adrian IV.
1155	Ireland bestowed on Henry II by Pope Adrian IV. Adrian IV restores papal authority in Rome. Arnold of Brescia is hanged as a heretic by Emperor Frederick. St Berthold founds the Carmelite order of monks.
1156	Austria made a duchy with special status by Emperor Frederick. William I of Sicily recovers Bari from the Greeks and makes his peace with Rome.
1157	Erik IX of Sweden conquers and forcibly converts Finland. Alfonso VII of Castile dies; he is succeeded by his sons Sancho III in Castile and Ferdinand II in León.
1158	Prince Vladislav of Bohemia elevated to king by Emperor Frederick. Sancho III of Castile dies, and is succeeded by his infant son Alfonso VIII.
1159	Pope Adrian IV dies, and is succeeded by Alexander III. John of Salisbury writes the *Policraticus*, a treatise on government.
1160	Emperor Frederick, incensed by witnessing the inhabitants of Crema dismembering their prisoners during his siege, hurls his own prisoners over the walls before entering and destroying the city.
1161	Edward the Confessor is canonized.
1162	Emperor Frederick destroys Milan. Thomas Becket is chosen as Archbishop of Canterbury. Danegeld – by now just a general tax – is collected in England for the final time.
1163	The Welsh rebel against Henry II, but the revolt is suppressed and Prince Rhys ap Gruffydd is imprisoned. Henry II and Thomas Becket quarrel over the Church's status vis-à-vis the monarch.
1164	Legal rights of Church and State codified by Henry II at the council of Clarendon; Becket rejects the code and is forced to flee after he is condemned at the council of Northampton. Héloïse dies and is buried next to Abelard.
1165	Emperor Manuel allies with Venice against Emperor Frederick. Malcolm IV of Scotland dies, and is succeeded by his brother William the Lion. Charlemagne is canonized.
1166	*The Song of Cnut* written down by a monk of Ely. The erection of jails in all English counties ordered by the Assize of Clarendon. William I of Sicily dies, and is succeeded by his son William II.
1167	Oxford University is created when English students are barred from attending Paris.
1168	Milan is rebuilt. Prince Andrei I Bogoliubsky of Vladimir-Suzdal sacks Kiev and assumes the title Grand Prince.
1169	Saladin becomes vizier to the Fatimid caliph al-'Adid of Cairo, effectively controlling Egypt. Norman-Welsh barons land at Wexford supporting King Dermot of Leinster's efforts to regain his throne.
1170	Henry II has his son Henry crowned joint-king (the 'Young King'). Richard Strongbow, earl of Pembroke, takes Waterford and marries Dermot of Leinster's daughter. Thomas Becket returns to Canterbury, but is murdered four weeks later.
1171	Dermot of Leinster dies, and is succeeded by his son-in-law Richard Strongbow, who is forced to accept Henry II as his overlord when Henry crosses to Ireland. Saladin abolishes the Fatimid caliphate and rules Egypt himself.
1172	Henry II receives homage from the Irish at Cashel, but his wife Eleanor raises Aquitaine against him, forcing him to seek a reconciliation with Pope Alexander at Avranches.
1173	Henry II's wife and sons revolt against him, supported by William the Lion of Scotland and Louis VII of France. Eleanor of Aquitaine is captured and imprisoned. Thomas Becket is canonized.
1174	Henry II does public penance for Becket's murder and subdues the revolt against him. Nur-ud-Din dies and a fight for power in the Arab world ensues. Saladin takes Damascus. Amalric I of Jerusalem dies, and is succeeded by his leper son Baldwin IV.
1175	By the treaty of Windsor Rory O'Connor recognized as High King of Ireland under Henry II's overlordship.
1176	The Lombard League defeats Emperor Frederick at Legnano. The first eisteddfod is held at Cardigan Castle. Construction starts at London Bridge.
1177	Baldwin IV of Jerusalem defeats Saladin at Ramleh. Angkor Wat, capital of the Khmer empire, falls to Champa invaders.
1178	Construction starts on the bridge at Avignon.
1179	The Waldensians, Roman Catholic reformers are forbidden to preach by the Pope without the permission of bishops. The Third Lateran Council rules that popes will henceforth be elected by a two-thirds majority of the College of Cardinals.
1180	Louis VII of France dies, and is succeeded by his son Philip Augustus. Emperor Manuel I dies, and is succeeded by his son Alexius II. Henry II reforms the English coinage.
1181	Pope Alexander III dies; Lucius III succeeds him.

1182	Valdemar I of Denmark dies, and is succeeded by his son Cnut VI. Revolts in Byzantium force Emperor Alexius II to make his father's cousin Andronicus co-Emperor.
1183	Emperor Alexius II murdered, and replaced by his co-emperor, Andronicus I. Emperor Frederick, the Pope and the Lombard League make the Peace of Constance. Saladin takes Aleppo. Henry the 'Young King', rebellious son of Henry II of England, dies.
1184	Cyprus gains freedom from Byzantium. Giorgi III of Georgia dies, and is succeeded by his daughter Thamar. Glastonbury Abbey burns down.
1185	Emperor Andronicus I killed by rioters and succeeded by Isaac II Angelus. Bulgarians under Peter and Ivan Asen revolt against Byzantium. Saladin takes Mosul. Prince John sent to govern Ireland, antagonizes the local lords and is recalled.
1186	Emperor Frederick marries his son Henry to Constance, heiress of Sicily, and has him crowned Caesar. Baldwin V of Jerusalem dies. The crown passes to Guy of Lusignan.
1187	Saladin defeats a crusader army at Hattin and takes Jerusalem. The Punjab conquered by the Ghaznavid Mohammad of Ghur. Bulgaria becomes independent under Ivan Asen.
1188	The Third Crusade is proclaimed; to this end the first general tax, the Saladin Tithe, is levied in France. Henry II quarrels with his son Richard and Philip II of France over his French lands and the succession.
1189	Henry II dies, and is succeeded by his son Richard, whose coronation is accompanied by a massacre of Jews. William II of Sicily dies; his bastard cousin Tancred takes the throne.
1190	Emperor Frederick I Barbarossa drowns in Cilicia whilst on crusade, he is succeeded by his son Henry VI. The Jews in York are massacred, but the city is fined.
1191	Richard I conquers Cyprus from the Byzantines and sells it to the Templars, before capturing Acre. Philip II returns to France after falling ill. Richard defeats Saladin at Arsuf. The Order of Germanic Hospitallers is founded at Acre. Zen Buddhism is introduced to Japan.
1192	Richard I, realizing he cannot win in Palestine, makes a truce with Saladin, ending the Third Crusade. On his return home, he is captured and imprisoned by Leopold, duke of Austria. Sultan Muhammad of Ghur captures Delhi, which becomes the Muslim capital in India. Yoritomo Minamoto becomes the first shogun (warlord) of Japan, effectively ruling under a figurehead emperor.
1193	Richard I is handed over to Emperor Henry VI, who demands ransom for his release. Prince John takes the opportunity to foment rebellion whilst Hubert Walter, archbishop of Canterbury, raises the sum. Saladin dies, and is succeeded in Cairo by his son Imad-ud-Din, whilst his relatives rule elsewhere in Arabia.
1194	The Yellow River changes course. Spitzbergen discovered by Norsemen. Richard I is freed after the ransom is paid, returns to England briefly to put down John's rebellion and leaves the country permanently for France. Emperor Henry VI conquers Sicily, deposing William III, son of Tancred. Prince Dafydd of Gwynedd dies, and is succeeded by his nephew Llywelyn ap Iorwerth the Great.
1195	Emperor Isaac II deposed, blinded and imprisoned by his brother Alexius III.
1196	Alfonso II of Aragon dies, and is succeeded by his son Pedro II. Bela III of Hungary dies; his son Imre succeeds him.
1197	Emperor Henry VI dies, sparking a succession dispute. Peter Asen of Bulgaria is murdered, and succeeded by his brother Kalojan. Prince Rhys of Deheubarth dies, and is succeeded by his son Gruffydd.
1198	Pope Celestine III dies. He is succeeded by Innocent III, who excommunicates Philip II of France for repudiating his wife Ingeborg of Denmark. Two rival emperors are established: Philip of Swabia, brother of Henry VI, and Otto, Duke of Saxony.
1199	Richard I dies after an injury at the siege of Chalus. He is succeeded by his brother John, although Philip II goes to war in France in support of John's nephew Arthur of Brittany. The Declaration of Speyer gives the German princes the right to elect their king.
1200	John of England and Philip II of France make peace at Le Goulet, with John confirmed in the Angevin lands in France under Philip's overlordship. Llywelyn the Great seizes Anglesey.
1201	The St Gotthard Pass is opened in Switzerland.
1202	The Fourth Crusade is proclaimed by Innocent III, with leadership given to Count Boniface III of Montferrat. The crusaders get into debt with Venice, whose doge, Enrico Dandolo, persuades them to take Zara for Venice. For this the crusaders are excommunicated by Innocent III.
1203	John murders his nephew, Arthur of Brittany, causing his French possessions to revolt. Crusaders and Venetians agree to help Isaac II regain the Byzantine throne from Alexius III, and are successful.
1204	Emperor Isaac II and his son Alexius IV deposed by Alexius V Ducas. The crusaders conquer Constantinople, and Alexius V flees to Morea, where he is captured and executed. Baldwin of Flanders is elected emperor, but the Byzantine empire disintegrates as relatives of the former ruling families set up independent states. Eleanor of Aquitaine dies. Normandy is captured by Philip Augustus.
1205	The Duchy of Athens is founded by Othon de la Roche. William of Champlitte founds the Principate of Achaea. Emperor Baldwin is defeated and executed by Kalojan of Bulgaria at Adrianople; he is succeeded by his brother Henry. Ladislas III of Hungary deposed by his uncle Andras II.
1206	The Mongol leader Temujin is proclaimed Genghis Khan at Karakorum. Qutb-ud-Din Aibak kills Sultan Muhammad and founds the Sultanate of Delhi. Theodore I Lascaris elected Legitimist Emperor at Nicaea.
1207	Marco I Sanudo founds the duchy of Naxos. Boniface of Montferrat, king of Thessalonica dies, and is succeeded by his son Demetrius.
1208	Philip of Swabia, pretender to the Holy Roman Empire, murdered by Otto of Wittelsbach, who is elected to succeed him and betrothed to his daughter. England placed under interdict by Innocent III. The Albigensian Crusade is proclaimed by Innocent III against Cathar heretics in Languedoc.
1209	The Albigensian fortress of Carcassonne is brutally taken by crusaders under Simon de Montfort. Otto of Wittelsbach crowned Emperor Otto IV in Rome. King John is excommunicated by Innocent III. Cambridge University founded by students leaving Oxford due to town and gown clashes.
1210	The order of the Friars Minor, founded by Francis of Assisi, approved by Innocent III. *Tristan und Isolde* written by Gottfried von Strassburg.

1211	Genghis Khan invades China. Sancho I of Portugal dies, and is succeeded by his son Alfonso II. Emperor Otto deposed by the German princes.
1212	Frederick II elected king by the German princes. Alfonso VIII of Castile decisively defeats the Moors at Las Navas de Tolosa. Stephen of Cloyes leads the Children's Crusade to its doom: many of the children who sail from Marseilles for the Holy Land end up in slavery.
1213	King John submits to the Papacy. Simon de Montfort invades Aragon, defeating the Aragonese at Muret and killing Pedro II, whose infant son James I is put into the care of the Templars.
1214	King John, Otto IV and other lords form alliance against Philip Augustus, who defeats the allied troops at Bouvines, Flanders. William the Lion of Scotland dies, and is succeeded by his son Alexander II.
1215	A revolt by barons in England leads to the signing under duress by King John of Magna Carta; rebel barons later capture Rochester Castle but John retakes it. Frederick II crowned emperor at Aachen. St Dominic founds the Dominican Order.
1216	Baronial revolts against King John gather force and the Dauphin Louis is invited to become king of England. John loses his baggage in the Wash and dies at Newark; he is succeeded by his son Henry III, with William Marshal, earl of Pembroke, proclaimed Regent. Pope Innocent III dies, and is succeeded by Honorius III.
1217	William Marshal defeats baronial rebels at Lincoln; the French fleet is later defeated off Sandwich and Prince Louis sues for peace. Henry III established as unchallenged king of England. The Fifth Crusade is launched under the leadership of John de Brienne.
1218	Persia overrun by Genghis Khan's Mongols. Deposed Emperor Otto IV dies, leaving Frederick II unchallenged. The Dannebrog is adopted as the flag of Denmark.
1219	Sultan Ka'us I of Rum dies, and is succeeded by his brother Kubadh I. Robert succeeds his mother Yolande as emperor in Constantinople. William Marshal dies.
1220	The Dresden Boys' choir founded. Building commences on Salisbury and Amiens cathedrals.
1221	Samarkand sacked by Genghis Khan. The Fifth Crusade ends in failure.
1222	University of Oxford establishes St George's Day, 23 April, as national holiday of England.
1223	Philip Augustus of France dies, and is succeeded by his son Louis VIII. Russians defeated by the Mongols at Kalka River. Alfonso II of Portugal dies, and is succeeded by his son Sancho II.
1224	The Jodo Shin (True Pure Land) sect founded in Japan by Shinran Shonin. Poitou and Gascony, possessions of Henry III of England, invaded by Louis VIII of France.
1225	Magna Carta is reissued in definitive form.
1226	Louis VIII of France dies, and is succeeded by his son Louis IX. St Francis of Assisi dies. The Teutonic Knights are commissioned to conquer and convert Prussia.
1227	Genghis Khan dies; his empire is divided among his three sons. Pope Honorius III dies, and is succeeded by Gregory IX. Frederick II embarks upon crusade, but is forced back by illness and excommunicated by Gregory IX for temporizing.
1228	Frederick II embarks upon crusade whilst Pope Gregory IX invades his realm. Francis of Assisi canonized.
1229	Frederick II reaches an agreement with Sultan Malik-al-Kamil, gaining Jerusalem, Bethlehem, Nazareth and an access corridor from Acre with a 15-year truce, and has himself crowned king of Jerusalem in Jerusalem. Returning from Palestine, Frederick defeats his enemies in Italy. The Balearic Islands conquered by Aragon.
1230	Frederick II and Pope Gregory IX reach an agreement at San Germano and Frederick's excommunication is lifted. Alfonso IX of León; dies his son Ferdinand III of Castile unites the two kingdoms.
1231	The Japanese shogun Fujiwara Yoritsune forbids the selling of children into slavery. Frederick II founds a medical school at Salerno.
1232	Muhammad I al-Ghalib comes to power in Granada, founding the Nasrid dynasty. Anthony of Padua canonized a year after his death.
1233	Pope Gregory IX founds the Papal Inquisition for the suppression of heresy and entrusts it to the Dominicans. The earl of Pembroke, aided by Llywelyn of Wales, leads a baronial revolt against Henry III.
1234	The earl of Pembroke is murdered in Ireland defending his Leinster estates against royalist attacks. Henry III and Llywelyn of Wales make peace.
1235	The Jin state in China falls to the Great Khan Ogedei's Mongols. Andras II of Hungary dies, and is succeeded by his son Bela IV.
1236	Alexander Nevsky succeeds to the Grand Duchy of Novgorod.
1237	The Mongols, led by Subutai and Ogedei, invade Russia, capture Moscow and devastate Poland.
1238	Moorish Valencia surrenders to James I of Aragon.
1239	Emperor Frederick II excommunicated again by Gregory IX.
1240	Prince Llywelyn of Gwynedd dies, and is succeeded by his son Dafydd. Richard of Cornwall and his brother-in-law Simon de Montfort lead a crusade to the Holy Land. The Mongol leader Batu, a grandson of Genghis Khan, takes and destroys Kiev.
1241	The Mongols advance into Eastern Europe, routing the Germans at Liegnitz in Silesia, but the death of Khan Ogedei saves Europe from invasion. Pope Gregory IX dies, and is succeeded by Celestine IV, who dies after seventeen days as Pontiff.
1242	Batu establishes the Golden Horde Mongols at Sarai on the Volga. Alexander Nevsky defeats the Teutonic Knights on the frozen Lake Peipus.
1243	Innocent IV elected Pope after an eighteen-month delay due to quarrels with Emperor Frederick II.
1244	Pasha Khwarazmi of Egypt recaptures Jerusalem for the Arabs. The Cathar stronghold of Montségur falls to Catholic besiegers and a mass execution of the defenders takes place outside.
1245	The Council of Lyon declares Frederick II deposed, causing civil war in Germany. Sancho II of Portugal deposed by Pope Innocent IV, who offers the throne to Sancho's brother Alfonso III.
1246	Landgrave Henry Raspe of Thuringia is elected German king. He defeats Frederick II's son Conrad at Nidda but is driven out of Thuringia by Conrad and Duke Otto II of Bavaria. Duke Frederick II of Austria dies; Emperor Frederick II seizes his duchy.

1247	Buda founded by Bela IV of Hungary to replace Pest, destroyed by the Mongols. With the demise of Henry of Thuringia, William II of Holland is elected anti-king in Germany.
1248	Louis IX of France sets off on the Seventh Crusade. Rhodes taken from the Byzantines by the Genoese. Moorish Seville falls after a two-year siege to Ferdinand III of Castile.
1249	The crusaders land in Egypt and take Damietta. Alexander II of Scotland dies, and is succeeded by his son Alexander III.
1250	Louis IX of France captured by Caliph Turan Shah of Egypt at the battle of Fariskur but released after paying ransom. The Mamluks depose and kill Turan Shah; Musa, a cousin of Turan Shah, becomes Caliph but rules in name only. Emperor Frederick II dies, and is succeeded by his son Conrad IV.
1251	Ottokar, margrave of Moravia, elected duke of Austria.
1252	Ferdinand III of Castile dies; his son Alfonso X succeeds him. Duke Andrei II of Vladimir deposed by the Great Khan Mongka in favour of his younger brother Alexander Nevsky.
1253	Wenceslas I of Bohemia dies, and is succeeded by his son Ottokar II, duke of Austria. The Buddhist monk Nichiren founds his own sect in Japan.
1254	Pope Innocent IV offers the Sicilian throne to Edmund, son of Henry III, who accepts on his behalf. Louis IX of France returns from crusade. Emperor Conrad IV dies. The succession of his infant son Conradin is blocked by opponents of the Hohenstaufens.
1255	Prince Llywelyn of Gwynedd ousts his brother Owen from joint rulership of the Principality.
1256	Venice and Genoa go to war. The order of Augustinian Hermits is founded. Hulagu, a grandson of Genghis Khan, conquers Persia.
1257	Richard, earl of Cornwall, is elected Holy Roman Emperor, but his election is disputed by Alfonso X of Castile.
1258	Hulagu Khan conquers Baghdad, killing Caliph al-Musta'sim and bringing the Abbasid Caliphate to an end. The Provisions of Oxford establish a form of parliamentary government in England. Manfred, regent of Sicily, crowns himself king, deposing his nephew Conradin, and is excommunicated by Pope Alexander IV.
1259	By the treaty of Paris Henry III gives up his claim to Normandy, Anjou and Poitou, and does homage for Gascony and Aquitaine to Louis IX.
1260	The Mamluk Baibars I becomes sultan in Egypt and defeats the Mongols at Ain Jalut in Palestine, saving Egypt from invasion and turning the tide of Mongol attacks. Kublai Khan comes to power in China.
1261	The Greeks reconquer Constantinople, driving the Latin Emperor Baldwin II from the city. The Nicaean Emperor Michael VIII Palaeologus succeeds him.
1262	Haakon IV of Norway unites Greenland and Iceland with his kingdom. Cadiz taken from the Moors.
1263	Alexander III of Scotland defeats Haakon IV of Norway at Largs and takes the Hebrides. Haakon dies on his way home and is succeeded by his son Magnus VI.
1264	Civil war erupts in England between Henry III and a baronial alliance led by Simon de Montfort; de Montfort defeats and captures Henry at Lewes, becoming de facto ruler of England.
1265	Charles of Anjou granted crusading privileges to conquer Sicily by Pope Clement IV. Simon de Montfort summons parliament, but is defeated and killed at Evesham by Prince Edward, who has escaped from imprisonment.
1266	Charles of Anjou defeats and kills Manfred of Sicily at Benevento and becomes king of Sicily. The Hebrides and the Isle of Man granted to Scotland by Norway under the terms of the Treaty of Perth.
1267	Llewelyn of Gwynedd, recognized as Prince of Wales by the treaty of Montgomery, pays homage to Henry III.
1268	Sultan Baibars captures Jaffa and Antioch. Conradin attempts to reclaim Sicily from Charles of Anjou, but is captured and executed. Pope Clement IV dies; the Papacy is left vacant.
1269	Louis IX of France orders Jews in his country to wear a purple wheel on their clothing.
1270	Louis IX of France dies in Tunisia whilst leading the Eighth Crusade; he is succeeded by his son Philip III. The poet Tannhäuser dies.
1271	Pope Gregory X elected to the three-years-vacant papal throne. Marco Polo accompanies his father and uncle to the Far East.
1272	Richard of Cornwall, king of the Romans, dies. Henry III of England dies, and is succeeded by his son Edward I, who is on crusade.
1273	Rudolf, count of Habsburg, elected German king and Holy Roman Emperor.
1274	Thomas Aquinas dies, leaving unfinished his *Summa Theologiae*. Kublai Khan sends an invasion fleet to Japan, but it is destroyed by a typhoon.
1275	Moses de León completes the Jewish mystical text the *Zohar*. Prince Llywelyn of Wales refuses homage to Edward I.
1276	Pope Gregory dies, followed by his successors Innocent V and Hadrian V; John XXI becomes 4th Pope of the year. Ottokar of Bohemia outlawed by Rudolf of Habsburg, but submits to him and is allowed to keep Bohemia and Moravia.
1277	Roger Bacon imprisoned for heresy. Sultan Baibars I of Egypt dies, and is succeeded by his son Baraka Khan. Llywelyn of Gwynedd forced to submit to Edward I by the treaty of Conway.
1278	Ottokar of Bohemia defeated and killed by Rudolf of Habsburg at Dürnkrut, he is succeeded by his son Wenceslas II. The glass mirror is invented.
1279	Alfonso III of Portugal dies near Macao, and is succeeded by his son Diniz. Kublai Khan defeats the Southern Song dynasty in a sea battle and reunites China under the rule of his Yuan dynasty.
1280	Magnus VI of Norway dies; his son Erik II succeeds him.
1281	When Kublai Khan sends a second invasion fleet to Japan it is again decimated by a typhoon, which the Japanese call *kamikaze*, divine wind.
1282	When his younger brother David starts a rebellion against Edward I, Llywelyn of Gwynedd is forced to take part, but is killed near Builth. His brother succeeds him. In the Sicilian Vespers, Sicilian nobles revolt

against Charles of Anjou, who flees whilst his countrymen are massacred. Pedro III of Aragon is offered the Sicilian crown and arrives to accept it.

1283   Prussia subdued by the Teutonic Knights. Edward I conquers Wales. Prince David of Gwynedd is surrendered by his men and executed by Edward.

1284   Kublai Khan invades Vietnam, but his army is destroyed by local guerrillas. Edward I settles Welsh affairs by the Statute of Rhuddlan and arranges for his son Edward to be born in Caernarfon castle.

1285   Charles of Anjou, king of Naples, dies whilst preparing to invade Sicily, succeeded by his son Charles II. Philip III of France dies, and is succeeded by his son Philip IV the Fair. Pedro III of Aragon and Sicily dies, to be succeeded in Aragon by his son Alfonso III and in Sicily by his son James.

1286   Alexander III of Scotland dies on a night ride; his heir is his granddaughter Margaret, the Maid of Norway.

1287   Kublai Khan invades Burma.

1288   Charles II of Naples is released from custody in Aragon on the condition that he accepts Aragonese rule in Sicily.

1289   Tripoli falls to Egyptian forces. Block printing is introduced to Europe at Ravenna.

1290   Edward I expels the Jews from England. Richard of Haldingham draws the *Mappa Mundi*. Margaret of Norway dies whilst on board ship to Scotland; the throne is vacant.

1291   Acre falls to Egyptian forces, ending crusader interest in Outremer. The Knights Hospitallers settle in Cyprus. Rudolf of Habsburg dies. The cantons of Uri, Schwyz and Unterwalden form the Everlasting League, the beginnings of Switzerland.

1292   Adolf, count of Nassau, elected German king. Edward I grants the Scottish throne to John de Balliol.

1293   Kublai Khan sends an expedition to take Java, but it fails.

1294   Philip IV of France confiscates Gascony; Edward I declares war but preparations are disrupted by revolt in Wales. Kublai Khan dies, and is succeeded by his grandson Temür.

1295   A Welsh revolt collapses after defeat at Maes Moydog. Scotland, resentful of a summons to help Edward I, forms the Auld Alliance with France. The Model Parliament convenes at Westminster.

1296   The Genoese defeat the Venetian fleet at Curzola; Marco Polo is amongst those captured. Edward I invades Scotland, forces John de Balliol to abdicate and takes the Stone of Scone, where Scottish kings are crowned, to Westminster.

1297   William Wallace leads a Scottish revolt against Edward I, defeating the English at Stirling Bridge and invading Northumberland and Cumberland. Giant moas become extinct on New Zealand's North Island.

1298   Adolf of Nassau is dethroned by his electors and killed at the battle of Göllheim; Albrecht of Austria, son of Rudolf of Habsburg, replaces him as German king. Edward I invades Scotland, defeating the Scots at Falkirk; Wallace flees abroad.

1299   Osman I, first of the Ottomans, becomes sultan of Turkey.

1300   Arnaud de Villeneuve distils brandy at Montpellier. Edward I invades Scotland again, but makes a truce after a Papal appeal to withdraw. Henry of Great Poland is deposed; Wenceslas II of Bohemia is elected to succeed him.

1301   Andras III of Hungary dies, ending the rule of the Arpad dynasty. Wenceslas II of Bohemia becomes king in his stead, but civil war breaks out. Edward I makes his son Edward Prince of Wales.

1302   The Black faction drive the Whites from Florence; Dante is exiled as a result. The Estates-General of France meet for the first time. Flemish burghers defeat the French at the battle of the Spurs.

1303   Philip IV of France sends Guillaume de Nogaret to capture Pope Boniface VIII and bring him to face trial in France. De Nogaret is thwarted by the Roman citizens, but Boniface dies a virtual prisoner and a broken man in the Vatican shortly after.

1304   The Scottish barons submit to Edward I at St Andrews whilst Stirling Castle only submits after a siege.

1305   Bertrand de Got, Archbishop of Bordeaux, elected Pope as Clement V. Wenceslas II of Bohemia, Poland and Hungary dies. He is succeeded in Bohemia and Poland by his son Wenceslas III, but in Hungary by Otto III of Bavaria. William Wallace is captured, tried and executed by the English.

1306   Wenceslas III of Bohemia and Poland is murdered. Albrecht of Austria invests his son Rudolf with Bohemia whilst Ladislas IV of Kujavia succeeds in Poland. Jews expelled from France. Rhodes purchased by the Knights Hospitallers. Robert Bruce murders John Comyn and is subsequently crowned king of Scots at Scone. The English invade Scotland and force Bruce to flee.

1307   Edward I of England dies, and is succeeded by his son Edward II, who creates Piers Gaveston earl of Cornwall. Philip IV seizes the property of the Knights Templar in France so as to replenish his treasury, but some of the Templar treasure is hidden away.

1308   The Templars are suppressed in England. Parliament forces Edward II to banish Piers Gaveston, who is created Lieutenant in Ireland. Albrecht of Austria is murdered on orders of his nephew John; Henry IV of Luxembourg is elected his successor.

1309   Clement V moves the Papacy to Avignon, thus beginning The 'Babylonian Captivity'.

1310   Parliament forces Edward II to appoint 21 Lords Ordainers to reform the government. A Council of Ten is appointed to rule Venice.

1311   The English Parliament orders baronial consent to appointments by Edward II. Robert Bruce raids Northumberland.

1312   The Knights Templar are abolished in France. Lyons is incorporated into France by the treaty of Vienne. Piers Gaveston is captured by barons and executed.

1313   Perth, Roxburgh, Edinburgh and the Isle of Man taken by the Scots, who besiege Stirling Castle. Emperor Henry VII dies.

1314   Jacques de Molay, Grand Master of the Knights Templar, is burned as a heretic; he curses Philip IV and Pope Clement V at the stake, both of whom die before the year is out. Edward II invades Scotland, but is routed at Bannockburn. Louis X succeeds his father Philip. Louis of Bavaria is elected German king, but a faction elects his rival Frederick of Austria as anti-king; civil war breaks out in Germany.

H
I
S
T
O
R
Y

1315	Edward Bruce, Robert's brother, is offered the High Kingship of Ireland; he sails to Ireland and defeats the Earl of Ulster near Connor.
1316	Edward Bruce, is crowned high king of Ireland. Louis X of France dies. He is briefly succeeded by his son Jean I, who dies soon after his father, and then by his brother Philip V. John XXII elected Pope after a two year hiatus.
1317	The Salic Law is adopted by the French royal family: from now on females and descendants of the female line may not inherit the crown or other titles.
1318	Edward Bruce is killed in the battle of Faughart.
1319	Scots raid into England, defeating an army at the battle of Myton-in-Swaledale; a truce is subsequently made between the English and Scots.
1320	Vladislav IV is crowned king of Poland. The Declaration of Arbroath asserts Scots independence and loyalty to Robert Bruce. Tughluq Shah I founds the Tughluq dynasty as rulers of the sultanate of Delhi, overthrowing Khusraw Shah of the Khalji dynasty.
1321	Parliament forces Edward II to banish his close supporters Hugh Despenser and his son, but he recalls them and raises an army. Dante Alighieri dies.
1322	Philip V of France dies, and is succeeded by his brother Charles IV. Edward II defeats his cousin Thomas, earl of Lancaster, at Boroughbridge; Lancaster is executed and Edward's opponents punished. Frederick of Austria defeated and taken prisoner by Louis of Bavaria at the battle of Mühldorf.
1323	Thomas Aquinas is canonized.
1324	Marco Polo dies. Charles IV of France invades Gascony.
1325	Tughluq Shah I of Delhi is murdered by his son Muhammad Shah I, who replaces him as Sultan. Louis of Bavaria accepts Frederick of Austria as co-regent of Germany, but the move is unsuccessful.
1326	Osman I of Turkey dies; his son Orkhan succeeds him. Queen Isabella of England and her lover Roger Mortimer invade England; Edward II is captured and the Despensers executed.
1327	Edward II is forced to abdicate in favour of his son Edward III, and is murdered 8 months later in Berkeley Castle. Munich is devastated by fire.
1328	Charles IV of France dies, and is succeeded by his cousin Philip VI, first of the Valois dynasty. Robert Bruce is recognized as king of the Scots by the treaty of Northampton; Pope John XXII also recognizes him.
1329	Robert Bruce dies of leprosy; he is succeeded by his son David II.
1330	Frederick of Austria dies; by the treaty of Hagenau Louis of Bavaria is recognized as emperor by the Habsburg faction. Edward III takes control of government in England, capturing and executing Roger Mortimer.
1331	Stephen Urosh III of Serbia is overthrown and murdered by his son Stephen Urosh IV Dushan, who replaces him as king.
1332	Lucerne joins the Swiss League. Edward Balliol invades Scotland, defeating loyalist forces at Dupplin Moor, and is crowned king, but is then defeated by loyalists and flees to England.
1333	Vladislav IV of Poland dies, and is succeeded by his son Casimir III the Great. Edward III and Edward Balliol besiege Berwick and defeat a relieving force at Halidon Hill. The Isle of Man is seized by England. The Black Death pandemic – a combination of bubonic and pneumonic plague passed on by fleas from infected rats – emerges in China.
1334	Casimir III of Poland encourages Jewish immigration. David II of Scotland flees to France and loyalist revolts break out. Berwick ceded to England by Edward Balliol. Pope John XXII dies, and is succeeded by Benedict XII.
1335	Emperor Andronicus III conquers Thessaly.
1336	Alfonso IV of Aragon dies, and is succeeded by his son Pedro IV. The Vijayanagar Empire is founded in southern India by Harihara I of the Yadava dynasty.
1337	Edward III claims the throne of France, thus precipitating the Hundred Years War.
1338	The French initiate hostilities against England, burning Portsmouth and Southampton. Edward III and Emperor Louis IV enter into an alliance. The university of Pisa is founded. Ashikaga Takaufi founds the Ashikaga shogunate.
1339	Venice conquers Treviso, thus gaining its first mainland possession.
1340	Waldemar IV, youngest son of the deposed Christopher II, ascends the Danish throne, ending eight years of anarchy. The English win a decisive naval victory over the French at Sluys.
1341	David II returns to Scotland, forcing the withdrawal of Edward Balliol. Emperor Andronicus III dies, and is succeeded by his 9-year-old son John V. When John's guardian, John Cantacuzene, attempts to set himself up as emperor, civil war erupts.
1342	Edward III conquers most of Brittany. Charles Robert, king of Hungary dies, and is succeeded by his son Louis I the Great.
1343	The Peruzzi banking house of Florence collapses as Edward III defaults on his loan repayments. The Black Death spreads amongst the Tartars in the Crimea.
1344	The Bardi banking house in Florence collapses. The Yellow River floods 16,000 square km of China and changes its course. Alfonso XI of Castile conquers Algeciras from the Moors.
1345	Stephen Urosh IV Dushan proclaims himself emperor of the Serbs and prepares to attack Byzantium.
1346	The French annihilated at Crécy by English bowmen. John of Luxembourg perishes in the battle, and is succeeded by his son Charles I, who is subsequently crowned German king. Scottish forces under David II invade England but are routed at Neville's Cross with David II taken prisoner.
1347	John Cantacuzene is victorious in the Byzantine civil war and reigns, nominally as co-emperor with John V, as John VI. Cola di Rienzi overthrows the Roman plutocracy, but attracts the enmity of Pope Clement VI and is forced to abdicate. Calais surrenders to Edward III after an 11-month siege. Emperor Louis IV dies during a bear hunt, and is succeeded by his rival Charles I of Luxembourg. The Black Death reaches the Black Sea, Sicily and Marseilles.

1348	The Black Death sweeps across Europe and has entered England by summer. Despite Pope Clement VI absolving them of blame, Jews are blamed in areas of France, Germany and Switzerland for the plague pandemic and are persecuted. Many leave for Poland and Russia which are more tolerant. Edward III founds the Order of the Garter.
1349	The Black Death reaches Scotland, Ireland and Poland. A flagellant movement appears as a response to the plague pandemic, but it is denounced and suppressed by Clement VI.
1350	Philip VI of France dies, and is succeeded by his son Jean II. Alfonso XI of Castile dies of the plague whilst besieging Gibraltar, and is succeeded by his son Pedro I the Cruel. Cola di Rienzi appears in Prague, where he is imprisoned by Charles of Luxembourg.
1351	Zurich joins the Swiss League. Florence and Milan go to war over Tuscany. The Statute of Labourers fixes wage rates and restricts movement of labourers in England, as a result of Black Death depopulation and the economic strain of war.
1352	Glarus and Zug join the Swiss League. The Black Death penetrates Russia. Cola di Rienzi is sentenced to death at Avignon, but is saved when Clement VI dies and his successor Innocent VI pardons him.
1353	Bern joins the Swiss League. Giovanni Boccaccio completes *The Decameron*.
1354	The Ottoman Turks take Gallipoli. Innocent VI grants Cola di Rienzi the title Senator and sends him to Rome, but he is killed in a riot within two months. The Genoese defeat a Venetian fleet at Sapienza.
1355	Stephen Urosh IV Dushan of Serbia dies, and is succeeded by his son Stephen Urosh V. The St Scholastica's Day riots in Oxford last three days, with many students killed in 'town and gown' clashes.
1356	Jean II of France captured by the English at the battle of Poitiers, where the Black Prince Edward Prince of Wales, gains a crushing victory.
1357	Parisian merchants, led by Etienne Marcel and Robert le Coq, revolt against the dauphin's administration. David II of Scotland ransomed by the treaty of Berwick.
1358	French peasants revolt in the Jacquerie uprising in the Beauvais but it is suppressed with English assistance. Etienne Marcel is assassinated in Paris by a supporter of the dauphin.
1359	Revolutionaries in red hats storm Bruges in an unsuccessful attempt to overthrow the patrician government. Ivan II of Muscovy dies, and is succeeded by his son Dimitri Donskoy.
1360	England and France sign the treaty of Brétigny, which gives England territorial gains and stipulates the payment of a ransom for Jean II. When the ransom cannot be raised Jean II voluntarily goes back into captivity. Sultan Orkhan of Turkey dies, and is succeeded by Murad I.
1361	Murad I takes Adrianople and makes it the Ottoman capital. The Black Death reappears in England and France.
1362	The Black Prince is appointed ruler of Aquitaine.
1363	Tughlug Timur, shah in Turkestan, dies; he is succeeded by his son Ilyas Khoja, establishing Zungarian Chaghatai rule.
1364	Jean II of France dies in captivity in England, and is succeeded by his son Charles V.
1365	By the Statute of Praemunire the English parliament repudiates Papal overlordship of the country and forbids appeals to the Papal court.
1366	Amadeus of Savoy takes Gallipoli as part of his crusade against the Turks. Pedro the Cruel of Castile is deposed in favour of his half-brother Henry of Trastamara.
1367	Pedro I of Portugal dies and is succeeded by his son Ferdinand. The Black Prince invades Castile in support of Pedro the Cruel, defeating Castilian and French forces at Najera and restoring Pedro's crown.
1368	Chinese Yuan Emperor Shundi is deposed by the Ming Zhu Yuanzhang, who takes the throne with the name Hongwu
1369	Pedro the Cruel of Castile offends the Black Prince, who abandons him. Besieged by Henry of Trastamara at Montiel, Pedro is defeated and killed by Henry who replaces him as king. France declares war on England.
1370	The Mongol ruler Timur the Lame (Tamburlaine) takes the throne of Samarkand. The Black Prince sacks Limoges. Casimir III of Poland dies in a hunting accident; the last Piast king, he is succeeded by his nephew Louis of Anjou, the king of Hungary.
1371	David II of Scotland dies; he is succeeded by his nephew Robert II, the first of the Stuarts. Sultan Murad I wins the battle of Chernomen – Macedonia, Bulgaria and the Byzantines are forced to admit his suzerainty.
1372	The English defeated by Castilian forces at sea off La Rochelle, which falls, along with Poitou, to the French.
1373	Brandenburg annexed by Emperor Charles IV from Otto V of Bavaria, and is given to his son Wenceslas to rule.
1374	A mysterious dancing craze affects Aix-La-Chapelle, when the inhabitants inexplicably dance themselves to exhaustion.
1375	England and France sign the truce of Bruges – English possessions in France much reduced as a result. The Mamluks take Sis from the Armenian King León V, ending Armenian independence.
1376	Edward, the Black Prince, dies. The Good Parliament is convened; Sir Peter de la Mare is chosen Speaker for the House of Commons.
1377	Pope Gregory XI returns the Papacy to Rome. Edward III dies, and is succeeded by his grandson Richard II; John of Gaunt becomes Regent. The French raid Sussex and Kent, burning Rye and Hastings.
1378	Pope Gregory XI dies. Urban VI is elected his successor but tries to reform the College of Cardinals, leading the French Cardinals to create Robert of Geneva Pope Clement VII at Anagni. He moves his Curia to Avignon and the Great Schism begins. Emperor Charles IV dies, and is succeeded by his son Wenceslas.
1379	Henry II of Castile dies, and is succeeded by his son Juan I.
1380	St Catherine of Siena dies. Charles V of France dies, and is succeeded by his son Charles VI the Mad. Dmitri III Donskoi, prince of Moscow, defeats the Mongols at Kulikovo.
1381	Wat Tyler and John Ball lead the Peasants' Revolt in England. Archbishop Sudbury is murdered outside the Tower by a mob but Tyler is stabbed to death by William Walworth, mayor of London, on meeting Richard II at Smithfield. Ball is executed and the rising is suppressed. Venice defeats Genoa in the war of Chioggia.

HISTORY

1382	The religious reformer John Wycliffe is condemned by Archbishop William Courtenay and barred from teaching at Oxford. Louis of Anjou, king of Hungary and Poland, dies, and is succeeded by his daughters Mary in Hungary and Jadwiga in Poland.
1383	The Bishop of Norwich leads the 'Norwich Crusade' to Flanders in support of Pope Urban VI, but is repulsed and impeached at home by Chancellor Michael de la Pole. Ferdinand of Portugal dies, and is succeeded by his daughter Beatrix.
1384	Juan I of Castile marries Beatrix of Portugal, but the Portuguese resist his claim to their throne. John Wycliffe dies.
1385	Scottish forces, aided by the French, raid Northumbria. Portuguese forces defeat Juan of Castile at the battle of Aljubarrota; João of Aviz, an illegitimate son of Pedro I, takes the kingship.
1386	England and Portugal sign the treaty of Windsor, sealed by the marriage of João I with John of Gaunt's daughter Philippa. Jadwiga of Poland marries Jagiello of Lithuania, who takes the name Vladislav V. Leopold III of Styria and Tyrol defeated and killed by the Swiss at the battle of Sempach; his 4 sons jointly succeed him.
1387	Olaf V of Denmark and Norway dies, and is succeeded by his mother Margaret I. Sigismund of Luxembourg, margrave of Brandenburg, marries Mary of Hungary, becoming king. Geoffrey Chaucer begins *The Canterbury Tales*.
1388	At the battle of Otterburn (Chevy Chase) the Scots under the earl of Douglas defeat and capture Henry 'Hotspur' Percy, though Douglas himself is killed.
1389	Margaret I of Denmark and Norway is offered the Swedish throne, invades and defeats King Albert II of Mecklenburg at Falköping, and thereby unites the Scandinavian thrones. Sultan Murad I defeats a Serb-led coalition at Kosovo and conquers Serbia. Murad is subsequently assassinated by the Serb noble Lazar, who is captured and put to death by Murad's son and successor Bayazid I.
1390	Byzantine Emperor John V is deposed by his grandson John VII, but his son Manuel restores him to the throne. Robert II of Scotland dies, and is succeeded by his son Robert III. Juan I of Castile dies, and is succeeded by his son Henry III.
1391	Emperor John V dies, and is succeeded by his son Manuel II. Jews persecuted in Andalusia and Barcelona, as scapegoats for plague. Gedun Truppa is the first Dalai Lama in Tibet.
1392	Charles VI of France suffers his first fit of madness. Yi Songgye founds the Yi Dynasty in Korea, supplanting the Koryo Dynasty and making Kyongsong (later known as Seoul) the capital.
1393	Bulgaria subdued by Sultan Bayazid I. Timur the Lame takes Baghdad. Emperor Wenceslas IV tortures and murders St John of Nepomuk in Prague.
1394	Emperor Wenceslas taken prisoner by his cousin Jobst of Moravia. Anti-Pope Clement VII dies, and is replaced by Benedict XXIII. Richard II goes to Ireland and sets the limit of the territory later known as 'The Pale'.
1395	Richard II receives the submission of 80 Irish chiefs and returns to England. Albert of Mecklenburg renounces the Swedish throne, confirming Margaret of Denmark as queen.
1396	England and France agree a 28-year truce. Sigismund of Hungary leads a Crusade to Nicopolis, where his army is routed by the Ottoman Turks. Gian Galeazzo Visconti buys the title Duke of Milan from Emperor Wenceslas.
1397	Scandinavian nobles assembled in the Union of Kalmar officially recognize the union of Denmark, Norway and Sweden under Queen Margaret. Sultan Bayazid besieges Constantinople but withdraws when Timur the Lame appears in his lands.
1398	Richard II orders a duel to settle the dispute between John of Gaunt's son Henry Bolingbroke and the duke of Norfolk; he then intercedes and banishes the pair. Timur the Lame conquers and sacks Delhi.
1399	John of Gaunt dies. Richard II confiscates the Lancastrian inheritance of Gaunt. Bolingbroke returns from exile, engineers the deposition of Richard II, and is crowned Henry IV in his stead.
1400	Richard II murdered in Pontefract Castle. Emperor Wenceslas is deposed for drunkenness and incompetence; Rupert III of the Palatinate elected to replace him. Owain Glyndwr attacks Lord Grey of Ruthin, proclaims himself prince of Wales and engineers a revolt in the Principality.
1401	Baghdad and Damascus fall to Timur the Lame.
1402	Sultan Bayazid defeated and captured by Timur the Lame at the battle of Ankara; Bayazid is forced to become Timur's footstool while his favourite wife Despina is made a naked waitress. Duke Gian Galeazzo Visconti of Milan dies whilst besieging Florence, and is succeeded by his son Giovanni Maria. The earl of Northumberland and his son Hotspur capture the earl of Douglas at the battle of Homildon Hill.
1403	Sultan Bayazid dies in captivity at Timur's camp; his sons Suleiman and Muhammad dispute the succession. The Doge of Venice imposes quarantine as an attempt to ward off the Black Death. The earl of Northumberland rebels against Henry IV but is defeated at Shrewsbury, where his son Hotspur perishes.
1404	Owain Glyndwr holds a Welsh parliament at Dolgellau.
1405	Timur the Lame dies, and is succeeded by his sons Miran Shah and Shah Rukh and by Miran Shah's son Khalil Sultan in his domains. Owain Glyndwr is defeated at Grosmont by John Talbot and at Usk by Henry, Prince of Wales. Richard Scrope, Archbishop of York, leads a revolt against Henry IV, but the rebellion collapses and Scrope is executed.
1406	Robert III of Scotland sends his son James to France for safety, fearing his brother Albany, but James is captured by the English at sea and imprisoned. Robert III dies and Albany becomes regent as James is kept captive.
1407	Louis, duke of Orléans, is assassinated on the orders of John the Fearless, duke of Burgundy, causing a feud between Burgundian and Armagnac followers in France.
1408	The last threat to Henry IV in England is extinguished by the Sheriff of Yorkshire's victory at Bramham Moor; the earl of Northumberland dies in the battle.
1409	Henry, prince of Wales, captures Harlech castle, kills Edmund Mortimer and subdues the Welsh revolt. In

an attempt to end the Great Schism a conclave of cardinals announces that both Gregory XII and Benedict XIII are deposed, and elects Alexander V in their stead. Both Gregory and Benedict refuse to accept this election, and there are now three contending popes. Dalmatia recovered by Venice.

1410   Anti-Pope Alexander V dies and John XXIII replaces him as the third pope. Emperor Rupert dies. Sigismund of Hungary, brother of the deposed Wenceslas, is elected to succeed him. The Teutonic Knights are decisively defeated by a Polish-Lithuanian force at Tannenberg.

1411   Portugal and Castile make peace. Poland and the Teutonic Knights make the Peace of Thorn.

1412   Duke Giovanni Visconti of Milan is assassinated, and succeeded by his brother Filippo Maria of Pavia. Margaret of Denmark, Sweden and Norway dies, and is succeeded by her great-nephew Erik of Pomerania.

1413   Henry IV of England dies; his son Henry V succeeds him. Civil war amongst the Ottomans ends when Muhammad I defeats and kills his brother Musa outside Constantinople.

1414   The Lollards, radical religious reformers, under Sir John Oldcastle, revolt against Henry V, but are suppressed. The Council of Constance is convened by John XXIII at the instigation of Sigismund of Hungary, in an attempt to end the Great Schism.

1415   The Council of Constance deposes John XXIII and accepts the abdication of Gregory XII, but Benedict XIII refuses to abdicate. Jan Hus is burnt for heresy, causing outrage in Bohemia. Henry V goes to war with France after the failure of negotiations to marry Catherine of Valois, and gains a crushing victory at Agincourt.

1416   Jerome of Prague, a follower of Hus, is burned for heresy. The Venetians defeat the Ottomans in the Dardanelles.

1417   Caen falls to Henry V. Oddo, Colonna is elected Pope, taking the name Martin V, and the Great Schism comes to an end, although Benedict XIII and a small number of clerics hold out.

1418   Madeira discovered by Portuguese explorers under the aegis of Henry the Navigator. John the Fearless of Burgundy takes control of the French government, but the Dauphin Charles sets up a rival administration at Bourges.

1419   Rouen, and subsequently Normandy fall to Henry V. Hussites rebel in Bohemia, defenestrating Catholic councillors in Prague. John the Fearless of Burgundy is assassinated by Armagnacs supporting Dauphin Charles, driving his successor Philip the Good to an alliance with England.

1420   The Anglo-Burgundian alliance makes the treaty of Troyes with Charles VI of France; Henry is made Charles' heir and marries his daughter Catherine. Chinese Emperor Yongle moves his capital to Dadu and renames it Beijing ('northern capital').

1421   Sultan Muhammad I dies, and is succeeded by his son Murad II. Florence buys the city of Livorno. The Zuider Zee is formed by an irruption of the North Sea; 100,000 perish in the process.

1422   Henry V dies, and is succeeded by his nine month-old son Henry VI. Charles VI of France dies and his son Charles VII declares himself king, but Henry VI is proclaimed king by Protector Bedford in the Anglo-Burgundian areas in accordance with the treaty of Troyes.

1423   Thessalonica is purchased from the Byzantines by Venice in an attempt to prevent the Ottomans taking it. James I of Scotland is freed from captivity by the treaty of London on payment of a ransom.

1424   Chinese Emperor Yongle dies and is succeeded by his son Hongxi. James I returns to Scotland and takes up government from his uncle Albany. The English defeat Charles VII at Verneuil.

1425   James I of Scotland executes his uncle Albany and his family. Emperor Manuel II dies, and is succeeded by his son John VIII. Le Mans falls to the English. Henry the Navigator takes the Canary Islands from Castile.

1426   Venice and Milan go to war.

1427   Yeshak of Ethiopia attempts to form an anti-Islamic alliance with Aragon and France.

1428   By the terms of the Treaty of Delft, Duke Phillip of Burgundy is made governor of Hainault, Holland and Zeeland and heir to Jacqueline of Bavaria, Countess of these lands.

1429   French lose to the English at Rouvray (battle of the Herrings) but under the leadership of Jeanne d'Arc relieve Orleans and are victorious at Patay, where Talbot is captured. Charles VII is crowned at Rheims.

1430   Thessalonica falls to the Ottomans of Murad II. Jeanne d'Arc is captured by the Burgundians at Compiègne and sold to the English, who imprison her at Rouen.

1431   A Lollard conspiracy led by 'Jack Sharp' is crushed by the duke of Gloucester. Jeanne d'Arc is burned as a witch at Rouen.

1432   The Azores are discovered by the Portuguese sailor Gonzalo Cabral. Sultan Murad II takes Albania.

1433   Lucca defeats Florence. Timbuktu falls to the Tuaregs. João I of Portugal dies, and is succeeded by his son Duarte. Duke Phillip of Burgundy forces Jacqueline of Bavaria to abdicate in Hainault, Holland and Zeeland after she had incited a failed revolt against him.

1434   The Khmer move their capital from Angkor to Phnom Penh. Cosimo de Medici is recalled from exile to rule Florence. Vladislav V of Poland dies, and is succeeded by his son Vladislav VI. Jan Van Eyck paints Giovanni Arnolfini and his wife.

1435   The Riksdag of Sweden meets for the first time and makes Engelbrecht Engelbrechtson regent for the ineffectual King Erik. Alfonso V of Aragon attempts to capture Naples, thus reuniting Naples and Sicily under one crown but is captured and later released. France and Burgundy are reconciled by the peace of Arras.

1436   The Compact of Iglau ends the Hussite wars in Bohemia and Emperor Sigismund is acknowledged king. Paris falls to the French. The Scots fail to capture Roxburgh Castle.

1437   James I of Scotland is murdered at Perth by Sir Robert Graham, who is executed for the deed. James II succeeds his father. Emperor Sigismund dies, and is succeeded by his son-in-law Albrecht II of Habsburg.

1438   Pahacutec founds the Inca dynasty in Peru. Erik of Denmark, Norway and Sweden flees from rebellions to Gotland, where he takes up piracy.

1439   Serbia falls to Sultan Murad II. The Council of Florence ratifies the union of Roman and Byzantine churches under Rome's primacy. German King Albrecht II dies, leaving his wife pregnant.

1440	Frederick III of Styria is elected German king. Ladislas Posthumus is born and succeeds his late father Albrecht in Austria and Bohemia; in Hungary Vladislav VI of Poland is invited to be king. Eton College is founded by Henry VI.
1441	The Churches of Rome and Ethiopia sign an act of union. The Portuguese sell Africans as slaves in Lisbon: from this the slave trade will develop.
1442	Eleanor Cobham, duchess of Gloucester, is divorced and imprisoned on charge of attempting to kill Henry VI by sorcery.
1443	The Ottomans defeated by the Hungarian hero Janos Hunyadi at Nish; George Castriota, governor of Albania, takes advantage of this defeat by declaring his province independent.
1444	Christians and Ottomans declare a truce at Adrianople and George Brankovich is restored to his principality of Serbia; Hungarians break the truce but are defeated at Varna; Vladislav VI of Poland perishes there and Ladislas Posthumus succeeds to the Hungarian throne.
1445	Cape Verde discovered by Diniz Diaz of Portugal. Copenhagen becomes the capital of Denmark.
1446	Corinth falls to the Ottomans. Janos Hunyadi is elected regent of Hungary for Ladislas.
1447	Casimir of Lithuania, a brother of the late Vladislav VI, is elected king of Poland. Milan becomes a republic on the death of Filippo Maria Visconti. Shah Rukh, Lord of Turkestan dies, and is succeeded by his son Ulugh Beg.
1448	With the death of Christopher of Bavaria, king of Sweden, Denmark and Norway, the Union of Kalmar dissolves. Christian of Oldenburg reigns in Denmark and Norway whilst Karl Knutsen is elected king of Sweden. Sultan Murad defeats the Hungarians under Janos Hunyadi at the second battle of Kosovo. Emperor John VIII dies, and is succeeded by his brother Constantine XI.
1449	Ulugh Beg, Lord of Turkestan, is executed by his son Abd al-Latif, who also puts his brother Abd al-Aziz to death. The Timurid provinces in Turkestan fragment as a result, and Babur ibn Baisonqur, a nephew of Ulugh Beg, takes power in Khurasan.
1450	Abd al-Latif dies; his cousin Abdullah Mirza succeeds him as Lord of Turkestan. Francesco Sforza overthrows the republic in Milan and makes himself duke. Normandy reconquered by France. Jack Cade leads a revolt in Kent and Sussex; it fails and Cade is killed, but Henry VI is forced to flee for safety to Kenilworth for a while.
1451	Gascony reconquered by the French. Sultan Murad II dies, and is succeeded by his son Muhammad II.
1452	Borso of Este is created duke of Modena by Emperor Frederick III. James II of Scotland murders the earl of Douglas at Stirling. John Talbot leads an expedition to Gascony and reconquers much of it.
1453	Constantinople falls to the Ottoman Sultan Muhammad II; Emperor Constantine XI perishes in the fighting and the Byzantine Empire is no more. The French win a decisive victory over the English at Castillon, where Talbot dies. Gascony is reconquered and the English hold only Calais in France. The Hundred Years War is thus brought to an end. Henry VI has a bout of insanity.
1454	The duke of York is appointed protector during Henry VI's incapacity. The Peace of Lodi is reached between Venice and Milan and their allies. Venice signs a treaty with Sultan Muhammad II.
1455	Henry VI recovers his sanity and dismisses the duke of York from the post of Protector. The Wars of the Roses begin when York and the earl of Warwick raise an army and defeat and capture Henry VI at St Albans. York is made Constable of England but pro-Lancastrian riots break out. Johannes Gutenberg produces the first printed Bible, using the movable metal type that he started to perfect in the 1450s.
1456	The Ottomans capture Athens but are repulsed from Belgrade by Janos Hunyadi, who dies soon after from plague. Vlad III the Impaler retakes the Wallachian throne from Vladislav II.
1457	Karl VIII of Sweden is driven out and replaced by Christian I of Denmark. Laszlo Hunyadi, son of Janos, is arrested and beheaded in Buda, sparking outrage in Hungary; Ladislas Posthumus is forced to flee to Prague, where he dies suddenly. Emperor Frederick III succeeds in Austria; George Podiebrad, leader of the Hussites, is elected king in Bohemia.
1458	Matthias Corvinus, second son of Janos Hunyadi, is elected king of Hungary. Alfonso V of Aragon dies, and is succeeded in Aragon and Sicily by his brother Juan II and in Naples by his bastard son Ferdinand.
1459	Civil war is renewed in England. The Yorkists are victorious at Blore Heath but defeated at Ludford Bridge. The Irish come out in support of the Yorkists.
1460	Henry VI defeated and captured by the Yorkists at Northampton; the duke of York is named heir to Henry but dies at the battle of Wakefield, where the Lancastrians are victorious. James II of Scotland dies when a cannon misfires at Roxburgh, and is succeeded by his son James III. Henry the Navigator dies.
1461	Yorkists victorious at Mortimer's Cross, where Owen Tudor is captured and executed, but defeated at St Albans. Henry VI is rescued by the Lancastrians. Edward of York deposes Henry VI and crushes the Lancastrians at Towton; Henry VI and his family flee to Scotland. Charles VII of France dies, and is succeeded by his son Louis XI. Trebizond falls to the Ottomans.
1462	Vlad III the Impaler of Wallachia is deposed and replaced by his pro-Turkish brother Radu III. Prince Vasili of Moscow dies, and is succeeded by his son Ivan III the Great.
1463	Bosnia conquered by the Ottomans, who go to war with the Venetians. England, France and Burgundy sign the Truce of Hesdin, the latter two recognizing Edward IV of York as king of England.
1464	Yorkists victorious at Hedgeley Moor and Hexham, and gain control of Northern England. Louis XI of France founds the *Poste Royale*. Cosimo de Medici dies, and is succeeded by his son Piero I.
1465	Henry VI captured in Ribblesdale and imprisoned in the Tower. Louis XI of France defeated by a coalition of royal dukes at Montlhéry and is forced to sign the treaty of Conflans.
1466	The Medicis form an alliance with the Vatican to finance alum mining in the Papal States. George Podiebrad, king of Bohemia, excommunicated by Pope Paul II.
1467	Philip the Good of Burgundy dies, and is succeeded by his son Charles the Bold.
1468	Zara Ya'kob Constantine of Ethiopia dies, and is succeeded by his son Ba'eda Maryam I. James III of Scotland contracts to marry Margaret, daughter of Christian of Denmark; the Orkneys and Shetlands are pledged as security for her dowry.

1469   Rebellion develops in England against Edward IV and the power of his wife's family. Edward is imprisoned after his army deserts him at Olney, and is released with a promise to appease the rebels. Piero de Medici dies; his sons Lorenzo the Magnificent and Giuliano succeed him. Ferdinand, heir to the throne of Aragon, marries Isabella, heiress of Castile.

1470   Portuguese seafarers reach the Gold Coast. Edward IV defeats a rebel army at Empingham, but Warwick and the Lancastrians reach an accord and invade, forcing Edward to flee to Burgundy. Henry VI is restored to the throne.

1471   Edward IV returns to England, defeats and kills Warwick at Barnet and then decisively defeats the Lancastrians at Tewkesbury, where Edward Prince of Wales perishes. Henry VI is murdered in the Tower. Louis XI of France and Charles the Bold of Burgundy go to war.

1472   Lopo Gonçalves is the first European to cross the Equator. Ivan III of Moscow marries Zoe, niece of Emperor Constantine XI, thus attempting to transfer imperial lustre to himself.

1473   Charles the Bold of Burgundy occupies Lorraine and Alsace. Cyprus falls under Venetian rule.

1474   The Union of Constance is formed against Charles the Bold of Burgundy, who makes an anti-French alliance, via the treaty of London, with Edward IV. Henry IV of Castile dies, and is succeeded by his half-sister Isabella and her husband Ferdinand, son of Juan II of Aragon.

1475   Edward IV invades France but is let down by his absent ally Charles the Bold and goes on to sign a 7-year truce with Louis XI via the treaty of Picquigny.

1476   Charles the Bold makes war on the Swiss, but is defeated at Granson, and later at Morat. Duke Galeazzo Sforza of Milan is assassinated by republicans, but is succeeded by his son Gian Galeazzo. William Caxton establishes the first English printing press.

1477   Edward IV bans early forms of skittles and cricket due to their interference with archery practice. Charles the Bold of Burgundy dies fighting the Swiss at the battle of Nancy; his state implodes and is effectively shared between Louis XI and Charles' son-in-law Maximilian, son of Emperor Frederick III.

1478   The duke of Clarence is drowned in a butt of Malmsey while imprisoned in the Tower of London. Novgorod subdued by Ivan the Great of Muscovy. Isabella of Castile unleashes the Inquisition on Jewish converts. Pope Sixtus VI and the Pazzi family plot to assassinate the Medicis; Giuliano is killed but Lorenzo escapes and decimates the Pazzis in revenge.

1479   Juan II of Aragon dies. His son Ferdinand succeeds him and the thrones of Castile and Aragon are thus united. The treaty of Constantinople ends the war between Venice and the Ottoman Empire.

1480   Ivan III frees Muscovy from Tartar domination. Duke René of Anjou dies; his domains, including Provence, are annexed by Louis XI. Otranto is taken by the Ottomans.

1481   Sultan Muhammad II dies, and is succeeded by his son Bayazid II. Alfonso V of Portugal dies, and is succeeded by his son João II.

1482   Venice goes to war with Ferrara. Louis XI and the Habsburgs make the Peace of Arras, partitioning the Burgundian domains.

1483   Edward IV dies, and is succeeded by his son Edward V, who disappears along with his brother Richard in the Tower. Their uncle Richard assumes the kingship. Louis XI of France dies, and is succeeded by his son Charles VIII. The Dominican Tomás de Torquemada takes control of the Spanish Inquisition.

1484   Diogo Cão discovers the mouth of the River Congo. Pope Innocent VIII issues the bull *Summis Desiderantes* against witchcraft.

1485   Emperor Frederick III expelled from Vienna by Matthias Corvinus of Hungary. Henry Tudor invades England against Richard III, defeats and kills him at Bosworth Field, and takes the throne. Caxton publishes Malory's *Morte d'Arthur.*

1486   Matthias Corvinus devises a law code for Hungary. Henry VII marries Elizabeth of York and unites the houses of Lancaster and York. Krämer and Spränger publish the *Malleus Maleficarum* attacking witches and witchcraft.

1487   Lambert Simnel leads revolt against Henry VII, claiming to be Edward IV's nephew, but is defeated at Stoke and sent to work in the royal kitchens. Bartholomew Diaz sails around the Cape of Good Hope, which he names the Cape of Storms.

1488   James III of Scotland is murdered; his son James IV succeeds him. Duke Francis of Brittany dies, and is succeeded by his daughter Anne. Johann Widmann develops the use of the symbols (+), (&), and (-). Bartholomew Diaz returns to Lisbon, where João II gives the Cape of Good Hope its name.

1489   Typhus is brought to Aragon by soldiers returning from Cyprus. Catherine Cornaro of Cyprus is forced to sell her kingdom to Venice. Henry VII signs the anti-French treaty of Redon with Brittany.

1490   Matthias Corvinus of Hungary dies without an heir, and is succeeded by Ladislas of Bohemia.

1491   Perkin Warbeck claims to be Richard, duke of York, and rallies support for his cause in France and Ireland. Charles VIII of France annexes Brittany by forcing Anne of Brittany to marry him.

1492   Granada, the last Moorish city, conquered by Ferdinand and Isabella; Spain effectively one country. Lorenzo the Magnificent of Florence dies, and is succeeded by his son Piero II. Casimir IV of Poland and Lithuania dies, and is succeeded by his sons John Albert in Poland and Alexander in Lithuania. Rodrigo Borgia elected Pope as Alexander VI. Henry VII invades France and is bought off by Charles VIII under the treaty of Étaples, with compensation for Brittany's annexation and the expulsion of Warbeck. Jews in Spain are ordered to convert or quit the country. Christopher Columbus discovers Cuba and Hispaniola.

1493   Columbus returns home from the Indies, and is sent back as governor of the new lands by Isabella of Castile, discovering Dominica. Pope Alexander VI publishes the bull *Inter Cetera Divina* dividing the New World between Spain and Portugal. Emperor Frederick III dies, and is succeeded by his son Maximilian I.

1494   Emperor Maximilian I recognizes Warbeck as king of England. Spain and Portugal divide the New World by the treaty of Tordesillas. Charles VIII of France invades Italy, deposes Piero de Medici in Florence and takes Rome. Duke Gian Galeazzo of Milan dies, probably poisoned by his uncle Lodovico, who succeeds him.

1495   Charles VIII of France expels Alfonso II of Naples and is crowned king of the state, but is forced to retreat by Alfonso's son Ferdinand II, who assumes the kingship. Syphilis strikes the state and the French soldiers are badly affected by it. The Diet of Worms is established to modernize the Holy Roman Empire. João II of Portugal dies, and is succeeded by his cousin Manuel the Fortunate. Warbeck received by James IV of Scotland. A dry-dock is built in Portsmouth, establishing the dockyard there.

1496   Henry VII commissions John Cabot to search for new lands. The Canary Islands conquered by Spain. Ferdinand II of Naples dies, and is succeeded by his uncle Frederick IV. James IV invades Northumberland in support of Warbeck. Manuel I of Portugal expels the Jews from his country.

1497   John and Sebastian Cabot reach Labrador and Newfoundland. The Cornish rebel against taxation but are defeated at Blackheath; Warbeck lands in Cornwall but is captured. John of Denmark defeats the Swedish at Brunkeberg and revives the Union of Kalmar. Savonarola stages a bonfire of vanities in Florence. Vasco da Gama rounds the Cape of Good Hope and gives Natal its name as he discovers it on Christmas Day.

1498   Charles VIII of France dies, and is succeeded by his second cousin once removed Louis XII, duke of Orléans. Savonarola burned at the stake for heresy. Vasco da Gama reaches Malindi in East Africa and then Calicut in India. Columbus embarks on a third voyage, discovering Trinidad and the Orinoco River.

1499   Louis XII of France divorces his wife Jeanne and marries Anne of Brittany to keep the duchy in French hands. Emperor Maximilian and the Swiss go to war; by the Peace of Basel, Swiss independence is granted. Venice and the Ottomans go to war; the Venetian fleet is defeated at Sapienza. Montenegro falls to the Ottomans. Louis XII takes Milan, forcing Ludovico Sforza to flee to the Tyrol. Perkin Warbeck is executed.

1500   Ludovico Sforza recaptures Milan, but the French return and capture Sforza on retaking the city. Pedro Cabral discovers Brazil when blown off course en route for India.

1501   Lithuania invaded by Ivan III of Moscow. Basel and Schaffhausen admitted to the Swiss Confederation. Frederick IV of Naples dies; Pope Alexander VI declares Louis XII Frederick's successor. Ismail I, sheikh of Ardabil, defeats Shah Alwand of Persia at Shurur and establishes Safavid rule in the country. Emperor Maximilian I recognizes the French conquests in Italy by the Peace of Trent.

1502   St Helena discovered by João de Nova. Arthur, prince of Wales, dies at Ludlow.

1503   Louis XII of France abandons his claim to the Neapolitan throne after his alliance with Ferdinand of Aragon collapses. Gonzalo de Cordoba defeats a French army and enters Naples. James IV of Scotland marries Margaret Tudor, daughter of Henry VII. Pope Alexander VI dies, and is succeeded briefly by Pius III, and then by Julius II.

1504   Albert of Bavaria defeats Rupert, son of the Elector Palatine in the Bavarian War, during which at Landshut the Frankonian knight Götz von Berlichingen loses his right hand and has it replaced by one of iron. Michelangelo's statue of *David* is put on display in Florence.

1505   Ivan III of Muscovy dies, and is succeeded by his son Vasili III.

1506   Niccolò Machiavelli forms a Florentine militia, the first national army established in Italy. Christopher Columbus dies. 4,000 Jews perish in a riot in Lisbon. Philip the Handsome, son of the Emperor Maximilian and husband of the de jure Castilian Queen Juana (Joanna) dies, sending his wife mad.

1507   Cesare Borgia dies whilst besieging Viana, in Spain.

1508   Juan Ponce de León colonizes Puerto Rico. Pope Julius II confirms that the German King will automatically become Holy Roman Emperor. Michelangelo starts painting the ceiling of the Sistine Chapel.

1509   Francisco de Almeida destroys a Muslim fleet at the battle of Diu, guaranteeing Portuguese control of the spice trade. Pope Julius II excommunicates the Venetian Republic, which is defeated by the French at Agnadello. Henry VII dies, and is succeeded by his son Henry VIII.

1510   Afonso de Albuquerque seizes Goa for Portugal. Sir Richard Empson and Edmund Dudley beheaded by Henry VIII for their unpopular fiscal policies under his father.

1511   Portuguese forces under Albuquerque seize Malacca, the centre of the spice trade. Julius II forms the Holy League with Venice to drive the French from Italy and enlists the support of Ferdinand of Aragon and Henry VIII.

1512   Forces of the Holy League are defeated by the French at Ravenna, but the French are then driven from Milan; Massimiliano Sforza, son of the deposed Duke Ludovico, becomes duke. Sultan Bayazid dies mysteriously after being deposed by his Janissaries; his son Selim I the Grim succeeds him.

1513   Juan Ponce de León discovers Florida. John of Denmark dies, and is succeeded by his son Christian II, who is rejected by the Swedes. Pope Julius II dies, and is succeeded by Leo X. Henry VIII invades France, where he and Emperor Maximilian are successful in the battle of Guinegatte (the Spurs). James IV of Scotland takes advantage of the English in France to invade, but his army is routed at Flodden and James is killed, to be succeeded by his infant son James V.

1514   The *Henry Grace a Dieu*, the largest warship in the world, is launched in England. Thomas Wolsey becomes Archbishop of York. The Ottoman Sultan Selim invades Persia and routs the Persian army at Chaldiran.

1515   Louis XII of France dies, and is succeeded by his son-in-law François I, who defeats the Swiss and Venetians at Marignano and takes Milan.

1516   Ferdinand II of Aragon dies, and is succeeded on the Spanish throne by his grandson Charles I. Pope Leo X and François I of France sign the Concordat of Bologna, giving France freedom in ecclesiastical appointments. Sultan Selim I defeats the Mamluks at Marjdabik and takes Syria. Thomas More publishes *Utopia*.

1517   Egypt falls to the Ottoman Turks, to whom the Sharif of Mecca submits, leaving Arabia under Ottoman control. Martin Luther nails 95 theses to the door of Wittenberg Cathedral attacking the sale of indulgences.

1518   Huldrych Zwingli forces the expulsion from Zurich of Barnardin Samson, a Franciscan seller of indulgences. Wolsey negotiates the Peace of London between England, France, the Holy Roman Empire, Spain and the Papacy; they agree to crusade against the Turks.

1519   Emperor Maximilian dies, and is succeeded by his grandson Charles V (I of Spain). Vasco de Balboa is beheaded in Panama as he loses the power struggle amongst the Spanish in Central America. Hernán

Cortés enters Tenochtitlán, the Aztec capital, and is received by Emperor Montezuma, whom he takes prisoner.

1520   Christian II of Denmark invades Sweden and is successful at Tiveden and Uppsala before taking Stockholm; despite proclaiming an amnesty he executes numerous leading Swedes. Henry VIII and François I meet at the Field of the Cloth of Gold near Calais. Cortés driven from Tenochtitlán by Cuauhtemoc. Sultan Selim I dies, and is succeeded by his son Suleiman I the Magnificent. Ferdinand Magellan sails through the Strait of Magellan and names the Pacific.

1521   Martin Luther is interrogated by the Diet of Worms; refusing to recant he is put in the castle of Wartburg for his own protection by Frederick of Saxony and begins a German translation of the Bible. Ferdinand Magellan dies in a skirmish in the Philippines. Cortés overthrows the Aztec empire; Montezuma II dies in the fighting. Sultan Suleiman I takes Belgrade. Henry VIII is awarded the title 'Defender of the Faith' by Leo X for an anti-Lutheran work.

1522   Luther returns to Wittenberg and initiates church services in German. Sultan Suleiman takes Rhodes from the Knights of St John. Juan Sebastiano del Cano returns home after finishing Magellan's circumnavigation of the world.

1523   Christian II of Denmark deposed by his nobles for cruelty and replaced by his uncle Frederick I. Gustavus Vasa takes advantage of the situation to be crowned king of Sweden. Sir Thomas More elected Speaker of the House of Commons. Zwingli publishes his 67 Articles in Zurich.

1524   Giovanni da Verrazano discovers New York Bay, naming Manhattan Angoulême. Denmark confirms Swedish independence by the treaty of Malmö. Shah Ismail I of Persia dies, and is succeeded by his son Tahmasp I.

1525   Emperor Charles V defeats François I of France at Pavia, imprisons him and establishes control over Italy. Albert von Brandenburg, Grand Master of the Teutonic Knights, makes himself duke of Prussia. A peasants' revolt in Germany is suppressed, and its leader Thomas Müntzer executed. Cardinal Wolsey gives Hampton Court to Henry VIII.

1526   François I of France signs the treaty of Madrid, ceding various lands to Charles V, but renounces it because the terms were extorted from him, and allies himself with Sultan Suleiman, who defeats and kills Louis II of Hungary at the battle of Mohacs. Ferdinand, brother of Emperor Charles V is chosen to succeed Louis II in Hungary and Bohemia, but the Hungarians elect John Zapolya as king. Zahir-ud-Din Babur defeats Sultan Ibrahim Lodi of Delhi at Panipat, takes Agra and founds the Mughal Empire.

1527   The Mughal Emperor Babur defeats Rajput forces at Kanvaha. England and France ally via the treaty of Westminster. Imperial troops sack Rome; Pope Clement VII is imprisoned in the Castel Sant' Angelo. Holbein paints Thomas More and his family.

1528   The physician and alchemist Paracelsus is forced from Basel due to his unorthodox medical opinions and treatments.

1529   François I of France and Emperor Charles V make peace via the treaty of Cambrai. Suleiman the Magnificent takes Buda and besieges Vienna but fails to take it. Cardinal Wolsey falls from power due to his inability to secure a divorce for Henry VIII from Catherine of Aragon. Sir Thomas More replaces him as Lord Chancellor, the first layman to hold the post.

1530   The Knights of St John are settled in Malta by Emperor Charles V. Melanchthon prepares the Confession of Augsburg as a statement of faith for the German Protestant princes, who form the Schmalkaldic League against Emperor Charles V. Cardinal Wolsey is arrested for treason, but dies whilst on his way to trial. The Mughal Emperor Babur dies, and is succeeded by his son Humayun.

1531   Lisbon is destroyed by an earthquake. The Catholic Swiss Cantons attack and defeat Zurich in the battle of Kappel; Zwingli dies in the fighting.

1532   The English clergy recognize Henry VIII as Supreme Head of the Church. Sultan Suleiman invades Hungary. The Inca chief Atahualpa seized by Pizarro, who reintroduces horses to South America. François Rabelais publishes Pantagruel.

1533   Henry VIII divorces Catherine of Aragon and marries Anne Boleyn with the sanction of Thomas Cranmer, newly appointed archbishop of Canterbury; this leads to Henry's excommunication. Pizarro executes Atahualpa by strangling and causes the downfall of the Incas. Holbein paints The Ambassadors. Vasili III of Moscow dies, and is succeeded by his son Ivan IV the Terrible.

1534   John of Leiden sets up the radical Protestant Anabaptist kingdom of Zion at Münster. Jacques Cartier sails for the New World by command of François I and reaches the Gulf of St Lawrence. Ignatius Loyola founds the Society of Jesus (Jesuits). The Act of Supremacy marks the final break between England and Rome, comfirming Henry VIII as Supreme Head of the Church of England.

1535   Jacques Cartier sails up the St Lawrence to Montreal. Thomas Cromwell is appointed Vicar-General to investigate religious houses in England. Francis of Waldeck retakes Münster from the Anabaptists. John Fisher, Bishop of Rochester, and Sir Thomas More executed for refusing to take an oath supporting Henry VIII's acts. Emperor Charles V conquers Tunis, defeating the pirate leader Khair ad-Din. Duke Francesco Sforza of Milan dies; the duchy reverts to Emperor Charles V.

1536   John of Leiden is executed in Münster. The Anabaptist Jacob Hutter is burned at the stake. Dissolution of the monasteries commences in England, leading to a rising under Robert Aske (the Pilgrimage of Grace). Henry VIII executes Anne Boleyn on the grounds of adultery and marries Jane Seymour. Wales is formally united with England. William Tyndale is executed for heresy.

1537   Pope Paul III prohibits enslavement of New World natives and excommunicates Catholic slave traders. Robert Aske is received by Henry VIII and Cromwell, but is later executed for treason. Jane Seymour dies after bearing the future Edward VI.

1538   Pope Paul III allies with Charles V and the Venetians in a Holy League against the Ottoman Empire, but the combined Venetian, Genoese and papal fleet is defeated at Prevesa by the Ottomans.

1539   Charles V and François I make peace with the treaty of Toledo. The Six Articles are passed in England, enforcing Catholic orthodoxy. Dissolution of the monasteries ends; the abbots of Reading, Colchester and Glastonbury are executed in the process.

1540   Henry VIII marries Anne of Cleves but quickly repudiates her. The marriage is annulled and he marries Catherine Howard. Thomas Cromwell falls from grace over the Cleves marriage and is executed. The Jesuits are recognized by Pope Paul III. The Norse colony of Greenland comes to an end, with the last colonist discovered dead outside his hut with a dagger in his hand.

1541   John Calvin sets up a theocratic government in Geneva. Henry VIII is accepted by the Irish Parliament as king of Ireland and head of the Irish Church.

1542   Henry VIII executes Catherine Howard for adultery. Pope Paul III establishes the Universal Inquisition to repress the Reformation. James V of Scotland raids Cumberland, but is defeated badly at Solway Moss. He dies soon after and is succeeded by his six-day-old daughter, Mary.

1543   Pope Paul III establishes an index of prohibited books. The Spanish Inquisition commences burning Protestants at the stake. Henry VIII marries Catherine Parr. Copernicus publishes his De revolutionibus orbium coelestrium, stating his belief that the planets orbit a stationary Sun.

1544   Henry VIII captures Boulogne, but subsequently retires from France when his ally Charles V and François I make peace with the treaty of Crépy-en-Valois.

1545   The Mary Rose capsizes off Portsmouth. Charles V and Suleiman the Magnificent make a truce with the treaty of Adrianople. The Council of Trent meets, in an attempt by the Catholic church to establish a Counter-Reformation.

1546   England and France make peace with the treaty of Ardres, by which England holds Boulogne for eight years before returning it to France. The Paris printer Etienne Dolet is executed for heresy and blasphemy as a result of publishing humanist works by the likes of Erasmus.

1547   Ivan IV the Terrible of Moscow crowned Tsar of Russia. Henry VIII dies, and is succeeded by his nine-year-old son Edward VI. François I laughs on receiving news of Henry's death, develops a fever and dies, to be succeeded by his son Henri II. John Knox is captured at St Andrews and sent to work on a French galley. Protector Somerset, ruling on behalf of his nephew Edward, invades Scotland and defeats the Scots at Pinkie.

1548   Francis Xavier founds a Jesuit mission in Japan. Sigismund I of Poland dies, and is succeeded by his son Sigismund II Augustus.

1549   Ivan IV summons the first Russian national assembly. The Protestant Book of Common Prayer is imposed in England, leading to risings in Devon and Cornwall. Robert Kett leads a revolt in Norfolk against land enclosures, but is defeated at Dussindale.

1550   England makes peace with France and Scotland by the treaty of Boulogne; Boulogne is returned to France and John Knox released from galley labour. Cricket is first referred to.

1551   Henri II of France disavows the Council of Trent and renews the war against Charles V. The Ottomans attack Malta, but are repulsed and take Tripoli instead.

1552   The duke of Somerset is executed. Tsar Ivan IV takes Kazan and attacks Astrakhan. The second Book of Common Prayer is introduced.

1553   Richard Chancellor opens a trade route to Moscow via the White Sea and Archangel. Edward VI dies, and is succeeded by his Catholic half-sister Mary, despite the duke of Northumberland's efforts to install Lady Jane Grey, his daughter-in-law, as a Protestant queen. Northumberland is later executed.

1554   Sir Thomas Wyatt leads revolt from Kent over Mary I's proposed marriage to Philip of Spain, but is defeated and executed. Lady Jane Grey is also executed, whilst Mary's half-sister Elizabeth is imprisoned in the Tower.

1555   Pope Julius III dies, his successor Marcellus II dies after a month, and Paul IV succeeds. Paul walls in Rome's Jewish quarter, creating a ghetto. John Knox returns to Scotland. Tobacco is brought to Europe from America. Mary I persecutes Protestants; Latimer and Ridley are burned at the stake in Oxford. Charles V hands sovereignty of the Netherlands to his son Philip.

1556   Thomas Cranmer is dismissed as Archbishop of Canterbury and burned at the stake. Emperor Charles V abdicates; his brother Ferdinand succeeds him as Emperor whilst his son Philip II succeeds in Spain. Indian Mughal emperor Humayun dies after falling from his library roof, and is succeeded by his son Jalal-ud-Din Akbar I.

1557   Tsar Ivan IV invades Poland. Macao founded by the Portuguese, whose King João III dies, and is succeeded by his grandson Sebastian. The Spanish drive the French from Italy after victory at the battle of St Quentin.

1558   Calais, England's last continental possession, falls to the French. Mary I dies, and is succeeded by her half-sister Elizabeth. William Cecil becomes Secretary of State. John Knox writes his First Blast of the Trumpet Against the Monstrous Regiment of Women.

1559   Christian III of Denmark dies, and is succeeded by his son Frederick II; Christian's imprisoned predecessor Christian II also dies. The Act of Supremacy restores the Church of England. The war between England, Spain and France is ended by the treaty of Cateau-Cambrésis. Henri II of France dies after a jousting accident, and is succeeded by his son François II.

1560   The treaty of Berwick is made between England and the Protestant Scottish lords against the French, whose troops are forced to return home; the Scots Parliament approves Knox's Calvinistic Confession of Faith. Louis de Bourbon organizes the Huguenot Conspiracy of Amboise against the Catholic Guises, but is thwarted by the Dowager Queen Catherine de Medici. François II of France dies, and is succeeded by his brother Charles IX.

1561   Philip II declares Madrid the capital of Spain. Persecution of French Huguenots suspended by the Edict of Orléans. Flemish Calvinist refugees settle in England. St Paul's Cathedral damaged by fire after a lightning strike.

1562   The duc de Guise orders the massacre of Huguenots at Vassy, thus precipitating the Wars of Religion in France. The English establish the 39 Articles of Religion.

1563   The duc de Guise is murdered by a Huguenot; Catherine de Medici is left in charge of the Catholic faction and grants limited toleration to the Huguenots by the Peace of Amboise, ending the First War of Religion. John Foxe's Book of Martyrs is published. The Council of Trent comes to an end.

1564   England and France make peace by the treaty of Troyes: in return for 220,000 crowns Elizabeth renounces claim to Calais. Emperor Ferdinand I dies, and is succeeded by his son Maximilian II.

1565   The Ottomans besiege Malta, but 700 Knights of St John under Jean de La Valette hold them off for 4 months before Spanish troops relieve them and force the Ottomans to withdraw. Mary Queen of Scots marries her cousin Henry, Lord Darnley.

1566   Mary Queen of Scots' secretary, David Rizzio, is murdered at Holyrood. Calvinists riot in the Netherlands and petition the Regent, Margaret of Palma, to abolish the Inquisition. Suleiman the Magnificent dies, and is succeeded by his son Selim II.

1567   Lord Darnley is murdered at Kirk o'Field; the earl of Bothwell, who is believed to have ordered the assassination, marries Mary Queen of Scots. The earl of Morton discovers the possibly fabricated Casket Letters incriminating Bothwell and Mary; the Scots Lords rebel against Mary, imprison her in Lochleven Castle and force her abdication in favour of her son James VI, with Moray as Regent. Philip II sends the duke of Alba to eliminate Protestant resistance in the Netherlands, where he begins a reign of terror. Regent Margaret resigns.

1568   The Second War of Religion in France is ended by the treaty of Longjumeau. Mary Queen of Scots escapes Lochleven, raises an army, but is defeated by Moray at Langside and flees to England. Alba beheads Counts Egmont and Hoorn in Brussels for opposing the Inquisition and confiscates the estates of those who failed to attend the Council of Blood. Erik XIV of Sweden is deposed due to mental illness and replaced by his brother John III. The first modern Eisteddfod is held at Caerwys.

1569   Elizabeth orders Mary of Scots' detention in Tutbury Castle and imprisons the duke of Norfolk, who seeks to marry Mary. Catholics under the duc d'Anjou defeat Huguenot forces at Jarnac. Mercator publishes his map of the world and establishes his projection. The Union of Lublin unites Poland and Lithuania. Catholic earls of Northumberland and Westmorland revolt, seize Durham, but are forced to flee by Baron Hunsdon. Cosimo de Medici is made the Grand duke of Tuscany by Pope Pius V.

1570   Regent Moray is assassinated; the earl of Lennox takes over the regency. Elizabeth I is excommunicated. The third War of Religion is ended by the Peace of St Germain-en-Laye. Tsar Ivan IV establishes a reign of terror in Great Novgorod and violently purges his government in Moscow. Denmark recognizes Swedish independence by the Peace of Stettin.

1571   Pope Pius V establishes the anti-Turkish Maritime League with Spain, Venice, Malta and Genoa; its fleet gains a decisive victory over the Turks at Lepanto. Roberto di Ridolfi plots to free Mary Queen of Scots and depose Elizabeth I, but the plots are exposed and fail. Sir Thomas Gresham's bourse is chartered as the Royal Exchange. Regent Lennox is murdered at Stirling; the earl of Mar replaces him.

1572   The duke of Norfolk is executed for treason in assisting the Ridolfi plot. Sigismund II of Poland dies without an heir; the Polish estates declare the crown elective. Catherine de Medici organises the Massacre of St Bartholomew's Day against the Huguenots; Admiral Gaspard de Coligny is disembowelled and defenestrated while still living. 3,000 Protestants die; Pope Gregory XIII congratulates Catherine. The fourth War of Religion commences. Regent Mar dies, replaced by the earl of Morton.

1573   The Peace of Constantinople ends the war between Venice and the Turks. Poland elects Henri, duc d'Anjou as king. The Edict of Boulogne ends the fourth War of Religion. Francis Walsingham is appointed Elizabeth's Secretary of State.

1574   The fifth War of Religion breaks out. Charles IX of France dies, and is succeeded by his brother Henri III, who abandons the Polish throne. Juan Fernandez discovers the Juan Fernandez Islands. Sultan Selim II dies after a fall in his bath, succeeded by his son Murad III.

1575   Dutch rebels fail to reach agreement with the Spanish Governor-General Requesens at Breda. The duc de Guise defeats the Huguenots at Dormans. Stephen Bathory of Transylvania is elected king of Poland.

1576   The Peace of Chastenoy ends the fifth War of Religion, but grants so many concessions to the Huguenots that the French Catholics ally with Philip II; Henri III outlaws Protestantism to appease them. Spanish troops rampage in the Netherlands, sacking Antwerp; the Pacification of Ghent allies the Lowland provinces in a pact for independence as a result. Emperor Maximilian II dies, and is succeeded by his son Rudolf II. Shah Tahmasp is murdered, and succeeded by his son Ismail II. The Theatre, England's first playhouse, is opened by Richard Burbage in Shoreditch.

1577   The sixth War of Religion breaks out; Catholic forces are victorious but to curb the power of the Holy League Henri III grants the Huguenots terms via the Peace of Bergerac. Don John of Austria arrives to take up the Governorship of the Netherlands, but his Perpetual Edict is rejected by William the Silent, who enters Brussels in triumph.

1578   Alessandro Farnese, duke of Parma, sent with an army to the Netherlands, where he defeats the Dutch at Gemblours and succeeds as governor on the death of Don John. Shah Isma'il II dies, and is succeeded by his brother Muhammad Kundabanda. King Sebastian of Portugal invades Morocco, but perishes along with most of his army at Al Kasr al Kebir, although the king of Fez is also killed. A cult develops around the dead king and four pretenders appear, who are all executed. Sebastian's great-uncle Henry succeeds him.

1579   The Union of Arras unites the Walloons of the Netherlands whilst the Dutch provinces unite under the Union of Utrecht and sign a military alliance with England. Francis Drake lands in California and claims English sovereignty over the area he calls 'New Albion'.

1580   The seventh War of Religion breaks out in France, but is ended by the treaty of Fleix. The Spanish invade Portugal led by the duke of Alva, defeat the Portuguese at Alcantara and conquer the country. Francis Drake completes a circumnavigation of the world.

1581   Stephen Bathory of Poland invades Russia. William the Silent appoints François, duc d'Alençon, king of the Netherlands. Tsar Ivan the Terrible kills his heir with his own hands. The Jesuit Edmund Campion is arrested, tortured, tried and executed.

1582   Tsar Ivan the Terrible makes peace with Poland and Sweden with the Peace of Jam-Zapolski and

	abandons Livonia and Estonia to Poland. James VI of Scotland kidnapped by pro-English nobles at Ruthven. Pope Gregory XIII introduces the Gregorian calendar, devised by Aloysius Lilius.
1583	James VI of Scotland escapes from his captors after 10 months. Humphrey Gilbert founds a colonial settlement in Newfoundland at St John's, but drowns on the return journey. Plots against Elizabeth I by John Somerville and Francis Throckmorton are foiled.
1584	Walter Raleigh founds a colony on Roanoke Island, Virginia. Tsar Ivan the Terrible dies, and is succeeded by his son Feodor I. François, duc d'Alencon dies, leaving Henri III with no direct heir; Henri of Navarre becomes nearest male heir. William the Silent is assassinated at Delft by Balthazar Gérard, but his son Maurice of Nassau continues the struggle against Spain.
1585	The Eighth War of Religion (the War of the Three Henris) breaks out in France as the Holy League under Henri, duc de Guise, attempt to stop Henri of Navarre from succeeding to the throne. The Netherlands are taken under English protection by the treaty of Nonsuch and a force under the earl of Leicester is sent to assist them.
1586	Kashmir annexed by the Emperor Akbar. Francis Drake raids Spanish New World colonies and rescues the survivors from the failed Roanoke settlement. Anglo-Dutch forces defeat the Spanish at Zutphen but Sir Philip Sidney dies as a result of a wound sustained there. Sir Anthony Babington plots against Elizabeth I, but Walsingham uncovers the plot and Babington is executed. Mary Queen of Scots is tried for her involvement and sentenced to death. Stephen Bathory of Poland dies.
1587	Mary Queen of Scots executed at Fotheringhay Castle. Sir Francis Drake raids Cadiz, 'singeing the king of Spain's beard' and disrupting preparations for the Armada. Sir Christopher Hatton is appointed Lord Chancellor. Poland elects Sigismund, son of John of Sweden, as king. Henri of Navarre defeats the Catholic League at Coutras.
1588	Frederick II of Denmark dies, and is succeeded by his son Christian IV. Henri, duc de Guise, enters Paris and forces Henri III to flee. The Spanish Armada sails for England under the duke of Medina Sidonia, but is defeated by the English and the weather. Although the tonnage of the 2 fleets was similar the Spanish lost nearly half of their 130 ships and the English none. Henri III arranges for Guise's assassination.
1589	The Russian Orthodox Church makes itself independent of Constantinople. Henri III of France is assassinated at St Cloud by Jacques Clément, a Dominican monk; he nominates Henri of Navarre as his successor, who founds the Bourbon line and defeats the Catholic League at Arques, whilst Sir John Harington invents the Ajax, a flushing toilet. The Rev. William Lee invents the first knitting machine.
1590	Shah Akbar conquers Orissa. Shah Abbas of Persia and Sultan Murad make peace, with Georgia, Azerbaijan and other provinces passing to the Turks. The Catholic League proclaim the cardinal Charles de Bourbon king of France; he dies soon after whilst Henri IV defeats them at Ivry. Edmund Spenser writes the first three books of *The Faerie Queene*. Shakespeare writes the *Henry VI* trilogy.
1591	The Tsar evich Dmitri is murdered, probably on order of the Regent Boris Godunov. Sir Richard Grenville dies after his ship, *Revenge*, battles a Spanish squadron single handed for 15 hours.
1592	Galileo Galilei is forced to move from Pisa to Padua after publishing his results on falling weights. The Japanese warlord Hideyoshi invades Korea and takes Seoul and Pyongyang. John III of Sweden dies, and is succeeded by his son Sigismund, king of Poland.
1593	The Chinese enter Korea and force Hideyoshi to retreat to the south coast. Christopher Marlowe is stabbed to death in Deptford by Ingram Frizer during a tavern brawl. Henri IV converts to Catholicism to win over his subjects (saying 'Paris is well worth a mass'). Salisbury Cathedral's organist strikes the Dean in a fit of rage and is dismissed from his post.
1594	Henri IV enters Paris and grants Huguenots freedom of worship by the Edict of St Germain-en-Laye. John Lancaster returns to Britain after sailing to the East Indies and establishes a spice trade. The philosopher Giordano Bruno is seized by the Vatican for espousing the Copernican theory of the Solar System.
1595	Sultan Murad III dies, and is succeeded by his son Muhammad III. Henri IV drives the Spanish from Burgundy after victory at Fontaine-Française. Spanish forces attack Cornwall, burning Penzance and Mousehole. Francis Drake and John Hawkins leave Plymouth to raid Panama; Hawkins dies en route near Puerto Rico.
1596	Francis Drake dies of dysentery off Panama. The tomato is introduced to England. The Catholic League submit to Henri IV, ending the Wars of Religion. Willem Barents discovers Spitsbergen. The English sack Cadiz whilst Spain captures Calais. The Ottomans defeat the Hungarians at Erlau and Keresztes.
1597	Philip II sends a second Armada to England, but it is scattered by storms and fails. Transylvania ceded to Emperor Rudolf II by Sigmund Bathory.
1598	Tsar Feodor I dies; his brother-in-law Boris Godunov seizes the throne and forces the national assembly to accept him. Henri IV of France grants rights to Huguenots by the Edict of Nantes. France and Spain make peace by the treaty of Vervins. Philip II of Spain dies, and is succeeded by his son Philip III.
1599	The Globe Theatre is built in London. The earl of Essex is made Lord Lieutenant of Ireland, but after signing an unauthorized truce with the earl of Tyrone returns to England and is arrested by Elizabeth I. The Swedish Diet deposes Sigismund III and makes Karl of Sodermanlund, uncle of Sigismund, regent for Sigismund's younger brother John.
1600	The East India Company is founded. Giordano Bruno is burned at the stake for heresy in Rome due to his support for the Copernican system. Ieyasu Tokugawa defeats his rivals at Sekigahara and takes control of Japan, moving the capital from Kyoto to Edo (Tokyo); the shipwrecked English mariner Will Adams becomes an adviser to him. Will Kemp morris-dances from London to Norwich.
1601	The earl of Essex leads a revolt against Elizabeth I, which fails and Essex is executed for treason. Moghul Emperor Akbar the Great annexes Berar, Ahmadnagar and Khandesh. A Spanish army lands in Ireland to support Tyrone's revolt.
1602	The Spaniards in Ireland surrender to Mountjoy at Kinsale. The Dutch East India Company is founded. Emperor Rudolf II suppresses the Moravian Brethren.
1603	Elizabeth I dies, her cousin twice removed; James VI of Scotland, succeeds her. Tyrone submits to

Mountjoy in Ireland, where James proclaims an amnesty. Walter Raleigh attempts to put Arabella Stuart on the throne rather than James, and is imprisoned for treason. Ieyasu founds the Tokugawa Shogunate in Japan. Sultan Muhammad III dies, and is succeeded by his son Ahmed I.

1604   The Hampton Court Conference convenes to discuss religious matters, and commissions an English translation of the Bible. Regent Karl becomes king of Sweden after his nephew John renounces the throne. England and Spain make peace. Ostend falls to the Spanish after a three-year siege.

1605   Tsar Boris Godunov dies; his son Feodor II succeeds him but is assassinated. A pretender, Dmitri, who claims to be a son of Ivan the Terrible, enters Moscow and is crowned Tsar. Akbar the Great dies, and is succeeded by his son Jahangir. Shogun Ieyasu retires in favour of his son Hidetada. Robert Catesby leads a plot to assassinate James I, but the plot fails and Guy Fawkes is caught red-handed under the House of Lords. Miguel de Cervantes publishes part one of *Don Quixote*.

1606   Tsar Dmitri is assassinated by the boyar (noble) Vasili Shuisky, who is elected Tsar. The Virginia Company is set up and 120 colonists leave London, led by Captain Christopher Newport. Shakespeare's *Macbeth* and *King Lear* are first performed.

1607   The English Parliament rejects the union of England and Scotland. Jamestown, Virginia is founded by Christopher Newport, who returns to England leaving Captain James Smith in charge; captured by the Algonquin, Smith's life is saved by the chief's daughter Pocahontas.

1608   Tsar Vasili Shuisky is defeated by a second 'False Dmitri', who advances on Moscow. Frederick IV of the Palatinate organizes a Protestant Union in Germany. Emperor Rudolf II is forced to cede Hungary, Austria and Moravia to his brother Matthias. The Jesuit state of Paraguay is established.

1609   Philip III of Spain signs a 12-year truce with the Dutch, effectively recognizing their independence. Duke Maximilian of Bavaria organizes a Catholic League to oppose the Protestant Union in Germany. John-William of Jülich-Cleves dies without an heir; Brandenburg and Neuburg quarrel over the territory. James I begins settling Protestants in Ulster.

1610   Galileo observes four moons orbiting Jupiter. Henri IV of France is assassinated by François Ravaillac; he is succeeded by his son Louis XIII. The Jamestown colonists abandon their settlement, but on meeting a ship of new settlers return and try again. Tsar Vasili Shuisky is deposed by Sigismund III of Poland and abducted to Warsaw; Vladislav, Sigismund's son, is offered the throne. Frederick IV of the Palatinate dies, and is succeeded by his son Frederick V.

1611   Henry Hudson is marooned by mutineers whilst searching for the North-west Passage and is never heard of again. Denmark declares war on Sweden. Emperor Rudolf II is forced to resign the Bohemian crown in favour of his brother Matthias. Karl IX of Sweden dies, and is succeeded by his son Gustavus II Adolphus.

1612   Emperor Rudolf II dies, and is succeeded as Holy Roman Emperor by his brother Matthias. Prince Dmitri Pojarsky forces the Polish in Moscow to surrender, thwarting Vladislav of Poland's claim for the throne. Henry, prince of Wales, dies of typhoid.

1613   Sweden and Denmark make the Peace of Knärod; Sweden gives up Finland. Mikhail Romanov, son of the Patriarch of Moscow, is elected Tsar by the boyars. The Globe Theatre burns down during a performance of Shakespeare's *Henry VIII*.

1614   Pocahontas marries John Rolfe, a settler. The 'Addled Parliament' meets, but is dissolved after clashes with James I over finance. The French parliament, the Estates-General convene, but is dismissed by the duc de Richelieu. The Virginian colonists resist French colonial attempts in Maine and Nova Scotia. Jülich-Cleves is divided between Brandenburg and Neuburg by the treaty of Xanten. John Napier publishes a book of logarithms.

1615   The Moluccas seized from the Portuguese by the Dutch, whilst the English defeat a Portuguese fleet off Bombay. Osaka falls to the Tokugawa shogunate. Lady Arabella Stuart starves herself to death in the Tower of London.

1616   Baffin Bay discovered by William Baffin. Francis Beaumont and Miguel de Cervantes die. William Shakespeare dies on his 52nd birthday. Manchurian Tartars invade China. Walter Raleigh is released from the Tower to search for El Dorado. James I sells peerages to raise funds. Maximilian of Tyrol and Archduke Albert renounce their claims to the Imperial throne in favour of Ferdinand of Styria. Galileo is arrested for heresy.

1617   Russia and Sweden make the Peace of Stolbovo; Novgorod is returned to Russia but Karelia is ceded to Sweden. Pocahontas is received by James I at court, but dies of smallpox soon after. Sultan Ahmad I dies, and is succeeded by his brother Mustafa I.

1618   Richelieu is exiled to Avignon after conspiring with the Queen Mother. Bohemian rebels throw the regents, Jaroslav von Martinitz and William Slawata, out of the Hradcany Palace in the Defenestration of Prague, an act which precipitates the Thirty Years War, as rebels led by Heinrich von Thurn advance on Austria and an Imperial army is raised to face them. Duke Albert Frederick of Prussia dies, his duchy passes to John Sigismund of Brandenburg. Francis Bacon is made Lord Chancellor. Walter Raleigh returns from his fruitless expedition to South America, and is executed by James I for treason to appease the Spaniards. Sultan Mustafa I is declared unfit to rule and is replaced by his nephew Osman II.

1619   Emperor Matthias dies. His cousin Ferdinand II of Styria succeeds him, but is deposed by the Bohemian Diet in favour of Frederick V of the Palatinate. A Bohemian army under Count von Thurn besieges Vienna, but is forced to withdraw. Louis XIII recalls Richelieu to subdue a revolt by Marie de Medici; the treaty of Angoulême ends the conflict. William Harvey establishes the circulation of the blood.

1620   Gustavus Adolphus of Sweden occupies Livonia after declaring war on Poland. The Pilgrim Fathers depart from Plymouth to America; the *Speedwell* is forced to turn back but the *Mayflower* arrives at Cape Cod; the settlement is called New Plymouth. Count Von Tilly leads a Catholic Union army to victory in the battle of the White Mountain against Frederick of Bohemia, who is deposed; the Bohemian revolt is suppressed by Emperor Frederick. Oliver Cromwell is denounced for playing cricket.

1621   Frederick V of the Palatinate is placed under Imperial Ban and his electorate invaded. The Huguenots rebel against Louis XIII. Philip III of Spain dies, and is succeeded by his son Philip IV, who resumes the war with the Netherlands. Count Olivares becomes chief minister of Spain. The Dutch West India Company is founded. Francis Bacon is impeached by Parliament for corruption, but is pardoned by James I.

1622   Richelieu is created a cardinal by Louis XIII, who makes peace with the Huguenots by reaffirming the Edict of Nantes. Count von Tilly is defeated at Wiesloch, but defeats Baden at Wimpfen and Brunswick at Höchst. Sultan Osman II is murdered by his Janissaries after planning to reform them and Mustafa I is restored to the throne.

1623   Abbas I of Persia takes Baghdad and Mosul from the Ottomans. Sultan Mustafa I is removed again from the throne and replaced by his nephew Murad IV. Count von Tilly defeats Brunswick at Stadtlohn and advances on Westphalia. Shogun Hidetada abdicates in favour of his son Iemitsu. Velázquez is appointed Court Painter to Philip IV of Spain. The First Folio of Shakespeare's plays is published.

1624   Cardinal Richelieu is made the chief minister of Louis XIII of France.

1625   James I dies, and is succeeded by his son Charles I. Sir William Courteen establishes a settlement on Barbados. Henri duc de Rohan leads a Huguenot rebellion against Louis XIII. Emperor Ferdinand II makes Wallenstein general of the Imperial forces and duke of Friedland. Breda falls to the Spanish after an eleven-month siege. Count von Tilly invades Saxony.

1626   Peter Minuit buys Manhattan from the Wappinger Confederacy for 60 guilders, founding New Amsterdam. The French colonise Madagascar. Louis XIII and the Huguenots make the Peace of La Rochelle. Wallenstein defeats a Protestant army at the Bridge of Dessau. The Duchy of Urbino is bequeathed to the Pope.

1627   Pirates attack Reykjavik. The Huguenots rise again; Richelieu besieges La Rochelle, which the duke of Buckingham tries but fails to relieve. Imperial forces conquer Silesia, Brunswick, Mecklenburg, Schleswig, Holstein and Jutland, forcing Christian IV of Denmark to retire from the war. Shah Jahangir dies, and is succeeded by his grandson Dawar Bakhsh.

1628   Wallenstein obtains the Duchy of Mecklenburg, assumes the title Admiral of the Baltic, but fails to take Stralsund. Shah Dawar Bahsh is removed from the throne by his uncle Shah Jahan I. Gustavus Adolphus enters the Thirty Years War. The duke of Buckingham is assassinated by John Fulton at Portsmouth. La Rochelle capitulates to Louis XIII. Ignatius Loyola is canonized.

1629   Shah Abbas of Persia dies, and is succeeded by his grandson Safi I. Charles I dissolves Parliament and assumes direct rule. Emperor Ferdinand II issues the Edict of Restitution, restoring Church estates and permitting freedom of worship only to adherents of the Confession of Augsburg, which the Catholic League ruthlessly enforces. Christian IV of Denmark regains his lands by the Peace of Lübeck, on condition he refrains from intervening in Imperial affairs. Sweden and Poland make the Peace of Altmark. Bethlen Gabor of Transylvania dies, and is succeeded by his wife Catherine of Brandenburg.

1630   Gustavus Adolphus invades Germany whilst Emperor Ferdinand II dismisses Wallenstein and replaces him with Tilly. Boston founded by John Winthrop. Sultan Murad IV defeats the Persians and captures Hamadan. Anglo-French hostilities are ended by the treaty of Madrid. George Rakoczy I is elected prince of Transylvania on the death of Stephen Bethlen.

1631   Richelieu and the German Protestant princes ally with Gustavus Adolphus against Emperor Ferdinand II. Urbino is annexed by the Papacy. Tilly brutally sacks Magdeburg, burns Halle and invades Saxony, but is defeated by Gustavus Adolphus at the battle of Breitenfeld. Gustavus Adolphus takes Frankfurt-am-Oder, Würzburg and Mainz. Wallenstein is reappointed by Emperor Ferdinand II.

1632   Gustavus Adolphus defeats Tilly, who is mortally wounded, at the Lech and takes Munich. At the battle of Lützen he defeats Walenstein but is killed in action. His daughter Christina succeeds him on the Swedish throne. Shah Jehan orders the destruction of Hindu temples. Charles I issues a charter for the colony of Maryland under the governorship of Lord Baltimore. The first coffee shop opens in London. Sigismund III of Poland dies, and is succeeded by his son Vladislav VII.

1633   Wallenstein defeats Bernard of Saxe-Weimar and a Swedish army at Steinau and occupies Bohemia. Galileo is forced by the Inquisition to abjure the theories of Copernicus.

1634   The Oberammergau Passion Play is enacted for the first time. Russia and Poland make peace via the treaty of Polianovska; Vladislav VII renounces his claim to Russia. Emperor Ferdinand II relieves Wallenstein of command, replacing him with Matthias Gallas. Wallenstein is assassinated soon after, whilst Imperial troops defeat the Swedes at Nördlingen and conquer Württemberg and Franconia.

1635   Cardinal Richelieu founds the Académie Française. Emperor Ferdinand II settles differences with Elector John George of Saxony via the Peace of Prague, after France and Sweden formally ally against him, formally bringing France into the Thirty Years War. Sweden and Poland agree a 20-year truce via the treaty of Stuhmsdorf. France and Saxe-Weimar ally by the treaty of St Germain-en-Laye. The first General Post Office in England opens in Bishopsgate, London.

1636   Persia and the Ottoman Empire make peace. Olivares invades Picardy. Swedish troops defeat the Saxons at the battle of Wittstock. Harvard College is founded in Cambridge, Massachusetts.

1637   Emperor Ferdinand II dies, and is succeeded by his son Ferdinand III. Bogislav XIV of Pomerania dies without an heir; his lands are divided between Sweden and Prussia. The Dutch under Frederick Henry of Orange recapture Breda.

1638   The Scottish Covenant is drawn up and signed, forcing Charles I to withdraw Laud's liturgy in Scotland. Bernhard of Saxe-Weimar takes Freiburg and Breisach. Sultan Murad IV retakes Baghdad from the Persians. Torture is abolished in England.

1639   The First Bishops' War erupts in Scotland between the Covenanters and Charles I. Peace comes by the Pacification of Berwick, and Charles I grants the Scots a General Assembly and Parliament, which he dissolves at the end of the year. Dutch admiral Maarten Tromp destroys a Spanish fleet in the decisive battle of the Downs.

1640   Catalonia revolts against Spanish taxes and control. Sultan Murad IV dies, and is succeeded by his brother Ibrahim. Charles I is forced to reconvene Parliament but the 'Short Parliament' refuses to authorize any taxes and is dissolved. The Scots revolt in the Second Bishops' War, defeating the English at Newburn. Thomas Wentworth is created earl of Strafford. The Great Council of Peers summoned by Charles I concludes the treaty of Ripon, paying off the Scots, and insists on the election of Parliament. The 'Long Parliament', is duly elected. João of Braganza is elected king of Portugal, which breaks free from Spain, but Spain refuses to recognize this. Elector George William of Brandenburg dies, and is succeeded by his son Frederick William, the 'Great Elector'. Strafford and Laud are impeached.

1641 Tsar Michael I forbids the sale and use of tobacco, yet makes the substance a State monopoly. Strafford is executed. Parliament abolishes the Star Chamber. Parliament sends the Grand Remonstrance to Charles I, who is infuriated. The comte de Soissons plots against Louis XIII, but Jean d'Orléans, the king's brother, exposes him. The Irish Catholics revolt.

1642 Charles I enters the House of Commons to arrest Hampden, Pym, Holles, Haselrig and Strode for treason, but the quintet have been warned and take refuge in the City of London. Charles I flees London, rejects Parliament's 19 Propositions and raises his standard in Nottingham, triggering the Civil War. Rupert of the Rhine defeats the Parliamentarians at Powick Bridge and Edgehill. Blaise Pascal invents an adding machine. Cardinal Richelieu dies; Cardinal Mazarin replaces him as first minister of France. Abel Tasman discovers Van Diemen's Land (Tasmania) and New Zealand.

1643 Evangelista Torricelli develops the barometer. Parliamentarians under Fairfax take Leeds. Cromwell is victorious at Grantham, but Hampden is defeated and killed at Chalgrove Field. Louis XIII of France dies, and is succeeded by his son Louis XIV. French troops defeat a combined Spanish, Italian, Dutch and Flemish army at the battle of Rocroi. Royalists are victorious at Roundway Down and take Bristol, but are defeated at Gloucester, Newbury and Winceby. John Pym dies of cancer. Olivares falls from power in Spain.

1644 Ming Emperor Chongzhen commits suicide as Peking falls to the bandit Li Zicheng, thus ending his dynasty's rule. Li proclaims himself emperor, but is driven out by the Manchus, who found the Qing dynasty with Shunzhi as Emperor. John Milton writes his pamphlet the *Areopagitica*, on press freedom. The Scottish Covenanters join the Civil War on the Parliamentarian side. After a Royalist victory at Cropredy Bridge, Cromwell heavily defeats Prince Rupert at Marston Moor and takes York. Scottish royalists under Montrose defeat the Covenanters at Tippermuir, Charles captures Fowey, whilst the second battle of Newbury is indecisive.

1645 Archbishop Laud is executed. Montrose defeats the Covenanters at Inverlochy. The Ottomans and Venice war over Crete. Armistice talks between Charles I and Parliament fail at Uxbridge. John Lilburne publicizes Leveller ideas. Swedish troops defeat the Imperial army at Jankau and take Moravia. The Dutch occupy St Helena. Parliament creates the New Model Army under Fairfax and Cromwell which decisively defeats the royalists at Naseby. Tsar Michael I dies, and is succeeded by his son Alexei. The French defeat the Bavarians at Nördlingen. Prince Rupert surrenders Bristol, incurring his uncle's wrath. Covenanters rout Montrose at Philiphaugh.

1646 The Swedes take Prague, and in concert with the French invade Bavaria. Royalist armies in Exeter and Oxford capitulate to Parliamentarians; Charles surrenders to the Covenanters at Southwell. Held in Newcastle, Charles fails to reach agreement with Parliament and tries, but fails, to escape.

1647 George Fox founds the 'Friends of the Truth', later to become the Quakers. Matthew Hopkins, the 'Witchfinder General' is found guilty of witchcraft himself and hanged. Bear baiting and folk dancing are banned in England. The Scots hand over Charles I to Parliament in return for £400,000. Stadtholder Frederick Henry of Holland dies, and is succeeded by his son William II. Naples revolts against Spanish rule. Bavaria and Cologne state their neutrality in the Thirty Years War by the treaty of Ulm, but Emperor Ferdinand III gains their support. Mainz and Hesse withdraw from the fray.

1648 Parliament loses patience with Charles I after he makes a secret treaty with the Scots, who rebel along with the Welsh. Spain reasserts its rule over Naples. Ukrainians under Bogdan Chmielnicki lead a pogrom of Jews in a bid to establish independence from Poland. Sultan Ibrahim is deposed and killed by his Janissaries for lifting the siege of Heraklion, and is succeeded by his son Muhammad IV. The Second Civil War is short-lived, Cromwell defeating the Scots at Preston, and Colonel Thomas Pride purges Parliament to ensure Charles I is put on trial. The Fronde riots break out in Paris asserting the rights of the Paris Parlement (Parliament). The Peace of Westphalia ends the Thirty Years War, but is condemned by Pope Innocent X.

1649 Charles I is tried by Parliament and executed; Parliament abolishes the monarchy and the House of Lords, proclaiming a 'Commonwealth'. The War of the Fronde is ended by the treaty of Rueil; however a second Fronde uprising breaks out. The Levellers and Diggers are suppressed. Royalists rebel in Ireland; Cromwell sacks Drogheda and Wexford.

1650 Mazarin allies himself with the leaders of the first Fronde, and imprisons the leaders of the second. René Descartes dies whilst in the service of Queen Christina. Montrose leads a Scottish uprising against Parliament but is defeated at Carbisdale, betrayed by Neil McLeod and hanged. Archbishop James Ussher calculates that the Earth was created in 4004 BC. Charles II arrives in Scotland. Cromwell invades Scotland and is victorious at Dunbar. Stadtholder William II dies of smallpox, leaving a posthumously born heir, William III. The Holy Roman Empire and Sweden reach an accord with the treaty of Nuremberg.

1651 Charles II is crowned at Scone and invades England but is defeated by Cromwell at Worcester, evades capture and flees to France. Thomas Hobbes publishes *Leviathan*, and John Playford *The English Dancing Master*. Paris Parlement votes for the release of the Great Condér, leader of the Fronde, forcing Mazarin from the country, but he returns with an army to suppress the rebellion. Shogun Iemitsu dies, and is succeeded by his son Ietsuna, who quickly suppresses two rebellions.

1652 Jan Van Riebeck founds Cape Town. The Great Condé defeats a royalist army at Bléneau and is welcomed in Paris, where a rebel government is formed; however, the government quarrels with the Parisian middle class, which lets Louis XIV into the city. Parliament publishes the reconciliatory Act of Pardon and Oblivion. Admiral Robert Blake defeats Maarten Tromp off Dover, and England and Holland go to war, but Blake is defeated off Dungeness.

1653 The pirate Zheng Chenkong ravages the Chinese coast in his war with the Manchus. Mazarin returns to Paris and suppresses the Fronde. Lorenzo Tonti devises the Tontine system of life insurance. The English fleet defeats the Dutch off Portland, North Foreland and Texel. Cromwell dissolves the Long Parliament, and after the unsuccessful Barebones Parliament is made Lord Protector. Izaak Walton publishes *The Compleat Angler.*

1654 The treaty of Westminster ends the Anglo-Dutch War. Queen Christina of Sweden abdicates, and is succeeded by her cousin Karl X. Bogdan Chmielnicki swears allegiance to Russia, which goes to war with Poland, taking Smolensk.

1655 Colonel Penruddock leads a rising against Cromwell in Wiltshire, which is suppressed. The English under Vice-Admiral Penn take Jamaica from the Spanish. Karl X of Sweden invades Poland, precipitating the first Northern War. Elector Frederick William of Brandenburg invades Prussia. Cromwell divides England into 11 districts, each governed by a major-general. Cromwell readmits Jews into England.

1656 Sweden and Prussia ally by the treaty of Königsberg, whilst Denmark, Russia and the Holy Roman Empire declare war on Sweden. Spain declares war on Britain. Sweden defeats Poland at the battle of Warsaw. Baruch Spinoza is excommunicated for heresy. João IV of Portugal dies, and is succeeded by his son Alfonso VI.

1657 Christiaan Huygens develops the pendulum clock. Cromwell rejects an offer of the crown and establishes a nominated House of Lords. Emperor Ferdinand dies, and is succeeded by his son Leopold I. Admiral Blake destroys a Spanish treasure fleet at Santa Cruz. Brandenburg allies with Poland against Sweden by the treaty of Bromberg.

1658 The stage coach service is established in England. Jan Swammerdam observes red blood cells for the first time. The treaty of Roskilde ends the first Northern War, but Charles X of Sweden starts a second by unsuccessfully attacking Copenhagen. An Anglo-French force defeats the Spanish at the battle of the Dunes and England acquires Dunkirk. Shah Jahan I is imprisoned by his son Aurangzeb Alamgir I, who replaces him as Mughal emperor. Oliver Cromwell dies; his son Richard becomes Lord Protector.

1659 Elector Frederick William of Brandenburg drives the Swedes from Prussia. Richard Cromwell resigns as Lord Protector; conflict between army and Parliament leads to a state of near-anarchy. France and Spain make the Peace of the Pyrenees.

1660 General Monck, commanding general in Scotland, leads his troops to London to call for a new Parliament, which meets and votes for the restoration of the monarchy under Charles II. Karl X of Sweden dies, and is succeeded by his son Karl XI. Charles II makes the Declaration of Breda promising religious toleration and returns to England. The Peace of Oliva ends the hostilities between Sweden, Poland, Brandenburg and the Holy Roman Empire. Denmark reaches peace with and cedes Skania to Sweden by the treaty of Copenhagen. The Royal Society for the Promotion of Natural Knowledge is founded. George Racoczy II of Transylvania dies in battle against the Turks.

1661 Michael Apafi I is elected to replace the deceased George Racoczy III as Prince of Transylvania. Chinese living within 10 miles of the coast are ordered to move inland in an attempt to deter pirate Zheng Chenkong. Cardinal Mazarin dies, letting Louis XIV begin personal rule. The Cavalier Parliament meets in England. The Peace of Kardis between Sweden and Russia finally ends the second Northern War. Tangier and Bombay are ceded to England by Portugal in a treaty of alliance.

1662 France and Holland ally against England. The revised Prayer Book is imposed on Anglicans. The Royal Society is granted a Royal Charter by Charles II. Dunkirk is sold to France by Charles II for £400,000.

1663 The Theatre Royal, Drury Lane, opens with a performance of John Fletcher's *The Humorous Lieutenant.* Colbert founds the Académie des Inscriptions et Belles Lettres in Paris. The Ottomans declare war on the Holy Roman Empire and invade Hungary. Colbert makes New France into a colony with Quebec as the capital.

1664 France and Saxony make an alliance. The Conventicle Act bans unauthorized religious meetings of more than 5 people in England, in an attempt to suppress nonconformism. Austrian troops defeat the Turks at St Gotthard on the Raab River and make the Truce of Vasvar. New Amsterdam under Peter Stuyvesant surrenders to the English, who rename it New York.

1665 The Great Plague hits London. The second Anglo-Dutch War opens; the Dutch are defeated off Lowestoft. Anglo-Portuguese forces defeat the Spanish at Villaviciosa and Montes Claros, securing Portuguese independence. Philip IV of Spain dies, and is succeeded by his son Charles II.

1666 Louis XIV founds a French Academy of Sciences. Holland allies with Brandenburg, Brunswick and Denmark to secure its safety, whilst France declares war on England. The English and Dutch fleets meet in the inconclusive Four Days Battle before an English victory at Orford Ness. London is ravaged by a Great Fire starting in Pudding Lane.

1667 Russia and Poland make peace with the treaty of Andrusovo, ending their 13-year war; Kiev, Smolensk and the Eastern Ukraine are ceded to Russia. John Milton's *Paradise Lost* is published. French troops invade Flanders and Hainault, starting the War of Devolution. The Dutch sail up the Medway to Chatham, sinking several ships and taking the English flagship back to Holland. England, Holland and France make peace by the treaty of Breda. The Medway débâcle leads to the fall of Clarendon, and the Cabal administration under Clifford, Arlington, Buckingham, Ashley and Lauderdale is formed. (Cabal is a mnemonic for its members but the word does not derive from them.) The Regent Pedro banishes Alfonso VI of Portugal to the Azores.

1668 England, Holland and Sweden ally by the treaty of the Hague. John Dryden is appointed the first Poet Laureate. Spain recognizes Portuguese independence by the treaty of Lisbon. The War of Devolution is ended by the Peace of Aix-La-Chapelle, whilst Louis XIV and Emperor Leopold I reach an agreement over future partition of Spanish realms. John Kasimir of Poland abdicates.

1669 The Lithuanian Michael Wisniowecki is elected king of Poland. The Mughal Aurangzeb bans Hinduism in India and destroys Hindu temples, leading to widespread revolts. Crete falls to the Ottomans. The Hanseatic League holds its last meeting. Antonio Stradivari makes his first violin. Samuel Pepys ceases writing his diary.

1670 Frederick III of Denmark dies, and is succeeded by his son Christian V. The Ukrainian Cossacks rebel against Polish rule, but are suppressed by Jan Sobieski. Gabriel Mouton, a French clergyman, proposes the establishment of decimal measurements. France and Bavaria make a defensive alliance, whilst Charles II makes the secret treaty of Dover with Louis XIV, pledging anti-Dutch collaboration and conversion to Roman Catholicism at an appropriate moment.

1671   The buccaneer Henry Morgan captures Panama City, is tried for piracy but pardoned and knighted by Charles II and later becomes Deputy Governor of Jamaica. The Ottomans declare war on Poland. The Don Cossacks under Stenka Razin revolt, but their rising is quelled and Razin executed. Milton publishes *Paradise Regained* and Aphra Behn *The Forced Marriage*.

1672   The Russian serfs rebel. Charles II issues the Declaration of Indulgence. Louis XIV declares war on the Dutch and sends his troops in; an English fleet defeats the Dutch at Southwold Bay. The Dutch Grand Pensionary Jan de Witt and his brother Cornelius are murdered by a mob, after William III of Orange has been appointed to the revived office of Stadtholder and put in charge of the Dutch army.

1673   Parliament forces Charles II to revoke the Declaration of Indulgence and instead passes the Test Act. Brandenburg pledges to refuse assistance to enemies of France by the treaty of Vossen, whilst Leopold I declares war on France. Michael Wisniowecki of Poland dies; the next day Jan Sobieski defeats the Ottomans at Khorzim.

1674   France devastates the Palatinate whilst Spain deters the anti-French coalition. Jan Sobieski is elected king of Poland. England and Holland make peace by the the treaty of Westminster. The bandit Sivaji Bhonsala founds a Marãthã state as independent from the Mughal Empire.

1675   France recovers Alsace after victory at Turkheim. Sweden goes to war with Denmark and Brandenburg, but is defeated by the latter at Fehrbellin. The Royal Greenwich Observatory is founded, with John Flamsteed as first Astronomer Royal.

1676   Tsar Alexis dies, and is succeeded by his son Feodor III. Jan Sobieski of Poland makes peace with the Ottomans under the treaty of Zuravno, ceding the Polish Ukraine. The Swedes defeat the Danes at Lunden.

1677   The Dutch are defeated by the French at Cassel, but with the Danes defeat a Swedish fleet at Öland. Jean Racine's tragedy *Phèdre* is first performed. Edmund Halley returns from St Helena, having catalogued the Southern Night Sky.

1678   France captures Ghent and Ypres. Russia joins the war against Sweden. France, Spain and Holland make the peace of Nijmegen; Holland regains its lost territories. False allegations made by Titus Oates and others of a 'Popish Plot' to kill Charles II lead to severe anti-Catholic measures. Hungarians under Emeric Tokolyi rebel against Imperial rule. Brandenburg takes Stralsund from the Swedes. The factional terms Whig and Tory enter use in Parliament.

1679   The Cavalier Parliament is dissolved. Archbishop Sharp of St Andrews murdered by Covenanters, whose rising is defeated by Monmouth at Bothwell Brig. Louis XIV forces the Peace of St Germain-en-Laye on Sweden and Brandenburg; the latter relinquishes its conquests. Sweden and Denmark make peace by the treaty of Lund. Henry Purcell is appointed organist of Westminster Abbey.

1680   Sivaji Bhonsala dies, and is succeeded by his son Sambhaji I, but Emperor Aurangzeb attempts to reconquer the Marathas. Shogun Ietsuna dies, and is succeeded by his brother Tsunayoshi.

1681   Charles II grants Pennsylvania as a nonconformist colony to William Penn. Emperor Kangxi suppresses the Rebellion of the Three Feudatories. France annexes Strasbourg. Bank cheques are issued for the first tiime in England.

1682   Louis XIV moves his court to Versailles. The Chelsea Hospital is founded. La Salle reaches the mouth of the Mississippi, names the surrounding area 'Louisiana' claiming it for France. Tsar Feodor III of Russia dies. His sister Sophia becomes regent for her younger brothers, Ivan V, who is mentally defective, and her half-brother Peter I, and seeks to kill Peter's supporters as a threat to her position.

1683   By the League of The Hague, Spain and the Holy Roman Empire join Holland and Sweden in an anti-French coalition. The Rye House Plot against Charles II and James, duke of York is unmasked; Lord William Russell and Algernon Sidney are executed for their roles in the plot and the earl of Essex commits suicide. Alfonso VI of Portugal dies, and is succeeded by his brother Pedro II. Ottomans besiege Vienna, but are forced to withdraw by Jan Sobieski of Poland and Charles, duke of Lorraine. China captures Formosa (Taiwan).

1684   The Japanese poet Saikaku composes 23,500 verses in 24 hours. The Holy Roman Empire, Poland and Venice form the Holy League of Linz against the Turks. Jews are expelled from Bordeaux.

1685   Charles II dies, and is succeeded by his brother James II, but his illegitimate son the duke of Monmouth leads an uprising which ends in defeat at Sedgemoor. Monmouth is beheaded and Judge Jeffreys conducts the 'Bloody Assizes' against Monmouth's followers. Louis XIV revokes the Edict of Nantes, forcing Huguenots to flee abroad and damaging the French economy.

1686   The Institut de Saint Louis is founded by Madame de Maintenon to educate the daughters of poor gentlefolk; the curriculum includes cookery; graduates are given a blue ribbon – the *cordon bleu*. The League of Augsburg is formed against Louis XIV by the Holy Roman Empire, Spain, Sweden, Saxony, Bavaria and the Palatinate. Buda is liberated from the Ottomans, whilst Russia declares war on them.

1687   Shogun Sunayoshi forbids the killing of animals in Japan. James II proclaims freedom of worship and receives the Papal Nuncio. Ottomans defeated by Charles of Lorraine at Mohács who expell them from Hungary, they lose the Greek Peloponnese and Athens to the Venetians. Sultan Muhammad IV is deposed by his Janissaries and replaced by his brother Suleiman III. Newton's *Principia* is published.

1688   Elector Frederick William of Brandenburg dies, and is succeeded by his son Frederick III. An heir to James II is born. To forestall a Catholic succession William of Orange is invited to replace James, which he does in the 'Glorious Revolution'. James II flees to exile in France. The Ottomans surrender Belgrade to the Austrians. France invades the Palatinate. A marine insurance society is founded in Edward Lloyd's Coffee House in London.

1689   Natal becomes a Dutch colony. Louis XIV declares war on Britain whilst James II arrives in Ireland and besieges Londonderry. A Jacobite rising in Scotland defeats a Covenanter army at Killiecrankie before being defeated at Dunkeld. Regent Sophia is deposed in Russia after conspiring to abduct Peter I, who is established as tsar. The Declaration of Rights is proclaimed in England.

1690   Marlborough captures Cork and Kinsale from Jacobite supporters. Spain and Savoy join the League of Augsburg, which is defeated at Fleurus. The French defeat an Anglo-Dutch fleet off Beachy Head and burn Teignmouth. William III defeats James II at the battle of the Boyne, forcing James back to France. Calcutta is founded by the East India Company. The Ottomans retake Transylvania, Serbia, Belgrade and Bulgaria.

1691   The first directory of addresses is published in Paris. Sultan Suleiman III dies, and is succeeded by his brother Ahmad II, whose reign starts poorly with defeat at Slankamen and expulsion from Hungary. The Irish Jacobites are defeated at Aughrim and pacified by the treaty of Limerick.

1692   The Campbells massacre the MacDonalds at Glencoe. Marlborough is briefly imprisoned for suspected treasonable contact with James II. The Salem witch trials commence. The English defeat a French invasion fleet at La Hogue, but an Anglo-Dutch army is defeated at Steenkirk. Ernst Augustus of Brunswick is made Elector of Hanover.

1693   William III borrows £1 million, instigating the National Debt. French fleet defeats an Anglo-Dutch one at Cape St Vincent and Lagos; French armies are also successful at Neerwinden and Marsaglia.

1694   William Paterson leads the founding of the Bank of England, with Sir John Houblon as its first Governor. Shah Suleiman I of Persia dies, and is succeeded by his son Husain I. Mary II of England dies.

1695   Princess Anne returns to court to act as hostess for her brother-in-law William III. Sultan Ahmad II dies, and is succeeded by his nephew Mustafa II. William Paterson helps found the Bank of Scotland. Peter the Great besieges Azov, but is forced to withdraw by the Turks with heavy losses. William III takes Namur.

1696   Jan Sobieski of Poland dies. Peter the Great takes Azov and conquers Kamchatka. The Window Tax is introduced in England, whilst John Locke and Isaac Newton reform the coinage.

1697   Peter the Great travels incognito from Russia to study European ways of life. Karl XI of Sweden dies, and is succeeded by his son Karl XII. Elector Frederick-Augustus I of Saxony is elected king of Poland, taking the title Augustus II. France, Britain, Spain and the Holy Roman Empire make peace by the treaty of Ryswick. Eugene of Savoy heavily defeats the Turks at Zenta.

1698   Elector Ernst Augustus of Hanover dies, and is succeeded by his son George. Leopold of Anhalt-Dessau introduces goose-stepping to the Prussian army. Whitehall Palace is largely destroyed by fire The Streltzy, elite musketeer regiments, revolt in Moscow, but the rising is quelled.

1699   Turkey signs the Peace of Karlowitz with Austria, to which it cedes Hungary, Croatia and Transylvania. Turkey also cedes its portion of the Ukraine to Poland, and Morea and Dalmatia to Venice. Christian V of Denmark dies, and is succeeded by his son Frederick IV. Denmark, Russia, Poland and Saxony sign the treaty of Preobrazhenskoe to carve up the Swedish Empire. William Dampier explores the western Australian coast. Henry Winstanley builds the first Eddystone Lighthouse.

1700   The German Protestant states adopt the Gregorian calendar. The Great Northern War opens with concerted attacks on Sweden; Saxony invades Livonia and Denmark invades Schleswig, but Sweden invades Zeeland, forces the Danes from the war by the treaty of Travendal, and defeats Russia at Narva. The duke of Gloucester dies, leaving no direct Stuart heir after Princess Anne (James Stuart being unacceptable). Charles II of Spain dies, the Habsburg line ends with him and the throne goes to Philip V, grandson of Louis XIV.

1701   Elector Frederick of Brandenburg makes himself king of Prussia; Emperor Leopold acquiesces in return for military aid. The War of the Spanish Succession opens; England, Holland and Savoy join the Holy Roman Empire in the Grand Alliance. Karl XII of Sweden invades Poland. Eugene of Savoy defeats the French at Carpi and Chiara. Antoine Cadillac founds Detroit. The Act of Settlement provides for the succession in England to pass to Electress Sophia of Hanover after Princess Anne. Jethro Tull develops the seed drill.

1702   William III dies, and is succeeded in England by his sister-in-law Anne, whilst in Holland the Stadtholdership is put into abeyance. The *Daily Courant* becomes London's first daily newspaper. Karl XII of Sweden takes Warsaw and Cracow. Marlborough captures Venlo, Roermond and Liège, and is raised from an earl to a Duke. Protestant peasants, the Camisards, revolt in the Cévennes.

1703   The Swedish defeat the Russians at Pulutsk. Marlborough takes Cologne and Bonn. Peter the Great founds St Petersburg. The Grand Alliance proclaims Archduke Charles of Austria king of Spain. Portugal joins the Grand Alliance and signs the Methuen treaty with England. The Eddystone Lighthouse is destroyed as a great storm hits Southern England.

1704   Sweden secures the deposition of Augustus II of Poland in favour of Stanislas Leszczynski. Gibraltar is captured by the English, who defeat a relieving force at Velez Malaga. Marlborough and Eugene of Savoy heavily defeat the French at Blenheim. Beau Nash becomes Master of Ceremonies at Bath.

1705   Edmund Halley predicts the return in 1758 of the comet that will bear his name. Emperor Leopold dies, and is succeeded by his son Joseph I. Peter the Great's westernization provokes revolts in Astrakhan. Barcelona falls to the Grand Alliance.

1706   Karl XII of Sweden defeats a Russo-Saxon army at Fraustadt. Marlborough defeats the French at Ramillies; Brussels, Antwerp, Ghent and Ostend quickly capitulate to him. Archduke Charles is installed in Madrid, but is driven out after 3 months by Philip V of Spain. Eugene of Savoy defeats the French at Turin and drives them from Lombardy. Augustus II of Poland abdicates, recognizing his usurper Stanislas I.

1707   Emperor Aurangzeb dies, and is succeeded by his son A'zam Shah, whose death soon after puts his brother Bahadur Shah I on the throne. A French army under the duke of Berwick defeats an Anglo-Portuguese force at Almanza. England and Scotland formally unite with the Act of Union. Prussia and Sweden sign a Perpetual Alliance. Admiral Sir Cloudesley Shovell's squadron runs aground in the Scillies, only one man survives. Fortnum & Mason's opens in Piccadilly.

1708   Marlborough and Eugene of Savoy defeat the French at Oudenarde; Marlborough subsequently captures Lille. Minorca captured by the British. The East India Company and the New East India Company merge. The Sikh guru Govind Singh is assassinated by order of the Mughal Bahadur Shah. Karl XII of Sweden invades the Ukraine.

1709   The *Tatler* is launched by Richard Steele and Joseph Addison. Tsar Peter defeats Karl XII of Sweden at
         Poltava, forcing Karl to take refuge in Anatolia and breaking Sweden's power. Augustus II takes advantage
         of this by driving Stanislas I from Poland and regaining the throne. Marlborough and Eugene of Savoy take
         Tournai and Mons and defeat the French at Malplaquet. Abraham Darby develops coke-fuelled iron
         smelting at Coalbrookdale.
1710   Stanhope is victorious at Almenara and Saragossa but is defeated and captured at Brihuega. Handel is
         appointed Kapellmeister to Elector George of Hanover. Christopher Wren completes St Paul's Cathedral.
1711   Addison and Steele launch the *Spectator*. Queen Anne establishes Ascot racecourse. Emperor Joseph I
         dies, and is succeeded by his brother Charles VI, who guarantees a Hungarian constitution by the Peace of
         Szathmar. Russia and Turkey sign the treaty of Pruth; Tsar Peter is forced to return Azov to the Turks. Rio
         de Janeiro is captured by the French. The South Sea Company is established. Marlborough is dismissed
         from command and replaced by Ormonde.
1712   Civil war breaks out in Switzerland; the Protestant cantons are victorious at Villmergen and peace is re-
         established by the treaty of Aarau. The Mughal Emperor Bahadur Shah I dies; his sons quarrel over the
         succession.
1713   Farrukhsiyar, grandson of Bahadur Shah, establishes himself as Mughal emperor. Karl XII of Sweden is
         taken prisoner by the Ottomans at Bender in Moravia. Frederick I of Prussia dies and is succeeded by his
         son Frederick William I. The treaties of Utrecht end the War of the Spanish Succession, with Philip V
         allowed to keep the throne, establishing the Bourbon dynasty in the country; the thrones of France and
         Spain are never to be united. Emperor Charles VI does not sign. Charles VI issues the Pragmatic Sanction,
         allowing female succession in Habsburg domains. Shogun Ienobu dies, and is succeeded by his infant son
         Ietsugu.
1714   The Board of Longitude promises a £20,000 reward for anybody who can discover a method of divining
         longitude. Russia gains control of Finland after victory at the battle of Storkyro. Charles VI makes peace
         with France at Rastatt and Baden. Queen Anne dies, and is succeeded by her second cousin George I, as
         his mother Sophia had died shortly before. Karl XII of Sweden is released by the Turks.
1715   Louis XIV dies, and is succeeded by his great-grandson Louis XV. Mir Vais, chief of Kandahar, dies; his son
         Mir Maahmoud succeeds him, but is assassinated by his uncle Mir Abdullah who takes power. The earl of
         Mar leads a Jacobite rising in Scotland; the Old Pretender James lands at Peterhead to support the rising,
         but his supporters are defeated at Sheriffmuir and Preston.
1716   The Old Pretender returns to France as the '15 rebellion fizzles out. Shogun Ietsugu dies aged seven and
         is succeeded by Yoshimune, a distant relation. Eugene of Savoy defeats the Ottomans at Peterwardein;
         Emperor Charles VI joins the war and Temesvar, the last Ottoman possession in Hungary, falls. The
         Tsarevich Alexei flees Russia and places himself under the protection of Charles VI.
1717   The Grand Lodge of the Freemasons is established at the Goose and Gridiron Tavern, Covent Garden.
         School attendance is made compulsory in Prussia. Lhasa is occupied by Mongols. Eugene of Savoy
         defeats the Ottomans at Belgrade.
1718   Edward Teach, Blackbeard, is killed in a fight in North Carolina. The first English banknotes are issued.
         Philip V of Spain sends troops into Sicily; the Quadruple Alliance of the Empire, France, England and
         Holland is formed to counter him. Tsarevich Alexei is killed by order of Peter the Great and his friends
         executed. Karl XII is killed at Fredriksten during an expedition into Norway, and is succeeded by his sister
         Ulrika.
1719   Liechtenstein becomes an independent principality under Count Hans von Liechtenstein, who has bought
         the territory. Herat rebels against Shah Hussein, and defeats an army sent to subdue the area. Sweden
         and Hanover make the Peace of Stockholm. The Mughal emperor Farrukhsiyar dies, creating a succession
         dispute which is eventually resolved when his cousin Muhammad ascends the throne.
1720   The Great Northern War is brought to an end as Sweden makes peace with her neighbours. Ulrika of
         Sweden abdicates in favour of her husband Frederick of Hesse. A plague outbreak in Marseille is the final
         time the Black Death pandemic strikes. The South Sea Company collapses (South Sea Bubble), as does
         John Law's Mississippi Company, bringing ruin to many. China makes Tibet a protectorate.
1721   A revolt in Formosa is suppressed by China. A regular postal service is established between London and
         New England. John Aislabie, Chancellor of the Exchequer, is dismissed and imprisoned for fraud. Robert
         Walpole is appointed First Lord of the Treasury by George I, becoming the first prime minister. Sweden and
         Russia sign the treaty of Nystadt; Russia gains Estonia. Peter the Great is proclaimed Emperor of All the
         Russias.
1722   Mir Mahmoud of Kandahar conquers Afghanistan, defeats the Persians at Gulnabad, and takes Isfahan.
         Shah Hussein abdicates in favour of his son Tahmasp, but Mahmoud proclaims himself Shah. Russia and
         the Ottoman Empire exploit the situation and invade; the Russians withdraw after an outbreak of ergotism.
         Hungary rejects Emperor Charles' Pragmatic Sanction. Jacob Roggeveen discovers Rapa Nui, naming it
         Easter Island.
1723   Louis XV of France attains his majority, ending the Regency period. Britain and Prussia sign the treaty of
         Charlottenburg, arranging marriages between the two royal houses.
1724   Philip V of Spain abdicates in favour of his son Luis, who dies some months after, and Philip returns to the
         throne. Russia and the Ottoman Empire make a treaty for the dismemberment of Persia, where Mir
         Mahmoud goes insane.
1725   Tsar Peter the Great dies, and is succeeded by his widow Catherine I. The Pragmatic Sanction is
         guaranteed by the treaty of Vienna. Tabriz falls to the Ottomans. Mir Mahmoud kills 39 Persian princes; the
         surviving nobles elect his cousin Ashraf to replace the insane Shah, who is murdered on order of Ashraf.
         The treaty of Hanover allies Britain, Prussia and France against Austria and Spain.
1726   Voltaire is exiled in England. General George Wade commences a programme of road-building in Scotland.
         Montevideo is founded. Cardinal Fleury becomes chief minister to Louis XV.
1727   Spain besieges Gibraltar, but does not formally declare war on Britain. Shah Ashraf defeats an Ottoman

army and the two powers make peace. Catherine I of Russia dies, and is succeeded by Peter II, a grandson of Peter I. George I dies of apoplexy, and is succeeded by his son George II.

1728   The Kiakhta treaty sets the border and terms of trade between China and Russia. Spain abandons its siege of Gibraltar when the Convention of the Prado settles a truce with Britain. Roman Catholics are disenfranchised in Ireland. Vitus Bering discovers the Bering Strait. The Empire and Prussia make the treaty of Berlin. A Freemasons' Lodge is founded in Madrid, but is quickly suppressed by the Inquisition.

1729   Emperor Yongzheng bans opium smoking in China. Corsica temporarily becomes independent of Genoa. France, Britain and Spain end hostilities with the treaty of Seville. Charles Wesley founds the Holy Club at Oxford with his brother John and George Whitehead.

1730   Peter II of Russia dies of smallpox; his cousin Anne takes power in a coup. Shah Ashraf is murdered after defeat near Shiraz; Tahmasp II returns to power. Viscount Townshend improves crop husbandry with the use of turnips after leaving Walpole's government. Crown Prince Frederick of Prussia is imprisoned at Küstrin after attempting to flee to England. Sultan Ahmad III is deposed, and replaced by his nephew Mahmud I. Frederick IV of Denmark dies, and is succeeded by his son Christian VI.

1731   John Hadley invents the reflecting quadrant. Shah Tahmasp is defeated by the Ottomans at Arijan and sues for peace, ceding large tracts of land to the Ottomans. Tahmasp is imprisoned by his brother-in-law Nadir Kuli and his infant son Abbas III set up as Shah. The Holy Roman Empire makes the treaty of Vienna with Britain, Holland and Spain, securing support for the Pragmatic Sanction.

1732   Genoa regains control of Corsica.

1733   James Oglethorpe establishes a colony at Savannah, founding the state of Georgia. John Kay invents a flying shuttle loom. Augustus II of Poland dies; France persuades Polish nobles to restore Stanislas I but Austria and Russia demand that Augustus' son, Frederick Augustus of Saxony, succeed his father. In the War of the Polish Succession, they invade Poland.

1734   Persia and the Ottoman Empire go to war. France and Spain defeat Austrian armies in Naples and Parma. Danzig falls to the invading Russian army, but Stanislas I escapes to Prussia.

1735   William Pitt is elected MP for Old Sarum. The treaty of Vienna ends the War of the Polish Succession, and Augustus III is established on the Polish throne. Russia allies with the Persian Nadir Kuli against the Ottoman Empire; Nadir defeats the Ottomans at Baghavand and takes Tiflis. John Harrison develops his chronometer. Linnaeus publishes *Systema naturae*, the origin of modern classification of plants and animals.

1736   Shah Abbas III dies, and Nadir Kuli succeeds him. Claudius Aymond performs the first successful appendectomy. Freemasonry is condemned by Pope Clement XII. Statutes against witchcraft are repealed in England. Emperor Yongzheng dies, and is succeeded by his son Qianlong.

1737   Benjamin Franklin creates the Philadelphia police force, the first of its kind. The Licensing Act orders all plays to submit to the Lord Chamberlain's censorship. Gian Gastone di Medici dies, last of his line. The Grand Duchy of Tuscany passes to Francis of Lorraine, whilst Lorraine passes to Stanislas I of Poland as a reward for renouncing his claim to the Polish throne.

1738   Orsova falls to the Ottomans, who drive the Imperial troops back to Belgrade. Jean H.L. Orry imposes the corvée, compulsory labour, to construct roads in France. John and Charles Wesley form the Methodist Society.

1739   Dick Turpin is hanged at York. Shah Nadir of Persia sacks Delhi, drastically diminishing Mughal power in India. Nadir seizes the Koh-i-Noor diamond. Emperor Charles VI makes peace with the Ottomans by the treaty of Belgrade, ceding the city to the Ottomans. England and Spain go to war (the War of Jenkins' Ear) over alleged Spanish transgressions. Porto Bello in Panama is seized by Admiral Vernon.

1740   Frederick William I of Prussia dies, and is succeeded by his son Frederick II the Great, who invades Silesia. Emperor Charles VI dies; he is succeeded in his kingdoms by his daughter Maria Theresa, but Saxony, Bavaria and Spain dispute her right to succeed and the War of the Austrian Succession begins. Tsarina Anna dies, and is succeeded by her infant great-nephew Ivan VI.

1741   Frederick the Great defeats the Austrians at Mollwitz and captures Brieg, Neisse, Glatz and Olmütz before the British mediate. Prague is occupied by a French, Bavarian and Saxon army. Elizabeth, daughter of Peter the Great, deposes Tsar Ivan VI and rules herself.

1742   Anders Celsius develops the centigrade thermometer system. Elector Charles Albert of Bavaria is elected to the vacant title of Holy Roman Emperor. Robert Walpole resigns as Prime Minister, replaced by the earl of Wilmington. Prussia defeats the Austrians at Chotusitz, before signing treaty of Berlin with Austria, gaining upper and lower Silesia. Britain and Prussia sign the treaty of Westminster, safeguarding Hanover.

1743   George II leads a multinational Pragmatic Army to victory over the French at Dettingen. Pogroms of Jews occur in Russia. Persia and the Ottoman Empire go to war. Austria and Saxony ally, whilst Bavaria is conquered by Austria.

1744   Frederick the Great invades Saxony and Bohemia, taking Prague before being driven back to Saxony. Maria Theresa launches a series of pogroms in Moravia and Bohemia against the Jews.

1745   Emperor Charles VII dies. Francis of Lorraine, grand duke of Tuscany and husband of Maria Theresa, is elected the new Emperor. The French defeat an army led by the duke of Cumberland at Fontenoy and advance into the Austrian Netherlands. The Prussians defeat the Austrians and Saxons at Hohenfriedberg and the Austrians at Soor. Charles Edward Stuart lands on Eriskay, proclaiming his father king. He gains support from various Scottish clans, takes Edinburgh and is victorious at Prestonpans, but loses his nerve on reaching Derby and withdraws.

1746   The retreating Jacobites are victorious at Falkirk but are routed by Cumberland at Culloden. The Young Pretender escapes, and helped by Flora MacDonald reaches Skye, from where he returns to France. Cumberland severely represses the Scots, and the wearing of tartan is outlawed. Canaletto moves to England. Philip V of Spain dies, and is succeeded by his son Ferdinand VI. France defeats Austria at Raucoux and takes the Austrian Netherlands.

1747   The Republic of the United Provinces is overthrown by the French and William IV of Orange-Nassau

<table>
<tr><td></td><td>resumes the post of Stadtholder. Prussia and Sweden form a defensive alliance. The French defeat an Anglo-Dutch army at Laufeld. Shah Nadir is murdered in Afghanistan; his nephew Adil succeeds him whilst Ahmed Shah Durrani takes advantage of the situation to establish an independent Afghanistan. Lord Lovat is beheaded for Jacobitism on Tower Hill, the last man to be executed there.</td></tr>
</table>

1748   The treaty of Aix-la-Chapelle ends the War of the Austrian Succession with a stalemate peace. This gives general recognition to the Pragmatic Sanction and the Prussian conquest of Silesia.

1749   Thomas Chippendale opens a workshop. Admiral Anson reforms the Royal Navy. Henry Fielding publishes *Tom Jones*.

1750   Henry Fielding and his brother John found the Bow Street Runners. Thomas Gray's 'Elegy Written in a Country Churchyard' is written in Stoke Poges. The Jockey Club is founded in the Star and Garter Coffee House, Pall Mall. J.S. Bach dies. João V of Portugal dies, and is succeeded by his son Jose I, who appoints the marquis of Pombal as his chief minister. Pombal strips the Inquisition of its power.

1751   China invades Tibet. Robert Clive seizes Arcot from the French. Stadtholder William IV dies, and is succeeded by his infant son William V. Britain adopts January 1 as the beginning of the New Year, instead of 25 March.

1752   Britain adopts the Gregorian calendar system; 11 days disappear from September. Benjamin Franklin invents the lightning conductor. Ahmed Shah of Afghanistan takes Lahore. Spain and the Holy Roman Empire sign the treaty of Aranjuez.

1753   Sir Hans Sloane dies; his legacy of books and collections are used to found the British Museum and British Library. The Marriage Act forbids unlicensed weddings in Britain. The Jewish Naturalization Act seeks to remove disabilities for Jews in Britain, but the hostility it engenders leads to its repeal.

1754   The Royal and Ancient Golf Club is founded at St Andrews, and codifies the rules of the sport. William Cookworthy pioneers English porcelain production. The first iron-rolling mill is built, in Fareham, Hampshire. In North America the Albany Convention is convened by several colonies and the Iroquois to form a joint defence against the French, who defeat two expeditions led by George Washington. The Convention agrees to Franklin's proposal for the union of the 13 colonies. Sultan Mahmud I dies while dismounting from his horse, and is succeeded by his brother Osman III.

1755   Casanova is imprisoned in Venice for spying. Pasquale de Paoli is elected general in Corsica, and leads a revolt against Genoa. In North America, General Braddock is killed in the battle of the Wilderness, as the French rout a British expedition, but the French are subsequently defeated at Lake George. Lisbon is devastated by an earthquake and tidal wave; 30,000 die.

1756   A porcelain factory is founded at Sèvres. John Smeaton builds a new Eddystone Lighthouse. England and Prussia ally by the treaty of Westminster. Minorca surrenders to Franco-Spanish forces after Admiral Byng breaks off a naval action. Britain declares war on France, but Montcalm drives the British from the Great Lakes. Siraj-ud-Daula, a French ally, seizes Calcutta, imprisoning 146 Britons in a small guardroom (Black Hole of Calcutta); according to English propaganda, only 23 emerge alive the next morning. Seven Years War erupts as Prussia invades Saxony, which has allied with France, Austria, Russia and Sweden against it.

1757   John Campbell invents the sextant. Ahmed Shah of Afghanistan takes Delhi and the Punjab. Robert Clive recovers Calcutta and defeats Siraj-ud-Daula at Plassey. For his role in losing Minorca, Admiral Byng is shot 'pour encourager les autres' at Portsmouth. Frederick the Great defeats the Austrians at Prague, but is defeated at Kolin before further victories at Rossback and Leuthen. Cumberland is routed by the French at Hastenbeck and is forced by the Convention of Klosterzeven to surrender Hanover to them. Sultan Osman III dies, and is succeeded by his cousin Mustafa III.

1758   Britain promises assistance to Prussia by the treaty of London. Samuel Johnson founds *The Idler*. Clive becomes governor of Bengal. An English army fighting for Frederick II of Prussia defeats the French at Krefeld, and Frederick crushes the Russians at Zorndorf but is defeated by the Austrians at Hochkirch. Fort Duquesne is captured from the French by George Washington and John Forbes and renamed Pittsburgh.

1759   Handel dies. Guadeloupe is captured by the British. Samuel Johnson publishes *Rasselas*. The French defeat Brunswick at Brunswick, but are defeated by an Anglo-Prussian army at Minden. Ferdinand VI of Spain dies, and is succeeded by his half-brother Charles III. Frederick the Great is defeated by an Austro-Russian army at Kunersdorf. General Wolfe defeats Montcalm on the Plains of Abraham outside Quebec; both generals die in battle. Quebec falls to the British. Admiral Hawke destroys a French squadron off Quiberon.

1760   Earl Ferrers is hanged at Tyburn, the last peer to be executed in Britain. Austria defeats Prussia at Landshut, but is defeated at Liegnitz. Amherst captures Montreal. Russian troops capture and burn Berlin. George II dies, and is succeeded by his grandson George III. Prussia defeats the Austrians at Torgau. John Harrison develops his H-4 chronometer.

1761   Ahmed Shah of Afghanistan defeats the Marathas at Panipat. Pondicherry, the French base in southern India, falls to Sir Eyre Coote. France and Spain invade Portugal; Portugal asks for British help. Spain and the Bourbon Italian states ally with France against Britain.

1762   Tsarina Elizabeth dies, and is succeeded by her nephew Peter III who withdraws from the Seven Years War and returns Pomerania to Prussia. St Vincent, Martinique Grenada and St Lucia seized by the British under Rodney. Jean-Jacques Rousseau writes the *Social Contract*. Sweden and Prussia ally by the treaty of Hamburg. Peter is assassinated on behalf of his wife, who succeeds him as Catherine II.

1763   The treaty of Paris ends the Seven Years War. Spain cedes Florida to Britain. The *Almanach de Gotha* is first published. Augustus III of Poland and Saxony dies; he is succeeded in Saxony only by his son Frederick-Christian, who also dies, and is succeeded by his son Frederick-Augustus III.

1764   James Hargreaves invents the spinning jenny. Stanislas Poniatowski is elected to the vacant Polish throne. Hyder Ali takes Mysore. Sir Hector Monro defeats the Nawab of Oudh at Buxar, and takes control of Bengal. Ex-Tsar Ivan VI is murdered in prison.

1765   Frederick the Great founds the Bank of Prussia. The Stamp Act imposes taxation on the American colonists, much to their disgust. Emperor Francis I dies, and is succeeded by his son Joseph II. The auto-da-fé is abolished in Lisbon.

1766   On the death of ex-king Stanislas, duke of Lorraine, the duchy reverts to France. The Stamp Act is repealed, but the Declaratory Act affirms the right of Parliament to tax the American colonists. Frederick V of Denmark dies, and is succeeded by his son Christian VII.

1767   Siam is invaded by the Burmese. Nevil Maskelyne, the Astronomer Royal, issues the first Nautical Almanac. Clive leaves India.

1768   The Royal Academy of Arts is founded, with Joshua Reynolds as the first president. The first edition of the *Encyclopaedia Britannica* is published. The Gurkha king Prithvi Naryan Shah makes Nepal a unitary kingdom. Corsica is bought by the French from Genoa. Austria renounces all claims to Silesia.

1769   Austria occupies the Lvov and Zips regions of Poland. Frederick the Great and Emperor Joseph II meet at Neisse to discuss the partition of Poland. Richard Arkwright develops the spinning frame. James Watt patents a steam engine. Josiah Wedgwood opens his pottery works at Etruria. Wellington, Napoleon, Ney and Soult are born.

1770   Joseph Cugnot constructs a steam-powered road vehicle in France. Lord North replaces Grafton as prime minister. The 'Boston Massacre', a brawl between civilians and troops, leaves 3 dead. All taxes, bar that on tea, on the American colonists are repealed. An Anglo-Spanish dispute over the Falklands is resolved by French mediation. Captain James Cook lands at Botany Bay, Australia. A Russian fleet defeats the Ottomans at the battle of Chesme.

1771   The Crimea is conquered by Russian Cossacks. Duke Charles-Emmanuel III of Savoy abolishes serfdom. Adolphus Frederick of Sweden dies, and is succeeded by his son Gustav III. The Marathas drive the Afghans from Delhi.

1772   The Danish nobility rebel against Count Johann von Struensee, who has held absolute power for a year, torturing and beheading him. George III secures the passage of the Royal Marriages Act to control whom the royal family may marry. Russia, Prussia and Austria perform the first partition of Poland. Gustav III of Sweden re-establishes absolute monarchy. Carl Wilhelm Scheele discovers oxygen (Priestley discovers it independently in 1774); Daniel Rutherford, Joseph Priestley, Henry Cavendish and Carl Wilhelm Scheele independently discover nitrogen.

1773   Emperor Joseph II expels the Jesuits, prompting Pope Clement XIV to dissolve the order. Tea is thrown into the sea in the protest known as the Boston Tea Party as a protest against the tea duty. The first Stock Exchange opens in London. Captain Cook enters the Antarctic Circle. Denmark cedes Oldenburg to Russia. Thomas Pritchard constructs the Ironbridge at Coalbrookdale.

1774   The Coercive Acts against Massachusetts include closing the port of Boston. Lord North is robbed by a highwayman at Chiswick. Louis XV of France dies, and is succeeded by his grandson Louis XVI. Sultan Mustafa III dies, and is succeeded by his brother Abdul-Hamid I. Russia acquires the northern Black Sea coast by the treaty of Kuchuk-Kainardji with Turkey. Joseph Priestley discovers oxygen. Austria occupies Bukovina. The Continental Congress, comprising all the America colonies bar Georgia, convenes, deciding to ban imports from and exports to Britain.

1775   Paul Revere rides to Lexington to warn of British troop movements. The American War of Independence opens. The colonists win victories at Concord, Fort Ticonderoga and Crown Point. The Second Continental Congress convenes and John Hancock is elected its president. The British defeat the rebels at Bunker Hill.

1776   Adam Smith publishes *The Wealth of Nations*. The St Leger is first run (founded by Colonel Barry St Leger). Grigori Potemkin organizes a Russian Black Sea Fleet. Russia and Denmark sign the treaty of Copenhagen. The American colonists issue the Declaration of Independence. After defeat at Long Island and on Lake Champlain they score a major victory at Trenton.

1777   Spain and Portugal settle their differences over their South American colonies. The Americans are victorious at Princeton, Ridgefield and Bennington, but lose at the Brandywine and Germantown before victory at Bemis Heights provokes Burgoyne to surrender at Saratoga. Elector Maximilian III of Bavaria dies; with no direct heir, the Electorship passes to Count Karl Theodor of the Palatine.

1778   Joseph Bramah patents an improved water closet. Captain Cook discovers and names the Sandwich Islands. France signs treaties of alliance with the United States. Frederick the Great opens the War of the Bavarian Succession by invading Bohemia. The British take Savannah.

1779   Samuel Crompton develops the spinning mule. Captain Cook is killed by natives in Hawaii. The Oaks is first run (named after the house at Epsom leased by the 12th earl of Derby). Warren Hastings sends British troops against the Marathas. The Peace of Teschen settles the War of the Bavarian Succession. British troops are defeated at Baton Rouge by an augmented American army. Spain declares war on Britain.

1780   Admiral Rodney defeats the Spanish off Cape St Vincent. Lord George Gordon whips up anti-Catholic hysteria in London into the Gordon riots. The Americans are defeated at Camden, but are victorious at Kings Mountain. Emperor Joseph II abolishes serfdom in Bohemia and Hungary. Maria Theresa dies, and is succeeded in Habsburg territories by her son Emperor Joseph. The Derby is first run. Peruvian Indians rebel against Spanish rule, led by the Inca descendant Tupac Amaru, who is executed next year as the revolt is suppressed.

1781   William Herschel discovers Uranus. Warren Hastings plunders the treasure of the Nabob of Oudh. Emperor Joseph II grants religious tolerance in the Holy Roman Empire and abolishes serfdom in Austria. General Cornwallis surrenders to the Americans at Yorktown, ending British military operations in America.

1782   Spain captures Minorca from Britain, and completes the conquest of Florida. Lord North resigns as prime minister, and is succeeded by Rockingham; on his death Shelburne replaces him, and Pitt the Younger becomes chancellor of the exchequer. Admiral Rodney defeats the French at the battle of the Saints. Rama I founds the Chakri dynasty as kings of Siam, ruling from Bangkok. The *Royal George* sinks off Portsmouth, with the loss of 800 men.

1783   Shelburne resigns as prime minister, succeeded by Portland, whose government falls; Pitt the Younger becomes prime minister at the age of 24. Henry Cort develops a method of puddling iron. The treaty of

Versailles recognizes American Independence and cedes Florida to Spain. The Montgolfier brothers make the first balloon flight at Annonay. Potemkin annexes the Crimea for Russia.

1784 Turkey is forced to accept the Russian annexation of the Crimea by the treaty of Constantinople. John Wesley draws up his 'Deed of Declaration', providing for the continuance of the Methodist movement. A revolt in Transylvania persuades Emperor Joseph II to suspend the Hungarian constitution. The East India Company is put under government control.

1785 Jean Blanchard and John Jefferies cross the English Channel by balloon. *The Daily Universal Register*, later renamed *The Times*, is founded. The prince of Wales secretly weds Maria Fitzherbert. Warren Hastings resigns as governor-general of India. The Diamond Necklace affair discredits Marie Antoinette and leads to the arrest of Cardinal de Rohan. Austria and Holland settle their differences by the treaty of Fontainebleau.

1786 Jacques Balmat and Michel-Gabriel Paccard make the first ascent of Mont Blanc. Penang is ceded by the Rajah of Kedah to Britain. Frederick the Great of Prussia dies, and is succeeded by his nephew Frederick William II.

1787 The Marylebone Cricket Club is founded, and Thomas Lord opens his first cricket ground. Warren Hastings is impeached by Edmund Burke. George Washington chairs a Constitutional Convention in America which draws up the constitution. Russia and Turkey go to war. Delaware, Pennsylvania and New Jersey are the first states to join the union of the United States.

1788 William Symington develops a workable steamboat. The First Fleet lands convicts at Botany Bay and Sydney is founded to house them. The trial for corruption of Warren Hastings begins. Gustavus III of Sweden invades Russian Finland. Louis XVI is persuaded to summon the Estates-General in France. George III suffers a bout of mental illness.

1789 Sultan Abdul Hamid I is poisoned and succeeded by his nephew Selim III. George Washington is elected the first president of the United States. A mutiny takes place, led by Fletcher Christian, on HMS *Bounty*; Christian and the mutineers settle on Pitcairn Island; Captain Bligh, set adrift, navigates across 3,600 miles of ocean to Timor. George III recovers from his illness The Estates-General meet at Versailles; the Third Estate declares itself a National Assembly and swears not to dissolve until a constitution is granted. The Paris mob storm the Bastille, starting a revolution. Feudalism is abolished in France. The National Assembly issues the Declaration of the Rights of Man. Louis XVI and his family are forced to go to Paris as the mob attacks Versailles. Belgrade and Bucharest are taken by Austria.

1790 Emperor Joseph II dies, and is succeeded by his brother Leopold II. Louis XVI accepts a revolutionary constitution. Philadelphia becomes the American capital. Alexander Hamilton founds Washington DC.

1791 Marie Harel develops Camembert cheese. The *Observer* begins publication. Boswell's *Life of Johnson* and Tom Paine's *Rights of Man* are published. John Wesley dies. The Canada Constitutional Act splits Canada into Upper and Lower Canada, with legislatures in Ontario and Quebec. Louis XVI flees Paris, but is captured at Varennes and forced to return. Mozart's *The Magic Flute* is 1st performed. The Bill of Rights, consisting of the first ten amendments to the American constitution, is codified.

1792 Denmark abjures slavery. The Democratic Republican and Federalist parties are founded in America. Russia and Turkey make the Peace of Jassy. Cornwallis defeats Tipu Sultan of Mysore at Seringapatam and takes half of Mysore. Emperor Leopold II dies, and is succeeded by his son Francis II. Gustavus III of Sweden is assassinated in Stockholm Opera House, and is succeeded by his son Gustavus IV. Prussia and Austria ally against France, which declares war on them and Sardinia. Prussia takes Verdun but the French are victorious at Valmy and conquer the Austrian Netherlands. The Paris mob storms the Tuileries; the Swiss Guard fire on them. Louis XVI is imprisoned in the Temple and the National Convention abolishes the monarchy. The Jacobins seize power and the guillotine is put into use.

1793 Louis XVI is executed, as are his cousin Philippe Égalité, duke of Orléans, and Queen Marie Antoinette. France declares war on Britain, Holland and Spain, which join the First Coalition against France. The Vendée rises against republican excesses, but a rebel army is routed at Savenay. America declares its neutrality, unable to decide which side to back. The Committee of Public Safety take power; Robespierre heads a government which embarks on the Reign of Terror. Prussia and Russia perform the Second Partition of Poland, seizing half of Poland's territory. Marat is murdered by Charlotte Corday. Toulon is occupied by the British, but recaptured by a force including Napoleon.

1794 King Kamehameha of Polynesia cedes Hawaii to George III, but the cession is not ratified. Shah Lutf Ali of Persia is defeated and killed by Agha Muhammad, who founds the Qajar dynasty. Kosciusko leads a rising of Polish patriots, which is suppressed by the Russians. The Reign of Terror reaches a height as Danton and Desmoulins are executed. Habeas Corpus is suspended in Britain. Admiral Howe defeats the French fleet on the 'Glorious First of June', but the French have revenge at Charleroi and Fleurus. Robespierre holds the Festival of the Supreme Being; Thermidorean moderates stage a coup – Robespierre and St Just are executed and the Jacobin Club closed.

1795 The French capture the Dutch fleet in the River Texel; Stadtholder William V is forced to flee to England and the French form the Batavian republic in the Netherlands. Prussia makes peace with France by the treaty of Basel. The Speenhamland magistrates devise a new form of poor relief. Warren Hastings is acquitted. The Chouan uprising occurs in Brittany. Cape Town and Trincomalee are taken by the British. The Directory, led by Barras, comes to power in France. Austria, Prussia, and Russia perform the Third Partition of Poland; Stanislas II is forced to abdicate as his country ceases to exist.

1796 Colombo is taken by the British, establishing British control over Ceylon. Emperor Qianlong abdicates, and is succeeded by his son Jiaqing. Napoleon leads an army into Italy; it defeats the Austrians at Millesimo, Lodi and Arcol and establishes the Lombard Republic. François Babeuf leads a conspiracy to overthrow the Directory, but it fails. Edward Jenner discovers a vaccine against smallpox. Elba is captured by Britain. Robert Burns dies aged 37. Spain and Britain go to war. Tsarina Catherine the Great dies, and is succeeded by her son Paul I.

1797 Napoleon defeats the Austrians at Rivoli, seizes Mantua, and founds the Ligurian republic in Genoa and the Cisalpine Republic. Trinidad and St Lucia are taken by the British from the French. Admiral Jervis defeats the Spanish at Cape St Vincent. French troops are landed at Fishguard, but are quickly captured. The first £1 banknotes are issued. John Adams succeeds George Washington as American President. The Royal Navy suffers mutinies at the Nore and Spithead, but defeats a Franco-Dutch fleet at Camperdown. Barras thwarts a royalist reaction by the coup d'état of Fructidor. By the Peace of Campo Formio, the Austrian Netherlands are annexed by France whilst Venice and its territories are passed to Austria; Venice thus loses its independence. Frederick William II of Prussia dies, and is succeeded by his son Frederick William III.

1798   Thomas Malthus produces his *Essay on the Principles of Population*. Coleridge and Wordsworth publish *Lyrical Ballads*. Napoleon captures Rome, proclaiming the Roman Republic and forcing Pope Pius VI into custody at Valence. The Helvetic Republic, encouraged by the French, is proclaimed in Bern. Napoleon then captures Malta en route to Egypt, where he defeats the Mamluks at the battle of the Pyramids, but Nelson destroys his fleet at the battle of the Nile. Irish rebels are defeated at Vinegar Hill, whilst French troops landing in support are forced to surrender at Ballinamuck. The Irish nationalist Wolfe Tone is captured, condemned, but commits suicide. Ferdinand IV of Naples enters Rome, but is driven out by the French and Naples overrun. Income Tax is introduced in Britain.

1799   Napoleon invades Syria, but is repulsed by Sir Sidney Smith at Acre. The Rosetta Stone is discovered. Britain and Hyderabad share Mysore after Tipu Sultan is killed at Seringapatam. The Second Coalition against France is organized by Pitt. Russian troops defeat the French at Zurich, but are eventually driven out; after victory at Cassano they overthrow the Cisalpine Republic. Napoleon defeats an Anglo-Turkish army at Aboukir. On 18 Brumaire Napoleon overthrows the Directory and becomes First Consul.

1800   The American capital is transferred from Philadelphia to Washington DC. The French defeat the Turks at Heliopolis. Austrian troops starve Genoa into submission, but are defeated at Marengo, giving Napoleon control of Italy. Malta is captured by the British.

1801   Great Britain and Ireland unite. France adopts a metric system of weights and measures. The Bank of France is founded. Austria and France make the peace of Lunéville, which destroys the viability of the Holy Roman Empire. Thomas Jefferson becomes American president. Pitt the Younger resigns as prime minister over Catholic Emancipation, and is replaced by Addington. Tsar Paul I is assassinated, succeeded by his son Alexander I. Nelson defeats the Danish fleet at Copenhagen (after the famous incident of him turning a blind eye to Parker's orders). The French troops in Egypt surrender to the English.

1802   William Cobbett founds the *Political Register*. The *Charlotte Dundas*, the world's first steamship, is built by William Symington. Madame Tussaud mounts her first waxworks exhibition in London. Napoleon becomes president of the Italian Republic, which has superseded the Cisalpine Republic. Britain and France make peace by the treaty of Amiens. Napoleon creates the Légion d'Honneur, is made First Consul for life and annexes Piedmont, Parma and Piacenza.

1803   The Swiss cantons regain their independence by the Act of Mediation. Henry Shrapnel develops an explosive shell. The United States purchase the Louisiana territory – over 800,000 sq. miles of land west of the Mississippi – from France. Thomas Telford commences building the Caledonian Canal. France and Britain resume hostilities; France occupies Hanover. Arthur Wellesley (the future duke of Wellington) leads British troops to victory against Sindhia of Gwalior in the Second Maratha War.

1804   Richard Trevithick develops a steam locomotive. The duc d'Enghien is executed for plotting a Bourbon restoration. The Code Napoleon comes into force. Addington is forced to resign by Pitt the Younger, who replaces him. Napoleon is proclaimed Emperor of the French, crowning himself in the presence of Pope Pius VII. A revolt forces the French to withdraw from Haiti. Former US treasury secretary Alexander Hamilton is killed in a duel with Vice-President Aaron Burr.

1805   Francis Beaufort devises the Beaufort Scale. Mungo Park explores the Upper Niger. Muhammad Ali is proclaimed Pasha of Egypt. Napoleon crowns himself king of Italy in Milan wih the old Lombard crown. Austria, Russia, Sweden and Britain form the Third Coalition against France. The British fleet is victorious at Trafalgar over a Franco-Spanish fleet, but Nelson is mortally wounded. On the same day Napoleon defeats an Austro-Russian army at Ulm, and is subsequently victorious at Austerlitz. France and Austria make peace by the treaty of Pressburg; Austria is forced to yield the Tyrol and her Italian possessions whilst Bavaria and Württemberg become kingdoms and Baden a grand duchy.

1806   Britain occupies the Cape of Good Hope. Pitt the Younger dies; Grenville forms a coalition, the 'Ministry of All the Talents', to replace him. Britain establishes a blockade of the European coastline; Napoleon retaliates by the Berlin Decree establishing the Continental System to bar European ports to British ships. Napoleon makes his brothers Joseph and Louis kings of Naples and Holland respectively. France organizes the Confederation of the Rhine; the Holy Roman Empire thus ceases to exist and Francis II is merely Emperor of Austria. Prussia joins the Third Coalition. Napoleon defeats the Prussians at Jena and Auerstadt and enters Berlin. Saxony becomes a kingdom by the Peace of Posen.

1807   Charles and Mary Lamb's *Tales from Shakespeare* is published; Charles is guardian to his sister, who stabbed their mother during a bout of insanity. Slavery is prohibited in Britain. Sultan Selim III is deposed by his Janissaries and succeeded by his cousin Mustapha IV. HMS *Leopard* takes deserters from USS *Chesapeake*, enraging the Americans. Napoleon meets Tsar Alexander at Tilsit and makes the peace by the treaty of Tilsit. Napoleon makes his brother Jerome king of Westphalia. Copenhagen is bombarded by the British. Baron von Stein becomes Prussian prime minister and emancipates the serfs there. France invades Portugal, which has refused to join the Continental System; the Portuguese royal family flees to Brazil.

1808   French troops under Murat invade Spain. Charles IV of Spain abdicates in favour of his son Ferdinand VII, but Napoleon orders Murat to force Joseph Bonaparte upon them. Spanish resistance puts Joseph to flight, but Napoleon takes Madrid and restores him. Grand Vizier Bairakdar attempts to restore Sultan Selim III, who is strangled by the janissaries. Bairakdar deposes and murders Sultan Mustafa IV, replacing him with his brother Mahmud II. Murat replaces Joseph as king of Naples.

1809   Sir John Moore is mortally wounded as British troops evacuate Corunna. Gustavus IV of Sweden is captured in a coup; the Duke of Sudermania forms a government and Gustavus is forced to abdicate. Gustavus IV's uncle Karl XIII eventually succeeds him. Britain and the Sikhs make a pact of friendship by the treaty of Amritsar. Napoleon annexes the Papal States, taking Pope Pius VII prisoner, and to further his dynastic ambitions, divorces Josephine. Wellington defeats Soult at Oporto and Jourdan at Talavera. Napoleon is defeated by the Austrians at Aspern, but is victorious at Wagram and makes peace with Austria by the treaty of Schönbrunn. Canning, British foreign secretary, and Castlereagh, war minister, fight a duel on Putney Heath and resign from office. Metternich becomes Austrian minister of foreign affairs. Austria joins the Continental System.

1810 Napoleon marries Marie Louise of Austria. Andreas Hofer leads an Austrian rebellion, but is executed at Mantua. Napoleon annexes Holland when his brother Louis abdicates, and later annexes Hanover and various German ports. Jean Bernadotte is invited to become heir to the Swedish throne as Karl XIII has no children. The Krupp steel works open in Essen.

1811 George III descends into madness and the prince of Wales is declared Regent. Belgrade is seized by the Russians. Pasha Muhammad Ali massacres the Mamluks at Cairo. Luddism erupts in the Midlands. Wellington defeats the French at Fuentes de Onoro and Albuera. Francisco de Miranda declares Venezuelan independence; Paraguay follows suit. William Harrison defeats the Shawnee at Tippecanoe.

1812 In Spain, Wellington takes Ciudad Rodrigo and Badajoz, defeats Marmont at Salamanca and enters Madrid. Prime minister Spencer Perceval is assassinated by John Bellingham, and is succeeded by the earl of Liverpool. America declares war on Britain. Napoleon leads his Grand Army into Russia. Britain, Russia and Sweden ally via the treaty of Örebro. De Miranda is made dictator of Venezuela after an earthquake, but is captured by the Spanish. After victory at Smolensk and an inconclusive outcome at Borodino Napoleon takes an evacuated Moscow, which is then burned down by Russian saboteurs. He orders a retreat, and has to suffer terrible losses in crossing the River Berezina. General Claude Malet attempts to depose Napoleon in his absence, but is executed as the conspiracy fails.

1813 The locomotive 'Puffing Billy' is developed by William Hedley. Prussia declares war on France, but is defeated, along with Russia, by Napoleon at Lützen, Bautzen and Wurschen. Wellington defeats Jourdan at Vittoria and crosses into France. Simon Bolívar becomes dictator of Venezuela. Austria declares war on France. Prusso-Russian troops defeat Napoleon at Grossbeeren and Wahlstatt, but are defeated at Dresden before further victory at Dennewitz. An Austro-Prusso-Russian army defeats Napoleon at Leipzig, and drives him back across Germany. Mexico declares independence from Spain. The French are expelled from Holland.

1814 Denmark cedes Heligoland to Britain by the treaty of Kiel. Murat deserts Napoleon and joins the Allies, who inflict defeats on Napoleon at La Rothière, Laon, Arcis and Fère-Champenoise before entering Paris. Wellington defeats the French at Toulouse. Napoleon abdicates, is banished to Elba, and is granted its sovereignty. Louis XVIII returns from exile. Ferdinand VII returns to the Spanish throne. The Austrian Netherlands and Holland unite to form the kingdom of the Netherlands. The White House is burned down by British troops.The Cape of Good Hope becomes a British colony. The Congress of Vienna opens. The treaty of Ghent ends hostilities between Britain and America.

1815 Napoleon returns from Elba, forcing Louis XVIII to flee to Ghent. His forces under Ney are victorious at Quatre Bras, but Wellington defeats him at Waterloo. After surrendering to the British, he is exiled to St Helena. Louis XVIII returns, Ney is executed and Murat deposed from Naples; he is executed when trying to regain his throne. Spanish troops reconquer Venezuela, forcing Bolívar to flee. To protect domestic growers against cheaper imports, the Corn Laws are passed in Britain. The treaty of Vienna draws up a new political map of Europe: Norway is passed to Denmark, the Rhineland to Prussia, Poland to Russia and various monarchs restored to their thrones.

1816 Argentina declares itself independent, as does Brazil under the Portuguese prince João, who succeeds to the Portuguese throne on the death of his mother Maria I, but remains in Brazil. The first Diet of the German Confederation opens in Frankfurt. Cobbett's *Political Register* increases its radical influence after a price cut to 2d.

1817 José de San Martín and Bernardo O'Higgins defeat the Spanish at Chacabuco and establish an independent Chile. The last major Luddite attack takes place in Loughborough. The 'Blanketeers' march from Manchester to protest against the suspension of the Habeas Corpus Act, but are halted at Stockport; there are similar riots elsewhere. Bolivar reestablishes an independent Venezuela. The Ottomans grant partial autonomy to the Serbs.

1818 The Rajput states and Indore come under British control by the treaty of Mundosir. Karl XIII of Sweden dies, and is succeeded by Bernadotte, who takes the name Karl XIV. The American-Canadian border is defined along the 49th parallel. James Blundell performs the first successful blood transfusion. At the Congress of Aix-la-Chapelle, the victorious allies agree to withdraw their troops from France, which has paid the war indemnity imposed in 1815.

1819 Stamford Raffles founds the city of Singapore. The United States take over Florida from Spain. The reactionary Karlsbad Decrees are promulgated in Germany. The Peterloo Massacre kills 11 people in Manchester, when yeomen attack a reformist crowd. The reactionary Six Acts are passed in England. Simon Bolivar becomes president of the newly independent Colombia.

1820 Liberia is founded for the repatriation of American Negroes. There are revolts in Spain, where Ferdinand VII is forced to restore the constitution of 1812, and in Portugal, demanding a constitution. George III dies, and is succeeded by his son George IV. The duc de Berry, heir to the French throne, is assassinated; a son, the comte de Chambord, is born posthumously. At the Congress of Troppau, Prussia, Austria and Russia discuss concerted action against revolutionary movements with Britain and France. The Cato Street Conspiracy to murder British cabinet ministers is discovered and its leaders executed. Keats publishes *Lamia, Isabella, The Eve of St Agnes and other Poems*.

1821 A Carbonarist uprising in Naples is put down by the Austrians, sanctioned by the Congress of Laibach. Bolívar defeats the Spanish at Carabobo, ensuring Venezuelan independence. Peru declares independence under José de San Martín. El Salvador, Honduras, Costa Rica, Guatemala and Panama follow suit. Greeks start an insurgence against the Ottomans in an attempt to gain independence. Victor Emmanuel of Piedmont is forced to abdicate in favour of his more liberal brother Charles Felix. The Austrians intervene, defeating the Piedmontese at Novara and reasserting control over the country.

1822   Viceroy Wellesley is attacked by Orangemen in Dublin in the 'Bottle Riots'. The Ottomans capture Chios and massacre its inhabitants. Agostín de Itúrbide is declared emperor of Mexico. A Greek flotilla burns an Ottoman fleet, bringing further reprisals. British foreign secretary Castlereagh commits suicide. Regent Pedro, son of João VI of Portugal, declares Brazil independent.

1823   Michael Faraday succeeds in liquefying chlorine. Emperor Agostín de Itúrbide is forced to abdicate as Mexico declares itself a republic. *The Lancet* is first published. A revolt in Spain is quelled with French assistance. President Monroe issues the Monroe Doctrine, closing the Americas to European colonialism.

1824   The RNLI is founded. The First Burmese War between Britain and Burma commences; Rangoon is taken by the British. Lord Byron dies at Missolonghi whilst assisting the Greeks. Beethoven's 9th Symphony is first performed. Louis XVIII of France dies, and is succeeded by his brother Charles X.

1825   Ferdinand I of the Two Sicilies dies, and is succeeded by his son Francis I. John Quincy Adams is elected American president by the House of Representatives after none of the four candidates gains a majority in the election. Bolivia under Jose de Sucre declares independence from Peru, and Uruguay, with Argentine support, from Brazil. The Stockton–Darlington railway opens, the first passenger-carrying line. The Erie Canal links the Hudson River to the Great Lakes and the American Midwest. Tsar Alexander I dies, and is succeeded by his brother Nicholas I, who is confronted by the Decembrist revolt of officers, which he puts down.

1826   The First Burmese War is ended by the treaty of Yandabo. João VI of Portugal dies, and is succeeded by his son Pedro IV, who abdicates in favour of his daughter Maria II and remains in Brazil. Persia and Russia go to war; the Russians are victorious at Ganja. Stamford Raffles founds the Royal Zoological Society in London.

1827   Peru secedes from Colombia. Count Kapodistrias is elected president of Greece as Britain, France and Russia sign the treaty of London pledging support for the Greeks; an allied fleet crushes an Ottoman and Egyptian fleet at Navarino. Russia defeats Persia and takes Yerevan.

1828   Wellington becomes prime minister. Russia makes peace with Persia by the treaty of Turkmanchai, and subsequently declares war on the Ottomans. Maria II of Portugal is deposed by her uncle, the Regent Dom Miguel, and flees to England as civil war breaks out. The treaty of Rio de Janeiro confirms Uruguayan independence. Thomas Arnold becomes headmaster of Rugby School.

1829   The Catholic Emancipation Act is passed in Britain. Wellington fights a duel with the earl of Winchelsea. The Metropolitan Police is founded by Robert Peel. The first Boat Race takes place at Henley. The London Protocol establishes Greek independence; the treaty of Adrianople ends Russo-Turkish hostilities. Stephenson's *Rocket* wins the Rainhill Trials. Slavery is abolished in Mexico.

1830   Joseph Smith founds the Church of Jesus Christ of Latter-Day Saints. The Swing riots, caused by the introduction of threshing machines and rural unemployment, start in Kent and spread west and north. George IV dies, and is succeeded by his brother William IV. Algeria is conquered by France, but an uprising in Paris forces Charles X to abdicate in favour of his grandson, however Louis-Philippe, duc d'Orléans, usurps the throne. Belgium secedes from the Kingdom of the Netherlands. Wellington is ousted as prime minister after a general election, and replaced by Earl Grey.

1831   Independence agitations in Italy are quelled by Austrian troops. Pedro I of Brazil abdicates, and is succeeded by his son Pedro II. A Polish revolt is put down after Russian troops are victorious at Ostroleka. Leopold of Saxe-Coburg is elected king of the Belgians. Charles Felix of Piedmont dies, and is succeeded by his distant relation Charles Albert. The Greek President Kapodistrias is assassinated. Faraday invents the dynamo. The defeat of Grey's Reform Bill in the Lords causes anti-clerical agitation. Mazzini founds Young Italy.

1832   The First Reform Act is passed, doubling the franchise. Otto of Bavaria is elected king of Greece.

1833   Britain annexes the Falkland Islands. The Convention of Kutahya passes control of Syria to Muhammad Ali of Egypt. Slavery is abolished in the British Empire. Ferdinand VII of Spain dies, and is succeeded by his infant daughter Isabella II. Santa Anna becomes President of Mexico whilst civil war looms in the country.

1834   The Zollverein customs union comes into operation in Germany. The Spanish Inquisition is abolished. To protect their constitutions, Portugal and Spain form a Quadruple Alliance with France and Britain. Don Carlos attempts to usurp the Spanish throne from his niece Isabella II, plunging the country into civil war, whilst in Portugal Dom Miguel is forced to flee as troops led by his brother Pedro restore Maria II to her throne. For forming a trade union, the Tolpuddle Martyrs are arrested and transported to Australia. Fire destroys the Houses of Parliament.

1835   Francis II of Austria dies, and is succeeded by his son Ferdinand I. Juan de Rosas becomes dictator of Argentina. The Boers begin the 'Great Trek'. Texas attempts to secede from Mexico.

1836   Santa Anna takes the Alamo at San Antonio; Davy Crockett and Jim Bowie are killed. Sam Houston defeats and captures Santa Anna at San Jacinto; Texas gains independence with Houston as president. Louis Napoleon Bonaparte attempts a revolt at Strasbourg, and is banished to America.

1837   William IV dies, and is succeeded in England by his niece Victoria and in Hanover by his brother Ernst Augustus, duke of Cumberland, who promptly cancels the constitution of 1833 there. Brunel launches the *Great Western*. Births, marriages and deaths are officially registered in England and Wales. Isaac Pitman develops shorthand. French Canadians revolt against British rule.

1838   Chopin begins his liaison with George Sand. Richard Cobden establishes the Anti-Corn Law League. The 'People's Charter' is published. Grace Darling assists in the rescue from the wreck of the *Forfarshire*. The First Afghan War begins; the British capture Kabul and imprison the Emir Dost Muhammad. The Boers defeat the Zulus at Blood River.

1839   The Rebecca Riots against the Poor Law Amendment Act take place in Wales (rioters disguise themselves as women). Goodyear discovers how to vulcanize rubber. Argentina and Uruguay go to war. The Ottomans invade Syria but are defeated by Ibrahim Pasha at Nezib. The treaty of London guarantees Belgian independence and neutrality. Sultan Mahmud II is poisoned, and succeeded by his son Abdul Mejid. Chinese attempts to stop the importation of opium lead to the Opium War with Britain. Frederick VI of Denmark dies, and is succeeded by his nephew, Christian VIII. Bradshaw's provides first railway timetables.

1840   The Maoris cede sovereignty of New Zealand to England by the treaty of Waitangi. Rowland Hill introduces the Penny Post. Frederick William III of Prussia dies, and is succeeded by his son Frederick William IV. Britain, Austria, Prussia and Russia ally against Muhammad Ali of Egypt by the treaty of London; after Beirut and Acre are captured, Muhammad agrees to return Syria to Ottoman rule. Lower and Upper Canada are united under a single legislature. Rafael Carrera becomes dictator of Guatemala. Louis Napoleon Bonaparte is imprisoned at Ham after another attempt to foment revolt fails. William I of Holland abdicates, and is succeeded by his son William II.

1841   Hong Kong is taken by the British. William Harrison dies after catching cold giving his inaugural address as US president, and is succeeded by John Tyler. Thomas Cook arranges his first excursion, to a temperance meeting. The Straits Convention closes the Bosporus to warships. Carlos Lopez becomes President of Paraguay. The first issue of Punch is published.

1842   Crawford W. Long performs the first operation under anaesthesia. British troops in Afghanistan are massacred. The second Chartist petition is rejected. Civil war erupts in Uruguay. The Webster-Ashburton treaty defines the US–Canadian border. The treaty of Nanking ends the Opium War; Hong Kong is ceded to Britain. Alexander Karageorgevich deposes Michael Obrenovich as prince of Serbia. Marx meets Engels. Britain withdraws from Afghanistan.

1843   The Thames Tunnel opens, first underwater tunnel in the world. Brunel launches the Great Britain. Sind is conquered by General Charles Napier. Hawaii becomes independent, with recognition from France and Britain.

1844   George Williams founds the YMCA. Karl XIV of Sweden dies, and is succeeded by his son Oscar I. The Factory Act fixes maximum workdays of 6½ hours for children, 12 hours for women. Samuel Morse transmits his first telegraph message. The Dominican Republic gains independence from Haiti. The Co-operative movement is founded in Rochdale.

1845   The Irish famine begins as the potato crop fails. Henry Newman converts to Catholicism. Sir John Franklin sets out with the Erebus and Terror to find the North-West Passage. British incursions in the Punjab and Kashmir cause the Anglo-Sikh War. The Sonderbund is formed when 7 Catholic cantons secede from the Confederation in Switzerland.

1846   The Anglo-Sikh War is ended by the treaty of Lahore. Cracow is annexed by Austria. Louis Napoleon Bonaparte escapes from prison and moves to London. The treaty of Washington settles the Oregon–Canada border along the 49th Parallel. America goes to war with Mexico after failing to purchase New Mexico; after victories at Palo Alto and Resaca de la Palma New Mexico is annexed by the United States. Peel repeals the Corn Laws, fatally splitting his party and forcing him to resign as prime minister; Lord John Russell replaces him. Charles Dickens founds the Daily News.

1847   Mexican troops under Santa Anna are defeated by the Americans at Buena Vista and Cerro Gordo. Liberia is proclaimed an independent republic. The Catholic cantons refuse to dissolve the Sonderbund, precipitating war in Switzerland.

1848   Christian VIII of Denmark dies, and is succeeded by his son Frederick III. Gold is discovered in California. The treaty of Guadalupe Hidalgo ends the conflict between America and Mexico, which is forced to yield its lands north of the Rio Grande. Marx and Engels publish the Communist Manifesto. Paris erupts in revolt, forcing Louis Philippe to abdicate. The Second French Republic is formed; a workers' revolt is put down (the June Days) and Louis Napoleon Bonaparte is elected President. The revolution in France inspires a wave of revolts across Europe: Metternich falls in Austria; Milan, Parma, Venice, Hungary and the Czechs revolt against Austrian dominion; liberals rise across Germany, creating a National Assembly; Rome rises against Papal war, forcing Pope Pius IX to flee to Gaeta. Piedmont declares war on Austria, but after victories at Goito and Pastrengo is defeated by Radetzky at Custozza. Windischgrätz suppresses the Czech rising; nevertheless, Emperor Ferdinand I is forced to abdicate in favour of his nephew Franz Josef. The Second Anglo-Sikh war breaks out. The third Chartist petition is presented amid a meeting which collapses in farce, and is rejected. Switzerland becomes a federal union. The Pre-Raphaelite Brotherhood is founded.

1849   The Sikhs are defeated by the British at Chillianwalla and forced to surrender at Rawalpindi; the Punjab is annexed by Britain. A Roman republic under Mazzini is formed, but French, Austrian, Spanish, Neapolitan and Tuscan troops capture Rome and restore Pope Pius IX. Radetzsky defeats the Piedmontese at Novara. Charles Albert of Piedmont abdicates in favour of his son Victor Emmanuel II and the Peace of Milan ends hostilities. The German National Assembly elects Frederick William IV 'Emperor of the Germans', but he refuses the title and the Assembly collapses in chaos. Hungary proclaims independence under Kossuth, but Russian troops invade and are victorious at Temesvar; Kossuth flees and Hungary returns to Austrian rule. Venice submits to the Austrians.

1850   Palmerston blockades Piraeus over the Don Pacifico Affair, forcing the Greeks to comply with his wishes, but is censured in parliament. Prussia and Denmark reach an accord on Schleswig-Holstein by the treaty of Berlin. Hong Xiuquan leads the Taiping rebellion in China. Count Camillo Cavour becomes chief minister of Piedmont.

1851   Danilo II succeeds Peter II in Montenegro and makes the state a principality. The Great Exhibition is held in Hyde Park. The Americas Cup yacht race is first held around the Isle of Wight. The Australian Gold Rush begins. Louis Napoleon Bonaparte stages a coup d'état in France.

1852   Juan Manuel de Rosas, Argentine dictator, is forced to flee after defeat by insurgents with Uruguayan and Brazilian help at Caseros. The Second Burmese War breaks out between Britain and Burma. Louis Napoleon Bonaparte proclaims the Second Empire, crowning himself Napoleon III.

1853	Pegu is taken by Britain as the Second Burmese War ends. Shogun Ieyoshi dies, and is succeeded by his son Iesada, who opens two Japanese ports to foreign trade. Russia invades the Ottoman Danubian principalities and destroys the Turkish fleet at Sinope. Maria II of Portugal dies, and is succeeded by her son Pedro V.
1854	The Convention of Bloemfontein leaves the Orange Free State free for the Boers and withdraws the British south of the Orange River. America makes the treaty of Kanagawa with Japan over trade and the Elgin treaty with Britain over Canadian trade. Britain and France declare war on Russia in support of Turkey and are victorious at the Alma, Balaklava (where the Charge of the Light Brigade takes place), and Inkerman, before besieging Sebastopol.
1855	Piedmont joins the anti-Russian alliance in the Crimean War by the treaty of Turin. Aberdeen resigns as prime minister over the conduct of the war, and is replaced by Palmerston. Tsar Nicholas I dies, and is succeeded by his son Alexander II. Britain and Afghanistan sign the anti-Persian treaty of Peshawar. The *Daily Telegraph* is first published. Sebastopol falls to the allied armies.
1856	The Victoria Cross is instituted. Britain annexes Oudh and establishes Natal as a Crown Colony. The Crimean War is ended by the treaty of Paris; the integrity of the Ottoman Empire is recognized and the Black Sea demilitarized. The Chinese board the *Arrow* off Canton over suspected piracy; British ships bombard Canton in response. Marthinius Pretorius establishes the Transvaal republic. Henry Bessemer introduces his steel-making converter.
1857	Britain forces Afghani independence on the Persians by the treaty of Paris. The Sepoys in Meerut revolt, sparking a general Indian Mutiny; the inhabitants of Cawnpore are massacred and Lucknow besieged for six months. Garibaldi forms the Italian National Association. British and French forces occupy Canton.
1858	Felice Orsini attempts to assassinate Napoleon III, causing Anglo-French tension and turning Napoleon's mind towards Italy; he has secret meetings at Plombières with Cavour. Anglo-Chinese hostilities are ended by the treaty of Tianjin. The Indian Mutiny is suppressed; the East India Company is wound up and its powers transferred to the British crown. Frederick William IV is declared insane; his brother William is made Regent. Alexander Karageorgevich is deposed by the Serbian Diet and replaced by Milos Obrenovich. France launches *La Gloire*, a naval vessel partially clad in iron.
1859	Piedmont traps Austria into war, and backed by Napoleon III is victorious at Magenta and Solferino. Ferdinand of the Two Sicilies dies, and is succeeded by his son Francis II. Napoleon III and Franz Josef of Austria make the Peace of Villafranca; Lombardy is passed to Piedmont. John Brown raids Harpers Ferry. Darwin publishes the *Origin of Species*. Queensland is established as a separate colony with Brisbane as its capital.
1860	Piedmont cedes Nice and Savoy to France by the treaty of Turin. Plebiscites in the Italian duchies favour union with Piedmont. Garibaldi and his 1,000 redshirts sail from Genoa to Sicily, take the island and then progress to Naples, where he proclaims Victor Emmanuel II of Piedmont king of Italy. Piedmontese troops invade the Papal States en route to the Two Sicilies, which Garibaldi hands to Victor Emmanuel II; Garibaldi retires to Caprera. South Carolina secedes from the Union in protest at the election of Abraham Lincoln as president. The Second Maori War breaks out in New Zealand. Richard Cobden negotiates an Anglo-French trade treaty. Anglo-French forces bombard Sinho, occupy the Tagu forts, defeat the Chinese army at Ba Lizhao and burn the Summer Palace in Peking in retaliation for Chinese treaty breaches and cruelty to captives; the treaty of Peking forces further concessions on the Chinese.
1861	Frederick William IV of Prussia dies and is succeeded by his brother Wilhelm I. Tsar Alexander II emancipates the Russian serfs. The kingdom of Italy is proclaimed, with its capital at Florence, as Rome refuses to join. The Confederate States of America are proclaimed at the Congress of Montgomery and go to war with the Union by bombarding Fort Sumter: the Civil War begins. The Confederates are victorious at Bull Run. Prince Albert dies. With the commissioning into the Royal Navy of the iron-hulled HMS *Warrior*, all other naval vessels are rendered effectively obsolete.
1862	In America the Union launches the ironclad USS *Monitor*, which fights the Confederate ironclad *Merrimack* to a draw in Hampton Roads. The battle of Shiloh is a bloody draw, whilst the Confederates are subsequently victorious at the second battle of Bull Run and Fredericksburg. Napoleon III sends French troops to establish a Catholic empire in Mexico, forcing the withdrawal of British and Spanish troops; the French are heavily defeated at Puebla. Bismarck is appointed prime minister of Prussia. A military revolt forces Otto I of Greece to abdicate and return to Bavaria.
1863	The first underground railway, from Farringdon Street to Paddington, is opened. The Greeks elect Prince Alfred of Britain as their new king, but he is forced to reject the position; William of Denmark is elected instead, taking the title George I. The Confederates are victorious at Chancellorsville, but are routed at Gettysburg, which proves a turning point. The Union has further victories at Vicksburg and Chattanooga but is defeated at Chickamauga. Lincoln gives the Gettysburg Address at the dedication of the cemetery there. Mexico City falls to the French, who invite Archduke Maximilian of Austria to become emperor of the country. Japan closes its ports and expels foreign traders, prompting Britain to bombard Kagoshima. Frederick VII of Denmark dies, and is succeeded by his nephew Christian IX, who incorporates Schleswig into the country after German pressure on the area. The English Football Association is founded.
1864	Austrian and Prussian troops invade Schleswig-Holstein, defeating the Danes at Düppel. A conference in London fails to settle the dispute, and Prussia and Austria force Denmark to cede the area by the treaty of Vienna. Archduke Maximilian accepts the Mexican crown. Brazil invades Uruguay after a dispute with Paraguay. The Taiping Rebellion is suppressed, with help from General Gordon's troops; Hong Xiuquan commits suicide. Ulysses S. Grant takes command of the Union army. In the Wilderness campaign in Virginia, the Union loses 60,000 of an army of over 100,000, the Confederacy 20,000 of its 60,000 men. Sherman takes Atlanta and Savannah as his Union army marches through Georgia. General George Thomas wipes out a Confederate army under J. B. Hood at Nashville.
1865	The Confederate states surrender to the Unionists at Appomattox; five days later Abraham Lincoln is assassinated by John Wilkes Booth. William Booth founds the Christian Revival Association (later the

Salvation Army). Edward Whymper climbs the Matterhorn. Edward Lister's use of carbolic acid founds modern antiseptic surgery. Lord Palmerston dies in office, and is succeeded as prime minister by Lord John Russell. Leopold I of Belgium dies, and is succeeded by his son Leopold II. The Thirteenth Amendment abolishes slavery in the US.

1866   Prince Alexander of Romania is dethroned and replaced by Carol I of Hohenzollern. Bismarck, with Italian assistance, engineers war against Austria and allied German states, defeating the Austrians at Sadowa, although the Italians are defeated at Custozza and the naval battle of Lissa. The Peace of Prague gives Prussia Hanover, Hesse, Nassau, Frankfurt and Holstein. Shogun Iemochi dies, and is succeeded by his kinsman Yoshinobu. The treaty of Vienna cedes Venetia to Italy.

1867   The Ausgleich creates the Dual Monarchy of Austria-Hungary. Alaska is sold by Russia to America. The Dominion of Canada is created. Emperor Maximilian of Mexico surrenders to insurgents after the French abandon him and is executed. Prussia forms the North German Confederation. The Second Reform Act doubles the British electorate. Garibaldi marches on Rome, but is defeated by a Franco-Papal army at Mentana and taken prisoner. The Queensberry Rules on boxing are drawn up.

1868   The Shogunate is abolished in Japan; by the Meiji Restoration power passes to Emperor Matsuhito. Disraeli becomes prime minister, but is defeated in a general election by Gladstone, who replaces him. Prince Michael of Serbia is assassinated, succeeded by his kinsman Milan II Isabella II of Spain is deposed after a revolution in Spain. The first Trades Union Congress meets in Manchester. The last public hangings in England take place.

1869   The first Nihilist Congress meets in Basel. The *Cutty Sark* is launched. Napoleon III reintroduces a parliamentary system to France. The Suez Canal is opened.

1870   Papal infallibility is proclaimed. Isabella II of Spain abdicates in favour of her son Alfonso XII but the throne is offered to Leopold of Hohenzollern, who is forced to decline it after French protests. These protests are edited by Bismarck into the 'Ems telegram' and used to foment war between France and Prussia. After a French victory at Saarbrücken, Prussia is victorious at Weissenberg, Wörth, Mars-la-Tour, Gravelotte and Sedan. Napoleon III surrenders and abdicates as Paris revolts and proclaims the Third Republic. Paris is besieged by the Prussians. Italian troops enter Rome and absorb it into the kingdom; it is made the capital. Amadeus of Savoy accepts the Spanish throne.

1871   Wilhelm I of Prussia is proclaimed emperor of a federal Germany at Versailles. Paris surrenders to the Prussians. The leftist Commune takes power there, and is repressed with the loss of 20,000 lives. The Convention of London abolishes the demilitarization of the Black Sea. Britain and America settle differences by the treaty of Washington. France and Germany make the Peace of Frankfurt; Alsace-Lorraine is ceded to Germany and an indemnity paid by France. Stanley meets Livingstone at Ujiji (now in Tanzania). Bank holidays are introduced.

1872   Wanderers win the first FA Cup final. Don Carlos invades Spain, but is routed at Oroquista and forced to withdraw. The secret ballot is introduced in Britain. Germany, Austria-Hungary and Russia form the Three Emperors League. The *Marie Celeste* is found deserted.

1873   A Spanish republic is proclaimed and Amadeus I forced to abdicate. Sultan Bargash Sayyid closes the slave markets in Zanzibar. The cities of Buda and Pest are united to form the Hungarian capital. W. C. Wingfield invents Sphairistike (lawn tennis).

1874   Disraeli defeats Gladstone in the General Election. Japan invades Formosa, and withdraws on payment of compensation by China. Fiji is annexed by Britain. Alfonso XII of Spain proclaims his reign at Sandhurst.

1875   Bismarck foments tension between Germany and France ('Is war in Sight?' article in the *Berlin Post*). Bosnia-Herzegovina revolts against Turkish rule. Matthew Webb swims the English Channel. Disraeli arranges the purchase of shares in the Suez Canal. Sir Joseph Bazalgette completes the London sewerage system. The MCC codifies the rules of lawn tennis.

1876   Korea becomes independent from China. Alexander Graham Bell patents the telephone. Bulgaria rises against Turkey, but is savagely repressed, drawing Gladstone out of retirement. Queen Victoria is proclaimed Empress of India and is officially inaugurated in January 1877. Sultan Abdul Aziz is deposed in favour of his nephew Murad V and commits suicide; Murad is himself deposed in favour of his brother Abdul Hamid II. General Custer is defeated and killed by the Sioux at the battle of Little Big Horn. Serbia and Montenegro declare war on Turkey, but the Serbs are routed at Alexinatz. Wild Bill Hickok is shot dead.

1877   Rutherford B. Hayes is elected American president after an electoral commission decides in his favour. Russia declares war on Turkey and takes Kars and Plevna. Britain warns Russia off taking Constantinople. Serbia also declares war on Turkey. Australia beats England in the first cricket Test match. The first Lawn Tennis Championships are held at Wimbledon.

1878   Victor Emmanuel II of Italy dies, and is succeeded by his son Umberto I. Russia takes Adrianople; the Turks capitulate and sign the treaty of San Stefano, in which Bulgarian, Romanian and Serbian independence is fully established. The provisions are unacceptable to other European powers; differences are resolved at the Congress of Berlin, where the San Stefano provisons are reduced in scale.

1879   The Irish Land League is founded. Britain goes to war with the Zulus, who massacre the British at Isandhlwana but are held at Rorke's Drift and defeated at Ulundi. Their king Cetewayo is captured and deported and the Zulu wars end; the Prince Imperial, heir of Napoleon III, is a casualty. Britain occupies the Khyber Pass by the treaty of Gandamak with Afghanistan and invades when the legation in Kabul is massacred, taking the city and deposing Emir Yakub. Khedive Ismail of Egypt is deposed in favour of his son Tewfik. The Tay Bridge collapses in a storm; 78 lives are lost as a train crossing the bridge falls into the river.

1880   Andrew Carnegie presents Dunfermline with a free library. Gladstone defeats Disraeli in the General Election. Tahiti is annexed by France. Morocco gains independence. Captain Boycott is ostracized by his tenants in County Mayo. Paul Kruger declares the Transvaal an independent republic.

1881   Boers repulse the British at Laing's Neck and defeat them at Majuba Hill; peace is made by the treaty of Pretoria, which recognizes an independent Transvaal as the South African Republic. James Garfield is inaugurated as American president but is shot and fatally wounded soon after. Tsar Alexander II is assassinated; he is succeeded by his son Alexander III, who responds by introducing repressive measures. Tunisia is made a French protectorate.

1882   Prince Milan II of Serbia declares himself king. The Hague Convention establishes a three-mile limit for territorial waters. The Fenians assassinate two British ministers in Phoenix Park, Dublin. Nationalist riots in Egypt led by Arabi Pasha lead to the British fleet bombarding Alexandria; Sir Garnet Wolseley defeats Arabi at Tel-el-Kebir and occupies Cairo.

1883   Paul Kruger becomes president of the South African Republic. Krakatoa erupts in spectacular fashion. Khedive Tewfik appoints a British agent to assist his government; Sir Evelyn Baring takes up the post. The Orient Express makes its first run. The Mahdi stirs up a revolt in Sudan and defeats an Anglo-Egyptian army at El Obeid.

1884   The Fabian Society is established. General Gordon reaches Khartoum intent on evacuating the city but decides to stay. China declares war on France after the latter bombards Formosa as a reprisal for China's refusal to acknowledge a French protectorate over Indo-China. The Third Reform Act is passed in Britain.

1885   Wolseley defeats the Mahdi's followers at Abu Klea but reaches Khartoum two days after its fall and Gordon's death. Wolseley is forced to withdraw and the news helps contribute to the fall of Gladstone's government. The Congo becomes the personal possession of Leopold II of Belgium. Germany annexes Tanganyika and Zanzibar. The Mahdi dies, but his successor Abdullah el Tasshi gains control over Sudan. Alfonso XII of Spain dies; his pregnant widow Maria Christina becomes regent.

1886   General Boulanger becomes French war minister. Gladstone's conversion to Irish Home Rule splits the Liberals; Joseph Chamberlain leads the Liberal Unionists into partnership with the Conservatives. Alfonso XIII of Spain is born king. France banishes the Bonaparte and Orléans families. Prince Alexander of Bulgaria abdicates after a coup. Randolph Churchill resigns as chancellor in a fit of pique and destroys his political career in the process. The discovery of gold in Transvaal transforms the politics of southern Africa.

1887   The First Colonial Conference opens in London. Germany and Russia make the secret Reinsurance Treaty. Zululand is annexed by Britain. Ferdinand of Saxe-Coburg is elected prince of Bulgaria. Italy and Abyssinia go to war; the Italians are routed at Dogali. Macao is ceded to Portugal.

1888   Kaiser Wilhelm I dies; his son Frederick III succeeds him, but dies soon after and is succeeded by his son Wilhelm II. Brazil frees its slaves. The Jack the Ripper murders take place in London. The first beauty contest is held in Spa, Belgium. The Suez Canal Convention, guaranteeing freedom of access to the canal, is signed in Constantinople.

1889   Urged by his supporters to stage a coup d'état, Boulanger refuses and flees abroad. Crown Prince Rudolf of Austria shoots his mistress and commits suicide at Mayerling. Milan II of Serbia abdicates in favour of his son Alexander II. Gustave Eiffel completes the Eiffel Tower for the Paris Exhibition. The first Pan-American Conference meets in Washington. The Brazilian army deposes King Pedro II and installs General Manuel de Fonseca as president.

1890   The Forth Railway Bridge opens. Kaiser Wilhelm forces Bismarck's resignation as Chancellor. Social insurance is introduced in Switzerland. Heligoland is exchanged for the German colonies of Zanzibar and Pemba by Britain. The first Japanese elections are held. William III of Holland dies, and is succeeded by his daughter Wilhelmina. Luxembourg separates from the Netherlands under Duke Adolf of Nassau. Sitting Bull is captured and killed; American troops massacre 200 Sioux at Wounded Knee.

1891   W.L. Judson invents the zip. President Fonseca of Brazil is ousted in favour of Vice-President Floriano Peixoto.

1892   Khedive Tewfik of Egypt dies, and is succeeded by his son Abbas II. Lizzie Borden murders her parents. Gladstone forms his fourth administration at the age of 82 after victory in the general election.

1893   The Independent Labour Party is founded in Bradford. Natal is granted self-government. The Matabele rise against the British South Africa Company, but Jameson crushes the revolt and takes Bulawayo, forcing King Lobengula into exile. Gladstone's Irish Home Rule Bill is defeated in the House of Lords. Transvaal annexes Swaziland.

1894   The Manchester Ship Canal is opened. Gladstone resigns from office, and is replaced as prime minister by Lord Rosebery. Uganda becomes a British protectorate. The Ottomans massacre thousands of Armenians in suppressing a revolt. President Carnot of France is assassinated by an Italian anarchist at Lyon. Korea and Japan declare war on China. Albert Dreyfus is arrested on a treason charge; convicted, he is imprisoned on Devil's Island.

1895   The treaty of Shimonoseki ends the Sino-Japanese War after the Japanese crush the Chinese at Wei hai wei; Formosa and Port Arthur are ceded to Japan but returned in exchange for an indemnity. Italy invades Abyssinia, but is defeated at Amba Alagi. The British South Africa Company's land south of the Zambezi is renamed Rhodesia. Premier Stamboulov of Bulgaria is assassinated. The Kiel Canal is opened. Wilhelm Röntgen discovers X-rays. The first public film show takes place. Jameson raids Transvaal, but fails to foment a rebellion against its Boer rulers.

1896   Jameson is captured by the Boers at Doorn Kop. Kaiser Wilhelm sends the Kruger Telegram, inflaming Anglo-German relations. Becquerel discovers radioactivity in uranium. Italy is defeated by the Abyssinians at Adowa and withdraws by the treaty of Addis Ababa. The first modern Olympic Games are held in Athens. Shah Nasir-ud-Din of Persia is assassinated; he is succeeded by his son Muzaffir-ud-Din. Marconi patents wireless telegraphy. Kitchener leads an Anglo-Egyptian force into the Sudan. Over 50,000 Armenians are massacred by the Turks.

1897   Crete proclaims union with Greece, prompting a war between Greece and Turkey; the Turks are victorious and the island stays under Turkish hands by the treaty of Constantinople. Hawaii is annexed by the United States. The first Zionist Congress meets in Basel.

1898   Zola publishes 'J'accuse' over the Dreyfus affair, proved to have been fabricated by anti-Semitic army officers. The USS *Maine* explodes in Havana harbour, Spanish involvement is suspected, and war breaks out between America and Spain; the Spanish fleet in Manila Bay is destroyed and the Americans are successful at San Juan and Santiago Bay; peace is made by the treaty of Paris, by which Spain cedes Cuba, Puerto Rico, Guam and the Philippines in return for $20m. Empress Elizabeth of Austria is murdered by an Italian anarchist. Kitchener defeats the Sudanese at Omdurman, retakes Khartoum and advances to Fashoda, where he discovers a French force which is ordered to withdraw after the British government protests to the French.

1899   The First Hague Peace Conference meets. Dreyfus is pardoned by presidential decree after being found guilty again in a second trial prompted by public opinion. Transvaal declares war on Britain; the Orange Free State allies with Transvaal. The Boers besiege Kimberley, Mafeking and Ladysmith and are victorious at Stormberg, Magersfontein and Colenso.

1900   The Boers are victorious at Spion Kop, but Kimberley, Ladysmith and Mafeking are relieved and Bloemfontein, Johannesburg and Pretoria are taken by the British, who annex the Orange Free State and Transvaal. Kruger flees to Germany but is refused an audience by Kaiser Wilhelm II. The Labour Representation Committee is established, with Ramsay MacDonald as secretary. The Boxer Rebellion against foreign influence in China breaks out; the German ambassador is murdered and the foreign legations in Beijing besieged, but are subsequently relieved. The first Zeppelin airship takes to the air. Umberto I of Italy is assassinated by an anarchist; his son Victor Emmanuel III succeeds him.

1901   The Commonwealth of Australia is created. The Boers begin guerrilla warfare against the British. The first British submarine, *Holland I*, is launched. Queen Victoria dies, and is succeeded by her son Edward VII. US President William McKinley is assassinated by an anarchist; Vice-President Theodore Roosevelt succeeds him. The Boxer Rebellion is ended by the Peace of Beijing. The first Nobel Prizes are awarded. Marconi, who is in Newfoundland receives a wireless message from Cornwall.

1902   Britain allies with Japan. St Pierre, Martinique, is destroyed by the eruption of Mount Pelée. The treaty of Vereeniging ends the Boer War with British sovereignty imposed. Trotsky escapes from prison in Siberia and flees to London, where he meets Lenin. The Order of Merit is established.

1903   King Alexander I and Queen Draga of Serbia are assassinated by supporters of the rival Karageorgevich dynasty, whose heir Peter I ascends the throne in their place. The first Tour de France takes place. The Russian Social Democratic Party splits into Mensheviks and Bolsheviks at its London conference. The Wright Brothers perform the first successful powered flight.

1904   The wireless distress signal CQD is adopted. The Japanese attack the Russians in Port Arthur, setting off war between the two countries; the Japanese are subsequently victorious at Liaoyang. Britain and France ally by the 'Entente Cordiale'. The Rolls-Royce motor company is founded. Vycheslav Plehve, Russian minister of the interior, is assassinated. The British enter Tibet by imposing the treaty of Lhasa; they aim to safeguard it from Russian penetration. The Russian fleet attacks Hull trawlers off the Dogger Bank, mistaking them for Japanese warships; the French mediate between Britain and Russia and the matter is resolved.

1905   Port Arthur surrenders to the Japanese; the resulting protests in St Petersburg are brutally crushed (Bloody Sunday); revolts flare up in Russia as a result, exacerbated by defeats at Mukden and the Tsushima Strait, where the navy is annihilated; the battleship *Potemkin* mutinies; the Russo-Japanese war is ended by the treaty of Portsmouth, a Soviet is established in St Petersburg and Tsar Nicholas II issues a liberal policy (the October Manifesto). Crete revolts against Turkish rule. Kaiser Wilhelm II visits Tangier, where he emphasizes German interests, to the alarm of other countries. Norway separates from Sweden; Prince Charles of Denmark is elected king, taking the name Haakon VII. The Conservative Party splits over tariff reform; Balfour resigns as PM as a result and Campbell-Bannerman replaces him. Albert Einstein publishes his special theory of relativity.

1906   The Liberals gain a landslide victory in the General Election. HMS *Dreadnought* is launched in Britain, making all other warships outdated and precipitating a naval arms race. The Algeciras Conference settles the Moroccan question and reduces European tension. San Francisco is hit by a severe earthquake. The Duma meets in Russia, but it is too liberal for the Tsar's liking and is dissolved. As the Tsar's control is re-established over the country, he backtracks on his liberal reforms. Dreyfus is rehabilitated in France and awarded the Légion d'Honneur. South Sinai is ceded to Egypt by the Turks under British pressure. Transvaal and the Orange River colonies are granted self-government.

1907   Sinn Fein ('We ourselves') is established. France and Japan reach agreement on an 'open door' policy in China. The Second Hague Peace Conference meets. Emperor Ko-jong of Korea is forced to abdicate by the Japanese, who establish a protectorate over the country with his son Sun-jong as a figurehead emperor. Britain and Russia reach an entente, forming the Triple Entente with France as a counterweight to the Triple Alliance of Germany, Italy and Austria-Hungary. New Zealand becomes a dominion.

1908   Carlos I of Portugal and his heir are assassinated; his younger son Manuel II succeeds him. The Young Turks revolt at Resina before gaining a majority in the new Ottoman parliament and introducing reforms. The first Ford Model T is sold. Bulgaria declares independence; Prince Ferdinand assumes the title of Tsar. Austria annexes Bosnia-Herzegovina, to international consternation. Crete declares union with Greece again.

1909   Turkey and Serbia are forced to accept the Austrian annexation of Bosnia-Herzegovina. Sultan Abdul Hamid II is deposed by the Young Turks in favour of his brother Muhammad V. Shah Muhammad Ali of Persia is deposed in favour of his son Ahmad by Ali Kuli Khan. Louis Blériot crosses the English Channel by aeroplane. The House of Lords rejects Lloyd-George's 'People's Budget', causing a constitutional crisis; Asquith calls a general election .

1910   Liberals and Tories tie in a General Election; Asquith's government depends on Labour and Irish Nationalist votes. Premier Boutros Ghali of Egypt is assassinated by a nationalist fanatic, whilst Islamic agitation increases. Edward VII dies, and is succeeded by his son George V, who inherits a constitutional crisis. South Africa becomes a dominion. Japan annexes Korea. Montenegro declares itself a kingdom under Nicholas I. Manuel II of Portugal is deposed by a revolution which declares Portugal a republic headed by Teofilo Braga. A second election produces another hung parliament.

1911	Electric escalators are installed for the first time at Earl's Court Station. Germany sends the gunboat *Panther* to Agadir, creating another international crisis. The Parliament Bill is passed by the Lords, under duress, settling the constitutional crisis. Italy declares war on Turkey as it attempts to invade Tripolitania (Libya). Sun Yat-sen leads a revolution overthrowing the Manchu monarchy in China and establishing a republic, with himself as its first president. The Mexican Civil War is ended by the establishment in power of the revolutionary, Francisco Madero. Roald Amundsen becomes the first man to reach the South Pole.
1912	The *Titanic* sinks on its maiden voyage, with the loss of over 1,500 lives. It becomes the first ship to use the newly adopted SOS distress signal. Emperor Meiji (Mutsuhito) of Japan dies, and is succeeded by his son Yoshihito. The treaty of Lausanne makes peace between Italy and Turkey, and accepts Italy's conquest of Tripolitania. The first Balkan War takes place when Serbia, Montenegro and Bulgaria declare war on Turkey, whose remaining European possessions are overrun.
1913	Greece joins the anti-Turkish alliance in the Balkans. George I of Greece is assassinated; his son Constantine I succeeds him. The great powers force the treaty of London on the combatants, which leaves none of them satisfied. Suffragette Emily Davison throws herself under the king's horse at the Derby. A Second Balkan War, precipitated by Bulgaria, erupts, with Serbia, Greece, Russia and Turkey against the country; this war is resolved by the treaty of Bucharest but tensions still simmer.
1914	Archduke Franz Ferdinand of Austria is assassinated by a Serb extremist in Sarajevo. Austria seeks to punish Serbia, but merely succeeds in dragging most of Europe into World War I. The British Expeditionary Force lands to support the French. Russia invades Germany, but is repulsed at Tannenberg and defeated at the Masurian Lakes. Germany invades Belgium and France, but is held at the Marne. The First battle of Ypres is a bloody draw and the trench system of warfare emerges on the Western Front. The British fleet is defeated by the Germans at Coronel but victorious at the Falkland Islands. Ireland is pushed to the brink of civil war over Home Rule, but the onset of war diverts attention away from the crisis. The Panama Canal opens.
1915	Germany uses poison gas for the first time at the Second battle of Ypres. The British attempt to surprise Turkey at Gallipoli, but are repulsed. German U-boat sinks the *Lusitania*, causing international outrage. Italy is enticed on to the Entente side in the war by the secret treaty of London and attacks Austria, but fails to advance. Edith Cavell is shot after accusations that she helped Allied soldiers escape from Brussels.
1916	The Mexican revolutionary Pancho Villa raids New Mexico. Germany and France fight a bloody draw over Verdun, which remains in French hands. Irish republicans stage the Easter Rising in Dublin, but the coup fails and the leaders are executed. American troops act as peacekeepers in the Dominican Republic. The British and German fleets fight the battle of Jutland, which proves indecisive but the German fleet withdraws to Kiel and remains there. Allied troops mount a major offensive on the Somme, which gains them some ground after 5 months of bloody battle. Emperor Franz Joseph of Austria dies, and is succeeded by his great-nephew Charles I. The Russian monk Rasputin is assassinated by a group of nobles concerned about his influence at court. Einstein publishes his general theory of relativity.
1917	The Orders of the Companions of Honour and of the British Empire are established. America, Cuba and China enter the war on the Allied side. The Allies are victorious at Arras and Passchendaele, although with much loss of life at the latter. Constantine I of Greece abdicates in favour of his son Alexander I. Mata Hari is executed as a spy. The Balfour Declaration over a Jewish homeland in Palestine is issued. Tanks are used for the first time with any effect at Cambrai. Troops mutiny in Russia; the worsening situation prompts Tsar Nicholas II to abdicate in favour of his brother Grand Duke Michael, who refuses the throne and the Tsardom collapses. A provisional government is set up, but fails to manage the war any better. Revolts against it in July are suppressed, as is Brusilov's coup attempt. However, the Bolsheviks succeed in a coup in November, forcing prime minister Kerensky to flee. Lenin is established in power.
1918	In Britain, a Representation of the People Act gives the vote to all men over 21 and all women over 30. Russia withdraws from the war by making the treaty of Brest-Litovsk with Germany; Finland, Poland and the Baltic States are given independence. A coalition of Bolshevik opponents declare war on them, starting civil war in Russia. The Bolsheviks murder the Tsar and his family. A German offensive is successful on the Western Front, but the Allies regroup and push them back, being victorious at the marne and Amiens. Ferdinand I of Bulgaria abdicates in favour of his son Boris III. The Austro-Hungarian Empire collapses; Emperor Charles I abdicates and the Empire becomes several republics. Allied forces remove the Turks from the Middle East. The Czechs declare independence under Tomas Masaryk. The German navy mutinies. Kaiser Wilhelm II abdicates; Germany becomes a republic. An armistice is signed ending action in World War I. The kingdom of Yugoslavia, under Peter I of Serbia, is proclaimed. A Spanish Influenza pandemic begins.
1919	The Eighteenth Amendment is passed, establishing Prohibition in America. The Allies convene in Paris to settle the world map after World War I; the treaties of Versailles with Germany, Saint-Germain with Austria and Neuilly with Bulgaria are imposed. The Bolsheviks establish the Third International. The League of Nations is founded. Alcock and Brown become the first men to fly the Atlantic. The German fleet is scuttled in Scapa Flow. In India, British troops kill 379 demonstrators in the Amritsar Massacre. Austria exiles the Habsburgs.
1920	Irish republicans begin guerrilla war against continued British rule. President Venustiano Carranza of Mexico is assassinated; he is succeeded by Adolfo de la Huerta. The treaties of Trianon with Hungary and Sèvres with Turkey are imposed. The International Court of Justice is established at The Hague. The Little Entente of Czechoslovakia and Yugoslavia (joined next year by Romania) is formed. King Alexander I of Greece dies; his father Constantine I resumes the throne.
1921	The first All-India parliament is opened in Delhi. Reza Khan Pahlevi organizes a coup d'etat in Persia. Ex-Emperor Charles fails to regain the Hungarian throne. The Bolsheviks are victors in the Russian Civil War, but the economy is ruined, forcing Lenin to adopt the New Economic Policy. The Allied Reparations Commission levies compensation of £6,650m on Germany. Britain and Irish republicans reach an accord; Northern Ireland is granted its own parliament with Sir James Craig as prime minister. Spanish troops in

Morocco are annihilated by Berber rebels, at Anual. Faisal I is elected king of Iraq after a plebiscite. Eduardo Iradier, prime minister of Spain is assassinated by an anarchist. Takashi Hara, prime minister of Japan, is assassinated.

1922   The treaties of Washington establish a Pacific status quo. The Irish Free State is established, but the IRA declares civil war against the government in Dublin and assassinates Prime Minister Michael Collins. The kingdom of Egypt is established under Fuad I. Mustafa Kemal evicts the Greeks from Smyrna. The Arabs in Palestine reject the British mandate. Constantine I of Greece abdicates again, in favour of his son George II. The Conservatives withdraw from the coalition government, bringing down Lloyd George. Bonar Law becomes prime minister. Mussolini leads the Fascists in a March on Rome and succeeds in forming a government. Mustafa Kemal proclaims Turkey a republic; Sultan Muhammad VI is deposed; his cousin Abdul-Majid II maintains the title Caliph. Howard Carter opens Tutankhamun's tomb. The BBC begins its radio broadcasts. The Union of Soviet Socialist Republics (USSR) is formed.

1923   The French occupy the Ruhr after the Germans default on reparations. Prime minister Stamboliski of Bulgaria is removed from office by a coup and shot while trying to escape. The treaty of Lausanne resolves the war between Greece and Turkey. President Warren Harding of America dies in office, and is succeeded by his laconic Vice-President Calvin Coolidge. Germany is hit by hyper-inflation. Primo de Rivera establishes a dictatorship in Spain with the approval of Alfonso XIII. Mustafa Kemal moves the Turkish capital to Ankara. Hitler mounts the 'Beer Hall Putsch'; it fails and he is imprisoned. The Greek army deposes George II.

1924   Venizelos becomes prime minister of Greece. Lenin dies; a triumvirate of Stalin, Kamenev and Zinoviev replaces him in power. After a general election produces a hung parliament, Ramsay MacDonald forms the first Labour government in Britain; he is defeated in a subsequent election, in which the Conservatives are helped by the forged Zinoviev Letter. Kemal abolishes the Caliphate and exiles the Ottomans from Turkey.

1925   Norway renames its capital Oslo and annexes Spitsbergen. Sun Yat-sen dies; Chiang Kai-shek is appointed his replacement by the Guomindang (Chinese Nationalist Party). Hindenburg is elected president of Germany. Hitler sets up the SS (Schutzstaffel) as his personal bodyguard. Reza Khan Pahlavi deposes Shah Ahmad of Persia and ascends the throne himself. The Locarno treaties are signed, guaranteeing the common borders of Belgium, France and Germany, and demilitarizing the Rhineland.

1926   Abdul-Aziz II Ibn Saud of Najd becomes king of the Hijaz. The General Strike is called in Britain, but fails to achieve much. Pilsudski stages a coup d'état in Poland. Lebanon is proclaimed a republic. Stalin forces the banishment of Trotsky and Zinoviev from Moscow as he assumes control of Russia. Emperor Yoshihito of Japan dies, and is succeeded by his son Hirohito. John Logie Baird develops television.

1927   Charles Lindbergh makes the first solo flight across the Atlantic. Trotsky is expelled from the Communist Party. Ferdinand I of Romania dies, and is succeeded by his infant nephew Michael.

1928   In Britain, all women receive the vote. The anti-war Kellogg-Briand Pact is signed. Albania becomes a kingdom under Ahmed Bey Zogu, who takes the title Zog I. The first Five Year Plan is outlined by Stalin. Chiang Kai-shek is formally elected president of China.

1929   Alexander I of Yugoslavia suppresses the constitution and proclaims a dictatorship. Italy and the Vatican make the Lateran Treaties, establishing an independent Vatican City. The St Valentine's Day Massacre of gangsters occurs in Chicago. Labour wins a general election for the first time and Ramsay MacDonald returns to office as prime minister. The Wall Street Crash leads to a collapse of share prices and the onset of severe economic depression in America.

1930   France starts work on the Maginot Line of defences. Primo de Rivera resigns office through ill health and dies soon after. Brüning forms a right-wing coalition government in Germany. Haile Selassie becomes king of Abyssinia. Carol II of Romania replaces his young son Michael as King. President Leguia of Peru is forced from office by a military coup. José Uriburu leads a military coup in Argentina. The R101 airship crashes and burns. Getulio Vargas leads a revolution in Brazil and is named President. The Youth Hostels Association is founded.

1931   Oswald Mosley leaves the Labour Party and forms the short-lived New Party. Alfonso XIII of Spain abdicates and leaves the country. The Credit-Anstalt bank of Austria collapses, creating a financial crisis in central Europe. The Invergordon mutiny over pay cuts occurs. Japan occupies Manchuria. MacDonald forms a National Government to deal with the deteriorating economic situation, but the Labour Party mostly splits from him. The Statute of Westminster defines dominion statutes and creates the Commonwealth.

1932   Gandhi is arrested after the Indian National Congress is declared illegal. President Doumer of France is assassinated by a Russian émigré. The Nazis win the German general election, but refuse to serve under President Hindenburg's nominee as Chancellor, Von Papen, who is later forced to resign. Iraq ceases to be a British mandate. Mosley founds the British Union of Fascists. Franklin D. Roosevelt defeats President Hoover in a landslide victory in the American presidential elections.

1933   Hitler is appointed German Chancellor. Prohibition is abolished in America. The Reichstag, Germany's parliament, building burns down; Communists are blamed. Chancellor Dollfuss of Austria rules by decree, provoking riots from Austrian Nazis. The first German concentration camps are opened. Hitler takes dictatorial powers; systematic persecution of Jews begins; the Gestapo is founded. Nadir Shah of Afghanistan is assassinated, succeeded by his son Muhammad Zahir Shah.

1934   Hitler purges the Nazi party in the 'Night of the Long Knives'. Austrian Nazis assassinate Dollfuss in a failed putsch; Schusnigg becomes chancellor. Hitler becomes German president on the death of Hindenburg. The USSR joins the League of Nations. King Alexander of Yugoslavia is assassinated together with the French foreign minister, Louis Barthou, at Marseille by a Croat revolutionary based in Hungary; he is succeeded by his son Peter II. Mao Zedong leads the Chinese Communists on the Long March. Sergei Kirov is assassinated in Leningrad, giving Stalin a pretext to purge the Russian Communists of his opponents.

1935   The Saar is returned to Germany after a plebiscite; Hitler repudiates the Versailles treaty and passes the Nuremberg decrees against Jews. Persia is renamed Iran by order of the Shah. Alcoholics Anonymous is established. Japan withdraws from the League of Nations. Italy invades Abyssinia; the League of Nations

H
I
S
T
O
R
Y

imposes sanctions against Italy but the Anglo-French Hoare–Laval plan proposes partial acquiescence in the conquest. George II of Greece returns to his throne. The US creates the Commonwealth of the Philippines, a step towards Filipino independence.

1936   George V dies, his son Edward VIII succeeds him but abdicates in favour of his brother George VI after falling in love with Wallis Simpson. The Japanese army attempts a coup, but fails. Germany reoccupies the Rhineland. King Fuad of Egypt dies, and is succeeded by his son Farouk. Italy completes its conquest of Abyssinia. Spanish generals, led by Franco, revolt against the Republican government; this leads to civil war. Television broadcasts start in Britain.

1937   Guernica is destroyed by aircraft of the German Condor Legion assisting Franco's rebels. The Peel Commission on Palestine proposes partition into Arab and Jewish states with a British mandate for Jerusalem and Bethlehem. Amelia Earhart disappears on a Pacific flight. Japan invades China, surprising the Chinese at the Marco Polo Bridge and capturing Beijing, Nanjing, Tianjin and Shanghai; the Chinese government moves to Chongqing. The legitimate Spanish government moves to Barcelona. Italy withdraws from the League of Nations.

1938   Austria is forced to unite with Germany (the Anschluss). Continuing his Great Purge of all potential opposition, Stalin tries and executes former colleagues including Buthasin, Rykor and Yagoda. The Sudeten Germans demand secession from Czechoslovakia; Britain and France appease Hitler at Munich and allow this, to much public disgust. Britain drops the Peel proposals on Palestine, prompting terrorist attacks in the area. Hungary annexes southern Slovakia. The anti-Jewish Kristallnacht takes place in Germany. Kemal Ataturk dies, and is succeeded as Turkish president by Ismet Inonu.

1939   Germany occupies the rump Czech lands and places Slovakia under protection. Franco's insurgents capture Madrid and are victorious in the Spanish Civil War. Italy invades Albania. Hungary and Spain quit the League of Nations. Germany and Russia conclude a non-aggression pact and carve up Poland between themselves. Poland is invaded by the two countries; Britain and France, who have pledged to guarantee Poland, declare war on Germany as a result. A German u-Boat sinks HMS *Royal Oak* in Scapa Flow. Russia invades Finland and the Baltic States and is expelled from the League of Nations. The *Graf Spee* is scuttled after losing the battle of the River Plate.

1940   Finland and Russia make peace. Germany invades Norway, Denmark, Benelux and France. Churchill replaces Chamberlain as prime minister. Allied troops are evacuated at Dunkirk. Italy declares war on Britain and France. The puppet Vichy France is established. The British destroy the French fleet at Mers-el-Kebir to prevent it falling into Vichy hands. The Home Guard is founded. A German aerial assault on Britain is repulsed (the Battle of Britain). Trotsky is assassinated in Mexico, possibly on Stalin's orders. Germany, Italy and Japan form the 'Axis'.

1941   British troops help the Abyssinians expel the Italians; Haile Selassie is restored to his throne. The pro-Nazi Regent Paul of Yugoslavia is deposed; Germany invades the country. Germany invades Russia. Reich Marshal Hermann Göring instructs Reinhard Heydrich, deputy chief of the SS, 'to carry out the final solution of the Jewish question'. Iran is invaded by Britain and Russia; Reza Shah abdicates in favour of his pro-Allied son Muhammad Reza. Mass deportations begin to death camps such as Auschwitz, Chelmno and Treblinka. Japan bombs Pearl Harbor and invades the Philippines; America thereby enters the war. Hong Kong falls to the Japanese.

1942   The Japanese take the Philippines, Dutch East Indies, Singapore and Burma, but lose the naval battles of the Coral Sea and Midway to the Americans. Two Czech resistance men sent from Britain assassinate Reinhard Heydrich; the Nazis burn Lidice as revenge. Rommel, after taking Tobruk, is defeated at El Alamein and forced to retreat across North Africa. The battle of Stalingrad begins.

1943   Churchill, Roosevelt and De Gaulle meet at Casablanca. The Germans surrender at Stalingrad and are driven back West. Guadalcanal falls to the US. Allied aircraft destroy a Japanese convoy at the Bismarck Sea. The Warsaw Ghetto is attacked by the Germans, falls after a siege, and survivors are deported to concentration camps. The Allies drive the Germans from North Africa and cross into Sicily and Italy. The Soviets score a major victory at Kursk in the largest ever tank battle. Mussolini is forced to resign and Badoglio replaces him. Italy signs an armistice with the Allies, but the Germans keep up the fight in the country. Churchill, Stalin and Roosevelt meet at Tehran.

1944   The Allies land at Anzio and take Rome. Leningrad is relieved by the Russians. The Solomon and Marshall Islands fall to the Americans, who defeat the Japanese at the Philippine Sea. The D-Day landings provide the springboard for the reconquest of France. Iceland gains independence from Denmark. Warsaw rises against the Germans. Guam falls to the Americans. The Russians enter Romania, Czechoslovakia, Bulgaria and Hungary. Stauffenberg leads a failed attempt on Hitler's life; Rommel is implicated and forced to commit suicide. The Germans fight back at the battle of the Bulge. North Burma is retaken by the British.

1945   The Allies enter Germany. The Americans take the Philippines and Okinawa. The League of Arab States is founded. F.D. Roosevelt dies, and is succeeded as American president by Truman. Mussolini is killed by partisans. Hitler commits suicide. Burma is recaptured by the British. Germany surrenders to the Allies. Churchill, Truman and Stalin meet at Potsdam to consider the future. Attlee replaces Churchill after a Labour landslide at the general election. America drops atomic bombs on Hiroshima and Nagasaki and Japan surrenders. Ho Chi Minh declares Vietnam an independent republic. The United Nations is founded. The Nuremberg trials commence. Peter II of Yugoslavia is deposed by the Communists.

1946   The United Nations convenes in London, as the League of Nations is formally wound up. Jewish terrorism recommences in Palestine. Juan Perón becomes president of Argentina. Mao Zedong proclaims war against the Guomindang regime in China. Victor Emmanuel III of Italy abdicates in favour of his son Umberto II, who is exiled when a referendum votes to abolish the monarchy. Transjordan becomes an independent state under King Abdullah. Bulgaria votes to abolish its monarchy and becomes a communist state. The Fourth Republic is established in France.

1947   The Dead Sea Scrolls are discovered. Mount Hekla erupts in Iceland. The Palestine question is passed to the United Nations for resolution after British partition proposals are rejected there. United Nations partition proposals are rejected by the Arabs. George II of Greece dies, and is succeeded by his brother Paul I. India, Pakistan and Burma become independent states. Michael of Romania is forced to abdicate by the communists.

1948   Gandhi is assassinated by a Hindu fundamentalist. The communists mount a coup in Czechoslovakia. The British leave Palestine once their mandate expires; Ben Gurion proclaims the state of Israel, which is immediately attacked by its Arab neighbours but fights them off. The Russians blockade West Berlin; the Allies respond by an airlift. Apartheid laws are passed in South Africa. Wilhelmina of Holland abdicates in favour of her daughter Juliana. Nehru sends Indian troops to force Hyderabad to join India, and the Nizam gives way under force.

1949   NATO is created. The Republic of Ireland is proclaimed. The Council of Europe is created. West and East Germany are created. Transjordan is renamed Jordan. The Chinese communists drive the Guomindang from China; it takes refuge on Formosa. Mao Zedong becomes the head of state of China. Indonesia is granted independence; Sukarno is elected president.

1950   North Korea invades South Korea, but the United Nations sends troops to defend it; when North Korea is forced to withdraw, China sends troops to assist it. Leopold III of Belgium returns from exile, but decides to abdicate after protests against him. China invades Tibet.

1951   MacArthur is replaced as UN commander in Korea, as the war develops into stalemate. The spies Burgess and Maclean flee to Moscow. King Abdullah of Jordan is assassinated, and is succeeded by his son Talal. Japan is granted independence after military occupation. A general election makes Churchill prime minister again.

1952   George VI dies, and is succeeded by his daughter Elizabeth II. Kenyatta heads the Mau Mau resistance to drive the British from Kenya. General Naguib leads a coup in Egypt; King Farouk is forced to abdicate in favour of his infant son Fa'ad II. King Talal of Jordan is deposed after being declared unfit to rule and is succeeded by his son Hussein. Britain produces an atomic bomb. America develops the H-bomb.

1953   Stalin dies; Malenkov succeeds to his posts; Khrushchev is appointed First Secretary. Hillary and Tensing achieve the first successful ascent of Mount Everest. A republic is proclaimed in Egypt and Naguib is granted dictatorial powers. The combatants in the Korean War sign an armistice at Panmunjon, ending the active war. The Federation of Rhodesia and Nyasaland is established.

1954   The Vietnamese communists defeat the French at Dien Bien Phu and occupy Hanoi. Alfredo Stroessner is elected president of Paraguay on the death of President Lopez. Vietnam is split into two at a conference in Geneva. SEATO is established. Rebellion breaks out in French Algeria. Colonel Nasser seizes power in Egypt from General Naguib. Laos gains independence from France.

1955   Malenkov resigns in Russia, and is replaced by Bulganin. Churchill resigns as prime minister, and is replaced by Eden. The Warsaw Pact is established as a communist counterweight to NATO. Austrian independence is restored by the Vienna Treaty. Juan Perón is ousted by a military coup in Argentina.

1956   The first Eurovision Song Contest is won by Switzerland. Sudan and Tunisia become independent republics. Morocco becomes an independent kingdom. Archbishop Makarios and Cypriot Enosis (union with Greece) agitators are deported to the Seychelles. Nasser nationalizes the Suez Canal. Imre Nagy is returned to power in Hungary after demonstrations, but proves too independent for Russia. Israel invades the Sinai, encouraged by Britain and France, who send troops to the Suez Canal to 'protect' it. Under international pressure, they withdraw when UN forces arrive. Russian troops are sent to Hungary; Nagy is seized and executed.

1957   Eden resigns as prime minister after the Suez fiasco, and is succeeded by Harold Macmillan. Ghana is granted independence. The European Economic Community is established by the treaty of Rome. Russia launches Sputnik I, the first space satellite. Mao Zedong decrees the disastrous Great Leap Forward in Chinese agriculture and rural industry.

1958   Egypt and Sudan unite as the United Arab Republic under Nasser. Khrushchev ousts Bulganin as Chairman of the Council of Ministers in Russia and has effective control of the government. The Fourth Republic in France collapses through the ramifications of the Algerian crisis; De Gaulle forms a government, establishes the Fifth Republic and is elected president. General Kassem stages a coup in Iraq, assassinating King Faisal, his son and the premier and taking power.

1959   Fidel Castro ousts President Batista from Cuba and creates a communist state there. The Dalai Lama is forced to flee Tibet as China represses the indigenous population. Mao Zedong resigns as China's head of state in favour of Liu Shaoqi, but remains in power as chairman of the communists. Singapore gains independence under prime minister Lee Kuan Yew. Cyprus is granted independence; Archbishop Makarios is elected president.

1960   The South African police fire on a protest in Sharpeville, killing 69. Gary Powers is shot down over Russia, causing US/Russian tension. Belgium grants independence to the Congo. Mrs Bandaranaike becomes prime minister in Ceylon, the first woman anywhere to hold such a post.

1961   Yuri Gagarin is launched into space in *Vostok 1*. Cuban rebels, assisted by America, land at the Bay of Pigs, but are repulsed by the Cuban army. South Africa leaves the Commonwealth. The Berlin Wall is constructed. UN Secretary-General Dag Hammarskjöld is killed in a plane crash in the Congo; U Thant is elected as his successor.

1962   Algeria is granted independence by France. Former SS administrator Adolf Eichmann is hanged by Israel for war crimes. Russia attempts to send arms to Cuba and establish a missile base there; President Kennedy blockades the island and forces Khrushchev to withdraw; for a few days the spectre of nuclear war looms large.

1963   Kim Philby flees to Moscow after his espionage activities are uncovered. The Profumo crisis develops in Britain, weakening Macmillan's government. Doctor Beeching's report initiates harsh cuts in the British railway system. The nuclear submarine USS *Thresher* sinks. A nuclear test ban treaty is signed by the US, USSR and Britain. Martin Luther King makes his 'I have a dream' speech. Macmillan resigns through ill health, and is replaced by Alec Douglas-Home. A military coup succeeds in South Vietnam. President Kennedy is assassinated; his assumed killer Lee Harvey Oswald is shot dead days later by Jack Ruby.

1964   Fighting breaks out in Cyprus between the Greek and Turkish communities; Greece refuses direct talks while the UN sends peacekeeping troops. King Paul of Greece dies, and is succeeded by his son Constantine II. Ian Smith becomes prime minister of Southern Rhodesia. Nelson Mandela, found guilty in the Rivonia treason trial, is sentenced to life imprisonment. Nyasaland gains independence as Malawi. America escalates operations against North Vietnam. Malta gains independence. Khrushchev is ousted from power in the USSR; Brezhnev and Kosygin take over. Northern Rhodesia becomes independent as Zambia.

1965   Nicolae Ceauçescu becomes premier of Romania. In reprisals after a failed communist coup, the Indonesian army kills half a million people. Rhodesia declares independence from Britain; sanctions are imposed on it as an illegal state. General Mobutu takes power in the Belgian Congo in a coup.

1966   Mrs Gandhi becomes prime minister of India. France withdraws from NATO. England win the football World Cup, defeating West Germany 4–2. South African prime minister Hendrik Verwoerd is assassinated, replaced by Vorster. Harold Wilson and Ian Smith discuss the Rhodesia affair on HMS *Tiger*, but the talks come to nothing.

1967   A military coup in Greece removes Constantine II from the throne; he is forced to flee as a counter-coup fails. Arab nations invade Israel, but Israel forces them back and captures Sinai, the West Bank and the Golan Heights in the Six Days War. Colour television begins in Britain. Jerusalem is proclaimed a united city under Israeli rule. General de Gaulle encourages the secession of Quebec whilst on a visit there, causing a diplomatic storm. Che Guevara is captured and shot in Bolivia. South Yemen gains independence.

1968   The communists begin the Tet Offensive in Vietnam. America commits the My Lai Massacre. Martin Luther King and Robert Kennedy are assassinated. Alexander Dubcek comes to power in Czechoslovakia, but his liberalization policies are unpopular in Russia, which sends in troops to re-establish a government more to its liking. Dubcek is arrested. Student riots in Paris destabilize the government, but de Gaulle uses his personal authority to reestablish effective government.

1969   Yasser Arafat is elected chairman of the PLO. General de Gaulle resigns as President of France, and is replaced by Georges Pompidou. America begins to withdraw troops from Vietnam. America lands men on the moon. Civil unrest in Northern Ireland spills over into fighting and terrorism; troops are sent to maintain order. Colonel Gaddafi deposes King Idris of Libya and assumes power.

1970   The Nigerian civil war ends with the capitulation of Biafra. Brazil win the football World Cup with the best team ever according to the popular press. The Portuguese dictator Salazar dies, and is succeeded as premier by Marcello Caetano. King Hussein of Jordan and Pope Paul VI survive assassination attempts. Salvador Allende is elected President of Chile. President Nasser of Egypt dies, and is succeeded by Anwar Sadat. The Japanese novelist Yukio Mishima commits suicide after failing to launch a military coup to purge the disgrace of defeat in 1945.

1971   Idi Amin seizes power in Uganda. The Vietnam war spreads into Laos and Cambodia. Decimal coinage is introduced in Britain. President François Duvalier of Haiti dies, and is succeeded by his son Jean-Claude (Baby Doc). Internment is introduced in Northern Ireland. The Congo is renamed Zaïre by President Mobutu. East Pakistan gains independence as Bangladesh.

1972   The Bloody Sunday shootings take place in Londonderry. President Nixon's visit to China initiates US-Chinese détente. Direct rule is imposed in Northern Ireland. Ceylon becomes the republic of Sri Lanka. The Democratic headquarters in the Watergate building, Washington are burgled; President Nixon is implicated, but is re-elected for a 2nd term. Palestinian terrorists seize and kill Israeli athletes at the Munich Olympics. Idi Amin expels Asians from Uganda.

1973   Britain, Ireland and Denmark join the EEC. A ceasefire is proclaimed in the Vietnam War, but fighting still continues in the area. The Cod War between Britain and Iceland develops. General Pinochet ousts President Allende of Chile in a violent coup, in which Allende perishes. Egypt and Syria attack Israel in the Yom Kippur War, but Israel repulses them. Vice-President Spiro Agnew of America resigns over income tax evasion; Gerald Ford replaces him. Arab oil producers embargo shipments to the West, which supports Israel in the war, causing an energy crisis. A coal strike in Britain forces the government to declare a three-day working week.

1974   After a coup in Portugal, Portuguese Guinea gains independence as Guinea-Bissau. Chancellor Willy Brandt of West Germany resigns when one of his aides is unmasked as an East German spy. Cypriot rebels overthrow Archbishop Makarios; Turkish forces invade Cyprus and occupy much of the north. The military junta in Greece resigns and a civilian government under Karamanlis is restored. President Nixon is forced to resign as a result of the Watergate affair; Gerald Ford replaces him and grants a pardon.

1975   North Vietnam overruns South Vietnam; America withdraws and Vietnam is reunited under a communist leadership. Portugal grants independence to Angola and Mozambique. Eritrean secessionists begin a guerrilla war in Ethiopia. King Faisal of Saudi Arabia is assassinated by his nephew Prince Faisal, who is beheaded for murder; the King's brother Khalid succeeds him. Chiang Kai-Shek dies, and is succeeded as President of Taiwan by Yan Jiangan. The Khmer Rouge declare Year Zero in Cambodia and embark on a programme of mass executions. General Franco dies; the country reverts to a monarchy under Juan Carlos I, grandson of Alfonso XIII.

1976   Chou En-lai and Mao Zedong die in China; the 'Gang of Four' attempt to take over but are arrested. Spain withdraws from Spanish Sahara, which is promptly seized by Morocco; Mauritania also takes a portion. Concorde enters regular passenger service. Harold Wilson resigns as prime minister and is succeeded by James Callaghan. Palestinian terrorists hijack an Air France plance, but Israeli commandos storm it at Entebbe.

1977   President Bante of Ethiopia and 10 aides are killed in a gun battle in a council meeting in Addis Ababa; Colonel Mengistu fills the void. Two Boeing 747s collide on the runway at Tenerife; 577 die. Deng Xiaoping assumes power in China. President Sadat of Egypt visits Israel. Jean Bedel Bokassa crowns himself Emperor of the Central African Empire (Republic) in an extravagant ceremony.

1978   Secessionist rebels, backed by Angola, Cuba and Russia, invade Katanga in Zaïre, but are repulsed with

American help. Red Brigade terrorists abduct and kill former Italian premier Aldo Moro. Communists seize control in South Yemen, and assassinate the President of North Yemen. Pope Paul VI dies, as does his successor John Paul I after 33 days; Karol Wojtyla is elected the first non-Italian Pope for 455 years and takes the name John Paul II. The first transatlantic balloon crossing is made. In Nicaragua the Sandinista guerrillas begin a campaign of violence against President Somoza. Israel and Egypt sign the Camp David accords. The Shah of Iran imposes martial law to curb dissent.

1979   The Khmer Rouge are overthrown in Cambodia. The Shah of Iran flees to Egypt and an Islamic fundamentalist regime under Ayatollah Khomeini is established; when the seriously ill Shah is allowed into America, extremists seize the American embassy in Tehran. Former prime minister Bhutto of Pakistan is hanged by the regime of General Zia. Margaret Thatcher comes to power in Britain. Saddam Hussein comes to power in Iraq, replacing Hassan al-Bakr. The Sandinistas overthrow Somoza and establish a junta in Nicaragua. Lord Mountbatten is assassinated by the IRA. Emperor Bokassa is deposed and the Central African Republic restored. Soviet troops enter Afghanistan, supposedly at the request of the government there, igniting civil war.

1980   Zimbabwe gains independence; Robert Mugabe comes to power. Queen Juliana of Holland abdicates in favour of her daughter Beatrix. President Tito of Yugoslavia dies, leaving a power vacuum. The SAS retake the Iranian Embassy, which had been taken by opponents of the Islamic regime. Mount St Helens erupts. The Moscow Olympic Games are boycotted by America and other countries in protest over Afghanistan. Solidarity is formed by shipyard workers in Gdansk. Iran and Iraq go to war.

1981   Ronald Reagan becomes US president. Iran releases the American Embassy hostages. The Space Shuttle makes its maiden space flight. Pope John Paul II is wounded in an assassination attempt in Rome by an extremist Turk. Several attacks on Iranian government officials leave many of the government dead, but it survives. President Sadat of Egypt is assassinated by extremists; Hosni Mubarak replaces him. Jerry Rawlings takes power in Ghana after a coup.

1982   Argentina invades the Falklands, but Britain sends a task force and retakes them; the military junta in Argentina falls as a result of this defeat. Israel withdraws from Sinai, but becomes enmeshed in Lebanon by trying to subdue the PLO's activities there. The Lebanese President Bashir Gemayel is assassinated; his brother Amin succeeds him. Leonid Brezhnev dies; Yuri Andropov replaces him as Soviet leader.

1983   Benigno Aquino is killed on returning to the Philippines in a government conspiracy to muzzle opposition. The Soviets shoot down a Boeing 747 that had strayed into Soviet airspace off Sakhalin. A coup in Grenada leaves prime minister Maurice Bishop and most of his cabinet dead; America sends troops in to restore order, to some anger in Britain.

1984   Yuri Andropov dies; Konstantin Chernenko replaces him as Soviet leader. Sikh extremists occupy the Golden Temple at Amritsar; over 200 die when Mrs Gandhi sends troops in to clear them. York Minster catches fire shortly after the modernist David Jenkins is enthroned as bishop of Durham. Britain agrees to hand Hong Kong back to China in 1997 on the expiration of the lease on the New Territories. Sikhs in revenge organize the assassination of Mrs Gandhi; her son Rajiv succeeds her as prime minister.

1985   Uruguay returns to civilian rule under President Sanguinetti. Chernenko dies; Mikhail Gorbachev succeeds him as Soviet leader and undertakes policies of openness (Glasnost) and reform (Perestroika). Brazil returns to civilian rule under President José Sarney. Enver Hoxha dies, and is succeeded by Ramiz Alia as President of Albania. A military coup removes Milton Obote from power in Uganda. The army, under General Babangida, takes power in Nigeria. The cruise liner *Achille Lauro* is hijacked by Palestinian guerrillas.

1986   All 7 crew die when the space shuttle *Challenger* explodes shortly after take-off. President Jean-Claude Duvalier of Haiti resigns and flees to Paris after revolts against his regime. The government of President Marcos of the Philippines falls; Cory Aquino is elected his successor. Prime minister Olof Palme of Sweden is mysteriously assassinated. America bombs Libya in reprisal for Libyan-sponsored terrorist actions. The nuclear power station in Chernobyl, Ukraine, suffers meltdown and explodes. The London Stock Exchange is computerized in the 'big bang'.

1987   Terry Waite is taken hostage in Lebanon whilst seeking to free others. *The Herald of Free Enterprise* capsizes outside Zeebrugge. A great storm crosses southern England, causing much damage. Boris Yeltsin is dismissed in Moscow for complaining at the slow pace of reform. An escalator catches fire at King's Cross; 31 die in the ensuing conflagration. America and Russia sign a nuclear weapons reduction treaty.

1988   The USSR begins withdrawal from Afghanistan. Iran and Iraq end their 8-year war. Iraq gasses dissident Kurds. General Zia of Pakistan is killed in a plane crash. Benazir Bhutto is subsequently elected prime minister of Pakistan. A terrorist bomb brings down a Pan-Am 747 over Lockerbie. USS *Vincennes* mistakenly shoots down an Iranian Airbus.

1989   Emperor Hirohito of Japan dies, and is succeeded by his son, Akihito. Alfredo Stroessner, dictator of Paraguay, is overthrown. General Noriega is defeated in the Panama general elections but ignores the result, causing the Americans to send in troops to remove him. Ayatollah Khomeini dies and Hojatolislam Rafsanjani becomes president of Iran. Communist governments collapse in Poland, Hungary, Czechoslovakia and Romania. The Berlin Wall comes down. President Ceauşescu is executed in Romania.

1990   Nelson Mandela is released from prison. Lithuania secedes from the USSR, which sends troops in an attempt to bring it to heel. East and West Germany are reunited. Iraq invades and annexes Kuwait. Sanctions are imposed by the UN, which sends troops to expel Iraq. The premiership of Mrs Thatcher collapses; John Major is elected to replace her.

1991   Somali rebels overthrow President Barre. The UN force expels Iraq from Kuwait, but leaves Saddam Hussein in power in Iraq. Rajiv Gandhi is assassinated by Tamil extremists while campaigning in the Indian general election. Croatia and Slovenia declare independence from Yugoslavia; Serbs and Croats begin a series of ethnic wars. Hard-line Communists attempt to overthrow President Gorbachev, but fail, and communism in Russia collapses. The Baltic states are granted independence. Gorbachev resigns as

Russian president and Boris Yeltsin is elected his successor. The USSR dissolves into its constituent parts.

1992   Algerian general elections are declared void when Islamic fundamentalists win; the latter begin a terrorist campaign. The sovereignty of Bosnia-Herzegovina is recognized by the EC and US, but Bosnian Serbs declare independence under Radovan Karadzic, and a vicious civil war develops; 'ethnic cleansing' kills thousands of Albanians and displaces hundreds of thousands. Hindu militants destroy the mosque at Ayodhya.

1993   Czechoslovakia splits into the Czech Republic and Slovakia. Israel and the PLO sign a peace accord. Cultists led by David Koresh kill American government officials at Waco and commit suicide after being besieged. President Premadasa of Sri Lanka is killed by a Tamil terrorist. The Russian communists rebel against President Yeltsin, but the revolt is quelled.

1994   Nelson Mandela is elected President of South Africa. The US invades Haiti. Jordan and Israel sign a peace treaty. Russia invades Chechnya.

1995   The World Trade Organization is founded. The Russians take the Chechen capital, Grozny; resistance continues elsewhere, but peace is agreed. Prime minister Yitzhak Rabin of Israel is assassinated by a Jewish fanatic; Shimon Peres succeeds him.

1996   Yasser Arafat is elected first president of Palestine. Benjamin Netanyahu defeats Shimon Peres in the Israeli general election; his hardline policies set back the peace process.

1997   Deng Xiaoping dies; Jiang Zemin takes power in China. Hong Kong is passed to China. Diana, Princess of Wales, is killed in a car crash. Labour wins a landslide victory in the general election; Tony Blair becomes prime minister. President Mobutu is overthrown in Zaïre, which the new government renames the Democratic Republic of Congo. The treaty of Amsterdam, providing for further European integration, is signed. Mother Teresa of Calcutta dies in her adopted city, aged 87. Jenny Shirley is sworn in as New Zealand's first woman prime minister.

1998   Frank Sinatra dies following a long illness. Frenchman Benoit Lecomte becomes the first man to swim the Atlantic; his 3,716-mile swim from Cape Cod to Quiberon, takes 72 days. Gerhard Schröder, the Social Democrat leader, replaces Christian Democrat leader Helmut Kohl as German Chancellor.

NB. The chronology above is a brief cross-section of British and world events of the last two thousand years. Some of the data will inevitably be duplicated in other sections but it is useful to be reminded of the order of events relative to other happenings of the day.

In a book that endeavours to seek the truth it seems incongruous to chronicle prehistorical events which by definition must be open to some doubt, even with all the latest DNA and radiocarbon dating techniques. The approach adopted is to give a brief overview of the order of events that are likely to be of interest to the reader and to chronicle other events, although still open to interpretation, of a more definite nature.

Every schoolchild learns to classify prehistory into Stone Age, Bronze Age and Iron Age but it is very difficult to be pedantic and say when one age started and another ended, in fact, of course the Stone and Bronze ages never really ended anyway. The Paleolithic Period or Old Stone Age is deemed to have commenced over two million years ago with evidence of the use of rudimentary chipped stone tools, probably by a distant relative of modern man. Fossil remains of this precursor of Homo Sapiens were found at Olduvai Gorge, Tanzania, in 1964 and variously assigned the names Homo Habilis, Australopithecus africanus, or Australopithecus robustus, although the latter two names are often applied to an even older relative of modern man thought to have existed millions of years earlier. Fossil remains of Peking Man and Java Man suggested another forerunner of modern man Homo Erectus and dated between over a million years ago until 300,000 years ago. From about 300,000 BC other species of early man evolved and were given the general name of Homo Sapiens. In 1856 the remains of a species of Homo Sapiens was discovered in the Neander Valley in Germany and dated between 200,000 BC and 30,000 BC. The species of Homo Sapiens that archaeologists and prehistorians call 'Modern Man' appears to date from circa 38,000 BC. The period from the identification of 'Modern Man' to the end of the Old Stone Age was characterised by the production of Paleolithic cave drawings, the oldest of which, the Chauvet paintings of southeast France, were discovered in 1994 and dated circa 29,000 BC making them circa 15,000 years older than the Lascaux paintings, Dordogne. This period also saw the beginning of organised tool-making industries beginning with the Aurignacian Culture and developing via the Gravettian (Périgordian), Solutrean, and Magdalenian Cultures to the Azilian industry which specialised in microlith tools for catching fish, birds and small mammals as the big game of the last ice age disappeared.

The next classification of prehistory is the Neolithic Period or New Stone Age characterised by stone tools shaped by polishing or grinding. This period of our history corresponds to the geological Holocene Epoch circa 8,000 BC, the most recent interval of the Earth's geological history. This period also corresponds to the end of the last ice age. In circa 10,400 BC a major climatic warming occurred, the Bolling interstadial, which lasted for approximately 400 years and this was followed by the Allerod interstadial between circa 9,800 BC and circa 9,000 BC. This intermittent global warming became constant in circa 8,000 BC and can be classified as the end of the last ice age, which began around the same time as the emergence of 'Modern Man', and the beginning of the New Stone Age. The first free standing stone buildings were built during the Neolithic Period, the oldest of which is Cgantija, a temple on the edge of the Xaghra plateau in the middle of the Maltese island of Gozo, circa 3,600 BC. The most recent archaeological find attributed to the Neolithic Period was the ice-man 'ötzi' discovered in the Otzal Alps on the Austrian-Italian border at an altitude of 3,210 metres, in 1991. Modern technology has established 'ötzi''s size, looks, apparel and enabled a reconstruction in the Museum of Archaeology in Bolzano, Italy, the country that claimed him. The consensus opinion is that 'ötzi' lived circa 3,300 BC. It is very difficult to approximate the beginning of the Bronze Age as there was a long period of quasi- copper based tools being produced. This period is referred to as the Chalcolithic (Copper-Stone) Age and even this period was precursed by the use of pure copper in Anatolia by 6,500 BC. The speculative classification of a Bronze Age perhaps can be dated to circa 3,000 BC when it was first established that the Greeks added tin to copper, although this practice only became widespread a thousand years later. The last technological and cultural period in our classification is the Iron Age which once again is very difficult to give a definite date of identification as there was a long period of overlapping with the Bronze Age. There is evidence of sparse use of iron in the Middle East as early as 3,000 BC but it did not replace bronze as a superior metal until circa 1,200 BC.

5508 The year of creation as adopted in Constantinople in 7th century and used by the Eastern Orthodox Church for 1,000 years.
5490 The year of creation as calculated by early Christians in Syria.
4004 James Ussher's 17th-century postulate as being the date of the creation of the universe.
3150 Egypt is united under Menes, the first king of the First Dynasty, and the first prehistoric human whose name we know. Sumerians invent a primitive writing system.
3100 Stonehenge is laid out.
3000 Egyptians pioneer the use of hieroglyphs.
2650 Pyramid of Zoser at Saqqara is built by Imhotep.
2566 The Great Pyramid of Khufu (aka Cheops), at Giza, is built and stands 480 feet high.
2500 A mysterious cult of 'Beaker folk' spreads throughout Europe, warriors being buried with their ornate cups.
2100 In Mesopotamia the first code of law is devised by Ur-Nammu and his son, Shulgi.
1700 Abraham, a prince of Ur, moves to Canaan and founds a religion.
1650 Jewish religion is developed by Abraham's grandson, Jacob.
1349 The young Pharaoh, Tutankhamun, is buried at Thebes.
1237 Ramesses II of Egypt dies and is succeeded by his son Merneptah.
1198 Ramesses III rallies the Egyptians against Mediterranean invaders known as 'Sea Peoples'.
1193 King Priam's city of Troy falls to the Greeks under Agamemnon.
1025 Samuel anoints Saul as king of Hebron.
1012 Saul and his son, Jonathan, are killed at the battle of Mount Gilboa, and succeeded by David.
1005 Jerusalem falls to King David who is anointed King of Judea by Samuel.
1000 The Rig Veda (Hindu hymns) are written.
 990 Absalom, 3rd son of King David, kills Amnon in revenge for the rape of his sister, Tamar, and is banished by David.
 978 Absalom leads a rebellion but is killed by David's nephew, Joab.
 961 David dies and is succeeded by his son, Solomon, who executes Joab for killing Absalom.
 922 Solomon is succeeded by his son, Rehoboam, but 10 northern tribes establish Israel, with Jeroboam as king.
 850 In Babylon an epic poem 'When on High' is dedicated to the great god, Marduk.
 800 The Vedas are written.
 776 The first Olympic Games are held in Olympia, Greece.
 753 Rome is founded by Romulus and Remus.
 750 Iliad and Odyssey become popular in Greece. Etruscans settle in Tuscany from the Middle East.
 722 Israel's capital since 879 BC, the Hill of Samaria, falls to Assyrian forces.
 721 The 27,000 Israelites are taken off by the Assyrians and become known as 'The Lost Tribes of Israel'.
 658 Byzantium is founded by Greek colonists from Megara.
 630 The Shi Jing (Book of Songs), an early book of Chinese poems is written.
 629 King Ashurbanipal of Assyria dies, leaving a library of over 25,000 books.
 621 The Athenian lawgiver Draco issues a code of laws that makes almost every offence punishable by death.
 597 Jerusalem falls to Nebuchadnezzar II, who exiles Jews in what becomes known as 'The Babylonian Captivity'.
 586 The transportation of Judaeans to Babylon, known as the Babylon Exile or Captivity.
 582 The first Pythian games are held.
 563 Siddhartha Gautama (Buddha) is born.
 550 The Temple of Artemis is built at Ephesus in Turkey.
 551 Kung Fu-tse (Confucius) is born.
 538 Cyrus allows the Jews to return to Jerusalem, thus ending the Babylonian Exile.
 528 Buddhism is founded in India.
 509 Tarquinius Superbus, King of Rome, is overthrown and Rome becomes a republic.
 490 Battle of Marathon gives Athens victory over the Persians.
 483 Siddhartha Gavtama (Budda) dies.
 480 Battle of Thermopylae gives the Persians, under Xerxes, victory over the Spartans and Thespians, under Leonidas. Battle of Salamis gives the Greeks (400 ships) victory over the Persians (1,000 ships).
 456 Aeschylus dies after writing 90 plays, of which only 7 are to survive.
 356 The Temple of Artenus, built by Croesus, king of Lydia, is burned by a madman, Herostratus.
 354 Mausoleum at Halicarnassus is built.
 336 Alexander the Great succeeds his father on the Macedonian throne.
 323 Alexander the Great dies, aged 32, in Babylon.
 276 First Syrian War begins.
 265 Archimedes invents his 'Archimedean Screw' for raising irrigation water.
 264 The First Punic War between Rome and Carthage begins.
 237 Hamilcar Barca leads a Carthaginian army in an invasion of Spain.
 228 Hamilcar Barca is killed and his command in Spain passes to his son-in-law Hasdrubal.
 221 Hasdrubal is assassinated and his command passes to Hannibal, the 26-year-old son of Hamilcar Barca.
 220 The Flaminian Way between Rome and Rimini is completed.
 218 The second Punic War begins.
 217 Battle of Lake Trasimene in Umbria gives Hannibal victory over Gaius Flaminius and 16,000 Romans.
 216 Battle of Cannae gives Hannibal a resounding victory over the Romans.

190   Battle of Magenta, near Smyrna, gives Rome a victory over Antiochus III of Syria.
183   Hannibal poisons himself.
160   Judas Maccabaeus is killed, his brother, Jonathan is destined to make Judaea a largely independent state.
149   Romans invade North Africa and besiege Carthage.
135   Rome's first Slave War begins.
102   Julius Caesar is born. (It is possible he was born upt ot 2 years later.)
83   Mark Antony is born.
73   Third Slave War breaks out under the leadership of Spartacus, a Thracian slave. Herod the Great is born.
63   Cicero, a Roman Consul, unmasks a conspiracy led by Catiline, the former governor of Africa.
60   The first Roman Triumvirate is formed by Julius Caesar, Pompey, and Crassus.
55   Julius Caesar's first invasion of Britain.
54   Julius Caesar's second invasion of Britain; Cassivellaunus agrees to pay tribute.
52   Gang warfare in Rome between supporters of Clodius and Milo results in the death of Clodius in a brawl.
49   Julius Caesar leads his legions across the Rubicon into Italy to begin the civil war.
47   Julius Caesar leads his legions across Asia Minor where he defeats Pharnaces III, King of Pontus, near Zela. announcing his victory in the dispatch 'Veni, Vidi, Vici' (I came, I saw, I conquered).
45   Julian calendar introduced by Sosigenes.
44   Julius Caesar is assassinated on the Ides of March.
43   The second Roman Triumvirate is formed by Octavian, Mark Antony, and Marcus Lepidus.
      Cicero is beheaded on the orders of Mark Antony.
42   Brutus and Cassius are defeated at Philippi in Macedonia; Cassius orders his shield-bearer to cut his throat, while Brutus runs on to the sword of his friend, Strato.
41   Mark Antony meets Cleopatra at Tarsus and as Julius Caesar had before him, he forms an alliance.
37   Herod the Great becomes King of Judea.
31   Battle of Actium gives victory to Octavian but Cleopatra escapes to Egypt.
30   Mark Antony commits suicide and Cleopatra follows soon after; her son, Caesarion is murdered. Egypt becomes a Roman province.
27   Augustus becomes the first Roman Emperor after changing his name from Octavian.

Modern History

Agent Orange   Notorious herbicide used by the US military machine in Vietnam in the 1960s and 1970s; its active ingredient 245-T was also used in weedkillers and caused devastation.

A6 Murder   Michael Gregsten and Valerie Storie were shot in their car in a lay-by off the A6 between Luton and Bedford in August 1961. Storie, who survived the shooting, picked out James Hanratty at an identity parade, which led to his hanging in April 1962. Journalist Paul Foot has campaigned on behalf of Hanratty pointing out that Peter Alphon confessed to the murder.

Balfour Declaration   A milestone on the way to establishing the state of Israel. Arthur Balfour the former Conservative PM, served as foreign secretary in 1916–19, and in November 1917 wrote to Lord Rothschild, leader of the British Jewish community, to the effect that Britain favoured a national home for the Jewish people provided that it did not prejudice the civil and religious rights of existing non-Jewish communities in Palestine.

Barlow Clowes   Fraudulent investment company, details of which came to light in 1988. Elizabeth Barlow disappeared but Peter Clowes was sentenced to 10 years imprisonment in 1992. The government at first refused to pay compensation, but the Ombudsman found maladministration by the Department of Trade and Industry so £150 m was provided.

Beveridge Report   Report laying down the framework for the development of the Welfare State. Published in 1942 and accepted by the coalition government in 1944, it became operational in 1948.

Big Bang   Transformation of the London Stock Exchange in October 1986 which reflected the advent of global stock and bond trading networks and of round-the-clock trading. It also abolished the different categories of stockbrokers and jobbers.

Birmingham Six   Patrick Hill, Richard McIlkenny, John Walker, William Power, Gerard Hunter and Hugh Callaghan wrongly imprisoned for IRA activities following the bombing of 2 public houses in Birmingham in November 1974. Their convictions were quashed in the Appeal Court in March 1991.

Bloody Sunday   A day of serious conflict in the Bogside area of Londonderry on 30 January 1972 when the security forces opened fire on a civil rights march, killing 13 civilians.

Blue Streak   British rocket which in the 1950s was expected to provide a nuclear delivery capability independent of US technological expertise; abandoned in 1960 in favour of the US Skybolt missile.

Bridgewater Four   Michael and Vincent Hickey, James Robinson and Patrick Molloy were convicted of killing newspaper delivery boy Carl Bridgewater at Yew Tree Farm in Staffordshire, largely because of a confession made by Molloy, who died in prison in 1981. The remaining 3 were released on 20 February 1997 after evidence of police corruption.

Chiltern Hundreds   British MPs cannot resign directly, but they may not hold an office of profit under the crown. The solution is to apply for the stewardship of various crown sinecures, of which the Chiltern Hundreds is the best-known.

Citizen's Charter   Government charter instigated by John Major in 1991 with the intention of improving standards of public services in the UK.

Cod War   A series of disputes between UK and Iceland in the 1960s over fishing rights.

Cuban Missile Crisis   US hostility towards the Cuban revolution, together with Castro's open espousal of communism, had brought Cuba into a close relationship with USSR. Following the US-sponsored Bay of Pigs invasion, Castro requested Soviet atomic weaponry to improve their defences. When US reconnaissance spotted missile sites being built, President Kennedy declared a blockade, on 22 October 1961. For several days a confrontation of superpowers appeared likely, but the Russians backed off, and the blockade ended on 20 November.

Dikko Affair   UK customs found the exiled Nigerian politician Umari Dikko drugged in a crate at Stansted airport in July 1984. Three Israelis and a Nigerian diplomat concealed in another crate were charged with kidnapping and administering drugs.

Doomsday Clock   Picture of a clock, the hands of which indicate the time estimated to remain before nuclear war (midnight), which has been printed in every issue of the *Bulletin of Atomic Scientists* since its founding in 1945. It stood at 11.58 during the cold war but was put back to 11.50 in 1989.

Echo 1   First US communications satellite; a large aluminium-coated balloon that reflected radio signals. Launched on 12 August 1960 by NASA as part of the US effort to close the satellite telecommunications lead achieved by the USSR with the Sputnik.

Elgin Marbles   Sculptures from the Parthenon obtained cheaply from the occupying Turks by the British Ambassador Lord Elgin in 1801 and later sold to the British Museum. The continuing Greek campaign for their return was spearheaded by Melina Mercouri as Minister for Culture and the injustice is often highlighted by the well-known television producer and quiz show host, William G Stewart.

Fourth Estate   Term used in modern times to describe the power of the press. The Middle Ages divided society into 3 estates: nobility, church and commons.

Fourth Man   Anthony Blunt was given this epithet when revealed as a spy in 1979 following the defections to the USSR of the spies Burgess and Maclean in 1951 and Kim Philby in 1963.

Gaza Strip   A 146-sq-mile area of land bordered by the Mediterranean, Israel and Egypt, captured by Israel from Egypt during the Six-Day War of 1967 and inhabited by 700,000 people, mostly stateless Palestinians living in refugee camps.

General Strike   Staged by the TUC from 3–13 May 1926 in an unsuccessful attempt to support coalminers. The strike provoked retaliatory legislation against trade unions.

Geneva Summit 1985   First of a series of bilateral superpower summit meetings held in the later 1980s involving Mikhail Gorbachev and Ronald Reagan (followed by George Bush).

Golan Heights   Range of strategic hills in south-west Syria overlooking northern Israel, captured by Israel from Syria in the Six-Day War of 1967.

Gold Standard   Economic system in which a country's paper currency is supported by gold, anyone having the right to demand from the national bank the same amount of gold as the face value of a banknote. Britain was on the gold standard from 1821–1914, partly returned to it in 1925 as a result of Churchill's wishes, but finally abandoned it in 1931 under the chancellorship of Philip Snowden.

Great Leap Forward   Campaign undertaken by Mao Zedong between 1957 and 1960 to organize China's vast population into large-scale rural communes and local manufacturing units, to meet the country's economic problems.

Guildford Four   Patrick Armstrong, Gerard Conlon,

Carole Richardson and Paul Hill were sentenced to life imprisonment in 1975 for the murder of 7 people in 1974 after the bombing of 2 public houses in Guildford and 1 in Woolwich. They were released on appeal in 1989 after police evidence was found to be misleading.

Herald of Free Enterprise   British car ferry owned by Townsend Thoresen which overturned and sank off the Belgian port of Zeebrugge on 6 March 1987 with the loss of 193 lives after the bow doors were left open.

Heysel Stadium Disaster   Death of 39 Belgian and Italian spectators on 29 May 1985 at the final of the European Cup football competition between Liverpool and Juventus in Belgium's Heysel Stadium when visiting British fans caused a wall and safety barriers to collapse.

Hiroshima   Southern Japanese city destroyed on 6 August 1945 by the first atomic bomb, nicknamed Little Boy and dropped from the US B-29 bomber *Enola Gay*.

Hiss Case   Legal case which typified US anti-communist paranoia. On 29 January 1950 Alger Hiss, accused by Whittaker Chambers of being a communist during the 1930s while working for the US State Department, was given a 5-year prison term.

Ho Chi Minh Trail   Network of concealed tracks through eastern Laos developed during the early stages of the Vietnam War as a supply route for North Vietnamese and Viet Cong forces in South Vietnam.

Holt Drowning   Disappearance and presumed death of Australian PM and Liberal Party leader Harold Holt while swimming at Portsea near Melbourne on 17 December 1967.

Human Shield   After Iraq's occupation of Kuwait in August 1990 Saddam Hussein used Western nationals captured there as a defence against possible action by the opposing coalition forces during operation Desert Shield.

100 Flowers Bloom   Political slogan adopted by Mao Zedong (Mao Tse-tung) in 1956 and launched as a movement in February 1957 to allow more free speech in Communist China. The high level of strikes that followed caused Mao to retract his original statement and suggested that the campaign was a means of identifying reactionary elements.

Hungarian Uprising   Popular uprising against Soviet domination in 1956 when after 4 days of demonstrations in Budapest, on 24 October the former communist PM, Imre Nagy, formed a revolutionary multi-party government and proclaimed Hungary's withdrawal from the Warsaw Pact. The Soviet Union crushed the uprising and Janos Kadar took over as head of a pro-Soviet regime and supervised the normalization policy. Nagy was executed by the new government in 1958.

In Place of Strife   Document published by the Labour government of the UK on 17 January 1969 setting out its policy for controlling industrial relations through legal sanctions.

Intifada   (Arabic: 'shaking off') Palestinian mass popular uprising in the Gaza Strip and West Bank which started in December 1987 with demonstrations, strikes and violent confrontation between Palestinian youths and Israeli occupying forces. Israel responded with an iron-fist approach which included beatings and deportations.

Iranian Embassy Siege   Storming of the Iranian

embassy in London by the SAS after it was seized on 30 April 1980 by Iranian dissidents seeking to draw attention to the plight of the Arab minority in Iran and demanding the release of 91 of their comrades imprisoned in Khuzestan.

Iron Curtain Frontier dividing the Eastern Europe of the communist bloc from the capitalist West. Winston Churchill popularized the phrase, using it in a 1946 speech at Westminster College, Fulton, Missouri when he said: 'From Stettin in the Baltic to Trieste in the Adriatic, an iron curtain has descended across the continent'. Joseph Goebbels has been credited with inventing the term.

ITT Scandal Scandal involving the activities of International Telephone and Telegraph in the USA and overseas. The scandal broke in 1972 when a plan to nationalize the Chilean Telephone Company (Chitelco) was sabotaged; ITT's collusion with the CIA culminated in the 1973 coup which overthrew the Allende government.

Jal Air Disaster World's worst air crash involving a single aircraft: a Boeing 747 on a Japan Airlines flight from Tokyo to Osaka crashed in mountainous terrain near Tokyo on 12 August 1985 and killed 520 of the 524 passengers and crew.

Jamahiriya Term coined by Colonel Gaddafi, who in 1977 changed the name of Libya to 'Socialist People's Libyan Arab Jamahiriya'. The word means 'State of the masses'.

Jonestown Massacre Mass death of 913 children, men and women at Jonestown, in the Guyana jungle, on 29 November 1978. The Rev. Jim Jones, founder of the People's Temple in Indianapolis in 1957, had set up a commune in Guyana in 1977. After murdering investigators, he led and apparently enforced a mass suicide.

Khaki Election General election of October 1900, called by Salisbury's Conservative-Unionist government, and named after the new khaki uniform worn by the British army in the Boer war.

Korean War War in 1950–3 between communist North Korea (supported by the USSR and China) and South Korea (supported by the USA and UN).

Lame-Duck President Term used to describe an outgoing US president between the elections in November and the beginning of the new president's term on 20 January the following year.

Lancaster House Agreement UK Foreign and Commonwealth Secretary Lord Carrington brokered this agreement which ended UDI and heralded the independence of Zimbabwe. It was signed on 21 December 1979 by former Rhodesian leader Ian Smith, PM Bishop Abel Muzorewa, Robert Mugabe and Joshua Nkomo, as well as by Carrington and Sir Ian Gilmour representing the British delegation. Lord Soames became governor during the transitional period.

LDC Least Developed Country, a category used by the UN to describe many of its poorer member states. According to UN estimates, over 500 million people lived in LDC's in 1990.

Limehouse Declaration Political statement issued on 25 January 1981 by four senior members of the British Labour Party, Roy Jenkins, David Owen, William Rodgers and Shirley Williams, who became popularly known as the gang of four, effectively launching the Social Democratic Party (SDP).

Lockerbie Scottish town on which a Pan Am airliner PA103 en route from London to New York crashed after a mid-air explosion on 21 December 1988,

killing all 259 passengers and crew as well as 11 townspeople. Two Libyans went on trial in Holland in 2000, accused of organizing the bombing. Abdelbaset Ali Mohamed Al Megrahi was found guilty and sentenced to life but Al Amin Khalifa Fhimah was freed due to lack of evidence.

Lockheed Scandal Political scandal which emerged in Japan in 1976, involving the acceptance of bribes by Kakuei Tanaka, PM 1972–4, from the Lockheed Aircraft Corporation.

Long March The 6,000-mile journey undertaken in 1934–5 by forces of the Chinese Communist Party from Jiangxi province to Yan'an in north Shaanxi to avoid encirclement by the forces of the nationalist Guomindang.

Los Angeles Riots Major disturbances which occurred in LA between 29 April and 4 May 1992 involving widespread destruction and ethnic violence that brought 58 deaths. The riots were sparked off when an all-white jury acquitted 4 white police officers who had been filmed beating black motorist Rodney King in March 1991.

Maastricht Netherlands town where the 12 EU member states met in December 1991 for the summit that concluded the treaty on European Union. They returned on 7 Feb 1992 for the formal signing of what became the Maastricht Treaty, which was an accord on European political union and on EMU (European Monetary Union).

MAD Mutually Assured Destruction, which would result from a full-scale nuclear war between the superpowers according to the theorists of deterrence by the 'balance of terror'.

Markov Affair Controversy associated with the death in London on 15 September 1978 of Georgi Markov, a Bulgarian journalist employed by the BBC World Service, who was injected with the poison from a specially adapted umbrella by an agent of the Bulgarian security service.

Marshall Plan Plan to assist the economic recovery of post-war Europe, proposed by US Secretary of State George Marshall in June 1947. The scheme offered US funding to European countries (eventually over $12 billion) if they co-operated with each other in drafting recovery programmes.

Mason-Dixon Line Boundary between the US states of Maryland and Pennsylvania which marks the border between former slave states of the south and northern states where slavery was illegal.

McCarthyism Anti-communist hysteria endemic in the USA in the early 1950s, built upon a foundation established by the House Committee on Un-American Activities. Senator Joseph McCarthy of Wisconsin made a speech in Wheeling, West Virginia, in February 1952 which began the series of anti-communist witch hunts.

Messina Conference June 1955 meeting between the foreign ministers of Belgium, France, Italy, Luxembourg, Netherlands and West Germany which led to the Rome Treaty of March 1957.

Mildenhall Treasure Hoard of Roman silver of the 4th century AD, discovered during ploughing in Suffolk in 1942. The main item of value is the 'Great Dish'.

Montgomery Bus Boycott Year-long boycott of the public transport system in Montgomery, Alabama, which provided a key early victory for the US civil rights movement. It began on 5 December 1955, after a black woman, Rosa Parks, was arrested for refusing to give up her seat on a bus to a white passenger.

Montreal Protocol Agreement signed in September 1987 by 24 countries which undertook to halve their CFC production by 1999. The protocol aims to reduce damage to the ozone layer.

Moro Affair Circumstances surrounding the kidnapping on 16 March 1978 of Aldo Moro, president of the Italian Christian Democratic Party, by the left-wing Brigate Rosse, and his assassination on 9 May after the government refused to meet the kidnappers' demands.

Nagasaki Target city on 9 August 1945 of the second atomic bomb which caused the Japanese surrender in World War II.

Normalization Sinister name for the programme aimed at stabilizing communist rule in Czechoslovakia after the suppression of the 1968 Prague Spring. Under Gustav Husak, Normalization featured a purge of tens of thousands of politically unreliable professionals and communist party members as well as an end to freedom of speech.

Pairing Convention whereby pairs of MPs, one each from the government and opposition sides, agree that if one is unable to be present to vote, the other will abstain.

Peacock Throne Metaphor for the pre-1979 Iranian monarchy and a reference to the throne used by the two Pahlavi shahs at their coronations. The original Peacock Throne was stolen by the Iranian conqueror Nadir Shah during a raid on the Mughal bastion, the Red Fort, in Delhi in 1793.

Perestroika Restructuring, slogan adopted by Soviet leader Mikhail Gorbachev in late 1986 to denote his policies of pragmatic reform.

Pieds Noirs (Black Feet) Term used to describe white French settlers resident in France's North African colonies, especially Algeria, and who returned to France after decolonization in the 1960s.

Ponting Affair Trial and acquittal of Clive Ponting in the UK in 1985 under the 1911 Official Secrets Act. Ponting, a high-flying civil servant in the MOD, was accused of leaking classified information to Labour MP Tam Dalyell, relating to the sinking of the Argentinian cruiser *Belgrano* during the 1982 Falklands War.

Potsdam Conference held from 17 July to 2 August 1945 between the USSR, UK and USA, the Big Three allied powers of World War II, to decide the treatment of defeated Germany.

Poulson Affair The events leading to the resignation on 18 July 1972 of Reginald Maudling as home secretary in the UK Conservative Cabinet. John Poulson was an architect who built up a major international practice in the 1960s and increased his standing through contacts with influential politicians. By the early 1970s he faced bankruptcy and was subsequently charged with corruption relating to bribes given to national and local politicians aimed at winning contracts. Poulson was sentenced to 7 years whilst Maudling, who had been chaiman of the Poulson company, resigned.

Profumo Affair Scandal leading to the resignation in 1963 of John Profumo as secretary of state for war in the UK Conservative Cabinet. Profumo had formed a liaison with Christine Keeler, who simultaneously was having a relationship with a Soviet military attaché in London, Eugene Ivanov.

Rivers of Blood Controversial speech made by UK Conservative MP Enoch Powell on 20 April 1968 in which he warned of what he saw as the social and economic consequences of continued immigration into the UK of black people from the Commonwealth. Powell compared himself to a Roman in Virgil's Aeneid who had a vision of the River Tiber foaming with blood.

Roe v Wade The landmark 1973 Supreme Court decision which made abortion legal in the USA.

Rosenbergs US couple, Julius and Ethel, who were executed in Sing Sing prison in 1953 for having allegedly supplied the Soviet Union with atomic bomb secrets.

San Francisco Conference International conference held April–June 1945 after which participants signed the UN charter. The conference was attended by 47 fully independent states as well as Byelorussia and Ukraine, which were Soviet constituents, and India and the Philippines, which had not at that stage achieved full independence.

Scarman Report Serious racial disturbances in South-East London in April 1981 led to Lord Scarman carrying out a thorough public inquiry, whose findings were published in November.

Schuman Plan Proposal advanced by French foreign minister Robert Schuman on 9 May 1950 which formed the European Coal and Steel Community.

Seles stabbing Tennis player Monica Seles was stabbed by a crazed fan of her rival, Steffi Graf, during a match in Hamburg on 30 April 1993.

Sellafield Site on the west coast of England, in Cumbria, run by British Nuclear Fuels. The first nuclear power station opened here, at Calder Hall, in 1956. At that time the area was known as Windscale, but on 10 October 1957 an atomic pile overheated, causing a near-catastrophe and some long-term fatalities. To protect the image of the industry the name of the site was changed.

Sharpeville Massacre In this South African township 50 miles from Johannesburg on 21 March 1960 the police killed 69 peaceful demonstrators protesting against the Pass Laws. The UN subsequently called for the abandonment of apartheid.

Six-Day War Threatened by a build-up of hostile Arab forces, between 5 and 10 July 1967 Israel attacked Egypt, Jordan and Syria and occupied the Sinai peninsular, the Gaza Strip, East Jerusalem, the West Bank and the Golan Heights, before declaring a ceasefire.

Social Contract Informal agreement between the UK Labour government and the TUC in the mid 1970s aiming to balance wage restraint against a loosening of legal restrictions on trade unions.

Spin Doctor In politics, a public relations expert working behind the scenes to have the media interpret events from the viewpoint favoured by a particular individual, faction of party.

Stockholm Syndrome Psychological condition in which hostages grow to empathize with their captors' political or personal convictions. The term derives from a bank robbery in Stockholm in 1973 when several people taken as hostages lent their support to the robbers.

Suez Crisis Middle East crisis precipitated by the nationalization of the mainly British and French-owned Suez Canal by Egyptian President Gamal Abdel Nasser on 26 July 1956. Nasser acted after the USA had reneged on a commitment to help finance the construction of the Aswan High Dam. Israel invaded on 29 October; acting in collusion, French and British forces intervened a week later, under guise of keeping the peace. By March 1957, all 3 had withdrawn under strong UN pressure.

HISTORY

Sutton Hoo Ship Burial Anglo-Saxon treasure unearthed in 1939 at Sutton Hoo in Suffolk and believed to have been the tomb of an Anglo-Saxon king buried about 625, possibly Raedwald. Mrs Pretty, who owned the land and hence the treasure, kindly donated the find to the British Museum.

TD Gaelic for Teachta Dála, a member of the Irish Dáil or lower house of parliament.

Territorial Waters The offshore area in which a coastal state claims sovereign jurisdiction, save for the customary rights of freedom of navigation for merchant shipping. At present 12 miles is the accepted boundary of territorial waters, with a few exceptions, mostly in Africa and Central and South America.

Third Man Kim Philby, a UK journalist and former intelligence officer who defected to the Soviet Union in January 1963, was given this epithet after the earlier defections of Guy Burgess and Donald Maclean in 1951.

Tiger Talks Negotiations held aboard HMS _Tiger_ off Gibraltar on 2–4 December 1966 between Harold Wilson and Ian Smith, which failed to end Rhodesian UDI.

Trident Multiple-warhead submarine-launched nuclear missile with a range of 4,500 miles, introduced in 1979 by the US Navy in refitted Poseidon submarines, and in larger _Ohio_-class submarines first delivered in 1981. A more powerful Trident 2 missile was introduced in 1990.

Union Carbide Disaster In December1984 a leak of toxic gas from Union Carbide pesticide plant near Bhopal, India, killed 2,500 and injured 200,000.

Vatican II The 2nd Vatican Council (the first was in 1869-70), which met in 4 sessions between 11 October 1962 and 8 December 1965. Launched by Pope John XXIII, it was concluded by his successor Pope Paul VI. Vatican II was the 21st Ecumenical Council in the history of the Roman Catholic Church and brought a reformist, liberalizing outlook to existing dogma.

Vietnam War The 1954–75 war between North and South Vietnam, the latter assisted from 1961 by the USA. The war resulted in victory for the North and the union of the two Vietnams in 1976.

Vincennes On 3 July 1988 the US warship _Vincennes_, serving in the Persian Gulf, mistook an Iran Air A3000 Airbus for an attacking bomber and shot it down, costing 290 civilian lives.

Waco Siege A 51-day siege of the HQ of the Branch Davidian religious cult near Waco, Texas, began on 28 February 1993 and ended on 19 April when the FBI stormed the compound and fire broke out, killing its leader David Koresh and 70 of its members.

Warnock Report UK report published in July 1984 on bio-ethics as well as the social and legal implications of recent and potential developments in the field of human-assisted reproduction. Chaired by Dame Mary Warnock, the committee recommended that certain forms of infertility treatment should be viewed as ethically acceptable.

Warren Commission Chaired by the head of the US Supreme Court, Chief Justice Earl Warren, the Commission investigated circumstances surrounding the assassination of President J. F. Kennedy in Dallas on 22 November 1963. The Commission's report concluded on 22 September 1964 that Lee Harvey Oswald had been solely responsible for the killing.

West Bank Territory of Palestine west of the River Jordan, claimed from 1949 to 1988 as part of Jordan, but occupied by Israel since the Six-Day War of 1967. The territory, excluding East Jerusalem, is widely referred to within Israel by its biblical names, Judea and Samaria, and is considered part of Eretz Israel. In September 1993 Israeli forces withdrew from the West Bank but the territory is still disputed by many Israelis.

Winter of Discontent Time of industrial unrest in the UK over the severe winter of 1978–9.

Wolfenden Report Report of the UK Committee on Homosexual Offences and Prostitution, chaired by Sir John Wolfenden, which recommended in particular the decriminalization of homosexual acts between consenting adult males and an increase in penalties for soliciting by prostitutes. The landmark report published on 4 Sepember 1957 led to the Street Offences Act of 1959 and to the Sexual Offences Act of 1967.

Year Zero Slogan adopted by the Khmer Rouge to denote the start of their 4-year period of rule in Cambodia in April 1975.

Yom Kippur War On 6 October 1973 Syria and Egypt mounted a surprise attack on Israel as it observed Yom Kippur (the Jewish Day of Atonement), aiming to regain territory lost during the Six-Day War of 1967. Although Israel was caught off guard initially, by 24 October the Israelis were advancing on Cairo and Damascus and a ceasefire was declared, restoring the status quo.

Zeebrugge Disaster see _Herald of Free Enterprise._

LANGUAGE

Foreign Words and Phrases

ab initio (L.) from the beginning

à bon marché (Fr.) a good bargain, cheap (lit. at a good market)

a cappella (It.) without instrumental accompaniment (lit. in chapel style)

à cheval (Fr.) on horseback (also denotes two roulette numbers)

achtung (Ger.) look out, beware, take heed (lit. attention)

ad astra (L.) to the stars

ad hoc (L.) for this special purpose (lit. to this)

ad libitum (L.) at pleasure

ad rem (L.) to the purpose, to the point (lit. to the matter)

à la carte (Fr.) each dish priced separately (lit. according to the menu)

à la mode (Fr.) according to custom or fashion

al dente (It.) firm when bitten (lit. to the teeth)

al fresco (It.) in the open air (lit. in the fresh)

Alma Mater (L.) applied to former school, university, or college, (lit. fostering or bounteous mother)

Angst (Ger.) anxiety

annus mirabilis (L.) a remarkable year (lit. year of wonder)

Anschauung (Ger.) point of view (lit. looking around)

Anschluss (Ger.) joining together

ante bellum (L.) before the war

a priori (L.) from cause to effect (lit. from the previous)

à propos (Fr.) to the purpose

auberge (Fr.) inn, tavern

au courant (Fr.) fully acquainted with (lit. in the current)

Aufklärung (Ger.) clarification, enlightenment

auf Wiedersehen (Ger.) till we meet again

au pair (Fr.) home-help from a foreign country (lit. on an equal basis)

au revoir (Fr.) till we meet again

auto-da-fé (Port.) act of faith

avant-garde (Fr.) progressive or radical artists and thinkers (lit. vanguard)

bain-marie (Fr.) a double saucepan (lit. bath of Maria)

baksheesh (Pers.) gratuity or tip (lit. a present)

banzai (Jap.) a Japanese battle-cry (lit. 10,000 years)

barrio (Sp.) district, suburb (lit. open country)

bas bleu (Fr.) literary woman, blue-stocking worker (lit. under blue)

batik (Malay) cloth dyeing method using wax, the cloth itself, (lit. painted)

bête noire (Fr.) a bugbear, pet aversion (lit. black beast)

bibelot (Fr.) trinket, curio, knick-knack (lit. small book)

bidet (Fr.) bestridable bath (lit. small horse)

Bildungsroman (Ger.) novel concerning early development of its central figure, (lit. education novel)

billet-doux (Fr.) love letter (lit. sweet note)

Blitzkrieg (Ger.) intense military attack (lit. lightning war)

Boche (Fr.) French slang for a German soldier (lit. rascal)

bois brûlé (Fr.) French-Canadian Indian (lit. burnt wood)

bona fide (L.) with good faith

bona-roba (It.) prostitute, wench (lit. good dress)

bona vacantia (L.) goods without any apparent owner and to which the Crown has the rights (lit. ownerless goods)

bonheur du jour (Fr.) small writing-table (lit. happiness of the day)

bonhomie (Fr.) good-nature (lit. good man)

bon mot (Fr.) witty remark (lit. good word)

bonsai (Jap.) miniature tree in a pot (lit. bowl growing)

bourgeois (Fr.) middle-class person (lit. town dweller)

cacoethes (Gr) bad habit, mania (lit. evil habit)

carabiniere (It.) member of Italian police force

carpe diem (L.) seize the day

carte blanche (Fr.) freedom of action, card hand with no court cards (lit. blank card)

caveat emptor (L.) let the buyer beware

cela va sans dire (Fr.) needless to say, that goes without saying

c'est la vie (Fr.) that's life

ceteris paribus (L.) other things being equal

cinquecento (Fr.) classical style of art of the 16th century (lit. five hundred)

cire perdue (Fr.) bronze casting using wax technique (lit. lost wax)

cogito, ergo sum (L.) I think, therefore I am

compos mentis (L.) sound of mind

corpus delicti (L.) body or substance of a crime

corregidor (Sp.) chief magistrate of a Spanish town (lit. to correct)

corrida (Sp.) a bullfight (lit. corral)

corrigenda (L.) things to be corrected

coup de foudre (Fr.) love at first sight, sudden event (lit. flash of lightning)

coup de grâce (Fr.) action that puts an end to something, (lit. stroke of mercy)

coup d'état (Fr.) sudden and violent change of government, (lit. stroke of state)

cri de coeur (Fr.) heartfelt appeal or protest (lit. cry from the heart)

cru (Fr.) French vineyard (lit. growth)

cucullus non facit monachum (L.) the cowl does not make the monk

cui bono (L.) to whose benefit

cul-de-sac (Fr.) road with one end blocked off, dead end (lit. bottom of the bag)

cum grano salis (L.) with a grain of salt

curriculum vitae (L.) course of life

dacha (Rus.) Russian country villa (lit. gift)

de facto (L.) in fact

déjà vu (Fr.) already seen

de jure (L.) by right (lit. from the law)

de profundis (L.) out of the depths

de rigueur (Fr.) required by etiquette (lit. of strictness)

Dei gratia (L.) by God's grace

Deo volente (L.) God willing

dernier cri (Fr.) latest fashion, last word (lit. last cry)

de trop (Fr.) superfluous, not wanted (lit. too much)

Doppelgänger (Ger.) wraith, look-a-like, (lit. double goer)

dos-à-dos (Fr.) a seat on which the users sit back to back, (lit. back to back)

dramatis personae (L.) cast of a play

duce (It.)   leader

duende (Sp.)   Imp, goblin, ghost

Dummkopf (Ger.)   dumb-head

e pluribus unum (L.)   one out of many

Ecce Homo (L.)   artistic representation of Christ crowned with thorns. From the words of Pontius Pilate to his accusers, (lit. behold the man)

echt (Ger.)   real, genuine, authentic

effendi (Turk.)   mister (lit. master)

emeritus (L.)   honourably retired (lit. meritorious)

ersatz (Ger.)   replacement, substitute, imitation

esprit de corps (Fr.)   pride in belonging to a group (lit. spirit of a body)

eureka (Gr.)   I have found it

ex officio (L.)   by virtue of his office (lit. out of duty)

fait accompli (Fr.)   thing already done (lit. accomplished fact)

fartlek (Swed.)   interval athletics training (lit. speed play)

fatwa (Arab.)   a legal decision

faux pas (Fr.)   social blunder, indiscretion (lit. false step)

Fidei Defensor (L.)   defender of the faith

flagrante delicto (L.)   in the act of a crime

floreat (L.)   let it flourish

force de frappe (Fr.)   French nuclear deterrent (lit. striking force)

Führer (Ger.)   leader

Gastarbeiter (Ger)   person with temporary permission to work, in a foreign country (lit. guest-worker)

Gauleiter (Ger.)   district leader

gestalt (Ger.)   organized whole in which each part affects every other part (lit. shape)

Gesundheit (Ger.)   your health (lit. healthy sound)

glasnost (Rus.)   openness

Götterdämmerung (Ger.)   In German mythology the final destruction of the world (lit. twilight of the gods)

goût (Fr.)   taste, artistic discernment

gravitas (L.)   solemn demeanour

gringo (Sp.)   term used by Latin-Americans for foreigners, (lit. foreigner)

Gulag (Rus.)   labour camp

habeas corpus (L.)   a writ to produce a prisoner before a court, (lit. you should have the body)

haiku (Jap.)   amusement verse

hajj (Arab.)   pilgrimage

Hakenkreuz (Ger.)   swastika (lit. hooked cross)

halal (Arab.)   cooked according to Muslim law (lit. lawful)

haute couture (Fr.)   high fashion (lit. high dressmaking)

haute cuisine (Fr.)   high-class cooking

haute école (Fr.)   classic style of riding (lit. high school)

hic et nunc (L.)   here and now

hic et ubique (L.)   here and everywhere

hic jacet (L.)   here lies

hic sepultus (L.)   here buried

hoi polloi (Gr.)   common people or rabble (lit. the many)

hominis est errare (L.)   to err is human

homme d'affaires (Fr.)   businessman

homme d'esprit (Fr.)   man of wit or genius

honi soit qui mal y pense (Fr.)   shamed be he who thinks evil

honores mutant mores (L.)   honours change manners

hors de combat (Fr.)   disabled or injured (lit. out of the fight)

hors d'oeuvre (Fr.)   savoury appetiser (lit. out of the course)

hwyl (W.)   fervour

Ibidem (L.)   In the same place

Ich dien (Ger.)   I serve

id est (L.)   that is

in camera (L.)   in secret (Lit. in the chamber)

incunabulum (L.)   book printed before 1501 (lit. from cradle), original Latin meaning was 'swaddling clothes'

in extremis (L.)   at the point of death (lit. in the last)

in flagrante delicto (L.)   in the act of a crime or red-handed, (lit. with the crime still ablaze), sometimes written 'flagrante delicto'

infra dig (L.)   beneath one's dignity

in loco parentis (L.)   in place of a parent

in petto (It.)   when a cardinal is selected by the pope but not yet anounced (lit. in the breast)

inshallah (Arab.)   equivalent to the term 'touch wood' (lit. if Allah wills)

inter alia (L.)   among other things

intra vires (L.)   within the powers of

in utero (L.)   before birth (lit. in the womb)

in vino veritas (L.)   drunken people often speak the truth, (lit. in wine, truth)

in vitro (L.)   in a test tube (lit. in glass)

ipso facto (L.)   by the fact itself

jacquerie (Fr.)   a peasants' revolt as in France in 1358 (lit. peasant)

j'adoube (Fr.)   I adjust (chess term)

je ne sais quoi (Fr.)   indefinable quality (lit. I know not what)

jeune premier (Fr.)   used in context of clinging on to youth (lit. first youth)

jeunesse dorée (Fr.)   rich and fashionable young people (lit. gilded youth)

jihad (Arab.)   a Muslim holy war (lit. conflict)

joie de vivre (Fr.)   joy of living

Jugendstil (Ger.)   art nouveau (lit. youth style)

Junker (Ger.)   class of Prussian land-owning aristocracy (lit. young lord)

juste milieu (Fr.)   happy medium or golden mean (lit. the right mean or the right course)

kamikaze (Jap.)   Japanese suicide pilots in WWII (lit. divine wind)

Kapellmeister (Ger.)   person in charge of an orchestra (lit. chapel master)

karaoke (Jap.)   Japanese entertainment of singing to backing tapes, (lit. empty orchestra)

Katzenjammer (Ger.)   colloquial term for a hangover (lit. cat's wailing)

kia ora (Maori)   good luck (lit. be well)

kibbutz (Heb.)   Jewish community in Israel (lit. gathering)

kibitzer (Yid.)   person who gives unwanted advice especially at a card game, (lit. lapwing or plover)

kitsch (Ger.)   worthless art

kolkhoz (Rus.)   Russian collective farm

kulak (Rus.)   land-owning peasant (lit. fist)

Kulturkampf (Ger.)   culture struggle

la dolce vita (It.)   the sweet life

laissez-faire (Fr.)   unrestricted commerce (lit. allow to do)

Langlauf (Ger.)   cross-country skiing (lit. long run)

lapsus linguae (L.)   slip of the tongue

lares et penates (L.)   household goods

l'chaim (Heb.)   a Jewish toast (lit. to life)

Lebensraum (Ger.)   territory needed by a state for its natural development, (lit. living space)

Lederhosen (Ger.)   leather trousers

lèse-majesté (Fr.)   high treason (lit. injured majesty)

lex scripta (L.)   written law

lex talionis (L.)   law of retaliation (lit. such law)

litterae humaniores (L.)   name given to study of

classics at Oxford University (lit. more humane letters)

locum tenens (L.)   a deputy (lit. place held)

locus classicus (L.)   authoritive and oft-quoted passage from a standard text (lit. classical place)

lycée (Fr.)   in France, a state secondary school (lit. pupil)

magnum opus (L.)   a great work of art or literature

maharishi (Hin.)   Hindu teacher of religious doctrine (lit. great sage)

mahatma (Sans.)   Brahman sage (lit. great soul)

maillot (Fr.)   tights worn for balet or gymnastics (lit. swaddling clothes)

mal de mer (Fr.)   seasickness

mañana (Sp.)   tomorrow

manqué (Fr.)   unfulfilled potential (lit. having missed)

maven (Yid.)   a connoisseur (lit. understanding)

mazel tov (Heb.)   congratulations or good luck (lit. good star)

mea culpa (L.)   by my own fault

memento mori (L.)   reminder of death

mene, mene, tekel, upharsin (Aram.)   words that appeared on the wall during Belshazzar's Feast (lit. numbered, numbered, weighed, divided)

mens rea (L.)   criminal intent (lit. guilty mind)

modus operandi (L.)   method of working

mot juste (Fr.)   appropriate word

multum in parvo (L.)   much in little

mutatis mutandis (L.)   with required changes

né(e) (Fr.)   born

ne plus ultra (L.)   extreme perfection (lit. not more beyond)

nil desperandum (L.)   never despair (lit. nothing to be despaired)

nisi (L.)   coming into effect unless otherwise stated (lit. unless)

noblesse oblige (Fr.)   obligation of nobility or privileged to be honourable (lit. nobility obliges)

nom de guerre (Fr.)   an assumed name (lit. name of war)

nom de plume (Fr.)   pen-name

non sequitur (L.)   statement that has no relevance to what went before (lit. it does not follow)

nota bene (L.)   note well

nuit blanche (Fr.)   sleepless night (lit. white night)

Nunc Dimittis (L.)   the Canticle of Simeon (Luke 2:29-32), (lit. now depart)

obiter dictum (L.)   said in passing

objet d'art (Fr.)   small object of artistic worth (lit. object of art)

objet trouvé (Fr.)   ordinary object seen from an artistic viewpoint, (lit. found object)

oeuvre (Fr.)   total output of an artist or writer

om mani padme hum (Sans.)   Tibetan Buddhists meditational chant. Aka Shadakshari mantra (lit. hail, jewel in the lotus)

omnia vincit amor (L.)   love conquers all

panem et circenses (L.)   bread and circuses (written by Juvenal of the loves of the typical Roman citizen)

parador (Sp.)   Inn or tavern

par avion (Fr.)   by airmail (lit. by air)

parvenu (Fr.)   an upstart or social climber (lit. to attain)

paterfamilias (L.)   male head of a household (lit. father of the family)

patois (Fr.)   dialect

pax vobiscum (L.)   peace be with you

per ardua ad astra (L.)   through adversity to the stars

perestroika (Rus.)   reconstruction

per se (L.)   In itself

persona non grata (L.)   unacceptable person

petit bourgeois (Fr.)   lower middle-class

petit four (Fr.)   small rich, sweet cakes, usually with icing (lit. little oven)

petit mal (Fr.)   mild form of epilepsy with short bouts of unconsciousness (lit. little illness)

pied à terre (Fr.)   temporary lodging (lit. foot to the ground)

pince-nez (Fr.)   spectacles without ear-pieces (lit. pinch nose)

pinxit (L.)   an inscription found after an artist's name on a painting (lit. painted)

pis aller (Fr.)   a compromise or last resort (lit. the worst going)

plongeur (Fr.)   washer-up (lit. plunger)

poco a poco (It.)   little by little

poilu (Fr.)   French equivalent of 'Tommy', an infantryman (lit. hairy)

posada (Sp.)   an inn in a Spanish-speaking country (lit. place for stopping)

pose plastique (Fr.)   theatrical presentation of the motionless nude female form (lit. flexible pose)

post meridiem (L.)   after midday

pousse-café (Fr.)   small glass of spirits especially brandy or a liqueur (lit. push-coffee)

prêt-à-porter (Fr.)   ready to wear or off the peg

prima donna (It.)   leading female operatic star (lit. first lady)

prima facie (L.)   at first sight (lit. first face)

primus inter pares (L.)   first among equals

pro tempore (L.)   for the time being

quattrocento (It.)   the 15th century especially in relation to Italian arts (lit. four hundred) short for milquattrocento '1400'

que será será (Sp.)   whatever will be will be

quidnunc (L.)   person eager to learn news or scandal, a gossipmonger, (lit. what now)

quid pro quo (L.)   one thing for another

quod erat demonstrandum (L.)   which was to be demonstrated

quod vide (L.)   usually seen as qv after a word treated more fully elsewhere (lit. which see)

raison d'être (Fr.)   reason for being

rapporteur (Fr.)   person appointed by a committee to prepare reports of meetings, (lit. reporter)

Realpolitik (Ger.)   ruthlessly realistic and opportunist approach to statesmanship

repechage (Fr.)   heat of a contest in which eliminated contestants compete again (lit. fishing out again)

res ipsa loquitur (L.)   the thing speaks for itself

rien ne va plus (Fr.)   roulette term meaning no more bets are to be placed (lit. nothing further goes)

Risorgimento (It.)   the 19th century movement for the political unification of Italy (lit. to rise again)

roman à clef (Fr.)   novel in which real people are depicted under disguised names (lit. novel with a key)

sang-froid (Fr.)   composure in the face of danger (lit. cold blood)

sanpaku (Jap.)   visibility of the white of the eye below the iris and on both sides (lit. three white)

sansculotte (Fr.)   low class Republican during the French Revolution (lit. without knee breeches)

sans souci (Fr.)   without cares

sasquatch   America's equivalent of the abominable snowman, aka big foot

satyagraha (Sans.)   a policy of non-violent resistance to British rule in India, (lit. truth pertinacity)

savoir-faire (Fr.)   knowing how to act

sayonara (Jap.)   goodbye

Schadenfreude (Ger.)   delighting in another's misfortune (lit. harm joy)

schlock (Yid.)   cheap or shoddy (lit. damaged merchandise)

LANGUAGE

schmaltz (Yid.) sentimentality (lit. melted fat)
schmuck (Yid.) contemptible person (lit. penis)
schweinhund (Ger.) term of abuse (lit. pig dog)
seicento (It.) the 17th century especially in relation to Italian arts (lit. six hundred) short for milseicento '1600'
semper eadem (L.) always the same (motto of Elizabeth I and Anne Boleyn)
seppuku (Jap.) the correct term in Japan for Hara-Kiri, which is a colloquialism (lit. cut open the stomach)
shiatsu (Jap.) acupuncture using fingers instead of needles (lit. finger pressure)
shmatte (Yid.) shabbiness especially of clothes (lit. rag)
sic (L.) bracketed insert in a text to indicate questionable word is correct (lit. thus or so)
sic transit gloria mundi (L.) thus passes the glory of the world
Sieg Heil (Ger.) Nazi salute accompanied by the raising of the right arm (lit. hail to victory)
sine die (L.) without a fixed date (lit. without a day)
sine prole (L.) without offspring
sine qua non (L.) an essential condition or requirement (lit. without which not)
son et lumière (Fr.) entertainment staged at night to set off a building artistically (lit. sound and light)
sotto voce (It.) musical term 'In an undertone' (lit. under voice)
soupçon (Fr.) slight suspicion of, small amount (lit. suspicion)
sputnik (Rus.) unmanned artificial earth satellite (lit. travelling companion)
stet (L.) literary mark in proofing meaning correction should be ignored (lit. let it stand)
Sturm und Drang (Ger.) late 18th century German literary style (lit. storm and stress)
subbotnik (Rus.) voluntary Saturday work to assist economy (lit. Saturday)
sub judice (L.) under consideration of a judge

sub poena (L.) writ compelling a court attendance (lit. under a penalty)
sub rosa (L.) in secret (lit. under the rose)
summa cum laude (L.) with the highest praise
table d'hôte (Fr.) fixed-price meal with set courses (lit. host's table)
tabula rasa (L.) clean slate (lit. scraped table)
tai chi (Chin.) Chinese system of callisthenics (lit. great fist)
tempus fugit (L.) time flies
tête-bêche (Fr.) double-headed stamp (lit. head to double-head)
tour de force (Fr.) masterly accomplishment (lit. show of strength)
trecento (It.) the 14th century especially in relation to Italian arts (lit. three hundred) short for miltrecento '1300'
tricoteuse (Fr.) woman who knitted at executions during French Revolution (lit. knitter)
trompe l'oeil (Fr.) appearance of reality in art (lit. deceives the eye)
ultra vires (L.) beyond the powers of
urbi et orbi (L.) to the city and the world
verbum sat sapienti (L.) a word is enough for a wise man
victor ludorum (L.) overall winner of a competition (lit. winner of the games)
videlicet (L.) namely
vis-à-vis (Fr.) in relation to (lit. face to face)
viva voce (L.) orally (lit. with the living voice)
vox populi (L.) voice of the people
Wanderjahr (Ger.) wonder year
Wehrmacht (Ger.) German forces 1921-45 (lit. defence force)
Wunderkind (Ger.) a highly talented child (lit. wonder child)
yordim (Heb.) emigrants from the state of Israel
Zaibatsu (Jap.) family business conglomerate (lit. wealthy clique)
Zeitgeist (Ger.) spirit of the times

Cockney Rhyming Slang

Cockney–Standard

Cockney	Standard	Cockney	Standard
Abergavenny	penny	bacon and eggs	legs
Adam and Eve	believe	ball of chalk	walk
airs and graces	faces	balloon car	saloon bar
	braces	band in the box	pox
	Epsom Races	band of hope	soap
alderman's nail	tail	Barnaby Rudge	judge
alligator	later	Barnet Fair	hair
almond rocks	socks	bat and wicket	ticket
Alphonse	ponce	Bath bun	son
Andy Cain	rain		sun
Anna Maria	fire	battle-cruiser	boozer
'apenny dip	ship	bazaar	bar (pub)
apple fritter	bitter (beer)	bear's paw	saw
apples and pears	stairs	Beecham's Pill	bill
April fools	stools		still (photo)
	tools	bees and honey	money
	football pools	beggar my neighbour	on the labour (dole)
April showers	flowers	bird lime	time
Aristotle	bottle	biscuits and cheese	knees
army and navy	gravy	bladder of lard	card
artful dodger	lodger	boat race	face
Auntie Ella	umbrella	Bob Squash	wash
Auntie Nellie	belly	Bo-Peep	sleep
babbling brook	cook	boracic lint	skint
	crook	bottle and glass	arse

Term	Meaning	Term	Meaning
bow and arrow	sparrow	gay and frisky	whisky
bread and butter	gutter	German bands	hands
bread and cheese	sneeze	ginger beer	queer
Bristol Cities	titties		engineer
Brussels sprouts	scouts	Glasgow Rangers	strangers
bubble and squeak	beak (magistrate)	God forbids	kids
	Greek	goose's neck	cheque
bucket and pail	jail	Gordon and Gotch	watch
bull and cow	row	grasshopper	copper
burnt cinder	window	greengages	wages
Burton-on-Trent	rent	Hampstead Heath	teeth
bushel and peck	neck	Hampton Wick	prick
Bushey Park	lark	Harry Randall	candle
butcher's hook	look	Harvey Nichols	pickles
Cain and Abel	table	hearts of oak	broke
canal boat	tote	hit and miss	kiss
Cape of Good Hope	soap		piss
Captain Cook	book	holy friar	liar
carving knife	wife	iron hoof	pouf
cash and carried	married	iron tank	bank
cat and mouse	house	Isle of Wight	right
Chalk Farm	arm	I suppose	nose
cheerful giver	liver	Jack and Jill	hill
Cherry Hogg	dog		bill
Chevy Chase	face		till
china plate	mate	jackdaw	jaw
chop sticks	six	Jack Jones	alone
clickety click	sixty-six	Jack Tar	bar
cobbler's awls	balls	Jack the Ripper	kipper
cock linnet	minute	jam jar	car
cockroach	coach	Jerry O'Gorman	Mormon
cock sparrow	barrow	Jimmy Riddle	piddle
cocoa	say so	Jim Skinner	dinner
Conan Doyle	boil	Joanna	piano
country cousin	dozen	Johnnie Horner	corner
crust of bread	head	Kate and Sydney	steak and kidney
cuddle and kiss	miss	Kate Karney	army
currant bun	son	Khyber Pass	arse
	sun	kidney punch	lunch
custard and jelly	telly	la-di-dah	car
cuts and scratches	matches	Lilian Gish	fish
daffydown dilly	silly	Lilley and Skinner	dinner
Daily Mail	tale		beginner
daisy roots	boots	linen draper	paper
dickory dock	clock	lion's lair	chair
dicky bird	word	loaf of bread	head
Dicky Dirt	shirt	loop the loop	soup
dig in the grave	shave	Lord Lovell	shovel
ding dong	song	Lord Mayor	swear
ding dong bell	hell	lousy brown	Rose and Crown
dinky doo	twenty-two	Lucy Locket	pocket
Doctor Crippen	dripping	macaroni	pony
dog and bone	phone	Marie Corelli	telly
do me goods	Woods (Woodbines)	Mickey Mouse	house
Duchess of Fife	wife	mince pies	eyes
Duke of York	chalk	Molly Malone	phone
	cork	monkeys' tails	nails
	fork	Mother Hubbard	cupboard
dustbin lids	kids	mother's ruin	gin
early hours	flowers	Mrs Chant	aunt
earwig	twig (understand)	Mutt and Jeff	deaf
eighteen pence	sense	nanny goat	boat
elephant's trunk	drunk		tote
field of wheat	street		coat
fife and drum	bum	near and far	bar
fine and dandy	brandy		car
fisherman's daughter	water	needle and pin	gin
flowery dell	cell	Nervo and Knox	pox
four by two	Jew		goggle box
frog and toad	road	Newington Butts	guts
front wheel skid	yid	Noah's ark	park
garden gate	magistrate		nark

north and south	mouth	Scapa Flow	go
oily rag	fag	Scotch pegs	legs
old pot and pan	old man	Sexton Blake	cake
Oliver Twist	fist		fake
on the floor	poor	skin and blister	sister
orchestra stalls	balls	sky rocket	pocket
Owen Nares	chairs	sorry and sad	bad
Oxford scholar	dollar	stammer and stutter	butter
peas in the pot	hot	stand at ease	cheese
pen and ink	stink	tea leaf	thief
piccolo and flute	suit	tea pot lid	yid
pig's ear	beer		quid
pimple and blotch	scotch		kid
pitch and toss	boss	tiddly wink	drink
plates of meat	feet	tit for tat	hat
pleasure and pain	rain	Tod Sloan	(on one's) own
potatoes in the mould	cold	Tom and Dick	sick
rabbit and pork	talk	Tommy Tucker	supper
read and write	fight	Tom Thumb	rum
Richard the Third	bird	trouble and strife	wife
Rory O'More	door	two and eight	state
Rosy Lee	tea	Uncle Bert	shirt
round the houses	trousers	Uncle Fred	bread
rub-a-dub-dub	pub	Uncle Ned	bed
Salford Docks	rocks	weasel and stoat	coat
salmon and trout	stout	weeping willow	pillow
sausage and mash	cash	whistle and flute	suit
	crash	you and me	tea

Cockney Rhyming Slang

Standard–Cockney

alone	Jack Jones	cake	Sexton Blake
arm	Chalk Farm	candle	Harry Randall
army	Kate Karney	car	jam jar
arse	bottle and glass		La-Di-Dah
	Khyber Pass		near and far
aunt	Mrs Chant	card	bladder of lard
bad	sorry and sad	cash	sausage and mash
balls	cobbler's awls	cell	flowery dell
	orchestra stalls	chair	lion's lair
bank	iron tank	chairs	Owen Nares
bar	Jack Tar	chalk	Duke of York
	near and far	cheese	stand at ease
bar (pub)	bazaar	cheque	goose's neck
barrow	cock sparrow	clock	dickory dock
beak (magistrate)	bubble and squeak	coach	cockroach
bed	Uncle Ned	coat	nanny goat
beer	pig's ear		weasel and stoat
beginner	Lilley and Skinner	cold	potatoes in the mould
believe	Adam and Eve	cook	babbling brook
belly	Auntie Nellie	copper	grasshopper
bill	Jack and Jill	cork	Duke of York
	Beecham's pill	corner	Johnnie Horner
bird	Richard the Third	crash	sausage and mash
bitter (beer)	apple fritter	crook	babbling brook
boat	nanny goat	cupboard	Mother Hubbard
boil	Conan Doyle	deaf	Mutt and Jeff
book	Captain Cook	dinner	Jim Skinner
boots	daisy roots		Lilley and Skinner
boozer	battle-cruiser	dog	Cherry Hogg
boss	pitch and toss	dollar	Oxford Scholar
bottle	Aristotle	door	Rory O'More
braces	airs and graces	dozen	country cousin
brandy	fine and dandy	drink	tiddly wink
bread	Uncle Fred	dripping	Doctor Crippen
broke	hearts of oak	drunk	elephant's trunk
bum	fife and drum	engineer	ginger beer
butter	stammer and stutter	Epsom Races	airs and graces

Term	Slang	Term	Slang
eyes	mince pies		dog and bone
face	boat race	piano	Joanna
	Chevy Chase	pickles	Harvey Nichols
faces	airs and graces	piddle	Jimmy Riddle
fag	oily rag	pillow	weeping willow
fake	Sexton Blake	piss	hit and miss
feet	plates of meat	pocket	sky rocket
fight	read and write		Lucy Locket
fire	Anna Maria	ponce	Alphonse
fish	Lilian Gish	pony	macaroni
fist	Oliver Twist	poor	on the floor
flowers	April showers	pouf	iron hoof
	early hours	pox	band in the box
football pools	April fools		Nervo and Knox
fork	Duke of York	prick	Hampton Wick
gin	needle and pin	pub	rub-a-dub-dub
	mother's ruin	queer	ginger beer
go	Scapa Flow	quid	tea pot lid
goggle box	Nervo and Knox	rain	Andy Cain
gravy	army and navy		pleasure and pain
greek	bubble and squeak	rent	Burton-on-Trent
guts	Newington Butts	right	Isle of Wight
gutter	bread and butter	road	frog and toad
hair	Barnet Fair	rocks	Salford Docks
hands	German bands	Rose and Crown	lousy brown
hat	tit for tat	row	bull and cow
head	crust of bread	rum	Tom Thumb
	loaf of bread	saloon bar	balloon car
hell	ding dong bell	saw	bear's paw
hill	Jack and Jill	say So	cocoa
hot	peas in the pot	scotch	pimple and blotch
house	cat and mouse	scouts	brussels sprouts
	Mickey Mouse	sense	eighteen pence
jail	bucket and pail	shave	dig in the grave
jaw	jackdaw	ship	'apenny dip
Jew	four by two	shirt	Dicky Dirt
judge	Barnaby Rudge		Uncle Bert
kid	tea pot lid	shovel	Lord Lovell
kids	dustbin lids	sick	Tom and Dick
	God forbids	silly	daffydown dilly
kipper	Jack the Ripper	sister	skin and blister
kiss	hit and miss	six	chop sticks
knees	biscuits and cheese	sixty-Six	clickety click
lark	Bushey Park	skint	boracic lint
later	alligator	sleep	Bo-Peep
legs	bacon and eggs	sneeze	bread and cheese
	Scotch pegs	soap	Cape of Good Hope
liar	holy friar		band of hope
liver	cheerful giver	socks	almond rocks
lodger	artful dodger	son	Bath bun
look	butcher's hook		currant bun
lunch	kidney punch	song	ding dong
magistrate	garden gate	soup	loop the loop
married	cash and carried	sparrow	bow and arrow
matches	cuts and scratches	stairs	apples and pears
mate	china plate	state	two and eight
minute	cock linnet	steak and kidney	Kate and Sydney
miss	cuddle and kiss	still (photo)	Beecham's pill
money	bees and honey	stink	pen and ink
Mormon	Jerry O'Gorman	stools	April fools
mouth	north and south	stout	salmon and trout
nails	monkeys' tails	strangers	Glasgow Rangers
nark	Noah's ark	street	field of wheat
neck	bushel and peck	suit	whistle and flute
nose	I suppose		piccolo and flute
old man	old pot and pan	sun	Bath bun
on the labour (dole)	beggar my neighbour		currant bun
(on one's) own	Tod Sloan	supper	Tommy Tucker
paper	linen draper	swear	Lord Mayor
park	Noah's ark	table	Cain and Abel
penny	Abergavenny	tail	alderman's nail
phone	Molly Malone	tale	Daily Mail

talk	rabbit and pork
tea	you and me
	Rosy Lee
teeth	Hampstead Heath
telly	Marie Corelli
	custard and jelly
thief	tea leaf
ticket	bat and wicket
till	Jack and Jill
time	bird lime
titties	Bristol Cities
tools	April fools
tote	nanny goat
	canal boat
trousers	round the houses
twenty-two	dinky doo

twig (understand)	earwig
umbrella	Auntie Ella
wages	greengages
walk	ball of chalk
wash	Bob Squash
watch	Gordon and Gotch
water	fisherman's daughter
whisky	gay and frisky
wife	Duchess of Fife
	trouble and strife
	carving knife
window	burnt cinder
Woods (Woodbines)	do me goods
word	Dicky Bird
yid	front wheel skid
	tea pot lid

Greek Alphabet

A	α	alpha	N	ν	nu
B	β	beta	Ξ	ξ	xi
Γ	γ	gamma	O	o	omicron
Δ	δ	delta	Π	π	pi
E	ε	epsilon	P	ρ	rho
Z	ζ	zeta	Σ	σ	sigma
H	η	eta	T	τ	tau
Θ	θ	theta	Y	υ	upsilon
I	ι	iota	Φ	ϕ	phi
K	κ	kappa	X	χ	chi
Λ	λ	lambda	Ψ	ψ	psi
M	μ	mu	Ω	ω	omega

Americanisms

English word	American equivalent	English word	American equivalent
A (film rating)	M (Mature film rating)	catapult	slingshot
AA (film rating)	R (Restricted film rating)	chat	confab
accumulator bet	parlay	chemist's shop	drug store
Akela	Den Mother	chest of drawers	bureau
Alf Garnett	Archie Bunker	chick-pea	garbanzo bean
Alsatian	German Shepherd	chimney	smokestack
aluminium	aluminum	chips	french fries
anorak	parka	chiropodist	podiatrist
approved school	reform school	commis waiter	bus boy
Armistice Day	Veteran's Day	condom	rubber
aubergine	eggplant	coriander	cilantro
autumn	fall	cos lettuce	romaine lettuce
baby's liquid feed	formula	courgette	zucchini
bag	sack	crisps	chips
big wheel	ferris wheel	cupboard	closet
biscuit	cookie	current account	checking account
Black Maria	patrol wagon	curriculum vitae	résumé
blue-eyed boy (pet)	fair-haired boy (pet)	curtains	drapes
bottom drawer	hope chest	dinner jacket	tuxedo
bowler hat	derby	directory inquiries	information
braces	suspenders	docker	longshoreman
budgerigar	parakeet	double cream	whipping cream
bum	fanny	drainpipe	downspout
bum-bag	fanny pack	draughts	checkers
by-law	ordinance	drawing pin	thumb tack
camp bed	cot	dressing gown	bathrobe
candy floss	cotton candy	dual carriageway	divided highway
car bonnet	hood	dustbin	garbage pail
car boot	trunk	elastic band	rubber band
car Park	parking lot	estate agent	realtor
caretaker	janitor	estate car	station wagon
cashier	teller	evening classes	night school

English word	American equivalent	English word	American equivalent
fan light	transom	pedestrian crossing	Crosswalk
fill In (a form)	fill out (a form)	pelmet	Valance
flannel	wash cloth	Perspex (trade name)	Plexiglas
flat (leased or owned)	apartment	petrol	gas
flat (owned)	condominium	petrol station	filling station
flautist	flutist	pharmacist	druggist
flex	wire	pimple	zit
flick knife	switchblade	plaster (medical dressing)	Band-Aid
flyover	overpass	policeman (uniformed)	patrolman
frying pan	skillet	post code	zip code
garage	bodyshop	pouffe	hassock
garden	yard	primary school	grade school
gardening	yard work	public convenience	comfort station
gear lever	gearshift	pushchair	stroller
girl guide	girl scout	queue	line
glow worm	lightning bug	quilt	comforter
goods van (train)	box car	railway porter	redcap
goods wagon (train)	freight car	reef knot	square knot
greaseproof paper	wax paper	refrigerator	icebox
green fingers	green thumbs	reserve price	upset price
guttering	eavestrough	rosé wines	blush wines
handbag	pocketbook	rota	roster
	purse	rubbish	garbage
Heath Robinson	Rube Goldberg	sack	fire
hire purchase	instalment plan	saloon Car	sedan
hob	burner	short-hand typist	stenographer
hot dog	weenie	short trousers	knee pants
housewife	homemaker	sideboards	sideburns
hymen	cherry	skipping rope	jumping pope
ice lolly	popsicle	skirting board	base board
icing sugar	confectionery sugar		mopboard
	powdered sugar	solicitor	attorney
income support	relief	sorbet	sherbet
influenza	grippe	spanner	wrench
jam	jelly	string	cord
jelly	jello	suitcase	valise
jemmy	jimmy	surgical spirit	rubbing alcohol
jug	pitcher	swede	rutabaga
jumble sale	rummage sale	sweet potato	yam
knacker's yard	glue factory	sweets	candy
ladder (in stockings)	run (in tights)	Swiss roll	jelly roll
ladybird	ladybug	tallboy	highboy
level crossing	grade crossing	tap	faucet
lift	elevator	telephone box	phone booth
lodger	roomer	tennis shoes	sneakers
long jump	broad jump	tie-pin	stick-pin
lorry	truck	tobacconist's shop	cigar store
lovebite	hickey	toilet (Domestic)	restroom
maize	corn	torch	flashlight
men's outfitter	haberdasher	tornado	twister
merry-go-round	carousel	tram	streetcar
minced meat	hamburger meat	trilby	fedora
	ground meat	trousers	pants
motorway	throughway	truncheon	nightstick
	freeway	U (Universal film rating)	G (General film rating)
	expressway	underground (tube)	subway
	superhighway	underpants	shorts
music-hall	vaudeville	undertaker	mortician
muslin	cheesecloth	up to you	down to you
Naafi	PX (Post Exchange)	verruca	planter's wart
nappy	diaper	vest	undershirt
notepad	scratchpad	waistcoat	vest
noughts & crosses	tic tac toe	wallet	billfold
offal	variety meat	washing up bowl	dishpan
okra	gumbo	wet paint	fresh paint
oven	range	wholemeal biscuit	graham cracker
paraffin	kerosene	windscreen	windshield
patience (card game)	solitaire	zed (z)	zee
pavement	sidewalk		

LANGUAGE

Forenames: Meanings

Aaron   high mountain/bright
Abdullah   servant of God
Abelard   resolute
Abel   breath
Abigail   father rejoices
Abner   father of light
Abraham   father on high/father of a multitude
Absalom   father of peace
Ada   noble/happy/prosperous
Adam   red earth
Adolph   noble wolf
Adrian   dark one of the Adriatic
Aesop   burnt faced
Agatha   good
Agnes   lamb/chaste
Ahab   uncle
Ajax   eagle
Akram   excellent
Alan   harmony/handsome
Alaric   ruler of all
Alastair   form of Alexander
Albert   nobly bright
Alexander   defender of men
Algernon   bearded
Ali   protected by God/the greatest
Alison   of noble kind
Alfred   elf/wise counsellor
Alma   apple/norishing/loving
Amadeus   lover of God
Amanda   fit to be loved
Ambrose   immortal
Amelia   hard-working
Amos   burden
Amy   beloved
Andrea   female form of Andrew
Andrew   manly
Angela   messenger/angel
Anita   grace, mercy
Anne   English form of Hannah
Anthea   flowery
Anthony   inestimable
April   name of a month
Arnold   eagle power
Arthur   bear/stone/valorous
Audrey   noble strength
Aziz   famous
Barbara   strange/foreign land
Barry   fair-headed/spear
Baruch   blessed
Basil   royal/kingly
Beatrice   bringer of joy
Belinda   beautiful and pretty
Benjamin   son of my right hand
Berenice   one who brings victory
Bernard   brave bear
Bertram   glorious raven
Beth   pet form of Elizabeth
Betty   pet form of Elizabeth
Bill   pet form of William
Bipin   forest
Bjorn   bear

Bob   pet form of Robert
Boris   fighter
Brandon   broom-covered hill
Brenda   burning/a flame
Bronwyn   white breasted
Bud   brother
Byron   from the cottage
Brian   hill/strength
Carl   man/husbandman
Cameron   crooked nose/awsome
Carmen   garden/song
Carol   female form of Charles
Casper   treasure
Catherine   pure
Cecilia   blind
Charles   man/husbandman
Cher   beloved
Christine   anointed
Christopher   carrier of Christ
Claire   bright/shining
Colin   form of Nicholas
Colette   victorious
Cordelia   jewel of the sea
Craig   rock
Cressida   golden
Cyril   lord
Damian   to tame
Daniel   God is my judge
Danielle   female form of Daniel
Darius   wealthy
Darren   beloved
David   beloved/friend
Dean   valley/leader
Deborah   bee/eloquent
Declan   man of prayer
Dennis   of Dionysus (Greek God of wine)
Derek   gifted ruler (form of Theodonic)
Dermot   free man
Derry   red-haired
Diane   divine
Donald   world ruler
Donna   lady
Donovan   dark warrior
Doris   gift of the sea
Dorothy   gift of God
Douglas   from the dark water
Dudley   of the people's meadows
Eamon   rich protector
Ebenezer   stone of help
Edward   prosperous guardian
Eileen   Irish form of Helen
Eldridge   wise ruler
Elijah   Jehovah is my God
Elizabeth   my God is bountiful
Elvis   all wise
Emily   industrious
Emma   all-embracing
Emmanuel   God with us
Enoch   dedicated
Eric   ruler of all
Erasmus   lovable

Esther star
Ethan firm/strong
Eugenie well born
Evelyn pleasant
Ezekial God will strengthen
Ezra helper
Felipe lover of horses
Felix fortunate
Ferdinand adventursome
Fidel faithful
Finlay fair hero
Floyd grey-haired
Frank Frenchman/freeman
Franklin freeholder
Frederick peaceful ruler
Gabriel God is my strength
Gail pet form of Abigail
Gareth gentle/firm spear
Garth protector
Gary spear/form of Gareth
Gavin hawk
Gemma gem
Geoffrey peaceful ruler/God's peace
George husbandman/farmer
Gerard bold spear
Gregory on the watch
Griselda grey battle maid
Gudrun God secret
Gulliver glutton
Guy lovely
Habib beloved
Hamish (variant of Jacob)
Hanif believer
Hans (variant of John)
Hannah grace/favour
Harold leader of armies
Harry pet form of Henry
Hayley hay-meadow
Hector steadfast
Helen bright/shining one
Henry household ruler
Hilary joyful
Hilda battle maid
Hiram most noble
Homer pledge
Horace keeper of the hours
Hortense gardener
Howard guardian
Hubert bright minded
Hugh heart/mind
Humphrey warrior peace
Ian Scottish form of John
Ichabod departed glory
Ida work
Imran strong
Ira watchful
Irene peace
Iris rainbow
Irvin handsome/fair
Isaac he will laugh
Isaiah God is salvation
Ishmael God will hear
Ivan his favour
Jacqueline female form of James

James one who takes by the heel
Jane female form of John
Jared descending
Jason to heal
Javier owner of a new horse
Jed hard
Jemima dove
Jennifer fair
Jeremy Jehovah exalts/appointed by God
Jess wealthy
Jessica God beholds
Jethro superabundance
Jezebel domination
Joab God is the father
Joachim God will judge
Joan helper
John Jehovah has been gracious
Jonathan Jehovah's gift
Joseph Jehovah adds
Joyce joyful
Julie descended from Jove/youthful
Karen from Katarina/pure
Katarina (form of Catherine)
Keir dark skinned
Keith of the forest
Kelly warlike one
Kenneth handsome; fair one or fire sprung
Kevin handsome at birth
Lakisha woman
Latoya Antonia
Laura bay/laurel
Leah gazelle
Lee of the meadow
Leila night
Leonard strong lion
Leslie of the grey, fortress
Letitia joy
Lilith of the night
Linda pretty
Lindsay pool on the island
Lloyd grey
Loretta pure
Lucille light
Lyn cascade
Madhur sweet
Madison warrior's son
Magnus great
Malcolm dove
Mandy much loved
Marcus war-like
Margaret pearl
Mario war-like
Mark Mars (god of war)
Martin Mars (god of war)
Marvin sea friend
Mary 'bitterness' or wished-for child
Matilda battle maiden
Matthew gift of the Lord
Maureen little Mary
Maurice dark-skinned
Melissa bee/honey
Merill famous
Michael like the Lord
Miranda fit to be wondered at

L
A
N
G
U
A
G
E

Moses   saved
Nadia   hope
Nancy   pet form of Anne
Natalie   birthday of the Lord
Neil   champion
Nicholas   victory of the people
Noah   rest/comfort
Omar   first son
Pamela   all honey
Patricia   noble
Paul   small
Peter   stone/rock
Philip   lover of horses
Quentin   fifth born child
Rachel   ewe
Randolph   edge wolf/house wolf
Raphael   God has healed
Raymond   counsel for the defence/wise protection
Rebecca   noose/one who brings peace
Rhoda   rose
Richard   strong ruler
Robert   bright fame
Roger   famous spear
Rolf   swift wolf
Ronald   counsel/power
Ronan   little seal
Rowan   red
Roxane   dawn
Ruth   vision of beauty
Samuel   heard/name of God
Sarah   princess
Saskia   protector of the universe
Sean   (form of John)
Sebastian   revered

Sharon   the plain
Shirley   bright clearing
Simon   listening attentively
Stacey   resurrection
Stephen   crown
Stuart   steward
Susan   lily
Sylvia   forest
Teresa   woman of Theresia/reaper
Theodoric   gifted ruler
Thomas   twin
Tiffany   manifestation of God
Timothy   honouring God
Tracy   pet form of Teresa
Trevor   big village/prudent
Tristan   the noisy one
Ursula   she bear
Vera   faith/truth
Victoria   victory
Vincent   conquer
Virgil   flourishing
Virginia   maiden
Vladimir   posess peace
Walter   ruling people
Wayne   wagon maker
William   helmet of resolution
Xavier   bright
Yuri   farmer
Yusuf   one chosen by God
Zachariah   God's remembrance
Zadok   just
Zia   enlightened
Zoe   life

LITERATURE

Autobiographies in Title Order

Title	Author
Absolutely Mahvelous	Billy Crystal
Absolutely Now	Lynn Franks
Accidental MP, An	Martin Bell
Actor and His Time, An	John Gielgud
Acts of Defiance	Jack Ashley
Acts of Faith	Adam Faith
Against Goliath	David Steel
Against the Grain	Boris Yeltsin
Alderman's Tale, The	Don Mosey
All Above Board	Wilfrid Brambell
Alliss in Wonderland	Peter Alliss
All My Yesterdays	Edward G Robinson
All Those Tomorrows	Mai Zetterling
Almost a Gentleman (1991)	John Osborne
Along My Line	Gilbert Harding
Also Known as Shirley (1987)	Shelley Winters
Always Playing	Nigel Kennedy
An American Comedy	Harold Lloyd
Animal Days	Desmond Morris
Another Part of the Wood (1974)	Kenneth Clark
Anything For a Quiet Life	Jack Hawkins
Apple Sauce	Michael Wilding
Arias and Raspberries	Sir Harry Secombe
As I Remember Them (1962)	Eddie Cantor
As I Walked Out One Midsummer's Morning	Laurie Lee (1929)
As It Happened (1954)	Clement, Attlee
As It Happens (1975)	Jimmy Savile
As It Seemed to Me	John Cole
Astronomer by Chance	Bernard Lovell
Backward Glance, A	Edith Wharton
Banjaxed	Terry Wogan
Bardot, Deneuve, and Fonda	Roger Vadim
Battling for Peace	Shimon Peres
Beam Ends (1934)	Errol Flynn
Beating Time	Antony Hopkins (conductor)
Before I Forget	James Mason
Before the Dawn	Gerry Adams
Beginning	Kenneth Branagh
Being Myself	Martina Navratilova
Beneath the Underdog	Charlie Mingus
Best of Times, Worst of Times	Shelley Winters
Better Class of Person, A (1981)	John Osborne
Blessings in Disguise (1985)	Alec Guinness
Bonus of Laughter, The	Leslie Crowther
Born Lucky	John Francome
Born to Believe (1953)	Lord Longford
Bound for Glory	Woody Guthrie
Boy	Roald Dahl
Bring on the Empty Horses	David Niven
British Picture, A (1985)	Ken Russell
Buried Day, The	Cecil Day Lewis
By Myself	Lauren Bacall
Can You Have It All	Nicola Horlick
Caught in the Act (1986)	Richard Todd
Change Lobsters and Dance	Lili Palmer
Changing	Liv Ullmann
Child of My Love	Sue Ryder
Choices	Liv Ullmann
Chronicles of Wasted Time	Malcolm Muggeridge
Cider With Rosie (1959)	Laurie Lee

Title	Author
Citizen Jane	Jane Fonda
Cleared for Take Off (1996)	Dirk Bogarde
Clear Water Stream, A (1958)	Henry Williamson
Closing Ranks (1997)	Dirk Bogarde
Coal Miner's Daughter, The	Loretta Lynn
Coming Attraction (1988)	Terence Stamp
Confessions	Jean-Jacques Rousseau
Confessions of an Actor	John Barrymore
Confessions of an Actor	Laurence Olivier
Confessions of an English Opium-Eater	Thomas De Quincey
Courting Triumph	Virginia Wade
Crying with Laughter	Bob Monkhouse
Cuban Rebel Girls (1959)	Errol Flynn
Dancing in the Light (1985)	Shirley MacLaine
Dancing in the Moonlight	Ronnie Barker
Dear Me	Peter Ustinov
Diet for Life	Lynn Redgrave
Don't Fall off the Mountain (1970)	Shirley MacLaine
Don't Laugh at Me	Norman Wisdom
Door Marked Summer, The	Michael Bentine
Double Feature (1989)	Terence Stamp
Drums under the Window (1945)	Sean O' Casey
Duke, The	David Nicholson
Ecstasy and Me	Hedy Lamarr
Ed Wynn's Son	Keenan Wynn
Eternal Male, The	Omar Sharif
Evening All	Ted Willis
Every Other Inch a Lady	Beatrice Lillie
Every Shot I Take	Davis Love III
Eye of the Tiger	Frank Bruno
Facing the Music	Jane Torvill & Christopher Dean
Falling towards England	Clive James
Farce about Face	Brian Rix
Final Dress (1983)	John Houseman
Fire over England (1994)	Ken Russell
First Interval	Donald Wolfit
Five Lives (1964)	Lord Longford
For Dogs and Angels	Chili Boucher
Free House, A	Walter Sickert
From a Bundle of Rags	Jim Bowen
Front and Center (1980)	John Houseman
Full Monty, The	Jim Davidson
Fun in a Chinese Laundry	Josef von Sternberg
Future Indefinite (1954)	Noel Coward
Gay Illiterate, The (1944)	Louella Parsons
Gift of Joy, A (1965)	Helen Hayes
Girl Power	Spice Girls
Glorious Uncertainty	Jenny Pitman
Good Vibrations	Jacqueline Gold (Ann Summers)
Good Vibrations	Evelyn Glennie
Goodbye to All That	Robert Graves
Goodness Had Nothing to Do with It	Mae West (1959)
Good, the Bad and the Bubbly, The	George Best
Grace Abounding	John Bunyan
Grain of Wheat (1974)	Lord Longford

Title	Author
Grand Inquisitor	Robin Day
Greatest Game of All, The (1969)	Jack Nicklaus
Great Meadow (1992)	Dirk Bogarde
Great Morning (1947)	Osbert Sitwell
Halfway Through the Door	Alan Arkin
Happy Go Lucky (1959)	Kenneth More
Happy Hooker, The	Xavier Hollander
Haunted Life, A	Anthony Perkins
Have Tux Will Travel (1958)	Bob Hope
Here Lies	Eric Ambler
His Eye Is on the Sparrow	Ethel Waters
Hitting across the Line	Viv Richards
Hollywood in a Suitcase (1980)	Sammy Davis Jnr
Hons and Rebels	Jessica Mitford
Hundred Different Lives, A	Raymond Massey
I Can't Stay Long (1975)	Laurie Lee
I.E. (1965)	Mickey Rooney
I Knock at the Door (1939)	Sean O' Casey
I Like What I Know	Vincent Price
I'm Still Here	Yvonne De Carlo
I'm Still Here (1989)	Eartha Kitt
In and Out of Character	Basil Rathbone
In Camera (1989)	Richard Todd
In Darkness and Light	Anthony Hopkins
Inishfallen Fare Thee Well (1949)	Sean O' Casey
In My Father's Court	Isaac Bashevis Singer
In My Mind's Eye (1983)	Michael Redgrave
In Search of History: A Personal Adventure	Theodore H. White
Inside the Third Reich	Albert Speer
Intermission	Anne Baxter
I Owe Russia $2000 (1963)	Bob Hope
I Paid Hitler	Baron Von Thyssen
I Reach for the Stars	Barbara Cartland
I Search for Rainbows (1967)	Barbara Cartland
I Seek the Miraculous (1978)	Barbara Cartland
I Was Born Greek	Melina Mercouri
Is It Me	Terry Wogan
Isthmus Years, The (1943)	Barbara Cartland
It Doesn't Take a Hero	Norman Schwarzkopf
It's All in the Playing (1987)	Shirley MacLaine
It's Been Fun (1949)	Anna Neagle
It's Me, O Lord! (1957)	A.E. Coppard
Jack of All Trades	Jack Warner
Jacob's Ladder	David Jacob
Jump Jockeys Don't Cry	Sharron Murgatroyd
Just Resting	Leo McKern
Just Williams	Kenneth Williams
Kentish Lad, A	Frank Muir
King's Story, A (1951)	Duke of Windsor
Kink	Dave Davies
Knock Wood	Candice Bergen
Last Christmas Show, The (1976)	Bob Hope
Laugh Is on Me, The	Phil Silvers
Laughter in the Next Room (1948)	Osbert Sitwell
Leaving a Doll's House	Claire Bloom
Left Hand: Right Hand (1944)	Osbert Sitwell
Let the Chips Fall	Rudy Vallee
Let's Get through Wednesday	Reginald Bosanquet
Life for Life's Sake	Richard Aldington
Life in Movies, A	Michael Powell
Life in Movies, A	Fred Zinneman
Life Is a Banquet	Rosalind Russell
Life Is Too Short (1991)	Mickey Rooney
Life Lines (1989)	Jill Ireland

Title	Author
Life of an American Workman, The	Walter Percy Chrysler
Life on Film (1971)	Mary Astor
Life, Sex and ESP (1975)	Mae West
Life Wish (1987)	Jill Ireland
Limelight and After	Claire Bloom
Little Clown, The	Reg Varney
Little Girl Lost	Drew Barrymore
Little Wilson and Big God (1987)	Anthony Burgess
Lonely Life, The (1962)	Bette Davis
Long Banana Skin, The	Michael Bentine
Long Walk to Freedom	Nelson Mandela
Lorenzo Goes to Hollywood	Edward Arnold
Love Is a Many-Splendoured Thing	Han Suyin
Love Is an Uphill Thing (1975)	Jimmy Savile
Man Who Listens to Horses, The	Monty Roberts
Martha, Jane and Me	Mavis Nicholson
Mask or Face (1958)	Michael Redgrave
Master of None	Gilbert Harding
Me	Katherine Hepburn
Mein Kampf	Adolf Hitler
Memoirs of a Professional Cad	George Sanders
Memories	Ethel Barrymore
Middle of My Century, The (1989)	Shelley Winters
Mingled Chime, A	Thomas Beecham
Minnie the Moocher and Me	Cab Calloway
Mirror in My House (1956)	Sean O' Casey
Moab is My Washpot	Stephen Fry
Moment of War, A	Laurie Lee
Moon's a Balloon, The	David Niven
More or Less (1978)	Kenneth More
Mother Goddam (1975)	Bette Davis
Movies, Mr Griffith and Me, The	Lilian Gish
Mr Nice	Howard Marks
Musician at Large	Steve Race
My American Journey	Colin Powell
My Days and Dreams	Edward Carpenter
My Double Life	Sarah Bernhardt
My Early Life (1981)	Ronald Reagan
My Life	Richard Wagner
My Life Line	Lady Isobel Barnett
My Lucky Stars: A Hollywood Memory (1989)	Shirley Maclaine
My Many Lives	Lotte Lehmann
My Name Escapes Me (1996)	Alec Guinness
My Story (1959)	Mary Astor
My Ten Years in the Studios (1940)	George Arliss
My Turn	Nancy Reagan
My Wicked Wicked Ways (1955)	Errol Flynn
Naked Civil Servant, The	Quentin Crisp
Nice One Cyril	Cyril Fletcher
Noa-Noa	Paul Gauguin
No Bed of Roses	Joan De Havilland
No Bells on Sunday	Rachel Roberts
Noble Essences (1950)	Osbert Sitwell
No Minor Chords	André Previn
Nostalgia Isnt What It Used to Be	Simone Signoret
Nothing's Impossible	Brian Blessed
Not the Whole Truth	Patrick Lichfield
Now and Then	Roy Castle
Oak and the Calf, The	Alexander Solzhenitsyn
Odd Man Out	Ronnie Biggs

Title	Author
Odd Woman Out	Muriel Box
On and Off the Fairway (1979)	Jack Nicklaus
One Day at a Time	Bernie Winters
One Hump or Two	Frank Worthington
One Man Tango	Anthony Quinn
One Small Footprint (1980)	Molly Weir
On My Way to the Club	Ludovic Kennedy
On Reflection (1969)	Helen Hayes
On the Other Hand	Fay Wray
On the Stage (1926)	George Arliss
Open Book, An	John Huston
Ordeal	Linda Lovelace
Orderly Man, An (1983)	Dirk Bogarde
Original Sin, The	Anthony Quinn
Other Half, The (1977)	Kenneth Clark
Other Side of the Street, The	Jean Alexander
Outline	Paul Nash
Out of Africa	Isak Dinesen / Karen Blixen
Out on a Limb	Heather Mills
Out on a Limb (1983)	Shirley MacLaine
Peacework (1991)	Spike Milligan
People	Edgar Wallace
Pictures in the Hallway (1942)	Sean O' Casey
Please Don't Hate Me	Dmitri Tiomkin
Point of View, A	Barry Took
Polly Wants a Zebra	Michael Aspel
Postillion Struck by Lightning, A (1977)	Dirk Bogarde
Precious Little Sleep	Wayne Sleep
Present Indicative (1937)	Noel Coward
Prick up Your Ears	Joe Orton
Quite Contrary	Mary Whitehouse
Ragman's Son, The	Kirk Douglas
Rebel with a Cause	Hans Eysenck
Reluctant Jester, The	Michael Bentine
Road to Hollywood (1977)	Bob Hope
Roamin' in the Gloaming	Sir Harry Lauder
Roar of the Crowd	Gentleman Jim Corbett
Runthrough (1972)	John Houseman
Scarlet Tree, The (1946)	Osbert Sitwell
Screening History	Gore Vidal
Second Act	Joan Collins
Self Consciousness	John Updike
Self Portrait	Gene Tierney
Shelley (1980)	Shelley Winters
Shoes Were for Sunday (1970)	Molly Weir
Shooting the Actor	Simon Callow
Short Walk from Harrods, A (1994)	Dirk Bogarde
Snakes and Ladders (1978)	Dirk Bogarde
Some Other Rainbow	John McCarthy and Jill Morrell
Spend Spend Spend	Vivian Nicholson
Stamp Album (1987)	Terence Stamp
Stand By Your Man	Tammy Wynette
Stare Back and Smile	Joanna Lumley
Steps in Time	Fred Astaire
Still Dancing	Lew Grade
Still on My Way to Hollywood	Ernie Wise
Story of a Bad Man	Thomas Aldrich
Story of a Soul, The	Thérèse of Lisieux
Straight Man, The	Nicholas Parsons
Straight Shooting	Robert Stack
Summoned by Bells	John Betjeman
Sunday Night at Seven	Jack Benny

Title	Author
Sunset and Evening Star (1955)	Sean O'Casey
Surprised by Joy	C.S. Lewis
Take It Like a Man	Boy George
Take My Life (1957)	Eddie Cantor
Taken on Trust	Terry Waite
Tall, Dark and Gruesome	Christopher Lee
Tell It to Louella (1962)	Louella Parsons
Testament of Youth	Vera Brittain
Testing Times	Graham Gooch
There's Always Tomorrow (1974)	Anna Neagle
There's Lovely	Johnny Morris
Things I Had to Learn, The	Loretta Young
Those Twentieth Century Blues	Michael Tippett
Thursday's Child	Eartha Kitt
Time and Chance	James Callaghan
Time to Declare	David Owen
To Hell and Back	Niki Lauda
To Hell and Back	Audie Murphy
To Keep the Ball Rolling	Anthony Powell
Travelling Player	Michael York
Tree Is a Tree, A	King Vidor
Twenty Questions	Norman Hackforth
Twice Over Lightly (1981)	Helen Hayes
Two-Way Story	Cliff Michelmore & Jean Metcalfe
Unreliable Memoirs	Clive James
Up in the Clouds, Gentlemen Please	John Mills
Up the Ladder to Obscurity	David Lodge
Up the Years from Bloomsbury (1927)	George Arliss
Vanished World, The (1969)	H.E. Bates
Vie d'Henri Brulard, La	Stendhal
Voyage (1978)	Sterling Hayden
Walking in the Shade	Doris Lessing
Walking Tall	Simon Weston
Wanderer (1963)	Sterling Hayden
Way I See It, The (1959)	Eddie Cantor
Wet Flanders Plain, The (1929)	Henry Williamson
What Falls Away	Mia Farrow
What's It All About	Michael Caine
When I Was Young	Raymond Massey
Where Have all the Bullets Gone (1985)	Spike Milligan
Where's Harry	Harry Carpenter
Where's the Rest of Me	Ronald Reagan
Why Me (1989)	Sammy Davis Jnr
Will This Do	Auberon Waugh
With Nails	Richard E. Grant
Words	Jean-Paul Sartre
World Elsewhere, A	Michael Hordern
World of Yesterday, The	Stefan Zweig
World Within World	Stephen Spender
Years of Opportunity, The (1947)	Barbara Cartland
Yes I Can (1966)	Sammy Davis Jnr
Yo Yo Man, The	Bill Maynard
You Can Get There from Here (1975)	Shirley MacLaine
Yours Indubitably	Robertson Hare
You've Had Your Time (1990)	Anthony Burgess
Zero to Hero	Frank Bruno

LITERATURE

NB: Dates are only provided when authors listed have more than one volume of autobiography or in instances where an author's identity may need clarification.

First lines of books and poems

Adams, Richard *Shardik* Even in the dry heat of summer's end, the great forest was never silent.

Agee, James *A Death in the Family* We are talking now of summer evenings in Knoxville, Tennessee in the time that I lived there so successfully disguised to myself as a child.

Alcott, Louisa May *Good Wives* In order that we may start afresh and go to Meg's wedding with free minds, it will be well to begin with a little gossip about the Marches.

Alcott, Louisa May *Little Men* Please, sir, is this Plumfield? asked a ragged boy of the man who opened the great gate at which the omnibus left him.

Alcott, Louisa May *Little Women* Christmas won't be Christmas without any presents, grumbled Jo, lying on the rug.

Angelou, Maya *I Know Why the Caged Bird Sings* When I was three and Bailey was four, we had arrived in the musty little town.

Arnold, Matthew 'Dover Beach' The sea is calm tonight. The tide is full, the moon lies fair.

Ashford, Daisy *The Young Visiters* Mr Salteena was an elderly man of 42 and was fond of asking peaple (sic) to stay with him.

Asimov, Isaac *Foundation* His name was Gaal Dornick and he was just a country boy who had never seen Trantor before.

Asimov, Isaac *I, Robot* I looked at my notes and I didn't like them. I'd spent three days at U.S. Robots and might as well have spent them at home with the Encyclopedia Tellurica.

Atwater, Richard & Florence *Mr. Popper's Penguins* It was an afternoon in late September. In the pleasant city of Stillwater, Mr. Popper, the house painter, was going home from work.

Atwood, Margaret *Cat's Eye* Time is not a line but a dimension, like the dimensions of space.

Auden, W.H. *Night Mail* This is the Night Mail crossing the border, bringing the cheque and the postal order.

Austen, Jane *Emma* Emma Woodhouse, handsome, clever, and rich, with a comfortable home and happy disposition, seemed to unite some of the best blessings of existence.

Austen, Jane *Mansfield Park* About thirty years ago, Miss Maria Ward of Huntingdon with only seven thousand pounds had the good luck to captivate Sir Thomas Bertram.

Austen, Jane *Northanger Abbey* No one who had ever seen Catherine Morland in her infancy would have supposed her born to be an heroine.

Austen, Jane *Persuasion* Sir Walter Elliot, of Kellynch Hall, in Somersetshire, was a man who, for his own amusement, never took up any book but the Baronetage . . .

Austen, Jane *Pride and Prejudice* It is a truth universally acknowledged, that a single man in possession of a good fortune, must be in want of a wife.

Austen, Jane *Sense and Sensibility* The family of Dashwood has long been settled in Sussex.

Baldwin, James *Go Tell It on the Mountain* Everyone had always said that John would be a preacher when he grew up, just like his father.

Banks, Lynne Reid *The Indian in the Cupboard* It

was not that Omri didn't appreciate Patrick's birthday present to him.

Barrie, J. M. *Peter Pan* All children, except one, grow up.

Barth, John *Giles Goat-Boy* George is my name; my deeds have been heard of in Tower Hall, and my childhood has been chronicled in the *Journal of Experimental Psychology*.

Barth, John *The Sot-Weed Factor* In the last years of the seventeenth century there was to be found among the fops & fools of the London coffee-houses one rangy, gangling flitch called Ebenezer Cooke, more ambitious than talented, and yet more talented than prudent.

Baum, Frank *The Wonderful Wizard of Oz* Dorothy lived in the midst of the great Kansas prairies, with Uncle Henry, who was a farmer, and Aunt Em, who was the farmer's wife.

Bellow, Saul *Herzog* If I am out of my mind, it's all right with me thought Moses Herzog.

Bellow, Saul *Humboldt's Gift* The book of ballads published by Von Humboldt Fleisher in the Thirties was an immediate hit.

Bemelmans, Ludwig *Madeline* In an old house in Paris that was covered with vines lived 12 little girls in two straight lines.

Benchley, Peter *Jaws* The great fish moved silently through the night water, propelled by short sweeps of its crescent tail.

Berryman, John *Homage to Mistress Bradstreet* The Governor your husband lived so long.

Bester, Alfred *The Stars My Destination* This was a Golden Age, a time of high adventure, rich living, and hard dying . . . but nobody thought so.

Betjeman, John 'A Subaltern's Love-Song' Miss J. Hunter Dunn, Miss J. Hunter Dunn, Furnish'd and burnish'd by Aldershot sun.

Blake, William 'Tyger!' Tyger! Tyger! burning bright In the forests of the night, What immortal hand or eye Could frame thy fearful symmetry?

Blatty, William Peter *The Exorcist* Like the brief doomed flare of exploding suns that registers dimly on blind men's eyes, the beginning of the horror passed almost unnoticed.

Böll, Heinrich *The Clown* It was dark by the time I reached Bonn, and I forced myself not to succumb to the series of mechanical actions which had taken hold of me in five years of travelling back and forth.

Boyle, T. Coraghessan *The Road to Wellville* Dr. John Harvey Kellogg, inventor of the cornflake and peanut butter, not to mention caramel-cereal coffee, Bromose, Nuttolene and some seventy-five other gastronomically correct foods, paused to level his gaze on the heavyset women in front of him.

Bradbury, Ray *Fahrenheit 451* It was a pleasure to burn.

Bradley, Marion Zimmer *Mists of Avalon* Even in high summer, Tintagel was a haunted place; Igraine, Lady of Duke Gorlois, looked out over the sea from the headland.

Braine, John *Life at the Top* She woke me up by lifting my eyelids; then she slipped under the bed clothes beside me and lay there smiling.

Brautigan, Richard *A Confederate General from Big Sur* When I first heard about Big Sur I didn't know that it was a member of the Confederate States of America.

Brontë, Anne   *Agnes Grey*   All true histories contain instruction, though in some, the treasure may be hard to find, and when found, so trivial in quantity that the dry shrivelled kernel scarcely compensates for the trouble of cracking the nut.

Brontë, Anne   *The Tenant of Wildfell Hall*   You must go back with me to the autumn of 1827.

Brontë, Charlotte   *Jane Eyre*   There was no possibility of taking a walk that day.

Brontë, Charlotte   *The Professor*   The other day, in looking over my papers, I found in my desk the following copy of a letter.

Brontë, Charlotte   *Villette*   My Godmother lived in a handsome house in the clean and ancient town of Bretton.

Brontë, Emily   *Wuthering Heights*   1801 – I have just returned from a visit to my landlord.

Brooke, Rupert   'The Soldier'   If I should die, think only this of me: That there's some corner of a foreign field That is forever England.

Brown, Margaret Wise   *Goodnight Moon*   In the great green room, there was a telephone and a red balloon.

Brown, Rita Mae   *Rubyfruit Jungle*   No one remembers her beginnings.

Brown, Rita Mae   *Venus Envy*   Dying's not so bad. At least I won't have to answer the telephone.

Browning, Elizabeth Barrett   'How Do I Love Thee'   How do I love thee? Let me count the ways. .

Browning, Robert   'Childe Roland to the Dark Tower Came'   My first thought was, he lied in every word.

Browning, Robert   'Home-Thoughts: from Abroad'   Oh, to be in England now that April's there . . .

Buchan, John   *The Thirty-Nine Steps*   I returned from the city about three o'clock on that May afternoon, pretty well disgusted with life.

Buck, Pearl   *The Good Earth*   It was Wang Lung's marriage day.

Bulwer-Lytton, Edward   *Paul Clifford*   It was a dark and stormy night and the rain fell in torrents – except at occasional intervals, when it was checked by a violent gust of wind which swept up the streets (for it is in London that our scene lies), rattling along the housetops, and fiercely agitating the scanty flame of the lamps that struggled against the darkness.

Bunyan, John   *The Pilgrim's Progress*   As I walked through the wilderness of this world, I !ighted on a certain place where was a Den, and I laid me down in that place to sleep: and, as I slept, I dreamed a dream.

Burgess, Anthony   *A Clockwork Orange*   What's it going to be then, eh?

Burgess, Anthony   *Earthly Powers*   It was the afternoon of my eighty-first birthday and I was in bed with my catamite when Ali announced that the Archbishop had come to see me.

Burnett, Frances Hodgson   *A Little Princess*   Once on a dark winter's day, when the yellow fog hung so thick and heavy in the streets of London that the lamps were lighted and the shop windows blazed with gas as they do at night, an odd-looking little girl sat in a cab with her father and was driven rather slowly through the big thoroughfares.

Burnett, Frances Hodgson   *The Secret Garden*   When Mary Lennox was sent to Misselthwaite Manor to live with her uncle everybody said she was the most disagreeable-looking child ever seen.

Burns, Robert   'A Red Red Rose'   O my luve's like a red, red rose, That's newly sprung in June.

Burns, Robert   'To a Field Mouse'   Wee, sleekit, cow'rin', tim'rous beastie, O what a panic's in thy breastie.

Butler, Samuel   *The Way of All Flesh*   When I was a small boy at the beginning of the century I remember an old man who wore knee-breeches and worsted stockings, and used to hobble about the street of our village with the help of a stick.

Byron, Lord   'She Walks in Beauty'   She walks in beauty, like the night Of cloudless climes and starry skies.

Caldwell, Taylor   *Great Lion of God*   He is very ugly, said his mother.

Camus, Albert   *The Stranger*   Mother died today. Or perhaps it was yesterday, I don't know.

Capote, Truman   *Breakfast at Tiffany's*   I am always drawn back to the places where I have lived, the houses & their neighborhoods.

Capote, Truman   *In Cold Blood*   The village of Holcomb stands on the high wheat plains of western Kansas, a lonesome area that other Kansans call 'out there'.

Carey, Peter   *Jack Maggs*   It was a Saturday night when the man with the red waistcoat arrived in London.

Carroll, Lewis   *Alice's Adventures in Wonderland*   Alice was beginning to get very tired of sitting by her sister on the bank, and of having nothing to do: once or twice she had peeped into the book her sister was reading, but it had no pictures or conversations in it, 'and what is the use of a book, thought Alice 'without pictures or conversation?'

Carroll, Lewis   *Through the Looking Glass and What Alice Found There;*   One thing was certain, that the *white* kitten had had nothing to do with it – it was the black kitten's fault entirely.

Castaneda, Carlos   *The Teachings of Don Juan*   My notes on my first session with don Juan are dated June 23,1961.

Cather, Willa   *My Ántonia*   I first heard of Ántonia on what seemed to me an interminable journey across the great midland plains of North America.

Cervantes, Miguel de   *Don Quixote*   At a village of La Mancha, whose name I do not wish to remember, there lived a little while ago one of those gentlemen who are wont to keep a lance in the rack, an old buckler, a lean horse and a swift greyhound.

Chandler, Raymond   *The Big Sleep*   It was about eleven o'clock in the morning, mid-October, with the sun not shining and a look of hard wet rain in the clearness of the foothills.

Chang, Jung   *Wild Swans*   At the age of fifteen my grandmother became the concubine of a warlord general.

Chaucer, Geoffrey   *The Canterbury Tales*   Whan that Aprill with his shoures soote The droghte of March hath perced to the roote.

Chesterton, G. K.   *The Man Who Was Thursday*   The suburb of Saffron Park lay on the sunset side of London, as red and ragged as a cloud of sunset.

Chesterton, G. K.   *The Donkey*   When fishes flew and forests walked and figs grew upon thorn.

Chopin, Kate   *The Awakening*   A green and yellow parrot, which hung in a cage outside the door, kept repeating over and over: 'Allez vous-en! Allez vous-en ! Sapristi ! That's all right !'

LITERATURE

Christie, Agatha *The Mirror Crack'd* Miss Jane Marple was sitting by her window.

Clarke, Arthur C. *Childhood's End* The Volcano that had reared Taratua up from the Pacific depths had been sleeping now for half a million years. Yet in a little while, thought Reinhold, the island would be bathed in fires fiercer than any that had attended its birth.

Clarke, Arthur C. *The City and the Stars* Like a glowing jewel, the city lay upon the breast of the desert. Once it had known change and alteration, but now time passed it by. Night and day fled across the desert's face, but in Diaspar it was always afternoon, and darkness never came.

Clarke, Arthur C. *2001: A Space Odyssey* The drought had lasted now for ten million years, and the reign of the terrible lizards had long since ended.

Cleland, John *Fanny Hill* Madam, I sit down to give you an undeniable proof of my considering your desires as indispensable orders.

Collins, Wilkie *The Moonstone* In the first part of Robinson Crusoe, at page one hundred and twenty-nine, you will find it thus written: 'Now I saw, though too late, the Folly of beginning a Work before we count the Cost, and before we judge rightly of our own strength to go through with it.'

Collins, Wilkie *The Woman in White* This is the story of what a Woman's patience can endure, and what a Man's resolution can achieve.

Condon, Richard *Prizzi's Honor* Corrado Prizzi's granddaughter was being married before the baroque altar of Santa Grazia de Traghetto, the lucky church of the Prizzi family.

Conrad, Joseph *Heart of Darkness* Nellie, a cruising yawl, swung to her anchor without a flutter of sails, and was at rest.

Conrad, Joseph *Lord Jim* He was an inch, perhaps two, under six feet, powerfully built, and he advanced straight at you with a slight stoop of the shoulders, head forward, and a fixed from-under stare which made you think of a charging bull.

Conrad, Joseph *Nostromo* In the time of Spanish rule, and for many years afterwards, the town of Sulaco – the luxuriant beauty of the orange gardens bears witness to its antiquity – had never been commercially anything more important than a coasting port with a fairly large local trade in ox-hides and indigo.

Conrad, Joseph *An Outcast of the Islands* When he stepped off the straight and narrow path of his peculiar honesty, it was with an inward assertion of unflinching resolve.

Conrad, Joseph *The Secret Agent* Mr Verloc, going out in the morning, left his shop nominally in charge of his brother-in-law.

Coolidge, Susan *What Katy Did Next* The September sun was glinting cheerfully into a pretty bedroom furnished with blue.

Cooper, James Fenimore *The Last of the Mohicans* It was a feature peculiar to the colonial wars of North America, that the toils and dangers of the wilderness were to be encountered before the adverse hosts could meet.

Crane, Stephen *The Red Badge of Courage* The cold passed reluctantly from the earth, and the retiring fogs revealed an army stretched out on the hills, resting.

Dahl, Roald *Charlie and the Chocolate Factory* These two very old people are the father and mother of Mr. Bucket.

Dante, Alighieri *Divine Comedy* Midway along the path of life.

Davies, Robertson *The Cunning Man* Should I have taken the false teeth?

Davies, W.H. 'Leisure' What is this life if, full of care, We have no time to stand and stare?

Defoe, Daniel *Robinson Crusoe* I was born in the year 1632, in the city of York, of a good family, though not of that country, my father being a foreigner of Bremen, who settled first at Hull. He got a good estate by merchandise, and leaving off his trade lived afterward at York, from whence he had married my mother, whose relations were named Robinson, a good family in that country, and from whom I was called Robinson Kreutznear.

Deighton, Len *Catch a Falling Spy* Smell that air, said Major Mann.

Deighton, Len *The Ipcress File* They came through on the hot line at about half past two in the afternoon.

De La Mare, Walter 'The Listeners' 'Is there anybody there?' said the Traveller, Knocking on the moonlit door.

Dick, Philip, K. *Do Androids Dream of Electric Sheep?* A merry little surge of electricity piped by automatic alarm from the mood organ beside his bed awakened Rick Deckard.

Dickens, Charles *Barnaby Rudge* In the year 1775, there stood upon the borders of Epping Forest, at a distance of about twelve miles from London – measuring the Standard in Cornhill, or rather from the spot on or near to which the Standard used to be in days of yore – a house of public entertainment called the Maypole; which fact was demonstrated to all such travellers as could neither read nor write (and at that time a vast number both of travellers and stay-at-homes were in this condition) by the emblem reared on the roadside over and against the house, which, if not of those goodly proportions that Maypoles were wont to present in olden times, was a fair young ash, thirty feet in height, and straight as any arrow that ever English yeoman drew.

Dickens, Charles *Bleak House* London. Michaelmas term lately over, and the Lord Chancellor sitting in Lincoln's Inn Hall.

Dickens, Charles *A Christmas Carol* Marley was dead, to begin with. There is no doubt whatever about that.

Dickens, Charles *David Copperfield* Whether I shall turn out to be the hero of my own life, or whether that station will be held by anybody else, these pages must show.

Dickens, Charles *Dombey and Son* Dombey sat in the corner of the darkened room in the great armchair by the bedside, and Son lay tucked up in a warm little basket bedstead, carefully disposed on a low settee immediately in front of the fire and close to it, as if his constitution were analogous to that of a muffin, and it was essential to toast him brown while he was very new.

Dickens, Charles *Great Expectations* My father's family name being Pirrip, and my christian name Philip, my infant tongue could make of both names nothing longer or more explicit than Pip.

Dickens, Charles *Hard Times* Now, what I want is Facts.

Dickens, Charles *Little Dorrit* Thirty years ago, Marseilles lay burning in the sun, one day.

Dickens, Charles *Martin Chuzzlewit* As no lady or

gentleman, with any claims to polite breeding, can possibly sympathise with the Chuzzlewit Family without being first assured of the extreme antiquity of the race, it is a great satisfaction to know that it undoubtedly descended in a direct line from Adam and Eve; and was, in the very earliest times, closely connected with the agricultural interest.

Dickens, Charles *The Mystery of Edwin Drood* An ancient English Cathedral Tower?.

Dickens, Charles *Nicholas Nickleby* There once lived, in a sequestered part of the county of Devonshire, one Mr Godfrey Nickleby: a worthy gentleman, who, taking it into his head rather late in life that he must get married, and not being young enough or rich enough to aspire to the hand of a lady of fortune, had wedded an old flame out of mere attachment, who in her turn had taken him for the same reason.

Dickens, Charles *The Old Curiosity Shop* Night is generally my time for walking.

Dickens, Charles *Oliver Twist* Among other public buildings in a certain town, which for many reasons it will be prudent to refrain from mentioning, and to which I will assign no fictitious name, there is one anciently common to most towns, great or small – to wit, a workhouse; and in this workhouse was born, on a day and date which I need not trouble myself to repeat, inasmuch as it can be of no possible consequence to the reader, in this stage of the business at all events, the item of mortality whose name is prefixed to the head of this chapter.

Dickens, Charles *Our Mutual Friend* In these times of ours, though concerning the exact year there is no need to be precise, a boat of dirty and disreputable appearance, with two figures in it, floated on the Thames, between Southwark Bridge which is of iron, and London Bridge which is of stone, as an autumn evening was closing in.

Dickens, Charles *Pickwick Papers* The first ray of light which illumines the gloom, and converts into a dazzling brilliancy that obscurity in which the earlier history of the public career of the immortal Pickwick would appear to be involved, is derived from the perusal of the following entry in the transactions of the Pickwick Club, which the editor of these papers feels the highest pleasure in laying before his readers as a proof of the careful attention, indefatigable assiduity, and nice discrimination, with which his search among the multifarious documents confided to him has been conducted.

Dickens, Charles *A Tale of Two Cities* It was the best of times, it was the worst of times, it was the age of wisdom, it was the age of foolishness, it was the epoch of belief, it was the epoch of incredulity, it was the season of Light, it was the season of Darkness, it was the spring of hope, it was the winter of despair, we had everything before us, we had nothing before us, we were all going direct to Heaven, we were all going direct the other way – in short, the period was so.

Dickinson, Emily untitled poem I heard a Fly buzz – when I died . . .

Doctorow, E. L. *Ragtime* In 1902 Father built a house at the crest of the Broadview Avenue hill in New Rochelle, New York.

Dos Passos, John *1919* Oh the infantree the infantree With the dirt behind their ears ARMIES CLASH AT VERDUN IN GLOBE'S GREATEST BATTLE 150,000 MEN AND WOMEN PARADE

but another question and a very important one is raised.

Dostoevsky, Fyodor *The Brothers Karamazov* Alexey Fyodorovitch Karamazov was the third son of Fyodor Pavlovitch Karamazov, a landowner well known in our district in his own day, and still remembered among us owing to his gloomy and tragic death, which happened thirteen years ago, and which I shall describe in its proper place.

Dostoevsky, Fyodor *Crime and Punishment* On an exceptionally hot evening early in July a young man came out of the garret in which he lodged in S. Place and walked slowly, as though in hesitation, towards K. bridge.

Doyle, Sir Arthur Conan *The Hound of the Baskervilles* Mr. Sherlock Holmes, who was usually very late in the mornings, save upon those not infrequent occasions when he was up all night, was seated at the breakfast table.

Dryden, John *Absalom and Achitophel* In pious times, ere priestcraft did begin. . .

Du Maurier, Daphne *The King's General* September 1653. The last of summer. The first chill winds of autumn.

Du Maurier, Daphne *Rebecca* Last night I dreamt I went to Manderley again.

Dumas, Alexandre *The Count of Monte Cristo* On the 24th of February, 1815, the lookout of Notre Dame de la Garde signalled the three-master, the *Pharaon*, from Smyrna, Trieste, and Naples. As usual, a pilot put off immediately, and rounding the Chateau d'If, got on board the vessel between Cape Morgion and the Isle of Rion.

Dumas, Alexandre *The Three Musketeers* On the first Monday of the month of April, 1625, the town of Meung, in which the author of The Romance of the Rose was born, appeared to be in a perfect state of revolution as if the Huguenots had just made a second Rochelle of it.

Eliot, George *Middlemarch* Miss Brooke had that kind of beauty which seems to be thrown into relief by poor dress.

Eliot, George *The Mill on the Floss* A wide plain, where the broadening Floss hurries on between its green banks to the sea, and the loving tide, rushing to meet it, checks its passage with an impetuous embrace.

Eliot, George *Silas Marner* In the days when the spinning-wheels hummed busily in the farmhouses – and even great ladies, clothed in silk and thread-lace, had their toy spinning-wheels of polished oak – there might be seen in districts far away among the lanes, or deep in the bosom of the hills, certain pallid undersized men, who, by the side of the brawny country-folk, looked like the remnants of a disinherited race.

Eliot, T.S. *East Coker* In my beginning is my end.

Eliot, T.S. 'The Love Song of J. Alfred Prufrock' Let us go then, you and I . . .

Ellison, Ralph *Invisible Man* I am an invisible man.

Farmer, Philip Jose *To Your Scattered Bodies Go* His wife had held him in her arms as if she could keep death away from him. He had cried out, 'My God, I am a dead man!'

Faulkner, William *Go Down, Moses* Isaac McCaslin, 'Uncle Ike', past seventy and nearer eighty than he ever corroborated any more, a widower now and uncle to half a country and father to one.

Faulkner, William *Sanctuary* From behind the screen of bushes which surrounded the spring, Popeye watched the man drinking.

Faulkner, William *The Sound and the Fury*
Through the fence, between the curling flower
spaces, I could see them hitting.

Fielding, Ian *Tom Jones* An author ought to
consider himself not as a gentleman who gives a
private or eleemosynary treat.

Fitzgerald, F. Scott *The Great Gatsby* In my
younger and more vulnerable years my father gave
me some advice that I've been turning over in my
mind ever since.

Flaubert, Gustave *Madame Bovary* We were in the
study-hall when the headmaster entered, followed by
a new boy not yet in school uniform and by the
handyman carrying a large desk.

Fleming, Ian *Chitty-Chitty-Bang-Bang* Most
motorcars are conglomerations (this is a long word
for bundles) of steel and wire and rubber and plastic,
and electricity and oil and gasoline and water, and
the toffee papers you pushed down the crack in the
back seat last Sunday.

Fleming, Ian *Goldfinger* James Bond, with two
double bourbons inside him, sat back in the final
departure lounge of Miami Airport and thought about
life and death.

Ford, Ford Madox *The Good Soldier* This is the
saddest story I have ever heard.

Forster, E.M. *A Passage to India* Except for the
Marabar Caves – and they are twenty miles off – the
city of Chandrapore presents nothing extraordinary.

Forsyth, Frederick *The Odessa File* Everybody
seems to remember what they were doing on
November 22nd 1963, when Kennedy was shot.

Fowles, John *The French Lieutenant's Woman* An
easterly is the most disagreeable wind in Lyme Bay –
Lyme Bay being that largest byte from the underside of
England's outstretched southwestern leg – and a
person of curiousity could at once have deduced
several strong probabilities about the pair who began
to walk down the quay at Lyme Regis, the small but
ancient eponym of the inbite, one incisively sharp and
blustery morning in the late March of 1867.

Gallico, Paul *The Poseidon Adventure* At seven
o'clock, the morning of the 26th of December, the
S.S. *Poseidon*, 81,000 tons, homeward bound for
Lisbon after a month-long Christmas cruise to African
and South American ports, suddenly found herself in
the midst of an unaccountable swell, 400 miles south-
west of the Azores, and began to roll like a pig.

Galsworthy, John *The Man of Property* Those
privileged to be present at a family festival of the
Forsythes have seen that charming and instructive
sight – an upper middle class family in full plumage.

Gardner, John *Grendel* The old ram stands looking
down over rockslides, stupidly triumphant.

Gibson, William *Neuromancer* The sky above the
port was the color of television, tuned to a dead
channel.

Gide, André *The Fruits of the Earth* Do not hope,
Nathaniel, to find God here or there – but
everywhere.

Gipson, Fred *Old Yeller* We called him Old Yeller.

Golding, William *Lord of the Flies* The boy with fair
hair lowered himself down the last few feet of rock
and began to pick his way towards the lagoon.

Golding, William *The Princess Bride* This is my
favorite book in all the world, though I have never
read it.

Goldman, William *Marathon Man* Everytime he
drove through Yorkville, Rosenbaum got angry, just
on general principles.

Goldsmith, Oliver 'Elegy on the Death of a Mad
Dog' Good people all, of every sort, Give ear unto
my song.

Grahame, Kenneth *The Wind in the Willows* The
Mole had been working very hard all the morning,
spring-cleaning his little home.

Grass, Günter *The Tin Drum* Granted: I am an
inmate of a mental hospital; my keeper is watching
me, he never lets me out of his sight; there's a
peephole in the door, and my keeper's eye is the
shade of brown that can never see through a blue-
eyed type like me.

Graves, Robert *I, Claudius* I, Tiberius Claudius
Drusus Nero Germanicus This-that-and-the-other
(for I shall not trouble you yet with all my titles) who
was once, and not so long ago either, known to my
friends and relatives and associates as 'Claudius the
Idiot', or 'That Claudius', or 'Claudius the
Stammerer', or 'Clau-Clau-Claudius' or at best as
'Poor Uncle Claudius', am now about to write this
strange history of my life; starting from my earliest
childhood and continuing year by year until I reach
the fateful point of change where, some eight years
ago, at the age of fifty-one, I suddenly found myself
caught in what I may call the 'golden predicament'
from which I have never since become disentangled.

Gray, Thomas 'Elegy Written in a Country
Churchyard' The curfew tolls the knell of parting
day . . .

Gray, Thomas 'The Progress of Poesy' Awake,
Aeolian lyre, awake

Greene, Graham *The Power and the Glory* Mr
Tench went out to look for his ether cylinder, into the
blazing Mexican sun.

Greene, Graham *The Quiet American* After dinner I
sat and waited for Pyle in my room over the rue
Catinat: he had said, 'I'll be with you at latest by ten,'
and when midnight had struck I couldn't stay quiet
any longer and went down into the street.

Guterson, David *Snow Falling on Cedars* The
accused man, Kabuo Miyamoto, sat proudly upright
with a rigid grace.

Høeg, Peter *Miss Smilla's Feeling for Snow* It's
freezing – an extraordinary 0º fahrenheit – and it's
snowing, and in the language that is no longer mine
the snow is qanik –

Haggard, H. Rider *King Solomon's Mines* It is a
curious thing that at my age, fifty-five last birthday, I
should find myself taking up a pen to try and write a
history.

Haggard, H. Rider *She* There are some events of
which each circumstance and surrounding detail
seem to be graven on the memory in such a fashion
that we cannot forget them.

Hailey, Arthur *Airport* At half-past six on a Friday
evening in January, Lincoln International Airport,
Illinois, was functioning, though with difficulty.

Haley, Alex *Roots* Early in the spring of 1750, in
the village of Juffure, four days upriver from the
coast of Gambia, West Africa, a manchild was born
to Omoro and Binta Kinte.

Hammett, Dashiell *The Maltese Falcon* Samuel
Spade's jaw was long and bony, his chin a jutting 'V'
under the more flexible 'V' of his mouth.

Hammett, Dashiell *The Thin Man* I was leaning
against a bar in a speak-easy on Fifty-second Street,
waiting for Nora to finish her Christmas shopping,
when a girl got up from the table where she had
been sitting.

Hardy, Thomas *Far from the Madding Crowd* When

Farmer Oak smiled, the corners of his mouth spread till they were within an unimportant distance of his ears, his eyes were reduced to chinks, and diverging wrinkles appeared round them, extending upon his countenance like the rays in a rudimentary sketch of the rising sun.

Hardy, Thomas *Jude the Obscure* The schoolmaster was leaving the village, and everybody seemed sorry.

Hardy, Thomas *The Mayor of Casterbridge* One evening of late summer, before the nineteenth century had reached one-third of its span, a young man and woman, the latter carrying a child, were approaching the large village of Weydon-Priors, in Upper Wessex, on foot.

Hardy, Thomas *Tess of the D'Urbervilles* On an evening in the latter part of May a middle-aged man was walking homeward from Shaston to the village of Marlott, in the adjoining Vale of Blakemore or Blackmoor.

Harris, Robert *Fatherland* Thick cloud had pressed down on Berlin all night and now it was lingering into what passed for morning.

Hartley, L.P. *The Go-Between* The past is a foreign country, they do things differently there.

Hawthorne, Nathaniel *The House of the Seven Gables* Halfway down a bystreet of one of our New England towns stands a rusty wooden house, with seven acutely peaked gables, facing towards various points of the compass, and a huge, clustered chimney in the midst.

Hawthorne, Nathaniel *The Scarlet Letter* A throng of bearded men, in sad-colored garments and gray, steeple-crowned hats, intermixed with women, some wearing hoods, and others bareheaded, was assembled in front of a wooden edifice, the door of which was heavily timbered with oak, and studded with iron spikes.

Heinlein, Robert *The Moon Is a Harsh Mistress* I see in *Lunaya Pravda* that Luna City Council has passed on first reading a bill to examine, license, inspect – and tax – public food vendors operating inside municipal pressure.

Heinlein, Robert *Stranger in a Strange Land* Once upon a time there was a Martian named Valentine Michael Smith.

Heller, Joseph *Catch-22* It was love at first sight.

Heller, Joseph *Something Happened* I get the willies when I see closed doors.

Hemans, Felicia 'Casabianca' The boy stood on the burning deck, Whence all but he had fled.

Hemingway, Ernest *The Old Man and the Sea* He was an old man who fished alone in a skiff in the Gulf stream and he had gone 84 days now without taking a fish.

Herrick, Robert 'To the Virgins, to Make Much of Time' Gather ye rosebuds while ye may, Old Time is still a-flying.

Hesse, Hermann *Siddhartha* In the shade of the house, in the sunshine on the river bank by the boats, in the shade of the sallow wood and the fig tree, Siddharta, the handsome Brahmin's son, grew up with his friend Govinda.

Higgins, Colin *Harold and Maude* Harold Chasen stepped up on the chair and placed the noose about his neck.

Hoban, Russell *Riddley Walker* On my naming day when I come 12 I gone front spear and kilt a wyld boar he parbly ben the las wyld pig on the Bundel.

Homer *The Odyssey* By now the other warriors, those that had escaped head-long ruin by sea or in a battle, were safely home.

Hopkins, Gerard Manley 'The Wreck of the Deutschland' Thou mastering me . . .

Hughes, Thomas *Tom Brown's Schooldays* The Browns have been illustrious by the pen of Thackeray and the pencil of Doyle.

Hugo, Victor *The Hunchback of Notre-Dame* It was three hundred forty-eight years, six months, and nineteen days ago today that the citizens of Paris were awakened by the pealing of all the bells in the triple precincts of the City, the University, and the Town.

Hugo, Victor *Les Misérables* In 1815, M. Charles-François-Bienvenu Myriel was Bishop of D—.

Hurston, Zora Neale *Their Eyes Were Watching God* Ships at a distance have every man's wish on board.

Huxley, Aldous *Brave New World* A squat gray building of only thirty-four stories. Over the main entrance the words CENTRAL LONDON HATCHERY AND CONDITIONING CENTRE, and in a shield the World State's motto, Community, Identity, Stability.

Huxley, Aldous *Crome Yellow* Along this particular stretch of line, no express had ever passed.

Irving, John *The Hotel New Hampshire* The summer my father bought the bear, none of us was born – we weren't even conceived: not Frank, the oldest; not Fanny, the loudest; not me, the next; and not the youngest of us, Lilly and Egg.

Irving, John *A Prayer for Owen Meany* I am doomed to remember a boy with a wrecked voice – not because of his voice, or because he was the smallest person I ever knew, or even because he was the instrument of my mother's death, but because he is the reason I believe in God; I am a Christian because of Owen Meany.

Irving, John *The World According to Garp* Garp's mother, Jenny Fields, was arrested in Boston in 1942 for wounding a man in a movie theater.

Jacques, Brian *Redwall* Mathias cut a comical figure as he hobbled his way along the cloisters, with his large sandals flip-flopping and his tail peeping from beneath the baggy folds of an oversized novice's habit.

James, Henry *The Turn of the Screw* The story had held us, round the fire, sufficiently breathless, but except the obvious remark that it was gruesome, as, on Christmas Eve in an old house, a strange tale should essentially be, I remember no comment uttered till somebody happened to say that it was the only case he had met in which such a visitation had fallen on a child.

Jong, Erica *Fear of Flying* There were 117 psychoanalysts on the Pan Am flight to Vienna and I'd been treated by at least six of them.

Jonson, Ben 'To Celia' Drink to me only with thine eyes: and I will pledge with mine.

Joyce, James *Dubliners* There was no hope for him this time: it was the third stroke.

Joyce, James *Portrait of the Artist as a Young Man* Once upon a time and a very good time it was there was a moocow coming down along the road and this moocow that was coming down along the road met a nicens little boy named baby tuckoo.

Joyce, James *Ulysses* Stately plump Buck Mulligan came from the stairhead, bearing a bowl of lather on which a mirror and a razor lay crossed.

Juster, Norton *The Phantom Tollbooth* There was a boy named Milo who didn't know what to do with himself . . .

Kafka, Franz 'Metamorphosis' As Gregor Samsa awoke one morning from uneasy dreams, he found himself transformed into a giant insect.

Kafka, Franz *The Trial* Someone must have been telling lies about Joseph K, for without having done anything wrong he was arrested one fine morning.

Keats, John 'La Belle Dame Sans Merci' Oh, What can ail thee, knight at arms Alone and palely loitering.

Keats, John *Hyperion* Deep in the shady sadness of a vale . . .

Keats, John 'On First Looking into Chapman's Homer' Much have I travell'd in the realms of gold, And many goodly states and kingdoms seen.

Keats, John 'To Autumn' Season of mists and mellow fruitfulness, close bosom-friend of the maturing sun.

Kennedy, William *Quinn's Book* I, Daniel Quinn, neither the first nor the last of a line of such Quinn's, set eyes on Maud the wondrous on a late December day in 1849 on the banks of the river of the aristocrats and paupers, just as the great courtesan Magdalena Colón, also known as La Última, a woman whose presence turned men into spittling, masturbating pigs, boarded a skiff to carry her across the river's icy water from Albany to Greenbush, her first stop en route to the city of Troy, a community of iron, where later that evening she was scheduled to enact, yet again, her role as the lascivious Lais, that fabled prostitute who spurned Demosthenes' gold and yielded free to Diogenes, the virtuous, impecunious tub-dweller.

King, Stephen *Carrie* Nobody was really surprised when it happened, not really, not on the subconscious level where savage things grow.

King, Stephen *Cujo* Not so long ago, a monster came to the small town of Castle Rock, Maine.

Kingsolver, Barbara *The Bean Trees* I have been afraid of putting air in a tire ever since I saw a tractor tire blow up and throw Newt Hardbines's father over the top of the Standard Oil sign.

Kingsolver, Barbara *Pigs in Heaven* Women on their own run in Alice's family.

Kipling, Rudyard 'Gunga Din' You may talk o'gin and beer, when you're quartered safe out 'ere.

Kipling, Rudyard 'If' If you can keep your head when all about you are losing theirs and blaming it on you.

Kipling, Rudyard *The Jungle Book* It was seven o'clock of a very warm evening in the Seeonee hills when Father Wolf woke up from his day's rest, scratched himself, yawned, and spread out his paws one after the other to get rid of the sleepy feeling in their tips.

Kipling, Rudyard *Kim* He sat in defiance of municipal orders, astride the gun of Zam-Zammeh on her brick platform opposite the old Ajaibgher – the Wonder House, as the natives called the Lahore Museum.

Kipling, Rudyard *Stalky and Co* In summer all right-minded boys built huts in the furze-hill behind the College – little lairs whittled out of the heart of the prickly bushes, full of stumps, odd root-ends, and spikes, but, since they were strictly forbidden, palaces of delight.

Knowles, John *A Separate Peace* I went back to the Devon School not long ago, and found it looking oddly newer than when I was a student there fifteen years before.

Kosinski, Jerzy *The Painted Bird* In the first weeks of World War II, in the fall of 1939, a six year old boy from a large city in Eastern Europe was sent by his parents, like thousands of other children, to the shelter of a distant village.

Kundera, Milan *The Unbearable Lightness of Being* The idea of eternal return is a mysterious one, and Nietzsche has often perplexed other philosophers with it: to think that everything recurs as we once experienced it, and that the recurrence itself recurs ad infinitum! What does this mad myth signify?

L'Engle, Madeline *A Wrinkle In Time* It was a dark and stormy night.

Lawrence, D. H. *Lady Chatterley's Lover* Ours is essentially a tragic age, so we refuse to take it tragically.

Lawrence, D. H. *Sons and Lovers* 'The Bottoms' succeeded to 'Hell Row'.

Lawrence, D. H. *Women In Love* Ursula and Gudrun Brangwen sat one morning in the window-bay of their father's house in Beldover, working and talking.

Le Carré, John *The Honourable Schoolboy* Afterwards, in the dusty little corners where London's secret servants drink together, there was argument about where the Dolphin case history should really begin.

Le Carré, John *The Spy Who Came in from the Cold* The American handed Leamas another cup of coffee and said, 'Why don't you go back and sleep? We can ring you if he shows up.'

Le Carré, John *Tinker, Tailor, Soldier, Spy* The truth is, if old Major Dover hadn't dropped dead at Taunton races Jim would never have come to Thursgood's at all.

Lee, Harper *To Kill a Mockingbird* When he was nearly thirteen, my brother Jem got his arm badly broken at the elbow.

Le Guin, Ursula *The Dispossessed* There was a wall.

Le Guin, Ursula *The Left Hand of Darkness* I'll make my report as if I told a story, for I was taught as a child on my homeworld that Truth is a matter of the imagination.

Leroux, Gaston *The Phantom of the Opera* It was the evening on which MM. Debienne and Poligny, the managers of the Opera, were giving a last gala performance to mark their retirement.

Levin, Ira *Rosemary's Baby* Rosemary and Guy Woodhouse had signed a lease on a five-room apartment in a geometric white house on First Avenue when they received word, from a woman named Mrs. Cortez, that a four-room apartment in Bramford had become available.

Lewis, C. S. *The Lion, the Witch and the Wardrobe* Once there were four children whose names were Peter, Susan, Edmond, and Lucy.

Lewis, Sinclair *Babbitt* The tower of Zenith aspired above the morning mist; austere towers of steel and cement and limestone, sturdy as cliffs and delicate as silver rods.

Lewis, Sinclair *Elmer Gantry* Elmer Gantry was drunk. He was eloquently drunk, lovingly and pugnaciously drunk.

Lewis, Sinclair *Main Street* This is America – a town of a few thousand, in a region of wheat and corn and dairies and little groves. The town is, in our tale, called 'Gopher Prairie, Minnesota.' But its Main Street is the continuation of Main Streets everywhere.

London, Jack *The Call of the Wild* Buck did not read the newspapers or he would have known that trouble was brewing.

Longfellow, Henry Wadsworth *The Song of Hiawatha* Should you ask me, whence these stories?

Longfellow, Henry Wadsworth 'The Village Blacksmith' Under a spreading chestnut tree The village smithy stands.

Lovecraft, H.P. *The Call Of Cthulhu* The most merciful thing in the world, I think, is the inability of the human mind to correlate all its contents.

Macaulay, Rose *The Towers of Trebizond* 'Take my camel dear', said my aunt Dot, as she climbed down from this animal on her return from High Mass.

McCloskey, Robert *Make Way for Ducklings* Mr. and Mrs. Mallard were looking for a place to live.

McCullough, Colleen *The First Man in Rome* Having no personal commitment to either of the new consuls, Gaius Julius Caesar and his son simply tacked themselves onto the procession which started nearest to their own house, the procession of the senior consul, Marcus Minucius Rufus.

McCullough, Colleen *The Thorn Birds* On December 8th, 1915, Meggie Cleary had her fourth birthday.

McCullough, Colleen *Caesar's Women* Brutus, I don't like the look of your skin. Come here to the light, please.

McCullers, Carson *The Heart Is a Lonely Hunter* In the town there were two mutes, and they were always together.

MacDonald, Betty *Mrs. Piggle Wiggle* I expect I might as well begin by telling you about Mrs. Piggle-Wiggle.

McEwan, Ian *Enduring Love* The beginning is simple to mark.

McKenna, Richard *The Sand Pebbles* Hello, ship, Jake Holman said under his breath.

McMillan, Terry *Waiting to Exhale* Right now I'm supposed to be all geeked up because I'm getting ready for a New Year's Eve party that some guy named Lionel invited me to.

McMurtry, Larry *Terms of Endearment* The success of a marriage invariably depends on the woman, Mrs. Greenway said.

Malamud, Bernard *The Fixer* From the small crossed window of his room above the stable in the brickyard, Yakov Bok saw people in their long overcoats running somewhere early that morning, everybody in the same direction.

Mann, Thomas *Buddenbrooks* And – and – what comes next? Oh, yes, yes, what the dickens does come next? C'est la question, ma très chère demoiselle! Frau Consul Buddenbrooks shot a glance at her husband and came to the rescue of her daughter.

Márquez, Gabriel García *One Hundred Years of Solitude* Many years later, as he faced the firing squad, Colonel Aureliano Buendía was to remember that distant afternoon when his father took him to discover ice.

Marvell, Andrew 'To His Coy Mistress' Had we but world enough, and time, This coyness, Lady, were no crime.

Masefield, John 'Sea-Fever' I must go down to the seas again, to the lonely sea and the sky, And all I ask is a tall ship and a star to steer her by . . .

Maugham, W. Somerset *Of Human Bondage* The day broke grey and dull.

Melville, Herman *Billy Budd* In the time before steamships, or then more frequently than now, a stroller along the docks of any considerable sea-port would occasionally have his attention arrested by a group of bronzed mariners, man-of-war's men or merchant-sailors in holiday attire ashore on liberty.

Melville, Herman *Moby-Dick* Call me Ishmael.

Metalious, Grace *Peyton Place* Indian summer is like a woman. Ripe, hotly passionate, but fickle, she comes and goes as she pleases so that one is never sure whether she will come at all, nor for how long she will stay.

Michener, James A. *The Source* On Tuesday the freighter steamed through the Straits of Gibraltar and for five days plowed eastward through the Mediterranean, past islands and peninsulas rich in history, so that on Saturday night the steward advised Dr. Cullinane, 'If you wish an early sight of the Holy Land you must be up at dawn.'

Miller, Henry *Tropic of Cancer* I am living at the Villa Borghese. There is not a crumb of dirt anywhere nor a chair misplaced. We are alone here and we are dead.

Miller Jr, Walter *A Canticle for Leibowitz* Brother Francis Gerard of Utah might never have discovered the blessed documents, had it not been for the pilgrim with girded loins who had appeared during that young novice's Lenten fast in the desert.

Milton, John *Lycidas* Yet once more, O ye laurels, and once more, Ye myrtles brown, with ivy never sere.

Milton, John 'On His Blindness' When I consider how my light is spent, Ere half my days, in this dark world and wide.

Milton, John *Paradise Lost* Of man's first disobedience, and the fruit Of that forbidden tree, whose mortal taste Brought death into the world, and all our woe, With loss of Eden.

Mitchell, Margaret *Gone with the Wind* Scarlett O'Hara was not beautiful, but men seldom realized it when caught by her charm as the Tarleton twins were.

Montgomery, Lucy Maud *Anne of Green Gables* Mrs. Rachel Lynde lived just where the Avonlea main road dipped down into a little hollow.

Morrison, Toni *Beloved* 124 was spiteful.

Morrison, Toni *Sula* In that place, where they tore the night shade and blackberry patches from their roots to make room for the Medallion City Golf Course, there was once a neighborhood.

Nabokov, Vladimir *Lolita* Lolita, light of my life, fire of my loins.

Naylor, Gloria *The Women of Brewster Place* Brewster Place was the bastard child of several clandestine meetings between the alderman of the sixth district and the managing director of the Unico Realty Company.

Niven, Larry *Ringworld* In the night time heat of Beirut in one of a row of general address transfer booths, Louis Wu flicked into reality.

Norton, Mary *The Borrowers* It was Mrs May who first told me about them.

Oates, Joyce Carol *Because It Is Bitter, and Because It Is My Heart* Little Red Garlock, sixteen years old, skull smashed soft as a rotted pumpkin and body dumped into the Cassadaga River near the

L
I
T
E
R
A
T
U
R
E

foot of Pitt Street, must not have sunk as deep as he'd been intended to sink, or floated as far.

Oates, Joyce Carol *Bellefleur* It was many years ago in that dark, chaotic, unfathomable pool of time before Germaine's birth (nearly twelve months before her birth), on a night in late September stirred by innumerable frenzied winds, like spirits contending with one another.

Oates, Joyce Carol *Expensive People* I was a child murderer.

O'Connor, Flannery *The Violent Bear It Away* Francis Marion Tarwater's uncle had been dead for only half a day when the boy got too drunk to finish digging his grave.

Orwell, George *1984* It was a bright cold day in April, and the clocks were striking thirteen.

Owen, Wilfred 'Anthem for Doomed Youth' What passing-bells for these who die as cattle?

Pasternak, Boris *Doctor Zhivago* On they went, singing 'Rest Eternal,' and whenever they stopped, their feet, the horses, and the gusts of wind seemed to carry on their singing.

Paterson, Katherine *Bridge to Terabitha* Ba-room, ba-room, ba-room, baripity, baripity, baripity, baripity – Good.

Piercy, Marge *Small Change* Beth was looking in the mirror of her mother's vanity.

Piper, Watty *The Little Engine That Could* Chug, chug, chug. Puff, puff, puff. Ding-dong, ding-dong.

Plath, Sylvia *The Bell Jar* It was a queer, sultry summer, the summer they electrocuted the Rosenbergs, and I didn't know what I was doing in New York.

Pohl, Frederik *Gateway* My name is Robinette Broadhead, in spite of which I am male.

Pope, Alexander *The Dunciad* The Mighty Mother, and her Son, who brings The Smithfield muses to the ear of kings, I sing.

Porter, Katherine Anne *Ship of Fools* August, 1931 – The port town of Veracruz is a little purgatory between land and sea.

Portis, Charles *True Grit* People do not give it credence that a fourteen-year-old girl could leave home and go off in the wintertime to avenge her father's blood.

Potok, Chaim *The Chosen* For the first fifteen years of our lives, Danny and I lived within five blocks of each other and neither of us knew of the other's existence.

Puzo, Mario *The Godfather* Amerigo Bonasera sat in New York Criminal Court Number 3 and waited for justice; vengeance on the men who had so cruelly hurt his daughter.

Pynchon, Thomas *Gravity's Rainbow* A screaming comes across the sky.

Rand, Ayn *Atlas Shrugged* Who is John Galt?.

Remarque, Erich Maria *All Quiet on the Western Front* We are five miles behind the front.

Renault, Mary *The King Must Die* The Citadel of Troizen, where the Palace stands, was built by giants before anyone remembers.

Rey, H.A. *Curious George* This is George. He lived in Africa.

Robbins, Tom *Even Cowgirls Get the Blues* Amoebae leave no fossils.

Robbins, Tom *Jitterbug Perfume* The beet is the most intense of vegetables.

Robbins, Tom *Still Life with Woodpecker* In the last quarter of the twentieth century, at a time when

Western civilization was declining too rapidly for comfort and yet too slowly to be exciting, much of the world sat on the edge of an increasingly expensive theater seat, waiting – with various combinations of dread, hope, and ennui – for something momentous to occur.

Robinson, Marilynne *Housekeeping* My name is Ruth. I grew up with my sister, Lucille, under the care of my grandmother,.

Rölvaag, O. E. *Giants in the Earth* Bright, clear sky over a plain so wide that the rim of the heavens cut down on it around the entire horizon.

Roth, Philip *Portnoy's Complaint* She was so deeply imbedded in my consciousness that for the first year of school I seemed to have believed that each of my teachers was my mother in disguise.

Rushdie, Salman *The Satanic Verses* To be born again, sang Gibreel Farishta tumbling from the heavens, 'first you have to die'.

Salinger, J.D. *The Catcher in the Rye* If you really want to hear about it, the first thing you'll probably want to know is where I was born, and what my lousy childhood was like.

Schaefer, Jack *Shane* He rode into our valley in the summer of '89.

Scott, Sir Walter *Old Mortality* 'Most Readers,' says the Manuscript of Mr Pattieson, 'must have witnessed with delight the joyous burst which attends the dismissing of a village-school on a fine summer evening.'

Segal, Erich *Love Story* What can you say about a 25 year old girl who died?

Selden, George *The Cricket in Times Square* A mouse was looking at Mario. The mouse's name was Tucker.

Service, Robert *The Shooting of Dan McGraw* A bunch of the boys were whooping it up in the Malarnute saloon.

Sewell, Anna *Black Beauty* The first place that I can well remember was a large pleasant meadow with a pond of clear water in it.

Shaw, Irwin *Rich Man, Poor Man* Mr. Donnelly, the track coach, ended the day's practice early because Henry Fuller's father came down to the high-school field to tell Henry that they had just got a telegram from Washington announcing that Henry's brother had been killed in action in Germany.

Shelley, Mary *Frankenstein* You will rejoice to hear that no disaster has accompanied the commencement of an enterprise which you have regarded with such evil forebodings.

Shelley, Percy Bysshe 'Ozymandias of Egypt' I met a traveller from an antique land . . .

Sholokhov, Mikhail *And Quiet Flows the Don* The Melekhov farm was right at the end of the Tatarsk village.

Shute, Nevil *On the Beach* Lt Commander Peter Holmes of the Royal Australian Navy woke soon after dawn.

Simak, Clifford *City* Gramp Stevens sat in a lawn chair, watching the mower at work, feeling the warm, soft sunshine seep into his bones.

Simak, Clifford *Way Station* The noise was ended now. The smoke drifted like thin gray wisps of fog above the tortured earth and the shattered fences.

Sims, George R. *In the Workhouse – Christmas Day* It is Christmas Day in the Workhouse.

Singer, Isaac Bashevis *Shosha* I was brought up on three dead languages – Hebrew, Aramaic, and

Yiddish (some consider the last not a language at all) – and in a culture that developed in Babylon: the Talmud.

Smith, Betty *A Tree Grows in Brooklyn* Serene was a word you could put to Brooklyn, New York.

Smith, Dodie *101 Dalmatians* Not long ago, there lived in London a young married couple of Dalmatian dogs named Pongo and Misses Pongo.

Solzhenitsyn, Alexander *The Gulag Archipelago* How do people get to this clandestine Archipelago?

Sontag, Susan *Death Kit* Diddy the Good was taking a business trip.

Spencer, Scott *Endless Love* When I was seventeen and in full obedience to my heart's most urgent commands, I stepped far from the pathway of normal life and in a moment's time ruined everything I loved – I loved so deeply, and when the love was interrupted, when the incorporeal body of love shank back in terror and my own body was locked away, it was hard for others to believe that a life so new could suffer so irrevocably.

Spenser, Edmund *The Faerie Queene* A Gentle Knight was pricking on the plaine.

Steinbeck, John *Cannery Row* Cannery Row in Monterey in California is a poem, a stink, a grating noise, a quality of light, a tone, a habit, a nostalgia, a dream.

Steinbeck, John *The Grapes of Wrath* To the red country and part of the gray country of Oklahoma, the last rains came gently, and they did not cut the scarred earth.

Steinbeck, John *Of Mice and Men* A few miles south of Soledad, the Salinas River drops in close to the hill-side bank and runs deep and green.

Steinbeck, John *The Pearl* Kino awakened in the near dark.

Stevenson, Robert Louis *The Strange Case of Dr Jekyll and Mr Hyde* Mr. Utterson the lawyer was a man of a rugged countenance, that was never lighted by a smile; cold, scanty and embarrassed.

Stevenson, Robert Louis *Kidnapped* I will begin the story of my adventures with a certain morning early in the month of June, the year of grace 1751, when I took the key for the last time out of the door of my father's house.

Stevenson, Robert Louis *Treasure Island* Squire Trelawney, Dr. Livesey, and the rest of these gentlemen having asked me to write down the whole particulars about Treasure Island.

Stevenson, R.L. & L. Osbourne *The Wrong Box* How very little does the amateur, dwelling at home at ease, comprehend the labours and perils of the author.

Stewart, Mary *The Crystal Cave* I am an old man now, but then I was already past my prime when Arthur was crowned King.

Stoker, Bram *Dracula* 3 May. Bistritz. – Left Munich at 8:35 P.M., on 1st May, arriving at Vienna early next morning; should have arrived at 6:46, but the train was an hour late. Buda-Pesth seems a wonderful place, from the glimpse which I got from the train and the little I could walk through the streets.

Stone, Irving *Lust for Life* Monsieur Van Gogh, it's time to wake up.

Stout, Rex *The Hand in Glove* It was not surprising that Sylvia Raffray, on that Saturday in September, had occasion for discourse with various men, none of them utterly ordinary, and with one remarkable young woman; it was not surprising that all this

happened without any special effort on Sylvia's part, for she was rich, personable to an extreme, an orphan, and six months short of twenty-one years.

Stowe, Harriet Beecher *Uncle Tom's Cabin* Late in the afternoon of a chilly day in February, two gentlemen were sitting alone over their wine, in a well-furnished dining parlour, in the town of P——, in Kentucky.

Sturgeon, Theodore *More Than Human* The idiot lived in a black and gray world, punctuated by the white lightning of hunger and the flickering of fear.

Styron, William *The Confessions of Nat Turner* To the public – The late insurrection in Southampton has greatly excited the public mind and led to a thousand idle, exaggerated and mischievous reports.

Swift, Jonathan *Gulliver's Travels* My father had a small estate in Nottinghamshire; I was the third of five sons.

Tan, Amy *The Hundred Secret Senses* My sister Kwan believes she has yin eyes.

Tan, Amy *The Joy Luck Club* My father asked me to be the fourth corner at the Joy Luck Club.

Thackeray, William M. *Vanity Fair* While the present century was in its teens, and on one sunshiny morning in June, there drove up to the great iron gate of Miss Pinkerton's academy for young ladies, on Chiswick Mall, a large family coach, with two fat horses in blazing harness, driven by a fat coachman in a three cornered hat and wig, at the rate of four miles an hour.

Theroux, Paul *The Mosquito Coast* We drove past Tiny Polski's mansion house to the main road, and then the five miles into Northampton, Father talking the whole way about savages and the awfulness of America – how it got turned into a dope-taking, door-locking, ulcerated danger zone of rabid scavengers and criminal millionaires and moral sneaks.

Thomas, Dylan *Under Milk Wood* To begin at the beginning, It is spring, moonless night in the small town, starless and bible-black . . .

Thoreau, Henry David *Walden* When I wrote the following pages, or rather the bulk of them, I lived alone, in the woods, a mile from any neighbor, in a house which I had built myself, on the shore of Walden Pond, in Concord, Massachusetts, and earned my living by the labor of my hands only.

Thurber, James *The Thirteen Clocks* Once upon a time, in a gloomy castle on a lonely hill, where there were thirteen clocks that wouldn't go, there lived a cold, aggressive Duke, and his niece, the Princess Saralinda.

Tolkien, J.R.R. *The Hobbit* In a hole in the ground there lived a hobbit.

Tolstoy, Leo *Anna Karenina* All happy families are alike, but an unhappy family is unhappy after its own fashion.

Tolstoy, Leo *War and Peace* Well, Prince, so Genoa and Lucca are now just family estates of the Buonapartes.

Travers, P.L. *Mary Poppins* If you want to find Cherry Tree Lane all you have to do is ask a policeman at the crossroads.

Twain, Mark *The Adventures of Huckleberry Finn* You don't know about me, without you have read a book by the name of *The Adventures of Tom Sawyer*, but that ain't no matter.

Twain, Mark *The Adventures of Tom Sawyer* TOM!

Tyler, Anne *Breathing Lessons* Maggie and Ira Moran had to go to a funeral in Deer Lick, Pennsylvania.

Undset, Sigrid *Kristin Lavransdatter* When the

L
I
T
E
R
A
T
U
R
E

lands and goods of Ivar Gjesling the younger, of Sundbu, were divided after his death in 1306, his lands in Sil of Gudbrandsdal fell to his daughter Ragnfrid and her husband Lavrans Björngulfsön.

Updike, John *Rabbit at Rest* Standing amid the tan, excited post-Christmas crowd at the Southwest Florida Regional Airport, Rabbit Angstrom has a funny sudden feeling that what he has come to meet, what's floating in unseen about to land, is not his son Nelson and daughter-in-law Pru and their two children but something more ominous and intimately his: his own death, shaped vaguely like an airplane.

Updike, John *Rabbit Is Rich* Running out of gas, Rabbit Angstrom thinks as he stands behind the summer-dusty windows of the Springer Motors display.

Updike, John *Rabbit Redux* Men emerge pale from the little printing plant at four sharp, ghosts for an instant, blinking, until the outdoor light overcomes the look of constant indoor light clinging to them.

Updike, John *Rabbit, Run* Boys are playing basketball around a telephone pole with a blackboard bolted to it.

Uris, Leon *Exodus* The airplane plip-plopped down the runway to a halt before the big sign: WELCOME TO CYPRUS.

Verne, Jules *Around the World in 80 Days* Mr Phileas Fogg lived, in 1872, at No. 7, Savile Row, Burlington Gardens, the house in which Sheridan died in 1814.

Vidal, Gore *Creation* I am blind. But I am not deaf. Becuase of the incompleteness of my misfortune, I was obliged yesterday to listen for nearly six hours to a self-styled historian whose account of what the Athenians call 'the Persian Wars' was nonsense of a sort that were I less old and more privileged, I would have risen in my seat at the Odeon and scandalized all Athens by answering him.

Vidal, Gore *Lincoln* Elihu B. Washburne opened his gold watch.

Vidal, Gore *Myra Breckinridge* I am Myra Breckinridge whom no man will ever possess.

Virgil *Aeneid* I sing of arms and the man.

Voltaire *Candide* In the country of Westphalia, in the castle of the most noble Baron of Thunder-ten-tronckh, lived a youth whom Nature had endowed with a most sweet disposition.

Vonnegut, Kurt *Breakfast of Champions* This is a tale of a meeting of two lonesome, skinny, fairly old white men on a planet which was dying fast.

Vonnegut, Kurt *Cat's Cradle* Call me Jonah.

Vonnegut, Kurt *Slapstick* To whom it may concern: It is springtime.

Vonnegut, Kurt *Slaughterhouse-Five* All this happened, more or less.

Walker, Alice *The Color Purple* You better not never tell nobody but God.

Walker, Alice *Possessing the Secret of Joy* I did not realize for a long time that I was dead.

Waller, Robert *The Bridges of Madison County* On the morning of August 8, 1965, Robert Kincaid locked the door to his small two-room apartment on the third floor of a rambling house in Bellingham, Washington.

Warren, Robert Penn *A Place To Come To* I was the only boy, or girl either, in the public school in the town of Dugton, Claxford County, Alabama, whose father had ever got killed in the middle of the night standing up in the front of his wagon to piss on the hindquarters of one of a span of mules and, being drunk, pitching forward on his head, still hanging

onto his dong, and hitting the pike in such a position and condition that both the left front and left rear wheels of the wagon rolled, with perfect precision, over his unconscious neck, his having passed out being, no doubt, the reason he took the fatal plunge in the first place.

Waugh, Evelyn *Brideshead Revisited* When I reached C Company lines, which were at the top of the hill, I paused and looked back at the camp, just coming into full view before me through the grey mist of early morning.

Waugh, Evelyn *Scoop* While still a young man, John Courteney Boot had, as his publisher proclaimed, 'achieved an assured and enviable position in contemporary letters'.

Wells, H.G. *The Island of Doctor Moreau* I do not propose to add anything to what has already been written concerning the loss of the 'Lady Vain'.

Wells, H.G. *The Time Machine* The Time Traveller (for so it will be convenient to speak of him) was expounding a recondite matter to us.

Wells, H.G. *The War of the Worlds* No one would have believed in the last years of the nineteenth century that this world was being watched keenly and closely by intelligences greater than man's and yet as mortal as his own; that as men busied themselves about their various concerns they were scrutinised and studied, perhaps almost as narrowly as a man with a microscope might scrutinise the transient creatures that swarm and multiply in a drop of water.

Welty, Eudora *The Optimist's Daughter* A nurse held the door open for them. Judge McKelva going first, then his daughter Laurel, then his wife Fay, they walked into the windowless room where the doctor would make his examination.

Wharton, Edith *Ethan Frome* I had the story, bit by bit, from various people, and, as generally happens in such cases, each time it was a different story.

White, E.B. *Charlotte's Web* Where's Papa going with that ax? said Fern to her mother as they were setting the table for breakfast.

White, E.B. *Stuart Little* When Mrs. Frederick C. Little's second son arrived, everybody noticed that he was not much bigger than a mouse.

Wibberley, Leonard *The Mouse That Roared* The Duchy of Grand Fenwick lies in a precipitous fold of the northern Alps and embraces in its tumbling landscape portions of three valleys, a river, one complete mountain with an elevation of two thousand feet and a castle.

Wilde, Oscar *The Ballad of Reading Gaol* He did not wear his scarlet coat.

Wilde, Oscar *The Picture of Dorian Gray* The studio was filled with the rich odour of roses, and when the light summer wind stirred amidst the trees of the garden there came through the open door the heavy scent of the lilac, or the more delicate perfume of the pink-flowering thorn.

Wilder, Thornton *The Bridge of San Luis Rey* On Friday noon, July the twentieth, 1714, the finest bridge in all Peru broke and precipitated five travelers into the gulf below.

Wolfe, Thomas *You Can't Go Home Again* It was the hour of twilight on a soft spring day toward the end of April in the year of Our Lord 1929, and George Webber leaned his elbows on the sill of his back window and looked out at what he could see of New York.

Wolfe, Thomas   *Look Homeward, Angel*   A destiny that leads the English to the Dutch is strange enough; but one that leads from Epsom into Pennsylvania, and thence into the hills that shut in Altamont above the proud coral cry of the cock, and the soft stone smile of the angel, is touched by that dark miracle of chance which makes new magic in a dusty world.

Woolf, Virginia   *Orlando*   He – for there could be no doubt of his sex, though the fashion of the time did something to disguise it – was in the act of slicing at the head of a Moor which swung from the rafters.

Wordsworth, William   *The Prelude*   Oh there is blessing in this gentle breeze.

Wouk, Herman   *The Winds of War*   Commander Victor Henry rode a taxi-cab home from the Navy building on Constitution Avenue, in a gusty gray March rainstorm that matched his mood.

Wright, Richard   *Native Son*   Brrrrrrriiiiiiiiiiiiiiiiiiiinng! An alarm clock clanged in the dark and silent room. A bed spring creaked. A woman's voice sang out impatiently. 'Bigger, shut that thing off!'

Wyndham, John   *The Day of the Triffids*   When a day that you happen to know is Wednesday starts off by sounding like Sunday, there is something seriously wrong somewhere.

Wyss, Johann   *The Swiss Family Robinson*   For many days we had been tempest-tossed.

Yeats, W.B.   'When You are Old'   When you are old and grey and full of sleep, And nodding by the fire, take down this book . . .

Zelazny, Roger   *Lord of Light*   His followers called him Mahasamatman and said he was a god. He preferred to drop the Maha- and the -atman, however, and called himself Sam.

NB: This is another section where it is only possible to list a good cross-section of works rather than a fully comprehensive catalogue. It is hoped that many of the better-known openings are included, as well as some more obscure but interesting ones. In the cases of works written in a foreign language and translated into English, the wording will vary according to the translator.

Closing Words of Books and Poems

Arnold, Mathew   'Dover Beach'   Swept with confused alarms of struggle and flight, where ignorant armies clash by night.

Arnold, Mathew   'The Scholar Gipsy'   Shy traffickers, the dark Iberians come, And on the beach undid his corded bales.

Asimov, Isaac   *I Robot*   She died last month at the age of Eighty Two.

Austen, Jane   *Emma*   But, in spite of these deficiencies, the wishes, the hopes, the confidence, the predictions of the small band of true friends who witnessed the ceremony, were fully answered in the perfect happiness of the union.

Austen, Jane   *Lady Susan*   I confess that I can pity only Miss Manwaring, who coming to town and putting herself to an expense in clothes, which impoverished her for two years, on purpose to secure him, was defrauded of her due by a woman ten years older than herself.

Austen, Jane   *Mansfield Park*   Fanny had never been able to approach but with some painful sensation of restraint or alarm, soon grew as dear to her heart, and as thoroughly perfect in her eyes, as everything else within the view and patronage of Mansfield Park had long been.

Austen, Jane   *Northanger Abbey*   I leave it to be settled by whomsoever it may concern, whether the tendency of this work be altogether to recommend parental tyranny or reward filial disobedience.

Austen, Jane   *Persuasion*   She gloried in being a sailor's wife, but she must pay the tax of quick alarm for belonging to that profession which is, if possible, more distinguished in its domestic virtues than in its national importance.

Austen, Jane   *Pride and Prejudice*   And they were both ever sensible of the warmest gratitude towards the persons who, by bringing her into Derbyshire, had been the means of uniting them.

Austen, Jane   *Sanditon*   It was impossible not to feel him hardly used; to be obliged to stand back in his own house and see the best place by the first constantly occupied by Sir Harry Denham.

Austen, Jane   *Sense and Sensibility*   Between Barton and Delaford, there was that constant communication which strong family affection would naturally dictate; and among the merits and the happiness of Elinor and Marianne, let it not be ranked as the least considerable, that though sisters and living almost within sight of each other, they could live without disagreement between themselves, or producing coolness between their husbands.

Austen, Jane   *The Watsons*   Emma was of course un-influenced, except to greater esteem for Elizabeth, by such representations – and the visitors departed without her.

Bellow, Saul   *Henderson the Rain King*   I guess I felt it was my turn now to move, and so went running – leaping, leaping, pounding, and tingling over the pure white lining of the gray Arctic silence.

Bennett, Arnold   *Clayhanger*   He braced himself to the exquisite burden to life.

Bennett, Arnold   *The Old Wives' Tale*   She glanced at the soup plate, and, on the chance that it might after all contain something worth inspection, she awkwardly balanced on her old legs and went to it again.

Brontë, Anne   *Agnes Grey*   And now I think I have said sufficient.

Brontë, Anne   *The Tenant of Wildfell Hall*   Till then, farewell, Gilbert Markham Staningley, June 10th 1847.

Brontë, Charlotte   *Jane Eyre*   Amen; even so come, Lord Jesus.

Brontë, Charlotte   *The Professor*   Papa, Come!

Brontë, Charlotte   *Villette*   Madame Walravens fulfilled her ninetieth year before she died. Farewell.

Brontë, Emily   *Wuthering Heights*   I lingered around them under that benign sky; watched the moths fluttering among the heath and harebells, listening to the soft wind breathing through the grass, and wondered how anyone could ever imagine unquiet slumbers for the sleepers in that quiet earth.

Buchan, John   *The Thirty-Nine Steps*   But I had done my best service, I think, before I put on khaki.

Carey, Peter   *Jack Maggs*   Affectionately Inscribed to

L
I
T
E
R
A
T
U
R
E

Percival Clarence Buckle, A man of letters, A patron of the arts.

Carroll, Lewis *Alice's Adventures in Wonderland* And how she would feel with all their simple sorrows, and find a pleasure in all their simple joys, remembering her own child-life, and the happy summer days.

Carroll, Lewis *Through the Looking Glass* But the provoking kitten only began on the other paw, and pretended it hadn't heard the question. Which do *you* think it was?

Cervantes, Miguel de *Don Quixote* Farewell.

Clarke, Arthur C. *2001* But he would think of something.

Cleland, John *Fanny Hill* I shall see you soon, and in the meantime think candidly of me, and believe me ever, madam, Yours, etc, etc, etc.

Collins, Wilkie *The Moonstone* Who can tell?

Conrad, Joseph *Lord Jim* While he waves his hand sadly at his butterflies.

Conrad, Joseph *An Outcast of the Islands* And Almayer, who stood waiting, with a smile of tipsy attention on his lips, heard no other answer.

Cookson, Catherine *The Maltese Angel* Oh, let me cry. Let me cry, my love.

Cookson, Catherine *The Year of the Virgins* Listen to me, Flo Coulson, your mother loves me. Do you hear that? Your mother loves me. Everything comes to him who waits. Your mother loves me.

Cooper, James Fennimore *The Pioneers* Who are opening the way for the march of the Nation across the Continent.

Defoe, Daniel *Robinson Crusoe* And here, resolving to harass myself no more, I am preparing for a longer journey than all these, having lived 72 years, a life of infinite variety, and learn'd sufficiently to know the value of retirement, and the blessing of ending our days in peace.

Dickens, Charles *David Copperfield* Oh Agnes, Oh my soul, so may thy face be by me when I close my life indeed; so may I, when realities are melting from me like the shadows which I now dismiss, still find thee near me, pointing upward!

Dickens, Charles *Great Expectations* And had given her a heart to understand what my heart used to be.

Dickens, Charles *Oliver Twist* These, and a thousand looks and smiles, and turns of thought and speech – I would fain recall them every one.

Dickens, Charles *Oliver Twist (supplementary)* I believe it none the less because that nook is in a church, and she was weak and erring.

Dickens, Charles *A Tale of Two Cities* It is a far, far better thing that I do, than I have ever done: it is a far, far better rest that I go to, than I have ever known.

Dostoevsky, Fyodor *Crime and Punishment* That might be the subject of a new story, but our present story is ended.

Doyle, Arthur Conan *The Hound of the Baskervilles* We can stop at Mancini's for a little dinner on the way.

Dumas, Alexander *The Three Musketeers* The opinion of those who thought themselves the best informed was that he was boarded and lodged in some royal castle at the expense of his generous eminence.

Fielding, Henry *Tom Jones* Who doth not most gratefully bless the day when Mr Jones was married to Sophia.

Greene, Graham *Brighton Rock* She walked rapidly in the thin June sunlight towards the worst horror of all.

Harris, Robert *Fatherland* Then he tugged the gun from his waistband, checked to make sure it was loaded and moved towards the silent trees.

Hartley, L.P. *Eustace and Hilda* But the cold crept onwards and he did not wake.

Heller, Joseph *Catch-22* The knife came down missing him by inches, and he took off.

Hughes, Thomas *Tom Brown's School Days* We can come to the knowledge of him in whom alone, the love and the tenderness, and the purity, and the strength, the courage, and the wisdom of all these, dwell for ever and ever in perfect fullness.

Huxley, Aldous *Crome Yellow* He climbed into the hearse.

Le Carré, John *The Honourable Schoolboy* And nor does Guillam, for George's sake.

Lewis, C.S. *The Lion, The Witch and The Wardrobe* But if the Professor was right it was only the beginning of the adventures of Narnia.

Lewis, Sinclair *Arrowsmith* We'll plug along on it for two or three years, and maybe we'll get something permanent – and probably we'll fail!

Longfellow, Henry Wadsworth 'The Villlage Blacksmith' Thus on its sounding anvil shaped Each burning deed and thought.

Longfellow, Henry Wadsworth 'The Wreck of the Hesperus' Christ saves us all from a death like this, on the reef of Norman's woe.

Lowry, Malcolm *Under the Volcano* Somebody threw a dead dog after him down the ravine.

Marvel, Andrew 'To His Coy Mistress' Thus though we cannot make our son, stand still, yet we will make him run.

McEwan, Ian *Enduring Love* So now, Rachael said. Tell Leo as well. Say it again slowly, that thing about the river.

Melville, Herman *Billy Budd* I am sleepy, and the oozy weeds about me twist.

Milton, John *On His Blindness* They also serve who only stand and wait.

Mitchell, Margaret *Gone With the Wind* After all, Tomorrow is another day.

O'Brien, Flann *At Swim-Two-Birds* He went home one evening and drank three cups of tea with three lumps of sugar in each, cut his jugular with a razor three times and scrawled with a dying hand on a picture of his wife, goodbye, goodbye, goodbye.

Service, Robert 'The Shooting of Dan McGraw' The woman that kissed him and pinched his poke, was the lady that's known as Lou.

Sewell, Anna *Black Beauty* I am still in the orchard at Birtwick standing with my old friends under the apple trees.

Shaw, Irwin *The Young Lions* Because he knew he had to deliver Noah Ackerman, personally, to Captain Green.

Solzhenitsyn, Alexander *One Day in the Life of Ivan Denisovich* The three extra days were because of the leap years.

Steel, Danielle *Kaleidoscope* He held her tightly in his arms and she knew he was telling the truth. 'Everything's going to be all right now.'

Steel, Danielle *Star* Home at last. Together.

Swift, Jonathan *Gulliver's Travels* And therefore, I here entreat those who have any tincture of this absurd vice, that they will not presume to appear in my sight.

Tolstoy, Leo *War and Peace* In the present case, it is an essential to surmount a consciousness of an unreal freedom and to recognise a dependence not perceived by our senses.

Tremain, Rose *Restoration* Before I have grown too

frail to climb the stairs – I shall bring you back.

Waugh, Evelyn   *Brideshead Revisited*   You're looking unusually cheerful today,' said the second-in-command.

Wilde, Oscar   *The Ballad of Reading Gaol*   The coward does it with a kiss, The brave man with a sword.

Wood, Mrs Henry   *East Lynne*   Oh Barbara, never forget – never forget that the only way to ensure peace in the end, is to strive always to be doing right, unselfishly, under God.

Wyndham, John   *The Day of the Triffids*   Until we have wiped the last one of them from the face of the land they have usurped.

NB: This section is much shorter than the opening lines, merely because closing lines tend to be less memorable than opening lines, and consequently, rarely crop up in any form of quiz.

Index of Books (in title order)

(* denotes author's first book)

Book	Author
Aaron's Rod	D.H. Lawrence
Absalom, Absalom!	William Faulkner
The Absentee	Maria Edgeworth
The Acid House	Irvine Welsh
The Actual	Saul Bellow
Adam Bede*	George Eliot
Adolphe	Benjamin Constant
The Aeneid	Virgil
Affliction	Fay Weldon
The African Queen	C.S. Forester
Afternoon Men*	Anthony Powell
Age of Innocence	Edith Wharton
The Age of Reason	Thomas Paine
Agnes Grey*	Anne Bronte
The Agony and the Ecstasy	Irving Stone
Airframe	Michael Crichton
Airport	Arthur Hailey
The Alexandria Quartet	Lawrence Durrell
Alias Grace	Margaret Atwood
Alice's Adventures in Wonderland	Lewis Carroll
Allan Quatermain	Henry Rider Haggard
All Quiet on the Western Front	Erich Maria Remarque
All the Conspirators*	Christopher Isherwood
Almayer's Folly*	Joseph Conrad
Alphabats	Paul Sellers
Altered States	Anita Brookner
The Ambassadors	Henry James
Amelia	Henry Fielding
An American Dream	Norman Mailer
American Pastoral	Philip Roth
American Psycho	Brett Easton Ellis
An American Tragedy	Theodore Dreiser
An Evil Cradling	Brian Keenan
And Quiet Flows the Don	Mikhail Sholokhov
Angel Pavement	J.B. Priestley
Angela's Ashes	Frank McCourt
Animal Farm	George Orwell
Anna Karenina	Leo Tolstoy
Anna of the Five Towns	Arnold Bennett
Anne of Green Gables*	L.M. Montgomery
Antic Hay	Aldous Huxley
Any Old Iron	Anthony Burgess
Appassionata	Jilly Cooper
Armageddon	Leon Uris
Around the World in 80 Days	Jules Verne
As I Lay Dying	William Faulkner
Atlas Shrugged	Ayn Rand
August 1914	Alexander Solzhenitsyn
The Awakening	Kate Chopin

Book	Author
An Awfully Big Adventure	Beryl Bainbridge
The Bad Place	Dean R. Koontz
The Ballad of Peckham Rye	Muriel Spark
The Ballad of the Sad Café	Carson McCullers
Bambi	Felix Salten
Barchester Towers	Anthony Trollope
Barnaby Rudge	Charles Dickens
Baron Münchhausen	R.E. Raspe
The Battle of the Books	Jonathan Swift
The Beach	Alex Garland
Beasts and Superbeasts	Hector Hugh Munro (Saki)
Beau Geste	P.C. Wren
The Beautiful and Damned	F. Scott Fitzgerald
The Beauty Myth	Naomi Wolf
Behind the Scenes at the Museum	Kate Atkinson
Belinda	Maria Edgeworth
The Bell Jar	Sylvia Plath
Beloved	Toni Morrison
Bend in the River	V.S. Naipaul
Bend Sinister	Vladimir Nabokov
Ben Hur	Lew Wallace
Beware of Pity	Stefan Zweig
The BFG	Roald Dahl
Biggles	Capt. W.E. Johns
The Big Sleep	Raymond Chandler
Big Sur	Jack Kerouac
Billy Budd	Herman Melville
Billy Bunter	Frank Richards
Billy Liar	Keith Waterhouse
Birds of Prey	Wilbur Smith
Birdsong	Sebastian Faulks
Black Ajax	George MacDonald Fraser
Black Beauty	Anna Sewell
The Black Prince	Iris Murdoch
The Black Stallion	Walter Farley
Bliss, and other stories	Katherine Mansfield
The Bloody Ground	Bernard Cornwell
Blott on the Landscape	Tom Sharpe
The Blue Angel	Heinrich Mann
Bluebeard	Charles Perrault
Bondage of Love	Catherine Cookson
The Bonfire of the Vanities	Tom Wolfe
Bonjour Tristesse	Françoise Sagan
The Book of Nonsense	Edward Lear
The Borrowers	Mary Norton
Bostonians, The	Henry James
The Bottle Factory Outing	Beryl Bainbridge
Box of Delights	John Masefield
Boyhood	Leo Tolstoy
Boys from Brazil	Ira Levin

LITERATURE

Book	Author	Book	Author
Branded Man	Catherine Cookson	Childhood	Leo Tolstoy
Brave New World	Aldous Huxley	Childhood	Maxim Gorky
Bravo Two Zero	Andy McNab	Children of the New Forest	Capt Frederick.
Breakfast at Tiffany's	Truman Capote		Marryat
Breaking Hearts	Simon Gray	The Children of Violence	Doris Lessing
Bride of Lammermoor	Walter Scott	Child Whispers*	Enid Blyton
Brideshead Revisited	Evelyn Waugh	Chitty Chitty Bang Bang	Ian Fleming
The Bridesmaid	Ruth Rendell	Chomolungma Sings the	Ed Douglas
The Bridge of San Luis Rey	Thornton Wilder	Blues	
Bridge on the River Kwai	Pierre Boulle	Christmas Carol, A	Charles Dickens
The Bridges of Madison	Robert James Waller	Chronicles of Thomas	Stephen Donaldson
County		Covenant	
Bridget Jones's Diary:	Helen Fielding	Cider With Rosie	Laurie Lee
A Novel		The Citadel	A.J. Cronin
A Brief History of Time	Stephen Hawking	The City and the Stars	Arthur C Clarke
Brigadier Gerard, The Exploits of	Arthur Conan Doyle	Clarissa	Samuel Richardson
Brighton Rock	Graham Greene	Claudia	Arnold Zweig
The British Museum Is Falling	David Lodge	Claudine (series)	Colette
Down		Clayhanger	Arnold Bennett
Broca's Brain	Carl Sagan	A Clockwork Orange	Anthony Burgess
The Brothers Karamazov	Fyodor Dostoyevsky	Cloister and the Hearth	Charles Reade
The Buccaneers	Edith Wharton	Close Relations	Deborah Moggach
Buddenbrooks*	Thomas Mann	Cocaine Nights	J.G. Ballard
The Buddha of Suburbia	Hanif Kureishi	Cold Mountain	Charles Frazier
Bulldog Drummond	Herman Cyril McNeile	The Collector	John Fowles
	(Sapper)	Colonel Sun	Robert Markham
Busman's Honeymoon	Dorothy L. Sayers	The Color Purple	Alice Walker
The Cabala*	Thornton Wilder	La Comédie Humaine	Honoré de Balzac
Cakes and Ale	William Somerset	The Comforters	Muriel Spark
	Maugham	Common Sense	Thomas Paine
Call for the Dead*	John Le Carré	Confessions of an English	Thomas De Quincey
Call of the Wild	Jack London	Opium Eater	
The Call of Wings	Agatha Christie	Coningsby	Benjamin Disraeli
The Camomile Lawn	Mary Wesley	A Cool Million	Nathanael West
Campbell's Kingdom	Ralph Hammond	Coral Island	R.M. Ballantyne
	Innes	The Corridors of Power	C.P. Snow
Cancer Ward	Alexander	The Count of Monte Cristo	Alexandre Dumas
	Solzhenitsyn		(Père)
Candide	Voltaire	The Country Diary of an	Edith Holden
The Canterbury Tales	Geoffrey Chaucer	Edwardian Lady	
The Captain and the Kings	Taylor Caldwell	The Country Girls	Edna O'Brien
Captain Corelli's Mandolin	Louis de Bernières	Cover Her Face*	P.D. James.
Captain Slaughterboard	Mervyn Peake	Cranford	Mrs Elizabeth
Drops Anchor*			Gaskell
The Carpetbaggers	Harold Robbins	Credo	Melvyn Bragg
The Carpet People*	Terry Pratchett	Crime and Punishment	Fyodor Dostoyevsky
The Case of the Velvet Claws	Earl Stanley Gardner	The Crocodile Bird	Ruth Rendell
The Castle	Franz Kafka	Crome Yellow	Aldous Huxley
The Castle of Otranto	Horace Walpole	Cross of St George	Alexander Kent
Castle Rackrent*	Maria Edgeworth	The Cruel Sea	Nicholas Monsarrat
The Casuarina Tree	William Somerset	Cry, the Beloved Country	Alan Paton
	Maugham	A Cure for Cancer	Michael Moorcock
Cat and Mouse	Günther Grass	Curtain	Agatha Christie
Catch-22	Joseph Heller	Daisy Miller	Henry James
Catcher in the Rye*	J.D. Salinger	Dame's Delight*	Margaret Forster
Catherine Herself*	James Hilton	A Dance to the Music of	Anthony Powell
Catriona	Robert Louis	Time (12 volumes)	
	Stevenson	Dangerous Davies	Leslie Thomas
The Cauldron	Colin Forbes	Dangerous Love	Ben Okri
Cause Celeb	Helen Fielding	The Dangling Man*	Saul Bellow
The Caves of Steel	Isaac Asimov	Daniel Deronda	George Eliot
A Celebration of Mass	Pope John Paul II	Dark Carnival*	Ray Bradbury
The Celestine Prophecy	James Redfield	The Dark Frontier*	Eric Ambler
Central Line – (short story)	Maeve Binchy	Darkness at Noon	Arthur Koestler
Centuries	Nostradamus	Dark Shadows Falling	Joe Simpson
A Certain Justice	P.D. James	The Darling Buds of May	H.E. Bates
Charity	Len Deighton	David Copperfield	Charles Dickens
Charlie and the Chocolate	Roald Dahl	The Day of the Jackal	Frederick Forsyth
Factory		The Day of the Locust	Nathanael West
Charlotte's Friends	Sarah Kennedy	The Day of the Triffids*	John Wyndham
Chérie	Colette	A Dead Cert	Dick Francis

LITERATURE

Book	Author	Book	Author
Gaudy Night	Dorothy L. Sayers	Headlong Hall	Thomas Love
The Tale of the Genji	Lady Murasaki		Peacock
Gentlemen Marry Brunettes	Anita Loos	Hearing Secret Harmonies	Anthony Powell
Gentlemen Prefer Blondes	Anita Loos	(A Dance to the Music of Time)	
George's Marvellous Medicine	Roald Dahl	The Heart is a Lonely	Carson McCullers
Georgy Girl	Margaret Forster	Hunter*	
Germinal	Émile Zola	Heart of Darkness	Joseph Conrad
Get Shorty	Elmore Leonard	Heart of Midlothian	Walter Scott
Ghost	Danielle Steele	The Heart of the Matter	Graham Greene
The Ghost in the Machine	Arthur Koestler	Heavy Weather	P.G. Wodehouse
The Ghost Road	Pat Barker	Heidi	Johanna Spyri
Gigi	Colette	Hemingway's Chair	Michael Palin
Gil Blas	Alain Le Sage	The History of Henry Esmond	W.M. Thackeray
The Ginger Man*	J.P. Donleavy	The Heretic's Apprentice	Ellis Peters
Giovanni's Room	James Baldwin	Hereward the Wake	Charles Kingsley
The Gladiators	Arthur Koestler	Herzog	Saul Bellow
The Glass Bead Game	Herman Hesse	High Fidelity	Nick Hornby
The Glass Key	Dashiell Hammett	High Rise	J.G. Ballard
The Go-Between	L.P. Hartley	A High Wind in Jamaica	Richard Hughes
The Godfather	Mario Puzo	The High Window	Raymond Chandler
The God of Small Things	Arundhati Roy	The Hireling	L.P. Hartley
God's Little Acre	Erskine Caldwell	A History of Tom Jones	Henry Fielding
The Golden Apples of the	Ray Bradbury	A Foundling	
Sun		The History Man	Malcolm Bradbury
The Golden Bowl	Henry James	The History of Mr Polly	H.G. Wells
Gone With the Wind	Margaret Mitchell	The Hitchhiker's Guide to the	Douglas Adams
Goodbye Mr Chips	James Hilton	Galaxy*	
Goodbye to Berlin	Christopher	HMS Ulysses*	Alistair MacLean
	Isherwood	The Hobbit	J.R.R. Tolkien
The Good Companions	J.B. Priestley	Hogfather	Terry Pratchett
The Good Earth	Pearl Buck	Hollywood Wives	Jackie Collins
The Good Soldier Schweyk	Jaroslav Hašek	The Honorary Consul	Graham Greene
Good Wives	Louisa May Alcott	Hope	Len Deighton
The Gormenghast Trilogy	Mervyn Peake	Hornblower (series)	C.S. Forester
Go Tell it on the Mountain	James Baldwin	The Hornet's Nest	Patricia Cornwell
Grapefruit	Yoko Ono	A Horseman Riding By	R.F. Delderfield
Grapes of Wrath	John Steinbeck	The Horse Whisperer	Nicholas Evans
The Grass is Singing*	Doris Lessing	Hotel	Arthur Hailey
Gravity's Rainbow	Thomas Pynchon	Hôtel du Lac	Anita Brookner
Great Apes	Will Self	Hound of Death	Agatha Christie
Great Expectations	Charles Dickens	The Hound of the Baskervilles	Arthur Conan Doyle
The Great Gatsby	F Scott Fitzgerald		
The Green Hat	Michael Arlen	A House Divided	Pearl Buck
Greenmantle	John Buchan	A House for Mr Biswas	V.S. Naipaul
Gridlock	Ben Elton	House of Cards*	Michael Dobbs
Grimus*	Salman Rushdie	Howards End	E.M. Forster
The Group	Mary McCarthy	How Green Was My Valley	Richard Llewellyn
Gulag Archipelago	Alexander	The Adventures of	Mark Twain
	Solzhenitsyn	Huckleberry Finn	
Gulliver's Travels	Jonathan Swift	Humboldt's Gift	Saul Bellow
The Gun Seller	Hugh Laurie	Hunchback of Notre Dame	Victor Hugo
The Gunpowder Plot: Terror	Antonia Fraser	Huntingtower	John Buchan
and Faith in 1605		Ice Station Zebra	Alistair Maclean
The Guns of Navarone	Alistair Maclean	I, Claudius	Robert Graves
Guys and Dolls	Damon Runyon	Icon	Frederick Forsyth
The Haj	Leon Uris	The Idiot	Fyodor Dostoyevsky
The Handmaid's Tale	Margaret Atwood	If This Is A Man	Primo Levi
Haphazard House	Mary Wesley	Immediate Action	Andy McNab
The Happy Return	C.S. Forester	The Immigrants	Howard Fast
Harper of Heaven	Robert Service	In a Free State	V.S. Naipaul
Harpoon at a Venture	Gavin Maxwell	In Camera	Jean-Paul Sartre
Harry Potter and the Chamber	J.K. Rowling	Incognita, or Love and Duty	William Congreve
of Secrets		Reconciled*	
Harry Potter and the Goblet	J.K. Rowling	Inside Mr Enderby	Anthony Burgess
of Fire		Insomnia	Stephen King
Harry Potter and the	J.K. Rowling	In the Beauty of the Lilies	John Updike
Philosopher's Stone		The Invisible Man	H.G. Wells
Harry Potter and the Prisoner	J.K. Rowling	The Ipcress File*	Len Deighton
of Azkaban		I, Robot	Isaac Asimov
Harvest	Celia Brayfield	Island in the Sun	Alec Waugh
Hatter's Castle*	A.J. Cronin	It	Stephen King

L
I
T
E
R
A
T
U
R
E

Book	Author	Book	Author
Manhattan Transfer	John Dos Passos	Nana	Émile Zola
Mansfield Park	Jane Austen	The Napoleon of Notting Hill	G.K. Chesterton
The Martian	George Du Maurier	National Velvet	Enid Bagnold
Martin Chuzzlewit*	Charles Dickens	Nausea	Jean-Paul Sartre
Mary Barton*	Elizabeth Gaskell	Neither Here Nor There	Bill Bryson
The Mary Deare	Ralph Hammond Innes	Never Love a Stranger	Harold Robbins
		The New Machiavelli	H.G. Wells
Mary Poppins	P.L. Travers.	Next of Kin	Joanna Trollope
The Mask of Dimitrios	Eric Ambler	Nexus	Henry Miller
Maskerade	Terry Pratchett	Nicholas Nickleby	Charles Dickens
Master and Commander	Patrick O'Brian	The Nigger of the Narcissus	Joseph Conrad
The Master and Margarita	Mikhail Bulgakov	Night and Day	Virginia Woolf
Matilda	Roald Dahl	The Night Manager	John Le Carré
The Mayor of Casterbridge	Thomas Hardy	Nightmare Abbey	Thomas Love Peacock
Meet the Tiger	Leslie Charteris		
Melincourt	Thomas Love Peacock	Night Train	Martin Amis
		The Nine Billion Names of God	Arthur C. Clarke
Memoirs of a Fox-Hunting Man	Siegfried Sassoon		
The Memory Game	Nicci French	The Nine Tailors	Dorothy L. Sayers
Men are From Mars, Women are From Venus	John Gray	Nineteen Eighty-Four	George Orwell
		Noble House	James Clavell
Men At Arms	Terry Pratchett	Noddy	Enid Blyton
Message from Malaga	Helen MacInnes	North and South	Mrs Elizabeth Gaskell
The Metamorphosis	Franz Kafka		
Metroland	Julian Barnes	Northanger Abbey	Jane Austen
The Midden	Tom Sharpe	Nostromo	Joseph Conrad
Midnight Cowboy	James Herlihy	Not a Penny More, Not a Penny Less*	Jeffrey Archer
Midnight's Children	Salman Rushdie		
The Midwich Cuckoos	John Wyndham	Notes From a Small Island	Bill Bryson
Miguel Street	V.S. Naipaul	Now We Are Six	A.A. Milne
Mildred Pierce	James M. Cain	The Oak and the Calf	Alexander Solzhenitsyn
The Mill on the Floss	George Eliot		
Miss Lonelyhearts	Nathaniel West	Oblomov	Ivan Goncharov
Moby-Dick	Herman Melville	The Odessa File	Frederick Forsyth
Moll Flanders	Daniel Defoe	An Occurrence at Owl Creek Bridge	Bierce Ambrose
A Month in the Country	Ivan Turgenev		
The Moon and Sixpence	William Somerset Maugham	Of Human Bondage	William Somerset Maugham
Moonstone	Wilkie Collins	Of Mice and Men	John Steinbeck
The Moor's Last Sigh	Salman Rushdie	O, How the Wheel Becomes It!	Anthony Powell
Mort	Terry Pratchett	The Old Curiosity Shop	Charles Dickens
Le Morte D'Arthur	Thomas Malory	The Old Devils	Kingsley Amis
Mother	Maxim Gorky	The Old Man and the Sea	Ernest Hemingway
Mother, Can You Hear Me?	Margaret Forster	Old Peter's Russian Tales	Arthur Ransome
Mother Goose	Charles Perrault	The Old Wives' Tale	Arnold Bennett
Mother Goose Treasury	Raymond Briggs	Oliver Twist	Charles Dickens
Mourning Doves	Helen Forrester	The Once and Future King	T.H. White
Mr Men	Roger Hargreaves	On the Road	Jack Kerouac
Mr Midshipman Easy	Capt. Frederick Marryat	One Day in the Life of Ivan Denisovich*	Alexander Solzhenitsyn
Mr Nice	Howard Marks	One Fat Englishman	Kingsley Amis
Mr Norris Changes Trains	Christopher Isherwood	One Hundred Years of Solitude	Gabriel Garcia Márquez
Mrs Dalloway	Virginia Woolf	One-Upmanship	Stephen Potter
Mr Sponge's Sporting Tour	Robert Smith Surtees	On the Beach	Nevil Shute
		Only When I Larf	Len Deighton
Murder Must Advertise	Dorothy L. Sayers	O Pioneers!	Willa Cather
The Murder of Roger Ackroyd	Agatha Christie	The Origin of Species	Charles Darwin
'The Murders in the Rue Morgue'	Edgar Allan Poe	Oroonoko	Aphra Behn
		Other Voices, Other Rooms*	Truman Capote
My Cousin Rachel	Daphne Du Maurier	Our Game	John Le Carré
My Family and Other Animals	Gerald Durrell	Our Man in Havana	Graham Greene
My Son, My Son	Howard Spring	Our Mutual Friend	Charles Dickens
The Mysterious Affair at Styles	Agatha Christie	An Outcast of the Islands	Joseph Conrad
The Mystery of Edwin Drood	Charles Dickens	Out of the Silent Planet	C.S. Lewis
The Mystic Masseur*	V.S. Naipaul	The Outsider	Albert Camus
My Universities	Maxim Gorky	Outskirts*	Hanif Kureishi
The Naked and the Dead*	Norman Mailer	The Overcoat	Nikolai Gogol
		Overture to Death	Ngaio Marsh
The Naked Lunch	William Burroughs	Paddy Clarke Ha Ha Ha	Roddy Doyle
The Name of the Rose	Umberto Eco	The Pallisers	Anthony Trollope

LITERATURE

Book	Author	Book	Author
The Screwtape Letters	C.S. Lewis	The Strange House*	Raymond Briggs
The Sea, The Sea	Iris Murdoch	Strangers and Brothers	C.P. Snow
Sea-Wolf	Jack London	Studs Lonigan Trilogy	James Farrell
The Second Sex	Simone de Beauvoir	Stuff	Joseph Connolly
Secret Diary of Adrian Mole	Sue Townsend	The Subjection of Women	John Stuart Mill
Aged 13 3/4*		A Suitable Boy	Vikram Seth
The Secret Garden	Frances Hodgson	A Summer Birdcage*	Margaret Drabble
	Burnett	The Sun Also Rises	Ernest Hemingway
The Secret Life of Walter Mitty	James Thurber	Superwoman	Shirley Conran
The Secret Seven	Enid Blyton	Swallows and Amazons	Arthur Ransome
The Seed and the Sower	Laurens	Swan	Naomi Campbell
	Van Der Post	Sweet William	Beryl Bainbridge
Seize the Day	Saul Bellow	The Swiss Family Robinson	Johann Wyss
The Selfish Gene	Richard Dawkins	The Sword in the Stone	T.H. White
Sense and Sensibility*	Jane Austen	Sword of Honour Trilogy	Evelyn Waugh
The Sentinel	Arthur C. Clarke	Sybil	Benjamin Disraeli
Seventh Avenue	Norman Bogner	The System of Logic	John Stuart Mill
79 Park Avenue	Harold Robbins	The Tailor of Panama	John Le Carré
Shadow Baby	Margaret Forster	Take a Girl Like You	Kingsley Amis
Shadow of a Sun*	A.S. Byatt	A Tale of a Tub	Jonathan Swift
Sharpe's Devil	Bernard Cornwell	The Tale of Jemima	Beatrix Potter
She	Henry Rider	Puddle-Duck	
	Haggard	The Tale of Mr Jeremy Fisher	Beatrix Potter
The Adventures of	Arthur Conan Doyle	The Tale of Squirrel Nutkin,	Beatrix Potter
Sherlock Holmes		A Tale of Two Cities	Charles Dickens
The Shipping News	Annie E. Proulx	Tales from Shakespeare	Charles and Mary
Shogun	James Clavell		Lamb
Shout at the Devil	Wilbur Smith	Tales of My Landlord	Walter Scott
The Sign of Four	Arthur Conan Doyle	Tales of the City	Armistead Maupin
Silas Marner	George Eliot	Tales of the South Pacific*	James Michener
The Silence of the Lambs	Thomas Harris	The Talisman	Walter Scott
Silmarillion	J.R.R. Tolkien	Talking to the Dead	Helen Dunmore
The Simisola	Ruth Rendell	Tancred	Benjamin Disraeli
Sins	Judith Gould	Tarka the Otter	Henry Williamson
Sir Charles Grandison	Samuel Richardson	Tarzan	Edgar Rice
Slaughterhouse-Five	Kurt Vonnegut		Burroughs
Sleepers	Lorenzo Carcaterra	A Taste of Honey	Shelagh Delaney
The Sleeping Beauty	Charles Perrault	Tenant of Wildfell Hall	Anne Bronte
Small Is Beautiful	Ernst Schumacher	Tender Is the Night	F. Scott Fitzgerald
A Small Town in Germany	John Le Carré	Tess of the D'Urbervilles	Thomas Hardy
The Snow Goose	Paul Gallico	Testament of Experience	Vera Brittain
The Snowman	Raymond Briggs	Testament of Friendship	Vera Brittain
Snow White and the Seven	Grimm Brothers	Testament of Youth	Vera Brittain
Dwarfs		That Uncertain Feeling	Kingsley Amis
Soldiers' Pay*	William Faulkner	Therapy	David Lodge
Some Other Rainbow	John McCarthy and	Thérèse Raquin	Émile Zola
	Jill Morrell	The Thin Man	Dashiell Hammett
Song of the Light: Rameses	Christian Jacq	The Third Man	Graham Greene
Sons and Lovers	D.H. Lawrence	The Third Twin	Ken Follett
Sophie's World	Jostein Gaarder	The Thirty-Nine Steps	John Buchan
The Sorrows of Young Werther	Johann Goethe	This Side of Paradise*	F. Scott Fitzgerald
The Sound and the Fury	William Faulkner	The Thorn Birds	Colleen McCullough
A Spell of Winter	Helen Dunmore	The Three Hostages	John Buchan
The Spirit Level	Seamus Heaney	Three Men in a Boat	Jerome K. Jerome
Spycatcher	Peter Wright	Three Men on the Bummel	Jerome K. Jerome
The Spy Who Came in	John Le Carré	The Three Musketeers	Alexandre Dumas
from the Cold			(Père)
Stamboul Train	Graham Greene	3001: The Final Odyssey	Arthur C. Clarke
The Stand	Stephen King	Through the Looking Glass	Lewis Carroll
Stanley and the Women	Kingsley Amis	Time for a Tiger*	Anthony Burgess
Stark*	Ben Elton	The Time Machine*	H.G. Wells
A Start in Life*	Anita Brookner	The Time of the Angels	Iris Murdoch
The State We're In	Will Hutton	A Time to Dance	Melvyn Bragg
Stay With Me Till Morning	John Braine	The Tin Drum*	Günther Grass
The Stepford Wives	Ira Levin	Tinker, Tailor, Soldier, Spy	John Le Carré
Steppenwolf	Herman Hesse	Titus Groan	Mervyn Peake
Still Life	A.S. Byatt	Tobacco Road	Erskine Caldwell
A Stone For Danny Fisher	Harold Robbins	To Cuba and Back	Richard Dana (Jr)
The Story of Esther Costello	Nicholas Monsarrat	To Kill A Mockingbird	Harper Lee
The Strange Case of Dr Jekyll	Robert Louis	Tom Brown's Schooldays	Thomas Hughes
and Mr Hyde	Stevenson	Tom Merry	Frank Richards

Book	Author	Book	Author
Tom Sawyer	Mark Twain	The War of the Worlds	H.G. Wells
Too Late the Phalarope	Alan Paton	Washington Square	Henry James
The Torrents of Spring*	Ernest Hemingway	The Wasp Factory	Iain Banks
Tortilla Flat	John Steinbeck	The Water-Babies	Charles Kingsley
To Serve Them All My Days	R.F. Delderfield	Watership Down	Richard Adams
To the Lighthouse	Virginia Woolf	Waverley	Walter Scott
Touching the Void	Joe Simpson	The Way of All Flesh	Samuel Butler
Tough Guys Don't Dance	Norman Mailer	A Weekend with Claud*	Beryl Bainbridge
The Town and the City*	Jack Kerouac	Weir of Hermiston	Robert Louis
A Town Like Alice	Nevil Shute		Stevenson
Toxic Shock	Sara Paretsky	The Well of Loneliness	Radcliffe Hall
The Toynbee Convector	Ray Bradbury	Westward Ho!	Charles Kingsley
Trainspotting	Irvine Welsh	What America Means to Me	Pearl Buck
The Treasure of the	Berick Traven	What Did You Do in the	Mavis Nicholson
Sierra Madre		War, Mummy	
The Treasure Seekers	Edith Nesbit	What Katy Did	Susan Coolidge
The Trial	Franz Kafka	What's Become of Waring?	Anthony Powell
Trilby	George Du Maurier	What's Bred in the Bone	Robertson Davies
The Life and Opinions of	Laurence Sterne	Wheels	Arthur Hailey
Tristram Shandy		When Eight Bells Toll	Alistair Maclean
Tropic of Cancer	Henry Miller	When the Lion Feeds*	Wilbur Smith
Tropic of Capricorn	Henry Miller	When the Wind Blows	Raymond Briggs
Tropic of Ruislip	Leslie Thomas	Where Eagles Dare	Alistair Maclean
The Trumpet Major	Thomas Hardy	Whisky Galore	Compton Mackenzie
The Turn of the Screw	Henry James	The White Company	Arthur Conan Doyle
Twenty Thousand Leagues	Jules Verne	White Eagles Over Serbia	Lawrence Durrell
Under the Sea		White Fang	Jack London
The Two Sisters*	H.E. Bates	The White Peacock*	D.H. Lawrence
2001: A Space Odyssey	Arthur C. Clarke	Whose Body?	Dorothy L. Sayers
2061: Odyssey Three	Arthur C. Clarke	A Wide Field	Günther Grass
2010: Odyssey Two	Arthur C. Clarke	Wild Swans	Jung Chang
Two Years Before the Mast	Richard Dana (Jr)	Wilhelm Meister's Apprenticeship	Johann Goethe
Typee*	Herman Melville	Wilhelm Meister's Travels	Johann Goethe
Ulysses	James Joyce	Wilt	Tom Sharpe
The Unbearable Bassington	Hector Hugh Munro	The Wind in the Willows	Kenneth Grahame
	(Saki)	A Window in Thrums	J.M. Barrie
The Unbearable Lightness	Milan Kundera	The Winds of War	Herman Wouk
of Being		Winnie-the-Pooh	A.A. Milne
Uncle Remus stories	Joel Chandler Harris	Winnie-the-Pooh: Now We	A.A. Milne
Uncle Tom's Cabin	Harriet Beecher	Are Six	
	Stowe	Winsome Winnie	Stephen Leacock
Under the Greenwood Tree	Thomas Hardy	The Witches of Eastwick	John Updike
Under the Net*	Iris Murdoch	The Witching Hour	Anne Rice
Under the Volcano	Malcolm Lowry	With These Hands	Pam Ayers
Under Western Eyes	Joseph Conrad	Witness for the Prosecution	Agatha Christie
Unnatural Exposure	Patricia Cornwell	The Woman in White	Wilkie Collins
The Upstart	Catherine Cookson	The Woman Who Walked into	Roddy Doyle
Utopia	Thomas More	Doors	
V	Thomas Pynchon	Women in Love	D.H. Lawrence
Valperga	Mary Shelley	The Wonderful Adventures of	Selma Lagerlöf
Vanity Fair: A Novel Without	W.M. Thackeray	Nils	
a Hero		Worrals of the WAAF	Capt. W.E. Johns
The Van	Roddy Doyle	Worst Fears	Fay Weldon
Vathek	William Beckford	Wreckers Must Breathe	Ralph Hammond
Vicar of Wakefield	Oliver Goldsmith		Innes
Victory	John Williams	Wuthering Heights	Emily Brontë
Villette	Charlotte Brontë	The X Files	Les Martin
The Virginians	W.M. Thackeray	A Year in Cricklewood	Alan Coren
The Virgin Soldiers*	Leslie Thomas	A Year in Provence	Peter Mayall
A Vision of Battlements*	Anthony Burgess	Year of the Tiger	Jack Higgins
Visitors	Anita Brookner	The Young Fur Traders	R.M. Ballantyne
Vivien Grey*	Benjamin Disraeli	The Young Man*	Stephen Potter
The Voyage Out*	Virginia Woolf	Youth	Leo Tolstoy
Walden, or Life in the Woods	Henry Thoreau	Zen and the Art of Motorcycle	Robert Pirsig
War and Peace	Leo Tolstoy	Maintenance	
The Warden	Anthony Trollope		

L
I
T
E
R
A
T
U
R
E

NB: The list above is a good cross-section of popular works, but by no means comprehensive. Many popular books are included and some interesting less-known works. For ease of reference, the list is re-sorted below by author.

Index of Books By Author

(* denotes author's first book)

L
I
T
E
R
A
T
U
R
E

Author	Book
	The Nigger of the Narcissus
	Nostromo
	An Outcast of the Islands
	Under Western Eyes
Shirley Conran	Lace
	Superwoman
Benjamin Constant	Adolphe
Catherine Cookson	Bondage of Love
	Branded Man
	Kate Hannigan*
	The Upstart
Susan Coolidge	What Katy Did
James Fenimore Cooper	The Last of the Mohicans
	Leatherstocking stories
	Precaution*
Jilly Cooper	Appassionata
	Emily*
Alan Coren	The Dog It Was That Died*
	A Year in Cricklewood
Bernard Cornwell	The Bloody Ground
	Excalibur
	Sharpe's Devil
Patricia Cornwell	The Hornet's Nest
	Unnatural Exposure
Stephen Crane	The Red Badge of Courage
Michael Crichton	Airframe
	Jurassic Park
	The Lost World
Richmal Crompton	Just William
A.J. Cronin	The Citadel
	Hatter's Castle*
	The Keys of the Kingdom
Edwina Currie	Parliamentary Affair
Roald Dahl	The BFG
	Charlie and the Chocolate Factory
	George's Marvellous Medicine
	James and the Giant Peach
	Matilda
Richard Dana Jr	To Cuba and Back
	Two Years Before the Mast
Charles Darwin	The Descent of Man
	The Origin of Species
Robertson Davies	What's Bred in the Bone
Richard Dawkins	The Selfish Gene
Simone De Beauvoir	The Second Sex
Daniel Defoe	A Journal of the Plague Year
	Moll Flanders
	Robinson Crusoe
Len Deighton	Charity
	Faith
	Funeral in Berlin
	Game, Set and Match
	Hope
	The Ipcress File*
	Only When I Larf
Shelagh Delaney	A Taste of Honey
R.F. Delderfield	A Horseman Riding By
	To Serve Them All My Days
Thomas De Quincey	Confessions of an English Opium Eater
Colin Dexter	Death Is Now My Neighbour

Author	Book
Charles Dickens	Barnaby Rudge
	Bleak House
	A Christmas Carol
	David Copperfield
	Dombey and Son
	Great Expectations
	Little Dorritt
	Martine Chuzzlewit
	The Mystery of Edwin Drood, (unfinished)
	Nicholas Nickleby
	The Old Curiosity Shop
	Oliver Twist
	Our Mutual Friend
	Pickwick Papers
	A Tale of Two Cities
James Dickey	Deliverance
Benjamin Disraeli	Coningsby
	Sybil
	Tancred
	Vivien Grey*
Michael Dobbs	House of Cards*
Stephen Donaldson	Chronicles of Thomas Covenant
J.P. Donleavy	A Fairytale of New York
	The Ginger Man*
Fyodor Dostoyevsky	The Brothers Karamazov
	Crime and Punishment
	The Idiot
Ed Douglas	Chomolungma Sings the Blues
Arthur Conan Doyle	The Exploits of Brigadier Gerard
	The Hound of the Baskervilles
	The Lost World
	The Adventures of Sherlock Holmes
	The Sign of Four
	The White Company
Roddy Doyle	Paddy Clarke Ha Ha Ha
	The Van
	The Woman Who Walked into Doors
Margaret Drabble	The Radiant Way
	The Garrick Year
	A Summer Birdcage*
Theodore Dreiser	An American Tragedy
Alexandre Dumas, (Père)	The Count of Monte Cristo
	The Three Musketeers
Alexandre Dumas, (Fils)	The Lady of the Camellias
Daphne Du Maurier	Frenchman's Creek
	Jamaica Inn
	My Cousin Rachel
	Rebecca
George Du Maurier	The Martian
	Trilby
Helen Dunmore	A Spell of Winter
	Talking to the Dead
Gerald Durrell	My Family and Other Animals
Lawrence Durrell	The Alexandria Quartet
	Pied Piper of Lovers*
	White Eagles Over Serbia
Umberto Eco	The Name of the Rose
	Foucault's Pendulum
Maria Edgeworth	The Absentee
	Belinda
	Castle Rackrent*

LITERATURE

Author	Book	Author	Book
Willis Hall	The Long and the Short and the Tall		Eyeless in Gaza
			Point Counter Point
Dashiell Hammett	The Glass Key	John Irving	A Prayer For Owen Meany
	The Maltese Falcon	Washington Irving	The Legend of Sleepy
	The Thin Man		Hollow
Ralph Hammond Innes	Campbell's Kingdom		Rip Van Winkle
	The Mary Deare		Salmagundi
	Wreckers Must Breathe	Christopher Isherwood	All the Conspirators*
Thomas Hardy	Desperate Remedies*		Goodbye to Berlin
	Far from the Madding Crowd		Mr Norris Changes Trains
			Prater Violet
	Jude the Obscure	Kazuo Ishiguro	The Remains of the Day
	The Mayor of Casterbridge	Christian Jacq	Song of the Light: Rameses
	The Return of the Native	Henry James	The Ambassadors
	Tess of the D'Urbervilles		The Bostonians
	The Trumpet Major		Daisy Miller
	Under the Greenwood Tree		The Golden Bowl
			The Portrait of a Lady
Roger Hargreaves	Mr Men		The Turn of the Screw
Joel Chandler Harris	Uncle Remus stories		Washington Square
Thomas Harris	The Silence of the Lambs	P.D. James	A Certain Justice
			Cover Her Face*)
L.P. Hartley	The Go-Between	Jerome K. Jerome	Three Men in a Boat
	The Hireling		Three Men on the Bummel
Stephen Hawking	A Brief History of Time		
Nathaniel Hawthorne	Fanshawe*	John McCarthy and Jill Morrell	Some Other Rainbow
	The Scarlet Letter		
Seamus Heaney	The Spirit Level	Capt. W.E. Johns	Biggles
Joseph Heller	Catch-22		Worrals of the WAAF
	Picture This	James Jones	From Here to Eternity
Ernest Hemingway	Death in the Afternoon	Erica Jong	Fear of Flying
	A Farewell to Arms	James Joyce	The Dubliners
	For Whom the Bell Tolls		Finnegans Wake
	The Garden of Eden		Portrait of the Artist As a Young Man
	The Old Man and the Sea		Ulysses
	The Sun Also Rises	Franz Kafka	The Castle
	Torrents of Spring*		Metamorphosis
Frank Herbert	Dune		The Trial
James Herbert	The Rats		An Evil Cradling
	The Fog	Brian Keenan	An Evil Cradling
James Herlihy	Midnight Cowboy	Sarah Kennedy	Charlotte's Friends
Herman Hesse	The Glass Bead Game	Alexander Kent	Cross of St George
	Peter Camenzind*	Jack Kerouac	Big Sur
	Steppenwolf		The Dharma Bums
Jack Higgins	The Eagle Has Landed		Doctor Sax
	The President's Daughter		On the Road
	The Year of the Tiger		The Town and the City*
Richard Hillary	The Last Enemy	Stephen King	Desperation
James Hilton	Catherine Herself*		Insomnia
	Goodbye Mr Chips		It
	Lost Horizon		The Stand
Edith Holden	The Country Diary of an Edwardian Lady	Charles Kingsley	Hereward the Wake
			The Water-Babies
A.M. Homes	The End of Alice		Westward Ho !
Anthony Hope	The Prisoner of Zenda	Rudyard Kipling	The Light That Failed
	Rupert of Hentzau	Arthur Koestler	Darkness at Noon
Nick Hornby	Fever Pitch*		The Ghost in the Machine
	High Fidelity		
E.W. Hornung	Raffles		The Gladiators
Richard Hughes	A High Wind in Jamaica	Dean R. Koontz	The Bad Place
Thomas Hughes	Tom Brown's Schooldays		Demon Seed
Victor Hugo	The Hunchback of Notre Dame	Judith Krantz	Princess Daisy
		Milan Kundera	The Unbearable Lightness of Being
	Les Misérables		
Will Hutton	The State We're In	Hanif Kureishi	The Buddha of Suburbia
Aldous Huxley	Antic Hay		Outskirts*
	Brave New World	Selma Lagerlöf	The Wonderful Adventures of Nils
	Crome Yellow		
	The Devils of Loudun	Charles and Mary Lamb	Tales from Shakespeare
	The Doors of Perception	Hugh Laurie	The Gun Seller

LITERATURE

Author	Book	Author	Book
Andrew Morton	Diana: Her New Life	Beatrix Potter	The Tale of Jemima
Hector Hugh Munro(Saki)	The Unbearable		Puddle-Duck
	Bassington		The Tale of Mr Jeremy
	Beasts and Superbeasts		Fisher
Murasaki Shikibu	The Tale of Genji		The Tale of Squirrel
Iris Murdoch	The Black Prince		Nutkin
	The Sea, The Sea	Stephen Potter	Gamesmanship
	The Time of the Angels		One-Upmanship
	Under the Net*		The Young Man*
Vladimir Nabokov	Bend Sinister	Anthony Powell	Afternoon Men*
	Lolita		A Dance to the Music of
V.S. Naipaul	Bend in the River		Time (12 Volumes)
	A House for Mr Biswas		The Fisher King
	In a Free State		Hearing Secret Harmonies
	Miguel Street		(last volume of Dance)
	The Mystic Masseur*		O, How the Wheel
Edith Nesbit	The Railway Children		Becomes It !
	The Lark		A Question of Upbringing
	The Treasure Seekers		(first volume of Dance)
Mavis Nicholson	What Did You Do in the		What's Become of
	War, Mummy?		Waring?
Mary Norton	The Borrowers	Terry Pratchett	The Carpet People*
Nostradamus	Centuries		Discworld
Patrick O'Brian	Master and Commander		Feet of Clay (Discworld
Edna O'Brien	The Country Girls		Series)
Ben Okri	Dangerous Love		Hogfather
Michael Ondaatje	The English Patient		The Last Continent
Yoko Ono	Grapefruit		Maskerade
Baroness Orczy	The Scarlet Pimpernel		Men At Arms
George Orwell	Animal Farm		Mort
	Down and Out in Paris	Sister Helen Prejean	Dead Man Walking
	and London	J.B. Priestley	Angel Pavement
	The Lion and the Unicorn		The Good Companions
	Nineteen Eighty-Four	Annie E. Proulx	The Shipping News
	The Road to Wigan Pier	Marcel Proust	Remembrance of Things
Thomas Paine	The Age of Reason		Past (novel cycle in 7
	Common Sense		parts
	Public Good	Alexander Pushkin	Eugene Onegin
	The Rights of Man	Mario Puzo	The Godfather
Michael Palin	Full Circle: A Pacific	Thomas Pynchon	Gravity's Rainbow
	Journey		V
	Hemingway's Chair	François Rabelais	Gargantua
Sara Paretsky	Toxic Shock		Pantagruel
John Dos Passos	Manhattan Transfer	Ayn Rand	Atlas Shrugged
Anna Pasternak	Princess in Love	Arthur Ransome	Old Peter's Russian Tales
Boris Pasternak	Doctor Zhivago*		Swallows and Amazons
Alan Paton	Cry, the Beloved Country	R.E. Raspe	Baron Münchhausen
	Too Late the Phalarope	Charles Reade	The Cloister and the
Thomas Love Peacock	Headlong Hall		Hearth
	Melincourt	James Redfield	Celestine Prophecy
	Nightmare Abbey	Erich Maria Remarque	All Quiet on the Western
Mervyn Peake	The Gormenghast Trilogy		Front
	Captain Slaughterboard	Ruth Rendell	The Bridesmaid
	Drops Anchor*		The Crocodile Bird
	Titus Groan		From Doon with Death*
Charles Perrault	The Sleeping Beauty		The Keys to the Street
	Bluebeard		Road Rage
	Little Red Riding Hood		Simisola
	Mother Goose	Anne Rice	The Witching Hour
	Puss in Boots	Frank Richards	Billy Bunter
Ellis Peters	The Heretic's Apprentice		Tom Merry
Robert Pirsig	Zen and the Art of Motor	Samuel Richardson	Clarissa
	cycle Maintenance		Pamela
Sylvia Plath	The Bell Jar		Sir Charles Grandison
Edgar Allan Poe	'The Fall of the House of	Harold Robbins	79 Park Avenue
	Usher'		The Carpetbaggers
	'The Murders in the Rue		The Dream Merchants*
	Morgue'		Never Love a Stranger
	'The Pit and the		A Stone For Danny Fisher
	Pendulum'	Monty Roberts	The Man Who Listens to
Pope John Paul II	A Celebration of Mass		Horses

LITERATURE

Author	Book	Author	Book
	Without a Hero	Alec Waugh	The Loom of Youth*
	The Virginians		Island in the Sun
D.M. Thomas	The Flute-Player	Auberon Waugh	The Foxglove Saga*
	The White Hotel	Evelyn Waugh	Brideshead Revisited
Dylan Thomas	Portrait of the Artist as a Young Dog		Decline and Fall*
Leslie Thomas	Dangerous Davies		Sword of Honour (Trilogy)
	Tropic of Ruislip	Fay Weldon	Affliction
	The Virgin Soldiers*		Down Among the Women
Flora Thompson	Lark Rise to Candleford		The Fat Woman's Joke*
Hunter S. Thompson	Fear and Loathing in Las Vegas		The Life and Loves of a She-Devil
Henry Thoreau	Walden, or Life in the Woods		Worst Fears
James Thurber	The Secret Life of Walter Mitty	H.G. Wells	The First Men in the Moon
J.R.R. Tolkien	The Hobbit		The History of Mr Polly
	The Lord of the Rings (Trilogy)		The Invisible Man
	The Silmarillion		The New Machiavelli
Leo Tolstoy	Anna Karenina		The Time Machine*
	Boyhood		The War of the Worlds
	Childhood	Irvine Welsh	The Acid House
	War and Peace		Ecstasy
	Youth		Trainspotting
Sue Townsend Adrian	The Secret Diary of Adrian Mole Aged 13¾*	Mary Wesley	The Camomile Lawn
			Haphazard House
Berick Traven	The Treasure of the Sierra Madre		Jumping the Queue
P.L. Travers	Mary Poppins	Nathanael West	A Cool Million
Robert Tressell	The Ragged Trousered Philanthropist		The Day of the Locust
Anthony Trollope	Barchester Towers		The Dream Life of Balso Snell
	Framley Parsonage		Miss Lonelyhearts
	The Macdermots of Ballycloran*	Edith Wharton	The Age of Innocence
	The Pallisers		The Buccaneers
	The Warden		Ethan Frome
Joanna Trollope	Next of Kin	Dennis Wheatley	The Devil Rides Out
Ivan Turgenev	Fathers and Sons	T.H. White	The Once and Future King
	A Month in the Country		The Sword in the Stone
Mark Twain	The Adventures of Huckleberry Finn	Oscar Wilde	The Picture of Dorian Gray
	The Adventures of Tom Sawyer	Thornton Wilder	The Bridge of San Luis Rey
Mark Updike	In the Beauty of the Lilies		The Cabala*
	Rabbit	John Williams (pictures by Tom Stoddart)	Victory
	The Witches of Eastwick	Henry Williamson	Salar the Salmon
Leon Uris	Armageddon		Tarka the Otter
	Exodus	Paul Wilson	Little Book of Calm
	The Haj	P.G. Wodehouse	Heavy Weather
Laurens Van Der Post	The Lost World of the Kalahari		Right Ho, Jeeves
	The Seed and the Sower	Tom Wolfe	The Bonfire of the Vanities
Jules Verne	Around the World in 80 Days	Naomi Wolf	The Beauty Myth
	Journey to the Centre of the Earth		Promiscuities
	Twenty Thousand Leagues Under the Sea	Virginia Woolf	Jacob's Room
Virgil	The Aeneid		Mrs Dalloway
Voltaire	Candide		Night and Day
Kurt Vonnegut	Player Piano*		To the Lighthouse
	Slaughterhouse 5		The Voyage Out*
Alice Walker	The Color Purple	Herman Wouk	The Winds of War
Lew Wallace	Ben Hur	P.C. Wren	Beau Geste
Robert James Waller	The Bridges Of Madison County	Peter Wright	Spycatcher
		Elizabeth Wurtzel	Prozac Nation
Horace Walpole	The Castle of Otranto	John Wyndham	The Day of the Triffids*
Keith Waterhouse	Billy Liar		The Kraken Wakes
			The Midwich Cuckoos
		Johann Wyss	The Swiss Family Robinson
		Émile Zola	Germinal
			J'Accuse
			Nana
			Thérèse Raquin
		Arnold Zweig	Claudia
		Stefan Zweig	Beware of Pity
			Kaleidoscope

Books: General Information

The Admirable Crichton   Master: Lord Loam. Ship: *The Bluebell.*

Alexandria Quartet   *Justine, Balthazar, Mountolive, Clea* (who had her right hand cut off to save her from drowning after it was pinned underwater by a harpoon gun).

Alice in Wonderland   In the croquet game, the mallets were flamingoes and the balls were hedgehogs.

Animal Farm   The manor farm was owned by Mr Jones, Napoleon the pig became the leader, Boxer was the horse.

Anna Karenina   Anna's death: She threw herself under a train.

Anne of Green Gables   Prince Edward Island was the setting for Anne Shirley's adventures.

Antic Hay   Title from *Edward II* by Christopher Marlowe.

Around the World in 80 Days   Central character is Phileas Fogg and his valet is Passepartout. They start and finish at the Reform Club in London. The Indian Widow is Aouda.

Bleak House   Court case was Jarndyce v Jarndyce, the rag and bone man was Krook (who died of spontaneous combustion).

Book of the Century   *Lord of the Rings* was voted Book of the Century in a survey of 25,000 people carried out in 1997 by Channel 4 and Waterstone's.

Bookshop   First WH Smith: Euston Station.

The Borrowers   The Names: Pod, Homily, Arrietty.

Brave New World   Title from *The Tempest* by William Shakespeare.

The Brothers Karamazov   Alyosha, Dmitry, Ivan, Smolykov.

Cakes and Ale   Title from *Twelfth Night* by William Shakespeare.

The Call of the Wild   Dog's name Buck.

Candide   Dr Pangloss's famous quote: 'All is for the best in the best of possible worlds.'

Canterbury Tales   The pilgrims met at the Tabard Inn, Southwark. The host on the pilgrimage was Harry Bailly. The summoner's tale tells of a corrupt mendicant friar who is tricked into accepting a donation of a fart.

Catch-22   Set in Pianosa in the Mediterranean. Captain Yossarian had the predicament. Kid Sampson died: cut in half by a low-flying aircraft. Catch-22 is the predicament faced by US bomber crews: You don't have to fly any more missions if you're crazy, but if you ask to be grounded you prove you're not crazy.

The Catcher in the Rye   Central character Holden Caulfield.

Children's Laureate   Quentin Blake became the first in 1999 and Ann Fine replaced him in May 2001

Clayhanger Trilogy   *Clayhanger, Hilda, Lessways, These Twain.* A fourth novel, *The Roll Call*, is loosely connected to the trilogy.

Cold Comfort Farm   Cows' names: *Aimless, Feckless, Graceless, Pointless.*

The Corridors of Power   War Minister was Roger Quaife.

The Count of Monte Cristo   The Count was Edmond Dantès, imprisoned in the Château D'if. He inherited a fortune left by Abbé Faria.

Crime and Punishment   Crime: murder of a female pawnbroker. Criminal: Raskolnikov. Investigating Inspector: Petrovitch.

David Copperfield   Headmaster of Salem House School: Mr Creakle. Aunt: Betsy Trotwood. Wives: Dora Spenlow and Agnes Wickfield.

Death in Venice   Gustav von Aschenbach dies of cholera.

Dickens   Only novel with female narrator: *Bleak House.*

Doctor Zhivago   Title character: Dr Yuri Zhivago. Wife: Tania Gromeko. Lover: Lara Antipova.

Dombey and Son   Captain Cuttle's famous quote: 'When found, make a note of.'

Don Quixote   Horse: Rosinante. Squire: Sancho Panza. Lady: Dulcinea.

East of Eden   Based on the story of Cain and Abel.

Emma   Emma Woodhouse marries Mr Knightley.

Every Man For Himself   Story of the *Titanic* disaster told by Morgan, a well connected young man.

Fair Stood the Wind for France   Title from 'Ballad of Agincourt' by Michael Drayton.

Far from the Madding Crowd   Bathsheba Everdene marries Sergeant Troy and Gabriel Oak. Title from 'Elegy Written in a Country Church-yard' by Thomas Gray.

Feet of Clay   Main character Commander Sir Samuel Vimes, head of Ankh-Morpork City Guard.

Finnegans Wake   Central character is Humphrey Chimpden Earwicker, a publican; the action takes place during one night.

Forsyte Saga Trilogy   *A Man of Property, In Chancery, To Let.*

For Whom the Bell Tolls   Title from a sermon by John Donne.

Foundation Trilogy   *Foundation, Foundation and Empire, Second Foundation.*

Gargantua and Pantagruel   Published under name 'Alcofri bas Nasier' (anagram of François Rabelais).

George Smiley   First appeared in *Call for the Dead.*

Glass of Blessings   (Barbara Pym)   Title from 'The Pulley' by George Herbert.

Gone with the Wind   Scarlett O'Hara marries Charles Hamilton, Frank Kennedy, Rhett Butler.

Gothic Novel: 1st   *The Castle of Otranto* by Horace Walpole (1764).

Grapes of Wrath   The Joad family – Tom, Al, Noah, Ruthie, Winfield and Rosasharn leave Oklahoma for California.

Gravity's Rainbow   Central character Tyrone Slothrop.

The Great Gatsby   Jay Gatsby loves Daisy Buchanan, cousin of narrator Nick Carraway.

Gulliver's Travels   Horses: Houyhnyms. Humans: Yahoos. Lands visited: Lilliput, Brobdingnag, Laputa, Blefuscu. Subtitle: 'Travels into Several Remote Nations of the World'.

Hardy's last novel   *Jude the Obscure.*

Harry Potter Books   Illustrated by Mary Grandpre. First in the series titled 'Harry Potter and the Sorcerer's Stone' in the USA.

Heavy Metal   Phrase coined by William Burroughs in *The Naked Lunch.*

The History Man   Title character Howard Kirk.

LITERATURE

Howard's End   House owners Mr and Mrs Wilcox.

Incunabula   Books printed before 1501 (means 'swaddling clothes').

Ivanhoe   Love interest: Lady Rowena.

James Bond books not by Fleming   *Colonel Sun* and *The James Bond Dossier* by Kingsley Amis, writing as Robert Markham.

Jane Eyre   Mr Rochester lives at Thornfield Hall. Jane's school is Lowood. Jane's bullying cousin is John Reed. Her home until aged 10 is Gateshead Hall. Dedicated to William Makepeace Thackery.

The Jewel in the Crown   First novel in the Raj Quartet. Plot revolves around the alleged rape in the Bibighar Gardens of Daphne Manners.

Jude the Obscure   Jude Fawley aspires to go to Christminster (Oxford), but fails to get into Sarcophagus College.

Kidnapped   Central character is David Balfour. His friend is the Jacobite Alan Breck. The ship that is meant to take David to the Carolina is the *Covenant*.

Kipps   Central character Arthur Kipps. Occupation: draper's assistant.

The Last Tycoon   Allegedly based on the Hollywood film producer Irving Thalberg.

Leather-Stocking stories   Hero: Natty Bumppo, also called 'Hawkeye' 'Pathfinder' and Deerslayer'. The Last of the Mohicans was Uncas and his father was Chingachgook.

Little Lord Fauntleroy   Title character: Cedric Errol.

Little Women   They are the March sisters: Amy, Beth, Jo and Meg.

Lolita   Title character: Dolores Haze.

The Longest Journey (E.M. Forster)   Title from *Epipsychidion* by Percy Bysshe Shelley.

Look Homeward, Angel (Thomas Wolfe)   from *Lycidas* by John Milton.

The Lord of the Rings   Setting: Middle Earth. Hobbit: Bilbo Baggins. Bilbo's nephew: Frodo, Maker of the One Ring: Sauron. Sauron's land: Mordor. Wizard: Gandalf. Gandalf's horse: Shadowfax. Books in the trilogy: *The Fellowship of the Ring*, *The Two Towers*, *The Return of the King*.

Madame Bovary   Title character neé Emma Rouault.

Mansfield Park   Heroine Fanny Price.

The Mayor of Casterbridge   Mayor: First Michael Henchard then Donald Farfrae. Setting: Wessex. 'Casterbridge' is Dorchester. Henchard sells his wife and daughter for five guineas.

The Memory Game   Nicci Gerrard and Sean French are co-writers.

The Mill on the Floss   Central characters: Tom and Maggie Tulliver. Setting: Dorlcote Mill.

Mirror Crack'd From Side to Side (Agatha Christie)   Title from 'The Lady of Shalott' by Alfred Lord Tennyson.

Moby Dick   Captain: Ahab. Narrator: Ishmael. Ship: Pequod.

The Moon and Sixpence   Inspired by the life of Paul Gauguin.

The Moonstone   Title is the name of a diamond.

Morse   Christian name Endeavour (revealed in *Death Is Now My Neighbour*).

Mort   Main character, Mort, is Death's hopelessly inept teenage apprentice.

Mr Weston's Good Wine (T.F. Powys)   Title from *Emma*, by Jane Austen.

My Son, My Son   Original title *Oh Absalom*.

Nicholas Nickleby   Nicholas marries Madeline Bray.

School: Dotheboys Hall. Schoolmaster: Wackford Squeers. Friend: Smike.

The Nine Tailors   are church bells that cause Geoffrey Deacon's death.

Nineteen Eighty-Four   Hero: Winston Smith. His lover: Julia (junior member of the anti-Sex League). Britain depicted as Airstrip One (part of Oceania).

Northanger Abbey   Heroine Catherine Morland.

Our Mutual Friend   Title character: John Harmon. Marries: Bella Wilfe. Villain: Silas Wegg the peg-leg.

Pale Fire (Nabokov)   Title from *Timon of Athens* by William Shakespeare.

A Passage to India   Setting: Chandrapore. Central characters: Dr Aziz and Cyril Fielding. Aziz accused of rape by Adela Quested.

Peter Rabbit's father   killed and made into a pie by Mrs McGregor.

The Pickwick Papers   Cricket match: Muggleton v Dingley Dell.

The Pilgrim's Progress   Hero: Christian. Castle: Doubting. Giant: Despair. Goal: Celestial City.

The Portrait of a Lady   Title character   Isabel Archer.

Power and the Glory   Set in Mexico.

The Prime of Miss Jean Brodie   Art teacher: Teddy Lloyd.

The Prince and the Pauper   Title characters – Prince: Edward, Prince of Wales, later Edward VI; Pauper: Tom Canty.

Prison: authors in

Brendan Behan for IRA activities.

William Blake in Chichester for fighting with a soldier.

John Bunyan in Bedford gaol for preaching without a licence.

Daniel Defoe after writing *The Shortest Way with Dissenters* (a satire on High Church attitudes to religious nonconformism).

John Donne in the Fleet for marrying Anne Moore (a minor) in 1576. Hence his comment: 'John Donne – Anne Donne – Undone.'

Fyodor Dostoyevsky was condemned to death for belonging to a revolutionary organization but was reprieved and served 4 years hard labour in Siberia.

Ben Jonson was imprisoned for killing Gabriel Spenser, but after pleading benefit of clergy was merely branded on the left thumb.

Ezra Pound was charged with treason for delivering radio broadcasts on behalf of the Axis powers during the Second World War, but was found unfit to plead and instead imprisoned in an asylum.

Alexander Solzhenitsyn spent 8 years in a prison camp for criticizing Stalin's conduct of the war against Nazi Germany.

Oscar Wilde was imprisoned for 2 years in Reading Gaol for homosexual offences. He wrote *De Profundis* while incarcerated, not *The Ballad of Reading Gaol*.

The Prisoner of Zenda   Title character: King Rudolf. Kingdom: Ruritania. Imprisoned by: Duke Michael.

Quentin Durward   Marries Isabelle de Croye.

Rabbit Tetralogy   *Rabbit, Run*; *Rabbit Redux*; *Rabbit Is Rich*; *Rabbit at Rest*.

The Railway Children   Names: Peter, Phyllis, Roberta.

The Raj Quartet   *The Jewel in the Crown*, *The Day of the Scorpion*, *A Division of the Spoils*, *The Towers of Silence*.

The Red and The Black (Stendhal's Le Rouge et le Noir). Colours symbolize respectively the Army and the Church.

The Red Badge of Courage Set in the American Civil War.

Rip Van Winkle Set in the Catskill Mountains. Rip sleeps for 20 years.

Room 101 In Orwell's Nineteen Eighty-Four, this room contained rats used to help interrogate Winston Smith, as they were his great fear.

The Scarlet Letter Central character: Hester Prynne. The Scarlet Letter: A for Adultery.

The Scarlet Pimpernel Title character: Sir Percy Blakeney.

Scriblerus Club Literary group including Swift, Pope, Gay, Arbuthnot and Thomas Parnell, which met from January to July 1714 to 'ridicule all the false tastes in learning'. Martinos Scriblerus was a pseudonym occasionally used by Pope.

The Seed and the Sower Filmed as *Merry Christmas Mr Lawrence*.

Sense and Sensibility Characters who represent these qualities: Sense – Elinor Dashwood. Sensibility – Marianne Dashwood.

Sherlock Holmes Housemaid: Mrs Hudson.

Shogun: Central character: John Blackthorne.

Slaughterhouse-Five Hero: Billy Pilgrim.

Sons and Lovers Son: Paul Morel.

The Sound and the Fury Title from: *Macbeth* by William Shakespeare. Family: Benjy, Caddy, Jason and Quentin Compson.

Spanish Civil War Served as stretcher bearer: W.H. Auden (for the Republicans).

The Spy Who Came in from the Cold Title character: Leamas.

Stammered Somerset Maugham.

Steppenwolf Central character: Harry Haller.

The Sun Also Rises Source of the term: 'The Lost Generation'.

Swiss Family Robinson Johann David Wyss wrote the story and his son Johann Rudolf completed and edited it. The Robinsons' names: Fritz, Ernest, Franz and Jack.

Sword of Honour Trilogy *Men at Arms, Officers and Gentlemen, Unconditional Surrender*.

The Tailor of Panama Tailor: Harry Pendel.

The Tale of Two Cities Cities: Paris and London. Sentenced to guillotine: Charles Darnay. Sacrificed himself in Darney's place: Sydney Carton.

Tender Is the Night Title from 'Ode to a Nightingale' by John Keats.

Tess of the D'Urbervilles Tess marries Angel Clare.

The Thirty-Nine Steps Hannay's servant: Paddock.

Three Men in a Boat Title characters: George, Harris, Montmorency (Dog).

Thrums Name given in J.M. Barrie to disguise Kirriemuir, his home town.

The Tin Drum Hero: Oskar Matzerath (a dwarf).

Tobacco Road Sharecropper: Jeeter Lester. Jeeter's wife: Ada.

Tom Jones Tom's wife: Sophia Western. Her servant: Mrs Honour.

The Trial Central character: Joseph K.

The Turn of the Screw Children: Miles and Flora. Ghosts: Miss Jessel and Peter Quint.

2001: A Space Odyssey Book based on the film of the same name.

Ulysses Central characters: Leopold and Molly Bloom and Stephen Daedalus. Set during 18 hours in Dublin on 16 June 1904.

Uncle Tom's Cabin Slave owner: Simon Legree.

Unnatural Exposure Plot: Bodies are being dumped in rubbish and bin men demand stress counselling.

Vanity Fair Central character: Becky Sharp marries: Rawdon Crawley. Becky's friend: Amelia Sedley. she marries: (1) George Osborne; (2) Captain Dobbin. School: Miss Pinkerton's. Illustrated by: W.M. Thackeray.

Victory (John Williams) Set during Tony Blair's campaign for the 1997 election (pictures by Tom Stoddart).

Villette Villette is a city based on Brussels.

The Water-Babies Set in Vendale.

Watership Down Rabbits Bigwig, Fiver, General Wormwort, Hazel.

The Well of Loneliness Originally banned for lesbian content.

Westward Ho! Hero: Amyas Leigh. His love: Rose of Torridge.

What Katy Did Heroine's full name: Katy Carr.

Whisky Galore Setting: Great and Little Todday.

White Fang offspring of a wolf-dog and a dog.

WH Smith *The End of Alice*, banned for its content of child abuse

The Wind in the Willows Characters: Badger, Mole, Toad, Water Rat.

Winnie-the-Pooh Title character: Edward (Pooh). Boy: Christopher Robin. Donkey: Eeyore. Elephant: Heffalump. Kidnapped baby: Roo (kangaroo). Illustrator: E. H. Shepard.

Woman publishers Virago (run by women for women).

Women in Love Gudrun Brangwen and Gerald Crich were based on Katherine Mansfield and John Middleton Murry.

Wuthering Heights Narrated by Mr Lockwood and Nelly Deane.

Wyss, Johann Rudolf Wrote the Swiss National Anthem 'Rufst du mein Vaterland'.

Zuleika Dobson (Max Beerbohm) Servant: Mélisande.

L
I
T
E
R
A
T
U
R
E

Plays and Playwrights

(* denotes playwright's first play)

Playwright	Play	Playwright	Play
Aeschylus	Oresteia Trilogy	J.M. Barrie	The Admirable Crichton
(c. 525–456 BC)	The Persians	(1860–1937)	The Boy David (last)
	Prometheus Bound		Dear Brutus
	Seven Against Thebes		Mary Knows
	Suppliants		Peter Pan
Edward Albee	The American Dream		Quality Street
(1928–)	A Delicate Balance		Walker, London*
	Three Tall Women		What Every Woman Knows
	Tiny Alice	H.E. Bates	The Last Bread
	Who's Afraid of Virginia	(1905–1974)	
Woolf?		Pierre Beaumarchais	The Barber of Seville
	The Zoo Story	(1732–1799)	Eugénie*
Maxwell Anderson	Anne of the Thousand Days		The Marriage of Figaro
(1888–1959)		Samuel Beckett	Breath
Jean Anouilh	Antigone	(1906–1989)	Endgame
(1910–1987)	Becket		Happy Days
	Eurydice		Ill Seen Ill Said
	The Lark (L'Alouette)		Not I
	L'Hermine*		Waiting for Godot
	L'Invitation au Château	Brendan Behan	The Hostage
	Thieves' Carnival	(1923–1964)	The Quare Fellow*
	Waltz of the Toreadors	Aphra Behn	The Feigned Courtizans
John Arden	All Fall Down*	(1640–89)	The Forced Marriage
(1930–)	Ironhand		The Rover
	Live Like Pigs	Alan Bennett	An Englishman Abroad
	Serjeant Musgrave's Dance	(1934–)	Forty Years On*
	Vandaleur's Folly		Getting On
	The Workhouse Donkey		Habeas Corpus
Aristophanes	The Acharnians		Kafka's Dick
(c448–388 BC)	The Birds		The Madness of George III
	Clouds		The Old Country
	Ecclesiazusae		On the Margin (1st TV play)
	The Frogs		A Question of Attribution
	The Knights		Talking Heads
	Lysistrata	Alan Bleasdale	Are You Lonesome Tonight?
	The Peace	(1946–)	Boys from the Blackstuff
	Plutus		Having a Ball
	Thesmophoriazusae		It's a Madhouse
	The Wasps		The Monocled Mutineer
Alan Ayckbourn	Absent Friends		No More Sitting on the Old
(1939–)	Absurd Person Singular		School Bench*
	Bedroom Farce		On the Ledge
	Callisto 5	Simon Block	Chimps
	A Chorus of Disapproval	Edward Bond	Early Morning
	Communicating Doors	(1934–)	Narrow Road to the Deep
	How the Other Half Loves		North
	Jeeves		The Pope's Wedding*
	Joking Apart	Dion Boucicault	The Colleen Bawn
	Just Between Ourselves	(c. 1820–1890)	The Corsican Brothers
	Living Together		London Assurance
	Man of the Moment		The Octoroon
	Mr Whatnot*		The Shaughraun
	The Norman Conquests	Bertolt Brecht	Baal
	Relatively Speaking	(1898–1956)	The Caucasian Chalk Circle
	Round and Round the		Drums in the Night*
	Garden		Fear and Misery in the Third
	Season's Greetings		Reich
	Sisterly Feelings		The Good Woman of
	A Small Family Business		Setzuan
	Table Manners		Mother Courage
	Ten Times Table		The Preventable Rise of
	Time and Time Again		Arturo Ui
	Time of My Life		The Threepenny Opera
	Way Upstream	Abe Burrows	Cactus Flower
	Woman in Mind	(1910–1985)	

Playwright	Play	Playwright	Play
Jim Cartwright (1958–)	Bed		Murder in the Cathedral
	The Rise and Fall of Little Voice		Old Possum's Book of Practical Cats
	Road		The Rock
Anton Chekhov (1860–1904)	The Bear		Sweeney Agonistes*
	The Cherry Orchard	Ben Elton	Gasping
	Ivanov*	(1959–)	Silly Cow
	The Island of Sakhalin	George Etherege	The Comical Revenge, or
	The Seagull	(c. 1635–92)	Love in a Tub
	The Three Sisters		The Man of Mode, or
	Uncle Vanya		Sir Fopling Flutter
	The Wood Demon		She Would If She Could
Caryl Churchill (1938–)	Cloud Nine	Euripides	Alcestis*
	Fen	(c. 484–406 BC)	Andromache
	Icecream		The Bacchae
	Light Shining*		Electra
	Light Shining in Buckinghamshire		Hecuba
	Serious Money		Helen
	Softcops		Hippolytus
	Top Girls		Ion
Jean Cocteau (1889–1963)	L'Aigle à deux têtes		Iphigenia in Aulis
	Les Mariés de la Tour Eiffel		Iphigenia in Tauris
	Orpheus		Medea
William Congreve (1670–1729)	The Double Dealer		The Phoenician Women
	Love for Love		The Trojan Women
	The Mourning Bride	George Farquhar	The Beaux' Stratagem
	The Old Bachelor*	(c. 1677–1707)	The Constant Couple
	The Way of the World		Love and a Bottle*
Pierre Corneille (1606–1684)	Andromède		The Recruiting Officer
	Le Cid	Georges Feydeau	An Absolute Turkey
	Cinna	(1862–1921)	A Flea in her Ear
	Clitandre		Hotel Paradiso
	La Galerie du Palais		Ladies' Tailor*
	Horace		Pig in a Poke
	The Liar (Le Menteur)	Eduardo de Filippo	Filumena
	Mélite*	(1900–1984)	La Grande Magia
	La Mort de Pompée		Saturday, Sunday, Monday
	Nicomède	Alistair Foot and	No Sex Please, We're British
	Polyeucte	Anthony Marriot	
	Pulchérie	John Ford	The Broken Heart
	Rodogune	(c. 1586–1640)	The Lady's Trial
	Théodore		The Lover's Melancholy
	La Veuve		Perkin Warbeck
Nöel Coward (1899–1973)	Bitter Sweet		'Tis Pity She's a Whore
	Blithe Spirit	Dario Fo	The Accidental Death of an
	Cavalcade	(1926–)	Anarchist
	Design for Living	Michael Frayn	Alphabetical Order
	Easy Virtue	(1933–)	Benefactors
	Fallen Angels		Clouds
	This Happy Breed		Donkeys' Years
	Hay Fever		Here
	I'll Leave it to You*		Look, Look
	Nude with Violin		Make and Break
	Peace in Our Time		Noises Off
	Post Mortem		The Sandboy
	Present Laughter	Brian Friel	The Two of Us*
	Private Lives	(1929–)	Dancing at Lughnasa
	Relative Values		The Enemy Within
	The Vortex		Faith Healer
John Dryden (1631–1700)	All for Love		The Freedom of the City
	The Indian Emperor		Molly Sweeney
	Marriage à-la-Mode		Philadelphia, Here I Come!
	The Rival Ladies		Translations
	The State of Innocence	Christopher Fry	Wonderful Tennessee
Alexander Dumas (Fils) (1824–1895)	Camille	(1907–)	The Boy With a Cart
			Curtmantle
T.S. Eliot (1888–1965)	The Cocktail Party		The Lady's Not for Burning
	The Confidential Clerk		A Phoenix Too Frequent
	The Elder Statesman		Thursday's Child
	The Family Reunion		The Tower
			Venus Observed

LITERATURE

Playwright	Play	Playwright	Play
John Galsworthy	The Silver Box		Racing Demon
(1867–1933)	The Skin Game		The Secret Rapture
Jean Genet	The Balcony		Slag*
(1910–1986)	The Maids	Richard Harris	The Business of Murder
	The Screens	(1934–)	Dead Guilty
John Godber	April in Paris		The Maintenance Man
(1956–)	Bouncers		Outside Edge
	Happy Families		Stepping Out
	Happy Jack	Harold Harwood	The Grain of Mustard Seed
	Lucky Sods	(1874–1959)	
	The Office Party	Ronald Harwood	After the Lions
	On the Piste	(1934–)	Another Time
	Salt of the Earth		Country Matters*
	September in the Rain		The Dresser
	Shakers		The Handyman
	Teechers		Poison Pen
	Up 'N' Under		Reflected Glory
Johann W. von Goethe	Götz von Berlichingen		Taking Sides
(1749–1832)	Die Mitschuldigen	Victor Hugo	Angelo
	Egmont	(1802–1885)	Cromwell
	Erwin und Elmire		Hernani
	Faust (Parts I & II)		Lucrèce Borgia
	Iphigenie auf Tauris		Marie Tudor
	Torquato Tasso		Marion Delorme
Nikolai Gogol	The Inspector General		Le Roi s'amuse
(1809–1852)			Ruy Blas
William Golding	The Brass Butterfly	Henrik Ibsen	An Enemy of the People
(1911–1993)		(1828–1906)	Catiline*
Oliver Goldsmith	She Stoops to Conquer		A Doll's House
(1728–1774)			Ghosts
Maxim Gorky	The Lower Depths		Hedda Gabler
(1868–1936)			John Gabriel Borkman
Harley Granville Barker	The Madras House		Love's Comedy
(1877–1946)	The Marrying of Ann Leete		The Master Builder
	The Voysey Inheritance		Peer Gynt
	Waste		The Wild Duck
Simon Gray	Butley Cell Mates	Eugène Ionesco	The Bald Prima Donna
(1936–)	The Common Pursuit	(1912–1994)	Rhinoceros
	Dog Days		The Lesson
	Dutch Uncle	Alfred Jarry	Ubu Roi
	Hidden Laughter	(1873–1907)	
	The Idiot	Terry Johnson	Dead Funny
	Life Support	(1955–)	Hysteria
	Molly		Imagine Drowning
	Otherwise Engaged		Insignificance
	Plaintiffs and Defendants		Unsuitable for Adults
	Quartermaine's Terms	Ben Jonson	The Alchemist
	The Rear	(1572–1637)	Bartholomew Fair
	Simply Disconnected		Catiline
	Sleeping Dog		Cynthia's Revels
	Spoiled		Every Man in His Humour
	Stagestruck		Every Man Out of His
	Two Sundays		Humour
	Wise Child*		The Poetaster
John Guare	The House of Blue Leaves		The Sad Shepherd
(1938–)	Six Degrees of Separation		(unfinished)
Patrick Hamilton	Gaslight (aka: Angel Street)		Sejanus
(1904–1962)	Rope (US title: Rope's End)		The Silent Woman
Christopher Hampton	After Mercer		Volpone
(1946–)	Les Liaisons Dangereuses	Tom Kempinski	Duet for One
	The Philanthropist	(1938–)	Separation
	Savages	Joseph Kesselring	Arsenic and Old Lace
	Total Eclipse	(1902–1967)	
	Treats	Thomas Kyd	The Spanish Tragedy
	When Did You Last See My	(1558–1594)	
	Mother?*	Mike Leigh	Abigail's Party
David Hare	The Absence of War	(1943–)	Babies Grow Old
(1947–)	Knuckle		Big Basil
	Licking Hitler (TV play)		The Box Play*
	Man Above Men (TV play)		Greek Tragedy
	Murmuring Judges		Individual Fruit Pies

Playwright	Play	Playwright	Play
	My Parents Have Gone to Carlisle		Daddy Kiss It Better
			A Day in the Death of Joe Egg*
	Nuts in May		Forget-Me-Not Lane
Alain-René Lesage (1668–1747)	Turcaret		The Freeway
Ira Levin (1929–)	Deathtrap		The Heart of the Country
	Veronica's Room		The National Health
Frederick Lonsdale (1881–1954)	Aren't We All?		Passion Play
	Canaries Sometimes Sing		A Piece of My Mind
	The Last of Mrs Cheyney		Poppy
	On Approval		Privates on Parade
Federico García Lorca (1898–1936)	Blood Wedding		Walk on the Grass (first TV play)
	The House of Bernarda Alba		When the Wind Blows
	Yerma	Edna O'Brien (1932–)	Flesh and Blood
Compton Mackenzie (1883–1972)	The Gentleman in Grey		Madame Bovary
			Virginia
Maurice Maeterlinck (1862–1949)	The Blue Bird	Sean O'Casey (1880–1964)	The Bishop's Bonfire
	La Princesse Maleine		Cockadoodle Dandy
	Mary Magdalene		Juno and the Paycock
	Pelléas et Mélisande		The Plough and the Stars
David Mamet (1947–)	American Buffalo		The Shadow of a Gunman
	The Cryptogram		The Silver Tassie
	Duck Variations	Clifford Odets (1906–1963)	Awake and Sing!
	Glengarry Glen Ross		Golden Boy
	A Life in the Theater		Till the Day I Die
	Oleanna		Waiting for Lefty
	Sexual Perversity in Chicago	Eugene O'Neill (1888–1953)	Ah, Wilderness
	The Shawl		Anna Christie
	Speed-the-Plow		Beyond the Horizon
Christopher Marlowe (1564–1593)	Doctor Faustus		Desire under the Elms
	Edward II		The Emperor Jones
	The Jew of Malta		The Great God Brown
	The Massacre at Paris		The Hairy Ape
	Tamburlaine the Great		The Iceman Cometh
Conor McPherson	The Weir		Lazarus Laughed
Thomas Middleton (c. 1570–1627)	Blurt		Long Day's Journey into Night
	The Changeling (with William Rowley)		Marco Millions
	A Game at Chess		Mourning Becomes Electra
	Master Constable		Strange Interlude
	The Spanish Gypsy (with William Rowley)		A Touch of the Poet
	Women Beware Women		The Web*
Arthur Miller (1915–)	After the Fall	Joe Orton (1933–1967)	Entertaining Mr Sloane*
	All My Sons*		The Erpingham Camp
	Broken Glass		Loot
	The Crucible		The Ruffian on the Stair
	Danger: Memory!		What the Butler Saw
	Death of a Salesman	John Osborne (1929–1994)	The Entertainer
	The Last Yankee		Epitaph for George Dillon
	The Man Who Had All the Luck		The Hotel in Amsterdam
			Inadmissible Evidence
	The Price		Jill and Jack (TV play)
	The Ride Down Mount Morgan		Look Back in Anger
	A View from the Bridge		Luther
Molière (1622–1673)	The Blue–Stockings		A Patriot for Me
	Le Bourgeois Gentilhomme		West of Suez (TV play)
	The Impostor	Arthur Wing Pinero (1855–1934)	The Cabinet Minister
	Le Malade Imaginaire		Dandy Dick
	Le Misanthrope		The Gay Lord Quex
	The Miser		His House in Order
	The School for Wives		The Magistrate
	Tartuffe		Mid-Channel
Nicholas Monsarrat (1910–1979)	The Visitors		The Profligate
			The Schoolmistress
John Mortimer (1923–)	The Dock Brief		The Second Mrs Tanqueray
	A Voyage Round My Father		The Squire
Peter Nichols (1927–)	Ben Spray		Trelawny of the 'Wells'
	Born in the Gardens		£200 a Year*
	Chez Nous	Harold Pinter (1930–)	Betrayal
			The Birthday Party

L
I
T
E
R
A
T
U
R
E

Playwright	Play
	The Caretaker
	The Homecoming
	Hothouse
	Moonlight
	No Man's Land
	One for the Road
	Other Places
	The Room*
Luigi Pirandello	Come Tu Mi Vuoi
(1867–1936)	Enrico IV
	Six Characters in Search of
	an Author
Sylvia Plath	Three Women
(1932–1963)	
J.B. Priestley	Dangerous Corner*
(1894–1984)	I Have Been Here Before
	An Inspector Calls
	Laburnum Grove
	The Linden Tree
	Time and the Conways
	When We Are Married
Alexander Pushkin	Boris Godunov
(1799–1837)	
Jean Racine	Alexandre le Grand
(1639–1699)	Andromaque
	Athalie
	Bajazet
	Bérénice
	Britannicus
	Esther
	Iphigénie
	La Thébaïde, ou Les Frères
	ennemis
	Mithridate
	Phèdre
Terence Rattigan	Adventure Story
(1911–1977)	The Browning Version
	Cause Célèbre
	The Deep Blue Sea
	Flare Path
	French Without Tears
	Harlequinade
	Ross
	Separate Tables
	The Winslow Boy
Edmond Rostand	Chantecler
(1868–1918)	Cyrano de Bergerac
William Rowley	A New Wonder: A Woman
(c. 1585–1642)	Never Vext
Willy Russell	Blind Scouse Trilogy*
(1947–)	Blood Brothers
	Boy with Transistor Radio
	Breezeblock Park
	Educating Rita
	I Read the News Today (radio)
	John, Paul, George
	Ringo . . . and Bert
	King of the Castle (TV play)
	One for the Road
	Our Day Out
	Shirley Valentine
	Stags and Hens
Jean-Paul Sartre	In Camera
(1905–1980)	The Condemned of Altona
James Saunders	Bodies
(1925–)	Making It Better
	Next Time I'll Sing to You
	Retreat
	A Scent of Flowers
Friedrich von Schiller	Demetrius (unfinished)
(1759–1805)	Don Carlos

Playwright	Play
	The Maid of Orleans
	Maria Stuart
	The Robbers*
	Wallenstein Trilogy
	William Tell
Anthony Shaffer	The Case of the Oily
(1926–)	Levantine
	Murderer
	Sleuth
Peter Shaffer	Amadeus
(1926–)	Black Comedy
	Equus
	Five-Finger Exercise*
	The Gift of the Gorgon
	Lettice and Lovage
	The Private Ear
	The Public Eye
	The Royal Hunt of the Sun
	Yonadab
George Bernard Shaw	Androcles and the Lion
(1856–1950)	Arms and the Man
	Back to Methuselah
	Caesar and Cleopatra
	Candida
	Captain Brassbound's
	Conversion
	The Devil's Disciple
	The Doctor's Dilemma
	Getting Married
	Heartbreak House
	John Bull's Other Island
	Major Barbara
	Man and Superman
	The Millionairess
	Mrs Warren's Profession
	Pygmalion
	Saint Joan
	Widowers' Houses
	You Never Can Tell
Sam Shepard	Buried Child
(1943–)	Cowboys*
	The Curse of the Starving
	Class
	Dog and Rocking Chair
	Fool for Love
	A Lie of the Mind
	The Rock Garden
	Simpatico
	The Tooth of Crime
	True West
Richard Brinsley	The Critic
Sheridan	Jupiter
(1751–1816)	The Rivals
	St Patrick's Day
	The School for Scandal
R.C. Sherriff	Home at Seven
(1896–1975)	Journey's End*
Alan Sillitoe (1928–)	All Citizens Are Soldiers
and Ruth Fainlight	
(1931–)	
Neil Simon	Barefoot in the Park
(1927–)	Biloxi Blues
	California Suite
	Come Blow Your Horn*
	The Gingerbread Lady
	The Good Doctor
	Last of the Red Hot Lovers
	Little Me
	Lost in Yonkers
	The Odd Couple
	Plaza Suite

Playwright	Play
	The Prisoner of Second Avenue
	Promises, Promises
	The Sunshine Boys
	Sweet Charity
	They're Playing Our Song
Sophocles (c. 496–405 BC)	Ajax
	Antigone
	Electra
	Ichneutae
	Oedipus at Colonus
	Oedipus Rex
	Philoctetes
	Trachiniae
Tom Stoppard (1937–)	After Magritte
	Albert's Bridge (radio)
	Dirty Linen
	The Dissolution of Dominic Boot (radio)
	Enter a Free Man
	Jumpers
	M Is for Moon Among Other Things (radio)
	Night and Day
	Professional Foul (TV play)
	The Real Inspector Hound
	Rosencrantz and Guildenstern Are Dead
	Separate Peace (first TV play)
	Travesties
	A Walk on the Water*
Tom Stoppard and André Previn (1929–)	Every Good Boy Deserves Favour
David Storey (1933–)	The Changing Room
	The Contractor
	Cromwell
	Early Days
	The Farm
	Home
	In Celebration
	Life Class
	The March on Russia
	Mother's Day
	The Restoration of Arnold Middleton*
	Sisters
August Strindberg (1849–1912)	The Creditors
	The Dance of Death
	A Dream Play
	The Father
	Master Olof
	Miss Julie
	To Damascus
J.M. Synge (1871–1909)	In the Shadow of the Glen
	The Playboy of the Western World
	Riders to the Sea
	The Tinker's Wedding

Playwright	Play
	The Well of the Saints
Peter Terson	Zigger Zagger
Brandon Thomas (1856–1914)	Charley's Aunt
Dylan Thomas (1914–1953)	Under Milk Wood
John Vanbrugh (1664–1726)	The Confederacy
	The Provok'd Husband
	The Provok'd Wife
	(both above completed by Colley Cibber)
	The Relapse, or Virtue in Danger
John Webster (1580–1625)	The Devil's Law Case
	The Duchess of Malfi
	The White Devil
Frank Wedekind (1864–1918)	Earth Spirit
	Pandora's Box
	Spring Awakening
Arnold Wesker (1932–)	Annie Wobbler
	Chicken Soup With Barley
	Chips With Everything
	I'm Talking About Jerusalem
	The Kitchen
	Roots
Hugh Whitemore (1936–)	The Best of Friends
	Breaking the Code
	It's Ralph
	Pack of Lies
	Stevie*
Oscar Wilde (1854–1900)	The Duchess of Padua
	An Ideal Husband
	The Importance of Being Ernest
	Lady Windermere's Fan
	Salome
	A Woman of No Importance
Thornton Wilder (1897–1975)	The Angel that Troubled the Waters
	The Long Christmas Dinner
	The Matchmaker
	Our Town
	The Skin of Our Teeth
	The Trumpet Shall Sound
Tennessee Williams (1911–1983)	Battle of Angels*
	Camino Real
	Cat on a Hot Tin Roof
	The Glass Menagerie
	The Night of the Iguana
	The Rose Tattoo
	A Streetcar Named Desire
	Suddenly Last Summer
	Sweet Bird of Youth
William Wycherley (1640–1716)	The Country Wife
	The Gentleman Dancing Master
	The Plain Dealer

LITERATURE

Plays and Playwrights (in Play Order)

(for playwrights' dates see previous section)

Play	Playwright	Play	Playwright
Abigail's Party	Mike Leigh	Absurd Person Singular	Alan Ayckbourn
The Absence of War	David Hare	The Accidental Death of an Anarchist	Dario Fo
Absent Friends	Alan Ayckbourn	The Acharnians	Aristophanes
An Absolute Turkey	Georges Feydeau		

Play	Playwright	Play	Playwright
The Admirable Crichton	J.M. Barrie	The Bishop's Bonfire	Sean O'Casey
Adventure Story	Terence Rattigan	Bitter Sweet	Nöel Coward
After Magritte	Tom Stoppard	Black Comedy	Peter Shaffer
After Mercer	Christopher Hampton	Blind Scouse Trilogy*	Willy Russell
After the Fall	Arthur Miller	Blithe Spirit	Nöel Coward
After the Lions	Ronald Harwood	Blood Brothers	Willy Russell
Ah, Wilderness	Eugene O'Neill	Blood Wedding	Federico García Lorca
Ajax	Sophocles	The Blue Bird	Maurice Maeterlinck
Albert's Bridge (radio)	Tom Stoppard	The Blue–Stockings	Molière
Alcestis*	Euripides	Blurt	Thomas Middleton
The Alchemist	Ben Jonson	Bodies	James Saunders
Alexandre le Grand	Jean Racine	Boris Godunov	Alexander Pushkin
All Citizens Are Soldiers	Alan Sillitoe and Ruth Fainlight	Born in the Gardens	Peter Nichols
		Bouncers	John Godber
All Fall Down*	John Arden	Le Bourgeois Gentilhomme	Molière
All for Love	John Dryden		
All My Sons*	Arthur Miller	The Box Play*	Mike Leigh
Alphabetical Order	Michael Frayn	The Boy David (last)	J.M. Barrie
Amadeus	Peter Shaffer	The Boy with a Cart	Christopher Fry
American Buffalo	David Mamet	Boy with Transistor Radio	Willy Russell
The American Dream	Edward Albee	Boys from the Blackstuff	Alan Bleasdale
An Enemy of the People	Henrik Ibsen	The Brass Butterfly	William Golding
An Englishman Abroad	Alan Bennett	Breaking the Code	Hugh Whitemore
Androcles and the Lion	George Bernard Shaw	Breath	Samuel Beckett
Andromache	Euripides	Breezeblock Park	Willy Russell
Andromaque	Jean Racine	Britannicus	Jean Racine
Andromède	Pierre Corneille	Broken Glass	Arthur Miller
The Angel that Troubled the Waters	Thornton Wilder	The Broken Heart	John Ford
		The Browning Version	Terence Rattigan
Angelo	Victor Hugo	Buried Child	Sam Shepard
Anna Christie	Eugene O'Neill	The Business of Murder	Richard Harris
Anne of the Thousand Days	Maxwell Anderson	Butley	Simon Gray
		The Cabinet Minister	Arthur Wing Pinero
Annie Wobbler	Arnold Wesker	Cactus Flower	Abe Burrows
Another Time	Ronald Harwood	Caesar and Cleopatra	George Bernard Shaw
Antigone	Jean Anouilh	California Suite	Neil Simon
Antigone	Sophocles	Callisto 5	Alan Ayckbourn
April in Paris	John Godber	Camille	Alexander Dumas, (Fils)
Are You Lonesome Tonight?	Alan Bleasdale	Camino Real	Tennessee Williams
		Canaries Sometimes Sing	Frederick Lonsdale
Aren't We All?	Frederick Lonsdale		
Arms and the Man	George Bernard Shaw	Candida	George Bernard Shaw
Arsenic and Old Lace	Joseph Kesselring	Captain Brassbound's Conversion	George Bernard Shaw
Athalie	Jean Racine		
Awake and Sing	Clifford Odets	The Caretaker	Harold Pinter
Baal	Bertolt Brecht	The Case of the Oily Levantine	Anthony Shaffer
Babies Grow Old	Mike Leigh		
The Bacchae	Euripides	Cat on a Hot Tin Roof	Tennessee Williams
Back to Methuselah	George Bernard Shaw	Catiline*	Henrik Ibsen
Bajazet	Jean Racine	Catiline	Ben Jonson
The Balcony	Jean Genet	The Caucasian Chalk Circle	Bertolt Brecht
The Bald Prima Donna	Eugène Ionesco		
The Barber of Seville	Pierre Beaumarchais	Cause Célèbre	Terence Rattigan
Barefoot in the Park	Neil Simon	Cavalcade	Nöel Coward
Bartholomew Fair	Ben Jonson	Cell Mates	Simon Gray
Battle of Angels*	Tennessee Williams	The Changeling	Thomas Middleton and William Rowley
The Bear	Anton Chekhov		
The Beaux' Stratagem	George Farquhar	The Changing Room	David Storey
Becket	Jean Anouilh	Chantecler	Edmond Rostand
Bed	Jim Cartwright	Charley's Aunt	Brandon Thomas
Bedroom Farce	Alan Ayckbourn	The Cherry Orchard	Anton Chekhov
Ben Spray	Peter Nichols	Chez Nous	Peter Nichols
Benefactors	Michael Frayn	Chicken Soup With Barley	Arnold Wesker
Bérénice	Jean Racine		
The Best of Friends	Hugh Whitemore	Chimps	Simon Block
Betrayal	Harold Pinter	Chips With Everything	Arnold Wesker
Beyond the Horizon	Eugene O'Neill	A Chorus of Disapproval	Alan Ayckbourn
Big Basil	Mike Leigh	Le Cid	Pierre Corneille
Biloxi Blues	Neil Simon	Cinna	Pierre Corneille
The Birds	Aristophanes	Claude Gueux	Victor Hugo
The Birthday Party	Harold Pinter	Clitandre	Pierre Corneille

Play	Playwright	Play	Playwright
Cloud Nine	Caryl Churchill	Duck Variations	David Mamet
Clouds	Michael Frayn	Duet for One	Tom Kempinski
Clouds	Aristophanes	Dutch Uncle	Simon Gray
Cockadoodle Dandy	Sean O'Casey	Early Days	David Storey
The Cocktail Party	T.S. Eliot	Early Morning	Edward Bond
The Colleen Bawn	Dion Boucicault	Earth Spirit	Frank Wedekind
Come Blow Your Horn*	Neil Simon	Easy Virtue	Nöel Coward
		Ecclesiazusae	Aristophanes
Come Tu Mi Vuoi	Luigi Pirandello	Educating Rita	Willy Russell
The Comical Revenge, or Love in a Tub	Sir George Etherege	Edward II	Christopher Marlowe
		Egmont	Johann Wolfgang von Goethe
The Common Pursuit	Simon Gray		
Communicating Doors	Alan Ayckbourn	The Elder Statesman	T.S. Eliot
The Condemned of Altona	Jean-Paul Sartre	Electra	Euripides
		Electra	Sophocles
The Confederacy	John Vanbrugh	The Emperor Jones	Eugene O'Neill
The Confidential Clerk	T.S. Eliot	Endgame	Samuel Beckett
The Constant Couple	George Farquhar	The Enemy Within	Brian Friel
The Contractor	David Storey	Enrico IV	Luigi Pirandello
The Corsican Brothers	Dion Boucicault	Enter a Free Man	Tom Stoppard
Country Matters*	Ronald Harwood	The Entertainer	John Osborne
The Country Wife	William Wycherley	Entertaining Mr Sloane*	Joe Orton
Cowboys*	Sam Shepard	Epitaph for George Dillon	John Osborne
The Creditors	August Strindberg	Equus	Peter Shaffer
The Critic	Richard Brinsley Sheridan	The Erpingham Camp	Joe Orton
Cromwell	David Storey	Erwin und Elmire	Johann Wolfgang von Goethe
Cromwell	Victor Hugo		
The Crucible	Arthur Miller	Esther	Jean Racine
The Cryptogram	David Mamet	Eugénie*	Pierre Beaumarchais
The Curse of the Starving Class	Sam Shepard	Eurydice	Jean Anouilh
		Every Good Boy Deserves Favour	Tom Stoppard and André Previn
Curtmantle	Christopher Fry		
Cynthia's Revels	Ben Jonson	Every Man in his Humour	Ben Jonson
Cyrano de Bergerac	Edmond Rostand	Every Man Out of his Humour	Ben Jonson
Daddy Kiss It Better	Peter Nichols		
The Dance of Death	August Strindberg	Faith Healer	Brian Friel
Dancing at Lughnasa	Brian Friel	Fallen Angels	Nöel Coward
Dandy Dick	Arthur Wing Pinero	The Family Reunion	T.S. Eliot
Dangerous Corner*	J.B. Priestley	The Farm,	David Storey
Danger: Memory!	Arthur Miller	The Father,	August Strindberg
A Day in the Death of Joe Egg*	Peter Nichols	Faust (Parts I & II)	Johann Wolfgang von Goethe
Dead Funny	Terry Johnson	Fear and Misery in the Third Reich	Bertolt Brecht
Dead Guilty	Richard Harris		
Dear Brutus	J.M. Barrie	The Feigned Courtizans	Aphra Behn
Death of a Salesman	Arthur Miller	Fen	Caryl Churchill
Deathtrap	Ira Levin	Filumena	Eduardo de Filippo
The Deep Blue Sea	Terence Rattigan	Five-Finger Exercise*	Peter Shaffer
A Delicate Balance	Edward Albee	Flare Path	Terence Rattigan
Demetrius (unfinished)	Friedrich von Schiller	A Flea in her Ear	Georges Feydeau
Design for Living	Nöel Coward	Flesh and Blood	Edna O'Brien
Desire under the Elms	Eugene O'Neill	Fool for Love	Sam Shepard
The Devil's Disciple	George Bernard Shaw	The Forced Marriage	Aphra Behn
The Devil's Law Case	John Webster	Forget-Me-Not Lane	Peter Nichols
Dirty Linen	Tom Stoppard	Forty Years On*	Alan Bennett
The Dissolution of Dominic Boot (radio)	Tom Stoppard	The Freedom of the City	Brian Friel
		The Freeway	Peter Nichols
The Dock Brief	John Mortimer	French Without Tears	Terence Rattigan
The Doctor's Dilemma	George Bernard Shaw	The Frogs,	Aristophanes
Dog and Rocking Chair	Sam Shepard	La Galerie du Palais	Pierre Corneille
Dog Days	Simon Gray	A Game at Chess	Thomas Middleton
A Doll's House	Henrik Ibsen	Gaslight (aka: Angel Street)	Patrick Hamilton
Don Carlos	Friedrich von Schiller		
Donkeys' Years	Michael Frayn	Gasping	Ben Elton
The Double Dealer	William Congreve	The Gay Lord Quex	Arthur Wing Pinero
Doctor Faustus	Christopher Marlowe	The Gentleman Dancing Master	William Wycherley
A Dream Play	August Strindberg		
The Dresser	Ronald Harwood	The Gentleman in Grey	Compton Mackenzie
Drums in the Night*	Bertolt Brecht	Getting Married	George Bernard Shaw
The Duchess of Malfi	John Webster	Getting On	Alan Bennett
The Duchess of Padua	Oscar Wilde	Ghosts	Henrik Ibsen

Play	Playwright
The Gift of the Gorgon	Peter Shaffer
The Gingerbread Lady	Neil Simon
The Glass Menagerie	Tennessee Williams
Glengarry Glen Ross	David Mamet
Golden Boy	Clifford Odets
The Good Doctor	Neil Simon
The Good Woman of Setzuan	Bertolt Brecht
Götz von Berlichingen	Johann W. von Goethe
The Grain of Mustard Seed	Harold Harwood
La Grande Magia	Eduardo de Filippo
The Great God Brown	Eugene O'Neill
Greek Tragedy	Mike Leigh
Habeas Corpus	Alan Bennett
The Hairy Ape	Eugene O'Neill
The Handyman	Ronald Harwood
This Happy Breed	Nöel Coward
Happy Days	Samuel Beckett
Happy Families	John Godber
Happy Jack	John Godber
Harlequinade	Terence Rattigan
Having a Ball	Alan Bleasdale
Hay Fever	Nöel Coward
The Heart of the Country	Peter Nichols
Heartbreak House	George Bernard Shaw
Hecuba	Euripides
Hedda Gabler	Henrik Ibsen
Helen	Euripides
Here	Michael Frayn
Hernani	Victor Hugo
Hidden Laughter	Simon Gray
Hippolytus	Euripides
His House in Order	Arthur Wing Pinero
Home	David Storey
Home at Seven	R.C. Sherriff
The Homecoming	Harold Pinter
Horace	Pierre Corneille
The Hostage	Brendan Behan
The Hotel in Amsterdam	John Osborne
Hotel Paradiso	Georges Feydeau
Hothouse	Harold Pinter
The House of Bernarda Alba	Federico García Lorca
The House of Blue Leaves	John Guare
How the Other Half Loves	Alan Ayckbourn
Hysteria	Terry Johnson
I Have Been Here Before	J.B. Priestley
I Read the News Today (radio)	Willy Russell
Icecream	Caryl Churchill
The Iceman Cometh	Eugene O'Neill
Ichneutae	Sophocles
An Ideal Husband	Oscar Wilde
The Idiot	Simon Gray
I'll Leave it to You*	Nöel Coward
Ill Seen Ill Said	Samuel Beckett
I'm Talking About Jerusalem	Arnold Wesker
Imagine Drowning	Terry Johnson
The Importance of Being Ernest	Oscar Wilde
The Impostor	Molière
In Camera	Jean-Paul Sartre
In Celebration	David Storey
In the Shadow of the Glen	J.M. Synge
Inadmissable Evidence	John Osborne

Play	Playwright
The Indian Emperor	John DrydeN
Individual Fruit Pies	Mike Leigh
Insignificance	Terry Johnson
An Inspector Calls	J.B. Priestley
The Inspector General	Nikolai Gogol
L'Invitation au Château	Jean Anouilh
Ion	Euripides
Iphigenia in Aulis	Euripides
Iphigenia in Tauris	Euripides
Iphigénie	Jean Racine
Iphigenie auf Tauris	Johann Wolfgang von Goethe
Ironhand	John Arden
The Island of Sakhalim	Anton Chekov
It's a Madhouse	Alan Bleasdale
It's Ralph	Hugh Whitemore
Ivanov*	Anton Chekhov
Jeeves	Alan Ayckbourn
The Jew of Malta	Christopher Marlowe
Jill and Jack (TV play)	John Osborne
John Bull's Other Island	George Bernard Shaw
John Gabriel Borkman	Henrik Ibsen
John, Paul, George, Ringo . . . and Bert	Willy Russell
Joking Apart	Alan Ayckbourn
Journey's End*	R.C. Sherriff
Jumpers	Tom Stoppard
Juno and the Paycock	Sean O'Casey
Jupiter	Richard Brinsley Sheridan
Just Between Ourselves	Alan Ayckbourn
Kafka's Dick	Alan Bennett
King of the Castle (TV play)	Willy Russell
The Kitchen	Arnold Wesker
The Knights	Aristophanes
Knuckle	David Hare
La Princess Maleine	Count Maurice Maeterlinck
Laburnum Grove	J.B. Priestley
Ladies' Tailor*	Georges Feydeau
Lady Windermere's Fan	Oscar Wilde
The Lady's Not for Burning	Christopher Fry
The Lady's Trial	John Ford
L'Aigle à deux têtes	Jean Cocteau
The Lark (L'Alouette)	Jean Anouilh
The Last Bread	H.E. Bates
Last of Mrs Cheyney	Frederick Lonsdale
The Last of the Red Hot Lovers	Neil Simon
The Last Yankee	Arthur Miller
Lazarus Laughed	Eugene O'Neill
Rhinoceros	Eugène Ionesco
Les Mariés de la Tour Eiffel	Jean Cocteau
Les Liaisons Dangereuses	Christopher Hampton
The Lesson	Eugène Ionesco
Lettice and Lovage	Peter Shaffer
L'Hermine*	Jean Anouilh
The Liar(Le Menteur)	Pierre Corneille
Licking Hitler (TV play)	David Hare
A Lie of the Mind	Sam Shepard
Life Class	David Storey
A Life in the Theater	David Mamet
Life Support	Simon Gray
Light Shining*	Caryl Churchill
Light Shining in Buckinghamshire	Caryl Churchill
The Linden Tree	J.B. Priestley
Little Me	Neil Simon
Live Like Pigs	John Arden

Play	Playwright	Play	Playwright
Living Together	Alan Ayckbourn	La Mort de Pompée	Pierre Corneille
London Assurance	Dion Boucicault	Mother Courage	Bertolt Brecht
The Long Christmas Dinner	Thornton Wilder	Mother's Day	David Storey
		Mourning Becomes Electra	Eugene O'Neill
Long Day's Journey into Night	Eugene O'Neill	The Mourning Bride	William Congreve
Look Back in Anger	John Osborne	Mr Whatnot*	Alan Ayckbourn
Look, Look	Michael Frayn	Mrs Warren's Profession	George Bernard Shaw
Loot	Joe Orton	Murder in the Cathedral	T.S. Eliot
Lost in Yonkers	Neil Simon	Murderer	Anthony Shaffer
Love and a Bottle*	George Farquhar	Murmuring Judges	David Hare
Love for Love	William Congreve	My Parents Have Gone to Carlisle	Mike Leigh
The Lover's Melancholy	John Ford		
Love's Comedy	Henrik Ibsen	Narrow Road to the Deep North	Edward Bond
The Lower Depths	Maxim Gorky		
Lucky Sods	John Godber	The National Health	Peter Nichols
Lucrèce Borgia	Victor Hugo	A New Wonder: Woman Never Vexed	William Rowley
Luther	John Osborne		
Lysistrata	Aristophanes	Next Time I'll Sing to You	James Saunders
M Is for Moon Among Other Things (radio)	Tom Stoppard	Nicomède	Pierre Corneille
		Night and Day	Tom Stoppard
Madame Bovary	Edna O'Brien	The Night of the Iguana	Tennessee Williams
The Madness of George III	Alan Bennett	No Man's Land	Harold Pinter
		No More Sitting on the Old School Bench*	Alan Bleasdale
The Madras House	Harley Granville Barker		
The Magistrate	Arthur Wing Pinero	No Sex Please, We're British	Alistair Foot and Anthony Marriot
The Maid of Orleans	Friedrich von Schiller		
The Maids	Jean Genet	Noises Off	Michael Frayn
The Maintenance Man	Richard Harris	Norman Conquests	Alan Ayckbourn
Major Barbara	George Bernard Shaw	Not I	Samuel Beckett
Make and Break	Michael Frayn	Nude with Violin	Nöel Coward
Making It Better	James Saunders	Nuts in May	Mike Leigh
Le Malade Imaginaire	Molière	The Octoroon	Dion Boucicault
Man Above Men (TV play)	David Hare	The Odd Couple	Neil Simon
		Oedipus at Colonus	Sophocles
Man and Superman	George Bernard Shaw	Oedipus Rex	Sophocles
The Man of Mode, or Sir Fopling Flutter	George Etherege	The Office Party	John Godber
		The Old Bachelor*	William Congreve
Man of the Moment	Alan Ayckbourn	The Old Country	Alan Bennett
The Man Who Had All the Luck,	Arthur Miller	Old Possum's Book of Practical Cats	T.S. Eliot
The March on Russia	David Storey	Oleanna	David Mamet
Marco Millions	Eugene O'Neill	On Approval	Frederick Lonsdale
Marie Tudor	Victor Hugo	On the Ledge	Alan Bleasdale
Marion Delorme	Victor Hugo	On the Margin (1st TV play)	Alan Bennett
The Marriage of Figaro	Pierre Beaumarchais		
Marriage à-la-Mode	John Dryden	On the Piste	John Godber
The Marrying of Ann Leete	Harley Granville Barker	One for the Road	Harold Pinter
		One for the Road	Willy Russell
Mary Knows	J.M. Barrie	Oresteia Trilogy	Aeschylus
Mary Magdalene	Maurice Maeterlinck	Orpheus	Jean Cocteau
Maria Stuart	Friedrich von Schiller	Other Places	Harold Pinter
The Massacre at Paris	Christopher Marlowe	Otherwise Engaged	Simon Gray
The Master Builder	Henrik Ibsen	Our Day Out	Willy Russell
Master Constable	Thomas Middleton	Our Town	Thornton Wilder
Master Olof	August Strindberg	Outside Edge	Richard Harris
The Matchmaker	Thornton Wilder	Pack of Lies	Hugh Whitemore
Medea	Euripides	Pandora's Box	Frank Wedekind
Mélite	Pierre Corneille	Passion Play	Peter Nichols
Mid-Channel	Arthur Wing Pinero	A Patriot for Me	John Osborne
The Millionairess	George Bernard Shaw	Peace in Our Time	Nöel Coward
Le Misanthrope	Molière	A Piece of My Mind	Peter Nichols
The Miser	Molière	The Peace	Aristophanes
Miss Julie	August Strindberg	Peer Gynt	Henrik Ibsen
Mithridate	Jean Racine	Pelléas et Mélisande	Count Maurice Maeterlinck
Die Mitschuldigen	Johann Wolfgang von Goethe	Perkin Warbeck	John Ford
		The Persians	Aeschylus
Molly	Simon Gray	Peter Pan	J.M. Barrie
Molly Sweeney	Brian Friel	Phèdre	Jean Racine
The Monocled Mutineer	Alan Bleasdale	Philadelphia Here I Come	Brian Friel
Moonlight	Harold Pinter	The Philanthropist	Christopher Hampton

LITERATURE

Play	Playwright	Play	Playwright
Philoctetes	Sophocles	Roots	Arnold Wesker
The Phoenician Women	Euripides	Rope (US title: Rope's End)	Patrick Hamilton
A Phoenix Too Frequent	Christopher Fry		
A Piece of My Mind	Peter Nichols	The Rose Tattoo	Tennessee Williams
Pig in a Poke	Georges Feydeau	Rosencrantz and Guildenstern Are Dead	Tom Stoppard
The Plain Dealer	William Wycherley		
Plaintiffs and Defendants	Simon Gray	Ross	Terence Rattigan
The Playboy of the Western World	J.M. Synge	Round and Round the Garden	Alan Ayckbourn
Plaza Suite	Neil Simon	The Rover	Aphra Behn
The Plough and the Stars	Sean O'Casey	The Royal Hunt of the Sun	Peter Shaffer
Plutus	Aristophanes	The Ruffian on the Stair*	Joe Orton
The Poetaster	Ben Jonson	Ruy Blas	Victor Hugo
Poison Pen	Ronald Harwood	The Sad Shepherd (unfinished)	Ben Jonson
Polyeucte	Pierre Corneille		
The Pope's Wedding*	Edward Bond	Saint Joan	George Bernard Shaw
Poppy	Peter Nichols	Saint Patrick's Day	Richard Brinsley Sheridan
Post Mortem	Nöel Coward	Salome	Oscar Wilde
Present Laughter	Nöel Coward	Salt of the Earth	John Godber
The Preventable Rise of Arturo Ui	Bertolt Brecht	The Sandboy	Michael Frayn
		Saturday, Sunday, Monday	Eduardo de Filippo
The Price	Arthur Miller	Savages	Christopher Hampton
The Prisoner of Second Avenue	Neil Simon	A Scent of Flowers	James Saunders
		The School for Scandal	Richard Brinsley Sheridan
The Private Ear	Peter Shaffer	The School for Wives	Molière
Private Lives	Nöel Coward	The Schoolmistress	Arthur Wing Pinero
Privates on Parade	Peter Nichols	The Screens	Jean Genet
Professional Foul (TV play)	Tom Stoppard	The Seagull	Anton Chekhov
		Season's Greetings	Alan Ayckbourn
The Profligate	Arthur Wing Pinero	The Second Mrs Tanqueray	Arthur Wing Pinero
Prometheus Bound	Aeschylus		
Promises, Promises	Neil Simon	The Secret Rapture	David Hare
The Provok'd Husband	John Vanbrugh (completed by Colley Cibber)	Sejanus	Ben Jonson
		Separate Peace (first TV Play)	Tom Stoppard
The Provok'd Wife	John Vanbrugh (completed by Colley Cibber)		
		Separate Tables	Terence Rattigan
The Public Eye	Peter Shaffer	Separation	Tom Kempinski
Pulchérie	Pierre Corneille	September in the Rain	John Godber
Pygmalion	George Bernard Shaw	Sergeant Musgrave's Dance	John Arden
Quality Street	J.M. Barrie		
The Quare Fellow*	Brendan Behan	Serious Money	Caryl Churchill
Quartermaine's Terms	Simon Gray	Seven Against Thebes	Aeschylus
A Question of Attribution	Alan Bennett	Sexual Perversity in Chicago	David Mamet
Racing Demon	David Hare		
The Real Inspector Hound	Tom Stoppard	The Shadow of a Gunman	Sean O'Casey
The Rear	Simon Gray	Shakers	John Godber
The Recruiting Officer	George Farquhar	The Shaughraun	Dion Boucicault
Reflected Glory	Ronald Harwood	The Shawl	David Mamet
The Relapse	John Vanbrugh	She Stoops to Conquer	Oliver Goldsmith
Relative Values	Nöel Coward	She Would If She Could	George Etherege
Relatively Speaking	Alan Ayckbourn	Shirley Valentine	Willy Russell
The Restoration of Arnold Middleton*	David Storey	The Silent Woman	Ben Jonson
		Silly Cow	Ben Elton
Retreat	James Saunders	The Silver Box	John Galsworthy
Rhinoceros	Eugène Ionesca	The Silver Tassie	Sean O'Casey
The Ride Down Mount Morgan	Arthur Miller	Simpatico	Sam Shepard
		Simply Disconnected	Simon Gray
Riders to the Sea	J.M. Synge	Single Spies	Alan Bennett
The Rise and Fall of Little Voice	Jim Cartwright	Sisterly Feelings	Alan Ayckbourn
		Sisters	David Storey
The Rival Ladies	John Dryden	Six Characters in Search of an Author	Luigi Pirandello
The Rivals	Richard Brinsley Sheridan		
Road	Jim Cartwright	Six Degrees of Separation	John Guare
The Robbers*	Friedrich von Schiller		
The Rock Garden	Sam Shepard	The Skin Game	John Galsworthy
The Rock	T.S. Eliot	The Skin of Our Teeth	Thornton Wilder
Rodogune	Pierre Corneille	Slag*	David Hare
Le Roi s'amuse	Victor Hugo	Sleeping Dog	Simon Gray
The Room*	Harold Pinter	Sleuth	Anthony Shaffer

Play	Playwright
A Small Family Business	Alan Ayckbourn
Softcops	Caryl Churchill
The Spanish Gypsy	Thomas Middleton and William Rowley
The Spanish Tragedy	Thomas Kyd
Speed-the-Plow	David Mamet
Spoiled	Simon Gray
Spring Awakening	Frank Wedekind
The Squire	Arthur Wing Pinero
Stagestruck	Simon Gray
Stags and Hens	Willy Russell
State of Innocence	John Dryden
Stepping Out	Richard Harris
Stevie*	Hugh Whitemore
Strange Interlude	Eugene O'Neill
A Streetcar Named Desire	Tennessee Williams
Suddenly Last Summer	Tennessee Williams
The Sunshine Boys	Neil Simon
Suppliants	Aeschylus
Sweeney Agonistes*	T.S. Eliot
Sweet Bird of Youth	Tennessee Williams
Sweet Charity	Neil Simon
Table Manners	Alan Ayckbourn
Taking Sides	Ronald Harwood
Talking Heads	Alan Bennett
Tamburlaine the Great	Christopher Marlowe
Tartuffe	Molière
Teechers	John Godber
La Thébaïde, ou Les Frères ennemis	Jean Racine
Ten Times Table	Alan Ayckbourn
Théodore	Pierre Corneille
Thesmophoriazusae	Aristophanes
They're Playing Our Song	Neil Simon
Thieves' Carnival	Jean Anouilh
The Three Sisters	Anton Chekhov
Three Tall Women	Edward Albee
Three Women	Sylvia Plath
The Threepenny Opera	Bertolt Brecht
Thursday's Child	Christopher Fry
Till the Day I Die	Clifford Odets
Time and the Conways	J.B. Priestley
Time and Time Again	Alan Ayckbourn
Time of My Life	Alan Ayckbourn
The Tinker's Wedding	J.M. Synge
Tiny Alice	Edward Albee
'Tis Pity She's a Whore	John Ford
To Damascus	August Strindberg
The Tooth of Crime	Sam Shepard
Top Girls	Caryl Churchill
Torquato Tasso	Johann Wolfgang von Goethe
Total Eclipse	Christopher Hampton
A Touch of the Poet	Eugene O'Neill
The Tower	Christopher Fry
Trachiniae	Sophocles
Translations	Brian Friel
Travesties	Tom Stoppard
Treats	Christopher Hampton
Trelawny of the 'Wells'	Arthur Wing Pinero
The Trojan Women	Euripides
True West	Sam Shepard
The Trumpet Shall Sound	Thornton Wilder

Play	Playwright
Turcaret	Alain-René Lesage
£200 a Year*	Arthur Wing Pinero
The Two of Us*	Michael Frayn
Two Sundays	Simon Gray
Ubu Roi	Alfred Jarry
Uncle Vanya	Anton Chekhov
Under Milk Wood	Dylan Thomas
Unsuitable for Adults	Terry Johnson
Up 'N' Under	John Godber
Vandaleur's Folly	John Arden
Venus Observed	Christopher Fry
Veronica's Room	Ira Levin
La Veuve	Pierre Corneille
A View from the Bridge	Arthur Miller
Virginia	Edna O'Brien
The Visitors	Nicholas Monsarrat
Volpone (The Fox)	Ben Jonson
The Vortex	Nöel Coward
A Voyage Round My Father	John Mortimer
The Voysey Inheritance	Harley Granville Barker
Waiting for Godot	Samuel Beckett
Waiting for Lefty	Clifford Odets
Walk on the Grass (first TV Play)	Peter Nichols
A Walk on the Water*	Tom Stoppard
Walker, London*	J.M. Barrie
Wallenstein Trilogy	Friedrich von Schiller
Waltz of the Toreadors	Jean Anouilh
The Wasps	Aristophanes
Waste	Harley Granville–Barker
The Way of the World	William Congreve
Way Upstream	Alan Ayckbourn
The Web*	Eugene O'Neill
The Weir	Conor McPherson
The Well of the Saints	J.M. Synge
West of Suez (TV play)	John Osborne
What Every Woman Knows	J.M. Barrie
What the Butler Saw	Joe Orton
When Did You Last See My Mother?*	Christopher Hampton
When the Wind Blows	Peter Nichols
When We Are Married	J.B. Priestley
The White Devil	John Webster
Who's Afraid of Virginia Woolf?	Edward Albee
Widowers' Houses	George Bernard Shaw
The Wild Duck	Henrik Ibsen
William Tell	Friedrich von Schiller
The Winslow Boy	Terence Rattigan
Wise Child*	Simon Gray
Woman in Mind	Alan Ayckbourn
A Woman of No Importance	Oscar Wilde
Women Beware Women	Thomas Middleton
Wonderful Tennessee	Brian Friel
The Wood Demon	Anton Chekhov
The Workhouse Donkey	John Arden
Yerma	Federico García Lorca
Yonadab	Peter Shaffer
You Never Can Tell	George Bernard Shaw
Zigger Zagger	Peter Terson
The Zoo Story	Edward Albee

LITERATURE

Theatre: General information

After the Fall Central character: Quentin. Former wife: Maggie (modelled on Marilyn Monroe).

Arms and the Man Setting: Bulgaria. Family: Petkoffs.

Banned by Lord Chamberlain *Early Morning* by Edward Bond (1968) was the last play to be banned by the Lord Chamberlain, whose office was abolished on 26 Sept. 1968.

The Birthday Party Party for: Stanley. Boarding house owners: Meg and Petey.

The Blue Bird Children: Mytyl and Tyltyl.

Broadway theatre named after Neil Simon is the only living American playwright to be so honoured.

Camille Central character Marguerite Gautier.

Candida Candida's husband: Reverend Morell. Poet: Marchbanks.

The Caretaker Title character Davies.

Cat on a Hot Tin Roof Title character: Maggie Pollitt. Husband: Brick. Location: St Louis.

Charley's Aunt Title character: Donna Lucia d'Alvadores. Charley's surname: Wykeham.

Chips with Everything Setting RAF.

Comedy Meaning: Revel-song.

Comedy of intrigue Founder: Sir George Etherege.

Death of a Salesman Salesman Willie Loman.

Doll's House Doll's name: Nora. Nora's husband: Torvald Helmer.

Entertainer Title character Archie Rice.

Equus Psychiatrist: Dysart. Stableboy: Alan Strang.

The Gingerbread Lady Filmed as: *Only When I Laugh.*

The Glass Menagerie Family: Wingfields.

Hedda Gabler Husband: Professor George Tessman.

The Iceman Cometh Salesman: Hickey. Setting: Harry Hope's saloon (NY).

The Importance of Being Ernest Title character: Jack Worthing (real name Ernest Moncrieff). Governess: Miss Prism. Jack found in handbag at station. Left in baby's place: novel. Algernon Moncrieff's fictional friend: Bunbury.

In Camera Setting: Hell. Characters: Garcin, Estelle, Inez.

The Inspector General Impostor: Khlestakov.

Japanese theatre Two main types: Nō (lit: talent) was developed in the 14th century from a court dance and the acrobatics of the sarugaku troupes. Kabuki (lit: singing and dancing art) was developed in the 17th century and was originally only performed by women. The costumes worn come from the Edo period (1603–1868).

The Jew of Malta Title character: Barabas.

Journey's End Setting: First World War.

Jumpers Professor: George Moore. George's Wife: Dotty.

Juno and the Paycock Paycock: Jack Boyle.

Killed by Tortoise Aeschylus was allegedly killed when an eagle dropped a tortoise on his head.

Killed fellow actor in duel Ben Jonson.

Le Bourgeois Gentilhomme Title character: Monsieur Jourdain.

Lady Windermere's Fan Mother: Mrs Erlynne.

The Lady's Not for Burning Setting: Cool Clary.

Famous Lines Brazil, Where the nuts come from (*Charley's Aunt*).

He is the very pineapple of politeness (Mrs Malaprop in *The Rivals*).

Heav'n has no rage, like love to hatred burn'd, Nor Hell a fury, like a woman scorned (*The Mourning Bride*).

Music hath charms to soothe a savage breast (*The Mourning Bride*).

Our civil community is founded on the pestiferous soil of falsehood (Dr Stockman in *An Enemy of the People*).

Very flat, Norfolk (*Private Lives*).

The Long Day's Journey into Night Family: Tyrones.

Look Back in Anger Central character: Jimmy Porter. Jimmy's wife: Alison.

Lyceum Managed by Sir Henry Irving 1878–99.

The Maids Title characters: Claire and Solange.

Le Misanthrope Title character: Alceste.

The Miser Lead character: Harpagon.

Mourning Becomes Electra Based on the Oresteia Trilogy by Aeschylus.

Norman Conquests *Table Manners, Round and Round the Garden, Living Together.*

Oresteia Trilogy (Aeschylus) Agamemnon, Choephoroe (*The Libation-Bearers*), Eumenides.

Peter Pan Children: John, Michael and Wendy Darling. Hook educated at Eton. Dog: Nana.

Phèdre Based on *Hippolytus* by Euripides.

The Playboy of the Western World Title character: Christie Mahon.

Prison Written in Our Lady of the Flowers by Jean Genet.

Private Lives Written for Gertrude Lawrence.

Pushkin's 'Little Tragedies' Mozart and Salieri, The Covetous Knight, The Stone Guest, The Feast during the Plague.

Pygmalion Professor: Henry Higgins. Flowergirl: Eliza Doolittle. Higgins home: Wimpole St. Scandal over: use of the word 'bloody'.

The Quare Fellow Set in a Dublin prison.

The Rivals Rivals: Captain Absolute (Ensign Beverley) and Sir Lucius O'Trigger (Bob Acres). Setting: Bath. Lady: Lydia Languish. Her Aunt: Mrs Malaprop,.

Roots Central character: Beatie Bryant. Setting: Norfolk.

Seagull Central characters: Irina, Nina, Trigorin the novelist.

Second Mrs Tanqueray Title character: Paula Ray.

She Stoops to Conquer Central character: Marlow. Marlow's love: Miss Hardcastle.

State of Innocence Based on *Paradise Lost* by John Milton.

A Streetcar Named Desire Central character: Blanche Du Bois. Blanche's sister: Stella. Stella's husband: Stanley Kowalsky. Setting: New Orleans.

Sturm and Drang (Storm and Stress) German literary movement that preceded Romanticism, taking its name from the play by Max Klinger *Der Wirrwarr, oder Sturm und Drang.*

Subtitle *Man and Superman* 'A Comedy and a Philosophy'.

Theatre of Cruelty Name given by Antonin Artaud to his use of lighting effects, screams and oversized puppets to induce audience reaction, as in *Les Cenci.*

Theatre of Fact Aka Documentary Theatre: a German movement founded in the early 1960s by Rolf Hochuth, Peter Weiss and Heinar Kipphardt, highlighting the political propaganda of post Second World War Germany.

Theatre of the Absurd   Name given to the pessimistic vision of humanity struggling vainly to find a purpose as depicted in works by Beckett (*Waiting for Godot*), Ionesco (*The Bald Soprano*), and such diverse dramatists as Jean Genet, Arthur Adamov and Harold Pinter.

The Three Sisters   Title characters: Irina, Masha, Olga.

Tragedy   Meaning: goat-song.

Travesties   Setting: Zurich.

Volpone   Servant: Mosca.

Waiting for Godot   Tramps: Vladimir (Didi), Estragon (Gogo).

Waiting for Lefty   Title character: Lefty Costello.

Wallenstein Trilogy   *Wallensteins Lager, Die Piccolomini, Wallensteins Tod.*

The Way of the World   Central characters: Mirabell, Millamant, Lady Wishford.

Wesker Trilogy   *Chicken Soup with Barley, Roots, I'm Talking About Jerusalem*

What the Butler Saw   Setting: Psychiatrist's clinic.

The Winslow Boy   Based on Archer–Shee case.

Poetry: By Poet

Anna Akhmatova
(1889–1966)
Anno Domini
White Flock

Matthew Arnold
(1822–1888)
Dover Beach
Empedocles on Etna
The Forsaken Merman
The Scholar Gypsy
Sohrab and Rustum
The Strayed Reveller
Thyrsis
Tristram and Iseult
The Circle Game

Margaret Atwood
(1939–)

W.H. Auden
(1907–1973)
About the House
The Age of Anxiety
Another Time
City Without Walls
The Double Man
Homage to Clio
In Memory of W.B. Yeats
Look, Stranger!
Miss Gee
New Year Letter
Night Mail
On This Island
The Orators
Paid on Both Sides
The Shield of Achilles
Spain
Stop All the Clocks

Richard Harris Barham
(1788–1845)
The Ingoldsby Legends
The Jackdaw of Rheims

Charles Baudelaire
(1821–1867)
Les Fleurs du mal

Hilaire Belloc
(1870–1953)
The Bad Child's Book of Beasts
Cautionary Tales
Matilda

John Betjeman
(1906–1984)
Continual Dew
Death in Leamington
A Few Late Chrysanthemums
Highland Low
The Metropolitan Railway
Mount Zion
New Bats in Old Belfries
A Nip in the Air
Old Lights for New Chancels
A Subaltern's Love Song
For the Fallen
Tristram's End

Laurence Binyon
(1869–1943)

William Blake
(1757–1827)
Jerusalem
Milton
The Sick Rose
Songs of Experience

Songs of Innocence
The Tyger

Aleksandr Blok
(1880–1921)
Nocturnal Hours
The Rose and the Cross
The Scythians
Songs About the Lady Fair
The Twelve

Edmund Blunden
(1896–1974)
Almswomen
Bonadventure
Pastorals
Undertones of War
The Waggoner

Wilfrid Scawen Blunt
(1840–1922)
The Old Squire

Gordon Bottomley
(1874–1948)
Poems of Thirty Years
To Ironfounders and Others

Robert Bridges
(1844–1930)
Eros and Psyche
The Growth of Love
London Snow
October
Prometheus the Firegiver
The Spirit of Man
The Testament of Beauty

Emily Brontë
(1818–1848)
Gondal
Last Lines
Plead for Me
Remembrance
To Imagination

Rupert Brooke
(1887–1915)
1914
The Old Vicarage, Grantchester
The Soldier

Elizabeth Barrett Browning
(1806–1861)
Aurora Leigh
The Battle of Marathon
Casa Guidi Windows
The Cry of the Children
How Do I Love Thee?
Poems before Congress
The Seraphim
Sonnets from the Portuguese

Robert Browning
(1812–1889)
Andrea del Sarto
Bells and Pomegranates
Childe Roland to the Dark Tower Came
Fra Lippo Lippi
Home Thoughts From Abroad
Home-Thoughts, from the Sea
How They Brought the Good News from Ghent to Aix
Men and Women
My Last Duchess

LITERATURE

	Paracelsus	(1874–1936)	*Greybeards at Play*
	Pauline		*The Wild Knight*
	The Pied Piper of Hamelin	John Clare	*First Love*
	Pippa Passes	(1793–1864)	*The Rural Muse*
	Rabbi Ben Ezra		*The Shepherd's Calendar*
	The Ring and the Book		*Village Minstrel*
	Soliloquy of the Spanish	Samuel Taylor	*The Ancient Mariner*
	Cloister	Coleridge (1772–1834)	*Christabel*
	Sordello		*Dejection: An ode*
John Bunyan	*The Pilgrim*		*Kubla Khan*
(1628–1688)			*Ode to France*
Robert Burns	*Address to a Mouse*		*The Rime of the Ancient*
(1759–1796)	*Auld Lang Syne*		*Mariner*
	Comin' Through the Rye	William Cory	*Heraclitus*
	The Cotter's Saturday Night	(1823–1892)	*Ionica*
	Death and Doctor Hornbook	William Cowper	*John Gilpin*
	Despondency	(1731–1800)	*The Task*
	Desolate and Pale Moonlight	George Crabbe	*The Borough*
	Epistle to Davie	(1754–1832)	*The Village*
	Ae Fond Kiss	Hart Crane	*The Bridge*
	For a' that and a' that	(1899–1932)	*White Buildings*
	Halloween	Dante Alighieri	*Banquet*
	The Holy Fair	(1265–1321)	*Canzoniere*
	Holy Willie's Prayer		*The Divine Comedy*
	The Jolly Beggars	W.H. Davies	*Leisure*
	Kilmarnock Poems	(1871–1940)	*Money*
	The Lament		*School's Out*
	A Red, Red Rose		*A Soul's Destroyer*
	Scots Musical Museum	Emily Dickinson	*A Bird Came Down the Walk*
	Tam O'Shanter	(1830–1886)	*A Narrow Fell in the Grass*
	To a Field Mouse		*Parting*
	The Twa Herds	Austin Dobson	*At the Sign of the Lyre*
Samuel Butler	*Hudibras*	(1840–1921)	*A Fancy From Fontenelle*
(1612–80)			*Proverbs in Porcelain*
Lord Byron	*Beppo*		*Vignettes in Rhyme*
(1788–1824)	*Childe Harold's Pilgrimage*	John Donne	*Anniversaries*
	The Destruction of	(c. 1572–1631)	*The Canonization*
	Sennacherib		*The Exstasie*
	Don Juan		*The Good-Morrow*
	Hours of Idleness		*Metempsychosis*
	Lara		*A Nocturnall upon St Lucies*
	The Prisoner of Chillon		*Day*
	She Walks in Beauty		*Song*
	The Siege of Corinth		*The Sun Rising*
	The Vision of Judgment		*A Valediction: Forbidding*
	We'll Go No More A-Roving		*Mourning*
Luis de Camoes	*The Lusiads*	Ernest Dowson	*Decorations*
(1524–1580)	*Rimas*	(1867–1900)	*Non Sum Qualis Eram*
Roy Campbell	*The Flaming Terrapin*		*Vitae Sumina Brevis*
(1901–1957)	*Flowering Rifle*	John Dryden	*Absalom and Achitophel*
	Soldier's Reply to the Poet	(1631–1700)	*Alexander's Feast*
	The Wayzgoose		*Annus Mirabilis: The Year of*
Lewis Carroll	*The Hunting of the Snark*		*Wonders, 1666*
(1832–1898)	*Jaberwocky*		*Astræ Redux*
	Phantasmagoria and other		*Fables, Ancient and Modern*
	Poems		*The Hind and the Panther*
	The Walrus and the		*The Medal*
	Carpenter		*Religio Laici*
Sydney Carter	*Lord of the Dance*		*A Song for St Cecilia's Day*
(1915–)			*Sylvia the Fair*
Charles Causley	*Farewell, Aggie Weston*	T.S. Eliot	*Ash Wednesday*
(1917–)	*Figure of 8*	(1888–1965)	*Four Quartets*
	RIJP		*Gerontion*
	Survivor's Leave		*The Hollow Men*
	Underneath the Water		*The Journey of the Magi*
	Union Street		*The Love Song of J. Alfred*
	The Young Man of Cury		*Prufrock*
Thomas Chatterton	*The Rowley Poems*		*The Waste Land*
(1752–1770)		Ralph Waldo Emerson	*Brahma*
Geoffrey Chaucer	*The Canterbury Tales*	(1803–1882)	*Give All to Love*
(c. 1343–1400)	*Troilus and Criseyde*		*May–Day*
G.K. Chesterton	*The Donkey*		*The Problem*

William Empson (1906–1984) — *The Gathering Storm*

Quintus Ennius (239–169 BC) — *Annales*

Gavin Ewart (1916–1995) — *Poets*

Edward Fitzgerald (1809–1883) — *The Rubaiyat of Omar Khayyam (translation from Persian)*

James Elroy Flecker (1884–1915)
- *The Bridge of Fire*
- *The Golden Journey to Samarkand*
- *The Old Ships*

Robert Lee Frost (1874–1963)
- *After Apple-Picking*
- *Birches*
- *A Boy's Will*
- *The Death of the Hired Man*
- *Dust of Snow*
- *Fire and Ice*
- *A Further Range*
- *The Gift Outright*
- *A Lone Striker*
- *Mountain Interval*
- *Mowing*
- *Neither Out Far Nor In Deep*
- *New Hampshire*
- *North of Boston*
- *The Oven Bird*
- *Pan With Us*
- *The Silken Tent*
- *Steeple Bush*
- *Stopping by Woods on a Snowy Evening*
- *The Tuft of Flowers*
- *West-Running Brook*
- *A Witness Tree*

Jean Genet (1910–1986) — *Chant Secret*

Allen Ginsberg (1926–1997)
- *Empty Mirror*
- *Howl**
- *Kaddish*
- *Planet News*
- *Reality Sandwiches*

Johann Wolfgang von Goethe (1749–1832)
- *Erlkönig*
- *Kennst du das Land*
- *Roman Elegies*

Oliver Goldsmith (1728–1774)
- *The Deserted Village*
- *Elegy on the Death of a Mad Dog*
- *The Traveller*

Robert Graves (1895–1985)
- *Fairies and Fusiliers*
- *Over the Brazier*
- *A Slice of Wedding Cake*

Thomas Gray (1716–1771)
- *The Bard*
- *The Descent of Odin*
- *Elegy Written in a Country Churchyard*
- *The Fatal Sisters*
- *Ode on a Distant Prospect of Eton College*
- *The Progress of Poesy*

Graham Greene (1904–1991) — *Bubbling April*

Julian Grenfell (1888–1915) — *Into Battle*

William Hamilton (1665–1751) — *Last Dying Words of Bonny Heck*

William Hamilton (1704–1754) — *The Braes of Yarrow*

Thomas Hardy (1840–1928)
- *The Darkling Thrush*
- *The Dynasts*
- *Wessex Poems*
- *Winter Words*

Seamus Heaney (1929–)
- *Beowulf (translation)*
- *Field Work*
- *Death of a Naturalist*
- *Door into the Dark*
- *Haw Lantern*
- *Seeing Things*
- *The Spirit Level (collection)*
- *Sweeney's Flight*

Felicia Hemans (1793–1835)
- *Casabianca*
- *The Landing of the Pilgrim Fathers*

William Henley (1849–1903)
- *England, My England*
- *For England's Sake*
- *Hawthorn and Lavender*
- *In Hospital*
- *Invictus*
- *A Song of Speed*
- *Song of the Sword*

Robert Herrick (1591–1674)
- *Cherry-Ripe*
- *Delight in Disorder*
- *To the Virgins, To Make Much of Time*
- *Upon Julia's Clothes*

Friedrich Holderlin (1770–1843)
- *Friedensfeier (Celebration of Peace)*

Homer (8th century BC)
- *The Iliad*
- *The Odyssey*

Thomas Hood (1799–1845)
- *Autumn, Ode to*
- *The Dream of Eugene Aram*
- *Faithless Sally Brown*
- *Lycus the Centaur*
- *National Tales*
- *Ruth*
- *The Song of the Shirt*
- *Tim Turpin*
- *Whims and Oddities*

Gerard Manley Hopkins (1844–1889)
- *Felix Randal*
- *Pied Beauty*
- *The Windhover*
- *The Wreck of the Deutschland*

A.E. Housman (1859–1936)
- *Epitaph on an Army of Mercenaries*
- *Fancy's Knell*
- *Last Poems*
- *More Poems*
- *A Shropshire Lad*

Ted Hughes (1930–)
- *Cave Birds*
- *Crow*
- *The Hawk in the Rain*
- *Lupercal*
- *Moortown*
- *The Remains of Elmet*
- *Wodwo*
- *Birthday Letters collection*

Victor Hugo (1802–1885)
- *Les Châtiments*
- *Les Contemplations*

James Leigh Hunt (1784–1859)
- *Abou Ben Adhem*
- *Jenny Kissed Me*
- *Juvenilia*
- *The Nile*

Henrik Ibsen (1828–1906) — *Brand*

Elizabeth Jennings (1926–)
- *The Animals' Arrival*
- *Lucidities*
- *One Flesh*
- *Relationships*
- *Song for a Birth or a Death*
- *A Way of Looking*

LITERATURE

Samuel Johnson	*London*
(1709–1784)	*The Vanity of Human Wishes*
Ben Jonson	*Drink to Me Only With Thine*
	Eyes
(1572–1637)	*To Celia*
John Keats	*Endymion*
(1795–1821)	*The Eve of St Agnes*
	Grecian Urn, Ode on a
	Hymn to Pan
	Hyperion
	Isabella or the Pot of Basil
	La Belle Dame Sans Merci
	Lamia
	Ode on Melancholy
	Ode to a Nightingale
	On First Looking into
	Chapman's Homer
	Ode to Psyche
	To Autumn
Rudyard Kipling	*The Ballad of East and West*
(1865–1936)	*Barrack-Room Ballads*
	The Betrothed
	Cities and Thrones and
	Powers
	The Female of the Species
	The Gods of the Copybook
	Headings
	Mandalay
	The Way Through the
	Woods
	The White Man's Burden
Walter Savage Landor	*Gebir*
(1775–1864)	*Rose Aylmer*
William Langland	*Piers Plowman*
(c. 1322–1400)	
Philip Larkin	*High Windows*
(1922–1985)	*The Less Deceived*
	The North Ship
	Toads Revisited
	The Whitsun Weddings
Emma Lazarus	*Admetus*
(1849–1887)	*By the Waters of Babylon*
	The New Colossus
Edward Lear	*The Owl and the Pussycat*
(1812–1888)	
Laurie Lee	*April Rise*
(1914–1997)	*The Bloom of Candles*
	My Many–Coated Man
	The Sun My Monument
Cecil Day Lewis	*Beechen Vigil*
(1904–1972)	*Overtures to Death*
C.S. Lewis	*Dymer*
(1898–1963)	
Henry Wadsworth	*The Belfry of Bruges*
Longfellow	*The Courtship of Miles*
(1807–1882)	*Standish*
	Evangeline
	Excelsior
	Kalevala
	The Golden Legend
	The Song of Hiawatha
	Paul Revere's Ride
	The Skeleton in Armour
	The Village Blacksmith
	Voices of the Night
	Wayside Inn, Tales of a
	The Wreck of the Hesperus
Federico García Lorca	*Canciones*
(1898–1936)	*Romancero Gitano*
Richard Lovelace	*To Althea*
(1618–1657)	*To Lucasta, On Going to the*
	Wars

Hugh MacDiarmid	*A Drunk Man Looks at the*
(1892–1978)	*Thistle*
	Sangschaw
Louis MacNeice	*Autumn Sequel*
(1907–1963)	*Bagpipe Music*
	Blind Fireworks
	The Burning Perch
	Solstices
Stéphan Mallarmé	*L'Aprés-midi d'un Faune*
(1842–1898)	
Osip Mandelstam Kamen	*Stone*
(1891–1938)	*Tristia*
Walter de la Mare	*The Listeners*
(1873–1956)	*O Lovely England*
	Peacock Pie
	Silver
	Songs of Childhood
	The Veil
Leo Marks	*Code Poem for the French*
	Resistance
Christopher Marlowe	*Come Live With Me and Be*
(1564–1593)	*My Love*
	Hero and Leander
	(unfinished)
	The Passionate Shepherd to
	His Love
Andrew Marvell	*The Definition of Love*
	The Garden
	An Horatian Ode
(1621–1678)	*To His Coy Mistress*
John Masefield	*Cargoes*
(1878–1967)	*Dauber*
	The Everlasting Mercy
	Gallipoli
	Nan
	Reynard the Fox
	Sea Fever
	Shakespeare
	The Widow in the Bye-
	Street
Vladimir Mayakovsky	*The Backbone Flute*
	A Cloud in Trousers
(1894–1930)	*150,000,000*
John McCrae	*In Flanders Fields*
(1872–1918)	
William McGonagall	*Poetic Gems*
(1830–1902)	*The Tay Bridge Disaster*
Alice Meynell	*Renouncement*
(1847–1922)	*The Shepherdess*
John Milton	*At a Solemn Music*
(1608–1674)	*Comus*
	De Doctrina Christiana
	Il Penseroso
	L'Allegro
	Let Us with a Gladsome
	Mind
	Lycidas
	Nativity Ode
	On His Blindness
	On the Late Massacre in
	Piedmont
	Paradise Lost
	Paradise Regained
	Samson Agonistes
E.G. Moll	*Returned Soldier*
(1900–)	
Clement Moore	*A Visit from St Nicholas*
(1779–1863)	
Thomas Moore	*Irish Melodies*
(1779–1852)	*Lalla Rookh*
	The Last Rose of Summer
	The Light of Other Days

L
I
T
E
R
A
T
U
R
E

Stevie Smith
(1902–1971)
Not Waving But Drowning

Charles Hamilton Sorley
(1895–1915)
All the Hills and Vales Along Marlborough

Robert Southey
(1774–1843)
The Battle of Blenheim
Bishop Bruno
Bishop Hatto
The Inchcape Rock
The Old Man's Comforts

Muriel Spark
(1918–)
The Fanfarlo

Edmund Spenser
(c. 1552–1599)
The Faerie Queene
Mother Hubberds Tale
The Shepheardes Calender

James Stephens
(1882–1950)
The Crock of Gold
In the Poppy Field
Insurrections

Robert Louis
Stevenson
(1850–1894)
A Child's Garden of Verses
A London Sabbath Morn
Underwoods
The Vagabond
The Woodman

John Still
(1543–1608)
Jolly Good Ale and Old

Rabindranath Tagore
(1861–1941)
The Crescent Moon
Gitanjali
The Golden Boat
Manasi

Ann Taylor (1782–1866)
and Jane Taylor
(1783–1824)
Twinkle Twinkle Little Star

Alfred, Lord Tennyson
(1809–1892)
The Charge of the Light Brigade
Crossing the Bar
Idylls of the King
In Memoriam
The Lady of Shalott
Locksley Hall
The Lotos-Eaters
Maud
Oenone
The Princess
The Revenge
Rizpah
Timbuctoo
To Virgil
Ulysses

William Makepeace
Thackeray
(1811–1863)
The Sorrows of Werther

Dylan Thomas
(1914–1953)
After the Funeral
Altarwise by Owl-Light
And Death Shall Have No Dominion
Deaths and Entrances
Do Not Go Gentle into That Good Night
Especially When the October Wind
In Country Sleep
In the White Giant's Thigh
I See the Boys of Summer
Light Breaks Where No Sun Shines
Over Sir John's Hill
Poem in October
We Lying by Seasand

Edward Thomas
(1878–1917)
Adlestrop

Henry David Thoreau
A Week on the Concord and Merrimack Rivers

Rose Thorpe
Curfew Must Not Ring Tonight

John Updike
(1932–)
The Carpentered Hen and Other Tame Creatures

Paul Valéry
(1871–1945)
La Jeune Parque

Edward de Vere
17th Earl of Oxford
(1550–1604)
What Cunning Can Express

Emile Verhaeren
(1855–1916)
Les Débâcles
Les Flamandes
La Multiple Splendeur

Paul Verlaine
(1844–1896)
La Bonne Chanson
Fêtes Galantes
Sagesse

François Villon
(1431–1463)
Battle des pendus
Le Grand Testament
Le Petit Testament

Virgil
(70–19 BC)
The Aeneid
The Bucolics
The Georgics (or Art of Husbandry)

Vincent Voiture
(1597–1648)
Vers de Société

Voltaire
(1694–1778)
La Henriade

Walt Whitman
(1819–1892)
Drum-Taps
Leaves of Grass
O Captain! My Captain!
Song of Myself
When Lilacs Last in the Dooryard Bloom'd

John Greenleaf Whittier
(1807–1892)
At Sundown
Barbara Frietchie
The Battle Autumn of 1862
In War Time
Laus deo
Snow-bound

Oscar Wilde
(1854–1900)
The Ballad of Reading Gaol
Ravenna
To Milton

Tennessee Williams
(1911–1983)
The Summer Belvedere
In the Winter of Cities

William Wordsworth
(1771–1855)
The Affliction of Margaret
The Borderers
To the Cuckoo
Daffodils
Ode to Duty
The Excursion
Guilt and Sorrow
Intimations of Immortality
I Wandered Lonely as a Cloud
The Lucy Poems
My Heart Leaps Up
Nutting
The Prelude
Resolution and Independence
She Was a Phantom of Delight
The Solitary Reaper
Tintern Abbey
Upon Westminster Bridge
Vaudracour and Julia

W.B. Yeats
(1865–1939)
Brown Penny
Byzantium
Ego Dominus Tuus
He Wishes For the Cloths of Heaven
An Irish Airman Foresees His Death
The Lake Isle of Innisfree
Sailing to Byzantium

Sergey Yesenin
(1895–1925)

When You Are Old
Confessions of a Hooligan
Moscow of the Taverns
Desolate and Pale Moonlight
The Black Man

Yevgeny Yevtushenko
(1933–)

Babi Yar
Heavy Soils
Ivan the Terrible
A Wave of the Hand
Zima Junction

Poetry: By Poem

(for poets' dates see previous section)

Abou Ben Adhem	James Leigh Hunt
About the House	W.H. Auden
Above the Barriers	Boris Pasternak
Absolom and Achitophel	John Dryden
Address to a Mouse	Robert Burns
Adlestrop	Edward Thomas
Admetus	Emma Lazarus
Adonais	Percy Bysshe Shelley
The Aeneid	Virgil
The Affliction of Margaret	William Wordsworth
L'Allegro	John Milton
After Apple-Picking	Robert Lee Frost
Aftermath	Siegfried Sassoon
After the Funeral	Dylan Thomas
The Age of Anxiety	W.H. Auden
Alastor	Percy Bysshe Shelley
Al Combate de Trafalgar	Manuel Quintana
Alexander's Feast	John Dryden
All the Hills and Vales Along	Charles Hamilton Sorley
Almswomen	Edmund Blunden
Altarwise by Owl-Light	Dylan Thomas
To Althea	Richard Lovelace
Amelia	Coventry Patmore
Amours	Pierre de Ronsard
And Death Shall Have No Dominion	Dylan Thomas
Andrea del Sarto	Robert Browning
The Animals' Arrival	Elizabeth Jennings
Annabel Lee	Edgar Allan Poe
Annales	Quintus Ennius
Anniversaries	John Donne
Anno Domini	Anna Akhmatova
Annus Mirabilis The Year of Wonders, 1666	John Dryden
Another Time	W.H. Auden
Anthem For Doomed Youth	Wilfred Owen
April Rise	Laurie Lee
Arcadia	Sir Philip Sidney
Argalus and Parthenia	Francis Quarles
Ariel	Sylvia Plath
Ash Wednesday	T.S. Eliot
Astræ Redux	John Dryden
Astrophel and Stella	Sir Philip Sidney
At a Solemn Music	John Milton
At Sundown	John Greenleaf Whittier
Attack	Siegfried Sassoon
At the Sign of the Lyre	Austin Dobson
Auld Lang Syne	Robert Burns
Aurora Leigh	Elizabeth Barrett Browning
Autumn Sequel	Louis MacNeice
Babi Yar	Yevgeny Yevtushenko
The Backbone Flute	Vladimir Mayakovsky
The Bad Child's Book of Beasts	Hilaire Belloc
Bagpipe Music	Louis MacNeice
Ballade des pendus	François Villon
Ballad of East and West	Rudyard Kipling
The Ballad of Reading Gaol	Oscar Wilde
Banquet	Dante Alighieri
Barbara Frietchie	John Greenleaf Whittier
The Bard	Thomas Gray
Barrack-Room Ballads	Rudyard Kipling
Le Bateau Ivre	Arthur Rimbaud
The Battle Autumn of 1862	John Greenleaf Whittier
The Battle of Blenheim	Robert Southey
The Battle of Marathon	Elizabeth Barrett Browning
Bed Riddance	Ogden Nash
Beechen Vigil	Cecil Day Lewis
The Belfry of Bruges	Henry Wadsworth Longfellow
Bells and Pomegranates	Robert Browning
The Bells	Edgar Allan Poe
Beppo	Lord George Byron
The Betrothed	Rudyard Kipling
Birches	Robert Lee Frost
A Bird Came Down the Walk	Emily Dickinson
A Birthday	Christina Rossetti
Bishop Bruno	Robert Southey
Bishop Hatto	Robert Southey
The Black Man	Sergey Yesenin
The Blessèd Damozel	Dante Gabriel Rossetti
Blind Fireworks	Louis MacNeice
On His Blindness	John Milton
The Bloom of Candles	Laurie Lee
Bocage	Pierre de Ronsard
Bonadventure	Edmund Blunden
La Bonne Chanson	Paul Verlaine
The Borderers	William Wordsworth
The Borough	George Crabbe
A Boy's Will	Robert Lee Frost
The Braes of Yarrow	William Hamilton
Brahma	Ralph Waldo Emerson
Brand	Henrik Ibsen
The Bridge of Fire	James Elroy Flecker
The Bridge	Hart Crane
The Bronze Horseman	Alexander Pushkin
Brown Penny	W.B. Yeats
Bubbling April	Graham Greene
The Bucolics	Virgil
The Burning Perch	Louis MacNeice
By the Waters of Babylon	Emma Lazarus
Byzantium	W.B. Yeats
Canciones	Federico Garcia Lorca
The Canonization	John Donne
The Canterbury Tales	Geoffrey Chaucer
The Cantos	Ezra Pound
Canzoniere	Dante Alighieri
Cargoes	John Masefield
Carpentered Hen and Other Tame Creatures	John Updike
Casa Guidi Windows	Elizabeth Barrett Browning
Casabianca	Felicia Hemans
Cautionary Tales	Hilaire Belloc
Cave Birds	Ted Hughes
Chant Secret	Jean Genet

LITERATURE

Field Work	Seamus Heaney	An Horatian Ode	Andrew Marvell
Figure of 8	Charles Causley	Hours of Idleness	Lord Byron
Fire and Ice	Robert Lee Frost	The House of Life	Dante Gabriel Rossetti
First Love	John Clare	How Do I Love Thee?	Elizabeth Barrett Browning
The Flaming Terrapin	Roy Campbell	Howl*	Allen Ginsberg
Flowering Rifle	Roy Campbell	How They Brought the	Robert Browning
The Flower of Old Japan	Alfred Noyes	Good News from	
Ae Fond Kiss	Robert Burns	Ghent to Aix	
For a' that and a' that	Robert Burns	Hudibras	Samuel Butler
For England's Sake	William Henley	Hugh Selwyn Mauberley	Ezra Pound
For Johnny	John Pudney	The Hunting of the Snark	Lewis Carroll
For the Fallen	Laurence Binyon	Hymn to Pan	John Keats
The Forest of Wild	Alfred Noyes	Hyperion	John Keats
Thyme		I See the Boys of Summer	Dylan Thomas
The Forsaken Merman	Matthew Arnold	I Wandered Lonely as a	William Wordsworth
Forty Singing Seamen	Alfred Noyes	Cloud	
Four Quartets	T.S. Eliot	Idylls and Songs	Francis Palgrave
Fra Lippo Lippi	Robert Browning	Idylls of the King	Alfred, Lord Tennyson
Friedensfeier (celebration	Friedrich Hölderlin	If This Be Treason	Ezra Pound
of peace		The Iliad	Homer
A Further Range	Robert Lee Frost	Il Penseroso	John Milton
Gallipoli	John Masefield	I'm a Stranger Here Myself	Ogden Nash
The Garden	Andrew Marvell	To Imagination	Emily Brontë
The Gathering Storm	William Empson	The Inchcape Rock	Robert Southey
Gebir	Walter Savage Landor	In Country Sleep	Dylan Thomas
The Georgics (or Art of	Virgil	The Ingoldsby Legends	Richard Harris Barham
Husbandry)		In Flanders Field	John McCrae
Gerontion	T.S. Eliot	In Hospital	William Henley
The Gift Outright	Robert Lee Frost	In Memoriam	Alfred, Lord Tennyson
Gitanjali	Rabindranath Tagore	In Memory of W.B. Yeats	W.H. Auden
Give All to Love	Ralph Waldo Emerson	Insurrections	James Stephens
Goblin Market	Christina Rossetti	In the Poppy Fields	James Stephens
The Gods of the Copybook	Rudyard Kipling	In the White Giant's Thigh	Dylan Thomas
The Golden Boat	Rabindranath Tagore	Intimations of Immortality	William Wordsworth
The Golden Journey to	James Elroy Flecker	Into Battle	Julian Grenfell
Samarkand		Invictus	William Henley
The Golden Legend	Henry Wadsworth	In War Time	John Greenleaf Whittier
	Longfellow	Ionica	William Cory
Gondal	Emily Brontë	An Irish Airman Foresees	W.B. Yeats
The Good Morrow	John Donne	His Death	
Le Grand Testament	François Villon	Irish Melodies	Thomas Moore
Greybeards at Play	G.K. Chesterton	Isabella or the Pot of Basil	John Keats
The Growth of Love	Robert Bridges	The Island Race	Henry Newbolt
Guilt and Sorrow	William Wordsworth	Israfel	Edgar Allan Poe
Halloween	Robert Burns	Ivan the Terrible	Yevgeny Yevtushenko
Haw Lantern	Seamus Heaney	Jaberwocky	Lewis Carroll
The Hawk in the Rain	Ted Hughes	The Jackdaw of Rheims	Richard Harris Barham
Hawthorn and Lavender	William Henley	Le Jardin des Tuileries	Oscar Wilde
He Wishes For the	W.B. Yeats	Jenny Kissed Me	James Leigh Hunt
Cloths of Heaven		Jerusalem	William Blake
Heavy Soils	Yevgeny Yevtushenko	La Jeune Parque	Paul Valéry
Hellas	Percy Bysshe Shelley	John Gilpin	William Cowper
La Henriade	Voltaire	The Jolly Beggars	Robert Burns
Heraclitus	William Cory	Jolly Good Ale and Old	John Still
Hero and Leander	Christopher Marlowe	The Journey of the Magi	T.S. Eliot
(unfinished)		Journeys and Places	Edwin Muir
The Song of Hiawatha	Henry Wadsworth	Julian and Maddalo	Percy Bysshe Shelley
	Longfellow	Juvenilia	James Leigh Hunt
High and Low	John Betjeman	Kaddish	Allen Ginsberg
The Highwayman	Alfred Noyes	Kamen	Osip Mandelstam
High Windows	Philip Larkin	Kalevala	Henry Wadsworth
The Hind and the Panther	John Dryden		Longfellow
The Hollow Men	T.S. Eliot	Kennst du das Land	Johann Wolfgang von
The Holy Fair	Robert Burns		Goethe
Holy Willie's Prayer	Robert Burns	Kilmarnock Poems	Robert Burns
Homage to Clio	W.H. Auden	The King's Tragedy	Dante Gabriel Rossetti
Homage to Sextus	Ezra Pound	Kubla Khan	Samuel Taylor Coleridge
Propertius		L'Apres-midi d'un Faune	Stéphane Mallarme
Home-Thoughts, from	Robert Browning	La Belle Dame Sans Merci	John Keats
Abroad		La Nymphe de la Seine	Jean Racine
Home-Thoughts, from	Robert Browning	The Labyrinth	Edwin Muir
the Sea		The Lady of Shallott	Alfred, Lord Tennyson

L
I
T
E
R
A
T
U
R
E

L
I
T
E
R
A
T
U
R
E

A Winter Ship	Sylvia Plath	The Wreck of the Deutschland	Gerard Manley Hopkins
Winter Trees	Sylvia Plath		
Winter Words	Thomas Hardy	The Wreck of the Hesperus	Henry Wadsworth Longfellow
The Witch of Atlas	Percy Bysshe Shelley		
A Witness Tree	Robert Lee Frost	The Young Man of Cury	Charles Causley
Wodwo	Ted Hughes	Zima Junction	Yevgeny Yevtushenko
The Woodman	Robert Louis Stevenson		

Poetry: General Information

alexandrine Iambic or trochaic hexameter (line of 12 syllables or 6 feet) with, usually, a caesura (break) at the 6th syllable.

allegory Narrative or description in prose or verse with an underlying meaning or moral message as in *The Faerie Queene* or *The Pilgrim's Progress*.

apocope Omission of the final letter, syllable or sound of a word, e.g. the poetic use of th' instead of the.

assonance Use of the same or similar vowel sounds close together for the sake of euphony, memorability or emotional effect, e.g. 'And deep asleep he seemed'.

asylum, committed to John Clare from 1837 until his death.

W.H. Auden Friend and collaborator: Christopher Isherwood.

The Ballad of Reading Gaol Famous extract: 'And all men kill the thing they love, by all let this be heard, Some do it with a bitter look, Some with a flattering word. The coward does it with a kiss, The brave man with a sword!'

ballade Poem of three eight-line stanzas, rhyming ababbcbc, and one four-line *envoi* (final stanza) rhyming bcbc, with a refrain at the end of each of its four sections. François Villon was a great exponent of the ballade in French, Hilaire Belloc in English.

Bastille Imprisoned for a year in 1717: Voltaire (François Marie Arouet).

bathos Anticlimax or sudden descent, intended or not, from the sublime to the commonplace, e.g. the last 2 lines of Tennyson's *Enoch Arden*: 'And when they buried him the little port, Had seldom seen a costlier funeral.'

Beat Poets Lawrence Ferlinghetti, Allen Ginsberg, Jack Kerouac, Gregory Corso.

Belloc Many of his works illustrated by G.K. Chesterton.

The Betrothed Extract: A woman is only a woman, but a good cigar is a Smoke.

Elizabeth Barrett Browning Pet name: She was affectionately known as 'My Little Portuguese' by her husband Robert Browning.

catachresis Misuse or incorrect application of a word, e.g. 'chronic' to mean 'severe', or 'refute' to mean 'deny'.

Christian Poet First English: Caedmon.

Clerihew Comic biographical poem in the form of a quatrain with lines of various length, rhyming aabb, named after its inventor Eric Clerihew Bentley (1875–1956). Example: The Art of Biography is different from Geography. Geography is about maps, Biography is about chaps.

Dithyramb Song or poem in honour of Dionysus.

The Donkey Describes itself as 'the devil's walking parody On all four-footed things'.

Dover Beach First lines 'The sea is calm tonight The tide is full.'

duels Ben Jonson killed fellow actor Gabriel Spencer. To defend his wife's honour, Alexander challenged and was killed by Baron d'Anthès.

Dymer CS Lewis published this work under the name of Clive Hamilton.

Elegy Written in a Country Churchyard Opening: 'The curfew tolls the knell of parting day, The lowing herd wind slowly o'er the lea . . .' Extract: 'Far from the madding crowd's ignoble strife . . .'

elision Suppression of a vowel or syllable in verse for the sake of metrical correctness, e.g. 'ta'en' (one syllable) replacing 'taken' (two).

enjambement Running-on of one line of verse into another without a grammatical break, e.g.: 'Nay, but this dotage of our general's O'erflows the measure . . .' (*Antony and Cleopatra*).

epigram Pointed, witty saying or verse that may be aphoristic, sarcastic, complimentary or amusing.

euphuism Highly elaborate prose style as found in John Lyly's *Euphues* (1580).

Four Quartets (T.S. Eliot) *Burnt Norton, East Coker, The Dry Salvages, Little Gidding.*

The Four Boileau, La Fontaine, Molière, Racine.

Georgian Poets Writing during the reign of *George V*: Lascelles Abercrombie, Hilaire Belloc, Rupert Brooke, W.H. Davies, Ernest Dowson, John Drinkwater, James Elroy Flecker, Robert Graves, Ralph Hodgson, John Masefield, Walter de la Mare, Harold Monro, Siegfried Sassoon, Sir John Squire, Edward Thomas.

The Golden Treasury of best songs and Lyrical poems in the English language Editor Francis Palgrave edited the classic book of poetic works (1861) with the help of his friend Tennyson, but controversially omitted all of William Blake's poems.

Griffin Poetry Prize Inaugurated in 2001 in Canada. $40,000 awarded to best Canadian collection and $40,000 to best international collection.

haiku Japanese verse form of seventeen syllables in three lines of five, seven and five syllables, encapsulating an idea, image or mood.

Home-Thoughts, From Abroad Opening: 'Oh, to be in England Now that April's there . . .'

Imagism Poetic movement and theory (1909–1917) which emphasized direct treatment of subject-matter, concreteness, extreme economy of language and the rhythm of phrases rather than the rhythm of regular metres. Poets include Richard Aldington, H.D., F.S. Flint, James Joyce, Amy Lowell and Ezra Pound.

Keats's epitaph By himself: 'Here lies one whose name was writ in water.'

Kubla Khan Sacred river: Alph.

Lake Poets Wordsworth, Coleridge and Southey.

Leisure Opening: 'What is this life if, full of care, We have no time to stand and stare?'

limerick Five-lined nonsense verse popularised by Edward Lear and following a rhyming scheme of aabba. Example: There was a young lady of Wilts Who walked up to Scotland on stilts When they said

LITERATURE

it was shocking To show so much stocking She answered "Then what about kilts."

The Listeners   First line: '"Is there anybody there?" said the traveller . . .'

Maud   Classic lines: Come into the garden, Maud, For the black bat, night, has flown . . .'

Metaphysical Poets   A group of English poets of the 17th century, who include John Donne, George Herbert, Henry Vaughan, Richard Crashaw and Andrew Marvell (term first used by Samuel Johnson, possibly influenced by a phrase of Dryden's).

metre   Measure of lines of verse which in English is basically accentual, determined by stress, each group of syllables, usually two or three, forms a metrical unit called a foot.

Milton called Athens   'Mother of arts and eloquence'.

The New Colossus   Lines from this sonnet, inscribed on the Statue of Liberty: 'Give me your tired, your poor, Your huddled masses, yearning to breathe free, The wretched refuse of your teeming shore. Send these, the homeless, tempest-tost to me, I lift my lamp beside the golden door'.

Night Mail   Opening: 'This is the Night Mail crossing the Border, Bringing the cheque and the postal order.'

Ode on a Distant Prospect of Eton College   Extract: 'Ye distant spires, ye antique towers . . .'

Ode to Autumn   Opening: 'Season of mists and mellow fruitfulness, Close bosom-friend of the maturing sun'.

Old English poem, 1st   *Beowulf* (probably composed orally in the 8th century; written down in 10th century).

The Old Vicarage, Grantchester   Details: Contains German and Greek lines (Jeffrey Archer purchased the property).

On his Blindness   First line: 'When I consider how my light is spent'.

Ozymandias   First line: 'I met a traveller from an antique land . . .'

pathetic fallacy   The ascription of human emotions to non-human objects and phenomena, e.g. 'the cruel sea'.

The Pilgrim's Progress   Extract: 'The name of the Slough was Despond'.

Pléiade, La   Group of seven French poets and writers of the 16th century, led by Pierre de Ronsard. The name was taken from that given by the Alexandrian critics to seven tragic poets of the reign of Ptolemy III Philadelphus (285–246BC). The other six members of La Pléiade were Joachim du Bellay, Jean-Antoine de Baif, Jean Dorat, Rémy Belleau, Etienne Jodelle and Pontis de Tyard.

Poet Laureate   Deposed: John Dryden, who became a Catholic in 1685 and was deposed in 1689 after the Glorious Revolution. Longest in office: Alfred, Lord Tennyson (1850–92).

Pott's disease   Suffered by Alexander Pope, who was only 4′ 6″ tall.

prisoner poets   François Villon – for his various criminal activities. James Leigh Hunt: 2 years (1813-15) for libelling the Prince Regent. Jean Genet: for theft, male prostitution, and other crimes. Richard Lovelace: in 1642, for being a Royalist.

The Rape of the Lock   Two Catholic families quarrel after a male member of one steals a lock of hair from a female member of the other.

Sally Brown (Thomas Hood)   Extract: 'They went and told the sexton, and The sexton toll'd the bell'.

Sea Fever   Opening: 'I must go down to the seas again, to the lonely sea and the sky, And all I ask is a tall ship and a star to steer her by . . .'

Shall I compare thee to a summer's day   Next lines: 'Thou art more lovely and more temperate. Rough winds do shake the darling buds of May, and summer's lease hath all to short a date . . .'

The Soldier   First line: 'If I should die think only this of me'.

Song (John Donne)   First line: 'Go and catch a falling star . . .'

Songs of Childhood   Published by Walter de la Mare using the pseudonym Walter Ramal.

sonnets   Three basic types: Spenserian, Shakespearian and Petrarchan.

Spenserian stanza   Eight iambic pentameters followed by one iambic hexameter, rhyming ababbcbcc.

spondee   Metrical foot consisting of two long or stressed syllables.

The Star-Spangled Banner   By Francis Scott Key (1779–1843). First line: 'Oh say can you see by the dawn's early light . . .'

Stella (From Astrophel and Stella)   Thought to be Penelope Devereux.

A Subaltern's Love-song   Beloved: Miss Joan Hunter Dunn. Towns mentioned: Aldershot and Camberley. Car mentioned: Hillman.

Tennyson quotes   'In the Spring a young man's fancy lightly turns to thoughts of love.'
'Man is the hunter; woman is his game . . .'
'"Tis better to have loved and lost Than never to have loved at all.'

tercet   Three-line stanza, particularly as used in terza rima.

terza rima   Verse-form of three-line stanzas rhyming aba, bcb, cdc, and so on, usually iambic pentameters, e.g. *Ode to the West Wind*.

To a Field Mouse   Opening: 'Wee, sleekit, cow'rin', tim'rous beastie, O what a panic's in thy breastie ! Extract: 'The best laid schemes o' mice an' men. Ganag aft a-gley.'

To a Skylark   Opening: 'Hail to thee, blithe Spirit'!

To the Virgins, To Make Much of Time   First line: 'Gather ye rosebuds while ye may . . .'

Transcendentalists   A mid 19th-century New England movement of writers, poets and philosophers who believed in the unity of all creation, the innate goodness of man and the supremacy of insight over logic and experience. Notable adherents were Ralph Waldo Emerson and Henry David Thoreau.

Upon Westminster Bridge   Opening: 'Earth has not anything to show more fair . . .'

The Village Blacksmith   Opening: Under the spreading chestnut tree The village smithy stands . . .'

A Visit from St Nicholas   Opening: '"Twas the night before Christmas . . .'

Whitbread Literary Award Winners

Category		Title	Author
1971	Novel	*The Destiny Waltz*	Gerda Charles
	Biography	*Henrik Ibsen*	Michael Meyer
	Poetry	*Mercia Hymns*	Geoffrey Hill
1972	Novel	*The Bird of Night*	Susan Hill
	Biography	*Trollope*	James Pope-Hennessy
	Children's book	*The Diddakoi*	Rumer Godden
1973	Novel	*The Chip-Chip Gatherers*	Shiva Naipaul
	Biography	*CB: A Life of Sir Henry Campbell-Bannerman*	John Wilson
	Children's book	*The Butterfly Ball & the Grasshopper's Feast*	Alan Aldridge and William Plomer
1974	Novel	*The Sacred and Profane Love Machine*	Iris Murdoch
	Biography	*Poor Dean Brendan*	Andrew Boyle
	Children's book (joint)	*How Tom Beat Captain Najork and His Hired Sportsmen*	Russell Hoban and Quentin Blake
		The Emperor's Winding Sheet	Jill Paton Walsh
1975	Novel	*Docherty*	William McIlvanney
	Autobiography	*In Our Infancy*	Helen Corke
	First book	*The Improbable Puritan: A Life of Bulstrode Whitelocke*	Ruth Spalding
1976	Novel	*The Children of Dynmouth*	William Trevor
	Biography	*Elizabeth Gaskell*	Winifred Gerin
	Children's book	*A Stitch in Time*	Penelope Lively
1977	Novel	*Injury Time*	Beryl Bainbridge
	Biography	*Mary Curzon*	Nigel Nicolson
	Children's book	*No End to Yesterday*	Shelagh Macdonald
1978	Novel	*Picture Palace*	Paul Theroux
	Biography	*Lloyd George: The People's Champion*	John Grigg
	Children's book	*The Battle of Bubble and Squeak*	Philippa Pearce
1979	Novel	*The Old Jest*	Jennifer Johnston
	Autobiography	*About Time*	Penelope Mortimer
	Children's novel	*Tulku*	Peter Dickinson
1980	Novel & Book of the Year	*How Far Can You Go?*	David Lodge
	Biography	*On the Edge of Paradise: A.C. Benson the Diarist*	David Newsome
	Children's novel	*John Diamond*	Leon Garfield
1981	Novel	*Silver's City*	Maurice Leitch
	Biography	*Monty: The Making of a General*	Nigel Hamilton
	Children's novel	*The Hollow Land*	Jane Gardam
	First novel	*A Good Man in Africa*	William Boyd
1982	Novel	*Young Shoulders*	John Wain
	Biography	*Bismarck*	Edward Crankshaw
	Children's novel	*The Song of Pentecost*	W.J. Corbett
	First novel	*On the Black Hill*	Bruce Chatwin
1983	Novel	*Fools of Fortune*	William Trevor
	Biography	*Vita*	Victoria Glendinning
	(joint)	*King George V*	Kenneth Rose
	Children's novel	*The Witches*	Roald Dahl
	First novel	*Flying to Nowhere*	John Fuller
1984	Novel	*Kruger's Alp*	Christopher Hope
	Biography	*T.S. Eliot*	Peter Ackroyd
	Children's novel	*The Queen of the Pharisees' Children*	Barbara Willard
	First novel	*A Parish of Rich Women*	James Buchan
	Short story	*Tomorrow is Our Permanent Address*	Diane Rowe
1985	Novel	*Hawksmoor*	Peter Ackroyd
	Biography	*Hugh Dalton*	Ben Pimlott
	Children's novel	*The Nature of the Beast*	Janni Howker
	First novel	*Oranges Are Not the Only Fruit*	Jeanette Winterson
	Poetry & Book of the Year	*Elegies*	Douglas Dunn
1986	Novel & Book of the Year	*An Artist of the Floating World*	Kazuo Ishiguro
	Biography	*Gilbert White*	Richard Mabey
	Children's novel	*The Coal House*	Andrew Taylor
	First novel	*Continent*	Jim Crace
	Poetry	*Stet*	Peter Reading
1987	Novel	*The Child in Time*	Ian McEwan
	Biography & Book of the Year	*Under the Eye of the Clock*	Christopher Nolan

Year	Category	Title	Author
	First novel	*The Other Garden*	Francis Wyndham
	Poetry	*The Haw Lantern*	Seamus Heaney
1988	Novel	*The Satanic Verses*	Salman Rushdie
	Biography	*Tolstoy*	A.N. Wilson
	Children's novel	*Awaiting Developments*	Judy Allen
	First novel & Book of the Year	*The Comforts of Madness*	Paul Sayer
	Poetry	*The Automatic Oracle*	Peter Porter
1989	Novel	*The Chymical Wedding*	Lindsay Clarke
	Biography and Book of theYear	*Coleridge: Early Visions*	Richard Holmes
	Children's novel	*Why Weeps the Brogan?*	Hugh Scott
	First novel	*Gerontius*	James Hamilton
	Poetry	*Shibboleth*	Michael Donaghy
1990	Novel & Book of the Year	*Hopeful Monsters*	Nicholas Mosley
	Biography	*A.A. Milne: His Life*	Ann Thwaite
	Children's novel	*A.K.*	Peter Dickinson
	First novel	*The Buddha of Suburbia*	Hanif Kureishi
	Poetry	*Daddy, Daddy*	Paul Durcan
1991	Novel	*The Queen of the Tambourine*	Jane Gardam
	Biography & Book of the Year	*A Life of Picasso*	John Richardson
	Children's novel	*Harvey Angell*	Diana Hendry
	First novel	*Alma Cogan*	Gordon Burn
	Poetry	*Gorse Fires*	Michael Longley
1992	Novel	*Poor Things*	Alasdair Gray
	Biography	*Trollope*	Victoria Glendinning
	Children's novel	*The Great Elephant Chase*	Gillian Cross
	First novel & Book of the Year	*Swing Hammer Swing!*	Jeff Torrington
	Poetry	*The Gaze of the Gorgon*	Tony Harrison
1993	Novel & Book of the Year	*Theory of War*	Joan Brady
	Biography	*Philip Larkin*	Andrew Motion
	Children's novel	*Flour Babies*	Anne Fine
	First novel	*Saving Agnes*	Rachel Cusk
	Poetry	*Mean Time*	Carol Ann Duffy
1994	Novel & Book of the Year	*Felicia's Journey*	William Trevor
	Biography	*The Married Man*	Brenda Maddox
	Children's novel	*Gold Dust*	Geraldine McCaughrean
	First novel	*The Longest Memory*	Fred D'Aguiar
	Poetry	*Out of Danger*	James Fenton
1995	Novel	*The Moor's Last Sigh*	Salman Rushdie
	Biography	*Gladstone*	Roy Jenkins
	Children's novel	*The Wreck of the Zanzibar*	Michael Morpurgo
	First novel & Book of the Year	*Behind the Scenes at the Museum*	Kate Atkinson
	Poetry	*Gunpowder*	Bernard O'Donoghue
1996	Novel	*Every Man for Himself*	Beryl Bainbridge
	Biography	*Thomas Cranmer: A Life*	Diarmaid MacCulloch
	First novel	*The Debt to Pleasure*	John Lancaster
	Poetry & Book of the Year	*The Spirit Level*	Seamus Heaney
	Children's Book of the Year	*The Tulip Touch*	Anne Fine
1997	Novel	*Quarantine*	Jim Crace
	Biography	*Victor Hugo*	Graham Robb
	First novel	*The Ventriloquist's Tale*	Pauline Melville
	Poetry & Book of the Year	*Tales from Ovid*	Ted Hughes
	Children's Book of the Year	*Aquila*	Andrew Norriss
1998	Novel	*Leading the Cheers*	Justin Cartwright
	Biography	*Georgiana, Duchess of Devonshire*	Amanda Foreman
	First novel	*The Last King of Scotland*	Giles Foden
	Children's Book of the Year	*Skellig*	David Almond
	Poetry & Book of the Year	*Birthday Letters*	Ted Hughes
1999	Novel	*Music and Silence*	Rose Tremain
	Biography	*Berlioz: Servitude and Greatness*	David Cairns
	First novel	*White City Bloc*	Tim Lott
	Children's Book of the Year	*Harry Potter and the Prisoner of Azkaban*	J.K. Rowling
	Poetry & Book of the Year	*Beowulf*	Seamus Heaney
2000	Novel & Book of the Year	*English Passengers*	Mathew Kneale
	Biography	*Bad Blood: A memoir*	Lorna Sage
	First novel	*White Teeth*	Zadie Smith
	Children's Book of the Year	*Coram Bay*	Jamila Gavin
	Poetry	*The Asylum Dance*	John Burnside

Pulitzer Prize for Fiction

Year	Book	Author	Year	Book	Author
1918	*His Family*	Ernest Poole	1961	*To Kill a Mockingbird*	Harper Lee
1919	*The Magnificent Ambersons*	Booth Tarkington	1962	*The Edge of Sadness*	Edwin O'Connor
1920	*No Award*		1963	*The Reivers*	William Faulkner
1921	*The Age of Innocence*	Edith Wharton	1964	*No Award*	
1922	*Alice Adams*	Booth Tarkington	1965	*The Keepers of the House*	Shirley Ann Grau
1923	*One of Ours*	Willa Cather	1966	*Collected Stories of*	Katherine Anne
1924	*The Able McLaughlins*	Margaret Wilson		*Katherine Anne Porter*	Porter
1925	*So Big*	Edna Ferber	1967	*The Fixer*	Bernard
1926	*Arrowsmith*	Sinclair Lewis			Malamud
1927	*Early Autumn*	Louis Bromfield	1968	*The Confessions of Nat*	William Styron
1928	*The Bridge at San Luis Rey*	Thornton Wilder		*Turner*	
1929	*Scarlet Sister Mary*	Julia Peterkin	1969	*House Made of Dawn*	N. Scott
1930	*Laughing Boy*	Oliver LaFarge			Momaday
1931	*Years of Grace*	Margaret Ayer	1970	*Collected Stories*	Jean Stafford
		Barnes	1971	*No Award*	
1932	*The Good Earth*	Pearl S. Buck	1972	*Angle of Repose*	Wallace Stegner
1933	*The Store*	T.S. Stribling	1973	*The Optimist's Daughter*	Eudora Welty
1934	*Lamb in his Bosom*	Caroline Miller	1974	*No Award*	
1935	*Now in November*	Josephine	1975	*The Killer Angels*	Michael Shaara
		Winslow	1976	*Humboldt's Gift*	Saul Bellow
		Johnson	1977	*No Award*	
1936	*Honey in the Horn*	Harold L. Davis	1978	*Elbow Room*	James Alan
1937	*Gone with the Wind*	Margaret Mitchell			McPherson
1938	*The Late George Apley*	John Phillips	1979	*The Stories of John*	John Cheever
		Marquand		*Cheever*	
1939	*The Yearling*	Marjorie Kinnan	1980	*The Executioner's Song*	Norman Mailer
		Rawlings	1981	*A Confederacy of Dunces*	John Kennedy
1940	*The Grapes of Wrath*	John Steinbeck			Toole
1941	*No Award*		1982	*Rabbit is Rich*	John Updike
1942	*In This Our Life*	Ellen Glasgow	1983	*The Color Purple*	Alice Walker
1943	*Dragon's Teeth*	Upton Sinclair	1984	*Ironweed*	William Kennedy
1944	*Journey in the Dark*	Martin Flavin	1985	*Foreign Affairs*	Alison Lurie
1945	*A Bell for Adano*	John Hersey	1986	*Lonesome Dove*	Larry McMurty
1946	*No Award*		1987	*A Summons to Memphis*	Peter Taylor
1947	*All the King's Men*	Robert Penn	1988	*Beloved*	Toni Morrison
		Warren	1989	*Breathing Lessons*	Anne Tyler
1948	*Tales of the South Pacific*	James A.	1990	*The Mambo King Plays*	Oscar Hijuelos
		Michener		*Songs of Love*	
1949	*Guard of Honor*	James Gould	1991	*Rabbit at Rest*	John Updike
		Cozzens	1992	*A Thousand Acres*	Jane Smiley
1950	*The Way West*	A.B. Guthrie Jr	1993	*A Good Scent from a*	Robert Olen
1951	*The Town*	Conrad Richter		*Strange Mountain*	Butler
1952	*The Caine Mutiny*	Herman Wouk	1994	*The Shipping News*	E. Annie Proulx
1953	*The Old Man and the Sea*	Ernest	1995	*The Stone Diaries*	Carol Shields
		Hemingway	1996	*Independence Day*	Richard Ford
1954	*No Award*		1997	*Martin Dressler: Tale of*	Steven
1955	*A Fable*	William Faulkner		*an American Dreamer*	Millhauser
1956	*Andersonville*	Mackinlay Kantor	1998	*American Pastoral*	Philip Roth
1957	*No Award*		1999	*The Hours*	Michael
1958	*A Death in the Family*	James Agee			Cunningham
1959	*The Travels of Jamie*	Robert Lewis	2000	*Interpreteur of Maladies*	Jhumpa Lahiri
	McPheeters	Taylor	2001	*The Amazing Adventures*	Michael Chabon
1960	*Advise and Consent*	Allen Drury		*of Kavalierd Clay*	

L
I
T
E
R
A
T
U
R
E

Booker Prize for Fiction

Year	Book	Author	Year	Book	Author
1969	*Something to Answer For*	P.H. Newby	1984	*Hotel Du Lac*	Anita Brookner
1970	*The Elected Member*	Bernice Rubens	1985	*The Bone People*	Keri Hulme
1971	*In a Free State*	V.S. Naipaul	1986	*The Old Devils*	Kingsley Amis
1972	*G*	John Berger	1987	*Moon Tiger*	Penelope Lively
1973	*The Siege of Krishnapur*	J.G. Farrell	1988	*Oscar and Lucinda*	Peter Carey
1974	*The Conservationist*	Nadine Gordimer	1989	*The Remains of the Day*	Kazuo Ishiguro
	Holiday	Stanley Middleton (joint)	1990	*Possession*	A.S. Byatt
			1991	*The Famished Road*	Ben Okri
			1992	*Sacred Hunger*	Barry Unsworth
1975	*Heat and Dust*	Ruth Prawer Jhabvala		*The English Patient*	Michael Ondaatje (joint)
1976	*Saville*	David Storey	1993	*Paddy Clarke Ha Ha Ha*	Roddy Doyle
1977	*Staying On*	Paul Scott	1994	*How Late it Was, How Late*	James Kelman
1978	*The Sea, The Sea*	Iris Murdoch	1995	*The Ghost Road*	Pat Barker
1979	*Offshore*	Penelope Fitzgerald	1996	*Last Orders*	Graham Swift
			1997	*The God of Small Things*	Arundhati Roy
1980	*Rites of Passage*	William Golding	1998	*Amsterdam*	Ian McEwan
1981	*Midnight's Children*	Salman Rushdie	1999	*Disgrace*	J.M. Coetzee
1982	*Schindler's Ark*	Thomas Keneally	2000	*The Blind Assassin*	Margaret Atwood
1983	*The Life and Times of Michael K*	J.M. Coetzee			

NB: The Booker McConnell Prize is awarded for a novel by a citizen of the UK, Eire, South Africa, or any Commonwealth country, with the proviso that it was first published in Britain.

Orange Prize for Fiction

The Orange Award was launched in January 1996 and is restricted to female novelists. As well as the annual prize of £30,000 the winner receives a bronze figurine created by Griznel Niven known as the 'Betsie'.

Winners	Year	Title
Helen Dunmore	1996	A Spell of Winter
Anne Michaels	1997	Fugitive Pieces
Carol Shields	1998	Larry's Party
Suzanne Berne	1999	A Crime in the Neighbourhood
Linda Grant	2000	When I Lived in Modern Times

Professions: Former and Alternative

Joseph Addison	MP for Malmesbury (1710–19)
Aesop	slave
Woody Allen	jazz clarinettist
Idi Amin	British Army Sergeant
Kingsley Amis	English lecturer at Swansea University
St Andrew	fisherman
John Arlott	policeman
Henry Armstrong	priest
Isaac Asimov	biochemist
Clement Attlee	social worker
W.H. Auden	stretcher bearer (Spanish Civil War)
Alfred Austin	lawyer
Alan Ayckbourn	BBC radio drama producer
Francis Bacon	MP for Liverpool (1588–92)
Hastings Banda	doctor
Roger Bannister	doctor
Brendan Behan	painter & decorator and labourer
Hilaire Belloc	MP for Salford (1906–9)
Alexander Graham Bell	speech teacher to deaf
Arnold Bennett	solicitor's clerk
R.D. Blackmore	lawyer
Cilla Black	coat checker In (Cavern)
Alexander Borodin	professor of Chemistry
John Buchan	MP for Scottish Universities (1927–35)
Robert Burns	excise officer
James Callaghan	civil servant (tax officer)
Geoff Capes	policeman
Lewis Carroll	mathematics lecturer
Jimmy Carter	peanut farmer
Joyce Cary	civil servant in Nigeria
Giacomo Casanova	librarian & spy
Fidel Castro	film extra
Miguel Cervantes	soldier
Geoffrey Chaucer	customs officer, MP and soldier
Lorrain Claude	pastry cook
William Cobbett	MP for Oldham (1832–35)
Edward Coke	MP for Aldeburgh (1589)
Perry Como	barber
Sean Connery	coffin polisher & RN sailor
Billy Connolly	shipyard worker
Gary Cooper	photographer & stuntman
André Courrèges	engineer

A.J. Cronin	inspector of mines
Dante Alighieri	embassy official
Christopher Dean	policeman
Dave Dee	policeman
Daniel Defoe	brickmaker & shopkeeper
Charles Dickens	court stenographer & factory shoe black
Benjamin Disraeli	novelist
John Donne	dean of St Pauls (1621–31)
Sir Arthur Conan Doyle	doctor (opthalmologist)
John Boyd Dunlop	vet
John Dyer	lawyer
Clint Eastwood	swimming instructor
Thomas Alva Edison	telegraph operator & newsboy
Albert Einstein	patent office clerk
T.S. Eliot	bank clerk
Juan Fangio	bus driver
Michael Faraday	bookseller & lab bottle washer
William Faulkner	postmaster
F. Scott Fitzgerald	Hollywood scriptwriter
Ian Fleming	intelligence officer
Errol Flynn	policeman (Tasmania)
Gerald Ford	male model
George Formby	jockey
Benjamin Franklin	printer
Billy Fury	tugboat worker
Clark Gable	lumberjack
Galileo Galilei	doctor
Greta Garbo	hat model
Graeme Garden	doctor
Giuseppe Garibaldi	candlemaker
James Garner	swimsuit model
Richard Gatling	doctor
Paul Gauguin	stockbroker & labourer (Panama canal)
Jean Genet	professional criminal
Edward Gibbon	MP for Liskeard (1774–80)
William Gilbert	barrister & cartoonist
Johann Goethe	fire chief & foreign minister
Sam Goldwyn	glove salesman
W.G. Grace	doctor
Kenneth Grahame	secretary to the Bank of England
Cary Grant	acrobat
Robert Graves	professor of English (Cairo University)
Fulke Greville	MP for Warwickshire
Zane Grey	dentist
Terry Griffiths	postman
Che Guevara	doctor
Gareth Hale	PE teacher
Thomas Hardy	architect's assistant
Bob Harris	policeman
Russell Harty	teacher
Alex Harvey	lion tamer
Nathaniel Hawthorne	American consul in Liverpool (1853–7)
A.P. Herbert	MP for Oxford University (1935)
William Herschel	music teacher
Benny Hill	milkman
Adolf Hitler	postcard painter
Ho Chi Minh	hotel cook
Bob Hope	boxer
Gerard Manley Hopkins	classics professor (University College Dublin)
Rod Hull	electrician
Gareth Hunt	seaman
Henrik Ibsen	pharmacist
David Jason	electrician
James Prescott Joule	brewer
James Robertson Justice	naturalist
Wassily Kandinsky	lawyer
Harvey Keitel	marine
Charles Kingsley	history professor
Alphonse de Lamartine	French foreign minister (1848)
Burt Lancaster	circus acrobat
Eddie Large	electrician
Philip Larkin	librarian of Hull University
Antoine Lavoisier	tax collector
Vladimir Lenin	lawyer
Franz Liszt	priest
Little Richard	priest
Syd Little	decorator
Henry Wadsworth Longfellow	Harvard lecturer
St Luke	doctor
John Lydgate	monk
Thomas Macaulay	MP for Calne (1830), Leeds (1831), Edinburgh (1839–47, 1852–6)
Harold Maurice Macmillan	publisher
Norman Mailer	candidate for NY mayor (4th of 5)
André Malraux	archaeologist
Walter de la Mare	oil company employee
John Marston	lawyer
Andrew Marvell	MP for Hull (1659–78)
Karl Marx	newspaper correspondent (NY Tribune)
Quentin Massys	blacksmith
St Matthew	tax collector
William Somerset Maugham	surgeon and wartime agent
Herman Melville	customs officer
Gregor Mendel	monk
Jonathan Miller	doctor
John Mills	toilet paper rep
Robert Mitchum	miner
Roger Moore	male model
Samuel Morse	artist
Arthur Mullard	boxer
Modeste Mussorgsky	civil servant
Bob Newhart	accountant
Paul Newman	motor racing driver
Isaac Newton	warden of Mint & MP for Cambridge University (1689, 1701–2)
Harold Nicolson	MP for West Leicester (1935–45)
David Niven	army officer
Sean O'Casey	building site labourer
George Orwell	policeman (Burma)
David Owen	doctor
Norman Pace	PE teacher
Thomas Love Peacock	chief examiner of East India company
Peter the Great	shipyard worker
St Peter	fisherman
Enoch Powell	professor of Greek
Magnus Pyke	nutritionist
Salvatore Quasimodo	engineer
Edgar Quinet	writer before politician
François Rabelais	doctor & monk
Walter Raleigh	MP for Devon (1585)
Ray Reardon	policeman & coal miner
Arthur Rimbaud	gun runner
Auguste Rodin	ornamental mason
Peter Roget	doctor

LITERATURE

Leonard Rossiter	insurance clerk	Margaret Thatcher	research chemist & lawyer
Henri Rousseau	customs officer	John Thaw	market porter
Sir Walter Scott	lawyer	J.R.R. Tolkien	professor of English (Oxford)
William Shakespeare	actor	Leo Tolstoy	army officer
R.B. Sheridan	MP for Stafford (1780–1806), Westminster (1806-7) and Ilchester (1807–12)	Anthony Trollope	post office employee
		Harry S. Truman	haberdasher
		Vincent Van Gogh	trainee priest
Nevil Shute	aircraft designer	John Vanbrugh	playwright before architect
Sir Philip Sidney	soldier	Lech Walesa	electrician
Delia Smith	hairdresser	Bradley Walsh	footballer (Brentford)
C.P. Snow	parliamentary sec. (Ministry of Technology)	George Washington	British Army colonel
		Chaim Weizmann	biochemist
Benjamin Spock	naval officer	Orson Welles	picador
Joseph Stalin	trainee monk	William Wilberforce	MP variously for Hull, Yorkshire and Bromber (1780–1825)
Freddie Starr	bricklayer		
Sir Richard Steele	MP for Stockbridge (1713)		
Tommy Steele	seaman	Ludwig Wittgenstein	hospital porter
Laurence Sterne	vicar	Terry Wogan	bank clerk
Wallace Stevens	insurance company executive	William Wordsworth	stamp distributor
		Harry Worth	miner
Rod Stewart	footballer (Brentford) & gravedigger	Christopher Wren	professor of astronomy
		Tammy Wynette	beautician
David Storey	Rugby League player	Boris Yeltsin	construction company director
Jonathan Swift	priest		
Jimmy Tarbuck	milkman	Brigham Young	carpenter, painter & glazier
Pyotr Tchaikovsky	civil servant	Émile Zola	clerk in publishing house

Fictional Literary Characters

Captain Absolute	*The Rivals*	Big Daddy	*Cat on a Hot Tin Roof*
Captain Ahab	*Moby Dick*	Bigwig (rabbit)	*Watership Down*
Benjamin Allen	*The Pickwick Papers*	Ernie Bilko	created by Nat Hiken
Roderick Alleyn	created by Ngaio Marsh	Mr Bingley	*Pride and Prejudice*
Charlie Allnutt	*The African Queen*	Stephen Blackpool	*Hard Times*
Squire Allworthy	*Tom Jones*	John Blackthorne	*Shogun*
Andy Capp	drawn by Reg Smythe	Modesty Blaise	created by Peter O'Donnell
Andy Pandy	created by Maria Bird	Sir Percy Blakeney	*The Scarlet Pimpernel*
Harry Angstrom	*The Rabbit Tetralogy*	Colonel Blimp	created by David Low
Lara Antipova	*Doctor Zhivago*	Leopold Bloom	*Ulysses*
Aouda	*Around the World in 80 Days*	Mr Boffin	*Our Mutual Friend*
John Appleby	created by Michael Innes	Prince Andrey Bolkonsky	*War and Peace*
Isobel Archer	*The Portrait of a Lady*	James Bond	created by Ian Flemming
Jack Aubrey	*Master and Commander (& others)*	Bosinney	*The Forsyte Saga*
Steve Austin	*Cyborg (by Martin Caidin)*	Josiah Bounderby	*Hard Times*
Ayesha	*She*	Boxer the Horse	*Animal Farm*
Dr Aziz	*A Passage to India*	Jack Boyle	*Juno and the Paycock*
Babar	created by Jean de Brunhoff	Lady Bracknell	*The Importance of Being Ernest*
Badger	*The Wind in the Willows*		
Bilbo Baggins	*The Hobbit, Lord of the Rings*	Ben Braddock	*The Graduate*
Major Bagstock	*Dombey and Son*	Colonel Brandon	*Sense and Sensibility*
David Balfour	*Kidnapped*	Sally Brass	*The Old Curiosity Shop*
Mrs Bardell	*The Pickwick Papers*	Sampson Brass	*The Old Curiosity Shop*
Barkis	*David Copperfield*	Madeline Bray	*Nicholas Nickleby*
The Baron (John Mannering)	created by Anthony Morton (John Creasey)	Alan Breck	*Kidnapped*
		Brer Rabbit	the *Uncle Remus Stories*
Oliver Barrett IV	*Love Story*	Dorothea Brooke	*Middlemarch*
Bastable Family	*The Treasure-Seekers* (by E. Nesbit)	Father Brown	created by GK Chesterton
		Pinkie Brown	*Brighton Rock*
Batman	created by Bob Kane	Mr Brownlow	*Oliver Twist*
Dr Jim Bayliss	*All My Sons*	Beatrice Bryant	*Roots*
Bazarov	*Fathers and Sons*	Daisy Buchanan	*The Great Gatsby*
Belinda	*The Rape of the Lock*	Bucket	*Bleak House*
Elizabeth Bennet	*Pride and Prejudice*	Charlie Bucket	*Charlie and the Chocolate Factory*
Inspector Bertozzo	*Accidental Death of an Anarchist*		
		Buck (the Dog)	*The Call of the Wild*
Rev. Edmund Bertram	*Mansfield Park*	Rosa Bud	*The Mystery of Edwin Drood*
Sir Thomas Bertram	*Mansfield Park*	Mr Bumble	*Oliver Twist*
Margot Beste-Chetwynde	*Decline and Fall*	Natty Bumppo	the *Leatherstocking stories*
		Sergeant Buzfuz	*The Pickwick Papers*

Albert Campion	created by Margery Allingham
Tom Canty	*The Prince and the Pauper*
Sir Danvers Carew	*Dr Jekyll and Mr Hyde*
William Carey	*Of Human Bondage*
James Carker	*Dombey and Son*
Katy Carr	*What Katy Did*
Richard Carstone	*Bleak House*
Sidney Carton	*A Tale of Two Cities*
Captain Cat	*Under Milk Wood*
Anne Catherick	*The Woman in White*
Catherine	*The Bell*
Holden Caulfield	*The Catcher in the Rye*
Jenny Cavillieri	*Love Story*
Mr Chadband	*Bleak House*
Professor Challenger	*The Lost World*
Canon Chasuble	*The Importance of Being Ernest*
Chauntecleer (the hen)	*Nun's Priest's Tale*
Cheeryble Brothers (Ned & Charles)	*Nicholas Nickleby*
Jack Chesney	*Charley's Aunt*
Edward Chester	*Barnaby Rudge*
Sir John Chester	*Barnaby Rudge*
Harvey Cheyne	*Captains Courageous*
Chichikov	*Dead Souls*
Chingachgook	the Leatherstocking stories
Mr Charles Chipping	*Goodbye, Mr Chips*
Christian	*The Pilgrim's Progress*
Frank Churchill	*Emma*
Petty Officer Claggart	*Billy Budd*
Ada Clare	*Bleak House*
Angel Clare	*Tess of the D'Urbervilles*
Eric Claudin	*The Phantom of the Opera*
Darius Clayhanger (printer)	*Clayhanger*
Clegg	*The Collector*
Arthur Clennam	*Little Dorrit*
Codlin & Short	*The Old Curiosity Shop*
Robert James Colley	*Rites of Passage*
Compson family	*The Sound and the Fury and Absalom, Absalom!*
Hugh Conway	*Lost Horizon*
Bob Cratchit	*A Christmas Carol*
Mr Crawford	*Mansfield Park*
Mr Creakle	*David Copperfield*
Mr Crisparkle	*The Mystery of Edwin Drood*
Guy Crouchback	*Men at Arms*
Lenina Crowne	*Brave New World*
Isabelle de Croye	*Quentin Durward*
Jerry Cruncher (body snatcher)	*A Tale of Two Cities*
Sergeant Cuff	*The Moonstone*
Curdie (miner)	*The Princess and the Goblin*
Captain Cuttle	*Dombey and Son*
Stephen Daedalus	*Ulysses*
Adam Dalgleish	created by P.D. James
Edmond Dantès	*Count of Monte Christo*
Mrs Danvers	*Rebecca*
Dapper	*The Alchemist*
Mr Fitzwilliam Darcy	*Pride and Prejudice*
Charles Darnay	*A Tale of Two Cities*
Dashwood family	*Sense and Sensibility*
Lady Dedlock	*Bleak House*
Sir Leicester Dedlock	*Bleak House*
Anne Deever	*All My Sons*
Danny Deever	*Barrack-Room Ballads*
Madame Defarge	*A Tale of Two Cities*
Maxim De Winter	*Rebecca*
James Dixon	*Lucky Jim*
Captain Dobbin	*Vanity Fair*
Eliza Doolittle	*Pygmalion*
Dowler	*The Pickwick Papers*
Paul Drake	created by Erle Stanley Gardner
Abel Drugger	*The Alchemist*
Bentley Drummie	*Great Expectations*
Blanche Du Bois	*A Streetcar Named Desire*
Lady Dulcinea	*Don Quixote*
Auguste Dupin	created by Edgar Allan Poe
Albus Dunbledore	Harry Potter Books
Dudley Dursley	Harry Potter Books
Catherine Earnshaw	*Wuthering Heights*
Humphrey Chimpden Earwicker	*Finnegans Wake*
Eeyore	*Winnie-the-Pooh*
Montague Egg	created by Dorothy L. Sayers
Anne Elliot	*Persuasion*
Sir Walter Elliot	*Persuasion*
Mrs Erlynne	*Lady Windermere's Fan*
Cedric Errol	*Little Lord Fauntleroy*
Esmeralda	*The Hunchback of Notre Dame*
Estella	*Great Expectations*
Estragon	*Waiting for Godot*
Etienne	*Germinal*
Bathsheba Everdene	*Far from the Madding Crowd*
Face	*The Alchemist*
Jane Fairfax	*Emma*
Jude Fawley	*Jude the Obscure*
Gervase Fenn	created by Edmund Crispin
Cyril Fielding	*A Passage to India*
Fiver	*Watership Down*
Pegeen Flaherty	*The Playboy of the Western World*
Flashman	*Tom Brown's Schooldays*
Henry Fleming	*The Red Badge of Courage*
Jeremiah Flintwinch	*Little Dorrit*
Phileas Fogg	*Around the World in 80 Days*
Fossil family	*Ballet Shoes* (Noel Streatfeild)
Frodo	*The Lord of the Rings*
Archdeacon Frollo	*The Hunchback of Notre Dame*
Sarah Gamp	*Martin Chuzzlewit*
Gandalf	*The Lord of the Rings*
Biddy Gargery	*Great Expectations*
Joe Gargery	*Great Expectations*
Mr Garland	*The Old Curiosity Shop*
James Gatz (Jay Gatsby)	*The Great Gatsby*
Marguerite Gautier	*Camille*
Walter Gay	*Dombey and Son*
Gerard	*The Cloister and the Hearth*
Inspector Ghote	created by H.R.F. Keating
Solomon Gills	*Dombey and Son*
Roderick Glossop (psychiatrist)	the Jeeves stories
Anthony Gloster (shipowner)	*The Mary Gloster* (Kipling)
Holly Golightly	*Breakfast at Tiffany's*
Gollum	*The Lord of the Rings*
Gowan Family	*Little Dorrit*
Thomas Gradgrind	*Hard Times*
Mary Graham	*Martin Chuzzlewit*
Edith Granger	*Dombey and Son*
Hermione Granger	Harry Potter Books
Cordelia Gray	created by P.D. James
Grendel	*Beowulf*
Mr Grewgious	*The Mystery of Edwin Drood*
Jack Grey	*Pale Fire*
Arthur Gride	*Nicholas Nickleby*
Joan Griffin	*The Invisible Man*
Clyde Griffiths	*An American Tragedy*

LITERATURE

Character	Work
Captain Grimes	*Decline and Fall*
Grip (raven)	*Barnaby Rudge*
Tania Gromeko	*Doctor Zhivago*
Gunga Din	created by Rudyard Kipling
Tod Hackett	*The Day of the Locust*
Harry Haller	*Steppenwolf*
Basil Hallward	*The Picture of Dorian Gray*
Ham	*David Copperfield*
Charles Hamilton	*Gone With the Wind*
Richard Hannay	*The Thirty-Nine Steps*
Miss Hardcastle	*She Stoops to Conquer*
Emma Haredale	*Barnaby Rudge*
Geoffrey Haredale	*Barnaby Rudge*
John Harmon (aka John Rokesmith)	*Our Mutual Friend*
James Harthouse	*Hard Times*
Miss Havisham	*Great Expectations*
Captain Hawdon	*Bleak House*
Hawkeye	the *Leatherstocking* stories
Bill Haydon (spy)	*Tinker, Tailor, Soldier, Spy*
Dolores Haze	*Lolita*
Hazel (rabbit)	*Watership Down*
Bradley Headstone	*Our Mutual Friend*
Uriah Heep	*David Copperfield*
Nora Helmer	*A Doll's House*
Michael Henchard	*The Mayor of Casterbridge*
Frederic Henry	*A Farewell to Arms*
Lizzy Hexam	*Our Mutual Friend*
Hickey	*The Iceman Cometh*
Henry Higgins	*Pygmalion*
Charles Highway	*The Rachel Papers*
Bridget Hitler	*Young Adolf* by Beryl Bainbridge
Mr Honeythunder	*The Mystery of Edwin Drood*
Captain Hook	*Peter Pan*
Houyhnhnms (horses)	*Gulliver's Travels*
Humbert Humbert	*Lolita*
Humpty Dumpty	*Through the Looking Glass*
Injun Joe	*Tom Sawyer*
Mr Jaggers	*Great Expectations*
John Jarndyce	*Bleak House*
John Jasper	*The Mystery of Edwin Drood*
Mrs Jennings	*Sense and Sensibility*
Mrs Jessel	*The Turn of the Screw*
Alfred Jingle	*The Pickwick Papers*
Tom Joad	*The Grapes of Wrath*
Jocasta	*Oedipus the King*
Victoria Jones	*Bhowani Junction* (John Masters)
Robert Jordan	*For Whom the Bell Tolls*
Monsieur Jourdain	*Le Bourgeois Gentilhomme*
Joseph K	*The Trial*
Alyosha Karamazov	*The Brothers Karamazov*
Dmitri Karamazov	*The Brothers Karamazov*
Ivan Karamazov	*The Brothers Karamazov*
Chris Keller	*All My Sons*
Frank Kennedy	*Gone With the Wind*
Khlestakov	*The Inspector General*
Kipps (draper's assistant)	*Kipps*
Howard Kirk	*The History Man*
Joseph Knecht	*The Glass Bead Game* aka (Magister Ludi)
Mr Knightley	*Emma*
Kostoglotov	*Cancer Ward*
Stanley Kowalsky	*A Streetcar Named Desire*
Krook	*Bleak House*
Helena Landless	*The Mystery of Edwin Drood*
Neville Landless	*The Mystery of Edwin Drood*
Lydia Languish	*The Rivals*
Leamas	*The Spy Who Came in from the Cold*
Simon Legree	*Uncle Tom's Cabin*
Amyas Leigh	*Westward Ho!*
Jeeter Lester	*Tobacco Road*
Adrian Leverkühn (composer)	*Doctor Faustus*
Levin	*Anna Karenina*
Ligia	*Quo Vadis?*
Little Emily	*David Copperfield*
Little Nell (Trent)	*The Old Curiosity Shop*
Teddy Lloyd	*The Prime of Miss Jean Brodie*
Lord Loam	*The Admirable Crichton*
Willy Loman	*Death of a Salesman*
Jarvis Lorry	*A Tale of Two Cities*
Lovewit	*The Alchemist*
Frank Lubey	*All My Sons*
Lucky	*Waiting for Godot*
Tertius Lydgate (surgeon)	*Middlemarch*
Lt Macaulay	*Bhowani Junction* (John Masters)
Abel Magwitch	*Great Expectations*
Christie Mahon	*The Playboy of the Western World*
Major Major	*Catch-22*
Mrs Malaprop	*The Rivals*
Draco Malfoy	Harry Potter Books
Captain Charles Mallison	*Lost Horizon*
Dr Manette	*A Tale of Two Cities*
Lucie Manette	*A Tale of Two Cities*
Daphne Manners	*The Jewel in the Crown*
Stephen Maturin	created by Patrick O'Brian
Oskar Matzerath	*The Tin Drum*
Meagles family	*Little Dorrit*
Oliver Mellors	*Lady Chatterley's Lover*
Mr Merdle	*Little Dorrit*
Merrylegs (pony)	*Black Beauty*
Messala	*Ben Hur*
Mr Micawber	*David Copperfield*
Duke Michael	*The Prisoner of Zenda*
Mildew	*Fungus the Bogeyman*
Millamant	*The Way of the World*
George Milton	*Of Mice and Men*
Minnehaha	*Hiawatha*
Mirabell	*The Way of the World*
Mold	*Fungus the Bogeyman*
Mole	*The Wind in the Willows*
Algernon Moncrieff	*The Importance of Being Ernest*
Montmorency (the dog)	*Three Men in a Boat*
Dr Monygham	*Nostromo*
Paul Morel	*Sons and Lovers*
Dean Moriarty	*On the Road*
Catherine Morland	*Northanger Abbey*
Mother's Younger Brother	*Ragtime* (E.L. Doctorow)
Mowgli	*The Jungle Book*
Matthew Mugg (catsmeat man)	*Doctor Dolittle*
Edward Murdstone	*David Copperfield*
Prince Myshkin	*The Idiot*
Mytyl	*The Blue Bird*
Nana	*Peter Pan*
Nancy	*Oliver Twist*
Napoleon the Pig	*Animal Farm*
Nawab of Satipur	*Heat and Dust* (Ruth Prawer Jhabvala)
Nayland-Smith	*Fu Manchu*
Captain Nemo	*Twenty Thousand Leagues Under the Sea*

Norah Nesbit	*Of Human Bondage*
Susan Nipper	*Dombey and Son*
Kit Nubbles	*The Old Curiosity Shop*
Mr Nupkins	*The Pickwick Papers*
Gabriel Oak	*Far from the Madding Crowd*
Kitty Oblonsky	*Anna Karenina*
Julia O'Brien	*Nineteen Eighty-Four*
Mrs Ogmore-Pritchard	*Under Milk Wood*
O-Lan	*The Good Earth*
Oompa Loompas	*Charlie and the Chocolate Factory*
George Osborne	*Vanity Fair*
Mr Palmer	*Sense and Sensibility*
Doctor Pangloss	*Candide*
Panurge	*Gargantua and Pantagruel*
Sancho Panza	*Don Quixote*
Passepartout	*Around the World in 80 Days*
Charity Pecksniff	*Martin Chuzzlewit*
Mercy Pecksniff	*Martin Chuzzlewit*
Seth Pecksniff	*Martin Chuzzlewit*
Clara Peggotty	*David Copperfield*
Daniel Peggotty	*David Copperfield*
Paul Pennyfeather	*Decline and Fall*
Pertelote (the cock)	*The Nun's Priest's Tale*
Ronald Osprey Petrefact	*Ancestral Vices* (Tom Sharpe)
Petrovitch	*Crime and Punishment*
Alexander Petrovsky	*Russian Hide-and-Seek* (Kingsley Amis)
Phaedrus	*Zen and the Art of*
Motorcycle	
	Maintenance
Aunt Peturia	Harry Potter Books
Piggy	*Lord of the Flies*
Billy Pilgrim	*Slaughterhouse-Five*
Ruth Pinch	*Martin Chuzzlewit*
Tom Pinch	*Martin Chuzzlewit*
Pip (Philip Pirrip)	*Great Expectations*
Captain Pissani	*Accidental Death of an Anarchist*
Herbert Pocket	*Great Expectations*
Maggie Pollitt	*Cat on a Hot Tin Roof*
Polynesia (parrot)	*Doctor Dolittle*
Ernest Pontifex	*The Way of All Flesh*
Jimmy Porter	*Look Back in Anger*
Claude (Mustard) Pott	created by P.G. Wodehouse
Pozzo	*Waiting for Godot*
Ford Prefect	*The Hitchhiker's Guide to the Galaxy*
Private Prewitt	*From Here to Eternity*
Fanny Price	*Mansfield Park*
Dr Primrose	*The Vicar of Wakefield*
Miss Prism	*The Importance of Being Ernest*
Dr Proudie	*Barchester Towers*
Mrs Proudie	*Barchester Towers*
Hester Prynne	*The Scarlet Letter*
Pushmi-Pullyu (two-headed llama)	*Doctor Doolittle*
Roger Quaife	*The Corridors of Power*
Quasimodo	*The Hunchback of Notre Dame*
Queen of Hearts	*Alice's Adventures in Wonderland*
Adela Quested	*A Passage to India*
Daniel Quilp	*The Old Curiosity Shop*
Quint	*The Turn of the Screw*
Ralph	*Lord of the Flies*
Elwin Ransome	*Perelandra* by C.S. Lewis
Raskolnikov	*Crime and Punishment*
Captain Rawdon	*Bleak House*
Paul Ray	*The Second Mrs Tanqueray*

Red Queen	*Through the Looking Glass*
Ignatius J. Reilly	*Confederacy of Dunces* (John K Toole)
Archie Rice	*The Entertainer*
Rico Bandello	*Little Caesar* (WR Burnett)
John Ridd	*Lorna Doone*
Rogue Riderhood	*Our Mutual Friend*
Sir Colenso Ridgeon	*The Doctor's Dilemma*
Monsieur Rigaud	*Little Dorrit*
Rikki Tikki Tavi	*The Jungle Book*
Christopher Robin	*Winnie-the-Pooh*
Fanny Robin	*Far from the Madding Crowd*
Mr Rochester	*Jane Eyre*
Mildred Rodgers	*Of Human Bondage*
Rose of Torridge	*Westward Ho!*
Emma Rouault	*Madame Bovary*
Lady Rowena	*Ivanhoe*
Roxane	*Cyrano de Bergerac*
Nicholas Rubashov	*Darkness at Noon*
King Rudolf	*The Prisoner of Zenda*
Mrs Rushworth	*Mansfield Park*
Captain Charles Ryder	*Brideshead Revisited*
Iris Aroon St Charles	*Good Behaviour* (Molly Keane)
Mr Sapsea	*The Mystery of Edwin Drood*
Sauron	*The Lord of the Rings*
Bob Sawyer	*The Pickwick Papers*
Rose Sayer	*The African Queen*
Scamper	*The Secret Seven*
Ebenezer Scrooge	*A Christmas Carol*
Basil Seal	*Black Mischief*
Amelia Sedley	*Vanity Fair*
John Francis Shade	*Pale Fire*
Shadowfax (horse)	*The Lord of the Rings*
Shalimar	*The Arabian Nights*
Becky Sharp	*Vanity Fair*
Anne Shirley	*Anne of Green Gables*
Bill Sikes	*Oliver Twist*
Napoleon Bonaparte Simpson	*The Spectacles* (Edgar Allan Poe)
Saleem Sinai	*Midnight's Children*
Dr Slop	*Tristram Shandy*
Obadiah Slope	*Barchester Towers*
Tyrone Slothrop	*Gravity's Rainbow*
Lennie Small	*Of Mice and Men*
Pavel Smedyakov	*The Brothers Karamzov*
Smike	*Nicholas Nickleby*
George Smiley	created by John le Carré
Smith	*Loneliness of the Long Distance Runner*
Winston Smith	*Nineteen Eighty-Four*
Lady Sneerwell	*The School for Scandal*
Augustus Snodgrass	*The Pickwick Papers*
Julian Sorel	*The Red and the Black*
Dora Spenlow	*David Copperfield*
Wackford Squeers	*Nicholas Nickleby*
Bertie Stanhope	*Barchester Towers*
James Steerforth	*David Copperfield*
Steerpike	*Titus Groan*
Alan Strang	*Equus*
Subtle	*The Alchemist*
Esther Summerson	*Bleak House*
Joseph Surface	*The School for Scandal*
Svengali	*Trilby*
Dick Swiveller	*The Old Curiosity Shop*
Tadzio	*Death in Venice*
John Tanner	*Man and Superman*
Mark Tapley	*Martin Chuzzlewit*
Mr Tartar	*The Mystery of Edwin Drood*
Tatiana	*Eugene Onegin*
Lady Teazle	*The School for Scandal*

LITERATURE

Professor George Tessman	Hedda Gabler	Alice Walker	The Color Purple
Becky Thatcher	Tom Sawyer	The Walrus and the Carpenter	Through the Looking Glass
Henry Tilney	Northanger Abbey	Wang Lung	The Good Earth
Timmy	The Famous Five	Maria Ward	Mansfield Park
Tinker Bell	Peter Pan	Mr Wardle	The Pickwick Papers
Tiny Tim	A Christmas Carol	Water Rat	The Wind in the Willows
Tiresias	Oedipus the King	Ronald Weasley	Harry Potter Books
Toad	The Wind in the Willows	Silas Wegg	Our Mutual Friend
Uncle Toby	Tristram Shandy	Sam Weller	The Pickwick Papers
Kenneth Marchal Toomey	Earthly Powers	Captain Wentworth	Persuasion
		Sophia Western	Tom Jones
Topsy	Uncle Tom's Cabin	Mr Weston	Emma
Tom Traddles	David Copperfield	Reg Wexford	created by Ruth Rendell
Rev. John Treherne	The Admirable Crichton	Ann Whitefield	Man and Superman
Trigorin	The Seagull	White Queen	Through the Looking Glass
Trilby (artist's model)	Trilby	Agnes Wickfield	David Copperfield
Disko Troop	Captains Courageous	Mr Wickham	Pride and Prejudice
Job Trotter	The Pickwick Papers	Bella Wilfer	Our Mutual Friend
Betsy Trotwood	David Copperfield	Ashley Wilkes	Gone With the Wind
Sergeant Troy	Far from the Madding Crowd	Joe Willett	Barnaby Rudge
Tulkinghorn	Bleak House	John Willett	Barnaby Rudge
Maggie Tulliver	The Mill on the Floss	Aaron Winthrop	Silas Marner
Tom Tulliver	The Mill on the Floss	Willy Nilly	Under Milk Wood
Tracy Tupman	The Pickwick Papers	Willy Wonka	Charlie and the Chocolate Factory
Tweedledum and Tweedledee	Through the Looking Glass	Nathaniel Winkle	The Pickwick Papers
Tyltyl	The Blue Bird	Nero Wolfe	created by Rex Stout
Uncas	the Leatherstocking stories	Dr Allan Woodcourt	Bleak House
Andrew Undershaft (arms maker)	Major Barbara	Emma Woodhouse	Emma
		Ernest Wooley	The Admirable Crichton
Jean Valjean	Les Misérables	Wormold	Our Man in Havana
Piet van der Valk	created by Nicolas Freeling	General Wormwort (rabbit)	Watership Down
Harriet Vane	created by Dorothy L. Sayers		
Dolly Varden	Barnaby Rudge	Jack Worthing	The Importance of Being Ernest
Gabriel Varden	Barnaby Rudge		
The Veneerings	Our Mutual Friend	Eugene Wrayburn	Our Mutual Friend
Lord Verisopht	Nicholas Nickleby	Jenny Wren	Our Mutual Friend
Uncle Vernon	Harry Potter Books	Charles Wykeham	Charley's Aunt
Vladimir	Waiting for Godot	Yahoos (humans)	Gulliver's Travels
Gustav Von Aschenbach	Death in Venice	Mary Yellan	Jamaica Inn
Voldemort	Harry Potter Books	Captain Yossarian	Catch-22
Count Vronsky	Anna Karenina	Falther Zossima	The Brothers Karamzov

Chaucer's Canterbury Pilgrims

1	The Knight's Tale	13	The Physician's Tale
2	The Miller's Tale	14	The Pardoner's Tale
3	The Reeve's Tale	15	The Shipman's Tale
4	The Cook's Tale	16	The Prioress's Tale
5	The Man of Law's Tale	17	Chaucer's Tale of Sir Thopas
6	The Wife of Bath's Tale	18	Chaucer's Tale of Melibeus
7	The Friar's Tale	19	The Monk's Tale
8	The Summoner's Tale	20	The Nun's Priest's Tale
9	The Clerk's Tale	21	The Second Nun's Tale
10	The Merchant's Tale	22	The Canon's Yeoman's Tale
11	The Squire's Tale	23	The Manciple's Tale
12	The Franklin's Tale	24	The Parson's Tale

NB: The Canterbury Tales was an unfinished collection of tales told in the course of a pilgrimage to Thomas Becket's shrine at Canterbury. In addition to the 22 story-tellers listed above, the party included a dyer, weaver, arrowmaker, haberdasher, carpenter, ploughman and guidesman, making a total of 29. Chaucer himself may be included as a pilgrim to give a definitive total of 30.

Poets Laureate

John Dryden (1668-88)
Thomas Shadwell (1688–92)
Nahum Tate (1692–1715)
Nicholas Rowe (1715–18)
Laurence Eusden (1718–30)
Colley Cibber (1730–57)
William Whitehead (1757–85)
Thomas Wharton (1785–90)
Henry James Pye (1790–1813)
Robert Southey (1813–43)

William Wordsworth (1843–50)
Alfred, Lord Tennyson (1850–92)
Alfred Austin (1896–1913)
Robert Bridges (1913–30)
John Masefield (1930–67)
Cecil Day-Lewis (1968–72)
Sir John Betjeman (1972–84)
Ted Hughes (1984–1998)
Andrew Motion (1999–

NB: Ben Jonson was the first to be granted a pension as poet, to James I (1616) and in 1630 Charles I added an annual butt of canary wine, which was discontinued by Henry Pye who preferred money. Sir William Davenant succeeded Jonson but the position was only made official in 1668. William Whitehead appointed after Thomas Gray declined the honour. Similarly Alfred Lord Tennyson became laureate after Samuel Rogers declined.

Servants (and Masters)

Lugg
Bunter
Miss Lemon
Mrs Hudson
Reginald Jeeves
Launcelot Gobbo
Passepartout
Sancho Panza
Mélisande
Paddock

Campion
Lord Peter Wimsey
Poirot
Sherlock Holmes
Bertie Wooster
Shylock
Phileas Fogg
Don Quixote
Zuleika Dobson
Richard Hannay

Francoise

Anatole
Mary Ann
Eurycleia
Feers

Mrs Honour
Corporal Trim

Marcel Family
(Remembrance of Things Past)
Aunt Dahlia (Jeeves Stories)
White Rabbit
Ulysses
Madame Ranevsky (Cherry Orchard)
Sophia Western (Tom Jones)
Uncle Toby (Tristram Shandy)

Other Literary Prizewinners

Crime Writers Association 1998
Crime Writers Association 1999

Crime Writers Association 2000

WH Smith Prize 1999
Mail on Sunday (John Llewellyn Rhys Prize) 1999
Cholmondeley Award 1999 (poetry)
Carnegie Prize 1999 (children's)
Kate Greenaway 1999 (children's illustrated)
Hugo Award 2000 (Hugo Gernsback)
   (Science Fiction Novel)
Orange Prize 2000 (women authors)
Parker Romantic Novel of the Year 1999
Parker Romantic Novel of the Year 2000
William Hill Sports Book of the Year 1999
Nestlé Smarties Prize 1999 (children's books)

Nestlé Smarties Prize 2000

Gold Dagger (Fiction) *Sunset Limited* by James Lee Burke
Gold Dagger (Fiction) *A Small Death in Lisbon* by Robert Wilson
Gold Dagger (Fiction) *Motherless Brooklyn* by Jonathan Lethem
Master Georgie by Christine Koning
The Ugliest House in the World by Peter H. Davis
Vicki Feaver, Geoffrey Hill, Elma Mitchell, Sheenagh Pugh
Skellig by David Almund
Pumpkin Soup by Helen Cooper
A Deepness in the Sky by Vernor Vinge

When I Lived in Modern Times by Linda Grant
Dancing in the Dark by Maureen Lee
Someone Like You by Cathy Kelly
A Social History of English Cricket by Derek Birley
Age 0–5 *The Gruffald* by Julia Donaldson
Age 6–8 *Snow White and the Seven Aliens* by Laurence Anholt
Age 9–11 *Harry Potter and the Prisoner of Azkaban* by J.K. Rowling
Age 0–5 *Max* by Bob Graham
Age 6–8 *Lizzie Zipmouth* by Jacqueline Wilson
Age 9–11 *The Wind Singer* by William Nicholson

LONDON

Theatres

Name	Address	Post	Details
Adelphi	Strand	WC2	Opened by John Scott in 1806 and originally called the Sans Pareil. First performance on 17 November 1806, *The Rout* recitations by Miss Jane M. Scott. Recently showing *Chicago* (Olivier Award: Best Musical 1998).
Albery	St Martin's Lane	WC2	Designed in 1903 by W.G.R. Sprague and called the New Theatre till 1923. Recently showing *Stepping Out: The Musical* (by Richard Harris).
Aldwych	Aldwych	WC2	Designed 1905 by W.G.R. Sprague. Home of Ben Traver's farces 1925–33.
Almeida	Almeida St	N1	Fringe theatre built for other purposes in 1837. Recently showing Jonathan Kent's *Ivanov* (Ralph Fiennes).
Apollo	Shaftesbury Ave	W1	Designed in 1901 by Lewen Sharp. Recently showing: *Popcorn* (by Ben Elton).
Apollo Victoria	Victoria	SW1	Opened in 1930 as a cinema; theatre since 1979. Recently showing: *Starlight Express* (since 1984).
Arts	Strand	WC2	Opened in 1927 as an avante-garde theatre challenging the censorial constraints of the Lord Chamberlain's Office. Recently showing *Carnaby Street*.
Barbican (and Pit)	Silk St	EC2	Opened in 1982, since when the London Symphony Orchestra has been in residence at Barbican Hall. Also home of the Royal Shakespeare Company
Bloomsbury	Off Tottenham Ct Rd	WC1	Fringe theatre that shows a wide spectrum of work.
Bridewell	Bride Lane	EC4	Fringe theatre recently showing *The Golem*.
Bush	Shepherds Bush	W12	Fringe theatre founded in 1972.
Cambridge	Earlham St	WC2	Designed in 1930. Recently showing *Grease* (transferred from the Dominion).
Coliseum	St Martin's Lane	WC2	Largest theatre in the West End, seating nearly 2500. Interior designed in 1904 by Frank Matcham. Home of the English National Opera since 1968.
Comedy	Panton St	SW1	Designed in 1881 by Thomas Verity. Recently showing *A Letter of Resignation*.
Criterion	Piccadilly	W1	Current home of the Reduced Shakespeare Company. Designed in 1874 by Thomas Verity.
Dominion	Tottenham Ct Rd	WC1	Built 1929 by William and T.R. Millburn.
Donmar Warehouse	Earlham St	WC2	Recently showing *The Front Page* with Griff Rhys Jones.
Drury Lane Theatre Royal	Catherine St	WC2	Designed in 1812 by Benjamin Wyatt. Designed in 1929 by Ewen Barr. Recently showing *Miss Saigon*.
Duchess	Catherine St	WC2	Recently showing *Scissor Happy*.
Duke of York's	St Martin's Lane	WC2	Designed by Walter Emden in 1892 and called the Trafalgar Square till 1895.
Fortune	Russell St	WC2	Designed in 1924 by Ernest Schaufelberg. Recently showing *The Woman in Black*.
Gaiety	Strand	WC2	Opened in 1868 and had England's first electric lighting system in 1878.
Garrick	Charing Cross Road	WC2	Designed by Walter Emden and C.J. Phipps in 1889.
Gate (Prince Albert Pub)	Pembridge Rd	W11	Reputation for high-quality productions of neglected European classics.
Gielgud	Shaftesbury Ave	W1	Designed 1906 by W.G.R. Sprague. Originally the Hick's Theatre: then the Globe (1909–95). Recently showing *The Things We Do for Love* by Alan Ayckbourn.
Greenwich	Crooms Hill	SE10	Open since 1969 in reconstructed Victorian music hall. Recently showing *Side by Side by Sondheim* with Dawn French.
Hampstead Theatre Club	Swiss Cottage	NW3	Fringe theatre recently showing *Terms of Abuse* by Jessica Townsend.
Her Majesty's	Haymarket	SW1	Original building designed by Sir John Vanbrugh in 1705; present theatre designed 1896 by C.J. Phipps. Recently showing *Phantom of the Opera*.
King's Head	Upper St	N1	Founded as a pub theatre in 1970. Recently showing *Journey's End*.
Lyceum	Wellington St	WC2	Designed by James Payne in 1771. Recently showing *Jesus Christ Superstar*.

Name	Address	Post	Details
Lyric	King St Hammersmith	W6	Designed in 1979.Usually performances of planned short-season runs.
Lyric	Shaftesbury Ave	W1	Designed in 1888 by C.J. Phipps. Recently showing *Marlene* (Siân Phillips).
Mayfair	Mayfair Hotel	W1	Part of the hotel complex.
Mermaid	Puddle Dock	EC4	Founded in 1959 by Sir Bernard Miles. Recently showing *Le Cercle Invisible* with Jean Baptiste Thierrée.
New Ambassadors	West St	WC2	Designed in 1913 by W.G.R. Sprague. Ivor Novello made debut here in *Deburau*.
New End	New End	NW3	Fringe theatre recently showing *An Empty Plate in the Café Du Grand Boeuf.*
New London	Drury Lane	WC2	Designed in 1973 by Paul Turkovic. Recently showing *Cats.*
Old Vic	Waterloo Rd	SE1	Designed 1818 by Rudolf Cabanel. Currently owned by the Old Vic Theatre Trust 2000 Ltd.
Palace	Cambridge Circus	WC2	Built by T.E. Collcutt and G.H. Holloway, opened in 1891 as The Royal English Opera House showing Sir Arthur Sullivan's *Ivanhoe.* Recently showing: *Les Misérables.*
Palladium	Argyll St	WC1	Opened in 1910 as a music hall. Recently showing *Oliver.*
Peacock	Portugal St	WC2	Sadler's Wells recently performing *Wallace and Gromit.*
Phoenix	Charing Cross Road	WC2	Designed by Giles Gilbert Scott and Bertie Crewe and opened in 1930 Recently showing *Blood Brothers.*
Piccadilly	Denman St	W1	Designed in 1928 by Bertie Crewe and Edward Stone. Recently showing *Cinderella.*
Players	Off Villiers St	SW1	Several locations since 1936. Now situated underneath Charing Cross arches.
Playhouse	Northumberland Ave	WC2	Designed by Sefton Parry in 1882
Prince Edward	Old Compton St	W1	Opened in 1930. Recently showing *Martin Guerre* (Alain Boublil & Claude-Michel Schönberg).
Prince of Wales	Coventry St	W1	Designed 1937 by Robert Cromie. Recently showing *Smokey Joe's Cafe* (songs of Leiber and Stoller.
Queen's	Shaftesbury Ave	W1	Interior designed 1907 by W.G.R. Sprague, new exterior redesigned by Bryan Westwood and Hugh Casson after bomb damage in 1940, reopened 1959.
Regent's Park (open air)	Regent's Park	NW1	Founded in 1932. Stages annual productions of *A Midsummer Night's Dream.*
Royal Court Downstairs	Sloane Square	SW3	Closed for refurbishment and temporarily using Duke of Yorks. Recently showing: The Weir by Conor McPherson.
Royal Court Upstairs	Sloane Square	SW3	Closed for refurbishment and temporarily using Ambassadors
Royal National Theatre	South Bank	SE1	Designed by Denys Lasdun, opened 1976. Three auditoriums, the Olivier (large and open-spaced), the Lyttelton and the Cottesloe. (proscenium arched) and the Cottesloe (small but flexible).
Royal Opera	Bow St	WC2	Designed by Edward Shepherd in 1732. Redesigned by E.M. Barry in 1858 and called The Covent Garden Opera Company. Renamed the Royal Opera House in 1968.
Sadler's Wells	Rosebery Ave	E1	Opened in 1683 by Thomas Sadler but sadly recently demolished.
Savoy	Strand	WC2	Designed in 1881 by C.J. Phipps and financed by Richard D'Oyly Carte for the production of Gilbert and Sullivan Operas. First public building to be lit by electricity, although the Gaiety theatre had experimented in 1878.
Shaftesbury	Shaftesbury Ave	WC1	Designed in 1911 by Bertie Crewe. Recently showing: Royal Opera (*The Merry Widow*).
Shakespeare's Globe	Southwark	SE1	Sam Wanamaker's dream of a theatre for all was opened in 1997 with Mark Rylance playing Henry V.
St Martins	West St	WC2	Designed in 1916 by W.G.R. Sprague. Recently showing *The Mousetrap.*
Strand	Aldwych	WC2	Designed 1905 by W.G.R. Sprague. Recently showing *Buddy.*
Theatre Royal, Haymarket	Haymarket	SW1	Built in 1821 by John Nash.
Theatre Royal, Stratford	Gerry Raffles Square	E15	Built in 1884 by James George Buckle. Recently showing *Throwaway* by Danny Miller.
Tricycle	Kilburn High Rd	NW6	Fringe theatre recently showing *Iced* by Ray Shell.
Unicorn	Great Newport St	WC2	Presently a travelling company following the closure of its theatre in Great Newport Street.
Vaudeville	Strand	WC2	Designed by C.J. Phipps 1870. Recently showing *Think No Evil of Us* (life of Kenneth Williams).
Victoria Palace	Victoria St	SW1	Designed in 1911 by Frank Hatcham. Recently showing *Always* (story of Edward VIII & Mrs Simpson).
Westminster	Palace St	SW1	Possibly the nearest theatre to Buckingham Palace
Whitehall	Whitehall	SW1	Built in 1930. Formerly to the design of E.A. Stone known for its farces.

LONDON

Name	Address	Post	Details
Wyndham's	Charing Cross Road	WC2	Designed by W.G.R. Sprague and opened in 1899. Recently showing *Art* (produced by Sean Connery).
Young Vic	The Cut	SE1	Built in 1970. Recently showing *Camino Real* by Tennessee Williams.

NB: Notable London fringe theatres (and pubs) not listed above include Half Moon, Old Red Lion, Orange Tree, Bird's Nest, Landor, Hen & Chickens, Pentameters, Albany, Etcetera, Oval House, Pleasance, Richmond (The Green) and Riverside Studios.

Statues

Site	Person(s) Depicted
Albert Hall (SW7)	*Prince Albert* by Joseph Durham (1863).
Bank of England (EC2)	Stone statues of *Sir John Soane* by Sir William Reid Dick (1937) and *King William III* by Sir Henry Cheere (1735).
Banqueting House, Whitehall (SW1)	Lead bust of *Charles I* by unknown sculptor.
Belgrave Square (SW1)	Bronze of *Simon Bolivar* by Hugo Daini (1974).
Birdcage Walk (SW1)	Bronze of *Field Marshal Earl Alexander of Tunis* by James Butler (1985).
Bloomsbury Square, (WC1)	*Charles James Fox* by Richard Westmacott (1816).
Cannon St (EC4)	Bronze mask of *Winston Churchill* by Frank Dobson (1959) over the entrance to Bracken House.
Carey St / Serle St (WC2)	Stone figure of *Sir Thomas More* by Robert Smith (1866).
Carlton Gardens (SW1)	Bronze of *General Charles de Gaulle* and *George VI* by William McMillan.
Cavendish Square (W1)	Bronze of *William George Bentinck* by Thomas Campbell (1851).
Charing Cross Rd (WC2)	Bronze of *Sir Henry Irving* by Thomas Brock (1910) by the St Martin's Place side of the National Portrait Gallery.
Chelsea Embankment (SW3)	Bronze of *Thomas Carlyle* by Sir Joseph Boehm (1882); seated bronze of *Sir Thomas More* by L. Cubitt Bevis (1969).
Chelsea Hospital (SW3)	*Bronze of King Charles II in Roman Costume*, by Grinling Gibbons (1676).
Chiswick House (W4)	Stone figure of *Inigo Jones* by John Rysbrack (1729).
City Rd (EC1)	*John Wesley* by John Adams-Acton (1891).
Cockspur St (SW1)	Bronze equestrian of *George III* by Matthew Cotes Wyatt.
Commercial Rd (E1)	Bronze of *Clement Attlee* by Frank Forster (1988) outside Limehouse Library.
Cornhill (No 32) EC3	Mahogany carving of *The Brontë sisters in Conversation with William Makepeace Thackeray* by Walter Gilbert (1939).
Crystal Palace Park (SE19)	Marble bust of *Sir Joseph Paxton* by W.F. Woodington (1869).
Downing St (SW1)	*Mountbatten* outside Foreign Office.
Euston Station (NW1)	Bronze of *Robert Stephenson* by Baron Marochetti (1871).
Festival Hall (SE1)	Bronze of *Frederic Chopin*, beside the Festival Hall, by B. Kubica (1975).
Fleet St (EC4)	Stone of *Elizabeth I* by William Kerwin (1586) over the vestry porch of St Dunstan in the West. This is the oldest statue of a monarch in London and, in fact, the oldest outdoor statue of any kind.
Fleet St (Nos 143–4) EC4	Stone of *Mary, Queen of Scots*, placed by an admirer, Sir John Tollemache Sinclair (1880).
Greenwich Park (SE10)	Samuel Nixon's Foggit Tor granite of *William IV*, erected in King William IV St in 1844 and moved to present site in 1938.
Grosvenor Gardens (SW1)	Bronze equestrian of *Marechal Foch* by G. Mallisard (1930).
Grosvenor Square (W1)	Bronze of *F.D. Roosevelt* by Sir William Reid Dick; bronze of *General Dwight D. Eisenhower* by Robert Dean (1989).
Guildhall (EC2)	Limewood carvings of mythical giants, *Gog and Magog*, by David Evans, replacing those burned in 1940.
Hamilton Gardens (W1)	Bronze of *George Gordon Byron* by Richard Belt (1880).
Hanover Square (W1)	Bronze of *William Pitt the Younger* by Francis Chantrey (1831).
Highgate Cemetery (N6)	Bronze of *Karl Marx* by Laurence Bradshaw (1956).
Holborn Circus (EC1)	Equestrian bronze of *Prince Albert* by Charles Bacon (1874).
Horse Guards Parade (SW1)	Bronze of *Field Marshal Earl Kitchener* by John Tweed (1926); bronze equestrian of *Field Marshal Viscount Wolseley* by Sir William Goscombe John (1920).
Houses of Parliament (SW1)	Equestrian bronze of *Richard I* in Old Palace Yard by Carlo Marochetti (1861); bronze of *Oliver Cromwell* outside Westminster Hall by Sir Hamo Thornycroft (1899). Statue of *George VI* stands opposite the *Richard I* outside the grounds and was sculpted by William Reid Dick (1947).
Hyde Park Corner (SW1)	Bronze of *The Duke of Wellington* on his horse, Copenhagen, by J.E. Boehm (1888).
Kensington Gardens (SW7)	Bronze of *Sir Winston and Lady Churchill* by Oscar Nemon (1981) situated near Hyde Park Gate; seated statue of *Queen Victoria* by her daughter, Princess Louise (1893); Albert Memorial designed by George Gilbert Scott, with seated statue of Albert begun by Baron Marochetti and completed in 1876 by John Foley.

Site	Person(s) Depicted
Kensington Palace (W8)	Bronze of *William III* by Heinrich Baucke (1907) presented by Kaiser Wilhelm II to his uncle, Edward VII.
King Charles Street (SW1)	Bronze figure of *Robert Clive* by John Tweed (1912).
King Edward Street (EC1)	Granite figure of *Sir Rowland Hill*, founder of the Penny Post, by R. Onslow Ford (1881).
Leicester Square: Centre (WC2)	Marble of *William Shakespeare* by Giovanni Fontana (1874); bronze of *Charlie Chaplin* by John Doubleday (unveiled by Ralph Richardson in 1981).
Leicester Square: Gates (WC2)	Memorial gates, to *John Hunter* by Thomas Woolner, *Isaac Newton* by William Calder Marshall, *Joshua Reynolds* by Henry Weekes (all 1874) and *William Hogarth* by Joseph Durham (1875), all of whom have commemorative busts.
The Mall (near Admiralty Arch, SW1)	Bronze of *Captain James Cook* by Sir Thomas Brock (1914).
	Seated marble statue of Queen Victoria by Sir Thomas Brock (1911).
Marylebone Rd (NW1)	Bronze of *John Fitzgerald Kennedy* by Jacques Lipchitz (1965).
Millbank (SW1)	Bronze of *Sir John Everett Millais* by Sir Thomas Brock (1904).
Old Bailey (EC4)	Gilt of *Justice* by F.W. Pomeroy (1907).
Park Crescent (W1)	Bronze of *Edward Augustus, Duke of Kent* (Queen Victoria's father) by S.S. Gahagen (1827).
Park Lane (W1)	*Achilles* (20′ bronze cast in 1822 by Sir Richard Westmacott) 'Erected by the women of England to Arthur, Duke of Wellington and his brave companions in arms'.
Parliament Square (SW1)	Bronzes of *George Canning*, in a toga, by Richard Westmacott (1832); *Sir Robert Peel* by Matthew Noble (1876); *Field Marshal Jan Christian Smuts* by Jacob Epstein (1958); *Abraham Lincoln* (copy of the statue by Augustus Saint-Gaudens in Chicago); *Winston Churchill* by Ivor-Roberts Jones(1973); *Benjamin Disraeli* by Mario Raggi (1883); *Lord Palmerston* by Thomas Woolner (1876).
Piccadilly Circus (W1)	*Shaftesbury Memorial Fountain*, better known as *Eros* although Alfred Gilbert's 1893 aluminium statue in fact depicts *The Angel of Christian Charity*, in honour of Lord Shaftesbury himself.
Pimlico Gardens (SW1)	Stone of *William Huskisson* in a Roman toga, by John Gibson (1836).
Prudential Assurance (Holborn EC1)	Cupronized plaster bust of *Charles Dickens* by Percy Fitzgerald (1907).
Red Lion Square (WC1)	Bronze bust of *Bertrand Russell* by Marcelle Quinton (1980).
Royal Exchange (EC2)	Equestrian bronze of *Wellington* begun by Francis Chantrey & completed by Henry Weekes (1844); and stone figure of *Richard Whittington* by J.E. Carew (1845).
Royal Geographical Society, Kensington Gore (SW7)	Bronzes of *David Livingstone* by T.B. Huxley-Jones (1953) and *Sir Ernest Shackleton* by C. Sarjeant Jagger (1932).
St Bartholomew's Hospital (EC1)	Stone figure of *Henry VIII*, the founder, by Francis Bird (1702) stands over the gateway.
St Giles Cripplegate	Memorial statue of *John Milton* by Montford (1904).
St James's Square (SW1)	*William III*, equestrian bronze by John Bacon the Elder (1808).
St Martin's Place (WC2)	Marble statue of *Edith Cavell* by Sir George Frampton (1920). Famous inscription reads: 'Patriotism is not enough. I must have no hatred or bitterness for anyone.'
St Thomas's Hospital (SE1)	Statue of *Sir Robert Clayton*, the hospital's benefactor. The only outdoor stone statue by Grinling Gibbons.
Savoy Place (WC2)	Bronze of *Michael Faraday* by J.H. Foley (1889) situated outside the Institution of Electrical Engineers.
Soho Square (W1)	Stone statue of *King Charles II* by Caius Gabriel Cibber once owned by W.S. Gilbert.
Somerset House, Strand (WC2)	Baroque fountain in bronze, including a figure of *King George III* by John Bacon the Elder (1788).
South Africa House (Trafalgar Square)	Large stone figure of *Bartholomew Diaz* by Coert Steynberg (1934).
South Square, Gray's Inn (WC1)	*Francis Bacon* by F.W. Pomeroy (1912).
Strand (WC2)	Bronzes of *Air Chief Marshal Lord Dowding* and *Sir Arthur 'Bomber' Harris* by Faith Winter (1988) opposite St Clement Danes, the RAF church, and *Dr Samuel Johnson* by Percy Fitzgerald (1910).
Tavistock Square (WC1)	Bronze of *Mahatma Gandhi* by Fredda Brilliant (unveiled by Harold Wilson in 1968).
Tooting Broadway (SW17)	Bronze of *King Edward VII* by L.F. Roselieb (1911).
Trafalgar Square (WC2)	Bronzes outside National Gallery of *George Washington* by Jean-Antoine Houdon and *James II* in Roman dress by Grinling Gibbons; *Sir Henry Havelock* by William Behnes (1861); bronze equestrians of *George IV* by Sir Francis Chantrey (1834) and *Charles I* by Hubert Le Sueur (1633); *Nelson's column* (170′ 2″), with statue of Nelson by E.H. Bailey (1843) and Landseer's lions cast in 1868 from guns recovered from the wreck of the *Royal George*. On the north wall of the Square are bronze busts of Admirals *Lord Beatty* by William McMillan (1984), *Lord Cunningham*, by Franta Belsky (1967) and *Lord Jellicoe* by Sir Charles Wheeler (1948).
University College London (WC1)	Bronze tablet and medallion of *Richard Trevithick* by L.S. Merrifield (1933).
Victoria Embankment (WC2)	*Isambard Kingdom Brunel* by Carlo Marochetti (1877); *Cleopatra's Needle* (68 ½′).

Site	Person(s) Depicted
Victoria Embankment Gardens (WC2)	Bronzes of *John Stuart Mill* by Thomas Woolner (1878); *Robert Burns* by Sir John Steel (1884); *Sir Arthur Sullivan* by W. Goscombe John (1903), with a mourning female on the plinth; *Robert Raikes* by Sir Thomas Brock (1880).
Victoria Tower Gardens, Westminster (SW1)	*Burghers of Calais* by Rodin, copy (installed 1915) of original in Calais, created 1895. Emmeline and Christabel Pankhurst by A.G. Walker (1930).
Waterloo Place (SW1)	*Duke of York Column* memorial to Frederick, 2nd son of George III, statue by Sir Richard Westmacott 1834; bronze equestrian of *King Edward VII* by Sir Bertram Mackennal (1922); bronze of *Captain Robert Falcon Scott* by Lady Scott (1915); *Florence Nightingale* by Walker.
Westminster Bridge (SE1)	Thomas Thornycroft's *Boadicea* at the north eastern end.
Whitehall (SW1)	Bronzes of *Sir Walter Raleigh* by William McMillan (1959); *Field Marshal Montgomery of Alamein* by Oscar Nemon (unveiled by Queen Mother in 1980); *Field Marshal the Viscount Alanbrooke* and *Field Marshal the Viscount Slim*, both by Ivor Roberts Jones.
Woodford Green (E18)	Bronze of *Winston Churchill* by David McFall (unveiled by Field Marshal Montgomery in October 1959).
Woolwich, Royal Arsenal (SE18)	Stone figure of *Wellington* by Thomas Milnes (1848).

Bridges

From East to West	Type	Opened	
Queen Elizabeth II	Road	1991	Clockwise route of M25; the Dartford Tunnel is the anti-clockwise route.
Tower	Road	1894	Built by John Wolfe-Barry to a design by Sir Horace Jones, the furthest bridge downstream in London.
London	Road	1831	Rebuilt by John Rennie but moved to Lake Havasu in 1967; new bridge opened by Queen Elizabeth II, 16 March 1973.
Alexandra	Rail	1866	Cannon St in the north to Clink St in the south.
Southwark	Road	1819	Built by John Rennie; rebuilt 1921.
Millennium	Foot	2000	Built by an amalgamation of Norman Foster, Anthony Caro and Ove Enge. Links St Paul's Cathedral and the Tate Modern.
Blackfriars	Rail	1864	Upper Thames St in the north to Southwark St in the south.
Blackfriars	Road	1769	Rebuilt 1869 and widened 1910.
Waterloo	Road	1817	Built by John Rennie but rebuilt by LCC between 1937 and 1944 to plans of Sir Giles Gilbert Scott, opened by Herbert Morrison 1945.
Hungerford	Rail & Foot	1863	Suspension bridge built by Brunel 1845 but rebuilt 1863 as Rail & Foot bridge designed by Sir John Hawkshaw.
Westminster	Road	1750	Leads from Westminster Abbey and Houses of Parliament to the former County Hall and St Thomas' Hospital. The bridge was rebuilt in 1862.
Lambeth	Road	1862	Leads from Millbank in the north to Lambeth Palace. Rebuilt in 1932.
Vauxhall	Road	1816	Leads from Millbank in the north to Kennington Lane. Rebuilt in 1906.
Grosvenor	Rail	1860	Rebuilt 1967.
Chelsea	Road	1934	Built 1858 but rebuilt as suspension bridge 1934 and widened 1937.
Albert	Road	1873	Restructured by Sir Joseph Bazalgette in 1884 and strengthened 1973.
Battersea	Road	1772	Built of wood by Henry Holland and rebuilt by Bazalgette 1890.
Battersea	Rail	1863	
Wandsworth	Road	1873	Rebuilt 1940.
Putney	Rail	1889	
Putney	Road	1729	Rebuilt by Bazalgette 1886.
Hammersmith	Road	1827	Rebuilt by Bazalgette 1887 and the first London suspension bridge.
Barnes	Rail & Foot	1849	Restructured 1893.
Chiswick	Road	1933	Built by Sir Herbert Baker and Alfred Dryland.
Kew	Rail	1869	
Kew	Road	1759	Rebuilt and renamed The King Edward VII Bridge 1903.
Richmond Lock	Foot	1894	
Twickenham	Road	1933	
Richmond	Rail	1848	Restructured 1908.
Richmond	Road	1777	Widened 1937.
Teddington Lock	Foot	1889	
Kingston	Road	1828	Widened 1914.
Hampton Court	Road	1753	Replaced by iron bridge 1865 and rebuilt 1933.

Postal Areas

E1	Whitechapel	SW1	Belgravia	SE1	Southwark		
E2	Bethnal Green	SW2	Brixton	SE2	Abbey Wood		
E3	Bow	SW3	Chelsea	SE3	Blackheath		
E4	Chingford	SW4	Clapham	SE4	Brockley		
E5	Clapton	SW5	Earls Court	SE5	Camberwell		
E6	East Ham	SW6	Fulham	SE6	Catford		
E7	Forest Gate	SW7	South Kensington	SE7	Charlton		
E8	Hackney	SW8	South Lambeth	SE8	Deptford		
E9	Homerton	SW9	Stockwell	SE9	Eltham		
E10	Leyton	SW10	West Brompton	SE10	Greenwich		
E11	Leytonstone	SW11	Battersea	SE12	Lee		
E12	Manor Park	SW12	Balham	SE13	Lewisham		
E13	Plaistow	SW13	Barnes	SE14	New Cross		
E14	Poplar	SW14	Mortlake	SE15	Peckham		
E15	Stratford	SW15	Putney	SE16	Rotherhithe		
E16	Victoria Docks	SW16	Streatham	SE17	Walworth		
E17	Walthamstow	SW17	Tooting	SE18	Woolwich		
E18	South Woodford	SW18	Wandsworth	SE19	Norwood		
		SW19	Wimbledon	SE20	Anerley		
N1	Islington	SW20	West Wimbledon	SE21	Dulwich		
N2	East Finchley			SE22	East Dulwich		
N3	Finchley (Church End)	W1	Mayfair	SE23	Forest Hill		
N4	Finsbury Park	W2	Paddington	SE24	Herne Hill		
N5	Highbury	W3	Acton	SE25	South Norwood		
N6	Highgate	W4	Chiswick	SE26	Sydenham		
N7	Holloway	W5	Ealing	SE27	West Norwood		
N8	Hornsey	W6	Hammersmith	SE28	Thamesmead		
N9	Lower Edmonton	W7	Hanwell	WC1	Bloomsbury		
N10	Muswell Hill	W8	Kensington	WC2	St James		
N11	New Southgate	W9	Maida Vale				
N12	North Finchley	W10	North Kensington	NW1	Camden Town		
N13	Palmers Green	W11	Notting Hill	NW2	Cricklewood		
N14	Southgate	W12	Shepherds Bush	NW3	Hampstead		
N15	South Tottenham	W13	West Ealing	NW4	Hendon		
N16	Stoke Newington	W14	West Kensington	NW5	Kentish Town		
N17	Tottenham			NW6	Kilburn		
N18	Upper Edmonton	EC1	Finsbury	NW7	Mill Hill		
N19	Upper Holloway	EC2	City	NW8	Marylebone		
N20	Whetstone	EC3	Spitalfields	NW9	Kingsbury		
N21	Winchmore Hill	EC4	Fleet St	NW10	Willesden		
N22	Wood Green			NW11	Golders Green		

L
O
N
D
O
N

General Information

Admiralty Arch (SW1) Built in 1910 to the design of Sir Aston Webb (who also designed the façade of Buckingham Palace) and consisting of 3 identical arches. Situated where the Mall leads into Trafalgar Square.

Alexandra Palace (N22) Sited in Muswell Hill and built in 1875 by Meeson and Johnson.

Alsop, William Designer of North Greenwich Jubilee Line Station.

Art galleries Tate Gallery, Millbank; National Gallery, Trafalgar Square; National Portrait Gallery, St Martin's Place; Wallace Collection, W1; Courtauld Institute, Strand; Sir John Soane's Museum, Lincoln's Inn Fields; William Morris Gallery, Forest Rd, E17.
Queen's Gallery in Buckingham Palace' Dulwich Picture Gallery built by Sir John Soane 1811–13. England's oldest public art gallery.

Banqueting House Designed by Inigo Jones in 1622 and the only part of Whitehall Palace still standing.

Belfast, HMS (SE1) Built in 1939 and situated at Symon's Wharf in Vine Lane, this 11,000-ton cruiser, the largest ever built was opened to the public in 1971.

Big Ben Housed in St Stephen's Tower within the Houses of Parliament (Palace of Westminster) Big Ben, weighing in at 13.5 tons, is the name of the large bell housed in the clock tower and named after, either Benjamin Caunt, a popular boxer of the day (1858), or more likely Sir Benjamin Hall, the Chief Commissioner of Works.

Billingsgate Market (EC3) Fish market in Lower Thames St, in use for over 7 centuries, which closed on 16 Jan 1982.

Billingsgate Market (E14) Opened on the Isle of Dogs 3 days after the original market closed.

Birdcage Walk (SW1) Here stood the aviary of James I.

Birkbeck College (WC1) Founded in 1823 as the London mechanics' Institution. Took its present name in 1907 and became part of the University of London in 1920. Situated in Malet Street.

Bishop of London, first   St Mellitus, c. AD 604.

Blackfriars Bridge   Roberto Calvi, an Italian banker, found hanging beneath it on 19 June 1982.

Blue Plaques   William Ewart had the idea of using these to commemorate famous people, and Lord Byron was the first to have a plaque conferred on the house where he was born in Holles St, Westminster.

British Library   Formed in 1973 from the amalgamation of the British Museum Library, National Central Library and National Lending Library. Now situated at St Pancras.

British Museum (WC1)   Founded in 1753, initially to house the collection of Hans Sloane (1660–1753), it was opened to the public in 1759 at Montague House. The present museum was built on the same site in 1823–47 to a design of Robert Smirke. The ethnographical department of the museum is called The Museum of Mankind. Among the best known of the museum's treasures are the Elgin Marbles, Portland Vase, Mildenhall Treasure, Rosetta Stone, Sutton Hoo, Lewis Chessman, and the Lindow Man. Recent millennium renovations include the museum's inner courtyard, hidden from the public for 150 years being turned into the '*Great Court*' covered with a spectacular glass and steel roof designed by Norman Foster.

British Telecom Tower   Designed by Eric Bedford and stands 580′ high with a 40′ mast giving an overall height of 620′. Originally called the Post Office Tower and nowadays simply the Telecom Tower.

Burghers of Calais replica   Sited in Victoria Tower Gardens.

Canary Wharf Tower   Designed by Cesar Pelli and at 850 feet exceeds the British Telecom Tower as Britain's tallest structure. Officially called No. 1 Canada Square.

Centre of London   Charing Cross is now used as the point for measuring distances to other places.

Charing Cross Station (WC2)   Situated just off the Strand and designed by Sir John Hawkshaw in 1864.

Clink Street (SE1)   Site of the Bishop of Winchester's London estate and synonymous with the name of his Ecclesiastical prison.

Clubs   Boodle's; Brooks's; Carlton; White's (all situated in St James's St, SW1); Beefsteak; Garrick; Pratt's (all the waiters are called George); Reform (Pall Mall), Athenaeum, Portland, Savile, Travellers, Groucho.

Coal Tax   Christopher Wren's 50 new churches were paid for by a tax on coal entering London.

Cockneys   Must be born within the sound of the church bells of St Mary le Bow.

Courtauld Institute of Art   Owned by the University of London and situated at Somerset House on the Strand.

Covent Garden Market (WC2)   London's main wholesale fruit, flower and vegetable market. Congestion in Central London caused its closure in 1974 after 340 years trading. The New Covent Garden Market was opened immediately at the former railway yard at Nine Elms, Battersea.

Denmark St   Aka Tin Pan Alley; home of the music publishing industry.

Docklands Light Railway   Opened in 1987 and now extended from the Isle of Dogs to Bank.

Drainage system   Designed by Joseph Bazalgette between 1859 and 1875 and still serving as the basis of London's sewage system.

Eel Pie Island, Twickenham   Joined to the mainland by an old rickety concrete bridge, about 3′ wide. Made famous in the 1960s when the Rolling Stones played a concert there.

Football clubs: oldest   Fulham (formed in 1879); Leyton Orient (1881); Spurs (1882); QPR (1885); Millwall (1885); Arsenal (1886); Brentford (1889); Wimbledon (1889); West Ham (1900); Chelsea (1905); Crystal Palace (1905); Charlton (1905).

Fulham Palace   Official residence of the Bishop of London until 1973.

Greater London   Consists of 31 boroughs and the cities of Westminster and London.

Greater London Council   Created in 1965, but abolished in 1986. Originally called the London County Council, formed 1889.

Greenwich Palace (SE10)   Built by Humphrey Deele of Gloucester in 1426 and now the site of the Royal Naval Hospital.

Gun salutes   A salute of 62 guns is fired at the Tower of London on the birthdays of HRH Prince Philip, HM Queen Elizabeth, the Queen Mother and HM the Queen, who also has a 62-gun salute on accession and coronatin day. A 42 gun salute is fired at the Tower of London and Hyde Park on other state occasions e.g. opening and dissolution of Parliament, the birth of a royal infant, or a royal procession through London.

Hampton Court Maze   Constructed for William and Mary (1690).

Highgate Hill   Dick Whittington supposedly 'turned' here and became Lord Mayor.

Hyde Park Corner (SW1)   Historic entrance to London from the west via the tollgate through Kensington and Knightsbridge.

Imperial War Museum   Opened in 1920, and since 1935 occupying the remaining part of the old Bethlem Royal Hospital, opened in 1815.

Livery Companies   Craft guilds set up to promote the various trades of London. The Weavers are the oldest established guild whilst the Mercers are thought of as the senior guild. At present there are 102 city guilds, The Water Conservators being the latest set up in 2000.

Lloyd's of London   Insurance underwriting corporation functional since the late 17th century, housed since 1986 in a headquarters designed by Richard Rogers.

London Eye   Situated on the South Bank between the Hungerford and Westminster bridges. The British Airways London Eye is administered by the Tusaud Group. The diameter of the wheel is 135 metres (450 feet) and the architects were David Marks and Julia Barfield.

London Gazette   Henry Muddiman started it in 1665. It is published on Tuesdays and Fridays, as the official organ of Britain's government. It was known as the Oxford Gazette for the first 23 bulletins.

London Stone   Now set in the wall of the Bank of China, Cannon St, and possibly once used by the Romans as a measuring point.

Marble Arch   Designed by John Nash to commemorate Nelson's victories, erected on side of Buckingham Palace in 1827, moved to Hyde Park in 1851.

Marylebone Road   Site of Madame Tussaud's and the Planetarium.

May Day Parade   Traditional parade through Hyde Park.

Mayor   Ken Livingstone.

Monument (EC2)   Contains 311 steps and commemorates the nearby spot in Pudding Lane where the Great Fire started in 1666. Designed by Christopher Wren, the total height is 202 feet.

Museum: Childhood   Situated in Bethnal Green. Administered by the Victoria and Albert Museum, opened in 1872.

Museum of London (EC2)   Opened in 1976 and illustrating the history of London from prehistoric times to the present day.

Museum: Wellington   Apsley House, Hyde Park Corner. Administered by the Victoria and Albert Museum.

National History Museum (SW7)   Situated near the V & A Museum in Cromwell Rd and opened in 1881 to a design of Alfred Waterhouse. Merged with the Ecological Museum in 1985.

National Maritime Museum (SE10)   Founded in 1932.

New Scotland Yard (SW1)   Metropolitan Police HQ situated near Victoria Street since 1967. The previous Scotland Yard building on the North Bank near Westminster Bridge was completed by Norman Shaw in 1890, after the original building at the top of Whitehall was damaged by a Fenian bomb in 1884..

Oldest club   White's, founded 1693.

Palace of Westminster (SW1)   The first palace was built for Edward the Confessor, not completed till 1858, but after the fire of 1834 its replacement was designed to become the home of both Houses of Parliament. Charles Barry's design was preferred to 96 other entrants, and he brought in Augustus Pugin to provide the Gothic interiors. The House of Commons was rebuilt by Giles Gilbert Scott after the bombing of 1941. St Stephen's Tower tops the Commons building, whilst the Victoria Tower stands at the southern end, at the other extreme from Big Ben.

Parks (central London)   Green, Hyde, Regent's, St James's, Kensington Gardens.

Pelicans   Live in St James's Park.

Peter Pan   Statue in Kensington Gardens sculpted by George Frampton in 1912.

Petticoat Lane (E1)   East London's long-established Sunday market (8am to 2pm) on Middlesex Street. Originally called Hog Lane Market in the 15th century. Given the name Petticoat Lane around 1600 because of its clothes stalls.

Piccadilly Circus   Junction of Haymarket, Regent St, Piccadilly, Shaftesbury Avenue, Coventry Street.

Planetarium   Opened in 1958 in Marylebone Rd, next to Madame Tussaud's.

Pool of London   A reach of Thames consisting of 2 parts: the Lower running from Limekiln Creek to Cherry Garden Pier, and the Upper, from Cherry Garden Pier to London Bridge. Tower Bridge divides the two.

Queen's House, Greenwich   Started by Inigo Jones during the reign of James I, as a gift to his wife Anne of Denmark; eventually completed in 1640. Now the centrepiece of the National Maritime Museum.

Ratcliff Highway Murders   Seven victims were murdered in 2 incidents on this street in present-day Stepney in Dec. 1811. John Williams, a lodger at the Pear Tree public house, was arrested but hanged himself before his trial. The incident was a spur to the eventual forming of the Metropolitan Police in 1829.

Richard II   Oldest painting of an English monarch from life (late 14th century), in Westminster Abbey.

Roman Gates of London Wall   Aldgate; Aldersgate; Bishopsgate; Cripplegate; Ludgate; Newgate.

Royal Academy   Founded by Joshua Reynolds in 1768, and originally site at Somerset House. Established in 1868 at Burlington House. Piccadilly Sackler Galleries added in 1990 by Norman Foster.

Royal Courts of Justice   Designed by George Street in 1868 and situated on the north side of the Strand, the courts hear civil cases and criminal appeals. Opened by Queen Victoria in 1882 the Supreme Court is made up of the High Court, Court of Appeal and Crown Court. The High Court has 3 divisions: Queen's Bench, Family and Chancery. There are over 150 judges in the Royal Courts of Justice, a corridor known as the Chicken Run, and a recent wing named after St Thomas More. A tributary of the River Fleet is reputed to run under the building.

Royal Exchange (EC3)   Founded by Thomas Gresham in 1566 as the 'Bourse' and proclaimed the Royal Exchange by Elizabeth I in 1570. First building destroyed in the Great Fire in 1666; second burned down in 1838; third completed 1842.

Royal National Theatre   Building on the South Bank opened in 1976 and designed by Denys Lasdun. Lyttelton was 1st of the 3 auditoria to open, followed by the Olivier and Cottesloe.

Science Museum (SW7)   Originally housed in the Victoria and Albert Museum but moved into its own building, across Exhibition Road, in 1913. The museum is the world's pre-eminent museum of science, medicine and technology. The Wellcome Wing, designed by Richard MacCormac, was opened in 2000 in partnership with the Wellcome Trust, Science Museum, and the Heritage Lottery Fund.

St James's Palace (SW1)   Built by Henry VIII.

St Paul's Cathedral   The new St Paul's Cathedral was built by Sir Christopher Wren between 1675 and 1710. The frescoes depicting the life of St Paul, above the Whispering Gallery on the underside of the dome are by James Thornhill. In the lower part of the south-west tower stands William Kempster's Geometrical Staircase and the clock room in the upper part houses Great Tom, the largest of three bells. The original St Paul's was built in 604 in the reign of St Ethelbert of Kent, the first Christian king in England, only to be destroyed by fire soon after. Two more rebuildings took place, culminating in the destruction by the Great Fire of 1666, when the only monument to survive was that of John Donne, the poet, who had been Dean of St Paul's for the last 10 years of his life. From pavement to the top of the cross on the tower of the dome, St Paul's is 365 feet high.

Silent Change   Annual ceremony to admit the new Lord Mayor.

Smithfield Market (EC1)   London's largest meat market which, although in decline, employs its own police force.

Somerset House   Designed by Sir William Chambers in the late 18th century and situated on the Strand.

Stock Exchange (EC2)   The new Stock Exchange opened in June 1973, replacing a building opened in 1888.

Strawberry Hill   Horace Walpole's Twickenham residence, built in 1748 and much extended, which is now the Roman Catholic St Mary's College of Higher Education.

Thames   No native name is known before Julius Caesar called the river 'Tamesis'. After Kent it is the

LONDON

oldest place name in England. Since 1996 it has been controlled by the Environment Agency.

Thames Embankments Victoria Embankment on the north side of the river, running from Westminster to Blackfriars, the Albert Embankment on the south side from Westminster Bridge to Vauxhall, and the Chelsea Embankment, from Chelsea Bridge to Battersea Bridge were constructed by Sir J.W. Bazalgette

Thames tunnels The first tunnel under the Thames, completed in 1843, and linking Wapping and Rotherhithe, was called the 'Thames Tunnel' and is still in existence as a railway tunnel. The oldest road tunnel is the old Blackwall, opened in 1897; other road tunnels include the new Blackwall (1967), Rotherhithe (1908), and Dartford (1963 and 1980). The only foot tunnel still in existence runs from Greenwich to the Isle of Dogs.

Thames reaches Starting from the mouth and proceeding upriver, the reaches are: Sea Reach (Yantlet Creek to West Blyth Buoy); Lower Hope (to Coalhouse Point); Gravesend (to Tilburyness); Northfleet Hope (to Broadness); St Clement's or Fiddlers' (to Stoneness); Long (to Dartford Creek); Erith Rands (to Coalharbour Point); Erith (to Jenningtree Point); Halfway (to Crossness); Barking (to Tripcock Point); Gallions (to Woolwich Hoba Wharf); Woolwich (to Lyle Park); Bugsby's (to Blackwell Point); Blackwall (to Dudgeon's Dock); Greenwich (to Deptford Creek); Limehouse (to Limekiln Creek); Lower Pool (to Cherry Garden Pier); Upper Pool (to London Bridge); London Bridge to Westminster Bridge and Westminster Bridge to Vauxhall Bridge (both nameless); Nine Elms (to Chelsea Bridge); Chelsea (to Battersea Bridge); Battersea (to Wandsworth Bridge); Wandsworth (to Putney Bridge); Barn Elms (to Hammersmith Bridge); Chiswick (to Chiswick Ferry); Corney (to Barnes Railway Bridge); and Mortlake (to Kew Bridge).

Theatre: largest Coliseum.

Tower of London: first foundation White Tower built by Gundul, bishop of Rochester, between 1078 and 1098.

Tower of London: Crown Jewels first housed During reign of Henry III.

Tower of London: last beheading Simon Fraser, Lord Lovat, in 1747. Last execution: Joseph Jacobs (15 Aug 1941).

Tower of London: last Monarch to occupy James I.

Tower of London: Towers Beauchamp; Bell; Bloody; Bowyer; Brick; Broad Arrow; Byward; Constable; Cradle; Devereux; Develin; Flint; Lanthorn; Martin; Middle; Salt; St Thomas's; Wakefield; Wardrobe (no longer standing); Well, White (the oldest).

Underground First stretch of underground electric railway between City and Stockwell opened in 1890. John Fowler and Sir Benjamin Baker engineered the work.

Other British Underground systems in Glasgow, Liverpool, and Newcastle.

Metropolitan Railway, using steam locomotives, opened in 1863 and ran from Paddington to Farringdon St. Harry Beck (1902–74) re-designed the map in 1931 and his use of straight lines and a colour-coding system for the different lines is still in use.

Underground Map Albert Stanley, Lord Ashfield, issued first map in 1908 to design of Harry Beck.

Unknown Warrior's Tomb Westminster Abbey.

Victoria and Albert Museum (SW7) The national museum of fine and applied art and design. Founded in 1852, and moved to its present site in 1857, being known then as the South Kensington Museum. The building was designed by Aston Webb and given its current name in 1899.

Wallace Collection Art collection in Hertford House, Manchester Squar, W1. Most famous work: *The Laughing Cavalier.*

Wardour St Once used as a term to denote the British film industry.

Westminster Abbey: founder St Edward the Confessor.

Westminster Abbey: Nave At the end of the Nave, just in front of the Great West Door, is a memorial to Winston Churchill and nearby is the grave of the Unknown Warrior, commemorating those who were killed in WW1. The graves and memorials in the Nave include those of David Livingstone, David Lloyd George, Clement Attlee, Ramsay MacDonald, Isaac Newton, Lord and Lady Baden-Powell and F.D. Roosevelt.

Westminster Abbey: Poets' Corner Graves and memorials of most of the major English poets and some writers and musicians. The foremost tomb is that of Geoffrey Chaucer, the first to be buried there, and the foremost memorial is that of William Shakespeare. Among the 20th-century poets commemorated are W.H. Auden, Dylan Thomas and T.S. Eliot. Gerard Manley Hopkins (1844–89), although buried in Glasnevin Cemetery, Dublin, has a commemorative plaque. Samuel Johnson, Charles Dickens, and G.F. Handel are also buried there, and Oscar Wilde has been commemorated on floor and window.

Westminster Abbey: Royal Tombs Elizabeth I; Mary I; Edward the Confessor; Henry VII; James I; Edward VI; George II; Henry III; Edward I; Edward III; Richard II; Henry V; Anne; Charles II; William III; Mary II and Mary Stewart; Queen of Scotland and France.

Westminster Abbey: Tomb of Elizabeth & Mary Latin inscription on their tomb reads: 'Consorts both in throne and grave, here sleep we two sisters, Elizabeth and Mary, in the hope of one resurrection.'

Westminster Cathedral (SW1) Roman Catholic Cathedral in Francis St, SW1, built of brick and Portland stone, to the design of John Francis Bentley and completed in 1903.

Westminster Hall Built by William Rufus between 1097 and 1099, home of the Royal Courts of Justice till they moved to the Strand in 1882, and incorporated in the Houses of Parliament.

White Lodge Built in 1727–8 in Richmond Park and formerly a royal residence, it is now the Royal Ballet School.

Whitehall Palace Tudor Palace much used by Henry VIII (died there in 1547) but William III found the river air exacerbated his asthma so transferred the royal residence to Kensington Palace. Only the Banqueting House, a later addition, survived the fire that destroyed the palace in 1698.

Zoo Founded by Sir Stamford Raffles; opened in 1828 after his death. Aviary designed by Lord Snowdon and opened in 1965.

MEDICINE

Medical Discoveries

Discovery	Date	Discoverer	Nationality
adrenal gland: function of	1856	Alfred Vulpian	French
adrenalin	1901	Jokichi Takamine	Japanese
AIDS	1981	Lost Angeles scientists	American
antisepsis	1865	Joseph Lister	British
blood circulation	1628	William Harvey	British
blood groups	1901	Karl Landsteiner	Austrian
chloroform	1847	James Simpson	British
chromosomes	1888	Thomas Morgan	American
corpuscles, red	1684	Antoni van Leeuwenhoek	Dutch
cortisone	1934	Edward Kendall	American
diabetes, cause of	1901	Eugene Opic	American
diphtheria bacillus	1884	Edwin Klebs and Friedrich Löffler	German
DNA, structure of	1953	Francis Crick and James Watson	British/American
Down's Syndrome, cause of	1959	Dr Jerome, Lejeune	French
electro-encephalogram	1929	Hans Berger	German
endorphins	1975	Hughes, Guillemin	American
enzymes	1833	Anselme Payen, Jean-François Persoz	French
ether as anaesthetic	1846	William Morton	American
heparin	1915	Jay McLean	American
heredity	1865	Gregor Mendel	Austrian
HIV virus, isolated	1983	Luc Montaigner (among others)	French
insulin, isolated	1921	F.G. Banting, C.H. Best, J.J.R. McLeod	Canadian
interferon	1957	A. Isaacs, J. Lindemann	UK/Swiss
leprosy bacillus	1869	Gerhard Hansen	Norwegian
microbes	1762	M.A. Plenciz	Austrian
morphine	1805	Friedrich Sertürner	German
nitrous oxide	1776	Joseph Priestley	British
nucleic acid	1869	J.F. Miescher	Swiss
penicillin	1928	Alexander Fleming	British
protozoa	1675	Antoni van Leeuwenhoek	Dutch
rabies vaccination	1885	Louis Pasteur	French
Rhesus factor	1939	Karl Landsteiner, A.S. Wiener	Austrian
scurvy, treatment of	1740	James Lind	British
sleeping sickness transmission	1895	David Bruce	British
smallpox vaccination	1796	Edward Jenner	British
streptomycin	1943	Selman Waksman	American
tomography	1915	André Bocage	French
tuberculosis bacillus	1882	Robert Koch	German
typhus bacillus	1880	Karl Eberth	German
vitamin A	1913	E. McCollum, M. Davis, T. Osborne, L. Mendel	American
vitamin B (niacin)	1913	Casimir Funk	Polish
vitamin B1 (thiamin)	1897	Christiaan Eijkman	Dutch
vitamin B2 (riboflavin)	1933	R. Kuhn, A. von Szent-Gyorgi, J. Wagner-Jauregg	Austrian/ Hungarian/ Austrian
vitamin B3	1937	Madden, Strong, Wooley, Elvehjem	British/American
vitamin B5	1933	R.J. Williams	American
vitamin B6	1936	Birch, A. von Szent-Gyorgi	US/Hungarian
vitamin B9	1938	Day	British
vitamin B12	1937	G.R. Minot, W.P. Murphy	British
vitamin C (isolated)	1928	A. von Szent-Gyorgi	Hungarian
vitamin D (isolated)	1924	Steenbock, Hess, Weinstock	German
vitamin E	1923	H.M. Evans, Bishop	American
vitamin K1	1934	Carl Peter Henrik Dam	Danish
vitamins, necessity of	1906	Sir Frederick Hopkins	British
X-rays	1892	Heinrich Hertz	German
X-rays, properties of	1895	Wilhelm Röntgen	German
yellow fever, mosquito transmission	1881	Ronald Ross	British

Bones in the Human Body

skull

occipital	1
parietal – 1 pair	2
sphenoid	1
ethmoid	1
inferior nasal conchae – 1 pair	2
frontal – 1 pair fused	1
nasal – 1 pair	2
lacrimal – 1 pair	2
temporal – 1 pair	2
maxilla – 1 pair	2
zygomatic – 1 pair	2
vomer	1
palatine – 1 pair	2
mandible – 1 pair fused	1
	22

arms

upper arm:	humerus – 1 pair	2
lower arm:	radius –1 pair	2
	ulna – 1 pair	2
carpus:	scaphoid – 1 pair	2
	lunate – 1 pair	2
	triquetral – 1 pair	2
	pisiform – 1 pair	2
	trapezium – 1 pair	2
	trapezoid – 1 pair	2
	capitate – 1 pair	2
	hamate – 1 pair	2
metacarpals – 5 pairs		10
phalanges:	1st digit – 2 pairs	4
	2nd digit – 3 pairs	6
	3rd digit – 3 pairs	6
	4th digit – 3 pairs	6
	5th digit – 3 pairs	6
		60

hip bones (pelvic girdle)

ilium fused with ischium and pubis – 1 pair	2

ears

malleus	2
incus	2
stapes	2
	6

Vertebrae

cervical	7
thoracic	12
lumbar	5
sacral – 5 fused to form sacrum	1
coccyx – fused joint	1
	26

ribs

true ribs – 7 pairs	14
false ribs – 5 pairs (2 floaters)	10
	24

sternum

manubrium	1
zternebrae	1
xiphisternum	1
	3

throat

hyoid	1

pectoral girdle

clavicle – 1 pair	2
scapula – 1 pair	2
	4

legs

upper leg:	femur – 1 pair	2
lower leg:	tibia – 1 pair	2
	fibula – 1 pair	2
tarsus:	talus – 1 pair	2
	calcaneus – 1 pair	2
	navicular – 1 pair	2
	medial cuneiform – 1 pair	2
	intermediate cuneiform – 1 pair	2
	lateral cuneiform – 1 pair	2
	cuboid – 1 pair	2
metatarsals – 5 pairs		10
phalanges	1st digit – 2 pairs	4
	2nd digit – 3 pairs	6
	3rd digit – 3 pairs	6
	4th digit – 3 pairs	6
	5th digit – 3 pairs	6
		58

Total

skull	22
arms	60
hips	2
ears	6
vertebrae	26
ribs	24
sternum	3
throat	1
pectoral girdle	4
legs	58
	206

General Information

acid in stomach   hydrochloric.

adrenal glands   glands that produce adrenalin, which prepares the body for stress by increasing heart rate and blood pressure. They also produce cortisone, which has a variety of metabolic effects.

allergy   term used by Clemens von Pirquet (1874–1929) in 1906 following his observations of the skin reaction to his test for tuberculosis.

allopathy   treatment of disease by conventional means – i.e. with drugs having opposite effects to the symptoms (opposite of homoeopathy).

Alzheimer's disease   serious disorder of the brain manifesting itself in premature senility. Named after the German neurologist, Alois Alzheimer (1864–1915), who first identified it.

analeptic drug   restores and invigorates.

anaphylaxis   an extreme, often life-threatening reaction to an antigen, e.g. to a bee sting, due to hypersensitivity following an earlier dose.

anatomy   The science of the bodily structure of animals and plants.

artery   tubular thick-walled muscular vessel that conveys oxygenated blood from the heart, the largest being the aorta.

Asperger's syndrome   mild variant of autism diagnosed in 1994. Sufferers may have extraordinary compensating talents, e.g. musical prodigy, Joseph Erber (born 1984).

axilla   anatomical name for the armpit.

biology   the study of living organisms.

blepharitis   inflammation of the eyelids.

blood: circulation time   23 seconds on average.

blood content in body   varies slightly, but average man has 12 pts (5.6 litres) and woman 7 pts (3.3 litres), making the average 9 pints in general. An approximate calculation for adults is 60 millilitres per kilogram of body weight.

blood groups   A, B, AB, O. Blood groups may also be divided into Rhesus negative and positive. The most common group is O, which is universally given, and AB can receive from any group.

blood pressure: readings   systolic is highest blood pressure reading; diastolic is lowest. Abnormally high or low conditions are called hypertension and hypotension respectively.

body builds   the classification system is called somatotype and consists of: ectomorph (tall), endomorph (fat), mesomorph (muscular).

bones   consist mainly of collagen, calcium phosphate and inorganic salts, mainly hydroxyapatite. The smallest is the stapes and the largest the femur. The only non-connected bone is the hyoid in the throat.

bradycardia   abnormally slow heart action.

brain   the brain contains 10,000 million nerve cells, each of which has a potential 25,000 inter-connections with other cells. Average weight of the brain is 3lb (1.4 kg). The left side is the rational side.

calcaneus   heel bone.

cells   the smallest cell in the human body is the male sperm, the largest is the female ovum.

central nervous system   brain and spinal cord (vertebrates).

Chinese restaurant syndrome   the so-called illness caused by monosodium glutamate. There is no evidence that the symptoms of dizziness and headaches affect but a tiny proportion of people.

cholangiography   X-ray examination of the bile ducts used to locate obstructions.

cholecystography   X-ray examination of the gall bladder used to detect the presence of gall stones.

chromosomes   there are 23 pairs in the human body, the female having two X sex chromosomes while the male has one XY pair. They carry the gene sequence and, therefore, full genetic blueprint.

collagen   protein of great tensile strength present in bones, cartilage, tendons, ligaments and the skin.

colostrum   mother's first breast-product after a birth before milk flow begins. Contains antibodies that bring important immunities.

comedo   medical name for a blackhead.

cornea   convex transparent membrane that forms the forward covering of the eyeball; it is the only part of the body devoid of blood supply.

couéism   form of auto-suggestion propagated by Emile Coué (1857–1926). A key phrase was: 'Every day, and in every way, I am becoming better and better.'

coxa (aka innominate bone)   hip bone or joint (contrast ilium).

Crohn's disease   chronic inflammatory disease of the intestines, especially the colon and ileum, causing ulcers and fistulae. Named after B.B. Crohn, US pathologist (1874–1983).

crural   of the leg.

cubital   of the forearm.

dentine   calcified tissue of tooth.

diaphragm   dome-shaped muscular partition that separates the abdominal and thoracic cavities.

disease: most widespread   tooth and gum disease.

Down's syndrome: cause   extra chromosome (three number 21s instead of the usual two, hence the medical name, Trisomy 21).

Economo's disease   trypanosomiasis (sleeping sickness).

English disease   aka bronchitis.

enuresis   Involuntary urination.

epiglottis   thin cartilaginous flap that covers the entrance to the larynx during swallowing, preventing food from entering the trachea.

epilepsy: categories   petit mal, grand mal, psychomotor.

epistaxis   a nose bleed.

erysipelas   aka St Anthony's Fire.

erythrocyte   red blood cell that contains the pigment haemoglobin and transports oxygen and carbon dioxide to and from the tissues.

eye chart, standard   Snellen chart.

folic acid   another name for vitamin B.

gland: largest   the liver.

glandular fever   infectious viral disease characterized by swelling of the lymph glands and prolonged lassitude. Aka infectious mononucleosis.

Government Chief Medical Officer   Professor Liam Donaldson.

Graves disease   exophthalmic goitre with characteristic swelling of the neck and protrusion of the eyes, resulting from an overactive thyroid gland.

haemoglobin   red oxygen-carrying protein containing iron and present in the red blood cells of vertebrates.

haemophilia   male-only disease that prevents the blood from clotting. Women may be carriers. Aka Royal Disease.

hallux   big toe.

hardest substance in body   tooth enamel.

Harefield   Britain's leading hospital for heart and heart-and-lung operations, situated 20 miles west of London.

hemicrania   migraine.

hernia   the projection of an organ through the lining of the cavity in which it is normally situated. The two most common forms of hernia are femoral (upper thigh) and inguinal (groin).

heroin: made from   morphine, an opium derivative.

herpes zoster   shingles, an acute painful inflammation of the nerve ganglia, with a skin eruption, often forming a girdle around the waist, and caused by the same virus as chickenpox.

homoeopathy   treatment of disease by minute doses of drugs that in a healthy person would produce symptoms of the disease. Opposite of allopathy.

hormones: female sex   oestrogen and progesterone.

hospice movement: founder   Dame Cicely Saunders.

housemaid's knee   inflammation and swelling of the bursa in front of the kneecap, often caused by

MEDICINE

continual kneeling on hard surfaces. Aka prepatellar bursitis.

humerus   bone extending from the shoulder to the elbow.

humours   obsolete name for the four chief fluids of the body, i.e. blood, phlegm, yellow bile and black bile, that were once thought to determine a person's physical and mental qualities. Aka cardinal humours.

Hurler's syndrome   defect in metabolism resulting in mental retardation, a protruding abdomen and bone deformities, including an abnormally large head. Aka gargoylism.

hypermetropia   the condition of having long sight.

illium   bone forming the upper part of each half of the human pelvis (contrast coxa).

inferiority complex   named by Alfred Adler.

innominate bone (aka coxa)   bone formed from the fusion of the ilium, ischium and pubis, aka the hip bone.

insulin: gland that produces   pancreas (in cells called the islets of Langerhans).

interferon   proteins made by cells in response to virus infection.

iridology   diagnosis by examination of the iris of the eye (used mainly in alternative medicine).

iris   the coloured muscular diaphragm that surrounds and controls the size of the pupil.

jaw bones   maxilla (upper jaw), mandible (lower jaw).

joints: lubricating fluid   synovial fluid.

keloid/cheloid   overgrown scar tissue.

kissing disease   glandular fever.

kyphosis   excessive outward curvature of the thoracic spine causing hunching of the back.

larynx   cartilaginous and muscular hollow organ forming part of the air passage to the lungs. Aka Adam's apple, voice-box.

Lassa fever   acute and often fatal febrile viral haemorrhagic disease of tropical Africa, named from the village in Nigeria where first reported.

Legionnaires' disease   form of bacterial pneumonia first identified after an outbreak at an American Legion meeting in Philadelphia in 1976 and spread by water droplets through air-conditioning systems and similar devices.

leucocyte   colourless amoeboid cell of blood and lymph, containing a nucleus and important in fighting disease. Aka white blood cell/white corpuscle.

leucoderma (aka vitiligo)   skin condition characterized by loss of melanin pigmentation.

leucoma   a white opacity in the cornea of the eye.

leucotomy   surgical cutting of white nerve fibres within the brain, especially prefrontal lobotomy.

leukaemia   malignant disease in which the bone marrow and other blood-forming organs produce too many leucocytes.

ligament   short band of tough flexible fibrous connective tissue linking bones together.

ligature   tie or bandage used in surgery for a bleeding artery.

lingua   the tongue.

lipids   organic compounds that are esters of fatty acids and are found in blood, cell membranes and elsewhere.

lithotomy   surgical removal of a calculus (stony secretion) from the bladder or urinary tract.

lithotripsy   removal of a calculus from the bladder or urinary tract by means of ultrasound techniques that

shatter the stone so that fragments passs naturally from the body.

liver: functions   production of bile to emulsify fat in the bowel. Reception of all the products of food absorption and the subsequent release as energy sources. Carbohydrates are stored as glycogen, and the liver uses insulin from the pancreas to control the body's glucose level. Purification of blood. Production of proteins needed for blood clotting.

liver transplants: hospital   Addenbrooke's Hospital near Cambridge was the pioneer.

lordosis   inward curvature of the spine.

lungs   the 700 million air sacs are called alveoli, and the right lung is heavier than the left.

lunula   crescent-shaped white area at the base of the fingernail.

lyme disease   form of arthritis caused by spirochaete bacteria transmitted by ticks. Named after a town in Connecticut, USA, where an outbreak occurred in 1975.

mantoux test   intradermal tuberculin test named after French physician Charles Mantoux 1877–1947.

mastoid process   conical prominence on the temporal bone behind the ear, to which muscles are attached.

Ménière's syndrome   inner ear disorder characterized by ringing in ear, dizziness and impaired hearing.

miner's disease   pneumoconiosis (caused by inhalation of coal dust).

mnemonic   for nerves in the superorbital tissue: Lazy French Tarts Lie Naked In Anticipation (Lacrimal, Frontal, Trochlear, Lateral, Nasociliary, Internal, Abduceris).

mons pubis   rounded mass of fatty tissue lying over the joint of the pubic bones.

mons veneris   Rounded mass of fatty tissue on a woman's abdomen above the vulva (Latin: Mount of Venus).

Moorfields   (London EC1) Britain's leading hospital specializing in eye injuries.

Munchausen's syndrome   medical name for feigned symptoms brought on with a view to gaining admission into hospital.

Munchausen's syndrome by proxy   mental condition in which a person seeks attention by inducing illness in another person, especially a child. Named after R.E. Raspe's literary hero.

muscae volitantes   moving black specks seen before the eyes, caused by opaque fragments floating in the vitreous humour ('floaters') or a defect in the lens.

muscle: not attached at both ends   tongue.

muscles: smile or frown debate   although smiling is more beneficial to one's wellbeing, in fact, frowning uses more muscles.

myeloid tissue   term for bone marrow, found in the or spinal cord and elsewhere.

myopia   short-sightedness.

naevus   birthmark in the form of a raised red patch on the skin.

nosology   branch of medical science dealing with the classification of diseases.

obstetrics   of or relating to childbirth and associated processes.

oedema   condition characterized by an excess of watery fluid collecting in the cavities or tissues of the body. Aka dropsy.

oesophagus   part of the alimentary canal between the pharynx and the stomach. Aka gullet.

olfactory   Of or relating to the sense of smell.

Paget's cancer   cancer of the nipple and surrounding tissue. Named after Sir James Paget (1814–99) the English surgeon and pathologist who described this disease.

Paget's disease   chronic disease of the bones characterized by inflammation and deformation. Aka *osteitis deformans*.

pancreas   gland secreting the hormone insulin, which regulates glucose levels in the body. Deficiency of insulin causes diabetes mellitus (sugar diabetes).

pathology   study of causes and nature of diseases.

phlegm: medical name   sputum.

plasma   clear yellowish fluid portion of blood or lymph in which the corpuscles and cells are suspended.

purkinje effect   As light intensity decreases red objects are perceived to fade faster than blue objects of similar brightness.

radius   outer and slightly shorter of the two bones of the forearm.

retina   light-sensitive portion of the eyeball.

retrovir   brand name of zidovudine (AZT), used in treating HIV and AIDS.

rubella   German measles.

rubeola   medical name for measles.

Schick test   identifies susceptibility to diptheria.

sclera   the white part of the eye.

sex change operation: first   George (Christine) Jorgensen (1952).

siamese twins: called after most famous conjoined twins to survive into adulthood Chang and Eng (1811–74), born in Siam.

singultus   hiccup.

skin   accounts for 16% of the body's weight and has an average surface area of 2,800 sq in (18,000 sq cm); as such, it is the largest and heaviest organ of the human body.

Stockholm syndrome   psychological term for process of bonding between hostage and captors.

Stoke Mandeville   Britain's leading hospital for the treatment of spinal injuries.

stomach capacity   about 2–2½ pints (0.94–1.18 litres).

stomatology   study of mouth diseases.

syncope   technical name for a faint.

talipes   club foot.

talus   the ankle bone.

tendon   cord or strand of strong fibrous tissue attaching a muscle to a bone.

testes   two glands that produce sperms and the male hormone testosterone.

test tube baby: first   Louise Brown in 1978 (doctors were Steptoe and Edwards).

thalassotherapy   ancient medical treatment of lying in sea water.

thorax   anatomical name for the chest.

thyroid gland   situated in the neck in front of the windpipe. Controls the metabolism.

tincture   medicinal extract in a solution of alcohol.

trachea   the windpipe.

trachoma   contagious disease of the eye with inflamed granulation on the inner surface of the lids, caused by chlamydiae.

trismus   variety of tetanus with tonic spasms of the jaw muscles causing the mouth to remain tightly closed. Aka lockjaw.

ulna   inner and longer of the two bones of the forearm.

urticaria   hives or nettle rash.

varicella   chickenpox.

variola   smallpox.

vascular   relating to blood vessels.

venereal disease: most common   gonorrhea.

vitiligo (aka leucoderma)   skin disease characterized by loss of melanin pigmentation.

vitamin   term coined by Casimir Funk (1884–1967) in 1911 for the unidentified substances present in food that could prevent the diseases scurvy, beriberi and pellagra.

Wasserman test: used for   testing for syphilis.

white death   tuberculosis.

yellow fever   tropical virus disease with fever and jaundice, transmitted by the mosquito and often fatal.

MEDICINE

Phobias

acero	sourness	**arachno**	spiders	**cheimai**	cold
achulo	darkness	**astheno**	weakness	**chero**	cheerfulness
acro	heights	**astra**	lightning	**chiono**	snow
aero	air	**ataxio**	disorder	**chrometo**	money
agora	open spaces	**ate**	ruin	**chromo**	colour
aichuro	points	**atelo**	imperfection	**chrono**	duration
ailuro	cats	**aulo**	flute	**chrystallo**	crystals
akoustico	sound	**aurora**	Northern Lights	**claustro**	closed spaces
alektoro	chickens	**automyso**	being dirty	**clino**	going to bed
algo	pain	**bacilli**	microbes	**cnido**	stings
amaka	carriages	**baro**	gravity	**coito**	sexual
amatho	dust	**baso**	walking		intercourse
amycho	being scratched	**batho**	depth	**cometo**	comets
andro	men	**batracho**	reptiles	**copro**	faeces
anemo	wind	**belono**	needles	**cremno**	precipices
angino	narrowness	**blenno**	slime	**cryo**	ice, frost
anglo	England and the	**bronto**	thunder	**cymo**	sea swell
	English	**caino**	novelty	**cyno**	dogs
anthropo	man	**carcino**	cancer	**cyprido**	venereal disease
antlo	flood	**cardio**	heart condition	**demo**	crowds
apeiro	infinity	**carno**	meat	**demono**	demons
api	bees	**chaeto**	hair	**dendro**	trees

dermato	skin	klepto	stealing	phengo	daylight
dermatosio	skin disease	koni	dust	phobo	fears
dike	injustice	kopo	fatigue	phono	speaking aloud
dipso	drinking	kristallo	ice		or noise
dora	fur	kypho	stooping	photo	light
dromo	crossing streets	lalo	stuttering	phronemo	thinking
dysmorpho	deformity	limno	lakes	phthisio	tuberculosis
eisoptro	mirror	linono	string	phyllo	leaves
electro	electricity	logo	words	pnigero	smothering
eleuthero	freedom	lysso	insanity	pogono	beards
emeto	vomiting	maieusio	pregnancy	poine	punishment
enete	pins	mania	insanity	poly	many things
entomo	insects	mastigo	flogging	potamo	rivers
eoso	dawn	mechano	machinery	poto	alcohol
eremo	solitude	merintho	being bound	pterono	feathers
ergasio	work	metallo	metals	pyro	fire
erythro	blushing	meteoro	meteors	rhabdo	being beaten
frigo	being cold	miso	contamination	russo	Russia
gallo	France and the	mono	being alone	rypo	soiling
	French	musico	music	satano	Satan
gameto	marriage	muso	mice	scio	shadows
geno	sex	myso	dirt	scopo	being stared at
genu	knees	myxo	slime	seia	flash
gephyro	crossing bridges	necro	corpses	sela	flashes
geuma	taste	negro	black people	sidero	stars
grapho	writing	nelo	glass	siderodromo	travelling by
gymno	nudity	neo	newness		train
gyno	women	nepho	clouds	sino	China
hade	Hell	nosema	illness	sito	food
haemato	blood	noso	disease	sperma	germs
hamartio	sin	nycto	darkness	spermato	germs
hapto	touch	ochlo	crowds	spermato	semen
harpaxo	robbers	ocho	vehicles	sphekso	wasps
hedono	pleasure	odonto	teeth	stasi	standing
helmintho	worms	oiko	home	stygio	hell
hiero	sacred things	olfacto	smell	syphilo	syphilis
hippo	horses	ombro	rain	tacho	speed
hodo	travel	ommeta	eyes	tapho	graves
homichlo	fog	oneiro	dreams	terato	monsters
homo	homosexuals	ophidio	snakes	terdeka	the number 13
horme	shock	ornitho	birds	thaaso	sitting
hyalinopygo	glass bottoms	osmo	odours	thalasso	sea
hydro	water	osphresio	body odours	thanato	death
hygro	dampness	ourano	Heaven	theo	God
hypegia	responsibility	paedi	children	thermo	heat
hypno	sleep	paedio	dolls	thixo	touching
hypso	high places	panto	everything	toco	childbirth
ideo	ideas	paralipo	neglect of duty	toxi	poison
io	rust	partheno	girls	traumato	injury
kakorraphia	failure	patho	disease	tremo	trembling
katagelo	Ridicule	patroio	heredity	triskaideka	the number 13
keno	void	peccato	sinning	trypano	injections
keraunothneto	fall of man-made	pediculo	lice	xeno	foreigners
	satellites	penia	poverty	zelo	jealousy
kineso	motion	phago	swallowing	zoo	animals
kineto	motion	phasmo	ghosts		

Operations: Military and Social

Accolade Unfulfilled 1943 plan for capture of Rhodes and other Aegean islands.

Acrobat Original name for Operation Torch and the name used in the 1943 film *Tunisian Victory*, it was the planned British operation to advance from Cyrenaica to Tripoli, 1941.

Adlertag (Eagle Day) Start of main German air offensive on 13 August 1940, which led to the Adlerangriff (German plan for Battle of Britain).

A Go Japanese plan for a counterattack against possible US recapture of the Marianas during 1944.

Alaric First German codename for their possible military takeover in Italy.

Allied Force Began on 24 March 1999 when United States military forces, acting with Nato allies, commenced air strikes against Serbian military targets in the former Yugoslavia. The multinational force was tasked by Nato to bring an end to crimes committed by the Federal Republic of Yugoslavia against ethnic Albanians in the southern province of Kosovo. On 20 June 1999 Operation Allied Force was officially terminated. This was in response to the departure of all FRY military and police forces from Kosovo in compliance with the Military Technical Agreement, which was signed by the Commander of KFOR and representatives of the FRY Government on 9 June 1940.

Alpen Veilchen (Alpine Violet) Proposed plan for Italians to break out from Albania into Greece. Cancelled on 19 January 1940.

Anakim First Allied plan for amphibious reconquest of Burma, abandoned in 1943.

Anton German occupation of Vichy France on 11 November 1942, first codenamed Attila.

Anvil Original codename for Allied landing on the French coast between Toulon and Cannes, later changed to Dragoon.

Aphrodite American scheme to load surplus bombers with explosives and fly them to the south coast of Britain, where the two-man crew would bail out and another plane would guide the plane to crash into a V-1 site. Joe Kennedy, elder brother of JFK, was blown up on a test run over Norfolk.

Apostle I Allied return to Norway on 10 May 1945.

Arcadia Codename for the conference between Churchill and F.D. Roosevelt in Washington, 22 December 1941–14 January 1942.

Aufbau Ost Prior to Barbarossa, this was the German buildup in the east.

Autumn Mist (Herbstrebel) Codename for the Ardennes Offensive (Battle of the Bulge) in 1944.

Avalanche US and British forces landing in the Gulf of Salerno causing the Germans to withdraw to the Gustav Line across the peninsula north of Naples, 9–19 September 1943.

Avonmouth Failed Allied expedition to Narvik May–June 1940.

Axis (Achse) Originally called 'Alaric', the disarming of the Italian army after their surrender to the Germans on 8 September 1943.

Babylon 7 June 1981, destruction of Osirak nuclear reactor in Iraq by Israeli F16s.

Badr 6 October 1973, Arab assault in Yom Kippur War.

Bagration Successful Soviet offensive in the central part of the German-occupied Russian Front, 23 June–29 August 1944.

Barbarossa German invasion of the USSR on 22 June 1941, supported by Romanian troops.

Battleaxe 15 June 1941, the first British offensive into 'Hellfire' (Halfaya) Pass, which failed to recapture Tobruk.

Baytown British landing at Reggio, 3 September 1943, and advance into the south-west Italian mainland, reaching Auletta on 19 September and Potenza on 20 September.

Bernhard Failed German plan to flood Britain with forged money during the Second World War, by means of an air drop, and thereby ruin the British economy.

Bigot Security classification for Normandy landing planning documents.

Birdcage Airborne leaflet drop on POW camps in the Far East announcing Japanese surrender.

Blackbuck 1 1 May 1982, bombing of Port Stanley runway by a Vulcan bomber.

Blackcock XII British Corps attack at Roermond, southeast Holland, 16–26 January 1945.

Black (Schwarz) The German occupation of Italy in 1943.

Blue Book Following an unexplained UFO sighting in Roswell, New Mexico, in 1947 the US Air Force set up a study group code-named Project Sign. Of the 147 reported sightings all but 12 were explained. A further rush of sightings prompted the set up of Project Grudge on 11 February 1949. The USAF attempted to explain every UFO sighting but of the 273 official sightings, 231 were classed as unidentified. In March 1952 Project Grudge went public as Project Blue Book and for the next 17 years remained the USAF's official UFO Study Program. Investigations ceased in 1969 as the US government advised the USAF that the project was no longer justifiable.

Bluecoat Normandy Operation of 30 July 1944, which concerned the initial British diversionary breakout from their American boundary, followed by the US 3rd Army, under Patton, breaking through the German defences at Avranches, the gateway from Normandy into Brittany.

Bodenplatte Luftwaffe offensive operation against Allied airfields in north-western Europe during December 1944.

Bodyguard Overall codename for multiple Allied deception tactics in 1944, but usually associated with the diversionary operation to deceive the Germans into thinking that the invasion was to be Kent-based and aimed at the Pas de Calais. Originally codenamed Jael.

Bolero The build up of US troops in the UK in 1942.

Bolo During Vietnam War, an ambush operation by American F-4 fighters, flying like bombers, which knocked out 7 North Vietnamese Migs in one go.

Brassard Allied amphibious landings launched from Corsica on Elba, 17 June 1944.

Brevity 15 May 1941, the first British offensive into Hellfire Pass.

Buckshot   Planned British attack in Libya, May 1942.

Bumblebee   Anti-burglary device instigated by the Metropolitan Police on 1 June 1993 and sponsored by Yellow Pages. Bumblebee has several aspects to its 'sting'. The aim is to target known burglars in an effort to 'fight back' against criminals. In 1995 the Bumblebee Imagining System was implemented whereby stolen property recovered by the police can be matched against photographs supplied by the victim. Bumblebee has also run a campaign to make people aware that covert police patrols are carried out at car boot sales. Another key factor in Bumblebee operations is the personalisation of belongings. The increase in computer and mobile phone companies having tracing methods has meant their products are no longer worth stealing.

Cartwheel Phase One   US troops recapture important islands in the Solomon Island Group from 1 July to 25 November 1943.

Cartwheel Phase Two   US and Australian forces invasion of north-east New Guinea from 4 September 1943 to 23 March 1944.

Catapult   3 July 1940, British naval attack on French fleet at Mers-el-Kebir, destroying or damaging most of its ships to prevent them from falling into German or Italian hands.

Catherine   British plan for forcing a passage into the Baltic to aid Poland, before the country's invasion by Germany and the Soviet Union in September 1939.

Cedar Falls   The US clearance of Vietcong from Iron Triangle, Vietnam, in 1967.

Centaur   Crackdown on Britain's 'black economy' by Customs and Excise from 1985 onwards. Lester Piggott was a famous catch.

Cerberus   Channel dash of the German ships *Scharnhorst*, *Prinz Eugen* and *Gneisenau* from Brest to Germany in February 1942.

Chariot   27–28 March 1942, British Commando raid on St Nazaire to destroy the Normandie Dock.

Charnwood   Normandy operation of 7 July 1944: attack north of Caen following a massive RAF bombardment.

Chastise   British bombers led by Wing-Commander Guy Gibson attacked three dams in the Ruhr region of Germany in May 1943, using the spinning or 'bouncing' bombs designed by Barnes Wallis. Two dams were breached. Aka the Dambusters' Raid.

Cheshire   British equivalent of Operation 'Provide Promise', i.e. the RAF flights into Sarajevo.

Chicken Little   Abortive attempt to predict time and place of Skylab's return to Earth in 1979.

Chromite   15 September 1950, General MacArthur's successful amphibious landing at Inchon during the Korean War.

Clean Hands   Launched by Milan magistrates in February 1992 to halt corruption in the city, especially collusion between the Mafia and the Christian Democratic Party.

Cobra   Allied Normandy USAAF breakout of July 25 1944, following massive bombardment by USAAF.

Cockade   Part of Allied deception plan to convince Germans that invasion of Europe would be anywhere but Normandy in summer of 1944. Brittany, northern Norway and the Pas de Calais were false objectives.

Colossus   First British airborne operation (unsuccessful), Tragino viaduct, Campagne, Italy, on 10 February 1941.

Compass   9 December 1940, British 8th Army attack at Sidi Barrani, Egypt, which began the destruction of the Italian 10th Army.

Corkscrew   Allied operations against the Mediterranean island of Pantelleria in June 1943.

Coronet   Proposed US invasion of Japanese island of Honshu in March 1946 overtaken by Japanese surrender the year before.

Corporate   British recapture of the Falklands in May/June 1982.

Countryman   Investigation into alleged corruption in the Metropolitan Police.

Cromwell   Not an operation but a British codeword for 'Invasion Imminent' used from 1940.

Crossbow   Operation using fighters, anti-aircraft batteries and barrage balloons against German V-1 flying bombs in 1944, and later to bomb the V-2 rocket launch sites.

Crusader   The 8th Army's first offensive (as 8th Army) in Libya, 18 November to 12 December 1941.

Culverin   Allied plan for recapture of northern Sumatra in 1943 – never carried out.

Deliberate Force   Nato's air campaign against Bosnian Serbs from 30 August to 14 September 1995.

Deny Flight   UN denial of Bosnian airspace to warring parties, began on 12 April 1993. On 28 February 1994 four Bosnian-Serb warplanes violating the no-fly zone were shot down by Nato aircraft. This was the first military engagement ever undertaken by the UN/NATO Alliance.

Desert Sabre   Official name for the ground war in the Persian Gulf January–February 1991, although US media often used the term 'Desert Sword'.

Desert Shield   US-led multi national force, whose establishment was formally announced on 9 November 1990 and whose aim was to secure the withdrawal of Iraqi troops from Kuwait.

Desert Storm   Air offensive launched by US-led allied forces on the night of 17 January 1991 against targets in Iraq and Iraqi-occupied Kuwait. The campaign lasted until 27 February 1991.

Detachment   US capture of the Japanese island of Iwo Jima from 19 February to 1 March 1945.

Diadem   Allied offensive that began on 11 May 1944, and broke the German Gustav Line, capturing Rome on 4 June 1944.

Dickens   The 3rd Battle of Cassino, Italy, 15 March 1944. The original codename was Bradman, a cricket reference.

Diver   British anti-V-1 measures.

Downfall   Projected Allied invasion of mainland Japan, planned for 1 November 1945 and never carried out.

Dragoon   Launched on 15 August 1944; Allied invasion of southern France, subsequent to Operation Anvil. When the US 7th Army and the French 1st Army landed on the French Riviera the Americans drove through the Alps to take Grenoble, while the French took Marseilles and advanced up the Rhône valley to rejoin the Americans near Lyons and move northeastward into Alsace in September 1944.

Dracula   Liberation of Rangoon completed on 3 May 1945.

Dynamo   Evacuation of Anglo-French forces from Dunkirk, 26 May to 4 June 1940.

Eclipse   Proposed dropping of Allied airborne army on Berlin in April 1945.

Edelweiss   German Army Group A's operations against Baku area of the Caucasus during the summer of 1942.

Eisenhammer Planned Luftwaffe attack on Soviet power stations during February 1945.

El Dorado Canyon 14 April 1986, 24 USAF F-111 bombers attacked Tripoli in reprisal raid.

Epsom Normandy operation in the last 5 days of June 1944, a british move to outflank Caen from the West.

Eureka Codename for the Tehran conference of November 1943 between Churchill, Roosevelt and Stalin.

Exporter British and Free French invasion of Vichy-ruled Lebanon and Syria from 8 June to 12 July 1941.

Felix Proposed German plan to capture Gibraltar and the Canary and Cape Verde Islands with Spanish aid in November 1940. Spain's neutrality ruled it out.

Firebrand Allied occupation of Corsica, largely by Free French forces, from September to October 1943.

Flash Codename for attempt on Hitler's life in March 1943 when a bomb placed in his plane by Fabian von Schlabrendorff failed to explode.

Flintlock US invasion of Marshall Islands and Kwajalein Atoll from 31 January to 7 February 1944.

Forager US invasion of the Marianas between J11 and 26 June 1944.

Fortitude, North and South Deception campaigns to suggest that invasion of Northern Europe would be directed at either Norway or the Pas de Calais in 1944.

Freeborn 8th Army provision for withdrawal to Egyptian frontier in 1941.

Frequent Wind US evacuation of Saigon, Vietnam, in April 1975.

Fritz Initial plan for German invasion of the Soviet Union in December 1940, precursor of Barbarossa.

Fuller Attempt to prevent the German warships *Scharnhorst* and *Gneisenau* escaping from Brest in December 1943.

Full Flow Greatest UK exercise since 1945 involving transfer of 57,000 troops from UK to Germany for Lionheart/Cold Fire exercises; began 3 September 1984.

Galvanic US occupation of Tarawa, Makin and Apamama, in the Gilbert Islands, on 20–21 November 1943.

Gemsbock Anti-partisan drive in Greece, July 1944.

Gomorrah RAF fire-storm raid on Hamburg, 25 July 1943, when anti-radar chaff, codenamed 'Window', was used for the first time.

Goodwood Normandy offensive of 18 July 1944: an attack by the British Second Army south-east of Caen following massive bombardment by RAF.

Granby British contribution to the Gulf War from Operation Desert Storm to the ceasefire on 11 April 1991.

Granite US offensive operations in the Central Pacific, beginning March 1944.

Grapeshot Allied attack on German-occupied northern Italy in 1944.

Grenade Operation that linked Lieutenant General William Simpson's 9th US Army to the Canadian offensive against the lower Rhine (Operation Veritable) in February 1945.

Gymnast Proposed British landings in Tunisia and Algeria in 1941, superseded by Torch.

Hammer Proposed Allied attack on Trondheim, central Norway, April 1940, abandoned as impracticable.

Hercules Proposed German airborne invasion of

Malta in the spring of 1942 involving airborne and sea landings. The operation was cancelled.

Horrido German anti-partisan drive in Yugoslavia during the spring of 1944.

Husky US and British troops landing in Sicily on 10 July 1943; total occupation achieved by 17 August 1943.

Icarus Proposed German invasion of Iceland in 1940; not carried out.

Iceberg US capture of Okinawa from 1 April to 22 June 1945.

I Go Japanese codename for naval counter-offensive in the Pacific during April 1943.

I – Go Sakusen Japanese air offensive in south-west Pacific, 7 to 16 April 1945 (aka Operation A).

Iltis German anti-partisan drive in Greece during March 1944.

Infatuate Allied operation to capture Walcheren Island in the Scheldt estuary on 1–18 November 1944.

Irma Media term for the airlift of some 40 people seriously injured in the war in Bosnia-Herzegovina to hospitals in the UK, Sweden and Italy in August 1993. Named after Irma Hadzimuratovic, a wounded 5-year-old whose plight was given huge media coverage after Prime Minister John Major arranged for her flight out of Sarajevo.

Ironclad British occupation of Diego Suarez, Madagascar, 8 May 1942.

Isabella (Ilona) Abortive German plans to occupy Atlantic coasts of Spain and Portugal in 1941.

Jael See Bodyguard.

Jericho RAF Mosquito raid on Amiens jail to release Resistance prisoners, 18 February 1944.

Joint Guardian In the aftermath of Operation Allied Force the Joint Guardian operation continues to pursue the ultimate goal of a peaceful multi-ethnic and democratic Kosovo. The original five-point plan of Allied Force was to stop the Serb offensive, force a Serb withdrawal, establish democratic self-government in Kosovo, allow a Nato-led peacekeeping force and to allow the safe return of Kosovar Albanian refugees.

Jubilee Disastrous Anglo-Canadian amphibious raid on Dieppe on 19 August 1942.

Junction City Only US para assault of Vietnam War, 22 February–14 May 1967.

Jupiter Projected Allied invasion of northern Norway in 1942; not carried out.

Just Cause Code name for the US military invasion of Panama between 20 December 1989 and 13 February 1990. It saw the first operational use of the stealth bomber.

Ka Go Japanese reinforcement of Guadalcanal in August 1942 resulting in the battle of the Eastern Solomons.

Kathleen A German-planned invasion of Ireland in the summer of 1940, with the support of the IRA. Preparing work on this plan was made by the IRA themselves, but aborted.

Konstantin German operation to seize control of Italian-controlled Balkans during September 1943.

Koralle German anti-partisan drive in Greece during July 1944.

Kreuzoller German anti-partisan drive in Greece during August 1944.

Kugelblitz German anti-partisan drive in Yugoslavia during latter half of 1943.

Kutuzov Soviet counter-offensive in the Kursk salient of July 1943.

M
I
L
I
T
A
R
Y

Leopard   German assault on the island of Leros, Greece, in 1943.

Lightfoot   General Montgomery's plan for the breakthrough phase of the 2nd Battle of El Alamein, 23 October 1942. It failed to break the German defenses.

Lila   German operation to seize the French fleet at Toulon. They found the fleet scuttled on 27 November 1942.

Limerick   British attack in Libya, June 1942.

Linebacker II   The 1972 Christmas bombing offensive against North Vietnam by US B-52 bombers.

Little Saturn   Soviet offensive against the German relief forces trying to break through to the encircled 6th Army at Stalingrad, launched on 16 December 1942.

Lumberjack   Advances by US First Army to the Rhine at Cologne and by US Third Army further south in February 1945.

Lustre   British transfer of forces from Western Desert to Greece in March 1941.

Luttich   German attempt to cut off the Americans breaking out of Normandy by attacking at Mortain 17 August 1944.

Magic   Name given to the overall US Intelligence programme before and during the Second World War devoted to breaking Japanese codes.

Magic Carpet   Airlift of some 50,000 Jews from Yemen to Israel in the late 1940s and early 1950s.

Magnet   Codename for the arrival of US forces in Northern Ireland in February 1942.

Mailfist   Planned Allied recapture of Singapore, in 1945.

Manhattan District   Cover name for the USA's atomic bomb project begun in June 1942.

Mannah   Dropping of food supplies to occupied Holland by RAF in April and May 1945. Also codename for British intervention in the Greek civil war in October 1944.

Marita   German assault on Yugoslavia and Greece in May 1941.

Maritime Monitor   Royal Navy blockade of Serbia.

Market Garden   The disastrous Allied airborne attack near Arnhem on 17 September 1944 which failed to link up with the British Second Army. Market was the airborne operation in which Allied paratroops were to seize key river crossings in advance of Second Army's tanks. Garden was the ground phase.

Menace   Failed Anglo-Free French attempt to capture Vichy Dakar in West Africa with help from De Gaulle in September 1940.

Mercury   German airborne assault on Crete in May 1941.

Midsummer Night's Dream   Probing attack by Rommel in Libya, 14 September 1941.

Millennium   RAF Bomber Command's 30/31 May 1942, 1,000-bomber raid on Cologne.

Mincemeat   Aka The Man Who Never Was. Precursor of Operation Husky, whereby the aim was to deceive the German general staff into believing the proposed Allied attack on Sicily was, in fact, to be on Sardinia and Corsica in the west and the Greek mainland in the east. The deception was the plan of two relatively junior officers, Squadron Leader Sir Archibald Cholmondley and intelligence officer Lt Cmdr Ewen Montagu. It was Cholmondley who first suggested planting a series of subtle clues on a dead body and ensuring the Germans would be privy to this information, and it was Montagu who gave the plan

its feasibility. The dead body, whose true identity was never revealed, was given the name of Captain (acting major) William Martin of the Royal Marines, and his mode of death was a plane crash at sea off the Spanish coast, where the Abwehr (German Intelligence) was known to be very active. The plan was a total success and 'Husky' gave the Allies control of the Mediterranean.

Mongoose   Operation launched by President John F. Kennedy and his brother Robert Kennedy, the Attorney-General, in December 1961, with the aim of overthrowing Fidel Castro of Cuba.

Moonlight Sonata   German air-raid on Coventry on 14 and 15 November 1940.

Moses   Secret airlift of Ethiopian Jews, or Falashas, to Israel from refugee camps in Sudan 1984–5.

Musketeer   Anglo-French assault on Suez on 5 November 1956, first ever use of helicopters in amphibious landing.

Myth   Soviet investigation into the death of Hitler in 1946, with aim of ensuring that he was in fact dead.

Neptun   German anti-partisan drive, Greece 1944.

Neptune   Naval side of Operation Overlord, involving 7,000 Allied ships.

No Ball   Air attacks on German rocket-launching sites in 1944–5.

Nordlicht (Northern Lights)   German operation against Leningrad during the summer of 1942.

Nordwind   German counter-attack in Alsace (west of Strasbourg) in January 1945.

Oak   Rescue of former prime minister Benito Mussolini from captivity in the Abruzzi mountains on 12 September 1943 by a small German force under Otto Skorzeny.

Olive   Allied attack on the Gothic Line, Italy, in August 1944.

Olympic   Proposed Allied plan to invade Kyushu in October 1945, precursor of projected Operation Downfall, the assault on Japan itself.

Overcast   US plan launched in July 1945 to spirit German weapon scientists away from Europe to work in US laboratories.

Overlord   Code name for the Allied invasion of Normandy in 1944. Originally planned for May, the day finally chosen was 5 June but the operation was delayed 24 hours by bad weather.

Panther   German anti-partisan drive in Yugoslavia during spring of 1944.

Paperclip   American project authorised by Harry S Truman in September 1946 whereby a selection of German scientists was brought to America to work on behalf of the US Government during the 'Cold War' following the end of the Second World War.

Paraquat   British recapture of South Georgia from Argentina on 25 April 1982.

Peace for Galilee   Codename for Israel's full-scale invasion of Lebanon in June 1982, launched with aim of eradicating the PLO from Lebanon.

Pedestal   British convoy to supply Malta in August 1942, involving 2 battleships (*Nelson* and *Rodney*), 3 aircraft carriers (*Victorious* and *Eagle* were sunk and *Indomitable* damaged), 2 ferry carriers (*Argus* and *Furious* carrying Spitfires), to Malta, 14 merchantmen (9 sunk, 5 arrived, including tanker, *Ohio* which was literally dragged into Malta sandwiched between 2 destroyers.

Pegasus   15 April 1968, relief by US and South Vietnamese forces of Khe Sanh combat base, Vietnam, besieged since mid-January.

Plan Blue (Fall Blau)   Originally, the name given to a 1938 study from the Luftwaffe about aerial warfare in England, but more commonly the German offensive in southern Russia in the spring of 1942. Aka 'Case Blue'.

Plan Green (Fall Grün)   In 1937 the plan to attack and occupy Czechoslovakia, which was executed without resistance in May 1938, after the Munich conference. In 1940 it was the name given to the plan for a frontal attack on the Maginot Line, later called Fall Braun.

Plan Red (Fall Rot)   In 1935 the Fall Rot was a study to defend against a surprise attack by France while defending the borders against Czechoslovakia and Poland. The 1937 version of Fall Rot included offensive operations against Czechoslovakia with the aim of preventing a prolonged two-front war. In 1940 it was the second part of the western campaign; after the destruction of the British Expeditionary Force and the northern army of France, it was, with Fall Braun, the attack on the rest of the French army, which was still entrenched in the Maginot Line.

Plan White (Fall Weiss)   German invasion of Poland in September 1939. Aka 'Case White'.

Plan Yellow (Fall Gelb)   German assault in the Low Countries and France launched on10 May 1940. Aka 'Case Yellow'.

Platinum   Part of 'Barbarossa' comprising operations towards Murmansk in the north.

Plunder   Montgomery's crossing of the Rhine at the head of the 21st Army Group on 23 March 1945.

Pointblank   Bombing campaign against German military, industrial and economic targets from May 1943.

Polar Bear   German assault on the island of Kos, Greece, in 1943.

Provide Assistance   Codename for the US relief operation launched on 23 July1994 to deliver humanitarian relief to Rwandan refugees in Zaïre, prompted by an outbreak of cholera, aka Operation Support Hope.

Provide Comfort   Code name for an emergency relief programme announced by Western allied forces on 16 April 1991, for the besieged Kurdish population of northern Iraq.

Provide Promise   USAF flights into Sarajevo during conflict. Began on 2 July 1992 with 21 nations forming a coalition to resupply a war-ravaged Sarajevo. The longest humanitarian airlift in history ended on 9 January 1996.

Puma   Proposed British operation to seize Canary Islands in 1941.

Punishment   German air attacks on Yugoslav capital of Belgrade from 6 to 8 April 1941.

Quadrant   Codename of the Quebec conference of August 1943, attended by Churchill and Roosevelt.

Rankin   Allied plans for return to European continent. Rankin A involved possible return in advance of scheduled Normandy invasion, B was response in case of German withdrawal from France or Norway, C in case of German unconditional surrender.

Ratweek   RAF and Yugoslav partisans launch attacks on roads and railways intending to prevent German withdrawal from Yugoslavia, September 1944.

Reckless   US operation against Hollandia, New Guinea, in April 1944.

Regenbogen (Rainbow)   Scuttling of German U-boats at the end of the Second World War. 231

scuttled during May 1945.

Restore Hope   Codename given to the December 1992 deployment of a US-led 35,000-strong multinational force in Somalia to ensure the safe delivery of international aid to Somalis who were starving as a result of the year-long civil war.

Rhine Exercise   The one and only cruise of the German battleship *Bismarck* from19 to 27 May 1941, when she sank in the Bay of Biscay.

Rhubarb   RAF Fighter Command sweeps over the English Channel and occupied French coastline from late 1940 onwards.

Richard   German plan for intervention in Spain in the event of a Republican victory in the Civil War.

Ring   Soviet operation to destroy encircled German 6th Army at Stalingrad in January 1943.

Rösselsprung (Knight's Move)   German attack on Tito's HQ, Hvar, Yugoslavia, 25 May 1944.

Rolling Thunder   Programme of sustained US bombing of North Vietnam mounted by administration of President Lyndon Johnson, March 1965–November 1968.

Rosario   Argentine invasion of the Falkland Islands on 3 April 1982.

Roundup   Allied plan to land in France between the Somme and the Seine (Dieppe and Le Havre) in spring 1943 by 30 US and 18 British divisions; replaced by Overlord.

Rumpelkammer (Junk Room)   German V1 campaign against UK 1944–5.

Rumyantsev   Soviet counter-offensive following Operation Citadel, August 1943, mounted at southern end of the Kursk salient.

Salmon Trap   Abortive German plan to cut Murmansk railway in 1942.

Sandstone   Codename for the US Army's nuclear testing series of 1948.

Schneesturm (Snowstorm)   German anti-partisan drive in Yugoslavia late 1943.

Scorcher   British occupation of Crete after withdrawal from Greece, May–June 1941.

Sea-Lion   Proposed German invasion of England in 1940.

Sextant   Cairo conference held just before and after the British–Soviet–US Tehran conference. At Cairo were US, British and Chinese heads of state, November and December 1943.

Sharp Guard   Nato-WEU restriction on shipping to the Federal Republic of Yugoslavia in 1994.

Sheepskin   Invasion of Anguilla in March 1969 by 300 British troops and 50 police to restore British rule from St Kitts-Nevis.

Shingle   Amphibious landing at Anzio, 22 January 1944, sealed off by Germans until Operation Diadem broke through the Gustav Line.

Sho Go (Victory)   Japanese defence plan in the summer of 1944, embracing several plans which could be put into effect once the axis of Allied advance became clear. Plan 1 provided for the defence of the Philippines, Plan 2 for the defence of Formosa and the Ryukyus, Plan 3 for the defence of Japan itself, Plan 4 for the defence of the Kuriles and Hokkaido. After Plan 1 was triggered, the Battle of Leyte Gulf ensued.

Shrapnel   Abortive British plan of 1940 to seize the Cape Verde Islands in the event of Spain entering the war on Germany's side and threatening Gibraltar.

Sickle   Cover name for the build-up of the US Eighth Air Force in Britain from 1942.

Slapstick British landing at Taranto on the heel of Italy and advance along the coast towards the German Gustav Line 9 September–30 November 1943.

Sledgehammer Proposed British–American contingency plan to invade Normandy and Brittany in Autumn 1942 if the Soviet Union appeared about to collapse.

Source British midget submarine attack on German battleship *Tirpitz*, 22 September 1943.

Spring Canadian breakout in Normandy July 1944, coordinated with Operations Goodwood and Cobra.

Starfish British deception plan early in the Second World War to simulate the effects of marker incendiaries dropped by bombers, and lure German bombers away from real targets.

Starkey Allied invasion practice in English Channel, September 1943, part of the Cockade deception plan.

Starvation US naval operation, launched in March 1945, to mine Japan's home waters.commenced March.

Steinadler German anti-partisan drive in Greece during July 1944.

Steinbock (Ibex) Luftwaffe bombing attacks on Britain in the spring of 1944.

Stosser German parachute operations during the Ardennes Offensive in 1944.

Strangle Air attacks destroying German communications in Italy before Operation Diadem in March 1944.

Student The German occupation of Rome in 1943. Part of Operation Black.

Sunrise Secret negotiations with the German command in Italy for surrender of German forces in May 1945.

Supercharge I British break-out in the 2nd Battle of El Alamein 2–4 November 1942.

Super-Gymnast Plan for an Allied landing in north-west Africa in 1942, which evolved into Operation Torch.

Symbol Anglo–American Casablanca Conference 14–23 January 1943.

Taxable RAF drop window off the Pas de Calais, as diversion for D-Day, 5–6 June 1944.

Terminal Allied conference at Potsdam 16 July to 2 August 1945.

Thunderbolt 3 July 1976, Israeli commando raid to release hostages from hijacked Palestinian terrorists to Entebbe. Thunderbolt was also codename in the Second World War for Luftwaffe cover for 'Cerberus'.

Thunderclap Plan favoured by 'Bomber' Harris for an all-out bombing assault on Germany, as a war winning *coup de grâce*, applied in particular to the bombing of Dresden in February 1945.

Tidal Wave USAAF bombing of the oil refineries at Ploesti, Romania, 1 August 1943.

Tiger British fast convoy loaded with war material which passed the length of the Mediterranean during May 1941, bringing tanks and fighter planes to the 8th Army in Egypt.

Torch Final codename for Allied landings in north-west Africa, 8 November 1942.

Totalize Normandy Operation of 7 Aug 1944, concerning Canadian attack towards Falaise, Normandy, aiming to link with US forces closing in from the south to trap German troops concentrated southward in the 'Falaise pocket'.

Tractable Canadian follow-up attack towards Falaise of 14 August 1944, an extension of Totalize.

Trident Anglo–American summit conference, Washington 12–25 May 1943. Operation Trident is also the name of a Metropolitan Police initiative begun in March 1998 to end a spate of shootings among the black communities in London.

Turquoise Codename for the French military operation in Rwanda launched on 23 June 1994 following the death in a plane crash of President Juvenal Habyarimana and the violence that followed.

Typhoon (Taifun) German push to capture Moscow, September–December 1941.

U Go Japanese drive on India, from Burma in March 1944.

UNOSOM II The aftermath of Operation Restore Hope in Somalia in 1994.

Uphold Democracy 19 September 1994, USA ousting of Haitian Junta in favour of exiled President Jean-Bertrand Aristide.

Uranus Soviet attack which trapped the Germans 6th Army in Stalingrad, November 1942.

Urgent Fury Codename for the military invasion of the Caribbean island of Grenada in October 1983 by 7,000 US Marines in order to rescue medical students embroiled in political chaos following the murder of PM Maurice Bishop by hardline Stalinists.

Valkyrie Codeword for anti-Nazi uprising planned to follow the failed assassination attempt on Adolf Hitler by Claus von Stauffenberg on 20 July 1944.

Varsity Airborne assault that accompanied Montgomery's crossing of the Rhine on 24 March 1945.

Velvet Unrealized offer made late in 1942, to base 20 Anglo–American air force squadrons in Soviet Caucasus.

Vengeance Assassination of Admiral Yamamoto, Japanese naval commander in chief, by American P-38 fighters on 18 April 1943.

Veritable Opening of the Allied Rhineland campaign on 8 February 1945 with Canadians driving south from Nijmegen in the Netherlands to capture land between the Rhine and Maas and so clear German troops from the west bank of the Upper Rhine.

Vittles US name for Berlin Airlift, 26 June 1948 to 30 September 1949.

Vulcan Final Allied offensive in Tunisia, 6 May 1943.

Warden RAF flights over northern Iraq, post Gulf War.

Watch on the Rhine The German counter-offensive in the Ardennes commencing 16 December 1944, aka the Battle of the Bulge.

Watchtower 7 August 1942, US capture of airstrip on Guadalcanal and the naval and seaplane base Tulagi in Solomon Isles, leading to a 6-month campaign to expel the Japanese from Guadalcanal.

Weiss 1 and 2 German anti-partisan drive in Bosnia, February 1943.

Weser Exercise The German invasion of Norway in April 1940.

Wilfred Proposed British plan to mine neutral Norwegian waters in April 1940, which was pre-empted by German invasion of Norway, though not before one minefield was laid.

Winter Storm General Von Manstein's unsuccessful operation to relieve Germany's encircled 6th Army at Stalingrad, December 1942.

Wolf German anti-partisan drive in Yugoslavia in the spring of 1944.

Zeppelin Abortive German plot to assassinate Stalin in July 1944.

Zipper   Projected British assault on Japanese-occupied Malaya in 1945, which was pre-empted by their surrender.

Zitadelle   German attack that led to the Battle of Kursk (central Russia) in July 1943. The largest tank battle in history.

Zorba   Codename for the ongoing investigation into Freemasonry within the Police Force.

General Information

aerobatics team: RAF   Red Arrows.

army: European country without one   Liechtenstein.

army: largest   China.

bugle calls   Reveille (first), Last Post (Penultimate), Lights Out (Last).

concentration camp: first   British in the Boer War.

decorations: highest UK civilian   George Cross.

decorations: highest UK military   Victoria Cross.

Foreign Legion   Founded by King Louis-Philippe (1831) as an aid to controlling French colonial possessions. The Legion's unofficial motto is *Legio Patria Nostra* (The Legion is Our Fatherland). Its monthly magazine is called *Képi Blanc* (White Kepi). Its HQ was formerly in Sidi Ben Abbas (Algeria) but is now in Aubagne, near Marseilles.

guards regiments   Grenadiers, Coldstream, Scots, Irish and Welsh.

home guard: original name   Local Defence Volunteers.

Household Cavalry regiments   Life Guards, Blues and Royals.

Marines: attached to   Admiralty (although classified as soldiers). The Royal Marines were founded in 1664.

Monty's double   Clifford James.

National Service   Commencing in 1947 and initially for men of 18+ and for a two-year term (lowered to 18 months); abolished in 1960. Last recruits passed out in 1962.

Officer Training School: Army   Sandhurst.

Officer Training School: Navy   Dartmouth.

Officer Training School: RAF   Cranwell.

Parachute Regiment: nickname   Red Devils.

private army: only force allowed in UK   Duke of Atholl Highlanders.

RAF: formed   Initially the Royal Flying Corps formed 13 May (1912) but amalgamated with the Royal Naval Air Service on 1 Apil 1918 to form the RAF.

salutes   Queen's Birthday 62 guns, opening of Parliament 42 guns.

SAS (Special Air Service): Founder   David Stirling.

Special Forces equivalents   Delta Force (US), SAS and SBS (Britain), Spetznaz (Russia).

US Air Force Academy (Colorado Springs)   Founded in 1954 and is the Officer Training School for the US Air Force.

US Marines: founded   1775.

US Military Academy (West Point)   Founded in 1802 and is the Officer Training School for the US Army.

US Naval Academy (Annapolis)   Founded in 1845 and is the Officer Training School for the US Navy and Marine Corps.

Victoria Cross: most won in a single action   Eleven at Rorke's Drift (22 January 1879) during the Zulu Wars.

M
I
L
I
T
A
R
Y

Comparative Ranks in the Armed Forces

Officers

Royal Navy	Army	RAF
Admiral of the Fleet	Field Marshal	Marshal of the Royal Air Force
Admiral	General	Air Chief Marshal
Vice-Admiral	Lieutenant-General	Air Marshal
Rear-Admiral	Major-General	Air Vice-Marshal
Commodore	Brigadier	Air Commodore
Captain	Colonel	Group Captain
Commander	Lieutenant-Colonel	Wing Commander
Lt-Commander	Major	Squadron Leader
Lieutenant	Captain	Flight Lieutenant
Sub-Lieutenant	Lieutenant	Flying Officer
Acting Sub-Lieutenant	Second Lieutenant	Pilot Officer

Noncommissioned Officers

Royal Navy	Army	RAF
Fleet Chief Petty Officer	Warrant Officer Class 1	Warrant Officer
	Warrant Officer Class 2	
Chief Petty Officer	Staff Sergeant	Flight Sergeant/Chief Technician
Petty Officer	Sergeant	Sergeant
Leading Rate	Corporal	Corporal
	Lance-Corporal	

Battles

Battle	War	Date	Details
Aachen	Second World War	21 Oct. 1944	Eight-day battle culminating in Allies capturing first major German city in the war.
Abensberg	Napoleonic Wars	20 Apr. 1809	French and Bavarians under Napoleon defeat Austrians under Archduke Charles.
Aberdeen	English Civil War	13 Sept. 1644	Royalists under marquis of Montrose defeated the Covenanters under Lord Burleigh.
Aboukir Bay/Nile	French Revolutionary Wars	1 Aug. 1798	Nelson destroyed 11 French ships in harbour, nullifying Napoleon's Egyptian land successes.
Abraham, Plains of	Seven Years' War	13 Sept. 1759	British secured Quebec; British and French leaders' James Wolfe and Marquis de Montcalm, were killed.
Actium	Second Triumvirate War	2 Sept. 31 BC	Octavia defeated Antony and Cleopatra on a promontory in Acarnania, Greece.
Adrianople	Roman/Visigoth War	9 Aug 378 AD	The Visigoth Fritigern defeated Romans led by Emperor Valens.
Adowa/Adwa	Italian Invasion of Ethiopia	1 Mar. 1896	King Menelik II's decisive defeat of General Baratieri forced Treaty of Addis Ababa on Italy, October 1896.
Adwalton Moor	English Civil War	30 June 1643	Royalists under the earl of Newcastle defeated Lord Fairfax's parliamentarians.
Aegospotami	Peloponnesian War	405 BC	The final battle of the Peloponnesian War in which the fleets of the two Greek rival powers fought a sea battle in the Hellespont and the Spartan leader Lysander using better tactics eventually defeated the Athenians under Conon.
Agincourt	Hundred Years' War	25 Oct. 1415	Henry V's archers laid foundations for defeat of French, under Constable Charles d'Albret.
Alamo	Texan/Mexican War	6 Mar. 1836	Col. Travis, Jim Bowie and Davy Crockett were among 183 Texans killed by Santa Anna's Mexican troops.
Åland	Great Northern War	July 1714	Russian fleet under Apraksin and Peter the Great defeated the Swedes under Ehrenskjold.
Alarcos	Spanish/Muslim Wars	18 July 1195	Moors under Yakub el Mansur defeated Spaniards under Alfonso VIII of Castile.
Aleppo	Tatar Invasion of Syria	11 Nov. 1400	Tatars under Tamerlane defeated Turks under the Syrian Emirs.
Alesia	Gallic Wars	c. 52 BC	Romans under Julius Caesar defeated Gauls under Vercingetorix.
Alexandria	British invasion of Egypt	21 Mar 1801	British under Sir Ralph Abercromby (killed) defeated French under General Menou.
Algeciras Bay	French Revolutionary Wars	8 July 1801	Two sea battles between British under Saumarez and French under Linois; the first was indecisive but the second won a victory for Saumarez.
Alicante	War of Spanish Succession	29 June 1706	Admiral Sir George Byng commanded a fleet of 5 ships that attacked the city walls causing severe damage.
Aliwal	First Anglo-Sikh War	28 Jan. 1846	General Sir Harry Smith led a joint British/Indian force to victory against Sikhs.
Alkmaar	Eighty Years' War	8 Oct. 1573	Siege was laid, 21 August 1573, by 1,000 Spaniards but Dutch defended successfully.
Alma	Crimean War	20 Sept. 1854	Indecisive battle between Russian and a joint British/French/Turkish army.
Alnwick	Anglo-Scottish Wars	13 Nov. 1093	Malcolm Canmore, king of Scotland, and his son Edward were both slain.
Alsen	Schleswig-Holstein War	29 June 1864	In this last engagement of the war, the Prussians defeated the Danes.
Amphipolis	Peloponnesian War	422 BC	Indecisive attempt by the Athenians under Cleon to recapture Amphipolis from the Spartans.
Ankara	Ottoman Wars	20th July 1402	Mongols under Tamerlane defeated Ottomans under the sultan Bayezid I.
Antietam	US Civil War	17 Sept. 1862	A decisive battle that halted the Confederates in their advance on Maryland.
Antioch	First Crusade	3 June 1098	Siege started on 21 October 1097; Saracens held out against crusaders for 7 months.
Antwerp	Eighty Years' War	4 Nov. 1576	Known as the Spanish Fury; Sancho d'Avila's Spaniards slaughtered 8,000 Walloons.

Battle	War	Date	Details
Anzio	Second World War	22 Jan. 1944	A surprise landing near Rome by nearly 50,000 British/American troops.
Appomattox	US Civil War	9 Apr. 1865	Confederate army was surrounded in the Court House and Lee surrendered to Grant.
Arausio	Teutonic Wars	105 BC	Germanic tribes defeated Romans under Quintus Servilius Caepio and Gnaeus Mallius Maximus.
Arbela	Alexander's Asiatic Wars	1 Oct. 331 BC	Macedonians defeated Persians under Darius, making Alexander master of Asia.
Arcot	Carnatic War	Aug. 1751	Robert Clive captured fortress and held it for 7 weeks, delaying French advance in India.
Ardennes	Second World War	16 Jan. 1945	Aka Battle of the Bulge (coined by Churchill), the last German offensive on the Western Front.
Armada	Anglo-Spanish War	July 1588	Spanish Armada of 130 ships defeated by English fleet of 197, under Lord Howard.
Arnhem	Second World War	17 Sept. 1944	While airborne US troops secured bridges over Maas and Waal, British Arnhem landing severely defeated.
Arques	French Religious Wars	21 Sept. 1589	Henry of Navarre, later King Henry IV, led Huguenots to victory against Catholic League.
Arsuf	Third Crusade	7 Sept. 1191	King Richard I gained notable tactical victory against the Saracens.
Ascalon/Ashqelon	First Crusade	19 Aug. 1099	Crusaders under Godefroi de Bouillon gained a victory against Saracens under Kilidj Arslan.
Ashdown	Danish invasion of Britain	8 Jan. 871	King Ethelred of Wessex aided by Alfred the Great defeated the Danes.
Ashingdon	Danish invasion of Britain	18 Oct. 1016	Canute of Denmark defeated Edmund Ironside which led to him becoming King.
Aspern	Napoleonic Wars	22 May 1809	French retreated to the island of Lobau in the Danube; they had few supplies and Napoleon rejected his generals' advice to retreat. Napoleon's first defeat, by an Austrian army.
Aughrim	War of English Succession	12 July 1691	William III's army led by Godert de Ginkel scattered a Jacobite army in Galway.
Auldearn	English Civil War	9 May 1645	Royalists under the marquis of Montrose defeated Covenanters east of Nairn.
Austerlitz	Napoleonic Wars	2 Dec. 1805	Aka Battle of the Three Emperors (Russian, French, Austrian). Napoleon defeated Kutuzov.
Bāhādurpur	Mughal Civil War	24 Feb 1658	Conflict between the four sons of Shāh Jehan, Mughal emperor of India, over the succession. The shah's second son, Shujā, set himself up as the governor of Bengal but was defeated in battle by the son of Dārā Shikoh, the eldest son of Shah Jehan. The third son, Aurangzeb, later executed his nephew, Sulaymān Shikoh.
Balaclava	Crimean War	25 Oct. 1854	Allied victory over the Russians, but disastrous charge of British Light Brigade prompted General Bosquet to say 'This is not war.'
Ball's Bluff	US Civil War	21 Oct. 1861	Confederates under General Evans defeated Union army under General Stone.
Baltimore	War of 1812	11 Sept. 1814	British under General Ross (killed) defeated Americans under General Winder.
Bannockburn	Scottish Independence	24 June 1314	Robert the Bruce defeated English invaders under King Edward II.
Barāri Ghāt	Afghan-Marāthā War	9 Jan. 1760	Afghan army under Ahmad Shāh Durrāni defeated the Marāthās under Dattāji Sindhia (died).
Barnet	Wars of the Roses	14 Apr. 1471	Yorkists under King Edward IV defeated Lancastrians under earl of Warwick (killed).
Beachy Head	War of English Succession	29–30 June 1690	English and Dutch under Lord Torrington defeated by French under Tourville.
Belleau Wood	First World War	6 June 1918	First major US – German clash of the war, a hard-won victory by General Bundy over Ludendorff.
Bellevue	Franco-Prussian War	18 Oct. 1870	Marshal Bazaine was driven back from Metz by Germans.
Berwick	Scottish Independence	28 Mar. 1296	Edward I's troops killed thousands after John de Balliol's refusal to supply men for Gascon War.
Beymaroo	First British-Afghan War	23 Nov.1841	General Elphinstone allowed only 1 gun for Brigadier Shelton to dislodge Afghans.

Battle	War	Date	Details
Bismarck	Second World War	27 May 1941	After sinking the cruiser *Hood*, Lutjens' battleship was sunk near Brest by British torpedo planes and warships.
Blenheim	War of Spanish Succession	13 Aug. 1704	Duke of Marlborough and Eugene of Savoy defeated French under Marshal Tallard in Bavarian town.
Blood River	Afrikaner-Zulu War	16 Dec. 1838	Zulus under King Dingaan (Dingane) were routed by the Transvaal Boers.
Blore Heath	Wars of the Roses	23 Sept. 1459	Yorkists under the earl of Salisbury dispersed Lancastrians under Lord Audley.
Borodino	Napoleonic Wars	7 Sept. 1812	Napoleon paved the way for his triumphant march on Moscow by defeating Kutuzov.
Bosworth Field	Wars of the Roses	21 Aug. 1485	Henry, Duke of Richmond, later Henry VII, defeated and killed Richard III to end wars.
Boudicca	Roman invasion of Britain	AD 61	Suetonius routed Queen Boudicca of the Iceni, who took poison on the battlefield.
Boyne	War of English Succession	1 July 1690	Decisive battle of the war; William III defeated James II.
Brandywine	US War of Independence	11 Sept. 1777	British under General Howe forced George Washington's troops to retreat.
Breitenfeld	Thirty Years' War	17 Sept. 1631	First major Protestant victory of the war, in which the Roman Catholic Habsburg emperor Ferdinand II and the Catholic League under Johan Isaclaes Graf von Tilly were defeated by the Swedish-Saxon army under King Gustavus II Adolphus of Sweden.
Brill	Eighty Years' War	1 Apr. 1572	De La Marck's *Wetergeuzen* (sea beggars) took Dutch port from Spain to gain first Dutch victory of war.
Britain	Second World War	June 1940 –Apr. 1941	German air raids intended to prepare for invasion of Britain but repulsed by RAF
Bronkhurst Spruit	First Boer War	20 Dec. 1880	Opening engagement of the war, a British column of 259 was ambushed and defeated.
Bull Run (Manassas) (First)	US Civil War	21July 1861	Beauregard defeated McDowell's Union army, Confederate General Jackson gained nickname 'Stonewall'.
Bull Run (Manassas) (Second)	US Civil War	29–30 Aug. 1862	Confederates Lee and Jackson routed troops under General Pope.
Bunker Hill	US War of Independence	17 June 1775	British troops under Howe gained Breed's Hill and Bunker Hill but suffered heavy losses.
Burlington Heights	War of 1812	5 May 1813	British under Col. Proctor attacked by Clay but eventually gained the day.
Bussaco	Peninsular War	27 Sept. 1810	Wellington defeated pursuing French army under Marshals Massna and Ney.
Buxar/Baksar	British/Bengal War	23 Oct.1764	Major Munro's victory over a confederation of Indian pirates gave the East India Company control of Bengal and Bihar.
Cadiz	Anglo-Spanish War	29 Apr. 1587	Drake destroyed over 100 ships in his famous singeing of the Spanish king's beard.
Caer Caradoc	Roman invasion of Britain	50 AD	Romans under Ostorius Scapula defeated Caratacus, king of the British tribe of Trinovantes.
Calais	Anglo-French Wars	6 Jan. 1558	Last English stronghold in France lost, causing Mary I to say 'When I am dead and opened, you shall find Calais will be writ on my heart'.
Cambodia	Vietnamese invasion	7 Jan. 1979	Vietnamese army captured Phnom Penh and formed People's Republic of Kampuchea.
Cambrai	First World War	20 Nov.– 7 Dec. 1917	Brig.-Gen. Elles led world's first massed tank attack: dramatic breakthrough but soon reversed.
Camden	US War of Independence	16 Aug. 1780	British under Cornwallis defeated Americans under General Gates.
Camperdown	French Revolutionary Wars	11 Oct.1797	British fleet under Duncan intercepted and routed a Dutch convoy on its way to support a French invasion of Ireland.
Campo Santo	War of Austrian Succession	8 Feb. 1743	Indecisive battle between Spaniards under Mortemar and Imperialists under Count Traum.
Camulodunum	Second Roman invasion of Britain	c. 43 AD	Romans under Emperor Claudius accepted surrender of local tribes after defeat on the Medway.

Battle	War	Date	Details
Cannae	Second Punic War	3 Aug. 216 BC	Hannibal gained a devastating victory over Romans under Varro due to superior cavalry.
Cape Matapan	Second World War	28 Mar. 1941	Small British fleet sank six or seven Italian ships off Cape Matapan, Greece (aka Cape Tainaron).
Cape St Vincent	French Revolutionary Wars	14 Feb. 1797	Spaniards were totally defeated by fleet of Sir John Jervis, who was made earl of St Vincent.
Carabobo	Latin American Wars	24 June 1921	South American rebels under Antonio Simon Bolivar defeated Spanish royalists under General La Torre.
Carbisdale	English Civil War	27 Apr. 1650	Marquis of Montrose captured by parliamentary force and executed the following month.
Carchemish	Syrian War	605 BC	Babylonian troops led by Crown Prince Nebuchadrezzar II captured Carchemish from the Egyptians.
Carlisle	Jacobite Rebellion of '45	9 Nov. 1745	Young Pretender, Charles Edward Stuart, Bonny Prince Charlie, defeated duke of Cumberland.
Carrhae	Roman/Mesopotamia War	53 BC	Romans under Marcus Licinius Crassus (killed) invaded Mesopotamia but were defeated by the Parthians.
Carrical	Seven Years' War	2 Aug. 1758	British under Admiral Pocock defeated French under Comte d'Ache but with little gains.
Cartagena	War of Austrian Succession	9 Mar. 1741	Port blockaded by British under Admiral Vernon but extensive losses forced his withdrawal.
Cassino	Second World War	Jan./May 1944	Fierce and protracted battle during which Allies blew up the Benedictine monastery, 15 February, believing it to be German-occupied.
Castillon	Hundred Years' War	17 July 1453	John Talbot, earl of Shrewsbury, was killed, and the English lost Gascony, in the last battle of the war.
Cedar Creek	US Civil War	19 Oct. 1864	Union General Sheridan defeated Confederates under General Early.
Cedar Mountain	US Civil War	9 Aug. 1862	Union Corps under Banks attacked Confederates under Jackson but forced to withdraw.
Cerignola	Franco-Spanish Wars	28 Apr. 1503	Spanish under Cordoba defeated French troops under Louis XII.
Chaeronea	Philippan Campaigns	338 BC	Macedonian army under Philip II defeated the joint Theban/Athenian army.
Chaldiran	Ottoman Wars	23 Aug.1514	Ottomans under Sultan Selim I defeated Safavid army under Shah Esma'il northeast of Lake Van.
Chalons	Attila Conquests	451 AD	Aka Battle of the Catalaunian Plains. Joint force of Romans and Visigoths defeated the Huns under Attila.
Chevy Chase	Scottish Independence	15 Aug. 1388	Aka Otterburn. Henry Percy's (Hotspurs) superior forces were soundly beaten by Scots.
Chickahominy	US Civil War	3 June 1864	General Lee's Confederates soundly repulsed Union attacks under Grant.
Chippenham	Danish Invasion of Britain	Jan. 878	Danes under Guthrum attacked King Alfred on 12th Night; he was forced to hide at Athelney.
Chongju	Russo-Japanese War	Apr. 1904	First land battle of war; Cossacks were driven back with few losses.
Chorillos	Peruvian-Chilean War	13 Jan. 1861	Chileans comprehensively defeated Peruvians.
Christianople	Danish-Swedish Wars	Autumn 1611	First military exploit of the 16-year-old King Gustavus Adolphus of Sweden was a total success.
Chrysler's Farm	War of 1812	11 Nov. 1813	British under Colonel Morrison defeated Americans under General Boyd.
Cold Harbour	US Civil War	3 June 1864	Grant's frontal attack on entrenched Confederate forces repulsed but counter-assault was disastrously defeated by Lee.
Colenso	Second Boer War	15 Dec. 1899	Sir Redvers Buller's first move to relieve Ladysmith repelled by Gen. Botha.
Copenhagen	French Revolutionary Wars	2 Apr. 1801	Nelson turned his blind eye to Admiral Hyde Parker's signal to retire and gained the day.
Coral Sea	Second World War	8 May 1942	Naval conflict fought mainly by aircraft from carriers. US carrier *Lexington* lost, but Japanese withdrew.
Coronel	First World War	1 Nov. 1914	Von Spee's *Scharnhorst* and *Gneisenau* sank the British ships *Monmouth* and *Good Hope*.

Battle	War	Date	Details
Corunna	Peninsular War	16 Jan. 1809	French under Marshal Soult defeated by British under Sir John Moore (killed).
Crécy	Hundred Years' War	26 Aug. 1346	Edward III's archers and cannon defeated French cavalry under Philip VI.
Cropredy Bridge	English Civil War	29 June 1644	Royalists under Charles I defeated Sir William Waller's parliamentarians near Banbury.
Cross Keys	US Civil War	8 June 1862	Confederates under Ewell fought successful rearguard action against Fremonts' Federals.
Cuba	Castro Revolt	26 July 1953	Fidel and Raul Castro led unsuccessful raid on armoury at Santiago and were imprisoned.
Culloden	Jacobite Rebellion of '45	16 Apr. 1746	Aka Drumossie Moor. Duke of Cumberland earned epithet 'Butcher' for treatment of Jacobite Rebels after his crushing victory.
Custoza (First)	Italian War of Independence	24 July 1848	Crushing defeat for the forces of Charles Albert, king of Sardinia-Piedmont by the Austrian veteran Field Marshal Joseph Radetzky.
Custoza (Second)	Italian War of Independence	24 June 1866	An 80,000-man Austrian army under Archduke Albert defeated a 120,000-man Italian army under Victor Emmanuel II.
Cyprus	Turkish Invasion	20 July 1974	Turkey invaded northern Cyprus and established a beachhead around Kyrenia.
D-Day	Second World War	6 June 1944	The launching of Operation Overlord, the Allied Invasion of Normandy, was a major turning point of the war.
Dettingen	War of Austrian Succession	27 June 1743	Anglo-Austrian-German victory over French; the last occasion that a British sovereign (George II) led his troops into battle.
Diamond Hill	Second Boer War	11 June 1900	Lord Roberts attacked General Botha near Pretoria and drove him from his position.
Dien Bien Phu	French-Vietnamese War	13 Mar.–7 May 1954	General Giap's siege and capture of key stronghold ended power in Indochina and French caused partition of Vietnam.
Dieppe	Second World War	19 Aug. 1942	Daytime Allied raid testing German Atlantic defences; 2nd Canadian Division suffered terrible losses.
Dingaan's Day	Afrikaner-Zulu War	16 Dec. 1838	Zulus under Dingaan were routed by the Transvaal Boers.
Dominica	US War of Independence	12 Apr. 1782	Aka Battle of Les Saintes. Admiral Rodney defeated French fleet, preserved British hold on Jamaica.
Dorylaeum	First Crusade	1 July 1097	Victory for Crusaders under Bohemond and Raymond of Toulouse over Seljuk Turks.
Douro	Peninsular War	12 May 1809	Wellington crossed the Douro and drove Marshal Soult's French troops out of Oporto.
Dover	Anglo-Dutch Wars	29 Nov. 1652	Dutch fleet under van Tromp victorious over Admiral Blake's English fleet at Dover and at Dungeness shortly after.
Dresden	Napoleonic Wars	26 Aug. 1813	Napoleon victorious over Russians, Prussians and Austrians.
Ebro River	Spanish Civil War	July-Nov. 1938	General Franco's Nationalists won a counter-offensive against Republicans under Modesto.
Edgecote	Wars of the Roses	26 July 1469	Lancastrian victory over Yorkists under the earl of Pembroke.
Edgehill	English Civil War	24 Oct. 1642	Indecisive first battle of Civil War between Charles I and parliamentarians under earl of Essex.
El Alamein	Second World War	Oct.-Nov. 1942	Montgomery's 8th Army drove Germans out of Egypt.
Elands River	Second Boer War	4 Aug. 1900	Australians under Col. Hore held out under fire until relieved by Kitchener.
Empingham	Wars of the Roses	12 Mar. 1470	Aka Losecoat Field. King Edward IV routed Sir Robert Welles's rebels.
Entholm	Northern Wars	11 June 1676	Swedes were defeated by Danish fleet under Admiral van Tromp.
Erbach	French Revolutionary Wars	15 May 1800	French under Sainte-Suzanne held out against Austrians under General Baron Kray.
Evesham	Second Barons' War	4 Aug. 1265	Prince Edward defeated the Barons, killed Simon de Montfort and restored Henry III.
Eylau	Napoleonic Wars	7–8 Feb. 1807	Indecisive battle between French troops under Napoleon and a joint Russian and Prussian army under Leonty Leontyevich Bennigsen.

Battle	War	Date	Details
Falkirk (First)	Scottish Independence	22 July 1298	English under Edward I defeated Scots under Sir William Wallace, who became a fugitive.
Falkirk (Second)	Jacobite Rebellion of '45	17 Jan. 1746	Jacobite army under Charles Edward Stuart (Young Pretender) defeated royalist forces under Henry Hawley.
Falkland Islands	First World War	8 Dec. 1914	Sturdee's squadron sank most of German Pacific squadron under von Spee (died).
Falkland Islands	British-Argentine War	2 Apr. 1982	Argentinian armed forces under General Galtieri invaded Falklands. On 3 April South Georgia was taken and on 5 April Rear Adm. Sandy Woodward led task force to free islands. On May 2 the *General Belgrano* was sunk by the sub *Conqueror*, and on 4 May the Destroyer *Sheffield* was hit and sank on 10 May. On 21 May 5000 troops under Major-Gen. Jeremy Moore went ashore at Port San Carlos, and Argentinian surrender terms were eventually signed on 14 June, 10 weeks and 3 days after invasion.
Ferrybridge	Wars of the Roses	28 Mar. 1461	Lancastrians under Lord Clifford defeated Yorkists under Lord Fitzwalter (killed).
Fisher's Hill	US Civil War	22 Sept. 1864	Union force under Sheridan defeated Confederates under General Early.
Five Forks	US Civil War	1 Apr.1865	Sheridan and Warren defeated Pickett's Confederates causing Lee's withdrawal from Richmond and surrender at Appomattox on 9 April.
Flodden	Anglo-Scottish Wars	9 Sept. 1513	English under the earl of Surrey (Thomas Howard) defeated Scots under James IV (killed).
Fontenoy	War of Austrian Succession	11 May 1745	French under Marshal de Saxe repulsed duke of Cumberland's abortive drive to relieve Tournai.
Formigny	Hundred Years' War	15 Apr. 1450	French under the comte de Clermont defeated English under Kyrielle restoring Normandy to France.
Fort Frontenac	Seven Years' War	27 Aug. 1758	Colonel Bradstreet defeated French under Noyan, who lost control of Lake Ontario.
Gebora	Peninsular War	19 Feb. 1811	Spaniards under Mendizabal were routed by French under Marshal Soult.
Gettysburg	US Civil War	1–3 July 1863	Greatest battle of the war between Meade's army of the Potomac and Lee's army of Virginia. Only a narrow Union victory, but it stopped Lee's invasion of the North.
Gibraltar	War of Spanish Succession	24 July 1704	British and Dutch fleet under Sir George Rooke defeated Spanish under marquis de Salinas and took Gibraltar.
Gitschin	Seven Weeks' War	29 June 1866	Prussians under Prince Frederick Charles defeated Austrians and Saxons under Clam-Gallas.
Glorious 1st of June	French Revolutionary Wars	1 June 1794	Aka Ushant. British under Lord Howe defeated French and sank the *Vengeur*.
Golden Spurs	Flemish War	11 July 1302	Aka Courtrai. Untrained Flemish guild workers defeated French cavalry in Flanders and took their spurs as a trophy of their victory.
Graf Spee	Second World War	17 Dec. 1939	The pride of the German fleet, the pocket battle ship *Graf Spee* was scuttled by Captain Hans Langsdorf after being harried by three British cruisers *Achilles*, *Ajax* and *Exeter* and forced into Montevideo harbour. The Uruguayan government ordered the ship to sea but, rather than face a certain defeat, Hitler himself ordered the scuttling and Langsdorf shot himself.
Granada	Moorish Wars	Jan. 1492	Moors under Boabdil were defeated and the city came under Catholic rule of Ferdinand II of Aragon and Isabella I of Castille.
Grant's Hill	Seven Years' War	14 Sept. 1758	Major Grant with 800 Highlanders defeated by French under de Ligneris at Fort Duquesne.
Gravelines	Franco-Spanish Wars	13 July 1558	Spanish under comte d'Egmont, backed by an English fleet, defeated French under Marshal de Thermes.

Battle	War	Date	Details
Guadalajara	Spanish Civil War	8 Mar. 1937	Republicans defeated Nationalists under Franco and Italian Fascists under General Roatta.
Guadalcanal	First World War	Aug. 1942–Jan 1943	Americans eventually gained victory over Japanese after 5 months' fighting on land and sea.
Guadeloupe	Second World War	3 July 1794	Sir John Jervis captured island but it was recaptured by the French on 10 December.
Guilford Courthouse	US War of Independence	15 Mar. 1781	British under Lord Cornwallis defeated Americans under General Greene.
Halidon Hill	Scottish Independence	19 July 1333	English troops under Edward III defeated Scottish forces attempting to relieve Berwick-upon-Tweed.
Han Ko/Hangö	Great Northern War	4–6 Aug. 1714	Peter the Great commanded a fleet against Swedes, the first major Russian victory at sea.
Harfleur	Hundred Years' War	Aug.–Sept. 1415	English under Henry V defeated the French troops after a 6-week siege of the port.
Harpers Ferry	US Civil War	15 Sept. 1862	Confederates under General Thomas Stonewall Jackson forced Union garrison to surrender.
Hastings	Norman Conquest	14 Oct. 1066	Aka Battle of Senlac Hill. Harold II of England (killed) defeated by William, duke of Normandy.
Hedgeley Moor	Wars of the Roses	25 Apr. 1464	Yorkist Lord Montagu routed Lancastrians under Margaret of Anjou and Ralph Percy (killed).
Heligoland	Napoleonic Wars	31 Aug. 1807	British squadron under Admiral Thomas Russell captured island from Danes.
Heligoland Bight	First World War	28 Aug. 1914	Admiral Beatty's battle cruiser *Lion* sank the German cruisers *Mainz* and *Koln*.
Heliopolis	French Revolutionary Wars	20 Mar. 1800	Turks in Egypt under Ibrahim Bey routed by French under General Kléber.
Herrings	Hundred Years War	12 Feb. 1429	Sir John Fastolfe defeated the comte de Clermont at Rouvray.
Hexham	Wars of the Roses	15 May 1464	Yorkists under Lord Montagu defeated and executed duke of Somerset.
Homildon Hill	Scottish Independence	14 Sept. 1402	English troops under Sir Henry Percy (Hotspur) defeated the Scots under the 4th earl of Douglas.
Hydaspes	Alexander's Asiatic Wars	326 BC	Fourth and last pitched battle fought by Alexander the Great during his Asiatic Campaign. Despite overwhelming numerical superiority of the Persian army led by Porus, and the 200 elephants that Porus had at his disposal, Alexander's tactical genius won the day.
Hyderabad	Conquest of Sind	24 Mar. 1843	British under Sir Charles Napier defeated Baluchis under Shir Mohammed.
Ilipa	Second Punic War	206 BC	Romans under Publius Cornelius Scipio (Africanus) defeated Carthaginians under Hasdrubal. Gisco and Mago in the Spanish town near Seville.
Imola	French Revolutionary Wars	3 Feb. 1797	French and Italian troops under Marshal Victor defeated Papal troops under General Colli.
Imphal	Second World War	29 Mar. 1944	Japanese troops besieged the city of Imphal in Assam, north-east India.
Inchon	Korean War	15 Sept. 1950	Amphibious landing by General Almond's X Corps drove the North Korean troops inland and seized Kimpo airfield.
Ingogo River	First Boer War	8 Feb. 1881	Boers defeated a small British column of 5 companies, 4 guns and a mounted force.
Inhlobane Mountain	Zulu War	28 Mar. 1879	British force of 1,300 under Cols Buller and Russell defeated by Zulus.
Inkerman	Crimean War	5 Nov. 1854	Russians under Prince Menshikov defeated by Franco-British troops under Raglan.
Ipsus	Macedonian-Egyptian War	301 BC	The combined forces of Lysimachus king of Thrace and Seleucus I Nicator of Babylon defeated the Macedonian army under Antigonus (killed) and his son Demetrius.
Isandhlwana	Zulu War	22 Jan. 1879	Six companies of 24th Regiment under Col. Durnford overwhelmed by Zulus under Matyana.
Issus	Alexander's Asiatic War	333 BC	Alexander the Great defeated Persians under King Darius.

Battle	War	Date	Details
Ivry	French Religious Wars	14 Mar. 1590	Henry IV's Huguenots defeated Catholic League under duc de Mayenne.
Iwo Jima	Second World War	19 Feb. 1945	General Schmidt's US V Amphibious Corps assaulted and secured the small island (8 sq miles) by 26 March.
Jajau	Mughal Civil War	12 June 1707	Family conflict to decide the successor to the Mughal emperor Aurangzeb; eventually his eldest surviving son Bahādur Shāh succeeded after a bloody battle with his brother Azam Shāh.
Jarnac	French Religious Wars	13 Mar. 1569	Catholics under the duke of Anjou defeated Huguenots under the prince de Condé.
Jena	Napoleonic Wars	14 Oct. 1806	Napoleon defeated the prince of Hohenlohe's Prussian army.
Jutland	First World War	31 May 1916	(Aka Skagerrak) Only major clash betwen British and German fleets in the war. British lost two ships, but German High Seas fleet did not seek battle thereafter.
Kadesh	Egyptian/Hittite War	1299 BC	Seeking to recapture the Syrian city of Kadesh, Ramses II engaged the Hittite leader Muwatallis without success and was forced to retreat; the Hittites moving southward into Damascus.
Kambula	Zulu War	29 Mar. 1879	British under Colonel Wood defeated Zulus under Cetewayo.
Karbalā	Muslim Wars	10 Oct. 680	Husayn ibn Ali, grandson of the Prophet Muhammad was defeated and killed by an army sent by the Umayyad Caliph Yazid I.
Karnāl	Mughal Civil Wars	24 Feb. 1739	Persian forces under Nāder Shāh defeated the Mughals under Emperor Muhammad Shāh.
Kemendine	First Burma War	10 June 1824	British under Sir Archibald Campbell defeated Burmese troops.
Khartoum	British-Sudan Campaign	26 Jan. 1885	General Gordon killed defending the city against the Mahdi after Beresford's troops were delayed.
Killiecrankie	Jacobite Rising	27 July 1689	Highland Jacobites under 'Bonny' Dundee defeated William III's troops under General Mackay, but Dundee's death undid the victory.
Kilsyth	English Civil War	15 Aug. 1645	Royalists under marquis of Montrose defeated Covenanters under General Baillie.
Kimberley	Second Boer War	15 Oct. 1899	Gen. French relieved town on 15 Feb. 1900 from Boer siege led by General Cronje.
Kioge	Northern War	July 1677	Danish fleet under Admiral Juel defeated Swedes under Admiral Horn.
Kissingen	Seven Weeks War	10 July 1866	Prussians under General Falkstein defeated Bavarians under General Zoller.
Kiu-lien-Cheng	Russo-Japanese War	1 May 1904	Japanese under Marshal Kuroki defeated Russians under General Sassulitch.
Königgrätz	Seven Weeks War	3 July 1866	Aka Battle of Sadowa. Decisive battle of the conflict in which Helmuth von Moltke's Prussian army defeated the Austrian army led by General Benedek, which led to Austria's exclusion from a Prussian-dominated Germany. The war was formally concluded on 23 August 1866 by the Treaty of Prague. Bismarck's alliance with Italy meant Venetia was ceded to the Italians.
Kosovo	Byzantine Wars	June 1389	Battle fought at Kosovo Polje (Field of the Blackbirds) between Serbs under Prince Lazar and Turks under Sultan Murad I, who gained a hard-fought victory.
Kursk Salient	Second World War	5–13 July 1943	Largest tank battle of the war, in which Russians smashed massive German offensive.
Ladysmith	Second Boer War	2 Nov. 1899	Sir George White defended against Boers until Redvers Buller relieved town 27 Feb. 1900.
Laings Nek	First Boer War	28 Jan. 1881	British under Gen Colley repulsed by Boers.
Lake Erie	War of 1812	10 Sept. 1813	Master Commandant Oliver Hazard Perry's fleet of 9 ships engaged 6 British warships under Captain Robert Heriot Barclay and although having to transfer from his flagship

MILITARY

Battle	War	Date	Details
			Lawrence to its sister ship *Niagara*, Perry sailed directly into the British line and firing broadsides as he went eventually forced the British to surrender.
Lake Trasimeno	Second Punic War	217 BC	The Carthaginian General Hannibal defeated the Roman army under Gaius Flaminius (killed) on the north shore of the Italian lake.
Landau	War of Spanish Succession	29 July 1702	French under de Melac lost the fortress to Prince Louis of Baden.
Langport	English Civil War	10 July 1645	Parliamentarians under Thomas Fairfax defeated Royalists under Lord Goring.
Langside	Anti-Marian Uprising	13 May 1568	Mary Queen of Scots's army was defeated by earl of Moray; Mary escaped to England.
Lansdowne	English Civil War	5 July 1643	Royalists under Sir Ralph Hopton defeated parliamentarians under Sir William Waller.
La Rochelle	Hundred Years' War	1372	A Castilian fleet under Bocanegra, acting in support of the French, defeated the English under Pembroke.
Lauffeld	War of Austrian Succession	2 July 1747	French under Marshal Saxe defeated allied Austrian and British army under Cumberland.
Leck	Thirty Years' War	5 Apr. 1632	Gustavus Adolphus's Swedish/German army defeated Imperialists under Tilly (mortally wounded).
Leghorn	Anglo-Dutch Wars	31 Mar. 1653	Admiral Van Gelen (killed) destroyed 6 English ships commanded by Commodore Appleton.
Leipzig	Napoleonic Wars	16–19 Oct. 1813	Napoleon defeated, and forced into decisive retreat, by Coalition of Blücher, Schwarzenberg and Bernadotte.
Le Mans	Franco-Prussian War	10–11 Jan. 1871	French under Chanzy were completely routed by Germans under Prince Frederick Charles.
Leningrad	Second World War	15 Jan. 1944	(Now St Petersburg) Russians relieved the 30-month blockade of the city after 5 days' fighting.
Lepanto	Cyprus War	7 Oct. 1571	Last major battle using oared ships brought decisive victory for the Holy League fleet under Don John of Austria over Ottoman Turks.
Leuctra	Boeotian-Athenian War	371 BC	Boeotian army under Epaminondas defeated a Spartan army under King Cleombrotus.
Lewes	English Barons' War	14 May 1264	Simon de Montfort defeated Henry III and Prince Edward and signed the Mise of Lewes.
Lexington	US War of Independence	19 Apr. 1775	First battle of the war resulted in minor victory for British troops under Lt-Col. Francis Smith.
Leyte Gulf	Second World War	24–26 Oct. 1944	Biggest ever naval battle. United States defeated Japanese comprehensively, losing 6 ships to Japan's 28.
Liaoyang	Russo-Japanese War	25 Aug.–3 Sept. 1904	Japanese army under Marshal Oyama forced Russians under General Kuropatkin to retreat.
Lille	War of Spanish Succession	12 Aug. 1708	French under Marshal de Boufflers surrendered to Prince Eugene on 25 Oct. 1708.
Lindley	Second Boer War	27 May 1900	Colonel Spragge surrendered to superior Boer force.
Little Bighorn	Sioux Rising	25 June 1876	Col. Custer (killed) and his 7th US Cavalry wiped out by Sioux and Cheyenne warriors under Sitting Bull.
Loudoun Hill	Scottish Independence	10 May 1307	Robert the Bruce defeated earl of Pembroke's cavalry by his spearmen's steadfastness.
Lucknow	Indian Mutiny	June–Nov. 1857	Siege relieved by General Sir Colin Campbell.
Lundy's Lane	War of 1812	25 July 1814	Americans under General Brown unsuccessfully attacked British under Sir George Drummond.
Lutzen	Thirty Years' War	16 Nov. 1632	Indecisive battle in which Gustavus II Adolphus of Sweden lost his life while engaging the Habsburg forces of Albrecht von Wallenstein.
Madrid	Spanish Civil War	7 Nov. 1936	Nationalists under General Mola attacked the Republican forces of General Miaja causing the government to flee to Valencia.
Mafeking	Second Boer War	Oct. 1899	Colonel Baden-Powell resisted Boers under General Cronje in siege not raised till 17 May 1900.
Magdeburg	Thirty Years' War	Mar. 1631	Imperialists under Field Marshal Tilly besieged the city and von Falkenberg was killed.

Battle	War	Date	Details
Magenta	Italian Independence Wars	4 June 1859	French under General MacMahon defeated Austrians under Marshal Gyulai.
Majuba Hill	First Boer War	27 Feb. 1881	Boers under General Joubert defeated British under Sir George Colley (killed).
Maldon	Danish Invasion of Britain	991 AD	Danish army under Tryggvason defeated Anglo-Saxons under Brithnoth.
Malplaquet	War of Spanish Succession	11 Sept. 1709	German and British forces under Marlborough defeated French under Villars in costly victory.
Malvern Hill	US Civil War	1 July 1862	Union repelled fierce Confederate attacks during 7 days' battle.
Mantineia	Peloponnesian War	418 BC	Spartan forces under King Agis defeated the Athenians.
Manzikert	Anatolian Wars	1071 AD	Byzantines under the emperor Romanus IV Diogenes were defeated by the Seljuq Turks led by Sultan Alp-Arslan.
Marathon	Persian-Greek Wars	Sept. 490 BC	Athenians under Miltiades, 10,000 in number, defeated 50,000 Persians.
Marengo	French Revolutionary Wars	14 June 1800	Napoleon with aid of General Desaix (killed) defeated Austrians under General Mélas.
Margate	Hundred Years' War	24 Mar. 1387	Earls of Arundel and Nottingham repelled invasion threat from Franco-Castilian force.
Marne	First World War	6–9 Sept. 1914 and July 1918	Two bloody battles. In both cases the Germans were forced to retreat.
Marston Moor	English Civil War	2 July 1644	Prince Rupert's royalists defeated by Cromwell's Ironsides under Fairfax and Manchester.
Medellín	Peninsular War	28 Mar. 1809	French under Marshal Victor comprehensively defeated Spanish under Cuesta.
Medway	Second invasion of Britain	c.43 AD	Romans under Emperor Claudius defeated Britons under Caractacus and his brother Togodumnus (died)
Megiddo	Palestinian War	c.1468 BC	The Palestinian town of Megiddo was captured by the Egyptian king Thutmosis III.
Metauro River	Second Punic War	207 BC	Romans under Marcus Livius Salinator and Claudius Nero defeated Carthaginians under Hasdrubal (died), the brother of Hannibal.
Midway	Second World War	3–6 June 1942	In battle fought mainly by aircraft, Japanese attack on US base repelled, US carrier *Yorktown* lost, but 4 Japanese carriers sunk.
Missolonghi (First)	Greek War of Independence	Jan. 1823	The Ottomans were forced to withdraw after failing to take the key fortress of Missolonghi (Mesolóngion).
Missolonghi (Second)	Greek War of Independence	23 Apr. 1826	Joint Turkish/Egyptian forces under Ibrahim Pasha defeated a smalll Greek garrison under Mavrocordatos.
Mohács	Ottoman Wars	29 Aug. 1526	Turks under Suleyman I defeated Hungarians under Louis II.
Molinos del Rey	Peninsular War	21 Dec. 1808	French under General St Cyr defeated Spanish under Reding.
Monongahela	French-Indian War	9 July 1755	British army under General Edward Braddock was routed by the joint French and Indian forces under Captain Daniel de Beaujeu and, after his death, by Captain Jean Dumas. The survivors of the battle near Fort Duquesne (Pittsburgh) included George Washington.
Mons Lactarius	Ostrogoth War	553 AD	Byzantine General Narses defeated the Goths under Teias (died), near Naples, Italy.
Morat	Swiss-Burgundy War	22 June 1476	Victory for the Swiss Confederation over the Burgundians under Charles the Bold.
Morgarten	Swiss War of Independence	15 Nov. 1315	Swiss Confederation's first military success against the Austrians under Leopold I.
Mortimer's Cross	Wars of the Roses	2 Feb. 1461	Edward, duke of York, defeated Lancastrians under earls of Pembroke and Wiltshire.
Mukden	Russo-Japanese War	19 Feb.–10 Mar. 1905	Russian stronghold in Manchuria that finally fell to the Japanese.
Munda	Roman Civil War	45 BC	Decisive battle of the Roman Civil War when Julius Caesar conclusively defeated the Pompeians.
Mylae	First Punic War	260 BC	Romans destroyed 50 Carthaginian ships.
Nahāvand	Arabian Wars	642 AD	Arab forces under Nu'mān defeated Sāsānian troops under Firuzan.

M
I
L
I
T
A
R
Y

Battle	War	Date	Details
Nancy	Swiss-Burgundy War	1477	Victory for the Swiss Confederation over the Burgundians under Charles the Bold (died).
Nanjing	Chinese Civil War	22 Apr. 1949	Communists captured Chiang Kai-shek's Nationalist capital, enabling communists under Mao Zedong to take control of China.
Naseby	English Civil War	14 June 1645	Parliamentarians under Fairfax routed Prince Rupert's royalists.
Nashville	US Civil War	15–16 Dec. 1864	Union army under General Thomas defeated Confederates under General Hood.
Navarino	Greek War of Independence	20 Oct. 1827	Last action between wooden ships. Britain, France and Russia defeated Turks and Egyptians.
Nemea	Corinthian War	394 BC	After the victory of Sparta in the Peloponnesian War against Athens it maintained its military superiority against a coalition of troops from Thebes, Corinth, Athens and Argos, largely due to their skill in hoplite warfare (use of heavy infantry).
Neva River	Swedish Holy War	15 July 1240	Novgorod army under Prince Alexander Yaroslavich defeated the Swedes under earl Birger on the banks of the Neva. Yaroslavich was given the name Nevsky in honour of his victory.
Neville's Cross	Anglo-Scottish Wars	17 Oct. 1346	Scots under David II routed by Henry de Percy and Ralph de Neville.
Newbury (First)	English Civil War	20 Sept. 1643	Charles I failed to prevent the parliamentarians under the earl of Essex from marching to London.
Newbury (Second)	English Civil War	27 Oct. 1644	Charles I's inconclusive encounter with parliamentary force under the earl of Manchester spurred formation of the New Model Army.
New Orleans	War of 1812	Jan. 1815	Andrew Jackson defeated English force under General Sir Edward Pakenham (killed).
New Orleans	US Civil War	Apr. 16th 1862	Union fleet under Commodore Farragut bombarded Forts Jackson and forced surrender of city.
Niagara	Seven Years' War	June 1759	British under General Prideaux (killed) besieged the Canadian fort and William Johnson successfully repulsed Ligneris.
Nicopolis	Ottoman Wars	25 Sept. 1396	Turks under Sultan Bayezid I defeated a Christian Allied army under Sigismund, king of Hungary.
Nile/Aboukir Bay	French Revolutionary Wars	1–2 Aug. 1798	French fleet destroyed and Admiral Brueys killed by Nelson, checking Napoleon's plans in Middle East.
Nong Sa Rai	Thai War of Independence	1593	The final battle between the Thai troops under Prince Naresuen and Burmese troops under King Nanda Bayin. The Burmese Crown Prince was slain by Naresuen and Thai independence was safe for 150 years.
Nördlingen	Thirty Years' War	5–6 Sept. 1634	Decisive victory for the Holy Roman Empire and Spain under Matthias Gallas over the Swedish army led by Gustav Karlsson Horn and Bernhard of Saxe-Weimar, which led to the dissolution of the Heilbronn alliance and forced Cardinal Richelieu to bring France into the war.
Northampton	Wars of the Roses	10 July 1460	Earl of March, later Edward IV, routed the Lancastrians, captured Henry VI and executed supporters, including Buckingham and Shrewsbury.
Novara	Italian War of Independence	23 Mar. 1849	Austrian troops under Marshal Joseph Radetzky routed Piedmontese army.
Okinawa	Second World War	1 Apr.–21 June 1945	US amphibious landing met fierce and protracted resistance inland, losing over 7,000 men to Japan's 100,000 killed. US and Japanese commanders Bruckner and Ushiima.
Omdurman	British-Sudan Campaigns	2 Sept. 1898	General Kitchener destroyed the Mahdi's army. Last full-scale cavalry charge by 21st Lancers, including Winston Churchill.

Battle	War	Date	Details
Opequan	US Civil War	19 Sept. 1864	Confederates under General Early defeated by General Sheridan and Lt-Col. George Custer.
Oporto	Peninsular War	28 Mar. 1809	French under Marshal Soult defeated Portuguese under Lima and Pareiras.
Orléans	Hundred Years' War	12 Oct. 1428–8 May 1429	Decisive siege in which English were forced to withdraw after Joan of Arc captured key siege forts.
Oswego	Seven Years' War	11 Aug. 1756	French under marquis of Montcalm took English fort held by Col. Mercer (killed).
Otterburn	Scottish Independence	15 Aug. 1388	Aka Chevy Chase. Scots under earls Douglas (killed) and Murray defeated Henry Percy (Hotspur).
Oudenarde	War of Spanish Succession	11 July 1708	British and Imperialists under Marlborough and Prince Eugene defeated French under Ventome and Burgundy.
Palo Alto	Mexican War	8 May 1846	First clash of the Mexican War in which the Americans under General Zachary Taylor defeated the Mexican army under General Mariano Arista.
Panipat (First)	Indian Wars	21 Apr. 1526	Mughal chief Bābur defeated Sultan Ibrāhīm Lodo of Delhi (died).
Panipat (Second)	Indian Wars	5 Nov. 1556	Bayram Khān, the guardian of Mughal emperor Akbar, defeated the Hindu General Hemu.
Panipat (Third)	Indian Wars	14 Jan. 1761	Afghan chief Ahmad Shāh Durrāni defeated the Marāthā army under the Bhāo Sahib.
Parma	War of Polish Succession	29 June 1734	French under Marshal de Coigny defeated Imperialists under Count Claudius de Mercy (killed).
Passchendaele	First World War	30 Oct. 1917	Aka 3rd Battle of Ypres. Canadian 3rd and 4th Division and British pushed back Germans but suffered heavy casualties.
Patay	Hundred Years War	18 June 1429	French under Joan of Arc and duc d'Alençon defeated English under Talbot and Fastolfe.
Pea Ridge	US Civil War	6–8 Mar. 1862	Aka Elk Horn Tavern. First key Union victory west of Mississippi. Confederate General Ben McCulloch killed.
Pearl Harbor	Second World War	7 Dec. 1941	Japanese carrier-based planes attacked US Pacific fleet without declaring war, sank 19 ships. USA forced into the war.
Pharsalus	Roman Civil War	48 BC	Julius Caesar defeated the much larger force of Pompey. Caesar, who had only minor losses exclaimed 'Hoc voluerunt' ('They would have it so').
Philippi	Brutus' Rebellion	42 BC	Republicans under Brutus and Cassius (both committed suicide) defeated by Octavian and Mark Antony, exposing Rome to autocratic rule.
Pichincha	Latin-American Wars	24 May 1822	South American rebels under Antonio José de Sucre overcame Spanish royalists.
Pinkie Cleugh	Anglo-Scottish Wars	10 Sept. 1547	Scots under the earls of Arran and Huntly defeated by English under Protector Somerset.
Plains of Abraham	Seven Years' War	13 Sept. 1759	French under Montcalm defeated by Wolfe and lost Quebec. Both generals killed.
Plassey	Seven Years' War	23 June 1757	British under Robert Clive defeated nawab of Bengal and assured East India Company's rule there.
Poitiers	Hundred Years' War	19 Sept. 1356	English archers under Edward the Black Prince defeated French under King John II.
Plataea	Persian-Greek Wars	479 BC	Greeks under Pausanias won a decisive victory over the Persians under Mardonius.
Port Arthur	Sino-Japanese War	21 Nov. 1894	(Now called Lushun.) Japanese defeated Chinese with very few casualties.
Port Arthur	Russo-Japanese War	8 Feb. 1904	Japanese fleet attacked Russian squadron without declaring war. Japan eventually won the port after almost a year's fighting (treaty of Portsmouth).
Preston	English Civil War	17–19 Aug. 1648	Cromwell's Roundheads defeated royalists under duke of Hamilton and Sir Marmaduke Langdale, ending the Second Civil War.
Preston	Jacobite Rebellion 1715	13 Nov. 1715	General Will Thomas's royalists defeated Jacobites under Thomas Forster.

Battle	War	Date	Details
Prestonpans	Jacobite Rebellion 1745	21 Sept. 1745	Aka Gladsmuir. Jacobites under Young Pretender Charles Edward Stuart defeated royalists in a 10-minute battle.
Princeton	US War of Independence	3 Jan. 1777	Americans under George Washington defeated British under Cornwallis.
Pydna	Third Macedonian War	22 June 168 BC	Romans under Lucius Aemilius Paullus defeated the Macedonians under king Perseus.
Pyramids	French Revolutionary Wars	21 July 1798	Napoleon defeated Mamelukes under Murad Bey and went on to occupy Cairo.
Quatre Bras	Napoleon's Hundred Days	16 June 1815	Marshal Ney engaged Wellington, causing his withdrawal to Waterloo.
Quebec	Seven Years' War	27 June 1759	First of two battles of Seven Years' War, which decided the future of Canada.
Queenston Heights	War of 1812	13 Oct. 1812	British in Canada under General Brock (killed) defeated Americans under General Van Rensselaer.
Quiberon Bay	Seven Years' War	20 Nov. 1759	British fleet under Admiral Hawke defeated French under Marshal de Conflans.
Radcot Bridge	Richard II's Barons' War	20 Dec. 1387	Earl of Derby, later Henry IV, defeated Richard II's supporter Robert de Vere, earl of Oxford.
Ramillies	War of Spanish Succession	23 May 1706	British and Imperialists under Marlborough defeated French under Villeroi.
Rieti	Italian War of Independence	7 Mar. 1821	Austrians defeated Pepe's Neapolitans, entered Naples and reinstated Ferdinand IV on throne.
Rio Salado		30 Oct. 1340	Castilian forces under Alfonso XI and Portuguese forces under Alfonso IV defeated Muslim Marinids of North Africa.
River Plate	Second World War	13 Dec. 1939	The battle in Uruguayan waters between British and German warships ended on 17 December with the scuttling of the German pocket battleship Graf Spee
Roanoke Island	US Civil War	7 Feb. 1862	Union General Burnside defeated Confederates under General Wise.
Rocroi	Thirty Years War	19 May 1643	French army under the Duc d'Enghien (later known as the Great Condé) routed a Spanish army under Don Francisco de Melo, ending the Spanish ascendency in Europe.
Rorke's Drift	Zulu-British War	22 Jan. 1879	Lts Chard and Bromhead led a company from 24th Regiment to repulse numerically far superior Zulu attack. 11 VCs awarded.
Ruhr Pocket	Second World WarI	1 Apr. 1945	US 9th Army surrounded remnants of Field Marshal Model's Army Group B, causing mass surrender and Model's suicide.
Sadowa	Seven Weeks' War	3 July 1866	See Königgrätz.
St Albans (First)	Wars of the Roses	22 May 1455	First battle in these wars. Duke of York defeated Lancastrians. Henry VI captured. Northumberland and Somerset killed.
St Albans (Second)	Wars of the Roses	17 Feb. 1461	Lancastrians under Margaret of Anjou defeated Yorkists and released Henry VI.
Saintes	US War of Independence	12 Apr. 1782	British under Admiral Sir George Rodney gained a decisive naval victory in the West Indies over a French fleet under the Comte de Grasse.
Salamanca	Peninsular War	22 July 1812	Wellington's Allied army defeated Marshal Auguste Marmont's force, the main French army in Spain.
Salamis (First)	Persian-Greek Wars	480 BC	Greeks under Themistocles won a naval victory over the Persians under Xerxes.
Salamis (Second)	Macedonian-Egyptian War	306 BC	Demetrius I Poliorcetes of Macedonia won a naval encounter with the Egyptians under Ptolemy I.
Salerno	Second World War	Sept. 1943	In Allied amphibious landing, 5th Army reinforced by US 82nd Airborne and British 7th Armoured took port and had entered Naples by 1 October.
Samaria	Palestinian War	722 BC	The capital of the Hebrew kingdom of Israel was destroyed by the Assyrians under Sargon II.
Samugarh	Mughal Civil War	29 May 1658	Decisive battle of the struggle for the Mughal throne between Aurangzeb and Murād Bakhsh, the third and fourth sons of Shah Jehan, on

Battle	War	Date	Details
			the one side, and the eldest son, Dārā Shikoh, on the other. Aurangzeb ultimately triumphed and began his long rule as emperor.
San Jacinto	Texan Rising	21 Apr. 1836	General Houston defeated Mexicans under Santa Anna, which led to admission to US states 1845.
Santa Cruz (First)	Anglo-Spanish Wars	1657	British fleet under Robert Blake destroyed the harboured Spanish fleet.
Santa Cruz (Second)	Anglo-Spanish Wars	1797	Horatio Nelson lost his right arm during his unsuccessful assault on the Tenerife port.
Saratoga (First)	US War of Independence	19 Sept. 1777	Aka Battle of Freeman's Farm. British army under General Burgoyne unsuccessfully attempted to gain access to Albany.
Saratoga (Second)	US War of Independence	7 Oct. 1777	Aka Battle of Bemis Heights or Second Battle of Freeman's Farm. General Burgoyne's continued engagement of American troops was thwarted by General Benedict Arnold.
Saratoga (Third)	US War of Independence	17 Oct. 1777	Decisive battle of the war whereby the British army under General Burgoyne was defeated by the Americans under Gates; the outcome encouraging the French into the war.
Sauchie Burn	Barons' Rebellion	18 June 1488	James III of Scotland (killed) defeated by rebel barons under the earl of Angus.
Sedan	Franco-Prussian War	1 Sept.1870	General von Moltke's German Army defeated French, Emperor Napoleon III surrendered, French Second Empire fell.
Sedgemoor	Monmouth's Rebellion	6 July 1685	Royal troops under the earl of Feversham defeated James, duke of Monmouth.
Selby	English Civil War	11 Apr. 1644	Sir Thomas Fairfax defeated royalists under Col. John Bellasis.
Seringapatam	Fourth Mysore War	1799	British army under Richard Wellesley defeated the Indians under Tipu Sultan (died).
Sevastopol	Crimean War	Sept. 1854–Sept. 1855	Successful Allied siege of Russian naval base.
Seven Days battle	US Civil War	26 June–2 July 1862	Confederates under General Lee staved off Union campaign to capture Richmond after a week-long series of battles.
Sevenoaks	Cade's Rebellion	18 June 1450	Rebels under Jack Cade defeated royal troops under Sir Humphrey Stafford (died).
Shanghai	Sino-Japanese War	8 Aug. 1937	Chinese defended this port for three months but eventually succumbed to Japanese.
Shannon and Chesapeake	War of 1812	1 June 1813	British frigate Shannon under Capt. Broke US frigate captured Chesapeake under Capt. Lawrence (killed).
Sheerness	Anglo-Dutch Wars	7 June 1667	Dutch fleet under Admiral de Ruyter sailed up the Medway to Upnor Castle and sank 7 ships.
Sheriffmuir	Jacobite Rebellion 1715	13 Nov. 1715	Indecisive battle between 10,000 Jacobite rebels under the earl of Mar and 3,300 loyalist Scots under the duke of Argyll.
Shiloh	US Civil War	6–7 Apr. 1862	Major engagement with even casualties, but Confederates under General Johnston (killed) eventually left the field to Grant's Federal troops.
Shirogawa	Satsuma Rebellion	24 Sept. 1876	Imperial army under Prince Taruhito defeated rebels under Takamori Saigo (killed).
Shrewsbury	Percy's Rebellion	21 July 1403	Royalists under Henry IV defeated Henry Percy (Hotspur), who was killed in battle.
Six Day War	Israeli–Arab War	5–10 June 1967	Victory over United Arab Republic, Syria and Jordan brought Israel control of Golan Heights, West Bank, Gaza Strip, Sinai Peninsula and the Old City of Jerusalem.
Sluys	Hundred Years' War	24 June 1340	English archers under Edward III defeated French in the Zwyn estuary in the main naval engagement of the war.
Solferino	Italian War of Independence	24 June 1859	Indecisive but bloody battle that led to the peace of Villafranca and the Austrian loss of Lombardy to Italy.
Solway Moss	Anglo-Scottish Wars	25 Nov. 1542	Scots under Oliver Sinclair were routed by English under Thomas Dacre and John Musgrave.

MILITARY

Battle	War	Date	Details
Somme	First World War	1 July–19 Nov.	Franco-British offensive cost over 1 million casualties, made small territory gains. First tank attack of war on 15 Sept. In 1918 Germans made the Somme target for their last offensive.
Stamford Bridge	Norse Invasion of Britain	25 Sept. 1066	English under Harold II defeated Norsemen under Harold Hardrada and Tostig (both killed).
Stirling Bridge	Scottish Independence	11 Sept. 1297	Scots under Sir William Wallace defeated the invading English under the earl of Surrey.
Stoke	Lambert Simnel's Rebellion	16 June 1487	Royal troops under Henry VII defeated rebels under John de la Pole, earl of Lincoln.
Talavera	Peninsular War	28 July 1809	Arthur Wellesley was made Viscount Wellington after defeating the French under King Joseph Bonaparte and Marchand Jourdan.
Tālikota	Muslim Wars	Jan. 1565	Muslim sultans of Bijāpur, Bidar, Ahmadnagar, and Golconda defeated the forces of the Hindu raja of Vijayanagar.
Tearless Battle	Spartan Wars	368 BC	Arcadians attempted to cut off Spartan army under Archidamus but no Spartans were killed.
Tel-el-Kebir	Egyptian Revolt	13 Sept. 1882	Sir Garnet Wolseley defeated Egyptian nationalists under Arabi Pasha.
Teutoberg Forest	German-Roman War	9 AD	The Germanic Cherusci tribe, led by the young German prince, Arminius, ambushed and slaughtered the Roman army under General Quinctilius Varus (died).
Tewkesbury	Wars of the Roses	4 May 1471	Yorkists under Edward IV defeated Lancastrians under Queen Margaret and Somerset. Prince Edward, son of Henry VI (killed).
Thapsus	Roman Civil War	6 Feb. 46 BC	Romans under Julius Caesar slaughtered the troops of Quintus Metellus Scipio, the father-in-law of Pompey the Great, and within weeks had conquered the rest of Roman Africa.
Thermopylae	Third Persian Invasion	19 Aug. 480 BC	Spartans and Thespians under Leonidas defeated by Persians under Xerxes.
Thorn	Great Northern War	22 Sept. 1702	Swedes under Charles XII defeated Poles and elected Stanislas Leszczynski king of Poland.
Tinchebrai	Norman Civil War	28 Sept. 1106	English under Henry I defeated his brother duke Robert of Normandy, annexing Normandy.
Toulon	French Revolutionary Wars	Aug.–Dec. 1793	Notable for being the engagement that earned Napoleon Bonaparte his reputation as a military tactician when he forced the withdrawal of the Anglo-Spanish fleet.
Tours/Poitiers	Muslim Invasion of France	10 Oct. 732	Franks under Charles Martel defeated Saracens under Abderrahman Ibn Abdillah (killed), halting Moorish conquest of Europe.
Towton	Wars of the Roses	29 Mar. 1461	Edward IV defeated Lancastrians under Henry VI and was crowned on 28 June.
Trafalgar	Napoleonic Wars	21 Oct. 1805	British fleet under Nelson (died) and Collingwood defeated Spanish and French under Villeneuve, losing no ships and capturing half of the enemy's.
Trenton	US War of Independence	26 Dec. 1776	Notable as the first success of George Washington in open warfare.
Tsushima Strait	Russo-Japanese War	27–28 May 1905	Admiral Togo routed Russian fleet under Rozlidestrenski, making first use of naval radio.
Ulm	Napoleonic Wars	20 Oct. 1805	Napoleon defeated Austrians under General Baron Mack von Leiberich (court-martialled).
Ulundi	Zulu-British War	4 July 1879	Final battle of the Anglo-Zulu War, in which Cetshwayo (Cetewayo) was defeated and taken prisoner.
Ushant			See Glorious 1st of June.
Valmy	French Revolutionary Wars	20 Sept. 1792	French under Dumouriez and Kellerman defeated Prussians under Duke of Brunswick.
Verdun	First World War	21 Feb.– 20 Dec. 1916	German General von Falkenhayn's war of attrition against French, with combined casualties of over 650,000 and no conclusive outcome.
Vienna	Ottoman Wars	Jul–Sept. 1683	The Siege of Vienna by the Turks against the Habsburg Holy Roman Emperor Leopold I. On 12 September a combined force led by John III Sobieski defeated the Turks.

Battle	War	Date	Details
Vinegar Hill	Irish Rebellion	21 June 1798	Irish loyalists under General Lake defeated Catholic rebels under Father Murphy.
Virginia Capes	US War of Independence	5 Sept. 1781	French naval victory over a British fleet under Admiral Thomas Graves near Chesapeake Bay.
Vitoria	Peninsular War	21 June 1813	British under Wellington defeated French and expelled Joseph Bonaparte from Spain.
Vyborg	Russo-Finnish War	24 Apr. 1918	General Mannerheim's Finnish White Army defeated Bolsheviks.
Wakefield	Wars of the Roses	30 Dec. 1460	Lancastrians under Somerset defeated Yorkists under Richard of York (killed).
Wandiwāsh	Seven Years' War	22 Jan. 1760	British under Sir Eyre Coote defeated the French under the Comte de Lally in what was the decisive battle in the Anglo-French conflict in southern India.
Warburg	Seven Years' War	31 July 1760	French under Chevalier du Muy forced to retire by joint Prussian/British force.
Waterloo	Napoleon's Hundred Days	18 June 1815	Wellington aided by Prussians under Blücher defeated Napoleon who abdicated on 22 June.
Worcester	English Civil War	3 Sept. 1651	Last pitched battle of civil war in which Cromwell defeated royalists under Charles II.
Yarmuk River	Palestinian Wars	20 Aug. 636	Arabian army under Khālid ibn al-Walid defeated a Byzantine army under Theodorus.
Yom Kippur	Israeli-Arab War	6–24 Oct. 1973	Syrian and Egyptian surprise offensive along Golan Heights and Suez Canal defeated after heavy fighting.
Yorktown	US War of Independence	19 Oct. 1781	General Cornwallis forced to surrender to US and French troops, ending war.
Ypres (First)	First World War	14 Oct.1914	General von Falkenhayn's push to reach ports of Calais and Dunkirk halted by the British Expeditionary Force under Sir John French.
Ypres (Second)	First World War	22 Apr.– late May 1915	General Falkenhayn used lethal chlorine gas for the first time, causing many Allied deaths and advancing about 3 miles.
Ypres (Third)	First World War		See Passchendaele.
Zama	Second Punic War	202 BC	Carthaginians under Hannibal were defeated by Romans under Scipio Africanus in final battle of this war.
Zenta	Ottoman Wars	11 Sept. 1697	Ottoman army under Sultan Mustafa II was engaged by an Austrian army under Prince Eugene of Savoy while crossing the Tisza river and comprehensively defeated.
Zutphen	Dutch War of Independence	22 Sept. 1586	Spanish victory over English force under Leicester notable for death of Sir Philip Sidney.

M
I
L
I
T
A
R
Y

MUSIC: CLASSICAL

Opera: Précis of Plots

Aida (Verdi, 1871)   Aida, a captive Ethiopian princess, is servant to the Egyptian princess Amneris. Both are in love with General Radamès, who loves Aida. Radamès goes to war against the Ethiopians, defeats them and is given Amneris's hand in marriage, but Radames is suspected of having betrayed his country in trying to help Aida and sentenced to death. Aida conceals herself in the tomb where both of them are buried alive, while above them, Amneris prays.

The Barber of Seville (Rossini, 1816)   Count Almaviva, aided by his barber Figaro, is pursuing Rosina. Her guardian, Bartolo, who wants to marry her himself, tries to stop them but is unsuccessful, and Rosina marries the count.

The Bartered Bride (Smetana, 1866)   Marenka loves Jenik, whose parents want to marry her to the halfwit son of Micha. Jenik is offered money to give her up, and accepts on condition she marries Micha's eldest son. This turns out to be Jenik himself; Marenka can marry him after all.

La Bohème (Puccini, 1896)   Mimi, who is consumptive, falls in love with a Bohemian poet, Rodolfo, and for a while they live together, but constant quarrels drive them apart. Then Rodolfo's friends discover that Mimi is dying and bring her to him, but it is too late and she dies in his arms.

Carmen (Bizet, 1875)   The soldier Don José deserts the army to follow the gypsy girl Carmen, who leaves him for the toreador Escamillo. Mad with jealousy, Don José follows her to the bullring and kills her.

Cavalleria Rusticana (Mascagni, 1890)   Brokenhearted because her lover, Turiddu, has abandoned her for another woman, Santuzza tells the other woman's husband what is going on. He kills Turiddu in a duel.

The Coronation of Poppaea (Monteverdi, 1643)   Emperor Nero resolves to marry his mistress Poppaea. One by one, he murders everyone who stands in their way until Poppaea is crowned empress.

Così fan tutte (Mozart, 1790)   The sisters Fiordiligi and Dorabella swear to be faithful to their lovers Ferrando and Guglielmo, so to try their fidelity the latter pretend to go off to the wars. But they return in disguise and each proceeds to make advances to the other's girl, who both respond. The men then reveal their disguise, but forgive their wayward sweethearts, and both couples are reunited.

Don Giovanni (Mozart, 1787)   Foiled in his attempts to seduce Donna Anna, the libertine Don Giovanni (aka Don Juan) kills her father, the Commendatore. Anna and her fiancé Don Ottavio vow to avenge him. They are joined by Donna Elvira, another former victim of the Don. In a gesture of defiance, Don Giovanni has confronted a statue of the Commendatore and invited him to dinner. The Commendatore duly accepts, arrives at the Don's house and drags him down to hell.

Eugene Onegin (Tchaikovsky, 1879)   Tatyana, young and open-hearted, falls in love with the worldly Eugene Onegin and confesses her feelings, but he rejects her. Years later they meet again and this time he falls in love with her, but by now she is married and, though still attracted to him, sends him away for ever.

Falstaff (Verdi, 1893)   Shakespeare's fat knight, Sir John Falstaff, is simultaneously wooing two wives of Windsor, Mistress Ford and Mistress Page, who discover what he is up to and contrive to pay him back, but Falstaff eventually takes it in good part and the opera finishes with a happy ending for a young couple involved in the plotting – Nannetta Ford and her lover, Fenton.

Faust (Gounod, 1859)   Faust has been given back his youth by the devil, Mephistopheles, so he can pursue the beautiful Marguerite. They fall in love and she has a child, but Faust then deserts her. She kills the child and is condemned to death. Faust returns to save her, but he is too late, and she dies and is borne to heaven.

Fidelio (Beethoven, 1805)   When Florestan is unjustly imprisoned, his wife Leonora disguises herself as a young man called Fidelio and gets a job inside the prison, from where she succeeds in getting him freed.

The Flying Dutchman (Wagner, 1843)   A Dutch sea captain has been condemned by the Devil to sail the seas for ever, unless he can find a woman who will love him until death. Once in every seven years he is allowed to land in search of her. He meets Senta, who declares her love for him, but leaves her owing to a misunderstanding, whereupon she throws herself into the sea and drowns, thus freeing him.

Gloriana (Britten, 1953)   The libretto was based on Lytton Strachey's *Elizabeth and Essex* and concerns the decline of Essex in the affections of Queen Elizabeth. The opening act tells of a fight between Essex and Lord Montjoy at the court of Elizabeth. They are rebuked, but the rebellious nature of Essex is recognized by the Queen. Essex is appointed Deputy of Ireland and given the charge of subduing Tyrone, but fails miserably. On his return to England the disgraced Essex rebels and is arrested as a traitor. At his trial at Whitehall, Essex is given a death sentence, which is eventually signed by Elizabeth after an injudicious word from Lady Rich. The final act depicts the Queen reflecting on her life to the audience.

Lohengrin (Wagner, 1850)   The heroine, Elsa, falsely accused, will lose her life if she cannot find a champion. When one appears (Lohengrin, a knight searching for the Holy Grail), he agrees to defend her so long as she never asks his name. Eventually they marry, but an enemy dupes her into asking her husband's name. Now she has broken her vow and he leaves her for ever.

Lucia di Lammermoor (Donizetti, 1835)   Lucy Ashton is in love with Edgar, but is tricked by her brother into marrying someone else. On her wedding night she goes mad and kills her husband. When he learns of her subsequent death, Edgar kills himself.

Madame Butterfly (Puccini, 1904)   The American naval Lieutenant Pinkerton has married the innocent Japanese girl Cio-Cio-San. He regards the arrangements as only temporary and leaves her when the time comes, but she loves him and longs for his return. When he does, with an American wife, Butterfly promises to give him their child and then kills herself.

The Magic Flute (Mozart, 1791) This is a contest between Good (the high priest Sarastro) and Evil (the Queen of the Night). Prince Tamino falls in love with the Queen of the Night's daughter, Pamina, and has to undergo many tests and temptations, helped by a gift of a magic flute, before he conquers Evil and wins the hand of his beloved.

Manon (Massenet, 1884) Manon Lescaut and the Chevalier Des Grieux fall in love and run away together, but she prefers luxury to poverty and leaves him for a rich man. She is eventually deported for being a prostitute. Des Grieux follows her, but she is overwhelmed by her suffering and dies in his arms.

The Marriage of Figaro (Mozart, 1786) Figaro, barber to the womanizing Count Almaviva, is about to be married to Susanna, the countess's maid, but discovers the count has designs on her. Figaro, Susanna, the countess and her page Cherubino hatch a plot to unmask the count, and all ends happily with the wedding of Figaro and Susanna.

The Mastersingers of Nuremberg (Wagner, 1868) The Mastersingers of Nuremberg are to hold a song contest, the prize being the hand of Eva. The knight Walther arrives, falls in love with Eva and decides to compete, coached by Hans Sachs the cobbler. Although his rival Beckmesser does his best to discredit him, he wins both the contest and Eva.

Norma (Bellini, 1831) The Druid priestess Norma has had two children by the Roman general Pollione, who has now fallen in love with a younger priestess, Adalgisa. Norma incites a Gallo-Roman war, Pollione is captured and sentenced to death, and they both go to be sacrificed together.

Otello (Verdi, 1887) Otello, the Moor of Venice, is tricked by the evil Iago into believing his wife, Desdemona, has been unfaithful to him. In a fit of jealousy he kills her, learns the truth, then kills himself.

I Pagliacci (Leoncavallo, 1893) A troupe of strolling players enact a real-life drama. The clown, Canio, does not know that his wife, Nedda, is having an affair with Silvio, a villager, although he is suspicious. At that night's performance, in which Canio plays a jealous husband, reality gets the better of him, the play becomes a real quarrel, and he stabs both Nedda and Silvio to death.

The Pearl Fishers (Bizet, 1863) Pearl fishers Zurga and Nadir have long loved the priestess, Leila, but have vowed not to let this destroy their friendship. Then Leila arrives to conduct a religious ceremony, and she and Nadir confess their love. They are discovered and sentenced to death. Zurga helps them escape but loses his own life as a result.

Peter Grimes (Britten, 1945) The lone fisherman, Peter Grimes, is an outsider in the East Coast fishing community where he lives. Already under suspicion after the mysterious death of his young apprentice, when a second boy dies unaccountably, Grimes is forced to take to sea and drowns himself.

Rigoletto (Verdi, 1851) The hunchback jester Rigoletto has helped his master, the Duke of Mantua, to seduce the daughter of the courtier Monterone, who curses him. The duke believes that Rigoletto has a mistress (actually his daughter), Gilda, and seduces her. In revenge, Rigoletto plots to have the duke murdered, but the plot misfires and Gilda is killed instead. The curse has been fulfilled.

The Ring Cycle (Wagner, 1876) *The Rhinegold*: The magic Rhinegold is at the bottom of the River Rhine, guarded by the Rhinemaidens. Alberich, the wicked dwarf, steals it and makes a ring from it to become all-powerful. Meanwhile, the god Wotan is looking for money to pay for his castle of Valhalla and plots to steal the gold. He tricks Alberich into parting with it, but it is cursed and results in a death. *The Valkyrie*: Wotan has fathered nine warrior-maidens, the Valkyries; his favourite is Brünnhilde. He also has a son and a daughter, Siegmund and Sieglinde, who were separated at birth. In a storm, Siegmund takes shelter in a hut where Sieglinde lives with her husband Hunding. The two fall in love and run away but are pursued by Hunding, who kills Siegmund. Brünnhilde carries Siegmund off to Valhalla in defiance of her father, who condemns her to sleep in a ring of fire until a hero comes to rescue her. *Siegfried*: Sieglinde has died giving birth to a son, Siegfried, who has been brought up by the dwarf Mime in the hope that he will one day get the Ring back. With the help of Wotan and Brünnhilde, Siegfried is led to the magic rock where he awakes Brünnhilde and they fall in love. *Twilight of the Gods*: Siegfried has taken the Ring from the dragon that was guarding it and now gives it to Brünnhilde while he goes in search of further adventure. He reaches the Hall of the Gibichungs, who hope to marry him to their sister Gutrune. Although Brünnhilde comes with the Ring to rescue him, he is killed. Brünnhilde builds a funeral pyre for him and climbs on to it herself. The Rhinemaidens arrive in a flood and snatch back the Ring, while Valhalla is consumed in flames. It is the end of the gods.

Der Rosenkavalier (Strauss, 1911) The young Count Octavian is having an affair with an older woman, the Marschallin, although she knows it cannot last. Octavian is sent to bear a silver rose as a symbol of the forthcoming marriage of the beautiful young Sophie von Faninal to a much older man, Baron Ochs. The two young people in love, their elders realize that it is better to let them go, and Octavian and Sophie face a future together.

Ruslan and Lyudmila (Glinka, 1842) Svyetozar is hosting a wedding celebration for his daughter Lyudmila, who is betrothed to the knight Ruslan. The bard Bayan sings but foretells of ill fortune for the newly-weds. A thunderclap followed by total darkness interrupts the festivities. Light returns but Lyudmila has disappeared. Lyudmila's former suitors search in vain. Ruslan encounters the wise magician Finn, who tells him of Lyudmila's abduction by the evil dwarf Chernomor. Ruslan acquires a magic sword and challenges Chernomor to a duel. The dwarf casts a sleeping spell on Lyudmila before encountering Ruslan, who defeats him by cutting off his beard, the source of power. Ruslan awakens Lyudmila with a magic ring.

The Tales of Hoffmann (Offenbach, 1881) The poet Hoffmann relates the stories of the three loves of his life, all destroyed by the same evil genius. First, there is Olympia, who, he does not realize until too late, is only a mechanical doll. Then the courtesan Giulietta, who leaves him for another, and finally Antonia, a pure young girl who knows she will die if she tries to sing but is tricked into doing so. The story of loss is about to be repeated with the opera singer Stella, and Hoffmann is left alone to drown his sorrows in beer.

MUSIC CLASSICAL

Tosca (Puccini, 1900)   The opera singer Floria Tosca is loved by the political agitator Cavaradossi and desired by the evil police chief, Scarpia. Cavaradossi is arrested, but Scarpia promises Tosca he will free him if she agrees to give herself to him. She kills Scarpia, but he has tricked her and Cavaradossi is shot, whereupon Tosca throws herself to her death from the prison battlements.

La Traviata (The Fallen Woman) (Verdi, 1853) Violetta, a courtesan, has fallen in love with a young aristocrat, Alfredo, but Alfredo's father begs her to break off the relationship as it will bring disgrace to his family, and she goes back to her old life. Alfredo confronts and denounces her, but she is dying of consumption, and when, too late, he returns to her side, she dies in his arms.

Tristan und Isolde (Wagner, 1865)   Isolde is to be married to King Mark of Cornwall and his nephew Tristan is sent to fetch her, but the two fall in love. After the wedding they meet, but they are discovered and Tristan is wounded. Isolde comes to him as he dies, then herself falls lifeless over his body.

Il Trovatore (The Troubadour) (Verdi, 1853)   Leonora is being serenaded by a mysterious troubador, regarded as a rival by Count di Luna, who is in love with her. The troubador turns out to be Manrico, apparently the son of the gypsy Azucena. But Azucena explains that years ago, in revenge for the agony of seeing her mother burned to death, she threw the Count's abducted baby brother into the flames – but by mistake threw her own baby instead. Manrico and Leonora run away but are pursued by the Count, who imprisons Manrico. Leonora agrees to marry the Count as the price of Manrico's freedom, but then kills herself. The Count executes Manrico, then is told by Azucena that he has killed his own brother.

Turandot (Busoni, 1917)   The cruel Chinese princess Turandot will marry only if a suitor prince can solve her three riddles. If he cannot, he will die. An unknown prince answers the riddles correctly but tells her that if she can discover his name by morning, he will agree to die. Turandot tortures the slave girl Liu, who knows the name but will not reveal it, and Liu eventually dies. The prince tells Turandot his name. It is 'Love,' and she accepts him as her husband.

NB: The above is only a small selection of operas but offers a flavour of the moods and emotions that can be explored in others.

Composers

Name	Principal works	Details
Hildegard of Bingen 1098–1179	Church music departing from traditional plainsong style	Saint and abbess
Pérotin c. 1160–c1205	Christmas and St Stephen's Day graduals (1198, 1199)	aka Perotinus Magnus; maître de chapelle at Notre Dame; exponent of *ars antiqua*
Adam de la Halle c. 1250–?1306	*Le jeu de Robin et de Marion* anticipated the genre of opéra comique	aka Adam the Hunchback; born Arras, France and died in Naples; court musician of the Comte d'Artois
Machaut, Guillaume de c. 1300–c.Y1377	*Messe de Notre Dame* (for four violins); *Voir Dit* (Tale of Truth), collection of ballads; 23 motets	Born and died in Reims; leading French composer of free-flowing *ars nova* style of 14th century; canon of Reims Cathedral
Landini, Francesco c. 1325–1397	Various madrigals; over 140 ballads	Born and died in Florence; blinded in youth from smallpox; noted for 'Landini Cadence' in which sixth degree octave is inserted between leading note and octave
Dunstable, John c. 1390–1453	Masses and motets	aka Dunstaple; internationally renowned in his day
Du Fay, Guillaume c. 1400–1474	8 masses; 87 motets; 59 French chansons	Composed earliest requiem mass; possibly originated Fauxbourdon style; canon of Cambrai
Ockeghem, Johannes c. 1430–1495	14 masses; 10 motets; 20 chansons	Born Flanders and died Tours; composer to 3 successive French kings: Charles VII, Louis XI, Charles VIII
Josquin des Prés c. 1445–1521	18 masses; 100 motets	Born Picardy and died Hainault; Luther called him 'Master of the Notes'
Isaac, Heinrich c. 1450–1517	36 masses; 'Innsbruck I Must Leave You' (song), reworked by J.S. Bach and Brahms	Born Brabant and died Florence; taught in household of Medici family
Taverner, John c. 1490–1545	8 masses (inc. *Westron Wynde*); other church music	Occasionally alleged to have given up music to persecute Catholics under Thomas Cromwell; subject of opera by Peter Maxwell Davies
Cabezón, Antonio de c. 1510–1566	'El Caballero variation'	Born Burgos and died Madrid; blind from birth
Tallis, Thomas c. 1510–1585	'Spem in alium nunquam habui' (In no other is my Hope) (motet)	Elizabeth I granted monopoly of sheet music to Tallis and William Byrd
Gabrieli, Andrea c. 1510–1586	7 masses and numerous motets	Born and died in Venice

MUSIC CLASSICAL

Name	Principal works	Details
Palestrina, Giovanni 1525–1594	Over 100 masses and 250 motets, including *Stabat Mater*	Took his name from his birthplace; lost his family in Italian plague
Lassus, Orlande 1532–1594	Wrote some 2,000 madrigals, motets, chansons, canzonas, masses, lieder, etc.	Born at Mons, died at Munich; preceded Palestrina as chapelmaster of Papal Church of St John Lateran, Rome
Byrd, William 1543–1623	Prolific composer and pioneer of madrigals but also composed motets, masses and music for organ and virginals, his most famous work being the collection of 42 virginal pieces *My Lady Nevells Book*	Pupil of Thomas Tallis and favoured by Queen Elizabeth despite being a Catholic; granted monopoly of all sheet music in England along with Tallis
Victoria Tomás Luis de 1548–1611	Composed in a similar style to that of Palestrina but distinguished by his use of Spanish melody. His total output consisted of church music including the motets *Vexilla Regis* and *Magnum Mysterium*, the acclaimed *Officium Hebdonadae Sanctae*, and the Requiem Mass composed at the death of Empress Maria	Spanish composer, born in Avila; studied for priesthood in Rome and in 1576 became chaplain to the widowed Empress Maria, sister of Philip II, returning with her to Madrid in 1583 to the convent of the Descalzas Reales, where he remained as choirmaster until his death
Morley, Thomas 1557–1602	Father of the English madrigal who edited the collection *The Triumphs of Oriana*; his last work was *The First Book of Ayres*	Pupil of Byrd who became organist at St Paul's Cathedral and Gentleman of the Chapel Royal in 1592
Sweelinck, Jan Pieterszoon 1562–1621	Wrote over 250 vocal works and 70 for keyboard. His fantasias were the first example of fully worked-out fugues. He founded the North German school which later included Diderik Buxtehude and J. S. Bach	Dutch composer, organist and harpsichordist. Succeeded his father as organist of the Oude Kerk (old church). Amsterdam in 1580, a position he held until his death
Bull, John c. 1562–1628	Although Bull's reputation was as a performer rather than a composer, he, along with William Byrd and Orlando Gibbons, published the first book of keyboard music in England, the aptly named *Parthenia* (Maidenhood), 1611. His other works include the virginal pieces *Walsingham* and *God Save the King*, although the attribution of our present National Anthem to Bull is perhaps not from this piece but a later untitled work	English musician. Appointed organist in the Queen's Chapel in 1586 and became the first music lecturer at Gresham College in 1597, and organist to James I in 1607. His Catholicism led him to flee England in 1613 to become organist of the Chapel Royal, Brussels and in 1615 became organist at Antwerp Cathedral, where he remained until his death
Dowland, John 1562–1626	Published 87 songs as well as *Lachrimae* (1604), 21 dance pieces containing 7 pavans, all beginning with the themeof Dowland's song 'Flow my tears'	Lutenist and singer/songwriter for the king of Denmark (1598–1606) and Lord Howard de Walden (1606–12) as well as Anne of Denmark and Charles I
Monteverdi, Claudio 1567–1643	First opera *La Favola d'Orfeo* (1607) is earliest opera in the regular repertoire; last opera: *L'Incoronazione di Poppea* (1642); many operas lost; other works listed in tables	Son of a barber/surgeon who wed the singer Claudia Cattaneo; he was a pupil of Ingegneri and was patronized by the duke of Mantua; took holy orders for a short time
Gibbons, Orlando 1583–1625	Composer of madrigals, e.g. 'The Silver Swan', and anthems, e.g. 'This is the Record of John'; also contributed to the first book of keyboard music printed in England, *Parthenia*	Organist of Chapel Royal from 1604 and Westminster Abbey from 1623
Frescobaldi, Girolamo 1583–1643	In 1612 he published 12 fantasias, and in 1624 a collection of 10 ricercari, five canzoni and 11 capriccios. Frescobaldi was a strong influence of the German Baroque school through the work of his pupils Froberger and Tunder	Italian virtuoso organist, born in Ferrara. Became organist at St Peter's, Rome, where 30,000 people are said to have attended his first performance

Composer	Works	Biography
Schütz, Heinrich 1585–1672	*Christmas Oratorio*; settings of the Passion	German composer and organist who studied law and was one of Bach's influences
Froberger, Johann Jakob 1616–67	Froberger was the first important German composer for the harpsichord and a leading light of early Baroque music	German composer, born in Stuttgart. He became a court organist in Vienna, 1637, and later that year travelled to Rome to study under Frescobaldi
Lully, Jean-Baptiste 1632–1687	Composed 20 operas and ballets, including *Alceste* (1684), *Psyché* (1678), *Roland* (1685), *Armide et Rénaud* (1686), *Achille et Polixène* (posthumous collaboration with Colasse) and *Le Bourgeois Gentilhomme* (collaboration with Molière)	Italian-born but took French nationality in 1661; from 1664 collaborated with Molière in series of comedy-ballets which were forerunners of French opera; danced role of the Mufti in *Le Bourgeois Gentilhomme*; died accidentally by stabbing himself in the foot with long pole used to conduct (wound turned gangrenous)
Buxtehude, Diderik c. 1637–1707	20 cantatas, of which the cycle of seven *Membra Jesu Nostri*, are the most famous. He also wrote toccatas, preludes, fugues and chaconnes. Most of his harpsichord music has been lost	Danish organist and composer. In 1688 he became organist Mary's Church, Lübeck, where his fame spread throughout Northern Germany. Handel visited him in 1703 and in 1705 J.S. Bach was known to have walked the 200 miles form Arnstadt to hear him play
Blow, John 1649–1708	Wrote over 100 anthems and 13 services but best known work was masque *Venus and Adonis* (1682)	One of the first choirboys of Chapel Royal after Restoration and organist at Westminster Abbey (1668–79), preceding Henry Purcell
Corelli, Arcangelo 1653–1713	First composition: Sonata for Violin and Lute. 60 sonatas (48 trio and 12 solo) 12 Concerti Grossi (published posthumously) the most famous being his *Christmas Concerto*	Italian violinist, conductor and composer. From 1687 he was under the patronage of Cardinal Pamphili. Corelli was a skilled conductor and is often thought of as a pioneer of modern orchestral direction
Purcell, Henry 1659–1695	Only opera *Dido and Aeneas* (1683); fantasias for strings (1680); 'My Heart is Inditing' for Coronation of James II (1685); semi-operas include *The Fairy Queen*, *King Arthur*, *The Tempest* and the unfinished *The Indian Queen*	Succeeded Matthew Locke as composer to the king's violins and John Blow as organist of Westminster Abbey (1679); in 1682 became one of the three organists of the Chapel Royal
Scarlatti, Alessandro 1660–1725	First of 115 operas *Gli Equivoci*; his greatest considered to be *Mitridate Eupatore* (1707); only comic opera *Il Trionfo dell'Onore* (1718); last opera *La Griselda* (1721)	Founder of Neapolitan School of composers; father of Domenico Scarlatti
Couperin, François 1668–1733	Composed 230 harpsichord pieces, also chamber music	Wrote textbook *The Art of Touching the Keyboard*; known as 'Couperin the Great' on account of quantity of musicians in the family
Vivaldi, Antonio 1678–1741	First opera *Ottone in Villa* (1713); first Venetian opera *Orlando Finto Pazzo*; best known opera *Orlando Furioso* (1727); most famous work *The Four Seasons* (1725); most famous oratorio *Juditha Triumphans* (1716)	Nicknamed the Red Priest after taking holy orders in 1703; taught violin at Ospedale della Pietà, an orphanage, from 1703; died and buried in a pauper's grave in Vienna; Peter Ryom catalogued works, Leipzig, 1974 with prefix RV (Ryom Verzeichnis)

Name	Principal works	Details
Telemann, Georg Philipp 1681–1767	Often considered the most prolific of all composers with 600 overtures and 44 passions to his name as well as 40 operas (best known being *Pimpinone*, 1725)	German composer and organist who had no formal training but studied Lully and André Campra; appointed Kantor at the Thomaskirche, Leipzig, in preference to J.S. Bach
Bach, Johann Sebastian 1685–1750	Orchestral and keyboard works include: *Brandenburg Concertos (Nos 1–6)* (1717); *The Well-Tempered Klavier* (48 preludes and fugues); *Goldberg Variations* (30 variations on original theme); English suites and French suites, as well as the unfinished *Die Kunst der Fuge* (The Art of Fugue); famous oratorios include *St John Passion*, *St Matthew Passion* and *Christmas Oratorio*	Born Eisenach and died in Leipzig; orphaned at age of 10 and lived with elder brother at Ohrdruf;married his cousin Maria Barbara Bach in 1707 and afterher death in 1720 married Anna Magdalena Wilcken (December 1721); almost totally blind during last year of life; Wagner described his work as 'The most stupendous miracle in all music'; catalogues have BWV nos (Bach Werke Verzeichnis)
Scarlatti, Domenico 1685–1757	About 550 harpsichord sonatas; also operas and oratorios	Long-time friend of Handel; powerful influence on modern keyboard technique
Handel, George Frederick 1685–1759	First opera *Almira* (1705) and last *Deidamia* (1740); other notable operas include *Agrippina* (1709), *Rinaldo* (1711), *Teseo* (1712), *Radamisto* (1720), *Tamerlano* (1724), *Orlando* (1733), *Ariodante* (1735), *Alcina* (1735), *Berenice* (1737), *Serse* (1738); orchestral works include *Water Music* (1717) and *Music for Royal Fireworks* (1749) played in Green Park to mark the Peace of Aix-la-Chapelle; oratorios include *Esther* (1732), *Athalia* (1733), *Alexander's Feast* (1736), *Israel in Egypt* (1739), *Messiah* (1741), *Judas Maccabaeus* (1746); church music includes *Dettingen Te Deum* (1743), *Chandos Anthems* (1718), *Zadok the Priest* (1737); other famous work is 5th Harpsichord Suite, nicknamed *The Harmonious Blacksmith* (1720)	Born in Halle and died in London; son of a barber/surgeon; studied law until his father died; became English citizen in 1726; received pension of £200 p.a. for life from Queen Anne (1712), which was increased to £600 by King George I for whom he wrote his famous. *Water Music* suite in 1717; blind for last 7 years of his life and aided by his agent and friend, John Christopher Smith
Arne, Thomas Augustine 1710–1778	First opera was *Rosamond* (1733); composed settings for Shakespeare songs including 'Under the Greenwood Tree', 'Where the Bee Sucks' and 'Blow Blow thou Winter Wind'; most famous work is 'Rule Britannia', originally written for *The Masque of Alfred*	Born and died in London; son of an upholsterer and educated at Eton; his sister was famous actress Mrs Cibber; son Michael wrote 'The Lass with a delicate air'; married a singer, Cecilia Young (1736)
Boyce, William 1711–1779	Most famously associated with the song 'Heart of Oak', composed in 1759 for pantomime *Harlequin's Invasion* to words by David Garrick; 8 symphonies and 12 overtures	Master of the King's Musick from 1755
Gluck, Christoph Willibald 1714–1787	First opera *Artaserse* (1741); best known opera is *Orfeo et Eurydice* (1762); other operas include *La Clemenza di Tito* (1752), *Alceste* (1767) and *Armide* (1777); his best known ballet is *Don Juan* (1761); opera comiques include *The Pilgrimage to Mecca*	Born Erasbach, Germany and died in Vienna; German composer under patronage of Prince Lobkowitz in his formative years; in 1754 Empress Maria Theresa appointed him opera Kapellmeister to court theatre in Vienna
Haydn, Franz Joseph 1732–1809	Composed 104 numbered symphonies; Symphony in D Major No 96 is called the 'Miracle' as it was thought that after its first performance the audience flocking to applaud him escaped injury	Austrian-born son of a farmer-wheelwright; precocious talent as a child; from 1761 was patronized by Prince Paul Esterházy, working as Vice-Kapellmeister at

Eisenstadt, Hungary; mutual admiration for Mozart influenced his work from 1781; Beethoven was his pupil for a short period; regarded as the father of the symphony only because of his prolific output; his works are often given Hob nos., after Anthony van Hoboken (1887–1983), who catalogued them

when a chandelier fell on their empty seats. In fact, this incident occurred on 2 February 1795 while his 102nd Symphony was playing; composed 20 operas, the first La Canterina 1766 and the last Orfeo ed Euridice (1791); other works include numerous masses, cantatas, sonatas, oratorios, concertos and chamber music

Cimarosa, Domenico
1749–1801

Court composer to Catherine II of Russia; in 1791 succeeded Salieri as Kapellmeister to Leopold II in Vienna; sentenced to death in 1799 for supporting French Republican army but reprieved on condition he left Naples

First of 65 operas was Le Stravaganze del Conti (1772); best known opera The Secret Marriage (1792); other operas include Artaserse (1784), Penelope (1795) and L'Apprensivo Raggirato (1798); also wrote 30 keyboard sonatas

Mozart, Wolfgang Amadeus
1756–1791

Born in Salzburg and died in Vienna; Johannes Chrysostomus Wolfgangus Theophilus was baptismal name; son of Leopold, Vice-Kapellmeister to Prince Archbishop of Salzburg; sister was Maria Anna (Nannerl; 1751–1829); in Rome in 1769 he heard Allegri's Miserere and wrote it out from memory; married Constance Weber in August 1782; his Requiem Mass for Count von Walsegg was completed after his death by Franz Süssmayr; work was catalogued by Ludwig von Köchel, an Austrian botanist and mineralogist

First opera was Apollo et Hyacinthus (1767); other operas include Bastien und Bastienne (1768), Idomeneo (1780), The Marriage of Figaro (1786), Don Giovanni (1787), Così fan tutte (1789), Die Zauberflöte (The Magic Flute) (1791); last opera La Clemenza di Tito (1791); of the 41 symphonies the last 3 were composed in a matter of a few weeks; also wrote numerous orchestral pieces and concertos for both piano and violin as well as horn concertos, string quartets, 40 songs and many sonatas; Eine kleine Nachtmusik (1787) is a popular orchestral piece, being theme tune for Brain of Britain quiz

Beethoven, Ludwig van
1770–1827

Born in Bonn and buried in Central Friedhof, Vienna; father was court singer to the elector of Cologne; dedicated his 3rd Symphony to Napoleon but retracted it on hearing he had made himself emperor; learned he was going deaf in 1798; mystery cloaks identity of his 'Immortal Beloved', although Antonie Brentano is a candidate as he dedicated his Diabelli Variations to her; freedom of Vienna bestowed on him in 1815

Only opera Fidelio (1805) was originally called Leonora; nine complete symphonies, but Dr Barry Cooper, a music lecturer at Aberdeen University, has pieced together, from sketches, a 10th Symphony by making projections of existing themes; composed 32 piano sonatas, including No. 14 in C sharp minor (Moonlight) and No. 15 in D major (Pastoral); best known piano concerto was No. 5 (Emperor); numerous songs, sonatas and masses; one violin concerto

Paganini, Niccolò
1782–1840

Born in Genoa, died of cancer of the larynx in Nice; regarded as greatest genius of the violin; successful gambler who owned a casino and lent money to struggling musicians, e.g. Berlioz; Mephistophelean looks fostered stories of satanic powers

Six violin concertos remain but various others lost; composed many variations on existing works, such as God Save the King, an aria from La Cenerentola and Witches' Dance, based on an air by Süssmayr; popular work is Variations on a Theme of Rossini and 24 Caprices; also wrote 12 sonatas for violin and guitar

Weber, Carl Maria
1786–1826

Born Eutin in Oldenburg, Germany, the son of a musician and actor-manager; died of tuberculosis while staying with Sir George Smart in his Great Portland St home and re-buried in Dresden in 1844

First of 9 operas Das Waldmädchen (1800); other operas include Silvana (1810), Abu Hassan (1811), Der Freischütz (1821), Euryanthe (1823) and his final opera Oberon (1826); also composed symphonies, songs and masses

Meyerbeer, Giacomo
1791–1864

German operatic composer, born in Berlin and originally named Jakob Liebmann Beer. He was a child prodigy pianist, playing a Mozart concerto at the age of 11. Meyerbeer's pageant-like operas were attacked by the anti-Semitism of Wagner

First opera Jephtas Gelübde (1812). Other notable operas include Robert le Diable (1831), Les Huguenots (1836), Le Prophète (1840), L'Etoile du Nord (1854) and L'Africaine (1864). Also wrote oratorio, marches, songs, and church music

Name	Principal works	Details
Rossini, Gioachino Antonio 1792–1868	First of 35 operas was *Demetrio e Polibio* (1806); best known operas include *Tancredi* (1813), *Otello* (1816), *Elizabeth of England* (1815), *La Gazza Ladia*, *Cinderella* (1817) and his last opera *William Tell* (1829); also composed cantatas, sonatas and orchestral works although retired completely from opera as a result of neurasthenia; late works include *Petite Messe Solennelle* and a variety of pieces he called 'Sins of my Old Age'; notable prodigy: 6 string sonatas date from his early teens	Born Pesaro in Italy, died in Paris; buried in Père Lachaise cemetary, but reinterred in Florence in 1887; son of a trumpeter and a singer; married soprano Isabella Colbran (1821) and then after divorcing her, Olympe Pélissier; court composer to Charles X of France in 1825; famous for his 'Samedi Soirs' performances; a gourmand: Tournedos Rossini is named after him; nicknamed Monsieur Crescendo
Schubert, Franz Peter 1797–1828	Wrote 9 numbered symphonies although 7th and 8th were unfinished, as were some unnumbered ones; first opera *Des Teufels Lustschloss* (1814); prolific output included over 600 songs of which 144 were written in 1815 (8 in one day); some popular songs include 'Death and the Maiden (1817)', the *Winterreise* (Winter Journey) song cycle (1827) and settings of Shakespearean songs, e.g. 'Who is Sylvia?' and 'Hark, Hark the Lark', *Lazarus* (1820), his setting of psalm 23, is best known, although 'Wanderer Fantasy' is popular; unusually did not compose any concertos	Born and died in Vienna, buried near to Beethoven at Währing, and later exhumed and reburied in the Central Cemetery of Vienna; father was schoolmaster and his first teacher; the celebrated baritone Michael Vogl sang many of his lieder; Schubert was a torchbearer at Beethoven's funeral in 1827; his works were catalogued by Otto Deutsch
Donizetti, Gaetano 1797–1848	First opera *Il Pigmalione* (1816); other operas include *Enrico di Borgogna* (1818), *Zoraide di Grenate* (1822), *Ann Boleyn* (1830), *Lucretia Borgia* (1833), *Lucia di Lammermoor* (1835), *Mary Stuart* (1835), *Roberto Devereux* (1837), *Don Pasquale* (1843) and (last) *Dom Sébastien* (1843); also wrote church music, string quartets and symphonies	Born and died in Bergamo; joined the Austrian army and composed in his spare time until 1822 when he left and became full-time composer; became insane in later life due to syphilis
Bellini, Vincenzo 1801–1835	First opera *Adelson e Salvini* (1825); others include *The Sleepwalker* (1831), *Norma* (1831) and, last opera, *I Puritani* (1835)	Born in Catania, Sicily, died in Puteaux, near Paris, reinterred in Catania 1876; studied under Niccolò Zingarelli at San Sebastiano in Naples
Berlioz, Hector 1803–1869	Operas: *Benvenuto Cellini* (1837), *Les Troyens* (1858) and *Béatrice et Bénédict* (1862); famous orchestral works include *Waverley* (1828), *King Lear* (1831), *Le Corsaire* (1831), *Rob Roy* (1832), *Harold in Italy* (1834), *Symphonie Funèbre et Triomphale* (1840); best known work is *Symphony Fantastique* (1830); famous dramatic cantata is *The Damnation of Faust*	Born Grenoble and died in Paris; son of a provincial doctor but dropped out of medical school for a music career; married Irish actress Harriet Smithson (1833); Paganini paid him 20,000 francs for *Harold in Italy*; formed liaison with singer Marie Recio (1841)
Strauss the Elder, Johann 1804–1849	Composed 251 works of which 152 were waltzes; *Radetzky March* (1848), named after an Austrian field-marshal, easily his best known work	Born and died (scarlet fever) in Vienna
Glinka, Mikhail 1804–1857	Two operas *Life for the Tsar* (1836) – aka Ivan Susanin – and *Ruslan and Lyudmila* (1842); orchestral works include *Kamarinskaya* (1848) and *Night in Madrid* (1848)	Born in Smolensk and died in Berlin; first Russian composer to be recognised outside Russia; worked in Communications Ministry 1824–8
Mendelssohn, Felix 1809–1847	Twelve early string symphonies, also 5 mature symphonies and concertos (e.g. for violin); dramatic works include *Midsummer Night's Dream* and the unfinished opera *Lorelei*; best known oratorios *Elijah* (1846)	Born Hamburg and died in Leipzig, probably due to overwork and blow of sister's death; grandson of philosopher Moses Mendelssohn; wrote *Hebrides Overture* (aka *Fingal's Cave*)

Composer	Biography	Works
(continued from previous page)	after visit to Britain in 1829; eldest sister was Fanny, a piano virtuoso; at 12 became friend of the 72-year-old Goethe	and *St Paul* (1836); hymns include 'Hear My Prayer' (1844), which contains the section 'O for the Wings of a Dove'
Chopin, Frédéric 1810–1849	Born in Zelazowa Wola, Poland, of French father and Polish mother; died in Paris; all works involve a piano; though a piano virtuoso, gave only about 30 public performances; lover of novelist George Sand (1837–47)	Piano works include the 'Funeral March' Sonata (1837), *Krakowiak Rondo* (1828) and *Là ci darem variations*; famous for his nocturnes, preludes, mazurks, études, written for solo piano; Waltz in D flat, known as the Minute Waltz
Schumann, Robert 1810–1856	Born in Zwickau and died in Endenich; studied law at Leipzig and Heidelberg; married Clara Wieck in 1840; attempted suicide in 1854 by throwing himself in the Rhine and was committed to an asylum	Only opera *Genoveva* (1849); incidental music to Byron's verse-drama *Manfred* 1849; 4 symphonies, songs and song-cycles, and numerous piano pieces, including *Abegg Variations* (dedicated to Meta Abegg and written using notes of her surname in 1830)
Liszt, Franz 1811–1886	Born Raiding in Hungary, died in Bayreuth; child prodigy who gave first piano recital aged 9; lived with Countess Marie d'Agoult from 1833 and had 3 children, one of whom, Cosima, first married Hans Bülow and then Wagner; Kapellmeister at Weiner court 1848–59, and championed Wagner and Berlioz; in 1865 he took minor orders and became Abbé Liszt	One opera *Don Sanche* (1825) in collaboration with Ferdinando Paer; 2 symphonies *Faust* (1857) and *Dante* (1856); piano works include 19 composed 'Hungarian Rhapsodies', 1846–85, *Annés de pèlerinage* (1848–77) and concertos; symphonic poems include *Les Préludes* (1848), *Orpheus* (1854), *Prometheus* (1850) and *Hamlet* (1858); also composed numerous études, songs and oratorios
Wagner, Richard 1813–1883	Born Leipzig and died in Venice, buried at Wahnfried; attended school in Dresden and Thomasschule in Leipzig; married actress Minna Planer in 1836 but had affair with Mathilde Wesendonck; King Ludwig of Bavaria became his patron; Minna died in 1866 and he started affair with Cosima, wife of Hans Bülow, who bore him 2 daughters (Isolde and Eva); Cosima's marriage was annulled in 1869 and she gave birth to Wagner's son, Siegfried; Wagner and Cosima were married in 1870	Composed only 1 symphony, in C (1832); first opera *Die Feen* (The Fairies 1834) although he did compose earlier work *Die Hochzeit* but destroyed it; other operas include *Rienzi, The Flying Dutchman, Lohengrin, Tannhäuser, Der Ring des Nibelungen, The Mastersingers of Nuremberg* and *Parsifal* (his last); the opera *Tristan und Isolde* reflected his emotional turmoil over Mathilde Wesendonck; orchestral works include overture based on 'Rule, Britannia', *Faust* overture, *Siegfried Idyll* and concert overture *Polonia*; also composed *7 Songs From Goethe's Faust*; as well as many books on music; pioneer of the Leitmotiv
Verdi, Giuseppe 1813–1901	Born Parma, died in Milan leaving bulk of his money to a home he had founded for elderly musicians; innkeeper's son first taught by local organist Antonio Barezzi, a wholesaler whose daughter he married; between 1838 and 1840 his wife and 2 children died; married soprano, Giuseppina Strepponi in 1859; in 1860, after Italianindependence from Austria, elected deputy in first National Parliament	First opera *Oberto, Conte di San Bonifacio* (1838) although an earlier one, *Rocester*, is lost; other operas include *Nabucco* (1841), *Ernani* (1843), *Attila* (1846), *Macbeth* (1847), *Luisa Miller* (1849), *Stiffelio* (1850), *Rigoletto* (1851), *Il Trovatore* (1852), *Otello* (1886) and *Falstaff* (1892); Verdi's *Requiem* composed in memory of poet Manzoni and played at funeral of Diana, Princess of Wales (1997)
Gounod, Charles 1818–1893	Born in Paris, died in St Cloud; won Grand Prix de Rome in 1839; studied for priesthood but chose a life in music	First opera *Sapho* (1851); best known *Faust* (1859); 3 symphonies and various oratorios and cantatas; also *Funeral March of a Marionette* (1872)
Offenbach, Jacques 1819–1880	Born in Deutz, near Cologne, and died in Paris; son of a cantor in Cologne synagogue; surname Offenbach came from the name of family's home town	First opera *Die Rheinnixen* (1864); only grand opera *The Tales of Hoffmann* (1881); only ballet *Le Papillon* (1860); operettas include *Orpheus in the Underworld* (1858), *La Belle Hélène* (1864) and *Daphnis et Chloé* (1860)

MUSIC CLASSICAL

Name	Principal works	Details
Bruckner, Anton 1824–1896	Ten symphonies, last unfinished; masses in D Minor (1864), E Minor (1869) and F Minor (1872) as well as cantatas and chamber music; many works edited by composer and others, and exist in various versions	Born in Ansfelden, died in Vienna; known internationally as a virtuoso organist; first (unnumbered) symphony written in his late thirties
Smetana, Bedrich 1824–1884	First opera *The Brandenburgers in Bohemia* (1863); other operas include *The Bartered Bride* (1866), *The Secret* (1878), *The Kiss* (1876) and *Two Widows* (1874); cycle of 6 symphonic poems, *Má Vlast* (My Country 1874–9)	Born in Litomysl, died in Prague; regarded as founder of Czech music; active in founding national opera house; venereal disease caused deafness and later insanity
Strauss the Younger, Johann 1825–1899	Composed nearly 400 waltzes of which the best known include *Blue Danube*, *Tales from the Vienna Woods* (1868), *Roses From the South* (1880) and *Emperor Waltz* (1888); most famous operetta *Die Fledermaus* (The Bat 1874); also composed various polkas and an unfinished ballet, *Cinderella* (completed by Joseph Bayer)	Born and died in Vienna; worked as a bank clerk in early career; known as the Waltz King; in 1848 revolution supported opposite side to his father
Borodin, Alexander 1833–1887	Only opera *Prince Igor* left unfinished and completed by Rimsky-Korsakov and Alexander Glazunov; 3 symphonies, the 3rd completed by Glazunov; 2 string quartets; tone poem *In The Steppes of Central Asia*; music used in Forrest and Wright's musical *Kismet*	Born and died in St Petersburg; illegitimate son of Russian prince; doctor and professor of chemistry; feminist who founded a school of medicine for women
Brahms, Johannes 1833–1897	Four symphonies and 4 concertos; orchestral works include *Tragic Overture* (1880), *Academic Festival Overture* (1880) and *Variations on a Theme by Haydn* (1873); key choral works, *German Requiem* (1866) and *Schickalslied* (1871); no operas, but nearly 200 songs as well as chamber music, organ works and piano works, including *Variations on a Theme by Paganini* (1866)	Born in Hamburg, died in Vienna; son of professional double-bass player; hailed as genius by Schumann in essay 'New Paths' 1853 and succeeded him as teacher to Princess Friederike of Lippe-Detmold
Saint-Saëns, Camille 1835–1921	First opera *La Princesse Jaune* (1872); most famous opera *Samson and Delilah* (1868); 3 symphonies (2 other symphonies were withdrawn); symphonic poems include *Danse Macabre* (1874); popular orchestral piece *Carnival of the Animals* (1886), its performance forbidden in the composer's lifetime (movement 13, 'The Swan', most popular piece); also composed *Variations on a Theme of Beethoven* (1874) and *Polonaise* for 2 pianos; various oratorios and masses include Psalm 150 (1907); 5 piano concertos, No. 2 best known	Born in Paris and died in Algiers; symphony No. 3 dedicated to Liszt's memory; wrote coronation march for Edward VII, 1902; *Carnival of the Animals* in 14 movements i.e. 'Royal March of the Lion', 'Hens & Cocks', 'Wild Asses', 'Tortoises', 'The Elephant', 'Kangaroos', 'Aquarium', 'Persons with Long Ears', 'Cuckoo in the Depths of Woods', 'Aviary', 'Pianists', 'Fossils', 'The Swan', 'Finale'; the tortoises are represented by the can-can in slow motion, the 'Dance of the Sylphs' on double-basses for the elephant and the fossils is a parody of *Danse Macabre*
Bizet, Georges 1838–1875	First opera *Le Docteur Miracle* (1856); last and most famous opera *Carmen* (1874); one symphony; orchestral suite *L'Arlésienne*	Born in Paris, died in Bougival; entered Paris Conservatory at age 9; Won Grand Prix de Rome in 1857
Mussorgsky, Modest 1839–1881	First opera *Salammbô* (unfinished); *Boris Godunov* (1869) only completed opera; piano works *Pictures at an Exhibition*; orchestral *A Night on the Bare Mountain*	Born in Karevo, Pskov, died in St Petersburg; one of the Russian 5 or Mighty Handful (the others: Balakirev, Cui, Borodin, Rimsky-Korsakov)
Tchaikovsky, Pyotr 1840–1893	First opera *Voyevoda* (1868); others include *Eugene Onegin* (1879) and *The Queen of Spades* (1890); last opera *Yolanta* (1891); 3 ballets *Swan Lake*	Born in Votkinsk, died in St Petersburg of cholera, although he may have taken poison to avoid a homosexual scandal; read

Law in St Petersburg and became civil servant; married Antonina Miliukova 1877 but left her a month later and attempted suicide in his guilt; Countess Nadezhda von Meck was his patron although they never met (it is said that he crossed the street once to avoid a meeting); it is said that he used to hold his head while conducting, lest it fall off!

(1876), *Sleeping Beauty* (1889) and *Nutcracker* (1892); other works include 6 symphonies, 2 piano concertos, a violin concerto, a number of tone poems including *Romeo and Juliet* and *Italian Caprice*, as well as an unnumbered *Manfred Symphony* (1885); *Rococo Variations* for cello and orchestra

Dvořák, Antonín
1841–1904

Born in Nelahozeves, Bohemia, died in Prague; son of a village butcher; joined National Theatre of Prague as viola player in 1866

Opera *Alfred* (1870); best known *Rusalka* (1900); last opera *Armida* (1903); 9 symphonies, including No. 9 in E Minor, *From the New World*; and other cello concertos

Sullivan, Arthur
1842–1900

Born in Lambeth and died, appropriately, on St Cecilia's Day, at Westminster; son of Irish bandmaster at Sandhurst; first to win Mendelssohn Scholarship of the Royal Academy of Music, 1856; knighted in 1883; *Thespis* in 1871 was 1st collaboration with Gilbert; Savoy Theatre, opened during run of *Patience*, specialized in Gilbert and Sullivan; the two fell out during a run of *The Gondoliers* supposedly over a choice of carpet for the theatre; they were reconciled for *Utopia Ltd* and *The Grand Duke* (1896)

Only grand opera *Ivanhoe* (1890); composed tune for hymn 'Onward Christian Soldiers'; 14 operettas in collaboration with W.S. Gilbert; songs include 'The Lost Chord'; first operetta *Cox and Box* (1866, librettist Burnand); last operetta *The Emerald Isle* left unfinished (completed by Edward German to Basil Hood's libretto); oratorios include *The Prodigal Son* (1869); cantatas include *Kenilworth* (1864); composed a symphony in E (the 'Irish'); incidental music to various Shakespeare plays

Grieg, Edvard
1843–1907

Born and died in Bergen; married his cousin, soprano Nina Hagerup, in 1867 when he also founded the Norweigen Academy of Music; Ibsen commissioned incidental music to Peer Gynt

Orchestral works include *Peer Gynt Suite* (1875), *Lyric Suite* (1904) and *Holberg Suite* (1884); wrote *Norwegian Dances* (4 hands) and numerous songs for piano; 1 symphony, 1 piano concerto

Rimsky-Korsakov, Nikolay
1844–1908

Born in Tikhvin, died in Lyubensk; navy cadet as child, hoping to become a sailor; slow movement of 1st Symphony written off Gravesend; wrote 1st opera whilst serving as a naval lieutenant; edited *100 Russian Folk-Songs* 1877

First opera *The Maid of Pskov* (aka: *Ivan the Terrible*) 1872; last opera (of 14) *The Golden Cockerel* (1907); 3 symphonies – first major Russian symphonies; famous orchestral works include *Spanish Caprice* (1887) and *Sheherazade* (1888)

Janáček, Leoš
1854–1928

Born in Moravia, died in Moravská, Ostrava; Czech composer who had his success late in life; inspired by an affair with Kamila Stösslova

First opera *Šárka* (1888); others *Jenůfa* (1904) and *From the House of the Dead* (1930: his last); Glagolitic Mass; rhapsody *Taras Balba*; 2 string quartets; song-cycle *Diary of One Who Disappeared*

Elgar, Edward
1857–1934

Born in Broadheath, Worcestershire, died in Worcester; son of an organist and music shop proprietor in Worcester; married General's daughter Caroline Roberts who died in 1920; knighted in 1904 as first English composer of International repute since Purcell

Composed 2 symphonies and an unfinished 3rd; cantata, *The Dream of the Gerontius* (1900); orchestral works *Pomp and Circumstance* marches (1901–30), *Enigma Variations* (1899); Violin Concerto in B Minor (1910); Cello Concerto in E Minor (1919); unfinished opera *The Spanish Lady*

Puccini, Giacomo
1858–1924

Born in Lucca, Italy, died in Brussels; came from a long line of church musicians

First opera *Le Villi* (The Willis) 1883; best known opera *Manon Lescaut* (1893), *La Bohème* (1896), *Tosca* (1900), *Madame Butterfly* (1904), *Turandot* (unfinished, but completed by Franco Alfano)

Name	Principal works	Details
Mahler, Gustav 1860–1911	Ten symphonies (one unfinished, completed by Deryck Cooke, 1st 8 of which Mahler conducted first performances); song symphony *Song of the Earth* (1909); song-cycle *Kindertotenlieder* (1904); cantata *Das Klagende Lied* (1880); only opera was completion of Weber's *The Three Pintos*	Born in Kalist, Bohemia, died in Vienna; brilliant conductor who headed Hamburg Opera from 1891; then Vienna State Opera, New York Metropolitan Opera, New York Philharmonic; converted from Judaism to Roman Catholicism 1897; married musician Alma Schindler in 1902
Debussy, Achille-Claude 1862–1918	Most famous opera *Pelléas et Mélisande*; Orchestral works *Prélude à l'après-midi d'un Faune* (1894); *La Mer* (1905); *Nocturnes* (1899)	Born in St Germain-en-Laye, died (cancer) in Paris; won Prix de Rome in 1884 with cantata *L'Enfant prodigue*; influenced by Javanese gamelan music at Paris Exposition; as well as by impressionist painters; married Lily Texier 1899 but left her 5 years later for a singer, Emma Bardac and married her in 1908; part of *La Mer* written in Eastborne
Delius, Frederick 1862–1934	First opera *Irmelin* (1892); last opera *Fennimore and Gerda* (1910); others *The Magic Fountain* (1895), *Koanga* (1897), *A Village Romeo and Juliet* (1901), and *Margot-la-Rouge* (1902); orchestral pieces *Brigg Fair* (1907), *On Hearing the First Cuckoo in Spring* (1912); choral works *Sea Drift* (1909), *A Mass of Life* (1909); various Norwegian songs, as well as concertos, piano pieces and melodramas	Born in Bradford, Yorkshire, died in Grez-sur-Loing; reinterred in May 1935 at Limpsfield, Surrey; until 1904 composed under name of Fritz Delius; influenced by lasting friendship with Grieg; married Jelka Rosen 1903 and lived near-Fontainebleau; became blind (probably due to syphilis) and continued composing helped by a young Yorkshire musician, Eric Fenby
Szymanowski, Karol 1882–1937	Operas *Hagith* (1913), *King Roger* (1924); 4 symphonies, 2 violin concertos, 2 ballets; voices and orchestra *Love Songs of Hafiz* (1911), *Stabat Mater* (1926); violin and piano, *Myths* (1915); also songs	Born in Tymoslowska, Ukraine, died in Lausanne; leading figure at turn of century in composer's association 'Young Poland in Music'; later influenced both by Stravinsky and by folk music of Tatra Mountains
Strauss, Richard 1864–1949	First of 15 operas *Guntram* (1893); others *Salome* (1905), *Electra* (1909), *Der Rosenkavalies* (1911), *Die Frau ohne Schatten* (1919); last opera *Capriccio* (1941); ballets include *Josephslegende* (1914); tone poems include *Till Eulenspiegel*, *Don Quixote* and *Also sprach Zarathustra*	Born in Munich, died in Garmisch-Partenkirchen; son of a horn player in Munich Court Orchestra; married soprano Pauline de Ahna, 1894; became Austrian citizen in 1947
Dukas, Paul 1865–1935	One opera *Ariane et Barbe-Bleu* (1906); 1 ballet *La Péri* (1912); most famous work, symphonic poem *The Sorcerer's Apprentice* (1897); 1 symphony, 1 piano sonata	Born and died in Paris; never prolific, he burned at least 15 years of unpublished work before he died; helped Saint-Saëns complete Guiraud's opera *Frédégonde*
Sibelius, Jean 1865–1957	Tone poem *Finlandia* became voice of his country; others *En Saga* (1901), *The Swan of Tuonela* (1893); 7 symphonies, 1 violin concerto	Born in Hämeenlinna (Tavastehus), died in Järvenpää; received State pension for life in 1897 to free him to compose; 5th Symphony written on his 50th birthday; did not compose for the last 27 years of his life
Nielsen, Karl 1865–1931	Six symphonies for violin, flut and clarinet; concertos, string quartets, piano music, songs; operas: *Saul and David* (1902), *Maskarade* (1906)	Born in Nootre-Lyndelse, Denmark, died in Copenhagen; wife a sculptor; developed 'progressive tonality' in which a work may change its key as it develops; in 5th symphony, sidedrummer is instructed to improvise so as to halt progress of orchestra

Satie, Erik
1866–1925

French composer and pianist, born in Honfleur, of a French father and Scottish mother. In 1893, he had a stormy affair with the artist Suzanne Valadon but lived as a recluse for some . years Satie parodied the orthodoxy and stiffness of established music using whimsical titles and musical directions. He was a major influence on many French composers including Debussy, Ravel and 'Les Six'

Three ballets *Parade* (1917), *Mercure*, and *Relâche* (1924). Parade was scored for typewriters, airplane propellers, sirens, ticker-tape, steamship whistle and lottery wheel. A marionette opera *Geneviève de Brabant* (1899). Piano pieces, include *Trois morceaux en forme de poire* (Three pear-shaped pieces) a work for four hands (1903) and *Gymnopédies* (1888) a trio of piano pieces Nos 1 and 3 orchestrated by Debussy and No. 2 by Roland-Manuel.

Vaughan Williams, Ralph
1872–1958

Born in Down Ampney, Gloucestershire, died in London; lived in Dorking in Surrey 1929–53

First opera *Hugh the Drover* (1914); last *The Pilgrim's Progress* (1951); orchestral works *In the Fen Country* (1904), *Fantasia on a Theme by Thomas Tallis* (1910); 9 symphonies, also concertos, ballets, songs and chamber music

Rachmaninoff, Sergei
1873–1943

Born in Semyonovo, Starorussky, died in Beverly Hills; virtuoso pianist; became US citizen in 1943; lifelong friend of the celebrated bass Chaliapin; underwent hypnosis when experiencing creative block – 2nd piano concerto dedicated to hypnotist

Three symphonies; 4 piano concertos, notably the 2nd in C minor; *Rhapsody on a Theme of Paganini* (1934) for piano and orchestra; many piano pieces; first opera *Aleko* (1892), last *Monna Vanna* (1907)

Holst, Gustav
1874–1934

Born in Cheltenham, died in London; worked as trombonist for Carl Rosa Opera (1898–1900); learned Sanskrit to translate hymns from *Rig Veda*

Best known for orchestral suite *The Planets* (1918); also for orchestra: *Egdon Heath* (1927), *Book Green Suite* (1933); first opera *Savitri* (1908), last opera *The Wandering Scholar* (1930)

Schoenberg, Arnold
1874–1951

Revolutionized music to reach atonality and serialism; had a phobia about the number 13, and "Moses und Aron" is spelled thus so as to only have 12 letters; teacher of Webern and Berg; became a US citizen in 1941

First opera (the monodrama): *Erwartung* (1909), last *Moses und Aron* (19051) other significant works include: *Gurrelieder, Pierrot Lunaire, A Survivor from Warsaw* and *Verklärte Nacht*

Ives, Charles
1874–1954

Born in Danbury, Connecticut, died in New York; wrote symphony while at Yale; formed his own insurance company (1907); 3rd symphony won Pulitzer Prize (1947)

Four symphonies and the so-called first orchestral set (New England Symphony); 'Universe' Symphony was never completed in his lifetime but Johnny Reinhard completed it and performed it in 1996; also wrote the song 'Shall We Gather at the River'

Ravel, Maurice
1875–1937

Born in Ciboure, died in Paris; orchestrated Mussorgsky's *Pictures at an Exhibition*; repeated failure to win Prix de Rome led to resignation of director of Paris Conservatoire, which awards it

Operas: *L'Heure Espagnole* (1907), *L'Enfant et les Sortilèges* (1925); ballets: *Daphnis et Chloé* (1911), *Boléro* (1928); 2 piano concertos (written simultaneously); also for piano: *Pavane pour une infante défunte* (1899), *Le Tombeau de Couperin* (1917); chamber music

Respighi, Ottorino
1879–1936

Born in Bolgna, died in Rome; studied under Rimsky-Korsakov in St Petersburg and Max Binch in Berlin

Roman trilogy of symphonic poems: *Pines of Rome, Fountains of Rome, Roman Festivals*; also *Three Botticelli Pictures*; concertos and operas

Bridge, Frank
1879–1941

Born in Brighton, died in Eastbourne; English composer, conductor, violist and violinist. In 1927 taught the 14-year-old Benjamin Britten. Conducted the New Symphony Orchestra from its inception at Covent Garden. Best known for his string quartets

One opera: *The Christmas Rose* (1929). Orchestral suite *The Sea* (1911) String Quartets: *Sir Roger de Coverley* (1922); *Scherzo Phantastick* (1901), and *Sally in our Alley* (1916)

MUSIC CLASSICAL

Name	Principal works	Details
Ireland, John 1879–1962	Orchestral prelude *The Forgotten Rite* (1913). Symphonic rhapsody *Mai Dun* (1921) the title refers to the prehistoric Dorset fortification, Maiden Castle. Comic overture *Satyricon* 1946). Tone poem *Sea Fever* (1913)	English composer and pianist, born in Bowden, Cheshire, and died in Washington, West Sussex. Established his reputation with his Violin Sonata in A (1917) but is best remembered for his settings of poems by Hardy, Houseman and Masefield
Bartók, Béla 1881–1945	*Music for Strings, Percussion and Celesta* (1936); *Concerto for Orchestra* (1943); only opera *Duke Bluebeard's Castle* (1911); ballets: *The Wooden Prince* (1911) and *The Miraculous Mandarin* (1919); 3 piano concertos; 2 violin concertos; 6 string quartets	Born in Nagyszentmiklós, Hungary (now Romania), died (leukaemia) in New York; dedicated collector of Hungarian and other East European folk music; anti-Nazi who emigrated to USA in 1940
Kodály, Zoltán 1882–1967	Three operas *Háry János* (1926), *Spinning Room* (1932), and *Czinka Panna* (1948). Choral and orchestral work *Psalmus Hungaricus* (1923) was based on text of Psalm 55 and commissioned for the 50th anniversary of the union of Buda and Pest. Two sets of Hungarian dances for orchestra *Marosszék Dances* (1930) and *Dances of Galánta* (1933)	Hungarian composer born in Kecskemét and died in Budapest. Wrote collections of folksongs with Béla Bartók between 1906 and 1921, although these were not published until 1951 as *Corpus Musicae Popularis Hungariae*. He carried out reforms in musical education and developed an evolutionary system of training and sight-singing
Stravinsky, Igor 1882–1971	Ballets include *The Firebird* (1910), *Petrushka* (1911), *The Rite of Spring* (1913), *Agon* (1953); first opera *The Nightingale* (1909), last *The Rake's Progress* (1951); important works in all the major forms include *Symphony of Psalms* (1930), *Ebony Concerto* (1946), *Septet* (1953), *Threni* (1958)	Born Oranienbaum, died New York; most influential classical composer of 20th century; became French citizen 1934, American 1945; first performance of *The Rite of Spring* in Paris caused famous riot by unattuned listeners
Webern, Anton 1883–1945	String quartet (1938); *Variations* for orchestra (1940); 3 cantatas; 1 symphony	Studied under Schoenberg and becoame rigorous exponent of serial music; born in Vienna, died in Mittersill after being shot accidentally by American sentry
Bax, Arnold 1883–1953	One ballet *Between Dusk and Dawn* (1917); seven symphonies. orchestral tone poem *Tintagel* (1919) first performed 1920; other orchestral works include *November Woods* (1917) and *Mourning Song* (1946)	Born in Streatham and died in Cork; english composer and pianist; master of the Kings/Queens; Music 1942–53. Knighted in 1937. His autobiography *Farewell My Youth* (1943) is an acclaimed work
Varèse, Edgard 1883–1965	Orchestral works include *Amériques* (1921), *Octandre* (1923) *Intégrales* (1925), *Arcana* (1927) and *Ionisation* (1931). Known for his experimental use of instrument combinations and unconventional percussion. His *Désert* (1954) employs tape-recorded sound; concentrated on electronic music after	French composer and conductor, born in Paris and died in New York. Became an American citizen in 1926. He organised the international Composers' Guild in 1921 and co-founded the Pan-American Association of Composers in 1927
Berg, Alban 1885–1935	Two operas, *Wozzeck* (1922) and *Lulu* (1935); *Lyric Suite* for string quartet (1926); violin concerto (1935)	Born and died in Vienna; (insect bite); quit civil servant career to compose; *Lulu* completetd by Friedrich Cerha, many years after Berg's death, due to reluctance of his widow
Prokofiev, Sergey 1891–1953	Seven symphonies, also concerti and string quartets; symphonic tale *Peter and the Wolf* (1936); ballets include *The Buffoon* (1920), *Age of Steel* (1926), *Romeo and Juliet* (1936); operas include *The Gambler* (1917), *Love for Three Oranges* (1919), *War and Peace* (1943)	Born Sontsovka, died in Moscow; lived in Paris 1920–33; wrote film scores, e.g. *Lieutenant Kijé* and *Alexander Nevsky*; died on the same day as Stalin

Bliss, Arthur
1891–1975

First opera *The Olympians* (1949); last opera *Tobias and the Angel* (1960); first ballet *Checkmate* (1937); last ballet *The Lady of Shalott* (1958); first symphony: *Colour Symphony*

Born and died in London; wrote music for Korda's film based on H.G. Wells's *Things to Come*; knighted in 1950; became master of the Queen's Musick in 1953

Hindemith, Paul
1895–1963

Operas include *Murder, the Hope of Women* (1919), *Mathis der Maler* (1935), *The Long Christmas Dinner* (1960); ballets: *Der Dämon* (1922), *Nobilissima Visione* (1938), *Hérodiade* (1944); several symphonies; a wealth of string quartets and sonatas

Born in Hannau, died in Frankfurt; married Gertrud Rottenberg in 1924; satirical opera *News of the Day* (1929) featured soprano singing in her bath; founded a music school in Ankara; associated with Gebrauchmusik ('utility' music, written for some social purpose)

Gershwin, George
1898–1937

First 'hit' song was 'Swanee' (1919); 1 opera: *Porgy and Bess*; *Rhapsody in Blue* for piano, jazz band and orchestra (1924); tone poem for *An American in Paris* (1928)

Born in Brooklyn, NY, died in Beverly Hills, California; turned pro musician aged 14; many collaborations with his elder brother, lyricist Ira Gershwin

Poulenc, Francis
1899–1963

First opera: *Les Mamelles des Tirésias* (1944), last *La Voix Humaine* (1958); ballet *Les Riches* (1923); solo piano works, concertos, sonatas and many songs; church music including *Gloria* and *Stabat Mater*

Born and died in Paris; had independent income (related to family in Rhône-Poulenc pharmaceuticals); longtime companion of baritone Pierre Bernac

Copland, Aaron
1900–1990

First ballet *Grohg* (1925); others *Billy the Kid* (1938), *Rodeo* (1942), *Appalachian Spring* (1944); 5 symphonies; orchestral work *El Salon Mexico* (1936); only opera *The Tender Land* (1954)

Born in Brooklyn, NY, died in New York; symphony finale based on *Fanfare for the Common Man*

Walton, William
1902–1983

Two symphonies; 4 concertos; oratorio *Belshazzar's Feet* (1931); 2 operas *Troilus and Cressida* (1954) and *The Bear* (1967); first ballet *The First Shoot* (1935)

Born in Oldham, died in Forio d'Ischia; son of choirmaster and singing teacher; wrote *Façade* to accompany Edith Sitwell; film scores include *First of the Few* and *Henry V*

Tippett, Michael
1905–1998

First opera *The Midsummer Marriage* (1955), also *The Knot Garden* (1969), *The Ice Break* (1976), last *New Year* (1989); 4 symphonies, 5 string quartets, concertos etc.; oratorio *A Child of Our Time* includes negro spirituals

Born and died in London; wrote own libretti; committed pacifist – acted as page-turner for Britten and Pears while imprisoned in Wormwood Scrubs as conscientious objector

Shostakovich, Dmitry
1906–1975

Fifteen symphonies, 15 string quartets, 6 concertos; piano preludes; first opera *The Nose* (1928); first ballet *The Age of Gold* (1930)

Born in St Petersburg, died in Moscow; twice severely criticized for formalism by Stalinist regime; fire fighter in Nazi siege of Leningrad 1941; wrote much film music

Messiaen, Olivier
1908–1992

One symphony *Turangalila* (premiered by Bernstein, 1948); *L'Ascension* for orchestra (1935); much organ music; 1 opera *St Francis of Assisi*

Born in Avignon, died in Paris; many works inspired by birdsong; *Quartet for the End of Time* (1941) written and premiered in POW camp

Carter, Elliott
1908–

Ballets *Pocahontas* (1939), *The Minotaur* (1947); concertos and symphonic works; many sonatas; *Night Fantasies* for piano (1980); 3 string quartets

Born in New York; encouraged by Ives; studied under Nadia Boulanger in Paris 1932–5

Barber, Samuel
1910–1981

Three operas and three symphonies; two ballets *Medea* (1946) revised as *Cave of the Heart* in 1947, and *Souvenirs* (1952); tone poem *Knoxville: Summer of 1915* (1947)

American composer and pianist; born in West Chester, Pennsylvania, and died in New York. Reputation made with his tone poem based on Arnold's 'Dover Beach' (1931)

MUSIC CLASSICAL

Name	Principal works	Details
Britten, Benjamin 1913–1976	First opera *Paul Bunyan* (1941); others include *Peter Grimes* (1945), *Billy Budd* (1951), *The Turn of the Screw* (1954) and last *Death in Venice* (1973); *Variations on a Theme of Frank Bridge* for string orchestra (1937); *War Requiem* for choir and orchestra (1961); only ballet *The Prince of the Pagodas* (1956)	Born at Lowestoft on St Cecilia's Day (22 Nov.) and died at Aldeburgh; lifelong friendship with Peter Pears; founded Aldeburgh Festival in 1948; became Lord Britten of Aldeburgh in 1976; first composer to be created life peer
Lutoslawski, Witold 1913–1994	Four symphonies; *Concerto for Orchestra* (1954); concertos for violin, cello, etc.; *Venetian Games* for orchestra (1961)	Warsaw café pianist in Second World War; regularly wrote controlled aleatory music, leaving certain things to chance; refused to write opera as could not see why people should sing rather than talk
Bernstein, Leonard 1918–1990	Three symphonies, 1 violin concerto (called *Serenade*); operas, *Trouble in Tahiti*, later became part of *A Quiet Place*; musicals: *On the Town, West Side Story, Candide*	Born in Lawrence, Massachusetts, died in New York; celebrated conductor and teacher; wrote film music for *On the Waterfront* (1954)
Simpson, Robert 1921–97	11 symphonies; two piano sonatas *Variations and Finale on a Theme of Haydn* (1948) and *Variations and Finale on a Theme of Beethoven* (1990)	English composer, musicologist and author; on BBC music staff 1951–80. Wrote books on several composers, including Carl Nielsen, Anton Bruckner and Jean Sibelius
Arnold, Malcolm 1921–	Nine symphonies; ballets: *Homage to the Queen* (1953), *Rinaldo and Armida* (1955) and *Electra* (1963); concert overture *Beckus the Dandipratt* (1948)	Born in Northampton; English composer, trumpeter, and conductor. Like Richard Rodney Bennett composed several film scores including *The Bridge on the River Kwai*; knighted in 1922
Boulez, Pierre 1921–	*Le Marteau sans Maître* for voice and chamber orchestra (1957); *Pli Selon Pli* for voice and orchestra (1962); *Eclats/Multiples* (1976)	Born in Montbrison; leader of French 12-tone music school; once suggested burning down opera houses, but now conducts in them regularly; continually revises a small number of works
Ligeti, György 1923–	Opera *Le Grand Macabre* (1978), *Kammerkonzert* (1970); 2 string quartets, piano etudes; various orchestral works	Born in Discószentmáron; left Hungary in 1956; music used in film 2001, though he only found out when he went to see it; one work is for 100 metronomes
Berio, Luciano 1925–	Orchestral music; many pieces for voice and various instruments include *Circles* (1960); operas include *La Vera Storia* (1982); most famous work *Sinfonia* (1969)	Exponent of serial and electronic music; one movement of *Sinfonia* mixes a movement of Mahler's *Resurrection* with much other music and spoken text
Henze, Hans Werner 1926–	Nine symphonies; prolific in most musical forms; first opera *Das Wundertheater* (1949), others include *Boulevard Solitude* (1951), *The Bassarids* (1965), *The English Cat* (1983); latest opera *Venus and Adonis* (1997)	Born in Gütersloh; equally at home with atonal, aleatory and conventional techniques; much influenced by Italy, living there for some years; many works have left-wing inspiration
Stockhausen, Karlheinz 1928–	Many works for varying ensembles, e.g. *Gruppen* for 3 orchestras and *Stimmung* for singers and tape; piano pieces, also electronic music; ongoing operatic project: *Licht* (cycle of 7 operas each linked to a day of the week)	Born in Mödrath, near Cologne; studied under Frank Martin, Messiaen and Milhaud; experimental works include a string quartet for players in helicopters

Rautavaara, Einojuhani
1928–

Born in Helsinki; a number of works invoke angels; *Cantus Arcticus* is a concerto for birds (recorded) and orchestra

Operas include *Vincent* (based on Van Gogh); latest opera *Aleksis Kivi* (1997); 7 symphonies, concertos, etc.

Sondheim, Stephen
1930–

Born in New York; writes lyrics and music; wrote lyrics for *West Side Story* and *Gypsy*; writes film scores, plays and film scripts; works often presented by opera companies

First musical *Saturday Night* (1957, but premiered in 1998); also *Company* (1970), *A Little Night Music* (1973), *Sweeney Todd* (1979); latest musical *Passion* (1995)

Górecki, Henryk
1933–

Born in Czernice, Poland; earlier work in a much more modern style; now exploring medieval influences

Three symphonies – the 3rd (*Symphony of Sorrowful Songs*) catapulted him to fame; also 2 string quartets, *Lerchenmusik, Kleines Requiem für ein Polka*, etc.

Maxwell Davies, Peter
1934–

Born in Salford, very prolific; many works inspired by Orcadian writer George Mackay Brown; surname is really Davies; universally known as Max; his 8th symphony, 'Antarctic Symphony' was composed after visiting the Antarctic peninsula between 20 December 1997 and 8 January 1998

Eight symphonies as of 2001; 10 Strathclyde Concertos for Scottish Chamber Orchestra, among other concertos; first opera *Taverner* (1970), latest *The Doctor of Myddfai* (1996); recent works include the tone poem *Mavis in Las Vegas and Mr Emmet Takes a Walk*

Birtwistle, Harrison
1934–

Born in Accrington; *Panic* (concertante work for saxophone and drum kit) commissioned for last night of centenary Prom season 1995; co-founded Pierrot Players with Maxwell Davies; knighted in 1998

First opera *Punch and Judy* (1967), latest *The Second Mrs Kong* (1994); one ballet: *Pulsefield* (1977); *Pulse Shadow* (1996) for soprano, ensemble and strings; *The Last Supper* (1999) for 14 soloists, chorus, orchestra and tape

Schnittke, Alfred
1934–1998

Born in Engels, USSR, died in Hamburg; Russian-born of German origin; name linked to 'polystylism', where many styles of music appear in one piece; symphony No. 5 is also Concerto Grosso No. 4

Eight symphonies, several concerti, including concerti grossi; first opera *Life with an Idiot* (1992), *The Eleventh Commandment* (1962), latest *Gesualdo* (1994); ballets include *Peer Gynt* (1986); also *Faust* cantata

Pärt, Arvo
1935–

Born in Paide, Estonia; emigrated to West Berlin in 1982; his early works were influenced by Shostakovich but developed his own austere style

Three symphonies, plus concerti; choral works include *St John's Passion* (1982), *Miserere* (1989) and *Berlin Mass* (1991)

Bennett, Richard Rodney
1936–

Born in Broadstairs, Kent; English composer and pianist educated at the Royal Academy of Music and in Paris under Pierre Boulez; ventured into the jazz field with his 1964 ballet *Jazz Calendar*, and followed this with *Jazz Pastoral* (1969); knighted in 1998.

Four operas; *The Ledge* (1961), *The Mines of Sulphur* (1965), *Penny for a Song* (1966), *Victory* (1969); ballets: *Jazz Calendar* (1964) and *Isadora* (1981); setting of poems by Kathleen Raine for soprano, chorus and orchestra *Spells* (1974)

Tavener, John
1944–

Born in London; recent work pervaded by religious sentiment of Greek Orthodox Church; claims descent from John Taverner

Operas include *Thérèse* (1979), *Mary of Egypt* (1992); many works for various instrumental groupings; *The Whale* (1967) was in first ever concert by London Sinfonietta; cello and strings piece *The Protecting Veil* (1987); choral work: *We Shall See Him as He Is* (1990)

Martland, Steven
1958–

English composer born in Liverpool; professed aim 'to return music to the streets'

Most famous orchestral work to date *Babi Yar* (1983); ensemble piece *Remembering Lennon* (1981)

MUSIC CLASSICAL

Adès, Thomas
1971–

Chamber Symphony (1990) first performed in 1993; *Five Eliot Landscapes* (1990): *The Origin of the Harp* (1994); *The Premises Are Alarmed* (1996) for the opening of the Bridgewater Hall in which the Hallé was conducted by Kent Nagano; *Powder Her Face* (1995) Chamber Opera; *Asyla* (1997)

English composer and pianist; second in piano section of the BBC Young Musician of the Year in 1989; graduated from Cambridge in 1992 with a double-starred first and established himself as a leading light both as a virtuoso and composer; Madehis Proms debut in 1998 and the following year conducted the BBC Symphony Orchestra in the London premiere of *Asyla*

Operatic Characters (by character)

Character	Opera	Composer	Role
Abdallo	Nabucco	Verdi	Nabucco's officer
Abdullah	Oberon	Weber	Pirate
Abigaille	Nabucco	Verdi	Nabucco's adopted daughter
Abimelech	Samson et Dalila	Saint-Saëns	Satrap of Gaza
Abraham	Háry János	Kodály	Innkeeper
Adalgisa	Norma	Bellini	Temple virgin
Adele	Die Fledermaus	Johann Strauss II	Eisenstein's maid
Adelma	Turandot	Busoni	Turandot's slave
Admetus	Alceste	Gluck	Alceste's husband
Adriano	Rienzi	Wagner	Colonna's son
Aegisth	Elektra	Richard Strauss	Klytemnestra's lover
Aeneas	Dido and Aeneas	Purcell	Trojan general
Agathe	Der Freischütz	Weber	Cuno's daughter
Ahmed	Marouf	Rabaud	Pastry cook
Aida	Aida	Verdi	Ethiopian princess
Alberich	Der Ring des Nibelungen	Wagner	Nibelung dwarf
Albert Herring	Albert Herring	Britten	Greengrocer's assistant
Albrecht von Brandenburg	Mathis der Maler	Hindemith	Archbishop of Mainz
Alceste	Alceste	Gluck	Wife of Admetus
Alcindoro	La Bohème	Puccini	Musetta's escort
Alfio	Cavalleria Rusticana	Mascagni	Teamster
Don Alfonso	Così fan tutte	Mozart	Don
Alfonso d'Este	Lucrezia Borgia	Donizetti	Lucrezia's third husband
Alfonso XI	La Favorita	Donizetti	King of Castile
Alfredo Germont	La Traviata	Verdi	Violetta's lover (a singer)
Ali	Marouf	Rabaud	Marouf's friend
Alice/Alisa	Lucia di Lammermoor	Donizetti	Lucy's companion
Alice Ford	Falstaff	Verdi	Citizen of Windsor
Alidoro	La Cenerentola	Rossini	Philosopher and magician
Almaviva	The Barber of Seville	Rossini	Count
Almaviva	The Marriage of Figaro	Mozart	Count
Emperor Altoum	Turandot	Puccini	Turandot's father
Don Alvaro	La Forza del Destino	Verdi	Leonora's lover
Alwa	Lulu	Berg	Writer
Amaryllus	The Poisoned Kiss	Vaughan Williams	Empress's son
Ambrogio	The Barber of Seville	Rossini	Bartolo's servant
Amelia	A Masked Ball	Verdi	Riccardo's lover, wife of Renato
Amfortas	Parsifal	Wagner	King of the Grail
Amina	The Sleepwalker	Bellini	The sleepwalking girl
Amneris	Aida	Verdi	Egyptian princess
Amonasro	Aida	Verdi	Aida's father (King of Ethiopia)
Amor	Orfeo ed Euridice	Gluck	God of love
Andromaque	The Trojans (Les Troyens)	Berlioz	Hector's widow
Angèle	The Tsar Has His Photograph Taken	Weill	Photographer
Angelica	The Poisoned Kiss	Vaughan Williams	Tormentilla's maid
Angelina	La Cenerentola	Rossini	Don Magnifico's step-daughter, Cinderella
Donna Anna	Don Giovanni	Mozart	Don Ottavio's fiancée
Annina	Der Rosenkavalier	Richard Strauss	Valzacchi's partner
Annina	La Traviata	Verdi	Violetta's confidante
Annius	La Clemenza di Tito	Mozart	Patrician
Antonio	The Marriage of Figaro	Mozart	Gardener
Apollyon	The Pilgrim's Progress	Vaughan Williams	Fallen angel
Arbace	Idomeneo	Mozart	Idomeneo's confidante
Mr Archdale	Porgy and Bess	Gershwin	White man
Arthur Bucklaw/Arturo	Lucia di Lammermoor	Donizetti	Lord
Arthur Jones	Billy Budd	Britten	Seaman
Ashby	The Girl of the Golden West	Puccini	Wells-Fargo agent
Avosmediano	Palestrina	Pfitzner	Bishop of Cadiz
Azucena	Il Trovatore	Verdi	Gypsy woman
Baba the Turk	The Rake's Progress	Stravinsky	Bearded lady
Babekan	Oberon	Weber	Saracen prince
Balthasar Zorn	The Mastersingers of Nuremberg	Wagner	Mastersinger and pewterer
Balthazar	La Favorita	Donizetti	Superior of the monastery
Barak	Turandot	Busoni	Servant

Character	Opera	Composer	Role
Barak	Die Frau ohne Schatten	Richard Strauss	Dyer
Barbarina	The Marriage of Figaro	Mozart	Antonio's daughter
Barnaba	La Gioconda	Ponchielli	Spy
Baron Ochs	Der Rosenkavalier	Richard Strauss	Sophie's would-be suitor
Baroncelli	Rienzi	Wagner	Roman citizen
Bartolo	The Barber of Seville	Rossini	Rosina's guardian
Basilio	The Barber of Seville	Rossini	Singing teacher
Don Basilio	The Marriage of Figaro	Mozart	Organist
Bayan	Ruslan and Lyudmila	Glinka	Bard
Sixtus Beckmesser	The Mastersingers of Nuremberg	Wagner	Mastersinger and town clerk
Beelzebub	Doktor Faust	Busoni	Spirit voice
Belinda	Dido and Aeneas	Purcell	Lady in waiting
Lady Bellows	Albert Herring	Britten	Elderly autocrat
Ben Budge	The Beggar's Opera	Pepusch	Highwayman
Benôit	La Bohème	Puccini	Landlord
Beppe	I Pagliacci	Leoncavallo	Harlequin
Berta	The Barber of Seville	Rossini	Housekeeper
Bess	Porgy and Bess	Gershwin	Porgy's mistress, formerly Crown's
Betty Doxy	The Beggar's Opera	Pepusch	Lady of the town
Bianca	The Rape of Lucretia	Britten	Nurse
Bianca	La Rondine	Puccini	Magda's friend
Lady Billows	Albert Herring	Britten	Elderly autocrat
Billy Budd	Billy Budd	Britten	Seaman and stammerer
Billy Jackrabbit	The Girl of the Golden West	Puccini	Red indian
Biterolf	Tannhäuser	Wagner	Knight
Dr Blind	Die Fledermaus	Johann Strauss II	Eisenstein's attorney
Bob Boles	Peter Grimes	Britten	Fisherman
Boniface	Le Jongleur de Notre Dame	Massenet	Cook
The Bonze	Madame Butterfly	Puccini	Priest
Brangäne	Tristan und Isolde	Wagner	Isolde's maid
Brünnhilde	Der Ring des Nibelungen	Wagner	Valkyrie
Brutus Jones	Emperor Jones	Gruenberg	Escaped convict, tribal ruler
Bussy	Zazà	Leoncavallo	Journalist
Calaf	Turandot	Busoni	Suitor to Turandot
Calaf	Turandot	Puccini	Suitor to Turandot
Canio	I Pagliacci	Leoncavallo	Pagliaccio (clown)
Wolfgang Capito	Mathis der Maler	Hindemith	Councillor
Cardillac	Cardillac	Hindemith	Goldsmith
Don Carlos	Don Carlos	Verdi	Heir to Spanish throne
Don Carlos	Ernani	Verdi	King of Castile
Carmen	Carmen	Bizet	Gypsy
Carolina	The Secret Marriage	Cimarosa	Geronimo's daughter
Cascart	Zazà	Leoncavallo	Music-hall performer
Cassio	Otello	Verdi	Lieutenant
Catarina	Madame Sans-Gêne	Giordano	Laundress
Cavaradossi	Tosca	Puccini	Painter
Sir Robert Cecil	Gloriana	Britten	Secretary to the Council
Celio	The Love for Three Oranges	Prokofiev	Magician
Cesare Angelotti	Tosca	Puccini	Escaped political prisoner
Charlemagne	Oberon	Weber	Emperor of the Franks
Charles Gérard	Andrea Chénier	Giordano	Revolutionary leader
Chernomor	Ruslan and Lyudmila	Glinka	An evil dwarf
Cherubino	The Marriage of Figaro	Mozart	Page
Chevalier des Grieux	Manon	Massenet	Manon's love
Chochenille	The Tales of Hoffmann	Offenbach	Spalanzani's servant
Chorèbe	The Trojans (Les Troyens)	Berlioz	Cassandra's lover
Christine	Intermezzo	Richard Strauss	Storch's wife
Chrysothemis	Elektra	Richard Strauss	Elektra's sister
Cio-Cio-San	Madame Butterfly	Puccini	Pinkerton's wife
Cirillo	Fedora	Giordano	Coachman
Claggart	Billy Budd	Britten	Master-at-arms
Claison	Capriccio	Richard Strauss	Actress
Clara	Porgy and Bess	Gershwin	Jake's wife
Princess Clarissa	The Love for Three Oranges	Prokofiev	King's niece
Clorinda	La Cenerentola	Rossini	Don Magnifico's daughter
Clotilde	Norma	Bellini	Norma's friend
Mrs Coaxer	The Beggar's Opera	Pepusch	Lady of the town
Comtesse de Coigny	Andrea Chénier	Giordano	Madeleine's mother
Cola Rienzi	Rienzi	Wagner	Papal legate
Collatinus	The Rape of Lucretia	Britten	Soldier
Colline	La Bohème	Puccini	Philosopher

Character	Opera	Composer	Role
Commendatore	Don Giovanni	Mozart	Donna Anna's father
Comte de Grieux	Manon	Massenet	Chevalier's father
Conrad Nachtigall	The Mastersingers of Nuremberg	Wagner	Mastersinger and bucklemaker
Coppelius	The Tales of Hoffmann	Offenbach	Scientist
Count de Luna	Il Trovatore	Verdi	Count of aragon
Crébillon	La Rondine	Puccini	Perichaud's friend
Creon	Oedipus Rex	Stravinsky	Jocasta's brother
Crown	Porgy and Bess	Gershwin	Stevedore
Don Curzio	The Marriage of Figaro	Mozart	Lawyer
Daland	The Flying Dutchman	Wagner	Sea captain
El Dancairo	Carmen	Bizet	Smuggler
Dandini	La Cenerentola	Rossini	Valet
Daniello	Johnny Spielt Auf	Krenek	Artist
Dansker	Billy Budd	Britten	Seaman
Dapertutto	The Tales of Hoffmann	Offenbach	Sorcerer
The Dark Fiddler	A Village Romeo and Juliet	Delius	Real owner of land
David	The Mastersingers of Nuremberg	Wagner	Hans Sachs' apprentice
David	L'Amico Fritz	Mascagni	Rabbi
de Bretigny	Manon	Massenet	A nobleman
Désiré	Fedora	Giordano	Valet
Despina	Così fan tutte	Mozart	Maid
Dickson	La Dame Blanche	Boieldieu	Tenant of the White Lady
Dido	Dido and Aeneas	Purcell	Queen of Carthage
Dimitri	Fedora	Giordano	Groom
Dipsacus	The Poisoned Kiss	Vaughan Williams	Magician
Dolly Trull	The Beggar's Opera	Pepusch	Lady of the town
Donald	Billy Budd	Britten	Seaman
Donner	Der Ring des Nibelungen	Wagner	Norse god
Dorabella	Così fan tutte	Mozart	Fiordiligi's sister
Douphol	La Traviata	Verdi	Baron
Duclou	Zazà	Leoncavallo	Stage manager
Mme Dufresne	Zazà	Leoncavallo	Milio's wife
Dumas	Andrea Chénier	Giordano	President of the tribunal
Earl of Essex	Gloriana	Britten	The Queen's favorite
Principessa Eboli	Don Carlos	Verdi	Lady-in-waiting
Edgar/Edgardo	Lucia di Lammermoor	Donizetti	Edgar of Ravenswood
Edmondo	Manon Lescaut	Puccini	Student
Elettra	Idomeneo	Mozart	Greek princess
Elektra	Elektra	Richard Strauss	Agamemnon's daughter
Elisabeth	Tannhäuser	Wagner	Hermann's niece
Elizabeth of England	Gloriana	Britten	Queen of England
Elisetta	The Secret Marriage	Cimarosa	Geronimo's older daughter
Ellen Orford	Peter Grimes	Britten	Schoolteacher
Elvino	The Sleepwalker	Bellini	Farmer, Amina's love
Elvira	Ernani	Verdi	Ernani's beloved
Donna Elvira	Don Giovanni	Mozart	Lady from Burgos
Enzo	La Gioconda	Ponchielli	Sea captain
Erda	Der Ring des Nibelungen	Wagner	Earth goddess
Ernesto	Don Pasquale	Donizetti	Don Pasquale's nephew
Eroshka	Prince Igor	Borodin	Gudok player
Escamillo	Carmen	Bizet	Bullfighter
Esmerelda	The Bartered Bride	Smetana	Dancer
Estrella	Háry János	Kodály	Lady-in-waiting
Euridice	Orfeo ed Euridice	Gluck	Orfeo's wife
Eva	The Mastersingers of Nuremberg	Wagner	Pogner's daughter
Fafner	Der Ring des Nibelungen	Wagner	Giant, builder of Valhalla
Dr Falke	Die Fledermaus	Johann Strauss II	Eisenstein's Friend
Faninal	Der Rosenkavalier	Richard Strauss	Sophie's father
Farfarello	The Love for Three Oranges	Prokofiev	A devil
Farlaf	Ruslan and Lyudmila	Glinka	Warrior, suitor to Lyudmila
Fasolt	Der Ring des Nibelungen	Wagner	Giant, builder of Valhalla
Fata Morgana	The Love for Three Oranges	Prokofiev	Witch
Fatima	Oberon	Weber	Reiza's companion
Fatimah	Marouf	Rabaud	Marouf's wife
Fenena	Nabucco	Verdi	Nabucco's daughter
Fenton	Falstaff	Verdi	In Love with Nanetta
Feodor	Boris Godunov	Mussorgsky	Son of Boris Godunov
Ferrando	Così fan tutte	Mozart	Dorabella's fiancé
Ferrando	Il Trovatore	Verdi	Captain of the Guard
Fidalma	The Secret Marriage	Cimarosa	Geronimo's sister
Figaro	The Barber of Seville	Rossini	Barber

Character	Opera	Composer	Role
Figaro	The Marriage of Figaro	Mozart	Servant to Almaviva
Filch	The Beggar's Opera	Pepusch	Pickpocket
Filipievna	Eugene Onegin	Tchaikovsky	Nurse
Finn	Ruslan and Lyudmila	Glinka	Wizard
Fiordiligi	Così fan tutte	Mozart	Dorabella's sister
Fiorello	The Barber of Seville	Rossini	Servant
Flamand	Capriccio	Richard Strauss	Musician
Flavio	Norma	Bellini	Centurion
Florestan	Fidelio	Beethoven	Spanish nobleman
Flosshilde	Der Ring des Nibelungen	Wagner	Rhinemaiden
Frank Ford	Falstaff	Verdi	Alice's husband
Frank	Die Fledermaus	Johann Strauss II	Prison governor
Frantz	The Tales of Hoffmann	Offenbach	Crespel's servant
Frasquita	Carmen	Bizet	Gypsy
Frasquita	Der Corregidor	Wolf	Tio Lucas' wife
Frazier	Porgy and Bess	Gershwin	Catfish Row 'lawyer'
Freia	Der Ring des Nibelungen	Wagner	Goddess of youth and beauty
Fricka	Der Ring des Nibelungen	Wagner	Wotan's wife
Fritz Kothner	The Mastersingers of Nuremberg	Wagner	Mastersinger and baker
Froh	Der Ring des Nibelungen	Wagner	Norse god
Frosch	Die Fledermaus	Johann Strauss II	Jailer
Gallanthus	The Poisoned Kiss	Vaughan Williams	Amaryllus's sister
Mr Gedge	Albert Herring	Britten	Vicar
Geneviève	Pelléas et Mélisande	Debussy	Mother of Pelléas
Gennaro	Lucrezia Borgia	Donizetti	Venetian nobleman, Lucrezia's son
Gennaro	The Jewels of the Madonna	Wolf-Ferrari	Blacksmith
Georges Brown	La Dame Blanche	Boieldieu	English officer
Gérald	Lakmé	Delibes	English officer
Gerhilde	Der Ring des Nibelungen	Wagner	Valkyrie
Geronimo	The Secret Marriage	Cimarosa	Citizen of Bologna
Gertrude	Hänsel and Gretel	Humperdinck	Mother of Hansel and Gretel
Gilda	Rigoletto	Verdi	Rigoletto's daughter
La Giaconda	La Giaconda	Ponchielli	Street singer, Enzo's love
Giorgetta	Il Tabarro	Puccini	Michele's wife
Godfrey	Lohengrin	Wagner	Elsa's brother
Golaud	Pelléas et Mélisande	Debussy	Arkel's grandson
Gorislava	Ruslan and Lyudmila	Glinka	Ratmir's lover
Goro	Madame Butterfly	Puccini	Marriage broker
Grech	Fedora	Giordano	Policeman
Prince Gremin	Eugene Onegin	Tchaikovsky	General
Grigorij	Boris Godunov	Mussorgsky	False Dimitri
Grimgerde	Der Ring des Nibelungen	Wagner	Valkyrie
Gubetta	Lucrezia Borgia	Donizetti	Servant to Lucrezia
Guglielmo	Così fan tutte	Mozart	Fiordiligi's fiancé
Gunther	Der Ring des Nibelungen	Wagner	Hagen's half-brother
Gutrune	Der Ring des Nibelungen	Wagner	Gunther's sister
Gzak	Prince Igor	Borodin	Polovtsian Khan
Hadji	Lakmé	Delibes	Nilakantha's servant
Hagen	Der Ring des Nibelungen	Wagner	Alberich's Descendant
Hans Foltz	The Mastersingers of Nuremberg	Wagner	Mastersinger and coppersmith
Hans Sachs	The Mastersingers of Nuremberg	Wagner	Mastersinger and cobbler
Hans Schwarz	The Mastersingers of Nuremberg	Wagner	Mastersinger and stocking weaver
Happy	The Girl of the Golden West	Puccini	Miner
Haroun al Rashid	Oberon	Weber	Caliph of Baghdad
Harry Paddington	The Beggar's Opera	Pepusch	Highwayman
Helmwige	Der Ring des Nibelungen	Wagner	Valkyrie
Henry Ashton	Ennio Lucia di Lammermoor	Donizetti	Lord of Lammermoor
Hermann	Tannhäuser	Wagner	Landgrave of Thuringia
Hermann	The Tales of Hoffmann	Offenbach	Student
Hermann Ortel	The Mastersingers of Nuremberg	Wagner	Mastersinger and soap boiler
Herod	Salome	Richard Strauss	Ruler of Galileo
Herodias	Salome	Richard Strauss	Herod's wife
Hob	The Poisoned Kiss	Vaughan Williams	Servant of Dipsacus
Hoffmann	The Tales of Hoffmann	Offenbach	Poet
Hunding	Der Ring des Nibelungen	Wagner	Siegmund's enemy
Hylas	The Trojans (Les Troyens)	Berlioz	Trojan sailor
Idamente	Idomeneo	Mozart	Idomeneo's son
Idomeneo	Idomeneo	Mozart	King of Crete
Ighino	Palestrina	Pfitzner	Palestrina's son
Prince Igor	Prince Igor	Borodin	Prince of Seversk
Ilia	Idomeneo	Mozart	Trojan princess

Character	Opera	Composer	Role
Ilka	*Háry János*	Kodály	Háry's fiancée
Incredible	*Andrea Chénier*	Giordano	Spy
Iopas	*The Trojans (Les Troyens)*	Berlioz	Poet
Irene	*Rienzi*	Wagner	Rienzi's sister
Isolde	*Tristan und Isolde*	Wagner	Irish princess
Jacquino	*Fidelio*	Beethoven	Rocco's assistant
Jago	*Ernani*	Verdi	Silva's squire
Jake	*Porgy and Bess*	Gershwin	Fisherman
Aunt Jane	*Hugh the Drover*	Vaughan Williams	Sister of the constable
Jaroslavna	*Prince Igor*	Borodin	Prince Igor's wife
Jean	*Le Jongleur de Notre Dame*	Massenet	A poor juggler
Jemmy Twitcher	*The Beggar's Opera*	Pepusch	Highwayman
Jenik	*The Bartered Bride*	Smetana	Micha's son
Jenny	*La Dame Blanche*	Boieldieu	Dickson's wife
Jenny Diver	*The Beggar's Opera*	Pepusch	Lady of the night
Jim	*Porgy and Bess*	Gershwin	Cotton picker
Jocasta	*Oedipus Rex*	Stravinsky	Wife of Oedipus
Joe	*The Girl of the Golden West*	Puccini	Miner
John	*Peter Grimes*	Britten	Peter's apprentice
John the Butcher	*Hugh the Drover*	Vaughan Williams	Mary's fiancé
John the Baptist	*Salome*	Richard Strauss	Jewish prophet
Johnny	*Johnny Spielt Auf*	Krenek	Artist
Don José	*Carmen*	Bizet	Corporal in the Guard
Juan Lopez	*Der Corregidor*	Wolf	Mayor
Judith	*Duke Bluebeard's Castle*	Bartók	Bluebeard's last wife
Junius	*The Rape of Lucretia*	Britten	Roman general
Justizrat	*Intermezzo*	Richard Strauss	Storch's friend
Kammersänger	*Intermezzo*	Richard Strauss	Storch's friend
Kate	*Madame Butterfly*	Puccini	Pinkerton's wife
Kathinka	*The Bartered Bride*	Smetana	Marenka's mother
Kecal	*The Bartered Bride*	Smetana	Marriage broker
King of Clubs	*The Love for Three Oranges*	Prokofiev	Ruler of the kingdom
Klingsor	*Parsifal*	Wagner	Magician
Kontchak	*Prince Igor*	Borodin	Polovtsian Khan
Kontchakovna	*Prince Igor*	Borodin	Kontchak's daughter
Kruschev	*Boris Godunov*	Mussorgsky	Boyard
Kundry	*Parsifal*	Wagner	Bewitched woman
Kunz Vogelgesang	*The Mastersingers of Nuremberg*	Wagner	Mastersinger and furrier
Kurvenal	*Tristan und Isolde*	Wagner	Tristan's retainer
Lakmé	*Lakmé*	Delibes	Nilakantha's daughter
Larina	*Eugene Onegin*	Tchaikovsky	Tatyana's mother
Larkens	*The Girl of the Golden West*	Puccini	Miner
Lartigen	*Zazà*	Leoncavallo	Monologist
Lawrence	*The Wreckers*	Smyth	Lighthouse keeper
Leandro	*The Love for Three Oranges*	Prokofiev	King of Spades and PM
Lenski	*Eugene Onegin*	Tchaikovsky	Olga's fiancé
Leonara di Gusman	*La Favorita*	Donizetti	King's mistress
Leonora	*Il Trovatore*	Verdi	Beloved of Manrico
Leonora	*Fidelio*	Beethoven	Florestan's wife
Leporello	*Don Giovanni*	Mozart	Servant
Lescaut	*Manon*	Massenet	A gambler
Lillas Pastia	*Carmen*	Bizet	Innkeeper
Lily	*Porgy and Bess*	Gershwin	Strawberry woman
Lindorf	*The Tales of Hoffmann*	Offenbach	Councillor of Nuremberg
Linette	*The Love for Three Oranges*	Prokofiev	Princess hidden in an orange
Lisette	*La Rondine*	Puccini	Magda's maid
Liù	*Turandot*	Puccini	Slave girl
Lob	*The Poisoned Kiss*	Vaughan Williams	Assistant of Dipsacus
Lockit	*The Beggar's Opera*	Pepusch	Jailer
Lodovico	*Otello*	Verdi	Venetian ambassador
Loge	*Der Ring des Nibelungen*	Wagner	Norse god
Lohengrin	*Lohengrin*	Wagner	Parsifal's son
Lola	*Cavalleria Rusticana*	Mascagni	Alfio's wife
Lorek	*Fedora*	Giordano	Surgeon
Loris Ipanov	*Fedora*	Giordano	Count
Lucia	*The Rape of Lucretia*	Britten	Lucretia's attendant
Lucretia	*Palestrina*	Pfitzner	Palestrina's wife
Lucretia	*The Rape of Lucretia*	Britten	Wife of Collatinus
Lucrezia Borgia	*Lucrezia Borgia*	Donizetti	Duchess of Ferrara
Lucy/Lucia	*Lucia di Lammermoor*	Donizetti	Ashton's sister
Lucy Lockit	*The Beggar's Opera*	Pepusch	Jailer's daughter

M U S I C   C L A S S I C A L

Character	Opera	Composer	Role
Luigi	Il Tabarro	Puccini	Stevedore, Giorgetta's father
Lulu	Lulu	Berg	Prostitute
Luther	The Tales of Hoffmann	Offenbach	Innkeeper
Lyudmila	Ruslan and Lyudmila	Glinka	A noblewoman
Macheath	The Beggar's Opera	Pepusch	Highwayman
MacIrton	La Dame Blanche	Boieldieu	Justice of the Peace
Mad Margaret	Ruddigore	Sullivan	Mad woman
Maddalena	Rigoletto	Verdi	Sparafucile's sister
Madeleine de Coigny	Andrea Chénier	Giordano	In Love with Andrea Chénier
Madelon	Andrea Chénier	Giordano	Old woman
Maffio Orsini	Lucrezia Borgia	Donizetti	Lucrezia's enemy
Magda	La Rondine	Puccini	Rambaldo's mistress
Magdalena	The Mastersingers of Nuremberg	Wagner	Nurse
Don Magnifico	La Cenerentola	Rossini	Baron of Montflagon
Mahomet	Der Rosenkavalier	Richard Strauss	Negro page
Dr Malatesta	Don Pasquale	Donizetti	Don Pasquale's friend
Maliella	The Jewels of the Madonna	Wolf-Ferrari	Gennaro's adopted sister
Mallika	Lakmé	Delibes	Lakmé's slave
Mama Lucia	Cavalleria Rusticana	Mascagni	Turiddu's mother
Manon	Manon	Massenet	Lescaut's cousin
Manrico	Il Trovatore	Verdi	Troubador
Duke of Mantua	Rigoletto	Verdi	Nobleman
Manuela	Der Corregidor	Wolf	Maid
Manz	A Village Romeo and Juliet	Delius	Farmer
Marcellina	Fidelio	Beethoven	Rocco's daughter
Marcellina	The Marriage of Figaro	Mozart	Housekeeper
Marcello	La Bohème	Puccini	Painter
Marco	Zazà	Leoncavallo	Dufresne's butler
Marenka	The Bartered Bride	Smetana	In love with Jenik
Marguerite	La Dame Blanche	Boieldieu	Servant
Marguérite	Faust	Gounod	Beloved of Faust
Maria	Porgy and Bess	Gershwin	Cookshop keeper
Marianne	Der Rosenkavalier	Richard Strauss	Sophie's duenna
Marie	Wozzeck	Berg	Prostitute
Marie-Louise	Háry János	Kodály	Napoleon's second wife
Marina Mnishek	Boris Godunov	Mussorgsky	Daughter of Voyevode of Sandomir
Mario Cavaradossi	Tosca	Puccini	Painter
King Marke	Tristan und Isolde	Wagner	King of Cornwall
Marlardot	Zazà	Leoncavallo	Music-Hall owner
Marouf	Marouf	Rabaud	Shoemaker
Marschallin	Der Rosenkavalier	Richard Strauss	Princess
Martha Schwerlein	Faust	Gounod	Marguérite's neighbour
Marti	A Village Romeo and Juliet	Delius	Farmer
Cavaliere Marullo	Rigoletto	Verdi	Courtier
Mary	Hugh the Drover	Vaughan Williams	Constable's daughter
Marzci	Háry János	Kodály	Marie's coachman
Masetto	Don Giovanni	Mozart	Peasant
Mat of the Mint	The Beggar's Opera	Pepusch	Highwayman
Mathieu	Andrea Chénier	Giordano	Waiter
Mathis	Mathis der Maler	Hindemith	Painter (Grünewald)
Matteo Borsa	Rigoletto	Verdi	Courtier
Matteo del Sarto	Arlecchino	Busoni	Tailor
Max	Johnny Spielt Auf	Krenek	Composer
Mélisande	Pelléas et Mélisande	Debussy	Golaud's wife
Melot	Tristan und Isolde	Wagner	Courtier
Melusine	Háry János	Kodály	Countess
Mercedes	Carmen	Bizet	Gypsy
Micaela	Carmen	Bizet	Village girl
Micha	The Bartered Bride	Smetana	Jenik's father
Michele	Il Tabarro	Puccini	Barge owner
Michelin	Zazà	Leoncavallo	Journalist
Milio Dufresne	Zazà	Leoncavallo	Zaza's lover
Mime	Der Ring des Nibelungen	Wagner	A Nibelung
Mimi	La Bohème	Puccini	Seamstress
Minnie	The Girl of the Golden West	Puccini	Barmaid
Dr Miracle	The Tales of Hoffmann	Offenbach	Doctor
Missail	Boris Godunov	Mussorgsky	Vagrant
Mistrust	The Pilgrim's Progress	Vaughan Williams	Neighbour
Molly Brazen	The Beggar's Opera	Pepusch	Lady of the town
Monostatos	The Magic Flute	Mozart	Servant

Character	Opera	Composer	Role
Montano	Otello	Verdi	Otello's predecessor
Morales	Carmen	Bizet	Officer of the Guard
Augustin Moser	The Mastersingers of Nuremberg	Wagner	Mastersinger and tailor
Muff	The Bartered Bride	Smetana	Comedian
Musetta	La Bohème	Puccini	In love with Marcello
Nabucco	Nabucco	Verdi	Nebuchadnezzar, King of Babylon
Naina	Ruslan and Lyudmila	Glinka	Witch
Namouna	Oberon	Weber	Fatima's grandmother
Nancy	Albert Herring	Britten	Baker's assistant
Nanetta	Falstaff	Verdi	Ford's daughter
Narbal	The Trojans (Les Troyens)	Berlioz	Dido's minister
Narraboth	Salome	Richard Strauss	Captain of the Guard
Natalia	Zazà	Leoncavallo	Zazà's maid
Nathanael	The Tales of Hoffmann	Offenbach	Student
Ned Keene	Peter Grimes	Britten	Apothecary
Nedda	I Pagliacci	Leoncavallo	Canio's wife
Nick	The Girl of the Golden West	Puccini	Bartender
Nicklaus	The Tales of Hoffmann	Offenbach	Hoffmann's friend
Nicola	Fedora	Giordano	Footman
Nicoletta	The Love for Three Oranges	Prokofiev	Princess hidden in an orange
Nilakantha	Lakmé	Delibes	Brahmin priest
Nimming Ned	The Beggar's Opera	Pepusch	Highwayman
Ninetta	The Love for Three Oranges	Prokofiev	Princess hidden in an orange
Norina	Don Pasquale	Donizetti	Widow
Norma	Norma	Bellini	Druid priestess
Norman	Lucia di Lammermoor	Donizetti	Follower of Ashton
Obstinate	The Pilgrim's Progress	Vaughan Williams	Neighbour
Octavian	Der Rosenkavalier	Richard Strauss	Bearer of the Rose
Oedipus	Oedipus Rex	Stravinsky	King of Thebes
Olga	Eugene Onegin	Tchaikovsky	Tatiana's sister
Olivier	Capriccio	Richard Strauss	Poet
Olympia	The Tales of Hoffmann	Offenbach	Mechanical doll
One-Arm	Die Frau ohne Schatten	Richard Strauss	Barak's brother
One-Eye	Die Frau ohne Schatten	Richard Strauss	Barak's brother
Orest	Elektra	Richard Strauss	Elektra's brother
Orfeo	Orfeo ed Euridice	Gluck	Singer-poet
Orlovsky	Die Fledermaus	Johann Strauss II	Rich Russian
Oroveso	Norma	Bellini	Norma's father
Ortlinde	Der Ring des Nibelungen	Wagner	Valkyrie
Ortrud	Lohengrin	Wagner	Wife of Frederick
Oscar	A Masked Ball	Verdi	Riccardo's page
Ovlour	Prince Igor	Borodin	Polovtsian traitor
Palestrina	Palestrina	Pfitzner	Composer
Pamina	The Magic Flute	Mozart	Daughter of Queen of the Night
Pang	Turandot	Puccini	Lord of Provisions
Pantalone	Turandot	Busoni	Minister
Pantaloon	The Love for Three Oranges	Prokofiev	King's friend
Panthée	The Trojans (Les Troyens)	Berlioz	Priest
Paolino	The Secret Marriage	Cimarosa	Carolina's secret husband
Paolo Orsini	Rienzi	Wagner	Patrician
Papagena	The Magic Flute	Mozart	Destined to be Papageno's wife
Papageno	The Magic Flute	Mozart	Bird catcher
Parpignol	La Bohème	Puccini	Toy vendor
Parsifal	Parsifal	Wagner	Knight of the Holy Grail
Peachum	The Beggar's Opera	Pepusch	Fence
Pelléas	Pelléas et Mélisande	Debussy	Arkel's grandson
Périchaud	La Rondine	Puccini	Rambaldo's friend
Peter	Porgy and Bess	Gershwin	Honey-man
Peter	Hänsel and Gretel	Humperdinck	Father of Hansel and Gretel
Peter Grimes	Peter Grimes	Britten	Fisherman
Pilgrim	The Pilgrim's Progress	Vaughan Williams	Pilgrim
Pimen	Boris Godunov	Mussorgsky	Hermit
Ping	Turandot	Puccini	Chinese Grand Chancellor
Lt Pinkerton	Madame Butterfly	Puccini	Lt in US Navy
Pittichinaccio	The Tales of Hoffmann	Offenbach	Giulietta's admirer
Don Pizarro	Fidelio	Beethoven	Prison governor
Pliable	The Pilgrim's Progress	Vaughan Williams	Neighbour
Veit Pogner	The Mastersingers of Nuremberg	Wagner	Mastersinger and goldsmith (Eva's father)
Pollione	Norma	Bellini	Proconsul of Rome

MUSIC CLASSICAL

Character	Opera	Composer	Role
Polly Peachum	The Beggar's Opera	Pepusch	Peachum's daughter, Macheath's wife
Polyxène	The Trojans (Les Troyens)	Berlioz	Priam's daughter
Pong	Turandot	Puccini	Lord of the Imperial Kitchen
Porgy	Porgy and Bess	Gershwin	A crippled beggar
Priam	The Trojans (Les Troyens)	Berlioz	King of Troy
Prince	Lulu	Berg	Traveller in Africa
Prince	The Love for Three Oranges	Prokofiev	Hypochondriac
Prunier	La Rondine	Puccini	Poet
Publius	La Clemenza di Tito	Mozart	Captain of Praetorian Guard
Queen Mother of Samarkand	Turandot	Busoni	Negress
Rafaele	The Jewels of the Madonna	Wolf-Ferrari	Leader of the Camorra
Raimondo	Rienzi	Wagner	Papal legate
Rambaldo	La Rondine	Puccini	Banker
Ramfis	Aida	Verdi	High priest
Don Ramiro	La Cenerentola	Rossini	Prince of Salerno
Jack Rance	The Girl of the Golden West	Puccini	Sheriff
Rangoni	Boris Godunov	Mussorgsky	Jesuit
Ratmir	Ruslan and Lyudmila	Glinka	Suitor to Lyudmila
Raymond/ Raimondo	Lucia di Lammermoor	Donizetti	Chaplain, Lucy's tutor
Mr Redburn	Billy Budd	Britten	First lieutenant
Red Whiskers	Billy Budd	Britten	Impressed seaman
Reinmar von Zweter	Tannhäuser	Wagner	Knight
Reiza	Oberon	Weber	Haroun el Rashid's daughter
El Remondado	Carmen	Bizet	Smuggler
Renato	A Masked Ball	Verdi	Riccardo's secretary
Repela	Der Corregidor	Wolf	Valet to magistrate
Rhadames	Aida	Verdi	Captain of the Guard
Riccardo	A Masked Ball	Verdi	Governor of Louisiana
Riedinger	Mathis der Maler	Hindemith	Rich Lutheran
Rigoletto	Rigoletto	Verdi	Gilda's father, a jester
Rocco	Fidelio	Beethoven	Chief jailer
Rodolfo	La Bohème	Puccini	Poet
Rosalinda	Die Fledermaus	Johann Strauss II	Eisenstein's wife
Rose	Lakmé	Delibes	An English lady
Rosina	The Barber of Seville	Rossini	Dr Bartolo's ward
Rossweisse	Der Ring des Nibelungen	Wagner	Valkyrie
Roucher	Andrea Chénier	Giordano	Andrea's friend
Ruggero	La Rondine	Puccini	Son of Rambaldo's childhood friend
Ruslan	Ruslan and Lyudmila	Glinka	Suitor to Lyudmila
Rustighello	Lucrezia Borgia	Donizetti	Alfonso's henchman
Sali	A Village Romeo and Juliet	Delius	Mary's daughter
Salome	Salome	Richard Strauss	Daughter of Herodias
Santuzza	Cavalleria Rusticana	Mascagni	In love with Turiddu
Sarastro	The Magic Flute	Mozart	High priest
Baron Scarpia	Tosca	Puccini	Chief of police
Dr Schön	Lulu	Berg	Editor
Senta	The Flying Dutchman	Wagner	Daland's daughter
Sharpless	Madame Butterfly	Puccini	US consul in Nagasaki
Sid	Albert Herring	Britten	Butcher's assistant
Siegfried	Der Ring des Nibelungen	Wagner	Son of Siegmund and Sieglunde
Sieglunde	Der Ring des Nibelungen	Wagner	Siegmund's twin sister
Siegmund	Der Ring des Nibelungen	Wagner	Mortal son of Wotan
Silvano	A Masked Ball	Verdi	A young sailor
Silvio	I Pagliacci	Leoncavallo	In love with Nedda
Sophie	Der Rosenkavalier	Richard Strauss	Daughter of von Faninal
Spalanzani	The Tales of Hoffmann	Offenbach	Inventor
Sportin' Life	Porgy and Bess	Gershwin	Dope dealer
Stella	The Tales of Hoffmann	Offenbach	Opera singer
Robert Storch	Intermezzo	Richard Strauss	Musical conductor
Suky Tawdry	The Beggar's Opera	Pepusch	Lady of the town
Susan B. Anthony	The Mother of Us All	Thomson	American suffragette
Susanna	The Marriage of Figaro	Mozart	Maid
Suzuki	Madame Butterfly	Puccini	Servant
Suzy	La Rondine	Puccini	Magda's friend
Svyetor	Ruslan and Lyudmila	Glinka	Lyudmila's father
Talpa	Il Tabarro	Puccini	Stevedore
Tannhäuser	Tannhäuser	Wagner	Knight
Tatiana	Eugene Onegin	Tchaikovsky	In love with Eugene
Telramund	Lohengrin	Wagner	Count of Brabant

Character	Opera	Composer	Role
Thisbe	La Cenerentola	Rossini	Don Magnifico's daughter
Timorous	The Pilgrim's Progress	Vaughan Williams	Neighbour
Tinca	Il Tabarro	Puccini	Stevedore
Tio Lucas	Der Corregidor	Wolf	Miller
Tiresias	Oedipus Rex	Stravinsky	Blind soothsayer
Titurel	Parsifal	Wagner	Father of Amfortas
Titus	La Clemenza di Tito	Mozart	Emperor of Rome
Tom Rakewell	The Rake's Progress	Stravinsky	The Rake
Tonio	I Pagliacci	Leoncavalo	Clown
Tonuelo	Der Corregidor	Wolf	Court messenger
Tormentilla	The Poisoned Kiss	Vaughan Williams	Daughter of Dipsacus
Tosca	Tosca	Puccini	Singer
Toto	Zazà	Leoncavallo	Dufresne's child
Mrs Trapes	The Beggar's Opera	Pepusch	Tally woman
Trim	The Girl of the Golden West	Puccini	Miner
Tristan	Tristan und Isolde	Wagner	Cornish knight
Trouble	Madame Butterfly	Puccini	Cio-Cio-San's child
Truchsess von Waldburg	Mathis der Maler	Hindemith	Leader of the army
Trulove	The Rake's Progress	Stravinsky	Anne's father
Princess Turandot	Turandot	Puccini	Daughter of Altoum
Turiddu	Cavalleria Rusticana	Mascagni	Soldier
Ulrica	A Masked Ball	Verdi	Fortune teller
Ulrich Eisslinger	The Mastersingers of Nuremberg	Wagner	Mastersingers and grocer
Mr Upfold	Albert Herring	Britten	Mayor
Ursula	Mathis der Maler	Hindemith	Riedinger's daughter
Valzacchi	Der Rosenkavalier	Richard Strauss	Scandalmonger
Varlaam	Boris Godunov	Mussorgsky	Vagrant
Vasek	The Bartered Bride	Smetana	Micha's second son
Venus	Tannhäuser	Wagner	Supernatural seductress
Captain Vere	Billy Budd	Britten	Ship's captain
Violetta Valery	La Traviata	Verdi	Courtesan
Vitellia	La Clemenza di Tito	Mozart	Daughter of deposed emperor
Vitellozzo	Lucrezia Borgia	Donizetti	Nobleman
Miss Vixen	The Beggar's Opera	Pepusch	Lady of the town
Vizier	Marouf	Rabaud	Sultan's adviser
Vladimir Igorevitch	Prince Igor	Borodin	Igor's son
Vladimir Yaroslavtitch	Prince Igor	Borodin	Yaroslavna's brother
Vreli	A Village Romeo and Juliet	Delius	Marti's daughter
Jake Wallace	The Girl of the Golden West	Puccini	Minstrel
Sir Walter Raleigh	Gloriana	Britten	Courtier
Walter von Stolzing	The Mastersingers of Nuremberg	Wagner	Franconian knight
Walther von der Vogelweide	Tannhäuser	Wagner	Knight
Waltraute	Der Ring des Nibelungen	Wagner	Valkyrie
Watchful	The Pilgrim's Progress	Vaughan Williams	Porter
Wellgunde	Der Ring des Nibelungen	Wagner	Rhine maiden
Woglinde	Der Ring des Nibelungen	Wagner	Rhine maiden
Wolfram	Tannhäuser	Wagner	Knight
Wotan	Der Ring des Nibelungen	Wagner	Norse god
Wowkle	The Girl of the Golden West	Puccini	Billy's squaw
Wozzeck	Wozzeck	Berg	Soldier
Xenia	Boris Godunov	Mussorgsky	Boris Godunov's daughter
Yamadori	Madame Butterfly	Puccini	Rich Japanese
Yniold	Pelléas et Mélisande	Debussy	Golaud's son
Yvette	La Rondine	Puccini	Magda's friend
Yvonne	Jonny Spielt Auf	Krenek	Chambermaid
Zaccaria	Nabucco	Verdi	High Priest of Jerusalem
Zazà	Zazà	Leoncavallo	Music-hall singer
Zerlina	Don Giovanni	Mozart	Engaged to Matteo
Zuniga	Carmen	Bizet	Captain of the Guard

Operatic Characters (by opera)

Opera	Composer	Character	Role
Aida	Verdi	Aida	Ethiopian princess
		Amneris	Egyptian princess
		Amonasro	Aida's father (King of Ethiopia)
		Ramfis	High priest
		Rhadames	Captain of the Guard
Albert Herring	Britten	Albert Herring	Greengrocer's assistant
		Lady Bellows	Elderly autocrat
		Mr Gedge	Vicar
		Mr Upfold	Mayor
		Nancy	Baker's assistant
		Sid	Butcher's assistant
Alceste	Gluck	Admetus	Alceste's husband
		Alceste	Wife of Admetus
L'Amico Fritz	Mascagni	David	Rabbi
Andrea Chénier	Giordano	Charles Gérard	Revolutionary leader
		Comtesse de Coigny	Madeleine's mother
		Dumas	President of the tribunal
		Incredible	Spy
		Madeleine de Coigny	In love with Andrea Chénier
		Madelon	Old woman
		Mathieu	Waiter
		Roucher	Andrea's friend
Arlecchino	Busoni	Matteo del Sarto	Tailor
The Barber of Seville	Rossini	Almaviva	Count
		Ambrogio	Bartolo's servant
		Bartolo	Rosina's guardian
		Basilio	Singing teacher
		Berta	Housekeeper
		Figaro	Barber
		Fiorello	Servant
		Rosina	Dr Bartolo's ward
The Bartered Bride	Smetana	Esmerelda	Dancer
		Jenik	Micha's son
		Kathinka	Marenka's mother
		Kecal	Marriage broker
		Marenka	In love with Jenik
		Micha	Jenik's father
		Muff	Comedian
		Vasek	Micha's second son
The Beggar's Opera	Pepusch	Ben Budge	Highwayman
		Betty Doxy	Lady of the town
		Dolly Trull	Lady of the town
		Filch	Pickpocket
		Harry Paddington	Highwayman
		Jemmy Twitcher	Highwayman
		Jenny Diver	Lady of the night
		Lockit	Jailer
		Lucy Lockit	Jailer's daughter
		Macheath	Highwayman
		Mat of the Mint	Highwayman
		Miss Vixen	Lady of the town
		Molly Brazen	Lady of the town
		Mrs Coaxer	Lady of the town
		Mrs Trapes	Tally woman
		Nimming Ned	Highwayman
		Peachum	Fence
		Polly Peachum	Peachum's daughter, Macheath's wife
		Suky Tawdry	Lady of the town
Billy Budd	Britten	Arthur Jones	Seaman
		Billy Budd	Seaman and stammerer
		Captain Vere	Ship's captain
		Claggart	Master-at-arms
		Dansker	Seaman
		Donald	Seaman
		Mr Redburn	First lieutenant
		Red Whiskers	Impressed seaman

Opera	Composer	Character	Role
La Bohème	Puccini	Alcindoro	Musetta's escort
		Benôit	Landlord
		Colline	Philosopher
		Marcello	Painter
		Mimi	Seamstress
		Musetta	In love with Marcello
		Parpignol	Toy Vendor
		Rodolfo	Poet
Boris Godunov	Mussorgsky	Feodor	Son of Boris Godunov
		Grigorij	False Dimitri
		Kruschev	Boyard
		Marina Mnishek	Daughter of Voyevode Sandomir
		Missail	Vagrant
		Pimen	Hermit
		Rangoni	Jesuit
		Varlaam	Vagrant
		Xenia	Boris Godunov's daughter
Capriccio	Richard Strauss	Claison	Actress
		Flamand	Musician
		Olivier	Poet
Cardillac	Hindemith	Cardillac	Goldsmith
Carmen	Bizet	Carmen	Gypsy
		Don José	Corporal in the Guard
		El Dancairo	Smuggler
		El Remondado	Smuggler
		Escamillo	Bullfighter
		Frasquita	Gypsy
		Lillas Pastia	Innkeeper
		Mercedes	Gypsy
		Micaela	Village girl
		Morales	Officer of the Guard
		Zuniga	Captain of the Guard
Cavalleria Rusticana	Mascagni	Alfio	Teamster
		Lola	Alfio's wife
		Mama Lucia	Turiddu's mother
		Santuzza	In love with Turiddu
		Turiddu	Soldier
La Cenerentola	Rossini	Alidoro	Philosopher and magician
		Angelina	Don Magnifico's stepdaughter, Cinderella
		Clorinda	Don Magnifico's daughter
		Dandini	Valet
		Don Magnifico	Baron of Montflagon
		Don Ramiro	Prince of Salerno
		Thisbe	Don Magnifico's daughter
La Clemenza di Tito	Mozart	Annius	Patrician
		Publius	Captain of Praetorian Guard
		Titus	Emperor of Rome
		Vitellia	Daughter of deposed emperor
Der Corregidor	Wolf	Frasquita	Tio Lucas' wife
		Juan Lopez	Mayor
		Manuela	Maid
		Repela	Valet to magistrate
		Tio Lucas	Miller
		Tonuelo	Court messenger
Così fan tutte	Mozart	Despina	Maid
		Don Alfonso	Don
		Dorabella	Fiordiligi's sister
		Ferrando	Dorabella's fiancé
		Fiordiligi	Dorabella's sister
		Guglielmo	Fiordiligi's fiancé
Dame Blanche La	Boieldieu	Dickson	Tenant of the White Lady
		Georges Brown	English officer
		Jenny	Dickson's wife
		MacIrton	Justice of the Peace
		Marguerite	Servant
Dido and Aeneas	Purcell	Aeneas	Trojan general
		Belinda	Lady-in-waiting
		Dido	Queen of Carthage
Don Carlos	Verdi	Don Carlos	Heir to Spanish throne
		Principessa Eboli	Lady in waiting

M
U
S
I
C

C
L
A
S
S
I
C
A
L

Opera	Composer	Character	Role
Don Giovanni	Mozart	Commendatore	Donna Anna's father
		Donna Anna	Don Ottavio's fiancée
		Donna Elvira	Lady from Burgos
		Leporello	Servant
		Masetto	Peasant
		Zerlina	Engaged to Matteo
Don Pasquale	Donizetti	Dr Malatesta	Don Pasquale's friend
		Ernesto	Don Pasquale's nephew
		Norina	Widow
Duke Bluebeard's Castle	Bartók	Judith	Blubeard's last wife
Elektra	Richard Strauss	Aegisth	Klytemnestra's lover
		Chrysothemis	Elektra's sister
		Elektra	Agamemnon's daughter
		Orest	Elektra's brother
Emperor Jones	Gruenberg	Brutus Jones	Escaped convict, tribal leader
Ernani	Verdi	Don Carlos	King of Castile
		Elvira	Ernani's beloved
		Jago	Silva's squire
Eugene Onegin	Tchaikovsky	Filipievna	Nurse
		Prince Gremin	General
		Larina	Tatyana's mother
		Lenski	Olga's fiancé
		Olga	Tatyana's sister
		Tatiana	In love with Eugene
Falstaff	Verdi	Alice Ford	Citizen of Windsor
		Fenton	In love with Nanetta
		Frank Ford	Alice's husband
		Nanetta	Ford's daughter
Faust	Gounod	Marguérite	Beloved of Faust
		Martha Schwerlein	Marguérite's neighbour
La Favorita	Donizetti	Alfonso XI	King of Castile
		Balthazar	Superior of the monastery
		Leonara di Gusman	King's mistress
Fedora	Giordano	Cirillo	Coachman
		Désiré	Valet
		Dimitri	Groom
		Grech	Policeman
		Lorek	Surgeon
		Loris Ipanov	Count
		Nicola	Footman
Fidelio	Beethoven	Don Pizarro	Prison governor
		Florestan	Spanish nobleman
		Jacquino	Rocco's assistant
		Leonora	Florestan's wife
		Marcellina	Rocco's daughter
		Rocco	Chief jailer
Die Fledermaus	Johann Strauss II	Adele	Eisenstein's maid
		Dr Blind	Eisenstein's attorney
		Dr Falke	Eisenstein's friend
		Frank	Prison governor
		Frosch	Jailer
		Orlovsky	Rich Russian
		Rosalinda	Eisenstein's wife
The Flying Dutchman	Wagner	Daland	Sea captain
		Senta	Daland's daughter
Die Frau ohne Schatten	Richard Strauss	Barak	Dyer
		One-Arm	Barak's brother
		One-Eye	Barak's brother
La Forza del Destino	Verdi	Don Alvaro	Leonora's lover
Der Freischütz		Agathe	Cuno's daughter
La Gioconda	Ponchielli	Barnaba	Spy
		Enzo	Sea captain
		La Giaconda	Street singer, Enzo's love
The Girl of the Golden West		Ashby	Wells-Fargo agent
		Billy Jackrabbit	Red Indian
		Happy	Miner
		Jack Rance	Sheriff
		Jake Wallace	Minstrel
		Joe	Mine
		Larkens	Miner
		Minnie	Barmaid

Opera	Composer	Character	Role
		Nick	Bartender
		Trim	Miner
		Wowkle	Billy's squaw
Gloriana	Britten	Earl of Essex	The Queen's favourite
		Elizabeth of England	Queen of England
		Sir Robert Cecil	Secretary to the Council
		Sir Walter Raleigh	Courtier
Hänsel and Gretel	Humperdinck	Gertrude	Mother of Hansel and Gretel
		Peter	Father of Hansel and Gretel
Háry János	Kodály	Abraham	Innkeeper
		Estrella	Lady-in-waiting
		Ilka	Háry's fiancée
		Marie-Louise	Napoleon's second wife
		Marzci	Marie's coachman
		Melusine	Countess
Hugh the Drover	Vaughan Williams	Aunt Jane	Sister of the constable
		John the Butcher	Mary's fiancé
		Mary	Constable's daughter
Idomeneo	Mozart	Arbace	Idomeneo's confidante
		Elettra	Greek princess
		Idamente	Idomeneo's son
		Idomeneo	King of Crete
		Ilia	Trojan princess
Intermezzo	Richard Strauss	Christine	Storch's wife
		Justizrat	Storch's friend
		Kammersänger	Storch's friend
		Robert Storch	Musical conductor
The Jewels of the Madonna	Wolf-Ferrari	Gennaro	Blacksmith
		Maliella	Gennaro's adopted sister
		Rafaele	Leader of the Camorra
Le Jongleur de Notre Dame	Massennet	Boniface	Cook
Jonny Spielt Auf	Krenek	Daniello	Artist
(Jonny Plays on)		Jonny	Artist
		Max	Composer
		Yvonne	Chambermaid
Lakmé	Delibes	Gérald	English officer
		Hadji	Nilakantha's servant
		Lakmé	Nilakantha's daughter
		Mallika	Lakmé's slave
		Nilakantha	Brahmin priest
		Rose	An English lady
Lohengrin		Godfrey	Elsa's brother
		Lohengrin	Parsifal's son
		Ortrud	Wife of Frederick
		Telramund	Count of Brabant
The Love for Three Oranges	Prokofiev	Celio	Magician
		Farfarello	A devil
		Fata Morgana	Witch
		King of Clubs	Ruler of the kingdom
		Leandro	King of Spades and prime minister
		Linette	Princess hidden in an orange
		Nicoletta	Princess hidden in an orange
		Ninetta	Princess hidden in an orange
		Pantaloon	King's friend
		Prince	Hypochondriac
		Princess Clarissa	King's niece
Lucia di Lammermoor	Donizetti	Alice/Alisa	Lucia's companion
		Arthur Bucklaw/Arturo	Lord
		Henry Ashton/Enrico	Lorn of Lammermoor
		Edgar/Edgardo	Edgar of Ravenswood
		Norman/Normando	Follower of Ashton
		Raymond/Raimondo	Chaplain, Lucy's tutor
Lucrezia Borgia	Donizetti	Alfonso d'Este	Duke of Ferrara, Lucrezia's third husband
		Gennaro	Venetian nobleman, Lucrezia's son
		Gubetta	Servant to Lucrezia
		Lucrezia Borgia	Duchess of Ferrara
		Maffio Orsini	Lucrezia's enemy
		Rustighello	Alfonso's henchman
		Vitellozzo	Nobleman, Gennaro's friend

Opera	Composer	Character	Role
Lulu	Berg	Alwa	Writer
		Dr Schön	Editor
		Lulu	Prostitute
		Prince	Traveller in Africa
Madame Butterfly	Puccini	The Bonze	Priest
		Cio-Cio-San	A geisha, Pinkerton's wife
		Goro	Marriage broker
		Kate	Pinkerton's American wife
		Lt Pinkerton	Lieutenant in US Navy
		Sharpless	US consul in Nagasaki
		Suzuki	Servant
		Trouble	Cio-Cio-San's child
		Yamadori	Rich Japanese
Madame Sans-Gêne	Giordano	Catarina	Laundress
The Magic Flute	Mozart	Monostatos	Servant
		Pamina	Daughter of Queen of the Night
		Papagena	Destined to be Papageno's wife
		Papageno	Bird catcher
		Sarastro	High priest
Manon	Massenet	Chevalier des Grieux	Manon's love
		Compte des Grieux	Chevalier's father
		de Bretigny	A nobleman
		Lescaut	A gambler
		Manon	Lescaut's cousin
Marouf	Rabaud	Ahmed	Pastry cook
		Ali	Marouf's friend
		Fatimah	Marouf's wife
		Marouf	Shoemaker
		Vizier	Sultan's adviser
The Marriage of Figaro	Mozart	Almaviva	Count
		Antonio	Gardener
		Barbarina	Antonio's daughter
		Cherubino	Page
		Don Basilio	Organist
		Don Curzio	Lawyer
		Figaro	Servant to Almaviva
		Marcellina	Housekeeper
		Susanna	Maid
A Masked Ball	Verdi	Amelia	Riccardo's love, wife of Renato
		Oscar	Riccardo's page
		Renato	Riccardo's secretary
		Riccardo	Governor of Louisiana
		Silvano	A young sailor
		Ulrica	Fortune teller
The Mastersingers of Nuremberg	Wagner	Augustin Moser	Mastersinger and tailor
		Balthasar Zorn	Mastersinger and pewterer
		Sixtus Beckmesser	Mastersinger and town clerk
		Conrad Nachtigall	Mastersinger and bucklemaker
		David	Hans Sachs's apprentice
		Eva	Pogner's daughter
		Fritz Kothner	Mastersinger and baker
		Hans Foltz	Mastersinger and coppersmith
		Hans Sachs	Mastersinger and cobbler
		Hans Schwarz	Mastersinger and stocking weaver
		Hermann Ortel	Mastersinger and soap boiler
		Kunz Vogelgesang	Mastersinger and furrier
		Magdalena	Nurse
		Ulrich Eisslinger	Mastersinger and grocer
		Veit Pogner	Mastersinger and goldsmith (Eva's father)
		Walter von Stolzing	Franconian knight
Mathis der Maler	Hindemith	Albrecht von Brandenburg	Archbishop of Mainz
		Mathis	Painter (Grünewald)
		Riedinger	Rich Lutheran
		Truchsess von Waldburg	Leader of the army
		Ursula	Riedinger's daughter
		Wolfgang Capito	Councillor
The Mother of Us All	Thomson	Susan B. Anthony	American suffragette
Nabucco	Verdi	Abdallo	Nabucco's officer
		Abigaille	Nabucco's adopted daughter

Opera	Composer	Character	Role
		Fenena	Nabucco's daughter
		Nabucco	Nebuchadnezzar, King of Babylon
		Zaccaria	High Priest of Jerusalem
Norma	Bellini	Adalgisa	Temple virgin
		Clotilde	Norma's friend
		Flavio	Centurion
		Norma	Druid priestess
		Oroveso	Norma's father
		Pollione	Proconsul of Rome
Oberon	Weber	Abdullah	Pirate
		Babekan	Saracen prince
		Charlemagne	Emperor of the Franks
		Fatima	Reiza's companion
		Haroun al Rashid	Calif of Baghdad
		Namouna	Fatima's grandmother
		Reiza	Haroun el Rashid's daughter
Oedipus Rex	Stravinsky	Creon	Jocasta's brother
		Jocasta	Wife of Oedipus
		Oedipus	King of Thebes
		Tiresias	Blind soothsayer
Orfeo et Euridice	Gluck	Amor	God of love
		Euridice	Orfeo's wife
		Orfeo	Singer poet
Otello	Verdi	Cassio	Lieutenant
		Lodovico	Venetian ambassador
		Montano	Otello's predecessor
I Pagliacci	Leoncavallo	Beppe	Harlequin
		Canio	Pagliaccio (clown)
		Nedda	Canio's wife
		Silvio	In love with Nedda
		Tonio	Clown
Palestrina	Pfitzner	Avosmediano	Bishop of Cadiz
		Ighino	Palestrina's son
		Lucretia	Palestrina's wife
		Palestrina	Composer
Parsifal	Wagner	Amfortas	King of the Grail
		King Titurel	Father of Amfortas
		Klingsor	Magician
		Kundry	Bewitched woman
		Parsifal	Knight of the Holy Grail
Pelléas et Mélisande	Debussy	Geneviève	Mother of Pelléas
		Golaud	Arkel's grandson
		Mélisande	Golaud's wife
		Pelléas	Arkel's grandson
		Yniold	Golaud's son
Peter Grimes	Britten	Bob Boles	Fisherman
		Ellen Orford	Schoolteacher
		John	Peter's apprentice
		Ned Keene	Apothecary
		Peter Grimes	Fisherman
The Pilgrim's Progress	Vaughan Williams	Apollyon	Fallen angel
		Mistrust	Neighbour
		Obstinate	Neighbour
		Pilgrim	Pilgrim
		Pliable	Neighbour
		Timorous	Neighbour
		Watchful	Porter
The Poisoned Kiss	Vaughan Williams	Amaryllus	Empress's son
		Angelica	Tormentilla's maid
		Dipsacus	Magician
		Gallanthus	Amaryllus's sister
		Hob	Servant of Dipsacus
		Lob	Assistant of Dipsacus
		Tormentilla	Daughter of Dipsacus
Porgy and Bess	Gershwin	Bess	Porgy's mistress, formerly Crown's
		Clara	Jake's wife
		Crown	Stevedore
		Frazier	Catfish row 'lawyer'
		Jake	Fisherman
		Jim	Cotton picker
		Lily	Strawberry woman

MUSIC CLASSICAL

Opera	Composer	Character	Role
		Maria	Cookshop keeper
		Mr Archdale	White man
		Peter	Honey-man
		Porgy	A crippled beggar
		Sportin' Life	Dope dealer
Prince Igor	Borodin	Eroshka	Gudok player
		Gzak	Polovtsian Khan
		Jaroslavna	Prince Igor's wife
		Kontchak	Polovtsian Khan
		Kontchakovna	Kontchak's daughter
		Ovlour	Polovtsian traitor
		Prince Igor	Prince of Seversk
		Vladimir Igorevitch	Igor's son
		Vladimir Yaroslavovitch	Yaroslavna's brother
The Rake's Progress	Stravinsky	Baba the Turk	Bearded lady
		Tom Rakewell	The Rake
		Trulove	Anne's father
The Rape of Lucretia	Britten	Bianca	Nurse
		Collatinus	Soldier
		Junius	Roman general
		Lucia	Lucretia's attendant
		Lucretia	Wife of Collatinus
Rienzi	Wagner	Adriano	Colonna's son
		Baroncelli	Roman citizen
		Cola Rienzi	Papal legate
		Irene	Rienzi's sister
		Paolo Orsini	Patrician
		Raimondo	Papal legate
Rigoletto	Verdi	Cavaliere Marullo	Courtier
		Duke of Mantua	Nobleman
		Gilda	Rigoletto's daughter
		Maddalena	Sparafucile's sister
		Matteo Borsa	Courtier
		Rigoletto	Gilda's father, a jester
Der Ring des Nibelungen	Wagner	Alberich	Nibelung dwarf
		Brünnhilde	Valkyrie
		Donner	Norse god
		Erda	Earth goddess
		Fafner	Giant, builder of Valhalla
		Fasolt	Giant, builder of Valhalla
		Flosshilde	Rhinemaiden
		Freia	Goddess of youth and beauty
		Fricka	Wotan's wife
		Froh	Norse god
		Gerhilde	Valkyrie
		Grimgerde	Valkyrie
		Gunther	Hagen's half-brother
		Gutrune	Gunther's sister
		Helmwige	Valkyrie
		Hunding	Siegmund's enemy
		Loge	Norse god
		Mime	A Nibelung
		Ortlinde	Valkyrie
		Rossweisse	Valkyrie
		Siegfried	Son of Siegmund and Sieglunde
		Sieglunde	Siegmund's twin sister
		Siegmund	Mortal son of Wotan
		Waltraute	Valkyrie
		Wellgunde	Rhine maiden
		Woglinde	Rhine maiden
		Wotan	Norse god
La Rondine	Puccini	Bianca	Magda's friend
		Crébillon	Perichaud's friend
		Lisette	Magda's maid
		Magda	Salon owner, Rambaldo's mistress
		Périchaud	Rambaldo's friend
		Prunier	Poet
		Rambaldo	Banker
		Ruggero	Son of Rambaldo's childhood friend
		Suzy	Magda's friend
		Yvette	Magda's friend

Opera	Composer	Character	Role
Der Rosenkavalier	Richard Strauss	Annina	Valzacchi's partner
		Baron Ochs	Sophie's would-be suitor
		Faninal	Sophie's father
		Mahomet	Negro page
		Marianne	Sophie's duenna
		Marschallin	Princess
		Octavian	Bearer of the Rose
		Sophie	Daughter of Faninal
		Valzacchi	Scandalmonger
Ruddigore	Sullivan	Mad Margaret	Mad woman
Ruslan and Lyudmila	Glinka	Bayan	Bard
		Chernomor	An evil dwarf
		Farlaf	Warrior
		Finn	Wizard
		Gorislava	Ratmir's lover
		Lyudmila	a noblewoman
		Naina	Witch
		Ratmir	Knight, suitor to Lyudmila
		Ruslan	Suitor to Lyudmila
		Svyetozer	Lyudmila's father
Salome	Richard Strauss	Herod	Ruler of Galilee
		Herodias	Herod's wife
		John the Baptist	Jewish prophet
		Narraboth	Captain of the Guard
		Salome	Daughter of Herodias
Samson et Dalila	Saint-Saëns	Abimilech	Satrap of Gaza
The Secret Marriage	Cimarosa	Carolina	Geronimo's daughter
		Elisetta	Geronimo's older daughter
		Fidalma	Geronimo's sister
		Geronimo	Citizen of Bologna
		Paolino	Carolina's secret husband
The Sleepwalker (La Sonnambula)	Bellini	Amina	The sleepwalking girl
		Elvino	Farmer
Il Tabarro	Puccini	Giorgetta	Michele's wife
		Luigi	Stevedore, Giorgetta's lover
		Michele	Barge owner
		Talpa	Stevedore
		Tinca	Stevedore
The Tales of Hoffmann	Offenbach	Chochenille	Spalanzani's servant
		Coppelius	Scientist
		Dapertutto	Sorcerer
		Dr Miracle	Doctor
		Frantz	Crespel's servant
		Hermann	Student
		Hoffmann	Poet
		Lindorf	Councillor of Nuremberg
		Luther	Innkeeper
		Nathanael	Student
		Nicklaus	Hoffmann's friend
		Olympia	Mechanical doll
		Pittichinaccio	Giulietta's admirer
		Spalanzani	Inventor
		Stella	Opera singer
Tannhäuser	Wagner	Biterolf	Knight
		Elisabeth	Hermann's niece
		Hermann	Landgrave of Thuringia
		Reinmar von Zweter	Knight
		Tannhäuser	Knight
		Venus	Supernatural seductress
		Walther von der Vogelweide	Knight
		Wolfram	Knight
Tosca	Puccini	Baron Scarpia	Chief of Police
		Cavaradossi	Painter
		Cesare Angelotti	Escaped political prisoner
		Mario Cavaradossi	Painter
		Tosca	Singer
La Traviata	Verdi	Alfredo Germont	Violetta's lover (a singer)
		Annina	Violetta's confidante
		Douphol	Baron
		Violetta Valery	Courtesan

Opera	Composer	Character	Role
Tristan und Isolde	Wagner	Brangäne	Isolde's maid
		Isolde	Irish princess
		King Marke	King of Cornwall
		Kurvenal	Tristan's retainer
		Melot	Courtier
		Tristan	Cornish knight
The Trojans (Les Troyens)	Berlioz	Andromaque	Hector's widow
		Chorèbe	Cassandra's lover
		Hylas	Trojan sailor
		Iopas	Poet
		Narbal	Dido's minister
		Panthée	Priest
		Polyxène	Priam's daughter
		Priam	King of Troy
Il Trovatore	Verdi	Azucena	Gypsy woman
		Count de Luna	Count of Aragon
		Ferrando	Captain of the Guard
		Manrico	Troubador
		Leonora	Beloved of Manrico
The Tsar Has His Photograph Taken	Weill	Angèle	Photographer
Turandot	Busoni	Adelma	Turandot's slave
		Barak	Servant
		Calaf	Suitor to Turandot
		Pantalone	Minister
		Queen Mother of Samarkand	Negress
Turandot	Puccini	Calaf	Suitor to Turandot
		Emperor Altoum	Turandot's father
		Liù	Slave girl
		Pang	Lord of Provisions
		Ping	Chinese Grand Chancellor
		Pong	Lord of the Imperial Kitchen
		Princess Turandot	Daughter of Altoum
A Village Romeo and Juliet	Delius	The Dark Fiddler	Real owner of land
		Manz	Farmer
		Marti	Farmer
		Sali	Manz's daughter
		Vreli	Marti's daughter
Wozzeck	Berg	Marie	Prostitute
		Wozzeck	Soldier
The Wreckers	Smyth	Lawrence	Lighthouse keeper
Zazà	Leoncavallo	Bussy	Journalist
		Cascart	Music-hall performer
		Duclou	Stage manager
		Mme Dufresne	Milio's wife
		Lartigen	Monologist
		Marco	Dufresne's butler
		Marlardot	Music-hall owner
		Michelin	Journalist
		Milio Dufresne	Zaza's lover
		Natalia	Zazà's maid
		Toto	Dufresne's child
		Zazà	Music-hall singer

Operas and Operettas

Operas and operettas	Composer	First performance	Librettist	General information
Adriana Lecouvreur	Francesco Cilea	1902	Milan	Colautti	
L'Africaine	Giacomo Meyerbeer	1865	London, Paris, New York	Scribe	
Agyptische Helena	Richard Strauss	1928	Dresden	Hofmannsthal	
Aida	Giuseppe Verdi	1871	Cairo	Ghislanzoni	
Akhnaten	Philip Glass	1984	Stuttgart	Glass (Richard Riddell, Robert Israel and Shalom Goldman helped with the libretto)	
Albert Herring	Benjamin Britten	1947	Glyndebourne	Crozier	
Alceste	Christoph Gluck	1767	Vienna	Calzabigi	
Aleko	Sergei Rachmaninov	1893	Moscow	Nemirovich-Danchenko	
Alfred	Thomas Arne	1740	London	Thomson and Mallet	Contains song 'Rule, Britannia'
Almira	George Frederick Handel	1705	Hamburg	Feustking	Handel's first opera
Alzira	Giuseppe Verdi	1845	Naples	Cammarano	
Amahl and the Night Visitors	Gian Carlo Menotti	1951	New York	Menotti	First opera written for TV
Amelia Goes to the Ball	Gian Carlo Menotti	1937	Berlin	Menotti	
L'Amico Fritz	Pietro Mascagni	1891	Rome	Daspuro	
Amleto (Hamlet)	Franco Faccio	1865	Genoa	Boito	
Andrea Chénier	Umberto Giordano	1896	Milan	Illica	
Aniara	Karl-Birger Blomdahl	1959	Stockholm	Lindegren	
Anne Boleyn	Gaetano Donizetti	1830	Milan	Romani	
Antar	Gabriel Dupont	1921	Paris	Dupont	
Antony and Cleopatra	Samuel Barber	1966	New York (Met)	Zeffirelli and Barber	
Arabella	Richard Strauss	1933	Dresden	Hofmannsthal	
Ariadne auf Naxos	Richard Strauss	1916	Vienna	Hofmannsthal	
Ariane et Barbe-bleu	Paul Dukas	1907	Paris	Maeterlinck	
Arlecchino (Harlequin)	Ferruccio Busoni	1917	Zurich	Busoni	
Armide	Christoph Gluck	1777	Paris	Quinault	
Artaxerxes	Thomas Arne	1762	London	Metastasio	
At the Boar's Head	Gustav Holst	1925	Manchester	Holst	
The Barber of Seville	Giovanni Paisiello	1782	St Petersburg	Petrosellini	
The Barber of Seville	Gioachino Rossini	1816	Rome	Sterbini	Based on Beaumarchais comedy
The Bartered Bride	Bedrich Smetana	1866	Prague	Sabina	
The Bassarids	Hans Werner Henze	1966	Salzburg	Auden and Kallman	
The Bear	William Walton	1967	Aldeburgh	Dehn	
Beatrice Cenci	Berthold Goldschmidt	1988	London	Esslin	Prizewinner in Festival of Britain Competition 1951
Béatrice et Bénédict	Hector Berlioz	1862	Baden-Baden	Berlioz	
The Beautiful Galathea	Franz von Suppe	1865	Vienna	Henrion	
The Beggar's Opera	Christoph Pepusch	1728	London	Gay	
Belfagor	Ottorino Respighi	1923	Milan	Morselli and Gaustalla	
Belisario	Gaetano Donizetti	1836	Venice	Cammarano	
La Belle Hélène	Jacques Offenbach	1864	Paris	Meilhac and Halevy	
The Bells of Corneville	Robert Planquette	1877	Paris and New York	Clairville and Gabet	
Benvenuto Cellini	Hector Berlioz	1838	Paris	Wailly and Barbier	

MUSIC CLASSICAL

Operas and operettas	Composer	First performance		Librettist	General information
Berenice	George Frederick Handel	1737	London	Salvi	
Billy Budd	Benjamin Britten	1951	London	Forster and Crozier	Ship: HMS *Indomitable*
The Black Mask	Krzysztof Penderecki	1986	Salzburg	Kupfer and Penderecki	
Blond Eckbert	Judith Weir	1994	London	Weir	
Boccaccio	Franz von Suppé	1879	Vienna	Zell and Génée	
La Bohème	Ruggiero Leoncavallo	1897	Venice	Leoncavallo	
La Bohème	Giacomo Puccini	1896	Turin	Giacosa and Illica	
The Bohemian Girl	Michael Balfe	1843	London	Bunn	Title translates as *La Bohème*, though not the same story
Boris Godunov	Modeste Mussorgsky	1874	St Petersburg	Mussorgsky	
Boulevard Solitude	Hans Werner Henze	1952	Hanover	Henze and Weil	
Die Brautwahl	Ferruccio Busoni	1912	Hamburg	Busoni, after Hoffmann	
The Burning Fiery Furnace	Benjamin Britten	1966	Orford	Plomer	
The Caliph of Baghdad	François Boieldieu	1800	Paris	Saint-Just	
La Calisto	Pietro Francesco Cavalli	1651	Venice	Faustini	
La Campana Sommersa	Ottorino Respighi	1927	Hamburg	Guastalla	Title translates as *The Submerged Bell*
Candide	Leonard Bernstein	1956	Boston	Hellmann	
El Capitan	John Philip Sousa	1896	New York and Boston	Klein	
Capriccio	Richard Strauss	1942	Munich	Krauss and Strauss	
I Capuleti e i Montecchi	Vincenzo Bellini	1830	Venice	Romani	The Capulets and the Montagues, i.e. Romeo and Juliet
Cardillac	Paul Hindemith	1926	Dresden	Lion	
Caritas	Robert Saxton	1991	Wakefield	Wesker	
Carmen	Georges Bizet	1875	Paris	Meilhac and Halévy	Carmen dies by stabbing (at the hands of Don José)
Castor and Pollux	Jean-Philippe Rameau	1737	Paris	Bernard	
The Catiline Conspiracy	Iain Hamilton	1974	Stirling	Hamilton	
Cavalleria Rusticana	Pietro Mascagni	1890	Rome	Menasci and Targioni-Tozzetti	
Cendrillon (Cinderella)	Nicolò Isouard	1810	Paris	Étienne	
Cendrillon (Cinderella)	Jules Massenet	1899	Paris	Henry Cain	
La Cenerentola (Cinderella)	Gioachino Rossini	1817	Rome	Ferretti	
Chérubin	Jules Massenet	1905	Monte Carlo	Henry Cain and Francis de Croisset	The story of Cherubino after the marriage of Figaro
Cheryomushki	Dmitry Shostakovich	1959	Moscow	Mass and Chervinsky	Shostakovich's only operetta
The Chocolate Soldier	Oscar Straus	1908	Vienna	Jacobson and Bernauer	Based on G.B. Shaw's play *Arms and the Man*
Christmas Eve	Nikolay Rimsky-Korsakov	1895	St Petersburg	Rimsky-Korsakov	Based on Gogol story
Le Cid	Jules Massenet	1885	Paris	D'Ennery, Gallet and Blau	
La Clemenza di Tito	Wolfgang Amadeus Mozart	1791	Prague	Metastasio	Mozart's last opera
Comedy on the Bridge	Bohuslav Martinu	1937	Prague (Radio)	Martinu	
Conchita	Riccardo Zandonai	1911	Milan	Vaucaire and Zangarini	
Confessions of a Justified Sinner	Thomas Wilson	1976	York	John Currie	Based on the novel by James Hogg
The Consul	Gian Carlo Menotti	1950	Philadelphia	Menotti	The Consul represents bureaucratic red tape
Le Coq d'Or	Nikolay Rimsky-Korsakov	1909	Moscow	Belsky	Rimsky-Korsakov's 14th and last opera
The Coronation of Poppaea	Claudio Monteverdi	1643	Venice	Busenello	Monteverdi's last opera

Operas and operettas	Composer	First performance		Librettist	General information
Der Corregidor (The Magistrate)	Hugo Wolf	1896	Mannheim	Mayreder	Based on The Three-Cornered Hat by Alarcón
Il Corsaro	Giuseppe Verdi	1848	Trieste	Piave	Based on Byron's poem The Corsair
Cosi fan tutte	Wolfgang Amadeus Mozart	1790	Vienna	da Ponte	Role of Fiordiligi long regarded as unsingable
The Count of Luxemburg	Franz Lehár	1909	Vienna	Wilner and Bodanzky	
Cox and Box	Arthur Sullivan	1867	London	Burnand	
The Cunning Little Vixen	Leoš Janáček	1924	Brno	Janáček	
Curlew River	Benjamin Britten	1964	Orford	Plomer	A church parable
Dafne	Jacopo Peri	1598	Florence	Rinuccini	Generally regarded to be the earliest opera
Dalibor	Bedrich Smetana	1868	Prague	Spindler	Translation of German text by Joseph Wenzig
La Dame Blanche (White Lady)	François Boieldieu	1825	Paris	Scribe	Based on Scott's The Monastery and Guy Mannering
Danton's Death	Gottfried Von Einem	1947	Salzburg	Blacher and Von Einem	Based on drama by Büchner
Daphne	Richard Strauss	1938	Dresden	Gregor	
Dardanus	Jean-Philipe Rameau	1739	Paris	De La Bruyère	
The Daughter of the Regiment	Gaetano Donizetti	1840	Paris	Saint-Georges and Bayard	
David	Darius Milhaud	1954	Jerusalem	Lunel	
Day of Peace (Friedenstag)	Richard Strauss	1938	Munich	Gregor	
Death in Venice	Benjamin Britten	1973	Aldeburgh	Myfanwy Piper	
Debora e Jaële	Ildebrando Pizzetti	1922	Milan	Pizzetti	
Deidamia	George Frederick Handel	1741	London	Rolli	Handel's last opera
The Deserted Island	Franz Joseph Haydn	1779	Eszterháza	Metastasio	Also the title of an opera by G. Scarlatti
Les Deux Journées (The Two Days)	Luigi Cherubini	1800	Paris	Bouilly	Known in Britain as The Water Carrier
Les Dialogues des Carmélites	Francis Poulenc	1957	Milan, Paris, San Francisco	Lavery	
Dido and Aeneas	Henry Purcell	1689	Chelsea	Nahum Tate	
A Dinner Engagement	Lennox Berkeley	1954	Aldeburgh	Paul Dehn	
Doctor Miracle	Georges Bizet	1857	Paris	Battu and Halévy	Joint winner of the Offenbach Prize with Lecocq
Doctor Miracle	Charles Lecocq	1857	Paris	Battu and Halévy	Joint winner of the Offenbach Prize with Bizet
The Doctor of Myddfai	Peter Maxwell Davies	1996	Cardiff	Pountney	
Doktor Faust	Ferruccio Busoni	1925	Dresden	Busoni	Completed after Busoni's death by Jarnach
Dollar Princess	Leo Fall	1907	Vienna	Willner and Grünbaum	
Don Carlos	Giuseppe Verdi	1867	Paris	Méry and Du Locle	Also known as Don Carlo
Don Giovanni	Wolfgang Amadeus Mozart	1787	Prague	Da Ponte	Based on Bertati's Don Juan (1775)
Don Pasquale	Gaetano Donizetti	1843	Paris and London	Ruffini	
Don Quixote	Jules Massenet	1910	Monte Carlo	Henry Cain	Based on Sheridan work
The Duenna	Roberto Gerhard	1949	BBC Radio	Gerhard and Hassall	Based on Sheridan work
The Duenna	Sergey Prokofiev	1946	Leningrad	Prokofiev and Mendelson	
Duke Bluebeard's Castle	Béla Bartók	1918	Budapest	Béla Balázs	
Duke of Alba	Gaetano Donizetti	1882	Rome	Scribe	Completed by Salvi
The Dwarf (Der Zwerg)	Alexander Zemlinsky	1922	Cologne	G.C. Klaren	Based on Oscar Wilde's The Birthday of the Infanta
Edgar	Giacomo Puccini	1889	Milan	Fontana	
Einstein on the Beach	Philip Glass	1976	Avignon	Knowles, Childs, Johnson	Composed in collaboration with Robert Wilson
Electrification of the Soviet Union	Nigel Osborne	1987	Glyndebourne	Craig Raine	Based on Pasternak's 'Last Summer' and 'Spectorsky'
Elegy for Young Lovers	Hans Werne Henze	1961	Schwetzingen	Auden and Kallman	

Operas and operettas	Composer	First performance	Librettist	General information
Elektra	Richard Strauss	1909 Dresden	Hofmannsthal	
L'Elisir d'Amore	Gaetano Donizetti	1832 Milan	Romani	
Elizabeth, Queen of England	Gioachino Rossini	1815 Naples	Giovanni Schmidt	Based on Sophia Lee's novel The Recess
The Emerald Isle	Arthur Sullivan	1901 London (Savoy)	Basil Hood	Posthumous comic opera completed by Edward German
The Emperor Jones	Louis Gruenberg	1933 New York	de Jaffa	
L'Enfant et les Sortilèges	Maurice Ravel	1925 Monte Carlo	Colette	
The English Cat	Hans Werner Henze	1983 Schwetzingen	Edward Bond	
Ernani	Giuseppe Verdi	1844 Venice	Piave	Based on Victor Hugo's play Hernani
Esclarmonde	Jules Massenet	1889 Paris	Blau and de Gramont	
L'Étoile (The Star)	Emmanuel Chabrier	1877 Paris	Leterrier and Vanloo	
L'Étoile du Nord (The North Star)	Giacomo Meyerbeer	1854 Paris	Scribe	
Eugene Onegin	Pyotr Tchaikovsky	1879 Moscow	Shilovsky and Tchaikovsky	
Euryanthe	Carl Maria Weber	1823 Vienna	Helmina von Chézy	
The Excursions of Mr Brouček	Leoš Janáček	1920 Prague	Janáček	
The Fair Maid of Perth	Georges Bizet	1867 Paris	St George and Adenis	Based on Sir Walter Scott's play of the same name
The Faithful Shepherd	George Frederick Handel	1712 London	Rossi	Based on Guarini's play
The Fall of the House of Usher	Claude Debussy	1977 New Haven	Debussy	Based on Edgar Allan Poe work but left unfinished and reconstructed by W. Harwood
Falstaff	Giuseppe Verdi	1893 Milan	Boito	Verdi's last opera
The Girl of the Golden West (La Fanciulla del West)	Giacomo Puccini	1910 New York (Met)	Civinini and Zangarini	Based on Belasco's play The Girl of the Golden West
Fanny Robin	Edward Harper	1975 Edinburgh	Harper	Based on Wessex poems and Far From the Madding Crowd
Faust	Ludwig Spohr	1816 Prague	J.K. Bernard	Not based on Goethe's Faust
Faust	Charles Gounod	1859 Paris	Barbier and Carré	Based on Carré's Faust et Marguerite and Goethe's Faust
La Favola d'Orfeo	Claudio Monteverdi	1607 Mantua	Striggio	
La Favorite	Gaetano Donizetti	1840 Paris	Royer, Vaëz and Scribe	
Fedora	Umberto Giordano	1898 Milan	Colautti	Based on Sardou's play of the same name
Die Feen (The Fairies)	Richard Wagner	1888 Munich	Wagner	Wagner's first opera
Fennimore and Gerda	Frederick Delius	1919 Frankfurt	Delius	Delius's 6th and last opera
Der Ferne Klang	Franz Schreker	1912 Frankfurt	Schreker	
La Fiamma	Ottorino Respighi	1934 Rome	Guastalla	
Fidelio, or the Triumph of Married Love	Ludwig van Beethoven	1805 Vienna	Josef Sonnleithner	Beethoven's only opera
Fidelity Rewarded	Franz Joseph Haydn	1781 Esterháza	G. Lorenzi	
The Fiery Angel	Sergey Prokofiev	1954 Paris	Prokofiev	Prokofiev's Symphony No. 3 uses themes from this opera
La Finta Giardiniera (The Feigned Garden Girl)	Wolfgang Amadeus Mozart	1775 Munich	Uncertain	Mozart's first significant opera
Die Fledermaus (The Bat)	Johann Strauss II	1874 Vienna and New York	Hafner and Genée	Opera in 3 acts although often played in one
The Flying Dutchman	Richard Wagner	1843 Dresden	Wagner	
Die Frau ohne Schatten	Richard Strauss	1919 Vienna	Hofmannsthal	English title: The Woman without a Shadow
From One Day to the Next	Arnold Schoenberg	1930 Frankfurt	Max Blonda	Max Blonda was Gertrud Schoenberg

Operas and operettas

Operas and operettas	Composer	First performance	Librettist	General information
From the House of the Dead	Leoš Janáček	1930 Brno	Janáček	Based on Dostoyevsky's novel
The Gambler	Sergey Prokofiev	1929 Brussels	Prokofiev	Based on Dostoyevsky's short story
The Gamblers	Dmitry Shostakovich	1978 Leningrad	Shostakovich	Unfinished opera completed by Krzysztof Meyer
Gawain	Harrison Birtwistle	1991 London	David Harsent	
Genoveva	Robert Schumann	1850 Leipzig	Reinick and Schumann	Also the name of an opera by Detlev Müller-Siemens
Gesualdo	Alfred Schnittke	1994 Vienna	Bletschacher	Based on life of the composer Gesualdo
Der Gewaltige Hahnrei	Berthold Goldschmidt	1992 Berlin	Goldschmidt	Composed in 1930
Gianni Schicchi	Giacomo Puccini	1918 New York	Forzano	The third part of Puccini's *Il Trittico*
La Gioconda	Amilcare Ponchielli	1876 Milan	'Tobia Gorrio' (Arrigo Boito)	Contains the ballet *Dance of the Hours* (Act 3)
Un Giorno di Regno	Giuseppe Verdi	1840 Milan	Romani	
Giuditta	Franz Lehár	1934 Vienna	Knepler and Löhner	Lehár's only opera
Gloriana	Benjamin Britten	1953 London	W. Plomer	Commissioned for coronation of Elizabeth II
Golem	John Casken	1989 London	Casken and Audi	
Golem	Larry Sitsky	1993 Sydney	Larry Sitsky	
The Gondoliers	Arthur Sullivan	1889 London	W.S. Gilbert	Aka: 'The King of Barataria'
Götterdämmerung (The Twilight of the Gods)	Richard Wagner	1876 Bayreuth	Wagner	Final opera in his tetralogy *Der Ring des Nibelungen*
The Government Inspector	Werner Egk	1957 Schwetzingen	Egk	Based on Gogol's story
Grande Duchesse de Gérolstein	Jacques Offenbach	1867 Paris, New York and London	Meilhac and Halévy	
The Grand Duke	Arthur Sullivan	1896 London and Berlin	W.S. Gilbert	Aka: 'The Statutory Duel'
The Grand Macabre	György Ligeti	1978 Stockholm	Meschke	
Greek	Mark-Anthony Turnage	1988 Munich	Turnage and Jonathan Moore	Based on Berkoff's play *Greek*
The Greek Passion	Bohuslav Martinů	1961 Zurich	Martinů and Kazantzakis	Based on Kazantzakis novel *Christ Recrucified*
Grisélidis	Jules Massenet	1901 Paris	Silvestre and Morand	Based on a story in Boccaccio's *Decameron*
The Growing Castle	Malcolm Williamson	1968 Dynevor	Williamson	Based on Strindberg's dream play
Guntram	Richard Strauss	1894 Weimar	Strauss	Strauss's first opera
Gwendoline	Emmanuel Chabrier	1886 Brussels	Mendès	
The Gypsy Baron (Zigeunerbaron)	Johann Strauss II	1885 Vienna	Schnitzer	
Halka	Stanislaw Moniuszko	1848 Vilnius (Wilno)	Wolski	
Hamlet (3 acts)	Humphrey Searle	1968 Hamburg	Searle	
Hamlet (5 acts)	Ambroise Thomas	1868 Paris	Barbier and Carré	Other operas on the subject by Scarlatti, Gasparini, Mercadante, Grandi, Szokolay
Hans Heiling	Heinrich Marschner	1833 Berlin	Devrient	
Hänsel and Gretel	Engelbert Humperdinck	1893 Weimar	Adelheid Wette	Based on the story by the Brothers Grimm
The Happy Prince	Malcolm Williamson	1965 Farnham	Williamson	
Harmony of the World	Paul Hindemith	1957 Munich	Hindemith	Based on life of Johann Kepler
Henry VIII	Camille Saint-Saëns	1883 Paris	Détroyat and Silvestre	
Hérodiade	Jules Massenet	1881 Brussels	Millet and Grémont	
L'Heure Espagnole	Maurice Ravel	1911 Paris	Franc-Nohain	
Higglety Pigglety Pop!	Oliver Knussen	1985 Glyndebourne	Knussen and Sendak	
Hin und Zurück (There and Back)	Paul Hindemith	1927 Baden Baden	Schiffer	
Hippolyte et Aricie	Jean-Philippe Rameau	1733 Paris	Abbé Pellegrin	
Historia von D. Johann Fausten	Alfred Schnittke	1995 Hamburg	Morgener and Schnittke	

Operas and operettas	Composer	First performance		Librettist	General information
HMS Pinafore	Arthur Sullivan	1878	London	W.S. Gilbert	Aka: 'The Lass That Loved a Sailor'
The Horseman	Aulis Sallinen	1975	Savonlinna	Haavikko	
Hugh the Drover	Ralph Vaughan Williams	1924	London	Harold Child	Aka: 'Love in the Stocks'
Les Huguenots	Giacomo Meyerbeer	1836	Paris	Scribe and Deschamps	
The Ice Break	Michael Tippett	1977	Covent Garden	Tippett	
Idomeneo, King of Crete	Wolfgang Amadeus Mozart	1781	Munich	G.B. Varesco	
Imeneo	George Frederick Handel	1740	London	Anonymous	
The Immortal Hour	Rutland Boughton	1914	Glastonbury	Boughton	
Importance of Being Earnest	Mario Castelnuovo-Tedesco	1975	New York	Castelnuovo-Tedesco	
L'Incoronazione di Poppea	Claudio Monteverdi	1642	Venice	Busenello	
The Indian Queen	Henry Purcell	1695	London	Dryden and R. Howard	Concerns Mexican–Peruvian rivalry
Inès de Castro	James MacMillan	1996	Edinburgh	Clifford	
L'Infedeltà delusa (Deceit Outwitted)	Franz Joseph Haydn	1773	Eszterháza	Coltellini	
Intermezzo	Richard Strauss	1924	Dresden	Strauss	Two main characters portrayed are Strauss and his wife
Intolleranza	Luigi Nono	1961	Venice	Nono	
The Invisible City of Kitezh	Nikolay Rimsky-Korsakov	1907	St Petersburg	Belsky	
Iolanthe	Arthur Sullivan	1882	London and New York	W.S. Gilbert	
Iphigénie en Aulide	Christoph Gluck	1774	Paris	Du Roullet	
Iphigénie en Tauride	Christoph Gluck	1778	Paris	Guillard and Du Roullet	
Iris	Pietro Mascagni	1898	Rome	Illica	
Irish Legend	Werner Egk	1955	Salzburg	Egk	Based on W.B. Yeat's 'Countess Cathleen'
Irmelin	Frederick Delius	1953	Oxford	Delius	
The Italian Girl in Algiers	Gioachino Rossini	1813	Venice	Anelli	Libretto taken from Mosca's opera of the same name
Ivan IV	Georges Bizet	1951	Bordeaux	F.H. Leroy and H. Trianon	
Ivanhoe	Arthur Sullivan	1891	London	J. Sturgis	Originally written for Gounod
The Jacobin	Antonin Dvořák	1889	Prague	M. Červinková-Riegrová	Based on Sir Walter Scott's novel
Jenůfa	Leoš Janáček	1904	Brno	Janáček	Retains title of 'Her Foster-Daughter' in Czech Republic
Jérusalem	Giuseppe Verdi	1847	Paris	Royer and Vaëz	
The Jewels of the Madonna	Ermanno Wolf-Ferrari	1911	Berlin	Golisciani and Zangarini	
The Jewess (La Juive)	Jacques Halévy	1835	Paris	Scribe	
Joan of Arc	Giuseppe Verdi	1845	Milan	Solera	
Le Jongleur de Notre Dame	Jules Massenet	1902	Monte Carlo	Léna	
Jonny Spielt Auf	Ernst Krenek	1927	Leipzig	Krenek	
The Journey to Rheims	Gioachino Rossini	1825	Paris	Balocchi	Full title: The Journey to Rheims or Inn of the Golden Lily
Judith	Arthur Honegger	1926	Monte Carlo	R. Morax	
Judith	Eugene Goossens	1929	London and Philadelphia	Arnold Bennett	
Juha	Aarre Merikanto	1958	Finland	Ackté and Aho	
Julien	Gustave Charpentier	1913	Paris	Charpentier	Sequel to Louise
Julietta	Bohuslav Martinů	1938	Prague	Martinu	
Julius Caesar in Egypt	George Frederick Handel	1724	London	N.F. Haym	Numerous other operas on the theme of Julius Caesar

Operas and operettas	Composer	First performance		Librettist	General information
The Jumping Frog of Calaveras County	Lukas Foss	1950	Indiana	J. Karsavina	Based on Mark Twain story
Der Junge Lord (The Young Lord)	Hans Werner Henze	1965	Berlin	I. Bachmann	
Der Kaiser von Atlantis	Viktor Ullmann	1943	Terezin	Kien	Premiere in Terezin prison camp banned
Kashchey the Immortal	Nikolay Rimsky-Korsakov	1902	Moscow	Rimsky-Korsakov	
Kate and the Devil	Antonín Dvořák	1899	Prague	A. Wenig	
Katerina Izmaylova	Dmitry Shostakovich	1934	Moscow	A. Preys and Shostakovich	Revision of 'Lady Macbeth of the Mtsensk District'
Die Kathrin	Erich Korngold	1939	Stockholm	Korngold	
Katya Kabanova	Leoš Janáček	1921	Brno	Janáček	Based on Ostrovsky's play The Storm
Khovanshchina (The Khovansky Affair)	Modest Mussorgsky	1886	St Petersburg	V. Stasov and Mussorgsky	Completed by Rimsky-Korsakov
King Arthur, or the British Worthy	Henry Purcell	1691	London	Dryden	Semi-opera, but in reality a play with extensive music
The King Goes Forth to France	Aulis Sallinen	1984	Savonlinna	P. Haavikko	
The King of Lahore	Jules Massenet	1877	Paris	L. Gallet	
The King of Ys	Édouard-Victor-Antoine Lalo	1888	Paris	Blau	
King Priam	Michael Tippett	1962	Coventry	Tippett	Based on Homer's Iliad
King Roger	Karol Szymanowski	1926	Warsaw	J. Iwaszkiewicz	
The King's Children	Engelbert Humperdinck	1897	Munich and London	Ernst Rosmer	Rosmer the pseudonym of Else Bernstein-Porges
The Kiss	Bedrich Smetana	1876	Prague	E. Krásnohorská	Based on story by Joanna Muzakova
Die Kluge (The Clever Girl)	Carl Orff	1943	Frankfurt	Orff	Aka The Wise Woman
The Knot Garden	Michael Tippett	1970	Covent Garden	Tippett	
Koanga	Frederick Delius	1904	Elberfeld	C.F. Keary	Based on G.W. Gable's novel The Grandissimes
König Hirsch (King Stag)	Hans Werner Henze	1956	Berlin	H. von Cramer	
Lady Macbeth of Mtsensk District	Dmitry Shostakovich	1963	Leningrad	A. Preys and Shostakovich	See Katerina Izmaylova
Lakmé	Léo Delibes	1883	Paris and Chicago	Gondinet and Gille	
The Lambton Worm	R. Sherlaw Johnson	1978	Oxford	Anne Ridler	
The Land of Smiles	Franz Lehár	1923	Vienna	L. Herzer and F .Löhner	
The Last Temptations	Joonas Kokkonen	1975	Helsinki	L. Kokkonen	Based on life of Finnish evangelist Paavo Ruotsalainen
Lear	Aribert Reimann	1978	Munich	Claus Henneberg	
The Legend of Tsar Sultan	Nikolay Rimsky-Korsakov	1900	Moscow	Belsky	Based on Pushkin poem; contains 'The Flight of the Bumble Bee'
Leonora, or Married Love	Pierre Gaveaux	1798	Paris	J.N. Bouilly	
Let's Make An Opera	Benjamin Britten	1949	Aldeburgh	Eric Crozier	
Das Liebesverbot	Richard Wagner	1836	Magdeburg	Wagner	Based on Shakespeare's Measure for Measure
Life for the Tsar	Mikhail Glinka	1836	St Petersburg	Baron Yegor Rosen	
Life with an Idiot	Alfred Schnittke	1992	Amsterdam	Erofeyev	
The Light Cavalry	Franz von Suppé	1866	Vienna	C. Costa	
The Lighthouse	Peter Maxwell Davies	1980	Edinburgh	Davies	
Linda di Chamounix	Gaetano Donizetti	1842	Vienna	Rossi	
The Lodger	Phyllis Tate	1960	London	David Franklin	
Lodoiska	Luigi Cherubini	1791	Paris	Fillette-Loraux	
Lohengrin	Richard Wagner	1850	Weimar	Wagner	Liszt was the conductor at the first performance
I Lombardi	Giuseppe Verdi	1843	Milan	Solera	
The Long Christmas Dinner	Paul Hindemith	1961	Mannheim	Thornton Wilder	

MUSIC CLASSICAL

Operas and operettas	Composer	First performance		Librettist	General information
Louise	Gustave Charpentier	1900	Paris	Charpentier	
The Love For Three Oranges	Sergey Prokofiev	1921	Chicago	Prokofiev	
The Love of Danae	Richard Strauss	1952	Salzburg	J. Gregor	
The Love of the Three Kings	Italo Montemezzi	1913	La Scala	Benelli	
Lowland (Tiefland)	Eugen D'Albert	1903	Prague	R. Lothar	
Lucia di Lammermoor	Gaetano Donizetti	1835	Naples	Cammarano	Based on Scott's novel Bride of Lammermoor (1819)
Lucio Silla	Wolfgang Amadeus Mozart	1772	Milan	G. da Gamerra	
Lucrezia Borgia	Gaetano Donizetti	1833	Milan	Romani	
Luisa Miller	Giuseppe Verdi	1849	Naples	Cammarano	
Lulu	Alban Berg	1937	Zurich	Berg	
Macbeth	Giuseppe Verdi	1847	Florence	Piave	
Macbeth	Ernest Bloch	1910	Paris	Edmond Fleg	
Macbeth	Lawrance Collingwood	1934	London	Collingwood	
Madame Angot's Daughter	Charles Lecocq	1872	Brussels	Clairville, Siraudin and Koning	
Madame Butterfly	Giacomo Puccini	1904	Milan	Giacosa and Illica	Based on Belasco's play
Madame Sans-Gêne	Umberto Giordano	1915	New York and Turin	Simoni	
Maddalena	Sergey Prokofiev	1978	Manchester	Prokofiev	Completed by Edward Downes
The Magic Flute	Wolfgang Amadeus Mozart	1791	Vienna	Schikaneder	
The Magic Fountain	Frederick Delius	1977	London	Jutta Bell and Delius	
The Magic Island (Die Zauberinsel)	Heinrich Sutermeister	1942	Dresden	Sutermeister	Based on Shakespeare's The Tempest
The Maid of Orleans	Pyotr Tchaikovsky	1881	St Petersburg	Tchaikovsky	
The Maid of Pskov	Nikolay Rimsky-Korsakov	1873	St Petersburg	Rimsky-Korsakov	
The Makropulos Affair	Leoš Janáček	1926	Brno	Janáček	Based on Karel Čapek's play
The Mamelles de Tirésias	Francis Poulenc	1947	Paris	Poulenc	Based on Apollinaire play
Manon	Jules Massenet	1884	Paris	Meilhac and Gille	Based on Prévost's novel Manon Lescaut
Manon Lescaut	Giacomo Puccini	1893	Turin	Giacosa, Illica, Ricordi, Praga and Oliva	
Margot la Rouge	Frederick Delius	1981	BBC Radio	Rosenval	Composed 1902
Maria di Rohan	Gaetano Donizetti	1843	Vienna	Cammarano	
Maria Golovin	Gian Carlo Menotti	1958	Brussels and New York	Menotti	
Maria Stuarda	Gaetano Donizetti	1835	Milan	G. Bardari	Based on Schiller's play
Maritana	Vincent Wallace	1845	London	E. Fitzball	
Marouf	Henri Rabaud	1914	Paris	Népoty	
The Marriage	Bohuslav Martinu	1954	Hamburg	Martinu	First airing was on American television (NBC) in 1953
The Marriage of Figaro	Wolfgang Amadeus Mozart	1786	Vienna	Da Ponte	Based on Beaumarchais play
The Marriage	Modest Mussorgsky	1917	Petrograd	Mussorgsky	
Martha, or Richmond Fair	Friedrich von Flotow	1847	Vienna	W. Friedrich	
The Martyrdom of St Magnus	Peter Maxwell Davies	1977	Kirkwall	Davies	First performance, St Magnus Cathedral, Kirkwall, Orkney
Mary of Egypt	John Tavener	1992	Aldeburgh	Mother Thekla	
Mary, Queen of Scots	Thea Musgrave	1977	Edinburgh	Musgrave	
The Mask of Orpheus	Harrison Birtwistle	1986	London	Peter Zinovieff	
Maskarade	Carl Nielsen	1906	Copenhagen	V. Andersen	Also the name of a ballet by John McCabe

Operas and operettas

Operas and operettas	Composer	First performance		Librettist	General information
A Masked Ball	Giuseppe Verdi	1859	Rome	Antonio Somma	
I Masnadieri (The Robbers)	Giuseppe Verdi	1847	London	Maffei	
Master Peter's Puppet Show	Manuel de Falla	1923	Seville	Falla	Based on incident in Cervantes' *Don Quixote*
The Mastersingers of Nuremberg	Richard Wagner	1868	Munich	Wagner	
Mathis der Maler (Matthias the Painter)	Paul Hindemith	1938	Zurich	Hindemith	Based on life of Matthias Grünewald
Mavra	Igor Stravinsky	1922	Paris	Kochno	
May Night	Nikolay Rimsky-Korsakov	1880	St Petersburg	Rimsky-Korsakov	Based on Gogol story
Mazeppa	Pyotr Tchaikovsky	1884	Moscow	Tchaikovsky and Burenin	
Medea (Médée)	Luigi Cherubini	1797	Paris	F.B. Hoffman	
The Medium	Gian Carlo Menotti	1946	Columbia University	Menotti	
Mephistopheles	Arrigo Boito	1868	Milan	Boito	Based on Goethe's *Faust*
Merrie England	Edward German	1902	London (Savoy)	Basil Hood	
The Merry Widow	Franz Lehár	1905	Vienna	V. Léon and L. Stein	Widow's name is Hanna Glawari
The Merry Wives of Windsor	Otto Nicolai	1849	Berlin	S.H. Mosenthal	
The Midsummer Marriage	Michael Tippett	1955	London	Tippett	
A Midsummer Night's Dream	Benjamin Britten	1960	Aldeburgh	Pears and Britten	
Mignon	Ambroise Thomas	1866	Paris	Barbier and Carré	Based on Goethe's novel *Wilhelm Meisters Lehrjahre*
The Mikado	Arthur Sullivan	1885	London	W.S. Gilbert	Aka: *The Town of Titipu*
The Mines of Sulphur	Richard Rodney Bennett	1965	London	Beverley Cross	
Mireille	Charles Gounod	1864	London and Paris	Carré	
The Miserly Knight	Sergei Rachmaninov	1906	Moscow	Rachmaninov	
Miss Donnithorne's Maggot	Peter Maxwell Davies	1974	Adelaide	Randolph Stow	
Miss Julie	Ned Rorem	1965	New York	Kenward Elmslie	Based on Strindberg's play
Miss Julie	William Alwyn	1976	Broadcast	Alwyn	Other version by Rorem and Bibalo
Mitridate, Rè di Ponto	Wolfgang Amadeus Mozart	1770	Milan	V.A. Cigna-Santi	
Mlada	Nikolay Rimsky-Korsakov	1892	St Petersburg	Rimsky-Korsakov	
Monday From Light	Karlheinz Stockhausen	1988	Milan	Stockhausen	
Monsieur Beaucaire	André Messager	1919	Birmingham	Lonsdale and Ross	Based on Booth Tarkington's story
The Moon (Der Mond)	Carl Orff	1939	Munich	Orff	
Moses und Aron	Arnold Schoenberg	1954	Hamburg	Schoenberg	
Moses in Egypt	Gioachino Rossini	1818	Naples	A.L. Tottola	
The Mother (Matka)	Alois Hába	1931	Munich	Hába	
The Mother of Us All	Virgil Thomson	1947	New York	Stein	Gertrude Stein and Virgil Thomson are characters
Mozart and Salieri	Nikolay Rimsky-Korsakov	1898	Moscow	Rimsky-Korsakov	
La Muette de Portici	Daniel Auber	1828	Paris	Scribe and Delavigne	Aka: *Masaniello*
Nabucco (Nebuchadnezzar)	Giuseppe Verdi	1842	Milan	T. Solera	
La Navarraise	Jules Massenet	1894	Covent Garden	Jules Claretie and Henri Cain	
Nelson	Lennox Berkeley	1953	London	Alan Pryce-Jones	
Nero (Nerone)	Arrigo Boito	1924	Milan	Boito	
Nero (Nerone)	Pietro Mascagni	1935	Milan	Targioni-Tozzetti	
Neues vom Tage (News of the Day)	Paul Hindemith	1929	Berlin	Marcellus Schiffer	
New Year	Michael Tippett	1989	Houston	Tippett	
A Night at the Chinese Opera	Judith Weir	1987	Cheltenham	Weir	

MUSIC CLASSICAL

Operas and operettas	Composer	First performance		Librettist	General information
The Night Bell	Gaetano Donizetti	1836	Naples	Donizetti	
A Night in Paris	Frederick Delius	1982	London	Rosenval	
A Night in Venice	Johann Strauss II	1883	Berlin	F. Zell (Camillo Walzel) and Genée	
The Nightingale (Le Rossignol)	Igor Stravinsky	1914	Paris and London	Stravinsky and S. Mitusov	
Nixon in China	John Adams	1987	Houston	Alice Goodman	
Norma	Vincenzo Bellini	1831	Milan	Romani	
The Nose	Dmitry Shostakovich	1930	Leningrad	Zamyatin, Yunin, Preys	Based Gogol story. Shostakovich wrote part of libretto
Notre Dame	Franz Schmidt	1914	Vienna	Leopold Wilk and Schmidt	
Noye's Fludde	Benjamin Britten	1958	Aldeburgh	Britten	Based on Chester miracle play
Oberon, or the Elf-King's Oath	Carl Maria Weber	1826	Covent Garden	J.R. Planché	
L'Oca del Cairo	Wolfgang Amadeus Mozart	1860	Frankfurt	Varesco	Unfinished opera buffa
Oedipus	George Enescu	1936	Paris	E. Fleg	
Oedipus Rex	Igor Stravinsky	1927	Paris	J. Cocteau	From Sophocles
The Olympians	Arthur Bliss	1949	London	J.B. Priestley	
The Opera Ball	Richard Heuberger	1898	Vienna	Léon and Waldeberg	Contains the aria 'Geh'n wir in's Chambre séparée'
The Oracle	Franco Leoni	1905	Covent Garden	C. Zanoni	Based on story The Cat and the Cherub by C.B. Fernald
Orfeo ed Euridice	Christoph Gluck	1762	Vienna	Calzabigi	
Orlando	George Frederick Handel	1733	London	Anon	Based on Ariosto's 16th-century poem, Orlando Furioso
Orlando Furioso	Antonio Vivaldi	1727	Venice	Braccioli	
Orlando Paladino	Franz Joseph Haydn	1782	Eszterháza	N. Porta	
Orpheus in the Underworld	Jacques Offenbach	1858	Paris	Crémieux and Halévy	
Osud (Fate)	Leoš Janáček	1958	Brno	Janáček	Janáček and Fedora Bartosová
Otello	Giuseppe Verdi	1887	Milan	Boito	
Ottone	George Frederick Handel	1723	London	N. Haym	
Our Man in Havana	Malcolm Williamson	1963	London	Sidney Gilliat	Based on Graham Greene's novel
Padmâvatî	Albert Roussel	1923	Paris	L. Laloy	Opera-ballet
I Pagliacci	Ruggiero Leoncavallo	1892	Milan	Leoncavallo	Famous aria 'Vesti la giubba' ('On with the motley') refers to clown's attire
Palestrina	Hans Pfitzner	1917	Munich	Pfitzner	
Paradise Lost	Krzysztof Penderecki	1978	Chicago	Christopher Fry	Based on Milton's poem
Paris and Helen	Christoph Gluck	1770	Vienna	Calzabigi	
Parisian Life (La Vie Parisienne)	Jacques Offenbach	1866	Paris	Meilhac and Halévy	
Parsifal	Richard Wagner	1882	Bayreuth	Wagner	Wagner's last opera
Partenope	George Frederick Handel	1730	London	Stampiglia	
Patience	Arthur Sullivan	1881	London	W.S. Gilbert	Aka: Bunthorne's Bride
Paul Bunyan	Benjamin Britten	1941	New York	W.H. Auden	
The Pearl Fishers	Georges Bizet	1863	Paris	Cormon and Carré	Action set in Ceylon (Sri Lanka)
Penelope	Rolf Liebermann	1954	Salzburg	H. Strobel	Based on the story of Ulysses' wife in Homer's Odyssey
Pénélope	Gabriel Fauré	1913	Monte Carlo and Paris	René Fauchois	

Operas and operettas	Composer	First performance		Librettist	General information
A Penny For a Song	Richard Rodney Bennett	1967	London	Colin Graham	
The Perfect Fool	Gustav Holst	1923	Covent Garden	Holst	
Peter Grimes	Benjamin Britten	1945	London	Montagu Slater	Based on George Crabbe's poem 'The Borough'
Peter Schmoll and his Neighbours	Carl Maria Weber	1803	Augsburg	Joseph Türk	
The Pilgrim's Progress	Ralph Vaughan Williams	1951	Covent Garden	Vaughan Williams	Christian's name in Bunyan's novel is changed to Pilgrim
The Pirate	Vincenzo Bellini	1827	Milan	Romani	
The Pirates of Penzance	Arthur Sullivan	1879	Paignton, Devon, and New York	W.S. Gilbert	Aka: *The Slave of Duty*
The Poacher or the Voice of Nature	Albert Lortzing	1842	Leipzig	Lortzing	
The Poisoned Kiss	Ralph Vaughan Williams	1936	London and Cambridge	Evelyn Sharp	Aka: *The Empress and the Necromancer*
Polly	Christoph Pepusch	1777	London	John Gay	
Porgy and Bess	George Gershwin	1935	Boston and New York	DuBose Heyward and Ira Gershwin	
Powder her Face	Thomas Adès	1995	Cheltenham		Shown on British television on Christmas Day 1999
Il Prigioniero (The Prisoner)	Luigi Dallapiccola	1949	Italy	Dallapiccola	
Prima Donna	Arthur Benjamin	1949	London	Cedric Cliffe	
Prima la Musica e Poe le Parole	Antonio Salieri	1786	Vienna	Casti	First performed in double bill with Mozart's *Der Schauspieldirektor*
Prince Igor	Alexander Borodin	1890	St Petersburg	Borodin	Completed by Rimsky-Korsakov and Glazunov
The Prince of Homburg	Hans Werner Henze	1960	Hamburg	Bachmann	
Princess Ida	Arthur Sullivan	1884	London and Boston	W.S. Gilbert	Aka: *Castle Adamant*
The Prodigal Son	Benjamin Britten	1968	Orford	Plomer	A church parable
Le Prophète	Giacomo Meyerbeer	1849	Paris and London	Scribe	
Punch and Judy	Harrison Birtwistle	1968	Aldeburgh	Stephen Pruslin	
Purgatory	Gordon Crosse	1966	Cheltenham	W.B. Yeats	
I Puritani (di Scozia)	Vincenzo Bellini	1835	London and Paris	C. Pepoli	Bellini's last opera
I Quattro Rusteghi (The Four Rustics)	Ermanno Wolf-Ferrari	1906	Munich	Sugano and Pizzolato	
The Queen of Sheba	Károly Goldmark	1875	Vienna	S H. Mosenthal	
The Queen of Spades (Pique Dame)	Pyotr Tchaikovsky	1890	St Petersburg	M. Tchaikovsky and Pyotr Tchaikovsky	
Quiet Flows the Don	Ivan Dzerzhinsky	1935	Leningrad	Dzerzhinsky	
A Quiet Place	Leonard Bernstein	1983	Houston	S. Wadsworth	Revised in 3 acts incorporating Bernstein's *Trouble in Tahiti*
Radamisto	George Frederick Handel	1720	London	N. Haym	
The Rajah's Diamond	Alun Hoddinott	1979	BBC TV	Myfanwy Piper	
The Rake's Progress	Igor Stravinsky	1951	Venice	Chester Kallman and W.H. Auden	
The Rape of Lucretia	Benjamin Britten	1946	Glyndebourne	Ronald Duncan	
The Red Line	Aulis Sallinen	1978	Helsinki	Sallinen	
Regina	Marc Blitzstein	1949	New Haven	Blitzstein	Based on Lilian Hellman's play *The Little Foxes*
Il Rè Pastore (The Shepherd King)	Wolfgang Amadeus Mozart	1775	Salzburg	Metastasio	
Resurrection	Peter Maxwell Davies	1987	Darmstadt	Maxwell Davies	
Das Rheingold (The Rhine Gold)	Richard Wagner	1869	Munich	Wagner	Became the prologue to the *The Ring* cycle
Richard the Lionhearted	André Grétry	1784	Paris	M.J. Sedaine	

Operas and operettas	Composer	First performance		Librettist	General information
Riders to the Sea	Ralph Vaughan Williams	1937	London	J.M. Synge	Faithful setting of Synge's play
Rienzi	Richard Wagner	1842	Dresden	Wagner	Based on Bulwer-Lytton's novel
Rigoletto	Giuseppe Verdi	1851	Venice	Piave	Based on Hugo's play Le Roi s'Amuse
Rinaldo	George Frederick Handel	1711	London	Rossi	Handel's first opera in England
Der Ring des Nibelungen	Richard Wagner	1876	Bayreuth	Wagner	
Der Ring des Polykrates	Erich Korngold	1916	Hamburg	J. Korngold	Composed 1914
The Rise and Fall of the City of Mahagonny	Kurt Weill	1930	Leipzig	Brecht	
The Rising of the Moon	Nicholas Maw	1970	Glyndebourne	Beverley Cross	
Il Ritorno d'Ulisse in Patria	Claudio Monteverdi	1640	Venice	G. Badoaro	English title: Ulysses' Return to His Native Land
Robert Devereux, Earl of Essex	Gaetano Donizetti	1837	Naples	Cammarano	
Robert the Devil	Giacomo Meyerbeer	1831	Paris	Scribe and Delavigne	
Rodelinda	George Frederick Handel	1725	London	Salvi and Haym	
Le Roi l'a dit	Léo Delibes	1873	Paris	Gondinet	
Le Roi malgré lui	Emmanuel Chabrier	1887	Paris	De Najac and Buroni	
Romeo and Juliet	Charles Gounod	1867	Paris, London and NY	Barbier and Carré	
Romeo and Juliet	Heinrich Sutermeister	1940	Dresden	Sutermeister	
La Rondine (The Swallow)	Giacomo Puccini	1917	Monte Carlo	Giuseppe Adami	
Der Rosenkavalier	Richard Strauss	1911	Dresden	Hofmannsthal	
The Royal Hunt of the Sun	Iain Hamilton	1977	London	Hamilton	Based on Peter Shaffer's play
Ruddigore	Arthur Sullivan	1887	London and New York	W.S. Gilbert	Aka: The Witch's Curse
Rusalka	Alexander Dargomyzhsky	1856	St Petersburg	Dargomyzhsky	
Rusalka	Antonin Dvořák	1901	Prague	J. Kvapil	
Ruslan and Lyudmila	Mikhail Glinka	1842	St Petersburg	Shirkov and Bakhturin	Based on Pushkin's poem
Ruth	Lennox Berkeley	1956	London	Crozier	
Sadko	Nikolay Rimsky-Korsakov	1898	Moscow	Rimsky-Korsakov, Stasov and Belsky	
St François d'Assise	Olivier Messiaen	1983	Paris	Messiaen	Messiaen's only opera
The Saint of Bleecker Street	Gian Carlo Menotti	1954	New York	Menotti	
Salome	Antoine Mariotte	1908	Lyons	Oscar Wilde	Based on Oscar Wilde's play
Salome	Richard Strauss	1905	Dresden	Hedwig Lachmann	Based on Wilde's play
Samson et Dalila	Camille Saint-Saëns	1877	Weimar	Lemaire	
Sapho	Jules Massenet	1897	Paris	Cain and Bernède	
Sárka	Zdeněk Fibich	1897	Prague	Schulzová	
Sárka	Leoš Janáček	1925	Brno	Zeyer	
Saturday from Light	Karlheinz Stockhausen	1984	Milan	Stockhausen	
Saul and David	Carl Nielsen	1902	Copenhagen	Christiansen	
Der Schauspieldirektor (The Impresario)	Wolfgang Amadeus Mozart	1786	Vienna	G. Stephanie	
Schwanda the Bagpiper	Jaromir Weinberger	1927	Prague	Kares and Brod	
Die Schweigsame Frau	Richard Strauss	1935	Dresden	Stefan Zweig	Translates as 'The Silent Woman'
The Secret Marriage	Domenico Cimarosa	1792	Vienna	G. Bertati	
The Secret	Bedřich Smetana	1878	Prague	Krásnohorská	
Semele	John Eccles	1964	Oxford	Congreve	Based on Ovid's Metamorphoses

Operas and operettas	Composer	First performance		Librettist	General information
Semele	George Frederick Handel	1744	London	Congreve	Includes aria 'Where'er you walk'
Semiramide	Gioachino Rossini	1823	Venice	G. Rossi	Many other operas based on Voltaire's Sémiramis
Semyon Kotko	Sergey Prokofiev	1940	Moscow	Prokofiev	
The Short Life (La Vida Breve)	Manuel De Falla	1913	Nice	Fernández Shaw	
The Sicilian Vespers	Giuseppe Verdi	1855	Paris	Scribe and Duveyrier	
The Siege of Corinth	Gioachino Rossini	1826	Paris	Balocchi and Soumet	
Siegfried	Richard Wagner	1876	Bayreuth	Wagner	Third part of Der Ring das Nibelungen
Sigurd	Ernest Reyer	1884	Brussels and London	Du Locle and Blau	
The Silken Ladder	Gioachino Rossini	1812	Venice	G.M. Foppa	
Simon Boccanegra	Giuseppe Verdi	1857	Venice	Piave and Montanelli	
Sir John in Love	Ralph Vaughan Williams	1929	London	Vaughan Williams	'Greensleeves' is sung by Mistress Ford in Act 3
The Sleepwalker	Vincenzo Bellini	1831	Milan and London	Romani	Italian title: La Sonnambula
The Small Venetian Square	Ermanno Wolf-Ferrari	1936	Milan	Ghisalberti	
The Snow Maiden (Snegurochka)	Nikolay Rimsky-Korsakov	1882	St Petersburg	Rimsky-Korsakov	
Die Soldaten (The Soldiers)	Bernd Alois Zimmermann	1965	Cologne	Zimmermann and Bernd Alois	
Son and Stranger	Felix Mendelssohn	1851	Leipzig	Klingemann	German title: Die Heimkehr aus der Fremde
The Sorcerer	Arthur Sullivan	1877	London	W.S. Gilbert	
Sorochintsy Fair	Modest Mussorgsky	1913	Moscow	Mussorgsky	Unfinished opera based on Gogol story
The Spanish Lady	Edward Elgar		Never performed	Elgar	Incomplete. Based on Jonson's The Devil Is an Ass
Stiffelio	Giuseppe Verdi	1850	Trieste	Piave	
The Stone Guest	Alexander Dargomyzhsky	1872	St Petersburg	Pushkin	Same story as Don Giovanni
The Story of a Real Man	Sergey Prokofiev	1948	Leningrad	Mira Mendelson and Prokofiev	
La Straniera	Vincenzo Bellini	1829	Milan	Romani	
Suor Angelica (Sister Angelica)	Giacomo Puccini	1918	New York	Forzano	The second part of Puccini's Il Trittico
Susanna's Secret	Ermanno Wolf-Ferrari	1909	Munich	Zangarini and Golisciani	Secret is that Susanna smokes
Il Tabarro (The Cloak)	Giacomo Puccini	1918	New York	Adami	The first part of Puccini's Il Trittico
A Tale of Two Cities	Arthur Benjamin	1957	London	Cedric Cliffe	
The Tales of Hoffmann	Jacques Offenbach	1881	Paris	Barbier and Carré	Three acts: Olympia, Antonia and Giulietta ('Barcarolle' in Act 3)
Tamerlane (Tamerlano)	George Frederick Handel	1724	London	N.F. Haym	
The Taming of the Shrew	Hermann Goetz	1874	Mannheim	J.V. Widmann	
Tancredi	Gioachino Rossini	1813	Venice	Rossi	
Tannhäuser	Richard Wagner	1845	Dresden	Wagner	Full title: Tannhäuser and the Singing Contest on the Wartburg
Taras Bulba	Arturo Berutti	1895	Buenos Aires	Berutti	
Taverner	Peter Maxwell Davies	1972	Covent Garden	Maxwell Davies	
The Telephone	Gian Carlo Menotti	1947	New York	Menotti	
The Tempest (Der Sturm)	Frank Martin	1956	Vienna	Martin	
The Tender Land	Aaron Copland	1954	New York	H. Everett	
Thaïs	Jules Massenet	1894	Paris	L. Gallet	Based on Anatole France novel (1890)
Theseus (Teseo)	George Frederick Handel	1713	London	N.F. Haym	
Thespis	Arthur Sullivan	1871	London	W.S. Gilbert	Aka: The Gods Grown Old

MUSIC CLASSICAL

Operas and operettas	Composer	First performance		Librettist	General information
The Thieving Magpie	Gioachino Rossini	1817	Milan	Gherardini	Italian title: La Gazza Ladra
The Threepenny Opera	Kurt Weill	1928	Berlin	Brecht	Based on The Beggar's Opera by John Gay and Christoph Pepusch
Tom Jones	Edward German	1907	London and Manchester	Thompson and Courtneidge	
Tom Jones	Stephen Oliver	1976	Snape	Oliver	
Tom Jones	François Philidor	1765	Paris	Poinsinet and Davesne	
Tosca	Giacomo Puccini	1900	London and Rome	Giacosa and Illica	Based on Sardou's play
Die Tote Stadt (The Dead City)	Erich Korngold	1920	Hamburg and Cologne	Paul Schott	Paul Schott is the pseudonym for Erich Korngold and his father Julius Korngold
The Travelling Companion	Charles Villiers Stanford	1925	Liverpool	Henry Newbolt	
La Traviata (The Fallen Woman)	Giuseppe Verdi	1853	Venice	Piave	Based on Dumas fils' novel Lady of the Camellias
Trial by Jury	Arthur Sullivan	1875	London	W.S. Gilbert	Only grand opera produced by the collaboration
The Trial (Der Prozess)	Gottfried von Einem	1953	Salzburg	Blacher and H. von Cramer	From Franz Kafka's novel
Tristan und Isolde	Richard Wagner	1865	Munich	Wagner	
Troilus and Cressida	William Walton	1954	Covent Garden	Christopher Hassall	Based on Chaucer's story, as opposed to Shakespeare's
The Trojans (Les Troyens)	Hector Berlioz	1863	Paris	Berlioz	
Trouble in Tahiti	Leonard Bernstein	1952	New York	Bernstein	
Il Trovatore (The Troubadour)	Giuseppe Verdi	1853	Rome	Cammarano and Bardare	Fourth act completed by Bardare, after death of Cammarano
The Tsarevich (Der Zarewitsch)	Franz Lehár	1927	Berlin	Reichart and Jenbach	
The Tsar has his Photograph Taken	Kurt Weill	1928	Leipzig	Kaiser	
The Tsar's Bride	Nikolay Rimsky-Korsakov	1899	Moscow	L.A. Mey	Adaptation of L.A. Mey's play, extra scene by Tumenev
Turandot	Ferruccio Busoni	1917	Zurich	Busoni	Based on Gozzi's play
Turandot (unfinished)	Giacomo Puccini	1926	Milan	Adami and Simoni	Final scene completed by Franco Alfano
Il Turco in Italia	Gioachino Rossini	1814	Milan	Romani	
The Turn of the Screw	Benjamin Britten	1954	Venice and London	Myfanwy Piper	Based on Henry James's story
The Twin Brothers	Franz Schubert	1820	Vienna	G. von Hofmann	
The Two Widows	Bedrich Smetana	1874	Prague	Emanuel Züngel	
Ulisse	Luigi Dallapiccola	1968	Berlin	Dallapiccola	Based on Homer
Ulysses	Reinhard Keiser	1722	Copenhagen	F.M. Lersner	
Ulysses	John C. Smith	1733	London	S. Humphreys	Based on Homer
Utopia Limited	Arthur Sullivan	1893	London	W.S. Gilbert	Aka: The Flowers of Progress
Vakula the Smith	Pyotr Tchaikovsky	1876	St Petersburg	Y. Polonsky	Based on Gogol's story Christmas Eve
Die Walküre (The Valkyrie)	Richard Wagner	1870	Munich	Wagner	The Valkyrie is Brünnhilde
The Vampire	Heinrich Marschner	1828	Leipzig	W.A. Wohlbrück	Based on John Polidori's story 'The Vampyre'
Vanessa	Samuel Barber	1958	New York	Menotti	Based on Dinesen's Seven Gothic Tales
Venus and Adonis	John Blow	1683	London	Anon	
La Vera Constanza (True Constancy)	Franz Joseph Haydn	1779	Eszterháza	F. Puttini	
Véronique	André Messager	1898	Paris	Vanloo and Duval	
Das Verratene Meer (The Sea Betrayed)	Hans Werner Henze	1990	Berlin	Treichel	
La Vestale	Gaspare Spontini	1807	Paris	De Jouy	
Victory	Richard Rodney Bennett	1970	Covent Garden	Beverley Cross	Based on Joseph Conrad's novel

Operas and operettas	Composer	First performance		Librettist	General information
A Village Romeo and Juliet	Frederick Delius	1907	Berlin	Delius	
Le Villi (The Willis)	Giacomo Puccini	1884	Milan	F. Fontana	
Violanta	Erich Korngold	1916	Munich	Müller	
The Violins of Saint-Jacques	Malcolm Williamson	1966	London	William Chappell	
The Visit of the Old Lady	Gottfried von Einem	1971	Vienna	Dürrenmatt	
The Voice of Ariadne	Thea Musgrave	1974	Snape Maltings	A. Elguera	
La Voix Humaine (The Human Voice)	Francis Poulenc	1959	Paris	Cocteau	
La Wally	Alfredo Catalani	1892	Milan	Illica	
The Wandering Scholar	Gustav Holst	1934	Liverpool	Clifford Bax	
War and Peace	Sergey Prokofiev	1944	Moscow	Mira Mendelson and Prokofiev	
Wat Tyler	Alan Bush	1974	Sadler's Wells	Nancy Bush	
We Come to the River	Hans Werner Henze	1976	London	Edward Bond	
The Wedding of the Camacho	Felix Mendelssohn	1827	Berlin	F. Voight	Based on an episode in Don Quixote
Werther	Jules Massenet	1892	Vienna	Blau, Milliet, Hartmann	Based on Goethe's novel The Sorrows of Young Werther
Where the Wild Things Are	Oliver Knussen	1980	Brussels	Maurice Sendak and Knussen	
William Tell	Gioachino Rossini	1829	Paris	De Jouy and Bis	André Grétry and B.A. Weber composed operas on same subject
The World on the Moon	Franz Joseph Haydn	1777	Eszterháza	Goldoni	
Wozzeck	Alban Berg	1925	Berlin	Berg	
The Wreckers	Ethel Smyth	1906	Leipzig	'H.B.' (Harry Brewster) Laforestier	
Das Wunder der Heliane	Erich Korngold	1927	Hamburg	Müller	
Wuthering Heights	Bernard Herrmann	1982	Portland, Oregon	Lucille Fletcher	
Xerxes (Serse)	George Frederick Handel	1738	London	Stampiglia	
Yan Tan Tethera	Harrison Birtwistle	1986	London	T. Harrison	
The Yeomen of the Guard	Arthur Sullivan	1888	London and NY	W.S. Gilbert	Aka: The Merryman and his Maid
Yolanta (Iolanta)	Pyotr Tchaikovsky	1892	St Petersburg	M. Tchaikovsky	
Zampa, or the Marble Bride	Ferdinand Hérold	1831	Paris	Mélesville	
Zar und Zimmermann	Albert Lortzing	1837	Leipzig	Lortzing	English translation: Tsar and Carpenter
Zaza	Ruggiero Leoncavallo	1900	Milan	Leoncavallo	

Operatic Suicides and Deaths

Character	Opera	Composer	Method
Aida	Aida	Verdi	Conceals herself in vault in which her lover is immured so as to share his death.
Andrey	Khovanshchina	Mussorgsky	Climbs a funeral pyre and perishes in the flames.
Brünnhilde	Götterdämmerung	Wagner	Rides her horse Grane on to Siegfried's funeral pyre.
Carmen	Carmen	Bizet	Stabbed by Don José.
Cio-Cio-San	Madame Butterfly	Puccini	Commits hara-kiri.
Cleopatra	Antony and Cleopatra	Barber	Presses an asp to her bosom.
Dido	Dido and Aeneas	Purcell	Stabs herself and mounts a funeral pyre.
Edgardo	Lucia di Lammermoor	Donizetti	Stabs himself with a dagger at Lucia's tomb.
Ernani	Ernani	Verdi	Stabs himself in fulfilment of a pledge to die when his enemy, Silva, sounds his horn.
Fenella	La Muette de Portici	Auber	Throws herself into the sea when she learns that her brother Masaniello has been killed.
Gioconda	La Gioconda	Ponchielli	Stabs herself to frustrate the lust of the spy Barnaba.
Gwendoline	Gwendoline	Chabrier	Stabs herself to join her Danish lover, Harald, in death.
Herman	Queen of Spades (Pique Dame)	Tchaikovsky	Stabs himself when he sees the ghost of an old countess whose death he has caused.
Iris	Iris	Mascagni	Throws herself into a sewer after unjustly being accused of becoming a geisha.
Katerina Ismailova	Lady Macbeth of Mtsensk District	Shostakovich	Drowns herself in a river en route to a Siberian prison camp.
La Wally	La Wally	Catalani	Throws herself from a precipice during an avalanche in the Alps.
Lakmé	Lakmé	Delibes	Poisons herself with the juice of an exotic flower when she loses her lover, Gerald.
Leonora	Il Trovatore	Verdi	Takes poison from a ring and swallows it rather than submit to the Count di Luna.
Liù	Turandot	Puccini	Stabs herself rather than reveal under torture the name of the Unknown Prince, Calaf.
Magda Sorel	The Consul	Menotti	Seals her kitchen and turns on the gas.
Manfredo	The Love of Three Kings	Montemezzi	Deliberately kisses the poisoned lips of his murdered wife Fiora in her tomb.
Marfa	Khovanshchina	Mussorgsky	Climbs a funeral pyre and perishes in the flames.
Margared	Le Roi d'Ys	Lalo	Leaps from precipice in remorse for aiding enemies to open dikes that protect city from sea.
Mizgir	The Snow Maiden (Snegurochka)	Rimsky-Korsakov	Flings himself into a lake when his beloved Snow Maiden is melted by a ray of sunlight.
Otello	Otello	Verdi	Stabs himself with a dagger following his murder of Desdemona.
Pollione	Norma	Bellini	Joins the Druid priestess on her funeral pyre.
Salome	Hérodiade	Massenet	Stabs herself upon learning that John the Baptist has been executed.
Selika	L'Africaine	Meyerbeer	Inhales the perfume of the manchinel tree, deadly to all who breathe it.
Seneca	L'Incoronazione di Poppea	Monteverdi	Opens his veins in the bath at the command of Emperor Nero.
Sister Angelica	Suor Angelica	Puccini	Swallows a poisonous potion she has concocted from the herbs in her convent's garden.
Tosca	Tosca	Puccini	Leaps to her death from parapet of the castle of Sant' Angelo in Rome after her lover is shot.
Violetta	La Traviata	Verdi	Dies of consumption.
Werther	Werther	Massenet	Shoots himself with a pistol.
Wozzeck	Wozzeck	Berg	Stabs his wife then walks into a pond and drowns.

Opera: General Information

aria (air)   Solo vocal piece in A-B-A form.

bleeding chunks   Operatic extracts played out of context. Term coined by Sir Donald Tovey.

burletta   A comic operetta.

Camerata   Society of 16th-century Florentine poets and musicians who developed opera.

canon   Counterpoint in which one melodic strand gives the rule to another.

cantata   Musical setting of a text, often religious, consisting of arias and choruses interspersed with recitatives.

canticle   Bible hymn, other than a psalm, used in church liturgy.

cantor   1) Leading singer in a synagogue. 2) Director of music in Lutheran Church.

caoine (pronounced 'keen')   Irish funeral song accompanied by wailing.

castrato   Male soprano or contralto whose voice was preserved by castration before puberty.

'Catalogue Aria'   Nickname for Leporello's aria in Act 1 Scene 2 of Mozart's *Don Giovanni* in which he recounts to Donna Elvira a list of his master Don Giovanni's conquests.

coloratura   Word applied both to a florid virtuoso aria and to the voice required for such a passage.

Don Giovanni: conquests   Italian 640, German 231, French 100, Turkish 91, Spanish 1003 = 2065 (according to Leporello, although in the opera he has none).

English National Opera   Assumed name in 1974, six years after moving into Coliseum in St Martin's Lane from previous London HQ at Sadler's Wells, Rosebery Avenue.

Gilbert and Sullivan: row over   Librettist and composer fell out over choice of carpet for the Savoy.

Gluck and Piccinni war   Divided Paris into French and Italian opera fans in the 1770s.

grand opera   Opera on a large scale, usually entirely sung.

intermezzo   Instrumental interlude used in course of an opera or play. Term also used for short opera performed between the acts of a larger one.

La Scala, Milan   Built in 1778 and named after Regina della Scala, wife of a Duke of Milan. The opera house (Lit. the staircase) opened on 3 August 1778 with operas of Salieri.

The Legend of Tsar Saltan   Orchestral interlude 'The Flight of the Bumble Bee' appears in Act 3.

leitmotif (leading theme)   Recurring theme written for a specific character or event in opera or television and film music.

libretto   The words of any vocal piece such as an oratorio, but particularly the text of an opera.

'Love-Death'   Wagner's name given to love duet in Act 2 of *Tristan und Isolde*, although more generally regarded as Isolde's aria at end of Act 3.

Mastersingers: thirteen   Sixtus Beckmesser – Town Clerk, Fritz Kothner – Baker, Balthasar Zorn – Pewterer, Ulrich Eisslinger – Grocer, Hans Sachs – Cobbler, Veit Pogner – Goldsmith, Kunz Vogelgesang – Furrier, Conrad Nachtigal – Bucklemaker, Augustin Mosler – Tailor, Hermann Ortel – Soap boiler, Hans Schwarz – Stocking weaver, Hans Foltz – Coppersmith, Walther von Stolzing – Unemployed.

Moody-Manners Opera Co   Touring opera company formed in 1898 by Charles Manners and his wife Fanny Moody but disbanded in 1916.

opera buffa (Fr. opera bouffe)   Comic opera; the opposite of *opera seria*.

opéra-comique   1) Second opera house of Paris; originally opened 1715; has a history of name changes and re-location; it is currently known as Salle Favart. 2) Term describing opera with spoken dialogue.

operetta   Light opera, sometimes of a comic nature, e.g. Gilbert and Sullivan operettas.

overture   Introductory music for an opera, oratorio or ballet.

Paris Opéra (Académie de Musique)   Latest building opened in 1875 and commonly known as Garnier or Salle Garnier, after its architect. After the opening of the Opéra Bastille in 1990, the Garnier Opéra is now used mainly for ballet. The term Paris Opéra is now used to mean the Garnier and the Bastille.

pasticcio/pastiche   Opera in which each act is by a different composer. Although these terms are often used synonymously, pastiche describes a work written in the style of another period or manner.

patter song   Rapid, sometimes tongue-twisting song often found in comic opera and now in pop music.

polo   Andalusian folk song accompanied with dance and performed in 3/8 with syncopations and vocal coloraturas on words, e.g. 'Ole' and 'Ay', as performed in several operas.

prima donna (first lady)   Most important female singer in an opera.

prologue   Introductory piece that presents the background for an opera.

Puccini: unfinished opera   Turandot (completed by Franco Alfano).

Rhinemaidens, three: Flosshilde, Wellgunde, Woglinde.

Singspiel   German light opera with spoken dialogue.

soubrette   Soprano comedienne.

surtitle   A printed translation of part of the text of an opera, usually projected on to a screen above the stage. This innovation was first used on 21 January 1983 by the Canadian Opera company for *Electra*.

travesti   Term used to describe operatic roles whereby character parts are sung by the opposite gender, e.g. Cherubino in *The Marriage of Figaro* or Prince Orlofsky in *Die Fledermaus*. Such parts are often called breeches or trouser-roles.

Turandot three riddles: What is born each night and dies each dawn...hope. What flickers red and warm like a flame, yet is not fire...blood. What is like ice but burns...Turandot.

TV opera: first   *Amahl and the Night Vistors* (Magi) by Menotti (1951).

Valkyries: Brünnhilde, Gerhilde, Grimgerde, Helmwige, Ortlinde, Rossweise, Schwertleite, Siegrune, Waltraute.

Venice Opera House   Teatro La Fenice, opened in 1792 and destroyed by fire 1836, rebuilt 1837 but seriously damaged again in 1996.

voice registers   Chest, head and middle voice; so called because the notes seem to come from these areas.

MUSIC CLASSICAL

Hymns, Anthems, Songs and Ballads

Abide With Me   Henry Francis Lyte.

America the Beautiful   Katherine Lee Bates (words); Samuel Augustus Ward (music).

America (My Country 'tis of Thee)   Samuel Francis Smith (tune of 'God Save the Queen').

Annie Laurie   William Douglas. First line: Maxwelton's braes are bonnie, where early fa's the dew.

Auld Lang Syne   Robert Burns.

Battle Hymn of the Republic   Julia Ward Howe. First line: Mine eyes have seen the glory of the coming of the Lord (tune of 'John Brown's body')

Beer Barrel Polka (Roll out the barrel)   Tune by Jaromir Vejvoda.

Caller Herrin'   Tune by Nathaniel Gow blends fishwives' cry with bells of St Andrew's Church; words by Lady Nairne.

Calm Sea and Prosperous Voyage   J.W. Goethe.

The Campbells are Coming   Anon.

Columbia, the Gem of the Ocean   Thomas à Becket (1808–90).

Eternal Father, Strong To Save   William Whiting (words); J.B. Dykes (music); aka 'The Navy's Hymn'. First line, 'O thou who bidd'st the ocean deep'.

Evening Hymn   Purcell (music); Fuller (words). First line, 'Now that the sun hath veiled his light'.

The Flowers that Bloom in the Springtime   W.S. Gilbert (words); Arthur Sullivan (music).

For the Fallen   3rd movement of Elgar's choral work *Spirit of England* with words by Laurence Binyon.

Funiculì Funiculà   Luigi Denza's song composed for the opening of the Naples funicular railway in 1880.

General William Booth Enters into Heaven   Ives (music); Vachel Lindsay (words).

Girl I Left Behind Me, The   Played in the British Army on occasions of departure and sometimes known as 'Brighton Camp'.

God Bless the Prince of Wales   Henry Brinley Richards (music); Ceiriog Hughes (words).

God Preserve the Emperor Francis (Emperor's Hymn)   Lorenz Haschka (words); Haydn (music); known as 'Austria' in hymn-books and became Austrian anthem. The German anthem 'Deutschland über Alles' adopted the tune.

Greensleeves   Old English tune popularly attributed to Henry VIII but no evidence of this is available, although it may have been written during his reign. Mentioned by Shakespeare in *The Merry Wives of Windsor* and tune used by Holst in *St Paul's Suite* and by Busoni in *Turandot*.

Habañera   Cuban song and dance of African origins, which became popular in Spain. Famous example is the habañera in Bizet's *Carmen*.

Happy Birthday to You   Composed in USA by Mildred Hill and published by Clayton F. Summy as 'Good Morning to All'.

Hark, the Herald Angels Sing   Words by Charles Wesley.

Hear My Prayer   Hymn by Mendelssohn containing section 'O for the wings of a dove'.

Heart of Oak   Written by actor David Garrick in 1759 to music by William Boyce. It was a topical song from the pantomime *Harlequin's Invasion* and commemorates the British victories at Minden, Quiberon Bay and Quebec.

Home, Sweet Home   Henry Bishop composed the music (1821) and the words were by J.H. Payne.

Internationale   Socialist song composed by P. Degeyter to words by Eugène Pottier; it was the official anthem of Communist Russia until 1 January 1944 and often confused with 'The Red Flag'.

Jerusalem   Music by Hubert Parry (1916); words by William Blake.

Jubilate   Psalm 100 (Anglican service), alternative to Benedictus; set to music by various composers.

Keel Row   Quoted by Debussy in the 3rd movement of his *Images*. This song, of unknown origin, first appeared in a collection of favourite Scots tunes and is principally identified with the North-east of England.

keen (caoine)   Irish funeral song with wailing. Represented in Vaughan Williams's opera *Riders to the Sea*.

Land of Hope and Glory   Finale of Elgar's *Coronation Ode* with words by A.C. Benson. The tune adapts the melody of the trio section of *Pomp and Circumstance March* No. 1 in D.

Land of My Fathers (Hen Wlad fy Nhadau)   National anthem of Wales (words by Evan James; music by his son James); originally called 'Glan Rhondda'.

Lass of Richmond Hill   James Hook (music); L. McNally (words). The song refers to Richmond in Yorkshire.

Last Rose of Summer, The   Adaption of R.A. Millihin's 'The Groves of Barley' by Thomas Moore (1779-1852), famously heard in Fredriech von Flotow's opera *Martha*.

Let Us Garlands Bring   Song-cycle by Gerald Finzi to words by Shakespeare, first performed in 1942 for the 70th birthday of Vaughan Williams. The five songs are 1) 'Come Away Death', 2) 'Who Is Sylvia?' 3) 'Fear No More the Heat O' the Sun', 4) 'O Mistress Mine', 5) 'It Was a Lover and His Lass'.

Lilliburlero   Song of unknown origin, which is the tune of Northern Ireland's 'Orange' party, set to different words as 'Protestant Boys'.

Lincoln, the Great Commoner   Song by Charles Ives; words by Edwin Markham.

Londonderry Air   Irish folk tune first published in the Petrie collection of 1855, the most famous words being those of 'Danny Boy' by F.E. Weatherly.

The Lost Chord   Song by Arthur Sullivan composed in 1877 in sorrow at his brother's death.

Magnificat   Canticle of the Virgin Mary, 'My Soul Doth Magnify the Lord', as it appears in St Luke's Gospel. Latin name is the first word of the Vulgate translation, i.e. Magnificat anima mea Dominum.

La Marseillaise   French national anthem, words and music by Claude Rouget de Lisle, written in 1792 under the title 'War Song For the Rhine Army'. Famously quoted in Tchaikovsky's *1812 Overture*.

Nearer, My God, to Thee   Hymn existing in British and American versions, both set to verses by Sarah Flower Adams. The English version was composed by John Dykes, and the American version is sung to the tune 'Bethany,' by Lowell Mason.

O Canada!   Canadian national anthem; originally a hymn in honour of St John the Baptist; music composed by Calixa Lavallée in 1880.

O Come All Ye Faithful   John Francis Wade wrote both the words and music in the early 1740s.

O God, Our Help in Ages Past   Based on Psalm 90 by Isaac Watts to a tune by William Croft, this hymn is particularly associated with Remembrance Day services.

Old Folks at Home   By Stephen Foster. First line: 'Way down upon the Swanee River, far, far away'.

Onward, Christian Soldiers   Reverend Sabine Baring-Gould published the words in 1868 and Arthur Sullivan the music in 1871.

***Pammelia* (All Honey)**   First collection of rounds, catches and canons published in England, by T. Ravenscroft in 1609.

Rock of Ages, Cleft For Me   Hymn; words by Reverend Augustus Montague Toplady; music by Richard Redhead.

Rule, Britannia!   Music by Thomas Arne to words of James Thomson and first played in *The Masque of Alfred* at Maidenhead on 1 August 1740. It has become a nationalistic English anthem and is also often considered to be the hidden theme of Elgar's *Enigma Variations*.

St Anne   English hymn tune of uncertain origin but possibly composed by William Croft. It is usually sung to the words 'O God, Our Help in Ages Past'.

Seven Gypsy Songs   Dvořák (music), Heyduk (words). 1) 'My Song Resounds', 2) 'My Triangle is Singing', 3) 'Silent the Woods', 4) 'Songs My Mother Taught Me', 5) 'Sound the Fiddle', 6) 'Clean Cotton Clothes', 7) 'To the Heights of Tatra'.

Sheep May Safely Graze   Air by J.S. Bach subsequently arranged by several composers, notably William Walton in *The Wise Virgins*.

Simple Gifts   Shaker hymn composed by Joseph Brackett (1848) and quoted by Copland in *Appalachian Spring*.

Song of Destiny (Schicksalsied)   Brahms (music); Hölderlin (words).

Song of the Fates (Gesang der Farzen)   Brahms (music); Goethe (words).

The Star-Spangled Banner   National anthem of USA. Words by Francis Scott Key (1814), written during the war of 1812, and music adapted from John Stafford Smith's *Anacreon in Heaven*.

Sumer is Icumen In (Summer is coming in)   Dating from *c.* 1240 and often quoted as the oldest extant canon. Aka 'The Reading Rota' as the author is thought to have been John of Fornsete, a monk of Reading Abbey.

Tea for Two   Song by Vincent Youmans, written for *No, No, Nanette* (1925). An orchestral version by Shostakovich (1928) was given the name 'Tahiti Trot'.

'Tis the Last Rose of Summer   Old Irish air originally called 'Castle Hyde'.

While Shepherds Watched Their Flocks   Words by Nahum Tate.

Ballets

Name	Music by	Choreographer	First performance	
The Age of Gold	Dmitry Shostakovich	Kaplan and Vaynonen	1930	Leningrad
Agon	Igor Stravinsky	Balanchine	1957	Los Angeles
El Amor brujo (Love the Magician)	Manuel de Falla	Falla (as pantomime) La Argentinita (as ballet in 1931)	1915	Madrid
Apollo Musagetes (Apollo, Leader of the Muses)	Igor Stravinsky	Bolm	1928	Washington
		Balanchine	1928	Paris
Appalachian Spring	Aaron Copland	Martha Graham	1944	Washington
L'Après-midi d'un faune	Claude Debussy	Nijinsky	1912	Paris
		Robbins	1946	New York
Bacchus and Ariadne	Albert Roussel	Lifar	1931	Paris
La Bayadère	Léon Minkus	Petipa	1877	St Petersburg
Les Biches	Francis Poulenc	Nijinskaya	1924	Monte Carlo
Billy the Kid	Aaron Copland	Loring	1938	Chicago
Boléro	Maurice Ravel	Nijinskaya	1928	Paris
The Bolt	Dmitry Shostakovich	Lopokov	1931	Leningrad
La Boutique Fantastique	Ottorino Respighi (arr. of Rossini's music)	Massine	1919	London
The Box of Toys	Claude Debussy	André Hellé	1919	Paris
Caroline Mathilde	Peter Maxwell Davies	Flindt	1991	Amsterdam
Checkmate	Arthur Bliss	de Valois	1937	Paris
Cinderella	Sergey Prokofiev	Ashton	1948	Moscow
Coppélia	Léo Delibes	Saint-Léon	1870	Paris
La Création du Monde	Darius Milhaud	Börlin	1923	Paris
The Creatures of Prometheus	Ludwig van Beethoven	Viganò	1801	Vienna
		Ashton	1970	Bonn
Daphnis et Chloé	Maurice Ravel	Fokine	1912	Paris
		Ashton	1957	London
Les Deux Pigeons	André Messager	Mérante	1886	Paris
Don Quixote	Léon Minkus	Petipa	1869	St Petersburg
Edward II	John McCabe	Bintley	1996	Stuttgart
Façade	William Walton	Ashton	1931	London
The Fairy's Kiss	Igor Stravinsky	Nijinskaya	1928	Paris
		MacMillan	1980	London
Fall River Legend	Morton Gould	de Mille	1948	New York
Fancy Free	Leonard Bernstein	Robbins	1944	New York
Le Festin de l'araignée (Spider's Banquet)	Albert Roussel	Staats	1913	Paris

Name	Music by	Choreographer	First Performance	
La Fille mal gardée (The Unchaperoned Girl)	John Lanchbery (arr. of Ferdinand Hérold's music)	Ashton	1960	London
Firebird	Igor Stravinsky	Fokine	1910	Paris
The Four Temperaments	Paul Hindemith	Balanchine	1946	New York
Gaîté Parisienne	Manuel Rosenthal (arr. of Offenbach's music)	Massine	1938	Monte Carlo
Gayane	Aram Khachaturian	Anisimova	1942	Leningrad
Giselle, or the Wilis	Adolphe Adam	Coralli and Perrot	1841	Paris
		Petipa	1884	St Petersburg
The Good-Humoured Ladies	Domenico Scarlatti (arr. by Tommasini)	Massine	1917	Rome
The Haunted Ballroom	Geoffrey Toye	de Valois	1934	London
Homage to the Queen	Malcolm Arnold	Ashton	1953	London (Coronation Night)
Horoscope	Constant Lambert	Ashton	1938	London
Jeux (Games)	Claude Debussy	Nijinsky	1913	Paris
Josephslegende (Legend of Joseph)	Richard Strauss	Fokine	1914	London and Paris
Madame Chrysanthème	Alan Rawsthorne	Ashton	1955	London
Les Mariés de la Tour Eiffel	Les Six (excluding Durey)	Börlin	1921	Paris
Miracle in the Gorbals	Arthur Bliss	Helpmann	1944	London
Miss Julie	Andrzej Panufnik	MacMillan	1970	Stuttgart
Nobilissima Visione	Paul Hindemith	Massine	1938	Monte Carlo
Nutcracker	Pyotr Tchaikovsky	Ivanov	1892	St Petersburg
Ondine (Undine)	Hans Werner Henze	Ashton	1958	London
Orpheus	Igor Stravinsky	Balanchine	1948	New York
Parade	Erik Satie	Massine	1917	Paris
Le Pas d'Acier	Sergey Prokofiev	Massine	1927	Paris
Paul Bunyan	William Bergsma	Ballet for puppets	1939	San Francisco
Peer Gynt	Alfred Schnittke	Neumeier	1986	Hamburg
The Peri	Paul Dukas	Clustine	1912	Paris
Perséphone	Igor Stravinsky	Jooss	1934	Paris
		Ashton	1962	London
Les Petits Riens	Wolfgang Amadeus Mozart	Jean Noverre	1778	Paris
Petrushka	Igor Stravinsky	Fokine	1911	Paris
Pineapple Poll	Arthur Sullivan (arr. by Mackerras)	Cranko	1951	Sadler's Wells
The Prince of the Pagodas	Benjamin Britten	Cranko	1957	Covent Garden
		MacMillan	1995	London
The Prodigal Son	Sergey Prokofiev	Balanchine	1929	Paris
Pulcinella	Igor Stravinsky	Massine	1920	Paris
The Rake's Progress	Gavin Gordon	de Valois	1935	London
Raymonda	Alexander Glazunov	Petipa	1898	Paris
The Rite of Spring	Igor Stravinsky	Nijinsky	1913	London and Paris
		MacMillan	1962	London
Rodeo	Aaron Copland	de Mille	1942	New York
Romeo and Juliet	Sergey Prokofiev	Psota	1938	Brno
		MacMillan	1965	London
Salome	Peter Maxwell Davies	Flindt	1978	Copenhagen
The Sanguine Fan	Edward Elgar	Hynd (1976 revival)	1917	London
Scaramouche	Jean Sibelius	Walbom	1922	Copenhagen
Scheherazade	Nikolay Rimsky-Korsakov	Fokine	1910	Paris
Schlagobers (Whipped Cream)	Richard Strauss	Kröller	1924	Vienna and Breslau
The Seven Deadly Sins	Kurt Weill	Balanchine	1933	Paris
The Sleeping Beauty	Pyotr Tchaikovsky	Petipa	1890	St Petersburg
The Song of the Earth	Gustav Mahler	MacMillan	1965	London
Spartacus	Aram Khachaturian	Jacobson	1956	Leningrad
Le Spectre de la Rose	Carl Maria Weber	Fokine	1911	Monte Carlo
The Stone Flower	Sergey Prokofiev	Lavrovsky	1954	Moscow
Swan Lake	Pyotr Tchaikovsky	Reisinger	1877	Moscow
		Petipa and Ivanov	1895	St Petersburg
Les Sylphides	Frederic Chopin	Mérante	1876	Paris
Sylvia, ou La Nymph de Diane	Léo Delibes	Fokine	1907	St Petersburg
		Ashton	1952	London
The Tales of Hoffman	Jacques Offenbach (arr. Lanchbery)	Darrell	1973	London
The Three-Cornered Hat	Manuel de Falla	Massine	1919	London
Tiresias	Constant Lambert	Ashton	1951	London
The Triumph of Neptune	Lord Berners	Balanchine	1926	London
La Ventana	Holm Lumbye	Bournonville	1854	Copenhagen

A Wedding Bouquet	Lord Berners	Ashton	1936	London
The Wedding (Les Noces)	Igor Stravinsky	Nijinskaya	1923	Paris
The Wise Virgins	William Walton	Ashton	1940	Sadler's Wells
The Wooden Prince	Bela Bartók	Balázs	1917	Budapest

NB: Where ballets have been re-choreographed, both original and better known modern versions are listed.

Ballet: General Information

ballet: first *Balet Comique de la Royne* (Paris 1581), produced by violinist Balthasar de Beaujoyeux.

Ballets Russes Founded in Paris in 1909 by Serge Diaghilev (Mikhail Fokine was his choreographer).

ballet terms Jeté – leap from one foot to another; arabesque – one leg raised behind and arms extended; entrechat – leap while striking heels together; pirouette – rapid whirling round on the point of one foot.

Bolshoi Theatre (Great Theatre) Oldest theatre in Moscow, originally called the Petrovsky, built by Maddox (1780), home of the Bolshoi Ballet.

classic ballet: first *Le Bourgeois Gentilhomme* (1670).

comédie-ballet French musico-dramatic entertainment devised by Molière and Lully in the late 17th century.

corps de ballet The ballet troupe excluding the principal dancers.

Dance Theatre of Harlem Founded by Arthur Mitchell (1968); first black classical ballet company; presented season at Covent Garden 1981.

defections from USSR Mikhail Baryshnikov while dancing with the Kirov in Toronto (1974); Natalia Makarova while dancing with the Kirov in London (1972); Rudolf Nureyev while dancing with the Kirov in Paris (1961).

La Fille mal gardée (*The Unchaperoned Girl*) Adaptation of a work based on French songs and airs originally produced in Bordeaux 1789.

Marie Taglioni (1804-1884) First ballerina to dance on points and to wear a tutu.

professional ballet dancer: first female La Fontaine in Lully's *Le Triomphe de l'Amour* at the Paris Opera House 1681.

Pulcinella Scenes and costumes by Picasso.

ritual dances: four dances (*The Midsummer Marriage*) 'The Earth in Autumn', 'Waters in Winter', 'Air in Spring', 'Fire in Summer'.

Ritual Fire Dance From Falla's *El Amor brujo* (*Love the Magician*).

Royal Ballet Name bestowed by Royal Charter in 1956 on the former Sadler's Wells Ballet, Covent Garden. Touring company originally known as Sadler's Wells Royal Ballet is now based in Birmingham and since 1991 is known as Birmingham Royal Ballet.

Le Spectre de la Rose Weber's *Invitation to the Dance* used as musical score.

Dance Types

allemande German dance, moderately paced in 4/4 rhythm, and performed in a cheerful fashion.

anglaise English country dance in quick duple metre.

apache French dance, often violent, imitating a Parisian gangster and his girlfriend.

badinage Playful dance or dance movement of a suite.

beguine Sensuous Latin ballroom dance originating in the Caribbean and danced to a bolero rhythm.

bergamasque (bergomask) Peasant dance of Bergamo, Italy, resembling a tarantella.

black bottom Popular dance of the late 1920s, originally in North America, involving lively rotation of the hips.

bolero Spanish dance in triple rhythm, said to have been invented in Cadiz around 1780.

bossa-nova Brazilian variation of the samba.

bourrée French dance, in quadruple time, performed in a lively style very like the gavotte.

branle French country dance of the 15th century characterized by a swaying motion and performed in a linked circle.

break bance Energetic solo dance frequently involving spinning on the floor on the back or head; originating in the USA in the 1980s.

cachucha Andalusian dance in triple metre similar to a bolero, for solo dancer.

cakewalk Popularized in the 1890s when black slaves parodied the white method of dance, a cake being awarded to best dancers.

calinda Negro dance, which was basis for an orchestral dance-interlude by Delius in his second opera *Koanga*.

calypso West Indian folk dance but better known in its sung form.

canaries Old 17th-century dance similar to a gigue and so called because it imitated Canary Island rituals.

can-can Boisterous Parisian dance of quadrille pattern originating in Algeria in the 1830s.

carmagnole Round dance, popular in the French Revolutionary period.

cha-cha-cha Cuban dance developed from the mambo in early 1950s.

chaconne Slow and dignified dance, probably originating in Spain.

Charleston Fast foxtrot named after Charleston, South Carolina, and popularized in New York in 1922.

conga Latin American dance of three steps and kick to the side, performed in chain with hands on the next person's hips.

cotillon Lively French formation dance of the 18th century similar to a quadrille.

courante From the French meaning 'running', a courante is moderate to lively in pace, with shifting rhythms.

csárdás Hungarian dance in two sections: 1) Slow and melancholy, 2) quick and lively.

cushion dance Dance where one partner dropped a cushion before the other, who then knelt on it and bestowed a kiss on the bearer.

danse champêtre French rustic dance performed in the open air.

divertissement Dance or ballet with or without lyric, included in an opera or play to add variety.

ezcudantza Basque festival dance for two performers with accompaniment of pipe and tabor.

fandango Old Spanish courtship dance in triple time.

farandole French line dance in 6/8 time usually to the accompaniment of galoubet and tambourin.

flamenco Spanish dance with lively toe and heel steps, usually accompanied by guitar and castanets.

foxtrot Ballroom dance in quadruple time combining short and long steps in various sequences, originated in North America in the early 20th century.

funk Style of popular dance music of US black origin, popularized by singers such as James Brown. The staccato body movements follow the heavy syncopation of the music.

galliard Spirited dance popular in Tudor times, performed in a gay, rollicking manner, in triple time.

galop (galopade) Mid 19th-century dance with lively rhythm, executed with hopping movements.

gavotte French dance in 4/4 time, starting on the third beat of the bar.

gigue Formal dance for two in the 16th and 17th centuries; derived from the jig and usually with violin accompaniment.

gitana Spanish gypsy dance.

gopak Lively Russian folk dance in duple time.

guajira Spanish dance with alternating rhythm between 6/8 and 3/4.

guaracha Spanish and Mexican folk dance in two sections, one in triple time and the other in duple. Dancer usually plays guitar.

habañera Cuban dance named after the city of Havana. Performed in 2/4 time.

halling Norwegian dance possibly originating in the Hallingdal. It is a frantic dance accompanied by Hardanger fiddle and other violins.

hanacca Moravian dance in simple triple time; a sort of quick polonaise.

haute danse Old term for a dance where feet are lifted, as opposed to *basse danse* in which they stay close to the floor.

hay Traditional country dance for two or more partners, with interweaving steps.

hob-and-nob Scottish country dance (1745) tune developed into 'The Campbells are Coming'.

hopak (gopak) Ukrainian folk dance, once for men only but later danced by couples. Steps are improvised but in 2/4 time.

hornpipe Lively English sailors' dance in 4/4 time.

jabo/jaleo Spanish dance for solo performer in a slow triple rhythm.

jarabe Spanish tap dance.

jig Lively British folk dance, usually in 6/8 time.

jitterbug Energetic dance, popular in the 1940s, performed chiefly to swing music.

jive Lively and jerky dance performed to jazz and, later, to rock and roll, popular in the 1940s and 1950s. Nowadays a generic term for any lively dance.

joropo Latin dance in rapid 3/4 time.

jota Spanish dance in rapid triple time with castanets and accompanied by guitar and voice.

krakoviak Polish dance from Krakow district, in lively 2/4 time.

kujawiak Polish dance for two, slower variant of the mazurka.

lambada Fast erotic Brazilian dance in which couples frequently touch hips. (Lit: A beating)

lancer Quadrille for 8 or 16 pairs, popular in 19th-century England.

Ländler Slow waltz originating in the Landel area of Austria.

lezginka Dance of the Lezghins, a Muslim tribe on the Iran border.

loure French dance, similar to a gigue but slower and graver, usually with bagpipe accompaniment.

malagueña Spanish dance from Málaga and Murcia, similar to fandango and exported to Mexico by Spanish settlers.

mambo Latin American ballroom dance.

matelotte Dutch sailors' dance similar to hornpipe but danced in clogs, with arms interlinked behind the dancers' backs.

maxixe Brazilian dance, precursor of the tango.

mazurka Polish national dance in triple time.

merengue Latin American ballroom dance.

minuet Stately court dance of 17th century in triple time. The style was adopted by classical composers in suites and overtures, and as third movement of symphonies and quartets.

morris English folk dance for men with accompaniment of fiddle, tabor, pipe, concertina and accordion, long associated with Whitsuntide. The dancers wear bells on their knees and often represent characters, e.g. the Fool or the Queen of the May.

musette Dance with a drone bass accompaniment.

nachtanz (after-dance) Term applied to the second of the two dance tunes which were commonly paired from the 15th to 16th centuries, i.e. pavane and salliard, sarabande and gigue, and passamezzo and salfarello.

new Jack swing Type of funk dance, often with rap.

paso doble Spanish dance with double steps in rapid 2/4 time.

passacaglia Almost indistinguishable from the chaconne in its slow triple-time steps.

passamezzo Italian dance of the 16th and 17th centuries, similar to pavane but faster and less serious.

passepied Lively minuet of Breton origin in triple time and popular in the 17th century.

pavane Slow, stately dance of Spanish origin, often danced in conjunction with the galliard.

polka Bohemian dance, popular in 19th century and comprising three steps and a hop in fast duple time.

polonaise Polish dance in 3/4 time performed as a march in a ceremonial style.

polska Scandinavian dance in simple triple time that derives from the Mazurka and dates from the union of the Polish and Swedish crowns (1587).

quadrille Square dance in five movements, for four or more couples.

quick-step Fast version of the foxtrot. Also a lively march in 2/4, also known as a quick march.

rant Old English 17th-century dance of the jig variety, originating in the north of England and Scotland.

redowa Bohemian dance resembling the Polish mazurka.

rigaudon (rigadoon) Light and graceful dance performed in 4/4 time and in a lively spirit, originating in Provence.

rondeña Fandango of southern Spain, named after Ronda in Andalusia.

rueda Spanish round dance in quintuple time, popular in Castile.

rumba Cuban dance in 8/8 time, originating in the 1920s and extending into the jazz age and into ballroom dancing.

running set English folk dance still popular in the Appalachian mountains of America.

salsa Latin American dance style combining Latin rhythms with rock.

saltarello Traditional Italian dance usually in compound duple time and as the name suggests incorporates a series of jumps and leaps.

samba Lively, modern ballroom dance from Brazil, developed from the maxixe. The samba was popularized in Britain in the 1940s and 1950s by Edmundo Ros.

saraband(e) Originating in 17th century Spain and performed in slow, dignified triple metre.

sardana National dance of Catalonia performed to the accompaniment of the fluvial.

schottische (Scottish) A 19th-century German dance resembling a slow polka. Introduced to England in 1848 and known as the 'German polka'.

seguidilla Andalusian national dance in fast triple metre.

Sir Roger de Coverley English country dance of uncertain origin.

springer Norwegian folk dance in 3/4 time.

Strathspey Scottish dance, slower than a reel, in 4/4 time using the Scotch snap rhythm.

tango Syncopated, faster version of habañera, originating in Argentina *c.* 1900; characterized by long gliding steps and sudden pauses.

tarantella Neapolitan peasant dance in 6/8 time.

tirana Spanish song/dance in 6/8 time, usually to guitar accompaniment; popular in Andalusia.

torch Dance (Fackeltanz) More often a torchlight procession to music, usually performed at weddings.

trepak Quick Russian dance in 2/4 time, most often associated with Cossacks.

veleta (valeta) Ballroom dance in triple-time. (Lit. weather-vane)

verbunkos Hungarian soldiers' dance used in the late 18th century to attract recruits for the army.

volta Lively Italian dance resembling a galliard and popular in the 16th and 17th centuries. Aslo known as lavolta. Britten's *Gloriana* includes a volta.

waltz Developed from the ländler around 1800 and performed in triple time whilst couples spin around the dance floor.

zamba Argentinian scarf dance (originated in Peru) in 6/8 time.

zapateado Spanish dance in triple time, characterised by rhythmic heel stamping.

zortziko Basque folk dance in 5/4 time, similar to the rueda.

zydeco Style of popular dance music that mixes cajun and Afro-Caribbean with rhythm and blues.

M
U
S
I
C

C
L
A
S
S
I
C
A
L

Organ Stops

Two types are flue pipes and reed pipes. Pipes may vary from 32 feet in length to less than an inch, giving the organ a range of nine octaves, larger than any other instrument. Below are listed some common stops.

Aeolina	Eighteenth	Jubal	Octavin	Seventeenth
Amoroso	Eleventh	Jula	Oiseau	Seventy-first
Bassoon	Eoline	Jungfernstime	Open Diapason	Third
Bible-Regal	Fernflöte (Distant	Keen Strings	Ottavina	Thiry-first
Bird Whistle	Flute)	Keraulophon	Parade Drum	Thunder
Block-flute	Fifteenth	Kerophone	Parforce	Tibia
Canary	Flageolet	Kleine Mixture	Pfeife	Twelfth
Carillon	Flûte à Pavillon	Koppel	Phoneuma	Tympani
Celesta	Forty-third	Labial Oboe	Piano	Ucceli
Clarabella	Furniture	Largo	Piccolo	Unda Maris (Wave
Clarinet Flute	Gamba	Larigot	Plein Jeu	of the Sea)
Clarion	Gedackt	Ludwigtone	Point-Flute	Untersatz
Cor de Nuit	Gemshorn	Magnaton	Portunal	Vidula
Corno di Bassetto	Grave Mixture	Major Bass	Quadragesima	Viola di Samba
Corno Dolce	Grobregal	Major Flute	Quincena	Vox Angelica
Cornopean	Hahn	Marimba	Quint	Vox Humana
Cor-Oboe	Harmonic Bass	Melodia	Racket	Wald Quint
Cremona	Harmonic Flute	Melophone	Rain	Woodland Flute
Crumhorn	Harmonic Piccolo	Mixture Stop	Reed Flute	Xylophone
Cuckoo	Harp	Montre	Resultant	Zauberflöte
Cymbel	Hautboy	Musette	Sackbut	Ziflot
Diaphone	Hohlflöte	Night Horn	Sadt	Zimbelstern
Docena	Horn Diapason	Nightingale	Salamine	Zünk
Doppelflöte	Hummel	Nineteenth	Salicional	
Dulciana Mixture	Infra Bass	Ninth	Scarf	
Duophone	Italian Principal	None	Septime	
Echo Gamba	Iula	Oboe	Serpent	

Ballet Dancers and Choreographers

Alvin Ailey Jr. (1931–89)
Alicia Alonso (1921–)
Frederick Ashton (1904–88)
George Balanchine (1904–83)
Mikhail Baryshnikov (1948–)
Maurice Béjart (1927–)
Svetlana Beriosova (1932–98)
David Bintley (1957–)
Carlo de Blaisis (1795–1878)
August Bournonville (1805–79)
Darcy Bussell (1969–)
Maria Anna de Camargo (1710–70)
Enrico Cecchetti (1850–1928)
Harold Christensen (1904–89)
Lew Christensen (1909–84)
John Cranko (1927–73)
Birgit Cullberg (1908–99)
Merce Cunningham (1919–)
Patrick Delcroix (1963–)
Agnes De Mille (1905–93)
Charles-Louis Didelot (1797–1837)
Anton Dolin (1904–83)
Anthony Dowell (1943–)
Nacho Duato (1957–)

Isadora Duncan (1878–1927)
Mats Elk (1945–)
Garth Fagan (1940–)
Suzanne Farrell (1945–)
Mikhail Fokine (1880–1942)
Margot Fonteyn (1919–91)
William Forsythe (1949–)
Loie Fuller (1862–1928)
Martha Graham (1894–1991)
Carlotta Grisi (1819–99)
Sylvie Guillem (1965–)
Hanya Holm (1893–1992)
Doris Humphrey (1895–1958)
Kurt Jooss (1920–)
Tamara Karsavina (1885–1978)
Gelsey Kirkland (1952–)
Jirì Kylàn (1947–)
Rudolf von Laban (1879–1958)
Serge Lifar (1905–86)
Paul Lightfoot (1966–)
Kenneth MacMillan (1929–)
Natalia Makarova (1940–)
Hans van Manen (1932–)
Alicia Markova (1910–)

Léonide Massine (1896–1979)
Mikhail Mordkin (1880–1944)
Bronislava Nijinska (1891–1972)
Vaclav Nijinsky (1890–1950)
Alwin Nikolais (1910–93)
Rudolf Nureyev (1939–93)
Gideon Obarzanek (1966–)
Anna Pavlova (1885–1931)
Marius Petipa (1818–1910)
Roland Petit (1924–)
Maya Plisetskya (1925–)
Jerome Robbins (1918–98)
Marie Sallé (1707–56)
Antoinette Sibley (1939–)
Maria Taglioni (1808–84)
Glen Tetley (1926–)
Twyla Tharp (1941–)
Antony Tudor (1908–87)
Galina Ulanova (1910–98)
Ninette de Valois (1898–2001)
Auguste Vestris (1760–1842)
Gaetano Vestris (1729–1808)
Charles Weidman (1901–75)
Mary Wigman (1886–1973)

Orchestral Positions
(can vary with conductor's preference)

Section	Position
First violins	Left of conductor and to the right of second violins
Second violins	Left of first violins and in front but slightly left of conductor
Cellos	Right of conductor and to the left of the violas
Violas	Right of cellos and in front but slightly right of the conductor
Double basses	Behind the violas and cellos
Trumpets	Behind the double basses and double bassoons
Horns	Behind the clarinets and bassoons
Harp	Behind the bass clarinet and in front of percussion
Piccolo	Left of second violin and in front of bass clarinet
Flutes	Left of piccolo and in front of clarinets
Cor anglais	Right of double basses and back of violas
Oboes	Right of cor anglais and left of the flutes
Bassoons	Behind the oboes and in front of the horns
Double bassoon	Behind the cor anglais and in front of the trumpets
Clarinets	Behind the flutes and in front of the horns
Bass clarinet	Behind the piccolo and to the left of second violins
Percussion	Behind the harp and to the right of timpani
Timpani	Behind the horns and between percussion and trombones
Trombones	Behind horns and trumpets
Tuba	Behind trumpets and to the left of trombones

NB: All positions are viewed relative to the section and not the front.

Master of the King's/Queen's Music

1625	Nicholas Lanier	1834	Christian Kramer
1666	Louis Grabu	1848	George Frederick Anderson
1674	Nicholas Staggins	1870	William George Cusins
1700	John Eccles	1893	Walter Parratt
1735	Maurice Greene	1924	Edward Elgar
1755	William Boyce	1934	Walford Davies
1779	John Stanley	1942	Arnold Bax
1786	William Parsons	1953	Arthur Bliss
1817	William Shield	1975	Malcolm Williamson

Classical Works

Music	Composer	Music	Composer
Abegg Variations	Robert Schumann	Éclats (Fragments)	Pierre Boulez
Academic Festival Overture	Johannes Brahms	Egdon Heath	Gustav Holst
		Eight Songs for a Mad King	Peter Maxwell Davies
An Alpine Symphony	Richard Strauss		
Also sprach Zarathustra (Thus Spake Zoroaster)	Richard Strauss	Eine Kleine Nachtmusik (A Little Night Music)	Wolfgang Amadeus Amadeus
Alto Rhapsody	Johannes Brahams	Elegy For JFK	Igor Stravinsky
The Apostles (oratorio)	Edward Elgar	Elijah Oratorio	Felix Mendelssohn
Appassionata Sonata	Ludwig van Beethoven	Emperor March (Kaisermarsch)	Richard Wagner
Archduke Trio	Ludwig van Beethoven		
Ariana a Naxos (cantata)	Franz Joseph Haydn	Emperor Waltz	Johann Strauss II
		The Enclosed Garden	Gabriel Fauré
The Art of Fugue	Johann Sebastian Bach	L'Enfant prodigue (cantata)	Claude Debussy
Asrael (symphony)	Josef Suk		
Aurora's Wedding	Pyotr Tchaikovsky	An English Suite	Parry, Hubert
Bergomask Suite	Claude Debussy	España	Emmanuel Chabrier
Brandenburg Concertos	Johann Sebastian Bach	Esther	George Frederick Handel
El Capitán (march)	John Philip Sousa	Façade	William Walton
Capriccio Espagnol	Nikolay Rimsky-Korsakov	The Fair Melusina	Felix Mendelssohn
Carmina Burana (part 1 of Trionfi trilogy)	Carl Orff	Fanfare for the Common Man	Aaron Copland
Carnaval	Robert Schumann	Fantasia on a Theme by Thomas Tallis	Ralph Vaughan Williams
Carnival	Antonín Dvořák		
The Carnival of Animals	Camille Saint-Saëns	Fantasia on a Theme of Handel	Michael Tippett
Catulli Carmina (cantata)	Carl Orff		
Caucasian Sketches	Mikhail Ippolitov-Ivanov	Fantasia on Christmas Carols	Ralph Vaughan Williams
Celtic Requiem	John Tavener		
Chagall Windows	John McCabe	Fantasia on Greensleeves	Ralph Vaughan Williams
Chamber Symphony (name of two works)	Arnold Schoenberg		
		Faust Overture	Richard Wagner
Chandos Anthems	George Frederick Handel	Fêtes galantes	Claude Debussy
A Child of Our Time	Sir Michael Tippett	Finlandia	Jean Sibelius
The Childhood of Christ	Hector Berlioz	Fireworks	Igor Stravinsky
Children's Corner	Claude Debussy	Fireworks Music	George Frederick Handel
A Children's Overture	Roger Quilter	Five Tudor Portraits	Ralph Vaughan Williams
Christmas Oratorio	Johann Sebastian Bach	The Flight of the Bumble Bee	Nikolay Rimsky-Korsakov
Clair de Lune	Claude Debussy		
The Cloud Messenger	Gustav Holst	Four Last Songs	Richard Strauss
Cockaigne (In London Town)	Edward Elgar	Four Sea Interludes	Benjamin Britten
		The Four Seasons	Antonio Vivaldi
Colonel Bogey	Kenneth Alford	Four Serious Songs	Johannes Brahms
Colour Symphony	Arthur Bliss	French Suites	Johann Sebastian Bach
Concertino Pastorale	John Ireland	Froissart	Edward Elgar
Construction in Metal (name of three works)	John Cage	From Stone to Thorn	Peter Maxwell Davies
		From the Diary of Virginia Woolf	Dominick Argento
Coronation Mass	Wolfgang Amadeus Mozart		
Coronation Ode	Edward Elgar	Funeral March of a Marionette	Charles Gounod
The Creation	Franz Joseph Haydn	The Garden of Fand	Arnold Bax
Crown Imperial	William Walton	Gaspard de la Nuit	Maurice Ravel
The Crown of India	Edward Elgar	A German Requiem	Johannes Brahms
The Crucifixion	John Stainer	The Girl With the Flaxen Hair	Claude Debussy
The Curlew (song cycle)	Peter Warlock		
The Damnation of Faust	Hector Berlioz	Gold and Silver (waltz)	Franz Lehár
Dance of Death (Totentanz)	Franz Liszt	The Golden Spinning Wheel	Antonín Dvořák
Danse Macabre	Camille Saint-Saëns	Golliwogg's Cakewalk	Claude Debussy
Dante Symphony	Franz Liszt	Good Friday Music	Richard Wagner
Davidde Penitente	Wolfgang Amadeus Mozart	Gymnopédies	Erik Satie
		Gypsy Songs (Zigeunerlieder)	Johannes Brahms
Death and the Maiden	Franz Schubert		
Death and Transfiguration	Richard Strauss	Habañera	Maurice Ravel
The Death of Cleopatra	Hector Berlioz	Hail to the Chief	James Sanderson
Deborah	George Frederick Handel	Hamlet (fantasy overture)	Pyotr Tchaikovsky
Diabelli Variations	Ludwig van Beethoven		
The Dream of Gerontius	Edward Elgar	Hamlet (symphonic poem)	Franz Liszt
Ebony Concerto	Igor Stravinsky		

Music	Composer	Music	Composer
Harold in Italy	Hector Berlioz	Lady Radnor's Suite	Hubert Parry
L'Heure Espagnole (The Spanish Hour)	Maurice Ravel	Land of the Mountain and the Flood	Hamish MacCunn
Hiawatha	Samuel Coleridge-Taylor	The Lark Ascending	Ralph Vaughan Williams
Hodie (On This Day)	Ralph Vaughan Williams	The Last Sleep of the Virgin	Jules Massenet
Holberg Suite	Edvard Grieg	Virgin	
The Holy Boy	John Ireland	Late Swallows	Frederick Delius
Holy Sonnets of John Donne	Benjamin Britten	Lazarus (oratorio)	Franz Schubert
Donne		The Legend of St Elizabeth	Franz Liszt
L'Horizon chimérique	Gabriel Fauré	Lélio, or the Return to Life	Hector Berlioz
Hungarian Dances	Johannes Brahms	Lie Strewn the White	Arthur Bliss
Hungarian Rhapsodies	Franz Liszt	Flocks (pastoral)	
The Hymn of Jesus	Gustav Holst	Lieutenant Kijé	Sergey Prokofiev
Hymn of Paradise	Herbert Howells	The Light of Life	Edward Elgar
Hymn to St Magnus	Peter Maxwell Davies	A Lincoln Portrait	Aaron Copland
Hymns from the Rig Veda	Gustav Holst	Little Suite	Claude Debussy
Iberia	Isaac Albéniz	Little Symphony	Charles Gounod
Imaginary Landscape	John Cage	A London Overture	John Ireland
In a Summer Garden	Frederick Delius	A London Symphony	Ralph Vaughan Williams
Indian Diary	Ferruccio Busoni	The Love Feast of the Apostles	Richard Wagner
Indian Fantasy	Ferruccio Busoni	Apostles	
In Honour of the City	George Dyson	Love-Dreams (Liebesträume)	Franz Liszt
In Honour of the City of London	William Walton	(Liebesträume)	
City of London		Love-Song Waltzes	Johannes Brahms
In the Faery Hills	Arnold Bax	The Magic Island	William Alwyn
In the South	Edward Elgar	Makrokosmos	George Crumb
In the Steppes of Central Asia	Alexander Borodin	Mantra	Karlheinz Stockhausen
Central Asia		The Mask of Time	Michael Tippett
Invitation to the Dance	Carl Maria Weber	Mass of Christ the King	Malcolm Williamson
In Windsor Forest	Ralph Vaughan Williams	A Mass of Life	Frederick Delius
Irish Symphony	Hamilton Harty	Má Vlast (My Country)	Bedřich Smetana
Islamey	Mily Balakirev	Mazeppa	Franz Liszt
The Island of Joy	Claude Debussy	Memento Vitae (Memory of Life)	Thea Musgrave
The Isle of the Dead	Sergei Rachmaninov	of Life)	
Israel in Egypt	George Frederick Handel	Mephisto Waltzes	Franz Liszt
Israel Symphony	Ernest Bloch	La Mer (The Sea)	Claude Debussy
Italian Caprice	Pyotr Tchaikovsky	Messiah (oratorio)	George Frederick Handel
Italian Serenade	Hugo Wolf	Metamorphosen	Richard Strauss
Jacob's Ladder	Arnold Schoenberg	A Midsummer Night's Dream (1826)	Felix Mendelssohn
Jamaican Rumba	Arthur Benjamin	Dream (1826)	
Jeux d'Eau (Fountains)	Maurice Ravel	A Midsummer Night's Dream	Carl Orff (1939)
Jeux d'Enfants (Children's Games)	Georges Bizet	Dream	
(Children's Games)		Mikrokosmos	Béla Bartók
Joan of Arc at the Stake (oratorio)	Arthur Honegger	The Miraculous Mandarin	Béla Bartók
Stake (oratorio)		Mládí (Youth)	Leoš Janáček
Joan of Arc at the Stake (concert aria)	Franz Liszt	Moby Dick (cantata)	Bernard Herrmann
Stake (concert aria)		Moby Dick (concertato)	Peter Mennin
Johannesburg Festival Overture	William Walton	Moby Dick (symphonic poem)	Douglas Moore
Overture		poem)	
Joshua	George Frederick Handel	Morning Heroes	Arthur Bliss
Judas Maccabaeus	George Frederick Handel	Mother Goose Suite	Maurice Ravel
Judith Triumphant	Antonio Vivaldi	Name Day (Namensfeier)	Ludwig van Beethoven
Judith (oratorio)	Thomas Arne (1761)	Natural Histories	Maurice Ravel
Judith (oratorio)	Hubert Parry (1888)	New England Holidays	Charles Ives
Kakadu Variations	Ludwig van Beethoven	Night and Dreams	Franz Schubert
Kamarinskaya (Wedding Song)	Mikhail Glinka	Night on the Bare Mountain	Modest Mussorgsky
(Wedding Song)		Mountain	
Karelia Suite	Jean Sibelius	Noble and Sentimental Waltzes	Maurice Ravel
Kinderscenen (Scenes From Childhood)	Robert Schumann	Waltzes	
From Childhood)		The Noonday Witch	Antonín Dvořák
King David	Arthur Honegger	Norfolk Rhapsody	Ralph Vaughan Williams
The Kingdom (oratorio)	Edward Elgar	North Country Sketches	Frederick Delius
King of Prussia Quartets	Wolfgang Amadeus Mozart	Nursery Suite	Edward Elgar
		The Oceanides	Jean Sibelius
King Stephen	Ludwig van Beethoven	Ode For St Cecilia's Day	Henry Purcell (1683–92)
Kontakte (Contacts)	Karlheinz Stockhausen	Ode For St Cecilia's Day	George Frederick Handel (1739)
Lachrimae	John Dowland		(1739)
Lachrymae	Benjamin Britten	Ode For St Cecilia's Day	Hubert Parry (1889)
Lady in the Dark	Kurt Weill	Ode to Death	Gustav Holst
The Lady of Shalott	Maurice Jacobson	Ode to Napoleon Bonaparte	Arnold Schoenberg
The Lady of Shalott	PhyllisTate	Bonaparte	

Music	Composer	Music	Composer
Odyssey	Nicholas Maw	Russian Easter Festival Overture	Nikolay Rimsky-Korsakov
Oiseaux Exotiques	Olivier Messiaen		
Omar Khayyám	Granville Bantock	Rustic Wedding	Károly Goldmark
On Hearing the First Cuckoo in Spring	Frederick Delius	Rustle of Spring	Christian Sinding
		St Anthony Variations	Johannes Brahms
Orb and Sceptre March	William Walton	St John Passion	Johann Sebastian Bach
Organ Solo Mass	Wolfgang Amadeus Mozart	St Ludmila	Antonín Dvořák
		St Matthew Passion	Johann Sebastian Bach
Orpheus	Franz Liszt	St Nicolas	Benjamin Britten
Othello	Antonín Dvořák	St Paul	Felix Mendelssohn
An Oxford Elegy	Ralph Vaughan Williams	St Paul's Suite	Gustav Holst
Pacific 231	Arthur Honegger	St Thomas Wake	Peter Maxwell Davies
Pan and Syrinx	Carl Nielsen	Samson (oratorio)	George Frederick Handel
Papillons (Butterflies)	Robert Schumann		
Paradise Lost (cantata)	Christopher Steel	Sarnia	John Ireland
Pavane	Gabriel Fauré	Satyricon	John Ireland
Pavane For a Dead Infanta	Maurice Ravel	Scapino	William Walton
Peacock Variations	Zoltán Kodály	Scaramouche	Darius Milhaud
Peasant Cantata	Johann Sebastian Bach	Scenes from the Bavarian Highlands	Edward Elgar
Peer Gynt	Edvard Grieg		
Pelléas et Mélisande	Gabriel Fauré	Scenes From the Saga of King Olaf	Edward Elgar
Pelléas et Mélisande	Arnold Schoenberg		
Pelléas et Mélisande	Jean Sibelius	Scottish Fantasy	Max Bruch
Peter and the Wolf	Sergey Prokofiev	Scythian Suite	Sergey Prokofiev
Phaëton	Camille Saint-Saëns	The Sea	Frank Bridge
Phoebus and Pan	Johann Sebastian Bach	Sea Drift	Frederick Delius
Pierrot Lunaire	Arnold Schoenberg	Sea Fever	John Ireland
Pines of Rome	Ottorino Respighi	Sea Pictures	Edward Elgar
The Planets	Gustav Holst	The Seasons	Franz Joseph Haydn
The Pleasure Dome of Kubla Khan	Charles Griffes	Serenade for Tenor, Horn and Strings	Benjamin Britten
Poet & Peasant Overture	Franz von Suppé	Severn Suite	Edward Elgar
Pohjola's Daughter	Jean Sibelius	Sheherazade	Nikolay Rimsky-Korsakov (1889)
Polovtsian Dances	Alexander Borodin		
Portsmouth Point	William Walton	Shéhérazade	Maurice Ravel (1904)
Prélude à l'Après-midi d'un faune	Claude Debussy	Shepherd Fennel's Dance	Balfour Gardiner
		Shylock	Gabriel Fauré
Préludes	Claude Debussy	Siegfried Idyll	Richard Wagner
Les Préludes	Ferencz Liszt	Simple Symphony	Benjamin Britten
Procession	Karlheinz Stockhausen	Slavonic Dances	Antonín Dvořák
The Prodigal Son	Benjamin Britten	Slavonic Rhapsodies	Antonín Dvořák
The Prodigal Son	Claude Debussy	The Soldier's Tale	Igor Stravinsky
The Prodigal Son (oratorio)	Arthur Sullivan	A Song for the Lord Mayor's Table	William Walton
Prometheus	Franz Liszt	The Song of Sorrow	Gustav Mahler
Queen Mary's Funeral Music	Henry Purcell	The Song of the Earth	Gustav Mahler
		Song of the Flea	Modest Mussorgsky
Quiet City	Aaron Copland	Song of the High Hills	Frederick Delius
Radetzky March	Johann Strauss the Elder	Song of the Young Boys	Karlheinz Stockhausen
Raft of the Medusa, The	Hans Werner Henze	Songs Without Words	Felix Mendelssohn
Rakastava (The Lover)	Jean Sibelius	Songs and Dances of Death	Modest Mussorgsky
Ramifications	György Ligeti		
Rapsodie Espagnole	Franz Liszt	Songs My Mother Taught Me	Antonín Dvořák
Rapsodie Espagnole (including Habañera)	Maurice Ravel		
		Songs of Travel	Ralph Vaughan Williams
Renard (The Fox)	Igor Stravinsky	The Sorcerer's Apprentice (based on Goethe poem)	Paul Dukas
Rhapsody in Blue	George Gershwin		
Rhapsody on a Theme of Paganini	Sergei Rachmaninov		
		The Spectre's Bride	Antonín Dvořák
Roman Festivals	Ottorino Respighi	The Spirit of England	Edward Elgar
Romeo and Juliet (fantasy overture)	Pyotr Tchaikovsky	Spitfire Prelude and Fugue	William Walton
		A Spring Symphony	Benjamin Britten
Romeo and Juliet (symphony)	Hector Berlioz	Spring (Printemps)	Claude Debussy
		The Starlight Express	Edward Elgar
Roses From the South	Johann Strauss II	La Stravaganza (The Extraordinary)	Antonio Vivaldi
Le Rouet d'Omphale	Camille Saint-Saëns		
Rugby	Arthur Honegger	Street Corner	Alan Rawsthorne
Ruins of Athens	Ludwig van Beethoven	Such a Day, Such a Night	Francis Poulenc
Rule, Britannia! (from The Masque Alfred)	Thomas Arne	Suite bergamasque	Claude Debussy
		Summer Night on the River	Frederick Delius
Running Set	Ralph Vaughan Williams		

Music	Composer	Music	Composer
Summer's Last Will and Testament	Constant Lambert	Ultimos Ritos (Last Rites)	John Tavener
The Swan of Tuonela	Jean Sibelius	Ulysses (cantata)	Mátyás Seiber
Swan Song	Franz Schubert	The Unanswered Question	Charles Ives
The Swan-Turner	Paul Hindemith	Universal Prayer	Andrzej Panufnik
Symphonia Domestica	Richard Strauss	Vallée d'Obermann	Franz Liszt
Symphonic Dances	Sergei Rachmaniniv	(Obermann Valley)	
Symphonic Metamorphosis of Themes by Weber	Paul Hindemith	La Valse (The Waltz)	Maurice Ravel
		Valse Triste (Sad Waltz)	Jean Sibelius
Symphonie Espagnole	Édouard-Victor-Antoine Lalo	Variations on a Rococo Theme	Pyotr Tchaikovsky
Symphonie Fantastique	Hector Berlioz	Variations on a Theme by Haydn	Johannes Brahms
Symphonie Funèbre et Triomphale	Hector Berlioz	Variations on a Theme of Frank Bridge	Benjamin Britten
Symphonies of Wind Instruments	Igor Stravinsky	Variations on a Theme of Hindemith	William Walton
Symphony in Three Movements	Igor Stravinsky	Venetian Games	Witold Lutoslawski
Symphony of Psalms	Igor Stravinsky	A Vision of Aeroplanes	Ralph Vaughan Williams
Syrinx	Claude Debussy	The Vision of Judgement	Peter Racine Fricker
Tahiti Trot	Dmitry Shostakovich	The Vision of St Augustine	Michael Tippett
Tales from the Vienna Woods	Johann Strauss II	Visions Fugitives (Fleeting Visions)	Sergey Prokofiev
Tam O'Shanter	Malcolm Arnold	The Wand of Youth	Edward Elgar
Taras Bulba	Leoš Janáček	War Requiem	Benjamin Britten
The Tempest	Pyotr Tchaikovsky (1873)	The Wasps	Ralph Vaughan Williams
The Tempest	Jean Sibelius (1925)	The Water Sprite	Antonín Dvořák
Theodora	George Frederick Handel	Water Music	George Frederick Handel
Three Pear-Shaped Pieces	Erik Satie	Wedding Day at Troldhaugen	Edvard Grieg
Three Places in New England	Charles Ives	Welles Raises Kane	Bernard Herrmann
Three Screaming Popes	Mark-Anthony Turnage	The Whale	John Tavener
Till Eulenspiegel	Richard Strauss	The White Peacock	Charles Griffes
Tintagel	Arnold Bax	Wine	Alban Berg
To the Children	Sergei Rachmaninov	Winterreise (Winter Journey)	Franz Schubert
The Tomb of Couperin	Maurice Ravel		
Tragic Overture	Johannes Brahms	The Wood Dove	Antonín Dvořák
Transcendental Studies	Franz Liszt	The Young Person's Guide to the Orchestra	Benjamin Britten
Turandot	Carl Maria Weber		
Tzigane (Gypsy)	Maurice Ravel	Zyklus (Cycle)	Karlheinz Stockhausen

Musical Instructions

a cappella   In the chapel style (unaccompanied).
accarezzevole   Caressingly.
accelerando   Becoming faster.
ad libitum   At will, improvised.
adagietto   Not quite as slow as adagio.
adagio   At ease. Slow tempo between largo (slower) and andante (faster).
adagissimo   Very slow.
addolorato   Sorrowfully.
à demi-jeu   With half the power.
à demi-voix   With half the voice, whispered.
affábile   Gently, pleasingly.
afflito   Sorrowfully, mournfully, sadly.
affrettando   Hurrying.
allegramente   Brightly, gaily.
allegretto   Moderately quick.
allegro   Quick.
ancora   Repeat, again.
andante   Moving along, flowing (slowish but not slow).
andantino   Diminutive of andante although nowadays usually means a little faster.
arcato   Bowed.

arpeggio   Playing of the notes of a chord individually in quick succession.
ballabile   In a dance style.
bariolage   Rapid alternation of open and stopped strings in violin playing.
barré   Playing a chord on the guitar with finger across all strings raising their pitch equally.
bisbigliando   Both hands playing adjacent strings of harp repeatedly pianissimo.
bouche fermée   Closed-mouth singing, i.e. humming.
brio   Vigour, spirit.
calando   Diminishing gradually – softer and slower.
calcando   Quickening gradually (literally, trampling).
col legno   With the wood; using the stick part of the bow to strike the string.
common time   4/4 metre.
comodo   Leisurely, moderate speed.
con brio   With vigour.
con fuoco   With fire; using both force and speed.
con lancio   With verve.
con sordini   On stringed instruments – with mutes; on keyboard instruments – with dampers.

coperti Covered; relates to drums being muted by being covered with a cloth.

crescendo Becoming louder.

da capo From the beginning (literally, from the head).

dal segno From the sign, meaning return to the sign and repeat.

diminuendo Becoming quieter.

diminution Opposite of augmentation, i.e shortening of the time-values of notes of melodic parts.

dolce Sweet, with an implication of 'soft'.

forte Loudly.

fortissimo Very loudly.

gedämpft (damped) Therefore muted for strings and horns; muffled for drums; soft-pedalled for piano.

giocoso Merry, playful.

grazioso Graceful.

jeté (flung) Bowing technique whereby the upper part of the bow is bounced on the string.

larghetto Slow tempo, a little faster than largo.

largo Broad, slow tempo.

legato Smoothly, with no breaks between successive notes.

lento Slow.

maestoso Majestically or stately.

martelé (hammered) Playing the violin with short strokes and never lifting the bow from the strings.

mezza voce Subdued tone between piano and forte (literally, middle voice).

moderato Moderate pace.

morendo Dying away, fading.

muta Direction to change keys, frequently found in timpani and horn parts.

piacere (pleasure) At the performer's discretion.

pianissimo (pp) Very soft.

pianississimo (ppp) Very, very soft.

piano (p) Soft.

pianoforte Soft-loud.

pizzicato (pinched) On string instruments, plucking the string.

poco a poco Little by little, gradually.

portamento Carrying, i.e. the carrying of the sound from one note to another (very legato).

portato Halfway between staccato and legato.

prestissimo Very, very fast; the fastest tempo.

presto Fast.

rake On guitar, dragging the pick across muted strings in an arpeggiated fashion.

rallentando Becoming gradually slower.

ritardando Delaying, becoming gradually slower.

rubato (robbed) Freely slowing down and speeding up the tempo without changing the basic pulse.

saltato (saltando) Bowing technique where the bow is bounced lightly on the string. Means 'jumping'.

scherzando (scherzhaft) Playful, light-hearted.

scherzo Piece in a lively tempo; 'joke'.

sostenuto Sustained.

sotto voce Under the voice, in a quiet soft voice.

spiccato (detached) Bouncing the bow on the strings.

stringendo Tightening, increasing the tension by hurrying the tempo.

strophic Describes a song that has identical music in each verse.

subito Suddenly, at once.

sul ponticello On the bridge: playing a stringed instrument with the bow as near as possible to the bridge.

sul tasto Instruction to take the bow over the fingerboard. Means 'on the fingerboard'.

sur la touche Bow over the fingerboard. Means 'on the touch', synonymous with *sul tasto*.

susurrando Whispering, murmuring.

tacet Stop playing and be silent.

tutti (all) Instruction for the whole orchestra to play.

una corda One string, i.e. the use of the soft pedal which causes the hammers of a piano to.strike only one string per note instead of three.

vibrato Rapid alteration of pitch or intensity of a note to impart 'expression'.

vivace Vivacious, i.e. fast and lively.

MUSIC CLASSICAL

Names and Nicknames of Symphonies

The Age of Anxiety	Bernstein's Symphony No. 2
Alleluiasymphonie	Haydn's Symphony No. 30 in C
America	Bloch's 'Epic Rhapsody' Symphony (1926)
Andante Cantabile	Tchaikovsky's Symphony No. 5 in E minor (2nd movement)
Antar	Rimsky-Korsakov's Symphony No. 2 Op. 9 (Oriental Suite)
Antarctica	Vaughan Williams' Symphony No. 7
Apocalyptic	Bruckner's Symphony No. 7
Asrael	Suk's Symphony No. 2 in C minor Op. 27
Babi Yar	Shostakovich's Symphony No. 13 in B flat minor Op. 113
The Bear (L'Ours)	Haydn's Symphony No. 82 in C
The Bells of Zlonice	Dvořák's Symphony No. 1 in C minor Op. 3
The Bell	Khachaturian's Symphony No. 2 in A minor
The Camp Meeting	Ives's Symphony No. 3
Capricieuse	Berwald's Symphony No. 2
Celestial Railroad	Ives's Symphony No. 4, 2nd movement, fantasy piece for piano
Cello Symphony	Britten's Opus 68 Symphony dedicated to Rostropovich
La Chasse (The Hunt)	Haydn's Symphony No. 73 in D
Choral	Beethoven's Symphony No. 9 in D minor Op. 125
Christmas	Haydn's Symphony No. 26 in D minor
Classical	Prokofiev's Symphony No. 1 in D Op. 25
Clock	Haydn's Symphony No. 101 in D
Decoration Day	Ives's 2nd Movement of his 'New England Holidays'
Deliciae Basiliensis	Honegger's Symphony No. 4
The Distraught Man	Haydn's Symphony No. 60 in C major

The Divine Poem	Scriabin's Symphony No. 3 in C minor Op. 43
Le Double	Dutilleux's Symphony No. 3
Dreams of Gandalf	Sallinen's Symphony No. 7
Drumroll	Haydn's Symphony No. 103 in E flat
Eroica	Beethoven's Symphony No. 3 in E flat major
Espansiva (Expansive)	Nielsen's Symphony No. 3
Fantaisies	Martinu's Symphony No. 6
Farewell (Abschied)	Haydn's Symphony No. 45 in F sharp minor
Fate	Beethoven's Symphony No. 5 in C minor Op. 67
Fate	Tchaikovsky's Symphony No. 4 in F minor Op. 36
Festive	Smetana's Symphony in E
Fire	Haydn's Symphony No. 59 in A
First of May	Shostakovich's Symphony No. 3 in E flat Op. 20
Four Seasons	Malipiero's Symphony No. 1
The Four Temperaments	Nielsen's Symphony No. 2 in C minor Op. 16
Fourth of July	Ives's 3rd Movement of his 'New England Holidays'
From a New Zealand Diary	Sallinen's Symphony No. 6
From the New World	Dvořák's Symphony No. 9 (formerly No. 5) in E minor
Funeral March	Beethoven's Symphony No. 3 in E flat Op. 55 (2nd movement)
Gothic	Havergal Brian's Symphony No. 1 in D minor
Great C Major	Schubert's Symphony No. 9 in C major
Great G Minor	Mozart's Symphony No. 40 in G minor, K550
Haffner	Mozart's Symphony No. 35 in D, K385
Heavenly Length	Schubert's Symphony No. 9 in C major
The Hen	Haydn's Symphony No. 83 in G minor
Holidays	Ives's Symphony (1904–13)
Horn Signal	Haydn's Symphony No. 31 in D
The Hunt (La Chasse)	Haydn's Symphony No. 73 in D
Hydriotaphia	Alwyn's Symphony No. 5
Hymn of Praise	Mendelssohn's Symphony No. 2 in B flat Op. 52
Ilya Murometz	Glière's Symphony No. 3
Imperial	Haydn's Symphony No. 53 in D
The Inextinguishable	Nielsen's Symphony No. 4, Op. 29
Irish	Stanford's Symphony No. 3 in F minor Op. 28
Irish	Sullivan's Symphony in E minor
Israel	Bloch's Symphony (1916)
Italian	Mendelssohn's Symphony No. 4 in A major Op. 90
Jeremiah	Bernstein's Symphony No. 1
Jupiter	Mozart's Symphony No. 41 in C major, K551
Kaddish	Bernstein's Symphony No. 3
Lamentations	Haydn's Symphony No. 26 in D minor
Largo	Dvořák's Symphony No. 5 (No. 9) in E minor (2nd movement)
Loudon	Haydn's Symphony No. 69 in C
Leningrad	Shostakovich's Symphony No. 7 in C major Op. 60
Linz	Mozart's Symphony No. 36 in C, K425
Little C Major	Schubert's Symphony No. 6 in C major
Little G Minor	Mozart's Symphony No. 25 in G minor, K183
Little Russian	Tchaikovsky's Symphony No. 2 in C minor Op. 17
Liturgique	Honegger's Symphony No. 3
Lobgesang (Hymn of Praise)	Mendelssohn's Symphony No. 2 in B flat Op. 52
London	Vaughan Williams's Symphony No. 2
London	Haydn's Symphony No. 104 in D
London Symphonies	Haydn's Symphonies Nos 93–104
Maria Theresia	Haydn's Symphony No. 48 in C
Mathis der Maler	Hindemith's Symphony (1934)
Le Matin (Morning)	Haydn's Symphony No. 6 in D
Mercury	Haydn's Symphony No. 43 in E flat
Michelangelo	Kancheli's Symphony No. 4
Le Midi (Noon)	Haydn's Symphony No. 7 in C
Military	Haydn's Symphony No. 100 in G
Miracle	Haydn's Symphony No. 96 in D
Mysterious Mountain	Hovahness' Symphony No. 2 Op. 132
New England Holidays	Ives's Symphony (1904–13)
New World	Dvořák's Symphony No. 9 (formerly No. 5) in E minor
1917 Symphony	Shostakovich's Symphony No. 12 in D minor
Nordic	Hanson's Symphony No. 1 in E minor Op. 21
Die Nullte	Bruckner's Symphony No. 0 in D minor
October	Shostakovichs' Symphony No. 2 in B major Op. 14
Ode to Joy	Beethoven's Symphony No. 9 in D Op. 125 (4th movement)
Organ	Saint-Saëns' Symphony No. 3 in C minor
L'Ours (The Bear)	Haydn's Symphony No. 82 in C
Oxford	Haydn's Symphony No. 92 in G

Palindrome	Haydn's Symphony No. 47 in G
Paris	Mozart's Symphony No. 31 in D, K297
Paris Symphonies	Haydn's Symphonies Nos 82–87
La Passione	Haydn's Symphony No. 49 in F minor
Pastoral	Beethoven's Symphony No. 6 in F major
Pastoral	Vaughan Williams Symphony No. 3
Pathétique	Tchaikovsky's Symphony No. 6 in B minor Op. 74
The Philosopher	Haydn's Symphony No. 22 in E flat
Pittsburgh	Hindemith's Symphony (1958)
Polish	Tchaikovsky's Symphony No. 3 in D Op. 29
La Poule (The Hen)	Haydn's Symphony No. 83 in G minor
Prague	Mozart's Symphony No. 38 in D, K504
Reformation	Mendelssohn's Symphony No. 5 in D minor
La Reine (The Queen)	Haydn's Symphony No. 85 in B flat
Requiem	Hanson's Symphony No. 4 Op. 34
Resurrection	Mahler's Symphony No. 2 in C minor
Resurrection	Rubbra's Symphony No. 9
Rhenish	Schumann's Symphony No. 3 in E flat major Op. 97
Romantic	Bruckner's Symphony No. 4 in E Flat major
Romantic	Hanson's Symphony No. 2 Op. 30
La Roxelane	Haydn's Symphony No. 63 in C major
Rustic Wedding	Goldmark's Symphony Op. 26
St Florian	Schnittke's Symphony No. 2
Salomon	Haydn's Symphony No. 104 in D
Salomon Symphonies	Haydn's Symphonies Nos 93–104
Schoolmaster	Haydn's Symphony No. 55 in E flat
Scotch (Scottish)	Mendelssohn's Symphony No. 3 in A minor Op. 56
Sea	Hanson's Symphony No. 7
Sea	Vaughan Williams's Symphony No. 1 in C
The Seasons	Spohr's Symphony No. 9 in B minor
Serena	Hindemith's Symphony (1946)
Sérieuse	Berwald's Symphony No. 1
Das Siegeslied	Brian's Symphony No. 4
Simple	Britten's Symphony Op. 4
Simple	Nielsen's Symphony No. 6
Sinfonia Antartica	See *Antartica*
Sinfonia Boreale	Holmboe's Symphony No. 8
Sinfonia da Requiem	Britten's Symphony Op. 20
Sinfonia di Sfere	Panufnik's Symphony No. 5
Sinfonia Elegiaca	Malipiero's Symphony No. 2
Sinfonia Elegiaca	Panufnik's Symphony No. 2
Sinfonia Mistica	Panufnik's Symphony No. 6
Sinfonia Rustica	Holmboe's Symphony No. 3
Sinfonia Rustica	Panufnik's Symphony No. 1
Sinfonia Sacra	Holmboe's Symphony No. 4
Sinfonia Sacra	Panufnik's Symphony No. 3
Sinfonia Sacra	Rubbra's Symphony No. 9
Sinfonia Votiva	Panufnik's Symphony No. 8
Singulière	Berwald's Symphony No. 3 in C minor
Le Soir (Evening)	Haydn's Symphony No. 8 in G
Song in the Night	Szymanowski's Symphony No. 3
Spring	Schumann's Symphony No. 1 in B flat Op. 38
Stimmen Verstummen	Gubaildulina's Symphony (1986)
Study	Bruckner's Symphony in F minor
Summer Music	Mathias's Symphony No. 2
Surprise	Haydn's Symphony No. 94 in G major
Symphony of a Thousand	Mahler's Symphony No. 8 in E flat major
Tempest	Haydn's Symphony No. 8 in G, Fourth movement
Tempora Mutantur	Haydn's Symphony No. 64 in A
Thanksgiving Day	Ives's 4th movement of his 'New England Holidays'
Titan	Mahler's Symphony No. 1 in D major
To the Memory of Lenin	Shostakovich's Symphony No. 12 in D minor Op. 112
Tragic	Schubert's Symphony No. 4 in C minor
Trauer (Mourning)	Haydn's Symphony No. 44 in E minor
Di Tre Re	Honegger's Symphony No. 5
Triumph	Smetana's Symphony in E
Ukrainian	Tchaikovsky's Symphony No. 2 in C minor
Unfinished	Schubert's Symphony No. 8 in B minor
Vigil	MacMillan's Symphony (1997)
Wagner	Bruckner's Symphony No. 3 in D minor
Washington Mosaics	Sallinen's Symphony No. 5
Washington's Birthday	Ives's 1st movement of his 'New England Holidays'

MUSIC

CLASSICAL

Waves	Kernis' Symphony No. 1
Winter Daydreams	Tchaikovsky's Symphony No. 1 in G minor Op. 13
The Year 1905	Shostakovich's Symphony No. 11 in G minor Op. 103
The Year 1917	Shostakovich's Symphony No. 12 in D minor Op. 112

Names and Nicknames of Symphonies (by composer)

Alwyn's Symphony No. 5	Hydriotaphia
Beethoven's Symphony No. 3 in E flat major	Eroica
Beethoven's Symphony No. 3 in E flat Op. 55 (2nd movement)	Funeral March
Beethoven's Symphony No. 5 in C minor Op. 67	Fate
Beethoven's Symphony No. 6 in F major	Pastoral
Beethoven's Symphony No. 9 in D minor Op. 125	Choral
Beethoven's Symphony No. 9 in D Op. 125 (4th movement)	Ode to Joy
Bernstein's Symphony No. 1	Jeremiah
Bernstein's Symphony No. 2	The Age of Anxiety
Bernstein's Symphony No. 3	Kaddish
Berwald's Symphony No. 1	Sérieuse
Berwald's Symphony No. 2	Capricieuse
Berwald's Symphony No. 3 in C major	Singulière
Bloch's 'Epic Rhapsody' Symphony (1926)	America
Bloch's Symphony (1916)	Israel
Brian's Symphony No. 1 in D minor	Gothic
Brian's Symphony No. 4	Das Siegeslied
Britten's Op. 68 dedicated to Rostropovich	Cello Symphony
Britten's Symphony Op. 20	Sinfonia da Requiem
Britten's Symphony Op. 4	Simple
Bruckner's Symphony in F minor	Study
Bruckner's Symphony No. 0 in D minor	Die Nullte
Bruckner's Symphony No. 3 in D minor	Wagner
Bruckner's Symphony No. 4 in E flat major	Romantic
Bruckner's Symphony No. 7	Apocalyptic
Dutilleux's Symphony No. 3	Le Double
Dvořák's Symphony No. 1 in C minor Op. 3	The Bells of Zlonice
Dvořák's Symphony No. 5 (No. 9) in E minor (2nd movement)	Largo
Dvořák's Symphony No. 9 (formerly No. 5) in E minor	From the New World
Glière's No. 3	Ilya Murometz
Goldmark's Symphony Op. 26	Rustic Wedding
Gubaildulina's Symphony (1986)	Stimmen Verstummen
Hanson's Symphony No. 1 in E minor Op. 21	Nordic
Hanson's Symphony No. 2 Op. 30	Romantic
Hanson's Symphony No. 4 Op. 34	Requiem
Hanson's Symphony No. 7	Sea
Haydn's Symphony No. 6 in D	Le Matin (Morning)
Haydn's Symphony No. 7 in C	Le Midi (Noon)
Haydn's Symphony No. 8 in G	Le Soir (Evening)
Haydn's Symphony No. 8 in G (4th movement)	Tempest
Haydn's Symphony No. 22 in E flat	The Philosopher
Haydn's Symphony No. 26 in D minor	Christmas
Haydn's Symphony No. 26 in D minor	Lamentation
Haydn's Symphony No. 30 in C	Alleluiasymphonie
Haydn's Symphony No. 31 in D	Horn Signal
Haydn's Symphony No. 43 in E flat	Mercury
Haydn's Symphony No. 44 in E minor	Trauer (Mourning)
Haydn's Symphony No. 45 in F sharp minor	Farewell (Abschied)
Haydn's Symphony No. 47 in G	Palindrome
Haydn's Symphony No. 48 in C	Maria Theresia
Haydn's Symphony No. 49 in F minor	La Passione
Haydn's Symphony No. 53 in D	Imperial
Haydn's Symphony No. 55 in E flat	Schoolmaster
Haydn's Symphony No. 59 in A	Fire
Haydn's Symphony No. 60 in C major	The Distraught Man
Haydn's Symphony No. 63 in C major	La Roxolane
Haydn's Symphony No. 64 in A	Tempora Mutantur
Haydn's Symphony No. 69 in C	Laudon
Haydn's Symphony No. 73 in D	The Hunt (La Chasse)
Haydn's Symphonies Nos 82–87	Paris Symphonies
Haydn's Symphony No. 82 in C	The Bear (L'Ours)
Haydn's Symphony No. 83 in G minor	The Hen (La Poule)
Haydn's Symphony No. 85 in B flat	La Reine (The Queen)

Haydn's Symphony No. 92 in G	Oxford
Haydn's Symphonies Nos 93–104	London Symphonies
Haydn's Symphonies Nos 93–104	Salomon Symphonies
Haydn's Symphony No. 94 in G major	Surprise
Haydn's Symphony No. 96 in D	Miracle
Haydn's Symphony No. 100 in G	Military
Haydn's Symphony No. 101 in D	Clock
Haydn's Symphony No. 103 in E flat	Drumroll
Haydn's Symphony No. 104 in D	London
Haydn's Symphony No. 104 in D	Salomon
Hindemith's Symphony (1934)	Mathis der Maler
Hindemith's Symphony (1946)	Serena
Hindemith's Symphony (1958)	Pittsburgh
Holmboe's Symphony No. 3	Sinfonia Rustica
Holmboe's Symphony No. 4	Sinfonia Sacra
Holmboe's Symphony No. 8	Sinfonia Boreale
Honegger's Symphony No. 3	Liturgique
Honegger's Symphony No. 4	Deliciae Basiliensis
Honegger's Symphony No. 5	Di Tre Re
Hovahness' Symphony No. 2 Op. 132	Mysterious Mountain
Ives's 1st movement of his 'New England Holidays'	Washington's Birthday
Ives's 2nd movement of his 'New England Holidays'	Decoration Day
Ives's 3rd movement of his 'New England Holidays'	Fourth of July
Ives's 4th movement of his 'New England Holidays'	Thanksgiving Day
Ives's Symphony No. 3	The Camp Meeting
Ives's Symphony No. 4, 2nd movement; fantasy piece for piano	Celestial Railroad
Ives's Symphony (1904–13)	Holidays
Ives's Symphony (1904–13)	New England Holidays
Kanchell's Symphony No. 4	Michelangelo
Kernis's Symphony No. 1	Waves
Khachaturian's Symphony No. 2 in A minor	The Bell
MacMillan's Symphony (1997)	Vigil
Mahler's Symphony No. 1 in D major	Titan
Mahler's Symphony No. 2 in C minor	Resurrection
Mahler's Symphony No. 8 in E flat major	Symphony of a Thousand
Malipiero's Symphony No. 1	Four Seasons
Malipiero's Symphony No. 2	Sinfonia Elegiaca
Martinu's Symphony No. 6	Fantaisies
Mathias's Symphony No. 2	Summer Music
Mendelssohn's Symphony No. 2 in B flat Op. 52	Lobgesang (Hymn of Praise)
Mendelssohn's Symphony No. 3 in A minor Op. 56	Scotch (Scottish)
Mendelssohn's Symphony No. 4 in A major Op. 90	Italian
Mendelssohn's Symphony No. 5 in D minor	Reformation
Mozart's Symphony No. 25 in G minor, K183	Little G Minor
Mozart's Symphony No. 31 in D, K297	Paris
Mozart's Symphony No. 35 in D, K385	Haffner
Mozart's Symphony No. 36 in C, K425	Linz
Mozart's Symphony No. 38 in D, K504	Prague
Mozart's Symphony No. 40 in G minor, K550	Great G Minor
Mozart's Symphony No. 41 in C major, K551	Jupiter
Nielsen's Symphony No. 2 in C minor Op. 16	The Four Temperaments
Nielsen's Symphony No. 3	Espansiva (Expansive)
Nielsen's Symphony No. 4, Op. 29	The Inextinguishable
Nielsen's Symphony No. 6	Simple
Panufnik's Symphony No. 1	Sinfonia Rustica
Panufnik's Symphony No. 2	Sinfonia Elegiaca
Panufnik's Symphony No. 3	Sinfonia Sacra
Panufnik's Symphony No. 5	Sinfonia di Sfere
Panufnik's Symphony No. 6	Sinfonia Mistica
Panufnik's Symphony No. 8	Sinfonia Votiva
Prokofiev's Symphony No. 1 in D Op. 25	Classical
Rimsky-Korsakov's Symphony No. 2 Op. 9 (Oriental Suite)	Antar
Rubbra's Symphony No. 9	Resurrection
Rubbra's Symphony No. 9	Sinfonia Sacra
Saint-Saëns's Symphony No. 3 in C minor	Organ
Sallinen's Symphony No. 5	Washington Mosaics
Sallinen's Symphony No. 6	From a New Zealand Diary
Sallinen's Symphony No. 7	Dreams of Gandalf
Schnittke's Symphony No. 2	St Florian
Schubert's Symphony No. 4 in C minor	Tragic
Schubert's Symphony No. 6 in C major	Little C Major
Schubert's Symphony No. 8 in B minor	Unfinished

MUSIC CLASSICAL

Schubert's Symphony No. 9 in C major	Great C Major
Schubert's Symphony No. 9 in C major, D944	Heavenly Length
Schubert's Symphony No. 1 in B flat Op. 38	Spring
Schubert's Symphony No. 3 in E flat major Op. 97	Rhenish
Scriabin's Symphony No. 3 in C minor Op. 43	The Divine Poem
Shostakovich's Symphony No. 2 in B major Op. 14	October
Shostakovich's Symphony No. 3 in E flat Op. 20	First of May
Shostakovich's Symphony No. 7 in C major Op. 60	Leningrad
Shostakovich's Symphony No. 11 in G minor Op. 103	The Year 1905
Shostakovich's Symphony No. 12 in D minor Op. 112	The Year 1917
Shostakovich's Symphony No. 12 in D minor Op. 12	To the Memory of Lenin
Shostakovich's Symphony No. 13 in B flat minor Op. 113	Babi Yar
Smetana's Symphony in E	Festive/Triumph
Spohr's Symphony No. 9 in B minor	Seasons
Stanford's Symphony No. 3 in F minor Op. 28	Irish
Suk's Symphony No. 2 in C minor Op. 27	Asrael
Sullivan's Symphony in E minor	Irish
Szymanowski's Symphony No. 3	Song in the Night
Tchaikovsky's Symphony No. 1 in G minor Op. 13	Winter Daydreams
Tchaikovsky's Symphony No. 2 in C minor Op. 17	Little Russian/Ukrainian
Tchaikovsky's Symphony No. 3 in D Op. 29	Polish
Tchaikovsky's Symphony No. 4 in F minor Op. 36	Fate
Tchaikovsky's Symphony No. 6 in B minor Op. 74	Pathétique
Vaughan Williams's Symphony No. 1 in C	Sea
Vaughan Williams's Symphony No. 2	London
Vaughan Williams's Symphony No. 3	Pastoral
Vaughan Williams's Symphony No. 7	Antarctica

Nicknames of Classical Works

Actus Tragicus	Bach's church cantata No. 106 ('God's time is the best')
Adieux Sonata	Beethoven's Piano Sonata No. 26 in E flat major, which he called 'The Farewell'
African	Saint-Saën's Piano Concerto No. 5
Air on the G String	Wilhelmj's arrangement of Bach Suite for Orchestra No. 3 in D (2nd movement)
American Quartet	Dvořák's String Quartet in F Op. 96
Andante Cantabile	Tchaikovsky's String Quartet No. 1 in D Op. 11 (2nd movement)
Appassionata Sonata	Beethoven's Piano Sonata No. 23 in F minor Op. 57
Archduke Trio	Beethoven's Piano Trio in B flat Op. 97, dedicated to Archduke Rudolf of Austria
Arpeggione	Schubert's Sonata in A minor for cello and piano
Basle Concerto	Stravinsky's Concerto in D for strings
Battle Symphony	Beethoven's orchestral work 'Wellington's Victory' Op. 91
The Bell	Haydn's String Quartet in D minor Op. 76 No. 2
The Bird	Haydn's String Quartet in C Op. 33 No. 3
The Black Mass	Scriabin's Piano Sonata No. 9 in F Op. 68
Black-key Étude	Chopin's Étude in G flat major for piano Op. 10 No. 5
Brandenburg Concertos	Bach's 6 concertos for various instruments, BWV 1046–1051
Bridal Chorus	Wagner's chorus from Act 3 of Lohengrin
Butterfly	Chopin's Étude in G flat for piano Op. 25 No. 9
Cat Waltz	Chopin's Waltz in F for piano Op. 34 No. 3
Cat's Fugue	Scarlatti's Fugue in G minor for harpsichord
La Chasse	Haydn's String Quartet in B flat Op. 1 No. 1
Chopsticks	Anonymous quick waltz tune for piano, first published in London 1877
Coffee Cantata	Bach's Cantata No. 211
Colas Breugnon	Kabalevsky's opera The Craftsman of Clamecy
Concord Sonata	Ives's Piano Sonata No. 2
Contemplation of Nothing Serious	Ives's orchestral piece Central Park in the Dark in the Good Old Summertime
Coronation Concerto	Mozart's Piano Concerto No. 26 in D, K537
The Cuckoo and the Nightingale	Handel's second set of six concertos for organ and orchestra
Dance Before the Golden Calf	Schoenberg's climax of Act 2 of his opera Moses und Aron
Dance of the Blessed Spirits	Gluck's slow dance in Act 2 of Orfeo ed Euridice, noted for its flute solo
Dance of the Comedians	Smetana's dance episode in Act 3 of The Bartered Bride, featuring clowns
Dance of the Hours	Episode, frequently played separately, in Act 3 of Ponchielli's La Gioconda and representing the conflict between darkness and light
Dance of the Seven Veils	Dance episode during Strauss's opera Salome
Dance of the Sylphs	Berlioz's orchestral episode during La Damnation de Faust, which forms part of Faust's dream on the banks of the Elbe

Dance of the Tumblers	Rimsky-Korsakov's episode during *The Snow Maiden* in which acrobats dance for the Tsar Berendey
Dead March in Saul	Handel's Funeral March from the oratorio *Saul*
Death and the Maiden	Schubert's String Quartet No. 14 in D minor
Dettingen Te Deum	Handel's *Te Deum* in D
Devil's Trill	Tartini's Violin Sonata in G minor
Diabelli Variations	Beethoven's 33 variations on a waltz by Diabelli in C for piano Op. 120
The Difficult Decision	Beethoven's String Quartet in F Op. 135 (4th movement)
Dissonance Quartet	Mozart's String Quartet No. 19 in C major, K465
Dog Waltz	Chopin's Waltz in D flat for piano Op. 64 No. 1
Dominicus Mass	Mozart's Mass in C, K66
Donkey Quartet	Haydn's String Quartet in D minor Op. 76 No. 2
Dorian Toccata and Fugue	Bach Toccata and Fugue in D minor for organ, BWV 538
A Dream	Haydn's String Quartet in F Op. 50 No. 5 (2nd movement)
Dumbarton Oaks	Stravinsky's Concerto in E flat for chamber ensemble
Dumky Trio	Dvořák's Piano Trio in E minor Op. 90
Ebony	Stravinsky's Concerto for clarinet and jazz band
Edward	Brahms's Ballade in D minor for piano Op. 10 No. 1
Eine Kleine Nachtmusik	Mozart's Divertimento in G for strings, K525
Eine Kleine Trauermusik	Schubert's Nonet in E flat minor for wind instuments
Elegy	Massenet's orchestral selection in E minor from his opera *Les Érinnyes*
Elvira Madigan	Mozart's Piano Concerto No. 21 in C
Emperor Concerto	Beethoven's Piano Concerto No. 5 in E flat major Op. 73
Emperor Quartet	Haydn's String Quartet in C major Op. 76 No. 3
English Suites	Bach's 6 Suites for harpsichord, BWV 806-811
Erdödy Quartets	Haydn's 6 String Quartets
Eroica Variations	Beethoven's 15 Variations and fugue on an Original Theme in E flat major Op. 76 Nos 75–80 for piano
Eyeglass Duo	Beethoven's Duo in E flat for viola and cello
Fall of Warsaw	Chopin's Étude in C minor for piano Op. 10 No. 12
Il Favorito	Vivaldi's Violin Concerto in E minor Op. 11 No. 2
Fiddle Fugue	Bach's Fugue in D minor for organ, BWV 539
Fifths	Haydn's String Quartet in D minor Op. 76 No. 2
Fingal's Cave	Mendelssohn's Overture for orchestra Op. 26, originally named *The Lonely Island*
The Forty-eight	Bach's *Well-Tempered Clavier*
The Four Seasons	Vivaldi's 4 Violin Concertos Op. 8 Nos 1–4
The Four Temperaments	Hindemith's Theme and Variations for string and piano: melancholic, sanguine, phlegmatic, choleric
French Suites	Bach's 6 Suites for harpsichord, BWV 812–817
The Frog	Haydn's String Quartet in D Op. 50 No. 6
From My Life	Smetana's String Quartets No. 1 in E minor (especially) and No. 2 in D minor
Funeral Anthem	Handel's anthem in G minor, *The Ways of Zion Do Mourn*
Funeral March	Chopin's Piano Sonata No. 2 in B flat minor Op. 35 (3rd movement)
Funeral March	Beethoven's Piano Sonata No. 12 in A flat Op. 26 (3rd movement)
Für Elise	Beethoven's Bagatelle in A minor for piano
Il Gardellino	Vivaldi's Flute Concerto in D Op. 10 No. 3
Gassenhauer Trio	Beethoven's Trio in B flat for clarinet, cello and piano Op. 11
German Suites	Bach's set of 6 keyboard partitas
Ghost Trio	Beethoven's Piano Trio in D major Op. 70 No. 1
The Girl With Enamel Eyes	Delibes 3-act ballet *Coppelia*
Goldberg Variations	Bach's Aria with Diverse Variations for harpsichord, BWV 988
Golden Sonata	Purcell's Sonata in F for two violins, viola da gamba and organ
Grand Duo	Schubert's Sonata in C major for piano (4 hands)
Grande Valse Brillante	Chopin's Waltz in E flat for piano Op. 18
Grazer Fantasie	Schubert's Fantasy in C for piano
Great Fugue	Beethoven's Fugue in B flat major for String Quartet Op. 133
Great Organ Mass	Haydn's Mass in E flat, Hob. XXII:4
Grief	Chopin's Étude in E for piano Op. 10 No. 3
Gypsy Rondo	Haydn's Piano Trio in G, Hob. XV:25 (3rd movement)
Haffner Serenade	Mozart's Suite in D major for orchestra, K250
Hallelujah Chorus	Handel's Chorus in D from his oratorio *Messiah*, No. 44
Hallelujah Concerto	Handel's Organ Concerto in B flat Op. 106
Hammerklavier	Beethoven's Piano Sonata No. 29 in B flat major Op. 106
Handel Variations	Brahms's Variations and Fugue on a Theme by Handel in B flat for Piano
Handel's Largo	Handel's aria 'Ombre mai fù', from his opera *Serse* (*Xerxes*)
Harmonious Blacksmith	Handel's Harpsichord Suite No. 5 in E (4th movement) Air with 5 variations
Harmonious Inspiration	Vivaldi's 12 concertos for various instruments Op. 3
Harmony Mass	Haydn's Mass No. 12 in B flat, H XXII:14
Harp Étude	Chopin's Étude in A flat for piano Op. 25 No. 1
Harp Quartet	Beethoven's String Quartet in E flat major Op. 74
Haydn Quartets	Mozart's 6 String Quartets Op. 10, K387–465

Haydn Variations	Brahms's Variations on a Theme by Joseph Haydn in B flat
The Hebrides	Mendelssohn's Overture for orchestra Op. 26
Heiliger Dankgesang	Beethoven's String Quartet in A minor Op. 132 (3rd movement)
Heiligmesse	Haydn's Mass in B flat, Hob. XXII:10
Hexenmenuet	Haydn's String Quartet in D minor Op. 76 No. 2 (3rd movement)
Hoffmeister Quartet	Mozart's String Quartet in D, K499
Hornpipe (aka Lark)	Haydn's String Quartet in D Op. 64 No. 5
Hornpipe Concerto	Handel's Concerto Grosso in B minor Op. 6, No. 12
Horn Trio	Brahms's Trio in E flat for violin, horn and piano Op. 40
Horseman (aka The Rider)	Haydn's String Quartet in G minor Op. 74 No. 3
Housatonic at Stockbridge	Ives's 'Three Places in New England' (3rd movement)
Humoresque	Dvořák's piano piece in G flat Op. 101 No. 7
Hunt Cantata	Bach Cantata 208 'Was mir behagt, ist nur die munter Jagd!'
The Hunt	Mozart's String Quartet No. 17 in B flat, K458
The Hunt	Haydn's String Quartet in B flat Op. 1 No. 1
Imperial Mass	Haydn's Mass No. 9 in D minor, Hob. XXII:11
Italian Concerto	Bach's Concerto for solo harpsichord, BWV 971
Jesu, Joy of Man's Desiring	Bach's chorale prelude from Cantata 147, 'Herz und Mund und Tat und Leben'
Jeunehomme Concerto	Mozart's Piano Concerto in E flat Op. 33 No. 2
Jig Fugue	Bach's Fugue in G for organ, BWV 577
The Joke	Haydn's String Quartet in E flat Op. 33 No. 2
Jungfernquartette	Haydn's 6 String Quartets Op. 33
Kaiser (aka Emperor)	Haydn's String Quartet in C Op. 76 No. 3
Kamennoi-Ostrov	Rubinstein's piece for piano in F sharp No. 22
Kettledrum Mass (Paukenmesse)	Haydn's Mass No. 7 in C major, Hob. XXII:9
Kreutzer Sonata	Beethoven's Violin Sonata No. 9 in A major Op. 47
Kreutzer Sonata Quartet	Janáček's String Quartet No. 1
Lark (aka Hornpipe)	Haydn's String Quartet in D Op. 64 No. 5
Late Quartets	Beethoven's String Quartets Op. 127, 130–133 and 135
Liebestraum	Liszt's Nocturne in A flat for piano; No. 3 of 3 of that title
Little Fugue in G Minor	Bach's Fugue for organ, BWV 578
Little Organ Mass	Haydn's Mass in B flat No. 5, Hob. XXII:7
Lobkowitz Quartets	Haydn's 2 String Quartets Op. 77 Nos 81–82
La Malinconia	Beethoven's String Quartet in B flat Op. 18 No. 6 (4th movement)
Manzoni Requiem	Verdi's *Requiem*, in memory of poet Alessandro Manzoni
Marche Militaire	Schubert's March in D for piano duet Op. 51 No. 1
Mariazell Mass	Haydn's Mass in C, Hob. XXII:8
Mass in Time of War	Haydn's Mass No. 7 in C, Hob. XXII:9
Mazeppa Études	Liszt's Transcendental Études for piano No. 4
Meditation	Massenet's selection in D for violin and orchestra from the opera *Thaïs*
Melody in F	Rubinstein's Piano Piece No. 1 of 2 melodies Op. 3
Military Polonaise	Chopin's Polonaise in A for piano Op. 40 No. 1
Minuet in G	Beethoven's 6 Minuets, WoO 10 No. 2
Minuet in G	Paderewski's Minuet for piano Op. 14 No. 1
Minuet in G	Bach's 'Notebook for Anna Magdalena Bach', 1st selection
Minute Waltz	Chopin's Waltz in D flat for piano Op. 64 No. 1
Missa Solemnis	Beethoven's Mass in D Op. 123
Moonlight Sonata	Beethoven's Piano Sonata No. 14 in C sharp minor Op. 27 No. 2
The Mount of Olives	Beethoven's Oratorio *Christ on the Mount of Olives* Op. 85
Mozartiana	Tchaikovsky's Suite No. 4 for orchestra
A Musical Joke	Mozart's Divertimento in F for chamber ensemble, K522
Muss es sein? Es muss sein! Es muss sein!	Beethoven's String Quartet in F major Op. 135 (4th movement)
Nelson Mass	Haydn's Mass No. 9 in D minor, Hob. XXII:11
New England	Ives's first orchestral set
Nicolai Mass	Haydn's Mass in G, Hob. XXII:6
Organ Solo Mass	Mozart's Mass in C, K259
Paganini Études	Liszt's 6 Études for piano on themes of Paganini
Paganini Variations	Brahms's *Variations on a Theme of Paganini* in A minor for piano
Pastoral Sonata	Beethoven's Piano Sonata No. 15 in D major Op. 28
Pastoral Symphony	Handel's interlude from his oratorio *Messiah*, No. 13
Pathétique	Beethoven's Piano Sonata No. 8 in C minor Op. 13
Paukenmesse (Kettledrum Mass)	Haydn's Mass in C, Hob. XXII:9
Peasant Cantata	Bach's Cantata 212 'Mer hahn en neue Oberkeet'
Pomp and Circumstance	Elgar's March in D major, from a set of 5 with that title, Op. 39 No. 1
Posthorn Serenade	Mozart's Serenade in D for orchestra, K320
Prelude in C	Bach's *Well-Tempered Clavier* Volume I, 1st selection
Prelude in C sharp minor	Rachmaninoff's Prelude for piano, Op. 3 No. 2
Prussian Quartets	Mozart's 3 String Quartets, K575, 589, 590
Prussian Quartets	Haydn's 6 String Quartets Op. 50 Nos 1–6
Quartetto Serioso	Beethoven's String Quartet in F minor Op. 95
Quartettsatz	Schubert's String Quartet No. 12 in C minor

Quintenquartett	Haydn's String Quartet in D minor Op. 76 No. 2
Rage over a Lost Penny	Beethoven's Rondo a Capriccio in G for piano Op. 129
Raindrop Prelude	Chopin's Prelude in D flat for piano Op. 28 No. 15
Rain Sonata	Brahms's Violin Sonata No. 1 in G Op. 78
Ratswahl Cantata	Bach's Cantata 71, 'Gott ist mein König'
Razor Quartet	Haydn's String Quartet in F minor Op. 55 No. 2
Razumovsky Quartets	Beethoven's 3 String Quartets Op. 59
Recitative	Haydn's String Quartet in G Op. 17 No. 5
Reliquie Sonata	Schubert's Piano Sonata No. 13 in C
Rêve Angélique	Rubinstein's piano piece in F sharp No. 22 from Kamennoi-Ostrov
Revolutionary Étude	Chopin's Étude in C minor for piano Op. 10 No. 12
The Rider (aka Horseman)	Haydn's String Quartet in G minor Op. 74 No. 3
Rondo a Capriccio	Beethoven's Piano Sonata in G Op. 129
Rondo alla Turca	Mozart's Piano Sonata in A, K331 (3rd movement)
Russian Quartets	Haydn's 6 String Quartets Op. 33 Nos 1–6
Russian Quartets	Beethoven's 3 String Quartets Op. 59
St Anne Fugue	Bach's Fugue in E flat for organ, BWV 552
St Anthony Chorale	Haydn's Divertimento in B flat for wind, instruments II:46 (2nd movement)
St Cecilia Mass	Haydn's Mass in C, XXII:5
St Joseph Mass	Haydn's Mass in E flat, Hob. XXII:4
Gli Scherzi	Haydn's 6 String Quartets Op. 33 Nos 37–42
Scherzoso	Beethoven's String Quartet in B flat Op. 130
Schübler Chorales	Bach's 6 Chorale Preludes for organ, BWV 645–50
Serenade	Haydn's String Quartet in F Op. 3 No. 5
Sheep May Safely Graze	Bach's Cantata 208, 'Was mir behagt ist nur die muntre Jagd'
Shepherd Boy Étude	Chopin's Étude in A flat for piano Op. 25 No. 1
Six-Four-Time Mass	Haydn's Mass in G, Hob. XXII:6
Solemn Vespers	Mozart's *Vesperae Solennes de Confessore* in C, K339
Sonata Facile	Mozart's Piano Sonata in C, K545
Sonata quasi una Fantasia	Beethoven's Piano Sonata No. 13 in E flat and No. 14 in C sharp minor
Spatzenmesse	Mozart's Mass in G, K220
Spaur Mass	Mozart's Mass in C, K258
Spring Sonata	Beethoven's Violin and Piano Sonata No. 5 in F Op. 24
Spring Song	Mendelssohn's 'Lied ohne Worte' (Song Without Words)
La Stravaganza	Vivaldi's 12 Violin Concertos Op. 4
Street Song Trio	Beethoven's Trio in B flat for clarinet, cello and piano Op. 11
Sun Quartets	Haydn's 6 String Quartets Op. 20 Nos 1–6
Sunrise Quartet	Haydn's String Quartet in B flat Op. 76 No. 4
Swedish Rhapsody	Alfvén's *Midsommarvaka* for orchestra Op. 19
Tempest	Beethoven's Piano Sonata No. 17 in D
Theresia Mass	Haydn's Mass No. 10 in B flat, Hob. XXII:12
Three Places in New England	Ives's first orchestral set
Timpani Mass	Haydn's Mass in C, Hob. XXII:9
To the Memory of an Angel	Berg's Violin Concerto
The Torrent	Chopin's Étude in C sharp Minor for piano Op. 10 No. 4
Tost Quartets	Haydn's 12 String Quartets Op. 54, 55, and 64
Trauer-Ode	Bach's Cantata 198, 'Lass, Fürstin, lass noch einen Strahl'
Ein Traum	Haydn's String Quartet in F Op. 50 No. 5 (2nd movement)
Triangle Concerto	Liszt's Piano Concerto No. 1 in E flat
Triple Concerto	Beethoven's Concerto in C for piano, violin and cello Op. 56
Tristesse	Chopin's Étude in E for piano Op. 10 No. 3
Trout Quintet	Schubert's Quintet in A for piano, violin, viola, cello and double bass
Trumpet Tune	Purcell's harpsichord piece in C
Trumpet Voluntary	Jeremiah Clarke's instrumental piece in D
Turkish March	Beethoven's incidental music to *The Ruins of Athens* for orchestra
Turkish Rondo	Mozart's Piano Sonata in A, K331 (3rd movement)
Twinkle Twinkle Variations	Mozart's Variation on 'Ah, vous dirai-je, maman' in C for piano
Two-Cello Quintet	Schubert's String Quintet in C Op. 163
Utrecht Jubilate	Handel's Jubilate in D
Utrecht Te Deum	Handel's Te Deum in D
Villanelle	Chopin's Étude in G flat for piano Op. 25 No. 9
Voces Intimae (Friendly Voices)	Sibelius' String Quartet in D minor Op. 56
Waisenhausmesse	Mozart's Mass in C minor, K139
Waldstein	Beethoven's Piano Sonata No. 21 in C major Op. 53
Wedding March	Mendelssohn's incidental music to *A Midsummer Night's Dream* for orchestra Op. 61 (9th movement)
Wedge Fugue	Bach's Fugue in E minor for organ
The White Mass	Scriabin's Piano Sonata No. 7 in F sharp Op. 64
Wind-Band Mass	Haydn's Mass No. 12 in B flat, Hob. XXII:14
Winter Wind Étude	Chopin's Etude in A minor for piano Op. 25 No. 11
Witches' Minuet	Haydn's String Quartet in D minor Op. 76 No. 2 (3rd movement)
WTC	Bach's *Well-Tempered Clavier*

MUSIC CLASSICAL

General Information

acciaccatura A short grace note played simultaneously with the principal note and released immediately.

Aldeburgh Festival Founded by Benjamin Britten in 1948, held in Aldeburgh, Suffolk, with concert hall, the Maltings, at nearby Snape.

Amati family Violin makers in Cremona, 16th–18th century. Nicola Amati taught Stradivari and Guarneri.

arpeggio Chord spread, i.e. notes played one after the other as on the harp.

Ars Antiqua (Old Art) Refers to music of 12th and 13th centuries derived from the school of Paris.

Ars Nova (New Art) Style of music developed in 14th-century France and Italy. Term coined by Philippe de Vitry.

attempted suicide: Debussy's wife Rosalie 'Lily' Texier shot herself during a bout of depression.

attempted suicide: Tchaikovsky Walked into the freezing River Neva at dead of night following his disastrous marriage in 1877.

Aurora's Wedding Divertissement of last act of *Sleeping Beauty*, sometimes performed separately.

bagatelle Short, plain composition especially for pianoforte e.g. Für Elise.

Baroque Musical era roughly from 1600 to around 1750.

Battle Symphony Beethoven's orchestral work *Wellington's Victory* Op. 91 (includes 'Rule, Britannia!' and 'God Save the King').

berceuse Lullaby.

Boehm system Theobald Boehm (1794–1881) devised an acoustically superior system of placing and sizing the holes in the flute, and of using the keys to cover them, now universally used.

Boosey and Hawkes Ltd London music publishers (amalgamated 1930).

Boston Symphony Orchestra Founded in October 1881 by Henry Lee Higginson.

Brahms: personal motto *Frei aber Froh* (free but happy). He used the initial letters as the thematic structure of his 3rd Symphony.

Brandenburg Concertos Bach's 6 Concerti Grossi dedicated to Christian Ludwig, Margrave of Brandenburg.

brindisi Drinking song usually accompanying a toast.

Canterbury degrees (Lambeth degrees) Music degrees conferred traditionally by the Archbishop of Canterbury.

capriccio Musical composition that has original and unexpected effects. Janáček and Stravinsky both wrote works called 'Capriccio'.

Carnegie Hall Largest concert-hall in New York, designed by W.B. Tuthill and opened in 1891.

castrato Male soprano castrated before puberty to preserve the voice.

cataloguers of works Schubert – Deutsch; Haydn – Hoboken; Scarlatti – Kirkpatrick (Longo numbers are also still used); Mozart – Köchel; Vivaldi – Ryom (Pincherle & Fanna also catalogued works); J.S. Bach – Schmieder (used initials BWV: Bach-Werke-Verzeichnis); Liszt – both R and S numbers; Nielsen – FS (Fog and Schousboe); Frank Bridge – H numbers; Holmboe – Rapoport (M for Meta numbers, after Holmboe's wife); Bartók – Sz numbers; Beethoven – Kinsky (used WoO

numbers for works without an opus) and Hess (used Hn numbers for other works); Purcell – Zimmerman; Handel – Baselt (HMV numbers); Dvorak – Burghauser; Donizetti – Inzaghi; Chopin – Brown.

catch Type of round whose words may sound comical when sung. A catch club was formed in London in 1761.

chamber music Term coined by Charles Burney in 1805 to describe music not intended for the church, theatre or public concert room, but now applied to ensemble music written for small groups, such as string quartets.

Cheltenham Festival Music festival started in 1945 as Festival of British Contemporary Music but since 1969 drawing music from international sources.

J. & W. Chester Ltd Music publishers founded in Brighton (1874) and specializing in Russian and other foreign composers.

Chetham's School of Music Founded in 1656, by a bequest from Humphrey Chetham (1580–1653), situated in Long Millgate, Manchester; Chetham's is Britain's only full-scale music school for children, with over 280 boys and girls aged 8–18.

Chicago Symphony Orchestra Founded in 1891 by Theodore Thomas; it is the third oldest orchestra in USA.

Children's Corner Six piano pieces dedicated by Debussy to his daughter: 1) Dr Gradus ad Parnassum, 2) Jimbo's Lullaby, 3) Serenade for the Doll, 4) Snow is Dancing, 5) The Little Shepherd, 6) Golliwogg's Cakewalk.

children: most born to one composer Twenty to J.S. Bach.

clam Playing a wrong note in a performance.

Classic FM: top 100, most popular work Max Bruch's 1st Violin Concerto (1996 and 1997).

Classical Period Ranges from the late 18th to the early 19th century.

Colour Symphony (Arthur Bliss): movements The four movements: *Purple*, *Red*, *Blue* and *Green*.

Composers' Guild of Great Britain Founded in 1944 to protect the rights of composers; affiliated to the Society of Authors. First president was Vaughan Williams.

concerto Work, usually in three movements, which contrasts and integrates a solo instrument with the orchestra.

conductor with 36 names Louis Julien (1812–60) was sponsored at his baptism by 36 members of the local philharmonic society.

coronach (corranach) Funeral dirge of Ireland and Highland Scotland.

Crossover Chart Established in 1996 and includes popular light classical pieces.

deaf composers Beethoven, Fauré, Fourenc, Smetana.

deaf percussionist Evelyn Glennie.

Diabelli Variations Beethoven's Thirty-Three Variations on a Waltz by Diabelli.

Dido's Lament Aria from Act 3 of Purcell's Dido and Aneneas, played annually at Remembrance Day service at the Cenotaph and beginning with the words 'When I am laid in earth'.

The Divine Poem Scriabin's Symphony No. 3 in C minor Op. 43 (three movements entitled *Struggles*, *Delights* and *Divine Play*).

Dvořák: son-in-law Josef Suk.

Early Music Consort Founded by David Munrow in 1967 to perform Renaissance and medieval music on original instruments.

Edinburgh Festival Founded in 1947 with Rudolf Bing as director. Three-week festival of music held in August–September now teems with other arts and entertainments.

Eighteen-Twelve (1812) Concert overture Op. 49 by Tchaikovsky commemorating the defeat of Napoleon's Grande Armée on its retreat from Moscow. It incorporates 'La Marseillaise'.

English Chamber Orchestra Founded in 1948 as the Goldsbrough Orchestra (after its founder); present name adopted in 1960.

English Folk Dance and Song Society Amalgamation in 1932 of Folk Song Society (founded 1898) and English Folk Dance Society (founded 1911); HQ in Cecil Sharp House, London, NW1 7AY.

Enigma Variations: musical portraits 1) Lady Elgar (C.A.E.); 2) Hew Steuart-Powell (H.D.S.-P.); 3) RB Townshend (R.B.T.); 4) W. Meath Baker (W.M.B.); 5) Richard P. Arnold (R.P.A.); 6) Isabel Fitton (Ysobel); 7) A. Troyte Griffith (Troyte); 8) Winifred Norbury (W.N.); 9) AJ Jaeger (Nimrod); 10) Dora Penny (Dorabella); 11) GR Sinclair (G.R.S.); 12) Basil Nevinson (B.G.N.); 13) Lady Mary Lygon; 14) Elgar (E.D.U.).

Estampes (Engravings) Three piano pieces by Debussy: *Pagodas*, *Evening in Granada*, and *Gardens in the Rain*.

étude (study) Composition intended to test and extend the performer's technique.

eurhythmics Method invented by Émile Jaques-Dalcroze (1865–1950) for expressing rhythmical aspect of music through gymnastic exercises.

Faust Symphony (Liszt) Movements portray three characters: *Faust*, *Gretchen* and *Mephistopheles*.

Fireworks Music Handel wrote the music to celebrate the Peace of Aix-La-Chapelle (1749); first played in Green Park, London.

First Post British Army bugle call, a summons back to the barracks, sounded at 9.30 p.m.

The Five (aka The Mighty Handful) Russian composers Balakirev, Borodin, Cui, Mussorgsky and Rimsky-Korsakov.

Frankfurt Group English composers who were pupils of Iwan Knorr in the 1890s; they were Norman O'Neill, Roger Quilter, Cyril Scott and Balfour Gardiner.

funeral marches Famous ones include Chopin's 3rd piano sonata; Handel's Dead March in *Saul*; 2nd movement of Beethoven's *Eroica*; Siegfried's Funeral March from Wagner's *Götterdämmerung*.

Gagliano family 18th-century family of violin-makers from Naples. Key members: Alessandro, his sons, Niccolò and Gennaro, and grandsons Ferdinando and Giuseppe.

gamelan A kind of orchestra widespread in south-east Asia, especially Indonesia, whose range of percussion includes gongs, drums, marimbas and chimes.

Gebrauchsmusik (utility music) Term associated in the 1920s with works by Hindemith, Weill and Krenek, influenced by Brecht and designed for social and educational purposes.

Gesamtkunstwerk Wagner's term for a dramatic work in which drama, music, poetry, song and painting would be united into a single artistic whole.

glee Vocal music for three or four parts, unaccompanied and homophonic, popular in late 18th- and early 19th-century England.

Goldberg Variations J.S. Bach's 30 variations on a theme for two-manual harpsichord.

Grove, Sir George English music writer (1820–1900) who, after training as a civil engineer, turned to musical studies and compiled *Grove's Dictionary of Music and Musicians*, then published in 4 volumes, now expanded into 20.

Guarneri Quartet American string quartet formed in 1964 in Vermont. Members are Arnold Steinhardt and John Dally (violins), Michael Tree (viola) and Peter Wiley (cello), who replaced founding member David Soyer in 2000.

Hail to the Chief March traditionally played at formal American events to announce the arrival of the President, first used at the inauguration of Martin Van Buren in 1837. The words came from Sir Walter Scott's *Lady of the Lake* but are no longer used. Derived from an old Gaelic tune, the melody was adapted by the English composer, James Sanderson (1769–1841) for a scene in Scott's play.

hairpins Nickname for the signs < (crescendo) and > (diminuendo).

Hallé Orchestra Founded in 1857 by Charles Hallé and based in Manchester. Sir John Barbirolli was the principal conductor from 1943 to his death in 1970. Kent Nagano has been the conductor since 1992.

Haydn's Symphony No. 45 Haydn directed his musicians to gradually leave the stage during the last movement, hence the nickname 'Farewell'.

Henry Wood: pseudonym Paul Klenovsky was the cryptic name (Klen means maple tree) under which Wood transcribed for orchestra Bach's Toccata and Fugue in D minor.

Hexameron Six variations for piano on a march from Bellini's *I Puritani*, each written by a different composer/pianist, i.e. Liszt, Pixis, Herz, Thalberg, Czerny and Chopin, each of whom played his variation at the first performance of the work in a charity concert in Paris in 1837 (first of the super groups one might say!).

humoresque Humorous or capricious instrumental piece. Famous examples are by Dvořák and Schumann.

Images Title used by Debussy for two works: 1) *Images* for Orchestra, including *Gigues*, *Ibéria* and *Rondes de Printemps*; 2) two sets for solo piano: *Reflets dans l'eau*, *Hommage à Rameau*, *Movement*, *Cloches à travers les feuilles*, *Et la lune descend sur le temple qui fut* and *Poissons d'or*.

Jena Symphony A work found by Fritz Stein in 1909 in Jena, Germany, and linked until 1957 with Beethoven; it turned out that Friedrich Witt was the composer.

La Jeune France (Young France) Group of four French composers (Yves Baudrier, André Jolivet, Daniel Lesur and Olivier Messiaen) who resolved in Paris in 1936 to carry out 'a return to the human' in composition.

jubilate Hymn of praise, usually based on Psalm 100 (in Roman Catholic Psalter, Psalm 99).

Juilliard Quartet Founded by William Schuman in New York in 1946; the line-up as at April 2001 is Joel Smirnoff and Ronald Copes (violins), Samuel Rhodes (viola) and Joel Krosnick (cello).

K numbers Named after the cataloguers of two composers: Mozart – Ludwig von Köchel; Scarlatti – Ralph Kirkpatrick.

karaoke (empty orchestra) Singing along with recorded accompaniment.

Kneller Hall Headquarters, founded in 1857 at Twickenham, Middlesex, of Royal Military School of Music.

La Scala (The Staircase) Milan opera house built in 1778 on the site of a church founded in the 18th century by Regina della Scala, wife of a Duke of Milan.

Last Post British Army bugle call sounded at 10.00 p.m. that ends the day. It is customary to play the Last Post at military funerals.

Leeds Piano Competition Established in 1963 by Fanny Waterman and Marion Thorpe and held triennially. The first winner was Michael Roll, and many placed pianists have won international reputations, notably Peter Donohoe, who was placed sixth in 1981.

Leitmotiv Term first used by A.W. Ambrose (c.1865) in an article about Wagner's operas and Liszt's symphonic poems; it was later used by F.W. Jähns, to denote a short and recurrent musical figure standing for an idea or character.

Les Six Term coined by Henri Collet in 1920 to describe the avant-garde French composers Georges Auric (1899–1983), Louis Durey (1888–1979), Arthur Honegger (1892–1955), Darius Milhaud (1892–1974), Francis Poulenc (1899–1963) and Germaine Tailleferre (1892–1983).

Leventritt Competition International competition alternately for pianists and violinists, established in 1939 by Leventritt Foundation, New York. Winner's prize consists of engagements with prominent orchestras and offer of recording contract.

Lincoln Center for the Performing Arts New York arts centre consisting of Metropolitan Opera House, Avery Fisher Hall, Juillard School and various theatres and societies.

London Philharmonic Orchestra Founded by Sir Thomas Beecham in 1932.

London Symphony Orchestra Founded by players who seceded from Henry Wood's Queen's Hall orchestra in 1904 and run by its own members ever since.

Má Vlast Cycle of 6 symphonic poems by Smetana: 1) The High Citadel (Vysehrad); 2) River Moldau (Vltava); 3) Sàrka; 4) From Bohemia's Meadows and Forests (Z Ceskych Luhu a Haju); 5) Tabor; 6) Blánik (The Valhalla of the Hussite heroes).

madrigal Song form for two or more voices developed in 13th- and 14th-century Italy, most often secular and unaccompanied; revived and enhanced during the Renaissance into an expressive, polyphonic form introduced into Elizabethan England.

Manchester School Name given to group of composers (Maxwell Davies, Harrison Birtwistle, Alexander Goehr and John Ogdon) taught in Manchester by Richard Hall in the late 1950s.

masque Courtly entertainment that evolved in 17th-century England, incorporating music, acting and spectacular costumes and scenery.

Mighty Handful (aka The Five) Alternative name for 'The Five' (coined by Vladimir Stasov).

minimalism Style of music that developed in the 1960s, involving repetition of short musical motifs in simple harmonic idiom. Prominent members include Philip Glass, Steve Reich and Terry Riley.

minuet Movement (usually the 3rd) in sonatas and symphonies of the classical period, derived from the dance of the same name.

Miserere Psalm 51 (50 in Roman Catholic Psalter) set to music by various composers.

most prolific composer Georg Philipp Telemann is often assigned this title; among his output are over 600 overtures, 44 Passions, 40 operas and numerous other works.

motet Choral composition, generally on a sacred text.

motif Short melodic pattern or musical idea that runs throughout a piece.

Mourning Music (Trauermusik) Paul Hindemith work composed within hours of the death of George V in 1936.

Mozart: wrote down on first hearing Gregorio Allegri's Miserere was supposedly sacrosanct to Vatican; Mozart went to a service there and went home and wrote it down from memory, thereby risking excommunication.

Mozart's Piano Concerto No. 21 in C Given nickname of 'Elvira Madigan' in 1967 because it was the theme tune of the film of that name.

Mozart's Piano Concerto No. 26 in D Given nickname of 'Coronation' because it was played at King Leopold II of Prussia's coronation.

Mozart's String Quartets 14–19 Dedicated to Haydn with the words 'I send my six sons to you'.

Mozart: work falsely attributed to Adélaïde violin concerto. In 1977 Marius Casadesus admitted he composed it.

musical epochs Medieval 600–1425; Renaissance 1425–1600; Baroque 1600–1750; Classical 1750–1825; Romantic 1820–80; Post-Romantic 1880–1910; Modern since 1910; some historians also identify a Nationalist epoch 1860–1910 and an Impressionist epoch 1890–1920.

musique concrète Music composed by manipulating recorded sounds, especially natural sounds rather than electronic.

National Gallery Recitals During the Second World War Dame Myra Hess founded and directed a series of lunchtime recitals, which became very popular and helped to sustain morale.

New Symphony Orchestra London orchestra founded by Sir Thomas Beecham in 1905 and became Royal Albert Hall Orchestra in 1920 and later disbanded.

New York Philharmonic Orchestra Oldest US symphony orchestra, founded in 1842 as Philharmonic Society of New York; merged with New York Symphony Orchestra in 1928 to become Philharmonic Symphony Society of New York; now known as the NYPO.

nocturne Night-piece, serenade.

notes of the scale: English to Italian A=la, B=si, C=do, D=re, E=mi, F=fa, G=sol.

octet A group of 8 musicians, or a piece of music written for such a group. A string octet is usually a double string quartet.

opus (work) Opus numbers are used to designate the order in which a given composer's works were written or published.

oratorio Musical setting for voices and orchestra of a text based on the Scriptures or an epic theme. Could be described as an opera without staging, scenery or costumes.

Parthenia   Title of the first book of keyboard music printed in England (1611), collecting pieces by William Byrd, John Bull and Orlando Gibbons.

pastorale   Either a musical play based on a rustic subject, or a composition with rustic overtones.

Performing Right Society   Association of composers, authors, and music publishers founded in Britain in 1914 to collect royalties for non-dramatic public performance and broadcasting of members' works.

Philharmonia Orchestra   English symphony orchestra founded in 1945 by Walter Legge.

piano quartet   Piano, violin, viola and cello.

piano quintet   Usually string quartet plus piano.

piano trio   Piano, violin, and cello.

Pictures at an Exhibition   Mussorgsky's versions in music of 10 pictures displayed at a memorial exhibition for Russian artist Victor Hartmann: 1) *The Gnome*; 2) *The Old Castle*; 3) *Tuileries*; 4) *Bydlo* (a farm cart); 5) *Unhatched Chickens*; 6) *Samuel Goldenberg and Shmuyle*; 7) *Market-Place at Limoges*; 8) *Catacombs*; 9) *Baba-Yaga (The Hut on Fowl's Legs)*; 10) *The Great Gate of Kiev*.

Pierrot Players   Instrument ensemble founded in 1967 by Maxwell Davies and Harrison Birtwistle, regrouped to form the Fires of London in 1970 before disbanding in 1987.

Pomp and Circumstance   Elgar's title (taken from Act 3 of *Othello*) for his set of five marches for symphony orchestra, the first of which was the basis for 'Land of Hope and Glory' (words by A.C. Benson).

Pre-classical   Term applied to composers such as C.P.E. Bach who are considered to be later than baroque and leading to the 'Classical' style of Haydn and Mozart.

Promenade Concerts   Although promenade concerts (at which listeners could saunter around) were put on in London as early as 1838, it was not until 1895 that they became a regular annual feature when Robert Newman began a series at Queen's Hall with Henry Wood as conductor. Wood's name became synonymous with the Proms, and after his death in 1944, Malcolm Sargent became principal conductor (1948–67). Royal Albert Hall became venue in 1941 on the destruction of Queen's Hall.

Proms: centenary   1995; Harrison Birtwistle composed *Panic*.

Proms: last four directors   Sir William Glock, Robert Ponsonby, Sir John Drummond and, the present incumbent, Nicholas Kenyon.

Queen's Hall   Once London's chief concert hall, situated in Langham Place, opened in 1893 and destroyed by fire in 1941.

rāga   Indian musical form that represents a mood, concept or occasion by one of many patterns of notes presented as an ascending and descending scale used as a basis for improvisation.

Ring Cycle   Full title *Der Ring des Nibelungen* (*The Ring of the Nibelung*). Often referred to as the tetralogy although Wagner himself called the first opera, *Das Rheingold*, the prologue. After it comes *Die Walküre* (*The Valkyrie*), followed by *Siegfried* and finally, *Götterdämmerung* (*Twilight of the Gods*).

Royal Academy of Music   Founded in London in 1822 and situated in Tenterden Street but moved to Marylebone Road in 1912. The RAM has about 700 students and 150 staff.

Royal College of Music   Founded in 1882 but moved to its present site at Prince Consort Road, South Kensington in 1894.

Royal Philharmonic Orchestra   Founded in 1946 by Sir Thomas Beecham, who was principal conductor until his death in 1961.

St Louis Symphony Orchestra   Founded in March 1881, the second oldest symphony orchestra in the USA.

Scottish Chamber Orchestra   Founded in 1974 with headquarters in Queen's Hall, Edinburgh.

secular music   Any music that is not sacred music.

septet   Make-up varies, but typical format would be violin, viola, French horn, clarinet, bassoon, cello and double bass.

sextet   Group of 6 musicians; a string sextet usually two each of violins, violas and cellos.

sonata   Instrumental composition usually in three or four movements for unaccompanied piano or, more rarely, for another stringed instrument with piano accompaniment.

stanza   One of a number of sections of a song, two or more lines long, characterized by a common metre, rhyme and number of lines.

string quartet   Violins (1st and 2nd), viola and cello.

string quintet   String quartet with added viola or cello.

string trio   Violin, viola and cello.

Sturm und Drang (Storm and Stress)   Term applied to a period (*c.*1760–80) of great emotional intensity in German literature and music. Musically, it is particularly associated with F. J. Haydn's works around the time of his Symphonies 40–59.

Suite bergamasque   Piano suite by Debussy, its 4 movements: *Prélude*, *Menuet*, *Clair de Lune*, and *Passepied*.

symphonic structure   In the Classical model, 4 movements: 1) a fast sonata; 2) a slow movement; 3) a minuet scherzo; 4) a fast movement, mostly a rondo.

Tchaikovsky Piano Competition   Quadrennial competition first held in Moscow in 1954. Famous winners include Van Cliburn, John Ogdon, Vladimir Ashkenazy.

Three Bs   Bach, Beethoven, Brahms (term coined by Hans von Bülow).

Three Choirs Festival   Annual meeting that rotates among the 3 cathedral choirs of Gloucester, Hereford and Worcester, held almost continuous since the early 18th century.

tonic sol-fa   System of sight-singing and notation devised by Sarah Ann Glover in England in the 1840s, though much the same system had been introduced in the USA by D. Sower in 1832.

toy symphony   Term for a symphony in which toy instruments are used as well as strings and piano; the most popular example is a work by Leopold Mozart, with toy instruments now thought to have been added by Michael Haydn.

train wreck   Colloquial term for what happens when the parts in an ensemble collide because the musicians are not playing together.

The Triumphs of Oriana   Collection of 5- and 6-part English madrigals by 24 composers assembled by Thomas Morley in 1601 in honour of Elizabeth I.

trumpet voluntary   Piece that imitates a trumpet but is, in fact, played using a similar sounding organ stop. The best known version is a transcription by Henry Wood of a piece originally ascribed to Purcell but now credited to Jeremiah Clarke. He called it 'The Prince of Denmark's March', but Wood's title has superseded Clarke's.

M
U
S
I
C

C
L
A
S
S
I
C
A
L

Tuning of Strings   Cello: C, G, D, A (octave lower than the viola). Violin: G, D, A, E. Double-bass: E, A, D, G. Banjo: 4 strings C, G, D, A; 5 strings G, D, G, B, D. Viola: C, G, D, A (5th lower than violin).

Tweedledum and Tweedledee   Name coined by John Byrom (1692–1763) to satirize the public feuding between composers G. F. Handel and G. Bononcini.

violinists: known for revealing garments   Vanessa Mae, Anne-Sophie Mutter, Linda Lampenius.

Wagner's patron   Ludwig II, King of Bavaria (1845–86).

The Walk to the Paradise Garden   Intermezzo before concluding scene of Delius's opera *A Village Romeo and Juliet*. The Paradise Garden is actually a public house.

Wedding March   Played at the end of Act 4 of Mendelssohn's *Midsummer Night's Dream* and traditionally used on exit from the church. The Bridal Chorus from *Lohengrin* commonly announces the entry.

Wigmore Hall   London concert hall in Wigmore Street, opened in 1901 as Bechstein Hall.

WoO   Werk ohne Op. zahl (work without opus number): system of catalogue numbers used to identify composer's works that lack opus numbers.

woodwind quintet   Usually flute, clarinet, oboe, French horn and bassoon.

Musical Instruments

accordion   Invented by Friedrich Buschmann of Berlin in 1822.

Aeolian harp   Box and strings that sound when hit by a current of air.

aeolina   Mouth organ.

angelica   Instrument of the lute family with 16 or 17 strings.

arpeggione   Six-stringed cello invented by G. Staufer of Vienna in 1823. Aka *guitare d'amour*.

aulos   Double-reed wind instrument of ancient Greece.

autoharp   Zither on which chord keys are pressed by one hand and strings strummed by the other.

Bach trumpet   Valveless trumpet in either C or D.

backfall   Part of an organ that connects the rods to the keyboard.

bagpipes   Ancient instrument popular throughout the world but particularly identified with Scotland. The Scottish Highland bagpipe has two tenor drones and a bass drone, tuned an octave apart. The chanter is the pipes that plays the tune. Versions of the bagpipe around the world include the Bulgarian *gaida*, the *cornemuse* of France and Belgium, the *gaita* of northwestern Spain and the Irish Uilleann pipes.

balalaika   Russian three-stringed instrument of the lute family with a triangular belly and moveable frets on the arm. The balalaika was developed in the 18th century from the *domra*.

bamboula   West Indian tambourine.

bandoneon   Argentinian variant of the accordian.

baritone horn   Brass instrument in B flat, related to the euphonium with a smaller bore and 3 valves.

baryton   Stringed instrument similar to viola da gamba but with sympathetic strings. Played by Prince Esterházy (Haydn's patron); it has made a revival in recent years.

Basque drum   Tambourine.

bassanello   Shawm-like woodwind instrument, no longer played.

bassoon   Bass member of the double-reed oboe family, pitched in C.

bell lyra   Type of portable glockenspiel.

bissex   Twelve-string guitar invented in 1770 by Vanhecke.

bodhran   Irish frame drum played with a double-ended stick.

bombard   Alto-pitched shawm.

bombardon   Form of bass tuba with 3 piston valves.

boobams   Percussion instrument using a varying number of bamboo tubes.

bottleneck   Tube that fits over a finger on the fretting hand used for slide-guitar playing.

bouzouki   Greek fretted string instrument with a long neck and 4 sets of strings.

cabaca/cabasa   Latin American percussion instrument, around or pear-shaped gourd covered with beads and fitted with a handle.

calliope   Literally meaning 'beautiful-voiced' after the Muse of epic poetry; US name for a steam-driven organ.

campanelle   Glockenspiel.

canale   Psaltery.

canntaireachd   Ancient Highland bagpipe notation, using syllables to represent a group of notes.

carillon   Alternative name for glockenspiel, so called by Handel in 1739 when he first used the instrument in *Saul*.

castanets   Twin cup-shaped clappers; name derives from the Spanish *castaña*, chestnut wood.

celesta   Small keyboard instrument patented by Auguste Mustel in 1886 and famously used in Tchaikovsky's 'Dance of the Sugar Plum Fairy'.

cello: full name   Violoncello.

cembalo   Short for clavicembalo, the Italian word for harpsichord.

cetera   Zither.

chalumeau   Forerunner of the clarinet with 6 to 8 finger-holes.

chanterelle   The E string on a violin, or the highest string on any instrument in the violin or lute family.

charivari   Cacophonous, extemporized music produced with any household utensil or object that will make a noise.

chitarrone   Lute similar to a theorbo but longer.

choke cymbal: aka   High-hat cymbal.

chromatic harp   Harp built by Pleyel in 1897; equipped with a string for every semitone, it needed no pedals.

cimbalom   Form of dulcimer native to Hungary, made up of a box on which strings are hit with mallets.

cittern   A 15th-century forerunner of the lute with metal strings tuned in pairs and plucked.

clapper   Striker in the middle of a bell.

clarinet   Single-reed woodwind instrument developed by JC Denner of Nuremberg in the late 17th century.

clàrsach   Ancient small Celtic harp having brass strings instead of gut or nylon ones.

clavecin   Harpsichord.

claves   Cuban percussion instruments consisting of round wooden sticks that are stuck together.

clavichord/clarichord   Small keyboard instrument invented in 14th century. Aka manichord or chekker.

colascione   European version of oriental long-necked lute popular in the Tudor period.

colophony   Bow rosin (named after Colophon in Asia Minor, the source of the best rosin).

concertina   Invented by Charles Wheatstone in 1829 as the 'Symphonium'. Similar to accordion but no keyboard.

console   Part of organ by which the musician operates the instrument.

cor Anglais   French for English horn, but in fact an alto oboe; invented by Ferlandis of Bergamo.

cor de chasse   Hunting horn developed in France in 17th century.

cornopean   Late 19th-century brass instrument similar to a trumpet.

crembalum   Type of Jew's harp.

crook   Tube inserted into a brass instrument to lengthen its tube and change its pitch.

crotales   Ancient Greek percussion instrument in form of a rattle or clapper.

crumhorn   Early and widely used Renaissance double-reed instrument. Name means 'curved horn'.

crwth   Welsh medieval instrument with 6 strings, a bowed lyre.

cuckoo   Two-note wind instrument imitating the bird.

damper   Felt piece that damps the vibration of the string on a piano until the key is depressed.

didjeridu (didgeridoo)   Native Australian wind instrument, which allows player to breathe through nose while playing.

digitorium   Small keyboard machine usually having 5 keys, which are sprung more severely than usual so as to strengthen fingers. Invented by Myer Marks in the mid-19th century.

domra   Type of early balalaika with a round body and two or three metal strings tuned a fourth apart.

double bass: aka   Bull-fiddle, doghouse.

Dudelsack   German form of bagpipe.

dulcimer   Ancient instrument with wire strings stretching over a shallow box which are struck with rods.

dulcitone   Instrument similar to celesta but with steel tuning forks instead of steel plates.

duplex-coupler piano   Invented by Emanuel Moór in 1921; has 2 keyboards, upper tuned an octave higher.

electronde   Electronic instrument invented by Martin Taubman in 1933, like the theramin but can create staccato effect.

embouchure   Mouthpiece of a brass instrument.

emicon   Electric instrument invented in USA in 1931 and producing notes from air in graded chromatic scale.

English flute: aka   Recorder.

English horn   Alto oboe, pitched a 5th lower and having a conical shape and bulbous bell.

euphonium   Tenor tuba in B flat. Also name of instrument made of glass plates and rods by Ernst Chladni in 1790.

fagotto   Bassoon.

fipple   Mouthpiece for all wind instruments.

flageolet   Small type of recorder.

flexatone   Patented in 1922 and consisting of a flexible metal sheet suspended in a wire frame with handle. Shaking produces a tremolo sound.

flugelhorn   Brass instrument in the cornet family but with a wider bore and larger bell.

flûte à bec (beak flute)   Type of recorder.

French harp   Harmonica.

French horn   Coiled brass wind intrument extending to 11ft when uncoiled with a bell of 14in diameter. Early form supposedly introduced to the orchestra by Lully; modern form uses valves introduced in the 1820s.

frog   On bowed instruments, the end of the bow that is held in the hand. Aka nut.

Geigenwerk   Type of hurdy-gurdy invented in Nurumberg in 1575 by Hans Haiden.

gekkin   Japanese instrument with circular body like banjo but with 9 frets and 4 strings tuned in pairs.

gemshorn   Type of flute made of horn, not used since 16th century. Aka chamois horn.

gittern   Medieval ancestor of guitar.

glochenspiel   (lit. bell play) Musical instrument consisting of hanging metal bars, which are struck with a hammer.

gong   Ancient percussion instrument first found in China, a metal disc generally with upturned edges, usually with indefinite pitch but sometimes tuned.

grelots   Little bells, e.g. sleigh bells, used as percussion.

gusla   One-stringed bowed instrument long popular in Slavonic cultures.

gusli   Ancient Russian instrument of the zither family.

harmonica   Mouth organ with metal reeds, first produced by Friedrich Buschman of Berlin in 1821 as the 'Mundäoline'. The two main types of harmonicas are the chromatic and the diatonic. The chromatic harmonica is preffered by blues players such as Bob Dylan and Neil Young. The diatonic harmonica has a wider range and more suited to the virtuoso such as Larry Adler.

harmonium   Small portable reed organ perfected by Alexandre Debain of Paris in the early 1840s.

harp   Forty-seven-stringed instrument whose modern orchestral version with a pedal mechanism was developed by Sébastien Érard.

harpsicord   Wing-shaped keyboard instrument in which the strings are mechanically plucked rather that struck with a hammer.

hautbois   French name for oboe, (lit. 'high wood').

Hawaiian guitar   Ukulele (also nickname of steel guitar) introduced by the Portuguese.

heckelphone   Double-reed, baritone oboe with a conical bore and bulbous bell.

helicon   Tuba with a circular construction that can be wrapped around the body for marching bands.

hellertion   Electric instrument developed in Frankfurt in 1936 by Bruno Helberger and Peter Lertes, similar to Theremin but with a range of 6 octaves.

hitschiriki   Japanese instrument like a bamboo flute with 7 finger-holes and 2 thumb-holes.

hityokin   Japanese vertical flute made of bamboo.

hornpipe   Wind instrument with a single reed and a cow's horn fitted on the end.

hummel   Swedish zither.

hurdy-gurdy   Medieval instrument resembling a viol but whose sound is produced by friction of hand-cranked wooden wheel on strings that could be stopped by keys.

huruk   Hourglass-shaped Indian drum.

hydraulis Ancient instrument, aka water organ, supposedly invented in Greece by Ktesibios in the 3rd century BC.

idiophone Term used for instrument whose own material makes a characteristic sound such as castanets, gongs, bells, etc.

Irish harp Small harp played while held in the lap.

Japanese fiddle One-stringed instrument played by street performers.

Jew's harp Folk instrument consisting of a metal frame that contains a flexible strip of metal. The frame is held between the player's teeth while the metal strip is twanged.

kazoo Short tube open at both ends, with a vibrating membrane in between, played by humming into it; a kind of mirliton.

kin Japanese string instrument, a small koto.

kithara Ancient but sophisticated Greek lyre, which is finger plucked.

klavier Keyboard instrument (with strings).

knollhorn Soft-sounding herald horn from the mid-western region of the US.

Korean temple block Oriental addition to the 20th-century dance-band drummer's equipment, constituting a skull-shaped hollow block of wood, in several sizes, and struck with a drumstick.

koto Japanese instrument resembling a zither, with 7 to 13 silk strings plucked by the fingers.

lira A 16th-century string instrument with drones, played with a bow.

loure French bagpipe.

lute Ancient musical instrument with a pear-shaped belly and a long, fretted fingerboard and played like a modern guitar.

lutherie The art of making string instruments – not only lutes, but also guitars and the violin family.

luthier One who practises lutherie.

lyra (lyre) Ancient Greek instrument with a 4-sided frame, encompassing strings attached from a soundbox to a crossbar. Played like a harp.

machete Portuguese 4-string folk guitar.

mandocello Bass mandolin.

mandola/mandora Small, early precursor of the lute and mandolin with 9 frets and up to 6 strings.

mandolin Instrument in the lute family, fretted and with 8 wire strings tuned in four pairs, G, D, A, E.

maracas Latin American percussion instrument consisting of two seed-filled gourds, which are shaken by handles.

mardakion Accordion-like instrument from the mid-west US.

marimba African percussion instrument introduced to Latin America, a deeper pitched version of the xylophone with metal resonators.

m'bira African 'thumb piano' made up of a number of metal or cane tongues held in position with a bar attached to a box or board. The free ends are twanged with the thumbs.

mellophone Variation of the French horn constructed for marching.

melodeon Related to the concertina, with 10 treble keys on the right, bellows and 4 bass keys on the left.

metallophone Percussion instrument consisting of tuned metal bars arranged in single or double rows.

mirliton Instrument containing a membrane to modify a sound made when the player hums or sings into or against it.

monochord Musical instrument with one string, used for determining the ratios of musical intervals.

Moog synthesizer Earliest commercial, voltage-controlled synthesizer, invented by Robert Moog in 1965.

mouth organ The term covers many instruments with metal reeds but nowadays is synonymous with the harmonica.

musetta Bellows-operated French bagpipe popular in the court of Louis XIV.

mute Device usually conical in shape, that muffles a brass instrument's sound.

nightingale Toy instrument used in by Scarlatti in an oratorio by Scarlatti and by Leopold Mozart in his *Toy Symphony*.

nose flute Originating in Polynesia, a bamboo flute blown through the nostrils.

nut On bowed instruments, device fitted on to the end of the bow that is held in the hand, and used to adjust the bow's tension.

oboe Double-reed woodwind instrument with a conical bore in C and a natural scale of D.

oboe d'amore Slightly bigger than the normal oboe, with a pear-shaped bell, and pitched a minor third lower.

ocarina (little goose) Small, round, wind instrument with finger holes, and made out of clay or porcelain; so named by Giuseppe Donati in mid-1800s; aka sweet potato.

oliphant Small medieval horn made from an elephant's tusk.

ondes Martenot Electronic keyboard instrument developed by Maurice Martenot in the 1920s; shaped like a spinet.

ophicleide Large, brass, keyed bass bugle played in the upright position, developed from the serpent (name is Greek for 'serpent with keys') but displaced by the bass tuba.

panharmonicon Mechanical orchestra invented by Johann Maelzel in 1805; inspiration of Beethoven's *Battle Symphony*.

panpipes (aka syrinx) Ancient wind instrument consisting of several pipes of graduated lengths bound together.

pegbox Box at the end of the neck on string instruments into which the pegs that adjust the strings are inserted.

phagotum Type of bellows-blown bagpipe invented by Canon Afranio of Ferrara in the early 1500s.

pianoforte Full name of the piano, with 88 keys, first made in Florence around 1700 by Bartolomeo Cristofori; name is Italian for soft-loud.

pianola Player piano manufactured in the early 1900s by the Aeolian Corporation; the first of the kind was the Welte-Mignon.

piccolo Small flute that sounds an octave higher than written (piccolo in C) or, less often, a minor ninth higher than written (piccolo in D flat).

point Tip of the bow of a string instrument.

poliphant Thirty-seven-stringed instrument of early 17th century; a cross between harp, lute and theorbo.

posthorn Cylindrical, valveless straight horn used by coachmen and mailcarriers to announce arrival.

psaltery Ancient string instrument, similar to the dulcimer.

purfling Decorative strip inlaid around the edges of a string instrument.

pyiba Pear-shaped, four-stringed, ancient Chinese lute.

racket Double-reed instrument consisting of short, thick cylinder of wood drilled along its length with a bore-holes connected into a single air channel.

raspa Cuban percussion instrument made out of gourd with notches that are scraped with a stick.

ratamacue Drum rudiment consisting of an alternating-hand sticking pattern.

ratchet/rattle Percussion instrument with a cogwheel that strikes one or more metal or wooden projections when twirled.

rebab An ancient North African and Middle Eastern short-necked fiddle with two strings.

rebec Small, pear-shaped, medieval bowed instrument, a development of the Arab rebab, with a short neck and three to five strings.

recorder End-blown wooden flute without keys, with a tapering bore.

reed(s) Clarinet is a single-reed instrument; oboe and bassoon are double-reed.

regal Portable reed organ of the 16th century.

Rhodes piano Electric piano developed by Harold Rhodes.

rhythmicon Keyboard percussion instrument using photoelectric cell and devised by Lev Theremin and Henry Cowell in 1931.

rosin Block of hardened tree resin that is rubbed across the bow hairs to enhance the friction.

rote (rotta) Lyre-type instrument from the Middle Ages.

sackbut Renaissance name for the slide trombone, which then had a smaller bell and narrower bore.

saddle On guitar, a thin strip of ivory, bone or plastic set into the bridge.

saltbox Charivari instrument used by flipping the lid and beating the side with a rolling pin or spoon.

samisen Flat-backed, long-necked lute from Japan with a skin-covered belly and three silk strings.

sarangi Northern Indian fiddle with short, thick neck and 3 to 4 bowed strings plus sympathetic strings.

sarod Indian instrument usually having 6 main strings and 12 to 15 sympathetic strings.

sarrusophone Double-reed woodwind instrument related to the oboe but made of brass, invented by French bandleader Sarrus in 1856.

saxophone Single-reed family of instruments, usually metal but sometimes plastic, invented by Adolphe Sax around 1840 and patented in 1846.

scordatura Changing the tuning of one or more strings from their standard pitch.

scroll Ornamental curled portion at the end of the pegbox on instruments of the violin family.

Scruggs picking Banjo finger-picking style developed by Earl Scruggs, using the thumb and two fingers.

serpent S-curved wooden horn with a conical bore, finger holes and a cup-shaped mouthpiece.

seven-string guitar Has an extra, high A string.

shakuhachi End-blown bamboo flute from Japan.

shawm Family of high-pitched, double-reed woodwind instruments of the Middle Ages; precursors of the oboe.

sheng Chinese mouth organ made up of wind chamber fitted with pipes with reeds that vibrate.

shofar Ancient Hebrew ceremonial wind instrument made of a ram's horn.

simandl bow For string basses; a bow configured to be held with the palm up.

sistrum Ancient percussion instrument made up of metal disc rattles threaded on rods.

sitar Long-necked Indian lute with moveable arched frets, a gourd resonator close to the pegboard, and 3 to 7 strings, below which are sympathetic strings, often as many as 12. Made popular in the West by Ravi Shankar.

skirl On bagpipe, the sounds made by the upper pipes.

sousaphone Tuba that encircles the body and made specifically for John Philip Sousa's band.

spinet Small Renaissance keyboard instrument with a plucking action like a harpsichord.

steel drums Made out of various-sized oil drums, with deeply incised patterns with different pitches.

stick chapman Electric 10-stringed (5 bass and 5 guitar) instrument that utilizes tapping technique on strings.

swell Mechanical device on some keyboard instruments for adjusting the volume of sound.

switch Percussion instrument, made up of wires bound at one end, that is struck against the hand.

sympathetic string String that vibrates in an instrument without being plucked in response to the vibrations of strings that are plucked, or to a percussion impact.

tablas Asymmetrical pair of conical, tuned, wooden Indian drums, beaten with the hands.

tabor Earliest form of the snare drum, which evolved into a military instrument.

talon The nut end of the bow used to play string instruments.

tambour Type of drum.

tambourine Percussion instrument of Arab origin consisting of a small, shallow, circular drum with metal discs inserted into its frame. The discs are known as jingles.

tambur(a) Long-necked, round-bodied lute. Indian tamburas have 4 strings, drones and a moveable ivory bridge to adjust pitch; Balkan tamburas are fretted.

tam-tam Large, flat, thin metal saucer suspended on a frame and struck with a soft beater.

theorbo Sixteenth-century arch-lute with numerous stopped and unstopped strings attached to separate pegbox.

Theremin Electronic instrument developed by Lev Theremin (1920); the hands do not touch the instrument but produce oscillations when they move around the antenna.

ti tzu Chinese flute with 6 finger-holes and a 7th hole covered with thin membrane whose vibration dictates the tone.

timbrel Ancient Middle Eastern tambourine, and its medieval European descendant.

tin whistle High-pitched, end-blown Irish flute with 6 holes, made out of metal.

tonette Wood or plastic end-blown flute with finger-holes.

tremolo arm Device that changes the pitch of the strings by moving the bridge with a type of spring action.

trombone Brass instrument, larger than a trumpet, and with a sliding tube to extend notes.

trumpet Brass wind instrument consisting of a long tubular central piece with a cup-shaped mouth-piece and wide, bell-shaped base. A trumpet has three valves.

tuba Bass instrument patented by W. Wieprecht and Moritz in Berlin (1835).

MUSIC CLASSICAL

tubular bells Percussion instrument in the form of suspended tubes, tuned to the diatonic scale, and struck with a hammer.

tuning-fork Two-pronged metal instrument invented in 1711 by the trumpeter John Shore. The pure tone that it emits when set vibrating helps to give the pitch to singers or instruments.

uilleann pipes Irish bagpipes worked by bellows held under one arm.

ukelele (ukulele) Four-stringed instrument developed in Hawaii in the 1870s from a kind of Portugese guitar

upright piano Piano in which strings are vertical. John Isaac Hawkins of Philadelphia first built iron-framed uprights in 1800.

vibraphone (vibes) Xylophone with metal bars and a wide vibrato effect produced by electrically operated fans.

vihuela Six-string Spanish instrument of the 1600s that looks like a guitar but is tuned as a lute.

vina Indian stringed instrument, those from northern India having a long stick-like unfretted fingerboard resting on two resonating gourds, those from southern India having a much broader fingerboard and a wooden body in place of one of the gourds.

viola da braccio Tenor viol played under the arm.

viola da gamba Bass viol played between the knees.

viola d'amore Unfretted tenor instrument with 7 strings and 7 to 14 sympathetic strings.

violin Treble stringed instrument with 4 strings tuned to G, D, A, E.

violoncello Tenor stringed instrument of the violin family, played between the knees, using bass clef, with 4 strings tuned to C, G, D, A.

virginal Small, soft-sounding harpsichord of the 16th and 17th centuries, with one string to a note.

Wagner tuba Invented by Richard Wagner specifically for his *Ring Cycle*; look is more of a horn than a tuba.

whammy bar Another name for tremolo arm.

woodwind Recorders, flutes, clarinets, saxophones, oboes, piccolos, cor anglais and bassoons (lowest pitch).

xylophone (lit. wood sound) Percussion instrument consisting of graduated, tuned wooden bars played by being struck with a hammer.

xylorimba Combination of xylophone and marimba.

zither Family of plucked string instruments including the dulcimer, hummel, koto, autoharp and psaltery, where the (up to 45) strings run the entire length of a flat body.

Famous Musicians

Bassoonists
Archie Camden
John Hebden
D. Kern Holoman
Jacques Hotteterre
Edwin James
John Lampe
William Waterhouse

Cellists
Hugo Becker
Luigi Boccherini
Pablo Casals
Gaspar Cassadó
Mischel Cherniavsky
Myung-Wha Chung
Robert Cohen
Karl Davidoff
Jean Louis Dufort
Jean Pierre Dufort
Jacqueline Du Pré
Maurice Eisenberg
Emanuel Feuermann
Amaryllis Fleming
Pierre Fournier
Auguste Franchomme
Carl Fuchs
Karine Georgian
Georg Goltermann
Bernard Greenhouse
Natalia Gutman
Lynn Harrell
Beatrice Harrison
Nicola Haym
John Hebden
Thomas Igloi
Steven Isserlis
Giuseppe Maria
  Jacchini

Ivor James
Antonio Janigro
Hans Kindler
Ralph Kirshbaum
Anton Kraft
Nicolaus Kraft
Robert Lindley
Julian Lloyd Webber
Martin Lovett
Antonio Lysy
Yo-Yo Ma
Enrico Mainardi
Mischa Maisky
António Meneses
Howard Mitchell
May Mukle
André Navarra
Charles Neate
Zara Nelsova
Arto Noras
Vladimir Orloff
Siegfried Palm
Stephen Paxton
Boris
  Pergamenschikov
Gregor Piatigorsky
Alfredo Piatti
Anthony Pini
William Pleeth
David Popper
Julius Rietz
Bernhard Romberg
Leonard Rose
Mstislav Rostropovich
Milos Sádlo
Felix Salmond
Samuil Samosud
Heinrich Schiff
Johann Schlick

Georg Schnéevoigt
Mátyás Seiber
Adrien François Servais
Raphael Sommer
William Henry Squire
János Starker
Guilhermina Suggia
Paul Tortelier
Yan Pascal Tortelier
Arturo Toscanini
Christopher Van
  Kampen
Alfred Wallenstein
Raphael Wallfisch
Moray Welsh
August Wenzinger
Hanus Wihan

Clarinettists
John Adams
Heinrich Bärmann
Jack Brymer
Louis Cahuzac
Benny Goodman
Woody Herman
Janet Hilton
Emma Johnson
Reginald Kell
Thea King
Hyacinth Klosé
Henry Lewis
Richard Mühlfeld
Gervase de Peyer
Artie Shaw
Anton Stadler
Richard Stolzman
Morton Subotnick
Frederick Thurston
Bernard Walton

Double Bass
Giovanni Bottesini
Ida Carroll
Eugene Cruft
Domenico Dragonetti
Barry Guy
Gary Karr
Franz Kotzwara
Serge Koussevitzky

Flautists
Richard Adeney
Bruno Bartoletti
Michel Blavet
Theobald Boehm
Giulio Briccialdi
Franz Doppler
Karl Doppler
Louis François Fleury
James Galway
Severino Gazzelloni
Geoffrey Gilbert
Dave Heath
Hans-Joachim
  Koellreutter
Hans-Martin Linde
Johann Bernhard
  Logier
Edward McGuire
Susan Milan
Gareth Morris
Marcel Moyse
Aurèle Nicolet
Johann Quantz
Jean-Pierre Rampal
Elaine Shaffer
Fritz Spiegl
Adolf Terschak
David Van Vactor

French Horn
Hermann Baumann
Aubrey Brain
Dennis Brain
Alan Civil
Anthony Halstead
David Pyatt
Barry Tuckwell

Guitarists
Julian Bream
Leo Brouwer
Cornelius Cardew
Ferdinando Carulli
Mauro Giuliani
Miguel Llobet
Carlos Montoya
Gaspar Sanz
Andrés Segovia
Philip Selby
Fernando Sor
Francisco Tárrega
Jason Vieaux
John Williams
Narciso Yepes

Harpists
Osian Ellis
Félix Godefroid
Marie Goossens
Sidonie Goossens
Alphonse Hasselmans
Ursula Holliger
Alfred Holý
Maria Korchinska
Johann Krumpholtz
François Naderman
Elias Parish-Alvars
John Parry
Nansi Richards
Marisa Robles
Carlos Salzédo
Marcel Tournier
Nicanor Zabaleta

Horns
David Amram
Johannes Amon
Adolph Borsdorf
Alan Civil
Louis-François Dauprat
John Denison
Heinrich Domnich
Anton Joseph Hampel
Maurice Handford
Ifor James
Ignaz Leutgeb
Giovanni Punto
Timothy Reynish
Franz Joseph Strauss
Barry Tuckwell

Mouth Organists
Larry Adler
Tommy Reilly

Oboists
Evelyn Barbirolli (née
  Rothwell)
Neil Black
Janet Craxton
John Cruft

Johann Fischer
Leon Goossens
Heinz Holliger
John Lancie
Ludwig August Lebrun
Charles Mackerras
Jean-Claude Malgoire
Friedrich Ramm
Ray Still
Edo de Waart

Organists
Herbert Andrews
Jennifer Bate
Jonathan Battishill
William Best
E. Power Biggs
John Birch
John Blitheman
John Blow
Léon Boëllmann
Georg Böhm
Kevin Bowyer
John Dykes Bower
Ernest Bullock
Charles Burney
John Camidge
Matthew Camidge
Thomas Camidge
Melville Cook
George Cunningham
Carlo Curley
John Danby
Thurston Dart
Christopher Dearnley
William Done
Maurice Dupré
Hermann Finck
Grattan Flood
Virgil Fox
Alfred Gaul
Nicolas Gigault
Eugène Gigout
Johann Goldberg
John Goss
Alan Gray
Nicolas de Grigny
Douglas Guest
George Guest
Christopher Herrick
Edward Hopkins
Karl Friedrich Horn
Francis Jackson
Geraint Jones
Johann Kerll
Jacob Kirckman
Leonhard Kleber
Carlmann Kolb
Johann Krebs
Jean Langlais
Philip Ledger
Edwin Lemare
Henry Ley
Gaston Litaize
Charles Lloyd
Vincent Lübeck
David Lumsden
André Marchal
Louis Marchand
Giovanni Martini
Olivier Messiaen
Georg Monn

James Nares
Edward Naylor
Martin Neary
Sydney Nicholson
Thomas Noble
Vincent Novello
Herbert Oakeley
Boris Ord
Johann Pachelbel
Jane Parker-Smith
Peter Pears
Simon Preston
Daniel Purcell
Henry Purcell
James Pyne
Helmuth Rilling
Edward Rimbault
Alec Robertson
Douglas Robinson
Lionel Rogg
Cyril Rootham
Barry Rose
Bernard Rose
Francisco de Salinas
Sir Malcolm Sargent
Heinrich Scheidemann
Samuel Scheidt
Albert Schweitzer
John Scott
George Sinclair
Johann Staden
Paul Steinitz
Leopold Stokowski
Karl Straube
Herbert Sumsion
Richard Terry
George Thalben-Ball
David Titterington
Thomas Trotter
David Tudor
Franz Tunder
Denis Vaughan
Louis Vierne
Helmut Walcha
William Walond
Henry Watson
Gillian Weir
Charles Wesley
Allan Wicks
Charles-Marie Widor
David Willcocks
Charles Lee Williams
Malcolm Williamson
Arthur Wills
Philipp Wolfrum
Leslie Woodgate
Henry Wood
Pietro Alessandro Yon
Pietro Ziani

Percussionists
James Blades
Evelyn Glennie
Stomu Yamastita

Pianists
Jacques Abram
Joaquin Achucarro
Thomas Ades
Daniel Adni
Roy Agnew
Martha Argerich

Vladimir Ashkenazy
Stefan Askenase
Victor Babin
Gina Bachauer
Paul Badura-Skoda
Daniel Barenboim
Hans Barth
Ethel Bartlett
Harold Bauer
Malcolm Bilson
Christian Blackshaw
Marc Blitzstein
Michel Block
Susan Bradshaw
Alfred Brendel
Yefim Bronfman
Bruno Canino
Teresa Carreño
Jean Casadesus
Robert Marcel
  Casadesus
Shura Cherkassky
Aldo Ciccolini
Van Cliburn
Harriet Cohen
Elizabeth Coolidge
Imogen Cooper
Joseph Cooper
Alfred Cortot
Johann Cramer
Paul Crossley
Clifford Curzon
Karl Czerny
György Cziffra
Michel Dalberto
Edward Dannreuther
Bella Davidovich
Peter Donohoe
Ania Dorfmann
Barry Douglas
Karl Engel
John Field
Margaret Fingerhut
Rudolf Firkusny
Annie Fischer
Edwin Fischer
Leon Fleisher
Myers Foggin
Andor Foldes
Hubert Foss
Ian Fountain
Fou Ts'ong
Philip Fowke
Homero Francesch
Samson François
Peter Frankl
Justus Frantz
Géza Frid
Ignaz Friedman
Benjamin Frith
Liza Fuchsova
Ossip Gabrilowitsch
Irwin Gage
Andrei Gavrilov
Walter Gieseking
Emil Gilels
Arabella Goddard
Leopold Godowsky
Anthony Goldstone
Richard Goode
Glenn Gould
Gary Graffman

Percy Grainger
Arthur de Greef
Gordon Green
Horacio Gutiérrez
Monique Haas
Ingrid Haebler
Charles Hallé
Mark Hambourg
Paul Hamburger
Iain Hamilton
Clara Haskil
Claude Helffer
Clifton Helliwell
Myra Hess
Rolf Hind
Alfred Hipkins
Ludwig Hoffman
Vladimir Horowitz
Colin Horsley
Louis Horst
Mieczyslaw Horszowski
Stephen Hough
Andrew Imbrie
John Ireland
Edward Isaacs
Leonard Isaacs
Michael Isador
Martin Isepp
Eugene Istomin
Paul Jacobs
Byron Janis
Grant Johannesen
Graham Johnson
Eileen Joyce
Terence Judd
Jeffrey Kahane
Joseph Kalichstein
Friedrich Kalkbrenner
William Kapell
Jean-Rodolphe Kars
Julius Katchen
Peter Katin
Mindru Katz
Wilhelm Kempff
John Kirkpatrick
Evgeny Kissin
Bernhard Klee
Walter Klien
Karl Klindworth
Zoltán Kocsis
Alfons Kontarsky
Aloys Kontarsky
Lili Kraus
Katia Labèque
Marielle Labèque
Frederic Lamond
Alicia de Larrocha
Philip Ledger
Yvonne Lefébure
Theodor Leschetizky
Oscar Levant
Raymond Lewenthal
Hans Leygraf
Josef Lhévinne
Rosina Lhévinne
John Lill
Eugene List
Kathleen Long
Marguérite Long
Alessandro Longo
Yvonne Loriod
Radu Lupu

Moura Lympany
Alexei Lyubimov
Joanna McGregor
Witold Malcuzynski
Leopold Mannes
Tobias Matthay
Denis Matthews
Florence May
Fanny Mendelssohn
Hephzibah Menuhin
Frank Merrick
Noel Mewton-Wood
Nina Milkina
Benno Moiseiwitsch
Federico Mompou
David Money
Stephen Montague
Gerald Moore
Angus Morrison
Ignaz Moscheles
Charles Neate
Marc Neikrug
Ivor Newton
Joaquin Nin
David Owen Norris
Lev Oborin
Noriko Ogawa
John Ogdon
Garrick Ohlsson
Mercedes Olivera
Georges Onslow
Ursula Oppens
Rafael Orozco
Leslie Orrey
Cristina Ortiz
George Osborne
Cécile Ousset
Vladimir Ovchinikov
Vladimir de Pachmann
Ignacy Jan Paderewski
Kun Woo Paik
Maria von Paradis
  (blind)
Jon Kimura Parker
Eric Parkin
Geoffrey Parsons
Leonard Pennario
Murray Perahia
Vlado Perlemuter
Egon Petri
Nikolai Petrov
Isidor Philipp
Maria-João Pires
Johann Peter Pixis
Artur Pizarro
Barbara von Ployer
Ivo Pogorelich
Maurizio Pollini
Jean-Bernard Pommier
Viktoria Postnikova
Leff Pouishnoff
Ferdinand Praeger
André Previn
Stephen Pruslin
Gwenneth Pryor
Anne Queffélec
Ruth Railton
Thomas Rajna
Dezsö Ránki
Clarence Raybould
Julius Reubke
Robert Riefling

Ferdinand Ries
Bernard Roberts
Rae Robertson
Pascal Rogé
Michael Roll
Martin Roscoe
Charles Rosen
Moriz Rosenthal
Mstislav Rostropovich
Anton Rubinstein
Arthur Rubinstein
Nikolay Rubinstein
Mikhail Rudy
Christian Rummel
Walter Rummel
Harold Rutland
Vasily Safonov
Harold Samuel
György Sándor
Jesús Maria Sanromá
Vasily Sapellnikov
Sir Malcolm Sargent
Irene Scharrer
Xaver Scharwenka
Ernest Schelling
Heinrich Schenker
Andras Schiff
Allan Schiller
Artur Schnabel
Karl Ulrich Schnabel
Irina Schnittke
Clara Schumann
Phyllis Sellick
Yitkin Seow
Peter Serkin
Rudolf Serkin
Shulamith Shafir
William Shakespeare
Howard Shelley
Maxim Shostakovich
Béla Siki
Constantin Silvestri
Abbey Simon
Leonard Slatkin
Jan Smeterlin
Cyril Smith
Ronald Smith
Yonty Solomon
Georg Solti
Peter Stadlen
Bernhard Stavenhagen
Wilhelm Stenhammar
Ronald Stevenson
Soulima Stravinsky
Walter Susskind
Roberto Szidon
Carl Tausig
André Tchaikowsky
Boris Tchaikovsky
Alec Templeton
Sigismond Thalberg
Jean-Yves Thibaudet
Michael Tilson Thomas
Martino Tirimo
Donald Tovey
Valerie Tryon
Norman Tucker
David Tudor
Rosalyn Tureck
Mitsuko Uchida
Sergio Varella-Cid
Tamás Vásáry

Bálint Vazsonyi
Isabelle Vengerova
Adela Verne
Mathilde Verne
Roger Vignoles
Ricardo Viñes
Lucille Wallace
Peter Wallfisch
Fanny Waterman
Sydney Watson
André Watts
Daniel Wayenberg
Joseph Weingarten
Erik Werba
Jósef Wieniawski
Earl Wild
David Wilde
Malcolm Williamson
Paul Wittgenstein
Roger Woodward
Enloc Wu
Friedrich Wührer
Marie Wurm
Jürg Wyttenbach
Théophile Ysaye
Carlo Zecchi
Géza Zichy
Alexander Ziloti
Krystian Zimerman
Jan Zimmer
Agnes Zimmermann

Trumpeters
Maurice André
Malcolm Arnold
Ernest Hall
Håkan Hardenberger
Philip Jones
Humphrey Lyttelton
Johann Petzold
Gerard Schwarz
Crispian Steel-Perkins
Edward Tarr
John Wilbraham

Tuba
Eleazar de Carvalho

Violists
Yuri Bashmet
Paul Doktor
Watson Forbes
Rivka Golani
Karel Hába
Nobuko Imai
Allan Pettersson
Jean Pougnet
Frederick Riddle
Hermann Ritter
Peter Schidlof
Bernard Shore
Lionel Tertis
Walter Trampler
Efrem Zimbalist

Violinists
Joseph Achron
Delphin Alard
Pierre Amoyal
Jelly Arányi
Alexandre-Joseph Artôt
Thomas Baltzar

John Banister
Angel Barrios
Richard Barth
Yuri Bashmet
Rudolf Baumgartner
Hugh Bean
Paul Beard
Boris Belkin
Joshua Bell
Norbert Brainin
George Bridgetower
Adolph Brodsky
Ole Bull
Alfredo Campoli
John Carrodus
Marius Casadesus
Arthur Catterall
Levon Chilingiran
Kyung-Wha Chung
Raymond Cohen
Béla Dekany
Gioconda De Vito
Augustine Dumay
John Ella
Mischa Elman
Devy Erlih
Adila Fachiri
Carlo Farina
Alfonso Ferrabosco
Christian Ferras
Michael Festing
Carl Flesch
Giovanni Fontana
Zino Francescatti
Miriam Fried
Joseph Fuchs
Mayumi Fujikawa
Ivan Galamian
Saschko Gawriloff
André Gertler
Rivka Golani
Szymon Goldberg
Stephane Grappelli
Hyam Greenbaum
Sidney Griller
Frederick Grinke
Ida Haendel
Marie Hall
Jascha Heifetz
Joseph Hellmesberger
Willy Hess
Ulf Hoelscher
Karl Hoffmann
Ralph Holmes

Henry Holst
Yuzuko Horigome
Jenö Hubay
Bronislaw Huberman
Monica Huggett
Shizuka Ishikawa
Feliks Janiewicz
Joseph Joachim
Leila Josefowicz
Joseph Kaminski
Mark Kaplan
Louis Kaufman
Hans Keller
Nigel Kennedy
Willem Kes
Isabelle van Keulen
Young-Uck Kim
Pawel Kochánski
Leonid Kogan
Franz Kotzwara
Fritz Kreisler
Gidon Kremer
Rodolphe Kreutzer
Wenzel Krumpholtz
Oleg Krysa
Jan Kubelik
Sigiswald Kuijken
Georg Kulenkampff
Franz Lamotte
Linda Lampenius
Jaime Laredo
Cho-Liang Lin
Tasmin Little
Alan Loveday
Mark Lubotsky
Anne Macnaghten
Vanessa Mae
André Mangeot
Mantovani
Alessandro Marcello
Silvia Marcovici
Johanna Martzy
Joseph Massart
Nicola Matteis
Eduard Melkus
Isolde Menges
Yehudi Menuhin
Goto Midori
Stoika Milanova
Nathan Milstein
Shlomo Mintz
Lydia Mordkovitch
Viktoria Mullover
Charles Munch

Anne-Sophie Mutter
Pietro Nardini
Yfrah Neaman
Wilma Neruda
Ginette Neveu
Sigmund Nissel
David Oistrakh
Igor Oistrakh
Raphael Oleg
Frantisek Ondncek
Igor Ozim
Niccolò Paganini
Manoug Parikian
György Pauk
Edith Peinemann
Itzhak Perlman
George Frederic Pinto
Adolf Pollitzer
Jean Pougnet
Maud Powell
William Primrose
Gaetano Pugnani
Giovanni Punto
Michael Rabin
John Ravenscroft
Ede Reményi
Vadim Repin
Ruggiero Ricci
Franz Anton Ries
Hubert Ries
Alexander Ritter
Andreas Jakob
  Romberg
Arnold Rosé
Carl Rosiers
Max Rostal
Christian Rummel
George Saint-George
Prosper Sainton
Johann Peter Salomon
Albert Sammons
Eugene Sarbu
Emile Sauret
Rosario Scalero
Anton Schindler
Alexander Schneider
Wolfgang Schneiderhan
Jaap Schröder
Franz Schubert
Ignaz Schuppanzigh
Otakar Sevcik
Emily Shinner
Oscar Shumsky
Joseph Silverstein

Dmitry Sitkovetzky
Camillo Sivori
Nikolay Sokoloff
Paolo Spagnoletti
Albert Spalding
Theodore Spiering
Johann Wenzel Stamitz
Simon Standage
Isaac Stern
Julius Stern
Frederick Stock
George Stratton
Josef Suk
Zoltán Székely
Henryk Szeryng
Josef Szigeti
Gabor Takács-Nagy
Václav Talich
Giuseppe Tartini
Vilmos Tátrai
Charles Taylor
Arve Tellefsen
Emil Telmányi
Henri Temianka
Klaus Tennstedt
Carlo Tessarini
Jacques Thibaud
César Thomson
Luigi Tomasini
Giuseppe Torelli
Roman Totenberg
Berthold Tours
Chrétien Urhan
Tibór Varga
Sándor Végh
Maxim Vengerov
Henri Verbrugghen
Henri Vieuxtemps
H. Waldo Warner
Joseph Miroslav Weber
Henryk Wieniawski
Wanda Wilkomirska
Marie Wilson
Michael Zacharewitsch
Christian Zacharias
Zvi Zeitlin
Jakob Zeugheer
Efrem Zimbalist
Frank Peter Zimmermann
Louis Zimmermann
Yossi Zivoni
Olive Zorian
Pinchas Zukerman
Paul Zukofsky

MUSIC CLASSICAL

Famous Singers

Sopranos
Aïno Ackté
Roberta Alexander
Jeannine Altmeyer
Elly Ameling
Marie Angel
Sheila Armstrong
Martina Arroyo
Florence Austral
Lilian Bailey
Isobel Baillie
Josephine Barstow

Kathleen Battle
Hildegard Behrens
Elizabeth Billington
Judith Blegen
Hannelore Bode
Barbara Bonney
Lucrezia Bori
Inge Borkh
Gré Brouwenstijn
Norma Burrowes
Montserrat Caballé
Teresa Cahill

Maria Callas
Emma Calvé
Maria Caniglia
Maria Caradori-Allan
Margherita Carosio
Katharina Cavalieri
Maria Cebotari
Maria Chiara
Gina Cigna
Mimi Coertse
Isabella Colbran
Elizabeth Connell

Mary Costa
Régine Crespin
Joan Cross
Lella Cuberli
Maud Cunitz
Toti Dal Monte
Suzanne Danco
Barbara Daniels
Gloria Davy
Anne Dawson
Lynne Dawson
Lisa Della Casa

Joséphine De Reszke
Emmy Destinn
Libuse Domaninska
Helen Donath
Dorothy Dorow
Dorothy Dow
Elizabeth Duparc
Denise Duval
Noël Eadie
Jean Eaglen
Emma Eames
Florence Easton
Christiane Eda-Pierre
Mary Ellis
Anne Evans
Carole Farley
Geraldine Farrar
Eileen Farrell
Helen Field
Sylvia Fischer
Kirsten Flagstad
Mirella Freni
Elizabeth Fretwell
Marya Freund
Marta Fuchs
Johanna Gadski
Amelita Galli-Curci
Mary Garden
Lesley Garrett
Catherine Gayer
Mechthild Gessendorf
Sona Ghazarian
Christel Goltz
Jill Gomez
Linda Esther Gray
Silvia Greenberg
Giulia Grisi
Reri Grist
Edita Gruberova
Nora Gruhn
Elisabeth Grümmer
Hilde Gueden
Nancy Gustafson
Marie Gutheil-Schoder
Alison Hagley
Joan Hammond
Heather Harper
Eiddwen Harrhy
Kathryn Harries
Elizabeth Harwood
Minnie Hauk
Cynthia Haymon
Lorna Haywood
Frieda Hempel
Elvira de Hidalgo
Judith Howarth
Karen Huffstodt
Rita Hunter
Maria Ivogün
Gundula Janowitz
Maria Jeritza
Sumi Jo
Eva Johannson
Gwyneth Jones
Ava June
Sena Jurinac
Raina Kabaivanska
Kiri Te Kanawa
Julie Kaufmann
Adelaide Kemble
Barbra Kemp
Yvonne Kenny

Adele Kern
Emma Kirkby
Dorothy Kirsten
Katharina Klafsky
Anny Konetzni
Hilde Konetzni
Annelies Kupper
Selma Kurz
Dora Labbette
Aloysia Lange
Nanny Larsén-Todsen
Magda Laszló
Marjorie Lawrence
Evelyn Lear
Lilli Lehmann
Liza Lehmann
Lotte Lehmann
Frida Leider
Adèle Leigh
Hellen Lemmens
Tiana Lemnitz
Mary Lewis
Miriam Licette
Caterina Ligendza
Jenny Lind
Berit Lindholm
Wilma Lipp
Pilar Lorengar
Victoria de Los Angeles
Felicity Lott
Germaine Lubin
Pauline Lucca
Sylvia McNair
Catherine Malfitano
Mathilde Mallinger
Blanche Marchesi
Lois Marshall
Margaret Marshall
Eva Marton
Valerie Masterson
Amalie Materna
Edith Mathis
Karita Mattila
Johanna Meier
Nellie Melba
Janine Micheau
Julia Migenes
Zinka Milanov
Anna von Mildenburg
Audrey Mildmay
Aprile Millo
Nelly Miricioiu
Martha Mödl
Anna Moffo
Fanny Moody
Grace Moore
Elsie Morison
Edda Moser
Maria Müller
Carol Neblett
Judith Nelson
Mignon Nevada
Agnes Nicholls
Birgit Nilsson
Christine Nilsson
Alda Noni
Elizabeth Norberg
Lillian Nordica
Jessye Norman
Clara Novello
Jarmila Novotná
Magda Olivero

Elaine Padmore
Felicity Palmer
Euphrosyne Parepa
Anne Pashley
Giuditta Pasta
Adelina Patti
Rose Pauly
Fanny Persiani
Roberta Peters
Helga Pilarczyk
Rosalind Plowright
Deborah Polaski
Lily Pons
Rosa Ponselle
Lucia Popp
Leontyne Price
Margaret Price
Yvonne Printemps
Ana Pusar
Ashley Putnam
Louisa Pyne
Rosa Raisa
Hildegard Ranczak
Judith Raskin
Aulikki Rautawaara
Delia Reinhardt
Maria Reining
Elisabeth Rethberg
Esther Réthy
Katia Ricciarelli
Margaret Ritchie
Faye Robinson
Joan Rodgers
Amanda Roocroft
Annaliese Rothenberger
Hermine Rudersdorff
Leonie Rysanek
Hilde Sadek
Sibyl Sanderson
Sylvia Sass
Bidú Sayão
Marianne Schech
Erna Schlüter
Elisabeth Schumann
Vera Schwarz
Elisabeth Schwarzkopf
Graziella Sciutti
Renata Scotto
Nadine Secunde
Irmgard Seefried
Meta Seinemeyer
Marcella Sembrich
Luciana Serra
Ellen Shade
Honor Sheppard
Margaret Sheridan
Amy Shuard
Margarethe Siems
Anja Silja
Dorothy Silk
Beverly Sills
Jeannette Sinclair
Victoria Sladen
Oda Slobodskaya
Elisabeth Söderström
Henriette Sontag
Elena Souliotis
Maria Stader
Eleanor Steber
Hanny Steffek
Sophie Stehle
Anna Steiger

Teresa Stich-Randall
Lilian Stiles Allen
Teresa Stolz
Anna Storace
Rosina Storchio
Teresa Stratas
Rita Streich
Cheryl Studer
Rosa Sucher
Elsie Suddaby
Susan Sunderland
Joan Sutherland
Helena Tattermuschová
Renata Tebaldi
Giusto Tenducci (male)
Milka Ternina
Margarete
  Teschemacher
Eva Tetrazzini
Luisa Tetrazzini
Maggie Teyte
Thérèse Tietjens
Pauline Tinsley
Anna Tomowa-Sintow
Helen Traubel
Carrie Tubb
Eva Turner
Dawn Upshaw
Viorica Ursuleac
Leontina Vaduva
Benita Valente
Anita Välkki
Ninon Vallin
Carol Vaness
Julia Varady
Astrid Varnay
Elizabeth Vaughan
Galina Vishnevskaya
Jennifer Vyvyan
Johanna Wagner
Yoko Watanabe
Claire Watson
Janice Watson
Lilian Watson
Aloysia Weber
Gillian Webster
Lucie Weidt
Ljuba Welitsch
Ruth Welting
Catherine Wilson
Marie Wittich
Sophie Wyss
Rachel Yakar
Mara Zampieri
Ruth Ziesak
Teresa Zylis-Gara

Mezzo-Soprano
Janet Baker
Agnes Baltsa
Cecilia Bartoli
Teresa Berganza
Faustina Bordoni
Olga Borodina
Marianne Brandt
Marie Brema
Grace Bumbry
Sally Burgess
Majorano Caffarelli
Sarah Jane Cahier
Susanna Cibber
Katherine Ciesinski

Cynthi Clarey
Girolamo Crescentini
Claire Croiza
Janice De Gaetani
Astra Desmond
Oralia Dominguez
Nancy Evans
Maria Ewing
Brigitte Fassbaender
Linda Finnie
Muriel Forster
Elena Gerhardt
Rita Gorr
Bernadette Greevy
Giuditta Grisi
Barbara Hendricks
Jane Henschel
Alfreda Hodgson
Grace Hoffman
Elisabeth Höngen
Marilyn Horne
Anne Howells
Eirian James
Della Jones
Fiona Kimm
Louise Kirkby-Lunn
Gillian Knight
Nadezda Kniplová
Kathleen Kuhlmann
Lotte Lenya
Marjana Lipovsek
Martha Lipton
Jean Madeira
Maria Malibran
Mathilde Marchesi
Waltraud Meier
Susanne Mentzer
Kerstin Meyer
Yvonne Minton
Diana Montague
Ann Murray
Hyacinth Nicholls
Elena Obraztsova
Maria Olczewska
Anne Sofie von Otter
Rosa Papier
Anna Pollak
Florence Quivar
Eva Randová
Nell Rankin
Regina Resnik
Anna Reynolds
Jean Rigby
Vera Rozsa
Trudeliese Schmidt
Hanna Schwarz
Constance Shacklock
Mitsuko Shirai
Giulietta Simionato
Monica Sinclair
Doris Soffel
Frederica von Stade
Risë Stevens
Ebe Stignani
Conchita Supervia
Gladys Swarthout
Klara Takács
Blanche Thebom
Kerstin Thorborg
Jennie Tourel
Zélia Trebelli
Tatiana Troyanos

Lucia Valentini-Terrani
Josephine Veasey
Shirley Verrett
Pauline Viardot-Garcia
Sieglinde Wagner
Edyth Walker
Penelope Walker
Sarah Walker
Carolyn Watkinson
Lucie Weidt
Eugenia Zareska
Delores Ziegler

Counter-tenors
James Bowman
Michael Chance
Alfred Deller
Jochen Kowalski
Andreas Scholl

Contraltos
Muriel Brunskill
Clara Butt
Giovanni Carestini
Kathleen Ferrier
Birgit Finnilä
Maureen Forrester
Louise Homer
Mary Jarred
Sigrid Onegin
Norma Procter
Gladys Ripley
Charlotte Sainton-Dolby
Ernestine
    Schumann-Heink
Antoinette Sterling
Caroline Unger
Lucia Elizabeth Vestris
Mary Wakefield
Helen Watts

Baritones
Pasquale Amato
Thomas Allen
Ettore Bastianini
Pierre Bernac
John Brownlee
Sesto Bruscantini
Renato Bruson
Delme Bryn-Jones
Renato Capecchi
Piero Cappuccilli
Clive Carey
Ulrik Cold
Brian Cooke
Peter Dawson
Giuseppe De Luca
Willi
    Domgraf-Fassbänder
Geraint Evans
Keith Falkner
David Ffrangcon-Davies
Dietrich Fischer-Dieskau
Lucien Fugère
Peter Glossop
Tito Gobbi
John Goss
Franz Grundheber
Hakan Hagegard
Derek Hammond-Stroud
Thomas Hampson
Percy Heming

Thomas Hemsley
Roy Henderson
George Henschel
Jason Howard
Neil Howlett
Gerhard Hüsch
Dmitri Hvorostovsky
Jorma Hynninen
Richard Jackson
Herbert Janssen
Phillip Joll
Dimitri Kharitonov
Peter Knapp
Otakar Kraus
Tom Krause
Jean-Louis Lassalle
Sergei Leiferkus
François Le Roux
George London
Benjamin Luxon
Donald McIntyre
James Maddalena
Victor Maurel
Donald Maxwell
Michael Maybrick
Yury Mazurok
Robert Merrill
Johannes Messchaert
Dennis Noble
John Noble
Alan Opie
Rolando Panerai
Charles Panzéra
Kostas Paskalis
Antonio Pini-Corsi
Juan Pons
Hermann Prey
Gino Quilico
Louis Quilico
Frederick Ranalow
John Rawnsley
Theodor Reichmann
Maurice Renaud
Marko Rothmüller
Titta Ruffo
Kennerley Rumford
Karel Salomon
Mario Sammarco
Charles Santley
Heinrich Schlusnus
Andreas Schmidt
Paul Schöffler
Antonio Scotti
William Shimell
John Shirley-Quirk
Paolo Silveri
Knut Skram
Russell Smythe
Gérard Souzay
Oley Speaks
Mariano Stabile
Thomas Stewart
Richard Stilwell
Julius Stockhausen
Jonathan Summers
Giuseppe Taddei
Carlo Tagliabue
Antonio Tamburini
Lawrence Tibbett
Alan Titus
Hermann Uhde
Theodor Uppman

Giuseppe Valdengo
Anton Van Rooy
Ramón Vinay
Michael Vogl
Eberhard Wächter
Ian Wallace
Jess Walters
William Warfield
Leonard Warren
Bernd Weikl
Willard White
Clarence Whitehill
David Wilson-Johnson
Ingvar Wixell
Ekkerhard Wlaschiha
Gregory Yurisich
Giorgio Zancanaro

Tenors
Valentin Adamberger
John Aler
John Alexander
Luigi Alva
Max Alvary
Francisco Araiza
John Beard
Karl Beck
Kim Begley
Jussi Björling
Beno Blachut
Rockwell Blake
Dino Borgioli
Stuart Burrows
José Carreras
Enrico Caruso
Richard Cassilly
Graham Clark
John Coates
Vinson Cole
Peter Cornelius
Jean Cox
Charles Craig
Richard Crooks
Hugues Cuénod
Arthur Davies
Ben Davies
Ryland Davies
Tudor Davies
Mario Del Monaco
François Delsarte
Fernando De Lucia
Gregory Dempsey
Jean De Reszke
Anton Dermota
Plácido Domingo
Nigel Douglas
Ronald Dowd
Warren Ellsworth
Poul Elming
Gervase Elwes
Karl Erb
Bruce Ford
Paul Frey
Manuel del Garcia
Nicolai Gedda
Giuseppe Giacomelli
Beniamino Gigli
Reiner Goldberg
Karl Graun
Donald Grobe
Jerry Hadley
Ben Heppner

MUSIC CLASSICAL

Martyn Hill
Joseph Hislop
Werner Hollweg
Hans Hopf
Walter Hyde
Hermann Jadlowker
Neil Jenkins
Siegfried Jerusalem
Edward Johnson
Parry Jones
Manfred Jung
Michael Kelly
Jan Kiepura
Waldemar Kmentt
Heinrich Knote
Alfredo Kraus
Werner Krenn
David Kuebler
Charles Kullman
Gary Lakes
Philip Langridge
Mario Lanza
Giacomo Lauri-Volpi
Jeffrey Lawton
Richard Leech
Keith Lewis
Richard Lewis
Luis Lima
Edward Lloyd
Max Lorenz
Veriano Lucheti
John McCormack
James McCracken
Giovanni Mario
Giovanni Martinelli
Yury Marusin
Helmut Melchert
Lauritz Melchior
Chris Merritt
Thomas Moser
Frank Mullings
Heddle Nash
Angelo Neumann
Albert Niemann
Adolphe Nourrit
Karl Oestvig
Alexander Oliver
Joseph O'Mara
Juan Oncina

Dennis O'Neill
Ian Partridge
Julius Patzak
Luciano Pavarotti
Peter Pears
Jan Peerce
Aureliano Pertile
Alfred Piccaver
Vilém Pribyl
Josef Protschka
Anton Raaff
Torsten Ralf
Thomas Randle
Sims Reeves
Alberto Remedios
David Rendall
Kenneth Riegel
Anthony Rolfe Johnson
Vladimir Rosing
Helge Roswaenge
Robert Rounseville
Giovanni-Battista
  Rubini
Thomas Salignac
Giovanni-Battista
  Sbriglia
Benedikt Schack
Aksel Schiotz
Tito Schipa
Erik Schmedes
Ludwig Schnorr
Rudolf Schock
Peter Schreier
Peter Seiffert
William Shakespeare
George Shirley
Léopold Simoneau
Leo Slezak
Fritz Soot
Gerhard Stolze
Kurt Streit
Ludwig Suthaus
Set Svanholm
Ferruccio Tagliavini
Francesco Tamagno
Enrico Tamberlik
Richard Tauber
John Templeton
Jess Thomas

Joseph Tichatschek
Richard Tucker
Fritz Uhl
Ragnar Ulfung
Georg Unger
Gerhard Unger
Jon Vickers
Ramón Vinay
Heinrich Vogl
Joseph Ward
Spas Wenkoff
Walter Widdop
Steuart Wilson
Gösta Winbergh
Wolfgang Windgassen
Hermann Winkelmann
Hermann Winkler
Ludwig Wüllner
Fritz Wunderlich
Alexander Young
Heinz Zednik
Giovanni Zenatello
Ivo Zidek

Castrato
Domenico Annibali
Majorano Caffarelli
Girolano Crescentini
Carlo Farinelli
Gaetano Guadagni
Domenico Mustafa
Senesino

Bass
Donald Adams
Paul Bender
Kurt Böhme
Kim Borg
Fyodor Chaliapin
Boris Christoff
Henry Cooke
Stafford Dean
Otto Edelmann
Signor Foli
David Franklin
Gottlob Frick
Manuel Garcia
Nicolai Ghiaurov
Nicola Ghiuselev

Josef Greindl
Paul Hillier
Robert Holl
Gwynne Howell
Marcel Journet
Manfred Jungwirth
Alexander Kipnis
Paul Knüpfer
Luigi Lablache
Charles Manners
Josef von Manowarda
Kurt Moll
Paolo Montarsolo
Yevgeny Nesterenko
Robert Newman
Siegmund Nimsgern
Ezio Pinza
Pol Plançon
Paul Plishka
Robert Radford
Ruggero Raimondi
Karl Ridderbusch
Michael Rippon
Paul Robeson
Forbes Robinson
Nicola Rossi-Lemeni
Joseph Rouleau
Kurt Rydl
Matti Salminen
Manfred Schenk
Andrew Shore
Cesare Siepi
Hans Sotin
Roger Soyer
Horace Stevens
Fyodor Stravinsky
Mihály Székely
Italo Tajo
Martti Talvela
Bryn Terfel
David Thomas
John Tomlinson
Richard Van Allan
José Van Dam
Norman Walker
Gustavus Waltz
David Ward
Ludwig Weber
Nicola Zaccaria

Conductors

Claudio Abbado
Komei Abe
Hermann Abendroth
Maurice Abravanel
Byron Adams
John Adams
Kurt Adler
Peter Adler
Yuri Ahronovitch
Gerd Albrecht
John Alldis
Antonio Almeida
Petr Altricher
Carl Alwin
Gilbert Amy
Karel Ancerl
Géza Anda
Karsten Andersen

Martin André
Volkmar Andreae
Paul Angerer
Enrique Arbós
Richard Armstrong
Vladimir Ashkenazy
David Atherton
Moshe Atzmon
Daniel Barenboim
Thomas Beecham
Jiri Belohlavek
Richard Bernas
Leonard Bernstein
Henry Bishop
Stanley Black
Richard Blackford
Nadia Boulanger
Pierre Boulez

Adrian Boult
Martyn Brabbins
Joly Braga-Santos
Nicholas Braithewaite
Warwick Braithwaite
Max Bruch
Hans Bülow
Fritz Busch
Ferruccio Busoni
Basil Cameron
Philip Cannon
Guido Cantelli
André Caplet
Franco Capuana
John Carewe
Mosco Carner
Jean-Claude
  Casadesus

Fritz Cassirer
Aldo Ceccato
Zdenek Chalabala
Harry Christophers
Myung-Whun Chung
Nicholas Cleobury
Stephen Cleobury
André Cluytens
Albert Coates
James Conlon
Emil Cooper
Michael Costa
Robert Craft
John Crosby
Edric Cundell
William Cusins
Henryk Czyz
Frank Damrosch

Leopold Damrosch
Walter Damrosch
Paul Daniel
Oskar Danon
Stephen Darlington
Dennis Russell Davies
Andrew Davis
Colin Davis
Jacques Delacôte
Norman Del Mar
Gaetano Delogu
John DeMain
Neville Dilkes
Christoph von Dohnányi
Antal Dorati
Clive Douglas
Edward Downes
Sian Edwards
Karl Elmendorff
Alberto Erede
Mark Ermler
Franco Faccio
Bryan Fairfax
Charles Farncombe
Robert Farnon
Vladimir Fedoseyev
Frederick Fennell
Arthur Fiedler
Max Fiedler
Adam Fischer
Ivan Fischer
Anatole Fistoulari
Grzegorz Fitelberg
Claus Peter Flor
Lawrence Foster
Myer Fredman
Ferenc Fricsay
Oskar Fried
Lionel Friend
Janos Fürst
Wilhelm Furtwängler
Piero Gamba
John Eliot Gardiner
Valery Gergiev
Alexander Gibson
Michael Gielen
Carlo Maria Giulini
Jane Glover
Daniel Godfrey
Walter Goehr
Georg Göhler
Vladimir Golschmann
Reginald Goodall
Roy Goodman
Ron Goodwin
Eugene Goossens
  (Belg.)
Eugene Goossens (Fr.)
Eugene Goossens (GB)
Hans Graf
Michael Graubart
Noah Greenberg
Bohumil Gregor
Charles Groves
Hermann Grunebaum
Marco Guidarini
Karl Haas
Robert Haas
François Habeneck
Alan Hacker
Hartmut Haenchen
Bernard Haitink

Charles Hallé
Louis Halsey
Simon Halsey
Maurice Handford
Vernon Handley
Nikolaus Harnoncourt
Trevor Harvey
László Heltay
Philippe Herreweghe
Bernard Herrmann
Alfred Hertz
Leslie Heward
Richard Hickox
Alfred Hill
Jun'ichi Hirokami
Irwin Hoffman
Christopher Hogwood
Heinrich Hollreiser
Imogen Holst
Bo Holten
Anthony Hopkins
John Hopkins
Jascha Horenstein
Milan Horvat
Anthony Hose
Elgar Howarth
Owain Arwel Hughes
Donald Hunt
George Hurst
Eliahu Inbal
Michiyoshi Inoue
Ernest Irving
Robert Irving
José Iturbi
Hiroyuki Iwaki
René Jacobs
Reginald Jacques
Jussi Jalas
Marek Janowski
Arvid Jansons
Mariss Jansons
Neeme Järvi
Paavo Järvi
Graeme Jenkins
Newell Jenkins
Eugen Jochum
Jullien Joly
Simon Joly
Enrique Jordá
Armin Jordan
James Judd
Louis Julien
Jürgen Jürgens
Robert Kajanus
Okko Kamu
Herbert von Karajan
Jacek Kasprzyk
Bernard Keeffe
Christopher Keene
Joseph Keilberth
Rudolf Kempe
Paul van Kempen
István Kertész
Willem Kes
Hans Kindler
Robert King
Bernhard Klee
Carlos Kleiber
Erich Kleiber
Otto Klemperer
Paul Kletzki
Berislav Klobucar

Hans Knappertsbusch
Kazuhiro Koizumi
Kyril Kondrashin
Franz Konwitschny
Kazimierz Kord
Zdenek Kosler
André Kostelanetz
Serge Koussevitzky
Jiri Kout
Karel Kovarovic
Clemens Krauss
Yakov Kreizberg
Jan Krenz
Henry Krips
Josef Krips
Jaroslav Krombholc
Karl Krueger
Rafael Kubelik
Gustav Kuhn
Efrem Kurtz
Franz Lachner
Charles Lamoureux
Michael Lankester
Joseph Lanner
Lars-Erik Larsson
Eduard Lassen
Ashley Lawrence
Alexander Lazarev
Philip Ledger
Michel Legrand
György Lehel
Erich Leinsdorf
Lawrence Leonard
Raymond Leppard
Hermann Levi
James Levine
Anthony Lewis
Henry Lewis
András Ligeti
Andrew Litton
Grant Llewellyn
David Lloyd-Jones
James Lockhart
Alain Lombard
Jesus Lopez-Cobos
James Loughran
Ferdinand Löwe
John Lubbock
Leighton Lucas
Leopold Ludwig
Alexandre Luigini
Peter Maag
Lorin Maazel
Zdenek Macal
Denis McCaldin
Nicholas McGegan
Charles Mackerras
Ernest MacMillan
Fritz Mahler
Gustav Mahler
Jerzy Maksymiuk
Jean-Claude Malgoire
Nikolay Malko
Luigi Mancinelli
August Manns
Mantovani
Gino Marinuzi
Neville Marriner
Odaline de la Martinez
Jean Martinon
Giuseppe Martucci
Diego Masson

Kurt Masur
Eduardo Mata
Lovro von Matacic
Muir Mathieson
John Mauceri
Peter Maxwell Davies
Zubin Mehta
Willem Mengelberg
Herbert Menges
Howard Mitchell
Bernardino Molinari
Francesco
  Molinari-Pradelli
Pierre Monteux
Kenneth Montgomery
Rudolf Moralt
Wyn Morris
Felix Mottl
Evgeny Mravinsky
Karl Muck
Michael Mudie
Leopoldo Mugnone
Charles Munch
Karl Münchinger
Riccardo Muti
Kent Nagano
Garcia Navarro
Boyd Neel
John Nelson
Woldemar Nelsson
Frantisek Neumann
Václav Neumann
Roy Newsome
Harry Newstone
Arthur Nikisch
Roger Norrington
David Oistrakh
Sakari Oramo
Eugene Ormandy
Tadaaki Otaka
Willem van Otterloo
Seiji Ozawa
Ettore Panizza
Paul Paray
Alain Paris
Andrew Parrott
Jules-Étienne
  Pasdeloup
Giuseppe Patanè
Bernhard Paumgartner
Emil Paur
Wilfrid Pelletier
Murray Perahia
Libor Pesek
Zoltán Peskó
Trevor Pinnock
Percy Pitt
Michel Plasson
Giorgio Polacco
Egon Pollak
John Poole
Frederik Prausnitz
Georges Prêtre
André Previn
Fernando Previtali
Brian Priestman
Klaus Pringsheim
John Pritchard
Felix Prohaska
Eve Queler
Peter Raabe
Ruth Railton

Karl Rankl
Simon Rattle
Clarence Raybould
Ernest Read
Hans Redlich
Leopold Reichwein
Fritz Reiner
Edouard van Remoortel
Timothy Reynish
Hans Richter
Karl Anton
  Rickenbacher
Kathleen Riddick
Hugo Rignold
Helmuth Rilling
Carlo Rizzi
James Robertson
Christopher Robinson
Stanford Robinson
Arthur Rodzinski
Landon Ronald
Karl Rosa
Hans Rosbaud
Albert Rosen
Joseph Rosenstock
Antoni Ros Marbá
Mario Rossi
Mstislav Rostropovich
Walter Rothwell
Tony Rowe
Witold Rowicki
Gennady
  Rozhdestvensky
Julius Rudel
Max Rudolf
Christian Rummel
Donald Runnicles
John Rutter
Paul Sacher
Vasily Safonov
Karel Salomon
Esa-Pekka Salonen
Samuil Samosud
Kurt Sanderling
Nello Santi
Gabriele Santini
Nino Sanzogno
Jukka-Pekka Saraste
Sir Malcolm Sargent
Wolfgang Sawallisch
Franz Schalk
Xaver Scharwenka
Hermann Scherchen
Heinrich Schiff

Anton Schindler
Thomas Schippers
Erich Schmid
Ole Schmidt
Hans Schmidt-Isserstedt
Georg Schnéevoigt
Alexander Schneider
Max Schönherr
Michael Schonwandt
Hans-Hubert Schönzeler
Peter Schreier
Ernst von Schuch
Ignaz Schuppanzigh
Carl Schuricht
Gerard Schwarz
Rudolf Schwarz
Claudio Scimone
Christopher Seaman
Uri Segal
Leif Segerstam
Karel Sejna
Jerzy Semkow
Tullio Serafin
Robert Shaw
Howard Shelley
Maxim Shostakovich
Oscar Shumsky
Joseph Silverstein
Constantin Silvestri
Geoffrey Simon
Yury Simonov
Vassily Sinaisky
George Sinclair
Dmitri Sitkovetsky
Stanislaw
  Skrowaczewski
Leonard Slatkin
Nicolas Slonimsky
Alexander Smallens
George Smart
Václav Smetácek
Nicholas Smith
Ethel Smyth
Nikolay Sokoloff
Georg Solti
Marc Soustrot
Theodore Spiering
Peter Stadlen
Simon Standage
Bernhard Stavenhagen
Erwin Stein
Fritz Stein
Horst Stein
Emil Steinbach

Fritz Steinbach
Pinchas Steinberg
William Steinberg
Markus Stenz
Fritz Stiedry
Frederick Stock
Leopold Stokowski
Josef Stransky
George Stratton
Karl Straube
Eduard Strauss I
Eduard Strauss II
Richard Strauss
Igor Stravinsky
Simon Streatfeild
Wolfgang Stresemann
Frank van der Stucken
Otmar Suitner
Walter Susskind
Yevgeny Svetlanov
Hans Swarowsky
Ward Swingle
Tadeusz Sygietynski
Georg Szell
Eugen Szenkar
Michel Tabachnik
Václav Talich
Egisto Tango
Jeffrey Tate
Vilem Tausky
Pyotr Tchaikovsky
Yuri Temirkanov
Klaus Tennstedt
Richard Terry
Christian Thielemann
Michael Tilson Thomas
Theodore Thomas
Bryden Thomson
Heinz Tietjen
Martino Tirimo
Paul Tortelier
Yan Pascal Tortelier
Arturo Toscanini
Geoffrey Toye
Barry Tuckwell
Rosalyn Tureck
Martin Turnovsky
Erik Tuxen
Heinz Unger
Eduard Van Beinum
André Vandernoot
Osmo Vanska
Silvio Varviso
Tamás Vásáry

Denis Vaughan
Sándor Végh
Henri Verbrugghen
Gilbert Vinter
Jaroslav Vogel
Hans Vonk
Edo de Waart
Roger Wagner
Siegfried Wagner
Alfred Wallenstein
Bruno Walter
Günter Wand
Volker Wangenheim
Guy Warrack
Akeo Watanabe
Sydney Watson
Joseph Miroslav Weber
Martin Wegelius
Bruno Weil
Felix Weingartner
George Weldon
Walter Weller
Franz Welser-Möst
August Wenzinger
Ian Whyte
Günther Wich
Allan Wicks
Mark Wigglesworth
David Wilde
Stephen Wilkinson
Jósef Wilkomirski
David Willcocks
Malcolm Williamson
Antoni Wit
Albert Wolff
Hugh Wolff
Henry Wood
David Wooldridge
Barry Wordsworth
Franz Wüllner
Jürg Wyttenbach
Arvid Yansons
Simone Young
Eugène Ysaye
Takuo Yuasa
Lothar Zagrosek
Carlo Zecchi
Hans Zender
Jakob Zeugheer
Alexander Ziloti
David Zinman
Pinchas Zukerman
Paul Zukofsky
Herman Zump

MUSIC: POP

Show and Film Songs: by Song

Song	Show/Film
Ac-cent-tchu-ate the Positive	Here Come the Waves
Adelaide	Guys and Dolls
Afraid to Dream	You Can't Have Everything
After the Ball	The Jolson Story
	A Trip to Chinatown (show)
	Lillian Russell
After You Get What You Want You Don't Want it	There's No Business Like Showbusiness
Again	Road House
Ain't Got a Dime to My Name	Road to Morocco
Ain't Got No – I Got Life	Hair
Ain't It a Shame About Mame	Rhythm on the River
Ain't Misbehavin'	Atlantic City
	Gentlemen Marry Brunettes
	You Were Meant For Me
	Hot Chocolates (show)
	The Strip
	Follow the Band
	Stormy Weather
Ain't She Sweet?	You Were Meant For Me
	You're My Everything
Alabamy Bound	With a Song in My Heart
	Broadway
	The Great American Broadcast
	Show Business
Alexander's Ragtime Band	Alexander's Ragtime Band
	There's No Business Like Show Business
Alice Blue Gown	Irene
All Alone	Alexander's Ragtime Band
All God's Chillun Got Rhythm	A Day at the Races
All I Ask of You	Phantom of the Opera (show)
All I Do Is Dream of You	Sadie McKee
	Broadway Melody of 1936
	The Boy Friend
	Singin' in the Rain
All My Loving	A Hard Day's Night
All of Me	Meet Danny Wilson
	Lady Sings the Blues
All of You	Silk Stockings
All or Nothing At All	Weekend Pass
All Over the Place	Sailors Three
All the Things You Are	Broadway Rhythm
	Because You're Mine
	Till The Clouds Roll By
All the Time in the World	On Her Majesty's Secret Service
All the Way (1957)	The Joker Is Wild

Song	Show/Film
All Through the Night	Anything Goes
All Time High	Octopussy
All You Need Is Love	Yellow Submarine
Almost Like Being in Love	Brigadoon
Always	Christmas Holiday
	Blue Skies
Always True to You in My Fashion	Kiss Me Kate
Among My Souvenirs	The Best Years of Our Lives
	Paris
And This Is My Beloved	Kismet
Animal Crackers in My Soup	Curly Top
The Anniversary Song	The Jolson Story
Another Brick in the Wall	The Wall
Another Suitcase in Another Hall	Evita (show)
Anything You Can Do	Annie Get Your Gun
Any Time's Kissing Time	Chu Chin Chow
Anywhere I Wander	Hans Christian Andersen
April in Paris	April in Paris
	Paris Holiday
	Both Ends of the Candle
April Played the Fiddle	If I Had My Way
April Showers	The Jolson Story
	Jolson Sings Again
	The Eddie Duchin Story
	April Showers
Aquarius	Hair
Arriverderci Darling	The Seven Hills of Rome
As I Love You	The Big Beat
As Long As He Needs Me	Oliver
As Time Goes By	Everybody's Welcome (show)
	Casablanca
At Last	Sun Valley Serenade
	The Glenn Miller Story
	Orchestra Wives
At Long Last Love	At Long Last Love
	You Never Know (show)
Auf Wiederseh'n	The Blue Paradise
	Deep in My Heart
Avalon	The Benny Goodman Story
	The Jolson Story
	Both Ends of the Candle
Baby Doll	The Belle of New York
Baby Face	Glorifying the American Girl
	Jolson Sings Again
	Thoroughly Modern Millie

Song	Show/Film	Song	Show/Film
Baby I Don't Care	Jailhouse Rock	Blue Skies	Glorifying the
Baby It's Cold Outside (1949)	Neptune's Daughter		American Girl
Bachelor Boy	Summer Holiday		The Jazz Singer
Bali Ha'i	South Pacific		Blue Skies
Basin Street Blues	The Glenn Miller Story		Alexander's Ragtime
	The Strip		Band
Baubles, Bangles and Beads	Kismet		White Christmas
Be a Clown	The Pirate	Boogie Woogie Bugle Boy	Swingtime Johnny
	Singin' in the Rain		Buck Privates
	(show)	Boots and Saddle	Call of the Canyon
Beale Street Blues	St Louis Blues	Born Free (1966)	Born Free
	It's Trad, Dad	The Boys in the Backroom	Destry Rides Again
Beat Out Dat Rhythm	Carmen Jones	Brazil	The Eddie Duchin
on a Drum			Story
Beautiful Dreamer	Swanee River		The Girl He Left
Be-Bop-A-Lula	The Girl Can't Help It		Behind
Be Careful, It's My Heart	Holiday Inn		Saludos Amigos
Because the Night	That Summer	The Breeze and I	Cuban Pete
Begin the Beguine	Broadway Melody of	Bright Eyes	Watership Down
	1940	Broken Hearted	The Best Things in Life
	Night and Day		Are Free
	Jubilee (show)	Brother, Can You Spare	Americana
Beginner's Luck	Shall We Dance	a Dime?	
Bei Mir Bist Du Schöhn	Love, Honour and	Buckle Down, Winsocki	Best Foot Forward
	Behave	Burlington Bertie from Bow	Mother Wore Tights
Be My Love	Looking For Love		Star
	The Toast of New	Bushel and a Peck	Guys and Dolls (show)
	Orleans	Bustopher Jones	Cats (show)
The Best Things In Life	The Best Things In Life	But Beautiful	Road to Rio
Are Free	Are Free	But Not for Me	Girl Crazy
	Good News	Buttons and Bows	The Paleface
Bewitched, Bothered	Pal Joey		Son of Paleface
and Bewildered		Button Up Your Overcoat	Follow Through
Bibbidi-Bobbidi-Boo	Cinderella		The Best Things in Life
Bidin' My Time	Girl Crazy		Are Free
	Rhapsody in Blue	Bye Bye Blackbird	Pete Kelly's Blues
	The Glenn Miller Story		The Eddie Cantor
Big Spender	Sweet Charity		Story
Bill	Showboat		Rainbow Round My
	The Man I Love		Shoulder
	Both Ends of the	By Strauss	An American in Paris
	Candle		The Show Is On (show)
The Birth of the Blues	Painting the Clouds	By the Light of the Silvery	The Jolson Story
	with Sunshine	Moon	Two Weeks with Love
	The Best Things in Life		The Birth of the Blues
	Are Free		Sunbonnet Sue
	The Birth of the Blues	By the Sleepy Lagoon	Sleepy Lagoon
The Black Bottom	George White's		
	Scandals (show)	Ça C'est l'Amour	Les Girls
	A Star Is Born	California, Here I Come	Lucky Boy
The Black Hills of Dakota	Calamity Jane		Jolson Sings Again
Bless Yore Beautiful Hide	Seven Brides for		With a Song in My
	Seven Brothers		Heart
Blow, Gabriel, Blow	Anything Goes		You're My Everything
Blueberry Hill	The Singing Hill		The Jolson Story
Blue Moon	This Could Be the Night		Rose of Washington
	Words and Music		Square
	Kiss Them for Me	Call Me	American Gigolo
	Grease	Call Me Irresponsible (1963)	Papa's Delicate
	Torch Song		Condition
	With a Song in My	Candy Kisses	Down Dakota Way
	Heart	Can I Forget You	High, Wide and
Blues in the Night	The Birth of the Blues		Handsome

Song	Show/Film	Song	Show/Film
The Canoe Song	Sanders of the River		Oh Kay (show)
Can't Buy Me Love	A Hard Day's Night		Both Ends of the
Can't Help Falling in Love	Blue Hawaii		Candle
Can't Help Lovin' Dat Man	Both Ends of the		Tea for Two
	Candle	Do I Love You Because	Cinderella (show)
	Show Boat	You're Beautiful	
	Till The Clouds Roll By	Do I Love You, Do I	Night and Day
Carolina in the Morning	The Dolly Sisters		DuBarry Was a Lady
	Jolson Sings Again	Doin' What Comes Naturally	Annie Get Your Gun
	April Showers	Do I Worry	Pardon My Sarong
	I'll See You in My	Dominique	The Singing Nun
	Dreams	The Donkey Serenade	The Firefly
C'est Magnifique	Can-Can	Don't Cry for Me, Argentina	Evita
C'est Si Bon	Latin Quarter (show)	Don't Ever Leave Me	Sweet Adeline
	New Faces		Both Ends of the
Charmaine	Sunset Boulevard		Candle
The Charm of You	Anchors Aweigh	Don't Fence Me In	Don't Fence Me In
Chattanooga Choo Choo	The Glenn Miller Story		Hollywood Canteen
	Springtime in the	Don't It Make My Brown Eyes	Convoy
	Rockies	Blue	
	Sun Valley Serenade	Don't Laugh at Me	Trouble in Store
Chattanooga Shoeshine Boy	Indian Territory	Don't Rain on My Parade	Funny Girl
Cheek to Cheek	Top Hat	Do-Re-Mi	The Sound of Music
Cheerful Little Earful	Sweet and Low (show)	Down among the Sheltering	That Midnight Kiss
Chica Chica Boom Chic	That Night in Rio	Palms	Some Like It Hot
Chim Chim Cheree (1964)	Mary Poppins	Do You Know Where You're	Mahogany
Clap Hands, Here Comes	Funny Lady	Going To?	
Charley		The Drinking Song	The Student Prince
Clap Yo' Hands	Oh Kay (show)	Duelling Banjos	Deliverance
	Rhapsody in Blue		
	Funny Face	Edelweiss	The Sound of Music
Cllmb Ev'ry Mountain	The Sound of Music	Eleanor Rigby	Yellow Submarine
Close as Pages in a Book	Up in Central Park	Embraceable You	An American in Paris
A Cock-Eyed Optimist	South Pacific		Girl Crazy
Colonel Bogey March	The Bridge on the		Nancy Goes to Rio
	River Kwai		Rhapsody in Blue
Come and Get It	The Magic Christian		Sincerely Yours
Come Back to Sorrento	Paramount on Parade		With a Song in My
Consider Yourself	Oliver		Heart
The Continental (1934)	The Gay Divorcee	Emotions	The Stud
Cool Water	Hands across the	Empty Chairs at Empty Tables	Les Misérables (show)
	Water	The Entertainer	The Sting
A Couple of Swells	Easter Parade	Evergreen	A Star is Born
		Everybody's Doing It	The Fabulous Dorseys
Dance to the Music	Woodstock		Alexander's Ragtime
Dancing in the Street	Cooley High		Band
Dancing on the Ceiling	Evergreen		Easter Parade
Dat's Love	Carmen Jones	Everybody's Talkin'	Midnight Cowboy
Day by Day	Godspell	Everything's Coming Up Roses	Gypsy
Days of Wine and Roses	Days of Wine and	Ev'ry Time We Say Goodbye	Seven Lively Arts
(1962)	Roses		(show)
The Deadwood Stage	Calamity Jane	Experiment	Nymph Errant (show)
Dear Little Cafe	Bitter-Sweet	Eye of the Tiger	Rocky III
Deep in the Heart of Texas	With a Song in My		
	Heart	Falling in Love Again	The Blue Angel
	Hi Neighbour	Falling in Love with Love	The Boys from
Delta Lady	Mad Dogs and		Syracuse
	Englishmen	Fame	Fame
Diamonds Are a Girl's	Gentlemen Prefer	Fascinating Rhythm	Girl Crazy
Best Friend	Blondes		Lady, Be Good!
Ding Dong the Witch Is Dead	The Wizard of Oz		Rhapsody in Blue
D.I.V.O.R.C.E.	Five Easy Pieces		Singin' in the Rain
Do Do Do	Star		(show)

M
U
S
I
C

P
O
P

Song	Show/Film	Song	Show/Film
Feather Your Nest	Tip Top (show)	Here Comes the Sun	John, Paul, George, Ringo and Bert
Feed the Birds	Mary Poppins		
A Fellow Needs a Girl	Allegro (show)	Here in My Arms	Tea for Two
Fever	Hey Boy! Hey Girl!	Hernando's Hideaway	The Pajama Game
Five Foot Two, Eyes of Blue	Has Anybody Seen My Gal?	Hi-Diddle-Dee-Dee (An Actor's Life For Me)	Pinocchio
Flash Bang Wallop	Half a Sixpence (show)	High Hopes (1959)	Hole in the Head
Flashdance – What a Feeling (1983)	Flashdance	High Noon (1952)	High Noon
		Hold the Line	Yesterday's Heroes
A Foggy Day	A Damsel in Distress	Honeysuckle Rose	Thousands Cheer
Foggy Mountain Breakdown	Bonnie and Clyde		Tin Pan Alley
The Folks Who Live on the Hill	High, Wide and Handsome	Hong Kong Blues	To Have and Have Not
For All We Know (1970)	Lovers and Other Strangers	Hopelessly Devoted to You	Grease
For Every Man There's a Woman	Casbah	Hound Dog	Grease
		How Are Things in Glocca Morra	Finian's Rainbow
For You, for Me, for Everyone	The Shocking Miss Pilgrim	How Could You Believe Me?	Wedding Bells
French Military Marching Song	The Desert Song	How High the Moon?	Two for the Show
Friendship	DuBarry Was a Lady	How Long Has This Been Going On	Funny Face
From the Top of Your Head	Two for Tonight		Rosalie (show)
		How to Handle a Woman	Camelot
Genie with the Light Brown Lamp	Aladdin and His Wonderful Lamp	I Cain't Say No	Oklahoma!
The Gentleman is a Dope	Allegro (show)	I Concentrate on You	Broadway Melody of 1940
Get Me to the Church on Time	My Fair Lady	I Could Have Danced All Night	My Fair Lady
Get Out and Get Under	Hullo Tango (show)	I Could Write a Book	Pal Joey
	The Pleasure Seekers (show)	Ida, Sweet as Apple Cider	Babes in Arms
			The Eddie Cantor Story
Get Out of Town	Leave It to Me (show)		Incendiary Blonde
Getting to Know You	The King and I	I Didn't Know What Time It Was	Pal Joey
Gigi (1958)	Gigi		Too Many Girls
The Gipsy in Me	Anything Goes (show)	I'd Do Anything	Oliver
Give Me the Moonlight	Hullo America	I Don't Know How to Love Him	Jesus Christ Superstar
	The Dolly Sisters	I Feel Pretty	West Side Story
The Glory of Love	Karate Kid II	If Ever I Would Leave You	Camelot
God on High	Les Misérables	If I Didn't Care	The Great American Broadcast
Gonna Build a Mountain	Stop the World – I Want To Get Off	If I Had a Talking Picture of You	The Best Things In Life Are Free
Good Morning Starshine	Hair		Sunny Side Up
Goodnight, Sweetheart	The Big Broadcast of 1936	If I Loved You	Carousel
		If I Ruled The World	Pickwick (show)
	You Were Meant for Me	If I Were A Bell	Guys and Dolls
		If I Were A Rich Man	Fiddler on the Roof
Happy Days Are Here Again	Chasing Rainbows Rain or Shine	I Get a Kick Out of You	Anything Goes
			Night and Day
Happy Holiday	Holiday Inn		Sunny Side of the Street
Happy Talk	South Pacific		
Harry Lime Theme	The Third Man	I Got Plenty of Nuttin'	Porgy and Bess
Have You Met Miss Jones	Gentlemen Marry Brunettes	I Got Rhythm	Girl Crazy
			Rhapsody in Blue
	Meet Me in St. Louis		An American in Paris
Have Yourself a Merry Little Christmas		I Got the Sun in the Morning	Annie Get Your Gun
The Heat Is on	Beverly Hills Cop	I Hate Men	Kiss Me, Kate
Hello, Hello, Who's Your Lady Friend?	The Story of Vernon and Irene Castle	I Just Called to Say I Love You (1984)	Woman in Red
Hello, Young Lovers	The King and I	I Know Him So Well	Chess (show)
Help	Help!	I Like to Recognize the Tune	Too Many Girls (show)
	John, Paul, George, Ringo and Bert		Meet the People

Song	Show/Film	Song	Show/Film
I'll Be with You in Apple Blossom Time	Buck Privates		I'll See You In My Dreams
I'll Build a Stairway to Paradise	Rhapsody in Blue Stop Flirting (show) An American in Paris George White's Scandals of 1922 (show)	It Might As Well Be Spring (1945)	Incendiary Blonde Show Business State Fair
		It's a Hap-Hap-Happy Day	Gulliver's Travels
		It's a Lovely Day Today	Call Me Madam
I'll Never Fall in Love Again	Promises, Promises (show)	It's All Right with Me	Can-Can
		It's d'Lovely	Anything Goes The Fleet's Lit Up (show) Red Hot and Blue (show)
I'll See You Again	Bitter-Sweet		
I'll See You in My Dreams	Follow the Boys I'll See You In My Dreams Pardon My Rhythm	It's Easy to Remember	Mississippi
		It's Only a Paper Moon	Too Young to Know Take a Chance
I Love a Piano	Easter Parade		
I Love Paris	Can-Can	I've Been a Bad Bad Boy	Privilege
I Love You (Archer and Thompson)	Little Jesse James (show) The Sun Also Rises	I've Got a Crush on You	Three for the Show Meet Danny Wilson Strike Up the Band (show) Both Ends of the Candle
I Love You (Porter)	Mexican Hayride		
I Love You, Samantha	High Society		
I'm Always Chasing Rainbows	The Dolly Sisters Oh, Look (show) The Ziegfeld Girl	I've Got a Gal in Kalamazoo	Kiss Them for Me Orchestra Wives
I'm Forever Blowing Bubbles	On Moonlight Bay	I've Got Five Dollars	Gentlemen Marry Brunettes
I'm Free	Tommy		
I'm Getting Sentimental over You	DuBarry Was a Lady	I've Got My Eyes on You	Broadway Melody of 1940
I'm Gonna Wash that Man Right out of My Hair	South Pacific	I've Got You on My Mind	The Gay Divorcee
		I've Got You under My Skin	Born to Dance Night and Day
I'm in Love With a Wonderful Guy	South Pacific		This Could Be the Night
I'm Looking over a Four-Leaf Clover	The Jazz Singer Jolson Sings Again	I've Grown Accustomed to Her Face	My Fair Lady
I'm Riding for a Fall	Thank Your Lucky Stars	I Wanna Be Loved by You	Gentleman Marry Brunettes Good Boy (show) Some Like It Hot Three Little Words
I'm Sitting on Top of the World	I'll Cry Tomorrow The Jolson Story Love Me Or Leave Me The Singing Fool		
The Impossible Dream	Man of La Mancha	I Want to Be Happy	No, No, Nanette Tea for Two
Indian Love Call	One Night of Love Rose Marie	I Whistle a Happy Tune	The King and I
Inka Dinka Doo	The Great Schnozzle This Time for Keeps Two Girls and a Sailor	I Wish I Didn't Love You So	The Perils of Pauline
		I Wish I Were in Love Again	Babes in Arms (show) Words and Music
In the Cool, Cool, Cool of the Evening (1951)	Here Comes the Groom	I Wonder Who's Kissing Her Now	I Wonder Who's Kissing Her Now Moonlight in Havana Prince for Tonight (show) The Time, the Place and the Girl
In the Mood	The Glenn Miller Story Sun Valley Serenade		
In the Still of the Night	Night and Day Rosalie		
I Remember You	The Fleet's In		
Irresistible You	Broadway Rhythm	I Won't Dance	Lovely to Look At Roberta Till the Clouds Roll By That Night in Rio
Isn't It Kinda Fun	State Fair		
Isn't It Romantic?	Love Me Tonight		
Isn't This a Lovely Day	Top Hat		
It Ain't Necessarily So	Porgy and Bess	I Yi Yi Yi Yi I Like You Very Much	
I Talk to the Trees	Paint Your Wagon		
It Could Happen to You	And the Angels Sing	The James Bond Theme	Doctor No
It Had to Be You	Her Kind of Man		

M
U
S
I
C

P
O
P

Song	Show/Film	Song	Show/Film
Jean	The Prime of Miss Jean Brodie		George White's Scandals of 1945
Jeepers Creepers	Going Places		The Jolson Story
Jenny	Lady in the Dark		The Man I Love
	Star		Rhapsody in Blue
Jezebel	The Seven Hills of Rome		Show Girl (show)
			Starlift
Johnny One Note	Words and Music	Long Ago and Far Away	Cover Girl
	Babes in Arms (show)		Till the Clouds Roll By
		Looking for a Boy	Tip-Toes (show)
June in January	Here Is My Heart	Look of Love	Casino Royale
June Is Busting Out All Over	Carousel	Louise	Innocents of Paris
Just in Time	Bells Are Ringing		The Stooge
Just One of Those Things	Can-Can	Love Changes Everything	Aspects of Love (show)
	The Eddie Duchin Story		
	Jubilee (show)	Love in Bloom	She Loves Me Not
	Lullaby of Broadway	Love Is a Many-Splendored Thing	Grease
	Night and Day		
	Panama Hattie	Love Is a Many-Splendored Thing	Love Is a Many-Splendored Thing
	Young at Heart		
		Love Is Sweeping the Country	Of Thee I Sing (show)
Keep the Home Fires Burning	Variety Jubilee		
Keep Young and Beautiful	Roman Scandals	Love Steals Your Heart	The Wicked Lady
Kiss in Your Eyes	The Emperor Waltz	Love Thy Neighbour	We're Not Dressing
Knockin' on Heaven's Door	Pat Garrett and Billy the Kid	Love Walked In	Rhapsody in Blue
			The Goldwyn Follies
The Lady Is a Tramp	Babes in Arms (show)	Luck Be a Lady Tonight	Guys and Dolls
	Pal Joey	Lucky in Love	Good News
	Words and Music		The Best Things in Life Are Free
The Lambeth Walk	Me and My Girl	Lucy in the Sky with Diamonds	John, Paul, George, Ringo and Bert
Lara's Theme (aka Somewhere My Love)	Dr Zhivago	Lullaby of Broadway	Gold Diggers of 1935
The Last Time I Saw Paris	Paris Holiday		Lullaby of Broadway
	Till the Clouds Roll By	Lulu's Back in Town	Broadway Gondolier
	Lady, Be Good!	Lydia the Tattooed Lady	At the Circus
Lavender Blue	So Dear to My Heart		
Leaning on a Lamp Post	Me and My Girl	Mack the Knife	The Threepenny Opera (show)
	Feather Your Nest		Satchmo the Great
Let Me Be Loved	The James Dean Story	Mad About the Boy	Words and Music (show)
Let's Be Buddies	Black Vanities (show)		Set to Music (show)
	Panama Hattie	Make Believe	Till the Clouds Roll By
Let's Call the Whole Thing Off	Shall We Dance?		Show Boat
Let's Do It (Let's Fall in Love)	Night and Day	The Man I Love	Both Ends of the Candle
	Can-Can		The Eddy Duchin Story
	Wake Up and Dream (show)		Lady Sings the Blues
	Paris (show)		The Man I Love
Let's Face the Music and Dance	Follow the Fleet		Rhapsody in Blue
			Sincerely Yours
Let's Hear It for the Boy	Footloose		Will o' the Whispers (show)
Life Is Just a Bowl of Cherries	George White's Scandals		Young at Heart
	The Best Things In Life Are Free	The March of the Siamese Children	The King and I
Little April Shower	Bambi		
Little Girl Blue	Jumbo	Maria	West Side Story
A Little Of What You Fancy	Variety Jubilee	Marta	The Big Broadcast
Living Doll	Serious Charge	Maybe	Oh Kay (show)
Liza	An American in Paris		

Song	Show/Film	Song	Show/Film
Me and My Shadow	Hold That Ghost	Oh, What a Circus	Evita
Memories Are Made of This	The Seven Hills of Rome	Oh, You Beautiful Doll	Wharf Angel
			Oh, You Beautiful Doll
Memory	Cats (show)		
Memo to Turner	Performance		The Story of Vernon and Irene Castle
Mimi	Love Me Tonight		
	Pepe		For Me and My Gal
Minnie the Moocher	The Big Broadcast	Ol' Man River	Show Boat
Miss Otis Regrets	Hi Diddle Diddle (show)		Till the Clouds Roll By
		Once upon a Dream	Play it Cool
	Night and Day	One Night in Bangkok	Chess (show)
Mister Snow	Carousel	Only a Rose	The Vagabond King
Mona Lisa (1950)	After Midnight	Only You	Rock around the Clock
Moonlight Becomes You	Road to Morocco	On the Atchison, Topeka and Santa Fe	The Harvey Girls
Moon River (1961)	Breakfast at Tiffany's		
The More I See You	The Diamond Horseshoe	On the Beach	Wonderful Life
		On the Good Ship Lollipop	Bright Eyes
The Most Beautiful Girl in the World	Jumbo	On the Street Where You Live	My Fair Lady
		On the Sunny Side of the Street	Swing Parade of 1946
Most Gentlemen Don't Like Love	Black Velvet (show)		Is Everybody Happy
	Leave it to Me (show)		Both Ends of the Candle
			The Benny Goodman Story
Mountain Greenery	Words and Music		
Mr Mistoffelees	Cats (show)		The Eddie Duchin Story
Mrs Robinson	The Graduate		
Music, Maestro, Please	These Foolish Things (show)		On the Sunny Side of the Street
Music of the Night	Phantom of the Opera (show)	Our Love Is Here to Stay	An American in Paris
			The Goldwyn Follies
My Baby Just Cares for Me	Whoopee		Lady Sings the Blues
My Favourite Things	Sound of Music	Out of My Dreams	Oklahoma!
My Funny Valentine	Pal Joey	Over My Shoulder	Evergreen
	Babes in Arms (show)	Over the Rainbow (1939)	The Wizard of Oz
	Gentlemen Marry Brunettes	Pack up Your Troubles in Your Old Kit Bag	Her Soldier Boy (show)
My Heart Belongs to Daddy	Let's Make Love		Wait Till the Sun Shines Nellie
	Love Thy Neighbour		
	Night and Day	People Will Say We're in Love	Oklahoma!
My Heart Stood Still	Words and Music	The Physician	Nymph Errant (show)
	A Connecticut Yankee		Star
My One and Only	Funny Face	Pinball Wizard	Tommy
My Resistance Is Low	Las Vegas Story	Please Do It Again	The French Doll (show)
My Romance	Jumbo		
My Sin	The Best Things in Life Are Free		Thoroughly Modern Millie
			Rhapsody in Blue
The Nearness of You	Romance in the Dark		Mayfair and Montmartre (show)
Never on Sunday (1960)	Never on Sunday		
New York, New York	On the Town	The Power of Love	Back to the Future
Nice Work If You Can Get it	An American in Paris	Put It There, Pal	Road to Utopia
	A Damsel in Distress	Puttin' on the Ritz	Blue Skies
Night and Day	Lady on a Train		Idiot's Delight
	The Gay Divorcee		Puttin' on the Ritz
	Night and Day		
	Reveille with Beverley	Que Sera, Sera (1956)	The Man Who Knew Too Much
The Night They Invented Champagne	Gigi		
Nobody Does It Better	The Spy Who Loved Me	Raindrops Keep Falling on My Head	Butch Cassidy and the Sundance Kid
Oh, Lady Be Good	Lady, Be Good!	Red Sails in the Sunset	Province Town Follies (show)
	Rhapsody in Blue		
Oh, What a Beautiful Morning	Oklahoma!		

M
U
S
I
C

P
O
P

Song	Show/Film
Return to Sender	Girls! Girls! Girls!
Rhapsody in Blue	The King of Jazz
	Rhapsody in Blue
Rhythm of Life	Sweet Charity
Rhythm of the Rain	The Man from the Folies Bergère
The Riff Song	The Desert Song
Right Back Where We Started From	The World is Full of Married Men
River Kwai March	The Bridge on the River Kwai
Road Runner	Cooley High
Rock around the Clock	Rock around the Clock
	The Blackboard Jungle
Roll Along, Prairie Moon	Here Comes the Band
Say You, Say Me (1985)	White Nights
Second-Hand Rose	Funny Girl
	My Man
	The Ziegfeld Follies of 1921 (show)
The Second Time Around	High Time
Secret Love (1953)	Calamity Jane
Send in the Clowns	A Little Night Music (show)
September Song	Knickerbocker Holiday
	Pepe
	September Affair
Seventy-Six Trombones	Music Man
The Shadow of Your Smile (1965)	The Sandpiper
Shaft (1971)	Shaft
Shall We Dance?	The King and I
The Sheik of Araby	Make it Snappy (show)
	Tin Pan Alley
She Loves You	A Hard Day's Night
She's So Beautiful	Time
Ship Without a Sail	Heads Up
Shoes with Wings On	The Barkleys of Broadway
Short'nin' Bread	Jericho
Sing For Your Supper	The Boys from Syracuse
Singin' in the Rain	Hollywood Revue of 1929
	Little Nellie Kelly
	Singin' in the Rain
Sit Down You're Rocking the Boat	Guys and Dolls
Slap That Bass	Shall We Dance?
Slaughter on Tenth Avenue	On Your Toes
	Words and Music
Smoke Gets in Your Eyes	Roberta
	Till the Clouds Roll By
	Lovely to Look At
So Am I	Lady Be Good! (show)
So in Love	Kiss Me Kate
Somebody Loves Me	George White's Scandals of 1924 (show)

Song	Show/Film
	Broadway Rhythm
	Pete Kelly's Blues
	Somebody Loves Me
	Lullaby of Broadway
	Rhapsody in Blue
Some Day	The Vagabond King
Some Day My Prince Will Come	Snow White and the Seven Dwarfs
Some Enchanted Evening	South Pacific
Someone to Watch over Me	Rhapsody in Blue
	Young at Heart
	Three for the Show
	Both Ends of the Candle
	Beau James
	Star
Something's Coming	West Side Story
Somewhere	West Side Story
Sonny Boy	The Singing Fool
	Jolson Sings Again
	The Best Things in Life Are Free
Soon	Strike Up the Band (show)
A Spoonful of Sugar	Mary Poppins
Spring Is Here	I Married an Angel
Stardust	The Eddie Duchin Story
Stay as Sweet as You Are	College Rhythm
Staying Alive	Saturday Night Fever
Straighten Up and Fly Right	Here Comes Elmer
	On Stage Everybody
Strange Music	Song of Norway
Stranger in Paradise	Kismet
Strangers in the Night	A Man Could Get Killed
Suicide Is Painless	M.A.S.H.
Summer Nights	Grease
Summertime	Porgy and Bess
Sunny Disposish	Americana (show)
Sunrise Sunset	Fiddler on the Roof
Supercalifragilisticexpiali-docious	Mary Poppins
The Surrey with the Fringe on Top	Oklahoma!
Swanee	Jolson Sings Again
	Sinbad (show)
	Rhapsody in Blue
	Jigsaw (show)
	The Glorious Days (show)
	The Jolson Story
	Sincerely Yours
	A Star Is Born
Sweeping the Clouds Away	Paramount on Parade
Sweet and Lowdown	Tip-Toes (show)
Sweet Georgia Brown	Some Like It Hot
Sweet Leilani (1937)	Waikiki Wedding
Swingin' on a Star (1944)	Going My Way
S'Wonderful	Funny Face
	Rhapsody in Blue
	An American in Paris
	Starlift

Song	Show/Film
Take My Breath Away (1986)	Top Gun
Talk to the Animals (1967)	Doctor Doolittle
Tara's Theme	Gone with the Wind
Tea for Two	With a Song in My Heart
	Sincerely Yours
	Jazz on a Summer's Day
	Tea for Two
	No, No, Nanette
Thank Heaven for Little Girls	Gigi
Thanks for the Memory (1938)	The Big Broadcast of 1938
That Certain Feeling	Tip-Toes (show)
	That Certain Feeling
That Old Black Magic	Star Spangled Rhythm
	Radio Stars on Parade
	Here Come the Waves
	Meet Danny Wilson
That's Amore	The Caddy
That's Entertainment	The Band Wagon
That's for Me	State Fair
There Is Nothing Like a Dame	South Pacific
There's A Small Hotel	On Your Toes (show)
	Words and Music
	Pal Joey
There's No Business Like Show Business	There's No Business Like Show Business
	Annie Get Your Gun
They All Laughed	Shall We Dance?
They Call the Wind Maria	Paint Your Wagon
They Can't Take That Away From Me	The Barkleys of Broadway
	Shall We Dance?
This Can't Be Love	Words and Music
	The Boys from Syracuse
	Jumbo
This Is My Song	Countess from Hong Kong
This Nearly Was Mine	South Pacific
Thou Swell	A Connecticut Yankee
	Words and Music
Three Coins in the Fountain (1954)	Three Coins in the Fountain
Till There Was You	Music Man
Time of My Life (1987)	Dirty Dancing
Together	The Best Things in Life Are Free
	Since You Went Away
To-Kay	Bitter-Sweet
To Keep My Love Alive	A Connecticut Yankee (show)
Tonight	West Side Story
Too Darn Hot	Kiss Me Kate
Trail of the Lonesome Pine	Way Out West
The Trolley Song	Meet Me in St Louis
True Love	High Society
Tubular Bells	The Exorcist
Tutti Frutti	Don't Knock the Rock
Two Little Blue Birds	Sunny

Song	Show/Film
The Ugly Duckling	Hans Christian Andersen
Up Where We Belong (1982)	An Officer and a Gentleman
Varsity Drag	Good News
Wanderin' Star	Paint Your Wagon
Wanting You	The New Moon
Watch the Birdie	Hellzapoppin
The Way We Were (1973)	The Way We Were
The Way You Look Tonight (1936)	Swing Time
We Kiss in the Shadow	The King and I
Welcome to My Dream	Road to Utopia
Well, Did You Evah?	High Society
	DuBarry Was a Lady (show)
We'll Gather Lilacs	Lilacs in the Spring
	Perchance to Dream (show)
We're in the Money	Painting the Clouds with Sunshine
	Gold Diggers of 1933
What is This Thing Called Love?	Starlift
	Wake Up and Dream
	Night and Day
	The Eddie Duchin Story
Whatever Lola Wants	What Lola Wants
	Damn Yankees (show)
What Kind of Fool Am I?	Stop the World – I Want to Get Off
What'll I Do?	Alexander's Ragtime Band
When I Fall in Love	Istanbul
	One Minute to Zero
When I Grow Too Old to Dream	The Night is Young
	Deep in My Heart
When I Take My Sugar to Tea	Monkey Business
When the Going Gets Tough	Jewel of the Nile
When the Red Red Robin	I'll Cry Tomorrow
	Has Anybody Seen My Gal?
	The Jolson Story
When Will I See You Again?	Black Joy
When You're Smiling	Meet Danny Wilson
When You Wish upon A Star	Pinocchio
Where or When	Words and Music
	Babes In Arms
Where's That Rainbow?	Words and Music
Where the Blue of the Night	The Big Broadcast
Whistle While You Work	Snow White and the Seven Dwarfs
White Christmas	White Christmas
	Blue Skies
	Holiday Inn
Who's Sorry Now?	Three Little Words
	A Night in Casablanca
Who Wants to Be a Millionaire?	High Society
Why Can't You Behave?	Kiss Me, Kate
Why Do I Love You?	Show Boat

M
U
S
I
C

P
O
P

Song	Show/Film	Song	Show/Film
Why Was I Born?	Sweet Adeline (show)	You'll Never Know (1943)	Hello, 'Frisco, Hello
Wind beneath My Wings	Beaches	You'll Never Walk Alone	Carousel
Windmills of Your Mind (1968)	The Thomas Crown Affair	You Light up My Life (1977)	You Light Up My Life
Wish Me Luck As You Wave Me Goodbye	Shipyard Sally	You Made Me Love You	Broadway Melody of 1938
With a Little Bit of Luck	My Fair Lady		Wharf Angel
With a Little Help from My Friends	Woodstock		The Jolson Story
	Stardust		Syncopation
	All This and World War II		Jolson Sings Again
	Sgt Pepper's Lonely Hearts Club Band		Love Me Or Leave Me
	Yellow Submarine	You Make Me Feel So Young	I'll Get By
With a Song in My Heart	Words and Music		Three Little Girls in Blue
	With a Song in My Heart	You Must Have Been a Beautiful Baby	Hard to Get
	This Is The Life		My Dream Is Yours
	Spring Is Here		The Eddie Cantor Story
	Painting the Clouds with Sunshine	Younger Than Springtime	South Pacific
	Young Man of Music	You're the Cream in My Coffee	The Cockeyed World
With Every Breath I Take	Here Is My Heart		The Best Things in Life Are Free
Won't You Come Home Bill Bailey?	The Five Pennies	You're the One That I Want	Grease
		You're the Top	Night and Day
Woodchoppers' Ball	What's Cooking?		Anything Goes
Wooden Heart	G.I. Blues	You Started Something	Moon over Miami
Wouldn't It Be Loverly	My Fair Lady	You Stepped out of a Dream	The Ziegfeld Girl
Wunderbar	Kiss Me, Kate	You Took Advantage of Me	Present Arms
			On Your Toes (show)
Yes Sir, That's My Baby	The Eddie Cantor Story		A Star Is Born
	Broadway (show)	You've Lost That Lovin' Feelin'	Stardust
You Are Beautiful	Flower Drum Song	Zip-a-dee-doo-dah (1947)	Song of the South
You'd Be So Nice to Come Home to	Something to Shout About	Zorba's Dance	Zorba the Greek

Show and Film Songs: by Show or Film

Show/Film	Song	Show/Film	Song
A Connecticut Yankee	My Heart Stood Still	All This and World War II	With a Little Help from My Friends
	Thou Swell		
A Connecticut Yankee (show)	To Keep My Love Alive	Allegro (show)	A Fellow Needs a Girl
A Damsel in Distress	A Foggy Day		The Gentleman Is a Dope
	Nice Work If You Can Get It	A Man Could Get Killed	Strangers in the Night
A Day at the Races	All God's Chillun Got Rhythm	American Gigolo	Call Me
After Midnight	Mona Lisa (1950)	Americana	Brother, Can You Spare a Dime
A Hard Day's Night	All My Loving	Americana (show)	Sunny Disposish
	Can't Buy Me Love	An American in Paris	By Strauss
	She Loves You		Embraceable You
Aladdin and His Wonderful Lamp	Genie With the Light Brown Lamp		I Got Rhythm
			I'll Build a Stairway to Paradise
Alexander's Ragtime Band	Alexander's Ragtime (1970) Band		Liza
	All Alone		Nice Work If You Can Get It
	Blue Skies		Our Love Is Here to Stay
	Everybody's Doing It		S'Wonderful
	What'll I Do	A Night in Casablanca	Who's Sorry Now?
A Little Night Music (show)	Send in the Clowns		

Show/Film	Song	Show/Film	Song
An Officer and a Gentleman	Up Where We Belong (1982)	Black Joy	When Will I See You Again?
Anchor's Aweigh	The Charm of You	Black Vanities (show)	Let's Be Buddies
And the Angels Sing	It Could Happen to You	Black Velvet (show)	Most Gentlemen Don't Like Love
Annie Get Your Gun	Anything You Can Do		
	Doin' What Comes Naturally	Blue Hawaii	Can't Help Falling in Love
	I Got the Sun in the Morning	Blue Skies	Always
	There's No Business Like Show Business		Blue Skies
			Puttin' on the Ritz
Anything Goes	All Through the Night		White Christmas
	Blow, Gabriel, Blow	Bonnie and Clyde	Foggy Mountain Breakdown
	I Get a Kick out of You	Born Free	Born Free (1966)
	It's d'Lovely	Born to Dance	I've Got You under My Skin
	You're the Top		
Anything Goes (show)	The Gipsy in Me	Both Ends of the Candle	April in Paris
April in Paris	April in Paris		Avalon
April Showers	April Showers		Bill
	Carolina in the Morning		Can't Help Loving Dat Man
Aspects of Love (show)	Love Changes Everything		Do Do Do
A Star Is Born	Evergreen (1976)		Don't Ever Leave Me
	The Black Bottom		I've Got a Crush on You
	Swanee		The Man I Love
	You Took Advantage of Me		On the Sunny Side of the Street
Atlantic City	Ain't Misbehavin'		Someone to Watch Over Me
At Long Last Love	At Long Last Love		
A Trip to Chinatown (show)	After the Ball	Breakfast at Tiffany's	Moon River (1961)
At the Circus	Lydia the Tattooed Lady	Bridge on the River Kwai	Colonel Bogey March
		Brigadoon	Almost Like Being in Love
Babes in Arms	Ida, Sweet as Apple Cider	Bright Eyes	On the Good Ship Lollipop
	Where or When	Broadway	Alabamy Bound
Babes in Arms (show)	I Wish I Were in Love Again	Broadway (show)	Yes, Sir, That's My Baby
	Johnny One Note	Broadway Gondolier	Lulu's Back in Town
	The Lady Is a Tramp	Broadway Melody of 1936	All I Do Is Dream of You
	My Funny Valentine	Broadway Melody of 1938	You Made Me Love You
Back to the Future	The Power of Love	Broadway Melody of 1940	Begin the Beguine
Bambi	Little April Shower		I Concentrate on You
The Band Wagon	That's Entertainment		I've Got My Eyes on You
The Barkleys of Broadway	They Can't Take That Away from Me	Broadway Rhythm	All the Things You Are
	Shoes With Wings On		Irresistible You
			Somebody Loves Me
Beaches	Wind beneath My Wings	Buck Privates	Boogie Woogie Bugle Boy
Beau James	Someone to Watch over Me		I'll Be with You in Apple Blossom Time
Because You're Mine	All the Things You Are	Butch Cassidy and the Sundance Kid	Raindrops Keep Falling On My Head
The Belle of New York	Baby Doll		
Bells Are Ringing	Just in Time		
Best Foot Forward	Buckle Down, Winsocki	Calamity Jane	The Black Hills of Dakota
The Best Things in Life Are Free	The Best Things in Life are Free		The Deadwood Stage
Beverly Hills Cop	The Heat Is On		Secret Love (1953)
Birth of the Blues	Blues in the Night		It's a Lovely Day Today
	By the Light of the Silvery Moon	Call Me Madam	Boots and Saddle
		Call of the Canyon	How to Handle a Woman
Bitter-Sweet	Dear Little Cafe	Camelot	
	I'll See You Again		If Ever I Would Leave You
	To-Kay		
The Blackboard Jungle	Rock around the Clock		

Show/Film	Song	Show/Film	Song
Can-Can	C'est Magnifique	DuBarry Was a Lady	Do I Love You, Do I
	I Love Paris		Friendship
	It's All Right with Me		I'm Getting Sentimental
	Just One of Those		over You
	Things	DuBarry Was a Lady (show)	Well, Did You Evah?
	Let's Do It (Let's Fall in		
	Love)	Easter Parade	A Couple of Swells
Careless Lady	All of Me		Everybody's Doing It
Carmen Jones	Beat Out Dat Rhythm		I Love a Piano
	on a Drum	Evergreen	Dancing on the Ceiling
	Dat's Love		Over My Shoulder
Carousel	If I Loved You	Everybody's Welcome (show)	As Time Goes By
	June Is Busting Out All	Evita	Don't Cry For Me,
	Over		Argentina
	Mister Snow		Oh, What a Circus
	You'll Never Walk Alone	Evita (show)	Another Suitcase in
Casablanca	As Time Goes By		Another Hall
Casbah	For Every Man There's		
	Woman	Fame	Fame (1980)
Casino Royale	The Look of Love	Feather Your Nest	Leaning on a Lamp Post
Cats	Bustopher Jones	Fiddler on the Roof	Sunrise, Sunset
	Mr Mistofolees		If I Were a Rich Man
	Memory	Finian's Rainbow	How Are Things in
Chasing Rainbows	Happy Days Are Here		Glocca Morra?
	Again	Five Easy Pieces	D.I.V.O.R.C.E.
Chess (show)	I Know Him So Well	Flashdance	Flashdance – What a
	One Night in Bangkok		Feeling (1983)
Christmas Holiday	Always	Flower Drum Song	You Are Beautiful
Chu Chin Chow	Any Time's Kissing	Follow the Band	Ain't Misbehavin'
	Time	Follow The Boys	I'll See You in My
Cinderella	Bibbidi-Bobbidi-Boo		Dreams
Cinderella (show)	Do I Love You Because	Follow the Fleet	Let's Face the Music
	You're Beautiful?		and Dance
College Rhythm	Stay as Sweet as You	Follow Through	Button Up Your
	Are		Overcoat
Convoy	Don't It Make My Brown	Footloose	Let's Hear It for the Boy
	Eyes Blue	For Me and My Gal	Oh, You Beautiful Doll
Cooley High	Dancing in the Street	Funny Face	Clap Yo' Hands
	Road Runner		How Long Has This
Countess from Hong Kong	This Is My Song		Been Going On?
Cover Girl	Long Ago and Far Away		My One and Only
Cuban Pete	The Breeze and I		S'Wonderful
Curly Top	Animal Crackers in My	Funny Girl	Don't Rain on My
	Soup		Parade
			Second-Hand Rose
Damn Yankees (show)	Whatever Lola Wants	Funny Lady	Clap Hands, Here
Days of Wine and Roses	Days of Wine and		Comes Charley
	Roses (1962)		
Deep in My Heart	Auf Wiederseh'n	Gentlemen Marry Brunettes	Have You Met Miss
	When I Grow Too Old to		Jones
	Dream		I Wanna Be Loved by
Deliverance	Duelling Banjos		You
Destry Rides Again	The Boys in the		I've Got Five Dollars
	Backroom		My Funny Valentine
Dirty Dancing	Time of My Life (1987)		Ain't Misbehavin'
Doctor Doolittle	Talk to the Animals	Gentlemen Prefer Blondes	Diamonds Are a Girl's
	(1967)		Best Friend
Doctor No	The James Bond Theme	George White's Scandals	Life Is Just a Bowl of
Don't Fence Me In	Don't Fence Me In		Cherries
Don't Knock the Rock	Tutti Frutti	George White's Scandals of	I'll Build a Stairway To
Down Dakota Way	Candy Kisses	1922 (show)	Paradise
Dr Zhivago	Lara's Theme (aka	George White's Scandals of	Somebody Loves Me
	Somewhere My Love)	1924 (show)	

Show/Film	Song	Show/Film	Song
George White's Scandals of 1945	Liza		When the Red Red Robin
George White's Scandals (show)	The Black Bottom	Heads Up	Ship Without a Sail
G.I. Blues	Wooden Heart	Hello, 'Frisco, Hello	You'll Never Know (1943)
Gigi	Gigi (1958)	Hellzapoppin	Watch the Birdie
	The Night They Invented Champagne	Help!	Help
	Thank Heaven for Little Girls	Here Comes Elmer	Straighten Up and Fly Right
Girl Crazy	Bidin' My Time	Here Comes the Band	Roll Along, Prairie Moon
	But Not for Me	Here Comes the Groom	In the Cool, Cool, Cool of the Evening
	Embraceable You	Here Come the Waves	That Old Black Magic
	Fascinating Rhythm		Ac-cent-tchu-ate the Positive
	I Got Rhythm	Here Is My Heart	June in January
Girls! Girls! Girls!	Return to Sender		With Every Breath I Take
Glorifying the American Girl	Baby Face	Her Kind of Man	It Had to Be You
	Blue Skies	Her Soldier Boy (show)	Pack Up Your Troubles in Your Old Kit Bag
Godspell	Day by Day	Hey Boy! Hey Girl!	Fever
Going My Way	Swingin' on a Star (1944)	Hi Diddle Diddle (show)	Miss Otis Regrets
Going Places	Jeepers Creepers	High Noon	High Noon (1952)
Gold Diggers of 1933	We're in the Money	High Society	I Love You, Samantha
Gold Diggers of 1935	Lullaby of Broadway		True Love
Gone with the Wind	Tara's Theme		Well, Did You Evah?
Good Boy (show)	I Wanna Be Loved by You		Who Wants to Be a Millionaire?
Good News	The Best Things in Life Are Free	High Time	The Second Time Around
	Lucky in Love	High, Wide and Handsome	Can I Forget You
	Varsity Drag		The Folks Who Live on the Hill
Grease	Blue Moon	Hi Neighbour	Deep in the Heart of Texas
	Hopelessly Devoted to You	Hold That Ghost	Me and My Shadow
	Hound Dog	Hole in the Head	High Hopes (1959)
	Love Is a Many-Splendored Thing	Holiday Inn	Be Careful, It's My Heart
	Summer Nights		Happy Holiday
	You're the One That I Want		White Christmas 1942)
Gulliver's Travels	It's A Hap-Hap-Happy Day	Hollywood Canteen	Don't Fence Me In
Guys and Dolls	Adelaide	Hollywood Revue of 1929	Singin' in the Rain
	If I Were a Bell	Hot Chocolates (show)	Ain't Misbehavin'
	Luck Be a Lady Tonight	Hullo America	Give Me the Moonlight
	Sit Down You're Rocking the Boat	Hullo Tango (show)	Get Out and Get Under
Guys and Dolls (show)	Bushel and a Peck	Idiot's Delight	Puttin' on the Ritz
Gypsy	Everything's Coming Up Roses	If I Had My Way	April Played the Fiddle
		I'll Cry Tomorrow	I'm Sitting on Top of the World
Hair	Ain't Got No – Got Life		When the Red Red Robin
	Aquarius	I'll Get By	You Make Me Feel So Young
	Good Morning Starshine	I'll See You in My Dreams	Carolina in the Morning
Half a Sixpence (show)	Flash Bang Wallop		I'll See You in My Dreams
Hands across the Water	Cool Water		It Had to Be You
Hans Christian Andersen	Anywhere I Wander	I Married an Angel	Spring Is Here
	The Ugly Duckling		
Hard to Get	You Must Have Been a Beautiful Baby		
Has Anybody Seen My Gal?	Five Foot Two, Eyes of Blue		

M
U
S
I
C

P
O
P

Show/Film	Song	Show/Film	Song
Incendiary Blonde	Ida, Sweet as Apple Cider	Knickerbocker Holiday	September Song
	It Had to Be You	Lady, Be Good!	Fascinating Rhythm
Indian Territory	Chattanoogie Shoeshine Boy		The Last Time I Saw Paris (1941)
Innocents of Paris	Louise		Oh, Lady Be Good
Irene	Alice Blue Gown	Lady, Be Good (show)	So Am I
Is Everybody Happy	On the Sunny Side of the Street	Lady in the Dark	Jenny
		Lady on a Train	Night and Day
Istanbul	When I Fall in Love	Lady Sings the Blues	All of Me
It's Trad, Dad	Beale Street Blues		The Man I Love
I Wonder Who's Kissing Her Now	I Wonder Who's Kissing Her Now		Our Love Is Here to Stay
		Las Vegas Story	My Resistance Is Low
Jailhouse Rock	Baby I Don't Care	Latin Quarter (show)	C'est Si Bon
Jazz on a Summer's Day	Tea for Two	Leave It to Me (show)	Get Out of Town
The Jazz Singer	I'm Looking Over a Four-Leaf Clover		Most Gentlemen Don't Like Love
Jericho	Short'nin' Bread	Les Misérables	Empty Chairs at Empty Tables
Jesus Christ Superstar	I Don't Know How to Love Him		God on High
Jewel of the Nile	When the Going Gets Tough	Les Girls	Ça C'est l'Amour
Jigsaw (show)	Swanee	Let's Make Love	My Heart Belongs to Daddy
John, Paul, George, Ringo and Bert	Help		We'll Gather Lilacs
	Here Comes the Sun	Lilacs in the Spring	After the Ball
	Lucy in the Sky with Diamonds	Lillian Russell	I Love You (Archer and Thompson)
Jolson Sings Again	April Showers	Little Jesse James (show)	Singin' in the Rain
	Baby Face	Little Nellie Kelly	Be My Love
	California, Here I Come	Looking for Love	Bei Mir Bist Du Schön
	Carolina in the Morning	Love, Honour and Behave	Love is a Many-Splendored Thing
	I'm Looking Over a Four-Leaf Clover	Love Is a Many-Splendored Thing	I Won't Dance
	Sonny Boy	Lovely to Look At	Smoke Gets in Your Eyes
	Swanee		
	You Made Me Love You	Love Me Or Leave Me	I'm Sitting on Top of the World
Jubilee (show)	Begin the Beguine		You Made Me Love You
	Just One of Those Things	Love Me Tonight	Isn't It Romantic?
Jumbo	Little Girl Blue		Mimi
	The Most Beautiful Girl in the World	Lovers and Other Strangers	For All We Know (1970)
	My Romance	Love Thy Neighbour	My Heart Belongs to Daddy
	This Can't Be Love	Lucky Boy	California, Here I Come
Karate Kid II	The Glory of Love	Lullaby of Broadway	Just One of Those Things
Kismet	And This Is My Beloved		Somebody Loves Me
	Baubles, Bangles and Beads		Lullaby of Broadway (1935)
	Stranger in Paradise		
Kiss Me, Kate	Always True to You in My Fashion	Mad Dogs and Englishmen	Delta Lady
	I Hate Men	Mahogany	Do You Know Where You're Going To?
	So in Love	Make It Snappy (show)	The Sheik of Araby
	Too Darn Hot	Man of La Mancha	The Impossible Dream
	Why Can't You Behave?		
	Wunderbar	Mary Poppins	Chim Chim Cheree (1964)
Kiss Them for Me	Blue Moon		
	I've Got a Gal in Kalamazoo		

MUSIC POP

Show/Film	Song	Show/Film	Song
	The Lady is a Tramp		Love Walked In
	My Funny Valentine		The Man I Love
	There's a Small Hotel		Oh, Lady Be Good
Panama Hattie	Just One of Those Things		Please Do It Again
			Rhapsody in Blue
	Let's Be Buddies		Somebody Loves Me
Papa's Delicate Condition	Call Me Irresponsible (1963)		Someone to Watch over Me
Paramount on Parade	Come Back to Sorrento		Swanee
	Sweeping the Clouds Away		S'Wonderful
		Rhythm on the River	Ain't It a Shame about Mame
Pardon My Rhythm	I'll See You in My Dreams	Road House	Again
Pardon My Sarong	Do I Worry	Road to Morocco	Ain't Got a Dime to My Name
Paris	Among My Souvenirs		
Paris (show)	Let's Do it (Let's Fall in Love)		Moonlight Becomes You
		Road to Rio	But Beautiful
Paris Holiday	April in Paris	Road to Utopia	Put It There, Pal
	The Last Time I Saw Paris		Welcome to My Dream
		Roberta	I Won't Dance
Pat Garrett and Billy the Kid	Knockin' on Heaven's Door		Smoke Gets in Your Eyes
Pepe	Mimi	Rock around the Clock	Only You
	September Song		Rock around the Clock
Perchance to Dream (show)	We'll Gather Lilacs	Rocky III	Eye of the Tiger
Performance	Memo to Turner	Romance in the Dark	The Nearness of You
Pete Kelly's Blues	Bye Bye Blackbird	Roman Scandals	Keep Young and Beautiful
	Somebody Loves Me		
Phantom of the Opera (show)	All I Ask of You	Rosalie	In the Still of the Night
	Music of the Night	Rosalie (show)	How Long Has This Been Going On
Pickwick (show)	If I Ruled the World		
Pinocchio	Hi-Diddle-Dee-Dee (An Actor's Life For Me)	Rose Marie	Indian Love Call
		Rose of Washington Square	California, Here I Come
	When You Wish upon a Star (1940)	Sadie McKee	All I Do Is Dream of You
Play It Cool	Once upon a Dream		
Porgy and Bess	I Got Plenty of Nuttin'	Sailors Three	All Over the Place
	It Ain't Necessarily So	St Louis Blues	Beale Street Blues
	Summertime	Saludos Amigos	Brazil
Present Arms	You Took Advantage of Me	Sanders of the River	The Canoe Song
		Satchmo the Great	Mack the Knife
Prince for Tonight (show)	I Wonder Who's Kissing Her Now	Saturday Night Fever	Staying Alive
		September Affair	September Song
Privilege	I've Been a Bad Bad Boy	Sergeant Pepper's Lonely Hearts Club Band	With a Little Help from My Friends
Promises, Promises (show)	I'll Never Fall in Love Again		
		Serious Charge	Living Doll
Province Town Follies (show)	Red Sails in the Sunset	Set to Music (show)	Mad about the Boy
Puttin' on the Ritz	Puttin' on the Ritz	Seven Brides for Seven Brothers	Bless Yore Beautiful Hide
Radio Stars on Parade	That Old Black Magic		
Rain or Shine	Happy Days Are Here Again	The Seven Hills of Rome	Arriverderci Darling
			Jezebel
Rainbow Round My Shoulder	Bye Bye Blackbird		Memories are Made of This
Red Hot and Blue (show)	It's d'Lovely		
Reveille with Beverley	Night and Day	Seven Lively Arts (show)	Ev'ry Time We Say Goodbye
Rhapsody in Blue	Bidin' My Time		
	Clap Yo' Hands	Shaft	Shaft (1971)
	Embraceable You	Shall We Dance?	Beginner's Luck
	Fascinating Rhythm		Let's Call the Whole Thing Off
	I Got Rhythm		Slap That Bass
	I'll Build a Stairway to Paradise		They All Laughed
	Liza		They Can't Take That Away from Me

Show/Film	Song	Show/Film	Song
	I Want to Be Happy		You Must Have Been a
	Tea for Two		Beautiful Baby
Thank Your Lucky Stars	I'm Riding for a Fall	The Eddie Duchin Story	April Showers
That Certain Feeling	That Certain Feeling		Brazil
That Midnight Kiss	Down among the		Just One of Those
	Sheltering Palms		Things
That Night in Rio	Chica Chica Boom		On the Sunny Side of
	Chic		the Street
	I Yi Yi Yi Yi I Like You		Stardust
	Very Much		What Is This Thing
That Summer	Because the Night		Called Love?
The Benny Goodman Story	Avalon		The Man I Love
	On the Sunny Side of	The Emperor Waltz	Kiss in Your Eyes
	the Street	The Exorcist	Tubular Bells
The Best Things in Life	The Birth of the Blues	The Fabulous Dorseys	Everybody's Doing It
Are Free	Broken Hearted	The Firefly	The Donkey Serenade
	Button Up Your	The Five Pennies	Won't You Come Home
	Overcoat		Bill Bailey
	If I Had a Talking Picture	The Fleet's In	I Remember You
	of You	The Fleet's Lit Up (show)	It's d'Lovely
	Life is Just a Bowl of	The French Doll (show)	Please Do It Again
	Cherries	The Gay Divorcee	The Continental
	Lucky in Love		I've Got You on My
	My Sin		Mind
	Sonny Boy		Night and Day
	Together		Be-Bop-A-Lula
	You're the Cream in My	The Girl Can't Help It	Brazil
	Coffee	The Girl He Left Behind	At Last
The Best Years of Our Lives	Among My Souvenirs	The Glenn Miller Story	Basin Street Blues
The Big Beat	As I Love You		Bidin' My Time
The Big Broadcast	Marta		Chattanooga Choo
	Minnie the Moocher		Choo
	Where the Blue of the		In the Mood
	Night	The Glorious Days (show)	Swanee
The Big Broadcast of 1936	Goodnight, Sweetheart	The Goldwyn Follies	Love Walked In
The Big Broadcast of 1938	Thanks for the Memory		Our Love Is Here to
	(1938)		Stay
The Blue Angel	Falling in Love Again	The Graduate	Mrs Robinson
The Blue Paradise	Auf Wiederseh'n	The Great American	Alabamy Bound
The Boy Friend	All I Do Is Dream of	Broadcast	
	You		If I Didn't Care
The Boys from Syracuse	Falling in Love with	The Great Schnozzle	Inka Dinka Doo
	Love	The Harvey Girls	On the Atchison, Topeka
	Sing for Your Supper		and Santa Fe
	This Can't Be Love	The James Dean Story	Let Me Be Loved
The Bridge on the River Kwai	River Kwai March	The Jazz Singer	Blue Skies
The Caddy	That's Amore	The Joker Is Wild	All the Way (1957)
The Cockeyed World	You're the Cream in My	The Jolson Story	After the Ball
	Coffee		The Anniversary Song
The Desert Song	French Military		April Showers
	Marching		Avalon
	Song		By the Light of the
	The Riff Song		Silvery Moon
The Diamond Horseshoe	The More I See You		California, Here I
The Dolly Sisters	Carolina in the Morning		Come
	Give Me the Moonlight		I'm Sitting on Top of the
	I'm Always Chasing		World
	Rainbows		Liza
The Eddie Cantor Story	Bye Bye Blackbird		Swanee
	Ida, Sweet as Apple		When the Red Red
	Cider		Robin
	Yes Sir, That's My		You Made Me Love
	Baby		You

Show/Film	Song	Show/Film	Song
The King and I	Getting to Know You	The Wall	Another Brick in the Wall
	The March of the Siamese Children	The Way We Were	The Way We Were (1973)
	Hello, Young Lovers	The Wicked Lady	Love Steals Your Heart
	I Whistle a Happy Tune	The Wizard of Oz	Over the Rainbow (1939)
	Shall We Dance?	The World Is Full of Married Men	Right Back Where We Started From
	We Kiss in the Shadow		
The King of Jazz	Rhapsody in Blue	The Ziegfeld Follies of 1921 (show)	Second-Hand Rose
The Magic Christian	Come and Get It		
The Man from the Folies Bergere	Rhythm of the Rain	The Ziegfeld Girl	I'm Always Chasing Rainbows
The Man I Love	Bill		You Stepped Out of a Dream
	Liza	There's No Business Like Show Business	Alexander's Ragtime Band
	The Man I Love		
The Man Who Knew Too Much	Que Sera, Sera (1956)		There's No Business Like Show Business
The New Moon	Wanting You		After You Get What You Want You Don't Want It
The Night Is Young	When I Grow Too Old to Dream		
The Pajama Game	Hernando's Hideaway	These Foolish Things (show)	Music, Maestro, Please
The Paleface	Buttons and Bows	This Could Be the Night	I've Got You under My Skin
The Perils of Pauline	I Wish I Didn't Love You So		Blue Moon
The Pirate	Be a Clown	This Is the Life	With a Song in My Heart
The Pleasure Seekers (show)	Get Out and Get Under		
The Prime of Miss Jean Brodie	Jean	This Time for Keeps	Inka Dinka Doo
		Thoroughly Modern Millie	Baby Face
The Sandpiper	The Shadow of Your Smile (1965)		Please Do It Again
The Seven Hills of Rome	Arriverderci Darling	Thousands Cheer	Honeysuckle Rose
	Memories Are Made of This	Three Coins in the Fountain	Three Coins in the Fountain (1954)
The Shocking Miss Pilgrim	For You, for Me, for Everyone	Three for the Show	I've Got a Crush on You
The Show Is On (show)	By Strauss		Someone to Watch over Me
The Singing Fool	I'm Sitting on Top of the World	Three Little Girls in Blue	You Make Me Feel So Young
	Sonny Boy		
The Singing Hill	Blueberry Hill	Three Little Words	I Wanna Be Loved by You
The Singing Nun	Dominique		Who's Sorry Now?
The Spy Who Loved Me	Nobody Does It Better	Till the Clouds Roll By	Long Ago and Far Away
The Sting	The Entertainer		All the Things You Are
The Stooge	Louise		Can't Help Loving Dat Man
The Story of Vernon and Irene Castle	Hello, Hello, Who's Your Lady Friend?		I Won't Dance
	Oh, You Beautiful Doll		The Last Time I Saw Paris
The Strip	Ain't Misbehavin'		Make Believe
	Basin Street Blues		Ol' Man River
The Stud	Emotions		Smoke Gets in Your Eyes
The Student Prince	The Drinking Song		She's So Beautiful
The Sun Also Rises	I Love You (Archer and Thompson)	Time	
		Tin Pan Alley	Honeysuckle Rose
The Third Man	Harry Lime Theme		The Sheik of Araby
The Thomas Crown Affair	Windmills of Your Mind (1968)	Tip-Toes (show)	Looking for a Boy
The Threepenny Opera (show)	Mack the Knife		Sweet and Lowdown
			That Certain Feeling
The Time, the Place and the Girl	I Wonder Who's Kissing Her Now	Tip Top (show)	Feather Your Nest
The Toast of New Orleans	Be My Love	To Have and Have Not	Hong Kong Blues
The Vagabond King	Only a Rose	Tommy	I'm Free
	Some Day		Pinball Wizard

Show/Film	Song	Show/Film	Song
Too Many Girls	I Didn't Know What Time It Was		Embraceable You
			Tea for Two
Too Many Girls (show)	I Like to Recognize the Tune		Alabamy Bound
			Blue Moon
Too Young to Know	It's Only a Paper Moon		With a Song in My Heart
Top Gun	Take My Breath Away (1986)	The Wizard of Oz	Ding Dong the Witch Is Dead
Top Hat	Cheek to Cheek		Over th Rianbow (1939)
	Isn't This a Lovely Day	Woman in Red	I Just Called to Say I Love You
Torch Song	Blue Moon		
Trouble in Store	Don't Laugh at Me	Wonderful Life	On the Beach
Two for the Show	How High the Moon?	Woodstock	Dance to the Music
Two for Tonight	From the Top of Your Head		With a Little Help from My Friends
Two Girls and a Sailor	Inka Dinka Doo	Words and Music	Slaughter on Tenth Avenue
Two Weeks with Love	By the Light of the Silvery Moon		Blue Moon
			I Wish I Were in Love Again
Up in Central Park	Close As Pages in a Book		Johnny One Note
			The Lady Is a Tramp
Variety Jubilee	Keep the Home Fires Burning		Mountain Greenery
	A Little of What You Fancy		My Heart Stood Still
			There's a Small Hotel
			This Can't Be Love
Waikiki Wedding	Sweet Leilani (1937)		Thou Swell
Wait Till the Sun Shines, Nellie	Pack Up Your Troubles in Your Old Kit Bag		Where or When
			Where's That Rainbow?
Wake Up and Dream	What Is This Thing Called Love?		With a Song in My Heart
Wake Up and Dream (show)	Let's Do It (Let's Fall in Love)	Words and Music (show)	Mad about the Boy
Watership Down	Bright Eyes	Yellow Submarine	All You Need Is Love
Way Out West	Trail of the Lonesome Pine		Eleanor Rigby
			With a Little Help from My Friends
Wedding Bells	How Could You Believe Me?	Yesterday's Heroes	Hold the Line
Weekend Pass	All or Nothing at All	You Can't Have Everything	Afraid to Dream
We're Not Dressing	Love Thy Neighbour	You Light Up My Life	You Light Up My Life (1977)
West Side Story	I Feel Pretty		
	Maria	You Never Know (show)	At Long Last Love
	Something's Coming	Young at Heart	Just One of Those Things
	Somewhere		The Man I Love
	Tonight		Someone to Watch over Me
Wharf Angel	Oh, You Beautiful Doll		
	You Made Me Love You	Young Man of Music	With a Song in My Heart
What Lola Wants	Whatever Lola Wants		
What's Cooking?	Woodchoppers' Ball	You're My Everything	Ain't She Sweet?
White Christmas	Blue Skies		California, Here I Come
	White Christmas	You Were Meant for Me	Ain't Misbehavin'
White Nights	Say You, Say Me (1985)		Ain't She Sweet?
Whoopee	My Baby Just Cares for Me		Goodnight, Sweetheart
Will o' the Whispers (show)	The Man I Love, California, Here I Come	Zorba the Greek	Zorba's Dance
With a Song in My Heart	Deep in the Heart of Texas		

Theme Songs or Signature Tunes

Song/Tune	Artiste	Song/Tune	Artiste
Back to Those Happy Days	Herman Darewski	Love in Bloom	Jack Benny
Be My Love	Mario Lanza	Love Is Like a Violin	Ken Dodd
Because of You	Tony Bennett	Lullaby of Broadway	George Shearing
Begin the Beguine	Leslie (Hutch) Hutchinson	Makin' Whoopee	Eddie Cantor
		Mañana Is Soon Enough For Me	Peggy Lee
Bei Mir Bist Du Schön	Andrews Sisters		
Bewitched Bothered and Bewildered	Bill Snyder	Marigold	Billy Mayerl
		Marta	Arthur Tracy (The Street Singer)
Bill	Helen Morgan		
Bugle Call Rag	Harry Roy	Minnie the Moocher	Cab Calloway
Ciribiribin	Harry James	Moonlight Serenade	Glenn Miller
Clap Hands Here Comes Charlie	Charlie Kunz	Mother Machree	John MacCormack
		Music, Maestro, Please	Harry Leader
Cocktails for Two	Carl Brisson	My Blue Heaven	Gene Austin
Coquette	Guy Lombardo	My Heart Belongs to Daddy	Mary Martin
Cry	Johnnie Ray	My Mammy	Al Jolson
Cuban Love Song	Edmundo Ros	My Time Is Your Time	Rudy Vallee
Dancing Time	Oscar Rabin	Near You	Francis Craig
Darling, Je Vous Aime Beaucoup	Hildegarde	Nightmare	Artie Shaw
		Oh Monah	Lew Stone
Dear Old Southland	Layton and Johnstone	O Mein Papa	Eddie Calvert
Deep Forest	Earl Hines	One O'Clock Jump	Count Basie
Dinah	Dinah Shore	On the Air	Carroll Gibbons
Don't Laugh at Me	Norman Wisdom	Over the Rainbow	Judy Garland
Dream	The Pied Pipers	Paper Doll	Mills Brothers
Dream Along with Me	Perry Como	Rags, Bottles or Bones	Syd Walker
Everybody Loves Somebody	Dean Martin	Red Sails in the Sunset	Suzette Tarri
Give Me the Moonlight	Frankie Vaughan	Rhapsody in Blue	Paul Whiteman
Give My Regards to Broadway	George M. Cohen	Rose of Washington Square	Fanny Brice
Goodbye (closing theme)	Benny Goodman	Sally	Gracie Fields
Goodnight	Cavan O'Connor	Say It With Music	Jack Payne
Goodnight, Sweetheart (closing theme)	Ray Noble	Sentimental Journey	Les Brown
		She's My Lovely	Billy Ternent
Here's to the Next Time	Henry Hall	Shine On Harvest Moon	Nora Bayes
How High the Moon	Les Paul and Mary Ford	Skyliner	Charlie Barnet
Hurry on Down	Nellie Lutcher	Sleepy Serenade	Cyril Stapleton
Ida, Sweet as Apple Cider	Eddie Cantor	Smoke Rings	Glen Gray
I Do Like to Be Beside the Seaside	Reginald Dixon	Some of These Days	Sophie Tucker
		Somebody Stole My Gal	Billy Cotton
I Don't Care	Eva Tanguay	So Rare (closing theme)	Jimmy Dorsey
If I Didn't Care	Ink Spots	So Tired	Russ Morgan
I Got Rhythm	Ethel Merman	Speak to Me of Love	Lucienne Boyer
I'll See You Again	Noël Coward	Stage Coach	Eric Winstone
I'll See You in My Dreams	Tony Martin	Stormy Weather	Lena Horne
I Love a Lassie	Harry Lauder	Straighten Up and Fly Right	Nat King Cole
I'm Getting Sentimental Over You	Tommy Dorsey	Sugar Blues	Clyde McCoy
		Summertime	Bob Crosby
Inka Dinka Doo	Jimmy Durante	Sunrise Serenade	Frankie Carle
In the Mood	Joe Loss	Sweet and Lovely	Russ Columbo
I Used to Sigh for the Silvery Moon	G.H.Elliott (Chocolate-coloured Coon)	Take Me to Your Heart Again	Edith Piaf
		Take the 'A' Train	Duke Ellington
J'Attendrai	Jean Sablon	Tenderly	Rosemary Clooney
Just an Old-Fashioned Girl	Eartha Kitt	Thanks for the Memory	Bob Hope
Just Like a Melody from Out of the Sky	Jay Wilbur	That Old Black Magic	Stanley Black
			Billy Daniels
La Mer	Charles Trenet	That's What I Like about The South	Phil Harris
Leaning on a Lamp Post	George Formby		
Let's Dance (opening theme)	Benny Goodman	The Dicky Bird Hop	Ronald Gourlay
Life Is Nothing without Music	Fred Hartley	The Donkey Serenade	Monte Rey
Louise	Maurice Chevalier	The Jolly Brothers	Albert Whelan

MUSIC POP

Song/Tune	Artiste	Song/Tune	Artiste
The Sweetest Music This Side of Heaven	Maurice Winnick	When My Baby Smiles At Me	Ted Lewis
The Very Thought of You (opening theme)	Ray Noble	When the Moon Comes Over the Mountain	Kate Smith
The Wheel of Fortune	Kay Starr	When You're Smiling	George Elrick
Tumbling Tumbleweeds	Sons of the Pioneers	Where the Blue of the Night	Bing Crosby
We'll Be Together Again	Frankie Laine	Whispering	Roy Fox
What's New	Billy Butterfield	Woodchoppers' Ball	Woody Herman
When Day Is Done	Ambrose	You're Dancing on My Heart	Victor Sylvester
When It's Sleepy Time Down South	Louis Armstrong	Yours	Vera Lynn

NB: The theme tunes or signature tunes above are the ones the people themselves considered to be so, and not always the one most readily identifiable with the artist. For example, few would consider 'Yours' to be more identifiable with Vera Lynn than 'The White Cliffs of Dover'. Similarly, 'Take Me To Your Heart Again' is certainly not the most famous Edith Piaf song.

It is probably a good idea at this stage to lay to rest once and for all the most common source of frustration for quiz players on the topic of signature tunes, i.e. is Glenn Miller's signature tune 'In the Mood' or 'Moonlight Serenade'? The problem arises because 'In the Mood' was one of Glenn Miller's most popular tunes and was featured in both *Sun Valley Serenade* and *The Glenn Miller Story*; however, Glenn Miller himself composed 'Moonlight Serenade' and always considered this to be his signature tune. Joe Loss did, in fact, record 'In the Mood' and subsequently adopted it as his signature.

TV and Radio Theme Tunes

Programme	Tune (and/or composer)	Programme	Tune (and/or composer)
Absolutely Fabulous	'This Wheel's on Fire' by Julie Driscoll	Dr Who	Theme by Ron Grainer
The Archers	'Barwick Green' (from '*My Native Heath*') suite written in 1922 by Arthur Wood	The Dukes of Hazzard	Theme tune by Waylon Jennings
		Eastenders	Theme tune by Simon May
Auf Wiedersehen Pet	'That's Living Alright' (sung by Joe Fagin)	Eastenders: vocal version	'Anyone Can Fall in Love' sung by Anita Dobson
The Avengers	Theme by Laurie Johnson	Equaliser	Theme tune by Stewart Copeland
Billy Cotton Band Show	'Somebody Stole My Gal'	Grand Prix	BBC – 'The Chain' by Fleetwood Mac
Blake's 7	Music by Dudley Simpson		
Blue Peter	'Barnacle Bill the Sailor' by Robison and Luther (famous adaptation by Mike Oldfield)	Great Antiques Hunt	Theme tune by the Brodsky Quartet
		Harry's Game	Theme by Clannad
Bonanza	Music by David Rose	Have Gun, Will Travel	'The Ballad of the Paladin'
Bootsie and Snudge	'Pop Goes the Weasel'	Hawaii Five O	Music by Morton Stevens
Brain of Britain	Mozart's *Eine kleine Nachtmusik*	Horse of the Year Show	Mozart's 40th Symphony
		Howards Way	Theme tune by Simon May
Captain Pugwash	'Hornblower' (played on the accordion by Tommy Edwards)	Howards Way: vocal version	'Always There' by Marti Webb
Crossroads	Theme by Tony Hatch and later adapted by Paul McCartney	I'm Sorry I'll Read That Again	'The Angus Prune Tune'
Dad's Army	'Who Do You Think You're Kidding, Mr Hitler?' sung by Bud Flanagan	Inspector Morse	Theme tune by Barrington Pheloung
		Ironside	Theme by Quincy Jones
Danger Man	Music by Edwin Astley	Jason King	Theme by Laurie Johnson
Desert Island Discs	'By the Sleepy Lagoon' by Eric Coates	Juke Box Jury	'Hit and Miss' by John Barry
Doctor Kildare	'Three Stars Will Shine Tonight (vocal version by Richard Chamberlain)	Just a Minute	*Minute Waltz* by Chopin
		The Killing Game	'Tom Hark' by the Piranhas

Programme	Tune (or composer)	Programme	Tune (or composer
Kojak	Theme by Billy Goldenberg	Ready Steady Go!	'I Can't Explain' (The Who)
		The Saint	Music by Edwin Astley
Life and Times of David Lloyd George	'Chi Mai' by Ennio Morricone	The Seven Faces of Woman	'She' (sung by Charles Aznavour)
Light of Experience	Theme by Doina De Jale	The Sky at Night	At the Castle Gate by Sibelius (from Pelléas et Mélisande)
The Lone Ranger	William Tell Overture by Rossini		
		The Snowman	'Walking in the Air' (sung by Aled Jones)
M.A.S.H.	'Suicide Is Painless' by Mash	South Bank Show	Variations on a Theme of Paganini by Julian Lloyd Webber
Mastermind	'Approaching Menace' by Neil Richardson		
Match of the Day	Drum Majorette	Star Trek	Music by Alexander Courage
Miami Vice	'Miami Vice Theme' and 'Crockett's Theme' (both by Jan Hammer)	Stingray	'Aquamarina' (sung by Garry Miller)
Minder	'I Could Be So Good For You' by Pat Waterman and Gerard Kenny	Supergran	Theme composed and sung by Billy Connolly
Mission Impossible	Theme by Lalo Schifrin	Test Match Special	'Cricket Calypso'
Mistral's Daughter	'Only Love' (sung by Nana Mouskouri)	That Was the Week That Was	Sung by Millicent Martin
Monty Python's Flying Circus	'Liberty Bell' by John Paul Souza	The Third Man	'Harry Lime Theme' by Anton Karas
Moonlighting	'Moonlighting Theme' by Al Jarreau	Tinker, Tailor, Soldier, Spy	Nunc Dimittis, arranged by Geoffrey Burgon
		Top of the Pops	'Yellow Pearl' by Phil Lynott (co-written by Lynott and Ray Davies); 'Whole Lotta Love' by ccs, 'The Wizard' by Paul Hardcastle
Neighbours	Theme by Tony Hatch		
Noddy	Paul K. Joyce		
No Honestly	'No Honestly' by Lynsey de Paul		
		Top Secret	'Sucu Sucu'
Onedin Line	Spartacus by Khatchaturian	Two-Way Family Favourites	'With a Song in My Heart' by Richard Rodgers
One Foot in the Grave	Composed and sung by Eric Idle		
Owen MD	'Sleepy Shores' by Johnny Pearson	Van Der Valk	'Eye Level' by Simon Park
		What the Papers Say	From the Cornish Dances by Malcolm Arnold
Perry Mason	Theme by Fred Steiner		
The Persuaders	Music by John Barry		
The Prisoner	Music by Ron Grainer	X Files	Music by Mark Snow
Prisoner Cell Block H	'On the Inside' (sung by Lynne Hamilton)		
Protectors	'Avenues and Alleyways' by Tony Christie	Yes Honestly	'Yes Honestly' by Georgie Fame
		Z Cars	'Theme from Z Cars' aka 'Johnny Todd' by the Johnny Keating Orchestra
Randall and Hopkirk (Deceased)	Music by Edwin Astley		
Rawhide	Theme sung by Frankie Laine		

M
U
S
I
C

P
O
P

Eurovision Song Contest Winners

Year	Song	Country (and Singer)	UK Entry	UK Posn
1956	Refrain	Switzerland (Lys Assia)	No entry	
1957	Net Als Toen	Holland (Corry Brokken)	All (Patricia Breden)	6th
1958	Dors, Mon Amour	France (André Claveau)	No entry	
1959	Een Beetje	Holland (Teddy Scholten)	Sing Little Birdie (Pearl Carr and Teddy Johnson)	2nd
1960	Tom Pillibi	France (Jacqueline Boyer)	Looking High, High, High (Bryan Johnson)	2nd
1961	Nous, les Amoureux	Luxembourg (Jean-Claude Pascal)	Are You Sure (Allisons)	2nd
1962	Un Premier Amour	France (Isabelle Aubret)	Ring-a-ding Girl (Ronnie Carroll)	4th
1963	Dansevise	Denmark (Grethe Jorgen Ingmann)	Say Wonderful Things (Ronnie Carroll)	4th
1964	Non Ho L'Eta (This Is My Prayer)	Italy (Gigliola Cinquetti)	I Say the Little Things (Matt Monro)	2nd
1965	Poupée de Cire, Poupée de Son	Luxembourg (France Gall)	I Belong (Kathy Kirby)	2nd
1966	Merci Chérie	Austria (Udo Jurgens)	A Man without Love (Kenneth McKellar)	7th
1967	Puppet on a String	UK (Sandie Shaw)	Puppet on a String	1st
1968	La La La	Spain (Massiel)	Congratulations (Cliff Richard)	2nd
1969	Viva Cantando	Spain (Salome)	Boom Bang-A-Bang	1st
	Boom Bang-A-Bang	UK (Lulu)		
	De Troubadour	Holland (Lennie Kuhr)		
	Un Jour Un Enfant	France (Frida Boccara)		
1970	All Kinds of Everything	Ireland (Dana)	Knock Knock (Mary Hopkin)	2nd
1971	Un Banc, Un Arbre, Une Rue	Monaco (Séverine)	Jack in the Box (Clodagh Rodgers)	4th
1972	Après Toi (Come What May)	Luxembourg (Vicky Leandros)	Beg, Steal or Borrow (New Seekers)	2nd
1973	Tu Te Reconnaîtras (Wonderful Dream)	Luxembourg (Anne-Marie David)	Power to all our Friends (Cliff Richard)	3rd
1974	Waterloo	Sweden (Abba)	Long Live Love (Olivia Newton-John)	4th
1975	Ding A Dong	Holland (Teach In)	Let Me Be the One (Shadows)	2nd
1976	Save Your Kisses for Me	UK (Brotherhood of Man)	Save Your Kisses For Me	1st
1977	L'Oiseau et L'Enfant	France (Marie Myriam)	Rock Bottom (Lynsey de Paul)	2nd
1978	A-ba-ni-bi	Israel (Izhar Cohen and the Alpha-Beta)	The Bad Old Days (Coco)	11th
1979	Hallelujah	Israel (Milk and Honey featuring Gali Atari)	Mary Ann (Black Lace)	7th
1980	What's Another Year?	Ireland (Johnny Logan)	Love Enough for Two (Prima Donna)	3rd
1981	Making Your Mind Up	UK (Buck's Fizz)	Making Your Mind Up	1st
1982	Ein Bisschen Frieden (A Little Peace)	Germany (Nicole)	One Step Further (Bardo)	7th
1983	Si la Vie Est Cadeau	Luxembourg (Corinne Hermes)	I'm Never Giving Up (Sweet Dreams)	6th
1984	Diggi loo-Diggi Ley	Sweden (Herreys)	Love Games (Belle and the Devotions)	7th
1985	La Det Swinge (Let it Swing)	Norway (Bobbysocks)	Love Is (Vikki)	4th
1986	J'aime la Vie	Belgium (Sandra Kim)	Runner in the Night (Ryder)	7th
1987	Hold Me Now	Ireland (Johnny Logan)	Only the Light (Rikki)	13th
1988	Ne Partez Pas Sans Moi	Switzerland (Celine Dion)	Go (Scott Fitzgerald)	2nd
1989	Rock Me	Yugoslavia (Riva)	Why Do I Always Get It Wrong (Live Report)	2nd
1990	Insieme:1992	Italy (Toto Cutugno)	Give a Little Love Back to the World (Emma)	6th
1991	Fångad Av En Stormvind	Sweden (Carola)	A Message to Your Heart (Samantha Janus)	10th

Year	Song	Country (and Singer)	UK Entry	UK Posn
1992	Why Me?	Ireland (Linda Martin)	One Step Out of Time (Michael Ball)	2nd
1993	In Your Eyes	Ireland (Niamh Kavanagh)	Better the Devil You Know (Sonia)	2nd
1994	Rock 'n' Roll Kids	Ireland (Paul Harrington and Charlie McGettigan)	We Will Be Free (Lonely Symphony) (Frances Ruffelle)	10th
1995	Nocturne	Norway (Secret Garden)	Love City Groove (Love City Groove)	10th
1996	The Voice	Ireland (Eimear Quinn)	Just a Little Bit (Gina G)	8th
1997	Love Shine a Light	UK (Katrina and the Waves)	Love Shine a Light	1st
1998	Diva	Israel (Dana International)	Where Are You? (Immari)	2nd
1999	Take me to our Leader	Sweden (Charlotte Nilsson)	Say It Again (Precious)	12th
2000	Fly on the Wings of Love	Denmark (Olsen Brothers)	Don't Play That Song Again (Nikki French)	16th
2001	Everybody	Estonia (Tanel Pader and Dave Benton)	No Dream Impossible (Lindsay Dracass)	15th

Classical-based Pop Tunes

Baubles, Bangles and Beads   Adapted from the String Quartet in D major by Alexander Borodin

Beat Out Dat Rhythm on a Drum   Based on 'The Gypsy Song' from the opera *Carmen* by Georges Bizet

Can Can (Bad Manners)   Adapted from *Orpheus in the Underworld* by Jaques Offenbach

Can't Help Falling in Love   Based on *Plaisir d'Amour* by Giovanni Martini

Capstick Comes Home   Based on Dvořák's Symphony No. 9 in E minor (2nd movement, Largo)

Danny Boy   Based on 'The Londonderry Air' by Frederick Weatherly

Dat's Love   Based on 'Habañera' from the opera *Carmen* by Georges Bizet

Fanfare for the Common Man (ELP)   Based on Aaron Copland's orchestral piece of the same name

Hello Muddah, Hello Fadduh   Adapted from 'Dance of the Hours', Act 3 of *La Gioconda* by Amilcare Ponchielli

Hot Diggity   Adapted from *España* (Spanish Rhapsody) by Emmanuel Chabrier

I Believe in Father Christmas   Adapted from the *Lieutenant Kijé Suite*, Op. 60 by Sergei Prokofiev

I'd Climb the Highest Mountain   Based on *Humoresque* Opus 101 No. 7 by Antonín Dvořák

If I Had Words   Adapted from the 3rd movement of Symphony No. 3 Op. 78 by Charles Camille Saint-Saëns

If You Are But a Dream   Adapted from *Romance* in E flat by Anton Rubinstein

I'm Always Chasing Rainbows   Adapted from *Fantaisie Impromptu* in C sharp minor Op. 66 by Frederic Chopin

In An Eighteenth-century Drawing Room   Adapted from Piano Sonata No. 3 in C by Wolfgang Amadeus Mozart

Joybringer   Adapted from the 4th movement of *The Planets Suite* Op. 32 by Gustav Holst ('Jupiter – Bringer of Jollity')

Kiss in Your Eyes   Adapted from *Une Chambre séparée* by Richard Heuberger

Lamp Is Low   Adapted from *Pavane pour une infante défunte* by Maurice Ravel

Land of Hope and Glory   Based on *Pomp and Circumstance March* No. 1 by Edward Elgar

Like I Do   Adapted from 'Dance of the Hours', Act 3 of *La Gioconda* by Amilcare Ponchielli

More Than Love   Adapted from the 2nd movement of the Sonata for Piano No. 8 in C minor, Op. 13 by Ludwig van Beethoven

Narcissus   Adapted from the *Water Scenes Suite*, Op. 13 No. 4 by Ethelbert Nevin

Nut Rocker   Adapted from the March from *Casse-noisette Suite*, Op. 71 by Tchaikovsky

Question and Answer   Adapted from *Petite Suite de Concert*, Op. 77 by Samuel Coleridge-Taylor

River Kwai March   Based on 'Colonel Bogey March' by Kenneth Alford

Rodrigo's Concerto   An arrangement of the 2nd movement of the *Concerto for Guitar and Orchestra in D major* by Joaquin Rodrigo

Sabre Dance   Adapted from *Gayaneh Ballet* by Aram Khatchaturian

So Deep Is the Night   Adapted from Etude in E minor, Op. 10 No. 3 by Frédéric Chopin

Song of India   Adapted from *Chanson indoue* by Nikolai Rimsky-Korsakov

The Story of a Starry Night   Based on the 1st movement of Symphony No. 6 by Tchaikovsky

Strange Music   Adapted from *Wedding-Day in Troldhaugen* by Edvard Greig

Stranger in Paradise   Adapted from a theme of the *Polovtsian Dances* by Alexander Borodin

Suddenly (Tony Bennett)   Adapted from *Une Chambre Séparée* by Richard Heuberger

Surrender (Elvis Presley)   Adapted from 'Torna A Surriento' by Ernesto De Curtis

The Things I Love   Based on Melodie in E flat major, Op. 42 No 3 by Tchaikovsky

Toccata and Fugue (Vanessa Mae)   Variation of a Toccata and Fugue by Johann Sebastian Bach

Under the Lilac Bough   Based on various pieces of music of Franz Schubert

Wagon Wheels   Adapted from the 2nd movement of Dvorak's Symphony No. 9 in E minor

Wild Horses   Based on 'Wilder Reiter' by Robert Schumann

Wooden Heart   Adapted from the German folk song 'Muss I denn'

M
U
S
I
C

P
O
P

Composers of Pop Songs and Tunes

Song	Composer	Song	Composer
Alexander's Ragtime Band	Irving Berlin	Easter Parade	Irving Berlin
Alfie	Burt Bacharach and Hal David	Eloise	Paul Ryan
All along the Watchtower	Bob Dylan	Fascinating Rhythm	George and Ira Gershwin
All of You	Cole Porter		
All the Young Dudes	David Bowie	First Cut Is the Deepest	Cat Stevens
Alternate Title	Mickey Dolenz	Floy Joy	William 'Smokey' Robinson
Always Something There To Remind Me	Burt Bacharach and Hal David	For the Good Times	Kris Kristofferson
And I Love You So	Don McLean		
Anything You Can Do	Irving Berlin	Genie with the Light Brown Lamp	Marvin, Welch, Bennett, Rostill (Shadows)
Automatically Sunshine	William 'Smokey' Robinson	Georgy Girl	Jim Dale and Tom Springfield
		Giving It All Away	Leo Sayer and David Courtney
Baby I Don't Care	Leiber and Stoller		
Bad To Me	Lennon and McCartney	Goldfinger	Tony Newley, John Barry and Leslie Bricusse
Batdance	Prince		
Beautiful Dreamer	Stephen Foster	Goodbye	Lennon and McCartney
Begin the Beguine	Cole Porter	Goodbye (Mary Hopkin)	Lennon and McCartney
Boat That I Row, The	Neil Diamond	Got to Get You into My Life	Lennon and McCartney
Born Free	Don Black and John Barry		
Bright Eyes	Mike Batt	Grease	Barry Gibb
Bring it on Home to Me	Sam Cooke	A Groovy Kind of Love	Carole Bayer Sager and Tony Wine
Brown Eyed Handsome Man	Chuck Berry		
		Halfway to Paradise	Gerry Goffin and Carole King
Carnival Is Over	Tom Springfield		
Chain Reaction	Bee Gees	Happy Holiday	Irving Berlin
Chantilly Lace	J.P. Richardson (The Big Bopper)	A Hard Rain's Gonna Fall	Bob Dylan
		Have I Told You Lately	Van Morrison
Cheek to Cheek	Irving Berlin	Help Me Make It through The Night	Kris Kristofferson
Close to You	Burt Bacharach and Hal David		
		Hey, Good Looking	Hank Williams
Come and Get It	Paul McCartney	Hopelessly Devoted to You	John Farrar
A Couple of Swells	Irving Berlin	The Hustle	Van McCoy
Cupid	Sam Cooke		
		I Don't Wanna Fight	Lulu
Dancing in the Street	Marvyn Gaye and William Stevenson	I Don't Want to Talk About it	Cat Stevens and Danny Whitten
Dancing on a Saturday Night	Barry Blue and Lynsey De Paul	If Not for You	Bob Dylan
		I Get a Kick Out of You	Cole Porter
The Day I Met Marie	Hank Marvin	I Got Plenty of Nuttin'	George and Ira Gershwin
Dick-A-Dum Dum (Kings Road)	Jim Dale	I Got Rhythm	George and Ira Gershwin
		I Got the Sun in the Morning	Irving Berlin
Do They Know It's Christmas?	Bob Geldof and Midge Ure		
Do You Know Where You're Going To?	Gerry Goffin and Michael Masser	I Just Don't Know What to do with Myself	Burt Bacharach and Hal David
Do You Love Me	Berry Gordy Jr	I'll Keep You Satisfied	Lennon and McCartney
Do You Want To Know a Secret	Lennon and McCartney	I'll Never Fall in Love Again	Burt Bacharach and Hal David
Doctorin' the Tardis	Gary Glitter, Ron Grainer, Chapman and Chinn	I'll Never Fall in Love Again (Tom Jones)	Lonnie Donegan and Jimmie Currie
Doin' What Comes Naturally	Irving Berlin	I Love You, Samantha	Cole Porter
Don't Cry Out Loud	Carole Bayer Sager and Peter Allen	I'm a Believer	Neil Diamond
		I'm a Tiger	Marty Wilde and Ronnie Scott
Don't Give Up On Us	Tony Macaulay		
Don't Sleep in the Subway	Tony Hatch and Jackie Trent	I'm into Something Good	Gerry Goffin and Carole King

Song	Composer
I Say a Little Prayer	Burt Bacharach and Hal David
I Shot the Sheriff	Bob Marley
Isn't This a Lovely Day	Irving Berlin
It Doesn't Matter Anymore	Paul Anka
It Don't Mean a Thing	Duke Ellington and Irving Mills
It Might as Well Rain until September	Gerry Goffin and Carole King
It's All in the Game	Charles Dawes and Carl Sigman
I've Got You under My Skin	Cole Porter
I Wanna Be Your Man	Lennon and McCartney
I Will Drink the Wine	Paul Ryan
Jackie Wilson Said	Van Morrison
Jambalaya	Hank Williams
The James Bond Theme	Monty Norman
Just Like a Woman	Bob Dylan
Killing Me Softly with His Song	Charles Fox and Norman Gimbel
Knockin' on Heaven's Door	Bob Dylan
Lady	Lionel Richie
The Lady is a Tramp	Rodgers and Hart
Leaning on a Lamp Post	Noel Gay
Leavin' on a Jet Plane	John Denver
Legend of the Glass Mountain	Nino Rota
Let's Call the Whole Thing Off	George and Ira Gershwin
Let's Do It (Let's Fall in Love)	Cole Porter
Let's Face the Music and Dance	Irving Berlin
Little Bit Me, Little Bit You	Neil Diamond
Living Doll	Lionel Bart
The Locomotion	Gerry Goffin and Carole King
Love and Marriage	Sammy Cahn and Jimmy Van Heusen
MacArthur Park	Jim Webb
Mack the Knife	Weill, Brecht, Blitzstein
Mad about the Boy	Noël Coward
Mad Dogs and Englishmen	Noël Coward
Magic Moments	Burt Bacharach and Hal David
Mama Told Me Not to Come	Randy Newman
The Man Who Sold the World	David Bowie
The March of the Siamese Children	Richard Rodgers
Mighty Quinn	Bob Dylan
Miss Otis Regrets	Cole Porter
Mr Tambourine Man	Bob Dylan
Money (That's What I Want)	Berry Gordy Jr and Janie Bradford
Mrs Brown You've Got a Lovely Daughter	Trevor Peacock

Song	Composer
My Guy	William 'Smokey' Robinson
My Heart Belongs to Daddy	Cole Porter
My Resistance Is Low	Hoagy Carmichael and Harold Adamson
Needles and Pins	Sonny Bono and Jack Nitzche
A Nice Cup Of Tea	A.P. Herbert
Night and Day	Cole Porter
Nothing Compares 2 U	Prince
Oh, Carol	Neil Sedaka and Howard Greenfield
Oh No, Not My Baby	Gerry Goffin and Carole King
Photograph	Ringo Starr and George Harrison
Pink Cadillac	Bruce Springsteen
The Purple People Eater	Sheb Wooley
Puttin' on the Ritz	Irving Berlin
Rhapsody in Blue	George Gershwin
River Kwai March	Malcolm Arnold
Roamin' in the Gloamin'	Harry Lauder
Rocket Man	Elton John and Bernie Taupin
Roll Over Beethoven	Chuck Berry
Running Bear	J.P. Richardson (The Big Bopper)
Saving All My Love for You	Gerry Goffin and Michael Masser
September Song	Maxwell Anderson and Kurt Weill
Simon Smith and His Amazing Dancing Bear	Randy Newman
Something's Gotten Hold of My Heart	Roger Cook and Roger Greenaway
Something Tells Me	Roger Cook and Roger Greenaway
Sophisticated Lady	Duke Ellington, Irving Mills and Mitchell Parish
Step Inside Love	Lennon and McCartney
The Stripper	David Rose
S'Wonderful	George and Ira Gershwin
Take Five	Paul Desmond and Lola Brubeck
Take Good Care of My Baby	Gerry Goffin and Carole King
Tara's Theme	Max Steiner
Tears of a Clown	Smokey Robinson, Stevie Wonder, Henry Cosby
This Guy's in Love With You	Burt Bacharach and Hal David
This is My Song	Charlie Chaplin
This Wheel's on Fire	Bob Dylan and Rick Danko

M
U
S
I
C

P
O
P

Throw Down A Line	Hank B. Marvin
To Keep My Love Alive	Rodgers and Hart
To Know Him is To Love Him	Phil Spector
To Love Somebody	Barry and Robin Gibb
Too Darn Hot	Cole Porter
Trains and Boats and Planes	Burt Bacharach and Hal David
True Love	Cole Porter
Twent-Four Hours from Tulsa	Burt Bacharach and Hal David
Twisting the Night Away	Sam Cooke
Up on the Roof	Gerry Goffin and Carole King
Up Where We Belong	Buffy St Marie, Jack Nitzche, William Jennings
We Are the World	Michael Jackson and Lionel Richie
Well, Did You Evah?	Cole Porter
What'll I Do	Irving Berlin
What's New, Pussycat?	Burt Bacharach and Hal David
When I'm Dead and Gone	Gallagher and Lyle
When I Need You	Carole Bayer Sager and Albert Hammond

Wherever I Lay My Hat	Marvin Gaye and Norman Whitfield
A Whiter Shade of Pale	Keith Richard and Gary Brooker
Who Wants to Be a Millionaire	Cole Porter
Wild Thing	Chip Taylor
Wild World	Cat Stevens
Will You Love Me Tomorrow	Gerry Goffin and Carole King
A Winter's Tale	Mike Batt
Wired for Sound	B.A. Robertson and Alan Tarney
Without You	Peter Ham and Tony Evans (Badfinger)
Wichita Lineman	Jim Webb
Woman in Love	Barry and Robin Gibb
Woodstock	Joni Mitchell
A World Without Love	Lennon and McCartney
Wunderbar	Cole Porter
You Make Me Feel So Young	Mack Gordon and Joseph Myrow
Your Cheating Heart	Hank Williams
You're the One That I Want	John Farrar
You're the Top	Cole Porter
You've Got Your Troubles	Roger Cook and Roger Greenaway

Derivations of Names

Group	Derivation	Where from
Abba (1972)	The initials of of its members Christian names	Sweden/Norway
Adam and the Ants (1977)	Adopted his surname as collective name for his group of four	London
A-Ha (1982)	Keyboardist Mags Furuholmen chose name as it was a universally accepted expression	Norway
Alice Cooper (1965)	Spelt out by a ouija board	USA
America (1967)	Met at London school; all 3 members were sons of US Air Force officers stationed in UK	USA
Archies (1967)	Named after a popular CBS cartoon series based on John Goldwater comic book characters	USA
Art of Noise (1983)	The name of an Italian futurist manifesto	UK
Aswad (1983)	Arabic for 'Black'	UK
Bachman-Turner Overdrive (1973)	Added name of a trucking magazine, *Overdrive*, to those of its founding members	Canada
Bad Company (1973)	From a Jeff Bridges film	UK
Bangles (1981)	Forced to change name from the Bangs because of existing band	Los Angeles
Bauhaus (1980)	Named after the German art movement	UK
Bay City Rollers (1970)	Chosen by sticking pin in map of USA and pricking Bay City	UK
Bee Gees (1959)	From the initials of their founder Barry Gibb. There is no substance to the myth that a racetrack promoter (Bill Goode) and a DJ (Bill Gates) inspired the name	Australia
B-52's	Southern US nickname for a bouffant hairstyle adopted by its female members	Georgia
Blondie (1975)	Lead singer's hair colour	New York
Boomtown Rats (1978)	Originally Nightlife Thugs; changed name to phrase in Woody Guthrie biography *Bound For Glory*	Dublin
Bread (1968)	Chosen after they were stuck behind a Wonder Bread truck in a traffic jam	Los Angeles
Buffalo Springfield (1966)	A make of steamroller	California
Canned Heat (1966)	From 1928 song by Mississipi bluesman Tommy Johnson, 'Canned Heat Blues'	Los Angeles
Captain And Tennille (1971)	Mike Love of the Beach Boys called Daryl Dragon 'Captain Keyboards' and the name stuck; other member Toni Tennille	San Francisco
CCS (1970)	Collective Consciousness Society, a collaboration between Alexis Korner, Mickie Most and John Cameron	UK
Clannad (1981)	Gaelic for 'Family'	Ireland
Commodores (1968)	Random choice from dictionary (nearly called the Commodes, so they say)	USA
Cream (1966)	Thought themselves the best so named themselves accordingly	UK
Creedence Clearwater Revival (1968)	Creedence was a friend of the band and Clearwater came from a beer commercial	USA
Crystals (1961)	After Crystal Bates, daughter of their first songwriter, Leroy Bates	USA
Cult (1982)	Originally called Southern Death Cult, taken from a newspaper headline	UK
Cure (1976)	Originally called the Easy Cure, a stock phrase of the day	Crawley
Damned (1976)	From the Dracula-style fancy dress worn by lead singer Dave Vanian	UK
Deacon Blue (1987)	From a Steely Dan record	UK
Dead Kennedys (1978)	Name was designed to shock, as it refers to the Kennedy brothers John and Robert	San Francisco
Deep Purple (1968)	Chosen as a contrast to Vanilla Fudge on whom they based their early music	UK
Def Leppard (1977)	Corruption of Deaf Leopard, proposed by band's lead singer Joe Elliott	Sheffield

Group	Derivation	Where from
Depeche Mode (1980)	From a French fashion magazine, meaning 'Fast Fashion'	UK
Devo (1972)	From video *Truth about De-evolution*, award winner at Ann Arbor Film Festival	Akron, Ohio
Dexy's Midnight Runners (1978)	Slang term for the pep pill Dexedrine	Birmingham
Dire Straits (1977)	From the financial plight of the group when formed	UK
Doobie Brothers (1970)	After 'doobie' the Californian nickname for a marijuana cigarette	San Jose, California
Doors (1965)	From Aldous Huxley book *The Doors of Perception* (Huxley took title from Blake work)	Los Angeles
Dr Feelgood (1971)	From 1962 US hit 'Doctor Feel-Good' by bluesman Piano Red	UK
Dr Hook (1968)	Prompted by the eye patch (as in Captain Hook) worn by lead singer Ray Sawyer	New Jersey
Duran Duran (1978)	First gig was at Barbarella's in Birmingham so used a name from the Jane Fonda film	Birmingham
Earth, Wind and Fire (1969)	Singer and drummer Maurice White named band after 3 of the ancient elements	USA
The Easybeats	From a BBC Light programme pop show hosted by Brian Matthews	USA
Echo and the Bunnymen (1977)	Echo was the nickname for their drum machine, which was replaced by Pete de Freitas	Liverpool
Eurythmics (1977)	Named in 1980 after 'Rhythm Gymnastics' style devised by Emile Jaques-Dalcroze	UK
Everything But the Girl (1982)	Took their misleading name from a local second-hand furniture store	Hull
Faces (1969)	Steve Marriott left the Small Faces to form Humble Pie and the 'Small' was dropped	London
Fairport Convention (1967)	After the house, 'Fairport', in which its guitarist Simon Nicol lived in Muswell Hill	London
Faith No More (1980)	After a greyhound on which they had a bet	Los Angeles
Fifth Dimension (1966)	Originally called Versatiles changed name to reflect being beyond the 4th dimension	Los Angeles
Fine Young Cannibals (1984)	From the Robert Wagner/Natalie Wood film *All the Fine Young Cannibals*	UK
Fixx (1980)	Originally called the Portraits but changed it to Fix then to Fixx because of drug slur	UK
Fleetwood Mac (1967)	From 2 members, drummer Mick Fleetwood and bassist John McVie	UK
Flock of Seagulls (1979)	From cult novel by Richard Bach, *Jonathan Livingstone Seagull* (1970)	Liverpool
Frankie Goes to Hollywood (1980)	Headline in *Variety* magazine about Sinatra moving from Las Vegas to Hollywood	Liverpool
Genesis (1965)	Originally 'Garden Wall'; Jonathan King renamed them in 1967 as they were being 'born'	London
Grateful Dead (1963)	Said to come from an Egyptian prayer book	San Francisco
Guess Who (1965)	Forerunner of Bachman-Turner Overdrive; name based on British band The Who	Canada
Guns N' Roses (1985)	Combination of former guitarist Tracii Guns and the lead singer's assumed name	Los Angeles
Harpers Bizarre (1963)	Variation on the magazine *Harper's Bazaar* (*Harper's and Queen*)	San Francisco
Headgirl (1981)	Motorhead and Girlschool united for one-hit wonder 'The St Valentine's Day Massacre'	UK
Heaven 17 (1980)	Named after a group in Anthony Burgess's novel *A Clockwork Orange*	Sheffield
Herman's Hermits (1961)	The Herman was derived from Sherman, the flying squirrel in *Rocky and Bullwinkle Show*	Manchester
Hollies (1962)	Tribute to Buddy Holly	Manchester
Hot Chocolate (1969)	Named by an agent from the Apple record company as a pun on their colour and style	London
Human League (1977)	From a science-fiction computer game	Sheffield
Humble Pie (1969)	Superstars Frampton and Marriott named band to contrast with their pop idol status	London
Icehouse (1980)	Originally Flowers; changed name to that of their 1st album so as not to clash with existing group	Sydney
INXS (1977)	Originally called Farriss Brothers after 3 members but changed to a pun on In Excess	Australia
Iron Maiden (1976)	From a medieval instrument of torture	London

Group	Derivation	Where from
Jefferson Airplane (1965)	Hippie jargon for a paper match split at one end to hold a reefer; subsequently changed name to Jefferson Starship (1974) then Starship (1985)	San Francisco
Jesus and Mary Chain (1983)	After Alan McGee's club in London, where they performed early hits	Scotland
Jethro Tull (1967)	From the famous agriculturist, author of *Horse Hoeing Husbandry*	Blackpool
Joy Division (1977)	Nazi slang term for a military brothel	UK
Judas Priest (1973)	From Bob Dylan song, 'Ballad of Frankie Lee and Judas Priest'	Birmingham
Kajagoogoo (1983)	Supposedly from original surname of film director Elia Kazan 'Kazanjoglou'	UK
KC and the Sunshine Band (1973)	Named after founder Harry Wayne Casey	Florida
Kinks (1963)	Named by pop impresario Larry Page, based on 'Kinky', a vogue word of swinging London	London
Kraftwerk (1970)	German for power plant referring to their electronic synthesisers	Düsseldorf
Level 42 (1980)	From the answer to the meaning of life in Douglas Adams's *The Hitch Hiker's Guide to the Galaxy*	UK
Lovin' Spoonful (1965)	From a line in a song by bluesman John Hurt	USA/Canada
Lynyrd Skynyrd (1966)	Named after the gym teacher who had expelled them from school	Jacksonville, Florida
Madness (1976)	From a Prince Buster song	UK
Mamas and the Papas (1965)	Named from 2 married couples in group, John and Michelle Phillips and Cass Elliot and John Hendricks	New York
Manhattan Transfer (1969)	From novel by Jon Dos Passos	New York
Men at Work (1979)	From road sign 'Danger Men at Work'	Melbourne
Metallica (1981)	Adopted a name to suit their particular type of rock music	Los Angeles
Mindbenders (1965)	The name of a Dirk Bogarde film	UK
Mothers of Invention (1965)	Originally called the Muthers but changed to echo proverb 'necessity is the ...'	Los Angeles
Motley Crue (1981)	Play on phrase motley crew, which was an apt name for their bizarre appearance	USA
Motorhead (1975)	Song written by Ian 'Lemmy' Kilminster for Hawkwind, group he was sacked from	UK
Mott the Hoople (1968)	From an obscure novel by Willard Manus published in 1967	Hereford
Move (1966)	From the 5 members various moves from their prior bands	Birmingham
New Kids on the Block (1984)	Named by manager Maurice Starr as a white equivalent to his other band, New Edition	Massachusetts
New Order (1980)	After suicide of Ian Curtis, Joy Division became New Order, which was also a Nazi term	UK
Pet Shop Boys (1981)	Named by its members for friends who worked in an Ealing pet shop	London
Pink Floyd (1965)	Named as tribute to bluesmen Pink Anderson and Floyd Council	London
Planxty (1972)	From an Irish folk dance	Ireland
Platters (1953)	Black American group took their name from the slang term for gramophone records	Los Angeles
Poco (1968)	Originally called Pogo after a comic strip but forced to amend it when creator objected	Los Angeles
Pogues (1983)	Original name was Pogue Mahone ('Kiss my arse'); changed after BBC banned them	UK/Ireland
Pretenders (1978)	Named by Chrissie Hynde after a Platters hit, 'The Great Pretender'	UK/USA
Pretty Things (1963)	After the Bo Diddley hit 'Pretty Thing'	Sidcup, Kent
Procul Harum (1967)	Originally called the Paramounts, said to have been renamed after someone's cat	Southend, Essex
Psychedelic Furs (1977)	From Velvet Underground hit 'Venus in Furs'	London
R.E.M. (1980)	Although an abbreviation for rapid eye movement, the name was arbitrarily arrived at	Athens, Georgia
REO Speedwagon (1967)	From an early make of fire engine, Ransom E. Olds Speedwagon	Champaign, Illinois

MUSIC POP

Group	Derivation	Where from
Righteous Brothers (1962)	Originally called Paramours; took their name from the slang for excellent performers	Anaheim, California
Rolling Stones (1962)	From the Muddy Waters song 'Rolling Stone'	London
Ronettes (1959)	From the nickname of Veronica Bennett (Ronnie), one of the founder members	New York
Roxy Music (1971)	Based on the Roxy cinema chain	London
Run DMC (1982)	Nicknames of their 2 lead singers, Joseph 'Run' Simmons and Darryl 'D' McDaniels	New York
Scritti Politti (1977)	Based on the Italian phrase for 'political writings'	Leeds
Searchers (1961)	Named after the John Wayne film	Liverpool
Selecter (1979)	From the 'B' side of their debut single 'Gangsters', written by Noel Davies	Coventry
Sex Pistols (1975)	Malcolm McLaren named them after his boutique 'Sex' and Shakespeare character	London
Shadows (1959)	Originally called the Drifters; Jet Harris changed name in a Ruislip pub in 1959	London
Shakatak (1980)	From a local boutique	London
Shakespears Sister (1989)	From a Smiths' song (spelt wrongly)	UK
Shalamar (1977)	Named after the Shalimar Gardens near Lahore in Pakistan	Los Angeles
Shirelles (1957)	Name based on their lead singer Shirley Owens	Passaic, New Jersey
Showaddywaddy (1973)	From 'Bop bop showaddywaddy' backing of 'Little Darlin' by the Diamonds	Leicester
Simple Minds (1977)	Self-deprecatory name adopted during the Punk era	Glasgow
Simply Red (1985)	Named after the red hair of its lead singer Mick Hucknall	Manchester
Slade (1969)	Originally Ambrose Slade among other names, shortened to Slade in 1969	Wolverhampton
Smiths (1982)	Suggests the anonymity its members are said to have sought	Manchester
Soft Cell (1979)	Pun on 'soft sell', a term used for selling by inducement	Leeds
Soft Machine (1966)	After the William Burroughs novel of 1961	Canterbury
Spandau Ballet (1979)	Name derived from 2 contrasting words as an oxymoron to give effect	London
Split Enz (1972)	Originally called Split Ends after hair that has split, but changed spelling in 1975	Auckland, NZ
Squeeze (1974)	From a Velvet Underground Album	London
Steeleye Span (1969)	Name adopted from the traditional Lincolnshire ballad 'Horkston Grange'	UK
Steely Dan (1972)	Name of steam-powered dildo in novel *The Naked Lunch* by William Burroughs	Los Angeles
Steppenwolf (1968)	From the Herman Hesse novel	USA/Canada
Stone Roses (1980)	Originally played as Patrol and English Rose ;chose similar name to Rolling Stones	Manchester
Stranglers (1974)	Originally the Guildford Strangler; shortened name when gaining following	Guildford
Strawbs (1967)	Originally the Strawberry Hill Boys, from the area of London they were from	London
Supertramp (1969)	From the W.H. Davies book *Autobiography of a Super-tramp*	London
Supremes (1959)	Originally called the Primettes as they supported the Primes (Temptations)	Detroit
Sweet (1966)	Originally called Wainwright's Gentlemen then Sweetshop	UK
Swinging Blue Jeans (1958)	Originally called Bluegenes changed name on gaining sponsorship from jeans company	Liverpool
Take That (1994)	From the caption beside a Madonna poster	UK
Talking Heads (1975)	From the television jargon for a kind of static presentation	New York
Teardrop Explodes (1978)	From a caption in Marvel the science fiction comic	Liverpool
Tears For Fears (1981)	From Arthur Janov's book on primal therapy *Prisoners of Pain*	UK

Group	Derivation	Where from
Ten cc (10cc) (1972)	Named by Jonathan King, implying that the average male semen ejaculation was 9 cc	Manchester
Ten Thousand Maniacs (1981)	Name resulted from mishearing of film title *12,000 Maniacs*	Jamestown, New York
Ten Years After (1965)	Originally called Jaybirds changed name in 1966 on 10th anniversary of rock 'n' roll	Nottingham
The The (1980)	Parody of the many rock groups whose name begins with 'The'	London
Thin Lizzy (1969)	From 'Tin Lizzy', colloquial name for an old car	Dublin
Thompson Twins (1977)	From the characters in the Tintin cartoons by Hergé	Sheffield
Three Dog Night (1968)	Australian expression for a cold night when 3 dogs are needed to keep warm	USA
Toto (1978)	Corruption of real name of lead singer, Toteaux, to give the name of dog in *The Wizard of Oz*	Los Angeles
T'Pau (1986)	Carol Decker named group from the high priestess of Vulcan, a character in *Star Trek*	London
U2 (1977)	Said to be suggestive of the words 'You too'	Dublin
UB40 (1978)	From designation of Unemployment Benefit form	Birmingham
Ultravox (1976)	Name means 'beyond the voice', but may also refer to founder John Foxx	London
Velvet Underground (1965)	From the title of a pornographic publication	London
Wet Wet Wet (1986)	From a lyric on a Scritti Politti record	UK
X (1977)	From group's lead singer Exene Cervenka, nicknamed X	Los Angeles
XTC (1977)	Suggests 'ecstasy', but last 2 letters are initials of their drummer Terry Chambers	Swindon
Yardbirds (1963)	From the jazzman Charlie Parker, nicknamed Yardbird	Kingston-upon-Thames
Yazoo (1982)	From an early blues record label	UK

MUSIC POP

Singles

(number in brackets = top chart position)

NB: The listings below include all number one singles and many of the Top 10 singles released since the inception of the charts in 1952, up to April 2001. Other records that did not make the Top 10 are included if they are regarded as 'classics' or have some other point of interest. Singles that reached the top of the charts are indicated by (1) after the title, and some other placings are indicated if the record has been covered by various artists or has some other merit. The alphabetical listings are compiled using first names; this is not in line with convention of listing by surname, but it is considered expedient to maintain consistency with the listing of groups.

Title	Group/Artiste	Title	Group/Artiste
A Certain Smile	Johnny Mathis	Ain't No Mountain High Enough	Diana Ross
A Dream's A Dream	Soul II Soul	Ain't No Stoppin' Us Now	McFadden and
A Fool Such As I (1)	Elvis Presley		Whitehead
A Good Heart (1)	Feargal Sharkey	Ain't Nothing Goin' On	Gwen Guthrie
A Hard Day's Night (1)	Beatles	But the Rent	
A Little Bit Me, A Little Bit You	Monkees	Ain't Nothing Like the	Elton John and
A Little Bit More	Dr Hook	Real Thing	Marcella Detroit
A Little Bit of Soap	Showaddywaddy	Ain't That a Shame	Fats Domino
A Little Bitty Tear (9)	Burl Ives	Ain't That Funny	Jimmy Justice
A Little Time (1)	Beautiful South	The Air That I Breathe	Hollies
A Message to You Rudy	Specials featuring	Airport	Motors
	Rico+	Albatross (1)	Fleetwood Mac
A Million Love Songs (7)	Take That	Alice, I Want You Just for Me	Full Force
A New England	Kirsty MacColl	All 4 Love	Color Me Badd
A Night To Remember	Shalamar	All Alone Am I	Brenda Lee
A Rockin' Good Way (5)	Shaky and Bonnie	All Along the Watchtower	Jimi Hendrix
A Teenager In Love (2)	Marty Wilde		Experience
A Trip to Trumpton	Urban Hype	All Around My Hat	Steeleye Span
A View to a Kill	Duran Duran	All Around the World (1)	Lisa Stansfield
A Walkin' Miracle	Limmie and the	All Around the World (1)	Oasis
	Family Cookin'	All Because of You	Geordie
Abacab	Genesis	All Cried Out	Alison Moyet
Abba-Esque (1)	Erasure	All Day and All of the Night (2)	Kinks
ABC	Jackson 5	All Day and All of the Night (7)	Stranglers
Abracadabra	Steve Miller	All for Love	Bryan Adams, Rod
	Fire		Stewart and Sting
Abraham, Martin and John	Marvin Gaye	All I Ever Need Is You	Sonny and Cher
Absolute Beginners (2)	David Bowie	All I Have to Do is Dream	Bobby Gentry and
Absolute Beginners (4)	Jam		Glen Campbell
Accidents (46)	Thunderclap	All I Have to Do Is Dream (1)	Everly Brothers
	Newman	All I Wanna Do	Sheryl Crow
Achy Breaky Heart (3)	Billy Ray Cyrus	All I Wanna Do Is Make	Heart
Achy Breaky Heart (53)	Alvin and the	Love to You	
	Chipmunks and	All I Want for Christmas Is You	Mariah Carey
	Billy Ray Cyrus	All Kinds of Everything	Dana
Act of War	Elton John and Millie	All Night Long (2)	Lionel Richie
	Jackson	All Night Long (5)	Rainbow
Activ 8 (Come with Me)	Altern 8	All of My Heart	ABC
Addams Groove	Hammer	All of My Life	Diana Ross
Addicted to Love	Robert Palmer	All of You	Diana Ross and Julio
Africa	Toto		Iglesias
African Waltz	Johnny Dankworth	All or Nothing (1)	Small Faces
After the Love Has Gone	Earth, Wind and	All Out of Love	Air Supply
	Fire	All Right Now	Free
Agadoo	Black Lace	All She Wants Is	Duran Duran
Against All Odds (1)	Mariah Carey and	All Shook Up (1)	Elvis Presley
	Westlife	All Stood Still	Ultravox
Against All Odds (Take a Look	Phil Collins	All That I Need (1)	Boyzone
at Me Now)		All That She Wants (1)	Ace of Base
Ain't Gonna Bump No More	Joe Tex	All the Love in the World (10)	Dionne Warwick
Ain't Got No – I Got Life (2)	Nina Simone	All the Way	Frank Sinatra
Ain't Nobody (1)	LL Cool J	All the Way from Memphis	Mott the Hoople
Ain't Nobody (6)	Rufus and Chaka	All the Young Dudes	Mott the Hoople
	Khan	All Time High	Rita Coolidge
Ain't Nobody Better	Inner City	All Together Now	Farm
Ain't No Doubt (1)	Jimmy Nail	All You Need Is Love (1)	Beatles
Ain't No Love	Sub Sub featuring	Almaz	Randy Crawford
	Melanie Williams	Almost There (2)	Andy Williams

Title	Group/Artiste	Title	Group/Artiste
Almost Unreal	Roxette	Anyway You Look	Northern Uproar
Alone Again (Naturally)	Gilbert O'Sullivan	Anywhere Is	Enya
Alone without You	King	Apache (1)	Shadows
Alphabet Street	Prince	Apeman	Kinks
Alright	Supergrass	Applejack	Jet Harris and Tony Meehan
Alright	Jamiroquai		
Alright Alright Alright	Mungo Jerry	April Love	Pat Boone
Also Sprach Zarathustra	Deodato	April Skies	Jesus and Mary Chain
Alternate Title	Monkees		
Always	Erasure	Are 'Friends' Electric? (1)	Tubeway Army
Always Look on the Bright Side of Life	Monty Python	Are You Gonna Go My Way	Lenny Kravitz
		Are You Lonesome Tonight (1)	Elvis Presley
Always on My Mind (1)	Pet Shop Boys	Are You Ready to Rock (8)	Wizzard
Always Something There to Remind Me (1)	Sandie Shaw	Are You Sure	Allisons
		Arms around the World	Louise
Always There	Incognito featuring Jocelyn Brown	Arms of Mary	Sutherland Brothers and Quiver
Always Yours (1)	Gary Glitter	The Arms of Orion	Prince with Sheena Easton
Amateur Hour	Sparks		
Amazing Grace (1)	Royal Scots Dragoon Guards	Around the World	Daft Punk
		Around the World (5)	Bing Crosby
Amazing Grace	Judy Collins	Around the World (8)	Gracie Fields
Americanos	Holly Johnson	Art for Art's Sake (5)	10cc
American Pie (2)	Don McLean	Arthur Daley (E's Alright)	Firm
American Pie (1)	Madonna	Arthur's Theme	Christopher Cross
Amigo	Black Slate	Ashes to Ashes (1)	David Bowie
Amoureuse	Kiki Dee	As I Love You (1)	Shirley Bassey
An Everlasting Love	Andy Gibb	As Long as You Love Me	Backstreet Boys
An Innocent Man	Billy Joel	As Tears Go By	Marianne Faithfull
And I Love You So	Perry Como	As Usual	Brenda Lee
And the Beat Goes On (2)	Whispers	As You Like It	Adam Faith
And the Birds Were Singing	Sweet People	At the Club	Drifters
Anfield Rap (Red Machine in Full Effect)	Liverpool FC	At the Hop	Danny and the Juniors
Angela Jones	Michael Cox	Atlantis (2)	Shadows
Angel Eyes (4)	Roxy Music	Atmosphere (7)	Russ Abbot
Angel Eyes/Voulez-Vous (3)	Abba	Atomic (1)	Blondie
Angel Face	Glitter Band	Attention to Me	Nolans
Angel Fingers (1)	Wizzard	Auberge	Chris Rea
Angel of Mine	Eternal	Auf Wiedersehen	Vera Lynn
Angels (4)	Robbie Williams	Autobahn	Kraftwerk
Angel (What Made Milwaukee Famous)	Rod Stewart	Automatic	Pointer Sisters
		Automatically Sunshine (10)	Supremes
Angie (5)	Rolling Stones	Automatic Lover	Dee D. Jackson
Angie Baby	Helen Reddy	Autumn Almanac	Kinks
Animal	Def Leppard	Avalon	Roxy Music
Animal Nitrate	Suede	Avenues and Alleyways	Tony Christie
Annie I'm Not Your Daddy	Kid Creole and the Coconuts	Axel F	Harold Faltermeyer
		Ay Ay Ay Ay Moosey	Modern Romance
Annie's Song (1)	John Denver	Babe (1)	Take That
Annie's Song (3)	James Galway	Babe (6)	Styx
Another Brick in the Wall (1)	Pink Floyd	Babooshka (5)	Kate Bush
Another Day	Paul McCartney	Baby Baby	Frankie Lymon and the Teenagers
Another Day in Paradise	Phil Collins		
Another One Bites the Dust	Queen	Baby Baby	Ami Grant
Another Rock and Roll Christmas	Gary Glitter	Baby Come Back (1)	Equals
		Baby Come Back (1)	Pato Banton
Another Step Closer To You	Kim Wilde and Junior	Baby Come to Me	James Ingram and Patti Austin
Another Suitcase in Another Hall	Barbara Dickson	Baby Face	Little Richard
		Baby I Know	Rubettes
Answer Me (1)	David Whitfield	Baby I Love You	Ramones
Answer Me (1)	Frankie Laine	Baby I Love You	Dave Edmunds
Answer Me (9)	Barbara Dickson	Baby I Love Your Way	Big Mountain
Anthem (8)	N-Joi	Baby I'm a Want You	Bread
Any Dream Will Do (1)	Jason Donovan	Baby It's You	Beatles
Anyone Can Fall in Love	Anita Dobson	Baby Jane (1)	Rod Stewart
Anyone Who Had a Heart (1)	Cilla Black	Baby Jump (1)	Mungo Jerry
Anything for You	Gloria Estefan and Miami Sound Machine	Babylon's Burning	Ruts
		Baby Love (1)	Supremes
Anyway Anyhow Anywhere	Who	Baby Make it Soon	Marmalade

M U S I C   P O P

Title	Group/Artiste
Baby Now That I've Found You	Foundations
Baby One More Time (1)	Britney Spears
Baby Please Don't Go (10)	Them
Back for Good (1)	Take That
Back Home (1)	England World Cup Squad (1970)
Back Off Boogaloo (2)	Ringo Starr
Back Street Luv	Curved Air
Back to Life (1)	Soul II Soul featuring Caron Wheeler
Bad	Michael Jackson
Bad Bad Boy	Nazareth
Bad Boy	Miami Sound Machine
Bad Boys	Wham
Bad Girl	Madonna
Bad Moon Rising	Creedence Clearwater Revival
Bad to Me (1)	Billy J. Kramer and the Dakotas
Badge	Cream
Bag It Up (1)	Geri Halliwell
Baggy Trousers	Madness
Baker Street	Gerry Rafferty
Baker Street (2)	Undercover
Ballad of a Landlord	Terry Hall
Ballad of Bonnie and Clyde	Georgie Fame
Ballad of Davy Crockett	Billy Hayes
The Ballad of Davy Crockett	Tennessee Ernie Ford
Ballad of John and Yoko (1)	Plastic Ono Band
Ballad of Paladin	Duane Eddy
Ball of Confusion (7)	Temptations
Ball Park Incident (6)	Wizzard
Ballroom Blitz (2)	Sweet
Banana Republic	Boomtown Rats
Banana Rock (9)	Wombles
Banana Splits	Dickies
Band of Gold (1)	Freda Payne
Band on the Run	Paul McCartney and Wings
Bang Bang	B.A. Robertson
Bangladesh	George Harrison
Banks of the Ohio	Olivia Newton-John
Banner Man	Blue Mink
Barbados (1)	Typically Tropical
Barbara Ann	Beach Boys
Barbie Girl (1)	Aqua
Barcelona	Freddie Mercury and Montserrat Caballe
Batdance	Prince
Beatles Movie Medley (10)	Beatles
Beatnik Fly	Johnny and the Hurricanes
Beautiful Day (1)	U2
Beauty and the Beast	Celine Dion and Peabo Bryson
Be Bop A Lula	Gene Vincent
Be Mine	Lance Fortune
Be My Baby	Vanessa Paradis
Be My Baby (4)	Ronettes
Be My Girl	Jim Dale
Be Quick Or Be Dead	Iron Maiden
Beat Dis	Bomb the Bass
Beat Surrender (1)	Jam
Beat the Clock	Sparks
Because of You	Dexy's Midnight Runners
Because the Night	Patti Smith Group
Because We Want To (1)	Billie
Because You're Mine	Mario Lanza

Title	Group/Artiste
Bed of Roses	Bon Jovi
Bed Sitter	Soft Cell
Beds Are Burning	Midnight Oil
Beetlebum (1)	Blur
Beg Steal or Borrow	New Seekers
Begin the Beguine (1)	Julio Iglesias
Behind a Painted Smile	Isley Brothers
Behind the Groove	Teena Marie
Being with You (1)	Smokey Robinson
Belfast Child (1)	Simple Minds
Believe (1)	Cher
Bell Bottom Blues	Alma Cogan
The Belle of St Mark	Sheila E
Bellissima	DJ Quicksilver
Ben	Michael Jackson
Ben (5)	Marti Webb
Bend It	Dave Dee, Dozy, Beaky, Mick and Tich
Bennie and the Jets	Elton John
Benny's Theme	Paul Henry and the Mayson Glen Orchestra
Bernadette	Four Tops
The Best Disco in Town	Ritchie Family
Best of My Love	Emotions
Best Thing That Ever Happened to Me	Gladys Knight and the Pips
The Best Things in Life Are Free	Bell Biv Devoe
The Best Things in Life Are Free	Luther Vandross and Janet Jackson
Best Years of Our Lives	Modern Romance
Better Love Next Time	Dr Hook
Better the Devil You Know	Sonia
Better the Devil You Know (2)	Kylie Minogue
Big Apple	Kajagoogoo
Big Bad John	Jimmy Dean
Big Eight	Judge Dread
Big Fun	Inner City featuring Kevin Saunderson
Big Fun	Gap Band
Big Girls Don't Cry	Four Seasons
Big in Japan	Alphaville
Big Log	Robert Plant
Big Man	Four Preps
Big Seven	Judge Dread
Big Six	Judge Dread
Big Yellow Taxi	Joni Mitchell
Billie Jean (1)	Michael Jackson
Billy Don't Be a Hero (1)	Paper Lace
Bimbo (7)	Ruby Wright
Bionic Santa	Chris Hill
Bird Dog	Everly Brothers
Birdhouse in Your Soul	They Might Be Giants
The Birdie Song	Tweets
Bitch	Meredith Brooks
The Bitch Is Back	Elton John
Bittersweet Symphony	The Verve
Black and White	Greyhound
Blackberry Way (1)	Move
Black Betty	Ram Jam
Black Coffee (1)	All Saints
Black Hills of Dakota	Doris Day
Black Is Black (1966)	Los Bravos
Black Is Black (1977)	La Belle Epoque
Black Night	Deep Purple
Black or White (1)	Michael Jackson
Black Skin Blue Eyed Boys	Equals
Black Superman (Muhammad Ali) (7)	Johnny Wakelin and the Kinshasa Band

Title	Group/Artiste	Title	Group/Artiste
Black Velvet	Alannah Myles	Boy from New York City	Darts
Black Velvet Band	Dubliners	A Boy from Nowhere	Tom Jones
Blame It on the Boogie	Big Fun	The Boys Are Back in Town (8)	Thin Lizzy
Blame It on the Boogie (15)	Mick Jackson	Boys Keep Swinging	David Bowie
Blame It on the Boogie (8)	Jackson 5	The Boys of Summer	Don Henley
Blame It on the Pony Express	Johnny Johnson and the Bandwagon	Boys (Summertime Love)	Sabrina
Blame It on the Weatherman (1)	B*witched	Brand New Friend	Lloyd Cole and the Commotions
Blanket on the Ground	Billy Jo Spears	Brand New Key	Melanie
Bless You	Tony Orlando	Brandy	Scott English
Blinded by the Light	Manfred Mann's Earth Band	Brass in Pocket (1)	Pretenders
		Brave New World	Toyah
Blockbuster (1)	Sweet	Bread and Butter	Newbeats
Block Rockin' Beats	Chemical Brothers	Break Away	Beach Boys
Blood on the Dance Floor (1)	Michael Jackson	Breakaway (4)	Tracey Ullman
Blow the House Down	Living in a Box	Breakdance Party	Break Machine
Blow Your Mind	Jamiroquai	Breakfast at Tiffany's (1)	Deep Blue Something
Blue (Da Ba Dee) (1)	Eiffel 65		
Blue Bayou	Roy Orbison	Breakfast in America	Supertramp
Blueberry Hill	Fats Domino	Breakfast in Bed (6)	UB40 featuring Chrissie Hynde
Blue Eyes	Elton John		
Blue Eyes	Don Partridge	Breakfast on Pluto	Don Partridge
Blue Guitar	Justin Hayward and John Lodge	Breakin' Down the Walls of Heartache	Johnny Johnson and the Bandwagon
Blue Hotel	Chris Isaak	Breaking Up Is Hard to Do	Neil Sedaka
Blue Jean (6)	David Bowie	Breaking Up Is Hard to Do (3)	Partridge Family
Blue Monday	New Order	Breakin' . . . There's No Stopping Us	Ollie and Jerry
Blue Moon (1)	Marcels		
Blue Room	Orb	Breakout	Swing Out Sister
Blue Savannah	Erasure	Breathe (1)	The Prodigy
Blue Suede Shoes (10)	Carl Perkins	Breathe Again	Toni Braxton
Blue Tango	Ray Martin	Breath of Life	Erasure
Blue Velvet (2)	Bobby Vinton	Breathless (1)	Corrs
Bo Diddley	Buddy Holly	Bridge of Sighs (3)	David Whitfield
The Boat That I Row	Lulu	Bridge Over Troubled Water (1)	Simon and Garfunkel
Bobby's Girl	Susan Maughan		
Body and Soul	Mai Tai	Bridget the Midget (The Queen of the Blues)	Ray Stevens
Bodyshakin'	911		
Body Talk	Imagination	Bright Eyes (1)	Art Garfunkel
Bohemian Rhapsody (1)	Queen	Brimful of Asha (1)	Cornershop
Boogie Nights	Heatwave	Bring a Little Water Sylvie	Lonnie Donegan
Boogie Oogie Oogie (3)	A Taste of Honey	Bring It All Back (1)	S Club 7
Boogie Wonderland	Earth, Wind and Fire with the Emotions	Bring Me Edelweiss	Edelweiss
Book of Days	Enya	Bring Your Daughter . . . To The Slaughter (1)	Iron Maiden
Book of Love	Mudlarks	Bringing On Back the Good Times	Love Affair
Boom Bang-A-Bang	Lulu		
Boombastic (1)	Shaggy	Broken Down Angel	Nazareth
Boom Boom Boom (1)	Outhere Brothers	Broken Wings	Mr Mister
Boom, Boom, Boom, Boom, (1)	Vergaboys	Broken Wings (1)	Stargazers
Boom! Shake the Room (1)	Jazzy Jeff and the Fresh Prince (Will Smith)	Broken Wings (6)	Art and Dotty Todd
		Brontosaurus	Move
		Brother Louie	Hot Chocolate
Bootie Call (1)	All Saints	Brother Louie (4)	Modern Talking
Born Free (6)	Vic Reeves and the Roman Numerals	Brothers in Arms	Dire Straits
		Brown Sugar (2)	Rolling Stones
Born in the USA/I'm on Fire	Bruce Springsteen	Brown-Eyed Handsome Man	Buddy Holly
Born to Be Wild (30)	Steppenwolf	Buffalo Gals	Malcolm McLaren and Supreme Team
Born to Make You Happy	Britney Spears		
Born to Be with You	Dave Edmunds	Buffalo Soldier	Bob Marley and the Wailers
Born Too Late	Poni-Tails		
Born with a Smile on My Face	Stephanie De Sykes	Build Me Up Buttercup	Foundations
Boss Drum	Shamen	Bump N' Grind	R. Kelly
Boss Guitar	Duane Eddy and the Rebelettes	The Bump	Kenny
		Buona Sera	Acker Bilk and his Paramount Jazz Band
The Bouncer	Kicks Like a Mule		
Bound 4 Da Reload (casualty) (1)	Oxide and Neutrino	Burlesque	Family
		Burning Bridges (5)	Status Quo
Bow Down Mister	Jesus Loves You (Boy George)	Burning Heart	Survivor
		Bushel and a Peck	Vivian Blaine
Boxer Beat	Jo Boxers		

Title	Group/Artiste	Title	Group/Artiste
But I Do	Clarence 'Frogman' Henry	Celebration	Kool and the Gang
		Centerfold	J. Geils Band
Butterfingers	Tommy Steele	C'est La Vie	Robbie Nevil
Butterfly (1)	Andy Williams	C'est La Vie (1)	B*withched
Bye Bye Baby (1)	Bay City Rollers	Cha Cha Heels	Eartha Kitt and Bronski Beat
Bye Bye Blues (24)	Bert Kaempfert		
Bye Bye Love	Everly Brothers	Chain Gang	Sam Cooke
Calendar Girl	Neil Sedaka	Chain Gang (9)	Jimmy Young
California Dreamin'	Mamas and the Papas	Chain Reaction (1)	Diana Ross
		Chains	Tina Arena
California Man	Move	Change	Tears for Fears
Call Me	Spagna	Changing Partners	Bing Crosby
Call Me (1)	Blondie	The Changingman	Paul Weller
Calling All the Heroes	It Bites	Chanson d'Amour (1)	Manhattan Transfer
Calling Your Name	Marilyn	Chant No. 1	Spandau Ballet
Camouflage	Stan Ridgway	Charlie Brown	Coasters
Can Can	Bad Manners	Charly	Prodigy
Can We Fix it (1)	Bob the Builder	Charmaine (6)	Bachelors
Candida	Dawn	Check Out the Groove	Bobby Thurston
Candle In the Wind 1997/ Something About the Way You Look Tonight	Elton John	Check This Out	L.A. Mix
		Chequered Love (4)	Kim Wilde
		Cherish (3)	Madonna
Candy Girl (1)	New Edition	Cherish (4)	Kool and the Gang
Candy Man (6)	Brian Poole and the Tremeloes	Cherry Pink and Apple Blossom White (1)	Eddie Calvert
Can't Buy Me Love (1)	Beatles	Cherry Pink and Apple Blossom White (1)	Perez Prado and Orchestra, King of Mambo
Can't Fight the Moonlight (1)	LeAnn Rines		
Can't Get By without You	Real Thing		
Can't Get Enough of Your Love Babe	Barry White	Chicka Boom	Guy Mitchell
		The Chicken Song	Spitting Image
Can't Get Used to Losing You (2)	Andy Williams	Children of the Revolution (2)	T Rex
		Chi Mai	Ennio Morricone
Can't Give You Anything (1)	Stylistics	China in Your Hand (1)	T'Pau
Can the Can (1)	Suzi Quatro	China Girl (2)	David Bowie
Can't Help Falling in Love (3)	Andy Williams	China Tea	Russ Conway
Can't Stand Losing You	Police	Chiquitita (2)	Abba
Can't Stay Away from You	Gloria Estefan and Miami Sound Machine	Chirpy Chirpy Cheep Cheep (1)	Middle of the Road
		Chocolate Salty Balls (PS I love you (1)	Chef
Can't Stop the Music (11)	Village People	The Chosen Few	Dooleys
Can't Take My Eyes off You (5)	Andy Williams	Christmas Alphabet (1)	Dickie Valentine
Can't Wait Another Minute	Five Star	Christmas in Dreadland	Judge Dread
Can We Talk	Code Red	Christmas Island (8)	Dickie Valentine
Can You Feel It	Jacksons	Church of the Poison Mind	Culture Club
Can You Feel the Force	Real Thing	Cigarettes and Alcohol	Oasis
Ça Plane Pour Moi	Plastic Bertrand	Cinderella Rockefella (1)	Esther and Abi Ofarim
Captain Beaky	Keith Michell		
The Captain of Her Heart	Double	Cindy Incidentally	Faces
Car Wash	Rose Royce	Cindy's Birthday	Shane Fenton and the Fentones
Cara Mia (1)	David Whitfield and Mantovani Orchestra		
		Circles	New Seekers
		The Circus	Erasure
Caravan of Love (1)	Housemartins	Clair (1)	Gilbert O'Sullivan
Careless Hands	Des O'Connor	The Clairvoyant	Iron Maiden
Careless Whisper (1)	George Michael	The Clapping Song (6)	Shirley Ellis
The Caribbean Disco Show	Lobo (Holland)	Classic	Adrian Gurvitz
Caribbean Queen	Billy Ocean	Classical Gas	Mason Williams
The Carnival Is Over (1)	Seekers	Close to You (7)	Maxi Priest
Carolina Moon (1)	Connie Francis	Close (to the Edit)	Art of Noise
Caroline (5)	Status Quo	Closer than Close	Rosie Gaines
Cars (1)	Gary Numan	Clouds across the Moon	Rah Band
Casanova (13)	Coffee	Club Fantastic	Wham
Casanova (9)	Levert	Club Tropicana	Wham
Cast Your Fate to the Wind	Sounds Orchestral	C'Mon Everybody (6)	Eddie Cochran
The Cat Crept In	Mud	C'Mon Everybody (3)	Sex Pistols
Catch a Falling Star	Perry Como	Co-Co	Sweet
Catch the Wind	Donovan	Coco Jamboo	Mr President
Catch Us If You Can	Dave Clark Five	Coconut	Nilsson
The Caterpillar	Cure	Cold Turkey	Plastic Ono Band
Cathy's Clown (1)	Everly Brothers	Colette	Billy Fury
Cats in the Cradle	Ugly Kid Joe	Colour of My Love	Jefferson

Title	Group/Artiste	Title	Group/Artiste
Dead Ringer for Love	Meatloaf	Does Your Mother Know (4)	Abba
Dear John (10)	Status Quo	Dog Eat Dog	Adam Ant
Dear Prudence	Siouxsie and the Banshees	Doing Alright with the Boys	Gary Glitter
		Do It Again	Beach Boys
Death of a Clown	Dave Davies	Dolce Vita	Ryan Paris
Debora	Tyrannosaurus Rex	Dolly My Love	Moments
December, '63 (Oh What a Night) (1)	Frankie Valli and the Four Seasons	Dominique	Singing Nun (Soeur Sourire)
Deck of Cards (13)	Max Bygraves	Domino Dancing	Pet Shop Boys
Deck of Cards (5)	Wink Martindale	Don Quixote	Nik Kershaw
Dedicated Follower of Fashion	Kinks	Donald Where's Your Troosers	Andy Stewart
Dedicated to the One I Love	Mamas and the Papas	Donna (2)	10cc
		Donna (3)	Marty Wilde
Deep	East 17	Don't Be a Stranger	Dina Carroll
Deep Deep Trouble	Simpsons featuring Bart and Homer	Don't Bring Me Down (10)	Pretty Things
		Don't Bring Me Down (6)	Animals
Deeper Underground (1)	Jamiroquai	Don't Call Me Baby (1)	Madison Avenue
Deeply Dippy	Right Said Fred	Don't Cry for Me, Argentina (1)	Julie Covington
Delilah (2)	Tom Jones	Don't Cry for Me, Argentina (5)	Shadows
Delilah (7)	Sensational Alex Harvey Band	Don't Do It Baby	Mac and Katie Kissoon
Delta Lady	Joe Cocker	Don't Ever Change	Crickets
Denis (2)	Blondie	Don't Give Me Your Life	Alex Party
Desiderata	Les Crane	Don't Give Up (9)	Peter Gabriel and Kate Bush
Desire (1)	U2		
Detroit City	Tom Jones	Don't Give Up (1)	Chicane featuring Bryan Adams
Devil Gate Drive (1)	Suzi Quatro		
Devil in Disguise (1)	Elvis Presley	Don't Give Up On Us (1)	David Soul
Devil Woman (5)	Marty Robbins	Don't Go Breaking My Heart	Elton John and Kiki Dee
The Devil's Answer	Atomic Rooster		
Devotion	Nomad	Don't Go (3)	Yazoo
Diamonds	Jet Harris and Tony Meehan	Don't It Make My Brown Eyes Blue	Crystal Gayle
Diamonds and Pearls	Prince and The New Power Generation	Don't It Make You Feel Good	Stefan Dennis
		Don't Know Much (2)	Linda Ronstadt (Aaron Neville uncredited)
Diana	Paul Anka		
Diane (1)	Bachelors		
Dick-A-Dum-Dum (Kings Road)	Des O'Connor	Don't Laugh at Me (3)	Norman Wisdom
		Don't Leave Me This Way (1)	Communards
Did You Ever	Nancy and Lee Hazlewood	Don't Leave Me This Way (5)	Harold Melvin and the Bluenotes
Died in Your Arms (I Just)	Cutting Crew	Don't Let It Die	Hurricane Smith
A Different Corner (1)	George Michael	Don't Let the Stars Get in Your Eyes	Perry Como
Dirty Cash	Adventures of Stevie V	Don't Let the Sun Catch You Crying	Gerry and the Pacemakers
Disappointed	Electronic		
D.I.S.C.O.	Ottawan	Don't Let the Sun Go Down On Me (1)	George Michael and Elton John
Disco Connection	Isaac Hayes Movement	Don't Look Back in Anger (1)	Oasis
Disco Duck	Rick Dees and His Cast of Idiots	Don't Miss the Party Line	Bizz Nizz
		Don't Play Your Rock 'N' Roll to Me	Smokey
Disco Stomp	Hamilton Bohannon		
Discoteque (1)	U2	Don't Sleep in the Subway (12)	Petula Clark
Distant Drums (1)	Jim Reeves	Don't Speak (1)	No Doubt
Divine Emotions	Narada	Don't Stand So Close to Me (1)	Police
D.I.V.O.R.C.E.	Tammy Wynette	Don't Stay Away Too Long	Peters and Lee
D.I.V.O.R.C.E. (1)	Billy Connolly	Don't Stop Me Now	Queen
Dizzy (1)	Vic Reeves and the Wonder Stuff	Don't Stop the Music	Yarbrough and Peoples
Dizzy (1)	Tommy Roe	Don't Stop Till You Get Enough	Michael Jackson
Do Anything You Wanna Do	Eddie and the Hotrods	Don't Stop (Wiggle Wiggle) (1)	Outhere Brothers
		Don't Take Away the Music	Tavares
The Dock of the Bay (3)	Otis Redding	Don't Talk Just Kiss	Right Said Fred, guest vocals Jocelyn Brown
Doctor Doctor (3)	Thompson Twins		
Doctorin' the House	Coldcut with Yazz and Plastic Population		
		Don't Talk to Me about Love	Altered Images
Doctorin' The Tardis	Timelords	Don't Throw Your Love Away (1)	Searchers
Doctor Jones (1)	Aqua	Don't Treat Me Like a Child	Helen Shapiro
Doctor's Orders	Sunny	Don't Turn Around	Aswad
Does Your Chewing Gum Lose It's Flavour	Lonnie Donegan	Don't Walk Away	Jade
		Don't Wanna Lose You	Gloria Estefan

Title	Group/Artiste	Title	Group/Artiste
Don't Waste My Time	Paul Hardcastle featuring Carol Kenyon	Easy	Commodores
		Easy Lover	Phil Collins and Philip Bailey
Don't Worry	Kim Appleby		
Don't Worry Be Happy	Bobby McFerrin	Ebeneezer Goode (1)	Shamen
Don't You (Forget About Me)	Simple Minds	Ebony and Ivory (1)	Paul McCartney with Stevie Wonder
Don't You Rock Me Daddy-O	Vipers Skiffle Group		
Don't You Think It's Time	Mike Berry	Echo Beach	Martha and the Muffins
Don't You Want Me (1)	Human League		
Don't You Want Me (6)	Felix	Edelweiss	Vince Hill
Doop (1)	Doop	E=MC2	Big Audio Dynamite
Do the Bartman	Simpsons	Egyptian Reggae	Jonathan Richman and the Modern Lovers
Do the Conga	Black Lace		
Do the Hucklebuck	Coast to Coast	Eighteen Strings	Tinman
Do They Know It's Christmas (1)	Band Aid	Eighteen with a Bullet	Pete Wingfield
Do They Know It's Christmas (1)	Band Aid II	Eighth Day	Hazel O'Connor
Double Barrel	Dave and Ansil Collins	Einstein A Go-Go	Landscape
		Elected (4)	Alice Cooper
Double Dutch	Malcolm McLaren	Elected (9)	Mr Bean and Smear Campaign: Bruce Dickinson
Do Wah Diddy Diddy (1)	Manfred Mann		
Do What You Do	Jermaine Jackson		
Down Down (1)	Status Quo	Election Day	Arcadia
Down on the Beach Tonight	Drifters	Electric Avenue	Eddy Grant
Down on the Street	Shakatak	Elegantly Wasted	INXS
Down to Earth	Curiosity Killed the Cat	Elenore	Turtles
		Elizabethan Reggae	Boris Gardiner
Down Under (1)	Men at Work	Eloise (2)	Barry Ryan
Down Yonder	Johnny and the Hurricanes	Eloise (3)	Damned
		Elusive Butterfly (5)	Bob Lind
Downtown (2)	Petula Clark	Embarrassment	Madness
Downtown Train	Rod Stewart	Emma	Hot Chocolate
Do You Know the Way to San José	Dionne Warwick	Emotional Rescue	Rolling Stones
		Encore Une Fois	Sash
Do You Love Me (1)	Brian Poole and the Tremeloes	Endless Love	Diana Ross and Lionel Richie
Do You Mind (1)	Anthony Newley	Endless Sleep	Marty Wilde
Do You Really Want To Hurt Me	Culture Club	End of the Line	Traveling Wilburys
Do You Remember	Phil Collins	End of the Road (1)	Boyz II Men
Do You Wanna Dance	Barry Blue	England Swings	Roger Miller
Do You Want Me (5)	Salt-N-Pepa	English Country Garden (5)	Jimmie Rodgers
Do You Want to Know a Secret	Billy J. Kramer and the Dakotas	Enjoy the Silence	Depeche Mode
		Enola Gay	Orchestral Manoeuvres in the Dark
Dr Beat	Miami Sound Machine		
Dr Kiss Kiss	5000 Volts		
Dragnet	Ted Heath	Enter Sandman	Metallica
Dreadlock Holiday (1)	10cc	Ernie (1)	Benny Hill
Dream a Little Dream of Me	Mama Cass	Erotica	Madonna
Dream Baby	Roy Orbison	Especially for You (1)	Kylie Minogue and Jason Donovan
Dreamboat (1)	Alma Cogan		
Dreamer (1)	Livin' Joy	Eternal Flame (1)	Bangles
Dreaming (2)	Blondie	Eternally	Jimmy Young
Dream Lover	Bobby Darin	The Eton Rifles	Jam
Dreams (1)	Gabrielle	Eve of Destruction	Barry McGuire
Drink Up Thy Zider	Adge Cutler and the Wurzels	Eve of the War (3)	Jeff Wayne's War of the Worlds
Drinking Song	Mario Lanza	Even the Bad Times Are Good	Tremeloes
Drive-In Saturday (3)	David Bowie		
Driven by You	Brian May	Everlasting Love (1)	Love Affair
Drowning in Berlin	Mobiles	Evermore	Ruby Murray
The Drugs Don't Work	The Verve	Every Breath You Take	Police
Dub Be Good To Me	Beats International	Every Day Hurts	Sad Cafe
Dude (Looks Like a Lady)	Aerosmith	Everyday Is Like Sunday	Morrissey
Duke of Earl	Darts	Every Little Thing She Does Is Magic	Police
Dyna-mite	Mud		
D'You Know What I Mean? (1)	Oasis	Every Loser Wins	Nick Berry
Each Time You Break My Heart	Nick Kamen	Every 1's a Winner	Hot Chocolate
Early in the Morning	Vanity Fare	Everyone's Gone to the Moon	Jonathan King
Earth Angel	Crew Cuts	(Backstreet's Back)	Backstreet Boys
Earth Song (1)	Michael Jackson	Everybody Hurts	R.E.M.
Ease On Down the Road	Michael Jackson and Diana Ross	Everybody Knows	Dave Clark Five

M
U
S
I
C

P
O
P

Title	Group/Artiste	Title	Group/Artiste
Everybody's Free	Rozalla	Ferry 'Cross The Mersey	Crowd
Everybody's Free (to Wear Sunscreen) (1)	Baz Luhrmann	Fever	Madonna
		Fever (5)	Peggy Lee
Everybody Wants to Rule the World (2)	Tears for Fears	Fields of Fire (400 Miles)	Big Country
		50 Ways to Leave Your Lover (23)	Paul Simon
Everybody Wants to Run the World (5)	Tears for Fears	Fill Me In (1)	Craig David
Everything about You	Ugly Kid Joe	The Final Countdown	Europe
Everything Changes (1)	Take That	Finally	Ce Ce Peniston
Everything Counts	Depeche Mode	Finchley Central	New Vaudeville Band
Everything I Am	Plastic Penny	Find My Love	Fairground Attraction
Everything I Do I Do It for You	Bryan Adams	Fine Time	Yazz
Everything I Own	Ken Boothe	Finger of Suspicion (1)	Dickie Valentine and the Stargazers
Everything I Own (1)	Boy George		
Everything Is Beautiful	Ray Stevens	Fire Brigade	Move
Everything Must Change	Paul Young	Firestarter (1)	Prodigy
Everything's Alright	Mojos	The First Time Ever I Saw Your Face	Roberta Flack
Every Time you Go Away	Paul Young		
Evil Hearted You	Yardbirds	The First Time	Adam Faith
The Evil That Men Do	Iron Maiden	5-4-3-2-1	Manfred Mann
Evil Woman	Electric Light Orchestra	Five Live (1)	George Michael, Queen, Lisa Stansfield
Excerpt from a Teenage Opera	Keith West		
Experiments with Mice	Johnny Dankworth	5-7-0-5	City Boy
Exterminate	Snap featuring Niki Harris	Flames of Paradise	Jennifer Rush and Elton John
Extremis	Gillian Anderson (speaking)	Flava (1)	Peter André
		Flash	B.B.E.
Eye Level	Simon Park	Flat Beat (1)	Mr Oizo
Eye of the Tiger (1)	Survivor	The Flintstones	B-52s
Fabulous	Charlie Gracie	FLM	Mel and Kim (Appleby)
Fade to Grey	Visage		
Fairground (1)	Simply Red	Float On	Floaters
Fairytale of New York	Pogues featuring Kirsty McColl	Floral Dance (21)	Terry Wogan
		Flowers in the Rain	Move
Faith	George Michael	Floy Joy (9)	Supremes
Faith Can Move Mountains	Johnnie Ray and the Four Lads	The Fly	U2
		Fly Away (1)	Lenny Kravitz
Falling	Roy Orbison	Flying Without Wings (1)	Westlife
Falling	Julee Cruise	Fog on the Tyne (Revisited)	Gazza and Lindisfarne
Falling in Love With You (1)	UB40		
Fame (17)	David Bowie	Foggy Mountain Breakdown	Lester Flatt and Earl Scruggs
Fancy Pants	Kenny		
Fanfare for the Common Man	Emerson, Lake and Palmer	Follow You Follow Me	Genesis
		Fool Again (1)	Westlife
Fantasy	Mariah Carey	Fool to Cry (6)	Rolling Stones
Fantasy Island	Tight Fit	Fool (If You Think It's Over)	Chris Rea
Farewell Is a Lonely Sound	Jimmy Ruffin	Foolish Beat	Debbie Gibson
Farewell My Summer Love	Michael Jackson	Footloose	Kenny Loggins
Far Far Away (2)	Slade	Footsee	Wigan's Chosen Few
Farmer Bill's Cowman (Kaiser Bill's Batman)	Wurzels	Footsteps	Steve Lawrence
		Foot Tapper (1)	Shadows
Fascinating Rhythm	Bass-O-Matic	For All Time	Catherine Zeta Jones
Fascination	Human League		
Fashion (5)	David Bowie	For America	Red Box
Fast Love (1)	George Michael	Forever and Ever (1)	Slik
Father and Son	Boyzone	Forever Autumn	Justin Hayward
Fattie Bum Bum	Carl Malcolm	Forever (8)	Roy Wood
Favourite Shirts (Boy Meets Girl)	Haircut 100	Forever Love (1)	Gary Barlow
FBI (6)	Shadows	Forget Me Not	Vera Lynn
Fear of the Dark	Iron Maiden	Forget Me Nots	Patrice Rushen
Feelings	Morris Albert	For Once in My Life	Stevie Wonder
Feel It (1)	Tamperer featuring Mayar	For the Good Times	Perry Como
		For Whom the Bell Tolls	Bee Gees
Feel Like Making Love	Roberta Flack	For Your Babies	Simply Red
Feel the Need in Me	Detroit Emeralds	For Your Eyes Only	Sheena Easton
Feels Like I'm in Love (1)	Kelly Marie	For Your Love	Yardbirds
Feet Up	Guy Mitchell	48 Crash	Suzi Quatro
Fernando (1)	Abba	I Fought the Law (33)	Bobby Fuller Four
Ferry across the Mersey	Gerry and the Pacemakers	Four Bacharach and David Songs (EP)	Deacon Blue

Title	Group/Artiste	Title	Group/Artiste
Go (Before You Break My Heart	Gigliola Cinquetti	Green Door (2)	Frankie Vaughan
God Gave Rock and Roll to You 11	Kiss	Green Green Grass of Home (1)	Tom Jones
God Only Knows	Beach Boys	The Green Manalishi With the Two-Prong Crown)	Fleetwood Mac
God Save the Queen (2)	Sex Pistols	Green Onions	Booker T. and the M.G.'s
Going Back to My Roots	Odyssey		
Going Home	Osmonds	Green Street Green	New Vaudeville Band
Going In with My Eyes Open (2)	David Soul	Green Tambourine	Lemon Pipers
Going Underground (1)	Jam	Grey Day	Madness
Gold	Spandau Ballet	Groove Is in the Heart	Deee-Lite
Golden Brown (2)	Stranglers	The Groove	Rodney Franklin
Golden Years (8)	David Bowie	Groovejet (If this Ain't Love (1)	Spiller
The Golden Years (EP)	Motorhead	The Groover (4)	T Rex
Goldie	Sarah Cracknell	Groovin'	Young Rascals
Gonna Get Along without You Now (8)	Viola Wills	Groovin' with Mr Bloe	Mr Bloe
		A Groovy Kind of Love (2)	Mindbenders
Gonna Make You A Star (1)	David Essex	Groovy Train	Farm
Gonna Make You an Offer You Can't Refuse	Jimmy Helms	Guaglione	Perez 'Prez' Prado and his Orchestra
Go Now (1)	Moody Blues	Guantanamera (7)	Sandpipers
Goodbye (1)	Spice Girls	Gudbuy T'Jane (2)	Slade
Goodbye My Love	Glitter Band	Guiding Star	Cast
Goodbye My Love (4)	Searchers	Guilty	Pearls
Goodbye Sam Hello Samantha	Cliff Richard	Guitar Boogie Shuffle	Bert Weedon
Goodbye Stranger	Pepsi and Shirlie	Guitar Tango (4)	Shadows
Goodbye Yellow Brick Road	Elton John	Gym and Tonic (1)	Spacedust
Good Golly Miss Molly	Little Richard	Gypsy Woman (La Da Dee)	Crystal Waters
Good Life	Inner City	Halfway Down the Stairs	Robin (Jerry Nelson), Kermit the Frog's nephew
Good Luck Charm (1)	Elvis Presley		
Good Morning Freedom	Blue Mink		
Good Morning Judge (5)	10cc		
Good Morning Starshine	Oliver	Halfway to Paradise	Billy Fury
Goodness Gracious Me	Peter Sellers and Sophia Loren	Hallelujah	Milk and Honey
		Handle With Care	Traveling Wilburys
Goodnight Girl (1)	Wet Wet Wet	Hand on Your Heart (1)	Kylie Minogue
Goodnight Midnight	Clodagh Rodgers	Hands to Heaven	Breathe
Good Thing	Fine Young Cannibals	Hands Up (Give Me Your Heart)	Ottawan
The Good, the Bad, and the Ugly (1)	Hugo Montenegro	Handy Man	Jimmy Jones
		Hanging Tough (1)	New Kids on the Block
Good Thing Going (4)	Sugar Minott		
Good Timin' (1)	Jimmy Jones	Hang on in There Baby	Curiosity Killed the Cat
Good Tradition	Tanita Tikaram		
A Good Year for the Roses	Elvis Costello	Hang on Sloopy	McCoys
Goody Two Shoes (1)	Adam Ant	Hanky Panky	Madonna
Google Eye	Nashville Teens	Happenin' All Over Again	Lonnie Gordon
Gossip Calypso	Bernard Cribbins	Happiness	Ken Dodd
Got My Mind Set on You	George Harrison	Happy Birthday (2)	Stevie Wonder
Gotta Be You	3T	Happy Birthday (2)	Altered Images
Gotta Have Something in the Bank Frank (8)	Frankie Vaughan and Kaye Sisters	Happy Birthday Sweet Sixteen	Neil Sedaka
		Happy Hour	Housemartins
Gotta Pull Myself Together	Nolans	H.A.P.P.Y Radio	Edwin Starr
Got 'Til It's Gone	Janet Jackson featuring Q-Tip and Joni Mitchell	Happy to Be on an Island in the Sun	Demis Roussos
		Happy Together	Turtles
Got to Be Certain	Kylie Minogue	Happy Wanderer	Obernkirchen Children's Choir
Got to Be There	Michael Jackson		
Got to Get	Rob 'N' Raz featuring Leila K	The Happy Whistler	Don Robertson
		Happy Xmas (War Is Over)	John and Yoko and the Plastic Ono Band
Go West	Pet Shop Boys		
Go Wild in the Country	Bow Wow Wow		
Grand Piano	Mixmaster	A Hard Rain's Gonna Fall	Bryan Ferry
Grandad (1)	Clive Dunn	Hard to Say I'm Sorry (4)	Chicago
Grandma's Party	Paul Nicholas	Harlem Shuffle	Bob and Earl
Grease (3)	Frankie Valli	Harper Valley PTA	Jeannie C. Riley
Great Balls of Fire (1)	Jerry Lee Lewis	Harvest for the World	Christians
Great Balls of Fire (45)	Tiny Tim	Harvest for the World (10)	Isley Brothers
Greatest Love of All	Whitney Houston	Hats Off to Larry	Del Shannon
The Great Pretender (4)	Freddie Mercury	Have I the Right (1)	Honeycombs
The Great Pretender (5)	Platters	Have I the Right (6)	Dead End Kids
The Great Pretender (9)	Jimmy Parkinson	Have You Ever Been in Love	Leo Sayer
Green Door (1)	Shakin' Stevens	Have You Seen Her	Chi-Lites

Title	Group/Artiste	Title	Group/Artiste
Have You Seen Your Mother Baby (5)	Rolling Stones	Hi-Fidelity	Kids from Fame with Valerie Landsberg
Hawkeye	Frankie Laine	High	Cure
Hazard	Richard Marx	High Class Baby	Cliff Richard
Head over Heels in Love	Kevin Keegan	High Energy	Evelyn Thomas
He Ain't Heavy, He's My Brother (1)	Hollies	High Hopes	Frank Sinatra
		High Noon	Frankie Laine
Heal the World	Michael Jackson	High Time	Paul Jones
Heart (1)	Pet Shop Boys	Hi-Hi Hi/C Moon	Wings
Heartache	Pepsi and Shirlie	Hi-Ho Silver	Jim Diamond
Heart and Soul	T'Pau	Hi-Ho Silver Lining	Jeff Beck
Heartbeat (3)	Ruby Murray	Hippy Chick	Soho
Heartbeat (7)	Showaddywaddy	Hippy Hippy Shake (2)	Swinging Blue Jeans
Heartbeat Tragedy(1)	Steps	His Latest Flame (1)	Elvis Presley
Heartbreaker (2)	Dionne Warwick	History (8)	Mai Tai
Heartbreak Hotel (2)	Elvis Presley	Hit and Miss	John Barry Orchestra
Heart Full of Soul	Yardbirds		
Hear the Drummer	Chad Jackson	Hit 'Em High	The Monstars
Heart of Glass (1)	Blondie	Hit Me with Your Rhythm Stick	Ian Dury and the Blockheads
Heart of Gold (10)	Neil Young		
Heart on My Sleeve	Gallagher and Lyle	Hold Back the Night	Trammps
Heart-Shaped Box	Nirvana	Holding Back the Years (2)	Simply Red
The Heat Is On	Glen Frey	Holding Out for a Hero (2)	Bonnie Tyler
Heaven Knows I'm Miserable Now	Smiths	Hold Me	Whitney Houston and Teddy Pendergrass
Heaven Must Be Missing an Angel	Tavares	Hold Me	P.J. Proby
		Hold Me Close (1)	David Essex
Heaven Must Have Sent You	Elgins	Hold Me Now	Johnny Logan
Hello (1)	Lionel Richie	Hold Me Thrill Me Kiss Me	Muriel Smith
Hello Goodbye (1)	Beatles	Hold Me Tight	Johnny Nash
Hello Hurray	Alice Cooper	Hold My Hand	Don Cornell
Hello I Love You	Doors	Hold On Tight	Electric Light Orchestra
Hello Little Girl	Fourmost		
Hello Mary Lou	Ricky Nelson	Hold On To My Love	Jimmy Ruffin
Hello This is Joanie	Paul Evans	Hold On (5)	En Vogue
Hell Raiser (2)	Sweet	Hold On (6)	Wilson Phillips
Help (1)	Beatles	Hold Tight	Dave Dee, Dozy, Beaky, Mick and Tich
Help Yourself	Tom Jones		
Here Comes Summer (1)	Jerry Keller		
Here Comes the Hotstepper	Ini Kamoze	Hold Your Head Up	Argent
Here Comes the Judge	Pigmeat Markham	Hole in My Shoe (2)	Traffic
Here Comes the Night (2)	Them	Hole in My Shoe (2)	Neil
Here Comes the Rain Again	Eurythmics	Hole in the Ground	Bernard Cribbins
Here Comes the Sun	Steve Harley	Holiday	Madonna
Here I Go Again (9)	Whitesnake	Holiday Rap	MC Miker 'G' and Deejay Sven
Here in My Heart (1)	Al Martino		
Here It Comes Again	Fortunes	Holidays in the Sun	Sex Pistols
Here We Go round the Mulberry Bush	Traffic	Holler/Let Love Lead the Way (1)	Spice Girls
		Holy Cow	Lee Dorsey
Hernando's Hideaway (1)	Johnston Brothers	Holy Smoke	Iron Maiden
Hersham Boys	Sham 69	Home Lovin' Man (7)	Andy Williams
He's Gonna Step on You Again	John Kongos	Homely Girl	Chi-Lites
He's in Town (3)	Rockin' Berries	Homely Girl (6)	UB40
He's Misstra Know It All	Stevie Wonder	Homeward Bound (9)	Simon and Garfunkel
He's the Greatest Dancer	Sister Sledge	Homing Waltz	Vera Lynn
Hey DJ I Can't Dance to That Music	Betty Boo	Honest Men	Electric Light Orchestra Part 2
Hey Girl	Small Faces	Honey	Bobby Goldsboro
Hey Girl Don't Bother Me (1)	Tams	Honey Honey (10)	Sweet Dreams
Hey Joe (1)	Frankie Laine	Hong Kong Garden	Siouxsie and the Banshees
Hey Joe (6)	Jimi Hendrix		
Hey Jude (16)	Wilson Pickett	Honky Cat	Elton John
Hey Jude (1)	Beatles	Honky Tonk Women (1)	Rolling Stones
Hey Little Girl	Del Shannon	Hooked on Classics	Royal Philharmonic Orchestra
Hey Now (Girls Just Want to Have Fun)	Cyndi Lauper		
		Hoots Mon (1)	Lord Rockingham's XI
Hey Paula	Paul and Paula		
Hey Rock and Roll (2)	Showaddywaddy	Hope of Deliverance	Paul McCartney
Hideaway	Dave Dee, Dozy, Beaky, Mick and Tich	Hopelessly Devoted to You	Olivia Newton-John
		Hotel California	Eagles
		Hot in the City	Billy Idol

Title	Group/Artiste
Hotlegs/I Was Only Joking (5)	Rod Stewart
Hot Love (1)	T Rex
Hot Toddy	Ted Heath
Hound Dog (2)	Elvis Presley
House Arrest	Krush
House of Fun (1)	Madness
House of Love	East 17
House of the Rising Sun (1)	Animals
House of the Rising Sun (4)	Frijid Pink
The House That Jack Built (4)	Alan Price Set
The House That Jack Built (9)	Tracie
How Am I Supposed To Live without You	Michael Bolton
How Come	Ronnie Lane and Slim Chance
How Deep Is Your Love (1)	Take That
How Deep Is Your Love (3)	Bee Gees
How Do You Do It? (1)	Gerry and The Pacemakers
How High	Charlatans
How Much is That Doggie in the Window	Lita Roza
How Much Is That Doggie in the Window	Patti Page
How Soon	Henry Mancini
Howzat	Sherbet
Human Nature	Gary Clail On-U Sound System
Humpin' Around	Bobby Brown
Hundred Mile High City	Ocean Colour Scene
A Hundred Pounds of Clay	Craig Douglas
Hungry Like the Wolf	Duran Duran
Hurry Up Harry	Sham 69
Hurt	Manhattans
Hush	Kula Shaker
The Hustle	Van McCoy and the Soul City Symphony
Hypnotize	Notorious B.I.G.
Hysteria	Def Leppard
I Am a Cider Drinker (Paloma Blanca) (3)	Wurzels
I Am Blessed	Eternal
I Am the Beat	Look
I Am . . . I Said	Neil Diamond
I Beg Your Pardon	Kon Kan
I Believe I Can Fly (1)	R. Kelly
I Believe (2)	Bachelors
I Believe (1)	Frankie Laine
I Believe (6)	EMF
I Believe in Father Christmas	Greg Lake
I Believe (in Love)	Hot Chocolate
I Believe/Up on the Roof (1)	Robson Green and Jerome Flynn
I Can Do It	Rubettes
I Can Hear Music	Beach Boys
I Can Hear the Grass Grow	Move
I Can Help	Billy Swan
I Can Make You Feel Good	Shalamar
I Can See Clearly Now	Johnny Nash
I Can't Control Myself (2)	Troggs
I Can't Dance	Genesis
I Can't Explain (8)	Who
I Can't Let Maggie Go	Honeybus
I Can't Stand It	Twenty 4 Seven and Captain Hollywood
I Can't Stand the Rain	Eruption
I Can't Stand Up for Falling Down	Elvis Costello
I Can't Wait	Nu Shooz

Title	Group/Artiste
I Close My Eyes and Count to Ten	Dusty Springfield
I Could Be Happy	Altered Images
I Could Be So Good for You (3)	Dennis Waterman and his Band
I Couldn't Live without You r Love	Petula Clark
I Did What I Did for Maria	Tony Christie
I Didn't Mean to Turn You On	Robert Palmer
I Die: You Die	Gary Numan
I Do I Do I Do I Do I Do (38)	Abba
I Do It For You	Fatima Mansions
I Don't Believe in If Anymore	Roger Whittaker
I Don't Care	Shakespears Sister
I Don't Wanna Dance (1)	Eddy Grant
I Don't Wanna Fight	Tina Turner
I Don't Want a Lover (8)	Texas
I Don't Want To	Tony Braxton
I Don't Want to Put a Hold on You	Berni Flint
I Don't Want To Talk about It	Everything ` the Girl
I Don't Want to Talk about It (1)	Rod Stewart
I Drove All Night (7)	Roy Orbison
I Drove All Night (7)	Cyndi Lauper
I Eat Cannibals	Toto Coelo
I Feel Fine (1)	Beatles
I Feel for You (1)	Chaka Khan
I Feel Like Buddy Holly	Alvin Stardust
I Feel Love (1)	Donna Summer
I Feel Love (Medley)	Marc Almond
I Feel the Earth Move	Martika
I Feel You (1)	Peter André
I Feel You	Depeche Mode
I Found Lovin'	Steve Walsh
I Get a Kick out of You	Gary Shearston
I Get a Little Sentimental over You	New Seekers
I Get So Lonely	Four Knights
I Go Ape	Neil Sedaka
I Got the Music in Me	Kiki Dee Band
I Got You Babe (1)	Sonny and Cher
I Got You Babe (1)	UB40 featuring Chrissie Hynde
I Guess That's Why They Call It the Blues	Elton John
I Have a Dream (1)	Westlife
I Have a Dream (2)	Abba
I Have Nothing	Whitney Houston
I Haven't Stopped Dancing Yet	Pat and Mick
I Hear You Knocking	Dave Edmunds
I Hear You Now	Jon and Vangelis
I Heard it through the Grapevine (1)	Marvin Gaye
I Honestly Love You	Olivia Newton-John
I Just Called to Say I Love You (1)	Stevie Wonder
I Just Can't Stop Loving You (1)	Michael Jackson
I Just Don't Know What to Do with Myself	Dusty Springfield
I Kissed You	Everly Brothers
I Knew You Were Waiting (for Me) (1)	Aretha Franklin and George Michael
I Know Him So Well (1)	Elaine Paige and Barbara Dickson
I Left My Heart in San Francisco	Tony Bennett
I Like it (1)	Gerry and The Pacemakers
I Love My Radio (6)	Taffy
I Love Rock 'N' Roll	Joan Jett and the Blackhearts

Title	Group/Artiste	Title	Group/Artiste
I'll Find My Way Home	Jon and Vangelis	In a Golden Coach	Billy Cotton
I'll Keep You Satisfied	Billy J. Kramer and the Dakotas	The In Betweenies	Goodies
		In Dreams	Roy Orbison
I'll Never Fall in Love Again (1)	Bobby Gentry	In Dulce Jubilo	Mike Oldfield
I'll Never Find Another You (1)	Seekers	In My Defence	Freddie Mercury
I'll Never Get Over You	Johnny Kidd and the Pirates	In My Own Time	Family
		In Summer	Billy Fury
I'll Pick a Rose for My Rose	Marv Johnson	In the Air Tonight	Phil Collins
I'll Take You Home Again Kathleen (7)	Slim Whitman	In the Army Now (2)	Status Quo
		In the Bad Bad Old Days	Foundations
Il Silenzio (1)	Dino Rosso	In the Closet	Michael Jackson
I'm a Believer (1)	Monkees	In the Country	Cliff Richard
I'm a Boy (2)	Who	In the Ghetto (2)	Elvis Presley
I'm a Man	Spencer Davis Group	In the Middle of Nowhere	Dusty Springfield
		In the Midnight Hour (12)	Wilson Pickett
I'm a Man Not a Boy	North and South	In the Navy (2)	Village People
I'm a Tiger	Lulu	In the Summertime (1)	Mungo Jerry
I'm a Wonderful Thing Baby	Kid Creole and the Coconuts	In the Year 2525 (Exordium and Terminus)	Zager and Evans
I'm Alive (1)	Hollies	In Yer Face	808 State
I'm Doing Fine Now	Pasadenas	In Your Care	Tasmin Archer
I'm Easy	Faith No More	In Your Eyes	George Benson
I'm Every Woman	Whitney Houston	In Zaïre (4)	Johnny Wakelin
I'm Every Woman (8)	Chaka Khan	Incommunicado	Marillon
I'm Free (5)	Soup Dragons featuring Junior Reid	Independence	Lulu
		Independent Women (1)	Destiny's Child
		Indestructible	Four Tops with Smokey Robinson
I'm Going Slightly Mad	Queen		
I'm Gonna Be	Proclaimers (Charles and Craig Reid)	Indiana Wants Me	R. Dean Taylor
		Indian Love Call (7)	Slim Whitman
I'm Gonna Be Strong	Gene Pitney	Indian Reservation	Don Fardon
I'm Gonna Get Me a Gun	Cat Stevens	Infinite Dreams	Iron Maiden
I'm Gonna Get You	Bizarre Inc	Infinity	Guru Josh
I'm Gonna Make You Love Me (3)	Diana Ross and Supremes with the Temptations	Informer	Snow
		Innuendo (1)	Queen
		Insanity	Oceanic
I'm Gonna Make You Mine	Lou Christie	Inside Out	Odyssey
I'm Gonna Run Away from You	Tami Lynn	Inside (1)	Stiltskin
I'm Gonna Tear Your Playhouse Down	Paul Young	Instant Karma	Lennon, Ono and Plastic Ono Band
I'm in the Mood for Dancing	Nolans	Instant Replay (10)	Yell!
I'm into Something Good (1)	Herman's Hermits	Instant Replay (8)	Dan Hartman
I'm Leaving It All up to You	Donny and Marie Osmond	Instinction	Spandau Ballet
		In Summer	Billy Fury
I'm Mandy Fly Me (6)	10cc	Interesting Drug	Morrissey
I'm Not in Love (1)	10cc	International Bright Young Thing	Jesus Jones
I'm Not Scared	Eighth Wonder	Into the Groove (1)	Madonna
I'm on Fire	5000 Volts	Into the Valley	Skids
I'm Real	James Brown featuring Full Force	Intuition	Linx
		Invisible Sun	Police
I'm So Excited	Pointer Sisters	Invisible Touch (Live)	Genesis
I'm So Glad I'm Standing Here Today	Crusaders (featuring Joe Cocker)	I.O.U.	Freez
		Ire Feelings	Rupie Edwards
I'm Still Standing	Elton John	The Irish Rover	Pogues and the Dubliners
I'm Still Waiting (1)	Diana Ross		
I'm Stone in Love with You	Stylistics	Iron Lion Zion	Bob Marley and the Wailers
I'm Stone in Love with You (10)	Johnny Mathis		
I'm Telling You Now	Freddie and the Dreamers	Island Girl	Elton John
		Island of Dreams	Springfields
I'm the Leader of the Gang (1)	Gary Glitter	Islands in the Stream	Kenny Rogers and Dolly Parton
I'm the One	Gerry and the Pacemakers	Isle of Innisfree	Bing Crosby
		Isn't It a Wonder	Boyzone
I'm the Urban Spaceman	Bonzo Dog Doo-Dah Band	Isn't She Lovely	David Parton
I'm Too Sexy	Right Said Fred	Israelites	Desmond Dekker and the Aces
I'm Walking behind You	Eddie Fisher with Sally Sweetland		
		Is She Really Going Out with him?	Joe Jackson
I'm Your Man (1)	Wham		
Imagine (1)	John Lennon	Is There Anybody Out There	Bassheads
Importance of Your Love	Vince Hill	Is There Something I Should Know (1)	Duran Duran
In a Broken Dream (3)	Python Lee Jackson		

Title	Group/Artiste	Title	Group/Artiste
Is This Love	Bob Marley and the Wailers	It's My Party (9)	Leslie Gore
		It's Not Unusual (1)	Tom Jones
Is This Love (9)	Whitesnake	It's Now or Never (1)	Elvis Presley
Is This Love?	Alison Moyet	It's Oh So Quiet	Björk
It Ain't Over Til It's Over	Lenny Kravitz	It's Only Make Believe (1)	Conway Twitty
It Ain't What You Do . . .	Fun Boy Three and Bananarama	It's Only Rock and Roll (10)	Rolling Stones
		It's Only Us/she's the One (1)	Robbie Williams
Itchycoo Park	M People	It's Over (1)	Roy Orbison
Itchycoo Park (3)	Small Faces	It's Over (8)	Funk Masters
It Doesn't Have to Be This Way	Blow Monkeys	It's Raining	Darts
It Doesn't Matter Anymore	Buddy Holly	It's Raining Men (2)	Weather Girls
It Don't Come Easy (4)	Ringo Starr	It's Still Rock and Roll to Me	Billy Joel
It Feels So Good (1)	Sonique	It's the Same Old Song	Four Tops
It Is Time to Get Funky	D Mob	It's Too Late	Carole King
It Isn't It Wasn't It Ain't Never Gonna Be	Whitney Houston and Aretha Franklin	It's Too Late (8)	Quartz introducing Dina Carroll
It Keeps Rainin'	Bitty McLean	It's Wonderful	Jimmy Ruffin
It Miek	Desmond Dekker and the Aces	It's You (9)	Freddie Starr
		It's Your Life	Smokie
It Might as Well Rain until September	Carole King	Itsy Bitsy Teeny Weeny Yellow Polka Dot Bikini (8)	Brian Hyland
It Must Be Love (14)	Labi Siffre	Itsy Bitsy Teeny Weeny Yellow Polka Dot Bikini (1)	Bombalurina featuring Timmy Mallett
It Must Be Love (4)	Madness	I've Been a Bad Bad Boy	Paul Jones
It Must Have Been Love	Roxette	I've Been Drinking	Jeff Beck and Rod Stewart
It Only Takes a Minute	100 Ton and A Feather (Jonathan King)	I've Been Thinking about You	Londonbeat
		I've Got a Little Something for You	MN8
It Only Takes a Minute (7)	Take That	I've Gotta Get a Message to You (1)	Bee Gees
It Oughta Sell a Million	Lyn Paul		
It Should Have Been Me	Yvonne Fair	I've Waited So Long	Anthony Newley
It Started With a Kiss	Hot Chocolate	Ivory Tower	Three Kayes
It Takes Two Baby (53)	Kershaw, Brookes, Jive Bunny and Londonbeat	Jackie (22)	Scott Walker
		Jackie Wilson Said	Dexy's Midnight Runners
It Takes Two (16)	Marvin Gaye and Kim Weston	Jack in the Box (4)	Clodagh Rodgers
		Jack in the Box (7)	Moments
It Takes Two (5)	Rod Stewart and Tina Turner	Jack Mix II/III	Mirage
		The Jack That House Built	Jack 'N' Chill
It Wasn't Me (1)	Shaggy featuring Ricardo 'RikRok' Ducent	Jack Your Body (1)	Steve 'Silk' Hurley
		Jailhouse Rock (1)	Elvis Presley
It's a Fine Day	Opus III	Jamming	Bob Marley and the Wailers
It's a Hard Life	Queen		
It's a Heartache (4)	Bonnie Tyler	January (1)	Pilot
Its a Love Thing	Whispers	Japanese Boy	Aneka
It's a Miracle	Culture Club	Jarrow Song	Alan Price
It's a Sin (1)	Pet Shop Boys	Jealous Guy (1)	Roxy Music
It's All in the Game (1)	Tommy Edwards	Jealous Mind (1)	Alvin Stardust
It's All in the Game (2)	Cliff Richard	Jealousy	Billy Fury
It's All Over Now (1)	Rolling Stones	The Jean Genie (2)	David Bowie
It's Almost Tomorrow (1)	Dreamweavers	Jeans On	David Dundas
It's Alright	East 17	Jeepster (2)	T Rex
It's Alright (5)	Pet Shop Boys	Je Ne Sais Pas Pourquoi	Kylie Minogue
It's Been So Long	George McCrae	Jennifer Eccles	Hollies
It's Different for Girls	Joe Jackson	Jennifer Juniper	Donovan
It's Four in the Morning	Faron Young	Je Suis Un Rock Star (14)	Bill Wyman
It's Getting Better	Mama Cass	Jesus to a Child (1)	George Michael
It's Gonna Be a Cold Cold Christmas	Dana	Jet	Paul McCartney and Wings
It's Good News Week	Hedgehoppers Anonymous	Je t'Aime (9)	Judge Dread
		Je t'Aime . . . Moi Non Plus (1)	Jane Birkin and Serge Gainsbourg
It's Grim Up North	Justified Ancients of Mu Mu	Jig a Jig	East of Eden
		Jilted John	Jilted John
It's Impossible	Perry Como	Jimmy Jimmy (16)	Undertones
It's in His Kiss	Linda Lewis	Joanna (2)	Kool and the Gang
It's Late	Ricky Nelson	Joanna (7)	Scott Walker
It's Like That	Run DMC vs Jason Nevins	Joan of Arc	Orchestral Manoeuvres in the Dark
It's My Life	Dr Alban		
It's My Party (1)	Dave Stewart with Barbara Gaskin	Joe Le Taxi	Vanessa Paradis

Title	Group/Artiste	Title	Group/Artiste
John I'm Only Dancing (12)	David Bowie	Killing Me Softly with His Song (6)	Roberta Flack
Johnny Come Home	Fine Young Cannibals	The Killing Moon	Echo and the Bunnymen
Johnny Reggae	Piglets	A Kind of Magic	Queen
Johnny Remember Me (1)	John Leyton	King of My Castle (1)	Wamdue Project
Join In and Sing Again	Johnston Brothers	King (4)	UB40
Join Together (9)	Who	The King of Rock 'N' Roll (7)	Prefab Sprout
The Joker (1)	Steve Miller Band	King of the Cops	Billy Howard
Jolene (7)	Dolly Parton	King of the Road	Roger Miller
Joy (4)	Soul II Soul	King of the Road (9)	Proclaimers
Joy and Pain	Donna Allen	Kingston Town	UB40
Joy Bringer	Manfred Mann's Earth Band	Kinky Afro	Happy Mondays
Joyride	Roxette	Kinky Boots	Patrick Macnee and Honor Blackman
Judge Fudge	Happy Mondays	Kiss (5)	Art of Noise featuring Tom Jones
Judy in Disguise (with Glasses)	John Fred and the Playboy Band	Kiss (6)	Prince and the Revolution
Judy Teen	Cockney Rebel	Kisses Sweeter Than Wine (7)	Jimmie Rodgers
Juke Box Jive	Rubettes	Kissin' in the Back Row of the Movies	Drifters
Julia Says	Wet Wet Wet	Kiss Me	Stephen 'Tin Tin' Duffy
Julie Do Ya Love Me	White Plains		
Juliet (1)	Four Pennies	Kites	Simon Dupree and the Big Sound
Jump (2)	Kriss Kross		
Jump (7)	Van Halen	Knock on Wood (6)	Amii Stewart
Jump (for My Love)	Pointer Sisters	Knock Three Times	Dawn
Jumping Jack Flash (1)	Rolling Stones	Knocked It Off	B.A. Robertson
Jump They Say	David Bowie	Knockin' on Heaven's Door (1)	Dunblane
Jump to the Beat	Dannii Minogue	Knockin' on Heaven's Door (2)	Guns N' Roses
Jump to the Beat	Stacy Lattisaw	Knowing Me Knowing You (1)	Abba
Jungle Rock	Hank Mizell	Kokomo	Beach Boys
Just an Illusion	Imagination	Kon Tiki (1)	Shadows
Just Another Day (5)	Jon Secada	Kowalski	Primal Scream
Just Another Night	Mick Jagger	Kung Fu Fighting (1)	Carl Douglas
Just Can't Get Enough	Depeche Mode	Kyrie	Mr Mister
Just Got Lucky	Jo Boxers	La Bamba (1)	Los Lobos
Justified and Ancient	KLF featuring Tammy Wynette	Labelled with Love	Squeeze
Just Like Eddie	Heinz	Labour of Love	Hue and Cry
Just Loving You	Anita Harris	La Dee Dah	Jackie Dennis
Just My Imagination (8)	Temptations	Ladies Night	Kool and the Gang
Just One More Night	Yellow Dog	Lady D'Arbanville	Cat Stevens
Just One Smile	Gene Pitney	Lady Eleanor	Lindisfarne
Just Say No	Grange Hill Cast	Lady Hear Me Tonight (1)	Medjo
Just the One	Levellers	Lady in Red	Chris De Burgh
Just the Way You Are	Billy Joel	Lady Madonna (1)	Beatles
Just the Way You Are (12)	Barry White	Lady Marmalade	Labelle
Just Walkin' in the Rain (1)	Johnnie Ray	Lady Marmalade	All Saints
Just What I Always Wanted	Mari Wilson	Lady Rose	Mungo Jerry
Just When I Needed You Most	Randy Vanwarmer	Lady Willpower	Union Gap featuring Gary Puckett
Karma Chameleon	Culture Club	La Isla Bonita (1)	Madonna
Kayleigh	Marillion	Lambada	Kaoma
Keep On Dancin' (8)	Gary's Gang	La Mer	Bobby Darin
Keep On Dancing	Bay City Rollers	Lamplight	David Essex
Keep On Loving You	REO Speedwagon	Last Christmas	Wham
Keep On Movin' (1)	5ive	Last Night in Soho	Dave Dee, Dozy, Beaky, Mick and Tich
Keep On Moving	Soul II Soul with Caron Wheeler		
Keep On Running (1)	Spencer Davis Group	Last of the Famous International Playboys	Morrissey
Keep On Walkin'	Ce Ce Peniston	The Last Time (1)	Rolling Stones
Keep Searchin'	Del Shannon	Last Train to Clarkesville (23)	Monkees
Keep the Faith	Bon Jovi	Last Train to San Fernando	Johnny Duncan and the Blue Grass Boys
The Key the Secret	Urban Cookie Collective		
Key to My Life	Boyzone	The Last Waltz	Engelbert Humperdinck
Kids in America (2)	Kim Wilde		
Killer	Adamski	Laugh at Me	Sonny
Killer (EP)	Seal	The Laughing Gnome (6)	David Bowie
Killer on the Loose	Thin Lizzy	Lavender	Marillion
Killer Queen	Queen	Lay All Your Love on Me (7)	Abba
Killing Me Softly (1)	The Fugees		

Title	Group/Artiste	Title	Group/Artiste
Lay Down Your Arms (1)	Anne Shelton	Let Your Yeah Be Yeah	Pioneers
Layla	Eric Clapton	Licence to Kill	Gladys Knight
Lay Lady Lay	Bob Dylan	Lick a Smurp for Christmas	Father Abraphart and
Lay Your Love on Me	Racey		the Smurps
Lazy Days (8)	Robbie Williams		(Jonathan King)
Lazy Sunday	Small Faces	Life Is a Long Song	Jethro Tull
Leader of the Pack	Joan Collins Fan Club	Life Is a Minestrone (7)	10cc
	(Julian Clary)	Life Is a Rollercoaster (1)	Ronan Keating
Leader of the Pack (3)	Shangri-Las	Life Is Too Short Girl	Sheer Elegance
Lean on Me (18)	Bill Withers	Lifeline	Spandau Ballet
Lean on Me (7)	Mud	Life on Mars (3)	David Bowie
Lean on Me (Ah-Li-Ayo) (3)	Red Box	Lift Me Up (1)	Geri Halliwell
Leave a Little Love	Lulu	Light My Fire (5)	Amii Stewart
Leave Me Alone	Michael Jackson	Light My Fire (6)	Jose Feliciano
Leave Them All Behind	Ride	Light My Fire (7)	Doors
Leavin' on a Jet Plane	Peter, Paul and Mary	Light of Experience (Doina	Georghe Zamfir
Leeds United	Leeds United FC	De Jale)	
Left to My Own Devices	Pet Shop Boys	Lightnin' Strikes	Lou Christie
Legend of Xanadu	Dave Dee, Dozy,	Like a Baby	Len Barry
	Beaky, Mick and	Like a Prayer (1)	Madonna
	Tich	Like a Rolling Stone	Bob Dylan
Lenny	Supergrass	Like a Virgin	Madonna
Les Bicyclettes de Belsize	Engelbert	Like Clockwork	Boomtown Rats
	Humperdinck	Like Sister and Brother	Drifters
Lessons in Love	Level 42	Like to Get to Know You Well	Howard Jones
Let 'Em In	Wings	Lily the Pink (1)	Scaffold
Let It Be (1)	Ferry Aid	Lily Was Here	David A. Stewart
Let It Be (2)	Beatles		featuring Candy
Let It Swing	Bobbysocks		Dulfer
Let Love Lead the Way/Holler (1)	Spice Girls	Linger	Cranberries
Let Me Be the One	Shadows	The Lion Sleeps Tonight (1)	Tight Fit
Let Me Be Your Fantasy (1)	Baby D	Lipstick on Your Collar	Connie Francis
Let Me Entertain You (3)	Robbie Williams	Liquidator	Harry J. All Stars
Let Me Go Lover (10)	Kathy Kirby	Listen to the Music	Doobie Brothers
Let Me Go Lover (3)	Dean Martin	Listen to What the Man Said	Wings
Let Me Go Lover (5)	Ruby Murray	Listen to Your Heart	Roxette
Let Me Go Lover (9)	Teresa Brewer	Listen to Your Heart	Sonia
Let Me In	Osmonds	Little Arrows	Leapy Lee
Let Me Try Again	Tammy Jones	Little Bird	Annie Lennox
Let's All Chant	Michael Zager Band	Little Children (1)	Billy J. Kramer and
Let's Dance (2)	Chris Montez		the Dakotas
Let's Dance (1)	David Bowie	Little Darlin'	Diamonds
Let's Get Ready to Rhumble	PJ and Duncan	Little Devil	Neil Sedaka
Let's Get Rocked	Def Leppard	Little Donkey (3)	Nina and Frederick
Let's Get Serious	Jermaine Jackson	Little Drummer Boy	Beverley Sisters
Let's Go All the Way	Sly Fox	Little Lies	Fleetwood Mac
Let's Go to San Francisco	Flowerpot Men	Little Man	Sonny and Cher
Let's Groove	Earth Wind and Fire	Little Miss Lonely	Helen Shapiro
Let's Hang On	Four Seasons with	A Little Peace	Nicole
	Sound of Frankie	Little Red Corvette/1999	Prince
	Valli	Little Red Rooster (1)	Rolling Stones
Let's Have a Quiet Night In (8)	David Soul	A Little Respect	Erasure
Let's Party (1)	Jive Bunny and the	Little Things	Dave Berry
	Mastermixers	Little Things Mean a Lot (1)	Kitty Kallen
Let's Spend the Night	Rolling Stones	Little Town Flirt	Del Shannon
Together (3)		Little White Bull	Tommy Steele
Let's Stay Together (6)	Tina Turner	Little Willy (4)	Sweet
Let's Stay Together (7)	Al Green	Live and Let Die (5)	Guns N' Roses
Let's Stick Together	Bryan Ferry	Live and Let Die (9)	Wings
Let's Talk about Sex (2)	Salt-N-Pepa featuring	Live Is Life	Opus
	Psychotropic	Live It Up	Mental as Anything
Let's Think about Living	Bob Luman	Liverpool Lou	Scaffold
Lets Wait Awhile	Janet Jackson	Living Daylights (5)	A-Ha
Let's Walk That-A-Way	Doris Day and	Living Doll (1)	Cliff Richard
	Johnnie Ray	Living Doll (1)	Cliff Richard with the
Let's Work	Mick Jagger		Young Ones and
The Letter	Boxtops		Hank Marvin
Letter from America	Proclaimers	Living in a Box	Living in a Box
Let There Be Drums	Sandy Nelson	Living in the Past	Jethro Tull
Let There Be Love	Simple Minds	Living Next Door to Alice	Smokie
Let Your Love Flow	Bellamy Brothers	Living on My Own (1)	Freddie Mercury

M
U
S
I
C

P
O
P

Title	Group/Artiste	Title	Group/Artiste
Living on the Ceiling	Blancmange	Lovefool	The Cardigans
Living on Video	Trans-X	Love Grows (1)	Edison Lighthouse
The Living Years	Mike and the	Love Guaranteed	Damage
	Mechanics	Love Hangover	Diana Ross
Livin' La Vida Loca (1)	Ricky Martin	The Love I Lost	West End featuring
Livin' on a Prayer	Bon Jovi		Sybil
Loadsamoney (Doin' Up	Harry Enfield	Love in an Elevator	Aerosmith
the House)		Love In the First Degree	Bananarama
Lock Up Your Daughters	Slade	Love Is a Battlefield	Pat Benatar
Loco in Acapulco	Four Tops	Love Is a Many-Splendored	Four Aces featuring Al
Locomotion (5)	Orchestral	Thing	Roberts
	Manoeuvres in the	Love Is a Stranger	Eurythmics
	Dark	Love Is All Around (1)	Wet Wet Wet
The Locomotion (2)	Kylie Minogue	Love Is All Around (5)	Troggs
Lola	Kinks	Love Is Contagious	Taja Sevelle
Lollipop	Chordettes	Love Is in the Air	John Paul Young
Lollipop (2)	Mudlarks	Love Is Like a Violin	Ken Dodd
London Calling	Clash	Love Is Like Oxygen (9)	Sweet
London Kid	Jean-Michel Jarre	Love Is the Drug	Roxy Music
	featuring Hank	Love Is the Law	Sea Horses
	Marvin	Love Kills	Freddie Mercury
London Nights	London Boys	Love Letters (4)	Alison Moyet
The Lone Ranger	Quantum Jump	Love Letters (4)	Ketty Lester
Lonely Boy	Paul Anka	Love Letters in the Sand	Pat Boone
Lonely Girl	Eddie Holman	Love Like a Man (10)	Ten Years After
Lonely This Christmas (1)	Mud	Love Like Blood	Killing Joke
Long-Haired Lover from	Little Jimmy Osmond	Lovely Day	Bill Withers
Liverpool (1)		Love Me	Yvonne Elliman
Long Live Love (1)	Sandie Shaw	Love Me Do (4)	Beatles
Long Shot Kick De Bucket	Pioneers	Love Me for a Reason (1)	Osmonds
Long Tall Sally	Little Richard	Love Me Love My Dog	Peter Shelley
Look at That Girl (1)	Guy Mitchell	Love Me or Leave Me	Sammy Davis Jnr
Look for a Star	Gary Mills	Love of My Life	Dooleys
Look Mama	Howard Jones	Love of the Common People (2)	Paul Young
Look Wot You Dun (4)	Slade	Love of the Common People (9)	Nicky Thomas
Looking After No. 1	Boomtown Rats	Love on a Mountain Top	Robert Knight
Looking for Linda	Hue And Cry	Love on your Side (9)	Thompson Twins
Looking High High High	Bryan Johnson	Love Plus One	Haircut 100
Looking Through the Eyes	Partridge Family	Love Really Hurts without You	Billy Ocean
of Love	starring David	Love Resurrection	Alison Moyet
	Cassidy	A Lover's Concerto	Toys
Looking through the Eyes of	Gene Pitney	Lovers of the World Unite	David and Jonathan
Love (3)		Love's Gotta Hold on Me	Dollar
Looking Up	Michelle Gayle	Love Shack	B-52's
Loop-De-Loop (5)	Frankie Vaughan	Love Shine a Light	Katrina and the
Loop di Love	Shag (Jonathan King)		Waves
Losing My Mind	Liza Minnelli	Lovesick Blues (1)	Frank Ifield
Losing You	Brenda Lee	Love Song	Simple Minds
Lost in France (9)	Bonnie Tyler	Love's Theme	Love Unlimited
Lost in Music	Sister Sledge		Orchestra
Love Action	Human League	Love Theme from A Star Is	Barbra Streisand
Love and Affection	Joan Armatrading	Born (Evergreen)	
Love and Kisses	Dannii Minogue	Love Theme from The Thorn	Juan Martin
Love and Marriage	Frank Sinatra	Birds	
Love and Pride	King	Love . . . Thy Will Be Done	Martika
Love Can Build a Bridge (1)	Cher, Chrissie Hynde,	Love to Hate You	Erasure
	Neneh Cherry,	Love to Love You Baby	Donna Summer
	Eric Clapton	Love Town	Booker Newbury III
Love Can't Turn Around	Farley 'Jackmaster'	Love Train	Holly Johnson
	Funk	Love Train	O'Jays
The Love Cats	Cure	Love Will Tear Us Apart	Joy Division
Love Changes Everything	Michael Ball	Love Won't Wait (1)	Gary Barlow
Love Changes (Everything)	Climie Fisher	The Love You Save	Jackson 5
Love City Groove	Love City Groove	Loving You	Minnie Riperton
Love Come Down	Evelyn 'Champagne'	Lovin' Things	Marmalade
	King	LSI	Shamen
Love Don't Cost a Thing (1)	Jennifer Lopez	Lucille (10)	Little Richard
Love Don't Live Here	Rose Royce	Lucille (1)	Kenny Rogers
Anymore (2)		Lucky Lips	Cliff Richard
Love Don't Live Here	Jimmy Nail	Lucky Number	Lene Lovich
Anymore (3)		Lucky Stars	Dean Friedman

Title	Group/Artiste	Title	Group/Artiste
Lucy in the Sky With Diamonds	Elton John	Mary's Prayer	Danny Wilson
Lullaby	Cure	Massachusetts (1)	Bee Gees
Lunatics (Have Taken Over the Asylum)	Fun Boy Three	The Masses against the Classes (1)	Manic Street Preachers
Lyin' Eyes	Eagles	Master and Servant	Depeche Mode
Ma Baker	Boney M	Masterblaster (Jammin')	Stevie Wonder
Macarthur Park (4)	Richard Harris	Material Girl	Madonna
Macarthur Park (5)	Donna Summer	Matthew and Son (2)	Cat Stevens
Mack the Knife (1)	Bobby Darin	Maybe Baby	Crickets
Mad about You	Bruce Ruffin	Me and Julio down by the Schoolyard	Paul Simon
Mad Passionate Love	Bernard Bresslaw		
Mad World	Tears for Fears	Me and Mrs Jones	Billy Paul
Maggie May (1)	Rod Stewart	Me and My Life	Tremeloes
Magic Fly	Space	Me and My Shadow	Frank Sinatra and Sammy Davis Jr
Magic Moments	Perry Como		
The Magic Number	De La Soul	Me and You and a Dog Named Boo	Lobo (US)
Magical Mystery Tour (double EP) (2)	Beatles		
		The Medal Song	Culture Club
Ma He's Making Eyes at Me (10)	Lena Zavaroni	Meet Me on the Corner	Lindisfarne
Ma He's Making Eyes at Me (2)	Johnny Otis Show	Megamix (6)	Technotronic
Mah Na Mah Na	Piero Umiliani	Mellow Yellow	Donovan
Maid of Orleans	Orchestral Manoeuvres in the Dark	Melody of Love	Inkspots
		Melting Pot	Blue Mink
		Memo from Turner	Mick Jagger
Make It Easy On Yourself (1)	Walker Brothers	Memories Are Made of This (1)	Dean Martin
Make It with You	Bread	Memories Are Made of This (5)	Dave King featuring the Keynotes
Make Love to Me (8)	Jo Stafford		
Make Me an Island	Joe Dolan	Memory	Elaine Paige
Make Me Smile (1)	Steve Harley and Cockney Rebel	Men in Black (1)	Will Smith
		Mercy Mercy Me – I Want You	Robert Palmer
Make the World Go Away	Eddy Arnold	Merry Christmas Everyone (1)	Shakin' Stevens
Making Up Again	Goldie	Merry Gentle Pops	Barron Knights
Makin' Love (9)	Floyd Robinson	Merry Xmas Everybody (1)	Slade
Male Stripper	Man 2 Man meet Man Parrish	The Message	Grandmaster Flash and the Furious Five
Malt and Barley Blues	McGuinness Flint	Message in a Bottle (1)	Police
Mama Used to Say	Junior	Message to Martha (Kentucky Bluebird)	Adam Faith
Mama Weer All Crazee Now (1)	Slade		
		A Message to Your Heart	Samantha Janus
Mama/Who Do You Think You Are	Spice Girls	Message Understood	Sandie Shaw
		Metal Guru (1)	T Rex
Mambo Italiano (No. 1 1954)	Rosemary Clooney	Me the Peaceful Heart	Lulu
Mambo No. 5 (A Little Bit of . . .)	Lou Bega	Mexicali Rose	Karl Denver
Mamma Mia (1)	Abba	Miami Vice Theme	Jan Hammer
Mammy Blue (31)	Roger Whittaker	Michael (1)	Highwaymen
Man with the Child in his Eyes	Kate Bush	Michael Caine	Madness
Mandy (11)	Barry Manilow	Michelle (1)	Overlanders
Maneater	Daryl Hall and John Oates	Mi Chico Latino (1)	Geri Halliwell
		Mickey	Toni Basil
Man from Nazareth	John Paul Joans	Midas Touch	Midnight Star
Manic Monday	Bangles	Midlife Crisis	Faith No More
Mannequin	Kids from Fame with Gene Anthony Ray	Midnight at the Oasis	Maria Muldaur
		Midnight in Moscow	Kenny Ball and his Jazzmen
Man of Mystery (5)	Shadows		
Man of the World	Fleetwood Mac	Midnight Rider	Paul Davidson
The Man That Got Away	Judy Garland	Midnight Train To Georgia	Gladys Knight and the Pips
The Man Who Sold the World	Lulu		
Man with the Child in his Eyes (6)	Kate Bush		
		Mighty Quinn (1)	Manfred Mann
March of the Siamese Children	Kenny Ball and his Jazzmen	Milk and Alcohol	Dr Feelgood
		Millennium (1)	Robbie Willliams
Marcheta	Karl Denver	Millennium Prayer (1)	Cliff Richard
Marguerita Time (3)	Status Quo	Mirror in the Bathroom	Beat
Maria	P.J. Proby	Mirror Man	Human League
Maria (1)	Blondie	Mirror Mirror	Pinkerton's Assorted Colours
Marrakesh Express	Crosby, Stills and Nash		
		Mirror Mirror	Dollar
Martha's Harbour	All about Eve	Misfit	Curiosity Killed the Cat
Mary Had a Little Boy	Snap		
Mary Had a Little Lamb	Wings	Mis-Shapes/Sorted for E's and Wizz	Pulp
Mary of the Fourth Form	Boomtown Rats		

M
U
S
I
C

P
O
P

Title	Group/Artiste	Title	Group/Artiste
Na Na Is the Saddest Word	Stylistics	Nobody's Diary	Yazoo
Na Na Na	Cozy Powell	Nobody's Fool	Haircut 100
Nairobi	Tommy Steele	No Matter How I Try	Gilbert O'Sullivan
Naked in the Rain	Blue Pearl	No Matter What	Badfinger
The Name of the Game (1)	Abba	No Milk Today	Herman's Hermits
Nathan Jones (5)	Supremes	No More Heroes (8)	Stranglers
Native New Yorker	Odyssey	No More 'I Love You's'	Annie Lennox
Natural Born Bugie	Humble Pie	No More Lonely Nights	Paul McCartney
Natural Sinner	Fair Weather	No More Mr Nice Guy	Alice Cooper
Naughty Girls	Samantha Fox featuring Full Force	No One But You	Billy Eckstine
		No One Is Innocent	Sex Pistols, Punk
Naughty Lady of Shady Lane	Dean Martin		Prayer by Ronald
Neanderthal Man	Hotlegs		Biggs
Needles and Pins (10)	Smokie	No Ordinary Love	Sade
Needles and Pins (1)	Searchers	No Other Love Have I (1)	Ronnie Hilton
Need You Tonight	INXS	No Particular Place To Go	Chuck Berry
Nellie the Elephant	Toy Dolls	No Regrets (7)	Walker Brothers
Nessun Dorma	Luciano Pavarotti	No Regrets (9)	Midge Ure
Never Be the Same Again (1)	Melanie C featuring Lisa Lopez	North Country Boy	Charlatans
		Northern Lights	Renaissance
Never Can Say Goodbye	Gloria Gaynor	No Sleep Till Brooklyn	Beastie Boys
Never-Ending Song of Love	New Seekers	No Son Of Mine	Genesis
Never-Ending Story	Limahl	Not Fade Away (3)	Rolling Stones
Never Ever (1)	All Saints	Nothing Can Divide Us	Jason Donovan
Never Forget (1)	Take That	Nothing Compares 2 U (1)	Sinead O'Connor
Never Gonna Give You Up	Rick Astley	Nothing Else Matters	Metallica
Never Gonna Give You Up (6)	Musical Youth	Nothing Rhymed	Gilbert O'Sullivan
Never Goodbye	Karl Denver	Nothing's Gonna Change My	Glenn Medeiros
Never Had a Dream come True (1)	SClub7	Love for You (1)	
		Nothings Gonna Stop Us	Starship
Never Knew Love Like This Before	Stephanie Mills	Now (1)	
		Notorious	Duran Duran
Never Let Her Slip Away (5)	Undercover	Now	Al Martino
Never Let Her Slip Away (5)	Andrew Gold	Now Is the Time	Jimmy James and
Never Never	Assembly		the Vagabonds
Never Too Late	Kylie Minogue	Now I've Found You	Sean Maguire
Never Trust a Stranger	Kim Wilde	No Woman No Cry (8)	Bob Marley and the
New Amsterdam	Elvis Costello		Wailers
New Song	Howard Jones	Now That We Found Love	Heavy D and the
New Year's Day (10)	U2		Boyz
New York Groove	Hello	Now That We've Found Love	Third World
New York, New York (43)	Gerard Kenny	Number One	Tremeloes
Night Birds	Shakatak	Numero Uno	Starlight
The Night Chicago Died	Paper Lace	Nutbush City Limits	Ike and Tina Turner
Night Fever (1)	Bee Gees	Ob-La-Di Ob-La-Da (1)	Marmalade
Night Games	Graham Bonnet	Oblivious	Aztec Camera
The Night Has a Thousand Eyes (3)	Bobby Vee	Off The Wall	Michael Jackson
		Oh Babe What Would You Say?	Hurricane Smith
Night of Fear	Move	Oh Boy	Crickets
Night Owl	Gerry Rafferty	Oh Boy (1)	Mud
The Night They Drove Old Dixie Down	Joan Baez	Oh Carol	Neil Sedaka
		Oh Carol (5)	Smokie
Nights in White Satin	Moody Blues	Oh Carolina (1)	Shaggy
Nights on Broadway	Candi Staton	Oh Happy Day	Edwin Hawkins
Nightshift	Commodores		Singers and
Nikita	Elton John		Dorothy Morrison
9 pm (Till I Come) (1)	ATB	Oh Happy Day (4)	Johnston Brothers
Nineteen (1)	Paul Hardcastle	Oh Julie (1)	Shakin' Stevens
Nineteenth Nervous Breakdown (2)	Rolling Stones	Oh Lori	Alessi
		Oh My Papa	Eddie Fisher
9 to 5	Sheena Easton	Oh No Not My Baby (6)	Rod Stewart
99 Red Balloons (1)	Nena	Oh Pretty Woman (1)	Roy Orbison
N-N-Nineteen Not Out	Commentators	Oh Well	Fleetwood Mac
No Charge	J.J. Barrie	Oh What a Circus	David Essex
No Doubt About It	Hot Chocolate	Oh Yeah (On the Radio)	Roxy Music
No Good	Prodigy	OK	Covington, Lenska,
No Honestly	Lynsey De Paul		Cornwell, Jones-
No Limit (1)	2 Unlimited		Davies
Nobody Does It Better (7)	Carly Simon	Okay!	Dave Dee, Dozy,
Nobody I Know	Peter and Gordon		Beaky, Mick and
Nobody's Child	Karen Young		Tich

Title	Group/Artiste	Title	Group/Artiste
O L'Amour	Dollar	Opposites Attract	Paula Abdul
Ol' Rag Blues (9)	Status Quo	Ordinary World	Duran Duran
Old Before I Die	Robbie Williams	Orinoco Flow (1)	Enya
Oldest Swinger In Town	Fred Wedlock	Ossie's Dream	Tottenham Hotspur
Ole Ola (Mulher Brasileira)	Rod Stewart and		FA Cup Final
	Scots World Cup		Squad
	Squad ('78)	O Superman	Laurie Anderson
Oliver's Army	Elvis Costello	Our House	Madness
On a Ragga Tip	SL2	Our Lips Are Sealed	Fun Boy Three
On a Slow Boat to China	Emile Ford and the	Out in the Fields	Gary Moore and Phil
	Checkmates		Lynott
On My Own	Patti Labelle and	Out of Space	Prodigy
	Michael McDonald	Out of Time	Chris Farlowe
On My Radio	Selecter	Outside of Heaven (1)	Eddie Fisher
On the Inside	Lynne Hamilton	Over Under Sideways Down	Yardbirds
On the Rebound	Floyd Cramer	Over You	Roxy Music
On the Street Where You Live	Vic Damone	Oxygene Part IV	Jean-Michel Jarre
Once Upon a Long Ago	Paul McCartney	Pacific	808 State
One (7)	U2	Paint It Black (1)	Rolling Stones
One and One Is One	Medicine Head	Pale Shelter	Tears For Fears
One Day At a Time (1)	Lena Martell	Paloma Blanca	George Baker
One Day I'll Fly Away	Randy Crawford		Selection
One Day in Your Life (1)	Michael Jackson	Pandora's Box	Orchestral
One in Ten	808 State versus		Manoeuvres in the
	UB40		Dark
One Love – People Get Ready	Bob Marley and the	Panic	Smiths
	Wailers	Papa Don't Preach (1)	Madonna
One Man Band	Leo Sayer	Papa's Got a Brand New Pigbag	Pigbag
One Moment In Time (1)	Whitney Houston	Paperback Writer (1)	Beatles
One More Try	George Michael	Paper Plane (8)	Status Quo
One Nation Under a Groove	Funkadelic	Paper Roses	Marie Osmond
One Night in Heaven	M People	Paper Roses (7)	Kaye Sisters
One Night (1)	Elvis Presley	Paper Sun	Traffic
10538 Overture	Electric Light	Paradise Lost	Herd
	Orchestra	Paranoid	Black Sabbath
One of Us (3)	Abba	Paranoid Android	Radiohead
One Step Beyond	Madness	Paranoimia	Art of Noise featuring
One Step Further	Bardo		Max Headroom
One Sweet Day	Mariah Carey and	Parisienne Walkways	Gary Moore
	Boyz 11 Men	Part of the Union (2)	Strawbs
1-2-3	Gloria Estefan and	Part Time Love	Elton John
	Miami Sound	Part Time Lover	Stevie Wonder
	Machine	Party Fears Two	Associates
1-2-3	Len Barry	Pasadena (4)	Temperance Seven
1-2-3 O'Leary	Des O'Connor	Passengers	Elton John
One Way Ticket	Eruption	Pass the Dutchie (1)	Musical Youth
Onion Song	Marvin Gaye and	Patricia	Perez Prado
	Tammi Terrell	Peace	Sabrina Johnston
Only Fools (Never Fall in Love)	Sonia	Peace in Our Time	Cliff Richard
Only Love	Nana Mouskouri	Peace on Earth – Little	David Bowie and Bing
Only One Road	Celine Dion	Drummer Boy	Crosby
Only One Woman	Marbles	Peaches	Stranglers
Only Sixteen (1)	Craig Douglas	Pearl in the Shell	Howard Jones
Only the Lonely (1)	Roy Orbison	Peek-A-Boo	New Vaudeville Band
Only You Can	Fox		featuring Tristram
Only You (1)	Flying Pickets	Peggy Sue	Buddy Holly
Only You (2)	Yazoo	Penny Lane/Strawberry	Beatles
Only You (4)	Praise	Fields Forever (2)	
Ooh Aah . . . Just a Little Bit (1)	Gina G	People Are People	Depeche Mode
Ooh La La La	Kool and the Gang	People Everyday	Arrested
Ooh to Be Ah	Kajagoogoo		Development
Ooh-Wakka-Doo-Wakka-Day	Gilbert O'Sullivan	Pepe	Duane Eddy and the
Ooh! What a Life	Gibson Brothers		Rebels
Ooops	808 State featuring	Pepper Box	Peppers
	Björk	Perfect (1)	Fairground Attraction
Ooops Up	Snap	Perfect Day (1)	BBC Allstars
Ooops! I Did It Again (1)	Britney Spears	Perfect Day (1)	Lou Reed and
Oops Up Side Your Head	Gap Band		Friends
Open Your Heart	M People	Perfect Moment (1)	Martine McCutcheon
Open Your Heart	Human League	Perfidia (4)	Ventures
Open Your Mind	Usura	Personality (6)	Anthony Newley

MUSIC POP

Title	Group/Artiste	Title	Group/Artiste
Rain Rain Rain	Frankie Laine and the Four Lads	Return of the Mack (1)	Mark Morrison
		Return to Innocence	Enigma
Rainy Day Women Nos 12 and 35	Bob Dylan	Return to Me	Dean Martin
		Return to Sender (1)	Elvis Presley
Rainy Night in Georgia	Randy Crawford	Reunited	Peaches and Herb
Rambling Rose	Nat King Cole	Reverence	Jesus and Mary Chain
Randy	Blue Mink		
Rapper's Delight	Sugarhill Gang	Reward	Teardrop Explodes
Rapture	Blondie	Rhythm Is a Dancer (1)	Snap
Rasputin	Boney M	Rhythm Is A Mystery	K-Klass
Rave On	Buddy Holly	Rhythm Is Gonna Get You	Gloria Estefan and Miami Sound Machine
Raving I'm Raving	Shut Up and Dance		
Rawhide	Frankie Laine		
Reach For the Stars (1)	Shirley Bassey	Rhythm of the Night	De Barge
Reach Out and Touch	Diana Ross	Richard III	Supergrass
Reach Out I'll Be There	Four Tops	Ricochet	Joan Regan with the Squadronaires
Reach Up (Papa's Got a Brand New Pig Bag)	Perfecto Allstarz		
		The Riddle	Nik Kershaw
Ready or Not	The Course	Ride a White Swan (2)	T Rex
Ready or Not (1)	The Fugees	Ride Like the Wind	East Side Beat
Real Gone Kid	Deacon Blue	Ride on Time	Black Box
Real Love (4)	Beatles	Riders in the Sky	Ramrods
The Real Slim Shady (1)	Eminem	Riders on the Storm	Doors
The Real Thing	Lisa Stansfield	Right Back Where We Started From	Sinitta
The Real Thing (1)	Tony di Bart		
Real Wild Child (Wild One)	Iggy Pop	Right Back Where We Started From	Maxine Nightingale
Really Free	John Otway and Wild Willy Barrett		
		Right by Your Side	Eurythmics
Really Saying Something	Bananarama with the Fun Boy Three	Right Here Waiting	Richard Marx
		Right Said Fred	Bernard Cribbins
Reason to Believe (19)	Rod Stewart	Ring My Bell (1)	Anita Ward
Reasons to Be Cheerful (Part 3)	Ian Dury	Ring Ring (32)	Abba
Rebel Rebel (5)	David Bowie	Ring Ring Ring	De La Soul
Rebel Yell	Billy Idol	Rio	Duran Duran
Red Balloon	Dave Clark Five	Rip It Up	Orange Juice
Red Dress (7)	Alvin Stardust	Rise (1)	Gabrielle
Red Light Spells Danger	Billy Ocean	The Rise and Fall of Flingel Bunt (5)	Shadows
Red Red Wine (1)	UB40		
Red River Rock	Johnny and the Hurricanes	Rise to the Occasion	Climie Fisher
		Riverdance	Bill Whelan featuring Anuna and the RTE
Reet Petite (1)	Jackie Wilson		
Reflections of My Life	Marmalade		
Reflections (5)	Diana Ross and the Supremes	River Deep Mountain High (11)	Supremes and the Four Tops
		River Deep Mountain High (3)	Ike and Tina Turner
The Reflex (1)	Duran Duran	The River of Dreams	Billy Joel
Reggae Like It Used to Be	Paul Nicholas	Rivers of Babylon	Boney M
Reggae Tune	Andy Fairweather Low	The River	Ken Dodd
§		Road Rage	Catatonia
Regret	New Order	Road Runner	Junior Walker and the All-Stars
Relax (1)	Frankie Goes to Hollywood		
		The Road to Hell (Part 2)	Chris Rea
Release Me (1)	Englebert Humperdinck	Road to Nowhere (6)	Talking Heads
		Robert De Niro's Waiting	Bananarama
Relight My Fire (1)	Take That featuring Lulu	Robin Hood	Gary Miller
		Robin (the Hooded Man)	Clannad
Remember Me	Diana Ross	Rock A Hula Baby (1)	Elvis Presley
Remember You're a Womble (3)	Wombles	Rock and Roll Waltz (1)	Kay Starr
Renaissance	M People	Rock and Roll (Parts 1 & 2)	Gary Glitter
Rent	Pet Shop Boys	Rock Around the Clock (1)	Bill Haley and his Comets
Renta Santa	Chris Hill		
Requiem (4)	London Boys	Rock Bottom	Lynsey De Paul and Mike Moran
Respect	Aretha Franklin		
Respectable (1)	Mel and Kim (Appleby)	Rock DJ	Robbie Williams
		Rock Island Line	Lonnie Donegan
Respect Yourself (7)	Bruce Willis	Rock Me Amadeus (1)	Falco
Restless	Gillan	Rock Me Gently	Andy Kim
Resurrection Shuffle	Ashton, Gardner and Dyke	Rock 'N' Roll (66)	John McEnroe, Pat Cash and Full Metal Rackets
Return of Django	Upsetters		
The Return of the Los Palmas Seven	Madness	Rock 'N' Roll (8)	Status Quo

Title	Group/Artiste	Title	Group/Artiste
Rock 'N' Roll Ain't Noise Pollution	AC / DC	Sabre Dance	Love Sculpture
		Sacrifice (1)	Elton John
Rock 'N' Roll Damnation	AC / DC	Sadness Part 1 (1)	Enigma
Rock 'N' Roll Mercenaries	Meat Loaf Featuring John Parr	Sad Songs (Say So Much)	Elton John
		Sad Sweet Dreamer (1)	Sweet Sensation
Rock 'N' Roll Winter (6)	Wizzard	The Safety Dance	Men without Hats
Rock On	David Essex	Sailing (1)	Rod Stewart
Rock-A-Billy (1)	Guy Mitchell	Sailing on the Seven Seas	Orchestral
Rocket Man	Elton John		Manoeuvres in the
Rockin' All Over the World (3)	Status Quo		Dark
Rockin' Around the Christmas Tree	Brenda Lee	Sail On	Commodores
		Sailor (10)	Anne Shelton
Rockin' Around the Christmas Tree (3)	Mel (Smith) and Kim Wilde	Sailor (1)	Petula Clark
		Sally	Gerry Monroe
Rockin' over the Beat (9)	Technotronic featuring Ya Kid K	Saltwater	Julian Lennon
		Sam	Olivia Newton-John
Rockin' Robin	Michael Jackson	Same Old Brand New (1)	A1
Rocking Goose	Johnny and the Hurricanes	San Francisco (1)	Scott McKenzie
		Sanctify Yourself	Simple Minds
Rockit	Herbie Hancock	Sandy (2)	John Travolta
Rocks	Primal Scream	Santa Claus Is Coming to Town (9)	Bruce Springsteen
Rock the Boat	Forrest		
Rock the Boat	Hues Corporation	Satisfaction (1)	Rolling Stones
Rock the Casbah	Clash	Satisfaction (29)	Bubblerock (Jonathan King)
Rock Your Baby (1)	George McCrae		
Rock Your Baby (8)	KWS	Saturday Love	Alexander O'Neal
Rodrigo's Guitar Concerto de Aranjuez	Manuel and his Music of the Mountains	Saturday Night (1)	Whigfield
		Saturday Night's Alright for Fighting	Elton John
Rok Da House	Beatmasters featuring Cookie Crew		
		Save a Prayer	Duran Duran
Roll Away the Stone	Mott the Hoople	Saved by the Bell	Robin Gibb
Rollercoaster (1)	B*witched	Save Me	Dave Dee, Dozy, Beaky, Mick and Tich
Rollin' Stone	David Essex		
Roll Over Beethoven (6)	Electric Light Orchestra		
		Save the Best for Last	Vanessa Williams
Roll Over Lay Down (9)	Status Quo	Save the Last Dance for Me	Drifters
Roll With It	Oasis	Save Your Love (1)	Renee and Renato
Romeo	Petula Clark	Saving All My Love for You (1)	Whitney Houston
Romeo	Mr Big (UK)	Saviour's Day (1)	Cliff Richard
Romeo and Juliet	Dire Straits	Say a Little Prayer (10)	Bomb the Bass featuring Maureen
Roobarb and Custard	Shaft		
Room in Your Heart	Living in a Box	Say Hello Wave Goodbye	Soft Cell
Rose Marie (1)	Slim Whitman	Say I'm Your No. 1	Princess
Roses Are Red (15)	Bobby Vinton	Say It Again	Jermaine Stewart
Roses of Picardy	Vince Hill	Say I Won't Be There	Springfields
Rosetta	Fame and Price Together	Say Say Say	Paul McCartney and Michael Jackson
		Say You Don't Mind	Colin Bluntstone
Rosie	Don Partridge	Say You'll Be There (1)	Spice Girls
Roulette	Russ Conway	Say You, Say Me	Lionel Richie
The Roussos Phenomenon (1)	Demis Roussos	Scarlett O'Hara	Jet Harris and Tony Meehan
Rubber Ball (4)	Bobby Vee		
Rubber Bullets (1)	10cc	Scatman (Ski-Ba-Bop-Ba-Dop-Bop)	Scatman John
Ruby Don't Take Your Love to Town	Kenny Rogers and the First Edition		
		School's Out (1)	Alice Cooper
Ruby Tuesday	Melanie	Scotch on the Rocks	Band of the Black Watch
Rumble in the Jungle	Fugees		
Runaway Boys	Stray Cats	Scream	Michael and Janet Jackson
Runaway Train	Elton John and Eric Clapton		
		Sea of Love (3)	Marty Wilde
Runaway (1)	Del Shannon	Sealed with a Kiss (1)	Jason Donovan
Run Baby Run	Newbeats	Sealed with a Kiss (3)	Brian Hyland
Running Bear (1)	Johnny Preston	Searchin'	Hazell Dean
Running in the Family	Level 42	Searching	China Black
Running Scared	Roy Orbison	Seaside Shuffle	Terry Dactyl and the Dinosaurs
Running Up That Hill (3)	Kate Bush		
Run Run Away	Slade	Seasons in the Sun (1)	Terry Jacks
Run to Him (6)	Bobby Vee	Seasons in the Sun (1)	Westlife
Run to the Hills	Iron Maiden	I Second That Emotion	Japan
Run to You (11)	Bryan Adams	Secret Love (1)	Doris Day
Run to You (3)	Rage	Secret Love (4)	Kathy Kirby
Rush Rush	Paula Abdul		

MUSIC
POP

Title	Group/Artiste	Title	Group/Artiste
See Emily Play	Pink Floyd	She's the One/It's Only Us (1)	Robbie Williams
See My Baby Jive (1)	Wizzard	She Wants to Dance with Me	Rick Astley
See the Day	Dee C Lee	She Wears My Ring	Solomon King
See You	Depeche Mode	She Wears Red Feathers (1)	Guy Mitchell
Self Control	Laura Branigan	Shifting Whispering Sands	Eamonn Andrews
Senses Working Overtime	XTC	Shindig (6)	Shadows
Sentinel	Mike Oldfield	Shine	Aswad
Senza Una Donna (Without a Woman)	Zucchero and Paul Young	Shining Star (EP)	INXS
Separate Lives	Phil Collins and Marilyn Martin	Shiny Happy People	R.E.M.
		Ship of Fools	Erasure
September	Earth, Wind and Fire	The Shoop Shoop Song (It's in His Kiss) (1)	Cher
Serious	Donna Allen	Shortsharpshock	Therapy
Sesame's Treet	Smart Es	Should I Stay or Should I Go	Clash
Set Adrift on Memory Bliss	PM Dawn	Shout (4)	Tears for Fears
Setting Sun (1)	The Chemical Brothers	Shout (7)	Lulu and the Luvvers
		Shout to the Top	Style Council
Set You Free	N-Trance	The Show	Doug E. Fresh and Get Fresh Crew
7 Days	Craig David		
Seven Drunken Nights	Dubliners	Show Me Heaven (1)	Maria McKee
Seven Little Girls Sitting in the Back Seat	Paul Evans and the Curls	Show Me Love	Robin S
Seven Little Girls Sitting in the Back Seat	Avons	Show Me the Way	Peter Frampton
		The Show Must Go On (2)	Leo Sayer
Seven Seas of Rhye	Queen	Show You the Way to Go (1)	Jacksons
7 Seconds	Youssou N'Dour featuring Neneh Cherry	Showing Out	Mel and Kim (Appleby)
		Sho' You Right (14)	Barry White
Seven Tears (1)	Goombay Dance Band	The Shuffle	Van McCoy
		Shut Up	Madness
7 Ways to Love	Cola Boy	Shy Boy	Bananarama
Seven Wonders	Fleetwood Mac	Shy Guy	Diana King
Sexcrime (Nineteen Eighty-Four)	Eurythmics	Side by Side	Kay Starr
Sexual Healing	Marvin Gaye	Side Saddle	Russ Conway
Sexy Eyes	Dr Hook	Sideshow	Barry Biggs
Sexy MF	Prince and the New Power Generation	The Sign	Ace of Base
		Sign 'O' the Times	Prince
Shaddap You Face (1)	Joe Dolce Music Theatre	Sign of the Times	Belle Stars
		Sign Your Name	Terence Trent D'Arby
Shake Your Love	Debbie Gibson	Signed Sealed Delivered I'm Yours	Stevie Wonder
Shakin' All Over	Johnny Kidd and the Pirates	Silence Is Golden (1)	Tremeloes
		Silent Night	Bing Crosby
Sha La La La Leee	Small Faces	Silhouettes	Cliff Richard
Shame Shame Shame	Shirley and Company	Silhouettes	Herman's Hermits
		Silly Games	Janet Kay
Shapes of Things	Yardbirds	Silly Love Songs	Wings
Shattered Dreams	Johnny Hates Jazz	Silly Thing	Sex Pistols
Shazam!	Duane Eddy and the Rebels	Silver Dream Machine	David Essex
		Silver Lady (1)	David Soul
She'd Rather Be With Me	Turtles	Silver Machine	Hawkwind
She Drives Me Crazy	Fine Young Cannibals	Silver Star	Four Seasons
		Simon Says	1910 Fruitgum Company
Sheela-Na-Gig	PJ Harvey		
Sheila	Tommy Roe	Simon Smith and His Amazing Dancing Bear	Alan Price Set
Sheila Take a Bow	Smiths		
She Loves You (1)	Beatles	Since Yesterday	Strawberry Switchblade
She Makes My Day	Robert Palmer		
She Means Nothing To Me	Cliff Richard and Phil Everly	Since You've Been Gone	Rainbow
		Sinful (13)	Pete Wylie with the Farm
Sherry	Four Seasons		
She's a Star	James	Singing the Blues (1)	Guy Mitchell
She's a Woman	Scritti Politti featuring Shabba Ranks	Singing the Blues (1)	Tommy Steele
		Single Girl	Sandy Posey
She Sells Sanctuary	Cult	Sir Duke	Stevie Wonder
She's Got Claws	Gary Numan	Sister Jane	New World
She's Leaving Home	Billy Bragg with Cara Tivey	Sisters Are Doin' It for Themselves	Eurythmics and Aretha Franklin
		Sit Down	James
She's Not There (12)	Zombies	16 Bars	Stylistics
She's Not You (1)	Elvis Presley	Sixteen Tons (1)	Tennessee Ernie Ford
She's On It	Beastie Boys		
She's out of My Life	Michael Jackson		

Title	Group/Artiste	Title	Group/Artiste
68 Guns	Alarm	Something's Happening	Herman's Hermits
Skin Deep	Ted Heath	Something Stupid (1)	Nancy Sinatra and Frank Sinatra
Skin Deep (7)	Duke Ellington		
Skweeze Me Pleeze Me (1)	Slade	Sometimes	Erasure
Sky High	Jigsaw	Somewhere	P.J. Proby
The Skye Boat Song	Roger Whittaker and Des O'Connor	Somewhere Out There	James Ingram and Linda Ronstadt
Slam Jam	WWF Superstars	Song for Guy	Elton John
Slap and Tickle	Squeeze	Song for Whoever	Beautiful South
Slave to Love	Bryan Ferry	Son of Hickory Holler's Tramp	O.C. Smith
Slave to the Rhythm	Grace Jones	Sorrow (3)	David Bowie
Sledgehammer	Peter Gabriel	Sorrow (4)	Merseys
Sleeping Satellite (1)	Tasmin Archer	Sorry I'm a Lady	Baccara
Sleepy Shores	Johnny Pearson	Sorry Suzanne	Hollies
The Slightest Touch	Five Star	So Strong	Labi Siffre
Slip Slidin' Away (36)	Paul Simon	Soul Clap '69	Booker T. and the M.G.s
Slowhand	Pointer Sisters		
Slow Rivers	Elton John and Cliff Richard	Soul Limbo	Booker T. and the M.G.s
Smarty Pants	First Choice	Soul Man	Sam and Dave
Smells Like Teen Spirit	Nirvana	Sound	James
Smoke Gets in Your Eyes (1)	Platters	Sound and Vision (3)	David Bowie
Smooth Criminal	Michael Jackson	The Sound of Silence (3)	Bachelors
Smooth Operator	Sade	Souvenir	Orchestral Manoeuvres in the Dark
The Smurf Song	Father Abraham and the Smurfs		
Snoopy vs The Red Baron	Hotshots	Sowing the Seeds of Love (5)	Tears for Fears
Snoopy vs The Red Baron	Royal Guardsmen	So You Win Again (1)	Hot Chocolate
Snot Rap	Kenny Everett	Spaceman (1)	Babylon Zoo
Snowbird	Anne Murray	Space Oddity (1)	David Bowie
So Emotional	Whitney Houston	Spanish Eyes (5)	Al Martino
So Far Away	Dire Straits	Spanish Flea	Herb Alpert
Softly Softly (1)	Ruby Murray	Spanish Hustle	Fat Larry's Band
So Good to Be Back Home Again	Tourists	Speak Like a Child	Style Council
So Hard	Pet Shop Boys	Speak to Me Pretty	Brenda Lee
Soldier Blue	Buffy Sainte-Marie	Special Brew	Bad Manners
Soley Soley	Middle of the Road	Speedy Gonzales	Pat Boone
Solid	Ashford and Simpson	Spice Up Your Life (1)	Spice Girls
		Spinning Around	Kylie Minogue
Solitaire (4)	Andy Williams	Spirit in the Sky (1)	Doctor and the Medics
So Long Baby	Del Shannon		
Solsbury Hill	Peter Gabriel	Spirit in the Sky (1)	Norman Greenbaum
So Macho	Sinitta	Spirits in the Material World	Police
Some Girls	Racey	Splish Splash (18)	Bobby Darin
Some Like It Hot	Power Station	Splish Splash (7)	Charlie Drake
Some Might Say (1)	Oasis	Squeeze Box (10)	Who
Some People (3)	Cliff Richard	S-S-S-Single Bed	Fox
Somebody Help Me (1)	Spencer Davis Group	St Elmo's Fire	John Parr
		St Valentine's Day Massacre	Girlschool and Motorhead (aka Headgirl)
Somebody Stole My Gal	Johnnie Ray		
Somebody to Love	Queen		
Somebody's Watching Me	Rockwell	Staccato's Theme	Elmer Bernstein
Someday	Ricky Nelson	Stairway to Heaven	Rolf Harris
Someday (I'm Coming Back)	Lisa Stansfield	Stairway to Heaven (8)	Far Corporation
Something About the Way You Look Tonight/Candle in the Wind 1997 (1)	Elton John	Stairway to Heaven (8)	Neil Sedaka
		Stan (1)	Eminem
		Stand and Deliver (1)	Adam and the Ants
Something about You	Level 42	Stand by Me (1)	Ben E. King
Something 'Bout You Baby I Like (9)	Status Quo	Stand by Me (2)	Oasis
		Stand by Me (39)	Kenny Lynch
Something/Come Together (4)	Beatles	Stand by Your Man (1)	Tammy Wynette
Something Else	Sex Pistols	Standing in the Road	Blackfoot Sue
Something Good	Utah Saints	Standing in the Shadows of Love	Four Tops
Something in the Air (1)	Thunderclap Newman		
		Standing on the Corner (4)	King Brothers
Something Old, Something New	Fantastics	Stand Up for Your Love Rights	Yazz
Something's Gotten Hold of My Heart (1)	Marc Almond featuring Gene Pitney	Star	Kiki Dee
		Stardust	David Essex
		Staring at the Sun	U2
Something's Gotten Hold of My Heart (5)	Gene Pitney	Starmaker	Kids from Fame
		Starman (10)	David Bowie

Title	Group/Artiste	Title	Group/Artiste
Star People 97	George Michael	Stutter Rap (No Sleep	Morris Minor and the
Starry Eyed	Michael Holliday	'til Bedtime)	Majors
Stars	Simply Red	Substitute	Liquid Gold
Stars on 45	Starsound	Substitute (5)	Who
Start (1)	Jam	Subterranean Homesick Blues	Bob Dylan
Start Me Up (7)	Rolling Stones	Suburbia	Pet Shop Boys
Starting Over (1)	John Lennon	Such a Night (1)	Johnnie Ray
Starting Together	Su Pollard	Sucu Sucu	Laurie Johnson
Star Trekkin' (1)	Firm	Suddenly You Love Me	Tremeloes
Star Wars Theme – Cantina	Meco	Suddenly (15)	Olivia Newton-John
Band			and Cliff Richard
State of Shock	Jacksons, Mick Jagger	Suddenly (3)	Angry Anderson
	and Michael	Suddenly (4)	Billy Ocean
	Jackson	Suedehead	Morrissey
Stay	Eternal	Sugar and Spice (2)	Searchers
Stay (1)	Shakespears Sister	Sugar Baby Love (1)	Rubettes
Stay (8)	Hollies	Sugarbush	Doris Day and
Stay Another Day (1)	East 17		Frankie Laine
Stay on These Roads (5)	A-Ha	Sugar Candy Kisses	Mac and Katie
Stay with Me	Faces		Kissoon
Stay with Me Till Dawn	Judie Tzuke	Sugar Me	Lynsey De Paul
Steam	Peter Gabriel	Sugar Moon	Pat Boone
Steamy Windows (13)	Tina Turner	Sugar Sugar	Sakkarin (Jonathan
Step by Step	New Kids on the		King)
	Block	Sugar Sugar (1)	Archies
Step It Up	Stereo MCs	Sugar Town	Nancy Sinatra
Step Off (Part 1)	Grandmaster Flash,	Suicide Blonde	INXS
	Melle Mel and	Sukiyaki	Kyu Sakamoto
	Furious Five	Sultans of Swing	Dire Straits
Steppin' Out	Joe Jackson	Summer Holiday (1)	Cliff Richard
Stick It Out	Right Said Fred and	Summer Holiday (50)	Kevin the Gerbil
	Friends	Summer in the City	Lovin' Spoonful
Still Haven't Found What	Chimes	Summerlove Sensation	Bay City Rollers
I'm Looking For		Summer Night City (5)	Abba
Stomp (1)	Steps	Summer Nights (10)	Marianne Faithull
Stoned Love (3)	Supremes	Summer Nights (1)	John Travolta and
The Stonk (1)	Hale and Pace and		Olivia Newton-John
	the Stonkers	Summer (the First Time)	Bobby Goldsboro
Stool Pigeon	Kid Creole and the	Summertime Blues	Eddie Cochran
	Coconuts	Summertime City	Mike Batt with the
Stop (2)	Spice Girls		New Edition
Stop in the Name of Love (7)	Supremes	The Sun Always Shines	A-Ha
Stop the Cavalry	Jona Lewie	on TV (1)	
Storm in a Teacup	Fortunes	Sunchyme	Dario G
The Story of My Life (1)	Michael Holliday	Sunday Girl (1)	Blondie
The Story of Tina	Al Martino	Sun Hits the Sky	Supergrass
Straight Up	Paula Abdul	Sunny Afternoon (1)	Kinks
Strange Kind of Woman	Deep Purple	Sunshine Girl	Herman's Hermits
Strange Little Girl (7)	Stranglers	Sunshine On a Rainy Day	Zoe
Stranger in Paradise	Tony Bennett	Sunshine Superman	Donovan
Stranger in Paradise (6)	Tony Martin	Super Trouper (1)	Abba
Stranger on the Shore	Acker Bilk and his	Superfly Guy	S Express
	Paramount Jazz	Superman (Gioca Jouer)	Black Lace
	Band	Sure (1)	Take That
Strangers in the Night (1)	Frank Sinatra	Surf City	Jan and Dean
Strawberry Fair	Anthony Newley	Surrender	Swing Out Sister
Street Dance	Break Machine	Surrender (1)	Elvis Presley
Street Fighting Man (21)	Rolling Stones	Surround Yourself With Sorrow	Cilla Black
Street Life	Crusaders (and	Suspicious Minds (2)	Elvis Presley
	Randy Crawford	Suspicious Minds (8)	Fine Young
	uncredited)		Cannibals
Street Life	Roxy Music	Swamp Thing	Grid
Streets of London (2)	Ralph McTell	Sway	Dean Martin
Streets of Philadelphia	Bruce Springsteen	Swear It Again (1)	Westlife
Strong (4)	Robbie Williams	Sweat (A La La La La Long)	Inner Circle
Street Tuff	Rebel MC and	Swedish Rhapsody	Ray Martin
	Double	Sweet Caroline	Neil Diamond
	Trouble	Sweet Child O' Mine	Guns N' Roses
Strut Your Funky Stuff	Frantique	Sweet Dream	Jethro Tull
Stuck in the Middle with You	Stealer's Wheel	Sweet Dreams (Are Made	Eurythmics
Stuck on You (9)	Trevor Walters	of This)	

Title	Group/Artiste
Sweet Harmony	Beloved
Sweet Inspiration	Johnny Johnson and the Bandwagon
Sweet Like Chocolate (1)	Shanks and Bigfoot
Sweet Lips	Monaco
Sweet Little Mystery	Wet Wet Wet
Sweetness	Michelle Gayle
Sweet Nothin's	Brenda Lee
Sweets for My Sweet (1)	Searchers
Sweet Surrender	Wet Wet Wet
Swingin' Shepherd Blues	Ella Fitzgerald
Swinging on a Star	Big Dee Irwin
Swing the Mood (1)	Jive Bunny and the Mastermixers
Swing Your Daddy	Jim Gilstrap
Swiss Maid	Del Shannon
Swords of a Thousand Men	Tenpole Tudor
Sylvia's Mother	Dr Hook
System Addict	Five Star
Tahiti	David Essex
Tainted Love (1)	Soft Cell
Take a Chance on Me (1)	Abba
Take a Message to Mary	Everly Brothers
Take Good Care of My Baby (3)	Bobby Vee
Take Good Care of Yourself	Three Degrees
Take It to the Limit	Eagles
Take Me Bak 'Ome (1)	Slade
Take Me to the Mardi Gras	Paul Simon
Take My Breath Away	Berlin
Take My Heart	Al Martino
Take On Me (1)	A1
Take On Me (2)	A-Ha
Take That Look off Your Face	Marti Webb
Tammy (2)	Debbie Reynolds
A Taste of Aggro	Barron Knights
Taxloss	Mansun
Teacher/Witch's Promise	Jethro Tull
Tea for Two Cha Cha	Tommy Dorsey and Warren Covington
Teardrops (3)	Womack and Womack
A Tear Fell	Teresa Brewer
Tears (1)	Ken Dodd
Tears Are Not Enough	ABC
Tears in Heaven	Eric Clapton
Tears of a Clown (1)	Smokey Robinson and the Miracles
Tears on My Pillow (1)	Kylie Minogue
Tears on My Pillow (1)	Johnny Nash
Tease Me	Chaka Demus and Pliers
Teddy Bear (4)	Red Sovine
Teenage Kicks (31)	Undertones
Teenage Rampage (2)	Sweet
A Teenager in Love (28)	Dion and the Belmonts
Teen Angel	Mark Dinning
Teen Beat	Sandy Nelson
Telegram Sam (1)	T Rex
Telephone Line	Electric Light Orchestra
Telephone Man	Meri Wilson
Teletubbies Say Eh-Oh (1)	Teletubbies
Tell Her about It	Billy Joel
Tell Him	Billie Davis
Tell Him	Hello
Tell It to My Heart	Taylor Dane
Tell Laura I Love Her (1)	Ricky Vallance
Tell Me a Story	Jimmy Boyd
Tell Me When	Applejacks
Telstar (1)	Tornados

Title	Group/Artiste
Temple of Love	Sisters of Mercy
Temptation	Heaven 17
Temptation (1)	Everly Brothers
The Tender Trap	Frank Sinatra
Tennessee Wig Walk	Bonnie Lou
Terry (4)	Twinkle
Thank U Very Much	Scaffold
Thank You for the Music (33)	Abba
That Doggie in the Window (1)	Lita Roza
That Girl Belongs to Yesterday	Gene Pitney
That'll Be the Day	Crickets
That Ole Devil Called Love	Alison Moyet
That Same Old Feeling	Pickettywitch
That's Amore	Dean Martin
That's Livin' Alright	Joe Fagin
That's the Way Love Goes	Janet Jackson
That's the Way Love Is	Ten City
That's the Way (I Like It)	KC and the Sunshine Band
That's What Friends Are For	Dionne Warwick and Friends
That's What Friends Are For (8)	Deniece Williams
That's What I Like (1)	Jive Bunny and the Mastermixers
The Anniversary Waltz –) Part 1 (2)	Status Quo
The Best (5)	Tina Turner
The Boxer (6)	Simon and Garfunkel
The Breeze and I (5)	Caterina Valente
The Dean and I (10)	10cc
The Earth Dies Screaming	UB40
The Edge of Heaven (1)	Wham
The Folk Singer	Tommy Roe
The Happening (6)	Supremes
The Last Farewell (2)	Roger Whittaker
The Logical Song	Supertramp
The Look	Roxette
The Look of Love	ABC
The Man from Laramie (1)	Jimmy Young
The Minute You're Gone (1)	Cliff Richard
The Most Beautiful Girl	Charlie Rich
The Next Time (1)	Cliff Richard
The One	Elton John
The One and Only (1)	Chesney Hawkes
The Only Rhyme That Bites	MC Tunes versus 808 State
The Only Way Is Up (1)	Yazz and the Plastic Population
The Race	Yello
The Rain	Oran 'Juice' Jones
The Size of a Cow	Wonder Stuff
The Special A.K.A. Live EP (1)	Special A.K.A.
The Story of the Blues (3)	Wah!
The Streak (1)	Ray Stevens
The Sun Ain't Gonna Shine Anymore (1)	Walker Brothers
The Sun Goes Down	Level 42
The Time of My Life (6)	Bill Medley and Jennifer Warnes
The Unforgettable Fire (6)	U2
The Wanderer (7)	Status Quo
The Way We Were	Gladys Knight and the Pips
The Wedding	Julie Rogers
The Whole of the Moon (3)	Waterboys
The Wombling Song (4)	Wombles
The Word Girl	Scritti Politti featuring Ranking Ann
The Young Ones (1)	Cliff Richard
Theme from a Summer Place	Percy Faith

MUSIC POP

Title	Group/Artiste	Title	Group/Artiste
Theme from Dixie	Duane Eddy and the Rebels	Thought I'd Died and Gone to Heaven	Bryan Adams
Theme from Exodus	Ferrante and Teicher	3 AM Eternal (1)	KLF with Children of the Revolution
Theme from Harry's Game	Clannad		
Theme from Mahogany	Diana Ross	Three Coins in the Fountain (1)	Frank Sinatra
Theme from M*A*S*H (Suicide Is Painless) (1)	MASH	Three Lions '98 (1)	Baddiel and Skinner and the Lightning Seeds
Theme From M.A.S.H. (Suicide Is Painless) (7)	Manic Street Preachers	Three Little Pigs	Green Jelly
Theme from New York, New York	Frank Sinatra	Three Steps to Heaven (2)	Showaddywaddy
		Three Steps To Heaven (No. 1 1960)	Eddie Cochran
Theme from S-Express (1)	S Express		
Theme from Shaft	Isaac Hayes	Three Times a Lady	Commodores
Theme from The Deer Hunter (Cavatina) (9)	Shadows	Thriller	Michael Jackson
		Through the Barricades	Spandau Ballet
Theme from the Saint	Orbital	Through the Storm	Aretha Franklin and Elton John
Theme from Z Cars	Johnny Keating		
Them Girls Them Girls	Zig and Zag	Throw Down a Line	Cliff and Hank
Then He Kissed Me	Crystals	Thunderbirds Are Go	FAB
There Are More Questions Than Answers	Johnny Nash	Ticket to Ride (1)	Beatles
		Tide Is High (1)	Blondie
There But for Fortune	Joan Baez	Tie a Yellow Ribbon round the Old Oak Tree	Dawn featuring Tony Orlando
There Goes My Everything	Engelbert Humperdinck		
		Tiger Feet (1)	Mud
There Goes My First Love	Drifters	Till	Tom Jones
There Is a Mountain	Donovan	Till I Loved You (Love Theme from Goya)	Barbra Streisand and Don Johnson
There It Is	Shalamar		
There Must Be an Angel (1)	Eurythmics	Time after Time	Cyndi Lauper
There She Goes	La's	Time (Clock of the Heart)	Culture Club
There There My Dear	Dexy's Midnight Runners	Time Is Tight	Booker T. and the M.G.s
There's a Ghost in My House	R. Dean Taylor	Times They Are A-Changing	Bob Dylan
There's a Kind of Hush	Herman's Hermits	Time to Say Goodbye	Sarah Brightman and Andrea Boceelli
There's a Whole Lot of Loving	Guys and Dolls		
There's No One Quite Like Grandma (1)	St Winifred's School Choir	The Time Warp	Damien
		Tin Soldier	Small Faces
There's No Other Way	Blur	Tired of Being Alone	Al Green
These Boots Are Made for Walking (1)	Nancy Sinatra	Tired of Waiting for You (1)	Kinks
		To All the Girls I've Loved Before	Julio Iglesias and Willie Nelson
They Don't Know (2)	Tracey Ullman		
They're Coming to Take Me Away Ha-Haaa!	Napoleon XIV	Tobacco Road	Nashville Teens
		To Be or Not to Be	B.A. Robertson
Things Can Only Get Better (1)	D-Ream	To Be with You	Mr Big (USA)
Things Can Only Get Better (6)	Howard Jones	Tocas Miracle (1)	Fragma
Things We Do for Love (6)	10cc	Toccata	Sky
Thinking about Your Love	Kenny Thomas	Toccata and Fugue	Vanessa Mae
Thinking of You	Colour Field	To Cut a Long Story Short	Spandau Ballet
Think Twice (1)	Celine Dion	Together	PJ Proby
This Charming Man	Smiths	Together Forever	Rick Astley
This Corrosion	Sisters of Mercy	Together in Electric Dreams	Giorgio Moroder and Phil Oakey
This Guy's In Love with You	Herb Alpert		
This Is It	Melba Moore	Together We Are Beautiful (1)	Fern Kinney
This Is It	Danii Minogue	To Know Him Is to Love Him (2)	Teddy Bears
This Is My Song (1)	Petula Clark		
This Is My Song (2)	Harry Secombe	To Know You Is to Love You	Peter and Gordon
This Is Not a Love Song	Public Image Ltd	Tokoloshe Man	John Kongos
This Is the World Calling	Bob Geldof	Tokyo Joe	Bryan Ferry
This Is to Mother You	Sinead O'Connor	Tokyo Melody	Helmut Zacharias
This Old Heart of Mine	Isley Brothers	To Love Somebody	Nina Simone
This Ole House (1)	Shakin' Stevens	To Love Somebody (8)	Jimmy Somerville
This Ole House (1)	Rosemary Clooney	Tom Dooley (5)	Kingston Trio
This One's for the Children	New Kids on the Block	Tom Hark (2)	Elias and his Zigzag Jive Flutes
This Time	England World Cup Squad (1982)	Tom Hark (6)	Piranhas
		Tomorrow	James
This Town Ain't Big Enough for Both of Us	Sparks	Tomorrow	Sandie Shaw
		Tomorrow People	Ziggy Marley and the Melody Makers
This Wheel's on Fire	Julie Driscoll, Brian Auger and the Trinity		
		Tom's Diner	DNA
Thorn in My Side	Eurythmics	Tom's Diner	Suzanne Vega
Those Were the Days (1)	Mary Hopkin	Tom Tom Turnaround	New World

Title	Group/Artiste	Title	Group/Artiste
Tom Traubert's Blues (Waltzing Matilda) (6)	Rod Stewart	The Twelfth of Never (1)	Donny Osmond
Tonight I Celebrate My Love	Peabo Bryson and Roberta Flack	20th Century Boy (3)	T Rex
		25 or 6 to 4	Chicago
Tonight I'm Yours (8)	Rod Stewart	Twenty-Four Hours from Tulsa	Gene Pitney
Too Blind to See It	Kym Sims	Twilight Zone (2)	2 Unlimited
Too Busy Thinking 'Bout My Baby	Marvin Gaye	Twist and Shout (1)	Chaka Demus, Pliers, Jack Radics
		Twist and Shout (4)	Salt-N-Pepa
Too Good to Be Forgotten	Amazulu	Twist and Shout (4)	Brian Poole and the Tremeloes
Too Late for Goodbyes	Julian Lennon		
Too Many Broken Hearts (1)	Jason Donovan	Twist in My Sobriety	Tanita Tikaram
Too Much (1)	Spice Girls	Twistin' the Night Away (6)	Sam Cooke
Too Much Love Will Kill You	Brian May	The Twist (Yo, Twist)	Fat Boys and Chubby Checker
Too Much Too Little Too Late	Johnny Mathis and Deniece Williams		
		2 Become 1 (1)	Spice Girls
Too Nice to Talk To	Beat	Two Can Play That Game	Bobby Brown
Too Shy (1)	Kajagoogoo	2-4-6-8 Motorway	Tom Robinson Band
Too Soon to Know	Roy Orbison	Two Kinds of Teardrop	Del Shannon
Too Young (5)	Donny Osmond	Two Little Boys (1)	Rolf Harris
Torch	Soft Cell	2 Minutes to Midnight	Iron Maiden
Torn between Two Lovers	Mary McGregor	2 Pints of Lager and a Packet of Crisps Please	Splodgenessa bounds
Tossing and Turning	Ivy League		
Total Eclipse of the Heart (1)	Bonnie Tyler	Two Princes	Spin Doctors
Touch Me (1)	Rui Dasilva featuring Cassandra	Two Tribes	Frankie Goes to Hollywood
Touch Me (3)	49'ers	U Can't Touch This	Hammer
Touch Me (All Night Long)	Cathy Dennis	U Got 2 Know	Cappella
Touch Me in the Morning	Diana Ross	U + Me = Love	Funky Worm
Touch Me (I Want Your Body)	Sam Fox	U R the Best Thing	D-Ream
Tower of Strength (1)	Frankie Vaughan	The Ugly Duckling (10)	Mike Reid
Town Called Malice (1)	Jam	'Ullo John Got a New Motor (15)	Alexei Sayle
Toy Balloons	Russ Conway	Um Um Um Um Um Um	Wayne Fontana and the Mindbenders
Toy Boy	Sinitta		
To You I Belong (1)	B*witched	Una Paloma Blanca	Jonathan King
Toy Soldiers	Martika	Un Banc, Un Arbre, Une Rue	Severine
Tracks of My Tears (9)	Smokey Robinson and the Miracles	Unbelievable	EMF
		Un-Break My Heart	Tony Braxton
Tracy	Cufflinks	Unchained Melody (1)	Righteous Brothers
Tragedy (1)	Bee Gees	Unchained Melody (1)	Jimmy Young
Tragedy (1)	Steps	Unchained Melody/White Cliffs of Dover(1)	Robson Green and Jerome Flynn
The Trail of the Lonesome Pine	Laurel and Hardy and the Avalon Boys		
		Unchain My Heart	Joe Cocker
Trains and Boats and Planes	Billy J. Kramer and the Dakotas	Under a Raging Moon	Roger Daltrey
		Under Pressure (1)	Queen and David Bowie
Trapped	Colonel Abrams		
Travellin' Light (1)	Cliff Richard	Under the Boardwalk (2)	Bruce Willis
Tribal Dance	2 Unlimited	Under the Bridge/Lady Marmalade (1)	All Saints
Tribute (Right On)	Pasadenas		
Trouble	Gillan	Under the Bridges of Paris	Eartha Kitt
True (1)	Spandau Ballet	Under the Moon of Love (1)	Showaddywaddy
True Blue (1)	Madonna	Under Your Thumb	Godley and Creme
True Colours	Cyndi Lauper	Underwater Love	Smoke City
True Faith	New Order	Union of the Snake	Duran Duran
True Love (2)	Elton John and Kiki Dee	United	Judas Priest
		Up around the Bend	Creedence Clearwater Revival
True Love (4)	Bing Crosby and Grace Kelly		
True Love Ways (2)	Peter and Gordon	Up on the Roof/I Believe (1)	Robson Green and Jerome Flynn
Truly	Lionel Richie		
Tubthumping	Chumbawamba	Up on the Roof (10)	Kenny Lynch
Tumbling Dice (5)	Rolling Stones	Upside down	Diana Ross
Tunnel of Love	Fun Boy Three	Up the Junction	Squeeze
Tunnel of Love	Dire Straits	Uptight	Stevie Wonder
Turn Back Time (1)	Aqua	Uptown Girl (1)	Billy Joel
Turn It On Again	Genesis	Uptown Girl (1)	Westlife
Turn On Tune In Cop Out	Freak Power	Up Up and Away	Johnny Mann Singers
Turn the Music Up	Players Association		
Turning Japanese	Vapors	Up Where We Belong	Joe Cocker and Jennifer Warnes
Turtle Power (1)	Partners in Kryme		
Tweedle Dee	Little Jimmy Osmond	Use It Up and Wear It Out (1)	Odyssey
Tweedle Dee Tweedle Dum	Middle of the Road	Vacation	Connie Francis
		Valentine	T'Pau

Title	Group/Artiste	Title	Group/Artiste
Valotte	Julian Lennon	War Baby	Tom Robinson
Vaya Con Dios	Les Paul and Mary Ford	The War Song	Culture Club
		Watching the Detectives	Elvis Costello
Venus (4)	Don Pablo's Animals	Waterfalls	TLC
Venus (8)	Shocking Blue	Waterloo	Doctor and the Medics (featuring Roy Wood)
Venus in Blue Jeans	Mark Wynter		
Victims	Culture Club		
Victims of Love	Erasure	Waterloo (1)	Abba
Vienna (2)	Ultravox	Waterloo Sunset	Kinks
Vienna Calling	Falco	Water Water	Tommy Steele
Vincent (1)	Don McLean	Way Down (1)	Elvis Presley
Violently Happy	Bjork	Way of Life	Family Dogg
Virginia Plain	Roxy Music	Way of the World	Tina Turner
Viva Bobby Joe	Equals	Wayward Wind (1)	Frank Ifield
Viva Forever	Spice Girls	Wayward Wind (8)	Tex Ritter
Viva Las Vegas	ZZ Top	Weak in the Presence of Beauty	Alison Moyet
Vogue (1)	Madonna		
Voice in the Wilderness (2)	Cliff Richard	We All Stand Together	Paul McCartney and the Frog Chorus
Volare (10)	Domenico Modugno		
Volare (2)	Dean Martin	We Are Detective (7)	Thompson Twins
Voodoo Chile (1)	Jimi Hendrix Experience	We Are Family	Sister Sledge
		We Are Glass	Gary Numan
Voyage Voyage	Desireless	We Are the Champions	Queen
Wait	Kym Mazelle	We Are the World (1)	USA for Africa
Waiting for a Girl Like You	Foreigner	Weather With You	Crowded House
Waiting for a Star to Fall	Boy Meets Girl	We Call It Acieed	D Mob
Waiting for a Train	Flash and the Pan	We Close Our Eyes	Go West
Waiting for An Alibi	Thin Lizzy	Wedding Bells	Godley and Creme
Wake Me Up before You Go Go (1)	Wham	We Didn't Start the Fire	Billy Joel
		We Do It	R & J Stone
Wake Up Boo!	Boo Radleys	We Don't Have To	Jermaine Stewart
Wake Up Little Suzie	Everly Brothers	We Don't Need Another Hero (3)	Tina Turner
Walk Away	Matt Monro	We Don't Talk Anymore (1)	Cliff Richard
Walk Away from Love	David Ruffin	Wee Rule	Wee Papa Girl Rappers
Walk Away Renee	Four Tops		
Walk Don't Run (8)	Ventures	We Got a Love Thang	Ce Ce Peniston
Walk Hand in Hand	Tony Martin	We Gotta Get Out of This Place	Animals
A Walk in the Black Forest	Horst Jankowski	We Have a Dream	Scottish World Cup Squad
Walk Like a Man	Four Seasons		
Walk Like an Egyptian	Bangles	We Have All the Time in the World	Louis Armstrong
Walk of Life	Dire Straits		
Walk On By (5)	Leroy Van Dyke	Welcome Home (1)	Peters and Lee
Walk On By (6)	Sybil	Welcome to My World	Jim Reeves
Walk On By (9)	Dionne Warwick	Welcome to the Pleasuredome	Frankie Goes to Hollywood
Walk On the Wild Side	Lou Reed		
Walk Right Back (1)	Everly Brothers	Welcome to Tomorrow	Snap featuring Summer
Walk Right In	Rooftop Singers		
Walk Tall	Val Doonican	We'll Bring the House Down (10)	Slade
Walk the Dinosaur	Was (Not Was)		
Walk This Way	Run D.M.C.	Well Did You Evah!	Deborah Harry and Iggy Pop
Walkin' Back to Happiness (1)	Helen Shapiro		
Walking in the Air	Aled Jones	Well I Ask You (1)	Eden Kane
Walking in the Rain	Partridge Family starring David Cassidy	We're All Alone	Rita Coolidge
		We're Going to Ibiza	Vengaboys
		We Should Be Together	Cliff Richard
Walking in the Rain (7)	Modern Romance	West End Girls	East 17
Walking on Broken Glass	Annie Lennox	West End Girls (1)	Pet Shop Boys
Walking on Sunshine	Katrina and the Waves	We Take Mystery	Gary Numan
		Wet Dream	Max Romeo
Walking on Sunshine (6)	Rocker's Revenge featuring Donnie Calvin	We've Got Tonight	Kenny Rogers and Sheena Easton
		We Will Make Love	Russ Hamilton
Walking on the Moon (1)	Police	We Will Rock You	Five and Queen
Walking on Thin Ice	Yoko Ono	Wham Rap	Wham
Walls Come Tumbling Down	Style Council	What a Difference a Day Makes	Esther Phillips
Wall Street Shuffle (10)	10cc		
The Wanderer	Dion	What a Waste	Ian Dury
Wanderin' Eyes	Charlie Gracie	What Are We Gonna Get 'Er Indoors (21)	Dennis Waterman and George Cole
Wannabe (1)	Spice Girls		
Wanted	Dooleys	What Are You Doing Sunday	Dawn featuring Tony Orlando
War (3)	Edwin Starr		

Title	Group/Artiste	Title	Group/Artiste
What Becomes of the Broken Hearted/Saturday Night at the Movies/You'll Never Walk Alone (1)	Robson and Jerome	When You're Young and in Love (7)	Flying Pickets
What Becomes of the Broken Hearted	Jimmy Ruffin	Whenever God Shines His Light	Van Morrison and Cliff Richard
What Becomes of the Broken Hearted (13)	Dave Stewart with Colin Blunstone	Whenever You Need Somebody	Rick Astley
What Can I Say	Boz Scaggs	Where Are You Baby	Betty Boo
What Can You Do for Me	Utah Saints	Where Are You Now (1)	Jackie Trent
What Do I Do	Phil Fearon and Galaxy	Where Can I Find Love	Livin Joy
What Do You Want (1)	Adam Faith	Where Did Our Love Go?(3)	Supremes
What Do You Want to Make Those Eyes at Me For (1)	Emile Ford and the Checkmates	Where Did Our Love Go? (8)	Donnie Elbert
		Where Do You Go	No Mercy
Whatever	Oasis	Where Do You Go to My Lovely (1)	Peter Sarstedt
Whatever I Do (Wherever I Go)	Hazell Dean	Where Is the Love	Roberta Flack and Donny Hathaway
Whatever Will Be Will Be (1)	Doris Day		
Whatever You Want (4)	Status Quo	Where the Streets Have No Name	Pet Shop Boys
What Have I Done to Deserve This	Pet Shop Boys and Dusty Springfield	Where the Streets Have No Name (4)	U2
What Have You Done for Me Lately	Janet Jackson	Where Will the Baby's Dimple Be	Rosemary Clooney
What Is Love	Haddaway	Wherever I Lay My Hat (1)	Paul Young
What Is Love	Howard Jones	Which Way You Goin' Billy	Poppy Family
What I've Got in Mind	Billy Jo Spears	Whiskey in the Jar (6)	Thin Lizzy
What Kind of Fool Am I	Anthony Newley	Whispering Grass	Windsor Davies and Don Estelle
What Took you so Long	Emma Bunton		
What's Another Year (1)	Johnny Logan	White Christmas (5)	Bing Crosby
What's Love Got to Do with It (3)	Tina Turner	White Christmas (6)	Mantovani
What's New Pussycat	Tom Jones	White Cliffs of Dover /Unchained Melody (1)	Robson Green and Jerome Flynn
What's the Frequency, Kenneth?	R.E.M.	White Horses	Jacky (Lee)
What's Up	4 Non Blondes	White Lines (Don't Don't Do It)	Grandmaster Flash and Melle Mel
Whatta Man	Salt-N-Pepa with En Vogue		
		White Room	Cream
What Would I Be	Val Doonican	Whiter Shade of Pale	Procol Harum
What You're Proposing (2)	Status Quo	A White Sport Coat	Terry Dene
Wheels	String-a-Longs	A White Sport Coat (6)	King Brothers
When (1)	Kalin Twins	White Wedding	Billy Idol
When (3)	Showaddywaddy	Who Do You Think You Are/Mama	Spice Girls
When a Child is Born (1)	Johnny Mathis	Whodunit	Tavares
When a Man Loves a Woman	Percy Sledge	Who Found Who	Jellybean featuring Elisa Fiorillo
When Am I Gonna Make a Living	Sade		
When Doves Cry	Prince	Who Killed Bambi (6)	Tenpole Tudor
When Forever Has Gone (2)	Demis Roussos	Who the F- - K Is Alice	Smokie featuring 'Chubby' Brown
When I Fall in Love	Donny Osmond		
When I Fall in Love	Nat King Cole	Whole Again (1)	Atomic Kitten
When I Need You (1)	Leo Sayer	Whole Lotta Shakin' Goin' On	Jerry Lee Lewis
When I Think of You	Janet Jackson	Whole Lotta Woman (1)	Marvin Rainwater
When I'm Dead and Gone	McGuinness Flint	A Whole New World (Aladdin's Theme)	Peabo Bryson and Regina Belle
When I'm Good and Ready	Sybil		
When Julie Comes Around	Cufflinks	Who Put the Lights Out	Dana
When Love and Hate Collide	Def Leppard	Who's Leaving Who	Hazell Dean
When Love Comes to Town (6)	U2 featuring BB King	Who's Sorry Now	Connie Francis
When Mexico Gave Up the Rhumba	Mitchell Torok	Who's That Girl?(1)	Madonna
		Who's That Girl?	Eurythmics
When My Little Girl Is Smiling	Jimmy Justice	Why	Annie Lennox
When the Going Gets Tough (1)	Billy Ocean	Why (10)	Carly Simon
When the Going Gets Tough (1)	Boyzone	Why (1)	Anthony Newley
When Will I See You Again (1)	Three Degrees	Why (3)	Donny Osmond
When Will You Say I Love You	Billy Fury	Why Can't I Wake Up With You	Take That
When You Ask About Love	Matchbox	Why Can't This Be Love (8)	Van Halen
When You Say Nothing at All Love Me (2)	Ronan Keating	Why Does It Always Rain on Me? (10)	Travis
When You Tell Me That You Love Me (2)	Diana Ross	Why Do Fools Fall in Love (1)	Teenagers featuring Frankie Lymon
		Why Do Fools Fall In Love (4)	Diana Ross
When You Walk in the Room (3)	Searchers	Why Oh Why Oh Why	Gilbert O'Sullivan
When You Were Young	Del Amitri	Wicked Game	Chris Isaak
When You're in Love with a Beautiful Woman	Dr Hook	Wide Boy	Nik Kershaw
		Wide Eyed and Legless	Andy Fairweather Low

Title	Group/Artiste
Wig-Wam Bam (4)	Sweet
Wild Boys	Duran Duran
Wild One (7)	Bobby Rydell
The Wild One (7)	Suzi Quatro
Wild Thing (21)	Tone Loc
Wild Thing (2)	Troggs
Wild Wind	John Leyton
Wild World	Jimmy Cliff
Wild World (5)	Maxi Priest
Will You	Hazel O'Connor
Willie Can	Beverley Sisters
Will You Love Me Tomorrow (4)	Shirelles
Wimoweh	Karl Denver
Winchester Cathedral	New Vaudeville Band
Wind Beneath My Wings (5)	Bette Midler
The Wind Cries Mary (6)	Jimi Hendrix Experience
Wind of Change	Scorpions
Winker's Song (Misprint)	Ivor Biggun and the Red Nosed Buglars
Winner Takes It All (1)	Abba
A Winter's Tale	David Essex
Wipe Out (5)	Surfaris
Wipeout (2)	Fat Boys and the Beach Boys
Wishful Thinking	China Crisis
Wishing	Buddy Holly
Wishing I Was Lucky	Wet Wet Wet
Wishing on a Star	Fresh 4 featuring Lizz E
Wishing on a Star	Rose Royce
Wishing Well	Terence Trent D'Arby
Wishing Well (7)	Free
Wishing (If I Had a Photograph of You)	A Flock of Seagulls
The Witch	Rattles
Witch Doctor	Don Lang
Witch Queen of New Orleans	Redbone
Witch's Promise/Teacher	Jethro Tull
With a Girl Like You (1)	Troggs
With a Little Help from My Friends (10)	Young Idea
With a Little Help from My Friends (1)	Joe Cocker
With A Little Help from My Friends (1)	Wet Wet Wet
With a Little Luck	Wings
With or without You (4)	U2
Without You (1)	Nilsson
Without You (1)	Mariah Carey
With You I'm Born Again	Billy Preston and Syreeta
Woman in Love (1)	Barbra Streisand
Woman in Love (3)	Three Degrees
A Woman In Love (1)	Frankie Laine
Woman (1)	John Lennon
Woman (7)	Jose Ferrer
Wombling Merry Christmas	Wombles
Wonderful Christmas Time	Paul McCartney
Wonderful Copenhagen	Danny Kaye
Wonderful Land (1)	Shadows
Wonderful Life	Black
Wonderful World Beautiful People	Jimmy Cliff
Wonderful World of the Young	Danny Williams
Wonderland	Big Country
The Wonder of You (1)	Elvis Presley
Wonderous Stories	Yes
Wonderwall (1)	Oasis
Wonderwall (2)	Mike Flowers Pops

Title	Group/Artiste
Won't Somebody Dance with Me	Lynsey De Paul
Wood Beez (Pray Like Aretha Franklin)	Scritti Politti
Wooden Heart (1)	Elvis Presley
Woodstock (1)	Matthews Southern Comfort
Wooly Bully	Sam the Sham and the Pharaohs
Words (1)	Boyzone
Words (2)	F.R. David
Words (8)	Bee Gees
Wordy Rappinghood	Tom Tom Club
Workaholic (4)	2 Unlimited
Workin' My Way Back to You	Four Seasons with Frankie Valli
Working in the Coalmine	Lee Dorsey
Working My Way Back to You	Detroit Spinners
Work That Body	Diana Ross
World	Bee Gees
World in Motion (1)	Englandneworder
World in Union (4)	Kiri Te Kanawa
A World of Our Own	Seekers
A World without Love (1)	Peter and Gordon
Would	Alice in Chains
Would I Lie To You (1)	Charles and Eddie
Wouldn't It Be Good	Nik Kershaw
Wuthering Heights	Kate Bush
Xanadu (1)	Olivia Newton-John and Electric Light Orchestra
Yah Mo B There	James Ingram and Michael McDonald
Yakety Yak	Coasters
Yeh Yeh	Georgie Fame
Yellow Pearl	Philip Lynott
Yellow River	Christie
Yellow Rose of Texas	Mitch Miller
Yellow Submarine/Eleanor Rigby (1)	Beatles
Yes My Darling Daughter	Eydie Gormé
Yes Sir I Can Boogie	Baccara
Yesterday (8)	Matt Monro
Yesterday (8)	Beatles
Yesterday Has Gone	Cupid's Inspiration
Yesterday Man	Chris Andrews
Yes Tonight Josephine (1)	Johnnie Ray
Ying Tong Song	Goons
YMCA	Village People
You (10)	Ten Sharp
You Ain't Seen Nothin' Yet	Bachman-Turner Overdrive
You Always Hurt the One You Love	Clarence 'Frogman' Henry
You Are Everything	Diana Ross and Marvin Gaye
You Are Not Alone (1)	Michael Jackson
You Are the Sunshine of My Life	Stevie Wonder
You Belong to Me (1)	Jo Stafford
You Better You Bet (9)	Who
You Can Call Me Al (4)	Paul Simon
You Can Do Magic	Limmie and the Family Cookin'
You Can Get It If You Really Want	Desmond Dekker
You Can Never Stop Me Loving You	Kenny Lynch
You Can't Hurry Love (3)	Supremes
You Can't Hurry Love (1)	Phil Collins

M
U
S
I
C

P
O
P

Singles: by Group/Artiste

Group/Artiste	Title	Group/Artiste	Title
A1	Same Old Brand New (1)	Alannah Myles	Black Velvet
	Take On Me (1)	Alan Price	Jarrow Song
Abba	Angel Eyes/Voulez-Vous (3)	Alan Price Set	The House That Jack Built (4)
	Chiquitita (2)		I Put a Spell on You
	Dancing Queen (1)		Simon Smith and His Amazing
	Does Your Mother Know (4)		Dancing Bear
	Fernando (1)	Alarm	68 Guns
	Gimme Gimme Gimme (A Man	Aled Jones	Walking in the Air
	after Midnight) (3)	Alessi	Oh Lori
	I Do I Do I Do I Do I Do (38)	Alex Party	Don't Give Me Your Life
	I Have a Dream (2)	Alexander O'Neal	Criticize
	Knowing Me Knowing You (1)		Saturday Love
	Lay All Your Love on Me (7)	Alexei Sayle	'Ullo John Got a New Motor
	Mamma Mia (1)		(15)
	Money Money Money (3)	Al Green	Let's Stay Together (7)
	The Name of the Game (1)		Tired of Being Alone
	One of Us (3)	Alice Cooper	Elected (4)
	Ring Ring (32)		Hello Hurray
	Summer Night City (5)		No More Mr Nice Guy
	Super Trouper (1)		Poison
	SOS (6)		School's Out (1)
	Take a Chance on Me (1)	Alice in Chains	Would
	Thank You for the Music (33)	Alison Moyet	All Cried Out
	Waterloo (1)		Is This Love?
	Winner Takes It All (1)		Love Letters (4)
ABC	All of My Heart		Love Resurrection
	Poison Arrow		That Ole Devil Called Love
	Tears Are Not Enough		Weak in the Presence of
	The Look of Love		Beauty
Abigail Mead and	Full Metal Jacket	Al Jarreau	Moonlighting Theme
Nigel Goulding		Al Jarreau and	The Music Of Goodbye
AC/DC	Rock 'N' Roll Ain't Noise Pollution	Melissa Manchester	(Out of Africa)
	Rock 'N' Roll Damnation	All about Eve	Martha's Harbour
Ace of Base	All That She Wants (1)	All-4-One	I Swear
	The Sign	Allisons	Are You Sure
Acker Bilk and his	Buona Sera	All Saints	Black Coffee (1)
Paramount Jazz	Stranger on the Shore (2)		Bootie Call (1)
Band			Under the Bridge/Lady
Adam and the Ants	Prince Charming (1)		Marmalade (1)
	Stand and Deliver (1)		Never Ever
Adam Ant	Dog Eat Dog		Pure Shores (1)
	Friend or Foe	Alma Cogan	Bell Bottom Blues
	Goody Two Shoes (1)		Dreamboat (1)
	Puss 'N' Boots	Al Martino	Here in My Heart (1)
	Young Parisians		Now
Adam Faith	As You Like It		Rachel
	The First Time		Spanish Eyes (5)
	Message to Martha (Kentucky		The Story of Tina
	Bluebird)		Take My Heart
	Poor Me (1)	Alphaville	Big in Japan
	What Do You Want (1)	Altered Images	Don't Talk to Me about Love
Adamski	Killer		Happy Birthday (2)
Adge Cutler and	Drink Up Thy Zider		I Could Be Happy
the Wurzels		Altern 8	Activ 8 (Come with Me)
Adrian Gurvitz	Classic	Alvin and the	Achy Breaky Heart (53)
Adventures of	Dirty Cash	Chipmunks and	
Stevie V		Billy Ray Cyrus	
Adverts	Gary Gilmore's Eyes	Alvin Stardust	I Feel Like Buddy Holly
Aerosmith	Dude (Looks Like a Lady)		I Won't Run Away
	Love in an Elevator		Jealous Mind (1)
A-Ha	Cry Wolf (5)		My Coo-Ca-Choo
	Living Daylights (5)		Pretend
	Stay on These Roads (5)		Red Dress (7)
	The Sun Always Shines on TV	Amazulu	Too Good to Be Forgotten
	(1)	Ami Grant	Baby Baby
	Take On Me (2)	Amii Stewart	Knock on Wood (6)
Air Supply	All Out of Love		Light My Fire (5)

Group/Artiste	Title
Andrea True Connection	More More More
Andrew Gold	Never Let Her Slip Away (5)
Andy Fairweather-Low	Reggae Tune
	Wide Eyed and Legless
Andy Gibb	An Everlasting Love
Andy Kim	Rock Me Gently
Andy Stewart	Donald Where's Your Troosers
Andy Williams	Almost There (2)
	Butterfly (1)
	Can't Get Used to Losing You (2)
	Can't Help Falling in Love (3)
	Can't Take My Eyes off You (5)
	Home Lovin' Man (7)
	Solitaire (4)
Aneka	Japanese Boy
Angry Anderson	Suddenly (3)
Animals	Don't Bring Me Down (6)
	House of the Rising Sun (1)
	We Gotta Get Out of This Place
Anita Dobson	Anyone Can Fall in Love
Anita Harris	Just Loving You
Anita Ward	Ring My Bell (1)
Anne Murray	Snowbird
Anne Shelton	Lay Down Your Arms (1)
	Sailor (10)
Annie Lennox	Little Bird
	No More 'I Love You's'
	Walking on Broken Glass
	Why
Annie Lennox and Al Green	Put a Little Love in Your Heart
Another Level	Freak Me (1)
Anthony Newley	Do You Mind (1)
	If She Should Come to You
	I've Waited So Long
	Personality (6)
	Pop Goes the Weasel
	Strawberry Fair
	What Kind of Fool Am I
	Why (1)
Applejacks	Tell Me When
Aqua	Barbie Girl (1)
	Doctor Jones (1)
	Turn Back Time (1)
Arcadia	Election Day
Archies	Sugar Sugar (1)
Aretha Franklin	I Say a Little Prayer
	Respect
Aretha Franklin and Elton John	Through the Storm
Aretha Franklin and George Michael	I Knew You Were Waiting (for Me) (1)
Argent	Hold Your Head Up
Armand Van Helden	You Don't Know Me (1)
Arnee and the Terminators	I'll Be Back
Arrested Development	Mr Wendal
	People Everyday
Art and Dotty Todd	Broken Wings (6)
Art Garfunkel	Bright Eyes (1)
	I Only Have Eyes for You (1)
Art of Noise	Close (To The Edit)
Art of Noise featuring Duane Eddy	Peter Gunn
Art of Noise featuring Max Headroom	Paranoimia
Art of Noise featuring Tom Jones	Kiss (5)
Ashford and Simpson	Solid

Group/Artiste	Title
Ashton, Gardner and Dyke	Resurrection Shuffle
Assembly	Never Never
Associates	Party Fears Two
Aswad	Don't Turn Around
	Give a Little Love (11)
	Shine
A Taste Of Honey	Boogie Oogie Oogie (3)
ATB	9PM (Till I Come) (1)
Atomic Kitten	Whole Again (1)
Atomic Rooster	The Devil's Answer
Average White Band	Pick Up the Pieces
Avons	Seven Little Girls Sitting in the Back Seat
Aztec Camera	Oblivious
B-52's	Love Shack
Baby D	Let Me Be Your Fantasy (1)
Babylon Zoo	Spaceman (1)
Baccara	Sorry I'm A Lady
	Yes Sir I Can Boogie
Bachelors	Charmaine (6)
	Diane (1)
	I Believe (2)
	I Wouldn't Trade You for the World (4)
	The Sound of Silence (3)
Bachman-Turner Overdrive	You Ain't Seen Nothin' Yet
Backstreet Boys	As Long as You Love Me
	Everybody (Backstreet's Back)
	I Want It That Way (1)
Baddiel and Skinner and the Lightning Seeds	3 Lions '98 (1)
Badfinger	Come and Get It
	No Matter What
Bad Manners	Can Can
	My Girl Lollipop
	Special Brew
Bananarama	Love in the first Degree
	Robert De Niro's Waiting
	Shy Boy
Bananarama with the Fun Boy Three	Really Saying Something
Band Aid	Do They Know It's Christmas (1)
Band Aid II	Do They Know It's Christmas (1)
Band of the Black Watch	Scotch on the Rocks
Bangles	Eternal Flame (1)
	Manic Monday
	Walk Like an Egyptian
Barbara Dickson	Another Suitcase in Another Hall
	Answer Me (9)
Barbra Streisand	Love Theme From a Star is Born (Evergreen)
	Woman in Love (1)
Barbra Streisand and Don Johnson	Till I Loved You (Love Theme from Goya)
Bardo	One Step Further
Barron Knights	Merry Gentle Pops
	Pop Go the Workers
	A Taste of Aggro
Barry Biggs	Sideshow
Barry Blue	Dancing on a Saturday Night
	Do You Wanna Dance
Barry Manilow	I Wanna Do It with You (10)
	Mandy (11)

Group/Artiste	Title
Barry McGuire	Eve of Destruction
Barry Ryan	Eloise (2)
Barry White	Can't Get Enough of Your Love Babe
	Just the Way You Are
	Sho' You Right (14)
	You're the First the Last My Everything (1)
Bassheads	Is There Anybody Out There
Bass-O-Matic	Fascinating Rhythm
Bay City Rollers	Bye Bye Baby (1)
	Give a Little Love (1)
	Keep On Dancing
	Money Honey
	Summerlove Sensation
Baz Luhrmann	Everybody's Free (to Wear Sunscreen) (1)
BC-52s	The Flintstones
Beach Boys	Barbara Ann
	Break Away
	Cottonfields
	Do It Again
	God Only Knows
	I Can Hear Music
	Kokomo
Beastie Boys	No Sleep Till Brooklyn
	She's on It
Beat	Mirror in the Bathroom
	Too Nice to Talk To
Beatles	All You Need Is Love (1)
	Baby It's You
	Beatles Movie Medley (10)
	Can't Buy Me Love (1)
	Day Tripper/We Can Work It Out (1)
	Free As a Bird
	From Me to You (1)
	A Hard Day's Night (1)
	Hello Goodbye (1)
	Help (1)
	Hey Jude (1)
	I Feel Fine (1)
	I Want to Hold Your Hand (1)
	Lady Madonna (1)
	Let It Be (2)
	Love Me Do (4)
	Magical Mystery Tour (double EP) (2)
	Paperback Writer (1)
	Penny Lane/Strawberry Fields Forever (2)
	Please Please Me (2)
	Real Love (4)
	She Loves You (1)
	Something/Come Together (4)
	Ticket to Ride (1)
	Yellow Submarine/Eleanor Rigby (1)
	Yesterday (8)
Beatles with Billy Preston	Get Back (1)
Beatmasters featuring Cookie Crew	Rok Da House
Beats International	Dub Be Good to Me
Beautiful South	A Little Time (1)
	Song for Whoever
	You Keep It All In
Bee Gees	For Whom the Bell Tolls
	How Deep is Your Love (3)
	I've Gotta Get a Message to You (1)

Group/Artiste	Title
	Massachusetts (1)
	Night Fever (1)
	Tragedy (1)
	Words (8)
	World
	You Win Again (1)
Bellamy Brothers	If I Said You Have a Beautiful Body
	Let Your Love Flow
Bell Biv Devoe	The Best Things in Life Are Free
Belle Stars	Sign of the Times
Beloved	Sweet Harmony
Ben E. King	Stand by Me (1)
Benny Hill	Ernie (1)
Berlin	Take My Breath Away
Bernard Bresslaw	Mad Passionate Love
Bernard Cribbins	Gossip Calypso
	Hole in the Ground
	Right Said Fred
Berni Flint	I Don't Want to Put a Hold on You
Bert Kaempfert	Bye Bye Blues (24)
Bert Weedon	Guitar Boogie Shuffle
Bette Midler	From a Distance
	Wind beneath My Wings (5)
Betty Boo	Hey DJ I Can't Dance to That Music
	Where Are You Baby
Beverley Craven	Promise Me
Beverley Sisters	I Saw Mommy Kissing Santa Claus
	Little Drummer Boy
	Willie Can
Big Audio Dynamite	E=MC^2
Big Country	Fields of Fire (400 Miles)
	Wonderland
Big Dee Irwin	Swinging on a Star
Big Fun	Blame It on the Boogie
Big Mountain	Baby I Love Your Way
Bill Haley and his Comets	Rock Around the Clock (1)
Billie	Because We Want To (1)
	Girlfriend (1)
	Day and Night (1)
Billie Davis	Tell Him
Bill Medley and Jennifer Warnes	The Time of My Life (6)
Bill Whelan featuring Anuna and RTE	Riverdance
Bill Withers	Lean on Me (18)
	Lovely Day (7)
Bill Wyman	Je Suis Un Rock Star (14)
Billy Bragg with Cara Tivey	She's Leaving Home
Billy Connolly	D.I.V.O.R.C.E.
Billy Cotton	Friends and Neighbours
	In a Golden Coach
Billy Eckstine	Gigi
	No One But You
Billy Fury	Colette
	Halfway to Paradise
	In Summer
	Jealousy
	When Will You Say I Love You
Billy Hayes	Ballad of Davy Crockett
Billy Howard	King Of the Cops
Billy Idol	Hot in the City
	Rebel Yell
	White Wedding

Group/Artiste	Title	Group/Artiste	Title
Billy J. Kramer and the Dakotas	Bad to Me (1)		Girls and Boys
	Do You Want to Know a Secret		There's No Other Way
	From a Window	Bob and Earl	Harlem Shuffle
	I'll Keep You Satisfied	Bob and Marcia	Young Gifted and Black
	Little Children (1)	Bobby Bloom	Montego Bay
	Trains and Boats and Planes	Bobby 'Boris' Pickett	Monster Mash (3)
Billy Joel	An Innocent Man	and the Crypt-	
	It's Still Rock and Roll to Me	Kickers	
	Just the Way You Are	Bobby Brown	Humpin' Around
	The River of Dreams		Two Can Play That Game
	Tell Her about It	Bobby Darin	Dream Lover
	Uptown Girl (1)		Mack the Knife (1)
	We Didn't Start the Fire		La Mer
Billy Jo Spears	Blanket on the Ground		Multiplication
	What I've Got in Mind		Splish Splash (18)
Billy Ocean	Caribbean Queen		You Must Have Been a
	Get outta My Dreams Get into		Beautiful Baby
	My Car	Bobby Fuller Four	I Fought the Law (33)
	Love Really Hurts without You	Bobby Gentry	I'll Never Fall in Love Again (1)
	Red Light Spells Danger	Bobby Gentry and	All I Have to Do Is Dream
	Suddenly (4)	Glen Campbell	
	When the Going Gets Tough (1)	Bobby Goldsboro	Honey
Billy Paul	Me and Mrs Jones		Summer (the First time)
Billy Preston and	With You I'm Born Again	Bobby McFerrin	Don't Worry Be Happy
Syreeta		Bobby Rydell	Wild One (7)
Billy Ray Cyrus	Achy Breaky Heart (3)	Bobbysocks	Let It Swing
Billy Swan	I Can Help	Bobby Thurston	Check Out the Groove
Bing Crosby	Around the World (5)	Bobby Vee	The Night Has a Thousand
	Changing Partners		Eyes (3)
	Isle of Innisfree		Rubber Ball (4)
	Silent Night		Run to Him (6)
	White Christmas (5)		Take Good Care of My Baby (3)
Bing Crosby and	True Love (4)	Bobby Vinton	Blue Velvet (2)
Grace Kelly			Roses Are Red (15)
Bing Crosby and	Zing a Little Zong	Bob Dylan	Lay Lady Lay
Jane Wyman			Like a Rolling Stone
Bitty McLean	It Keeps Rainin'		Positively Fourth Street
Bizarre Inc	I'm Gonna Get You		Rainy Day Women Nos 12 and
	Playing with Knives		35
Bizz Nizz	Don't Miss the Party Line		Subterranean Homesick Blues
Björk	It's Oh So Quiet		The Times They Are A
	Violently Happy		Changing
Black	Wonderful Life	Bob Geldof	This Is the World Calling
Black Box	Ride on Time	Bob Lind	Elusive Butterfly (5)
Blackfoot Sue	Standing in the Road	Bob Luman	Let's Think about Living
Black Lace	Agadoo	Bob Marley and	Buffalo Soldier
	Do the Conga	the Wailers	Iron Lion Zion
	Superman (Gioca Jouer)		Is This Love
Black Legend	You See The Trouble With Me		Jamming
	(1)		No Woman No Cry
Black Sabbath	Paranoid		One Love – People Get Ready
Black Slate	Amigo	Bob the Builder	Can We Fix It (1)
Blancmange	Living on the Ceiling	Bomb the Bass	Beat Dis
Blondie	Atomic (1)	Bomb the Bass	
	Heart of Glass (1)	featuring Maureen	Say a Little Prayer (10)
	Rapture	Bombalurina with	Itsy Bitsy Teeny Weeny Yellow
	Call Me (1)	Timmy Mallett	Polka Dot Bikini (1)
	Denis (2)	Boney M	Daddy Cool (6)
	Dreaming (2)		Ma Baker
	Maria (1)		Rasputin
	Sunday Girl (1)		Rivers of Babylon
	Tide is High (1)	Bon Jovi	Bed of Roses
Blow Monkeys	It Doesn't Have to Be This Way		Keep the Faith
Bluebells	Young at Heart (1)		Livin' on a Prayer
Blue Mink	Banner Man		Please Come Home for
	Good Morning Freedom		Christmas
	Melting Pot	Bonnie Lou	Tennessee Wig Walk
	Randy	Bonnie Tyler	Holding Out for a Hero (2)
Blue Pearl	Naked in the Rain		It's A Heartache (4)
Blur	Beetlebum (1)		Lost in France (9)
	Country House (1)		Total Eclipse of the Heart (1)

MUSIC POP

Group/Artiste	Title	Group/Artiste	Title
Bonzo Dog Doo-Dah Band	I'm the Urban Spaceman	Bryan Ferry	A Hard Rain's Gonna Fall
			Let's Stick Together
Booker Newbury III	Love Town		Slave to Love
Booker T. and the M.G.s	Green Onions		Tokyo Joe
	Soul Clap '69	Bryan Johnson	Looking High High High
	Soul Limbo	Bubblerock (Jonathan King)	Satisfaction (29)
	Time Is Tight		
Boomtown Rats	Banana Republic	Buddy Holly	Bo Diddley
	Like Clockwork		Brown-Eyed Handsome Man
	Looking After No. 1		It Doesn't Matter Anymore
	Mary of the Fourth Form		Peggy Sue
Boo Radleys	Wake Up Boo!		Rave On
Boris Gardiner	Elizabethan Reggae		Wishing
	I Want to Wake Up with You (1)	Buffy Sainte-Marie	Soldier Blue
Bound 4 Da Reload	Oxide and Neutrino (1)	Burl Ives	A Little Bitty Tear (9)
Bow Wow Wow	Go Wild in the Country	B.A. Robertson	Bang Bang
Boxtops	Cry Like a Baby		Knocked It Off
	The Letter		To Be or Not to Be
Boy George	Everything I Own (1)	B.B.E.	Flash
Boy Meets Girl	Waiting for a Star to Fall	B*witched	Blame It on the Weatherman (1)
Boyz II Men	End of the Road (1)		C'est la Vie (1)
Boyzone	All That I Need (1)		Rollercoaster (1)
	A Different Beat		To You I Belong (1)
	Father and Son	Candi Staton	Nights on Broadway
	Isn't It a Wonder		Young Hearts Run Free
	Key to My Life	Cappella	U Got 2 Know
	No Matter What (1)	Cardigans	Lovefool
	When the Going Gets Tough (1)	Carl Douglas	Kung Fu Fighting (1)
	Words (1)	Carl Malcolm	Fattie Bum Bum
	You Needed Me (1)	Carl Perkins	Blue Suede Shoes (10)
Boz Scaggs	What Can I Say	Carly Simon	Coming Around Again
Bread	Baby I'm a Want You		Nobody Does It Better (7)
	Make It with You		Why (10)
Break Machine	Breakdance Party		You're So Vain (3)
	Street Dance	Carole Bayer Sager	You're Moving Out Today
Breathe	Hands to Heaven	Carole King	It Might As Well Rain Until September
Brenda Lee	All Alone Am I		
	As Usual		It's Too Late
	I Want to Be Wanted	Cast	Free Me
	Losing You		Guiding Star
	Rockin' around the Christmas Tree	Cat Stevens	I'm Gonna Get Me a Gun
			Lady D'Arbanville
	Speak to Me Pretty		Matthew and Son (2)
	Sweet Nothin's		Morning Has Broken
Brian Hyland	Itsy Bitsy Teeny Weeny Yellow Polka Dot Bikini (8)	Catatonia	Mulder and Scully
			Road Rage
	Sealed with a Kiss (3)	Caterina Valente	The Breeze and I (5)
Brian May	Driven by You	Catherine Zeta Jones	For All Time
	Too Much Love Will Kill You	Cathy Dennis	Touch Me (All Night Long)
Brian Poole and the Tremeloes	Candy Man (6)	Ce Ce Peniston	Finally
	Do You Love Me (1)		Keep On Walkin'
	Twist and Shout (4)		We Got a Love Thang
Britney Spears	Baby One More Time (1)	Celine Dion	Only One Road
	Born to Make You Happy (1)		My Heart Will Go On (1)
	Oops I Did It Again (1)		Think Twice (1)
Bruce Ruffin	Mad about You	Celine Dion and Peabo Bryson	Beauty and the Beast
	Rain		
Bruce Springsteen	Born in the USA/I'm On Fire	Chad Jackson	Hear the Drummer
	Dancing in the Dark	Chaka Demus and Pliers	Tease Me
	Santa Claus Is Coming to Town (9)		
		Chaka Demus, Pliers, Jack Radics and Taxi Gang	Twist and Shout (1)
	Streets of Philadelphia		
Bruce Willis	Respect Yourself (7)		
	Under the Boardwalk (2)	Chaka Khan	I Feel for You (1)
Bryan Adams	Everything I Do I Do It for You		I'm Every Woman (8)
	Please Forgive Me	Charlatans	How High
	Run to You (11)		North Country Boy
	Thought I'd Died and Gone To Heaven	Charles and Eddie	Would I Lie to You (1)
		Charles McDevitt Skiffle and Nancy Whiskey	Freight Train
Bryan Adams, Rod Stewart and Sting	All for Love		

M
U
S
I
C

P
O
P

Group/Artiste	Title	Group/Artiste	Title
Craig Douglas	A Hundred Pounds of Clay	Damien	The Time Warp
	Only Sixteen (1)	Damned	Eloise (3)
	Pretty Blue Eyes	Dan Hartman	Instant Replay (8)
Craig McLachlan and Check 1-2	Mona	Dana	All Kinds of Everything
			It's Gonna Be a Cold Cold Christmas
Cranberries	Linger		Please Tell Him That I Said Hello
	Zombie		
Crash Test Dummies	MMM MMM MMM MMM		Who Put the Lights Out
Cream	Badge	Dannii Minogue	Jump to the Beat
	White Room		Love and Kisses
Creedence Clearwater Revival	Bad Moon Rising		This Is It
	Proud Mary	Danny and the Juniors	At the Hop
	Up Around the Bend	Danny Kaye	Wonderful Copenhagen
Crew Cuts	Earth Angel	Danny Mirror	I Remember Elvis Presley
Crickets	Don't Ever Change	Danny Williams	Moon River (1)
	Maybe Baby		Wonderful World of the Young
	Oh Boy	Danny Wilson	Mary's Prayer
	That'll Be the Day	Dario G	Sunchyme
Crispian St Peters	Pied Piper	Darts	Boy from New York City
	You Were on My Mind		Come Back My Love
Crosby, Stills and Nash	Marrakesh Express		Daddy Cool (6)
Crowd	Ferry 'Cross the Mersey		Duke of Earl
Crowded House	Weather with You		It's Raining
Crown Heights Affair	You Gave Me Love	Daryl Hall and John Oates	Maneater
Crusaders featuring Joe Cocker	I'm So Glad I'm Standing Here Today	Dave and Ansil Collins	Double Barrel
Crusaders (and Randy Crawford uncredited)	Street Life		Monkey Spanner
Crystal Gayle	Don't It Make My Brown Eyes Blue	Dave Berry	The Crying Game
			Little Things
Crystals	Da Doo Ron Ron	Dave Clark Five	Catch Us If You Can
	Then He Kissed Me		Everybody Knows
Crystal Waters	Gypsy Woman (La Da Dee)		Red Balloon
Cufflinks	Tracy	Dave Davies	Death of a Clown
	When Julie Comes Around	Dave Dee, Dozy, Beaky, Mick and Tich	Bend It
Cult	She Sells Sanctuary		Hideaway
Culture Beat	Mr Vain (1)		Hold Tight
Culture Club	Church of the Poison Mind		Last Night in Soho
	Do You Really Want To Hurt Me		Legend of Xanadu
	It's a Miracle		Okay!
	Karma Chameleon		Save Me
	The Medal Song		Zabadak!
	Move Away	Dave Edmunds	Baby I Love You
	Time (Clock of the Heart)		Born to Be with You
	Victims		Girls Talk
	The War Song		I Hear You Knocking
Cupid's Inspiration	Yesterday Has Gone		Queen of Hearts
Cure	The Caterpillar	Dave Edmunds and the Stray Cats	The Race Is On
	Friday I'm in Love	Dave King featuring the Keynotes	Memories Are Made of This (5)
	High		
	The Love Cats	Dave Stewart (and Colin Blunstone)	What Becomes of the Broken Hearted (13)
	Lullaby		
Curiosity Killed the Cat	Down to Earth	Dave Stewart with Barbara Gaskin	It's My Party (1)
	Misfit		
	Hang on in There Baby	David and Jonathan	Lovers of the World Unite
Curtis Mayfield	Move On Up	David A. Stewart (& Candy Dulfer)	Lily Was Here
Curtis Stigers	I Wonder Why		
	You're all That Matters to Me	David Bowie	Absolute Beginners (2)
Curved Air	Back Street Luv		Ashes To Ashes (1)
Cutting Crew	Died in Your Arms (I Just)		Blue Jean (6)
Cyndi Lauper	Girls Just Want to Have Fun		Boys Keep Swinging (7)
	Hey Now (Girls Just Want to Have Fun)		China Girl (2)
			Drive-In Saturday (3)
	I Drove All Night (7)		Fame (17)
	Time after Time		Fashion (5)
	True Colours		Golden Years (8)
C.W. McCall	Convoy		The Jean Genie (2)
Daft Punk	Around the World		John I'm Only Dancing (12)
Damage	Love Guaranteed		

Group/Artiste	Title	Group/Artiste	Title
	Jump They Say		Hysteria
	The Laughing Gnome (6)		Let's Get Rocked
	Let's Dance (1)		When Love and Hate Collide
	Life on Mars (3)	Del Amitri	When You Were Young
	Modern Love (2)	Del Shannon	Hats Off to Larry
	Rebel Rebel (5)		Hey Little Girl
	Sorrow (3)		Keep Searchin'
	Sound and Vision (3)		Little Town Flirt
	Space Oddity (1)		Runaway (1)
	Starman (10)		So Long Baby
David Bowie and	Peace on Earth – Little		Swiss Maid
Bing Crosby	Drummer Boy		Two Kinds of Teardrop
David Bowie and	Dancing in the Street (1)	Demis Roussos	Happy to Be on an Island in the
Mick Jagger			Sun
David Dundas	Jeans On		The Roussos Phenomenon (1)
David Essex	Gonna Make You a Star (1)		When Forever Has Gone (2)
	Hold Me Close (1)	Deniece Williams	Free (1)
	Lamplight		That's What Friends Are For (8)
	Oh What a Circus	Denise La Salle	My Toot Toot
	Rock On	Dennis Waterman and	What Are We Gonna Get 'Er
	Rollin' Stone	George Cole	Indoors (21)
	Silver Dream Machine	Dennis Waterman and	
	Stardust	His Band	I Could Be So Good for You (3)
	Tahiti	Deodato	Also Sprach Zarathustra
	A Winter's Tale	Depeche Mode	Enjoy the Silence
David Parton	Isn't She Lovely		Everything Counts
David Ruffin	Walk Away from Love		I Feel You
David Soul	Don't Give Up on Us (1)		Just Can't Get Enough
	Going in with My Eyes Open (2)		Master and Servant
	Let's Have a Quiet Night In (8)		People Are People
	Silver Lady (1)		See You
David Whitfield	Answer Me (1)	Desireless	Voyage Voyage
	Bridge of Sighs (3)	Desmond Dekker	You Can Get It If You Really
David Whitfield and	Cara Mia (1)		Want
Mantovani Orchestra		Desmond Dekker	Israelites
Dawn	Candida	and the Aces	It Miek
	Knock Three Times	Des O'Connor	1-2-3 O'Leary
Dawn featuring	Tie A Yellow Ribbon Round the		Careless Hands
Tony Orlando	Old Oak Tree		Dick-A-Dum-Dum (King's Road)
	What Are You Doing Sunday		I Pretend (1)
Dawn Penn	You Don't Love Me	Des'ree	You Gotta Be
De Barge	Rhythm of the Night	Destiny's Child	Independent Women (1)
De La Soul	The Magic Number	Detroit Emeralds	Feel the Need in Me
	Ring Ring Ring	Detroit Spinners	Cupid – I've Loved You for a
Deacon Blue	Four Bacharach and David		Long Time
	Songs (EP)		Ghetto Child
	Real Gone Kid		Working My Way Back to You
Dead End Kids	Have I the Right (6)	Dexy's Midnight	Because of You
Dead or Alive	You Spin Me Round	Runners	Come on Eileen (1)
Dean Friedman	Lucky Stars		Geno (1)
Dean Martin	Gentle on My Mind		Jackie Wilson Said
	Let Me Go Lover (3)		There There My Dear
	Memories Are Made of This (1)	Diamonds	Little Darlin'
	Naughty Lady of Shady Lane	Diana King	Shy Guy
	Return to Me	Diana Ross	Ain't No Mountain High Enough
	Sway		All of My Life
	That's Amore		Chain Reaction (1)
	Volare (2)		I'm Still Waiting (1)
Debbie Gibson	Foolish Beat		Love Hangover
	Shake Your Love		My Old Piano
Debbie Reynolds	Tammy (2)		Reach Out and Touch
Deborah Harry	French Kissin' in the USA		Remember Me
Deborah Harry and	Well Did You Evah!		Theme from Mahogany
Iggy Pop			Touch Me in the Morning
Dee C. Lee	See the Day		Upside Down
Dee D. Jackson	Automatic Lover		When You Tell Me That You
Deee-Lite	Groove Is in the Heart		Love Me (2)
Deep Blue Something	Breakfast at Tiffanys (1)		Why Do Fools Fall in Love (4)
Deep Purple	Black Night		Work That Body
	Strange Kind of Woman	Diana Ross and Julio	All of You
Def Leppard	Animal	Iglesias	

Group/Artiste	Title	Group/Artiste	Title
Diana Ross and Lionel Richie	Endless Love		Breakfast on Pluto Rosie
Diana Ross and Marvin Gaye	You Are Everything	Don Robertson Donald Peers	The Happy Whistler Please Don't Go
Diana Ross and Michael Jackson	Ease On Down the Road	Donna Allen	Joy and Pain Serious
Diana Ross and the Supremes	Reflections (5)	Donna Summer	I Feel Love (1) Love to Love You Baby
Diana Ross and the Supremes with The Temptations	I'm Gonna Make You Love Me (3)	Donnie Elbert Donny and Marie Osmond	Macarthur Park (5) Where Did Our Love Go? (8) I'm Leaving It All up to You Morning Side of the Mountain
Diana Ross, Marvin Gaye, Smokey Robinson, Stevie Wonder	Pops We Love You	Donny Osmond	Puppy Love (1) Too Young (5) The Twelfth of Never (1)
Diane Decker	Poppa Piccolino		When I Fall in Love
Dickie Valentine	Christmas Alphabet (1) Christmas Island (8)		Why (3) Young Love (1)
Dickie Valentine and the Stargazers	Finger of Suspicion (1)	Donovan	Catch the Wind Colours
Dickies	Banana Splits		Jennifer Juniper
Dina Carroll	Don't Be a Stranger		Mellow Yellow
Dion	The Wanderer		Sunshine Superman
Dion and the Belmonts	A Teenager in Love (28)	Doobie Brothers	There Is a Mountain Listen to the Music
Dionne Warwick	All the Love in the World (10)	Dooleys	The Chosen Few Love of My Life
	Do You Know the Way to San José	Doop	Wanted Doop (1)
	Heartbreaker (2)	Doors	Hello I Love You
	Walk On By (9)		Light My Fire (7)
Dionne Warwick and Friends	That's What Friends Are For	Doris Day	Riders on the Storm Black Hills of Dakota
Dire Straits	Brothers in Arms		My Love and Devotion
	Money for Nothing		Secret Love (1)
	Private Investigations		Whatever Will Be Will Be (1)
	Romeo and Juliet	Doris Day and Frankie Laine	Sugarbush
	So Far Away		
	Sultans of Swing	Doris Day and Johnnie Ray	Let's Walk That-A-Way
	Tunnel of Love	Double	The Captain of her Heart
	Walk of Life	Doug E. Fresh and Get Fresh Crew	The Show
	Your Latest Trick		
Disco Tex and the Sex-O-Lettes	Get Dancing	Dr Alban D-Ream	It's My Life Things Can Only Get Better (1)
Divinyls	I Touch Myself		U R the Best Thing
Dixie Cups	Iko Iko (23)	Dreamweavers	It's Almost Tomorrow (1)
DJ Quicksilver	Bellissima	Drifters	At the Club
D Mob	It Is Time to Get Funky		Come On over to My Place
	Put Your Hands Together		Down on the Beach Tonight
	We Call It Acieed		Kissin' in the Back Row of the Movies
DNA	Tom's Diner		Like Sister and Brother
Doctor and the Medics	Spirit in the Sky (1)		Save the Last Dance for Me There Goes My First Love
Doctor and the Medics featuring Roy Wood	Waterloo		You're More Than a Number in My Little Red Book
Dollar	I Wanna Hold Your Hand	Dr Feelgood	Milk and Alcohol
	Love's Gotta Hold on Me	Dr Hook	A Little Bit More
	Mirror Mirror		Better Love Next Time
	O L'Amour		If Not You
Dolly Parton	Jolene (7)		Sexy Eyes
Domenico Modugno	Volare (10)		Sylvia's Mother
Don Cornell	Hold My Hand		When You're in Love With a Beautiful Woman
Don Fardon	Indian Reservation		
Don Henley	The Boys of Summer	Duane Eddy	Ballad of Paladin
Don Lang	Witch Doctor	Duane Eddy and the Rebelettes	Boss Guitar
Don McLean	American Pie (2)		Dance with the Guitar Man
	Crying (1)		Play Me Like You Play Your Guitar
	Vincent (1)		
Don Pablo's Animals	Venus (4)		
Don Partridge	Blue Eyes		

Group/Artiste	Title
Duane Eddy and the Rebels	Pepe
	Peter Gunn Theme (6)
	Shazam!
	Theme from Dixie
Dubliners	Black Velvet Band
	Seven Drunken Nights
Duke Ellington	Skin Deep (7)
Dunblane	Knockin' On Heaven's Door (1)
Duran Duran	A View to a Kill
	All She Wants Is
	Girls on Film
	Hungry Like the Wolf
	Is There Something I Should Know (1)
	Notorious
	Ordinary World
	The Reflex (1)
	Rio
	Save a Prayer
	Union of the Snake
	Wild Boys
Dusty Springfield	I Close My Eyes and Count to Ten
	I Just Don't Know What to Do with Myself
	In the Middle of Nowhere
	I Only Want to Be with You
	You Don't Have to Say You Love Me (1)
Eagles	Hotel California
	Lyin' Eyes
	Take It to the Limit
Eamonn Andrews	Shifting Whispering Sands
Earth, Wind and Fire	After the Love Has Gone
	Let's Groove
	September
Earth Wind and Fire with the Emotions	Boogie Wonderland
Eartha Kitt	Under the Bridges of Paris
Eartha Kitt and Bronski Beat	Cha Cha Heels
East of Eden	Jig a Jig
East 17	Deep
	House of Love
	It's Alright
	Stay Another Day (1)
	West End Girls
East Side Beat	Ride Like the Wind
Easybeats	Friday on My Mind (6)
Echo and the Bunnymen	The Cutter
	The Killing Moon
Eddie and the Hotrods	Do Anything You Wanna Do
Eddie Calvert	Cherry Pink and Apple Blossom White (1)
Eddie Cochran	C'Mon Everybody (6)
	Summertime Blues
	Three Steps To Heaven
Eddie Fisher	Oh My Papa
	Outside of Heaven (1)
Eddie Fisher with Sally Sweetland	I'm Walking behind You
Eddie Holman	Lonely Girl
Eddy Arnold	Make the World Go Away
Eddy Grant	Electric Avenue
	Gimme Hope Jo'anna
	I Don't Wanna Dance (1)
Edelweiss	Bring Me Edelweiss
Eden Kane	Get Lost
	Well I Ask You (1)
Edison Lighthouse	Love Grows (1)

Group/Artiste	Title
Edmund Hockridge	Young and Foolish
Edwin Hawkins Singers and Dorothy Morrison	Oh Happy Day
Edwin Starr	H.A.P.P.Y. Radio
	War (3)
Eiffel 65	Blue (Da Ba Dee)
Eighth Wonder	I'm Not Scared
808 State	Cubik
	In Yer Face
	Pacific
808 State featuring Björk	Ooops
808 State versus UB40	One in Ten
Elaine Paige	Memory
Elaine Paige and Barbara Dickson	I Know Him So Well (1)
Electric Light Orchestra	10538 Overture
	Evil Woman
	Hold On Tight
	Mr Blue Sky
	Roll Over Beethoven (6)
	Telephone Line
Electric Light Orchestra Part 2	Honest Men
Electronic	Disappointed
Elgins	Get the Message
	Heaven Must Have Sent You
Elias and his Zigzag Jive Flutes	Tom Hark (2)
Ella Fitzgerald	Swingin' Shepherd Blues
Elmer Bernstein	Staccato's Theme
Elton John	Bennie and the Jets
	The Bitch Is Back
	Blue Eyes
	Candle In the Wind (1)
	Crocodile Rock
	Goodbye Yellow Brick Road
	Honky Cat
	I Guess That's Why They Call It The Blues
	I'm Still Standing
	Island Girl
	Lucy In the Sky With Diamonds
	Nikita
	Part Time Love
	Passengers
	Pinball Wizard (7)
	Rocket Man
	Sacrifice (1)
	Sad Songs (Say So Much)
	Saturday Night's Alright for Fighting
	Song for Guy
	The One
	Your Song
Elton John and Cliff Richard	Slow Rivers
Elton John and Eric Clapton	Runaway Train
Elton John and Kiki Dee	Don't Go Breaking My Heart
	True Love (2)
Elton John and Marcella Detroit	Ain't Nothing Like the Real Thing
Elton John and Millie Jackson	Act of War
Elton John Band	Philadelphia Freedom
Elton John, J. Lennon and Muscle Shoals Horns	I Saw Her Standing There (40)

MUSIC POP

Group/Artiste	Title	Group/Artiste	Title
Elvis Costello	A Good Year for the Roses		Sometimes
	I Can't Stand Up for Falling Down		Victims of Love
		Eric Clapton	Layla
	New Amsterdam		Tears in Heaven
	Oliver's Army	Erma Franklin	Piece of My Heart
	Watching the Detectives	Eruption	I Can't Stand the Rain
Elvis Presley	All Shook Up (1)		One Way Ticket
	Are You Lonesome Tonight (1)	Esther and Abi Ofarim	Cinderella Rockefella (1)
	Crying in the Chapel (1)	Esther Phillips	What a Difference a Day Made
	Devil in Disguise (1)	Eternal	Angel of Mine
	A Fool Such As I (1)		I Am Blessed
	Girl of My Best Friend (9)		Stay
	Good Luck Charm (1)	Eternal featuring Bebe Winans	I Wanna Be the Only One (1)
	Heartbreak Hotel (2)		
	His Latest Flame (1)	Europe	The Final Countdown
	Hound Dog (2)	Eurythmics	Here Comes the Rain Again
	In the Ghetto (2)		Love Is a Stranger
	It's Now or Never (1)		Right by Your Side
	Jailhouse Rock (1)		Sexcrime (Nineteen Eighty-Four)
	My Boy (5)		
	My Way (9)		Sweet Dreams (Are Made of This)
	One Night (1)		
	Return to Sender (1)		There Must Be an Angel (1)
	Rock A Hula Baby (1)		Thorn in My Side
	She's Not You (1)		Who's That Girl?
	Surrender (1)	Eurythmics and Aretha Franklin	Sisters Are Doin' It For Themselves
	Suspicious Minds (2)		
	Way Down (1)	Evelyn 'Champagne' King	Love Come Down
	The Wonder of You (1)		
	Wooden Heart (1)	Evelyn Thomas	High Energy
Emerson, Lake and Palmer	Fanfare for the Common Man	Everly Brothers	All I Have to Do Is Dream (1)
			Bird Dog
EMF	I Believe (6)		Bye Bye Love
	Unbelievable		Cathy's Clown (1)
Emile Ford and the Checkmates	On a Slow Boat to China		I Kissed You
	What Do You Want to Make Those Eyes at Me For (1)		Problems
			Take a Message to Mary
Eminem (Marshal Mathers)	Stan (1)		Temptation (1)
	The Real Slim Shady (1)		Wake Up Little Suzie
Emma Bunton	What Took You So Long (1)		Walk Right Back (1)
Emotions	Best of My Love	Everything but the Girl	I Don't Want to Talk about It
Englebert Humperdinck	The Last Waltz		Missing
	Les Bicyclettes de Belsize		New York
	Release Me (1)	Eydie Gormé	Yes My Darling Daughter
	There Goes My Everything	FAB	Thunderbirds Are Go
England World Cup Squad (1970)	Back Home (1)	Faces	Cindy Incidentally
			Pool Hall Richard
England World Cup Squad (1982)	This Time		Stay With Me
		Fair Weather	Natural Sinner
Englandneworder	World in Motion (1)	Fairground Attraction	Find My Love
Enigma	Return to Innocence		Perfect (1)
	Sadness Part 1 (1)	Faith No More	I'm Easy
Ennio Morricone	Chi Mai		Midlife Crisis
En Vogue	Free Your Mind	Falco	Rock Me Amadeus (1)
	Give It Up, Turn It Loose		Vienna Calling
	Hold On (5)	Fame and Price Together	Rosetta
	My Lovin'		
Enya	Anywhere Is	Family	Burlesque
	Book of Days		In My Own Time
	Orinoco Flow (1)	Family Dogg	Way of Life
Equals	Baby Come Back (1)	Family Stand	Ghetto Heaven
	Black Skin Blue Eyed Boys	Fantastics	Something Old, Something New
	Viva Bobby Joe	Far Corporation	Stairway to Heaven (8)
Erasure	Abba-Esque (1)	Farley 'Jackmaster' Funk	Love Can't Turn Around
	Always		
	Blue Savannah	Farm	All Together Now
	Breath of Life		Groovy Train
	The Circus	Faron Young	It's Four in the Morning
	A Little Respect	Fat Boys and Chubby Checker	The Twist (Yo, Twist)
	Love to Hate You		
	Ship of Fools		

Group/Artiste	Title
Fat Boys and the Beach Boys (2)	Wipeout (2)
Fat Boy Slim	Praise You (1)
Fat Larry's Band	Zoom
Father Abraham and the Smurfs	The Smurf Song
Father Abraphart and the Smurps (Jonathan King)	Lick a Smurp for Christmas
Fatima Mansions	I Do It for You
Fats Domino	Ain't That a Shame
	Blueberry Hill
Feargal Sharkey	A Good Heart (1)
	You Little Thief
Felix	Don't You Want Me (6)
Fern Kinney	Together We Are Beautiful (1)
Ferrante and Teicher	Theme from Exodus
Ferry Aid	Let It Be (1)
Fiddler's Dram	Day Trip to Bangor
Fine Young Cannibals	Good Thing
	Johnny Come Home
	She Drives Me Crazy
	Suspicious Minds (8)
Firm	Arthur Daley (E's Alright)
	Star Trekkin' (1)
First Choice	Smarty Pants
Five	Keep on Moving (1)
Five and Queen	We Will Rock You (1)
Five Star	Can't Wait Another Minute
	Rain or Shine
	The Slightest Touch
	System Addict
5000 Volts	Dr Kiss Kiss
	I'm on Fire
Flash and the Pan	Waiting For a Train
Fleetwood Mac	Albatross (1)
	Green Manalishi (with the Two-Prong Crown)
	Little Lies
	Man of the World
	Oh Well
	Seven Wonders
Fleetwoods	Come Softly to Me
Floaters	Float On
A Flock of Seagulls	Wishing (If I Had a Photograph of You)
Flowerpot Men	Let's Go to San Francisco
Floyd Cramer	On the Rebound
Floyd Robinson	Makin' Love (9)
Flying Lizards	Money (5)
Flying Pickets	Only You (1)
	When You're Young and in Love (7)
Foo Fighters	Monkey Wrench
Foreigner	I Want to Know What Love Is (1)
	Waiting for a Girl Like You
Forrest	Rock the Boat
Fortunes	Here It Comes Again
	Storm in a Teacup
	You've Got Your Troubles
49'ers	Touch Me (3)
Foundations	Baby Now That I've Found You
	Build Me Up Buttercup
	In the Bad Bad Old Days
Four Aces	Mr Sandman
Four Aces featuring Al Roberts	Love Is a Many-Splendored Thing
Four Knights	I Get So Lonely
Fourmost	Hello Little Girl

Group/Artiste	Title
4 Non Blondes	What's Up
Four Pennies	Juliet (1)
Four Preps	Big Man
Four Seasons	Big Girls Don't Cry
	Sherry
	Silver Star
	Walk Like a Man
Four Seasons with Frankie Valli	Workin' My Way Back to You
Four Seasons with Sound of Frankie Valli	Let's Hang On
	Rag Doll
Four Tops	Bernadette
	If I Were a Carpenter
	It's the Same Old Song
	Loco in Acapulco
	Reach Out I'll Be There
	Standing in the Shadows of Love
	Walk Away Renee
Four Tops featuring Smokey Robinson	Indestructible
Fox	Only You Can
	S-S-S-Single Bed
Foxy Brown	I'll Be
Fragma	Toca's Miracle
Frank Ifield	Confessin' (1)
	I Remember You (1)
	Lovesick Blues (1)
	Wayward Wind (1)
Frank Sinatra	All the Way
	High Hopes
	Love and Marriage
	Strangers in the Night (1)
	The Tender Trap
	Theme from New York, New York
	Three Coins in the Fountain (1)
Frank Sinatra and Sammy Davis Jr	Me and My Shadow
Frankie Goes to Hollywood	The Power of Love (1)
	Rage Hard
	Relax (1)
	Two Tribes
	Welcome to the Pleasuredome
Frankie Laine	Answer Me (1)
	Hawkeye
	Hey Joe (1)
	High Noon
	I Believe (1)
	Rawhide
	Woman in Love, A (1)
Frankie Laine and the Four Lads	Rain Rain Rain
Frankie Lymon and the Teenagers	Baby Baby
Frankie Miller	Darlin'
Frankie Valli	Grease (3)
	My Eyes Adored You
Frankie Valli and the Four Seasons	December '63 (Oh What a Night) (1)
Frankie Vaughan	Garden of Eden (1)
	Green Door (2)
	Loop-De-Loop (5)
	Tower of Strength (1)
Frankie Vaughan and the Kaye Sisters	Gotta Have Something in the Bank Frank (8)
Frantique	Strut Your Funky Stuff
F.R. David	Words (2)
Freak Power	Turn On Tune In Cop Out

M
U
S
I
C

P
O
P

Group/Artiste	Title	Group/Artiste	Title
Fred Wedlock	Oldest Swinger In Town	Gene Pitney	I'm Gonna Be Strong
Freda Payne	Band of Gold (1)		Just One Smile
Freddie and the Dreamers	If You Gotta Make a Fool of Somebody		Looking Through the Eyes of Love (3)
	I'm Telling You Now		Princess in Rags
	I Understand		Something's Gotten Hold of My Heart (5)
	You Were Made for Me		That Girl Belongs to Yesterday
Freddie Mercury	The Great Pretender (4)		Twenty-Four Hours from Tulsa
	In My Defence	Genesis	Abacab
	Living on My Own (1)		Follow You Follow Me
	Love Kills		I Can't Dance
Freddie Mercury and Montserrat Caballe	Barcelona		Invisible Touch (Live)
			No Son of Mine
Freddie Starr	It's You (9)		Turn It On Again
Free	All Right Now	Gene Vincent	Be Bop A Lula
	My Brother Jake	Geordie	All Because of You
	Wishing Well (7)	George Baker Selection	Paloma Blanca
Freez	I.O.U.		
Fresh 4 featuring Lizz E	Wishing on a Star	George Benson	Give Me the Night
			In Your Eyes
Frijid Pink	House of the Rising Sun (4)	George Harrison	Bangladesh
Fugees	Killing Me Softly (1)		Give Me Love
	Ready or Not (1)		Got My Mind Set on You
	Rumble in the Jungle		My Sweet Lord (1)
Full Force	Alice I Want You Just for Me	George McCrae	It's Been So Long
Fun Boy Three	The Lunatics (Have Taken Over the Asylum)		Rock Your Baby (1)
		George Michael	Careless Whisper (1)
	Our Lips Are Sealed		A Different Corner (1)
	Tunnel of Love		Faith
Fun Boy Three and Bananarama	It Ain't What You Do ...		Fast Love (1)
			Funky
Funk Masters	It's Over (8)		I Want Your Sex
Funkadelic	One Nation under a Groove		Jesus to a Child (1)
Funky Worm	U + Me = Love		One More Try
Gabrielle	Dreams (1)		Praying for Time
	Rise (1)		Star People 97
Gala	Freed from Desire		You Have Been Loved (2)
Galaxy featuring Phil Fearon	Dancing Tight	George Michael and Elton John	Don't Let the Sun Go Down on Me (1)
Gallagher and Lyle	Heart on My Sleeve	George Michael, Queen, Lisa Stansfield	Five Live (1)
	I Wanna Stay With You		
Gap Band	Big Fun		
	Oops Up Side Your Head	Georghe Zamfir	Light of Experience (Doina De Jale)
Gary Barlow	Forever Love (1)		
	Love Won't Wait (1)	Georgie Fame	Ballad of Bonnie and Clyde
Gary Clail On-U Sound System	Human Nature		Get Away
			Yeh Yeh
Gary Glitter	Always Yours (1)	Gerard Kenny	New York, New York (43)
	Another Rock and Roll Christmas	Geri Halliwell	Bag It Up (1)
			Lift Me Up (1)
	Doing Alright with the Boys		Mi Chico Latino (1)
	I Love You Love Me Love (1)	Gerry Monroe	My Prayer
	I'm the Leader of the Gang (1)		Sally
		Gerry Rafferty	Baker Street
	Rock and Roll (Parts 1 & 2)		Night Owl
Gary Miller	Robin Hood	Gerry and The Pacemakers	Don't Let the Sun Catch You Crying
Gary Mills	Look For a Star		
Gary Moore	Parisienne Walkways		Ferry across the Mersey
Gary Moore and Phil Lynott	Out in the Fields		How Do You Do It? (1)
			I Like It (1)
Gary Numan	Cars (1)		I'm the One
	Complex		You'll Never Walk Alone (1)
	I Die: You Die	Gibson Brothers	Ooh! What a Life
	She's Got Claws		Que Sera Mi Vida (If You Should Go)
	We Are Glass		
	We Take Mystery	Gigliola Cinquetti	Go (Before You Break My Heart)
Gary Shearston	I Get a Kick out of You		
Gary 'US' Bonds	Quarter to Three	Gilbert O'Sullivan	Alone Again (Naturally)
Gary's Gang	Keep on Dancin' (8)		Clair (1)
Gazza	Geordie Boys (Gazza Rap)		Get Down (1)
Gazza and Lindisfarne	Fog on the Tyne (Revisited)		

Group/Artiste	Title
	No Matter How I Try
	Nothing Rhymed
	Ooh-Wakka-Doo-Wakka-Day
	Why Oh Why Oh Why
Gillan	Restless
	Trouble
Gillian Anderson (speaking)	Extremis
Gina G	Fresh
	Ooh Aah ... Just A Little Bit (1)
Giorgio Moroder and Phil Oakey	Together in Electric Dreams
Girlschool & Motorhead (aka Headgirl)	St Valentine's Day Massacre
Gladys Knight	Licence to Kill
Gladys Knight and the Pips	Best Thing That Ever Happened to Me
	Midnight Train to Georgia
	The Way We Were
Glen Frey	The Heat Is On
Glenn Medeiros	Nothing's Gonna Change My Love for You (1)
Glitter Band	Angel Face
	Goodbye My Love
Gloria Estefan	Cuts Both Ways
	Don't Wanna Lose You
	Go Away
Gloria Estefan and Miami Sound Machine	Anything for You
	Can't Stay Away from You
	1-2-3
	Rhythm Is Gonna Get You
Gloria Gaynor	I Will Survive
	Never Can Say Goodbye
Godley and Creme	Under Your Thumb
	Wedding Bells
Golden Earring	Radar Love
Goldie	Making Up Again
Goodies	Funky Gibbon
	The In Betweenies
Goombay Dance Band	Seven Tears (1)
Goons	Ying Tong Song
Gordon Lightfoot	If You Could Read My Mind
Go West	We Close Our Eyes
Grace Jones	Slave to the Rhythm
Gracie Fields	Around the World (8)
Graham Bonnet	Night Games
Grandmaster Flash and Melle Mel	White Lines (Don't Don't Do it)
Grandmaster Flash and The Furious Five	The Message
Grandmaster Flash, Melle Mel and Furious 5	Step Off (Part 1)
Grange Hill Cast	Just Say No
Green Jelly	Three Little Pigs
Greg Lake	I Believe in Father Christmas
Greyhound	Black and White
Grid	Swamp Thing
Gun	Race with the Devil
Guns N' Roses	Knockin' on Heaven's Door (2)
	Live and Let Die (5)
	Sweet Child O' Mine
Guru Josh	Infinity
Guy Mitchell	Chicka Boom
	Feet Up
	Look at That Girl (1)
	Pretty Little Black Eyed Susie
	Rock-A-Billy (1)
	She Wears Red Feathers (1)
	Singing the Blues (1)

Group/Artiste	Title
Guys and Dolls	There's a Whole Lot of Loving
Gwen Guthrie	Ain't Nothing Goin' On but the Rent
Haddaway	What Is Love
Haircut 100	Favourite Shirts (Boy Meets Girl)
	Love Plus One
	Nobody's Fool
Hale and Pace and the Stonkers	The Stonk (1)
Hamilton Bohannon	Disco Stomp
Hammer	Addams Groove
	U Can't Touch This
Hank Locklin	Please Help Me I'm Falling
Hank Mizell	Jungle Rock
Hanson	Mmm Bop (1)
Happy Mondays	Judge Fudge
	Kinky Afro
Harold Faltermeyer	Axel F
Harold Melvin and the Bluenotes	Don't Leave Me This Way (5)
	If You Don't Know Me By Now (9)
Harry Enfield	Loadsamoney (Doin' Up the House)
Harry J. All Stars	Liquidator
Harry Secombe	This Is My Song (2)
Hawkwind	Silver Machine
Hazell Dean	Searchin'
	Whatever I Do (Wherever I Go)
	Who's Leaving Who
Hazel O'Connor	D-Days
	Eighth Day
	Will You
Hear'say	Pure and Simple
Heart	All I Wanna Do Is Make Love to You
	You're the Voice (56)
Heatwave	Boogie Nights
Heaven 17	Temptation
Heavy D. and the Boyz	Now That We Found Love
Hedgehoppers Anonymous	It's Good News Week
Heinz	Just Like Eddie
Helen Reddy	Angie Baby
Helen Shapiro	Don't Treat Me Like a Child
	Little Miss Lonely
	Walkin' Back to Happiness (1)
	You Don't Know (1)
Hello	New York Groove
	Tell Him
Helmut Zacharias	Tokyo Melody
Henry Mancini	How Soon
Herb Alpert	Spanish Flea
	This Guy's in Love with You
Herbie Hancock	Rockit
Herd	From the Underworld
	Paradise Lost
Herman's Hermits	I'm into Something Good (1)
	No Milk Today
	Silhouettes
	Something's Happening
	Sunshine Girl
	There's a Kind of Hush
Highwaymen	Michael (1)
Hollies	The Air That I Breathe
	He Ain't Heavy, He's My Brother (1)
	I'm Alive (1)
	Jennifer Eccles

M
U
S
I
C

P
O
P

Group/Artiste	Title	Group/Artiste	Title
	Sorry Suzanne		Holy Smoke
	Stay (8)		Infinite Dreams
Holly Johnson	Americanos		Run to the Hills
	Love Train		2 Minutes to Midnight
Honeybus	I Can't Let Maggie Go	Isaac Hayes	Theme from 'Shaft'
Honeycombs	Have I the Right (1)	Isaac Hayes	Disco Connection
Horst Jankowski	A Walk in the Black Forest	Movement	
Hot Butter	Popcorn	Isley Brothers	Behind a Painted Smile
Hot Chocolate	Brother Louie		Harvest for the World (10)
	Emma		This Old Heart of Mine
	Every 1's a Winner	It Bites	Calling All the Heroes
	Girl Crazy	Ivor Biggun and the	Winker's Song (Misprint)
	I Believe (In Love)	Red Nosed Burglars	
	It Started with a Kiss	Ivy League	Funny How Love Can Be
	No Doubt About It		Tossing and Turning
	So You Win Again (1)	Jackie Dennis	La Dee Dah
	You Sexy Thing	Jackie Trent	Where Are You Now (1)
Hotlegs	Neanderthal Man	Jackie Wilson	Reet Petite (1)
Hotshots	Snoopy vs the Red Baron	Jack 'N' Chill	The Jack That House Built
Housemartins	Caravan Of Love (1)	Jackson 5	ABC
	Happy Hour		Blame It on the Boogie (8)
Howard Jones	Like to Get to Know You Well		I Want You Back
	Look Mama		I'll Be There
	New Song		The Love You Save
	Pearl in the Shell	Jacksons	Can You Feel It
	Things Can Only Get Better (6)		Show You the Way to Go (1)
	What Is Love	Jacksons, Mick Jagger	State Of Shock
Hudson-Ford	Pick Up the Pieces	and Michael Jackson	
Hue and Cry	Labour of Love	Jacky (Lee)	White Horses
	Looking for Linda	Jade	Don't Walk Away
Hues Corporation	Rock the Boat	Jaki Graham and	Could It Be I'm Falling in Love
Huey Lewis and the	The Power of Love (9)	David Grant	
News		Jam	Absolute Beginners (4)
Hugo Montenegro	The Good, the Bad and the		Beat Surrender (1)
	Ugly (1)		The Eton Rifles
Human League	Don't You Want Me (1)		Going Underground (1)
	Fascination		Start (1)
	Love Action		Town Called Malice (1)
	Mirror Man	James	She's a Star
	Open Your Heart		Sit Down
Humble Pie	Natural Born Bugie		Sound
Hurricane Smith	Don't Let It Die		Tomorrow
	Oh Babe What Would You Say?	James Brown	I'm Real
Ian Dury	Reasons to Be Cheerful (Part 3)	featuring Full Force	
	What a Waste	James Galway	Annie's Song (3)
Ian Dury and the	Hit Me With Your Rhythm Stick	James Ingram and	Somewhere Out There
Blockheads		Linda Ronstadt	
Iggy Pop	Real Wild Child (Wild One)	James Ingram and	Yah Mo B There
Ike and Tina Turner	Nutbush City Limits	Michael McDonald	
	River Deep Mountain High (3)	James Ingram and	Baby Come To Me
Imagination	Body Talk	Patti Austin	
	Just an Illusion	James Taylor	You've Got a Friend (4)
Incognito featuring	Always There	Jamiroquai	Alright
Jocelyn Brown			Blow Your Mind
Ini Kamoze	Here Comes the Hotstepper		Deeper Underground (1)
Inkspots	Melody of Love	Jan and Dean	Surf City
Inner Circle	Sweat (A La La La La Long)	Jan Hammer	Crockett's Theme
Inner City	Ain't Nobody Better		Miami Vice Theme
	Good Life	Jane Birkin and Serge	Je T'Aime... Moi Non Plus (1)
Inner City featuring	Big Fun	Gainsbourg	
Kevin Saunderson		Janet Jackson	Let's Wait Awhile
INXS	Elegantly Wasted		That's the Way Love Goes
	Need You Tonight		What Have You Done for Me
	Shining Star (EP)		Lately
	Suicide Blonde		When I Think of You
Iron Maiden	Be Quick or Be Dead	Janet Jackson	Got 'Til It's Gone
	Bring Your Daughter ... to the	featuring Q-Tip and	
	Slaughter (1)	Joni Mitchell	
	The Clairvoyant	Janet Kay	Silly Games
	The Evil That Men Do	Japan	Ghosts
	Fear of the Dark		I Second That Emotion

Group/Artiste	Title
Jason Donovan	Any Dream Will Do (1)
	Nothing Can Divide Us
	Sealed With a Kiss (1)
	Too Many Broken Hearts (1)
Jazzy Jeff and the Fresh Prince (Will Smith)	Boom! Shake the Room (1)
Jean-Michel Jarre	Oxygene Part IV
Jean-Michel Jarre featuring Hank Marvin	London Kid
Jeannie C. Riley	Harper Valley PTA
Jeff Beck	Hi-Ho Silver Lining
Jeff Beck and Rod Stewart	I've Been Drinking
Jeff Wayne's War of the Worlds	Eve of the War (3)
Jefferson	Colour of My Love
Jellybean featuring Elisa Fiorillo	Who Found Who
Jennifer Lopez	Love Don't Cost a Thing (1)
Jennifer Rush	The Power of Love, (1)
Jennifer Rush and Elton John	Flames of Paradise
Jermaine Jackson	Do What You Do
	Let's Get Serious
Jermaine Stewart	Say It Again
	We Don't Have To
Jerry Keller	Here Comes Summer (1)
Jerry Lee Lewis	Great Balls of Fire (1)
	Whole Lotta Shakin' Goin' On
Jesus and Mary Chain	April Skies
	Reverence
Jesus Jones	International Bright Young Thing Thing
Jesus Loves You (Boy George)	Bow Down Mister
Jet Harris and Tony Meehan	Applejack
	Diamonds
	Scarlett O'Hara
Jethro Tull	Life Is a Long Song
	Living in the Past
	Sweet Dream
	Teacher/The Witch's Promise
Jets	Crush on You
J. Geils Band	Centrefold
Jigsaw	Sky High
Jilted John	Jilted John
Jim Dale	Be My Girl
Jim Diamond	Hi Ho Silver
	I Should Have Known Better (1)
Jim Gilstrap	Swing Your Daddy
Jimi Hendrix	Hey Joe (6)
Jimi Hendrix Experience	All along the Watchtower
	Purple Haze
	Voodoo Chile (1)
	The Wind Cries Mary (6)
Jimmie Rodgers	English Country Garden (5)
	Kisses Sweeter Than Wine (7)
Jimmy Boyd	Tell Me a Story
Jimmy Cliff	Wild World
	Wonderful World Beautiful People
Jimmy Dean	Big Bad John
Jimmy Helms	Gonna Make You an Offer You Can't Refuse
Jimmy James and The Vagabonds	Now Is the Time
Jimmy Jones	Good Timin' (1)
	Handy Man

Group/Artiste	Title
Jimmy Justice	Ain't That Funny
	When My Little Girl Is Smiling
Jimmy Nail	Ain't No Doubt (1)
	Crocodile Shoes
	Love Don't Live Here Anymore (3)
Jimmy Parkinson	The Great Pretender (9)
Jimmy Ruffin	Farewell Is a Lonely Sound
	Hold on to My Love
	It's Wonderful
	What Becomes of the Broken Hearted (4)
Jimmy Somerville	To Love Somebody (8)
	You Make Me Feel
Jimmy Young	Chain Gang (9)
	Eternally
	The Man from Laramie (1)
	More (4)
	Unchained Melody (1)
Jim Reeves	Distant Drums (1)
	I Love You Because
	I Won't Forget You
	Welcome to My World
Jive Bunny and the Mastermixers	Let's Party (1)
	Swing the Mood (1)
	That's What I Like (1)
J. J. Barrie	No Charge
Jo Boxers	Boxer Beat
	Just Got Lucky
Jo Stafford	Make Love to Me (8)
	You Belong to Me (1)
Joan Armatrading	Love and Affection
Joan Baez	The Night They Drove Old Dixie Down
	There but for Fortune
Joan Collins Fan Club (Julian Clary)	Leader of the Pack
Joan Jett and the Blackhearts	I Love Rock 'N' Roll
Joan Regan with the Squadronaires	Ricochet
Joe Cocker	Delta Lady
	Unchain My Heart
	With a Little Help from My Friends (1)
Joe Cocker and Jennifer Warnes	Up Where We Belong
Joe Dolan	Make Me an Island
Joe Dolce Music Theatre	Shaddap You Face (1)
Joe Fagin	That's Livin' Alright
Joe Jackson	Is She Really Going Out with Him?
	It's Different for Girls
	Steppin' Out
Joe South	Games People Play
Joe Tex	Ain't Gonna Bump No More
John and Yoko and the Plastic Ono Band	Happy Xmas (War Is Over)
John Barry Orchestra	Hit and Miss
John Cooper Clarke	Gimmix! Play Loud
John Denver	Annie's Song (1)
John Farnham	You're the Voice (6)
John Fred and the Playboy Band	Judy in Disguise (with Glasses)
John Kongos	He's Gonna Step on You Again
	Tokoloshe Man
John Lennon	Imagine (1)
	Starting Over (1)
	Woman (1)

Group/Artiste	Title
John Lennon and the Plastic Ono Band	Power to the People
John Leyton	Johnny Remember Me (1)
	Wild Wind
John McEnroe, Pat Cash and Full Metal Rackets	Rock 'N' Roll (66)
John Miles	Music
Johnnie Ray	Just Walkin' in the Rain (1)
	Somebody Stole My Gal
	Such a Night (1)
	Yes Tonight Josephine (1)
Johnnie Ray and the Four Lads	Faith Can Move Mountains
Johnny and the Hurricanes	Beatnik Fly
	Down Yonder
	Red River Rock
	Rocking Goose
Johnny Dankworth	African Waltz
	Experiments with Mice
Johnny Duncan and the Blue Grass Boys	Last Train to San Fernando
Johnny Hates Jazz	Shattered Dreams
Johnny Johnson and the Bandwagon	Blame it On the Pony Express
	Breakin' Down the Walls of Heartache
	Sweet Inspiration
Johnny Keating	Theme from Z Cars
Johnny Kidd and the Pirates	I'll Never Get over You
	Shakin' All Over
Johnny Logan	Hold Me Now
	What's Another Year (1)
Johnny Mann Singers	Up Up and Away
Johnny Mathis	A Certain Smile
	I'm Stone in Love with You (10)
	When a Child is Born (1)
Johnny Mathis and Deniece Williams	Too Much too Little too Late
Johnny Nash	Cupid
	Hold Me Tight
	I Can See Clearly Now
	Tears on My Pillow (1)
	There Are More Questions Than Answers
	You Got Soul
Johnny Otis Show	Ma He's Making Eyes at Me (2)
Johnny Pearson	Sleepy Shores
Johnny Preston	Cradle of Love (2)
	Running Bear (1)
Johnny Tillotson	Poetry in Motion (1)
Johnny Wakelin	In Zaïre (4)
Johnny Wakelin and the Kinshasa Band	Black Superman (Muhammad Ali) (7)
John Otway and Wild Willy Barrett	Really Free
John Parr	St Elmo's Fire
John Paul Joans	Man from Nazareth
John Paul Young	Love Is in the Air
John Rowles	If I Only Had Time
Johnston Brothers	Hernando's Hideaway (1)
	Join In and Sing Again
	Oh Happy Day (4)
John Travolta	Sandy (2)
John Travolta and Olivia Newton-John	Summer Nights (1)
	You're the One That I Want (1)
John Waite	Missing You (9)
Jon and Vangelis	I Hear You Now
	I'll Find My Way Home
Jona Lewie	Stop the Cavalry
Jonathan King	Everyone's Gone to the Moon
	Una Paloma Blanca

Group/Artiste	Title
Jonathan Richman and the Modern Lovers	Egyptian Reggae
Joni Mitchell	Big Yellow Taxi
Jon Secada	Just Another Day (5)
Jose Feliciano	Light My Fire (6)
Jose Ferrer	Woman (7)
Joyce Sims	Come into My Life
Joy Division	Love Will Tear Us Apart
JT and the Big Family	Moments in Soul
Juan Martin	Love Theme from The Thorn Birds
Judas Priest	United
Judge Dread	Big Eight
	Big Seven
	Big Six
	Christmas in Dreadland
	Je t'Aime (9)
Judie Tzuke	Stay with Me Till Dawn
Judy Collins	Amazing Grace (No. 5 1970)
Judy Garland	The Man That Got Away
Julee Cruise	Falling
Julian Lennon	Saltwater
	Too Late For Goodbyes
	Valotte
Julie Covington	Don't Cry for Me Argentina (1)
Julie Driscoll, Brian Auger and the Trinity	This Wheel's on Fire
Julie Rogers	The Wedding
Julio Iglesias	Begin the Beguine (1)
Julio Iglesias and Willie Nelson	To All the Girls I've Loved Before
Junior	Mama Used to Say
Junior Walker and the All-Stars	Road Runner
Justified Ancients of Mu Mu	It's Grim Up North
Justin Hayward	Forever Autumn
Justin Hayward and John Lodge	Blue Guitar
Kajagoogoo	Big Apple
	Ooh to Be Ah
	Too Shy (1)
Kalin Twins	When (1)
Kaoma	Lambada
Karen Young	Nobody's Child
Karl Denver	Marcheta
	Mexicali Rose
	Never Goodbye
	Wimoweh
Kate Bush	Babooshka (5)
	Man with the Child in His Eyes (6)
	Running up That Hill (3)
	Wuthering Heights (1)
Kate Bush and Peter Gabriel	Don't Give Up (9)
Kate Robbins and Beyond	More Than in Love (2)
Kathy Kirby	Let Me Go Lover (10)
	Secret Love (4)
Katrina and the Waves	Love Shine a Light
	Walking on Sunshine
Kaye Sisters	Paper Roses (7)
Kay Starr	Comes A-Long A-Love (1)
	Rock and Roll Waltz (1)
	Side By Side
KC and the Sunshine Band	Give It Up (1)
	Please Don't Go (3)
	Queen of Clubs
	That's the Way (I Like It)

Group/Artiste	Title
kd lang	Constant Craving
Keith Michell	Captain Beaky
Keith West	Excerpt from a Teenage Opera
Kelly Marie	Feels Like I'm in Love (1)
Ken Barrie	Postman Pat
Ken Boothe	Everything I Own
Ken Dodd	Happiness
	Love Is Like a Violin
	Promises
	The River
	Tears (1)
Kenny	The Bump
	Fancy Pants
Kenny Ball and his Jazzmen	March of the Siamese Children
	Midnight in Moscow
Kenny Everett	Snot Rap
Kenny Loggins	Footloose
Kenny Lynch	Stand by Me (39)
	Up on the Roof (10)
	You Can Never Stop Me Loving You
Kenny Rogers	Coward of the County (1)
	Lucille (1)
Kenny Rogers and Dolly Parton	Islands in the Stream
Kenny Rogers and Sheena Easton	We've Got Tonight
Kenny Rogers and the First Edition	Ruby Don't Take Your Love to Town
Kenny Thomas	Thinking about Your Love
Kershaw, Brookes, Jive Bunny and Londonbeat	It Takes Two Baby (53)
Ketty Lester	Love Letters (4)
Kevin Keegan	Head over Heels in Love
Kevin the Gerbil	Summer Holiday (50)
Kicks Like a Mule	The Bouncer
Kid Creole and the Coconuts	Annie I'm Not Your Daddy
	I'm a Wonderful Thing Baby
	Stool Pigeon
Kids from Fame	Starmaker
Kids from Fame featuring Gene Anthony Ray	Mannequin
Kids from Fame featuring Valerie Landsberg	Hi-Fidelity
Kiki Dee	Amoureuse
	Star
Kiki Dee Band	I Got the Music in Me
Killing Joke	Love Like Blood
Kim Appleby	Don't Worry
Kim Wilde	Chequered Love (4)
	Four Letter Word
	If I Can't Have You
	Kids in America (2)
	Never Trust a Stranger
	You Keep Me Hangin' On (2)
Kim Wilde and Junior	Another Step Closer to You
King	Alone without You
	Love and Pride
King Brothers	Standing on the Corner (4)
	A White Sport Coat (6)
Kingston Trio	Tom Dooley (5)
Kinks	All Day and All of the Night (2)
	Apeman
	Autumn Almanac
	Dedicated Follower of Fashion
	Lola
	Sunny Afternoon (1)
	Tired of Waiting for You (1)

Group/Artiste	Title
	Waterloo Sunset
	You Really Got Me (1)
Kiri Te Kanawa	World in Union (4)
Kirsty MacColl	A New England
Kiss	Crazy Crazy Nights
	God Gave Rock and Roll to You II
Kitty Kallen	Little Things Mean a Lot (1)
K-Klass	Rhythm Is a Mystery
KLF featuring Tammy Wynette	Justified and Ancient
KLF Featuring the Children of the Revolution	3 AM Eternal (1)
Knack	My Sharona
Kon Kan	I Beg Your Pardon
Kool and the Gang	Celebration
	Cherish (4)
	Joanna (2)
	Ladies Night
	Ooh La La La
Kraftwerk	Autobahn
	Computer Love/The Model (1)
Kriss Kross	Jump (2)
Krush	House Arrest
K7	Come Baby Come
Kula Shaker	Hush
KWS	Please Don't Go (1)
	Rock Your Baby (8)
Kylie Minogue	Better the Devil You Know (2)
	Confide in Me
	Give Me Just a Little More Time (2)
	Got to Be Certain
	Hand on Your Heart (1)
	I Should Be So Lucky (1)
	Je Ne Sais Pas Pourquoi
	The Locomotion (2)
	Never Too Late
	Spinning Around (1)
	Tears on My Pillow (1)
Kylie Minogue and Jason Donovan	Especially for You (1)
Kym Mazelle	Wait
Kym Sims	Too Blind to See It
Kyu Sakamoto	Sukiyaki
Labelle	Lady Marmalade
La Belle Epoque	Black Is Black (1977)
Labi Siffre	It Must Be Love (14)
	So Strong
Lambrettas	Poison Ivy
L.A. Mix	Check This Out
Lance Fortune	Be Mine
Landscape	Einstein A Go-Go
La's	There She Goes
Laura Branigan	Gloria (6)
	Self Control
Laurel and Hardy and the Avalon Boys with Chill Wills	The Trail of the Lonesome Pine
Laurie Anderson	O Superman
Laurie Johnson	Sucu Sucu
Laurie Lingo and the Dipsticks	Convoy GB
LeAnn Rimes	Can't Fight the Moonlight
Leapy Lee	Little Arrows
Lee Dorsey	Holy Cow
	Working in the Coalmine
Leeds United FC	Leeds United
Leif Garrett	I Was Made for Dancin'
Lemon Pipers	Green Tambourine

Group/Artiste	Title	Group/Artiste	Title
Len Barry	1-2-3	Living in a Box	Blow the House Down
	Like a Baby		Living in a Box
Lena Martell	One Day at a Time (1)		Room in Your Heart
Lena Zavaroni	Ma He's Making Eyes at Me (10)	Livin' Joy	Dreamer (1)
Lene Lovich	Lucky Number		Where Can I Find Love
Lennon, Ono and the	Instant Karma	Liza Minnelli	Losing My Mind
Plastic Ono Band		LL Cool J	Ain't Nobody (1)
Lenny Kravitz	Are You Gonna Go My Way		I Need Love
	Fly Away (1)	Lloyd Cole and the	Brand New Friend
	It Ain't Over Til It's Over	Commotions	
Leo Sayer	Have You Ever Been in Love	Lobo (Holland)	The Caribbean Disco Show
	Moonlighting (2)	Lobo (US)	I'd Love You to Want Me
	More Than I Can Say (2)		Me and You and a Dog Named
	One Man Band		Boo
	The Show Must Go On (2)	London Boys	London Nights
	When I Need You (1)		Requiem (4)
	You Make Me Feel Like	Londonbeat	I've Been Thinking about You
	Dancing	Lonnie Donegan	Bring a Little Water Sylvie
Leroy Van Dyke	Walk On By (5)		Cumberland Gap (1)
Les Crane	Desiderata		Does Your Chewing Gum Lose
Leslie Gore	It's My Party (9)		It's Flavour
Les Paul and Mary	Vaya Con Dios		Gambling Man (1)
Ford			My Old Man's a Dustman (1)
Lester Flatt and Earl			Rock Island Line
Scruggs	Foggy Mountain Breakdown	Lonnie Gordon	Happenin' All Over Again
Let Loose	Crazy for You	Look	I Am the Beat
Level 42	Lessons in Love	Lord Rockingham's XI	Hoots Mon (1)
	Running in the Family	Los Bravos	Black Is Black (1966)
	Something about You	Los Lobos	La Bamba (1)
	The Sun Goes Down	Lou Bega	Mambo No. 5 (1)
Levellers	Just the One	Lou Christie	I'm Gonna Make You Mine
Levert	Casanova (9)		Lightnin' Strikes
Lieutenant Pigeon	Mouldy Old Dough (1)	Louis Armstrong	We Have All the Time in the
Lighthouse Family	Raincloud		World
Lightning Seeds	You Showed Me	Louise	Arms around the World
Lil' Louis	French Kiss	Lou Rawls	You'll Never Find Another Love
Limahl	Never Ending Story		Like Mine
Limmie and the	A Walkin' Miracle	Lou Reed	Walk on the Wild Side
Family Cookin'	You Can Do Magic	Lou Reed and	Perfect Day (1)
Linda Lewis	It's in His Kiss	Friends	
Linda Ronstadt (and	Don't Know Much (2)	Love Affair	Bringing On Back the Good
Aaron Neville			Times
uncredited)			Everlasting Love (1)
Lindisfarne	Lady Eleanor		Rainbow Valley
	Meet Me On the Corner	Love City Groove	Love City Groove
Linx	Intuition	Love Sculpture	Sabre Dance
Lionel Richie	All Night Long (2)	Love Unlimited	Love's Theme
	Dancing on the Ceiling	Orchestra	
	Hello (1)	Lovin' Spoonful	Daydream
	My Destiny		Summer in the City
	Say You, Say Me	Luciano Pavarotti	Nessun Dorma
	Truly	Lulu	The Boat That I Row
Lipps Inc	Funkytown		Boom Bang-A-Bang
Liquid Gold	Dance Yourself Dizzy		I'm a Tiger
	Substitute		Independence
Lisa Lisa and Cult	I Wonder if I Take You Home		Leave a Little Love
Jam with Full Force			The Man Who Sold the World
Lisa Stansfield	All Around the World (1)		Me the Peaceful Heart
	The Real Thing	Lulu and the Luvvers	Shout (7)
	Someday (I'm Coming Back)	Luther Vandross and	The Best Things in Life Are
Lita Roza	That Doggie in the Window (1)	Janet Jackson	Free
Little Jimmy Osmond	Long Haired Lover from	Lynne Hamilton	On the Inside
	Liverpool (1)	Lyn Paul	It Oughta Sell a Million
	Tweedle Dee	Lynsey De Paul	No Honestly
Little Richard	Baby Face		Sugar Me
	The Girl Can't Help It		Won't Somebody Dance with
	Good Golly Miss Molly		Me
	Long Tall Sally	Lynsey De Paul and	Rock Bottom
	Lucille (10)	Mike Moran	
Liverpool FC	Anfield Rap (Red Machine in	Lynyrd Skynyrd	Free Bird
	Full Effect)	M	Pop Muzik

Group/Artiste	Title	Group/Artiste	Title
Mac and Katie Kissoon	Don't Do it Baby	Manuel and his Music of the Mountains	Rodrigo's Guitar Concerto de Aranjuez
	Sugar Candy Kisses	Marbles	Only One Woman
Madison Avenue	Don't Call Me Baby (1)	Marc Almond	The Days of Pearly Spencer
Madness	Baggy Trousers		I Feel Love (Medley)
	Embarrassment		Tainted Love
	Grey Day	Marc Almond featuring Gene Pitney	Something's Gotten Hold of My Heart (1)
	House of Fun (1)		
	It Must Be Love (4)	Marcello Minerbi	Zorba's Dance
	Michael Caine	Marcels	Blue Moon (1)
	My Girl	Mari Wilson	Just what I Always Wanted (8)
	One Step Beyond		
	Our House	Maria McKee	Show Me Heaven (1)
	The Return of the Los Palmas Seven	Maria Muldaur	Midnight at the Oasis (21)
		Mariah Carey	All I Want For Christmas Is You
	Shut Up		Fantasy
Madonna	American Pie (1)		Without You (1)
	Bad Girl	Mariah Carey and Boyz II Men	One Sweet Day
	Cherish (3)		
	Erotica	Mariah Carey and Westlife	Against All Odds (1)
	Fever		
	Frozen (1)	Marianne Faithfull	As Tears Go By
	Hanky Panky		Summer Nights (10)
	Holiday	Marie Osmond	Paper Roses
	Into the Groove (1)	Marillion	Incommunicado
	La Isla Bonita (1)		Kayleigh
	Like a Prayer (1)		Lavender
	Like a Virgin	Marilyn	Calling Your Name
	Material Girl	Marilyn McCoo and Billy Davis Jr	You Don't Have To Be a Star
	Music (1)		
	Papa Don't Preach (1)	Marino Marini and his Quartet	Come Prima
	Rain		
	True Blue (1)	Mario Lanza	Because You're Mine
	Vogue (1)		Drinking Song
	Who's That Girl (1)	Mari Wilson	Just What I Always Wanted
Mai Tai	Body and Soul	Mark Dinning	Teen Angel
	History (8)	Mark Morrison	Moan and Groan
Malcolm McLaren	Double Dutch		Return of the Mack (1)
Malcolm McLaren and Supreme Team	Buffalo Gals	Mark Wynter	Go Away Little Girl
			Venus in Blue Jeans
Mama Cass	Dream a Little Dream of Me	Marmalade	Baby Make It Soon
	It's Getting Better		Cousin Norman
Mamas and the Papas	California Dreamin'		Lovin' Things
			Ob-La-Di Ob-La-Da (1)
	Creeque Alley		Rainbow
	Dedicated to the One I Love		Reflections of My Life
	Monday Monday	M/A/R/R/s	Pump up the Volume (1)
Manchester Utd Football Squad	Come On You Reds (1)	Marshall Hain	Dancing in the City
		Martha and the Muffins	Echo Beach
Manfred Mann	Do Wah Diddy Diddy (1)		
	5-4-3-2-1	Martha Reeves and the Vandellas	Dancing in the Street (4)
	Fox on the Run (5)		
	Mighty Quinn (1)	Martika	I Feel the Earth Move
	My Name Is Jack		Love ... Thy Will Be Done
	Pretty Flamingo (1)		Toy Soldiers
	Ragamuffin Man	Martine McCutcheon	Perfect Moment (1)
Manfred Mann's Earth Band	Blinded by the Light	Marti Webb	Ben (5)
	Davy's on the Road Again		Take That Look off Your Face
	Joy Bringer		
Manhattans	Hurt	Marty Robbins	Devil Woman (5)
Manhattan Transfer	Chanson d'Amour (1)	Marty Wilde	A Teenager In Love (2)
Manic Street Preachers	If You Tolerate This Your Children Will be Next (1)		Donna (3)
			Endless Sleep
	Theme from M.A.S.H. (Suicide Is Painless) (7)		Sea of Love (3)
		Marv Johnson	I'll Pick a Rose for My Rose
	The Masses Against the Classes (1)		You Got What It Takes
Mansun	Taxloss	Marvin Gaye	Abraham, Martin and John
Man 2 Man meet Man Parrish	Male Stripper		I Heard It Through the Grapevine (1)
Mantovani	Moulin Rouge (1)		
	White Christmas (6)		

M
U
S
I
C

P
O
P

Group/Artiste	Title	Group/Artiste	Title
	Sexual Healing	Miami Sound Machine	Bad Boy
	Too Busy Thinking 'Bout My Baby		Dr Beat
Marvin Gaye and Kim Weston	It Takes Two (16)	Mica Paris	My One Temptation
Marvin Gaye and Tammi Terrell	Onion Song	Michael and Janet Jackson	Scream
Marvin Rainwater	Whole Lotta Woman (1)	Michael Ball	Love Changes Everything
Mary Hopkin	Those Were the Days (1)	Michael Bolton	How Am I Supposed to Live Without You
Mary McGregor	Torn between Two Lovers	Michael Cox	Angela Jones
Mary Wells	My Guy (5)	Michael Crawford	The Music of the Night
MASH	Theme from M*A*S*H (Suicide Is Painless) (1)	Michael Holliday	Starry Eyed
Mason Williams	Classical Gas		The Story of My Life (1)
Matchbox	When You Ask about Love	Michael Jackson	Bad
Matt Monro	Portrait of My Love (3)		Ben
	Walk Away		Billie Jean (1)
	Yesterday (8)		Black or White (1)
Matthews Southern Comfort	Woodstock (1)		Blood on the Dance Floor (1)
Max Bygraves	Deck of Cards (13)		Don't Stop Till You Get Enough
Maxi Priest	Close to You (7)		Earth Song (1)
	Wild World (5)		Farewell My Summer Love
Maxine Nightingale	Right Back Where We Started From		Give In to Me
Max Romeo	Wet Dream		Got to Be There
Maxx	Get-A-Way		Heal the World
MC Hammer	Pray (8)		I Just Can't Stop Loving You (1)
MC Miker 'G' and Deejay Sven	Holiday Rap		In the Closet
MC Tunes versus 808 State	The Only Rhyme That Bites		Leave Me Alone
McCoys	Hang On Sloopy		Off the Wall
McFadden and Whitehead	Ain't No Stoppin' Us Now		One Day in Your Life (1)
McGuinness Flint	Malt and Barley Blues		Rockin' Robin
	When I'm Dead and Gone		She's Out of My Life
Meat Loaf	Dead Ringer for Love		Smooth Criminal
	I'd Do Anything for Love (But I Won't Do That) (1)		Thriller
Meat Loaf featuring John Parr	Rock 'N' Roll Mercenaries		You Are Not Alone (1)
Meco	Star Wars Theme – Cantina Band	Michael Jackson and Paul McCartney	The Girl Is Mine
Medicine Head	One and One Is One	Michael Jackson and Diana Ross	Say Say Say
Mel and Kim (Appleby)	F.L.M.		Ease On Down the Road
	Respectable (1)	Michael Jackson and Stevie Wonder	Get It
	Showing Out	Michael Zager Band	Let's All Chant
Melanie	Brand New Key	Michelle Gayle	Looking Up
	Ruby Tuesday		Sweetness
Melanie B featuring Missy 'Misdemeanour' Elliot	I Want You Back (1)	Mick Jackson	Blame It on the Boogie (15)
		Mick Jagger	Just Another Night
Melanie C	I Turn to You (1)		Let's Work
Melanie C featuring Lisa Lopes	Never Be the Same Again (1)		Memo from Turner
Melba Moore	This Is It	Middle of the Road	Chirpy Chirpy Cheep Cheep (1)
Mel (Smith) and Kim Wilde	Rockin' around the Christmas Tree (3)		Soley Soley
Mel Tormé	Mountain Greenery		Tweedle Dee Tweedle Dum
Men at Work	Down Under (1)	Midge Ure	If I Was (1)
Mental As Anything	Live it Up		No Regrets (9)
Men without Hats	The Safety Dance	Midnight Oil	Beds Are Burning
Meredith Brooks	Bitch	Midnight Star	Midas Touch
Meri Wilson	Telephone Man	Migil Five	Mockingbird Hill
Merseybeats	I Think of You	Mike and the Mechanics	The Living Years
Merseys	Sorrow (4)	Mike Batt with the New Edition	Summertime City
Metallica	Enter Sandman	Mike Berry	Don't You Think It's Time
	Nothing Else Matters	Mike Flowers Pops	Wonderwall (2)
		Mike Oldfield	In Dulce Jubilo
			Portsmouth
			Sentinel
		Mike Oldfield with Maggie Reilly	Moonlight Shadow
		Mike Reid	The Ugly Duckling (10)

Group/Artiste	Title
Mike Sarne with Wendy Richard	Come Outside (1)
Milk and Honey	Hallelujah
Millie	My Boy Lollipop (2)
Milli Vanilli	Girl I'm Gonna Miss You
	Girl You Know It's True
Mindbenders	A Groovy Kind of Love (2)
Minnie Riperton	Loving You
Mirage	Jack Mix II/III
Mitch Miller	Yellow Rose of Texas
Mitchell Torok	When Mexico Gave up the Rumba
Mixmaster	Grand Piano
Mixtures	The Pushbike Song
MN8	I've Got a Little Something for You
Mobiles	Drowning in Berlin
Modern Romance	Ay Ay Ay Ay Moosey
	Best Years of Our Lives
	Walking in the Rain (7)
Modern Talking	Brother Louie (4)
Modjo	Lady (Hear Me Tonight) (1)
Mojos	Everything's Alright
Moments	Dolly My Love
	Jack in the Box (7)
Moments and Whatnauts	Girls
Monaco	Sweet Lips
Monkees	Alternate Title
	Daydream Believer
	I'm a Believer (1)
	Last Train to Clarkesville (23)
	A Little Bit Me, A Little Bit You
Monstars	Hit 'Em High
Monty Python	Always Look on the Bright Side of Life
Moody Blues	Go Now (1)
	Nights in White Satin
	Question
Morris Albert	Feelings
Morris Minor and the Majors	Stutter Rap (No Sleep 'til Bedtime)
Morrissey	Everyday Is Like Sunday
	Interesting Drug
	Last of the Famous International Playboys
	The More You Ignore Me the Closer I Get
	Suedehead
Motorhead	The Golden Years (EP)
Motors	Airport
Mott the Hoople	All the Way from Memphis
	All the Young Dudes
	Roll Away the Stone
Mouth and MacNeal	I See a Star
Move	Blackberry Way (1)
	Brontosaurus
	California Man
	Fire Brigade
	Flowers in the Rain
	I Can Hear the Grass Grow
	Night of Fear
M People	Itchycoo Park
	Moving On Up
	One Night in Heaven
	Open Your Heart
	Renaissance
Mr Bean and Smear Campaign: Bruce Dickinson	Elected (9)

Group/Artiste	Title
Mr Big (UK)	Romeo
Mr Big (USA)	To Be with You
Mr Blobby	Mr Blobby (1)
Mr Bloe	Groovin' with Mr Bloe
Mr Mister	Broken Wings
	Kyrie
Mr Oizot	Flat Beat (1)
Mr President	Coco Jamboo
Mud	The Cat Crept In
	Dyna-mite
	Lean on Me (7)
	Lonely This Christmas (1)
	Moonshine Sally
	Oh Boy (1)
	Tiger Feet (1)
Mudlarks	Book of Love
	Lollipop (2)
Mungo Jerry	Alright Alright Alright
	Baby Jump (1)
	In the Summertime (1)
	Lady Rose
Muriel Smith	Hold Me Thrill Me Kiss Me
Musical Youth	Never Gonna Give You Up (6)
	Pass the Dutchie (1)
Nana Mouskouri	Only Love
Nancy and Lee Hazlewood	Did You Ever
Nancy Sinatra	Sugar Town
	These Boots Are Made For Walking (1)
Nancy Sinatra and Frank Sinatra	Something Stupid (1)
Napoleon XIV	They're Coming to Take Me Away Ha-Haaa!
Narada Michael Walden	Divine Emotions
	I Shoulda Loved Ya
Nashville Teens	Google Eye
	Tobacco Road
Natalie Cole	Miss You Like Crazy
	Pink Cadillac
Natasha	Iko Iko (10)
Nat King Cole	Rambling Rose
	When I Fall in Love
Nazareth	Bad Bad Boy
	Broken Down Angel
	My White Bicycle
Ned Miller	From a Jack to a King
Neil	Hole in My Shoe (2)
Neil Diamond	Cracklin' Rosie
	I Am ... I Said
	Sweet Caroline
Neil Diamond and Barbra Streisand	You Don't Bring Me Flowers
Neil Reid	Mother of Mine
Neil Sedaka	Breaking Up Is Hard to Do
	Calendar Girl
	Happy Birthday Sweet Sixteen
	I Go Ape
	Little Devil
	Oh Carol
	Stairway to Heaven (8)
Neil Young	Heart of Gold (10)
Nena	99 Red Balloons (1)
Newbeats	Bread and Butter
	Run Baby Run
New Edition	Candy Girl (1)
New Kids on the Block	Cover Girl
	Hanging Tough (1)
	If You Go Away
	Step by Step

M
U
S
I
C

P
O
P

Group/Artiste	Title	Group/Artiste	Title
	This One's for the Children		Roll With It
	You Got It (1)		Some Might Say (1)
New Order	Blue Monday		Stand by Me (2)
	Regret		Whatever
	True Faith		Wonderwall (1)
New Seekers	Beg Steal or Borrow	Obernkirchen	Happy Wanderer
	Circles	Children's Choir	
	I'd Like to Teach the World to	Ocean Colour Scene	Hundred Mile High City
	Sing (1)	Oceanic	Insanity
	I Get a Little Sentimental over	O.C. Smith	Son of Hickory Holler's
	You		Tramp
	Never Ending Song of Love	Odyssey	Going Back to My Roots
	You Won't Find Another Fool		If You're Looking for a Way
	Like Me (1)		Out
New Vaudeville	Finchley Central		Inside Out
Band	Green Street Green		Native New Yorker
	Winchester Cathedral		Use It Up and Wear It
New Vaudeville	Peek-A-Boo		Out (1)
Band with		Offspring	Pretty Fly (for a White
Tristram			Guy) (1)
New World	Sister Jane	Ohio Express	Yummy Yummy Yummy
	Tom Tom Turnaround	O'Jays	Love Train
Nick Berry	Every Loser Wins (1)	Oleta Adams	Get Here
Nick Kamen	Each Time You Break My	Olive	You're Not Alone (1)
	Heart	Oliver	Good Morning Starshine
Nick Lowe	I Love the Sound of Breaking	Olivia Newton-John	Banks of the Ohio
	Glass		Hopelessly Devoted to You
Nicky Thomas	Love of the Common People		If Not for You
	(9)		I Honestly Love You
Nicole	A Little Peace		Physical
Nightcrawlers	Push the Feeling On		Sam
Nik Kershaw	Don Quixote	Olivia Newton-John	Suddenly (15)
	I Won't Let the Sun Go Down on	and Cliff Richard	
	Me	Olivia Newton-John	Xanadu (1)
	The Riddle	and Electric Light	
	Wide Boy	Orchestra	
	Wouldn't It Be Good	Ollie and Jerry	Breakin' ... There's No Stopping
Nilsson	Coconut		Us
	Without You (1)	One Hundred Ton	It Only Takes a Minute
Nina and Frederick	Little Donkey (3)	and a Feather	
Nina Simone	Ain't Got No – I Got Life (2)	(Jonathan King)	
	My Baby Just Cares for Me	Opus	Live Is Life
	To Love Somebody	Opus III	It's a Fine Day
911	A Little Bit More (1)	Orange Juice	Rip It Up
	Bodyshakin'	Oran 'Juice' Jones	The Rain
1910 Fruitgum	Simon Says	Orb	Blue Room
Company		Orbital	The Theme from The Saint
Nini Rosso	Il Silenzio	Orchestral	Enola Gay
Nirvana	Come as You Are	Manoeuvres in	Joan of Arc
	Heart-Shaped Box	the Dark	Locomotion (5)
	Smells Like Teen Spirit		Maid of Orleans
N-Joi	Anthem (8)		Pandora's Box
No Doubt	Don't Speak		Sailing on the Seven Seas
No Mercy	Where Do You Go		Souvenir
Nolans	Attention to Me	Osmonds	Crazy Horses
	Gotta Pull Myself Together		Going Home
	I'm in the Mood for Dancing		Let Me In
Nomad	Devotion		Love Me for a Reason (1)
Norman Greenbaum	Spirit in the Sky (1)		The Proud One (1)
Norman Wisdom	Don't Laugh at Me (3)	Otis Redding	The Dock of the Bay (3)
North and South	I'm a Man Not a Boy	Ottawan	D.I.S.C.O.
Northern Uproar	Anyway You Look		Hands Up (Give Me Your
Notorious B.I.G.	Hypnotize		Heart)
N-Trance	Set You Free	Our Kid	You Just Might See Me Cry
Nu Shooz	I Can't Wait	Outhere Brothers	Boom Boom Boom (1)
Oasis	All around the World (1)		Don't Stop (Wiggle Wiggle)
	Cigarettes and Alcohol		(1)
	Don't Look Back in Anger (1)		Michelle (1)
	D'You Know What I	Overlanders	My Favourite Waste of Time
	Mean? (1)	Owen Paul	Bound 4 Da Reload (Casualty)
	Go Let It Out (1)	Oxide and Neutrino	(1)

Group/Artiste	Title	Group/Artiste	Title
Paper Lace	Billy Don't Be a Hero (1)		Me and Julio Down by the Schoolyard
	The Night Chicago Died		Mother and Child Reunion
Partners in Kryme	Turtle Power (1)		Slip Slidin' Away (36)
Partridge Family	Breaking Up Is Hard to Do (3)		Take Me to the Mardi Gras
	I Think I Love You		You Can Call Me Al (4)
Partridge Family Starring David Cassidy	Looking Through the Eyes Of Love	Paul Weller	The Changingman
		Paul Young	Come Back and Stay
	Walking in the Rain		Everything Must Change
Pasadenas	I'm Doing Fine Now		Every Time You Go Away
	Tribute (Right On)		I'm Gonna Tear Your Playhouse Down
Pat and Mick	I Haven't Stopped Dancing Yet		I Wish You Love
Pat Benatar	Love Is a Battlefield		Love of the Common People (2)
Pat Boone	April Love		Wherever I Lay My Hat (1)
	Friendly Persuasion	Paula Abdul	Opposites Attract
	I'll Be Home		Rush Rush
	Love Letters in the Sand		Straight Up
	Speedy Gonzales	Peabo Bryson and Regina Belle	A Whole New World (Aladdin's Theme)
	Sugar Moon		
Pato Banton	Baby Come Back (1)	Peabo Bryson and Roberta Flack	Tonight I Celebrate My Love
Patrice Rushen	Forget Me Nots		
Patrick Macnee and Honor Blackman	Kinky Boots	Peaches and Herb	Reunited
		Pearls	Guilty
Patsy Cline	Crazy (14)	Pebbles	Girlfriend
Patsy Gallant	From New York to L.A.	Peggy Lee	Fever (5)
Patti Labelle and Michael McDonald	On My Own		Mr Wonderful
		Peppers	Pepper Box
Patti Page	How Much Is That Doggie in the Window	Pepsi and Shirlie	Goodbye Stranger
			Heartache
Patti Smith Group	Because the Night	Percy Faith	Theme from A Summer Place
Paul and Paula	Hey Paula		
	Young Lovers	Percy Sledge	When a Man Loves a Woman
Paul Anka	Diana		
	Lonely Boy	Perez Prado and Orchestra, King of Mambo	Cherry Pink and Apple Blossom White (1)
Paul Anka (featuring Odia Coates)	You're Having My Baby		
Paul Davidson	Midnight Rider	Perez Prado	Patricia
Paul Evans	Hello This Is Joanie	Perez 'Prez' Prado and his Orchestra	Guaglione
Paul Evans and the Curls	Seven Little Girls Sitting in the Back Seat		
		Perfecto Allstarz	Reach Up (Papa's Got a Brand New Pig Bag)
Paul Hardcastle	Nineteen (1)		
Paul Hardcastle featuring Carol Kenyon	Don't Waste My Time	Perry Como	And I Love You So
			Catch a Falling Star
Paul Henry and the Mayson Glen Orchestra	Benny's Theme		Don't Let the Stars Get in Your Eyes
			For the Good Times
Paul Jones	High Time		It's Impossible
	I've Been a Bad Bad Boy		Magic Moments
Paul McCartney	Another Day	Peter and Gordon	Nobody I Know
	Hope of Deliverance		To Know You Is to Love You
	No More Lonely Nights		True Love Ways (2)
	Once Upon a Long Ago		A World without Love (1)
	Pipes of Peace (1)	Peter Andre	Flava
	Wonderful Christmas Time		I Feel You
	Young Boy	Peter Frampton	Show Me the Way
Paul McCartney and the Frog Chorus	We All Stand Together	Peter Gabriel and Kate Bush	Don't Give Up (9)
Paul McCartney and Wings	Band on the Run	Peter Gabriel	Games without Frontiers
	Jet		Sledgehammer
	My Love (9)		Solsbury Hill
Paul McCartney with Stevie Wonder	Ebony and Ivory (1)		Steam
		Peter, Paul and Mary	Leavin' on a Jet Plane
Paul McCartney and Michael Jackson	The Girl Is Mine	Peters and Lee	Don't Stay Away Too Long
	Say Say Say		Welcome Home (1)
Paul Nicholas	Dancing with the Captain	Peter Sarstedt	Frozen Orange Juice
	Grandma's Party		Where Do You Go to My Lovely (1)
	Reggae Like It Used to Be		
Paul Simon	50 Ways to Leave Your Lover (23)	Peter Sellers and Sophia Loren	Goodness Gracious Me

Group/Artiste	Title
Peter Shelley	Gee Baby
	Love Me Love My Dog
Peter Skellern	You're a Lady
Pete Wingfield	Eighteen With a Bullet
Pete Wylie with the Farm	Sinful (13)
Pet Shop Boys	Always on My Mind (1)
	Domino Dancing
	Go West
	Heart (1)
	It's Alright (5)
	It's A Sin (1)
	Left to My Own Devices
	Rent
	So Hard
	Suburbia
	West End Girls (1)
	Where the Streets Have No Name
Pet Shop Boys and Dusty Springfield	What Have I Done to Deserve This
Petula Clark	Don't Sleep in the Subway (12)
	Downtown (2)
	I Couldn't Live without Your Love
	Romeo
	Sailor (1)
	This Is My Song (1)
PhD	I Won't Let You Down
Phil Collins	Against All Odds (Take a Look at Me Now) (2)
	Another Day in Paradise
	Do You Remember
	In the Air Tonight
	You Can't Hurry Love (1)
Phil Collins and Marilyn Martin	Separate Lives
Phil Collins and Philip Bailey	Easy Lover
Phil Fearon and Galaxy	What Do I Do
Philip Lynott	Yellow Pearl
Phyllis Nelson	Move Closer (1)
Pickettywitch	That Same Old Feeling
Piero Umiliani	Mah Na Mah Na
Pigbag	Papa's Got a Brand New Pigbag
Piglets	Johnny Reggae
Pigmeat Markham	Here Comes the Judge
Pilot	January (1)
Pinkees	Danger Games
Pinkerton's Assorted Colours	Mirror Mirror
Pink Floyd	Another Brick in the Wall (1)
	See Emily Play
Pioneers	Let Your Yeah Be Yeah
	Long Shot Kick De Bucket
Pipkins	Gimme Dat Ding
Piranhas	Tom Hark (6)
Piranhas featuring Boring Bob Grover	Zambesi
PJ and Duncan	Let's Get Ready to Rhumble
PJ Harvey	Sheela-Na-Gig
PJ Proby	Hold Me
	Maria
	Somewhere
	Together
Plastic Bertrand	Ça Plane Pour Moi
Plastic Ono Band	Ballad of John and Yoko (1)

Group/Artiste	Title
	Cold Turkey
	Give Peace a Chance
Plastic Penny	Everything I Am
Platters	The Great Pretender (5)
	My Prayer (4)
	Smoke Gets in Your Eyes (1)
Players Association	Turn the Music Up
Pluto Shervington	Dat
PM Dawn	Set Adrift on Memory Bliss
Pogues and the Dubliners	The Irish Rover
Pogues featuring Kirsty McColl	Fairytale of New York
Pointer Sisters	Automatic
	I'm So Excited
	Jump (for My Love)
	Slowhand
Police	Can't Stand Losing You
	De Do Do Do, De Da Da Da
	Don't Stand So Close to Me (1)
	Every Breath You Take
	Every Little Thing She Does IsMagic
	Invisible Sun
	Message in a Bottle (1)
	Spirits in the Material World
	Walking on the Moon (1)
Poni-Tails	Born too Late
Pop Will Eat Itself	Get the Girl! Kill the Baddies!
Poppy Family	Which Way You Goin' Billy
Power Station	Get It On (22)
	Some Like It Hot
Praga Khan featuring Jade 4 U	Free Your Body
Praise	Only You (4)
Prefab Sprout	The King of Rock 'N' Roll(7)
Pretenders	Brass in Pocket (1)
Pretty Things	Don't Bring Me Down (10)
Primal Scream	Kowalski
	Rocks
Primitives	Crash
Prince	Alphabet Street
	Batdance
	Little Red Corvette/1999
	The Most Beautiful Girl in the World (1)
	Sign 'O' the Times
	When Doves Cry
Prince and the New Power Generation	Gett Off
	Sexy MF
	Diamonds and Pearls
Prince and the Revolution	Kiss (6)
	Purple Rain
Prince with Sheena Easton	The Arms of Orion
Princess	Say I'm Your No. 1
Proclaimers	King of the Road (9)
	Letter from America
Proclaimers (Charles and Craig Reid)	I'm Gonna Be
Procol Harum	Whiter Shade of Pale (1)
Prodigy	Breathe (1)
	Charly
	Firestarter (1)
	No Good
	Out of Space
Pseudo Echo	Funky Town
Psychedelic Furs	Pretty in Pink
Public Image Ltd	This Is Not a Love Song

M
U
S
I
C

P
O
P

Group/Artiste	Title	Group/Artiste	Title
Robin Beck	First Time (1)		Nineteenth Nervous Breakdown (2)
Robin Gibb	Saved by the Bell		Not Fade Away (3)
Robin (Jerry Nelson), Kermit the Frog's Nephew	Halfway Down the Stairs		Paint It Black (1)
			Satisfaction (1)
Robin S	Show Me Love		Start Me Up (7)
Robin Sarstedt	My Resistance Is Low (3)		Street Fighting Man (21)
Robson Green and Jerome Flynn	I Believe/Up on the Roof (1)		Tumbling Dice (5)
	Unchained Melody (1)	Ronan Keating	Life Is a Rollercoaster (1)
	White Cliffs of Dover		When You Say Nothing at All (1)
	Up on the Roof/What Becomes of the Broken Hearted/You'll Never Walk Alone (1)	Ronettes	Be My Baby (4)
Rocker's Revenge featuring Donnie Calvin	Walking on Sunshine (6)	Ronnie Hilton	No Other Love (1)
		Ronnie Lane and Slim Chance	How Come
Rockin' Berries	He's in Town (3)	Rooftop Singers	Walk Right In
	Poor Man's Son (5)	Rose Royce	Car Wash
Rockwell	Somebody's Watching Me		Love Don't Live Here Anymore (2)
Rodney Franklin	The Groove		Wishing on a Star
Rod Stewart	Angel (What Made Milwaukee Famous ...)	Rosemary Clooney	Mambo Italiano (No. 1 1954)
	Baby Jane (1)		This Ole House (1)
	Da Ya Think I'm Sexy (1)		Where Will the Baby's Dimple Be
	Downtown Train	Rosie Gaines	Closer Than Close
	Hotlegs/I Was Only Joking (5)	Roxette	Almost Unreal
	I Don't Want to Talk about It (1)		It Must Have Been Love
	Maggie May (1)		Joyride
	Oh No Not My Baby (6)		Listen to Your Heart
	Reason to Believe (19)		The Look
	Sailing (1)	Roxy Music	Angel Eyes (4)
	Tom Traubert's blues (Waltzing Matilda)(6)		Avalon
	Tonight I'm Yours (8)		Dance Away (2)
	You Wear It Well (1)		Jealous Guy (1)
	You're in My Heart (3)		Love Is the Drug
Rod Stewart and Tina Turner	It Takes Two (5)		More Than This
Rod Stewart and Scots World Cup Squad (1978)	Ole Ola (Mulher Brasileira)		Oh Yeah (On the Radio)
			Over You
			Pyjamarama
Roger Daltrey	Giving It All Away		Street Life
	Under a Raging Moon		Virginia Plain
Roger Miller	England Swings	Royal Guardsmen	Snoopy vs the Red Baron
	King of the Road	Royal Philharmonic Orchestra	Hooked on Classics
Roger Whittaker	I Don't Believe In If Anymore	Royal Scots Dragoon Guards	Amazing Grace (1)
	Mammy Blue (31)		
	The Last Farewell (2)	Roy Orbison	Blue Bayou
Roger Whittaker and Des O'Connor	The Skye Boat Song		Dream Baby
Rolf Harris	Stairway to Heaven		Falling
	Two Little Boys (1)		I Drove All Night (7)
Rolling Stones	Angie (5)		In Dreams
	Brown Sugar (2)		It's Over (1)
	Come On (21)		Oh Pretty Woman (1)
	Emotional Rescue		Only the Lonely (1)
	Fool to Cry (6)		Pretty Paper
	Get off of My Cloud (1)		Running Scared
	Have You Seen Your Mother Baby (5)		Too Soon to Know
	Honky Tonk Women (1)		You Got It
	I Wanna Be Your Man (12)	Roy Orbison and kd lang	Crying (13)
	It's All Over Now (1)	Roy Wood	Forever (8)
	It's Only Rock and Roll (10)	Rozalla	Everybody's Free
	Jumping Jack Flash (1)	Rubettes	Baby I Know
	The Last Time (1)		I Can Do It
	Let's Spend the Night Together (3)		Juke Box Jive
	Little Red Rooster (1)		Sugar Baby Love (1)
	Miss You (3)	Ruby Murray	Evermore
			Heartbeat (3)
			Let Me Go Lover (5)
			Softly Softly (1)
		Ruby Wright	Bimbo (7)

Group/Artiste	Title
Rufus and Chaka Khan	Ain't Nobody
Rui Da Silva featuring Cassandra	Touch Me (1)
Run-DMC	Walk This Way
Run-DMC vs Jason Nevins	It's Like That (1)
Rupie Edwards	Ire Feelings
Russ Abbot	Atmosphere (7)
Russ Conway	China Tea
	Roulette
	Side Saddle
	Toy Balloons
Russ Hamilton	We Will Make Love
Ruts	Babylon's Burning
Ryan Paris	Dolce Vita
Sabrina	Boys (Summertime Love)
Sabrina Johnston	Peace
Sacha Distel	Raindrops Keep Falling on My Head
Sad Cafe	Every Day Hurts
Sade	No Ordinary Love
	Smooth Operator
	When Am I Gonna Make a Living
	Your Love Is King
Sailor	Girls Girls Girls
	Glass of Champagne
Sakkarin (Jonathan King)	Sugar Sugar
Salt-N-Pepa	Do You Want Me (5)
	Push It (2)
	Twist and Shout (4)
	You Showed Me (15)
Salt-N-Pepa with Psychotropic	Let's Talk About Sex (2)
Salt-N-Pepa with En Vogue	Whatta Man
Sam and Dave	Soul Man
Sam Cooke	Chain Gang
	Twistin' the Night Away (6)
Samantha Fox	Touch Me (I Want Your Body)
Samantha Fox featuring Full Force	Naughty Girls
Samantha Janus	A Message to Your Heart
Sammy Davis Jnr	Love Me or Leave Me
Sam the Sham and the Pharaohs	Wooly Bully
Sandie Shaw	Always Something There to Remind Me (1)
	Girl Don't Come
	Long Live Love (1)
	Message Understood
	Monsieur Dupont
	Puppet on a String (1)
	Tomorrow
Sandpipers	Guantanamera (7)
Sandy Nelson	Let There Be Drums
	Teen Beat
Sandy Posey	Single Girl
Sarah Brightman and Andrea Bocelli	Time to Say Goodbye
Sash	Encore Une Fois
Scaffold	Lily the Pink (1)
	Liverpool Lou
	Thank U Very Much
Scatman John	Scatman (Ski-Ba-Bop-Ba-Dop-Bop)
S Club 7	Bring It All Back (1)
	Never Had a Dream Come True (1)

Group/Artiste	Title
Scorpions	Wind of Change
Scott English	Brandy
Scott Fitzgerald, Y. Keeley, St Thomas Moore Choir	If I Had Words
Scottish World Cup Squad	We Have a Dream
Scott McKenzie	San Francisco (1)
Scott Walker	Jackie (22)
	Joanna (7)
Scritti Politti	Wood Beez (Pray Like Aretha Franklin)
Scritti Politti featuring Ranking Ann	The Word Girl
Scritti Politti featuring Shabba Ranks	She's a Woman
Sea Horses	Love Is the Law
Seal	Crazy (2)
	Killer (EP)
Sean Maguire	Now I've Found You
Searchers	Don't Throw Your Love Away (1)
	Goodbye My Love (4)
	Needles and Pins (1)
	Sugar and Spice (2)
	Sweets for My Sweet (1)
	When You Walk in the Room (3)
Seekers	The Carnival Is Over (1)
	Georgy Girl
	I'll Never Find Another You (1)
	Morningtown Ride
	A World of Our Own
Selecter	On My Radio
Sensational Alex Harvey Band	Delilah (7)
Severine	Un Banc, Un Arbre, Une Rue
Sex Pistols	C'Mon Everybody (3)
	God Save the Queen (2)
	Holidays in the Sun
	Pretty Vacant (6)
	Silly Thing
	Something Else
Sex Pistols, Punk Prayer by Ronald Biggs	No One Is Innocent
S Express	Superfly Guy
	Theme From S-Express (1)
Shabba Ranks	Mr Loverman
Shadows	Apache (1)
	Atlantis (2)
	Dance On (1)
	Don't Cry for Me, Argentina (5)
	FBI (6)
	Foot Tapper (1)
	Frightened City (3)
	Guitar Tango (4)
	Kon Tiki (1)
	Let Me Be the One
	Man of Mystery (5)
	The Rise and Fall of Flingel Bunt (5)
	Shindig (6)
	Theme from The Deer Hunter (Cavatina) (9)
	Wonderful Land (1)
Shaft	Roobarb and Custard
Shaggy	Boombastic (1)
	It Wasn't Me (1)
	Oh Carolina (1)
Shag (Jonathan King)	Loop di Love
Shakatak	Down on the Street
	Night Birds

Group/Artiste	Title	Group/Artiste	Title
Shakatak featuring Al Jarreau	Day by Day (53)		If You Don't Know Me by Now (2)
Shakespears Sister	I Don't Care		Stars
	Stay (1)	Simpsons	Do the Bartman
	You're History	Simpsons featuring Bart and Homer	Deep Deep Trouble
Shakin' Stevens	Green Door (1)		
	Merry Christmas Everyone (1)	Sinead O'Connor	Nothing Compares 2 U (1)
	Oh Julie (1)		This Is to Mother You
	This Ole House (1)	Singing Nun (Soeur Sourire)	Dominique
	You Drive Me Crazy (2)		
Shaky and Bonnie	A Rockin' Good Way (5)	Sinitta	Cross My Broken Heart
Shalamar	Dead Giveaway		Right Back Where We Started From
	I Can Make You Feel Good		So Macho
	A Night to Remember		Toy Boy
	There It Is	Siouxsie and the Banshees	Dear Prudence
Shamen	Boss Drum		Hong Kong Garden
	Ebeneezer Goode (1)	Sister Sledge	Frankie (1)
	LSI		He's the Greatest Dancer
	Move Any Mountain		Lost in Music
	Phorever People		We Are Family
Sham 69	Hersham Boys	Sisters of Mercy	Temple of Love
	Hurry Up Harry		This Corrosion
	If the Kids Are United	Skids	Into the Valley
Shane Fenton and the Fentones	Cindy's Birthday	Sky	Toccata
		SL2	On a Ragga Tip
Shangri-Las	Leader of the Pack (3)	Slade	Coz I Luv You (1)
Shanice	I Love Your Smile		Cum on Feel the Noize (1)
Shanks and Bigfoot	Sweet Like Chocolate (1)		Far Far Away (2)
Sheb Wooley	Purple People Eater		Gudbuy T'Jane (2)
Sheena Easton	For Your Eyes Only		Lock up Your Daughters
	Modern Girl (8)		Look Wot You Dun (4)
	9 to 5		Mama Weer All Crazee Now (1)
Sheer Elegance	Life Is Too Short Girl		Merry Xmas Everybody (1)
Sheila E	The Belle of St Mark		My Friend Stan (2)
Sherbet	Howzat		Run Run Away
Sheryl Crow	All I Wanna Do		Skweeze Me Pleeze Me (1)
Shirelles	Will You Love Me Tomorrow (4)		Take Me Bak 'Ome (1)
Shirley and Company	Shame Shame Shame		We'll Bring the House Down (10)
Shirley Bassey	As I Love You (1)	Slik	Forever and Ever (1)
	Reach for the Stars (1)	Slim Dusty	A Pub with No Beer
Shirley Ellis	The Clapping Song (6)	Slim Whitman	I'll Take You Home Again Kathleen (7)
Shocking Blue	Venus (8)		Indian Love Call (7)
Shola Ama	You Might Need Somebody		Rose Marie (1)
Showaddywaddy	Dancin' Party (4)	Sly and the Family Stone	Dance to the Music
	Heartbeat (7)		
	Hey Rock and Roll (2)	Sly Fox	Let's Go All the Way
	A Little Bit of Soap	Small Faces	All or Nothing (1)
	Pretty Little Angel Eyes		Hey Girl
	Three Steps to Heaven (2)		Itchycoo Park (3)
	Under the Moon of Love (1)		Lazy Sunday
	When (3)		My Mind's Eye
	You Got What It Takes (2)		Sha La La La Leee
Shut Up and Dance	Raving I'm Raving		Tin Soldier
Silver Convention	Get Up and Boogie	Smart Es	Sesame's Treet
Simon and Garfunkel	The Boxer (6)	Smiths	Heaven Knows I'm Miserable Now
	Bridge over Troubled Water (1)		Panic
	Homeward Bound (9)		Sheila Take a Bow
	Mrs Robinson		This Charming Man
Simon Dupree and the Big Sound	Kites	Smoke City	Underwater Love
		Smokey	Don't Play Your Rock 'N' Roll To Me
Simon Park	Eye Level		If You Think You Know How to Love Me
Simple Minds	Belfast Child (1)		
	Don't You (Forget about Me)		
	Let There Be Love		
	Love Song		
	Sanctify Yourself	Smokey Robinson	Being with You (1)
Simply Red	Fairground (1)	Smokey Robinson and the Miracles	Tears of a Clown (1)
	For Your Babies		Tracks of My Tears (9)
	Holding back the Years (2)	Smokie	It's Your Life

M
U
S
I
C

P
O
P

Group/Artiste	Title	Group/Artiste	Title
Stereo Mc's	Connected		The Happening (6)
	Step It Up		Nathan Jones (5)
Steve Harley	Here Comes the Sun		Stoned Love (3)
Steve Harley and	Make Me Smile (1)		Stop in the Name of
Cockney Rebel			Love (7)
Steve Harley and	The Phantom of the Opera		Where Did Our Love
Sarah Brightman			Go (3)
Steve Lawrence	Footsteps		You Can't Hurry Love (3)
Steve Miller Band	Abracadabra		You Keep Me Hangin'
	The Joker(1)		On (7)
Steve 'Silk' Hurley	Jack Your Body (1)	Supremes and the	River Deep Mountain
Steve Walsh	I Found Lovin'	Four Tops	High (11)
Stevie Wonder	For Once in My Life	Surfaris	Wipe Out (5)
	Happy Birthday (2)	Survivor	Burning Heart
	He's Misstra Know It All		Eye of the Tiger (1)
	I Just Called to Say I Love	Susan Maughan	Bobby's Girl
	You (1)	Sutherland Brothers	Arms of Mary
	I Was Made to Love Her	and Quiver	
	Masterblaster (Jammin')	Suzanne Vega	Tom's Diner
	My Cherie Amour	Suzi Quatro	Can the Can(1)
	Part Time Lover		Devil Gate Drive (1)
	Signed Sealed Delivered I'm		48 Crash
	Yours		If You Can't Give Me Love
	Sir Duke		The Wild One (7)
	Uptight	Sweet	Ballroom Blitz (2)
	You Are the Sunshine of My		Blockbuster (1)
	Life		Co-Co
Stiltskin	Inside (1)		Fox on the Run (2)
Stock Aitken	Mr Sleaze		Hell Raiser (2)
Waterman			Little Willy (4)
Stranglers	All Day and All of the		Love Is Like Oxygen (9)
	Night (7)		Teenage Rampage (2)
	Golden Brown (2)		Wig-Wam Bam (4)
	No More Heroes (8)	Sweet Dreams	Honey Honey (10)
	Peaches	Sweet People	And the Birds Were Singing
	Strange Little Girl (7)	Sweet Sensation	Sad Sweet Dreamer (1)
Strawberry	Since Yesterday	Swinging Blue Jeans	Hippy Hippy Shake (2)
Switchblade			You're No Good
Strawbs	Part of the Union (2)	Swing Out Sister	Breakout
Stray Cats	Runaway Boys		Surrender
String-a-Longs	Wheels	Sybil	Walk On By (6)
Style Council	My Ever Changing		When I'm Good and Ready
	Moods (5)	Sydney Youngblood	If Only I Could
	Shout to the Top	Sylvester	You Make Me Feel (Mighty
	Speak Like a Child		Real) (8)
	Walls Come Tumbling	Sylvia	Y Viva Espana (4)
	Down	Tab Hunter	Young Love (1)
Stylistics	Can't Give You Anything (1)	Taffy	I Love My Radio (6)
	I'm Stone in Love with You	Taja Sevelle	Love Is Contagious
	Na Na Is the Saddest Word	Take That	Back for Good (1)
	16 Bars		Could It Be Magic (4)
	You Make Me Feel Brand		Everything Changes (1)
	New		How Deep is Your Love (1)
Styx	Babe (6)		It Only Takes a Minute (7)
Sub Sub with Melanie	Ain't No Love		A Million Love Songs (7)
Williams			Never Forget (1)
Suede	Animal Nitrate		Pray (1)
Sugar Minott	Good Thing Going (4)		Promises
Sugarhill Gang	Rapper's Delight		Sure (1)
Sunny	Doctor's Orders		Why Can't I Wake Up with
Supergrass	Alright		You Babe (1)
	Lenny	Take That featuring	Relight My Fire (1)
	Richard III	Lulu	
	Sun Hits the Sky	Talking Heads	Road to Nowhere (6)
Supertramp	Breakfast in America	Tami Lynn	I'm Gonna Run Away from You
	The Logical Song	Tammy Jones	Let Me Try Again
Su Pollard	Starting Together	Tammy Wynette	D.I.V.O.R.C.E.
Supremes	Automatically Sunshine		Stand by Your Man (1)
	(10)	Tamperer featuring	Feel It (1)
	Baby Love (1)	Maya	
	Floy Joy (9)	Tams	Hey Girl Don't Bother Me (1)

Group/Artiste	Title
Tanita Tikaram	Good Tradition
	Twist in My Sobriety
Tasmin Archer	In Your Care
	Sleeping Satellite (1)
Tavares	Don't Take Away the Music
	Heaven Must Be Missing an Angel
	More Than a Woman
	Whodunit
Taylor Dane	Prove Your Love
	Tell It to My Heart
Teardrop Explodes	Reward
Tears for Fears	Change
	Everybody Wants to Rule the World (2)
	Everybody Wants to Run the World (5)
	Mad World
	Pale Shelter
	Shout (4)
	Sowing the Seeds of Love (5)
Technotronic	Megamix (6)
Technotronic featuring Felly	Pump Up the Jam (2)
Technotronic featuring Reggie	Move That Body (12)
Technotronic featuring Ya Kid K	Get Up (2)
	Rockin' over the Beat (9)
Teddy Bears	To Know Him Is to Love Him (2)
Ted Heath	Dragnet
	Hot Toddy
	Skin Deep
Teena Marie	Behind the Groove
Teenagers featuring Frankie Lymon	Why Do Fools Fall in Love (1)
Teletubbies	Teletubbies Say Eh-Oh (1)
Telly Savalas	If (1)
Temperance Seven	Pasadena (4)
	You're Driving Me Crazy (1)
Temptations	Ball of Confusion (7)
	Just My Imagination (8)
	My Girl (2)
10cc	Art for Art's Sake (5)
	The Dean and I (10)
	Donna (2)
	Dreadlock Holiday (1)
	Good Morning Judge (5)
	I'm Mandy Fly Me (6)
	I'm Not in Love (1)
	Life Is a Minestrone (7)
	Rubber Bullets (1)
	Things We Do for Love (6)
	Wall Street Shuffle (10)
Ten City	That's the Way Love Is
Ten Sharp	You (10)
Ten Years After	Love Like a Man (10)
Tennessee Ernie Ford	The Ballad of Davy Crockett
	Give Me Your Word (1)
	Sixteen Tons (1)
Tenpole Tudor	Swords of a Thousand Men
	Who Killed Bambi (6)
Terence Trent D'Arby	If You Let Me Stay
	Sign Your Name
	Wishing Well
Teresa Brewer	Let Me Go Lover (9)
	A Tear Fell
Terry Dactyl and the Dinosaurs	Seaside Shuffle
Terry Dene	A White Sport Coat
Terry Hall	Ballad of a Landlord

Group/Artiste	Title
Terry Jacks	Seasons in the Sun (1)
Terry Wogan	Floral Dance (21)
Texas	I Don't Want a Lover (8)
Tex Ritter	Wayward Wind (8)
Them	Baby Please Don't Go (10)
	Here Comes the Night (2)
Therapy	Shortsharpshock
They Might Be Giants	Birdhouse in Your Soul
Thin Lizzy	The Boys Are Back in Town (8)
	Killer on the Loose
	Waiting for An Alibi
	Whiskey in the Jar (6)
Third World	Dancing on the Floor
	Now That We've Found Love
Thompson Twins	Doctor Doctor (3)
	Love on Your Side (9)
	We Are Detective (7)
	You Take Me Up (2)
Three Degrees	My Simple Heart
	Take Good Care of Yourself
	When Will I See You Again (1)
	Woman in Love (3)
Three Kayes	Ivory Tower
3T	Gotta Be You
Thunderclap Newman	Accidents (46)
	Something in the Air (1)
Tiffany	Could've Been (4)
	I Saw Him Standing There (8)
	I Think We're Alone Now (1)
Tight Fit	Fantasy Island
	The Lion Sleeps Tonight (1)
Timelords	Doctorin' the Tardis
Tina Arena	Chains
Tina Turner	I Don't Wanna Fight
	Let's Stay Together (6)
	Steamy Windows (13)
	The Best (5)
	Way of the World
	We Don't Need Another Hero (3)
	What's Love Got to Do with It (3)
Tinman	Eighteen Strings
Tin Tin Out (with Tony Hadley)	Dance with Me
Tiny Tim	Great Balls of Fire (45)
TLC	Waterfalls
Tom Jones	A Boy from Nowhere
	Daughter of Darkness
	Delilah (2)
	Detroit City
	Green Green Grass of Home (1)
	Help Yourself
	I Was Born to Be Me
	It's Not Unusual (1)
	Till
	What's New Pussycat
	The Young New Mexican Puppeteer
Tommy Dorsey and Warren Covington	Tea For Two Cha Cha
Tommy Edwards	It's All in the Game (1)
Tommy James and the Shondells	Mony Mony (1)
Tommy Roe	Dizzy (1)
	Sheila
	The Folk Singer
Tommy Steele	Butterfingers

Group/Artiste	Title	Group/Artiste	Title
	Little White Bull		Telegram Sam (1)
	Nairobi		20th Century Boy (3)
	Singing the Blues (1)	Trini Lopez	If I Had a Hammer (4)
	Water Water	Trio	Da Da Da
Tom Robinson	War Baby	Troggs	I Can't Control Myself (2)
Tom Robinson Band	2-4-6-8 Motorway		Love Is All Around (5)
Tom Tom Club	Wordy Rappinghood		Wild Thing (2)
Tone Loc	Funky Cold Medina		With a Girl Like You (1)
	Wild Thing (21)	Tubeway Army	Are Friends Electric (1)
Toni Basil	Mickey	Turtles	Elenore
Toni Braxton	Breathe Again		Happy Together
Tony Bennett	I Left My Heart in San		She'd Rather Be with Me
	Francisco	Tweets	The Birdie Song
	Stranger in Paradise	Twenty 4 Seven with	I Can't Stand It
Tony Braxton	I Don't Want To	Captain Hollywood	
	Un-Break My Heart	Twinkle	Terry (4)
Tony Christie	Avenues and Alleyways	2 Unlimited	Get Ready for This (2)
	I Did What I Did for Maria		No Limit (1)
Tony di Bart	The Real Thing (1)		Tribal Dance
Tony Martin	Stranger in Paradise (6)		Twilight Zone (2)
	Walk Hand in Hand		Workaholic (4)
Tony Orlando	Bless You	Tymes	Ms Grace (1)
Topol	If I Were a Rich Man	Typically Tropical	Barbados (1)
Tori Amos	Cornflake Girl	Tyrannosaurus Rex	Debora
	Professional Widow (1)	UB40	Falling in Love with You (1)
Tornados	Globetrotter		Homely Girl (6)
	Telstar (1)		King (4)
Toto	Africa		Kingston Town
Toto Coelo	I Eat Cannibals		Red Red Wine (1)
Tottenham Hotspur	Ossie's Dream		The Earth Dies Screaming
Cup Final Squad		UB40 featuring	Breakfast in Bed (6)
Tourists	I Only Want to Be with You	Chrissie Hynde	I Got You Babe (1)
	So Good to Be Back Home	Ugly Kid Joe	Cats in the Cradle
	Again		Everything about You
Toy Dolls	Nellie the Elephant	Ultra Nate	Free
Toyah	Brave New World	Ultravox	All Stood Still
	Four from Toyah EP		Dancing with Tears in My
	I Want to Be Free		Eyes
Toys	A Lover's Concerto		Vienna (2)
T'Pau	China in Your Hand (1)	Undercover	Baker Street (2)
	Heart and Soul		Never Let Her Slip Away (5)
	Valentine	Undertones	Jimmy Jimmy (16)
Tracey Ullman	Breakaway (4)		My Perfect Cousin
	Move Over Darling (8)		Teenage Kicks (31)
	They Don't Know (2)	Union Gap featuring	Lady Willpower
Tracie	The House That Jack Built (9)	Gary Puckett	Young Girl (1)
Traffic	Here We Go Round the	Unit Four Plus Two	Concrete and Clay (1)
	Mulberry Bush	Upsetters	Return of Django
	Hole in My Shoe (2)	Urban Cookie	The Key the Secret
	Paper Sun	Collective	
Trammps	Hold Back the Night	Urban Hype	A Trip to Trumpton
Transvision Vamp	I Want Your Love	USA for Africa	We Are the World (1)
Trans-X	Living On Video	Usher	You Make Me Wanna (1)
Traveling Wilburys	End of the Line	Usura	Open Your Mind
	Handle with Care	Utah Saints	Something Good
Travis	Why Does It Always Rain on		What Can You Do for Me
	Me? (10)	U2	Beautiful Day (1)
Tremeloes	Even the Bad Times Are		Desire (1)
	Good		Discotheque (1)
	Me and My Life		The Fly
	Number One		I Still Haven't Found What I'm
	Silence Is Golden (1)		Looking For (6)
	Suddenly You Love Me		New Year's Day (10)
Trevor Walters	Stuck on You (9)		One (7)
T Rex	Children of the Revolution (2)		Pride (In the Name of
	Get It On (1)		Love) (3)
	The Groover (4)		Staring at the Sun
	Hot Love (1)		The Unforgettable Fire (6)
	Jeepster (2)		Where the Streets Have No
	Metal Guru (1)		Name (4)
	Ride a White Swan (2)		With or Without You (4)

Group/Artiste	Title
U2 featuring BB King	When Love Comes to Town (6)
Val Doonican	If the Whole World Stopped Loving
	Walk Tall
	What Would I Be
Vanessa Mae	Toccata and Fugue
Vanessa Paradis	Be My Baby
	Joe Le Taxi
Vanessa Williams	Save the Best for Last
Van Halen	Jump (7)
	Why Can't This Be Love 98)
Vanilla Ice	Ice Ice Baby (1)
	Play That Funky Music (10)
Vanity Fare	Early in the Morning
Van McCoy	The Shuffle
Van McCoy with theSoul City Symphony	The Hustle
Van Morrison and Cliff Richard	Whenever God Shines His Light
Vapors	Turning Japanese
Vengaboys	Boom, Boom, Boom, Boom (1)
	We're Going to Ibiza (1)
Ventures	Perfidia (4)
	Walk Don't Run (8)
Vera Lynn	Auf Wiedersehen
	Forget Me Not
	Homing Waltz
Vera Lynn with Frank Weir and Orchestra	My Son My Son (1)
The Verve	Bittersweet Symphony
	The Drugs Don't Work (1)
Vic Damone	On the Street Where You Live
Vicky Leandros	Come What May
Vic Reeves and the Roman Numerals	Born Free (6)
Vic Reeves and the Wonder Stuff	Dizzy (1)
Village People	Can't Stop the Music (11)
	In the Navy (2)
	YMCA
Vince Hill	Edelweiss
	Importance of Your Love
	Roses of Picardy
Viola Wills	Gonna Get Along without You Now (8)
Vipers Skiffle Group	Cumberland Gap (10)
	Don't You Rock Me Daddy-O (10)
Visage	Fade to Grey
Vivian Blaine	Bushel and a Peck
Wah!	The Story of the Blues (3)
Waldo de los Rios	Mozart Symphony No. 40 in G Minor
Walker Brothers	Make It Easy on Yourself (1)
	My Ship Is Coming In (3)
	No Regrets (7)
	The Sun Ain't Gonna Shine Anymore (1)
Wamdue Project	King of My Castle (1)
Was (Not Was)	Walk the Dinosaur
Waterboys	The Whole of the Moon (3)
Wayne Fontana and the Mindbenders	Game Of Love
	Um Um Um Um Um Um
Weather Girls	It's Raining Men (2)
Wedding Present	Come Play with Me (10)
Wee Papa Girl Rappers	Wee Rule
West End featuring Sybil	The Love I Lost

Group/Artiste	Title
Westlife	Flying without Wings (1)
	Fool Again (1)
	If I Let You Go (1)
	I Have a Dream/Seasons in the Sun (1)
	My Love (1)
	Swear It Again (1)
	Uptown Girl (1)
Westlife and Mariah Carey	Against All Odds (1)
Wet Wet Wet	Goodnight Girl (1)
	If I Never See You Again
	Julia Says
	Love Is All Around (1)
	Sweet Little Mystery
	Sweet Surrender
	Wishing I Was Lucky
	With a Little Help from My Friends (1)
Wham	Bad Boys
	Club Fantastic
	Club Tropicana
	Freedom (1)
	I'm Your Man (1)
	Last Christmas
	The Edge of Heaven (1)
	Wake Me up before You Go Go (1)
	Wham Rap
	Young Guns (3)
Whigfield	Saturday Night (1)
Whispers	And the Beat Goes On (2)
	It's a Love Thing
Whistling Jack Smith	I Was Kaiser Bill's Batman
White Plains	Julie Do Ya Love Me
Whitesnake	Here I Go Again (9)
	Is This Love (9)
White Town	Your Woman
Whitney Houston	Greatest Love of All
	I Have Nothing
	I Wanna Dance with Somebody (1)
	I Will Always Love You (1)
	I'm Every Woman
	One Moment in Time (1)
	Saving All My Love for You (1)
	So Emotional
Whitney Houston and Aretha Franklin	It Isn't It Wasn't It Ain't Never Gonna Be
Whitney Houston and Teddy Pendergrass	Hold Me
Who	Anyway Anyhow Anywhere
	I Can't Explain (8)
	I'm a Boy (2)
	Join Together (9)
	My Generation (2)
	Pinball Wizard (4)
	Squeeze Box (10)
	Substitute (5)
	You Better You Bet (9)
Wigan's Chosen Few	Footsee
William Bell and Judy Clay	Private Number
Will Smith	Men in Black (1)
Wilson Phillips	Hold On (6)
	Hey Jude (16)
Wilson Pickett	In the Midnight Hour (12)
Windsor Davies and Don Estelle	Whispering Grass

MUSIC POP

Group/Artiste	Title	Group/Artiste	Title
Wings	Give Ireland Back to the Irish		For Your Love
	Hi Hi Hi/C Moon		Heart Full of Soul
	Let 'Em In		Over Under Sideways Down
	Listen to What the Man Said		Shapes of Things
	Live and Let Die (9)	Yazoo	Don't Go (3)
	Mary Had a Little Lamb		Nobody's Diary
	Mull of Kintyre (1)		Only You (2)
	Silly Love Songs	Yazz	Fine Time
	With a Little Luck		Stand Up for Your Love Rights
Wink Martindale	Deck of Cards (5)	Yazz and the Plastic	The Only Way Is Up (1)
Wizzard	Angel Fingers (1)	Population	
	Are You Ready to Rock (8)	Yell!	Instant Replay (10)
	Ball Park Incident (6)	Yello	The Race
	I Wish It Could Be Christmas	Yellow Dog	Just One More Night
	Everyday (4)	Yes	Wonderous Stories
	Rock 'N' Roll Winter (6)	Yoko Ono	Walking on Thin Ice
	See My Baby Jive (1)	Young Idea	With a Little Help from My
Womack and	Celebrate the World (19)		Friends (10)
Womack	Love Wars (14)	Young Rascals	Groovin'
	Teardrops (3)	Youssou N'Dour	7 Seconds
Wombles	Banana Rock (9)	featuring Neneh	
	Remember You're a Womble (3)	Cherry	
	Wombling Merry Christmas	Yvonne Elliman	If I Can't Have You
	The Wombling Song (4)		Love Me
Wonder Stuff	The Size of a Cow	Yvonne Fair	It Should Have Been Me
Wurzels	Combine Harvester (Brand	Zager and Evans	In the Year 2525 (Exordium
	New Key) (1)		and Terminus)
	Farmer Bill's Cowman (Kaiser	Zig and Zag	Them Girls Them Girls
	Bill's Batman)	Ziggy Marley and the	Tomorrow People
	I Am a Cider Drinker (Paloma	Melody Makers	
	Blanca) (3)	Zoe	Sunshine on a Rainy Day
WWF Superstars	Slam Jam	Zombies	She's Not There (12)
Xpansions	Move Your Body (7)	Zucchero and	Senza Una Donna (Without
XTC	Senses Working Overtime	Paul Young	a Woman)
Yarbrough and	Don't Stop the Music	ZZ Top	Gimme all Your Lovin'
Peoples			Viva Las Vegas
Yardbirds	Evil Hearted You		

Christmas No. 1s

1952	Here in My Heart – Al Martino	1977	Mull of Kintyre/Girls' School – Wings
1953	Answer Me – Frankie Laine	1978	Mary's Boy Child – Boney M
1954	Let's Have Another Party – Winifred Atwell	1979	Another Brick in the Wall – Pink Floyd
1955	The Christmas Alphabet – Dickie Valentine.	1980	There's No One Quite Like Grandma – St
1956	Just Walkin' in the Rain – Johnnie Ray		Winifred's School Choir
1957	Mary's Boy Child – Harry Belafonte	1981	Don't You Want Me – Human League
1958	It's Only Make Believe – Conway Twitty	1982	Save Your Love – Renee and Renato
1959	What Do You Want to Make Those Eyes at	1983	Only You – Flying Pickets
	Me For – Emile Ford and the Checkmates	1984	Do They Know It's Christmas – Band Aid
1960	I Love You – Cliff Richard and the Shadows	1985	Merry Christmas Everyone – Shakin'
1961	Moon River – Danny Williams		Stevens
1962	Return to Sender – Elvis Presley	1986	Reet Petite – Jackie Wilson
1963	I Want to Hold Your Hand – Beatles	1987	Always on My Mind – Pet Shop Boys
1964	I Feel Fine – Beatles	1988	Mistletoe and Wine – Cliff Richard
1965	Day Tripper/We Can Work It Out – Beatles	1989	Do They Know It's Christmas? – Band Aid II
1966	Green Green Grass of Home – Tom Jones	1990	Saviour's Day – Cliff Richard
1967	Hello Goodbye – Beatles	1991	Bohemian Rhapsody / These Are the Days
1968	Lily the Pink – Scaffold		of Our Lives – Queen
1969	Two Little Boys – Rolf Harris	1992	I Will Always Love You – Whitney Houston
1970	I Hear You Knockin' – Dave Edmunds	1993	Mr. Blobby – Mr. Blobby
1971	Ernie (The Fastest Milkman in the West) –	1994	Stay Another Day – East 17
	Benny Hill	1995	Earth Song – Michael Jackson
1972	Long Haired Lover from Liverpool – Little	1996	2 Become 1 – Spice Girls
	Jimmy Osmond	1997	Too Much – Spice Girls
1973	Merry Xmas Everybody – Slade	1998	Goodbye – Spice Girls
1974	Lonely This Christmas – Mud	1999	I Have a Dream/Seasons in the Sun –
1975	Bohemian Rhapsody – Queen		Westlife
1976	When a Child Is Born – Johnny Mathis	2000	Can We Fix It – Bob The Builder

LPs

Title	Group/artiste	Title	Group/artiste
Abacab	Genesis	Blue Is the Colour	Beautiful South
Abbey Road	Beatles	Blue Sky on Mars	Matthew Sweet
According to My Heart	Jim Reeves	Bookends	Simon and Garfunkel
Achtung Baby	U2	Both Sides	Phil Collins
Actually	Pet Shop Boys	Boys and Girls	Bryan Ferry
Adrenalize	Def Leppard	Breakfast In America	Supertramp
Affection	Lisa Stansfield	Bridge of Spies	T'Pau
Afterburner	ZZ Top	Bridge Over Troubled Water	Simon and Garfunkel
Aftermath	Rolling Stones	British Steel	Judas Priest
The Age of Consent	Bronski Beat	Brothers in Arms	Dire Straits
Agent Provocateur	Foreigner	Buddah and the Chocolate Box	Cat Stevens
Aja	Steely Dan	Bursting at the Seams	Strawbs
Aladdin Sane	David Bowie	Business as Usual	Men at Work
Album of the Year	Faith No More	Cafe Bleu	Style Council
Alf	Alison Moyet	Can't Slow Down	Lionel Richie
All Change	Cast	Captain Fantastic and the	Elton John
All Things Must Pass	George Harrison	Brown Dirt Cowboy	
Ancient Heart	Tanita Tikaram	Captain Paralytic and the	
Andromeda Heights	Prefab Sprout	Brown Ale Cowboy	Mike Harding
Another Time, Another Place	Bryan Ferry	Caribou	Elton John
Anthem	Toyah	Carry On up the Charts	Beautiful South
The Anvil	Visage	Catch Bull at Four	Cat Stevens
Appetite for Destruction	Guns N' Roses	China Town	Thin Lizzy
Are You Experienced?	Jimi Hendrix	Chorus	Erasure
	Experience	Circle of One	Oleta Adams
Are You Gonna Go My Way	Lenny Kravitz	The Circus	Erasure
Argus	Wishbone Ash	Cloud Nine	George Harrison
Armed Forces	Elvis Costello	Colour	Christians
Arrival	Abba	The Colour and the Shape	Foo Fighters
Astral Weeks	Van Morrison	Colour By Numbers	Culture Club
Atlantic Crossing	Rod Stewart	The Colour of My Love	Celine Dion
Atom Heart Mother	Pink Floyd	Coming Up	Suede
Attack of the Grey Lantern	Mansun	Communique	Dire Straits
Auberge	Chris Rea	Connected	Stereo MCs
Autobahn	Kraftwerk	Conscience	Womack and
Automatic for the People	R.E.M.		Womack
Avalon	Roxy Music	Conversation Peace	Stevie Wonder
Babylon and On	Squeeze	Cosmo's Factory	Creedence
Back in Black	AC/DC		Clearwater
Back to Front (1)	Gilbert O'Sullivan		Revival
	(1972)	Crazy You	G.U.N.
Back to Front (1)	Lionel Richie	Cricklewood Green	Ten Years After
	(1992)	Crime of the Century	Supertramp
Bad	Michael Jackson	Crocodiles	Echo and the
Bagsy Me	Wannadies		Bunnymen
Band of Gypsies	Jimi Hendrix	Cross of Changes	Enigma
Band on the Run	Wings	Crossroads	Tracy Chapman
Batman	Prince	Culture Club	Colour by Numbers
Bat Out Of Hell	Meat Loaf	Cuts Both Ways	Gloria Estefan
Before the Rain	Eternal	Dancin' in the Key of Life	Steve Arrington
Beggars Banquet	Rolling Stones	Dangerous	Michael Jackson
Be Here Now (1)	Oasis	Dare	Human League
Behind the Mask	Fleetwood Mac	Dark Side of the Moon	Pink Floyd
Big Bang	We've Got a Fuzzbox	A Day at the Races	Queen
	and We're Gonna	Daydream	Mariah Carey
	Use it	Days of Future Passed	Moody Blues
Big River	Jimmy Nail	Destination Anywhere	Jon Bon Jovi
Billion Dollar Babies	Alice Cooper	Destiny	Gloria Estefan
Black Tie White Noise	David Bowie	Diamond Dogs	David Bowie
Blast	Holly Johnson	Diamond Life	Sade
Blonde on Blonde	Bob Dylan	A Different Beat	Boyzone
Blondes Have More Fun	Rod Stewart	Different Class	Pulp
Blood on the Dance Floor (1)	Michael Jackson	Dig Your Own Hole	Chemical Brothers
Blood Sugar Sex Magik	Red Hot Chilli	Discovery	Electric Light
	Peppers		Orchestra
Bloody Tourists	10cc	Disraeli Gears	Cream
Blue for You	Status Quo	Diva	Annie Lennox

M
U
S
I
C

P
O
P

Title	Group/artiste	Title	Group/artiste
The Division Bell	Pink Floyd	Goodbye	Cream
Dizzy Heights	Lightning Seeds	Goodbye Cruel World	Elvis Costello
Do It Yourself	The Seahorses	Goodbye Yellow Brick Road	Elton John
Don't Be Cruel	Bobby Brown	Goodnight Vienna	Ringo Starr
Don't Shoot Me, I'm Only the		Graceland	Paul Simon
Piano Player	Elton John	Graffiti Bridge	Prince
Double Fantasy	John Lennon	The Great Escape	Blur
Down Drury Lane to Memory	One Hundred and	Great Expectations	Tasmin Archer
Lane	One Strings	The Great Rock 'n' Roll Swindle	Sex Pistols
Drag	kd lang	Guilty	Barbra Streisand
Dreamland	Robert Miles	Happy Nation	Ace of Base
Dreams Are Nothin' More	David Cassidy	Harvest	Neil Young
Than Wishes		Headquarters	Monkees
Dr Feelgood	Motley Crue	The Healing Game	Van Morrison
Duke	Genesis	Hearsay	Alexander O'Neal
Eat to the Beat	Blondie	Heaven and Hell	Vangelis
Electric Ladyland	Jimi Hendrix	Heavy Soul (1)	Paul Weller
	Experience	Hedgehog Sandwich	Not the 9 O'Clock
Electric Warrior	T Rex		News Cast
Elegantly Wasted	INXS	Hello	Status Quo
Eliminator	ZZ Top	Help!	Beatles
Emergency on Planet Earth	Jamiroquai	Hergest Ridge	Mike Oldfield
Emotional Rescue	Rolling Stones	High on the Happy Side	Wet Wet Wet
Endless Flight	Leo Sayer	Highway 61 Revisited	Bob Dylan
English Settlement	X-Ray Specs	History – Past Present and	Michael Jackson
Enjoy Yourself	Kylie Minogue	Future Book	
Every Good Boy Deserves	Moody Blues	Hit	Wannadies
Favour		Horses	Patti Smith
Every Picture Tells a Story	Rod Stewart	Hotel California	Eagles
Everybody Else Is Doing it,	Cranberries	Hot Rats	Frank Zappa
So Why Can't We		Hounds of Love	Kate Bush
Everything Changes	Take That	Houses of the Holy	Led Zeppelin
Everything Must Go	Manic Street	Human Racing	Nik Kershaw
	Preachers	Human's Lib	Howard Jones
Exile on Main Street	Rolling Stones	Human Touch	Bruce Springsteen
Extra Virgin	Olive	Hunky Dory	David Bowie
Façades	Sad Cafe	Hunting High and Low	A-Ha
Face Value	Phil Collins	The Hurting	Tears for Fears
Falling Into You	Celine Dion	Hypnotised	Undertones
Fantastic!	Wham!	Hysteria (1)	Def Leppard
Faster Than the Speed of Night	Bonnie Tyler	Hysteria (3)	Human League
The Fat of the Land (1)	The Prodigy	I Am	Eath Wind and Fire
Fear of the Dark	Iron Maiden	I Do Not Want What I	Sinead O'Connor
Fever In Fever Out	Luscious Jackson	Haven't Got	
The Final Cut	Pink Floyd	If the Beatles Had Read	Wonder Stuff
Fireball	Deep Purple	Hunter . . . The Singles	
Flaming Pie (1)	Paul McCartney	The Immaculate Collection	Madonna
Flesh and Blood	Roxy Music	In Blue	Corrs
Flowers in the Dirt	Paul McCartney	In It for the Money	Supergrass
Flying Colours	Chris De Burgh	Innervisions	Stevie Wonder
Fog on the Tyne	Lindisfarne	An Innocent Man	Billy Joel
Foreign Affair	Tina Turner	The Innocents	Erasure
Forever	Damage	Innuendo	Queen
Forever Changes	Love	In Search of the Lost Chord	Moody Blues
461 Ocean Boulevard	Eric Clapton	In Square Circle	Stevie Wonder
Four Symbols	Led Zeppelin	In Through the Out Door	Led Zeppelin
Foxtrot	Genesis	Into the Gap	Thompson Twins
Fresh	Gina G	Invisible Touch	Genesis
Fresh Cream	Cream	I Say I Say I Say	Erasure
From the Cradle	Eric Clapton	I Should Coco	Supergrass
The Game	Queen	It Doesn't Matter Anymore	Supernaturals
Germ Free Adolescents	X-Ray Specs	It's Better to Travel	Swing Out Sister
Ghost in the Machine	Police	It's Great When You're	Black Grape
The Gift	Jam	...Straight Yeah!	
Give Me the Reason	Luther Vandross	I've Been Expecting You	Robbie Williams
Glittering Prize	Simple Minds	Jam	Little Angels
Goat's Head Soup	Rolling Stones	John Wesley Harding	Bob Dylan
Going for the One	Yes	Jollification	Lightning Seeds
Going to a Go-Go	Smokey Robinson	The Joshua Tree	U2
	and the Miracles	Journey Through the Secret	Stevie Wonder
Gold Blade	Hometurf	Life of Plants	

Title	Group/artiste	Title	Group/artiste
Journey to the Centre of the Earth	Rick Wakeman	Nashville Skyline	Bob Dylan
Ju Ju	Siouxsie and the Banshees	Natural	Peter Andre
		Never a Dull Moment	Rod Stewart
Junction Seven	Steve Winwood	Never for Ever	Kate Bush
K	Kula Shaker	Never Mind the Bollocks Here's the Sex Pistols	Sex Pistols
Kaleidoscope	Siouxsie and the Banshees	New Boots and Panties!!	Ian Dury & the Blockheads
Kavana	Kavana	A New Flame	Simply Red
Keep the Faith	Bon Jovi	New Jersey	Bon Jovi
Kimono My House	Sparks	A New World Record	Electric Light Orchestra
Kings of the Wild Frontier	Adam Ant		
Koo Koo	Debbie Harry	A Night at the Opera	Queen
L	Steve Hillage	Night Birds	Shakatak
Labour of Love	UB40	Night Flight to Venus	Boney M
La Passione	Chris Rea	A Night on the Town	Rod Stewart
The Last Waltz	The Band	Night Owl	Gerry Rafferty
L.A. Woman	Doors	Nine Lives	Aerosmith
Legend	Bob Marley and the Wailers	1982	Status Quo
		Nobody Else	Take That
Let It Bleed	Rolling Stones	A Nod's as Good as a Wink To a Blind Horse	Faces
The Lexicon of Love	ABC		
Lie	Charles Manson	No Jacket Required	Phil Collins
Life	Simply Red	No More Heroes	Stranglers
Life Thru a Lens	Robbie Williams	No Need to Argue	Cranberries
Lil' Darlin'	Thomas Ribeiro	No Parlez	Paul Young
The Lion and the Cobra	Sinead O'Connor	No Sleep till Hammersmith	Motorhead
Little Creatures	Talking Heads	Nothing Like the Sun	Sting
Live at the BBC	Beatles	The Number of the Beast	Iron Maiden
Live in the City of Light	Simple Minds	Ocean Drive	Lighthouse Family
Liverpool	Frankie Goes to Hollywood	Oceans of Fantasy	Boney M
		Odds and Sods	Who
Living in Oz	Rick Springfield	Off the Wall	Michael Jackson
Living in the Material World	George Harrison	Ogden's Nut Gone Flake	Small Faces
Living in the Past	Jethro Tull	OK Computer (1)	Radiohead
The Lone Ranger	Suggs	Old New Borrowed and Blue	Slade
Love at the Greek	Neil Diamond	Older	George Michael
Love de Luxe	Sade	Once Upon a Star	Bay City Rollers
Love Hurts	Cher	Once Upon a Time	Simple Minds
Love over Gold	Dire Straits	One Hot Minute	Red Hot Chili Peppers
Lovesexy	Prince	On Every Street	Dire Straits
Machine Head	Deep Purple	On the Level	Status Quo
Mad Dogs and Englishmen	Joe Cocker	On the Threshold of a Dream	Moody Blues
Made in Heaven	Queen	Only Human	Dina Carroll
Make It Big	Wham!	Only Yesterday	Carpenters
Makin' Movies	Dire Straits	Ooh-La-La	Faces
Manifesto	Roxy Music	Open Road (1)	Gary Barlow
The Man Who	Travis	Our Favourite Shop	Style Council
Meat is Murder	Smiths	Out of Time	R.E.M.
Meaty, Beaty, Big and Bouncy	Who	Outlandos d'Amour	Police
Medusa	Annie Lennox	Oxygene	Jean-Michel Jarre
Middle of Nowhere (1)	Hanson	Parallel Lines	Blondie
The Miracle	Queen	Paranoid	Black Sabbath
Mirror Ball	Neil Young	Parklife	Blur
Misplaced Childhood	Marillion	Pastpresent	Clannad
Missing .... Presumed Having a Good Time	Notting Hillbillies	Pearl	Janis Joplin
		Pearls	Elkie Brooks
Mondo Bongo	Boomtown Rats	Pet Sounds	Beach Boys
Monster	R.E.M.	Phuq	Wildhearts
The More Things Change	Machine Head	Physical Graffiti	Led Zeppelin
Morning Glory	Oasis	Picture This	Wet Wet Wet
Mother Nature Calls	Cast	Pills 'N' Thrills and Bellyaches	Happy Mondays
Mr Fantasy	Traffic	Pin-Ups	David Bowie
Mr Wonderful	Fleetwood Mac	Piper at the Gates of Dawn	Pink Floyd
Mud Slide Jim and the Blue Horizon	James Taylor	Pisces, Aquarius, Capricorn and Jones Ltd	Monkees
Music Box	Mariah Carey	Play (1)	Moby
Music for the Jilted Generation	Prodigy	The Pleasure Principle	Gary Numan
Music from Big Pink	The Band	Pocketful of Kryptonite	Spin Doctors
My Aim Is True	Elvis Costello	Pop	U2
Naked	Talking Heads	Popped in Souled Out	Wet Wet Wet

Title	Group/artiste	Title	Group/artiste
Porcupine	Echo and the Bunnymen	So	Peter Gabriel
Pornography	Cure	So Far So Good	Bryan Adams
Postcard	Mary Hopkin	Solitude Standing	Suzanne Vega
Pot Luck	Elvis Presley	So Long So Wrong	Alison Krauss and Union Station
Presence	Led Zeppelin		
Private Collection	Cliff Richard	Some Friendly	Charlatans
Private Dancer	Tina Turner	The Song Remains the Same	Led Zeppelin
Promises and Lies	UB40	Songs in the Key of Life	Stevie Wonder
Prophets, Seers and Sages	T, Rex	Songs of Faith and Devotion	Depeche Mode
Protection	Massive Attack	The Soul Cages	Sting
Pulse	Pink Floyd	Soul Provider	Michael Bolton
Pump	Aerosmith	Sound of Lies	The Jayhawks
Pump Up the Jam	Technotronic	Sparkle in the Rain	Simple Minds
Push	Bros	Spartacus	Farm
A Question of Balance	Moody Blues	Speak and Spell	Depeche Mode
Quick Step and Side Kick	Thompson Twins	Spellbound	Paula Abdul
Rage	T'Pau	Spirits Having Flown	Bee Gees
Rage in Eden	Ultravox	Sports Car	Judie Tzuke
Ram	Paul and Linda McCartney	Standing Stone	Paul McCartney
		Stand Up	Jethro Tull
Rattle and Hum	U2	Stanley Road	Paul Weller
The Raw and the Cooked	Fine Young Cannibals	Staring at the Sun	U2
Real Things	2 Unlimited	Stars	Simply Red
Red River Valley	Slim Whitman	Station to Station	David Bowie
Regatta de Blanc	Police	Stay on These Roads	A-Ha
Reload	Tom Jones	Steel Wheels	Rolling Stones
Reminiscing	Buddy Holly and the Crickets	Steeltown	Big Country
		Step by Step	New Kids on the Block
Replicas	Tubeway Army		
Republic	New Order	Sticky Fingers	Rolling Stones
Return of the Space Cowboy	Jamiroquai	Still Crazy after All These Years	Paul Simon
Return to Fantasy	Uriah Heep	Still Waters	Bee Gees
Revenge	Eurythmics	Stranded	Roxy Music
Revolver	Beatles	The Stranger	Billy Joel
Rhythm of the Saints	Paul Simon	Street Fighting Years	Simple Minds
The Riddle	Nik Kershaw	String of Hits	Shadows
Rising from the East	Bally Sagoo	Stripped	Rolling Stones
Rubber Soul	Beatles	Stupidity	Dr Feelgood
Rumours	Fleetwood Mac	Supernatural	Santana
Rum, Sodomy and the Lash	Pogues	Surrealistic Pillow	Jefferson Airplane
Runaway Horses	Belinda Carlisle	Sweet Baby James	James Taylor
Said and Done	Boyzone	Symbol	Prince
Saturday Night	Zhane	Synchronicity	Police
Savage	Eurythmics	Take Two	Robson and Jerome
Scary Monsters and Super Creeps	David Bowie	Tales from Topographic Oceans	Yes
		Talking Back to the Night	Steve Winwood
Script for a Jester's Tear	Marillion	Talking Book	Stevie Wonder
The Secret of Association	Paul Young	Talking with the Taxman about Poetry	Billy Bragg
The Seeds of Love	Tears for Fears		
Sensational	Michelle Gayle	Tango in the Night	Fleetwood Mac
Sentimental Journey	Ringo Starr	Tanx	T Rex
Sergeant Pepper's Lonely Hearts Club Band	Beatles	Tapestry	Carole King
		A Tapestry of Dreams	Charles Aznavour
Seven and the Ragged Tiger	Duran Duran	Tarkus	Emerson, Lake and Palmer
Seventh Son of a Seventh Son	Iron Maiden		
Share My World	Mary J. Blige	Tears and Laughter	Johnny Mathis
Shaved Fish	John Lennon	Tease Me	Chaka Demus and Pliers
Shelter	Brand New Heavies		
Shepherd Moons	Enya	Teaser and the Firecat	Cat Stevens
She's So Unusual	Cyndi Lauper	Technique	New Order
She's the Boss	Mick Jagger	Telekon	Gary Numan
Silk and Steel	Five Star	Tell Me on a Sunday	Marti Webb
Singles	Alison Moyet	Tellin' Stories	The Charlatans
The Six Wives of Henry VIII	Rick Wakeman	10	Wet Wet Wet
Sleeping with the Past	Elton John	Ten Good Reasons	Jason Donovan
The Slider	T Rex	Tennis	Chris Rea
Slowhand	Eric Clapton	The Man and His Music	Sam Cooke
Smiler	Rod Stewart	Thriller	Michael Jackson
The Smoker You Drink The Player You Get	Joe Walsh	Through the Barricades	Spandau Ballet
		Thunder and Lightning	Thin Lizzy
		Time for Healing	Sounds of Blackness

Title	Group/artiste	Title	Group/artiste
Timeless	Sarah Brightman	Wanted	Yazz
To the Extreme	Vanilla Ice	War	U2
To the Faithful Departed	Cranberries	Water Sign	Chris Rea
Touch	Eurythmics	Watermark	Enya
Tragic Kingdom	No Doubt	We All Had Doctors' Papers	Max Boyce
Transformer	Lou Reed	We Can Make It	Peters and Lee
Travelling without Moving	Jamiroquai	We Can't Dance	Genesis
Trout Mask Replica	Captain Beefheart and his Magic Band	We Have All the Time in the World	Louis Armstrong
True Stories	Talking Heads	We Too Are One	Eurythmics
Tubular Bells	Mike Oldfield	Welcome to the Pleasuredome	Frankie Goes to Hollywood
Tuesday Night Music Club	Sheryl Crow		
Tug of War	Paul McCartney	Welcome to Wherever You Are	INXS
Tunnel of Love	Bruce Springsteen	Whatever You Want	Status Quo
Turn Back the Clock	Johnny Hates Jazz	When the World Knows Your Name	Deacon Blue
Turn It Upside Down	Spin Doctors		
Tusk	Fleetwood Mac	Whipped Cream and Other Delights	Herb Alpert and the Tijuana Brass
12 Gold Bars	Status Quo		
21 Today	Cliff Richard	White Feathers	Kajagoogoo
U.F. Orb	Orb	White on Blonde	Texas
Ultra	Depeche Mode	The Whole Story	Kate Bush
Under the Pink	Tori Amos	Wicked Game	Chris Isaak
The Unforgettable Fire	U2	Wild!	Erasure
Universal Soldier	Donovan	Wild Wood	Paul Weller
Up	Right Said Fred	Wish	Cure
Upstairs at Eric's	Yazoo	Wish You Were Here	Pink Floyd
Urban Hymns (1)	Verve	Women and Captain First	Captain Sensible
Use Your Illusion	Guns N' Roses	Words of Love	Buddy Holly and the Crickets
Vauxhall and I	Morrissey		
Very	Pet Shop Boys	Wu-Tang Forever	Wu-Tang Clan
Viva Hate	Morrissey	You and Me Both	Yazoo
Voice of Love	Diana Ross	Young Americans	David Bowie
Voices from the Holy Land	Aled Jones	Your Secret Love	Luther Vandross
Voodo Lounge	Rolling Stones	You Showed Me	Lightning Seeds
Voulez-Vous	Abba	Youthquake	Dead or Alive
Wake Up!	Boo Radleys	Zenyatta Mondatta	Police
Waking Up the Neighbours	Bryan Adams	Zooropa	U2
Walking Wounded	Everything But the Girl		
Walthamstow	East 17		

M
U
S
I
C

P
O
P

Nationalities of Pop Groups and Soloists

Abba   Sweden and Norway
AC/DC   UK and Australia
Adamski   UK
Air Supply   UK and Australia
Alphaville   Germany
Aneka   UK
Angry Anderson   Australia
Anthrax   USA
Aphrodite's Child   Greece
Aqua   Denmark
Baccara   Spain
Basia   Poland
Belle Stars   UK
Black Box   Italy
Boney M   Jamaica, Antilles, Montserrat
Boris Gardiner   Jamaica
Cappella   Italy
Catatonia   Wales
Chicory Tip   UK
Crowded House   Australia and New Zealand
Curved Air   UK
Cutting Crew   UK and Canada
Danny Mirror   Holland
Darts   UK
Deee-Lite   USA, Russia and Japan

Del Amitri   UK
Eddy Grant   Guyana
Edmund Hockridge   Canada
Emile Ford   UK
Enigma   Germany and Romania
Enya   Ireland
Europe   Sweden
Father Abraham   Holland
Fleetwood Mac   UK and USA
Foreigner   UK and USA
Fox   UK and USA
FPI Project   Italy
Funkadelic   USA
Gallagher and Lyle   UK
Gibson Brothers   Martinique
Go-Gos   USA
Golden Earring   Holland
Greyhound   Jamaica
Guess Who   Canada
Hawkwind   UK (German dancer)
Helmut Zacharias   Germany
Hothouse Flowers   Ireland
Human Resource   Holland
Icehouse   New Zealand
Incognito   UK and France

Inner Circle   Jamaica
Jam and Spoon   Germany
Jam Machine   Italy
Jam Tronik   Germany
Jan Hammer   Czechoslovakia
John Farnham   Australia
John Parr   UK
John Paul Young   Australia
JT and the Big Family   Italy
Kaoma   France
Kraftwerk   Germany
Lobo (70s band)   USA
Lobo (80s band)   Holland
Mai Tai   Holland
Manfred Mann   South Africa
M/A/R/R/S   UK
Martha and the Muffins   Canada
Martika   USA
Men at Work   Australia
Men Without Hats   Canada
Mental As Anything   Australia
Metallica   USA and Denmark
Mezzoforte   Iceland
Midnight Oil   Australia
Milk and Honey   Israel
Millie   Jamaica
Milli Vanilli   France and Germany
Mixmaster   Italy
Modern Talking   Germany
Mouth and MacNeal   Holland
New Seekers   UK
Norman Greenbaum   USA
Opus   Austria
Ottawan   France
Pasadenas   UK
Patsy Gallant   Canada
Peppers   France

Percy Faith   Canada
Perez Prado   Cuba
Plastic Bertrand   Belgium
Poppy Family   Canada
Praga Khan   Belgium
Prefab Sprout   UK
Pseudo Echo   Australia
Python Lee Jackson   Australia
Rob 'N' Raz   (featuring Leila K)   Sweden
Roxette   Sweden
Rozalla   Zimbabwe
Rush   Canada
Shocking Blue   Holland
Silver Convention   Germany and USA
Snap   Germany and USA
Soeur Sourire   (Singing Nun)   Belgium
Spagna   Italy
Split Enz   New Zealand and UK
Starlight   Italy
Starsound   Holland
Stereophonics   Wales
Sweet People   France
Sylvia   Sweden
Teach-In   Holland
Technotronic   Belgium
Ten Sharp   Holland
Third World   Jamaica
Thomas Dolby   UK
Thompson Twins   New Zealand and UK
2 Unlimited   Holland
Vanessa Paradis   France
Van Halen   Holland and USA
Whigfield   Denmark
Wigan's Chosen Few   USA
Yello   Switzerland
Zucchero   Italy

General Information

album charts: first No. 1   *South Pacific, Original Soundtrack.*

album charts: started   1958.

Asia: members   formed in 1981 by Carl Palmer, John Wetton (King Crimson and Roxy Music), Steve Howe (Yes) and Geoff Downes (Yes/Buggles).

Beatles   Joint holders, with Elvis Presley, of most No. 1 records (17), including 11 consecutive No. 1s

B sides: famous   'I Talk to the Trees' by Clint Eastwood, B side of 'Wand'rin Star'; 'I Do it For You' by Fatima Mansions, B side of 'Theme from Mash' by Manic Street Preachers.

Blind Faith: members   Eric Clapton (Cream), Steve Winwood (Traffic), Rick Grech, Ginger Baker (Cream).

bongo player on 'Apache'   Cliff Richard.

Booker T. and the M.G.s: MG stands for Memphis Group.

charts: symbol indicating rise or fall   Bullet.

crowd (Ferry 'Cross the Mersey)   Christians, Holly Johnson, Paul McCartney, Gerry Marsden and Stock Aitken Waterman.

David Bowie   First TV appearance on *Gadzooks! Its All Happening* in 1965 with the Manish Boys who were nearly banned because of the length of Bowie's hair. Other groups he formed included King Bees, Kon-Rads, Feathers, Hype, and the Lower Third.

Emerson, Lake and Palmer (ELP)   Keith Emerson (The Nice), Greg Lake (King Crimson) and Carl Palmer (Atomic Rooster and the Crazy World of Arthur Brown).

Fine Young Cannibals: members   Roland Gift, Andy Cox (The Beat), David Steele (The Beat).

Five Star: family name   Pearson.

Led Zeppelin: members   Robert Plant, Jimmy Page, John Paul Jones, John Bonham.

Madonna: Father of her children Carlos Leon, actor and personal trainer, Guy Ritchie, film director (husband).

Missing star   Richey Edwards of Manic Street Preachers went missing in 1995.

Monkees   Advertisement in the Los Angeles *Daily Vanity* in September 1965 by Bob Rafelson and Bert Schneider led to the formation of the band. Of the 437 hopefuls who were auditioned, Stephen Stills, Charles Manson and Danny Hutton (later of Three Dog Night) were among those turned down.

most weeks on LP charts   *Bat Out of Hell* (472 weeks to date but only reached No. 9).

No. 1 in LP charts throughout year   *South Pacific, Original Soundtrack* (1959).

Notting Hillbillies: members   Mark Knopfler,

Brendan Croker, Steve Phillips, Guy Fletcher, Ed Bicknall (Knopfler's manager).

pop star thrown off plane in Germany   Keith Flint of Prodigy.

Single charts: first No. 1   'Here in My Heart' by Al Martino (November 1952).

Single charts: started   14 November 1952 (12 records).

Single: wrong name on label   'Elizabethan Reggae' by Boris Gardiner originally had 'Byron Lee' on label.

Spice Girls: nicknames   Emma Bunton – Baby Spice, Mel Brown – Scary Spice, Mel Chisholm – Sporty Spice, Victoria Adams – Posh Spice, Geri Halliwell – Ginger Spice.

Spice Girls: No. 1s   Apart from the nine No. 1

records as a group, as at April 2001, all four members have had solo No. 1 singles.

That's What Friends Are For   Dionne Warwick and Friends featuring Elton John, Stevie Wonder and Gladys Knight.

Top of the Pops: theme tunes   'Whole Lotta Love', 'Yellow Pearl' (Phil Lynott), 'The Wizard' (Paul Hardcastle), 'Get out of That' (Tony Gibber).

Vice-President of USA wrote: No. 1 Hit   Charles Dawes adapted his 'Melodie' with Carl Sigman, which became 'It's all in the game'.

Vince Clarke: bands involved with   Depeche Mode, Yazoo (with Alison Moyet) and Erasure (with Andy Bell).

Westlife: No. 1s   First seven records all reached No. 1.

Previous Names of Groups

The Alarm   Toilets, 17
America   Daze
Applejacks   Jaguars, Crestas
Badfinger   Iveys
Bangles   Supersonic Bangs, The Bangs
Bauhaus   Bauhaus 1919
Beachboys   Carl and the Passions
Beatles   Silver Beatles, Quarrymen, Beatals, Beat Brothers
Black Sabbath   Earth
Boomtown Rats   Nightlife Thugs
The Christians   Natural High
The Commodores   Mighty Mystics
The Cult   Southern Death Cult
Culture Club   In Praise of Lemmings, Sex Gang Children
The Cure   The Easy Cure
Deep Purple   Roundabout
Depeche Mode   Composition of Sound
Dire Straits   Cafe Racers
Doobie Brothers   Pud
Dr Hook   Chocolate Papers
Eurythmics   The Catch, Tourists
Faces   Quiet Melon, Small Faces
Family   Farinas
Fifth Dimension   Versatiles
The Fixx   Portraits, The Fix
The Fourmost   Blue Jays, Four Jays
The Four Seasons   Variatones, Four Lovers
The Four Tops   Four Aims
Frankie Goes to Hollywood   Hollycaust
Freddie and the Dreamers   Kingfishers
Genesis   Garden Wall
Gerry and the Pacemakers   Mars Bars
The Grateful Dead   Warlocks
Herman's Hermits   Heartbeats
Hollies   Fourtones, Deltas
Human League   Dead Daughters, Future
Icehouse   Flowers
INXS   Farriss Brothers

Led Zeppelin   New Yardbirds, Birmingham Water Buffalo Society
Madness   The Invaders
Mamas and the Papas   The New Journeymen, Mugwumps
Manfred Mann   Mann-Hugg Blues Brothers
Marillion   Silmarillion
The Mission   Sisters of Mercy
Mothers of Invention   Muthers, Mothers
Mott the Hoople   Silence
New Order   Joy Division
Orchestral Manoeuvres in the Dark (OMD)   VCL XL
Pogo   Poco
Pogues   Pogue Mahone
Procol Harum   Paramounts
Righteous Brothers   Paramours
Shadows   Drifters
Simon and Garfunkel   Tom and Jerry
Simply Red   Frantic Elevators
Slade   Ambrose Slade, 'N Betweens
Sonny and Cher   Caesar and Cleo
Spice Girls   Touch (without Emma Bunton)
Split Enz   Split Ends
Starship   Jefferson Airplane, Jefferson Starship
Status Quo   Spectres, Traffic Jam
Stone Roses   Patrol, English Rose
Stranglers   Guildford Stranglers
Strawbs   Strawberry Hill Boys
Supremes   Primettes
Sweet   Wainwright's Gentlemen, Sweetshop
Swinging Blue Jeans   Bluegenes
Talking Heads   Portable Crushers, Vague Dots
Ten Years After   Jaybirds
T Rex   Tyrannosaurus Rex
Ultravox   Zips, Innocents, London Soundtrack, Fire of London
Wham   Executive (Paul Ridgeley and David Mortimer in line-up)
The Who   High Number

MUSIC POP

Dubbed Singing Voice of Well Known Actors

Actor	Voice and film
Ann Blyth	Gogi Grant (Both Ends of the Candle)
Audrey Hepburn	Marni Nixon (My Fair Lady)
Christopher Plummer	Bill Lee (Sound of Music)
Cyd Charisse	India Adams (The Band Wagon)
Deborah Kerr	Marni Nixon (King and I)
Diahann Carroll	Bernice Peterson (Carmen Jones)
Dorothy Dandridge	Marilyn Horne (Carmen Jones)
Edmund Purdom	Mario Lanza (The Student Prince)
Franco Nero	Gene Merlina (Camelot)
Harry Belafonte	LeVerne Hutcherson (Carmen Jones)
Jean Seberg	Anita Gordon (Paint Your Wagon)
Jeanne Crain	Anita Ellis (Gentlemen Marry Brunettes)
Joan Leslie	Louanne Hogan (Rhapsody in Blue)
Joe Adams	Marvin Hayes (Carmen Jones)

Actor	Voice and film
John Kerr	Bill Lee (South Pacific)
Juanita Hall	Muriel Smith (South Pacific)
Larry Parks	Al Jolson (The Jolson Story)
Lucille Bremer	Trudy Erwin (Till the Clouds Roll By)
Natalie Wood	Marni Nixon (West Side Story)
Ned Beatty	Vernon Midgley (Hear My Song)
Peter O'Toole	Simon Gilbert (Man of La Mancha)
Richard Beymer	Jim Bryant (West Side Story)
Rita Moreno	Leona Gordon (King and I)
Rita Moreno	Betty Wand (West Side Story)
Rossano Brazzi	Giorgio Tozi (South Pacific)
Sophia Loren	Renata Tebaldi (Aida)
Susan Hayward	Jane Froman (With a Song in My Heart)
Vera-Ellen	Carole Richards (Call Me Madam)

Mythology and Legend

Deities

Role	Greek	Roman	Egyptian	Norse	Sumerian
Principal god	Zeus	Jupiter	Am(m)on	Odin	An
Principal goddess	Hera	Juno	Mut	Frigg	Inanna
Messenger of the gods	Hermes	Mercury	Thoth	Hermod	Uncertain
God of agriculture	Cronus	Saturn	Osiris	Uncertain	Emesh
Goddess of agriculture	Demeter	Ceres	Renenutet	Rindr	Nisaba
Goddess of childbirth	Eileithyia	Juno	Apet	Uncertain	Ninhursaga
Goddess of the dawn	Eos	Aurora	Uncertain	Uncertain	Anahita
God of the dead	Thanatos	Mors	Anubis	Odin	Nergal
Goddess of death	Hecate	Libitina	Nephthys	Hel	Uncertain
God of destruction	Ares	Mars	Seth	Uncertain	Uncertain
God of dreams	Morpheus	Morpheus	Uncertain	Uncertain	Uncertain
God of the Earth	Aesculapius	Aesculapius	Geb	Uncertain	Uncertain
Goddess of the Earth	Gaia	Tellus	Maat	Nerthus	Ki
God of fertility	Priapus	Faunus	Ing	Frey	Ninurta
Goddess of fertility	Artemis	Diana	Bastet	Gefjon	Inanna
God of fire	Hephaestus	Vulcan	Ptah	Loki	Gerra
Goddess of flowers	Hestia	Flora	Qudshu	Nanna	Uncertain
Goddess of health	Hygeia	Salus	Meresger	Uncertain	Nininsina Dazimus
Goddess of the hearth	Hestia	Vesta	Uncertain	Sigyn	Uncertain
God of heaven	Zeus	Jupiter	Ptah	Uncertain	An
Goddess of the hunt	Artemis	Diana	Neith	Skadi	Uncertain
Goddess of justice	Themis	Uncertain	Maat	Forseti	Uncertain
God of love	Eros	Cupid	Uncertain	Uncertain	Uncertain
Goddess of love	Aphrodite	Venus	Hathor	Freya	Inanna
Goddess of magic/ witchcraft	Hecate	Uncertain	Isis	Uncertain	Uncertain
God of marriage	Hymen	Hymen	Bes	Uncertain	Uncertain
God of the Moon	Apollo	Apollo	Neferhotep	Uncertain	Nanna
Goddess of the Moon	Selene	Luna	Isis	Mani	Ningal
Goddess of motherhood	Rhea	Ops	Taweret	Uncertain	Uncertain
God of music	Apollo	Apollo	Uncertain	Bragi	Uncertain
Goddess of night	Nyx	Uncertain	Nephthys	Nott	Uncertain
Goddess of peace	Irene	Pax	Uncertain	Uncertain	Uncertain
God of poetry	Apollo	Apollo	Thoth	Odin/Bragi	Uncertain
Goddess of the rainbow	Iris	Uncertain	Uncertain	Uncertain	Uncertain
God of the sea	Poseidon	Neptune	Nun	Aegir/Njord	Apsu
Goddess of the sea	Amphitrite	Salacia	Tefenet	Ran	Nammu
God of the sky	Uranus	Jupiter	Uncertain	Odin	An
Goddess of the sky	Hera	Juno	Nut	Uncertain	Inanna
God of sleep	Hypnos	Somnus	Uncertain	Uncertain	Uncertain
Goddess of spring	Persephone	Proserpine	Renpet	Uncertain	Ninkasi
God of the sun	Helios	Sol	Ra (Re)	Sol	Utu
God of thunder	Hephaestus	Jupiter	Seth	Thor	Adad
Goddess of truth	Themis	Justitia	Maat	Uncertain	Uncertain
God of the Underworld	Pluto/Hades	Orcus/Dis	Osiris	Villi	Endugukka
Goddess of the Underworld	Hecate	Proserpine	Hathor	Hel	Ereshkigal
Goddess of victory	Nike	Victoria	Apet	Uncertain	Uncertain
God of war	Ares	Mars	Seth	Tyr/Odin	Ninurta
Goddess of war	Athene	Minerva	Sekhmet	Uncertain	Inanna
God of water	Ganymede	Uncertain	Hapi	Uncertain	Enki
God of wine	Dionysus	Bacchus/Liber	Bes	Uncertain	Uncertain
God of wisdom	Apollo	Apollo	Thoth	Odin	Enki
Goddess of wisdom	Athene	Minerva	Neith	Uncertain	Hea
God of woods	Pan	Silvanus	Min	Uncertain	Ashnan
Goddess of youth	Hebe	Juventas	Renpet	Uncertain	Uncertain

Deities of Lesser Mythologies

Role	Babylonian	Hindu	Phoenician	Celtic	Aztec
King of the gods	Marduk	Indra	Kumarbi/El	Dagda	Tezcatlipoca
God of agriculture	Tammuz	Sita	Telepinu	Amaethon	Centeotl
Goddess of childbirth	Uncertain	Shashti	Ashtaroth	Brigit	Chihuacoatl
Goddess of the dawn	Aja	Ushas	Shachar	Uncertain	Uncertain
God of the Dead	Uncertain	Yama	Mot	Dagda	Mictlantecuhtli
Goddess of death	Uncertain	Kali	Uncertain	Morrígan	Mictlantecuhtli
God of destruction	Uncertain	Shiva	Uncertain	Balor	Itzlacoliuhqui
God of the Earth	Apsu	Uncertain	Uncertain	Dagda	Ometecuhtli
Goddess of the Earth	Tiamat	Pitthivi	Beruth	Danu	Coatlicue
God of fertility	Hadad	Dyaus	Baal	Cernunnos	Tlaloc
Goddess of fertility	Ishtar	Prithivi	Anath/Astarte	Danu	Chalchiuhtlicue
God of fire	Uncertain	Agni	Uncertain	Belenus	Xiuhtecuhtli
Goddess of flowers	Uncertain	Uncertain	Uncertain	Olwen	Xochiquetzal
God of heaven	Apsu	Dyaus	Anu	Uncertain	Ometeotl
Goddess of the hunt	Uncertain	Minakshi	Uncertain	Abnoba	Uncertain
God of love	Uncertain	Kama	Uncertain	Angus	Huehuecoyotl
Goddess of love	Ishtar	Rati	Astarte	Aine	Xochiquetzal
Goddess of magic/witchcraft	Uncertain	Dursa	Kamrusepa	Bodhbh	Malinalxochi
God of the Moon	Sin	Chandra	Yarikh	Uncertain	Uncertain
Goddess of the Moon	Anunitu	Candi	Nikkal	Arianrhod	Coyolxauhqui
Goddess of motherhood	Nintur	Devi	Hannahanna	Danu	Chalchiuhtlicue
God of music	Uncertain	Uncertain	Uncertain	Maponus	Macuilxochitl
Goddess of night	Uncertain	Ratri	Shalim	Uncertain	Itzlacoliuhqui
God of poetry	Uncertain	Uncertain	Uncertain	Ogma	Huitzilopochtli
God of the sea	Uncertain	Varuna	Yamm	Manannan	Uncertain
Goddess of the sea	Tiamat	Uncertain	Asherat	Don	Chalchiuhtlicue
God of the sky	Anu	Dyaus	Teshub	Camulus	Tlaloc
Goddess of the sky	Tiamat	Aditi	Shapash	Don	Uncertain
God of the sun	Shamash	Surya	Nergal	Lug	Tonatiuh
God of thunder	Hadad	Indra	Taru	Taranis	Tlaloc
God of war	Uncertain	Karttikeya	Astabis	Uncertain	Huitzilopochtli
Goddess of war	Ishtar	Durga	Astarte	Morrígan	Clhvacoatl
God of water	Ea	Varuna	Uncertain	Nechtan	Tlaloc
God of wine	Uncertain	Uncertain	Uncertain	Uncertain	Tepoztecatl
God of wisdom	Ea	Ganes(h)a	Uncertain	Uncertain	Uncertain
Goddess of wisdom	Uncertain	Uncertain	Uncertain	Sul	Uncertain

NB: There are a number of points that should be borne in mind when studying the above tables.

First, it should be remembered that in many instances there would be more than one representation of a god for a particular subject. For example, as well as Aegir, both Njord and Vili are often described as Norse gods of the sea. In all cases I have listed the main god who is usually identified with the subject.

Second, there is often a transposition of gods in some mythologies, and in particular the Middle East should be treated with some care. Babylonian mythology is often called Assyrian, Akkadian or Persian, while Phoenician can also be called Hittite as well as Assyrian and Akkadian.

Third, where there is controversy over an entry or there is no god who represents a subject, the word 'Uncertain' has been entered; this does not mean, for instance, that there was no Egyptian god of love but merely that there is not a single god who unequivocally fits the criteria of being both universally accepted and identifiable.

Groups

Muses (9)	of	Literal meaning	Pleiades (7)	7 against Thebes
Thalia	Comedy	Good cheer/plenty	Maia	Polynices
Clio	History	Fame	Taygete	Tydeus
Melpomene	Tragedy	Singing	Elektra	Adrastus
Urania	Astronomy	Celestial	Alkyone	Capaneus
Polyhymnia	Song and mime	Many songs	Asterope	Hippomedon
Erato	Love poetry	Lovely	Kelaino	Parthenopaeus
Euterpe	Lyric poetry	Joy	Merope	Amphiarus
Calliope	Epic poetry	Beautiful voice		
Terpsichore	Dance	Joyful dance		

Sages of India (7)

Atri
Bharadvaja
Gautama
Jamadagni
Kashyapa
Vasistha
Vishvamitra

Hills of Rome (7)

Capitoline
Quirinal
Viminal
Esquiline
Caelian
Aventine
Palatine

> Useful mnemonic:
> Can Queen Victoria Eat
> Cold Apple Pie?

Titans (12)

Brontes
Atlas
Astraeus
Cronus
Hyperion
Oceanus
Rhea
Coeus
Helios
Arges
Phoebe
Thema

> Useful mnemonic:
> BAA CHOP CHAPS

Underworld Rivers (5)

Cocytus (wailing)
Lethe (forgetfulness)
Acheron (grief)
Styx (hate)
Phlegethon (fire)

> Useful mnemonic:
> CLASP

Furies (3) (Erinyes or Eumenides)

Tisiphone (avenger of
murder)
Alecto (relentless)
Megaera (resentful)

> Useful mnemonic:
> Furies aren't TAMe

Graces (3) (Charites)

Euphrosyne (good cheer)
Aglaia (splendour or
bright one)
Thaleia (jollity)

> Useful mnemonic:
> Say Grace before you
> EAT

Fates (3) (Moerae)

Clotho (spun the thread of
life)
Atropos (cut off the thread
of life)
Lachesis (measured out
the thread of life)

> Useful mnemonic:
> CAL(L) the fates in
> times of trouble

Gorgons (3)

Medusa
Euryale
Stheno

> Useful mnemonic:
> Medusa's hair was a
> MESs

MYTHOLOGY AND LEGEND

Twelve Labours of Heracles

The killing of the Nemean lion Heracles beat the lion senseless and throttled it; he then skinned the lion with its own claws and donned the pelt to render himself invulnerable.

The killing of the Lernaean Hydra Iolaus cauterized the neck of the Hydra to prevent the two new heads growing each time that Heracles chopped off one of its nine heads.

The capture of the Hind on Mt Ceryneia Heracles chased the Hind for a year, for its golden horns and bronze hoofs. He blamed Eurystheus for its capture so as not to bring the wrath of Artemis on himself.

The capture of the Boar of Mt Erymanthus Heracles returned with the Boar to Tiryns, and Eurystheus hid in an urn at the sight of it.

The cleansing of the Augean stables Heracles cleaned the stables, which had not been cleaned in 30 years, by diverting the rivers Alpheus and Peneus through them.

The killing of the Birds of Lake Stymphalos Heracles scared the Birds from the trees with bronze castanets and shot them with arrows one by one.

The capture of the Cretan Bull Heracles captured the Bull and returned it to Greece.

The capture of the Mares of Diomedes Heracles slew Diomedes, fed him to the Mares and tamed them.

The capture of the Girdle of Hippolyte Heracles slew the queen of the Amazons and took the Girdle for Eurystheus' daughter.

The capture of Geryon's Cattle Heracles slew Geryon and returned to Greece with the Cattle.

The capture of the Apples of the Hesperides Heracles slew Ladon, the dragon that guarded the tree tended by the Hesperides, and took the Golden Apples (later returned by Athene).

The capture of Cerberus Heracles entered the underworld to capture the 3-headed dog.

General Information

Abderus Friend of Heracles in whose care Heracles left the mares of Diomedes. The horses ate him and Heracles founded a town in Thrace in his honour.

Abnoba The goddess of the hunt in the mythology of Gaul. Identified with the Roman Diana.

Acheloüs Greek river god, the son of Oceanus and Tethys.

Achilles Greek hero, born in Thessaly, son of Peleus and the goddess Thetis. When he was a baby his mother dipped him in the Styx, making him invulnerable save for his right heel, by which she held him.

Actaeon Greek hero, grandson of Cadmus, changed into a stag by Artemis and killed by his own hounds because he spied her bathing.

Admetus In Greek mythology the king of Pherae in Thessaly. Apollo served him for a year and introduced him to Alcestis.

Adonis Syrian god, the son of Myrrha and her father Cinyras. He was born from the bark of a tree and brought up by Persephone and forced to spend a third of his time with her and a third with Aphrodite. He was mortally wounded by a wild boar sent by a hostile god or goddess.

Aeacus Son of Zeus and Aegina and king of the Myrmidones. The Myrmidones were originally ants, transformed into men by Zeus at the request of Aeacus. He had two sons, Peleus and Telamon, by his wife Endeis and was also the father of Phocus by a Nereid. Aeacus was one of the three judges of the Underworld.

Aeëtes In Greek mythology, the king of Colchis and possessor of the Golden Fleece sought by Jason.

Aegeus Greek king of Athens and father of Theseus by Aethra, daughter of Pittheus, king of Troezen. Aethra brought Theseus up secretly at her father's court, during which time Aegeus married Medea. When Theseus finally returned to his father's court, Medea fled. Before Theseus went to slay the Minotaur he and Aegeus agreed that he would hoist a white sail when returning to Athens to signal his success. On returning, Theseus forgot to do this and Aegeus, seeing a black sail on his son's ship, supposed him dead and, in grief, threw himself into the sea, henceforth called the Aegean.

Aegisthus In Greek mythology the seducer of Clytemnestra, the wife of his cousin Agamemnon, whom the two lovers conspired to kill. Agamemnon's son Orestes avenged the assassination by killing Aegisthus and Clytemnestra.

Aeneas Trojan hero, son of Aphrodite and Anchises, bravest of the Trojans after Hector and, according to some Roman lines of mythology, the founder of Rome. Aeneas was the lover of Dido, queen of Carthage.

Aeneid Virgil's unfinished epic poem in 12 volumes recounting the deeds of Aeneas, supposed ancestor of Emperor Augustus of Rome. The epic begins after the fall of Troy and ends with the defeat of Turnus the Rutulian prince and the subsequent marriage of Aeneas and Lavinia, the Latin princess.

Aeolus Greek god of the winds and son of Poseidon who gave Odysseus a sack containing all the winds.

Aesculapius Roman god of medicine. Greek counterpart is Asclepius.

Aesir Norse race of warlike gods, who lived in Asgardthey included Odin, Thor, Tyr, Baldu and Frigg (see Vanir).

Aetolus Conqueror of Aetolia. The son of Endymion, king of Elis, he was banished across the Corinthian Gulf after accidentally killing Apis in a chariot race.

Agamemnon Greek king of Argos, murdered by his wife Clytemnestra.

Aganippe Fountain at the foot of Mt Helicon, sacred to the Muses, who are sometimes called the Aganippides.

Ajax (the greater) Greek hero, a giant of a man, the son of Telamon. Killed himself in fury at not receiving Achille's armour after his death.

Ajax (the lesser) Greek hero, son of Oileus. Raped King Priam's daughter Cassandra on the altar of Athene.

Alcestis Greek heroine who saved her husband Admetus by offering her own life.

Alcheringa According to Australian aboriginal mythology, the Golden Age when the first ancestors were created.

Alcides Another name for Heracles, whose grandfather was reputed to be Alcaeus.

Alcmene Wife of Amphitrion, son of Alcaeus. Alcmene mothered Heracles by Zeus in the guise of her husband. Married Rhadamanthus after Amphitrion's death.

Alphito Greek barley goddess of Argos.

Amalthea She-goat. Zeus broke off one of Amalthea's horns to make the Cornucopia (Horn of Plenty).

Amazons Warrior women of Greek mythology who removed a breast to give free play to bow arm.

Amphitrion In Greek mythology king of Tiryns and husband of Alcmene.

Amphitrite Daughter of Nereus, leader of the Nereids. Mothered Triton by Poseidon.

Anchises According to Greek and Roman mythology, the Trojan father of Aeneas by Aphrodite.

Androcles Roman slave who aided and befriended a lion that later saved his life when he was thrown to the lions for attempting to escape.

Andromache In Greek mythology, the wife of Hector and slave of Neoptolemus.

Andromeda According to Greek mythology, daughter of king Cepheus and queen Cassiopeia; she was rescued by Perseus from a sea-monster and subsequently married him.

Angels Nine choirs divided into three ranks: Seraphim, Cherubim and Thrones; Dominions, Powers and Virtues; Principalities, Archangels and Angels.

Antaeus Libyan giant, son of Poseidon and Ge, who was an invincible wrestler until Hercules – realizing he drew his strength from his mother, Earth – held him in the air and squeezed him to death.

Antigone In Greek mythology the daughter of Oedipus and Jocasta and sister of Ismene.

Anubis Egyptian god who guides souls to the world beyond. Often depicted with the head of a jackal.

Aphrodite Greek goddess of love and beauty and wife of Hephaestus.

Apis Egyptian god of strength, represented as a bull.

Apollo Greek and Roman god of prophecy, music, youth, archery and healing, and son of Zeus and Leto (Jupiter and Latona in Roman myth).

Arachne According to Greek mythology, a weaver from Lydia who was changed into a spider by Athena.

Ares Greek god of war, son of Zeus and Hera and lover of Aphrodite.

Arethusa Greek goddess of springs and fountains.

Argo The 50-oared longship which carried Jason and the Argonauts to Colchis in their quest for the Golden Fleece.

Argonauts The band of heroes chosen by Jason to man the Argo and sail in search of the Golden Fleece. The Argonauts included Argus, Atalanta, Calais, Castor and Polydeuces, Heracles, Meleager, Orpheus, Peleus, Telamon and Zetes.

Argus (1) Greek watchman with 100 eyes who watched over Io but was killed by Hermes. His eyes were placed in the peacock's tail by Hera. (2) The faithful hound of Odysseus/Ulysses. (3) The builder of the *Argo*.

Ariadne In Greek mythology, the daughter of King

Minos of Crete and wife of Dionysus after Theseus abandoned her.

Artemis   Greek goddess of fertility and the hunt, daughter of Zeus and Leto and twin sister of Apollo.

Arthur   Legendary British king, son of Uther Pendragon and Igraine, said to have lived in the 6th century. He was born in Tintagel and buried in Glastonbury; Arthur's court was at Camelot (Winchester, according to Malory's *Morte d'Arthur*).

Aruna   The Hindu god of dawn and charioteer of the sun, often identified with the Greek and Roman goddesses Eos and Aurora. Aruna was also known as Rumra (lit. rosy).

Aruru   One of the names of the Sumerian goddess of childbirth, Ninhursaga (lit. germ loosener).

Asclepius   Greek god of healing.

Asgard   In Norse mythology the realm of the gods in heaven and connected to the earth by the rainbow bridge, Bifrost, which was guarded by Heimdall.

Ask   In Norse mythtology the ash tree from which man was hewn.

Asphodel, Plain of   That part of Hades reserved for the great proportion of the dead. There they continued a shadowy existence in continuance of their former lives since they were bodiless.Contrast Elysium and Tartarus.

Ataentsic   According to Iroquois and Huron mythology, the first woman and ancestor of the human race.

Atalanta   Greek heroine who refused to marry any man unless he could beat her in a foot race. Milanion became her husband after Aphrodite helped him defeat her. Atalanta was the sole female Argonaut.

Aten   Egyptian god; took the form of a solar disc.

Athene   According to Greek mythology, the daughter of Zeus and Metis who sprang from her father's head fully armed. Among her titles was Parthenos (Virgin), from which the Parthenon was named.

Atlas   Titan that bears up the earth. Son of Iapetus and Clymene and brother of Prometheus.

Attis   Greek god of vegetation.

Autolycus   Son of Hermes and Chione and grandfather of Odysseus.

Baba Yaga   Witch or ogress in Slav mythology.

Bacchae   Female followers of the cult of Bacchus or Dionysus.

Bacchus   Roman mythological counterpart of the Greek Dionysus, god of wine and ecstasy.

Baldur   Norse favourite of the gods and son of Odin and Frigg. Baldur was invulnerable to everything except mistletoe, and Loki tricked the blind god Hoder into throwing a mistletoe dart that killed him.

Balmung   Siegfried's sword, according to the *Nibelungenlied*.

Basilisk   Greek monster also called a Cockatrice, that killed with a stare.

Bastet   According to Egyptian mythology, the cat-headed goddess of fertility, love and sex.

Befana   Good fairy of Italian children who is supposed to fill their stockings with toys on Twelfth Night.

Belenus   The Celtic god of healing and light, referred to as 'The Shining One'. He was in charge of the

welfare of sheep and cattle. His wife is the goddess Belisama; they are often compared to the Roman Apollo and Minerva.

Bellerophon   Greek hero who tamed Pegasus and killed the Chimera.

Bellona   Greek goddess of war.

Beowulf   Norse warrior prince who killed the man-eating monster Grendel in a wrestling match.

Berserker   Norse warrior who fought with great ferocity; hence the phrase 'to go berserk'.

Bifrost   In Norse mythology, the rainbow bridge that led from Asgard to Earth. Literally means quivering path.

Biton and Cleobis   Sons of a priestess of Hera in Argos who drew their mother's chariot several miles to the goddess's temple when no oxen could be found.

Bor (Burr)   Norse god who married the giantess Bestla. She bore him three sons, Odin, Villi and Vé.

Boreas   Greek god of the north wind.

Bragi   Norse god of poetry and music, son of Odin.

Briareus   One of the Hecatoncheires. Aka Aegaeon.

Brigit   Celtic goddess of the poetic arts, childbirth and divination.

Bunyip   In Australian aboriginal mythology, monster who was the source of evil.

Cadmus   In Greek mythology, the son of Agenor, king of Phoenicia and grandson of Poseidon. When Zeus carried off his sister Europa, he went to look for her but was told by the Delphic oracle to relinquish the search and to follow a magical cow. Where the cow lay down he was to found a city, the future city of Thebes. Cadmus married Harmonia.

Caishen   Chinese god of wealth.

Calais   Twin brother of Zetes. The winged sons of Boreas and Oreithyia, they accompanied the Argonauts and drove off the Harpies.

Calchas   Renegade Trojan seer who helped the Greeks at Troy and foretold that Troy would not fall without Achilles' presence and that the sacrifice of Iphigenia was necessary to secure a favourable wind.

Callisto   Daughter of Lycaon, who became one of Artemis's huntresses. She bore Arcas to Zeus, who sought to conceal their affair from his wife Hera by turning Callisto into a bear.

Calypso (Hidden)   Nymph of the island of Ogygia who tended Odysseus there for 8 years until Zeus ordered him home to Ithaca.

Cassandra   Greek heroine given the gift of prophecy by Apollo with the proviso that, although telling the truth, she would not be believed.

Cassiopeia   Wife of Cepheus and mother of Andromeda.

Castor and Pollux   Roman counterpart of Castor and Polydeuces.

Castor and Polydeuces   Aka the Dioscuri, sons of Zeus and Leda. Castor was an expert horseman and Polydeuces was the best boxer in Greece. Some versions have the mortal Castor as son of Tyndareus (Leda lay with both Zeus and Tyndareus). They were transformed into the Gemini constellation

M
Y
T
H
O
L
O
G
Y

A
N
D

L
E
G
E
N
D

Centaur   In Greek mythology the hybrid offspring of Centaurus, son of Ixion, and the mares of Mt Pelion in Thessaly.

Cepheus   In Greek mythology, the husband of Cassiopeia and father of Andromeda.

Cerberus   According to Greek mythology, the three-headed dog that guards the entrance to the Underworld. Offspring of Echidna and Typhon.

Chac   Maya god of rain and lightening.

Chaos   In Greek creation myth, Chaos was the infinite space existing before creation, from which Ge (the Earth) sprang.

Charon   According to Greek mythology, the ferryman of the underworld. Offspring of Erebos and Nyx. Greeks to this day place a coin in the mouth of corpses to pay for the ferry charge.

Charybdis   Greek mythological monster resembling a giant whirlpool which infested the Strait of Messina together with Scylla.

Chimera   Greek monster with the head of lion, the body of a goat and the tail of a serpent. Offspring of Echidna and Typhon.

Chiron   Centaur who was untypically wise and civilized. When Chiron died he became the constellation Sagittarius.

Circe   Greek sorceress who turned Odysseus's men into swine. Daughter of Helios and Perse.

Clytemnestra   Greek twin sister of Helen and wife of Agamemnon.

Conán the Bald   According to Celtic mythology, a warrior and follower of the hero Finn Mac Cumhall. Conán was the son of Morna and brother of Goll.

Conchobar   Celtic king of Ulster and illegitimate son of Nessa, queen of Ulster, and the druid Cathbhadh.

Consus   Roman god of seed sowing.

Cressida   According to Greek mythology, she deserted Troilus, a Trojan prince, for Diomedes.

Cretan bull   Magnificent white bull sent by Poseidon to Minos for sacrifice. Minos's wife Pasiphaë so admired the bull that she had Daedalus construct a hollow cow for her to get inside and mate with the bull – that was how she came to bear the Minotaur. The bull was captured by Heracles, freed by Eurystheus and finally recaptured by Theseus at Marathon and sacrificed to Athene.

Croesus   Last king of Lydia, famous for his vast wealth.

Cronus   Greek god of agriculture and father of Zeus.

Cuchulainn   In Celtic mythology the legendary Irish hero, called the 'Hound of Culann' because, having accidentally slain the watchdog of the smith, Culann, he subsequently took the animal's place as penance. He was brought up in the court of King Conchobar of Ulster, whose kingdom he defended against all invaders. Cuchulainn's parents were the sun god Lug, and Dechtire, the wife of an Ulster chieftain. Although Cuchulainn was a handsome youth, in battle he would turn into a frenzied monster, with one eye receding into his head while the other stood out huge and red on his cheek.
Cuchulainn's wife was Emer, daughter of the chieftain Forgall. Women continued to fall in love with Cuchulainn after his marriage, and his eventual death was as a result of rebuffing the war goddess

Morrigan, who assaulted him with innumerable foes.

Cupay   In the mythology of the Peruvian Inca people, the god of death. He is sometimes known as Supay.

Cybele   Greek goddess of the earth and lover of Attis.

Cyclops   One-eyed giants descended from Gaia and Uranus. Polyphemus is most famous for his capture of Odysseus, who blinded him.

Daedalus   In Greek mythology the greatest of mortal craftsmen who made wings out of wax and feathers for himself and his son Icarus to escape imprisonment in the Creton labyrinth. However, Icarus flew too near the sun and fell to his death when the wax melted.

Damocles   Member of the court of Dionysius I, tyrant of Syracuse. Cicero tells how the tyrant had him eat a sumptuous dinner while a sword was suspended by a hair over his head, to show him the limits of rank and power.

Danu (Dana)   The Celtic earth-mother goddess, also identified with fertility, wisdom and the wind. In Welsh versions she is known as Don and is associated with the air and the sea.

Daphne   Greek heroine turned into a laurel bush to evade Apollo.

Daphnis   Son of Hermes and a nymph. The originator of pastoral poetry.

Deianeira   Greek princess, the daughter of King Oenus and Queen Althaea of Aetolia, and the second wife of Heracles, whom she killed by mistake when she smeared his garment with a centaur's poisonous blood, thinking it was a love charm.

Deidamia   Maiden who fell in love with Achilles and bore him Neoptolemus.

Deirdre   According to Irish legend, she killed herself after being forced to marry King Conchobar.

Delphi   Site of Apollo's Dorian shrine and oracle, the most famous centre of his worship.

Deucalion   Greek hero, son of Prometheus, who repopulated the earth with his wife Pyrrha after Zeus's flood.

Devi (Mahadevi)   In Hindu mythology the wife of S(h)iva. Originally there were several goddesses acknowledged as the wives of S(h)iva by different Hindu castes, but eventually they merged into the one manifestation, Devi. Other forms of Devi include, Bhairavi, Chandi, Durga, Gauri (Jagadgauri), Jaganmata, Kali, Parvati, Sati and Uma.

Dian-Cecht   The Celtic god of medicine and healing, and the grandfather of the sun god Lug.

Dido   Greek heroine, daughter of the King of Tyre, who founded Carthage. Virgil told of her suicide when abandoned by her lover, Aeneas.

Dioscuri (sons of Zeus)   Zeus had intercourse with Leda in the form of a swan and she produced two eggs. From one came Castor and Clytemnestra and from the other came Polydeuces and Helen.

Draupnir   Odin's magic ring.

Dryad   In classical mythology a tree-nymph, sometimes called a hamadryad, which was supposed to die when the tree died. Oak trees were usually favoured by dryads.

Durga   In Hindu mytholog a fierce form of Devi who was born fully grown and beautiful; she was immediately armed by the gods and sent forth against the buffalo demon Mahisha. Although blessed with beautiful golden skin, Durga had a fixed, menacing expression and rode upon a tiger. In each of her 10 hands she held one of the god's weapons, i.e. Agni's flaming dart, Indra's thunderbolt, Kubera's club, Shesha's garland of snakes, S(h)iva's trident, Surya's quiver and arrow, Varuna's conch shell, Vayu's bow, Vishnu's discus and Yama's iron rod.

Echidna In Greek mythology, she was the offspring of the earth goddess Gaia and her brother Tartarus. Echidna had the upper body of a nymph and the lower body of a serpent.

Echo Greek nymph who pined away till she was only a voice for the love of Narcissus.

Edda Norse collection of mythological and heroic lays. Also the title of a manual of mythology compiled by the Icelandic historian Snorri Sturluson (1178–1241).

Egeria Roman goddess of fountains and childbirth.

Electra Daughter of Agamemnon and Clytemnestra, and sister of Orestes and Iphegenia.

Electryon Son of Perseus and Andromeda, king of Mycenae and father of Alcmene, the wife of Amphitrion.

Elysian Fields (Elysium) Greek mythological paradise to which the great and virtuous went after death.

Embla In Norse mythology the elm tree from which woman was hewn.

Endymion King of Elis who was visited by Selene while sleeping in a cave and forced into an endless sleep so she could admire his beauty.

Enlil In Sumerian mythology one of the triad of creator-gods with Enki and An.

Epeius Cowardly son of Panopeus who built the Trojan horse.

Epigoni Greek sons of the 7 against Thebes who succeeded in destroying the city.

Epimetheus In Greek mythology, the brother of Prometheus and husband of Pandora.

Epona Roman goddess of horses.

Erebus (Darkness) Son of Chaos and father of Aether and Hemera by Night, his sister.

Eros (Desire) Greek god of love, the offspring of Aphrodite and Ares.

Eshmun The Phoenician god of healing, identified with the Greek Asclepius and Roman Aesculapius.

Europa According to Greek mythology, the daughter of King Agenor and Queen Telephassa of Phoenicia. Zeus wooed Europa as a bull and had intercourse with her in the guise of an eagle. She bore him three sons: Minos, Rhadamanthus and Sarpedon. Europa married the Cretan king Asterius.

Eurus South-east wind, son of Astraeus and Eos.

Eurydice Greek dryad, wife of Orpheus. She was lost forever after Orpheus looked back to make sure she was following as he led her out of Hades.

Eurystheus King of the Argolid region of the Peloponnese, son of King Sthenelus and Queen Nicippe of Mycenae. Heracles was sentenced to serve him for 12 years as penance for killing his wife, Megara. Eurystheus subsequently set him the twelve labours.

Fafnir In Germanic mythology a dragon who guarded the Nibelung hoard of treasure.

Fauna Roman goddess of fertility.

Faunus Roman god of crops, herds and woodlands.

Fenrir In Norse mythology a monstrous wolf who was the offspring of Loki.

Ferghus Irish hero of superhuman size and strength. King of Ulster before Conchobar, Ferghus was the lover of Nessa, the mother of Conchobar.

Feronia Roman goddess of spring flowers.

Fides Roman god of honesty.

Finn mac Cumhal Irish hero who possessed the gift of foresight when biting his thumb.

Fintan In Irish mythology the salmon of knowledge, which Finn mac Cumhal tasted accidentally. He burned his thumb on the flesh as he turned it on a spit. Once he sucked the thumb he became a sage.

Fjorgyn Norse goddess, mother of Thor.

Fortuna Roman goddess of chance and fate.

Frey Norse god of fertility.

Freyja Norse goddess of love, twin sister of Frey.

Frigg Norse goddess of fertility, wife of Odin.

Ganesha Hindu god depicted with the head of an elephant; the offspring of Parvati, the wife of S(h)iva.

Ganymede Greek god of rain and cupbearer to the gods; the son of King Tros of Troy.

Garang The first man according to the Dinka people of the Sudan.

Genius Roman protective god, one for every individual, group and State.

Geryon Three-bodied monster living on the island of Erythia who owned cattle guarded by Eurytion.

Gilgamesh Sumerian king of Uruk, son of the goddess Ninsun and a mortal. His story is told in the Gilgamesh epic, the oldest extant work of literature (c. 2000 BC), which tells of his search for the secret of eternal life.

Gimli In Norse mythology the highest heavenly abode that was not consumed in Ragnarok.

Ginnungagap In Norse mythology the 'Yawning Gap' or primeval emptiness, which held all the potential energy of creation.

Glaucus (1) King of Corinth, son of Sisyphus and Merope and father of Bellerophon. He fed his horses on human flesh but Aphrodite caused them to devour Glaucus himself because he mocked her.

Glaucus (2) Grandson of Bellerophon who fought for the Trojans and was slain by Ajax.

Glaucus (3) Son of Minos and Pasiphaë who was drowned in a barrel of honey.

Glaucus (4) Boeotian fisherman who pursued Scylla and was turned into a sea god on eating a magic herb.

Golden Age Concept of the Greek poet Hesiod, who listed Golden, Silver, Bronze and Iron as the four ages of man in his *Works and Days*.

Golden Bough A gift Aeneas had to take to Proserpina before he could enter the underworld.

Golden Fleece Fleece of the golden ram of Colchis, kept by King Aeëtes of Colchis and guarded by an unsleeping dragon.

Gorgons Three sisters–Eurydale, Medusa and Scheno–offspring of Phorcys and Ceto. Medusa was

MYTHOLOGY AND LEGEND

the mortal sister killed by Perseus. The Gorgons were the sisters of the Graiae.

Götterdämmerung Literally means 'Twilight of the Gods'; in Germanic mythology the equivalent of the Norse final battle, Ragnarok.

Graces Daughters of Zeus and the sea nymph Eurynome.

Graiae In Greek mythology, three sisters who had one eye and one tooth between them; sisters of the Gorgons.

Great Mother of the Gods Oriental and Greco-Roman deity, known as Cybele in Latin literature. Her full Roman name was Mater Deum Magna Idaea (Great Idaean Mother of the Gods). Her Phrygian name was Agdistis or Dindymus.

Griffin Greek monster with lion's body and eagle's head and wings.

Gula In Babylonian mythology the goddess of healing corresponding to the Sumerian Bau.

Hades In Greek mythology the son of Cronus and Rhea, and brother of Zeus and Poseidon. The three brothers drew lots for their realms and Hades drew the underworld. Although this nether world was not originally given a name, it became known by the name of its chief god Hades (unseen). The god Hades was also known as Pluto (rich), and the Roman equivalent was Dis or Orcus. The realm of Hades can be sub-divided into Elysium, Tartarus and the Plain of Asphodel.

Hamadryad See Dryad.

Hanuman In Indian mythology the monkey that became the most loyal companion of Rama and his consort Sita.

Harpies Greek spirits with heads of women and bodies of birds.

Hebe Greek goddess of youth and spring, daughter of Zeus and Hera, and wife of Heracles after his death.

Hecate Greek goddess of the underworld and daughter of Coeus and Phoebe.

Hector According to Greek mythology, the bravest Trojan and son of Priam; the brother of Paris and husband of Andromache. Killed by Achilles.

Hecuba Wife of King Priam of Troy and mother of Hector, Paris, Troilus and Cassandra.

Heimdall Norse god, and guardian of the bridge, Bifrost. Born of nine mothers.

Hekatoncheires (100 hands) In Greek mythology, the name of three giants with 100 hands and 50 heads each: Briareus, Cottus and Gyges. They were the offspring of Gaia and Uranus.

Helen Greek heroine, daughter of Zeus and Leda, sister of Clytemnestra and Castor and Pollux.

Hephaestus Son of Zeus and Hera who was thrown from Olympia by his mother and landed in the sea. Hephaestus made the armour for Achilles.

Hera Greek goddess of marriage and childbirth and queen of the gods.

Heracles Greek hero who performed the Twelve Labours of Eurystheus. Offspring of Zeus and Alcmene.

Hercules Roman equivalent of Heracles.

Hermaphroditus Son of Hermes and Aphrodite. Salmacis embraced him so closely that they became fused as one, with a woman's breasts and a man's genitals.

Hermes Son of Zeus and Maia. Hermes invented the lyre soon after birth.

Hermione Daughter of Helen and Menelaus.

Hermod Norse god, son of Odin.

Hero Greek high priestess and lover of Leander, who swam the Hellespont every night to see her but was eventually drowned causing Hero to throw herself in the sea.

Hesperides In Greek mythology, the daughters of the evening star who guarded the Golden Apples together with the dragon Ladon.

Hindu myth and religion Of all the world's leading mythologies, by far the most complex and expansive are Hindu beliefs. Even the term 'mythology' does not sit easily with a body of culture that is still revered today. It is beyond the scope of this work to trace the roots of Hindu beliefs and philosophy with its many tributaries, which themselves form a whole, separate strata of mythology. Many of the gods have personifications under differing names, and others have re-incarnations (avatars), which may bring with them a whole new substrata of mythology. Hindu mythology does not lend itself to fall comfortably within the table of comparative gods, indeed, the choice of Indra as principal god, or king of the gods, can only be loosely adhered to as a comparative to Zeus or Jupiter. Hindu mythology can be further divided into pre-Vedic, late-Vedic, post-Vedic, pre-Aryan post-Aryan and Classical, all of which has its own version of the creation. In the late-Vedic period, *c.*1200 BC, Brahma might have been considered the most important Hindu god, but he was gradually eclipsed by Vishnu and S(h)iva. Strict adherence to the Veda would place Prajapati (Lord of Creatures) as the creator god. In another version, the Prajapatis are the 10 'mind-born' children of Brahma. The traditional Trimurti of Brahma, Vishnu and S(h)iva, would be considered the most important Hindu gods, but it is true to say that Indra is the equivalent of Zeus in Greek mythology or Jupiter in Roman.

Hippolyte Queen of the Amazons and sister of Antiope.

Hoder Blind Norse god who killed Baldur.

Horus Egyptian god of light with a falcon's head, son of Osiris and Isis.

Huitzilopochtli Chief Aztec god, linked with the sun, fire, war and human sacrifice.

Hyacinthus Peloponnesian youth loved by Apollo who was killed when the jealous Zephyrus diverted a discus to hit him.

Hydra Greek monster usually depicted with 9 heads; slain by Heracles.

Hyperion Greek Titan, son of Uranus and Gaia.

Iapetus Greek Titan, father of Prometheus and Atlas, grandfather of Deucalion.

Icarus Son of Daedalus; he flew too near the sun while escaping from Crete and fell into the Aegean Sea and drowned.

Idavold In Norse mythology the playground of the gods.

Idomeneus King of Crete who contributed 100 ships to the expedition against Troy.

Idunn   Norse goddess of the golden apples of youth,
wife of Bragi.

Iliad   Homer's epic poem on the siege of Troy.

Imhotep   The Egyptian god of medicine and healing.

Io   Greek heroine turned into a heifer by Zeus to save
her from the wrath of Hera.

Iphigenia   Daughter of Agamemnon and
Clytemnestra, sacrificed by her father at Aulis to
gain a favourable wind for the Greek fleet sailing to
Troy.

Isis   Egyptian goddess of magic and mother of
Horus.

Ismene   Daughter of Oedipus and Jocasta. She followed her father and her sister, Antigone, into exile.

Isthmian Games   Quadrennial games held at Corinth
in honour of Poseidon.

Ithaca   Island home of Odysseus, one of the Ionian
Islands.

Ixion   Greek king of Thessaly who was the first to
murder a kinsman, his father-in-law; he was bound
to a wheel of fire in Tartarus for trying to rape Hera.

Janus   Roman god of entrances, travel and the
dawn, depicted as a man with two faces.

Jason   Son of Aeson, the Aeolian King of Iolcos.
Aeson's half-brother Pelias usurped the throne and
Queen Alcimede was forced to smuggle her son to
safety, entrusting him to the care of Chiron, the
centaur. Jason returned to Iolcis to regain his
father's kingdom and was told by Pelias that he
would step down in return for the golden fleece of a
ram, which hung from a tree in Colchis, and was
guarded by a dragon. Jason engaged Argus to
build a large galley for the journey and successfully
attained his goal with the help of some legendary
Greek heroes. During his adventures he married
the sorceress, Medea, but whether he ever attained
the throne of Iolcos is doubtful. Jason eventually
died when the decaying prow of the Argo fell
on him.

Jimmu-tenno   Legendary first Emperor of Japan, aka
Kamu-yamato-iware-biko.

Jocasta   Wife of King Laius and mother of Oedipus.

Jotunheim   In Norse mythology the land of the race
of giants, said to lie among the roots of Yggdrasil.

Jumala   Finnish supreme god.

Juno   Roman goddess of marriage, childbirth and
light, and queen of the gods.

Jupiter   Originally a Roman sky god, but then regarded by the Romans as *Dies Pater* (Father Day), and
later still became the Roman equivalent of Zeus.

Kama   Hindu god of love and pleasure.

Khnum   Egyptian goddess of creation.

Khonsou   Egyptian god, son of Ammon.

Kvasir   Norse god of wisdom.

Laertes   King of Ithaca and father of Odysseus by
Anticleia.

Lakshmi   In Hindu mythology, also known as Sri,
attained importance as the consort of Vishnu under
each of his incarnations; when he became Rama
she was faithful Sita, and when he became Krishna
she became his wife, Rukmini.

Lapithes   Mythological race that fought a famous war
with the centaurs.

Lares   Roman gods of the house and fertility.

Leander   Mythical youth of Abydos who drowned
while swimming the Hellespont to meet Hero.

Leda   Seduced by Zeus in the form of a swan and
gave birth to Helen and Polydeuces in one egg and
Castor and Clytemnestra in another. Other versions
record that Helen and Polydeuces were children of
Zeus and that Castor and Clytemnestra were children of her husband, Tyndareus.

Leviathan   Sea monster mentioned in the book of
Job, resembling a crocodile.

Liber Pater   Roman god of agriculture and human
fertility.

Libitina   Roman goddess of funeral rites.

Lilith   Demonic first wife of Adam in Hebrew mytholgy.

Lohengrin   In Germanic legend, the son of Parsifal.

Loki   Norse god of mischief.

Lorelei   In German mythology a siren said to dwell
on a rock at the edge of the Rhine, south of
Koblenz, who lures boatmen to destruction.

Lud(d)   Mythical king of Britain whose temple in
Roman London was near St Paul's Cathedral. Ludd
was also the name of a Celtic god of the sea.

Llyr (Lir)   A Celtic god of waters and the sea; the
father of Manannan.

Maat   Egyptian goddess of sterility, truth and justice.

Mabinogion   A collection of stories written in Welsh
in medieval times, the principal source of ancient
Welsh and British Myths.

Macha   In Celtic mythology a collective name for the
trinity of war goddesses Macha, Morrígan, and
Nemain. As an individual, Macha was sometimes
known as Dana (crow) or Badb (raven).

Mahabharata   Sanskrit verse epic composed
between 400 BC and AD 400. It relates a dynastic
feud between the Pandavas and their cousins the
Kauravas, respectively gods and demons.

Maia   Roman goddess of fertility.

Manasa   Serpent goddess of Hindu mythology.

Manitou   Supreme deity of the Algonquian people fo
North American.

Marduk   Supreme god of Babylon.

Mazda   Persian god of wisdom.

Medea   In Greek mythology a princess of Colchis and
powerful sorceress; deserted by Jason after helping
him to steal the Golden Fleece, she killed their two
children.

Megara   Daughter of King Creon of Thebes and first
wife of Heracles, who killed her in a fit of madness
caused by the goddess Hera.

Megingjord   Name of Thor's belt, which magnifies his
strength.

Meleager   In Greek mythology the heir of King
Oeneus of Calydon. The Fates appeared to his
mother, Althaea, when he was seven days old,
they pointed to a burning stick in the fireplace and
told her that her son's life would last as long as the
stick would burn. Althaea snatched the stick from
the fire and hid it away. His father incurred the
wrath of Artemis and she sent a wild boar to
Calydon to ravage his crops. Meleager offered the
boar's pelt and tusks to anyone who could deliver
the death blow. Many of his fellow Argonauts joined
the hunt, including Atalanta, who he was besotted
by. Although Meleager himself delivered the final

death thrust, he gave the pelt to Atalanta, which upset his two uncles. In a rage he killed them both, and his mother, seeing the corpses of her brothers, threw the stick into the fire, and Meleager's life drained away

Menelaus King of Sparta, younger brother of Agamemnon and husband of Helen.

Merope A Pleiad and wife of Sisyphus.

Metis In Greek mythology the daughter of Oceanus and Tethys and first wife of Zeus.

Mictlan Aztec land of the dead.

Midas Mythical king of Phygian. In one story, Apollo burdens him with ass's ears for fudging badly in a music contest. In another, he receives but manages to shed the gift of turning all he touches to gold.

Midgard In Norse mythology the dwelling place of mankind, formed from the body of the giant Ymir and linked to Asgard by Bifrost, the rainbow bridge.

Milo Champion wrestler in Greek mythology.

Mimir Norse giant who guarded the well of wisdom near the roots of Yggdrasil.

Minos In Greek mythology the son of Europa and Zeus and brother to Sarpedon and Rhadamanthys. Following a dispute with his two brothers, Minos succeeded to the throne of Crete. The issue of the succession was decided when, having prayed for a divine sign, Poseidon sent Minos a magnificent bull from the sea. However, because Minos neglected to sacrifice the bull, Poseidon cursed him, causing his wife, Pasiphaë, to fall madly in love with the creature. With the help of the craftsman Daedalus, Pasiphaë was able to satisfy her lust by hiding in a decoy cow. The offspring of this union was the Minotaur, a monster with the head of a bull but the body of a man. Minos commissioned Daedalus to construct a labyrinth to house the Minotaur, and each year 9 boys and 9 girls were brought from Athens as food for the monster. One year the Greek hero Theseus was chosen for sacrifice and slew the Minotaur with the help of Minos's daughter Ariadne, who supplied him with a thread to enable him to retrace his steps after the slaying. King Minos followed Daedalus to Sicily with his mind set on revenge, but Daedalus was warned of his presence and arranged for boiling oil to kill the king when he took a bath at Kamikos.

Minotaur Greek monster, son of Pasiphaë and a bull, kept in a labyrinth on Crete by King Minos.

Mithra(s) Persian god of light, justice and war.

Mjollnir Thor's hammer, said to cause lightning.

Mnemosyne Greek Titan who was the mother of all the Muses.

Morrígan Irish war goddess whose name means phantom queen; also the collective name of the trinity of war goddesses Macha, Morrígan, and Nemain.

Muses Sacred to Mount Helicon. See listing on p. 782.

Myrmidons People of Aegina, created by Zeus for King Aeacus; some of them fought for Achilles at Troy.

Myth The term was first used by the Greek historian Herodotus (c.484 BC – c.420 BC) to describe a body of knowledge or beliefs that have no foundation in fact and so must be distinguished from history although recorded fact can take mythical proportions due to historical interpretation.

Nabu (Nebo) Babylonian Mythology. Son of Marduk, and the scribe and herald of the gods.

Naiads Freshwater nymphs in Greek mythology.

Nanna Norse goddess, wife of Baldur.

Narcissus Greek hero whom Nemesis caused to fall in love with his own reflection.

Nataraja Title of the Hindu god S(h)iva, meaning lord of the dance.

Nehallenia Norse goddess of plenty.

Nemesis Greek goddess of destiny, the daughter of Oceanus.

Nereids Fifty beautiful sea nymphs, the daughters of Nereus and Doris, of whom the most famous were Amphitrite and Thetis.

Nereus Greek god of the sea.

Nessus Greek centaur whose blood caused the death of his killer, Heracles.

Nestor King of Pylos and only one of Neleus's 12 sons spared by Heracles. The oldest of the Greeks at Troy and the only one to return home without mishap.

Nibelung In German legend, any of the race of dwarfs who possessed a treasure hoard stolen by Siegfried.

Nibelungenlied Heroic epic of unknown authorship written in the early 13th centruy and based on German history and legend.

Niflheim In Norse mythology the abode of the dead, sometimes identified with hell.

Niobe In Greek mythology queen of Thebes, wife of King Amphion and daughter of Tantalus and Dione.

Njord Norse god, father of Frey and Freyja.

Norns Norse goddesses of destiny: Urdr – the past, Verdandi – the present, and Skuld – the future.

Notus Greek mythology. South-west wind known to the Romans as Auster. Son of Astraeus and Eos.

Numa Pompilius Legendary second King of Rome who succeeded Romulus.

Nun In Egyptian mythology, the dark primeval ocean of chaos, which existed before the first gods.

Nymph Any one of a class of mythological, youthful female divinities inhabiting woods, springs, mountains or the sea. Although nymphs were not immortal, their life span was usually several thousand years.

Oceanid(e)s Greek sea-nymphs, daughters of Oceanus and Tethys.

Oceanus Greek god of the River Oceanus and son of Gaia and Uranus.

Odysseus (aka Ulysses) Greek hero, the son of Laertes and Anticlea, king and queen of Ithaca, a key figure in Homer's *Iliad* and central in the *Odyssey*.

Oedipus (swollen foot) Greek hero, king of Thebes, who inadvertently killed his father and married his mother.

Oisin In Celtic mythology, a warrior and poet, son of Finn mac Cumhall and Sadb.

Ops Roman goddess of the harvest, and consort of Saturn.

Oread A Greek mountain-nymph.

Orestes In Greek mythology the king of Argos and Sparta, son of Agamemnon and Clytemnestra.

Orion In Greek mythology a giant hunter, son of Poseidon and Euryale.

Orpheus Greek musician and poet, son of King Oeagrus of Thrace and Calliope. He married Eurydice, failed to rescue her from Hades after she was killed by a snake, and was finally torn to pieces by the women of Thrace.

Osiris Egyptian god of vegetation, brother of Seth and husband of Isis.

Otr Norse otter god.

Otus and Ephialtes Twin sons of Iphimedeia and Poseidon.

Pales Roman goddess of flocks.

Palladium Mythical statue of Athene given to Dardanus by Zeus to ensure the protection of Troy.

Pan Greek god of male sexuality, herds and woods.

Pandora In Greek mythology the first woman on earth. When her dowry box was opened it released all the world's ill and retained only hope.

Paris A prince of Troy, the son of Priam. He abducted Helen, the wife of Menelaus, so causing the Trojan War.

Parvati In Hindu mythology Parvati (the mountaineer) was one of the forms of Devi and as such, the mother of the elephant-headed god of wisdom, Ganes(h)a. Parvati became the golden-skinned Gauri.

Pasiphaë In Greek mythology the daughter of Helios and mother of the Minotaur.

Patroclus Greek warrior who, while wearing Achilles's armour, was killed by Hector during the seige of Troy.

Pegasus Greek winged horse that sprang from the body of Medusa after her death.

Pelasgus The first man, according to one version of the Greek creation myth.

Peleus In Greek mythology the King of Phythia in Thessaly. He married Thetis and fathered Achilles.

Penates Roman gods of food and drink.

Penelope The wife of Odysseus. During his long absence after the Trojan war, she tricked the suitors who were plaquing her to marry by unravelling a shroud every night, having promised to make her decision when she had finished weaving it.

Persephone Greek goddess of the underworld, corn and the spring.

Perse Daughter of Oceanus and wife of Helios, to whom she bore Circe, Pasiphaë, Aeëtes and Perses.

Perses (1) Son of Perseus and Andromeda. Said to have given his name to Persia.

Perses (2) Son of Helios and Perse and father of Hecate.

Perseus Greek hero, son of Zeus and Danaë; he slew the Gorgon Medusa and married Andromeda.

Phaeton Greek hero, son of Helios and Clymene. Killed by a thunderbolt from Zeus after losing control of the sun-chariot and endangering the safety of the world. Phaeton's body fell into the river Eridanus (Po).

Philoctetes Greek hero who killed Paris.

Pleiades In Greek mythology the 7 daughters of Atlas and Pleione.

Plutus Greek god of wealth.

Polybus In Greek mythology the king of Corinth, husband of Merope and adoptive father of Oedipus.

Pomona Roman goddess of fruit trees.

Portunus Roman god of husbands and harbours.

Poseidon Greek god of the sea and earthquakes.

Priam In Greek mythology the king of Troy, son of King Laomedon and Queen Strymo.

Priapus Son of Dionysus and Aphrodite, a fertility god, often portrayed with a grotesquely large phallus.

Procrustes (Stretcher) In Greek mythology an innkeeper who killed travellers on the road between Athens and Eleusis by lopping or stretching their bodies to fit his bed. Theseus killed him by decapitation.

Prometheus In Greek mythology a Titan, sometimes credited with making mankind out of clay. Because he stole fire from the gods and gave it to man, Zeus bound him to a rock for an eagle to peck out his liver, which always regrew because Prometheus was immortal.

Proserpine Roman goddess of the Underworld, corn and the spring.

Proteus Sea god, the son of Oceanus and Tethys. Proteus was a seer but would take any form to avoid questioning.

Psyche In Greek mythology the soul, often portrayed as a butterfly. Personified as a woman, she fell in love with Eros and suffered many ordeals before they were united.

Ptah Egyptian god of creation.

Pygmalion In Greek mythology the king of Cyprus who fell in love with a statue.

Pyrrha Daughter of Epimetheus and Pandora and wife of Deucalion with whom she repopulated the earth after the flood.

Quetzalcoatl Toltec and Aztec god of vegetation and the wind, sometimes depicted as a bearded man wearing a mask, sometimes as a feathered serpent..

Quirinus Roman god of war, after whom a hill of Rome was named.

Ragnarok Final destruction of the Norse gods in a battle to the death with evil.

Ramayana One of the two great Sanskrit verse epics (along with the *Mahabharata*) dating back to the 3rd century BC, the story of Prince Rama, his struggle for the throne of Ajodhya, and his war with the demon Ravana to rescue his abducted wife Sita, with Hanuman's help

Remus See Romulus and Remus.

Rhadamanthus Son of Europa and Zeus and brother to Minos and Sarpedon. After death he became a judge in the underworld.

Rhea Greek goddess of motherhood; sister and wife of Cronus.

Rhesus Thracian king who helped the Trojans but was slain by Odysseus.

Rhiannon In Welsh Celtic mythology, the daughter of the King of the Otherworld and wife of Pwyll, prince of Dyfed.

Romulus and Remus Twin sons of Mars, and legendary founders of Rome.

Round Table In Arthurian legend the great table of Camelot that seated King Arthur's knights. The Siege Perilous (dangerous seat) remained vacant

MYTHOLOGY AND LEGEND

because only the bringer of the Holy Grail could use it without coming to harm.

Rumina Roman goddess of nursing mothers.

Sarpedon In Greek mythology the son of Europa and Zeus and brother to Minos and Rhadamanthus.

Satyr A Greek mythological creature, part man, part goat; the satyrs were followers of Dionysus.

Scaean (Left-Hand) Gate Situated in the walls of Troy; the spot where Achilles fell.

Scylla Greek sea monster; originally the daughter of Poseidon, she was turned into a monster by Amphitrite. in Straits of Messina opposite Charybdis depicted as snake with 6 heads that lived in a cave.

Sekmet Egyptian goddess of power and battle, depicted with the head of a lioness.

Selene Greek goddess of the moon, daughter of Hyperion and Thea; she was most notably the lover of Endymion.

Semiramis In Assyrian mythology the wife of Ninus and co-founder with him of Nineveh.

Set Egyptian god of evil.

Seven against Thebes Greek champions – Adrasius, Amphiaraüs, Capaneus, Hippomedon, Parthenopaeus, Polynices and Tydeus – who failed to overthrow Eteocles from his Kingship.

Seven Kings of Rome Romulus (753–715 BC), Numa Pompilius (715–673 BC), Tullius Hostilius (673–642 BC), Ancus Marcius (642–616 BC), Tarquin the Elder (616–579 BC), Servius Tullius (579–534 BC), Tarquinius Superbus (Proud Tarquin) (534–510 BC).

Shu Egyptian god of Air.

Sibyl Roman prophetess.

Sibylline Books Roman tradition tells how a sibyl offered Tarquinius Priscus 9 prophetic books which he refused to buy at the price. She destroyed three and he still refused them; she burned three more and he took the remaining three at the price demanded for the nine. Special priests kept them and they were consulted only when the Senate authorized it in time of need. In 83 BC the originals were destroyed by fire. The original books instructed the Romans to convey the sacred stone of Cybele to Rome.

Sif Norse goddess, wife of Thor.

Sigmund In Germanic legend the son of Volsung who won the divine sword Gram by extracting it from a tree trunk.

Sigurd In Germanic legend the son of Sigmund and Hjordis and owner of the horse, Grani.

Sigyn Norse goddess, wife of Loki.

Silvanus Roman god of trees and forests.

Siren In Homer's *Odyssey* one of a group of creatures, half woman and half bird, who lure sailors to their death by their singing. Odysseus and the Argonauts withstood their fatal charms, the latter because Orpheus outsang them.

Sisyphus In Greek mythology a Corinthian king destined in Hades to roll a large stone up a hill for evermore, only for it to keep rolling back when it reaches the top.

Skadi In Norse mythology the wife of Njord.

Skan Lakota god embodying the sky.

Sleipnir Odin's 8-legged horse.

Sobek Egyptian crocodile god.

Soma In Hindu mythology an intoxicating drink. Soma was also an early god of the moon.

Spartoi (sown men) Sprang up fully armed when Cadmus sowed the dragon's teeth and killed each other until five remained: Echion, Udaeus, Chthonius, Hyperenor and Pelorus.

Sphinx Greek monster with a woman's head and lion's body.

Stentor Greek herald during the Trojan War, famous for his very loud voice.

Stymphalian birds In Greek mythology a flock of man-eating birds, which infested Lake Stymphalos in Arcadia. Killed by Heracles.

Surabhi In Indian mythology a divine cow of plenty.

Syrinx Greek nymph of Arcadia. She was pursued by Pan, who made the first pan-pipes from her embodiment, as a bed of reeds was the only way she could escape him.

Tantalus Greek mythological king of Sipylos in Lydia, who stole the food of the gods and was condemned to stand thirsty and hungry forever in a pool that receded when he bent down to drink, beneath fruit trees whose branches retreated when he reached to pick their fruit.

Tarpeian Rock Named after Tarpeia, the traitor daughter of the keeper of the Roman citadel. Became the rock from which Roman traitors were thrown.

Tartarus That part of Hades reserved for those that offended the gods during their lifetime.

Taweret Egyptian protector goddess of women and children, often depicted as part crocodile, part lion and part hippopotamus.

Telamon Son of Aeacus and brother of Peleus; Telamon fathered Ajax by Periboea.

Telemachus Greek hero, son of Odysseus and Penelope.

Tenes Son of Apollo who gave his name to the Greek island of Tenedos.

Themis Daughter of Ge and Uranus and sister of Cronus. The wife of Zeus before Hera.

Theseus Mythical Greek hero, king of Athens and son of King Aegeus and Queen Aethra; it was Theseus who defeated the Minotaur in its labyrinth home in Crete.

Thetis Greek goddess and mother of Achilles.

Thunderbird Totem figure of Native Americans from the north-west. Aka Skyamsen.

Tiresias Legendary blind prophet of Thebes who had been both male and female and estimated that women had 9 times more pleasure during intercourse than men.

Tonalpohualli Aztec sacred calendar consisting of 260 days which were divided into 20 weeks of 13 days.

Trimurti Trinity of Hindu gods: Brahma(n) the Creator, Vishnu the Preserver and S(h)iva the Destroyer.

Tristan and Isolde Celtic legend. Tristan was a harpist and Isolde was the daughter of the king of Ireland. They drank a love potion together by mistake and fell irretrievably in love.

Triton Son of Poseidon and Amphitrite. He was a

merman, the upper half human, the lower half fish. Triton used a conch shell trumpet to calm the waves.

Troilus In Greek mythology, the young son of Priam, slain by Achilles. His romance with Cressida is a medieval invention.

Ull Norse god and stepson of Thor.

Valhalla In Norse mythology the great hall of Odin in Asgard, where warriors who died as heroes in battle dwelled eternally.

Valkyries Norse warrior handmaidens to Odin.

Vanir Norse race of benelovent gods including Njörd, Frey and Freyja. The Vanir warred with the Aesir and were eventually absorbed into their number.

Varuna In Hindu mythology Varuna was at one time the upholder of heaven and earth and often associated with Surya as the creator of the sun. In post-Vedic mythology he became god of the seas and rivers.

Vertumnus Roman god of fertility.

Vestal virgins College of priestesses of the Roman cult of Vesta, the hearth goddess. Originally four of them; later 6 (generally considered as the number); and finally 7.

Vidar Norse god, a son of Odin and slayer of the wolf Fenir.

Vishnu's Incarnations The 10 avatars of Vishnu are 1. Matsya, 2. Kurma, 3. Varaha, 4. Narasinha,

5. Vamana 6. Paras(h)urama, 7. Ramachandra (Rama), 8. Krishna, 9. Buddha, 10. Kalki.

Völund In Norse mythology, a smith and artificer and king of the elves. In Germanic legends he appears as Wieland; in English folklore as Wayland Smith.

Wyvern Mythical beast with a dragon's head, a serpent's tail and a body with wings and two legs.

Yggdrasil In Norse mythology, the ash tree that binds the heavens, earth and the underworld with it's roots and branches. It shelters the remnants of humanity when Raganrok destroys the gods and sets the world on fire.

Ymir The first being and forefather of all the Norse giants. Slain by Odin, who made the earth from his flesh, the water from his blood and the sky from his skull.

Zephyrus West Wind, the son of Astraeus and Eus and father of Xanthus and Balius, the talking horses of Achilles. Roman counterpart was Favonius.

Zetes Twin brother of Calais. Winged sons of Boreas and Oreithyia, they accompanied the Argonauts and drove off the Harpies.

Zeus's conquests The supreme god of the Greek parthenon took many forms in his amorous pursuit of goddesses, nymphs and humans.

Zeus's Conquests

Conquest	Form	Offspring
Alcmene	Amphitryon	Heracles
Antiope	Satyr	Amphion and Zetheus
Danaë	Shower of gold	Perseus
Demeter	Himself	Persephone
Europa	Bull and eagle	Minos, Sarpedon and Rhadamanthus
Eurynome	Himself	Graces
Ganymede	Eagle	None
Io	Cloud	Epaphos
Leda	Swan	Helen, Clytemnestra, Castor and Pollux
Leto	Quail	Apollo and Artemis
Maia	Himself	Hermes
Mnemosyne	Himself	Moses
Rhea	Serpent	None
Semele	Mortal	Dionysus
Thetis	Himself	None

Famous Horses of Myth and History

Name	Owner	Horse's owner's identity	Name	Owner	Horse's owner's identity
Arvak	Sol	Norse maiden	Babieca	El Cid	Spanish hero
Abaster	Pluto	Greek god	Balios	Achilles	Greek hero
Abatos	Pluto	Greek god	Barbary Roan	Richard II	English king
Abraxa	Aurora	Roman goddess	Bayard	Renaud de Montanbau	Legendary Frankish knight
Actaeon	Helios	Greek sun god			
Aethon	Helios	Greek sun god	Black Agnes	Mary Queen of Scots	Scottish queen
Aeton	Pluto	Greek god	Black Bess	Dick Turpin	Literary creation
Al Borak	Mohammed	Founder of Islam	Brigliadoro	Orlando	Legendary character
Alfana	Gradasso	Literary creation			
Alsvid	Sol	Norse maiden	Bronte	Helios	Greek sun god
Amethea	Helios	Greek sun god	Bucephalus (Ox-Head)	Alexander the Great	Macedonian ruler
Arion	Hercules	Mythological hero			
Arundel	Bevis of Hampton	Literary creation	Carman	Chevalier de Bayard	French knight

Name	Owner	Horse's owner's identity	Name	Owner	Horse's owner's identity
Celer	Lucius Verus	Roman emperor	Lampos	Helios	Greek sun god
Cerus	Adrastus	Mythological king of Argos	Lamri	King Arthur	Legendary Anglo-Saxon king
Champion	Gene Autry	TV cowboy			
Comanche	US cavalry	Only survivor of Little Big Horn	Marengo	Napoleon	French emperor
Copenhagen	Duke of Wellington	Soldier and statesman	Marocco	Mr Banks	Elizabethan horseman
Cyllaros	Castor and Pollux	Roman mythological twins	Marsala	Garibaldi	Italian patriot
			Nonios	Pluto	Greek god
			Pegasus	Bellerophon	Greek hero
Dapple	Sancho Panza	Literary character	Phaeton	Aurora	Roman goddess
Diablo	Cisco Kid	Literary creation	Phallus (stallion)	Heraclius	Byzantine emperor
Dinos	Diomedes	Mythological king of Argos	Phlegon	Helios	Greek sun god
			Phrenicos	Hiero of Syracuse	Winner of 73rd olympiad
Doublet	Princess Anne	Royal Olympian	Podarge (Swift Foot)	Hector	Trojan hero
Eos	Aurora	Roman goddess			
Erythreos	Helios	Greek sun god	Purocis	Helios	Greek sun god
Ethon	Hector	Trojan hero	Rosabelle	Mary Queen of Scots	Scottish queen
Fadda (mule)	Mohammed	Founder of Islam			
Ferrant d'Espagne	Oliver	Legendary Frankish knight	Rosinante	Don Quixote	Literary creation
			Savoy	Charles VIII	French king
Foxhunter	Colonel Harry Llewellyn	Olympic champion	Scout	Tonto	TV creation
			Sefton	Metropolitan Police	Bomb victim
Galathe	Hector	Trojan hero	Shibdiz	Chosroes II	Persian ruler
Grani	Siegfried	German legendary character	Silver	Lone Ranger	TV creation
			Skinfaxi (Shining Mane)	Dagr	Horse of Day (Norse myth)
Grizzle	Dr Syntax	Literary creation			
Haizum	Gabriel	Archangel	Sleipnir	Odin	Norse supreme god
Harpagus	Castor and Pollux	Roman mythological twins			
			Sorrel	William III	British king
			Strymon	Xerxes	Persian king
Hercules	The Steptoes	TV creation	Tachebrune	Ogier the Dane	Hero of chansons de geste
Hippocampus	Neptune	Roman god			
Hrimfaxi (Frost Mane)	Nott	Horse of Night (Norse myth)	Tony	Tom Mix	Film cowboy
			Topper	Hopalong Cassidy	Film cowboy
Incitatus	Caligula	Roman emperor	Trebizond	Guarinos	French knight at Roncesvalles
Kantanka	Prince Gautama	The Buddha			
Lampon	Diomedes	Mythological king of Argos	Trigger	Roy Rogers	TV cowboy
			White Surrey	Richard III	English king
			Xanthus	Achilles	Greek hero

Famous Dogs   (Fact and Fiction)

Name	Owner or details	Name	Owner or details
Arctophonos	Orion's dog (bear-killer)	Diamond	Isaac Newton
Argos	Ulysses	Digby	Biggest dog in the world in 1973 film
Asta	*Thin Man* series	Dizzie	Michael Foot
Blondie	Hitler	Dougal	Character in *Magic Roundabout*
Boatswain	Lord Byron	Dragon	Aubry of Montdidier
Boot	Old English sheepdog in *The Perishers* (cartoon strip)	Flush	Elizabeth Barrett Browning
		Freeway	Jonathan and Jennifer Hart
Bounce	Alexander Pope	Gargittios	One of Geryon's dogs slain by Hercules
Boy	Prince Rupert's dog, killed at Marston Moor		
		Geist	Matthew Arnold's dachshund
Bran	Finn mac Cumhal	Gelert	Prince Llewellyn's greyhound
Brutus	Landseer's greyhound (invader of the larder)	Giallo	Walter Savage Landor
		Gnasher	Dennis the Menace
Cabal (Cavall)	King Arthur's favourite hound	Greyfriars Bobby	Watched over owner's grave for 14 years
Cerberus	Three-headed dog that guards Hades		
		Hamlet	Sir Walter Scott's black greyhound
Chequers	Richard Nixon	Hodain (aka Leon)	Tristan
Daisy	Blondie		
Dash	Charles Lamb	K9	Robot in *Dr Who*

Name	Owner or details
Kaiser	Matthew Arnold's dachshund
Katmir	Dog of the Seven Sleepers
Laelaps	Procris
Laika	Fox terrier that was the first dog in space
Lassie	Actually a female dog named Pal
Luath	Cuchulainn
Luath	Robert Burns
Lucy	David Blunkett
Lufra	Douglas's hound in Scott's *Lady of the Lake*
Maera (Glistener)	Icarius
Maida	Sir Walter Scott's deerhound
Mathe	Richard II's greyhound
Montmorency	Three Men in a Boat
Nana	Darling family (*Peter Pan*)
Nigger	Guy Gibson
Nipper	Fox terrier logo for His Master's Voice (HMV)
Offa	David Blunkett
Olaf	Snoopy's brother
Orthos	One of Geryon's dogs slain by Hercules

Name	Owner or details
Paddy	Harold Wilson
Pearl	Beryl the Peril
Peritas	Alexander the Great
Petra	*Blue Peter*
Pickles	Found the World Cup
Ptoophagos	Orion's dog (glutton of Ptoon, in Boeotia)
Rin Tin Tin	Died in Jean Harlow's arms
Rufus	Sir Winston Churchill's poodle
Sandy	Little Orphan Annie
Scamper	Secret Seven
Sceolang	Finn mac Cumhal
Shep	John Noakes
Snoopy	Beagle in *Peanuts* (cartoon strip)
Snowy	Tintin
Soda	Chris Patten
Spike	Snoopy's brother
Spottie	*The Woodentops*
Theron	Roderick the Goth
Timmy	Famous Five member
Toby	Punch
Whisky	Chris Patten
Won Ton Ton	Saved Hollywood in 1976 film

Living Creatures (except birds)

aardvark nocturnal mammal, inhabiting the grasslands of Africa south of the Sahara and feeding on ants and termites. It is the sole member of its family (Orycteropodidae) and order (Tubulidentata). The aardvark is also called an ant bear. Sp.: *Orycteropus afer.*

aardwolf nocturnal mammal, inhabiting the plains of east and southern Africa, feeding on termites and insect larvae. Family: Hyaenidae (Hyenas) and Order: Carnivora. Sp.: *Proteles cristatus.*

abalone gastropod mollusc with a shallow, ear-shaped shell lined with mother-of-pearl.Gen.: *Haliotis.*

albacore long-finned tunny fish. Sp.: *Thunnus alalunga.*

alewife fish of the north-west Atlantic related to the herring. Sp.: *Alosa pseudoharengus.*

alligator either of two crocodilian reptiles of the family Alligatoridae (alligators and caymans) and distinguished from true crocodiles by their shorter and broader snouts. The American alligator (*Alligator mississippiensis*), the larger of the two species, can grow to a length of almost 6 metres, and the Chinese alligator (*Alligator sinensis*), about a quarter of that length.

alpaca South American herbivore mammal of the Andes with long shaggy hair, related to the llama. Sp.: *Lama pacos.*

anchovy small marine food fish of the herring family. Sp.: *Engraulis encrasicholus.*

ant small social insect of the order Hymenoptera, typically living in organized colonies of winged males (drones), wingless sterile females (workers) and fertile females (queens). The body of an ant has three segments, i.e. head, abdomen and thorax. Family: Formicidae.

ant: Amazon ant which captures pupae of other ant species to raise as slaves. Gen.: *Polyergus.*

antelope bovid mammals of Africa and Asia that include bushbucks, elands, gnus, gazelles, impalas, springboks, dik-diks, blackbucks, oryxes, gerenuks and nilgai. Antelopes have unbranched horns, which they do not shed. Family: Boridae.

ape primates characterized by long arms and the absence of a tail. Great apes are the chimpanzee, gorilla and orang-utan (Family: Pongidae). Lesser apes are the various gibbons (Family: Hylobatidae).

argalis large Asiatic wild sheep with massive horns. Sp.: *Ovis ammon.*

armadillo nocturnal insect-eating but generally omnivorous edentate mammal native to the southern USA and Central and S. America, with large claws for digging and a body covered in bony plates, often rolling itself into a ball when threatened. They range from 3- to as many as 13-banded. Burmeister's and pink fairy armadillos are endangered species. Family: Dasypodidae.

axolotl aquatic newt-like salamander from Mexico, which in natural conditions retains its larval form for life but is able to breed. Name means 'water servant'. Sp.: *Ambystoma mexicanum.*

aye-aye nocturnal arboreal prosimian primate of Madagascar related to the lemurs. Sp.: *Daubentonia madagascariensis.*

babirusa wild hog with upturned tusks native to the Malay archipelago. Sp.: *Babyrousa babyrussa.*

baboon primate of the family Cercopithecidae, characterized by its fox-like muzzle and long tail. Gen.: *Papio.*

badger (American) stout-bodied carnivore with greyish to reddish coat and black facial stripes. Sp.: *Taxidea taxus.*

badger (Eurasian) stout-bodied carnivore with greyish coat and black and white facial stripes. All badgers are members of the family Mustelidae. Sp.: *Meles meles.*

badger (honey) aka ratel. Musteline mammal inhabiting wooded regions of Africa and Asia. Sp.: *Mellivora capensis.*

bandicoot any small, agile terrestrial marsupial of the family Peramelidae of Australia and New Guinea. Bandicoots typically have long, pointed muzzles, large ears and long tails, and feed mainly on small invertebrates.

bandicoot rat large, dark brown, burrowing rat of the family Muridae, order Rodentia, of India and Sri Lanka, sometimes known as a mole rat. The bandicoot rat makes a grunting noise similar to that of a pig. Sp.: *Bandicota indica.*

barnacle small marine crustacean of the subclass Cirripedia that, as an adult, lives head-down attached to rocks or the bottom of the hull of a ship.

barnacle: goose common barnacle found worldwide, living attached by a stalk to driftwood. Gen.: *Lepas.*

bear large plantigrade, omnivorous mammal of the family Ursidae, order Carnivora. The smallest species is the Malaysian sun bear (*Helarctos malayanus*), and the largest is the Kodiak bear (*Ursus arctos middendorffi*).

beluga large kind of Russian sturgeon from which caviar is obtained. Sp.: *Huso huso.*

bib light brown European marine gadoid food fish. Aka pout. Sp.: *Gadus luscus.*

binturong arboreal civet of southern. Asia with a shaggy black coat and a prehensile tail. Sp.: *Arctictis binturong.*

bison: American ox-like grazing mammal with short-haired body and longer, darker hair on its head. Aka plains buffalo. Sp.: *Bison bison.*

black widow any venomous spider of the family Theridiidae, inhabiting warm climates throughout the world. The venom of the spider causes sharp pain and some muscle cramping but is usually only temporary and never fatal. The female is characterized by its dark colour and red hourglass marking on its abdomen. The males are rarely seen as they are often eaten by the female after mating. Black widows are known as button spiders in South Africa, redbacks in Australia and katipos in New Zealand. Gen.: *Latrodectus.*

bobcat small Northern American lynx with a spotted, reddish-brown coat and a short tail. Sp.: *Felis rufus.*

bonito one of several small, tuna-like marine food fishes of the family Scombridae (tunnies and mackerels) inhabiting warm Atlantic and Pacific waters. Gen.: *Sarda.*

boomslang   venomous tree-snake native to sub-Saharan Africa. Sp.: *Dispholidus typus.*

brachiosaurus   herbivorous dinosaurs, probably the largest land animals ever known (80 tons+). Gen.: *Brachiosaurus.*

brandling   red earthworm with rings of a brighter colour, which is often found in manure and used as fishing bait. Sp.: *Eisenia foetida.*

brown recluse   North American venomous spider with a dark brown body of about 3 centimetres long with a distinct violin-shaped design on its back. Sp.: *Loxosceles reclusa.*

buffalo (African)   large, black, sparsely haired animal weighing up to 700kg. Sp.: *Syncerus caffer.*

buffalo (Indian)   aka water buffalo or carabao. Southeast Asian domestic beast of burden weighing up to 1200kg. Sp.: *Bubalus bubalis.*

bullfrog   large frog native to North America and Mexico and known for its loud croak. Sp.: *Rana cateseiana.*

bumble-bee   large social bee with a loud hum. Aka humble-bee. Gen.: *Bombus.*

bummalo   small fish of south Asian coasts, dried and used as food, especially Bombay duck. Sp.: *Harpodon nehereus.*

bush baby   small nocturnal tree-dwelling African primate with very large eyes. Aka galago. Six species of the family Lorisidae.

cacomistle   raccoon-like animal of North America with a dark ringed tail. Sp.: *Bassariscus sumichrasti.*

callop   gold-coloured freshwater fish of Australia. Aka golden perch. Sp.: *Plectroplites ambiguus.*

camel: Arabian   camel with one hump native to the deserts of North Africa and the Near East (aka dromedary). Sp.: *Camelus dromedarius.*

camel: Bactrian   camel with two humps native to central Asia. Sp.: *Camelus bactrianus.*

capelin   small smeltlike fish of the North Atlantic used as food and as bait for catching cod. Sp.: *Mallotus villosus.*

capuchin   monkey of the family Cebidae, characterized by its head hair suggestive of a cowl. Gen.: *Cebus.*

capybara   very large, semi-aquatic rodent (up to 65 kg) native to South America east of the Andes. Sp.: *Hydrochoerus hydrochaeris.*

caracal   lynx native to Norht Africa and south-west. Asia. Sp.: *Felis caracal.*

caribou   large deer of Arctic regions of North America, having large branched antlers in the male and female, the only species of deer to do so. The caribou is known as a reindeer in Eurasia. Sp.: *Rangifer tarandus.*

carpenter ant   large ant which bores into wood to nest. Gen.: *Camponotus.*

cat: domestic   small feline mammal often kept as household pet. The cat is thought to have originated in Egypt. Unusual breeds include the Angora, which is usually deaf, the Manx, which is tailless, and the Siamese, which has blue eyes. Cats move in the same way as the camel and giraffe, i.e. by moving first the front and back legs on one side, then the front and back legs on the other side. Most cats have 18 toes, 5 on the front foot and 4 on the back. Sp.: *Felis domesticus.*

cat: wild   feline mammal living in the wild. Sp.: *Felis silvestris.*

cattle   dairy breeds include Ayrshire, Danish Red, Friesian, Guernsey, Jersey and Kerry. Beef cattle include Aberdeen Angus, Blonde d'Aquitaine, Blue Grey, Charolais, Chianina, Devon, Galloway, Hereford, Highland, Limousin, Lincoln Red, Luing, Maine-Anjou, Shorthorn and Sussex. Dual-purpose breeds include Dexter, Meuse-Rhine-Ijssel, Red Poll, Dairy Shorthorn, Simmental, South Devon and Welsh Black. Gen.: *Bos.*

cavy   any small South American rodent of the family Caviidae, especially of the genus *Cavia.*

cayman (caiman)   reptile of the family Alligatoridae (alligators and caymans), inhabiting riverbanks of Central and South America.

centipede   carnivorous arthropod, having a body of between 14 and 190 segments, each bearing one pair of legs. The common house centipede, order Scutigerida, is 25 millimetres (1 inch) long with a black striped body and 15 pairs of legs. Class: Chilopoda.

chamois   agile goat-antelope native to the mountains of Europe and Asia. Sp.: *Rupicapra rupicapra.*

cheese-fly   small black fly that breeds in cheese. Sp.: *Piophila casei.*

cheetah   fastest-running feline with a leopard-like spotted coat and non-retractable claws. Sp.: *Acinonyx jubatus.*

chigger   tropical flea of which females burrow under people's skin, causing painful sores. Aka chigoe, sand flea and jigger. Sp.: *Tunga penetrans.*

chimpanzee   tailless primate of the family Pongidae, inhabiting forests and savannahs of tropical west and central Africa. The two species are the common chimpanzee (*Pan troglodytes*) and the pygmy chimpanzee (*Pan paniscus*).

chinchilla   small South American rodent of the family Chinchillidae, which is bred in captivity for its soft grey fur. Chinchillas resemble long-tailed rabbits, although their ears are smaller. Sp.: *Chinchilla laniger.*

Chinese water deer   along with the musk deer, one of only two species of deer that do not have antlers. Sp.: *Hyfropotes inermis.*

chipmunk   North American ground squirrel having alternate light and dark stripes running down the body. Gen.: *Tamias.*

cicada   any of 1,500 varieties of winged-insects of the order Homoptera. The dog-day cicada of the genus *Tibicen,* is typically 3 centimetres long with greenish head and wings, acting as a canopy over its abdomen and thorax. The so-called periodic cicadas of the genus *Magicicada,* including the 17-year and 13-year cicadas, are darker in colour and have red eyes.

civet   cat-like mammals of Africa and Southern Asia with spotted fur, noted for the powerful-smelling fluid from their anal glands from which they bear their name. Family: Viverridae.

clouded leopard   large spotted arboreal cat of Southeast Asia. Sp.: *Neofelis nebulosa.*

coati   raccoon-like, omnivorous mammals of Central and South America with a long flexible snout and a long, usually ringed, tail. Gen.: *Nasua* and *Nasuella.*

coelacanth   primitive lobe-finned fish of the Indian Ocean, thought to be extinct until a living specimen was caught in 1938. Sp.: *Latimeria chalumnae.*

colugo   see flying lemur.

coral   any of a variety of invertebrate marine organisms of the phylum Cnidaria, class Anthozoa, characterized by having spikey, leathery or stonelike skeletons. Stony coral, of the order Madreporaria, form reefs and islands. Red coral, of the genus *Corallium,* also known as precious coral, is used to make ornaments and jewellery.

N
A
T
U
R
E

cougar see puma.

coyote aka prairie wolf. Predatory canine mammal of North America, smaller than the wolf. Sp.: *Canis latrans*.

crane-fly large two-winged flies with very long legs. Aka daddy-long-legs or leatherjacket. Family: Tipulidae.

crayfish small lobster-like freshwater crustacean. Aka spiny lobster. Gen.: *Astacus*.

cribo large, non-venomous American snake. Aka indigo snake or gopher snake. Sp.: *Drymarchon corais*.

crocodile any reptile of the family Crocodilidae, typically having a broad head, tapering snout, massive jaws, and a thick outer covering of boney scales. The salt water crocodile may grow up to 7 metres long and is the world's largest reptile. The sex of a crocodile is decided during incubation, a male is born if the egg is maintained at a constant 31.6 ° Celsius, hotter or colder and the sex is female. Gen.: *Crocodilus*.

crown of thorns starfish that feeds on coral polyps and has increasingly threatened Australia's Great Barrier Reef. The species can grow up to 50 centimetres, has numerous red spines and may have up to 19 arms. Sp.: *Acanthaster planci*.

dace freshwater fish related to the carp. Sp.: *Leuciscus leuciscus*.

death's-head hawk-moth Large dark hawk-moth with yellowish underwings and skull-like markings on the back of the thorax. Sp.: *Acherontia atropos*.

death-watch beetle small beetle which makes a sound like a watch ticking, once supposed to portend death, and whose larva bores in dead wood. Sp.: *Xestobium rufovillosum*.

deer any ruminant quadruped of the family Cervidae, distinguished in the male by the presence of deciduous branching horns or antlers, and in the young by the presence of spots. The furry covering of the newly formed antlers is given the name velvet.

devil's coach-horse large rove beetle. Sp.: *Ocypus olens*.

devil's darning needle alternative name for a dragonfly or damselfly. Order: Odonata.

dhole fierce canine pack-hunting mammal of the forests of central and South-east Asia. Sp.: *Cuon alpinus*.

dik-dik dwarf antelope native to Africa. Gen.: *Madoqua*.

dingo wild dog of the family Canidae, generally light brown in colour with long muzzle and bushy tail. The dingo, also known as the warrigal, can be found throughout mainland Australia and Tasmania. It is a scavenging carnivore and has a distinct howl but does not bark. Sp.: *Canis dingo*.

diplodocus four-legged plant-eating dinosaur with the longest known tail of all dinosaurs (11 metres). Gen.: *Diplodocus*.

dog domesticated carnivorous mammal. Sp.: *Canis familiaris*.

dolphin any of various marine cetacean mammals of the family Delphinidae, which are typically larger than porpoises but smaller than whales. Sp.: *Delphinus delphis*.

dolphin: bottle-nosed inhabiting all the world's oceans and named after its beak-like snout, which is shaped like a bottle and gives the impression of having a permanent smile. Sp.: *Tursiops truncatus*.

dormouse: common nocturnal squirrel-like rodent with bushy tail. Sp.: *Muscardinus avellanarius*.

dormouse (edible) aka fat dormouse. Largest of the dormice, once prized as food by the Romans. Sp.: *Glis glis*.

douroucouli nocturnal monkey of South America having large, staring eyes. Aka night monkey or owl monkey. Sp.: *Aotus trivirgatus*.

dragonet Any scaleless, spiny marine fish of the family Callionymidae, the males of which are brightly coloured.

dragonfly predatory insect of the suborder Anisoptera, order Odonata, having a large head and eyes, long slender body and two pairs of iridescent wings, which may have a span in excess of 15 centimetres. Sp.: *Libellula forensis*. Alternative names of the dragonfly include devil's darning needle and devil's arrow.

drosophila small fruit fly used extensively in genetic research because of its large chromosomes, numerous varieties and rapid rate of reproduction. Gen.: *Drosophila*.

duck-billed platypus amphibious egg-laying mammal of eastern Australia, having dense fur, a broad flat bill and tail and webbed feet. The platypus and echidna are the only two members of the order Monotremata, i.e. mammals that lay eggs. The male has a toxic horny spur on both hind legs, the venom of which is powerful enough to kill a dog and cause excruciating pain to humans. An excellent swimmer, the platypus has a buoyant body so always swims in a downward tract and is capable of being submerged for up to 10 minutes if resting. Sp.: *Ornithorhynchus anatinus*.

dugong large marine mammal of the order Sirenia, closely related to the manatee; the sole extant member of the family Dugongidae. The dugong is shorter than the manatee and darker skinned but has the same body shape. Manatees inhabit the waters of the Caribbean, South America and West Africa, while the dugongs are found in East African and Australian waters. Like the manatee, the dugong is also sometimes called a sea cow because of its grass-eating habits. Sightings of dugongs and manatees by early explorers gave rise to the mythology of mermaids and sirens. Sp.: *Dugong dugon*.

duiker mostly forest-dwelling African antelopes having a crest of long hair between their horns. Gen.: *Cephalophus* and *Sylvicapra*.

eagle ray large ray with long pointed pectoral fins. Family: Myliobatidae.

earth worm any of various species of ground worms of the phylum Annelida, class Oligochaeta, especially members of the genera *Lumbricus*, *Allolobophora* and *Eisenia*.

echidna egg-laying insectivorous mammals native to Australia and New Guinea, with a covering of spines, a long snout and long claws. Aka spiny anteater. Family: Tachyglossidae.

eel teleost fish having long, snake-like body, smooth slimy skin and reduced fins. Gen.: *Anguilla*.

eland antelope native to Africa, having spirally twisted horns. The giant eland is the largest of living antelopes. Gen.: *Tragelaphus*.

elephant: African larger of the two species of elephant. Sp.: *Loxodonta africana*.

elephant: Indian smaller of the two species of elephant. Gen.: *Elephas maximus*.

emperor moth large moth related to the silk moths

with eye-spots on all four wings. Sp.: *Saturnia pavonia*.

eyra   reddish-brown variety of jaguarondi. Sp.: *Felis yagouaroundi*.

fallfish   freshwater fish of North America resembling the chub. Sp.: *Semotilus corporalis*.

fallow deer   small deer having a white-spotted reddish-brown coat in the summer. Sp.: *Dama dama*.

false gavial (gharial)   Southeast Asian reptile of the family Crocodilidae with long straight snout, giving the impression of being a gavial. Sp.: *Tomistoma schlegeli*.

fennec   smallest fox, native to North Africa and Arabia, having large pointed ears. Sp.: *Vulpes zerda*.

fer-de-lance   large, highly venomous pit viper of tropical South America and the West Indies. Sp.: *Bothrops atrox*.

ferret   domesticated albino variety of the polecat, bred for hunting rats and rabbits. Sp.: *Mustela putorius*.

fly   member of the insect order Diptera, containing over 85,000 species divided into the suborders Nematocera (midges, gnats, crane flies and mosquitoes), Brachycera (bee flies, robber flies and horse flies) and Cyclorrhapha (house flies, fruit flies, blow flies, and leafminers). Dipterans are distinguished from other insects (such as dragonflies and mayflies) by their wing structure, the so-called 'true' flies being characterized by the use of only one pair of wings for flight, the second pair becoming fixed and being used for balance. The smallest two-winged flies are midges, and the largest are robber flies of the family Asilidae, which can attain lenths of up to 8 centimetres.

flying fish   warm-water fish with wing-like pectoral fins for gliding through the air. Family: Exocoetidae.

flying fox   fruitbats with fox-like heads, largest species with wingspan approaching 2 metres. Family: Pteropodidae.

flying lemur   either of two lemur-like mammals of South-east Asia, having a membrane between the fore and hind limbs for gliding from tree to tree. Aka colugo. Gen.: *Cynocephalus*.

flying lizard   long-tailed lizard of S.E. Asia with elongated ribs supporting membranes for gliding. Gen.: *Draco*.

flying squirrel   any squirrel with skin joining the fore and hind limbs for gliding from tree to tree. Gen.: *Aeromys, Belomys, Eupetdurus, Glaucomys, Hylopetes, Petaurista, Petinomys, Pteromys, Pteromyscus, Trogopterus*.

fox   various members of the dog family, Canidae, typically small in stature with a bushy tail known as a brush. They include the African Sand, Bat-eared, Bengal, Black, Blanford's, Brant, Chama, Corsac, Hoary, Indian, Kit, Pale, Rüppell's, Samson, Sand, Silver, Steppe, Swift and Tibetan Sand. Gen.: *Vulpes, Dusicyon, Alopex, Otocyon*.

frog   several families of the order Anura, mainly insectivorous amphibians having a short, tailless body with long hind legs for hopping. The European common frog is Sp.: *Rana temporaria*.

furniture beetle   beetle whose larvae bore into wood and are known as 'woodworm'. Sp.: *Anobium punctatum*.

galago   see bush baby.

galliwasp   West Indian lizard. Sp.: *Diploglossus monotropis*.

garfish   marine fish having long, beak-like jaws with sharp teeth. Aka needlefish. Family: Belonidae.

gavial (gharial)   long-snouted reptile of the order Crocodilia, and the only species of the family Gavialidae. The gavial inhabits the rivers of northern India and grows to a length of up to 5 metres. Sp.: *Gavialis gangeticus*.

gazelle   antelope of Asia or Africa. Gen.: *Gazella, Antilope, Antidoreas, Procapra, Ammodoreas, Litocranius*.

gecko   nocturnal lizards found in warm climes, with adhesive feet for climbing purposes, the only lizards with voices. Family: Gekkonidae.

gelada   brownish baboon with a bare red patch on its chest, native to Ethiopia. Sp.: *Theropithecus gelada*.

gemsbok   large antelope of south-west and east Africa. Sp.: *Oryx gazella*.

genet (genette)   cat-like mammal native to Africa and Southern Europe with spotted fur and a long, ringed, bushy tail. Gen.: *Genetta*.

gerbil   various genera of mouse-like desert rodents. The species often kept as a pet is *Meriones ungulculatus*, the Mongolian gerbil.

gerenuk   antelope native to east Africa, with a very long neck and small head. Sp.: *Litocranius walleri*.

giant anteater   edentate (toothless) mammal of Central and South America with long snout used for feeding on termites. Sp.: *Myrmecophaga tridactyla*.

gila monster   venomous lizard of southwest USA and northwestern Mexico. The gila monster is stout-bodied with black and pink markings and grows to about 45 centimetres (18 inches). Sp.: *Heloderma suspectum*.

giraffe   ruminant mammal of Africa with a long neck and forelegs and a skin of dark patches separated by lighter lines. It is the tallest living animal (over 5 metres). Sp.: *Giraffa camelopardalis*.

gnu   two antelope species of the genus *Connochaetes*, native to southern Africa, Kenya, Tanzania and Zambia, with a large, erect head and brown stripes on the neck and shoulders. Aka wildebeest.

goat   males are called rams or billies and females are does or nannies. Domesticated breeds include Angora, Kashmir, Nubian, Saanen and Toggenburg. Sp.: *Capra hircus*.

goldfish   freshwater cyprinid fish of eastern Europe and Asia, especially China. Sp.: *Carassius auratus*.

gopher   burrowing rodents of the family Geomyidae native to North America, having food pouches on the cheeks. Aka pocket gopher.

gopher tortoise   tortoise native to southern USA, that excavates tunnels to shelter from the sun. Gen.: *Gopherus*.

gorilla   largest anthropoid ape, native to central Africa. Sp.: *Gorilla gorilla*.

gourami   large freshwater fish native to South-east Asia. Aka labyrinth fish. Sp.: *Osphronemus goramy*.

grampus   dolphin with a blunt snout and long, pointed black flippers. Aka Risso's dolphin. Sp.: *Grampus griseus*.

grasshopper   any orthopterous insect of the families Acrididae (short-horned grasshoppers) and Tettigoniidae (long-horned grasshoppers). The grasshopper frequents semi-arid regions and grasslands. Many species are green in colour, although some are brownish-grey with red or yellow markings. The upper hind legs of a grasshopper are elongated, and the males tend to produce a buzzing sound by rubbing the femur against its wings. The young of a grasshopper is called a nymph.

N
A
T
U
R
E

grayling silver-grey freshwater fish with a long, high dorsal fin. Gen.: *Thymallus*.

grayling butterfly having wings with grey undersides and bright eye-spots on the upper side. Sp.: *Hipparchia semele*.

greenbottle fly of the genus *Lucilia*, which lays eggs in the flesh of sheep.

grunion slender Californian silverside fish, which spawns on beaches. Sp.: *Leuresthes tenuis*.

gudgeon small European freshwater fish, often used as bait. Sp.: *Gobio gobio*.

guinea pig domesticated Southern American cavy kept as a pet or for research in biology. Sp.: *Cavia porcellus*.

haddock edible marine fish of the north Atlantic, similar to cod but smaller. Sp.: *Melanogrammus aeglefinus*.

hairstreak species of butterfly of the family Lycaenidae, distinguished by the hair-like markings on the underside of their wings. Usually brown or grey in colour but occasionally red and black. Gen.: *Callophrys*.

hamadryas large, powerful monkey of the plains and open-rock areas of southern Arabia and northeast Africa. Aka sacred baboon or Arabian baboon. Sp.: *Papio hamadryas*.

hamster: common Eurasian rodent of the subfamily Cricetinae, having a short tail and large cheek pouches for storing food. Sp.: *Cricetus cricetus*.

hamster: golden Eurasian rodent of the subfamily Cricetinae, having a short tail and large cheek pouches for storing food and often kept as a pet or as a laboratory animal. Sp.: *Mesocricetus auratus*.

hanuman Indian langur venerated by Hindus. Aka wanderoo. Sp.: *Semnopithecus entellus*.

hare larger than a rabbit, with longer ears, its habitat is called a form. Sp.: *Lepus europaeus*.

harp seal earless seal of the family Phocidae, found in the North Atlantic and Arctic oceans. The typical male is golden-grey with dark markings on its back and face and can grow up to 2 metres long and weigh in excess of 200 kilograms (440 pounds). A young harp seal is variously named bedlamer, beater or greyback, depending on its age and development. Sp.: *Pagophilus groenlandicus*.

hartebeest large African antelope with ringed horns bent back at the tips. Gen.: *Alcelaphus*.

harvest mouse small mouse with a prehensile tail, which nests in the stalks of growing grain. Sp.: *Micromys minutus*.

hedgehog Old World mammal of the order Insectivora with spiny back and very small tail. The common western European species is *Erinaceus europaeus*.

hellbender large, brownish-grey North American salamander measuring up to 75 centimetres in length, with a flat head, short stout legs and a wrinkled fold of skin down its sides. Sp.: *Cryptobranchus alleganiensis*.

hercules beetle large South American beetle with two horns extending from its head. Sp.: *Dynastes hercules*.

herring soft-finned fish of northern seas with elongated scaled body and smooth head. Sp.: *Clupea harengus*.

horned toad South-east Asian toads with horn-shaped extensions over the eyes. Family: Pelobatidae.

horned toad American lizard covered with spiny scales. Gen.: *Phrynosoma*.

hornet large wasp with brown and yellow striped body, capable of inflicting a severe sting. Sp.: *Vespa crabro*.

horseshoe bat bat of the Old World with a horseshoe-shaped ridge on the nose. Family: Rhinolophidae.

horseshoe crab large marine arthropod with a horseshoe-shaped shell and a long tail-spine. Gen.: *Limulus*.

house mouse very common grey mouse, which scavenges around human dwellings. Often kept as pets or used in laboratory experiments. Sp.: *Mus musculus*.

housefly fly of the family Muscidae, breeding in decaying organic matter and often entering houses. Sp.: *Musca domestica*.

hyena (spotted) long-legged, carnivorous, dog-like mammal of Africa. Aka laughing hyena. Sp.: *Crocuta crocuta*.

ibex wild goat of mountainous areas of Europe, north Africa and Asia, with a beard and thick, curved, ridged horns. Sp.: *Capra ibex*.

iguanodon large, herbivorous, long-tailed bipedal dinosaur of the Cretaceous period. Gen.: *Iguanodon*.

impala medium-size antelope of South and East Africa capable of long high jumps. Sp.: *Aepyceros melampus*.

indigo snake see cribo.

jackal four species of African or South Asian canine mammals of the genus *Canis*.

jackrabbit North American hare with long hind legs and large ears. The white-tailed jackrabbit is *Lepus townsendii*.

jaguar large feline mammal of south-west USA and Central and South America, similar to the leopard but with a shorter tail and larger spots on its coat. Sp.: *Panthera onca*.

jaguarondi North and South American small grey cat with short legs and long tail. Sp.: *Felis yagouaroundi*.

jellyfish marine coelenterate of the class Scyphozoa having an umbrella-shaped, jelly-like body and stinging tentacles.

kalong fruit-eating bat. Aka flying fox. Sp.: *Pteropus edulis*.

kangaroo any of up to 50 species of Australasian marsupial mammals of the family Macropodidae. Kangaroos may grow to a height in excess of 2.5 metres and leap a distance of over 13 metres in a single bound at a speed of 50 km per hour.

katipo venomous spider of New Zealand, usually black with a red or orange stripe on its abdomen. Sp.: *Latrodectus katipo*.

katydid orthopterous insect of the family Tettigoniidae (long-horned grasshopper). The katydid is usually coloured green and lives among the foliage of North American trees. Its name derives from the cry of 'katydid, katy didn't' which is heard throughout the night and produced by the insect rubbing its wings together.

kiang wild ass of a race native to Tibet with a thick furry coat, a subspecies of the Asiatic ass, *Equus hemionus*.

killer whale actually a kind of dolphin, with a black back, white belly and prominent dorsal fin. Sp.: *Orcinus orca*.

king cobra world's largest venomous snake (up to 5.5 metres), found from southern China to the

Philippines and Indonesia. Aka hamadryad. Sp.: *Ophiophagus hannah*.

kinkajou nocturnal fruit-eating mammal of Central and South America, with a prehensile tail and a very long tail. Sp.: *Potos flavus*.

kissing gourami small, brightly coloured freshwater fish, a popular aquarium pet. Sp.: *Helostoma temminckii*.

koala slow-moving, arboreal marsupial of eastern Australia, having grey fur and feeding on eucalyptus leaves and bark. The koala is also known as a koala bear although not related to the Ursidae family. Sp.: *Phascolarctos cinereus*.

kolinsky Siberian and Asian weasel with a rich brown coat. Sp.: *Mustela sibirica*.

Komodo dragon predatory lizard native to the East Indies, largest of all surviving lizards. Sp.: *Varanus komodoensis*.

kouprey rare grey ox, native to forests in Indo-China. Sp.: *Bos sauveli*.

krait any venomous snake of the Asiatic genus *Bungarus*.

lamprey mostly parasitic, eel-like fish of the family Petromyzontidae, without scales, paired fins or jaws, but having a sucker mouth with horny teeth and a rough tongue.

land crab crab that lives in burrows inland and migrates in large numbers to the sea to breed. Sp.: *Cardisoma guanhumi*.

langur any of various agile arboreal Old World monkeys of the family Cercopithecidae.

laughing hyena see hyena (spotted).

leafcutter ant ant of tropical America, which cuts pieces from leaves to cultivate fungus. Gen.: *Atta*.

leafcutter bee solitary bee, which lines its nest with leaf fragments. Family: Megachilidae.

lemon sole flatfish of the plaice family. Sp.: *Microstomus kitt*.

lemur any Madagascan prosimian primate of the family Lemuridae.

leopard large African or Asian feline mammal with either a black-spotted yellowish fawn or all-black coat. Aka panther. Sp.: *Panthera pardus*.

limpet marine gastropod mollusc with a shallow conical shell and a broad muscular foot that sticks tightly to rocks. The common limpet is *Patella vulgata*.

lion large predatory feline mammal of Africa and north-west India, often called the king of beasts. Sp.: *Panthera leo*.

llama South American ruminant related to the camel, kept as a beast of burden and for its soft woolly fleece. Sp.: *Lama glama*.

loach small, edible freshwater fish of the family Cobitidae.

locust orthopterous insect of the family Acrididae (short-horned grasshopper), which is prone to multiply quickly and migrate long distances in destructive swarms.

loris: slender and slow small slow-moving nocturnal tree-dwelling primates with small ears and a very short tail. The slender loris, *Loris tardigradus*, is found in southern India. The slow loris, *Nycticebus coucang*, is found in south-west Asia and the East Indies.

louse wingless insect parasitic on a wide range of birds and mammals. Those that infest the human hair and skin and transmit various diseases are *Pediculus humanus*.

lynx short-tailed cat inhabiting forests of Europe, Asia and North America. The lynx is distinguished by its tufted ears, hairy soles, broad short head and mottled fur. Sp.: *Felis lynx*.

macaque medium-sized monkey of the Old World genus *Macaca*, including the rhesus monkey and barbary ape, typically having a rather long face with cheek pouches.

mackerel (common) North Atlantic marine fish with a greenish-blue body, used for food. Sp.: *Scomber scombrus*.

magpie moth white geometrid moth with black and yellow markings whose caterpillars feed on fruit bushes. Sp.: *Abraxas grossulariata*.

Malayan stink badger aka teledu or skunk badger. Strong-smelling, dark coat is key feature. Sp.: *Mydaus javanensis*.

mamba any venomous African snake of the genus *Dendroaspis*, especially the green and black mambas, *Dendroaspis angusticeps* and *Dendroaspis polylepis*.

mammoth large, extinct elephant of the Pleistocene period. Gen.: *Mammuthus*.

mammoth (woolly) large extinct elephant of the Pleistocene period having a hairy coat and long tusks. Sp.: *Mammuthus primigenius*.

manatee large, aquatic, plant-eating, sirenian mammal with paddle-like forelimbs, no hind limbs and a powerful tail. Aka sea cow. Gen.: *Trichechus*.

mandrill large West African baboon, the adult of which has a brilliantly coloured face and blue-coloured buttocks. Sp.: *Papio sphinx*.

mangabey various small long-tailed West and Central African monkeys of the genus *Cercocebus*. Named after a region of Madagascar.

marbled white whitish butterfly with black markings. Sp.: *Melanargia galathea*.

margay small wild Central and South American cat. Sp.: *Felis wiedii*.

markhor large, spiral-horned wild goat of Central Asia. Sp.: *Capra falconeri*.

marmoset tropical American monkeys having a long silky coat and a bushy tail. Gen.: *Callithrix*.

marmot burrowing, hibernating rodents of the squirrel family with a heavy-set body and short bushy tail, living in colonies in Europe, Asia and the Americas. Gen.: *Marmota*.

marten any weasel-like carnivore of the genus *Martes*, having valuable fir.

massasauga small North American rattlesnake named from corruption of Mississagi River, Ontario. Sp.: *Sistrurus catenatus*.

mastodon extinct, elephant-like proboscidean mammal common in the Miocene period. Gen.: *Mammut*.

mayfly insects with an acquatic nymph and a fragile-winged adult, which lives only briefly in spring. Aka green drake. Order: Ephemeroptera.

meadow brown common brown butterfly with eye-spots on the upper wing. Sp.: *Maniola jurtina*.

megaloceros giant deer whose antlers had a 3.5 metre span, it lived in Eurasia during the last Ice Age. Gen.: *Megaloceros*.

megalosaurus flesh-eating dinosaur, the first to receive a scientific name. Gen.: *Megalosaurus*.

Mexican bearded lizard related to the gila monster and inhabiting the same territory, the Mexican bearded lizard is similar in colour but grows to about 80 centimetres (32 inches). Together they are the only species of poisonous lizards. Sp.: *Heloderma horridum*.

miller's thumb   small, spiny, freshwater fish with a large head. Aka bullhead. Sp.: *Cottus gobio*.

millipede   herbivorous arthropod of the class Diplopoda, which can have up to 200 pairs of legs.

mink: American   semi-aquatic musteline mammal having slightly webbed feet, often hunted for their valuable fur. Sp.: *Mustela vison*.

mink: European   slightly smaller version of the American mink. Sp.: *Mustela lutreola*.

mites   small parasitic arachnid of the order Acarina, similar to ticks but distinguished by the lack of a sensory pit, known as Haller's organ, on the end segment of the first of four pairs of legs.

mola   (ocean sunfish, headfish) large grey heavy ocean fish with short body, flattened sideways. Aka Sp.: *Mola mola*.

mole   small burrowing mammals of the order Insectivora, family Talpidae, found in Europe, Asia and North America. The British mole is *Talpa europaeus*.

mongoose   small predatory mammals of Africa, southern Europe and Asia, having long tail and brindled coat. Two sub-families: Galidinae and Herpestinae.

monkey   any of numerous primates of a group including the families Cebidae (capuchins), Callithricidae (marmosets and tamarins) and Cercopithecidae (baboons and macaques), especially any of the long-tailed varieties.

moonfish   see opah.

moose   North American elk. Sp.: *Alces alces*.

mouf(f)lon   wild mountain sheep of South Europe. Sp.: *Ovis musimon*.

mud puppy   large, grey, neotenous aquatic salamander of eastern USA with conspicuous red feathery gills. Sp.: *Necturus maculosus*.

mudskipper   any small goby of the family Periophthalmidae, found along the coasts of the Indian and Pacific oceans, able to leave the water and scramble over mud.

mulloway   large Australian marine fish used as food. Sp.: *Argyrosomos hololepidotus*.

muntjac   any small deer of the genus *Muntiacus*, native to South-east Asia, the male having tusks and small antlers.

musk deer   three species of small Asian deer of the genus *Moschus*, having no antlers and in the male having long protruding canine teeth. The musk gland of the male is valued for its use in perfume and medicines.

musk ox   large goat-antelope native to North America with a thick, shaggy coat and small, curved horns. Sp.: *Ovibos moschatus*.

muskellunge   large North American pike particularly inhabiting the Great Lakes. Aka maskinonge. Sp.: *Esox masquinongy*.

muskrat   large aquatic rodent of the vole tribe, native to North America, having a musky smell. Aka musquash. Gen.: *Ondata zibethicus*.

narwhal   small Arctic whale, the male of which has a long, straight, spirally twisted tusk developed from one of its teeth. Sp.: *Monodon monoceros*.

natterjack   toad of western Eurasia with a bright yellow stripe down its back and moving by running not hopping. Sp.: *Bufo calamita*.

newt   any of more than 40 species of tailed amphibian of the order Urodela and family Salamandridae. Aquatic newts have smooth moist skins, while terrestrial species have rough skin and are known as efts. British newts are of the genera *Triturus* (tritons), the most common being the smooth newt (*Triturus vulgaris*).

nilgai   large short-horned Indian antelope. Sp.: *Boselaphus tragocamelus*.

Norway lobster   small European lobster or scampi. Aka Dublin Bay prawn. Sp.: *Nephrops norvegicus*.

numbat   small western Australian termite-eating marsupial with a bushy tail and black and white striped back. Sp.: *Myrmecobius fasciatus*.

ocelot   medium-size cat native to the Americas, having a deep yellow or orange coat with black striped and spotted markings. Sp.: *Felis pardalis*.

octopus   any cephalopod mollusc of the order Octopoda, varying in size from 1 centimetre to almost 6 metres, with an armspan of almost 9 metres. Octopuses (or octopi) have 8 tentacles and eject an inky fluid when attacked. The largest species is the North Pacific octopus (*Octopus dofleini*) and the smallest is the Californian octopus (*Octopus micropyrsus*). The common octopus (*Octopus vulgaris*) reaches an average size of 1 metre. The octopus has the most complex brain of any invertebrate, having both long-term and short-term memories.

opah   large, rare, deep-sea fish having a silver-blue back with white spots and crimson fins. Aka moonfish. Sp.: *Lampris guttatus*.

opossum   any mainly tree-living marsupial of the family Didelphidae, native to North and South America, and having a prehensile tail and hind feet with an opposable thumb.

orang-utan   large, red, long-haired, tree-living ape native to Borneo and Sumatra. Aka wild man of the woods. Sp.: *Pongo pygmaeus*.

orfe   freshwater cyprinid fish of Europe that occurs in two colour varieties i.e. golden and silver. Orfes are often called goldfish. Sp.: *Idus idus*.

oribi   small African grazing antelope having reddish-fawn back and white underparts. Sp.: *Ourebia ourebi*.

oryx   large African antelope having long straight nearly upright horns. Gen.: *Oryx*.

otter   freshwater carnivorous mammals of Europe, Asia, Africa and the Americas, with smooth fur and webbed feet. Sub-family Lutrinae.

ounce   see snow leopard.

paddlefish   primitive bony fish of the Mississippi and Yangtze rivers, leaden grey, with a long flat snout. Sp.: *Polyodon spathula* and *Psephurus gladius*

paddymelon (pademelon)   small wallaby of coastal scrubby regions of Australia. Gen.: *Thylogale*.

painted lady   orange-red butterfly with black and white spots. Sp.: *Cynthia cardui*.

panda: giant   large, rare, bear-like mammal native to certain mountain bamboo forests of China, having characteristic black and white markings. Sp.: *Ailuropoda melanoleuca*.

panda: red   Himalayan raccoon-like mammal with reddish-brown fur and a long, bushy tail. Sp.: *Ailurus fulgens*.

pangolin   various mammal species native to Asia and Africa covered with overlapping horny scales and having a small head with elongated snout and tongue, with which they feed on ants, and a tapering tail. Aka scaly anteater. Gen.: *Manus*.

peacock butterfly   butterfly with eye-like markings on its wings. Sp.: *Inachis io*.

pearl-oyster   any of various marine bivalve molluscs of the genus *Pinctada*, bearing pearls.

peccary   three species of American, wild, pig-like mammals of the family Tayassuidae. Sp.: *Tayassu tajacu, Tayassu pecari* and *Catagonus wagneri*.

Père David's deer   large, slender-antlered deer, named after Father A. David, French missionary and naturalist (d. 1900). Sp.: *Elaphurus davidiensis*.

phalanger   any of various species of Australasian marsupial mammals of the family Phalangeridae, also known as possums on the Australian mainland and Tasmania.

plaice   European flatfish having a brown back with orange spots and a white underside, much used for food. Sp.: *Pleuronectes platessa*.

polar bear   white carnivorous bear of coastal regions of the North Pole. Sp.: *Ursus maritimus*.

polecat (European)   small, brownish-black, fetid flesh-eating mammal of the weasel family. Sp.: *Mustela putorius*.

porpoise   any of various marine cetacean mammals of the families Delphinidae and Phocoenidae, which are typically smaller than dolphins and with chubbier shape and blunter snout. Sp.: *Phocoena phocoena*.

possum   any member of the Phalangeridae family of marsupial mammals native to Australasia. Possums are tree-dwellers. The brush-tailed possum (*Trichosurus vulpecula*) is the most common marsupial in Australia.

potto   short-tailed prosimian primate, of the family Lorisidae, having vertebral spines protruding through its neck. The potto is often confused with the kinkajou, as it is a slow-moving, nocturnal, arboreal mammal.

prawn   any of various marine decapod crustaceans of the genera *Palaemon* and *Penaeus*, similar to shrimps but having two pairs of pincers.

pterodactyl   extinct flying reptile of the late Jurassic, having membranous wings supported on an elongated 4th digit. Gen.: *Pterodactylus*.

puma   largest American feline mammal, resembling a lion. It is the best jumper of the cat family. Aka cougar or mountain lion. Sp.: *Felis concolor*.

pygmy white-toothed shrew   smallest member of the mouse-like, long-snouted mammals of the family Soricidae. Sp.: *Suncus etruseus*.

quokka   small marsupial resembling a wallaby, primarily inhabiting Rottnest Island off the coast of Perth, Western Australia. Sp.: *Setonix brachyurus*.

rabbit   burrowing leporid mammal which is smaller than a hare and has much shorter ears. The European rabbit is *Oryctolagus cuniculus*.

raccoon   omnivorous mammal of the genus *Procyon* occupying diverse habitats in North and South America. It has a pointed muzzle, long tail and greyish-black fur with black bands around the tail and across the face. The common raccoon of North America is *Procyon lotor*.

ratel   see badger (honey).

red deer   forest-dweller of Europe and western to central Asia. Males are called harts and females, hinds. Harts with 12 tines are known as 'Royal' and one with 14 tines is a 'Wilson'. Sp.: *Cervus elaphus*.

reindeer   see caribou.

Rocky Mountain goat   massive, yellowish-white goat-antelope inhabiting mountains in western North America. Sp.: *Oreamnos americanus*.

roe deer   small, graceful woodland deer of Eurasia, the males having small antlers and a reddish-brown summer coat. Sp.: *Capreolus capreolus*.

ring-tailed lemur   rock-dwelling lemur with elongated hind legs and a long tail with brown and white ringed markings. Sp.: *Lemur catta*.

sable   marten of northern Asian and Japanese forests, with dark brown luxuriant fur. Sp.: *Martes zibellina*.

sabre-toothed tiger   extinct, lion-size mammal of the cat family (only distantly related to the tiger) with long, curved, upper canine teeth. Aka sabre-toothed cat. Gen.: *Smilodon*.

salamander   any tailed amphibian of the order Urodela that most commonly inhabit freshwater and damp woodlands. Salamanders resemble lizards but are related to newts in the family Salamandridae, and can be aquatic, semi-aquatic, or terrestrial. They are generally very small (10–15 centimetres) but giant salamanders may attain a length of up to 180 centimetres. The semi-aquatic Chinese giant salamander (*Andrias davidianus*) grows in excess of 1 metre but the largest salamander is the Japanese giant salamander (*Andrias japonicus*).

sand lizard   small, green-grey-brown Eurasian lizard with long clawed digits. Sp.: *Lacerta agilis*.

scorpion   arachnid of the order Scorpionida, having an elongated body and a segmented, upwardly curving tail that is tipped with a venomous stinger. During mating the male and female perform a courtship dance and after copulation the female often devours the male.

seal: eared   carnivorous pinniped (paddle-footed) aquatic mammal of the family Otariidae, which comes to shore to breed. Eared seals swim by 'rowing' with their front flippers and can turn their hindflippers forward to walk on land.

seal: elephant   large seal, the male having an inflatable snout. Aka sea elephant. Gen.: *Mirounga*.

seal: true   carnivorous pinniped (paddle-footed) aquatic mammal of the family Phocidae, which comes to shore to breed. They are earless, swim with their hindflippers, and hump along on land, unable to use their hindflippers as support.

sea lion   any of five species of eared seal of the South Atlantic and Pacific. The Californian sea lion (*Zalophus californianus*) is the species trained for circus performances.

sea squirt   any small primitive marine animal of the class Ascidiacea, having a sac-like body with openings through which water enters and leaves. Sea squirts are sedentary and sessile and can be found on coral reefs, pier pilings, ships' hulls, rocks and seashells. Peculiarly, they can be found on the backs of some species of crabs, while other species of crabs may dwell inside the cavities of a sea squirt.

serval   slender feline mammal of the African savanna, having an orange-brown coat with black spots, large ears and long legs. Sp.: *Felis serval*.

sheep   any of various bovid mammals having ribbed horns and a narrow face. Domesticated breeds, genus *Ovis*, include Border Leicester, Cheviot, Clun Forest, Cobb 101, Cotswold, Dartmoor, Devon Longwool, Dorset Down, Dorset Horn, Exmoor Horned, Hampshire, Herdwick, Ile-de-France, Karakul, Kerry Hill, Leicester, Lincoln, The Lonk, Masham, Merino, Oxford, Rambouillet, Romney, Roscommon, Ryeland, Scottish Blackface, Shropshire, Southdown, Suffolk, Swaledale, Welsh Mountain, Wensleydale and Wiltshire Horned.

NATURE

shrew small, mouse-like, long-snouted mammals of the order Insectivora, family Soricidae. The European common shrew is *Sorex araneus*. Aka shrewmouse.

shrew: elephant small, insect-eating mammals native to Africa, having a long snout and long hind limbs Family: Macroscelididae.

shrimp any of various marine decapod crustaceans of the genus *Crangon*, having a slender flattened body, long tail and a single pair of pincers. Although large shrimps in excess of 5 millimetres are sometimes called prawns, this is misleading as a prawn is a distinct species with two sets of pincers. The two most important shrimps are the common shrimp (*Crangon vulgaris*) and the edible shrimp (*Peneus setiferus*).

skunk American musteline mammals of the subfamily Mephitinae, typically having a black and white coat and bushy tail.They eject a foul-smelling fluid from the anal gland when attacked. The familiar striped skunk is *Mephitis mephitis*.

slender-tailed meerkat see suricate.

sloth shaggy-coated, arboreal edentate mammals of Central and South America that hang upside down by their arms. Three-toed sloths, genus Bradypus; two-toed sloths, genus *Choloepus*.

slow worm Eurasian legless lizard with brownish-grey, snake-like body. Sp.: *Anguis fragilis*.

snake (grass) non-venomous European snake having brownish-green body. Sp.: *Natrix natrix*.

snow leopard large, feline, mammal of mountainous regions of central Asia, having a long, pale brown coat marked with black rosettes. Aka ounce. Sp.: *Panthera uncia*.

solenodon rare, shrew-like, nocturnal mammal of the West Indies, having a long hairless tail and an elongated snout. Cuban species, *Solenodon cubanus*; Hispaniola species, *Solenodon paradoxus*.

spectacled bear solitary South American species of the family Ursidae and inhabiting mountainous terrain, which gives it an alternative name of Andean bear. It grows up to 180 centimetres long (6 feet) and has a dark brown coat, with whitish markings around its eyes and facial circumference. Sp.: *Tremarctos ornatus*.

sponge any member of primitive multicellular aquatic animals of the phylum Porifera, which have porous, baglike bodies with a skeleton of hard spicules or elastic fibres. The dried skeleton of sponges are procured for commercial purposes as bathroom sponges because of their ability to hold water.

squirrel (grey) grey-furred squirrel native to eastern North America but found worldwide. Sp.: *Sciurus carolinensis*.

squirrel (red) reddish-brown squirrel inhabiting woodlands of Europe and Asia. Sp.: *Sciurus vulgaris*.

starfish any echinoderm of the classes Asteroidea (sea stars) and Ophiuroidea (brittle stars), typically having a flat body and 5 tentacles, although some species may have many more.

stoat small, long-bodied carnivorous mammal of the weasel family having reddish-brown upper parts and a black-tipped tail and in northern areas turning white in winter, when it is known as ermine. Sp.: *Mustela erminea*.

sturgeon primitive bony fish of temperate waters of the northern hemisphere, valued as a source of caviar and isinglass. Family: Acipenseridae.

sugar glider Australian possum that glides from tree to tree by means of a fold of skin that joins its front and hind legs. The sugar glider is also known as the flying possum or flying phalanger. Sp.: *Petaurus breviceps*.

suricate southern African mongoose which has a lemur-like face. Aka slender-tailed meerkat. Sp.: *Suricata suricatta*.

swallowtail butterfly member of the subfamily Papilioninae, order Lepidoptera. Swallowtails are found worldwide and are named for the tail-like extensions of their hindwings. Gen.: *Papilio*.

taipan large highly venomous snake of north-east Australia, dark brown with a creamy-colored head. Sp.: *Oxyuranus scutellatus*.

tapeworm any of various parasitic flatworms of the order Cestoda, which attack the liver and digestive tract of vertebrates.

tapir four species of forest-dwelling perissodactyl mammals of South and Central America and South-east Asia, having an elongated snout, three-toed hind legs and four-toed forelegs. Genus *Tapirus*.

tarpon large, silvery, game fish of warm Atlantic waters, having a compressed, scaled body. *Tarpon atlanticus* is the best-known species.

Tasmanian devil small, ferocious, carnivorous marsupial having black fur with pale markings, strong jaws and short legs. Aka ursine dasyure. Sp.: *Sarcophilus harrisi*.

Tasmanian wolf see thylacine.

tayra large, arboreal, musteline mammal of Central and South America, having a dark brown body and paler head. Sp.: *Eira barbata*.

teledu see Malayan stink badger.

tenrec: tailless small mammal of Madagascar (but largest insectivore), resembling a hedgehog or shrew. Sp.: *Tenrec ecaudatus*.

termites whitish, ant-like insect of the order Isoptera. The two main species are 'ground' termites and 'drywood' termites. Termites feed on cellulose, which is found in wood and wood products. They are social insects, and a typical colony would include workers, soldiers, winged reproductives, and a king and queen. The alternative name for a termite is 'white ant', although there are subtle differences between the body shape of an ant and a termite. An ant has a tapered abdomen, while that of a termite is straight. The ant also has bent antennae whereas the termites are straight. The winged reproductives are similar to flying ants, although their double wings are even in size while the ant's double wings are uneven in size.

terrapin web-footed chelonian reptile that lives on land or in fresh water. Family: Emydidae.

thylacine presumed extinct, dog-like carnivorous marsupial of Tasmania, having greyish-brown fur with dark vertical stripes on the back. Aka Tasmanian wolf. Sp.: *Thylacinus cynocephalus*.

tick small parasitic arachnid of the families Ixodidae and Nuttalliellidae (hard ticks) and Argasidae (soft ticks). Ticks dwell on the skin of warm-blooded animals and feed on the blood and tissues of their hosts.

tiger large Asian feline mammal with yellowy coat and black stripes. Sp.: *Panthera tigris*.

timber rattlesnake heavy-bodied snake with a broad head that is distinct from its narrow neck. The rattlesnake inhabits the prairies of North America, where it feeds on a variety of small mammals, which are killed by its venomous bite. Humans are not under threat from rattlesnakes as 60 per cent of all bites are dry, and even venomous bites rarely cause more than temporary discomfort. The rattlesnake is generally golden-brown with black markings except for the head, which is plain brown, and its rattler, at the tip of its tail, which is dark black. Sp.: *Crotalus horridus*.

toad anuran amphibian, secreting a poisonous fluid, similar to frogs but more terrestrial, having drier, warty skin. The Eurasian common toad is *Bufo bufo*.

tokay large (35 cm) grey gecko with orange and deep blue spots, of South-east Asia. Sp.: *Gekko gecko*.

tortoise herbivorous chelonian reptile found in warm regions worldwide except Australia. Family: Testudinidae.

tree frog arboreal frog of the family Hylidae, with sucker-like pads to aid in climbing. Tree frogs are also known as tree toads.

triceratops rhinoceros-like herbivorous dinosaur of the Cretaceous period, having three horns and a short armoured neck frill. Gen.: *Triceratops*.

turtle aquatic chelonian reptiles with a flattened shell and flipper-like limbs for swimming. Several families of the order Chelonia.

tyrannosaurus rex 14 metre long, 6 metre tall, flesh-eating dinosaur with relatively small 2-fingered hands. Gen.: Tyrannosaurus.

unau aka Linné's two-toed sloth. Sp.: *Choloepus didactylus*.

vervet small, yellowish-grey, African, long-tailed monkey. Sp.: *Cercopithecus aethiops*.

vicuña South American mammal of the high Andes related to the llama, with fine silky wool. Sp.: *Vicugna vicugna*.

viscacha large South American burrowing rodent related to the chinchillas. Gen.: *Lagidium* and *Lagostomus*.

vole (field) small, rodent of the family Cricetidae with stocky body, short tail and small ears. Sp.: *Microtus agrestis*.

vole (water) large amphibious vole of Eurasian river banks. Sp.: *Arvicola terrestris*.

wallaby (hare) small rodent-like herbivorous marsupial of Australia and New Guinea, family Macropodidae. Gen.: *Lagorchestes*.

wallaby (rock) herbivorous marsupial of Australia and New Guinea, resembling a small kangaroo, of the family Macropodidae. Gen.: *Protemnodon*.

walrus large, tusked, aquatic mammal of the Arctic, a bottom feeder – mainly on molluscs – related to the eared seals. Its family, Odobenidae, has only one species: *Odobenus rosmarus*.

wapiti big North American deer, which is now considered as a larger race of the red deer. Sp.: *Cervus canadensis*.

warble fly any of various flies of the genus *Hypoderma*, whose larvae infest the skin of cattle and horses.

warthog African wild pig with a large head, warty lumps on its face and large curved tusks. Sp.: *Phacochoerus aethiopicus*.

wasp stinging insect of the order Hymenoptera, with black and yellow stripes and a very thin waist.

water moccasin (cottonmouth) poisonous, semi-aquatic snake of south-eastern USA. Sp.: *Agkistrodon piscivorus*.

water opossum semi-aquatic tropical American opossum with dark-banded grey fur. Aka yapok. Sp.: *Chironectes minimus*.

weasel (European common) small, brown and white carnivorous mammal with a slender body, related to the stoat. Gen.: *Mustela nivalis*.

whale any of the larger marine mammals of the order Cetacea, having a streamlined body and horizontal tail, and breathing air through a blowhole on the head. Gen.: *Cetacea*.

whale shark large, tropical whale-like shark feeding close to the surface. Sp.: *Rhincodon typus*.

white admiral mottled brown butterfly with a white splashed band down its wings. Sp.: *Limenitis camilla*.

wildcat wild cat of Eurasia and Africa with a grey and black coat and a bushy tail. Sp.: *Felis silvestris*.

wildebeest see gnu.

wisent the European bison. Sp.: *Bison bonasus*.

witch North Atlantic flatfish resembling the lemon sole. Sp.: *Glyptocephalus cynoglossus*.

wobbegong (spotted) carpet shark of the family Orectolobidae, inhabiting Australian waters and having a richly patterned brown and white skin. Sp.: *Orectolobus maculatus*.

wolf (grey) wild, flesh-eating mammal of the northern hemisphere, ancestor of the domestic dog. Gen.: *Canis lupus*.

wolf-fish large, voracious blenny of the North Atlantic. Family: Anarhichadidae.

wolverine large, musteline mammal of northern forests of Eurasia and North America, a predator and scavenger, having dark very thick water-resistant fur. Aka glutton. Sp.: *Gulo gulo*.

wombat (common) Australian bear-like terrestrial marsupial with coarse dark hair and small ears. Sp.: *Vombatus ursinus*.

wombat (hairy nosed) two marsupial species of Queensland and central south Australia, with fine grizzled fur and longer ears than the common wombat. Sp.: *Lasiorhinus krefftii* and *Lasiorhinus latifrons*.

woodchuck reddish-brown and grey North American burrowing marmot. Aka groundhog. Sp.: *Marmota monax*.

woodlouse small, terrestrial, isopod crustacean of the order Oniscoidea, feeding on rotten wood and plant matter, some of them (pill bugs) able to roll into a ball. The common woodlouse is *Oniscus asellus*.

yapok see water opossum.

yellowfin tuna fish of warm seas with yellowish fins, widely fished for food. Sp.: *Thunnus albacares*.

yellowtail game fish of coastal waters of southern California and Mexico, having a yellow tail fin. Sp.: *Seriola dorsalis*.

zebra (plains) African quadruped related to the ass and horse, with black and white stripes. Sp.: *Equus burchelli*.

zebu domestic humped ox of India, East Asia and Africa. Sp.: *Bos indicus*.

zorilla flesh-eating African mammal of the weasel family, aka African polecat. Sp.: *Ictonyx striatus*.

N
A
T
U
R
E

Miscellaneous Information

abranchiate   having no gills.

amphibian: largest   Japanese giant salamander.

anadromous   of a fish (e.g. the salmon), swimming up a river from the sea to spawn.

anthrax   fatal bacterial disease of sheep and cattle, transmissible to humans and affecting the skin and lungs; aka wool-sorters' disease.

ants: noses   five.

apatosaurus: aka   Brontosaurus.

ape: smallest   gibbon (apes have no tails).

artiodactyl   any placental ungulate mammal whose hoofs have an even number of toes – e.g. pigs, sheep, camels, deer, cattle, antelope and hippopotamuses.

batrachian   of or relating to frogs or toads.

bees: eyes   five.

braxy   acute and usually fatal bacterial disease of sheep characterized by high fever, coma and inflammation of the fourth stomach, caused by infection with *Clostridium septicum*.

butterfly: largest   Queen Alexandra's birdwing of Papua New Guinea has a wingspan of up to 25 centimetres (10 inches).

butterfly: tastes with   back feet.

carnivore: largest   the dinosaur Tyrannosaurus is the largest so far known; today the Kodiak bear is largest. The badger is the largest British carnivore.

carnivores: largest molars   giant panda.

catadromous   of a fish (e.g. the eel), swimming down a river to the sea to spawn.

chelonian   reptiles including turtles, terrapins and tortoises, having upper and lower shells of bony plates – the carapace and plastron – covered with horny scales.

cladistics   method of classifying animals and plants on the basis of shared characteristics that indicate the relative recency of common ancestry.

class   major taxonomic division of animals that contain one or more orders e.g. Amphibia, Mammalia and Reptilia. The class Mammalia includes the orders Carnivora, Primates and Rodentia.

coarse fish   any freshwater fish other than salmon and trout.

crab: lives in cast-off mollusc shell   hermit crab.

cricket: ears   situated on front legs.

crops: damage   boll weevil (cotton); Colorado beetle (potato); locust (most vegetation); phylloxera (vine).

daddy-long-legs: aka   cranefly or harvestman (US); the larvae are called leatherjackets.

death-watch beetle   the ticking is caused by knocking its head against wood.

dinosaur: heaviest   Brachiosaurus (up to 100 tons).

dinosaur: longest   Diplodocus (up to 30 metres).

dog licences: year abolished   1988.

droppings   deer – crotties, hare – currants, otter – spraints.

elephant: teeth number   four.

elytron   either of the two wing cases of a beetle.

family   major taxonomic division of animals that contain one or more genera e.g. Canidae (dogs) and Felidae (cats). The family Canidae includes the genus *Vulpes* (foxes).

fish: fastest   cosmopolitan sailfish.

fish: most poisonous   stone fish.

fly: wings   trues flies (including craneflies, gnat, mosquitos) have two; the four-winged caddis flies, dragonflies, etc., are not true flies.

genus   major taxonomic division of animals that contain one or more species e.g. *Vulpes* (foxes). The genus *Vulpes* (foxes) includes the species *Vulpes bengalensis* (Bengal fox).

giant panda: related to   raccoons (family Procyonidae).

glanders   contagious and fatal disease of horses, mules and donkeys, caused by the bacterium *Actinobacillus mallei* and characterized by swellings below the jaw and mucous discharge from the nostrils.

hedgehog: fleas   one hedgehog may have up to 500 fleas, but the hedgehog flea (*Archaeopsylla erinacei*) does not bite humans.

hedgehog: no. of spines   usually about 5,000.

hinny   offspring of a female donkey and a male horse.

horse: colours   bay – brown with black mane and legs; chestnut – reddish-brown; dun – sandy with black mane; palomino – golden with pale mane; piebald – black and white; skewbald – brown and white; strawberry roan – chestnut and white.

insect: heaviest   goliath beetle.

insects: segments   head, abdomen, thorax (mnemonic: insects wear HATs).

invertebrate: largest   giant squid.

kangaroo: name means   'I don't understand'.

kingdom   any of the three groups into which natural objects may be divided i.e. animals, plants and minerals.

koala: name means   'no drink' (feeds on eucalyptus leaves).

lobster: colour   Bluish but goes red when cooked.

louping-ill   viral disease of animals, especially sheep, transmitted by ticks and causing staggering and jumping.

males give birth   seahorse, from a pouch where the femlae deposits her eggs.

mallenders   dry, scabby eruption behind a horse's knee.

metazoan   any animal of the subkingdom Metazoa, having multicellular and differentiated tissues and comprising all animals except Protozoa and Parazoa (sponges).

mirror: response to   the chimpanzee is the only animal, apart from humans, able to recognize itself in a mirror.

mule   cross between a male horse and a donkey.

murrain   infectious disease of cattle caused by parasites.

octopus: hearts   three.

omasum   the third stomach of a ruminant.

ophidian   reptile of the suborder Serpentes, comprising snakes.

order   Major taxonomic division of animals that contain one or more families e.g. Carnivora, Primates and Rodentia. The order Carnivore includes the families Canidae (dogs) and Felidae (cats).

pandas: born   January (feed on bamboo shoots).

perissodactyl   any placental ungulate mammal whose hoofs have an odd number of toes – e.g. horses, tapirs and rhinoceroses.

pets: legal age to buy   in Britain 12 years old is the minimum legal age to purchase a pet.

phylum major taxonomic division of animals that contain one or more classes e.g. Arthropoda and Chordata. The phylum Arthropoda includes the classes, Arachnids, Centipedes, Crustaceans and insects. The phylum Chordata includes the classes, Amphibia, Mammilia and Reptilia.

pinnipeds: definition carnivorous aquatic mammals with flippers for feet (name means wing-foot).

pismire Middle English name for an ant deriving from the smell of an anthill.

reproduces: young axolotl often reproduces before reaching adult stage itself.

rhinoceros: number of horns Indian and Javan, one; Black, Sumatran and White, two.

rodents: largest capybara (in world), beaver (in Europe), coypu (in UK).

ruminant herbivorous animal that chews the cud.

scrapie fatal disease of sheep and goats, a spongiform encephalopathy producing degeneration of the central nervous system, caused by changes in prion proteins.

sex: changes annually oyster.

silkworm: food mulberry leaves.

snake: heaviest South American anaconda.

spavin disease of a horse's hock with a hard bony swelling or excrescence.

species any of the taxomic groups into which a genus is divided e.g. the genus *Vulpes* (foxes) has many different species, such as *Vulpes bengalensis* (Bengal fox) and *Vulpes pallida* (pale fox). Species are denoted by two words, the first being the genus and the second the species.

spider: eyes eight.

stomach: turns inside out starfish.

strangles acute bacterial disease of horses caused by infection with *Streptococcus equi*, characterized by inflammation of the mucous membranes of the respiratory tract. Aka equine distemper.

sunburn: suffers from the pig is the only non-human animal to suffer from sunburn.

taxonomy the branch of biology concerned with the classification of organsims into groups based on similarities of structure, origin and type. Carolus Linneaus (1707–78) was the first person to structure principles for defining genera and species of organsims and to create a uniform system for naming them. The seven tiers of the hierarchy are kingdom, phylum, class, order, family, genus and species. The first six ranks use a single word to describe its members, but the names of species are binomial. Various intermediary divisions of the seven main ranks have been necessitated by the continuing discovery of new species, and the prefixes sub-, super- and infra- are often applied to create new categories, and further tiers are established by using headings such as tribe or cohort. All intermediary divisions use a single word to describe its members, but subspecies become trinomial. Conventionally, the names of superfamilies end in 'oidea', families in idae', subfamilies in 'inaw' and tribes in 'ini'

taxonomy: mnemonic Kingdom, Phylum, Class, Order, Family, Genus, Species (Kent Play Cricket On Fridays, Girls Spectate).

turning sickness affliction of wildebeest whereby loss of balance faculties cause a never-ending walking in circles until death; it happens when bot-flies lay eggs in their nose and larvae find their way into the brain.

twins: consistent production armadillos and salamanders always give birth to twins.

ungulates all mammals with hoofs; they are divided into odd-toed (perissodactyl) and even-toed (artiodactyl).

vision: rear-view giraffes have ability to see behind them without turning.

woodlouse: legs fourteen.

WWF: symbol World Wide Fund for Nature symbol is a giant panda.

zoophyte plantlike animal, e.g. coral, sea anemone or sponge.

NATURE

Gestation Periods

Animal	Days	Animal	Days	Animal	Day
aardvark	210	chimpanzee	235	goat	150
alpaca	345	civet	80	gorilla	260
anteater, giant	190	coati	77	guinea pig	63
antelope	280	coyote	63	hamster	25
armadillo	60–120	deer, fallow	230	hare	32
ass	350	deer, musk	170	hare, mountain	50
baboon	180	dhole	61	hedgehog	30
badger	100–360	dingo	63	hippopotamus	240
bear, grizzly	230	dog, domestic	60	horse	350
polar bear	240	dog, African wild	72	hyena	93
beaver	105	dolphin	350	jackal	63
bison	280	dormouse	30	jaguar	100
boar, wild	115	dromedary	400	kangaroo	180–335
bobcat	63	elephant, Asiatic	608	koala	36
buffalo	310	ermine	28	lemming	21
bush baby	110–193	ferret	60	lemur	60–160
capybara	150	fox, red	63	leopard	100
cat, domestic	52	gazelle	188	lion	110
cattle	283	gerbil	28	llama	360
chamois	165	gibbon	230	lynx	63
cheetah	95	giraffe	460	macaque	180

Animal	Days	Animal	Days	Animal	Day
marmoset	150	puma	93	tiger	103
mink	50	rabbit	30	vole	90
mole	35	raccoon	63	wallaby	40
mongoose	60	rat, black	21	walrus	460
moose	264	reindeer	225	warthog	172
mouse	25	rhinoceros, black	450	weasel	40
narwhal	435	seal, common	245	whale	350
ocelot	70	seal, eared	360	whale, beluga	435
opossum	12	sea lion	350	whale, sperm	435
orang-utan	240	sheep	148	wolf	62
otter	55	shrew	18	wolverine	270
panda, giant	138	skunk	63	yak	258
pig	115	sloth	180–340	zebra	340
porcupine	210	squirrel	40	zorilla	43
porpoise	183	tapir	370		

Maximum Life Spans

Species	Years	Species	Years	Species	Years
Marion's tortoise	152	slow-worm	54	giant panda	27
quahog	150	gorilla	53	red deer	26
man	123	domestic goose	50	tiger	26
spur thighed tortoise	116	Indian rhinoceros	49	grey squirrel	23
deep sea clam	100	European brown bear	47	domestic goat	20
killer whale	90	grey seal	46	blue sheep	20
sea anemone	90	blue whale	45	queen ant	18
European eel	88	goldfish	41	common rabbit	18
lake sturgeon	82	common boa	40	hedgehog	16
freshwater mussel	80	common toad	40	land snail	15
Asiatic elephant	78	Cape giraffe	36	guinea pig	14
tuatara	77	Bactrian camel	35	capybara	12
Andean condor	72	Hoffmann's sloth	34	tree shrew	11
African elephant	70	domestic cat	34	giant centipede	10
great eagle owl	68	canary	34	golden hamster	10
American alligator	66	American bison	33	fat dormouse	8
blue macaw	64	bobcat	32	millipede	7
horse	62	red kangaroo	30	house mouse	6
ostrich	62	domestic dog	29	moonrat	4
orang-utan	57	budgerigar	29	monarch butterfly	1
chimpanzee	56	lion	29	bedbug	0.5
pike	55	theraphosid spider	28	house fly	0.04
hippopotamus	54	domestic pig	27		

Animal Cries

Animal	Cry	Animal	Cry	Animal	Cry
apes	gibber	chickens	peep	frogs	croak
asses	bray	cocks	crow	geese	cackle, hiss
bears	growl	cows	moo, low	grasshoppers	chirp, pitter
bees	hum	crows	caw	guineafowls	come back
beetles	drone	cuckoos	cuckoo	guineapigs	squeak
bitterns	boom	deer	bell	grouse	drum
blackbirds	whistle	dogs	bark, bay,	hares	squeak
blackcaps	chick-chack		howl, yelp	hawks	scream
bulls	bellow	doves	coo	hens	cackle,
calves	bleat	ducks	quack		cluck
cats	mew, purr,	eagles	scream	horses	neigh,
	caterwaul,	falcons	chant		whinny
	swear	flies	buzz	hyenas	laugh
chaffinches	chirp, pink	foxes	bark, yelp	jays	chatter

Animal	Cry	Animal	Cry	Animal	Cry
kittens	mew	owls	hoot,	sheep	bleat, baa
lambs	bleat, baa		screech	snakes	hiss
linnets	chuckle	oxen	low, bellow	sparrows	chirp
lions	roar, growl	parrots	talk	stags	bellow, call
magpies	chatter	peacocks	scream	swallows	twitter
mice	squeak,	peewits	peewit	swans	cry, sing
	squeal	pigs	grunt,	(before death)	
monkeys	chatter,		squeak,	thrushes	whistle
	gibber		squeal	tigers	roar, growl
nightingales	pipe,	pigeons	coo	turkeys	gobble
	warble,	ravens	croak	vultures	scream
	jug-jug	rooks	caw	whitethroat	chirr
				wolves	howl

Animal Habitations

Animal	Habitation	Animal	Habitation	Animal	Habitation
ant	formicary,	hare	form, down	squirrel	drey
	ant-hill	horse	stable	tiger	lair
ape	tree-nest	lion	den	wasp	vespiary,
badger	set, earth	mole	fortress		nest
bear	den, lair	mouse	hole, nest	wolf	lair
beaver	lodge	otter	holt		
bee	apiary, hive	penguin	rookery		
bird	nest, aviary	rabbit	burrow,		
eagle	eyrie		warren		
fox	earth, lair	spider	web		

Animals: Young

Animal	Young	Animal	Young	Animal	Young
ass	foal, hinny	fox	cub	pigeon	squab
bear	cub	frog	tadpole,	pike	jack
beaver	kitten		froglet	rabbit	kit
cat	kitten	gnat	bloodworm	roe deer	kid
cod	codling	goat	kid	salmon	parr, smolt,
cow	calf, heifer	goose	gosling		grilse
crane-fly	leather	grouse	poult	seal	pup
	jacket	hare	leveret	sheep	lamb
deer	fawn	hippopotamus	calf	squirrel	kitten
duck	duckling	horse	foal	swan	cygnet
eagle	eaglet	kangaroo	joey	whale	calf
eel	elver	lion	cub	zebra	foal
elephant	calf	otter	whelp		
fish	fry	pig	piglet		

Plants and Trees

abele the white poplar. Sp.: *Populus alba*.

alder betuluceous tree having toothed leaves and cone-like fruits. The bark is used in dying and tanning and the wood for bridges (as it resists underwater rot). Gen.: *Alnus*.

alfalfa leguminous plant with clover-like leaves and flowers, grown for fodder and as a salad vegetable. Aka lucerne. Sp.: *Medicago sativa*.

almond small rosaceous tree native to western Asia with pink flowers and green fruit containing edible nut. Sp.: *Prunus amygdalus*.

aloe vera Caribbean aloe yielding a gelatinous substance used in cosmetics as an emollient. Sp.: *Aloe vera*.

alsike species of clover named after Swedish town. Sp.: *Trifolium hybridum*.

anise umbelliferous plant having aromatic seeds. Sp.: *Pimpinella anisum*.

arum lily tall, lily-like, aroid plant found mainly in Southern Africa. Sp.: *Zantedeschia aethiopica*.

ash oleaceous tree with compound leaves, winged seeds and clusters of greenish flowers. Gen.: *Fraxinus*.

aspen poplar tree with especially tremulous leaves. Sp.: *Populus tremula*.

NATURE

balsa bombacaceous tree of tropical America, distinguished by its very light wood. Sp.: *Ochroma lagopus.*

banyan moraceous tree of tropical India and the East Indies, having aerial roots that grow down into the soil, forming additional trunks. Sp.: *Ficus benghalensis.*

baobab African tree with an enormously thick trunk and large, edible, pulpy fruit hanging down on stalks. Sp.: *Adansonia digitata.*

barley erect, annual, temperate grass with short leaves and bristly flowers used for grain. Sp.: *Hordeum vulgares.*

bayberry North American shrub having aromatic leaves and bearing berries covered in a wax coating. Sp.: *Myrica cerifera and Myrica cerifera.*

beech hardwood tree having smooth, greyish bark. Gen.: *Fagus.*

bee orchid European and North Africa orchid with bee-shaped flowers. Sp.: *Ophrys apifera.*

betony purple-flowered plant. Sp.: *Stachys officinalis.*

bilberry hardy dwarf shrub of North Europe growing on heaths and mountains and having red drooping flowers and dark blue berries. Sp.: *Vaccinium myrtillus.*

birch hardwood, close-grained tree with thin, peeling bark. Gen.: *Betula.*

black bryony climbing plant with dark tubers and poisonous red berries. Sp.: *Tamus communis.*

black-eyed Susan flower with yellow petals and a dark centre. Gen.: *Rudbeckia.*

bladderwort aquatic plant whose leaves have small bladders for trapping and digesting insects. Gen.: *Utricularia.*

bladderwrack common brown seaweed with fronds containing air bladders that give buoyancy. Sp.: *Fucus vesiculosus.*

bleeding heart plant with heart-shaped, rose pink flowers hanging from an arched stem. Sp.: *Dicentra spectabilis.*

borage plant with bright blue flowers and hairy leaves used as flavouring. Sp.: *Borago officinalis.*

brookweed small, white-flowered plant of the primrose family growing in wet ground. Sp.: *Samolus valerandi.*

buckbean bog plant with white or pinkish hairy flowers. Sp.: *Menyanthes trifoliata.*

buckthorn (common) thorny shrub with berries formerly used as a cathartic. Sp.: *Rhamnus cathartica.*

buckwheat cereal plant with seeds used for fodder and for flour to make bread. Sp.: *Fagopyrum esculentum.*

burdock plant with prickly flowers and dock-like leaves. Gen.: *Arctium.*

busy Lizzie East African plant with abundant red, pink or white flowers, often grown as bedding or house plants. Sp.: *Impatiens walleriana.*

butterbur waterside plant with pale purple flowers and large, soft leaves formerly used to wrap butter. Gen.: *Petasites.*

buttercup yellow-flowered meadow plant of Europe and North America. Gen.: *Ranunculus.*

butterfly bush common name given to buddleia bush. Sp.: *Buddleia davidii.*

calabash tree evergreen tree, bearing fruit in the form of large gourds, native to tropical America. Sp.: *Crescentia cujete.*

calluna common heather native to Europe and North Africa. Sp.: *Calluna vulgaris.*

carambola small tree native to South-east Asia bearing golden-yellow ribbed fruit. Aka star fruit. Sp.: *Averrhoa carambola.*

cashew bushy evergreen tree native to Central and North America bearing kidney-shaped nuts attached to fleshy fruits. Sp.: *Anacardium occidentale.*

cassava (bitter) plant of the spurge family having starchy tuberous roots. Aka manioc tapioca. Sp.: *Manihot esculenta.*

catmint plant with downy leaves, purple-spotted white flowers, and a mint-like smell attractive to cats. Sp.: *Nepeta cataria.*

cedar coniferous tree having spreading branches, needle-like evergreen leaves and cones. Gen.: *Cedrus.*

celery pine Australasian tree with branchlets like celery leaves. Sp.: *Phyllocladus trichomanoides.*

charlock a wild mustard with yellow flowers. Sp.: *Sinapis arvensis.*

checkerberry North American evergreen shrub of the health family with spiny, scented leaves, white flowers and crimson fruits. Aka wintergreen. Sp.: *Gaultheria procumbens.*

cherry plum tree native to south-western Asia with solitary white flowers and red fruit. Sp.: *Prunus cerasifera.*

chervil umbelliferous plant with small white flowers; its aniseed flavoured leaves used as a herb for flavouring soup and salads. Sp.: *Anthriscus cereifolium.*

chestnut broad-leaved tree, which produces flowers in long catkins and nuts in a prickly bur. Gen.: *Castanea.*

chickpea leguminous plant with short, swollen pods containing yellow-beaked edible seed. Aka garbanza. Sp.: *Cicer arietinum.*

chicory blue-flowered plant cultivated for its salad leaves and its root, which is ground for coffee. Sp.: *Cichorium intybus.*

Chinese water chestnut sedge with rushlike leaves arising from a corm, which is used as food. Sp.: *Eleocharis tuberosa.*

chives small allium with purple-pink flowers and dense tufts of long tubular leaves, which are used as a herb. Sp.: *Allium schoenoprasum.*

Christmas rose small, white-flowered, winter-blooming plant. Sp.: *Helleborus niger.*

cinchona evergreen trees of South America, of the madder family, having fragrant flowers; the bark of this tree contains quinine. Gen.: *Cinchona.*

cineraria plant cultivated for its bright flowers. Sp.: *Pericallis cruenta.*

cloudberry small mountain bramble with a white flower and an orange-coloured fruit. Sp.: *Rubus chamaemorus.*

coco de mer palm tree of the Seychelles producing a large fruit containing a two-lobed, edible nut (world's largest seed). Sp.: *Lodoicea maldivica.*

coltsfoot plant of the daisy family with large leaves and yellow flowers. Sp.: *Tussilago farfara.*

columbine an aquilegia with purple-blue flowers. Sp.: *Aquilegia vulgaris.*

cork oak evergreen Mediterranean oak. Sp.: *Quercus suber.*

cowbane poisonous plant found in marshes. Sp.: *Cicuta virosa.*

cow parsley hedgerow plant having lacelike umbels of flowers. Sp.: *Anthriscus sylvestris.*

cowslip primula with fragrant yellow flowers, which grows in pastures and meadows. Sp.: *Primula veris.*

cranebill any of various plants of the genus *Geranium*, having pink or purple flowers and long, slender, beaked fruit.

cuckoo flower meadow plant with pale lilac flowers. Aka lady's smock. Sp.: *Cardamine pratensis.*

cuckoo pint wild arum with arrow-shaped leaves and scarlet berries. Sp.: *Arum maculatum.*

daffodil bulbous plant with a yellow, trumpet-shaped corona. Sp.: *Narcissus pseudonarcissus.*

daisy small, low-growing European plant having a rosette of white leaves and yellow centre. Sp.: *Bellis perennis.*

dawn redwood Chinese deciduous coniferous tree of a genus first known only from fossils. Sp.: *Metasequoia glyptostroboides.*

dead man's fingers species of orchid, *Orchis mascula.*

deadly nightshade highly poisonous plant with drooping purple flowers and black, cherry-like fruit. Sp.: *Atropa belladonna.*

death cap poisonous toadstool of deciduous woodland. Sp.: *Amanita phalloides.*

deodar Himalayan cedar with drooping branches bearing large barrel-shaped cones. Tallest of the cedar family. Sp.: *Cedrus deodara.*

destroying angel poisonous white toadstool. Sp.: *Amanita virosa.*

dewberry shrub with bluish fruit similar to a blackberry. Sp.: *Rubus caesius.*

dill umbelliferous herb with yellow flowers and aromatic seeds. Sp.: *Anethum graveolens.*

divi-divi tree native to tropical America, bearing curved pods, which are a source of tannin. Sp.: *Caesalpinia coriaria.*

dog's tooth violet plant of the Liliaceae family with speckled leaves, purple flowers and a toothed perianth. Sp.: *Erythronium dens-canis.*

Douglas fir large conifer over 100m tall of western North America. Sp.: *Pseudotsuga menziesii.*

doum palm tree with edible fruit. Sp.: *Hyphaene thebaica.*

dove's foot type of cranesbill. Sp.: *Geranium molle.*

dragon tree palm-like tree of the Canary Islands. Sp.: *Dracaena draco.*

durian large tree native to South-east Asia, bearing oval spiny fruit containing a creamy pulp with a fetid smell but an agreeable taste. Sp.: *Durio zibethinus.*

Dutchman's breeches plant of eastern North America with white flowers and finely divided leaves. Sp.: *Dicentra cucullaria.*

Dutchman's pipe climbing vine of eastern North America with hooked tubular flowers. Sp.: *Aristolochia durior.*

ebony tree with hard, dark wood often used for cabinetwork. Sometimes called persimmon. Sp.: *Diospyros ebenum.*

eglantine wild rose with small fragrant leaves and flowers. Sp.: *Rosa eglanteria.*

elm tree with serrated leaves and winged fruits (samaras), the wood being hard and heavy. Gen.: *Ulmus.*

endive curly-leaved plant used in salads. Sp.: *Cichorium endivia.*

eucalyptus myrtaceous tree native to Australia; species include blue gum and ironbark. Gen.: *Eucalyptus.*

false acacia the locust tree, often grown for ornament. Sp.: *Robinia pseudoacacia.*

felwort purple-flowered gentian. Sp.: *Gentianella amarella.*

fennel yellow-flowered umbelliferous plant with fragrant seeds and fine leaves used as flavourings. Sp.: *Foeniculum vulgare.*

fenugreek leguminous plant with aromatic seeds, which are often used in curry powder. Sp.: *Trigonella foenum-graecum.*

fern pteridophyte plant having roots, stems and fronds and reproducing by spores formed in structures (sori) on the fronds. Division: Pteridophyta (syn. Filicinophyta).

fever tree yellow-flowered southern African tree. Sp.: *Acacia xanthophloea.*

feverfew aromatic, bushy plant with feathery leaves and white, daisy-like flowers, used to treat migraine and formerly to reduce fever. Sp.: *Tanacetum parthenium.*

figwort plant of the genus *Scrophularia* with dull, purplish-brown flowers, once believed to be useful against scrofula.

flax-lily New Zealand plant of the agave family yielding valuable fibre. Sp.: *Phormium tenax.*

forget-me-not plant with small, yellow-eyed, bright blue flowers. Gen.: *Myosotis.*

foxglove tall plant with erect spikes of purple or white bell-shaped flowers. Sp.: *Digitalis purpurea.*

fraxinella aromatic plant of rue family having foliage that emits an ethereal inflammable oil. Aka burning bush. Sp.: *Dictamnus albus.*

gentian plants found in mountainous regions, having violet or blue trumpet-shaped flowers. Gen.: *Gentiana.*

gerbera any plant of the genus *Gerbera*, of Africa or Asia, especially the Transvaal daisy. Gen.: *Gerbera.*

germander any of varions plants of the genus *Teucrium*, typically being a mildly aromatic, white felted perenial shrublet with a compact domed shape. The flowers, which appear between April and July, are reddish or purplish in colour. Germander was used in Cypriot folk-medicine as a cure for stomach ailments and jaundice.

germander speedwell creeping plant with germander-like leaves and blue flowers. US name: bird's-eye speedwell. Sp.: *Veronica chamaedrys.*

ginger hot, spicy root, which can be powdered for use in cooking, or preserved in syrup, or candied. Sp.: *Zingiber officinale.*

gladiolus plants of *Iridaceae* family with sword-shaped leaves and brightly coloured flower spikes. Gen.: *Gladiolus.*

goatsbeard Eurasian plant with woolly stems and large heads of yellow-rayed flowers surrounded by large, green bracts. Sp.: *Tragopogon pratensis.*

goatsbeard American rosaceous plant with long spikes of small white flowers. Gen.: *Aruncus.*

goat's-rue Eurasian leguminous plant cultivated for its white, mauve or pinkish flowers. Sp.: *Galega officinalis.*

goat's-rue North American leguminous plant with pink-and-yellow flowers. Sp.: *Tephrosia virginiana.*

good King Henry weed of the goosefoot family. Sp.: *Chenopodium bonus-henricus.*

goosefoot plant that has small greenish flowers and leaves like the foot of a goose. Gen.: *Chenopodium.*

gopher North American tree, yielding yellowish timber; not to be confused with the arident field gopher tree from which Noah's Ark was reputedly built. Sp.: *Cladrastis lutea.*

grass monocotyledonous plants encompassing all the cereal plants as well as reeds and bamboos. Family *Gramineae.*

greenheart tropical American evergreen tree of the laurel family. Gen.: *Ocotea rodiaei.*

guaiacum trees native to tropical America with hard, dense, oily timber. Gen.: *Guaiacum.*

guava small tropical American tree bearing an edible, pale orange fruit with pinky, juicy flesh. Sp.: *Psidium guajava.*

guelder rose deciduous shrub with round bunches of creamy-white flowers. Sp.: *Viburnum opulus.*

guernsey lily nerine, originally from South Africa, with large, pink, lily-like flowers. Sp.: *Nerine sarniensis.*

hare's-foot clover with soft hair around the flowers. Sp.: *Trifolium arvense.*

hart's tongue fern with narrow undivided fronds. Sp.: *Phyllitis scolopendrium.*

hawthorn thorny shrub or tree with white, red or pink blossom and small, dark red fruit or haws. Sp.: *Crataegus monogyna.*

hazel small tree bearing round brown edible nuts. Sp.: *Corylus avellana.*

henbane poisonous herbaceous plant with sticky hairy leaves and an unpleasant smell. Sp.: *Hyoscyamus niger.*

henna tropical shrub having small pink, red or white flowers; the reddish dye from its shoots and leaves is used to colour hair. Sp.: *Lawsonia inermis.*

herb Christopher white-flowered baneberry. Sp.: *Actaea spicata.*

herb Paris plant with a single flower and four leaves in a cross shape on an unbranched stem. Sp.: *Paris quadrifolia.*

herb Robert common cranesbill with red-stemmed leaves and pink flowers. Sp.: *Geranium robertianum.*

holly evergreen tree with prickly leaves and red berries, often used as Christmas decorations. Gen.: *Ilex.*

hop climbing plant cultivated for the cones borne by the female, used in brewing. Sp.: *Humulus lupulus.*

hornbeam tree of the genus *Carpinus* with a smooth bark and a hard tough wood. Gen.: *Carpinus.*

horse chestnut Eurasian tree with palmate leaves and inedible nuts enclosed in a spiky bur (conkers). Sp.: *Aesculus hippocastanum.*

horse mushroom large, edible mushroom. Sp.: *Agaricus arvensis.*

horseradish cruciferous plant with long, lobed leaves. Sp.: *Armoracia rusticana.*

hortensia kind of hydrangea (distinct from lacecap) with large, round, infertile flower heads. Sp.: *Hydrangea macrophylla.*

huckleberry North American shrub with blue or black soft fruit. Gen.: *Gaylussacia.*

Iceland poppy Arctic poppy with white or yellow flowers. Sp.: *Papaver nudicaule.*

Indian hemp strong-smelling Asian moraceous plant. Aka marijuana, Cannabis. Sp.: *Cannabis indica.*

ivy climbing plants having lobed evergreen leaves and black, berry-like fruits. Gen.: *Hedera.*

jack-by-the-hedge white-flowered cruciferous plant of shady places. Sp.: *Alliaria petiolata.*

jackfruit East Indian tree bearing fruit resembling breadfruit. Sp.: *Artocarpus heterophyllus.*

japonica flowering shrub with round white, green or yellow, edible fruit and bright red flowers. Sp.: *Chaenomeles speciosa.*

jarrah the Western Australian mahogany gum tree. Sp.: *Eucalyptus marginata.*

jasmine oleaceous shrub or climbing plant whose fragrant flowers are used in perfumery. Gen.: *Jasminum.*

kangaroo paw Australian plant with irregular woolly flowers. Floral emblem of Western Australia. Sp.: *Anigozanthos manglesii.*

kangaroo vine evergreen climbing plant with serrated leaves. Sp.: *Cissus antarctica.*

kidney vetch yellow-flavoured leguminous plant found in grassland. Aka lady's finger. Sp.: *Anthyllis vulneraria.*

knotweed fast-growing Japanese plant. Sp.: *Fallopia japonica.*

ladino large type of white clover native to Italy and cultivated for fodder. Sp.: *Trifolium repens.*

lamb's ears garden plant with whitish, woolly leaves. Sp.: *Stachys byzantina.*

lemon balm bushy plant with leaves smelling and tasting of lemon. Sp.: *Melissa officinalis.*

lemon geranium lemon-scented pelargonium. Sp.: *Pelargonium crispum.*

lemon verbena shrub with lemon-scented leaves. Aka lemon plant. Sp.: *Aloysia triphylla.*

leopard's bane any plant of the genus *Doronicum* with large, yellow, daisy-like flowers. Sp.: *Doronicum.*

live oak American evergreen tree. Sp.: *Quercus virginiana.*

loquat tree of the Rosaceae family, bearing small, yellow, egg-shaped fruit. Sp.: *Eriobotrya japonica.*

love-in-a-mist blue-flowered garden plant with many delicate green bracts. Sp.: *Nigella damascena.*

love-lies-bleeding garden plant with drooping spikes of purple-red blooms. Sp.: *Amaranthus caudatus.*

lungwort Eurasian plant with spotted leaves and clusters of blue or purple flowers. Sp.: *Pulmonaria officinalis.*

lungwort (sea) boraginaceous plant of the northern temperate genus *Mertensia*, with drooping clusters of tubular, usually blue flowers. Aka oyster plant. Gen.: *Mertensia maritima.*

madder plant with small yellow flowers and a red fleshy root. Gen.: *Rubia.*

mahogany tropical tree yielding a hard, reddish-brown wood used for furniture making. Sp.: *Swietenia mahagoni.*

mandrake poisonous plant with white, or purple flowers and large yellow fruit, having emetic and narcotic properties and possessing a root once thought to resemble the human form and to shriek when plucked. Sp.: *Mandragora officinarum.*

mangosteen Malaysian tree bearing a white juicy-pulped fruit with a thick, reddish-brown rind. Sp.: *Garcinia mangostana.*

mangrove any tropical tree or shrub of the genus *Rhizophora* growing in shore-mud with many tangled roots above ground. Gen.: *Rhizophora.*

Manila hemp Philippine plant with a strong fibre used for rope-making. Sp.: *Musa textilis.*

manuka small New Zealand tree with aromatic leaves and hard timber. Sp.: *Leptospermum scoparium.*

maple any tree or shrub of the genus *Acer,* grown for shade, ornament, wood, or sugar.

marsh mallow   herbaceous plant, the roots of which were formerly used to make a sweet confection. Sp.: *Althaea officinalis.*

marsh marigold   golden-flowered plant, which grows in moist pastures. Sp.: *Caltha palustris.*

martagon   lily with small, purple, turban-like flowers. Sp.: *Lilium martagon.*

marvel of Peru   showy garden plant with flowers opening at dusk. Sp.: *Mirabilis jalapa.*

mayapple   American herbaceous plant bearing a yellow, egg-shaped fruit in May. Sp.: *Podophyllum peltatum.*

mayflower   In North America trailing arbutus that blooms in May. Sp.: *Epigaea repens.*

maz(z)ard   the wild sweet cherry of Europe. Sp.: *Prunus avium.*

meadow rue   plants of the buttercup family with small yellow or purple flowers. Gen.: *Thalictrum.*

meadow saffron   meadow plant resembling a crocus and producing lilac flowers in autumn, while still leafless. Sp.: *Colchicum autumnale.*

meadowsweet   plant of the Rosaceae family, common in meadows and damp places, with creamy-white fragrant flowers. Also the name of a North American plant of the genus *Spiraea.* Sp.: *Filipendula ulmaria.*

medlar   tree of the rose family bearing small brown apple-like fruits, which are best eaten when over-ripe. Sp.: *Mespilus germanica.*

mignonette   plants of the genus *Reseda,* some having aromatic grey-green flowers.

mimosa   Leguminous shrub having globular yellow flowers and sensitive leaflets, which droop when touched. Sp.: *Mimosa pudica.*

mistletoe   parasitic plant growing on apple and other trees and bearing white, glutinous berries in winter. Americans have a related plant of the genus *Phoradendron.* Sp.: *Viscum album.*

mock pennyroyal   North American aromatic plant. Sp.: *Hedeoma pulegioides.*

moneywort   trailing evergreen plant with round glossy leaves and yellow flowers. Sp.: *Lysimachia nummularia.*

monkey flower   short creeping plant with bright yellow flowers. Sp.: *Mimulus guttatus.*

monkey-puzzle   coniferous tree native to Chile with downward-pointing branches and small, close-set leaves. Aka Chile pine. Sp.: *Araucaria araucana.*

montbretia   hybrid plant of genus *Crocosmia* with bright, orange-yellow, trumpet-shaped flowers.

morning glory   any of various twining plants, with trumpet-shaped flowers, of the genus *Ipomoea.*

mother-in-law's tongue   plant with long, erect, pointed leaves. Sp.: *Sansevieria trifasciata.*

mung bean   leguminous plants of the genus *Vigna,* native to India and yielding a small bean used as food.

musk-rose   rambling rose with large, white flowers smelling of musk. Sp.: *Rosa moschata.*

musk thistle   nodding thistle whose flowers have a musky fragrance. Sp.: *Carduus nutans.*

musk tree   Australian tree with a musky smell. Sp.: *Olearia argyrophylla.*

mustard   plant eaten at the seedling stage, often with cress, and whose seeds are crushed and made into a paste and used as a spicy condiment. Sp.: *Sinapis alba.*

mustard   plant with slender pods and yellow flowers. Sp.: *Brassica nigra.*

myrtle   evergreen shrub with aromatic foliage and white flowers with purple-black ovoid berries. Sp.: *Myrtus communis.*

narcissus   yellow, orange or white flowered plants with crown surrounded by spreading segments. Gen.: *Narcissus*

nardoo   clover-like plant of Australian origin. Sp.: *Marsilea drummondii.*

nasturtium   Any cruciferous plant of the genus Nasturtium, including watercress. Trailing plants of the Americas with rounded edible leaves and bright orange, yellow or red flowers of the genus *Tropaeolum.*

nopal   cactus having yellow flowers and purple fruits, sometimes called prickly pear. Gen.: *Opuntia.*

oak   any tree of the genus *Quercus,* having lobed leaves and bearing acorns.

obeche   West African tree. Sp.: *Triplochiton scleroxylon.*

okra   African edible plant of the mallow family. Aka gumbo or ladies' fingers. Sp.: *Abelmoschus esculentus.*

orpin(e)   succulent, herbaceous, purple-flowered plant. Sp.: *Sedum telephium.*

ox-eye daisy   plant of the daisy family, with large white flowers with yellow centres. Sp.: *Leucanthemum vulgare.*

oxlip   woodland primula. Sp.: *Primula elatior.*

ox-tongue   plant of the daisy family with bright yellow flowers. Gen.: *Picris.*

palmyra   Asian palm with fan-shaped leaves used for matting. Sp.: *Borassus flabellifer.*

parsley   biennial herb with white flowers and crinkly aromatic leaves. Sp.: *Petroselinum crispum.*

parsley fern   fern with leaves like parsley. Sp.: *Cryptogramma crispa.*

passion flower   any climbing plant of the genus *Passiflora* with a flower that was supposed to suggest the instruments of the Crucifixion.

patchouli   strongly scented south Asian shrub from which a perfume is made. Gen.: *Pogostemon.*

peanut   leguminous plant bearing pods that ripen underground and contain seeds used as food and yielding oil. Sp.: *Arachis hypogaea.*

pedunculate oak   a common oak in which clusters of acorns are borne on long stalks. Sp.: *Quercus robur.*

peepul (pipal)   moraceous tree of tropical India and the East Indies, resembling the banyan, and thought of as sacred by Buddhists because the founder of the religion is said to have found enlightenment while sitting under its branches. Sp.: *Ficus religiosa.*

pennyroyal   creeping mint cultivated for its supposed medicinal properties. Sp.: *Mentha pulegium.*

periwinkle   tropical shrub native to Madagascar. Sp.: *Catharanthus roseus.*

periwinkle   any of several Eurasian apocynaceous evergreen plants of the genus *Vinca,* having trailing stems and blue flowers. Aka creeping myrtle or trailing myrtle (USA).

pine   coniferous evergreen with long, needle-shaped leaves and brown cones. Gen.: *Pinus.*

pinkster flower   the pink azalea. Sp.: *Rhododendron periclymenoides.*

piripiri   plant of the rose family native to New Zealand and having prickly burs. Sp.: *Acaena anserinifolia.*

poplar   salicaceous tree with triangular leaves, light, soft wood and flowers borne in catkins. Gen.: *Populus.*

prickly pear   cactus of the genus *Opuntia*, native to arid regions of America and bearing barbed bristles and large, pear-shaped, prickly fruits.

ragged robin   pink-flowered campion with spiky, tattered-looking petals. Aka cuckoo flower. Sp.: *Lychnis flos-cuculi.*

rose   shrub or climbing plant having prickly stems and fragrant flowers. Gen.: *Rosa.*

rowan   tree with delicate pinnate leaves and scarlet berries. Sp.: *Sorbus aucuparia.*

rue   dwarf shrub with bipinnate or tripinnate glaucous leaves and yellow flowers. Gen.: *Ruta.*

salsify   Mediterranean plant having grass-like leaves, purple flower heads and a long, white edible taproot. Aka oyster plant or vegetable oyster. Sp.: *Tragopogon porrifolius.*

shaddock   tree named after Captain Shaddoch who brought the seed to Barbados. Aka pomelo. Sp.: *Citrus maxima.*

shamrock   most common shamrock is the wood sorrel, *Oxalis acetosella*, and this is the plant worn on St Patrick's Day. Other trifoliate shamrocks include black medic (*Medicago lupulina*) and white clover (*Trifolium repens*).

snake's head   bulbous plant with bell-shaped, pendent flowers. Sp.: *Fritillaria meleagris.*

southernwood   bushy kind of wormwood. Sp.: *Artemisia abrotanum.*

sweet marjoram   one of two aromatic herbs (the other being wild marjoram) whose fresh dried leaves are used as a flavouring in cookery. Sp.: *Majorana hortensis.*

teak   large, verbenaceous tree of East Indies yielding a hard, valuable yellow-brown wood. Sp.: *Tectona grandis.*

tobacco   solanaceous plant having hairy leaves, and funnel-shaped, fragrant flowers. Gen.: *Nicotiana.*

tomatillo   Mexican ground cherry bearing purplish, edible fruit. Sp.: *Physalis philadelphica.*

tomato   plant of the nightshade family bearing glossy red or yellow pulpy edible fruit. Sp.: *Lycopersicon esculentum.*

toothwort   parasitic plant with toothlike, root scales. Sp.: *Lathraea squamaria.*

toquilla   palm-like tree native to South America. Sp.: *Carludovica palmata.*

trailing arbutus   see mayflower.

Transvaal daisy   plant of the Asteraceae family. Gen.: *Gerbera.*

traveller's joy   wild clematis. Aka old man's beard. Sp.: *Clematis vitalba.*

tree mallow   tall, woody-stemmed European mallow of cliffs and rocks. Sp.: *Lavatera arborea.*

tree tomato   South American shrub with egg-shaped, red fruit. Sp.: *Cyphomandra betacea.*

tulip   bulbous, spring-flowering plant of a variety of colours. The word tulip is derived from the Turkish *Tülbend*, meaning turban, from the shape of the expanded flower. Gen.: *Tulipa.*

tulip tree   North American tree with tulip-like flowers and lobed leaves. Gen.: *Liriodendron tulipifera.*

tumbleweed   plant of arid areas of North America and Australia, which forms a globular bush that breaks off in late summer and is tumbled about by the wind. Gen.: *Amaranthus alba.*

turmeric   tropical Asian plant of the Zingiberaceae family, yielding aromatic rhizomes used as a spice and for yellow dye. Sp.: *Curcuma longa.*

umbrella plant   African sedge having large umbrella-like whorls of slender leaves and widely grown as an ornamental water plant. Sp.: *Cyperus alternifolius.*

umbrella tree   North American magnolia having long leaves clustered into an umbrella formation at the ends of the branches and unpleasant-smelling, white flowers. Sp.: *Magnolia tripetala.*

vetch   plant largely used for silage and fodder. Sp.: *Vicia sativa.*

violet   low-growing plant characterized by horizontal petals and purple, cordate leaves. Gen.: *Viola.*

viper's bugloss   stiff bristly blue-flowered plant. Sp.: *Echium vulgare.*

wall fern   an evergreen polypody with very large leaves. Sp.: *Polypodium vulgare.*

wallflower   spring-flowering garden plant with fragrant yellow, orange-red or dark red flowers. Sp.: *Cheiranthus cheiri.*

wall germander   European germander having two-lipped pinkish-purple flowers with a very small upper lip. Sp.: *Teucrium chamaedrys.*

wall rue   small fern with leaves like rue, growing on walls and rocks. Aka spleewort. Sp.: *Asplenium ruta-muraria.*

walnut   tree having aromatic leaves and drooping catkins, the nut of which contains a wrinkled edible kernel in two halves and enclosed in a green fruit. Gen.: *Juglans.*

wandering jew   climbing plant with stemless, variegated leaves. Gen.: *Tradescantia albiflora.*

water chestnut   aquatic plant bearing an edible seed. Sp.: *Trapa natans.*

water hyacinth   tropical American aquatic plant which is a serious weed of waterways in warm countries. Sp.: *Eichhornia crassipes.*

watercress   hardy perennial cress growing in running water, with pungent leaves used in salad. Sp.: *Nasturtium officinale.*

wayfaring tree   white-flowered European and Asian shrub, common along roadsides, with berries turning from green through red to black. Sp.: *Viburnum lantana.*

wild marjoram   one of two aromatic herbs (the other being sweet marjoram) whose fresh dried leaves are used as a flavouring in cookery. Sp.: *Origanum vulgare.*

wild pansy   Eurasian plant having purple, yellow, and pale mauve spurred flowers, aka heartsease, love-in-idleness. Sp.: *Viola tricolor.*

willow   white-wood tree with graceful flexible branches and catkins. Gen.: *Salix.*

wintergreen   low-growing plants with drooping spikes of white, bell-shaped flowers. Gen.: *Pyrola.*

witch alder   American shrub with leaves like that of the alder. Sp.: *Fothergilla gardenii.*

witch hazel   North American shrub with yellow flowers, the leaves and bark used to treat bruises. Gen.: *Hamamelis virginiana.*

woad   glaucous, yellow-flowered cruciferous plant formerly grown for its blue dye. Sp.: *Isatis tinctoria.*

wolfsbane   various ranunculaceous plants with hooded purple or yellow flowers. Aka aconite, monkshood. Gen.: *Aconitum.*

wood anemone   wild spring-flowering, anemone. Sp.: *Anemone nemorosa.*

woodruff   white-flowered plant grown for the fragrance of its whorled leaves when dried or crushed. Sp.: *Galium odoratum.*

woody nightshade   scrambling woody Eurasian plant with purple flowers and recurved petals with protruding cone of yellow anthers and poisonous, red, berrylike fruits. Aka bittersweet. Sp.: *Solanum dulcamara*.

wych elm   Eurasian elm with large rough leaves and pliant branches. Sp.: *Ulmus glabra*.

yellow archangel   Eurasian yellow-flowered nettle. Sp.: *Lamiastrum galeobdolon*.

yellow flag   yellow-flowered iris with slender, sword-shaped leaves. Sp.: *Iris pseudacorus*.

yellow rattle   yellow-flowered herb, which is partly parasitic. Sp.: *Rhinanthus minor*.

yellow toadflax   plant with narrow leaves like flax and spurred yellow flowers. Sp.: *Linaria vulgaris*.

yerba buena (good herb)   North American trailing plant with lilac flowers formally used by Californian

Americans to make a medicinal tea. Sp.: *Satureja douglasii*.

yerba santa   North American shrub whose leaves are used medicinally. Lit. 'holy herb'. Sp.: *Eriodictyon californicum*.

yew   Dark-leaved evergreen coniferous tree having seeds enclosed in a fleshy red aril, and often planted in churchyards. Gen.: *Taxus*.

yiang-ylang / iiang-ilang.   Malaysian tree from which a fragrant perfume is distilled. Sp.: *Cananga odorata*.

Yorkshire fog   fodder grass. Sp.: *Holcus lanatus*.

yucca   plant of Agavaceae family with woody stem and sword-shaped leaves. Aka Adam's needle. Gen.: *Yucca*.

Miscellaneous Information

agriculture: soilless   hydroponics.

allogamy   cross-fertilization in plants.

angiosperm   flower-producing plants that reproduce by seeds enclosed within a carpel, including herbaceous plants, herbs, shrubs, grasses and most trees.

carnations: types of   self (one colour), fancy (multi coloured), picotee (pale with darker edge).

carnivorous plants   pitcher plant, sundew, venus fly trap.

deciduous conifer   larch, swamp cypress.

Dutch elm disease   disease of elms, often fatal, caused by the fungus *Ceratocystis ulmi* and spread by bark beetles.

entomophily   pollination by insects.

entophyte   plant growing inside a plant or animal.

epiphyte   plant growing on another but not parasitic on it, e.g. a moss on a tree trunk.

fastest growth   bamboo (about 38 cm, 15 inches a day).

flower parts   female part: pistil   male part: stamen   Perfect flower: contains male and female parts. Stigma: mouth of the pistil, which receives the pollen in impregnation. Style: neck of the pistil, which contains the stigma. Ovary: swollen basal part of the pistil containg the ovules.

frond   the compound leaf of a fern or a palm.

garden city: First   Letchworth in Herts (1903), founded by Ebenezer Howard.

gymnosperm   any of various plants having seeds unprotected by an ovary, including conifers, cycads and ginkgo.

halophyte   plant adapted to saline conditions.

largest living thing   a Californian redwood tree, *Sequoia sempervirens*, nicknamed the General Sherman. (275 feet high and 1,385 tons in weight)

leaves: types of   bract, stipule and pinnate.

mulch   half-rotten vegetable matter used to prevent soil erosion.

nettle sting: cause   formic acid.

oak apples: caused by   wasp eggs.

oldest tree   a bristlecone pine (*Pinus longaera*) nicknamed Old Methuselah. Approx 5,000 years old and situated in the White Mountains, California.

osmosis   the passage of a solvent through a semipermeable membrane from a less concentrated to a more concentrated solution until both solutions are of the same concentration. Wilhelm Pfeffer, a

German plant physiologist, first studied osmosis in 1877, although the term was introduced by the British chemist Thomas Graham in 1854. Osmosis is the method used by plants for water absorption.

pergola   arbour or covered walk, formed of growing plants trained over trellis-work.

plant families   apple – rose (Rosaceae); ash – olive (Oleaceae); asparagus – lily (Liliaceae); aubergine – nightshade (Solanum); avocado – laurel (Lauraceae); bamboo - grass (Gramineae); barley – grass (Gramineae); blackberry – rose (Rosaceae); bluebell – lily (Liliaceae); breadfruit – mulberry (Moraceae); broccoli – cabbage (Brassica); brussels sprout – cabbage (Brassica); buckwheat – dock (Polygonaceae); camellia – tea (Theaceae); carrot – parsley (Apiaceae); cauliflower – cabbage (Brassica); celery – parsley (Apiaceae); cherry – rose (Rosaceae); chives – lily (Liliaceae); cinnamon – laurel (Lauraceae); coffee – madder (Rubiaceae); cork oak – beech (Fagacrab); cotton – mallow (Malvaceae); dandelion – daisy (Compositae); elder – honeysuckle (Caprifoliaceae); fig – mulberry (Moraceae); garlic – lily (Liliaceae); gooseberry – Grossulariaceae; guelder Rose – (Caprifoliaceae); hemlock – parsley (Apiaceae); hemp - mulberry (Moraceae); hop – mulberry (Moraceae); hyacinth – lily (Liliaceae); jasmine –olive (Oleaceae); Jerusalem artichoke – daisy (Compositae); knotgrass (Aka Allseed) – dock (Polygonaceae); leek – lily (Liliaceae); lemon – rue (Rutaceae); lettuce – daisy (Compositae); lilac – olive (Oleaceae); lime – rue (Rutaceae); maize – grass (Gramineae); marijuana – mulberry (Moraceae); mustard – cabbage (Brassica); okra – mallow (Malvaceae); onion – lily (Liliaceae); orange – rue (Rutaceae); parsnip – parsley (Apiaceae); peach – rose (Rosaceae); pear – rose (Rosaceae); plum – rose (Rosaceae); potato – nightshade (Solanum); privet – olive (Oleaceae); radish – cabbage (Brassica); rape – cabbage (Brassica); raspberry – rose (Rosaceae); rhubarb – dock (Polygonaceae); rye – grass (Gramineae); shallot – lily (Liliaceae); sorrel – dock (Polygonaceae); strawberry – rose (Rosaceae); swede – cabbage (Brassica); thistle – daisy (Compositae); tobacco – nightshade (Solanum); tomato – nightshade (Solanum); tulip – lily (Liliaceae); turnip – cabbage (Brassica); vanilla – orchid (Orchidaceae); wheat – grass (Gramineae).

plants: products from   agar agar – seaweed; amber – pine tree resin; aspirin – willow tree (originally);

NATURE

atropine – deadly nightshade; cocaine – coca plant; cochineal – beetles; copra – coconut; digitalis – foxglove; frankincense (*Olibanum*) – tree bark resin (*Boswellia*); henna dye – leaves of henna plant; heroin – opium poppy; hessian – plant root; linen – spun flax; linseed oil – seeds of flax plant; madder – plant root; morphine – opium poppy; myrrh – myrrh tree resin; opium – opium poppy (*Papaver somniferum*); quinine – cinchona bark; raffia – palm; saffron – crocus; semolina – wheat; tapioca – cassava root; turmeric – curcuma plant; turpentine – coniferous trees (especially pine).

pomegranate: varieties   paper-shell, Spanish ruby, wonderful.

roots: types of   adventitious, aerial, climbing, contratile, lateral, preumatophore, prop.

Royal Horticultural Society   Founded in 1804 and in its centenary year of 1904 established Wisley as its Show Garden.

sacking: fibre used for   jute.

scandents   climbing plants.

sweet pea: from   Sicily.

tallest tree   Douglas fir.

taxonomy   classification of living organisms into groups in an organized hierarchy. The largest group is the kingdom – e.g. Plants (Plantore); Animals (Animalia). Below the Kingdom; in desending order, come: Phylum, Class, Subclass; Order, Family, Genus, Species.

toadstool: most poisonous   deathcap.

tomato: original name   love apple.

tudor rose   conventionalized 5-lobed figure of a rose; the white and the red rose were adopted as the symbols of the Houses of York and Lancaster during the Wars of the Roses.

tulip: named from   the Turkish turban *Tülbend*.

underwater: grows   rice.

vanilla: family   orchid family.

variegation   different colourings of a leaf.

xerophyte   plant, such as cacti, that grows in dry conditions.

yucca tree: pollination   only by the yucca moth, *Pronuba* (Tegetierila) *yuccasella*.

Alternative Names of Flowers, Plants and Trees

Aaron's beard	rose of Sharon, althaea
adder's tongue	dogtooth violet
abele	white poplar
abelmosk	musk mallow
althaea	Aaron's beard
amaryllis	belladonna lily
antirrhinum	snapdragon
aquilegia	columbine
arum lily	calla lily
Australian sword lily	kangaroo paw
autumn crocus	meadow saffron
baby's breath	gypsophila
baobab	monkey bread tree
bayberry	wax myrtle
bergenia	elephant's ear
belladonna lily	amaryllis
belladonna	deadly nightshade, dwale
bluebell	wild hyacinth
bog myrtle	sweet gale
bo tree	peepul
bogbean	buckbean
buckbean	bogbean
burning bush	Fraxinella
calla lily	arum lily
cardinal flower	scarlet lobelia
carnation	gillyflower
catmint	catnip
catnip	catmint
charlock	field mustard
checkerberry	wintergreen
Chile pine	monkey puzzle
Chinese eddo	elephant's ear
chionodoxa	glory-of-the-snow
chlorophytum	spider plant
clematis	traveller's joy
columbine	aquilegia
cow parsley	Queen Anne's lace
cowbane	water hemlock
cowslip	marsh marigold (USA)
cranberry	fen-berry
creeping myrtle	periwinkle
cuckoo flower	ragged Robin, lady's smock
cuckoo pint	jack-in-the-pulpit, lords and ladies, wake-Robin
dasheen	elephant's ear
deadly nightshade	belladonna
delphinium	larkspur
dittany	Fraxinella
dogtooth violet	adder's tongue
dwale	belladonna
eddo	elephant's ear
eglantine	sweet brier
elephant's ear	bergenia, Chinese eddo, eddo, dasheen, taro
fen-berry	cranberry
field mustard	charlock
fleur-de-lis	iris
fraxinella	dittany, burning bush, gas plant
French lilac	goat's-rue (Eurasian plant)
gas plant	fraxinella
gillyflower	carnation
ginkgo	maidenhair tree

gladiolus
glory-of-the-snow
goatsbeard (Eurasian plant)

goat's-rue (Eurasian plant)
golden chain
guaiacum
guelder Rose
gumbo
gypsophilia
hawthorn

heartsease
Indian cress
iris
Jack-go-to-bed-at-noon

Jack-in-the-pulpit
Japanese quince
japonica

Johnny-jump-up (USA)
kangaroo paw

kidney vetch
kingcup
laburnum
ladies' fingers
lady's finger
lad's love
lady's smock
larkspur
lignum vitae
lime tree
linden tree
livelong
lords and ladies
love-in-idleness
lungwort
maidenhair tree
mandrake
marsh marigold
marsh marigold (USA)
may
may apple
mayflower
meadow saffron

moneywort
monkey bread tree
monkey puzzle
mountain ash

sword lily
chionodoxa
Jack-go-to-bed-
  at-noon
French lilac
laburnum
lignum vitae
snowball tree
okra
baby's breath
may
quickthorn
whitethorn
Johnny-jump-up
  (USA)
love-in-idleness
wild pansy
nasturtium
fleur-de-lis
goatsbeard
  (Eurasian plant)
cuckoo pint
japonica
Japanese
  quince
heartsease
Australian sword
  lily
lady's finger
marsh marigold
golden chain
okra
kidney vetch
southernwood
cuckoo flower
delphinium
guaiacum
linden tree
lime tree
orpin(e)
cuckoo pint
heartsease
oyster-plant
ginkgo
may apple
kingcup
cowslip
hawthorn
mandrake
trailing arbutus
autumn crocus
naked ladies
naked boys
wandering sailor
baobab
Chile pine
rowan

musk mallow
naked boys
naked ladies
nasturtium
okra

old man's beard
orpin(e)
oyster-plant

pandanus
peepul
periwinkle

pink azalea
pinkster flower
Queen Anne's lace
quickthorn
ragged Robin
Rose of Sharon

rowan
salsify

scarlet lobelia
screw – pine
snapdragon
snowball tree
southernwood
spider plant
sweet brier
sweet gale
sword lily
taro
trailing arbutus
trailing myrtle
traveller's joy
vegetable oyster
Virginia creeper
wake-Robin
wandering sailor
water hemlock
wax myrtle
white poplar
whitethorn
wild Honeysuckle
wild hyacinth
wild pansy
winter cress
wintergreen
woodbine

woodbine (USA)
yellow rocket

abelmosk
meadow saffron
meadow saffron
Indian cress
gumbo
ladies' fingers
traveller's joy
livelong
lungwort
salsify
screw-pine
bo tree
creeping myrtle
trailing myrtle
pinkster flower
pink azalea
cow parsley
hawthorn
cuckoo flower
Aaron's beard
althaea
mountain ash
oyster-plant
vegetable oyster
cardinal flower
pandanus
antirrhinum
guelder rose
lad's love
chlorophytum
eglantine
bog myrtle
gladiolus
elephant's ear
mayflower
periwinkle
clematis
salsify
woodbine (USA)
cuckoo pint
moneywort
cowbane
bayberry
abele
hawthorn
woodbine
bluebell
heartsease
yellow rocket
checkerberry
wild
  honeysuckle
Virginia creeper
winter cress

N
A
T
U
R
E

NB: All the alternatives have been listed alphabetically for ease of reference.

Birds: Miscellaneous Information

altricial of a young bird or animal requiring care and feeding by the parents after hatching or birth

arctic tern: migrates to Antarctica

backwards-flying the hummingbird is the only bird that can fly backwards

beaks: characteristics insect eating birds usually have pointed bills while carnivorous birds have hooked bills

bird: smallest bee hummingbird

bird of paradise: from New Guinea and nearby islands (birds of paradise hang upside down)

bird of prey: largest Andean condor

bird of prey: largest UK golden eagle

British bird: biggest mute swan

British bird: fastest runner pheasant (up to 21 mph)

British bird: highest flier whooper swans on migration have been sighted at 27,000 feet

British bird: largest egg mute swan

British bird: longest-lived Manx shearwater (29.82 years)

British bird: most common wren

British bird: smallest goldcrest

British bird: smallest egg goldcrest

British Isles: exclusive to red grouse and Scottish crossbill do not migrate and are found only in the UK

carinate of a bird having a keeled breastbone; opposite of ratite

deepest diving bird emperor penguin

drops bones on rocks to break the bearded vulture (lammergeyer)

ducks: sex that quacks only females

egg: smallest hummingbird

extinct birds dodo lived on the island of Mauritius and became extinct in the late 17th century; great auk or Atlantic pigeon became extinct in the mid-19th century; moa of New Zealand became totally extinct by early 19th century

falconry breeding and training of hawks for sporting purposes. The female is called a falcon, the male is a tiercel

fastest bird peregrine falcon has been timed at 217 mph during swoop as part of the courtship display. The golden eagle has reached speeds exceeding 150 mph during a vertical dive, but the fastest bird in level flight, with recorded speeds exceeding 110 mph, is the Alpine swift

fastest runner ostrich

first known bird archaeopteryx (name means 'ancient wing')

gizzard muscular thick-walled part of a bird's stomach, used for grinding food, usually with the help of grit

grallatorial of or relating to long-legged wading birds e.g. flamingos and storks (from Latin *grallator*, 'stiltwalker')

guano excrement of seabirds found on islands off South America, Africa and the West Indies and used as manure

hangs upside down birds of paradise of Papua New Guinea frequently adopt this position

largest birds ostrich is clearly the largest living bird (moas extinct); the largest flying bird is more contentious but is possibly the kori bustard of sub-Saharan Africa

longest migration Arctic tern (11,222 miles from Anglesey to Australia)

nests at end of riverbank tunnels kingfisher

nests in water crested grebe

New World: definition term used to differentiate between the time before and after the Americas were discovered. New World relates to the Americas: the western hemisphere

nostrils at tip of beak kiwi

Old World: definition term used to differentiate between the time before and after the Americas were discovered. The Old World consists of Europe, Asia and Africa: the eastern hemisphere

owl: smallest elf owl

painter of USA birds John Audubon

palmiped web-footed bird

ratite of a bird having a keelless breastbone and therefore unable to fly; opposite of carinate

sacred birds quetzal (Aztecs), ibis (Egyptians)

seabird: largest emperor penguin

smells when excited the hoopoe raises its crest when excited and emits a foul-smelling liquid

smell: keenest sense of kiwi

snail shells: breaks with stone thrush

sonar-equipped the guacharo, or oilbird, is capable of flying in total darkness in a similar way to bats

steals food in flight skua often steals food from other birds whilst in flight

strigiformes order of birds that solely include owls

underwater: longest emperor penguin (up to 18 minutes)

underwater: walks dipper

web-footed bird: smallest petrel

white stork: UK breeding in 1416 a nest was found on St Giles Cathedral, Edinburgh, the only known UK breeding occurrence

wingspan: longest albatross, although the largest wings belong to the Andean condor

Birds

alcid bird of the auk famil, Sp.: *Alcidae*.

Andean condor world's largest bird of prey with a wingspan of 3 meters and body weight of up to 15 kilograms., Sp.: *Vultur gryphus*.

avadavat: green and red South Asian waxbills (aka amadavat). Sp.: *Amandava formosa* and *Amandava amandava*.

avocet white bird with black-patterned head and back; its most notable feature is the upcurved bill. Sp.: *Recurvirostra avosetta*.

bateleur short-tailed African eagle. Sp.: *Terathopius ecaudatus*.

bean goose similar to the pink-footed goose but distinguished by its orange bill and feet. Sp.: *Anser fabalis*.

bee-eater exotic European bird with yellow throat and multi-coloured plumage. Sp.: *Merops apiaster*.

bittern bird of the heron family with a brown and buff plumage barred with black, and famous for its booming call. Sp.: *Botaurus stellaris*.

black grouse spectacular bird with a lyre-shaped tail, the cocks having black plumage and the hens, grey. The black grouse is famous for its courtship display during the mating season. Sp.: *Lyrurus tetrix*.

blackbird black bird of the thrush family having a yellow beak, the female having a dark brown plume. Sp.: *Turdus merula*.

blackcap small songbird, nicknamed 'the monk' in Germany because of its grey plumage and distinct black cap. Sp.: *Sylvia atricapilla*.

bobolink North American oriole originally called Bob o' Lincoln. Sp.: *Dolichonyx oryzivorus*.

boobook brown spotted owl, native to Australia and New Zealand. Sp.: *Ninox novaeseelandiae*.

booby tropical marine bird, similar to a gannet, with a straight, stout bill and white plumage with darker markings. Gen.: *Sula*.

bowerbird bird native to Australia and New Guinea; the males construct elaborate bowers of feathers, grasses and shells. Family *Ptilonorhynchidae*.

budgerigar small, green parakeet native to Australia, bred in coloured varieties and often kept as cage birds. Sp.: *Melopsittacus undulatus*.

bulbul Asian or African songbird of dull plumage with contrasting bright patches. Family *Pycnonotidae*.

bullfinch small plump finch with black head, grey-blue back and red breast. Sp.: *Pyrrhula pyrrhula*.

bunting: corn. seed-eating bird related to the finches with a streaked, sparrow-like plumage. Sp.: *Emberiza calandra*.

bustard: great large, mainly terrestrial bird with long neck, long legs and stout tapering body. Sp.: *Otis tarda*.

buzzard predatory bird of the hawk family with broad wings, well adapted for soaring flight. Sp.: *Buteo buteo*.

capercaillie largest of the grouse family and extinct in Britain from the late 18th until mid-19th century. Sp.: *Tetrao urogallus*.

cassowary large, flightless bird of Australia and the Malay Archipelago, with heavy body, stout legs, a wattled neck and a bony crest on its forehead. Gen.: *Casuarius*.

chaffinch common European finch, the male of which has a blue-grey head with pinkish cheeks and breast. Sp.: *Fringilla coelebs*.

chough large black bird of the crow family, seen in Europe, Asia and Africa, with a long, downward-curving red bill and red legs. Sp.: *Pyrrhocorax pyrrhocorax*.

chukar red-legged Eurasian partridge. Sp.: *Alectoris chukar*.

collared turtle dove similar to the turtle dove but with a black half moon on the back of its neck, which gives rise to the name. Sp.: *Streptopelia decaocto*.

coot resembles an oversized moorhen, although the breast is grey-black and the beak is white rather than yellow and red. Sp.: *Fulica atra*.

cormorant diving seabird with lustrous black plumage. Sp.: *Phalacrocorax carbo*.

corncrake rail with a rasping call, inhabiting grassland and nesting on the ground. Sp.: *Crex crex*.

cotinga any member of the large and varied New World tropical family Cotingidae, many with vivid plumage and unuasally modified heel feathers.

cowbird North American oriole which often eats insects stirred up by grazing cattle and is known to lay its eggs in other birds' nests. Gen.: *Molothrus*.

crane long-legged, long-necked wading bird, which inhabits marshes and plains in most parts of the world except South America. Sp.: *Grus grus*.

crested lark often kept as a cage bird, not only for its own song but also for its ability to imitate the calls and cries of other birds. Sp.: *Galerida cristata*.

crossbill finch having a bill with crossed mandibles with which it opens pine cones. Gen.: *Loxia curvirostra*.

crow: carrion common predatory and scavenging European crow, similar to the rook but having a pure black bill. Sp.: *Corvus corone*.

crow: hooded highly intelligent bird with jet black and ashen grey plumage. Sp.: *Corvus cornix*.

cuckoo known as the harbinger of spring, the adult birds are slate blue-grey above, white underneath with dark grey barring. The cuckoo builds no nest of its own but parasitizes other birds by laying in their nests. Sp.: *Cuculus canorus*.

curlew bird with brownish plumage that is barred and patterned, and bill that is long and slightly curved downwards. Sp.: *Numenius arquata*.

demoiselle small crane native to Asia and North Africa Sp.: *Anthropoides virgo*.

dipper diving bird of mountain streams. Aka water ouzel. Gen.: *Cinclus*.

dotterel small migratory plover named from the ease with which it is caught (word supposedly signifying stupidity). Sp.: *Eudromias morinellus*.

dowitcher wading bird breeding in North America and related to sandpipers. Gen.: *Limnodromus*.

drongo any insect-eating bird of the family Dicruridae, possessing a long, forked tail, native to Asia, Africa and Australia.

duiker long-tailed cormorant. Sp.: *Phalacrocorax africanus*.

dunlin long-billed sandpiper. Sp.: *Calidris alpina*.

dunnock small European songbird with brown and grey plumage. Sp.: *Prunella modularis*.

eagle large bird of prey with keen vision and powerful flight. Family *Accipitridae*.

eider sea duck of which the female's brownish plumage is the source of eiderdown, while the male plumage is white and black.Sp.: *Somateria mollissima*.

emu Australian flightless bird, secound in size only to the ostrich, which it resembles, although the emu has three-toed feet as opposed to the ostriches two-toed. Sp.: *Dromains novachsllandiae*.

falcon any diurnal bird of prey of the family Falconidae, having long pointed wings and sometimes trained to hunt small game for sport.

fieldfare large Old World thrush having a pale grey head and rump, brown wings and back and a blackish tail. Sp.: *Turdus pilaris*.

finch any small seed-eating songbird of the family Fringillidae, including canaries, crossbills and chaffinches.

finch: zebra small Australian waxbill with black and white stripes on face, popular as a cage bird. Sp.: *Poephila guttata*.

frigate bird: magnificent seabird found in tropical seas, with a wide wingspan and deeply forked tail. Sp.: *Fregata magnificens*.

fulmar gull-like seabird, Britain's longest-lived bird, often reaching 40 years of age. Sp.: *Fulmarus glacialis*.

gadwall brownish-grey freshwater duck. Sp.: *Anas strepera*.

gannet   heavily built marine bird, a spectacular diver for fish, having a long stout bill and typically white plumage with dark markings. Sp.: *Sula bassana*.

garganey   small duck, the drake of which has a white stripe from the eye to the neck. Sp.: *Anas querquedula*.

gerfalcon (gyrfalcon)   large falcon of cold northern regions. Sp.: *Falco rusticolus*.

glaucous gull   large gull with typical brown and white speckled plumage, of Arctic coasts. Sp.: *Larus hyperboreus*.

go-away bird   any of several touracos of the genus *Corythaixoides*.

godwit   wading bird with long legs and a long, straight or slightly upcurved bill. Gen.: *Limosa*.

goldcrest   smallest British and European bird, usually growing to a maximum of about 9cm (3½in), with an olive green plumage and yellow or orange crest. Sp.: *Regulus regulus*.

golden eagle   large eagle with yellow-tipped head-feathers. Sp.: *Aquila chrysaetos*.

golden-eye   black-and-white diving duck of northern waters. Sp.: *Bucephala clangula*.

golden-eye   black-and-white diving duck, slightly larger than the above. Sp.: *Bucephala islandica*.

goldfinch   exotically coloured bird with an unusual tinkling, twittering song, often compared to little bells. Sp.: *Carduelis carduelis*.

goosander   large diving duck with a narrow serrated bill. Sp.: *Mergus merganser*.

goose   any of various large waterbirds of the family Anatidae, with short legs, webbed feet and a broad bill.

goose: barnacle   an Arctic goose which winters in northern Europe. Sp.: *Branta leucopsis*.

goose: Brent   small migratory Arctic-breeding goose with black, grey and white plumage. Sp.: *Branta bernicla*.

goose: Canada   wild goose with brownish-grey plumage and white cheeks and breast, native to northern America. Sp.: *Branta canadensis*.

goshawk   large, short-winged hawk often used in falconry. Sp.: *Accipiter gentilis*.

great crested grebe   large Old World grebe with a crest and ear-tufts. Sp.: *Podiceps cristatus*.

greenfinch   finch with green and yellow plumage. Sp.: *Carduelis chloris*.

greylag   goose native to Europe. Sp.: *Anser anser*.

grosbeak   Any of various finches and cardinals having stout conical bills and brightly coloured plumage. The largest species is the pine grosbea,. *Pinicola enucleator*.

guillemot   narrow-billed auk, nesting on cliffs or islands. Sp.: *Uria aalge*.

guinea fowl   African fowl with slate-coloured white-spotted plumage. Sp.: *Numida meleagris*.

hammerhead   heron-like African and Arabian marsh bird with a heavy black bill and an occipital crest. Sp.: *Scopus umbretta*.

harpy eagle   South American crested bird of prey, one of the largest of eagles. Sp.: *Harpia harpyja*.

harrier   any bird of prey of the genus *Circus* with long wings for swooping over the ground.

hawk   any of various diurnal birds of prey of the family Accipitridae, having a characteristic curved beak, rounded short wings and a long tail.

heron: grey   long-necked wading bird with a blue-grey plumage and yellow beak. Sp.: *Ardea cinerea*.

herring gull   becomes progressively greyer as it matures and also changes colour from winter to summer. Sp.: *Larus argentatus*.

hobby   small, long-winged falcon, which catches prey on the wing. Sp.: *Falco subbuteo*.

hoopoe   Eurasian bird whose crest is held erect at moments of excitement. Sp.: *Upupa epops*.

hornbill   tropical Old World bird with a horn-like excrescence on its large curved bill. Family Bucerotidae.

house martin   black and white swallow-like bird, which builds a mud nest under the eaves of houses. Sp.: *Delichon urbica*.

ibis   any wading bird of the family Threskiornithidae, with a long down-curved bill, long neck and long legs, and nesting in colonies.

Iceland gull   although many spend the winter in Iceland the Iceland gull breeds in Greenland and north Alaska. Sp.: *Larus glaucoides*.

jabiru   large black-necked stork of Central and South America, with mainly white plumage. Sp.: *Ephippiorhynchus mycteria*.

jacamar   small insect-eating bird with partly iridescent plumage, of the tropical South American family Galbulidae.

jacana   tropical wading bird with elongated toes and hind claws, which enable them to walk on floating leaves. Family Jacanidae.

jack snipe   small snipe often seen in marshy areas. Sp.: *Lymnocryptes minimus*.

jackdaw   small grey-headed crow often frequenting rooftops and nesting in tall buildings and noted for its inquisitiveness and magpie tendencies to thieve bright objects. Sp.: *Corvus monedula*.

Java sparrow   waxbill native to Java and Bali. Sp.: *Padda oryzivora*.

jay   brownish-pink bird of crow family, whose wings are decorated with flashes of blue. Sp.: *Garrulus glandarius*.

kaka   large New Zealand parrot with olive-brown plumage. Sp.: *Nestor meridionalis*.

kestrel   a resident of Great Britain and our most com-mon true falcon; often mistaken for a sparrowhawk, but is a hoverer rather than a glider and is far less ferocious. Sp.: *Falco tinnunculus*.

killdeer   large North American plover with a plaintive song. Sp.: *Charadrius vociferus*.

kingfisher   slightly larger than the house sparrow and brilliantly plumed, the kingfisher is a swift flying, swooping bird that feeds on insects and small fish. Sp.: *Alcedo atthis*.

kittiwake   small gull that nests on sea cliffs of the north Atlantic and Arctic oceans. Sp.: *Rissa tridactyla*.

kiwi   flightless New Zealand birds with hairlike feathers and a long bill, nesting in burrows. Gen.: *Apteryx*.

knot   small northern sandpiper with a short bill and grey plumage. Sp.: *Calidris canutus*.

lammergeier   large vulture of Africa, central Asia and southern Europe, with a very large wingspan and dark, beard-like feathers on either side of its beak. Sp.: *Gypaetus barbatus*.

lapwing   plover with black and white plumage, crest-ed head, and a shrill cry. Sp.: *Vanellus vanellus*.

lesser whitethroat   slightly smaller than its namesake and tends to be somewhat shyer. Sp.: *Sylvia curruca*.

limpkin   wading marsh bird of the Americas whose name derives from its limping gait. Aka courlan. Sp.: *Aramus guarauna*.

linnet small European songbird; grey-brown plumage with red forehead and breast in summer; famous for its wide range of singing voice. Sp.: *Acanthis cannabina.*

little auk small Arctic auk. Sp.: *Plautus alle.*

little grebe small waterbird of the grebe family. Sp.: *Tachybaptus ruficollis.*

lory any of various brightly coloured Australasian and South-east Asian parrots of the subfamily Loriinae.

lorikeet any of various small brightly coloured parrots of the subfamily Loriinae.

lovebird any of various African and Madagascan parrots. Gen.: *Agapornis.*

lyre-bird either of two Australian birds of the family Menuridae, the male of which has a lyre-shaped tail.

macaw any long-tailed, brightly coloured parrot of the genus *Ara* or *Anodorhynchus,* native to South and Central America.

magpie black and white plumed bird of the crow family, often regarded as a pest by farmers as it has thieving tendencies, especially for bright shiny objects. Sp.: *Pica pica.*

magpie lark Australian bird of the family Grallinidae, in particular a common long-legged black and white bird, Sp.: *Grallina cyanoleuca.*

mallard duck which is common over most of the northern hemisphere, the drake having a bottle green head and rufous markings. The mallard is thought to be the ancestor of all domestic breeds of duck. Sp.: *Anas platyrhynchos.*

mandarin duck originally from eastern Asia but introduced in many other regions; although the female has typical looks, the drake is exotically coloured. sp.: *Aix galericulata.*

Manx shearwater European oceanic bird with long slender wings and black and white plumage. Sp.: *Puffinus puffinus.*

marabou large West African stork whose down is used as a trimming for hats. Sp.: *Leptoptilos crumeniferus.*

meadow pipit common pipit native to Europe, Asia and Africa. Sp.: *Anthus pratensis.*

meadowlark North American songbirds with a yellow breast. Sp.: *Sturnella magna* and slightly smaller *Sturnella reglecta.*

merganser any of various diving fish-eating northern ducks of the genus *Mergus,* with a long narrow serrated hooked bill.

merlin small European or N. American falcon that hunts small birds. Sp.: *Falco columbarius.*

mistle (missel) thrush large thrush with a spotted breast that feeds on mistletoe berries. Sp.: *Turdus viscivous.*

mockingbird long-tailed songbirds of the American family Mimidae noted as mimics of other birds' calls. The common mokingbird of the eastern USA is *Mimus polyglottos.*

Montagu's harrier slender migratory Eurasian bird of prey named after George Montagu 1751–1815, a British naturalist. Sp.: *Circus pygargus.*

moorhen waterside bird having black plumage with blue-green breast and a white line along the flanks. Sp.: *Gallinula chloropus.*

Muscovy musk duck tropical American duck, having a small crest and red markings on its head. Sp.: *Cairina moschata.*

musk duck Australian duck, having a musky smell. Sp.: *Biziura lobata.*

mutton-bird various southern hemisphere birds of the genus *Puffinus,* especially the short-tailed shearwater. Sp.: *Puffinus tenuirostris.*

nightingale loud songbird with dark brown plumage and lighter underparts. Sp.: *Luscinia megarhynchos.*

nightjar nocturnal birds with a cryptic plumage and large eyes, which feed on insects. Sp.: *Caprimulgus.*

nutcracker forest-dwelling Old World bird of the crow family, having speckled plumage. Sp.: *Nucifraga caryocatactes.*

nuthatch small songbird that climbs up and down tree trunks and feeds on nuts and insects. Sp: Sitta europaea.

oriole: golden yellow-plumed Eurasian bird with black wings and red beak. Sp.: *Oriolus oriolus.*

osprey bird of prey with a dark back and whitish head and underparts praying on fish. Sp.: *Pandion haliaetus.*

ostrich world's largest living bird can weigh in excess of 180 kilograms and stand 2.5 meters high. The ostrich can attain running speed of 40 mph, which it can sustain for up to 30 minutes. The ostrich lays the largest egg, weighing up to 2 kilograms and measuring 15 centimeters in diameter. Sp.: *Struttiio camelus.*

ovenbird any Central or South American bird of the family Furnariidae, which build domed nests out of clay or tunnel underground to lay their eggs.

owl: barn type of owl that likes to nest in barns and other accessable rural buildings. Sp.: *Tyto alba.*

owl: eagle large Eurasian owl with long ear-tufts. Sp.: *Bubo bubo.*

owl: horned North American owl with hornlike feathers over the ears. Sp.: *Bubo virginianus.*

owl: little small owl of Africa and Eurasia, with speckled plumage. Sp.: *Athene noctua.*

owl: long-eared known for its peculiar barking cry, broken by 'yaps'; its long ears are in reality tufts of feathers. Sp.: *Asio otus.*

owl: tawny familiar owl with rich brown plumage, barred and checked with darker bars and streaks. Sp.: *Strix aluco.*

oystercatcher wading bird with black and white plumage and long laterally compressed orange-red bill. Sp.: *Haematopus ostralegus.*

partridge game bird with light grey plumage, barred and streaked with chestnut. Sp.: *Perdix perdix.*

penguin flightless seabird of the southern hemisphere with black upper parts and white underparts, and wings developed into scaly flippers for swimming underwater. Family Spheniscidae.

penguin: Adélie Most common species of penguin. Sp.: *Pygoscelis adeliae.*

penguin: emperor largest species of penguin, which can grow to a height of 120 cm (4 ft). Sp.: *Aptenodytes forsteri.*

penguin: fairy smallest species of penguin, average height of 41 cm (16 in). Aka little blue penguin. Sp.: *Eudyptula minor.*

penguin: Galápagos unlike the emperor and the Adélie, the Galápagos penguin is confined to the tropics of South America. Sp.: *Spheniscus mendiculus.*

penguin: gentoo abundant in the Falkland and other Atlantic islands. Sp.: *Pygoscelis papua.*

peregrine falcon powerful falcon, breeding on coastal cliffs and much used for falconry. Sp.: *Falco peregrinus.*

petrel small wave-hanging seabirds, blackish with a white rump. Family: Hydrobihdar.

NATURE

petrel: Wilson's common petrel that breeds around Antarctica but is often seen in the Atlantic. Sp.: *Oceanites oceanicus*.

phalarope any small wading bird or swimming bird of the family Phalaropodidae, with a straight bill and lobed feet.

pheasant game bird introduced to Britain from its native home in south-eastern Europe and central Asia; the cock birds show a wide colour variation, with brown and buff common specimens, although some almost black birds have been sighted in recent years. Sp.: *Phasianus colchicus*.

pipit: tree light brown plumed bird of the wagtail family. Sp.: *Anthus trivialis*.

plover: golden a wader noted for its musical but sad rising whistle, the golden plover is a golden speckled colour with a white or sometimes black underparts. Sp.: *Pluvialis apricaria*.

plover: ringed small chunky wader with brown plumage, white underparts and a black ring round the neck. Sp.: *Charadrius hiaticula*.

pochard familiar diving duck, the male having silvery plumage with chestnut head and black underparts whilst the females are silvery-brown. Sp.: *Aythya ferina*.

ptarmigan high mountain grouse whose grey-brown and black plumage changes to white in the winter. Sp.: *Lagopus mutus*.

puffin Britain's most recognizable seabird, with its large multicoloured bill and awkward movement; the main colonies are in north Scotland, the largest on St Kilda, west of the Outer Hebrides. Sp.: *Fratercula arctica*.

quail game bird, which looks like a miniature partridge although its plumage is a red-buff carrying streaks of cream and black. The quail is rarely sighted, due largely to its habit of taking refuge in grassland when spotted. Sp.: *Coturnix coturnix*.

quetzal spectacular tree bird of central America, a member of the trogon family, with green back and crimson and white under parts; the male's green tail plumes grow to 60 cm (2 feet). SP.: *Pharomachons mocinno*.

raven large passerine bird of the crow family, having a large,straight, black bill, long, wedge-shaped tail and black plumage. Sp.: *Corvus corax*.

razorbill common auk of the north Atlantic which typically nests in colonies on cliffs. Sp.: *Alca torda*.

red kite once a common scavenger in the streets during Elizabethan and the early Stuart period, this bird of prey gradually died out but has been reintroduced into England and Wales. Sp.: *Milvus milvus*.

redpoll soft striped brown plumed songbird of the finch family. Sp.: *Acanthis flammea*.

redstart similar in size and habit to the robin, with a grey plumage and black throat. Sp.: *Phoenicurus phoenicurus*.

redstart: black darker than its namesake but has similar feeding habits of taking insects, mainly on the wing. Sp.: *Phoenicurus ochruros*.

redwing small European thrush, having a speckled breast, reddish flanks and brown back. Sp.: *Turdus iliacus*.

rhea either of two large flightless birds of South Africa, *Rhea americana* and *Pterocieia pennara*, similar to ostrich but hairy, three-toed feet.

ring ouzel thrush with a white crescent across its breast. Sp.: *Turdus torquatus*.

robin well-loved bird with brown plumage and red breast with yellow throat. Sp.: *Erithacus rubecula*.

roller beautifully coloured migrant from Africa. The plumage shows a brown back, with blue wing coverts, greenish-blue head, blue undersurface and purplish tail and wings. Sp.: *Coracias garrulus*.

rook most common member of the crow family, notable for its jet black plumage and depredations among the eggs of smaller birds. Sp.: *Corvus frugilegus*.

ruff Eurasian member of the sandpiper family. The males' communal dancing display is called 'lekking'. The female is called a reeve. Sp.: *Philomachus pugnax*.

Sabine's gull fork-tailed seabird breeding on islets and marshy tundra in Arctic Greenland, Alaska and northern Siberia. Sp.: *Larus sabini*.

sanderling small busy sandpiper of the genus *Calidris* that frequents sandy shores. Sp.: *Calidris alba*.

sand martin slightly smaller than the house martin, with dark brown plumage and a brown band across its white breast. Sp.: *Riparia riparia*.

sandpiper various smallish members of the family Scolopacidae, walkers with long legs and long slender bills, which include the curtar, durilin and snipe.

shag very similar to the cormorant but smaller and darker green, no white marking on face and more of a crest. Sp.: *Phalacrocorax aristotelis*.

shoveler duck with spoon-shaped bill, a blue patch on each wing, and in the male a green head, white breast and reddish-brown body. Sp.: *Anas clypeata*.

shrike: red-backed chestnut-backed bird with grey head and rump and black ear coverts. Aka butcher bird. Sp.: *Lanius collurio*.

siskin small finch with brownish-green back with yellow shades and black cap. Sp.: *Carduelis spinus*.

skua: Arctic smaller member of this predatory seabird genus with dark plumage and a hooked bill, all of them famous for harassing terns or gulls into dropping or disgorging fish they have caught. Sp.: *Stercorarius parasiticus*.

skua: great heavy, broad-winged seabird with brown plumage and wings with white bar on wings. Sp.: *Stercorarius skua*.

skylark like the cuckoo, this ground-dwelling songbird is often thought of as a harbinger of spring; it has a dull brown plumage with white ribbing. Sp.: *Alauda arvensis*.

smew merganser of north Europe and Asia with white plumage with black markings. Sp.: *Mergus albellus*.

snipe bird of the sandpiper family inhabiting marshy areas. Collective noun is a 'wisp'. Sp.: *Gallinago gallinago*.

snow bunting bunting of northern and arctic regions having a white plumage with dark markings on the wings, back and tail. Sp.: *Plectrophenax nivalis*.

social weaver small gregarious Old World passerine songbird of the chiefly African family Ploceidae, having a short thick bill and a dull plumage. The name derives from the bird's characteristic of building covered nests in trees and living in communities of hundreds. Sp.: *Philetairus socius*.

song thrush song bird with brown plumage and white underparts speckled with brown; its repetitive refrain sounds rather like 'Come out, come out, come out'. Sp.: *Turdus philomelos*.

sparrowhawk fiercest of our native hawks, identified by its rapid flight with long gliding intervals and sudden swoops on prey. Sp.: *Accipiter nisus*.

sparrow: house small common brown and grey bird which nests in the eaves and roofs of houses. Sp.: *Passer domesticus.*

spoonbill wading bird of warm regions, having white plumage and a long, horizontally flattened bill. Sp.: *Platalea leucorodia.*

spotted flycatcher sparrow-sized grey-brown bird with a whitich breast, able to catch insects in flight. Sp.: *Muscicapa striata.*

starling distinctly coloured bird with black, iridescently green-tinged plumage, white flecks throughout its cover, and a yellow beak. Sp.: *Sturnus vulgaris.*

stock dove similar to the wood-pigeon but smaller. Sp.: *Columba oenas.*

storm(y) petrel small petrel of the north Atlantic, Europe's smallest seabird. Sp.: *Hydrobates pelagicus.*

swallow streamlined insect-hunter with a distinctive blue sheen on the back and wings, chestnut throat and white breast. Sp.: *Hirunda rustica.*

swan: Bewick's smallest swan, rarely seen in England outside the Slimbridge Wildfowl Trust and the Ouse Washes. Sp.: *Cygnus columbianus.*

swan: mute commonest Eurasian swan, having white plumage and an orange-red bill with a swollen black base. Sp.: *Cygnus olor.*

swan: trumpeter large North American wild swan. Sp.: *Cygnus buccinator.*

swan: whooper black bill with yellow nose, most of Britain's winter whoopers are from Iceland. Sp.: *Cygnus cygnus.*

swift fast-flying bird with dark brown plumage; it is a summer bird in Britain and spends its winters in Africa. Sp.: *Apus apus.*

teal smallest of Europe's wintering ducks, appearing like a smaller wigeon. Sp.: *Anas crecca.*

tern graceful, slender-winged seabird that dives headlong after small fish. Gen.: *Sterna.*

tern: Arctic greyer than the common or sandwich tern, can be seen at close hand on the Farne Islands. Sp.: *Sterna paradisaea.*

tern: common most familiar tern, with grey-white plumage, black cap and red bill. Sp.: *Sterna hirundo.*

tern: little small tern distinguished from other terns by its yellow bill. Sp.: *Sterna albifrons.*

tern: roseate rare bird with white plumage, black cap and extra long tail streamers. Sp.: *Sterna dougallii.*

tern: Sandwich largest of the terns found regularly in Britain, distinguished from other terns by its pale white plumage and black bill with yellow tip. Sp.: *Sterna sandvicensis.*

tit: bearded Eurasian songbird common in reed beds; it has a tawny back and tail and, in the male, a grey and black head. Sp.: *Panurus biarmicus.*

tit: blue gymnastic bird with bright blue cap and yellow underparts, often seen hanging upside down while hunting for food. Sp.: *Parus caeruleus.*

tit: crested chubby bird with dull brown plumage and white crest marked with black, in Britain restricted to the Scottish Highlands but more common on the Continent. Sp.: *Parus cristatus.*

tit: great Eurasian songbird with black-and-white head markings. Sp.: *Parus major.*

tit: long-tailed black and white plumed tit distinguished from other tits by its long tail. Sp.: *Aegithalos caudatus.*

tit: marsh grey-backed tit that inhabits woods and hedges. Sp.: *Parus palustris.*

tit: penduline southern European bird that derives its name from the hanging nest characteristic of the species. Sp.: *Remiz pendulinis.*

tit: willow Eurasian black-capped tit. Sp.: *Parus montanus.*

touraco (turaco) any brightly coloured crested arboreal African bird of the family Musophagidae.

tragopan tree-dwelling Asian pheasant; the male displays erect fleshy horns on its head. Gen.: *Tragopan.*

tree sparrow two distinct species. *Passer montanus* is a Eurasian sparrow inhabiting agricultural land. *Spizella arborea* is a North American sparrow-like bird of the bunting family, breeding on the edge of the tundra.

treecreeper small passerine songbirds of the family Certhiidae of the northern hemisphere, having a brown-and-white plumage and slender downward-curving bill. Named from their characteristic of creeping up trees to feed on insects. Gen.: *Certhia.*

turkey buzzard American vulture, unrelated to the Old World vultures, so called because of its bare reddish head and dark plumage. Sp.: *Cathartes aura.*

turtle dove small slim dove with thin neck, protruding round white head, deep chest and brownish-grey plumage with black marks. Sp.: *Streptopelia turtur.*

umbrella bird cotinga of tropical America, with a large, black, overhanging crest and a long feathered wattle. Gen.: *Cephalopterus.*

Victoria crowned pigeon large blue crested pigeon of New Guinea. Sp.: *Goura victoria.*

vulture any of various large birds of prey of the distinct Old and New World families Accipitridae and Cathartidae, with the head and neck more or less bare of feathers, feeding mainly on carrion and reputed to gather with others in anticipation of a death.

wagtail: white terrestrial bird, named from the up and down waggings of the tail at each halt that accompany its short darting rushes in a zigzag course. Sp.: *Motacilla alba alba.*

wandering albatross very large white albatross of southern oceans, having very long and narrow black-tipped wings. Sp.: *Diomedea exulans.*

warbler: barred arrives in Europe, from Africa, later than the other warblers and rarely visits Britain. Sp.: *Sylvia nisoria.*

warbler: Cetti's named after an 18th-century Italian Jesuit; it is the only European passerine with 10 tail feathers, rather than 12. Sp.: *Cettia cetti.*

warbler: Dartford until recently Britain's only resident warbler; it was first described from Bexley Heath, near Dartford in Kent, in 1773. Sp.: *Sylvia undata.*

warbler: great reed migrant bird seen frequently in the reed beds of East Anglia and the southern coast. Sp.: *Acrocephalus arundinaceus.*

warbler: icterine migratory warbler with brownish plumage and olive green underparts. Sp.: *Hippolais icterina.*

warbler: reed inconspicuous bird with overall brown colouring with lighter underparts. Sp.: *Acrocephalus scirpaceus.*

water ouzel see dipper.

water rail highly nervous and secretive bird, more often heard than seen; it hides in its reed-bed home at the slightest disturbance. Sp.: *Rallus aquaticus.*

wattlebird various Australian honeyeaters with a

NATURE

wattle hanging from each cheek. Gen.: *Anthochaera* and *Melidectes*. Also various New Zealand songbirds of the family Callaeidae, with wattles hanging from the base of the bill, e.g. the saddleback. Sp.: *Creadion carunculatus*.

waxbill any small finch-like bird of the family Estrildidae, with a red bill resembling sealing wax in colour.

waxwing any of three species of crested perching birds of the genus *Bombycilla*, with small tips like red sealing wax to some wing feathers.

weka large flightless New Zealand rail. Sp.: *Gallirallus australis*.

whale-headed stork grey African stork with a large bill shaped like a clog. Sp.: *Balaeniceps rex*.

wheatear small northern thrush having a grey back, black wings and tail, white rump and pale brown underparts. Sp.: *Oenanthe oenanthe*.

whimbrel small migratory curlew with a striped crown and trilling call. Sp.: *Numenius phaeopus*.

whinchat Old World songbird having mottled brown-and-white plumage with pale cream underparts; it is a member of the subfamily of thrushes. Sp.: *Saxicola rubetra*.

white stork widely protected in Europe, a pure white bird with black wing tips and long red beak and legs. Sp.: *Ciconia ciconia*.

Whitethroat warbler with greyish plumage, rusty wings and white underparts. Sp.: *Sylvia communis*.

wi(d)geon gregarious duck, the male of which has a reddish-brown head and chest, and grey and white back and wings. Sp.: *Anas penelope*.

woodchat shrike shrike of southern Europe, north Africa and the Middle East, having black and white plumage with a chestnut head. Sp.: *Lanius senator*.

woodcock any game bird of the genus *Scolopax* that inhabits woodlands. The common Eurasian species is *Scolopax rusticola*.

woodpecker any bird of the family Picidae that climbs and taps tree trunks in search of insects.

woodpecker: black largest of the European wood-peckers; the jet-black plumage is broken only by its red cap. Sp.: *Dryocopus martius*.

woodpecker: great spotted black and white plumage with a large red patch on the nape of the neck (male only); noted for its repeated drumming on the trunks of trees. Sp.: *Dendrocopos major*.

woodpecker: green large green and yellow European woodpecker with a red crown. Sp.: *Picus viridis*.

woodpecker: pileated large North American wood-pecker with a red-topped head. Sp.: *Dryocopus pileatus*.

wood pigeon large pigeon, having white patches like a ring round its neck. Sp.: *Columba palumbus*.

wren small light brown bird famous for its building of more than one nest, the hen making her choice and the 'spares' used as roosting spots in bad weather. Sp.: *Troglodytes troglodytes*.

wryneck small bird of the woodpecker family, able to turn its head over its shoulder. Sp.: *Jynx torquilla*.

yellowhammer bunting of which the male has a yellow head, neck and breast. Sp.: *Emberiza citrinella*.

yellowlegs: greater and lesser two migratory sand-pipers with yellow legs. Sp.: *Tringa melanoleuca* and *Tringa flavipes*.

Alternative or Poetic Names of Birds

adjutant bird	stork	fish hawk	osprey
aepyornis	elephant bird	(North America)	
apteryx	kiwi	frigate bird	man-of-war bird
ash-coloured falcon	Montagu's harrier	goatsucker	nightjar
barn owl	yellow owl	goldcrest	woodcock pilot
	white owl		golden-crested wren
bearded tit	reedling	golden-crested wren	goldcrest
blackbird	merle	gowk	cuckoo
blackcap	monk	grackle	crow blackbird
black guillemot	puffinet	great grey shrike	white whisky john
blue tit	tinnock	great skua	bonxie
	tom tit	green cormorant	shag
bonxie	great skua	greenfinch	green linnet
	skua	green linnet	greenfinch
bullbat	nighthawk	green plover	lapwing
bullfinch	nope	green woodpecker	yaffle
butcher bird	shrike (esp. red-backed)	halcyon	kingfisher
chaffinch	sheld apple	hedge sparrow	dunnock
corncrake	land rail	horned grebe	Slavonian grebe
crow blackbird	grackle	kestrel	windhover
cuckoo	gowk	kingfisher	halcyon
cushat	wood pigeon	kiwi	apteryx
	ring dove	kotuku	white heron
dabchick	little grebe	land rail	corncrake
dipper	water crake	lapwing	peewit (pewit)
dunnock	hedge sparrow		green plover
elephant bird	aepyornis	lark	laverock

laverock	lark	sheld apple	chaffinch
little grebe	dabchick	shrike	butcher bird (esp. red-backed)
man-of-war bird	frigate bird	shoebill	whale-headed stork
mavis	song thrush	skua	bonxie
merganser	sawbill	Slavonian grebe	horned grebe
merle	blackbird	smew	white nun
mock nightingale	sedge warbler	song thrush	mavis
monk	blackcap		throstle
Montagu's harrier	ash-coloured falcon	stork	adjutant bird
moorhen	water hen	storm petrel	Mother Carey's chicken
mosquito hawk	nighthawk		witch
Mother Carey's chicken	storm petrel	tawny owl	wood owl
		throstle	song thrush
mountain Linnet	twite	tinnock	blue tit
nighthawk	bullbat	tit lark	pipit
	mosquito hawk	tom tit	blue tit
nightingale	philomel	turkey buzzard	turkey vulture
nightjar	goatsucker (North America)	turkey vulture	turkey buzzard
nope	bullfinch	twite	mountain linnet
osprey	fish hawk	water crake	dipper
peewit (pewit)	lapwing	water hen	moorhen
philomel	nightingale	whale-headed stork	shoebill
pipit	tit lark	white heron	kotuku
puffin	sea parrot	white nun	smew
puffinet	black guillemot	white owl	barn owl
reedling	bearded tit	white whisky john	great grey shrike
ring dove	cushat	windhover	kestrel
robin	ruddock	witch	storm petrel
ruddock	robin	woodcock pilot	goldcrest
sawbill	merganser	wood owl	tawny owl
Scotch nightingale	sedge warbler	wood pigeon	cushat
sea parrot	puffin	yaffle	green woodpecker
sedge warbler	Scotch nightingale	yellow bunting	yellowhammer
	mock nightingale	yellowhammer	yellow bunting
shag	green cormorant	yellow owl	barn owl

NB: For ease of reference, the alternatives have been listed alphabetically.

Collective Nouns

BY GROUPS

actors cast, company, troupe
aeroplanes flight, squadron, wing
angels host
antelopes herd
ants colony, army
apes shrewdness
arms pile
arrows sheaf, quiver
asparagus bundle
asses pace
badgers cete
barley crop
barracuda battery
baseball team
bass fleet
bears sleuth, sloth
beaters squad
beauties galaxy
beavers colony
bees swarm, grist

bells peal
birds flock
bishops bench
bitterns sedge, siege
bloodhounds sute
boars sounder
books library
bowls set
boy scouts jamboree
boys blush
bread batch, caste
bucks brace, leash
budgerigars chatter
butlers draught
camels caravan, flock
capercaillie tok
capitalists syndicate
cards pack, deck
cars fleet
cats clowder
cattle herd, drove
chickens brood

children class
chocolates box
choughs chattering
cigarettes packet
clams bed
clergy assemblage, convocation
clothes outfit
colts rag
coots covert
corn sheaf
cranes sedge, siege
cricket team eleven
crockery service
crows murder
cubs litter
curlews herd
dancers troupe
deer herd
dogs show, kennel
donkeys drove
dottrel trip

ducks (in flight)
flush, pump, team
ducks (on ground)
badelynge
ducks (in water) paddling
dunlins flight
eagles convocation
eels swarm
eggs clutch
elk gang
falcons cast
ferrets fesnyng, business
finches charm
firewood bundle
fish shoal
flamingos flurry, regiment
flies swarm
flowers bunch, bouquet, nosegay, posy
foresters stalk

foxes skulk, earth
frogs army, colony
fruit orchard
geese (in flight) skein
geese (on ground) gaggle
girls bevy
gnats swarm, cloud
goats herd, tribe, trip
goldfinches charm
goldfish troubling
golf-clubs set
grapes bunch, cluster
grass tuft
grouse (several broods) pack
grouse (single brood) covey
guardians board
guillemots bazaar
gulls colony
guns battery, park
hares down, husk
harpists melody
hawks cast
hay truss
hedgehogs array
hermits observance
herons sedge, siege
hooligans gang
horses haras
hounds pack, mute
hunters blast
hunting dogs cry
ibis crowd
islands archipelago, chain
jellyfish smuck
kangaroos troop
kittens kindle
knaves rayful

labourers gang
lapwings deceit
larks exaltation
leopards leap
lions pride
magistrates bench
magpies tiding, tittering
majors morbidity
mallards flush
mares stud
martens richesse
mice nest
minstrels troupe
moles labour
monkeys troop
mules barren
music library
musicians band, orchestra
nightingales watch
onions rope
owls parliament
oxbirds fling
oxen yoke, team
papers budget
parrots company
partridges covey
passenger pigeons roost
peacocks muster
pearls string, rope
peas pod
penguins rookery, colony
people assembly, clique, audience, community
pheasants nye
pictures exhibition
pigs litter, drove
plovers congregation, wing

plums basket
pochards rush
polecats chine
police posse. detachment
politicians caucus
porpoises school
poultry run
pups litter
quail bevy
rabbits nest
race horses string
rags bundle
ravens unkindness
rhinoceros crash
roes bevy
rooks clamour, building
ruffs hill
runners field
sailors crew, watch
sails outfit
saints community
sandpipers fling
sardines family
savages horde
seals herd, pod
sergeants subtiltie
servants staff
sheep flock
sheldrakes dopping
ships fleet, flotilla
slaves gang
smelt quantity
snakes den, pit
snipe wisp, walk
soldiers detachment
spiders cluster, clutter
stamps collection
starlings murmuration
stars cluster, constellation

steps flight
sticks faggot
strawberries punnet
subalterns simplicity
swans herd, bevy
swifts flock
swine sounder, drift, dryet
swine (tame) doylt
teals spring
thieves gang
thrush mutation
tigers ambush
toads knot, knab
trees clump, orchard, spinney, thicket
troops brigade, division
trout hover
turkeys rafter
turtles bale, dole
turtle doves pitying
wasps nest
whales school, pod, gam
whelps litter
whiskey case
whiting pod
wigeon company
wild cats dout
wildfowl plump, sord, sute
wine vintage
witches coven
wolves pack
women bevy
woodcock fall, plump
woodpeckers descent
worshippers congregation.

BY NAMES

ambush tigers
archipelago islands
army frogs, ants
array hedgehogs
assemblage clergy
assembly people
audience people
badelynge ducks (on ground)
bale turtles
band musicians
barren mules
basket plums
batch bread
battery guns, barracuda
bazaar guillemots
bed clams
bench magistrates, bishops

bevy quail, girls, women, roes, swans
blast hunters
blush boys
board guardians
bouquet flowers
box chocolates
brace bucks
brigade troops
brood chickens
budget papers
building rooks
bunch grapes, flowers
bundle firewood, asparagus, rags
business ferrets
caravan camels
case whiskey

cast hawks, actors, falcons
caste bread
caucus politicians
cete badgers
chain islands
charm goldfinches
chatter budgerigars
chattering choughs
chine polecats
clamour rooks
class children
clique people
cloud gnats
clowder cats
clump trees
clutch eggs

clutter spiders
collection stamps
colony gulls, frogs, penguins, ants, beavers
community people, saints
company actors, wigeon, parrots
congregation plovers, worshippers
constellation stars
convocation eagles, clergy
coven witches
covert coots
covey partridges, grouse (single brood)
crew sailors
crash rhinoceros

crew sailors
crop barley
crowd ibis
cry hunting dog
deceit lapwings
deck cards
den snakes
descent woodpeckers
detachment soldiers, police
division troops
dole turtles
dopping sheldrakes
dout wild cats
down hares
doylt swine (tame)
draught butlers
drift swine
drove donkeys, cattle, pigs
dryet swine
earth foxes
eleven cricket team
exaltation larks quiver
exhibition pictures
faggot sticks
fall woodcock
family sardines
fesnyng ferrets
field runners
fleet cars, ships
flight dunlins, aeroplanes, steps
fling oxbirds, sandpipers
flock swifts, birds, sheep
flotilla ships
gaggle geese (on ground)
galaxy beauties
gam whales
gang labourers, hooligans,
   thieves, slaves, elk
gleam herring
grist bees
haras horses
herd deer, goats, cattle, curlews,
   antelopes, seals, swans
hill ruffs
horde savages
host angels
hover trout
husk hares
jamboree boy scouts
kennel dogs

kindle kittens
knab toads
knot toads
labour moles
leap leopards
leash bucks
library music, books
litter pups, whelps, pigs, cubs
melody harpists
morbidity majors
murder crows
murmuration starlings
muster peacocks
mutation thrush
mute hounds
nest mice, rabbits, wasps
nosegay flowers
nye pheasants
observance hermits
orchard fruit, trees
orchestra musicians
outfit sails, clothes
pace asses
pack hounds, cards, wolves,
   grouse (several broods)
packet cigarettes
paddling ducks (in water)
park guns
parliament owls
peal bells
pile arms
pit snakes
pitying turtle doves
plump woodcock, wildfowl
pod peas, whiting, whales, seals
posse police
posy flowers
pride lions
pump ducks (in flight)
punnet strawberries
quantity smelt
quiver arrows
rafter turkeys
rag colts
rayful knaves
richesse martens
rookery penguins
roost passenger pigeons
rope onions, pearls
run poultry

rush pochards
school porpoises, whales
sedge cranes, bitterns, herons
service cockery
set golf-clubs, bowls
sheaf corn, arrows
shoal fish
show dogs
shrewdness apes
siege bitterns, cranes, herons
simplicity subalterns
skein geese (in flight)
skulk foxes
sleuth bears
sloth bears
smuck jellyfish
sord wildfowl
sounder swine, boars
spinney trees
spring teals
squad beaters
squadron aeroplanes
staff servants
stalk foresters
string race horses, pearls
stud mares
subtiltie sergeants
sute bloodhounds, wildfowl
swarm gnats, bees, flies
syndicate capitalists
team ducks (in flight), baseball,
   oxen
thicket trees
tiding magpies
tittering magpies
tok capercaillie
tribe goats
trip goats
troop kangaroos, monkeys
troubling goldfish
troupe minstrels, actors, dancers
truss hay
tuft grass
unkindness ravens
vintage wine
walk snipe
watch sailors, nightingales
wing aeroplanes, plovers
wisp snipe
yoke oxen

N
A
T
U
R
E

NEWSPAPERS

National Newspapers

Name	Location	Founded	Details
Belfast News Letter	Belfast	1737	Britain's oldest surviving daily newspaper
Courier	Dundee	1816	Founded as the *Dundee Courier and Argus*
Daily Courant	London	1702	First successful daily newspaper
Daily Express	London	1900	Founded by C. Arthur Pearson
Daily Herald	London	1911	Merged into the *Sun* in 1964
Daily Mail	London	1896	Founded by Alfred Harmsworth (Lord Northcliffe)
Daily Mirror	London	1903	Founded by Alfred Harmsworth (Lord Northcliffe)
Daily Sketch	London	1909	Merged into the *Daily Mail* in 1971
Daily Star	London	1978	Owned by United Newspapers (Express Group)
Daily Telegraph	London	1855	Amalgamated in 1937 with the *Morning Post*
European	London	1990	Founded by Robert Maxwell and sold on Thursdays
Evening Standard	London	1827	Part of the 'Mail' Group of Newspapers
Financial News	London	1884	Merged with *Financial Times* in 1945
Financial Times	London	1888	Adopted its pink paper in 1893
Guardian	London	1821	Founded as the *Manchester Guardian* and became a daily in 1855
Herald	Glasgow	1783	Founded as *Glasgow Advertiser*, changed name to *Glasgow Herald* 1802–1992
Independent	London	1986	Originally part of the Mirror Group and founded by three *Daily Telegraph* journalists
Independent on Sunday	London	1990	Originally part of the Mirror Group
Mail on Sunday	London	1982	Sister paper to the *Daily Mail*
News of the World	London	1843	Founded by John Browne Bell
Observer	London	1791	Founded by Irishman W.S. Bourne
People	London	1881	Founded to support the Conservative cause originally
Press and Journal	Aberdeen	1748	Founded by James Chalmers as *Aberdeen's Journal*
Scotland on Sunday	Edinburgh	1988	Sister paper to the *Scotsman*
Scotsman	Edinburgh	1817	First non-London newspaper to open an office in Fleet Street
Sun	London	1964	Founded in 1911 as the *Daily Herald*
Sunday Express	London	1918	Founded by Lord Beaverbrook
Sunday Mirror	London	1963	Founded by Harold Harmsworth as the *Sunday Pictorial* in 1915
Sunday Post	Glasgow	1914	Launched as the Post Sunday Special, it is the leading Scottish Sunday paper
Sunday Telegraph	London	1961	Sister paper to the *Daily Telegraph*
Sunday Times	London	1822	Launched as *The New Observer* and then *The Independent Observer* in 1821
Times	London	1785	Founded by John Walter
Today	London	1986	Founded by Eddie Shah

International Newspapers

(location and date founded)

ABC   Madrid   1905
Al-Akhbar   Cairo   1944
Apogevmatini   Athens   1952
Avriani   Athens   1980
Berlingske Tidende   Copenhagen   1749
Bild am Sonntag   Hamburg   1956
Boston American   Boston   1904
B.T.   Copenhagen   1916
Chicago Sun   Chicago   1941
Corriere della Sera   Milan   1876
Diario Popular   Lisbon   1942
Ethnos   Athens   1891
Evening Herald   Dublin   1891
Evening Press   Dublin   1954

Le Figaro   Paris   1828
L'Humanité   Paris   1904
Irish Independent   Dublin   1905
Irish Times   Dublin   1859
Izvestiya   Petrograd   1917
La Lanterne   Brussels   1944
La Libre   Brussels   1884
Il Messaggero   Rome   1878
Le Monde   Paris   1944
Morgunbladid   Reykavik   1913
Die Neue Zeitung   Munich   1945
Neue Zurcher Zeitung   Zurich   1789
New York Post   New York   1801
New York Times   New York   1851

New York World   New York   1860
L'Osservatore Romano   Vatican   1929
El Pais   Madrid   1976
Plain Dealer   Cleveland   1842
Politiken   Copenhagen   1884
Pravda   Moscow   1912
La Repubblica   Rome   1976
Le Soir   Brussels   1887
La Stampa   Turin   1867
Süddeutsche Zeitung   Munich   1945
Sunday Independent   Dublin   1905
Sunday Press   Dublin   1949

Sunday World Dublin 1973
Svenska Dagbladet Stockholm
  1884
Tagesspiegel Berlin 1945
Tägliche Rundschau Berlin
  1945

De Telegraaf Amsterdam 1893
Tribune Chicago 1847
La Vanguardia Barcelona 1881
Wall Street Journal New York
  1889

Washington Post Washington
  DC 1877
Die Welt Hamburg 1945
Ya Madrid 1935

Regional Newspapers

Name	Location	Name	Location	Name	Location
Argus	Brighton	Evening News	Bolton	News and Star	Carlisle
Burton Mail	Burton-on Trent		Cambridge	The News	Portsmouth
			Edinburgh	Northern Echo	Darlington
Chronicle	Bath		Manchester	Northamptonshire	Kettering
Chronicle and Echo	Northamptons		Norwich Scarborough	Evening Telegraph	
Courier and Advertiser	Dundee	Evening Post	Bristol Nottingham	Observer	Crawley
			Reading	Oxford Mail	Oxford
Citizen	Gloucester		Wigan	Paisley Daily Express	Glasgow
Daily Echo	Bournemouth	Evening Telegraph	Coventry		
Daily Examiner	Huddersfield		Derby	Post	Birmingham
Daily Mail	Hull		Dundee	Sentinel	Stoke
Daily Post	Liverpool		Grimsby	Shropshire Star	Telford
Daily Record	Glasgow		Peterborough	South Wales Evening Post	Swansea
Dorset Echo	Weymouth		Scunthorpe	Southern Daily Echo	Southampton
East Anglian Daily Times	Ipswich	Evening Times	Glasgow	Star	Sheffield
Eastern Daily Press	Norwich	Express and Echo	Exeter		Barnsley
		Express Star	Wolverhampton		Doncaster
Echo	Liverpool	The Gazette	Blackpool		
	Lincoln		South Shields	Telegraph	Belfast
	Sunderland	Gloucestershire Echo	Cheltenham	Telegraph and Argus	Bradford
Essex Chronicle	Chelmsford				
Evening Advertiser	Swindon	Greenock Telegraph	Dunfermline	Western Daily Press	Bristol
Evening Chronicle	Oldham	Heartland Evening News	Nuneaton	Western Mail	Cardiff
	Newcastle	Herald Express	Torquay	Western Morning News	Plymouth
Evening Courier	Halifax	Kent Today	Aylesford		
Evening Echo	Weymouth	The Journal	Newcastle	Yorkshire Evening Post	Leeds
	Basildon	Lancashire Evening Post	Preston	Yorkshire Post	Leeds
Evening Express	Aberdeen	Lancashire Evening Telegraph	Blackburn		
Evening Gazette	Colchester Middlesbrough	Mercury	Leicester		
Evening Herald	Plymouth				
Evening Mail	Birmingham				

Editors (as at May 2001)

Daily Mail Paul Dacre
Daily Mirror Piers Morgan
Daily Sport Jeff McGowan
Daily Star Peter Hill (previously Phil Walker)
Daily Telegraph Charles Moore
Evening Standard Max Hastings
Express Christopher Williams (previously Rosie Boycott)
Guardian Alan Rusbridger
Independent Simon Kelner (previously Andrew Marr)
Independent on Sunday Janet Street Porter (previously Kim Fletcher and before her Rosie Boycott)
Mail on Sunday Peter Wright (previously Jonathan Holborow)
Metro Timothy Jotishky

News of the World Rebekah Wade (previously Phil Hall)
Observer Roger Alton (previously Will Hatton, now Editor-in-Chief)
People Neil Wallis
Spectator Boris Johnson
Racing Post Alan Byrne
Sun David Yelland (previously Stuart Higgins)
Sunday Express Michael Pilgrim (previously Richard Addis)
Sunday Mirror Tina Weaver (previously Colin Myler)
Sunday Telegraph Dominic Lawson
Sunday Times John Witherow
Times Peter Stothard
Tribune Mark Seddon
Vogue Alexandra Shulman

Agony Aunts, Horoscopes, Crosswords

Agony Aunts

Virginia Ironside *Independent*
Jane O'Gorman *Daily Star*
Eve Pollard *Daily Mirror*
Deidre Sanders *Sun*
Kate Saunders *Express*
Miriam Stoppard *Daily Mirror*

Horoscopes

Jonathan Cainer *Daily Mirror*
Russell Grant *Daily Mirror*
Sally Kirkman *Daily Star*
Marjorie Orr *Express*
Mystic Meg *Sun*
Shelley von Strunckel *Evening Standard; Sunday Times*
Justin Toper *Daily Mirror*

Crosswords

Peter Watson *Daily Mail*
Aelred *Independent*
Aquila *Independent*
Araucaria *Guardian*
Azed *Observer*
Beelzebub *Sunday Independent*
Bunthorne *Guardian*
Columba *Independent*
Enigmatist *Guardian*
Gemini *Guardian*
Monk *Independent*
Pasquale *Guardian*
Phi *Independent*
Quixote *Sunday Independent*
Rufus *Guardian*
Spurios *Independent*

Newspaper Cartoons and Cartoonist(s)

Alisdair *Times* Pugh and Way
Andy Capp *Daily Mirror* and *Sunday Mirror* Reg Smythe
Augusta *Evening Standard* Angus McGill and Dominic Poelsma
Austin *Guardian* Austin
Badlands *Sun* Steve McGarry
Beau Peep *Daily Star* Kettle and Christine
Ben and Katie *Daily Star* Doug Baker and Roca
Bill Caldwell (cartoonist) *Daily Star*
Bogart *Daily Mail* Peter Plant
Bristow *Evening Standard* Frank Dickens
Clogger F.C. *Daily Star* Bill Caldwell
Colonel Blimp *Evening Standard* David Low
Dilbert *Daily Telegraph* and *Express* Scott Adams
Doonesbury *Guardian* Garry Trudeau
Dreadnoughts, The *Sun* Martin Fish
Faith, Hope and Sue *Express* Lisa Wild
Flook (1949–84) *Daily Mail* Trog (Wally Fawkes)
Fred Basset *Daily Mail* Alex Graham
Gambols *Express* Barry Appleby
Garfield *Evening Standard* and *Express* Jim Davis
Giles Daily and Sunday *Express* Carl Ronald Giles
Griffin *Express* Griffin
Hagar the Horrible *Sun* Chris Browne
Heath *Daily Telegraph* Heath
Hector Breeze *Express* Hector Breeze

Horace *Daily Mirror* Kettle and Christine
I Don't Believe It *Daily Mail* Dick Millington
If *Guardian* Steve Bell
Jane *Daily Mirror* Norman Pett (originally)
Judge Dredd of 2000 AD *Daily Star* Smith and Rennie
Kipper Williams (cartoonist) *Guardian*
Liberty Meadows *Express* Frank Cho
Livvy *Sun* Bob Maher
Mandy Capp *Daily Mirror* Carla Ostrer and Mahoney
Matt *Daily Telegraph* Matt
Modesty Blaise *Evening Standard* Peter O'Donnell
Peanuts *Daily Mail* Charles Schulz
Perishers *Daily Mirror* Bill Mevin and Maurice Dodd
Peter Brookes *Times* Peter Brookes
Psycops *Sun* Wilbur
Real Life *Daily Mirror* Johnston
Rupert Bear *Express* Mary Tourtel (1920–48)
Scorer *Daily Mirror* Gillatt and Tomlinson
Steve Bell (cartoonist) *Guardian*
Striker *Sun* Pete Marsh
The Stringalongs *Times* (originally) Mark Boxer
Teenage Mum *Daily Star* Graham Hey
Tim *Independent*
Weber Family *Guardian* Posy Simmonds
Wizard of Id *Evening Standard* Parker and Hart

General Information

Asahi Shimbun Japan's leading newspaper has been produced 'untouched by human hands' since 24 September 1980.
***Avanti*: famous editor** Benito Mussolini edited the Milan based socialist paper from 1912 to 1914. Mussolini subsequently founded the newspaper *Il Popolo d'Italia* in 1914.
***Boy's Own*: founded** in 1879 by the Religious Tract Society and ceased in 1967.

cartoon: first drawn by John Wesley Jarvis in 1814 for the Washington Federal Republican.
cartoon: first UK 'The Unknown Tongue' (printed in *Bell's New Weekly Messenger*) 8 Jan. 1832.
Children's Newspaper founded by Arthur Mee in 1919.
***Christian Science Monitor*: founder** Mary Baker Eddy in Boston 1908.
clock on *Times* Diary page always set on 4.30.

colour supplement: first four-page section of the *New York World* 19 November 1893.

colour supplement: first UK Sunday Times Colour Section (became Sunday Times Magazine) 4 February 1962.

comic strip: first *Yellow Kid* by R.F. Outcault (published in the *New York World* in 1896).

Corriere della Sera although this newspaper translates as 'Evening Courier', it is a morning daily newspaper.

crossword puzzle: first compiled by Liverpool-born Arthur Wynne (published in *New York World* Sunday 21 December 1913).

crossword puzzle: first UK *Sunday Express* 2 November 1924.

crossword puzzle: first *Times* 1 February 1930 and compiled by Adrian Bell (father of ex-MP Martin Bell).

crusader logo introduced on the *Express* by Lord Beaverbrook in 1930.

Daily Express **column: famous** 'By the Way' (J.B. Morton under the name of 'Beachcomber').

famous sale Max Aitken sold the Express group to Trafalgar House on 30 June 1977 (subsequently sold to United Newspapers 1985).

daily newspaper: first UK *The Perfect Diurnall* Feb. 1660 (*Daily Courant* of 1702 was first successful daily).

daily poem *Independent*.

Daily Sketch: **merger** in May 1971 the *Daily Sketch* merged into the *Daily Mail*.

Daily Telegraph **editor: former** W.F. (Bill) Deedes.

Daily Telegraph: news first published on front page 1969.

Daily Worker Communist newspaper founded in 1932. Name changed to *Morning Star* in 1966 but *Daily Worker* revived in 1992.

Der Spiegel the German news magazine was founded in 1947.

Edinburgh Gazette Scottish equivalent of the *London Gazette*, founded in 1699 and appearing twice a week.

Evening News: **merger** on 31 October 1980 the *Evening News* was merged into the *Evening Standard*.

evening newspaper: first *Dawks's News-Letter* (published in London) 23 June 1696.

famous columnists *Daily Mirror* political cartoonist Vicky and columnist Cassandra.

Foreign newspapers *El Pais* – Argentina, *Avanti* - Milan, *Exame* – Brazil, *Feral Tribune* – Croatia, *Hihon Keizai Shimbun* – Japan, *La Presse* – Quebec, *Moderna Tider* – Stockholm, *Qianshao* – Hong Kong.

founded as women's paper *Daily Mirror*.

Globe the British paper was suppressed in November 1915 for spreading false rumours about Lord Kitchener's resignation.

Good Housekeeping: **founded** the British magazine was founded in 1922, although the US version was founded much earlier.

Harijan: **founder** Mahatma Gandhi founded the Indian weekly publication in 1933.

Hearst, William Randolph: famous castle San Simeon, California.

Hearst: famous newspapers *Examiner* (1887 his first), *Morning Journal* (1895 later became *Journal-American*).

Hitler diaries extracts published by *Stern* magazine in May 1983 and considered authentic by historian Hugh Trevor-Roper, but later exposed as a fake produced by a dealer in Nazi memorabilia.

Independent: launched by Andreas Whittam-Smith and associates on 7 Oct. 1986 and subsequently acquired by a consortium led by Mirror Group Newspapers, 18 March 1994.

John Bull: **date commenced** 1906, although the character first appeared in 1712 in a pamphlet by John Arbuthnot (1667–1735).

The Liberator influential anti-slavery weekly newspaper of Abolitionist crusader William Lloyd Garrison between 1831 and 1865, published in Boston.

Life **magazine: first published** 1936 by Henry Luce, publisher of *Time*. *Life* magazine ceased on 29 December 1972 but was relaunched in October 1978.

Listener: **founded** by the BBC in 1929 and closed in January 1991.

London Daily News: **founded by** Robert Maxwell in February 1987 but it folded in July when the *Evening News* was temporarily relaunched.

London Gazette Government's bulletin in which official announcements are made. Founded in 1665 as the *Oxford Gazette* and appearing 4 times a week.

magazine: shortest title *Ms*, the American feminist magazine founded in 1972, may lay claim to that title.

Manchester Guardian: **renamed** In 1960 the *Manchester Guardian* was renamed *The Guardian*.

Marie-Claire: **founded** the French women's magazine was founded in 1954.

Messenger Group: launched by The free newspapers were launched by Eddie Shah in Warrington in 1983 and produced by non-union workers.

New Republic: **founded by** the American paper was founded by H.D. Croly in 1914.

New Society: **founded** the weekly sociology magazine was founded in 1962 and merged into the *New Statesman* in 1988.

newspaper: best-selling *News of the World* is Britain's largest-selling newspaper (approx 4.8 million).

newspaper: first *Acta Diurna* (Daily Events) dating from 59 BC and attributed to Julius Caesar.

newspaper: first surviving English *Weekly News* 1622 (Newspapers were printed before this date but none survive.)

New Statesman: **founded by** Beatrice and Sidney Webb in 1913 and aided by leading Fabians such as G.B. Shaw.

Now: **founder** the magazine was founded by James Goldsmith in September 1979 and ceased in March 1981.

page 3 girls: year started 1970.

People: **famous libel case** an article in 1909 alleged that chancellor David Lloyd George had committed adultery and had paid £20,000 to keep the case out of court.

Picture Post: **first published** 1938 and founded by Edward Hulton. It closed in 1957.

Playboy: **founded by** Hugh Hefner, December 1953.

Post: **launched by** Eddie Shah in November 1988 and folded after 33 issues.

Press Council: founded 1953 (replaced by the Press Complaints Commission 1 January 1991).

Private Eye: **founded** In February 1962 and saved from financial ruin by Peter Cook in April 1962.

Punch   first published in 1841 and ceased production on 8 Aril 1992. Aka *The London Charivari*.

Radio Times: **founded**   1923.

Radio Times: **first woman editor**   Sue Robinson.

Reader's Digest: **founded**   DeWitt Wallace and his wife Lila Acheson published the first issue in Greenwich Village, New York 5 February 1922.

Scottish Daily News: **founded**   launched by a workers' co-operative 5 May 1975 but closed in Oct. 1975 despite intervention by Robert Maxwell.

Sun: **founded**   15 September 1964 when the TUC sold its shares in the *Daily Herald*.

Sunday Correspondent: **launched**   on 17 September 1989 and closed in Nov. 1990.

Sunday Herald: **founded**   in 1915 and subsequently renamed the *Sunday Graphic*; closed down in 1960.

Tatler: founded by Richard Steele in 1709 and assisted by Joseph Addison until its closure in 1711. It was replaced by the non-political *Spectator* in 1711 but the name was revived in 1901 for an illustrated monthly magazine which is still published today.

Telegraph Group   moved from Fleet Street to Docklands in 1987 and printed in London and new site (1986) in Manchester.

Time **magazine: founded by**   Henry A. Luce and Briton Hadden in 1923.

Times: **previous name**   *Daily Universal Register* until 1788.

Times: nickname   *The Thunderer* (the nickname of Thomas Barnes, editor of the *Times* 1817–41).

Times: news first appeared on front page   3 May 1966.

Today: **date commenced**   launched by Eddie Shah 4 March 1986 as Britain's first full-colour, low-cost tabloid, its sales failed to achieve targets and it was subsequently sold to Tiny Rowland's Lonrho Co.

Wapping: exodus to   *Times*, *Sunday Times*, *Sun* and *News of the World* moved overnight to a new plant in Wapping 25 Jan. 1986.

yellow journalism   term coined to describe the sensationalistic reporting and frenzied promotional schemes adopted in the fierce circulation wars between William Randolph Hearst's *Journal* and Joseph Pulitzer's *World*.

Nobel Prize Winners

	Physics	Chemistry	Literature	Medicine	Peace	Economics
1901	Wilhelm Röntgen (Ger.) Discovery of X-rays	Jacobus van't Hoff (Neth.) Laws of chemical dynamics and osmotic pressure	René Sully-Prudhomme (Fr.) Poet	Emil von Behring (Ger.) Work on serum therapy Pioneer in immunology	Jean Henri Dunant (Switz.) Frédéric Passy (Fr.)	
1902	Hendrik Lorentz (Neth.) Pieter Zeeman (Neth.) Magnetism on radiation	Emil Fischer (Ger.) Work on sugar and purine syntheses	Theodor Mommsen (Ger.) Historian	Sir Ronald Ross (Brit.) Discovery of how malaria enters an organism	Elie Ducommun (Switz.) Charles Gobat (Switz.)	
1903	Antoine-Henri Becquerel (Fr.) Pierre and Marie Curie (Fr.) Radioactivity	Svante Arrhenius (Swed.) Theory of electrolytic dissociation	Björnsterne Björnson (Nor.) Novelist, poet, dramatist	Niels Finsen (Den.) Phototherapy	Sir William Cremer (Brit.) Founder of Workmen's Peace Association	
1904	Lord Rayleigh (Brit.) Discovery of argon	Sir William Ramsay (Brit.) Discovery of inert gases	Frédéric Mistral (Fr.) Poet J. Echegaray Eizaguirre (Sp.)	Ivan Pavlov (Russ.) Physiology of digestion	Institute of International Law (founded 1873)	
1905	Philipp Lenard (Ger.) Research on cathode rays	Adolf von Baeyer (Ger.) Work on organic dyes	H. Sienkiewicz (Pol.) Novelist	Robert Koch (Ger.) Tuberculosis research	Bertha von Suttner (Austria)	
1906	Sir J.J. Thomson (Brit.) Research into electrical conductivity of gases	Henri Moissan (Fr.) Isolation of fluorine Moissan furnace	Giosuè Carducci (Ita.) Poet	Camillo Golgi (Ita.) and S. Ramon y Cajal (Sp.) Structure of nervous system	Theodore Roosevelt (US)	
1907	A.A. Michelson (US) Spectroscopic and metrological investigations	Eduard Buchner (Ger.) Discovery of non-cellular fermentation	Rudyard Kipling (Brit.) Poet and novelist	Alphonse Laveran (Fr.) Discovery of the role of protozoa in diseases	Ernesto T. Moneta (Ita.) Louis Renault (Fr.)	
1908	Gabriel Lippman (Fr.) Photographic reproduction of colours	Lord Rutherford (Brit.) Disintegration of elements Chemistry of radioactivity	Rudolf Eucken (Ger.) Philosopher	Paul Ehrlich (Ger.) Ilya Mechnikov (Russ.) Work on immunity	Klas P. Arnoldson (Swed.) Fredrik Bajer (Den.)	
1909	Guglielmo Marconi (Ita.) Karl Braun (Ger.) Wireless telegraphy	Wilhelm Ostwald (Ger.) Pioneer work on catalysis, chemical equilibrium and reaction velocities	Selma Lagerlöf (Swed.) Novelist	Emil Kocher (Switz.) Physiology, pathology and surgery of thyroid gland	Baron d'Estournelles de Constant (Fr.) Auguste Beernaert (Belg.)	
1910	J. van Der Waals (Neth.) Gas and liquid equation	Otto Wallach (Ger.) Alicyclic combinations	Paul von Heyse (Ger.) Poet and novelist	Albrecht Kossel (Ger.) Cellular chemistry research	International Peace Bureau (founded 1891)	

	Physics	Chemistry	Literature	Medicine	Peace	Economics
1911	Wilhelm Wien (Ger.) Discoveries regarding laws governing heat radiation	Marie Curie (Fr.) Discovered/isolated radium Discovered Polonium	Maurice Maeterlinck (Belg.) Dramatist	Allvar Gullstrand (Swed.) Work on dioptrics of the eye	Tobias Asser (Neth.) Alfred Fried (Austria)	
1912	Nils Gustaf Dalén (Swed.) Invention of automatic regulators for lighting coastal beacons and light buoys	Victor Grignard (Fr.) Paul Sabatier (Fr.) Discovery of Grignard reagents and hydrogenating organic compounds	Gerhart Hauptmann (Ger.) Dramatist	Alexis Carrel (Fr.) Work on vascular suture Transplantation of organs	Elihu Root (US)	
1913	H. Kamerlingh Onnes (Neth.) Liquid helium production Low temperature properties	Alfred Werner (Switz.) Work on the linkage of atoms in molecules	Sir R. Tagore (India) Poet	Charles Richet (Fr.) Work on anaphylaxis	Henri Lafontaine (Belg.)	
1914	Max von Laue (Ger.) Discovery of diffraction of X-rays by crystals	Theodore Richards (US) Accurate determination of atomic weights of elements	no award	Robert Barany (Austria) Work on vestibular apparatus	no award	
1915	Sir William Bragg (Brit.) Sir Lawrence Bragg (Brit.) Analysis of crystals by means of X-rays	Richard Willstätter (Ger.) Pioneer researches on plant pigments, especially chlorophyll	Romain Rolland (Fr.) Novelist	no award	no award	
1916	no award	no award	V. von Heidenstam (Swed.) Poet	no award	no award	
1917	Charles Barkla (Brit.) Discovery of characteristic X-radiation of elements	no award	Karl Gjellerup (Den.) H. Pontoppidan (Den.) Novelists	no award	International Red Cross Committee (founded 1863)	
1918	Max Planck (Ger.) Elemental quantum theory	Fritz Haber (Ger.) Synthesis of ammonia	no award	no award	no award	
1919	Johannes Stark (Ger.) Doppler effect in positive ions and spectral line division	no award	Carl Spitteler (Switz.) Poet and novelist	Jules Bordet (Belg.) Discoveries in regard to immunity	Woodrow Wilson (US)	
1920	Charles Guillaume (Switz.) Discovery of anomalies in alloys	Walther Nernst (Ger.) Work in thermochemistry	Knut Hamsun (Nor.) Novelist	August Krogh (Den.) Discovery of capillary motor regulating mechanism	Léon Bourgeois (Fr.)	

	Physics	Chemistry	Literature	Medicine	Peace	Economics
1921	Albert Einstein (Switz.) Services to theoretical physics	Frederick Soddy (Brit.) Chemistry of radioactive substances and occurrence and nature of isotopes	Anatole France (Fr.) Novelist	no award	Karl Branting (Swed.) Christian Louis Lange (Nor.)	
1922	Niels Bohr (Den.) Investigation of atomic structure and radiation	Francis Aston (Brit.) Work with mass spectrograph	Jacinto Benavente y Martinez (Spa.) Dramatist	Archibald Hill (Brit.) Discovery relating to heat production in muscles	Fridtjof Nansen (Nor.)	
1923	Robert Millikan (US) Work on elementary electric charge	Fritz Pregl (Austria) Method of microanalysis of organic substances	W.B. Yeats (Ire.) Poet	Sir F.G. Banting (Can.) J.J.R. Macleod (Brit.) Discovery of insulin	no award	
1924	Karl Siegbahn (Swed.) Work in X-ray spectroscopy	no award	Wladyslaw Reymont (Pol.) Novelist	Willem Einthoven (Neth.) Discovery of electro-cardiogram mechanism	no award	
1925	James Franck (Ger.) Gustav Hertz (Ger.) Discovery of laws governing impact of electrons upon an atom	Richard Zsigmondy (Austria) Elucidation of hetero-geneous nature of colloidal solutions	George Bernard Shaw (Ire.) Dramatist	no award	Austen Chamberlain (Brit.) Charles G. Dawes (US)	
1926	Jean-Baptiste Perrin (Fr.) Work on discontinuous structure of matter	Theodor Svedberg (Swed.) Work on disperse systems	Grazia Deledda (Ita.) Novelist	Johannes Fibiger (Den.) Contributions to cancer research	Aristide Briand (Fr.) Gustav Stresemann (Ger.)	
1927	Arthur Holly Compton (US) Discovery of wave change in diffused X-rays Charles Wilson (Brit.) Visibility of electric particles	Heinrich Wieland (Ger.) Researches into the constitution of bile acids	Henri Bergson (Fr.) Philosopher	J. Wagner-Jauregg (Austria) Work on malaria inoculation in dementia paralytica	Ferdinand Buisson (Fr.) Ludwig Quidde (Ger.)	
1928	Owen Richardson (Brit.) Richardson's Law	Adolf Windaus (Ger.) Sterols + vitamin connection	Sigrid Undset (Nor.) Novelist	Charles Nicolle (Fr.) Work on typhus	no award	
1929	Louis de Broglie (Fr.) Discovery of the wave nature of electrons	Sir Arthur Harden (Brit.) H. von Euler-Chelpin (Swed.) Fermentation of sugars and connective enzymes	Thomas Mann (Ger.) Novelist	Christiaan Eijkman (Neth.) Antineuritic vitamin Sir F. Hopkins (Brit.) Growth stimulating vitamins	Frank B. Kellogg (US)	
1930	Sir C. Raman (India) Work on light diffusion	Hans Fischer (Ger.) Chlorophyll research	Sinclair Lewis (US) Novelist	Karl Landsteiner (US) Human blood grouping	Nathan Söderblom (Swed.)	

	Physics	Chemistry	Literature	Medicine	Peace	Economics
1931	no award	Karl Bosch (Ger.) Friedrich Bergius (Ger.) High pressure methods	Erik Axel Karlfeldt (Swed.) Poet	Otto Warburg (Ger.) Discovery of nature and action of respiratory enzyme	Jane Addams (US) Nicholas Murray Butler (US)	
1932	Werner Heisenberg (Ger.) Indeterminacy principle of quantum mechanics	Irving Langmuir (US) Discoveries in surface chemistry	John Galsworthy (Brit.) Novelist	Edgar D. Adrian (Brit.) Sir C. Sherrington (Brit.) Neuron investigations	no award	
1933	P.A.M. Dirac (Brit.) Erwin Schrödinger (Austria) Intro of wave equations in quantum mechanics	no award	Ivan Bunin (USSR) Novelist	Thomas Hunt Morgan (US) Heredity transmission functions of chromosomes	Sir Norman Angell (Brit.)	
1934	no award	Harold Urey (US) Discovery of heavy hydrogen	Luigi Pirandello (Ita.) Dramatist	George R. Minot (US) William P. Murphy (US) George H. Whipple (US) Anaemia treatments	Arthur Henderson (Brit.)	
1935	Sir James Chadwick (Brit.) Discovery of the neutron	Frédéric Joliot-Curie (Fr.) Irène Joliot-Curie (Fr.) Radioactive element theory	no award	Hans Spemann (Ger.) Organizer effect in embryo	Carl von Ossietzky (Ger.)	
1936	Victor Hess (Austria) Cosmic radiation discovery Carl Anderson (US) Positron discovery	Peter Debye (Neth.) Work on dipole moments and diffraction of X-rays and electrons in gases	Eugene O'Neill (US) Dramatist	Sir H.H. Dale (Brit.) Otto Loewi (Ger.) Work on chemical transmission of nerve impulses	Carlos S. Lamas (Arg.)	
1937	Clinton Davisson (US) George P. Thomson (Brit.) Interference phenomenon in crystals irradiated by electrons	Walter Haworth (Brit.) Research on carbohydrates and vitamin C Paul Karrer (Switz.) Research on Carotenoids	Roger Martin du Gard (Fr.) Novelist	Albert Szent-Györgyi (Hung.) Work on biological combustion	Viscount Cecil of Chelwood (Brit.)	
1938	Enrico Fermi (Ita.) Artificial radioactive element by neutron irradiation	Richard Kuhn (Ger.) Research on carotenoids (declined)	Pearl Buck (US) Novelist	Corneille Heymans (Belg.) Discovery of sinus role in respiration regulation	Nansen International Office for Refugees (founded 1931)	
1939	Ernest Lawrence (US) Invented cyclotron	Adolf Butenandt (Ger.) Work on sexual hormones (declined) Leopold Ružička (Switz.) Polymethylenes research	Frans Eemil Sillanpää (Fin.) Novelist	Gerhard Domagk (Ger.) Antibacterial effect of Prontosil (declined)	no award	

	Physics	Chemistry	Literature	Peace	Medicine	Economics
1940	no award	no award	no award	no award	no award	
1941	no award	no award	no award	no award	no award	
1942	no award	no award	no award	no award	no award	
1943	Otto Stern (US) Discovery of the magnetic moment of the proton	George de Hevesy (Hung.) Use of isotopes as tracers in chemical research	no award	no award	Henrik Dam (Den.) Discovery of vitamin K Edward A. Doisy (US) Chemical nature of vitamin K	
1944	Isidor Rabi (US) Resonance method for registration of magnetic properties of atomic nuclei	Otto Hahn (Ger.) Discovery of the fission of heavy nuclei	J.V. Jensen (Den.) Novelist	International Red Cross Committee (founded 1863)	Joseph Erlanger (US) Herbert S. Gasser (US) Research on differentiated functions of nerve fibres	
1945	Wolfgang Pauli (Austria) Discovery of the exclusion principle	Artturi Virtanen (Fin.) Invention of fodder preservation method	Gabriela Mistral (Chile) Poet	Cordell Hull (US)	Sir Alexander Fleming (Brit.) Ernst B. Chain (Brit.) Lord Florey (Aus.) Penicillin discovery	
1946	Percy Bridgman (US) Discoveries in the domain of high-pressure physics	James Sumner (US) Wendell Stanley (US) John Northrop (US) Enzyme research	Herman Hesse (Switz.) Novelist	Emily Greene Balch (US) John R. Mott (US)	Hermann J. Muller (US) Production of mutations by X-ray irradiation	
1947	Edward Appleton (Brit.) Discovery of Appleton layer in upper atmosphere	Robert Robinson (Brit.) Investigations on alkaloids and other plant products	Andre Gide (Fr.) Novelist and essayist	American Friends Service Committee (US) Friends Service Council (London)	Carl F. Cori (US) Gerty T. Cori (US) Bernardo Houssay (Arg.) Glycogen conversion	
1948	Patrick Blackett (Brit.) Discoveries in the domain of nuclear physics analysis; serum proteins	Arne Tiselius (Swed.) Researches on electrophoresis and adsorption	T.S. Eliot (Brit.) Poet and critic	no award	Paul Müller (Switz.) Properties of DDT	
1949	Yukawa Hideki (Jap.) Prediction of the existence of mesons	William Giauque (US) Behaviour of substances at extremely low temps	William Faulkner (US) Novelist	Lord Boyd-Orr (Brit.)	Walter Rudolf Hess (Switz.) Middle-brain function Antonio Egas Moniz (Port.) Leucotomy research	
1950	Cecil Powell (Brit.) Photographic method of studying nuclear processes; discoveries about mesons	Otto Diels (Ger.) Kurt Alder (Ger.) Discovery and development of diene synthesis	Bertrand Russell (Brit.) Philosopher	Ralph Bunche (US)	Philip S. Hench (US) Edward C. Kendall (US) Tadeus Reichstein (Switz.) Cortex hormones research	

	Physics	Chemistry	Literature	Medicine	Peace	Economics
1951	John Cockcroft (Brit.) Ernest Walton (Ire.) Atomic nuclei research	Edwin McMillan (US) Glenn Seaborg (US) Transuranium element work	Pär Lagerkvist (Swed.) Novelist	Max Theiler (SA) Yellow fever research	Léon Jouhaux (Fr.)	
1952	Felix Bloch (US) Edward Purcell (US) Discovery of nuclear magnetic resonance in solids	Archer Martin (Brit.) Richard Synge (Brit.) Development of partition chromatography	François Mauriac (Fr.) Poet, novelist, dramatist	Selman A. Waksman (US) Discovery of streptomycin	Albert Schweitzer (Alsace)	
1953	Frits Zernike (Neth.) Method of phase contrast microscopy	Hermann Staudinger (Ger.) Work on macromolecules	Winston Churchill (Brit.) Historian and orator	Fritz A. Lipman (US) H.A. Krebs (Brit.) Discovery of coenzyme A	George C.Marshall (US)	
1954	Max Born (Brit.) Wave functions studies Walther Bothe (Ger.) Coincidence method	Linus Pauling (US) Study of the nature of the chemical bond	Ernest Hemingway (US) Novelist	John F. Enders (US) Thomas H. Weller (US) Frederick Robbins (US) Polio virus in tissue culture	Office of the UN High Commisioner for Refugees (founded 1951)	
1955	Willis Lamb Jnr (US) Hydrogen spectrum study Polykarp Kusch (US) Magnetic electron study	Vincent du Vigneaud (US) First synthesis of a polypeptide hormone	Halidor Laxness (Ice.) Novelist	Axel Hugo Theorell (Swed.) Nature and mode of action of oxidation enzymes	no award	
1956	William Shockley (US) John Bardeen (US) Walter Brattain (US) Discovery of transistor effect	Nikolay Semyonov (USSR) Cyril Hinshelwood (Brit.) Work on the kinetics of chemical reactions	Juan Ramon Jimenez (Spa.) Poet	Werner Forssman (Ger.) Dickinson Richards (US) André F. Cournand (US) Heart catheterization	no award	
1957	Tsung-Dao Lee (China) Chen Ning Yang (China) Principle of parity research	Alexander Todd (Brit.) Work on nucleotides and nucleotide coenzymes	Albert Camus (Fr.) Novelist and dramatist	Daniel Bovet (Ita.) Production of curare	Lester B. Pearson (Can.)	
1958	Pavel A. Cherenkov (USSR) Ilya M. Frank (USSR) Igor Y. Tamm (USSR) Discovery and interpretation of Cherenkov effect	Frederick Sanger (Brit.) Determination of structure of the insulin molecule	Boris Pasternak (USSR) Novelist and poet (declined)	George W. Beadle (US) Edward L. Tatum (US) Joshua Lederberg (US) Research in genetics	Dominique G. Pire (Belg.)	
1959	Emilio Segrè (US) Owen Chamberlain (US) Antiproton research	Jaroslav Heyrovsky (Czech) Discovery + development of polarography	Salvatore Quasimodo (Ita.) Poet	Severo Ochoa (US) Arthur Kornberg (US) Nucleic acids research	Philip Noel-Baker (Brit.)	

	Physics	Chemistry	Literature	Medicine	Peace	Economics
1960	Donald Glaser (US) Development of the bubble chamber	Willard Libby (US) Development of radio-carbon dating	Saint-John Perse (Fr.) Poet	Macfarlane Burnet (Aus.) Peter B. Medawar (Brit.) Tissue transplant research	Albert Lutuli (SA)	
1961	Robert Hofstadter (US) Atomic nucleon research Rudolf Mössbauer (Ger.) Mössbauer effect	Melvin Calvin (US) Study of chemical steps that take place during photosynthesis	Ivo Andrić (Yug) Novelist	Georg von Békésy (US) Functions of the inner ear	Dag Hammarskjöld (Swed.)	
1962	Lev D. Landau (USSR) Research into condensed state of matter	John C. Kendrew (Brit.) Max F. Perutz (Brit.) Hemoprotein research	John Steinbeck (US) Novelist	Francis H.C. Crick (Brit.) James D. Watson (US) Maurice Wilkins (Brit.) DNA molecular structure	Linus Pauling (US)	
1963	J.H.D. Jensen (Ger.) Maria Goeppert Mayer (US) Eugene Paul Wigner (US) Atomic nuclei research	Giulio Natta (Ita.) Karl Ziegler (Ger.) Research into polymers in the field of plastics	George Seferis (Gre.) Poet	Sir John Eccles (Aus.) Alan Lloyd Hodgkin (Brit.) Andrew Huxley (Brit.) Nerve fibre research	International Red Cross and League of Red Cross (HQ of both in Geneva)	
1964	Charles H.Townes (US) Nikolay G.Basov (USSR) Aleksandr Prokhorov (USSR) Maser/laser research	Dorothy Hodgkin (Brit.) Determining the structure of biochemical compounds used to control pernicious anaemia	Jean-Paul Sartre (Fr.) Philosopher and dramatist (declined)	Konrad Bloch (US) Feodor Lynen (Ger.) Cholesterol research	Martin Luther King Jr (US)	
1965	Julian Schwinger (US) Richard Feynman (US) Tomonaga Shin'ichiro (Jap.) Quantum electrodynamics	Robert B. Woodward (US) Synthesis of chlorophyll	Mikhail Sholokhov (USSR) Novelist	François Jacob (Fr.) Jacques Monod (Fr.) André Lwolf (Fr.) Body cells research	UN Children's Fund (founded 1946)	
1966	Alfred Kastler (Fr.) Optical methods for studying Hertzian resonances in atoms	Robert S. Mulliken (US) Research into electronic structure of molecules	Shmuel Yosef Agnon (Isr.) Nelly Sachs (Swed.) Novelist and poet	Charles B. Huggins (US) Francis Peyton Rous (US) Cancer research	no award	
1967	Hans A. Bethe (US) Discoveries concerning the energy production of stars	Manfred Eigen (Ger.) Ronald G.W. Norrish (Brit.) George Porter (Brit.) Chemical reaction research	Miguel Angel Asturias (Guat.) Novelist	Haldan Keffer Hartline (US) George Wald (US) Ragnar A. Granit (Swed.) Eye research	no award	
1968	Luis W. Alvarez (US) Discovered resonance states	Lars Onsager (US) Work on theory of thermodynamics of irreversible processes	Kawabata Yasunari (Jap.) Novelist	Robert W. Holley (US) H. Gobind Khorana (US) Marshall Nirenberg (US) Genetic code deciphering	Rene Cassin (Fr.)	

	Physics	Chemistry	Literature	Peace	Medicine	Economics
1969	Murray Gell-Mann (US) Discoveries concerning the classification of elementary particles	Derek H.R. Barton (Brit.) Odd Hassel (Nor.) Organic compound research	Samuel Beckett (Ire.) Novelist and dramatist	International Labour Organization (founded 1919)	Max Delbrück (US) Alfred D. Hershey (US) Salvador E. Luria (US) Research of viruses	Ragnar Frisch (Nor.) Jan Tinbergen (Neth.) Work in econometrics
1970	Hannes Alfvén (Swed.) Louis Néél (Fr.) Work in magnetohydro-dynamics and magnetism	Luis Leloir (Arg.) Discovery of sugar nucleo-tides and their role in the biosynthesis of carbohydrates	A. Solzhenitsyn (USSR) Novelist	Norman Borlaug (US)	Julius Axelrod (US) Bernard Katz (Brit.) Ulf von Euler (Swed.) Nerve transmission research	Paul Samuelson (US) Work in scientific analysis of economic theory
1971	Dennis Gabor (Brit.) Holography invention	Gerhard Herzberg (Can.) Molecule structure research	Pablo Neruda (Chile) Poet	Willy Brandt (Ger.)	Earl W. Sutherland Jr (US) Action of hormones	Simon Kuznets (US) Economic growth of nations
1972	John Bardeen (US) Leon N. Cooper (US) John R. Schrieffer (US) Superconductivity theory	Christian B. Anfinsen (US) Stanford Moore (US) William H. Stein (US) Enzyme chemistry research	Heinrich Böll (Ger.) Novelist	no award	Gerald M. Edelman (US) Rodney Porter (Brit.) Research on the chemical structure of antibodies	John Hicks (Brit.) Kenneth J. Arrow (US) Welfare theory and economic equilibrium theory
1973	Leo Esaki (Jap.) Ivar Giaever (US) Brian Josephson (Brit.) Superconductivity research	Ernst Fischer (Ger.) Geoffrey Wilkinson (Brit.) Organometallic chemistry	Patrick White (Aus.) Novelist	Henry Kissinger (US) Le Duc Tho (N. Viet.) (declined)	Karl von Frisch (Austria) Konrad Lorenz (Austria) Nikolaas Tinbergen (Neth.) Animal behaviour patterns	Wassily Leontief (US) Input analysis
1974	Sir Martin Ryle (Brit.) Antony Hewish (Brit.) Work in radio astronomy	Paul J. Flory (US) Studies of long-chain molecules	Eyvind Johnson (Swed.) Harry Martinson (Swed.) Novelist and poet	Sato Eisaku (Jap.) Sean MacBride (Ire.)	Albert Claude (US) Christian R. de Duve (Belg.) George E. Palade (US) Cell structure research	Gunnar Myrdal (Swed.) Friedrich von Hayek (Brit.) Economic, social and institutional phenomena
1975	Aage Bohr (Den.) Ben R. Mottelson (Den.) L. James Rainwater (US) Atomic nucleus research paved way for nuclear fusion	J.W. Cornforth (Brit.) Vladimir Prelog (Switz.) Work in stereochemistry	Eugenio Montale (Ita.) Poet	Andrey D. Sakharov (USSR)	Renato Dulbecco (US) Howard M. Temin (US) David Baltimore (US) Tumour viruses research	Leonid Kantorovich (USSR) Tjalling Koopmans (US) Contribution to the theory of optimum allocation of resources
1976	Burton Richter (US) Samuel C.C. Ting (US) Elementary particles research	William Lipscomb (US) Structure of boranes	Saul Bellow (US) Novelist	Mairead Corrigan (N. Ire.) Betty Williams (N. Ire.)	Baruch Blumberg (US) D. Carleton Gajdusek (US) Infectious diseases research	Milton Friedman (US) Consumption analysis and monetary theory

	Physics	Chemistry	Literature	Medicine	Peace	Economics
1977	Philip W. Anderson (US) Sir Nevill Mott (Brit.) John H. Van Vleck (US) Studies into behaviour of electrons in magnetic non-crystalline solids	Ilya Prigogine (Belg.) Widening the scope of thermodynamics	Vicente Aleixandre (Spa.) Poet	Rosalyn S. Yalow (US) Roger Guillemin (US) Andrew Schally (US) Development of radio-immunoassay, research on pituitary hormones	Amnesty International (founded 1961)	Bertil Ohlin (Swed.) James Meade (Brit.) Contributions to theory of international trade
1978	Pyotr L. Kapitsa (USSR) Invention of helium liquefier Robert W. Wilson (US) Arno A. Penzias (US) Discovery of cosmic micro-wave background radiation	Peter D. Mitchell (Brit.) Formulation of a theory of energy transfer processes in biological systems	Isaac Bashevis Singer (US) Novelist	Werner Arber (Switz.) Daniel Nathans (US) Hamilton O. Smith (US) Discovery of enzymes that fragment DNAs	Menachem Begin (Isr.) Anwar Sadat (Egy.)	Herbert A. Simon (US) Decision-making processes in economic organizations
1979	Sheldon Glashow (US) Abdus Salam (Pak.) Steven Weinberg (US) Establishment of analogy between electromagnetism and subatomic particles	Herbert C. Brown (US) Georg Wittig (Ger.) Introduction of compounds of boron and phosphorus in the synthesis of organic substances	Odysseus Elytis (Greece) Poet	Allan M. Cormack (US) Godfrey N. Hounsfield (Brit.) Development of computed axial tomography scan	Mother Teresa of Calcutta (India)	W. Arthur Lewis (Brit.) Theodore W. Schultz (US) Analyses of economic processes in developing nations
1980	James W. Cronin (US) Val L. Fitch (US) Demonstration of simultaneous violation of both charge-conjugation + parity inversion symmetries	Paul Berg (US) 1st preparation of hybrid DNA Walter Gilbert (US) Frederick Sanger (Brit.) Development of chemical analysis of DNA structure	Czeslaw Milosz (US) Poet	Baruj Benacerraf (US) George D. Snell (US) Jean Dausset (Fr.) Investigations of genetic control of the response of immunological system to foreign substances	Adolfo Pérez Esquivel (Arg.)	Lawrence R. Klein (US) Development and analysis of empirical models of business fluctuations
1981	Kai M. Siegbahn (Swed.) Nicolaas Bloembergen (US) Electron spectroscopy for chemical analysis Arthur L. Schawlow (US) Applications of lasers in spectroscopy	Fukui Kenichi (Jap.) Roald Hoffmann (US) Orbital symmetry interpretation of chemical reactions	Elias Canetti (Bulg.) Novelist and essayist	Roger W. Sperry (US) Functions of the cerebral hemispheres Torsten N. Wiesel (Swed.) David H. Hubel (US) Processing of visual information by the brain	Office of the United Nations High Commissioner for Refugees (founded 1951)	James Tobin (US) Empirical macro-economic theories
1982	Kenneth G. Wilson (US) Analysis of continuous phase transitions	Aaron Klug (Brit.) Determination of structure of biological substances	Gabriel G. Márquez (Col.) Novelist, journalist and social critic	Sune K. Bergström (Swe.) Bengt I. Samuelsson (Swe.) John R. Vane (Brit.) Prostaglandins research	Alva Myrdal (Swed.) Alfonso G. Robles (Mex.)	George Stigler (US) Economic effects of governmental regulation

	Physics	Chemistry	Literature	Medicine	Peace	Economics
1983	S. Chandrasekhar (US) William A. Fowler (US) Research into stars	Henry Taube (Can.) Study of electron transfer reactions	William Golding (Brit.) Novelist	Barbara McLintock (US) Discovery of mobile plant genes affecting heredity	Lech Walesa (Pol.)	Gerard Debreu (US) Mathematical proof of supply and demand theory
1984	Carlo Rubbia (Ita.) Simon van der Meer (Neth.) Discovery of subatomic particles W and Z which supports electro weak theory	Bruce Merrifield (US) Development of a method of polypeptide synthesis	Jaroslav Seifert (Czech.) Poet	Niels K. Jerne (Den.) Georges JF Kohler (Ger.) Cesar Milstein (Arg.) Study of monoclonal antibodies	Desmond Tutu (SA)	Richard Stone (Brit.) Development of national income accounting system
1985	Klaus von Klitzing (Ger.) Discovery of quantized Hall effect concerning exact measurement of electrical resistance	Herbert A. Hauptman (US) Jerome Karle (US) Mapping chemical structure of small molecules	Claude Simon (Fr.) Novelist	Michael S. Brown (US) Joseph L. Goldstein (US) Cholesterol metabolism cell receptors	International Physicians for the Prevention of Nuclear War (founded 1980)	Franco Modigliani (US) Financial market theory and household savings
1986	Ernst Ruska (Ger.) Gerd Binnig (Ger.) Heinrich Rohrer (Switz.) Electron microscopes	Dudley Herschbach (US) Yuan T. Lee (US) John C. Polyani (Can.) Analytical methodology	Wole Soyinka (Nigeria) Playwright and poet	Stanley Cohen (US) Rita Levi-Montalcini (Ita.) Discovery of regulatory agents concerning cell growths	Elie Wiesel (Fr.)	James M. Buchanan (US) Political theories advocating limited government role in the economy
1987	J. Georg Bednorz (Ger.) K. Alex Müller (Switz.) Discovery of new superconducting materials	Charles J. Pedersen (US) Donald J. Cram (US) Jean-Marie Lehn (Fr.) molecule development	Joseph Brodsky (US) Poet and essayist	Tonegawa Susumu (Jap.) Study of genetic aspects of antibodies	Oscar Arias Sanchez (Costa Rica)	Robert M. Solow (US) Economic growth theory
1988	Leon Lederman (US) Melvin Schwartz (US) Jack Steinberger (US) Subatomic particle research	Johann Deisenhofer (Ger.) Robert Huber (Ger.) Hartmut Michel (Ger.) Photosynthesis research	Naguib Mahfouz (Egypt) Novelist	James W. Black (Brit.) Gertrude B. Elion (US) George H. Hitchings (US) Drug research	UN Peacekeeping Forces	Maurice Allais (Fr.) Market theory
1989	Hans Dehmelt (US) Wolfgang Paul (Ger.) Norman Ramsey (US)	Sydney Altman (US) Thomas Cech (US) RNA research	Camilo Jose Cela (Spa.) Poet and novelist	J Michael Bishop (US) Harold E. Varmus (US)	Tenzin Gyatso (Tib.) Dalai Lama XIV	Trygve Haavelmo (Nor.) Quantitative economics
1990	Jerome Friedman (US) Henry Kendall (US) Richard Taylor (Can.) Quark model theory	Elias James Corey (US) Retrosynthetic analysis	Octavio Paz (Mex.) Poet	Joseph E. Murray (US) E. Donnall Thomas (US)	Mikhail Gorbachev (Rus.)	Harry M. Markowitz (US) Merton Miller (US) William Sharpe (US) Financial economic theory

	Physics	Chemistry	Literature	Peace	Medicine	Economics
1991	Pierre-Gilles de Gennes (Fr.) Superconductivity theory	Richard R. Ernst (Switz.) Spectroscopy development	Nadine Gordimer (SA)	Aung San Suu Kyi (Burma)	Erwin Neher (Ger.) Bert Sakmann (Ger.) Patch-clamp technique	Ronald Coase (Brit.) Transaction cost theory
1992	George Charpak (Fr.) Elementary particle study	Rudolph A. Marcus (US) Electron transfer	Derek Walcott (St Lucia) Poet	Rigoberta Menchú (Guat.)	Edmond H. Fischer (US) Edwin G. Krebs (US) Protein regulation	Gary S. Becker (US) Microeconomic analysis
1993	Russell Hulse (US) Joseph Hooton Taylor (US) Discovery of new type of pulsar	Kary Banks Mullis (US) Polymerase chain reaction Michael Smith (Can.) Mutagenesis theory	Toni Morrison (US) Novelist	Nelson Mandela (SA) F.W. de Klerk (SA)	Richard Roberts (Brit.) Phillip Allen Sharp (US) Mosaic genes discovery	Robert Fugel (US) Douglas North (US) Quantitative methods as reasons for economic change
1994	Clifford Shull (US) Bertram Brockhouse (Can.) Study of neutron beams	George Olah (US) Carbocations	Kenzaburo Oe (Jap.) Novelist	Yasser Arafat (Pal.) Shimon Peres (Isr.) Yitzhak Rabin (Isr.)	Martin Rodbell (US) Alfred G. Gilman (US) Discovery of G protein	John Nash (US) John Harsanyi (US) Reinhard Selten (Ger.) Games theory
1995	Martin L. Pearl (US) Tau lepton discovery Frederick Reines (US) Neutrino detection	F Sherwood Rowland (US) Mario Molina (Mex.) Paul Crutzen (Ned.) Ozone layer research	Seamus Heaney (Ire.) Poet	Joseph Rotblat (Brit.) Pugwash Conferences on Science and World Affairs	Edward B. Lewis (US) Eric F. Wieschaus (US) C. Nüsslein-Volhard (Ger.) Genes theory	Robert E. Lucas (US) Macroeconomic analysis
1996	David M. Lee (US) Douglas D. Osheroff (US) Robert C. Richardson (US) Discovery of superfluidity in helium-3	Harry Kroto (Brit.) Robert Curl (US) Richard Smalley (US) Discovery of C_{60} molecule	Wislawa Szymborska (Pol.) Poet	Jose Ramos-Horta (E. Timor) Bishop Carlos Belo of Dili	Peter C. Doherty (Aus.) Rolf M. Zinkernagel (Switz.)	James Mirrlees (Brit.) William Vickrey (Can.)
1997	Steven Chu (US) Claude Cohen-Tannoudji (Fr.) William D. Phillips (US) Atom research	John Walker (Brit.) Paul Boyer (US) Jens Skou (Den.) Molecular biology research	Dario Fo (Ita.) Playwright	Ms Jodie Williams (US) and International Campaign to Ban Landmines	Stanley B. Prusiner (US) Discovery of prions	Robert Merton (US) Myron Scholes (US) Fischer Black (US) Contribution to economic theory
1998	Robert B. Laughlin (US) Horst L. Stormer (Ger.) Daniel C. Tsui (US) Quantum fluids	John Pople (Brit.) Walter Kohn (USA) Quantum theory application to molecules	José Saramago (Port.) Novelist	John Hume (N. Ire.) David Trimble (N. Ire.) For 'Good Friday' Agreement	Robert S. Furghgott (US) Louis J. Ignarro (US) Ferid Murad (US) Cardiovascular research	Amartya Sen (India) Welfare economics
1999	Gerardus T. Hooft (Neth.) Martinus J. G. Veltman (Neth.) Study of electro-weak interactions	Ahmed Zewai (Egypt) Femtosecond spectroscopy	Günter Grass (Ger.) Novelist	Médecins Sans Frontières (Belg.)	Günter Blobel (Ger.) Study of proteins	Robert A. Mundell (Can.) Fiscal policy analysis

NOBEL PRIZE WINNERS

| 2000 | Herbert Kroemer (Ger.)
Zhores Alferov (Ger.)
Developing semiconductor
heterostructures
Jack S. Kilby (US)
Invention of the integrated
circuit | Alan J. Heeger (US)
Alan G. MacDiarmid (US)
Hideki Shirakawa (Japan)
Discovery of conductive
polymers | Gao Xingjian (China) | Arvid Carlsson (Sweden)
Paul Greengard (US)
Eric Kandel (US)
Research into signal
transduction in the nervous
system | Kim Dae Jung (S. Korea)
Work in reconciliation with
North Korea | James J. Heckman (Ger.)
Daniel L. McFadden (US)
Contribution to economic
theory and analysis |

NB: Many of the award winners listed above have dual nationalities. The nationality given is therefore not necessarily the country of birth.

General Information
Royal Swedish Academy of Sciences awards the Physics, Chemistry and Economics Prizes.
Swedish Karolinska Institute awards the Medicine Prize.
Swedish Academy of Arts awards the Literature Prize.
The Peace Prize is awarded by a committee of 5 members of the Norwegian Storting.
Nils Dalen, the 1912 Nobel Prizewinner for Physics, was blinded in 1913 by an explosion whilst conducting an experiment.
William and Lawrence Bragg were the only father and son to win a prize when they were joint winners of the 1915 Physics Prize.
A woman has never won the Economics Prize.

ORGANIZATIONS

Chief Executives or Chairmen (as at June 2001)

Abbey National Ian Harley (CE); Christopher Tugendhat (C)

Aberdeen Football Club Stuart Milne (C)

Adidas-Salomon Herbert Hainer (CE)

Airtours David Crossland (C); Tim Byrne (CE)

Alfred McAlpine Terence Harrison (C); Oliver Whitehead (CE)

Allders Brian Fidler (C); Harvey Lipsith (CE)

Alliance & Leicester John R. Windeler (C)

Allied Domecq Philip Bowman (CE); Sir Christopher Hogg (C)

Antisoma Glyn Edwards (CE)

AOL Steve Case (C); Jerry Levin (CE)

AorTech International Eddie McDaid (CE); James Gordon Wright (C)

Arena Leisure Martin Pope (C)

Arsenal Football Club P. D. Hill-Wood (C)

Arts Council Gerry Robinson (C)

Asda Dave Ferguson (CE)

Associated British Foods Harold W. Bailey (C); Peter J. Jackson (CE)

Aston Villa Football Club Herbert Douglas Ellis (C); Herbert Douglas Ellis (CE)

BA Rod Eddington (CE); Lord Marshall of Knightsbridge (C)

BAA Lawrence Urquhart (C); Mike S. Hodgkinson (CE)

BAE Systems Richard Evans (C); John P. Weston (CE)

Bank of England Sheila V. Masters (C)

Bank of Scotland Peter Burt (CE)

Barclays Sir Peter Middleton (C); Matthew W. Barrett (CE)

Bass Ian Prosser (C); Tim Clarke (CE)

BAT (British American Tobacco) Martin F. Broughton (C)

BG Group Frank Chapman (CE); Richard V. Giordano (C)

BICC Alan Jones (CE)

Billiton Brian Gilbertson (C)

Blacks Leisure Simon Bentley (CE); David Bernstein (C)

Blue Circle Rt. Hon. The Lord Christopher Tugendhat (C); Richard Haythornthwaite (CE)

BMW Joachim Milberg (C)

BOC Tony Isaac (CE); Sir David G. John (C)

Body Shop Patrick Gournay (CE); Anita L. Roddick (JC); T. Gordon Roddick (JC)

Boeing Phil Condit (C)

Boosey & Hawkes Richard Holland (CE); Gerry Mortimer (C)

Boots John McGrath (C); Steve G. Russell (CE)

Bradford & Bingley Lindsay MacKinlay (C); Christopher Rodrigues (CE)

Britannia Harold Cottam (C); Brian H. Shaw (CE)

British Aerospace Sir Richard Evans (C)

British Airways Rod Eddington (CE); Lord Marshall of Knightsbridge (C)

British Banker's Association Ian Mullen (C)

British Energy Peter Hollins (CE); John Robb (C)

British Midland Sir Michael Bishop (C)

British Petroleum Sir John Browne (CE); Peter Sutherland (C)

British Telecom Sir Christopher Bland (C); Sir Peter Bonfield (CE)

British Tourist Authority David Quarmby (C)

Brown & Jackson Johan Visser (CE)

BSkyB Tony Ball (CE)

Budgens Clive T. Clague (C); Martin Hyson (CE)

BUPA Bryan Nicholson (C)

Burger King John Dasburg (C); John Dasburg (CE)

Cable & Wireless Ralph Robbins (C); Graham Wallace (CE)

Cadbury Schweppes Derek Bonham (C); John Sunderland (CE)

Camelot Sir George Russell (C); Diane Thompson (CE)

Cannons Harm Tegelaars (CE)

Carpetright Lord Philip Charles Harris of Peckham (C)

Carlton Communications Gerry Murphy (CE); Michael Green (C)

Centrica Roy Gardner (CE); Sir Michael Perry (C)

CGNU Insurance Richard Harvey (CE)

Channel 4 Michael Jackson (CE); Vanni Treves (C)

Chelsea Village Michael Russell (CE); Ken Bates (C)

Chelsfield Elliott Bernerd (C)

Chiroscience Hugh Collum (C)

Chrysalis Group Richard Huntingford (CE); Chris Wright (C)

Chubb Robert L. Gasparini (CE)

Cisco Systems John Chambers (CE)

Citadel Technology Victor K. Kiam (C)

Claims Direct Colin Poole (CE); Tony Sullman (C)

Clearstream André Lussi (CE)

Coca Cola Douglas Ivester (C); Douglas Ivester (CE)

Compass Mike Bailey (CE); Francis MacKay (C)

Consignia (formerly Post Office) Neville Bain (C); John Roberts (CE)

Co-operative Bank Graham Bennett (C); Mervyn Pedelty (CE)

Coral Eurobet Robert Scott (CE)

Cordiant Communications Michael Bungey (CE); Charles Scott (C)

Corus (formerly British Steel) Sir Brian Moffatt (C)

Courts Paul C. Cohen (C)

Coutts and Company Sir Ewen Fergusson (C); Andrew Fisher (CE)

Daily Mail Viscount Rothermere IV (C); Charles Sinclair (CE)

Debenhams Belinda Earl (CE); Peter Jarvis (C)

De La Rue Brandon Gough (C); Ian Much (CE)

Deutsche Bank Rolf Breuer (C)

De Vere Group Lord Daresbury (C); Paul Dermody (CE)

Diageo (Guinness & Grand Met) Lord Blyth (C); Paul Walsh (CE)

Dixons John Clare (CE); Sir Stanley Kalms (C)

Easyjet Stelios Haji-Ioannou (C); Ray Webster (CE)

e-comsport (proposed name: Podia) David Giampaolo (C); Scott Poulter (CE)

Economist Group, The Dominic Cadbury (C)

Egg Mike Harris (CE); Roberto Mendoza (C)

Elementis Lyndon Cole (CE); Jonathan Fry (C)

EMAP Kevin Hand (CE); Robin Miller (C)

EMI Eric L. Nicoli (C); Eric L. Nicoli (CE)

Energis Gordon Owen (C); David Wickham (CE)

Equitable Life Assurance Society Charles Thomson (CE); Vanni Treves (C)

Eurotunnel PLC Philippe Lazare (CE); Charles MacKay (C)

Express Dairies Neil Davidson (CE); Christopher Haskins (C)

Financial Times Group David Bell (C); Stephen Hill (CE)

Findel K. Chapman (C); D. Johnson (CE)

First Choice Holidays Ian Clubb (C); Peter Long (CE)

FirstGroup Martin Gilbert (C); Moir Lockhead (CE)

Fitness First Christopher Pearce (C)

Freeserve John Charles Clare (C)

Galen Holdings John King (C); Roger Biossonneault (CE)

Geest R. Ian Menzies-Gow (C)

George Wimpey Peter Johnson (CE); John Robinson (C)

GKN C.K. Chow (CE); Sir David Lees (C)

Glaxo Wellcome Jean-Pierre Garnier (CE); Sir Richard Sykes (C)

Goshawk Insurance David Hooker (C)

Granada Group Charles Lamb Allen (CE); Gerry Robinson (C)

Greene King Timothy Bridge (CE); David McCall (C)

GUS Sir Victor Blank (C); John Peace (CE)

Habitat Terence Conran (C)

Halifax James Crosby (CE); Lord Stevenson of Coddenham (C)

Hamleys Simon Burke (C)

Harland and Wolff Bryngulv Mugaas (CE)

Harrods Mohamed Al Fayed (C)

Hays Ronnie Frost (C)

Hilton Group John Jackson (C); David Michels (CE)

HMV Media Group Alan Giles (CE); Timothy Waterstone (C)

Homebase John Lovering (C); Rob Templeman (CE)

Hornby Frank Martin (CE)

House of Fraser John Coleman (CE); Michael Wemms (C)

HSBC John Bond (C); Keith Whitson (CE)

Imperial Chemical Industries Charles Miller-Smith (C); Brendan O'Neill (CE)

I Feel Good Holdings J. K. H. Brown (CE); Felix Dennis (C)

Imperial Tobacco Derek Bonham (C); Gareth Davis (CE)

Invensys Colin Marshall (C); Allen Yurko (CE)

J. D. Wetherspoon Tim Martin (C)

Johnson Matthey H. Michael P. Miles (C); C. R. N. Clark (CE)

John Lewis Partnership Stuart Hampson (C); Stuart Hampson (CE)

John Menzies David MacKay (CE); Gavin Reed (C)

J. Sainsbury George Bull (C); Sir Peter Davis (CE)

Kenwood Appliances Colin Gordon (CE)

Kingfisher Sir John Banham (C); Sir Geoffrey Mulcahy (CE)

Lastminute.com Brent Hoberman (CE); Allan Leighton (C)

Laura Ashley Khoo Kay Peng (C); Ng Kwan Cheong (CE)

Legal & General Sir Christopher Harding (C)

Lego Kjeld Kristiansen (CE)

Leicester City Football Club Rodney Walker (C)

LIFFE Hugh Freedberg (CE); R. Brian Williamson (C)

Littlewoods J. M. Barry Gibson (CE); James Ross (C)

Lloyd's of London Nicholas E. T. Prettejohn (CE); Saxon Riley (C)

Lloyds - TSB Peter Ellwood (CE); Maarten A. van den Bergh (C)

London Bridge Software Gordon Crawford (C)

London Scottish Bank P. T. Furlong (C); Roy Reese (CE)

London Stock Exchange Don Cruickshank (C); Clara Furse (CE)

London Transport Sir Malcolm Bates (C)

LucasVarity Victor Rice (CE)

Luminar Keith Hamill (C); Steven Thomas (CE)

LVMH Bernard Arnault (C)

Manchester United PLC Peter Kenyon (CE); Sir Roland Smith (C)

Matalan John Hargreaves (C)

Marconi John Mayo (CE); Lord Simpson (C)

Marks & Spencer Luc Vandevelde (C); Luc Vandevelde (CE)

Méridien Hotels Juergen Bartels (CE); Guy Hands (C)

Merrill Lynch HSBC Margaret Barrett (CE)

Microsoft Bill Gates (CE)

Money Channel PLC T. H. Hobman (CE); Paul Killik (C)

Mothercare Chris Martin (CE); Alan Smith (C)

Motorola Christopher B. Galvin (C); Christopher B. Galvin (CE)

NASDAQ Wick Simmons (CE)

National Air Traffic Services Sir Roy McNulty (C)

National Lottery Commission Mark Harris (CE); Helena Shovelton (C)

National Power Keith Henry (CE)

National Westminster Bank Sir David Rowland (C)

Nationwide Building Society Brian Davis (CE); Charles Nunneley (C)

N Brown David Alliance (C); Jim Martin (CE)

Newcastle United PLC Alfred Olding Fletcher (CE)

News Corp K. R. Murdoch (C); K. R. Murdoch (CE)

Next Sir Brian Pitman (C); Simon Wolfson (CE)

Nottingham Forest PLC M. A. Arthur (CE); E. M. Barnes (C)

Novartis Healthcare Daniel Vasella (C); Daniel Vasella (CE)

ONdigital Stuart Prebble (CE)

Orange Michel Bon (C); Jean-Francois Pontal (CE)

Orchestream Alan Bates (C); Ashley Ward (CE)

Pearson PLC Marjorie Scardino (CE); Lord Stevenson of Coddenham (C)

Pearson Television Richard Eyre (CE)

Persimmon Duncan Davidson (C); John White (CE)

Pilkington Nigel Rudd (C); Paolo Scaroni (CE)

Pizza Express Ian Eldridge (CE); David Page (C)

Powderject Pharmaceuticals Paul Drayson (C); Paul Drayson (CE)

Powergen Nick Baldwin (CE); Edmund Wallis (C)

Preston North End PLC B. M. Gray (C); A. J. Scholes (CE)

Prudential Jonathan Bloomer (CE); Sir Martin Jacomb (C)

Railtrack Steve Marshall (CE); John Robinson (C)

Rangers Football Club PLC David Murray (C)

Rank Mike Smith (CE)

Ranks Hovis McDougall Paul Wilkinson (C)

Reed International Morris Tabakslat (C)

Rentokil Initial Henry E. St L. King (C); Sir Clive Thompson (CE)

Reuters Group Sir Christopher Hogg (C); Peter Job (CE)

Rio Tinto R. Leigh Clifford (CE); Robert Wilson (C)

Rolls-Royce PLC John Rose (CE); Sir Ralph Robins (C)

Royal & Sun Alliance Sir Patrick Gillam (C); Bob Mendelsohn (CE)

Royal Bank of Scotland Fred Goodwin (CE)

Royal Doulton Hamish Grossart (C)

Royal Opera House Sir Colin Southgate (C)

Safeway Carlos Criado-Perez (CE); David Webster (C)

Sage Group Michael Jackson (C); Paul Walker (CE)

Schroders David Salisbury (CE); I. Peter Sedgwick (C)

Scoot.com Robert Bonnier (CE); Richard Eykel (C)

Scottish & Newcastle Brian Stewart (C)

Scottish Power Ian Russell (CE); Charles Miller Smith (C)

Selfridges W. Alun Cathcart (C); Vittorio Radice (CE)

Severn Trent Water T. David G. Arculus (C); Robert Walker (CE)

Shaftesbury Jonathan Lane (CE); Peter Levy (C)

Shell Transport & Trading Sir Mark Moody-Stuart (C); Phil Watts (CE)

Signet Group Terry Burman (CE); James McAdam (C)

Slough Estates Sir Nigel Mobbs (C); Derek Wilson (CE)

Somerfield Alan Smith (CE); John von Spreckelsen (C)

Stagecoach Holdings Keith Cochrane (CE); Brian Souter (C)

Standard Chartered Sir Patrick Gillam (C); Gurvirendra Talwar (CE)

Sun Life & Provincial Lord Douro (C); Mark Wood (CE)

Tate and Lyle David Lees (C); Larry Pillard (CE)

Taylor Woodrow Keith Egerton (CE); Robert Hawley (C)

Telewest Communications Adam Singer (CE); Anthony Stenham (C)

Tesco Terry Leahy (CE); John Gardiner (C)

Thames Water Bill Alexander (CE); Roger Carr (C)

Thomas Cook Holdings John Donaldson (C); John Donaldson (CE)

3i Group Brian P. Larcombe (CE); Sir George Russell (C); Baroness Hogg (from 1/1/02) (C)

Tote Peter Jones (C)

Tottenham Hotspur PLC Sir Alan Sugar (C)

Tussauds Group Michael Jolly (C); Michael Jolly (CE)

Ultraframe David Moore (CE); Rod Sellers (C)

Unilever Niall FitzGerald (JC); Antony Burgmans (JC)

United Biscuits Holdings Malcolm Ritchie (C); Malcolm Ritchie (CE)

Virgin Group Sir Richard Branson (C)

Viridian Group Patrick Haren (CE); Philip Rogerson (C)

Vodafone Chris Gent (CE); Lord MacLaurin of Knebworth (C)

Wal-Mart Lee Scott (CE)

Weetabix Richard George (C)

Wellcome Trust Sir Dominic Cadbury (C)

Wembley PLC Claes Hultman (C); Nigel Potter (CE)

West Bromwich Albion PLC P. Thompson (C); J. D. Wile (CE)

WH Smith Richard Handover (CE); Martin Taylor (C)

Whitbread Sir John Banham (C); David Thomas (CE)

William Hill Organization John Brown (C); David Harding (CE)

Wireless Group Kelvin Mackenzie (C); Kelvin Mackenzie (CE)

Wolseley Charlie Banks (CE)

Woolwich Lynne Peacock (CE)

Xenova Group John Jackson (C); David Oxlade (CE)

Yorkshire-Tyne Tees TV Ward Thomas (C)

Zara Amancio Ortega (C)

Zeneca Sir David Barnes (CE); Sir M. S. Lipworth (C)

Key

CE = Chief Executive
C = Chairman
JC = Joint Chairman

Organizations, Movements and Bodies

ACP the 68 African, Caribbean and Pacific countries which have special trade relations with the European Union.

Action Directe leftwing French revolutionary group formed in 1979 and responsible for numerous bombings.

Agenda 21 blueprint for action adopted at the 1992 Earth Summit in Rio setting out requirements for sustainable development.

Aipac American Israel Public Affairs Committee, Israel's official lobbying arm in the USA and as such part of the influential US Jewish lobby. Based in Washington, DC.

Akali Dal supreme political organization of the Indian Sikh community. Founded in December 1920 and based in the Punjab.

Alawi Islamic sub-sect signifying followers of the Caliph Ali, revered by Shias. Prominent in Syria, Lebanon and Turkey.

Alfaro Vive Carajo! translates as 'Alfaro Lives, Dammit!' Ecuadorean left-wing nationalist guerrilla group named in memory of the President 1895–1901, 1906–11.

Al-Fatah (Arabic: victory) Movement for the National Liberation of Palestine. Mainstream component of the PLO founded by Yasser Arafat in 1958.

Alpha 66 paramilitary group of anti-Castroites based in Miami. Formed in 1962 and named after its 66 founder members.

Amazon Pact signed in July 1978 by Bolivia, Brazil, Colombia, Ecuador, Guyana, Peru, Surinam and Venezuela. Committed to preserving ecological balance of the Amazon region.

Amnesty International founded in 1961 by Peter Benenson and Sean Macbride Kropotkin, it campaigns for the release of prisoners of conscience.

ANC African National Congress, South Africa's principal anti-apartheid organization, banned 1960–90 but now the majority party in ruling coalition.

Angry Brigade small anarchistic group in the UK in existence in 1968–71, which carried out several bombings.

Anti-Nazi League leftwing organization in the UK formed in the 1970s to combat racist parties and more recently the British National Party.

Anzus security pact between Australia, NZ and the USA signed in San Francisco on 1 September 1951. Initially formed as deterrent to Japan but no longer operational.

Apostles Cambridge University Conversation Society founded in 1820. Guy Burgess and Anthony Blunt were recruited from the Apostles by Soviet Intelligence.

Arab League organization formed in 1945 originally for mutual economic aid but more recently dealing with the Middle East peace process.

ASEAN Association of South East Asian Nations. Founded in 1967, members include Indonesia, Malaysia, Singapore, Thailand, Philippines and Brunei.

Baader-Meinhof Gang   extremist leftwing terrorist group active in Germany in the late 1960s; later became the Rote Armee Fraktion (RAF).

Ba'ath   movement founded in Syria in the 1940's by Michel Aflaq with the aim of creating a single socialist Arab nation.

Band Aid   charity formed by Bob Geldof and Midge Ure in December 1984 for the purpose of famine relief in Ethiopia.

BCCI   Bank of Credit and Commerce International which collapsed in July 1991. Lord Justice Bingham criticized the Bank of England's supervisory role.

Benelux   grouping of Belgium, Netherlands and Luxembourg for a mutually advantageous economic climate. Founded in 1932 by the Convention of Ouchy.

Black Berets   élite paramilitary police force formed by the Soviet Interior Ministry in 1987. Aka Omon, they had a reputation for ruthlessness, especially in the Baltic States.

Black Sash   South African liberal women's anti-apartheid organization originally formed in 1955 as the Women's Defence of the Constitution League in response to the removal of the vote for coloureds. The black sash was worn as a peaceful protest against violation of rights.

Black September   Palestinian terrorist group, named in memory of the Jordanian expulsion of Palestinians in Sepember 1970. Responsible for the Munich Olympic massacre of Israeli athletes.

B'Nai B'rith   international Jewish organization founded in 1843 and based in Washington, DC.

BND   the German Federal Intelligence Service, founded in 1956 under the ex-Nazi Reinhard Gehlen and based in Munich.

Boss   Bureau of State Security, a now defunct branch of the South African Intelligence Service. Founded in 1969 by PM J.B. Vorster.

Boundaries Commission   UK body responsible for defining the boundaries of parliamentary constituencies.

Boys Brigade   founded by William Smith in 1883.

Boys' Clubs   although boys' clubs were in existence in major British cities in the 19th century, the National Association was founded in 1925.

BRA   Bougainville Revolutionary Army, a guerrilla force fighting for independence for the mineral-rich island of Bougainville from the state of Papua New Guinea.

Brigate Rosse (Red Brigades)   leftwing urban guerrillas responsible for a spate of kidnappings and bombings in the 1970s culminating in the murder of former PM Aldo Moro in 1978.

British Academy   Established in 1901; its full title being 'British Academy for the Promotion of Historical, Philosophical and Philological Studies'.

British Council   Established in 1934 and funded by the government for the purpose of representing British culture abroad. With offices in more than 80 countries, it arranges for visits by British artists, lecturers and performers, mounts exhibitions, teaches English and provides libraries of British books.

Brookings Institution   Influential US think-tank based in Washington, DC, and comprised of distinguished figures from various fields.

Bruges Group   Informal Conservative grouping of 'Eurosceptics', named from a speech made in the Belgian city of Bruges on 20 September 1988 by Margaret Thatcher.

Camorra   Network of groups engaged in organized crime in the Naples region.

Caricom   Caribbean Community and Common Market, an alliance of English-speaking Caribbean countries promoting economic, political and cultural unity.

Central African Federation   Federation of the British colonies of Northern Rhodesia (Zambia), Southern Rhodesia (Zimbabwe) and Nyasaland (Malawi). Established in 1953 and dissolved in 1963.

Central Committee   Leading organ in the Communist Party of the Soviet Union whose full members elected the powerful Politburo and secretariat.

CERM   Centre d'Exploitation du Rnseigment Militaire (Centre for exploitation of Military intelligence). French internal security agency, formerly called Deuxième Bureau until 10 Dec. 1971.

CERN   European Centre for Nuclear Research, a co-operative agency with 12 member countries founded in 1952 and located outside Geneva.

Charter 88   Pressure group in the UK that demands a new constitutional settlement guaranteeing political, civil and human rights.

Chetniks   Serbian nationalist army of resistance led by Draza Mihailovic, which occupied parts of east and south Yugoslavia during the second world war. Term now applies to all Serb irregulars.

CHOGM   Commonwealth Heads of Government Meeting, the main policy-making body of the Commonwealth. A CHOGM is convened every 2 years.

CIA   Central Intelligence Agency, often referred to internally as 'The Company'. Its HQ is at Langley, Virginia.

Civic Forum   Czech coalition of parties formed during the Velvet Revolution in November 1989 as the focus of democratic opposition to the communist regime.

Club of Rome   non-governmental association of industrialists, policy analysts and scientists, seeking to bring their different perspectives to bear on problems of the global economy.

CND   Campaign for Nuclear Disarmament, a British organisation which mobilized mass opposition to nuclear weapons in general and the UK's independent nuclear deterrent in particular. Founder members in 1958 include Bertrand Russell.

Comecon   Informal name for the Council for Mutual Economic Assistance (CMEA), founded in 1949 as a response to the USA's Marshall Plan. Members included Warsaw Pact countries (excluding Albania) and Cuba, Mongolia and Vietnam.

Committee of 100   Militant offshoot of CND, formed in 1960 and headed by Bertrand Russell; its main weapon was 'sit down' protests.

Commonwealth of Nations   Voluntary association of 53 independent states (Mozambique being latest member) which evolved from the British Empire, latterly concerned with postcolonial economic and cultural development. Originated with the 1931 Statute of Westminster. Elizabeth II is head of 16 Commonwealth states.

Confederation of British Industry   CBI, formed in 1965 via merger of Federation of British Industries, British Employers' Confederation and National Association of British Manufacturers.

Congress   Bicameral legislature of the USA consisting of a 100-member senate elected for 6 years, with one third being renewed every 2 years, and a 435-member House of Representatives (lower chamber) elected for 2 years. Each state sends 2 senators to the upper house.

Contadora Group Latin American peace initiative in Central America set up by Colombia, Mexico, Panama and Venezuela in January 1983; controversially recognizes Nicaraguan Sandinistas.

Contras Nicaraguan counter-revolutionary forces financed during the 1980s by the US Reagan administration, in part illegally, as revealed by the Iran-Contra affair. Many Contras offered allegiance to the dictator Anastasio Somoza, ousted in 1979.

Council of Europe Intergovernmental organization with its HQ in Strasbourg. Founded on 5 May 1949 to promote civil society and human rights.

CPLA Cordillera People's Liberation Army, a guerrilla group operating in the Philippines until it signed a ceasefire with President Corazon Aquino on 13 Sept. 1986.

Creep Committee to Re-elect the President. Established in advance of the November 1972 US Presidential elections, its aim was to re-elect Richard Nixon by orchestrating a dirty tricks campaign against his Democratic opponents, which ultimately led to the Watergate scandal.

Dáil Éireann 166-seat lower house of the legislature of Eire. Members are elected for 5-year term on the basis of proportional representation. Translates as 'Assembly of Ireland'.

Death Squads Rightwing paramilitary groups often associated with conniving governments who assassinate those deemed a threat to the state. Term was coined in the 1960s in Brazil, when the police force used such squads, perhaps financed by the CIA.

Dergue Military ruling body in Ethiopia between 1973 and 1991, most closely associated with the Marxist-Leninist regime of Lt-Col. Mengistu Haile Mariam.

Deuxième Bureau French internal security agency run by the Ministry of the Interior and Administative Reform. Changed its name to CERM in 1971.

DGSE Direction Générale de la Sécurité Extérieure (General Directorate for External Security), the French foreign secret service established on 4 April 1982.

Diet Japanese bicameral legislature consisting of a House of Representatives (lower chamber) elected for a 4-year term and a House of Councillors (upper chamber), half of whose members are elected every years.

Dina Chilean secret police serving the military junta during the 1970s.

DST Direction de la Surveillance de Territoire. The French counterpart to the FBI or MI5.

Duma The name of the parliament of Imperial Russia but now referring to the lower house of the new Russian parliament or Federal Assembly.

Earth Day Annual worldwide effort on 22 April by pressure groups to focus public attention on environmental issues.

Earth Summit World environmental conference also known as the UN Conference on Environment and Development (UNCED), held in Rio de Janeiro on 3–14 June 1992 and billed as the largest ever gathering of world leaders.

EBRD European Bank for Reconstruction and Development, founded in May 1990 by 39 countries (including USA and Soviet Union), plus the European Commission and the European Investment Bank. Conceived by French president François Mitterrand to aid the Eastern European transition to a market economy.

Economic and Social Council ECOSOC, one of the 6 principal organs of the UN, established under Chapter X of the UN Charter, responsible for co-ordination of UN specialized agencies.

ECSC European Coal and Steel Community, which brought Italy and Benelux countries into Franco-German co-operation framework of 1950 Schuman Plan, forerunner of EEC.

EEC European Economic Community, founded under Treaty of Rome in March 1957 by France, Germany, Italy and Benelux countries; came into operation in January 1958.

EFTA European Free Trade Association, set up in 1960 under the Stockholm Convention. Its 7 original members were UK, Denmark (left in 1973 to join the EC), Portugal (left 1986), Austria, Switzerland, Norway and Sweden.

EMS European Monetary System, an arrangement for closer monetary co-operation within the EC, operational from March 1979.

EMU European Monetary Union, dating back to the Werner report of 1971; works to promote the smooth operation of capital transfers within participating countries.

EOKA National Organization of Cypriot Fighters, Greek Cypriot movement which from 1955 until the independence of Cyprus in 1960 fought a guerrilla campaign against British rule.

ERM Exchange Rate Mechanism, regarded as the core of the EMS but badly damaged when the UK and Italy pulled out as a result of Black Wednesday in September 1992.

ESA European Space Agency, formed in 1973 as a result of the merger of the European Space Research Organization and the European Launcher Development Organization and committed to a European Space policy.

ETA Basque Fatherland and Freedom, militant separatist organization which fights for the independence of the Basque country from Spain.

EU European Union, currently existing of 15 member states, the original 6 (Belgium, France, West Germany, Italy, Luxemburg, The Netherlands) plus Denmark, Eire, UK, Portugal, Spain, Greece, Austria, Sweden and Finland.

European Communities more generally referred to as the EU since 1 November 1993, the date on which the Maastricht Treaty on the European Union came into force.

European Court of Justice set up in Luxembourg under 1958 Treaty of Rome and responsible for ruling on whether EU member countries are acting in accord with Community Law.

European Parliament one of 3 principal institutions of the EU, with the Council of Ministers and European Commission. Elections held every 5 years and parliament meets in Strasbourg.

Falange Spain's rightwing nationalist party formed in 1937 by General Francisco Franco and formally abolished on 1 April 1977.

Falashas name assigned to Ethiopian Jews, which they themselves reject in favor of the name Beta Israel (House of Israel).

FAO Food and Agricultural Organization, one of the largest of the UN specialized agencies founded in 1945, it aims to combat malnutrition and hunger.

Fascism a 20th-century ideology which has been interpreted as rightwing or centrist in orientation. Derived from the Latin fasces (bundle of rods sometimes including an axe used by Roman magistrates as a symbol of authority), term became prominent following Mussolini's 'March on Rome' in 1922.

ORGANIZATIONS

FBI Federal Bureau of Investigation, part of the US Justice Department and responsible for violations of federal law; has its HQ in Washington DC.

FCO Foreign and Commonwealth Office, UK government department responsible for external relations and representation. The FCO was created in 1968 through the merger of the original Foreign Office (formed in 1782) and the Commonwealth Office.

FLN Front de Libération Nationale (National Liberation Front), political organization during Algeria's independence struggle (1954–62). Founded 1954 under leadership of Ahmed Ben Bella.

FLNC Front de Libération Nationale de la Corse (Corsican National Liberation Front). Formed in May 1976, it is a clandestine extremist group fighting for self-determination from France.

Force De Frappe independent French nuclear weapons strike force instigated by Charles de Gaulle in December 1960 as a protest at the special relationship between the UK and USA.

Four D's democratization, disarmament, decartelization and denazification, implemented against the defeated Germans by the Allies and agreed at Potsdam.

Friends of the Earth international environmental pressure group, originating in the USA as an offshoot of the Sierra Club. It supports research on environmental issues, lobbies policy makers, and has been most successful in increasing public awareness.

G7 Group of 7 most powerful industrialized countries: Canada, France, Germany, Italy, Japan, USA and the UK.

GCHQ Government Communications Headquarters, part of the UK intelligence machinery which provides government departments and military commands with signals intelligence. Established in 1946 as the successor to the Government Code and Cipher School.

Geneva Conventions body of international humanitarian laws adopted in Geneva on 12 August 1949 and endorsed by the UN, which are intended to protect and assist war victims.

Gleneagles Agreement the 1977 decision by Commonwealth heads of government to ban official sporting links with South Africa until the dismantling of apartheid. Named after the golf club in Scotland which was the venue for the meeting.

Gosplan Soviet Union's State Planning Committee established in 1921 to work out a single state economic plan and methods and means of implementing it.

Greenpeace environmental pressure group whose members, now organized internationally with a headquarters in Amsterdam, engage in non-violent action to disrupt environmentally damaging projects. Founded in 1971 when nuclear tests on Amchitka Island, Alaska were disrupted.

Grey Panthers US pressure group organized to promote the interests of the elderly and retired. Name derived humorously from the Black Panthers.

Guardian Angels US volunteer group founded in 1979 to fight crime in New York City. Wearing red berets they have been accused of being vigilantes.

Gulag Soviet acronym, Chief Directorate of Labour Camps. Established in 1930, estimates put number of inmates in the 1940s at over 8 million, of whom 85% were political prisoners.

Haganah Jewish defence force which operated from 1920 until the creation of Israel in 1948 to defend Jewish settlements in Palestine.

Hallstein Doctrine West German policy in 1950s and 1960s of severing diplomatic relations with any state recognizing East Germany and refusing relations with any communist country except the Soviet Union.

Hamas acronym for Islamic Resistance Movement, a radical islamic group operating in Israeli-occupied territories. Founded in February 1988 by Sheikh Ahmed Ismail Yassin.

harkis Algerian Muslim auxiliary soldiers in the service of the French army during the French occupation of Algeria 1938–62.

Hezbollah Party of God. The main fundamentalist, Shia movement in Lebanon, operating in the south against Israel.

Human Rights Watch US-based international human rights organization, the second largest worldwide after Amnesty International. Originated in 1978 with HQ in New York.

IAEA International Atomic Energy Agency, autonomous organization within the UN which aims to promote the peaceful use of nuclear energy; founded in 1957, and based in Vienna..

IBRD International Bank for Reconstruction and Development, a UN specialized agency more commonly known as the World Bank. Based in Washington, DC, and established in 1945 following the Bretton Woods conference, it is the largest single source of lending for development by its worldwide members.

ICAO International Civil Aviation Organization, UN specialized agency which aims to establish international standards necessary for the safety and security of air transport.

ICRC International Committee of the Red Cross, founded in 1863 by Swiss philanthropist Henry Dunant after witnessing the battle of Solferino in 1859.

IMF International Monetary Fund, usually deemed synonymous with the World Bank, but to gain access to IBRD funds, member states must be members of the IMF.

Inkatha Zulu word meaning 'Mystical Coil', a reference to the coil worn by African women to help them carry heavy weights on their heads. Conservative South African organization led by Chief Mangosuthu Buthelezi, founded in 1976 and based in Kwazulu-Natal.

International Court of Justice based at The Hague and founded in 1946, the ICJ is the principal judicial organ of the UN and is authorized to resolve disputes between UN member states. It is assisted by a governing body composed of 15 judges of differing nationalities, elected for a 9-year term.

Interpol International Criminal Police Organization established in 1923 and based in Lyon.

IRA Irish Republican Army, currently the main militant republican movement in Northern Ireland, originally formed in 1919 to fight for Irish independence.

John Birch Society extreme rightwing group founded in the USA in 1958 by Robert H.W. Welch, its name deriving from an American intelligence worker killed by Chinese communists in 1945.

KGB Komitet Gosudarstvennoy Bezopasnosti (Committee of State Security), Soviet Union's security police established in 1954. The KGB was scrapped after the August coup of 1991 and replaced in Russia in Jan. 1994 by the Federal Counterintelligence Service.

Knesset   The Israeli unicameral legislature, located in Jerusalem.

KNU   Karen National Union, a guerrilla organization in Myan Mar (Burma), which has fought for a separate Karen state since the late 1940s.

Ku Klux Klan   US white racist paramilitary organization with long history of violence against blacks. Established in Tennessee at the end of the US Civil War in 1865 and still active.

Lok Sabha   lower house of the Indian Parliament; the upper chamber is the Rajya Sabah.

Mafia   in Italy, the network of organized crime, including the Sicilian Mafia, the Neapolitan Camorra and the Calabrian 'Ndrangheta'.

Matrix Churchill   UK machine tool company at the centre of the events that led to the Scott inquiry established on 15 February 1996, into defence-related exports to Iraq. Paul Henderson, Trevor Abrahams and Peter Allen, executives of the Iraqi-owned Matrix Churchill, were arrested in October 1990 and charged with illegally exporting machine tools to Iraq. All three were acquitted and it emerged that Henderson had acted as an MI6 agent.

Mau Mau   secret political society in Kenya which developed into a violent anti-colonial rebellion in the 1950s.

Médecins Sans Frontières   founded in Paris by a group of French doctors in 1971 to provide emergency medical aid worldwide, it is funded by donations. MSF has offices in 20 countries worldwide, the international office being in Brussels.

MI5   the UK Security Service. The counterintelligence service was originally established in 1909 to assess and combat threats to UK security.

MI6   UK's Secret Intelligence Service. Formed in 1909, its role is to gather intelligence abroad in support of the government's security, defence, foreign and economic policies.

Monday Club   right-wing grouping of the UK Conservative Party, formed in 1960. Established in reaction to Harold Macmillan's wind of change speech, the Club was characterized by support for the South African regime, and subsequently the Rhodesian UDI regime, by advocacy of voluntary repatriation of black Commonwealth immigrants, and by opposition to anti-apartheid activities such as sporting boycotts.

Moral Rearmament   revivalist movement established in the UK in 1938 by the US-born Lutheran pastor Frank Buchman, which succeeded Buchman's previous 'Oxford Movement', based its teachings on the 4 absolutes of purity, unselfishness, honesty and love, and on the importance of 'life-change'.

Mossad   the most important, powerful and prominent of the Israeli intelligence agencies. Founded in 1951 by Isser Harel, who served as its director until 1963, it concerns itself with matters of espionage, intelligence gathering and covert political operations in foreign countries.

Mujaheddin-I-Khalq   lay guerrilla organization representing leftwing Muslim groups in Iran. Founded in the early 1970s, it was banned after the Islamic Revolution for its espousal of a variant of Islamic socialism and its criticism of the regime of Ayatollah Khomeini.

NASA   National Aeronautics and Space Administration, the US government agency created in 1958 to co-ordinate civilian activities in space.

National Front   fringe UK racist party founded in 1967 from small neo-fascist groups, including League of Empire Loyalists, British National Party, and Racial Preservation Society.

National Health Service   UK's state health care system. The architect of the service was Aneurin Bevan, health minister in the Labour government of Clement Attlee, drawing on the Beveridge Report of 1942 on the welfare state. The NHS was officially inaugurated on 5 July 1948.

National Trust   National Trust for Places of Historic Interest or Natural Beauty, founded by Octavia Hill in 1895.

Nato   North Atlantic Treaty Organisation, based in Brussels and formed in April 1949. Nato came into being during the Soviet blockade of Berlin, taking as its basic tenet that an armed attack on any Nato country would be seen as an attack on them all.

New Jewel Movement   leftwing party founded in Grenada in 1973 which in 1979 overthrew the government of Sir Eric Gairy and set up a People's Revolutionary Government under PM Maurice Bishop.

1922 Committee   body consisting of all Conservative back-bench MPs in the UK House of Commons. The name commemorates the decision in 1922, forced on the party leadership by Tory backbenchers, to bring down Lloyd George's coalition government. Sir Archibald S. Hamilton is the chairman as at the time of writing.

Non-Proliferation Treaty   arms control agreement approved by the UN in June 1968 and effective from March 1970.

OECD   Organization for Economic Co-Operation and Development, formed in 1961 as the instrument for international co-operation among industrialized member states on economic and social policies. HQ in Paris.

Oireachtas   bicameral legislature of the Republic of Ireland, comprising the 166-seat lower house, the Dáil Éireann, and the 60-seat upper house or Senate, the Seanad Éireann.

OPEC   Organization of Petroleum Exporting Countries, Established in Sept. 1960 by Iran, Iraq, Kuwait, Saudi Arabia and Venezuela, subsequently enlarged to include Qatar, Indonesia, Libya, Abu Dhabi, Algeria, Nigeria, Ecuador and Gabon. It aims to unify petroleum policies among member countries in order to ensure stable prices. Ecuador left OPEC in 1993.

Organization of African Unity   established in 1963 by 32 African countries to promote continental unity and solidarity of African states. Headquarters are in Addis Ababa, Ethiopia.

OSS   Office for Strategic Services, US intelligence organization which was the predecessor of the CIA. Established in June 1942.

Oxfam   Oxford Committee for Famine Relief, founded in 1942 to aid women and children in nazi-occupied Greece and based in Oxford, it now has 40 overseas field offices.

PDSA   People's Dispensary for Sick Animals, founded by Mary Dickin in 1917.

Pearce Commission   UK government body established in Nov. 1971 to investigate whether proposals to settle the dispute with Rhodesia over UDI (Unilateral Declaration of Independence) were acceptable to the Rhodesian people.

Pentagon   HQ, in Arlington, VA, of the US Defence Department and the Departments of the Army, Navy and Airforce.

ORGANIZATIONS

Phalange main rightwing Maronite Christian movement in Lebanon. The Phalangist Party and its militias spearheaded the Christian side in the Lebanese civil war 1975–91, during which they were allied with Israel.

PLO Palestine Liberation Organization, founded in 1964 as spokesman for all matters concerning the Palestinian people. Yasser Arafat has led the PLO since 1969.

Politburo key committee in the leadership structures of most communist parties, elected in the case of the Soviet Union by the central committee of the CPSU.

Quai d'Orsay term used for the French Ministry of Foreign Affairs, whose HQ is located in this street alongside the River Seine in Paris.

Radio Free Europe broadcasting operation covering the countries of Eastern and Central Europe, funded by the US government and operating from Munich under US management. Founded in 1949, it merged with Radio Liberty in 1976 and its aims are to broadcast non-partisan information.

Red Army Russian army formed in 1917 by the Bolsheviks and organized by Leon Trotsky to fight the anti-communist white armies.

Red Guards groups composed of students and schoolchildren in China who as 'Red Guards of the Cultural Revolution' had the task of unmasking revisionists and promoting Maoism. Emerging in 1966, the Red Guard operated for over a year before being disbanded.

Risorgimento the 19th-century movement for the political unification of Italy.

Royal Academy (of Arts) founded in 1768 at Somerset House but eventually moved to Burlington House. First president was Joshua Reynolds.

Royal Automobile Club founded in 1897 and responsible for many aspects of motoring safety and control.

Royal Exchange founded by Thomas Gresham in 1568 and home to various financial institutions. The present building was built by William Tite in 1844.

Royal Geographical Society founded in 1830 as the Geographical Society of London, it has been sited at Kensington Gore since 1912 in a house designed by Norman Shaw.

Royal Horticultural Society established in 1804 and awarded its royal charter in 1861, the RHS holds many shows but is primarily concerned with the Chelsea Flower Show held in Ranelagh Gardens since 1913. The Society has gardens at Wisley, Rosemoor near Great Torrington, Devon, and Hyde Hall, Essex.

Royal Institution (of GB) established in 1799 by Count Rumford (Benjamin Thompson), this scientific organization still has its headquarters in Albemarle St, London W1.

Royal Scottish Academy founded in 1826 and occupying a Greek Revival building in Edinburgh built by William Playfair.

Royal Society founded in 1660, early members included Christopher Wren and Samuel Pepys. Isaac Newton was president 1703–27.

SALT Strategic Arms Limitation Talks, held between USSR and USA 1969–79. Salt I, 1969–72, and Salt II, 1973–4, were between Nixon and Brezhnev and Salt II talks were concluded in 1979 by Carter and Brezhnev in Vienna, after which the SALT talks were renamed START.

Sandinista leftwing Nicaraguan revolutionary movement that overthrew President Anastasio Somoza in 1979. Founded in 1961 and named in honour of Augusto César Sandino, the leader of a small peasant army that waged a campaign (1926–33) against the US occupation of Nicaragua.

SAVAK defunct Iranian security organization established in 1957 with the aid of USA and Israeli intelligence services, and used to crush opposition to Mohammad Reza Shah Pahlavi.

Save the Children Fund founded by Eglantyne Jebb, an Englishwoman, who saw starving children in Austria (1919). The Princess Royal is the President.

Schengen Group European mainland countries within the EU which are party to the Schengen Agreement on abolishing border controls between their territories while improving police co-operation. The original group which met in Schengen in Luxembourg in June 1985 consisted of the Benelux countries and France and Germany; Spain and Portugal soon ratified the treaty, followed by Italy, Greece and Austria.

Securitate communist Romania's security police which mounted a brutal defence of the regime of Nicolae Ceausescu during the December 1989 revolution.

Sejm the lower house of the Polish National Assembly, comprising 460 directly elected members.

SHAPE Supreme Headquarters Allied Powers Europe, the NATO military HQ of Allied Command Europe. SHAPE was moved from Paris to near Mons in Belgium in 1967, after De Gaulle's decision to withdraw France from NATO.

Shin Bet the Israeli internal security agency, aka the General Security Service.

Sierra Club probably the world's first environmental pressure group, formed in 1892 in California by naturalist John Muir.

Sinn Fein (ourselves alone) prominent revolutionary party fighting initially for the republican independence of Ireland, and, since partition, for the reunification of the country.

Snowdrop Campaign founded after the killing of 16 children in Dunblane on 13 March 1996 and named after the only flower in bloom that day. The campaign, backed by international film star Sean Connery, aims to ban civilian ownership of firearms.

Solidarity Polish trade union and opposition movement founded in 1980 by striking workers at the Gdansk shipyard. Its first leader was the future President Lech Walesa.

Stasi the Ministry of State Security of communist East Germany, which operated from 1950 to 1990.

Stern Gang British name for the Zionist guerrilla group founded in Palestine in 1940 by Abraham Stern and responsible till 1949 for several terrorist attacks.

Stormont the Northern Ireland parliament buildings in Belfast, the seat of the N.I. parliament from 1932 until the introduction of direct rule in 1972.

Tamil Tigers militant organization formed in 1976 aiming to achieve and independent Tamil state in northern Sri Lanka.

TASS Soviet Union's state news agency.

Tontons Macoutes (from a Creole word meaning 'Uncle Knapsack', a bogeyman), the notorious Haitian right-wing secret police, set up in 1958 by Papa Doc Duvalier.

TUC   Trades Union Congress, the key umbrella employees' organization in the UK, founded in 1868.

Tupamaros   Uruguayan guerrilla group named after an 18th-century Peruvian Indian chief Tupac Amarú, and founded in 1962 by Raúl Antonaccio, an activist in sugar cane cutters' strikes. The group is still active today under the name 'National Liberation Movement'.

Tynwald   parliament of the Isle of Man, a UK Crown Dependency. The principal chamber of Tynwald is the 24-member directly elected House of Keys. Tynwald celebrated its millennium in 1979; only the Althing of Iceland claims to be older (dating back to at least 930).

UN General Assembly   established under Chapter IV of the UN Charter to act as the organization's plenary body, representing all member states, it oversees the work of the UN's subsidiary bodies.

UN Secretariat   listed in Chapter III of its Charter, the Secretariat, and the functions of the Secretary-General, are covered in detail in Chapter XV of the Charter. Elected by the Security Council. Secretariatship is usually for a term of 5 years with an automatic option to carry on unless vetoed by a member of the Council. Trygve Lie of Norway took office in Feb. 1946 and his term was extended until he resigned in November 1952, despite a Soviet veto. Other holders have been Dag Hammarskjöld of Sweden (April 1953 until his death in the Congo in September 1961), U Thant of Burma (1961–71), Kurt Waldheim of Austria (1972–81), Javier Pérez de Cuéllar of Peru (1982–91), Boutros Boutros-Ghali of Egypt (1 January 1992 – 1 January 1997, US vetoed continuation) and the incumbent Kofe Anan of Ghana.

UN Security Council   established under Chapter V of the Charter, the Security Council has primary responsibility for the maintenance of international peace and security. It presently has 15 member states, 10 non-permanent members plus China, France, Russia, UK and USA, which are permanent members and carry power of veto.

UNESCO   Paris-based UN Educational, Scientific and Cultural Organization, founded in 1946 to promote international collaboration in those fields of endeavour. USA, UK and Singapore are not members at present after suggestions of financial mismanagement.

UNITA   National Union for the Total Independence of Angola. Led by Jonas Savimbi, UNITA fought alongside the Popular Movement for the Liberation of Angola during the struggle against colonial rule, but following the Portuguese withdrawal in 1975 it

began a rivalry with the MPLA, backed by South Africa and the USA and not yet concluded.

United Arab Republic   political union of Egypt and Syria proclaimed between 1958 and 1961. Egypt retained the title of UAR until 1971, when it took the name Arab Republic of Egypt.

United Nations   Established on 24 Oct. 1945 with its HQ completed in New York in 1952, the UN replaced the inter-war League of Nations, and its 111 articles of the Charter were proposed at the San Francisco Conference from 25 April – 25 June 1945. Its 6 principal organs are the General Assembly, Security Council, Economic and Social Council, Trusteeship Council, International Court of Justice and the Secretariat. Membership has risen from 51 at inception to 188 as at 30 September 1998.

United Nations Budget   Top 7 countries contributing to the UN are USA (25%), Japan (18%), Germany (9.6%), Russia (2.9%), France (6.5%), UK (5.1%) and Italy (5.4%) as at 30 September 1998.

Universal Postal Union   UN specialized agency based in Berne, Switzerland, first established in 1875 and taken over by the UN in 1948, charged with promoting international collaboration in postal services.

UNPROFOR   UN Protection Force, established in January 1992 and dispatched to Croatia in March 1992 to monitor a ceasefire between Croatia and Krajina Serbs.

Velvet Revolution   near-bloodless overthrow of Czech communist regime in November–December 1989 resulting in the ousting of the leader, Milos Jakes, and subsequent presidency of Vaclav Havel.

Warsaw Pact   Warsaw Treaty Organization, which was the communist counterpart to NATO during the cold war. Original signatories in May 1955 were Albania, Bulgaria, Czechoslovakia, East Germany, Hungary, Poland, Romania and the USSR. Albania withdrew in 1968 and following the collapse of communism in central and Eastern Europe the Warsaw Pact was dissolved in February 1991.

Women's Institute   founded in 1897 at Stoney Creek, Canada.

World Health Organization   UN specialized agency based in Geneva and founded in 1948 with the aim of attaining the highest level of health for mankind.

World Wide Fund for Nature   known until 1988 as the World Wildlife Fund, it was formed in 1961 and raises funds for a variety of conservation projects.

Yakuza   Japanese criminal organization comparable to US mafia-type syndicates.

O
R
G
A
N
I
Z
A
T
I
O
N
S

PERFUME

Animal Sources

ambergris found floating on the sea (particularly the Indian Ocean) in oily grey lumps. It is excreted by the sperm whale after feeding on cuttlefish and is used as a base for perfumes.

castoreum comes from the follicles in the genital areas of both male and female beavers; used as a fixative.

civet comes from a pouch beneath the tails of both male and female civet cats; used as a fixative.

hyraceum excreted by the hyrax, a small rabbit-like animal found in the Middle East. It was used in ancient Arabic perfumes but is rarely used nowadays.

musk comes from the preputial follicle of the male musk deer. It is used as a fixative and is also thought to be an aphrodisiac. Chinese courtesans were fed bland foods perfumed with musk, so that when aroused the warmth of their bodies released the scent.

propolis a sticky brown fixative which bees collect from trees to use as a cement in their hives.

sweet hoof or onycha an ingredient of incense that comes from the shells of marine snails found around India and the Red Sea.

Plant, Mineral and Synthetic Sources

angelica root of the holy ghost (*Angelica archangelica*). It has a strong musky aroma.

bdellium myrrh (see also opoponax), an aromatic gum.

ben oil an essential oil from the winged seeds of the horseradish tree, used as a base oil for perfumes.

burning bush white dittany. The oil from the plant can vaporize in hot weather and catch fire without harming the plant itself. The fragrant essential oil is used in pot-pourri.

cherry pie heliotrope, used in pot-pourri and in modern perfumes such as 'Lou Lou' (Cacharel).

coumarin a white crystalline substance with a scent of new-mown hay, found in withered herbs and fruits. It is also manufactured synthetically from coal tar.

devil's dung asafoetida, a tall evil-smelling plant used as a fixative.

farnesol manufactured synthetically, but also found in musk. It gives a scent of lily of the valley.

frangipani the first plant to be named after a perfume. In 15th-century Rome, one of the Frangipani family made the perfume from orris, spices, civet and musk digested in wine alcohol. Later, French colonists in the West Indies found a bush (*Plumeria alba*) which had the same smell and named it frangipani.

galbanum small drops of it ooze from the stems of the giant fennel. It is mentioned in the Old Testament. It has a spicy-green scent with a hint of musk and is used in the 'top notes' of quality perfumes like Chanel No. 19.

handflower wallflower. The name 'handflower' comes from the practice, stemming from ancient Greece, of carrying the flowers in the hand as a nosegay during festivals.

indole the synthetic material derived from coal tar used to produce the scent of jasmine and neroli.

ionone the synthetic material used to make the scent of violets.

isoeugenol the synthetic material used to make the scent of carnations.

labdanum comes from rock-rose shrubs found around the Mediterranean; often gathered by combing the beards of goats which have browsed on the bushes. It was thought to have aphrodisiac qualities. Assyrian kings liked young women who had spent time soaking during a six-month period in baths of labdanum or bdellium, after six months soaking in myrrh.

linalol the synthetic material used to make the scents of lilac, lily and honeysuckle.

love-in-the-mist nigella, a hardy annual which grows to a height of about 1.5 m and has a fragrance of ambrette seeds.

malabathrum a dried aromatic leaf from a species of cinnamon, used by the Romans in the making of unguents.

muguet lily of the valley. It is used in many 'quality' perfumes such as 'Opium' (Yves St Laurent), and 'Florissa' (Floris). Its fragrance is manufactured synthetically as farnesol.

olibanum frankincense, a fragrant gum resin often used as an incense and, in perfumes, as a fixative.

opoponax myrrh (probably the Biblical myrrh collected from the land of Punt). Its oil, with a scent of fenugreek, is distilled from the yellowish lumps which occur on the plant. It is used mainly for incense and pot-pourri.

orris comes from iris roots; has a violet-like scent.

storax originally from the bark of the liquidamber tree which grows in Turkey, Asia Minor and Rhodes, but now manufactured synthetically. It has a smell of cinnamon, and is used as a fixative.

syringa lilac. The flowers are used mainly in pot-pourri, and its oil is used in 'quality' perfumes such as 'Chamade' (Guerlain), 'Florissa' (Floris) and 'Soir de Paris' (Bourjois).

verbena holy wort. The leaves have a lemon scent. It is used mainly in cosmetics and soaps and the leaves are sometimes dried for use in sachets.

Perfumes and Perfume Houses

Alliage	Estée Lauder (1972)	Knowing	Estée Lauder (1988)
Amarige	Givenchy (1991)	L'Aimant	Coty (1927)
Anaïs Anaïs	Cacharel (1978)	L'Air du Temps	Nina Ricci (1948)
Arpège	Lanvin (1927; relaunched 1994)	L'Egoïste	Chanel (1990)
		Le Jardin	Max Factor (1986)
Bal à Versailles	Jean Desprez (1962)	Lou Lou	Cacharel (1987)
Beautiful	Estée Lauder (1985)	Ma Griffe	Carven (1946)
Brut	Fabergé (1964)	Mon Parfum	Paloma Picasso / L'Oréal (1984)
Cabochard	Grès (1959)		
Calandre	Paco Rabanne (1969)	Must	Cartier (1981)
Chamade	Guerlain (1969)	Obsession	Calvin Klein (1985)
Charlie	Revlon (1973)	Old Spice	Shulton (1937)
Cheap and Chic	Moschino (1996)	Only	Julio Iglesias / Myrurgia (1989)
Chlöe	Lagerfeld (1975)		
Chypre	Coty (1917)	Opium	Yves St Laurent (1977)
CKOne	Calvin Klein (1994)	Paris	Yves St Laurent (1983)
Devin	Aramis (1978)	Parure	Guerlain (1975)
Diva	Ungaro (1983)	Pleasures	Estée Lauder (1996)
Drakkar Noir	Guy Laroche (1982)	Poême	Lancôme (1995)
Dune	Christian Dior (1991)	Poison	Christian Dior (1985)
Eau de Bonpoint	Annick Goutal (1989)	Polo	Ralph Lauren (1978)
Eau Sauvage	Dior (1966)	Red	Giorgio Beverly Hills (1989)
Eden	Cacharel (1994)		
Escape	Calvin Klein (1991)	Red Door	Elizabeth Arden (1990; relaunched 1996)
Eternity	Calvin Klein (1988)		
Fahrenheit	Dior (1988)	Rive Gauche	Yves St Laurent (1971)
Femme	Rochas (1944)	Samsara	Guerlain (1989)
Fidgi	Guy Laroche (1962)	Shalimar	Guerlain (1925)
Fleurs de Fleurs	Nina Ricci (1980)	Shocking	Schiaparelli (1936)
Gentleman	Givenchy (1974)	So Pretty	Cartier (1995)
Imprévu	Coty (1965)	Special No. 127	Floris (1890)
Intimate	Revlon (1955)	Trésor	Lancôme (1990)
Ivoire	Balmain (1979)	Tweed	Lenthéric (1933)
Jardins de Bagatelle	Guerlain (1983)	Vent Vert	Balmain (1947)
Je Reviens	Worth (1932)	Youth Dew	Estée Lauder (1953)
Jicky	Guerlain (1889)	Ysatis	Givenchy (1984)
Joy	Patou (1930)		

Notable Perfumes

aqua angeli   a perfumed water made from aloewood, nutmeg, clove, storax, benzoin and rosewater, first made for scenting the shirts of Louis XIV of France.

eau-de-Cologne   first developed by Paul Feminis in Cologne in the early 18th century. Its main ingredients were lavender and citrus, neroli, bergamot and lemon. 4711 Mullhens of Cologne still uses the original formula.

Chanel No. 5   named because the fragrance chosen by Coco Chanel from specimens supplied by Ernest Beauxs was sample No. 5. The first aldehyde perfume.

Chanel No. 19   named for Coco Chanel's birthday (19 August).

damask water   popular in 16th-century England. It is made mainly from rosewater.

Eau de Bonpoint   by Annick Goutal (1989). The first fragrance for babies.

Imperial Leather   first made in 1768 by Bayleys, the court perfumers in London, as a result of a challenge by the Russian Count Orloff, to make a perfume with the scent of worn leather. It became a favourite of Catherine the Great, under the name 'Eau de Cologne Imperiale Russe'. Cussons took over Bayleys and renamed the perfume Imperial Russian Leather, but dropped 'Russian' in 1939.

L'Interdit   launched for Audrey Hepburn in 1957. It was Givenchy's first perfume. The name means 'the forbidden one' – forbidden, at first, to all but Audrey Hepburn, whose face graced the advertisement.

Jicky   the first 'modern' perfume, created in 1889 by Aimé Guerlain.

Joy   the most expensive perfume on the market soon after its manufacture by Jean Patou in 1930.

Only   launched in 1989 by Myrurgia in association with singer Julio Iglesias.

Special No. 127   created by Floris in 1890 for Grand Duke Orloff of Russia. No. 127 was the page in Floris' Book where he wrote formulae which were created uniquely for individual customers.

Vent Vert   launched in 1947 by Balmain. It was the first 'green' perfume.

Notable Perfumers

Baur   Albert Baur was patenter of the first synthetic musk perfume, Musk Baur, in 1988.

Beaux   Ernest Beaux developed the first aldehyde-based perfume, Chanel No. 5.

Carles   Jean Carles, of Grasse, insured his nose for $1 million. His creations include 'Canoe' in 1935 (for Dana) and 'Shocking' in 1936 (for Schiaparelli). He founded the School of Perfumery in Grasse, Provence.

Farina   Jean-Marie Farina opened a shop in Paris in 1806 to sell eau-de-Cologne. He sold his business in 1840 to Léonce Collas, who passed it on in 1862 to his cousins, Messrs Roger & Gallet.

Floris   the oldest perfume house in the world, founded in 1730 as a barber's shop in Jermyn Street, London, by Juan Floris from Minorca.

Hermès   arose from a harness-making, then glove-making business. Many of its perfumes are named after horse and carriage parts, for example 'Calèche' (a four-wheeled horse-drawn carriage).

Perkin   William Perkin found out how to synthesize coumarin from coal tar, a much-used ingredient with a new-mown-hay fragrance. This was one of the first major discoveries in synthetic perfumery.

Miscellaneous

Abir   perfumed powder used in India, usually sprinkled on linen. Its ingredients include sandalwood, aloes, cardamon, cloves, civet and rose.

Aldehyde   a group of alcohol-derived chemicals which form other groups of chemicals known as benzoid compounds. Their discovery led to the manufacture of synthetic perfume ingredients.

chypre   originally a famous Roman perfume made in Cyprus (hence the name). Nowadays used to describe perfumes with fresh top notes of bergamot, with other citrus ingredients such as neroli, lemon and orange, with middle notes of jasmin and rose and a base of oakmoss, with labdanum, storax, civet, patchouli and musk. The first modern chypre perfume was 'Chypre by Coty' (1917).

khaluq   an unguent made by early Arabs which men were forbidden to use.

kyphi   an incense made by the ancient Egyptians, based on wine, honey, raisins, herbs, frankincense, myrrh and juniper berries.

kypros   an ancient Greek perfume which contained wine and cardamon and a sweet-scented substance called aspalathus.

magma   the dried dregs from unguent bottles which the ancient Greeks and Romans added to scented powders.

olla-podrida   pot-pourri made by perfume-makers from their waste materials with which they mixed herbs and lavender and rose petals.

perfumer's organ   not his or her nose! It is the work bench and surrounding ingredients and equipment.

pomander   a solid ball of perfumed material, such as crushed petals bound with a gum. In Tudor times they were carried to mask unpleasant smells and to ward off infection. In the 16th century it became popular to make them from oranges with cloves pushed into them, then baked. People fastened them to their belts or wrists. Nowadays they are sometimes used to perfume wardrobes.

tussie-mussie   a nosegay dating from Elizabethan times, when it was originally made from flowers and herbs chosen for their symbolic meanings, e.g. rosemary for remembrance, daisy for faithfulness etc.

unguent cone   cone made from perfumed fat (usually ox-tallow), which was fixed on to the hair or head-dress so that it melted and ran down the hair and body, perfuming them as it did so.

Strengths and Forms of Perfume in Descending Order According to Strength

Concentration	Name
15–30% in high-grade alcohol	extrait
15–18% in 80–90% grade alcohol	eau de parfum
4–8% in alcohol	eau de toilette
3–5% in 70% alcohol/water	eau de Cologne
3% in 80% pure alcohol	eau fraiche

Containers

acerra   small box used by the Romans to contain incense burned in temples.

alabastrum   pot, usually made from alabaster, agate or onyx, used by the Romans to contain perfumed oils.

aryballos / ampulla   small flask used by the ancient Greeks to contain perfumed oils, often carried hanging from the wrist by a small strap.

pouncet box   box used since Elizabethan times to contain perfumed powders placed between bedlinen. Originally used to hold pumice stone which was needed in the preparation of parchment for writing.

vinaigrette   small metal box whose inner lid was pierced, popular in 18th/19th-century Europe. It held a sponge soaked in aromatic vinegar and was used as a smelling bottle.

Founders

Amouage   The Hamood family of the Sultanate of Oman (1983).

Avon   David McConnell (1886), Suffern, California. He was a travelling book-salesman who liked to give his customers free gifts of inexpensive perfume. Originally called the California Perfume Co., its name changed to Avon (after Stratford-on-Avon) in 1959.

Cacharel   Jean Bosquet (1962), Paris. The name comes from a wild duck found in Provence.

Charles of the Ritz   Charles Jundt (1934), New York.

Coty   François Sputorno (1905), Paris.

Elizabeth Arden   Florence Graham (1910), New York. Name derived from the title of the book *Elizabeth and Her German Garden* by Elizabeth von Arnim.

Fragonard   Eugene Fuchs (1783), Grasse, Provence. Named after the painter Fragonard.

Lancôme   Armand Petitjean (1935), Paris.

Mary Chess   Grace Mary Chess Robinson (1932), London.

Revlon   Charles and Joseph Revson and Charles Lachmann (1932), Boston, originally to market nail varnish.

Perfume Families or Classification

Perfumes are usually classified according to seven 'family' groups which form a continuum from floral to fougère.

floral   mainly made from flower oils. These are light, daytime perfumes, e.g. 'Anaïs Anaïs' (Cacharel), 'L'Air du Temps' (Nina Ricci).

green   giving an impression of new-mown grass. Fresh-smelling perfumes which include among their ingredients mosses, ferns, citrus fruits and herbs, e.g. 'Alliage' (Estée Lauder), 'Chanel No. 19' (Chanel).

aldehydic   based on synthetic aldehydes. They range from floral through woody to powdery, e.g. 'Chanel No. 5' (Chanel), 'White Linen' (Estée Lauder).

chypre   their fragrance is floral or green but with a heavy base such as ambergris, e.g. 'Cabochard' (Grès), 'Chypre' (Coty).

oriental   their fragrance is spicy, strong and exotic and has a heavy sweetness which comes from ingredients such as musk, vanilla and sandalwood, e.g. 'Poison' (Christian Dior) and 'Opium' (Yves St Laurent).

tobacco / leather   they have a hint of tobacco, leather and woody aromas, e.g. 'Antaeus' (Chanel) and 'Cuir de Russie' (Chanel).

fougère   their fragrance is fresh, with a note of lavender, herbs, oakmoss, coumarin and new-mown hay, e.g. 'Drakkar Noir' (Guy Laroche), 'Brut' (Fabergé).

PHOTOGRAPHY

Photography and Cinematography

Ansel Easton Adams (1902–84) American photographer who co-founded Group f/64 with Edward Weston (1932) and helped set up the Department of Photography at the New York Museum of Modern Art (1940). His publications include *Taos Pueblo* (1930) and *Born Free and Equal* (1944).

Diane Arbus (1923–71) American photographer famous for her intense portraits of American social outcasts.

Eugène Atget (1857–1927) French photographer famous for recording the streets and scenes of old Paris; his unusual images of the commonplace inspired the Surrealists.

Richard Avedon (1923–) Photographer who made his name as a fashion photographer with *Harper's Bazaar*. His first sitter was Russian pianist-composer Sergei Rachmaninov.

David Royston Bailey (1938–) English photographer who started his professional life as a fashion photographer but developed as a portraitist during the 1960s, specializing in nudes. His 1965 collection *David Bailey's Box of Pin-ups* (1965) included pictures of celebrities of the day, from the Beatles to the Krays.

Billy Bitzer (1874–1944) US motion picture cameraman who, in partnership with the pioneer director D.W. Griffiths, developed camera techniques that set the standard for all future motion pictures. He was the first cameraman to use artificial lighting for his work, and his other innovations included the use of soft-focus photography, using a light-diffusion screen in front of the camera lens, the fade-out, and the iris shot, in which the frame is either gradually blacked out in a shrinking circle, thereby ending a scene, or gradually opened in a widening circle, beginning a scene.

Margaret Bourke-White (1904–71) American photojournalist who was employed by *Fortune* magazine in 1929 and subsequently became staff photographer and associate editor on *Life* magazine (1936). She was the first woman photographer to be attached to the US armed forces, producing outstanding reports of the siege of Moscow in 1941, and the opening of the concentration camps in 1944. Bourke-White married the American author Erskine Caldwell in 1939 but was divorced in 1942.

Mathew Brady (1823–96) New York-born photographer famous for his record of the American Civil War with the Union armies.

Bill Brandt (1904–83) English photographer who studied with Man Ray in London before working for the Ministry of Information and recording conditions during the Blitz. Brandt subsequently found fame with his landscapes and nudes. His publications include *The English at Home* (1936), *Perspective of Nudes* (1961) and *Shadows of Light* (1966).

Brassaï (1899–1984) Professional name of Gyula Halász, the Hungarian-born French painter and photographer. His photography included the nightlife of 1930s Paris.

Henri Cartier–Bresson (1908–) French photographer who initially studied painting with André Lhote before working as an assistant to film director Jean Renoir. His publications include *The Decisive Moment* (1952) and *The Europeans* (1955).

Julia Margaret Cameron (1815–79) British photographer who pioneered portrait photography.

Louis Jacques Mandé Daguerre (1787–1851) French painter and physicist who invented the daguerreotype, i.e. the first practical process of photography. Though the first permanent photograph was made in 1826 by Niépce, it was of poor quality and required about 8 hours exposure time as opposed to Daguerre's process which took 20 to 30 minutes.

Terence Donovan (1936–96) London-born photographer and film director whose work covered a wide spectrum of contemporary life. He worked for *Vogue*, *Harpers & Queen*, *Elle*, and *Marie Claire*.

George Eastman (1854–1932) US manufacturer who introduced the Kodak camera (1888) and Brownie camera (1900). Contrary to popular belief he was unrelated to Linda Eastman.

Walker Evans (1903–75) American photographer who produced a powerful record of the faces, homes and lives of America's 1930s rural poor.

Roger Fenton (1819–69) English photographer who was famous for his Crimean War pictures.

William Henry Fox Talbot (1800–77) English chemist, linguist and photographer who in 1839 invented the photographic negative and whose *The Pencil of Nature* (1844) was the first photographic book.

William Friese-Greene (1855–1921) British photographer who is often credited with the invention of cinematography, although Thomas Edison would appear to have a stronger claim. Friese-Greene did however pioneer stereoscopic and colour cinematography, but once again lacked the technical knowledge necessary to bring his ideas to fruition. A 1951 feature film, *The Magic Box*, was based on his life.

John Heartfield (1891–1968) Originally named Helmut Herzfelde, German pioneer of the photomontage, e.g. *Hurrah, the Butter is Finished* (1935).

Lewis Wickes Hine (1874–1940) American photographer who studied sociology before making a photographic study of Ellis Island immigrants and child labourers. Hine worked for the American Red Cross in WW1 and recorded the construction of the Empire State Building in his survey *Men at Work* (1932).

James Wong Howe (1899–1976) Chinese-born American cinematographer who started work in 1917 as assistant cameraman to Cecil B. De Mille and in 1922 became chief cameraman for *Famous Players*. Howe pioneered the use of the wide-angle lens, deep focus, and ceilinged sets to replicate shipboard claustrophobia. He won Oscars for his work on *The Rose Tattoo* (1955) and *Hud* (1963).

Yousuf Karsh (1908–) Armenian-born Canadian photographer who was appointed official portrait photographer to the Canadian government in 1935. His reputation was made with a 1941 portrait of Sir Winston Churchill, and he continued to photograph all the world's leading statesmen.

André Kertész (1894–1985) Hungarian-born American photographer famous for his pioneering use of the small hand-held camera, the well-observed social scene, the surreal figure study, still life, and later the fashion image.

Edwin Herbert Land (1909–91)   US inventor and physicist whose invention of the Polaroid (one-step) process for developing and printing photographs culminated in a revolution in photography unparalleled since the advent of roll film.

Dorothea Lange (1895–1965)   US photographer who started as a society photographer but became famous for her social records of migrant workers during the 1930s depression.

Lord Patrick Lichfield (1939–)   British aristocratic photographer whose reputation was built around his royal photographs and his nude calendars.

Auguste Lumière (1862–1954), Louis Lumière (1864–1948)   French chemist brothers who invented the first successful cine camera and projector (1895) and a process of colour photography. They also produced the first film newsreels, and the first movie, *La Sortie des usines Lumière* (1895).

László Moholy-Nagy (1895–1946)   Hungarian-born American photographer famous for his constructivist-inspired, semi-abstract images, and his inspiring teaching at the Bauhaus.

Eadweard Muybridge (1830–1904)   Original name Edward James Muggeridge. English photographer famous for his early experiments in capturing motion in photographic images and for his landscapes of the American West. Muybridge was employed by the railroad magnate Leland Stanford in 1872 to prove that during a particular moment in trotting, all four legs of a horse are off the ground simultaneously. His studies were interrupted while he was tried for the murder of his wife's lover, but after his acquittal he developed a special shutter that gave an exposure of 2/1,000 of a second which proved Stanford's theory.

Nadar (1820–1910)   Professional name of Gaspard-Félix Tournachon, French artist and photographer whose Paris studio became a favourite haunt of the intelligentsia. In 1886 he produced the first photo interview, a series of 21 photographs of the centenarian scientist Eugène Chevreul, each captioned with the sitter's replies to Nadar's questions. He pioneered the use of aerial photographs for map-making and in 1858 took the first pictures from a balloon.

Joseph-Nicéphore Niépce (1765–1833)   French inventor who was the first to make a permanent photographic image (1826).

Man Ray (1890–1976)   American photographer, painter and film-maker, born Emanuel Rabinovich, who was a leading light in the development of Modernism. He founded the New York Dadaist movement with Marcel Duchamp and Francis Picabia before moving to Paris and working with René Clair. Man Ray pioneered the use of photographic images made without a camera, 'Rayographs'.

Henry Peach Robinson (1830–1901)   English photographer who opened a studio at Leamington Spa in 1857 and specialized in images of costumed models and painted settings. He was a founder member of the Linked Ring (1892), a group of photographers seeking to excel in artistic creation.

Alexander Rodchenko (1891–1956)   Soviet photographer and photomontagist who introduced 'New Photography' to post-revolutionary Russia.

Erich Salomon (1886–1944)   German photojournalist who was master of the candid shot whereby he

caught politicians and celebrities off guard for new magazines of the 1920s. He died in Auschwitz.

August Sander (1876–1964)   German photographer celebrated for his ambitious project 'Man in the Twentieth Century', a picture of the doomed Weimar Republic through the faces of its people.

Aaron Siskind (1903–)   American photographer who began his career while teaching English in New York (1932). His subjects showed the usual American depiction of the depression of the 1930s, but unlike other documentaries of the period his *Dead End: The Bowery* and *Harlem Document* show as much concern for pure design as for the plight of the subjects. Siskind developed an abstract approach to his art and began photographing mundane subjects and architectural ruins. He became professor of photography at the Institute of Design of the Illinois Institute of Technology in Chicago (1951–71) and held a similar post at Rhode Island School of Design from 1971.

W. Eugene Smith (1918–78)   US photojournalist noted for his impassioned documentary photographs from around the world, seen mostly in *Life* magazine in the 1940s and 50s.

Edward Steichen (1879–1973)   Luxembourg-born American photographer who became a member of the Linked Ring in England and made his reputation with his studies of the nude. In 1902 he co-founded the American Photo-Secession Group with Alfred Stieglitz. In WW1 he served as commander of the photographic division of the US army. In the 1920s Steichen developed a New Realism style and became heavily involved in fashion photography. He was head of US Naval Film Services during WW2, and director of photography at the New York Museum of Modern Art from 1945 to 1962, where he put on the 'Family of Man' exhibition in 1955.

Alfred Stieglitz (1864–1946)   American photographer who founded the Photo-Secession Group in 1902 with Edward Steichen. He was a major figure in establishing photography as an art form and his gallery of modern art at 291 Fifth Avenue, NY, was the linchpin of his work.

Paul Strand (1890–1976)   US photographer and documentary film-maker who studied under Lewis Hine. In 1933 he was appointed chief of photography and cinematography in the government Secretariat of Education in Mexico. Known for his still lifes, architectural studies and photographic books on regions of the world.

Edward Weston (1886–1958)   American photographer who made his reputation in his Glendale studio but moved to Mexico in 1923, where he developed his modernist style. In 1932 he joined Ansel Adams and others in forming the 'straight photography' purists Group *f*/64 in California. His close-up studies of inanimate objects such as shells and vegetables exemplified his vision of detailed form and the richness of his control of tone. He produced notable landscapes of the Mojave Desert, and in 1937, with the first-ever award of a Guggenheim Fellowship to a photographer, travelled the American West before touring the Eastern States to illustrate an edition of Walt Whitman's *Leaves of Grass*.

Minor White (1908–76)   American photographer and editor who was greatly influenced by Edward Weston and Alfred Stieglitz. In 1946 he moved to San Francisco and worked with Ansel Adams, whom he followed as director of the photographic department in the California School of Fine Art (1947–52). White was appointed professor of creative photography at the Massachusetts Institute of Technology

P
H
O
T
O
G
R
A
P
H
Y

(1965–76) and founded the periodicals *Aperture* and *Image*.

Garry Winogrand (1928–84) American photographer who created a highly influential brand of urban street photography, fusing the 'snapshot' approach with a sense of energy and crowded events in his images.

Politics

Country – Name of Governmental Chambers – Type of Government

NB The upper chambers of bicameral parliaments are listed first in this table, and the name of parliaments are the most commonly accepted, e.g. the parliament of Algeria is bicameral, the upper house being the Majlis el-Umma and the lower house the National Assembly. The combined assemblies are generally referred to as the Majlis (council). Parliaments are generally elected for a term of years but in some bicameral assemblies the two chambers may have differing lengths of term. In our example of Algeria, the lower house is elected for a five-year term but the upper house has a third of its members elected for six years, a third elected for three years, and the remaining third at the president's discretion. The membership is the statutory capacity as at June 2001.

Country	Name of Governmental Chambers	Name of Parliament	Years of Office
Afghanistan	Shura (Ruling Council) (10 members)	Shura	varies
Albania	National Assembly (155 members)	National Assembly	4
Algeria	Majlis el-Umma (Council of the Nation) (144 members)	Majlis	varies
	National Assembly (380 members)		5
Andorra	General Council of the Valleys (28 members)	General Council of the Valleys	4
Angola	National Assembly (220 members)	National Assembly	5
Antigua and Barbuda	Senate (17 members)	Parliament	varies
	House of Representatives (17 members)		5
Argentina	Senate (72 members)	Congress	varies
	Chamber of Deputies (257 members)		varies
Armenia	Azgayin Zhoghov (National Assembly) (131 members)	Azgayin Zhoghov	5
Australia	Senate (76 members)	Federal Parliament	6
	House of Representatives (148 members)		3
Austria	Bundesrat (Federal Council) (64 members)	National Assembly	varies
	Nationalrat (National Council) (183 members)		4
Azerbaijan	Melli-Majlis (National Council) (125 members)	Melli-Majlis	varies
Bahamas	Senate (16 members)	Parliament	varies
	House of Assembly (40 members)		5
Bahrain	Consultative Council (30 members)	Parliament	4
Bangladesh	Jatiya Sangsad (house of the nation) (300 members)	Jatiya Sangsad	5
Barbados	Senate (21 members)	Parliament	varies
	House of Assembly (28 members)		5
Belarus	Council of the Republic (64 members)	National Assembly	5
	House of Representatives (110 members)		5
Belgium	Senate (71 members)	Federal Parliament	varies
	Chamber of Representatives (150 members)		4
Belize	Senate (8 members)	National Assembly	varies
	House of Representatives (29 members)		5
Benin	National Assembly (83 members)	National Assembly	4
Bhutan	Tshogdu (National Assembly) (150 members)	Tshogdu	3
Bolivia	Senate (27 members)	Congress	5
	Chamber of Deputies (130 members)		5
Bosnia-Herzegovina	Chamber of Peoples (15 members i.e. 5 Croat, 5 Muslim, 5 Serb)	National Assembly	2
	Chamber of Representatives (42 members)		2
Botswana	House of Chiefs (15 members)	National Assembly	5
	National Assembly (47 members)		5
Brazil	Senate (81 members)	Congress	8
	Chamber of Deputies (513 members)		4
Brunei	There are no political parties or elections, the Sultan ruling since a revolt in December 1962.		
Bulgaria	National Assembly (240 members)	National Assembly	4
Burkina Faso	Assembly of People's Deputies (111 members)	National Assembly	5
	Chamber of Representatives (178 members)		3
Burundi	National Transition Assembly (121 members)	National Assembly	5
Cambodia	Senate (61 members)	National Assembly	5
	National Assembly (122 members)		5
Cameroon	National Assembly (180 members)	National Assembly	5
Canada	Senate (105 members)	Federal Parliament	varies
	House of Commons (301 members)		5
Cape Verde	National Assembly (72 members)	National Assembly	5

Country	Name of Governmental Chambers	Name of Parliament	Years of Office
Central African Republic	National Assembly (109 members)	National Assembly	5
Chad	National Assembly (125 members)	National Assembly	4
Channel Islands (less Sark)	States of Deliberation (132 members)	The States	4
– Sark	Chief Pleas (5 members)	Chief Pleas	4
Chile	Senate (48 members)	Congress	8
	Chamber of Deputies (120 members)		4
China	National People's Congress (2,984 members)	National People's Congress	5
Colombia	Senate (102 members)	Congress	4
	House of Representatives (161 members)		4
Comoros	Senate (15 members)	Federal Assembly	6
	Legislative Council (42 members)		4
Congo, Dem. Rep. of the	New constitution yet to be finalized.	To be arranged	T. B. A.
Congo, Republic of the	Supreme Council of the Republic (153 members)	Supreme Council	T. B. A.
Costa Rica	Legislative Assembly (57 members)	Legislative Assembly	4
Côte D'Ivoire	National Assembly (175 members)	National Assembly	5
Croatia	Chamber of Counties (65 members)	Sabor (parliament)	4
	House of Representatives (151 members)		4
Cuba	National Assembly of People's Power (601 members)	National Assembly	5
Cyprus	House of Representatives (80 members)	Parliament	5
Czech Republic	Senate (81 members)	Federal Assembly	6
	Chamber of Deputies (200 members)		4
Denmark	Folketing (179 members including 2 for Greenland and the Faroes)	Folketing (parliament)	4
Djibouti	Chamber of Deputies (65 members)	National Assembly	5
Dominica	House of Assembly (30 members)	National Assembly	5
Dominican Republic	Senate (30 members)	Congress	4
	Chamber of Deputies (149 members)		4
Ecuador	National Congress (125 members)	Congress	4
Egypt	Majlis Ash-Sha'Ab (People's Assembly) (454 members)	Majlis	5
El Salvador	Legislative Assembly (84 members)	Legislative Assembly	3
Equatorial Guinea	National Assembly (80 members)	National Assembly	5
Eritrea	Hagerawi Baito (National Assembly) (150 members)	Hagerawi Baito	4
Estonia	Riigikogu (National Assembly) (101 members)	Riigikogu	4
Ethiopia	Federation Council (120 members)	Parliament	5
	Council of People's Representatives (550 members)		5
Fiji Islands	Senate (32 members)	Parliament	varies
	House of Representatives (71 members)		5
Finland	Eduskunta (parliament) (200 members)	Eduskunta	4
France	Senate (321 members)	Parliament	varies
	National Assembly (577 members)		5
Gabon	Senate (91 members)	Parliament	6
	National Assembly (120 members)		5
Gambia	National Assembly (49 members)	National Assembly	5
Georgia	Parliament (235 members)	Parliament	4
Germany	Bundesrat (Federal Council) (69 members)	Parliament	varies
	Bundestag (Federal Assembly) (669 members)		4
Ghana	Parliament (200 members)	Parliament	4
Greece	Vouli Ton Ellinon (Chamber of Deputies) (300 members)	Vouli	4
Grenada	Senate (13 members)	Parliament	5
	House of Representatives (15 members)		5
Guatemala	National Congress (113 members)	Congress	4
Guinea	National Assembly (114 members)	National Assembly	5
Guinea-Bissau	National People's Assembly (102 members)	National People's Assembly	4
Guyana	National Assembly (65 members)	National Assembly	5
Haiti	Senate (27 members)	National Assembly	6
	Chamber of Deputies (82 members)		4
Honduras	National Congress (128 members)	Congress	4
Hungary	Országgyülés (National Assembly) (386 members)	Országgyülés	4
Iceland	Althingi (Parliament) (63 members)	Althingi	4

Country	Name of Governmental Chambers	Name of Parliament	Years of Office
India	Rajya Sabha (Council of States) (245 members)	Sansad (Parliament)	6
	Lok Sabha (House of the People) (545 members)		5
Indonesia	Dewan Perwakilan Rakyat (H. of Representatives) (500 members)	Dewan Perwakilan Rakyat	5
Iran	Majles Shoraye Eslami (Islamic Ruling Council) (290 members)	Majles	4
Iraq	Majlis Watani (Council of the Nation) (250 members)	Majlis	4
Ireland	Seanad Eireann (Senate) (60 members)	Oireachtas (parliament)	5
	Dáil Eireann (House of Representatives) (166 members)		5
Israel	Knesset (Assembly) (120 members)	Knesset	4
Italy	Senate (315 members)	Parliament	5
	Chamber of Deputies (630 members)		5
Jamaica	Senate (21 members)	Parliament	5
	House of Representatives (60 members)		5
Japan	Sangiin (House of Councillors) (252 members)	Kokkai (Diet)	6
	Shugiin (House of Representatives) (500 members)		4
Jordan	Al-Aayan (Senate) (40 members)	Majlis Al-Umma	4
	Al-Nuwaab (House of Representatives) (80 members)		4
Kazakhstan	Senate (39 members)	Mazhilis	5
	Mazhilis (Council) (77 members)		5
Kenya	Bunge (National Assembly) (210 members)	Bunge	5
Kiribati	Maneaba Ni Maungatabu (House of Assembly) (41 members)	Unicameral	4
Korea South	Kuk Hoe (National Assembly) (299 members)	Kuk Hoe	4
Korea North	Supreme People's Assembly (687 members)	National Assembly	5
Kuwait	Majlis Al-Umma (Council of the Nation) (65 members)	Majlis	4
Kyrgyzstan	Myizam Chygaru Palatasay (Legislative Assembly) (60 members)	Jogorku Kenesh (High Council)	5
	El Okuldor Palatasay (People's Assembly) (45 members)		5
Laos	Sapha Heng Xat (National Assembly) (99 members)	Sapha Heng Xat	5
Latvia	Saeima (Supreme Council) (100 members)	Saeima	4
Lebanon	Majlis Al-Nuwwab (Council of Deputies) (128 members)	Majlis	4
Lesotho	Senate (33 members)	Parliament	5
	National Assembly (79 members)		5
Liberia	Senate (26 members)	National Assembly	9
	House of Representatives (64 members)		6
Liechtenstein	Landtag (25 members)	Landtag	4
Lithuania	Seimas (Supreme Council) (141 members)	Seimas	4
Luxembourg	Chamber of Deputies (60 members)	Parliament	5
Macedonia	Sobranie (Assembly) (120 members)	Sobranie	4
Madagascar	National Assembly (150 members)	National Assembly	5
Malawi	National Assembly (193 members)	National Assembly	5
Malaysia	Dewan Negara (Senate) (69 members)	Majlis	3
	Dewan Rakyat (House of Representatives) (193 members)		5
Maldives	Majlis (50 members)	Majlis	5
Mali	National Assembly (147 members)	National Assembly	5
Malta	Il-Kamra Tad-Deputati (House of Representatives) (65 members)	Il-Kamra Tad-Deputati	5
Marshall Islands	Nitijela (House of Assembly) (33 members)	Nitijela	4
Mauritania	Majlis-Al-Chouyoukh (Senate) (56 members)	National Assembly	6
	Al Jamiya-Al-Wataniya (National Assembly) (79 members)		5
Mauritius	National Assembly (70 members)	National Assembly	5
Mexico	Senate (128 members)	Congress	6
	Chamber of Deputies (500 members)		3
Micronesia (Federated States)	Congress (14 members, four of whom are elected for four years)	Congress	2
Moldova	Parliament (104 members)	Parliament	4

Country	Name of Governmental Chambers	Name of Parliament	Years of Office
Monaco	National Council (18 members)	National Council	5
Mongolia	Ulsyn Ikh Khural (The Great Hural) (76 members)	Ulsyn Ikh Khural	4
Montenegro	National Assembly (85 members)	National Assembly	5
Morocco	Majlis Nawab (Chamber of Representatives) (325 members)	Majlis	6
	Majlis al-Mustacharin (Chamber of Counsellors) (270 members)		9
Mozambique	People's Assembly (200 members)	National Assembly	5
Myanmar (Burma)	Constitutional Convention (706 members)	Constitutional Convention	T. B. A.
Namibia	National Council (26 members)	Parliament	6
	National Assembly (78 members)		5
Nauru	Parliament (19 members)	Parliament	3
Nepal	Rastriya Sabha (National Council) (60 members)	Parliament	6
	Pratinidhi Sabja (House of Representatives) (205 members)		5
Netherlands	First Chamber (75 members)	States General	4
	Second Chamber (150 members)		4
New Zealand	House of Representatives (120 members)	Parliament	3
Nicaragua	National Assembly (93 members)	National Assembly	6
Niger	National Assembly (83 members)	National Assembly	5
Nigeria	Senate (109 members)	National Assembly	4
	House of Representatives (360 members)		4
Norway	Lagting (25% of Storting membership)	Storting(et) (165 members)	4
	Odelsting (75% of Storting membership)		4
Oman	Majlis al Shura (Council of State) (60 members)	Majlis	varies
Pakistan	Senate (87 members)	Majlis	3
	Majlis as-Shoora (National Assembly) (217 members)		5
Palau	Senate (14 members)	Olbiil Era Kelulau (Congress)	4
	House of Delegates (16 members)		4
Panama	Legislative Assembly (72 members)	Legislative Assembly	5
Papua New Guinea	National Parliament (109 members)	Parliament	5
Paraguay	Senate (45 members)	Congress	5
	Chamber of Deputies (80 members)		5
Peru	National Congress (120 members)	Congress	5
Philippines	Senate (24 members)	Congress	6
	House of Representatives (250 members)		3
Poland	Senate (100 members)	Sejm	4
	Sejm (Parliament) (460 members)		4
Portugal	Assembly of the Republic (230 members)	Assembly of the Republic	4
Qatar	No established parliament although the Amir is advised by a 30-member Council of Ministers		
Romania	Senate (140 members)	Parliament	4
	Chamber of Deputies (345 members)		4
Russia	Soviet Federation (178 members)	Federal Assembly	varies
	Duma (450 members)		4
Rwanda	National Transitional Assembly (74 members)	National Transitional Assembly	5
Saint Kitts and Nevis	National Assembly (15 members)	National Assembly	5
Saint Lucia	Senate (11 members)	National Assembly	5
	National Assembly (18 members)		5
Saint Vincent and Grenadines	National Assembly (21 members)	National Assembly	5
Samoa	Legislative Assembly (49 members)	Legislative Assembly	5
San Marino	Consiglio grande e generale (60 members)	Consiglio grande e generale	5
Sao Tome and Principe	National Assembly (55 members)	National Assembly	4
Saudi Arabia	Majlis al Shura (Council of State) (100 members)	Majlis	varies
Senegal	National Assembly (140 members)	National Assembly	5
Serbia	National Assembly (250 members)	National Assembly	5
Seychelles	National Assembly (34 members)	National Assembly	5
Sierra Leone	Parliament (80 members)	Parliament	5
Singapore	Parliament (93 members)	Parliament	5
Slovakia	National Council (150 members)	National Council	4
Slovenia	State Council (40 members)	National Assembly	5
	National Assembly (90 members)		4
Solomon Islands	Parliament (50 members)	Parliament	5

Country	Name of Governmental Chambers	Name of Parliament	Years of Office
Somalia	Transitional National Assembly	To be arranged	T. B. A.
South Africa	National Council of Provinces (90 members)	Volksraad	5
	Volksraad (National Assembly) (400 members)		5
Spain	Congress Senate (259 members)	Cortes Generales	4
	Congress of Deputies (350 members)		4
Sri Lanka	Parliament (225 members)	Parliament	6
Sudan	Majlis Watani (Council of the Nation) (360 members)	Majlis	4
Suriname	National Assembly (51 members)	National Assembly	5
Swaziland	Senate (30 members)	Libandla (Parliament)	5
	House of Assembly (65 members)		5
Sweden	Riksdag (349 members)	Riksdag(en)	4
Switzerland	Council of States (46 members)	Federal Assembly	4
	National Council (200 members)		4
Syria	Majlis Al-Chaab (250 members)	Majlis	4
Tadzhikstan	Majlisi Milliy (34 members)	Majlis Oli (Supreme Council)	5
	Majlisi Namoyandogon (63 members)		5
Taiwan	Yuan (225 members)	Yuan	3
Tanzania	Bunge (National Assembly) (275 members)	Bunge	5
Thailand	Wuthisapha (Senate) (200 members)	Rathasapha (Parliament)	6
	Saphaphuthan Ratsadon (National Assembly) (500 members)		4
Togo	National Assembly (81 members)	National Assembly	5
Tonga	Fale Alea (Legislative Assembly) (30 members)	Fale Alea	3
Trinidad and Tobago	Senate (31 members)	Parliament	5
	House of Representatives (36 members)		5
Tunisia	Majlis Al-Nuwwab (Council of Deputies) (182 members)	Majlis	5
Turkey	Millet Meclisi (National Assembly) (550 members)	Millet Meclisi	5
Turkmenistan	Mejlis (Council) (50 members)	Mejlis	5
Tuvalu	Parliament (15 members)	Parliament	4
Uganda	Parliament (281 members)	Parliament	5
Ukraine	Verkhovna Rada (Supreme Council) (450 members)	Verkhovna Rada	4
United Arab Emirates	Majlis Watani Itihad (Federal National Council) (360 members)	Majlis	2
United Kingdom	House of Lords (675 members as at 31 May 2001)	Parliament	varies
	House of Commons (659 members)		5
USA	Senate (Upper House of 100 members serve for 6 yrs)	Congress	6
	House of Representatives (435 members serve for 2 yrs)		2
Uruguay	Senate (31 members)	Congress	5
	Chamber of Deputies (99 members)		5
Uzbekistan	Oliy Majlis (Supreme Assembly) (250 members)	Majlis	5
Vanuatu	Parliament (52 members)	Parliament	4
Venezuela	National Assembly (165 members)	National Assembly	5
Vietnam	Quoc Hoi (National Assembly) (450 members)	Quoc Hoi	5
Yemen	Majlis Annowab (Council of Representatives) (301 members)	Majlis	4
Yugoslavia	Vece Republika (Chamber of the Republics) (40 members)	Skupstina SRJ	5
	Vece Gradjana (Chamber of Citizens) (138 members)		4
Zambia	House of Assembly (158 members)	National Assembly	5
Zimbabwe	House of Assembly (150 members)	National Assembly	5

British Prime Ministers

Name	Term of Office	Party	Education	Constituency	Marriage(s)	Buried
1 Sir Robert Walpole (earl of Orford) (1676–1745)	1721–1742	Whig	Eton & Cambridge (King's)	Castle Rising (1701–2), King's Lynn (1702–42)	Catherine Shorter, Maria Skerrett	Houghton, Norfolk
2 Sir Spencer Compton (earl of Wilmington) (1673–1743)	1742–1743	Whig	St Pauls & Oxford (Trinity)	Rye (1698–1710), East Grinstead (1713–15), Sussex (1715–28)	Unmarried	Compton Wynates, Warwickshire
3 Henry Pelham (1696–1754)	1743–1754	Whig	Westminster & Oxford (Hart Hall)	Seaford (1717–22), Sussex (1722–54)	Catherine Manners	Laughton Church, nr Lewes, E. Sussex
4 Thomas Pelham-Holles (duke of Newcastle) (1693–1768)	1754–1756	Whig	Westminster & Cambridge (Clare)	House of Lords	Henrietta Godolphin	Laughton Church, nr Lewes, E. Sussex
5 William Cavendish (duke of Devonshire) (1720–1764)	1756–1757	Whig	private education	Derbyshire (1741–51)	Baroness Clifford	Derby Cathedral
6 Thomas Pelham-Holles (duke of Newcastle) (1693–1768)	1757–1762	Whig	Westminster & Cambridge (Clare)	House of Lords	Henrietta Godolphin	Laughton Church, nr Lewes, E. Sussex
7 John Stuart (earl of Bute) (1713–1792)	1762–1763	Tory	Eton	House of Lords	Mary Wortley-Montagu	Rothesay, Bute
8 George Grenville (1712–1770)	1763–1765	Whig	Eton & Oxford (Christ Church)	Buckingham (1741–70)	Elizabeth Wyndham	Wotton, Bucks
9 Charles Watson Wentworth (marquis of Rockingham) (1730–1782)	1765–1766	Whig	Westminster & Cambridge (St John's)	House of Lords	Mary Bright	York Minster
10 Augustus Henry Fitzroy (duke of Grafton) (1735–1811)	1766–1770	Whig	Westminster & Cambridge (Peterhouse)	Bury St Edmunds	Anne Liddell, Elizabeth Wrottesley	Euston, Suffolk
11 Lord Frederick North (earl of Guildford) (1732–1792)	1770–1782	Tory	Eton, Oxford (Trinity), Leipzig	Banbury (1754–90)	Anne Speke	All Saints, Wroxton, Oxfordshire
12 Charles Watson Wentworth (marquis of Rockingham) (1730–1782)	1782	Whig	Westminster & Cambridge (St John's)	House of Lords	Mary Bright	York Minster
13 William Petty (earl of Shelburne) (1737–1805)	1782–1783	Whig	Oxford (Christ Church)	Chipping Wycombe (1760–61)	Sophia Carerett, Louisa FitzPatrick	High Wycombe
14 William Henry Cavendish-Bentinck (duke of Portland) (1738–1809)	1783	Coalition	Westminster & Oxford (Christ Church)	Weobley, Herefordshire (1761–2) (as Whig)	Dorothy Cavendish	St Marylebone, London
15 William Pitt the Younger (1759–1806)	1783–1801	Tory	Cambridge (Pembroke Hall)	Appleby (1781–1806)	Unmarried	Westminster Abbey
16 Henry Addington (Viscount Sidmouth) (1757–1844)	1801–1804	Tory	Cheam, Winchester, Lincoln's Inn & Oxford (Brasenose)	Devizes (1783–1805)	Ursula Mary Hammond, Marianne Townshend	Mortlake
17 William Pitt the Younger (1759–1806)	1804–1806	Tory	Cambridge (Pembroke Hall)	Appleby (1781–1806)	Unmarried	Westminster Abbey
18 William Wyndham Grenville (1759–1834)	1806–1807	Coalition	Eton, Oxford (Christ Church), Lincoln's Inn	Buckingham (1782–4), Buckinghamshire (1784–90)	Anne Pitt	Burnham, Bucks
19 William Henry Cavendish-Bentinck (duke of Portland) (1738–1809)	1807–1809	Tory	Westminster & Oxford (Christ Church)	Weobley, Herefordshire (1761–2) (as Whig)	Dorothy Cavendish	St Marylebone, London
20 Spencer Perceval (1762–1812)	1809–1812	Tory	Harrow & Cambridge (Trinity)	Northampton	Jane Spencer-Wilson	Charlton

Name	Term of Office	Party	Education	Constituency	Marriage(s)	Buried
21 Robert Banks Jenkinson (earl of Liverpool) (1770–1828)	1812–1827	Tory	Charterhouse & Oxford (Christ Church)	Rye (1796–1803) elected for Appleby 1790 too young see note 4 below	Louisa Theodosia Hervey Mary Chester	Hawkesbury
22 George Canning (1770–1827)	1827	Tory	Eton, Oxford (Christ Church), Lincoln's Inn		Joan Scott	Westminster Abbey
23 Frederick John Robinson (Viscount Goderich) (1782–1859)	1827–1828	Tory	Harrow, Cambridge (St John's), Lincoln's Inn	Carlow (1806–7) & Ripon (1807–27)	Sarah Hobart	Nocton, Lincs
24 Arthur Wellesley duke of Wellington) (1769–1852) (	1828–1830	Tory	Browns Seminary, King's Rd, Chelsea, Eton, Brussels & Angers Military Acad.	Rye (1806), Newport IOW (1807–9) St Michael (1807)	Catherine Pakenham	St Paul's Cathedral
25 Charles Grey (Earl Grey) (1764–1845)	1830–1834	Whig	Eton, Cambridge (Trinity) & Middle Temple	Northumberland (1786–1807) Appleby (1807), Tavistock (1807)	Mary Elizabeth Ponsonby	Howick House, Northumberland
26 Henry William Lamb (Viscount Melbourne) (1779–1848)	1834	Whig	Eton, Cambridge (Trinity), Glasgow, Lincoln's Inn	see n.4 below	Caroline Ponsonby	Hatfield
27 Robert Peel (1788–1850)	1834–1835	Tory	Harrow, Oxford (Christ Church), Lincoln's Inn	see n.4 below	Julia Floyd	Drayton Bassett
28 Henry William Lamb (Viscount Melbourne) (1779–1848)	1835–1841	Whig	Eton, Cambridge (Trinity), Glasgow, Lincoln's Inn	see n.4 below	Caroline Ponsonby	Hatfield
29 Robert Peel (1788–1850)	1841–1846	Conservative	Harrow, Oxford (Christ Church), Lincoln's Inn	see n.4 below	Julia Floyd	Drayton Bassett
30 John Russell (Earl Russell) (1792–1878)	1846–1852	Whig	Westminster & Edinburgh	see n.4 below	Adelaide Lister Frances E. M. Kynynmound	Chenies, Bucks
31 Edward George Stanley (earl of Derby) (1799–1869)	1852	Conservative	Eton & Oxford (Christ Church)	see n.4 below	Emma Wilbraham-Bootle	Knowsley, Lancs
32 George Hamilton Gordon (earl of Aberdeen) (1784–1860)	1852–1855	Conservative (Peelite)	Harrow & Cambridge (St John's)	House of Lords	Catherine Hamilton Harriet Douglas	Stanmore, Gtr London
33 Henry John Temple (Viscount Palmerston) (1784–1865)	1855–1858	Liberal	Harrow, Edinburgh, Cambridge (St John's)	see n.4 below	Emile Lamb the Dowager Countess Cowper	Westminster Abbey
34 Edward George Stanley (earl of Derby) (1799–1869)	1858–1859	Conservative	Eton & Oxford (Christ Church)	see n.4 below	Emma Wilbraham-Bootle	Knowsley, Lancs
35 Henry John Temple (Viscount Palmerston) (1784–1865)	1859–1865	Liberal	Harrow, Edinburgh, Cambridge (St John's)	see n.4 below	Emile Lamb the Dowager Countess Cowper	Westminster Abbey
36 John Russell (Earl Russell) (1792–1878)	1865–1866	Liberal	Westminster & Edinburgh	see n.4 below	Adelaide Lister Frances E. M. Kynynmound	Chenies, Bucks

POLITICS

Name	Term of Office	Party	Education	Constituency	Marriage(s)	Buried
37 Edward George Stanley (earl of Derby) (1799–1869)	1866–1868	Conservative	Eton & Oxford (Christ Church)	see n.4 below	Emma Wilbraham-Bootle	Knowsley, Lancs
38 Benjamin Disraeli (earl of Beaconsfield) (1804–1881)	1868	Conservative	Lincoln's Inn	Maidstone (1837–41), Shrewsbury (1841–7), Buckinghamshire (1847–76)	Mrs Wyndham Lewis née Mary Ann Evans	Hughenden Manor, Buckinghamshire
39 William Ewart Gladstone (1809–1898)	1868–1874	Liberal	Seaforth Vicarage, Eton, Oxford (Christ Church)	see n.4 below	Catherine Glynne	Westminster Abbey
40 Benjamin Disraeli (earl of Beaconsfield) (1804–1881)	1874–1880	Conservative	Lincoln's Inn	Maidstone (1837–41), Shrewsbury (1841–7), Buckinghamshire (1847–76)	Mrs Wyndham Lewis née Mary Ann Evans	Hughenden Manor, Buckinghamshire
41 William Ewart Gladstone (1809–1898)	1880–1885	Liberal	Seaforth Vicarage, Eton, Oxford (Christ Church)	see n.4 below	Catherine Glynne	Westminster Abbey
42 Robert Arthur Talbot Cecil (marquis of Salisbury) (1830–1903)	1885–1886	Conservative	Eton & Oxford (Christ Church)	Stamford (1853–68)	Georgiana Alderson	Hatfield
43 William Ewart Gladstone (1809–1898)	1886	Liberal	Seaforth Vicarage, Eton, Oxford (Christ Church)	see n.4 below	Catherine Glynne	Westminster Abbey
44 Robert Arthur Talbot Cecil (marquis of Salisbury) (1830–1903)	1886–1892	Conservative	Eton & Oxford (Christ Church)	Stamford (1853–68)	Georgiana Alderson	Hatfield
45 William Ewart Gladstone (1809–1898)	1892–1894	Liberal	Seaforth Vicarage, Eton, Oxford (Christ Church)	see n.4 below	Catherine Glynne	Westminster Abbey
46 Archibald Philip Primrose (earl of Rosebery) (1847–1929)	1894–1895	Liberal	Eton & Oxford (Christ Church)	House of Lords	Hannah de Rothschild	Dalmeny
47 Robert Arthur Talbot Cecil (marquis of Salisbury) (1830–1903)	1895–1902	Conservative	Eton & Oxford (Christ Church)	Stamford (1853–68)	Georgiana Alderson	Hatfield
48 Arthur Balfour (earl of Balfour) (1848–1930)	1902–1905	Conservative	Eton & Cambridge (Trinity)	Hertford (1874–85), E. Manchester (1885–1906), London (1906–22)	Unmarried	Whittinghame, East Lothian
49 Henry Campbell-Bannerman (1836–1908)	1905–1908	Liberal	Glasgow & Cambridge (Trinity)	Stirling (1868–1908)	Sarah Charlotte Bruce	Meigle, Scotland
50 Herbert Henry Asquith (earl of Oxford) (1852–1928)	1908–1916	Liberal	City of London & Oxford (Balliol)	East Fife (1886–1918), Paisley (1920–4)	Helen Kelsall Melland Emma Tennant	Sutton Courtney Church, Bucks
51 David Lloyd George (earl of Dwyfor) (1863–1945)	1916–1922	Coalition	Llanystumdwy Church School	Caernarvon (1890–1945)	Margaret Owen Frances Stevenson	Bank of River Dwyfor
52 Andrew Bonar Law (1858–1923)	1922–1923	Conservative	Gilbertfield in Hamilton & Glasgow High School	see n.4 below	Annie Pitcairn	Westminster Abbey
53 Stanley Baldwin (1867–1947) (Earl Baldwin of Bewdley)	1923–1924	Conservative	Harrow & Cambridge (Trinity)	Bewdley, Worcs (1908–37)	Lucy Ridsdale	Worcester Cathedral
54 James Ramsay MacDonald (1866–1937)	1924	Labour	Drainie Parish Board School	see n.4 below	Margaret Gladstone	Spynie Churchyard, Lossiemouth

Name	Term of Office	Party	Education	Constituency	Marriage(s)	Buried
55 Stanley Baldwin (1867–1947) (Earl Baldwin of Bewdley)	1924–1929	Conservative	Harrow & Cambridge (Trinity)	Bewdley, Worcs (1908–37)	Lucy Ridsdale	Worcester Cathedral
56 James Ramsay MacDonald (1866–1937)	1929–1935	Labour	Drainie Parish Board School	see n.4 below	Margaret Gladstone	Spynie Churchyard, Lossiemouth
57 Stanley Baldwin (1867–1947) (Earl Baldwin of Bewdley)	1935–1937	National	Harrow & Cambridge (Trinity)	Bewdley, Worcs (1908–37)	Lucy Ridsdale	Worcester Cathedral
58 Neville Chamberlain (1869–1940)	1937–1940	National	Rugby & Mason College (later Birmingham University)	Ladywood, Birmingham (1918–29) Edgbaston (1929–40)	Annie Vere Cole	Westminster Abbey (ashes)
59 Winston Leonard Spencer Churchill (1874–1965)	1940–1945	Coalition	Harrow & Royal Military College, Sandhurst	see n.4 below	Clementine Ogilvy Hozier	Bladon, Oxfordshire
60 Clement Attlee (1883–1967)	1945–1951	Labour	Haileybury Coll. & Oxford (University)	Limehouse, Stepney (1922–50) West Walthamstow (1950–5)	Violet Millar	Westminster Abbey
61 Winston Leonard Spencer Churchill (1874–1965)	1951–1955	Conservative	Harrow & Royal Military College, Sandhurst	see n.4 below	Clementine Ogilvy Hozier	Bladon, Oxfordshire
62 Anthony Eden (earl of Avon) (1897–1977)	1955–1957	Conservative	Eton & Oxford (Christ Church)	Warwick & Leamington (1923–57)	Beatrice Beckett Anne Spencer-Churchill	Alvediston, Wiltshire
63 Maurice Harold Macmillan (earl of Stockton) (1894–1986)	1957–1963	Conservative	Eton & Oxford (Balliol)	Stockton on Tees (1924–9 & 1931–45), Bromley (1945–64)	Dorothy Cavendish	Horsted Keynes
64 Alexander Frederick Douglas-Home (Lord Home of the Hirsel) (1903–1995)	1963–1964	Conservative	Eton & Oxford (Christ Church)	S. Lanark (1931–45), Lanark (1950–1), Kinross & West Perthshire (1963–74)	Elizabeth Alington	Coldstream
65 James Harold Wilson (1916–1995) (Lord Wilson of Rievaulx)	1964–1970	Labour	Milnsbridge, Royds Hall, Wirral, Oxford (Jesus)	Ormskirk (1945–50) Huyton (1950–83)	Gladys Mary Baldwin	Scilly Isles
66 Edward Heath (1916–)	1970–1974	Conservative	Chatham House, Ramsgate, Oxford (Balliol)	Bexley (1950–74), Bexley–Sidcup (1974–2001)	Unmarried	
67 James Harold Wilson (1916–1995) (Lord Wilson of Rievaulx)	1974–1976	Labour	Milnsbridge, Royds Hall, Wirral, Oxford (Jesus)	Ormskirk (1945–50) Huyton (1950–83)	Gladys Mary Baldwin	Scilly Isles
68 Leonard James Callaghan (Lord Callaghan of Cardiff) (1912–)	1976–1979	Labour	Portsmouth Northern Sec.	South Cardiff (1945–50), SE Cardiff (1950–83)	Audrey Moulton	
69 Margaret Hilda Thatcher (1925–) (Baroness Thatcher of Kesteven)	1979–1990	Conservative	Kesteven & Grantham, Oxford (Somerville)	Finchley (1959–74), Barnet, Finchley (1974–92)	Denis Thatcher	
70 John Major (1943–)	1990–1997	Conservative	Rutlish Grammar	Huntingdon (1983 to present)	Norma Johnson	
71 Tony Blair (1953–)	1997–	Labour	Durham Choristers, Fettes (Edinburgh), Oxford (St John's)	Sedgefield (1983 to present)	Cherie Booth	

Notes

1 Prime Minister Although the office of prime minister is traditionally stated as commencing in 1721, in fact there were chief ministers given this label long before this date, and conversely there have been chief ministers subsequent to this date who did not bear the title of prime minister, e.g. William Pitt the Elder and Charles James Fox, in the mid- and late 18th century. To confuse matters further, Walpole was designated First Lord of the Treasury until 1730, as were some other future prime ministers of the 18th and 19th centuries. It was not until 1905 that the title of prime minister became official.

2 Party A second point of conjecture concerns the designation of the ruling party of the day. Until the first Electoral Reform Act of 1832 and the subsequent rise of the Conservative and Liberal parties, the government of the day was often a coalition of sorts, and the ruling party is given as the party of the prime minister in power, unless unaffiliated.

3 Chief ministers not listed above Sir William Pulteney, earl of Bath, actually kissed the hand of George II on 10 Feb. 1746, but within three days was unable to form a government. James Waldegrave kissed the hand of George II on 8 June 1757 but returned seals on 12 June, unable to form a ministry. Charles James Fox and his erstwhile enemy Lord North were the de facto heads of government in 1783, while the duke of Portland was merely the nominal prime minister. William Pitt the Elder, earl of Chatham, although not included in the table above, was in effect the prime minister from 1756 to 1761 during most of the Seven Years' War, although never taking up official office. From 1766 to 1768 Pitt was also Head of the Government but chose the secondary post of Lord Privy Seal; gout prevented him serving in anything but name for this second term.

4 Constituencies: See numbers in table above

(22) George Canning's constituencies: Newport IOW (1793–6 & 1806–7), Wendover (1796–1802), Tralee (1802–6), Hastings (1807–12), Liverpool (1812–23), Harwich (1823–6), Newport IOW (1826–7) & Seaford (1827).

(26) Viscount Melbourne's constituencies: Leominster (1806), Haddington Borough (1806–7), Portarlington (1807–12), Peterborough (1816–19), Hertfordshire (1819–26) Newport IOW (1827), Bletchingley (1827–8).

(27) Robert Peel's constituencies: Cashel (Tipperary) (1809–12), Chippenham (1812–17), Oxford University (1817–29), Westbury (1829–30), Tamworth (1830–50).

(30) Earl Russell's constituencies: Tavistock (1813–17, 1818–20, 1830–1), Huntingdonshire (1820–6), Bandon (1826–30), Devon (1831–2), South Devon (1832–5), Stroud (1835–41), London (1841–61).

(31) Earl of Derby's constituencies: Stockbridge (1822–6), Preston (1826–30), Windsor (1831–2), North Lancs (1832–44).

(33) Viscount Palmerston's constituencies: Newport IOW (1807–11), Cambridge University (1811–31), Bletchingley (1831–2), South Hants (1832–4), Tiverton (1835–65).

(39) William Gladstone's constituencies: Newark (1832–45 as Tory), Oxford University (1847–65 as Peelite until 1859 then Liberal), South Lancs (1865–8), Greenwich (1868–80), Midlothian (1880–95).

(52) Andrew Bonar Law's constituencies: Blackfriars, Glasgow (1900–6), Dulwich (1906–10), Bootle (1911–18), Central Glasgow (1918–23).

(54) Ramsay MacDonald's constituencies: Leicester (1906–18), Aberavon (1922–9), Seaham, Co. Durham (1929–31), Scottish Universities (1936–7).

(59) Winston Churchill's constituencies: Oldham (1900–6, Conservative until 1904 then Liberal), NW Manchester (1906–8), Dundee (1908–22), Epping (1924–45), Woodford, Essex (1945–64 as Conservative).

5 Miscellaneous information

(2) Sir Spencer Compton was a Tory until 1704.

(8) George Grenville was nicknamed the Gentle Shepherd.

(9) Charles Watson Wentworth repealed the Stamp Act.

(10) Augustus Henry Fitzroy, the duke of Grafton, was a victim of the *pseudonymous* Junius letters which attacked various government ministers in the London *Public Advertiser* (1769–72), although the identity of Junius remains unknown. Sir Philip Francis is a possible candidate.

(11) Lord Frederick North became a Whig in 1783.

(13) William Petty, the earl of Shelburne, was nicknamed Malagrida, after a notorious scheming Jesuit.

(18) William Wyndham Grenville's administration of February 1806–March 1807 was known as 'The Ministry of All the Talents' and comprised followers of Charles James Fox. Its greatest achievement was the abolition of slavery in March 1807.

(20) Spencer Perceval was assassinated by John Bellingham in the lobby of the Commons.

(24) Arthur Wellesley, duke of Wellington, was known as Arthur Wesley until 1804.

(27) Robert Peel died after a fall from a horse.

(30) Adelaide Lister, the wife of Lord John Russell, became Baroness Ribblesdale.

(31) Edward George Stanley, the earl of Derby, became a Tory in 1835 (previously a Whig).

(33) Henry John Temple, Viscount Palmerston, was a Tory until 1829, then a Whig, and finally a Liberal.

(49) Henry Campbell-Bannerman died at 10 Downing Street, last PM to die in office.

(50) Herbert Henry Asquith's administration was a coalition from 1915.

(52) Andrew Bonar Law was born in New Brunswick, Canada.

(59) Winston Churchill's first administration became Conservative from 23 May 1945.

Members of Cabinet

(Formed by the Rt. Hon. Tony Blair on 8 June 2001)

Tony Blair	Prime Minister, First Lord of the Treasury and Minister for the Civil Service
John Prescott	Deputy Prime Minister and First Minister of State
Gordon Brown	Chancellor of the Exchequer
Jack Straw	Secretary of State for Foreign and Commonwealth Affairs
	Previous incumbent Robin Cook (May 1997 to June 2001)
Lord (Derry) Irvine of Lairg	Lord Chancellor
David Blunkett	Secretary of State for the Home Department
	Previous incumbent Jack Straw (May 1997 to June 2001)
Estelle Morris	Secretary of State for Education and Skills
	Previous incumbent David Blunkett (May 1997 to June 2001 when Education and Employment)
Robin Cook	President of the Council and Leader of the House of Commons
	Previous incumbents Ann Taylor (May 1997 to July 1998) and Margaret Beckett (July 1998 to June 2001)
Helen Liddell	Secretary of State for Scotland
	Previous incumbents Donald Dewar (1997 to 1999) and Dr John Reid (1999 to 2001)
Geoff Hoon	Secretary of State for Defence
	Previous incumbent Lord George Robertson (May 1997 to Oct. 1999)
Alan Milburn	Secretary of State for Health
	Previous incumbent Frank Dobson (May 1997 to Oct. 1999)
Hilary Armstrong	Chief Whip (Parliamentary Secretary to the Treasury)
	Previous incumbent Nick Brown (May 1997 to July 1998) and Ann Taylor (July 1998 to June 2001)
Tessa Jowell	Secretary of State for Culture, Media and Sports
	Previous incumbent Chris Smith (May 1997 to June 2001)
Alistair Darling	Secretary of State for Work and Pensions
	Previous incumbent Harriet Harman (May 1997 to July 1998 when Social Security) and Alistair Darling (July 1998 to June 2001 when Social Security)
Dr John Reid	Secretary of State for Northern Ireland
	Previous incumbents Mo Mowlam (May 1997 to Oct. 1999) and Peter Mandelson (Oct. 1999 to Jan. 2001)
Paul Murphy	Secretary of State for Wales
	Previous incumbents Ron Davies (May 1997 to 1998) and Alun Michael (1998 to 1999)
Clare Short	Secretary of State for International Development
Lord Williams of Mostyn	Leader of the House of Lords
	Previous incumbents Lord Richard of Ammanford (May 1997 to July 1998) and Baroness Jay of Paddington (July 1998 to June 2001)
Patricia Hewitt	Secretary of State for Trade and Industry
	Previous incumbents Margaret Beckett (May 1997 to July 1998), Peter Mandelson (July to Dec. 1998) and Stephen Byers (Dec. 1998 to June 2001)
Andrew Smith	Chief Secretary to the Treasury
	Previous incumbents Alastair Darling (May 1997 to July 1998), Stephen Byers (July to Dec. 1998) and Alan Milburn (Dec. 1998 to Oct. 1999)
Margaret Beckett	Secretary of State for Environment, Food and Rural Affairs
	Previous incumbents Jack Cunningham (May 1997 to July 1998) when Agriculture, Fisheries and Food and Nick Brown (July 1998 to June 2001) when Agriculture, Fisheries and Food
Stephen Byers	Secretary of State for Transport, Local Government and the Regions
	Previous incumbent Dr John Reid as Minister for Transport (1998 to 1999)
Charles Clarke	Minister Without Portfolio and Party Chairman

also attending Cabinet meetings

Nick Brown	Minister of State for Work
Lord Carter	Lords Chief Whip and Captain of the Gentlemen at Arms
John Spellar	Minister for Transport

Departments of State and Ministers

Defence

Secretary of State – The Rt. Hon. Geoff Hoon, MP
Minister of State – The Rt. Hon. Adam Ingram, MP
Parliamentary Under-Secretaries of State – The Lord Bach and Dr Lewis Moonie, MP

Education and Skills

Secretary of State – The Rt. Hon. Estelle Morris, MP
Minister of State for Schools – Stephen Timms, MP

Minister of State for Universities – Margaret Hodge, MP
Parliamentary Secretary of State – Baroness Ashton of Upholland
Parliamentary Under-Secretaries of State – Ivan Lewis, MP, and John Healey, MP

Environment, Food and Rural Affairs

Secretary of State – The Rt. Hon. Margaret Beckett, MP
Minister for the Environment – The Rt. Hon. Michael Meacher, MP
Minister for Rural Affairs – The Rt. Hon. Alun Michael, MP
Parliamentary Under-Secretaries of State – Elliot Morley, MP, and The Lord Whitty

Foreign and Commonwealth Office

Secretary of State – The Rt. Hon. Jack Straw, MP
Minister for Foreign and Commonwealth Affairs – Baroness Symons of Vernham Dean
Minister for Europe – Peter Hain, MP
Ministers of State – Ben Bradshaw, MP, Baroness Amos, Dr Denis Macshane, MP

Health

Secretary of State – The Rt. Hon. Alan Milburn, MP
Ministers of State – John Hutton, MP, and Jacqui Smith, MP
Parliamentary Secretary of State – Lord Hunt of Kings Heath
Parliamentary Under-Secretaries of State – Hazel Blears, MP, and Yvette Cooper, MP

Home Office

Secretary of State – The Rt. Hon. David Blunkett, MP
Minister of State Police, Courts and Drugs – John Denham, MP
Minister of Prisons – Keith Bradley, MP
Minister of Asylum and Immigration – Jeff Rooker
Parliamentary Secretary of State – Bev Hughes, MP
Parliamentary Under-Secretaries of State – Angela Eagle, MP, and Robert Ainsworth, MP

International Development

Secretary of State – The Rt. Hon. Clare Short, MP
Parliamentary Secretary – Hilary Benn, MP

Law Officers' Department

Attorney General – Lord Goldsmith, QC
Solicitor General – The Rt. Hon. Harriet Harman, MP
Advocate General for Scotland – Dr Lynda Clark, QC, MP

Lord Chancellor's Department

Lord Chancellor – The Rt. Hon. The Lord Irvine of Lairg, QC
Parliamentary Secretary – Baroness Scotland of Asthal, QC
Parliamentary Under-Secretaries of State – Michael Willis, MP, and Rosie Winterton, MP

Culture, Media and Sports

Secretary of State – The Rt. Hon. Tessa Jowell, MP
Minister of State for Sport – The Rt. Hon. Richard Caborn, MP
Minister of State for the Arts – The Rt. Hon. Baroness Blackstone
Parliamentary Secretary – Dr Kim Howells, MP

Northern Ireland Office

Secretary of State – The Rt. Hon. Dr John Reid, MP
Minister of State – Jane Kennedy, MP
Parliamentary Secretary – Des Browne, MP

Cabinet Office

Deputy Prime Minister and First Secretary of State – The Rt. Hon. John Prescott, MP
Minister and Chancellor of the Duchy of Lancaster – The Rt. Hon. Lord MacDonald of Tradeston
Previous incumbents David Clark (May 1997 to July 1998) Dr Jack Cunningham (July 1998 to Oct. 1999) and Mo Mowlam (Oct. 1999 to June 2001)
Minister Without Portfolio and Party Chairman – The Rt. Hon. Charles Clarke, MP
Minister of State – Barbara Roche, MP
Minister of State, Women's Minister in the Lords – Sally Morgan
Previous Ministers for Women Harriet Harman (May 1997 to July 1998) and Baroness Jay of Paddington (July 1998 to June 2001)
Parliamentary Secretary – Christopher Leslie, MP

Scottish Office

Secretary of State – The Rt. Hon. Helen Liddell, MP
Minister of State – George Foulkes, MP

Works and Pensions

Secretary of State for Works and Pensions – Rt. Hon. Alistair Darling, MP
Minister for Work – The Rt. Hon. Nick Brown, MP
Minister for Pensions – The Rt. Hon. Ian McCartney, MP
Parliamentary Secretary of State – The Baroness Hollis of Heigham
Parliamentary Under-Secretaries of State – Maria Eagle, MP, and Malcolm Wicks, MP

Transport, Local Government and the Regions

Secretary of State for Transport, Local Government and the Regions – Rt. Hon.
Stephen Byers, MP
Minister for Transport – The Rt. Hon. John Spellar, MP
Minister for Local Government – The Rt. Hon. Nick Raynsford, MP
Minister for Housing and Planning – Lord Falconer of Thoroton, QC
Under-Secretaries of State – David Jamieson, MP, Sally Keeble, MP, Dr Alan
Whitehead, MP

Trade and Industry

Secretary of State for Trade and Industry – The Rt. Hon. Patricia Hewitt, MP
Minister for E-Commerce and Competitiveness – Douglas Alexander, MP
Minister for Trade – Baroness Symons of Vernham Dean
Minister for Industry and Energy – Brian Wilson, MP
Minister for Employment and the Regions – Alan Johnson, MP
Under-Secretaries of State – Lord Sainsbury of Turville, Melanie Johnson, MP, Nigel
Griffiths, MP

Treasury

Prime Minister, First Lord of the Treasury and Minister for Civil Service – Rt. Hon. Tony
Blair, MP
Chancellor of the Exchequer – Rt. Hon. Gordon Brown, MP
President of the Council, and Leader of the Commons – Rt. Hon. Robin Cook, MP
Financial Secretary – The Rt. Hon. Paul Boateng, MP
Paymaster General – Dawn Primarolo, MP
Economic Secretary – Ruth Kelly, MP
Parliamentary Secretary and Government Chief Whip – Rt. Hon. Hilary Armstrong, MP
Parliamentary Under-Secretary of State – Stephen Twigg, MP
Lords Commissioners – Anne McGuire, MP, John Heppell, MP, Tony McNulty, MP, Nick
Ainger, MP, and Graham Stringer, MP
Assistant Whips – Fraser Kemp, MP, Ian Pearson, MP, Angela Smith, MP, Ivor Caplin,
MP, Jim Fitzpatrick, MP, Philip Woolas, MP, Dan Norris, MP
Prime Minister's Parliamentary Private Secretary – David Hanson, MP

Welsh Office

Secretary of State – The Rt. Hon. Paul Murphy, MP
Parliamentary Secretary – Don Touhig, MP

Her Majesty's Household

Lord Chamberlain – Rt. Hon. Lord Luce, GCVO
Lord Steward – The Duke of Abercorn
Master of the Horse – The Lord Vestey
Mistress of the Robes – The Duchess of Grafton, GCVO
Deputy Chief Whip and Treasurer – Keith Hill, MP
Comptroller – Thomas McAvoy, MP
Vice-Chamberlain – Gerry Sutcliffe, MP
Lord Chief Whip and Capt of the Honourable Corps of Gentlemen-At-Arms – Rt. Hon.
The Lord Carter
Deputy Chief Whip and Captain of the Queen's Yeoman of the Guard – The Lord
McIntosh of Haringey
Lords-in-Waiting – The Lord Davies of Oldham, Bruce Grocott, Lord Filkin, Lord
Bassam of Brighton
Baronesses-in-Waiting – Baroness Farrington of Ribbleton and Baroness Ramsay of
Cartvale

Downing Street Staff

Chief of Staff – Jonathan Powell
Prime Minister's Principal Private Secretary – Jeremy Heywood
Director of Communications and Strategy – Alastair Campbell
Head of Government Relations – Anji Hunter
Political Secretary – Robert Hill
Prime Minister's Official Spokesmen – Godric Smith and Tom Kelly

NB Following the June 2001 General Election, the basic salary of Cabinet ministers was increased to £99,793. The Prime Minister's basic salary was increased to £163,418 and the Lord Chancellor's to £167,760.
The First Minister of Scotland is Henry McLeish, representing Fife Central in the Scottish Parliament.
The First Minister of Wales is Rhodri Morgan, representing Cardiff West in the Welsh Assembly.
The First Minister of Northern Ireland is David Trimble, who represents Upper Bann both at Stormont and Westminster.

General Election Results by Candidate: 7 June 2001

Abbott, Diane	*Hackney North & Stoke Newington*	Labour
Adams, Gerry	*Belfast West*	Sinn Fein
Adams, Irene	*Paisley North*	Labour
Ainger, Nick	*Carmarthen West & Pembrokeshire South*	Labour
Ainsworth, Bob	*Coventry North East*	Labour
Ainsworth, Peter	*Surrey East*	Conservative
Alexander, Douglas	*Paisley South*	Labour Co-Op
Allan, Richard	*Sheffield Hallam*	Liberal Democrat
Allen, Graham	*Nottingham North*	Labour
Amess, David	*Southend West*	Conservative
Ancram, Michael	*Devizes*	Conservative
Anderson, Donald	*Swansea East*	Labour
Anderson, Janet	*Rossendale & Darwen*	Labour
Arbuthnot, James	*Hampshire North East*	Conservative
Armstrong, Hilary	*Durham North West*	Labour
Atherton, Candy	*Falmouth & Camborne*	Labour
Atkinson, David	*Bournemouth East*	Conservative
Atkinson, Peter	*Hexham*	Conservative
Atkins, Charlotte	*Staffordshire Moorlands*	Labour
Austin, John	*Erith & Thamesmead*	Labour
Bacon, Richard	*Norfolk South*	Conservative
Bailey, Adrian	*West Bromwich West*	Labour Co-Op
Baird, Vera	*Redcar*	Labour
Baker, Norman	*Lewes*	Liberal Democrat
Baldry, Tony	*Banbury*	Conservative
Banks, Tony	*West Ham*	Labour
Barker, Greg	*Bexhill & Battle*	Conservative
Barnes, Harry	*Derbyshire North East*	Labour
Baron, John	*Billericay*	Conservative
Barrett, John	*Edinburgh West*	Liberal Democrat
Barron, Kevin	*Rother Valley*	Labour
Battle, John	*Leeds West*	Labour
Bayley, Hugh	*York, City of*	Labour
Beard, Nigel	*Bexleyheath & Crayford*	Labour
Beckett, Margaret	*Derby South*	Labour
Beggs, Roy	*Antrim East*	Ulster Unionist
Begg, Anne	*Aberdeen South*	Labour
Beith, Alan	*Berwick-upon-Tweed*	Liberal Democrat
Bellingham, Henry	*Norfolk North West*	Conservative
Bell, Stuart	*Middlesborough*	Labour
Bennett, Andrew	*Denton & Reddish*	Labour
Benn, Hilary	*Leeds Central*	Labour
Benton, Joe	*Bootle*	Labour
Bercow, John	*Buckingham*	Conservative
Beresford, Sir Paul	*Mole Valley*	Conservative
Berry, Roger	*Kingswood*	Labour
Best, Harold	*Leeds North West*	Labour
Betts, Clive	*Sheffield Attercliffe*	Labour
Blackman, Elizabeth	*Erewash*	Labour
Blair, Tony	*Sedgefield*	Labour
Blears, Hazel	*Salford*	Labour
Blizzard, Bob	*Waveney*	Labour
Blunkett, David	*Sheffield Brightside*	Labour
Blunt, Crispin	*Reigate*	Conservative
Boateng, Paul	*Brent South*	Labour
Borrow, David	*Ribble South*	Labour
Boswell, Tim	*Daventry*	Conservative
Bottomley, Peter	*Worthing West*	Conservative
Bottomley, Virginia	*Surrey South West*	Conservative
Bradley, Keith	*Manchester Withington*	Labour
Bradley, Peter	*Wrekin, The*	Labour

Bradshaw, Ben	*Exeter*	Labour
Brady, Graham	*Altrincham & Sale West*	Conservative
Brake, Tom	*Carshalton and Wallington*	Liberal Democrat
Brazier, Julian	*Canterbury*	Conservative
Breed, Colin	*Cornwall South East*	Liberal Democrat
Brennan, Kevin	*Cardiff West*	Labour
Brinton, Helen	*Peterborough*	Labour
Brooke, Annette	*Dorset Mid & Poole North*	Liberal Democrat
Browne, Des	*Kilmarnock & Loudoun*	Labour
Browning, Angela	*Tiverton & Honiton*	Conservative
Brown, Gordon	*Dunfermline East*	Labour
Brown, Nick	*Newcastle upon Tyne East & Wallsend*	Labour
Brown, Russell	*Dumfries*	Labour
Bruce, Malcolm	*Gordon*	Liberal Democrat
Bryant, Chris	*Rhondda*	Labour
Buck, Karen	*Regent's Park & Kensington*	Labour
Burden, Richard	*Birmingham Northfield*	Labour
Burgon, Colin	*Elmet*	Labour
Burnett, John	*Devon West & Torridge*	Liberal Democrat
Burnham, Andrew	*Leigh*	Labour
Burnside, David	*Antrim South*	Ulster Unionist
Burns, Simon	*Chelmsford West*	Conservative
Burstow, Paul	*Sutton and Cheam*	Liberal Democrat
Burt, Alastair	*Bedfordshire North East*	Conservative
Butterfill, John	*Bournemouth West*	Conservative
Byers, Stephen	*Tyneside North*	Labour
Cable, Dr Vincent	*Twickenham*	Liberal Democrat
Caborn, Richard	*Sheffield Central*	Labour
Cairns, David	*Greenock & Inverclyde*	Labour
Calton, Patsy	*Cheadle*	Liberal Democrat
Cameron, David	*Witney*	Conservative
Campbell, Alan	*Tynemouth*	Labour
Campbell, Anne	*Cambridge*	Labour
Campbell, Gregory	*Londonderry East*	Democratic Unionist
Campbell, Menzies	*Fife North East*	Liberal Democrat
Campbell, Ronnie	*Blyth Valley*	Labour
Cann, Jamie	*Ipswich*	Labour
Caplin, Ivor	*Hove*	Labour
Carmichael, Alistair	*Orkney & Shetland*	Liberal Democrat
Casale, Roger	*Wimbledon*	Labour
Cash, William	*Stone*	Conservative
Caton, Martin	*Gower*	Labour
Cawsey, Ian	*Brigg & Goole*	Labour
Challen, Colin	*Morley & Rothwell*	Labour
Chapman, Ben	*Wirral South*	Labour
Chapman, Sir Sydney	*Chipping Barnet*	Conservative
Chaytor, David	*Bury North*	Labour
Chidgey, David	*Eastleigh*	Liberal Democrat
Chope, Christopher	*Christchurch*	Conservative
Clapham, Michael	*Barnsley West and Penistone*	Labour
Clappison, James	*Hertsmere*	Conservative
Clarke, Charles	*Norwich South*	Labour
Clarke, Kenneth	*Rushcliffe*	Conservative
Clarke, Paul	*Gillingham*	Labour
Clarke, Tom	*Coatbridge & Chryston*	Labour
Clark, Lynda	*Edinburgh Pentlands*	Labour
Clark, Tony	*Northampton South*	Labour
Clelland, David	*Tyne Bridge*	Labour
Clifton-Brown, Geoffrey	*Cotswold*	Conservative
Clwyd, Ann	*Cynon Valley*	Labour
Coaker, Vernon	*Gedling*	Labour
Coffey, Ann	*Stockport*	Labour
Cohen, Harry	*Leyton & Wanstead*	Labour
Coleman, Iain	*Hammersmith & Fulham*	Labour
Collins, Tim	*Westmorland & Lonsdale*	Conservative
Colman, Tony	*Putney*	Labour
Connarty, Michael	*Falkirk East*	Labour
Conway, Derek	*Old Bexley & Sidcup*	Conservative
Cook, Frank	*Stockton North*	Labour
Cook, Robin	*Livingston*	Labour
Cooper, Yvette	*Pontefract & Castleford*	Labour
Corbyn, Jeremy	*Islington North*	Labour

POLITICS

Cormack, Sir Patrick	Staffordshire South	Conservative
Corston, Jean	Bristol East	Labour
Cotter, Brian	Weston-Super-Mare	Liberal Democrat
Cousins, Jim	Newcastle upon Tyne Central	Labour
Cox, Tom	Tooting	Labour
Cranston, Ross	Dudley North	Labour
Cran, James	Beverley & Holderness	Conservative
Crausby, David	Bolton North East	Labour
Cruddas, Jon	Dagenham	Labour
Cryer, Ann	Keighley	Labour
Cryer, John	Hornchurch	Labour
Cummings, John	Easington	Labour
Cunningham, Jack	Copeland	Labour
Cunningham, Jim	Coventry South	Labour
Cunningham, Tony	Workington	Labour
Curry, David	Skipton & Ripon	Conservative
Curtis-Thomas, Claire	Crosby	Labour
Daisley, Paul	Brent East	Labour
Dalyell, Tam	Linlithgow	Labour
Darling, Alistair	Edinburgh Central	Labour
Davey, Edward	Kingston & Surbiton	Liberal Democrat
Davey, Valerie	Bristol West	Labour
David, Wayne	Caerphilly	Labour
Davidson, Ian	Glasgow Pollok	Labour Co-Op
Davies, Denzil	Llanelli	Labour
Davies, Geraint	Croydon Central	Labour
Davies, Quentin	Grantham & Stamford	Conservative
Davis, David	Haltemprice & Howden	Conservative
Davis, Terry	Birmingham Hodge Hill	Labour
Dawson, Hilton	Lancaster & Wyre	Labour
Dean, Janet	Burton	Labour
Denham, John	Southampton Itchen	Labour
Dhanda, Parmjit	Gloucester	Labour
Dismore, Andrew	Hendon	Labour
Djanogly, Jonathan	Huntingdon	Conservative
Dobbin, Jim	Heywood & Middleton	Labour Co-Op
Dobson, Frank	Holborn & St Pancras	Labour
Dodds, Nigel	Belfast North	Democratic Unionist
Doherty, Pat	Tyrone West	Sinn Fein
Donaldson, Jeffrey	Lagan Valley	Ulster Unionist
Donohoe, Brian	Cunninghame South	Labour
Doran, Frank	Aberdeen Central	Labour
Dorrell, Stephen	Charnwood	Conservative
Doughty, Sue	Guildford	Liberal Democrat
Dowd, Jim	Lewisham West	Labour
Drew, David	Stroud	Labour Co-Op
Drown, Julia	Swindon South	Labour
Duncan Smith, Iain	Chingford & Woodford Green	Conservative
Duncan, Alan	Rutland & Melton	Conservative
Duncan, Peter	Galloway & Upper Nithsdale	Conservative
Dunwoody, Gwyneth	Crewe & Nantwich	Labour
Eagle, Angela	Wallasey	Labour
Eagle, Maria	Liverpool Garston	Labour
Edwards, Huw	Monmouth	Labour
Efford, Clive	Eltham	Labour
Ellman, Louise	Liverpool Riverside	Labour
Ennis, Jeff	Barnsley East & Mexborough	Labour
Etherington, Bill	Sunderland North	Labour
Evans, Nigel	Ribble Valley	Conservative
Ewing, Annabelle	Perth	Scottish Nationalists
Fabricant, Michael	Lichfield	Conservative
Fallon, Michael	Sevenoaks	Conservative
Farrelly, Paul	Newcastle-under-Lyme	Labour
Field, Frank	Birkenhead	Labour
Field, Mark	Cities of London & Westminster	Conservative
Fisher, Mark	Stoke-on-Trent Central	Labour
Fitzpatrick, Jim	Poplar & Canning Town	Labour
Fitzsimons, Lorna	Rochdale	Labour
Flight, Howard	Arundel & South Downs	Conservative
Flint, Caroline	Don Valley	Labour
Flook, Adrian	Taunton	Conservative
Flynn, Paul	Newport West	Labour

Follett, Barbara	Stevenage	Labour
Forth, Eric	Bromley & Chislehurst	Conservative
Foster, Derek	Bishop Auckland	Labour
Foster, Don	Bath	Liberal Democrat
Foster, Michael	Worcester	Labour
Foster, Michael	Hastings & Rye	Labour
Foulkes, George	Carrick, Cumnock & Doon	Labour Co-Op
Fox, Dr Liam	Woodspring	Conservative
Francis, Hywel	Aberavon	Labour
Francois, Mark	Rayleigh	Conservative
Gale, Roger	Thanet North	Conservative
Galloway, George	Glasgow Kelvin	Labour
Gapes, Mike	Ilford South	Labour Co-Op
Gardiner, Barry	Brent North	Labour
Garnier, Edward	Harborough	Conservative
George, Andrew	St Ives	Liberal Democrat
George, Bruce	Wallsall South	Labour
Gerrard, Neil	Walthamstow	Labour
Gibb, Nick	Bognor Regis & Littlehampton	Conservative
Gibson, Dr Ian	Norwich North	Labour
Gidley, Sandra	Romsey	Liberal Democrat
Gildernew, Michelle	Fermanagh & South Tyrone	Sinn Fein
Gillan, Cheryl	Chesham & Amersham	Conservative
Gilroy, Linda	Plymouth Sutton	Labour Co-Op
Godsiff, Roger	Birmingham Sparkbrook & Small Heath	Labour
Goggins, Paul	Wythenshawe & Sale East	Labour
Goodman, Paul	Wycombe	Conservative
Grayling, Chris	Epsom and Ewell	Conservative
Gray, James	Wiltshire North	Conservative
Greenway, John	Ryedale	Conservative
Green, Damien	Ashford	Conservative
Green, Matthew	Ludlow	Liberal Democrat
Grieve, Dominic	Beaconsfield	Conservative
Griffiths, Jane	Reading East	Labour
Griffiths, Nigel	Edinburgh South	Labour
Griffiths, Win	Bridgend	Labour
Grogan, John	Selby	Labour
Gummer, John	Suffolk Coastal	Conservative
Hague, William	Richmond (Yorks)	Conservative
Hain, Peter	Neath	Labour
Hall, Mike	Weaver Vale	Labour
Hall, Patrick	Bedford	Labour
Hamilton, David	Midlothian	Labour
Hamilton, Fabian	Leeds North East	Labour
Hammond, Philip	Runnymede & Weybridge	Conservative
Hancock, Mike	Portsmouth South	Liberal Democrat
Hanson, David	Delyn	Labour
Harman, Harriet	Camberwell & Peckham	Labour
Harris, Dr Evan	Oxford West & Abingdon	Liberal Democrat
Harris, Tom	Glasgow Cathcart	Labour
Harvey, Nick	Devon North	Liberal Democrat
Haselhurst, Sir Alan	Saffron Walden	Conservative
Havard, Dai	Merthyr Tydfil & Rhymney	Labour
Hawkins, Nicholas	Surrey Heath	Conservative
Hayes, John	South Holland & The Deepings	Conservative
Heald, Oliver	Hertfordshire North East	Conservative
Healey, John	Wentworth	Labour
Heal, Sylvia	Halesowen & Rowley Regis	Labour
Heathcoat-Amory, David	Wells	Conservative
Heath, David	Somerton & Frome	Liberal Democrat
Henderson, Doug	Newcastle upon Tyne North	Labour
Henderson, Ivan	Harwich	Labour
Hendrick, Mark	Preston	Labour Co-Op
Hendry, Charles	Wealden	Conservative
Hepburn, Stephen	Jarrow	Labour
Heppell, John	Nottingham East	Labour
Hermon, Sylvia	Down North	Ulster Unionist
Hesford, Stephen	Wirral West	Labour
Hewitt, Patricia	Leicester West	Labour
Heyes, David	Ashton-under-Lyne	Labour
Hill, Keith	Streatham	Labour
Hinchcliffe, David	Wakefield	Labour

Hoban, Mark	Fareham	Conservative
Hodge, Margaret	Barking	Labour
Hoey, Kate	Vauxhall	Labour
Hogg, Douglas	Sleaford & North Hykeham	Conservative
Holmes, Paul	Chesterfield	Liberal Democrat
Hood, Jimmy	Clydesdale	Labour
Hoon, Geoff	Ashfield	Labour
Hope, Phil	Corby	Labour Co-Op
Hopkins, Kelvin	Luton North	Labour
Horam, John	Orpington	Conservative
Howard, Michael	Folkestone & Hythe	Conservative
Howarth, Alan	Newport East	Labour
Howarth, George	Knowsley North & Sefton East	Labour
Howarth, Gerald	Aldershot	Conservative
Howells, Dr Kim	Pontypridd	Labour
Hoyle, Lindsay	Chorley	Labour
Hughes, Beverley	Stretford & Urmston	Labour
Hughes, Kevin	Doncaster North	Labour
Hughes, Simon	Southwark North & Bermondsey	Liberal Democrat
Humble, Joan	Blackpool North & Fleetwood	Labour
Hume, John	Foyle	SDLP
Hunter, Andrew	Basingstoke	Conservative
Hurst, Alan	Braintree	Labour
Hutton, John	Barrow & Furness	Labour
Iddon, Brian	Bolton South East	Labour
Illsley, Eric	Barnsley Central	Labour
Ingram, Adam	East Kilbride	Labour
Jackson, Glenda	Hampstead and Highgate	Labour
Jackson, Helen	Sheffield Hillsborough	Labour
Jackson, Robert	Wantage	Conservative
Jack, Michael	Fylde	Conservative
Jamieson, David	Plymouth Devonport	Labour
Jenkins, Brian	Tamworth	Labour
Jenkin, Bernard	Essex North	Conservative
Johnson, Alan	Hull West & Hessle	Labour
Johnson, Boris	Henley	Conservative
Johnson, Melanie	Welwyn Hatfield	Labour
Jones, Dr Lynne	Birmingham Selly Oak	Labour
Jones, Helen	Warrington North	Labour
Jones, Kevan	Durham North	Labour
Jones, Martyn	Clwyd South	Labour
Jones, Nigel	Cheltenham	Liberal Democrat
Jowell, Tessa	Dulwich and West Norwood	Labour
Joyce, Eric	Falkirk West	Labour
Kaufman, Gerald	Manchester Gorton	Labour
Keeble, Sally	Northampton North	Labour
Keen, Alan	Feltham & Heston	Labour Co-Op
Keen, Ann	Brentford & Isleworth	Labour
Keetch, Paul	Hereford	Liberal Democrat
Kelly, Ruth	Bolton West	Labour
Kemp, Fraser	Houghton & Washington East	Labour
Kennedy, Charles	Ross, Skye & Inverness West	Liberal Democrat
Kennedy, Jane	Liverpool Wavertree	Labour
Key, Robert	Salisbury	Conservative
Khabra, Piara	Ealing Southall	Labour
Kidney, David	Stafford	Labour
Kilfoyle, Peter	Liverpool Walton	Labour
King, Andy	Rugby & Kenilworth	Labour
King, Oona	Bethnal Green & Bow	Labour
Kirkbride, Julie	Bromsgrove	Conservative
Kirkwood, Archy	Roxburgh & Berwickshire	Liberal Democrat
Knight, Greg	Yorkshire East	Conservative
Knight, Jim	Dorset South	Labour
Kumar, Dr Ashok	Middlesborough South & Cleveland East	Labour
Ladyman, Dr Stephen	Thanet South	Labour
Laing, Eleanor	Epping Forest	Conservative
Lait, Jacqui	Beckenham	Conservative
Lamb, Norman	Norfolk North	Liberal Democrat
Lammy, David	Tottenham	Labour
Lansley, Andrew	Cambridgeshire South	Conservative
Lawrence, Jackie	Preseli Pembrokeshire	Labour
Laws, David	Yeovil	Liberal Democrat

Laxton, Bob	Derby North	Labour
Lazarowicz, Mark	Edinburgh North & Leith	Labour
Leigh, Edward	Gainsborough	Conservative
Lepper, David	Brighton Pavilion	Labour Co-Op
Leslie, Christopher	Shipley	Labour
Letwin, Oliver	Dorset West	Conservative
Levitt, Tom	High Peak	Labour
Lewis, Dr Julian	New Forest East	Conservative
Lewis, Ivan	Bury South	Labour
Lewis, Terry	Worsley	Labour
Liddell-Grainger, Ian	Bridgwater	Conservative
Liddell, Helen	Airdrie and Shotts	Labour
Lidington, David	Aylesbury	Conservative
Lilley, Peter	Hitchen & Harpenden	Conservative
Linton, Martin	Battersea	Labour
Lloyd, Tony	Manchester Central	Labour
Llwyd, Elfyn	Meirionnydd Nant Conwy	Plaid Cymru
Lord, Michael	Suffolk Central & Ipswich North	Conservative
Loughton, Tim	Worthing East & Shoreham	Conservative
Love, Andy	Edmonton	Labour Co-Op
Lucas, Ian	Wrexham	Labour
Luff, Peter	Worcestershire Mid	Conservative
Luke, Iain	Dundee East	Labour
Lyons, John	Strathkelvin & Bearsden	Labour
MacDonald, Calum	Western Isles	Labour
MacDougall, John	Fife Central	Labour
Mackay, Andrew	Bracknell	Conservative
MacKinlay, Andrew	Thurrock	Labour
MacLean, David	Penrith & The Border	Conservative
MacShane, Denis	Rotherham	Labour
MacTaggart, Fiona	Slough	Labour
Mahmood, Khalid	Birmingham Perry Barr	Labour
Mahon, Alice	Halifax	Labour
Malins, Humfrey	Woking	Conservative
Mallaber, Judy	Amber Valley	Labour
Mallon, Seamus	Newry & Armagh	SDLP
Mandelson, Peter	Hartlepool	Labour
Mann, John	Bassetlaw	Labour
Maples, John	Stratford-on-Avon	Conservative
Marris, Robert	Wolverhampton South West	Labour
Marsden, Gordon	Blackpool South	Labour
Marsden, Paul	Shrewsbury & Atcham	Labour
Marshall-Andrews, Robert	Medway	Labour
Marshall, David	Glasgow Shettleston	Labour
Marshall, Jim	Leicester South	Labour
Martin, Michael	Glasgow Springburn	Labour
Martlew, Eric	Carlisle	Labour
Mates, Michael	Hampshire East	Conservative
Maude, Francis	Horsham	Conservative
Mawhinney, Sir Brian	Cambridgeshire North West	Conservative
May, Theresa	Maidenhead	Conservative
McAvoy, Tommy	Glasgow Rutherglen	Labour Co-Op
McCabe, Stephen	Birmingham Hall Green	Labour
McCafferty, Christine	Calder Valley	Labour
McCartney, Ian	Makerfield	Labour
McDonagh, Siobhain	Mitcham & Morden	Labour
McDonnell, John	Hayes & Harlington	Labour
McFall, John	Dumbarton	Labour Co-Op
McGrady, Eddie	Down South	SDLP
McGuinness, Martin	Ulster Mid	Sinn Fein
McGuire, Anne	Stirling	Labour
McIntosh, Anne	Vale of York	Conservative
McIsaac, Shona	Cleethorpes	Labour
McKechin, Ann	Glasgow Maryhill	Labour
McKenna, Rosemary	Cumbernauld & Kilsyth	Labour
McLoughlin, Patrick	Derbyshire West	Conservative
McNamara, Kevin	Hull North	Labour
McNulty, Tony	Harrow East	Labour
McWalter, Tony	Hemel Hempstead	Labour Co-Op
McWilliam, John	Blaydon	Labour
Meacher, Michael	Oldham West & Royton	Labour
Meale, Alan	Mansfield	Labour

Mercer, Patrick	Newark	Conservative
Merron, Gillian	Lincoln	Labour
Michael, Alun	Cardiff South & Penarth	Labour Co-Op
Milburn, Alan	Darlington	Labour
Miliband, David	South Shields	Labour
Miller, Andrew	Ellesmere Port & Neston	Labour
Mitchell, Andrew	Sutton Coldfield	Conservative
Mitchell, Austin	Great Grimsby	Labour
Moffatt, Laura	Crawley	Labour
Moonie, Lewis	Kirkcaldy	Labour Co-Op
Moore, Michael	Tweeddale, Ettrick & Lauderdale	Liberal Democrat
Moran, Margaret	Luton South	Labour
Morgan, Julie	Cardiff North	Labour
Morley, Elliot	Scunthorpe	Labour
Morris, Estelle	Birmingham Yardley	Labour
Moss, Malcolm	Cambridgeshire North East	Conservative
Mountford, Kali	Colne Valley	Labour
Mudie, George	Leeds East	Labour
Mullin, Chris	Sunderland South	Labour
Munn, Meg	Sheffield Heeley	Labour
Murphy, Denis	Wansbeck	Labour
Murphy, Jim	Eastwood	Labour
Murphy, Paul	Torfaen	Labour
Murrison, Andrew	Westbury	Conservative
Naysmith, Doug	Bristol North West	Labour Co-Op
Norman, Archie	Tunbridge Wells	Conservative
Norris, Dan	Wansdyke	Labour
O'Brien, Mike	Warwickshire North	Labour
O'Brien, Stephen	Eddisbury	Conservative
O'Brien, William	Normanton	Labour
O'Hara, Eddie	Knowsley South	Labour
O'Neill, Martin	Ochil	Labour
Oaten, Mark	Winchester	Liberal Democrat
Olner, Bill	Nuneaton	Labour
Opik, Lembit	Montgomeryshire	Liberal Democrat
Organ, Diana	Forest of Dean	Labour
Osborne, George	Tatton	Conservative
Osborne, Sandra	Ayr	Labour
Ottaway, Richard	Croydon South	Conservative
Owen Jones, John	Cardiff Central	Labour Co-Op
Owen, Albert	Yns Mon	Labour
Page, Richard	Hertfordshire South West	Conservative
Paice, James	Cambridgeshire South East	Conservative
Paisley, Rev. Ian	Antrim North	Democratic Unionist
Palmer, Nick	Broxtowe	Labour
Paterson, Owen	Shropshire North	Conservative
Pearson, Ian	Dudley South	Labour
Perham, Linda	Ilford North	Labour
Picking, Anne	East Lothian	Labour
Pickles, Eric	Brentwood & Ongar	Conservative
Pickthall, Colin	Lancashire West	Labour
Pike, Peter	Burnley	Labour
Plaskitt, James	Warwick & Leamington	Labour
Pollard, Kerry	St Albans	Labour
Pond, Chris	Gravesham	Labour
Pope, Greg	Hyndburn	Labour
Portillo, Michael	Kensington & Chelsea	Conservative
Pound, Stephen	Ealing North	Labour
Powell, Sir Raymond	Ogmore	Labour
Prentice, Bridget	Lewisham East	Labour
Prentice, Gordon	Pendle	Labour
Prescott, John	Hull East	Labour
Price, Adam	Carmarthen East & Dinefwr	Plaid Cymru
Primarolo, Dawn	Bristol South	Labour
Prisk, Mark	Hertford & Stortford	Conservative
Prosser, Gwynn	Dover	Labour
Pugh, John	Southport	Liberal Democrat
Purchase, Ken	Wolverhampton North East	Labour Co-Op
Purnell, James	Stalybridge & Hyde	Labour
Quinn, Lawrie	Scarborough & Whitby	Labour
Quin, Joyce	Gateshead East & Washington West	Labour
Rammell, Bill	Harlow	Labour

Randall, John	*Uxbridge*	Conservative
Rapson, Syd	*Portsmouth North*	Labour
Raynsford, Nick	*Greenwich & Woolwich*	Labour
Redwood, John	*Wokingham*	Conservative
Reed, Andy	*Loughborough*	Labour
Reid, Alan	*Argyll & Bute*	Liberal Democrat
Reid, Dr John	*Hamilton North & Bellshill*	Labour
Rendel, David	*Newbury*	Liberal Democrat
Robathan, Andrew	*Blaby*	Conservative
Robertson, Angus	*Moray*	Scottish Nationalist
Robertson, Hugh	*Faversham & Kent Mid*	Conservative
Robertson, John	*Glasgow Aniesland*	Labour
Robertson, Laurence	*Tewkesbury*	Conservative
Robinson, Geoffrey	*Coventry North West*	Labour
Robinson, Iris	*Strangford*	Democratic Unionist
Robinson, Peter	*Belfast East*	Democratic Unionist
Roche, Barbara	*Hornsey & Wood Green*	Labour
Roe, Marion	*Broxbourne*	Conservative
Rooney, Terry	*Bradford North*	Labour
Rosindell, Andrew	*Romford*	Conservative
Ross, Ernie	*Dundee West*	Labour
Roy, Frank	*Motherwell & Wishaw*	Labour
Ruane, Chris	*Vale of Clwyd*	Labour
Ruddock, Joan	*Lewisham Deptford*	Labour
Ruffley, David	*Bury St Edmunds*	Conservative
Russell, Bob	*Colchester*	Liberal Democrat
Russell, Christine	*Chester, City of*	Labour
Ryan, Joan	*Enfield North*	Labour
Salmond, Alex	*Banff & Buchan*	Scottish Nationalist
Salter, Martin	*Reading West*	Labour
Sanders, Adrian	*Torbay*	Liberal Democrat
Sarwar, Mohammad	*Glasgow Govan*	Labour
Savidge, Malcolm	*Aberdeen North*	Labour
Sawford, Philip	*Kettering*	Labour
Sayeed, Jonathan	*Bedfordshire Mid*	Conservative
Sedgemore, Brian	*Hackney South & Shoreditch*	Labour
Selous, Andrew	*Bedfordshire South West*	Conservative
Shaw, Jonathan	*Chatham & Aylesford*	Labour
Sheerman, Barry	*Huddersfield*	Labour Co-Op
Shephard, Gillian	*Norfolk South West*	Conservative
Shepherd, Richard	*Aldridge-Brownhills*	Conservative
Sheridan, James	*Renfrewshire West*	Labour
Shipley, Debra	*Stourbridge*	Labour
Short, Clare	*Birmingham Ladywood*	Labour
Simmonds, Mark	*Boston & Skegness*	Conservative
Simon, Sion Llewelyn	*Birmingham Erdington*	Labour
Simpson, Alan	*Nottingham South*	Labour
Simpson, Keith	*Norfolk Mid*	Conservative
Singh, Marsha	*Bradford West*	Labour
Skinner, Dennis	*Bolsover*	Labour
Smith, Andrew	*Oxford East*	Labour
Smith, Angela	*Basildon*	Labour Co-Op
Smith, Chris	*Islington South & Finsbury*	Labour
Smith, Geraldine	*Morecambe & Lunesdale*	Labour
Smith, Jacqui	*Redditch*	Labour
Smith, John	*Vale of Glamorgan*	Labour
Smith, Llew	*Blaenau Gwent*	Labour
Smith, Sir Robert	*Aberdeenshire West & Kincardine*	Liberal Democrat
Smyth, Rev. Martin	*Belfast South*	Ulster Unionist
Soames, Nicholas	*Sussex Mid*	Conservative
Soley, Clive	*Ealing Acton & Shepherd's Bush*	Labour
Southworth, Helen	*Warrington South*	Labour
Spellar, John	*Warley*	Labour
Spelman, Caroline	*Meriden*	Conservative
Spicer, Sir Michael	*Worcestershire West*	Conservative
Spink, Robert	*Castle Point*	Conservative
Spring, Richard	*Suffolk West*	Conservative
Squire, Rachel	*Dunfermline West*	Labour
Stanley, Sir John	*Tonbridge & Malling*	Conservative
Starkey, Phyllis	*Milton Keynes South West*	Labour
Steen, Sir Anthony	*Totnes*	Conservative
Steinberg, Gerry	*Durham, City of*	Labour

Stevenson, George	*Stoke-on-Trent South*	Labour
Stewart, David	*Inverness East, Nairn & Lochaber*	Labour
Stewart, Ian	*Eccles*	Labour
Stinchcombe, Paul	*Wellingborough*	Labour
Stoate, Howard	*Dartford*	Labour
Strang, Dr Gavin	*Edinburgh East & Musselburgh*	Labour
Straw, Jack	*Blackburn*	Labour
Streeter, Gary	*Devon South West*	Conservative
Stringer, Graham	*Manchester Blackley*	Labour
Stuart, Gisela	*Birmingham Edgbaston*	Labour
Stunell, Andrew	*Hazel Grove*	Liberal Democrat
Sutcliffe, Gerry	*Bradford South*	Labour
Swayne, Desmond	*New Forest West*	Conservative
Swire, Hugo	*Devon East*	Conservative
Syms, Robert	*Poole*	Conservative
Tami, Mark	*Alyn & Deeside*	Labour
Tapsell, Sir Peter	*Louth & Horncastle*	Conservative
Taylor, Ann	*Dewsbury*	Labour
Taylor, Dari	*Stockton South*	Labour
Taylor, David	*Leicestershire North West*	Labour
Taylor, Ian	*Esher & Walton*	Conservative
Taylor, John	*Solihull*	Conservative
Taylor, Matthew	*Truro & St Austell*	Liberal Democrat
Taylor, Richard	*Wyre Forest*	Independent
Taylor, Sir Teddy	*Rochford & Southend East*	Conservative
Thomas, Gareth	*Harrow West*	Labour
Thomas, Gareth	*Clwyd West*	Labour
Thomas, Simon	*Ceredigion*	Plaid Cymru
Thurso, John	*Caithness, Sunderland & Easter Ross*	Liberal Democrat
Timms, Stephen	*East Ham*	Labour
Tipping, Paddy	*Sherwood*	Labour
Todd, Mark	*Derbyshire South*	Labour
Tonge, Dr Jenny	*Richmond Park*	Liberal Democrat
Touhig, Don	*Islwyn*	Labour Co-Op
Tredinnick, David	*Bosworth*	Conservative
Trend, Michael	*Windsor*	Conservative
Trickett, Jon	*Hemsworth*	Labour
Trimble, David	*Upper Bann*	Ulster Unionist
Truswell, Paul	*Pudsey*	Labour
Turner, Andrew	*Isle of Wight*	Conservative
Turner, Dennis	*Wolverhampton South East*	Labour Co-Op
Turner, Desmond	*Brighton Kemptown*	Labour
Turner, Neil	*Wigan*	Labour
Twigg, Derek	*Halton*	Labour
Twigg, Stephen	*Enfield Southgate*	Labour
Tyler, Paul	*Cornwall North*	Liberal Democrat
Tynan, Bill	*Hamilton South*	Labour
Tyrie, Andrew	*Chichester*	Conservative
Vaz, Keith	*Leicester East*	Labour
Viggers, Peter	*Gosport*	Conservative
Vis, Rudi	*Finchley & Golders Green*	Labour
Walley, Joan	*Stoke-on-Trent North*	Labour
Walter, Robert	*Dorset North*	Conservative
Ward, Claire	*Watford*	Labour
Wareing, Robert	*Liverpool West Derby*	Labour
Waterson, Nigel	*Eastbourne*	Conservative
Watkinson, Angela	*Upminster*	Conservative
Watson, Tom	*West Bromwich East*	Labour
Watts, Dave	*St Helens North*	Labour
Webb, Professor Steven	*Northavon*	Liberal Democrat
Weir, Michael	*Angus*	Scottish Nationalist
Whitehead, Alan	*Southampton Test*	Labour
White, Brian	*Milton Keynes North East*	Labour
Whittingdale, John	*Maldon & Chelmsford East*	Conservative
Wicks, Malcolm	*Croydon North*	Labour
Widdecombe, Ann	*Maidstone & The Weald*	Conservative
Wiggin, Bill	*Leominster*	Conservative
Wilkinson, John	*Ruislip Northwood*	Conservative
Willetts, David	*Havant*	Conservative
Williams, Alan	*Swansea West*	Labour
Williams, Betty	*Conwy*	Labour
Williams, Hywel	*Caernarfon*	Plaid Cymru

Williams, Roger	Brecon & Radnorshire	Liberal Democrat
Willis, Phil	Harrogate & Knaresborough	Liberal Democrat
Wills, Michael	Swindon North	Labour
Wilshire, David	Spelthorne	Conservative
Wilson, Brian	Cunninghame North	Labour
Winnick, David	Walsall North	Labour
Winterton, Ann	Congleton	Conservative
Winterton, Nicholas	Macclesfield	Conservative
Winterton, Rosie	Doncaster Central	Labour
Wishart, Peter	Tayside North	Scottish Nationalist
Woodward, Shaun	St Helens South	Labour
Wood, Mike	Batley & Spen	Labour
Woolas, Phil	Oldham East & Saddleworth	Labour
Worthington, Tony	Clydebank & Milngavie	Labour
Wray, Jimmy	Glasgow Bailliestown	Labour
Wright, David	Telford	Labour
Wright, Dr Anthony	Cannock Chase	Labour
Wright, Tony	Great Yarmouth	Labour
Wyatt, Derek	Sittingbourne & Sheppey	Labour
Yeo, Tim	Suffolk South	Conservative
Younger-Ross, Richard	Teignbridge	Liberal Democrat
Young, Sir George	Hampshire North West	Conservative

General Election Results by Constituency: 7 June 2001

Aberavon	Francis, Hywel	Labour
Aberdeen Central	Doran, Frank	Labour
Aberdeen North	Savidge, Malcolm	Labour
Aberdeen South	Begg, Anne	Labour
Aberdeenshire West & Kincardine	Smith, Sir Robert	Liberal Democrat
Airdrie and Shotts	Liddell, Helen	Labour
Aldershot	Howarth, Gerald	Conservative
Aldridge-Brownhills	Shepherd, Richard	Conservative
Altrincham & Sale West	Brady, Graham	Conservative
Alyn & Deeside	Tami, Mark	Labour
Amber Valley	Mallaber, Judy	Labour
Angus	Weir, Michael	Scottish Nationalist
Antrim East	Beggs, Roy	Ulster Unionist
Antrim North	Paisley, Rev. Ian	Democratic Unionist
Antrim South	Burnside, David	Ulster Unionist
Argyll & Bute	Reid, Alan	Liberal Democrat
Arundel & South Downs	Flight, Howard	Conservative
Ashfield	Hoon, Geoff	Labour
Ashford	Green, Damien	Conservative
Ashton-under-Lyne	Heyes, David	Labour
Aylesbury	Lidington, David	Conservative
Ayr	Osborne, Sandra	Labour
Banbury	Baldry, Tony	Conservative
Banff & Buchan	Salmond, Alex	Scottish Nationalist
Barking	Hodge, Margaret	Labour
Barnsley Central	Illsley, Eric	Labour
Barnsley East & Mexborough	Ennis, Jeff	Labour
Barnsley West and Penistone	Clapham, Michael	Labour
Barrow & Furness	Hutton, John	Labour
Basildon	Smith, Angela	Labour Co-Op
Basingstoke	Hunter, Andrew	Conservative
Bassetlaw	Mann, John	Labour
Bath	Foster, Don	Liberal Democrat
Batley & Spen	Wood, Mike	Labour
Battersea	Linton, Martin	Labour
Beaconsfield	Grieve, Dominic	Conservative
Beckenham	Lait, Jacqui	Conservative
Bedford	Hall, Patrick	Labour
Bedfordshire Mid	Sayeed, Jonathan	Conservative
Bedfordshire North East	Burt, Alastair	Conservative
Bedfordshire South West	Selous, Andrew	Conservative
Belfast East	Robinson, Peter	Democratic Unionist
Belfast North	Dodds, Nigel	Democratic Unionist
Belfast South	Smyth, Rev. Martin	Ulster Unionist
Belfast West	Adams, Gerry	Sinn Fein

P
O
L
I
T
I
C
S

Berwick-upon-Tweed	Beith, Alan	*Liberal Democrat*
Bethnal Green & Bow	King, Oona	*Labour*
Beverley & Holderness	Cran, James	*Conservative*
Bexhill & Battle	Barker, Greg	*Conservative*
Bexleyheath & Crayford	Beard, Nigel	*Labour*
Billericay	Baron, John	*Conservative*
Birkenhead	Field, Frank	*Labour*
Birmingham Edgbaston	Stuart, Gisela	*Labour*
Birmingham Erdington	Simon, Sion Llewelyn	*Labour*
Birmingham Hall Green	McCabe, Stephen	*Labour*
Birmingham Hodge Hill	Davis, Terry	*Labour*
Birmingham Ladywood	Short, Clare	*Labour*
Birmingham Northfield	Burden, Richard	*Labour*
Birmingham Perry Barr	Mahmood, Khalid	*Labour*
Birmingham Selly Oak	Jones, Dr Lynne	*Labour*
Birmingham Sparkbrook & Small Heath	Godsiff, Roger	*Labour*
Birmingham Yardley	Morris, Estelle	*Labour*
Bishop Auckland	Foster, Derek	*Labour*
Blaby	Robathan, Andrew	*Conservative*
Blackburn	Straw, Jack	*Labour*
Blackpool North & Fleetwood	Humble, Joan	*Labour*
Blackpool South	Marsden, Gordon	*Labour*
Blaenau Gwent	Smith, Llew	*Labour*
Blaydon	McWilliam, John	*Labour*
Blyth Valley	Campbell, Ronnie	*Labour*
Bognor Regis & Littlehampton	Gibb, Nick	*Conservative*
Bolsover	Skinner, Dennis	*Labour*
Bolton North East	Crausby, David	*Labour*
Bolton South East	Iddon, Brian	*Labour*
Bolton West	Kelly, Ruth	*Labour*
Bootle	Benton, Joe	*Labour*
Boston & Skegness	Simmonds, Mark	*Conservative*
Bosworth	Tredinnick, David	*Conservative*
Bournemouth East	Atkinson, David	*Conservative*
Bournemouth West	Butterfill, John	*Conservative*
Bracknell	Mackay, Andrew	*Conservative*
Bradford North	Rooney, Terry	*Labour*
Bradford South	Sutcliffe, Gerry	*Labour*
Bradford West	Singh, Marsha	*Labour*
Braintree	Hurst, Alan	*Labour*
Brecon & Radnorshire	Williams, Roger	*Liberal Democrat*
Brent East	Daisley, Paul	*Labour*
Brent North	Gardiner, Barry	*Labour*
Brent South	Boateng, Paul	*Labour*
Brentford & Isleworth	Keen, Ann	*Labour*
Brentwood & Ongar	Pickles, Eric	*Conservative*
Bridgend	Griffiths, Win	*Labour*
Bridgwater	Liddell-Grainger, Ian	*Conservative*
Brigg & Goole	Cawsey, Ian	*Labour*
Brighton Kemptown	Turner, Desmond	*Labour*
Brighton Pavilion	Lepper, David	*Labour Co-Op*
Bristol East	Corston, Jean	*Labour*
Bristol North West	Naysmith, Doug	*Labour Co-Op*
Bristol South	Primarolo, Dawn	*Labour*
Bristol West	Davey, Valerie	*Labour*
Bromley & Chislehurst	Forth, Eric	*Conservative*
Bromsgrove	Kirkbride, Julie	*Conservative*
Broxbourne	Roe, Marion	*Conservative*
Broxtowe	Palmer, Nick	*Labour*
Buckingham	Bercow, John	*Conservative*
Burnley	Pike, Peter	*Labour*
Burton	Dean, Janet	*Labour*
Bury North	Chaytor, David	*Labour*
Bury South	Lewis, Ivan	*Labour*
Bury St Edmunds	Ruffley, David	*Conservative*
Caernarfon	Williams, Hywel	*Plaid Cymru*
Caerphilly	David, Wayne	*Labour*
Caithness, Sunderland & Easter Ross	Thurso, John	*Liberal Democrat*
Calder Valley	McCafferty, Christine	*Labour*
Camberwell & Peckham	Harman, Harriet	*Labour*
Cambridge	Campbell, Anne	*Labour*
Cambridgeshire North East	Moss, Malcolm	*Conservative*

Cambridgeshire North West	Mawhinney, Sir Brian	*Conservative*
Cambridgeshire South	Lansley, Andrew	*Conservative*
Cambridgeshire South East	Paice, James	*Conservative*
Cannock Chase	Wright, Dr Anthony	*Labour*
Canterbury	Brazier, Julian	*Conservative*
Cardiff Central	Owen Jones, John	*Labour Co-Op*
Cardiff North	Morgan, Julie	*Labour*
Cardiff South & Penarth	Michael, Alun	*Labour Co-Op*
Cardiff West	Brennan, Kevin	*Labour*
Carlisle	Martlew, Eric	*Labour*
Carmarthen East & Dinefwr	Price, Adam	*Plaid Cymru*
Carmarthen West & Pembrokeshire South	Ainger, Nick	*Labour*
Carrick, Cumnock & Doon	Foulkes, George	*Labour Co-Op*
Carshalton and Wallington	Brake, Tom	*Liberal Democrat*
Castle Point	Spink, Robert	*Conservative*
Ceredigion	Thomas, Simon	*Plaid Cymru*
Charnwood	Dorrell, Stephen	*Conservative*
Chatham & Aylesford	Shaw, Jonathan	*Labour*
Cheadle	Calton, Patsy	*Liberal Democrat*
Chelmsford West	Burns, Simon	*Conservative*
Cheltenham	Jones, Nigel	*Liberal Democrat*
Chesham & Amersham	Gillan, Cheryl	*Conservative*
Chesterfield	Holmes, Paul	*Liberal Democrat*
Chester, City of	Russell, Christine	*Labour*
Chichester	Tyrie, Andrew	*Conservative*
Chingford & Woodford Green	Duncan Smith, Iain	*Conservative*
Chipping Barnet	Chapman, Sir Sydney	*Conservative*
Chorley	Hoyle, Lindsay	*Labour*
Christchurch	Chope, Christopher	*Conservative*
Cities of London & Westminster	Field, Mark	*Conservative*
Cleethorpes	McIsaac, Shona	*Labour*
Clwyd South	Jones, Martyn	*Labour*
Clwyd West	Thomas, Gareth	*Labour*
Clydebank & Milngavie	Worthington, Tony	*Labour*
Clydesdale	Hood, Jimmy	*Labour*
Coatbridge & Chryston	Clarke, Tom	*Labour*
Colchester	Russell, Bob	*Liberal Democrat*
Colne Valley	Mountford, Kali	*Labour*
Congleton	Winterton, Ann	*Conservative*
Conwy	Williams, Betty	*Labour*
Copeland	Cunningham, Jack	*Labour*
Corby	Hope, Phil	*Labour Co-Op*
Cornwall North	Tyler, Paul	*Liberal Democrat*
Cornwall South East	Breed, Colin	*Liberal Democrat*
Cotswold	Clifton-Brown, Geoffrey	*Conservative*
Coventry North East	Ainsworth, Bob	*Labour*
Coventry North West	Robinson, Geoffrey	*Labour*
Coventry South	Cunningham, Jim	*Labour*
Crawley	Moffatt, Laura	*Labour*
Crewe & Nantwich	Dunwoody, Gwyneth	*Labour*
Crosby	Curtis-Thomas, Claire	*Labour*
Croydon Central	Davies, Geraint	*Labour*
Croydon North	Wicks, Malcolm	*Labour*
Croydon South	Ottaway, Richard	*Conservative*
Cumbernauld & Kilsyth	McKenna, Rosemary	*Labour*
Cunninghame North	Wilson, Brian	*Labour*
Cunninghame South	Donohoe, Brian	*Labour*
Cynon Valley	Clwyd, Ann	*Labour*
Dagenham	Cruddas, Jon	*Labour*
Darlington	Milburn, Alan	*Labour*
Dartford	Stoate, Howard	*Labour*
Daventry	Boswell, Tim	*Conservative*
Delyn	Hanson, David	*Labour*
Denton & Reddish	Bennett, Andrew	*Labour*
Derby North	Laxton, Bob	*Labour*
Derby South	Beckett, Margaret	*Labour*
Derbyshire North East	Barnes, Harry	*Labour*
Derbyshire South	Todd, Mark	*Labour*
Derbyshire West	McLoughlin, Patrick	*Conservative*
Devizes	Ancram, Michael	*Conservative*
Devon East	Swire, Hugo	*Conservative*
Devon North	Harvey, Nick	*Liberal Democrat*

POLITICS

Devon South West	Streeter, Gary	*Conservative*
Devon West & Torridge	Burnett, John	*Liberal Democrat*
Dewsbury	Taylor, Ann	*Labour*
Don Valley	Flint, Caroline	*Labour*
Doncaster Central	Winterton, Rosie	*Labour*
Doncaster North	Hughes, Kevin	*Labour*
Dorset Mid & Poole North	Brooke, Annette	*Liberal Democrat*
Dorset North	Walter, Robert	*Conservative*
Dorset South	Knight, Jim	*Labour*
Dorset West	Letwin, Oliver	*Conservative*
Dover	Prosser, Gwynn	*Labour*
Down North	Hermon, Sylvia	*Ulster Unionist*
Down South	McGrady, Eddie	*SDLP*
Dudley North	Cranston, Ross	*Labour*
Dudley South	Pearson, Ian	*Labour*
Dulwich and West Norwood	Jowell, Tessa	*Labour*
Dumbarton	McFall, John	*Labour Co-Op*
Dumfries	Brown, Russell	*Labour*
Dundee East	Luke, Iain	*Labour*
Dundee West	Ross, Ernie	*Labour*
Dunfermline East	Brown, Gordon	*Labour*
Dunfermline West	Squire, Rachel	*Labour*
Durham, City of	Steinberg, Gerry	*Labour*
Durham North	Jones, Kevan	*Labour*
Durham North West	Armstrong, Hilary	*Labour*
Ealing Acton & Shepherd's Bush	Soley, Clive	*Labour*
Ealing North	Pound, Stephen	*Labour*
Ealing Southall	Khabra, Piara	*Labour*
Easington	Cummings, John	*Labour*
East Ham	Timms, Stephen	*Labour*
East Kilbride	Ingram, Adam	*Labour*
East Lothian	Picking, Anne	*Labour*
Eastbourne	Waterson, Nigel	*Conservative*
Eastleigh	Chidgey, David	*Liberal Democrat*
Eastwood	Murphy, Jim	*Labour*
Eccles	Stewart, Ian	*Labour*
Eddisbury	O'Brien, Stephen	*Conservative*
Edinburgh Central	Darling, Alistair	*Labour*
Edinburgh East & Musselburgh	Strang, Dr Gavin	*Labour*
Edinburgh North & Leith	Lazarowicz, Mark	*Labour*
Edinburgh Pentlands	Clark, Lynda	*Labour*
Edinburgh South	Griffiths, Nigel	*Labour*
Edinburgh West	Barrett, John	*Liberal Democrat*
Edmonton	Love, Andy	*Labour Co-Op*
Ellesmere Port & Neston	Miller, Andrew	*Labour*
Elmet	Burgon, Colin	*Labour*
Eltham	Efford, Clive	*Labour*
Enfield North	Ryan, Joan	*Labour*
Enfield Southgate	Twigg, Stephen	*Labour*
Epping Forest	Laing, Eleanor	*Conservative*
Epsom and Ewell	Grayling, Chris	*Conservative*
Erewash	Blackman, Elizabeth	*Labour*
Erith & Thamesmead	Austin, John	*Labour*
Esher & Walton	Taylor, Ian	*Conservative*
Essex North	Jenkin, Bernard	*Conservative*
Exeter	Bradshaw, Ben	*Labour*
Falkirk East	Connarty, Michael	*Labour*
Falkirk West	Joyce, Eric	*Labour*
Falmouth & Camborne	Atherton, Candy	*Labour*
Fareham	Hoban, Mark	*Conservative*
Faversham & Kent Mid	Robertson, Hugh	*Conservative*
Feltham & Heston	Keen, Alan	*Labour Co-Op*
Fermanagh & South Tyrone	Gildernew, Michelle	*Sinn Fein*
Fife Central	MacDougall, John	*Labour*
Fife North East	Campbell, Menzies	*Liberal Democrat*
Finchley & Golders Green	Vis, Rudi	*Labour*
Folkestone & Hythe	Howard, Michael	*Conservative*
Forest of Dean	Organ, Diana	*Labour*
Foyle	Hume, John	*SDLP*
Fylde	Jack, Michael	*Conservative*
Gainsborough	Leigh, Edward	*Conservative*
Galloway & Upper Nithsdale	Duncan, Peter	*Conservative*

Gateshead East & Washington West	Quin, Joyce	*Labour*
Gedling	Coaker, Vernon	*Labour*
Gillingham	Clarke, Paul	*Labour*
Glasgow Aniesland	Robertson, John	*Labour*
Glasgow Bailliestown	Wray, Jimmy	*Labour*
Glasgow Cathcart	Harris, Tom	*Labour*
Glasgow Govan	Sarwar, Mohammad	*Labour*
Glasgow Kelvin	Galloway, George	*Labour*
Glasgow Maryhill	McKechin, Ann	*Labour*
Glasgow Pollok	Davidson, Ian	*Labour Co-Op*
Glasgow Rutherglen	McAvoy, Tommy	*Labour Co-Op*
Glasgow Shettleston	Marshall, David	*Labour*
Glasgow Springburn	Martin, Michael	*Labour*
Gloucester	Dhanda, Parmjit	*Labour*
Gordon	Bruce, Malcolm	*Liberal Democrat*
Gosport	Viggers, Peter	*Conservative*
Gower	Caton, Martin	*Labour*
Grantham & Stamford	Davies, Quentin	*Conservative*
Gravesham	Pond, Chris	*Labour*
Great Grimsby	Mitchell, Austin	*Labour*
Great Yarmouth	Wright, Tony	*Labour*
Greenock & Inverclyde	Cairns, David	*Labour*
Greenwich & Woolwich	Raynsford, Nick	*Labour*
Guildford	Doughty, Sue	*Liberal Democrat*
Hackney North & Stoke Newington	Abbott, Diane	*Labour*
Hackney South & Shoreditch	Sedgemore, Brian	*Labour*
Halesowen & Rowley Regis	Heal, Sylvia	*Labour*
Halifax	Mahon, Alice	*Labour*
Haltemprice & Howden	Davis, David	*Conservative*
Halton	Twigg, Derek	*Labour*
Hamilton North & Bellshill	Reid, Dr John	*Labour*
Hamilton South	Tynan, Bill	*Labour*
Hammersmith & Fulham	Coleman, Iain	*Labour*
Hampshire East	Mates, Michael	*Conservative*
Hampshire North East	Arbuthnot, James	*Conservative*
Hampshire North West	Young, Sir George	*Conservative*
Hampstead and Highgate	Jackson, Glenda	*Labour*
Harborough	Garnier, Edward	*Conservative*
Harlow	Rammell, Bill	*Labour*
Harrogate & Knaresborough	Willis, Phil	*Liberal Democrat*
Harrow East	McNulty, Tony	*Labour*
Harrow West	Thomas, Gareth	*Labour*
Hartlepool	Mandelson, Peter	*Labour*
Harwich	Henderson, Ivan	*Labour*
Hastings & Rye	Foster, Michael	*Labour*
Havant	Willetts, David	*Conservative*
Hayes & Harlington	McDonnell, John	*Labour*
Hazel Grove	Stunell, Andrew	*Liberal Democrat*
Hemel Hempstead	McWalter, Tony	*Labour Co-Op*
Hemsworth	Trickett, Jon	*Labour*
Hendon	Dismore, Andrew	*Labour*
Henley	Johnson, Boris	*Conservative*
Hereford	Keetch, Paul	*Liberal Democrat*
Hertford & Stortford	Prisk, Mark	*Conservative*
Hertfordshire North East	Heald, Oliver	*Conservative*
Hertfordshire South West	Page, Richard	*Conservative*
Hertsmere	Clappison, James	*Conservative*
Hexham	Atkinson, Peter	*Conservative*
Heywood & Middleton	Dobbin, Jim	*Labour Co-Op*
High Peak	Levitt, Tom	*Labour*
Hitchen & Harpenden	Lilley, Peter	*Conservative*
Holborn & St Pancras	Dobson, Frank	*Labour*
Hornchurch	Cryer, John	*Labour*
Hornsey & Wood Green	Roche, Barbara	*Labour*
Horsham	Maude, Francis	*Conservative*
Houghton & Washington East	Kemp, Fraser	*Labour*
Hove	Caplin, Ivor	*Labour*
Huddersfield	Sheerman, Barry	*Labour Co-Op*
Hull East	Prescott, John	*Labour*
Hull North	McNamara, Kevin	*Labour*
Hull West & Hessle	Johnson, Alan	*Labour*
Huntingdon	Djanogly, Jonathan	*Conservative*

P
O
L
I
T
I
C
S

Hyndburn	Pope, Greg	*Labour*
Ilford North	Perham, Linda	*Labour*
Ilford South	Gapes, Mike	*Labour Co-Op*
Inverness East, Nairn & Lochaber	Stewart, David	*Labour*
Ipswich	Cann, Jamie	*Labour*
Isle of Wight	Turner, Andrew	*Conservative*
Islington North	Corbyn, Jeremy	*Labour*
Islington South & Finsbury	Smith, Chris	*Labour*
Islwyn	Touhig, Don	*Labour Co-Op*
Jarrow	Hepburn, Stephen	*Labour*
Keighley	Cryer, Ann	*Labour*
Kensington & Chelsea	Portillo, Michael	*Conservative*
Kettering	Sawford, Philip	*Labour*
Kilmarnock & Loudoun	Browne, Des	*Labour*
Kingston & Surbiton	Davey, Edward	*Liberal Democrat*
Kingswood	Berry, Roger	*Labour*
Kirkcaldy	Moonie, Lewis	*Labour Co-Op*
Knowsley North & Sefton East	Howarth, George	*Labour*
Knowsley South	O'Hara, Eddie	*Labour*
Lagan Valley	Donaldson, Jeffrey	*Ulster Unionist*
Lancashire West	Pickthall, Colin	*Labour*
Lancaster & Wyre	Dawson, Hilton	*Labour*
Leeds Central	Benn, Hilary	*Labour*
Leeds East	Mudie, George	*Labour*
Leeds North East	Hamilton, Fabian	*Labour*
Leeds North West	Best, Harold	*Labour*
Leeds West	Battle, John	*Labour*
Leicester East	Vaz, Keith	*Labour*
Leicester South	Marshall, Jim	*Labour*
Leicester West	Hewitt, Patricia	*Labour*
Leicestershire North West	Taylor, David	*Labour*
Leigh	Burnham, Andrew	*Labour*
Leominster	Wiggin, Bill	*Conservative*
Lewes	Baker, Norman	*Liberal Democrat*
Lewisham Deptford	Ruddock, Joan	*Labour*
Lewisham East	Prentice, Bridget	*Labour*
Lewisham West	Dowd, Jim	*Labour*
Leyton & Wanstead	Cohen, Harry	*Labour*
Lichfield	Fabricant, Michael	*Conservative*
Lincoln	Merron, Gillian	*Labour*
Linlithgow	Dalyell, Tam	*Labour*
Liverpool Garston	Eagle, Maria	*Labour*
Liverpool Riverside	Ellman, Louise	*Labour*
Liverpool Walton	Kilfoyle, Peter	*Labour*
Liverpool Wavertree	Kennedy, Jane	*Labour*
Liverpool West Derby	Wareing, Robert	*Labour*
Livingston	Cook, Robin	*Labour*
Llanelli	Davies, Denzil	*Labour*
Londonderry East	Campbell, Gregory	*Democratic Unionist*
Loughborough	Reed, Andy	*Labour*
Louth & Horncastle	Tapsell, Sir Peter	*Conservative*
Ludlow	Green, Matthew	*Liberal Democrat*
Luton North	Hopkins, Kelvin	*Labour*
Luton South	Moran, Margaret	*Labour*
Macclesfield	Winterton, Nicholas	*Conservative*
Maidenhead	May, Theresa	*Conservative*
Maidstone & The Weald	Widdecombe, Ann	*Conservative*
Makerfield	McCartney, Ian	*Labour*
Maldon & Chelmsford East	Whittingdale, John	*Conservative*
Manchester Blackley	Stringer, Graham	*Labour*
Manchester Central	Lloyd, Tony	*Labour*
Manchester Gorton	Kaufman, Gerald	*Labour*
Manchester Withington	Bradley, Keith	*Labour*
Mansfield	Meale, Alan	*Labour*
Medway	Marshall-Andrews, Robert	*Labour*
Meirionnydd Nant Conwy	Llwyd, Elfyn	*Plaid Cymru*
Meriden	Spelman, Caroline	*Conservative*
Merthyr Tydfil & Rhymney	Havard, Dai	*Labour*
Middlesborough	Bell, Stuart	*Labour*
Middlesborough South & Cleveland East	Kumar, Dr Ashok	*Labour*
Midlothian	Hamilton, David	*Labour*
Milton Keynes North East	White, Brian	*Labour*

Milton Keynes South West	Starkey, Phyllis	*Labour*
Mitcham & Morden	McDonagh, Siobhain	*Labour*
Mole Valley	Beresford, Sir Paul	*Conservative*
Monmouth	Edwards, Huw	*Labour*
Montgomeryshire	Opik, Lembit	*Liberal Democrat*
Moray	Robertson, Angus	*Scottish Nationalist*
Morecambe & Lunesdale	Smith, Geraldine	*Labour*
Morley & Rothwell	Challen, Colin	*Labour*
Motherwell & Wishaw	Roy, Frank	*Labour*
Neath	Hain, Peter	*Labour*
New Forest East	Lewis, Dr Julian	*Conservative*
New Forest West	Swayne, Desmond	*Conservative*
Newark	Mercer, Patrick	*Conservative*
Newbury	Rendel, David	*Liberal Democrat*
Newcastle-under-Lyme	Farrelly, Paul	*Labour*
Newcastle upon Tyne Central	Cousins, Jim	*Labour*
Newcastle upon Tyne East & Wallsend	Brown, Nick	*Labour*
Newcastle upon Tyne North	Henderson, Doug	*Labour*
Newport East	Howarth, Alan	*Labour*
Newport West	Flynn, Paul	*Labour*
Newry & Armagh	Mallon, Seamus	*SDLP*
Norfolk Mid	Simpson, Keith	*Conservative*
Norfolk North	Lamb, Norman	*Liberal Democrat*
Norfolk North West	Bellingham, Henry	*Conservative*
Norfolk South	Bacon, Richard	*Conservative*
Norfolk South West	Shephard, Gillian	*Conservative*
Normanton	O'Brien, William	*Labour*
Northampton North	Keeble, Sally	*Labour*
Northampton South	Clark, Tony	*Labour*
Northavon	Webb, Professor Steven	*Liberal Democrat*
Norwich North	Gibson, Dr Ian	*Labour*
Norwich South	Clarke, Charles	*Labour*
Nottingham East	Heppell, John	*Labour*
Nottingham North	Allen, Graham	*Labour*
Nottingham South	Simpson, Alan	*Labour*
Nuneaton	Olner, Bill	*Labour*
Ochil	O'Neill, Martin	*Labour*
Ogmore	Powell, Sir Raymond	*Labour*
Old Bexley & Sidcup	Conway, Derek	*Conservative*
Oldham East & Saddleworth	Woolas, Phil	*Labour*
Oldham West & Royton	Meacher, Michael	*Labour*
Orkney & Shetland	Carmichael, Alistair	*Liberal Democrat*
Orpington	Horam, John	*Conservative*
Oxford East	Smith, Andrew	*Labour*
Oxford West & Abingdon	Harris, Dr Evan	*Liberal Democrat*
Paisley North	Adams, Irene	*Labour*
Paisley South	Alexander, Douglas	*Labour Co-Op*
Pendle	Prentice, Gordon	*Labour*
Penrith & The Border	MacLean, David	*Conservative*
Perth	Ewing, Annabelle	*Scottish Nationalist*
Peterborough	Brinton, Helen	*Labour*
Plymouth Devonport	Jamieson, David	*Labour*
Plymouth Sutton	Gilroy, Linda	*Labour Co-Op*
Pontefract & Castleford	Cooper, Yvette	*Labour*
Pontypridd	Howells, Dr Kim	*Labour*
Poole	Syms, Robert	*Conservative*
Poplar & Canning Town	Fitzpatrick, Jim	*Labour*
Portsmouth North	Rapson, Syd	*Labour*
Portsmouth South	Hancock, Mike	*Liberal Democrat*
Preseli Pembrokeshire	Lawrence, Jackie	*Labour*
Preston	Hendrick, Mark	*Labour Co-Op*
Pudsey	Truswell, Paul	*Labour*
Putney	Colman, Tony	*Labour*
Rayleigh	Francois, Mark	*Conservative*
Reading East	Griffiths, Jane	*Labour*
Reading West	Salter, Martin	*Labour*
Redcar	Baird, Vera	*Labour*
Redditch	Smith, Jacqui	*Labour*
Regent's Park & Kensington	Buck, Karen	*Labour*
Reigate	Blunt, Crispin	*Conservative*
Renfrewshire West	Sheridan, James	*Labour*
Rhondda	Bryant, Chris	*Labour*

POLITICS

Ribble South	Borrow, David	*Labour*
Ribble Valley	Evans, Nigel	*Conservative*
Richmond Park	Tonge, Dr Jenny	*Liberal Democrat*
Richmond (Yorks)	Hague, William	*Conservative*
Rochdale	Fitzsimons, Lorna	*Labour*
Rochford & Southend East	Taylor, Sir Teddy	*Conservative*
Romford	Rosindell, Andrew	*Conservative*
Romsey	Gidley, Sandra	*Liberal Democrat*
Rossendale & Darwen	Anderson, Janet	*Labour*
Ross, Skye & Inverness West	Kennedy, Charles	*Liberal Democrat*
Rother Valley	Barron, Kevin	*Labour*
Rotherham	MacShane, Denis	*Labour*
Roxburgh & Berwickshire	Kirkwood, Archy	*Liberal Democrat*
Rugby & Kenilworth	King, Andy	*Labour*
Ruislip Northwood	Wilkinson, John	*Conservative*
Runnymede & Weybridge	Hammond, Philip	*Conservative*
Rushcliffe	Clarke, Kenneth	*Conservative*
Rutland & Melton	Duncan, Alan	*Conservative*
Ryedale	Greenway, John	*Conservative*
Saffron Walden	Haselhurst, Sir Alan	*Conservative*
Salford	Blears, Hazel	*Labour*
Salisbury	Key, Robert	*Conservative*
Scarborough & Whitby	Quinn, Lawrie	*Labour*
Scunthorpe	Morley, Elliot	*Labour*
Sedgefield	Blair, Tony	*Labour*
Selby	Grogan, John	*Labour*
Sevenoaks	Fallon, Michael	*Conservative*
Sheffield Attercliffe	Betts, Clive	*Labour*
Sheffield Brightside	Blunkett, David	*Labour*
Sheffield Central	Caborn, Richard	*Labour*
Sheffield Hallam	Allan, Richard	*Liberal Democrat*
Sheffield Heeley	Munn, Meg	*Labour*
Sheffield Hillsborough	Jackson, Helen	*Labour*
Sherwood	Tipping, Paddy	*Labour*
Shipley	Leslie, Christopher	*Labour*
Shrewsbury & Atcham	Marsden, Paul	*Labour*
Shropshire North	Paterson, Owen	*Conservative*
Sittingbourne & Sheppey	Wyatt, Derek	*Labour*
Skipton & Ripon	Curry, David	*Conservative*
Sleaford & North Hykeham	Hogg, Douglas	*Conservative*
Slough	MacTaggart, Fiona	*Labour*
Solihull	Taylor, John	*Conservative*
Somerton & Frome	Heath, David	*Liberal Democrat*
South Holland & The Deepings	Hayes, John	*Conservative*
South Shields	Miliband, David	*Labour*
Southampton Itchen	Denham, John	*Labour*
Southampton Test	Whitehead, Alan	*Labour*
Southend West	Amess, David	*Conservative*
Southport	Pugh, John	*Liberal Democrat*
Southwark North & Bermondsey	Hughes, Simon	*Liberal Democrat*
Spelthorne	Wilshire, David	*Conservative*
St Albans	Pollard, Kerry	*Labour*
St Helens North	Watts, Dave	*Labour*
St Helens South	Woodward, Shaun	*Labour*
St Ives	George, Andrew	*Liberal Democrat*
Stafford	Kidney, David	*Labour*
Staffordshire Moorlands	Atkins, Charlotte	*Labour*
Staffordshire South	Cormack, Sir Patrick	*Conservative*
Stalybridge & Hyde	Purnell, James	*Labour*
Stevenage	Follett, Barbara	*Labour*
Stirling	McGuire, Anne	*Labour*
Stockport	Coffey, Ann	*Labour*
Stockton North	Cook, Frank	*Labour*
Stockton South	Taylor, Dari	*Labour*
Stoke-on-Trent Central	Fisher, Mark	*Labour*
Stoke-on-Trent North	Walley, Joan	*Labour*
Stoke-on-Trent South	Stevenson, George	*Labour*
Stone	Cash, William	*Conservative*
Stourbridge	Shipley, Debra	*Labour*
Strangford	Robinson, Iris	*Democratic Unionist*
Stratford-on-Avon	Maples, John	*Conservative*
Strathkelvin & Bearsden	Lyons, John	*Labour*

Streatham	Hill, Keith	*Labour*
Stretford & Urmston	Hughes, Beverley	*Labour*
Stroud	Drew, David	*Labour Co-Op*
Suffolk Central & Ipswich North	Lord, Michael	*Conservative*
Suffolk Coastal	Gummer, John	*Conservative*
Suffolk South	Yeo, Tim	*Conservative*
Suffolk West	Spring, Richard	*Conservative*
Sunderland North	Etherington, Bill	*Labour*
Sunderland South	Mullin, Chris	*Labour*
Surrey East	Ainsworth, Peter	*Conservative*
Surrey Heath	Hawkins, Nicholas	*Conservative*
Surrey South West	Bottomley, Virginia	*Conservative*
Sussex Mid	Soames, Nicholas	*Conservative*
Sutton and Cheam	Burstow, Paul	*Liberal Democrat*
Sutton Coldfield	Mitchell, Andrew	*Conservative*
Swansea East	Anderson, Donald	*Labour*
Swansea West	Williams, Alan	*Labour*
Swindon North	Wills, Michael	*Labour*
Swindon South	Drown, Julia	*Labour*
Tamworth	Jenkins, Brian	*Labour*
Tatton	Osborne, George	*Conservative*
Taunton	Flook, Adrian	*Conservative*
Tayside North	Wishart, Peter	*Scottish Nationalist*
Teignbridge	Younger-Ross, Richard	*Liberal Democrat*
Telford	Wright, David	*Labour*
Tewkesbury	Robertson, Laurence	*Conservative*
Thanet North	Gale, Roger	*Conservative*
Thanet South	Ladyman, Dr Stephen	*Labour*
Thurrock	MacKinlay, Andrew	*Labour*
Tiverton & Honiton	Browning, Angela	*Conservative*
Tonbridge & Malling	Stanley, Sir John	*Conservative*
Tooting	Cox, Tom	*Labour*
Torbay	Sanders, Adrian	*Liberal Democrat*
Torfaen	Murphy, Paul	*Labour*
Totnes	Steen, Sir Anthony	*Conservative*
Tottenham	Lammy, David	*Labour*
Truro & St Austell	Taylor, Matthew	*Liberal Democrat*
Tunbridge Wells	Norman, Archie	*Conservative*
Tweeddale, Ettrick & Lauderdale	Moore, Michael	*Liberal Democrat*
Twickenham	Cable, Dr Vincent	*Liberal Democrat*
Tyne Bridge	Clelland, David	*Labour*
Tynemouth	Campbell, Alan	*Labour*
Tyneside North	Byers, Stephen	*Labour*
Tyrone West	Doherty, Pat	*Sinn Fein*
Ulster Mid	McGuinness, Martin	*Sinn Fein*
Upminster	Watkinson, Angela	*Conservative*
Upper Bann	Trimble, David	*Ulster Unionist*
Uxbridge	Randall, John	*Conservative*
Vale of Clwyd	Ruane, Chris	*Labour*
Vale of Glamorgan	Smith, John	*Labour*
Vale of York	McIntosh, Anne	*Conservative*
Vauxhall	Hoey, Kate	*Labour*
Wakefield	Hinchcliffe, David	*Labour*
Wallasey	Eagle, Angela	*Labour*
Wallsall South	George, Bruce	*Labour*
Walsall North	Winnick, David	*Labour*
Walthamstow	Gerrard, Neil	*Labour*
Wansbeck	Murphy, Denis	*Labour*
Wansdyke	Norris, Dan	*Labour*
Wantage	Jackson, Robert	*Conservative*
Warley	Spellar, John	*Labour*
Warrington North	Jones, Helen	*Labour*
Warrington South	Southworth, Helen	*Labour*
Warwick & Leamington	Plaskitt, James	*Labour*
Warwickshire North	O'Brien, Mike	*Labour*
Watford	Ward, Claire	*Labour*
Waveney	Blizzard, Bob	*Labour*
Wealden	Hendry, Charles	*Conservative*
Weaver Vale	Hall, Mike	*Labour*
Wellingborough	Stinchcombe, Paul	*Labour*
Wells	Heathcoat-Amory, David	*Conservative*
Welwyn Hatfield	Johnson, Melanie	*Labour*

POLITICS

Wentworth	Healey, John	*Labour*
West Bromwich East	Watson, Tom	*Labour*
West Bromwich West	Bailey, Adrian	*Labour Co-Op*
West Ham	Banks, Tony	*Labour*
Westbury	Murrison, Andrew	*Conservative*
Western Isles	MacDonald, Calum	*Labour*
Westmorland & Lonsdale	Collins, Tim	*Conservative*
Weston-Super-Mare	Cotter, Brian	*Liberal Democrat*
Wigan	Turner, Neil	*Labour*
Wiltshire North	Gray, James	*Conservative*
Wimbledon	Casale, Roger	*Labour*
Winchester	Oaten, Mark	*Liberal Democrat*
Windsor	Trend, Michael	*Conservative*
Wirral South	Chapman, Ben	*Labour*
Wirral West	Hesford, Stephen	*Labour*
Witney	Cameron, David	*Conservative*
Woking	Malins, Humfrey	*Conservative*
Wokingham	Redwood, John	*Conservative*
Wolverhampton North East	Purchase, Ken	*Labour Co-Op*
Wolverhampton South East	Turner, Dennis	*Labour Co-Op*
Wolverhampton South West	Marris, Robert	*Labour*
Woodspring	Fox, Dr Liam	*Conservative*
Worcester	Foster, Michael	*Labour*
Worcestershire Mid	Luff, Peter	*Conservative*
Worcestershire West	Spicer, Sir Michael	*Conservative*
Workington	Cunningham, Tony	*Labour*
Worsley	Lewis, Terry	*Labour*
Worthing East & Shoreham	Loughton, Tim	*Conservative*
Worthing West	Bottomley, Peter	*Conservative*
Wrekin, The	Bradley, Peter	*Labour*
Wrexham	Lucas, Ian	*Labour*
Wycombe	Goodman, Paul	*Conservative*
Wyre Forest	Taylor, Richard	*Independent*
Wythenshawe & Sale East	Goggins, Paul	*Labour*
Yeovil	Laws, David	*Liberal Democrat*
Yns Mon	Owen, Albert	*Labour*
Yorkshire East	Knight, Greg	*Conservative*
York, City of	Bayley, Hugh	*Labour*

Miscellaneous Information: After 2001 General Election

Composition of the House of Commons (541 men, 118 women = 659)	Labour 412 (317 men, 95 women), Conservatives 166 (152 men, 14 women).
	Liberal Democrats 52 (47 men, 5 women), Ulster Unionists 6 (5 men, 1 woman).
	Scottish Nationalists 5 (4 men, 1 woman), Dem. Unionists 5 (4 men, 1 woman).
	Plaid Cymru 4 (4 men), Sinn Fein 4 (3 men, 1 woman), SDLP 3 (3 men).
	Independent 1 (man) and Michael Martin (speaker) who does not vote in divisions except when the voting is tied.
husband and wife MPs	Ann and Nicholas Winterton; Julie Kirkbride and Andrew Mackay.
largest majority	John Cummings (Easington) had a majority of 21,949.
mother and son MPs	Ann Cryer (Keighley) is the mother of John Cryer (Hornchurch).
Muslim MP: first	Mohammad Sarwar (first elected in 1997). Khalid Mahmood (first in England).
overseas born MPs	Paul Beresford (NZ), Gisella Stuart (Germany), Rudi Vis (Holland).
quickest result	South Sunderland result announced at 10.42, the fastest ever.
smallest majority	Patsy Calton (LD) defeated Stephen Day (C) by 33 votes.
sons of ex MP	Dominic Grieve is the son of Percy Grieve, former MP for Solihull.
	Hilary Benn is the son of Tony Benn former MP for Chesterfield.
twins	Angela and Maria Eagle, MPs for Wallasey and Liverpool Garston.

PROVERBS

Biblical Proverbs (from the Book of Proverbs)

A wise man will hear, and will increase learning: and a man of understanding shall attain unto wise counsels (1.5).

Listen to the discipline of your father and do not forsake the law of your mother (1.8).

Happy is the man that has found wisdom, and the man that has discernment (3.13).

Do not hold back good from those to whom it is owing, when it happens to be in the power of your hand to do [it] (3.27).

Do not fabricate against your fellow man anything bad, when he is dwelling in a sense of security with you (3.29).

Do not quarrel with a man without cause, if he has rendered no bad to you (3.30).

Do not become envious of a man of violence, nor choose any of his ways (3.31).

Into the path of wicked ones do not enter, and do not walk straight on into the way of bad ones (4.14).

Remove from yourself the crookedness of speech, and the deviousness of lips put far away from yourself (4.24).

Smooth out the course of your foot, and may all your own ways be firmly established (4.26).

Go to the ant, see its ways and become wise (6.6).

Do not reprove a ridiculer, that he may not hate you. Give a reproof to a wise person and he will love you (9.8).

A wise son is one that makes a father rejoice, and a stupid son is the grief of his mother (10.1).

He that is walking in integrity will walk in security, but he that is making his ways crooked will make himself known (10.9).

Hatred is what stirs up contentions, but love covers over even all transgressions (10.12).

The tongue of the righteous person is choice silver, whilst the heart of the wicked one is worth little (10.20).

Deception is in the heart of those fabricating mischief, but those counselling peace have rejoicing (12.20).

A prudent man concealeth knowledge (12.23).

He that walketh with wise men shall be wise: but a companion of fools shall be destroyed (13.20).

He that spareth his rod hateth his son (13.24).

Pride goeth before destruction, and an haughty spirit before a fall (16.18).

General Proverbs

All roads lead to Rome.
An old poacher makes the best keeper.
Beauty is potent but money is omnipotent.
Better be stung by a nettle than pricked by a rose.
Between two stools one falls to the ground.
A bird in the hand is worth two in the bush.
Caesar's wife must be above suspicion.
Cards are the devil's books.
All cats are grey in the dark.
Caveat emptor (Let the buyer beware).
Diligence is the mother of good luck.
A drowning man will catch at a straw.
Enough is as good as a feast.
Every cloud has a silver lining.
Experience is the mistress of fools.
Faint heart never won fair lady.
A fair exchange is no robbery.
Fair words butter no parsnips.
Far fowls have fair feathers.
The folly of one man is the fortune of another.
A fool may ask more questions in an hour than a wise man can answer in seven years.
The fool wanders, the wise man travels.
Give a dog a bad name and hang him.
Go to bed with the lamb, and rise with the lark.
The hand that rocks the cradle rules the world.
He is a fool who makes his doctor his heir.
He should have a long spoon that sups with the devil.
He that sings on Friday will weep on Sunday.
He was a bold man that first ate an oyster.
A heavy purse makes a light heart.
A hedge between keeps friendship green.

If ifs and ans were pots and pans, there'd be no trade for tinkers.
If St Vitus's day [15 June] be rainy weather, it will rain for 30 days together.
If you run after two hares, you will catch neither.
If you sing before breakfast, you'll cry before night.
If you swear, you'll catch no fish.
Keep a thing seven years and you will find a use for it.
Knowledge is power.
A light purse makes a heavy heart.
Lose an hour in the morning and you'll be all day hunting for it.
A mackerel sky is never long dry.
Magpies: one's sorrow, two's mirth, three's a wedding, four's a birth, five's a christening, six a dearth, seven's heaven, eight is hell, and nine's the devil his ane sel'.
March comes in like a lion and goes out like a lamb.
Mighty oaks from little acorns grow.
Monday's child is fair of face,/Tuesday's child is full of grace,/Wednesday's child is full of woe,/Thursday's child has far to go,/Friday's child is loving and giving,/Saturday's child works hard for living. But the child who is born on the Sabbath day is lucky and happy and good and gay.
Nature abhors a vacuum.
Necessity is the mother of invention.
Needs must when the devil drives.
Never is a long day.
Never trouble trouble till trouble troubles you.
A nod is as good as a wink to a blind horse.
Out of debt, out of danger.
Penny wise, pound foolish.

Prevention is better than cure.

Procrastination is the thief of time

Promises and pie-crusts are made to be broken.

The proof of the pudding is in the eating.

Providence is better than rent.

Rain before seven, fine before eleven.

Red sky at night shepherd's delight, red sky in the morning shepherd's warning.

The road to hell is paved with good intentions.

Salmon and sermon have their season in Lent.

Save your breath to cool your porridge.

Sloth is the key to poverty.

Sneeze on a Monday you sneeze for danger, sneeze on a Tuesday you kiss a stranger, sneeze on a Wednesday you sneeze for a letter, sneeze on a Thursday for something better, sneeze on a Friday you sneeze for sorrow, sneeze on a Saturday see your sweetheart tomorrow, sneeze on a Sunday your safety seek, the devil will have you the whole of the week.

Spare the rod and spoil the child.

Speak well of your friend, of your enemy say nothing.

Still waters run deep.

A tale twice told is cabbage twice sold.

Talk of the devil, and he'll appear.

Tell that to the marines.

Thrift is good revenue.

Time and tide wait for no man.

Virtue is its own reward.

Virtue never grows old.

What can't be cured must be endured.

When the sun is highest he casts the least shadow.

When the wind is in the east it's good for neither man nor beast./When the wind is in the north the skilful fisher goes not forth./When the wind is in the south it blows the bait in the fish's mouth./When the wind is in the west the weather is at the best.

Who knows most says least.

Whom God wishes to destroy, he first makes mad *(Quos Deus vult perdere, prius dementat)*.

A wild goose never laid a tame egg.

A wonder lasts but nine days.

You cannot make an omelette without breaking eggs.

You cannot make a silk purse out of a sow's ear.

You cannot teach an old dog new tricks.

Young men may die, old men must.

Zeal without knowledge is fire without light.

Zeal without prudence is frenzy.

NB Some of the proverbs above are corruptions of biblical proverbs. Others were coined by great thinkers and philosophers, and yet others have simply come into general usage through time.

QUOTATIONS

Quotations (in Alphabetical Order)

All Gaul is divided into three parts. — Julius Caesar

All hope abandon ye who enter. (from *Divine Comedy*) — Dante Alighieri

All is for the best in the best of possible worlds. (from *Candide*) — Voltaire

An archaeologist is the best husband any woman can have – the older she gets the more interested he is in her. — Agatha Christie

And so to bed. — Samuel Pepys

And therefore never send to know for whom the bell tolls; It tolls for thee. — John Donne

Arms and the man I sing. (from the *Aeneid*) — Virgil

Art for art's sake. — Victor Cousin

Attila the hen. (speaking about Margaret Thatcher) — Clement Freud

Balance of power. — Sir Robert Walpole

Bank is a place that will lend you money if you can prove that you don't need it, A. — Bob Hope

Because it's there. (when asked why he wanted to climb Mt Everest) — George Mallory

Better to err with Pope, than shine with Pye. — Lord George Byron

Bigger they come the harder they fall, The. — Robert Fitzsimmons

Blood is thicker than water. — Commodore Tattnall

Boy stood on the burning deck, The. (from 'Casablanca') — Felicia Hemans

Bread and circuses. (*Panem et circenses*, alluding to what the people desired) — Juvenal

Buck stops here, The. — Harry S Truman

Bumping pitch and a blinding light, an hour to play and the last man in, A. — Sir Henry Newbolt

Candy is dandy. But liquor is quicker. — Ogden Nash

Carthage must be destroyed. — Senator Cato

Cauliflower is nothing but cabbage with a college education. (from Pudd'nhead Wilson's calendar) — Mark Twain

Child is father of the man, The. — William Wordsworth

Claret is the liquor for boys, Port for men, but he who aspires to be a hero must drink brandy. — Dr Samuel Johnson

Classic is something that everybody wants to have read and nobody wants to read, A. — Mark Twain

Comedian does funny things; a good comedian does things funny, A. — Buster Keaton

Cook was a good cook as cooks go; and as cooks go she went, The. — Saki

Cough and the world coughs with you. Fart and you stand alone. — Trevor Griffiths

Desiccated calculating machine, A. (writing about Hugh Gaitskell) — Aneurin Bevan

Die is cast, The (on crossing the Rubicon in 49 BC) — Julius Caesar

Don't count your chickens before they are hatched. — Aesop

Don't get mad, get even. — Senator Everett Dirksen

Don't one of you fire until you see the whites of their eyes. (at Bunker Hill in 1775) — US General Israel Putnam

Each man kills the thing he loves. (from *The Ballad of Reading Gaol*) — Oscar Wilde

Ears made him look like a taxi cab with both doors open. (writing about Clark Gable) — Howard Hughes

East is East and West is West and never the twain shall meet. — Rudyard Kipling

England is a nation of shopkeepers. — Napoleon Bonaparte

Eureka (I have found it). — Archimedes

Every man over forty is a scoundrel. — G.B. Shaw

Experience is the name everyone gives to his mistakes. (from *Lady Windermere's Fan*) — Oscar Wilde

Fair stood the wind for France. — Michael Drayton

Father, I cannot tell a lie, I did it with my little hatchet. — George Washington

Female of the species is more deadly than the male, The. — Rudyard Kipling

Fools rush in where angels fear to tread, For. — Alexander Pope

From the sublime to the ridiculous there is only one step. (after the retreat from Moscow in 1812) — Napoleon Bonaparte

Generals January and February. (referring to his chief allies against Britain and France in the Crimea) — Tsar Nicholas I

Genius is one per cent inspiration and ninety-nine per cent perspiration. — Thomas Alva Edison

Ghost in the machine, The. — Gilbert Ryle

Give a man a free hand and he'll run it all over you. — Mae West

Give me a lever long enough and I will move the world. — Archimedes

Give us the tools and we will finish the job. — Winston Churchill

Go and catch a falling star. — John Donne

Go West, young man, and grow up with the country. — Horace Greeley

God made the country, and man made the town. — William Cowper

God moves in a mysterious way, his wonders to perform. — William Cowper

God's in his heaven – all's right with the world. — Robert Browning

Golf is a good walk spoiled. — Mark Twain

Gondola of London, The. (referring to the hansom cab) — Benjamin Disraeli

Good Americans, when they die, go to Paris. — Thomas Gold Appleton

Grain, which in England is generally given to horses but in Scotland supports the people, A. (definition of oats)	Dr Samuel Johnson
Great Cham of literature Samuel Johnson, That. (in a letter to John Wilkes)	Tobias Smollett
Great fleas have little fleas upon their backs to bite 'em, and little fleas have lesser fleas and so ad infinitum.	Augustus De Morgan
Greatest happiness of the greatest number, The.	Jeremy Bentham
He can run but he can't hide.	Joe Louis
He makes no friend who never made a foe.	Lord Alfred Tennyson
He nothing common did, or mean, Upon that memorable scene. ('An Horatian Ode upon Cromwell's Return from Ireland')	Andrew Marvell
He speaks to me as if I were a public meeting. (referring to William Gladstone)	Queen Victoria
Heaven has no rage like love to hatred turned, Nor hell a fury like a woman scorned.	William Congreve
Hell is other people.	Jean-Paul Sartre
Here Skugg lies snug as a bug in a rug.	Benjamin Franklin
History is bunk.	Henry Ford
History of the world is but the biography of great men, The.	Thomas Carlyle
Hope springs eternal in the human breast.	Alexander Pope
How can they tell? (on being told Calvin Coolidge was dead)	Dorothy Parker
I am his Highness' dog at Kew; Pray tell me sir, whose dog are you?	Alexander Pope
I am just going outside and may be some time.	Capt. Lawrence Oates
I am the State (*L'État, c'est moi*).	Louis XIV
I awoke one morning and found myself famous.	Lord George Byron
I beseech you in the bowels of Christ, think it possible you may be mistaken.	Oliver Cromwell
I can resist everything except temptation. (from *Lady Windermere's Fan*)	Oscar Wilde
I fear the Greeks even when they bring gifts. (from the *Aeneid*)	Virgil
I have always thought that every woman should marry, and no man.	Benjamin Disraeli
I have been poor and I have been rich. Rich is better.	Sophie Tucker
I have nothing to declare but my genius. (at US customs)	Oscar Wilde
I have nothing to offer but blood, toil, tears and sweat.	Winston Churchill
I know I have the body of a weak and feeble woman, but I have the heart and stomach of a King.	Elizabeth I
I look upon the world as my parish.	Wesley, John
I married beneath me, all women do.	Nancy Astor
I never trust a man unless I've got his pecker in my pocket.	Lyndon B. Johnson
I think, therefore I am (*cogito ergo sum*).	René Descartes
I want to be the white man's brother, not his brother-in-law.	Martin Luther King
Ich bin ein Berliner.	John F. Kennedy
I'd like that translated, if I may. (reacting to Nikita Khruschev's banging of shoe on table at the UN)	Harold Macmillan
If God did not exist, it would be necessary to invent him.	Voltaire
If I have seen further it is by standing on the shoulders of giants.	Isaac Newton
If you can keep your head when all about you are losing theirs and blaming it on you. (from 'If')	Rudyard Kipling
If you can meet with triumph and disaster and treat those two impostors just the same (from 'If')	Rudyard Kipling
If you pay peanuts, you get monkeys.	Sir James Goldsmith
Ignorance is bliss.	Thomas Gray
Ignorance, Madam, pure ignorance. (when asked why he defined pastern as a knee of a horse in his dictionary).	Dr Samuel Johnson
I'm going to spend, spend, spend.	Viv Nicholson
I'm not really a Jew, just Jew-ish, not the whole hog. (*Beyond the Fringe* sketch)	Dr Jonathan Miller
I'm only a beer teetotaller not a champagne teetotaller. (from *Candida*)	G.B. Shaw
In my sport the quick are too often listed among the dead.	Jackie Stewart
In the future everyone will be famous for fifteen minutes.	Andy Warhol
In the long run we are all dead.	J.M. Keynes
In this country [England] it is good to kill an admiral from time to time, to encourage the others. (re: shooting of Byng)	Voltaire
In two words, Impossible.	Sam Goldwyn
Include me out.	Sam Goldwyn
Indomitable in retreat; invincible in advance; insufferable in victory. (writing of Field-Marshal Montgomery)	Winston Churchill
Into each life some rain must fall.	Henry Wadsworth Longfellow
Into the valley of death rode the six hundred.	Lord Alfred Tennyson
It is better to die on your feet than to live on your knees.	La Pasionaria
It is magnificent but it is not war. (referring to the Charge of the Light Brigade)	General Pierre Bousquet
It is true that liberty is precious – so precious that it must be rationed.	Lenin
It matters not how a man dies, but how he lives.	Dr Samuel Johnson
It's not the size of the dog in the fight – it's the size of the fight in the dog.	Dwight D. Eisenhower
Keep a diary and one day it'll keep you.	Mae West
Kind hearts are more than coronets.	Lord Alfred Tennyson
Knowledge is Power.	Francis Bacon

Lady's not for turning, The.	Margaret Thatcher
Lamps are going out all over Europe, The.	Edward Gray
Laugh and the world laughs with you; Weep and you weep alone. (from her poem 'Solitude')	Ella Wheeler Wilcox
Let them eat cake.	Marie Antoinette
Let us never negotiate out of fear, but let us never fear to negotiate.	John F. Kennedy
Lies, damned lies and statistics.	Benjamin Disraeli
Lion and the calf shall lie down together, but the calf won't get much sleep, The.	Woody Allen
Little learning is a dangerous thing, A.	Alexander Pope
Love is like the measles, we all have to go through it.	Jerome K. Jerome
Love's young dream.	Thomas Moore
Macmillan's role as a poseur was itself a pose.	Harold Wilson
Mad is he? Then I hope he will bite some of my other generals. (on being told General Wolfe was mad)	George II
Man is born free; and everywhere he is in chains. (first line of *The Social Contract*)	Jean-Jacques Rousseau
Man is by nature a civic animal.	Aristotle
Man is only as old as the woman he feels, A.	Groucho Marx
Man is the hunter, woman is his game.	Lord Alfred Tennyson
Man who knows the price of everything and the value of nothing, A. (definition of a cynic)	Oscar Wilde
Manners maketh man.	William of Wykeham
Marriage is a wonderful invention, but then again, so is the bicycle repair kit.	Billy Connolly
Medium is the message, The.	Marshall McLuhan
Meek shall inherit the earth, but not its mineral rights, The.	J. Paul Getty
Men seldom make passes at girls who wear glasses.	Dorothy Parker
Modest little man with much to be modest about, A. (writing of Clement Attlee)	Winston Churchill
Moving finger writes and having writ moves on, The.	Omar Khayyam
Mr Balfour's poodle. (referring to the House of Lords)	Lloyd George
Music hath charms to soothe a savage breast.	William Congreve
Never in the field of human conflict was so much owed by so many to so few. (referring to Battle of Britain pilots)	Winston Churchill
Never trust a man with short legs – brains too near their bottom.	Noël Coward
Nice guys finish last. (referring to his baseball team)	Leo Durocher
Night has a thousand eyes and the day but one, The.	Francis Bourdillon
No man but a blockhead ever wrote except for money.	Dr Samuel Johnson
No man is an island.	John Donne
No man is justified in doing evil on the ground of expediency.	Theodore Roosevelt
None but the brave deserves the fair.	John Dryden
Nothing is certain but death and taxes.	Benjamin Franklin
Nuts! (replying to von Manteuffel's surrender call during the Battle of the Bulge)	Brigadier General McAuliffe
O what a tangled web we weave when first we practise to deceive.	Sir Walter Scott
Oh liberty! what crimes are committed in your name!	Madame Roland
Old soldiers never die, they simply fade away.	General MacArthur
Once upon a midnight dreary, while I pondered weak and weary. (from 'The Raven')	Edgar Allan Poe
One man's wage rise is another man's price increase.	Harold Wilson
One swallow does not make a summer.	Aristotle
Only good Indians I ever saw were dead, The.	General Philip Sheridan
Only reason so many people showed up was to make sure that he was dead, The. (of Louis Mayer's funeral)	Sam Goldwyn
Only thing we have to fear is fear itself, The.	F.D. Roosevelt
Open my heart and you will see graved inside of it, 'Italy'.	Robert Browning
Patriotism is not enough. I must have no hatred or bitterness towards anyone.	Edith Cavell
Patriotism is the last refuge of a scoundrel.	Dr Samuel Johnson
Peace for our time. (on returning from Munich in 1938)	Neville Chamberlain
Peccavi. ('I have sinned' from a telegram sent after capturing Sind in 1834)	Sir Charles Napier
Pen is mightier than the sword, The.	Bulwer Lytton
Penny Punch and Judy show, A. (referring to television)	Winston Churchill
Politics is the art of the possible.	R.A. Butler
Power tends to corrupt and absolute power corrupts absolutely.	Lord Acton
Power without responsibility, the privilege of the harlot throughout the ages (referring to the press)	Stanley Baldwin
Procrastination is the thief of time.	Edward Young
Property is theft.	Pierre-Joseph Proudhon
Public, be damned, The.	Cornelius Vanderbilt
Publish and be damned.	Duke of Wellington
Put your trust in God and keep your powder dry.	Oliver Cromwell
Quoth the Raven, 'Nevermore'. (from 'The Raven')	Edgar Allan Poe
Religion is the opium of the people.	Karl Marx
Remedy is worse than the disease, The.	Francis Bacon
Remember that time is money.	Benjamin Franklin

Reports of my death have been greatly exaggerated. — Mark Twain

Riddle wrapped in a mystery inside an enigma, A. (referring to the Soviet Union) — Winston Churchill

Rose is a Rose is a Rose, A. — Gertrude Stein

Seagreen incorruptible, The. (referring to Robespierre) — Thomas Carlyle

Secret of success is sincerity, once you can fake that you've got it made, The. — Arthur Bloch

Seize the present day (*carpe diem*) — Horace

She is the best man in England. (referring to Margaret Thatcher) — Ronald Reagan

Sheep in sheep's clothing, A. (writing of Clement Attlee) — Winston Churchill

Sic transit gloria mundi (So passes away the glory of the world). — Thomas à Kempis

Single death is a tragedy, a million deaths is a statistic, A. — Joseph Stalin

Speak softly and carry a big stick. — Theodore Roosevelt

Speech is silvern, Silence is golden. — Thomas Carlyle

Stone walls do not a prison make, Nor iron bars a cage. (from 'To Althea from Prison') — Richard Lovelace

Sucker born every minute, There's a. — P.T. Barnum

Sweet Swan of Avon. (referring to William Shakespeare) — Ben Jonson

Television is an invention that permits you to be entertained in your living room by people you wouldn't have in your home. — Sir David Frost

Tell me the old, old story. — Katherine Hankey

There are two things no man will admit he can't do well: drive and make love. — Stirling Moss

There is no terror in a bang – only in the anticipation of it. — Alfred Hitchcock

There is properly no history; only biography. — Ralph Waldo Emerson

There never was a good war or a bad peace. — Benjamin Franklin

There's no such thing as a free lunch. (also used by J.K. Galbraith) — Milton Friedman

They also serve who only stand and wait. — John Milton

Thy need is greater than mine. (on giving his water to a soldier at Zutphen) — Sir Philip Sydney

'Tis better to have loved and lost, than never to have loved at all. (from 'In Memoriam') — Lord Alfred Tennyson

To err is human, to forgive, divine. — Alexander Pope

Trouble with Freud is that he never played the Glasgow Empire Saturday night, The. — Ken Dodd

Turn on, Tune in, Drop out. — Timothy Leary

Unpleasant and unacceptable face of Capitalism. (referring to Lonrho) — Edward Heath

Unspeakable in pursuit of the uneatable, The. (referring to foxhunting) — Oscar Wilde

Variety's the spice of life. — William Cowper

Veni, Vidi, Vici (I came, I saw, I conquered). (from a letter written after his victory at Zela in Asia Minor) — Julius Caesar

Verbal contract isn't worth the paper it's written on, A. — Sam Goldwyn

War is hell. — General Sherman

Warts and everything. — Oliver Cromwell

We are American at puberty. We die French. — Evelyn Waugh

We are not amused. — Queen Victoria

We must indeed all hang together or, most assuredly, we shall all hang separately (on signing the Declaration of Independence) — Benjamin Franklin

Week is a long time in politics, A. — Harold Wilson

What you said hurt me very much. I cried all the way to the bank. (replying to critics) — Liberace

When a man is tired of London he is tired of life. — Dr Samuel Johnson

When a man knows he is to be hanged in a fortnight it concentrates his mind wonderfully. — Dr Samuel Johnson

When the eagles are silent the parrots begin to jabber. — Winston Churchill

Where law ends, tyranny begins. — William Pitt (1st Earl of Chatham)

Whoever is not against us is with us. — Janos Kadar

Will no one rid me of this turbulent priest? (referring to Thomas à Becket) — Henry II

Wind of change is blowing through the continent, The. (speaking to South African Parliament in 1960) — Harold Macmillan

Winning is not everything. It's the only thing. — Vince Lombardi

Wisest fool in Christendom, The. (speaking of James I of England and VI of Scotland) — Henry IV of France

Woman is only a woman, but a good cigar is a smoke, A. (from 'The Betrothed') — Rudyard Kipling

Women should be obscene and not heard. — John Lennon

Wonders will never cease. — Sir Henry Bate Dudley

World must be made safe for democracy, The — Woodrow Wilson

Worth seeing, yes; but not worth going to see. (speaking about the Giant's Causeway) — Dr Samuel Johnson

Would you buy a second-hand car from this man? (writing about Richard Nixon) — Mort Sahl

Writer of dictionaries, a harmless drudge, A. (definition of a lexicographer) — Dr Samuel Johnson

Ye distant spires, ye antique towers. (from 'Ode on a Distant Prospect of Eton') — Thomas Gray

You can fool all the people some of the time, and some of the people all the time, but you cannot fool all the people all of the time. — Abraham Lincoln

You can have it any colour as long as it's black. — Henry Ford

You can make a throne from bayonets but you can't sit on it long. — Boris Yeltsin

You're either part of the solution or part of the problem. — Eldridge Cleaver

You're not drunk if you can lie on the floor without holding on. — Dean Martin

Youth is wasted on the young. — G.B. Shaw

NB Details of the quotation are given in brackets above but will need to be cross-referenced if the alphabetical table by person is being used. The same caveat as in the 'Dying Sayings' applies. It is doubtful that many of these utterances were original thoughts; for instance, the Milton Friedman entry may have been a corruption of a phrase from a Robert Heinlein novel *The Moon is a Harsh Mistress* and the MacArthur entry was almost certainly from a popular song of the 1920s. Some popular attributions, e.g. 'An Iron Curtain Descending', have also been omitted because of doubts about their origins.

Quotations (in Alphabetical Order by Person)

Acton, Lord	Power tends to corrupt and absolute power corrupts absolutely.
Aesop	Don't count your chickens before they are hatched.
Allen, Woody	The lion and the calf shall lie down together, but the calf won't get much sleep.
Antoinette, Marie	Let them eat cake.
Appleton, Thomas Gold	Good Americans, when they die, go to Paris.
Archimedes	*Eureka* (I have found it).
	Give me a lever long enough and I will move the world.
Aristotle	Man is by nature a civic animal.
	One swallow does not make a summer.
Astor, Nancy	I married beneath me, all women do.
Bacon, Francis	Knowledge is Power.
	The remedy is worse than the disease.
Baldwin, Stanley	Power without responsibility, the privilege of the harlot throughout the ages.
Barnum, P.T.	There's a sucker born every minute.
Bentham, Jeremy	The greatest happiness of the greatest number.
Bevan, Aneurin	A desiccated calculating machine.
Bloch, Arthur	The secret of success is sincerity, once you can fake that you've got it made.
Bonaparte, Napoleon	England is a nation of shopkeepers.
	From the sublime to the ridiculous there is only one step.
Bourdillon, Francis	The night has a thousand eyes and the day but one.
Bousquet, General Pierre	It is magnificent but it is not war.
Browning, Robert	God's in his heaven – all's right with the world.
	Open my heart and you will see graved inside of it, 'Italy'.
Butler, R.A.	Politics is the art of the possible.
Byron, Lord George	Better to err with Pope, than shine with Pye.
	I awoke one morning and found myself famous.
Caesar, Julius	All Gaul is divided into three parts.
	The die is cast.
	Veni, Vidi, Vici (I came, I saw, I conquered).
Carlyle, Thomas	Speech is silvern, Silence is golden.
	The history of the world is but the biography of great men.
	The seagreen incorruptible.
Cato, Senator	Carthage must be destroyed.
Cavell, Edith	Patriotism is not enough. I must have no hatred or bitterness towards anyone.
Chamberlain, Neville	Peace for our time.
Christie, Agatha	An archaeologist is the best husband any woman can have – the older she gets the more interested he is in her.
Churchill, Winston	A modest little man with much to be modest about.
	A penny Punch and Judy show.
	A riddle wrapped in a mystery inside an enigma.
	A sheep in sheep's clothing.
	Give us the tools and we will finish the job.
	I have nothing to offer but blood, toil, tears and sweat.
	Indomitable in retreat; invincible in advance; insufferable in victory.
	Never in the field of human conflict was so much owed by so many to so few.
	When the eagles are silent the parrots begin to jabber.
Cleaver, Eldridge	You're either part of the solution or part of the problem.
Congreve, William	Heaven has no rage like love to hatred turned, Nor hell a fury like a woman scorned.
	Music hath charms to soothe a savage breast.
Connolly, Billy	Marriage is a wonderful invention, but then again, so is the bicycle repair kit.
Cousin, Victor	Art for art's sake.
Coward, Noël	Never trust a man with short legs – brains too near their bottom.
Cowper, William	God made the country, and man made the town.
	God moves in a mysterious way, his wonders to perform.
	Variety's the spice of life.
Cromwell, Oliver	I beseech you in the bowels of Christ, think it possible you may be mistaken.
	Put your trust in God and keep your powder dry.
	Warts and everything.
Dante Alighieri	All hope abandon ye who enter.

De Morgan, Augustus	Great fleas have little fleas upon their backs to bite 'em, and little fleas have lesser fleas and so ad infinitum.
Descartes, René	I think, therefore I am (*cogito ergo sum*).
Dirksen, Senator Everett	Don't get mad, get even.
Disraeli, Benjamin	I have always thought that every woman should marry, and no man.
	Lies, damned lies and statistics.
	The gondola of London.
Dodd, Ken	The trouble with Freud is that he never played the Glasgow Empire Saturday night.
Donne, John	And therefore never send to know for whom the bell tolls/; it tolls for thee.
	Go and catch a falling star.
	No man is an island.
Drayton, Michael	Fair stood the wind for France.
Dryden, John	None but the brave deserves the fair.
Dudley, Sir Henry Bate	Wonders will never cease.
Durocher, Leo	Nice guys finish last.
Edison, Thomas Alva	Genius is one per cent inspiration and ninety-nine per cent perspiration.
Eisenhower, Dwight D.	It's not the size of the dog in the fight – it's the size of the fight in the dog.
Elizabeth I	I know I have the body of a weak and feeble woman, but I have the heart and stomach of a King.
Emerson, Ralph Waldo	There is properly no history; only biography.
Fitzimmons, Robert	The bigger they come the harder they fall.
Ford, Henry	History is bunk.
	You can have it any colour as long as it's black.
Franklin, Benjamin	Here Skugg lies snug as a bug in a rug.
	Nothing is certain but death and taxes.
	Remember that time is money.
	There never was a good war or a bad peace.
	We must indeed all hang together or, most assuredly, we shall all hang separately.
Freud, Clement	Attila the hen.
Friedman, Milton	There's no such thing as a free lunch.
Frost, Sir David	Television is an invention that permits you to be entertained in your living room by people you wouldn't have in your home.
George II	Mad is he? Then I hope he will bite some of my other generals.
George, Lloyd	Mr Balfour's poodle.
Getty, J. Paul	The meek shall inherit the earth, but not its mineral rights.
Goldsmith, Sir James	If you pay peanuts, you get monkeys.
Goldwyn, Sam	A verbal contract isn't worth the paper it's written on.
	In two words, Impossible.
	Include me out.
	The only reason so many people showed up was to make sure that he was dead.
Gray, Thomas	Ignorance is bliss.
	Ye distant spires, ye antique towers.
Greeley, Horace	Go West, young man, and grow up with the country.
Grey, Edward	The lamps are going out all over Europe.
Griffiths, Trevor	Cough and the world coughs with you. Fart and you stand alone.
Hankey, Katherine	Tell me the old, old story.
Heath, Edward	Unpleasant and unacceptable face of Capitalism.
Hemans, Felicia	The boy stood on the burning deck.
Henry II	Will no one rid me of this turbulent priest?
Henry IV of France	The wisest fool in Christendom.
Hitchcock Alfred	There is no terror in a bang – only in the anticipation of it.
Hope, Bob	A bank is a place that will lend you money if you can prove that you don't need it.
Horace	Seize the present day (*carpe diem*).
Hughes, Howard	Ears made him look like a taxi cab with both doors open.
Jerome, Jerome K.	Love is like the measles, we all have to go through it.
Johnson, Dr Samuel	A grain, which in England is generally given to horses but in Scotland supports the people.
	A writer of dictionaries, a harmless drudge.
	Claret is the liquor for boys, Port for men, but he who aspires to be a hero must drink brandy.
	Ignorance, Madam, pure ignorance.
	It matters not how a man dies, but how he lives.
	No man but a blockhead ever wrote except for money.
	Patriotism is the last refuge of a scoundrel.
	When a man is tired of London he is tired of life.
	When a man knows he is to be hanged in a fortnight it concentrates his mind wonderfully.
	Worth seeing, yes; but not worth going to see.
Johnson, Lyndon B.	I never trust a man unless I've got his pecker in my pocket.
Jonson, Ben	Sweet Swan of Avon.
Juvenal	Bread and circuses (*Panem et circenses*).
Kadar, Janos	Whoever is not against us is with us.

Keaton, Buster	A comedian does funny things; a good comedian does things funny.
Kempis, Thomas à	*Sic transit gloria mundi* (so passes away the glory of the world).
Kennedy, John F.	Ich bin ein Berliner.
	Let us never negotiate out of fear, but let us never fear to negotiate.
Keynes, J.M.	In the long run we are all dead.
Khayyam, Omar	The moving finger writes and having writ moves on.
King, Martin Luther	I want to be the white man's brother, not his brother-in-law.
Kipling, Rudyard	A woman is only a woman, but a good cigar is a smoke.
	East is East and West is West and never the twain shall meet.
	If you can keep your head when all about you are losing theirs and blaming it on you.
	If you can meet with triumph and disaster and treat those two impostors just the same.
	The female of the species is more deadly than the male.
Leary, Timothy	Turn on, Tune in, Drop out.
Lenin	It is true that liberty is precious – so precious that it must be rationed.
Lennon, John	Women should be obscene and not heard.
Liberace	What you said hurt me very much. I cried all the way to the bank.
Lincoln, Abraham	You can fool all the people some of the time, and some of the people all of the time, but you cannot fool all the people all the time.
Lombardi, Vince	Winning is not everything. It's the only thing.
Longfellow, Henry Wadsworth	Into each life some rain must fall.
Louis XIV	I am the State (*L'État, c'est moi*).
Louis, Joe	He can run but he can't hide.
Lovelace, Richard	Stone walls do not a prison make, Nor iron bars a cage.
Lytton, Bulwer	The pen is mightier than the sword.
MacArthur, General	Old soldiers never die, they simply fade away.
Macmillan, Harold	I'd like that translated, if I may.
	The wind of change is blowing through the continent.
Mallory, George	Because it's there.
Martin, Dean	You're not drunk if you can lie on the floor without holding on.
Marvell, Andrew	He nothing common did, or mean, Upon that memorable scene.
Marx, Groucho	A man is only as old as the woman he feels.
Marx, Karl	Religion is the opium of the people.
McAuliffe, Brigadier General	Nuts!
McLuhan, Marshall	The medium is the message.
Miller, Dr Jonathan	I'm not really a Jew, just Jew-ish, not the whole hog.
Milton, John	They also serve who only stand and wait.
Moore, Thomas	Love's young dream.
Moss, Stirling	There are two things no man will admit he can't do well: drive and make love.
Napier, Sir Charles	Peccavi (I have sinned).
Nash, Ogden	Candy is dandy. But liquor is quicker.
Newbolt, Sir Henry	A bumping pitch and a blinding light, an hour to play and the last man in.
Newton, Isaac	If I have seen further it is by standing on the shoulders of giants.
Nicholas I, Tsar	Generals January and February.
Nicholson, Viv	I'm going to spend, spend, spend.
Oates, Capt. Lawrence	I am just going outside and may be some time.
Parker, Dorothy	How can they tell?
	Men seldom make passes at girls who wear glasses.
Pasionaria, La	It is better to die on your feet than to live on your knees.
Pepys, Samuel	And so to bed.
Pitt, William (1st Earl of Chatham)	Where law ends, tyranny begins.
Poe, Edgar Allan	Once upon a midnight dreary, while I pondered weak and weary.
	Quoth the Raven, 'Nevermore'.
Pope, Alexander	A little learning is a dangerous thing.
	For fools rush in where angels fear to tread.
	Hope springs eternal in the human breast.
	I am his Highness' dog at Kew; Pray tell me sir, whose dog are you?
	To err is human, to forgive, divine.
Proudhon, Pierre-Joseph	Property is theft.
Putnam, US General Israel	Don't one of you fire until you see the whites of their eyes.
Reagan, Ronald	She is the best man in England.
Roland, Madame	Oh liberty! what crimes are committed in your name!
Roosevelt, F.D.	The only thing we have to fear is fear itself.
Roosevelt, Theodore	No man is justified in doing evil on the ground of expediency.
	Speak softly and carry a big stick.
Rousseau, Jean-Jacques	Man is born free, and everywhere he is in chains.
Ryle, Gilbert	The ghost in the machine.
Sahl, Mort	Would you buy a second-hand car from this man?
Saki	The cook was a good cook as cooks go; and as cooks go she went.
Sartre, Jean-Paul	Hell is other people.

QUOTATIONS

Scott, Sir Walter	O what a tangled web we weave when first we practise to deceive.
Shaw, G.B.	Every man over forty is a scoundrel.
	I'm only a beer teetotaller not a champagne teetotaller.
	Youth is wasted on the young.
Sheridan, General Philip	The only good Indians I ever saw were dead.
Sherman, General	War is hell.
Sidney, Sir Philip	Thy need is greater than mine.
Smollett, Tobias	That great Cham of literature Samuel Johnson.
Stalin, Joseph	A single death is a tragedy, a million deaths is a statistic.
Stein, Gertrude	A Rose is a Rose is a Rose.
Stewart, Jackie	In my sport the quick are too often listed among the dead.
Tattnall, Commodore	Blood is thicker than water.
Tennyson, Lord Alfred	He makes no friend who never made a foe.
	Into the valley of death rode the six hundred.
	Kind hearts are more than coronets.
	Man is the hunter, woman is his game.
	'Tis better to have loved and lost, than never to have loved at all.
Thatcher, Margaret	The lady's not for turning.
Truman, Harry S.	The buck stops here.
Tucker, Sophie	I have been poor and I have been rich. Rich is better.
Twain, Mark	A classic is something that everybody wants to have read and nobody wants to read.
	Cauliflower is nothing but cabbage with a college education.
	Golf is a good walk spoiled.
	Reports of my death have been greatly exaggerated.
Vanderbilt, Cornelius	The public, be damned.
Queen Victoria	We are not amused.
	He speaks to me as if I were a public meeting.
Virgil	Arms and the man I sing.
	I fear the Greeks even when they bring gifts.
Voltaire	All is for the best in the best of possible worlds.
	If God did not exist, it would be necessary to invent him.
	In this country [England] it is good to kill an admiral from time to time, to encourage the others.
Walpole, Sir Robert	Balance of power.
Warhol, Andy	In the future everyone will be famous for fifteen minutes.
Washington, George	Father, I cannot tell a lie, I did it with my little hatchet.
Waugh, Evelyn	We are American at puberty. We die French.
Wellington, Duke of	Publish and be damned.
Wesley, John	I look upon the world as my parish.
West, Mae	Give a man a free hand and he'll run it all over you.
	Keep a diary and one day it'll keep you.
Wilcox, Ella Wheeler	Laugh and the world laughs with you; Weep and you weep alone.
Wilde, Oscar	A man who knows the price of everything and the value of nothing.
	Each man kills the thing he loves.
	Experience is the name everyone gives to his mistakes.
	I can resist everything except temptation.
	I have nothing to declare but my genius.
	The unspeakable in pursuit of the uneatable.
William of Wykeham	Manners maketh man.
Wilson, Harold	A week is a long time in politics.
	Macmillan's role as a poseur was itself a pose.
	One man's wage rise is another man's price increase.
Wilson, Woodrow	The world must be made safe for democracy.
Wordsworth, William	The child is father of the man.
Yeltsin, Boris	You can make a throne from bayonets but you can't sit on it long.
Young, Edward	Procrastination is the thief of time.

Nursery Rhymes

As I was going to St Ives I met a man with seven wives, each wife had seven sacks, each sack had seven cats, each cat had seven kits, kits, cats, sacks and wives, how many going to St Ives?

Baa baa black sheep have you any wool? Yes sir, yes sir, three bags full; one for the master, and one for the dame, and one for the little boy who lives down the lane.

Bobby Shafto's gone to sea, silver buckles on his knee,

he'll come back and marry me, bonny Bobby Shafto.

Dance to your daddy, my little babby, dance to your daddy, my little lamb; you shall have a fishy, in a little dishy, you shall have a fishy, when the boat comes in.

Ding, dong, bell, pussy's in the well. Who put her in? Little Johnny Green. Who pulled her out? Little Tommy Stout.

Doctor Foster went to Gloucester, in a shower of rain;

he stepped in a puddle, right up to his middle, and never went there again.

Georgie Porgie pudding and pie, kissed the girls and made them cry; when the boys came out to play, Georgie Porgie ran away.

Goosey, goosey gander, where shall I wander? Upstairs and downstairs, in my lady's chamber. There I met an old man who would not say his prayers, I took him by the left leg and threw him down the stairs.

Hark, hark, the dogs do bark, the beggars are coming to town; some in rags, and some in jags, and one in a velvet gown.

Hey diddle diddle, the cat and the fiddle, the cow jumped over the moon; the little dog laughed to see such sport, and the dish ran away with the spoon.

Hickory, dickory dock, the mouse ran up the clock. The clock struck one, the mouse ran down, hickory, dickory dock.

Humpty Dumpty sat on a wall, Humpty Dumpty had a great fall; all the king's horses and all the king's men couldn't put Humpty together again.

I had a little nut tree, nothing would it bear, but a silver nutmeg, and a golden pear.

If all the world were paper, and all the sea were ink, if all the trees were bread and cheese, what should we have to drink?

Jack be nimble, Jack be quick, Jack jump over the candle stick.

Jack Sprat could eat no fat, his wife could eat no lean, and so between them both, you see, they licked the platter clean.

Little Bo-Peep has lost her sheep, and doesn't know where to find them; leave them alone and they will come home, dragging their tails behind them.

Little Boy Blue, come blow your horn, the sheep's in the meadow, the cow's in the corn. Where is the boy who looks after the sheep? He's under a haystack fast asleep.

Little Jack Horner sat in the corner, eating a Christmas pie; he put in his thumb, and pulled out a plum, and said, What a good boy am I.

Little Miss Muffet sat on a tuffet, eating her curds and whey; along came a spider, who sat down beside her, and frightened Miss Muffet away.

Little Polly Flinders, sat among the cinders, warming her pretty little toes; her mother came and caught her, and whipped her little daughter, for spoiling her nice new clothes.

Little Tommy Tucker sings for his supper; what shall we give him? White bread and butter. How shall he cut it without a knife? How will he marry without a wife?

Lucy Locket lost her pocket, Kitty Fisher found it; not a penny was there in it, only ribbon round it.

Mary had a little lamb, its fleece was white as snow; and everywhere that Mary went the lamb was sure to go.

Mary, Mary, quite contrary, how does your garden grow? With silver bells and cockle shells, and pretty maids all in a row.

Old King Cole was a merry old soul, and a merry old soul was he; he called for his pipe, and he called for his bowl, and he called for his fiddlers three.

Old Mother Hubbard went to the cupboard, to fetch her poor dog a bone; but when she came there, the cupboard was bare, and so the poor dog had none.

On the twelfth day of Christmas my true love sent to me twelve lords a-leaping, eleven ladies dancing, ten pipers piping, nine drummers drumming, eight maids a-milking, seven swans a-swimming, six geese a-laying, five gold rings, four colly birds, three French hens, two turtle doves, and a partridge in a pear tree.

One, two, three, four, five, once I caught a fish alive; six, seven, eight, nine, ten, then I let it go again. Why did you let it go? Because it bit my finger so. Which finger did it bite? This little finger on the right.

Oranges and lemons, say the bells of St Clement's. You owe me five farthings, say the bells of St Martin's. When will you pay me? say the bells of Old Bailey. When I grow rich, say the bells of Shoreditch. When will that be? say the bells of Stepney. I'm sure I don't know, says the great bell at Bow. Here comes the candle to light you to bed, here comes a chopper to chop off your head.

Pat-a-cake, pat-a-cake baker's man, bake me a cake as fast as you can; pat it and prick it and mark it with B, put it in the oven for baby and me.

Pease porridge hot, pease porridge cold, pease porridge in the pot, nine days old.

Polly put the kettle on, Polly put the kettle on, Polly put the kettle on, we'll all have tea. Sukey take it off again, Sukey take it off again, Sukey take it off again, they've all gone away.

Pussy cat, pussy cat, where have you been? I've been to London to visit the Queen. Pussy cat, pussy cat, what did you there? I frightened a little mouse under her chair.

Ride a cock horse to Banbury Cross, to see a fine lady upon a white horse; rings on her fingers and bells on her toes, and she shall have music wherever she goes.

Ring-a-ring o'roses, a pocket full of posies, A-tishoo, A-tishoo, we all fall down.

Rub-a-dub-dub, three men in a tub, and how do you think they got there? The butcher, the baker, the candlestick maker, they all jumped out of a rotten potato, 'twas enough to make a man stare.

See-saw Margery Daw, Johnny shall have a new master; Johnny shall have but a penny a day, because he can't work any faster.

Simple Simon met a pieman, going to the fair; said Simple Simon to the pieman, let me taste your ware. Said the pieman to Simple Simon, show me first your penny; said Simple Simon to the pieman, indeed I have not any.

Sing a song of sixpence, a pocket full of rye; four and twenty blackbirds baked in a pie. When the pie was opened the birds began to sing; wasn't that a dainty dish to set before the king? The king was in his counting-house, counting out his money, the queen was in the parlour, eating bread and honey, the maid was in the garden, hanging out the clothes, along came a blackbird and pecked off her nose.

Solomon Grundy, born on Monday, christened on Tuesday, married on Wednesday, took ill on Thursday, worse on Friday, died on Saturday, buried on Sunday, this is the end of Solomon Grundy.

Taffy was a Welshman, Taffy was a thief, Taffy came to my house and stole a leg of beef. I went to Taffy's house, Taffy wasn't in, I jumped upon his Sunday hat, and poked it with a pin.

The Grand Old Duke of York, he had ten thousand men, he marched them up to the top of the hill, and he marched them down again; and when they were up they were up, and when they were down they were down, and when they were only halfway up, they were neither up nor down.

The man in the moon came down too soon, and asked

the way to Norwich; he went by the south, and burnt his mouth, with supping cold plum porridge.

The north wind doth blow, and we shall have snow, and what will poor Robin do then, poor thing? He'll sit in a barn, and keep himself warm, and hide his head under his wing, poor thing.

The Queen of Hearts she made some tarts, all on a summer's day. The Knave of Hearts he stole the tarts, and took them clean away. The King of Hearts called for the tarts, and beat the knave full sore. The Knave of Hearts brought back the tarts, and vowed he'd steal no more.

There was a crooked man, who walked a crooked mile, he found a crooked sixpence against a crooked stile, he bought a crooked cat, which caught a crooked mouse, and they all lived together in a little crooked house.

There was a man lived in the moon, lived in the moon, lived in the moon, and his name was Aiken Drum, and he played upon a ladle, a ladle, a ladle.

There was an old woman who lived in a shoe, she had so many children she didn't know what to do; she gave them some broth without any bread, she whipped them all soundly and sent them to bed.

This little piggy went to market, this little piggy stayed at home, this little piggy had roast beef, this little piggy had none, and this little piggy went wee-wee-wee, all the way home.

Tom, Tom, the piper's son, stole a pig and away he run; the pig was eat, and Tom was beat, and Tom went howling down the street.

Twinkle, twinkle, little star, how I wonder what you are! Up above the world so high, like a diamond in the sky.

Wee Willie Winkie runs through the town, upstairs and downstairs in his night-gown, rapping at the window, crying through the lock, are the children all in bed, it's past eight o' clock.

What are little boys made of? . . . Snips and snails and puppy-dog tails. What are little girls made of? . . . Sugar and spice and all things nice.

Who killed Cock Robin? I, said the sparrow, with my bow and arrow, I killed Cock Robin. Who saw him die? I, said the fly, with my little eye, I saw him die.

Yankee Doodle came to town, riding on a pony; stuck a feather in his cap, and called it macaroni.

NB There are slight corruptions of wording in some nursery rhymes, usually dependent on region. For example, little boys can be made of 'frogs and snails'.

Popes

Popes and antipopes	Dates	Original name, feast day or miscellaneous information
1 St Peter	To 64	feast day 29 June
2 St Linus	c. 67–76/79	feast day 23 September
3 St Anacletus	c. 76/79–88/91	feast day 26 April
4 St Clement I	c. 88/92–97/101	feast day 23 November
5 St Evaristus	c. 97–c107	feast day 6 October
6 St Alexander I	c. 105/9–115/19	feast day 3 May
7 St Sixtus I	c. 115–c125	feast day 3 April
8 St Telesphorus	c. 125–c136	feast day 5 January (Greek)
9 St Hyginus	c. 136–c140	feast day 11 January (Greek)
10 St Pius I	c. 140–c155	feast day 11 July
11 St Anicetus	c. 155–c166	feast day 17 April (Syria)
12 St Soter	c. 166–c175	feast day 22 April
13 St Eleutherius	c. 175–c189	feast day 26 May
14 St Victor I	c. 189–c199	feast day 28 July (African)
15 St Zephyrinus	c. 199–c217	feast day 26 August
16 St Calixtus I	217–222	feast day 14 October
17 Hippolytus	217–235	first antipope
18 St Urban I	222–230	feast day 25 May
19 St Pontian	230–235	feast day 19 November
20 St Anterus	235–236	feast day 3 January (Greek)
21 St Fabian	236–250	feast day 20 January
22 St Cornelius	251–253	feast day 16 September
23 Novatian	251	Novatianus (antipope)
24 St Lucius I	253–254	feast day 4 March
25 St Stephen I	254–257	feast day 2 August
26 St Sixtus II	257–258	feast day 6 August (Greek)
27 St Dionysius	259–268	feast day 6 December (Greek)
28 St Felix I	269–274	feast day 30 May
29 St Eutychian	275–283	feast day 7 December
30 St Gaius	283–296	feast day 22 April (Dalmatian)
31 St Marcellinus	296–304	feast day 26 April
32 St Marcellus I	308–309	feast day 16 January
33 St Eusebius	309–310	feast day 17 August (Greek)
34 St Miltiades	311–314	feast day 10 December
35 St Sylvester I	314–335	feast day 31 December
36 St Mark	336	feast day 7 October
37 St Julius I	337–352	feast day 12 April
38 Liberius	352–366	
39 Felix II	355–358	antipope 357–8
40 St Damasus I	366–384	feast day 11 December (Latin Mass)
41 Ursinus	366–367	Antipope
42 St Siricius	384–399	feast day 26 November
43 St Anastasius I	399–401	feast day 19 December
44 St Innocent I	401–417	feast day 28 July
45 St Zosimus	417–418	feast day 26 December (Greek)
46 St Boniface I	418–422	feast day 4 September
47 Eulalius	418–419	antipope
48 St Celestine I	422–432	feast day 27 July
49 St Sixtus III	432–440	feast day 28 March
50 St Leo I	440–461	feast day 11 April (Leo the Great)
51 St Hilary	461–468	feast day 28 February
52 St Simplicius	468–483	feast day 10 March
53 St Felix III	483–492	feast day 1 March
54 St Gelasius I	492–496	feast day 21 November
55 Anastasius II	496–498	
56 St Symmachus	498–514	feast day 19 July
57 Laurentius	498	antipope
58 Laurentius	501–505	antipope
59 St Hormisdas	514–523	feast day 6 August
60 St John I	523–526	feast day 27 May
61 Felix IV	526–530	feast day 30 January
62 Dioscorus	530	Egyptian
63 Boniface II	530–532	
64 John II	533–535	Mercurius (first pope to change name)

	Popes and antipopes	Dates	Original name, feast day or miscellaneous information
65	St Agapetus I	535–536	feast day 22 April
66	St Silverius	536–537	feast day 20 June
67	Vigilius	537–555	
68	Pelagius I	556–561	
69	John III	561–574	Catelinus
70	Benedict I	575–579	
71	Pelagius II	579–590	
72	St Gregory I	590–604	feast day 12 March
73	Sabinian	604–606	
74	Boniface III	607	
75	St Boniface IV	608–615	
76	St Deusdedit	615–618	feast day 8 November (aka Adeodatus I)
77	Boniface V	619–625	
78	Honorius I	625–638	
79	Severinus	638–640	
80	John IV	640–642	Dalmatian
81	Theodore I	642–649	Jerusalem
82	St Martin I	649–655	feast day 12 November
83	St Eugenius I	654–657	feast day 2 June
84	St Vitalian	657–672	
85	Adeodatus II	672–676	
86	Donus	676–678	
87	St Agatho	678–681	feast day 10 January
88	St Leo II	681–683	feast day 3 July
89	St Benedict II	684–685	feast day 8 May
90	John V	685–686	Syrian
91	Conon	686–687	
92	St Sergius I	687–701	feast day 8 September
93	Theodore	687	antipope
94	Paschal	687	antipope
95	John VI	701–705	Greek
96	John VII	705–707	Greek
97	Sisinnius	708	
98	Constantine	708–715	
99	St Gregory II	715–731	feast day 11 February
100	St Gregory III	731–741	feast day 28 November (Syrian)
101	St Zacharias	741–752	feast day 15 March
102	Stephen II	752	died after two days
103	Stephen III	752–757	Papal States founder
104	St Paul I	757–767	feast day 28 June
105	Constantine II	767–768	antipope
106	Philip	768	antipope
107	Stephen IV	768–772	
108	Adrian I	772–795	
109	St Leo III	795–816	feast day 12 June (Crowned Charlemagne)
110	Stephen V	816–817	
111	St Paschal I	817–824	feast day 14 May
112	Eugenius II	824–827	
113	Valentine	827	feast day 14 February
114	Gregory IV	827–844	created 1 November All Saints day
115	John	844	antipope
116	Sergius II	844–847	
117	St Leo IV	847–855	feast day 17 July
118	Benedict III	855–858	
119	Anastasius	855	Anastasius the Librarian (antipope)
120	St Nicholas I	858–867	
121	Adrian II	867–872	
122	John VIII	872–882	crowned Charles the Fat Emperor
123	Marinus I	882–884	
124	St Adrian III	884–885	feast day 8 July
125	Stephen VI	885–891	
126	Formosus	891–896	
127	Boniface VI	896	
128	Stephen VII	896–897	
129	Romanus	897	
130	Theodore II	897	
131	John IX	898–900	
132	Benedict IV	900–903	
133	Leo V	903	
134	Christopher	903–904	antipope
135	Sergius III	904–911	

	Popes and antipopes	Dates	Original name, feast day or miscellaneous information
136	Anastasius III	911–913	
137	Lando	913–914	
138	John X	914–928	
139	Leo VI	928	
140	Stephen VIII	929–931	
141	John XI	931–935	
142	Leo VII	936–939	
143	Stephen IX	939–942	
144	Marinus II	942–946	
145	Agapetus II	946–955	
146	John XII	955–964	Ottaviano (crowned Emperor Otto)
147	Leo VIII	963–965	
148	Benedict V	964–966	Benedict the Grammarian
149	John XIII	965–972	
150	Benedict VI	973–974	
151	Boniface VII	974	Franco (first term)
152	Benedict VII	974–983	
153	John XIV	983–984	Pietro Canepanova
154	Boniface VII	984–985	Franco (second term)
155	John XV	985–996	
156	Gregory V	996–999	Bruno of Carinthia (first German pope)
157	John XVI	997–998	Giovanni Filagato (antipope)
158	Sylvester II	999–1003	Gerbert of Aurillac (French)
159	John XVII	1003	Secco
160	John XVIII	1004–1009	Fasano
161	Sergius IV	1009–1012	Pietro Buccaporci
162	Gregory VI	1012	antipope
163	Benedict VIII	1012–1024	Teofilatto
164	John XIX	1024–1032	Romano (crowned Emperor Conrad II)
165	Benedict IX	1032–1044	Teofilatto (12 yrs old)
166	Sylvester III	1045	John of Sabina
167	Benedict IX	1045	Teofilatto (second term)
168	Gregory VI	1045–1046	Giovanni Graziano
169	Clement II	1046–1047	Suidger
170	Benedict IX	1047–1048	Teofilatto (third term)
171	Damasus II	1048	Poppo (Bavarian)
172	St Leo IX	1049–1054	feast day 19 April (aka Bruno of Egisheim)
173	Victor II	1055–1057	Gebhard of Hirschberg
174	Stephen X	1057–1058	Frederick of Lorraine
175	Benedict X	1058–1059	Giovanni Mincio (antipope)
176	Nicholas II	1058–1061	Gerard of Burgundy
177	Alexander II	1061–1073	Anselm of Baggio
178	Honorius II	1061–1072	Cadelo (antipope)
179	St Gregory VII	1073–1085	feast day 25 May 25 (aka Hildebrand)
180	Clement III	1080–1100	Guibert (antipope)
181	Victor III	1086–1087	feast day 16 September
182	Urban II	1088–1099	Odo of Lagery
183	Paschal II	1099–1118	Raniero
184	Theodoric	1100–1102	antipope
185	Albert/Aleric	1102	antipope
186	Sylvester IV	1105–1111	Maginulfo (antipope)
187	Gelasius II	1118–1119	Giovanni da Gaetan
188	Gregory VIII	1118–1121	Maurice Bourdin (antipope)
189	Calixtus II	1119–1124	Guy of Burgundy
190	Honorius II	1124–1130	Lamberto Scannabecchi
191	Celestine II	1124	Theobald Buccapecus
192	Innocent II	1130–1143	Gregorio Papareschi
193	Anacletus II	1130–1138	Pietro Pierleoni (antipope)
194	Victor IV	1138	Gregory Conti (antipope)
195	Celestine II	1143–1144	Guido de Castellis
196	Lucius II	1144–1145	Gherardo Caccianemici
197	Eugenius III	1145–1153	feast day 8 July (aka Bernard of Pisa)
198	Anastasius IV	1153–1154	Corrado di Suburra
199	Adrian IV	1154–1159	Nicholas Breakspear (only English pope)
200	Alexander III	1159–1181	Rolando Bandinelli
201	Victor IV	1159–1164	Ottaviano de Monticello (antipope)
202	Paschal III	1164–1168	Guido da Crema (antipope)
203	Calixtus III	1168–1178	John of Struma (antipope)
204	Innocent III	1179–1180	Lando di Sezze (antipope)
205	Lucius III	1181–1185	Ubaldo Allucingoli
206	Urban III	1185–1187	Uberto Crivelli

RELIGION

Popes and antipopes		Dates	Original name, feast day or miscellaneous information
207	Gregory VIII	1187	Alberto de Morra
208	Clement III	1187–1191	Paolo Scolari
209	Celestine III	1191–1198	Giacinto Bobo-Orsini
210	Innocent III	1198–1216	Lothair di Segni
211	Honorius III	1216–1227	Cencio Savelli
212	Gregory IX	1227–1241	Ugolino di Segni (excommunicated Frederick II)
213	Celestine IV	1241	Goffredo Castiglioni
214	Innocent IV	1243–1254	Sinibaldo Fieschi
215	Alexander IV	1254–1261	Rinaldo Deisegni
216	Urban IV	1261–1264	Jacques Pantaleon
217	Clement IV	1265–1268	Guido Fulcodi
218	Gregory X	1271–1276	Tebaldo Visconti
219	Innocent V	1276	feast day June 22nd (first Dominican pope)
220	Adrian V	1276	Ottobono Fieschi
221	John XXI	1276–1277	Pedro Hispano (Portuguese)
222	Nicholas III	1277–1280	Giovanni Orsini
223	Martin IV	1281–1285	Simon de Brion
224	Honorius IV	1285–1287	Giacomo Savelli
225	Nicholas IV	1288–1292	Girolamo Masci
226	St Celestine V	1294	feast day 19 May (first pope to abdicate)
227	Boniface VIII	1294–1303	Benedict Caetani
228	Benedict XI	1303–1304	feast day 7 July
229	Clement V	1305–1314	Bertrand de Got (Avignon from 1309)
230	John XXII	1316–1334	Jacques Duese (Babylonian Captivity 1309–77)
231	Nicholas V	1328–1330	Pietro Rainalducci (antipope)
232	Benedict XII	1334–1342	Jacques Fournier (Avignon)
233	Clement VI	1342–1352	Pierre Roger (Avignon)
234	Innocent VI	1352–1362	Etienne Aubert (Avignon)
235	Urban V	1362–1370	feast day 19 December (Avignon)
236	Gregory XI	1370–1378	Pierre de Beaufort (Avignon till 1377)
237	Urban VI	1378–1389	Bartolomeo Prignano (Western Schism 1378–1417)
238	Clement VII	1378–1394	Robert of Geneva (antipope)
239	Boniface IX	1389–1404	Pietro Tomacelli
240	Benedict XIII	1394–1423	Pedro de Luna (antipope)
241	Innocent VII	1404–1406	Cosimo de Migliorati
242	Gregory XII	1406–1415	Angelo Correr
243	Alexander V	1409–1410	Peter of Candia (antipope)
244	John XXIII	1410–1415	Baldassare Cossa (antipope)
245	Martin V	1417–1431	Oddone Colonna
246	Clement VIII	1423–1429	Gil Sanchez Munoz (antipope)
247	Benedict XIV	1425–1433	The Hidden Pope (counter antipope)
248	Eugenius IV	1431–1447	Gabriele Condulmer
249	Felix V	1439–1449	Amadeus VIII the Peaceful (antipope)
250	Nicholas V	1447–1455	Tommaso Parentucelli
251	Calixtus III	1455–1458	Alfonso di Borgia (uncle of Rodrigo)
252	Pius II	1458–1464	Enea Piccolomini
253	Paul II	1464–1471	Pietro Barbo
254	Sixtus IV	1471–1484	Francesco Dellarovere
255	Innocent VIII	1484–1492	Giovanni Battista Cibo
256	Alexander VI	1492–1503	Rodrigo Borgia (father of Lucretia)
257	Pius III	1503	Francesco Piccolomini
258	Julius II	1503–1513	Giuliano Dellarovere (patron of Michelangelo)
259	Leo X	1513–1521	Giovanni de Medici (excommunicated Luther 1521)
260	Adrian VI	1522–1523	Adrian Florenz Boeyens (only Dutch pope)
261	Clement VII	1523–1534	Giulio de Medici
262	Paul III	1534–1549	Alessandro Farnese (called Council of Trent)
263	Julius III	1550–1555	Giovanni del Monte
264	Marcellus II	1555	Marcello Cervini
265	Paul IV	1555–1559	Gian Pietro Carafa
266	Pius IV	1559–1565	Giovanni de Medici (concluded Council of Trent)
267	St Pius V	1566–1572	Antonio Ghislieri (excommunicated Elizabeth I 1570)
268	Gregory XIII	1572–1585	Ugo Boncompagni (Gregorian calendar)
269	Sixtus V	1585–1590	Felice Peretti (excommunicated Henry of Navarre)
270	Urban VII	1590	Giambattista Castagna
271	Gregory XIV	1590–1591	Niccolo Sfondrato
272	Innocent IX	1591	Giovanni Facchinetti
273	Clement VIII	1592–1605	Ippolito Aldobrandini
274	Leo XI	1605	Alessandro de Medici
275	Paul V	1605–1621	Camillo Borghese
276	Gregory XV	1621–1623	Alessandro Ludovisi
277	Urban VIII	1623–1644	Maffeo Barberini (patron of sculptor Bernini)

Popes and antipopes		Dates	Original name, feast day or miscellaneous information
278	Innocent X	1644–1655	Giovanni Pamphili
279	Alexander VII	1655–1667	Fabio Chigi
280	Clement IX	1667–1669	Giulio Rospiglioso
281	Clement X	1670–1676	Emilio Altieri
282	Innocent XI	1676–1689	feast day 13 August
283	Alexander VIII	1689–1691	Pietro Ottoboni
284	Innocent XII	1691–1700	Antonio Pignatelli
285	Clement XI	1700–1721	Giovanni Albani
286	Innocent XIII	1721–1724	Michelangelo dei Conti (recognized Old Pretender)
287	Benedict XIII	1724–1730	Pietro Maria Orsini
288	Clement XII	1730–1740	Lorenzo Corsini (condemned Freemasonry)
289	Benedict XIV	1740–1758	Prospero Lambertini
290	Clement XIII	1758–1769	Carlo Rezzonico
291	Clement XIV	1769–1774	Giovanni Ganganelli (dissolved Jesuits 1773)
292	Pius VI	1775–1799	Giannangelo Braschi
293	Pius VII	1800–1823	Barnaba Chiaramonti (revived Jesuits 1814)
294	Leo XII	1823–1829	Annibale Della Genga
295	St Pius VIII	1829–1830	Francesco Castiglioni
296	Gregory XVI	1831–1846	Bartolomeo Cappellari (Austrian)
297	Pius IX	1846–1878	Giovanni Mastai-Ferretti (longest reign, 32 yrs)
298	Leo XIII	1878–1903	Vincenzo Pecci
299	St Pius X	1903–1914	feast day 3 September (last to be canonized)
300	Benedict XV	1914–1922	Giacomo Della Chiesa
301	Pius XI	1922–1939	Ambrogio Damiano Ratti
302	Pius XII	1939–1958	Eugenio Maria Pacelli
303	John XXIII	1958–1963	Angelo Giuseppe Roncalli (second Vatican Council)
304	Paul VI	1963–1978	Giovanni Battista Montini (first to visit Asia)
305	John Paul I	1978	Albino Luciani (reigned 34 days)
306	John Paul II	1978–	Karol Wojtyla (Polish: first non-Italian since Adrian VI)

Popes: Miscellaneous Information

antipope	an alternative claimant to the bishop of Rome who has just cause in disputing the papacy.	Felix X was the last elected antipope.
		last non-Italian	Adrian VI (1522) Dutch
assassinated	26	last to be canonized	Pius X on 29 May 1954
boy pope	Benedict IX (12 yrs old)	letters to churches	encyclicals
Britain: first to visit	John Paul II (1982)	longest reign	Pius IX (32 yrs)
British Pope	Adrian IV (Nicholas Breakspear)	new pope: how known	White smoke from Vatican chimney
Cadaver Synod	Formosus (896) tried and executed after his death!	non-existent pope	John XX, due to error in numbering in 10th century
Celestine II	Theobald Buccapecus, elected pope in 1124, resigned after a few days and is often omitted in lists, hence the duplication.	Pacem in Terris	encyclical of John XXIII (Peace on Earth)
		Pilgrim Pope	Paul VI (because of his great travelling)
Council of Trent	19th ecumenical council of RC Church; 1545–63 in northern Italy	pope's blessing	Urbi et Orbi (To the city and the world)
		pope: also called	Sovereign of Vatican City
crushed to death	John XXI; ceiling of papal palace at Viterbo collapsed		Vicar of Christ on Earth Bishop of Rome Patriarch of the West
directives called	Papal Bull		Primate of Italy
double name: first	John Paul I (named after two predecessors)	pope: elected by	College of Cardinals: two-thirds majority required
female pope	Joan (fictional)	pope: means	father
Humanae Vitae	encyclical of Paul VI condemning birth control (1968)	Redemptor Hominus	encyclical of John Paul II about respect for man
		Sacerdotalis Caelibatus	encyclical of Paul VI concerning priestly celibacy
Infallibility	doctrine promulgated in July 1870, reaffirmed 1973	throne	Sedes Gestatoria
		Vatican Council: first	1869–70 (convoked by Pius IX)
John Paul II	archbishop of Cracow		
last antipope	the count of Savoy took holy orders and set himself up as Clement XV in 1969 but was never recognized outside his own small circle.	Vatican Council: second	1962–65 (convoked by John XXIII)

Popes (Alphabetical Order)

1	Adeodatus II	672–676	69	Clement I	c. 88/92–97/101
2	Adrian I	772–795	70	Clement II	1046–1047
3	Adrian II	867–872	71	Clement III	1080–1100
4	Adrian III	884–885	72	Clement III	1187–1191
5	Adrian IV	1154–1159	73	Clement IV	1265–1268
6	Adrian V	1276	74	Clement V	1305–1314
7	Adrian VI	1522–1523	75	Clement VI	1342–1352
8	Agapetus I	535–536	76	Clement VII	1378–1394
9	Agapetus II	946–955	77	Clement VII	1523–1534
10	Agatho	678–681	78	Clement VIII	1423–1429
11	Albert/Aleric	1102	79	Clement VIII	1592–1605
12	Alexander I	c. 105/9–115/19	80	Clement IX	1667–1669
13	Alexander II	1061–1073	81	Clement X	1670–1676
14	Alexander III	1159–1181	82	Clement XI	1700–1721
15	Alexander IV	1254–1261	83	Clement XII	1730–1740
16	Alexander V	1409–1410	84	Clement XIII	1758–1769
17	Alexander VI	1492–1503	85	Clement XIV	1769–1774
18	Alexander VII	1655–1667	86	Conon	686–687
19	Alexander VIII	1689–1691	87	Constantine	708–715
20	Anacletus	c. 76/79–88/91	88	Constantine II	767–768
21	Anacletus II	1130–1138	89	Cornelius	251–253
22	Anastasius	855	90	Damasus I	366–384
23	Anastasius I	399–401	91	Damasus II	1048
24	Anastasius II	496–498	92	Deusdedit	615–618
25	Anastasius III	911–913	93	Dionysius	259–268
26	Anastasius IV	1153–1154	94	Dioscorus	530
27	Anicetus	c. 155–c. 166	95	Donus	676–678
28	Anterus	235–236	96	Eleutherius	c. 175–c. 189
29	Benedict I	575–579	97	Eugenius I	654–657
30	Benedict II	684–685	98	Eugenius II	824–827
31	Benedict III	855–858	99	Eugenius III	1145–1153
32	Benedict IV	900–903	100	Eugenius IV	1431–1447
33	Benedict V	964–966	101	Eulalius	418–419
34	Benedict VI	973–974	102	Eusebius	309–310
35	Benedict VII	974–983	103	Eutychian	275–283
36	Benedict VIII	1012–1024	104	Evaristus	c. 97–c. 107
37	Benedict IX	1032–1044	105	Fabian	236–250
38	Benedict IX	1045	106	Felix I	269–274
39	Benedict IX	1047–1048	107	Felix II	355–358
40	Benedict X	1058–1059	108	Felix III	483–492
41	Benedict XI	1303–1304	109	Felix IV	526–530
42	Benedict XII	1334–1342	110	Felix V	1439–1449
43	Benedict XIII	1394–1423	111	Formosus	891–896
44	Benedict XIII	1724–1730	112	Gaius	283–296
45	Benedict XIV	1425–1433	113	Gelasius I	492–496
46	Benedict XIV	1740–1758	114	Gelasius II	1118–1119
47	Benedict XV	1914–1922	115	Gregory I	590–604
48	Boniface I	418–422	116	Gregory II	715–731
49	Boniface II	530–532	117	Gregory III	731–741
50	Boniface III	607	118	Gregory IV	827–844
51	Boniface IV	608–615	119	Gregory V	996–999
52	Boniface V	619–625	120	Gregory VI	1012
53	Boniface VI	896	121	Gregory VI	1045–1046
54	Boniface VII	974	122	Gregory VII	1073–1085
55	Boniface VII	984–985	123	Gregory VIII	1118–1121
56	Boniface VIII	1294–1303	124	Gregory VIII	1187
57	Boniface IX	1389–1404	125	Gregory IX	1227–1241
58	Calixtus I	217–222	126	Gregory X	1271–1276
59	Calixtus II	1119–1124	127	Gregory XI	1370–1378
60	Calixtus III	1168–1178	128	Gregory XII	1406–1415
61	Calixtus III	1455–1458	129	Gregory XIII	1572–1585
62	Celestine I	422–432	130	Gregory XIV	1590–1591
63	Celestine II	1124	131	Gregory XV	1621–1623
64	Celestine II	1143–1144	132	Gregory XVI	1831–1846
65	Celestine III	1191–1198	133	Hilary	461–468
66	Celestine IV	1241	134	Honorius I	625–638
67	Celestine V	1294	135	Honorius II	1061–1072
68	Christopher	903–904	136	Honorius II	1124–1130

137	Honorius III	1216–1227
138	Honorius IV	1285–1287
139	Hormisdas	514–523
140	Hyginus	c. 136–c. 140
141	Innocent I	401–417
142	Innocent II	1130–1143
143	Innocent III	1179–1180
144	Innocent III	1198–1216
145	Innocent IV	1243–1254
146	Innocent V	1276
147	Innocent VI	1352–1362
148	Innocent VII	1404–1406
149	Innocent VIII	1484–1492
150	Innocent IX	1591
151	Innocent X	1644–1655
152	Innocent XI	1676–1689
153	Innocent XII	1691–1700
154	Innocent XIII	1721–1724
155	John	844
156	John I	523–526
157	John II	533–535
158	John III	561–574
159	John IV	640–642
160	John V	685–686
161	John VI	701–705
162	John VII	705–707
163	John VIII	872–882
164	John IX	898–900
165	John X	914–928
166	John XI	931–935
167	John XII	955–964
168	John XIII	965–972
169	John XIV	983–984
170	John XV	985–996
171	John XVI	997–998
172	John XVII	1003
173	John XVIII	1004–1009
174	John XIX	1024–1032
175	John XXI	1276–1277
176	John XXII	1316–1334
177	John XXIII	1410–1415
178	John XXIII	1958–1963
179	John Paul I	1978
180	John Paul II	1978–
181	Julius I	337–352
182	Julius II	1503–1513
183	Julius III	1550–1555
184	Lando	913–914
185	Laurentius	498
186	Laurentius	501–505
187	Leo I	440–461
188	Leo II	681–683
189	Leo III	795–816
190	Leo IV	847–855
191	Leo V	903
192	Leo VI	928
193	Leo VII	936–939
194	Leo VIII	963–965
195	Leo IX	1049–1054
196	Leo X	1513–1521
197	Leo XI	1605
198	Leo XII	1823–1829
199	Leo XIII	1878–1903
200	Liberius	352–366
201	Linus	c. 67–76/79
202	Lucius I	253–254
203	Lucius II	1144–1145
204	Lucius III	1181–1185
205	Marcellinus	296–304
206	Marcellus I	308–309
207	Marcellus II	1555
208	Marinus I	882–884

209	Marinus II	942–946
210	Mark	336
211	Martin I	649–655
212	Martin IV	1281–1285
213	Martin V	1417–1431
214	Miltiades	311–314
215	Nicholas I	858–867
216	Nicholas II	1058–1061
217	Nicholas III	1277–1280
218	Nicholas IV	1288–1292
219	Nicholas V	1328–1330
220	Nicholas V	1447–1455
221	Novatian	251
222	Paschal	687
223	Paschal I	817–824
224	Paschal II	1099–1118
225	Paschal III	1164–1168
226	Paul I	757–767
227	Paul II	1464–1471
228	Paul III	1534–1549
229	Paul IV	1555–1559
230	Paul V	1605–1621
231	Paul VI	1963–1978
232	Pelagius I	556–561
233	Pelagius II	579–590
234	Peter	to c. 64
235	Philip	768
236	Pius I	c. 140–c. 155
237	Pius II	1458–1464
238	Pius III	1503
239	Pius IV	1559–1565
240	Pius V	1566–1572
241	Pius VI	1775–1799
242	Pius VII	1800–1823
243	Pius VIII	1829–1830
244	Pius IX	1846–1878
245	Pius X	1903–1914
246	Pius XI	1922–1939
247	Pius XII	1939–1958
248	Pontian	230–235
249	Romanus	897
250	Sabinian	604–606
251	Sergius I	687–701
252	Sergius II	844–847
253	Sergius III	904–911
254	Sergius IV	1009–1012
255	Severinus	638–640
256	Silverius	536–537
257	Simplicius	468–483
258	Siricius	384–399
259	Sisinnius	708
260	Sixtus I	c115–c125
261	Sixtus II	257–258
262	Sixtus III	432–440
263	Sixtus IV	1471–1484
264	Sixtus V	1585–1590
265	Soter	c. 166–c. 175
266	Stephen I	254–257
267	Stephen II	752
268	Stephen III	752–757
269	Stephen IV	768–772
270	Stephen V	816–817
271	Stephen VI	885–891
272	Stephen VII	896–897
273	Stephen VIII	929–931
274	Stephen IX	939–942
275	Stephen X	1057–1058
276	Sylvester I	314–335
277	Sylvester II	999–1003
278	Sylvester III	1045
279	Sylvester IV	1105–1111
280	Symmachus	498–514

RELIGION

281	Telesphorus	c. 125–c. 136		294	Ursinus	366–367
282	Theodore	687		295	Valentine	827
283	Theodore I	642–649		296	Victor I	c. 189–c. 199
284	Theodore II	897		297	Victor II	1055–1057
285	Theodoric	1100–1102		298	Victor III	1086–1087
286	Urban I	222–230		299	Victor IV	1138
287	Urban II	1088–1099		300	Victor IV	1159–1164
288	Urban III	1185–1187		301	Vigilius	537–555
289	Urban IV	1261–1264		302	Vitalian	657–672
290	Urban V	1362–1370		303	Zacharias	741–752
291	Urban VI	1378–1389		304	Zephyrinus	c. 199–c. 217
292	Urban VII	1590		305	Zosimus	417–418
293	Urban VIII	1623–1644				

General Information

Adam's first wife Lilith (according to Jewish folklore).

Adulterer's Bible edition of the Bible of 1631, with the misprinted commandment 'thou shalt commit adultery'. Aka Wicked Bible.

ahimsa law of Reverence for, and non-violence to, every form of life (Hindu, Buddhist and Jainist philosophy).

Black Friars Dominicans (Friar Preachers are a mendicant order founded in 1215).

Black Monks Benedictines (established c. AD 535–540).

Buddhism founded by Siddhartha Gautama in the sixth century BC. Buddha means 'Enlightened One'.

Two main divisions are Theravada Buddhism and Mahayana Buddhism.

The third minor division is Vajrayana or Tantric Buddhism.

The Buddha's teachings are described as the Four Noble Truths.

The Middle or Noble Eightfold Path is the finding of truth and leads to Nirvana.

The ten precepts include five for laymen, i.e. prohibiting killing, stealing, lying, sexual misconduct and drinking intoxicating liquor, and five for monastic novices, i.e. not to eat at certain hours, not to take part in festivals, not to use garlands or perfumes, not to use a luxurious bed and not to accept money for oneself. The birth of the Buddha is celebrated in the festival of Vesak/Wesak. The Buddha's first sermon is celebrated in the festival of Dhamma-cakka.

Cathari Manichean order that flourished in western Europe during the 12th and 13th centuries. The name derives from the Greek 'Katharos' meaning pure.

Christadelphians founded by John Thomas in 1848, although the name was adopted during the US Civil War.

Christian Scientists founded in Boston, Massachusetts, by Mary Baker Eddy (1879).

Church Army founded by Wilson Carlile (1882) in the slums of London.

Grey Friars Franciscans (founded c. 1207 and affiliated with the Poor Clares since 1212).

Hinduism originated about 4,000 years ago in the land of the Indus River.

The Veda is the most ancient body of religious literature.

The power of the Brahmans (priest class) is central to the belief.

Ahimsa is the doctrine of non-injury or the absence of the desire to harm.

Brahma (creator), Vishnu (protector) and Siva (destroyer and restorer) constitute the Trimurti.

Islam founded by Mohammed in AD 622 when he fled from Mecca to Medina (flight known as the Hegira).

Koran (Qur'ān) is regarded as the word of God given to Mohammed by the angel Gabriel.

Koran consists of 114 surahs (chapters).

Five pillars of Islamic faith are: the Shahādah – there is no god but God and Mohammed is the prophet of God; the salat – the five daily prayer sessions; the zakat – the tax that constitutes the giving of alms; the saum – fasting during daylight hours of Ramadan; hajj – the pilgrimage to Mecca that every Muslim should take at least once in their lifetime. The two major branches of Islam are the Sunnites (largest) and the Shi'ites.

Jainism founded in India in the sixth century BC by Mahavira. Jains practise Ahimsa.

Jehovah's Witnesses founded by Charles Taze Russell (1881).

Jerusalem centre of Islam, Judaism and Christianity. The Wailing Wall is sacred to the Jews, the Dome of the Rock is sacred to Muslims and Church of the Holy Sepulchre is sacred to Christians.

Jesse son of Obed, and father of David.

Judaism the body of Jewish civil and ceremonial law is contained in the Talmud, which comprises the Mishnah and the Gemara. The Hebrew Bible comprises 24 books. The civil calendar begins with the month of Tishri, the first day of which is the holiday of Rosh Hashana (New Year). Other Jewish holidays include Shavuot or Pentecost, which commemorates the revelation of the Torah (Law) at Sinai; Yom Kippur (Day of Atonement), which ends the ten days of penitence from Rosh Hashana; and Sukkot (Tabernacles), in remembrance of the Israelites' wanderings after the Exodus. Yom Kippur, Rosh Hashana, and Sukkot are celebrated in the Jewish month of Tishri. Purim celebrates the story of Esther and is celebrated in the month of Adar.

Israeli Jews are divided equally among Ashkenazi (Germanic) and Sephardic (strictly speaking, descendants of Spanish Jews pre-1492; more loosely, non-Ashkenazi), although the Ashkenazim constitute more than 80% of all Jews in the world.

Manich(a)eism religious order founded by the Persian prophet Mani (c. 216–274) based on the conflict between goodness and evil. Manicheism also describes any heretical philosophy involving dualistic doctrines.

Menorah seven-branched candelabrum that is now an emblem of Judaism and badge of Israel.

Methodism   founded by John Wesley (1738).

Mormons   aka Church of Jesus Christ of Latter-Day Saints, founded by Joseph Smith in 1830 and not Brigham Young, who merely led them to Salt Lake City, Utah, in 1847.

Panchen Lama   one of the two great Lamas of Tibet. (The other is the Dalai Lama.)

Penitential Psalms   seven psalms (i.e. 6, 32, 38, 51, 102, 130, 143) all expressing penitence.

Plymouth Brethren   founded in Dublin by the Reverend John Nelson Darby (1827) and named after the Devon town.

Potiphar   Pharaoh's official who bought Joseph as a slave.

Premonstratensians   religious sect founded in the twelfth century by St Norbert.

religious journals   Christian Scientists – *Citadel*, *Monitor*; Jehovah's Witnesses – *Watchtower*; Roman Catholics – *Tabrel, Universe, Herald*; Salvation Army – *War Cry*.

Salvation Army   founded by William Booth (1865) as the New Christian Mission; name changed in 1878. Motto: Blood and Fire.

Seven Sorrows of Mary

1 The prophecy of Simeon (that a sword would pierce her soul).

2 The flight into Egypt.

3 The loss of the holy child in Jerusalem.

4 Meeting with the Lord on the road to Calvary.

5 The Crucifixion (when she stood at the foot of the cross).

6 The Deposition (taking down of Christ from the cross).

7 The Entombment (burial of Christ).

Shakers   founded by James Wardley and Jane Wardley (1747).

Shinto   founded in Japan in the eighth century AD and divided into groups of which the best-known are Jinja and Kyoha.

The sacred texts are *Kojiki* and *Nihonshoki*.

Shinto literally means 'the teaching' or 'the way of the Gods'.

Sikhism   founded by the Guru Nanak in the fifteenth century; the holy book is the Adi Granth.

Society of Friends   founded by George Fox (1650); aka Quakers.

Society of Jesus   founded by Ignatius Loyola (1534).

Stations of the Cross   There are fourteen Stations of the Cross (aka Way of the Cross). They depict the final events in the Passion of Christ. Usually seen portrayed in churches but may also be found in cemeteries, hospitals and on mountainsides.

1 Jesus is condemned to death.

2 Jesus is made to bear his cross.

3 Jesus falls the first time.

4 Jesus meets his mother.

5 Simon of Cyrene is made to bear the cross.

6 Veronica wipes Jesus' face.

7 Jesus falls the second time.

8 Women of Jerusalem weep over Jesus.

9 Jesus falls the third time.

10 Jesus is stripped of his garments.

11 Jesus is nailed to the cross.

12 Jesus dies on the cross.

13 Jesus is taken down from the cross.

14 Jesus is placed in the sepulchre.

Ten Commandments   listed in Exodus and Deuteronomy.

1 Thou shalt have no other gods before me.

2 Thou shalt not make any graven images or likeness of anything in Heaven.

3 Thou shalt not take the name of the Lord thy God in vain.

4 Remember the Sabbath day, to keep it holy.

5 Honour thy father and thy mother.

6 Thou shalt not kill.

7 Thou shalt not commit adultery.

8 Thou shalt not steal.

9 Thou shalt not bear false witness against thy neighbour.

10 Thou shalt not covet thy neighbour's house, wife, manservant, ox or ass.

Unification Church   founded by the Reverend Sun Myung Moon (1954).

Visitation   the visit of the Virgin Mary to her cousin Elizabeth, mother of John the Baptist.

White Friars   Carmelites (mendicant order established *c.* 1155 and approved in 1226 by Pope Honorius III).

White Monks   Cistercians (founded in 1098).

R
E
L
I
G
I
O
N

Archbishops of York

734	Egberht	1061	Ealdred	1306	William Greenfield
767	Æthelberht	1070	Thomas I of Bayeux	1317	William Melton
780	Eanbald I	1100	Gerard	1342	William de la Zouche
796	Eanbald II	1109	Thomas II	1352	John Thoresby
808	Wulfsige	1119	Thurstan	1374	Alexander Neville
837	Wigmund	1143	William Fitzherbert	1388	Thomas Arundel
854	Wulfhere	1147	Henry Murdac	1396	Robert Waldby
900	Æthalbald	1153	William Fitzherbert	1398	Richard le Scrope
928	Hrothweard	1154	Roger of Pont l'Eveque	1407	Henry Bowet
931	Wulfstan I	1191	Geoffrey Plantagenet	1426	John Kempe
956	Osketel	1215	Walter de Gray	1452	William Booth
971	Oswald	1256	Sewal de Bovill	1464	George Nevill
971	Edwald	1258	Godfrey Ludham	1476	Lawrence Booth
992	Ealdwulf	1266	Walter Giffard	1480	Thomas Rotherham
1003	Wulfstan II	1279	William Wickwane	1501	Thomas Savage
1023	Ælfric Puttoc	1286	John Romanus	1508	Christopher Bainbridge
1041	Æthelric	1298	Henry Newark	1514	Thomas Wolsey
1051	Cynesige	1300	Thomas Corbridge	1531	Edward Lee

1545	Robert Holgate	1683	John Dolben	1863	William Thomson
1555	Nicholas Heath	1688	Thomas Lamplugh	1891	William Connor Magee
1561	Thomas Young	1691	John Sharp	1891	William Dalrymple
1570	Edmund Grindal	1714	William Dawes		Maclagan
1577	Edwin Sandys	1724	Lancelot Blackburn	1909	Cosmo Gordon Lang
1589	John Piers	1743	Thomas Herring	1929	William Temple
1595	Matthew Hutton	1747	Matthew Hutton	1942	Cyril Forster Garbett
1606	Tobias Matthew	1757	John Gilben	1956	Arthur Michael Ramsey
1628	George Montaigne	1761	Roben Hay Drumond	1961	Frederick Donald Coggan
1629	Samuel Harsnett	1777	William Markham	1975	Stuart Yarwonh Blanch
1632	Richard Neile	1808	Edward Venables Vernon	1983	John Stapylton Habgood
1641	John Williams		Harcourt	1995	David Michael Hope
1660	Accepted Frewen	1847	Thomas Musgrave		
1664	Richard Sterne	1860	Charles Thomas Longley		

Patron Saints

accountants	Matthew	church	Joseph
actors	Genesius, Vitus	carpenters	Joseph
advertising	Bernardino of Siena	children	Nicholas
airmen	Our Lady of Loretto, Theresa	chorea	Vitus
animals	Francis of Assisi	civil servants	Thomas More
archers	Sebastian	clergy	Gabriel Possenti
architects	Thomas, Barbara	coffin bearers	Joseph of Arimathea
Argentina	Our Lady of Lujan	colleges	Thomas Aquinas
army	Maurice	comedians	Vitus
artists	Luke	condemned criminals	Dismas
astronauts	Joseph of Cupertino	cooks	Lawrence, Martha
astronomers	Dominic	craftsmen	Elegius
athletes	Sebastian	crippled	Giles
Australia	Our Lady Help of Christians	Cuba	Our Lady of Charity
Austria	Leopold	Cyprus	Barnabas
authors	Francis of Sales	Czech Republic	Wenceslas
bakers	Elizabeth of Hungary, Nicholas of Torentino, Zita	dairy workers	Bridgid of Ireland
		dancers	Vitus
bankers	Matthew	deacons	Stephen
barbers	Cosmas, Damian, Louis	deaf	Francis of Sales
bastards	John Francis Regis	death	Archangel Michael, Margaret of Antioch
battle	Archangel Michael		
beekeepers	Ambrose	Denmark	Asgar/Canute
beggars	Martin of Tours	dentists	Apollonia
Belgium	Joseph	dieticians	Martha
blacksmiths	Dunstan	disabled	Giles
Bolivia	Our Lady of Capucclana	disasters	Genevieve
bookkeepers	Matthew	doctors	Luke
booksellers	John of God	domestics	Zita
Brazil	Peter of Alcantara	Dominican Republic	Our Lady of Mercy
brewers	Augustine of Hippo, Luke, Nicholas of Myra	doubters	Thomas
		drunkards	Martin of Tours
bricklayers	Stephen	dyers	Maurice
brides	Nicholas of Myra	earthquakes	Francis Borgia, Gregory the Wonderworker
bridges	John Nepomucen		
broadcasters	Archangel Gabriel	ecologists	Francis of Assisi
Brussels	Michael	eczema	Anthony the Abbot
butchers	Anthony the Abbot, Luke, Adrian of Nicomedia	Edinburgh	Giles
		editors	John Bosco
button-makers	Louis	Egypt	Mark
builders	Vincent Ferrer, Barbara, Thomas	El Salvador	Our Lady of Peace
		engineers	Patrick, Ferdinand III
cab-drivers	Fiacre	England	George
Canada	Joseph, Anne (mother of Mary)	epilepsy	Dympna, Vitus
cancer victims	Peregrine Laziosi	Europe	Cyril, Benedict
caretakers	Joseph of Arimathea	examination candidates	Joseph of Cupertino
candle-makers	Ambrose		
cavalry	Martin of Tours	farmers	George, Isidore
chaplains	John of Capistrano	fathers	Joseph
charcoal burners	Alexander	Finland	Henry
childbirth	Gerard Majella, Margaret of Antioch	firemen	Florian
		flying	Joseph of Cupertino
choirboys	Dominic Savio	fishermen	Peter, Andrew

Florence	John the Baptist	Norway	Olaf
florists	Dorothea, Therese	numismatists	Eligius
France	Denis	nurses	Agatha, Raphael,
funeral directors	Joseph of Arimathea, Dysmas		Camillus of Lellis
gardeners	Adelard, Phocas, Tryphon,	orphans	Ivo of Kermartin
	Dorothea, Fiacre	Oslo	Halivard
Germany	Boniface	painters	Luke
Glasgow	Kentigern (aka Mungo)	Pakistan	Thomas, Francis Xavier
goldsmiths	Dunstan	pallbearers	Joseph of Arimathea
gravediggers	Anthony, Joseph	Papua New Guinea	Archangel Michael
Greece	Andrew, Nicholas, Paul	paralysed	Giles
grocers	Michael	paratroopers	Archangel Michael
Guatemala	James the Greater	Paris	Geneviève
gunners	Barbara	pawnbrokers	Nicholas
haemorrhoids	Fiacre	perfumers	Nicholas of Myra
hairdressers	Martin of Porres	Peru	Joseph, Rose of Lima
Haiti	Our Lady of Perpetual Help	pilots	Mary, Our Lady of Loreto
headaches	Teresa of Avila, Denis	physicians	Luke
heart patients	John of God	pig herders	Anthony
hernia sufferers	Cathal	plasterers	Bartholomew
Holland	Willibrord	poets	Cecilia, David, Columbia
horseriders	Martin of Tours	Poland	Stanislaus, Casimir
horses	Eligius, Hippolytus	policemen	Michael
hospitals	John of God, Camillus de	politicians	Thomas More
	Lellis, Vincent de Paul	poor	Anthony of Padua, Lawrence
hoteliers	Gentian, Amand	Portugal	George, Anthony
housewives	Anne, Martha, Zita	postal workers	Archangel Gabriel
Hungary	Stephen	pregnancy	Gerard Majella, Raymond
hunters	Eustace, Hubert		Nonnatus
ice skaters	Edwina	printers	Augustine of Hippo, John of
Iceland	Olaf		God
India	Our Lady of the Assumption	prison officers	Hippolytus
infantrymen	Maurice	quantity surveyors	Thomas
innkeepers	Amand, Martin of Tours, Gentian	Quebec	John the Baptist
Ireland	Patrick	rabies victims	Hubert
Italy	Francis of Assisi	radio	Archangel Gabriel
jewellers	Eligius (Eloi)	radiologists	Archangel Michael
Jordan	John the Baptist	Ripon	Wilfred
journalists	Francis of Sales	Rome	Peter
judges	John of Capistrano	Russia	Andrew, Nicholas
jumping	Venantius	sailors	Christopher, Cuthbert, Francis
lame	Giles		of Paolo, Dhocas
lawyers	Genesius, Ivo, Thomas More	scholars	Bede, Bridgit, Jerome
lepers	Giles	scientists	Albert
librarians	Jerome, Catherine of Alexandria	Scotland	Andrew
lighthouse keepers	Clement, Venerius	scouts	George
Lisbon	Vincent	sculptors	Claude
London	Paul	secretaries	Genesius
lost articles	Anthony of Padua	shoemakers	Crispin
lost causes	Jude	singers	Gregory
lovers	Valentine	skiers	Bernard of Montjoux
Madagascar	Vincent de Paul	skin diseases	Anthony
Madrid	Isidore	soldiers	George, Joan of Arc, Sebastian
magistrates	Ferdinand III of Castille	South Africa	Our Lady of the Assumption
Malta	Paul	Spain	James
marriage	John Francis Regis	speleologists	Benedict
masons	Thomas	stamp collectors	Archangel Gabriel
mental illness	Dymphna	statesmen	Thomas More
messengers	Archangel Gabriel	students	Thomas Aquinas
metalworkers	Anastasius, Eligius	surgeons	Cosmas, Damian
Mexico	Joseph	Sweden	Bridget, Eric
midwives	Raymond Nonnatus	swimmers	Adjutor
milliners	James the Greater	Switzerland	Nicholas
miners	Barbara, Anne (mother of Mary)	tailors	Homobonus
Moscow	Boris	tax collectors	Matthew
motorcyclists	Our Lady of Grace	teachers	Catherine, Gregory
motorists	Christopher, Frances of Rome	teenagers	Maria Goretti
motorways	John the Baptist	telecommunications	Archangel Gabriel
musicians/singers	Cecilia, Dunstan, Gregory	telephone	Gabriel
neurological	Vitus	television	Clare
disorders		thieves	Dismas
New Zealand	Our Lady Help of Christians	throat disorders	Blaise

RELIGION

toothache	Apollonia	Wales	David
travellers	Christopher	West Indies	Gertrude
undertakers	Dismas	wine merchants	Amand, Vincent
unmarried women	Nicholas of Myra	wine growers	Vincent
venereal disease	Fiacre	wool combers	Blaise
Venice	Mark	workers	Joseph
vets	Eligius (Eloi)	writers	Francis of Sales
Vietnam	Joseph	yachtsmen	Adjutor
volcanoes	Agatha		

NB Almost everyone, everything and everywhere can be included under the auspices of a patron saint. Sometimes the affiliation lies in historical events and sometimes in ancient folklore and, more frequently still, homage is often paid to a particular saint for convenience, for example, cab-drivers call on St Fiacre as their protector because the Hotel St Fiacre in Paris was the first establishment to offer coaches for hire. Confusion often arises in this field as to why a particular saint has been adopted by a particular group. For example, St Martin of Tours is identified with innkeepers and drunks but is often depicted as a young mounted soldier. It should also be noted that many occupations have more than one recognized patron saint, and extra care should therefore be taken when compiling questions on this subject. For example, do not ask who is the patron saint of soldiers unless you are prepared to accept any of the three possible answers.

Archbishops of Canterbury

1	Augustine	597–604		47	Boniface of Savoy	1241–70
2	Lawrence (Laurentius)	604–619		48	Robert Kilwardby	1272–78
3	Mellitus	619–624		49	John Pecham	1279–92
4	Justus	624–627		50	Robert Winchelsey	1293–1313
5	Honorius	627–653		51	Walter Reynolds	1313–27
6	Deusdedit	655–664		52	Simon Mepham	1327–33
7	Theodore (Theodorus) of Tarsus	668–690		53	John Stratford	1333–48
				54	Thomas Bradwardine	1348–49
8	Berhtwald (Beorhtweald)	693–731		55	Simon Islip	1349–66
9	Tatwine	731–734		56	Simon Langham	1366–68
10	Nothelm	735–739		57	William Whittlesey	1368–74
11	Cuthbert (Cuthbeorht)	740–760		58	Simon Sudbury	1375–81
12	Bregowine (Breguwine)	761–764		59	William Courtenay	1381–96
13	Jaenberht (Jaenbeorht)	765–792		60	Thomas Arundel	1396–97
14	Aethelheard	793–805		61	Roger Walden	1397–99
15	Wulfred	805–832		60	Thomas Arundel (restored)	1399–1414
16	Feologild	832		62	Henry Chichele	1414–43
17	Ceolnoth	833–870		63	John Stafford	1443–52
18	Aethelred	870–889		64	John Kempe	1452–54
19	Piegmund	890–914		65	Thomas Bourchier	1454–86
20	Aethelhelm	914–923		66	John Morton	1486–1500
21	Wulfhelm	923–942		67	Henry Deane	1501–03
22	Oda	942–958		68	William Warham	1503–32
23	Aelfsige	959		69	Thomas Cranmer	1533–56
24	Beorhthelm	959		70	Reginald Pole	1556–58
25	Dunstan	960–988		71	Matthew Parker	1559–75
26	Aethelgar	988–990		72	Edmund Grindal	1575–83
27	Sigeric Serio	990–994		73	John Whitgift	1583–1604
28	Aelfric	995–1005		74	Richard Bancroft	1604–10
29	Aelfheah	1005–12		75	George Abbot	1611–33
30	Lyfing	1013–20		76	William Laud	1633–45
31	Aethelnoth	1020–38		77	William Juxon	1660–63
32	Eadsige	1038–50		78	Gilbert Sheldon	1663–77
33	Robert of Jumièges	1051–52		79	William Sancroft	1677–90
34	Stigand	1052–70		80	John Tillotson	1691–94
35	Lanfranc	1070–89		81	Thomas Tenison	1694–1715
36	Anselm	1093–1109		82	William Wake	1715–37
37	Ralph d'Escures	1114–22		83	John Potter	1737–47
38	William of Corbeil	1123–36		84	Thomas Herring	1747–57
39	Theobald	1138–61		85	Matthew Hutton	1757–58
40	Thomas à Becket	1162–70		86	Thomas Secker	1758–68
41	Richard of Dover	1174–84		87	Frederick Cornwallis	1768–83
42	Baldwin	1184–90		88	John Moore	1783–1805
43	Hubert Walter	1193–1205		89	Charles Manners Sutton	1805–28
44	Stephen Langton	1206–28		90	William Howley	1828–48
45	Richard le Grant	1229–31		91	John Bird Sumner	1848–62
46	Edmund Rich	1233–40		92	Charles Thomas Longley	1862–68

93	Archibald Campbell Tait	1868–82
94	Edward White Benson	1883–96
95	Frederick Temple	1896–1902
96	Randall Thomas Davidson	1903–28
97	Cosmo Gordon Lang	1928–42
98	William Temple	1942–44
99	Geoffrey Francis Fisher	1945–61

100	Arthur Michael Ramsey	1961–74
101	Frederick Donald Coggan	1974–80
102	Robert Alexander Runcie	1980–90
103	George Carey	1990

Miscellaneous Information

Archbishop of Canterbury: 100th	Arthur Michael Ramsey
Archbishop: remained bishop	Stigand remained bishop of Worcester
Aristotle philosophies: taught at Oxford	Edmund of Abingdon: first to do so
Augustine landed: where	Isle of Thanet AD 597
buried	SS Peter and Paul (later St Augustine's), Canterbury
converted King	King Aethelbert of Kent
founded church	Christ Church Canterbury
order of monks	Benedictines
Roman prior of	St Andrews Benedictine monastery
welcomed by	King Aethelbert of Kent
Book of Common Prayer: drew up	Thomas Cranmer
born on Greek island	Frederick Temple
Carthusian monk	Boniface of Savoy
Catholic archbishop: last	Reginald Pole
Charles I: ministered on scaffold	William Juxon
Edmund Rich: also known as	Edmund of Abingdon
English-born archbishop: first	Berhtwald
Father and son: only holders	Frederick and William Temple
Henry Chichele: founded	St John's and All Souls colleges at Oxford 1437
heresy: convicted of	Thomas Cranmer (burned at stake)
high treason: accused of	William Laud (beheaded on Tower Hill)
investiture controversy: resolved by	Synod of Rockingham (temporarily)
Lambeth Conference	decennial meeting of Anglican bishops
Lanfranc: originally trained as	lawyer
secured Crown for	William II (Rufus)
Laurentius' dream	dream of St Peter reminded him of his mission
Lombardy: born	Lanfranc and Anselm
Maidstone Hospital: founder	Boniface of Savoy
married Oliver Cromwell's niece	John Tillotson 1664
Mellitus: prayer legend	caused wind to divert fire from Canterbury church
Morton's Fork:	rich pay taxes; poor are considered to be concealing wealth
murdered in Canterbury Cathedral	Thomas à Becket
murdered during Peasant's Revolt	Simon Sudbury (first beheading on Tower Hill)
nicknames: John Whitgift	Little black husband (by Elizabeth I)
Matthew Parker	Nosey Parker
official residence	Lambeth Palace, and Old Palace Canterbury
pallium	a mantle, and symbol of papal approval of archiepiscopal appointment
Piers Gaveston excommunicated by	Robert Winchelsey
plague: died of	Thomas Bradwardine
plot against William I: detected	Lanfranc
position created by	Pope Gregory I
Primate of	All England
prior of Bec Benedictine monastery	Lanfranc, Anselm, Theobald
Protestant archbishop: first	Thomas Cranmer
published Antiquities of Greece	John Potter
Queen Elizabeth II: crowned	Geoffrey Fisher
refused oath of allegiance	William Sancroft: to William and Mary
Repton School: former headmasters	William Temple and Geoffrey Fisher
Richard I: governor in absentia	Hubert Walter
Rochester: first bishop of	St Justus
Scholasticism: founder of	St Anselm
Sheldonian Theatre, Oxford: built	Gilbert Sheldon
son-in-law of Archbishop Tait	Randall Thomas Davidson
St Dunstan: secured crown for	St Edward the Martyr AD 975
Stigand: excommunicated by	Pope Nicholas II 1059. Uncanonical behaviour caused Pope to support William I's invasion
succeeded Thomas Arnold at Rugby	Archibald Campbell Tait
Synod of Whitby 663/664	Northumbria decided to follow Roman Church
Tarsus: born in	Theodore

RELIGION

The Bible

Genesis   God creates Adam from dust.
Garden of Eden planted.
Trees of Life and Knowledge.
Adam names all living beasts.
Eve is created from Adam's rib.
Serpent deceives Eve into eating forbidden fruit.
Birth of Cain and Abel.
Cain becomes tiller of the soil, and Abel a shepherd.
Cain kills Abel and when asked by the Lord as to his whereabouts replies, 'Am I my brother's keeper?'
Cain is 'marked' by God and flees to the land of Nod.
Cain's wife gives birth to a son, Enoch, and builds a city in his name.
Adam's third son Seth is fathered at the age of 130 and Adam dies at age 930.
Methuselah is sired by Enoch (descendant of Seth, not Cain) and lives for 969 years.
Methuselah sires Lamech who subsequently sires Noah.
Noah begets three sons: Shem, Ham, and Japheth. He was 500 years old.
God destroys man by bringing great flood but reprieves Noah.
Noah (aged 600) builds an ark of gopher wood (300 x 50 cubits, and 30 cubits high), three storeys in total.
God directs Noah to take aboard seven of each type of clean beast but just two of each unclean.
There were eight humans on the ark, i.e. Noah and his sons plus their wives.
Ark comes to rest on Mt Ararat.
Noah sends forth a raven and then a dove, which comes back with an olive leaf to show that the rains have ceased.
Noah becomes the first 'drunken man' after planting a vineyard.
Noah lives for 350 years after the flood and dies aged 950.
Noah's great grandson, Nimrod, begins to be a mighty one on the earth.
Nimrod's kingdom begins with Babel, Erech, Accad, Calneh and Shinar.
The whole earth is of one language, one speech.
After the tower of Babel is built, the Lord scatters the people abroad to confound their language.
The Lord calls unto Abram and blesses him.
Abram, with his wife Sarai and nephew Lot, journey into the land of Canaan.
Abram and Lot return from Egypt, after Sarai is taken by the Pharaoh.
Lot moves to live in Sodom, but the men of Sodom are wicked and sinners.
Then comes the 'Battle of the Kings'.
At the battle in the vale of Siddim, the kings of Sodom and Gomorrah are beaten and fall into slimepits.
Lot is taken prisoner by the victors.
Abram attacked at Hobah, and gains the release of Lot, all his goods, the women and the people.
Abram's wife Sarai cannot bear him children; she therefore gives Abram her maid Hagar, who bears him a child, Ishmael.
Abram is 86 years old when he fathers Ishmael.
The Lord renames Abram – Abraham.
The Lord makes a covenant with Abraham which states that every male child is to be circumcised at eight days old.
The Lord renames Sarai – Sarah.
At the age of 90, Sarah bears Abraham a son, Isaac.
Two angels come to see Lot at the gates of Sodom.
The men of Sodom are struck blind.
Lot, his wife and two daughters leave Sodom.
They are told not to look behind them.
Sodom and Gomorrah are destroyed by the Lord.
Lot's wife looks behind her and is turned into a pillar of salt.
Lot's two daughters get him drunk so that they may 'lie' with him to preserve his seed.
Lot's elder daughter has a son, Moab.
Lot's younger daughter also has a son called Ben-ammi.
Abraham tells Abimelech, king of Gerar, that Sarah is his sister, and she is taken by Abimelech.
Abraham casts Hagar and his son Ishmael away.
Abimelech makes a covenant with Abraham and returns to the land of the Philistines.
Abraham has his faith tested by the Lord.
Sarah dies at the age of 127.
A wife is sought for Isaac.
Abraham's servant finds and meets Rebekah.
Rebekah consents to go to Isaac; she then becomes his wife.

Abraham takes a second wife, Keturah.

Keturah bears him Zimran, Jokshan, Medan, Midian, Ishbak and Shuah.

Abraham dies aged 175.

Ishmael dies aged 137.

Ishmael has twelve sons – Nebajoth, Kedar, Adbeel, Mibsam, Mishma, Dumah, Massa, Hadar, Tems, Jetur, Naphish and Kedemah.

Rebekah gives birth to twins – Esau (a hunter) and Jacob (a tent-maker).

Esau sells his birthright to Jacob for a mess of pottage (bread and lentil stew).

Jacob deceives his father, Isaac, into believing that he is his brother Esau.

When Esau finds out about the deceit he threatens Jacob.

While searching for a wife, Jacob dreams of the ladder reaching from earth to the heavens.

Jacob dreams of the Angels of God ascending and descending on the ladder.

Jacob meets Rachel.

Jacob works for seven years in order to win Rachel.

Jacob takes both Rachel and her younger sister Leah as his wives.

Rachel is barren, but Leah bears Jacob a son, Reuben.

Leah later bears Simeon, Levi and Judah.

Rachel gives Jacob her handmaiden, Bilhah, to take as a wife.

Bilhah bears Dan and Naphtali.

Leah gives her maid, Zilpah, to Jacob to take as a wife.

Zilpah bears Gad and Asher.

Leah bears Jacob a fifth son, Issachar, a sixth, Zebulun, and a daughter, Dinah.

Rachel herself then conceives and bears a son, Joseph.

Jacob becomes very rich, with many cattle, maidservants, menservants, camels and asses.

Jacob has a vision at Mahanaim.

Jacob sends messengers to Esau, requesting his return to Laban.

Esau comes to meet him with 400 men.

Jacob sends a present to Esau of various animals.

When Jacob meets Esau, Jacob bows seven times.

Esau runs to meet Jacob, and embraces him. They both weep.

Jacob builds an altar at Shalem, and calls it El-elohe-Israel.

Dinah is defiled by Shechem, son of Hamor, the Hivite.

Simeon and Levi slay all the males of the city, and take Dinah from Shechem's house.

Jacob is unhappy with his sons, because the Canaanites and Perizzites will now rise against him.

God tells Jacob to move to Beth-el.

Jacob and his household journey to Beth-el, build an altar and call it El-beth-el.

Jacob is renamed Israel.

Rachel dies while giving birth to Benjamin.

While away from his household, Reuben lies with Bilhah, his father's concubine.

Jacob's sons now number twelve.

Jacob goes to his father, Isaac, at Hebron, where Isaac dies, aged 180.

Jacob favours Joseph over his brothers.

Joseph has dreams which cause his brothers to hate him.

At first Joseph's brothers plot to kill him.

Joseph's brothers sell him into slavery with the Ishmaelites.

The brothers dip Joseph's long garment in goat's blood, and take it to Jacob.

Jacob mourns his son's death.

Judah meets and takes the daughter of a Canaanite, named Shuah.

Shuah bears three sons: Er, Onan and Shelah.

Judah takes a wife for Er, whose name is Tamar.

Er displeases the Lord and He slays him.

Judah tells Onan to marry Tamar, his brother's widow.

Onan spills his seed on the ground; this displeases the Lord also and He slays Onan.

Judah tells Tamar to live in his house and wait until Shelah is grown.

Tamar deceives Judah into thinking she is a harlot.

When Judah hears that Tamar is pregnant, he orders her to be burnt.

She is spared when Judah realizes he is the father of her child.

Tamar has twins, Pharez and Zarah.

Joseph is sold in Egypt to Potiphar, an officer of the Pharaoh.

Joseph is promoted to overseer.

Joseph's master's wife asks him to lie with her, but Joseph refuses.

She later pulls his garment off him and Joseph flees.

She lies to Potiphar, saying that Joseph came to her to force her to lie with him.

Joseph is imprisoned in the King's prison.

He interprets the dreams of the Pharaoh's officers.

After being in prison for two years, the Pharaoh has a dream and is told of Joseph.

Joseph interprets the Pharaoh's dream.

Joseph foretells the famine.

Joseph is released from prison and lives in the Pharaoh's house.

The famine is worldwide, but Egypt has stockpiled corn.

All the countries of the world come to Egypt to buy corn.

Jacob sends Joseph's brothers to Egypt to buy corn.

Joseph is now governor of the land.

His brothers come and bow before him.

Joseph recognizes his brothers but they not him.

Joseph accuses his brothers of being spies.

Joseph supplies them with food and returns all their money to them.

At an inn the brothers realize that Joseph has returned their money.

Joseph insists that his brothers bring Benjamin to him.

Israel sends all the brothers to Egypt.

All the brothers are taken to Joseph's house for a feast.

Again Joseph fills their sacks with food and also returns their money.

Joseph puts his silver cup in the sack of Benjamin, the youngest brother.

Joseph's stewards find the silver cup and accuse the brothers of theft.

Judah petitions Joseph, asking that Benjamin be allowed to return to his father.

Joseph weeps and makes himself known to his brothers.

Pharaoh commands the brothers to bring back to Egypt all their families.

They tell Israel that Joseph is alive, but Israel does not believe them.

When Israel sees the wagons that Pharaoh has given to them, he believes.

Israel and his entire family return to Egypt to see Joseph.

Joseph meets his father at Goshen.

Israel is given Goshen by Pharaoh.

When people run out of money to buy bread, Joseph sells bread in exchange for livestock.

Joseph buys all the land of Egypt, except the land of the priests.

Joseph gives the people seed to grow their own crops.

The people must give one-fifth of their crops to Pharaoh.

Joseph takes his two sons, Manasseh and Ephraim, to Israel, where Israel blesses them.

Israel prophesies to his twelve sons, then dies, aged 147.

Israel insists that he be buried with his ancestors.

Pharaoh allows Joseph to travel to Canaan for the burial.

Afterwards Joseph and his brothers return to Egypt.

The brothers think that now Israel is dead, Joseph may seek retribution.

Joseph reassures them.

Joseph dies aged 110 and is buried in Egypt.

Exodus   Israel and his sons enter Egypt, each with his household.

Joseph is already in Egypt.

Their offspring multiply at an extraordinary rate until the land is filled with them.

A new king of Egypt becomes worried that the sons of Israel are growing so numerous.

The sons of Israel are oppressed.

The more they are oppressed, the more they multiply.

Eventually the Egyptians make the sons of Israel slaves.

The king of Egypt orders the Hebrew midwives, Shiphrah and Puah, to put to death any male child at birth.

Fearing God, the midwives disobey the Egyptian king.

Finally Pharaoh orders all his people to throw every newborn son into the River Nile.

A man from the house of Levi takes a daughter of Levi, and she becomes pregnant.

She conceals her son for three months.

She then places him in a basket, in the reeds, on the River Nile.

Pharaoh's daughter finds him, and realizes he is a child of the Hebrews.

The child grows up and becomes a son to the daughter of Pharaoh.

She names him Moses.

Moses sees an Egyptian striking a Hebrew; he strikes the Egyptian down and kills him.

Pharaoh hears about it and tries to kill Moses.

Moses runs away to the land of Midian.

Moses meets the priest of Midian, who gives his daughter Zipporah to him.

Zipporah bears Moses a son, Gershom.

Moses becomes a shepherd.

While with the flock, Moses comes to Horeb. Here, an Angel appears to him in a flaming bush.

God speaks to Moses, instructing him to bring the sons of Israel out of Egypt.

Moses wants a sign that this is God.

God tells Moses to throw his rod on to the ground and it becomes a serpent.

God then tells Moses to grab the serpent by its tail, and it becomes a rod.

God gives Moses other signs, turning his hand into a leper's hand and restoring it and turning water from the Nile into blood.

Moses meets Aaron, his brother.

Moses returns to Egypt with his wife and family.

Moses and Aaron meet with the elders of the sons of Israel.

Moses and Aaron meet with Pharaoh and ask that the Hebrews may go into the wilderness for a festival.

Pharaoh refuses permission for the Hebrews to go into the wilderness.

Pharaoh makes the sons of Israel work harder.

The officers of the sons of Israel blame Moses and Aaron for this harsh treatment.

Moses promises to deliver the sons of Israel from this oppression.

Moses and Aaron again meet with Pharaoh; Moses is now 80 years old and Aaron 83.

Aaron throws down his rod in front of Pharaoh and it becomes a serpent.

The magic-practising priests of Egypt do the same thing.

Aaron's rod swallows their rods.

Moses meets Pharaoh on the bank of the Nile, strikes the water with his rod and turns the water into blood.

The magic-practising priests proceed to do the same thing.

Moses tells Pharaoh that unless the people are allowed to go into the wilderness, there will be a plague of frogs. Aaron waves his staff over the Nile and a plague of frogs come to land.

The magic-practising priests do the same thing.

Aaron strikes the dust of Egypt, and it all becomes a swarm of gnats.

The magic practising priests attempts to do the same but they fail.

Moses tells Pharaoh that if the people are not released into the wilderness, gadfly will infest every house.

Gadfly infest every house in Egypt.

Finally Pharaoh calls Moses and Aaron and tells them to take their people into the wilderness.

The gadfly disappear, so Pharaoh does not allow the people to go into the wilderness.

Moses tells Pharaoh that if the people are not released, a pestilence will strike every animal in Egypt.

Moses takes a handful of soot, throws it in the air, in sight of Pharaoh, and it becomes boils and blisters upon man and beast.

The magic-practising priests are unable to attempt to copy this because the boils are affecting them.

Moses again goes to Pharaoh and promises a hailstorm that will kill every man and beast in the field .

The next day, a storm of hail, thunder and lightning strikes Egypt.

Pharaoh now calls Moses and Aaron and release the people to go into the wilderness.

Once the storm stops, Pharaoh again refuses to release the people into the wilderness.

Moses and Aaron see Pharaoh and tell him that a plague of locusts will appear tomorrow unless the people are released.

Locusts covers all of the land of Egypt.

Moses stretches out his arm and darkness falls all over Egypt.

The firstborn of every family in Egypt is threatened with death.

Instructions for the feast of the Passover are given to Moses by the Lord.

At midnight, the firstborn of every man and every beast dies.

Finally Pharaoh tells the people to leave.

The exodus takes place.

The people of Israel reach the Red Sea.

A pillar of cloud by daytime and a pillar of fire by night lead them into the wilderness.

Pharaoh proceeds to give chase when he realizes that the people are escaping.

When Pharaoh reaches the people they are camped by the sea.

Moses stretches his hand over the sea and it parts, allowing the sons of Israel to walk through the Red Sea.

The Egyptians follows them into the Red Sea.

Moses again stretches his hand over the sea and the water returns to its normal state, drowning the Egyptians.

Moses leads the people into the wilderness for three days; they reach Marrah, but cannot drink the water because it is bitter.

The Lord directs Moses to a tree, which he throws into the water and the water becomes sweet.

At the wilderness of Sin, the sons of Israel begin to murmur against Moses and Aaron.

Quails arrive in the evening, and in the morning the wilderness is covered in bread.

By collecting double bread on the sixth day, and resting on the seventh, the Sabbath law is observed.

The sons of Israel eat the manna for 40 years.

At Massah, Moses is instructed to strike a stone with his rod, and water comes out of the rock.

The Amalekites attack the sons of Israel.

Moses instructs Joshua to choose men to go and fight the Amalekites.

Moses watches from the top of a hill.

When Moses lifts his rod, the Israelites are superior.

When Moses lowers his rod, the Amalekites are superior.

Moses' father-in-law, Jethro, along with his wife Zipporah, his two children, Gershom and Eliezer, and Moses' two sons, visits Moses in the wilderness.

Jethro advised Moses to appoint Judges.

Moses takes his advice.

The people go to meet their God on Mount Sinai.

The Lord calls Moses to the top of the mountain.

Moses then returns down the mountain to take Aaron back to the top with him.

Moses is given the Ten Commandments.

Rules on how slaves are treated, including 'eye for eye'.

Further rules covering theft, seduction, sorcery, bestiality, bribery and many more are given to Moses.

Three times a year the Israelites must celebrate a festival to the Lord.

Boundary of the 'promised land' is set, from the Red Sea to the Sea of the Philistines and from the wilderness to the river.

Moses goes up the mountain to receive the stone tablets.

Moses stays on the mountain for 40 days and 40 nights.

The people are instructed to build an ark of acacia wood, two and a half cubits in length, and one and a half cubits deep.

The ark must be overlaid with gold, both inside and outside.

The ark must have four gold rings, two either side.

The people must make two poles of acacia wood and overlay them with gold.

These poles go through the rings in order for the ark to be carried.

The poles must not be removed from the rings.

The commandments must be placed within the ark.

The people are instructed to build a tabernacle, with all its utensils.

The design of the garments to be worn by priests is given to Moses.

Instructions for the installation of priests are given.

Instructions for keeping the Sabbath are given.

When the Lord finishes speaking with Moses on Mount Sinai, he gives to Moses two tablets of stone.

The people are frustrated because Moses is on Mount Sinai for so long.

The people persuade Aaron to make a 'God' for them.

After melting down the people's jewellery, he makes a golden calf.

The making of the golden calf angers the Lord.

When Moses sees the golden calf, he is so angry he smashes the two tablets and destroys the golden calf.

Moses seeks out the loyal people and the sons of Levi gather themselves to him.

Moses sends the sons of Levi back into the camp to kill the sinners; they kill about 3,000.

Moses moves his tent outside the camp and calls it a tent of meeting.

Whenever Moses enters the tent, a pillar of cloud descends and stands at the entrance.

The Lord instructs Moses to carve out two tablets of stone and the Lord will rewrite the commandments.

The Lord will not allow Moses to see his face.

The Lord repeats the terms of the covenant between himself and the people of Israel.

Moses again comes down from Mount Sinai with the two tablets.

The people contribute gifts to the Lord.

Bezalel and Oholiab are selected for special teachings and wisdom.

The people begin to make the cloth and other finery for the tabernacle.

Once completed, the Lord's glory fills the tabernacle.

Leviticus   Instructions for offerings of animals and grain are given to the people of Israel.

All grain offerings must be seasoned with salt.

A young bull must be sacrificed for a sin of a priest.

A young goat must be sacrificed for a sin of a chieftain.

Other sins demand other offerings.

Even unintentional sins must be paid for with offerings.

The eating of fat or blood is forbidden.

Aaron and his sons are installed as priests.

Nadab and Abihu, sons of Aaron, make an offering to the Lord that was not prescribed.

Fire from heaven consumes both.

Instructions as to which animals and fish are clean or unclean are given.

Instructions for the purification of women are given.

Priests are to make leprosy tests; anybody with leprosy is declared unclean.

Garments worn by lepers are also unclean.

Instructions for offerings in the case of a cleansed leper are given.

Uncleanliness in the case of male and female discharges is explained.

Atonement Day procedures are given.

The laws regarding incest are given.

Similarly laws regarding sodomy and bestiality are given.

Laws regarding gleaning of crops are given.

Laws regarding slander, interbreeding, fruit trees and magic are given.

Similarly, laws regarding spiritism, respect of parents and adultery are given.

The law that priests are to be undefiled is explained.

Laws regarding Sabbath, Pentecost, Day of Atonement, festival of Booths and loaves of showbread explained.

The fiftieth year is to become a Jubilee.

The Jubilee year is also a year of restorations. For example, if a man sells his house, he must repurchase it in the fiftieth year.

Laws regarding the help to be given to the poor are explained.

Regarding the poor, money given must bear no usury or interest charges.

No idols or images of the Lord are to be worshipped.

The Lord explains the blessings that the people will enjoy if they keep his laws and commandments.

The Lord explains the chastisements that the people will suffer if they do not keep his laws and commandments.

Values are put on sanctifying your soul, animal, house, field, etc. to the Lord.

Numbers   (Numbers is Bemidbar in Hebrew and means 'In the wilderness'.)

The Lord tells Moses to register every male over 20 years of age.

The Lord also names the assembly; all are chieftains of the tribes of Israel.

The tribes are registered for the army.

All are registered except the Levites.

Moses is told to appoint the Levites over the tabernacle and all the utensils.

When the people set up camp, each tribe must camp with its (three-tribe) division.

Each tribe is designated a place to camp, starting with the (three-tribe) division of Judah eastmost.

The other tribes are designated a place in camp working westwards.

The tribe of Levi must minister to Aaron, and must keep their obligation to him.

Moses registers all the male Levites from the age of one month upwards.

Each of the families of Levi are given a task to perform regarding the tabernacle and the utensils.

Following instructions from Moses, all lepers, persons with discharges and anyone unclean are sent out of the camp.

A water test is explained, to test for jealousy.

If a man or woman takes a special vow to live as a Nazirite, they must stay away from grapes, wine and intoxicating liquor.

Also during the time of living as a Nazirite, no razor should touch a hair.

The further rules of the special vows of living as a Nazirite are explained.

The wording of the Lord's blessing is given to Moses. It is: May the Lord bless you and keep you, May the Lord make his face shine toward you and may he favour you, May the Lord lift up his face toward you and assign peace to you.

Having had all the laws and commandments explained to him, Moses now anoints the tabernacle.

All the chieftains make offerings of grain and cattle, of silver bowls, of other animals, which Moses accepts.

These offerings continue for eleven days.

On the twelfth day an offering by Naphtali is made; this is the inaugural offering at the altar.

The Lord tells Moses to instruct Aaron to light the seven lamps.

Moses is instructed to take the Levites among the people and cleanse them.

Instructions for the cleansing are given.

The Lord explains to Moses the preparation for the Passover.

The Lord instructs Moses to make two trumpets of silver.

These are to be used for convening the assembly or breaking up the camp.

If one trumpet is blown, the chieftains meet with Moses.

If two trumpets are blown, the whole assembly must meet with Moses.

On the twentieth day of the second month, of the third year, the cloud lifts and the people begin to leave the wilderness.

Moses asks Hobab to join the people going to Israel, but Hobab says that he wants to return to his own people.

Moses pleads with Hobab, and he joins Moses and the people.

Some of the people begin to complain about being in the wilderness.

This angers the Lord, and He sends down fire.

The people begin to cry for meat and fish.

Moses asks the Lord for help, because he feels he cannot cope.

The Lord tells Moses to select 70 of the oldest men, take them to the meeting tent, and He will place some of the spirit on them.

The spirit also falls on Eldad and Medad, who were not in the meeting tent, and they begin acting as prophets.

A wind blows quails from the coast to the camp.

Those people who showed selfish craving are slaughtered by the Lord.

Miriam and Aaron begin opposing Moses.

The Lord tells Moses to take Miriam and Aaron to the meeting tent, where He will speak with them.

The Lord is so angry that Miriam is struck with leprosy.

Moses pleads for mercy, and after seven days in quarantine, she is allowed back into the camp.

Moses sends out a man from each tribe, each a chieftain, to spy out the land of Canaan.

After 40 days they return to Moses; ten spies give bad reports.

The people begin to rebel.

The Lord is very angry that the people do not respect Him; He tells Moses that He will strike them with pestilence.

Moses pleads on their behalf.

The punishment for rebellion is to remain in the wilderness for 40 years.

Some of the people decide to leave the camp without Moses and the ark.

These people are defeated by the Amalekites and Canaanites.

Moses is instructed to tell the people of Isreal how they must render up burnt offerings on entering the promised land.

Moses is instructed to tell the people how they must atone for a sin by mistake.

Anyone who commits a deliberate sin must die.

A man collecting pieces of wood on the Sabbath is stoned to death.

Korah, Dathan and Abiram, together with 250 rebels, rise against Moses.

All the rebels are instructed to attend a meeting, each carrying a fire holder.

The earth swallows up Korah, Dathan and Abiram, their households and anything belonging to them.

A fire comes from the Lord and consumes the 250 rebels.

Some of the people still complain, so the Lord brings forth a scourge on them.

Moses tells Aaron to go among them and atone for their sins.

This Aaron does, and eventually stops the scourge.

This scourge kills 14,700 people.

A rod is taken from each of the twelve houses of Israel, placed in the meeting tent, and the Lord chooses one rod to bud.

Aaron's rod, for the house of Levi, has budded.

The Lord explains to Aaron the obligations of Levi.

Moses is instructed again regarding cleansing, especially regarding a man who dies in a tent.

The people move into the wilderness of Zin.

Here Miriam dies and is buried.

The people now have no water and reproach Moses and Aaron.

The Lord instructs Moses to strike a rock and water will come forth.

Moses strikes the rock twice and water enough for all the people and beasts comes forth.

These waters are called the Waters of Meribah.

Moses sends messengers to the king of Edom, to seek permission to pass through his land.

The king of Edom refuses.

The people turn away and travel to Mount Hor.

On Mount Hor, Moses strips Aaron of his clothes and places them on Eleazar (Aaron's son).

Aaron then dies.

The people weep for Aaron for 30 days.

The Canaanite king of Arad begins to attack the people and takes some captives.

The Lord intervenes and strikes down the Canaanites.

The people continue to trek around the land of Edom, but are not happy.

Some of the people rebel, so the Lord sends poisonous serpents among them and many die.

Moses is instructed to make a copper serpent and place it on a pole.

Anyone who was bitten by the serpents will look at the copper serpent and will live.

Moses sends messengers to Sihon, king of the Amorites, requesting permission to pass through his land.

Sihon refuses, and gathers his people and begins to fight the Israelites at Jahaz.

Sihon is defeated and the Israelites take possession of his land.

The Israelites now attack Ogm, the king of Bashan; they defeat him and take possession of his land.

Moab now grows very frightened of the Israelites.

Balak, the king of Moab, sends messengers to Balaam.

Balaam refuses to help.

Balak sends more messengers, more important messengers than at first.

Balaam goes with them to Balak, but on the journey meets with the Lord's angel, which only Balaam's she-ass sees.

Balaam beats his she-ass, and passes by the angel by walking in a field.

The angel reappears at a narrow place; again only Balaam's she-ass sees the angel.

Balaam beats his she-ass and he passes the angel by walking alongside the wall.

The angel reappears at a place where he cannot pass by; the she-ass lies down in the road.

Balaam beats his she-ass again.

The Lord makes the she-ass speak.

She asks Balaam, 'Why have you beaten me three times?'

Balaam says that if he had a sword he would have killed her.

The angel appears to Balaam and asks why he beats his she-ass.

Balaam continues his journey to Moab.

Balaam begins to speak the words that the Lord has put into his mouth.

He orders Balak to build seven altars.

He also orders him to provide seven bulls and seven rams.

A bull and a ram are offered on each altar.

Balaam refuses to help Balak.

Balaam proceeds to utter four proverbial statements, all the word of the Lord.

Balak is foiled.

Israel abides in Shittim and the people begin to commit whoredom with the daughters of Moab.

Israel joins himself unto Baal-peor and the anger of the Lord is blazed against him.

The Lord tells Moses to take the heads of the people and hang them up before him.

Zimri, a child of Israel, brings a Midianite woman into the sight of Moses.

Phinehas, son of Eleazar, son of Aaron, pierces both the man and woman and the plague is scourged.

The Lord tells Moses to vex the Midianites and smite them.

After the plague the Lord tells Moses and Eleazar to take the children of Israel, from 20 years onwards, out of Egypt.

Reuben and his descendants, numbering 250, are swallowed by the earth and become a sign.

The sons of Korah do not die.

Census is taken of eight more tribes and the land is divided.

Joshua is appointed to succeed Moses.

The procedures for various feast days and solemn days are established.

Moses equips an army to slay the Midianites.

The Lord speaks to Moses on the plains of Moab, by the Jordan at Jericho, and tells him to dwell in Canaan.

Deuteronomy   The fifth book of the Old Testament is written in the form of a farewell address by Moses to the Israelites before they enter the Promised Land of Canaan. The speeches recall Israel's past, reiterate laws and. emphasize that observance of these laws is essential for the well-being of the people. The title Deuteronomy derives from the Greek meaning 'copy' although the Hebrew translation means 'words'.

Joshua   The book of Joshua was written while the people of Israel were exiles in Babylonia. It can be divided into three sections, i.e. the conquest of Canaan, the distribution of the land and Joshua's farewell address and death.

This book contains the destruction of the Wall of Jericho.

Judges	The book of Judges was written at about the same time as the book of Joshua and the Judges were the leaders of Israel. Noteworthy events are the death of Joshua and the birth and death of Samson.
Ruth	The central character is a Moabite woman who marries the son of a Judaean couple living in Moab. Ruth moves to Judah with her mother-in-law, Naomi, and becomes the wife of Boaz. She bears Obed, the grandfather of David, although these events are thought to be doubtful.
Samuel, first book	Samuel anoints Saul as the first King of Israel and the book tells further of the exploits of his son Jonathan. The book continues with the story of David conquering Goliath and his great friendship with Jonathan. The book concludes with Abigail giving good counsel to David, Saul visiting the Witch of Endor, and the ultimate death of both Saul and Jonathan on Mount Gilboa.
Samuel, second book	David is anointed king at age 30. He rules for a further 40 years. David commits adultery with Bathsheba, the wife of Uriah the Hittite, and plots his death so he can marry her himself. The Lord sends Nathan, the anointer of David, to reprove him for his deed by telling him a parable of a ewe lamb. The Lord takes the life of the first-born of David and Bathsheba as penance. David and Bathsheba soon have another child, Solomon, and he is loved by the Lord. David's son Absalom plots the death of his brother Amnon, for forcing his sister Tamar. Absalom is killed during the civil war and is mourned by David.
Kings, first book	Zadok the Priest anoints Solomon as king. David eventually dies. The Lord appears to Solomon in a dream and grants a request and is pleased that he asks for wisdom. Solomon builds a great temple as a place of worship to the Lord and also a great house for himself. Queen of Sheba visits King Solomon and is impressed by his demeanour and they exchange gifts. Solomon's heart moves away from the Lord in his old age and he is told the kingship will be removed from his son. Solomon dies and is succeeded by his son, Rehoboam. The Lord's words come true as Jeroboam replaces Rehoboam as king of all Israel except Judah. The divided kingdom of Israel is eventually ruled by Ahab, son of Omri. Ahab takes Jezebel for a wife and sets up an altar to Baal in Samaria. Elijah the Tishbite informs Ahab there will be a drought and indeed no rain falls for 3½ years. Ahab tries to buy the vineyard of Naboth the Jezreelite but is refused. Ahab's wife Jezebel plots the death of Naboth to gain possession of his vineyard. Ahab is slain in battle with the Syrians.
Kings, second book	Elijah is taken up into heaven by a whirlwind and is succeeded by his pupil, Elisha. Jezebel is thrown out of a window and killed. Elisha dies and is buried; a dead man laid on his bones comes to life. The Lord is incensed by the Israelites and removes them, leaving only the tribe of Judah. Nebuchadnezzar II, the king of Babylon, destroys Jerusalem.
Chronicles, first book	The first book of Chronicles details genealogies from Adam up to and including the reign of David. The chronicler used the books of Samuel and Kings as his main source, although modifications were made.
Chronicles, second book	The second book of Chronicles details the reign of Solomon to the end of the Babylonian exile. The chronicler has ignored the northern kingdom of Samaria.
Ezra	Ezra continues the history of Israel from the end of the Babylonian exile. The chronicler details the rising of the Persian Empire from its first king, Cyrus the Great.
Nehemiah	The chronicler continues the story of Israel in the time of another Jewish leader, Nehemiah, who was released from captivity in c. 444 BC, during the reign of Artaxerxes, king of Persia. The rebuilding of Jerusalem is highlighted and the great wall is built.
Esther	Esther is the Jewish wife of the Persian King Ahasuerus (Xerxes I). Esther persuades the king to retract an order for the general annihilation of Jews throughout the Empire. The book explains how the feast of Purim came to be celebrated by the Jews, although the story is largely apocryphal.
Job	The book of Job is written in the form of a series of speeches whereby Job disputes with three friends and the Lord. Job proclaims his innocence and injustice of his suffering while his friends (Job's comforters) blame his sin. Job personifies poverty and patience.

R
E
L
I
G
I
O
N

Psalms   The book of Psalms consists of 150 sacred poems, which are meant to be sung.
Usually divided into five sections, i.e. psalms 1–41, 42–72, 73–89, 90–106, 107–150.
The best-known psalm is no. 23, 'The Lord is my Shepherd'.
Psalm 51 is often called the 'Neck' verse as its recitation would save the neck of those
claiming Benefit of Clergy.
Although the authors are of doubtful origin, 73 psalms are attributed to David.

Proverbs   Book of wisdom with moral and ethical relevance, in a similar vein to the book of Job but with
more finite thoughts.
At the start of the text the proverbs are attributed to Solomon but it is known that many of them
were written after his time.

Ecclesiastes Another book of wisdom, which takes a fatalistic view of life and asks man not to question
God's love.
Once again the book alludes to Solomon as being the author, but this is doubtful because of
chronologies in the text.

Song of   Collection of love poems spoken alternately by a man and a woman.
Solomon   This book is the festival scroll for Passover, which celebrates the Exodus of the Israelites from
Egypt.
The authorship is unknown and Solomon's name was added at a later date.

Isaiah   The prophet Isaiah, son of Amos, reflects on the blasphemy of his people in the eyes of the Lord.
Isaiah calls for a return to the worship of the Lord and talks of 'beating swords into ploughshares'.
Isaiah talks further of peace and his vision of the wolf residing with the lamb.
Isaiah's prophecy of the falling of Babylon comes true.

Jeremiah   The Judaean prophet Jeremiah lived during the reign of King Josiah and his ministry lasted until
the Babylonian conquest.
Chapters 1–25 consist of prophecies against Judah and Jerusalem.
Chapters 26–45 consist of narratives about Jeremiah and may have been composed by Baruch.
Chapters 46–51 consist of prophecies against foreign nations and chapter 52 is a historical
appendix.

Lamentations The poems are laments over the destruction of Judah, Jerusalem and the Temple by the
Babylonians in 586 BC.
Lamentations is often called 'Lamentations of Jeremiah', although authorship is uncertain.

Ezekiel   The prophet Ezekiel was active during the first quarter of the sixth century BC.
The book was written in exile and is valuable for understanding the lives of exiles in Babylon.

Daniel   Daniel interprets Nebuchadnezzar's dream.
Nebuchadnezzar throws Shadrach, Meshach and Abednego into a fiery furnace but the Lord
sends an angel to help them.
Belshazzar holds a feast and Daniel interprets the writing on the wall, 'mene, mene, tekel, parsin'.
The interpretation means that the Lord has numbered the days of the Babylonian kingdom and it
is to be divided.
King Darius reluctantly throws Daniel into the lions' den but the Lord sends an angel to help Daniel

Hosea   The last twelve books of the Old Testament bear the name of the minor prophets and are sometimes
known as 'the Twelve'.
The first chapter is a biographical report of the prophet Hosea's marriage to Gomer, a harlot.
A similar marriage is described in Chapter 3, which is thought to allude to the Lord's love for Israel.

Joel   Joel reiterates the concept that salvation will come to Judah and Jerusalem only when the people
turn to the Lord.

Amos   Amos, a Judaean prophet from Tekoa, was active during the reign of Jeroboam II.
Most of the chapters form a collection of individual sayings and reports of visions.
Much of the rest of the text is by way of a moral judgement on the rich and self-indulgent.
The book ends with a promise of restoration for Israel.

Obadiah   Shortest book of the Bible, with one chapter of 21 verses.
The book announces that the Day of Judgement is nigh for all nations and that Jews will be
restored to their native land.

Jonah   The book of Jonah recounts the story of the prophet.
The Lord calls for Jonah to go to the Assyrian city of Nineveh to prophesy.
Jonah is concerned that the city will repent and be forgiven, and tries to escape his bidding.
Jonah is caught in a storm at sea while escaping and is thrown overboard at his own request.
The Lord appoints a great fish to swallow Jonah and he remains in the fish's maw for three days
and nights.

Jonah prays for deliverance and is vomited out of the fish and once again told to go to Nineveh.
Jonah becomes angry as his fears of repentance are realized and he sits outside the city awaiting its destruction.
A plant springs up overnight to give him shelter from the heat but it is destroyed by a great worm.
Jonah is bitter about the destruction but the Lord chastises him for his care for a plant rather than people.

Micah
The Judaean prophet Micah was active during the last half of the eighth century BC.
Micah's threats and promises are a reiteration of many of the other minor prophets.

Nahum
The book is an oracle concerning Nineveh and is attributed to the vision of Nahum of Elkosh.
The fall of the city of Nineveh is the theme of the prophetic oracle.

Habakkuk
Similar to the book of Nahum; it is written in a liturgical style and portrays a moral theme.

Zephaniah
The dominant theme of the book is the 'Day of the Lord', which the prophet sees as imminent due to the sins of Judah.
The 'Humble' and 'Lowly' will be saved through purification by judgement.

Haggai
The book comprises four prophecies delivered over a four-month period in the second year of the reign of Darius I.

Zechariah
Chapters 1–8 contain the prophecies of Zechariah; the rest of the book is of unknown attribution.
Zechariah was active from 520 to 518 BC and was a contemporary of Haggai.
He shared the concern of Haggai that the Temple of Jerusalem must be rebuilt.

Malachi
Last of the twelve Old Testament books that bear the name of the minor prophets and, indeed, the last book of the OT.
The book comprises four chapters, each in the form of a question-and-answer discussion.
Malachi was probably written in the first half of the fifth century BC and its authorship is unknown.

NB The first five books of the Old Testament are usually called the Pentateuch, or Books of Moses. The contents of the first four of these books have been catalogued in the order that the events took place in the text of the Bible. The remaining books have important events highlighted but have no other great detail about them. The New Testament has been dealt with in a similar manner. The author does not wish to upset any religious denomination and it should be noted that texts can differ slightly from Bible to Bible. There are 39 books of the Old Testament and 27 of the New Testament, totalling 66 in all.

New Testament

Matthew
The first of the four New Testament Gospels recounting the life and death of Jesus Christ.
Matthew, Mark and Luke are known as Synoptic Gospels, as they share a similar general view.
The Gospel was composed in Greek c. AD 70 and is traditionally attributed to the Apostle Matthew the tax-collector.
Chapters 5–7 describe Jesus's Sermon on the Mount, which includes the Beatitudes and the Lord's Prayer.

Mark
The Gospel is attributed to John Mark (Acts 12:12; 15:37), a disciple of Peter and associate of Paul.
Mark is the shortest and earliest of the four Gospels and was probably used by Matthew and Luke to compose their accounts.
More than 90 per cent of the content of Mark's Gospel appears in Matthew's and more than 50 per cent in the Gospel of Luke.

Luke
Luke was known as the beloved physician and was a close associate of the Apostle Paul.
Luke gives details of Jesus' infancy and the Ascension as well as Caesar Augustus' census.
Parables include the Good Samaritan and the Prodigal Son.

John
John was known as the beloved disciple of Jesus.
John's Gospel covers a different time span than the others, concentrating on Jesus' ministry in Judea.
John's account differs in that it does not record many of the symbolic acts of Jesus but rather portrays Jesus as God's son.

Acts of the Apostles
Acts was traditionally written by Luke, whose Gospel concludes where Acts begins, that is, with Christ's Ascension into heaven.
The early chapters describe the descent of the Holy Spirit on the Apostles at Pentecost, which was the birth of the Church.
Chapter 3 describes Peter's healing of a lame man and chapter 5 the death of Ananias for his false tongue.
Chapter 7 describes the stoning of Stephen.

RELIGION

Chapter 9 describes the healing of Aeneas by Peter and the conversion of Saul to Paul on the road to Damascus.

Chapters 27 and 28 describe Paul's shipwreck in Malta and his successful teaching in Rome.

The underlying theme is the spreading of Christianity to the Gentile world under the influence of the Holy Spirit.

Romans

The proper and full title of this book is 'The Epistle of Paul the Apostle to the Romans'.

The book was probably composed at Corinth in *c.* AD 57 and was addressed to the Christian Church at Rome.

The letter is largely a morality and cautionary tale but is considered important in Lutheran teaching.

Corinthians, first book

The proper and full title of this book is 'The First Letter of Paul the Apostle to the Corinthians'.

Written *c.* AD 53 at Ephesus, Asia Minor, and addresses the problems of the early years of the Church.

Paul begins his letter with a reminder that all are servants of Christ and stewards of the mysteries of God.

Paul goes on to address questions of immorality, marriage and celibacy as well as the worthy reception of the Eucharist.

In chapter 13 Paul explains that no gift of God has meaning unless accompanied by love.

Corinthians, second book

The proper and full title of this book is 'The Second Letter of Paul the Apostle to the Corinthians'.

Written *c.* AD 55 in Macedonia, possibly after an unsatisfactory visit by Paul to Corinth.

Paul urges the Corinthians to assist the poor of Jerusalem and is gratified when Titus reveals their repentance.

Galatians

The proper and full title of this book is 'The Letter of Paul the Apostle to the Galatians'.

In this book, Paul defends his credentials as a true Apostle of Jesus Christ.

Ephesians

The proper and full title of this book is 'The Letter of Paul the Apostle to the Ephesians'.

Traditionally supposed to have been written while Paul was in prison, but this is doubtful.

The text is in the form of an affirmation that there is one Lord, one faith, one baptism, one God and father of us all.

Philippians

The proper and full title of this book is 'The Letter of Paul the Apostle to the Philippians'.

There is more evidence that this letter was in fact written by Paul in prison (*c.* AD 62) than in the case of his letter to the Ephesians.

His address to the Macedonian people was probably stirred by thoughts of his own mortality as he pondered execution.

Colossians

The proper and full title of this book is 'The Letter of Paul the Apostle to the Colossians'.

Addressed to Christians at Colossae, Asia Minor, whose congregation was founded by Epaphras.

The letter is in the form of a reminder of God's love and a call for repentance for their wayward ways.

Thessalonians, first book

The proper and full title of this book is 'The First Letter of Paul the Apostle to the Thessalonians'.

First letter was written after his co-worker, Timothy, returned from Thessalonia to report that the new converts were steadfast.

Thessalonians, second book

The proper and full title of this book is 'The Second Letter of Paul the Apostle to the Thessalonians'.

The second letter explains that the final day will not come until after the Antichrist appears and proclaims himself God.

Timothy, first book

The proper and full title of this book is 'The First Letter of Paul the Apostle to Timothy'.

The book deals with Church administration and the growth of heresies.

Timothy, second book

The proper and full title of this book is 'The Second Letter of Paul the Apostle to Timothy'.

The letter urges Timothy to 'guard the truth that has been entrusted to you by the Holy Spirit'.

The letter urges Timothy to visit soon, although the writer believes he is 'on the point of being sacrificed'.

Titus

The proper and full title of this book is 'The Letter of Paul the Apostle to Titus'.

Titus was a close friend of Paul and was the organizer of the Church in Crete.

The letter urges Titus to appoint worthy elders to positions of responsibility and to preach sound doctrine.

The letter also warns against the disruptive influence of 'Jewish myths', especially those of the 'circumcision party'.

Philemon

The proper and full title of this book is 'The Letter of Paul the Apostle to Philemon'.

The letter was written to Philemon, a wealthy Christian from Colossae, on behalf of Onesimus, Philemon's former slave.

Hebrews   The proper and full title of this book is 'The Letter of Paul the Apostle to the Hebrews'.
                     The letter was addressed to a Christian community whose faith was faltering because of strong
                         Jewish influences.
                     The author concludes that Christianity is superior to Judaism.

James   The letter of James, a Christian Jew, is a moralistic reflection on early Jewish Christianity.
                     The letter covers topics such as cursing, boasting, oaths, prayers, poverty and endurance under
                         persecution.

Peter,   The first letter urges persecuted Christians to emulate the suffering Christ in their distress.
first book   He reminded them that after his Passion and death, Jesus rose from the dead and is now in glory.

Peter,   The second letter is principally concerned with the Second Coming of Christ.
second book   Peter also warns against false teachers, whose conduct is as immoral as their words are
                         deceptive.

John,   The John in question is the disciple John the Evangelist, son of Zebedee.
first book   His first letter urges the Christian community to repudiate heretical teachings.

John,   The writer of both the second and the third letters calls himself 'presbyter', i.e. elder.
second book

John,   Addressed to a certain Gaius and complaining of Diotrephes, who lies to put himself first.
third book

Jude   The letter of Jude, brother of James and a servant of Jesus Christ, warns against false gods.

Revelation   The proper and full title of this book is 'The Revelation of St John the Divine'.
                     Attributed to John, the beloved disciple, and possibly written at Patmos in the Aegean Sea.
                     The number 7 is used in a symbolic sense to represent totality or perfection.
                     Chapter 6 describes the Four Horsemen of the Apocalypse.
                     Chapter 7 describes the 12 tribes of Israel, which were sealed 12,000 of each, totalling 144,000.
                     Chapter 13 gives the number of the beast, i.e. 666.
                     Chapter 14 describes the 144,000 virgins who will have their place in heaven.

R
E
L
I
G
I
O
N

SCIENCE

Chemical Elements

Name	Symbol	No.	Name source	Discovered or isolated by
actinium	Ac	89	beam	André-Louis Debierne 1899
aluminium	Al	13	alum	Hans Christian Oersted 1825
americium	Am	95	America	Glenn Seaborg, Ralph James, Leon Morgan and Albert Ghiorso at the University of Chicago 1944
antimony	Sb	51	antimonium	known to the ancients, its extraction from stibrite was first discovered by Basil Valentine c.1450, although its properties were first described by Nicholas Lémery in 1707
argon	Ar	18	inactive	Lord Rayleigh and W. Ramsay 1894
arsenic	As	33	yellow orpiment	Albertus Magnus in the 13th century
astatine	At	85	unstable	Berkeley University, California, 1940
barium	Ba	56	heavy	Humphry Davy 1808
berkelium	Bk	97	university	Berkeley University, California, 1949
beryllium	Be	4	beryl	Nicolas Louis Vauquelin 1797
bismuth	Bi	83	uncertain	Basil Valentine 1450
boron	B	5	borax and carbon	Gay-Lussac, Thenard and Davy 1808
bromine	Br	35	stench	Antoine-Jérôme Balard 1826
cadmium	Cd	48	zinc ore	Friedrich Stromeyer 1817
caesium	Cs	55	silvery white	Robert Bunsen and G. Kirchhoff 1860
calcium	Ca	20	lime	Humphry Davy 1808
californium	Cf	98	California	Berkeley University, California, 1950
carbon	C	6	charcoal	prehistoric
cerium	Ce	58	asteroid Ceres	Hisinger, Klaproth and Berzelius 1803
chlorine	Cl	17	greenish yellow	Humphry Davy 1810
chromium	Cr	24	colour	Nicolas Louis Vauquelin 1797
cobalt	Co	27	goblin	Georg Brandt 1735
copper	Cu	29	Cyprus	prehistoric
curium	Cm	96	Pierre and Marie Curie	Berkeley University, California, 1944
dysprosium	Dy	66	hard to get at	P.E. Lecoq de Boisbaudran 1886
einsteinium	Es	99	Einstein	Albert Ghiorso, Berkeley 1952
erbium	Er	68	Ytterby (Sweden)	Carl Gustav Mosander 1843
europium	Eu	63	Europe	Eugène-Anatole Demarçay 1901
fermium	Fm	100	Enrico Fermi	Albert Ghiorso, Berkeley 1952
fluorine	F	9	flowing	Henri Moissan 1886
francium	Fr	87	France	Marguerite Perey 1939
gadolinium	Gd	64	Johan Gadolin	P.E. Lecoq de Boisbaudran 1886
gallium	Ga	31	cock	P.E. Lecoq de Boisbaudran 1875
germanium	Ge	32	Germany	Clemens Winkler 1886
gold	Au	79	colour gold	prehistoric
hafnium	Hf	72	Copenhagen	Dirk Coster and G. von Hevesy 1923
hahnium	Ha	105	Otto Hahn	disputed by Russia and USA
helium	He	2	sun	William Ramsay 1895
holmium	Ho	67	Stockholm	Soret, Delafontaine and Cleve 1878/9
hydrogen	H	1	water-producing	Cavendish 1766 but Lavoisier named it
indium	In	49	indigo	Ferdinand Reich and Theo Richter 1863
iodine	I	53	violet	Bernard Courtois 1811
iridium	Ir	77	rainbow (iris)	Smithson Tennant 1804
iron	Fe	26	Anglo-Saxon word	prehistoric
krypton	Kr	36	hidden	W. Ramsay and Morris W. Travers 1898
lanthanum	La	57	lie unseen	Carl Gustav Mosander 1839
lawrencium	Lr	103	Ernest Lawrence	Berkeley University, California, 1961
lead	Pb	82	Anglo-Saxon word	prehistoric
lithium	Li	3	stone	Johan August Arfvedson 1817
lutetium	Lu	71	Paris	Carl Auer von Welsbach and G. Urbain 1907/8
magnesium	Mg	12	magnesia	Humphry Davy 1808
manganese	Mn	25	magnet	Carl W. Scheele and Johan Gahn 1774
mendelevium	Md	101	D.I. Mendeleyev	Berkeley University, California, 1955
mercury	Hg	80	planet Mercury	prehistoric
molybdenum	Mo	42	lead	Peter Jacob Hjelm 1782
neodymium	Nd	60	new twin	Carl Auer von Welsbach 1885
neon	Ne	10	new	W. Ramsay and Morris W. Travers 1898
neptunium	Np	93	planet Neptune	Edwin McMillan and Philip Abelson 1940
nickel	Ni	28	copper demon	Baron Axel Frederik Cronstedt 1751

Name	Symbol	No.	Name source	Discovered or isolated by
niobium	Nb	41	Tantalus's daughter	discovered by Charles Hatchett 1801; first isolated by C.W. Blomstrand
nitrogen	N	7	nitre-forming	Daniel Rutherford 1772
nobelium	No	102	Nobel Inst. Stockholm	Berkeley University, California, 1958
osmium	Os	76	smell	Smithson Tennant 1804
oxygen	O	8	Acid-producing	Scheele/Priestley 1772/4; Lavoisier name
palladium	Pd	46	asteroid Pallas	William Hyde Wollaston 1803
phosphorus	P	15	light-bringer	Hennig Brand 1669
platinum	Pt	78	silvery element	known to the ancients; first reported by A. de Ulloa in South America 1736
plutonium	Pu	94	planet Pluto	Berkeley University, California, 1940
polonium	Po	84	Poland	Marie Curie 1898
potassium	K	19	potash	Humphry Davy 1807
praseodymium	Pr	59	green twin	Carl Auer von Welsbach 1885
promethium	Pm	61	Prometheus	Marinsky, Glendenin and Coryell 1947
protactinium	Pa	91	first actinium	Kasmir Fajans and D. Göhring 1913
radium	Ra	88	ray	Pierre and Marie Curie and G. Bemont 1898
radon	Rn	86	radium	F. Dorn 1901
rhenium	Re	75	rhine	I. Tacke, W. Noddack and O. Berg 1925
rhodium	Rh	45	rose	William Hyde Wollaston 1803
rubidium	Rb	37	dark red	R. Bunsen and Gustav Kirchhoff 1861
ruthenium	Ru	44	Russia	Karl Klaus 1844 but named by G. Osann in its impure form in 1827
rutherfordium	Rf	104	Ernest Rutherford	disputed by Soviet and US scientists
samarium	Sm	62	samarskite	P.E. Lecoq de Boisbaudran 1879
scandium	Sc	21	Scandinavia	Lars Nilson and Per Teodor Cleve 1879
selenium	Se	34	moon	Jons Jacob Berzelius 1817
silicon	Si	14	hard stone	Jons Jacob Berzelius 1824
silver	Ag	47	colour silver	prehistoric
sodium	Na	11	soda	Humphry Davy 1807
strontium	Sr	38	Strontian (Scotland)	Humphry Davy 1808
sulphur	S	16	sulphur	known to the ancients; first recognized as an element by Antoine Lavoisier 1777
tantalum	Ta	73	Tantalus	Anders Gustaf Ekeberg 1802
technetium	Tc	43	man-made	discovered by C. Perrier and E.G. Segrè of Italy in a sample of molybdenum at Berkeley University, California, 1937
tellurium	Te	52	Earth	Franz J. Müller von Reichenstein 1782
terbium	Tb	65	Ytterby (Sweden)	Carl Gustav Mosander 1843
thallium	Tl	81	green shoot	discovered by Sir William Crookes 1861
thorium	Th	90	Thor	Jons Jacob Berzelius 1828
thulium	Tm	69	Thule	Per Teodor Cleve 1879
tin	Sn	50	Anglo-Saxon word	prehistoric
titanium	Ti	22	Titans	discovered by William Gregor 1771; rediscovered by Martin Heinrich Klaproth (who gave it its present name) 1795
tungsten	W	74	heavy stone	Juan Jose and Fausto Elhuyar 1783
uranium	U	92	planet Uranus	Martin Heinrich Klaproth 1789
vanadium	V	23	Norse goddess	Nils Gabriel Sefström 1830
xenon	Xe	54	stranger	W. Ramsay and Morris W. Travers 1898
ytterbium	Yb	70	Ytterby (Sweden)	J.C.G. de Marignac 1878
yttrium	Y	39	Ytterby (Sweden)	Johan Gadolin 1794
zinc	Zn	30	German word	known in China and India before 1500
zirconium	Zr	40	golden	discovered by Martin Heinrich Klaproth 1789; isolated by J.J. Berzelius in 1824

S
C
I
E
N
C
E

Periodic Table of Elements

No.	Name	Symbol	Form	No.	Name	Symbol	Form
1	hydrogen	H	gas	10	neon	Ne	gas
2	helium	He	gas	11	sodium	Na	metallic solid
3	lithium	Li	metallic solid	12	magnesium	Mg	metallic solid
4	beryllium	Be	metallic solid	13	aluminium	Al	metallic solid
5	boron	B	metallic solid	14	silicon	Si	metallic solid
6	carbon	C	non-metallic solid	15	phosphorous	P	non-metallic solid
7	nitrogen	N	gas	16	sulphur	S	non-metallic solid
8	oxygen	O	gas	17	chlorine	Cl	gas
9	fluorine	F	gas	18	argon	Ar	gas

No.	Name	Symbol	Form	No.	Name	Symbol	Form
19	potassium	K	metallic solid	62	samarium	Sm	metallic solid
20	calcium	Ca	metallic solid	63	europium	Eu	metallic solid
21	scandium	Sc	metallic solid	64	gadolinium	Gd	metallic solid
22	titanium	Ti	metallic solid	65	terbium	Tb	metallic solid
23	vanadium	V	metallic solid	66	dysprosium	Dy	metallic solid
24	chromium	Cr	metallic solid	67	holmium	Ho	metallic solid
25	manganese	Mn	metallic solid	68	erbium	Er	metallic solid
26	iron	Fe	metallic solid	69	thulium	Tm	metallic solid
27	cobalt	Co	metallic solid	70	ytterbium	Yb	metallic solid
28	nickel	Ni	metallic solid	71	lutetium	Lu	metallic solid
29	copper	Cu	metallic solid	72	hafnium	Hf	metallic solid
30	zinc	Zn	metallic solid	73	tantalum	Ta	metallic solid
31	gallium	Ga	metallic liquid	74	tungsten	W	metallic solid
32	germanium	Ge	metalloid solid	75	rhenium	Re	metallic solid
33	arsenic	As	metalloid solid	76	osmium	Os	metallic solid
34	selenium	Se	non-metallic solid	77	iridium	Ir	metallic solid
35	bromine	Br	non-metallic liquid	78	platinum	Pt	metallic solid
36	krypton	Kr	gas	79	gold	Au	metallic solid
37	rubidium	Rb	radioactive semi-solid	80	mercury	Hg	metallic liquid
				81	thallium	Tl	metallic solid
38	strontium	Sr	metallic solid	82	lead	Pb	metallic solid
39	yttrium	Y	metallic solid	83	bismuth	Bi	metallic solid
40	zirconium	Zr	metallic solid	84	polonium	Po	radioactive solid
41	niobium	Nb	metallic solid	85	astatine	At	from bismuth
42	molybdenum	Mo	metallic solid	86	radon	Rn	gas
43	technetium	Tc	from molybdenum	87	francium	Fr	radioactive liquid
44	ruthenium	Ru	metallic solid	88	radium	Ra	radioactive solid
45	rhodium	Rh	metallic solid	89	actinium	Ac	from uranium
46	palladium	Pd	metallic solid	90	thorium	Th	metallic solid
47	silver	Ag	metallic solid	91	protactinium	Pa	from thorium
48	cadmium	Cd	metallic solid	92	uranium	U	metallic solid
49	indium	In	metallic solid	93	neptunium	Np	from plutonium
50	tin	Sn	metallic solid	94	plutonium	Pu	from uranium-238
51	antimony	Sb	metallic solid	95	americium	Am	from plutonium
52	tellurium	Te	non-metallic solid	96	curium	Cm	from plutonium
53	iodine	I	solid but sublimates	97	berkelium	Bk	from americium
54	xenon	Xe	gas	98	californium	Cf	from cerium
55	caesium	Cs	metallic liquid	99	einsteinium	Es	from plutonium
56	barium	Ba	metallic solid	100	fermium	Fm	from plutonium
57	lanthanum	La	metallic solid	101	mendelevium	Md	from einsteinium
58	cerium	Ce	metallic solid	102	nobelium	No	from cerium
59	praseodymium	Pr	metallic solid	103	lawrencium	Lr	from californium
60	neodymium	Nd	metallic solid	104	rutherfordium	Rf	synthetic metal
61	promethium	Pm	from uranium	105	hahnium	Ha	from californium

Chemistry: General Information

atom and molecule: difference atoms are the smallest part of an element that can take part in a chemical reaction; molecules are the smallest particle of either an element or compound that can exist independently and at the same time keep the properties of the original substance, e.g. the smallest unit of water is the water molecule, which is made up of two atoms of hydrogen and one of oxygen.

atom: meaning indivisible.

chemical bonds there are two main types of chemical bonding, covalent and ionic, and two more specialized types, metallic and hydrogen bonding.

chemical groups there are various ways elements can be subdivided, the most common being metallic and non-metallic. Metallic elements, or their oxides, dissolve in acids to form positively charged ions called cations. Non-metallic elements can be further subdivided into the unreactive noble gases, the reactive halogens, and others.

chemical matter: three types compound, mixture or element.

chemistry: definition chemistry is the scientific study of substances.

isotopes atoms of a given element which have the same number of protons and electrons and the same chemical properties, but have a different number of neutrons in their nuclei, and consequently different atomic masses. Isotopes may be either stable or radioactive.

organic compounds all compounds that contain carbon. All other compounds are inorganic.

polymers polymers are long-chain molecules in which a group of atoms are repeated. They can be natural – e.g. cellulose, DNA, fats, proteins and starches – or artificial – e.g. nylon, polystyrene, polythene, PVC, and in fact all by-products of 'plastics'.

states of matter solid, liquid or gas.

sub-atomic particles chemical properties of elements depend on the structure of their atoms, which are made up of three sub-atomic particles, protons (positive charge), neutrons and electrons (negative charge). Protons and neutrons are situated in the nucleus of the atom and the electrons orbit this nucleus. The number of protons in the nucleus of an element determines the atomic number used in the periodic table.

sublimation occurs when chemical matter changes directly from a solid to a gas without first melting into a liquid.

valency property of atoms or groups, equal to the number of atoms of hydrogen that the atom or group will combine with or displace in forming compounds.

Geochemical Abundances of the Elements

		%		Mohs scale of hardness
Lithosphere	oxygen	46.60	1	talc
	silicon	27.72	2	gypsum
	aluminium	8.13	3	calcite
	iron	5.00	4	fluorite
			5	apatite
Hydrosphere	oxygen	85.70	6	orthoclase
	hydrogen	10.80	7	quartz
	chlorine	1.935	8	topaz
	sodium	1.078	9	corundum
			10	diamond
Halogens*	fluorine	**Noble gases†**	helium	
	astatine		argon	
	bromine		radon	
	iodine		krypton	
	chlorine		xenon	
			neon	

* Mnemonic: Fab(r)ic all end ine.

† Also called inert or rare gases.

NB The table listing the chemical elements in alphabetical order contains the name of the person who discovered or first isolated the element. This may be different from the person who first prepared the chemical e.g. chlorine was first prepared (from hydrochloric acid and manganese dioxide) by Carl Wilhelm Scheele in 1774 and was considered a compound until Sir Humphry Davy showed that it could not in fact be decomposed and that muriatic (hydrochloric) acid consists of hydrogen and another true element that he named chlorine.

SCIENCE

Mathematics: General Information

algebra method of solving mathematical problems by the use of symbols when figures are inadequate due to their size or unknown nature.

angles less than 90° = acute; more than 90° = obtuse; more than 180° = reflex.

Archimedes' principle physical law of buoyancy stating that any body submerged in a fluid at rest is acted upon by an upward force equal to the weight of the fluid displaced.

binary numbers a comparison of decimal and binary numbers (decimal first) 1 = 1, 2 = 10, 3 = 11, 4 = 100, 5 = 101, 6 = 110, 7 = 111, 8 = 1000, 9 = 1001, 10 = 1010.

books Euclid – *Elements*; Bertrand Russell (in collaboration with A.N. Whitehead) – *Principia Mathematica*; Sir Isaac Newton – *Principia*.

calculus branch of mathematics that permits the manipulation of continuously varying quantities. It is subdivided into integral and differential. Calculus (which is Latin for pebble) was independently invented by Gottfried Leibniz and Isaac Newton.

circle: parts of *chord* = a line that joins two points of a circle; *diameter* = the longest chord of a circle; *radius* = point from centre of circle to perimeter; *sector* = portion of circle between centre and two points on perimeter; *segment* = portion of a circle

between a chord and the perimeter (it is important to know the distinction between a sector and a segment as this is an often-asked question). Circumference of a circle = 2 × pi × the radius (or pi × the diameter); the area of a circle = pi × radius².

complex number number having a real and an imaginary part, e.g. 5 + 3i is a complex number.

coordinates the technical names for graph coordinates are abscissa (the horizontal *x* coordinate) and ordinate (the vertical *y* coordinate).

cylinder solid figure with straight sides and a circular section.

The area of a cylinder = 2 × pi × radius × height + 2 × pi × radius squared.

The volume = the area of the base × the height.

ellipse an ellipse is a closed conic section with the appearance of a flattened circle. It is formed by an inclined plane that does not intersect the base of the cone.

factorial the factorial of a number is the product of all the whole numbers inclusive between 1 and the number itself; the symbol is ! e.g. 6! = 1×2×3×4×5×6 = 720.

factors a factor is a number that divides exactly into another number, e.g. 6 divides exactly into 48 eight times; thus both 6 and 8 are factors of 48.

Fibonacci numbers   sequence of numbers in which each number is the sum of its two predecessors, e.g. 1, 1, 2, 3, 5, 8, 13, etc.

game theory   branch of mathematics used to analyse competitive situations whose outcomes depend not only on one's own choices, and perhaps chance, but also on the choices made by other parties, or 'players'. Modern game theory was created practically at one stroke by the publication in 1944 of *Theory of Games and Economic Behaviour* by the mathematician John von Neumann and the economist Oskar Morgenstern.

geometry   branch of mathematics concerned with the properties and relations of points, lines, surfaces, and solids. Euclid's *Elements*, written about 330 BC, is the definitive origin of the subject.

hexadecimal system   base 16, uses digits 0–9 plus letters A–F to denote numbers 10 to 15.

imaginary number   the square root of –1 is denoted by the letter i, so $i^2 = -1$; real multiples of i, such as 3i, 2.3i, etc., are known as imaginary numbers.

line: definition   a line is length without breadth.

logarithms   system invented by John Napier whereby multiplication and division of large numbers are made simple by substituting the operations of addition and subtraction.

matrix   set of numbers arranged in rows and columns so as to form a rectangular array.
The numbers are called the elements, or entries, of the matrix.
The term matrix was introduced by the 19th-century English mathematician Arthur Cayley, who developed the algebraic aspect of matrices.

mean   in a series of values in a distribution the mean is the average value of all the values: e.g. in a series such as 1, 4, 4, 5, 7, 9, 12 the mean would be 6.

median   in a series of values in a distribution the median is the middle value in order of size: e.g. in a series such as 1, 4, 4, 5, 7, 9, 12 the median would be 5.

mode   in a series of values in a distribution the mode is the most frequently occurring value: e.g. in a series such as 1, 4, 4, 5, 7, 9, 12 the mode would be 4.

numbers   chiliad – 1,000; myriad – 10,000; lakh – 100,000; crore – 10,000,000; billion – 1,000,000,000,000 (USA 1,000,000,000); googol – one followed by a hundred noughts; googolplex – one followed by a googol of noughts.

octal system   base 8; uses digits 0–7: e.g. 31 in base 10 would be 37 in base 8.

parabola   curve formed by cutting a right circular cone with a plane parallel to the sloping side of the cone.

parallelogram   quadrilateral with opposite pairs of sides equal in length and parallel. When all sides are of the same length it is known as a rhombus. The area of a parallelogram is base × height.

perfect numbers   perfect numbers are equal to the sum of all their factors excluding the number itself, e.g. 6, whose factors are 1, 2, and 3. The first five perfect numbers are 6, 28, 496, 8,128, and 33,550,336.

pi (π)   pi has been measured to many thousands of decimal places but to six places = 3.141592. It is a transcendental number.

polygons   the sum of the interior angles = $(2n - 4) \times 90°$ where n = the number of sides. The sum of the exterior angles of any polygon = 360° regardless of the number of sides (an exterior angle of a polygon

is the angle between one side extended and the adjacent side): e.g. triangle = 180°; quadrilateral = 360°; pentagon = 540°; hexagon = 720°; octagon = 1080°; nonagon = 1260°; decagon = 1440°; hendecagon = 1620°; dodecagon = 1800°; icosagon = 3240°.

polyhedron   solid figure with four or more plane faces.

prime number   a natural number (over 1) that has no proper factors, i.e. which cannot be divided by any natural numbers other than itself and 1 – e.g. 2, 3, 5, 7, 11, 13, 17...

prism   solid figure (polyhedron) with two equal polygonal faces in parallel planes, other faces being parallelograms. The volume of a prism = the area of either end × the perpendicular distance between the ends.

pyramid   a solid figure whose base is a polygon and whose apex is joined to each vertex of the base. Therefore all its faces, apart from the base, are triangles. Any pyramid can be fitted inside a prism so that the base of the pyramid is one end of the prism, and the apex of the pyramid is on the other end of the prism. The volume of a pyramid on a rectangular base = ⅓ length × breadth × height.

Pythagoras' theorem   in a right-angled triangle, the square of the hypotenuse is equal to the sum of the squares of the other two sides.

quadratic equation   equation containing as its highest power the square of a single unknown variable.
General formula is $ax^2 + bx + c = 0$, in which a, b, and c are constants and only the coefficient a cannot equal 0.

rational number   number that can be written in the form % (a over b), where a and b are integers and b is not equal to zero.

reciprocal   of a quantity, that quantity divided into 1; thus the reciprocal of 2 is ½.

rhombus   diamond-shaped plane figure, a parallelogram with four equal sides and no right angles. The area of a rhombus = ½ the product of the diagonals.

simultaneous equations   two or more algebraic equations that contain two or more unknown quantities and are simultaneously true, e.g. x + 3y = 6 and 3y – 2x = 4. The solution is to eliminate one of the variables by multiplying the first equation by 2 and adding the two equations to give 9y = 16.

sine   in trigonometry, of an angle in a right-angled triangle, the ratio of the length of the side opposite the angle to the length of the hypotenuse.

sphere   circular solid with all points on its surface the same distance from its centre. The surface area = 4 × pi × radius squared. Volume = ⅔ pi × radius cubed A little-known fact about the sphere is that the area of any zone of its curved surface lying between two parallel planes is exactly equal to the curved surface of the surrounding cylinder between the same two planes.

standard deviation   in statistics, a measure of the variability (dispersion or spread) of any set of numerical values about their arithmetic mean. It is specifically defined as the square root of the arithmetic mean of the squared deviations.

tetrahedron   solid figure with four triangular faces, i.e. a pyramid on a triangular base. The volume of a tetrahedron = ⅓ (the area of the triangular base x height).

topology   branch of geometry which deals with those

properties of a figure which remain unchanged even when the figure is continuously transformed. A famous topological problem was to prove that only three colours are needed to produce a map to give adjoining areas different colours.

transcendental number real number that is not a root of a polynomial equation with integer coefficients.

trapezium four-sided plane figure quadrilateral with two parallel sides of unequal length. The area of a trapezium = ½ the sum of the parallel sides x the perpendicular distance between them. To find the area three measurements have to be taken, i.e. the height between the pair of parallel sides and the length of both of the parallel sides. If a and b are the two parallel sides the formula would be ½ (a + b)h.

triangle Three-sided plane figure; *scalene* triangles

have no two sides equal; *isosceles* triangles have two equal sides and angles, *equilateral* triangles have three equal sides and angles. The area of a triangle = ½ base × height, however it is possible to calculate the area from the length of its sides using an Archimedean formula square root of (s(s − a) (s − b) (s − c)) where s = half the sum of the sides.

trigonometry branch of mathematics which solves problems relating to plane and spherical triangles.

vector physical quantity that has both magnitude and direction, such as velocity or acceleration of an object.

Venn diagrams diagram representing a set or sets and the logical relationships between them. Sets are drawn as circles whose overlap contains elements that are common to both sets and thus represent a third set.

NB The information on mathematics is merely an overview of basic relevant information on the subject. No attempt has been made to show functions of matrices or calculus, for example, as these are beyond the scope of this book.

Physics: SI Units
(*Système International d'Unités*)

Base units

Quantity	Unit	Symbol	Definition
length	metre	m	1,650,763.73 wavelengths in vacuum of the red-orange light given out by the krypton-86 isotope.
mass	kilogram	kg	Mass of international prototype of the kilogram, at the Bureau International des Poids et Mésures at Sèvres, near Paris.
time	second	s	Duration of 9,192,631,770 periods of the radiation corresponding to the transition between the two hyperfine levels of the ground state of the caesium-133 atom.
electric current	ampere	A	That constant current which, if maintained in two straight parallel conductors of infinite length of negligible circular cross-section, and placed 1 metre apart in a vacuum, would produce between these conductors a force equal to 2×10^{-7} newtons per metre of length.
thermodynamic temperature	kelvin	K	The fraction $\frac{1}{273.16}$ of the thermodynamic temperature of the triple point of water. The triple point of water is the point where water, ice and water vapour are in equilibrium.
luminous intensity	candela	cd	The luminous intensity, in a given direction, of a source that emits monochromatic radiation of frequency 540×10^{12} Hz, and has a radiant intensity in that direction of $\frac{1}{683}$ watts per steradian.
amount of substance	mole	mol	Amount of substance of a system that contains as many elementary entities (atoms, molecules, ions, etc.) as there are atoms in 0.012 kilogram of carbon-12.

Supplementary units

Quantity	Unit	Symbol	Definition
plane angle	radian	rad	The plane angle between two radii of a circle that cut off on the circumference an arc equal in length to the radius.
solid angle	steradian	sr	The solid angle that, having its vertex in the centre of a sphere, cuts off an area of the surface of the sphere equal to that of a square having sides of length equal to the radius of the sphere.

S
C
I
E
N
C
E

Derived Units

Quantity	Unit	Symbol	Other SI Units
area	square metre	m^2	
volume	cubic metre	m^3	
velocity	metre per second	$m \cdot s^{-1}$	
angular velocity	radian per second	$rad\ s^{-1}$	
acceleration	metre per second squared	$m \cdot s^{-2}$	
angular acceleration	radian per second squared	$rad\ s^{-2}$	
frequency	hertz	Hz	s^{-1}
density	kilogram per cubic metre	$kg \cdot m^{-3}$	
momentum	kilogram metre per second	$kg \cdot m \cdot s^{-1}$	
angular momentum	kilogram metre squared per second	$kg \cdot m^2 \cdot s^{-1}$	
moment of inertia	kilogram metre squared	$kg \cdot m^2$	
force	newton	N	$kg \cdot m \cdot s^{-2}$
pressure (stress)	pascal	Pa	$N \cdot m^{-2} = kg \cdot m^{-1} \cdot s^{-2}$
work (energy)	joule	J	$N \cdot m = kg \cdot m^2 \cdot s^{-2}$
power	watt	W	$J \cdot s^{-1} = kg \cdot m^2 \cdot s^{-3}$
surface tension	newton per metre	$N \cdot m^{-1}$	$kg \cdot s^{-2}$
dynamic viscosity	newton second per metre squared	$N \cdot s \cdot m^{-2}$	$kg \cdot m^{-1} \cdot s^{-1}$
kinematic viscosity	metre squared per second	$m^2 \cdot s^{-1}$	
temperature	degree Celsius	$°C$	
thermal coefficient of linear expansion	per degree Celsius (or kelvin)	$°C^{-1}, K^{-1}$	
thermal conductivity	watt per metre degree Celsius	$W \cdot m^{-1} \cdot °C^{-1}$	$kg \cdot m \cdot s^{-3} \cdot °C^{-1}$
heat capacity	joule per kelvin	$J \cdot K^{-1}$	$kg \cdot m^2 \cdot s^{-2} \cdot K^{-1}$
specific heat capacity	joule per kilogram kelvin	$J \cdot kg^{-1} \cdot K^{-1}$	$m^2 \cdot s^{-2} K^{-1}$
specific latent heat	joule per kilogram	$J \cdot kg^{-1}$	$m^2\ s^{-2}$
electrical charge	coulomb	C	$A \cdot s$
electromotive force (potential difference)	volt	V	$W \cdot A^{-1} = kg \cdot m^2 \cdot s^{-3} \cdot A^{-1}$
electrical resistance	ohm	Ω	$V \cdot A^{-1} = kg \cdot m^2 \cdot s^{-3} \cdot A^{-2}$
electrical conductance	siemens	S	$A \cdot V^{-1} = kg^{-1} \cdot m^{-2} \cdot s^3 \cdot A^2$
electrical capacitance	farad	F	$A \cdot s \cdot V^{-1} = kg^{-1} \cdot m^{-2} \cdot s^4 \cdot A^2$
inductance	henry	H	$V \cdot s \cdot A^{-1} = kg \cdot m^2 \cdot s^{-2} \cdot A^{-2}$
magnetic flux	weber	Wb	$V \cdot s = kg \cdot m^2 \cdot s^{-2} \cdot A^{-1}$
magnetic flux density	tesla	T	$Wb \cdot m^{-2} = kg \cdot s^{-2} \cdot A^{-1}$
magnetomotive force	ampere	A	
luminous flux	lumen	Lm	$cd \cdot sr$
illumination	lux	Lx	$lm \cdot m^{-2} = cd \cdot sr \cdot m^{-2}$
radiation activity	becquerel	Bq	s^{-1}
radiation absorbed dose	gray	Gy	$J \cdot kg^{-1} = m^2 \cdot s^{-2}$

Physics: General Information

Avogadro's law   law stating that equal volumes of gases at the same temperature and pressure contain equal numbers of molecules.

Avogadro's constant   the number of atoms or molecules in one mole of a substance.

baryon   subatomic particle that has a mass equal to or greater than that of a proton.

Bernoulli's principle   the principle that in a liquid flowing through a pipe the pressure difference that accelerates the flow when the bore changes is equal to the product of half the density times the change of the square of the speed, provided friction is negligible. Named after Daniel Bernoulli, Swiss mathematician and physician 1700–82.

Coriolis effect   an effect whereby a mass moving in a rotating system is accelerated perpendicular to its motion and to the axis of rotation, which helps to explain why wind patterns are clockwise in the northern hemisphere and anticlockwise in the southern. Named after French engineer G.G. Coriolis 1792–1843.

Doppler effect   phenomenon observed for sound waves and electromagnetic radiation, characterized by a change in the apparent frequency of a wave as a result of relative motion between the observer and the source.

entropy   measure of the unavailability of a system's thermal energy for conversion into mechanical work, often interpreted as a measure of the degree of disorder or randomness in the system.

fermion   any of several subatomic particles with half-integral spin, e.g. nucleons.

Feynman diagram   diagram of interactions between subatomic particles. Named after Richard Feynman, US physicist (1918–88).

Foucault's pendulum   pendulum which rotates in relation to the Earth's surface and thus changes its plane in relation to the position of the Earth's rotational plane. The pendulum swings in a clockwise plane in the northern hemisphere and anticlockwise in the southern, and on the equator would therefore be stationary. This mathematical effect explains the trajectory of moving objects through the air. Named after Jean Bernard Foucault (1819–68), who set up the first pendulum.

General relativity   Einstein's theory that the effects of acceleration and gravity were equivalent.

Heisenberg uncertainty principle   principle that the momentum and position of a particle cannot both be precisely determined at the same time.

Latent heat   heat required to convert a solid into a liquid or vapour, or a liquid into vapour, without change of temperature.

Matter: four fundamental forces   interactions between matter can be explained by four forces.

1) Gravitational: weakest of the four forces, whereby masses mutually attract. Gravity is the force that holds solar systems and galaxies together.

2) Electromagnetic: force maintaining the magnetic field and the electron-nucleus structure of an atom.

3) Strong: about 100 times stronger than the electromagnetic force, it holds together the protons and neutrons within an atomic nucleus.

4) Weak: force associated with the radioactive beta-decay of some nuclei.

Matter: three fundamental states   gas, solid, liquid.

Newton's three laws of motion   1) A body will remain stationary or travelling at a constant velocity unless it is acted upon by an external force.

2) The resultant force exerted on a body is directly proportional to the acceleration produced by the force and takes place in the direction of the force.

3) To every action there is an equal and opposite reaction.

Pauli exclusion principle   the assertion that no two electrons in an atom can occupy the same energy state simultaneously, or in other words, that no two fermions can have the same quantum number. Named after Wolfgang Pauli, Austrian physicist (1900–58).

Physics: definition   physics is the study of the basic laws that govern matter.

Quantum theory   describes the behaviour of particles within atoms and the absorption and emission of electromagnetic radiation by matter in its various states.

Schrödinger's cat   hypothetical situation whereby a cat is placed inside a box for one hour with a radioactive atom whose probability of decay is 50% per hour. If the atom decays a Geiger counter triggers a mechanism breaking a cyanide capsule and killing the cat. If the atom does not decay the cat remains alive. Quantum theory suggests that until the box is opened at the end of the hour, the cat is neither alive nor dead.

Special relativity   states that nothing can exceed the speed of light, which is the same in all inertial time frames, and that all inertial time frames are equally good for carrying out experiments.

Thermodynamics: three laws   1) First law states that the total amount of energy in any closed system always remains the same.

2) Second law states that heat will always flow from a hotter object to a colder one and not the other way round.

3) Third law states that on approaching absolute zero, extracting energy from a system becomes increasingly harder.

Venturi tube   device for measuring fluid flow, consisting of a tube so constricted that the pressure differential produced by fluid flowing through the constriction gives a measure of the rate of flow.

Wheatstone bridge   apparatus for measuring electrical resistances by equalizing the potential at two points of a circuit.

Young's modulus   measure of elasticity equal to the ratio of the stress acting on a substance to the strain produced. Named after Thomas Young, English scientist (1773–1829).

Zeeman effect   the splitting of the spectrum line into several components by a magnetic field. Named after Pieter Zeeman, Dutch physicist (1865–1943).

S
C
I
E
N
C
E

SHAKESPEARE

Plays

1 All's Well That Ends Well

The Persons of The Play

The Dowager COUNTESS of Roussillon
BERTRAM, Count of Roussillon, her son
HELEN, an orphan, attending the Countess
LAVATCH, a clown, the Countess's servant
REYNALDO, the Countess's steward
PAROLES, Bertram's companion
LAFEU, an old lord
The KING of France

FIRST LORD DUMAINE
SECOND LORD DUMAINE, his brother
INTERPRETER, a French soldier
The DUKE of Florence
WIDOW Capilet
DIANA, her daughter
MARIANA, a friend of the widow
Lords, attendants, soldiers, citizens

Quotations

	Spoken by
A young man married is a man that's marr'd.	Paroles
From lowest place when virtuous things proceed.	King of France
I have an answer will serve all men.	Lavatch
Love all, trust a few, do wrong to none.	Countess of Roussillon
Oft expectation fails and most oft there where most it promises.	Helen
Our remedies oft in ourselves do lie which we ascribe to heaven.	Helen
Praising what is lost makes the remembrance dear.	King of France
The hind that would be mated by the lion must die for love.	Helen
The web of our life is of a mingled yarn.	First Lord Dumaine
There's a place and means for every man alive.	Paroles
'Twere all one that I should love a bright particular star.	Helen

Précis of plot

Helen, the daughter of a poor physician, Gerard de Narbonne, falls in love with Bertram, son of her guardian the Countess of Roussillon. Helen uses her magic to cure the King of France and as a reward he brings about the marriage of Helen and Bertram. The marriage is doomed to fail when Bertram takes flight to the Tuscan wars, and it is only consummated when Bertram seduces Helen in the guise of the Florentine maiden Diana.

Setting

France and Italy in the 14th century

2 Antony and Cleopatra

Mark ANTONY, Triumvir of Rome
Friends and followers of Antony:
VENTIDIUS
SILIUS
EROS
CAMIDIUS
SCARUS
DECRETAS
Domitius ENOBARBUS
DEMETRIUS
PHILO
SELEUCUS
Octavius CAESAR, Triumvir of Rome
OCTAVIA, his sister
Friends and followers of Caesar:
MAECENAS
AGRIPPA
TAURUS
DOLABELLA
THIDIAS
GALLUS
PROCULEIUS

LEPIDUS, Triumvir of Rome
Sextus POMPEY (Pompeius)

Friends of Pompey:
MENECRATES
MENAN
VARRIUS

CLEOPATRA, Queen of Egypt
Cleopatra's attendants:
CHARMIAN
IRAS
ALEXAS
DIOMED

MARDIAN, a eunuch

SOOTHSAYER
AMBASSADOR
MESSENGERS
BOY who sings
SENTRY and men of his WATCH
Men of the GUARD
EGYPTIAN
CLOWN
SERVANTS
SOLDIERS
Attendants, eunuchs, soldiers

Quotations

	Spoken by
Age cannot wither her, nor custom stale her infinite variety.	Enobarbus
Celerity is never more admired than by the negligent.	Cleopatra
Come thou monarch of the vine, plumpy Bacchus with pink eyne!	Boy (sung)
Dost thou not see my baby at my breast.	Cleopatra
Finish, good lady; the bright day is done, and we are for the dark.	Iras

Give me my robe, put on my crown; I have immortal longings in me.	Cleopatra
He wears the rose of youth upon him.	Antony
His biting is immortal; those that do die of it seldom or never recover.	Clown
His legs bestrid the ocean: his rear'd arm crested the world: his voice was propertied.	Cleopatra
I am dying, Egypt, dying; only I here importune death a while until of many thousand kisses the poor last I lay upon thy lips.	Antony
I found you as a morsel cold upon dead Caesar's trencher.	Antony
I have yet room for six scotches more.	Scarus
I saw her once hop forty paces through the public street; and having lost her breath, she spoke, and panted, that she did make defect perfection.	Enobarbus
I wish you joy o' the worm.	Clown
If thou and nature can so gently part, the stroke of death is as a lover's pinch.	Cleopatra
In nature's infinite book of secrecy little can I read.	Soothsayer
In time we hate that which we often fear.	Charmian
It is well done, and fitting for a princess descended of so many royal kings.	Charmian
Let's have one other gaudy night.	Antony
My salad days, when I was green in judgement, cold in blood.	Cleopatra
Now boast thee, death, in thy possession lies a lass unparalleled.	Charmian
Out, fool – I forgive thee for a witch.	Charmian
O, wither'd is the garland of the war. The soldier's pole is fall'n: young boys and girls are level now with men. The odds is gone.	Cleopatra
Sometime we see a cloud that's dragonish, a vapour sometime like a bear or lion, a towered citadel, a pendant rock, a fork'd mountain, or blue promontory with trees upon't.	Antony
The barge she sat in, like a burnish'd throne, burn'd on the water.	Enobarbus
The nature of bad news infects the teller.	Messenger
There's beggary in the love that can be reckon'd.	Antony
Though I am mad I will not bite him. Call!	Cleopatra
Though it be honest, it is never good to bring bad news.	Cleopatra
To business that we love we rise betime, and go to't with delight	Antony
Unarm, Eros; the long day's task is done, and we must sleep	Antony
What's brave, what's noble, let's do it after the high Roman fashion, and make death proud to take us.	Cleopatra
Where's my serpent of old Nile.	Cleopatra

Précis of plot
The second triumvirate is disintegrating and Mark Antony becomes infatuated with Cleopatra, Queen of Egypt. The play tells of the sea fight between Antony and Octavius near Actium and Antony's subsequent suicide, believing Cleopatra dead. Cleopatra too commits suicide rather than be captured by Octavius.

Setting
Rome and Alexandria in the 1st century BC.

3 As You Like It

DUKE SENIOR, living in banishment	ORLANDO, Oliver's brother
ROSALIND, his daughter, later disguised as Ganymede	ADAM, a former servant of Sir Rowland
AMIENS, Lord attending on Duke Senior	DENIS, Oliver's servant
JAQUES, Lord attending on Duke Senior	SIR OLIVER MARTEXT, a country clergyman
TWO PAGES	CORIN, an old shepherd
DUKE FREDERICK	SILVIUS, a young shepherd, in love with Phoebe
CELIA, his daughter, later disguised as Aliena	PHOEBE, a shepherdess
LE BEAU, a courtier attending on Duke Frederick	WILLIAM, a countryman, in love with Audrey
CHARLES, Duke Frederick's wrestler	AUDREY, a goatherd, betrothed to Touchstone
TOUCHSTONE, a jester	HYMEN, God of marriage
OLIVER, eldest son of Sir Rowland de Bois	Lords, pages, and other attendants
JAQUES, Oliver's brother	

Quotations	Spoken by
All the world's a stage, and all the men and women merely players. They have their exits and their entrances and one man in his time plays many parts, his acts being seven ages.	Jaques
And rail'd on Lady Fortune in good terms	Jaques
And so, from hour to hour, we ripe and ripe, and then from hour to hour, we rot and rot; and thereby hangs a tale.	Jacques
An ill-favoured thing, sir, but mine own.	Touchstone
Ay, now am I in Ardenne; the more fool I. When I was at home I was in a better place; but travellers must be content.	Touchstone
Beauty provoketh thieves sooner than gold.	Rosalind
Blow, blow, thou winter wind, thou are not so unkind as man's ingratitude.	Amiens (sung)
But whate'er you are that in this desert inaccessible under the shade of melancholy boughs, lose and neglect the creeping hours of time.	Orlando

Chewing the food of sweet and bitter fancy.	Oliver
Dead shepherd, now I find thy saw of might, 'Who ever loved that loved not at first sight?'	Phoebe (quoting Marlowe's 'Hero and Leander')
Down on your knees, and thank heaven, fasting, for a good man's love.	Rosalind
Do you not know I am a woman? when I think I must speak, sweet, say on.	Rosalind
Every one fault seeming monstrous till his fellow-fault came to match it.	Rosalind
Fleet the time carelessly, as they did in the golden world.	Charles
For in my youth I never did apply hot and rebellious liquors to my blood	Adam
Hast any philosophy in thee, shepherd?	Touchstone
He that wants money, means and content is without three good friends.	Corin
He uses his folly like a stalking-horse and under the presentation of that he shoots his wit.	Duke Senior
How now, wit! whither wander you?	Celia
I am not a slut, though I thank the gods I am foul.	Audrey
I can suck melancholy out of a song, as a weasel sucks eggs.	Jaques
I do desire we may be better strangers.	Orlando
If ever – as that ever may be near – you meet in some fresh cheek the power of fancy, then shall you know the wounds invisible that love's keen arrows make.	
If it be true that good wine needs no bush 'tis true that a good play needs no epilogue.	Rosalind
If thou remember'st not the slightest folly that ever love did make thee run into, thou hast not loved.	Silvius
I had rather have a fool to make me merry than experience to make me sad.	Rosalind
I must have liberty withal, as large a charter as the wind, to blow on whom I please.	Jaques
It is a melancholy of mine own, compounded of many simples, extracted from many objects, and indeed the sundry contemplation of my travels, in which my often rumination wraps me in a most humorous sadness.	Jaques
It is meat and drink to me to see a clown.	Touchstone
It is to be all made of faith and service.	Silvius
It is to be all made of fantasy, all made of passion.	Silvius
It is to be all made of sighs and tears.	Silvius
Men are April when they woo, December when they wed, maids are May when they are maids, but the sky changes when they are wives.	Rosalind
Men have died from time to time and worms have eaten them, but not for love.	Rosalind
Most friendship is feigning, most loving mere folly.	Amiens (sung)
Motley's the only wear.	Jaques
My lungs began to crow like chanticleer, that fools should be so deep-contemplative, and I did laugh sans intermission an hour by his dial.	Jaques
My pride fell with my fortunes.	Rosalind
'No sir,' quoth he, 'Call me not fool till heaven hath sent me fortune' and then he drew a dial from his poke, and, looking on it with lack-lustre eye, says very wisely 'it is ten o' clock thus we may see,' quoth he, 'how the world wags.'	Jaques
No sooner met but they looked; no sooner looked but they loved; no sooner loved but they sighed; no sooner sighed but they asked one another the reason, no sooner knew the reason but they sought the remedy.	Rosalind
O, how bitter a thing it is to look into happiness through another man's eyes!	Orlando
O, how full of briers is this working-day world!	Rosalind
O Sir, we quarrel in print, by the book; as you have books for good manners. I will name you the degrees. The first, the Retort Courteous; the second, the Quip Modest; the third, the Reply Churlish; the fourth, the Reproof Valiant; the fifth, the Countercheck Quarrelsome; the sixth, the Lie with Circumstance; the seventh, the Lie Direct.	Touchstone
O wonderful, wonderful, and most wonderful! and yet again wonderful, and after that, out of all whooping!	Celia
Sans teeth, sans eyes, sans taste, sans everything.	Jaques
Speak, sad brow and true maid.	Rosalind
Sweep on, you fat and greasy citizens.	First Lord
Sweet are the uses of adversity, which like the toad, ugly and venomous, wears yet a precious jewel in its head; and this our life exempt from public haunt, finds tongues in trees, books in the running brooks, sermons in stones, and good in everything.	Duke Senior
The big round tears coursed one another down his innocent nose in piteous chase.	First Lord
The fair, the chaste and unexpressive she.	Orlando
The horn, the horn, the lusty horn is not a thing to laugh to scorn.	Lords (sung)
Therefore my age is as a lusty winter, frosty, but kindly.	Adam
The 'why' is plain as way to parish church.	Jaques
This is the very false gallop of the verses.	Touchstone
Thou mak'st a testament as worldlings do, giving thy sum of more to that which had too much.	First Lord
Time travels in divers paces with divers persons.	Rosalind

Truly, I would the gods had made thee poetical.	Touchstone
Truly thou art damned, like an ill-roasted egg all on one side.	Touchstone
Under the greenwood tree, who loves to lie with me, and turn his merry note, unto the sweet bird's throat, Come hither, come hither, come hither. Here shall he see: no enemy, but winter and rough weather.	Amiens (sung)
Very good orators, when they are out, they will spit.	Rosalind
We'll have a swashing and a martial outside, as many other mannish cowards have, that do outface it with their semblances.	Rosalind
Well said: that was laid on with a trowel.	Celia
We that are true lovers run into strange capers.	Touchstone
Who doth ambition shun and loves to live i' the sun seeking the food he eats and pleased with what he gets.	Chorus
Your 'if' is the only peacemaker; much virtue in 'if'.	Touchstone

Précis of plot
The story of the love between a high-born maiden, Rosalind, oppressed by her uncle Duke Frederick, who has usurped his elder brother's dukedom, and Orlando, the third and youngest son of Duke Frederick's enemy Sir Rowland de Bois, himself oppressed by his tyrannical elder brother Oliver. Sub-plots include the romantic liaisons between Touchstone and Audrey, Celia and Oliver, and Silvius and Phoebe.

Setting
The Forest of Arden (possibly Ardenne).

4 The Comedy of Errors

Solinus, DUKE of Ephesus	ANGELO, a goldsmith
EGEON, father of the Antipholus twins	BALTHASAR, a merchant
ANTIPHOLUS OF EPHESUS, Egeon's son	A COURTESAN
ANTIPHOLUS OF SYRACUSE, twin brother	Doctor PINCH, a schoolmaster and exorcist
DROMIO OF EPHESUS	MERCHANT OF EPHESUS
DROMIO OF SYRACUSE, his twin brother	SECOND MERCHANT, Angelo's creditor
ADRIANA, wife of Antipholus of Ephesus	EMILIA, an abbess at Ephesus
LUCIANA, her sister	Officers and attendants
NELL, Adriana's kitchen-maid	Jailer, messenger, headsman

Quotations

	Spoken by
A wretched soul, bruised with adversity.	Adriana
The pleasing punishment that women bear.	Egeon

Précis of plot
The Comedy of Errors is a true farce, in as much as the unlikely situations stretch the imagination of the audience. But the play itself is probably the most classically constructed of any of Shakespeare's works. The action all takes place within a few hours and revolves around the mistaken identity of twin brothers and their bondmen, who also happen to be twins. The audience are further tested intellectually by the long-lost brothers sharing the same names as do their servants.

Setting
Ephesus circa 14th century.

5 Coriolanus

Caius MARTIUS, later surnamed CORIOLANUS	His LIEUTENANT
MENENIUS Agrippa	His SERVINGMEN
Titus LARTIUS, a General	CONSPIRATORS with Aufidius
COMINIUS, a General	Volscian LORDS
VOLUMNIA, Coriolanus' mother	Volscian CITIZENS
VIRGILIA, his wife	SOLDIERS in the Volscian army
YOUNG MARTIUS, his son	ADRIAN, a Roman
VALERIA, a chaste lady of Rome	NICANOR, a Volscian
SICINIUS Velutus, tribune	A Roman HERALD
Junius BRUTUS, tribune	MESSENGERS
CITIZENS of Rome	AEDILES
SOLDIERS in the Roman army	Gentlewoman, usher, Volscian Senators,
Tullus AUFIDIUS, General of the Volscian army	Roman Captains, officers and lictors

Quotations

	Spoken by
Bid them wash their faces and keep their teeth clean.	Coriolanus
Chaste as the icicle that's candied by the frost from purest snow and hangs on Diana's temple.	Coriolanus
Hear you this Triton of the minnows?	Coriolanus
His nature is too noble for the world. He would not flatter Neptune for his trident.	Menenius
If you have writ your annals true, 'tis there that, like an eagle in a dove-cote, I fluttered your Volscians in Corioles. Alone I did it. 'Boy'!	Coriolanus

I thank you for your voices, thank you, your most sweet voices.	Third citizen
Look, sir, my wounds, I got them in my country's service when some certain of your brethren roar'd and ran from the noise of our own drums.	Coriolanus
My gracious silence, hail!	Coriolanus
O, a kiss long as my exile, sweet as my revenge!	Coriolanus
You common cry of curs! whose breath I hate.	Coriolanus

Précis of plot

Caius Marcius is granted the cognomen of Coriolanus for his fearlessness in the Roman struggle against the neighbouring Volsci, but this brave but tyrannical warrior ultimately rebels and the subsequent intrigues form the basis of the plot.

Setting

Rome circa 5th century BC, Corioli, Antium.

6 Cymbeline, King of Britain

CYMBELINE, King of Britain	Filario's friends:
Princess INNOGEN, his daughter	FRENCHMAN
GUIDERIUS, Cymbeline's son, known as Polydore	DUTCHMAN
ARVIRAGUS, Cymbeline's son, known as Cadwal	SPANIARD
QUEEN, Cymbeline's wife, Innogen's stepmother	GIACOMO, an Italian
Lord CLOTEN, the Queen's son	
BELARIUS, a banished Lord, calling himself Morgan	Caius LUCIUS, ambassador, later General
CORNELIUS, a physician	Two Roman SENATORS
HELEN, a lady attending on Innogen	Roman TRIBUNES
Two LORDS, attending on Cloten	Philharmonus, a SOOTHSAYER
Two GENTLEMEN	JUPITER
Two British CAPTAINS	Ghost of SICILIUS Leonatus, father of Posthumus
Two JAILERS	Ghost of the MOTHER of Posthumus
POSTHUMUS Leonatus, Innogen's husband	Ghosts of the BROTHERS of Posthumus
PISANIO, his servant	Lords attending Cymbeline, ladies attending the
FILARIO, a friend of Posthumus	Queen, musicians, messengers, soldiers

Quotations

	Spoken by
Fear no more the heat o' th' sun, nor the furious winter' rages. Thou thy worldly task hast done, home art gone and ta'en thy wages. Golden lads and girls all must, as chimney-sweepers, come to dust.	Guiderius
Hark, hark! the lark at heaven's gate sings, and Phoebus gins arise.	Musician (sung)
I have not slept one wink.	Pisanio
Prouder than rustling in unpaid-for silk.	Belarius
Slander, whose edge is sharper than the sword, whose tongue outvenoms all the worms of Nile, whose breath rides on the posting winds and doth belie all corners of the world.	Pisanio
The natural bravery of your isle, which stands as Neptune's park, ribbed and paled in, with banks unscalable and roaring waters.	Queen
There will be many Caesars, ere such another Julius. Britain's a world by itself, and we will nothing pay for wearing our own noses.	Cloten
Thersites body is as good as Ajax when neither is alive	Guiderius
The sceptre, learning, physic, must all follow this, and come to dust	Arviragus
Weariness can snore upon the flint, when resty sloth finds the down pillow hard.	Belarius
With fairest flowers whilst summer lasts and I live here Fidele, I'll sweeten thy sad grave; thou shalt not lack the flower that's like thy face, pale primrose, nor the azured harebell, like thy veins, no, nor the leaf of eglantine, whom not to slander, out-sweeten'd not thy breath.	Arviragus

Précis of plot

Cymbeline is a tragicomedy full of intrigues and sub-plots, the most notable concerning the wager between Giacomo and Posthumus regarding the chastity of Posthumus' wife Innogen. The subsequent 'death' and awakening of Innogen are central to the events that happily conclude this fantasy.

Setting

Britain and Rome circa 1st century AD.

NB Cymbeline's daughter's name is given in the folio as Imogen, but this is thought to be a misprint.

7 Hamlet

Prince HAMLET, son of King Hamlet and Queen Gertrude	Courtiers:
GHOST of Hamlet, late King of Denmark	VALTEMAND
KING CLAUDIUS, his brother	CORNELIUS
QUEEN GERTRUDE of Denmark, wife of Claudius	OSRIC
POLONIUS, a Lord	GENTLEMEN
LAERTES, son of Polonius	
OPHELIA, a daughter of Polonius	SAILOR
REYNALDO, servant of Polonius	PRIEST
FORTINBRAS, Prince of Norway	
A CAPTAIN in his army	HORATIO
AMBASSADORS from England	ROSENCRANTZ
PLAYERS, who play the Prologue, King and Queen, and	GUILDENSTERN
Lucianus, in 'The Mousetrap'	Soldiers:
Lords, messengers, attendants, guards, soldiers	FRANCISCO
followers of Laertes, sailors	BARNARDO
Two CLOWNS, gravedigger and his companion	MARCELLUS

Quotations

	Spoken by
A beast, that wants discourse of reason, would have mourned longer.	Hamlet
A certain convocation of political worms are e'en at him.	Hamlet
A countenance more in sorrow than in anger.	Horatio
A king of shreds and patches.	Hamlet
Alas, poor Yorick. I knew him, Horatio – a fellow of infinite jest, of most excellent fancy.	Hamlet
A little more than kin, and less than kind.	Hamlet
A man may fish with the worm that hath eat of a king, and eat of the fish that hath fed of that worm.	Hamlet
A man that fortune's buffets and rewards, hath ta'en with equal thanks.	Hamlet
And then it started like a guilty thing upon a fearful summons.	Horatio
And these few precepts in thy memory keep.	Polonius
And to my mind – though I am native here, and to the manner born, it is a custom more honoured in the breach than the observance.	Hamlet
Angels and ministers of grace defend us.	Hamlet
Assume a virtue, if you have it not.	Hamlet
A was a man. Take him for all in all, I shall not look upon his like again.	Hamlet
Ay, springes to catch woodcocks.	Polonius
Be all my sins remembered.	Hamlet
Beggar that I am, I am even poor in thanks.	Hamlet
Be somewhat scanter of your maiden presence.	Polonius
Be thou as chaste as ice, as pure as snow, thou shalt not escape calumny. Get thee to a nunnery, go, farewell.	Hamlet
Beware of entrance to a quarrel, but being in, bear't that the opposed may be aware of thee.	Polonius
Brevity is the soul of wit.	Polonius
But I am pigeon-liver'd and lack gall to make oppression bitter.	Hamlet
But I have that within which passeth show – these but the trappings and the suits of woe.	Hamlet
But in the gross and scope of my opinion, this bodes some strange eruption to our state.	Horatio
But, look, the morn, in russet mantle clad, walks o'er the dew of yon high eastern hill.	Horatio
But soft! methinks I scent the morning air.	Ghost
But that I am forbid to tell the secrets of my prison-house, I could a tale unfold.	Ghost
Come, give us a taste of your quality.	Hamlet
Cudgel thy brains no more about it.	First Clown
Cut off even in the blossoms of my sin.	Ghost
Do not, as some ungracious pastors do, show me the steep and thorny way to heaven.	Ophelia
Doubt thou the stars are fire; doubt that the sun doth move; doubt truth to be a liar; but never doubt I love.	Polonius
For this relief much thanks; tis bitter cold and I am sick at heart.	Francisco
Frailty thy name is woman.	Hamlet
Give it an understanding but no tongue.	Hamlet
Give me that man that is not passion's slave, and I will wear him in my heart's core, ay, in my heart of heart, as I do thee.	Hamlet
God's bodykins, man, much better. Use every man after his desert, and who should 'scape whipping?	Hamlet
Hath oped his ponderous and marble jaws.	Hamlet
His greatness weighed, his will is not his own.	Laertes
How now, a rat? dead for a ducat, dead.	Hamlet
I am but mad north-north-west; when the wind is southerly, I know a hawk from a handsaw.	Hamlet
I do not set my life at a pin's fee.	Hamlet
I doubt some foul play.	Hamlet

S
H
A
K
E
S
P
E
A
R
E

I have heard of your paintings too, well enough. God hath given you one face, and you make yourselves another.	Hamlet
I have thought some of nature's journeymen had made men and not made them well, they impersonated humanity so abominably.	Hamlet
Imperious Caesar, dead, and turn'd to clay. Might stop a hole to keep the wind away.	Hamlet
I must be cruel only to be kind.	Hamlet
In my mind's eye, Horatio.	Hamlet
In the dead waste and middle of the night.	Horatio
It goes so heavily with my disposition that this goodly frame, the earth, seems to me a sterile promontory.	Hamlet
It is not nor it cannot come to good. But break, my heart, for I must hold my tongue.	Hamlet
It out-Herods Herod.	Hamlet
It was as I have seen it in his life, a sable silver'd.	Horatio
It will discourse most excellent music.	Hamlet
I will speak daggers to her, but use none.	Hamlet
Look with what courteous action, it wafts you to a more removed ground.	Marcellus
Marry, this is miching *malhecho*. That means mischief.	Hamlet
More matter, with less art.	Queen Gertrude
Murder most foul, as in the best it is.	Ghost
Must, like a whore, unpack my heart with words.	Hamlet
My words fly up, my thoughts remain below.	King Claudius
Neither a borrower, nor a lender be.	Polonius
Now cracks a noble heart. Goodnight, sweet prince, and flight of angels sing thee to thy rest.	Horatio
O Hamlet, what a falling off was there!	Ghost
O, my offence is rank! it smells to heaven.	King Claudius
O my prophetic soul! mine uncle?	Hamlet
On fortune's cap we are not the very button.	Guildenstern
O, that this too too solid flesh would melt, thaw and resolve itself into a dew	Hamlet
O villain, villain, smiling, damned villain!	Hamlet
O, what a noble mind is here o'erthrown!	Ophelia
O, what a rogue and peasant slave am I.	Hamlet
Rest, rest, perturbed spirit!	Hamlet
Seems, madam? nay, it is; I know not 'seems'.	Hamlet
So excellent a king, that was, to this, Hyperion to a satyr: so loving to my mother, that he might not beteem the winds of heaven visit her face too roughly.	Hamlet
Some say that ever 'gainst that season comes, wherein our saviour's birth is celebrated, the bird of dawning singeth all night long.	Marcellus
Something is rotten in the state of Denmark.	Marcellus
Speak the speech, I pray you, as I pronounced it to you.	Hamlet
Still harping on my daughter.	Polonius
Suit the action to the word, the word to the action.	Hamlet
Take these again; for to the noble mind, rich gifts wax poor when givers prove unkind.	Ophelia
Tear a passion to tatters, to very rags, to split the ears of the groundlings.	Hamlet
That he is mad, 'tis true; 'tis true 'tis pity and pity 'tis 'tis true.	Polonius
The best actors in the world, either for tragedy, comedy, history pastoral, pastorical-comical, historical-pastoral, tragical-historical, tragical-comical-historical-pastoral, scene individable, or poem unlimited. Seneca cannot be too heavy, nor Plautus too light.	Polonius
The chariest maid is prodigal enough if she unmask her beauty to the moon.	Laertes
The glow-worm shows the matin to be near.	Ghost
The lady doth protest too much, methinks.	Queen Gertrude
The mobled queen.	Hamlet
The play, I remember, pleased not the million; 'twas caviare to the general.	Hamlet
The play's the thing wherein I'll catch the conscience of the King.	Hamlet
There are more things in heaven and earth, Horatio, than are dreamt of in your philosophy.	Hamlet
There is nothing either good or bad, but thinking makes it so.	Hamlet
There's rosemary, that's for remembrance. Pray, love, remember. And there is pansies; that's for thoughts.	Ophelia
The rest is silence. O, O, O, O!	Hamlet
These are but wild and whirling words, my lord.	Horatio
The time is out of joint. O cursed spite, that ever I was born to set it right.	Hamlet
They are the abstract and brief chronicles of the time.	Hamlet
This is the very coinage of your brain.	Queen Gertrude
This sweaty haste doth make the night joint-labourer with the day.	Marcellus
Though this be madness, yet there is method in't.	Polonius
Thou know'st 'tis common; all that lives must die.	Queen Gertrude
Thrift, thrift, Horatio! the funeral baked meats did coldly furnish forth the marriage tables.	Hamlet
'Tis now the very witching time of night, when churchyards yawn and hell itself breathes out contagion to this world.	Hamlet
To be, or not to be; that is the question: whether 'tis nobler in the mind to suffer the slings and arrows of outrageous fortune, or to take arms against a sea of troubles, and,	Hamlet

by opposing, end them. To die, to sleep – no more, and by a sleep to say we end the heartache and the thousand natural shocks that flesh is heir to – 'tis a consummation devoutly to be wished. To die, to sleep. To sleep, perchance to dream. Ay, there's the rub, for in that sleep of death what dreams may come when we have shuffled off this mortal coil must give us pause.

Unhand me, gentlemen; by heaven, I'll make a ghost of him that lets me.	Hamlet
Very like a whale.	Polonius
We do it wrong, being so majestical, to offer it the show of violence.	Marcellus
We know what we are, but know not what we may be.	Ophelia
What, frighted with false fire?	Hamlet
What may this mean, that thou, dead corpse, again in complete steel, revisit'st thus the glimpses of the moon, making night hideous.	Hamlet
What's Hecuba to him or he to Hecuba, that he should weep for her?	Hamlet
What should such fellows as I do, crawling between earth and heaven.	Hamlet
When sorrows come, they come not single spies, but in battalions.	King Claudius
Whether in sea or fire, in earth or air, the extravagant and erring spirit hies to his confine.	Horatio
While memory holds a seat in this distracted globe.	Hamlet
While one with moderate haste might tell a hundred.	Horatio
Whose sore task does not divide the Sunday from the week.	Marcellus
Why, let the stricken deer go weep, the hart ungalled play, for some must watch, while some must sleep, so runs the world away.	Hamlet
Why, she would hang on him, as if increase of appetite had grown by what it fed on.	Hamlet
With devotion's visage and pious action we do sugar o'er the devil himself.	Polonius
With one auspicious and one dropping eye, with mirth in funeral and with dirge in marriage.	King Claudius

Précis of plot
King Hamlet has been murdered by his brother Claudius, who has usurped the throne and married Gertrude, the King's widow. Prince Hamlet gains his revenge by feigning madness and ultimately killing his would-be assassins and Claudius.

Setting
Denmark.

8   Henry IV Part 1

KING HENRY IV	SIR JOHN Oldcastle
PRINCE HARRY, Prince of Wales, Henry's son	Edward (Ned) POINS
Lord JOHN OF LANCASTER, Henry's son	RUSSELL
Earl of WESTMORLAND	HARVEY
Sir Walter BLUNT	Earl of DOUGLAS
Earl of WORCESTER	FRANCIS, a drawer
Percy, Earl of NORTHUMBERLAND, his brother	VINTNER
Henry Percy, known as HOTSPUR, Northumberland's son	GADSHILL
Kate, LADY PERCY, Hotspur's wife	CARRIERS
Lord Edmund MORTIMER, called Earl of March	CHAMBERLAIN
LADY MORTIMER, his wife	OSTLER
OWAIN GLYNDWR, Lady Mortimer's father	TRAVELLERS
Mistress Quickly, HOSTESS of an Eastcheap inn	SHERIFF
Sir Richard VERNON	MESSENGERS
Scrope, ARCHBISHOP of York	SERVANT
SIR MICHAEL, member of the Archbishop's household	Lords and soldiers

Quotations   **Spoken by**

A fellow of no mark nor likelihood.	King Henry
And such a deal of skimble-skamble stuff.	Hotspur
A plague of all cowards, I say.	Sir John
A plague of sighing and grief, it blows a man up like a bladder.	Sir John
Banish plump Jack, and banish all the world.	Sir John
By heaven, methinks it were an easy leap.	Hotspur
Came there a certain lord, neat and trimly dressed, fresh as a bridegroom, and his chin, new reaped, showed like a stubble-land at harvest-home. He was perfumed like a milliner, and 'twixt his finger and his thumb he held a pouncet-box, which ever and anon he gave his nose and took't away again.	Hotspur
Company, villainous company hath been the spoil of me.	Sir John
Domesday is near: die all, die merrily.	Hotspur
Farewell, the latter spring; farewell, All-hallown summer.	Prince Harry
He made me mad, to see him shine so brisk, and smell so sweet, and talk so like a waiting-gentlewoman, of guns and drums and wounds, God save the mark! and telling me the sovereign'st thing on earth was parmacity for an inward bruise.	Hotspur
He was but as the cuckoo is in June, heard, not regarded.	King Henry
I am bewitched by the rogue's company.	Sir John
I am not in the role of common men.	Glyndwr

I am not yet of Percy's mind, the Hotspur of the North – he that kills me some six or seven dozen of Scots at a breakfast, washes his hands, and says to his wife, 'Fie upon this quiet life! I want work.'	Prince Harry
I could brain him with his lady's fan.	Hotspur
If all the year were playing holidays, to sport would be as tedious as to work.	Prince Harry
If reasons were as plentiful as blackberries.	Sir John
In those holy fields, over whose acres walk'd those blessed feet; which fourteen hundred years ago were nailed, for our advantage, on the bitter cross.	King Henry
I saw young Harry, with his beaver on.	Vernon
It would be argument for a week, laughter for a month, and a good jest forever.	Prince Harry
I understand thy kisses, and thou mine.	Mortimer
Let us be Diana's foresters, gentlemen of the shade, minions of the moon.	Sir John
Look down into the pomegranate, Ralph!	Francis
O, the blood more stirs to rouse a lion than to start a hare!	Hotspur
Old father antic, the law.	Sir John
So shaken as we are, so wan with care.	King Henry
O, thou hast damnable iteration, and art indeed able to corrupt a saint.	Sir John
O, monstrous! eleven buckram men grown out of two!	Prince Harry
Tell truth and shame the devil.	Hotspur
There lives not three good men unhanged in England, and one of them is fat and grows old.	Sir John
There's neither honesty, manhood, nor good fellowship in thee.	Sir John
'Tis my vocation, Hal. 'Tis no sin for a man to labour in his vocation.	Sir John
Two stars keep not their motion in one sphere	Prince Harry
What, in thy quips and thy quiddities.	Sir John
You rogue, they were bound every man of them, or I am a jew else, an Hebrew jew.	Sir John

Précis of plot
The main plot tells of the rebellions against King Henry by Worcester, Hotspur and Glyndwr. However, the sub-plots highlighting the characters of the young Prince Hal and the reprobate Sir John Oldcastle (Falstaff) lend the real substance to the play.

Setting
England in the early 15th century.

9 Henry IV Part 2

KING HENRY IV	Ensign PISTOL
PRINCE HARRY, later crowned King Henry V	PETO
PRINCE JOHN of Lancaster, Henry IV's son	DOLL TEARSHEET, a whore
SIR JOHN Falstaff	GOWER, a messenger
Bardolf	Sir John Blunt
Poins	Sir John Coleville
Falstaff's Page	Lord Hastings
Humphrey, Duke of GLOUCESTER, Henry IV's son	SNARE, a sergeant
Thomas, Duke of CLARENCE, Henry IV's son	FANG, a sergeant
Percy, Earl of NORTHUMBERLAND, of the rebels' party	Neville, Earl of WARWICK
NORTHUMBERLAND'S WIFE	Earl of SURREY
KATE, their son Hotspur's widow	Earl of WESTMORLAND
TRAVERS, Northumberland's servant	HARCOURT
MORTON, a bearer of news from Shrewsbury	Ralph MOULDY
Scrope, ARCHBISHOP of York	Simon SHADOW
Thomas, Lord MOWBRAY, the Earl Marshal	Thomas WART
MISTRESS QUICKLY, hostess of a tavern	Francis FEEBLE
PORTER of Northumberland's household	Peter BULLCALF
Robert SHALLOW, a country justice	DRAWERS
DAVY, Shallow's servant	BEADLES
SILENCE, a country justice	GROOMS
Sneak and other musicians	MESSENGER
Lord Chief Justice's men, soldiers and attendants	

Quotations

	Spoken by
A foutre for the world and worldlings base! I speak of Africa and golden joys.	Pistol
A joint of mutton, and any pretty little tiny kickshaws.	Shallow
A man can die but once.	Feeble
A rascally yea-forsooth knave.	Sir John
An habitation giddy and unsure, hath he that buildeth on the vulgar heart.	Archbishop of York
Away, you scullion, you rampallian, you fustilarian! I'll tickle your catastrophe.	Page
By my troth, captain, these are very bitter words.	Mistress Quickly
Death, as the psalmist saith, is certain to all; all shall die. How a good yoke of bullocks at Stamford fair?	Shallow
Even such a man, so faint, so spiritless, so dull, so dead in look, so woe-begone, drew Priam's curtain in the dead of night.	Northumberland
For my voice, I have lost it with hallowing and singing of anthems.	Sir John

He hath eaten me out of house and home.	Mistress Quickly
He was indeed the glass wherein the noble youth did dress themselves.	Lady Percy
I am not only witty in myself, but the cause that wit is in other men.	Sir John
I beseek you now, aggravate your choler.	Mistress Quickly
I can get no remedy against this consumption of the purse. Borrowing only lingers and lingers it out, but the disease is incurable.	Sir John
If I do, fillip me with a three-man beetle.	Sir John
Is it not strange that desire should so many years outlive performance.	Poins
I know thee not old man, fall to thy prayers.	King Harry
It was always yet the trick of our English nation, if they have a good thing, to make it too common.	Sir John
Let the end try the man.	Prince Harry
Lord, Lord, how subject we old men are to this vice of lying.	Sir John
O, sleep, O gentle sleep, nature's soft nurse, how have I frighted thee, that thou no more wilt weigh my eyelids down, and steep my senses in forgetfulness.	King Henry
Past and to come seems best; things present, worst.	Archbishop of York
Thou didst swear to me, upon a parcel-gilt goblet, sitting in my Dolphin-chamber, at the round table, by a sea coal fire, upon Wednesday in Wheeson week.	Mistress Quickly
Under which king, Besonian? speak, or die.	Pistol
Uneasy lies the head that wears a crown.	King Henry
We have heard the chimes at midnight, Master Shallow.	Sir John
We that are in the vanguard of our youth, I must confess, are wags too.	Sir John
Wilt thou upon the high and giddy mast, seal up the ship-boy's eyes, and rock his brains.	King Henry
With all appliances, and means to boot.	King Henry
Yet the first bringer of unwelcome news hath but a losing office, and his tongue sounds ever after as a sullen bell remembered knolling a departing friend.	Northumberland

Précis of plot
The plot of the first part of Henry IV is continued, although there are subtle changes made to certain characters and the historical content is not so highlighted. Hal is still plagued with rebellions, albeit from different spheres, but his anxieties over Prince Harry's behaviour are eventually alleviated in a touching scene, and this change of character is shown to the full in Harry's rejection of Sir John after his crowning.

Setting
England in the early 15th century.

10 Henry V

KING HARRY V of England, claimant to French throne	Sir Thomas ERPINGHAM
Duke of GLOUCESTER, the King's brother	John BATES
Duke of CLARENCE, the King's brother	Alexander COURT
Duke of EXETER, his uncle	Michael WILLIAMS
KING CHARLES VI of France	HERALD
ISABEL, his wife and queen	Duke of YORK
The DAUPHIN, their son and heir	SALISBURY
CATHERINE, their daughter	WESTMORLAND
Archbishop of CANTERBURY	WARWICK
ALICE, an old gentlewoman	Bishop of ELY
Richard, Earl of CAMBRIDGE	Sir Thomas GREY
Henry, Lord SCROPE of Masham	Duke of BOURBON
The CONSTABLE of France	Duke of ORLÉANS
MONTJOY, the French Herald	Duke of BERRI
GOVERNOR of Harfleur	Lord RAMBURES
French AMBASSADORS to England	Lord GRANDPRÉ
BOY, formerly Falstaff's page	Duke of BURGUNDY
HOSTESS, formerly Mistress Quickly, now Pistol's wife	PISTOL
Captain GOWER, an Englishman	NIM
Captain FLUELLEN, a Welshman	BARDOLPH
Captain MACMORRIS, an Irishman	CHORUS
Captain JAMY, a Scot	

Quotations

	Spoken by
All hell shall stir for this.	Pistol
And gentlemen in England now abed, shall think themselves accursed they were not here, and hold their manhoods cheap while any speaks, that fought with us upon Saint Crispin's day.	King Harry
And make your chronicle as rich with praise, as is the ooze and bottom of the sea.	Canterbury
As 'tis ever common that men are merriest when they are from home.	King Harry
Base is the slave that pays.	Pistol
But if it be a sin to covet honour, I am the most offending soul alive.	King Harry
Can this cock-pit hold the vasty fields of France? or may we cram, within this wooden O the very casques that did affright the air at Agincourt?	Chorus
Consideration like an angel came, and whipp'd the offending Adam out of him.	Canterbury
Cry, 'God for Harry! England and Saint George.'	King Harry

Every subject's duty is the king's; but every subject's soul is his own.	King Harry
For so work the honey-bees, creatures that by a rule in nature teach the act of order to a peopled kingdom.	Canterbury
For these fellows of infinite tongue, that can rhyme themselves into ladies' favours, they do always reason themselves out again.	King Harry
From camp to camp through the foul womb of night.	Chorus
He's in Arthur's bosom, if ever man went to Arthur's bosom.	Hostess
I dare not fight, but I will wink and hold out mine iron.	Nim
I see you stand like greyhounds in the slips.	King Harry
If he be not fellow with the best king, thou shalt find the best king of good fellows.	King Harry
If we are marked to die, we are enough to do our country loss; and if to live, the fewer men, the greater share of honour.	King Harry
I thought upon one pair of English legs did march three Frenchmen.	King Harry
Men of few words are the best men.	Boy
Now all the youth of England are on fire, and silken dalliance in the wardrobe lies.	Chorus
O that we now had here, but one ten thousand of those men in England that do no work today!	Warwick
Old men forget, yet all shall be forgot; but he'll remember with advantages, what feats he did that day.	King Harry
Once more unto the breach, dear friends, once more.	King Harry
On, on, you noblest English, whose blood is fet from fathers of war-proof. Fathers that, like so many Alexanders, have in these parts from morn til even fought, and sheathed their swords for lack of argument.	King Harry
Self love, my liege, is not so vile a sin as self neglecting.	Dauphin
Tennis balls, my liege.	Exeter
Then shall our names, familiar in his mouth as household words – Harry the King, Bedford and Exeter, Warwick and Talbot, Salisbury and Gloucester – be in their flowing cups, freshly remember'd.	King Harry
There is occasions and causes why and wherefore in all things.	Fluellen
There is some soul of goodness in these evils.	King Harry
This day is called the feast of Crispian. He that outlives this day and comes safe home will stand a-tiptoe when this day is named, and rouse him of the name of Crispian.	King Harry
Though patience be a tired mare, yet she will plod.	Nim
Trust none, for oaths are straws, men's faiths are wafer-cakes, and hold-fast is the only dog, my duck.	Pistol
Turn him to any cause of policy, the Gordian knot of it he will unloose.	Canterbury
We few, we happy few, we band of brothers.	King Harry

Précis of plot
The war against France dominates the play, although Shakespeare stayed loyal to many characters from the two parts of Henry IV to create comic diversion.

Setting
England and France 1414 to 1420.

11 Henry VI Part 1

KING HENRY VI	BASSET
Duke of GLOUCESTER, Lord Protector, uncle of Henry	A LAWYER
Duke of BEDFORD, regent of France	A LEGATE
Duke of EXETER	Earl of WARWICK
Bishop of WINCHESTER (later Cardinal), uncle of Henry	Earl of SALISBURY
Duke of SOMERSET	Earl of SUFFOLK
RICHARD PLANTAGENET, later DUKE OF YORK	Edmund MORTIMER
Duke of BURGUNDY, uncle of King Henry	Duke of ALENÇON
GENERAL of the French garrison at Bordeaux	BASTARD of Orléans
RENÉ, Duke of Anjou, King of Naples	Lord TALBOT
MARGARET, his daughter	JOHN Talbot
Sir William GLASDALE	COUNTESS of Auvergne
Sir Thomas GARGRAVE	MASTER GUNNER of Orléans
Sir John FASTOLF	A BOY, his son
Sir William LUCY	JOAN la Pucelle
CHARLES, Dauphin of France	A SHEPHERD, father of Joan
WOODVILLE, Lieutenant of the Tower of London	MAYOR of London
Porter, French sergeant, sentinels, scout, herald, officers	VERNON
Governor of Paris, fiends and soldiers, servingmen	
Messengers and keepers of the Tower of London	

Quotations

	Spoken by
And while I live, I'll ne'er fly from a man.	Joan
Between two hawks, which flies the higher pitch.	Warwick
Between two dogs, which hath the deeper mouth.	
Between two blades, which bears the better temper.	
Between two horses, which doth bear him best.	

Between two girls, which hath the merriest eye.
I have perhaps some shallow spirit of judgement.   Joan
Christ's mother helps me, else I were too weak.   Bedford
Unbidden guests are often welcomest when they are gone.

Précis of plot
The first part of Henry VI covers the period between the funeral of Henry V and the end of the Hundred Years
War, between England and France. As in many of the Shakespearian plays, the historical accuracy comes
second to the plot.

Setting
England 1422 to 1453.

12 Henry VI Part 2

KING HENRY VI and QUEEN MARGARET	Gloucester's SERVANTS
William de la Pole, Marquis, later Duke of SUFFOLK	Two SHERIFFS of London
Duke Humphrey of GLOUCESTER, the Lord Protector	Sir John STANLEY
Dame Eleanor Cobham, the DUCHESS of Gloucester	HERALD
CARDINAL BEAUFORT, Bishop of Winchester	Two MURDERERS
Duke of BUCKINGHAM	COMMONS
Duke of SOMERSET	CAPTAIN of a ship
Old Lord CLIFFORD and YOUNG CLIFFORD, his son	MASTER of that ship
Duke of YORK	The Master's MATE
EDWARD, Earl of March, the Duke's son	Walter WHITMORE
Crookback RICHARD, the Duke's son	Two GENTLEMEN
Earl of SALISBURY and Earl of WARWICK, his son	Jack CADE, a Kentishman
Emmanuel, the CLERK of Chatham	Dick the BUTCHER
Two or three PETITIONERS	Smith the WEAVER
Thomas HORNER, an armourer	A sawyer
PETER Thump, his man	JOHN
Three NEIGHBOURS, who drink to Horner	REBELS
Three PRENTICES, who drink to Peter	Sir Humphrey STAFFORD
Sir John HUME, a priest	STAFFORD'S BROTHER
John SOUTHWELL, a priest	Lord SAYE
Margery Jordan, a WITCH	Lord SCALES
Roger BOLINGBROKE, a conjurer	Matthew Gough
ASNATH, a spirit	A SERGEANT
Three or four CITIZENS of London	A BEADLE of Saint Albans
Simon SIMPCOX and SIMPCOX'S WIFE	Townsmen of Saint Albans
The MAYOR of Saint Albans	VAUX, a messenger
Alexander IDEN, who kills Cade	A POST
Aldermen of Saint Albans	MESSENGERS
Attendants, guards, servants, soldiers, falconers	A SOLDIER

Quotations

	Spoken by
Could I come near your beauty with my nails, I'd set my ten commandments in your face.	Duchess
Is not this a lamentable thing that of the skin of an innocent lamb should be made parchment? that parchment being scribbled o'er should undo a man?	Cade
Sir, he made a chimney in my father's house, and the bricks are alive at this day to testify.	Weaver
Smooth runs the water where the brook is deep.	Suffolk
The first thing we do let's kill all the lawyers.	Dick the Butcher
The gaudy, blabbing, and remorseful day, is crept into the bosom of the sea.	Captain
There shall be in England seven halfpenny loaves sold for a penny, the three-hooped pot shall have ten hoops and I will make it a felony to drink small beer.	Cade
Thou hast most traitorously corrupted the youth of the realm in erecting a grammar school; and, whereas before, our forefathers had no books but the score and tally, thou hast caused printing to be used and, contrary to the King, his crown and dignity, thou hast built a paper mill.	Cade
What stronger breastplate than a heart untainted.	King Henry

Précis of plot
The original title of this play was *The First Part of the Contention of the Two Famous Houses of York and
Lancaster*, and Shakespeare has stayed true, to a great extent, to this period of history, which includes the
Kentish rebellion led by Jack Cade, and ultimately leads to the Wars of the Roses.

Setting
England 1445 to 1455.

SHAKESPEARE

13 Henry VI Part 3

KING HENRY VI
QUEEN MARGARET
PRINCE EDWARD, their son
Duke of SOMERSET
Duke of EXETER
Earl of NORTHUMBERLAND
Earl of WESTMORLAND
Lord CLIFFORD
Lord Stafford
SOMERVILLE
Henry, young Earl of Richmond
A SOLDIER who has killed his father
A HUNTSMAN who guards King Edward
The divided House of Neville:
Earl of WARWICK
Marquis of MONTAGUE, his brother
Earl of OXFORD, their brother-in-law
Lord HASTINGS, their brother-in-law
Of the Duke of York's party:
Richard Plantagenet, Duke of YORK
EDWARD, Earl of March, his son, later KING EDWARD IV
LADY GRAY, a widow, later Edward's wife and queen
Earl RIVERS, Lady Gray's brother

GEORGE, later DUKE OF CLARENCE
RICHARD, later DUKE OF GLOUCESTER
Earl of RUTLAND, Edward's brother
Rutland's TUTOR, a chaplain
SIR JOHN Mortimer, York's uncle
Sir Hugh Mortimer, his brother
Duke of NORFOLK
Sir William Stanley
Earl of Pembroke
Sir John MONTGOMERY
A NOBLEMAN
Two GAMEKEEPERS
Three WATCHMEN
LIEUTENANT of the Tower

The French:
KING LOUIS
LADY BONA, his sister-in-law
Lord Bourbon, the French High Admiral

A SOLDIER who has killed his son
Mayor of Coventry
MAYOR of York
Aldermen of YORK
Soldiers, messengers and attendants

Quotations

	Spoken by
Didst thou never hear that things ill got had ever bad success?	King Henry
Down, down to hell, and say I sent thee thither.	Richard of Gloucester
Gives not the hawthorn bush a sweeter shade, to shepherds looking on their seely sheep, than doth a rich embroider'd canopy, to Kings that fear their subjects' treachery?	King Henry
My crown is in my heart, not on my head.	King Henry
O God! methinks it were a happy life, to be no better than a homely swain, to sit upon a hill, as I do now; to carve out dials quaintly, point by point, thereby to see the minutes how they run. How many makes the hour full complete, how many hours bring about the day, how many days will finish up the year, how many years a mortal man may live.	King Henry
Oh tiger's heart wrapp'd in a woman's hide!	York
Suspicion always haunts the guilty mind, the thief doth fear each bush an officer.	Richard of Gloucester

Précis of plot

This play chronicles the substantive episodes in the War of the Roses, although the usual Shakespearian anachronisms do not detract from the play's subtleties.

Setting

England 1455 to 1471.

14 Henry VIII (All Is True)

PROLOGUE
KING HENRY VIII
Duke of BUCKINGHAM
Lord ABERGAVENNY
Earl of SURREY
Duke of NORFOLK
Duke of SUFFOLK
LORD CHAMBERLAIN
LORD CHANCELLOR
Lord SANDS (aka Sir William Sands)
Sir Thomas LOVELL
Sir Anthony DENNY
Sir Henry GUILDFORD
CARDINAL WOLSEY
Two SECRETARIES
Buckingham's SURVEYOR
CARDINAL CAMPEIUS
GARDINER, King's secretary, later Bishop of Winchester
His PAGE
Thomas CROMWELL
CRANMER, Archbishop of Canterbury
QUEEN KATHERINE, later KATHERINE, Princess Dowager
GRIFFITH, her gentleman usher
PATIENCE, her waiting woman

Archbishop of Canterbury
Bishop of LINCOLN
Bishop of Ely
Bishop of Rochester
Bishop of Saint Asaph
Two priests
Serjeant-at-arms
Two noblemen
A CRIER
Appearing in the Coronation:
Three GENTLEMEN
Two judges
Choristers
Lord Mayor of London
Garter King of Arms
Marquis of Dorset
Four Barons of the Cinque Ports
Stokesley, Bishop of London
Old Duchess of Norfolk
Countesses

A MESSENGER
Lord CAPUTIUS
ANNE Boleyn

Other WOMEN
Six spirits who dance before Katherine in a vision
At Cranmer's trial:
A DOOR-KEEPER
Doctor BUTTS, the King's physician
Pursuivants, pages, footboys, grooms
BRANDON
SERJEANT-AT-ARMS
Sir Nicholas VAUX
Tipstaves, Halberdiers and common people
Appearing at the Legatine Court:
Two vergers
Ladies, gentlemen, a SERVANT, attendants

An OLD LADY
At the Christening:
A PORTER
His MAN
Two aldermen
Lord Mayor of London
GARTER King of Arms
Six noblemen
Old Duchess of Norfolk, godmother
Princess Elizabeth, the child
Marchioness Dorset, godmother

EPILOGUE
Two SCRIBES

Quotations

	Spoken by
A peace above all earthly dignities, a still and quiet conscience.	Cardinal Wolsey
Cromwell, I charge thee, fling away ambition. By that sin fell the angels.	Cardinal Wolsey
Had I but serv'd my God with half the zeal I served my King, he would not in mine age have left me naked to mine enemies.	Cardinal Wolsey
Heaven is above all yet – there sits a judge that no king can corrupt.	Queen Katherine
He gave his honours to the world again, his blessed part to heaven, and slept in peace.	Griffith
He was a man of an unbounded stomach.	Katherine
Love thyself last. Cherish those hearts that hate thee.	Cardinal Wolsey
He was a scholar, and a ripe and good one.	Griffith
Men's evil manners live in brass; their virtues we write in water	Griffith
So farewell – to the little good you bear me. Farewell, a long farewell, to all my greatness!	Cardinal Wolsey
So may he rest, his faults lie gently on him.	Katherine
Those twins of learning that he raised in you, Ipswich and Oxford.	Griffith
'Tis better to be lowly born, and range with humble livers in content, than to be perk'd up in a glistering grief and wear a golden sorrow.	Anne
Vain pomp and glory of this world, I hate ye!	Cardinal Wolsey

Précis of plot
The reign of Henry VIII from the opening description of the Field of the Cloth of Gold, of 1520, to the christening of Princess Elizabeth, in 1533.

Setting
England 1521 to 1533.

15 Julius Caesar
Julius CAESAR
CALPURNIA, his wife
Marcus BRUTUS, a noble Roman, opposed to Caesar
PORTIA, his wife
LUCIUS, his servant
Officers and soldiers in Brutus' army:
LUCILLIUS
MESSALA
VARRUS
CLAUDIO
YOUNG CATO
STRATO
VOLUMNIUS
FLAVIUS
DARDANIUS
CLITUS
Rulers of Rome after Caesar's death:
Mark ANTONY
OCTAVIUS Caesar
LEPIDUS

PINDARUS, Cassius' bondman
TITINIUS, an officer in Cassius' army
POPILLIUS Laena, a Senator
Senators, soldiers and attendants

ARTEMIDORUS
CINNA the Poet
Opposed to Caesar:
Caius CASSIUS
CASCA
TREBONIUS
DECIUS Brutus
METELLUS Cimber
CINNA
Caius LIGARIUS

FLAVIUS, a tribune
MURELLUS, a tribune
CICERO, a Senator
PUBLIUS, a Senator

A POET
GHOST of Caesar
A COBBLER
A CARPENTER
Other PLEBEIANS
A MESSENGER
SERVANTS
SOOTHSAYER

Quotations

	Spoken by
As Caesar loved me, I weep for him.	Brutus
As proper men as ever trod upon neat's leather have gone upon my handiwork.	Cobbler

Between the acting of a dreadful thing and the first motion, all the interim is like a phantasma, or a hideous dream.	Brutus
Beware the ides of March.	Soothsayer
But for your words, they rob the Hybla bees, and leave them honeyless.	Cassius
But I am constant as the Northern Star, of whose true fixed and resting quality, there is no fellow in the firmament.	Caesar
But when I tell him he hates flatterers; he says he does being then most flattered.	Decius
But yesterday the word of Caesar might have stood against the world. Now lies he there, and none so poor to do him reverence.	Antony
Caesar said to me 'Darest thou, Cassius, now leap in with me into this angry flood, and swim to yonder point?' Upon the word, accoutred as I was I plunged in and bade him follow.	Cassius
Cowards die many times before their deaths; the valiant never taste of death but once.	Caesar
Cry 'havoc' and let slip the dogs of war.	Antony
Et tu, Brute? – then fall Caesar.	Caesar (last words)
Fierce fiery warriors fight upon the clouds, in ranks and squadrons and right form of war.	Calpurnia
For Brutus is an honourable man; so are they all, all honourable men.	Antony
For he will never follow anything that other men begin.	Brutus
For I have neither wit, nor words, nor worth, action nor utterance, nor the power of speech, to stir men's blood.	Antony
Friends, Romans, countrymen, lend me your ears.	Antony
He reads much, he is a great observer, and he looks quite through the deeds of men.	Caesar
His life was gentle, and the elements so mixed in him that nature might stand up and say to all the world, 'This was a man'.	Antony
How hard it is for women to keep counsel!	Portia
How many ages hence, shall this our lofty scene be acted over, in states unborn and accents yet unknown.	Cassius
I am no orator as Brutus is; but as you know me all, a plain blunt man.	Antony
I am not gamesome; I do lack some part of that quick spirit that is in Antony.	Brutus
If you have tears, prepare to shed them now.	Antony
I had rather be a dog and bay the moon than such a Roman.	Brutus
Let me have men about me who are fat.	Caesar
Let's carve him as a dish fit for the gods.	Brutus
Lowliness is young ambition's ladder, whereto the climber upward turns his face; but when he once attains the upmost round, he then unto the ladder turns his back, looks in the clouds, scorning the base degrees by which he did ascend.	Brutus
Now in the name of all the gods at once, upon what meat doth this our Caesar feed, that he is grown so great?	Cassius
O judgement, thou art fled to brutish beasts, and men have lost their reasons!	Antony
O pardon me, thou bleeding piece of earth, that I am meek and gentle with these butchers!	Antony
See what a rent the envious Casca made.	Antony
Set honour in one eye and death i'th'other, and I will look on both indifferently.	Brutus
There is a tide in the affairs of men, which, taken at the flood, leads on to fortune.	Brutus
There was a Brutus once that would have brooked the eternal devil to keep his state in Rome, as easily as a king.	Cassius
This was the most unkindest cut of all.	Antony
This was the noblest Roman of them all.	Antony
Well, honour is the subject of my story. I cannot tell what you and other men think of this life; but, for my single self, I had as lief not be, as live to be in awe of such a thing as I myself.	Cassius
When beggars die, there are no comets seen; the heavens themselves blaze forth the death of princes.	Calpurnia
When love begins to sicken and decay, it useth an enforced ceremony.	Brutus
Why, he that cuts off twenty years of life, cuts off so many years of fearing death.	Casca
Why, man, he doth bestride the narrow world like a Colossus.	Cassius
Yet Brutus says he was ambitious, and Brutus is an honourable man.	Antony
Yond Cassius has a lean and hungry look. He thinks too much. Such men are dangerous.	Caesar
You are my true and honourable wife, as dear to me as are the ruddy drops that visit my sad heart.	Brutus
You blocks, you stones, you worse than senseless things!	Murellus

Précis of plot

The play depicts the events that led to the assassination of Julius Caesar and the aftermath thereof. As in many Shakespearian History plays, facts are often altered and rearranged in the interests of dramatic economy and effectiveness.

Setting

Rome, Sardis and near Philippi 44 to 42 BC.

16 King John

KING JOHN of England
QUEEN ELEANOR, his mother
LADY FALCONBRIDGE
Philip the BASTARD, later knighted as Richard Plantagenet,
her illegitimate son by King Richard I
Robert FALCONBRIDGE, her legitimate son
James GURNEY, her attendant
Lady BLANCHE of Spain, niece of King John
PRINCE HENRY, son of King John
HUBERT, a follower of King John
KING PHILIP of France
LOUIS THE DAUPHIN, his son
ARTHUR, Duke of Brittaine, nephew of King John
Lady CONSTANCE, his mother
Duke of AUSTRIA (Limoges)
CHÂTILLON, ambassador
Cardinal PANDOLF, a legate from the Pope
PETER OF POMFRET, a prophet
Lords, soldiers, attendants

Earl of SALISBURY
Earl of PEMBROKE
Earl of ESSEX
Lord BIGOT
A CITIZEN of Angers
HERALDS
EXECUTIONERS
MESSENGERS
SHERIFF

Quotations	Spoken by
And oftentimes excusing of a fault doth make the fault the worser by th' excuse.	Pembroke
Another lean unwashed artificer cuts off his tale, and talks of Arthur's death.	Hubert
For courage mounteth with occasion.	Duke of Austria
Heat me these irons hot.	Hubert
Here is my throne; bid kings come bow to it.	Constance
How oft the sight of means to do ill deeds, make deeds ill done!	King John
Life is as tedious as a twice-told tale, vexing the dull ear of a drowsy man.	Louis the Dauphin
Lord of thy presence, and no land beside?	Queen Eleanor
Saint George that swinged the dragon, and e'er since sits on his horseback at mine hostess' door.	Bastard
This England never did, nor never shall, lie at the proud foot of a conqueror.	Bastard
To gild refined gold, to paint the lily.	Salisbury
When Fortune means to men most good, she looks upon them with a threatening eye.	Pandolf
Zounds! I never was so bethumped with words, since first I called my brother's father, dad.	Bastard

Précis of plot

Selected events from King John's reign are portrayed, although Shakespeare concentrates on Philip Falconbridge, the illegitimate son of Richard I, for his sub-plot; and significant events such as Magna Carta are ignored.

Setting

England and France 1199 to 1216.

17 King Lear

LEAR, King of Britain
GONERIL, Lear's eldest daughter
Duke of ALBANY, her husband
REGAN, Lear's second daughter
Duke of CORNWALL, her husband
CORDELIA, Lear's youngest daughter
King of FRANCE, a suitor of Cordelia
Duke of BURGUNDY, a suitor of Cordelia
Earl of KENT, later disguised as Caius
Earl of GLOUCESTER

EDGAR, later disguised as Tom o' Bedlam
EDMOND, bastard son of Gloucester
OLD MAN, Gloucester's tenant
Lear's FOOL
OSWALD, Goneril's steward
A SERVANT of Cornwall
A KNIGHT
A HERALD
A CAPTAIN
Gentlemen, servants, soldiers, attendants

Quotations	Spoken by
And my fool is hanged. No, No, no life? Why should a dog, a horse, a rat have life and thou no breath at all?	Lear
As flies to wanton boys are we to the gods, they kill us for their sport	Gloucester
A still soliciting eye, and such a tongue.	Cordelia
Blow, winds, and crack your cheeks! rage, blow, you cataracts and hurricanoes, spout.	Lear
Drinks the green mantle of the standing pool.	Edgar
Fie, foe, and fum; I smell the blood of a British man.	Edgar
Fortune, good night; smile once more; turn thy wheel.	Kent
Howl, howl, howl, howl! O, you are men of stones.	Lear
How sharper than a serpent's tooth it is to have a thankless child.	Lear
I am a man more sinned against than sinning.	Lear
I have seen better faces in my time than stands on any shoulder that I see before me at this instant.	Kent

SHAKESPEARE

I have seen the day, with my good biting falchion.	Lear
I'll talk a word with this same learned Theban.	Lear
Ingratitude, thou marble-hearted fiend.	Lear
I tax you not, you elements, with unkindness.	Lear
Mastiff, greyhound, mongrel grim.	Edgar
My cue is villainous melancholy, with a sigh like Tom o' Bedlam.	Edmond
O, that way madness lies. Let me shun that.	Lear
Out-paramoured the Turk.	Edgar
Poor naked wretches, whereso'er you are.	Lear
Poor Tom's a-cold.	Edgar
So young and so untender?	Lear
Take physic, pomp, expose thyself to feel what wretches feel.	Lear
The gods are just, and of our pleasant vices, make instruments to plague us.	Edgar
The little dogs and all, Tray, Blanch, and sweetheart see, they bark at me.	Lear
The prince of darkness is a gentleman.	Edgar
These late eclipses in the sun and moon portend no good to us.	Gloucester
The wheel has come full circle.	Edmond
The worst is not so long as we can say 'This is the worst'.	Edgar
Things that love night, love not such nights as these.	Kent
This is the excellent foppery of the world; that when we are sick in fortune – often the surfeits of our own behaviour – we make guilty of our disasters the sun, the moon, and stars, as if we were villains by necessity, fools by heavenly compulsion, knaves, thieves, and treachers by spherical predominance, drunkards, liars, and adulterers by an enforced obedience of planetary influence; and all that we are evil in by a divine thrusting on.	Edmond
This is the foul fiend Flibbertigibbet; he begins at curfew, and walks 'til the first cock.	Edgar
Thou whoreson Z, thou unnecessary letter.	Kent
'Tis a naughty night to swim in.	Fool
Vex not his ghost, O let him pass.	Kent
You are not worth the dust which the rude wind blows in your face.	Albany

Précis of plot
The story of a king who, angry with the failure of his virtuous youngest daughter, Cordelia, to compete for his favour in a love-test, divides his kingdom between her two malevolent sisters. The sub-plot depicts Lear's madness and the blinding of Gloucester, as well as Edgar's loyalty to his father.

Setting
Britain.

18 Love's Labour's Lost

Ferdinand, KING of Navarre
Lords attending on the King:
BIRON
LONGUEVILLE
DUMAINE

PRINCESS of France
Ladies attending on the Princess:
ROSALINE
KATHERINE
MARIA

BOYET
Two other LORDS
COSTARD, a Clown
JAQUENETTA, a country wench
Sir NATHANIEL, a curate
HOLOFERNES, a schoolmaster
Anthony DULL, a constable
MERCADÉ, a messenger
A FORESTER
Don Adriano de ARMADO, a Spanish
braggart
MOTE, his page

Quotations

	Spoken by
A jest's prosperity lies in the ear of him that hears it, never in the tongue of him that makes it.	Rosaline
A lover's eyes will gaze an eagle blind; a lover's ear will hear the lowest sound.	Biron
At Christmas I no more desire a rose, than wish a snow in May's new-fangled mirth.	Biron
A very beadle to a humorous sigh.	Biron
Devise wit, write pen, for I am for whole volumes, in folio.	Armado
He draweth out the thread of his verbosity finer than the staple of his argument.	Holofernes
He hath never fed of the dainties that are bred in a book.	Nathaniel
In the posteriors of this day, which the rude multitude call the afternoon.	Armado
Light, seeking light, doth light of light beguile.	Biron
Remuneration – O, that's the Latin word for three-farthings.	Costard
Spite of cormorant devouring time.	King
Study is like the heavens' glorious sun, that will not be deep-searched with saucy looks. Small have continual plodders ever won, save base authority from others' books.	Biron
This wimpled, whining, purblind, wayward boy.	Biron
Why, all delights are vain; but that most vain, which with pain purchased, doth inherit pain.	Biron

Précis of plot
The young King of Navarre, and three of his friends, vow to devote the following three years to austere self-improvement, forgoing the company of women. The ensuing farce is both sophisticated and cleverly staged.

Setting
Navarre circa 14th century.

19 Macbeth

KING DUNCAN of Scotland	Scottish Thanes:
MALCOLM, King Duncan's son	LENNOX
DONALBAIN, King Duncan's son	ROSS
A CAPTAIN in Duncan's army	ANGUS
MACBETH, Thane of Glamis, later Thane Cawdor,	CAITHNESS
then King of Scotland	MENTEITH
LADY MACBETH, Macbeth's wife	
A DOCTOR, attending on Lady Macbeth	Six WITCHES
A Waiting-GENTLEWOMAN, attending on Lady Macbeth	An English DOCTOR
BANQUO, a Scottish Thane	A SPIRIT LIKE A CAT
FLEANCE, his son	Three APPARITIONS:
MACDUFF, Thane of Fife	an armed head
LADY MACDUFF, his wife	a bloody child
MACDUFF'S SON	a child crowned
SIWARD, Earl of Northumberland	Other SPIRITS
YOUNG SIWARD, his son	An OLD MAN
HECATE, Queen of the Witches	A MESSENGER
A PORTER at Macbeth's castle	MURDERERS
Three MURDERERS attending on Macbeth	SERVANTS
SEYTON, servant of Macbeth	soldiers, drummers
A show of eight kings, Lords and Thanes	

Quotations

Quotation	Spoken by
All the perfumes of Arabia will not sweeten this little hand.	Lady Macbeth
Angels are bright still, though the brightest fell.	Malcolm
Be innocent of the knowledge, dearest chuck.	Macbeth
Blow wind, come wrack, at least we'll die with harness on our back.	Macbeth
But screw your courage to the sticking-place, and we'll not fail.	Lady Macbeth
By the pricking of my thumbs, something wicked this way comes.	Second Witch
Canst thou not minister to a mind diseased.	Macbeth
Come what, come may, time and the hour runs through the toughest day.	Macbeth
Consider it not so deeply.	Lady Macbeth
Double, double, toil and trouble, fire burn, and cauldron bubble.	Three Witches
Hang out our banners on the outward walls.	Macbeth
How now, you secret, black, and midnight hags.	Macbeth
I am in blood stepped in so far that, should I wade no more, returning were as tedious as go o'er.	Macbeth
I dare do all that may become a man; who dares do more is none.	Macbeth
If you can look into the seeds of time, and say which grain will grow and which will not.	Banquo
I 'gin to be aweary of the sun.	Macbeth
I had most need of blessing, and Amen stuck in my throat.	Macbeth
I must become a borrower of the night, for a dark hour or twain.	Banquo
Infirm of purpose! give me the daggers.	Lady Macbeth
Is this a dagger which I see before me? the handle towards my hand? come let me clutch thee.	Macbeth
It was the owl that shrieked, the fatal bellman.	Lady Macbeth
I would applaud thee to the very echo.	Macbeth
Look like the innocent flower, but be the serpent under't.	Lady Macbeth
Might be the be-all and the end-all here.	Macbeth
Now good digestion wait on appetite, and health on both.	Macbeth
O, I could play the woman with mine eyes, and braggart with my tongue!	Macduff
Or have we eaten on the insane root, that takes the reason prisoner.	Banquo
Out, damned spot; out, I say.	Lady Macbeth
Shake off this downy sleep, death's counterfeit, and look on death itself!	Macduff
Sleep shall neither night nor day, hang upon his pent-house lid.	First Witch
Stands not within the prospect of belief.	Macbeth
That no compunctious visitings of nature shake my fell purpose.	Lady Macbeth
That which hath made them drunk hath made me bold.	Lady Macbeth
The attempt and not the deed confounds us.	Lady Macbeth
The earth hath bubbles, as the water has, and these are of them.	Banquo
The labour we delight in physics pain.	Macbeth
There's husbandry in heaven, their candles are all out.	Banquo
The Thane of Cawdor lives; why do you dress me in borrow'd robes.	

S
H
A
K
E
S
P
E
A
R
E

The weird sisters hand in hand.	Three Witches
This castle hath a pleasant seat; the air nimbly and sweetly recommends itself unto our gentle senses.	King Duncan
Throw physic to the dogs; I'll none of it.	Macbeth
To-morrow, and to-morrow, and to-morrow, creeps in this petty pace from day to day, to the last syllable of recorded time, and all our yesterdays have lighted fools the way to dusty death. Out, out, brief candle! Life's but a walking shadow, a poor player that struts and frets his hour upon the stage and then is heard no more: It is a tale told by an idiot, full of sound and fury, signifying nothing.	Macbeth
We have scotched the snake, not killed it.	Macbeth
What, all my pretty chickens and their dam, at one fell swoop.	Macduff
What are these, so wither'd and so wild in their attire, that look not like the inhabitants o' the earth, and yet are on't.	Banquo
What bloody man is that?	King Duncan
Who can be wise, amazed, temperate and furious, loyal and neutral, in a moment?	Macbeth
Yet I do fear thy nature; it is too full o'th' milk of human kindness.	Lady Macbeth
Yet who would have thought the old man to have had so much blood in him.	Lady Macbeth
Your face, my thane, is as a book where men may read strange matters.	Lady Macbeth

Précis of plot

A story of witchcraft, murder, and retribution, which can also be seen as a study in the philosophy and psychology of evil.

Setting

Scotland and England 1039 to 1057.

20 Measure for Measure

Vincentio, the DUKE of Vienna	A PROVOST
ANGELO, appointed his deputy	ELBOW, a simple constable
ESCALUS, an old Lord	A JUSTICE
CLAUDIO, a young gentleman	ABHORSON, an executioner
JULIET, betrothed to Claudio	BARNARDINE, a dissolute condemned prisoner
ISABELLA, Claudio's sister	MARIANA, betrothed to Angelo
LUCIO, 'a fantastic'	A BOY, attendant on Mariana
Two other such GENTLEMEN	FRIAR PETER
FROTH, a foolish gentleman	FRANCESCA, a nun
MISTRESS OVERDONE, a bawd	VARRIUS, a Lord, friend to the Duke
POMPEY, her clownish servant	Lords, officers, citizens, servants

Quotations	**Spoken by**
Ay, but to die, and go we know not where; to lie in cold obstruction, and to rot.	Claudio
But man, proud man, dressed in a little brief authority, most ignorant of what he's most assured, his glassy essence, like an angry ape, plays such fantastic tricks before high heaven as makes the angels weep.	Isabella
Condemn the fault, and not the actor of it.	Angelo
Every true man's apparel fits your thief.	Abhorson
Heaven doth with us as we with torches do.	Duke of Vienna
If I must die, I will encounter darkness as a bride, and hug it in my arms.	Claudio
I hold you as a thing enskied and sainted.	Lucio
No ceremony that to great ones 'longs. Not the king's crown, nor the deputed sword, the marshal's truncheon, nor the judge's robe, become them with one half so good a grace, as mercy does.	Isabella
O, it is excellent to have a giant's strength, but it is tyrannous to use it like a giant.	Isabella
Our doubts are traitors, and makes us lose the good we oft might win.	Lucio
Some rise by sin, and some by virtue fall.	Escalus
That in the captain's but a choleric word, which in the soldier is flat blasphemy.	Isabella
The jury passing on the prisoner's life, may in the sworn twelve have a thief or two, guiltier than him they try.	Angelo
The miserable have no other medicine; but only hope.	Claudio
They say, best men are moulded out of faults; and for the most, become much more the better, for being a little bad.	Mariana
This will last out a night in Russia, when nights are longest there.	Angelo
Virtue is bold, and goodness never fearful	Duke of Vienna

Précis of plot

The central action revolves around the dilemma of Isabella, a novice nun, whose brother is to be executed unless she succumbs to the attentions of Angelo. *Measure for Measure* is a morality play with similar sentiments to *The Merchant of Venice*, but is far more explicitly concerned with sex, and death.

Setting

Vienna circa 1500.

21 The Merchant of Venice

ANTONIO, a merchant of Venice
BASSANIO, his friend and Portia's suitor
LEONARDO, Bassanio's servant
LANCELOT, a clown and servant
GOBBO, his father
Prince of MOROCCO, Portia's suitor
Prince of ARAGON, Portia's suitor
PORTIA, an heiress
NERISSA, her waiting-gentlewoman
BALTHASAR, Portia's servant
STEFANO, Portia's servant
Jailer, attendants, servants, magnificoes of Venice

SHYLOCK, a Jew
JESSICA, his daughter
LORENZO
GRAZIANO
SALERIO
SOLANIO
DUKE of Venice
TUBAL, a Jew

Quotations

	Spoken by
A Daniel come to judgement, yea, a Daniel!	Shylock
All that glisters is not gold.	Morocco
And when I ope my lips, let no dog bark.	Graziano
But love is blind and lovers cannot see.	Jessica
But ships are but boards, sailors but men. There be land rats and water rats, water thieves and land thieves.	Shylock
How like a fawning publican he looks. I hate him for he is a Christian.	Shylock
How sweet the moonlight sleeps upon this bank!	Lorenzo
I am never merry when I hear sweet music	Jessica
I dote on his very absence.	Portia
If you prick us do we not bleed? If you tickle us do we not laugh? If you poison us do we not die? and if you wrong us shall we not revenge?	Shylock
It is a wise father that knows his own child.	Lancelot
I would not have given it for a wilderness of monkeys.	Shylock
Mislike me not for my complexion, the shadowed livery of the burnished sun.	Morocco
The quality of mercy is not strained. It droppeth as the gentle rain from heaven, upon the place beneath.	Portia
You call me misbeliever, cut-throat, dog, and spit upon my Jewish gaberdine.	Shylock
You taught me first to beg, and now methinks, you teach me how a beggar should be answered.	Portia

Précis of plot

The central plot involves an irascible Jewish money-lender and his efforts to exact full payment for a debt. The sub-plot involves the method of an heiress, Portia, of testing her suitors. The comedy is created by Shylock, the Jew's, strict adherence to the letter of the law and his ultimate downfall by being hoist by his own petard.

Setting

Venice and Belmont circa 14th century.

22 The Merry Wives of Windsor

MISTRESS Margaret PAGE
Master George PAGE, her husband
ANNE and WILLIAM Page, their children
MISTRESS Alice FORD
Master Frank FORD, her husband
Doctor CAIUS, a French physician
MISTRESS QUICKLY, his housekeeper
John RUGBY, his servant
Master FENTON, in love with Anne Page
Master Abraham SLENDER
Robert SHALLOW, his uncle, a justice
The HOST of the Garter Inn
Sir Hugh EVANS, a Welsh parson
Peter SIMPLE, Slender's servant
Children of Windsor, appearing as fairies

ROBIN, Sir John's page
JOHN, a servant
ROBERT, a servant
SIR JOHN Falstaff
BARDOLPH
PISTOL
NIM

Quotations

	Spoken by
A man of my kidney.	Sir John
Faith, thou hast some crotchets in thy head now.	Mistress Ford
Here will be an old abusing of God's patience and the King's English.	Mistress Quickly
I cannot tell what the dickens his name is.	Mistress Page
I have a kind of alacrity in sinking.	Sir John
I hope good luck lies in odd numbers.	Sir John
I will make a Star Chamber matter of it.	Shallow
O, what a world of vile ill-favoured faults.	Anne
There was the rankest compound of villainous smell that ever offended nostril.	Sir John
Vengeance of Jenny's case!	Mistress Quickly

S
H
A
K
E
S
P
E
A
R
E

| We burn daylight. Here: read, read. | Mistress Ford |
| Why then, the world's mine oyster, which I with sword will open. | Pistol |

Précis of plot
The central plot tells of Sir John Falstaff's unsuccessful attempts to seduce Mistress Page and Mistress Ford, and of the unfounded jealousy of Master Ford. The sub-plot revolves around the wooing of Anne Page and ultimate success of Master Fenton.

Setting
Windsor mid-15th century.

23 A Midsummer Night's Dream

THESEUS, Duke of Athens
HIPPOLYTA, Queen of the Amazons
EGEUS, father of Hermia
HERMIA, daughter of Egeus
LYSANDER, loved by Hermia
DEMETRIUS, suitor to Hermia
HELENA, in love with Demetrius
OBERON, King of the Fairies
TITANIA, Queen of the Fairies
ROBIN GOODFELLOW, a puck
Peter QUINCE, a carpenter
Nick BOTTOM, a weaver
Francis FLUTE, a bellows-mender
Robin STARVELING, a tailor
Attendant Lords and fairies

SNUG, a joiner
Tom SNOUT, a Tinker

Four Fairies:
COBWEB
MOTE
MUSTARDSEED
PEASEBLOSSOM

Quotations

Quotations	Spoken by
A calendar, a calendar! look in the almanac; find out moonshine, find out moonshine.	Bottom
A lion among ladies is a most dreadful thing; for there is not a more fearful wild-fowl than your lion living.	Bottom
A part to tear a cat in.	Bottom
A proper man, as one shall see in a summer's day.	Quince
And the imperial votaress passed on, in maiden meditation, fancy-free, yet marks I where the bolt of Cupid fell: It fell upon a little western flower, before milk-white, now purple with love's wound, and maidens call it love-in-idleness.	Oberon
Bless thee, Bottom! bless thee! thou are translated.	Quince
But earthlier happy is the rose distilled than that which, withering on the virgin thorn, grows, lives, and dies in single blessedness.	Theseus
He bravely broach'd his boiling bloody breast.	Quince (as prologue)
I am slow of study.	Snug
I have a reasonable good ear in music. Let's have the tongs and the bones.	Bottom
I have an exposition of sleep come upon me.	Bottom
I know a bank where the wild thyme blows, where oxlips and the nodding violet grows, quite over-canopied with luscious woodbine, with sweet musk-roses and with eglantine.	Oberon
Ill met by moonlight, proud Titania.	Oberon
I'll put a girdle round the earth in forty minutes.	Puck
I will roar you as gently as any sucking dove; I will roar you as 'twere any nightingale.	Bottom
Lord, what fools these mortals be.	Puck
Love looks not with the eyes, but with the mind; and therefore is wing'd Cupid painted blind.	Helena
Masters, spread yourselves.	Bottom
My hounds are bred out of the Spartan kind, so flew'd, so sanded, and their heads are hung, with ears that sweep away the morning dew; crook-knee'd, and dew-lapp'd like Thessalian bulls; slow in pursuit, but match'd in mouth like bells.	Theseus
Oh hell! to choose love by another's eyes.	Hermia
Or in the night, imagining some fear, how easy is a bush supposed a bear.	Theseus
She was a vixen when she went to school; and though she be but little, she is fierce.	Helena
Since once I sat upon a promontory, and heard a mermaid on a dolphin's back uttering such dulcet and harmonious breath that the rude sea grew civil at her song and certain stars shot madly from their spheres, to hear the sea-maid's music.	Oberon
So we grew together, like to a double cherry, seeming parted, but yet an union in partition; two lovely berries moulded on one stem.	Helena
Swift as a shadow, short as any dream, brief as the lightning in the collied night, that, in a spleen, unfolds both heaven and earth, and ere a man hath power to say 'Behold' the jaws of darkness do devour it up.	Lysander
That is the true beginning of our end.	Quince (as prologue)
The best in this kind are but shadows; and the worst are no worse, if imagination amend them.	Theseus
The course of true love never did run smooth.	Lysander

The iron tongue of midnight hath told twelve.	Theseus
The jaws of darkness do devour it up: so quick bright things come to confusion.	Lysander
The lover, all as frantic, sees Helen's beauty in a brow of Egypt. The poet's eye,	Theseus
in a fine frenzy rolling, doth glance from heaven to earth, from earth to heaven.	
The lunatic, the lover and the poet, are of imagination all compact.	Theseus
This is 'erc'les' vein.	Bottom
Very tragical mirth.	Lysander (reads)
What hempen homespuns have we swaggering here.	Puck

Précis of plot
Theseus, Duke of Athens, prepares to marry Hippolyta, Queen of the Amazons. The sub-plots include the tangled web of love between Lysander, Hermia, Demetrius and Helena, and the production of a play, *Pyramus and Thisbe* (based on Ovid's *Metamorphoses*), for the Duke's wedding.

Setting
Athens and a nearby wood.

24 Much Ado About Nothing

DON PEDRO, Prince of Aragon
BALTHASAR, attendant on Don Pedro, a singer
DON JOHN, the bastard brother of Don Pedro
BORACHIO, follower of Don John
CONRAD, follower of Don John
LEONATO, Governor of Messina
HERO, his daughter
BEATRICE, an orphan, his niece
ANTONIO, an old man, brother of Leonato
MARGARET, attendant on Hero
URSULA, attendant on Hero
DOGBERRY, constable in charge of Watch
VERGES, the Headborough, Dogberry's partner

BENEDICK, of Padua
CLAUDIO, of Florence
FRIAR Francis
A SEXTON
WATCHMEN
A BOY, serving Benedick
Attendants and messengers

Quotations	**Spoken by**
Are you good men and true?	Dogberry
But then there was a star danced, and under that was I born.	Beatrice
Comparisons are odorous.	Dogberry
Disdain and scorn ride sparkling in her eyes.	Hero
Flat burglary, as ever was committed.	Dogberry
For there was never yet philosopher, that could endure the toothache patiently.	Leonato
Friendship is constant in all other things, save in the office and affairs of love.	Claudio
He hath indeed better bettered expectation.	Messenger
He is a very valiant trencherman, he has an excellent stomach.	Beatrice
He wears his faith but as the fashion of his hat.	Beatrice
I have a good eye, uncle, I can see a church by daylight.	Beatrice
I was not born under a rhyming planet.	Benedick
O that he were here to write me down an ass!	Dogberry
O, what men dare do! what men may do! what men daily do, not knowing what they do!	Claudio
Patch grief with proverbs, make misfortune drunk.	Leonato
Taming my wild heart to thy loving hand.	Beatrice
To be a well-favoured man is the gift of fortune, but to write and read comes by nature.	Dogberry
Well, everyone can master a grief but he that has it.	Benedick
What, my dear Lady Disdain! are you yet living?	Benedick
Yes, I thank God, I am as honest as any man living that is an old man and no honester than I.	Verges

Précis of plot
The central plot concerns Don John's deception whereby Claudio believes his beloved Hero unfaithful. However, the sub-plot of the relationship between Beatrice and Benedick adds the real substance to the play, and the gradual realization of their love for each other has spawned countless works.

Setting
Messina in Sicily.

25 Othello

OTHELLO, the Moor of Venice
DESDEMONA, his wife
Michael CASSIO, his lieutenant
BIANCA, a courtesan, in love with Cassio
IAGO, the Moor's Ensign
EMILIA, Iago's wife
A CLOWN, servant of Othello
BRABANZIO, Desdemona's father, a senator

The DUKE of Venice
SENATORS of Venice
A HERALD
A MESSENGER

SHAKESPEARE

GRAZIANO, Brabanzio's brother
LODOVICO, kinsman of Brabanzio
RODERIGO, Venetian in love with Desdemona
MONTANO, Governor of Cyprus
Attendants, officers, sailors, gentlemen, musicians

Quotations

	Spoken by
A fellow almost damned in a fair wife, that never set a squadron in the field.	Iago
Alas, what ignorant sin have I committed?	Desdemona
And of the cannibals that each other eat, the Anthropophagi, and men whose heads do grow beneath their shoulders.	Othello
Be sure thou prove my love a whore. Be sure of it. Give me the ocular proof.	Othello
But I will wear my heart upon my sleeve, for daws to peck at.	Iago
But men are men, the best sometimes forgot.	Iago
But this denoted a foregone conclusion.	Othello
Excellent wretch! Perdition catch my soul.	Othello
He hath a daily beauty in his life that makes me ugly.	Iago
He that is robbed, not wanting what is stol'n, let him not know it and he's not robbed at all.	Othello
How poor are they that ha' not patience! what wound did ever heal but by degrees?	Iago
I am not merry, but I do beguile.	Desdemona
I do perceive here a divided duty.	Desdemona
If she be black, and thereto have a wit; she'll find a white that shall her blackness fit.	Iago
I have very poor and unhappy brains for drinking, I could well wish courtesy would invent some other custom of entertainment.	Cassio
I would have him nine years a-killing. A fine woman, a fair woman, a sweet woman.	Othello
Keep up your bright swords, for the dew will rust 'em.	Othello
My story being done, she gave me for my pains a world of kisses.	Othello
No hinge, nor loop to hang a doubt on.	Othello
O beware, my lord, of jealousy; it is the green-eyed monster which doth mock the meat it feeds on.	Iago
O God, that men should put an enemy in their mouths to steal away their brains.	Cassio
O most lame and impotent conclusion.	Desdemona
On horror's head horrors accumulate.	Othello
Potations pottle-deep.	Iago
Pride, pomp and circumstance of glorious war!	Othello
Reputation, reputation, reputation! O, I have lost my reputation! I have lost the immortal part of myself, and what remains is bestial.	Cassio
Silence that dreadful bell – It frights the isle from her propriety.	Othello
Take note, take note, O world, to be direct and honest is not safe.	Iago
Then must you speak of one that loved not wisely but too well.	Othello
'Tis neither here nor there.	Emilia
To mourn a mischief that is past and gone, is the next way to draw new mischief on.	Duke of Venice
To suckle fools, and chronicle small beer.	Iago
Your daughter and the Moor are now making the beast with two backs.	Iago
You are one of those that will not serve God, if the devil bids you.	Iago

Précis of plot

The story of a Moorish commander deluded by his ensign into believing that his young wife has been unfaithful to him with another soldier. By subtle innuendo and apparent physical proof, Iago convinces Othello that Desdemona has slept with Cassio, his lieutenant; his deceit results in tragedy.

Setting

Venice and Cyprus circa 1570.

26 Pericles, Prince of Tyre

John GOWER, the Presenter
ANTIOCHUS, King of Antioch
His DAUGHTER
PERICLES, Prince of Tyre
MARINA, Pericles' daughter
CLEON, governor of Tarsus
DIONIZA, his wife
LEONINE, a murderer
CERIMON, a physician of Ephesus
PHILEMON, his servant
KING SIMONIDES of Pentapolis
THAISA, his daughter
Three FISHERMEN, his subjects
Five PRINCES, suitors of Thaisa
LYSIMACHUS, Governor of Mytilene
Lords, ladies, pages, messengers, sailors and gentlemen

THALIART, a villain
HELICANUS
AESCHINES
A MARSHAL
LICHORIDA, Thaisa's nurse
A BAWD
A PANDER
BOULT, a leno
DIANA, Goddess of chastity

Quotations

	Spoken by
Master, I marvel how the fishes live in the sea.	Third Fisherman
Why, as men do a-land; the great ones eat up the little ones.	First Fisherman (reply)
O you gods! why do you make us love your goodly gifts and snatch them straight away?	Pericles
See where she comes, apparell'd like the spring!	Pericles
'Tis time to fear when tyrants seem to kiss.	Pericles

Précis of plot

Pericles, Prince of Tyre, flees from the court of the King of Antioch after solving a riddle that incriminates the King in an incestuous relationship with his daughter. The play chronicles the ensuing travels of Pericles and culminates in his reunion with his long lost daughter, Marina.

Setting

Antioch, Tyre, Tarsus, Pentapolis, Ephesus, Mitylene.

27 Richard II

KING RICHARD II	Followers of King Richard:
The QUEEN, his wife	GREEN
JOHN OF GAUNT, Duke of Lancaster, Richard's uncle	BAGOT
Harry BOLINGBROKE, his son, later HENRY IV	BUSHY
DUCHESS OF GLOUCESTER	
Duke of YORK, King Richard's uncle	Lord BERKELEY
DUCHESS OF YORK	Lord FITZWATER
Duke of AUMERLE, their son	Duke of SURREY
Thomas MOWBRAY, Duke of Norfolk	Lord WILLOUGHBY
	ABBOT OF WESTMINSTER
Of Bolingbroke's party:	Sir Piers EXTON
Percy, Earl of NORTHUMBERLAND	LORD MARSHAL
HARRY PERCY, his son	HERALDS
Lord ROSS	CAPTAIN of the Welsh army
Of King Richard's party:	LADIES attending the Queen
Earl of SALISBURY	GARDENER
BISHOP OF CARLISLE	Gardener's MEN
Sir Stephen SCROPE	Exton's MEN
	Lords, soldiers, attendants
KEEPER of the prison at Pomfret	
GROOM of King Richard's stable	

Quotations

	Spoken by
A jewel in a ten-times barred-up chest is a bold spirit in a loyal breast	Mowbray
Can sick men play so nicely with their names?	King Richard
For God's sake let us sit upon the ground, and tell sad stories of the death of kings: how some have been deposed; some slain in war; some haunted by the ghost they have deposed; some poisoned by their wives; some sleeping kill'd; all murder'd.	King Richard
How long a time lies in one little word!	Bolingbroke
Methinks I am a prophet new-inspired.	John of Gaunt
Mount, mount, my soul; thy seat is up on high, whilst my gross flesh sinks downward, here to die.	Richard (last words)
Not all the water in the rude rough sea, can wash the balm from an anointed king.	King Richard
O call back yesterday, bid time return.	Salisbury
Of comfort no man speak. Let's talk of graves, of worms and epitaphs.	King Richard
Peace shall go sleep with Turks and infidels.	Bishop of Carlisle
That which in mean men we entitle patience is pale cold cowardice in noble breasts.	Duchess of Gloucester
The daintiest last, to make the end most sweet.	Bolingbroke
Things sweet to taste prove in digestion sour.	John of Gaunt
This must my comfort be: the sun that warms you here shall shine on me.	Bolingbroke
This royal throne of kings, this sceptred isle, this earth of majesty, this seat of Mars, this other Eden, demi-paradise, this fortress built by nature for herself against infection and the hand of war, this happy breed of men, this little world, this precious stone set in the silver sea, which serves it in the office of a wall, or as a moat defensive to a house against the envy of less happier lands; this blessed plot, this earth, this realm, this England.	John of Gaunt
Truth hath a quiet breast.	Mowbray
We were not born to sue, but to command.	King Richard
You may my glories and my state depose, but not my griefs; still am I king of those.	Richard

Précis of plot

This tragical history play centres around the time of Richard's enforced abdication. The substance of the play is historically accurate, although elements of fiction do exist to some degree, for example, the murder of Richard by Sir Piers Exton.

Setting

England and Wales at the turn of the 15th century.

SHAKESPEARE

28 Richard III

KING EDWARD IV
DUCHESS OF YORK, his mother
PRINCE EDWARD, Edward IV's son
Richard, the young Duke of YORK, Edward IV's son
George, Duke of CLARENCE
RICHARD, Duke of Gloucester, later KING RICHARD
Clarence's SON
Clarence's DAUGHTER
QUEEN ELIZABETH, King Edward's wife
Anthony Woodville, Earl RIVERS, her brother
Marquis of DORSET, her son
Lord GRAY, her son
Sir Thomas VAUGHAN
GHOST OF KING HENRY the Sixth
QUEEN MARGARET, his widow
GHOST OF PRINCE EDWARD, his son
LADY ANNE, Prince Edward's widow
William, LORD HASTINGS, Lord Chamberlain
Lord STANLEY, Earl of Derby, his friend
HENRY EARL OF RICHMOND, later KING HENRY VII
Sir Robert BRACKENBURY, Lieutenant of the Tower

Sir James BLUNT
Sir Walter HERBERT
Duke of BUCKINGHAM
Duke of NORFOLK
Sir Richard RATCLIFF
Sir William CATESBY
Sir James TIRREL
Two MURDERERS
A PAGE
CARDINAL
Bishop of ELY
John, a PRIEST
CHRISTOPHER, a priest
Earl of OXFORD
Lord MAYOR of London
A SCRIVENER
Hastings, a PURSUIVANT
SHERIFF
Aldermen and citizens
Attendants, two bishops,
messengers and soldiers

Quotations

	Spoken by
A horse, a horse, my kingdom for a horse!	King Richard
And thus I clothe my naked villainy, with odd old ends stol'n forth of holy writ, and seem a saint, when I most play the devil.	Richard Gloucester
But soft, here come my executioners.	Richard Gloucester
High-reaching Buckingham grows circumspect.	King Richard
Now is the winter of our discontent, made glorious summer by this son of York.	Richard Gloucester
O coward conscience, how dost thou afflict me?	King Richard
Slave, I have set my life upon a cast, and I will stand the hazard of the die. I think there are six Richmonds in the field. Five have I slain today, instead of him. A horse, a horse, my kingdom for a horse.	King Richard (last words)
So wise so young, they say, do never live long.	Richard Gloucester
Their lips were four red roses on a stalk, and in their summer beauty kissed each other.	Tyrrell
Was ever woman in this humour wooed? Was ever woman in this humour won?	Richard Gloucester

Précis of plot

In this play, Shakespeare demonstrates a more complete artistic control of his historical material than in its predecessors, and historical events are freely manipulated in the interests of an overriding design. The play chronicles the period of about twelve years before Richard's reign, highlighting his bloody progress to the crown and his short two-year reign, culminating in his defeat at Bosworth.

Setting

England 1471 to 1485.

29 Romeo and Juliet

CHORUS
ROMEO
MONTAGUE, his father
MONTAGUE'S WIFE
BENVOLIO, Montague's nephew
ABRAHAM, Montague's servingman
BALTHASAR, Romeo's man
JULIET
CAPULET, her father
CAPULET'S WIFE
TYBALT, her nephew
His page
Escalus, PRINCE of Verona
Other CITIZENS OF THE WATCH
Masquers, guests, gentlewomen, followers

PETER
SAMSON
GREGORY
Other SERVINGMEN
MUSICIANS
PETRUCCIO
MERCUTIO
PARIS
PAGE to Paris
FRIAR LAURENCE
FRIAR JOHN
An APOTHECARY
CHIEF WATCHMAN
CAPULET'S COUSIN
Juliet's NURSE

Quotations

	Spoken by
A pair of star-crossed lovers take their life.	Chorus
A plague o' both your houses.	Mercutio
For you and I are past our dancing days.	Capulet
I do not bite my thumb at you sir, but I bite my thumb, sir.	Samson
Nay, I am the very pink of courtesy.	Mercutio
O happy dagger, this is thy sheath! there rust, and let me die	Juliet (last words)

One pain is lessened by another's anguish.	Benvolio
O Romeo, Romeo, wherefore art thou Romeo.	Juliet
O then I see Queen Mab hath been with you.	Mercutio
Parting is such sweet sorrow.	Juliet
See how she leans her cheek upon her hand. O, that I were a glove upon that hand, that I might touch that cheek.	Romeo
Thus with a kiss I die.	Romeo (last words)
True, I talk of dreams, which are the children of an idle brain, begot of nothing but vain fantasy.	Mercutio
What's in a name? That which we call a rose by any other word would smell as sweet.	Juliet
When well-apparelled April on the heel of limping winter treads.	Capulet
With Rosaline, my ghostly father? No, I have forgot that name and that name's woe.	Romeo

Précis of plot
This play tells of the bitter feud between the Montagues and Capulets. Romeo, a Montague, falls in love with Juliet, a Capulet, but their love is doomed from the outset as death and tragedy befall both families.

Setting
Verona and Mantua early in the 14th century.

30 The Taming of the Shrew

In the Induction:
CHRISTOPHER SLY, beggar and tinker
A HOSTESS
A LORD
BARTHOLOMEW, his page
HUNTSMEN, SERVANTS AND PLAYERS
In the play-within-the-play:
BAPTISTA Minola, a gentleman of Padua
KATHERINE, his elder daughter
BIANCA, his younger daughter
PETRUCHIO, a gentleman of Verona, suitor of Katherine
VINCENTIO, Lucentio's father
A PEDANT, schoolmaster from Mantua
Other servants of Baptista and Petruchio
LUCENTIO, disguised as Cambio, a teacher

GREMIO, suitor of Bianca
HORTENSIO, another suitor
TRANIO, a servant
BIONDELLO, a servant
GRUMIO, a servant
CURTIS, a servant
A WIDOW
A TAILOR
A HABERDASHER
An OFFICER
NATHANIEL, a servingman
PHILIP, a servingman
JOSEPH, a servingman
PETER, a servingman

Quotations

	Spoken by
And as the sun breaks through the darkest clouds, so honour peereth in the meanest habit.	Petruccio
A woman moved is like a fountain troubled, muddy, ill seeming, thick, bereft of beauty.	Katherine
No profit grows where is no pleasure ta'en.	Tranio
This is a way to kill a wife with kindness.	Petruccio

Précis of plot
The play has three main strands. The first shows how a drunken tinker, Christopher Sly, is made to believe himself a lord for whose entertainment a play is to be presented. The second strand is the central plot of the play performed for Sly, in which the shrewish Katherine is wooed, won, and tamed by the fortune-hunting Petruchio. The third strand involves Lucentio, Gremio, and Hortensio, all of them suitors for the hand of Katherine's sister, Bianca.

Setting
Padua and Petruchio's house circa 14th century.

31 The Tempest

PROSPERO, the rightful Duke of Milan
MIRANDA, his daughter
ANTONIO, his brother, the usurping Duke of Milan
ALONSO, King of Naples
SEBASTIAN, his brother
FERDINAND, Alonso's son
GONZALO, an honest old counsellor of Naples
ADRIAN, a Lord
FRANCISCO, a Lord
ARIEL, an airy spirit attendant upon Prospero
CALIBAN, a savage and deformed native, who is also Prospero's slave
TRINCULO, Alonso's jester
STEFANO, Alonso's drunken butler

The MASTER of a ship
BOATSWAIN
MARINERS
SPIRITS
The Masque
Spirits appearing as:
IRIS
CERES
JUNO
Nymphs and reapers

Quotations

	Spoken by
A very ancient and fish-like smell.	Trinculo
Be not afeard. The isle is full of noises, sounds and sweet airs, that give delight and hurt not.	Caliban

Fie, what a spendthrift is he of his tongue!	Antonio
Full fathom five thy father lies. Of his bones are coral made.	Ariel (sung)
He that dies pays all debts.	Stefano
How beauteous mankind is! O brave new world, that has such people in't!	Miranda
In the dark backward and abyss of time?	Prospero
Knowing I loved my books, he furnished me from mine own library with volumes that	Prospero
I prize above my dukedom.	
Misery acquaints a man with strange bedfellows.	Trinculo
My library was dukedom large enough.	Prospero
They'll take suggestions as a cat laps milk.	Antonio
We are such stuff as dreams are made on, and our little life is rounded with a sleep.	Prospero
Where the bee sucks, there suck I.	Ariel
You taught me language, and my profit on't is I know how to curse.	Caliban

Précis of plot

The central plot of *The Tempest* is one of witchcraft and connivance. The action takes place on an island after a shipwreck, as Prospero explains to his daughter, Miranda, how they came to the island, some twelve years earlier, and how the shipwreck has brought his enemies, Alonso, King of Naples, and Prospero's own brother, Antonio, face to face with their wrongdoings. The action takes place within a few hours, as in *The Comedy of Errors*.

Setting

A small island off the coast of Tunis.

32 Timon of Athens

TIMON of Athens	FOOL
LUCILIUS, a servant	PAGE
An OLD ATHENIAN	CAPHIS
LORDS and SENATORS of Athens	ISIDORE'S SERVANT
VENTIDIUS, one of Timon's false friends	POET
ALCIBIADES, an Athenian Captain	PAINTER
APEMANTUS, a churlish philosopher	JEWELLER
One dressed as CUPID in the Masque	MERCHANT
LADIES dressed as Amazons in the Masque	Mercer
FLAVIUS, Timon's steward	LUCULLUS' SERVANT
FLAMINIUS, a servant	LUCIUS' SERVANT
SERVILIUS, a servant	TITUS' SERVANT
Other SERVANTS of Timon	HORTENSIUS' SERVANT
LUCULLUS, a flattering Lord	PHILOTUS' SERVANT
LUCIUS, a flattering Lord	PHRYNIA, a whore
SEMPRONIUS, a flatterring Lord	TIMANDRA, a whore
Three STRANGERS, one called Hostilius	The banditti, THIEVES
SOLDIER of Alcibiades' army	
Two of VARRO'S SERVANTS	
Messengers, attendants, soldiers	

Quotations

	Spoken by
I wonder men dare trust themselves with men.	Apemantus
'Tis not enough to help the feeble up, but to support him after.	Timon

Précis of plot

Timon is a misanthrope because his friends flattered and sponged on him in prosperity but abandoned him in poverty. Timon finds gold once more and his friends return.

Setting

Athens and neighbouring woods.

33 Titus Andronicus

SATURNINUS, later Emperor	CAPTAIN
BASSIANUS, his brother	AEMILIUS
TITUS ANDRONICUS, general against the Goths	Sons of Titus:
SEMPRONIUS, kinsman of Titus	LUCIUS
VALENTINE, kinsman of Titus	QUINTUS
TAMORA, Queen of the Goths, wife of Saturninus	MARTIUS
Her sons:	MUTIUS
ALARBUS	
DEMETRIUS	NURSE
CHIRON	CLOWN
AARON, a Moor, her lover	
LAVINIA, daughter of Titus	
YOUNG LUCIUS, a boy, son of Lucius	
MARCUS ANDRONICUS, a tribune, Titus' brother	

PUBLIUS, his son
Senators, tribunes, Romans, Goths, soldiers and attendants

Quotations
She is a woman, therefore may be wooed; she is a woman, therefore may be won;
she is Lavinia, therefore must be loved.
Sweet mercy is nobility's true badge.

Spoken by
Demetrius

Tamora

Précis of plot
Tamora, Queen of the Goths, seeks revenge on her captor, Titus, for the ritual slaughter of her son, Alarbus; she achieves it when her other sons, Chiron and Demetrius, rape and mutilate Titus' daughter, Lavinia. Later, Titus himself seeks revenge on Tamora and her husband Saturninus, after Tamora's black lover, Aaron, has falsely led him to believe that he can save his sons' lives by allowing his own hand to be chopped off. Though he is driven to madness, Titus, with his brother Marcus and his last surviving son, Lucius, achieves a spectacular sequence of vengeance in which he cuts Tamora's sons' throats, serves their flesh baked in a pie to their mother, kills Lavinia to save her from her shame, and stabs Tamora to death. Then in rapid succession, Saturninus kills Titus and is himself killed by Lucius, who, as the new Emperor, is left with Marcus to bury the dead, to punish Aaron, and to 'heal' Rome.

Setting
Rome 4th century AD.

34 Troilus and Cressida
HELEN, wife of Menelaus, now living with Paris
ALEXANDER, servant of Cressida
Servants of Troilus, musicians
soldiers and attendants
Greeks:
AGAMEMNON, Commander-in-Chief
MENELAUS, his brother
NESTOR
ULYSSES
ACHILLES
PATROCLUS, his companion
DIOMEDES
AJAX
THERSITES
MYRMIDONS, soldiers of Achilles
Servants of Diomedes, soldiers
CASSANDRA, Priam's daughter, a prophetess
ANDROMACHE, wife of Hector
AENEAS, a commander
ANTENOR, a commander
PANDARUS, a Lord
CRESSIDA, his niece
CALCHAS, her father, who has joined the Greeks

PROLOGUE
Trojans:
PRIAM, King of Troy
His sons:
HECTOR
DEIPHOBUS
HELENUS, a priest
PARIS
TROILUS
MARGARETON, a bastard

Quotations
For to be wise and love exceeds man's might.
I am giddy. Expectation whirls me round. The imaginary relish is so sweet, that it enchants my sense.
I have had my labour for my travail.
One touch of nature makes the whole world kin.
The baby figure of the giant mass of things to come at large.
Welcome ever smiles, and farewell goes out sighing.

Spoken by
Cressida
Troilus

Pandarus
Ulysses
Nestor
Ulysses

Précis of plot
The war between Greece and Troy has been provoked by the abduction of the Greek, Helen, by the Trojan hero Paris, son of King Priam. Shakespeare's play opens when the Greek forces, led by Menelaus' brother Agamemnon, have already been besieging Troy for seven years. Shakespeare concentrates on the opposition between the Greek hero Achilles and the Trojan Hector. Shakespeare also shows how the war, caused by one love affair, destroys another. The story of the love between the Trojan, Troilus, and the Grecian, Cressida, encouraged by her uncle Pandarus, and of Cressida's desertion of Troilus for the Greek Diomedes.

Setting
Troy and the Greek camp during the Trojan War.

35 Twelfth Night
ORSINO, Duke of Illyria
VALENTINE, attending Orsino
CURIO, attending Orsino
VIOLA, a lady, later disguised as Cesario

SIR ANDREW AGUECHEEK
MALVOLIO, Olivia's steward
FABIAN, a member of Olivia's household
FESTE, the clown, her jester
FIRST OFFICER

SEBASTIAN, her twin brother
ANTONIO, a sea-captain
OLIVIA, a Countess
MARIA, her waiting-gentlewoman
SIR TOBY BELCH, Olivia's kinsman

SECOND OFFICER
CAPTAIN
PRIEST
SERVANT of Olivia
Musicians, sailors, lords, attendants

Quotations

	Spoken by
Be not afraid of greatness. Some are born great, some achieve greatness, and some have greatness thrust upon 'em.	Malvolio
Cressida was a beggar.	Feste
Farewell, fair cruelty.	Viola
He does it with a better grace, but I do it more natural.	Sir Andrew
He plays o'th' viol-de-gamboys, and speaks three or four languages word for word without book.	Sir Toby
I am a great eater of beef, and I believe that does harm to my wit.	Sir Andrew
I am all the daughters of my father's house, and all the brothers too.	Viola
I am sure care's an enemy to life.	Sir Toby
If music be the food of love, play on.	Orsino
Is it a world to hide virtues in?	Sir Toby
Love sought is good, but given unsought, is better.	Olivia
Many a good hanging prevents a bad marriage.	Feste
My purpose is indeed a horse of that colour.	Maria
No more cakes and ale.	Sir Toby
Not to be a-bed after midnight is to be up betimes.	Sir Toby
O world, how apt the poor are to be proud!	Olivia
Still you keep o'th' windy side of the law.	Fabian
What is the opinion of Pythagoras concerning wildfowl?	Feste
Wherefore are these things hid?	Sir Toby
Why, this is very midsummer madness.	Olivia

Précis of plot
The main plot is of a shipwrecked girl, Viola, who, disguised as a boy, Cesario, serves a young Duke, Orsino, and undertakes love-errands on his behalf to a noble lady, Olivia, who falls in love with her but mistakenly betrothes herself to her twin brother Sebastian.

Setting
Illyria

36 The Two Gentlemen of Verona

DUKE of Milan
SILVIA, his daughter
PROTEUS, a gentleman of Verona
LANCE, his clownish servant
VALENTINE, a gentleman of Verona
SPEED, his clownish servant
THURIO, a foolish rival to Valentine
EGLAMOUR, agent for Silvia in her escape

ANTONIO, father of Proteus
PANTHINO, his servant
JULIA, beloved of Proteus
LUCETTA, her waiting-woman
HOST, where Julia lodges
OUTLAWS
Servants and musicians

Quotations

	Spoken by
How use doth breed a habit in a man!	Valentine
I have no other but a woman's reason, I think him so because I think him so.	Lucetta
O heaven, were man but constant, he were perfect.	Proteus
Who is Silvia? What is she, that all our swains commend her?	Host (sung)

Précis of plot
This play tells of the friendship of Valentine and Proteus and the strain their relationship is put under when they both fall in love with Silvia, the daughter of the Duke of Milan.

Setting
Verona, Milan, and Mantua.

37 The Two Noble Kinsmen

THESEUS, Duke of Athens
HIPPOLYTA, Queen of the Amazons
EMILIA, her sister
PIRITHOUS, friend of Theseus
PALAMON, a noble kinsman
ARCITE, a noble kinsman
Hymen, God of marriage
ARTESIUS, an Athenian soldier
Three QUEENS, widows of kings killed in Thebes
VALERIUS, a Theban

PROLOGUE
A SERVANT
A BOY, who sings
A HERALD
MESSENGERS
A DOCTOR
EPILOGUE

WOMAN, attending Emilia
An Athenian GENTLEMAN
Six KNIGHTS, attending Arcite and Palamon
A JAILER, in charge of Theseus' prison
The WOOER of the jailer's daughter
Two FRIENDS of the jailer
Six COUNTRYMEN, one dressed as a baboon
GERALD, a schoolmaster
NELL, a country wench
Four other country wenches:
Fritz, Madeleine, Luce and Barbara
Timothy, a TABORER

Quotations	**Spoken by**
New plays and maidenheads are near akin.	Prologue
Your grief is written on your cheek.	Emilia

Précis of plot
This play is based on Chaucer's Knight's Tale, on which Shakespeare had already drawn for episodes of *A Midsummer Night's Dream*. It tells of the conflicting claims of love and friendship between Palamon and Arcite, the Two Noble Kinsmen of the title, who, as in *The Two Gentlemen of Verona*, both fall in love with the same woman, but unlike the earlier play, decide to fight for their love. The play is sometimes not listed as a Shakespearian play, as there is a body of thought that believes it to be, at best, a collaboration with John Fletcher; unlike *Henry VIII*, their other joint work, it was not listed in the 1623 folio of Shakespeare's works.

Setting
Athens.

38 The Winter's Tale

LEONTES, King of Sicily	A JAILER
HERMIONE, his wife	A MARINER
MAMILLIUS, his son	CAMILLO, a Lord
PERDITA, his daughter	ANTIGONUS, a Lord
POLIXENES, King of Bohemia	CLEOMENES, a Lord
FLORIZEL, his son, in love with Perdita, aka Doricles	DION, a Lord
ARCHIDAMUS, a Bohemian Lord	CLOWN, his son
AUTOLYCUS, a rogue, once in the service of Florizel	
PAULINA, Antigonus's wife	Other shepherds and shepherdesses
EMILIA, a lady attending on Hermione	Twelve countrymen disguised as satyrs
MOPSA, a shepherdess	Other Lords and gentlemen, ladies,
DORCAS, a shepherdess	Officers and servants at Leontes' court
SERVANT of the old shepherd	TIME, as chorus

Quotations	**Spoken by**
A sad tale's best for winter.	Mamillius
A snapper up of unconsidered trifles.	Autolycus
Exit, pursued by a bear.	Stage direction
For you there's rosemary and rue.	Perdita
Good sooth, she is the queen of curds and cream.	Camillo
I would there were no age between ten and three-and twenty, or that youth would sleep out the rest; for there is nothing in the between but getting wenches with child, wronging the ancientry, stealing, fighting.	Old Shepherd
Jog on, jog on, the footpath way.	Autolycus (sung)
Lawn as white as driven snow.	Autolycus (sung)
Let me have no lying. It becomes none but tradesmen.	Autolycus
We were as twinned lambs that did frisk i' th' sun, and bleat the one at th' other.	Polixenes
When daffodils begin to peer.	Autolycus (sung)

Précis of plot
The improbable tale of King Leontes' suspicions of his wife's adultery with King Polixenes, his childhood friend. Leontes expels his new-born daughter, Perdita, thinking her the fruit of this unholy alliance, and she is brought up as a shepherdess. Perdita falls in love with Florizel, son of Polixenes, her supposed father, but she is eventually re-united with her true father.

Setting
Sicily and Bohemia circa 14th century.

S
H
A
K
E
S
P
E
A
R
E

Chronology of
Shakespeare's Plays

1589–92	Henry VI Parts 1, 2, and 3
1592–93	Richard III, The Comedy of Errors
1593–94	Titus Andronicus, The Taming of the Shrew
1594–95	The Two Gentlemen of Verona, Love's Labour's Lost, Romeo and Juliet
1595–96	Richard II, A Midsummer Night's Dream
1596–97	King John, The Merchant of Venice
1597–98	Henry IV Part 1 and 2
1598–99	Much Ado About Nothing, Henry V
1599–1600	Julius Caesar, As You Like It
1600–01	Hamlet, The Merry Wives of Windsor
1601–02	Twelfth Night, Troilus and Cressida
1602–03	All's Well That Ends Well
1604–05	Measure for Measure, Othello
1605–06	King Lear, Macbeth
1606–07	Antony and Cleopatra
1607–08	Coriolanus, Timon of Athens
1608–09	Pericles
1609–10	Cymbeline
1610–11	The Winter's Tale
1611–12	The Tempest
1612–13	Henry VIII, The Two Noble Kinsmen

Other Works

1592–93	Venus and Adonis (narrative poem)
1593–94	The Rape of Lucrece (narrative poem)
1593–1600	Sonnets (154 in total)
1600–01	The Phoenix and the Turtle (67-line elegy)
1609 circa	A Lover's Complaint (329-line poem)
	Various poems (attributed)

Original Titles

Henry VI Part 2 – The First Part of the Contention
Henry VI Part 3 – Richard Duke of York
Henry VIII – All Is True

Full Titles

Cymbeline, King of Britain
Hamlet, Prince of Denmark
Othello, the Moor of Venice
Pericles, Prince of Tyre
Twelfth Night, or What You Will

NB Shakespeare is generally credited with having penned 37 plays, but it can be argued that this figure could perhaps be just as easily 36, or 38, depending on the treatment given to the final two works, Henry VIII and The Two Noble Kinsmen. These plays are thought to be collaborations between Shakespeare and John Fletcher, although only Henry VIII appears in the First Folio of 1623. Therefore, when one is asked which was the last play Shakespeare wrote, it is true to say that it would be impossible to give an unqualified answer unless the question is very specific. The last play wholly credited to Shakespeare is The Tempest; the last play cited in the First Folio is Henry VIII; and the last play that Shakespeare wrote ignoring these two provisos is The Two Noble Kinsmen. The author of this work was asked this question by Anne Robinson on The Weakest Link and was not impressed when I informed her there were three possible answers. I referred her to my book but was quickly voted off.

It should also be noted that as well as doubts as to the degree of Shakespeare's involvement in one or two of the plays, there are also doubts as to their chronological order. There is evidence to suggest, for instance, that Shakespeare's first play was probably not Henry VI Part 1, but, Henry VI Part 2. However, an answer of Henry VI would seem to be the most equitable solution to this one.

Films Based on Shakespearian Works

All Night Long – 1961	based on Othello directed by Basil Dearden
An Honourable Murder – 1959	based on Julius Caesar directed by Godfrey Grayson
Chimes at Midnight – 1966	based on Henry V directed by Orson Welles
Forbidden Planet – 1956	based on The Tempest directed by Fred M. Wilcox
Kiss Me Kate – 1953	musical based on The Taming of the Shrew directed by George Sidney
Men of Respect – 1990	based on Macbeth directed by William Reilly
Prospero's Books – 1991	based on The Tempest directed by Peter Greenaway
Ran – 1985	Japanese version of King Lear three sons cast instead of three daughters written and directed by Akiro Kurosawa
Rosencrantz and Guildenstern Are Dead – 1990	based on Hamlet written and directed by Tom Stoppard
The Boys from Syracuse – 1940	musical based on The Comedy of Errors directed by Edward A. Sutherland

Throne of Blood – 1957   Japanese version of Macbeth
                                      directed by Akiro Kurosawa
West Side Story – 1961   based on *Romeo and Juliet*
                                      directed by Robert Wise

NB The list above includes only films that do not specifically mention the title of the Shakespeare work: e.g. *Joe Macbeth* is a gangster film that follows a very similar plot to *Men of Respect* but includes a reference to Macbeth in the title. There are many films that allude to characters in Shakespeare but do not follow the plot closely enough to be included here. The Orson Welles film *Chimes at Midnight* is sometimes called *Falstaff*.

General Information

As You Like It	seven ages of man: 1) infant; 2) schoolboy; 3) lover; 4) soldier; 5) justice; 6) old age; 7) second childhood.
born	23 April 1564 in Stratford-upon-Avon. This may or may not be the actual date, but St George's Day seemed apt.
children	three: Susanna, Judith and Hamnet. Susanna born 1582, and twins Hamnet and Judith born 1585. Hamnet died in 1596, aged 11½. Susanna married Dr John Hall and Judith married Thomas Quiney. Shakespeare's line ended in 1670 with the death of Elizabeth, Susanna's daughter.
christened	26 April 1564 at Holy Trinity Church, Stratford-upon-Avon.
chronicler	Francis Meres' *Palladis Tamia* listed Shakespeare's works up to 1598.
collaborators	John Fletcher and various others.

death	23 April 1616 in Stratford-upon-Avon. Shakespeare therefore, traditionally, died on his birthday, aged 52. There are no names on Shakespeare's gravestone, but these words:
	    Good friend, for Jesus' sake forbear
	    To dig the dust enclosed here.
	    Blest be the man that spares these stones,
	    And curst be he that moves my bones.
	Shakespeare's family erected a monument in Holy Trinity church, Stratford, 1623.

dedicatee	Henry Wriothesley, the 3rd Earl of Southampton, had the narrative poems *Venus and Adonis* and *The Rape of Lucrece* dedicated to him.
Falstaff, Sir John	based on Sir John Oldcastle, the Protestant martyr. Shakespeare was forced to change the name from Oldcastle to Falstaff after complaints from relatives. *Henry IV* Part 1 is here quoted using the original name. The original names of Sir John's associates Bardolph and Peto have also been listed in *Henry IV* Part 1 in their original form, i.e. Russell and Harvey.
father	John Shakespeare, a glover, wool dealer, and sometime Mayor; died 1601.
First Folio	John Heminges and Henry Condell produced First Folio 1623.
first play	*Henry VI* (see notes at end of plays).
great tragedy	the 'four great tragedies' are often listed as *Hamlet*, *King Lear*, *Macbeth*, and *Othello*.
home	bought 'New Place' Stratford in 1597 Bishopsgate, and also lived with a French Huguenot family called Mountjoy for a short while during 1604, at Cripplegate.
July: takes place in	*Romeo and Juliet.*
kin	William was one of eight children of which he was the third child and first son. Only three brothers and a sister survived infancy. William's brother Edmund was also an actor.
last play	*The Tempest*, *Henry VIII*, or *The Two Noble Kinsmen* (see notes at end of plays).
lines: most	Hamlet has the most lines spoken by any one character in a single play but is only third on the overall list if one takes into consideration other plays that a character may appear in. Richard III has more lines taking into account his appearances in *Henry VI*, but the most lines are spoken by Sir John Falstaff, if one considers that Shakespeare's folio of 1623 had by then changed the name of Sir John Oldcastle in *Henry IV* Part 1.
longest play	this can be contentious due to disputed passages, but taking the 1623 folio as the basis of the question, then *Hamlet* is longest followed by *Richard III.*
married	Anne Hathaway, a farmer's daughter, from Shottery, near Stratford, 28 November 1582. He was 18, she 26 and pregnant. Anne died in 1623.
mother	Mary Arden, from Wilmcote, Warwickshire; died in 1609.
portraits	Martin Droeshout's engraving of Shakespeare, first published on the title-page of the First Folio 1623, is one of only two likenesses of Shakespeare; the other is the bust of Shakespeare in his monument, designed by Gheerart Janssen. It is unclear whether these are true likenesses, as it was common practice of many artists to use stencils, and it is thought possible that Droeshout may have used a common stencil of the day, possibly that of Elizabeth I.
shortest play	given the criteria used for deciding the longest play, the shortest play is clearly *The Comedy of Errors.*
sobriquet	the Sweet Swan of Avon, coined by Ben Jonson.
sonnets	published in 1609 by Thomas Thorpe, and dedicated to 'Mr W.H.' The sonnets pertain to a young man, a dark lady, and a rival poet. Sonnets 1 to 17 exhort a young man to marry; Sonnets 1 to 126 are all about a young man; Sonnets 127 to 154 are about the dark lady; Sonnet 126 is not in sonnet form, as it has only 12 lines.
theatres	Globe was built in 1599 on Bankside, south of the Thames. James Burbage founded the Lord

S
H
A
K
E
S
P
E
A
R
E

Chamberlain's Company within the Globe and his son Richard Burbage was the principal actor. Shakespeare bought an interest in the Globe, and also a half share in the Blackfriars Theatre, in 1608, and from then on Shakespeare produced winter plays at the Blackfriars and summer plays at the Globe. The Lord Chamberlain's Men became the King's Men on James I's accession. Opposition to the King's Men came mainly from Edward Alleyne's 'Admiral's Men'. John Fletcher became chief dramatist of the King's Men after Shakespeare. Will Kempe was the leading comedy actor of the King's Men. Richard Tarleton was the leading comedy actor of the rival Admiral's Men. Forerunners of the Lord Chamberlain's Men were the Queen's Men. The Chamberlain's Men first performed at the 'Theatre', in Shoreditch, and then at the 'Curtain'. The Globe caught fire and was destroyed in 1613 during performance of *Henry VIII*.

First Lines of Shakespeare's Plays

Play	*First line*	*Spoken by*
C All's Well That Ends Well	In delivering my son from me I bury a second husband.	Dowager Countess of Roussillon
T Antony and Cleopatra	Nay, but this dotage of our General's o'erflows the measure.	Philo
C As You Like It	As I remember, Adam, it was upon this fashion.	Orlando
C The Comedy of Errors	Proceed, Solinus, to procure my fall.	Egeon
T Coriolanus	Before we proceed any further, hear me speak.	first Citizen
C Cymbeline, King of Britain	You do not meet a man but frowns.	first Gentleman
T Hamlet	Who's there?	Barnardo
H Henry IV Part 1	So shaken as we are, so wan with care.	King Henry IV
H Henry IV Part 2	Open your ears; for which of you will stop.	Rumour
H Henry V	O for a muse of fire.	Chorus (as Prologue)
H Henry VI Part 1	Hung be the heavens with black!	Bedford
H Henry VI Part 2	As by your high imperial majesty.	Suffolk
H Henry VI Part 3	I wonder how the King escaped our hands.	Warwick
H Henry VIII (All Is True)	I come no more to make you laugh.	Prologue
T Julius Caesar	Hence, home, you idle creatures, get you home.	Flavius
H King John	Now say, Châtillon, what would France with us?	King John
T King Lear	I thought the King had more affected the Duke of Albany than Cornwall.	Earl of Kent
C Love's Labour's Lost	Let fame, that all hunt after in their lives.	King Ferdinand
T Macbeth	When shall we three meet again? In thunder, lightning, or in rain?	First Witch
C Measure for Measure	Escalus.	Vincentio, Duke of Vienna
C The Merchant of Venice	In sooth, I know not why I am so sad.	Antonio
C The Merry Wives of Windsor	Sir Hugh, persuade me not. I will make a Star Chamber matter of it.	Shallow
C A Midsummer Night's Dream	Now, fair Hippolyta, our nuptial hour draws on apace.	Theseus
C Much Ado About Nothing	I learn in this letter that Don Pedro of Aragon comes this night to Messina.	Leonato
T Othello	Tush, never tell me!	Roderigo
C Pericles, Prince of Tyre	To sing a song that old was sung.	Gower, as Chorus
H Richard II	Old John of Gaunt, time-honoured Lancaster.	King Richard II
H Richard III	Now is the winter of our discontent.	Richard Gloucester
T Romeo and Juliet	Two households, both alike in dignity in fair Verona.	Chorus (as Prologue)
C The Taming of the Shrew	I'll feeze you, in faith.	Christopher Sly
C The Tempest	Boatswain!	Master of a ship
T Timon of Athens	Good day, sir.	Poet
T Titus Andronicus	Noble patricians, patrons of my right.	Saturninus
C Troilus and Cressida	In Troy there lies the scene. From isles of Greece.	Prologue
C Twelfth Night	If music be the food of love, play on.	Orsino
C The Two Gentlemen of Verona	Cease to persuade, my loving Proteus.	Valentine
C The Two Noble Kinsmen	New plays and maidenheads are near akin.	Prologue
C The Winter's Tale	If you shall chance, Camillo, to visit Bohemia.	Archidamus

Play	Last line	Spoken by
C All's Well That Ends Well	The bitter past, more welcome is the sweet.	The King of France (n.b. Epilogue follows)
T Antony and Cleopatra	High order in this great solemnity.	Octavius Caesar
C As You Like it	Proceed, proceed. We'll so begin these rites as we do trust they'll end, in true delights.	Duke Senior (nb Epilogue follows)
C The Comedy of Errors	And now let's go hand in hand, not one before another.	Dromio of Ephesus
T Coriolanus	Yet he shall have a noble memory. Assist.	Aufidius
C Cymbeline, King of Britain	Ere bloody hands were washed, with such a peace.	Cymbeline
T Hamlet	Go, bid the soldiers shoot.	Fortinbras
H Henry IV Part 1	Let us not leave till all our own be won.	King Henry IV
H Henry IV Part 2	Come, will you hence?	Prince John (nb Epilogue follows)
H Henry V	And may our oaths well kept and prosp'rous be.	King Harry (nb Epilogue follows)
H Henry VI Part 1	But I will rule both her, the King, and realm.	Suffolk
H Henry VI Part 2	And more such days as these to us befall!	Warwick
H Henry VI Part 3	For here, I hope, begins our lasting joy.	King Edward IV
H Henry VIII (All Is True)	This little one shall make it holiday.	King Henry VIII (nb Epilogue follows)
T Julius Caesar	To part the glories of this happy day.	Octavius
H King John	If England to itself do rest but true.	Philip the Bastard
T King Lear	Shall never see so much, nor live so long.	Edgar
C Love's Labour's Lost	The words of Mercury are harsh after the songs of Apollo. You that way, we this way.	Armado
T Macbeth	Whom we invite to see us crowned at Scone.	Malcolm
C Measure for Measure	What's yet behind that's meet you all should know.	Vincentio, Duke of Vienna
C The Merchant of Venice	Well, while I live I'll fear no other thing so sore as keeping safe Nerissa's ring.	Graziano
C The Merry Wives of Windsor	For he tonight shall lie with Mistress Ford.	Master Ford
C A Midsummer Night's Dream	Meet me all by break of day.	Oberon (nb Epilogue follows)
C Much Ado About Nothing	Think not on him till tomorrow, I'll devise thee brave punishments for him. Strike up, pipers.	Benedick
T Othello	This heavy act with heavy heart relate.	Lodovico
C Pericles, Prince of Tyre	New joy wait on you. Here our play has ending.	Gower
H Richard II	In weeping after this untimely bier.	King Henry IV
H Richard III	That she may long live here, God say 'Amen'.	King Henry VII
T Romeo and Juliet	For never was a story of more woe than this of Juliet and her Romeo.	Escalus
C The Taming of the Shrew,	'Tis a wonder, by your leave, she will be tamed so.	Lucentio
C The Tempest	Please you, draw near.	Prospero (nb Epilogue follows)
T Timon of Athens	Let our drums strike.	Alcibiades
T Titus Andronicus	And being dead, let birds on her take pity.	Lucius
C Troilus and Cressida	Hope of revenge shall hide our inward woe.	Troilus
C Twelfth Night	And we'll strive to please you every day.	Feste
C The Two Gentlemen of Verona	One feast, one house, one mutual happiness.	Valentine
C The Two Noble Kinsmen	And bear us like the time.	Theseus (nb Epilogue follows)
C The Winter's Tale	We were dissevered. Hastily lead away.	Leontes

NB C = Comedy **H** = History **T** = Tragedy

Shakespearian Characters

Character	Play	Character	Play
AARON, a Moor	Titus Andronicus	ADRIANA	The Comedy of Errors
ABERGAVENNY, Lord	Henry VIII	AEDILES	Coriolanus
ABHORSON, an executioner	Measure for Measure	AEMILIUS	Titus Andronicus
ABRAHAM, Montague's servingman	Romeo and Juliet	AENEAS, a commander	Troilus and Cressida
		AESCHINES	Pericles, Prince of Tyre
ACHILLES	Troilus and Cressida	AGAMEMNON, commander in chief	Troilus and Cressida
ADAM, a former servant of Sir Rowland	As You Like It		
		AGRIPPA	Antony and Cleopatra
ADRIAN, a Lord	The Tempest	AGUECHEEK, Sir Andrew	Twelfth Night
ADRIAN, a Roman	Coriolanus	AJAX	Troilus and Cressida

Character	Play
ALARBUS, son of Tamora	Titus Andronicus
ALBANY, Duke of, Goneril's husband	King Lear
ALCIBIADES, an Athenian Captain	Timon of Athens
ALENÇON, Duke of	Henry VI Part 1
ALEXANDER, servant of Cressida	Troilus and Cressida
ALEXAS	Antony and Cleopatra
ALICE, an old gentlewoman	Henry V
ALONSO, King of Naples	The Tempest
AMIENS, Lord attending on Duke Senior	As You Like It
ANDROMACHE, wife of Hector	Troilus and Cressida
ANGELO, a goldsmith	The Comedy of Errors
ANGELO, appointed Vincentio's deputy	Measure for Measure
ANGUS, a Thane	Macbeth
ANNE, Lady	Richard III
ANTENOR, a commander	Troilus and Cressida
ANTIGONUS, a Lord	The Winter's Tale
ANTIOCHUS, King of Antioch	Pericles, Prince of Tyre
ANTIPHOLUS OF EPHESUS	The Comedy of Errors
ANTIPHOLUS OF SYRACUSE	The Comedy of Errors
ANTONIO, a merchant of Venice	The Merchant of Venice
ANTONIO, a sea-captain	Twelfth Night
ANTONIO, an old man	Much Ado About Nothing
ANTONIO, father of Proteus	The Two Gentlemen of Verona
ANTONIO, Prospero's brother	The Tempest
ANTONY, Mark	Antony and Cleopatra, Julius Caesar
APEMANTUS, a churlish philosopher	Timon of Athens
APOTHECARY	Romeo and Juliet
ARAGON, Prince of	The Merchant of Venice
ARCHBISHOP of York, Scrope	Henry IV Parts 1 and 2
ARCHIDAMUS, a Bohemian Lord	The Winter's Tale
ARCITE, a noble kinsman	The Two Noble Kinsmen
ARIEL, an airy spirit	The Tempest
ARMADO, Don Adriano de	Love's Labour's Lost
ARTEMIDORUS	Julius Caesar
ARTESIUS, an Athenian soldier	The Two Noble Kinsmen
ARTHUR, Duke of Brittaine	King John
ARVIRAGUS	Cymbeline, King of Britain
ASNATH, a spirit	Henry VI Part 2
AUDREY, a goatherd	As You Like It
AUFIDIUS, General	Coriolanus
AUMERLE, Duke of	Richard II
AUSTRIA (Limoges), Duke of	King John
AUSTRINGER	All's Well That Ends Well
AUTOLYCUS, a rogue	The Winter's Tale
BAGOT	Richard II
BALTHASAR, a merchant	The Comedy of Errors
BALTHASAR, a singer	Much Ado About Nothing
BALTHASAR, Portia's servant	The Merchant of Venice
BALTHASAR, Romeo's man	Romeo and Juliet

Character	Play
BANDITTI, thieves	Timon of Athens
BANQUO, a Scottish Thane	Macbeth
BAPTISTA MINOLA	The Taming of the Shrew
BARDOLPH	Henry IV Part 2 and Henry V The Merry Wives of Windsor
BARNARDINE	Measure for Measure
BARNARDO	Hamlet
BARTHOLOMEW, a page	The Taming of the Shrew
BASSANIO	The Merchant of Venice
BASSET	Henry VI Part 1
BASSIANUS, Saturninus' brother	Titus Andronicus
BASTARD of Orleans	Henry VI Part 1
BATES, John	Henry V
BAWD	Pericles, Prince of Tyre
BEADLE of Saint Albans	Henry VI Part 2
BEATRICE, an orphan	Much Ado About Nothing
BEAUFORT, Cardinal Bishop of Winchester	Henry VI Part 2
BEDFORD, Duke of, regent of France	Henry VI Part 1
BELARIUS, a banished Lord	Cymbeline, King of Britain
BELCH, Sir Toby, Olivia's kinsman	Twelfth Night
BENEDICK, of Padua	Much Ado About Nothing
BENVOLIO, Montague's nephew	Romeo and Juliet
BERKELEY, Lord	Richard II
BERRI, Duke of	Henry V
BIANCA, a courtesan	Othello
BIANCA, Baptista's youngest daughter	The Taming of the Shrew
BIGOT, Lord	King John
BIONDELLO, a servant	The Taming of the Shrew
BIRON	Love's Labour's Lost
BLANCHE, Lady, of Spain	King John
BLUNT, Sir James	Richard III
BLUNT, Sir Walter	Henry IV Part 1
BOATSWAIN	The Tempest
BOLEYN, Anne	Henry VIII
BOLINGBROKE, Harry, Duke of Hereford	Richard II
BOLINGBROKE, Roger, a conjurer	Henry VI Part 2
BONA, Lady	Henry VI Part 3
BORACHIO, follower of Don John	Much Ado About Nothing
BOTTOM, a weaver	A Midsummer Night's Dream
BOULT	Pericles, Prince of Tyre
BOURBON, Duke of	Henry V
BOY who sings	Antony and Cleopatra
BOY who sings	The Two Noble Kinsmen
BOY, attendant on Mariana	Measure for Measure
BOY, formerly Falstaff's page	Henry V
BOY, serving Benedick	Much Ado About Nothing
BOYET	Love's Labour's Lost
BRABANZIO, a senator of Venice	Othello
BRACKENBURY, Sir Robert	Richard III
BRANDON	Henry VIII
BRUTUS, Marcus, a noble Roman	Julius Caesar

Character	Play	Character	Play
BRUTUS, tribune	Coriolanus	CITIZENS OF THE WATCH	Romeo and Juliet
BUCKINGHAM, Duke of	Henry VIII	CLARENCE, Duke of	Henry V
BUCKINGHAM, Duke of	Henry VI Part 2 and	CLARENCE, Duke of	Richard III
	Richard III	CLAUDIO	Julius Caesar
BULLCALF, Peter	Henry IV Part 2	CLAUDIO, a young	Measure for Measure
BURGUNDY, Duke of	Henry V and	gentleman	
	Henry VI Part I	CLAUDIO, of Florence	Much Ado About
BURGUNDY, Duke of	King Lear		Nothing
BUSHY	Richard II	CLEOMENES, a Lord	The Winter's Tale
BUTTS, the King's physician	Henry VIII	CLEON, Governor of	Pericles, Prince of Tyre
CADE, Jack	Henry VI Part 2	Tarsus	
CAITHNESS, a Thane	Macbeth	CLEOPATRA, Queen of	Antony and Cleopatra
CAIUS, a French physician	The Merry Wives of	Egypt	
	Windsor	CLIFFORD, Lord	Henry VI Part 3
CALCHAS, Cressida's father	Troilus and Cressida	CLIFFORD, Old Lord	Henry VI Part 2
CALIBAN, a deformed	The Tempest	CLIFFORD, the younger	Henry VI Part 2
savage		CLITUS	Julius Caesar
CALPURNIA	Julius Caesar	CLOTEN, the Queens' son	Cymbeline, King of
CAMBRIDGE, Richard,	Henry V		Britain
Earl of		CLOWN	Antony and Cleopatra
CAMIDIUS	Antony and Cleopatra	CLOWN	Titus Andronicus
CAMILLO, a Lord	The Winter's Tale	CLOWN, Autolycus' son	The Winter's Tale
CANTERBURY,	Henry V	CLOWN, servant of Othello	Othello
Archbishop of		CLOWNS	Hamlet
CANTERBURY,	Henry VIII	COBBLER	Julius Caesar
Archbishop of		COBHAM, Dame Eleanor	Henry VI Part 2
CAPHIS	Timon of Athens	COBWEB	A Midsummer Night's
CAPTAIN	King Lear		Dream
CAPTAIN	Titus Andronicus	COLEVILLE, Sir John	Henry IV Part 2
CAPTAIN	Twelfth Night	COMINIUS, a General	Coriolanus
CAPTAIN in Duncan's army	Macbeth	CONRAD	Much Ado About
CAPTAIN of a ship	Henry VI Part 2		Nothing
CAPTAIN of the Welsh army	Richard II	CONSTABLE of France	Henry V
CAPULET'S COUSIN	Romeo and Juliet	CONSTANCE, Lady	King John
CAPULET'S WIFE	Romeo and Juliet	CORDELIA	King Lear
CAPULET, Juliet's father	Romeo and Juliet	CORIOLANUS	Coriolanus
CAPUTIUS, Lord	Henry VIII	CORIN, an old shepherd	As You Like It
CARDINAL	Richard III	CORNELIUS	Hamlet
CARDINAL CAMPEIUS	Henry VIII	CORNELIUS, a physician	Cymbeline, King of
CARDINAL WOLSEY	Henry VIII		Britain
CARLISLE, Bishop of	Richard II	CORNWALL, Duke of	King Lear
CARPENTER	Julius Caesar	COSTARD, a Clown	Love's Labour's Lost
CARRIERS	Henry IV Part 1	COUNTESS of Auvergne	Henry VI Part 1
CASCA	Julius Caesar	COURTESAN	The Comedy of Errors
CASSANDRA, a prophetess	Troilus and Cressida	COURT, Alexander	Henry V
CASSIO, Michael, a	Othello	CRANMER, Archbishop	Henry VIII
Lieutenant		of Canterbury	
CASSIUS	Julius Caesar	CRESSIDA, Pandarus'	Troilus and Cressida
CATESBY, Sir William	Richard III	niece	
CATHERINE	Henry V	CRIER	Henry VIII
CELIA, later disguised as	As You Like It	CROMWELL, Thomas	Henry VIII
Aliena		CUPID	Timon of Athens
CERES, a spirit	The Tempest	CURIO, attending Orsino	Twelfth Night
CERIMON, a physician	Pericles, Prince of Tyre	CURTIS, a servant	The Taming of the
of Ephesus			Shrew
CHAMBERLAIN	Henry IV Part 1	CYMBELINE, King of Britain	Cymbeline, King of
CHARLES, Dauphin	Henry VI Part 1		Britain
of France		DARDANIUS	Julius Caesar
CHARLES, Duke	As You Like It	DAUPHIN, of France	Henry V
Frederick's wrestler		DAVY, Shallow's servant	Henry IV Part 2
CHARMIAN	Antony and Cleopatra	DE LA POLE, William	Henry VI Part 2
CHÂTILLON, an	King John	DECIUS BRUTUS	Julius Caesar
ambassador		DECRETAS	Antony and Cleopatra
CHIEF WATCHMAN	Romeo and Juliet	DEIPHOBUS, son of Priam	Troilus and Cressida
CHILDREN of WINDSOR	The Merry Wives of	DEMETRIUS	A Midsummer Night's
	Windsor		Dream
CHIRON, son of Tamora	Titus Andronicus	DEMETRIUS	Antony and Cleopatra
CHRISTOPHER, a priest	Richard III	DEMETRIUS	Titus Andronicus
CICERO, a senator	Julius Caesar	DENIS, Oliver's servant	As You Like It
CINNA the conspirator	Julius Caesar	DENNY, Sir Anthony	Henry VIII
CINNA the poet	Julius Caesar	DESDEMONA	Othello

S
H
A
K
E
S
P
E
A
R
E

Character	Play	Character	Play
DIANA	All's Well That Ends Well		The Merry Wives of
DIANA, Goddess of chastity	Pericles, Prince of Tyre		Windsor
DICK the BUTCHER	Henry VI Part 2	FANG, a sergeant	Henry IV Part 2
DIOMED	Antony and Cleopatra	FASTOLF, Sir John	Henry VI Part 1
DIOMEDES	Troilus and Cressida	FEEBLE, Francis	Henry IV Part 2
DIONIZA, wife of Cleon	Pericles, Prince of Tyre	FENTON, Master	The Merry Wives of
DION, a Lord	The Winter's Tale		Windsor
DOCTOR to Lady Macbeth	Macbeth	FERDINAND	The Tempest
DOCTOR, an Englishman	Macbeth	FERDINAND, King of	Love's Labour's Lost
DOGBERRY, the constable	Much Ado About	Navarre	
	Nothing	FESTE, the clown	Twelfth Night
DOLABELLA	Antony and Cleopatra	FILARIO	Cymbeline, King of
DOLL TEARSHEET, a	Henry IV Part 2		Britain
whore		FIRST LORD DUMAINE	All's Well That Ends Well
DONALBAIN	Macbeth	FIRST OFFICER	Twelfth Night
DON JOHN	Much Ado About	FITZWATER, Lord	Richard II
	Nothing	FIVE PRINCES	Pericles, Prince of Tyre
DON PEDRO, Prince of	Much Ado About	FLAMINIUS, a servant	Timon of Athens
Aragon	Nothing	FLAVIUS	Timon of Athens
DOOR-KEEPER	Henry VIII	FLAVIUS, a tribune	Julius Caesar
DORCAS, a shepherdess	The Winter's Tale	FLEANCE	Macbeth
DORSET, Marchioness of	Henry VIII	FLORENCE, Duke of	All's Well That Ends Well
DORSET, Marquis of	Henry VIII	FLORIZEL, aka Doricles	The Winter's Tale
DORSET, Marquis of	Richard III	FLUELLEN, Captain, a	Henry V
DOUGLAS, Earl of	Henry IV Part 1	Welshman	
DROMIO OF EPHESUS	The Comedy of Errors	FLUTE, a bellows-mender	A Midsummer Night's
DROMIO OF SYRACUSE	The Comedy of Errors		Dream
DULL, Anthony, a constable	Love's Labour's Lost	FOOL	King Lear
DUMAINE	Love's Labour's Lost	FOOL	Timon of Athens
DUNCAN, King of Scotland	Macbeth	FORD, Master Frank	The Merry Wives of
DUTCHMAN	Cymbeline, King of		Windsor
	Britain	FORD, Mistress Alice	The Merry Wives of
EARL RIVERS	Henry VI Part 3		Windsor
EDGAR, aka Tom o' Bedlam	King Lear	FORESTER	Love's Labour's Lost
EDMOND	King Lear	FORTINBRAS, Prince	Hamlet
EDWARD IV, King	Richard III	of Norway	
EDWARD, Earl of March	Henry VI Parts 2 and 3	FRANCESCA, a nun	Measure for Measure
EGEON, merchant of	The Comedy of Errors	FRANCIS, a drawer	Henry IV Part 1
Syracuse		FRANCISCO	Hamlet
EGEUS, father of Hermia	A Midsummer Night's	FRANCISCO, a Lord	The Tempest
	Dream	FREDERICK, Duke	As You Like It
EGLAMOUR	The Two Gentlemen of	FRENCHMAN	Cymbeline, King of
	Verona		Britain
EGYPTIAN	Antony and Cleopatra	FRIAR FRANCIS	Much Ado About
ELBOW, a simple constable	Measure for Measure		Nothing
ELIZABETH, Princess	Henry VIII	FRIAR JOHN	Romeo and Juliet
ELY, Bishop of	Henry V	FRIAR LAURENCE	Romeo and Juliet
ELY, Bishop of	Henry VIII	FRIAR PETER	Measure for Measure
ELY, Bishop of	Richard III	FROTH	Measure for Measure
EMILIA	The Two Noble Kinsmen	GADSHILL	Henry IV Part 1
EMILIA, a lady	The Winter's Tale	GALLUS	Antony and Cleopatra
EMILIA, an abbess	The Comedy of Errors	GARDENER	Richard II
EMILIA, Iago's wife	Othello	GARDINER, later Bishop	Henry VIII
EMMANUEL, Clerk	Henry VI Part 2	of Winchester	
of Chatham		GARGRAVE, Sir Thomas	Henry VI Part 1
ENOBARBUS, Domitius	Antony and Cleopatra	GARTER King of Arms	Henry VIII
EROS	Antony and Cleopatra	GENERAL of French	Henry VI Part 1
ERPINGHAM, Sir Thomas	Henry V	garrison	
ESCALUS, an old Lord	Measure for Measure	GEORGE, Duke of	Richard III
ESCALUS, Prince of Verona	Romeo and Juliet	Clarence	
ESSEX, Earl of	King John	GEORGE, later Duke	Henry VI Part 3
EVANS, Sir Hugh, a Welsh	The Merry Wives of	of Gloucester	
parson	Windsor	GERALD, a schoolmaster	The Two Noble Kinsmen
EXETER, Duke of	Henry V	GERTRUDE, Queen of	Hamlet
EXETER, Duke of	Henry VI Part 1	Denmark	
EXETER, Duke of	Henry VI Part 3	GHOST of Caesar	Julius Caesar
EXTON, Sir Piers	Richard II	GHOST of Hamlet	Hamlet
FABIAN	Twelfth Night	GHOST of King Henry VI	Richard III
FALCONBRIDGE, Lady	King John	GHOST of Mother of	Cymbeline, King of
FALCONBRIDGE, Robert	King John	Posthumus	Britain
FALSTAFF, Sir John	Henry IV Part 2	GHOST of Prince Edward	Richard III

Character	Play
GHOST of Sicilius Leonatus	Cymbeline, King of Britain
GHOSTS of brothers of Posthumus	Cymbeline, King of Britain
GIACOMO, an Italian	Cymbeline, King of Britain
GLASDALE, Sir William	Henry VI Part 1
GLOUCESTER, Duchess of	Richard II
GLOUCESTER, Duke Humphrey of	Henry VI Part 2
GLOUCESTER, Duke of	Henry V
GLOUCESTER, Duke of	Henry VI Part 1
GLOUCESTER, Earl of	King Lear
GLOUCESTER, Humphrey, Duke of	Henry IV Part 2
GOBBO	The Merchant of Venice
GONERIL	King Lear
GONZALO	The Tempest
GOODFELLOW, Robin, a puck	A Midsummer Night's Dream
GOUGH, Matthew	Henry VI Part 2
GOVERNOR of Harfleur	Henry V
GOWER, a messenger	Henry IV Part 2
GOWER, Captain, an Englishman	Henry V
GOWER, John, the Presenter	Pericles, Prince of Tyre
GRANDPRÉ, Lord	Henry V
GRAY, Lady	Henry VI Part 3
GRAY, Lord	Richard III
GRAZIANO	Othello
GRAZIANO	The Merchant of Venice
GREEN	Richard II
GREGORY	Romeo and Juliet
GREMIO	The Taming of the Shrew
GREY, Sir Thomas	Henry V
GRIFFITH, a gentleman usher	Henry VIII
GROOM of King Richard's stable	Richard II
GRUMIO, a servant	The Taming of the Shrew
GUIDERIUS, known as Polydore	Cymbeline, King of Britain
GUILDENSTERN	Hamlet
GUILDFORD, Sir Henry	Henry VIII
GURNEY, James	King John
HABERDASHER	The Taming of the Shrew
HAMLET, Prince	Hamlet
HARCOURT	Henry IV Part 2
HARVEY	Henry IV Part 1
HASTINGS, a pursuivant	Richard III
HASTINGS, Lord	Henry IV Part 2
HASTINGS, Lord	Henry VI Part 3
HECATE, Queen of Witches	Macbeth
HECTOR	Troilus and Cressida
HELEN	Cymbeline, King of Britain
HELEN	Troilus and Cressida
HELENA	A Midsummer Night's Dream
HELENUS, a priest	Troilus and Cressida
HELEN, an orphan	All's Well That Ends Well
HELICANUS	Pericles, Prince of Tyre
HENRY IV, King	Henry IV Parts 1 and 2
HENRY V, King	Henry V
HENRY VI, King	Henry VI Parts 1, 2 and 3
HENRY VIII, King	Henry VIII

Character	Play
HENRY, Earl of Richmond	Richard III
HENRY, Lord Scrope of Masham	Henry V
HERBERT, Sir Walter	Richard III
HERMIA	A Midsummer Night's Dream
HERMIONE	The Winter's Tale
HERO	Much Ado About Nothing
HIPPOLYTA, Queen of the Amazons	A Midsummer Night's Dream
HIPPOLYTA, Queen of the Amazons	The Two Noble Kinsmen
HOLOFERNES, a schoolmaster	Love's Labour's Lost
HORATIO	Hamlet
HORNER, Thomas, an armourer	Henry VI Part 2
HORTENSIO, a teacher	The Taming of the Shrew
HORTENSIUS' SERVANT	Timon of Athens
HOST of the Garter Inn	The Merry Wives of Windsor
HOST, where Julia lodges	The Two Gentlemen of Verona
HOSTESS, formerly Mistress Quickly	Henry V
HOTSPUR, Henry Percy	Henry IV Part 1
HUBERT	King John
HUME, Sir John, a priest	Henry VI Part 2
HUNTSMAN	Henry VI Part 3
HYMEN, God of marriage	The Two Noble Kinsmen
HYMEN, God of marriage	As You Like It
IAGO, the Moor's ensign	Othello
IDEN, Alexander	Henry VI Part 2
INNOGEN, Princess	Cymbeline, King of Britain
INTERPRETER, a French soldier	All's Well That Ends Well
IRAS	Antony and Cleopatra
IRIS, a spirit	The Tempest
ISABEL	Henry V
ISABELLA	Measure for Measure
ISIDORE'S SERVANT	Timon of Athens
JAILER	The Two Noble Kinsmen
JAILER'S BROTHER	The Two Noble Kinsmen
JAILER'S DAUGHTER	The Two Noble Kinsmen
JAMY, Captain, a Scot	Henry V
JAQUENETTA, a country wench	Love's Labour's Lost
JAQUES, Lord	As You Like It
JESSICA	The Merchant of Venice
JEWELLER	Timon of Athens
JOAN la Pucelle	Henry VI Part 1
JOHN	Henry VI Part 2
JOHN OF GAUNT, Duke of Lancaster	Richard II
JOHN OF LANCASTER	Henry IV Part 1
JOHN, a priest	Richard III
JOHN, a servant	The Merry Wives of Windsor
JOHN, King of England	King John
JOSEPH, a servingman	The Taming of the Shrew
JULIA	The Two Gentlemen of Verona
JULIET	Measure for Measure
JULIET	Romeo and Juliet
JULIUS CAESAR	Julius Caesar
JUNO, a spirit	The Tempest
JUPITER	Cymbeline, King of

Character	Play	Character	Play
	Britain	LYSANDER	A Midsummer Night's Dream
JUSTICE	Measure for Measure		
KATE	Henry IV Part 2	LYSIMACHUS, Governor of Mytilene	Pericles, Prince of Tyre
KATE, Lady Percy	Henry IV Part 1		
KATHERINE	Love's Labour's Lost	MACBETH, Lady	Macbeth
KATHERINE	The Taming of the Shrew	MACBETH, Thane of Glamis	Macbeth
KEEPER of the prison	Richard II	MACDUFF, Lady	Macbeth
KENT, Earl of	King Lear	MACDUFF, Thane of Fife	Macbeth
KING CHARLES VI of France	Henry V	MACDUFF'S SON	Macbeth
		MACMORRIS, Captain	Henry V
KING CLAUDIUS	Hamlet	MAECENAS	Antony and Cleopatra
KING of France	All's Well That Ends Well	MALCOLM, King	Macbeth
KING of France	King Lear	MALVOLIO, Olivia's steward	Twelfth Night
KING PHILIP of France	King John	MAMILLIUS	The Winter's Tale
KING SIMONIDES of Pentapolis	Pericles, Prince of Tyre	MARCELLUS	Hamlet
		MARCUS ANDRONICUS, a tribune	Titus Andronicus
LAERTES	Hamlet		
LAFEU, an old lord	All's Well That Ends Well	MARDIAN, a eunuch	Antony and Cleopatra
LANCE	The Two Gentlemen of Verona	MARGARET	Henry VI Part 1
		MARGARET	Much Ado About Nothing
LANCELOT, a clown	The Merchant of Venice		
LARTIUS, a General	Coriolanus	MARGARETON, a bastard	Troilus and Cressida
LAVATCH, a clown	All's Well That Ends Well	MARIA	Love's Labour's Lost
LAVINIA	Titus Andronicus	MARIA, a waiting-gentlewoman	Twelfth Night
LEAR, King of Britain	King Lear		
LE BEAU	As You Like It	MARIANA	All's Well That Ends Well
LEGATE	Henry VI Part 1	MARIANA	Measure for Measure
LENNOX, a Thane	Macbeth	MARINA	Pericles, Prince of Tyre
LEONARDO	The Merchant of Venice	MARINER	The Winter's Tale
LEONATO, governor of Messina	Much Ado About Nothing	MARSHAL	Pericles, Prince of Tyre
		MARTEXT, Sir Oliver, a clergyman	As You Like It
LEONINE, a murderer	Pericles, Prince of Tyre	MARTIUS	Titus Andronicus
LEONTES, King of Sicily	The Winter's Tale	MASTER GUNNER of Orleans	Henry VI Part 1
LEPIDUS	Antony and Cleopatra, Julius Caesar		
		MASTER of a ship	Henry VI Part 2
LICHORIDA, Thaisa's nurse	Pericles, Prince of Tyre	MASTER of a ship	The Tempest
LIEUTENANT of the Tower	Henry VI Part 3	MATE of a ship	Henry VI Part 2
LIGARIUS	Julius Caesar	MAYOR of London	Henry VI Part 1
LINCOLN, Bishop of	Henry VIII	MAYOR of Saint Albans	Henry VI Part 2
LODOVICO	Othello	MAYOR of York	Henry VI Part 3
LONGUEVILLE	Love's Labour's Lost	MELUN, Count	King John
LORD CHAMBERLAIN	Henry VIII	MENAN	Antony and Cleopatra
LORD CHANCELLOR	Henry VIII	MENECRATES	Antony and Cleopatra
LORD CHIEF JUSTICE	Henry IV Part 2	MENELAUS	Troilus and Cressida
LORD MARSHAL	Richard II	MENENIUS Agrippa	Coriolanus
LORD MAYOR OF LONDON	Henry VIII	MENTEITH, a Thane	Macbeth
LORD MAYOR OF LONDON	Richard III	MERCADE, a messenger	Love's Labour's Lost
LORENZO	The Merchant of Venice	MERCHANT OF EPHESUS	The Comedy of Errors
LOUIS THE DAUPHIN	King John	MERCUTIO	Romeo and Juliet
LOUIS, King	Henry VI Part 3	MESSALA	Julius Caesar
LOVELL, Sir Thomas	Henry VIII	METELLUS CIMBER	Julius Caesar
LUCENTIO, from Pisa	The Taming of the Shrew	MICHAEL, Sir	Henry IV Part 1
		MILAN, Duke of	The Two Gentlemen of Verona
LUCETTA, a waiting-woman	The Two Gentlemen of Verona		
		MIRANDA	The Tempest
LUCIANA	The Comedy of Errors	MONTAGUE, Marquis of	Henry VI Part 3
LUCILIUS, a servant	Timon of Athens	MONTAGUE, Romeo's father	Romeo and Juliet
LUCILLIUS	Julius Caesar		
LUCIO, 'a fantastic'	Measure for Measure	MONTAGUE'S WIFE	Romeo and Juliet
LUCIUS	Titus Andronicus	MONTANO, Governor of Cyprus	Othello
LUCIUS, a flattering Lord	Timon of Athens		
LUCIUS, a servant	Julius Caesar	MONTGOMERY, Sir John	Henry VI Part 3
LUCIUS, an ambassador	Cymbeline, King of Britain	MONTJOY, the French Herald	Henry V
LUCIUS' SERVANT	Timon of Athens	MOPSA, a shepherdess	The Winter's Tale
LUCULLUS' SERVANT	Timon of Athens	MOROCCO, Prince of	The Merchant of Venice
LUCULLUS, a flattering Lord	Timon of Athens	MORTIMER, aka Earl of March	Henry IV Part 1
LUCY, Sir William	Henry VI Part 1	MORTIMER, Edmund	Henry VI Part 1

Character	Play
MORTIMER, Lady	Henry IV Part 1
MORTIMER, Sir Hugh	Henry VI Part 3
MORTIMER, Sir John	Henry VI Part 3
MORTON	Henry IV Part 2
MOTE	A Midsummer Night's Dream
MOTE, a page	Love's Labour's Lost
MOULDY, Ralph	Henry IV Part 2
MOWBRAY, Thomas, Duke of Norfolk	Richard II
MURELLUS, a tribune	Julius Caesar
MUSTARDSEED	A Midsummer Night's Dream
MUTIUS	Titus Andronicus
MYRMIDONS	Troilus and Cressida
NATHANIEL, a servingman	The Taming of the Shrew
NATHANIEL, Sir, a curate	Love's Labour's Lost
NELL, a country wench	The Two Noble Kinsmen
NELL, a kitchen-maid	The Comedy of Errors
NERISSA, a waiting-gentlewoman	The Merchant of Venice
NESTOR	Troilus and Cressida
NICANOR, a Volscian	Coriolanus
NIM	Henry V
NIM	The Merry Wives of Windsor
NORFOLK, Duke of	Henry VIII
NORFOLK, Duke of	Henry VI Part 3 and Richard III
NORFOLK, old Duchess of	Henry VIII
NORTHUMBERLAND, Earl of	Henry VI Part 3
NORTHUMBERLAND'S WIFE	Henry IV Part 2
OBERON, King of the Fairies	A Midsummer Night's Dream
OCTAVIA	Antony and Cleopatra
OCTAVIUS Caesar	Julius Caesar
OCTAVIUS CAESAR	Antony and Cleopatra
OLD ATHENIAN	Timon of Athens
OLDCASTLE, Sir John	Henry IV Part 1
OLD MAN	Macbeth
OLD MAN, Gloucester's tenant	King Lear
OLIVER	As You Like It
OLIVIA, a Countess	Twelfth Night
OPHELIA	Hamlet
ORLANDO	As You Like It
ORLÉANS, Duke of	Henry V
ORSINO, Duke of Illyria	Twelfth Night
OSRIC	Hamlet
OSTLER	Henry IV Part 1
OSWALD, Goneril's steward	King Lear
OTHELLO, the Moor of Venice	Othello
OVERDONE, Mistress, a bawd	Measure for Measure
OWAIN GLYNDWR	Henry IV Part 1
OXFORD, Earl of	Henry VI Part 3 and Richard III
PAGE, Anna	The Merry Wives of Windsor
PAGE, Master George	The Merry Wives of Windsor
PAGE, Mistress Margaret	The Merry Wives of Windsor
PAGE, William	The Merry Wives of Windsor
PAINTER	Timon of Athens

Character	Play
PALAMON, a noble kinsman	The Two Noble Kinsmen
PANDARUS, a Lord	Troilus and Cressida
PANDER	Pericles, Prince of Tyre
PANDOLF, Cardinal	King John
PANTHINO, a servant	The Two Gentlemen of Verona
PARIS	Romeo and Juliet
PARIS	Troilus and Cressida
PAROLES	All's Well That Ends Well
PATIENCE, a waiting woman	Henry VIII
PATROCLUS	Troilus and Cressida
PAULINA	The Winter's Tale
PEASEBLOSSOM	A Midsummer Night's Dream
PEDANT, schoolmaster from Mantu	The Taming of the Shrew
PEMBROKE, Earl of	King John
PERCY, Earl of Northumberland	Henry IV Parts 1 and 2
PERCY, Earl of Northumberland	Richard II
PERCY, Harry	Richard II
PERDITA	The Winter's Tale
PERICLES, Prince of Tyre	Pericles, Prince of Tyre
PETER	Romeo and Juliet
PETER, a servingman	The Taming of the Shrew
PETER OF POMFRET, a prophet	King John
PETER THUMP	Henry VI Part 2
PETO	Henry IV Part 2
PETRUCCIO	Romeo and Juliet
PETRUCHIO, a gentleman of Verona	The Taming of the Shrew
PHILEMON, Cerimon's servant	Pericles, Prince of Tyre
PHILIP, a servingman	The Taming of the Shrew
PHILIP the BASTARD	King John
PHILO	Antony and Cleopatra
PHILOTUS' SERVANT	Timon of Athens
PHOEBE, a shepherdess	As You Like It
PHRYNIA, a whore	Timon of Athens
PINCH, Doctor, a schoolmaster	The Comedy of Errors
PINDARUS	Julius Caesar
PIRITHOUS	The Two Noble Kinsmen
PISANIO, a servant	Cymbeline, King of Britain
PISTOL, Ensign	Henry V The Merry Wives of Windsor Henry IV Part 2
POET	Julius Caesar
POET	Timon of Athens
POINS, Edward	Henry IV Parts 1 and 2
POLIXENES, King of Bohemia	The Winter's Tale
POLONIUS, a Lord	Hamlet
POMPEY (Pompeius)	Antony and Cleopatra
POMPEY, a clownish servant	Measure for Measure
POPILLIUS Laena, a senator	Julius Caesar
PORTER	Henry IV Part 2
PORTER at Macbeth's castle	Macbeth

Character	Play	Character	Play
PORTER, at the christening	Henry VIII	SALISBURY	Henry V
		SALISBURY, Earl of	Henry VI Parts 1, and 2
PORTIA, an heiress	The Merchant of Venice	SALISBURY, Earl of	King John
PORTIA, Brutus's wife	Julius Caesar	SALISBURY, Earl of	Richard II
POSTHUMUS Leonatus	Cymbeline, King of Britain	SAMSON	Romeo and Juliet
		SANDS, Lord	Henry VIII
PRIAM, King of Troy	Troilus and Cressida	SATURNINUS	Titus Andronicus
PRIEST	Hamlet	SAWYER	Henry VI Part 2
PRIEST	Twelfth Night	SAYE, Lord	Henry VI Part 2
PRINCE EDWARD	Henry VI Part 3 and Richard III	SCALES, Lord	Henry VI Part 2
		SCARUS	Antony and Cleopatra
PRINCE HAL	Henry IV Parts 1 and 2	SCRIVENER	Richard III
PRINCE HENRY	King John	SCROPE, Sir Stephen	Richard II
PRINCE JOHN of Lancaster	Henry IV Part 2	SEBASTIAN	The Tempest
PRINCESS of France	Love's Labour's Lost	SEBASTIAN	Twelfth Night
PROCULEIUS	Antony and Cleopatra	SECOND LORD DUMAINE	All's Well That Ends Well
PROSPERO	The Tempest	SECOND MERCHANT	The Comedy of Errors
PROTEUS, a gentleman of Verona	The Two Gentlemen of Verona	SECOND OFFICER	Twelfth Night
		SELEUCUS	Antony and Cleopatra
PROVOST	Measure for Measure	SEMPRONIUS	Titus Andronicus
PUBLIUS	Titus Andronicus	SEMPRONIUS, a flattering Lord	Timon of Athens
PUBLIUS, a senator	Julius Caesar		
QUEEN, Cymbeline's wife	Cymbeline, King of Britain	SENIOR, Duke	As You Like It
		SENTRY and men of his WATCH	Antony and Cleopatra
QUEEN, wife of Richard II	Richard II		
QUEEN ELEANOR	King John	SERGEANT	Henry VI Part 2
QUEEN ELIZABETH	Richard III	SERJEANT-AT-ARMS	Henry VIII
QUEEN KATHERINE	Henry VIII	SERVANT of Cornwall	King Lear
QUEEN MARGARET	Henry VI Parts 2 and 3	SERVANT of Olivia	Twelfth Night
QUEEN MARGARET	Richard III	SERVANT of the old shepherd	The Winter's Tale
QUICKLY, Mistress	Henry IV Parts 1 and 2		
QUICKLY, Mistress	The Merry Wives of Windsor	SERVILIUS, a servant	Timon of Athens
		SEXTON	Much Ado About Nothing
QUINCE, a carpenter	A Midsummer Night's Dream	SEYTON, servant of Macbeth	Macbeth
QUINTUS	Titus Andronicus	SHADOW, Simon	Henry IV Part 2
RAMBURES, Lord	Henry V	SHALLOW, Robert, a country justice	Henry IV Part 2
RATCLIFF, Sir Richard	Richard III		The Merry Wives of Windsor
REGAN	King Lear		
RENÉ, King of Naples	Henry VI Part 1	SHEPHERD, father of Joan	Henry VI Part 1
REYNALDO, a servant	Hamlet	SHERIFF	Henry IV Part 1
REYNALDO, a steward	All's Well That Ends Well	SHERIFF	King John
RICHARD II, King	Richard II	SHERIFF	Richard III
RICHARD PLANTAGENET	Henry VI Part 1	SHYLOCK, a Jew	The Merchant of Venice
RICHARD PLANTAGENET	Henry VI Part 3	SICINIUS Velutus, tribune	Coriolanus
RICHARD, Crookback	Henry VI Part 2	SILENCE, a country justice	Henry IV Part 2
RICHARD, Duke of Gloucester	Richard III	SILIUS	Antony and Cleopatra
		SILVIA	The Two Gentlemen of Verona
RICHARD, the young	The Merry Wives of Windsor		
		SILVIUS, a young shepherd	As You Like It
ROBIN, Sir John's page	The Merry Wives of Windsor	SIMPCOX'S WIFE	Henry VI Part 2
		SIMPCOX, Simon	Henry VI Part 2
ROCHESTER, Bishop of	Henry VIII	SIMPLE, Peter, Slender's servant	The Merry Wives of Windsor
RODERIGO, a Venetian gentleman	Othello		
		SIWARD, Earl of Northumberland	Macbeth
ROMEO	Romeo and Juliet		
ROSALIND	As You Like It	SIWARD, the younger	Macbeth
ROSALINE	Love's Labour's Lost	SIX COUNTRYMEN	The Two Noble Kinsmen
ROSENCRANTZ	Hamlet	SIX KNIGHTS	The Two Noble Kinsmen
ROSS, a Thane	Macbeth	SIX SPIRITS	Henry VIII
ROSS, Lord	Richard II	SIX WITCHES	Macbeth
ROUSILLON, Bertram, Count of	All's Well That Ends Well	SLENDER, Master Abraham	The Merry Wives of Windsor
ROUSILLON, Countess of	All's Well That Ends Well	SLY, Christopher, beggar and tinker	The Taming of the Shrew
RUGBY, John	The Merry Wives of Windsor		
		SMITH the WEAVER	Henry VI Part 2
RUMOUR, the Presenter	Henry IV Part 2	SNARE, a sergeant	Henry IV Part 2
RUSSELL	Henry IV Part 1	SNOUT, a tinker	A Midsummer Night's Dream
RUTLAND, Earl of	Henry VI Part 3		
SAINT ASAPH, Bishop of	Henry VIII	SNUG, a joiner	A Midsummer Night's Dream
SALERIO	The Merchant of Venice		

Character	Play
SOLANIO	The Merchant of Venice
SOLDIER of Alcibiades' army	Timon of Athens
SOLDIER who has killed his father	Henry VI Part 3
SOLDIER who has killed his son	Henry VI Part 3
SOLINUS, Duke of Ephesus	The Comedy of Errors
SOMERSET, Duke of	Henry VI Parts 1, 2 and 3
SOMERVILLE	Henry VI Part 3
SOOTHSAYER	Antony and Cleopatra
SOOTHSAYER	Julius Caesar
SOOTHSAYER, called Philarmonus	Cymbeline, King of Britain
SOUTHWELL, John, a priest	Henry VI Part 2
SPANIARD	Cymbeline, King of Britain
SPEED	The Two Gentlemen of Verona
SPIRIT LIKE A CAT	Macbeth
STAFFORD'S BROTHER	Henry VI Part 2
STAFFORD, Sir Humphrey	Henry VI Part 2
STANLEY, Lord, Earl of Derby	Richard III
STANLEY, Sir John	Henry VI Part 2
STARVELING, a tailor	A Midsummer Night's Dream
STEFANO, Alonso's drunken butler	The Tempest
STEFANO, Portia's servant	The Merchant of Venice
STOKESLEY, Bishop of London	Henry VIII
STRATO	Julius Caesar
SUFFOLK, Duke of	Henry VIII
SUFFOLK, Earl of	Henry VI Part 1
SURREY, Duke of	Richard II
SURREY, Earl of	Henry IV Part 2
SURREY, Earl of	Henry VIII
TABORER, called Timothy	The Two Noble Kinsmen
TAILOR	The Taming of the Shrew
TALBOT, John	Henry VI Part 1
TAMORA, Queen of the Goths	Titus Andronicus
TAURUS	Antony and Cleopatra
THAISA	Pericles, Prince of Tyre
THALIART, a villain	Pericles, Prince of Tyre
THERSITES	Troilus and Cressida
THESEUS, Duke of Athens	A Midsummer Night's Dream
THESEUS, Duke of Athens	The Two Noble Kinsmen
THIDIAS	Antony and Cleopatra
THOMAS, Duke of Clarence	Henry IV Part 2
THOMAS, Lord Mowbray	Henry IV Part 2
THREE APPARITIONS	Macbeth
THREE FISHERMEN	Pericles, Prince of Tyre
THREE MURDERERS	Macbeth
THREE NEIGHBOURS	Henry VI Part 2
THREE PRENTICES	Henry VI Part 2
THREE QUEENS	The Two Noble Kinsmen
THREE STRANGERS	Timon of Athens
THURIO	The Two Gentlemen of Verona
TIMANDRA, a whore	Timon of Athens
TIME, as chorus	The Winter's Tale
TIMON of Athens	Timon of Athens
TIRREL, Sir James	Richard III
TITANIA, Queen of the Fairies	A Midsummer Night's Dream

Character	Play
TITINIUS, a Roman officer	Julius Caesar
TITUS ANDRONICUS	Titus Andronicus
TITUS' SERVANT	Timon of Athens
TOUCHSTONE, a jester	As You Like It
TRANIO, a servant	The Taming of the Shrew
TRAVERS, Northumberland's servant	Henry IV Part 2
TREBONIUS	Julius Caesar
TRINCULO, Alonso's jester	The Tempest
TROILUS	Troilus and Cressida
TUBAL, a Jew	The Merchant of Venice
TUTOR, of Rutland, a chaplain	Henry VI Part 3
TWELVE COUNTRYMEN	The Winter's Tale
TYBALT	Romeo and Juliet
ULYSSES	Troilus and Cressida
URSULA, attendant on Hero	Much Ado About Nothing
VALENTINE, a gentleman of Verona	The Two Gentlemen of Verona
VALENTINE, attending Orsino	Twelfth Night
VALENTINE, kinsman of Titus	Titus Andronicus
VALERIA	Coriolanus
VALERIUS, a Theban	The Two Noble Kinsmen
VALTEMAND	Hamlet
VARRIUS	Antony and Cleopatra
VARRIUS, a Lord	Measure for Measure
VARRUS	Julius Caesar
VAUGHAN, Sir Thomas	Richard III
VAUX, a messenger	Henry VI Part 2
VAUX, Sir Nicholas	Henry VIII
VENICE, Duke of	Othello
VENICE, Duke of	The Merchant of Venice
VENTIDIUS	Antony and Cleopatra
VENTIDIUS	Timon of Athens
VERGES, the Headborough	Much Ado About Nothing
VERNON	Henry VI Part 1
VERNON, Sir Richard	Henry IV Part 1
VINCENTIO, Lucentio's father	The Taming of the Shrew
VINCENTIO, The Duke of Vienna	Measure for Measure
VINTNER	Henry IV Part 1
VIOLA, a lady	Twelfth Night
VIRGILIA	Coriolanus
VOLUMNIA	Coriolanus
VOLUMNIUS	Julius Caesar
WAITING-GENTLEWOMAN	Macbeth
WART, Thomas	Henry IV Part 2
WARWICK	Henry V
WARWICK, Earl of	Henry VI Parts 1, 2 and 3
WARWICK, Neville, Earl of	Henry IV Part 2
WATCHMEN	Much Ado About Nothing
WESTMINSTER, Abbot of	Richard II
WESTMORLAND	Henry V
WESTMORLAND, Earl of	Henry IV Parts 1, 2 and 3
WHITMORE, Walter	Henry VI Part 2
WIDOW	The Taming of the Shrew
WIDOW CAPILET	All's Well That Ends Well
WILLIAM, a countryman	As You Like It
WILLIAM, Lord Hastings	Richard III
WILLIAMS, Michael	Henry V
WILLOUGHBY, Lord	Richard II

Character	Play	Character	Play
WINCHESTER, Bishop of	*Henry VI Part 1*	YORK, Duchess of	*Richard II*
WITCH, Margery Jordan	*Henry VI Part 2*	YORK, Duchess of	*Richard III*
WOMAN, attending Emilia	*The Two Noble Kinsmen*	YORK, Duke of	*Henry V*
WOODVILLE, Anthony, Earl RIVERS	*Richard III*	YORK, Duke of	*Henry VI Part 2*
		YORK, Duke of	*Richard II*
WOODVILLE, Lieutenant of Tower	*Henry VI Part 1*	YOUNG CATO	*Julius Caesar*
		YOUNG LUCIUS, a boy	*Titus Andronicus*
WOOER of the jailer's daughter	*The Two Noble Kinsmen*	YOUNG MARTIUS	*Coriolanus*
WORCESTER, Earl of	*Henry IV Part 1*		

First Lines of Shakespearian Sonnets

No.

1 From fairest creatures we desire increase
2 When forty winters shall besiege thy brow
3 Look in thy glass, and tell the face thou viewest
4 Unthrifty loveliness, why dost thou spend
5 Those hours that with gentle work did frame
6 Then let not winter's ragged hand deface
7 Lo, in the orient when the gracious light
8 Music to hear, why hear'st thou music sadly?
9 Is it for fear to wet a widow's eye
10 For shame deny that thou bear'st love to any
11 As fast as thou shalt wane, so fast thou grow'st
12 When I do count the clock that tells the time
13 O that you were yourself! But, love, you are
14 Not from the stars do I my judgement pluck
15 When I consider every thing that grows
16 But wherefore do not you a mightier way
17 Who will believe my verse in time to come
18 Shall I compare thee to a summer's day?
19 Devouring time, blunt thou the lion's paws
20 A woman's face with nature's own hand painted
21 So is it not with me as with that muse
22 My glass shall not persuade me I am old
23 As an unperfect actor on the stage
24 Mine eye hath played the painter, and hath steeled
25 Let those who are in favour with their stars
26 Lord of my love, to whom in vassalage
27 Weary with toil I haste me to my bed
28 How can I then return in happy plight
29 When, in disgrace with fortune and men's eyes
30 When to the sessions of sweet silent thought
31 Thy bosom is endeared with all hearts
32 If thou survive my well-contented day
33 Full many a glorious morning have I seen
34 Why didst thou promise such a beauteous day
35 No more be grieved at that which thou hast done
36 Let me confess that we two must be twain
37 As a decrepit father takes delight
38 How can my muse want subject to invent
39 O, how thy worth with manners may I sing
40 Take all my loves, my love, yea, take them all
41 Those pretty wrongs that liberty commits
42 That thou hast her, it is not all my grief
43 When most I wink, then do mine eyes best see
44 If the dull substance of my flesh were thought
45 The other two, slight air and purging fire
46 Mine eye and heart are at a mortal war
47 Betwixt mine eye and heart a league is took
48 How careful was I when I took my way
49 Against that time – if ever that time come
50 How heavy do I journey on the way
51 Thus can my love excuse the slow offence
52 So am I as the rich whose blessed key
53 What is your substance, whereof are you made

54 O how much more doth beauty beauteous seem
55 Not marble nor the gilded monuments
56 Sweet love, renew thy force. Be it not said
57 Being your slave, what should I do but tend
58 That god forbid, that made me first your slave
59 If there be nothing new, but that which is
60 Like as the waves make towards the pebbled shore
61 Is it thy will thy image should keep open
62 Sin of self-love possesseth all mine eye
63 Against my love shall be as I am now
64 When I have seen by time's fell hand defaced
65 Since brass, nor stone, nor earth, nor boundless sea
66 Tired with all these, for restful death I cry
67 Ah, wherefore with infection should he live
68 Thus is his cheek the map of days outworn
69 Those parts of thee that the world's eye doth view
70 That thou are blamed shall not be thy defect
71 No longer mourn for me when I am dead
72 O, lest the world should task you to recite
73 That time of year thou mayst in me behold
74 But be contented when that fell arrest
75 So are you to my thoughts as food to life
76 Why is my verse so barren of new pride
77 Thy glass will show thee how thy beauties wear
78 So oft have I invoked thee for my muse
79 Whilst I alone did call upon thy aid
80 O, how I faint when I of you do write
81 Or I shall live your epitaph to make
82 I grant thou wert not married to my muse
83 I never saw that you did painting need
84 Who is it that says most which can say more
85 My tongue-tied muse in manners holds her still
86 Was it the proud full sail of his great verse
87 Farewell – thou art too dear for my possessing
88 When thou shalt be disposed to set me light
89 Say that thou didst forsake me for some fault
90 Then hate me when thou wilt, if ever, now
91 Some glory in their birth, some in their skill
92 But do thy worst to steal thyself away
93 So shall I live supposing thou art true
94 They that have power to hurt and will do none
95 How sweet and lovely dost thou make the shame
96 Some say thy fault is youth, some wantonness
97 How like a winter hath my absence been
98 From you have I been absent in the spring
99 The forward violet thus did I chide
100 Where art thou, muse, that thou forget'st so long
101 O truant muse, what shall be thy amends
102 My love is strengthened, though more weak in seeming
103 Alack, what poverty my muse brings forth
104 To me, fair friend, you never can be old
105 Let not my love be called idolatry

First Lines of Sonnets: Alphabetical Order

SHAKESPEARE

SOVEREIGNS

General Information on Sovereigns of England and Great Britain

William I Domesday Book of 1086 contained details of the land settlement of England and its purpose was to maximize the land tax yield. It received its name in the 12th century to signify that, like the day of judgement, there could be no appeal from its verdict.

Hereward the Wake ('Watchful One'), a Lincolnshire squire, raided Peterborough Abbey in 1070 as a protest against William's appointment of a Norman abbot. He took refuge on the Isle of Ely and eventually escaped through the Fens.

Bishop Odo of Bayeux was William's half-brother and it was he who commissioned the Bayeux Tapestry (embroidery).

Of William's four sons, Robert became duke of Normandy and Richard died in infancy.

William was Edward the Confessor's cousin by way of his mother Emma, who was the sister of William's grandfather, Count Richard II. Edward the Confessor was Harold II's brother-in-law by way of his marriage to Edith, Harold's sister.

William's invasion forces assembled at the mouth of the Dives river in September 1066 but adverse winds prevented a due-north sailing to the Isle of Wight, so he regrouped at St Valéry on Somme and sailed on 27 September to the south coast of England and took Pevensey and Hastings unchallenged. Harold was victorious against Tostig and Harald Hardraade at Stamford Bridge, near York, on 25 September and met William at the Battle of Hastings on 14 October. William only had about 7,000 troops but his archers won the day and, when Harold was killed, the English gave up.

William II William was called Rufus because of his ruddy complexion.

Malcolm III of Scotland (Malcolm Canmore, aka Great Head) became king of Scotland in 1057 on the death of Macbeth, who had killed Malcolm's father, Duncan, in 1040. He invaded England five times between 1061 and 1093 and was killed at Alnwick in Northumberland. Four of his sons succeeded him – Duncan, Edgar, Alexander and David.

Traditionally William was shot by an arrow fired by a Norman knight called Walter Tirel, although many believe that William's younger brother Henry was the instigator.

Henry I Henry was the only English-born son of William I.

His brother Robert was paid a pension of 3,000 marks to resign his claim to the English throne and concentrate his attentions on Normandy, but in 1105–6 Henry was forced to make war against his brother's maladministration. Robert was defeated at Tinchebrai in 1106, and was kept a prisoner for life.

In 1120, Henry's only legitimate son, William, was drowned on his way from Normandy to England in what is now known as the *White Ship* disaster.

Matilda Matilda was pledged the throne in 1127 but Stephen became king in 1135. Matilda invaded the kingdom in 1139, landed at Arundel and established a stronghold in the West Country with her half-brother Robert of Gloucester. She captured Stephen at Lincoln and pronounced herself 'Lady of the English'. Her forces were defeated September 14 1141 while besieging the royalist-held Wolvesey Castle in what is known as the 'Rout of Winchester'. Robert Earl of Gloucester was taken prisoner and exchanged for King Stephen. Matilda was never crowned and her six months' reign is often disregarded.

Stephen Stephen usurped the crown by declaring Matilda illegitimate, as her father had remarried.

Henry II Henry was the first Plantagenet king of England.

He systematically destroyed the adulterine (unlicensed) castles which had sprung up during the reign of his predecessor.

Henry's conflict with Thomas à Becket was over a written statement made by Henry at Clarendon, near Salisbury, on 30 January 1164 whereby he wanted the benefit of clergy to be lifted and have lay authorities try clerks taking holy orders.

The English pope, Adrian IV, gave Henry authority over the whole of Ireland.

Incited by Queen Eleanor, Prince John and Richard rebelled against Henry and their cause was espoused by the kings of France and Scotland. William the Lion of Scotland was taken prisoner at Alnwick and forced to sign the Treaty of Falaise, 1174, thereby swearing allegiance to Henry.

Henry, the first son of Henry II, died in 1183 and his second son, Geoffrey, was killed in a tournament in Paris in 1185.

Henry's mistress, the fair Rosamond, daughter of Walter Clifford, was said to have borne him two sons – William Longsword, earl of Salisbury, and Geoffrey, archbishop of York – but this is unlikely.

Henry and his two sons were known as Angevin kings, and although Plantagenet was the other name for this royal House, subsequent members are not Angevin. To confuse matters further, although Richard II was traditionally the last king of the House of Plantagenet, the Yorkist Richard III was the last of the direct line.

Henry's second son, Henry (aka FitzHenry), was crowned on 14 June 1170, to rule in association with his father, and was known as Henry III or Henry the Young King; he died of dysentery in 1183.

Richard I

Richard was given the Duchy of Aquitaine aged 11, and was enthroned as duke of Aquitaine at Poitiers in 1172.

He departed for the Holy Land to fight the third Crusade in 1190.

Richard made a truce for three years with Saladin but was captured on his way home by Duke Leopold in December 1192. He was imprisoned at the duke's castle at Durnstein on the Danube and then handed over to Henry VI of Germany. Richard was released in February 1194 after paying a ransom of nearly 150,000 marks.

Richard left Hubert Walter as virtual ruler of England while he was away.

John

John became count of Mortain on Richard's accession in 1189.

When Richard recognized his nephew, Arthur, duke of Brittany, as his heir in October 1190, John broke his oath to Richard not to enter England while he was away at the Crusades.

Richard finally accepted John as his heir in 1196.

John's first marriage to Isabella of Gloucester was dissolved on the grounds of consanguinity, both parties being great-grandchildren of Henry I. John's second marriage, to Isabella of Angoulême, was largely responsible for the loss of many French territories.

Pope Innocent III excommunicated John in November 1209 because of his refusal to accept Stephen Langton as archbishop of Canterbury.

The Barons' War of 1215–17 ensued after John sealed the Magna Carta of 15 June 1215 but did not abide by it. Magna Carta comprises a preamble and 63 clauses. The most famous clauses are (39), guaranteeing every free man security from illegal interference in his person or property, (40), which guaranteed justice to all, and (12), which stated that the king was not to levy taxes without reference to the 'common council'.

Henry III

Henry was 9 years old when he became king, so William Marshal, First Earl of Pembroke and Striguil, acted as his regent for the first three years, followed by Hubert de Burgh for the next eight years.

Henry was forced to agree to the Provisions of Oxford, 1258, which created a council of fifteen barons and formed the first judicial Parliament.

The civil war between Henry III and his barons, led by Simon de Montfort, was called the Second Baron's War (1264–7).

Edward I

Edward won great renown as a knight on the eigth, and last, Crusade of 1270 and did not return home for his coronation until 1274.

He campaigned against Llewelyn ap Gruffud, of Gwynedd, and finally forced him into submission in 1276; and after his death in 1282 the principality was formally annexed to the English Crown by the Statute of Wales, 1284.

In 1289 Edward betrothed his infant son to Margaret, the infant Queen of Scotland (Maid of Norway), in order to unite England and Scotland, but Margaret died the following year.

Edward called the 'Model Parliament' of 1295 to allay discontent at home and the following year marched north, stripped John Balliol of his crown and carried the Stone of Scone back to England. He had a setback at Stirling Bridge in 1297, but the following year he trounced William Wallace at Falkirk.

Edward II

In 1301 Edward became the first English Prince of Wales.

His favourite was Piers Gaveston, whom he made duke of Cornwall. When Gaveston was executed in 1312, Edward chose Hugh le Despenser and his son as his new favourites, and they aided in the overthrow of Thomas, earl of Lancaster, in 1321.

Edward was defeated by Robert the Bruce at Bannockburn, 24 June 1314.

Edward's wife, Isabella, despised him and took a lover in Roger de Mortimer. In 1326 she landed on the coast of Suffolk, executed the Despensers and forced Edward to abdicate. Edward was murdered the following year in Berkeley Castle, Gloucestershire, probably by Isabella and Roger de Mortimer. Edward III was crowned in January 1327, eight months before his father died.

Edward III

In 1328 Edward married Phillipa of Hainault and two years later put Mortimer to death and banished his mother to Castle Rising.

Charles IV of France died without a son in 1328 and Edward claimed his kingdom by right of his mother, who was Charles's sister. He declared war against Philip VI in 1337, which was in effect the start of the Hundred Years War.

Accompanied by his eldest son, Edward the Black Prince, Edward had a great victory at Crécy in 1346 and another at Poitiers in 1356, where it is said the Black Prince gained his spurs.

Edward's mistress from 1366 onwards was Alice Perrers, his wife's lady-in-waiting, who let the government slip into the hands of Edward's fourth son, John of Gaunt.

The Black Prince died in 1376 and his son by Joan, the Fair Maid of Kent, succeeded Edward III, as Richard II.

Richard II

Although a council of twelve was officially entrusted to govern during Richard's minority, in effect John of Gaunt was the regent.

Poll tax of 1380 created national unrest and led to the Peasants' Revolt of 1381, when rebels under Wat Tyler took Rochester Castle in Kent and then marched on London with fellow radicals from Essex. Richard saw the Essex men at Mile End and made extensive promises, and the next day, 14 June, met Wat Tyler's men at Smithfield. Tyler was struck down by the mayor of London, William Walworth, in revenge for the atrocities of the previous day when the archbishop of Canterbury, Simon of Sudbury, was murdered.

John of Gaunt died in 1399 and his son succeeded him as duke of Lancaster. Richard went to Ireland in May 1399 and on 4 July Henry, duke of Lancaster, landed back in England. Although Richard hurried back to England, he submitted to his cousin at Flint on 19 August and was put in the Tower. On 29 September 1399 he resigned the Crown in favour of Henry and he seems to have been murdered at Pontefract Castle, Yorkshire, early in 1400.

Richard was the first British monarch to abdicate.

Henry IV

Henry was the first king of the House of Lancaster.

His surname of Bolingbroke came from his birthplace in Lincolnshire.

Henry defeated Harry Hotspur at Shrewsbury on 21 July 1403, when Hotspur was slain.

Henry V

Henry had Richard II's body buried in Westminster Abbey.

Henry thought he had a good claim to the French crown through his great-grandfather, Edward III.

Henry's famous victory at Agincourt was on 25 October 1415.

In 1420 Henry became regent of France via the 'Perpetual Peace' of Troyes.

Henry persecuted the Lollards, would-be Church reformers who had become the first group of English heretics to represent a political threat.

Henry VI

Henry was less than a year old when he became king of England, and on the death of his maternal grandfather, King Charles VI, he became king of France when just over 1 year of age. He was officially crowned king of England in 1429 and of France in 1431.

By 1453 the Hundred Years War was effectively over, with England expelled from all France except Calais.

Cade's Rebellion of 1450 was a revolt by Kentish gentry against the high taxes and alleged corruption in Henry's council. On 18 June Cade defeated a royal army at Sevenoaks and then marched on London. He was eventually killed attempting to evade arrest at Heathfield, Sussex.

Edward IV

Richard, duke of York, became protector while Henry VI suffered temporary madness in 1454. Richard had in fact a better title to the crown than Henry, as he was descended from Lionel, duke of Clarence, third son of Edward III. When Henry recovered, Richard refused to hand back the throne. He defeated Henry at St Albans on 22 May 1455, thereby starting the Wars of the Roses. Although in the ascendant, York did not claim the Crown until 1460, when he became Henry's heir, resulting in Edward Prince of Wales being disinherited. Richard was killed at Wakefield soon after but his son claimed the Crown as Edward IV, after his victory at Mortimer's Cross, and the second battle at St Albans. After a series of victories at Towton, Hedgeley Moor and Hexham, Edward married Elizabeth Woodvillle and the opposition to this family briefly restored Henry VI to the throne in 1470. Undeterred, Edward regrouped and with only 2,000 men, defeated the Lancastrians and killed Warwick at Barnet on 14 April 1471. Edward carried on to Tewkesbury and on 4 May 1471 his decisive victory and the death of Edward, Prince of Wales, effectively ended the Lancastrian resistance. Henry VI was killed soon after in the Tower of London.

Edward V

The 12-year-old King Edward V was escorted from Ludlow by Earl Rivers but Richard, duke of Gloucester, the future Richard III, intercepted him at Northampton, brought him to London on 4 May 1483 and was then made protector. In June, Edward's brother, Richard, duke of York, joined him in the Tower of London and they were never seen again. In 1674 some bones were found and re-interred as theirs in Westminster Abbey.

Richard III

Richard became duke of Gloucester in 1461.

On the death of Edward IV on 9 April 1483, Richard became Protector of the Realm for Edward's son and successor, the 12-year-old King Edward V, whom he imprisoned in the Tower of London along with his younger brother Richard on the premise that Edward IV's marriage was invalid and therefore his sons were illegitimate. Richard was proclaimed king in June 1483.

It is possible that Richard had a hand in the murder of Henry VI in the Tower of London on the night of 21 May 1471.

Richard's chief supporter had been Henry Stafford, 2nd duke of Buckingham, but soon after Richard's coronation he entered into a plot with friends of Henry, earl of Richmond, the future Henry VII. The attempt failed and Buckingham was executed. Henry landed at Milford Haven on 7 August 1485. Richard met him at Bosworth on 22 August, and there lost his kingdom and his life. He was the last British monarch to die in battle.

Henry VII

Henry was the first Tudor monarch of England. His claim to the throne became definite on the deaths of Henry VI's only son, Edward, and Henry VI himself, which made Henry Tudor the last surviving male heir of the House of Lancaster.

Henry's victory at Bosworth owed a great deal to his stepfather, Lord Stanley, deserting to him. Henry united the houses of York and Lancaster by way of his marriage to Elizabeth of York.

In 1487 Lambert Simnel, the son of a baker, under the influence of a priest named William Symonds, claimed to be Edward Plantagenet, son of George, duke of Clarence. He was crowned in Dublin in 1487, but his followers were defeated at Stoke and Henry gave Simnel a job in his kitchens. In 1491 Perkin Warbeck impersonated Richard, duke of York, one of the princes presumed dead in the Tower. Warbeck invaded south-west England in 1498 but was caught by Henry and eventually hanged.

Henry VIII

The six wives of Henry VIII were:

Catherine of Aragon (1485–1536), daughter of Ferdinand II of Spain and Isabella I of Castile. Married 11 June 1509, Chapel of the Observant Friars.

Anne Boleyn (1507–36), marchioness of Pembroke, daughter of Thomas Boleyn. Married 25 January 1533.

Jane Seymour (1509–37), daughter of Sir John Seymour. Married 30 May 1536, Queen's Closet, York Place, London.

Anne of Cleves (1515–57), daughter of John, duke of Cleves. Married 6 January 1540, Greenwich.

Catherine Howard (1521–42), daughter of Lord Edmund Howard. Married 28 July 1540, Oatlands.

Catherine Parr (1512–48), daughter of Sir Thomas Parr. Married 12 July 1543, Hampton Court.

Henry met Francis I in a field near Calais in June 1520, and although the display of friendship was short-lived, the lavish ceremonies became known as the Field of the Cloth of Gold.

Henry accused Thomas Wolsey (1475–1530), Lord Chancellor England 1515–29, of high treason for failing to obtain the pope's permission for the king's divorce from Catherine of Aragon. Wolsey died on the journey from York to London and was succeeded by Thomas More (1478–1535), who was executed in 1535 for refusing to swear the oath to the Act of Succession and thereby denying papal supremacy. Thomas Cromwell now became Henry's most trusted aide. After arranging Henry's divorce from Catherine in 1533 he organized the dissolution of the monasteries, 1536–9, but was ultimately executed on a trumped-up charge of treason in 1540.

Edward VI

Edward was 10 years old when he became king and his uncle, Edward Seymour, duke of Somerset, acted as his first Lord Protector, followed by John Dudley, earl of Warwick.

Lady Jane Grey

Jane was married against her will to the son of the Lord Protector, John Dudley, earl of Warwick, who connived to put her on the throne because she was the great-granddaughter of Henry VII, through her mother Lady Frances Brandon, whose own mother was Mary, the younger of King Henry VIII's two sisters. Jane ruled for only nine days and was beheaded with her husband on 12 February 1554 after her father was found to be involved in the Wyatt Rebellion.

Mary I

Mary was known as Bloody Mary because of her policy of burning heretics.

After she lost Calais in 1554 she was reported to have said that when she died, Calais would be found writ on her heart.

Elizabeth I

Elizabeth was linked romantically with Robert Dudley, earl of Leicester, and later in life with Robert Devereux, earl of Essex, whom she was forced to execute for treason.

Two important conspiracies against Elizabeth were the Ridolfi Plot (1571) and the Babington Plot (1586), which ultimately caused the execution of Mary, Queen of Scots, in 1587.

Elizabeth's chief minister for most of her reign was William Cecil, Lord Burghley.

Elizabeth had a first-class intelligence network which was the envy of Europe; her minister in charge was Francis Walsingham.

James I

James was also James VI of Scotland (1567–1625), after his mother, Mary, Queen of Scots, was forced to abdicate.

James's slogan was 'No Bishop, No King', which was used to reassure the people that Elizabethan Church settlements were to be maintained and that he believed the Anglican Church and the monarchy to be interdependent.

The leader of the Gunpowder Plot of 5 November 1605 was Robert Catesby, and his fellow conspirators included Thomas Winter, John Wright and Guido/Guy Fawkes, all staunch Roman Catholics. The plot was against James's stance on religion, and the aim was to blow up him, his family and all the lords present. The plot failed when Francis Tresham, a newly enrolled conspirator, warned his brother-in-law, Lord Monteagle, not to attend parliament that day.

James's parliament of April–June 1614 was called the 'Addled' because it was dissolved without passing any bills.

Before he became king of England, James was thought to be having a homosexual affair with Esmé Stuart.

The 'Main' plot of 1603 was an attempt to put Arabella Stuart on the throne.

Charles I

The 'Five Members' that Charles attempted to arrest on 4 January 1642 were John Pym, John Hampden, Denzil Holles, Arthur Hesilrige and William Strode.

Charles's parliaments were: the 'Short', 13 April–5 May 1640, in which he demanded money for the Bishops' War against the Scottish covenanters, and the 'Long', in which Charles impeached Strafford and Laud and which ran from 1640 to 1660 but became the 'Rump' after Pride's purge of about 140 royalist MPs on 6 December 1648.

The Bishops' Wars of 1639–40 were provoked by the attempts of Charles to impose Anglicanism on Scotland. The English prayer book was refused and episcopacy was abolished in Scotland. Charles summoned the Short Parliament in order to obtain supplies for the resumption of the war. After the 'Grand Remonstrance', whereby parliament voiced its dissatisfaction with the monarchy, and the incident of the 'Five Members', civil war was imminent and Charles eventually raised his standard at Nottingham on 22 August 1642. After the indecisive battle of Edgehill, 23 October 1642, Charles was forced to retreat at Turnham Green, London, and for the duration of the Civil War based his capital at Oxford. After many more indecisive battles, the formation of the New Model Army in February 1645, commanded by Fairfax and Cromwell, and the royalist defeat at Naseby, June 1645, spelt the end for Charles.

Charles II   James, duke of Monmouth, was the illegitimate son of Charles II and Lucy Walter.

The incident of Charles hiding up an oak tree to escape capture occurred during the Battle of Worcester in 1651.

General George Monk organized the restoration of the monarchy, and Charles entered London in triumph on his birthday, 29 May 1660, after issuing his Declaration of Breda promising a general amnesty and liberty of conscience.

In 1678 anti-Catholic feeling was stoked to fever-point by the trumped-up revelations of Titus Oates about a supposed Popish plot to murder Charles. In 1683 the Rye House Plot was a conspiracy to murder Charles and his brother James, duke of York, as they travelled from Newmarket races to London past Rye House in Hertfordshire. Monmouth, Algernon, Sidney and several prominent Whigs were implicated.

James II   In 1685 the Monmouth Rebellion was crushed and Judge Jeffreys' Bloody Assizes followed.

James was forced to abdicate because of his Catholic tendencies and was succeeded by the Protestant William of Orange.

Aided by a small body of French troops, James invaded Ireland and made an abortive attempt to reclaim his throne, but was defeated at the battle of the Boyne, 1690, and returned to St Germain.

William III   William landed at Torbay on 5 November 1688, following an invitation from the 'Immortal Seven' noblemen to protect the Protestant religion. When James fled to France, William and Mary were declared joint sovereigns. Jacobite resistance was ended by the battles of Killiecrankie, July 1689, and the Boyne, 1690.

William died after his horse stumbled at seeing a mole run out from his hill, causing him to fall and break his right collarbone. Complications set in when William caught an infection and he died on 8 March 1702.

Anne   Only one of Anne's children survived infancy, William, duke of Gloucester, who died in 1700 at the age of 12.

Sarah Churchill, later duchess of Marlborough, was the lifelong friend and confidante of Anne, and when corresponding they often used the names Mrs Freeman and Mrs Morley. Sarah Churchill's cousin, Abigail Masham, née Hill, later became Anne's favourite.

In 1704 a fund was set up by Anne for the benefit of the poorer clergy and this 'Queen Anne's Bounty' was amalgamated into the Church Commissioners when it was set up in 1948.

George I   The Act of Settlement of 1701 ensured the Crown for George.

George married his cousin Sophia Dorothea of Zell in 1682, but divorced her in 1694 for adultery with a Swedish nobleman and kept her imprisoned in the castle of Ahlden until her death in 1726.

The '15' rebellion (1715) was an attempt by Jacobites to put James Edward Stuart, the Old Pretender (son of James II and Mary of Modena), on the throne.

George's unpopularity was not helped by the fact that he never learnt to speak fluently in English.

George II   George was the last British sovereign to lead an army into battle, in 1743 at Dettingen, which he won.

The '45' rebellion (1745) was an attempt to put Charles Edward Stuart, the Young Pretender (son of James Edward Stuart), on the British throne. It was ruthlessly put down by William Augustus, the duke of Cumberland, the second son of George, at Culloden.

George III   George is said to have had a child by Hannah Lightfoot, a Quaker, and it is possible he even married her, although this is extremely doubtful.

George had long periods of insanity and the Prince of Wales, later George IV, was appointed Regent from 1811 onwards.

George IV   George had a much-publicized affair with an actress, Mrs Robinson, when aged 18; his ceremony of marriage with Mrs Maria Fitzherbert, when aged 23, was deemed unlawful in England.

William IV   William was called the Sailor King.

He lived with an actress, Dorothy Jordan, from 1790 to 1811 and she bore him ten children.

SOVEREIGNS

Victoria   Under Salic law, Victoria could not claim her dominion over Hanover, and this title passed to her uncle, Ernest Augustus, duke of Cumberland.

She became Empress of India in 1876, although officially this title was conferred on her on 1 January 1877.

Victoria published *Leaves from the Journal of our Life in the Highlands (1869)* and *More Leaves (1884).*

Victoria was the first monarch to live in Buckingham Palace.

Edward VII   Edward's Christian name was Albert but he used his second name in deference to Queen Victoria.

Edward was cited in a divorce scandal of 1870.

George V   George instigated the monarch's Christmas Day broadcasts to the nation in 1932.

Edward VIII   Abdicated to marry a divorcee and became Governor of the Bahamas in WW2.

George VI   George was a keen tennis player and played in the Wimbledon Championships of 1926.

He substituted the title of Head of the Commonwealth for Emperor of India in 1947.

George's Christian name was Albert but he used his fourth name in deference to Queen Victoria.

Elizabeth II   On 13 June 1996, Elizabeth II had ruled longer than Elizabeth I.

Elizabeth was in Kenya when she heard she was Queen.

The Queen's actual birthday is 21 April; her official birthday falls on the second Saturday in June.

NB The list above contains information on sovereigns since the Norman invasion, which tends to be 90 per cent of any school history curriculum; other sovereigns, either of the whole or part of England, are listed below.

House of Wessex

802–839	Egbert (became ruler of all the English kingdoms from 829–30)
839–858	Aethelwulf (son of Egbert)
858–860	Aethelbald (son of Aethelwulf)
860–865	Aethelbert (brother of Aethelbald)
865–871	Aethelred I (brother of Aethelbert)
871–899	Alfred (the Great, brother of Aethelred I)
899–924	Edward (the Elder, son of Alfred)
924–924	Aelfweard (son of Edward)
924–939	Aethelstan (brother of Aelfweard)
939–946	Edmund I (brother of Aethelstan)
946–955	Eadred (brother of Edmund)
955–959	Eadwig (son of Edmund)
959–975	Edgar (the Peaceful, brother of Eadwig)
975–978	St Edward (the Martyr, son of Edgar)
978–1016	Aethelred II (the Unready or Ill-Advised, brother of St Edward)
1013–1014	Swein Forkbeard (deposed Aethelred II in this year)
1016–1016	Edmund II (Ironside, son of Aethelred II)
1042–1066	St Edward (the Confessor, son of Aethelred II)
1066–1066	Harold II (Godwinson)

House of Denmark

1016–1035	Cnut (the Great, son of Swein Forkbeard)
1037–1040	Harold I (Harefoot, son of Cnut)
1040–1042	Harthacnut (brother of Harold)

Kings and Queens of England and Great Britain

	Reign	Date of accession	Born	Died	Marriage(s)
William I aka the Bastard, the Conqueror	1066–1087	25 Dec.	Falaise, France, c. 1028, illegitimate son of Robert I, 6th duke of Normandy, by Herleva/Arlette, daughter of Fulbert the Tanner.	Abdominal injury while riding via Mantes, died 5 weeks later on 9 Sept. 1087 at Rouen. Buried at the Abbey of St Stephen, Caen.	Matilda (died 1083), daughter of Baldwin V, count of Flanders; 4 sons, 5 daughters. Married at Eu c. 1053.
William II Rufus	1087–1100	26 Sept.	Normandy, c. 1056, 3rd son of William I and Matilda.	Arrow wound while hunting in the New Forest, nr Brockenhurst, Hants, 2 Aug. 1100. Buried in Winchester Cathedral.	Unmarried.
Henry I Beauclerc	1100–1135	5 Aug.	Selby, Yorkshire, 1068, 4th son of William I and Matilda. Buried at Reading Abbey. 1 Dec. 1135.	Fever, St Denis-le-Ferment, Grisors. Aged 67,	Edith (aka Matilda), died 1118, daughter of Malcom III and Margaret. Wed Westminster Abbey, Nov. 1100. Adela, died 1151, daughter of Godfrey VII, count of Louvaine (granddaughter of Edmund Ironside); 1 son, 1 daughter.
Matilda 'Empress Maud'	1141		London, Feb. 1102, only legitimate daughter of Henry I.	Natural causes, Rouen, Normandy. Buried at Fontenvaud Abbey church, Anjou.	Henry V, Emperor of Germany, married in 1114, died in 1125. Geoffrey V, count of Anjou; 3 sons. Married 1128, died 1151.
Stephen	1135–1154	22 Dec.	Blois, France, c. 1096, 3rd son of Stephen aka Henry, count of Blois, and Adela, 5th daughter of William I.	Heart attack, St Martin's Priory, Dover, 25 Oct. 1154. Buried at Faversham Abbey.	Matilda, died 1151, daughter of count of Boulogne and Mary, sister of Matilda (wife of Henry I); 3 sons, 2 daughters. Married 1125.
Henry II Plantagenet Fitzempress Curtmantle	1154–1189	19 Dec.	Le Mans, France, 5 March 1133, eldest son of Geoffrey V, count of Anjou, and Matilda, only daughter of Henry I.	Fever, castle of Chinon, Tours, 6 July 1199. Buried at Fontrevraud Abbey in Anjou, reburied Westminster Abbey.	Eleanor (1122–1204), daughter of duke of Aquitaine and divorced wife of Louis VII of France; 5 sons, 3 daughters. Married at Bordeaux, 1152.
Richard I aka Lionheart	1189–1199	3 Sept.	Oxford, 8 Sept. 1157, 3rd son of Henry II and Eleanor.	Arrow wound while besieging the castle of Chalus, Limousin, France, 6 April 1199. Buried at Fontrevraud Abbey in Anjou, reburied Westminster Abbey.	Berengaria died c.1230, daughter of Sancho VI of Navarre. No ssue. Married at Limassol, Cyprus, 1191.
John aka Lackland	1199–1216	27 May	Beaumont Palace, Oxford, 24 Dec. 1167, 5th son of Henry II and Eleanor.	Dysentery, Newark Castle, Notts, Oct. 1216. Buried at Worcester Cathedral.	Isabel, died 1217. Married 1191 at Marlborough, Wilts; no issue. Isabella, died 1246, daughter of count of Angoulême; 2 sons, 3 daughters. Married at Angoulême, Aug. 1200.

	Reign	Date of accession	Born	Died	Marriage(s)
Henry III aka the Builder	1216–1272	28 Oct.	Winchester, 1 Oct. 1207, elder son of John and Isabella of Angoulême.	Natural causes, Westminster, aged 65, 16 Nov. 1272. Buried Westminster Abbey Church.	Eleanor, died 1291, daughter of count of Provence, Raymond Berengar. Married at Canterbury, 1236; 2 sons, 3 daughters.
Edward I aka Longshanks, Hammer of the Scots	1272–1307	20 Nov.	Westminster, 17 June 1239; eldest son (to survive infancy) of Henry III and Eleanor of Provence. Buried at Westminster Abbey.	Natural causes, Burgh-on-the-Sands nr Carlisle, 7 July 1307, aged 68.	Eleanor, died 1290, daughter of king of Castile, Ferdinand III, 4 sons, 7 daughters. Married Las Huelgas, Oct. 1254. Margaret (1282–1317), daughter of King Philip III of France; 2 sons, 1 daughter. Married Canterbury Sept. 1299.
Edward II	1307–1327	8 July	Caernarfon Castle, Wales, 25 April 1284; 4th and only surviving son of Edward I and Eleanor of Castile.	Murdered Berkeley Castle, Sept. 1327. Buried Gloucester Cathedral.	Isabella (1292–1358), daughter of King Philip IV of France; 2 sons, 2 daughters. Married Boulogne, Jan. 1308.
Edward III	1327–1377	25 Jan.	Windsor Castle, 13 Nov. 1312; elder son of Edward II and Isabella.	Natural causes, Sheen, 21 June 1377. Buried at Westminster Abbey.	Philippa (1314–69) daughter of count of Hainault and Holland; 7 sons, 5 daughters. Married at York, 24 June 1328.
Richard II	1377–1399	22 June	Bordeaux, France, 6 Jan. 1367; 2nd but only surviving son of Edward, the Black Prince, and Joan, the Fair Maid of Kent (granddaughter of Edward I).	Neurasthenia, Pontefract Castle. Buried at Westminster Abbey.	Anne of Bohemia (1366–94), daughter of Emperor Charles I. No issue. Wed St Stephens Chapel, 1382. Isabelle (1389–1409), daughter of Charles VI of France. No issue. Wed St Nicholas, Calais, 1396.
Henry IV aka Bolingbroke	1399–1413	30 Sept.	Bolingbroke Castle, Lincolnshire, April 1366; eldest son of John of Gaunt, 4th son of Edward III and Blanche, great-granddaughter of Henry III.	Eczema and gout, Jerusalem Chamber, Westminster. Buried at Westminster Abbey.	Mary de Bohun (1368–94), daughter of Humphrey of Hereford; 5 sons, 2 daughters. Wed Rochford, Essex, 1380. Joan (1370–1437), 2nd daughter of King Charles II of Navarre. No issue. Married Winchester, Feb. 1403.
Henry V aka Harry	1413–1422	21 March	Monmouth, Wales, 16 Sept. 1387; 2nd and eldest surviving son of Henry IV and Lady Mary de Bohun.	Dysentery, Bois de Vincennes, aged 34. Buried in Chapel of the Confessor, Westminster Abbey.	Catherine of Valois (1401–37), daughter of Charles VI of France; 1 son. Wed church of St John, Troyes, 2 June 1420.

	Reign	Date of accession	Born	Died	Marriage(s)
Henry VI	1422–1461	1 Sept.	Windsor, 6 Dec. 1421; only son of Henry V and Catherine of Valois.	Murdered by stabbing, Tower of London, 21 May 1471. Buried at Windsor.	Margaret (1430–82), daughter of René, duke of Anjou; 1 son. Wed Tichfield Abbey, April 1445.
Edward IV	1461–1470	4 March	Rouen, France, 28 April 1442; eldest son of Richard, 3rd duke of York and the Lady Cecily Nevill, daughter of Ralph, earl of Westmorland.	Pneumonia, Westminster, April 1483. Buried at Windsor.	Elizabeth (1437–92), daughter of Sir Richard Woodville; 3 sons, 7 daughters. Wed Grafton, Northants, 1464.
Henry VI	1470–1471	6 Oct.	As above.		As above.
Edward IV	1471–1483	11 April	As above.		As above.
Edward V	1483	9 April	Westminster, 2 Nov. 1470, eldest son of Edward IV and Elizabeth Woodville.	Tower of London?	Unmarried.
Richard III aka Crookback	1483–1485	26 June	Fotheringay, Northants, 2 Oct. 1452; 4th and only surviving son of Richard, 3rd duke of York (the Protector), and Cecily Nevill.	Killed Bosworth 22 Aug.1485. Buried at the Abbey of the Grey Friars, Leicester.	Anne (1456–85), daughter of Richard Nevill, earl of Warwick, and widow of Edward, prince of Wales; 1 son. Married 12 July 1472.
Henry VII	1485–1509	22 Aug.	Pembroke Castle, 27 Jan. 1457; only child of Edmund Tudor, 1st earl of Richmond, and Margaret Beaufort, great-great-granddaughter of Edward III.	Rheumatoid arthritis and gout, 21 April, at Richmond. Buried in his own chapel at Westminster.	Elizabeth (1466–1503), daughter of Edward IV; 3 sons, 4 daughters. Wed Westminster, Jan. 1486.
Henry VIII aka Bluff King Hal, Old Copper Nose	1509–1547	22 April	Greenwich, 28 June 1491; 2nd and only surviving son of Henry VII and Elizabeth.	Sinusitis and periostitis of the leg at Palace of Westminster, 21 April 1509. Buried at Windsor.	See separate entry.
Edward VI	1547–1553	28 Jan.	Hampton Ct, 12 Oct. 1537; only surviving son of Henry VIII by Jane Seymour.	Tuberculosis at Greenwich. Buried in Henry VII's Chapel, Westminster Abbey.	Unmarried.
Jane aka Nine-Day Queen	1553	10 July	Bradgate Park, Leics, Oct. 1537; eldest daughter of Henry Grey, 3rd marquess of Dorset, and Frances, daughter of Mary Tudor, sister of Henry VIII.	Beheaded Tower of London Feb. 1554. Buried St Peter ad Vincula within the Tower.	Guilford Dudley, son of John Dudley, duke of Northumberland. Wed Durham Hse, London, May 1533.
Mary I aka Bloody Mary	1553–1558	19 July	Greenwich, 18 Feb. 1516; only surviving child of Henry VIII and Catherine of Aragon.	Influenza in London. Buried Westminster Abbey.	Philip, son of Emperor Charles V and later king of Spain in 1554.
Elizabeth I aka Virgin Queen	1558–1603	17 Nov.	Greenwich, 7 Sept. 1533; daughter of Henry VIII and Anne Boleyn.	Sepsis from tonsillar abscess at Richmond. Buried Westminster Abbey.	Unmarried.

SOVEREIGNS

	Reign	Date of Accession	Born	Died	Marriage(s)
James I	1603–1625	26 March	Edinburgh Castle, 19 June 1566; son of Mary queen of Scots (daughter of James V) and Henry Darnley.	Bright's disease, Theobalds Park, Herts. Buried Westminster Abbey.	Anne, daughter of Frederick II of Denmark. Married 20 Aug. 1589, by proxy.
Charles I	1625–1649	27 March	Dunfermline Palace, 19 Nov. 1600; only surviving son of James I and Anne of Denmark.	Beheaded at Whitehall, Jan 1649. Buried at Windsor.	Henrietta Maria, daughter of Henry IV of France. Paris, 1 May 1625, by proxy.
Charles II aka Old Rowley	1660–1685	29 May	St James Palace, 29 May 1630; eldest son of Charles I and Henrietta Maria.	Uraemia and mercurial poisoning, Whitehall. Buried Henry VII's Chapel, Westminster.	Catherine of Braganza, daughter of John. Wed Portsmouth, 21 May 1662.
James II	1685–1688	6 Feb.	St James Palace, 14 Oct. 1633; only surviving son of Charles I and Henrietta Maria.	Cerebral haemorrhage, St Germain, France. Remains were interred at 5 different venues in France. All are now lost except for those at the parish church at St Germain.	Anne Hyde, daughter of Edward Hyde, Worcester Hse, Strand, 3 Sept. 1660. Mary D'este, daughter of duke of Modena. Wed Modena, 30 Sept. 1673, by proxy.
William III	1688–1702	13 Feb.	The Hague, 4 Nov. 1650; only son of William II, Prince of Orange, and Mary Stuart, daughter of Charles I.	Pleuro-pneumonia following fracture of right collarbone after falling from his horse near Kensington. Buried Henry VII's Chapel, Westminster.	Mary, daughter of James II and Anne Hyde. Wed St James's Palace, 4 Nov. 1677.
Mary II	1688–1694	13 Feb.	St James Palace, 30 April 1662.	Smallpox at Kensington, 28 Dec. 1694. Buried Henry VII's Chapel, Westminster.	William III.
Anne aka Brandy Nan	1702–1714	8 March	St James Palace, 6 Feb. 1665, daughter of James II and Anne Hyde.	Brain haemorrhage, Kensington. Buried Henry VII's Chapel, Westminster.	George of Denmark (1653–1708), son of Frederick III of Denmark. Chapel Royal, St James's Palace, 1683.
George I	1714–1727	1 Aug.	Osnabrück, 28 May 1660; son of Ernest, duke of Brunswick-Lüneburg and elector of Hanover, and Sophia, daughter of Elizabeth, queen of Bohemia, eldest daughter of James I.	Thrombosis, Ibbenburen. Buried Hanover.	Sophia Dorothea, daughter of George William, duke of Lüneburg-Celle. Wed 21 Nov. 1682, divorced 1694.
George II	1727–1760	11 Jun.	Hanover, 30 Oct. 1683; son of George I and Sophia Dorothea.	Thrombosis, Palace of Westminster. Buried Henry VII's Chapel, Westminster.	Wilhelmina Charlotte Caroline of Ansbach (1683–1737), daughter of John Frederick, margrave of Brandenburg-Ansbach, 22 Aug. 1705.
George III aka Farmer George	1760–1820	25 Oct.	Norfolk House, London, 24 May 1738; son of Frederick Lewis, prince of Wales, and Princess Augusta of Saxe-Gotha.	Senility, Windsor. St George's Chapel, Windsor.	Charlotte Sophia (1744–1818), daughter of Charles Louis Frederick, duke of Mecklenburg-Strelitz, 8 Sept. 1761.

1761.

	Reign	Date of Accession	Born	Died	Marriage(s)
George IV	1820–1830	29 Jan.	St James's Palace, 12 Aug. 1762; eldest son of George III and Charlotte.	Stomach rupture and dropsy, Windsor. Buried St George's Chapel, Windsor.	Maria Fitzherbert, 1785, without king's consent and denied by George IV. Caroline of Brunswick, 8 April 1795, Chapel Royal, St James's Palace.
William IV aka Sailor King	1830–1837	26 June	Buckingham Palace, 21 Aug. 1765; son of George III and Charlotte.	Pneumonia/cirrhosis, Windsor. Buried St George's Chapel, Windsor.	Adelaide, daughter of duke of Saxe-Meiningen, 11 July 1818, Kew.
Victoria	1837–1901	20 June	Kensington Palace, 24 May 1819; daughter of Edward duke of Kent, 4th son of George III, and Victoria, daughter of Francis of Saxe-Coburg-Saalfeld.	Senility, Osborne House, IoW. Buried at Frogmore nr Windsor.	Francis Albert (1819–61), 2nd son of Ernest I of Saxe-Coburg-Gotha, 10 Feb. 1840, St James's Palace.
Edward VII aka Denmark, Peacemaker	1901–1910	22 Jan.	Buckingham Palace, 9 Nov. 1841; eldest son of Victoria and Albert.	Bronchitis, Buckingham Palace. Buried at St George's Chapel, Windsor.	Alexandra, daughter of Christian IX of Denmark, 10 March 1863, St George's Chapel.
George V	1910–1936	6 May	Marlborough House, London, 3 June 1865; 2nd son of Edward and Alexander.	Bronchitis, Sandringham. Buried at St George's Chapel, Windsor.	Mary, daughter of Francis, duke of Teck, 6 July 1893, St James's Palace.
Edward VIII aka People's King, France	1936	20 Jan.	White Lodge, Richmond Park, 23 June 1894; eldest son of George V and Mary.	Throat cancer, Paris, 28 May 1972. Buried at Frogmore, Windsor.	Wallis Simpson née Warfield, 3 June 1937, Château de Candé, near Tours.
George VI	1936–1952	11 Dec.	York Cottage, Sandringham, 14 Dec. 1895; second son of George V and Mary.	Lung cancer, Sandringham. Buried at St George's Chapel, Windsor.	Elizabeth Bowes-Lyon, daughter of 14th earl of Strathmore and Kinghorne, 26 April 1922.
Elizabeth II	1952–	6 Feb.	17 Bruton St, London, 21 April 1926; elder daughter of George VI and Elizabeth.	Reigned since 6 Feb. 1952.	Philip, son of Prince Andrew of Greece and Princess Alice. Married in Westminster Abbey, 20 Nov. 1947.

SOVEREIGNS

British Royalty: Miscellaneous Details

abdicated: first Richard II

Alexandra Rose Day inaugurated in 1912 by Queen Alexandra

Angevin kings Henry II, Richard I, John

Andrew, Prince married Sarah Ferguson in 1986

Anne, Princess Princess Royal since 1987
  attempted kidnapping by Ian Ball in 1974 in the Mall
  house Gatcombe Park

annus horribilis Queen Elizabeth's name for 1992

anti-smoking tract: published James I

Babington Plot Roman Catholic plot against Elizabeth I in 1586

bald as a young woman Elizabeth I

baldness revealed after execution Mary, queen of Scots

bathed every three months Elizabeth I

battle: died in; last sovereign Richard III

battle: led troops in; last George II (Dettingen)

bigamist George IV

Bill of Rights Act barring Catholics from succession

bodyguard scandal Commander Michael Trestrail resigned as the Queen's bodyguard (19 July 1982) after admitting a homosexuality scandal

Buckingham Palace: first to live in Queen Victoria
  bought by George III in 1762

burnt the cakes (traditionally) King Alfred

Cabal advisors to Charles II: Clifford, Ashley, Buckingham, Arlington and Lauderdale

Cabinet meetings: attended most Queen Anne

Cavalier Parliament Charles II (aka Pensionary Parliament) first English Parliament 8 May 1661

Charles II: illegitimate son duke of Monmouth, son of Lucy Walter

Charles, Prince married 1981, divorced 1996
  Prince of Wales title bestowed in 1958; inaugurated in 1969
  houses Highgrove and Chevening
  Cherry B incident of 1963 Charles bought while under-age, in Outer Hebrides
  aka Lord of the Isles, Steward of Scotland, duke of Cornwall
  children's nanny Tiggy Legg Bourke

cherry brandy drinker George IV

children: most Henry I (20 acknowledged bastards plus two legitimate)
  most legitimate Edward I (18)

Christian: first Ethelbert

Clarence, duke of: last Albert, eldest son of Edward VII

commoner; first to wed Henry IV

crowned: battlefield Henry VII

crowned: twice Charles II

Defender of the Faith: first Henry VIII

deposed James II

divorced: first John

dukes: royal Cornwall, Edinburgh, Gloucester, Kent, Wessex, York

education Prince Philip (Cheam and Gordonstoun) Prince Charles (Cheam, Gordonstoun, Cambridge) The Prince of Wales also spent the 1966 school year as an exchange student at the Geelong Church of England Grammar School in

Melbourne, Australia.
  Princess Anne (Beneden, in Kent)
  Prince William (Eton College)
  Prince Harry (Eton College)
  Princess Beatrice (Aiglon College in Switzerland)

Edward VII: House of Lords speech housing speech given while Prince of Wales

Edward VIII abdication speech written by Walter Monckton

Eleanor Crosses: 12 Marking resting place of Eleanor of Castile's cortege; crosses at Lincoln, Grantham, Stamford, Stratford, Woburn, Dunstable, St Albans, Cheapside, Northampton Geddington and Waltham still standing; last, Charing Cross, is a replica

Elizabeth I: favourite Robert Dudley, earl of Leicester

Elizabeth II coronation day 2, June 1953
  biographer Sarah Bradford (1996)
  royal arms insignia Dieu et Mon Droit
  aka Lord High Admiral of England
  married 20 Nov. 1947

fattest king George IV

finger: extra Anne Boleyn

Five Members Pym, Hampden, Heselrige, Holles and Strode, whom Charles I attempted to arrest on 4 Jan. 1642, as well as Lord Mandeville

heirs to throne males are heirs apparent; females are heirs presumptive

Henry VIII: fate of wives divorced, beheaded, died, divorced, beheaded, died

honours: awarded on New Year's Day and the Queen's official birthday

Irish state coach used by British monarchs for coronations

jewellers, Crown Garards

Kent, duke and duchess of three children: Helen Taylor Windsor, Lord Nicholas and George, Earl St Andrews
  Duchess of Kent Katherine Worsley

king over the water Jacobite term for pretenders

Lancaster: House of Henry IV, V, VI

Lollards: suppressed Henry V

mad king George III

madness: bouts of Henry VI

mad queen Caroline of Brunswick

Margaret, Princess married 1960 to Anthony Armstrong Jones

married kings of England and France Eleanor of Aquitaine (Louis VII and Henry II)

murdered by queen and her lover Edward II

oldest: accession William IV (64)

oldest royal residence Windsor Castle

Parliament: first; in the reign of Henry III

pawned Crown jewels Richard II (to pay for wedding)

Plantagenet: first Henry II
  last Richard II, although later kings from Plantagenet line

Popish Plot fictitious Jesuit plot of Titus Oates and Israel Tonge against Charles II resulting in the execution of Oliver Plunket, primate of Ireland

premier duke of Scotland dukes of Hamilton

pretenders: Henry VII's reign Perkin Warbeck (1498), hanged for treason; Lambert Simnel (1487), became kitchen hand

prince of Wales: longest Edward VII (59 yrs)

last before Charles Edward VIII

last Welsh Llewellyn

Prince Philip aka duke of Edinburgh, earl of Merioneth. Birthday, 10 June. Parents, Prince Andrew and Princess Alice of Greece

queen never set foot in England Berengaria, wife of Richard I

Richards all died violently

Ridolfi Plot Catholic plot against Elizabeth I in 1571

Roman Catholic monarch: last James II

royal allowance Civil List

rugby Peter Phillips, son of the Princess Royal, played rugby for Scottish schools

Rye House Plot plot to murder Charles II and his brother on the way home from Newmarket races

Sarah Armstrong-Jones married Daniel Chatto

shortest queen Matilda, wife of William I

spoke little English George I

stammered George VI

St Edward's crown made for Charles II's coronation

toilet: died on George II

two queens: father of James II (Mary and Anne)

urinated in font Ethelred the Unready

USA: first to go to George VI

Victoria's gillie John Brown

White Ship disaster William, son of Henry I, drowned at Barfleur, 25 Nov. 1120

wife: met at altar George III (Charlotte Sophia)

Wimbledon: played at George VI

wisest fool in Christendom James I (coined by Henry IV of France)

write name: first to do so Richard II

York, House of Edward IV, V, Richard III

Order of Precedence (England and Wales)

The sovereign	Lord President of the Council
The Prince Philip, duke of Edinburgh	Speaker of the House of Commons
The Prince of Wales	Lord Privy Seal
The sovereign's younger sons	Ambassadors and High Commissioners
The sovereign's grandsons	Lord Great Chamberlain
The sovereign's cousins	Earl Marshal
Archbishop of Canterbury	Lord Steward of the Household
Lord High Chancellor	Lord Chamberlain of the Household
Archbishop of York	Master of the Horse
The Prime Minister	Then dukes, marquesses, earls, viscounts, barons

NB The order of precedence has been included in this section purely to show the distinction between order of precedence and succession. Precedence is a traditional ceremonial observation and, although closely following the order of succession in some areas, it is in fact a separate and distinct list.

Order of Succession

1	HRH Prince Charles, The Prince of Wales	11	HRH Princess Margaret, countess of Snowdon
2	HRH Prince William of Wales	12	Viscount Linley, David Armstrong-Jones
3	HRH Prince Henry of Wales	13	Lady Sarah Chatto (née Armstrong-Jones)
4	HRH Prince Andrew, duke of York	14	Samuel Chatto
5	HRH Princess Beatrice of York	15	HRH Richard, duke of Gloucester
6	HRH Princess Eugenie of York	16	The earl of Ulster
7	HRH Prince Edward	17	Lady Davina Windsor
8	HRH Princess Anne, Princess Royal	18	Lady Rose Windsor
9	Peter Phillips, son of Princess Anne	19	HRH Edward, duke of Kent
10	Zara Phillips, daughter of Princess Anne	20	Baron Downpatrick

Rulers of the British Isles

Kings and Queens of Scotland

House of Alpin

842–858	Kenneth I (MacAlpin)
858–862	Donald I
862–877	Constantine I
877–878	Aed
878–889	Giric and Eochaid
889–900	Donald II
900–943	Constantine II
943–954	Malcolm I
954–962	Indulf
962–966	Duf
966–971	Culén
971–995	Kenneth II
995–997	Constantine III
997–1005	Kenneth III
1005–1034	Malcolm II

House of Dunkeld

1034–1040	Duncan I

House of Moray

1040–1057	Macbeth
1057–1058	Lulach

House of Dunkeld

1058–1093	Malcolm III (Canmore, aka Big Head)
1093–1097	Donald III
1094	Duncan II
1097–1107	Edgar
1107–1124	Alexander I (the Fierce)
1124–1153	David I (the Saint)
1153–1165	Malcolm IV (the Maiden)
1165–1214	William I (the Lion)

SOVEREIGNS

| 1214–1249 | Alexander II |
| 1249–1286 | Alexander III |

House of Norway

| 1286–1290 | Margaret (Maid of Norway) |
| 1290–1292 | interregnum (disputed by 13 competitors) |

House of Balliol

| 1292–1296 | John Balliol |
| 1296–1306 | interregnum |

House of Bruce

| 1306–1329 | Robert I (the Bruce) |
| 1329–1371 | David II |

House of Balliol

| 1332–1356 | Edward (son of John, abdicated) |

House of Stewart

1371–1390	Robert II (Stewart)
1390–1406	Robert III
1406–1437	James I
1437–1460	James II
1460–1488	James III
1488–1513	James IV
1513–1542	James V
1542–1567	Mary
1567–1625	James VI

Rulers of the Principality of Wales

Kingdom of Gwynedd

825–844	Merfyn the Freckled
844–878	Rhodri I (the Great)
878–916	Anarawd
916–942	Idwal the Bald
942–950	Hywel I (the Good)
950–979	Iago I
979–985	Hywel II

985–986	Cadwallon
986–999	Maredudd
999–1005	Cynan I
1005–1023	Llywelyn I
1023–1039	Iago II
1039–1063	Gruffydd I
1081–1137	Gruffydd II
1137–1170	Owain
1170–1174	Cynan II
1174–1194	David I (East Gwynedd)
1174–1195	Rhodri II (West Gwynedd)
1174–1200	Gruffydd III (South Gwynedd)
1194–1240	Llywelyn II (The Great)
1240–1246	David II

Principality of Wales

| 1246–1282 | Llywelyn III (ap Gruffydd) |
| 1282–1283 | David III |

NB Although Llywelyn ap Gruffydd is invariably quoted as the last native prince of Wales, in fact it is true to say that his brother, David ap Gruffydd, was the last native prince of Wales. This confusion arises simply because England did not recognize anyone except Llywelyn as ruler. The Welsh would recognize David as their last prince, and the English Llywelyn. In 1301 the future Edward II became prince of Wales, and subsequently the eldest son of the reigning monarch has been given this title.

The High Kingship of Ireland

House of Ui Néill

445–452	Niall of the Nine Hostages
819–833	Conchobar
1002–1014	Brian Bóruma (king of Munster)
1166–1186	Ruaidri

NB The short list above includes the first and last kings of Ireland and two other famous kings. Many of the other rulers are obscure and were not recognized as such until at least the 9th century.

Other Important Historical Rulers

Israel

1020–1010 BC	Saul
1010–970 BC	David
970–931 BC	Solomon

Kingdom of Judah

| 930–914 BC | Rehoboam (son of Solomon) |

Kingdom of Israel

| 931–910 BC | Jeroboam I (son of Solomon) |

Lydia: last king

| 560–547 BC | Croesus |

Persian Empire

559–530 BC	Cyrus the Great
529–522 BC	Cambyses
522 BC	Smerdis (Bardiya)
521–486 BC	Darius I (The Great)
485–465 BC	Xerxes I
464–424 BC	Artaxerxes I
424 BC	Xerxes II
424 BC	Sogdianus
423–405 BC	Darius II
404–359 BC	Artaxerxes II
358–338 BC	Artaxerxes III

| 337–336 BC | Arses |
| 335–330 BC | Darius III |

Macedonia (selected kings)

399–397 BC	Orestes
359–336 BC	Philip II
336–323 BC	Alexander III (the Great)
179–168 BC	Perseus (the last king)

Visigoth kingdom

| 395–410 | Alaric I (first king of the Visigoths) |
| 711–714 | Agila II (last king of the Visigoths) |

Anglo-Saxon kingdoms

455–488	Hengest (first ruler of kingdom of Kent)
823–825	Baldred (last ruler of kingdom of Kent)
547–559	Ida (first ruler of Bernicia)
585–592	Hussa (last ruler of Bernicia)
569–599	Aelle (first ruler of Deira)
599–604	Aethelric (last ruler of Deira)
592–616	Aethelfrith (Northumberland: Bernicia and Deira)

913–927	Aldred (last ruler of Northumberland)
633–655	Penda (first ruler of Mercia)
757–796	Offa (kingdom of Mercia)
918–919	Aelfwyn (last ruler of Mercia)
519–534	Cerdic (first ruler of Wessex)
802–839	Egbert (last ruler of Wessex)

Kingdom of France (selected)
Carolingian House

751–768	Pepin the Short (first king of France)
768–814	Charlemagne (Holy Roman Emperor, 800)
840–877	Charles I (the Bald)
877–879	Louis II (the Stammerer)
885–888	Charles II (the Fat)
893–923	Charles III (the Simple)
986–987	Louis V (the Sluggard)

Capetian House

987–996	Hugh Capet
996–1031	Robert II (the Pious)
1108–1137	Louis VI (the Fat)
1137–1180	Louis VII (the Younger)
1223–1226	Louis VIII (the Lion)
1285–1314	Philip IV (the Fair)
1314–1316	Louis X (the Stubborn)
1316–1322	Philip V (the Tall)
1322–1328	Charles IV (the Fair)

House of Valois

1328–1350	Philip VI
1350–1364	John II (the Good)
1364–1380	Charles V (the Wise)
1380–1422	Charles VI (the Mad)
1422–1461	Charles VII (the Victorious)
1483–1498	Charles VIII

House of Angoulême

1515–1547	Francis I
1547–1559	Henry II
1559–1560	Francis II (husband of Mary of Scots)
1560–1574	Charles IX
1574–1589	Henry III

House of Bourbon

1589–1610	Henry IV (Paris is worth a mass)
1610–1643	Louis XIII
1643–1715	Louis XIV (the Sun King)
1715–1774	Louis XV
1774–1792	Louis XVI

First Empire

1804–1814	Napoleon I (king of Italy, 1805)

Second Empire

1852–1870	Napoleon III

Kingdom of Italy

1849–1878	Victor Emmanuel II
1878–1900	Humbert I
1900–1946	Victor Emmanuel III
1946–1946	Humbert II

NB Although Victor Emmanuel III is often thought to be the last king of Italy, in fact, he was the last 'crowned' king. Humbert II (Umberto) was the last incumbent.

Kingdom of Spain (selected)
House of Habsburg

1516–1556	Charles I (Holy Roman Emperor, 1519–58)
1556–1598	Philip II (husband of Bloody Mary)

House of Bourbon

1700–1724	Philip V (grandson of Louis XIV of France)

House of Bonaparte

1808–1813	Joseph Napoleon

House of Bourbon

1975–	Juan Carlos I

Kingdom of Portugal (selected)

1139–1185	Afonso I

House of Avis

1385–1433	John I (the Bastard)
1578–1580	Henry (the Cardinal)

House of Braganza

1640–1656	John IV
1706–1750	John V (the Magnanimous)
1834–1853	Maria II

House of Saxe-Coburg-Gotha

1853–1861	Pedro V
1908–1910	Manuel II

Kingdom of Norway (selected)

858–928	Harald I
1957–1991	Olav V
1991–	Harald V

Kingdom of Denmark (selected)

940–986	Harald I
1972–	Margaret II

Kingdom of Sweden (selected)

980–995	Erik the Victorious

House of Vasa

1523–1560	Gustavus I
1560–1568	Erik XIV
1568–1592	John III
1592–1599	Sigismund

House of Bernadotte

1818–1844	Charles XIV
1973–	Charles XVI Gustavus

Kingdom of Netherlands (selected)

1572–1584	William I (the Silent)
1806–1810	Louis Napoleon
1890–1948	Wilhelmina
1948–1980	Juliana
1980–	Beatrix

Tsars/Tsarinas of Russia

1533–1584	Ivan IV (the Terrible)
1598–1605	Boris Godunov
1462–1505	Ivan III (the Great)
1613–1645	Michael Romanov
1682–1725	Peter I (the Great)
1725–1727	Catherine I (Martha)
1762–1796	Catherine II (the Great, Sophi of Anhalt)
1894–1917	Nicholas II

Inca Empire

1532–1533	Atauhualpa
1571–1572	Tupac Amaru

Aztec Empire

1372–1391	Acamapichtli
1427–1440	Itzcoatl

Japanese Empire

0–10 BC	Jimmu
1623–1651	Iemitsu
1713–1716	Ietsugu
1853–1858	Iesada
1867–1868	Keiki (Yoshinobu)

Chinese dynasties

18th–12th cent. BC	Shang
1111–255 BC	Chou
770–221 BC	Tung
221–206 BC	Ch'in
206–220 AD	Han
581–618	Sui
618–907	T'ang

960–1279	Sung
1206–1368	Yüan
1368–1644	Ming
1644–1912	Manchu (Ch'ing)

Last kings/queens of

Romania	Michael (1940–47)
Bulgaria	Simeon II (1943–46)
Albania	Zog I (1928–39)
Afghanistan	Muhammad Zahir Shah (1933–73)
Korea	Sunjong (1907–10)
Burma	Thibaw (1878–85)
Laos	SavangVatthana (1959–75)
Cambodia	Sihanouk (1941–55) Monarchy re-established on 23 Sept. 1993
Ethiopia	Asfa Wossen (1974–75)
Madagascar	Ranavalona (1883–96)
Zululand	Dinuzulu (1884–87)
Hawaii	Liliuokalani (1891–93)
Hungary	John Sigismund (1540–70)
Poland	Stanislas II Augustus (1764–95)
Bohemia	Ferdinand I (1526–64)

Holy Roman Emperors

Charlemagne (Charles I)	800–814	William of Holland	1247–1256
Louis I (the Pious)	814–840	Conrad IV	1250–1254
civil war	840–843	great interregnum	1254–1273
Lothair I	843–855	Richard	1257–1272
Louis II	855–875	Alfonso	1257–1275
Charles II (the Bald)	875–877	Rudolf I	1273–1291
interregnum	877–881	Adolf	1292–1298
Charles III (the Fat)	881–887	Albert I	1298–1308
interregnum	887–891	Henry VII	1308–1313
Guido of Spoleto	891–894	Frederick III	1314–1326
Lambert of Spoleto	892–898	Louis IV	1314–1346
Arnulf	898–899	Charles IV	1346–1378
Louis III (the Blind)	901–905	Wenceslas	1378–1400
Conrad I	911–918	Rupert	1400–1410
Berengar	915–924	Jobst	1410–1411
Henry I	919–936	Sigismund	1410–1437
Otto I (the Great)	936–973	Albert II	1438–1439
Otto II	973–983	Frederick III	1440–1493
Otto III	983–1002	Maximillian I	1493–1519
Henry II (the Saint)	1002–1024	Charles V	1519–1556
Conrad II	1024–1039	Ferdinand I	1556–1564
Henry III (the Black)	1039–1056	Maximillian II	1564–1576
Henry IV	1056–1106	Rudolf II	1576–1612
Rudolf	1077–1080	Matthias	1612–1619
Hermann	1081–1093	Ferdinand II	1619–1637
Conrad	1093–1101	Ferdinand III	1637–1657
Henry V	1106–1125	Leopold I	1658–1705
Lothair II	1125–1137	Joseph I	1705–1711
Conrad III	1138–1152	Charles VI	1711–1740
Frederick I (Barbarossa)	1152–1190	interregnum	1740–1742
Henry VI	1190–1197	Charles VII	1742–1745
Philip	1198–1208	Francis I	1745–1765
Otto IV	1198–1214	Joseph II	1765–1790
Frederick II	1215–1250	Leopold II	1790–1792
Henry VII	1220–1235	Francis II	1792–1806
Henry Raspe	1246–1247		

Roman Kings

Romulus	753–715 BC		Tarquinius Priscus	616–578 BC
Numa Pompilius	715–673 BC		Servius Tullius	578–534 BC
Tullus Hostilius	673–642 BC		Tarquinius Superbus	534–509 BC
Ancus Marcius	642–616 BC			

NB The traditional seven kings of Rome as listed above are of extremely dubious factual exactitude and nowadays are only observed as truth in the context of being a very popular quiz question, and to this end the ones to remember are the first, Romulus, and the last, Tarquinius Superbus (Proud Tarquin).

Roman Emperors

Augustus	27 BC–AD 14	Probus	276–282
Tiberius	14–37	Carus	282–283
Caligula	37–41	Numerian (east)	283–284
Claudius	41–54	Carinus (west)	283–285
Nero	54–68	Postumus (Gaul)	260–269
Galba	68–69	Laelian (Gaul)	269
Otho	69	Marius (Gaul)	269
Vitellius	69	Victorinus (Gaul)	269–271
Vespasian	69–79	Tetricus (Gaul)	271–274
Titus	79–81	Diocletian (see below)	284–305
Domitian	81–96	Maximian (see below)	286–305
Nerva	96–98	Constantius I (see below)	305–306
Trajan	98–117	Galerius (see below)	305–311
Hadrian	117–138	Severus (west)	306–307
Antoninus Pius	138–161	Maxentius (west)	307–312
Marcus Aurelius	161–180	Constantine I (west until 324)	307–337
Commodus	180–192	Licinius (Pannonia and east)	308–324
Pertinax	193	Maximinus II (east)	310–313
Didius Julianus	193	Valerius Valens	316–317
Septimius Severus	193–211	Martinian	324
Geta	211	Constantine II (Gaul, Britain, Spain)	337–340
Caracalla	211–217	Constans (west)	337–350
Macrinus	217–218	Constantius II (east)	337–361
Diadumenian	218	Magnentius (west)	350–353
Elagabalus	218–222	Julian the Apostate (Gaul until 361)	360–363
Severus Alexander	222–235	Jovian	363–364
Maximinus the Thracian	235–238	Valentinian I (west)	364–375
Gordian I	238	Valens (east)	364–378
Gordian II	238	Gratian (west)	375–383
Balbinus	238	Valentinian II	375–392
Pupienus Maximus	238	Theodosius I (the Great) (east)	379–395
Gordian III	238–244	Maximus (west)	383–388
Philip I the Arabian	244–249	Victor (west)	387–388
Philip II	247–249	Eugenius (west)	392–394
Decius	249–251		
Herennius Etruscus	251		
Hostilian	251		
Trebonianus Gallus (co-ruler with			
Misson Volusian)	251–253		
Volusian	251–253		
Aemilian	253		
Valerian (east)	253–260		
Gallienus (west)	253–268		
Saloninus	260		
Claudius II	268–270		
Quintillus	270		
Aurelian	270–275		
Tacitus	275–276		
Florian	276		

After a short interregnum the Empire split into east and west. Selected entries are as follows:

Western Roman Emperors

Honorius	395–423 (the first)
Romulus Augustus	475–476 (the last)

Eastern Roman Emperors

Arcadius	395–408 (the first)
Justinian I (the Great)	527–565
Constantine XI	1449–1453 (the last)

Turkish capture of Constantinople ultimately ended the Byzantine Empire.

NB The names used in the above table are the ones familiarly adopted by history. The full names are complex and can be depicted in an imperial style or in Latin. It became increasingly impractical to rule over the whole of the Roman Empire and although the empire was not officially split until AD 395 , many joint emperors divided their territories between east and west, with further subdivisions into Gaul, Britain, Illyria etc. To use the Diocletian tetrarchy as an example, Galerius, residing in Sirmium, administered Illyria, Achaea, and the Danubian provinces; Maximian, residing in Milan, administered Italy, Sicily, and Africa; Constantius I, residing in Trier, governed Gaul, Spain, and Britain; and Diocletian, residing in Nicomedia, watched over Thrace, Asia, and Egypt.

AD 69 is often referred to as the year of the four emperors but in AD 238 there were six emperors. Maximinus became the first soldier who had started from the ranks to become Roman emperor, he was replaced by the aged proconsul Gordian, who ruled jointly with his son. Gordian committed suicide on learning of the death of his son in a battle with Capellianus, governor of Numidia. The Roman Senate then proclaimed two elderly senators Balbinus and Pupienus Maximus joint emperors. The imperial guards murdered the Senate's nominees and the grandson of Gordian became emperor as Gordian III, at the age of 13. Valentinian II was proclaimed emperor in Budapest (Aquincum) at the age of 4, and ruled Italy, Africa, Illyricum, through his mother. He was found dead in his palace at Vienna, probably murdered by agents of Arbogast, the usurper in Gaul. In areas likely to confuse, I have added the administrative area in parenthesis.I have omitted usurpers such as Vetranio (abdicated in AD 351) and Procopius (reigned in Constantinople AD 365–6), as this would only confuse matters further.

SPORT & LEISURE

American Football

	Superbowl winners			Runners up
1967	Green Bay Packers	NFC	35-10	Kansas City Chiefs
1968	Green Bay Packers	NFC	33-14	Oakland Raiders
1969	New York Jets	AFC	16-7	Baltimore Colts
1970	Kansas City Chiefs	AFC	23-7	Minnesota Vikings
1971	Baltimore Colts	AFC	16-13	Dallas Cowboys
1972	Dallas Cowboys	NFC	24-3	Miami Dolphins
1973	Miami Dolphins	AFC	14-7	Washington Redskins
1974	Miami Dolphins	AFC	24-7	Minnesota Vikings
1975	Pittsburgh Steelers	AFC	16-6	Minnesota Vikings
1976	Pittsburgh Steelers	AFC	21-7	Dallas Cowboys
1977	Oakland Raiders	AFC	32-14	Minnesota Vikings
1978	Dallas Cowboys	NFC	27-10	Denver Broncos
1979	Pittsburgh Steelers	AFC	35-31	Dallas Cowboys
1980	Pittsburgh Steelers	AFC	31-19	Los Angeles Raiders
1981	Oakland Raiders	AFC	27-10	Philadelphia Eagles
1982	San Francisco 49ers	NFC	26-21	Cincinnati Bengals
1983	Washington Redskins	NFC	27-17	Miami Dolphins
1984	Los Angeles Raiders	AFC	38-9	Washington Redskins
1985	San Francisco 49ers	NFC	38-16	Miami Dolphins
1986	Chicago Bears	NFC	46-10	New England Patriots
1987	New York Giants	NFC	39-20	Denver Broncos
1988	Washington Redskins	NFC	42-10	Denver Broncos
1989	San Francisco 49ers	NFC	20-16	Cincinnati Bengals
1990	San Francisco 49ers	NFC	55-10	Denver Broncos
1991	New York Giants	NFC	20-19	Buffalo Bills
1992	Washington Redskins	NFC	37-24	Buffalo Bills
1993	Dallas Cowboys	NFC	52-17	Buffalo Bills
1994	Dallas Cowboys	NFC	30-13	Buffalo Bills
1995	San Francisco 49ers	NFC	49-28	San Diego Chargers
1996	Dallas Cowboys	NFC	27-17	Pittsburgh Steelers
1997	Green Bay Packers	NFC	35-21	New England Patriots
1998	Denver Broncos	AFC	31-24	Green Bay Packers
1999	Denver Broncos	AFC	34-19	Atlanta Falcons
2000	St Louis Rams	AFC	23-16	Tennessee Titans
2001	Baltimore Ravens	AFC	34-7	New York Giants

(AFC = American Football Conference. NFC = National Football Conference.)

American Football: General Information

field goals: points score	3
most valuable player award	Jim Thorpe Trophy
players: number	11 a side on pitch at any one time
playing area	grid iron
playing period	60 minutes
rules played	Harvard Rules
safety touch: points score	2
Super Bowl	championship game of the National Football League played by the winners of league's American Football Conference and National Football Conference
touchdown: points score	6
trophy played for	Vince Lombardi trophy
World Bowl 2000 winner	Rhein Fire beat Scottish Claymores 13-10
World League: teams	Barcelona Dragons, London Monarchs, Amsterdam Admirals, Scottish Claymores, Frankfurt Galaxy, Rhein Fire

Angling: British Freshwater Records (as at June 2001)

Barbel	17 lb 4oz	Ray Walton	Rudd	4 lb 8oz		Rev. E.C. Alston
Bleak	4oz 9dm	Dennis Flack	Salmon	64 lb		Georgina Ballatine
Bream	16 lb 10oz	Lee McManus	Tench	14 lb 7oz		Gordon Beaven
Carp (Mary)	56 lb 6oz	Kevin Cummins	Natural Trout:			
Carp: Crucian	4 lb 5oz 8dm	Adrian Eves	Brown	25 lb 5oz 12dm		A. Finlay
Carp: Grass	31 lb	Derek Smith	Cultivated Trout:			
Catfish	62 lb	Rob Garner	Brown	28 lb 1oz		D. Taylor
Chub	8 lb 10oz	Peter Smith	Natural Trout:			
Dace	1 lb 4oz 4dm	J. Gasson	Rainbow	36 lb 14oz 8dm		C. White
Eel	11 lb 2oz	Steve Terry	Cultivated Trout:			
Golden Orfe	7 lb 14oz 8dm	Mick Pardoe	Rainbow	24 lb 1oz 4dm		J. Hammond
Perch	5 lb 9oz	John Shayler	Trout: Sea	28 lb 5oz		J. Farrent
Pike	46 lb 13oz	Ray Lewis	Zander	19 lb 5oz 8dm		Dave Lavender
Roach	4 lb 3oz	Ray Clarke				

Angling: Freshwater Champions

	Individual	*Team*
1959	Robert Tesse (France)	France
1960	Robert Tesse (France)	Belgium
1961	Ramon Legogue (France)	E. Germany
1962	Raimondo Tedasco (Italy)	Italy
1963	William Lane (England)	France
1964	Joseph Fontanet (France)	France
1965	Robert Tesse (France)	Romania
1966	Henri Guiheneuf (France)	France
1967	Jacques Isenbaert (Belgium)	Belgium
1968	Gunter Grebenstein (W. Germany)	France
1969	Robin Harris (England)	Holland
1970	Marcel Van den Eynde (Belgium)	Belgium
1971	Dino Bassi (Italy)	Italy
1972	Hubert Levels (Netherlands)	France
1973	Pierre Michiels (Belgium)	Belgium
1974	Aribert Richter (W. Germany)	France
1975	Ian Heaps (England)	France
1976	Dino Bassi (Italy)	Italy
1977	Jean Mainil (Belgium)	Luxembourg
1978	Jean-Pierre Fourgeat (France)	France
1979	Gérard Heulard (France)	France
1980	Wolf-Rudiger Kremkus (W. Germany)	W. Germany
1981	Dave Thomas (England)	France
1982	Kevin Ashurst (England)	Holland
1983	Wolf-Rudiger Kremkus (W. Germany)	Belgium
1984	Bobby Smithers (Ireland)	Luxembourg
1985	Dave Roper (England)	England
1986	Lud Wever (Netherlands)	Italy
1987	Clive Branson (Wales)	England
1988	Jean-Pierre Fourgeat (France)	England
1989	Tom Pickering (England)	Wales
1990	Bob Nudd (England)	France
1991	Bob Nudd (England)	England
1992	David Wesson (Australia)	Italy
1993	Mario Barros (Portugal)	Italy
1994	Bob Nudd (England)	England
1995	Paul Jean (France)	France
1996	Alan Scotthorne (England)	Italy
1997	Alan Scotthorne (England)	Italy
1998	Alan Scotthorne (England)	England
1999	Bob Nudd (England)	Spain
2000	Jacob Falsini (Italy)	Italy

World Fly Fishing Champions

Individual		Team	Individual		Team
1981	C. Wittkamp (Netherlands)	Netherlands	1991	Brian Leadbetter (England)	NZ
1982	Viktor Diez (Spain)	Italy	1992	Perluigi Coccito (Italy)	Italy
1983	S. Fernandez (Spain)	Italy	1993	Russell Owens (Wales)	England
1984	Tony Pawson (England)	Italy	1994	Pascal Cognard (France)	Czechoslovakia
1985	Leslaw Frasik (Poland)	Poland	1995	Jeremy Herrmann (England)	England
1986	Slivoj Svoboda (Czechoslovakia)	Italy	1996	Perluigi Coccito (Italy)	Czecholsovakia
1987	Brian Leadbetter (England)	England	1997	Pascal Cognard (France)	France
1988	John Pawson (England)	England	1998	T. Starychfolta (Czechoslovakia)	Czechoslovakia
1989	Wladislaw Trzebuinia (Poland)	Poland	1999	Ross Steward (Australia)	Australia
1990	Franciszek Szajnik (Poland)	Czechoslovakia	2000	Pascal Cognard (France)	France

Archery: Target World Champions

	Men	Team	Women	Team
1931	M. Sawicki (Poland)	France	J. Kurkowska (Poland)	——
1932	L. Reith (Belgium)	Poland	J. Kurkowska (Poland)	——
1933	D. McKenzie (USA)	Belgium	J. Kurkowska (Poland)	Poland
1934	H. Kjellson (Sweden)	Sweden	J. Kurkowska (Poland)	Poland
1935	A van Kohlen (Belgium)	Belgium	Ina Catani (Sweden)	GB
1936	E. Heilborn (Sweden)	Czechoslovakia	J. Kurkowska (Poland)	Poland
1937	G de Rons (Belgium)	Poland	Ingo Simon (GB)	GB
1938	F. Hadas (Czechoslovakia)	Czechoslovakia	N.-Weston Martyr (GB)	Poland
1939	R. Beday (France)	France	J. Kurkowska (Poland)	Poland
1946	E.T. Holbek (Denmark)	Denmark	N. de Wharton Burr	GB
1947	H. Deutgen (Sweden)	Czechoslovakia	J. Kurkowska (Poland)	Denmark
1948	H. Deutgen (Sweden)	Sweden	N. de Wharton Burr	Czechoslovakia
1949	H. Deutgen (Sweden)	Czechoslovakia	B. Waterhouse (GB)	GB
1950	H. Deutgen (Sweden)	Denmark	Jean Lee (USA)	Finland
1952	S. Andersson (Sweden)	Sweden	Jean Lee (USA)	USA
1953	B. Lundgren (Sweden)	Sweden	Jean Richards (USA)	Finland
1955	N. Andersson (Sweden)	Sweden	K. Wisniowska (Poland)	GB
1957	O. Smathers (USA)	USA	C. Meinhart (USA)	USA
1958	S. Thysell (Sweden)	Finland	S. Johansson (Sweden)	USA
1959	J. Caspers (USA)	USA	Ann Corby (USA)	USA
1961	J. Thornton (USA)	USA	N. Vanderheide (USA)	USA
1963	C. Sandlin (USA)	USA	V. Cook (USA)	USA
1965	M. Haikonen (Finland)	USA	M. Lindholm (Finland)	USA
1967	Ray Rogers (USA)	USA	M. Maczynska (Poland)	Poland
1969	Hardy Ward (USA)	USA	D. Lidstone (Canada)	USSR
1971	J. Williams (USA)	USA	E. Gapchenko (USSR)	Poland
1973	V. Sidoruk (USSR)	USA	Linda Myers (USA)	USSR
1975	Darrell Pace (USA)	USA	Z. Rustamova (USSR)	USSR
1977	R. McKinney (USA)	USA	Luann Ryon (USA)	USA
1979	Darrell Pace (USA)	USA	Kim Jin-ho (Korea)	Korea
1981	K. Laasonen (Finland)	USA	N. Butuzova (USSR)	USSR
1983	R. McKinney (USA)	USA	Kim Jin-ho (Korea)	Korea
1985	R. McKinney (USA)	Korea	I. Soldatova (USSR)	USSR
1987	V. Yesheyev (USSR)	W. Germany	Ma Xiaojun (China)	USSR
1989	S. Zabrodskiy (USSR)	USSR	Kim Soo-nyung (Korea)	Korea
1991	S. Fairweather (Australia)	Korea	Kim Soo-nyung (Korea)	Korea
1993	K. Park (Korea)	France	K. Hyo-Jung (Korea)	Korea
1995	Lee Kyung-Chul (Korea)	Korea	N. Valeeva (Moldovia)	Korea
1997	Kim Kyung-Ho (Korea)	Korea	Kim Du-Ri (Korea)	Korea
1999	Chil Hong Sung (Korea)	Italy	Lee Evn Kyung (Korea)	Italy

Athletics: Olympic Games 1996

	Men			Women	
100m	Donovan Bailey (Canada)	9.84	100m	Gail Devers (USA)	10.94
	Frankie Fredericks (Namibia)	9.89		Merlene Ottey (Jamaica)	10.94
	Ato Boldon (Trinidad)	9.90		Gwen Torrance (USA)	10.96
200m	Michael Johnson (USA)	19.32	200m	Marie-Jose Pérec (France)	22.12
	Frankie Fredericks (Namibia)	19.68		Merlene Ottey (Jamaica)	22.24
	Ato Boldon (Trinidad)	19.80		Mary Onyali (Nigeria)	22.38
400m	Michael Johnson (USA)	43.49	400m	Marie-Jose Pérec (France)	48.25
	Roger Black (GB)	44.41		Cathy Freeman (Australia)	48.63
	Davis Kamoga (Uganda)	44.53		Falilat Ogunkoya (Nigeria)	49.10
800m	Vebjorn Rodal (Norway)	1:42.58	800m	Svetlana Masterkova (Russia)	1:57.73
	Hezekiel Sepeng (SA)	1:42.74		Ana Fidelia Quirot (Cuba)	1:58.11
	Fred Onyancha (Kenya)	1:42.79		Maria Lurdes Mutola (Zambia)	1:58.71
1500m	Noureddine Morceli (Algeria)	3:35.78	1500m	Svetlana Masterkova (Russia)	4:00.83
	Fermin Cacho (Spain)	3:36.40		Gabriela Szabo (Romania)	4:01.54
	Stephen Kipkorir (Kenya)	3:36.72		Theresia Kiesl (Austria)	4:03.02
5000m	Venuste Niyongabo (Bur)	13:07.96	5000m	Wang Junxia (China)	14:59.88
10000m	Haile Gebrselassie (Ethiopia)	27:07.34	10000m	Fernando Ribeiro (Portugal)	31:01.63
Marathon	Josia Thugwane (SA)	2:12.36	Marathon	Fatuma Roba (Ethiopia)	2:26.05
3000m S/chase	Joseph Keter (Kenya)	8:07.12	100m Hurdles	Lyudmila Engquist (Sweden)	12.58
			400m Hurdles	Deon Hemmings (Jamaica)	52.82
110m Hurdles	Allen Johnson (USA)	12.95	High Jump	Stefka Kostadinova (Bulgaria)	2.05m
400m Hurdles	Derrick Adkins (USA)	47.54	Long Jump	Chioma Ajunwa (Nigeria)	7.12m
Pole Vault	Jean Galfione (France)	5.92m	Triple Jump	Inessa Kravets (Ukraine)	15.33m
High Jump	Charles Austin (USA)	2.39m	Shot Putt	Astrid Kumbernuss (Germany)	20.56m
Long Jump	Carl Lewis (USA)	8.50m	Discus	Ilke Wyludda (Germany)	69.66m
Triple Jump	Kenny Harrison (USA)	18.09m	Javelin	Heli Rantanen (Finland)	67.94m
Shot Putt	Randy Barnes (USA)	21.62m	Heptathlon	Ghada Shouaa (Syria)	6780
Discus	Lars Riedel (Germany)	69.40m	10k Walk	Yelena Nikolayeva (Russia)	41.49
Hammer	Balazs Kiss (Hungary)	81.24m	800m	Louise Sauvage (Australia)	1:54.90
Javelin	Jan Zelezny (Czechoslovakia)	88.16m	Wheelchair:		
Decathlon	Dan O'Brien (USA)	8824	4x100	United States	41.95
20k Walk	Jefferson Perez (Ecuador)	1:20.07	4x400	United States	3:20.91
50k Walk	Robert Korzeniowski (Poland)	3:43.30			
1500m Wheelchair:	Claude Issorat (France)	3:15.18			
4x100	Canada	37.69			
4x400	United States	2:55.99			

Athletics: Olympic Games 2000

	Men			Women		Team
100m	M. Greene (US)	9.87	100m	M. Jones (US)	10.75	
	A. Boldon (Tri)	9.99		E. Thanou (Gr)	11.12	
	O. Thompson (Bar)	10.04		T. Lawrence (Jam)	11.18	
200m	K. Kenteris (Gr)	20.09	200m	M. Jones (US)	21.84	
	D. Campbell (GB)	20.14		P. Davis-Thompson (Bah)	22.27	
	A. Boldon (Tri)	20.20		S. Jayasinghe (S. Lanka)	22.28	
400m	M. Johnson (US)	43.84	400m	C. Freeman (Aus)	49.11	
	A. Harrison (US)	44.40		L. Graham (Jam)	49.58	
	G. Haughton (Jam)	44.70		K. Merry (GB)	49.72	
800m	N. Schumann (Ger)	1:45.08	800m	M. Mutola (Moz)	1:56.15	
	W. Kipketer (Den)	1:45.14		S. Graf (Aus)	1:56.64	
	A. D. Said-Guerni (Alg)	1:45.16		K. Holmes (GB)	1:56.80	
1500m	N. Ngeny (Ken)	3:32.07	1500m	N. Merah-Benida (Alg)	4:05.10	
	H. El Guerrouj (Mor)	3:32.32		V. Szekely (Rom)	4:05.15	
	B. Lagat (Ken)	3:32.44		G. Szabo (Rom)	4:05.27	
5000m	M. Wolde (Eth)	13:35.49	5000m	G. Szabo (Rom)	14:40.79	
	A. Saidi-Sief (Alg)	13:36.20		S. O' Sullivan (Ire)	14:41.02	
	B. Lahlafi (Mor)	13:36.47		G. Wami (Eth)	14:42.23	
10000m	H. Gebrselassie (Eth)	27:18.20	10000m	D. Tulu (Eth)	30:17.49	
	P. Tergat (Ken)	27:18.29		G. Wami (Eth)	30:22.48	
	A. Mezgebu (Eth)	27:19.75		F. Ribeiro (Por)	30:22.88	
Marathon	G. Abera (Eth)	2:10:11	Marathon	N. Takahashi (Jap)	2:23:14	
	E. Wainaina (Ken)	2:10:31		L. Simon (Rom)	2:23:22	
	T. Tola (Eth)	2:11:10		J. Chepchumba (Ken)	2:24:45	

	Men			Women	Team
3000m S/Chase	R. Kosgei (Ken)	8:21.43	100m Hurdles	O. Shishigina (Kaz)	12.65
	W. B. Kipketer (Ken)	8:21.77		G. Alozie (Nig)	12.68
	A. Ezzine (Mor)	8:22.15		M. Morrison (US)	12.76
110m Hurdles	A. Garcia (Cub)	13.00	400m Hurdles	I. Privalova (Rus)	53.02
	T. Trammell (US)	13.16		D. Hemmings (Jam)	53.45
	M. Crear (US)	13.22		N. Bidouane (Mor)	53.57
400m Hurdles	A. Taylor (US)	47.50	Pole Vault	S. Dragila (US)	4.60
	H. S. Somayli (Saudi)	47.53		T. Grigorieva (Aus)	4.55
	L. Herbert (SA)	47.81		V. Flosadottir (Ice)	4.50
Pole Vault	N. Hysong (US)	5.90	High Jump	Y. Yelesina (Rus)	2.01
	L. Johnson (US)	5.90		H. Cloete (SA)	2.01
	M. Tarasov (Rus)	5.90		K. Bergqvist (Swe)	1.99
High Jump	S. Kliugin (Rus)	2.35		O. Pantelimon (Rom)	1.99
	J. Sotomayor (Cub)	2.32	**note**	Joint gold medallists	
	A. Hammad (Alg)	2.32		and joint bronze medallists	
Long Jump	I. Pedroso (Cub)	8.55	Long Jump	H. Drechsler (Ger)	6.99
	J. Taurima (Aus)	8.49		F. May (Ita)	6.92
	R. Schurenko (Ukr)	8.31		M. Jones (US)	6.92
Triple Jump	J. Edwards (GB)	17.71	Triple Jump	T. Marinova (Bul)	15.20
	Y. Garcia (Cub)	17.47		T. Lebedeva (Rus)	15.00
	D. Kasputin (Rus)	17.46		O. Hovorova (Ukr)	14.96
Shot Putt	A. Harju (Fin)	21.29	Shot Putt	Y. Korolchik (Bela)	20.56
	A. Nelson (US)	21.21		L. Peleshenko (Rus)	19.92
	J. Godina (US)	21.20		A. Kumbernuss (Ger)	19.62
Discus	V. Alekna (Lith)	69.30	Discus	E. Zvereva (Bela)	68.40
	L. Riedel (Ger)	68.50		A. Kelesidou (Gr)	65.71
	F. Kruger (SA)	68.19		I. Yatchenko (Bela)	65.20
Hammer	S. Ziolkowski (Pol)	80.02	Hammer	K. Skolimowska (Pol)	71.16
	N. Vizzoni (Ita)	79.64		O. Kuzenkova (Rus)	69.77
	I. Astapkovich (Bela)	79.17		K. Muenchow (Ger)	69.28
Javelin	J. Zelezny (Cz)	90.17	Javelin	T. Hattestad (Nor)	68.91
	S. Backley (GB)	89.85		M. Maniani-Tzelili (Gr)	67.51
	S. Makarov (Rus)	88.67		O. Menendez (Cub)	66.18
Decathlon	E. Nool (Est)	8641	Heptathlon	D. Lewis (GB)	6584
	R. Sebrle (Cz)	8606		Y. Prokhorova (Rus)	6531
	C. Huffins (US)	8595		N. Sazanovich (Bela)	6527
20 Walk	R. Korzeniowski (Pol)	1:18:59	20k Walk	Wang Liping (China)	1:29:05
	N. Hernandez (Mex)	1:19:03		K. Plaetzer (Nor)	1:29:33
	V. Andreyev (Rus)	1:19:27		M. Vasco (Esp)	1:30:23
50 Walk	R. Korzeniowski (Pol)	3:42.22			
	A. Fadejevs (Lat)	3:43.40			
	J. Sanchez (Mex)	3:44.36			
4x100	USA	37.61	4x100	Bahamas	41.95
	Brazil	37.90		Jamaica	42.13
	Cuba	38.04		USA	42.20
4x400	USA	2:56.35	4x400	United States	3:22.62
	Nigeria	2:58.35		Jamaica	3:23.25
	Jamaica	2:58.78		Russia	3:23.46

SPORT & LEISURE

Athletics: General Information

Amateur Athletic Association   AAA founded in 1880 from the Amateur Athletic Club of 1866.

Decathlon: order of events   100m, Long Jump; Shot; High Jump; 400m; 110m Hurdles; Discus; Pole Vault; Javelin; 1500m.

discus: weight and dimensions   Men's: 2kg (4 lb 6½ oz),   Women's: 1kg   Circle: 2½m (8 feet 2½ in).

5000m: first under 13 minutes   Said Aouita (Morocco).

four-minute mile: first   Roger Bannister wearing No. 41 ran 3 mins 59.4 secs at Iffley Rd, Oxford (6 May 1954).

four-minute mile: second   John Landy.

hammer: weight   16 lb.

Heptathlon: order of events   100m Hurdles; High Jump; Shot; 200m (first day); Long Jump; Javelin and 800m (second day).

High Jump: first to 2m (woman)   Rosie Ackerman (Germany).

first to 6′ (man)   Marshall Jones Brooks (1876).

first to 6′ (woman)   Debbie Brill (1970).

first to 7′ (man)   Charles Dumas (1956).

100m: first (man) under 10 seconds   Armin Hary (1960).

100 Yards: first (man) under 10 seconds   J. P. Tennent (1868).

110 Hurdles: first (man) under 13 seconds   Renaldo Nehemiah.

Hurdles men's   110m H: 3′ 6″ (106.7 cm). Women's 100 H: 2′ 9″ (83.8 cm) Men's 400 H: 3′ high (91.4cm) and 35m between. Women's 400 H: 2′ 6″ high (26.2cm) 35m between.

javelin: weight and dimensions   Men's: 800 grams

(1 lb 12 oz), minimum length 260 cm. Women's: 600 grams (1lb 5oz), minimum length 220 cm.

Marathon: distance   26 miles 385 yards.

Marathon: origin   distance run by Pheidippides to relay news of battle of Marathon (extra 385 yards added in 1908 Olympics so as to finish race in front of Royal Box).

Mile: first man under 3 minutes 50 seconds   John Walker (1975).

Mile: first woman under 5 minutes   Diane Leather (1955).

Pentathlon: ancient   running, jumping, discus, javelin, wrestling.

Pentathlon: modern   riding, fencing, shooting, swimming, cross country run.

Pentathlon: women   200m; 100 Hurdles; Shot; High Jump; Long Jump (800m and Javelin added for Heptathlon).

Pole Vault: first man over 6m   Sergey Bubka (1985).

shot: dimensions   Men's: 7.26 kg (16 lb). Women's: 4kg (8 lb 13 oz). Circle: 2.134m (7 feet).

Steeplechase: waterjump   not jumped on first lap so seven times in all.

World Championships: won first six   Sergey Bubka won the first six World Championship pole vault events (1983, 1987, 1991, 1993, 1995, 1997).

world record holders: became MPs   Chris Chataway and Sebastian Coe.

world records: five in a day   Jesse Owens (1935).

world records: not broken at Olympics   only the Men's Discus record has never been broken at an Olympic Games.

World Record Holders (as at 30/05/01)

Men

100m	Maurice Greene (USA)	9.79
200m	Michael Johnson (USA)	19.32
300m	Michael Johnson (USA)	30.85
400m	Michael Johnson (USA)	43.18
800m	Wilson Kipketer (Ken)	1:41.11
1000m	Noah Ngeny (Ken)	2:11.96
1500m	Hicham El Guerrouj (Mor)	3:26.00
Mile	Hicham El Guerrouj (Mor)	3:43.13
2 Miles	Daniel Komen (Ken)	7:58.61
2000m	Hicham El Guerrouj (Mor)	4:44.79
3000m	Daniel Komen (Ken)	7:20.67
5000m	Haile Gebrselassie (Eth)	12:39.36
10000m	Haile Gebrselassie (Eth)	26:22.75
20000m	Arturo Barrios (Mex)	56:55.60
1 Hour	Arturo Barrios (Mex)	21,101m
Half Marathon	Paul Tergat (Ken)	59:05
25000m	Toshihiko Seko (Jap)	1:13:55.80
30000m	Toshihiko Seko (Jap)	1:29:18.80
Marathon	Khalid Khannouchi (Mor)	2:05:42
3000m S/Chase	Bernard Barmasai (Ken)	7:55.72
110m Hurdles	Colin Jackson (GB)	12.91
400m Hurdles	Kevin Young (USA)	46.78
Pole Vault	Sergey Bubka (UKR)	6.14
High Jump	Javier Sotomayor (Cub)	2.45
Long Jump	Mike Powell (USA)	8.95
Triple Jump	Jonathan Edwards (GB)	18.29
Shot Putt	Randy Barnes (USA)	23.12
Discus	Jürgen Schult (Ger)	74.08
Hammer	Yury Sedykh (URS)	86.74
Javelin	Jan Zelezny (CZ)	98.48
Decathlon	Roman Sebrle (Czech)	9026
4x100	USA	37.40
4x200	Santa Monica Track Club	1:18.68
4x400	USA	2:54.20
4x800	GB (Eliott, Cook, Cram, Coe)	7:03.89
4x1500	Germany	14:38.80

Women

100m	Florence Griffith-Joyner (USA)	10.49
200m	Florence Griffith-Joyner (USA)	21.34
400m	Marita Koch (Ger)	47.60
800m	Jarmila Kratochvilova (TCH)	1:53.28
1000m	Svetlana Masterkova (RUS)	2:28.98
1500m	Qu Yunxia (Chn)	3:50.46
2000m	Sonia O'Sullivan (Ire)	5:25.36
Mile	Svetlana Masterkova (RUS)	4:12.56

Women

3000m	Wang Junxia (Chn)	8:06.11
5000m	Jiang Bo (China)	14:28.09
10000m	Wang Junxia (Chn)	29:31.78
20000m	Tegla Loroupe (Ken)	1:05:26.06
25000m	Karolina Szabo (Hung)	1:29:29.20
3000m S/chase	Cristina Iloc-Casandra (Romania)	9:40.20
1 Hour	Silvana Cruciata (Ita)	18,084m
Half Marathon	I. Kristiansen (Nor)	1:06:40
Marathon	Tegla Loroupe (Ken)	2:20:43
30000m	Karolina Szabo (Hung)	1:47:05.06
100m Hurdles	Yordanka Donkova (Bul)	12.21
400m Hurdles	Kim Batten (USA)	52.61
Pole Vault	Stacy Dragila (USA)	4.63
High Jump	Stefka Kostadinova (Bul)	2.09
Long Jump	Galina Chistyakova (URS)	7.52
Triple Jump	Inessa Kravets (UKR)	15.50
Shot Putt	Natalya Lisovskaya (URS)	22.63
Discus	Gabriele Reinsch (Ger)	76.80
Hammer	Mihaela Melinte (Rom)	75.97
Javelin (pre 1999)	Petra Felke (Ger)	80.00
Javelin (post 1999)	Trine Hattestad (Nor)	69.48
Heptathlon	Jackie Joyner-Kersee (USA)	7291
4x100	East Germany	41.37
4x200	USA	1:27.46
4x400	Soviet Union	3:15.17
4x800	Soviet Union	7:50.17

NB Marathon and half marathon records are officially 'World Bests' rather than World Records due to the non-standardization of courses.

Baseball: World Series

Winners				*Runners-up*	
1903	Boston Red Sox (AL)		5–3	Pittsburgh Pirates (NL)	
1904	no series				
1905	New York Giants (NL)		4–1	Philadelphia Athletics (AL)	
1906	Chicago White Sox (AL)		4–2	Chicago Cubs (NL)	
1907	Chicago Cubs (NL)		4–0	Detroit Tigers (AL)	
1908	Chicago Cubs (NL)		4–1	Detroit Tigers (AL)	
1909	Pittsburgh Pirates (NL)		4–3	Detroit Tigers (AL)	
1910	Philadelphia Athletics (AL)		4–1	Chicago Cubs (NL)	
1911	Philadelphia Athletics (AL)		4–2	New York Giants (NL)	
1912	Boston Red Sox (AL)		4–3	New York Giants (NL)	
1913	Philadelphia Athletics (AL)		4–1	New York Giants (NL)	
1914	Boston Braves (NL)		4–0	Philadelphia Athletics (AL)	
1915	Boston Red Sox (AL)		4–1	Philadelphia Phillies (NL)	
1916	Boston Red Sox (AL)		4–1	Brooklyn Dodgers (NL)	
1917	Chicago White Sox (AL)		4–2	New York Giants (NL)	
1918	Boston Red Sox (AL)		4–2	Chicago Cubs (NL)	
1919	Cincinnati Reds (NL)		5–3	Chicago White Sox (AL)	
1920	Cleveland Indians (AL)		5–2	Brooklyn Dodgers (NL)	
1921	New York Giants (NL)		5–3	New York Yankees (AL)	
1922	New York Giants (NL)		4–0	New York Yankees (AL)	
1923	New York Yankees (AL)		4–2	New York Giants (NL)	
1924	Washington Senators (AL)		4–3	New York Giants (NL)	
1925	Pittsburgh Pirates (NL)		4–3	Washington Senators (AL)	
1926	St Louis Cardinals (NL)		4–3	New York Yankees (AL)	
1927	New York Yankees (AL)		4–0	Pittsburgh Pirates (NL)	
1928	New York Yankees (AL)		4–0	St Louis Cardinals (NL)	
1929	Philadelphia Athletics (AL)		4–1	Chicago Cubs (NL)	
1930	Philadelphia Athletics (AL)		4–2	St Louis Cardinals (NL)	
1931	St Louis Cardinals (NL)		4–3	Philadelphia Athletics (AL)	
1932	New York Yankees (AL)		4–0	Chicago Cubs (NL)	
1933	New York Giants (NL)		4–1	Washington Senators (AL)	
1934	St Louis Cardinals (NL)		4–3	Detroit Tigers (AL)	
1935	Detroit Tigers (AL)		4–2	Chicago Cubs (NL)	
1936	New York Yankees (AL)		4–2	New York Giants (NL)	
1937	New York Yankees (AL)		4–1	New York Giants (NL)	

Winners			*Runners-up*
1938	New York Yankees (AL)	4–0	Chicago Cubs (NL)
1939	New York Yankees (AL)	4–0	Cincinnati Reds (NL)
1940	Cincinnati Reds (NL)	4–3	Detroit Tigers (AL)
1941	New York Yankees (AL)	4–1	Brooklyn Dodgers (NL)
1942	St Louis Cardinals (NL)	4–1	New York Yankees (AL)
1943	New York Yankees (AL)	4–1	St Louis Cardinals (NL)
1944	St Louis Cardinals (NL)	4–2	St Louis Browns (AL)
1945	Detroit Tigers (AL)	4–3	Chicago Cubs (NL)
1946	St Louis Cardinals (NL)	4–3	Boston Red Sox (AL)
1947	New York Yankees (AL)	4–3	Brooklyn Dodgers (NL)
1948	Cleveland Indians (AL)	4–2	Boston Braves (NL)
1949	New York Yankees (AL)	4–1	Brooklyn Dodgers (NL)
1950	New York Yankees (AL)	4–0	Philadelphia Phillies (NL)
1951	New York Yankees (AL)	4–2	New York Giants (NL)
1952	New York Yankees (AL)	4–3	Brooklyn Dodgers (NL)
1953	New York Yankees (AL)	4–2	Brooklyn Dodgers (NL)
1954	New York Giants (NL)	4–0	Cleveland Indians (AL)
1955	Brooklyn Dodgers (NL)	4–3	New York Yankees (AL)
1956	New York Yankees (AL)	4–3	Brooklyn Dodgers (NL)
1957	Milwaukee Braves (NL)	4–3	New York Yankees (AL)
1958	New York Yankees (AL)	4–3	Milwaukee Braves (NL)
1959	Los Angeles Dodgers (NL)	4–2	Chicago White Sox (AL)
1960	Pittsburgh Pirates (NL)	4–3	New York Yankees (AL)
1961	New York Yankees (AL)	4–1	Cincinnati Reds (NL)
1962	New York Yankees (AL)	4–3	San Francisco Giants (NL)
1963	Los Angeles Dodgers (NL)	4–0	New York Yankees (AL)
1964	St Louis Cardinals (NL)	4–3	New York Yankees (AL)
1965	Los Angeles Dodgers (NL)	4–3	Minnesota Twins (AL)
1966	Baltimore Orioles (AL)	4–0	Los Angeles Dodgers (NL)
1967	St Louis Cardinals (NL)	4–3	Boston Red Sox (AL)
1968	Detroit Tigers (AL)	4–3	St Louis Cardinals (NL)
1969	New York Mets (NL)	4–1	Baltimore Orioles (AL)
1970	Baltimore Orioles (AL)	4–1	Cincinnati Reds (NL)
1971	Pittsburgh Pirates (NL)	4–3	Baltimore Orioles (AL)
1972	Oakland Athletics (AL)	4–3	Cincinnati Reds (NL)
1973	Oakland Athletics (AL)	4–3	New York Mets (NL)
1974	Oakland Athletics (AL)	4–1	Los Angeles Dodgers (NL)
1975	Cincinnati Reds (NL)	4–3	Boston Red Sox (AL)
1976	Cincinnati Reds (NL)	4–0	New York Yankees (AL)
1977	New York Yankees (AL)	4–2	Los Angeles Dodgers (NL)
1978	New York Yankees (AL)	4–2	Los Angeles Dodgers (NL)
1979	Pittsburgh Pirates (NL)	4–3	Baltimore Orioles (AL)
1980	Philadelphia Phillies (NL)	4–2	Kansas City Royals (AL)
1981	Los Angeles Dodgers (NL)	4–2	New York Yankees (AL)
1982	St Louis Cardinals (NL)	4–3	Milwaukee Brewers (AL)
1983	Baltimore Orioles (AL)	4–1	Philadelphia Phillies (NL)
1984	Detroit Tigers (AL)	4–1	San Diego Padres (NL)
1985	Kansas City Royals (AL)	4–3	St Louis Cardinals (NL)
1986	New York Mets (NL)	4–3	Boston Red Sox (AL)
1987	Minnesota Twins (AL)	4–3	St Louis Cardinals (NL)
1988	Los Angeles Dodgers (NL)	4–1	Oakland Athletics (AL)
1989	Oakland Athletics (AL)	4–0	San Francisco Giants (NL)
1990	Cincinnati Reds (NL)	4–0	Oakland Athletics (AL)
1991	Minnesota Twins (AL)	4–3	Atlanta Braves (NL)
1992	Toronto Blue Jays (AL)	4–2	Atlanta Braves (NL)
1993	Toronto Blue Jays (AL)	4–2	Philadelphia Phillies (NL)
1994	no series		
1995	Atlanta Braves (NL)	4–2	Cleveland Indians (AL)
1996	New York Yankees (AL)	4–2	Atlanta Braves (NL)
1997	Florida Marlins (NL)	4–3	Cleveland Indians (AL)
1998	New York Yankees (AL)	4–0	San Diego Padres (NL)
1999	New York Yankees (AL)	4–0	Atlanta Braves (NL)
2000	New York Yankees (AL)	4–1	New York Mets (NL)

(AL = American League.   NL = National League.)

Baseball: General Information

ball: weight between 5 and 5¼ oz.

bat: dimensions maximum length of 42 inches, maximum thickness of 2¾ inches.

Black Sox scandal eight members of the Chicago White Sox were accused of accepting bribes to throw the 1919 World Series. Although subsequently found not guilty the players were suspended for life from the 1921 season onwards.

Black Sox scandal: judge Kenesaw Mountain Landis.

commissioner: first Kenesaw Mountain Landis.

Continental League: inaugurated 27 July 1959.

first match under Cartwright Rules (1846) New York Nine (23) v Knickerbocker Club (1).

Hall of Fame founded in 1936 in Cooperstown, NY.

innings per game nine.

inventor of game Abner Doubleday, a Civil War general, credited with invention in 1839 although it was more likely derived from the game of rounders in the 18th century.

number in team nine.

playing area diamond.

rules codified by Alexander Joy Cartwright (1845).

Ruth: George Herman nicknamed 'Babe' and 'The Sultan of Swat'.

umpires four umpires run a game positioned near the home plate and the three bases.

World Series: contestants winners of the American League and National League.

Cricket – Trophy Winners from 1946

County Championship		Sunday League	Benson and Hedges Cup	NatWest Trophy (Gillette Cup 1963–81)
1946	Yorkshire	–	–	–
1947	Middlesex	–	–	–
1948	Glamorgan	–	–	–
1949	Middlesex/Yorkshire	–	–	–
1950	Lancashire/Surrey	–	–	–
1951	Warwickshire	–	–	–
1952	Surrey	–	–	–
1953	Surrey	–	–	–
1954	Surrey	–	–	–
1955	Surrey	–	–	–
1956	Surrey	–	–	–
1957	Surrey	–	–	–
1958	Surrey	–	–	–
1959	Yorkshire	–	–	–
1960	Yorkshire	–	–	–
1961	Hampshire	–	–	–
1962	Yorkshire	–	–	–
1963	Yorkshire	–	–	Sussex
1964	Worcestershire	–	–	Sussex
1965	Worcestershire	–	–	Yorkshire
1966	Yorkshire	–	–	Warwickshire
1967	Yorkshire	–	–	Kent
1968	Yorkshire	–	–	Warwickshire
1969	Glamorgan	Lancashire	–	Yorkshire
1970	Kent	Lancashire	–	Lancashire
1971	Surrey	Worcestershire	–	Lancashire
1972	Warwickshire	Kent	Leicestershire	Lancashire
1973	Hampshire	Kent	Kent	Gloucestershire
1974	Worcestershire	Leicestershire	Surrey	Kent
1975	Leicestershire	Hampshire	Leicestershire	Lancashire
1976	Middlesex	Kent	Kent	Northamptonshire
1977	Kent/Middlesex	Leicestershire	Gloucestershire	Middlesex
1978	Kent	Hampshire	Kent	Sussex
1979	Essex	Somerset	Essex	Somerset
1980	Middlesex	Warwickshire	Northamptonshire	Middlesex
1981	Nottinghamshire	Essex	Somerset	Derbyshire
1982	Middlesex	Sussex	Somerset	Surrey
1983	Essex	Yorkshire	Middlesex	Somerset
1984	Essex	Essex	Lancashire	Middlesex
1985	Middlesex	Essex	Leicestershire	Essex
1986	Essex	Hampshire	Middlesex	Sussex
1987	Nottinghamshire	Worcestershire	Yorkshire	Nottinghamshire
1988	Worcestershire	Worcestershire	Hampshire	Middlesex
1989	Worcestershire	Lancashire	Nottinghamshire	Warwickshire
1990	Middlesex	Derbyshire	Lancashire	Lancashire
1991	Essex	Nottinghamshire	Worcestershire	Hampshire
1992	Essex	Middlesex	Hampshire	Northamptonshire

County Championship	Sunday League	Benson and Hedges Cup	NatWest Trophy (Gillette Cup 1963–81)
1993 Middlesex	Glamorgan	Derbyshire	Warwickshire
1994 Warwickshire	Warwickshire	Warwickshire	Worcestershire
1995 Warwickshire	Kent	Lancashire	Warwickshire
1996 Leicestershire	Surrey	Lancashire	Lancashire
1997 Glamorgan	Warwickshire	Surrey	Essex
1998 Leicestershire	Lancashire	Essex	Lancashire
1999 Surrey	Lancashire	Gloucestershire	Gloucestershire
2000 Surrey	Gloucestershire	Gloucestershire	Gloucestershire

Cricket: General Information

ball: weight Between 5½ and 5¾ ounces (159.9–163g).

bat throwing controversy Dermot Reeves (Warks) threw bat away to avoid bat and pad catch.

Benson and Hedges Cup in 1999, the Benson and Hedges Super Cup replaced the old format, but the original format was reverted to in 2000.

best Test Match bowling figures Jim Laker 19 for 90, England v Australia at Old Trafford (1956). (Tony Locke took other wicket).

best Test Match bowling figures in single innings Jim Laker 10 for 53 v Australia at Old Trafford (1956).

Bodyline Series of 1932/3 (Australia v England) the leading bowler was Harold Larwood (33 wickets) and the England captain was Douglas Jardine, who instructed Larwood to bowl at the leg stump and into the batsman's body.

Bosie Aussie name for googly (named after its inventor B.J.T. Bosanquet, father of newsreader, Reginald).

brothers: seven played for Worcestershire Foster brothers: Basil, Henry, Maurice, Neville, Reginald, Geoffrey, Wilfrid.

captain of England also Olympic boxing gold medallist J.W.H.T. Douglas.

Chinaman googly bowled by a left-hander i.e. ball that breaks from off to leg.

county captain: longest tenure W.G. Grace for Gloucester (1871–99).

county championship officially constituted in 1890, although counties existed prior to that date and claimed a sort of unofficial title. The 1890 championship was contested by eight counties, Gloucestershire, Kent, Lancashire, Middlesex, Nottinghamshire, Surrey, Sussex, and Yorkshire. The title was won in 1890, and the following two seasons, by Surrey. The sponsors for the 2001 season are Cricinfo and previous sponsors were Schweppes (1977–83), Britannic Assurance (1984–98) and PPP Healthcare (1999–2000). The only two counties to join the championship since World War One are Glamorgan (1921) and Durham (1992).

County Cricket: Grounds Derbyshire – Nottingham Road, Derby; Durham – Riverside Ground, Chester-le-Street; Essex – New Writtle St, Chelmsford; Glamorgan – Sophia Gardens, Cardiff; Gloucestershire – Nevil Road, Bristol; Hampshire – Northlands Road, Southampton; Kent – St Lawrence Ground, Canterbury; Lancashire – Old Trafford, Manchester; Leicestershire – Grace Road, Leicester; Middlesex – Lord's, London; Northants – Wantage Road, Northampton; Nottinghamshire – Trent Bridge, Nottingham; Somerset – St James's Street, Taunton; Surrey – Foster's Oval, Kennington; Sussex – Eaton Road, Hove; Warwickshire – Edgbaston, Birmingham; Worcestershire – New Road, Worcester; Yorkshire – Headingley, Leeds.

CGU National League nicknames Derbyshire (Scorpions), Durham (Dynamos), Essex (Eagles), Glamorgan (Dragons), Gloucestershire (Gladiators), Hampshire (Hawsk), Lancashire (Lightning), Leicestershire (Foxes), Middlesex (Crusaders), Northamptonshire (Steelbacks), Nottinghamshire (Outlaws), Somerset (Sabres), Surrey (Lions), Sussex (Sharks), Warwickshire (Bears), Worcestershire (Royals), Yorkshire (Phoenix).

dismissal: methods bowled, caught, handled the ball, hit the ball twice, hit wicket, leg before wicket (lbw), obstructing the field, run out, stumped, timed out.

double: first to complete (1000 runs and 100 wickets in a season) W.G. Grace.

Douglas, J.W.H.T. : nickname Johnny Wont Hit Today. Douglas also won a gold medal for Great Britain in the 1908 Olympics at Middleweight Boxing.

ECB (England and Wales Cricket Board): chairman Lord MacLaurin of Knebworth.

fifty: slowest first class Trevor Bailey.

googly off break bowled with a leg break action.

highest scorer in first class cricket Brian Lara 501 not out v Durham.

highest scorer in test cricket Brian Lara 375 v England.

hundred: first recorded John Minshull, 107 for Duke of Dorset's XI v Wrexham (1769).

last man to take hattrick in Test Match for England Darren Gough v Australia at Sydney (1998–99).

Lords: three locations present site: St John's Wood, London.

monarch made cricket illegal Edward IV in 1477 (revoked in 1748).

Olympic champions Great Britain.

one day internationals: fastest century Shahid Afridi (Pakistan) scored 100 in 37 balls against Sri Lanka in 1997.

run: distance for completion of 58ft (17.68m).

six 6's in over: first Gary Sobers (for Notts v Glamorgan, bowler: Malcolm Nash); Ravi Shastri was the second man to accomplish the feat.

stumps: height 28 inches (71.1cm).

Sunday League CGU National League since 1999.

Sunday League: double century Ally Brown of Surrey.

swearing incident Mike Gatting at umpire Shakoor Rana (1987).

TCCB: name change in 1996 ECB (England and Wales Cricket Board).

Test cricket: oldest player Wilfred Rhodes (52).

Test cricket: youngest English player Brian Close (18).

Test cricket: youngest player Hasan Raza (Pakistan) was 14 yrs 227 days old when he played against Zimbabwe in 1996–97.

Test Match century: fewest balls Viv Richards (56).

Test Match: first Australia v England, Melbourne Cricket Ground 1877.

Test Match: tied Australia v West Indies (1960) and Australia v India (1986).

university grounds Cambridge – Fenner's Oxford – The Parks.

West Indies: three Ws Weekes, Worrell, Walcott.

Wisden: colour yellow.

World Cup football winner played County Cricket Geoff Hurst.

World Cup winners West Indies beat Australia (1975); West Indies beat England (1979); India beat West Indies (1983); Australia beat England (1987); Pakistan beat England (1991); Sri Lanka beat Australia (1996); Australia beat Pakistan (1999).

World Cup: defeated West Indies Kenya bowled West Indies out for 93 in group match of 1996 World Cup.

Darts: World Champions

	Winner		Runner-up
1978	Leighton Rees	11–7	John Lowe
1979	John Lowe	5–0	Leighton Rees
1980	Eric Bristow	5–3	Bobby George
1981	Eric Bristow	5–3	John Lowe
1982	Jocky Wilson	5–3	John Lowe
1983	Keith Deller	6–5	Eric Bristow
1984	Eric Bristow	7–1	Dave Whitcombe
1985	Eric Bristow	6–2	John Lowe
1986	Eric Bristow	6–0	Dave Whitcombe
1987	John Lowe	6–4	Eric Bristow
1988	Bob Anderson	6–4	John Lowe
1989	Jocky Wilson	6–4	Eric Bristow
1990	Phil Taylor	6–1	Eric Bristow
1991	Dennis Priestley	6–0	Eric Bristow
1992	Phil Taylor	6–5	Mike Gregory
1993	John Lowe	6–3	Alan Warriner
1994	John Part (Canada)	6–0	Bobby George
	Dennis Priestley	6–1	Phil Taylor
1995	Richie Burnett	6–3	Ray Barneveld (Netherlands)
	Phil Taylor	6–2	Rod Harrington
1996	Steve Beaton	6–3	Richie Burnett
	Phil Taylor	6–4	Dennis Priestley
1997	Les Wallace	6–3	Marshall James
	Phil Taylor	6–3	Dennis Priestley
1998	Ray Barneveld (Netherlands)	6–5	Richie Burnett
	Phil Taylor	6–0	Dennis Priestley
1999	Ray Barneveld (Netherlands)	6–5	Ronnie Baxter
	Phil Taylor	6–2	Peter Manley
2000	Ted Hankey	6–0	Ronnie Baxter
	Phil Taylor	7–3	Dennis Priestley
2001	John Walton	6–2	Ted Hankey
	Phil Taylor	7–0	John Part

NB First named winners are Embassy BDO champions. Second named winners are WDC champions (now called PDC).

Darts: General Information

BDO: stands for	British Darts Organization
News of the World Competition	1991–7 suspended sponsorship
News of the World: best of legs	best of three throughout competition
PDC: stands for	Professional Darts Council
venues: Embassy	Lakeside CC, Frimley Green, Surrey
	Heart of Midlands Club, Notts (1978)
	Jollees Night Club, Stoke (1979–85)
venue: PDC	Circus Tavern, Purfleet
WDC: stands for	World Darts Council
World Champions: nine-dart legs	John Lowe won £102,000 for achieving the first nine-dart 501 leg
	Paul Lim (USA) was second man to achieve a nine-dart leg

SPORT & LEISURE

Darts: News of the World Champions

1948	Harry Leadbetter	1960	Tom Reddington	1972	Brian Netherton	1982	Roy Morgan
1949	Jack Boyce	1961	Alec Adamson	1973	Ivor Hodgkinson	1983	Eric Bristow
1950	Dixie Newberry	1962	Eddie Brown	1974	Peter Chapman	1984	Eric Bristow
1951	Harry Perryman	1963	Robbie Rumney	1975	Derek White	1985	Dave Lee
1952	Tommy Gibbons	1964	Tom Barrett	1976	Bill Lennard	1986	Bobby George
1953	Jimmy Carr	1965	Tom Barrett	1977	Mick Norris	1987	Mike Gregory
1954	Oliver James	1966	Wilf Ellis	1978	Stefan Lord	1988	Mike Gregory
1955	Tom Reddington	1967	Wally Seaton		(Sweden)	1989	Dave Whitcombe
1956	Trevor Peachey	1968	Bill Duddy	1979	Bobby George	1990	Paul Cook
1957	Alwyn Mullins	1969	Barry Twomlow	1980	Stefan Lord	1997	Phil Taylor
1958	Tommy Gibbons	1970	Henry Barney		(Sweden)		
1959	Albert Welch	1971	Dennis Filkins	1981	John Lowe		

Football: English League Winners

	Division 1	Division 2	Division 3	Division 3 South
1889	Preston North End	—	—	—
1890	Preston North End	—	—	—
1891	Everton	—	—	—
1892	Sunderland	—	—	—
1893	Sunderland	Small Heath	—	—
1894	Aston Villa	Liverpool	—	—
1895	Sunderland	Bury	—	—
1896	Aston Villa	Liverpool	—	—
1897	Aston Villa	Notts County	—	—
1898	Sheffield United	Burnley	—	—
1899	Aston Villa	Manchester City	—	—
1900	Aston Villa	The Wednesday	—	—
1901	Liverpool	Grimsby Town	—	—
1902	Sunderland	West Bromwich Albion	—	—
1903	The Wednesday	Manchester City	—	—
1904	The Wednesday	Preston North End	—	—
1905	Newcastle United	Liverpool	—	—
1906	Liverpool	Bristol City	—	—
1907	Newcastle United	Nottingham Forest	—	—
1908	Manchester United	Bradford City	—	—
1909	Newcastle United	Bolton Wanderers	—	—
1910	Aston Villa	Manchester City	—	—
1911	Manchester United	West Bromwich Albion	—	—
1912	Blackburn Rovers	Derby County	—	—
1913	Sunderland	Preston North End	—	—
1914	Blackburn Rovers	Notts County	—	—
1915	Everton	Derby County	—	—
1916	not held	not held	—	—
1917	not held	not held	—	—
1918	not held	not held	—	—
1919	not held	not held	—	—
1920	West Bromwich Albion	Tottenham Hotspur	—	—
1921	Burnley	Birmingham City	Crystal Palace	—
	Division 1	Division 2	Division 3 North	Division 3 South
1922	Liverpool	Nottingham Forest	Stockport County	Southampton
1923	Liverpool	Notts County	Nelson	Bristol City
1924	Huddersfield Town	Leeds United	Wolverhampton Wanderers	Portsmouth
1925	Huddersfield Town	Leicester City	Darlington	Swansea Town
1926	Huddersfield Town	The Wednesday	Grimsby Town	Reading
1927	Newcastle United	Middlesbrough	Stoke City	Bristol City
1928	Everton	Manchester City	Bradford Park Avenue	Millwall
1929	The Wednesday	Middlesbrough	Bradford City	Charlton Athletic
1930	Sheffield Wednesday	Blackpool	Port Vale	Plymouth Argyle
1931	Arsenal	Everton	Chesterfield	Notts County
1932	Everton	Wolverhampton Wanderers	Lincoln City	Fulham
1933	Arsenal	Stoke City	Hull City	Brentford
1934	Arsenal	Grimsby Town	Barnsley	Norwich City
1935	Arsenal	Brentford	Doncaster Rovers	Charlton Athletic
1936	Sunderland	Manchester United	Chesterfield	Coventry City
1937	Manchester City	Leicester City	Stockport County	Luton Town

1938	Arsenal	Aston Villa	Tranmere Rovers	Millwall
1939	Everton	Blackburn Rovers	Barnsley	Newport County
1940	not held	not held	not held	not held
1941	not held	not held	not held	not held
1942	not held	not held	not held	not held
1943	not held	not held	not held	not held
1944	not held	not held	not held	not held
1945	not held	not held	not held	not held
1946	not held	not held	not held	not held
1947	Liverpool	Manchester City	Doncaster Rovers	Cardiff City
1948	Arsenal	Birmingham City	Lincoln City	Queen's Park Rangers
1949	Portsmouth	Fulham	Hull City	Swansea Town
1950	Portsmouth	Tottenham Hotspur	Doncaster Rovers	Notts County
1951	Tottenham Hotspur	Preston North End	Rotherham United	Nottingham Forest
1952	Manchester United	Sheffield Wednesday	Lincoln City	Plymouth Argyle
1953	Arsenal	Sheffield United	Oldham Athletic	Bristol Rovers
1954	Wolverhampton Wanderers	Leicester City	Port Vale	Ipswich Town
1955	Chelsea	Birmingham City	Barnsley	Bristol City
1956	Manchester United	Sheffield Wednesday	Grimsby Town	Leyton Orient
1957	Manchester United	Leicester City	Derby County	Ipswich Town
1958	Wolverhampton Wanderers	West Ham United	Scunthorpe United	Brighton & Hove Albion

	Division 1	**Division 2**	**Division 3**	**Division 4**
1959	Wolverhampton Wanderers	Sheffield Wednesday	Plymouth Argyle	Port Vale
1960	Burnley	Aston Villa	Southampton	Walsall
1961	Tottenham Hotspur	Ipswich Town	Bury	Peterborough United
1962	Ipswich Town	Liverpool	Portsmouth	Millwall
1963	Everton	Stoke City	Northampton Town	Brentford
1964	Liverpool	Leeds United	Coventry City	Gillingham
1965	Manchester United	Newcastle United	Carlisle United	Brighton & Hove Albion
1966	Liverpool	Manchester City	Hull City	Doncaster Rovers
1967	Manchester United	Coventry City	Queen's Park Rangers	Stockport County
1968	Manchester City	Ipswich Town	Oxford United	Luton Town
1969	Leeds United	Derby County	Watford	Doncaster Rovers
1970	Everton	Huddersfield Town	Orient	Chesterfield
1971	Arsenal	Leicester City	Preston North End	Notts County
1972	Derby County	Norwich City	Aston Villa	Grimsby Town
1973	Liverpool	Burnley	Bolton Wanderers	Southport
1974	Leeds United	Middlesbrough	Oldham Athletic	Peterborough United
1975	Derby County	Manchester United	Blackburn Rovers	Mansfield Town
1976	Liverpool	Sunderland	Hereford United	Lincoln City
1977	Liverpool	Wolverhampton Wanderers	Mansfield Town	Cambridge United
1978	Nottingham Forest	Bolton Wanderers	Wrexham	Watford
1979	Liverpool	Crystal Palace	Shrewsbury Town	Reading
1980	Liverpool	Leicester City	Grimsby Town	Huddersfield Town
1981	Aston Villa	West Ham United	Rotherham United	Southend United
1982	Liverpool	Luton Town	Burnley	Sheffield United
1983	Liverpool	Queen's Park Rangers	Portsmouth	Wimbledon
1984	Liverpool	Chelsea	Oxford United	York City
1985	Everton	Oxford United	Bradford City	Chesterfield
1986	Liverpool	Norwich City	Reading	Swindon Town
1987	Everton	Derby County	Bournemouth	Northampton Town
1988	Liverpool	Millwall	Sunderland	Wolverhampton Wanderers
1989	Arsenal	Chelsea	Wolverhampton Wanderers	Rotherham United
1990	Liverpool	Leeds United	Bristol Rovers	Exeter City
1991	Arsenal	Oldham Athletic	Cambridge United	Darlington
1992	Leeds United	Ipswich Town	Brentford	Burnley

	Premier League	**Division 1**	**Division 2**	**Division 3**
1993	Manchester United	Newcastle United	Stoke City	Cardiff City
1994	Manchester United	Crystal Palace	Reading	Shrewsbury Town
1995	Blackburn Rovers	Middlesbrough	Birmingham City	Carlisle United
1996	Manchester United	Sunderland	Swindon Town	Preston North End
1997	Manchester United	Bolton Wanderers	Bury	Wigan Athletic
1998	Arsenal	Nottingham Forest	Watford	Notts County
1999	Manchester United	Sunderland	Fulham	Brentford
2000	Manchester United	Charlton	Preston North End	Swansea City
2001	Manchester United	Fulham	Millwall	Brighton

S
P
O
R
T
&
L
E
I
S
U
R
E

Football: English League Clubs

Club	League debut	Nickname(s)	Ground	Previous name(s)
Arsenal	1893	Gunners	Arsenal Stadium, Highbury	Dial Square, Royal Arsenal, Woolwich Arsenal
Aston Villa	1888	Villans	Villa Park	none
Barnet	1991	Bees	Underhill	Barnet Alston FC (relegated in 2001)
Barnsley	1898	Tykes, Reds, Colliers	Oakwell	Barnsley St Peter's
Birmingham City	1892	Blues	St Andrew's	Small Heath Alliance, Small Heath, Birmingham
Blackburn Rovers	1888	Rovers	Ewood Park	none
Blackpool	1896	Seasiders	Bloomfield Road	Blackpool St Johns, Blackpool South Shore
Bolton Wanderers	1888	Trotters	The Reebok Stadium	Christ Church FC
AFC Bournemouth	1923	Cherries	Dean Court	Boscombe St John's, Boscombe, Bournemouth & Boscombe Athletic
Bradford City	1903	Bantams	The Pulse Stadium, Valley Parade	none
Brentford	1920	Bees	Griffin Park	none
Brighton & Hove Albion	1920	Seagulls	Withdean Stadium	Brighton & Hove Rangers, Brighton & Hove United
Bristol City	1901	Robins	Ashton Gate	Bristol South End
Bristol Rovers	1920	Pirates	Memorial Ground	Black Arabs, Eastville Rovers, Bristol Eastville Rovers
Burnley	1888	Clarets	Turf Moor	Burnley Rovers
Bury	1894	Shakers	Gigg Lane	none
Cambridge United	1970	The 'U's'	Abbey Stadium	Abbey United
Cardiff City	1920	Bluebirds	Ninian Park	Riverside, Riverside Albion
Carlisle United	1928	Cumbrians, Blues	Brunton Park	amalgamation of Shaddongate United and Carlisle Red Rose
Charlton Athletic	1921	Haddicks, Valiants, Robins	The Valley	none
Chelsea	1905	Blues	Stamford Bridge	none
Cheltenham Town	1999	Robins	Whaddon Road	none
Chester City	1931	Blues, City	Deva Stadium (Bumpers Lane)	King's School Old Boys and Chester Rovers, Chester (relegated in 2000)
Chesterfield	1899	Spireites, Blues	Recreation Ground, Saltergate	Chesterfield Town
Colchester United	1950	The 'U's'	Layer Road	Colchester Town
Coventry City	1919	Sky Blues	Highfield Road	Singers FC
Crewe Alexandra	1892	Railwaymen	Gresty Road	none
Crystal Palace	1920	Eagles	Selhurst Park	none
Darlington	1921	Quakers	Feethams Ground	none
Derby County	1888	Rams	Pride Park	none
Doncaster Rovers	1901	Rovers	Belle Vue	none (relegated in 1998)
Everton	1888	Toffees	Goodison Park	St Domingo FC
Exeter City	1920	Grecians	St James Park	amalgamation of St Sidwell's United and Exeter United
Fulham	1907	Cottagers	Craven Cottage	Fulham St Andrew's
Gillingham	1920	Gills	Priestfield Stadium	Excelsior, New Brompton
Grimsby Town	1892	Mariners	Blundell Park	Grimsby Pelham
Halifax	1921	Shaymen	Shay Stadium	none (relegated in 1993, promoted back in 1998)
Hartlepool United	1921	Pool	Victoria Park	Hartlepools United, Hartlepool
Huddersfield Town	1910	Terriers	Alfred McAlpine Stadium, Leeds Rd	none
Hull City	1905	Tigers	Boothferry Park	none
Ipswich Town	1938	Blues, Town	Portman Road	Ipswich Association FC
Kidderminster Harriers	2000	Harriers	Aggborough Stadium	none
Leeds United	1920	United	Elland Road	formed after Leeds City disbanded by FA order
Leicester City	1894	Foxes, Filberts	City Stadium, Filbert Street	Leicester Fosse
Leyton Orient	1905	The 'O's'	Leyton Stadium, Brisbane Road	Glyn Cricket & Football Club, Eagle FC, Orient, Clapton Orient
Lincoln City	1892	Red Imps	Sincil Bank	none

Club	League debut	Nickname(s)	Ground	Previous name(s)
Liverpool	1893	Reds, Pool	Anfield Road	none
Luton Town	1897	Hatters	Kenilworth Road	amalgamation of Luton Town Wanderers and Excelsior
Macclesfield Town	1997	Silkmen	Moss Rose	none
Manchester City	1892	Citizens, Blues	Maine Road	Ardwick FC
Manchester United	1892	Red Devils	Old Trafford	Newton Heath
Mansfield Town	1931	Stags	Field Mill	Mansfield Wesleyans
Middlesbrough	1899	Boro	Cellnet Riverside Stadium	none
Millwall	1920	Lions	New Den	Millwall Rovers, Millwall Athletic
Newcastle United	1893	Magpies	St James' Park	Stanley, Newcastle East End
Northampton Town	1920	Cobblers	Sixfields Stadium	none
Norwich City	1920	Canaries	Carrow Road	none
Nottingham Forest	1892	Forest, Reds	City Ground	none
Notts County	1888	Magpies	County Ground, Meadow Lane	Notts FC
Oldham Athletic	1907	Latics	Boundary Park	Pine Villa
Oxford United	1962	The 'U's'	Manor Ground	Headington, Headington United
Peterborough United	1960	Posh	London Road Ground	formed after Peterborough and Fletton disbanded
Plymouth Argyle	1920	Pilgrims	Home Park	Argyle Athletic Club
Portsmouth	1920	Pompey	Fratton Park	none
Port Vale	1892	Valiants	Vale Park	Burslem Port Vale
Preston North End	1888	Lilywhites, North End	Deepdale	none
Queen's Park Rangers	1920	Rangers, 'R's'	Rangers Stadium, Loftus Road	St Jude's
Reading	1920	Royals, Biscuitmen	Modejski	none
Rochdale	1921	Dale	Spotland	none
Rotherham United	1893	Merry Millers	Millmoor	Thornhill United, Rotherham County, Rotherham Town
Rushden and Diamonds	2001	Diamonds	Nene Park	formed from a merger between Rushden Town and Diamonds in 1992
Scarborough	1987	Boro	McCain Stadium, Seamer Road	Scarborough Cricketers' FC (relegated 1999)
Scunthorpe United	1950	The Iron	Glanford Park	Scunthorpe & Lindsey United
Sheffield United	1892	Blades	Bramall Lane	none
Sheffield Wednesday	1892	Owls	Hillsborough	The Wednesday
Shrewsbury Town	1950	Shrews, Town	Gay Meadow	none
Southampton	1920	Saints	The Dell	Southampton St Mary's
Southend United	1920	Shrimpers, Blues	Roots Hall	none
Stockport County	1900	County, Hatters	Edgeley Park	Heaton Norris Rovers
Stoke City	1888	Potters	The Britannia Stadium	Stoke
Sunderland	1890	Rokerites	The Stadium of Light	Sunderland and District Teachers Association FC
Swansea City	1920	Swans	Vetch Field	Swansea Town
Swindon Town	1920	Robins	County Ground	Spartans and St Mark's Young Men's Friendly Society (amalgamation)
Torquay United	1927	Gulls	Plainmoor	Torquay Town
Tottenham Hotspur	1908	Spurs	White Hart Lane	Hotspur FC
Tranmere Rovers	1921	Rovers	Prenton Park	Belmont AFC
Walsall	1892	Saddlers	Bescot Stadium	Walsall Town Swifts
Watford	1920	Hornets	Vicarage Road	West Herts
West Bromwich Albion	1888	Throstles, Baggies, Albion	The Hawthorns	West Bromwich Strollers
West Ham United	1919	Hammers, Irons	Boleyn Ground, Upton Park	Thames Ironworks FC
Wigan Athletic	1978	Latics	JJB Stadium	none
Wimbledon	1977	Dons	Selhurst Park	Wimbledon Old Centrals
Wolverhampton Wanderers	1888	Wolves	Molineux	St Luke's
Wrexham	1921	Robins	Racecourse Ground	none
Wycombe Wanderers	1993	Chairboys, Blues	Adams Park	North Town Wanderers
York City	1929	Minstermen	Bootham Crescent	none

SPORT & LEISURE

Football: Scottish League Clubs

Club	Ground	Nickname(s)
Aberdeen	Pittodrie Stadium	The Dons
Airdrieonians	Skyberry Excelsior Stadium	The Diamonds/Waysiders
Albion Rovers	Cliftonhill Stadium, Coatbridge	The Wee Rovers
Alloa Athletic	Recreation Park	The Wasps
Arbroath	Gayfield Park	The Red Lichties
Ayr United	Somerset Park	The Honest Men
Berwick Rangers	Shielfield Park	The Borderers
Brechin City	Glebe Park	City
Celtic	Celtic Park	The Bhoys
Clyde	Broadwood Stadium	The Bully Wee
Clydebank	Cappielow Park	The Bankies
Cowdenbeath	Central Park	Blue Brazil
Dumbarton	Cliftonhill Stadium	The Sons
Dundee	Dens Park	The Dark Blues/Dee
Dundee United	Tannadice Park	The Terrors
Dunfermline Athletic	East End Park	The Pars
East Fife	Bayview Park, Methil	The Fifers
East Stirling	Firs Park, Falkirk	The Shire
Elgin City	Borough Briggs	City/Black & Whites
Falkirk	Brockville Park	The Bairns
Forfar Athletic	Station Park	The Loons/Sky Blues
Greenock Morton	Cappielow Park	The Ton
Hamilton Academical	Firhill Stadium	The Accies
Heart of Midlothian	Tynecastle Park	The Jam Tarts
Hibernian	Easter Road	The Hi-Bees
Inverness Caledonian Thistle	Caledonian Stadium, East Longman	Caley/The Jags
Kilmarnock	Rugby Park	The Killies
Livingston	West London Courier Stadium	Thistle/Wee Jags
Montrose	Links Park	The Gable Endies
Motherwell	Fir Park	The Well
Partick Thistle	Firhill Park	The Jags
Peterhead	Balmoor Stadium	Blue Toon
Queen of the South	Palmerston Park, Dumfries	The Doonhamers/Queens
Queen's Park	Hampden Park	The Spiders
Raith Rovers	Stark's Park, Kirkcaldy	The Rovers
Rangers	Ibrox Stadium	The Blues/Gers
Ross County	Victoria Park, Dingwall	County
St Johnstone	McDiarmid Park, Perth	The Saints
St Mirren	St Mirren Park, Love Street, Paisley	The Buddies
Stenhousemuir	Ochilview Park	The Warriors
Stirling Albion	Forthbank Stadium	The Binos
Stranraer	Stair Park	The Blues

NB Dumbarton are currently sharing Albion Rovers' stadium. Elgin City are now the most northerly club in the Football League.

European Nations Championship

Date	Venue	Winners		Runners-up
1960	Paris	Soviet Union	2–1	Yugoslavia
1964	Madrid	Spain	2–1	Soviet Union
1968	Rome	Italy	2–0	Yugoslavia (replay after 1–1 draw)
1972	Brussels	West Germany	3–0	Soviet Union
1976	Belgrade	Czechoslovakia	2–2	West Germany (5–3 on penalties)
1980	Rome	West Germany	2–1	Belgium
1984	Paris	France	2–0	Spain
1988	Munich	Holland	2–0	Soviet Union
1992	Gothenburg	Denmark	2–0	Germany
1996	London	Germany	2–1	Czech Republic (golden goal after 1–1)
2000	Rotterdam	France	2–1	Italy (golden goal after 1–1)

PFA Young Player of the Year

Kevin Beattie (Ipswich)	1974
Mervyn Day (West Ham)	1975
Peter Barnes (Manchester City)	1976
Andy Gray (Aston Villa)	1977
Tony Woodcock (Notts Forest)	1978
Cyrille Regis (WBA)	1979
Glenn Hoddle (Tottenham)	1980
Gary Shaw (Aston Villa)	1981
Steve Moran (Southampton)	1982
Ian Rush (Liverpool)	1983
Paul Walsh (Luton)	1984
Mark Hughes (Manchester Utd)	1985
Tony Cottee (West Ham)	1986
Tony Adams (Arsenal)	1987
Paul Gascoigne (Newcastle)	1988
Paul Merson (Arsenal)	1989
Matt Le Tissier (Southampton)	1990
Lee Sharpe (Manchester Utd)	1991
Ryan Giggs (Manchester Utd)	1992
Ryan Giggs (Manchester Utd)	1993
Andy Cole (Newcastle)	1994
Robbie Fowler (Liverpool)	1995
Robbie Fowler (Liverpool)	1996
David Beckham (Manchester Utd)	1997
Michael Owen (Liverpool)	1998
Nicolas Anelka (Arsenal)	1999
Harry Kewell (Leeds)	2000

PFA Player of the Year

Norman Hunter (Leeds)
Colin Todd (Derby County)
Pat Jennings (Tottenham)
Andy Gray (Aston Villa)
Peter Shilton (Notts Forest)
Liam Brady (Arsenal)
Terry McDermott (Liverpool)
John Wark (Ipswich)
Kevin Keegan (Southampton)
Kenny Dalglish (Liverpool)
Ian Rush (Liverpool)
Peter Reid (Everton)
Gary Lineker (Everton)
Clive Allen (Tottenham)
John Barnes (Liverpool)
Mark Hughes (Manchester Utd)
David Platt (Aston Villa)
Mark Hughes (Manchester Utd)
Gary Pallister (Manchester Utd)
Paul McGrath (Aston Villa)
Eric Cantona (Manchester Utd)
Alan Shearer (Blackburn)
Les Ferdinand (Newcastle)
Alan Shearer (Newcastle)
Dennis Bergkamp (Arsenal)
David Ginola (Tottenham Hotspur)
Roy Keane (Manchester Utd)

World Footballer of the Year

Lothar Matthäus (Germany and Inter Milan) (1991)	Ronaldo (Brazil and Inter Milan) (1996)
Marco Van Basten (Holland and AC Milan) (1992)	Ronaldo (Brazil and Inter Milan) (1997)
Robert Baggio (Italy and Juventus) (1993)	Zinédine Zidane (France and Juventus) (1998)
Romario (Brazil and Barcelona) (1994)	Rivaldo (Brazil and Barcelona) (1999)
George Weah (Liberia and AC Milan (1995)	Zinédine Zidane (France and Juventus) (2000)

Football Writers' Player of the Year

1948	Stanley Matthews (Blackpool)	1974	Ian Callaghan (Liverpool)
1949	Johnny Carey (Manchester Utd)	1975	Alan Mullery (Fulham)
1950	Joe Mercer (Arsenal)	1976	Kevin Keegan (Liverpool)
1951	Harry Johnston (Blackpool)	1977	Emlyn Hughes (Liverpool)
1952	Billy Wright (Wolves)	1978	Kenny Burns (Notts Forest)
1953	Nat Lofthouse (Bolton)	1979	Kenny Dalglish (Liverpool)
1954	Tom Finney (Preston North End)	1980	Terry McDermott (Liverpool)
1955	Don Revie (Manchester City)	1981	Frans Thijssen (Ipswich)
1956	Bert Trautmann (Manchester City)	1982	Steve Perryman (Tottenham)
1957	Tom Finney (Preston North End)	1983	Kenny Dalglish (Liverpool)
1958	Danny Blanchflower (Tottenham)	1984	Ian Rush (Liverpool)
1959	Syd Owen (Luton)	1985	Neville Southall (Everton)
1960	Bill Slater (Wolves)	1986	Gary Lineker (Everton)
1961	Danny Blanchflower (Tottenham)	1987	Clive Allen (Tottenham)
1962	Jimmy Adamson (Burnley)	1988	John Barnes (Liverpool)
1963	Stanley Matthews (Stoke City)	1989	Steve Nicol (Liverpool)
1964	Bobby Moore (West Ham)	1990	John Barnes (Liverpool)
1965	Bobby Collins (Leeds)	1991	Gordon Strachan (Leeds)
1966	Bobby Charlton (Manchester Utd)	1992	Gary Lineker (Tottenham)
1967	Jackie Charlton (Leeds)	1993	Chris Waddle (Sheffield Wednesday)
1968	George Best (Manchester Utd)	1994	Alan Shearer (Blackburn Rovers)
1969	Tony Book (Manchester City) and	1995	Jürgen Klinsmann (Tottenham)
	Dave Mackay (Derby County)	1996	Eric Cantona (Manchester Utd)
1970	Billy Bremner (Leeds)	1997	Gian Franco Zola (Chelsea)
1971	Frank McLintock (Arsenal)	1998	Dennis Bergkamp (Arsenal)
1972	Gordon Banks (Stoke City)	1999	David Ginola (Tottenham)
1973	Pat Jennings (Tottenham)	2000	Roy Keane (Manchester Utd)

SPORT & LEISURE

European Footballer of the Year

1956	Stanley Matthews (Blackpool)		1978	Kevin Keegan (SV Hamburg)
1957	Alfredo Di Stefano (Real Madrid)		1979	Kevin Keegan (SV Hamburg)
1958	Raymond Kopa (Real Madrid)		1980	Karl-Heinz Rummenigge (Bayern Munich)
1959	Alfredo Di Stefano (Real Madrid)		1981	Karl-Heinz Rummenigge (Bayern Munich)
1960	Luis Suarez (Barcelona)		1982	Paolo Rossi (Juventus)
1961	Omar Sivori (Juventus)		1983	Michel Platini (Juventus)
1962	Josef Masopust (Dukla Prague)		1984	Michel Platini (Juventus)
1963	Lev Yashin (Moscow Dynamo)		1985	Michel Platini (Juventus)
1964	Denis Law (Manchester Utd)		1986	Igor Belanov (Dynamo Kiev)
1965	Eusebio (Benfica)		1987	Ruud Gullit (AC Milan)
1966	Bobby Charlton (Manchester Utd)		1988	Marco Van Basten (AC Milan)
1967	Florian Albert (Ferencvaros)		1989	Marco Van Basten (AC Milan)
1968	George Best (Manchester Utd)		1990	Lothar Matthäus (Inter Milan)
1969	Gianni Rivera (AC Milan)		1991	Jean-Pierre Papin (Marseille)
1970	Gerd Muller (Bayern Munich)		1992	Marco Van Basten (AC Milan)
1971	Johann Cruyff (Ajax)		1993	Roberto Baggio (Juventus)
1972	Franz Beckenbauer (Bayern Munich)		1994	Hristo Stoichkov (Barcelona)
1973	Johann Cruyff (Barcelona)		1995	George Weah (AC Milan)
1974	Johann Cruyff (Barcelona)		1996	Matthias Sammer (Borussia Dortmund)
1975	Oleg Blokhin (Dynamo Kiev)		1997	Ronaldo (Inter Milan)
1976	Franz Beckenbauer (Bayern Munich)		1998	Zinédine Zidane (Juventus)
1977	Allan Simonsen (Borussia Moenchengladbach)		1999	Rivaldo (Barcelona)
			2000	Luis Figo (Real Madrid)

NB In 1955–1994 the award was restricted to Europeans. Since 1995 it is for all players in European clubs regardless of nationality.

Football: General Information

Arsenal tube station: former name	Gillespie Road (one of the innovative Herbert Chapman's ideas).
artificial turf: 1st team to use	Queen's Park Rangers (1981). Luton followed soon after.
ball: circumference	between 27 and 28 inches (69–71cm).
Black: 1st English international	Viv Anderson (1978).
caps 1st awarded for internationals	1886.
city that never had Premier (Div. 1) team	Hull.
crossbar introduced	1875.
England team from one club	In 1894 Corinthians supplied all eleven players for England v Wales at Wrexham.
England: 1st home loss to foreign side	In 1953 Hungary defeated England 6–3.
England: 1st loss to foreign side	In 1929 Spain beat England 4–3 in Madrid.
European Footballer of the Year: 1st	Stanley Matthews.
FA Charity Shield: contestants	FA Cup winners v League winners.
FA Cup Final: 1st monarch to attend	King George V (1914).
FA Cup: 15 original teams	Barnes, Civil Service, Clapham Rovers, Crystal Palace (not the present one), Donnington School (Spalding), Great Marlow, Hampstead Heathens, Harrow Chequers, Hitchin, Maidenhead, Queen's Park, Reigate Priory, Royal Engineers (Chatham), Upton Park, Wanderers.
FA Cup: 1st floodlit tie	Kidderminster v Brierley Hill (1955).
1st player sent off in final	Kevin Moran of Manchester Utd (1985).
1st replay (Wembley)	1970 (draw at Wembley, replayed at Old Trafford).
1st scorer	M.P. Betts (a Harrow Chequer) scored the first goal in an FA Cup tie.
broke neck in final	Bert Trautmann of Manchester City (1956).
horse cleared pitch	PC George Storey on a white horse cleared overcrowded pitch at Wembley's first Cup Final (1923).
non-League winner	Tottenham Hotspur (1901).
played every year	Great Marlow (now Marlow) and Maidenhead have played in every FA Cup since 1872.
stolen	1895 (from a Birmingham shop).
floodlit game: 1st	1887.
floodlit: international 1st	England v Spain at Wembley (1955).
Football Association: address	16 Lancaster Gate, London W2 3LW; Tel: 020 7 262 4542.
Football Association: set up at	Freemason's Tavern, Lincoln's Inn Fields (1863).
goal nets: used for 1st time	1891 (North v South match).
goal: dimensions	height: 8 feet (2.4m), width: 8 yards (7.3m).
home internationals: 1st played	1883 (Scotland v Ireland was the first match).
home internationals: last played	1984 (Ireland won on goal difference after all four teams finished on 3 points).

international: first official	England v Scotland (1872).
Irish club: lst founded	Cliftonville (1879).
Irish FA: when formed	1880.
League and Cup double: 1st	Preston North End won FA Cup without conceding a goal and League without losing a game (1889).
numbering of players	introduced by Herbert Chapman, manager of Arsenal (1928).
oldest club: when founded	Sheffield (1857).
oldest League club: when founded	Notts County (1862).
oldest Scottish club: when founded	Queen's Park (1867).
Olympic Games: UK victory	White City (1908) and Stockholm (1912).
penalty kick introduced	1891 (at request of the Irish FA).
penalty spot: distance from goal	12 yards (11m).
points: first club to score over 100 in League	York City (101) 1983/4 season.
points: League record	Sunderland (105) 1998/9.
Rangers: won every league match	1898/9 season.
religious support: Glasgow	traditionally Catholics follow Celtic and Protestants follow Rangers.
rules: codified	at Cambridge University (1846).
Scottish FA: when formed	1873.
shinguards introduced	1874.
stadiums: famous world football	Amsterdam Arena, Amsterdam (Ajax); Azteca Stadium, Mexico; Bernabeu, Madrid (Real Madrid); Giuseppe Meazza, San Siro (AC and Inter Milan); Lansdowne Rd, Dublin; Maracana, Rio de Janeiro; Noucamp, Barcelona; Olympic Stadium, Munich (Bayern Munich); Parc des Princes, Paris (St Germain); Stade de France, St Denis; Stadio Delle Alpi, Torino (Juventus); Stadium of Light, Lisbon (Benfica); Windsor Park, Belfast (Linfield).
stadium: largest capacity	Maracana Stadium, Rio de Janeiro.
Sunday football: 1st League game	20 Jan. 1974 (Millwall v Fulham).
televised football: 1st	29 Aug. 1936 (Arsenal v Everton). BBC showed same evening.
televised football: 1st live	30 April 1938, Wembley FA Cup final, shown by BBC.
3 points: 1st played	1981/2 season.
3 points: 1st played Scotland	1994/5 season.
tragedies: Bolton	9 March 1946 (wall and barrier collapsed, 33 killed) Bolton v Stoke.
Bradford	11 May 1985 (3rd Division game between Bradford City and Lincoln City), fire in main stand, 56 died.
Heysel (Brussels)	29 May 1985 (European Cup final Liverpool v Juventus), Liverpool fans on rampage, 41 died.
Hillsborough	15 April 1989 (Notts Forest v Liverpool, FA Cup semi-final), Leppings Lane end, 96 died.
Ibrox	5 April 1902 (stand collapsed, 25 killed) Scotland v England. 2 Jan. 1971 (Celtic v Rangers who equalized in final minute, causing mayhem, 66 died).
transfer: 1st £1,000	A. Common from Sunderland to Middlesbrough (1905).
1st £10,000	D. Jack from Bolton to Arsenal (1928).
1st £50,000	D. Law from Huddersfield to Manchester City (1960).
1st £100,000	D. Law from Torino to Manchester Utd (1962).
1st £100,000 (English clubs)	A. Ball from Blackpool to Everton (1966) (actual transfer price £110,000).
1st £200,000	M. Peters from West Ham to Spurs (1970).
1st £500,000	D. Mills from Middlesbrough to West Brom (1979).
1st £1 million	T. Francis from Birmingham to Nottingham Forest (1979).
1st £2 million	P. Gascoigne from Newcastle to Spurs (1988).
1st £10 million and £15 million	A. Shearer from Blackburn to Newcastle (1996).
two-handed throw introduced	1895.
war started by football match	El Salvador v Honduras (1969).
Welsh FA: when formed	1876.
white ball legalized	1950.
World Cup: England 1st played	in 1950 (England were beaten in the qualifying competition in Brazil).
World Cup: most tournaments	Antonio Carbajal, the Mexican goalkeeper (5). Lothar Matthäus, Germany (5).
World Cup: top scorer in single tournament	Just Fontaine of France (13), 1958.

SPORT&LEISURE

Football Association Cup

Date	Winner		Runner-up
1872	Wanderers	1–0	Royal Engineers
1873	Wanderers	2–0	Oxford University
1874	Oxford University	2–0	Royal Engineers
1875	Royal Engineers	1–1, 2–0	Old Etonians
1876	Wanderers	1–1, 3–0	Old Etonians
1877	Wanderers	2–1 aet	Oxford University
1878	Wanderers	3–1	Royal Engineers
1879	Old Etonians	1–0	Clapham Rovers
1880	Clapham Rovers	1–0	Oxford University
1881	Old Carthusians	3–0	Old Etonians
1882	Old Etonians	1–0	Blackburn Rovers (first appearance of a Northern club in the final)
1883	Blackburn Olympic	2–1 aet	Old Etonians (last appearance of English amateur finalists)
1884	Blackburn Rovers	2–1	Queen's Park
1885	Blackburn Rovers	2–0	Queen's Park
1886	Blackburn Rovers	0–0, 2–0	West Bromwich Albion
1887	Aston Villa	2–0	West Bromwich Albion
1888	West Bromwich Albion	2–1	Preston North End
1889	Preston North End	3–0	Wolverhampton Wanderers
1890	Blackburn Rovers	6–1	The Wednesday
	William Townley scored first-ever Cup Final hat-trick		
1891	Blackburn Rovers	3–1	Notts County
1892	West Bromwich Albion	3–0	Aston Villa
1893	Wolverhampton Wanderers	1–0	Everton
1894	Notts County (first 2nd Division team to win the FA Cup)	4–1	Bolton Wanderers
1895	Aston Villa	1–0	West Bromwich Albion
	trophy was stolen on 11/9/95 and was never recovered		
1896	The Wednesday	2–1	Wolverhampton Wanderers
	new trophy was an exact replica of the original		
1897	Aston Villa (second team to do 'the double')	3–2	Everton
1898	Nottingham Forest	3–1	Derby County
1899	Sheffield United	4–1	Derby County
1900	Bury	4–0	Southampton
1901	Tottenham Hotspur	2–2, 3–1	Sheffield United
	Tottenham – only non-League team to win the FA Cup since the League started in 1988/9 – also started the tradition of decorating the cup with ribbons in the colours of the winning team		
1902	Sheffield United	1–1, 2–1	Southampton
1903	Bury (record winning margin in FA Cup Final)	6–0	Derby County
1904	Manchester City	1–0	Bolton Wanderers
1905	Aston Villa	2–0	Newcastle United
1906	Everton	1–0	Newcastle United
1907	The Wednesday	2–1	Everton
1908	Wolverhampton Wanderers	3–1	Newcastle United
1909	Manchester United	1–0	Bristol City
1910	Newcastle United	1–1, 2–0	Barnsley
	after this final it was discovered that the trophy had not been copyrighted and it had been copied for another tournament, so the trophy was presented to Lord Kinnaird and a new one was commissioned		
1911	Bradford City	0–0, 1–0	Newcastle United
	first winners of new (present) trophy made by Fattorini & Sons of Bradford		
1912	Barnsley	0–0, 1–0 aet	West Bromwich Albion
1913	Aston Villa	1–0	Sunderland
1914	Burnley	1–0	Liverpool
1915	Sheffield United	3–0	Chelsea
1916	not held		
1917	not held		
1918	not held		
1919	not held		
1920	Aston Villa	1–0 aet	Huddersfield Town
1921	Tottenham Hotspur	1–0	Wolverhampton Wanderers
1922	Huddersfield Town	1–0	Preston North End
1923	Bolton Wanderers	2–0	West Ham United

Date	Winner		Runner-up
	first Wembley Final – official crowd figure 126,047 – actual figure 180,000–200,000		
1924	Newcastle United	2–0	Aston Villa
1925	Sheffield United	1–0	Cardiff City
1926	Bolton Wanderers	1–0	Manchester City (1st team to reach the Cup Final and be relegated in same season)
1927	Cardiff City (only non-English team to win the Cup)	1–0	Arsenal
1928	Blackburn Rovers	3–1	Huddersfield Town
1929	Bolton Wanderers	2–0	Portsmouth
1930	Arsenal	2–0	Huddersfield Town
1931	West Bromwich Albion	2–1	Birmingham City
1932	Newcastle United	2–1	Arsenal
1933	Everton	3–0	Manchester City
1934	Manchester City	2–1	Portsmouth
1935	Sheffield Wednesday	4–2	West Bromwich Albion
1936	Arsenal	1–0	Sheffield United
1937	Sunderland	3–1	Preston North End
1938	Preston North End	1–0 aet	Huddersfield Town
1939	Portsmouth	4–1	Wolverhampton Wanderers
1940	not held		
1941	not held		
1942	not held		
1943	not held		
1944	not held		
1945	not held		
1946	Derby County	4–1 aet	Charlton Athletic
	the ball burst during the final – also this was the only season when two-legged matches were played in the FA Cup – prior to the semi-final stage		
1947	Charlton Athletic	1–0 aet	Burnley
	the ball burst again		
1948	Manchester United	4–2	Blackpool
	only time winners have played against a team from top flight in every round		
1949	Wolverhampton Wanderers	3–1	Leicester City
1950	Arsenal	2–0	Liverpool
1951	Newcastle United	2–0	Blackpool
1952	Newcastle United	1–0	Arsenal
1953	Blackpool	4–3	Bolton Wanderers
	'The Matthews Final' – Stan Mortensen hat-trick – winner scored by Bill Perry		
1954	West Bromwich Albion	3–2	Preston North End
1955	Newcastle United	3–1	Manchester City
1956	Manchester City	3–1	Birmingham City
1957	Aston Villa	2–1	Manchester United
1958	Bolton Wanderers	2–0	Manchester United
1959	Nottingham Forest	2–1	Luton Town
1960	Wolverhampton Wanderers	3–0	Blackburn Rovers
1961	Tottenham Hotspur (3rd team to do 'the double' – first in 20th century)	2–0	Leicester City
1962	Tottenham Hotspur	3–1	Burnley
1963	Manchester United	3–1	Leicester City
1964	West Ham United	3–2	Preston North End
	Howard Kendall was the then youngest finalist in 20th century)		
1965	Liverpool	2–1 aet	Leeds United
1966	Everton	3–2	Sheffield Wednesday
1967	Tottenham Hotspur	2–1	Chelsea
	first all-London Wembley final		
1968	West Bromwich Albion	1–0 aet	Everton
1969	Manchester City	1–0	Leicester City
1970	Chelsea	2–2, 2–1 aet	Leeds United
1971	Arsenal (4th team to do 'the double')	2–1 aet	Liverpool
1972	Leeds United	1–0	Arsenal
1973	Sunderland (first 2nd division team to win the Cup since West Brom in 1931)	1–0	Leeds United
1974	Liverpool	3–0	Newcastle United
1975	West Ham United	2–0	Fulham
	Bobby Moore played for Fulham against West Ham		
1976	Southampton	1–0	Manchester United
1977	Manchester United	2–1	Liverpool

Date	Winner		Runner-up
1978	Ipswich Town (only team to play in every round of Cup including preliminary)	1–0	Arsenal
1979	Arsenal	3–2	Manchester United
1980	West Ham United (most recent 2nd Division Cup winners Paul Allen beat Howard Kendall's 20th century record as youngest player)	1–0	Arsenal
1981	Tottenham Hotspur	1–1, 3–2	Manchester City
1982	Tottenham Hotspur	1–1, 1–0	Queen's Park Rangers
1983	Manchester United	2–2, 4–0	Brighton & Hove Albion
1984	Everton	2–0	Watford
1985	Manchester United	1–0 aet	Everton
1986	Liverpool	3–1	Everton
1987	Coventry City	3–2 aet	Tottenham Hotspur
1988	Wimbledon	1–0	Liverpool
1989	Liverpool	3–2 aet	Everton
1990	Manchester United	3–3, 1–0	Crystal Palace
1991	Tottenham Hotspur	2–1 aet	Nottingham Forest
1992	Liverpool	2–0	Sunderland
1993	Arsenal Arsenal also beat Sheffield Wednesday in the League Cup final	1–1, 2–1 aet	Sheffield Wednesday
1994	Manchester United (6th team to do 'the double')	4–0	Chelsea
1995	Everton	1–0	Manchester United
1996	Manchester United (1st team to do a second 'double') Eric Cantona 1st foreign player to captain the FA Cup winners	1–0	Liverpool
1997	Chelsea	2–0	Middlesbrough
1998	Arsenal	2–0	Newcastle United
1999	Manchester United (3rd double – also 1st team to do a 'treble' of League, FA Cup and European Champions Cup)	2–0	Newcastle United
2000	Chelsea	1–0	Aston Villa
2001	Liverpool	2–1	Arsenal

European Cup Winners' Cup

Date	Winner		Runners-up	Venue
1961	Fiorentina	4–1 on agg.	Glasgow Rangers	Glasgow, Florence
1962	Atletico Madrid	1–1, 3–0	Fiorentina	Glasgow, Stuttgart
1963	Tottenham Hotspur	5–1	Atletico Madrid	Rotterdam
1964	Sporting Lisbon	3–3,1–0	MTK Budapest	Brussels, Antwerp
1965	West Ham United	2–0	Munich 1860	Wembley
1966	Borussia Dortmund	2–1 aet	Liverpool	Glasgow
1967	Bayern Munich	1–0 aet	Glasgow Rangers	Nuremberg
1968	AC Milan	2–0	SV Hamburg	Rotterdam
1969	Slovan Bratislava	3–2	Barcelona	Basle
1970	Manchester City	2–1	Gornik Zabrze	Vienna
1971	Chelsea	1–1, 2–1 aet	Real Madrid	Athens, Athens
1972	Glasgow Rangers	3–2	Dynamo Moscow	Barcelona
1973	AC Milan	1–0	Leeds United	Salonika
1974	Magdeburg	2–0	AC Milan	Rotterdam
1975	Dynamo Kiev	3–0	Ferencvaros	Basle
1976	Anderlecht	4–2	West Ham United	Brussels
1977	SV Hamburg	2–0	Anderlecht	Amsterdam
1978	Anderlecht	4–0	Austria Vienna	Paris
1979	Barcelona	4–3 aet	Fortuna Düsseldorf	Basle
1980	Valencia	0–0, 5–4 on pens	Arsenal	Brussels
1981	Dynamo Tbilisi	2–1	Carl Zeiss Jena	Düsseldorf
1982	Barcelona	2–1	Standard Liège	Barcelona
1983	Aberdeen	2–1 aet	Real Madrid	Gothenburg
1984	Juventus	2–1	FC Porto	Basle
1985	Everton	3–1	Rapid Vienna	Rotterdam
1986	Dynamo Kiev	3–0	Atletico Madrid	Lyon
1987	Ajax	1–0	Lokomotiv Leipzig	Athens
1988	Mechelen	1–0	Ajax	Strasbourg
1989	Barcelona	2–0	Sampdoria	Berne
1990	Sampdoria	2–0	Anderlecht	Gothenburg
1991	Manchester United	2–1	Barcelona	Rotterdam
1992	Werder Bremen	2–0	AS Monaco	Lisbon
1993	Parma	3–1	Royal Antwerp	London (Wembley)
1994	Arsenal	1–0	Parma	Copenhagen

Date	Winner		Runners-up	Venue
1995	Real Zaragoza	2–1	Arsenal	Paris
1996	Paris St-Germain	1–0	Rapid Vienna	Brussels
1997	Barcelona	1–0	Paris St-Germain	Rotterdam
1998	Chelsea	1–0	VFB Stuttgart	Stockholm
1999	Lazio	2–1	Real Majorca	Birmingham

NB The European Cup Winners' Cup was established in 1960 and is contested by national Cup winners or the runners-up if the winners were in the European Cup. 1999 was the last competition. As from 1999/2000 national Cup winners will compete in an expanded VEFA Cup.

European Champion Clubs' Cup

Date	Winner		Runners-up	Venue
1956	Real Madrid	4–3	Stade de Reims	Paris
1957	Real Madrid	2–0	Fiorentina	Madrid
1958	Real Madrid	3–2, aet	AC Milan	Brussels
1959	Real Madrid	2–0	Stade de Reims	Stuttgart
1960	Real Madrid	7–3	Eintracht Frankfurt	Glasgow
1961	Benfica	3–2	Barcelona	Berne
1962	Benfica	5–3	Real Madrid	Amsterdam
1963	AC Milan	2–1	Benfica	London
1964	Inter Milan	3–1	Real Madrid	Vienna
1965	Inter Milan	1–0	Benfica	Milan
1966	Real Madrid	2–1	Partizan Belgrade	Brussels
1967	Celtic	2–1	Inter Milan	Lisbon
1968	Manchester United	4–1, aet	Benfica	London
1969	AC Milan	4–1	Ajax	Madrid
1970	Feyenoord	2–1, aet	Celtic	Milan
1971	Ajax	2–0	Panathinaikos	London
1972	Ajax	2–0	Inter Milan	Rotterdam
1973	Ajax	1–0	Juventus	Belgrade
1974	Bayern Munich	1–1, 4–0	Atletico Madrid	Brussels
1975	Bayern Munich	2–0	Leeds United	Paris
1976	Bayern Munich	1–0	St Etienne	Glasgow
1977	Liverpool	3–1	Borussia Moenchengladbach	Rome
1978	Liverpool	1–0	FC Bruges	London
1979	Nottingham Forest	1–0	Malmo	Munich
1980	Nottingham Forest	1–0	SV Hamburg	Madrid
1981	Liverpool	1–0	Real Madrid	Paris
1982	Aston Villa	1–0	Bayern Munich	Rotterdam
1983	SV Hamburg	1–0	Juventus	Athens
1984	Liverpool	1–1, 4–2 on pens	AS Roma	Rome
1985	Juventus	1–0	Liverpool	Brussels
1986	Steaua Bucharest	0–0, 2–0 on pens	Barcelona	Seville
1987	FC Porto	2–1	Bayern Munich	Vienna
1988	PSV Eindhoven	0–0, 6–5 on pens	Benfica	Stuttgart
1989	AC Milan	4–0	Steaua Bucharest	Barcelona
1990	AC Milan	1–0	Benfica	Vienna
1991	Red Star Belgrade	0–0, 5–3 on pens	Marseille	Bari
1992	Barcelona	1–0, aet	Sampdoria	London
1993	Marseille*	1–0	AC Milan	Munich
1994	AC Milan	4–0	Barcelona	Athens
1995	Ajax	1–0	AC Milan	Vienna
1996	Juventus	1–1, 4–2 on pens	Ajax	Rome
1997	Borussia Dortmund	3–1	Juventus	Munich
1998	Real Madrid	1–0	Juventus	Amsterdam
1999	Manchester United	2–1	Bayern Munich	Barcelona
2000	Real Madrid	3–0	Valencia	Paris
2001	Bayern Munich	1–1, 5–4 on pens	Valencia	Milan

*Marseille were subsequently stripped of title following bribery scandal concerning Bernard Tapié, the club president.

NB The European Cup was established in 1955 and was contested by the respective League champions of the member countries of the Union of European Football Associations (UEFA).

In recent seasons, clubs finishing second, third and fourth in the League of those countries with the highest VEFA points coefficients can qualify for the European Champions Cup.

SPORT & LEISURE

European Super Cup

1972	Ajax		1987	FC Porto
1973	Ajax		1988	Mechelen
1974	not contested		1989	Milan
1975	Kiev Dynamo		1990	Milan
1976	Anderlecht		1991	Manchester Utd
1977	Liverpool		1992	Barcelona
1978	Anderlecht		1993	Parma
1979	Notts Forest		1994	Milan
1980	Valencia		1995	Ajax
1981	not contested		1996	Juventus
1982	Aston Villa		1997	Barcelona
1983	Aberdeen		1998	Chelsea
1984	Juventus		1999	Lazio
1985	not contested		2000	Galatasaray
1986	Steaua			

Original 12 Football League Clubs

Accrington	Everton
Aston Villa	Notts County
Blackburn Rovers	Preston North End
Bolton Wanderers	Stoke City
Burnley	West Bromwich Albion
Derby County	Wolverhampton Wanderers

Women's World Championship

1991	USA
1995	Norway
1999	USA

Asian Cup

Date	Winner		Date	Winner		Date	Winner
1956	South Korea		1972	Iran		1988	Saudi Arabia
1960	South Korea		1976	Iran		1992	Japan
1964	Israel		1980	Kuwait		1996	Saudi Arabia
1968	Iran		1984	Saudi Arabia			

African Champions Cup

Date	Winner		Date	Winner
1964	Oryx Douala (Cameroon)		1983	Asante Kotoko (Ghana)
1965	not held		1984	Zamalek (Egypt)
1966	Stade Abidjan (Ivory Coast)		1985	FAR Rabat (Morocco)
1967	TP Englebert (Zaïre)		1986	Zamalek (Egypt)
1968	TP Englebert (Zaïre)		1987	Al Ahly (Egypt)
1969	Al Ismaili (Egypt)		1988	EP Setif (Algeria)
1970	Asante Kotoko (Ghana)		1989	Raja Casablanca (Morocco)
1971	Canon Yaoundé (Cameroon)		1990	JS Kabylie (Algeria)
1972	Hafia Conakry (Ghana)		1991	Club Africain (Algeria)
1973	AS Vita Kinshasa (Zaïre)		1992	Wydad Casablanca (Morocco)
1974	CARA Brazzaville (Congo)		1993	Zamalek (Egypt)
1975	Hafia Conakry (Ghana)		1994	Esperance (Tunisia)
1976	MC Algiers (Algeria)		1995	Orlando Pirates (South Africa)
1977	Hafia Conakry (Ghana)		1996	Zamalek (Egypt)
1978	Canon Yaoundé (Cameroon)		1997	Raja Casablanca (Morocco)
1979	Union Douala (Cameroon)		1998	ASEC Abidjan (Ivory Coast)
1980	Canon Yaoundé (Cameroon)		1999	Raja Casablanca (Morocco)
1981	JE Tizi-Ouzou (Algeria)		2000	Hearts of Oato (Ghana)
1982	Al Ahly (Egypt)			

African Nations Cup

1957	Egypt	1980	Nigeria
1959	Egypt	1982	Ghana
1962	Ethiopia	1984	Cameroon
1963	Ghana	1986	Egypt
1965	Ghana	1988	Cameroon
1968	Zaïre	1990	Algeria
1970	Sudan	1992	Ghana
1972	Congo	1994	Nigeria
1974	Zaïre	1996	South Africa
1976	Morocco	1998	Egypt
1978	Ghana	2000	Cameroon

World Club Cup

Date	Winner	Date	Winner
1960	Real Madrid	1981	Flamengo (Rio)
1961	Peñarol (Montevideo)	1982	Peñarol (Montevideo)
1962	Santos (São Paulo)	1983	Gremio (Porto Alegre, Brazil)
1963	Santos (São Paulo)	1984	Independiente (Argentina)
1964	Internazionale (Milan)	1985	Juventus (Turin)
1965	Internazionale (Milan)	1986	River Plate (Buenos Aires)
1966	V (Montevideo)	1987	FC Porto (Oporto)
1967	Racing Club (Arg)	1988	Nacional (Montevideo)
1968	Estudiantes (La Plata, Argentina)	1989	AC Milan
1969	AC Milan	1990	AC Milan
1970	Feyenoord (Rotterdam)	1991	Red Star Belgrade
1971	Nacional (Montevideo)	1992	São Paulo
1972	Ajax (Amsterdam)	1993	São Paulo
1973	Independiente (Argentina)	1994	Velez Sarsfield (Argentina)
1974	Atletico Madrid	1995	Ajax (Amsterdam)
1975	not played	1996	Juventus (Turin)
1976	Bayern Munich	1997	Borussia Dortmund
1977	Boca Juniors (Buenos Aires)	1998	Real Madrid
1978	not played	1999	Cointhians (Brazil)
1979	Olimpia (Paraguay)	2000	Real Madrid
1980	Nacional (Montevideo)		

NB From 1960 to 1979 the competition was decided on points, not goal difference. From 1980 to 1998 it was played in Tokyo. Since 1999 it has been a World Cup Championship, held in Brazil, for champions of all Continental Associations.

Copa America
South American Championship

Date	Winner	Date	Winner
1910	Argentina	1947	Argentina
1916	Uruguay	1949	Brazil
1917	Uruguay	1953	Paraguay
1919	Brazil	1955	Argentina
1920	Uruguay	1956	Uruguay
1921	Argentina	1957	Argentina
1922	Brazil	1959	Argentina
1923	Uruguay		Uruguay
1924	Uruguay	1963	Bolivia
1925	Argentina	1967	Uruguay
1926	Uruguay	1975	Peru
1927	Argentina	1979	Paraguay
1929	Argentina	1983	Uruguay
1935	Uruguay	1987	Uruguay
1937	Argentina	1989	Brazil
1939	Peru	1991	Argentina
1941	Argentina	1993	Argentina
1942	Uruguay	1995	Uruguay
1945	Argentina	1997	Brazil
1946	Argentina	1999	Brazil

S
P
O
R
T
&
L
E
I
S
U
R
E

Copa Libertadores
South American Club Cup

Date	Winner	Date	Winner
1960	Peñarol (Montevideo, Uruguay)	1987	Peñarol (Montevideo, Uruguay)
1964	Independiente (Buenos Aires, Argentina)	1989	Atlético Nacional (Medellín, Colombia)
1965	Independiente (Buenos Aires, Argentina)	1990	Olimpia (Asunción, Paraguay)
1969	Estudiantes (La Plata, Argentina)	1991	Colo Colo (Santiago, Chile)
1970	Estudiantes (La Plata, Argentina)	1995	Gremio (Pôrto Alegre, Brazil)
1972	Independiente (Buenos Aires, Argentina)	1996	River Plate (Buenos Aires, Argentina)
1974	Independiente (Buenos Aires, Argentina)	1997	Cruzeiro (Belo Horizonte, Brazil)
1975	Independiente (Buenos Aires, Argentina)	1998	Vasco Da Gama (Rio, Brazil)
1976	Cruzeiro (Belo Horizonte, Brazil)	1999	Palmeiras (São Paulo, Brazil)
1978	Boca Juniors (Buenos Aires, Argentina)	2000	Boca Juniors (Buenos Aires, Argentina)
1985	Argentinos Juniors (Buenos Aires, Argentina)		

NB The competition has been held every year since 1960. Only the winners that did not go on to win the World Club Cup are listed.

Scottish Cup Finals

Winners			Runners-up	Winners			Runners-up
1874	Queen's Park	2–0	Clydesdale	1917	not held		
1875	Queen's Park	3–0	Renton	1918	not held		
1876	Queen's Park	1–1, 2–0	Third Lanark	1919	not held		
1877	Vale of Leven	0–0,1–1, 3–2	Rangers	1920	Kilmarnock	3–2	Albion Rovers
1878	Vale of Leven	1–0	Third Lanark	1921	Partick Thistle	1–0	Rangers
1879	Vale of Leven	1–1, walkover	Rangers	1922	Morton	1–0	Rangers
1880	Queen's Park	3–0	Thornlibank	1923	Celtic	1–0	Hibernian
1881	Queen's Park	3–1	Dumbarton	1924	Airdrieonians	2–0	Hibernian
1882	Queen's Park	2–2, 4–1	Dumbarton	1925	Celtic	2–1	Dundee
1883	Dumbarton	2–2, 2–1	Vale of Leven	1926	St Mirren	2–0	Celtic
1884	Queen's Park	walkover	Vale of Leven	1927	Celtic	3–1	East Fife
1885	Renton	0–0, 3–1	Vale of Leven	1928	Rangers	4–0	Celtic
1886	Queen's Park	3–1	Renton	1929	Kilmarnock	2–0	Rangers
1887	Hibernian	2–1	Dumbarton	1930	Rangers	0–0, 2–1	Partick Thistle
1888	Renton	6–1	Cambuslang	1931	Celtic	2–2, 4–2	Motherwell
1889	Third Lanark	2–1	Celtic	1932	Rangers	1–1, 3–0	Kilmarnock
1890	Queen's Park	1–1, 2–1	Vale of Leven	1933	Celtic	1–0	Motherwell
1891	Hearts	1–0	Dumbarton	1934	Rangers	5–0	St Mirren
1892	Celtic	5–1	Queen's Park	1935	Rangers	2–1	Hamilton
1893	Queen's Park	2–1	Celtic	1936	Rangers	1–0	Third Lanark
1894	Rangers	3–1	Celtic	1937	Celtic	2–1	Aberdeen
1895	St Bernard's	2–1	Renton	1938	East Fife	1–1, 4–2	Kilmarnock
1896	Hearts	3–1	Hibernian	1939	Clyde	4–0	Motherwell
1897	Rangers	5–1	Dumbarton	1940	not held		
1898	Rangers	2–0	Kilmarnock	1941	not held		
1899	Celtic	2–0	Rangers	1942	not held		
1900	Celtic	4–3	Queen's Park	1943	not held		
1901	Hearts	4–3	Celtic	1944	not held		
1902	Hibernian	1–0	Celtic	1945	not held		
1903	Rangers	0–0, 1–1, 2–0	Hearts	1946	not held		
1904	Celtic	3–2	Rangers	1947	Aberdeen	2–1	Hibernian
1905	Third Lanark	0–0, 3–1	Rangers	1948	Rangers	1–1, 1–0	Morton
1906	Hearts	1–0	Third Lanark	1949	Rangers	4–1	Clyde
1907	Celtic	3–0	Hearts	1950	Rangers	3–0	East Fife
1908	Celtic	5–1	St Mirren	1951	Celtic	1–0	Motherwell
1909	cup withheld (see below)			1952	Motherwell	4–0	Dundee
				1953	Rangers	1–1, 1–0	Aberdeen
1910	Dundee	2–2, 0–0, 2–1	Clyde	1954	Celtic	2–1	Aberdeen
1911	Celtic	0–0, 2–0	Hamilton	1955	Clyde	1–1, 1–0	Celtic
1912	Celtic	2–0	Clyde	1956	Hearts	3–1	Celtic
1913	Falkirk	2–0	Raith Rovers	1957	Falkirk	1–1, 2–1	Kilmarnock
1914	Celtic	0–0, 4–1	Hibernian	1958	Clyde	1–0	Hibernian
1915	not held			1959	St Mirren	3–1	Aberdeen
1916	not held			1960	Rangers	2–0	Kilmarnock

Winners			Runners-up	Winners			Runners-up
1961	Dunfermline	0–0, 2–0	Celtic	1983	Aberdeen	1–0 aet	Rangers
1962	Rangers	2–0	St Mirren	1984	Aberdeen	2–1 aet	Celtic
1963	Rangers	1–1, 3–0	Celtic	1985	Celtic	2–1	Dundee
1964	Rangers	3–1	Dundee				United
1965	Celtic	3–2	Dunfermline	1986	Aberdeen	3–0	Hearts
1966	Rangers	0–0, 1–0	Celtic	1987	St Mirren	1–0 aet	Dundee
1967	Celtic	2–0	Aberdeen				United
1968	Dunfermline	3–1	Hearts	1988	Celtic	2–1	Dundee
1969	Celtic	4–0	Rangers				United
1970	Aberdeen	3–1	Celtic	1989	Celtic	1–0	Rangers
1971	Celtic	1–1, 2–1	Rangers	1990	Aberdeen	0–0, 9–8 pens	Celtic
1972	Celtic	6–1	Hibernian	1991	Motherwell	4–3 aet	Dundee
1973	Rangers	3–2	Celtic				United
1974	Celtic	3–0	Dundee	1992	Rangers	2–1	Airdrieonians
			United	1993	Rangers	2–1	Aberdeen
1975	Celtic	3–1	Airdrieonians	1994	Dundee United	1–0	Rangers
1976	Rangers	3–1	Hearts	1995	Celtic	1–0	Airdrieonians
1977	Celtic	1–0	Rangers	1996	Rangers	5–1	Hearts
1978	Rangers	2–1	Aberdeen	1997	Kilmarnock	1–0	Falkirk
1979	Rangers	0–0, 0–0, 3–2	Hibernian	1998	Hearts	2–1	Rangers
1980	Celtic	1–0	Rangers	1999	Rangers	1–0	Celtic
1981	Rangers	0–0, 4–1	Dundee	2000	Rangers	4–0	Aberdeen
			United	2001	Celtic	3–0	Hibernian
1982	Aberdeen	4–1 aet	Rangers				

NB In 1879 Vale of Leven awarded cup as Rangers failed to appear for replay after 1–1 draw.
In 1881 Dumbarton protested the first result in which Queen's Park won 2–1.
In 1884 Queen's Park awarded the cup after Vale of Leven failed to appear.
In 1889 Scottish FA ordered a replay because of playing conditions after Third Lanark won match 3–0.
In 1892 both teams protested about first game in which Celtic won 1–0.
In 1909 Celtic v Rangers 2–2, 1–1 with riot in extra time – clubs refused to play a third match – cup was withheld by Scottish FA.

SPORT & LEISURE

World Cup

	Winner		Runners-up		Venue
1930	Uruguay	4–2	Argentina		Uruguay
1934	Italy	2–1	Czechoslovakia	after extra time	Italy
1938	Italy	4–2	Hungary		France
1950	Uruguay	2–1	Brazil	deciding match of pool	Brazil
1954	West Germany	3–2	Hungary		Switzerland
1958	Brazil	5–2	Sweden		Sweden
1962	Brazil	3–1	Czechoslovakia		Chile
1966	England	4–2	West Germany	after extra time	England
1970	Brazil	4–1	Italy		Mexico
1974	West Germany	2–1	Holland		West Germany
1978	Argentina	3–1	Holland	after extra time	Argentina
1982	Italy	3–1	West Germany		Spain
1986	Argentina	3–2	West Germany		Mexico
1990	West Germany	1–0	Argentina		Italy
1994	Brazil	0–0	Italy	Brazil won 3–2 on penalties	USA
1998	France	3–0	Brazil		France

Inter-Cities Cup (became UEFA Cup in 1972)

	Winners		Runners-up
1955–58	Barcelona	8–2 agg.	London
1958–60	Barcelona	4–1 agg.	Birmingham City
1961	AS Roma	4–2 agg.	Birmingham City
1962	Valencia	7–3 agg.	Barcelona
1963	Valencia	4–1 agg.	Dynamo Zagreb
1964	Real Zaragoza	2–1 (in Barcelona)	Valencia
1965	Ferencvaros	1–0 (in Turin)	Juventus
1966	Barcelona	4–3 agg.	Real Zaragoza
1967	Dynamo Zagreb	2–0 agg.	Leeds United
1968	Leeds United	1–0 agg.	Ferencvaros

	Winners		*Runners-up*
1969	Newcastle United	6–2 agg.	Ujpest Dozsa
1970	Arsenal	4–3 agg.	Anderlecht
1971	Leeds United	3–3 agg., away goals	Juventus
1972	Tottenham Hotspur	3–2 agg.	Wolverhampton Wanderers
1973	Liverpool	3–2 agg.	Borussia Moenchengladbach
1974	Feyenoord	4–2 agg.	Tottenham Hotspur
1975	Borussia Moenchengladbach	5–1 agg.	Twente Enschede
1976	Liverpool	4–3 agg.	FC Bruges
1977	Juventus	2–2 agg., away goals	Athletic Bilbao
1978	PSV Eindhoven	3–0 agg.	Bastia
1979	Borussia Moenchengladbach	2–1 agg.	Red Star Belgrade
1980	Eintracht Frankfurt	3–3 agg., away goals	Borussia Moenchengladbach
1981	Ipswich Town	5–4 agg.	AZ67 Alkmaar
1982	IFK Gothenburg	4–0 agg.	SV Hamburg
1983	Anderlecht	2–1 agg.	Benfica
1984	Tottenham Hotspur	2–2 agg., 4–3 on pens	Anderlecht
1985	Real Madrid	3–1 agg.	Videoton
1986	Real Madrid	5–3 agg.	Cologne
1987	IFK Gothenburg	2–1 agg.	Dundee United
1988	Bayer Leverkusen	3–3 agg., 3–2 on pens	Espanol
1989	Napoli	5–4 agg.	Stuttgart
1990	Juventus	3–1 agg.	Fiorentina
1991	Inter Milan	2–1 agg.	AS Roma
1992	Ajax	2–2 agg., away goals	Torino
1993	Juventus	6–1 agg.	Borussia Dortmund
1994	Inter Milan	2–0 agg.	Casino Salzburg
1995	Parma	2–1 agg.	Juventus
1996	Bayern Munich	5–1 agg.	Bordeaux
1997	Schalke 04	1–1 agg., 4–1 on pens	Inter Milan
1998	Inter Milan	3–0 (Paris)	Lazio
1999	Parma	3–0 (Moscow)	Marseille
2000	Galatasaray	0–0, 4–1 on pens	Arsenal
2001	Liverpool	5–4 on golden goal (Dortmund)	Alaves

NB The 1998 UEFA Cup in Paris was held over one leg for the first time.

Football League Cup

	Winners		*Runners-up*
1961	Aston Villa	3–2 on agg. aet	Rotherham United
1962	Norwich City	4–0 on agg.	Rochdale
1963	Birmingham City	3–1 on agg.	Aston Villa
1964	Leicester City	4–3 on agg.	Stoke City
1965	Chelsea	3–2 on agg.	Leicester City
1966	West Bromwich Albion	5–3 on agg.	West Ham United
1967	Queen's Park Rangers	3–2	West Bromwich Albion
1968	Leeds United	1–0	Arsenal
1969	Swindon Town	3–1	Arsenal
1970	Manchester City	2–1	West Bromwich Albion
1971	Tottenham Hotspur	2–0	Aston Villa
1972	Stoke City	2–1	Chelsea
1973	Tottenham Hotspur	1–0	Norwich City
1974	Wolverhampton Wanderers	2–1	Manchester City
1975	Aston Villa	1–0	Norwich City
1976	Manchester City	2–1	Newcastle United
1977	Aston Villa	0–0, 1–1, 3–2 aet	Everton
1978	Nottingham Forest	0–0, 1–0 aet	Liverpool
1979	Nottingham Forest	3–2	Southampton
1980	Wolverhampton Wanderers	1–0	Nottingham Forest
1981	Liverpool	1–1, 2–1	West Ham United
1982	Liverpool	3–1 aet	Tottenham Hotspur
1983	Liverpool	2–1 aet	Manchester United
1984	Liverpool	0–0, 1–0 aet	Everton
1985	Norwich City	1–0	Sunderland
1986	Oxford United	3–0	Queen's Park Rangers
1987	Arsenal	2–1	Liverpool
1988	Luton Town	3–2	Arsenal
1989	Nottingham Forest	3–1	Luton Town
1990	Nottingham Forest	1–0	Oldham Athletic
1991	Sheffield Wednesday	1–0	Manchester United
1992	Manchester United	1–0	Nottingham Forest

	Winners		Runners-up
1993	Arsenal	2–1	Sheffield Wednesday
1994	Aston Villa	3–1	Manchester United
1995	Liverpool	2–1	Bolton Wanderers
1996	Aston Villa	3–0	Leeds United
1997	Leicester City	1–1, 1–0 aet	Middlesbrough
1998	Chelsea	1–0	Middlesbrough
1999	Tottenham	1–0	Leicester City
2000	Leicester	2–1	Tranmere Rovers
2001	Liverpool	1–1, 5–4 on pens.	Birmingham

Scottish League Cup

	Winners		Runners-up		Winners		Runners-up
1947	Rangers	4–0	Aberdeen	1976	Rangers	1–0	Celtic
1948	East Fife	1–1, 4–1	Falkirk	1977	Aberdeen	2–1	Celtic
1949	Rangers	2–0	Raith Rovers	1978	Rangers	2–1	Celtic
1950	East Fife	3–0	Dunfermline	1979	Rangers	2–1	Aberdeen
1951	Motherwell	3–0	Hibernian	1980	Dundee Utd	0–0, 3–0	Aberdeen
1952	Dundee	3–2	Rangers	1981	Dundee Utd	3–0	Dundee
1953	Dundee	2–0	Kilmarnock	1982	Rangers	2–1	Dundee Utd
1954	East Fife	3–2	Partick Thistle	1983	Celtic	2–1	Rangers
1955	Hearts	4–2	Motherwell	1984	Rangers	3–2	Celtic
1956	Aberdeen	2–1	St Mirren	1985	Rangers	1–0	Dundee Utd
1957	Celtic	0–0, 3–0	Partick Thistle	1986	Aberdeen	3–0	Hibernian
1958	Celtic	7–1	Rangers	1987	Rangers	2–1	Celtic
1959	Hearts	5–1	Partick Thistle	1988	Rangers	3–3, 5–3 on penalties	Aberdeen
1960	Hearts	2–1	Third Lanark				
1961	Rangers	2–0	Kilmarnock	1989	Rangers	3–2	Aberdeen
1962	Rangers	1–1, 3–1	Hearts	1990	Aberdeen	2–1	Rangers
1963	Hearts	1–0	Kilmarnock	1991	Rangers	2–1	Celtic
1964	Rangers	5–0	Morton	1992	Hibernian	2–0	Dunfermline
1965	Rangers	2–1	Celtic	1993	Rangers	2–1	Aberdeen
1966	Celtic	2–1	Rangers	1994	Rangers	2–1	Hibernian
1967	Celtic	1–0	Rangers	1995	Raith Rovers	2–2, 6–5 on penalties	Celtic
1968	Celtic	5–3	Dundee				
1969	Celtic	6–2	Hibernian	1996	Aberdeen	2–0	Dundee
1970	Celtic	1–0	St Johnstone	1997	Rangers	4–3	Hearts
1971	Rangers	1–0	Celtic	1998	Celtic	3–0	Dundee Utd
1972	Partick Thistle	4–1	Celtic	1999	Rangers	2–1	St Johnstone
1973	Hibernian	2–1	Celtic	2000	Celtic	2–0	Aberdeen
1974	Dundee	1–0	Celtic	2001	Celtic	3–0	Kilmarnock
1975	Celtic	6–3	Hibernian				

Scottish League Champions

	Dumbarton/Rangers				
1892	Dumbarton	1913	Rangers	1937	Rangers
1893	Celtic	1914	Celtic	1938	Celtic
1894	Celtic	1915	Celtic	1939	Rangers
1895	Hearts	1916	Celtic	1947	Rangers
1896	Celtic	1918	Rangers	1948	Hibernian
1897	Hearts	1920	Rangers	1949	Rangers
1898	Celtic	1921	Rangers	1950	Rangers
1899	Rangers	1922	Celtic	1951	Hibernian
1900	Rangers	1923	Rangers	1952	Hibernian
1901	Rangers	1924	Rangers	1953	Rangers
1902	Rangers	1925	Rangers	1954	Celtic
1903	Hibernian	1926	Celtic	1955	Aberdeen
1904	Third Lanark	1927	Rangers	1956	Rangers
1905	Celtic	1928	Rangers	1957	Rangers
1906	Celtic	1929	Rangers	1958	Hearts
1907	Celtic	1930	Rangers	1959	Rangers
1908	Celtic	1931	Rangers	1960	Hearts
1909	Celtic	1932	Motherwell	1961	Rangers
1910	Celtic	1933	Rangers	1962	Dundee
1911	Rangers	1934	Rangers	1963	Rangers
1912	Rangers	1935	Rangers	1964	Rangers
		1936	Celtic	1965	Kilmarnock

S P O R T & L E I S U R E

1966	Celtic	1978	Rangers	1990	Rangers
1967	Celtic	1979	Celtic	1991	Rangers
1968	Celtic	1980	Aberdeen	1992	Rangers
1969	Celtic	1981	Celtic	1993	Rangers
1970	Celtic	1982	Celtic	1994	Rangers
1971	Celtic	1983	Dundee Utd	1995	Rangers
1972	Celtic	1984	Aberdeen	1996	Rangers
1973	Celtic	1985	Aberdeen	1997	Rangers
1974	Celtic	1986	Celtic	1998	Celtic
1975	Rangers	1987	Rangers	1999	Rangers
1976	Rangers	1988	Celtic	2000	Rangers
1977	Celtic	1989	Rangers	2001	Celtic

Golf: Majors

Year	British Open	US Open	US PGA	US Masters
1860	W. Park	—	—	—
1861	T. Morris Snr	—	—	—
1862	T. Morris Snr	—	—	—
1863	W. Park	—	—	—
1864	T. Morris Snr	—	—	—
1865	A. Strath	—	—	—
1866	W. Park	—	—	—
1867	T. Morris Snr	—	—	—
1868	T. Morris Jnr	—	—	—
1869	T. Morris Jnr	—	—	—
1870	T. Morris Jnr	—	—	—
1871	not held	—	—	—
1872	T. Morris Jnr	—	—	—
1873	T. Kidd	—	—	—
1874	M. Park	—	—	—
1875	W. Park	—	—	—
1876	R. Martin	—	—	—
1877	J. Anderson	—	—	—
1878	J. Anderson	—	—	—
1879	J. Anderson	—	—	—
1880	R. Ferguson	—	—	—
1881	R. Ferguson	—	—	—
1882	R. Ferguson	—	—	—
1883	W. Fernie	—	—	—
1884	J. Simpson	—	—	—
1885	R. Martin	—	—	—
1886	D. Brown	—	—	—
1887	W. Park Jnr	—	—	—
1888	J. Burns	—	—	—
1889	W. Park Jnr	—	—	—
1890	J. Ball	—	—	—
1891	H. Kirkcaldy	—	—	—
1892	H. Hilton	—	—	—
1893	W. Auchterlonie	—	—	—
1894	J. Taylor	—	—	—
1895	J. Taylor	H. Rawlins	—	—
1896	H. Vardon	J. Foulis	—	—
1897	H. Hilton	J. Lloyd	—	—
1898	H. Vardon	F. Herd	—	—
1899	H. Vardon	W. Smith	—	—
1900	J. Ball	H. Vardon	—	—
1901	H. Kirkcaldy	W. Anderson	—	—
1902	A. Herd	L. Auchterlonie	—	—
1903	H. Vardon	W. Anderson	—	—
1904	J. White	W. Anderson	—	—
1905	J. Braid	W. Anderson	—	—
1906	J. Braid	A. Smith	—	—
1907	A. Massy (France)	A. Ross	—	—
1908	J. Braid	F. McLeod	—	—
1909	J. Taylor	G. Sargent	—	—
1910	J. Braid	A. Smith	—	—
1911	H. Vardon	J. McDermott	—	—
1912	Ted Ray	J. McDermott	—	—
1913	J. Taylor	F. Ouimet	—	—

Year	British Open	US Open	US PGA	US Masters
1914	H. Vardon	W. Hagen	—	—
1915	not held	J. Travers	—	—
1916	not held	C. Evans Jnr	J. Barnes	—
1917	not held	not held	not held	—
1918	not held	not held	not held	—
1919	not held	W. Hagen	J. Barnes	—
1920	G. Duncan	Ted Ray (GB)	J. Hutchison	—
1921	J. Hutchison	J. Barnes	W. Hagen	—
1922	W. Hagen	G. Sarazen	G. Sarazen	—
1923	A. G. Havers	B. Jones	G. Sarazen	—
1924	W. Hagen	C. Walker	W. Hagen	—
1925	J. Barnes	W. McFarlane	W. Hagen	—
1926	B. Jones	B. Jones	W. Hagen	—
1927	B. Jones	T. Armour	W. Hagen	—
1928	W. Hagen	J. Farrell	L. Diegel	—
1929	W. Hagen	B. Jones	L. Diegel	—
1930	B. Jones	B. Jones	T. Armour	—
1931	T. Armour	B. Burke	T. Creavy	—
1932	G. Sarazen	G. Sarazen	O. Dutra	—
1933	D. Shute	J. Goodman	G. Sarazen	—
1934	T. Cotton	O. Dutra	P. Runyan	H. Smith
1935	A. Perry	S. Parks Jnr	J. Revolta	G. Sarazen
1936	A. Padgham	T. Manero	D. Shute	H. Smith
1937	T. Cotton	R. Guldahl	D. Shute	B. Nelson
1938	R. Whitcombe	R. Guldahl	P. Runyan	H. Picard
1939	R. Burton	B. Nelson	H. Picard	R. Guldahl
1940	not held	L. Little	B. Nelson	J. Demaret
1941	not held	C. Wood	V. Ghezzi	C. Wood
1942	not held	not held	S. Snead	B. Nelson
1943	not held	not held	not held	not held
1944	not held	not held	B. Hamilton	not held
1945	not held	not held	B. Nelson	not held
1946	S. Snead	L. Mangrum	B. Hogan	H. Keiser
1947	F. Daly	L. Worsham	J. Ferrier	J. Demaret
1948	T. Cotton	B. Hogan	B. Hogan	C. Harmon
1949	B. Locke	C. Middlecoff	S. Snead	S. Snead
1950	B. Locke	B. Hogan	C. Harper	J. Demaret
1951	M. Faulkner	B. Hogan	S. Snead	B. Hogan
1952	B. Locke	J. Boros	J. Turnesa	S. Snead
1953	B. Hogan	B. Hogan	W. Burkemo	B. Hogan
1954	P. Thompson	E. Furgol	C. Harbert	S. Snead
1955	P. Thompson	J. Fleck	D. Ford	C. Middlecoff
1956	P. Thompson	C. Middlecoff	J. Burke	J. Burke Jnr
1957	B. Locke	D. Mayer	L. Hebert	D. Ford
1958	P. Thompson	T. Bolt	D. Finsterwald	A. Palmer
1959	G. Player	W. Casper	B. Rosburg	A. Wall Jnr
1960	K. Nagle	A. Palmer	J. Hebert	A. Palmer
1961	A. Palmer	G. Littler	J. Barber	G. Player
1962	A. Palmer	J. Nicklaus	G. Player	A. Palmer
1963	R. Charles	J. Boros	J. Nicklaus	J. Nicklaus
1964	T. Lema	K. Venturi	B. Nicholls	A. Palmer
1965	P. Thompson	G. Player	D. Marr	J. Nicklaus
1966	J. Nicklaus	W. Casper	A. Geiberger	J. Nicklaus
1967	R. de Vicenzo	J. Nicklaus	D. January	G. Brewer
1968	G. Player	L. Trevino	J. Boros	B. Goalby
1969	A. Jacklin	O. Moody	R. Floyd	G. Archer
1970	J. Nicklaus	A. Jacklin	D. Stockton	W. Caspar
1971	L. Trevino	L. Trevino	J. Nicklaus	C. Coody
1972	L. Trevino	J. Nicklaus	G. Player	J. Nicklaus
1973	T. Weiskopf	J. Miller	J. Nicklaus	T. Aaron
1974	G. Player	H. Irwin	L. Trevino	G. Player
1975	T. Watson	L. Graham	J. Nicklaus	J. Nicklaus
1976	J. Miller	J. Pate	D. Stockton	R. Floyd
1977	T. Watson	H. Green	L. Wadkins	T. Watson
1978	J. Nicklaus	A. North	J. Mahaffey	G. Player
1979	S. Ballesteros	H. Irwin	D. Graham (Australia)	F. Zoeller
1980	T. Watson	J. Nicklaus	J. Nicklaus	S. Ballesteros
1981	W. Rogers	D. Graham (Australia)	L. Nelson	T. Watson
1982	T. Watson	T. Watson	R. Floyd	C. Stadler
1983	T. Watson	L. Nelson	H. Sutton	S. Ballesteros
1984	S. Ballesteros	F. Zoeller	L. Trevino	B. Crenshaw

S P O R T & L E I S U R E

Year	British Open	US Open	US PGA	US Masters
1985	S. Lyle	A. North	H. Green	B. Langer (Germany)
1986	G. Norman	R. Floyd	B. Tway	J. Nicklaus
1987	N. Faldo	S. Simpson	L. Nelson	L. Mize
1988	S. Ballesteros	C. Strange	J. Sluman	S. Lyle
1989	M. Calcavecchia	C. Strange	P. Stewart	N. Faldo
1990	N. Faldo	H. Irwin	W. Grady (Australia)	N. Faldo
1991	I. Baker-Finch	P. Stewart	J. Daly	I. Woosnam
1992	N. Faldo	T. Kite	N. Price	F. Couples
1993	G. Norman	L. Janzen	P. Azinger	B. Langer
1994	N. Price	E. Els	N. Price	J. M. Olazabal
1995	J. Daly	C. Pavin	S. Elkington	B. Crenshaw
1996	T. Lehman	S. Jones	M. Brooks	N. Faldo
1997	J. Leonard	E. Els	D. Love III	T. Woods
1998	M. O'Meara	L. Janzen	V.J. Singh	M. O'Meara
1999	P. Lawrie	P. Stewart	T. Woods	J.M. Olazabal
2000	T. Woods	T. Woods	T. Woods	V.J. Singh
2001	D. Duval	R. Goosen	D. Toms	T. Woods

Golf: World Matchplay Championship

Year	Winner	Runner-up	Year	Winner	Runner-up
1964	Arnold Palmer	Neil Coles	1983	Greg Norman	Nick Faldo
1965	Gary Player	Peter Thomson	1984	S.Ballesteros	B. Langer
1966	Gary Player	Jack Nicklaus	1985	S.Ballesteros	B. Langer
1967	Arnold Palmer	Peter Thomson	1986	Greg Norman	S. Lyle
1968	Gary Player	Bob Charles	1987	Ian Woosnam	S. Lyle
1969	Bob Charles	Gene Littler	1988	S. Lyle	Nick Faldo
1970	Jack Nicklaus	Lee Trevino	1989	Nick Faldo	Ian Woosnam
1971	Gary Player	Jack Nicklaus	1990	Ian Woosnam	Mark McNulty
1972	Tom Weiskopf	Lee Trevino	1991	S.Ballesteros	Nick Price
1973	Gary Player	Graham Marsh	1992	Nick Faldo	Jeff Sluman
1974	Hale Irwin	Gary Player	1993	Corey Pavin	Nick Faldo
1975	Hale Irwin	Al Geiberger	1994	Ernie Els	C.Montgomerie
1976	David Graham	Hale Irwin	1995	Ernie Els	S.Elkington
1977	Graham Marsh	Ray Floyd	1996	Ernie Els	Vijay Singh
1978	Isao Aoki	Simon Owen	1997	Vijay Singh	Ernie Els
1979	Bill Rogers	Isao Aoki	1998	Mark O'Meara	Tiger Woods
1980	Greg Norman	S. Lyle	1999	Colin Montgomerie	Mark O'Meara
1981	S. Ballesteros	Ben Crenshaw	2000	Lee Westwood	Colin Montgomerie
1982	S.Ballesteros	S. Lyle			

Golf: Ryder Cup

Year	Winner	Venue	Year	Winner	Venue
1927	USA	Worcester, Massachusetts	1967	USA	Houston, Texas
1929	GB	Moortown, North Yorkshire	1969	tie	Royal Birkdale, Lancashire
1931	USA	Scioto, Ohio	1971	USA	St Louis, Missouri
1933	GB	Southport & Ainsdale, Lancashire	1973	USA	Muirfield, Scotland
			1975	USA	Laurel Valley, Pennsylvania
1935	USA	Ridgewood, New Jersey	1977	USA	Royal Lytham, Lancashire
1937	USA	Southport & Ainsdale, Lancashire	1979	USA	Greenbrier, Virginia
			1981	USA	Walton Heath
1947	USA	Portland, Oregon	1983	USA	Palm Beach
1949	USA	Ganton, Yorkshire	1985	Europe	Belfry
1951	USA	Pinehurst, North Carolina	1987	Europe	Muirfield Village
1953	USA	Wentworth, Surrey	1989	tie	Belfry
1955	USA	Thunderbird G & C, California	1991	USA	Kiawah Island
1957	GB	Lindrick, Yorkshire	1993	USA	Belfry
1959	USA	Eldorado CC, California	1995	Europe	Oak Hill CC
1961	USA	Royal Lytham, Lancashire	1997	Europe	Valderrama
1963	USA	Atlanta, Georgia	1999	USA	Boston, Massachusetts
1965	USA	Royal Birkdale, Lancashire			

NB Since 1979 the Ryder Cup has been contested by USA and Europe.

Golf: General Information

British Open: oldest winner	Old Tom Morris (46)
youngest winner	Young Tom Morris (17)
youngest winner 20th century	Seve Ballesteros (22)
clubs: maximum allowed	14
Curtis Cup	Biennial tournament instituted in 1932 and played between amateur ladies teams from the United States and Great Britain and Ireland. Teams consist of six players, two substitutes and a captain.
golf balls: pimples	332
Ryder Cup: father and sons played	Percy and Peter Alliss, Antonio and Ignacio Garrido
Samuel Ryder: profession	seed-merchant
Solheim Cup	Biennial tournament instituted in 1990 and played between professional ladies teams from the United States and Europe. It takes its name from Karsten Solheim, owner of golf club manufacturer Ping. Teams consist of 12 players and a non-playing captain.
US Masters: oldest winner	Jack Nicklaus (46)
youngest winner	Tiger Woods (21)
US Open: oldest winner	Hale Irwin (45)
youngest winner	John McDermott (19)
US PGA: oldest winner	Julius Boros (48)
youngest winner	Gene Sarazen (20)
US Women's Open: first UK winner	Laura Davies (1987)
Walker Cup	Inaugurated in 1921 and played between amateur teams from the United States and the British Isles. It was proposed by George Walker, the then president of the USGA, as the International Challenge Trophy but took its present name in 1922. It became a biennial event in 1924. Teams consist of eight players, two substitutes and a captain.

SPORT&LEISURE

Horse Racing: British Classics and Grand National Winners

	St Leger		Oaks		Derby	
Year	Horse	Jockey	Horse	Jockey	Horse	Jockey
1776	Allabaculia	J. Singleton	—	—	—	—
1777	Bourbon	J. Cade	—	—	—	—
1778	Hollandaise	G. Hearon	—	—	—	—
1779	Tommy	G. Lowrey Snr	Bridget	R. Goodison	—	—
1780	Ruler	J. Mangle	Teetotum	R. Goodison	Diomed	S. Arnull
1781	Serina	R. Forster	Faith	R. Goodison	Young Eclipse	C. Hindley
1782	Imperatrix	G. Searle	Ceres	S. Chifney Snr	Assassin	S. Arnull
1783	Phoenomenon	A. Hall	Maid of Oakes	S. Chifney Snr	Saltram	C. Hindley
1784	Omphale	J. Kirton	Stella	C. Hindley	Sergeant	J. Arnull
1785	Cowslip	G. Searle	Trifle	J. Bird	Aimwell	C. Hindley
1786	Paragon	J. Mangle	Perdita by Tanden	J. Edwards	Noble	J. White
1787	Spadille	J. Mangle	Annette	Fitzpatrick	Sir Peter Teazle	S. Arnull
1788	Young Flora	J. Mangle	Nightshade	Fitzpatrick	Sir Thomas	W. South
1789	Pewett	J. Singleton	Tag	S. Chifney Snr	Skyscraper	S. Chifney Snr
1790	Ambidexter	G. Searle	Hippolyta	S. Chifney Snr	Rhadamanthus	J. Arnull
1791	Young Traveller	J. Jackson	Portia	J. Singleton	Eager	Stephenson
1792	Tartar	J. Mangle	Volante	C. Hindley	John Bull	F. Buckle
1793	Ninety-three	W. Peirse	Caelia	J. Singleton	Waxy	W. Clift
1794	Beningborough	J. Jackson	Hermione	S. Arnull	Daedalus	F. Buckle
1795	Hambletonian	Boyes	Platina	Fitzpatrick	Spreadeagle	A. Wheatley
1796	Ambrosio	J. Jackson	Parissot	J. Arnull	Didelot	J. Arnull
1797	Lounger	J. Shepherd	Nike	F. Buckle	Brown c by fidget	J. Singleton
1798	Symmetry	J. Jackson	Bellissima	F. Buckle	Sir Harry	S. Arnull
1799	Cockfighter	T. Fields	Bellina	F. Buckle	Archduke	J. Arnull
1800	Champion	F. Buckle	Ephemera	Fitzpatrick	Champion	W. Clift
1801	Quiz	J. Shepherd	Eleanor	Saunders	Eleanor	Saunders
1802	Orville	J. Singleton Jnr	Scotia	F. Buckle	Tyrant	F. Buckle
1803	Remembrancer	B. Smith	Theophania	F. Buckle	Ditto	W. Clift
1804	Sancho	F. Buckle	Pellisse	W. Clift	Hannibal	W. Arnull
1805	Staveley	J. Jackson	Meteora	F. Buckle	Cardinal Beaufort	Fitzpatrick
1806	Fyldener	T. Carr	Bronze	W. Edwards	Paris	J. Shepherd
1807	Paulina	W. Clift	Briseis	S. Chifney	Election	J. Arnull
1808	Petronius	B. Smith	Morel	W. Clift	Pan	Collinson
1809	Ashton	B. Smith	Maid of Orleans	J. Moss	Pope	T. Goodison

	St Leger		Oaks		Derby	
Year	Horse	Jockey	Horse	Jockey	Horse	Jockey
1810	Octavian	W. Clift	Oriana	W. Peirse	Whalebone	W. Clift
1811	Soothsayer	B. Smith	Sorcery	S. Chifney	Phantom	F. Buckle
1812	Ottrington	R. Johnson	Manuella	W. Peirse	Octavius	W. Arnull
1813	Altisidora	J. Jackson	Music	T. Goodison	Smolensko	T. Goodison
1814	William	J. Shepherd	Medora	Barnard	Blucher	W. Arnull
1815	Filho da Puta	J. Jackson	Minuet	T. Goodison	Whisker	T. Goodison
1816	The Duchess	B. Smith	Landscape	S. Chifney	Prince Leopold	W. Wheatley
1817	Ebor	R. Johnson	Neva	F. Buckle	Azor	J. Robinson
1818	Reveller	R. Johnson	Corinne	F. Buckle	Sam	S. Chifney Jnr
1819	Antonio	J. Nicholson	Shoveler	S. Chifney	Tiresias	W. Clift
1820	St Patrick	J. Johnson	Caroline	H. Edwards	Sailor	S. Chifney Jnr
1821	Jack Spiggot	W. Scott	Augusta	J. Robinson	Gustavus	S. Day
1822	Theodore	J. Jackson	Pastille	H. Edwards	Moses	T. Goodison
1823	Barefoot	T. Goodison	Zinc	F. Buckle	Emilius	F. Buckle
1824	Jerry	B. Smith	Cobweb	J. Robinson	Cedric	J. Robinson
1825	Memnon	W. Scott	Wings	S. Chifney	Middleton	J. Robinson
1826	Tarrare	G. Nelson	Lilias	T. Lye	Lap-dog	G. Dockeray
1827	Matilda	J. Robinson	Gulnare	F. Boyce	Mameluke	J. Robinson
1828	The Colonel	W. Scott	Turquoise	J.B. Day	Cadland	J. Robinson
1829	Rowton	W. Scott	Green Mantle	G. Dockeray	Frederick	Forth
1830	Birmingham	P. Conolly	Variation	G. Edwards	Priam	S. Day
1831	Chorister	J.B. Day	Oxygen	J.B. Day	Spaniel	W. Wheatley
1832	Margrave	J. Robinson	Galata	P. Conolly	St Giles	W. Scott
1833	Rockingham	S. Darling	Vespa	J. Chapple	Dangerous	J. Chapple
1834	Touchstone	G. Calloway	Pussy	J.B. Day	Plenipotentiary	P. Conolly
1835	Queen of Trumps	T. Lye	Queen of Trumps	T. Lye	Mundig	W. Scott
1836	Elis	J.B. Day	Cyprian	W. Scott	Bay Middleton	J. Robinson
1837	Mango	S. Day Jnr	Miss Letty	J. Holmes	Phosphorus	G. Edwards
1838	Don John	W. Scott	Industry	W. Scott	Amato	J. Chapple
1839	Charles the Twelfth	W. Scott	Deception	J.B. Day	Bloomsbury	S. Templeman
1840	Launcelot	W. Scott	Crucifix	J.B. Day	Little Wonder	Macdonald
1841	Satirist	W. Scott	Ghuznee	W. Scott	Coronation	P. Conolly
1842	Blue Bonnett	T. Lye	Our Nell	T. Lye	Attila	W. Scott
1843	Nutwith	J. Marson	Poison	F. Butler	Cotherstone	W. Scott
1844	Foig a Ballagh	H. Bell	The Princess	F. Butler	Orlando	E. Flatman
1845	The Baron	F. Butler	Refraction	H. Bell	The Merry Monarch	F. Bell
1846	Sir Tatton Sykes	W. Scott	Mendicant	S. Day	Pyrrhus the First	S. Day
1847	Van Tromp	J. Marson	Miami	S. Templeman	Cossack	S. Templeman
1848	Surplice	E. Flatman	Cymba	S. Templeman	Surplice	S. Templeman
1849	Flying Dutchman	Marlow	Lady Evelyn	F. Butler	Flying Dutchman	Marlow
1850	Voltigeur	J. Marson	Rhedycina	F. Butler	Voltigeur	J. Marson
1851	Newminster	S. Templeman	Iris	F. Butler	Teddington	J. Marson
1852	Stockwell	J. Norman	Songstress	F. Butler	Daniel O'Rourke	F. Butler
1853	West Australian	F. Butler	Catherine Hayes	Marlow	West Australian	F. Butler
1854	Knight of St George	Basham	Mincemeat	Charlton	Andover	A. Day
1855	Saucebox	J. Wells	Marchioness	S. Templeman	Wild Dayrell	R. Sherwood
1856	Warlock	E. Flatman	Mincepie	A. Day	Ellington	Aldcroft
1857	Imperieuse	E. Flatman	Blink Bonny	Charlton	Blink Bonny	Charlton
1858	Sunbeam	L. Snowden	Governess	Ashmall	Beadsman	J. Wells
1859	Gamester	Aldcroft	Summerside	G. Fordham	Musjid	J. Wells
1860	St Albans	L. Snowden	Butterfly	J. Snowden	Thormanby	H. Custance
1861	Caller Ou	T. Challoner	Brown Duchess	L. Snowden	Kettledrum	Bullock
1862	The Marquis	T. Challoner	Feu de Joie	T. Challoner	Caractacus	J. Parsons
1863	Lord Clifden	J. Osborne	Queen Bertha	Aldcroft	Macaroni	T. Challoner
1864	Blair Atholl	J. Snowden	Fille de l'Air	A. Edwards	Blair Atholl	J. Snowden
1865	Gladiateur	H. Grimshaw	Regalia	Norman	Gladiateur	H. Grimshaw
1866	Lord Lyon	H. Custance	Tormentor	J. Mann	Lord Lyon	H. Custance
1867	Achievement	T. Challoner	Hippia	J. Daley	Hermit	J. Daley
1868	Formosa	T. Challoner	Formosa	G. Fordham	Blue Gown	J. Wells
1869	Pero Gomez	J. Wells	Brigantine	T. Cannon	Pretender	J. Osborne
1870	Hawthornden	J. Grimshaw	Gamos	G. Fordham	Kingcraft	T. French
1871	Hannah	C. Maidment	Hannah	C. Maidment	Favonius	T. French
1872	Wenlock	C. Maidment	Reine	G. Fordham	Cremorne	C. Maidment
1873	Marie Stuart	T. Osborne	Marie Stuart	T. Cannon	Doncaster	F. Webb
1874	Apology	J. Osborne	Apology	J. Osborne	George Frederick	H. Custance

	St Leger		Oaks		Derby	
Year	Horse	Jockey	Horse	Jockey	Horse	Jockey
1875	Craig Millar	T. Challoner	Spinaway	F. Archer	Galopin	Morris
1876	Patriarch	J. Goater	Enguerrande	Hudson	Kisber	C. Maidment
1877	Silvio	F. Archer	Placida	H. Jeffrey	Silvio	F. Archer
1878	Jannette	F. Archer	Jannette	F. Archer	Sefton	H. Constable
1879	Rayon d'Or	J. Goater	Wheel of Fortune	F. Archer	Sir Bevys	G. Fordham
1880	Robert the Devil	T. Cannon	Jenny Howlet	J. Snowden	Bend Or	F. Archer
1881	Iroquois	F. Archer	Thebais	G. Fordham	Iroquois	F. Archer
1882	Dutch Oven	F. Archer	Geheimnis	T. Cannon	Shotover	T. Cannon
1883	Ossian	J. Watts	Bonny Jean	J. Watts	St Blaise	C. Wood
1884	The Lambkin	J. Watts	Busybody	T. Cannon	St Gatien/ Harvester	C.Wood/Loates
1885	Melton	F. Archer	Lonely	F. Archer	Melton	F. Archer
1886	Ormonde	F. Archer	Miss Jummy	J. Watts	Ormonde	F. Archer
1887	Kilwarlin	W. Robinson	Reve d'Or	C. Wood	Merry Hampton	J. Watts
1888	Seabreeze	W. Robinson	Seabreeze	W. Robinson	Ayrshire	F. Barrett
1889	Donovan	F. Barrett	L'Abbesse de Jouarre	J. Woodburn	Donovan	T. Loates
1890	Memoir	J. Watts	Memoir	J. Watts	Sainfoin	J. Watts
1891	Common	G. Barrett	Mimi	F. Rickaby	Common	G. Barrett
1892	La Fleche	J. Watts	La Fleche	G. Barrett	Sir Hugo	Allsopp
1893	Isinglass	T. Loates	Mrs Butterwick	J. Watts	Isinglass	T. Loates
1894	Throstle	M. Cannon	Amiable	W. Bradford	Ladas	J. Watts
1895	Sir Visto	S. Loates	La Sagesse	S. Loates	Sir Visto	S. Loates
1896	Persimmon	J. Watts	Canterbury Pilgrim	F. Rickaby	Persimmon	J. Watts
1897	Galtee More	C. Wood	Limasol	W. Bradford	Galtee More	C. Wood
1898	Wildfowler	C. Wood	Airs and Graces	W. Bradford	Jeddah	O'Madden
1899	Flying Fox	M. Cannon	Musa	O. Madden	Flying Fox	M. Cannon
1900	Diamond Jubilee	H. Jones	La Roche	M. Cannon	Diamond Jubilee	H. Jones
1901	Doricles	K. Cannon	Cap and Bells II	M. Henry	Volodyovski	L. Reiff
1902	Sceptre	F.W. Hardy	Sceptre	H. Randall	ard Patrick	J. Martin
1903	Rock Sand	D. Maher	Our Lassie	M. Cannon	Rock Sand	D. Maher
1904	Pretty Polly	W. Lane	Pretty Polly	W. Lane	St Amant	K. Cannon
1905	Challacombe	O. Madden	Cherry Lass	H. Jones	Cicero	D. Maher
1906	Troutbeck	G. Stern	Keystone II	D. Maher	Spearmint	D. Maher
1907	Wool Winder	W. Halsey	Glass Doll	H. Randall	Orby	J. Reiff
1908	Your Majesty	W. Griggs	Signorinetta	W. Bullock	Signorinetta	W. Bullock
1909	Bayardo	D. Maher	Perola	F. Wootton	Minoru	H. Jones
1910	Swynford	F. Wootton	Rosedrop	C. Trigg	Lemberg	B. Dillon
1911	Prince Palatine	F. O'Neill	Cherimoya	F. Winter	Sunstar	G. Stern
1912	Tracery	G. Bellhouse	Mirska	J. Childs	Tagalie	J. Reiff
1913	Night Hawk	E. Wheatley	Jest	F. Rickaby Jnr	Aboyeur	E. Piper
1914	Black Jester	W. Griggs	Princess Dorrie	W. Huxley	Dubar II	M. MacGee
1915	Pommern	S. Donoghue	Snow Marten	Walter Griggs	Pommern	S. Donoghue
1916	Hurry On	C. Childs	Fifinella	J. Childs	Fifinella	J. Childs
1917	Gay Crusader	S. Donoghue	Sunny Jane	O. Madden	Gay Crusader	S. Donoghue
1918	Gainsborough	J. Childs	My Dear	S. Donoghue	Gainsborough	J. Childs
1919	Keysoe	B. Carslake	Bayuda	J. Childs	Grand Parade	F. Templeman
1920	Caligula	A. Smith	Charlebelle	A. Whalley	Spion Kop	F. O'Neill
1921	Polemarch	J. Childs	Love in Idleness	J. Childs	Humorist	S. Donoghue
1922	Royal Lancer	R. Jones	Pogram	E. Gardner	Captain Cuttle	S. Donoghue
1923	Tranquil	T. Weston	Brownhylda	V. Smyth	Papyrus	S. Donoghue
1924	Salmon-Trout	B. Carslake	Straitlace	F. O'Neill	Sansovino	T. Weston
1925	Solario	J. Childs	Saucy Sue	F. Bullock	Manna	S. Donoghue
1926	Coronach	J. Childs	Short Story	R.A. Jones	Coronach	J. Childs
1927	Book Law	H. Jellis	Beam	T. Weston	Call Boy	C. Elliot
1928	Fairway	T. Weston	Toboggan	T. Weston	Felstead	H. Wragg
1929	Trigo	M. Beary	Pennycomequick	H. Jelliss	Trigo	J. Marshall
1930	Singapore	G. Richards	Rose of England	G. Richards	Blenheim	H. Wragg
1931	Sandwich	H. Wragg	Brulette	E.C. Elliot	Cameronian	F. Fox
1932	Firdaussi	F. Fox	Udaipur	M. Beary	April the Fifth	F. Lane
1933	Hyperion	T. Weston	Chatelaine	S. Wragg	Hyperion	T. Weston
1934	Windsor Lad	C. Smirke	Light Brocade	B. Carslake	Windsor Lad	C. Smirke
1935	Bahram	C. Smirke	Quashed	H. Jelliss	Bahram	F. Fox
1936	Boswell	P. Beasley	Lovely Rosa	T. Weston	Mahmoud	C. Smirke
1937	Chulmleigh	G. Richards	Exhibitionist	S. Donoghue	Mid-day Sun	M. Beary
1938	Scottish Union	B. Carslake	Rockfel	H. Wragg	Bois Roussel	C. Elliot
1939	no race held		Galatea II	R.A. Jones	Blue Peter	E. Smith
1940	Turkhan	G. Richards	Godiva	D. Marks	Pont L'Eveque	S. Wragg

	St Leger		Oaks		Derby	
Year	Horse	Jockey	Horse	Jockey	Horse	Jockey
1941	Sun Castle	G. Bridgland	Commotion	H. Wragg	Owen Tudor	W. Nevett
1942	Sun Chariot	G. Richards	Sun Chariot	G. Richards	Watling Street	H. Wragg
1943	Herringbone	H. Wragg	Why Hurry	C. E. Elliot	Straight Deal	T. Carey
1944	Tehran	G. Richards	Hycilla	G. Bridgland	Ocean Swell	W. Nevett
1945	Chamossaire	T. Lowrey	Sun Stream	H. Wragg	Dante	W. Nevett
1946	Airborne	T. Lowrey	Steady Aim	H. Wragg	Airborne	T. Lowrey
1947	Sayajirao	E. Britt	Imprudence	W.R. Johnstone	Pearl Diver	G. Bridgland
1948	Black Tarquin	E. Britt	Masaka	W. Nevett	My Love	W. Johnstone
1949	Ridge Wood	M. Beary	Musidora	E. Britt	Nimbus	C. Elliot
1950	Scratch II	W.R. Johnstone	Asmena	W.R. Johnstone	Galcador	W.R. Johnstone
1951	Talma II	W.R. Johnstone	Neasham Belle	S. Clayton	Arctic Prince	C. Spares
1952	Tulyar	C. Smirke	Frieze	E. Britt	Tulyar	C. Smirke
1953	Premonition	E. Smith	Ambiguity	J. Mercer	Pinza	G. Richards
1954	Never Say Die	C. Smirke	Suncap	W.R. Johnstone	Never Say Die	L. Piggott
1955	Meld	W.H. Carr	Meld	W.H. Carr	Phil Drake	F. Palmer
1956	Cambremer	F. Palmer	Sicarelle	F. Palmer	Lavandin	W.R. Johnstone
1957	Ballymoss	T.P. Burns	Carrozza	L. Piggott	Crepello	L. Piggott
1958	Alcide	W. Carr	Bella Paola	M. Garcia	Hard Ridden	C. Smirke
1959	Cantelo	E. Hide	Petite Etoile	L. Piggott	Parthia	W. Carr
1960	St Paddy	L. Piggott	Never Too Late	R. Poincelet	St Paddy	L. Piggott
1961	Aurelius	L. Piggott	Sweet Solera	W. Rickaby	Psidium	R. Poincelet
1962	Hethersett	W. Carr	Monade	Y. Saint-Martin	Larkspur	N. Sellwood
1963	Ragusa	G. Bougoure	Noblesse	G. Bougoure	Relko	Y. Saint-Martin
1964	Indiana	J. Lindley	Homeward Bound	G. Starkey	Santa Claus	A. Breasley
1965	Provoke	J. Mercer	Long Look	J. Purtell	Sea Bird II	T.P. Glennon
1966	Sodium	F. Durr	Valoris	L. Piggott	Charlottown	A. Breasley
1967	Ribocco	L. Piggott	Pia	E. Hide	Royal Palace	G. Moore
1968	Ribero	L. Piggott	La Lagune	G. Thiboeuf	Sir Ivor	L. Piggott
1969	Intermezzo	R. Hutchinson	Sleeping Partner	J. Gorton	Blakeney	E. Johnson
1970	Nijinsky	L. Piggott	Lupe	A. Barclay	Nijinsky	L. Piggott
1971	Athens Wood	L. Piggott	Altesse Royale	G. Lewis	Mill Reef	G. Lewis
1972	Boucher	L. Piggott	Ginevra	A. Murray	Roberto	L. Piggott
1973	Peleid	F. Durr	Mysterious	G. Lewis	Morston	E. Hide
1974	Bustino	J. Mercer	Polygamy	P. Eddery	Snow Knight	B. Taylor
1975	Bruni	A. Murray	Juliet Marny	L. Piggott	Grundy	P. Eddery
1976	Crow	Y. Saint-Martin	Pawneese	Y. Saint-Martin	Empery	L. Piggott
1977	Dunfermline	W. Carson	Dunfermline	W. Carson	The Minstrel	L. Piggott
1978	Julio Mariner	E. Hide	Fair Salinia	G. Starkey	Shirley Heights	G. Starkey
1979	Son of Love	A. Lequeux	Scintillate	P. Eddery	Troy	W. Carson
1980	Light Cavalry	J. Mercer	Bireme	W. Carson	Henbit	W. Carson
1981	Cut Above	J. Mercer	Blue Wind	L. Piggott	Shergar	W. Swinburn
1982	Touching Wood	P. Cook	Time Charter	W. Newmes	Golden Fleece	P. Eddery
1983	Sun Princess	W. Carson	Sun Princess	W. Carson	Teenoso	L. Piggott
1984	Comanche Run	L. Piggott	Circus Plume	L. Piggott	Secreto	C. Roche
1985	Oh So Sharp	S. Cauthen	Oh So Sharp	S. Cauthen	Slip Anchor	S. Cauthen
1986	Moon Madness	P. Eddery	Midway Lady	R. Cochrane	Shahrastani	W. Swinburn
1987	Reference Point	S. Cauthen	Unite	W. Swinburn	Reference Point	S. Cauthen
1988	Minster Son	W. Carson	Diminuendo	S. Cauthen	Kayhasi	R. Cochrane
1989	Michelozzo	S. Cauthen	Snow Bride	S. Cauthen	Nashwan	W. Carson
1990	Snurge	A. Quinn	Salsabil	W. Carson	Quest for Fame	P. Eddery
1991	Toulon	P. Eddery	Jet Ski Lady	C. Roche	Generous	A. Munro
1992	User Friendly	G. Duffield	User Friendly	G. Duffield	Dr Devious	J. Reid
1993	Bobs Return	P. Robinson	Intrepidity	M. Roberts	Commander-in-Chief	M.J. Kinane
1994	Moonax	P. Eddery	Balanchine	L. Dettori	Erhaab	W. Carson
1995	Classic Cliché	L. Dettori	Moonshell	L. Dettori	Lammtara	W. Swinburn
1996	Shantou	L. Dettori	Lady Carla	P. Eddery	Shaamit	M. Hills
1997	Silver Patriarch	P. Eddery	Reams of Verse	K. Fallon	Benny the Dip	W. Ryan
1998	Nedawi	J. Reid	Shahtoush	M.J. Kinane	High Rise	O. Peslier
1999	Mutafaweq	R. Hills	Ramruma	K. Fallon	Oath	K. Fallon
2000	Millenary	T. Quinn	Love Divine	T. Quinn	Sinnclar	J. Murtagh
2001	Milan	M.J. Kinane	Imagine	M.J. Kinane	Galileo	M.J. Kinane

	2000 Guineas		1000 Guineas		Grand National	
Year	Horse	Jockey	Horse	Jockey	Horse	Jockey
1809	Wizard	W. Clift	—	—	—	—
1810	Hephestion	F. Buckle	—	—	—	—
1811	Trophonius	S. Barnard	—	—	—	—
1812	Cwrw	S. Chifney	—	—	—	—

Year	2000 Guineas Horse	Jockey	1000 Guineas Horse	Jockey	Grand National Horse	Jockey
1813	Smolensko	H. Miller	—	—	—	—
1814	Olive	W. Arnold	Charlotte	W. Clift	—	—
1815	Tigris	W. Arnold	Brown foal by Selim	W. Clift	—	—
1816	Nectar	W. Arnold	Rhoda	S. Barnard	—	—
1817	Manfred	W. Wheatley	Neva	W. Arnold	—	—
1818	Interpreter	W. Clift	Corinne	F. Buckle	—	—
1819	Antar	E. Edwards	Catgut	F. Buckle	—	—
1820	Pindarrie	F. Buckle	Rowena	F. Buckle	—	—
1821	Reginald	F. Buckle	Zeal	F. Buckle	—	—
1822	Pastille	F. Buckle	Whizgig	F. Buckle	—	—
1823	Nicolo	W. Wheatley	Zinc	F. Buckle	—	—
1824	Schariar	W. Wheatley	Cobweb	J. Robinson	—	—
1825	Enamel	J. Robinson	Tontine	W. Alkover	—	—
1826	Dervise	J.B. Day	Problem	J. Day	—	—
1827	Turcoman	F. Buckle	Arab	F. Buckle	—	—
1828	Cadland	J. Robinson	Zoe	J. Robinson	—	—
1829	Patron	F. Boyce	B. foal by Godolphin	Arnull	—	—
1830	Augustus	P. Conolly	Charlotte West	J. Robinson	—	—
1831	Riddlesworth	J. Robinson	Galantine	P. Conolly	—	—
1832	Archibald	Pavis	Galata	Arnull	—	—
1833	Clearwell	J. Robinson	Tarantella	Wright	—	—
1834	Glencoe	J. Robinson	May-Day	J. Day	—	—
1835	Ibrahim	J. Robinson	Preserve	E. Flatman	—	—
1836	Bay Middleton	J. Robinson	Destiny	J. Day	—	—
1837	Achmet	E. Edwards	Chapeau d'Espagne	J. Day	The Duke (Maghull)	Mr Potts
1838	Grey Momus	J.B. Day	Barcarolle	E. Edwards	Sir Henry (Maghull)	T. Olliver
1839	The Corsair	Wakefield	Cara	G. Edwards	Lottery (Liverpool)	Jem Mason
1840	Crucifix	J.B. Day	Crucifix	J. Day	Jerry	Mr Bretherton
1841	Ralph	J.B. Day	Potentia	J. Robinson	Charity	Mr Powell
1842	Meteor	W. Scott	Firebrand	S. Rogers	Gaylad	T. Olliver
1843	Cotherstone	W. Scott	Extempore	S. Chifney	Vanguard	T. Olliver
1844	The Ugly Buck	J. Day Jnr	Sorella	J. Robinson	Discount	Crickmere
1845	Idas	E. Flatman	Pic-nic	W. Abdale	Cure-all	W.G. Loft
1846	Sir Tatton Sykes	W. Scott	Mendicant	S. Day	Pioneer	Taylor
1847	Conyngham	J. Robinson	Clementina	E. Flatman	Matthew	D. Wynne
1848	Flatcatcher	J. Robinson	Canezou	F. Butler	Chandler	Capt. Little
1849	Nunnykirk	F. Butler	Flea	A. Day	Peter Simple	T. Cunningham
1850	Pitsford	A. Day	Chestnut foal by Slane	F. Butler	Abdel Kader	C. Green
1851	Hernandez	E. Flatman	Aphrodite	J. Marson	Abdel Kader	T. Abbot
1852	Stockwell	Norman	Kate	A. Day	Miss Mowbray	Mr A. Goodman
1853	West Australian	F. Butler	Mentmore Lass	Charlton	Peter Simple	T. Olliver
1854	The Hermit	A. Day	Virago	J. Wells	Bourton	Tasker
1855	Lord of the Isles	Aldcroft	Habena	S. Rogers	Wanderer	J. Hanlon
1856	Fazzaletto	E. Flatman	Manganese	J. Osborne	Freetrader	G. Stevens
1857	Vedette	J. Osborne	Imperieuse	E. Flatman	Emigrant	C. Boyce
1858	Fitz-Roland	J. Wells	Governess	Ashmall	Little Charley	W. Archer
1859	The Promised Land	A. Day	Mayonnaise	G. Fordham	Half Caste	C. Green
1860	The Wizard	Ashmall	Sagitta	Aldcroft	Anatis	Mr Thomas
1861	Diophantus	A. Edwards	Nemesis	G. Fordham	Jealousy	J. Kendall
1862	The Marquis	Ashmall	Hurricane	Ashmall	Huntsman	H. Lamplugh
1863	Macaroni	T. Challoner	Lady Augusta	A. Edwards	Emblem	G. Stevens
1864	General Peel	Aldcroft	Tomato	J. Wells	Emblematic	G. Stevens
1865	Gladiateur	H. Grimshaw	Siberia	G. Fordham	Alcibiade	Capt. Coventry
1866	Lord Lyon	Thomas	Repulse	T. Cannon	Salamander	Mr A. Goodman
1867	Vauban	G. Fordham	Achievement	H. Custance	Cortolvin	J. Page
1868	Moslem	T. Challoner	Formosa	G. Fordham	The Lamb	Mr Edwards
1869	Pretender	J. Osborne	Scottish Queen	G. Fordham	The Colonel	G. Stevens
1870	Macgregor	J. Daley	Hester	J. Grimshaw	The Colonel	G. Stevens
1871	Bothwell	J. Osborne	Hannah	C. Maidment	The Lamb	Mr Thomas
1872	Prince Charlie	J. Osborne	Reine	H. Parry	Casse Tete	J. Page
1873	Gang Forward	T. Challoner	Cecilia	J. Morris	Disturbance	J.M. Richardson
1874	Atlantic	F. Archer	Apology	J. Osborne	Reugny	J.M. Richardson
1875	Camballo	J. Osborne	Spinaway	F. Archer	Pathfinder	Mr Thomas
1876	Petrarch	Luke	Camelia	T. Glover	Regal	J. Cannon
1877	Chamant	J. Goater	Belphoebe	H. Jeffery	Austerlitz	Mr F.G. Hobson
1878	Pilgrimage	T. Cannon	Pilgrimage	T. Cannon	Shifnal	J. Jones

	2000 Guineas		1000 Guineas		Grand National	
Year	Horse	Jockey	Horse	Jockey	Horse	Jockey
1879	Charibert	F. Archer	Wheel of Fortune	F. Archer	The Liberator	G. Moore
1880	Petronel	G. Fordham	Elizabeth	C. Wood	Empress	T. Beasley
1881	Peregrine	F. Webb	Thebais	G. Fordham	Woodbrook	T. Beasley
1882	Shotover	T. Cannon	St Marguerite	C. Wood	Seaman	Lord Manners
1883	Galliard	F. Archer	Hauteur	G. Fordham	Zoedone	Count Kinsky
1884	Scot-free	Platt	Busybody	T. Cannon	Voluptuary	Mr E.P. Wilson
1885	Paradox	F. Archer	Farewell	G. Barrett	Roquefort	Mr E.P. Wilson
1886	Ormonde	G. Barrett	Miss Jummy	J. Watts	Old Joe	T. Skelton
1887	Enterprise	T. Cannon	Reve d'Or	C. Wood	Gamecock	W. Daniells
1888	Ayrshire	J. Osborne	Briar-root	W. Warne	Playfair	Mawson
1889	Enthusiast	T. Cannon	Minthe	J. Woodburn	Frigate	T. Beasley
1890	Surefoot	Liddiard	Semolina	J. Watts	Ilex	A. Nightingall
1891	Common	G. Barrett	Mimi	F. Rickaby	Come Away	H. Beasley
1892	Bonavista	W. Robinson	La Fleche	G. Barrett	Father O'Flynn	Capt. Owen
1893	Isinglass	T. Loates	Siffleuse	T. Loates	Cloister	Dollery
1894	Ladas	J. Watts	Amiable	W. Bradford	Why Not	A. Nightingall
1895	Kirkconnel	J. Watts	Galeottia	F. Pratt	Wildman From Borneo	J. Widger
1896	St Frusquin	T. Loates	Thais	J. Watts	The Soarer	D. Campbell
1897	Galtee More	C. Wood	Chelandry	J. Watts	Manifesto	T. Kavanagh
1898	Disraeli	S. Loates	Nun Nicer	S. Loates	Drogheda	J. Gourley
1899	Flying Fox	M. Cannon	Sibola	J.T. Sloan	Manifesto	G. Williamson
1900	Diamond Jubilee	H. Jones	Winifreda	S. Loates	Ambush II	A. Anthony
1901	Handicapper	W. Halsey	Aida	D. Maher	Grudon	A. Nightingall
1902	Sceptre	H. Randall	Sceptre	H. Randall	Shannon Lass	D. Read
1903	Rock Sand	J.H. Martin	Quintessence	H. Randall	Drumcree	P. Woodland
1904	St Amant	K. Cannon	Pretty Polly	W. Lane	Moifaa	A. Birch
1905	Vedas	H. Jones	Cherry Lass	G. McCall	Kirkland	F. Mason
1906	Gorgos	H. Jones	Flair	B. Dillon	Ascetic's Silver	Hon A. Hastings
1907	Slieve Gallion	W. Higgs	Witch Elm	B. Lynham	Eremon	A. Newey
1908	Norman III	O. Madden	Rhodora	L. Lyne	Rubio	H.B. Bletsoe
1909	Minoru	H. Jones	Electra	B. Dillon	Lutteur III	G. Parfrement
1910	Neil Gow	D. Maher	Winkipop	B. Lynham	Jenkinstown	R. Chadwick
1911	Sunstar	G. Stern	Atmah	F. Fox	Glenside	J.R. Anthony
1912	Sweeper II	D. Maher	Tagalie	L.H. Hewitt	Jerry M	E. Piggott
1913	Louvois	J. Reiff	Jest	F. Rickaby Jnr	Covetcoat	P. Woodland
1914	Kennymore	G. Stern	Princess Dorrie	W. Huxley	Sunloch	W.J. Smith
1915	Pommern	S. Donoghue	Vaucluse	F. Rickaby Jnr	Ally Sloper	J.R. Anthony
1916	Clarissimus	J. Clark	Canyon	F. Rickaby Jnr	Vermouth	J. Reardon
1917	Gay Crusader	S. Donoghue	Diadem	F. Rickaby Jnr	Ballymacad	E. Driscoll
1918	Gainsborough	J. Childs	Ferry	B. Carslake	Poethlyn	E. Piggott
1919	The Panther	R. Cooper	Roseway	A. Whalley	Poethlyn	E. Piggott
1920	Tetratema	B. Carslake	Cinna	W. Griggs	Troytown	J.R. Anthony
1921	Craig An Eran	J. Brennan	Bettina	G. Bellhouse	Shaun Spadah	F.B. Rees
1922	St Louis	G. Archibald	Silver Urn	B. Carslake	Music Hall	F.B. Rees
1923	Ellangowan	C. Elliot	Tranquil	E. Gardner	Sgt Murphy	Capt. Bennet
1924	Diophon	G. Hulme	Plack	E.C. Elliott	Master Robert	R. Trudgill
1925	Manna	S. Donoghue	Saucy Sue	F. Bullock	Double Chance	Major Wilson
1926	Colorado	T. Weston	Pillion	R. Perryman	Jack Horner	W. Watkinson
1927	Adam's Apple	J. Leach	Cresta Run	A. Balding	Sprig	T.E. Leader
1928	Flamingo	C. Elliot	Scuttle	J. Childs	Tipperary Tim	W.P. Dutton
1929	Mr Jinks	H. Beasley	Taj Mah	W. Sibbritt	Gregalach	R. Everett
1930	Diolite	F. Fox	Fair Isle	T. Weston	Shaun Goilin	T. Cullinan
1931	Cameronian	J. Childs	Four Course	E.C. Elliott	Grakle	R. Lyall
1932	Orwell	R. Jones	Kandy	E.C. Elliott	Forbra	J. Hamey
1933	Rodosto	R. Brethes	Brown Betty	J. Childs	Kellsboro Jack	D. Williams
1934	Colombo	W. Johnstone	Campanula	H. Wragg	Golden Miller	G. Wilson
1935	Bahram	F. Fox	Mesa	W. R. Johnstone	Reynoldstown	F.C. Furlong
1936	Pay Up	R. Dick	Tide-Way	R. Perryman	Reynoldstown	F.T. Walwyn
1937	Le Ksar	C. Semblat	Exhibitionist	S. Donoghue	Royal Mail	E. Williams
1938	Pasch	G. Richards	Rockfel	S. Wragg	Battleship	Bruce Hobbs
1939	Blue Peter	E. Smith	Galatea II	R. A. Jones	Workman	T. Hyde
1940	Djebel	C. Elliot	Godiva	D. Marks	Bogskar	M. Jones
1941	Lambert Simnel	C. Elliot	Dancing Time	R. Perryman	no race	—
1942	Big Game	G. Richards	Sun Chariot	G. Richards	no race	—
1943	Kingsway	S. Wragg	Herringbone	H. Wragg	no race	—
1944	Garden Path	H. Wragg	Picture Play	E. C. Elliott	no race	—
1945	Court Martial	C. Richards	Sun Stream	H. Wragg	no race	—
1946	Happy Knight	T. Weston	Hypericum	D. Smith	Lovely Cottage	Capt. R. Petre
1947	Tudor Minstrel	G. Richards	Imprudence	W. R. Johnstone	Caughoo	E. Dempsey

Year	2000 Guineas Horse	Jockey	1000 Guineas Horse	Jockey	Grand National Horse	Jockey
1948	My Babu	C. Smirke	Queenpot	G. Richards	Sheila's Cottage	A.P. Thompson
1949	Nimbus	C. Elliot	Musidora	E. Britt	Russian Hero	L. McMorrow
1950	Palestine	C. Smirke	Camaree	W.R. Johnstone	Freebooter	J. Power
1951	Ki Ming	A. Breasley	Belle Of All	G. Richards	Nickel Coin	J.A. Bullock
1952	Thunderhead II	R. Poincelet	Zabara	K. Gethin	Teal	A.P Thompson
1953	Nearula	E. Britt	Happy Laughter	E. Mercer	Early Mist	B. Marshall
1954	Darius	E. Mercer	Festoon	A. Breasley	Royal Tan	B. Marshall
1955	Our Babu	D. Smith	Meld	W.H. Carr	Quare Times	P. Taaffe
1956	Gilles de Retz	F. Barlow	Honeylight	E. Britt	E.S.B.	D.V. Dick
1957	Crepello	L. Piggott	Rose Royale II	C. Smirke	Sundew	F. Winter
1958	Pall Mall	D. Smith	Bella Paola	S. Boullenger	Mr What	A.R. Freeman
1959	Taboun	G. Moore	Petite Etoile	D. Smith	Oxo	M. Scudamore
1960	Martial	R. Hutchinson	Never Too Late	R. Poincelet	Merryman II	G. Scott
1961	Rockavon	N. Stirk	Sweet Solera	W. Rickaby	Nicolaus Silver	R. Beasley
1962	Privy Councillor	W. Rickaby	Abermaid	W. Williamson	Kilmore	F. Winter
1963	Only For Life	J. Lindley	Hula Dancer	R. Poincelet	Ayala	P. Buckley
1964	Baldric II	W. Pyers	Pourparler	G. Bougoure	Team Spirit	W. Robinson
1965	Niksar	D. Keith	Night Off	W. Williamson	Jay Trump	T. Smith
1966	Kashmir II	J. Lindley	Glad Rags	P. Cook	Anglo	T. Norman
1967	Royal Palace	G. Moore	Fleet	G. Moore	Foinavon	J. Buckingham
1968	Sir Ivor	L. Piggott	Caergwrle	A. Barclay	Red Alligator	B. Fletcher
1969	Right Tack	G. Lewis	Full Dress II	R. Hutchinson	Highland Wedding	E. Harty
1970	Nijinsky	L. Piggott	Humble Duty	L. Piggott	Gay Trip	P. Taaffe
1971	Brigadier Gerard	J. Mercer	Altesse Royale	Y. Saint-Martin	Specify	J. Cook
1972	High Top	W. Carson	Waterloo	E. Hide	Well To Do	G. Thorner
1973	Mon Fils	F. Durr	Mysterious	G. Lewis	Red Rum	B. Fletcher
1974	Nonoalco	Y. Saint-Martin	Highclere	J. Mercer	Red Rum	B. Fletcher
1975	Bolkonski	G. Dettori	Nocturnal Spree	J. Roe	L'Escargot	T. Carberry
1976	Wollow	G. Dettori	Flying Water	Y. Saint-Martin	Rag Trade	J. Burke
1977	Nebbiolo	G. Curran	Mrs McArdy	E. Hide	Red Rum	T. Stack
1978	Roland Gardens	F. Durr	Enstone Spark	E. Johnson	Lucius	R. Davies
1979	Tap on Wood	S. Cauthen	One in a Million	J. Mercer	Rubstic	M. Barnes
1980	Known Fact	W. Carson	Quick as Lightning	B. Rouse	Ben Nevis	C. Fenwick
1981	To-Agori-Mou	G. Starkey	Fairy Footsteps	L. Piggott	Aldaniti	R. Champion
1982	Zino	F. Head	On the House	J. Reid	Grittar	R. Saunders
1983	Lomond	P. Eddery	Ma Biche	F. Head	Corbiere	B. De Haan
1984	El Gran Señor	P. Eddery	Pebbles	P. Robinson	Hallo Dandy	N. Doughty
1985	Shadeed	L. Piggott	Oh So Sharp	S. Cauthen	Last Suspect	H. Davies
1986	Dancing Brave	G. Starkey	Midway Lady	R. Cochrane	West Tip	R. Dunwoody
1987	Don't Forget Me	W. Carson	Miesque	F. Head	Maori Venture	S. Knight
1988	Doyoun	W. Swinburn	Ravinella	G. Moore	Rhyme 'n Reason	B. Powell
1989	Nashwan	W. Carson	Musical Bliss	W. Swinburn	Little Polveir	J. Frost
1990	Tirol	M. Kinane	Salsabil	W. Carson	Mr Frisk	Mr M. Armytage
1991	Mystiko	M. Roberts	Shadayid	W. Carson	Seagram	N. Hawke
1992	Rodrigo De Triano	L. Piggott	Hatoof	W. Swinburn	Party Politics	C. Llewellyn
1993	Zafonic	P. Eddery	Sayyedati	W. Swinburn	no race	—
1994	Mr Baileys	J. Weaver	Las Meninas	J. Reid	Minnehoma	R. Dunwoody
1995	Pennekamp	T. Jarnet	Harayir	R. Hills	Royal Athlete	J. Titley
1996	Mark of Esteem	L. Dettori	Bosra Sham	P. Eddery	Rough Quest	M. Fitzgerald
1997	Entrepreneur	M.J. Kinane	Sleepytime	K. Fallon	Lord Gyllene	A. Dobbin
1998	King of Kings	M.J. Kinane	Cape Verdi	L. Dettori	Earth Summit	C. Llewellyn
1999	Island Sands	L. Dettori	Wince	K. Fallon	Bobbyjo	P Carberry
2000	King's Best	K. Fallon	Lahan	R. Hills	Papillon	R. Walsh
2001	Golan	K. Fallon	Ameerat	P. Robinson	Red Marauder	R. Guest

Horse Racing: General Information

all weather tracks: UK	Lingfield, Southwell, Wolverhampton
autumn double	Cesarewitch and Cambridgeshire
champion jockey: 13 times in a row	E. Flatman (1840–52) and Fred Archer (1874–86)
champion jockey: shot himself	Fred Archer (aged 31)
Cheltenham Gold Cup: won five times in row	Golden Miller (1932–36)
classics: jockey won most	Lester Piggott (30)
crash helmets: made compulsory	1924
Derby: inaugurated by	Sir Charles Bunbury
Derby: longest winning distance	Shergar (10 lengths)

S P O R T & L E I S U R E

Derby: where run during WW2	Newmarket (1940–45)
flat jockey: champion most times	Gordon Richards (26)
Fred Archer: nickname	The Tinman
French Derby: run	Chantilly
Gary Bardwell: nickname	The Angry Ant
Grand National winner: future monarch owned	Ambush II (King Edward VII in 1900)
Grand National: 1st woman jockey	Charlotte Brew (1977)
Grand National: 1st woman jockey to complete	Geraldine Rees
Grand National: number of fences	30
Grand National: royal horse that collapsed	Devon Loch, ridden by Dick Francis
Grand National: where run during WW1	Gatwick (1916–18) as 'War National Chase' (1917–18), and 'Race Course Association Chase' 1916
Grand National: youngest winning rider	Bruce Hobbs on Battleship in 1938 aged 17
harness racing: gaits	trotting (striding with horse's left front and right rear leg synchronized)
	pacing (moving both legs on one side of body at the same time)
harness racing: vehicle pulled	sulky
Harry Wragg: nickname	The Headwaiter
Irish Classics: run	all at the Curragh
Irish Grand National: run	Fairyhouse
Irish Grand National: woman jockey won	Ann Ferris
jockeys: not allowed to wear	beards
jockey: 1st knighted	Gordon Richards
Lester Piggott: 1st winner	The Chase (1948)
Lester Piggott: nickname	The Long Fellow
mare: age filly becomes	five
Melbourne Cup: run	Flemington Park
Oaks: where run during WW2	Newmarket (1940–45)
pacing: US Triple Crown	William H. Cane Futurity (1955); Messenger Stake (1957); Little Brown Jug (1946)
racehorse birthdays	1 January (Northern Hemisphere) and 1 August (Southern Hemisphere)
racehorses: maximum letters in name	18
racing colours: Her Majesty the Queen	purple, gold braid, scarlet sleeves, black velvet cap with gold fringe
racing colours: Queen Elizabeth the Queen Mother	blue, buff stripes, blue sleeves, black cap, gold tassel
Scottish Grand National: run	Ayr
spring double	Lincoln and Grand National
stallion: age colt becomes	five
starting stalls: 1st used in UK	Newmarket in 1965 (8 July)
thoroughbred: ancestry	Darley Arabian, Byerly Turk, Godolphin Arabian (aka barb)
trotting: US Triple Crown	Hambleton (commenced 1926); Yonkers Futurity (1958); Kentucky Futurity (1893)
US Triple Crown	Kentucky Derby (1st of the season), Preakness Stakes, Belmont Stakes (1st of the season)
Welsh Grand National: run	Chepstow

Motor Racing: Formula 1 World Champions

Year	Winning driver	Country	Car	Runner-up	Constructor Championship
1950	Giuseppe Farina	Italy	Alfa Romeo	Juan Manuel Fangio	—
1951	Juan Manuel Fangio	Argentina	Alfa Romeo	Alberto Ascari	—
1952	Alberto Ascari	Italy	Ferrari	Giuseppe Farina	—
1953	Alberto Ascari	Italy	Ferrari	Juan Manuel Fangio	—
1954	Juan Manuel Fangio	Argentina	Maserati/Mercedes	Jose Gonzalez (Argentina)	—
1955	Juan Manuel Fangio	Argentina	Mercedes-Benz	Stirling Moss (GB)	—
1956	Juan Manuel Fangio	Argentina	Lancia-Ferrari	Stirling Moss (GB)	—
1957	Juan Manuel Fangio	Argentina	Maserati	Stirling Moss (GB)	—
1958	Mike Hawthorn	UK	Ferrari	Stirling Moss (GB)	Vanwall
1959	Jack Brabham	Australia	Cooper-Climax	Tony Brooks (GB)	Cooper-Climax
1960	Jack Brabham	Australia	Cooper-Climax	Bruce McLaren (NZL)	Cooper-Climax
1961	Phil Hill	USA	Ferrari	Wolfgang von Trips (W. Germany)	Ferrari
1962	Graham Hill	UK	BRM	Jim Clark	BRM
1963	Jim Clark	UK	Lotus-Climax	Graham Hill	Lotus-Climax
1964	John Surtees	UK	Ferrari	Graham Hill	Ferrari
1965	Jim Clark	UK	Lotus-Climax	Graham Hill	Lotus-Climax
1966	Jack Brabham	Australia	Brabham-Repco	John Surtees	Brabham-Repco
1967	Denny Hulme	New Zealand	Brabham-Repco	Jack Brabham	Brabham-Repco

Year	Winning driver	Country	Car	Runner-up	Constructor Championship
1968	Graham Hill	UK	Lotus-Ford	Jackie Stewart	Lotus-Ford
1969	Jackie Stewart	UK	Matra-Ford	Jacky Ickx (Belgium)	Matra-Ford
1970	Jochen Rindt	Austria	Lotus-Ford	Jacky Ickx (Belgium)	Lotus-Ford
1971	Jackie Stewart	UK	Tyrrell-Ford	Ronnie Peterson (Sweden)	Tyrrell-Ford
1972	Emerson Fittipaldi	Brazil	Lotus-Ford	Jackie Stewart	Lotus-Ford
1973	Jackie Stewart	UK	Tyrrell-Ford	Emerson Fittipaldi	Lotus-Ford
1974	Emerson Fittipaldi	Brazil	McLaren-Ford	Clay Regazzoni (Switzerland)	McLaren-Ford
1975	Niki Lauda	Austria	Ferrari	Emerson Fittipaldi	Ferrari
1976	James Hunt	UK	McLaren-Ford	Niki Lauda	Ferrari
1977	Niki Lauda	Austria	Ferrari	Jody Scheckter	Ferrari
1978	Mario Andretti	USA	Lotus-Ford	Ronnie Peterson (Sweden)	Lotus-Ford
1979	Jody Scheckter	South Africa	Ferrari	Gilles Villeneuve (Canada)	Ferrari
1980	Alan Jones	Australia	Williams-Ford	Nelson Piquet	Williams-Ford
1981	Nelson Piquet	Brazil	Brabham-Ford	Carlos Reutemann (Argentina)	Williams-Ford
1982	Keke Rosberg	Finland	Williams-Ford	J. Watson (GB) and D. Pironi (France)	Ferrari
1983	Nelson Piquet	Brazil	Brabham-BMW	Alain Prost	Ferrari
1984	Niki Lauda	Austria	McLaren-TAG	Alain Prost	McLaren-TAG
1985	Alain Prost	France	McLaren-TAG	Michele Alboreto (Italy)	McLaren-TAG
1986	Alain Prost	France	McLaren-TAG	Nigel Mansell	Williams-Honda
1987	Nelson Piquet	Brazil	Williams-Honda	Nigel Mansell	Williams-Honda
1988	Ayrton Senna	Brazil	McLaren-Honda	Alain Prost	McLaren-Honda
1989	Alain Prost	France	McLaren-Honda	Ayrton Senna	McLaren-Honda
1990	Ayrton Senna	Brazil	McLaren-Honda	Alain Prost	McLaren-Honda
1991	Ayrton Senna	Brazil	McLaren-Honda	Nigel Mansell	McLaren-Honda
1992	Nigel Mansell	UK	Williams-Renault	Ricardo Patrese (Italy)	Williams-Renault
1993	Alain Prost	France	Williams-Renault	Ayrton Senna	Williams-Renault
1994	Michael Schumacher	Germany	Benetton-Ford	Damon Hill	Williams-Renault
1995	Michael Schumacher	Germany	Benetton-Renault	Damon Hill	Williams-Renault
1996	Damon Hill	UK	Williams-Renault	Jacques Villeneuve	Williams-Renault
1997	Jacques Villeneuve	Canada	Williams-Renault	Michael Schumacher	Williams-Renault
1998	Mika Hakkinen	Finland	McLaren-Mercedes	Michael Schumacher	McLaren Mercedes
1999	Mika Hakkinen	Finland	McLaren-Mercedes	Eddie Irvine	Ferrari
2000	Michael Schumacher	Germany	Ferrari	Mika Hakkinen	Ferrari

Motor Racing: General Information

circuits: Formula 1 — Argentinian – Buenos Aires; Australian – Adelaide, Melbourne; Austrian – A1 Ring, Spielberg; Belgian – Spa-Francorchamps, Zolder; Brazilian – Sao Paolo, Interlagos (Rio de Janeiro); British – Silverstone; Canadian – Montreal; Dutch – Zandvoort; French – Magny Cours, Dijon; German – Hockenheim; Hungarian – Budapest; Italian – Monza; Japanese – Suzuka; Luxembourg – Nurburgring, Germany; Malaysian – Sepang; Mexican – Mexico City; Monaco – Monte Carlo; Portuguese – Estoril; San Marino – Imola; Spanish – Catalunya Montjuich (Barcelona); US – Detroit, Long Beach, Indianapolis.
Nurburgring is no longer used for German GP but has been the venue of the European GP in recent years. Similarly, Aida in Japan is no longer used for its own GP but has been the venue for Pacific GP.

Formula 1: flags — black – disqualification of a driver; black and white chequered – end of race; blue – car about to overtake; red – premature end of race; yellow – danger, no overtaking; yellow and red diagonal stripes – oil on track.

Formula 1: most consecutive wins — Alberto Ascari (9).

Formula 1: oldest champion — Juan Manuel Fangio (46).

Formula 1: posthumous champion — Jochen Rindt (1970).

Formula 1: woman driver first — Lella Lombardi (1975).

fuel: used in Formula 1 — nitro-methane.

Indianapolis 500: first winner — Ray Harroun in Marmon Wasp (1911).

Indianapolis 500: laps — 200, (although the race is 500 miles in length, hence the name).

Indianapolis 500: Formula 1 winners — Jim Clark (1965), Graham Hill (1966), Mario Andretti (1969), E. Fittipaldi (1989 and 1993), J. Villeneuve (1995).

land speed record: holder — Andy Green in Thrust SSC (714 mph).
first over 100 mph: Louis Rigolly in 1904.

Monaco GP: five times winner — Graham Hill.

motor cycling: nine championships — Giacomo Agostini of Italy (eight consecutive from 1965–72 and 1975 in the 500 cc class).

speedway championships — raced over four laps, the short track world championships commenced in 1936 and long track in 1971.

UK motor racing circuit: first — Brooklands.

Olympic Games: Venues

1896	Athens, Greece
1900	Paris, France
1904	St Louis, USA
1908	London, UK
1912	Stockholm, Sweden
1920	Antwerp, Belgium
1924	Paris, France
1928	Amsterdam, Holland
1932	Los Angeles, USA
1936	Berlin, Germany
1948	London, UK
1952	Helsinki, Finland
1956	Melbourne, Australia
1960	Rome, Italy
1964	Tokyo, Japan
1968	Mexico City
1972	Munich, Germany
1976	Montreal, Canada
1980	Moscow, USSR
1984	Los Angeles, USA
1988	Seoul, South Korea
1992	Barcelona, Spain
1996	Atlanta, USA
2000	Sydney, Australia
2004	Athens, Greece

Winter Olympics: Venues

1924	Chamonix, France
1928	St Moritz, Switzerland
1932	Lake Placid, NY, USA
1936	Garmisch Partenkirchen, Germany
1948	St Moritz, Switzerland
1952	Oslo, Norway
1956	Cortina, Italy
1960	Squaw Valley, California, USA
1964	Innsbruck, Austria
1968	Grenoble, France
1972	Sapporo, Japan
1976	Innsbruck, Austria
1980	Lake Placid, NY, USA
1984	Sarajevo, Yugoslavia
1988	Calgary, Canada
1992	Albertville, France
1994	Lillehammer, Norway
1998	Nagano, Japan
2002	Salt Lake City, USA

Olympics: General Information

ancient Olympics: in honour of	Zeus.
appearances: most	Raymondo d'Inzeo (8).
black power salute	Tommie Smith and John Carlos 1968. (Other man on rostrum was Peter Norman of Australia.)
Briton took part in Summer and Winter Olympics	Derek Allhusen.
British peer gold medallist	The Marquess of Exeter (Lord Burghley) 1928, 400m Hurdles.
cancelled games: intended hosts	1916 – Berlin; 1940 – Tokyo (then Helsinki); 1944 – London.
champions: father and son	Imre Nemeth (Hammer) and Miklos Nemeth (Javelin).
champion: five times in row	Steve Redgrave (Rowing 1984–2000).
champion: four times in row	Al Oerter (Discus 1956–68).
cheat: Modern Pentathlon	Boris Onischenko in Fencing discipline (1976).
country contested every games	UK (both Summer and Winter).
diplomas awarded to	fourth to eighth places.
equestrian events: 1956	held in Stockholm.
extra lap run in error	Steeplechase 1932.
father and son rowing gold medallists	Charles and Richard Burnell.
flag: colours	blue, yellow, black, green, red rings on a white background. (Rings represent the five major continents.)
gold medals: last given	1912 was the last time solid gold medals were given.
gold medal: received by post	Harold Abrahams (1924).
golds: most in single games	Mark Spitz (7) (Swimming 1972).
high jump: youngest champion	Ulrike Mayfarth (16), who was also the oldest winner aged 28.
host country: no golds	Canada (1976).
IOC: presidents	Dimitrios Vikélas (1894–96); Baron de Coubertin (1896–1925); Henri de Baillet-La Tour (1925–42); J. Sigfrid Edström (1946–52); Avery Brundage (1956–72); Michael Morris, Lord Killanin (1972–80); Juan António Samaranch (1980–2001).
marathon: barefoot winner	Abebe Bikila (1960).
marathon: distance standardized	1924 (although first run as 26 miles 385 yds in 1908).
medal withheld for professionalism	Jim Thorpe in 1912 (he was reinstated in 1973).
modern Olympics: instigator	Baron Pierre de Coubertin.
Munich massacre	Black September terrorists killing of Israeli athletes (1972).
oldest Briton to win gold medal	Jerry Milner (60 years old in 1908 when winning Shooting gold).
Olympiad: definition	in ancient Greece the time between games was an Olympiad (four years).
Olympic motto	Citius Altius Fortius (Faster, Higher, Stronger).
opening parade	always led by Greece and completed by the host country.
original location	Olympia (776 BC–AD 393, abolished by Emperor Theodosius I).

POW in World War Two	Harold Cassells (1920 Hockey gold medallist).
sex testing: year began	1968.
swimming: first 100m under 1 minute	Johnny Weismuller (1924) (59 seconds).
walkover: champion	Wyndham Halswelle in the 400m (1908).
woman gold medallist: first	Charlotte Cooper (GB) when she won Tennis Singles (1900).
woman: running, throwing, jumping medals	Mildred 'Babe' Didrikson won gold in 80m Hurdles and Javelin and silver medal in High Jump (1932).
Zatopek gold medal treble	In 1952 Emil Zatopek won 5k, 10k and Marathon.

Olympics: British Gold Medal Winners

Name	*Date*	*Sport*	*Event*
Abrahams, Harold	1924	Athletics	4 x 100m Relay
Ainslie, Ben	2000	Sailing	Laser Class
Ainsworth-Davis, Jack	1920	Athletics	4 x 400m Relay
Allhusen, Derek	1968	Equestrian	3-Day Event – Team
Amoore, Edward	1908	Shooting	Small-Bore Rifle Team
Applegarth, Willie	1912	Athletics	4 x 100m Relay
Aspin, John	1908	Yachting	12 Metres Class
Astor, J.J.	1908	Rackets	Doubles
Atkin, Charles	1920	Hockey	
Attrill, Louis	2000	Rowing	Coxed Eight
Bacon, Stanley	1908	Wrestling	Middleweight Freestyle
Badcock, Felix	1932	Rowing	Coxless Fours
Bailey, Horace	1908	Football	
Baillon, Louis	1908	Hockey	
Barber, Paul	1988	Hockey	
Barrett, Edward	1908	Tug of War	
Barrett, Frederick	1920	Polo	
Barrett, Roper	1908	Lawn Tennis	Indoor Men's Doubles
Barridge, J.E.	1900	Football	
Bartlett, Charles	1908	Cycling	100km Track Race
Batchelor, Steve	1988	Hockey	
Beachcroft, Charles	1900	Cricket	
Beesly, Richard	1928	Rowing	Coxless Fours
Belville, Miles	1936	Yachting	6 Metres Class
Bennett, Charles	1900	Athletics	1500m
	1900	Athletics	5000m Team
Bennett, John	1920	Hockey	
Bentham, Isaac	1912	Swimming	Water Polo Team
Beresford, Jack	1924	Rowing	Single Sculls
	1932	Rowing	Coxless Fours
	1936	Rowing	Double Sculls
Beresford, John	1900	Polo	
Berry, Arthur	1908	Football	
	1912	Football	
Bevan, Edward	1928	Rowing	Coxless Fours
Bhaura, Kulbir	1988	Hockey	
Bingley, Norman	1908	Yachting	7 Metres Class
Birkett, Arthur	1900	Cricket	
Blackstaffe, Harry	1908	Rowing	Single Sculls
Boardman, Chris	1936	Yachting	6 Metres Class
Boardman, Chris	1992	Cycling	4000m Pursuit
Bond, David	1948	Yachting	Swallow Class
Bowerman, Alfred	1900	Cricket	
Braithwaite, Bob	1968	Shooting	Clay Pigeon
Brasher, Chris	1956	Athletics	3000m Steeplechase
Brebner, Ron	1912	Football	
Brown, Godfrey	1936	Athletics	4 x 400m Relay
Buchanan, John	1908	Yachting	12 Metres Class
Buckenham, Claude	1900	Football	
Buckley, George	1900	Cricket	
Bucknall, Henry	1908	Rowing	Eights
Budgett, Richard	1984	Rowing	Coxed Fours
Bugbee, Charlie	1912	Swimming	Water Polo Team
	1920	Swimming	Water Polo Team
Bullen, Jane	1968	Equestrian	3-Day Event Team
Bunten, James	1908	Yachting	12 Metres Class
Burchell, Francis	1900	Cricket	
Burgess, Edgar	1912	Rowing	Eights

SPORT&LEISURE

Name	Date	Sport	Event
Burghley, Lord David	1928	Athletics	400m Hurdles
Burn, Tom	1912	Football	
Burnell, Charles	1908	Rowing	Eights
Burnell, Richard	1948	Rowing	Double Sculls
Bushnell, Bertie	1948	Rowing	Double Sculls
Butler, Guy	1920	Athletics	4 x 400m Relay
Campbell, Charles	1908	Yachting	8 Metres Class
Campbell, Colin	1920	Hockey	
Canning, George	1920	Tug of War	
Carnell, Arthur	1908	Shooting	Small-Bore Rifle
Cassels, Harold	1920	Hockey	
Chalk, Alfred	1900	Football	
Chapman, Frederick	1908	Football	
Christian, Fred	1900	Cricket	
Christie, Linford	1992	Athletics	100m
Clift, Robert	1988	Hockey	
Clive, Lewis	1932	Rowing	Coxless Pairs
Coales, Bill	1908	Athletics	3 Miles Team
Cochrane, Blair	1908	Yachting	8 Metres Class
Coe, Sebastian	1980	Athletics	1500m
	1984	Athletics	1500m
Coe, Tom	1900	Swimming	Water Polo Team
Coleman, Robert	1920	Yachting	7 Metres Class
Cook, Stephanie	2000	Rowing	Coxless Fours
Cooke, Harold	1920	Hockey	
Cooper, Charlotte	1900	Lawn Tennis	Women's Singles
	1900	Lawn Tennis	Mixed Doubles
Cooper, Malcolm	1984	Shooting	Small-Bore Rifle, three positions
	1988	Shooting	Small-Bore Rifle, three positions
Corbett, Walter	1908	Football	
Corner, Harry	1900	Cricket	
Cornet, George	1908	Swimming	Water Polo Team
	1912	Swimming	Water Polo Team
Cracknell, James	2000	Modern Pentathlon	Individual Event
Crichton, Charles	1908	Yachting	6 Metres Class
Crockford, Eric	1920	Hockey	
Cross, Martin	1984	Rowing	Coxed Fours
Crummack, Rex	1920	Hockey	
Cudmore, Collier	1908	Rowing	Coxless Fours
Cuming, Fred	1900	Cricket	
Currie, Lorne	1900	Yachting	Open Class
	1900	Yachting	0.5–1 Ton Class
Daly, Denis	1900	Polo	
D'Arcy, Vic	1912	Athletics	4 x 100m Relay
Davies, Chris	1972	Yachting	Flying Dutchman Class
Davies, Lynn	1964	Athletics	Long Jump
De Relwyskow, George	1908	Wrestling	Lightweight Freestyle
Deakin, Joe	1908	Athletics	3 Miles Team Race
Dean, Billy	1920	Swimming	Water Polo Team
Dennis, Simon	2000	Rowing	Coxed Eight
Derbyshire, Rob	1900	Swimming	Water Polo Team
	1908	Swimming	4 x 200m Freestyle Relay
Dines, Joe	1912	Football	
Dixon, Charles	1912	Lawn Tennis	Indoor Mixed Doubles
Dixon, Richard	1908	Yachting	7 Metres Class
Dod, William (brother of Lottie)	1908	Archery	York Round
Dodds, Richard	1988	Hockey	
Doherty, Laurie	1900	Lawn Tennis	Men's Singles
	1900	Lawn Tennis	Men's Doubles
Doherty, Reggie	1900	Lawn Tennis	Men's Doubles
(brother of Laurie Doherty)	1900	Lawn Tennis	Mixed Doubles
	1908	Lawn Tennis	Men's Doubles
Donne, William	1900	Cricket	
Douglas, Johnny	1908	Boxing	Middleweight
Douglas, Rowley	2000	Rowing	Coxed Eight
Downes, Arthur	1908	Yachting	12 Metres Class
Downes, Henry (Arthur's brother)	1908	Yachting	12 Metres Class
Dunlop, David	1908	Yachting	12 Metres Class
Easte, Philip	1908	Shooting	Clay Pigeon Team
Eastlake-Smith, Gladys	1908	Lawn Tennis	Indoor Women's Singles
Edwards, Jonathan	2000	Athletics	Triple Jump

Name	Date	Sport	Event
Edwards, Jumbo	1932	Rowing	Coxless Pairs
	1932	Rowing	Coxless Fours
Eley, Maxwell	1924	Rowing	Coxless Fours
Elliot, Launceston	1896	Weightlifting	One-Handed Lift
Ellison, Adrian	1984	Rowing	Coxed Fours (cox)
Etherington-Smith, Raymond	1908	Rowing	Eights
Exshaw, William	1900	Yachting	2–3 Ton Class
Faulds, Richard	2000	Shooting	Double Trap
Faulkner, David	1988	Hockey	
Fenning, John	1908	Rowing	Coxless Pairs
Field-Richards, John	1908	Motor Boating	8 Metres Class
Finnegan, Chris	1968	Boxing	Middleweight
Fleming, John	1908	Shooting	Small-Bore Rifle, moving target
Fleming, Philip	1912	Rowing	Eights
Fletcher, Jennie	1912	Swimming	4 x 100m Freestyle Relay
Forsyth, Charlie	1908	Swimming	Water Polo Team
Foster, Bill	1908	Swimming	4 x 200m Freestyle Relay
Foster, Tim	2000	Rowing	Coxless Fours
Fox, Jim	1976	Modern Pentathlon	Team Event
Freeman, Harry	1908	Hockey	
Garcia, Russell	1988	Hockey	
Garton, Stanley	1912	Rowing	Eights
George, Rowland	1932	Rowing	Coxless Fours
Gillan, Angus	1908	Rowing	Coxless Fours
	1912	Rowing	Eights
Gladstone, Albert	1908	Rowing	Eights
Glen-Coats, Thomas	1908	Yachting	12 Metres Class
Godfree, Kitty	1920	Lawn Tennis	Women's Doubles
Goodfellow, Fred	1908	Tug of War	
Goodhew, Duncan	1980	Swimming	100m Breaststroke
Gordon-Watson, Mary	1972	Equestrian	3-Day Event Team
Gore, Arthur	1908	Lawn Tennis	Indoor Men's Singles
	1908	Lawn Tennis	Indoor Men's Doubles
Gosling, William	1900	Football	
Grace, Fred	1908	Boxing	Lightweight
Green, Eric	1908	Hockey	
Green, Tommy	1932	Athletics	50km Walk
Gretton, John (serving MP)	1900	Yachting	Open Class
	1900	Yachting	0.5–1 Ton Class
Griffiths, Cecil	1920	Athletics	4 x 400m Relay
Grimley, Martyn	1988	Hockey	
Grinham, Judy	1956	Swimming	100m Backstroke
Grubor, Luka	2000	Rowing	Coxed Eight
Gunn, Dick	1908	Boxing	Featherweight
Gunnell, Sally	1992	Athletics	400m Hurdles
Halswelle, Wyndham	1908	Athletics	400m
Hampson, Tommy	1932	Athletics	800m
Hannam, Edith	1912	Lawn Tennis	Indoor Women's Singles
	1912	Lawn Tennis	Indoor Mixed Doubles
Hanney, Ted	1912	Football	
Hardman, Harry	1908	Football	
Harmer, Russell	1936	Yachting	6 Metres Class
Harrison, Audley	2000	Boxing	Super Heavyweight
Haslam, A.	1900	Football	
Haslam, Harry	1920	Hockey	
Hawkes, Robert	1908	Football	
Hemery, David	1968	Athletics	400m Hurdles
Herbert, Garry	1992	Rowing	Coxed Pairs (cox)
Hill, Albert	1920	Athletics	800m
	1920	Athletics	1500m
Hill, Arthur	1912	Swimming	Water Polo Team
Hill, Bertie	1956	Equestrian	3-Day Event Team
Hillyard, George	1908	Lawn Tennis	Men's Doubles
Hirons, Bill	1908	Tug of War	
Hoare, Gordon	1912	Football	
Hodge, Percy	1920	Athletics	3000m Steeplechase
Holman, Fred	1908	Swimming	200m Breaststroke
Holmes, Andy	1984	Rowing	Coxed Fours
	1988	Rowing	Coxless Pairs
Holmes, Fred	1920	Tug of War	
Horsfall, Ewart	1912	Rowing	Eights

S
P
O
R
T
&
L
E
I
S
U
R
E

Name	Date	Sport	Event
Humby, Harry	1908	Shooting	Small-Bore Rifle Team
Humphreys, Fred	1908	Tug of War	
	1920	Tug of War	
Hunt, Kenneth	1908	Football	
Hunt-Davis, Ben	2000	Rowing	Coxed Eight
Ireton, Albert	1908	Tug of War	
Jacobs, David	1912	Athletics	4 x 100m Relay
Jarvis, John Arthur	1900	Swimming	1000m Freestyle
	1900	Swimming	4000m Freestyle
Johnson, Victor	1908	Cycling	One-Lap Race
Johnstone, Banner	1908	Rowing	Eights
Jones, Ben	1908	Cycling	5000m Track Race
	1908	Cycling	Three-Lap Pursuit
Jones, Ben	1968	Equestrian	3-Day Event Team
Jones, Chris	1920	Swimming	Water Polo Team
Jones, J.H.	1900	Football	
Keene, Foxhall	1900	Polo	
Kelly, Fred	1908	Rowing	Eights
Kemp, Peter	1900	Swimming	Water Polo Team
Kerly, Sean	1988	Hockey	
Kingsbury, Clarrie	1908	Cycling	20km Track Race
	1908	Cycling	Three-Lap Pursuit
Kinnear, Wally	1912	Rowing	Single Sculls
Kirby, Alister	1912	Rowing	Eights
Kirkwood, Jimmy	1988	Hockey	
Knight, Arthur	1912	Football	
Lambert-Chambers, Dolly	1908	Lawn Tennis	Women's Singles
Lance, Tommy	1920	Cycling	2000m Tandem
Lander, John	1928	Rowing	Coxless Fours
Larner, George	1908	Athletics	3500m and 10 Mile Walk
Laurie, Ran	1948	Rowing	Coxless Pairs
Laws, Gilbert	1908	Yachting	6 Metres Class
Leaf, Charles	1936	Yachting	6 Metres Class
Leighton, Arthur	1920	Hockey	
Leman, Richard	1988	Hockey	
Lessimore, Edward	1912	Shooting	Small-Bore Rifle Team, 50m
Lewis, Denise	2000	Athletics	Heptathlon
Liddell, Eric	1924	Athletics	400m
Lindsay, Andrew	2000	Rowing	Coxed Eight
Lindsay, Robert	1920	Athletics	4 x 400m Relay
Lister, Bill	1900	Swimming	Water Polo Team
Littlewort, Henry	1912	Football	
Llewellyn, Sir Harry (Foxhunter)	1952	Equestrian	Prix des Nations Team
Lockett, Vivian	1920	Polo	
Logan, Gerald	1908	Hockey	
Lonsbrough, Anita	1960	Swimming	200m Breaststroke
Lowe, Douglas	1924	Athletics	800m
	1928	Athletics	800m
McBryan, Jack	1920	Hockey	
MacDonald-Smith, Iain	1968	Yachting	Flying Dutchman Class
McGrath, George	1920	Hockey	
Macintosh, Henry	1920	Athletics	4 x 100m Relay
McIntyre, Mike	1988	Yachting	Star Class
McKenzie, John	1908	Yachting	12 Metres Class
Mackay, Frank (USA born)	1900	Polo	
MacKinnon, Duncan	1908	Rowing	Coxless Fours
Mackworth-Praed, Cyril	1924	Shooting	Running Deer (double shot)
MacLagen, Gilchrist	1908	Rowing	Eights
McMeekin, Tom	1908	Yachting	6 Metres Class
Macnabb, James	1924	Rowing	Coxless Fours
McNair, Winifred	1920	Lawn Tennis	Women's Doubles
McTaggart, Dick	1956	Boxing	Lightweight
McWhirter, Douglas	1912	Football	
Maddison, W.J.	1920	Yachting	7 Metres Class
Mallin, Harry	1920	Boxing	Middleweight
(retired undefeated 300 fights)	1924	Boxing	Middleweight
Marcon, Sholto	1920	Hockey	
Martin, Albert	1908	Yachting	12 Metres Class
Martin, Leonard	1936	Yachting	6 Metres Class
Martin, Steve (played 1 minute)	1988	Hockey	
Matthews, Ken	1964	Athletics	20km Walk

Name	Date	Sport	Event
Matthews, M.K.	1908	Shooting	Small-Bore Rifle Team
Maunder, Alex	1908	Shooting	Clay Pigeon Team
Meade, Richard	1968	Equestrian	3-Day Event Team
	1972	Equestrian	3-Day Event and Team
Melvill, Tim	1920	Polo	
Meredith, Leon	1908	Cycling	Three-Lap Pursuit
Merriman, Fred	1908	Tug of War	
Miller, Charles	1908	Polo	
Miller, George (brother of Charles)	1908	Polo	
Millner, Jerry	1908	Shooting	Free Rifle
Mills, Edwin	1908	Tug of War	
	1920	Tug of War	
Mitchell, Harry	1924	Boxing	Light-Heavyweight
Moore, Bella	1912	Swimming	4 x 100m Freestyle Relay
Moore, F.W.	1908	Shooting	Clay Pigeon Team
Moorhouse, Adrian	1988	Swimming	100m Breaststroke
Morris, Stewart	1948	Yachting	Swallow Class
Morrison, Robert	1924	Rowing	Coxless Fours
Morton, Lucy	1924	Swimming	200m Breaststroke
Murray, Robert	1912	Shooting	Small-Bore Rifle Team
Neame, Philip	1924	Shooting	Running Deer (double shot)
(only man to be awarded Victoria Cross, knighthood and Olympic gold)			
Nevinson, George	1908	Swimming	Water Polo Team
Newall, Queenie	1908	Archery	National Round
Nicholas, J.	1900	Football	
Nickalls, Guy	1908	Rowing	Eights
Nickalls, Patteson	1908	Polo	
Nightingale, Danny	1976	Modern Pentathlon	Team Event
Noble, Alan	1908	Hockey	
Noel, Evan	1908	Rackets	Singles
O'Kelly, Con	1908	Wrestling	Heavyweight, Freestyle
Oldman, Albert	1908	Boxing	Heavyweight
Osborn, John	1976	Yachting	Tornado Class
Ovett, Steve	1980	Athletics	800m
Packer, Ann	1964	Athletics	800m
Page, Edgar	1908	Hockey	
Palmer, Charles	1908	Shooting	Clay Pigeon Team
Pappin, Veryan	1988	Hockey	
Parker, Adrian	1976	Modern Pentathlon	Team Event
Parker, Bridget	1972	Equestrian	3-Day Event Team
Pattisson, Rodney	1968	Yachting	Flying Dutchman Class
	1972	Yachting	Flying Dutchman Class
Payne, Ernest	1908	Cycling	Three-Lap Pursuit
(known as the Worcester Wonder, Payne changed sports to become a Manchester Utd footballer)			
Peacock, Bill	1920	Swimming	Water Polo Team
Pennell, Vane	1908	Rackets	Doubles
Pepe, Joseph	1912	Shooting	Small-Bore Rifle Team, 50m
Percy, Iain	2000	Sailing	Finn Class
Perry, Herbert	1924	Shooting	Running Deer (double shot)
Peters, Mary	1972	Athletics	Pentathlon
Phillips, Mark	1972	Equestrian	3-Day Event Team
Pike, J.F.	1908	Shooting	Clay Pigeon Team
Pimm, William	1908	Shooting	Small-Bore Rifle Team
	1912	Shooting	Small-Bore Rifle Team, 50m
Pinsent, Matthew	1992	Rowing	Coxless Pairs
	1996	Rowing	Coxless Pairs
	2000	Rowing	Coxless Fours
Postans, J.M.	1908	Shooting	Clay Pigeon Team
Potter, Jonathan	1988	Hockey	
Powlesland, Alfred	1900	Cricket	
Pridmore, Reggie	1908	Hockey	
Purcell, Noel	1920	Swimming	Water Polo Team
(Purcell was also an Irish rugby international)			
Purnell, Clyde	1908	Football	
Quash, Bill	1900	Football	
Queally, Jason	2000	Cycling	Kilometre Sprint
Radmilovic, Paul	1908	Swimming	Water Polo Team

Name	Date	Sport	Event
	1908	Swimming	4 x 200m Freestyle Relay
	1912	Swimming	Water Polo Team
	1920	Swimming	Water Polo Team
Rampling, Godfrey	1936	Athletics	4 x 400m Relay
Rand, Mary	1964	Athletics	Long Jump
(Mary won the full set of medals with			
silver in Pentathlon and bronze in the relay)			
Rawlinson, Alfred	1900	Polo	
Rawson, Ronald	1920	Boxing	Heavyweight
Redgrave, Steve	1984	Rowing	Coxed Fours
	1988	Rowing	Coxless Pairs
	1992	Rowing	Coxless Pairs
	1996	Rowing	Coxless Pairs
	2000	Rowing	Coxless Fours
Redwood, Bernard	1908	Motor Boating	8 Metres Class
	1908	Motor Boating	Under 60-Foot Class
Rees, Percy	1908	Hockey	
Rhodes, John	1908	Yachting	8 Metres Class
Rimmer, J.T.	1900	Athletics	4000m Steeplechase
	1900	Athletics	5000m Team Race
Ritchie, Major	1908	Lawn Tennis	Men's Singles
Rivett-Carnac, Charles	1908	Yachting	7 Metres Class
Rivett-Carnac, Frances	1908	Yachting	7 Metres Class
(wife of Charles)			
Roberts, Bill	1936	Athletics	4 x 400m Relay
Robertson, Arthur	1908	Athletics	Three Miles Team Race
Robertson, Arthur	1900	Swimming	Water Polo Team
Robertson, Shirley	2000	Sailing	Europe Dinghy Class
Robinson, Eric	1900	Swimming	Water Polo Team
Robinson, John	1908	Hockey	
Robinson, Sidney	1900	Athletics	5000m Team Race
Rook, Laurence	1956	Equestrian	3-Day Event Team
Russell, Arthur	1908	Athletics	3200m Steeplechase
Ryan, Harry	1920	Cycling	2000m Tandem
Sanders, Terence	1924	Rowing	Coxless Fours
Sanderson, Ronald	1908	Rowing	Eights
Sanderson, Tessa	1984	Athletics	Javelin
Scarlett, Fred	2000	Rowing	Coxed Eight
Searle, Greg	1992	Rowing	Coxed Pairs
Searle, Jonny	1992	Rowing	Coxed Pairs
Sewell, John	1912	Tug of War	
	1920	Tug of War	
Sharpe, Ivan	1912	Football	
Sheen, Gillian	1956	Fencing	Individual Foil
Shepherd, John	1908	Tug of War	
	1920	Tug of War	
Sherwani, Imran	1988	Hockey	
Shoveller, Stanley	1908	Hockey	
	1920	Hockey	
Smith, Charles	1908	Swimming	Water Polo Team
	1912	Swimming	Water Polo Team
	1920	Swimming	Water Polo Team
Smith, Faulder	1920	Hockey	
Smith, Herbert	1908	Football	
Somers-Smith, John	1908	Rowing	Coxless Fours
Southwood, Dick	1936	Rowing	Double Sculls
Spackman, F.G.	1900	Football	
Spiers, Annie	1912	Swimming	4 x 100m Freestyle Relay
Spinks, Terry	1956	Boxing	Flyweight
Stamper, Harry	1912	Football	
Stapley, Henry	1908	Football	
Steer, Irene	1912	Swimming	4 x 100m Freestyle Relay
Stewart, Douglas	1952	Equestrian	Prix des Nations Team
(only British man to have competed at			
Olympic eventing and show jumping competitions)			
Stiff, Harry	1920	Tug of War	
Strode-Jackson, Arnold	1912	Athletics	1500m
Styles, William	1908	Shooting	Small-Bore disappearing target
Sutton, Henry	1908	Yachting	8 Metres Class
Swann, Sidney	1912	Rowing	Eights
Symes, John	1900	Cricket	

Name	Date	Sport	Event
Tait, Gerald	1908	Yachting	12 Metres Class
Taylor, Henry	1908	Swimming	400m Freestyle
	1908	Swimming	1500m Freestyle
	1908	Swimming	4 x 200m Freestyle Relay
Taylor, Ian	1988	Hockey	
Thomas, Harry	1908	Boxing	Bantamweight
Thompson, Daley	1980	Athletics	Decathlon
	1984	Athletics	Decathlon
Thompson, Don	1960	Athletics	50km Walk
Thomson, Gordon	1908	Rowing	Coxless Pairs
Thorne, Ernie	1920	Tug of War	
Thornycroft, Tom	1908	Motor Boating	8 Metres Class
	1908	Motor Boating	Under 60-Foot Class
Thould, Tom	1908	Swimming	Water Polo Team
	1912	Swimming	Water Polo Team
Toller, Montague	1900	Cricket	
Trapmore, Steve	2000	Rowing	Coxed Eight
Turnbull, Noel	1920	Lawn Tennis	Men's Doubles
Turner, R.R.	1900	Football	
Tysoe, Alf	1900	Athletics	800m
	1900	Athletics	5000m Team Race
Vaile, Bryn	1988	Yachting	Star Class
Voigt, Emil	1908	Athletics	Five Miles
Walden, Harry (also music-hall comic)	1912	Football	
Warriner, Michael	1928	Rowing	Coxless Fours
Weldon, Frank	1956	Equestrian	Three-Day Event Team
(born in India, Weldon was the only			
British Olympic gold medal winner to escape from Colditz)			
Wells, Allan	1980	Athletics	100m
Wells, Henry	1912	Rowing	Eights (cox)
West, Kieran	2000	Rowing	Coxed Eight
White, Reg	1976	Yachting	Tornado Class
White, Wilf	1952	Equestrian	Prix des Nations Team
Whitlock, Harold	1936	Athletics	50km Walk
Whitty, Allen	1924	Shooting	Running Deer (double shot)
Wilkie, David	1976	Swimming	200m Breaststroke
Wilkinson, Cyril	1920	Hockey	
Wilkinson, George	1900	Swimming	Water Polo Team
	1908	Swimming	Water Polo Team
	1912	Swimming	Water Polo Team
Wilson, Herbert	1908	Polo	
Wilson, Jack	1948	Rowing	Coxless Pairs
Wodehouse, Lord John	1920	Polo	
Wolff, Freddie	1936	Athletics	4 x 400m Relay
Wood, Arthur	1908	Yachting	8 Metres Class
Wood, Harvey	1908	Hockey	
Woodward, Vivian	1908	Football	
	1912	Football	
Woosnam, Max	1920	Lawn Tennis	Men's Doubles
(also played football for England and			
golf and cricket for Cambridge)			
Wormald	1912	Rowing	Eights
Wright, Cyril	1920	Yachting	7 Metres Class
Wright, Dorothy	1920	Yachting	7 Metres Class
(wife of Cyril)			
Wright, Gordon	1912	Football	
Zealey, Jim	1900	Football	

S
P
O
R
T
&
L
E
I
S
U
R
E

Tennis: Wimbledon Champions

	Men	Women	Men's Doubles	Women's Doubles
1877	S.W. Gore (GB)	—	—	—
1878	P.F. Hadow (GB)	—	—	—
1879	J.T. Hartley (GB)	—	—	—
1880	J.T. Hartley (GB)	—	—	—
1881	W. Renshaw (GB)	—	—	—
1882	W. Renshaw (GB)	—	—	—
1883	W. Renshaw (GB)	—	—	—
1884	W. Renshaw (GB)	M. Watson (GB)	W. Renshaw / E. Renshaw	—
1885	W. Renshaw (GB)	M. Watson (GB)	W. Renshaw / E. Renshaw	—
1886	W. Renshaw (GB)	B. Bingley (GB)	W. Renshaw / E. Renshaw	—
1887	H.F. Lawford (GB)	C. Dod (GB)	W. Wilberforce / P.B. Lyon	—
1888	E. Renshaw (GB)	C. Dod (GB)	W. Renshaw / E. Renshaw	—
1889	W. Renshaw (GB)	B. Bingley Hillyard (GB)	W. Renshaw / E. Renshaw	—
1890	W.J. Hamilton (GB)	H. Rice (GB)	J. Pim / F.O. Stoker	—
1891	W. Baddeley (GB)	C. Dod (GB)	W. Baddeley / H. Baddeley	—
1892	W. Baddeley (GB)	C. Dod (GB)	E.W. Lewis / H.S. Barlow	—
1893	J. Pim (GB)	C. Dod (GB)	J. Pim / F.O. Stoker	—
1894	J. Pim (GB)	B. Hillyard (GB)	W. Baddeley / H. Baddeley	—
1895	W. Baddeley (GB)	C. Cooper (GB)	W. Baddeley / H. Baddeley	—
1896	H.S. Mahony (GB)	C. Cooper (GB)	W. Baddeley / H. Baddeley	—
1897	R.F. Doherty (GB)	B. Hillyard (GB)	R.F. Doherty / L.H. Doherty	—
1898	R.F. Doherty (GB)	C. Cooper (GB)	R.F. Doherty / L.H. Doherty	—
1899	R.F. Doherty (GB)	B. Hillyard (GB)	R.F. Doherty / L.H. Doherty	—
1900	R.F. Doherty (GB)	B. Hillyard (GB)	R.F. Doherty / L.H. Doherty	—
1901	A.W. Gore (GB)	C. Cooper Sterry (GB)	R.F. Doherty / L.H. Doherty	—
1902	L.H. Doherty (GB)	M.E. Robb (GB)	S.H. Smith / F.L. Riseley	—
1903	L.H. Doherty (GB)	D.K. Douglass (GB)	R.F. Doherty / L.H. Doherty	—
1904	L.H. Doherty (GB)	D.K. Douglass (GB)	R.F. Doherty / L.H. Doherty	—
1905	L.H. Doherty (GB)	M. Sutton (US)	R.F. Doherty / L.H. Doherty	—
1906	L.H. Doherty (GB)	D.K. Douglass (GB)	S. Smith / F. Riseley	—
1907	N.E. Brookes (Aus)	M. Sutton (US)	N.E. Brookes / A.F. Wilding	—
1908	A.W. Gore (GB)	C. Sterry (GB)	A.F. Wilding / M.J.G. Ritchie	—
1909	A.W. Gore (GB)	D.P. Boothby (GB)	A.W. Gore / H. Roper Barrett	—
1910	A.F. Wilding (NZ)	D.K. Douglass Chambers (GB)	A.F. Wilding / M.J.G. Ritchie	—
1911	A.F. Wilding (NZ)	D.K. Douglass Chambers (GB)	A.H. Gobert / M. Decugis	—
1912	A.F. Wilding (NZ)	E.W. Larcombe (GB)	H. Roper Barrett / C.P. Dixon	—
1913	A.F. Wilding (NZ)	D.K. Douglass Chambers (GB)	H. Roper Barrett / C.P. Dixon	R.J. McNair / D.P. Boothby
1914	N.E. Brookes (Aus)	D.K. Douglass Chambers (GB)	N.E. Brookes / A.F. Wilding	E. Ryan / A.M. Morton
1915	not held	not held	not held	not held
1916	not held	not held	not held	not held
1917	not held	not held	not held	not held
1918	not held	not held	not held	not held
1919	G.L. Patterson (Aus)	S. Lenglen (Fr)	R.V. Thomas / P. O'Hara Wood	S. Lenglen / E. Ryan
1920	W.T. Tilden (US)	S. Lenglen (Fr)	R.N. Williams / C.S. Garland	S. Lenglen / E. Ryan
1921	W.T. Tilden (US)	S. Lenglen (Fr)	R. Lycett / M. Woosnam	S. Lenglen / E. Ryan
1922	G.L. Patterson (Aus)	S. Lenglen (Fr)	J.O. Anderson / R. Lycett	S. Lenglen / E. Ryan
1923	W.M. Johnston (US)	S. Lenglen (Fr)	L.A. Godfree / R. Lycett	S. Lenglen / E. Ryan
1924	J. Borotra (Fr)	K. McKane (GB)	F.T. Hunter / V. Richards	H. Wightman / H.N. Wills
1925	R. Lacoste (Fr)	S. Lenglen (Fr)	J. Borotra / R. Lacoste	S. Lenglen / E. Ryan
1926	J. Borotra (Fr)	K. McKane Godfree (GB)	J. Brugnon / H. Cochet	M.K. Browne / E. Ryan
1927	H. Cochet (Fr)	H.N. Wills (US)	F.T. Hunter / W.T. Tilden	H.N. Wills / E. Ryan
1928	R. Lacoste (Fr)	H.N. Wills (US)	J. Brugnon / H. Cochet	P. Saunders / M. Watson
1929	H. Cochet (Fr)	H.N. Wills (US)	W.L. Allison / J. Van Ryn	P. Saunders Michell / M. Watson
1930	W.T. Tilden (US)	H.N. Wills Moody (US)	W.L. Allison / J. Van Ryn	H.N. Wills Moody / E. Ryan
1931	S.B. Wood (US)	C. Aussem (Ger)	G.M. Lott / J. Van Ryn	P. Mudford / D. Shepherd-Barron
1932	H.E. Vines (US)	H.N. Wills Moody (US)	J. Borotra / J. Brugnon	D. Metaxa / J. Sigart
1933	J.H. Crawford (Aus)	H.N. Wills Moody (US)	J. Borotra / J. Brugnon	E. Ryan / R. Mathieu
1934	F.J. Perry (GB)	D.E. Round (GB)	G.M. Lott / L.R. Stoefen	E. Ryan / R. Mathieu
1935	F.J. Perry (GB)	H.N. Wills Moody (US)	J.H. Crawford / A.K. Quist	F. James / K.E. Stammers

	Men	Women	Men's Doubles	Women's Doubles
1936	F.J. Perry (GB)	H.H. Jacobs (US)	G.P. Hughes / C.R.D. Tuckey	F. James / K.E. Stammers
1937	J.D. Budge (US)	D.E. Round (GB)	J.D. Budge / G. Mako	S. Mathieu / B. Yorke
1938	J.D. Budge (US)	H.N. Wills Moody (US)	J.D. Budge / G. Mako	S. Palfrey Fabyan / A. Marble
1939	R.L. Riggs (US)	A. Marble (US)	E.T. Cooke / R.L. Riggs	S. Palfrey Fabyan / A. Marble
1940	not held	not held	not held	not held
1941	not held	not held	not held	not held
1942	not held	not held	not held	not held
1943	not held	not held	not held	not held
1944	not held	not held	not held	not held
1945	not held	not held	not held	not held
1946	Y. Petra (Fr)	P.M. Betz (US)	T. Brown / J.A. Kramer	L.A. Brough / M. Osborne
1947	J. Kramer (US)	M.E. Osborne (US)	R. Falkenburg / J.A. Kramer	R.B. Todd / D.J. Hart
1948	B. Falkenburg (US)	A.L. Brough (US)	J.E. Bromwich / F.A. Sedgman	A.L. Brough / M.E.Osborne du Pont
1949	T. Schroeder (US)	A.L. Brough (US)	R.A. Gonzales / F.A. Parker	A.L. Brough / M. du Pont
1950	B. Patty (US)	A.L. Brough (US)	J.E. Bromwich / A.K. Quist	A.L. Brough / M. du Pont
1951	D. Savitt (US)	D.J. Hart (US)	K.B. McGregor / F.A. Sedgman	D.J. Hart / S.J. Fry
1952	F. Sedgman (Aus)	M. Connolly (US)	K.B. McGregor / F.A. Sedgman	D.J. Hart / S.J. Fry
1953	V. Seixas (US)	M. Connolly (US)	L.A. Hoad / K.R. Rosewall	D.J. Hart / S.J. Fry
1954	J. Drobny (Cze)	M. Connolly (US)	R.N. Hartwig / M.G. Rose	A.L. Brough / M. du Pont
1955	M.A. Trabert (US)	A.L. Brough (US)	R.N. Hartwig / L.A. Hoad	A. Mortimer / J.A. Shilcock
1956	L.A. Hoad (Aus)	S.J. Fry (US)	L.A. Hoad / K.R. Rosewall	A. Buxton / A. Gibson
1957	L.A. Hoad (Aus)	A. Gibson (US)	J.E. Patty / G. Mulloy	A. Gibson / D.R. Hard
1958	A.J. Cooper (Aus)	A. Gibson (US)	S. Davidson / U. Schmidt	M.E. Bueno / A. Gibson
1959	A. Olmedo (Per)	M.E. Bueno (Braz)	R. Emerson / N.A. Fraser	J. Arth / D.R. Hard
1960	N.A. Fraser (Aus)	M.E. Bueno (Braz)	R.H. Osuna / R.D. Ralston	M.E. Bueno / D.R. Hard
1961	R.G. Laver (Aus)	A. Mortimer (GB)	R. Emerson / N.A. Fraser	K. Hantze / B.J. Moffitt
1962	R.G. Laver (Aus)	K. Hantze Susman (US)	R.A.J. Hewitt / F.S. Stolle	B.J. Moffitt / K. Hantze Susman
1963	C.R. McKinley (US)	M. Smith (Aus)	R.H. Osuna / A. Palafox	M.E. Bueno / D.R. Hard
1964	R.S. Emerson (Aus)	M.E. Bueno (Braz)	R.A.J. Hewitt / F.S. Stolle	M. Smith / L.R. Turner
1965	R.S. Emerson (Aus)	M. Smith (Aus)	J.D. Newcombe / A.D. Roche	M.E. Bueno / B.J. Moffitt
1966	M. Santana (Spa)	B.J. Moffitt King (US)	K.N. Fletcher / J.D. Newcombe	M.E. Bueno / N. Richey
1967	J.D. Newcombe (Aus)	B.J. King (US)	R.A.J. Hewitt / F.D. McMillan	R. Casals / B.J. Moffitt King
1968	R.G. Laver (Aus)	B.J. King (US)	J.D. Newcombe / A.D. Roche	R. Casals / B.J. King
1969	R.G. Laver (Aus)	A. Haydon Jones (GB)	J.D. Newcombe / A.D. Roche	M. Smith Court / J.A.M. Tegart
1970	J.D. Newcombe (Aus)	M. Smith Court (Aus)	J.D. Newcombe / A.D. Roche	R. Casals / B.J. King
1971	J.D. Newcombe (Aus)	E.F. Goolagong (Aus)	R.S. Emerson / R.G. Laver	R. Casals / B.J. King
1972	S.R. Smith (US)	B.J. King (US)	R.A.J. Hewitt / F.D. McMillan	B.J. King / B. Stove
1973	J. Kodes (Cze)	B.J. King (US)	J.S. Connors / I. Nastase	R. Casals / B.J. King
1974	J.S. Connors (US)	C.M. Evert (US)	J.D. Newcombe / A.D. Roche	E.F. Goolagong / M. Michel
1975	A.R. Ashe (US)	B.J. King (US)	V. Gerulaitis / A. Mayer	A. Kiyomura / K. Sawamatsu
1976	B. Borg (Swe)	C.M. Evert (US)	B.E. Gottfried / R. Ramirez	C.M. Evert / M. Navratilova
1977	B. Borg (Swe)	S.V. Wade (GB)	R.L. Case / G. Masters	H. Gourlay Cawley / J.C. Russell
1978	B. Borg (Swe)	M. Navratilova (Cze)	R.A.J. Hewitt / F.D. McMillan	K. Reid / W. Turnbull
1979	B. Borg (Swe)	M. Navratilova (US)	J.P. McEnroe / P. Fleming	B.J. King / M. Navratilova
1980	B. Borg (Swe)	E.F. Goolagong Cawley (Aus)	P. McNamara / P. McNamee	K. Jordan / A.E. Smith
1981	J.P. McEnroe (US)	C.M. Evert Lloyd (US)	J.P. McEnroe / P. Fleming	M. Navratilova / P.H. Shriver
1982	J.S. Connors (US)	M. Navratilova (US)	P. McNamara / P. McNamee	M. Navratilova / P.H. Shriver

SPORT & LEISURE

	Men	Women	Men's Doubles	Women's Doubles
1983	J.P. McEnroe (US)	M. Navratilova (US)	J.P. McEnroe / P. Fleming	M. Navratilova / P.H. Shriver
1984	J.P. McEnroe (US)	M. Navratilova (US)	J.P. McEnroe / P. Fleming	M. Navratilova / P.H. Shriver
1985	B. Becker (Ger)	M. Navratilova (US)	H.P. Gunthardt / B. Taroczy	K. Jordan / E. Smylie
1986	B. Becker (Ger)	M. Navratilova (US)	J. Nystrom / M. Wilander	M. Navratilova / P.H. Shriver
1987	P. Cash (Aus)	M. Navratilova (US)	R. Seguso / K. Flach	C. Kohde-Kilsch / H. Sukova
1988	S. Edberg (Swe)	S. Graf (Ger)	R. Seguso / K. Flach	S. Graf / G. Sabatini
1989	B. Becker (Ger)	S. Graf (Ger)	J.B. Fitzgerald / A. Jarryd	J.Novotna/H.Sukova
1990	S. Edberg (Swe)	M. Navratilova (US)	R. Leach / J. Pugh	J.Novotna/H.Sukova
1991	M. Stich (Ger)	S. Graf (Ger)	J.B. Fitzgerald / A. Jarryd	L. Savchenko / N. Zvereva
1992	A. Agassi (US)	S. Graf (Ger)	J.P. McEnroe / M. Stich	G. Fernandez / N. Zvereva
1993	P. Sampras (US)	S. Graf (Ger)	T. Woodbridge / M. Woodforde	G. Fernandez / N. Zvereva
1994	P. Sampras (US)	C. Martinez (Spa)	T. Woodbridge / M. Woodforde	G. Fernandez / N. Zvereva
1995	P. Sampras (US)	S. Graf (Ger)	T. Woodbridge / M. Woodforde	J. Novotna / A. Sanchez-Vicario
1996	R. Krajicek (Ned)	S. Graf (Ger)	T. Woodbridge / M. Woodforde	M. Hingis / H. Sukova
1997	P. Sampras (US)	M. Hingis (Swi)	T. Woodbridge / M. Woodforde	G. Fernandez / N. Zvereva
1998	P. Sampras (US)	J. Novotna (Cze)	J. Eltingh / P. Haarhuis	M. Hingis / J. Novotna
1999	P. Sampras (US)	L. Davenport (US)	M. Bhupathi / L. Paes	L. Davenport / C. Morariu
2000	P. Sampras (US)	V. Williams (US)	T. Woodbridge/M. Woodforde	V. Williams / S. Williams
2001	G. Ivanisevic (Cro)	V. Williams (US)	D. Johnson / J. Palmer	L. Raymond / R. Stubbs

Tennis: US Open

	Men	Women	Men's Doubles	Women's Doubles
1881	R.D. Sears (US)	—	C.M. Clark / F.W. Taylor	—
1882	R.D. Sears (US)	—	R.D. Sears / J. Dwight	—
1883	R.D. Sears (US)	—	R.D. Sears / J. Dwight	—
1884	R.D. Sears (US)	—	R.D. Sears / J. Dwight	—
1885	R.D Sears (US)	—	R.D. Sears / J.S. Clark	—
1886	R.D Sears (US)	—	R.D. Sears / J. Dwight	—
1887	R.D Sears (US)	E. Hansell (US)	R.D. Sears / J. Dwight	—
1888	H.W. Slocum (US)	B.L. Townsend (US)	O.S. Campbell / V.G. Hall	—
1889	H.W. Slocum (US)	B.L. Townsend (US)	H.W. Slocum / H.A. Taylor	M. Ballard / B.L. Townsend
1890	O.S. Campbell (US)	E.C. Roosevelt (US)	V.G. Hall / C. Hobart	E.C. Roosevelt / G.W. Roosevelt
1891	O.S. Campbell (US)	M.E. Cahill (US)	O.S. Campbell / R.P. Huntington	M.E. Cahill / W.F. Morgan
1892	O.S. Campbell (US)	M.E. Cahill (US)	O.S. Campbell / R.P. Huntington	M.E. Cahill / A.M. McKinley
1893	R.D. Wrenn (US)	A.M. Terry (US)	C. Hobart / F.H. Hovey	A.M. Terry / H. Butler
1894	R.D. Wrenn (US)	H.R. Hellwig (US)	C. Hobart / F.H. Hovey	H.R. Hellwig / J.P. Atkinson
1895	F.H. Hovey (US)	J.P. Atkinson (US)	M.G. Chace / R.D. Wrenn	H.R. Hellwig / J.P. Atkinson
1896	R.D. Wrenn (US)	E.H. Moore (US)	C.B. Neel / S.R. Neel	E.H. Moore / J.P. Atkinson
1897	R.D. Wrenn (US)	J.P. Atkinson (US)	L.E. Ware / G.P. Sheldon	J.P. Atkinson / K. Atkinson
1898	M.D. Whitman (US)	J.P. Atkinson (US)	L.E. Ware / G.P. Sheldon	J.P. Atkinson / K. Atkinson
1899	M.D. Whitman (US)	M. Jones (US)	H. Ward / D.F. Davis	J.W. Craven / M. McAteer
1900	M.D. Whitman (US)	M. McAteer (US)	H. Ward / D.F. Davis	E. Parker / H. Champlin
1901	W.A. Larned (US)	E.H. Moore (US)	H. Ward / D.F. Davis	J.P. Atkinson / M. McAteer
1902	W.A. Larned (US)	M. Jones (US)	R.F. Doherty / H.L. Doherty	J.P. Atkinson / M. Jones
1903	H.L. Doherty (GB)	E.H. Moore (US)	R.F. Doherty / H.L. Doherty	E.H. Moore / C.B. Neely
1904	H. Ward (US)	M.G. Sutton (US)	H. Ward / B.C. Wright	M.G. Sutton / M. Hall
1905	B.C. Wright (US)	E.H. Moore (US)	H. Ward / B.C. Wright	H. Homans / C.B. Neely
1906	W.J. Clothier (US)	H. Homans (US)	H. Ward / B.C. Wright	L.S. Coe / D.S. Platt
1907	W.A. Larned (US)	Evelyn Sears (US)	F.B. Alexander / B.C. Wright	M. Wimer / C.B. Neely
1908	W.A. Larned (US)	M. Barger-Wallach (US)	F.B. Alexander / H.H. Hackett	Evelyn Sears / M. Curtis
1909	W.A. Larned (US)	H. Hotchkiss (US)	F.B. Alexander / H.H. Hackett	H.V. Hotchkiss / E.E. Rotch
1910	W.A. Larned (US)	H. Hotchkiss (US)	F.B. Alexander / H.H. Hackett	H.V. Hotchkiss / E.E. Rotch
1911	W.A. Larned (US)	H. Hotchkiss (US)	R.D. Little / G.F. Touchard	H.V. Hotchkiss / Eleanora Sears
1912	M.E.McLoughlin (US)	M.K. Browne (US)	M.E. McLoughlin / T.C. Bundy	D. Greene / M.K. Browne
1913	M.E.McLoughlin (US)	M.K. Browne (US)	M.E. McLoughlin / T.C. Bundy	M.K. Browne / L. Williams
1914	R.N. Williams (US)	M.K. Browne (US)	M.E. McLoughlin / T.C. Bundy	M.K. Browne / L. Williams
1915	W.M. Johnston (US)	M. Bjurstedt (Nor)	W.M. Johnston / C.J. Griffin	H.V. Hotchkiss Wightman / Eleanora Sears
1916	R.N. Williams (US)	M. Bjurstedt (Nor)	W.M. Johnston / C.J. Griffin	M. Bjurstedt / Eleanora Sears
1917	R.L. Murray (US)	M. Bjurstedt (Nor)	F.B. Alexander / H.A.Throckmorton	M. Bjurstedt / Eleanora Sears
1918	R.L. Murray (US)	M. Bjurstedt (Nor)	W.T. Tilden / V. Richards	M. Zinderstein / E.E. Goss
1919	W.M. Johnston (US)	H. Hotchkiss Wightman (US)	N.E. Brookes / G.L. Patterson	M. Zinderstein / E.E. Goss
1920	W.T. Tilden (US)	M. Bjurstedt Mallory (US)	W.M. Johnston / C.J. Griffin	M. Zinderstein / E.E. Goss
1921	W.T. Tilden (US)	M. Mallory (US)	W.T. Tilden / V. Richards	M.K. Browne / L. Williams
1922	W.T. Tilden (US)	M. Mallory (US)	W.T. Tilden / V. Richards	M. Zinderstein Jessup / H.N. Wills
1923	W.T. Tilden (US)	H.N. Wills (US)	W.T. Tilden / B.I.C. Norton	K. McKane / P.L. Howkins Covell
1924	W.T. Tilden (US)	H.N. Wills (US)	H.O. Kinsey / R.G. Kinsey	H. Wightman / H.N. Wills
1925	W.T. Tilden (US)	H.N. Wills (US)	R.N. Williams / V. Richards	M.K. Browne / H.N. Wills
1926	R. Lacoste (Fr)	M. Mallory (US)	R.N. Williams / V. Richards	E. Ryan / E.E. Goss
1927	R. Lacoste (Fr)	H.N. Wills (US)	W.T. Tilden / F.T. Hunter	K. McKane Godfree / E.H. Harvey
1928	H. Cochet (Fr)	H.N. Wills (US)	G.M. Lott / J.F. Hennessey	H. Wightman / H.N. Wills
1929	W.T. Tilden (US)	H.N. Wills (US)	G.M. Lott / J.H. Doeg	P. Watson / P. Michel
1930	J.H. Doeg (US)	B. Nuthall (GB)	G.M. Lott / J.H. Doeg	B. Nuthall / S. Palfrey
1931	H.E. Vines (US)	H.N. Wills Moody (US)	W.L. Allison / J. Van Ryn	B. Nuthall / E. Bennett Whittingstall

S P O R T & L E I S U R E

	Men	Women	Men's Doubles	Women's Doubles
1932	H.E. Vines (US)	H.H. Jacobs (US)	H.E. Vines / K. Gledhill	H.H. Jacobs / S. Palfrey
1933	F.J. Perry (GB)	H.H. Jacobs (US)	G.M. Lott / L.R. Stoefen	B. Nuthall / F. James
1934	F.J. Perry (GB)	H.H. Jacobs (US)	G.M. Lott / L.R. Stoefen	H.H. Jacobs / S. Palfrey
1935	W.L. Allison (US)	H.H. Jacobs (US)	W.L. Allison / J. Van Ryn	H.H. Jacobs / S. Palfrey Fabyan
1936	F.J. Perry (GB)	A. Marble (US)	J.D. Budge / G. Mako	M. Van Ryn / C.A. Babcock
1937	J.D. Budge (US)	A. Lizana (Chile)	G. Von Cramm / H. Henkel	S. Palfrey Fabyan / A. Marble
1938	J.D. Budge (US)	A. Marble (US)	J.D. Budge / G. Mako	S. Palfrey Fabyan / A. Marble
1939	R.L. Riggs (US)	A. Marble (US)	A.K. Quist / J.E. Bromwich	S. Palfrey Fabyan / A. Marble
1940	W.D. McNeill (US)	A. Marble (US)	J.A. Kramer / F.R. Schroeder	S. Palfrey Fabyan / A. Marble
1941	R.L. Riggs (US)	S. Palfrey Cooke (US)	J.A. Kramer / F.R. Schroeder	S. Palfrey Cooke / M.E. Osborne
1942	F.R. Schroeder (US)	P.M. Betz (US)	G. Mulloy / W.F. Talbert	A.L. Brough / M.E. Osborne
1943	J.R. Hunt (US)	P.M. Betz (US)	J.A. Kramer / F.A. Parker	A.L. Brough / M.E. Osborne
1944	F.A. Parker (US)	P.M. Betz (US)	W.D. McNeill / R. Falkenburg	A.L. Brough / M.E. Osborne
1945	F.A. Parker (US)	S. Palfrey Cooke (US)	G. Mulloy / W.F. Talbert	A.L. Brough / M.E. Osborne
1946	J.A. Kramer (US)	P.M. Betz (US)	G. Mulloy / W.F. Talbert	A.L. Brough / M.E. Osborne
1947	J.A. Kramer (US)	A.L. Brough (US)	J.A. Kramer / F.R. Schroeder	A.L. Brough / M.E. Osborne
1948	R.A. Gonzales (US)	M.E. Osborne du Pont (US)	G. Mulloy / W.F. Talbert	A.L. Brough / M.E. Osborne du Pont
1949	R.A. Gonzales (US)	M.E. du Pont (US)	J. Bromwich / O.W. Sidwell	A.L. Brough / M.E. du Pont
1950	A. Larsen (US)	M.E. du Pont (US)	J. Bromwich / F.A. Sedgeman	A.L. Brough / M.E. du Pont
1951	F.A. Sedgeman (Aus)	M. Connolly (US)	K.B. McGregor / F.A. Sedgeman	D.J. Hart / S.J. Fry
1952	F.A. Sedgeman (Aus)	M. Connolly (US)	M.G. Rose / E.V. Seixas	D.J. Hart / S.J. Fry
1953	M.A. Trabert (US)	M. Connolly (US)	R.N. Hartwig / M.G. Rose	D.J. Hart / S.J. Fry
1954	E.V. Seixas (US)	D.J. Hart (US)	E.V. Seixas / M.A. Trabert	D.J. Hart / S.J. Fry
1955	M.A. Trabert (US)	D.J. Hart (US)	K. Kamo / A. Miyagi	A.L. Brough / M.E. du Pont
1956	K.R. Rosewall (Aus)	S.J. Fry (US)	L.A. Hoad / K.R. Rosewall	A.L. Brough / M.E. du Pont
1957	M.J. Anderson (Aus)	A. Gibson (US)	A.J. Cooper / N.A. Fraser	A.L. Brough / M.E. du Pont
1958	A.J. Cooper (Aus)	A. Gibson (US)	A. Olmedo / H. Richardson	J.M. Arth / D.R. Hard
1959	N.A. Fraser (Aus)	M.E. Bueno (Braz)	N.A. Fraser / R.S. Emerson	J.M. Arth / D.R. Hard
1960	N.A. Fraser (Aus)	D.R. Hard (US)	N.A. Fraser / R.S. Emerson	M.E. Bueno / D.R. Hard
1961	R.S. Emerson (Aus)	D.R. Hard (US)	C. McKinley / R.D. Ralston	D.R. Hard / L. Turner
1962	R.G. Laver (Aus)	M. Smith (Aus)	R.H. Osuna / A. Palafox	M.E. Bueno / D.R. Hard
1963	R.H. Osuna (Mex)	M.E. Bueno (Braz)	C. McKinley / R.D. Ralston	R. Ebbern / M. Smith
1964	R.S. Emerson (Aus)	M.E. Bueno (Braz)	C. McKinley / R.D. Ralston	B.J. Moffitt / K. Hantze Susman
1965	M. Santana (Spa)	M. Smith (Aus)	R.S. Emerson / F.S. Stolle	C.A. Graebner / N. Richey
1966	F.S. Stolle (Aus)	M.E. Bueno (Braz)	R.S. Emerson / F.S. Stolle	M.E. Bueno / N. Richey
1967	J.D. Newcombe (Aus)	B.J. Moffitt King (US)	J.D. Newcombe / A.D. Roche	R. Casals / B.J. Moffitt King
1968	A.R. Ashe (US)	S.V. Wade / B.M. Smith Court (Aus)	R.C. Lutz / S.R. Smith	M.E. Bueno / B.M. Smith Court
1969	R.G. Laver (Aus) / S.R. Smith (US)	B.M. Court (Aus)	K.R. Rosewall / F.S. Stolle D. Crealy / A. Stone	F. Durr / D.R. Hard B.M. Court / S.V. Wade
1970	K.R. Rosewall (Aus)	B.M. Court (Aus)	P. Barthes / N. Pilic	B.M. Court / J.A.M. Dalton
1971	S.R. Smith (US)	B.J. King (US)	J.D. Newcombe / R. Taylor	R. Casals / J.A.M. Dalton
1972	I. Nastase (Rom)	B.J. King (US)	C.E. Drysdale / R. Taylor	F. Durr / B. Stove
1973	J.D. Newcombe (Aus)	B.M. Court (Aus)	O.K. Davidson / J.D. Newcombe	B.M. Court / S.V. Wade
1974	J.S. Connors (US)	B.J. King (US)	R.C. Lutz / S.R. Smith	R. Casals / B.J. King
1975	M. Orantes (Spa)	C.M. Evert (US)	J.S. Connors / I. Nastase	B.M. Court / S.V. Wade
1976	J.S. Connors (US)	C.M. Evert (US)	T.S. Okker / M.C. Riessen	L. Boshoff / I. Kloss
1977	G. Vilas (Arg)	C.M. Evert (US)	R.A.J. Hewitt / F.D. McMillan	M. Navratilova / B. Stove

	Men	Women	Men's Doubles	Women's Doubles
1978	J.S. Connors (US)	C.M. Evert (US)	R.C. Lutz / S.R. Smith	B.J. King / M. Navratilova
1979	J.P. McEnroe (US)	T.A. Austin (US)	J.P. McEnroe / P. Fleming	W.M. Turnbull / B. Stove
1980	J.P. McEnroe (US)	C.M. Evert Lloyd (US)	R.C. Lutz / S.R. Smith	B.J. King / M. Navratilova
1981	J.P. McEnroe (US)	T.A. Austin (US)	J.P. McEnroe / P. Fleming	K. Jordan / A. Smith
1982	J.S. Connors (US)	C.M. Evert Lloyd (US)	K. Curren / S. Denton	R. Casals / W.M. Turnbull
1983	J.S. Connors (US)	M. Navratilova (US)	J.P. McEnroe / P. Fleming	M. Navratilova / P.H. Shriver
1984	J.P. McEnroe (US)	M. Navratilova (US)	J.B. Fitzgerald / T. Smid	M. Navratilova / P.H. Shriver
1985	I. Lendl (Cze)	H. Mandlikova (Cze)	K. Flach / R. Seguso	C. Kohde-Kilsch/ H. Sukova
1986	I. Lendl (Cze)	M. Navratilova (US)	A. Gomez / S. Zivojinovic	M. Navratilova / P.H. Shriver
1987	I. Lendl (Cze)	M. Navratilova (US)	S. Edberg / A. Jarryd	M. Navratilova / P.H. Shriver
1988	M. Wilander (Swe)	S. Graf (Ger)	S. Casal / E. Sanchez	G. Fernandez / R. White
1989	B. Becker (Ger)	S. Graf (Ger)	J.P. McEnroe / M. Woodforde	H. Mandlikova / M. Navratilova
1990	P. Sampras (US)	G. Sabatini (Arg)	P. Aldrich / D. Visser	G. Fernandez / M. Navratilova
1991	S. Edberg (Swe)	M. Seles (Yug)	J.B. Fitzgerald / A. Jarryd	P.H. Shriver / N. Zvereva
1992	S. Edberg (Swe)	M. Seles (Yug)	J. Grabb / R. Reneberg	G. Fernandez / N. Zvereva
1993	P. Sampras (US)	S. Graf (Ger)	K. Flach / R. Leach	A. Sanchez-Vicario / H. Sukova
1994	A. Agassi (US)	A. Sanchez-Vicario (Spa)	J. Eltingh / P. Haarhuis	J. Novotna / A. Sanchez-Vicario
1995	P. Sampras (US)	S. Graf (Ger)	T. Woodbridge / M. Woodforde	G. Fernandez / N. Zvereva
1996	P. Sampras (US)	S. Graf (Ger)	T. Woodbridge / M. Woodforde	G. Fernandez / N. Zvereva
1997	P. Rafter (Aus)	M. Hingis (Swi)	Y. Kafelnikov / D. Vacek	J. Novotna / L. Davenport
1998	P. Rafter (Aus)	L. Davenport (US)	S. Stolle / C. Suk	M. Hingis / J. Novotna
1999	A. Agassi (US)	S. Williams (US)	S. Lateau / A. O'Brien	S. Williams / V. Williams
2000	M. Safin (Rus)	V. Williams (US)	L. Hewitt / M. Mirnyi	A. Sugiyama / J. Halard-Decugis

Tennis: Australian Open

	Men	Women		Men	Women
1905	R.W. Heath (Aus)	—	1935	J.H. Crawford (Aus)	D.E. Round (GB)
1906	A.F. Wilding (NZ)	—	1936	A.K. Quist (Aus)	J. Hartigan (Aus)
1907	H.M. Rice (Aus)	—	1937	V.B. McGrath (Aus)	N.M. Wynne (Aus)
1908	F.B.. Alexander (US)	—	1938	J.D. Budge (US)	D.M. Bundy (US)
1909	A.F. Wilding (NZ)	—	1939	J.E. Bromwich (US)	E. Westacott (Aus)
1910	R.W. Heath (Aus)	—	1940	A.K. Quist (Aus)	N.M. Wynne Bolton (Aus)
1911	N.E. Brookes (Aus)	—			
1912	J.C. Parke (GB)	—	1941	not held	not held
1913	E.F. Parker (Aus)	—	1942	not held	not held
1914	A. O'Hara Wood (Aus)	—	1943	not held	not held
1915	F.G. Lowe (GB)	—	1944	not held	not held
1916	not held	—	1945	not held	not held
1917	not held	—	1946	J.E. Bromwich (US)	N.M. Bolton (Aus)
1918	not held	—	1947	D. Pails (Aus)	N.M. Bolton (Aus)
1919	A.R.F. Kingscote (GB)	—	1948	A.K. Quist (Aus)	N.M. Bolton (Aus)
1920	P. O'Hara Wood (Aus)	—	1949	F.A. Sedgman (Aus)	D.J. Hart (US)
1921	R.H. Gemmell (Aus)	—	1950	F.A. Sedgman (Aus)	L.A. Brough (US)
1922	J.O. Anderson (Aus)	M. Molesworth (Aus)	1951	R. Savitt (US)	N.M. Bolton (Aus)
			1952	K.B. McGregor (Aus)	T. Long (Aus)
1923	P. O'Hara Wood (Aus)	M. Molesworth (Aus)	1953	K.R. Rosewall (Aus)	M. Connolly (US)
			1954	M.G. Rose (Aus)	T. Long (Aus)
1924	J.O. Anderson (Aus)	S. Lance (Aus)	1955	K.R. Rosewall (Aus)	B. Penrose (Aus)
1925	J.O. Anderson (Aus)	D.S. Akhurst (Aus)	1956	L.G. Hoad (Aus)	M. Carter (Aus)
1926	J.B. Hawkes (Aus)	D.S. Akhurst (Aus)	1957	A.J. Cooper (Aus)	S.J. Fry (US)
1927	G.L. Patterson (Aus)	E.F. Boyd (Aus)	1958	A.J. Cooper (Aus)	A. Mortimer (GB)
1928	J. Borotra (Fr)	D.S. Akhurst (Aus)	1959	A. Olmedo (Per)	M. Carter Reitano (Aus)
1929	J.C. Gregory (GB)	D.S. Akhurst (Aus)			
1930	E.F. Moon (Aus)	D.S. Akhurst (Aus)	1960	R.G. Laver (Aus)	M. Smith (Aus)
1931	J.H. Crawford (Aus)	C. Buttsworth (Aus)	1961	R.S. Emerson (Aus)	M. Smith (Aus)
1932	J.H. Crawford (Aus)	C. Buttsworth (Aus)	1962	R.G. Laver (Aus)	M. Smith (Aus)
1933	J.H. Crawford (Aus)	J. Hartigan (Aus)	1963	R.S. Emerson (Aus)	M. Smith (Aus)
1934	F.J.Perry (GB)	J. Hartigan (Aus)	1964	R.S. Emerson (Aus)	M. Smith (Aus)

SPORT & LEISURE

	Men	Women		Men	Women
1965	R.S. Emerson (Aus)	M. Smith (Aus)			(US)
1966	R.S. Emerson (Aus)	M. Smith (Aus)	1983	M. Wilander (Swe)	M. Navratilova (US)
1967	R.S. Emerson (Aus)	N. Richey (US)	1984	M. Wilander (Swe)	C.M. Evert Lloyd
1968	W.W. Bowrey (Aus)	B.J. Moffitt King			(US)
		(US)	1985	S. Edberg (Swe)	M. Navratilova (US)
1969	R.G. Laver (Aus)	M. Smith Court	1986	not held	not held
		(Aus)	1987	S. Edberg (Swe)	H. Mandlikova (Cze)
1970	A.R. Ashe (US)	M. Court (Aus)	1988	M. Wilander (Swe)	S. Graf (Ger)
1971	K.R. Rosewall (Aus)	M. Court (Aus)	1989	I. Lendl (Cze)	S. Graf (Ger)
1972	K.R. Rosewall (Aus)	V.S. Wade (GB)	1990	I. Lendl (Cze)	S. Graf (Ger)
1973	J.D. Newcombe (Aus)	M. Court (Aus)	1991	B. Becker (Ger)	M. Seles (Yug)
1974	J.S. Connors (US)	E. Goolagong (Aus)	1992	J. Courier (US)	M. Seles (Yug)
1975	J.D. Newcombe (Aus)	E. Goolagong (Aus)	1993	J. Courier (US)	M. Seles (Yug)
1976	M. Edmondson (Aus)	E. Goolagong	1994	P. Sampras (US)	S. Graf (Ger)
		Cawley (Aus)	1995	A. Agassi (US)	M. Pierce (Fra)
1977 (Jan)	R. Tanner (US)	K. Reid (Aus)	1996	B. Becker (Ger)	M. Seles (US)
1977 (Dec)	V. Gerulaitas (US)	E. Cawley (Aus)	1997	P. Sampras (US)	M. Hingis (Swi)
1978	G. Vilas (Arg)	C. O'Neill (Aus)	1998	P. Korda (Cze)	M. Hingis (Swi)
1979	G. Vilas (Arg)	B. Jordan (US)	1999	Y. Kafelnikov (Rus)	M. Hingis (Swi)
1980	B. Teacher (US)	H. Mandlikova (Cze)	2000	A. Agassi (US)	L. Davenport (US)
1981	J. Kriek (SA)	M. Navratilova (US)	2001	A. Agassi (US)	J. Capriati (US)
1982	J. Kriek (SA)	C.M. Evert Lloyd			

Tennis: French Open

	Men	Women		Men	Women
1891	H. Briggs	—	1932	H. Cochet (Fr)	H.N. Wills (US)
1892	J. Schopfer (Fr)	—	1933	J.H. Crawford (Aus)	M.C. Scriven (GB)
1893	L. Riboulet (Fr)	—	1934	G. von Cramm (Ger)	M.C. Scriven (GB)
1894	A. Vacherot (Fr)	—	1935	F.J. Perry (GB)	H. Sperling (Den)
1895	A. Vacherot (Fr)	—	1936	G. von Cramm (Ger)	H. Sperling (Den)
1896	A. Vacherot (Fr)	—	1937	H. Henkel (Ger)	H. Sperling (Den)
1897	P. Aymé (Fr)	C. Masson (Fr)	1938	J.D. Budge (US)	S. Mathieu (Fr)
1898	P. Aymé (Fr)	C. Masson (Fr)	1939	W.D. McNeill (US)	S. Mathieu (Fr)
1899	P. Aymé (Fr)	C. Masson (Fr)	1940	not held	not held
1900	P. Aymé (Fr)	Y. Prévost (Fr)	1941	not held	not held
1901	A. Vacherot (Fr)	P. Girod (Fr)	1942	not held	not held
1902	A. Vacherot (Fr)	C. Masson (Fr)	1943	not held	not held
1903	M. Decugis (Fr)	C. Masson (Fr)	1944	not held	not held
1904	M. Decugis (Fr)	K. Gillou (Fr)	1945	not held	not held
1905	M. Germot (Fr)	K. Gillou (Fr)	1946	M. Bernard (Fr)	M.E. Osborne (US)
1906	M. Germot (Fr)	K. Fenwick	1947	J. Asboth (Hung)	P. Todd (US)
1907	M. Decugis (Fr)	M. de Kermel (Fr)	1948	F.A. Parker (US)	N. Landry (Belg)
1908	M. Decugis (Fr)	K. Fenwick	1949	F.A. Parker (US)	M.E. Osborne du
1909	M. Decugis (Fr)	J. Mattey (Fr)			Pont (US)
1910	M. Germot (Fr)	J. Mattey (Fr)	1950	J.E. Patty (US)	D.J. Hart (US)
1911	A.H. Gobert (Fr)	J. Mattey (Fr)	1951	J. Drobny (Cze)	S.J. Fry (US)
1912	M. Decugis (Fr)	J. Mattey (Fr)	1952	J. Drobny (Cze)	D.J. Hart (US)
1913	M. Decugis (Fr)	M. Broquedis (Fr)	1953	K.R. Rosewall (Aus)	M. Connolly (US)
1914	M. Decugis (Fr)	M. Broquedis (Fr)	1955	M.A. Trabert (US)	M. Connolly (US)
1915	not held	not held	1955	M.A. Trabert (US)	A. Mortimer (GB)
1916	not held	not held	1956	L.A. Hoad (Aus)	A. Gibson (US)
1917	not held	not held	1957	S. Davidson (Swe)	S.J. Bloomer (GB)
1918	not held	not held	1958	M. Rose (Aus)	S. Kormoczy
1919	not held	not held			(Hung)
1920	A.H. Gobert (Fr)	S. Lenglen (Fr)	1959	N. Pietrangeli (Ita)	C.C. Truman (GB)
1921	J. Samazeuilh (Fr)	S. Lenglen (Fr)	1960	N. Pietrangeli (Ita)	D.R. Hard (US)
1922	H. Cochet (Fr)	S. Lenglen (Fr)	1961	M. Santana (Spa)	A.S. Haydon (GB)
1923	P. Blanchy (Fr)	S. Lenglen (Fr)	1962	R.G. Laver (Aus)	M. Smith (Aus)
1924	J. Borotra (Fr)	D. Vlasto (Fr)	1963	R.S. Emerson (Aus)	L.R. Turner (Aus)
1925	R. Lacoste (Fr)	S. Lenglen (Fr)	1964	M. Santana (Spa)	M. Smith (Aus)
1926	H. Cochet (Fr)	S. Lenglen (Fr)	1965	F.S. Stolle (Aus)	L.R. Turner (Aus)
1927	R. Lacoste (Fr)	K. Bouman (Ned)	1966	A.D. Roche (Aus)	A.S. Haydon Jones
1928	H. Cochet (Fr)	H.N. Wills (US)			(GB)
1929	R. Lacoste (Fr)	H.N. Wills (US)	1967	R.S. Emerson (Aus)	F. Durr (Fr)
1930	H. Cochet (Fr)	H.N. Wills Moody	1968	K.R. Rosewall (Aus)	N. Richey (US)
		(US)	1969	R.G. Laver (Aus)	M. Smith Court (Aus)
1931	J. Borotra (Fr)	C. Aussem (Ger)	1970	J. Kodes (Cze)	M. Court (Aus)

Men		Women	
1971	J. Kodes (Cze)	E. Goolagong (Aus)	
1972	A. Gimeno (Spa)	B.J. Moffitt King (US)	
1973	I. Nastase (Rom)	M. Court (Aus)	
1974	B. Borg (Swed)	C.M. Evert (US)	
1975	B. Borg (Swed)	C.M. Evert (US)	
1976	A. Panatta (Ita)	S. Barker (GB)	
1977	G. Vilas (Arg)	M. Jausovec (Yug)	
1978	B. Borg (Swed)	V. Ruzici (Rom)	
1979	B. Borg (Swed)	C.M. Evert Lloyd (US)	
1980	B. Borg (Swed)	C.M. Evert Lloyd (US)	
1981	B. Borg (Swed)	H. Mandlikova (Cze)	
1982	M. Wilander (Swe)	M. Navratilova (US)	
1983	Y. Noah (Fr)	C.M. Evert Lloyd (US)	
1984	I. Lendl (Cze)	M. Navratilova (US)	
1985	M. Wilander (Swe)	C.M. Evert Lloyd (US)	
1986	I. Lendl (Cze)	C.M. Evert Lloyd (US)	
1987	I. Lendl (Cze)	S. Graf (Ger)	
1988	M. Wilander (Swe)	S. Graf (Ger)	

Men		Women	
1989	M. Chang (US)	A. Sanchez-Vicario (Spa)	
1990	A. Gomez (Ecu)	M. Seles (Yug)	
1991	J. Courier (US)	M. Seles (Yug)	
1992	J. Courier (US)	M. Seles (Yug)	
1993	S. Bruguera (Spa)	S. Graf (Ger)	
1994	S. Bruguera (Spa)	A. Sanchez-Vicario (Spa)	
1995	T. Muster (Aut)	S. Graf (Ger)	
1996	Y. Kafelnikov (Rus)	S. Graf (Ger)	
1997	G. Kuerten (Braz)	I. Majoli (Croat)	
1998	C. Moya (Spa)	A. Sanchez-Vicario (Spa)	
1999	A. Agassi (US)	S. Graf (Ger)	
2000	G. Kuerten (Braz)	M. Pierce (Fra)	
2001	G. Kuerten (Braz)	J. Capriati (US)	

Tennis: General Information

Australian Open: venue	Flinders Park, Melbourne, since 1988.
Davis Cup: inaugurated	1900.
most wins	USA.
official title	The International Men's Team Championship of the World.
Federation Cup	women's equivalent of the Davis Cup. Inaugurated in 1963. The United States defeated Australia 2–1 in the first final.
'Four Musketeers'	Jean Borotra, Jacques ('Toto') Brugnon, Henri Cochet, René Lacoste.
French Championships: made Open	before 1925 the French Championships were open only to members of French clubs.
French Open: venue	Roland Garros Stadium, Paris, since 1928.
Grand Slam: definition	winning the four major titles consecutively irrespective of calendar year (formerly had to be achieved in the calendar year).
holders	Donald Budge, Maureen Connolly, Margaret Court, Steffi Graf, Rod Laver (twice) and Martina Navratilova.
junior winner	Earl Buchholz won all four junior titles in 1958 followed by Stefan Edberg in 1983.
Hopman Cup	international mixed teams event first held between 28 December 1988 and 1 January 1989, Czechoslovakia beating Australia in the first championship.
net: height in middle	3 feet (91cm).
nicknames: Bounding Basque	Jean Borotra.
Poker Face	Helen Wills Moody.
Rocket	Rod Laver.
The Ghost	Harold Mahony.
The Two Helens	Helen Wills Moody and Helen Jacobs (great rivals and born on the same street in Berkeley, California).
Olympic champions: 1996	Lindsay Davenport (US) and Andre Agassi (US).
Olympic Games: ice hockey player	Jaroslav Drobny (Cze, 1948).
tennis challenge: battle of the sexes	Bobby Riggs had beaten Margaret Court but was then beaten by Billie Jean King (and famously presented with a pig).
tennis: original name	sphairistiké.
'Three Musketeers'	Jean Borotra, Henri Cochet, René Lacoste.
US Open: venue	Flushing Meadows, New York, since 1978.
Wimbledon champion: 1st black man	Arthur Ashe (1975).
1st black person	Althea Gibson (1957).
Mixed Doubles: brother and sister	John and Tracy Austin won the 1981 Championship.
man and wife	Mr and Mrs L.A. Godfree won the 1926 Championship.
boycott year	1973 (due to suspension of Nikki Pilic of Yugoslavia).
champion at first and only attempt	Bobby Riggs (1939) won all three titles on his only appearance at the Championships.
first professional champion	Rod Laver (1968).
last amateur champion	John Newcombe (1967).
longest match	5 hours 12 minutes: Pancho Gonzales beat Charlie Pasarell (22–24, 1–6, 16–14, 6–3, 11–9) in 1969 (this match hastened the need for the tie-break system).
oldest men's champion	Arthur Gore (41).

S P O R T & L E I S U R E

champion later represented Brazil in Davis Cup	Robert Falkenburg.	
unseeded champion	Boris Becker (1985).	
unseeded player in two finals	Kurt Nielsen (Den) beaten in 1953 and 1955.	
youngest champion	Lottie Dod (GB) aged 15.	
youngest men's champion	Boris Becker (Ger) aged 17.	

Sporting Trophies

Name	Sport	Details	First held
Admirals Cup	yachting	biennial international competition for sailing yachts	1957
Air Canada Silver Broom	curling	formerly the Scotch Whisky Cup, became Air Canada in 1959	1968
America's Cup	yachting	originally called 100 Guineas Cup and raced around the Isle of Wight	1851
Ashes	cricket	England v Australia test matches (since 1882 called 'Ashes')	1877
Baron Matsui Inter-Club Cup	judo	club competition named after the Japanese Ambassador	1928
Beefeater's Gin	rowing	Oxford and Cambridge Boat Race	1829
Bledisloe Cup	rugby union	New Zealand v Australia	1931
Bologna Trophy	swimming	England v Scotland v Wales speed swimming contest	1929
Borg-Warner Trophy	motor racing	winner of the Indianapolis 500	1932
Bowring Bowl	rugby union	annual Oxbridge Varsity match	1872
Britannia Cup	yachting	for small yachts (under 32ft) of any country to challenge the holder	1951
Britannia Shield	speedway	inter-club challenge competition	1957
Calcutta Cup	rugby union	England v Scotland	1870
Camanachd Cup	shinty	championship of Scotland	1896
Canada Cup	golf	world team championship (two per team)	1953
Cole Cup	fencing	men's sabre	1922
Cowdray Park Gold Cup	polo	international competition	1956
Currie Cup	cricket	South African Provincial competition	1889
Currie Cup	rugby union	South African Provincial Championship	1892
Curtis Cup	golf	amateur women – USA v Great Britain and Ireland	1932
Davis Cup	tennis	The International Lawn Tennis Challenge Trophy	1900
Dewar Cup	rifle shooting	small-bore shooting competition	1909
Diamond Challenge	rowing	blue riband of single sculling	1884
Doggetts Coat & Badge	rowing	sculling contest on the Thames between ex-passenger skiffs	1715
Eisenhower Trophy	golf	biennial international competition	1958
Federation Cup	tennis	women's world amateur team championship	1963
George Hearn Cup	diving	awarded to England's most successful diver	1954
Goldberg-Vass Memorial Trophy	judo	London open competition	1956
Gordon Bennett Trophy	motor racing	forerunner of the Grand Prix	1901
Grand Challenge Cup	rowing	Henley Regatta – eights	1839
Grey Cup	Canadian football	championship game between winners of Eastern and Western Conferences	1909
G. Melville Clark Trophy	diving	awarded to England's most successful diving club	1951
Harry Sunderland Trophy	rugby league	man of the Premiership final. T. Fogarty of Halifax first winner	1965
Heisman Memorial Trophy	American football	awarded annually by the Downtown Athlete Club of New York City to the outstanding college football player of the United States	1935
Henry Benjamin Trophy	swimming and water polo	awarded to England's most successful swimming and water polo club	1910
Iroquois Cup	lacrosse	English club championship	1890
Jules Rimet Trophy	football	world cup	1930
King George V Gold Cup	showjumping	men's international competition at Hickstead	1934
Name	Sport	Details	First held
Kinnaird Cup	Eton fives	public schools' competition	1926
Lance Todd Award	rugby league	man of the match award in Challenge Cup final	1897
Lapham Trophy	squash	Canada v USA	1921
Londonderry Cup	squash	public schools' Old Boys' competition	1934
Lonsdale Belt	boxing	British title – won outright for winning three title fights at the same weight	1909

Lugano Trophy	walking	world championship of race walking	1961
MacRobertson International Shield	croquet	international competition	1925
Manuel Avilla Camacho Cup	polo	Mexico v USA	1941
Marcel Corbillon Cup	table tennis	women's world table tennis team championships	1934
Marchant Cup	rugby fives	London grammar schools competition	1929
Middleton Cup	bowls	inter-county championship	1911
Philadelphia Gold Cup	rowing	Olympic single sculling trophy	1908
Pilkington Cup	rugby union	English club knockout cup (prev. National Cup)	1972
Presidents Trophy	golf	USA v Rest of World (Men)	1994
Prince of Wales Cup	yachting	international 14 ft dinghy championship	1927
Prince Rainier Cup	fencing	awarded tothe nation with best results in World Championships	1950
Princess Elizabeth Cup	rowing	Henley Regatta – eights for public schools	1946
Queen Elizabeth II Cup	showjumping	women's international competition at Hickstead	1949
Queen's Prize	rifle shooting	open competition first competed for at Wimbledon	1860
Ranfurly Shield	rugby union	NZ rugby trophy for provincial teams	1902
Regal Trophy	rugby league	formerly sponsored by John Player, became Regal Trophy in 1989	1971
Ryder Cup	golf	men – USA v Europe (USA v GB and I before 1979)	1927
Scottish Tennant's Cup	rugby union	Scottish club knockout cup	1996
Seawanhaka Cup	yachting	For small yachts (under 25ft) of any country to challenge the holder	1895
Silver Goblets & Nickalls Cup	rowing	Henley Regatta: coxless pairs amateur international	1845
Sir William Burton Trophy	yachting	national 12 ft dinghy championship	1936
Solheim Cup	golf	women – USA v Europe	1990
Stanley Cup	ice hockey	North American ice hockey championship	1894
Strathcona Cup	curling	Canada v Scotland international competition	1903
Subalterns' Cup	polo	inter-services competition	1896
Super 12 Trophy	rugby union	Southern Hemisphere provincial championship	1995
SWALEC Cup	rugby union	Welsh club knockout cup (prev. Welsh Cup, Schweppes Cup)	1972
Swaythling Cup	table tennis	men's world table tennis team championships	1927
Talbot Handicap	crown green bowls	Blackpool-based open competition	1882
Thomas Cup	badminton	men's world badminton team championship	1949
Über Cup	badminton	women's world badminton team championships	1957
Val Barker Trophy	boxing	most stylish boxer at an Olympic Games	1904
Vince Lombardi Trophy	American football	superbowl	1967
Volvo World Cup	showjumping	world championship competition	1979
Walker Cup	golf	amateur men – USA v Great Britain and Ireland	1922
Waterloo Cup	coursing	the 'Derby' of coursing, named after a Liverpool hotel	1836
Waterloo Cup	crown green bowls	Blackpool-based open competition	1907
Webb Ellis Trophy	rugby union	world cup	1987
Westchester Cup	polo	Great Britain v USA	1886
Wheeler-Schebber	motor racing	awarded to the leader of the Indianapolis 500 after 400 miles (160 laps), replaced in 1932 by the Borg-Warner Trophy	
Wightman Cup	tennis	annual team competition between USA and England	1923
Wolfe-Noel Cup	squash	USA v GB women's match	1933
Worrell Trophy	cricket	West Indies v Australia	1931
Wyfold Challenge Cup	rowing	Henley Regatta	1847
Yeaden Memorial Trophy	swimming	awarded to the English swimmer whose performance is adjudged the best	1938

NB The inaugural dates given are for the competition; in some cases the trophy has been renamed.

S
P
O
R
T
&
L
E
I
S
U
R
E

Sporting Trophies: Supplements

Britannia Cup	rowing	James Norris Trophy	ice hockey
Camrose Trophy	yachting	Leekes British Open	squash
Corble Cup	fencing	Leonard Trophy	bowls
Courtney Trophy	rugby League	Little Brown Jug	harness racing
Eden Cup	fencing	Melrose Trophy	rugby union
Espirito Santo Trophy	golf	Peall Trophy	car rallying
Gordon Bennett Cup	ballooning	Prince Philip Cup	rowing
Halford Hewitt Cup	golf	Prince Philip Trophy	showjumping
Hambleton	harness racing	Russell-Cargill Trophy	rugby union
Harmsworth Trophy	powerboat racing	Sam McGuire Trophy	Gaelic football
Hummel Super Cup	handball	Sheffield Shield	cricket
Hummel Super League	handball	Stewards Cup	rowing
Hurlingham Champion Cup	polo	Veuve Cliquot Gold Cup	polo
Ipswich Cup	fencing	Yetton Trophy	bowls

Television Sports Personality of the Year

Chris Chataway	1954	Steve Ovett	1978
Gordon Pirie	1955	Sebastian Coe	1979
Jim Laker	1956	Robin Cousins	1980
Dai Rees	1957	Ian Botham	1981
Ian Black	1958	Daley Thompson	1982
John Surtees	1959	Steve Cram	1983
David Broome	1960	Torvill and Dean	1984
Stirling Moss	1961	Barry McGuigan	1985
Anita Lonsbrough	1962	Nigel Mansell	1986
Dorothy Hyman	1963	Fatima Whitbread	1987
Mary Rand	1964	Steve Davis	1988
Tommy Simpson	1965	Nick Faldo	1989
Bobby Moore	1966	Paul Gascoigne	1990
Henry Cooper	1967	Liz McColgan	1991
David Hemery	1968	Nigel Mansell	1992
Ann Jones	1969	Linford Christie	1993
Henry Cooper	1970	Damon Hill	1994
HRH Princess Anne	1971	Jonathan Edwards	1995
Mary Peters	1972	Damon Hill	1996
Jackie Stewart	1973	Greg Rusedski	1997
Brendan Foster	1974	Michael Owen	1998
David Steele	1975	Lennox Lewis	1999
John Curry	1976	Steve Redgrave	2000
Virginia Wade	1977		

Commonwealth Games: Venues

Hamilton, Canada	1930	Christchurch, NZ	1974
London, England	1934	Edmonton, Canada	1978
Sydney, Australia	1938	Brisbane, Australia	1982
Auckland, NZ	1950	Edinburgh, Scotland	1986
Vancouver, Canada	1954	Auckland, NZ	1990
Cardiff, Wales	1958	Victoria, Canada	1994
Perth, Australia	1962	Kuala Lumpur, Malaysia	1998
Kingston, Jamaica	1966	Manchester, England	2002
Edinburgh, Scotland	1970		

Number of Players in a Team

		Details
polo	4	Up to 8 chukkas of $7^{1}/_{2}$ min
basketball	5	4 periods
ice hockey	6	3 periods of 20 min
volleyball	6	Court size: 30ft x 60ft
netball	7	4 periods of 15 min

water polo	7	blue or white caps (red for goalkeepers)
baseball	9	9 innings
		Details
rounders	9	2 innings
American football	11	1 hour
football	11	2 halves of 45 min
cricket	11	see relevant section
hockey	11	field size: 100 yd x 60 yd (goal 4 yd x 7 ft high)
		men's, 2 halves of 35 min; women's, 2 of 30 min
stoolball	11	girls' game resembling cricket
lacrosse (men's)	10	4 periods of 15 min
lacrosse (women's)	12	4 periods of 15 min
Canadian football	12	field size: 110 yd x 65 yd
shinty	12	field size: 160 yd x 80 yd
rugby league	13	no wing forwards
rugby union	15	2 halves of 40 min
Gaelic football	15	2 periods of 30 min
hurling	15	women's version called 'camogie'
Australian rules	18	4 periods of 25 min

Sportspeople

Ackland, Janet	**bowls**
Adams, Neil	**judo**
Allan, Alister	**shooting**
Alsop, Fred	**triple jump**
Altwegg, Jeannette	**figure skating**
Angus, Howard	**rackets and real tennis**
Aoki, Haruchika (Jpn)	**motor cycling (125cc)**
Appleyard, Bob	**cricket**
Armstrong, Gary	**rugby union**
Ashton, Eric	**rugby league**
Aspinall, Nigel	**croquet**
Astbury, Andrew	**swimming**
Atkins, Geoffrey	**rackets**
Atkins, John	**cyclo cross**
Baddeley, Steve	**badminton**
Baddeley, Wilfred and Herbert	**tennis**
Baerlein, Edgar	**rackets and real tennis**
Bailey, Bill	**cycling**
Bailey, McDonald	**athletics**
Bailey, William James	**cycling**
Baillieu, Chris	**rowing**
Baker, Edwin Percy	**bowls**
Baker, Philip Noel	**athletics (1959 Nobel Peace Prize)**
Bakewell, Enid	**cricket**
Balashov, Alexandr (Rus)	**ice speedway**
Balding, Gerald	**polo**
Balding, Gerald Matthews	**polo**
Ball, John	**golf**
Barber, Paul	**hockey**
Barnato, Woolf	**motor racing**
Barrichello, Rubens (Braz)	**motor racing (Formula 1)**
Barry, Ernest	**rowing**
Barton, Pam	**golf**
Beamish, George	**rugby union**
Beck, Margaret	**badminton**
Bedell-Sivright, Darkie	**rugby union**
Bell, Diane	**judo**
Beresford, Jack	**rowing**
Besford, Jack	**swimming**
Biaggi, Massimiliano (Ita)	**motor cycling (250cc)**
Bickers, Dave	**motocross**
Black, Ian	**swimming**
Blenkinsop, Ernie	**football**
Boocock, Nigel	**speedway**
Boone, Willie	**rackets**

Bourne, Teddy	**fencing**
Bowman, George	**carriage driving**
Bradley, Caroline	**show jumping**
Bradshaw, Harry	**golf**
Braid, James	**golf**
Braithwaite, Bob	**shooting**
Briggs, Johnny	**cricket**
Briggs, Karen	**judo**
Brinkley, Brian	**swimming**
Brittin, Janette	**cricket**
Brockway, John	**swimming**
Bromfield, Percy	**table tennis**
Bullen, Jane	**three-day event**
Butcher, Don	**squash**
Cadalora, Luca (Ita)	**motor cycling (250cc and 125cc)**
Caira, Philip Mario	**weightlifting**
Capirossi, Loris (Ita)	**motor cycling (125cc and 250cc)**
Carnill, Denys	**hockey**
Cazelet, Victor	**squash**
Chapman, Vera	**hockey**
Cheape, Leslie	**polo**
Cheeseborough, Susan	**gymnastics**
Chester, Frank	**cricket**
Chifney, Sam	**horse racing**
Childs, Joe	**horse racing**
Clark, Gillian	**badminton**
Clark, Roger	**rallying**
Cobb, John	**motor racing**
Cockett, John	**hockey**
Colclough, Maurice	**rugby union**
Colledge, Cecilia	**figure skating**
Collins, Peter (1931–58)	**motor racing**
Collins, Peter (1954–)	**speedway**
Cooper, Charlotte	**tennis**
Cooper, Malcolm	**shooting**
Cotter, Edmond	**croquet**
Covey, Fred	**real tennis**
Craven, Peter	**speedway**
Creus, Julian	**weightlifting**
Cripps, Norwood	**rackets and real tennis**
Cronshey, John Dennis	**speed skating**
Crooks, Lee	**rugby league**
Crooks, Tim	**rowing**
Cumming, Arthur	**figure skating**
Curry, Joan	**squash and tennis**

Cutler, David	bowls
Daly, Fred	golf
Davidge, Chris	rowing
Davies, Terry	rugby union
Davis, Howard	hockey
Dawes, Alison	show jumping
De Beaumont, Charles	fencing
De Wharton Burr, Nilla	archery
Dear, Jim	rackets, real tennis, squash
Dempsey, Jack 'Nonpareil'	boxing
Denny, Doreen	ice dancing
Disley, John	steeplechaser
Dixon, Charles	tennis
Dixon, Karen	three-day event
Dixon, Robin	bobsleigh
Dod, Willie	archery
Doherty, Reggie	tennis
Donaldson, Walter	snooker
Doohan, Michael (Aus)	motor cycling (500cc)
Doyle, Tony	cycling
Driffield, Leslie	billiards
Drummond, Des	rugby league
Drummond-Hay, Anneli	show jumping
Duke, Geoff	motor cycling (500cc)
Dugard, Martin	speedway
Edwards, Hugh 'Jumbo'	rowing
Edwards, Margaret	swimming
Egan, Joe	rugby league
Elford, Vic	motor racing
Ellaby, Alf	rugby league
Elliot, Douglas	rugby union
Elliot, Helen	table tennis
Elliot, Launceston	weightlifting
Elwell, Keith	rugby league
Erhardt, Carl	ice hockey
Evans, Mal	bowls
Everts, Stefan (Bel)	motocross
Fairbrother, Nicola	judo
Fairs, Punch	real tennis
Farndon, Tom	speedway
Farr, Judy	walking
Ferris, Liz	diving
Ferris, Sam	marathon
Figg, James	boxing
Flockhart, Ron	motor racing
Ford, Bernard	ice dancing
Ford, Horace	archery
Ford, Trevor	football
Fordham, George	football
Foster, Jimmy	ice hockey
Fox, Jim	modern pentathlon
Fox, Neil	rugby league
Fox, Richard	canoeing
Freeman, Alfred 'Tich'	cricket
Frentzen, Heinz-Harold (Ger)	motor racing (Formula 1)
Frith, Frederick	motor cycling
Fulford, Robert	croquet
Fulton, Arthur	shooting
Furrer, Carl	trampolining
Galica, Davina	skiing and motor racing
Gallie, Christine	judo
Gee, Kenneth	rugby league
George, Walter	athletics
Giles, Jack	squash
Glen Haig, Mary	fencing
Gower, Lily	croquet
Grace, Edward Mills	cricket
Green, Tommy	walking
Guthrie, Jimmy	motor cycling

Haining, Peter	rowing
Hale, Jack	swimming
Hall, Darren	badminton
Hallam, Ian	cycling
Hallard, Steve	archery
Halliday, Jim	weightlifting
Hamill, Billy (USA)	speedway
Hancock, Greg (USA)	speedway
Hand, Tony	ice hockey
Harding, Phyllis	swimming
Hardisty, Alan	rugby league
Hardstaff, Joe	cricket
Harper, Ernie	marathon
Harris, Lord George	cricket
Harris, Reg	cycling
Hatfield, Jack	swimming
Hathorn, Gina	skiing
Havelock, Gary	speedway
Hawke, Lord Martin	cricket
Healey, Donald	rallying
Heatley, Basil	marathon
Heatly, Peter	diving
Helme, Gerry	rugby league
Hendren, Patsy	cricket
Herriott, Maurice	steeplechaser
Hicks, Humphrey	croquet
Hide, Molly	cricket
Hill, Albert	athletics
Hiller, Bob	rugby union
Hipwood, Julian	polo
Hocking, Gary (Zim)	motor cycling (500cc)
Hodgson, Neil	superbike racing
Holden, Jack	marathon
Holmes, Andrea	trampolining
Holmes, Terry	rugby union
Horgan, Denis	shot putter
Hoskyns, Bill	fencing
Howland, Bonzo	shot putter
Hume, Donald	badminton
Inman, Melbourne	billiards
Ireland, Innes	motor racing
Ivy, Bill	motor cycling (125cc)
James, Carwyn	rugby union
Jameson, Andrew	swimming
Jameson, Tommy	squash
Jarrett, Keith	rugby union and league
Jarvis, John	swimming
Jay, Allan	fencing
Jeeps, Dickie	rugby union
Johnson, Ralph	fencing
Johnson, Tebbs Lloyd	walking
Jones, Cliff (1914–90)	rugby union
Jones, Cliff (1935–)	football
Jones, Courtney	ice dancing
Jones, Mandy	cycling
Jordan, Tony	badminton
Kane, Peter	boxing
Karalius, Vince	rugby league
Keane, Moss	rugby union
Keenan, Peter	boxing
Kelly, Sean	cycling
Kelly-Hohmann, Margaret	swimming
Kelsey, Jack	football
Kendall-Carpenter, John	rugby union
Kerly, Sean	hockey
Kershaw, Cecil	rugby union
King, Norman	bowls
King, Shayne (NZ)	motocross
Kitchen, Bill	speedway
Knight, Billy	tennis

Kocinski, John (USA)	motor cycling (250cc and superbikes)	Meredith, Leon	cycling
Laidlaw, Roy	rugby union	Miles, Eustace	rackets and real tennis
Langton, Eric	speedway	Milford, David	rackets
Larcombe, Ethel	tennis	Millar, Robert	cycling
Larner, George	walking	Miller, Sammy	motor cycling
Latham, Peter	rackets and real tennis	Millward, Roger	rugby league
		Minter, Derek	motor cycling
Lawler, Ivan	canoeing	Mitchell, Abe	golf
Lawton, Barbara	high jumper	Mitchell, Beryl	rowing
Leather, Diane	athletics	Mitchell, William	billiards
Leden, Judy	hang gliding	Monaghan, Terry	speed skating
Lee, George	gliding	Montgomerie, Robert	fencing
Lee, Michael	speedway	Moore, Ann	show jumping
Lee, Sidney	billiards	Moore, Steve	water skiing
Legh, Alice	archery	Morgan, Janet	squash
Leman, Richard	hockey	Morris, Stewart	yachting
Le Moignan, Martine	squash	Morton, Lucy	swimming
Lennox, Avril	gymnastics	Moss, Pat	rallying
Lerwill, Alan	long jumper	Mould, Marion	show jumping
Lessing, Simon	triathlon	Muckelt, Ethel	figure skating
Line, Peter	bowls	Mynn, Alfred	cricket
Lloyd, Emrys	fencing	Nash, Tony	bobsleigh
Long, Liz	swimming	Neale, Denis	table tennis
Lorum, Mark	speedway	Neligan, Gwen	fencing
Loris, Chris	speedway	Nettleton, Louise	archery
Lucas, Muriel	badminton	Nevett, Bill	jockey
Lumb, Margot	squash	Newall, Queenie	archery
Lumley, Penny	real tennis	Newman, Tom	billiards
Lunn family	skiing	Nicholas, Alison	golf
Lunn, Gladys	athletics	Nielsen, Hans (Den)	speedway
Lycett, Randolph	tennis	Nieto, Angel (Esp)	motor cycling (125cc)
Lynch, Benny	flyweight boxer	Noel, Susan	squash
Mace, Jem	middleweight boxer	Norman, Wendy	modern pentathlon
Mack, Curly	badminton	Obolensky, Alex	rugby union
Mackey, Mick	hurling	Obree, Graeme	cycling
Mackinnon, Esmé	skiing	O'Dell, George	motor cycling
Mahoney, Harold	tennis	O'Keefe, Dan	Gaelic football
Male, James	rackets and real tennis	Oliver, Alan	show jumping
		Oliver, Eric	sidecar racing
Mallin, Frederick	middleweight boxer	Opie, Lisa	squash
Mallin, Harry	middleweight boxer	O'Reilly, Wilf	speed skating
Mannion, Wilf	football	Ottley, Dave	javelin
Mansergh, Terence	hockey	Paish, Geoff	tennis
Mapple, Andy	water skiing	Palmer, Charles	judo
Marques, David	rugby union	Palmer, Thomas 'Pedlar'	bantamweight boxer
Marshall, Peter	squash	Panis, Olivier (Fra)	motor racing (Formula 1)
Martin, Louis	weightlifting		
Martin, Stephen	hockey	Parke, James	tennis and rugby union
Matthews, Ken	walking	Parker, Jack	speedway
McAuliffe, Jack	lightweight boxer	Paterson, Alan	high jumper
McAvoy, Jock	light-heavyweight boxer	Pattisson, Rodney	yachting
		Patton, Peter	ice hockey
McCoig, Robert	badminton	Paul, René	fencing
McConnell, William	hockey	Payne, Howard	hammer thrower
McEvoy, Freddie	bobsleigh	Payne, Rosemary	discus thrower
McGregor, Yvonne	cycling	Paynter, Eddie	cricket
McIntyre, Bob	motor cycling	Peall, W.J.	billiards
McKechnie, Neil	swimming	Peck, Geoff	orienteering
McKenzie, George	Wrestling	Petersen, Jack	light-heavyweight boxer
McKiernan, Catherina	athletics		
McKinlay, Ken	speedway	Phelps, Brian	diving and trampolining
McLean, William	hockey		
McLeod, Hugh	rugby union	Phelps, Richard	modern pentathlon
McNeill, Carol	orienteering	Phelps, Ted	rowing
McRae, Alister	rallying	Phillips, Mollie	figure skating
McRae, Colin	rallying	Pickering, Jean	long jumper
McRae, Jimmy	rallying	Pickering, Karen	swimming
McTigue, Mike	boxing	Pilch, Fuller	cricket
Meade, Richard	three-day event	Pinching, Evie	skiing
Menu, Alain (Switz)	touring cars	Platt, Susan	javelin
Meredith, Billy	football	Porter, Hugh	cyclist

Potter, Jon	hockey	Simmers, Max	rugby union
Potter, Martin	surfing	Simmonds, Dave	motor cycling
Prenn, John	rackets		(125cc)
Price, Berwyn	athletics	Simpson, Cyril	rackets
Price, Tommy	speedway	Simpson, Tommy	cycling
Probyn, Jeff	rugby union	Sixsmith, Janet	hockey
Pullin, John	rugby union	Slawinski, Kendra	netball
Radford, Peter	athletics	Smith, Charles	water polo
Radmilovic, Paul	swimming and water	Smith, Sydney	tennis
	polo	Smithies, Karen	cricket
Rainey, Wayne (USA)	motor cycling (500cc)	Snode, Chris	diving
Ray, Ted	golf	Snow, Julian	real tennis
Read, Phil	motor cycling (125cc	Snowball, Betty	cricket
	and 250cc)	Solomon, John	croquet
Redman, Jim (Zim)	motor cycling (250cc)	Sopwith, Sir Tommy	yachting
Reece, Tom	billiards	Springman, Sarah	triathlon
Rendle, Sharon	judo	Stammers, Kay	tennis
Renshaw, William	tennis	Starbrook, Dave	judo
Rhodes, Ronald	canoeing	Steel, Dorothy	croquet
Richards, Gordon W.	horse racing	Steele, Mavis	bowls
(1930–98)		Stevens, Ray	badminton
Richards, Sir Gordon	horse racing	Stewart-Wood, Jeannette	water skiing
(1904–86)		Stoop, Adrian	rugby union
Richards, Tom	marathon	Sturgess, Colin	cycling
Richardson, Peter	cricket	Sturgess, William	walking
Richardson, T.D.	figure skating	Surtees, William	rackets
Richmond, Ken	wrestling and judo	Talbot, Derek	badminton
Ring, Christy	hurling	Tancred, Bill	discus
Ringer, Anthony	shooting	Tanner, Haydn	rugby union
Riseley, Frank	tennis	Tarleton, Nelson	boxing
Ritchie, Margaret	discus	Tate, Maurice	cricket
Roberts, John	billiards	Tatum, Kelvin	speedway
Roberts, Philippa	water skiing	Taylor, Ian	hockey
Robinson, Brian	cycling	Terry, Simon	archery
Robinson, Jem	horse racing	Thomas, Neil	gymnastics
Robinson, Val	hockey	Thompson, Don	walking
Rogers, Iris	badminton	Thompson, Ian	marathon
Ronaldson, Chloe	roller skating	Thomson, Andy	bowls
Round, Dorothy	tennis	Thorpe, Dave	motocross
Rowe, Arthur	shot putter	Tisdall, Bob	400m hurdler
Rowe, Diana	table tennis	Tomes, Alan	rugby union
Rowe, Rosalind	table tennis	Tomlins, Freddie	figure skating
Russell-Vick, Mary	hockey	Tortelli, Sébastien (USA)	motocross
Rutherford, Monica	gymnastics	Towler, Diane	ice dancing
Salo, Mika (Fin)	motor racing	Tredgett, Mike	badminton
	(Formula 1)	Tredgold, Roger	fencing
Salvadori, Roy	motor racing	Trew, Billy	rugby union
Sandford, Cecil	motor cycling (125cc	Troke, Helen	badminton
	and 250cc)	Tucker, Andrew	shooting
Saunders, Vivien	golf	Tucker, Sam	rugby union
Savage, David	hockey	Tuckey, Raymond	tennis
Saville, Sammy	hockey	Tyler, Dorothy	high jumper
Schofield, Garry	rugby league	Ubbiali, Carlo (Ita)	motor cycling (125cc
Schwantz, Kevin (USA)	motor cycling		and 250cc)
	(500cc)	Uber, Betty	badminton
Scotland, Ken	rugby union	Ulyett, George	cricket
Scott, Peter	yachting and gliding	Verstappen, Jos (Neth)	motor racing
Scriven, Peggy	tennis		(Formula 1)
Seaman, Dick	motor racing	Vickers, Stan	walking
Searle, Greg and Johnny	rowing	Wagstaff, Harold	rugby league
Seaton, Paul	water skiing	Wallace, Shaun	cycling
Segrave, Henry	motor racing	Warburg, David	real tennis
Seligman, Edgar	fencing	Ward, Pat	tennis
Sharpe, Graham	figure skating	Wardrop, Jack	swimming
Shaw, Norma	bowls	Warner, Sir Pelham	cricket
Sheen, Gillian	fencing	Waterman, Split	speedway
Sheil, Norman	cycling	Watson, Maud	tennis
Sheridan, Eileen	cycling	Watson, Willie	cricket and football
Shilcock, Anne	tennis	Webster, Steve	motor cycling
Shotton, Sue	trampolining		(sidecars)
Shoveller, Stanley	hockey	Weetman, Harry	golf
Shrubb, Alf	athletics	Welsh, Freddie	boxing

Westwood, Jean	**ice dance**	Wills, Philip	**gliding**
White, Belle	**diving**	Wonderful Terrific	**baseball**
White, Wilf	**show jumping**	Mons III (USA)	
Whiteley, Johnny	**rugby league**	Wooderson, Sydney	**athletics**
Whitford, Arthur	**gymnastics**	Woodgate, W.B.	**rowing**
Whitlock, Harold	**walking**	Woodward, Clive	**rugby union**
Whittle, Harry	**athletics**	Woodward, Vivian	**football**
Wigg, Simon	**speedway**	Wooller, Wilf	**rugby union**
Wilkinson, Diana	**swimming**	Woosnam, Max	**tennis and football**
Wilkinson, George	**water polo**	Yardley, Norman	**cricket**
Williams, Freddie	**speedway**		

NB The table above is merely a list of perhaps less well-known sports people, due either to their practising a minority sport or to the time elapsed since their success. A more thorough record of their achievements is beyond the scope of this book. Sportspeople listed are British unless stated otherwise.

Sporting Terms

adolph *trampolining* three-and-a-half front twisting somersault.

airshot *golf* complete missing of ball which constitutes a stroke (unless mulligan awarded).

albatross *golf* score of 3 under par on a particular hole.

appel *fencing* beating or stamping of foot during contest.

apron *golf* grass cut short between fairway and approach to the green.

Arab spring *gymnastics* cartwheel with a quarter turn.

assist *basketball* final pass given to shooter of a basket.

axel *ice skating* a one-and-a-half turn jump from the forward outside edge of one skate to the backward outside edge of the other (named after Norwegian skater Axel Rudolph Paulser).

back alley *badminton* the area at the back of the court.

bai-hou *karate* white crane stance with one knee raised high (popularized in *Karate Kid* films).

balestra *fencing* attack after an appel.

barani *trampolining* front somersault with half twist.

battery *baseball* originally a term for the pitcher but now incorporates the pitcher and catcher.

baulk *billiards* line from which game begins.

ba(u)lk *baseball* illegal action by a pitcher.

beamer *cricket* ball bowled higher than a full toss so endangering the batsman.

besom *curling* type of broom used to sweep the ice to gain more distance.

bib *netball* tie-up over top with player's position labelled.

birdie *golf* score of 1 under par on a hole.

blind side *rugby* short side between scrum and touch line.

block *volleyball* basic return at the net to counter the opponent's spike.

blocking *basketball* illegal personal contact that impedes the progress of an opponent who does not have the ball.

bogey *golf* score of 1 over par on a hole.

bonk *cycling* tiredness caused by lack of food.

bonspiel *curling* term used for an important match.

boom *yachting* long spar or pole hinged at one end, securing the bottom of a ship's sail.

bosey / bosie *cricket* Australian name for a googly

(named after B.J.T. Bosanquet 1877–1936, an English cricketer).

Boston crab *wrestling* manoeuvre whereby one fighter sits on the back of the other with legs tucked under his arms.

bouncer *cricket* ball bowled short and fast in order to cause batsman to take evasive action.

bowling crease *cricket* line extended from the stumps sideways and four feet behind the popping crease; the ball must be delivered between these two lines.

brakeman *bobsleigh* person who operates the brakes in the sleigh.

Brill bend *high jumping* named after Debbie Brill, equivalent to the Fosbury flop.

brush *curling* implement for sweeping the ice, thereby causing the stone to travel further.

bunt *baseball* to let the ball hit the bat without swinging at it.

burgee *yachting* ornamental flag which serves no other purpose.

buttonhook *American football* type of pass for the receiver running straight downfield and then doubling back a few steps to receive it.

bye *cricket* extra gained by batting side when the batsmen run or the ball crosses the boundary after no contact with bat has taken place.

calx *Eton wall game* area behind the goal-line.

caman *shinty* stick used for striking.

cannon *billiards* object ball hitting opponent's ball and the red ball (scores 3 points).

capriole *dressage* horse jumps straight upward with its forelegs drawn in, kicking back with its hind legs horizontal.

catch *real tennis* obsolete former name for the game.

catch a crab *rowing* to get an oar trapped underwater or to miss the water with a stroke.

catenaccio system *football* sweeper system.

checking *ice hockey* legal manoeuvre of physical contact to gain control of puck.

chicane *motor racing* sharp double-bend.

chinaman *cricket* left-handed bowler's googly to a right-handed batsman.

chistera *pelota / jaïï alaïï* curved glove with a chestnut or ash frame, aka Cesta.

christiania *skiing* turn in which the skis are kept in parallel, used for stopping short. Aka christie.

Christmas tree *drag racing* starting system.

Christmas tree *football* descriptive formation.

chui *judo* warning with 3 points deducted.

chukka *polo* each of the 7½-minute periods into which a game is divided. Also spelt 'chucker' or 'chukker'.

close-hauled *wind surfing* area 45 degrees each side of wind direction.

conversion *Canadian football* method of adding to score after touchdown has been scored.

conversion *rugby* method of adding to score after try has been scored (2 points score).

courbet / curvet *dressage* jump forward at the levade.

cover *cricket* fielding position midway between infield and outfield in which a good fielder may save a single.

cover point *cricket* fielding position on the off side and nearer the batsman than the non-striker.

crampon *curling* device formerly used to enable a steady delivery but now obsolete.

crampon *rock-climbing* frame with 10 or 12 metal spikes, strapped to boots to give a firmer footing.

cross buttock *wrestling* throw in which a wrestler throws an opponent head first over his or her hip.

crosse *lacrosse* stick between 40–72 inches long and 4–10 inches wide.

crucifix *gymnastics (rings)* basic position with the arms held outstretched to the sides.

curve ball *baseball* ball which deviates from the path it would otherwise take, because of the spin imparted by the pitcher.

cut line *squash* line above which a served ball must strike the wall.

dan *martial arts* each of the numbered grades of the advanced level of proficiency in many martial arts.

diamond *baseball* the area formed by the four bases within the infield.

dig *volleyball* defensive motion of digging the ball up from below the net height with two hands to counter a spike.

ditch *bowls* the channel around the rink.

dog-leg *golf* hole that bends sharply to one side, so ensuring a positional shot is played.

domestiques *cycling* team members of tour teams who will sacrifice their position for team leaders.

double eagle *golf* score of 3 under par on a particular hole (US term).

down *American football* each of a fixed number of attempts to advance the ball 10 yards.

drop-kick *rugby* kick made by dropping the ball and kicking it as it rebounds from the ground.

drop-out *rugby* a drop-kick made from within the defending team's 22-metre (formerly 25yds) line in order to restart play after the ball has gone dead.

drop-line *angling* weighted fishing-line for fishing near the bottom of a waterway.

dropped goal *rugby* goal scored with a drop-kick that propels the ball over the crossbar.

dummy, sell a *rugby* to successfully feign a pass.

dunk *basketball* shoot a basket by jumping so that the hands are above the ring and the ball is dunked down through the hoop.

eagle *American football* defensive formation.

eagle *golf* score of 2 under par on a hole.

egg position *skiing* tucked position that ensures a good fast glide.

en garde *fencing* call to a fencer to adopt a defensive stance in readiness for an attack or bout.

end *bowls* division of a match whereby after all woods are bowled the next 'end' is played from the other end of the rink.

end *curling* division of a match whereby after all stones are bowled the next 'end' is played from the other end of the rink.

English *pool* north American term for using 'side' on the cueball.

Eskimo roll *canoeing* a 360-degree roll starting and finishing above water but 180 degrees of which is underwater.

expedite *table tennis* rule whereby a match is brought to a conclusion after a series of long rallies or deuces by setting a limit to the number of strokes per point.

extras *cricket* generic name for all types of byes and penalty runs scored other than by the batsman hitting the ball.

face-off *ice hockey* start of game.

fairway *golf* part of golf course between tee and green in which the grass is cut short to reward accuracy.

feng taidu *kung fu* phoenix stance keeping low on one leg ready to rise.

fine leg *cricket* fielding position between wicket keeper and square leg but deeper.

flèche *archery* obsolete name for an arrow.

flèche *fencing* a running attack.

flic flac *gymnastics* simple back flip.

fliffis *trampolining* double front somersault with twist.

flying mare *wrestling* throw in which one wrestler throws the other over his or her back using the other's arm as a lever.

Fosbury flop *high jumping* technique named after Dick Fosbury, whereby head and shoulders are thrown over the bar first, chest upwards and with legs pulled back to ensure economical clearance.

free throw *basketball* free shot at basket due to an infringement by the opposition.

fukuro shinai *kendo* wooden sword often covered in cloth or leather.

full-nelson *wrestling* two-handed hold whereby the arms are placed under the arms of the opponent and interlocked behind his neck, immobilizing the upper body.

gaff *yachting* spar situated on the after side of a mast and supporting the head of a fore-and-aft sail.

garryowen *rugby* another name for an up and under.

genoa *yachting* large jib with a low foot.

gojo-ryu *karate* hard / soft technique.

gokuhi *martial arts* techniques and 'secrets' of masters relayed to gifted students.

googly *cricket* off-break ball bowled with apparent leg-break action.

goosewinged *yachting* square-rigged boats having the topsail spread for scudding under when the wind is strong, the bunt of the sail being hauled up to the yard.

gridiron *American football* the field of play.

gully *cricket* fielding position a little wider than the slips.

gybe *yachting* of a fore-and-aft sail or its boom, to swing from one side of a vessel to the other.

hack *curling* notch made in the ice used to steady the foot when delivering a stone.

hackamore *horse racing* bitless bridle with a hard oval noseband which allows pressure to be exerted on the nose by means of the reins attached just in front of a heavy counterbalancing knot.

half-nelson *wrestling* hold whereby the arm of the opponent is bent behind his back and pushed upwards.

halyard *yachting* rope or tackle for raising or lowering a sail.

hammer grip *table tennis* rarely used method of holding the bat whereby no fingers touch its face.

hand-in *squash* the server.

hand-out *squash* when player loses a point on his service he becomes hand-out.

haute école *dressage* advanced training methods (high school).

head *bowls* the grouping of the woods around the jack.

hecht *gymnastics* dismount from the asymmetric bars head and body first between bars.

held ball *basketball* called when two opponents have one or two hands so firmly upon the ball that neither can gain possession.

herringboning *skiing* method of climbing a slope by walking with the skis pointing outwards.

hikiwake *kendo* a draw in a competitive match.

hog line *curling* line behind which the stone must be delivered.

hog's back *equestrianism* sharp-ridged natural mound for jumping.

honk *cycling* cycling out of the saddle.

hooker *rugby* front row of scrum position player supported between the two props who attemps to hook ball back with his feet to be used by his team.

hoop *basketball* the metal ring of the 'basket'.

hoop *croquet* arch through which the ball must be driven.

house *curling* the round target area of concentric circles.

I formation *American football* offensive formation.

in touch *rugby* out of play.

ippon *judo* full point in Japan (scores 10 points in competition).

Irish whip *wrestling* one-handed throw whereby the arm is whipped back and forth forcing a somersault in the air by the opponent.

jack *bowls* white ball which is the target for the woods.

jib *yachting* triangular staysail stretching from the outer end of the jib-boom to the fore-topmast.

judoka *judo* judo player.

jugogi *judo* judo suit.

jump ball *basketball* method of putting the ball into play whereby the referee tosses it up between two opponents who try to tap it to a teammate.

katame-waza *judo* basic hold.

keikoku *judo* judge's warning with 7 points deducted.

kinsa *judo* 3 point scoring technique.

kip *gymnastics* movement whereby the body is straightened from a piked position by pushing the hips forward and the legs back.

knock-on *rugby* illegal move that knocks the ball forward and on to the ground with hand or arm.

koka *judo* hold between 10 and 20 seconds.

kyu *martial arts* student.

laundry *drag racing* the parachute that slows the cars down.

leg-bye *cricket* run scored after the ball has touched any part of the batsman but his hand.

leg side *cricket* the side of the wicket on which the receiving batsman stands.

levade *dressage* horse raises and draws in its forelegs, standing balanced on its bent hind legs.

line-out *rugby* method of throwing ball back into play between two lines of opposing forwards after it has gone out over the touchline.

lock *rugby* one of two forwards in second row of scrum.

long bomb *roller hockey* long pass from defence to set up sudden counter-attack.

long dong *kung fu* eastern dragon position with one hand in front of forehead (palm out) and the other covering abdomen (palm down).

long hop *cricket* ball that is bowled flat and short so as to almost bounce twice before reaching batsman.

luff *yachting* the edge of a fore-and-aft sail next to the mast or stay (among other definitions it is also a term for obstructing the opposition attempting to pass on the windward side by sailing closer to the wind).

lutz *ice skating* jump in which the skater takes off from the outside back edge of one skate and lands, after full rotation, on the outside back edge of the other.

maiden *cricket* an over in which no runs have been scored.

mallet *croquet* the striking implement used to manoeuvre the ball through the hoops.

mashie *golf* obsolete colloquial name for a no. 5 iron.

mashie-niblick *golf* obsolete colloquial name for a no. 7 iron.

mata *judo* break of a hold.

maul *rugby* distinguished from ruck by ball being held off the ground.

men *kendo* the armour that covers the head and face.

mid-off *cricket* fielding position on the side opposite to where the facing batsman stands; in the case of a right-handed batsman, to the left of the bowler during his run-up.

mid-on *cricket* fielding position on the side where the facing batsman stands; in the case of a right-handed batsman, to the right of the bowler during his run-up.

mid-wicket *cricket* self-explanatory fielding position whereby if an equilateral triangle was plotted using the 22 yards between the stumps, mid-wicket would lie on the apex.

monkey climb *wrestling* move whereby one wrestler climbs up and wraps himself around the other to immobilize him.

mulligan *golf* free stroke awarded informally after a poor shot, usually an air shot.

nage-waza *judo* basic throw.

niblick *golf* obsolete colloquial name for a sand wedge or sometimes a wedge.

night watchman *cricket* lower-order batsman who comes in up the order to protect a key player if a wicket is lost near close of play.

no side *rugby* official name for end of the game, no longer commonly used.

nock *archery* notch at end of bow to run string through.

nocking point *archery* point of a bowstring to which the notch of an arrow is applied.

Notre Dame shift *American football* offensive move

SPORT & LEISURE

whereby the backs move just before the snap of the ball from their T-formation.

nunchaku *kung fu* rice flail used in exhibitions.

nutmeg *football* to play the ball between the legs of a defender and run around him to collect it.

O'Brien shift *shot putting* common gliding technique named after Parry O'Brien.

Oklahoma *American football* defensive formation.

oxer *equestrianism* brush fence with a guard rail on one side.

ozeki *sumo* the second rank after yokozuna (means 'great barrier').

painter *yachting* short rope or chain by which the shank of an anchor is held fast.

parallelogram *Gaelic football* playing area.

parry *fencing* warding off an attack especially with a counter.

passage *dressage* cadenced high-stepping trot.

pebble *curling* another name for a stone.

penholder grip *table tennis* method of holding the bat like a pencil popularized by the Chinese; quick footwork is essential as backhands are impossible to play. Aka eastern grip.

penthouse *real tennis* sloping roof of the corridor or gallery running around three sides of the court.

piaffe *dressage* a trot in place.

pick *basketball* action of a player who, without causing contact, delays or prevents an opponent from reaching his desired position.

pick-up *sprinting* second phase of race after the start during which the head is raised and relaxation starts.

pile-driver *wrestling* up-ending the opponent and driving his head into the canvas.

pinch-hitter *baseball* less technically accomplished player capable of hitting out forcefully.

piste *fencing* total fencing area.

piste *skiing* total skiing area.

pitcher *baseball* specialist thrower of the ball towards the opposing batter.

piton *rock-climbing* eye peg hammered into rock so that a rope can be attached.

pivot *basketball* movement in which a player with the ball steps once or more in any direction with the same foot while the other foot is kept at its point of contact with the floor.

plastron *fencing* padded, leather-covered breastplate.

point *cricket* off-side fielding position wide of gully.

popping crease *cricket* line four feet in front of and parallel to the wicket within which the batsmen must remain unless the ball is dead or they are running.

press *basketball* defensive technique of harassing players into hurried play.

prop *rugby* one of the two forwards in the front row of the scrum who support hooker.

puck *ice hockey* flat rubber disc used in place of ball.

puissance *show jumping* high jump event.

punt *rugby* kick made by dropping the ball and kicking before it hits the ground.

putout *baseball* self-explanatory term meaning to cause a batter or base runner to be out.

quarterback *American football* player stationed behind the centre who directs a team's attacking play.

rack *pool* implement used for setting the red balls at the start of a frame (also the name used for an individual frame).

randolph (randi) *trampolining* two-and-a-half twisting front somersault.

repechage *rowing* a second chance for the best of the losing rowers in eliminating heats to progress to a final.

return crease *cricket* the lines either side of the wicket at right angles to the bowling crease.

riposte *fencing* a lunge or quick thrust after parrying.

rocker *ice skating* a skate with a curved blade.

roquet *croquet* to strike another player's ball with your own.

rover *American football* defensive linebacker assigned to move about to anticipate opponents' plays.

rover *archery* target chosen at random and at an undetermined range (also a mark for long-distance shooting).

rover *Australian rules football* player forming part of the ruck.

rover *croquet* ball that has passed through all the hoops but not pegged out (also a name for a player whose ball has done this).

ruck *rugby* occurs when progress of the ball is checked and two or more players struggle to gain possession. Distinguished from maul by ball being on the ground and legally playable only with the feet.

rush *ice hockey* sudden attack on goal often from a defensive position.

salchow *ice skating* full-turn jump from the inside back edge of one skate to the outside back edge of the other.

schuss *skiing* starting gate or housing.

scissors *high jump* training technique of clearing bar with legs only and no rotation of hips.

scissors *rugby* change of direction of attack by player running in diagonally opposite to the line of attacking play when receiving ball.

screen *basketball* another name for 'pick'.

scrimmage *American football* offense and defense facing each other.

scrum *rugby* formed by eight forwards of each side in three ranks for purpose of gaining possession with the feet. Note: rugby league scrummages contain six players.

serpentine *dressage* series of half-circles alternately to right and left.

shido *judo* judge's warning with no point deducted.

shime-waza *judo* strangulation technique.

shinai *kendo* sword made up of four bamboo sticks bound together.

shobu-ari *kendo* the end of a match.

shopping, going *billiards* potting your opponent's ball.

short leg *cricket* fielding position close to the batsman and on the leg side.

shotgun *American football* offensive formation.

shroud *yachting* set of ropes supporting the mainsail.

shukokai *karate* a karate school.

shuriken *karate* one of various designs of small throwing weapons often eight-sided and sharp.

side *billiards* off-centre striking of the cueball to make false angle in positional play.

silly mid-off *cricket* close fielding position short of mid-off.

silly mid-on *cricket* close fielding position short of mid-on.

sleeper *wrestling* application of pressure on the nerves in the neck which can cause loss of consciousness.

slip   *cricket*   fielding position next to the wicket-keeper.

snap   *American football*   put the ball into play on the ground by a quick backward movement.

soigneur   *cycling*   general dogsbody of team responsible for its physical and mental preparation.

soop   *curling*   assist the progress of a curling stone by sweeping the ice in front of it.

southpaw   *boxing*   boxer who leads with his right hand.

space lob   *roller hockey*   use of end boards to pass to team mates.

spare   *ten pin bowling*   knocking down all the pins with two successive bowls.

spider   *billiards, snooker*   implement used when bridging directly over a ball.

spider   *darts*   wire frame around the board.

spike   *volleyball*   one-handed attacking shot from above and across the net. Spike serves are common at the higher levels.

spinnaker   *yachting*   large triangular sail carried forward of or opposite the mainsail.

spinner   *angling*   real or artificial bait or lure fixed so as to revolve when pulled through the water.

spinnerama   *roller hockey*   complicated tactical move to deceive opposition.

spinning   *cycling*   US term for twiddling now commonly used in UK.

split   *ten pin bowling*   attempt to knock down pins which are wide apart.

split   *weightlifting*   action of thrusting forward with one foot and backward with the other to aid leverage during lift.

split T   *American football*   offensive formation.

spoon   *angling*   artificial bait in the shape of the bowl of a spoon, used in spinning or trolling.

spoon   *golf*   any club with a slightly concave wooden head, but often refers to a 3 wood specifically.

stealing bases   *baseball*   reaching bases without the striker hitting the ball.

stone   *curling*   the heavy 'top' with a handle which is aimed at the house.

straddle   *high jump*   similar to western roll, but the straddle jumper keeps legs wide apart and body straight.

strike   *baseball*   complete miss of the ball.

strike   *ten pin bowling*   knocking all the pins down with one ball.

suicide squad   *American football*   specialist players who deliberately block attacks.

sulky   *harness racing*   vehicle used in harness racing.

sweeper   *curling*   team member who sweeps the ice to gain distance for stone.

swingtime   *trampolining*   a series of different moves performed between bounces.

switch-hitting   *boxing*   changing from orthodox to southpaw during a bout.

tack   *equestrianism*   saddle, bridle and bit.

tack   *yachting*   zigzag movement of a boat.

tagged out   *baseball*   self-explanatory term.

tame-shiwari   *karate*   exercise for toughening using breaking techniques.

taw   *marbles*   line from which a player shoots; also another name for the actual game and formerly a name for a large marble.

tee   *curling*   centre point of the house.

tee   *golf*   small peg on which to rest the ball when driving; also the name for the area where the initial drive is made.

T formation   *American football*   offensive formation.

third man   *cricket*   fielding position deep behind the slip area.

tice   *cricket*   obsolete term for a yorker.

tice   *croquet*   stroke tempting an opponent to aim at one's ball.

tiger country   *golf*   deep rough usually on high ground.

tin   *squash*   the lower line on the wall above which all shots must be played.

tkachyov   *gymnastics*   one-handed 360-degree swing on horizontal (high) bar.

tolley   *marbles*   portmanteau word from 'taw' and 'alley'.

touchdown   *American football*   equivalent of a try in rugby, except that the ball need not touch the ground when carried or received inside the opponents' end zone (6 points score).

touché   *fencing*   an acknowledgment that a scoring hit has been made in a bout.

toucher   *bowls*   wood that has touched the jack in its travels.

tram lines   *tennis*   the outer lines at each side of the court which become part of the court in doubles matches.

trapeze   *yachting*   sliding support used for outboard balancing on a yacht.

travelling   *basketball*   running with the ball without bouncing it.

triangle   *angling*   set of three hooks fastened together so that the barbs form a triangle.

triangle   *snooker*   implement used for setting the red balls at the start of a frame.

troll   *angling*   fish by drawing bait along in the water.

try   *rugby*   scoring method by means of touching the ball down in the opponents' goal area behind their goal line (5 points score).

tsuba   *kendo*   guard of the sword.

tsuka   *kendo*   handle of the sword.

tsukahara   *gymnastics*   vault consisting of a quarter or half turn on to the horse followed by one and half somersaults off.

turkey   *ten pin bowling*   gaining three strikes in successive bowls.

turnover   *basketball*   loss of possession of the ball by a team before any member has been able to try for a basket.

twiddling   *cycling*   pedalling fast in a gear with no pressure asserted.

up and under   *rugby*   kicking the ball up field high and long to make time for the kicker and attacking players to reach the point where it comes down.

uwate-dashi-nage   *sumo*   one-handed throw.

uwate-nage   *sumo*   hip throw using both hands.

veer attack   *American football*   offensive formation.

volley   *volleyball*   two-handed shot that may go over the net or to another team member to spike.

vorlage   *skiing*   position in which the skier leans forward without lifting the heels from the skis. It is also a common name for skiing trousers when pluralized.

vorlaufer   *skiing*   literally meaning 'run on ahead' in German, it is a term used for the pre-competition skiers who test the safety and degree of difficulty of a ski course.

walkover *horse racing* horse having the formality of walking over the line as it is the only entrant in a race.

wall pass *football* pass from one player to another and back to save having to face a defender (also called one-two).

warner single wing *American football* offensive formation.

wazari-ni-chikai-waza *judo* 5-point score (two make an ippon).

wazari *judo* almost point in Japanese (scores 7 points in competition).

western grip *table tennis* traditional method of holding a bat with fingers on face of bat.

western roll *high jumping* technique, rarely used today, whereby the front leg is thrown high over the bar and the body and other leg roll over and parallel to the bar.

wicket maiden *cricket* an over during which no runs have been scored and a wicket has been taken.

wide *cricket* extra given to batting side due to ball being bowled too wide of the batsman.

wipe out *surfing* tumbling off the board, often due to unforeseen wave.

wired *croquet* prevented from taking a particular course by an intervening hoop or peg.

wishbone *yachting* boom composed of two halves that curve outward from the mast on either side of the sail and in again, the clew of the sail between them being attached to the point where they meet aft.

yamashita *gymnastics* flat handspring over the vaulting horse.

yokozuna *sumo* grand champion.

yori kiri *sumo* strong forward push.

yorker *cricket* ball bowled at feet of batsman whether playing back or forward.

yuko *judo* hold between 20 and 25 seconds.

NB This is far from being an exhaustive listing of sporting terminology. Dictionaries of terms are available on many individual sports and so it would be impossible to catalogue all known terms. What I have tried to do is give a good cross-section of technical terms over many sports. I should also point out that some terms will relate to other sports, e.g billiard based sports or running ball sports.

Some Late Additions (Without Definitions)

Term	Sport	Term	Sport
button	curling	merlin rocket	yachting
button	rowing	miller	trampolining
catalina	synchronized swimming	planche	gymnastics
flying wedge	American football	RS 400	yachting
follower	Australian rules football	rudolph (rudy)	trampolining
hash marks	American football	sliothar	hurling
hooking	hockey	spearing	hockey
hurl	hurling	stutz	gymnastics
hurley	hurling	surfboard	wrestling
International 14	yachting	sweeper	football
keyhole	basketball	tinsica	gymnastics
kiggle-kaggle	curling	triangle and sausage	yachting
kyokushinkai	karate	votte	dressage
Laser 5000	yachting	wishbone	American football

Other Sports
Greyhound Racing

Derby Winners

1980	Indian Joe	1991	Ballinderry Ash
1981	Parkdown Jet	1992	Farloe Melody
1982	Laurie's Panther	1993	Ringa Hustle
1983	I'm Slippy	1994	Moral Standards
1984	Whisper Wishes	1995	Moaning Lad
1985	Pagan Swallow	1996	Shanless Slippy
1986	Tico	1997	Some Picture
1987	Signal Spark	1998	Tom's the Best
1988	Hit the Lid	1999	Chart King
1989	Lartigue Note	2000	Rapid Lad
1990	Slippy Blue	2001	Rapid Lad

Rugby League – Man of Steel

1977	David Ward (Leeds)	1990	Shaun Edwards (Wigan)
1978	George Nicholls (St Helens)	1991	Gary Schofield (Leeds)
1979	Doug Laughton (Widnes)	1992	Dean Bell (Wigan)
1980	George Fairbairn (Wigan)	1993	Andy Platt (Wigan)
1981	Ken Kelly (Warrington)	1994	Jonathan Davies (Warrington)
1982	Mick Morgan (Carlisle)	1995	Denis Betts (Wigan)
1983	Allan Agar (Featherstone Rovers)	1996	Andy Farrell (Wigan)
1984	Joe Lydon (Widnes)	1997	James Lowes (Bradford Bulls)
1985	Ellery Hanley (Bradford Northern)	1998	Iestyn Harris (Leeds Rhinos)
1986	Gavin Miller (HKR)	1999	Adrian Vowles (Castleford Tigers)
1987	Ellery Hanley (Wigan)	2000	Sean Long (St Helens)
1988	Martin Offiah (Widnes)		
1989	Ellery Hanley (Wigan)		

Rugby Union Six Nations Championships

1977	France	1990	Scotland
1978	Wales	1991	England
1979	Wales	1992	England
1980	England	1993	France
1981	France	1994	Wales
1982	Ireland	1995	England
1983	France / Ireland	1996	England
1984	Scotland	1997	France
1985	Ireland	1998	France
1986	France / Scotland	1999	Scotland (last Five Nations Championship)
1987	France	2000	England
1988	France / Wales	2001	England
1989	France		

Miscellaneous Information: Sport

Acque Minerale and Tamburello	features of Imola and San Marino motor racing circuits.
archery: target colours	gold (centre), red, blue, black, white.
Australian rules football: inventor	George Ligowsky.
backwards: sports where competitors move	back-stroke swimming; rowing; tug of war.
badminton: All-England champion seven successive years	Rudy Hartono (1968–74).
badminton: family won 35 All-England titles	Frank Devlin and his daughters Judy and Sue.
badminton: origin	originally called Shuttlecock and Battledore and named after the country estate of the Duke of Beaufort, where it originated in 1873. It was popularized by army officers in India who played it as an outdoor game.
bagatelle: brief description	similar to bar billiards but board has nine holes and nine balls are used (four red, four white and a black ball that scores double).
bagatelle: variations	cannon game; Mississippi; sans égal.
basketball: court size	50′ × 94′.
basketball: famous US teams	Boston Celtics; Houston Rockets; Los Angeles Lakers; Milwaukee Bucks; New York Knickerbockers; Philadelphia 76ers; Phoenix Suns; Portland Trail Blazers; Seattle Supersonics; St Louis Hawks; Washington Bullets.
basketball: inventor	Dr James Naismith invented basketball at the YMCA training school in Springfield, Mass. (1891).
beard: not allowed	jockeys.
billiards: World Matchplay champion 1998	Mike Russell of England defeated Peter Gilchrist of England 8–5.
boat race: dead heat	1877.

SPORT & LEISURE

boat race: first woman cox	Susan Brown in 1981.
boat race: reserve crews	Cambridge – Goldie, Oxford – Isis.
bowls: first world champion in 1966	David Bryant (Eng).
bowls: invented by	flat green bowls in its modern form began in 1848 when William Mitchell, a Glasgow solicitor, drew up the rules.
bowls: 2001 world indoor champion	Paul Foster (Scot) beat Richard Corsie (Scot).
boxing: amateur weight limits	light fly – 106lb/48kg; fly – 112lb/51kg; bantam – 119lb/54kg; feather – 126lb/57kg; light – 132lb/60kg; light welter – 140lb/63.5kg; welter – 148lb/67kg; light middle – 157lb/71kg; middle – 165lb/75kg; light heavy – 179lb/81kg; heavy – 201lb/91kg; super heavy – 201lb+/91kg+.
champion at five weights	Sugar Ray Leonard.
first champion	James Figg is generally regarded as the first modern champion when he set up his school in 1719.
first East European professional	Laszlo Papp.
first fight with gloves	Gentleman Jim Corbett defeated John L. Sullivan in 1892.
first million dollar gate	Jack Dempsey v Georges Carpentier in 1921.
four main governing bodies	World Boxing Association (WBA), founded 1920; World Boxing Council (WBC), founded 1963; International Boxing Federation (IBF), founded 1983; World Boxing Organization (WBO), founded 1988.
heavyweight champion longest reign	Joe Louis (1937–49).
last bareknuckle champion	John L. Sullivan.
oldest and youngest world champions	light heavyweight, Archie Moore (48); light welterweight, Wilfredo Benitez (17).
professional weight limits	straw/mini-fly – 105lb/48kg; light fly/jnr fly – 108lb/49kg; fly – 112lb/51kg; super fly/jnr bantam – 115lb/52kg; bantam – 118lb/54kg; super bantam/jnr feather – 122lb/55kg; feather – 126lb/57kg; super feather/jnr light – 130lb/59kg; light – 135lb/61kg; super light/jnr welter – 140lb/64kg; welter – 147lb/67kg; super welter/jnr middle – 154lb/70kg; middle – 160lb/73kg; super middle – 168lb/76kg; light heavy – 175lb/79kg; jnr heavy/cruiser – 190lb/86kg; heavy – 190lb+/86kg+.
Queensberry Rules: first fight under	Jim Corbett beat John L. Sullivan (1892).
initiated by	Jack Broughton devised first rules in 1743, but they were not codified until 1867 by 8th marquess of Queensberry.
undefeated heavyweight champion	Rocky Marciano (49 fights).
undisputed heavyweight champions	John L. Sullivan (1882); James J. Corbett (1892); Bob Fitzsimmons (1897); James J. Jeffries (1899); Marvin Hart (1905); Tommy Burns (1906); Jack Johnson (1908); Jess Willard (1915); Jack Dempsey (1919); Gene Tunney (1926); Max Schmeling (1930); Jack Sharkey (1932); Primo Carnera (1933); Max Baer (1934); James J. Braddock (1935); Joe Louis (1937); Ezzard Charles (1949); Jersey Joe Walcott (1951); Rocky Marciano (1952); Floyd Patterson (1956); Ingemar Johansson (1959); Floyd Patterson (1960); Sonny Liston (1962); Cassius Clay (1964); Joe Frazier (1970); George Foreman (1973); Muhammad Ali (1974); Leon Spinks (1978); Mike Tyson (1987).
youngest world heavyweight champion	Mike Tyson.
bullfighting: barbed sticks	banderillas.
cape	muleta (red one side and yellow the other).
term used for a pass	veronica.
terms for fighters	matador – principal fighter appointed to kill the bull; picador – horseman who pricks the bull with a banderilla to weaken it; toreador – stock name for any fighter.
chess: mens world champions 2001	Alexander Khalifman (FIDE); Vladimir Kramnik (PCA World Champion).
croquet	four balls used; two to a team; red and yellow play against blue and black; six hoops are used.
cycling: oldest British sprint champion	Reg Harris (aged 54).
terms	honking – cycling off the saddle; spinning – turning an easy gear very quickly with no effort.
Tour de France, first non-European winner	Greg Lemond of USA in 1986.
Tour de France, five times winners	Eddie Merckx, Jacques Anquetil, Bernard Hinault.
darts: sponsors	Embassy sponsor the BDO World Championship while Skol sponsor the WDC Championship.

Eton fives: 2000 county champions	Kent beat Berkshire 3–0.
fatalities: sport with highest rate of	angling (fish rather than folk!).
fencing: caught cheating	Boris Onischenko of USSR in Modern Pentathlon (1976).
heaviest weapon	Épée.
target areas	foil – body only; épée – no restriction; sabre – over waist.
technical term for guard	coquille.
weapons used by women	traditionally foil only but nowadays championships exist for sabre and épée.
frisbee: two forms of	Ultimate and Guts.
golf: British amateur champion 2001	Michael Hoey (Ireland)
gong: banged for J. Arthur Rank	Bombardier Billy Wells (1889–1967), British heavyweight boxing champion, was succeeded by Ken Richmond, the wrestling gold medalist at the 1954 Commonwealth Games.
Greyhound Grand National: triple winner	Sherry's Prince.
greyhound racing: most consecutive wins	Ballyregan Bob (32).
trap colours	red – 1; blue – 2; white – 3; black – 4; orange – 5; black and white striped – 6.
grouse shooting: season	Glorious Twelfth (August) to 10 December.
gymnastics: exercises for men	floor, horizontal bar, parallel bars, pommel horse, rings, vault (lengthwise).
exercises for women	floor, asymmetric bars, beam, vault (widthwise).
first perfect score of 10	Nadia Comaneci in 1976.
ice hockey: 1998 world champions	Sweden beat Finland 1–0.
Stanley Cup 1998	Detroit beat Washington 4–0.
ice skating: British champions 1997	Steven Cousins (men) and Jane Arrowsmith (women).
world champions 1998	Alexei Yagudin (men), Michelle Kwan (women), Elena Berezhnaya and Anton Sikharulidze (pairs), and Anjelika Krylova and Oleg Ovsyannikov (dance).
judo: 1997 British world champion	Kate Howey (middleweight).
London Marathon organizers	John Disley and Chris Brasher organized first London Marathon in 1981.
martial arts: meanings	tae kwon do – way of the foot and fist; judo – gentle way; aikido – way of spirit harmony; karate – way of the empty hand; kyudo – way of the bow; kung fu – leisure time/hobby.
Olympic Games: famous competitors	Philip Noel Baker was an Olympic finalist at 1500m in 1912 and silver medallist in 1920 before winning the Nobel Peace Prize in 1959. Noel Harrison, who took part in Skiing in 1952, is the actor son of Rex Harrison. Harry Llewellyn, who won gold medal for Equestrianism in 1952, is father of Roddy Llewellyn. Charles Simmons, who took part in Gymnastics 1952, is father of Jean Simmons. John Kelly, who won gold medal for Rowing in 1920, was father of Grace Kelly. Prince Albert of Monaco took part in bobsleigh events in 1988. Godfrey Rampling, who ran in the 4 x 400m Relay in 1936, was the father of Charlotte Rampling. Bill Nankeville who ran in the 1500m in 1948, is the father of Bobby Davro. Ioannis Theodoracopulous, who was a hurdler in 1936, was the father of Taki. Arthur Porritt, who accompanied Harold Abrahams in the 1924 Games, was father of Jonathon Porritt the Green politician.
pelota vasca (jai alai): origins	invented in Italy as 'longue paume' and introduced to France in 13th century. It is the fastest ball game in the world.
pheasant shooting: season	1 October to 1 February.
polo: pitch dimensions	polo has the largest pitch of any sport with a maximum length of 300 yards and width of 200 yards.
rackets: 2001 world champion	J. Malc (GB) defeated N. Smith (GB).
racketball: inventors	American racketball devised by Joe Sobek in 1949; British racketball was devised by Ian Wright in 1976.
real tennis: origins	developed from 'jeu de paume' (game of the palm) and played in Australia, England, France, Scotland and USA. First world champion in 1740 was a Frenchman named Clergé.

SPORT & LEISURE

roller skating: first rink opened	Newport, Rhode Island, in 1866.
rowing: skimming of oar across water	feathering.
rugby league: nicknames	Australia – Kangaroos; New Zealand – Kiwis; Widnes – Chemics; Warrington – Wires.
rugby union: jersey colours	Australia – gold; Barbarians – black and white hoops; England – white; France – blue; Ireland – green; New Zealand – black; Scotland – blue; Wales – red.
nicknames	Argentina – Pumas; Australia – Wallabies; New Zealand – All Blacks; South Africa – Springboks.
played both codes at same time	Martin Offiah left Wigan August 1996 to play union for Bedford and league for London Broncos.
skiing: Olympic champions who won all titles	Toni Sailer (1956) and Jean-Claude Killy (1968).
piste grading	black – difficult run; red – intermediate run; blue – easy run; green – beginners' slope.
snooker: first televised 147 maximum by	Steve Davis (1982 Lada Classic).
first to make 147 in World Championships	Cliff Thorburn (1983).
women's Embassy World Champion 2001	Lisa Quick (GB).
world champions at the Crucible	John Spencer (1977), Ray Reardon (1978), Terry Griffiths (1979), Cliff Thorburn (1980), Steve Davis (1981), Alex Higgins (1982), Steve Davis (1983–84), Dennis Taylor (1985), Joe Johnson (1986), Steve Davis (1987–89), Stephen Hendry (1990), John Parrott (1991), Stephen Hendry 1992–96), Ken Doherty (1997), John Higgins (1998), Stephen Hendry (1999), Mark Williams (2000), Ronnie O'Sullivan (2001).
softball: inventor	George Hancock invented the indoor version of baseball in 1887 in Chicago.
speedway: laps	four
1998 world champion	Tony Rickardsson of Sweden.

sport stars

Baird, Charlotte	surfing
Clarke, Chris	croquet
Fogarty, Carl	superbike racing
Heaney, Julz	water skiing
Heaney, Nick	water skiing
Simmonite, Rachael	rallying
Simmonite, Stephanie	rallying
Smith, Lawrie	yachting.

squash: origins	Harrow school.
world champion sixteen years running	Heather McKay Blundell of Australia.
stop on line: competitors do not pass finishing line	swimming.
substitutes: allowed while game in play	ice hockey.
suicides: famous sportsmen	Fred Archer (1857–86), champion jockey for 13 years 1874–86, shot himself aged 29. George O'Dell (1945–81), a double world champion in side-car racing, took his own life aged 35. Recent sporting suicides include the Yorkshire cricketer David Bairstow and footballer Justin Fashanu.
table tennis: ball dimensions	from 2001 season ball diameter increased to 40mm.
expedite rule	comes into play in long game and means point must be won within so many strikes or server is awarded the point.
2001 world champions: men's	Wang Liqin
women's	Wang Nam
ten pin bowling: maximum score in one game	300.
tennis champs: British, venue	Telford.
Vasaloppet	Swedish marathon ski race over 85km between Sälen and Mora, first run in 1922.
volleyball: former name	invented in 1895 by William Morgan of Massachusetts and called 'Mintonette'.
weightlifting: Olympic lifts	clean and jerk, snatch.
weightlifting: power lifts	bench press, dead lift, squat.
wrestling: two styles	freestyle and Greco-Roman.

yachting: famous champion	Peter Scott, son of explorer Robert Falcon Scott, won bronze medal in 1936 Olympics and became British gliding champion in 1963.
Olympic classes	Europe, Finn (solo class), 470, Laser, Mistral, Star, Tornado (catamaran), Soling (three-man crew).

Games: Miscellaneous

baccarat	gambling card game the object of which is to hold cards with values as near to nine as possible.
backgammon	dice number: 5; counters: 15 per player; points on board: 24.
bezique	played with a 64-card double piquet deck, i.e. all cards below 7, except the ace, are removed from two standard 52-card decks.
canasta	played with two standard decks of 52 cards, plus four jokers, totalling 108 cards. Hands are played until one partnership reaches 5000 points.
	Canasta was developed in Uruguay and passed via Argentina to the USA in 1949.
card games: names	boston, briscola, calabrasella, écarté, imperial, klaberjass, loo, michigan, napoleon, oh hell, Pope Joan, skat, vint, beggar my neighbour, donkey, old maid, Persian pasha.
cards: Queen depicted	Elizabeth of York (wife of Henry VII).
charades	parlour game whereby one person mimes and the other players guess the title.
chess: right-hand corner	the right-hand corner square as white sets up is white (important to remember).
chicane	bridge hand without trumps or without cards of any one suit.
Cluedo: characters	Colonel Mustard, Professor Plum, Reverend Green, Mrs Peacock, Miss Scarlet, Mrs White, Dr Black (victim).
weapons	knife, revolver, spanner, lead pipe, rope, and candlestick.
crambo	game in which a player gives a word or verse line to which each of the others must find a rhyme.
cribbage	developed by poet, Sir John Suckling, in the early 17th century and usually played to 121 points.
dominoes	28 tiles in a set with a total of 168 pips (seven doubles).
El Gordo	Spanish National Lottery (largest in the world).
euchre	played with a 32-card deck (cards below 7 are removed).
fan-tan	chinese gambling game in which players try to guess the remainder after the banker has divided a number of hidden objects into four groups.
faro	gambling card game in which bets are placed on the order of appearance of the cards. This is the game in which Count Rostov lost a fortune in Tolstoy's *War and Peace*.
frisbee: original name	Pluto Platter.
go	Japanese board game using terms: false eyes, eyes and armies. Played on a grid of 19 horizontal and 19 vertical lines forming 361interactions.
jai alai	South American version of pelota played with large curved wicker baskets.
mah jongg	Chinese game using terms: pung, kong and chow. 144 tiles are usually used (36 bamboos, 36 circles, 36 characters, 12 honours, 16 winds, 8 flowers and seasons). The name was coined and copyrighted by Joseph P. Babcock.
Monopoly: inventor	Charles Darrow, a heating engineer.
properties	brown: Old Kent Road (cheapest), Whitechapel; light blue: Angel Islington (pub), Euston Road, Pentonville Road; mauve: Pall Mall, Whitehall, Northumberland Avenue; orange: Bow Street, Marlborough Street, Vine Street (statistically the most 'landed on' square); red: Strand, Fleet Street, Trafalgar Square; yellow: Leicester Square, Coventry Street, Piccadilly; green: Regent Street, Oxford Street, Bond Street; dark blue: Park Lane, Mayfair (most expensive).
stations	King's Cross, Marylebone, Fenchurch Street, Liverpool Street.
corners	Go, Just Visiting, Free Parking, Go to Jail.
USA version	Atlantic City, New Jersey, is used, with 'Boardwalk' the most expensive property.
ombre	card game for three players that was popular throughout Europe in the 17th and 18th centuries.

SPORT & LEISURE

pall-mall	game in which a ball is driven by a mallet along an alley and through an iron ring.
patzer	poor player at chess.
pelota	Basque and Spanish game played in a walled court with a ball and 'basket-like' rackets attached to the hand. Pelota is thought to be the fastest of ball sports outside golf.
pinochle	pronounced 'pea knuckle', and played with 48 cards (two decks stripped of cards below 9). Within the game, pinochle stands for the Jack of Diamonds and Queen of Spades. The 9 of trumps is called the dix. Winner is player who first reaches 1000 points.
piquet	given the name by Charles I of England to honour Henrietta Maria, his French wife. Piquet deck is 32 cards with all cards below 7 stripped from deck.
poker: best hand	royal flush (ace to 10 in the same suit).
roulette: numbers	European wheels have 37 divisions (0–36), American wheels have 38 including a double zero.
Scrabble: inventor	James Brunot in 1949, first used the name scrabble.
made by	Spear Games.
tile values	highest Q and Z (10), J and X (8), K (5), Y H V W F (4), P M C B (3), D G (2), others 1 point except blank (0).
original name	criss cross (designed by Alfred M. Butts, an architect, in 1931).
vigoro	Australian ball game combining elements of cricket and baseball.
Yarborough	whist or bridge hand with no card above a 9. Named afer the earl of Yarborough who died in 1897, and was said to have bet against its occurrence.
tarot	originally 22 cards (the Major Arcana: see below). The Venetians added 56 cards (the Minor Arcana) split into 4 suits: the clubs, symbolizing money matters; cups (hearts), symbolizing love and friendship; swords (spades), symbolizing ill fortune; denari (diamonds), symbolizing business and travel.

0	Fool/Joker	11	Fortitude / Strength
1	Magician / Montebank	12	Hanged Man
2	High Priestess / Popess	13	Death
3	Empress	14	Temperance
4	Emperor	15	Devil
5	Hierophant / Pope	16	Tower
6	Lovers	17	Star
7	Chariot	18	Moon
8	Justice	19	Sun
9	Hermit	20	Judgement
10	Wheel of Fortune	21	World / Universe

NB In some versions of the Major Arcana nos. 8 and 11 are reversed.

Stamps: First Issues

Country	Year	Country	Year	Country	Year
Aden	1937	Brazil	1843	Dominica	1874
Afghanistan	1870	British Indian Ocean	1968	Dominican Republc	1865
Andorra	1928	Territory		Ecuador	1865
Antigua and Barbuda	1862	British Solomon Isles	1907	Egypt	1866
Argentina	1858	Brunei	1906	El Salvador	1867
Armenia	1920	Bulgaria	1879	Estonia	1918
Ascension	1922	Burma/Myanmar	1937	Ethiopia	1894
Australia	1902	Canada	1851	Faroe Isles	1940
Austria	1850	Cape of Good Hope	1853	Fiji	1870
Azerbaijan	1919	Cayman Islands	1900	Finland	1856
Bahamas	1859	Channel Isles	1941	France	1849
Bahrain	1933	Chile	1853	Gambia	1869
Bangladesh	1971	China	1878	Georgia	1919
Barbados	1852	Cook Isles	1892	Germany	1872
Barbuda	1922	Crete	1900	Ghana	1875
Belgium	1849	Cuba	1855	Gibraltar	1886
Belize	1866	Cyprus	1880	Great Britain	1840
Bermuda	1865	Czech Republic	1918	Greece	1861
Bolivia	1866	Danish West Indies	1855	Greenland	1938
Bosnia-Hercegovina	1879	Danzig	1920	Grenada	1861
Botswana	1886	Denmark	1851	Guatemala	1871

Guyana	1850	Palestine	1918
Haiti	1881	Panama	1878
Hawaii	1851	Papua	1901
Heligoland	1867	Papua New Guinea	1952
Honduras	1866	Paraguay	1870
Hong Kong	1862	Philippines	1854
Hungary	1871	Pitcairn Isles	1940
Iceland	1873	Portugal	1853
India	1852	Queensland	1860
Ionian Isles	1859	Rhodesia	1890
Ireland	1922	Rhodesia and Nyasaland	1954
Isle of Man	1973	Russia	1857
Israel	1948	Sabah (North Borneo)	1883
Italy	1862	San Marino	1877
Jamaica	1860	Sarawak	1869
Japan	1871	Saudi Arabia	1916
Jordan	1920	Serbia	1866
Kenya	1890	Seychelles	1890
Kiribati	1911	Sierra Leone	1860
Latvia	1918	South Africa	1910
Lebanon	1924	South Australia	1855
Leeward Isles	1890	Southern Rhodesia	1924
Liberia	1860	South West Africa	1923
Liechtenstein	1912	South Yemen	1963
Lithuania	1918	Spain	1850
Luxembourg	1852	Sri Lanka	1857
Malawi	1891	St Helena	1856
Malaysia	1867	Sudan	1897
Maldives	1906	Swaziland	1889
Malta	1860	Sweden	1855
Mauritius	1847	Switzerland	1843
Mexico	1856	Syria	1919
Monaco	1885	Tasmania	1853
Mongolia	1924	Thailand	1883
Montserrat	1876	Tokelau Isles	1948
Natal	1857	Tonga	1886
Nauru	1915	Transvaal	1869
Nepal	1881	Turkey	1863
Netherlands	1852	Uganda	1895
New Guinea	1914	Uruguay	1856
New South Wales	1850	USA	1845
New Zealand	1855	USA: Confederacy	1861
Nicaragua	1862	Victoria	1850
Nigeria	1914	Western Australia	1854
Norfolk Isles	1947	Yemen	1926
Northern Rhodesia	1925	Zambia	1964
Norway	1855	Zanzibar	1895
Orange Free State	1868	Zimbabwe	1979
Pakistan	1947	Zululand	1888

SPORT & LEISURE

TELEVISION

Programmes

A For Andromeda Julie Christie (Christine/A for Andromeda).

Absolutely Fabulous Jennifer Saunders (Edina Monsoon), Joanna Lumley (Patsy Stone), Julia Sawalha (Saffron), Jane Horrocks (Bubble), June Whitfield (Mother). Shopped at Harvey Nichols and based on Lynne Franks.

Adam Adamant Lives! Gerald Harper (Adam Llewellyn De Vere Adamant), Juliet Harmer (Georgina Jones), Peter Ducrow (the Face). Entombed from 1902 to 1966.

Addams Family, The Carolyn Jones (Morticia), John Astin (Gomez), Jackie Coogan (Uncle Fester Frump), Ted Cassidy (Lurch and Thing), Blossom Rock, sister of Jeanette McDonald (Grandmama). Lived in Cemetery Ridge with assortment of pets including octopus called Aristotle, black widow spider called Homer, man-eating African strangler called Cleopatra.

Adventures of Black Beauty, The Judi Bowker (Victoria Gordon), William Lucas (Dr James Gordon).

Adventures of Robin Hood, The Richard Greene (Robin), Bernadette O'Farrell and Patricia Driscoll (Maid Marian), Archie Duncan and Rufus Cruikshank (Little John), Alexander Gauge (Friar Tuck), Alan Wheatley (Sheriff of Nottingham). Theme sung by Dick James.

Adventures of Tugboat Annie, The Minerva Urecal (Tugboat Annie Brennan, Capt. of *Narcissus*), Walter Sande (Capt. Bullwinkle).

Adventures of William Tell, The Conrad Phillips (Tell), Jennifer Jayne (Hedda), Willoughby Goddard (Landburgher Gessler).

After Henry Prunella Scales (Sarah France), Joan Sanderson (Eleanor Prescott). Originally a BBC radio series, it was transferred to television with the same two stars.

Agony Maureen Lipman (Jane Lucas), Simon Williams (Laurence Lucas). Magazine: *Person Series*. Created by Anna Raeburn and Len Richmond.

Airwolf Jan-Michael Vincent (Stringfellow Hawke, a keen cellist), Ernest Borgnine (Dominic Santini).

Alf Alien Life Form (Michu Meszaros wore furry suit and Paul Fusco was the voice of ALF), Max Wright (Willie Tanner). Home planet: Melmac. Neighbours: Ochmoneks. Tanners' pet cat was called Lucky.

Alias Smith and Jones Pete Duel (Hannibal Heyes/Joshua Smith), Ben Murphy (Jed 'Kid' Curry/Thaddeus Jones). Roger Davis was narrator of first series but took over from Pete Duel after he committed suicide and Ralph Story took over voice-overs.

All Creatures Great and Small Christopher Timothy (James Herriot), Robert Hardy (Siegfried Farnon), Tricki Woo (Pekinese), Peter Davison (Tristan Farnon), Carol Drinkwater and Lynda Bellingham (Helen Alderson/Herriot).

All Gas and Gaiters Derek Nimmo (Rev. Mervyn Noote), William Mervyn (Bishop), Robertson Hare (Archdeacon).

All in the Family Carroll O'Connor (Archie Bunker), Jean Stapleton (Edith 'Dingbat' Bunker), Rob Reiner (Mike 'Meathead' Stivic the Pole), Sally Struthers (Gloria). America's answer to Alf Garnett.

All Our Yesterdays Presenters: James Cameron, Brian Inglis, Bernard Braden.

'Allo 'Allo Gordon Kaye (René Artois), Carmen Silvera (Edith), Vicki Michelle (Yvette), Guy Siner (Lt Gruber), Nicholas Frankou (Flying Officer Carstairs), John D. Collins (Flying Officer Fairfax), Kirsten Cooke (Michelle), Richard Gibson (Herr Flick), Richard Marner (Colonel Von Strohm), Kim Hartman (Helga Geerhart). Created by Jeremy Lloyd and David Croft.

Ally McBeal Calista Flockhart (Ally McBeal), Gil Bellows (Billy Thomas), Courtney Thorne-Smith (Georgia Thomas), Greg Germann (Richard Fish), Peter MacNicol (John Cage), Lucy Liv (Ling Woo).

And Mother Makes Three Wendy Craig (Sally Harrison/Redway). Follow-up series called *And Mother Makes Five*.

Andromeda Breakthrough, The Susan Hampshire (Christine/A for Andromeda). Follow-on series from *A For Andromeda*.

Andy Pandy Created by Freda Lingstrom and Maria Bird. Friends: Teddy and Looby Loo.

Angels Fiona Fullerton (Patricia Rutherford), Julie Dawn Cole (Jo Longhurst), Shirley Cheriton (Kathy Betts), Pauline Quirke (Vicky Smith). Hospital: St Angela's, Battersea.

Animal Hospital Rolf Harris, Shauna Lowry (Hamden Veterinary Hospital in Aylesbury).

Animal Magic Presenters: Johnny Morris, Terry Nutkins.

Antiques Roadshow Presenters: Angela Rippon, Bruce Parker, Arthur Negus, Hugh Scully. See *Going For A Song*.

Aquarius Presenters: Humphrey Burton, Russell Harty, Peter Hall.

Are You Being Served? John Inman (Mr Humphries), Mollie Sugden (Mrs Slocombe), Arthur Brough (Mr Grainger), Frank Thornton (Capt. Peacock), Nicholas Smith (Mr Rumbold), Arthur English (Mr Harman), Wendy Richard (Miss Brahms), Mike Berry (Mr Spooner), Trevor Bannister (Mr Lucas). Sequel: *Grace and Favour*.

Army Game, The William Hartnell (CSM Bullimore), Bill Fraser (Sgt Claude Snudge), Michael Medwin (Corporal Springer), Harry Fowler (Corporal 'Flogger' Hoskins), Charles Hawtrey (Pte 'Prof' Hatchett), Bernard Bresslaw (Pte 'Popeye' Popplewell), Alfie Bass (Pte 'Excused Boots' Bisley), Norman Rossington (Pte 'Cupcake' Cook), Frank Williams (Capt. Pocket), Mario Fabrizi (Lance Corporal Ernest 'Moosh' Merryweather), Dick Emery (Pte 'Chubby' Catchpole). Base: Hut 29 of the Surplus Ordnance Depot at Nether Hopping, Staffordshire.

Around the World in 80 Days Michael Palin's reconstruction of Phileas Fogg's journey.

Arthur of the Britons Oliver Tobias (Arthur), Rupert Davies (Cerdig), Jack Watson (Llud), Brian Blessed (Mark of Cornwall), Michael Gothard (Kai).

A-Team, The George Peppard (Col. John 'Hannibal' Smith), Lawrence 'Mr T' Tureaud (Sgt Bosco 'BA'

Baracus), Dwight Schultz (Capt. HM 'Howling Mad' Murdock), Dirk Benedict (Lt Templeton 'Faceman' Peck), Melinda Culea (Amy Amanda Allen alias Triple A). 'BA' stood for Bad Attitude.

At Last the 1948 Show   John Cleese, Tim Brooke-Taylor, Graham Chapman, Marty Feldman, Aimi Macdonald.

Auf Wiedersehen Pet   Tim Healy (Denis Patterson), Jimmy Nail ('Oz' Osbourne), Kevin Whately (Neville Hope), Gary Holton (Wayne), Pat Roach (Bomber), Timothy Spall (Barry Taylor), Christopher Fairbank (Moxey). Gary Holton died during filming of the follow-up series in Spain.

Avengers, The   Patrick MacNee (John Steed), Honor Blackman (Cathy Gale), Diana Rigg (Emma Peel), Linda Thorson (Tara King), Patrick Newell (Mother). Steed lived at 3 Duchess Mews, London. Originally called *Police Surgeon*, starring Ian Hendry as Dr David Keel.

A.J. Wentworth, BA   Arthur Lowe played the absent-minded teacher.

Bagpuss   Bagpuss owned by Emily. Narrator and writer: Oliver Postgate.

Ballykissangel   Niall Tobin (Father MacAnally), Gary Whelan (Brendan Kearney), Peter Caffrey (Padraig Kelly), Deirdre Donnelly (Siobhan Mehigan), Birdy Sweeney (Eamon), Victoria Smurfit (Orla), Don Wycherley (Father Aidan), Aine Ni Mhuiri (Kathleen), Joe Savino (Liam), Tina Kellegher (Niamh Egan), Lorcan Cranitch (Sean Dillon), Frankie McCafferty (Donal). Original series starred Stephen Tompkinson (Father Clifford) and Dervla Kirwan (Assumpta Fitzgerald) and the late Tony Doyle.

Banacek   George Peppard (Thomas Banacek).

Banana Splits, The   Voices: Fleegle (Paul Winchell), Bingo (Daws Butler), Drooper (Allan Melvin), Snorky (Don Messick).

Batman   Adam West (Batman/Bruce Wayne), Burt Ward (Robin/Dick Grayson), Frank Gorshin and John Astin (Riddler), Julie Newmar, Eartha Kitt, Lee Meriwether (Catwoman), Vincent Price (Egg Head), Tallulah Bankhead (Black Widow), Burgess Meredith (Penguin), Carolyn Jones (Queen of Diamonds), Liberace (Chandel), Cliff Robertson (Shame), Van Johnson (Minstrel), Shelley Winters (Ma Parker), Ida Lupino (Dr Cassandra), Otto Preminger, George Sanders and Eli Wallach (Mr Freeze), Cesar Romero (Joker), Yvonne Craig (Batgirl alias Barbara Gordon).

Battlestar Galactica   Lorne Greene (Commander Adama), Dirk Benedict (Lt Starbuck).

Baywatch   David Hasselhoff (Lt Mitch Bucannon), Pamela Denise Anderson (C.J. Parker), Erika Eleniak (Shauni McLain), Nicole Eggert (Summer Quinn), Yasmin Bleeth (Caroline Holden). Story of Los Angeles County Lifeguards working on Malibu Beach. Spin-off from 1989 TV film *Panic at Malibu Beach*, starring David Hasselhoff.

Beauty and the Beast   Vincent (Ron Perlman), Assistant DA Catherine Chandler (Linda Hamilton), Roy Dotrice (Father), Stephen McHattie (Gabriel).

Beiderbecke Affair   James Bolam (Trevor Chaplin), Barbara Flynn (Jill Swinburne). The Beiderbecke of the title was Bix Beiderbecke the jazz great, whose music was played by Kenny Baker. Sequels were *The Beiderbecke Tapes* and *The Beiderbecke Connection*.

Ben Casey   Vince Edwards (Ben), Sam Jaffe (Dr David Zorba), Ben Piazza (Dr Mike Rogers).

Hospital: County General. Produced by Bing Crosby Productions, which discovered Vince Edwards.

Bergerac   John Nettles (Det. Sgt Jim Bergerac), Terence Alexander (Charlie Hungerford), Lisa Goddard (Philippa Vale). Story of an alcoholic policeman in Jersey.

Beverly Hillbillies   Buddy Ebsen (Jed Clampett), Irene Ryan (Daisy Moses alias Granny), Donna Douglas (Elly May), Max Baer Jnr (Jethro Bodine and Jethrene Bodine), Nancy Kulp (Jane Hathaway), Sharon Tate (Janet Trego).

Beverly Hills 90210   Shannen Doherty (Brenda Walsh), Jason Priestley (Brandon Walsh). Title is a Zip code.

Bewitched   Elizabeth Montgomery (Samantha Stephens), Dick York and Dick Sargent (Darren), Agnes Moorhead (Endora), Marion Lorne (Aunt Clara), David White (Larry Tate).

Big Big Talent Show, The   Jonathan Ross hosts the star-spotting talent show.

Big Break   Snooker-based game show hosted by Jim Davidson and John Virgo.

Big Brother   Launched in July 2000. The original ten housemates were Anna, Andrew, Caroline, Craig, Darren, Melanie, Nick, Nichola, Sada and Thomas. Nick Bateman was evicted for cheating and replaced by Claire Strutton. The three finalists were Craig Philips, Anna Nolan and Darren Ramsey. The winner of the £70,000 first prize was Craig. Marjorie was the pet chicken, Juanita the toy baby, and Davina McCall the presenter.

Birds of a Feather   Pauline Quirke (Sharon Theodopolopoudos), Linda Robson (Tracey Stubbs), Lesley Joseph (Dorien Green), Peter Polycarpou and David Cardy (Chris Theodopolopoudos). Series created by Laurence Marks and Maurice Gran.

Blackadder   Various series written by Rowan Atkinson, Richard Curtis and Ben Elton. Characters included Baldrick (Tony Robinson), Queen Elizabeth I (Miranda Richardson), Melchett (Stephen Fry), Captain Darling/Percy (Tim McInnerny).

Blake's 7   Gareth Thomas (Blake), Paul Darrow (Kerr Avon), Sally Knyvette (Jenna Stannis), Michael Keating (Vila Restal), Jan Chappell (Cally from Auron), Josette Simon (Dayna Mellanby), David Jackson (Gan Olag), Steven Pacey (Capt. Del Tarrant), Peter Tuddenham (voice of Zen and Orac), Glynis Barber (Soolin), Jacqueline Pearce (Servalan). Spacecraft: Liberator and Scorpio Penal Colony, Cygnus Alpha. Dictatorship name: The Federation. Creator: Terry Nation. Gan Olag was implanted with a 'Brain Limiter' to stop him killing.

Blooming Marvellous   Sarah Lancashire (Liz), Clive Mantle (Jack).

Blot on the Landscape   David Suchet (Blott), George Cole (Sir Giles Lynchwood MP), Simon Cadell (Dundridge). Adaption by Malcolm Bradbury of Tom Sharpe's black comic novel. Filmed at Stanage Park, near Ludlow.

Blue Peter   Original presenters in 1958: Leila Williams and Christopher Trace. Other presenters include Valerie Singleton, Peter Purves, John Noakes, Lesley Judd, Simon Groom, Sarah Greene, Peter Duncan, Janet Ellis, Michael Sundin, Anthea Turner, Diane-Louise Jordan, Caron Keating, John Leslie, Mark Curry and Yvette Fielding.

Bonanza   Lorne Greene (Ben Cartwright), Michael Landon (Little Joe Cartwright), Dan Blocker (Eric 'Hoss' Cartwright, Norwegian for good luck), Pernell Roberts (Adam), Victor Sen Yung (Hop Sing), Ray

Teal (Sheriff Ray Coffee), David Canary (Mr 'Candy' Canaday), Tim Matheson (Griff King). The three sons had different mothers.

Boon   Michael Elphick (Ken Boon), Neil Morrissey (Rocky Cassidy).

Boss Cat   Cartoon characters include: Benny the Ball, Choo Choo, Spook, The Brain, Fancy-Fancy, Officer Dibble. Series called *Top Cat* outside UK.

Bottom   Rik Mayall (Richie Richard), Adrian Edmondson (Eddie Hitler).

Bouquet of Barbed Wire   Frank Finlay (Peter Manson), Sheila Allen (Cassie), Susan Penhaligon (Prue), James Aubrey (Gavin Sorenson).

Boyd QC   Michael Denison.

Boys from the Blackstuff   Bernard Hill (Yosser Hughes), Michael Angelis (Chrissie Todd), Julie Walters (Angie Todd). Written by Alan Bleasdale. Famous catchphrase: Gi's a job.

Boys from the Bush   Tim Healy (Reg Toomer), Chris Haywood (Dennis Tontine).

Brains Trust, The   Chairmen: Hugh Ross Willliams, Michael Flanders.

Branded   Chuck Connors (Jason McCord), only survivor of Indian massacre at the Battle of Bitter Creek in Wyoming and thought therefore to be a coward. Opening court martial scene is memorable.

Brass   Timothy West (Bradley Hardacre), Caroline Blakiston (Patience), Geoffrey Hinsliff and Geoffrey Hutchings (George Fairchild). Set in Utterley.

Bread   Peter Howitt and Graham Bickley (Joey Boswell), Jean Boht (Nellie), Ronald Forfar (Freddie), Victor McGuire (Jack), Gilly Coman and Melanie Hill (Aveline), Jonathan Morris (Adrian), Nick Conway (Billy), Rita Tushingham (Celia Higgins). Series created by Carla Lane.

Brideshead Revisited   Anthony Andrews (Lord Sebastian Flyte), Jeremy Irons (Charles Ryder), Diana Quick (Lady Julia Flyte), Laurence Olivier (Lord Marchmain), John Gielgud (Edward Ryder), Claire Bloom (Lady Ryder).

Brittas Empire, The   Chris Barrie (Gordon), Pippa Heywood (Helen), Julia St John (Laura Lancing). Leisure centre: Whitbury Newtown Leisure Centre.

Brothers, The   Jean Anderson (Mary Hammond), Glyn Owen and Patrick O'Connell (Edward Hammond), Gabrielle Drake (Jill Hammond), Colin Baker (Paul Merroney), Liza Goddard (April Merroney), Kate O' Mara (Jane Maxwell). Type of business: haulage.

Brush Strokes   Karl Howman (Jacko), Mike Walling (Eric), Nicky Croydon (Jean), Howard Lew Lewis (Elmo Putney), Gary Waldhorn (Lionel Bainbridge).

Buck Rogers in the 25th Century   Gil Gerard (Buck), Felix Silla (Twiki: voiced by Mel Blanc, Bob Elyea), Henry Silva and Michael Ansara (Kane), Wilfred Hyde-White (Dr Goodfellow), Pamela Hensley (Princess Ardala). Year 2491. Space capsule: Ranger 3, launched in 1987. City: New Chicago. Rivals: Draconians.

Budgie   Adam Faith (Budgie Bird), Iain Cuthbertson (Charlie Endell), Lynn Dalby (Hazel), Georgina Hale (Jean Bird), John Rhys-Davies (Laughing Spam Fritter), Rio Fanning (Grogan). Writers: Keith Waterhouse and Willis Hall.

Buffy the Vampire Slayer   Sarah Michelle Gellar (Buffy Summers), Alyson Hannigan (Willow Rosenberg), Nicholas Brendon (Xander Harris), Anthony Head (Rupert Giles), Emma Caulfield (Anya), Seth Green (Oz), Marc Blucas (Riley Finn), David Boreanaz (Angel), Charisma Carpentes

(Cordelia), James Marsters (Spike).

Bulman   Don Henderson (George Bulman). Character first appeared in *The XYY Man* and then in *Strangers*. His quirky nature included his wearing of fingerless gloves, constant use of an inhaler and carrying of a plastic bag whose contents we rarely saw.

Busman's Holiday   Presenters: Julian Pettifer, Sarah Kennedy, Elton Welsby.

Butterflies   Wendy Craig (Ria Parkinson), Geoffrey Palmer (Ben Parkinson, a dentist), Andrew Hall (Russell Parkinson), Nicholas Lyndhurst (Adam Parkinson). Series created by Carla Lane.

By the Sword Divided   Sharon Mughan (Anne Lacey/Fletcher), Julian Glover (Sir Martin Lacey), Tim Bentinck (Sir Thomas Lacey). Plot: a family is torn apart by the English Civil War.

Cagney and Lacey   Tyne Daly (Mary Beth Lacey), Meg Foster and Sharon Gless (Christine Cagney).

Call My Bluff   Presenters: Robert Robinson, Bob Holness.

Callan   Edward Woodward (Callan), Russell Hunter (Lonely), Ronald Radd, Michael Goodliffe, Derek Bond, William Squire (Hunter), Anthony Valentine (Toby Meres), Patrick Mower (Cross). Series started as an Armchair Theatre production, *A Magnum For Schneider*, with Peter Bowles playing Toby Meres.

Camberwick Green   Took over Monday *Watch with Mother* slot from 'Picture Box'. Characters included Capt. Snort, Sgt Major Grout, Windy Miller of Colley's Mill, Mickey Murphy the baker, Dr Mopp, Thomas Tripp the milkman, Mrs Dingle the postmistress, Mrs Honeyman, PC McGarry (No. 452).

Campion   Peter Davison (Albert Campion), Brian Glover (Magersfontein Lugg, Campion's manservant).

Candid Camera   Presenters: Bob Monkhouse, Jonathan Routh, Peter Dulay.

Captain Pugwash   Characters included Capt. Horatio Pugwash (Skipper of the *Black Pig*), Able Seamen Barnabas and Willy, Master Bate, Tom and Cutthroat Jake. Theme music 'The Hornblower', performed by Tommy Edmonson. Narrator: Peter Hawkins.

Captain Scarlet and the Mysterons   Voices: Francis Matthews (Paul Metcalfe/Capt. Scarlet), Donald Gray (Charles Gray/Col. White), Ed Bishop (Adam Svenson/Capt. Blue), Paul Maxwell (Bradley Holden/Capt. Grey), Sylvia Anderson (Magnolia Jones/Melody Angel), Liz Morgan (Juliette Pointon/Destiny Angel), Janna Hill (Karen Wainwright/Symphony Angel), Liz Morgan (Diane Sims/Rhapsody Angel), Lian-Shin (Chan Kwan/Harmony Angel), Donald Gray (Conrad Turner/Capt. Black), Charles Tingwell (Edward Wilkie/Dr Fawn), Gary Files (Patrick Donaghue/Capt. Magenta), Jeremy Wilkin (Richard Frazier/Capt. Ochre), Cy Grant (Seymour Griffiths/Lt Green), Paul Maxwell (World President). Year: 2068. Spectrum base: Cloudbase Angel. Interceptor aircraft codeword: SIG Spectrum is Green.

Casey Jones   Alan Hale Jnr (John Luther 'Casey' Jones). Worked for Illinois Central Railroad. Engine name: Cannonball Express. His faithful dog was called Cinders.

Cathy Come Home   Carol White (Cathy Ward), Ray Brooks (Reg Ward). Written by Jeremy Sandford, directed by Ken Loach. This drama brought Shelter, a campaign for the homeless, to the awareness of many.

Catweazle Geoffrey Baildon (Catweazle), Robin Davis (Carrot Bennett). Story of an 11th-century wizard stranded in the 20th century.

Champions Stuart Damon (Craig Stirling), William Gaunt (Richard Barrett), Alexandra Bastedo (Sharon McCready). Worked for Nemesis, based in Geneva.

Changing Rooms Hosted by Carol Smillie. Designers include Graham Wynne and Linda Barker. DIY expert: Andy Kane.

Charlie's Angels Kate Jackson (Sabrina Duncan), Farrah Fawcett-Majors (Jill Munroe), Jaclyn Smith (Kelly Garrett), Cheryl Ladd (Kris Munroe), Shelley Hack (Tiffany Welles), Tanya Roberts (Julie Rogers). Voice of Charlie Townshend: John Forsythe.

Cheers Ted Danson (Sam Malone), Shelley Long (Diane Chambers), Rhea Perlman (Carla Tortelli/Le Bec), Georg Wendt (Norm the accountant), John Ratzenberger (Cliff the mailman), Kelsey Grammer (Frasier Crane the psychiatrist), Woody Harrelson (Woody), Kirstie Alley (Rebecca Howe).

Chef Lenny Henry (Gareth Blackstock), Caroline Lee Johnson (Janice), Roger Griffiths (Everton). Chef of Le Château Anglais in the Oxfordshire Cotswolds.

Cheyenne Clint Walker (Cheyenne Bodie). Replaced for short time by Ty Hardin as Bronco Lane, who eventually gained his own series.

Chigley Described as a hamlet near Camberwick Green, Trumptonshire. Characters included Mr Clutterbuck the Builder, Chipppy Minton the Carpenter, Lord Belborough, Mr Cresswell the owner of the biscuit factory, Harry Farthing the Potter, Mr Brackett the Butler.

Chinese Detective, The David Yip (Det. Sgt Johnny Ho).

Chips Erik Estrada (Francis 'Ponch' Poncherello), Larry Wilcox (Jonathan Baker). Story of two Los Angeles police motorcyclists working for the California Highway Patrol (Chips).

Circus Boy Notable for the casting of Mickey Braddock (formerly and latterly Dolenz) as Corky.

Cisco Kid, The Duncan Renaldo (Cisco), Leo Carrillo (Pancho). Cisco's horse: Diablo. Pancho's horse: Loco. Pancho was expert with a whip. Based on stories by O'Henry.

Citizen James Sid James (Sidney Balmoral James), Bill Kerr (William 'Bill' Kerr), Liz Fraser (Liz Fraser).

Citizen Smith Robert Lindsay (Walter Henry 'Wolfie' Smith), Mike Grady (Ken), Tony Millan (Tucker), Cheryl Hall (Shirley), Peter Vaughan and Tony Steedman (Charlie Johnson). Leader of the Tooting Popular Front with his catchphrase 'Power to the People'.

Clangers, The Clangers were the pink and woolly, mouse-like creatures who took their names from the sound made when they battened down their dustbin-lid hatches and retreated underground. Other inhabitants of the planet were the Froglets, Soup Dragon and Iron Chicken.

Cleopatras, The Actresses who played the Cleopatras included Michelle Newell, Elizabeth Shepherd, Caroline Mortimer, Sue Holderness, Amanda Boxer, Prue Clarke, Pauline Moran.

Colditz Jack Hedley (Lt Col. John Preston), Robert Wagner (Flt Lt/Major Phil Carrington), David McCallum (Flt Lt Simon Carter), Bernard Hepton (Kommandant), Anthony Valentine (Major Horst Mohn).

Come Dancing Presenters include McDonald Hobley, Angela Rippon, David Jacobs, Terry Wogan, Rosemarie Ford, Noel Edmonds, Judith Chalmers,

Keith Fordyce, Michael Aspel, Peter West and Peter Dimmock.

Compact Ronald Allen (Ian Harmon), Carmen Silvera (Camilla Hope), Vincent Ball (David Rome). Created by Hazel Adair and Peter Ling of *Crossroads* fame.

Cool For Cats Britain's first pop music show in 1956 and hosted by Ker Robertson and then Kent Walton.

Cosby Show Bill Cosby (Heathcliff Huxtable, an obstetrician), Phylicia Ayres-Allen/Rashad (Clair, a lawyer). Their children: Sondra, Rudy, Denise, Theo, Vanessa.

Countdown Words-and-numbers game hosted by Richard Whiteley and Carol Vorderman. First programme on Channel 4. *Countdown* has the most professional production team of any show on the box – it includes three *Countdown* champions and producer Mark Nyman is a former World Scrabble Champion. The author has happy memories of the show although beaten on the conundrum on his second appearance.

Cracker Robbie Coltrane (Eddie 'Fitz' Fitzgerald). Created by Jimmy McGovern.

Crackerjack Hosts: Eamonn Andrews, Leslie Crowther, Michael Aspel, Ed Stewart, Stu Francis. Stooges: Peter Glaze, Don Maclean, Leslie Crowther. Game: Double or Drop.

Crime Traveller Michael French (David Wicks in *EastEnders*) starred in this time machine series.

Criss Cross Quiz Popular quiz show hosted by Jeremy Hawk (father of actress Belinda Lang). Derived its format from the American *Tic Tac Dough*.

C.A.T.S. Eyes Jill Gascoigne (Maggie Forbes), Rosalyn Landor (Pru Standfast), Leslie Ash (Frederica 'Fred' Smith). C.A.T.S. stood for Covert Activities Thames Section.

Dad's Army Arthur Lowe (Capt. George Mainwaring, a bank manager), John Le Mesurier (Sgt Arthur Wilson), Clive Dunn (L/Corporal Jack Jones, a butcher), John Laurie (Pte James Frazier, an undertaker), James Beck (Pte James Walker, a spiv), Ian Lavender (Pte Frank Pike, a silly boy), Arnold Ridley (Pte Charles Godfrey), Bill Pertwee (ARP Warden William Hodges, a greengrocer), Frank Williams (the vicar), Colin Bean (Pte Sponge), Pamela Cundell (Mrs Fox). Created by Jimmy Perry and David Croft and set in Walmington-on-Sea (supposedly Bexhill).

Dalziel and Pascoe Warren Clarke (Det. Supt Andrew Dalziel), Colin Buchanan (Det. Insp. Peter Pascoe). Written by Stephen Lowe and based on Reginald Hill's books.

Dangermouse Voices: Dangermouse (David Jason), Penfold (Terry Scott), Stiletto Mafioso (Brian Trueman), Baron Greenback (Edward Kelsey). Created by Mike Harding and Brian Trueman. Written by Brian Trueman and Angus Allen. Narrated by David Jason.

Darling Buds of May, The David Jason (Sidney Charles 'Pop' Larkin), Pam Ferris (Ma Larkin), Catherine Zeta Jones (Mariette Larkin/Charlton), Philip Franks (Cedric 'Charley' Charlton).

Defenders, The E.G. Marshall (Lawrence Preston), Robert Reed (Kenneth Preston). Father and son lawyers.

Dempsey and Makepeace Michael Brandon (Lt James Dempsey), Glynis Barber (Det. Sgt Harriet Makepeace). Dept: S110.

Department S Peter Wyngarde (Jason King), Joel Fabiani (Stewart Sullivan), Rosemary Nichols

TELEVISION

(Annabelle Hurst). Department S was a department of Interpol.

Desmond's Norman Beaton (Desmond Ambrose), Carmen Munroe (Shirley Ambrose), Ram John Holder (Pork Pie). Life in a Peckham barber's shop.

Detectives, The Jasper Carrott (Bob Louis), Robert Powell (Dave Briggs), George Sewell (Supt Frank Cottam).

Dial 999 Robert Beatty (Canadian Mountie Mike Maguire), seconded to London on work experience.

Dick Van Dyke Show, The Dick Van Dyke (Rob Petrie), Mary Tyler Moore (Laura), Larry Matthews (Ritchie), Rose Marie (Sally Rogers), Carl Reiner (Alan Brady), Morey Amsterdam (Maurice 'Buddy' Sorrell).

Dinnerladies Victoria Wood (Bren), Thelma Barlow (Dolly), Celia Imrie (Philippa), Maxine Peake (Twinkle), Anne Reid (Jean), Duncan Preston (Stan), Andrew Dunn (Tony), Shobna Gulati (Anita), Julie Walters (Petula), Christopher Greet (Mr Michael), Jane Hazlegrove (Lisa), Sue Devaney (Secretary).

Doctor Finlay Tannochbrae 20 years on (real-life Auchtermuchty in Fife), with Dr Finlay played by David Rintoul and the character's Christian name changed to John.

Dr Finlay's Casebook Bill Simpson (Dr Alan Finlay), Andrew Cruickshank (Dr Angus Cameron), Barbara Mullen (Janet). Set in 1920s Tannochbrae (real-life Callander), the base for practice was Arden House. The stories were based on *The Adventures of a Black Bag* by A.J. Cronin.

Doctor in the House Barry Evans (Michael Upton), Robin Nedwell (Duncan Waring), Geoffrey Davies (Dick Stuart-Clark), George Layton (Paul Collier). Based on the books by Richard Gordon.

Don't Wait Up Nigel Havers (Dr Tom Latimer), Tony Britton (Dr Toby Latimer). Writer: George Layton.

Doomwatch John Paul (Dr Spencer Quist), Simon Oates (Dr John Ridge), Robert Powell (Tobias 'Toby' Wren).

Dotto Game show hosted by Robert Gladwell, Jimmy Hanley and Shaw Taylor during its two-year run. Based on American show which was taken off as part of the 'Quiz Show Scandal'.

Dr Kildare Richard Chamberlain (Dr James Kildare), Raymond Massey (Dr Leonard Gillespie). Based on Max Brand books. Richard Chamberlain had a hit with the vocal version of the theme tune, 'Three Stars Will Shine Tonight'. Hospital: Blair General.

Dr Who First Dr Who was William Hartnell, followed by Patrick Troughton, Jon Pertwee, Tom Baker, Peter Davidson, Colin Baker, Sylvester McCoy. Other Dr Who's have included Richard Hurndall, who took William Hartnell's part in *The Five Doctors*, Paul McGann who played the Doctor in a television film, and Peter Cushing, who appeared as the Doctor in two feature films. The original crew were William Russell (Ian Chesterton), Jacqueline Hill (Barbara Wright) and Carole Ann Ford (Susan Foreman, the Doctor's granddaughter). Other assistants included Peter Purves (Steven Taylor), Nicola Bryant (Perpugillian 'Peri' Brown), Sophie Aldred (Ace), Frazer Hines (Jamie McCrimmon), Janet Fielding (Tegan Jovanka), Elizabeth Sladen (Sarah Jane Smith), Katy Manning (Jo Grant), Sarah Sutton (Nyssa). The Doctor is from the planet Gallifrey. The five actors who played the Master were (1) Roger Delgado (2) Peter Pratt (3) Geoffrey Beevers (4) Anthony Ainley (5) Eric Roberts. Tardis:

Time And Relative Dimensions In Space.

Dragnet Jack Webb (Joe Friday). Episodes began: 'The story you are about to see is true, only the names have been changed to protect the innocent.' Set in Los Angeles. Badge no.: 714.

Drop the Dead Donkey Robert Duncan (Gus), Neil Pearson (Dave), Jeff Rawle (George), Stephen Tompkinson (Damien), David Swift (Henry), Victoria Wicks (Sally). Written by Andy Hamilton and Guy Jenkin. Original working title for the show was 'Dead Belgians Don't Count'.

Duchess of Duke Street, The Gemma Jones (Louisa Trotter), Christopher Cazenove (Charles Tyrrell). Loosely based on the life story of Rosa Lewis, a kitchen maid who became manageress of the Cavendish Hotel in Jermyn Street. Hotel in series: Bentinck.

Dukes of Hazzard, The Catherine Bach (Daisy Duke), Tom Wopat (Luke Duke), John Schneider (Bo Duke), Sorrell Booke (Jefferson Davis 'Boss' Hogg). The Dukes were the Robin Hoods of Hazzard County, driving around in their 1969 Dodge Charger named The General Lee. Narration and theme tune by Waylon Jennings.

Dustbinmen, The John Woodvine and Brian Wilde (Bloody Delilah), Bryan Pringle (Cheese and Egg), Graham Haberfield (Winston Platt), Trevor Bannister (Heavy Breathing). Created and produced by Jack Rosenthal. Lorry called Thunderbird Three.

Edge of Darkness Bob Peck (Ronald Craven), Joanne Whalley (Emma Craven), Joe Don Baker (Darius Jedburgh). Music by Eric Clapton.

Edward and Mrs Simpson Edward Fox (Edward), Cynthia Harris (Mrs Wallis Warfield Simpson), Peggy Ashcroft (Queen Mary), David Waller (Stanley Baldwin).

Edward the Seventh Timothy West (Edward as an adult), Charles Sturridge (Edward as a teenager), Annette Crosbie (Queen Victoria), Robert Hardy (Prince Albert).

Elizabeth R Glenda Jackson (Elizabeth), Robert Hardy (Robert Dudley), Ronald Hines (William Cecil), Daphne Slater (Mary Tudor), Vivian Pickles (Mary, Queen of Scots), John Woodvine (Sir Francis Drake), Nicholas Selby (Sir Walter Raleigh).

Emergency Ward 10 Jill Browne (Carole Young), Charles Tingwell (Dr Alan Dawson), Desmond Carrington (Dr Chris Anderson), John Carlisle (Mr Lester Large), Ray Barrett (Dr Don Nolan), Jane Rossington (Nurse Kate Ford), Paul Darrow (Mr Verity), John Alderton (Dr Richard Moone), Pik-Sen Lim (Nurse Kwai).

Empire Road Norman Beaton (Everton Bennett).

Equalizer, The Edward Woodward (Robert McCall).

ER George Clooney (Dr Douglas Ross), Noah Wyle (Dr John Carter), Eriq La Salle (Dr Peter Benton), Julianna Margulies (Nurse Hathaway), Alex Kingston (Dr Elizabeth Corday), Anthony Edwards (Dr Mark Greene), Paul McCrane (Dr Robert Romano), Ming-Na (Dr Jing-Mai Chen), Michael Michele (Dr Cleo Finch), Maura Tiernay (Nurse Abby Lockheart), Laura Innes (Dr Kerry Weaver), Goran Visnjie (Dr Luka Kovac), Erik Palladino (Dr Dave Malucci). Set in Cook County Hospital, Chicago.

Ever-Decreasing Circles Richard Briers (Martin Brice), Penelope Wilton (Ann Brice), Stanley Lebor (Howard Hughes). Creators: John Esmonde and Bob Larbey.

Expert, The Marius Goring (Dr John Hardy).

Face to Face Presenter: John Freeman.

Fairly Secret Army Geoffrey Palmer (Major Harry Kitchener Wellington Truscott). Army called Queen's Own West Mercian Lowlanders.

Fall and Rise of Reginald Perrin, The Leonard Rossiter (Reginald Iolanthe Perrin/Martin Wellbourne), Pauline Yates (Elizabeth), John Barron (CJ), Sue Nicholls (Joan Greengross), Geoffrey Palmer (Jimmy), John Horsley (Doc Morrissey), Bruce Bould (David Harris-Jones). Created by David Nobbs. Companies: Sunshine Desserts/Grot.

Fame Debbie Allen (Lydia Grant), Erica Gimpel (Coco Hernandez), Gene Anthony Ray (Leroy Johnson), Lori Singer (Julie Miller), Janet Jackson (Cleo Hewitt).

Family at War, A Colin Douglas (Edwin Ashton), Barbara Flynn (Freda Ashton), Coral Atkins (Sheila Ashton), John Nettles (Ian McKenzie).

Family Fortunes Presenters include Bob Monkhouse, Max Bygraves and Les Dennis.

Family, The Fly-on-the-wall look at the Wilkins family from Reading.

Fantasy Football Presenters: Frank Skinner and David Baddiel.

Fantasy Island Ricardo Montalban (Mr Roarke), Herve Villechaize (Tattoo).

Far Pavilions, The Ben Cross (Ashton Pelham-Martyn), Amy Irving (Princess Anjuli), Christopher Lee (Kaka-Ji-Rao), Omar Sharif (Koda Dad), John Gielgud (Cavagnari), Rossano Brazzi (the Rana of Bhithor).

Father Dear Father Patrick Cargill (Patrick Glover), Natasha Pyne (Anna Glover), Ann Holloway (Karen Glover), Noel Dyson (Matilda 'Nanny' Harris).

Fawlty Towers John Cleese (Basil), Prunella Scales (Sybil), Andrew Sachs (Manuel), Connie Booth (Polly Sherman), Ballard Berkeley (Major Gowen). Set in Torquay.

FBI, The Efrem Zimbalist Jnr (Inspector Lewis Erskine).

Fifteen to One General knowledge quiz hosted by William G. Stewart. Series winners include Jon Goodwin, Anthony Martin, Kevin Ashman, Mal Collier, Thomas Dyer, Andrew Francis, Barbara Thompson, Leslie Booth, Julian Allen, Martin Riley, Ian Potts, Arnold O'Hara, Trevor Montague, Stanley Miller, Glen Binnie, Bill Francis, Mike Kirby, Nick Terry, Doug Griffiths and Bill McKaig. Mal Collier won the Champion of Champions event held at Christmas 1997. The author was sued by William G. Stewart for the return of his prizes and all his expenses incurred during his eight appearances on the show. The suit was brought by Mr Stewart because a breach of his rules took place whereby contestants are not allowed to take part a second time unless he invites them. The judge commented that 'Mr Stewart was very easily upset'.

Filthy, Rich and Catflap Nigel Planer (Filthy Ralph), Rik Mayall (Richard Rich), Adrian Edmondson (Eddie Catflap). Written by Ben Elton.

Fire Crackers Joe Baker (Jumbo). Inept local firemen working in Cropper's End.

Fireball XL5 Characters include Colonel Steve Zodiac, Professor Matthew Matic, Venus Commander Zero, Lt 90, Zoonie, Robert the Robot.

Flintstones Characters include Fred, Wilma and Pebbles Flintstone, Barney, Betty and Bamm Bamm Rubble, and Dino the pet dinosaur.

Flipper Luke Halpin (Sandy Ricks), Brian Kelly (Porter Ricks). Last star dolphin of seven, called Bebe, died 4 May 1997, aged 40.

Flowerpot Men, The Characters included Bill and Ben, Little Weed and Slowcoach the Tortoise.

Follyfoot Gillian Blake (Dora), Arthur English (Slugger), Desmond Llewellyn (the Colonel), Steve Hodson (Steve).

Food and Drink Presenters include Chris Kelly, Henry Kelly, Susan Grossman, Jilly Goolden, Michael Barry, Oz Clarke, Paul Heiney.

Forsyte Saga, The Kenneth More (Jolyon Forsyte), Eric Porter (Soames Forsyte), Nyree Dawn Porter (Irene Heron/Forsyte).

Fortunes of War Kenneth Branagh (Guy Pringle), Emma Thompson (Harriet Pringle).

Fosters, The Notable for an early performance by Lenny Henry as Sonny Foster.

Four Feather Falls Voice of Tex Tucker: Nicholas Parsons. One feather allowed Tex's dog Dusty to speak; another gave speech to his horse, Rocky; the last two controlled the accuracy of his pistols.

Four Just Men, The Jack Hawkins (Ben Manfred MP), Dan Dailey (Tim Collier), Richard Conte (Jeff Ryder), Vittorio De Sica (Ricco Poccari).

Frasier Kelsey Grammer (Frasier Crane), David Hyde Pierce (Niles Crane), Bebe Neuwirth (Lilith), John Mahoney (Martin Crane), Jane Leeves (Daphne Moon), Peri Gilpin (Roz Doyle).

Friends Lisa Kudrow (Phoebe), Matt Le Blanc (Joey), Courtney Cox (Monica), Jennifor Aniston (Rachel Green), David Schwimmer (Ross), Matthew Perry (Chandler).

F Troop Ken Berry (Captain Wilton Parmenter), Forrest Tucker (Sgt Morgan O'Rourke), Larry Storch (Corporal Randolph Agarn), John Mitchum (Trooper Hoffenmuller).

Fugitive, The David Janssen (Dr Richard Kimble), Barry Morse (Lt Philip Gerard), Bill Raisch (Fred Johnson alias the one-armed man).

Game for a Laugh Presenters include Matthew Kelly, Henry Kelly, Sarah Kennedy, Jeremy Beadle, Rustie Lee, Martin Daniels, Debbie Rix, Lee Peck.

Generation Game Hosts include Bruce Forsyth, Larry Grayson and Jim Davidson.

Gentle Touch, The Jill Gascoigne (DI Maggie Forbes), Derek Thompson (Det. Sgt Jimmy Fenton).

Get Smart Don Adams (Maxwell Smart, Agent 86), Barbara Feldon (Agent 99). Cover: salesman for Pontiac Greeting Card Co. Series created by Mel Brooks.

Girl From Uncle, The Stefanie Powers (April Dancer), Noel Harrison (Mark Slate), Leo G. Carroll (Mr Waverly).

Girls on Top Tracey Ullman (Candice), Dawn French (Amanda), Jennifer Saunders (Jennifer), Ruby Wax (Shelley), Joan Greenwood (Lady Carlton).

Give Us a Break Robert Lindsay (Mickey Noades), Paul McGann (Mo Morris).

Gladiators Presenters: John Fashanu, Jeremy Guscott, Ulrika Jonsson.

Gnomes of Dulwich Terry Scott and Hugh Lloyd continuing their partnership as a big and small gnome. John Clive played the third 'old' gnome.

Going For a Song Presenter: Max Robertson.

Golden Girls, The Beatrice Arthur (Dorothy Zbornak), Rue McClanahan (Blanche Devereaux), Betty White (Rose Nylund), Estelle Getty (Sophia Petrillo).

Golden Shot, The Presenters included Jackie Rae, Bob Monkhouse, Norman Vaughan, Charlie Williams.

TELEVISION

Good Afternoon Channel 5 daytime programme featuring the hospital documentary series Liverpool Mums, Pets Go Public, where contestants have to match pets with their owners, and Cryptogram, a general knowledge and word game of which the author has pleasant memories.

Good Life, The Richard Briers (Tom Good), Felicity Kendall (Barbara), Penelope Keith (Margo Leadbeatter), Paul Eddington (Jerry Leadbeatter). Goat: Geraldine.

Goodnight Sweetheart Nicholas Lyndhurst (Gary Sparrow), Dervla Kirwan (Phoebe Bamford), Victor McGuire (Ron Wheatcroft), Christopher Ettridge (PC Reg Deadman), Michelle Holmes (Yvonne Sparrow). Elizabeth Carling and Emma Amos took over leading female roles.

Good Old Days, The Transmitted from the Leeds City Varieties Theatre, compered by Leonard Sachs (originally Don Gemmell). Every show ended with a rendition of 'Down at the Old Bull and Bush'.

Grange Hill Todd Carty (Peter 'Tucker' Jenkins), Susan Tully (Suzanne Ross), Letitia Dean (Lucinda), Peter Moran (Pogo Patterson), Gwyneth Powell (Bridget McCluskey), Mark Savage (Gripper Stebson), Sean Maguire (Tegs Ratcliffe).

Great Antiques Hunt, The Host: Jilly Goolden.

Grimleys, The Brian Conley (Digby), Amanda Holden (Geraldine), Noddy Holder, James Bradshaw.

Gunsmoke/Gun Law James Arness (Matt Dillon), Amanda Blake (Kitty Russell), Milburn Stone (Dr Galen 'Doc' Adams), Dennis Weaver (Chester Goode), Burt Reynolds (Quint Asper).

Happy Days Henry Winkler (Arthur Fonzarelli), Ron Howard (Richie Cunningham), Scott Baio (Charles 'Chachi' Arcola), Suzi Quattro (Leather Tuscadero), Robin Williams (Mork).

Hark at Barker Ronnie Barker (Lord Rustless), David Jason (Dithers).

Harry Enfield Show Characters include the Slobs: Wayne and Waynetta and children Frogmella and Spudulike.

Hart to Hart Robert Wagner (Jonathan Hart), Stefanie Powers (Jennifer Hart), Lionel Stander (Max), Freeway the dog. Occupations: businessman and journalist.

Have Gun Will Travel Richard Boone (Paladin), Kam Tong (Hey Boy), Lisa Lu (Hey Girl).

Have I Got News for You Hosted by Angus Deayton. Team captains are Paul Merton and Ian Hislop.

Hawaii Five-O Jack Lord (Steve Garrett), James MacArthur ('Danno' Williams), Kam Fong (Chin Ho Kelly).

Hawkeye and the Last of the Mohicans John Hart (Nat 'Hawkeye' Cutler), Lon Chaney Jnr (Chingachgook).

Hazell Nicholas Ball (James Hazell), Roddy McMillan (Choc Minty). Created by Terry Venables and Gordon Williams.

Heartbeat Nick Berry (PC Nick Rowan), Derek Fowlds (Sgt Oscar Blaketon), Bill Maynard (Claude Jeremiah Greengrass). Set in 1964 Yorkshire.

Hector's House Adventures of a dog (Hector), a cat (Zaza) and a frog (Mrs Kiki).

Herbs, The Garden owners: Sir Basil and Lady Rosemary. Other characters include Constable Knapweed, Mr Onion the schoolteacher and his pupils, the Chives, Bayleaf the gardener, Aunt Mint, Sage the owl, Tarragon the dragon, Pashana Bedi

the snake-charmer, and Belladonna. The real stars were Dill the dog and Parsley the lion. Gordon Rollings was the narrator and the magic word that opened the gate was 'Herbidacious'.

Here's Lucy Lucille Ball (Lucy Carter), Gale Gordon (Harrison Carter).

Hergé's Adventures of Tin Tin Narrator: Peter Hawkins. Characters include Snowy the white fox-terrier, Captain Haddock, the Thompson Twins, Professor Calculus and General Alcazar.

Hi-De-Hi Paul Shane (Ted Bovis), Ruth Madoc (Gladys Pugh), Simon Cadell (Jeffrey Fairbrother), David Griffin (Squadron Leader Clive Dempster), Jeffrey Holland (Spike Dixon), Su Pollard (Peggy Ollerenshaw). Holiday camp: Maplins at Crimpton-on-Sea.

Highway to Heaven Michael Landon (Jonathan Smith), Victor French (Mark Gordon).

Hill Street Blues Daniel J.Travanti (Captain Frank Furillo), Veronica Hamel (Joyce Davenport), Robert Prosky (Sgt Stanislaus Jablonski).

Hitch-Hiker's Guide to the Galaxy, The Simon Jones (Arthur Dent), David Dixon (Ford Prefect), Sandra Dickinson (Trillian), David Learner (Marvin), Stephen Moore (Marvin's voice), Mark Wing-Davey (Zaphod Beeblebrox), Peter Jones (the book voice).

Hogan's Heroes Bob Crane (Colonel Robert Hogan), Werner Klemperer (Colonel Wilhelm Klink), John Banner (Sgt Hans Schulz), Larry Hovis (Sgt Andrew Carter), Ivan Dixon (Corporal James Kinchloe).

Holiday Presenters include Frank Bough, Des Lynam, Cliff Michelmore, Joan Bakewell, Jill Dando, Anneka Rice, Eamonn Holmes.

House of Cards Ian Richardson (Francis Urquhart). Based on Michael Dobbs's novel.

How/How 2 Presenters include Fred Dineage, Jack Hargreaves, Jon Miller, Bunty James, Marian Davies, Carol Vorderman, Gareth Jones.

Howard's Way Maurice Colbourne (Tom Howard), Jan Harvey (Jan Howard), Glyn Owen (Jack Rolfe), Stephen Yardley (Ken Masters), Tony Anholt (Charles Frere), Nigel Davenport (Sir Edward Frere), Kate O'Mara (Laura Wilde). Created by Gerard Glaister and Allan Prior. Yard name: Mermaid.

How Do They Do That? Presenters: Esther McVeigh and Eamonn Holmes.

HR Pufnstuff Jack Wild (Jimmy), Billie Hayes (Witchiepoo).

Huckleberry Hound Show, The Characters included Pixie and Dixie, Jinks the Cat, Yogi Bear and Boo Boo, Hokey Wolf and Ding a Ling. Huckleberry used to sing 'Clementine' constantly.

Human Jungle, The Herbert Lom (Dr Roger Corder), Sally Smith (Jennifer Corder), Mary Yeomans (Nancy Hamilton).

I Claudius Derek Jacobi (Claudius), Siân Phillips (Livia), Brian Blessed (Octavian/Augustus), George Baker (Tiberius), John Hurt (Caligula), Patrick Stewart (Sejanus), Chris Biggins (Nero).

I Love Lucy Lucille Ball (Lucy Ricardo), Desi Arnaz (Ricky Ricardo), Vivian Vance (Ethel Mertz), William Frawley (Fred Mertz). First sit-com to be filmed live in front of a studio audience.

In at the Deep End Chris Searle and Paul Heiney took it in turn to learn new skills.

Inside George Webley Roy Kinnear played the depressive character created by Keith Waterhouse and Willis Hall.

Inspector Alleyn Mysteries, The   Patrick Malahide (Chief Insp. Roderick Alleyn). Character created by Ngaio Marsh.

Inspector Morse   John Thaw (Chief Insp. Endeavour Morse), Kevin Whately (Det. Sgt Robbie Lewis).

Interpol Calling   Charles Korvin (Insp. Paul Duval), Edwin Richfield (Insp. Mornay).

Invaders, The   Roy Thinnes (David Vincent, an architect). Narrator: William Conrad.

Invisible Man, The   In the original series Dr Peter Brady's voice was that of Tim Turner although no actor was billed. David McCallum played the character of Daniel Westin in the 1975 series.

I Spy   Robert Culp (Kelly Robinson, tennis pro), Bill Cosby (Alexander Scott, tennis trainer).

It Ain't Half Hot Mum   Windsor Davies (RSM B.L. Williams), Melvyn Hayes (Bombardier 'Gloria' Beaumont), George Layton (Bombardier Solomons), Michael Bates (Rangi Ram), Don Estelle (Gunner 'Lofty' Sugden).

It Takes a Thief   Robert Wagner (Alexander Mundy), Fred Astaire (Alister Mundy).

Ivor the Engine   Narrated by David Edwards, Anthony Jackson, Olwen Griffiths and Oliver Postgate, who also wrote the stories. Railway: Merioneth and Llantissily Rail Traction Company. Driver: Jones the Steam. Other characters included Owen the Signal and Dai Station, the man who looked after Llaniog Station. Ivor's boiler was fired by Idris the dragon. Jones always aspired to sing in the choir like his pal Evans the Song. Peter Firmin drew all the pictures.

Jackanory   First story told by Lee Montague ('Cap of Rushes'). Most prolific story teller: Bernard Cribbins.

Jane   Glynis Barber played the wartime cartoon character in the 1982 television adaption.

Jemima Shore Investigates   Patricia Hodge played the TV reporter created by Lady Antonia Fraser.

Jesus of Nazareth   Robert Powell (Jesus as an adult), Immad Cohen (Jesus as a boy), Olivia Hussey (Virgin Mary), Anne Bancroft (Mary Magdalene), Ian McShane (Judas Iscariot), Rod Steiger (Pontius Pilate), James Mason (Joseph of Arimathea), Peter Ustinov (Herod the Great), Michael York (John the Baptist), Stacy Keach (Barabbas), Laurence Olivier (Nicodemus).

Jetsons, The   Jetsons lived in the 21st century in Orbit City. George Jetson worked at Spacely Space Sprockets. The family pet dog was Astro.

Jewel in the Crown, The   Peggy Ashcroft (Barbie Batchelor), Geraldine James (Sarah Layton), Stuart Wilson (Major Clark), Tim Pigott-Smith (Ronald Merrick), Art Malik (Hari Kumar), Susan Wooldridge (Daphne Manners), Charles Dance (Sgt Guy Perron), Josephine Welcome (Mira). Based on Paul Scott's novels.

Joe 90   Joe McClaine, alias Joe 90, worked for WIN, the World Intelligence Network, using his father's invention BIGRAT (Brain Impulse Galvanoscope Record And Transfer).

Joking Apart   Robert Bathurst (Mark Taylor), Tracie Bennett (Tracy), Fiona Gillies (Becky Taylor).

Jonathan Creek   Alan Davies (Jonathan Creek), Caroline Quentin (Madeline Magellan).

Juke Box Jury   First panel: Alma Cogan, Susan Stranks, Gary Miller and Pete Murray. The three presenters were David Jacobs, Noel Edmonds and Jools Holland.

Juliet Bravo   Stephanie Turner (Insp. Jean Darblay), Anna Carteret (Insp. Kate Longton). Fictional town: Hartley in Lancashire.

Junior Criss Cross Quiz   Hosts included Jeremy Hawk, Bob Holness, Mike Sarne, Bill Grundy and Danny Blanchflower.

Just Good Friends   Paul Nicholas (Vince Pinner), Jan Francis (Penny Warrender).

Kavanagh QC   John Thaw (James Kavanagh QC), Geraldine James (Eleanor Harker QC).

Keeping Up Appearances   Patricia Routledge (Hyacinth Bucket), Geoffrey Hughes (Onslow). Created by Roy Clarke.

Knight Rider   David Hasselhoff (Michael Knight, formerly Michael Long), William Daniels (voice of Kitt, the Knight Industries Two Thousand).

Kojak   Telly Savalas (Lt Theo Kojak), Dan Frazer (Capt. Frank McNeil), Kevin Dobson (Lt Bobby Crocker), George Savalas (Stavros), Mark Russell (Saperstein). Worked in Manhattan South 13th Precinct.

Krypton Factor, The   Tough quiz testing both physical and mental faculties. Gordon Burns's name was synonymous with the series.

Kung Fu   David Carradine (Kwai Chang Caine), Keye Luke (Master Po), Radames Pera (Caine as a boy). Bruce Lee was rejected for the role and died soon after.

KYTV   Angus Deayton (Mike Channel), Geoffrey Perkins (Mike Flex), Helen Atkinson Wood (Anna Daptor).

LA Law   Richard Dysart (Leland McKenzie), Harry Hamlin (Michael Kuzak), Corbin Bernsen (Arnie Becker), Michael Tucker (Stuart Markowitz), Diana Muldaur (Rosalind Shays).

Laramie   John Smith (Slim Sherman), Robert Fuller (Jess Harper), Hoagy Carmichael (Jonesy), Spring Byington (Daisy Cooper).

Larry Sanders Show, The   Garry Shandling (Larry Sanders), Rip Torn (Arthur), Jeffrey Tambor (Hank Kingsley).

Last of the Summer Wine   Peter Sallis (Norman Clegg), Bill Owen (Compo Seminite), Michael Bates (Blamire), Brian Wilde (Foggy Dewhurst), Michael Aldridge (Seymour Utterthwaite), Kathy Staff (Nora Batty), Jean Alexander (Auntie Wainwright). Filmed in Holmfirth in Yorkshire. Written by Roy Clarke.

League of Gentlemen, The   Jeremy Dyson, Mark Gatiss, Steve Pemberton, Reece Shearsmith. Set in Royston Vazey (the real name of comedian Roy 'chubby' Brown).

Life and Loves of a She Devil, The   Julie T. Wallace (Ruth Patchett), Dennis Waterman (Bobbo Patchett), Patricia Hodge (Mary Fisher).

Likely Lads, The   James Bolam (Terry Collier), Bob Ferris (Rodney Bewes), Sheila Fearn (Audrey Collier), Brigit Forsyth (Thelma Ferris). Written by Dick Clement and Ian La Frenais. Sequel: *Whatever Happened to the Likely Lads*.

Little House on the Prairie   Michael Landon (Charles Ingalls), Karen Grassle (Caroline Ingalls), Melissa Gilbert (Laura Ingalls/Wilder), Melissa Sue Anderson (Mary Ingalls/Kendall).

Liver Birds, The   Polly James (Beryl Hennessey), Nerys Hughes (Sandra Hutchinson/Paynton), Pauline Collins (Dawn, the original flatmate of Beryl), Elizabeth Estensen (Carol Boswell), Mollie Sugden (Mrs Hutchinson), John Nettles (Paul), Jonathan Lynn (Robert).

London's Burning   Mark Arden (Roland 'Vaseline' Cartwright), Glen Murphy (George Green), James Hazeldine (Mike 'Bayleaf' Wilson), Richard Walsh (Bert 'Sicknote' Quigley), Gerard Horan (Leslie

T
E
L
E
V
I
S
I
O
N

'Charisma' Appleby), Ben Onwukwe (Stuart 'Recall' Mackenzie), Heather Peace (Sally 'Gracie' Fields), Edward Peel (John Coleman), Michael Garner (Geoffrey 'Poison' Pearce), Fuman Dar (Ronnie 'Hi-Ho' Silver), Connor Byrne (Rob 'Hyper' Sharpe), Sam Callis (Adam Benjamin), Al Hunter Ashton (Pit bull). Firefighters of Blue Watch B25, Blackwall, created by Jack Rosenthal.

Lone Ranger, The Initially played by Clayton Moore and then by John Hart before he left to play Hawkeye. Jay Silverheels always played the faithful Tonto. Lone Ranger's horse: Silver. (He would often say 'Hi-ho, Silver, away' when in a hurry.) Tonto's horse: Scout. (Tonto would often call his friend Kemo Sabe, which meant Trusty Scout.) The Lone Ranger's real name was John Reid, a Texas Ranger ambushed and left for dead. It is often said that if you can listen to Rossini's 'William Tell Overture' without thinking of the Lone Ranger (same tune) then you are a real classical music aficionado.

Lord Peter Wimsey Ian Carmichael (Lord Peter Wimsey), Glyn Houston (Bunter, his manservant).

Lost in Space Guy Williams (Professor John Robinson), Jonathan Harris (Zachary Smith), Bob May (the robot), Dick Tufeld (voice of the robot). Spaceship: Jupiter 11. Pet space monkey: the Bloop.

Lotus Eaters, The Ian Hendry (Erik Shepherd), Wanda Ventham (Ann Shepherd). Drama set on Crete.

Lou Grant Edward Asner (Lou), Robert Walden (Joe Rossi). Spin-off from the *Mary Tyler Moore Show*. Newspaper: *Los Angeles Tribune*.

Love Hurts Adam Faith (Frank Carver), Zoë Wanamaker (Tessa Piggott), Jane Lapotaire (Diane Warburg), Tony Selby (Max Taplow).

Love Me Do Game show in which three couples vie for the chance to wed. Host: Shane Richie.

Love Thy Neighbour Jack Smethurst (Eddie Booth), Kate Williams (Joan), Rudolph Walker (Bill Reynolds), Nina Baden Semper (Barbie), Keith Marsh (Jacko Jackson). Jacko's famous saying: 'I'll 'ave 'alf.'

Lovejoy Ian McShane (Lovejoy), Dudley Sutton (Tinker Deal), Chris Jury (Eric Catchpole), Phyllis Logan (Lady Jane Felsham). Lovejoy's Morris Minor: Miriam.

Lovers, The Richard Beckinsale (Geoffrey), Paula Wilcox (Beryl).

Lucy Show, The Lucille Ball (Lucy Carmichael), Gale Gordon (Theodore J. Mooney), Vivian Vance (Vivian Bagley).

Lytton's Diary Peter Bowles (Neville Lytton). Incidents in the life of a newspaper diarist.

Magic Roundabout Characters include Dougal (the dog), Ermintrude (the cow), Brian (the snail), Mr Rusty, Mr McHenry, Zebedee, Dylan (the rabbit), Florence. Created by Serge Danot and narrated by Eric Thompson and Nigel Planer.

Magnificent Evans, The Ronnie Barker (Plantagenet Evans), Dyfed Thomas (Home Rule O'Toole), Myfanwy Talog (Bron).

Magnum PI Tom Selleck (Thomas Sullivan Magnum), John Hillerman (Jonathan Quayle Higgins III), Roger E. Mosley (Theodore 'TC' Calvin), Orson Welles (voice of Robin Masters).

Magpie Presenters include Susan Stranks, Pete Brady, Tony Bastable, Mick Robertson, Jenny Hanley, Tommy Boyd, Douglas Rae.

Main Chance, The John Stride (David Main), Kate O'Mara (Julia Main). Story of a young, successful lawyer.

Making Out Margi Clarke (Queenie), Shirley Stelfox (Carol May), Tracie Bennett (Norma), Melanie Kilburn (Jill), Keith Allen (Rex), Brian Hibbard (Chunky).

Man About the House Richard O'Sullivan (Robin Tripp), Paula Wilcox (Chrissy Plummer), Sally Thomsett (Jo), Brian Murphy (George Roper), Yootha Joyce (Mildred Roper). Spin-off series were *Robin's Nest* and *George and Mildred*.

Man at the Top Kenneth Haigh (Joe Lampton). Feature film of the same name followed.

Man Called Ironside, A Raymond Burr (Chief Robert T. Ironside), Don Galloway (Det. Sgt Ed Brown), Barbara Anderson (Eve Whitfield), Don Mitchell (Mark Sanger), Elizabeth Baur (Fran Belding).

Man From Atlantis Patrick Duffy (Mark Harris; had green eyes), Belinda J. Montgomery (Dr Elizabeth Merrill), Victor Buono (Mr Schubert), Robert Lussier (Brent). Submersible name: Cetacean.

Man From Uncle, The Robert Vaughan (Napoleon Solo, agent no. 11), David McCallum (Ilya Kuryakin, agent no. 2), Leo G. Carroll (Alexander Waverly, agent no. 1). UNCLE: United Network Command for Law and Enforcement. Secret office: behind Del Floria's Tailor Shop. Enemy: Thrush.

Manhunt Alfred Lynch (Jimmy Porter), Peter Barkworth (Vincent), Cyd Hayman (Nina). Heroic tales of French Resistance in WW2. Theme tune: Beethoven's Fifth Symphony.

Man in a Suitcase Richard Bradford (McGill).

Man in Room 17, The Richard Vernon (Oldenshaw), Michael Aldridge (Dimmock). Criminologists working in an office near the Houses of Parliament.

Marcus Welby MD Robert Young (Welby), James Brolin (Dr Steven Kiley).

Mark Saber Donald Gray (Saber), Michael Balfour (Barny O'Keefe). Story of the one-armed detective.

Marriage Lines Richard Briars (George Starling), Prunella Scales (Kate).

Mary Tyler Moore Show Mary Tyler Moore (Mary Richards), Ed Asner (Lou Grant), Valerie Harper (Rhoda Morgenstern), Cloris Leachman (Phyllis Lindstrom). Based in TV Station WJM-TV.

M.A.S.H. Alan Alda (Capt. Benjamin Franklin 'Hawkeye' Pierce), Wayne Rogers (Capt. 'Trapper John' McIntyre), Loretta Swit (Maj. Margaret 'Hot Lips' Houlihan), Larry Linville (Maj. Frank Burns), Gary Burghoff (Corporal Walter 'Radar' O'Reilly), William Christopher (Father Francis Mulcahy), Jamie Farr (Corporal Maxwell Klinger). Hawkeye's tent known as the Swamp. M.A.S.H.: Mobile Army Surgical Hospital.

Mastermind Ran from 1972 to 1997 with Magnus Magnusson as 'Interrogator' throughout the run. Producer/director David Mitchell. Other producers include Bill Wright, Roger MacKay, Peter Massey, Penelope Cowell Doe. Main researcher: Dee Wallace. Winners: Nancy Wilkinson (1972), Patricia Owen (1973), Elizabeth Horrocks (1974), John Hart (1975), Roger Pritchard (1976), Sir David Hunt (1977), Rosemary James (1978), Dr Philip Jenkins (1979), Fred Housego (1980), Leslie Grout (1981), Sir David Hunt (1982), Christopher Hughes (1983), Margaret Harris (1984), Ian Meadows (1985), Jennifer Keaveney (1986), Dr Jeremy Bradbrooke (1987), David Beamish (1988), Mary-Elizabeth Raw (1989), David Edwards (1990), Stephen Allen

(1991), Steve Williams (1992), Gavin Fuller (1993), George Davidson (1994), Kevin Ashman (1995), Richard Sturch (1996), Anne Ashurst (1997).

Maverick   James Garner (Brett Maverick), Jack Kelly (Bart Maverick), Roger Moore (Cousin Beau).

May to December   Anton Rodgers (Alec Callender), Eve Matheson/Lesley Dunlop (Zoe Angell/Callender).

McCloud   Dennis Weaver (Sam McCloud), seconded to New York from Taos, New Mexico.

McMillan and Wife   Rock Hudson (Commissioner Stewart McMillan), Susan Saint James (Sally McMillan). Based in San Francisco.

Me and My Girl   Richard O'Sullivan (Simon Harrap), Joanne Ridley (Samantha Harrap), Joan Sanderson (Nell Cresset), Tim Brooke-Taylor (Derek Yates). Advertising agency: Eyecatchers. Theme song sung by Peter Skellern.

Meet the Wife   Thora Hird (Thora Blacklock), Freddie Frinton (Freddie Blacklock). Stemmed from a Comedy Playhouse production called *The Bed*.

Me Mammy   Milo O'Shea (Bunjy Kennefick), Anna Manahan (Mrs Kennefick), Yootha Joyce (Miss Argyll), David Kelly (Cousin Enda), Ray McAnally (Father Patrick).

Men Behaving Badly   Martin Clunes (Gary), Neil Morrissey (Tony), Leslie Ash (Deborah), Caroline Quentin (Dorothy). The first series featured Harry Enfield as Dermot but Neil Morrissey replaced him for series two Although originally an ITV series, by series three it was screened on BBC 1. The writer was Simon Nye, who also created Frank Stubbs.

Metal Mickey   The robot Mickey was invented by Ken Wilberforce and played by Ashley Knight. This series is best remembered for the fact that Mickey Dolenz was the producer/director.

Miami Vice   Don Johnson (James 'Sonny' Crockett), Philip Michael Thomas (Ricardo Tubbs), Edward James Olmos (Lt Martin Castillo), Sheena Easton (Caitlin Davies).

Midnight Caller   Gary Cole (Jack 'Nighthawk' Killian).

Millennium   Lance Henriksen (Frank Black), Megan Gallagher (Catherine Black), Chris Ellis (Penseyres). Created by Chris Carter of *X Files* fame.

Minder   George Cole (Arthur Daly), Dennis Waterman (Terry McMann), Glynn Edwards (Dave), Patrick Malahide (Det. Sgt Albert 'Charlie' Chisholm), Peter Childs (Sgt Rycott). The theme tune, 'I Could Be So Good For You', was sung by Dennis Waterman.

Mind Your Language   Barry Evans (Jeremy Brown), François Pascal (Danielle Favre), Pik-Sen-Lim (Chung Su-Lee).

Miss Marple   Joan Hickson (Miss Marple).

Mission Impossible   Peter Graves (Jim Phelps), Leonard Nimoy (Paris), Barbara Bain (Cinnamon Carter), Martin Landau (Rollin Hand), Greg Morris (Barney Collier), Steven Hill (Daniel Briggs), Lesley Ann Warren (Dana Lambert), Peter Lupus (Willie Armitage). Voice on the tape: Bob Johnson. Catchprase: 'This tape will self-destruct in five seconds' (occasionally ten seconds).

Mister ED   Alan Young (Wilbur Post). Story of a talking horse.

Mogul   Series about an oil company, which later changed it's title to *The Troubleshooters*.

Moment of Truth   Cilla Black hosted the show in which three contestants have a week to master a given task.

Monkees, The   TV Series about a pop group. Micky Dolenz, Mike Nesmith, Peter Tork and Davy Jones.

Monty Python's Flying Circus   Messrs Cleese, Idle, Gilliam, Jones, Palin, Chapman and Carol Cleveland.

Moonlighting   Bruce Willis (David Addison), Cybill Shepherd (Maddie Hayes). Detective agency: Blue Moon.

Mork and Mindy   Robin Williams (Mork from Ork), Pam Dawber (Mindy McConnell), Jonathan Winters (Mearth). Mork gave birth to Mearth, who called Mindy 'Shoe' and Mork 'Mommy'. Series was a spin-off from an episode of *Happy Days*.

Moviedrome   Presenters Alex Cox, Mark Cousins.

Mr and Mrs   The alternating presenters were Alan Taylor and Derek Batey.

Mr Magoo   Voice of Magoo (Jim Backus); Waldo was his nephew.

Mr Pastry   Richard Hearne, an actor, acrobat and dancer, invented this character. Popular for over 20 years.

Muffin the Mule   Presenter: Annette Mills. Puppeteer: Ann Hogarth.

Munsters, The   Fred Gwynne (Herman), Yvonne De Carlo (Lily), Al Lewis (Grandpa), Butch Patrick (Eddie), Beverley Owen/Pat Priest (Marilyn). Lived at: 1313 Mockingbird Lane, Mockingbird Heights.

Muppet Show, The   Characters include Miss Piggy Lee, Kermit T. Frog, Statler and Waldorf, Animal, Gonzo, Fozzie Bear, Zoot, Swedish Chef, Dr Teeth, Robin the Frog. First seen in *Sesame Street*. Created by Jim Henson and Frank Oz.

My Favorite Martian   Ray Walston (Uncle Martin), Bill Bixby (Tim O'Hara).

Nearest and Dearest   Hylda Baker (Nellie Pledge), Jimmy Jewel (Eli), Madge Hindle (Lily), Edward Malin (Walter).

Never the Twain   Donald Sinden (Simon Peel), Windsor Davies (Oliver Smallbridge), Honor Blackman (Veronica).

New Avengers   Joanna Lumley (Purdey), Gareth Hunt (Mike Gambit), Patrick MacNee (John Steed).

New Statesman, The   Rik Mayall (Alan Beresford B'Stard), Terence Alexander (Sir Greville), Marsha Fitzalan (Sarah).

Nice Time   Germaine Greer, Jonathan Routh and Kenny Everett in wacky sketch show produced by John Birt.

Night Fever   Channel 5 karaoke programme hosted by Suggs.

99–1   Leslie Grantham (Mick Raynor), Robert Stephens (Commander Oakwood).

No Hiding Place   Sequel to *Crimesheet* and *Murder Bag*. Raymond Francis (Superintendent Lockhart), Eric Lander (Sergeant Baxter), Johnny Briggs (Det. Sgt Russell).

No, Honestly   John Alderton (Charles 'CD' Danby), Pauline Collins (Clara Danby).

No Place Like Home   William Gaunt (Arthur Crabtree), Martin Clunes (Nigel Crabtree), Patricia Garwood (Beryl).

No – That's Me Over Here   Ronnie Corbett (Ronnie), Rosemary Leach (Rosemary), Henry McGee (Henry).

Not in Front of the Children   Wendy Craig (Jennifer Corner), Paul Daneman/Ronald Hines (Henry Corner).

Not Only But Also   Peter Cook and Dudley Moore.

Not the Nine O'Clock News   Rowan Atkinson, Chris

Langham (replaced by Griff Rhys-Jones), Mel Smith, Pamela Stephenson.

NYPD Blue Dennis Franz (Det. Andy Sipowicz), Rick Schroder (Det. Danny Sorenson), James McDaniel (Lt. Arthur Fancy), Nicholas Turturro (Det. James Martinez), Sharon Lawrence (Asst. DA Sylvia Costas Sipowicz), Gordon Clapp (Det. Greg Medavoy). Co-created by Steven Bochco and David Milch. NYPD is New York Police Department.

Oh Brother/Oh Father Derek Nimmo (Brother/Father Dominic), Felix Aylmer (Father Anselm).

Oh, Doctor Beeching! Su Pollard (Ethel Schumann), Paul Shane (Jack Skinner), Jeffrey Holland (Cecil Parkin), Stephen Lewis (Harry Lambert), Julia Deakin (May Skinner).

Old Grey Whistle Test/Whistle Test Bob Harris, Anne Nightingale, Andy Kershaw, Mark Ellen, Ian Whitcomb, Richard Skinner.

One Foot in the Grave Richard Wilson (Victor Meldrew), Annette Crosbie (Margaret), Angus Deayton (Patrick).

Onedin Line, The Peter Gilmore (Capt. James Onedin), Jane Seymour (Emma Callon), Jill Gascoigne (Letty Gaunt). First ship: *Charlotte Rose*.

Only Fools and Horses David Jason (Del Boy Trotter), Nicholas Lyndhurst (Rodney), Lennard Pearce (Grandad), Buster Merryfield (Uncle Albert), Tessa Peake-Jones (Raquel), Gwyneth Strong (Cassandra), Roger Lloyd Pack (Trigger), John Challis (Boycie), Sue Holderness (Marlene). Pub: Nag's Head. Trotters' address: 368 Nelson Mandela House, Peckham. Company name: Trotter's Independent Trading Transport. Features Del's yellow Reliant Robin. Title from the adage 'Only fools and horses work'. Writer: John Sullivan.

Only When I Laugh James Bolam (Roy Figgis), Peter Bowles (Archie Glover), Richard Wilson (Dr Gordon Thorpe).

On Safari Presenters Armand and Michaela Denis.

On the Buses Reg Varney (Stan Butler), Stephen Lewis (Blakey), Anna Karen (Olive), Michael Robbins (Arthur), Bob Grant (Jack). Bus company: Luxtons.

On the Move Bob Hoskins (Alf), Donald Gee (Bert).

On the Up Dennis Waterman (Tony Carpenter), Sam Kelly (Sam), Joan Sims (Mrs Fiona Wembley).

Opportunity Knocks Presenters: Hughie Green, Bob Monkhouse, Les Dawson.

Other 'Arf, The Lorraine Chase (Lorraine Watts), John Standing (Charles Lattimer), Pat Hodge (Sybil Howarth).

OTT (Over The Top) Adult version of *TISWAS*, with variations such as the three naked balloon dancers.

Our Man at St Mark's Leslie Phillips (Rev. Andrew Parker), Donald Sinden (Rev. Stephen Young).

Outside Edge Robert Daws (Roger Dervish), Brenda Blethyn (Miriam, 'Mim'), Timothy Spall (Kevin Costello), Josie Lawrence (Maggie).

Pallisers, The Susan Hampshire (Lady Glencora McCluskie/Palliser), Philip Latham (Plantagenet Palliser), Jeremy Irons (Frank Tregear), Anthony Andrews (Earl of Silverbridge), Derek Jacobi (Lord Fawn).

Panorama Presenters include Pat Murphy, Richard Dimbleby, Malcolm Muggeridge, David Dimbleby.

Paradise Club Leslie Grantham (Danny Kane), Don Henderson (Frank Kane).

Partridge Family Shirley Jones (Shirley), David Cassidy (Keith), Susan Dey (Laurie), Danny Bonaduce (Chris).

Peak Practice Kevin Whately (Dr Jack Kerruish), Amanda Burton (Dr Beth Glover), Gray O'Brien (Tom Deneley), Gary Mavers (Andrew Attwood), Maggie O'Neill (Alex Redman), Joseph Millson (Sam Morgan). Set in Cardale, Peak District.

Pebble Mill at One Presenters: Bob Langley, Donny MacLeod, Jan Leeming, Anna Ford, Paul Coia, Magnus Magnusson. Pebble Mill was revived after a short break with presenters including Judi Spiers, Alan Titchmarsh, Gloria Hunniford and Ross King.

Pennies From Heaven Bob Hoskins (Arthur Parker), Cheryl Campbell (Eileen), Gemma Craven (Joan Parker). Written by Dennis Potter.

Perfect Scoundrels Peter Bowles (Guy Buchanan), Bryan Murray (Harry Cassidy). Series created by its stars.

Perry Mason Raymond Burr (Perry Mason), Barbara Hale (Della Street), William Hopper (Paul Drake), William Talman (Hamilton Burger), Ray Collins (Lt Tragg). Set in Los Angeles.

Persuaders, The Tony Curtis (Danny Wilde), Roger Moore (Lord Brett Sinclair), Laurence Naismith (Judge Fulton).

Peter Principle, The Jim Broadbent (Peter), Claire Skinner (Susan), Stephen Moore (Geoffrey), Tracy Keating (Brenda), David Schneider (Bradley), Daniel Flynn (Dave), Janette Legge (Iris). Tale of inept bank manager.

Petrocelli Barry Newman (Tony Petrocelli), Susan Howard (Maggie). Set in fictional San Remo.

Peyton Place Ryan O'Neal (Rodney Harrington), Mia Farrow (Allison McKenzie), Ed Nelson (Dr Mike Rossi), Dorothy Malone (Constance McKenzie), Christopher Connelly (Norman Harrington).

Phil Silvers Show Phil Silvers (Master Sgt Ernest Bilko), Maurice Gosfield (Pte Duane Doberman), Joe E. Ross (Sgt Rupert Ritzik), Billy Sands (Pte Dino Paparelli), Paul Ford (Colonel John Hall), Allan Melvin (Cpl Henshaw), Harvey Lembeck (Cpl Rocco Barbella), Elizabeth Fraser (Joan). Rocco Barbella was the real name of boxer Rocky Graziano, the casting director.

Pie in the Sky Richard Griffiths stars as masterchef and ace detective Henry Crabbe.

Pinky and Perky Creators: Jan and Vlasta Dalibor.

Plane Makers, The Patrick Wymark (John Wilder), Barbara Murray/Ann Firbank (Pamela Wilder), Jack Watling (Don Henderson). Aircraft factory name: Scott Furlong. Follow-on series was called *The Power Game*.

Please Sir John Alderton (Bernard 'Privet' Hedges), Deryck Guyler (Norman Potter), Peter Cleall (Eric Duffy), Joan Sanderson (Doris Ewell), David Barry (Frankie Abbott), Richard Davies (Mr Price), Jill Kerman (Penny Wheeler/Hedges), Spin-off series: *The Fenn Street Gang*.

Poldark Robin Ellis (Ross Poldark), Angharad Rees (Demelza), Ralph Bates (George Warleggan). Based on novels by Winston Graham.

Police Woman Angie Dickinson (Sgt Suzanne 'Pepper' Anderson), Earl Holliman (Lt Bill Crowley).

Popstars Auditions of thousands of young budding pop stars in the quest to put together a five-piece all singing and dancing supergroup. The five winners were Danny Foster, Myleene Klass, Noel Sullivan, Kym Marsh and Suzanne Shaw who became

Hear'Say. The show's executive producer was 'Nasty' Nigel Lythgoe.

Porridge Ronnie Barker (Norman Stanley Fletcher), Richard Beckinsale (Lennie Godber), Fulton MacKay (Mr MacKay), Peter Vaughan (Groutie), David Jason (Blanco), Brian Wilde (Mr Barrowclough), Patricia Brake (Ingrid), Chris Biggins (Lukewarm), Maurice Denham (Judge Rawley), Tony Osoba (McLaren), Sam Kelly (Warren). Prison setting: HMP Slade. Sentence: five years. Sequel: *Going Straight.*

Porterhouse Blue David Jason (Skullion), Ian Richardson (Sir Godber Evans), Griff Rhys-Jones (Cornelius Carrington).

Postman Pat Characters include Jess the cat, Mrs Goggins the postmistress and twins Katie and Tom Pottage.

Pot Black Half-hour snooker programme which popularized the game as a television medium. Ran from 1969 to 1986, Ray Reardon was the first champion and Jimmy White the last. The theme tune was 'Ivory Rag'. *Pot Black* was briefly revived for one series. A *Masters Pot Black* was held in 1997, the winner being Joe Johnson.

Potter Arthur Lowe (Redvers Potter), replaced by Robin Bailey when Arthur Lowe died between series.

Price is Right, The Presenters: Leslie Crowther and Bruce Forsyth.

Pride and Prejudice Colin Firth (Fitzwilliam Darcy), Jennifer Ehle (Elizabeth Bennet), Alison Steadman (Mrs Bennet), Julia Sawalha (Lydia Bennet).

Prisoner, The Patrick McGoohan (No. 6). Filmed in Portmeirion, Wales.

Professionals, The Gordon Jackson (George Cowley), Lewis Collins (William Bodie), Martin Shaw (Ray Doyle).

Protectors, The Robert Vaughan (Harry Rule), Nyree Dawn Porter (Contessa di Contini), Tony Anholt (Paul Buchet).

Quantum Leap Scott Bakula (Dr Sam Beckett), Dean Stockwell (Al Calavicci).

Quatermass Reginald Tate/André Morell/John Robinson/John Mills (Professor Bernard Quatermass). Written by Nigel Kneale.

Question of Sport, A Presenters: David Vine, David Coleman, Sue Barker.

Rab C. Nesbit Gregor Fisher's character first appeared in *Naked Video.* Children are Gash and Burney.

Rag Trade, The Peter Jones (Mr Fenner), Reg Varney (Reg), Miriam Karlin (Paddy), Sheila Hancock (Carole), Esma Cannon (Little Lil), Barbara Windsor (Judy), Wanda Ventham (Shirley). A revival series starred Anna Karen as the character she played in *On the Buses.*

Randall and Hopkirk (Deceased) Mike Pratt (Jeff Randall), Kenneth Cope (Marty Hopkirk), Annette Andre (Jean Hopkirk). Revived in the 1990s with Reeves and Mortimer playing Marty and Jeff.

Rawhide Eric Fleming (Gil Favor), Clint Eastwood (Rowdy Yates), Paul Brinegar (Wishbone), Sheb Wooley (Pete Nolan), James Murdock (Harkness 'Mushy' Mushgrove).

Ready Steady Go Presenters Keith Fordyce, Cathy McGowan, David Gell, Michael Aldred.

Red Dwarf Chris Barrie (Arnold J. Rimmer BSc, SSC), Craig Charles (Dave Lister), Danny John-Jules (Cat), Norman Lovett/Hattie Hayridge (Holly), David Ross/Robert Llewellyn (Kryten).

Remington Steele Pierce Brosnan, Stephanie Zimbalist (Laura Holt, the owner of Remington Steele Investigations).

Rhoda Valerie Harper (Rhoda Morgenstern/Gerard), Julie Kavner (Brenda Morgenstern), Lorenzo Musoc (Carlton the doorman, voice only). Spin-off from the *Mary Tyler Moore Show.*

Rich Man Poor Man First of the TV 'Best Sellers', based on an Irwin Shaw novel and starring Peter Strauss and Nick Nolte.

Rifleman, The Chuck Connors (Lucas McCain), Johnny Crawford (Mark McCain).

Right to Reply Presenters include: Gus MacDonald, Linda Agran, Brian Hayes, Rory McGrath, Sheena McDonald, Roger Bolton.

Rings on Their Fingers Martin Jarvis (Oliver Pryde), Diane Keen (Sandy Bennett/Pryde).

Rising Damp Leonard Rossiter (Rigsby), Richard Beckinsale (Allan), Frances de la Tour (Miss Jones), Don Warrington (Philip), Vienna the cat. Based on a one-act play, *The Banana Box.*

Robin Hood Short-lived series of 1953 in which Patrick Troughton (second Dr Who) took the lead role.

Robin of Sherwood Michael Praed (Robin of Loxley), Jason Connery (Robert of Huntingdon), Clive Mantle (Little John), Ray Winstone (Will Scarlet), Judi Trott (Maid Marian). Music by Clannad.

Robin's Nest Richard O'Sullivan (Robin Tripp), Tessa Wyatt (Victoria Nicholls), Tony Britton (James Nicholls), David Kelly (Albert Riddle, the one-armed washer-up), Honor Blackman/Barbara Murray (Marion).

Rock Follies Charlotte Cornwell, Julie Covington (Devonia Dee Rhoades), Rula Lenska. Group name: The Little Ladies.

Rockford Files, The James Garner, Noah Beery Jnr (Joseph 'Rocky' Rockford), Joe Santos (Det. Sgt Dennis Becker).

Room 101 Original presenter Nick Hancock, who was followed by Paul Merton.

Roseanne Roseanne Barr (Roseanne Conner), John Goodman (Dan), George Clooney (Booker Brooks).

Royle Family, The Caroline Aherne (Denise Best), Ricky Tomlinson (Jim Royle), Sue Johnston (Barbara Royle), Craig Cash (Dave Best), Ralf Little (Anthony Royle), Liz Smith (Norma Speakman).

Rumpole of the Bailey Leo McKern (Horace Rumpole), Patricia Hodge (Phyllida Trant/Erskine-Brown), Peter Bowles (Guthrie Featherstone), Bill Fraser (Justice Bullingham). Wife: Hilda (She who must be obeyed). Winebar: Pomeroy's. Drink: Château Fleet Street).

Saint, The Roger Moore (Simon Templar alias the Saint). Car: Volvo P1800S. Inspector: Claude Eustace Teal. Sequel: *Return of the Saint,* starring Ian Ogilvy.

Sea Hunt Lloyd Bridges (Mike Nelson). Boat: the *Argonaut.*

Secret Army Jan Francis (Lisa Colbert; codename Yvette), Bernard Hepton (Albert Foiret), Clifford Rose (Sturmbannführer Ludwig Kessler). Underground movement: Lifeline.

Secret Diary of Adrian Mole, Aged 13¾ Gian Sammarco (Adrian), Stephen Moore (Mr Mole), Julie Walters and Lulu (Pauline Mole), Lindsey Stagg (Pandora). Based on the Sue Townsend novels.

Seinfeld Jerry Seinfeld (Jerry), Jason Alexander

(George), Michael Richards (Kramer), Julia Louis Dreyfus (Elaine).

September Song Michael Williams (Billy Balsam), Russ Abbot (Ted Fenwick), Michael Angelis (Arnie).

77 Sunset Strip Efrem Zimbalist Jnr (Stuart Bailey), Roger Smith (Jeff Spencer), Ed Byrnes (Kookie). Much of the action took place outside Dean Martin's restaurant, Dino's.

Sexton Blake Laurence Payne (Sexton Blake), Roger Foss (Tinker), Dorothea Phillips (Mrs Bardell). Bloodhound: Pedro. White Rolls Royce nicknamed the Grey Panther.

Sharpe Sean Bean (Richard Sharpe), Daragh O'Malley (Sgt Pat Harper), Peter Postlewaite (Hakeswill), Philip Whitchurch (Frederickson), Liz Hurley (Isabella), Assumpta Sema (Teresa, the first Mrs Sharpe), Abigail Cruttenden (Lady Jane, the second Mrs Sharpe), Cecile Paoli (Lucille Dubert, the third Mrs Sharpe), Louise Germaine (Sally Clayton), John Tams (Hagman) also co-wrote the music. Based on novels by Bernard Cornwell.

Shillingbury Tales Robin Nedwell (Peter Higgins), Diane Keen (Sally Higgins), Lionel Jeffries (Major Langton), Bernard Cribbins (Cuffy), Jack Douglas (Jake).

Shine On Harvey Moon Kenneth Cranham/Nicky Henson (Harvey Moon), Linda Robson (Maggie Moon), Nigel Planer (Lou Lewis), Elizabeth Spriggs (Nan), Pauline Quirke (Veronica), Maggie Steed (Rita Moon). Harvey's occupation: professional footballer.

Simpsons, The Characters include: Homer and Marge Simpson and their children Bart, Lisa and Maggie. The pet dog is called Santa's Little Helper. Other characters include Montgomery Burns, Waylon Smithers, Professor John Frink, Millhouse van Houten, Sideshow Bob, Krusty the Clown, and Chief Wiggum and his son Ralph. Series is set in Springfield and started life as a cartoon short on the *Tracy Ullman Show.*

Singing Detective, The Michael Gambon (Philip E. Marlow), Joanne Whalley (Nurse Mills/Carlotta), Patrick Malahide (Mark Binney/Mark Finney/Raymond Binney), Jim Carter (Mr Marlow), Alison Steadman (Beth Marlow/Lili). Hospital ward: Sherpa Tensing. Illness: psoriasis. Written by Dennis Potter.

Sir Francis Drake Terence Morgan (Drake), Jean Kent (Queen Elizabeth), Michael Crawford (John Drake).

Six-Five Special Presenters: Pete Murray, Josephine Douglas, Freddie Mills, Jim Dale. Jack Good was the original producer and Adam Faith made his debut on his way to stardom.

Six Million Dollar Man Lee Majors (Steve Austin), Richard Anderson (Oscar Goldman), Lyndsay Wagner (Jaime Sommers). The opening sequence showing Steve Austin's crash in the Mojave Desert was in fact Donald Campbell's fatal accident while attempting the world water-speed record on Coniston Water.

64,000 Dollar Question, The Questions were guarded every week by Detective Fabian. Bob Monkhouse hosted the British version.

Six Wives of Henry VIII, The Keith Michell (Henry), Annette Crosbie (Catherine of Aragon), Dorothy Tutin (Anne Boleyn), Anne Stallybrass (Jane Seymour), Elvi Hale (Anne of Cleves), Angela Pleasance (Catherine Howard), Rosalie Crutchley

(Catherine Parr), Patrick Troughton (Duke of Norfolk). Narrator: Anthony Quayle.

Sliders John Rhys-Davies (Maximillian Arturo), Jerry O'Connell (Quinn Mallory), Sabrina Lloyd (Wade Wells), Cleavant Derricks (Rembrandt Brown). Sliding is the term used for entering parallel universes.

Slinger's Day Bruce Forsyth (Cecil Slinger). The untimely death of Leonard Rossiter precipitated the arrival of Bruce Forsyth to take over the role of the put-upon supermarket manager, his name changed from Tripper to Slinger.

Soap Katherine Helmond (Jessica Tate), Cathryn Damon (Mary Dallas Campbell), Billy Crystal (Jodie Dallas), Robert Guillaume (Benson Dubois), Robert Mandan (Chester Tate).

Soldier, Soldier Jerome Flynn (Paddy Garvey), Robson Green (Dave Tucker), David Haig (Mjr Tom Cadman).

Some Mothers Do 'Ave 'Em Michael Crawford (Frank Spencer), Michele Dotrice (Betty). Daughter: Jessica.

Sopranos, The James Gondolfini (Tony Soprano), Edie Falco (Carmela Soprano), Nancy Marchand (Livia Soprano), Lorraine Bracco (Dr Jennifer Melfi), Jamie-Lynn Sigler (Meadow Soprano), Robert Iler (A.J. Soprano), Aida Turturro (Janice 'Parvati' Soprano), Dominic Chianese (Corrado Soprano), Tony Sirico (Paulie Walnuts), Steve van Zandt (Silvio Dante), John Ventimiglia (Artie Bucco).

Sorry! Ronnie Corbett (Timothy Lumsden, a librarian), Barbara Lott (Mrs Phyllis Lumsden).

South Park Adult cartoon series. Characters include Kenny (who is invariably killed), Kyle, Stan, Cartman, Chef, Mr Garrison, Ned, Uncle Jimbo and Officer Barbrady.

Space: 1999 Martin Landau (John Koenig), Barbara Bain (Dr Helena Russell), Catherine Schell (Maya), Barry Morse (Professor Victor Bergman). Crew of Moonbase Alpha stranded in space.

Space Patrol Voices: Capt. Larry Dart (Dick Vosburgh), Husky and Slim (Ronnie Stevens), Gabblerdictum (Libby Morris), Colonel Raeburn (Murray Kash). Ship: Galasphere 347. Year: 2100. The Space Patrol was the active unit of the United Galactic Organization. Libby Morris was Raeburn's super-efficient blonde secretary from Venus; fortunately there is no such thing as a dumb blonde on Venus.

Special Branch George Sewell (Det. Chief Insp. Alan Craven), Patrick Mower (Det. Chief Insp. Tom Haggerty), Derren Nesbitt (Det. Insp. Jordan), Fulton Mackay (Det. Supt Inman).

Spender Jimmy Nail, Sammy Johnson (Stick), Paul Greenwood (Supt Yelland).

Spenser For Hire Robert Urich (Spenser), Avery Brooks (Hawk), Barbara Stock (Susan Silverman).

Spitting Image Created by Peter Fluck, Roger Law and Michael Lambie-Martin.

St Elsewhere Ed Flanders (Donald Westphall), William Daniels (Mark Craig), Ed Begley Jnr (Victor Ehrlich). Hospital: St Elegius, Boston.

Star Trek William Shatner (James Tiberius Kirk), Leonard Nimoy (Mr Spock – his mother is T'Pau, a Vulcan), De Forest Kelly (Dr Leonard 'Bones' McCoy), James Doohan (Scottie), George Takei (Mr Sulu), Nichelle Nichols (Lt Uhura), Walter Koenig (Ensign Pavel Chekov), Majel Barrett (Nurse Chapel). Crew size: 430. Decks: 8. Five-year mission to boldly go where no man has gone before.

Enterprise no.: NCC 1701A. Shuttle: Galileo. Spock's blood colour: green (T positive).

Star Trek: The Next Generation   Patrick Stewart (Captain Jean-Luc Picard), Jonathan Frakes (Commander William Ryker), LeVar Burton (Lt Geordi La Forge), Michael Dorn (Lt Worf), Denise Crosby (Lt Tasha Yar), Gates McFadden (Dr Bev Crusher), Marina Sirtis (Deanna Troi), Brent Spiner (Lt Cmdr Data), Wil Wheaton (Wesley), Diana Muldaur (Dr Katherine Pulaski), Whoopi Goldberg (Guinan). Original *Star Trek* set in the 23rd century; this series was set 78 years later. Enterprise no.: NCC 1701D.

Stars in Their Eyes   Presenters: Leslie Crowther, Matthew Kelly.

Starsky and Hutch   David Soul (Ken Hutchinson), Paul Michael Glaser (Dave Starsky), Antonio Fargas (Huggie Bear).

Steptoe and Son   Harry H. Corbett (Harold), Wilfred Bramble (Albert), Hercules the horse. American spin-off: *Sandford and Son.*

Stingray   Troy Tempest, George 'Phones' Sheridan, Atlanta Shore, Titan, Agent X20. Marina was the mute daughter of Emperor Aphony from Pacifica and her pet seal was called Oink. Organization: WASP, World Aquanaut Security Patrol, in Marineville. Year: 2000.

Streets of San Francisco, The   Karl Malden (Det. Lt Mike Stone), Michael Douglas (Insp. Steve Keller).

Sunday Night at the London Palladium   Comperes included: Tommy Trinder, Bruce Forsyth, Des O'Connor, Jimmy Tarbuck, Norman Vaughan, Jim Dale, Hughie Green, Alfred Marks, Robert Morley, Dave Allen, Roger Moore, Don Arrol, Arthur Haynes, Dickie Henderson.

Supercar   Mike Mercury, Professor Popkiss, Dr Beaker, Masterspy, Mitch the monkey, Zarin.

Supergran   Gudrun Ure (Granny Smith), Iain Cuthbertson (Scunner Campbell). Set in Chisleton.

Superman   Original series starred George Reeves, who committed suicide after being typecast in this role. The more recent series stars Dean Cain as Superman and Teri Hatcher as Lois Lane.

Surgical Spirit   Nichola McAuliffe (Dr Sheila Sabatini), Duncan Preston (Dr Jonathan Haslam). Gillies Hospital.

Sutherland's Law   Iain Cuthbertson played Procurator Fiscal Sutherland.

Sweeney, The   John Thaw (Det. Inspector Jack Regan), Dennis Waterman (Det. Sgt George Carter).

Sykes   Eric Sykes and Hattie Jacques (lived at Sebastopol Terrace), Derek Guyler (Korky), Richard Wattis (Mr Brown).

Sylvania Waters   Australian fly-on-the-wall story of the Baker-Donaher family by Paul Watson (*The Family*).

Taggart   Mark McManus (Det. Chief Insp. Jim Taggart), Neil Duncan (Det. Sgt Peter Livingstone), Blythe Duff (Det. Sgt. Jackie Reid).

Take Three Girls   Angela Down, Liza Goddard, Susan Jameson.

Take Your Pick   Presenters: Michael Miles, Des O'Connor. Original man with the gong: Alec Dane.

Taxi   Judd Hirsch (Alex Reiger), Jeff Conaway (Bobby Wheeler), Danny de Vito (Louis de Palma), Marilu Henner (Elaine Nardo), Tony Danza (Tony Banta), Andy Kaufman (Latka Gravas), Christopher Lloyd (Reverend Jim 'Iggie' Ignatowski). Cab company: Sunshine Cabs.

Teletubbies   Tinky Winky, Dipsy, Laa Laa, Po. Babygros open to reveal televisions. Created by Anne Wood. Looked after by a vacuum cleaner called Noo Noo. Voices include Eric Sykes and Toyah Wilcox.

Tenko   Stephanie Beacham (Rose Millar), Stephanie Cole (Dr Beatrice Mason), Bert Kwouk (Yamauchi).

Thank Your Lucky Stars   Presenters: Brian Matthews, Jim Dale and Keith Fordyce.

Third Man   Michael Rennie (Harry Lime). Popular theme tune played on the zither by Shirley Abicaire.

This Morning   Popular daytime magazine hosted live by Richard Madeley and Judy Finnegan.

Thomas the Tank Engine   Narrators: Ringo Starr, Michael Angelis. Thomas is a blue engine; Gordon is green. Written by the Reverend Awdry. The Fat Controller became Sir Topham Hat.

1000 to One   Quiz show hosted by Dale Winton in which, over five weeks, 1000 contestants were whittled down to one winner who scooped 1000 prizes. Your author was one of the five winners but alas narrowly failed to hit the jackpot.

Thunderbirds   Thunderbird 1 pilot Scott Tracy (usually first at the scene because of its high-speed capability); Thunderbird 2 pilot Virgil (pod carrier for Thunderbird 4 and any special equipment required); Thunderbird 3 pilot Alan (rocket back-up) – Alan manned the Spacestation occasionally; Thunderbird 4 pilot Gordon (underwater machine which had great versatility); Thunderbird 5 pilot John (the stationery Spacestation). Jeff Tracy was the father and co-ordinator and Kyrano was his oriental assistant. GB agent was Lady Penelope Creighton-Ward and her butler was Parker. Her Rolls Royce had the registration FAB1; her yacht was FAB2. Technical expert was Hiram Hackenbacker (Brains). Set in the year 2063. The Hood (Kyrano's half-brother) was the arch-enemy who regularly appeared.

Till Death Us Do Part   Warren Mitchell (Alf Garnett), Anthony Booth (Mike), Dandy Nichols (Else), Una Stubbs (Rita), Patrica Hayes (Min Reed). Written by Johnny Speight.

Time Tunnel, The   James Darren (Dr Tony Newman), Robert Colbert (Dr Doug Phillips), Lee Meriwether (Dr Ann McGregor).

Tinker Tailor Soldier Spy   Alec Guinness (George Smiley), Bernard Hepton (Toby Esterhase), Beryl Reid (Connie Sachs).

TISWAS   Today is Saturday, Watch (wear a) and Smile. Presenters included Chris Tarrant, John Asher, Trevor East, Sally James, Lenny Henry, John Gorman, Clive Webb, Sylvester McCoy, Frank Carson, Fogwell Flax and Bob Carolgees and Spit the dog.

Today's the Day   Current affairs quiz programme hosted by Martyn Lewis. Your author, with his chum, won the 1997 series.

To the Manor Born   Penelope Keith (Audrey Fforbes-Hamilton), Peter Bowles (Richard de Vere), Michael Bilton (Ned), Angela Thorne (Marjory Frobisher), John Rudling (Brabinger), Daphne Heard (Mrs Polouvicka).

Tonight   Presenter: Cliff Michelmore. Catchphrase: The next Tonight will be tomorrow night. Notable reporters included Trevor Philpott, Julian Pettifer, Magnus Magnusson, Alan Whicker and the hugely popular Fyfe Robertson.

Top Gear   Presenters include William Woolard, Angela Rippon, Barrie Gill, Noel Edmonds, Sue

TELEVISION

Baker, Jeremy Clarkson, Quentin Willson, Tiff Needell, Chris Goffey, Tony Mason, Janet Trewin, Michele Newman.

Triangle Kate O'Mara (Katherine Laker), Michael Craig (John Anderson), Larry Lamb (Matt Taylor). Company: Triangle Lines. Short-lived soap notable for the bikini-clad posing of its star.

Tripper's Day Leonard Rossiter (Norman Tripper); see *Slinger's Day*.

Trumpton Spin-off series from *Camberwick Green* but the action moved from Pippin Fort. Captain Flack's local firemen: Hugh, Pugh, Barney McGrew, Cuthbert, Dibble and Grubb.

Tutti Frutti Robbie Coltrane (Danny McGlone), Emma Thompson (Suzie Kettles). Band: The Majestics.

TW3 That Was The Week That Was, presented by David Frost and produced by Ned Sherrin.

Twin Peaks Kyle MacLachlan (Agent Dale Cooper), Michael Ontkean (Sheriff Harry S. Truman), Ray Wise (Leland Palmer), Sheryl Lee (Laura Palmer/Madeleine Ferguson), Piper Laurie (Catherine Martell), Dana Ashbrook (Bobby Briggs), Sherilyn Fenn (Audrey Horne). Characters included a dwarf who talked backwards, the Log Lady and Audrey, who tied knots in cherry stalks with her tongue. Killer was Laura's father, Leland, possessed by 'Bob'.

Two Fat Ladies Jennifer Paterson and Clarissa Dickson. Oversize chefs who ride in a combination motorcycle.

2 Point 4 Children Belinda Lang (Bill Porter), Gary Olsen (Ben Porter).

Two's Company Elaine Stritch (Dorothy McNab), Donald Sinden (Robert Hiller).

UFO Ed Bishop (Commander Edward Straker), George Sewell (Colonel Alec Freeman), Peter Gordeno (Peter Karlin, the captain of the Vipers), Gabrielle Drake (Lt Gay Ellis), Michael Billington (Colonel Paul Foster), Wanda Ventham (Colonel Virginia Lake). Defence unit: SHADO (Supreme Headquarters Alien Defence Organization). Reconnaissance satellite: S.I.D. (Space Intruder Detector). Location: beneath the Harlington-Straker film studios just outside London (and Moonbase).

Upstairs Downstairs Gordon Jackson (Mr Angus Hudson), Angela Baddeley (Mrs Kate Bridges), Jean Marsh (Rose), David Langton (Lord Richard Bellamy), Simon Williams (Capt. James Bellamy), Nicola Pagett (Elizabeth Bellamy/Kirkbridge), Lesley-Anne Down (Georgina Worsley), Jacqueline Tong (Daisy), Christopher Beeny (Edward), Pauline Collins (Sarah), John Alderton (Thomas). Address: 165 Eaton Place. Spin-off series: *Thomas and Sarah*.

V Marc Singer (Mike Donovan), Jane Badler (Diana: famous scene where she swallowed a mouse), Jenny Beck and Jennifer Cooke (Elizabeth), Michael Ironside (Ham Tyler), Blair Tefkin (Robin Maxwell, who gave birth to Elizabeth).

Very Peculiar Practice, A Peter Davison (Dr Stephen Daker), David Troughton (Dr Bob Buzzard), Barbara Flynn (Dr Rose Marie), Michael J. Shannon (Jack B. Daniels). Set at Lowlands University. Written by Andrew Davies.

Virginian, The James Drury (Virginian), Doug McClure (Trampas), Lee J. Cobb (Judge Henry Garth), Gary Clarke (Steve Hill), John McIntire (Clay Grainger), Stewart Grainger (Alan MacKenzie), Lee

Majors (Roy Tate). Series set on the Shiloh Ranch, Medicine Bow, Wyoming.

Vision On Presenters include Tony Hart, Larry Parker, Sylvester McCoy, Pat Keysell, Ben Benison, Wilf Lunn, David Cleveland.

Voyage to the Bottom of the Sea Richard Basehart (Admiral Harriman Nelson), David Hedison (Captain Lee Crane). Nuclear submarine: the *Seaview*. Set in the year 1984.

Wacky Races Eleven cars lined up to win the title 'The World's Wackiest Racer'. Car 1: Boulder Mobile; Rock and Gravel Slag. Car 2: Creepy Coupé; Big and Little Gruesome. Car 3: Ring-a-Ding Convert-a-Car; Prof. Pat Pending. Car 4: Crimson Haybailer; Red Max. Car 5: Compact Pussycat; Penelope Pitstop. Car 6: Army Surplus Special; Gen. Sgt and Private Pinkley. Car 7: Bulletproof Bomb; Clyde and Anthill Mob. Car 8: Arkansas Chugabug; Luke and Blubber Bear. Car 9: Turbo Terrific; All-American Peter Perfect. Car 10: Buzz Wagon; Rufus Ruffcut and Sawtooth. Car 00: Mean Machine driven by Dick Dastardly and his dog Muttley. Spin-off series were *The Perils of Penelope Pitstop* and *Dastardly and Muttley in their Flying Machines*, in which they tried to 'Stop the Pigeon'.

Waltons, The Ralph Waite (John), Michael Learned (Olivia), and their seven children: Richard Thomas and Robert Wightman (John Boy), Judy Norton Taylor (Mary Ellen), Jon Walmsley (Jason), Mary Elizabeth McDonough (Erin), David W. Harper (J. Robert 'Jim Bob'), Eric Scott (Ben), Kami Cotler (Elizabeth). Their grandparents were played by Will Geer (Zeb) and Ellen Corby (Esther).

Washington Behind Closed Doors Jason Robards (President Richard Monckton).

Watch With Mother Original five: Picture Book (Patricia Driscoll), Andy Pandy, Bill and Ben, Rag, Tag and Bobtail, The Woodentops. Ran from 1952 to 1980. Others included Tales of the Riverbank, Pogles Wood, Bizzy Lizzy and Barnaby.

Watchdog Presenters include Nick Ross, Lynn Faulds Wood, John Stapleton, Anne Robinson, Alice Beer.

Water Margin, The Set in the water margins of Lian Shan Po. The hero was Lin Chung who, with his wife Hsiao, warred against evil in 14th-century China.

Weakest Link, The Presenter Anne Robinson's catchphrase of 'You are the weakest link, goodbye' soon became the ultimate put-down. The popular daytime BBC2 quiz show was given a prime-time slot on BBC1 due to its record viewing figures. Highlights include Ms Robinson's strange pronunciation and inability to cope with answers not exactly corresponding to what's on her card. Your author lasted a mere two rounds and was voted off after answering all his questions correctly. Please refer to the Shakespeare section for further details.

Whack-O! Jimmy Edwards (Prof. James Edwards), Arthur Howard and Julian Orchard (Mr Oliver Pettigrew). School name: Chiselbury.

What's My Line Presenters include Eamonn Andrews, Emma Forbes, Penelope Keith, David Jacobs. Original panel: Isobel Barnett, David Nixon, Gilbert Harding, Barbara Kelly.

What the Papers Say Presenters include Kingsley Martin, Brian Inglis and Stuart Hall.

When the Boat Comes In James Bolam (Jack Ford), Susan Jameson (Jessie Seaton).

Whiplash Peter Graves (Christopher Cobb). Set in the outback of Australia with a memorable theme tune.

Who Wants to Be a Millionaire? Presenter Chris Tarrant's catchphrases include 'D'you wanna phone a friend?', '50/50', and 'Ask the audience'. The first winner was Judith Keppel and the first man to win the million was David Edwards.

Whoops! Apocalypse Barry Morse (Johnny Cyclops), Richard Griffiths (Premier Dubienkin), Ed Bishop (Jay Garrick), Alexei Sayle (Commissar Solzhenitsyn), Peter Jones (Kevin Pork), John Cleese (Lacrobat).

Wind in the Willows, The Voices were Michael Hordern (Badger), David Jason (Toad), Peter Sallis (Rat), Richard Pearson (Mole).

Winds of War, The Robert Mitchum (Commander Victor 'Pug' Henry), Victoria Tennant (Pamela Tudsbury), Ali MacGraw (Natalie Jastrow), Jan-Michael Vincent (Byron Henry), Ben Murphy (Warren Henry), Howard Lang (Winston Churchill), Gunter Meisner (Hitler). Written by Herman Wouk.

Winston Churchill – The Wilderness Years Robert Hardy (Winston), Siân Phillips (Clementine), Peter Barkworth (Stanley Baldwin), Eric Porter (Neville Chamberlain).

Win, Lose or Draw Hosts: Danny Baker, Shane Richie, Bob Mills.

WKRP in Cincinnati Gary Sandy (Andy Travis), Gordon Jump (Arthur Carlson, 'Big Guy'), Loni Anderson (Jennifer Marlowe), Tim Reid (Gordon Sims, 'Venus Flytrap'), Howard Hesseman (Johnny Caravella, 'Dr Johnny Fever').

Woodentops, The Characters included Daddy and Mummy Woodentop, their twin children Jenny and Willy, Baby Woodentop, Mrs Scrubbit, Sam (the man who helped out in the garden), Buttercup the cow and Spotty the mischievous dog.

World at War World War Two history researched by Noble Frankland, produced by Jeremy Isaacs and narrated by Laurence Olivier.

World's End Short-lived soap opera set around the Mulberry public house, Chelsea, and starring Harry Fowler, Michael Angelis, Paul Brooke, Neville Smith, Primi Townsend.

Worzel Gummidge Jon Pertwee (Worzel), Una Stubbs (Aunt Sally), Geoffrey Bayldon (the Crowman), Lorraine Chase (Dolly Clothes-Peg), Joan Sims (Mrs Bloomsbury-Barton). Written by Keith Waterhouse and Willis Hall from an adaption of Barbara Euphan Todd novels. Worzel was found in Ten Acre Field on Scatterbrook Farm by John and Sue Peters.

Wyatt Earp, The Life and Legend of Hugh O'Brian (Wyatt Earp), Mason Alan Dinehart III (Bat Masterson, Earp's deputy), Douglas Fowley and Myron Healey (Doc Holliday), Lash La Rue (Sheriff John Behan).

Wycliffe Jack Shepherd (Det. Supt Wycliffe), Helen Masters (Det. Insp. Lane), Jimmy Yuill (Det. Insp. Kersey).

Xena: Warrior Princess Lucy Lawless (Xena), New Zealand-made off-shoot series from *Hercules*.

X Files, The David Duchovny (Fox Mulder), Gillian Anderson (Dana Scully), Mitch Pileggi (Skinner), William B. Davis (the Cigarette-Smoking Man [C.G.B. Spender]).

XYY Man, The Stephen Yardley (William 'Spider' Scott, who had an extra 'Y' chromosome which appeared to give him a liking for dangerous pursuits, sometimes criminal), Don Henderson (Det. Sgt George Bulman).

Year in Provence, A John Thaw (Peter Mayle), Lindsay Duncan, Christian Luciani.

Yes Minister/Prime Minister Paul Eddington (Jim Hacker, Minister of Administrative Affairs/Prime Minister), Nigel Hawthorne (Sir Humphrey Appleby), Derek Fowlds (Bernard Wooley). Created by Antony Jay and Jonathan Lynn.

You Rang, M'Lord Paul Shane (Alf Stokes), Su Pollard (Ivy Teesdale), Jeffrey Holland (James Twelvetrees). Title song sung by Paul Shane and Bob Monkhouse.

Young Ones, The Rik Mayall (Rick), Nigel Planer (Neil), Adrian Edmondson (Vyvyan), Christopher Ryan (Mike), Alexei Sayle (Jerzy Balowski, and his family). Saying: For Cliff's sake.

You've Been Framed Presenters include Jeremy Beadle and Lisa Riley.

Z Cars Stratford Johns (Det. Chief Insp. Barlow), Frank Windsor (Det. Sgt John Watt), Brian Blessed (PC William 'Fancy' Smith), Joseph Brady (PC John 'Jock' Weir), James Ellis (Sgt Herbert 'Bert' Lynch), Jeremy Kemp (PC Bob Steele), Terence Edmond (PC Ian Sweet), Colin Welland (PC David Graham), Leonard Rossiter (Det. Insp. Bamber), John Slater (Det. Sgt Tom Stone), Alison Steadman (WPC Bayliss). Theme tune based on folk song 'Johnny Todd'. Spin-off series *Softly Softly*, set in Wyvern.

Zoo Gang, The John Mills (Tommy Devon), Brian Keith (Stephen Halliday), Barry Morse (Alec Marlowe), Lili Palmer (Manouche Roget).

Zoo Time Presenters were Desmond Morris, Chris Kelly and Harry Watt.

Zorro Guy Williams (Don Diego de la Vega, 'Zorro'), Gene Sheldon (Bernardo). Zorro means fox in Spanish.

T
E
L
E
V
I
S
I
O
N

Soap Operas: Cast of Characters

Character	Actor/Actress	Character	Actor/Actress
Albion Market (set in Manchester)		**Brookside (creator Phil Redmond; set in Liverpool)**	
Derek Owen	David Hargreaves		
Lisa O'Shea	Sally Baxter	Annabelle Collins	Doreen Sloane
Ly Nhu Chan	Pik-Sen Lim	Anthea Dixon	Barbara Hatwell
Lynne Harrison	Noreen Kershaw	Barry Grant	Paul Usher
Miriam Ransome	Carol Kaye	Bel Simpson	Lesley Nightingale
Morris Ransome	Bernard Spear	Beth Jordache	Anna Friel
Roy Harrison	Jonathan Barlow	Billy Corkhill	John McArdle
Ted Pilkington	Anthony Booth	Bobby Grant	Ricky Tomlinson
Tony Fraser	John Michie	Chrissy Rogers	Eithne Browne
Viv Harker	Helen Shapiro	Damon Grant	Simon O'Brien
		Dan Simpson	Andrew Butler

Character	Actor/Actress	Character	Actor/Actress
David 'Bing' Crosbie	John Burgess	Bet Lynch/Gilroy	Julie Goodyear
D-D Dixon	Irene Marot	Betty Turpin/Williams	Betty Driver
Diana Spence/Corkhill	Paula Frances	Bill Webster	Peter Armytage
Diane Murray	Bernie Nolan	Billy Walker	Ken Farrington
Doreen Corkhill	Kate Fitzgerald	Blanche Hunt	Maggie Jones
Emily Shadwick	Jennifer Ellison	Chris Collins	Matthew Marsden
Georgia Simpson	Helen Grace	Concepta Hewitt	Doreen Keogh
Heather Huntington/Haversham/	Amanda Burton	David Barlow	Alan Rothwell
Black		Deirdre Hunt/Layton/Barlow/	Anne Kirkbride
Jackie Corkhill	Sue Jenkins	Rachid	
Jacqui Dixon	Alexandra Fletcher	Dennis Tanner	Philip Lowrie
Jerome Johnson	Leon Lopez	Derek Wilton	Peter Baldwin
Jimmy Corkhill	Dean Sullivan	Dev Alaham	Jimmie Harkiskin
Julia Brogan	Gladys Ambrose	Eddie Yeats	Geoffrey Hughes
Karen Grant	Shelagh O'Hara	Elsie Tanner/Howard	Pat Phoenix
Katie Rogers	Diane Burke	Emily Bishop	Eileen Derbyshire
Katrina Evans	Ann Marie Davies	Ena Sharples	Violet Carson
Leo Johnson	Steven Cole	Ernest Bishop	Stephen Hancock
Madge Richmond	Shirley Stelfox	Fiona Middleton	Angela Griffin
Mandy Jordache	Sandra Maitland	Florrie Lindley	Betty Alberge
Max Farnham	Steve Pinder	Fred Elliott	John Savident
Mick Johnson	Louis Emerick	Fred Gee	Fred Feast
Mike Dixon	Paul Byatt	Gail Platt	Helen Worth
Nat Simpson	John Sandford	Gary Mallett	Ian Mercer
Nicholas Black	Alan Rothwell	Gordon Clegg	Bill Kenwright
Ollie Simpson	Michael J. Jackson	Harry Hewitt	Ivan Beavis
Peter Phelan	Sam Kane	Hayley Patterson/Cropper	Julie
Rachel Dixon	Tiffany Chapman		Hesmondhalgh
Ray Hilton	Kenneth Cope	Hilda Ogden	Jean Alexander
Rod Corkhill	Jason Hope	Irma Ogden	Sandra Gough
Roger Huntington	Rob Spendlove	Jack Duckworth	Bill Tarmey
Ron Dixon	Vince Earl	Jack Walker	Arthur Leslie
Sheila Grant/Corkhill	Sue Johnston	Janice Battersby	Vicky Entwistle
Susannah Farnham/Morrisey	Karen Drury	Jed Stone	Kenneth Cope
Thomas 'Sinbad' Sweeney	Michael Starke	Jerry Booth	Graham Haberfield
Tinhead Tim O'Leary	Philip Olivier	Jez Quigley	Lee Boardman
Tracy Corkhill	Justine Kerrigan	Jim McDonald	Charles Lawson
Trevor Jordache	Brian Murray	Judy Mallett	Gaynor Faye
		Ken Barlow	William Roache
Casualty (set in Holby City Hospital)		Kevin Webster	Michael Le Vell
Adam Osman	Pal Aron	Leanne Tilsley	Jane Danson
Amy Howard	Rebecca Wheatley	Len Fairclough	Peter Adamson
Charlie Fairhead	Derek Thompson	Leonard Swindley	Arthur Lowe
Chloe Hill	Jan Anderson	Les Battersby	Bruce Jones
Clive King	George Harris	Linda Sykes	Jacqueline Pirie
Dr Barbara 'Baz' Samuels Hayes	Julia Watson	Liz McDonald	Beverley Callard
Dr Ewart Plimmer	Bernard Gallagher	Lucille Hewitt	Jennifer Moss
Dr Mike Barratt	Clive Mantle	Martha Longhurst	Lynne Carol
Elizabeth Straker	Maureen O'Brien	Martin Platt	Sean Wilson
Holly Miles	Sandra Huggett	Maud Grimes	Elizabeth Bradley
Josh Griffiths	Ian Bleasdale	Maxine Peacock	Tracy Shaw
Lisa 'Duffy' Duffin	Catherine Shipton	Mike Baldwin	Johnny Briggs
Liz Harker	Sue Devaney	Minnie Caldwell	Margot Bryant
Matt Hawley	Jason Merrells	Myra Booth	Susan Jameson
Max Gallagher	Robert Gwilym	Natalie Horrocks/Barnes	Denise Welch
Megan Roach	Brenda Fricker	Norman 'Curly' Watts	Kevin Kennedy
Penny Hutchens	Donna Alexander	Ray Langton	Neville Buswell
Sean Maddox	Gerald Kyd	Rita Sullivan	Barbara Knox
Tina Seabrook	Claire Goose	Roy Cropper	David Neilson
Tony Walker	Eamonn Boland	Sally Webster	Sally Whittaker
		Samantha Failsworth	Tina Hobley
Coronation Street (set in Weatherfield)		Spider Nugent	Martin Hancock
Alan Bradley	Mark Eden	Stan Ogden	Bernard Youens
Alan Howard	Alan Browning	Steve McDonald	Simon Gregson
Alan McKenna	Glenn Hugill	Tanya Pooley	Eva Pope
Albert Tatlock	Jack Howarth	Toyah Battersby	Georgia Taylor
Alec Gilroy	Roy Barraclough	Valerie Barlow	Anne Reid
Anna Baldwin/Halliwell	Amanda Barrie	Vera Duckworth	Elizabeth Dawn
Angie Freeman	Deborah McAndrew	Vikram Sorrell	James Gaddas
Annie Walker	Doris Speed	Vinnie Desai	Chris Bisson
Audrey Roberts	Sue Nicholls		

Character	Actor/Actress
Crossroads	
Adam Chance	Tony Adams
Amy Turtle	Ann George
Anne-Marie Wade	Dee Hepburn
Barbara Brady/Hunter	Sue Lloyd
Benny Hawkins	Paul Henry
Carlos Raphael	Anthony Morton
Clifford Leyton	Johnny Briggs
David Hunter	Ronald Allen
Diane Lawton/Hunter/Parker	Susan Hanson
Doris Luke	Kathy Staff
Jill Richardson/Harvey/Chance	Jane Rossington
Marilyn Gates/Hope	Sue Nicholls
Meg Richardson/Mortimer	Noele Gordon
Miranda Pollard	Claire Faulkenbridge
Myrtle Cavendish	Gretchen Franklin
Nicola Freeman	Gabriella Drake
Paul Ross	Sandor Elès
Rosemary Hunter	Janet Hargreaves
Sandra Gould	Diane Keen
Sandy Richardson	Roger Tonge
Sharon Metcalfe	Carolyn Jones
Shughie McFee	Angus Lennie
Sid Hooper	Stan Stennett
Valerie Pollard	Heather Chasen
Vera Downend	Zeph Gladstone
Vince Parker	Peter Brookes
Dallas	
Ben Stivers/Wes Parmalee	Steve Forrest
Bobby Ewing	Patrick Duffy
Carter McKay	George Kennedy
Clayton Farlow	Howard Keel
Cliff Barnes	Ken Kercheval
Don Lockwood	Ian McShane
Dusty Farlow	Jared Martin
Eleanor Southworth Ewing/Farlow (Miss Ellie)	Barbara Bel Geddes and Donna Reed
Gary Ewing	David Ackroyd and Ted Shackelford
Jenna Wade	Morgan Fairchild, Francine Tacker, Priscilla Presley
Jock Ewing	Jim Davis
John Ross 'JR' Ewing	Larry Hagman
Katherine Wentworth	Morgan Brittany
Kristin Shepard	Colleen Camp and Mary Crosby
LeeAnn De La Vega	Barbara Eden
Lucy Ewing/Cooper	Charlene Tilton
Pamela Barnes/Ewing	Victoria Principal
Ray Krebbs	Steve Kanaly
Stephanie Rogers	Lesley Anne Down
Sue Ellen Ewing	Linda Gray
Valene Ewing	Joan Van Ark
Willard 'Digger' Barnes	David Wayne and Keenan Wynn
Dynasty (set in Denver, Colorado)	
Adam Carrington/ Michael Torrance	Gordon Thomson
Alexis Carrington/Colby/Dexter	Joan Collins
Amanda Carrington	Catherine Oxenberg and Karen Cellini
Ben Carrington	Christopher Cazenove
Blake Carrington	John Forsythe
Caress Morell	Kate O'Meara
Dominique Deveraux	Diahann Carroll

Character	Actor/Actress
Dr Nick Toscanni	James Farentino
Fallon Carrington/Colby	Pamela Sue Martin and Emma Samms
Jeff Colby	John James
Krystle Jennings/Carrington	Linda Evans
Monica Colby	Tracy Scoggins
Prince Michael	Michael Praed
Sable Colby	Stephanie Beacham
Sammy Jo	Heather Locklear
Steven Carrington	Al Corley and Jack Coleman
EastEnders (set in Walford)	
Ali Osman	Nejdet Salih
Andy O'Brien	Ross Davidson
Angie Watts	Anita Dobson
Annie Palmer	Nadia Sawalha
Arthur Fowler	Bill Treacher
Barry Evans	Shaun Williamson
Beppe di Marco	Michael Greco
Bianca Butcher	Patsy Palmer
Big Ron	Ron Tarr
Billy Mitchell	Perry Fenwick
David Wicks	Michael French
Debbie Wilkins	Shirley Cheriton
Dennis Watts	Leslie Grantham
Diane Butcher	Sophie Lawrence
Dot Cotton	June Brown
Dr Harold Legg	Leonard Fenton
Eddie Royle	Michael Melia
Ethel Skinner	Gretchen Franklin
Frank Butcher	Mike Reid
George 'Lofty' Holloway	Tom Watt
George Palmer	Paul Moriarty
Grant Mitchell	Ross Kemp
Hattie Tavernier	Michelle Gayle
Ian Beale	Adam Woodyatt
Jamie Mitchell	Jack Ryder
Janine Butcher	Charlie Brooks
Jim Branning	John Bardon
Joe Wicks	Paul Nicholls
Kat Slater	Jessie Wallace
Kathy Mitchell	Gillian Taylforth
Laura Dunn	Hannah Waterman
Lisa Shaw	Lucy Benjamin
Lorraine Wicks	Jacqueline Leonard
Lou Beale	Anna Wing
Lynne Slater	Elaine Lordan
Mark Fowler	David Scarboro and Todd Carty
Melanie Healy	Tamzin Outhwaite
Michelle Fowler/Holloway	Susan Tully
Mo Harris	Laila Morse
Natalie Evans	Lucy Speed
Nick Cotton	John Altman
Nigel Bates	Paul Bradley
Pat Butcher/Evans	Pam St Clement
Pauline Fowler	Wendy Richard
Peggy Mitchell/Butcher	Jo Warne and Barbara Windsor
Pete Beale	Peter Dean
Phil Mitchell	Steve McFadden
Polly Becker	Victoria Gould
Ricky Butcher	Sid Owen
Robbie Jackson	Dean Gaffrey
Roy Evans	Tony Caunter
Sam Mitchell/Butcher	Danniella Westbrook
Sandra di Marco	Clare Wilkie
Sharon Watts/Mitchell	Letitia Dean

TELEVISION

Character	Actor/Actress	Character	Actor/Actress
Simon Wicks	Nick Berry	Steve Marchant	Paul Opacic
Sonia Jackson	Natalie Cassidy	Terry Woods	Billy Hartman
Steve Owen	Martin Kemp	Vic Windsor	Alun Lewis
Sue Osman	Sandy Ratcliff	Viv Windsor	Deena Payne
Tiffany Mitchell	Martine	Zak Dingle	Steve Halliwell
	McCutcheon	Zoe Tate	Leah Bracknell
Tom Clements	Donald Tandy		
Tony Hills	Mark Homer	**Home and Away (set in Summer Bay near Sydney)**	
Zoe Slater	Michelle Ryan	Ailsa Hogan/Stewart	Judy Nunn
		Casey	Rebecca Croft
Eldorado (set in Los Barcos)		Chloe	Kristy Wright
Blair Lockhead	Josh Nathan	Curtis	Shane Ammann
Dieter Schultz	Kai Maurer	Emma Jackson	Dannii Minogue
Drew Lockhead	Campbell Morrison	Fisher	Norman Coburn
Gwen Lockhead	Patricia Brake	Grant Mitchell	Craig McLachlan
Joy Slater	Leslee Udwin	Isobel	Lorrae Desmond
Nessa Lockhead	Julie Fernandez	Jesse	Ben Unwin
Stanley Webb	William Lucas	Kelly	Katrina Hobbs
Trish Valentine	Polly Perkins	Pippa	Debra Lawrance
		Rebecca	Belinda Emmett
Emmerdale (set in Beckindale)		Selina	Tempany Deckert
Adam Forrester	Tim Vincent	Shannon	Isla Fisher
Alan Turner	Richard Thorp	Travis	Nic Testoni
Albert Dingle	Bobby Knutt		
Amos Brearly	Ronald Magill	**Knots Landing (set in California)**	
Andy Hopwood/Sugden	Kelvin Fletcher	Abby Cunningham/Ewing/Sumner	Donna Mills
Annie Sugden/Kempinski	Sheila Mercier	Charles Scott	Michael York
Ashley Thomas	John Middleton	Gary Ewing	Ted Shackleford
Bernice Blackstock	Samantha Giles	Gregory Sumner	William Devane
Betty Eagleton	Paula Tilbrook	Joshua Rush	Alec Baldwin
Biff Fowler	Stuart Wade	Karen Fairgate/MacKenzie	Michele Lee
Butch Dingle	Paul Loughran	Patrick 'Mack' MacKenzie	Kevin Dobson
Carlos Diaz	Gary Turner	Peter Hollister	Hunt Block
Christopher Tate	Peter Amory	Ruth Galveston	Ava Gardner
Des Bartenshaw	Tony Barton	Valene Ewing/Gibson/Waleska	Joan Van Ark
Diane Blackstock	Elizabeth Estensen		
Dolly Arcaster/Skilbeck	Katherine Barker	**Neighbours (set in Erinsborough)**	
	and Jean Rogers	Annalise Hartman	Kimberley Davies
Donna Windsor	Verity Rushworth	Brenda Riley	Genevieve Lemon
Edna Birch	Shirley Stelfox	Brett Stark	Brett Blewitt
Emily Dingle	Kate McGregor	Bronwen Davies	Rachel Friend
Eric Pollard	Christopher Chittell	Charlene Mitchell/Robinson	Kylie Minogue
Frank Tate	Norman Bowler	Darren Stark	Todd MacDonald
Henry Wilks	Arthur Pentelow	Debbie Martin	Marnie
Jack Sugden	Andrew Burt and		Reece-Wilmore
	Clive Hornby	Des Clarke	Paul Keane
Jan Glover	Roberta Kerr	Dr Beverly Marshall	Lisa Armytage and
Jason Kirk	James Carlton		Shaunna O'Grady
Joe Sugden	Frazer Hines	Dr Clive Gibbons	Geoff Paine
Kathy Bates/Merrick/Tate/Glover	Malandra Burrows	Gail Lewis/Robinson	Fiona Corke
Kelly Windsor	Adele Silva	Hannah Martin	Rebecca Ritters
Kim Tate/Barker	Claire King	Harold Bishop	Ian Smith
Linda Fowler	Tonicha Jeronimo	Helen Daniels	Anne Haddy
Lisa Clegg	Jane Cox	Henry Mitchell Ramsay	Craig McLachlan
Mandy Dingle	Lisa Riley	Jim Robinson	Alan Dale
Mark Reynolds	Anthony Lewis	Joe Mangel	Mark Little
Marlon Dingle	Mark Charnock	Julie Robinson/Martin	Vikki Blanche and
Matt Skilbeck	Jo Kendall		Julie Mullins
Ned Glover	Johnny Leeze	Karl Kennedy	Alan Fletcher
Paddy Kirk	Dominic Brent	Lance Wilkinson	Andrew Bibby
Pat Merrick/Sugden	Helen Weir	Libby Kennedy	Kym Valentine
Rachel Hughes	Glenda McKay	Lou Carpenter	Tom Oliver
Rebecca Cairns	Sarah Neville	Lucy Robinson	Kylie Flinker,
Rev. Donald Hinton	Hugh Manning		Sasha Close and
Robert Sugden	Christopher Smith		Melissa Bell
Roy Glover	Nicky Evans	Madge Mitchell/Ramsay/Bishop	Anne Charleston
Sam Dingle	James Hooton	Malcolm Kennedy	Benji McNair
Sarah Sugden	Alyson Spiro	Max Ramsay	Francis Bell
Scot Windsor	Ben Freeman	Melanie Pearson/Mangel	Lucinda Cowden
Seth Armstrong	Stan Richards	Mike Young	Guy Pearce
Sophie Wright	Jane Cameron	Nell Mangel/Worthington	Vivean Gray

Character	Actor/Actress	Character	Actor/Actress
Paul Robinson	Stefan Dennis	Sgt Bob Cryer	Eric Richard
Philip Martin	Ian Rawlings	WPC Martella	Nula Conwell
Rosemary Daniels	Joy Chambers	WPC Cathy Marshall	Lynne Miller
Scott Robinson	Darius Perkins and	WPC Claire Brind	Kelly Lawrence
	Jason Donovan	WPC Hagen	Samantha Robson
Shane Ramsay	Peter O'Brien	WPC June Ackland	Trudie Goodwin
Sky Bishop/Mangel	Miranda Fryer	WPC Norika Datta	Seeta Indrani
Toadfish	Ryan Moloney	WPC Polly Page	Lisa Geoghan
Toby Mangel	Finn Greentree		
	Keene		

Colbys, The (spin-off from *Dynasty* and set in Los Angeles)

Character	Actor/Actress
Bliss Colby	Claire Yarlett

The Bill (set in Sun Hill)

Character	Actor/Actress	Character	Actor/Actress
Chief Insp. Cato	Philip Whitchurch	Constance Colby	Barbara Stanwyck
Chief Insp. Derek Conway	Ben Roberts	Fallon Carrington/Colby	Emma Samms
Chief Supt Charles Brownlow	Peter Ellis	Francesca Scott Colby	Katherine Ross
DC Alfred 'Tosh' Lines	Kevin Lloyd	Jason Colby	Charlton Heston
DC Glaze	Karl Collins	Miles Colby	Maxwell Caulfield
DCI Meadows	Simon Rouse	Monica Colby	Tracy Scoggins
DC Jim Carver	Mark Wingett	Sable Scott Colby	Stephanie
DC Lennox	George Rossi		Beacham
DC Mike Dashwood	Jon Iles	Zachary Powers	Ricardo Montalban
DC Woods	Tom Cotcher		
Det. Chief Insp. Kim Reid	Carolyn Pickles	**The Newcomers (set in Angleton)**	
Det. Insp. Chris Deakin	Shaun Scott	Andrew Kerr	Robin Bailey
Det. Insp. Frank Burnside	Christopher Ellison	Ellis Cooper	Alan Browning
Det. Insp. Roy Galloway	John Salthouse	Joyce Harker	Wendy Richard
Det. Sgt Danny Pearce	Martin Marquez	Julie Robertson	Deborah Watling
Det. Sgt Don Beech	Billy Murray	Maria Cooper	Judy Geeson
Det. Sgt Ted Roach	Tony Scannell	Robert Malcolm	Conrad Phillips
PC Barry Stringer	Jonathan Dow	Vivienne Cooper	Maggie Fitzgibbon
PC Dave Litten	Gary Olsen		
PC Dave Quinnan	Andrew Paul	**The Sullivans**	
PC Francis 'Taffy' Edwards	Colin Blumenau	Dave Sullivan	Paul Cronin
PC George Garfield	Huw Higginson	Geoff Sullivan	Jamie Higgins
PC Jarvis	Stephen Beckett	Grace Sullivan	Lorraine Bayly
PC Reg Hollis	Jeff Stewart	Harry Sullivan	Michael Caton
PC Robin Frank	Ashley Gunstock	Jack Fletcher	Reg Gorman
PC Ron Smollett	Nick Stringer	Jim Sullivan	Andy Anderson
PC Steve Loxton	Tom Butcher	John Sullivan	Andrew McFarlane
PC Timothy Able	Mark Haddigan	Kitty Sullivan	Susan Hannaford
PC Tony Stamp	Graham Cole	Maggie Baker	Vikki Hammond
PC Tony 'Yorkie' Smith	Robert Hudson	Terry Sullivan	Richard Morgan
Sgt Bayden	Tony O'Callaghan	Tom Sullivan	Steven Tandy

TELEVISION

Television, Radio and Media Adverts

A diamond is forever　De Beer Consolidated Mines

Aah . . . Bisto

All human life is there　News of the World

All the news that's fit to print　*New York Times*

And all because the lady loves . . .　Milk Tray

Any time, any place, anywhere　Martini (coined by Barry Day)

Are you with . . . No, I'm with the　Woolwich

Ask the man from the . . .　Pru (Prudential Assurance Co. Ltd)

A . . . works wonders　Double Diamond

Bank that likes to say Yes　TSB

Beanz meanz . . .　Heinz

Beats as it sweeps as it cleans　Hoover vacuum cleaners

Beer that made Milwaukee famous　Schlitz

B . . . O . . .　Lifebuoy soap

Builds bonny babies　Glaxo

Buy some for Lulu　Smarties

. . . calling!　Avon

Can you tell . . . from butter?　Stork margarine

Chocolates with the less fattening centres　Maltesers

Chocolates? No . . .　Maltesers

Cleans a big, big carpet for less than half a crown　1001

Clunk click, every trip　Jimmy Savile's seat belt campaign (from 1971)

Cool as a mountain stream　Consulate cigarettes

Cuts cleaning time in half　Flash

Does she or doesn't she?　Clairol hair colouring (coined by Shirley Polykoff)

Don't ask the price. It's a penny　Marks & Spencer (when first opened)

Don't be vague, ask for . . .　Haig whisky

Don't say brown, say . . .　Hovis

Don't you just love being in control　British Gas, and Mrs Merton and her son, Malcolm

Fingerlickin' good　Kentucky Fried Chicken

First truly feminine cigarette　Eve

Fly the flag　British Airways

Forces grey out, forces white in   Fairy Snow

Fortifies the over forties   Phyllosan

Fresh as the moment when the pod went pop   Birds Eye peas

Full of Eastern promise   Fry's Turkish Delight

Getting there is half the fun   Cunard Steamship Line

Gives a meal man appeal   Oxo

Good to the last drop   Maxwell House coffee

Gordon's gin (first scented advert)   Shown in May 1997 when juniper berries could be smelt in cinema

Go to work on an . . .   Egg (slogan is often attributed to Fay Weldon)

Graded grains make finer flour   Homepride

Hands that do dishes are as soft as your face with mild, green Fairy Liquid

Have a break, bave a . . .   KitKat

Helps you work, rest and play   A Mars a day (possibly attributed to Murray Walker)

Hold it up to the light, not a stain and shining bright   Surf

I dreamed I . . . in my   Maidenform bra

I think you probably are   Cockburns Port

I was so impressed I bought the company Remington (said by Victor Kyam)

If you see Sid, tell him   British Gas slogan during privatization

I'm only here for the beer   Double Diamond

I'm . . . fly me   National Airlines

. . . is good for you   Guinness

Is she or isn't she?   Harmony hair spray

It's for yoo-hoo!   British Telecom

It's the real thing   Coca-Cola

It's what your right arm's for   Courage beer

Keep your schoolgirl complexion   Palmolive

Keynsham – spelt K-E-Y-N-S-H-A-M   Horace Batchelor's phrase on Luxembourg's pools advisory service

Kills 99% of all household germs   Domestos

Let's face the music and dance   Allied Dunbar

Let your fingers do the walking   Yellow Pages (Kirsty MacColl's version of 'Days' was popular theme)

Looks good, tastes good and by golly it does you good   Mackeson

Loudest noise comes from the electric clock Rolls Royce

Make tea bags make tea   Tetley's

Makes exceedingly good cakes   Mr Kipling

Means happy motoring   Esso (sign)

Melts in your mouth, not in your hands   Treets

Milk from contented cows   Carnation

Mint with the hole   Polo

Minty bit stronger   Trebor Mints

Naughty but nice   Original advert about cream cakes (Salman Rushdie coined the phrase)

Nice 'ere 'innit?   Campari (Lorraine Chase)

Nice face, shame about the breath   Listerine mouthwash

Nice one, Cyril   Wonderloaf

Nicole . . . Papa   Renault Clio

99 44/100 % Pure   Ivory soap

Nissan Almira   Parodies of *The Sweeney* and *The Professionals*

Nissan Micra   'No No No' by Nancy Nova

Nothing acts faster than . . .   Anadin

Nuts! Whole hazelnuts   Cadbury's Wholenut

One degree under? Try . . .   Aspro

Pizza Hut   Jonathan Ross, Caprice, Gareth Southgate, Damon Hill, Mikhail Gorbachev, Pamela Anderson

Plink plink fizz   Alka Seltzer

Prevents that sinking feeling   Bovril

Probably the best lager in the world   Carlsberg

Prolongs active life   Pal dog food

Promise her anything, but give her . . .   Arpège (coined by Edouard Cournand, president of Lanvin Perfumes)

Pure genius   Guinness

Put a tiger in your tank   Esso

Puts the 'T' in Britain   Typhoo tea

Refreshes the parts other beers cannot reach Heineken (coined by Terry Lovelock)

Ring of confidence   Colgate toothpaste

. . . satisfy   Senior Service cigarettes

Schhh . . . you know who   Schweppes

Seven pieces of heaven   Fry's Chocolate Cream

Simply years ahead   Philips

'Singing in the Rain' (rap version)   McDonald's

Snap! crackle! and pop!   Kellogg's Rice Crispies

Solutions for a small planet   IBM

Splash it on all over   Brut

Spreads straight from the fridge   Blueband margarine

Stays sharp till the bottom of the glass   Harp lager

Stop me and buy one   Wall's ice cream

Sweet you can eat between meals   Milky Way (without spoiling your appetite)

Takes good care of you   BOAC

Tested by dummies, driven by the intelligent Volvo

The appetizer   Tizer

The bank that listens   Midland

The bright one, the right one, it's . . .   Martini

The cereal that's shot from guns   Quaker Puffed Wheat

The drive of your life   Peugeot 106

The real smell of . . .   Brut

The shirt you don't iron   Rael Brook Toplin

The soluble aspirin   Disprin

They grow on you   Roses chocolates

They're bootiful   Bernard Matthews's turkeys

They're grrrreat!   Frosties

Things go better with . . .   Coke (Coca-Cola)

To fly, to serve   British Airways

Too good to hurry mints   Murray Mints

To our members we're the fourth emergency service   Automobile Association

Top people read the . . .   Times

Try a little VC 10derness   British Airways

Vorsprung durch Technik   Audi

Watch out there's a Humphrey about   Milk

We never forget you have a choice   British Caledonian

We try harder   Avis Car Rentals (coined by Doyle, Dane & Bernbach)

We'll take more care of you   British Airways

Were you truly wafted here from Paradise? Nah! Luton Airport   Campari (Lorraine Chase)

When you fancy a fruity treat, unzip a . . .   Banana

When you've got it, flaunt it   Braniff Airways

Which twin has the Toni? Toni Home Perms
Why does the man in the mask drink . . . Metz
Wodka from Warrington Vladivar
World's favourite airline British Airways
Wot a lot I got Smarties
Would you give me your last . . .? Rolo
You know what comes between me and my Calvins? Calvin Klein jeans (15-year-old Brooke Shields in 1980)
You'll look a little lovelier each day with fabulous pink Camay soap

You'll wonder where the yellow went . . . when you brush your teeth with Pepsodent
You make it what it is BBC
You press the button, we do the rest Kodak
Your country needs you WW1 army recruitment poster (Kitchener pointing with right hand)
You're never alone with a . . . Strand (coined by John May)
You too can have a body like mine Charles Atlas (Angelo Siciliano)

Television and Radio: Miscellaneous Information

advertisement: first Gibbs SR toothpaste.
advertisement: shown after death Yul Brynner made anti-smoking advert with the message, 'Hullo, I'm dead; smoking killed me.'
Any Questions/Answers Presenters: Freddy Grisewood, David Jacobs.
Archers First broadcast on BBC on 1 January 1951, although first heard on a local station in the Midlands in 1950. The Archers lived on Brookfield Farm in Ambridge, just south of Borchester, Borsetshire. Many weddings during the series have been recorded at Hanbury Church in Worcestershire. Princess Margaret as President of the NSPCC visited Ambridge for a fashion show (1984). Eddie Grundy famously got drunk in Britt Ekland's dressing room at the Christmas pantomime (1992). Billing: Everyday story of country folk. Local pub: The Bull.
aspect ratio Normal: 4 x 3. Wide screen: 16 x 9.
BAFTA TV Awards: 2001
   Best Actress   Judi Dench (*Last of the Blonde Bombshells*)
   Best Actor   Michael Gambon (*Longitude*)
   Best Light Entertainment Performance   Graham Norton (*So Graham Norton*)
   Best Comedy Performance   Sacha Baron Cohen (*Da Ali G Show*)
   Best Single Drama   *Care* (Kieran Prendiville and Antonia Bird)
   Best Drama Serial   *Longitude*
   Best Factual Series   *Britain at War in Colour*
   Best Comedy Programme   *Da Ali G Show*
   Best Situation Comedy   *Black Books*
   Best Soap   *Emmerdale*
BBC announcer: first Leslie Mitchell.
BBC Choice First new BBC channel for 34 years (Clive Anderson opened the proceedings on 23 September 1998).
BBC Director General: first Lord Reith.
BBC Director of Radio Jenny Abramsky took over from Matthew Bannister on 19 November 1998.
BBC Radio controllers Radio 5 Live – Bob Shennan; Radio 4 – Helen Boaden; Radio 3 – Roger Wright; Radio 2 – James Moir; Radio 1 – Andy Parfitt.
BBC Television controllers BBC 1 – Lorraine Heggessey; BBC 2 – Jane Root.
BBC Television executives Chairman is Sir Christopher Bland and Director General is Greg Dyke.
BBC 2 Commenced 20 April 1964; mascots were Hullabaloo and Custard (two kangaroos).

Beyond Our Ken Billed as 'A sort of radio show' and starred Kenneth Horne.
Brain of Britain Hosted by Robert Robinson and produced by Richard Eades. Questions set by Ian Gillies (Mycroft). Winners: Martin Dakin (1954), Arthur Maddock (1955), Anthony Carr (1956), Rosemary Watson (1957), David Keys (1958), Dr Reginald Webster (1959), Patrick Bowing (1960), Irene Thomas (1961), Henry Button (1962), Ian Barton (1963), Ian Gillies (1964), Robert Crampsey (1965), Richard Best (1966), Lt Cmdr Loring (1967), Ralph Raby (1968), T.D. Thomson (1969), Ian Matheson (1970), Fred Morgan (1971), A. Lawrence (1972), Glyn Court (1973), Roger Pritchard (1974), Winifred Lawson (1975), Thomas Dyer (1976), Martin Gostelow (1977), James Nesbitt (1978), Arthur Gerard (1979), Tim Paxton (1980), Peter Barlow (1981), John Pusey (1982), Sue Marshall (1983), Peter Bates (1984), Richard Fife (1985), Stephen Gore (1986), Ian Sutton (1987), Paul Monaghan (1988), Barbara Thompson (1989), Jim Eccleson (1990), Chris Wright (1991), Mike Billson (1992), Geoffrey Colton (1993), Ian Wynn-Mackenzie (1994), Ian Kinloch (1995), Kevin Ashman (1996), Daphne Fowler (1997), Guy Herbert (1998), Leslie Duncalf (1999), Mike Smith-Rawnsley (2000).
Brains Trust The first panel were Julian Huxley, C.E.M. Joad and Cmdr A.B. Campbell. The chairman was Donald McCullough, who was replaced by Gilbert Harding.
Breakfast Television Started 17 January 1983 (*BBC Breakfast Time*).
Broadcasting Standards Authority: first chairman Lord Rees Mogg.
BSkyB: controller Elizabeth Murdoch.
Byker Grove: setting Newcastle upon Tyne.
Carlton TV: fine Carlton Television was fined £2m for faking the documentary *The Connection*.
Channel 4 Started in 1982 (first programme: *Countdown*).
Channel 4: chief executive Michael Jackson (chairman: Michael Bishop).
Channel 5 Launched on 30 March 1997 by Dawn Airey and the Spice Girls.
Channel 5: chief executive David Elstein.
chefs on television Jane Asher, Susan Brooks, Robert Carrier, Fanny Craddock, Anton Edelman, Keith Floyd, Philip Harbin, Ainsley Harriott, Graham Kerr, Anton Mossiman, Jamie Oliver, Paul Rankin, Gary Rhodes, Delia Smith, Rick Stein, Brian Turner, Antony Worrall Thompson.
Classic FM: chief executive Ralph Bernard.

TELEVISION

colour television Started in 1967.

Crookes Tube: function Produced cathode rays.

Desert Island Discs: first guest Vic Oliver.

Desert Island Discs: presenters Roy Plomley, Michael Parkinson, Sue Lawley.

digital television: advantages Traditional broadcasting is based on electronic signals that rise and fall to represent the shades of black, white and colour in the TV picture. The continuously varying signal is a direct analogue of the image it represents, just as the variations in the grooves of an LP, picked up by the stylus, are an analogue of the music. Analogue broadcasting is spendthrift in its use of the radio spectrum. There is a limited range of frequencies that can be used for TV transmissions, and each analogue station needs a healthy chunk of that space (approx 8 megahertz). Transmitters using the same frequency must be a long way apart, otherwise they interfere with one another, so transmitters closer than a few hundred kilometres to each other must employ different frequencies. As a result, it takes 44 frequencies in the UHF band to provide the four terrestrial channels. Digital broadcasting alters the rules. Instead of representing the image by a continuously variable signal, digital TV encodes it in the same language used by computers, a long stream of binary digits, or 'bits', each of which is either 0 or 1, a pulse or a non-pulse. It takes an enormous number of such bits to encode a TV picture, but it is easier to distinguish a pulse from a non-pulse than it is to discern the varying waveform of an analogue signal. This means that transmitters can be run at a much lower signal strength and still provide a decent picture. This in turn reduces the interference problem for terrestrial broadcasters so that better use can be made of the available frequencies, and picture quality is greatly improved. A full TV picture requires about 216 million bits per second but only the changes from one picture to the next are encoded so as to enable the data to fit into the frequency band.

Golden Rose of Montreux: 1999 *The League of Gentlemen.*

Hamish Macbeth: setting Plockton, on the west coast of Scotland.

House of Lords: first televised 1985.

iconoscope: inventor Vladimir Zworykin (1923).

ITMA (It's That Man Again) Tommy Hanley was the title character and Dorothy Summers played Mrs Mopp.

ITN newscaster: first Chris Chataway.

ITV: managing director David Liddiment.

Just a Minute Chairman Nicholas Parsons. Panellists have included: Kenneth Williams, Derek Nimmo, Peter Jones, Clement Freud, Paul Merton, Graham Norton, Lance Percival and Sheila Hancock. The aim is to talk for one minute on a given topic without Hesitation, Deviation or Repetition.

Life with the Lyons Ben Lyon and Bebe Daniels and their children Barbara and Richard.

local radio stations Aire – Leeds, Beacon – Wolverhampton, BRMB – Birmingham, Centre – Leicester, Chiltern – Luton/Bedford, City – Liverpool, Hallam – Sheffield, Hereward – Peterborough, Mercia – Coventry, Mercury – Crawley, Orwell – Ipswich, Pennine – Bradford, Piccadilly – Manchester, Trent – Nottingham, 2CR – Bournemouth, West – Bristol, Wyvern – Hereford and Worcester.

Men from the Ministry, The Wilfrid Hyde Whyte (Roland Hamilton-Jones), Richard Murdock (Richard Lamb).

Nielsens US equivalent of BARB showing American audience ratings.

OnDigital TV service 30-channel service launched by Ulrika Jonsson on 15 November 1998.

pirate radio station: first Radio Caroline, from 1964 to 1967.

radio play: caused panic Orson Welles's *War of the Worlds* broadcast in 1938.

radio stations: formerly called Radio 4 (Home), Radio 3 (Third), Radio 2 (Light). These were the three main stations. Radio 1 commenced in 1967.

Round Britain Quiz Hosted by Nick Clarke.

satellite TV: reception areas Known as Footprints.

S4C: full name Sianel Pedwar Cymru.

SkyDigital Launched on 1 October 1998.

soap opera: first on television *The Appleyards* ran from 1952 to 1957 and is truly the first example of a televised British soap opera. The first adult British soap opera was *The Grove Family* (1954–7). The first daily soap opera was *Sixpenny Corner* (set in the new town of Springwood). This is another controversial area that requires careful attention. *The Appleyards* was shown fortnightly and was a children's soap, while *The Groves* was broadcast weekly and was for adults.

soap opera: why called Term derived from the American radio of the 1930s when soap and detergent companies sponsored the 15-minute daily radio programmes. Proctor and Gamble were a leading light in this field.

Sony Radio Academy Awards 2001

Comedy Award *Dead Ringers* (Radio 4). Cast includes Jon Colshaw, Jan Ravens, Mark Perry and Kevin Connelly.

Drama Award Alpha (BBC World Service). Central performance by David Calder.

2000 Award Terry Wogan (for adding half a million new listeners to BBC Radio 2).

Station of the Year BBC Radio 2.

Gold Award Chris Tarrant (lifetime career achievements including his 14 years as London's most popular breakfast presenter with Capital FM).

Sports Award The Wembley Live Obituary Show (BBC Sport for Five Live).

Interactive Award The Stephen Rhodes Consumer Programme (BBC Three Counties Radio)

Feature Award Thirteen Ways of Looking at a Blackbird (BBC Radio 3).

News Broadcaster Award Jon Gaunt (BBC Three Counties Radio).

Breakfast Music Award Daryl Denham in the Morning (100.7 Heart FM).

Music Broadcaster Award Stuart Maconie (BBC Radio 2).

Steve Coogan Creations Alan Partridge, Paul Calf, Pauline Calf, Tony Farino.

stripping Showing of programme at the same time every day of every week.

swear word: first to use Kenneth Tynan was the first to use the 'f' word on television.

Teletext BBC – Ceefax; ITV – Oracle.

television companies Anglia TV, based in Norwich, started in 1959 (logo is a series of triangles in shape of an 'A'). Associated Television (ATV) first broadcast in September 1955, at weekends only. The BBC formed in London in 1922 as a radio station and in 1936 started television broadcasts. BSkyB formed in 1990 by merger of Sky TV and British Satellite Broadcasting. Border Television formed in 1961 (logo is ovoid shape with an inverted 'Y' running through the centre). Carlton Television formed in 1992. Central Television formed in 1982 and is now part of the Carlton Network (logo is a 12-part sphere). Grampian Television formed in 1961 (logo is a saltire cross on a television screen). Granada Television formed in 1955 and is the only original franchise holder still broadcasting. Harlech Television formed in 1968. ITC (Independent Television Corporation) formed as an alternative to the BBC. LWT (London Weekend Television) started in 1967 from Fridays at 6.00 p.m. to Sunday nights. Meridian Television replaced TVS as franchise holder for the south and south-east on 1 January 1993 (logo is a sunny face). Rediffusion started broadcasting on weekdays only in September 1955. Scottish Television formed in 1957. Southern Television formed in 1958. Thames Television formed when ABC merged with Associated Rediffusion in the late 1960s. Tyne Tees formed in 1959 and is now owned by Granada Media. Ulster Television formed in 1959. Westcountry Television formed in 1993 and is owned by Carlton Communications. Yorkshire Television formed in 1968 and is owned by Granada Media.

television: inventor   John Logie Baird created his first televisor, a contraption made from a tea-chest,

a biscuit box and darning needles, in 1923, and gave a first public demonstration in 1926. In 1928 he produced a crude colour system.

television licences: first   Licences were first issued in 1946 at £2 each. Cost of a colour licence at July 2000 is £109; black and white is £35.50.

test card girl: famous   Carol Hersey (billed as the most seen person on television).

TV am: launched by   David Frost, Michael Parkinson, Robert Kee, Anna Ford, Angela Rippon.

Twenty Questions: presenters   Stewart McPherson, Gilbert Harding, Kenneth Horne, Cliff Michelmore.

Twenty Questions: mystery voice   Norman Hackforth.

Ulster TV: chairman   John B. McGuckian.

Ulster TV: location   Havelock House, Belfast.

Variety Playhouse: MC   Vic Oliver.

Virgin Radio: chairman   David Campbell.

weather   Laura Greene (ITV), Ian McCaskill, Bill Giles, Suzanne Charlton, Helen Young, John Ketley, Peter Cockcroft, Michael Fish (BBC).

weather: hurricane announcement   Michael Fish gave us the good news on 15 October 1987 that the person who rang up saying a hurricane was likely for tomorrow was completely wrong!

Wogan: appeared drunk on in 1990   George Best.

World Service Radio: controller   Mark Byford.

World Service Television   BBC channel launched in 1991.

T
E
L
E
V
I
S
I
O
N

TRANSPORT: AIRCRAFT

Chronology

1300 Marco Polo reports man-carrying kites in use in China.

1500 Leonardo da Vinci designs helicopters and ornithopters.

1709 A model hot-air balloon demonstrated by Father Laurenço de Gusmao at the court of King John V of Portugal (8 Aug.).

1783 First manned balloon flight by Pilâtre de Rozier and the marquis d'Arlandes in the Bois de Boulogne (21 Nov.). First flight of hydrogen balloon by Professor Jacques Charles (1 Dec.).

1784 First British balloon flight (4 Oct.).

1785 First crossing of the English Channel by balloon piloted by Jean-Pierre Blanchard and John Jeffries (7 Jan.).

1799 Sir George Cayley designs his first glider.

1810 Cayley publishes a paper on the theory of the airplane.

1843 The 'Steam Airplane' patented by William Samuel Henson.

1849 Cayley's 'Boy-Lifter' glider succeeds in lifting a small boy off the ground.

1852 Henri Giffard makes first semi-controlled powered flight in airship (24 Sept.).

1853 Cayley succeeds in making his coachman fly his glider.

1861 Balloons used by Union forces in American Civil War.

1870 Leon Gambetta escapes from a besieged Paris by balloon (7 Oct.).

1890 Clément Ader's *Eole* aircraft makes a short 'hop' near Paris (9 Oct.).

1891 Otto Lilienthal makes his first glider flight.

1894 Sir Hiram Maxim's biplane makes brief uncontrolled ascent (31 July).

1896 Otto Lilienthal dies after glider crash (10 Aug.).

1899 Glider pioneer Percy Pilcher dies following glider crash (2 Oct.).

1900 LZ1 makes first rigid airship flight (Count Zeppelin) (2 July).

1900 Wright brothers begin glider experiments (1 Dec.).

1903 Lebaudy airship makes first fully controlled flight in history (8 May). Samuel Langley's *Aerodrome* aircraft narrowly fails to make first powered flight (7 Oct.). Wright brothers make first powered flight (Orville at the controls) in *Flyer* (17 Dec.).

1906 Alberto Santos-Dumont makes first powered flight in Europe (23 Oct.). French company, Voisin Frères, established for the production of powered aircraft (Nov.).

1907 Breguet gyroplane makes first helicopter 'hop' (19 Sept.). Paul Cornu's helicopter makes first 'hop' (13 Nov.). Lt Thomas W. Selfridge became first person killed in a plane crash when he and Orville Wright crash at Fort Meyer, Virginia (17 Sept.).

1908 Samuel Cody makes first powered flight in Britain (16 Oct.).

1909 Louis Blériot makes first flight across the English Channel (25 July).

1910 Harry Houdini, the celebrated escapologist and illusionist, makes the first successful flight on the Australian continent in a Voisin biplane (18 March).

1911 Eugene Ely lands Curtiss biplane on USS *Pennsylvania* (18 Jan.). First mail carried by air in UK (9 Sept.). First aerial warfare by Italian Army Aviation Corps over Libya (23 Oct.). Lt Giulio Gavotti makes the first air raid by dropping a 4½ lb bomb on Turks at Ain Zara (1 Nov.). Aircraft used in Mexican Revolution.

1912 Royal Flying Corps (RFC) formed (13 April). Death of Wilbur Wright (30 May). Bulgarian M. Popoff becomes first pilot killed in warfare, during a reconnaissance flight (3 Nov.).

1914 Lts V. Waterfall and C.G.G. Bayley first British fliers killed in action (22 Aug.). Paris becomes the first capital city to be bombed from the air (30 Aug.). Japanese seaplanes attack the Austro-German fleet at Kiaochow, causing the first ship to be sunk from the air (17 Sept.). HMS *Ark Royal* becomes the world's first aircraft carrier (9 Dec.).

1915 LZ38 airship makes the first air raid on London (31 May). Flt Sub-Lt R.A. Warneford (VC) downs the LZ37, the first Zeppelin to be shot down (7 June). Katherine Stinson becomes first woman to loop the loop (18 July). Roland Garros is captured in Belgium (20 April). Garros was the first Frenchman to cross the Mediterranean by air, and working with Raymond Saulnier invented deflector plates to enable him to fire a machine gun through the propeller.

1916 Death of Ernst Mach (19 Feb.). Boeing formed as Pacific Aero Products Co (15 July). SL11 airship shot down in North London by Lt W. Leefe-Robinson (VC) (2 Sept.). World's first flying bomb, the Hewitt-Sperry, built by Curtiss, is tested (12 Sept.). The airship ace Heinrich Mathy is killed when LZ72 is shot down over Potters Bar (2 Oct.). First British airline, Aircraft Transport &Travel Ltd, registered (5 Oct.).

1917 Baron von Richthofen awarded the 'Pour le Mérite' medal (16 Jan.). Death of Count von Zeppelin (8 March). Billy Mitchell became the first US Army officer to fly over German lines (24 April). Albert Ball killed in France (7 May), awarded posthumous VC (3 June). Sopwith Camel goes into service with Royal Flying Corps (RFC) in France (July). First flight of the Vickers Vimy (30 Nov.).

1918 Air Ministry established and Lord Rothermere is first Sec. of State for Air (2 Jan.). Royal Flying Corps and Royal Naval Air Service combine to create the Royal Air Force (1 April). Baron von Richthofen shot down (21 April). Hermann Goering takes over as leader of

Richthofen's squadron (7 July). HMS *Furious*, adapted from cruiser to aircraft carrier, launched six Sopwith Camels against Zeppelin sheds (19 July). Peter Strasser, German commander of airships, shot down in L70 off Cromer (5 Aug.). Roland Garros killed when his SPAD XIII breaks up during a dogfight (5 Oct.). Handley Page 0/400 becomes first plane to fly from Egypt to India (12 Dec.).

1919 Britain's first scheduled air service inaugurated (10 May). US Navy Curtiss flying boat flown by Lt Cmdr Albert Read becomes first aircraft to fly the Atlantic (in stages) (27 May). Alcock and Brown make first non-stop crossing of the Atlantic in a Vickers Vimy (15 June). German Zeppelin fleet scuttled (23 June). First flight of Junkers F13, the first all-metal monoplane airliner (25 June). London's first airport opens at Hounslow Heath (1 July). British airship R34 makes first two-way Atlantic crossing (13 July). Edward Mannock, Britain's most successful ace, posthumously awarded VC (18 July). First flight over the Canadian Rockies by Capt. Ernest Hoy (7 Aug.). KLM founded (7 Oct.). Handley Page Transport provide first in-flight meals (11 Oct.). Ross and Keith Smith make first flight from Britain to Australia in a Vickers Vimy (10 Dec.) .

1920 First flight from Britain to South Africa (20 March). Croydon Airport begins operations, taking over from Hounslow (29 March). Juan de la Cierva is granted a patent for the Autogiro (27 Aug.). Dayton-Wright RB Racer aircraft flown with retractable landing gear. Qantas (Queensland and Northern Territory Aerial Services) founded (16 Nov.). First British airline disaster: Handley Page 0/400 crashes at Cricklewood, killing four (14 Dec.). Airline AT & T goes into liquidation (15 Dec.).

1921 First free flight of a helicopter since 1907, assisted by a balloon (15 Jan.). Orly aerodrome opened in Paris (1 March). Croydon Airport officially opened (31 March). Vickers Vernon, first troop-carrying aircraft, delivered to RAF (1 Aug.). First aerial crop-dusting takes place in Ohio, USA, by Lt John B. Macready in a Curtiss JN6 (3 Aug.). Airship R38 crashes in Hull, killing many of Britain's most experienced airshipmen (24 Aug.).

1922 Formation of RAF reserve announced (9 Feb.). Jack Sanderson became first airline steward (2 April). First mid-air collision, between Farman Goliath and Daimler DH18, over Poix in northern France (7 April). First night flight by Grands Express from Le Bourget to Croydon (9 June). First air crossing of South Atlantic by S. Cabral and G. Coutinho of Portugal (16 June). Dr Albert Taylor and Leo Young make first successful detections of objects by radio observation (23 Sept.). QANTAS flies its first scheduled service, the first passenger being Mr A. Kennedy (2 Nov.). First instance of skywriting 'Smoke Lucky Strikes' (28 Nov.).

1923 First public flight of Juan de la Cierva's Autogyro (9 Jan.). First drop tank used (Boeing MB-3A) (5 March). First air troop-transport took place during Kurdish uprising when 280 Sikhs were flown from Kingarban to Kirkuk (April).

Etienne Ochmichen makes world's first helicopter closed-circuit flight (1 May). Amelia Earhart receives pilot's certificate from NAA, the first woman to do so (16 May). Sabena Airlines formed in Belgium (23 May). Formation of New Zealand Air Force (14 June). First flight of US airship *Shenandoah* (3 Sept.). Dixmunde disaster over the Mediterranean: 52 killed in airship explosion (21 Dec.).

1924 Royal Canadian Air Force formed (1 April). First sustained forward flight of a helicopter made by Etienne Ochmichen (14 April). Fleet Air Arm established (April). Start of first aeroplane flight round the world by Lts L.H. Smith and Erik Nelson (24 April–28 Sept.). Formation of Imperial Airways (28 April). First circumnavigation of Australia: Goble and McIntyre in a Fairey IIID (19 May). First flight around Japan: Goto and Yonezawa in a Kawanishi K-6 (31 July). First aerial circumnavigation by two Douglas world cruisers of the US Army Air Service: Smith and Arnold in *Chicago*, Nelson and Harding in *New Orleans* (28 Sept.).

1925 First production DH60 Moth delivered (21 July), maiden flight 22 Feb. First flight of M-17 ELLO, the first Messerschmitt aircraft (16 Aug.). *Shenandoah* breaks up in mid-air over Ohio; 29 dead (3 Sept.).

1926 Alan Cobham flies his DH-50 over Victoria Falls on the way to Cape Town (24 Jan.). Robert Goddard launches first liquid-fuelled rocket (16 March). Formation of Deutsche Luft Hansa A.G. (6 April). Richard G. Byrd flies over North Pole in Fokker F.VII (9 May). Amundsen makes first flight over North Pole in an airship (14 May). US Army Air Service becomes US Army Air Corps (2 July). First aircraft launched and recovered by submarine, US *S-1* (28 July). Alan Cobham completes epic flight from London to Australia and back (1 Oct).

1927 Lindbergh makes first non-stop solo Atlantic crossing in *Spirit of St Louis* (21 May). Lt Dick Bentley makes first solo flight from Britain to Cape Town (28 Sept.).

1928 Inauguration of Flying Doctor service in Australia (15 May). Nobile's *Italia* airship crashes in the Arctic (25 May). Charles Kingsford Smith flies Pacific in *Southern Cross* (9 June). Amelia Earhart becomes first woman to fly the Atlantic (as passenger 18 June). JAL formed in Japan (30 Oct.).

1929 Formation of LOT in Poland (1 Jan.). First scheduled passenger flight from London to India (6 April). First stowaway on transatlantic flight (journalist Arthur Shreiber, 14 June). *Graf Zeppelin* completes first circumnavigation of the globe (29 Aug.). Schneider Trophy retained by Britain, Flying Officer H.R.D. Waghorn in Supermarine S-6B (7 Sept.). Testing of first wireless guidance system for aircraft (1 Oct.). R101 unveiled at Cardington (2 Oct.). First flight of R100 from Howden (16 Nov.).

1930 Whittle applies for patent for his turbojet (16 Jan.). Jack Northrop flies experimental 'Flying Wing', with tail boom (1 May). Ellen Church, a registered nurse from Iowa, became the first air hostess (15 May). Amy Johnson makes first solo flight to Australia by a woman (24 May). Formation of TWA (16 July). Death of Glen Curtiss (23 July). R101 receives Certificate of Airworthiness (2 Oct.). R101 crashes and explodes at Beauvais, France, on way to India (5 Oct.). First demonstration of Handley Page HP42 (17 Nov.).

1931 Iraqi airforce makes inaugural flight (8 April). Wiley Post makes flight around Northern Hemisphere in Lockheed Vega *Winnie Mae* (1 July). 400 mph barrier broken by Flt Lt George Stainforth in Supermarine SGB (29 Sept.). USS *Akron* aircraft carrier airship commissioned (2 Nov.).

1932 Asian mainland attacked from the air for the first time by Japanese bombers (26 Feb.). Aeroflot formed in Moscow (25 March). Amy Johnson and Jim Mollison announce their engagement (9 May). Amelia Earhart becomes first woman to fly Atlantic non-stop solo (21 May). Santos-Dumont commits suicide (23 July). First flight of Model 17, Beech Aircraft Corporation's first aircraft (4 Nov.).

1933 Maiden flight of Boeing 247 (8 Feb.). Formation of Indian airforce (1 April). French Armée de l'Air created (1 April). First flight over Everest (Westland PV3 piloted by marquis of Douglas and Westland Wallace piloted by David McIntyre (3 April). USS *Akron* crashes into the Atlantic off New Jersey; 70 killed (5 April). USS *Macon* (*Akron*'s replacement) commissioned (23 June). First flight of Douglas DC-1 (1 July). Air France inaugurated (31 Oct.).

1934 Deutsche Luft Hansa becomes Lufthansa (1 Jan.). First flight of Boeing P-26 (10 Jan.). DC-2 goes into service with TWA (11 May). De Havilland Comet wins England–Australia air race (24 Oct.).

1935 Amelia Earhart becomes first woman to fly the Pacific alone (12 Jan.). Death of Hugo Junkers (3 Feb.). USS *Macon* crashes into the sea off California (12 Feb.). Goering named as chief of the new Luftwaffe (10 March). First flight of Messerschmitt BF 109 (28 March). Swissair begins regular scheduled service to London (1 April). First flight of privately funded Bristol 142 (Blenheim) (12 April). Successful radar experiment in Suffolk (24 July). First flight of Boeing 299 (Flying Fortress) (28 July). Deaths of Wiley Post and Will Rogers in Alaskan air crash (15 Aug.). First flight of Hurricane (6 Nov.). Charles Kingsford Smith disappears over Indian Ocean (9 Nov.). First air traffic control centre opens in US (1 Dec.). First flight of Douglas DST (DC-3) (12 Dec.).

1936 Death of Billy Mitchell (19 Feb.). Maiden flight of *Hindenburg* (4 March). Supermarine Spitfire makes first flight piloted by Mutt Summers (5 March). Gatwick Airport officially opened (6 June). First flight of Westlander Lysander (10 June). First flight of Vickers Wellington (by Mutt Summers) (15 June). Formation of RAF Volunteer Reserve (30 July). Death of Blériot (8 Aug.). First Short Empire C-Class flying boat goes into service (30 Oct.). DC-2 crashes at Croydon killing 14 including Juan de la Cierva (9 Dec.).

1937 Saab established (2 April). First trials of Whittle's turbojet (13 April). Guernica bombed (26 April). *Hindenburg* explodes at Lakehurst; 36 killed (6 May). Death of R.J. Mitchell (11 June). Amelia Earhart disappears over the Pacific while attempting a round-the-world flight (navigator: Fred Noonan) (2 July).

1938 First in-flight refuelling of an airliner (Short Empire Flying Boat) (20 Jan.). Short-Mayo composite aircraft separates in flight for the first time (6 Feb.). First flight of Bell XP-3A Airacobra, the first US fighter to feature a cannon (6 April). First flight of Douglas DC-4 (7 June). Spitfire goes into RAF service (4 Aug.). Japanese aircraft shoot down a Chinese DC-2 airliner, the first civil airliner to be lost to hostile air attack (24 Aug.). First flight of Westland Whirlwind (11 Oct.). Germany launches its first aircraft carrier, *Graf Zeppelin* (8 Dec.). First flight of Boeing Stratoliner, the first pressurized airliner (31 Dec.).

1939 First flight of XP-38, Lockheed Lightning (27 Jan.). First flight of Mitsubishi Zero (1 April). Chain Home radar system goes online (4 April). First flight of Short Stirling (14 May). First flight of Focke-Wulf FW 190 (1 June). First flight of rocket-powered Heinkel He 176 at Peenemünde (20 June). Formation of Women's Auxiliary Air Force (28 June). First flight of Bristol Beaufighter (17 July). Formation of BOAC from British Airways and Imperial Airways (4 Aug.). First flight of jet aircraft, Heinkel He 178 (23 Aug.). RAF mobilized (1 Sept.). German paratroops make first-ever offensive parachute drop in Poland (3 Sept.). First 'bombing' raid (of leaflets) by RAF against Germany (4 Sept.). First 'kills' by RAF against German bombers (16 Oct.). First German bomber brought down on British soil since 1918 (28 Oct.). First flight of Heinkel He 177 (19 Nov.). First flight of Consolidated XB-24, Liberator (29 Dec.).

1940 First flight of Hawker Typhoon (24 Feb.). Sikorsky VS-300 helicopter makes first free flight (13 May). First flight of North American B-25 Mitchell (19 Aug.). First RAF raid on Berlin (25 Aug.). Caproni-Campini N.I. experimental jet makes first flight (28 Aug.). Battle of Britain Day; entire strength of RAF Fighter Command committed against Luftwaffe attack (15 Sept.). Eagle Squadron of RAF formed by US volunteer pilots at Church Fenton (19 Sept.). First flight of North American NA-73 (P-51 Mustang) (20 Oct.). First major Italian air raid on Britain (11 Nov.). Twenty Fairy Swordfish from HMS *Eagle* and HMS *Illustrious* successfully attack Italian fleet at Taranto (12 Nov.). Coventry bombed (14 Nov.). First flight of DH 98 Mosquito (25 Nov.). First test flight of HS-293A guided bomb (18 Dec.).

1941 Death of Amy Johnson when her Airspeed Oxford crashes in Thames Estuary (5 Jan.). First flight of Avro Lancaster (9 Jan.). First flight of the Heinkel He 280, the world's first multi-jet aircraft (2 April). First flight of Republic P-47 Thunderbolt (6 May). Rudolf Hess parachutes into Scotland from a Messerschmitt Me110 (10 May). First British jet aircraft, a Gloster E-28/39, makes its maiden flight (15

May). Opening of Washington National Airport (16 June). First successful rocket assisted take-off in California (July). Heini Dittmar pilots a Messerschmitt Me 163A Komet at a speed of 623.85 mph (2 Oct.). Japanese attack Pearl Harbor (7 Dec.).

1942 Arthur Harris takes charge of Bomber Command (22 Feb.). First Lancaster mission (3 March). Doolittle raid against Japanese B 25s from USS *Hornet* (21 April). Battle of the Coral Sea (8 May). Battle of Midway (6 June). First flight of Grumman Hellcat (26 June). First flight of Me 262 jet fighter (18 July). First flight of Hawker Tempest (2 Sept.). First flight of B29 Super Fortress (21 Sept.). First flight of Bell XP-59 Airacomet, the first US jet aircraft (1 Oct.). Brabazon Committee (postwar airliners) established (23 Dec.).

1943 First flight of Gloster Meteor, the first British jet fighter (5 March). RAF breaches Mohne and Eder dams using 'bouncing' bomb designed by Barnes Wallis (16 May). Leslie Howard shot down in KLM DC-3 over the English Channel (1 June). First flight of Arado Ar 234, the world's first jet bomber (15 June). *Memphis Belle* becomes first B-17 to complete 25 missions in Europe (19 June). First use by RAF of 'Window', the strips of metal foil dropped to jam radar systems (24 July).

1944 First B29 raid (on Bangkok) (5 June). First V1 hits London (13 June). Mariana's Turkey Shoot – Japanese lose 480 aircraft and 3 carriers (20 June). First use of napalm (by Lockheed Lightnings against Coutances, France (17 July). International Civil Aviation conference in Chicago; 52 countries attend. Gives rise to Chicago Convention (1 Nov.–7 Dec.). *Tirpitz* sunk by RAF Lancasters of 617 Squadron (12 Nov.). Glenn Miller disappears in a UC-64 over the English Channel (5 Dec.).

1945 22,000 lb Grand Slam, the heaviest bomb ever dropped, used successfully against the Bielefeld Viaduct (14 March). International Air Transport Association (IATA) formed in Havana (19 April). Atomic bomb tested at Alamogordo (16 July). Atomic bomb 'Little Boy' dropped on Hiroshima by B29 *Enola Gay* (6 Aug.). Atomic bomb 'Fat Man' dropped on Nagasaki by B29 *Bock's Car* (9 Aug.). First flight of turboprop-powered aircraft, a modified Gloster Meteor (20 Sept.). Absolute speed record taken to 606 mph by Gloster Meteor (7 Nov.).

1946 Civil Aviation Act establishes BOAC, BEA and BSAA (British South American Airways), their first commercial departure, made from London Heathrow, a BSAA Lancastrian (1 Jan.). First Pan-Am flight to London from New York (1 June). Air India formed from TATA airlines (29 July). Scandinavian Airline Systems (SAS) formed (31 July). First flight of Convair B-36 (8 Aug.). Aerolinee Italiane Internazionali (Alitalia) established (16 Sept.). Cathay Pacific Airways formed in Hong Kong (24 Sept.). First artificial snowstorm caused by cloud seeding (13 Nov.).

1947 Last DC-3 built by Douglas; it is sold to Sabena but on 2 March 1948 it crashes at Heathrow with loss of 19 lives. First round-the-world air service operated by Pan-Am (12 June).

Kenneth Arnold sees nine aircraft moving 'as a saucer would if you skimmed it over the water' at high speed near Mt Rainier, Washington (24 June). First flight of Boeing Stratocruiser (8 July). Last DC-4 built by Douglas delivered to South African Airways (and still in service) (9 Aug.). USAF established as a separate armed service (18 Sept). Captain Charles Yeager becomes first man to break the sound barrier flying at Mach 1.015 at 42,000′ in Bell X-1 (14 Oct.). BEA makes last scheduled flight from Croydon Airport (1 Nov.). Hughes H-4 Hercules (*Spruce Goose*), the largest aircraft in the world, is flown for the first and only time by Howard Hughes, for one mile (2 Nov.).

1948 Death of Orville Wright (30 Jan.). Thirty killed when a Pan-Am Lockheed Constellation crashes near Shannon (15 April). First action by Israeli airforce (20 May). Start of Operation Vittles – the Berlin Airlift (26 June). Thirty-nine killed at Northolt when an RAF Avro York collides with an SAS DC-6 (4 July). First flight of Vickers Viscount (16 July). Idlewild Airport (now JFK) opens in New York (31 July). John Derry breaks sound barrier in UK in a DH 108 (6 Sept.). El Al comes into being (15 Nov.). Wright Flyer goes on display at the Smithsonian Institute (17 Dec.).

1949 Israeli airforce Messerschmitt 109s shoot down four RAF Spitfires near the Egyptian border (7 Jan.). First non-stop round-the-world flight completed by USAF B-50A *Lucky Lady II* (2 March). First flight of English Electric Canberra (13 May). First flight of De Havilland Comet, the world's first jet airliner (27 July). BOAC absorbs BSAA (30 July). First flight of Bristol Brabazon, largest aircraft ever built in Britain (4 Sept.).

1950 World's worst aircrash: 80 killed when Avro Tudor carrying rugby fans crashes in a field near Cardiff (12 March). First glider crossing of the English Channel (Lorne Welch, 12 April). HMS *Ark Royal* launched (3 May). First North Korean aircraft shot down in Korean war by Twin Mustang (27 June). First helicopter rescue of downed pilot behind enemy lines in Korea (4 Sept.). First flight of Lockheed Super Constellation (13 Oct.). Twenty-eight killed as BEA Viking crashes in fog at Heathrow (31 Oct.). World's first jet-against-jet dogfight, F-80 versus Mig-15, the F-80 being successful (8 Nov.). Bell Model 47 helicopters arrive at MASH units in Korea (1 Dec.).

1951 First non-stop unrefuelled crossing of Atlantic by jet, RAF Canberra (21 Feb.). First flight of Vickers Valiant (18 May). First in-flight refuelling under combat conditions in Korea (6 July). First in-flight sweeping of wings – Bell X-5 research aircraft (16 July). JAL reformed in Tokyo (1 Aug.). First flight of Supermarine Swift (5 Aug.). USAF orders nuclear-powered aircraft from Convair (5 Sept.). First mass movement of troops to battlefront by helicopter, in Korea (21 Sept.). Last DC-6 completed and delivered to Braniff Airways (2 Nov.). First flight of Gloster Javelin (26 Nov.). First interception of aircraft by missile at White Sands, New Mexico (27 Nov.). First turbine-engined helicopter,

TRANSPORT AIRCRAFT

Kaman K-225, makes its maiden flight (10 Dec.). First airline flight over North Pole by Alaska Air (12 Dec.).

1952 First flight of Bristol type 173 twin rotor helicopter (3 Jan.). De Havilland Comet 1 gets first certificate of airworthiness for a jet airliner (22 Jan.). First flight of B-52 (15 April). First successful landing of an aircraft at the North Pole (USAF C-47) (3 May). First scheduled passenger jet service: BOAC Comet 1 from London (3 May). BOAC begins a weekly service from London to Colombo with Comet 1 (11 Aug.). First flight of Bristol Britannia (16 Aug.). First flight of Avro Vulcan (30 Aug.). John Derry and 28 spectators killed when his DH110 crashes at Farnborough (6 Sept.). First doubts about Comet safety after take-off accident in Rome (26 Oct.). First flight of Handley Page Victor (24 Dec.).

1953 Lufthansa revived in Germany (6 Jan.). BOAC Comet crashes near Calcutta killing 43 (2 May). First flight of DC-7 (18 May). Dan-Air established (21 May). 129 killed when USAF C-124 Globemaster II crashes on take-off in Japan (18 June). Neville Duke breaks absolute speed record (727.48 mph) in Hawker Hunter (7 Sept.).

1954 First flight of Lockheed Starfighter (7 Jan.). BOAC Comet *Yoke Peter* crashes off Elba, killing 35 (10 Jan.). Last operational flight of a RAF Spitfire (1 April). South African Airways Comet crashes off Stromboli (8 April). Churchill orders the grounding of all Comets (12 April). First flight of Jet Provost (26 June). First flight of Boeing Model 367-80, prototype of the 707 (15 July). First flight of the Rolls Royce Thrust Measuring Rig, 'The Flying Bedstead' (3 Aug.). First flight of Lockheed Hercules (23 Aug.). Court of Inquiry into Comet crashes concludes that metal fatigue is to blame (19 Oct.).

1955 Pakistan International Airlines (PIA) established (10 Jan.). First operational departure from the central complex at Heathrow (17 April). Fifty-eight killed when a Lockheed Constellation of El Al is shot down by Bulgarian Airforce Mig-15s near the Greek border (27 July). First flight of Republic Thunderchief (22 Oct.). Forty-four killed aboard a United Airlines DC-6B after it blows up in mid-air. It is subsequently proven that the explosion was caused by a bomb, planted to perpetrate an insurance fraud. (Arthur Hailey's *Airport* was based on this incident) (1 Nov.). First flight of Fokker Friendship (24 Nov.).

1956 Death of Lord Trenchard (10 Feb.). Peter Twiss flies Fairey Delta 2 at 1,131.76 mph to take official airspeed record (10 March). First flight of Dassault Super Mystère (15 May). 128 killed when a United Airlines DC-3 collides with a TWA Constellation over the Grand Canyon (30 June). First flight of Fiat G-91 (9 Aug.). First human flight over 100,000': Iven Kincheloe in Bell X-2 (125,907') (7 Sept.). Luftwaffe re-established (24 Sept.). First flight of Convair B-58 Hustler (11 Oct.). UK's first atomic bomb dropped in Australia (11 Oct.). Last RAF Lancaster retired (15 Oct.). First aircraft landing at the South Pole: US Navy R4D-5

Skytrain *Que Sera Sera* (31 Oct.). First flight of Dassault Mirage III (17 Nov.).

1957 World's first long-haul airliner, Bristol Britannia, enters service with BOAC (1 Feb.). Death of Richard Byrd (12 March). First flight of Short SC-1 (2 April). UK's first hydrogen bomb dropped near Christmas Island (15 May). First flight of Fairey Rotodyne (6 Nov.). First flight of Boeing 707 (production model) (21 Dec.).

1958 Death of Ernst Heinkel (Jan.). Munich air crash: seven Manchester Utd players killed (7 Feb.). First flight of De Havilland Comet 4 (27 April). First flight of Blackburn Buccaneer (30 April). First flight of McDonnell F-4 Phantom (27 May). First flight of DC-8 (30 May). New Gatwick Airport opens (9 June). First flight of Westland Wessex (20 June). Death of Henri Farman (17 July). NASA created (29 July). Last flying boat operations in UK (Aquila Airways: Southampton to Madeira) (30 Sept.). First jet airliner on Atlantic route (BOAC Comet 4: London–New York–London) (4 Oct.). Last DC-6 built delivered to JAT (Jugoslavian Airlines) (17 Nov.). First production Fokker Friendship delivered to Aer Lingus (29 Nov.).

1959 First flight of A.W. Argosy (8 Jan.). First flight of Convair 880 (27 Jan.). Buddy Holly, Richie Valens and the Big Bopper killed when their Beechcraft Bonanza crashes in Mason City, Iowa (3 Feb.). First flight of Alouette III (28 Feb.). First scheduled passenger flight of Sud-Aviation Caravelle (6 May). Last operational flight of RAF Sunderland (15 May). First flight of X-15 (8 June). First flight of Mirage IV A (17 June). First flight of Northrop F-5 (30 July). Jacqueline Auriol becomes first woman to exceed Mach 2 (in Mirage III) (26 Aug.). Croydon Airport closed (30 Sept.). De Havilland merges with Hawker Siddeley (17 Dec.).

1960 First flight of Grumman A-6 Intruder (19 April). Gary Powers shot down in Lockheed U-2 over Siberia (1 May). Captain Joseph Kittinger free-falls from 102,800' to 17,500', the highest parachute jump ever (16 Aug.). First flight of Hawker P-1127 (prototype of Harrier) (21 Oct.). 132 killed when TWA Super Constellation and United DC-8 collide over New York (16 Dec.).

1961 Seventy-three killed when Sabena 707 crashes in Brussels (15 Feb.). VIASA begins operations in Caracas (1 April). Yuri Gagarin becomes first man in space (12 April). X-15 flown at 3,074 mph and 105,100' by Major Robert White (21 April). Alan Shepherd becomes first US astronaut (5 May). First flight across the Channel by VTOL aircraft, Short SC-1 (27 May). First flight of Aviation Traders ATL-98 Carvair (21 June). Air Congo established (28 June). First flight of Handley Page HP-115 (17 Aug.). Mirage III jet slices through a cable car wire killing six at Chamonix (30 Aug.). Dag Hammarskjöld's DC-6B crashes near Ndola, Northern Rhodesia (18 Sept.).

1962 First flight of Hawker Siddeley Trident (9 Jan.). First use of Agent Orange in defoliant raids in SE Asia (12 Jan.). First US helicopter shot down in Vietnam (4 Feb.). 111 killed when British Caledonian DC-7C crashes at Douala,

Cameroon (4 Mar). First flight of Bristol T-188 (14 April). Death of Sir Frederick Handley Page (21 April). First flight of A-12 (prototype of SR-71 Blackbird) (26 April). 130 killed when Air France 707 crashes at Orly (3 June). Air France 707 crashes in Guadeloupe, killing 113 (21 June). X-15A flies at 4,159 mph (27 June). First flight of Vickers VC-10 (29 June). X-15 goes into space: Major Robert White flies it to 314,750', earning himself 'Astronauts' Wings' (17 July). First flight of HS 125 (13 Aug.). First flight of Aerospace Lines 'Pregnant Guppy' (19 Sept.).

1963 First reference to Anglo-French supersonic airliner as 'Concorde', in speech by De Gaulle (13 Jan.). First flight of Boeing 727 (2 Feb.). BEA introduces first stand-by fares (1 April). Last RAF Mosquitoes retired (8 May). First flight of BAC III (20 Aug.). First flight of HS-748 (21 Dec.). Idlewild Airport renamed John F. Kennedy (24 Dec.).

1964 First flight of Short Belfast (5 Jan.). Death of Maurice Farman (25 Feb.). Jerrie Mock completes first solo aerial circumnavigation by a woman (17 April). VC-10 enters airline service (29 April). First flight of BAC 221 (Concorde research aircraft) (1 May). Actor Roger Moore becomes Air France's 8,000,000th passenger (21 May). First flight of North American XB-70 Valkyrie (21 Sept.). First flight of BAC TSR2 (27 Sept.). First flight of General Dynamics F-111 (21 Dec.). First flight of Lockheed SR-71 (22 Dec.).

1965 First flight of Mirage III V-01 (VTOL aircraft) (12 Feb.). First flight of Douglas DC-9 (25 Feb.). TSR2 cancelled by Wilson government (6 April). Death of Sir Geoffrey De Havilland (26 May).

1966 Four hydrogen bombs fall from a B-52 over southern Spain following a collision with KC-135 tanker; all four are recovered (17 Jan.). Laker Airways launched (8 Feb.). France leaves NATO (7 March). Death of Sir Sydney Camm (12 March). North American XB-70 crashes after colliding with a chase aircraft (8 June). Sheila Scott completes first round-the-world solo flight by a British woman (20 June). X-15 flies at 4,250 mph (Mach 6.33) (18 Nov.).

1967 First flight of Saab 37 Viggen (8 Feb.). Wrecked oil tanker the *Torrey Canyon* bombed by RAF and Royal Navy aircraft (18 March). First flight of Boeing 737 (9 April). First flight of HS Nimrod (23 May). DC-4 charter plane crashes in the Pyrenees, killing 88 (3 June). British Midland Argonaut crashes at Manchester, killing 72 (4 June). Six-day war begins with Israeli air strikes against Egypt, Syria and Jordan (5 June). X-15 attains its fastest speed, 4,534 mph (Mach 6.72), flown by Major William Knight (3 Oct.). Concorde rolled out at Toulouse (11 Dec.).

1968 Last Handley Page Hastings retires from RAF (5 Jan.). Yuri Gagarin is killed when his Mig-15 crashes near Moscow (27 March). 121 survive crash of BOAC 707 at Heathrow (8 April). Last Avro Anson retires from RAF after 32 years (28 June). First flight of Sepecat Jaguar (8 Sept.). First flight of TU-144 'Concordski' (31 Dec.).

1969 First flight of Boeing 747 (9 Feb.). First flight of Concorde (001 at Toulouse) (2 March). First flight of Concorde (002 in UK) (9 April). RAF Strike Command formed from Bomber and Fighter Command (30 April). Concorde goes supersonic for the first time (1 Oct.). Nigeria Airways VC-10 crashes in the jungle; 87 killed (20 Nov.).

1970 First wide-bodied airliner landing at Heathrow (Boeing 747 of Pan-Am) (12 Jan.). Death of Mikhail Mil (31 Jan.). Death of Lord Hugh Dowding (15 Feb.). Last Dakota retires from RAF service (4 April). Tullamarine Airport in Melbourne opens (1 July). First flight of McDonnell Douglas DC-10 (29 Aug.). Black September blow up TWA 707, Swissair DC-8 and BOAC VC-10 at Dawson's Field, and a Pan-Am 747 at Cairo (12 Sept.). Concorde 002 lands at Heathrow (13 Sept.). Concorde 001 flies at Mach 2 (4 Nov.). First flight of Lockheed Tristar (16 Nov.). Death of Artem Mikoyan (15 Dec.). Airbus Industrie formally established (18 Dec.). Jeanne M. Holm becomes first USAF female general (31 Dec.).

1971 Four members of the Red Arrows killed when two Folland Gnats collide at RAF Kemble (20 Jan.). London Air Traffic Control Centre opens at West Drayton (31 Jan.). First flight of Westland Lynx (21 March). Federal Express founded (17 April). Southwest Airlines begin operations (18 June). 162 killed when ANA Boeing 707 collides with a fighter in Japan (30 July). DC-10 enters airline service (5 Aug.). Civil Aviation Authority established in London (5 Aug.). First flight of Shackleton AEW (30 Sept.). BEA Vanguard breaks up over Belgium; 55 killed (2 Oct.). D.B. Cooper successfully hijacks a Northwest Boeing 727, demands $200,000 and escapes by parachute (24 Nov.).

1972 President Nixon announces that the space shuttle will be developed (5 Jan.). British Airways Board takes over BOAC, BEA and their subsidiaries (1 April). Lockheed Tristar enters airline service (26 April). First fly-by-wire in the USA: Phantom II (29 April). First flight of Fairchild A-10 (10 May). Japanese terrorists kill 25 at Lod Airport (30 May). 118 killed at Staines when BEA Trident crashes after take-off, Britain's worst air disaster until Lockerbie (18 June). First flight of McDonnell Douglas F15 Eagle (27 July). Ilyushin IL-62 crashes in Berlin; 156 killed (14 Aug.). Prince William of Gloucester is killed when his Piper Cherokee crashes during the Goodwood Trophy air race at Wolverhampton (28 Aug.). Death of Igor Sikorsky (26 Oct.). Death of Andrei Tupolev (23 Dec.).

1973 Libyan Airlines 727 shot down by Israeli fighters over Sinai; 74 killed (21 Feb.). TU-144 crashes at the Paris Air Show following mid-air breakup; 14 killed (3 June). 123 die at Orly when a Varig 707 burns after an emergency landing (11 July). Death of Sir Alan Cobham (21 Oct.). First flight of Dassault-Bregeu Dornier Alpha jet (26 Oct.).

1974 First flight of General Dynamics F-16 (2 Feb.). Last Comet in airline service retires (12 Feb.). World's worst air disaster: 346 killed when a

T
R
A
N
S
P
O
R
T

A
I
R
C
R
A
F
T

Turkish Airlines DC-10 crashes near Paris (worst until 27 March 1977) (3 March). Airbus A300 enters airline service (23 May). Death of Charles Lindbergh (26 Aug.). First flight of Panavia Tornado (14 Aug.). Fifty-nine killed when Lufthansa 747 crashes in Nairobi, the first ever 747 crash (20 Nov.). First flight of Rockwell B-1 Bomber (23 Dec.).

1975 Death of Air Chief Marshal Sir Keith Park (6 Feb.). Death of Adrienne Bolland (18 March). First flight of DHC Dash 7 (27 March). US helicopters airlift last personnel from embassy roof in Saigon (30 April). First flight of Boeing 747 SP (4 July). Last Lockheed Constellation in airline service retires (16 July). Concorde becomes first aircraft to make four Atlantic crossings in one day (1 Sept.). Graham Hill killed when his aircraft crashes near Elstree (29 Nov.).

1976 First commercial flight of Concorde (Paris–Rio and London–Bahrain) (21 Jan.). Death of Howard Hughes (5 April). Air France and British Airways Concordes land together at Dulles Airport, Washington (24 May). Israeli commandos rescue over 100 passengers from Palestinian terrorists at Entebbe, Uganda (4 July). Viktor Belenko defects to the West in a Mig-25 in Japan (6 Sept.). Worst ever mid-air collision: 176 killed when BA Trident and Yugoslav DC-9 collide over Croatia (10 Sept.).

1977 Death of Sergei Ilyushin (7 Feb.). World's worst ever aircraft disaster: two 747s (KLM and Pan-Am) collide on the ground in Tenerife, 575 killed (27 March). Death of Werner von Braun (16 June). Rockwell B-1 cancelled by President Carter (30 June). First gliding flight of space shuttle *Enterprise* (released from 747) (13 Aug.). Bryan Allen flies *Gossamer Condor*, the first successful man-powered aircraft (23 Aug.). Freddie Laker launches his Skytrain service from London to New York (26 Sept.). GSG 9 successfully storm a hijacked Lufthansa 737 at Mogadishu; 86 saved (17 Oct.).

1978 213 killed when Air India Boeing 747 explodes in mid-air over Bombay (1 Jan.). British Aerospace takes control of British Aircraft Corporation, Hawker Siddeley and Scottish Aviation (1 Jan.). Narita Airport opens in Tokyo amid environmental protests (22 May). First crossing of Atlantic by balloon: *Double Eagle II* (17 Aug.). Death of German aircraft engineer Willy Messerschmitt (15 Sept.). Collision between Pacific Southwest 727 and Cessna in San Diego; 144 killed (25 Sept.). Icelandair DC-8 crashes in Sri Lanka, 202 killed (16 Nov.).

1979 All DC-10 aircraft grounded following crash at Chicago on 25 May which killed 279 (6 June). Bryan Allen flies man-powered aircraft, *Gossamer Albatross*, across the Channel (13 June). Death of Emile Dewoitine (5 July). Death of Sir Barnes Wallis (30 Oct.). 257 killed in Antarctica when Air New Zealand DC-10 crashes near Mt Erebus (29 Nov.).

1980 Air UK formed from British Island Airways and Air Anglia (16 Jan.). Air Zimbabwe created from Air Rhodesia (18 April). Operation Eagle Claw aborted in Iranian desert following collision of CH-53 helicopter with Hercules transport. The operation was intended to free US hostages in Tehran (25 April). HMS *Ark Royal* makes its final voyage, to the breakers yard (22 Sept.). Last commercial flight of Comet 4, a round trip for enthusiasts (9 Nov.).

1981 Last Boeing 707 in Pan-Am service retires (3 Jan.). Death of Donald Douglas (1 Feb.). Death of Jack Northrop (18 Feb.). First flight of Rockwell Space Shuttle *Columbia* (12 April). Israeli airforce bombs Iraqi nuclear reactor at Osirak (7 June). Gulf of Sirte/Sidra incident: two US Navy F-14s shoot down two Libyan SU-22s (19 Aug.). First flight of Boeing 767 (26 Sept.). First flight of Hughes Notar helicopter, i.e. No Tail Rotor (17 Dec.).

1982 Eighty killed when Air Florida 737 crashes into the icy Potomac River in Washington, after wings ice up before take-off (13 Jan.). First flight of Boeing 757 (19 Feb.). First flight of Airbus A310 (3 April). RAF Vulcans take part in the longest bombing runs in history (7,860 miles) from Ascension Island against targets in the Falklands (April–May). Braniff International Airlines files for bankruptcy (13 May). Last Boeing 707 in British Airways service retires (24 May). Last Boeing 707 in Air France service retires (28 Oct.). Last British V-Bomber Squadron disbanded (21 Dec.).

1983 269 killed when a Soviet SU-15 shoots down a Korean Airlines 747 over Sakhalin Island (2 Sept.).

1984 Inaugural flight of Virgin Atlantic Airways (22 June). Last Boeing 727 completed (14 Aug.). First flight of ATR 42 feeder airliner (16 Aug.). First flight of Rockwell B-1B (18 Oct.). First flight of MD-83 (17 Dec.).

1985 TWA 727 hijacked in Rome by AMAL guerrillas; all bar one of the hostages are subsequently released (15 June). 329 killed after an Air India 747 explodes over the Atlantic en route to London (23 June). 520 when JAL 747 crashes into a mountain in Japan (13 Aug). Fifty-four killed at Manchester when a British Airtours 737 catches fire (22 Aug.).

1986 Armed police begin patrolling Heathrow Airport (8 Jan.). *Challenger* disaster: all seven crew are killed when space shuttle explodes shortly after launch (28 Jan.). Terminal 4 opens at Heathrow (12 April). USAF F-IIIs execute air strikes against targets in Libya (15 April). Death of Marcel Bloch (18 April). BA privatized (21 Oct.). Forty-five killed when a BA Chinook ferrying oil workers crashes in the Shetlands (6 Nov.). Dick Rutan and Jeana Yeager fly around the world non-stop and unrefuelled, in specially designed aircraft *Voyager* (23 Dec.).

1987 First flight of Airbus A320 (22 Feb.). Last airworthy Bristol Blenheim crashes at Denham (21 June). BAA privatized (16 July). Richard Branson and Per Lindstrand complete first hot-air balloon crossing of the Atlantic (3 July). BA takes over British Caledonian (16 July). BA takes on first female pilots (31 Oct.). London City Airport opens (5 Nov.).

1988 First ever aircraft registration number retired by FAA, i.e. Amelia Earhart's Lockheed Electra which vanished in July 1937 (8 Feb.). North Terminal opens at Gatwick Airport (18 March). First flight of 'Super-Jumbo' Boeing 747-400 (29 April). Airbus A320 crashes in trees at Mulhouse air show; four killed (26 June). 290 killed when USS Vincennes shoots down Iranian Airbus (3 July). Thirty-three killed at Ramstein when Frecce Tricolori (Italian National Aerobatic Team) aircraft collide above spectators at air show (28 Aug.). Death of Sheila Scott (20 Oct.). F-117A Stealth aircraft formally unveiled by USAF (10 Nov.). Lockerbie disaster: 270 killed after bomb causes Pan-Am Jumbo to crash on houses; worst air disaster in British history (21 Dec.).

1989   Thirty-two killed when British Midland 737 crashes on to the M1 at Kegworth (8 Jan.). First flight of Northrop B-2 Spirit Flying Wing Stealth Bomber (17 July). 107 killed at Sioux City, Iowa, when United Airlines DC-10 crashes on landing (19 July). Death of Alexander Yakovlev (22 Aug.). Bell/Boeing Vertol V-22 Osprey tilt rotor aircraft makes first transition to level flight (14 Sept.).

1990   First flight of Northrop/McDonnell Douglas YF-23 (subsequently dropped in favour of Lockheed YF-22) (27 Aug.). First flight of Rockwell/MBB X-31A low-speed experimental aircraft (11 Oct.). United Airlines takes over Pan-Am's London routes (23 Oct.). Osaka Airport opens in Japan (9 Nov.).

1991   First Boeing 727 retires after 27 years with United Airlines (13 Jan.). Air Europe, based at Gatwick Airport, ceases to operate (17 Jan.). Operation Desert Storm makes large-scale use of Stealth aircraft for the first time (Jan.). First scheduled United Airlines flight to London (4 April). Boeing finally ends production of 707 after 37 years (1 Sept.). First flight of McDonnell Douglas C-17 (15 Sept.). First flight of Airbus A-340 (25 Oct.). First MD-11 delivered (to Finnair) (29 Nov.). Pan-Am ceases operations (4 Dec.).

1992   TWA announces that it is bankrupt (11 Jan.). Piper declared bankrupt (1 April). Plans for MD-12 (4-engine, 600-seat airliner) announced (30 April). BAA announces plans for Terminal 5 at Heathrow (12 May).

1995   First Boeing 777 begins operations at Heathrow (United Airlines) (July).

Airports: UK

Airport	Location	Airport	Location	Airport	Location
Aldergrove	Belfast	**Kidlington**	Oxford	**Staverton**	Gloucestershire
Baltasound	Unst, Shetlands	**Kirkwall**	Orkneys	**Stornoway**	Hebrides
Barton	Manchester	**Leuchars**	Fife	**Stronsay**	Orkneys
Benbecula	Hebrides	**Linley Hill**	Beverley	**Sumburgh**	Shetlands
Booker	Wycombe, Bucks	**Manston**	Kent	**Sywell**	Northampton
Brize Norton	Oxford	**North Bay**	Barra, Hebrides	**Teeside**	Cleveland
Brough	East Yorkshire	**North Denes**	Great Yarmouth	**Tingwall**	Lerwick, Shetlands
City	Belfast	**North Ronaldsay**	Orkneys		
City	London	**Papa Westray**	Orkneys	**Tiree**	Hebrides
Compton Abbas	Dorset	**Port Ellen**	Islay, Hebrides	**Tresco**	Scillies
Conington	Peterborough	**Prestwick**	Ayrshire	**Turnhouse**	Edinburgh
Coventry	West Midlands	**Rhoose**	Cardiff	**Unst**	Shetlands
Dalcross	Inverness	**Roborough**	Plymouth	**Walney Island**	Barrow, Cumbria
Dyce	Aberdeen	**Ronaldsway**	Isle of Man	**West Freugh**	Dumfries
East Midlands	Derbyshire	**St Angelo**	Enniskillen, Fermanagh	**West Midlands**	Birmingham
Eday	Orkneys			**Westray**	Orkneys
Eglinton	Londonderry	**St Just**	Land's End	**Whalsay**	Shetlands
Fair Isle	Shetlands	**St Mary's**	Scilly Isles	**Wick**	Caithness
Flotta	Orkneys	**Sanday**	Orkneys	**Wickenby**	Lincolnshire
Full Sutton	North Yorkshire	**Sandown**	Isle of Wight	**Woodford**	Greater Manchester
Gatwick	West Sussex	**Scatsa**	Shetlands		
Glenegedale	Islay	**Scone**	Perth	**Woodvale**	Merseyside
Goodwood	Chichester	**Sibson**	Peterborough	**Yeovilton**	Somerset
Grimsetter	Orkney	**Silverstone**	Northants		
Heathrow	London	**Stansted**	NE London		
		Stapleford	Essex		

Airlines

Name	Country	Name	Country	Name	Country
ACES	Colombia	**Aerolineas**	Argentina	**Alia**	Jordan
Aer Lingus	Ireland	**Air Littoral**	France	**Alitalia**	Italy
Aeroflot	Russia	**Air UK**	UK (Stansted)	**American Airlines**	USA

Name	Country	Name	Country	Name	Country
ANA	All Nippon Airways	Frontie Airlines	USA	Pan-Am	USA
Augusta Airways	Australia	Garuda	Indonesia	PIA	Pakistan
Avianca	Colombia	Gronlandsfly	Greenland	Qantas	Australia
Bell-Air	New Zealand	Iberia	Spain	Republic Airlines	USA
Britannia	UK (Luton)	Interflug	East Germany	RyanAir	Ireland
British Airways	UK	JAL	Japanese Airlines	Sabena	Belgium
Cathay Pacific	Hong Kong	JAT	Yugoslavia	Sansa	Costa Rica
Continental Airlines	USA	KLM	Netherlands	SAS	Denmark, Norway, Sweden
CP Air	Canada	Kyrnair	Corsica		
Crossair	Switzerland	Ladeco	Chile	TAP	Portugal
CSA	Czech Republic	LAP	Paraguay	THY	Turkey
		Linjeflyg	Sweden	Tower Air	USA
Delta Airlines	USA	LOT	Poland	Transavia Airlines	Netherlands
DETA	Mozambique	Lufthansa	Germany	Transworld Airlines	USA
Dragonair	Hong Kong	Malev	Hungary	United Airlines	USA
Eastern Airlines	USA	NFD	Germany	Varig	Brazil
El Al	Israel	Norontair	Canada	VIASA	Venezuela
Flitestar	South Africa	Northwest Airlines	USA	Virgin	UK (Gatwick)
		Olympic	Greece	Western Airlines	USA

Airport Codes

Code	Airport	Location	Code	Airport	Location	Code	Airport	Location
ABD	Abadan	Iran	BZV	Brazzaville	Congo			Islands
ABJ	Abidjan	Ivory Coast	CAJ	Cairo	Egypt	FNI	Nîmes	France
ABS	Abu Simnel	Egypt	CCS	Caracas	Venezuela	FRA	Frankfurt	Germany
ABZ	Aberdeen	Scotland	CCU	Calcutta	India	GBE	Gaborone	Botswana
ACE	Arecife	Lanzarote	CDG	Charles de Gaulle	Paris	GCI	Guernsey	UK
ACI	Alderney	Channel Islands	CER	Cherbourg	France	GNB	Grenoble	France
ACK	Nantucket, MA	USA	CFN	Donegal	Eire	GOA	Genoa	Italy
ACT	Waco, Texas	USA	CFR	Caen	France	GOH	Nuuk (Godthaab)	Greenland
ADD	Addis Ababa	Ethiopia	CFU	Kerkyra	Greece	GOI	Goa	India
AGP	Malaga	Spain	CHC	Christchurch	New Zealand	GPS	Galapagos Isles	Ecuador
AKL	Auckland	New Zealand	CMN	Casablanca	Morocco	HAJ	Hanover	Germany
ALC	Alicante	Spain	CPT	Cape Town	South Africa	HBA	Hobart	Tasmania
ALH	Albany, WA	Australia	CXI	Christmas Island	Kiribati	HDO	Hyderabad	Pakistan
ALP	Aleppo	Syria				HFA	Haifa	Israel
ALY	Alexandria	Egypt	DCA	Washington	USA	HKT	Phuket	Thailand
AMA	Amarillo, Texas	USA	DLH	Duluth	Minnesota	HLZ	Hamilton	New Zealand
ANR	Antwerp	Belgium	DOL	Deauville	France			
ASD	Andros	Bahamas	DTM	Dortmund	Germany	HND	Haneda	Tokyo
AUH	Abu Dhabi	UAE	DUD	Dunhedin	New Zealand	HYD	Hyderabad	India
BBQ	Barbuda	Leeward Isles	DUS	Düsseldorf	Germany	IAD	Dulles International	Washington
BEB	Benbecula	Scotland	DXB	Dubai	UAE	IBZ	Ibiza	Spain
BEY	Beirut	Lebanon	DYU	Dushanbe	Tadzhikstan	IEV	Kiev	Ukraine
BFS	Belfast	N. Ireland	EGC	Bergerac	France	IOM	Isle of Man	UK
BGO	Bergen	Norway	EVN	Yerevan	Armenia	IOR	Inishmore	Eire
BHX	Birmingham	England	EWR	Newark, NJ	USA	IPC	Easter Island	Chile
BJL	Bangui	Gambia	EYW	Key West	Florida	JDH	Jodhpur	India
BKK	Bangkok	Thailand	FAO	Faro	Portugal	JFK	John F. Kennedy	New York
BKO	Bamako	Mali	FBU	Fornebu	Oslo			
BLZ	Blantyre	Malawi	FCO	Fiumicino	Rome	JNU	Juneau	Alaska
BRN	Berne	Switzerland	FIE	Fair Isle	Scotland	JRS	Jerusalem	Israel
BSL	Basle	Switzerland	FIH	Kinshasa	Dem Rep. of Congo	KEF	Keflavik	Iceland
BTZ	Bursa	Turkey				KEL	Kiel	Germany
BUH	Bucharest	Romania	FNA	Freetown	Sierra Leone	KHI	Karachi	Pakistan
BXO	Bissau	Guinea-Bissau	FNC	Funchal	Madeira	KLU	Klagenfurt	Austria
						KRK	Krakow	Poland

Code	Airport	Location	Code	Airport	Location	Code	Airport	Location
KTP	Kingston	Jamaica	MOW	Moscow	Russia			Samoa
KTW	Katowice	Poland	MPM	Maputu	Mozambique	PRJ	Capri	Italy
LAS	McCarran	Las Vegas	MRS	Marseille	France	PRY	Pretoria	South Africa
LAX	Los Angeles	California	MXL	Mexicali	Mexico	RBA	Rabat	Morocco
LCA	Larnaca	Cyprus	NBO	Nairobi	Kenya	REK	Reykjavik	Iceland
LEH	Le Havre	France	NCE	Nice	France	RUH	Riyadh	Saudi
LFW	Lomé	Togo	NCL	Newcastle	England			Arabia
LGW	Gatwick	London	NDY	Sanday	Scotland	SEL	Seoul	South Korea
LHE	Lahore	Pakistan	NQY	Newquay	England	SNN	Shannon	Eire
LHR	Heathrow	London	NRT	Narita	Tokyo	SPK	Sapporo	Japan
LIG	Limoges	France	NSI	Nsimalen,	Cameroon	STR	Stuttgart	Germany
LTN	Luton	Bedfordshire		Yaoundé		THR	Tehran	Iran
LUN	Lusaka	Zambia	NTE	Nantes	France	TIA	Tirana	Albania
LWK	Lerwick	Shetlands	NTY	Sun City	South Africa	URO	Rouen	France
LXR	Luxor	Egypt	ODE	Odense	Denmark	VRN	Verona	Italy
MAA	Madras	India	OPO	Oporto	Portugal	WAW	Warsaw	Poland
MBJ	Montego Bay	Jamaica	ORD	O'Hare	Chicago	WLG	Wellington	New
MCM	Monte Carlo	Monaco	ORK	Cork	Eire			Zealand
MDL	Mandalay	Burma	ORN	Oran	Algeria	YXY	Whitehorse	Canada
		(Myanmar)	PAP	Port au Prince	Haiti	YYC	Calgary	Canada
MEB	Melbourne	Australia	PFO	Paphos	Cyprus	YZF	Yellowknife	Canada
MFN	Milford Sound	New	PGF	Perpignan	France	ZAZ	Zaragosa	Spain
		Zealand	PID	Paradise Island	Bahamas	ZRH	Zurich	Switzerland
MLH	Mulhouse	France	PMO	Palermo	Italy			
MMA	Malmö	Sweden	PNQ	Poona	India			
MME	Teesside	England	PPG	Pago Pago	American			

NB The airport codes above are a small-cross section of the thousands of abbreviations used internationally. Most of the codes represent the location of the airport but others denote the name.

Airports: International

Name	Location	Name	Location	Name	Location
Abadan	Iran	Benina	Benghazi, Libya	Changi	Singapore
Adana	Turkey	Benito Juarez	Mexico City	Charleroi	Belgium
Agno	Lugano, Switzerland	Bierset	Liège, Belgium	Charles de Gaulle	Paris
Albany County	New York	Bilund	Denmark	Charlotte	North Carolina
Alexander Hamilton	St Croix, W. Indies	Blackburne/ Plymouth	Montserrat	Chek Lap Kok	Hong Kong (New)
Alfonso Bonilla		Blagnac	Toulouse	Chiang Kai Shek	Taipei, Taiwan
Aragon	Cali, Colombia	Bole	Addis Ababa	Ciampino	Rome
Amborovy	Majunga, Madagascar	Bonriki	Kiribati	Cointrin	Geneva
		Boukhalef	Tangier, Morocco	Collinstown	Dublin
Amilcar Cabral	Cape Verde	Bourgas	Bulgaria	Congonhas	São Paulo, Brazil
Aminu	Kano, Nigeria	Bradley	Hartford, Connecticut	Coolidge	Antigua
Arlanda	Stockholm			Costa Smeralda	Olbia, Sardinia
Arnos Vale	St Vincent	Brnik	Ljubljana	Cotonou	Benin
Arrecife	Lanzarote	Bromma	Stockholm	Cristoforo Colombo	Genoa
Arturo Marino Benitez	Santiago, Chile	Bulawayo	Zimbabwe		
		Butmir	Sarajevo	Crown Point	Scarborough, Tobago
Atuona	Hiva Oa, French Polynesia	Byrd Field	Richmond, Virginia		
		Cairns	Queensland	Cuscatlan	El Salvador
Augusto Co Sandino	Managua, Nicaragua	Calabar	Nigeria	Dalaman	Turkey
		Cancun	Mexico	Deurne	Antwerp
Balice	Kracow, Poland	Cannon	Reno, Nevada	D.F. Malan	Cape Town
Baneasa	Bucharest	Canton	Akron, Ohio	Domodedovo	Moscow
Barajas	Madrid	Capodichino	Naples	Dorval	Montreal
Basle-Mulhouse (Euro Airport)	Basle, Switzerland	Cardiff	Rhoose	Douala	Cameroon
		Carrasco	Montevideo	Dulles	Washington
Beira	Mozambique	Cebu	Philippines	Dum Dum	Calcutta
Ben Gurion	Tel Aviv				

Name	Location	Name	Location	Name	Location
Ecterdingen	Stuttgart		PNG		Massachusetts
Eduardo Gomes	Manaus, Brazil	James M. Cox	Dayton, Ohio	Long Beach	California
El Alto	La Paz, Bolivia	J.F. Kennedy	La Paz	Loshitsa	Minsk,
El Dorado	Bogotá, Colombia	John F. Kennedy	New York		Byelorussia
Elat	Israel	John Foster	Washington DC	Louis Botha	Durban
Elmas	Cagliari	Dulles		Lourdes/Tarbes	Juillan, France
Eppley Airfield	Omaha,	John Wayne	Los Angeles,	Lubbock	Texas
	Nebraska		California	Lungi	Freetown, Sierra
Esenboga	Ankara	Jorge Chavez	Lima, Peru		Leone
Ezeiza	Buenos Aires	Jose Martí	Havana, Cuba	Lupepau'u	Tonga
Faaa	Tahiti	Kai Tak	Hong Kong (old)	Luqa	Malta
Faleolo	Apia, Samoa	Kamazu	Lilongwe, Malawi	Mactan	Cebu,
F.D. Roosevelt	St Eustatius,	Kastrup	Copenhagen,		Philippines
	W. Indies		Denmark	Mahon	Menorca
Ferihegy	Budapest	Katunayake	Colombo, Sri	Mais Gate	Haiti
Findel	Luxembourg		Lanka	Malpensa	Milan
Fiumicino		Keflavik	Reykjavik,	Marco Polo	Venice
(Leonardo da	Rome		Iceland	Mariscal Sucre	Quito, Ecuador
Vinci)		Kent County	Grand Rapids,	Marsh Harbour	Abaco Island,
Flamingo Field	Bonaire		Michigan		Bahamas
Flesland	Bergen, Norway	Kerkyra	Corfu	Matsapha	Manzini,
Fontanarossa	Catania, Sicily	Khoramaksar	Aden		Swaziland
Fornebu	Oslo	Khwaja Rawash	Kabul,	Maturin	Venezuela
Fort Myers	Florida		Afghanistan	Maxglan	Salzburg, Austria
Fort Worth	Dallas, Texas	Kimpo	Seoul, South	Maya Maya	Brazzaville,
Freeport	Bahamas		Korea		Congo
Fua'amotu	Tonga	King Khaled	Riyadh, Saudi	McCarran	Las Vegas
Fuenterrabia	San Sebastián		Arabia	McCoy	Orlando, Florida
Fuerteventura	Canary Islands	Kingsford Smith	Sydney, Australia	McNary Field	Salem, Oregon
Fuhlsbüttel	Hamburg	Kitsap	Washington,	Meenambakkam	Madras, India
Galileo Galilei	Pisa		USA	Mehrabad	Tehran, Iran
G'Bessia	Conakry	Klagenfurt	Austria	Melita	Djerba, Tunisia
General Manuel		Kloten	Zurich	Melsbroek	Brussels
Marquez de	Mexico	Kota Kinabulu	Sabah, Malaysia	Melville Hall	Dominica
Leon		Kotoka	Accra, Ghana	Menara	Marrakesh,
General Mitchell	Milwaukee	Kranebitten	Innsbruck		Morocco
Gillot	Réunion	Kuching	Sarawak,	Mercedita	Puerto Rico
G. Marconi	Bologna		Malaysia	Midway	Chicago
Golden Rock	St Kitts	Kungsangen	Norrköping,	Ministro Pistarini	Buenos Aires
Grantley Adams	Barbados		Sweden	Mirabel	Montreal
Hahaya	Moroni, Comoros	La Aurora	Guatemala	Monroe County	Rochester, NY
Halim	Djakarta	La Coruña	Spain	Morelos	Mexico
Perdanakusama		La Guardia	New York	Münster/	
Hanan	Niue	La Mesa	San Pedro Sula,	Osnabrück	Germany
Hancock Field	Syracuse, NY		Honduras	Murtala	Lagos,
Haneda	Tokyo	Landvetter	Göteborg,	Muhammed	Nigeria
Hartsfield	Atlanta, Georgia		(Gothenburg)	Nadi	Fiji
Hato	Curaçao		Sweden	Naha	Okinawa (Japan)
Hellenikon	Athens	Larnaca	Cyprus	Narita	Tokyo
Henderson Field	Honiara,	Las Americas	Dominican	Narssarsuaq	Greenland
	Solomon Isles		Republic	N'Djili	Kinshasa, Congo
Heraklion	Crete	Las Palmas	Gran Canaria		Democratic
Hewanorra	St Lucia	Le Bourget	Paris		Republic
Hongqiao	Shanghai	Le Lamentin	Martinique	Nejrab	Aleppo, Syria
Hopkins	Cleveland, Ohio	Leonardo da	Rome	Newark	New York
Indira Gandhi	New Delhi	Vinci (Fiumicino)		Newcastle	Nevis Island
Inezgane	Agadir, Morocco	Le Raizet	Guadeloupe	Ninoy Aquino	Manila,
Isla Verde	San Juan,	Les Angades	Oujda, Morocco		Philippines
	Puerto Rico	Lesquin	Lille, France	Nis	Yugoslavia
Ivanka	Bratislava	Lester B.	Toronto	Norman Manley	Kingston,
Ivato	Antananarivo,	Pearson			Jamaica
	Madagascar	Linate	Milan	North Front	Gibraltar
Izmir	Turkey	Lindbergh	San Diego,	Nouadhibou	Mauritania
Jackson Field	Port Moresby,		California	Oakland	California
		Logan	Boston,		

Name	Location	Name	Location	Name	Location
O'Hare	Chicago	Sainte Foy	Quebec	Tacoma	Seattle
Okecie	Warsaw	Sale	Rabat, Morocco	Tamatve	Madagascar
Olaya Herrera	Medellín, Colombia	Salgado Filho	Brazil	Tarbes (Lourdes)	Juillan, France
Oran	Algeria	Salote Pilolevu	Tonga	Tegal	Berlin
Orebro	Sweden	Sangster	Montego Bay, Jamaica	Tempelhof	Berlin
Orly	Paris			Thalerhof	Graz, Austria
Osaka	Japan	San Pablo	Seville	Theodore Francis Green	Rhode Island
Osnabrück (Münster)	Germany	Santa Caterina	Funchal, Madeira		
		Santa Cruz	Bombay	Timehri	Georgetown, Guyana
Osvaldo Vieira	Guinea Bissau	Santa Isabel	Malabo, Guinea		
Otopeni	Bucharest	Santos Dumont	Rio	Toncontin	Tegucigalpa, Honduras
Owen Roberts	Grand Cayman	Schipol	Amsterdam		
Paphos	Cyprus	Schwechat	Vienna	Tontouta	New Caledonia
Paradisi	Rhodes	Seeb	Oman	Torslanda	Göteborg (Gothenburg)
Patenga	Bangladesh	Seewoosagur Ramgoolam	Mauritius		
Patrick Henry	Norfolk, Virginia			Totegegie	Gambier Island
Pearson	Toronto	Senou	Mali	Townsville	Australia
Pekoa	Vanuatu	Sfax	Tunisia	Treasure Cay	Abaco Island, Bahamas
Peretola	Florence	Sharjah	United Arab Emirates		
Peshawar	Pakistan			Tribhuyan	Nepal
Peterson Field	Colorado	Sheremetyevo	Moscow	Trivandrum	India
Piarco	Trinidad	Silvio Pettirossi	Paraguay	Truax Field	Wisconsin
Pochentong	Cambodia	Simon Bolivar	Ecuador	Tullamarine	Melbourne
Point Noire	Congo	Simon Bolivar	Caracas, Venezuela	Turku	Finland
Point Salines	Grenada			Ulemiste	Estonia
Polonia	Indonesia	Sir Seretse Khama	Botswana	Unokovo	Moscow
Port Bouet	Ivory Coast	Skanes	Morocco	Uplands	Ottawa
Port Harcourt	Nigeria	Sky Harbour	Phoenix, Arizona	V.C. Bird	Antigua
Portland	Maine	Snilow	Ukraine	Vagar	Faeroe Islands
Princess Beatriz	Aruba	Sola	Stavanger, Norway	Vantaa	Helsinki
Provence	Marseille			Vigie	St Lucia
Pula	Yugoslavia	Sondica	Bilbao	Viracopos	São Paulo, Brazil
Pulkovo	St Petersburg	Søndre Srømfjord	Greenland	Wall Blake	Anguilla
Punta Raisi	Palermo, Sicily			Washington	Baltimore, Maryland
Queen Alia	Jordan	Spilve	Latvia		
Ras Al Khaimah	United Arab Emirates	Spokane	Washington	Wattay	Laos
		Standiford Field	Louisville, Kentucky	West End	Bahamas
Rebiechowo	Gdansk, Poland			Wichita	Kansas
Reina Beatrix	Aruba	Stapleton	Denver, Colorado	Will Rogers	Oklahoma
Reina Sofia	Tenerife			William B. Hartsfield	Atlanta, Georgia
Riem	Munich	St Thomas	Virgin Islands		
Robert Mueller	Austin, Texas	Sturup	Malmö, Sweden	William P. Hobby	Houston, Texas
Roberts	Monrovia, Liberia	Subang	Malaysia	Yoff	Senegal
Rochambau	French Guiana	Sunan	North Korea	Yundam	Gambia
Ruzyne	Prague	Sylmet	Dhaka, Bangladesh	Zaventem	Brussels
				Zia	Bangladesh

TRANSPORT AIRCRAFT

TRANSPORT: CARS

Makes and Models

AC Cars Ace, Aceca, Cobra Sportster

Alfa Romeo GTV, 156, Spider

Aston Martin DB5, DB7 (David Brown), V8

Audi A3, 80, Cabriolet, Quattro

Austin A90, Healey, Maestro, Metro

Bentley Arnage Mulsanne, Brooklands, Continental T

BMW 528i, M3, 328i, Z3

Cadillac Allante, Evoq, Fleetwood, La Salle

Citroën Berlingo, Dyane, Mehari, Saxo 2CV, VTS, Xantia, Xsara

Daewoo (Korea) Cielo, Espero, Lanos, Leganza, Matiz, Nexia, Nubira

Daihatsu (Japan) Applause, Cuore, Move

Dodge Charger, Coronet, Power Wagon, Viper

Ferrari Berlinetta, F355, Maranello, 360 Modena, 360 Spider, Testarossa

Fiat Barchetta, Brava, Bravo, Cinquecento, Doblo, Ducato, Fiorino, Marea, Multipla, Punto, Scudo, Seicento, Spider, Stilo, Tempra, Tipo, Ulysse, Uno

Ford Aerostar, Anglia, Aspire, Bronco, Capri, Contour, Cortina, Cougar, Edsel, Escort, Explorer, Fiesta, Focus, Galaxy, Granada, Ka, Maverick, Model T, Mondeo,

Mustang, Pinto, Probe, Ranger, Sapphire, Scorpio, Taurus, Torino, Thunderbird, Victoria

Honda Accord, Aerodeck, Civic, CR-V, J-VX, Legend, Odyssey, Passport, Prelude

Hyundai (Korea) Accent, Avatar, Elantra, Santa Fe, Sonata, Tiburon

Jaguar E-Type, S-Type, XJ12, XK120, XK8

Lada Niva, Riva, Samara

Landrover Defender, Discovery, Freelander

Lincoln Blackwood, Navigator

Lotus Elan, Elise, Esprit, Exige

Maserati Ghibil

Mercedes C180, CLK, Malaya, Necar 3, SLK Roadster, Vision SLR

Mitsubishi Diamante, Eclipse, Mirage, Montero, Salent, Shogun

Nissan Almira, Frontier, Maxima, Micra, Pathfinder, Patrol, Primera, Quest, QX, Serena, Skyline, 300 ZX, Tirano

Peugeot Boxer, 406, Partner, 205

Porsche Boxster, Carrera, 911, 924, Varrera minivan

Proton Perdana, Persona, Satria

Renault Clio, Espace, Extra, Fuego, Kangoo, Laguna, Master, Mégane Alizé, Mégane Scenic, Safranes, Spider, Trafic, Twingo

Rolls Royce Camargue,

Corniche, Phantom, Silver Cloud, Silver Dawn, Silver Ghost, Silver Seraph, Silver Shadow, Silver Spirit, Silver Wraith

Rover Ascot, 800, Relax, 200

Saab Carlsson, Sonett

Seat Alhambra, Arosa, Malaga, Marbella

Skoda Felicia

Subaru Justy, Legacy, Loyale

Suzuki Alto, Baleno, Capuccino, Swift, Vitaras

Toyota Avalon, Camry Solara, Celica, Corolla, Highlander, Lexus, Prius, RAV4, Sequoia, Sienna, Supra, Tacoma, Tercel, Tundra

TVR Cerbera, Chimaera

Vauxhall Astra SRi, Belmont SRi, Calibra, Carlton, Cavalier (became Vectra), Chevette, Corsa, Frontera, Monterrey, Nova, Omega, Senator, Tigra Bermuda, Vectra

Vauxhall (van) Arena, Astravan, Brava, Combo, Corsavan

Volkswagen Beetle, Cabrio, Cabriolet, Corrado, Fox, Golf GTi, Jetta, Passat, Polo, Scirocco, Sharan, Thing, Vento

Volvo C70, 850, 340, S60, S80, V40, V70

Yugo 55A GL

Motorways

M1	London to Leeds	M32	Bristol to M4	M66	Manchester to Rochdale
M2	Rochester to Faversham	M40	London to Birmingham	M67	Hyde Bypass
M3	Sunbury to Southampton	M41	London to West Cross	M69	Coventry to Leicester
M4	London to Swansea	M42	Bromsgrove to Measham	M73	Glasgow
M5	Birmingham to Exeter	M45	M1 to A45 (Coventry)	M74	Glasgow to Lesmahagow
M6	Rugby to Carlisle	M50	Ross to Tewkesbury	M77	Ayr
M8	Edinburgh to Erskine Bridge	M53	Chester to Birkenhead	M80	Stepps Bypass
M9	Edinburgh to Dunblane	M54	M6 to Telford	M90	Dunfermline to Perth, Bonnybridge to Kincardine Bridge
M10	M1 to St Albans	M55	Preston to Blackpool		
M11	London to Cambridge	M56	Manchester to Queensferry	M180	M18 to Humber Bridge
M18	Rotherham to Goole	M57	Liverpool outer ring road		
M20	Swanley to Folkestone	M58	Liverpool to Wigan		
M23	Hooley (Surrey) to Crawley (Sussex)	M61	Manchester to Preston	**NB** The first UK motorway was the Preston Bypass in 1958, now part of the M6.	
M25	London Orbital	M62	Liverpool to Hull		
M26	Sevenoaks to Tonbridge	M63	Manchester south ring road		
M27	Southampton Bypass	M65	Calder Valley from M6		

International Car Registration Plates

A	Austria	ETH	Ethiopia	MA	Morocco	RSM	San Marino
AFG	Afghanistan	F	France	MAL	Malaysia	RU	Burundi
AL	Albania	FJI	Fiji	MC	Monaco	RWA	Rwanda
AND	Andorra	FL	Liechtenstein	MEX	Mexico	S	Sweden
AUS	Australia	FR	Faeroe	MS	Mauritius	SD	Swaziland
B	Belgium		Islands	MW	Malawi	SF	Finland
BD	Bangladesh	GB	United	N	Norway	SGP	Singapore
BDS	Barbados		Kingdom	NA	Netherlands	SME	Surinam
BG	Bulgaria	GBA	Alderney		Antilles	SN	Senegal
BH	Belize	GBG	Guernsey	NIC	Nicaragua	SWA	Namibia
BR	Brazil	GBJ	Jersey	NL	Netherlands	SY	Seychelles
BRN	Bahrain	GBM	Isle of Man	NZ	New Zealand	SYR	Syria
BRU	Brunei	GBY	Malta	P	Portugal	T	Thailand
BS	Bahamas	GBZ	Gibraltar	PA	Panama	TG	Togo
BUR	Burma	GCA	Guatemala	PAK	Pakistan	TN	Tunisia
	(Myanmar)	GH	Ghana	PE	Peru	TR	Turkey
C	Cuba	GR	Greece	PL	Poland	TT	Trinidad and
CDN	Canada	GUY	Guyana	PNG	Papua New		Tobago
CH	Switzerland	H	Hungary		Guinea	USA	USA
CI	Ivory Coast	HK	Hong Kong	PY	Paraguay	V	Vatican City
CL	Sri Lanka	HKJ	Jordan	RA	Argentina	VN	Vietnam
CO	Colombia	I	Italy	RB	Botswana	WAG	Gambia
CR	Costa Rica	IL	Israel	RC	Taiwan	WAL	Sierra Leone
CS	Czech Republic	IND	India	RCA	Central	WAN	Nigeria
CY	Cyprus	IR	Iran		African Rep.	WD	Dominica
D	Germany	IRL	Ireland	RCB	Congo	WG	Grenada
DK	Denmark	IRQ	Iraq	RCH	Chile	WL	St Lucia
DOM	Dominican	IS	Iceland	RH	Haiti	WS	Western
	Republic	J	Japan	RI	Indonesia		Samoa
DY	Benin	JA	Jamaica	RIM	Mauritania	WV	St Vincent and
DZ	Algeria	K	Cambodia	RL	Lebanon		Grenadines
E	Spain	KWT	Kuwait	RM	Madagascar	YU	Yugoslavia
EAK	Kenya	L	Luxembourg	RMM	Mali	YV	Venezuela
EAT	Tanzania	LAO	Laos	RN	Niger	Z	Zambia
EAZ	Zanzibar	LAR	Libya	RO	Romania	ZA	South Africa
EC	Ecuador	LB	Liberia	ROK	Korea	ZRE	Dem. Rep. of
ES	El Salvador	LS	Lesotho	ROU	Uruguay		Congo
ET	Egypt	M	Malta	RP	Philippines	ZW	Zimbabwe

TRANSPORT CARS

General Information

Automobile Association founded in 1905; originally formed to warn members of police patrols.

Breathalyzer introduced in 1967 by Minister of Transport, Barbara Castle.

car founders and designers: Fiat – Agnelli family; Jaguar – William Lyons; Lotus – Colin Chapman.

driving test initiated in 1935 and L-plates issued in the same year.

Mini introduced in 1959 and designed by Alex Issigonis.

MoT (Ministry of Transport) testing established in 1960 and compulsory for vehicles over three years old.

number plates first issued in 1903, the first being A1 to Lord Russell.

parking meters first seen in the UK in 1958, the same year that London saw its first traffic wardens.

petrol pumps were first used in 1919 in the UK.

Route 66 runs from Chicago (Illinois) to Los Angeles (California).

Royal Automobile Club founded in 1897, the second largest motoring organization after the AA.

veteran cars are those built up to the end of 1918; contrast Vintage cars, 1919–30.

TRANSPORT: SHIPS

Famous Ships – Miscellaneous

Aaron Manby   first iron steamship, launched in 1822.

Achille Lauro   formerly *Willem Ruys*, Italian cruise ship dogged by disaster. Collided with a fishing boat 1971, one crew member killed; fire broke out on board 1981, two passengers killed; hijacked between Alexandria and Port Said by the PLO Oct. 1985, one passenger murdered; gutted by fire and sank in the Indian Ocean Nov. 1994, two passengers killed.

Amoco Cadiz   super-tanker that ran aground off the coast of Brittany (March 1978) spilling 220,000 tons of crude oil.

Ancon   first ship through the Panama Canal.

Andrea Doria   Italian ship which collided with a Swedish ship and sank (1956).

Archimedes   first large sea-going steamship driven by a screw-propeller, it weighed 237 tons (Nov. 1838).

Argonaut   first submarine to navigate extensively in the open sea. Built in 1897 by the US engineer and naval architect Simon Lake, it was fitted with wheels for travel on the bottom of the sea. In 1898 the *Argonaut* travelled from Norfolk, Virginia, to New York, through heavy storms, proving the seaworthiness of this type of submarine construction.

Black Pig   vessel captained by Captain Pugwash in the children's series.

Braer   oil tanker that ran aground off the Shetlands (Jan. 1993) spilling 85,000 tons of crude oil.

Britannia   launched in April 1953, the Royal Yacht *Britannia* was finally laid to rest in December 1997.

Britannic   sister ship of the *Titanic*, sank after hitting a mine in 1916 in the Aegean while employed as a hospital ship.

Californian   Leyland liner, accused of ignoring *Titanic*'s distress calls but subsequently found to have no radio operator on duty.

Canberra   P&O cruise ship, affectionately nicknamed 'The Great White Whale'; entered service 1961; served as a hospital ship in the Falklands 1982; last cruise 1997.

Carnival Destiny   largest passenger ship in history: 893' long, 116' wide, weighs 101,353 tons and too wide to go through Panama Canal.

Carpathia   ship that came to the rescue of the *Titanic* when it sank.

Charlotte Dundas   first commercially successful paddle-steamer launched in Scotland, 1802, by William Symington for Lord Dundas.

Charlotte Rhodes   James Onedin's ship in the TV series *The Onedin Line*.

Christina   Aristotle Onassis' yacht named after his daughter.

Cutty Sark   famous tea and wool clipper built in 1869, the name deriving from the witch in Burns's *Tam O'Shanter*. It has been on display at Greenwich since 1957.

Don Juan   boat in which Percy Bysshe Shelley was drowned in 1822.

Elise   first steamboat to cross the English Channel (1816).

ENZA   New Zealand catamaran with eight-man crew led by Peter Blake and Robin Knox-Johnston which won the Jules Verne Trophy for sailing non-stop round the world in a record time of 74 days 22 hrs 17 mins, returning on 1 April 1994.

Estonia   Swedish-owned ferry that sank in the Baltic in September 1994 when the bow doors broke open, costing 852 lives; the worst postwar maritime disaster.

Exxon Valdez   super-tanker that ran aground off Alaskan coast (March 1989) spilling 12,000,000 gallons of crude oil.

Forfarshire   steamer wrecked off the Farne Islands in 1838, Grace Darling famously helping in the rescue.

Francis Smith   first British steamboat fitted with screw-propellers and built by Francis Pettit Smith, a farmer from Hendon (1836). It was 25' long and weighed 5 tons.

Grand Princess   the P&O liner is currently being built in Fincantieri, Italy, and is expected to be 951' long and weigh 109,000 tons to exceed the *Carnival Destiny* as the largest ever passenger ship.

Great Britain   built by Isambard Kingdom Brunel (1843), it was the first iron-hulled screw-propeller steamship. Since being towed from the Falklands in 1970, where it had been scuttled in 1937, it has been on display in Bristol.

Great Eastern   built by Isambard Kingdom Brunel (1858). At 666' long, it was the world's largest ship until 1899. In 1866, it laid the transatlantic cable. Sold for scrap in 1888.

Great Western   built by Isambard Kingdom Brunel (1838), It was the first wooden steamship to make regular transatlantic crossings.

Gypsy Moth IV   Francis Chichester became the first Englishman to sail single-handed round the world in this yacht (1966/7). Now on display at Greenwich.

Happy Giant   formerly named the *Seawise Giant* and with a deadweight tonnage of 564,763 tons, this was the largest ship afloat, but after extensive damage in the Gulf in Dec. 1987 and May 1988 has been refitted and reduced to 420,000 tons.

Helias Fos   this steam-turbine oil tanker is the current largest ship afloat at a deadweight tonnage of 550,051 tons.

Herald of Free Enterprise   Townsend Thoresen-owned cross-Channel ferry which capsized near the Belgian port of Zeebrugge due to the bow doors being insecure (6 March 1987); 188 lives were lost as a result.

Hispaniola   fictional ship in Robert Louis Stevenson's *Treasure Island*, skippered by Captain Smollet and owned by Squire Trelawney.

Lady Ghislaine   yacht owned by Robert Maxwell and named after his daughter, from which he went overboard and drowned (Nov. 1991).

Lake Champlain   first British liner with ship's radio (1901), it communicated with the SS *Lucania* mid-Atlantic.

Lenin   first nuclear-powered ship. This Soviet naval ice-breaker was launched in 1957.

Little Juliana   first steamboat fitted with screw-propellers (May 1804).

Lively Lady   yacht in which Alec Rose sailed single-handed round the world, returning to Portsmouth after nearly a year (4 July 1968).

Lusitania   Cunard liner sunk by German torpedo off the Irish coast (7 May 1915) with the loss of about 1,200 lives. This was a major factor in the USA's entry into the First World War.

Maiden   British yacht with all-female crew skippered by Tracy Edwards; won its class in Whitbread Round the World Race (1989).

Marchioness   Thames pleasure steamer rammed and sunk by the dredger *Bowbelle* at Southwark (August 1989); 51 lives were lost.

Mary Celeste   US brigantine under command of Ben Briggs, found in Atlantic (1872) with no sign of crew or struggle; cargo was secure.

Mauretania   sister ship of the *Lusitania*, built in 1907.

Mayflower   carried the 102 Pilgrim Fathers from Plymouth to Cape Cod, Massachusetts (1620), to found the first New England colony. Oceanus Hopkins was born on board the *Mayflower*.

Morning Cloud   yacht owned and captained by Edward Heath.

Nautilus   Captain Nemo's submarine in Jules Verne's novel *20,000 Leagues Under the Sea*.

Normandie   passenger liner destroyed by fire in New York harbour in 1941.

Norway   largest passenger liner ever built (formerly called *France*).

Olympic   sister ship of the *Titanic*.

Pequod   whaling ship captained by Captain Ahab and destroyed by Moby Dick in Melville's novel.

Pyroscaphe   first practical steamboat. Built near Lyon in 1783, it was a 138'-long paddle steamer and weighed 182 tons.

Queen Anne's Revenge   Edward Teach's (Blackbeard) ship captured in the Caribbean in 1717 and used for piracy until Jan. 1718.

Queen Elizabeth   built in 1938, the *Queen Elizabeth* (Seawise University) was destroyed in Hong Kong Harbour in Jan. 1972.

QEII   built in 1968, it is the largest passenger liner in service between Southampton and New York.

Queen Mary   now a floating hotel in Long Beach, California, it was built in 1936 and was the flagship of the Cunard line.

Rainbow Warrior   Greenpeace ship which was sunk in Auckland Harbour in July 1985 by French intelligence agents, killing one member of the crew.

Rising Star   first ship to cross the Atlantic from east to west (1821/2).

Savannah   first steamship to cross the Atlantic (1819).

Savannah   first commercially successful nuclear-powered ship, launched 1959.

Sea Empress   oil tanker which ran aground off Milford Haven (Feb. 1996) spilling 72,000 tons of crude oil.

Speedwell   sister ship of the *Mayflower* which left Southampton for New England but was forced into harbour at Plymouth, Devon.

Suhaili   yacht in which Robin Knox-Johnston became first man to circumnavigate the world non-stop and single-handed; he returned in April 1969.

Talitha G   motor yacht owned by John Paul Getty.

Titanic   White Star's unsinkable flagship which hit an iceberg on its maiden voyage on the night of 14 April 1912 and capsized in the early hours of 15 April with the loss of 1,513 lives. Wreck was found in 1985.

Torrey Canyon   ran aground off Land's End (March 1967) spilling its cargo of 100,000 tons of crude oil.

Turbinia   built and demonstrated by Charles Parsons at Spithead (1897), it was the first ship to use turbine engines.

Victoria and Albert   name given to three royal yachts; the first was a paddle-steamer of 1843; the last was built in 1899 and used until replaced by *Britannia*.

T
R
A
N
S
P
O
R
T

S
H
I
P
S

Famous Ships – Naval

Agamemnon   64-gun ship launched in 1781, commanded by Nelson from 1793 and his favourite ship. Abandoned in 1809 when it ran aground at Maldonado Bay.

Amethyst   frigate which in July 1949 escaped under cover of night along the flooded Yangtze.

Arethusa   launched 1849; last Royal Navy ship to go into action entirely under sail, at Sebastopol in 1855. From 1874 to 1933 it was a training ship at Greenhithe.

Argus   first aircraft carrier, completed in 1918.

Arizona   said to be the first US battleship sunk at Pearl Harbor on 7 Dec. 1941.

Ark Royal   many ships have had the name but the most famous were probably the flagship of the British Fleet against the Spanish Armada (1588), although it was only the nickname, the aircraft carrier sunk by an Italian torpedo in November 1941, and the present aircraft carrier which is the Royal Navy's largest fighting ship.

Association   flagship of Sir Cloudesley Shovell, wrecked off the Scilly Isles in 1707 with all hands lost.

Belfast   Europe's largest surviving WW2 warship, displacing 11,500 tons. Commissioned 1939, paid off 1971. The cruiser is now on display on the Thames.

Bellerophon   Napoleon Bonaparte surrendered to the British aboard this ship (15 July 1815) after the Battle of Waterloo.

Birmingham   US light-cruiser from which Eugène Ely took off in a 50 hp Curtiss pusher biplane (10 Nov. 1910) while it was at anchor in Chesapeake Bay, so making it the first ship with a temporary flight-deck.

Bismarck   German battleship sunk in the North Atlantic after it had sunk the British cruiser HMS *Hood* (May 1941).

Bonhomme Richard   John Paul Jones's 40-gun warship, blown in two off Flamborough Head in 1779.

Bounty   ship that while carrying breadfruit trees from Tahiti was the scene of a mutiny (28 April 1789) by Fletcher Christian (settled on Pitcairn Island). Captain William Bligh and 18 crew were set adrift in the Pacific.

Captain   experimental British turret ship of 1870 designed by Captain Cowper Coles; sank in the Bay of Biscay shortly after commissioning with the loss of 472 lives.

Constitution   American ship of the line, launched 1798. Nicknamed 'Old Ironsides'; on display in Boston.

Coventry   sister ship of the *Sheffield* and also sunk by an Argentinian Exocet missile during the Falklands War.

Devastation   launched 1871; first British capital ship which did not require sails.

Dreadnought   British battleship launched 1906 which revolutionized naval warfare in the early decades of the 20th century.

Dreadnought   Britain's first nuclear submarine, launched in 1960.

Elizabeth Bonaventure   Drake's flagship in the raid on Cadiz in 1587.

Enterprise   first nuclear-powered aircraft carrier.

Excellent   home to the naval gunnery school established in 1830; since 1891, a shore base on Whale Island, Portsmouth.

Ganges   last British ship of the line; launched 1821, paid off 1861. From 1866 a training ship. Name passed to a shore base near Ipswich in 1905; closed 1976.

General Belgrano   Argentine cruiser sunk by the British submarine *Conqueror* during Falklands War (2 May 1982).

Graf Spee   German pocket battleship scuttled by her captain off Montevideo Harbour after being harried across the River Plate by the cruisers, *Ajax*, *Achilles* and *Exeter* (Dec. 1939).

Henry, Grâce de Dieu   Henry VIII's flagship, built 1514 and carried 186 guns.

Hermes   aircraft carrier, last of the old-style carriers operated by the Royal Navy, which was flagship during the Falklands War.

Invincible   the second aircraft carrier that was sent to the Falklands after the Argentine invasion (2 April 1982).

Lightning   first purpose-built torpedo boat (1877).

Long Beach   first nuclear warship, launched in Quincy, Massachusetts (14 July 1959).

Maine   American armoured cruiser of 1886; blew up in Havana 1898, resulting in the Spanish-American War.

Mary Rose   Henry VIII's favourite ship, launched 1509, sank 1545 but was raised in 1982 and is still being restored at Portsmouth.

Merrimack   steam frigate scuttled in Norfolk harbour by Union forces, then raised by the Confederates and converted to an ironclad; fought a draw with the *Monitor* in Hampton Roads in 1862 and destroyed by her own captain shortly afterwards.

Missouri   Japanese surrender terms were signed aboard this ship in Tokyo Bay (2 Sept. 1945).

Monarch   First British turret-gunned ship, launched 1868.

Monitor   US iron-hulled warship with single gun turret, fought *Merrimack* in Hampton Roads 1862; capsized in a gale shortly after.

Nautilus   world's first nuclear-powered submarine, launched by the USA in 1954. The name derived from an early submarine designed by Robert Fulton for Napoleon (1800).

Northumberland   third-rate ship of the line which took Napoleon Bonaparte to St Helena in 1815.

PT 109   John F. Kennedy's torpedo boat during World War II.

Revenge   Drake's ship used during the attack by the Spanish Armada (1588). In 1591, captained by Sir Richard Grenville, fought a fifteen-hour battle single-handedly against 53 Spanish ships off Flores.

Royal George   100-gun ship of 1756; carried Hawke's flag at Quiberon Bay in 1759; capsized at Spithead in 1782 with loss of 900 lives.

Royal Oak   British battleship sunk at Scapa Flow (Orkneys) by a German torpedo (Oct. 1939) with the loss of 833 lives.

Scharnhorst   German battlecruiser which escaped from Brest with the *Gneisenau* and *Prinz Eugen* (Feb. 1942) but was sunk at the Battle of North Cape (Dec. 1943).

Sheffield   British destroyer hit by an Exocet missile on 4 May 1982 with the loss of 20 lives.

Squirrel   Sir Humphrey Gilbert's ship used during the attack by the Spanish Armada (1588).

Temeraire   98-gun ship launched in 1798; fought at Trafalgar; broken up on the Thames 1838 and immortalized on canvas by Turner.

Tiger   the ship used by Harold Wilson and Ian Smith during their UDI discussions (1966).

Tirpitz   German battleship sunk by RAF bombers in April 1944.

Trincomalee   built 1817, renamed *Foudroyant* in 1892 and a training ship in Portsmouth Harbour until 1987 when she was towed to Hartlepool for restoration and given back her original name.

Vanguard   iron-hulled frigate accidentally rammed and sunk by her sister ship *Iron Duke* in 1875.

Vanguard   Britain's largest battleship. Decommissioned 1960 and ran aground on leaving Portsmouth to be scrapped.

Vasa   flagship of Gustavus Adolphus of Sweden. Sank in harbour in 1628; recovered intact from seabed and now on display.

Victoria   launched 1859; last wooden battleship built for the Royal Navy. Paid off 1867; name used by British battleship of 1887 which sank off Tripoli in 1893 when flagship of Admiral George Tryon. It was accidentally rammed by *Camperdown*, flagship of Tryon's second-in-command, Alfred Markham.

Victory   launched at Chatham 1765, Horatio Nelson's flagship at the battle of Trafalgar (21 Oct. 1805); flagship of C-in-C Portsmouth since 1835. Dry-docked and restored in 1922, the *Victory* is now on display at Portsmouth.

Warrior   first iron-hulled battleship (and last surviving); built at Blackwall on the Thames (1859/60). When commissioned in 1861, it made every other naval vessel obsolete. On display in Portsmouth since 1987.

Wilton   first plastic warship, launched in Southampton 18 Jan. 1972.

Famous Ships – Voyages of Exploration

Adventure   James Cook's consort ship to the *Resolution* during his Antarctic voyage 1772–5; converted from a Whitby collier.

Arktika   first ship to reach the North Pole, in 1977.

Beagle   Charles Darwin's ship which surveyed South American islands and in particular Galapagos (1831–6). Darwin was the science officer, the captain was Robert Fitzroy.

Calypso   most famous submarine of Jacques Cousteau.

Challenger   Royal Navy survey ship, sailed 79,000 miles from 1872 to 1876, adding greatly to knowledge of the seas. Most recent RN ship of that name also an oceanographic vessel.

Discovery   Captain James Cook sought the Northwest Passage in 1776–9 with the *Resolution* and the *Discovery*. He was slain on the beach at Kealakekua, Hawaii, by Polynesian natives (1779).

Discovery   Robert Falcon Scott's ship used in his British National Antarctic Expedition of 1901–4 in which he was accompanied by Ernest Shackleton. Now on display in Dundee.

Endeavour   James Cook's voyage to Australia and New Zealand (1768–71), on which Joseph Banks was chief scientist, was carried out on this converted collier, originally called *Earl of Pembroke*.

Endurance   Ernest Shackleton's ship on his Antarctic voyage of 1914–16; sank in the Weddell Sea but since raised and on display in Dundee.

Erebus   one of the two ill-fated ships (the other was the *Terror*) used by Sir John Franklin in his search for the Northwest Passage (1845–6).

Fram   Norwegian explorer Fridtjof Nansen's ship used on his Arctic explorations (1893–6). Roald Amundsen sailed in *Fram* (which meant 'Forward') on his successful expedition of 1911–12 to the South Pole.

Gjöa   Roald Amundsen's ship in which he sailed the Northwest Passage (1902–6) and found the magnetic North Pole.

Golden Hind   ship on which Francis Drake became first Englishman to circumnavigate the globe (1580); originally called *Pelican*.

Grenville   the schooner that James Cook commanded while surveying the coast of Newfoundland 1763–68.

Kon Tiki   Thor Heyerdahl's single-sailed balsa-wood raft on which he crossed the Pacific (1947).

Matthew   John Cabot discovered Newfoundland and Nova Scotia (1497) in this 50-ton ship.

Mazurek   carried Krystyna Choynowska-Liskievicz on the first female solo circumnavigation of the globe in 1978.

Morning   Supply ship that accompanied the *Discovery* in Scott's Antarctic expedition of 1901–4.

Ernest Shackleton was invalided home on this ship.

Nimrod   Ernest Shackleton's ship on the voyage (1907–9) in which he located the magnetic South Pole, and climbed Mt Erebus but only came within 97 miles of the South Pole.

Quest   ship on which Ernest Shackleton died during his third Antarctic voyage (Grytviken, South Georgia 1922).

RA II   Thor Heyerdahl's papyrus raft on which he crossed the Atlantic (1970).

Resolute   one of Edward Belcher's ships sent to seek the missing (and already dead) John Franklin in 1852; abandoned in 1854 after being locked in ice off Melville Island; found 1,000 miles away in Davis Strait in 1855, still perfectly seaworthy.

Resolution   James Cook's flagship during his voyage to Antarctica 1772–5. Cook sought the Northwest Passage 1776–9 in this ship.

Roebuck   William Dampier's ship on his voyage to Australia and New Guinea (1699–1700).

Santa Maria   Christopher Columbus's flagship caravel during his expedition to the New World (1492–3), accompanied by the *Niña* and *Pinta*.

Spray   Joshua Slocum's boat in which he circumnavigated the earth, the first man to do so solo (1895–8).

Terra Nova   Captain Robert Falcon Scott's ship used on his ill-fated Antarctic expedition 1910–12.

Terror   one of the two ships (the other was *Erebus*) used by Sir John Franklin in his search for the Northwest Passage (1845–6).

Theodore Roosevelt   Robert Peary's ship used when he became first person to reach the North Pole (6 April 1909). Peary's former friend, Frederick Cook, was found to have fraudulently reported his own earlier reaching of the Pole.

Tigris   Thor Heyerdahl's third raft.

Trieste   bathysphere submarine which holds the record for the deepest descent (10,916 m) on 23 Jan. 1960.

Vega   first ship to achieve the Northeast Passage, in 1878–9, under Nils Nordenskjöld.

Victoria   first ship to circumnavigate the globe (1522). Although Ferdinand Magellan set out with five ships (the flagship *Trinidad*, *San Antonio*, *Concepción*, *Santiago* and *Victoria*) four were lost and he himself was killed in the Philippines (1521). The circumnavigation was completed by Juan Sebastián del Cano.

Viking   Norwegian explorer Fridtjof Nansen's first exploratory ship (1888) in which he first sailed to Greenland.

Windward   British Arctic explorer Frederick Jackson's ship on which Fridtjof Nansen briefly journeyed back to Norway in Aug. 1896.

Ships – General Information

binnacle   the casing in which the ship's compass is kept.

box the compass   to name the points of the compass in proper order.

breeches buoy   life-saving device run on a rope stretched from a wrecked vessel to a place of safety.

bulwark   that part of the sides of a ship which rises above the upper deck.

caïque   long, narrow, light rowing skiff used on the Bosporus.

clipper ship: first   *Rainbow* (1845).

dahabeah/dahabeeyah   houseboat used on the Nile (from Arabic: the Golden One).

dhow   single-masted ship with a very long yard and a lateen sail, used on the Arabian sea.

diesel-powered ship: first   *Petit-Pierre*.

distress signals   SOS – Morse (formerly CQD, Come Quickly Danger); Mayday – vocal distress shout.

extremities of ship   front – bow; back – stern; left side looking front – port (formerly larboard); right side looking front – starboard.

felucca   small vessel used in the Mediterranean, propelled by oars or lateen sails, or both.

flotsam   goods lost in shipwreck and found floating.

gondola   long, narrow Venetian boat with peaked ends, propelled by one oar.

gunwale   upper edge of a ship's side next to the bulwarks.

hull: plank types   clinker-built – built with overlapping planks fastened with clinched nails; carvel-built – having the planks flush at the edges.

hydrofoil   invented by Comte de Lambert in 1897 and developed by Enrico Forlanini in 1898.

jetsam   goods thrown overboard in order to lighten a ship in distress, and subsequently washed ashore.

junk   flat-bottomed vessel with lugsails, used in the Chinese seas.

kayak   Inuit and Alaskan canoe, made of sealskins stretched on a light wooden framework.

kitchen or cook-house   galley.

knot   one nautical mile per hour. The British nautical mile was 6,080 feet but in 1970 the International nautical mile of 1,852 metres was adopted. The measurement was devised by Richard Norwood in 1673.

lighthouses: UK authority   Trinity House.

lights   starboard – green; port – red; top at night – white.

masts: how many   sloop and cutter (1); ketch, brig, brigantine, yawl (2); barque (3 or more); schooner (2 or more).

P&O: meaning   Peninsular and Oriental.

pipe down   naval colloquialism derived from the boatswain's call of this name, meaning 'Hands turn in', i.e. 'Lights out'.

piping the side   traditional ceremony of blowing the boatswain's pipe when royalty arrive or depart from battleship.

plimsoll line   maximum loading mark on hull of ship, named after Samuel Plimsoll (1824–98), promoter of the Merchant Shipping Act 1876.

ports: famous   Athens – Piraeus; London – Tilbury; Rome – Ostia.

ports: general   biggest – New York; busiest – Rotterdam; largest inland – Montreal.

PT Boat: meaning   Patrol Torpedo Boat.

Q-ship   merchant ship with concealed guns, used to decoy enemy ships into the range of its weapons. Q stood for 'Query'.

rudder: invented by   Chinese, 1st century BC.

sails   lateen – triangular.

ships: register of   Lloyd's.

ship: largest   oil tanker *Jahre Viking* at 1,504′ long and weighing over 564,000 tonnes.

steam turbine: inventor   Charles Parsons (1897).

V-shaped hull: pioneer   Uffa Fox (who instructed HRH Prince Philip, the Duke of Edinburgh, in the finer points of yachting).

Venice: water bus   vaporetto.

watches at sea   first watch – 8pm to midnight; middle watch – midnight to 4am; morning watch – 4am to 8am; forenoon – 8am to midday; afternoon watch – midday to 4pm; first dog watch – 4pm to 6pm; second dog watch – 6pm to 8pm.

xebec / zebec   small three-masted Mediterranean vessel with both square and lateen sails, formerly used by Algerian pirates.

yachts: famous   *Talitha G* – John Paul Getty; *Saratoga* – Humphrey Bogart; *Saxara* – Mohamed Al Fayed.

Railway Tunnels: World's Longest

	Span	Built	Railway	Length (mile)
Seikan	Honshu–Hokkaido	1988	Japan Rail	33.5
Channel	Cheriton–Fréthun	1994	BR/French National	30.7
Daishimizu	Jōmō-Kogen–Echigo	1980	Japan Rail	13.9
Simplon No. 2	Brig–Iselle	1922	Swiss Federal	12.4
Simplon No. 1	Brig–Iselle	1906	Swiss Federal	12.3
Shin Kanmon	Honshu–Kyushu	1975	Japan Rail	11.6
Apennine	Florence–Bologna	1934	Italian State	11.5
Rokko	Osaka–Shinkobe	1972	Japan Rail	10.1
Furka Base	Oberwald–Realp	1982	Furks-Oberalp Switzerland	9.6
Haruna	Jōmō-Kogen–Echigo	1982	Japan Rail	9.5
Gotthard	Göschenen–Airolo	1882	Swiss Federal	9.3
Mt Macdonald	Selkirk Mts–British Columbia	1989	CP Rail, Canada	9.1

Longest railway tunnel on the Indian sub-continent is the Kojak Tunnel at Shelabagh, Pakistan (2½ miles). The Lyttelton Tunnel (1.6 miles) was the first railway tunnel in NZ and the only one through an extinct volcano. Longest overland railway tunnel in the UK is the Severn Tunnel.

Railway Bridges: World's Longest

	Location	Opened	Length (ft)
Huey P. Long	New Orleans, USA	1935	23,235
Yangtze River	Nanjing, China	1968	22,218
Hell Gate	New York, USA	1917	19,233
Greenwich	London, England	1836	19,000
Orvieto Viaduct	Paglia River	1980	17,634
Savannah River	S. Carolina, USA	1909	13,000
Lower Zambesi	Mozambique	1934	12,064
Venice Viaduct	Italy	1846	11,821
Tay	Scotland	1887	11,653
Storstrom	Denmark	1937	10,537

World's oldest railway bridge is the Tanfield Arch in County Durham, designed by Ralph Wood and built in 1727. World's highest railway bridge, above water, is the Hanging Bridge above the Arkansas River, Colorado, at 1,053′.

London Underground Stations: Name Changes

Current name	Previous name
Acton Town	Mill Hill Park
Arsenal	Gillespie Road
Becontree	Gale Street Halt
Charing Cross	Strand
Debden	Chigwell Road
Embankment	Charing Cross
Euston Square	Gower Street
Fulham Broadway	Walham Green
Green Park	Dover Street
Kensington (Olympia)	Addison Road
Ladbroke Grove	Notting Hill
Marylebone	Great Central
Moor Park	Sandy Lodge
Oakwood	Enfield West
Ravenscourt Park	Shaftesbury Road
South Woodford	George Lane
St Paul's	Post Office
Tooting Bec	Trinity Road
Tower Hill	Mark Lane
West Kensington	North End (Fulham)
White City	Wood Lane
Woodside Park	Torrington Park, Woodside

Rail Companies: Since BR Privatized

Anglia Railway   Cardiff Railway Co.   Central Trains   Chiltern Railway Co.   Connex South Central   Connex South Eastern   Eurostar   Gatwick Express   Island Line   LTS Rail (London, Tilbury South)   Mersey Rail   Midland Mainline   North London Rail   North Western Trains   Regional Railways North East   Scot Rail   South Wales and West   South West Trains   South West Trains (Stagecoach)   Thames   Thameslink   Virgin West   West Anglia Great Northern   West Coast Railway Co.

Railway Stations: Locations

Anhalter	Berlin	**King's Cross**	London	**Saint Lazare**	Paris
Bank Top	Darlington	**Lime Street**	Liverpool	**Shrub Hill**	Worcester
Buchanan Street	Glasgow	**Liverpool Street**	London	**Snow Hill**	Birmingham
Charing Cross	London	**London Rd**	Leicester	**Spa**	Bath
Citadel	Carlisle	**Low Level**	Wolverhampton	**St David's**	Exeter
Connolly	Dublin	**Marine**	Dover	**St Enoch**	Glasgow
Euston	London	**Midland**	Derby	**Temple Meads**	Bristol
Foregate Street	Worcester	**Mumps**	Oldham	**Thorpe**	Norwich
Forster Square	Bradford	**New Street**	Birmingham	**Trent Valley**	Nuneaton
Gare du Nord	Paris	**Paddington**	London	**Union**	Washington
Grand Central	New York	**Paragon**	Hull	**Victoria**	London,
Harbour	Folkestone,	**Parkway**	Bristol		Manchester,
	Portsmouth	**Piccadilly**	Manchester		Bombay
Haymarket	Edinburgh	**Priory**	Dover	**Waterloo**	London
High Level	Wolverhampton	**Queen Street**	Cardiff,	**Waverley**	Edinburgh
High Street	Swansea		Glasgow	**Yaroslavl**	Moscow

Railways: General Information

accident: first caused by moving train Rt Hon William Huskisson MP was run down by the *Rocket* at the opening of the Liverpool & Manchester Railway 15 Sept. 1830. He was rushed to Eccles Hospital on the *Northumbrian*. A runaway wagon caused the death of two boys in a Tyne coalpit in 1650. Unfortunately numerous incidents of this kind took place but were not really the work of trains in the accepted sense of the word.

air-brake: designer George Westinghouse (1846–1914) developed the air-brake from the simple non-automatic system of 1866 into the fully automatic (i.e. the brakes are automatically applied should any break in the train air pipe occur). System still in use in most countries. Most British railways used the vacuum brake, which had nothing to do with Westinghouse.

APT BR Advanced Passenger Train ran from London to Glasgow in 3 hrs 52 mins 45 secs at an average speed of 103 mph (12 Dec. 1984). This service was abandoned in 1986 due to numerous problems.

broad-gauge railway: last train the *Cornishman* was the last broad-gauge passenger train to run, on 21 May 1892, from Paddington to Penzance.

Chicago rail system nicknamed the 'El', which is short for elevated (several other cities, notably New York, also had elevated railways known as 'Els').

diesel locomotive: first the first diesel locomotive to go into regular service was a Swedish-built metre-gauge Bo Bo type put into operation by Tunisian Railways in 1921.

dining car: first first buffet cars were put into service on the Philadelphia, Wilmington & Baltimore Railroad in 1863.

electric railway: first Brighton seafront, built by Magnus Volk (1851–1937), still known as Volk's Electric Railway.

electrification of railways modern standard system of railway electrification at 25 kV 50 Hz was first used in France in 1950 and in England on the Colchester– Clacton–Walton lines in 1959.

fare-paying customers: first to carry Oystermouth Railway built a railway from Swansea to Mumbles

and on 25 March 1807 became first to convey fare-paying passengers. This railway closed in 1960.

father of railways George Stephenson.

father of the locomotive Richard Trevithick.

horse-drawn railways Middleton Railway, Leeds, in 1758 was the first to be built under its own Act of Parliament, although other horse-worked railways had been operating in the Tyne coalfield on private land for many years previously.

horse-drawn railways: public the Surrey Iron Railway from Wandsworth to Croydon (opened 26 July 1803) was the first horse-drawn railway opened to the public, inasmuch as it accepted consignments. Passengers were not carried (at least not officially!).

locomotive railway: first Stockton and Darlington, opened in 1825.

locomotive railway: first passenger line Liverpool to Manchester, opened in 1830.

London railway: first Spa Road to Deptford, part of London & Greenwich Railway, opened 8 Feb. 1836.

London Underground: first automatic barrier Stamford Brook.

London Underground: first line Metropolitan Line, from Bishop's Road to Farringdon Street, 10 Jan. 1863.

longest platform in Great Britain Colchester, at 1981'.

Mallard LNER 'A4' Class Pacific No. 4468 *Mallard* reached a speed of just over 126 mph for a few seconds on a brake-test trial run between Grantham and Peterborough (3 July 1938). *Mallard* can be seen at the National Railway Museum, York.

monorail: first Charles Lartique's monorail system was used on a short demonstration line in France and then on the Listowel and Ballybunion Railway in Ireland, 1883. It was not a true monorail but comprised a single rail raised about 4' above the ground on an A-frame with two guiding rails about 1' off the ground.

National Railway Museum museum opened in York in 1975 and combining the holdings of the British Transport Commission's museum at Clapham and the LNER museum at York.

nationalization railways were nationalized from 1 Jan. 1948 and were divided into five regions: 1) Scottish, 2) North Eastern, 3) London Midland, 4) Eastern, 5) Western and Southern. (The Eastern and North Eastern were amalgamated on 1 Jan. 1967.)

platforms: most UK Waterloo main line.

Puffing Billy world's first steam locomotive running on smooth rails instead of the previous rack rails. Designed by William Hedley and first put into operation in 1813 from Wylam colliery in Northumberland to the river Tyne. The *Wylam Dilly* was made at much the same time. Note: Trevithick's Penydarren engine had smooth iron wheels running on smooth cast-iron tram plates!

railcar: designer William Bridges Adams designed the 6-wheeled steam railcar *Fairfield* (named after the road in Bow, London, where he operated from).

railtrack: longest in straight line Nullarbor Plain, Australia.

railway: first private opened in June 1789 by the Loughborough & Nanpanton Railway Co.

railway king George Hudson.

Railways Act 1921 from 1 Jan. 1923 the amalgamation of the railways meant that four major companies were formed: 1) The Great Western Railway, 2) The London, Midland & Scottish Railway, 3) The London and North Eastern Railway, 4) The Southern Railway.

railways: USA operating co. Amtrak.

Rainhill Trials competition held on 6–14 Oct. 1829 near Liverpool to choose the design of locomotive for Liverpool & Manchester Railway. Robert Stephenson's *Rocket* won the £500 prize by beating Timothy Hackworth's *Sans Pareil* and John Braithwaite and John Ericsson's *Novelty*.

RKB code: meaning the code RKB refers to a single item of rolling stock containing a restaurant seating portion, a buffet counter and a kitchen.

San Francisco rail system BART (Bay Area Rapid Transit).

Schools-Class locomotives introduced by Southern Railway in 1930 and named after famous schools, first being called *Eton*.

Scottish railway: first Kilmarnock and Troon Railway was the first 'proper' railway in Scotland. Opened 6 July 1812.

sleeping cars: European wagons lits.

sleeping car: first the *Chambersburg*, introduced by the Cumberland Valley Railroad on its Pennsylvanian Harrisburg–Chambers route, was the first example of a sleeping car (1836).

standard gauge first used on Willington Colliery wagonway near Newcastle upon Tyne in 1764 and set at 4′ 8½″ or 1,435 mm, this being an average of the wagon ways in this area. It is thought that the average gauge of between 4′ 6″ and 4′ 9″ was the width of the track required for two horses abreast.

station: largest Grand Central, New York.

station: largest UK Clapham Junction.

station: most northerly in Great Britain Thurso.

steam locomotive: first Richard Trevithick built the first locomotive and ran it on the Penydarren Railway, near Merthyr Tydfil, on 6 Feb. 1804.

TGV Train à Grande Vitesse; began a regular hourly service between Paris and Lyon, the 265-mile journey taking 2 hrs 40 mins.

third-class travel redesignated as second class by British Rail in 1956. (The old second class had largely fallen out of use by the turn of the century.)

timetable: national *Bradshaw's Railway Companion* was the first national railway timetable in 1839.

underground: British four British cities with underground railways: London, Glasgow, Liverpool and Newcastle (Metro).

most passengers Moscow.

most stations New York.

names Berlin – U Bahn; Rome – Metropolitana; Stockholm – T-Bana; Paris – Métro.

USSR: terms for first and second class Soft and Hard class.

wheel configurations: nicknames Atlantic (4-4-2): name originally applied to a batch of 4-4-2s built by Baldwin of Philadelphia for the Atlantic Coast Railroad in 1894. In the UK, Atlantics were in use for hauling express passenger trains on the Great Northern, North Eastern, North British and London, Brighton & South Coast Railways. It should be borne in mind that the term 'Atlantic' properly describes a 4-4-2 locomotive with a separate tender; thus 4-4-2 tank engines, such as were in widespread use in the UK, are not true Atlantics but are more analogous to a 4-4-0 with an additional axle to support a rear bunker. **Mogul (2-6-0):** first true Mogul, with a leading two-wheel Bissell truck, was built by Baldwin of Philadelphia for the Louisville & Nashville Railroad in 1860. In the UK in the twentieth century Moguls were in extensive use on all four of the post-1923 mainline railways, and after 1948, in all regions of British Railways. The term Mogul properly applies to a 2-6-0 with outside cylinders, so that the inside-cylindered 2-6-0s of the Caledonian and Glasgow, and South Western Railways were not true Moguls, being essentially large 0-6-0-s with a leading truck for increased front-end stability. **Pacific (4-6-2):** name seems to have originated because the engines concerned were obviously bigger than Atlantics. In the UK, Pacifics were in general express service on the LNER from the mid-Twenties, the LMS from 1933 and the Southern Railway from 1941. The Great Western Railway had actually built the first UK Pacific (No. 111 *The Great Bear*) in 1908 but found it something of a white elephant. It was scrapped in 1924, and various mechanical components were incorporated in a new 'Castle' class 4-6-0, No. 111 *Viscount Churchill*. **Baltic (4-6-4):** name appears to be of Germanic origin. (To an American, a 4-6-4 is a Hudson.) Only one 4-6-4 tender engine ever ran in the UK. This was Gresley's experimental high-pressure water-tube boiler 4-cylinder compound No. 10000, built for the LNER in 1929. It was rebuilt as a conventional 3-cylinder simple expansion engine and ran until 1959, latterly as British Railways No. 60700. This engine was not a true Baltic, since the rear carrying axles were disposed as a Cartazzi axle and a separate two-wheel radial truck, making the engine technically a 4-6-2-2. Around 1920, however, there was a vogue, particularly on the London Brighton & South Coast, Lancashire & Yorkshire and Glasgow & South Western Railways, for extremely large 4-6-4 tank engines, which, while not true Baltics (*vide supra* under Atlantic), were referred to as Baltics consistently enough to legitimize the usage. **Prairie (2-6-2):** name applied in the American Midwest after first examples were built in 1900 for the Chicago, Burlington & Quincy Railroad. Apart from one curious 8-cylinder experimental engine built as a semi-private venture by Cecil Paget at Derby in 1908, the only 2-6-2 tender engines to run in the UK were Gresley's extremely successful V2-class built from

1936 onwards for the LNER, and his lightweight V4 design of 1941, of which only two examples were built before his death. In the 20th century, several hundred 2-6-2 tank engines were built in the UK, particularly by the Great Western Railway, and, although not true Prairies (being actually Moguls with a rear bunker), they were generally referred to as Prairie tanks. **Consolidation (2-8-0):** name is that carried by the first example of this type, built in 1865 for the Lehigh & Mahanoy Railroad. The name was not much used to describe British 2-8-0s, but it does seem to have attached itself to the 2-8-0 freight locomotives built at Swindon for the Great Western Railway by G.J. Churchward and his successors. This may be due to Churchward's close following of American locomotive practice resulting in an essentially American designation attaching itself to his engines of the 2-8-0 type. **Mikado (2-8-2):** so named because the first examples were made in the USA for export to Japan. In the UK, the only 2-8-2 tender engines were built by Gresley for the LNER. First, the two heavy freight engines of class P1, built in 1925. These were mechanically a cross between an A1-class Pacific and an O2-class Consolidation. As a small, non-standard class they were both withdrawn in 1945. Second was the magnificent class P2, six examples of which were built 1934–36, for working express passenger trains to Scotland. They were rebuilt as very mediocre Pacifics after Gresley's death. **Decapod:** a curiosity – to an American, a Decapod is a 2-10-0. The only two classes of engines of this type to run in the UK were the 251 examples of the standard-class 9F, built by British Railways between 1954 and 1960, and 25

examples bought secondhand from the Ministry of Supply after WW2. These, however, were never referred to as Decapods (except, presumably, by Americans!). The Decapod, however, was a huge 0-10-0 tank engine built by the Great Eastern Railway in 1903 as part of an experiment in the drastic acceleration of suburban trains. It did everything which was expected of it, but was far too heavy for the track and bridges. It was broken up shortly afterwards and a few components incorporated in a 0-8-0 goods engine. **NB** The following type names are largely in American use only, generally because no locomotives of the type referred to ever ran in the UK. **American (4-4-0):** applies only to the classic outside-cylindered, bar-framed three-point suspension locomotive familiar from countless Western films. **Ten Wheeler (4-6-0):** strictly an American term only. (Casey Jones was driving Illinois Central ten-wheeler No. 382 when he met his death at Vaughan, Mississippi, on 29 April 1900.) **Mastodon (4-8-0):** there were actually two 4-8-0 tender engines on the narrow-gauge Londonderry & Lough Swilly Railway in Ireland. They were used on the desolate Burtonport extension line in north-west Donegal, where I doubt if anyone ever referred to them as Mastodons. **Berkshire (2-8-4):** pronounced 'BurkSHIRE'. **Mountain (4-8-4) Santa Fe (2-10-2):** introduced by the Atchison, Topeka & Santa Fe Railroad in 1903, for working over the Raton Pass. **Texas (2-10-4):** called this in the USA but called 'Selkirk' in Canada.

World's longest railway: Trans-Siberian   running from Moscow (Yaroslavl Station) to Vladivostok (5,801 miles); opened 3 Nov. 1901.

Presidents

	President		Birthplace	Life span	Party	In office
1	Washington	George	Virginia	1732–1799	Federalist	1789–1797
2	Adams	John	Massachusetts	1735–1826	Federalist	1797–1801
3	Jefferson	Thomas	Virginia	1743–1826	Republican	1801–1809
4	Madison	James	Virginia	1751–1836	Republican	1809–1817
5	Monroe	James	Virginia	1758–1831	Republican	1817–1825
6	Adams	John Quincy	Massachusetts	1767–1848	Republican	1825–1829
7	Jackson	Andrew	South Carolina	1767–1845	Democratic	1829–1837
8	Van Buren	Martin	New York	1782–1862	Democratic	1837–1841
9	Harrison	William Henry	Virginia	1773–1841	Whig	1841
10	Tyler	John	Virginia	1790–1862	Whig	1841–1845
11	Polk	James Knox	North Carolina	1795–1849	Democratic	1845–1849
12	Taylor	Zachary	Virginia	1784–1850	Whig	1849–1850
13	Fillmore	Millard	New York	1800–1874	Whig	1850–1853
14	Pierce	Franklin	New Hampshire	1804–1869	Democratic	1853–1857
15	Buchanan	James	Pennsylvania	1791–1868	Democratic	1857–1861
16	Lincoln	Abraham	Kentucky	1809–1865	Republican	1861–1865
17	Johnson	Andrew	North Carolina	1808–1875	Union	1865–1869
18	Grant	Ulysses Simpson	Ohio	1822–1885	Republican	1869–1877
19	Hayes	Rutherford Birchard	Ohio	1822–1893	Republican	1877–1881
20	Garfield	James Abram	Ohio	1831–1881	Republican	1881
21	Arthur	Chester Alan	Vermont	1830–1886	Republican	1881–1885
22	Cleveland	Stephen Grover	New Jersey	1837–1908	Democratic	1885–1889
23	Harrison	Benjamin	Ohio	1833–1901	Republican	1889–1893
24	Cleveland	Grover	New Jersey	1837–1908	Democratic	1893–1897
25	Mckinley	William	Ohio	1843–1901	Republican	1897–1901
26	Roosevelt	Theodore	New York	1858–1919	Republican	1901–1909
27	Taft	William Howard	Ohio	1857–1930	Republican	1909–1913
28	Wilson	Thomas Woodrow	Virginia	1856–1924	Democratic	1913–1921
29	Harding	Warren Gamaliel	Ohio	1865–1923	Republican	1921–1923
30	Coolidge	Calvin	Vermont	1872–1933	Republican	1923–1929
31	Hoover	Herbert Clark	Iowa	1874–1964	Republican	1929–1933
32	Roosevelt	Franklin Delano	New York	1882–1945	Democratic	1933–1945
33	Truman	Harry S.	Missouri	1884–1972	Democratic	1945–1953
34	Eisenhower	Dwight David	Texas	1890–1969	Republican	1953–1961
35	Kennedy	John Fitzgerald	Massachusetts	1917–1963	Democratic	1961–1963
36	Johnson	Lyndon Baines	Texas	1908–1973	Democratic	1963–1969
37	Nixon	Richard Milhous	California	1913–1995	Republican	1969–1974
38	Ford	Gerald Rudolph	Nebraska	1913–	Republican	1974–1977
39	Carter	James Earl	Georgia	1924–	Democratic	1977–1981
40	Reagan	Ronald Wilson	Illinois	1911–	Republican	1981–1989
41	Bush	George Herbert Walker	Massachusetts	1924–	Republican	1989–1993
42	Clinton	William Jefferson	Arkansas	1946–	Democratic	1993–2001
43	Bush	George Walker	Connecticut	1946–	Republican	2001–

Vice Presidents

Vice President		Birthplace	In office	Vice President to
Adams	John	Massachusetts	1789–1797	Washington
Jefferson	Thomas	Virginia	1797–1801	Adams
Burr	Aaron	New Jersey	1801–1805	Jefferson
Clinton	George	New York	1805–1812	Jefferson/Madison
Gerry	Elbridge	Massachusetts	1813–1814	Madison
Tompkins	Daniel D.	New York	1817–1825	Monroe
Calhoun	John Caldwell	South Carolina	1825–1832	Adams/Jackson
Van Buren	Martin	New York	1833–1837	Jackson
Johnson	Richard Mentor	Kentucky	1837–1841	Van Buren
Tyler	John	Virginia	1841	Harrison
Dallas	George Mifflin	Pennsylvania	1845–1849	Polk
Fillmore	Millard	New York	1849–1850	Taylor
King	William Rufus De Vane	North Carolina	1853	Pierce
Breckinridge	John Cabell	Kentucky	1857–1861	Buchanan
Hamlin	Hannibal	Maine	1861–1865	Lincoln
Johnson	Andrew	North Carolina	1865	Lincoln
Colfax	Schuyler	New York	1869–1873	Grant

Vice President		Birthplace	In office	Vice President to
Wilson	Henry	New Hampshire	1873–1875	Grant
Wheeler	William A.	New York	1877–1881	Hayes
Arthur	Chester A.	Vermont	1881	Garfield
Hendricks	Thomas A.	Ohio	1885	Arthur
Morton	Levi Parsons	Vermont	1889–1893	Harrison
Stevenson	Adlai E.	Kentucky	1893–1897	Cleveland
Hobart	Garret A.	New Jersey	1897–1899	McKinley
Roosevelt	Theodore	New York	1901	McKinley
Fairbanks	Charles Warren	Ohio	1905–1909	Roosevelt
Sherman	James Schoolcraft	New York	1909–1912	Taft
Marshall	Thomas R.	Indiana	1913–1921	Wilson
Coolidge	Calvin	Vermont	1921–1923	Harding
Dawes	Charles Gates	Ohio	1925–1929	Coolidge
Curtis	Charles	Kansas	1929–1933	Hoover
Garner	John Nance	Texas	1933–1941	Roosevelt
Wallace	Henry Agard	Iowa	1941–1945	Roosevelt
Truman	Harry S.	Missouri	1945	Roosevelt
Barkley	Alben W.	Kentucky	1949–1953	Truman
Nixon	Richard Milhous	California	1953–1961	Eisenhower
Johnson	Lyndon Baines	Texas	1961–1963	Kennedy
Humphrey	Hubert H.	South Dakota	1965–1969	Johnson
Agnew	Spiro T.	Maryland	1969–1973	Nixon
Ford	Gerald Rudolph	Nebraska	1973–1974	Nixon
Rockefeller	Nelson Aldrich	Maine	1974–1977	Ford
Mondale	Walter F.	Minnesota	1977–1981	Carter
Bush	George Herbert Walker	Massachusetts	1981–1989	Reagan
Quayle	J. Danforth	Indiana	1989–1993	Bush, G.H.W.
Gore	Albert	Washington DC	1993–2001	Clinton
Cheney	Richard B.	Nebraska	2001	Bush, G.W.

Presidents and Vice Presidents: Miscellaneous Information

assassinated Lincoln, Garfield, McKinley, Kennedy.

attempts Ford (Sarah Jane Moore) 1975, Reagan (John Hinckley) 1981.

bachelor James Buchanan.

bald Martin Van Buren and Dwight Eisenhower.

bath: got stuck in William Howard Taft.

broccoli: hated George Bush.

Camelot: nickname of John F. Kennedy's regime.

China: first to visit Richard Nixon.

Clinton's cat: named Socks (belonged to daughter Chelsea).

Confederate states: president Jefferson Davis.

cried on television during campaign Edmund Muskie.

Declaration of Independence: drafted by Thomas Jefferson.

Democrat-turned-Republican: first Ronald Reagan.

Democratic Party Headquarters Tammany Hall, New York.

Democratic Party symbol Donkey.

Democratic split during Vietnam War Hawks and Doves.

died in office W. Harding, W. Harrison, F.D. Roosevelt, Z. Taylor.

divorced: first Ronald Reagan.

duel: killed opponent in Andrew Jackson.

elected for four terms F.D. Roosevelt.

elected unanimously by Electoral College George Washington.

elected with one vote against James Monroe.

father and son John Adams and his son John Quincy Adams.

ex-director of the CIA George Bush.

father was UK ambassador John F. Kennedy's father Joseph.

fireside chats: radio broadcasts F.D. Roosevelt.

four freedoms Speech, worship, freedom from fear and want. Roosevelt's basis for UN Charter, San Francisco 1945.

Fourteen Points Woodrow Wilson.

Garfield: assassinated by Charles Guiteau 1881.

Gettysburg Address Lincoln's speech of 1863.

grandfather and grandson William Harrison and Benjamin Harrison.

Grand Old Party (GOP) Republican party nickname.

Great Triumvirate of statesmen John Calhoun, Henry Clay, Daniel Webster.

hospital: first born in Jimmy Carter.

illegitimate child: accused of having Stephen Grover Cleveland.

impeachment: only one, in 1868 Andrew Johnson; breaching Tenure of Office Act. Senate vote fell one short of two-thirds majority.

imprisoned by British Andrew Jackson (during War of Independence).

Jefferson: holiday retreat Poplar Row.

Kennedy's attorney general Robert Kennedy, his brother.

Kennedy: assassinated by Lee Harvey Oswald, 1963 (shot by Jack Ruby).

kitchen cabinet Andrew Jackson's unofficial advisers.

knighted by Britain Eisenhower.

Lincoln assassinated by John Wilkes Booth (an actor), 1865. Samuel Mudd jailed for setting Booth's leg. Lincoln died in Peterson House, Washington DC.

longest term F.D. Roosevelt, 12 years.

male model: former Gerald Ford.

McKinley assassinated by   Leon Czolgosz, 1901.

minister to Great Britain: first   John Adams.

Monroe Doctrine: allegedly drafted by   John Quincy Adams.

Monroe: lived   Oak Hill.

New Deal   F.D. Roosevelt's 1930s recovery plan.

newspaper publisher   Warren Harding – Marion *Star*.

nicknames   J. Carter – Hot Shot & Toadsy; G. Bush – Wimp; Andrew Jackson – Old Hickory; Clinton – Comeback Kid.

Nobel Peace Prize   Theodore Roosevelt, 1906; Woodrow Wilson, 1919.

not elected as President   Gerald Ford (was also not elected Vice President).

occupation: most common   lawyer.

oldest to take office   Ronald Reagan, aged 69.

pneumonia: died of   William Henry Harrison.

President for the day   David Atchison – Zachary Taylor would not be sworn in on a Sunday.

prison; presidential candidate ran from   Eugene Debs in 1912.

Quakers   Herbert Hoover, Richard Nixon.

qualifications required   native born,14 years' residence, 35 years old.

re-elected: after losing office   Stephen Grover Cleveland.

Republican Party symbol   elephant.

residence   White House.

resigned   Richard Nixon.

resigned as Vice President   Spiro Agnew; income tax evasion charge.

Roman Catholic: first   John F. Kennedy.

Roughriders   Roosevelt second in command to Col. Leonard Wood.

Secretary of State   Eisenhower's – John Foster Dulles; Nixon's – Henry Kissinger; Carter's – Cyrus Robert Vance.

shirt advertisement: appeared in   Ronald Reagan.

shortest term   William Henry Harrison, about a month.

slogans: presidential   Full Dinner Pail – McKinley; Great Society – Lyndon Johnson; New Deal – F.D. Roosevelt; New Frontier – Kennedy.

slogans: other   'Would you buy a used car from this man?' – said by anti-Nixon protesters. 'The buck stops here' – Truman. 'No taxation without representation' – during dispute with Britain over taxation.

State of the Union   presidential speech given annually in January.

stood against   Bush – Michael Dukakis; Clinton – Ross Perot and George Bush; Hayes – Samuel Tilde; Hoover – Al Smith; Truman – Thomas Dewey.

terms limitation   two, under the 22nd Amendment to Constitution.

Vice President: born James Colbath   Henry Wilson.

Crédit Mobilier scandal   Schuyler Colfax.

Confederate general   John Cabell Breckinridge.

killed Alexander Hamilton   Aaron Burr.

letters from London   George Mifflin Dallas.

lives at   Admiralty Building, Washington.

Nobel Peace Prize 1925   Charles Dawes.

treason trial   Aaron Burr.

wrote no. 1 hit single   Charles Dawes ('It's all in the Game').

vice-presidential candidate: first female   Geraldine Ferraro in 1984.

Virginia plan   James Madison.

Washington: lived   Mount Vernon.

Watergate scandal   burglary of Democratic HQ in Washington.

White House: designer   James Hoban.

White House: first occupier   John Adams.

wives of presidents   George Washington – Martha Custis; Abraham Lincoln – Mary Todd; F.D. Roosevelt – Eleanor Roosevelt; J.F. Kennedy – Jaqueline Bouvier; Ronald Reagan – Nancy Davis; George Bush – Barbara Pierce; Bill Clinton – Hilary Rodham.

youngest president   Theodore Roosevelt (took office following assassination of McKinley).

youngest elected president   John F. Kennedy.

U
N
I
T
E
D

S
T
A
T
E
S

States

State	Nickname	Motto	State tree	State bird	State flower	State capital	Zip code
Alabama (Ala.)	Cotton Yellowhammer Heart of Dixie	We dare defend our rights	southern pine	yellowhammer	camelia	Montgomery	AL
Alaska (Alas.)	Last Frontier Land of the Midnight Sun	North to the future	Sitka spruce	willow ptarmigan	forget-me-not	Juneau	AK
Arizona (Ariz.)	Grand Canyon Apache	God enriches	paloverde	cactus wren	saguaro cactus blossom	Phoenix	AZ
Arkansas (Ark.)	Land of Opportunity Bear Wonder	The people rule	pine	mockingbird	apple blossom	Little Rock	AR
California (Cal.)	Golden	I have found it	Californian redwood	Californian valley quail	golden poppy	Sacramento	CA
Colorado (Colo.)	Centennial	Nothing without providence	Colorado blue spruce	lark bunting	Rocky Mountain columbine	Denver	CO
Connecticut (Conn.)	Constitution Nutmeg	He who transplanted still sustains	white oak	American robin	mountain laurel	Hartford	CT
District of Columbia	DC	Justice for all	scarlet oak	woodthrush	American beauty rose		
Delaware (Del.)	First Diamond	Liberty and independence	American holly	blue hen chicken	peach blossom	Dover	DE
Florida (Fla.)	Sunshine Peninsular	In God we trust	sabal palm	mockingbird	orange blossom	Tallahassee	FL
Georgia (Ga.)	Empire State of the South Peach	Wisdom, justice and moderation	live oak	brown thrasher	Cherokee rose	Atlanta	GA
Hawaii (Hi.)	Aloha	The life of the land is perpetuated in righteousness	kukui (candlenut)	nene (Hawaiian goose)	hibiscus	Honolulu	HI
Idaho (Ida.)	Gem Gem of the Mountains	Let it be perpetual	western white pine	mountain bluebird	syringa	Boise	ID
Illinois (Ill.)	Prairie Land of Lincoln	State sovereignty – national union	white oak	cardinal	native violet	Springfield	IL
Indiana (Ind.) Iowa (Ia.)	Hoosier Hawkeye Corn	Crossroads of America Our liberties we prize and our rights we will maintain	tulip tree (yellow poplar) oak	cardinal eastern goldfinch	peony wild rose	Indianapolis Des Moines	IN IA
Kansas (Kan.)	Sunflower Jayhawker	To the stars through difficulties	cottonwood	western meadowlark	native sunflower	Topeka	KS
Kentucky (Ky.)	Blue Grass	United we stand, divided we fall	tulip tree (yellow poplar)	cardinal	goldenrod	Frankfort	KY

State	Nickname	Motto	State tree	State bird	State flower	State capital	Zip code
Louisiana (La.)	Pelican, Creole, Sugar, Bayou	Union, justice and confidence	bald cypress	eastern brown pelican	magnolia	Baton Rouge	LA
Maine (Me.)	Pine Tree	I direct	eastern white pine	chickadee	white pine cone and tassel	Augusta	ME
Maryland (Md.)	Free, Old Line	Manly deeds, womanly words	white oak	Baltimore oriole	black-eyed Susan	Annapolis	MD
Massachusetts (Mass.)	Bay, Old Colony	By the sword we seek peace, but peace only under liberty	American elm	chickadee	mayflower (trailing arbutus)	Boston	MA
Michigan (Mich.)	Wolverine, Water Wonderland	If you seek a pleasant peninsular, look about you	white pine	robin	apple blossom	Lansing	MI
Minnesota (Minn.)	North Star, Gopher, Land of 10,000 Lakes, Land of Sky-Blue Waters	The North Star	red, or Norway pine	loon	pink and white lady's slipper	St Paul	MN
Mississippi (Miss.)	Magnolia	By valor and arms	magnolia	mockingbird	magnolia	Jackson	MS
Missouri (Mo.)	Show Me	The welfare of the people shall be the supreme law	dogwood	bluebird	hawthorn	Jefferson City	MO
Montana (Mont.)	Treasure, Big Sky Country	Gold and silver	ponderosa pine	western meadowlark	bitterroot	Helena	MT
Nebraska (Nebr.)	Cornhusker, Beef, Tree Planters	Equality before the law	cottonwood	western meadowlark	goldenrod	Lincoln	NB
Nevada (Nev.)	Sagebrush, Silver, Battle Born	All for our country	single-leaf piñon	mountain bluebird	sagebrush	Carson City	NV
New Hampshire (NH)	Granite	Live free or die	white birch	purple finch	purple lilac	Concord	NH
New Jersey (NJ)	Garden	Liberty and prosperity	red oak	eastern goldfinch	purple violet	Trenton	NJ
New Mexico (N. Mex)	Land of Enchantment, Sunshine	It grows as it goes	piñon (nut pine)	roadrunner	yucca flower	Santa Fe	NM
New York (NY)	Empire	Ever upward	sugar maple	bluebird	rose	Albany	NY
North Carolina (NC)	Tar Heel, Old North	To be rather than to seem	longleaf pine	cardinal	dogwood	Raleigh	NC
North Dakota (N.Dak.)	Flickertail, Sioux	Liberty and union, now and forever, one and inseparable	American elm	western meadowlark	wild prairie rose	Bismarck	ND

UNITED STATES

State	Nickname	Motto	State tree	State bird	State flower	State capital	Zip code
Ohio (Oh.)	Buckeye	With God, all things are possible	buckeye	cardinal	scarlet carnation	Columbus	OH
Oklahoma (Okla.)	Sooner	Labour conquers all things	redbud	scissor-tailed flycatcher	mistletoe	Oklahoma City	OK
Oregon (Oreg.)	Beaver	The Union	Douglas fir	western meadowlark	Oregon grape	Salem	OR
Pennsylvania (Pa.)	Keystone	Virtue, liberty, and independence	hemlock	ruffed grouse	mountain laurel	Harrisburg	PA
Rhode Island (RI)	Little Rhody Plantation	Hope	red maple	Rhode Island red	violet	Providence	RI
South Carolina (SC)	Palmetto	Prepared in mind and resources	cabbage palmetto	Carolina wren	Yellow jessamine	Columbia	SC
South Dakota (S. Dak.)	Coyote Sunshine	Under God the people rule	Black Hills spruce	ring-necked pheasant	pasqueflower	Pierre	SD
Tennessee (Tenn.)	Volunteer	Agriculture and commerce	tulip poplar	mockingbird	iris	Nashville	TN
Texas (Tex.)	Lone Star	Friendship	pecan	mockingbird	bluebonnet	Austin	TX
Utah (Ut.)	Beehive	Industry	blue spruce	sea gull	sego lily	Salt Lake City	UT
Vermont (Vt.)	Green Mountain	Freedom and unity	sugar maple	hermit thrush	red clover	Montpelier	VT
Virginia (Va.)	Mother of Presidents Old Dominion Cavalier	Thus always to tyrants	flowering dogwood	cardinal	dogwood	Richmond	VA
Washington (Wash.)	Evergreen Chinook	By and by	western hemlock	willow goldfinch	western rhododendron	Olympia	WA
West Virginia (W. Va.)	Mountain Panhandle	Mountaineers are always free	sugar maple	cardinal	big rhododendron	Charleston	WV
Wisconsin (Wis.)	Badger America's Dairyland	Forward	sugar maple	robin	wood violet	Madison	WI
Wyoming (Wyo.)	Equality	Equal rights	cottonwood	meadowlark	Indian paintbrush	Cheyenne	WY

State: Bordered by

Alabama Tennessee, Georgia, Mississippi, Florida.
Alaska None.
Arizona California, Nevada, Utah, New Mexico, Colorado.
Arkansas Tennessee, Mississippi, Louisiana, Missouri, Texas, Oklahoma.
California Arizona, Nevada, Oregon.
Colorado Utah, Wyoming, Arizona, New Mexico, Nebraska, Kansas, Oklahoma.
Connecticut Massachusetts, Rhode Island, New York.
Delaware Pennsylvania, New Jersey, Maryland.
Florida Georgia, Alabama.
Georgia South Carolina, Florida, Alabama, Tennessee, North Carolina.
Hawaii None.
Idaho Utah, Nevada, Washington, Wyoming, Oregon, Montana.
Illinois Kentucky, Missouri, Indiana, Wisconsin, Iowa.
Indiana Illinois, Michigan, Ohio, Kentucky.
Iowa Nebraska, Missouri, Illinois, Wisconsin, Minnesota, South Dakota.
Kansas Colorado, Oklahoma, Missouri, Nebraska.
Kentucky Tennessee, Illinois, Virginia, West Virginia, Missouri, Ohio, Indiana.
Louisiana Mississippi, Arkansas, Texas.

Maine New Hampshire.
Maryland Pennsylvania, Virginia, West Virginia, Delaware.
Massachusetts Vermont, New Hampshire, Rhode Island, New York, Connecticut.
Michigan Indiana, Ohio, Wisconsin.
Minnesota North Dakota, South Dakota, Iowa, Wisconsin.
Mississippi Louisiana, Arkansas, Tennessee, Alabama.
Missouri Iowa, Illinois, Kentucky, Tennessee, Arkansas, Oklahoma, Kansas, Nebraska.
Montana Idaho, Wyoming, North Dakota, South Dakota.
Nebraska Colorado, Wyoming, Iowa, South Dakota, Kansas, Missouri.
Nevada California, Utah, Arizona, Idaho, Oregon.
New Hampshire Maine, Massachusetts, Vermont.
New Jersey New York, Pennsylvania, Delaware.
New Mexico Colorado, Oklahoma, Texas, Arizona, Utah.
New York Vermont, Massachusetts, Connecticut, New Jersey, Pennsylvania.
North Carolina South Carolina, Virginia, Georgia, Tennessee.
North Dakota Montana, Minnesota, South Dakota.
Ohio Michigan, Indiana, Kentucky, West Virginia, Pennsylvania.

Oklahoma Texas, Arkansas, Kansas, Missouri, New Mexico, Colorado.
Oregon Washington, Idaho, California, Nevada.
Pennsylvania Delaware, New Jersey, New York, Maryland, West Virginia, Ohio.
Rhode Island Connecticut, Massachusetts.
South Carolina North Carolina, Georgia.
South Dakota North Dakota, Minnesota, Iowa, Nebraska, Wyoming, Montana.
Tennessee Kentucky, Alabama, Mississippi, Missouri, Arkansas, Georgia, Virginia, North Carolina.
Texas Louisiana, New Mexico, Oklahoma, Arkansas.
Utah Colorado, New Mexico, Arizona, Nevada, Wyoming, Idaho.
Vermont Massachusetts, New York, New Hampshire.
Virginia Maryland, West Virginia, Kentucky, Tennessee, North Carolina.
Washington Oregon, Idaho.
West Virginia Virginia, Kentucky, Ohio, Pennsylvania, Maryland.
Wisconsin Illinois, Michigan, Minnesota, Iowa.
Wyoming Montana, South Dakota, Nebraska, Colorado, Utah, Idaho.

UNITED STATES

Statistical Information

Order of Admission to the Union

1st	Delaware (1787)	18th	Louisiana (1812)	35th	West Virginia (1863)
2nd	Pennsylvania (1787)	19th	Indiana (1816)	36th	Nevada (1864)
3rd	New Jersey (1787)	20th	Mississippi (1817)	37th	Nebraska (1867)
4th	Georgia (1788)	21st	Illinois (1818)	38th	Colorado (1876)
5th	Connecticut (1788)	22nd	Alabama (1819)	39th	North Dakota (1889)
6th	Massachusetts (1788)	23rd	Maine (1820)	40th	South Dakota (1889)
7th	Maryland (1788)	24th	Missouri (1821)	41st	Montana (1889)
8th	South Carolina (1788)	25th	Arkansas (1836)	42nd	Washington (1889)
9th	New Hampshire (1788)	26th	Michigan (1837)	43rd	Idaho (1890)
10th	Virginia (1788)	27th	Florida (1845)	44th	Wyoming (1890)
11th	New York (1788)	28th	Texas (1845)	45th	Utah (1896)
12th	North Carolina (1789)	29th	Iowa (1846)	46th	Oklahoma (1907)
13th	Rhode Island (1790)	30th	Wisconsin (1848)	47th	New Mexico (1912)
14th	Vermont (1791)	31st	California (1850)	48th	Arizona (1912)
15th	Kentucky (1792)	32nd	Minnesota (1858)	49th	Alaska (1959)
16th	Tennessee (1796)	33rd	Oregon (1859)	50th	Hawaii (1959)
17th	Ohio (1803)	34th	Kansas (1861)		

Largest: by size

1st	Alaska	18th	North Dakota	35th	Tennessee
2nd	Texas	19th	Oklahoma	36th	Virginia
3rd	California	20th	Missouri	37th	Kentucky
4th	Montana	21st	Washington	38th	Indiana
5th	New Mexico	22nd	Wisconsin	39th	Maine
6th	Arizona	23rd	Georgia	40th	South Carolina
7th	Nevada	24th	Florida	41st	West Virginia
8th	Colorado	25th	Illinois	42nd	Maryland
9th	Wyoming	26th	Iowa	43rd	Vermont
10th	Michigan	27th	Arkansas	44th	New Hampshire
11th	Oregon	28th	New York	45th	Massachusetts
12th	Minnesota	29th	North Carolina	46th	Hawaii
13th	Utah	30th	Alabama	47th	New Jersey
14th	Idaho	31st	Louisiana	48th	Connecticut
15th	Kansas	32nd	Mississippi	49th	Delaware
16th	Nebraska	33rd	Pennsylvania	50th	Rhode Island
17th	South Dakota	34th	Ohio		

Largest: by population

1st	California	18th	Maryland	35th	New Mexico
2nd	New York	19th	Washington	36th	Utah
3rd	Texas	20th	Louisiana	37th	Nebraska
4th	Florida	21st	Minnesota	38th	Maine
5th	Pennsylvania	22nd	Alabama	39th	Hawaii
6th	Illinois	23rd	Kentucky	40th	New Hampshire
7th	Ohio	24th	Arizona	41st	Nevada
8th	Michigan	25th	South Carolina	42nd	Idaho
9th	New Jersey	26th	Colorado	43rd	Rhode Island
10th	North Carolina	27th	Oklahoma	44th	Montana
11th	Georgia	28th	Connecticut	45th	South Dakota
12th	Virginia	29th	Iowa	46th	North Dakota
13th	Massachusetts	30th	Oregon	47th	Delaware
14th	Indiana	31st	Mississippi	48th	Alaska
15th	Missouri	32nd	Kansas	49th	Vermont
16th	Tennessee	33rd	Arkansas	50th	Wyoming
17th	Wisconsin	34th	West Virginia		

General Information

Alamo: killed in siege of 1836 Davy Crockett and Jim Bowie. **site of siege** Franciscan Mission Hall in San Antonio, Texas. **dates of siege** 23 February to 6 March 1836. **Mexican leader** Santa Anna. **meaning of** poplar (Spanish) or cottonwood tree.

Alaska: purchased from Russia, 1867; known as Seward's Folly.

America: named after Amerigo Vespucci.

anti-communist witch hunts 1950s Senator Joseph McCarthy.

Back to Africa Movement leader Marcus Garvey.

Bay Area Rapid Transit (BART) San Francisco.

Black Muslims: developed movement Elijah Muhammad 1934.

Borders with eight other states Missouri and Tennessee.

Boss Tweed Corrupt leader of Tammany Hall Democrats, New York.

Boston Mountains Arkansas and Oklahoma (Ozarks).

Boston Tea Party: date of 16 December 1773. **reason for destruction of tea** protest against British

tea tax. **owners of tea** British East India Company. **British retaliation** Intolerable Acts (shut down port, pending payment).

Bretton Woods Conference, NH, 1944: formed IMF and International Bank for Reconstruction.

bus boycott of Montgomery, Alabama: caused by Rosa Parks refusing to give up seat in Dec. 1955.

California: largest city Los Angeles.

Californian gold rush: first prospector James Wilson Marshall, 1848.

first major strike J.A. Sutter, a Swiss settler, 1849.

capital of America before Washington DC Philadelphia, 1783–9.

Central Park: designers Frederick Law Olmstead and Calvert Vaux.

child: first born of English parents Virginia Dare.

civil rights demo: troops called in Selma, Alabama,1956; Autherine Lucy expelled.

Civil War: dates of outbreak and surrender 15 April 1861 to 9 April 1865. **started: where** Fort Sumter in Charleston Harbour, SC, April 1861.

Lee surrender to Grant: where Appomattox Court House, Virginia, 9 April 1865. **official ending: on surrender of** Gen. Richard Taylor, 4 May 1865. **first state to secede from Union** South Carolina, December 1860. **second state to secede** Mississippi, January 1861. **antebellum: meaning of** period before the war. **battle above the clouds** Lookout Mountain, Chattanooga, Tennessee. **Confederate capital** Richmond, Virginia.

Colin Powell: autobiography *My American Journey*.

commonwealths: officially called Massachusetts, Kentucky and Virginia.

commonwealth: self-styled Pennsylvania.

Confederate states: antebellum Alabama, Florida, Georgia, Louisiana, Mississippi, South Carolina, Texas. **four joined at outbreak of Civil War** Arkansas, North Carolina, Tennessee, Virginia. **President** Jefferson Davis.

Congress: first woman Jeanette Rankin, 1916.

Constitution of the USA: ratified by New Hampshire's ninth vote, 1788.

Constitutional amendments Abolition of Slavery, 13th. Presidential Terms, 22nd. Prohibition, 18th. Votes for Blacks, 15th. Votes for Women, 19th.

coterminous states: high and low point Mt Whitney and Death Valley, both in California.

Coxey's Army unemployed march to Washington DC, 1894.

Dakota: named after Sioux Indian tribe.

Declaration of Independence 4 July 1776.

Delaware: three counties New Castle, Kent, Sussex.

Delaware: largest city Wilmington.

District of Columbia: ceded by Maryland, 1791.

Emancipation proclamation freeing of slaves during Civil War.

Essex Junto: leader Timothy Pickering. **term coined by** John Hancock, 1778. **supported** Alexander Hamilton. **based** Massachusetts.

First state to join Union Delaware, 7 Dec. 1787.

Florida: largest city Jacksonville.

Four corners touching Utah, Colorado, New Mexico, Arizona.

Gadsden purchase of land for USA in 1853 land bought from Mexico, now New Mexico and Arizona.

Georgia: marched through during Civil War General Sherman.

gold on land caused rush 1849 John Sutter.

good neighbour policy 1928 Latin American policy of F.D. Roosevelt.

Grape Workers Union leader led boycott Cesar Chavez, 1968.

Hartford Convention of 1814–15 began demise of Federalist Party.

Hawaii: European discoverer Captain James Cook, 1778.

Hawaii: former name Sandwich Islands.

Haymarket Massacre of 1886 police fire on crowd at May Day Rally in Chicago.

Homestead Act 1862: Lincoln's aim to provide land free to settlers to cultivate.

Honolulu: island situated Oahu.

honorary citizenship Winston Churchill.

Indian chief surrendered to General Miles Geronimo.

Intolerable Acts enforced embargo of Boston until compensation paid.

Irangate scandal: USA accused of arms for Iran in return for funds to Nicaraguan Contras. **famous testimony** Oliver North.

Ivy League: nickname for The top eight universities and colleges of USA. **members** Harvard (1636), Yale (1701), Pennsylvania (1740), Princeton (1746), Columbia (1754), Brown (1764), Dartmouth (1769), Cornell (1853).

Kent State University, Ohio, 1970 National Guard shot dead four students during anti-war demo.

Ku Klux Klan: formed Pulaski, Tennessee, 1866.

Lend-lease Pact: March 1941 Roosevelt signed with Britain for WW2 aid.

Lewis and Clark expedition 1804–6 exploration of western America.

Lewis and Clark: state governors of Louisiana and Missouri Territory respectively.

Los Angeles: name when founded, 1781 the Town of the Queen of the Angels.

Louisiana purchase Mississippi valley bought from France 1803.

Louisiana: largest city New Orleans.

Louisiana: named in honour of Louis XIV.

Mammoth Cave Kentucky.

Manhattan Island: bought from Indian tribes for 60 guilders.

Manhattan Island: purchaser Peter Minuit.

mapped America Samuel de Champlain, 1605; John Smith, 1614.

Maryland named in honour of wife of Charles I: Henrietta Maria.

Mason–Dixon line: boundaries Pennsylvania–Maryland; border of North and South.

Mason–Dixon line: why drawn disputes of Penn and Calvert families in 1760s.

Mayflower: sister ship *Speedwell*; deemed unseaworthy.

Mexican ceded states of 1848 Texas, New Mexico, California.

Mexican ceded states: clerk responsible Nicholas Trist.

Michigan: two land masses joined by Mackinac Bridge (Big Mac), built 1957.

Michigan: borders on Great Lakes all except Ontario.

Mississippi University: first black to enter James Meredith.

Montana: name means mountain (Spanish).

Mormon Church: founded at Fayette, New York, in 1830.

mountain: highest in America Mount McKinley, Alaska, 20,320′ (6,194 m).

Nat Turner insurrection 1831 slave uprising in Virginia.

Naval Academy Annapolis, Maryland.

Nebraska: name means flat water.

Nevada: name means snow-clad (Spanish).

New England: named by John Smith, 1614. **six states** Connecticut, Maine, Massachusetts, New Hampshire, Rhode Island, Vermont.

New Hampshire: named after English county of Hampshire, 1629.

New Orleans: same parallel as Cairo, Delhi, Shanghai.

New York named in honour of duke of York, later James II.

New York City: five boroughs Queens, Bronx, Manhattan, Brooklyn, Richmond County and Staten Island.

UNITED STATES

New York State: capital's former name   Fort
Orange, 1624; became Albany.

New York: political differences   upstate is
Conservative, downstate is Liberal.

North Dakota: largest city   Fargo.

Oklahoma: name means   red people.

oldest American town   St Augustine, Florida, 1565.

Pilgrim Fathers: ship   *Mayflower*. **landed**
Provincetown in Massachusetts, November 1620.
first to land   John Alden. **established**   Plymouth
Colony. **Indian interpreter**   Squanto. **Indian welcomed them**   Samoset, a Pemaquid from Maine.

Portsmouth, New Hampshire   treaty ended Russo-
Japanese war, 1905.

presidential primary: earliest   New Hampshire.

rectangular-shaped states   Wyoming and Colorado.

Rhode Island: official name   The State of Rhode
Island and Providence Plantations.

Richmond County: named in honour of   Charles
Lennox, duke of Richmond, son of Charles II.

Russia: closest point to   Diomede Islands, Bering
Strait.

San Francisco meeting of United Nations   April
1945.

school integration: Federal troops enforced   Little
Rock, Arkansas, 1957.

Sea Islands: sub-tropical islands of   South
Carolina.

senator: first black   Edward Brooke.

Seneca Falls Convention, 1848   Women's Rights'
Movement began.

size of USA doubled by   Louisiana purchase.

slave abolitionist leader   Harriet Tubman, former
slave.

slavery: abolished   1863. **escape network to the
North**   underground railroad. **last state to abolish**
Mississippi.

Spindletop oil well, Texas   blew 1901.

Tammany Hall (New York)   byword for municipal corruption.

Tarpon Springs, Florida   centre for Greek Orthodox
religion and sponge industry.

Teapot Dome Affair, aka Elk Hills Scandal   Sec. of
Interior Albert Fall jailed for corruption.

territories: overseas   American Virgin Islands,
Commonwealth of Puerto Rico, Guam, Samoa.

terrorism: executed 1927 but pardoned 1977
Sacco and Vanzetti.

Texas: annexed by America, in   1845. **former capital**   Houston, until 1839, then Austin. **largest city**
Houston.

Townshend Acts 1767   British taxes that sparked
revolt.

Vietnam: secret documents   Pentagon papers
showed USA involvement. **secret documents
revealed by**   Daniel Ellsberg, 1971.

Virginia: named in honour of   Elizabeth I.

War of Independence: started   Lexington,
Massachusetts, April 1775. **ended**   Yorktown,
Virginia, October 1781. **rode to warn of British
approach**   Paul Revere. **traitor for British**
Benedict Arnold. **American general**   George
Washington. **British general**   Charles Cornwallis.
Washington's ally   Marquis of Lafayette.

Washington: capital since   1789.

Watts riots   Los Angeles, 1965.

witchcraft trials   Salem, Massachusetts, 1692 (20
executed).

wobblies   Industrial Workers of the World, trade
union.

Yellowstone National Park: three states   Wyoming,
Montana, Idaho.

NB More detailed information pertaining to rivers, mountains and other geographical features of the USA can be
found in the geography section.

MISCELLANEOUS ITEMS OF INTEREST

Units of Length

link (surveying)	7.92 inches (100th part of chain)
span	9 inches (approx span of hand)
hand	4 inches (horse measurement)
cubit	18 inches (biblical measurement)
pace	30 inches (from the stride)
cable	120 fathoms (720 feet; a fathom equals six feet)
nautical mile	6,080 feet (1 sec of arc at Equator) (now 1,852 metres)

Paper Sizes

A0	841 x 1189 mm (33⅛ × 46¾ inches)
A1	594 x 841 mm (23⅜ × 33⅛ inches)
A2	420 x 594 mm (16½ × 23⅜ inches)
A3	297 x 420 mm (11¾ × 16½ inches)
A4	210 x 297 mm (8¼ × 11¾ inches)
A5	148 x 210 mm (5⅞ × 8¼ inches)
A6	105 x 148 mm (4⅛ × 5⅞ inches)
A7	74 x 105 mm (2¹⁵⁄₁₆ × 4⅛ inches)
A8	52 x 74 mm (2¹⁄₁₆ × 2¹⁵⁄₁₆ inches)
A9	37 x 52 mm (1¹⁵⁄₃₂ × 2¹⁄₁₆ inches)
A10	26 x 37 mm (1¹⁄₃₂ × 1¹⁵⁄₃₂ inches)
Elephant	584 x 711 mm (23 × 28 inches)

Book Sizes

Crown Quarto	246 × 189 mm
Crown Octavo	186 × 123 mm
Demy Quarto	276 × 219 mm
Demy Octavo	216 × 138 mm
Royal Quarto	312 × 237 mm
Royal Octavo	234 × 156 mm

Morse Code

A	dot dash	**H**	dot dot dot dot	**O**	dash dash dash	**V**	dot dot dot dash
B	dash dot dot dot	**I**	dot dot	**P**	dot dash dash dot	**W**	dot dash dash
C	dash dot dash dot	**J**	dot dash dash dash	**Q**	dash dash dot dash	**X**	dash dot dot dash
D	dash dot dot	**K**	dash dot dash	**R**	dot dash dot	**Y**	dash dot dash dash
E	dot	**L**	dot dash dot dot	**S**	dot dot dot	**Z**	dash dash dot dot
F	dot dot dash dot	**M**	dash dash	**T**	dash		
G	dash dash dot	**N**	dash dot	**U**	dot dot dash		

Mnemonics

Types of cedars Atlas – Ascending branches, deodar – drooping branches, lebanon – level branches.

Can Queen Victoria eat cold apple pie? The seven hills of Rome: Capitoline, Quirinal, Viminal, Esquiline, Caelian, Aventine, Palatine.

Did Mary ever visit Brighton Beach? Order of Nobility: Duke, Marquess, Earl, Viscount, Baron, Baronet.

Bless my dear Aunt Sally Order of operations in algebraic expressions: Brackets, Multiply, Divide, Add, Subtract.

BROM 4689 (Duke of Marlborough's Telephone No.) Marlborough's battles: Blenheim (1704), Ramilies (1706), Oudenarde (1708), Malplaquet (1709).

Men very easily make jugs serve useful nocturnal purposes Planets from the sun: Mercury, Venus, Earth, Mars, Jupiter, Saturn, Uranus, Neptune, Pluto.

Spring forward, fall back Mnemonic to remember whether to put clock forward or back.

Virgins are rare Ohm's Law: Volts = Amps x Resistance.

How I want a drink alcoholic of course after the heavy chapters involving quantum mechanics Mnemonic for remembering pi to 14 places: 3.14159265358979.

No plan like yours to study history wisely British ruling houses: Norman, Plantagenet, Lancaster, York, Tudor, Stuart, Hanover, Windsor

NB This last little section on mnemonics is a reminder in itself that a sound general knowledge base can only be achieved if facts are committed to memory. There is no shortcut to success in the quiz world; of course, a keen interest taken in things going on around you is desirable, as is a basic level of intelligence, but given that most people share those basic requirements then the secret of success is the amount of data consumed and the way that data is processed. The rate at which information is consumed varies depending on the level of commitment of the reader, but the way that information is stored can be the vital edge required to recall that seemingly long-forgotten nugget or that either/or situation so often encountered by quiz buffs. Mnemonics are an invaluable aid to quiz players, and should be used in some form or other when memorizing lists. It does not matter how silly, rude, outlandish or downright inarticulate the mnemonic is, all that matters is that it works.

Colours

alabaster	White	elephant	Grey	olive	Greyish-Green
amaranth	Purple	emerald	Green	or	Gold
amber	Yellow	fallow	Yellow	peridot	Green (yellowish-green)
argent	Silver	fawn	Yellowish-Brown		
ash	Pale Grey	flame	Orangey-Red	pillar-box	Bright Red
auburn	Reddish-Brown	foxy	Reddish-Brown	plum	Reddish-Purple
aureate	Golden	gamboge	Yellow	primrose	Pale Yellow
azure	Sky Blue	gentian	Violet	puce	Purple-Brown
bamboo	Yellowish-Brown	gridelin	Grey-Violet	russet	Reddish-Brown
bay	Reddish-Brown	grizzly	Grey	rust	Reddish-Brown
bice	Blue	gules	Red	sable	Black
bistre	Brown	hazel	Reddish-Brown	saffron	Orange-Yellow
bronze	Yellowish-Brown	heliotrope	Mauve (light purple)	sandy	Yellowish-Red
brunette	Dark Brown			sanguine	Blood Red
buff	Pale Yellow	honey	Yellow	sapphire	Blue
cardinal	Red (scarlet)	indigo	Violet Blue	scarlet	Bright Red tinged with Orange
carmine	Red (crimson)	ivory	Creamy-White		
carnation	Rosy Pink	jonquil	Yellow		
celandine	Yellow	jupiter	Blue	sepia	Reddish-Brown
cerise	Red	khaki	Brownish-Yellow	sienna	Yellowish-Brown
cerulean	Blue	lake	Crimson	solferino	Crimson
chestnut	Reddish-Brown	lapis lazuli	Blue	sorrel	Reddish-Brown
chocolate	Brown	lavender	Pale Blue (with a trace of red)	straw	Pale Yellow
chrome	Yellow			tan	Yellowish-Brown
cinereous	Ash-Grey	lilac	Pinkish-Violet	teak	Reddish-Brown
cinnabar	Vermilion	lily	White	teal	Greenish-Blue
cinnamon	Yellowish-Brown	livid	Bluish-Purple	topaz	Yellow
citrine	Lemon Yellow	magenta	Mauve (mauvish-crimson)	turquoise	Greenish-Blue
cobalt	Blue			ultramarine	Blue
cochineal	Scarlet	malachite	Green	umber	Reddish-Brown
cornelian	Reddish-White	maroon	Brownish-Crimson	verd-antique	Green
cornflour	Blue	mazarine	Blue	vermilion	Red
crimson	Purplish-Red	moon	White	violet	Bluish-Purple
damask	Pinkish-Red	murrey	Purplish-Red	viridescent	Green
dun	Greyish-Brown	nacarat	Orangey-Red	xanthin	Yellow
ebony	Brownish-Black	ochre	Yellow (light browny yellow)		

Angles

	Angles in regular polygon	Total angles	Sides	Formula
triangle	60°	180°	3	(2 × 3–4) × 90 = 180
quadrilateral	90°	360°	4	(2 × 4–4) × 90 = 360
pentagon	108°	540°	5	(2 × 5–4) × 90 = 540
hexagon	120°	720°	6	(2 × 6–4) × 90 = 720
heptagon	129°	900°	7	(2 × 7–4) × 90 = 900
octagon	135°	1080°	8	(2 × 8–4) × 90 = 1080
nonagon	140°	1260°	9	(2 × 9–4) × 90 = 1260
decagon	144°	1440°	10	(2 × 10–4) × 90 = 1440
dodecagon	150°	1800°	12	(2 × 12–4) × 90 = 1800
hendecagon	162°	3240°	20	(2 × 20–4) × 90 = 3240

NB Sum of the interior angles of a polygon = (2n–4) × 90 degrees where n = the number of sides.

Adjectives

Objects

acicular	needle-like	hastate	spear-shaped
acinaciform	scimitar-shaped	lenticular	lens-shaped
		ligneous	wood-like
aciniform	grape-like	linguiform	tongue-shaped
alaric	wing-shaped		
allantoic	sausage-shaped	lunate	crescent-shaped
		marmoreal	marble-like
amygdaloid	almond-shaped	navicular	boat-shaped
		oculiform	eye-shaped
annular	ring-shaped	odontoid	tooth-shaped
arcuate	bow-shaped	oviform	egg-shaped
baculiform	rod-like	palmate	palm-shaped
cancroid	crab-like	pinnate	feather-like
clavate	club-shaped	pyriform	pear-like
cordate	heart-shaped	reniform	kidney-shaped
cricoid	ring-shaped	sagittate	arrow-shaped
crinoidal	lily-like	saponaceous	soap-like
cuneal	wedge-shaped	scutate	shield-shaped
cyprinoid	carp-like	stellate	star-shaped
decussate	cross-shaped	toroid	doughnut-shaped
dendroid	tree-shaped	trochal	wheel-shaped
dentoid	tooth-shaped	unciform	hook-shaped
ethmoid	sieve-like	verticillate	whorl-shaped
falciform	sickle-shaped	xiphoid	sword-shaped
ganoid	scale-like		

Animals

anguine	snake-like	lupine	wolf-like
anserine	goose-like	murine	mouse-like
apian	bee-like	ovine	sheep-like
aquiline	eagle-like	ophidian	snake-like
asinine	ass-like	passerine	sparrow-like
avian	bird-like	pavanine	peacock-like
bovine	ox-like	piscine	fish-like
canine	dog-like	porcine	pig-like
caprine	goat-like	psittacine	parrot-like
cervine	deer-like	saurian	lizard-like
columbine	dove-like	simian	ape-like
corvine	crow-like	squaloid	shark-like
equine	horse-like	taurine	bull-like
feline	cat-like	turdine	thrush-like
hircine	goat-like	ursine	bull-like
leonine	lion-like	vaccine	cow-like
leporine	hare-like	vulpine	fox-like

Alphabets

	No. of characters	Description
Albanian	36	based on the Tosk language since 1945.
Arabic	28	all consonants; written from right to left.
Aramaic	22	all consonants; written from right to left.
Armenian	38	31 consonants and 7 vowels.
Balinese	27	the Latin alphabet is now used in Bali.
Bassa	29	formerly used in Liberia.
Batak	30	20 consonants, 10 vowels, written from bottom to top.
Braille	63	each made up of 1–6 raised dots arranged in six-position matrix.
Buhid	48	used to write the Tagalog language of the Philippines.
Bulgarian	30	adaptation of the Cyrillic alphabet.
Cyrillic	32	nowadays synonymous with the Russian alphabet.
Ethiopic	26	all consonants; 7 variations of each letter.
Etruscan	20	16 consonants, 4 vowels written left to right then right to left.
Gaelic	18	no J, K, Q, V, W, X, Y, Z.
Georgian	33	used by about 3.5 million people.
Gothic	27	original Gothic alphabet had 25 letters.
Grantha	35	30 consonants and 5 vowels; written left to right.
Greek	24	17 consonants and 7 vowels.
Gujarati	41	34 consonants, 7 vowels each having two variants.
Hebrew	22	all consonants; written from left to right.
Latin (Roman)	26	alphabet used by English speakers. J, U, W not in original Roman alphabet.
Mongolian	33	adaptation of the Cyrillic alphabet.
Ogham	29	also known as beth luis, or beth luis nion.
Phoenician	22	no vowels.
Runic	24	also known as fu(th)ark from its first six letters.
Russian	33	adaptation of the Cyrillic alphabet.
Serbian	29	adaptation of the Cyrillic alphabet.
Tamil	36	24 consonants, 12 vowels.
Telego	51	35 consonants, 16 vowels.
Ugaritic	30	cuneiform alphabet of 27 consonants and 3 vowels.
Ukrainian	33	adaptation of the Cyrillic alphabet.

MISCELLANEOUS

Roman Roads

Aemilian Way	Rimini to Milan	**Fosse Way**	Lincoln to Exeter
Akeman Street	Alchester to Cirencester	**Icknield Way**	Wash to Salisbury Plain
Appian Way	Rome to Brindisi	**Salarian Way**	Rome to Ancona
Aurelian Way	Rome to Genoa	**Stane Street (1)**	London to Chichester
Casinge Street	Dover to London	**(2)**	Braughing in Hertfordshire to Colchester
Cassian Way	Rome to Florence		
Dere Street	Risingham to Hadrian's Wall	**Watling Street (1)**	London to Wroxeter via St Albans
Ermine Street	London to York		
Flaminian Way	Rome to Rimini	**Watling Street (2)**	Wroxeter to Abergavenny

US Money

All US bills have a portrait of a famous American on the front and a design on the back as follows:

	Front	Back		Front	Back
$1	Washington	Great Seal of USA	$100	Franklin	Independence Hall
$2	Jefferson	Signers of Declaration	$500	McKinley	Ornate Design
$5	Lincoln	Lincoln Memorial	$1,000	Cleveland	Ornate Design
$10	Hamilton	US Treasury	$5,000	Madison	Ornate Design
$20	Jackson	White House	$10,000	Chase	Ornate Design
$50	Grant	US Capitol	$100,000	Wilson	Ornate Design

British Money

Until 1943 there were white bank notes for values of £10, £20, £50, £100, £500 and £1,000 but these ceased to be legal tender in 1945. The old white £5 note issued between 1945 and 1956 ceased to be legal tender in 1961. The £5 note issued between 1957 and 1963 that coincided with the term of office of Harold MacMillan, and bearing a portrait of Britannia, ceased to be legal tender in 1967. The £5 note issued between 1963 and 1971 was the first of the series to bear a portrait of the Queen. The first note with a portrait of the Queen on the front was a £1 note issued in 1960. The 10 shilling note was replaced by the 50p coin in 1969 and ceased to be legal tender in 1970 (they could however be redeemed if presented at the Head Office of the Bank of England). The £1 note was replaced by a coin in 1983 and ceased to be legal tender in 1988.

The current notes as at August 2001 portray famous people as follows:

£5	George Stephenson (1781–1848) and his 'Rocket'
£10	Charles Darwin (1809–82) and the Beagle
£20	Sir Edward Elgar (1857–1934) and Worcester Cathedral
£50	Sir John Houblon (1632–1712) the Bank of England gatekeeper. The current Chief Cashier of the Bank of England is Merlyn Lowther who replaced G.E.A. Kentfield.

Previous portraits on notes are as follows:

£5	Duke of Wellington
£10	Charles Dickens and before him Florence Nightingale
£20	Michael Faraday and before him William Shakespeare
£50	Sir Christopher Wren

British coins ceased to be legal tender as follows:

Farthing (¼d)	1960
Pre-decimal halfpenny	1969
Half-crown (2s 6d)	1970
Threepenny bit	1971
Sixpence (6d = 2½p)	1980
Decimal halfpenny	1984

Confusion often arises when one considers which was the first decimal coin brought into circulation. In 1968 the shilling and two shilling coins were replaced by a new 5p and 10p coin. This pre- empted decimalization in 1971 and was an exercise in the public becoming used to the new system. The coins were of the same value as previously and did not alter the public perception in any way. In 1969 the new 50p coin was introduced replacing the ten shilling note which of course was a vastly different form hence it often being considered as the first decimal coin introduced.

In 1971 the ½p, 1p, and 2p coins were introduced and in 1982 the 20p coin followed. In 1983 the £1 coin replaced the £1 note and in 1986 the first £2 coin was minted. Decimal coins minted before 1982 had their value in 'New' pence.

UK Telephone STD Codes

0121	Birmingham
0131	Edinburgh
0141	Glasgow
0151	Liverpool
0161	Manchester
0191	Newcastle upon Tyne

Recent changes to STD codes

Cardiff was 01222 now 02920
Coventry was 01203 now 02476
London was 0171 now 0207
London was 0181 now 0208
Portsmouth was 01705 now 02392
Southampton was 01703 now 02380

NB All Northern Ireland numbers have been changed to six-digit numbers, all of which begin 028.